The Classic Food of Northern Italy

ANNA DEL CONTE

The Classic Food of Northern Italy

PAVILION

FOR ELEANOR

First published in Great Britain in 1995 by
Pavilion Books Limited
26 Upper Ground
London SE1 9PD

Home Economist: Caroline Liddell
Stylist: Helen Payne
Map artworks by Alec Hurzer

Ⓥ Indicates recipes suitable for vegetarians

Designed by Andrew Barron & Collis Clements Associates

A CIP catalogue record for this book is available from the British Library

ISBN 1-85793-239 0

Typeset in Galliard by Servis Filmsetting Ltd.
Printed and bound in Great Britain by
Butler & Tanner Ltd, Frome and London

10 9 8 7 6 5 4 3 2 1

This book may be ordered by post direct from the publisher.
Please contact the Marketing Department. But try your bookshop first.

Contents

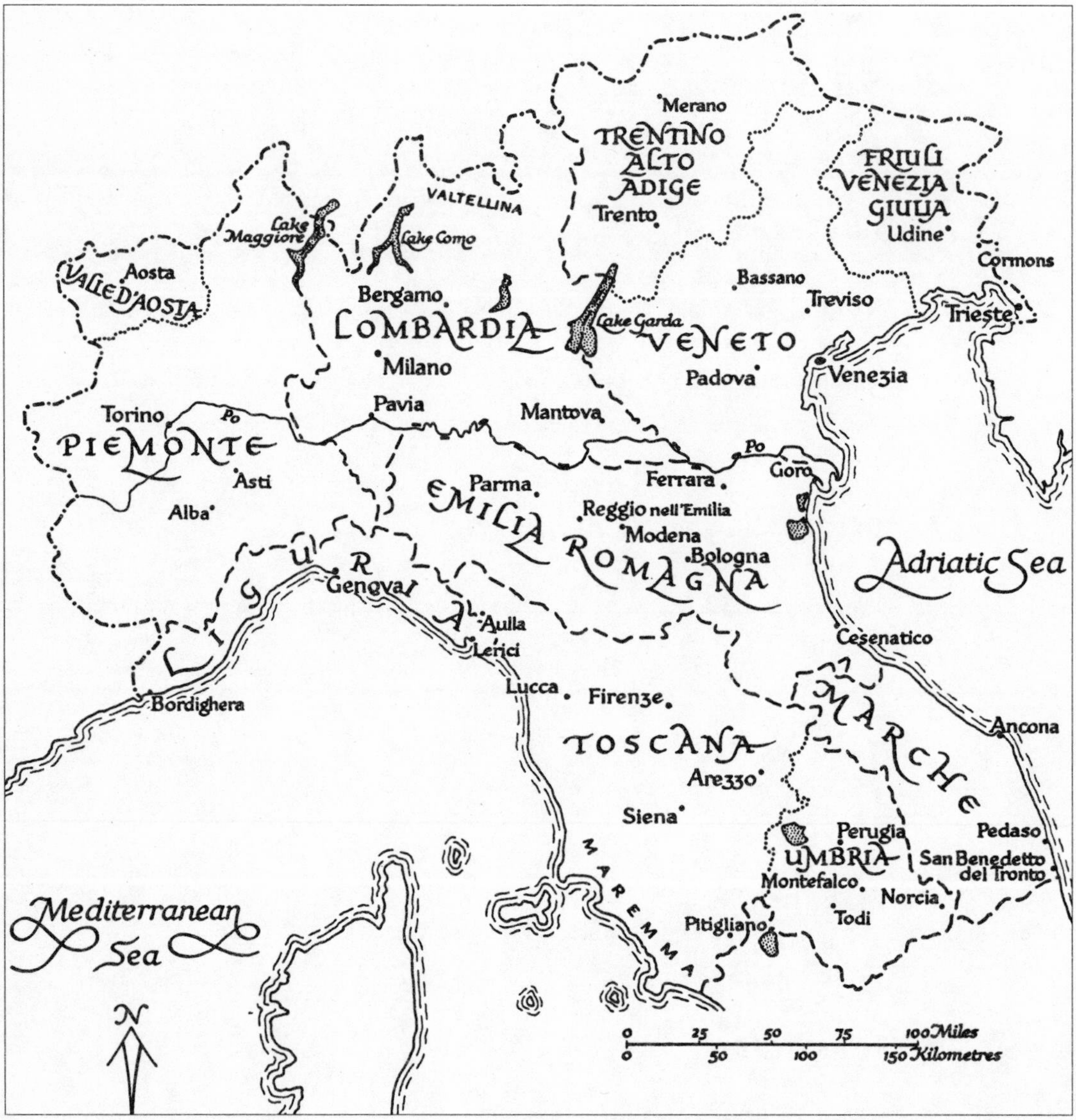
Merano
TRENTINO ALTO ADIGE
Trento
FRIULI VENEZIA GIULIA
Udine
Cormons
Trieste
VALTELLINA
Lake Maggiore
Lake Como
Lake Garda
Aosta
VALLE D'AOSTA
Bergamo
LOMBARDIA
Milano
Pavia
Mantova
Bassano
Treviso
VENETO
Padova
Venezia
Torino
Po
PIEMONTE
Asti
Alba
Parma
EMILIA ROMAGNA
Reggio nell'Emilia
Modena
Bologna
Ferrara
Goro
Adriatic Sea
LIGURIA
Genova
Aulla
Lerici
Bordighera
Cesenatico
Lucca
Firenze
TOSCANA
Arezzo
Siena
MARCHE
Ancona
Perugia
UMBRIA
Pedaso
San Benedetto del Tronto
Montefalco
Norcia
Todi
Pitigliano
MAREMMA
Mediterranean Sea
N
0 25 50 75 100 Miles
0 50 100 150 Kilometres

Foreword

It is England's good fortune that an accomplished Italian food writer fell in love with, and married, an Englishman. Anna Del Conte was born and reared a Milanese and is a true daughter of that special breed of Northern Italians who share an innate and intense passion on the subject of food.

Living in this country, but keeping strong links with Italy and her family, Anna's writing and culinary enthusiasm have been a beacon of true light among greyer shades of the misrepresentations that predominate in cookbooks and magazines under the heading *Italian*.

Anna is a purist. She will not countenance anything that isn't in the strictest sense authentic. So, with this in mind, I am here to recommend to you what surely must be the best researched and presented book on Northern Italian food yet published. If you want to grasp and understand the real thing, it is here on every page. With this book you will not only be able to cook authentic Italian food, you will also be able to go on an exciting journey of discovery throughout the whole of Northern Italy.

I personally have been waiting for this book for some time. Thank you, Anna, for all the hard work and research that has gone into it, and for making real Italian cooking and eating accessible to all of us.

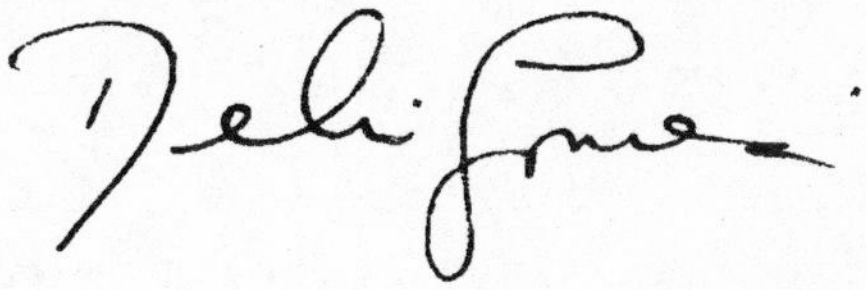

Introduction

History and geography have both played their part in making the cooking of Italy so strongly regional. For all the hundreds of years between the fall of the Roman Empire and the middle of the last century (1861 to be precise) the Italian peninsula was divided into independent, sovereign – and often hostile – states. That these states were frequently under foreign domination was another factor that pitted one state against another.

The degree to which this regionality still exists today can hardly be exaggerated. 'Where are you from?' is the first thing one Italian asks another when they meet for the first time. Before my husband had grown used to this *campanilismo*, he was struck by hearing me say, in surprised tones, 'She's from Florence . . . but she's very nice.' The Florentines have never been bosom friends of the Lombards!

It is only natural that this regionality, and the foreign domination, should have had a profound effect on Italian cooking. After the Napoleonic débâcle, for instance, the Spanish Bourbons returned to Naples and Sicily, the Vatican continued to govern central Italy, and the Hapsburgs were sitting happily all over Veneto and Lombardy. Meanwhile the Dukes of Savoia (the future kings of Italy) were becoming more and more powerful in Piedmont, and the charming Grand Duchess Marie Louise, Napoleon's widow, was teaching her subjects in Parma how to make cakes à l'Autrichienne.

So it is that, to this day, Parma boasts some of the best dolci in Italy, Venetian cooking has strong Hungarian and Eastern influences, the cooking of Lombardy prides itself on some of the best dishes of braised meat which the Austrians brought south, while the French taught the Milanese the use of butter and cream.

Although the same basic ingredients are used throughout northern Italy, they are cooked in different ways in each region. A fish soup from Ancona on the Adriatic, delicately flavoured with saffron, would be very different from the fish soup of Tuscany, a fiery cacciucco, and specifically from Livorno, on the Mediterranean, whose cooking has been strongly influenced by its spice trade with North Africa.

Another excellent example concerns the various ways of cooking *baccalà* and *stoccafisso* – salt cod and stockfish. This preserved fish was first brought to Sicily at the beginning of the millennium by the Normans. In the old days fish could not be kept or transported and, during some months of the year, could not even be caught. Thus, because of the Italians' partiality for fish, this preserved cod became very popular all over the peninsula. It was always available, was plentiful and – unlike now – was cheap.

There are a great number of recipes for baccalà or stoccafisso in any regional cookery book. The same fish, yes, but cooked with local flavourings and local methods. Liguria offers baccalà with spinach or Swiss chard, while in Tuscany baccalà is coated with flour, fried first and then *insaporito* – made tasty – in a tomato sauce, as are the Tuscans' red mullet and their cardoons. But it is in Veneto that the most famous recipes for stoccafisso have been created. The stockfish, succulent with melting onions, is cooked in milk with local potatoes and plenty of garlic and parsley, but never with the southern tomatoes. There and in Lombardy, baccalà and stoccafisso are always served with the Alpine staple, polenta.

Polenta and rice illustrate another aspect of the regionality of Italian food. They are both grown in northern Italy, and it is there that recipes for them abound. The risotti are lavishly dressed with butter, the local fat. Indeed, one used to talk of the 'butter line', which ran from west to east, to the north of Tuscany and south of Emilia-Romagna. North of this line, butter was the cooking fat, to the south it was oil.

These divisions result from the country's geography and climate, and they are sharpened by the contrast between the sea and the mountains. The northern part of the 1200 kilometre-long peninsula is fastened to continental Europe by the uninterrupted chain of the Alps. The country's only plain is here in the North, the huge Po valley, rich and fertile, where cattle graze and rice grows. Another massive chain cuts the country across vertically, the Apennines, from which countless valleys run down to the Adriatic sea on the eastern side and the Tyrrenian on the western.

Up to the Second World War these valleys, dotted with olive trees and covered with vines, were not connected by roads, and their inhabitants pursued their cultures and cooking unaware of what was going on 20 kilometres away on the other side of the mountains. Two such valleys, which run south almost next to each other, from Liguria into Tuscany, are the Lunigiana and the Garfagnana. I have found that many of the dishes of one of these valleys are quite unknown in the other. Another example from my own experience: when in a restaurant near Siena recently I suggested to the chef that I would like a soup of *farro* – emmer wheat. He told me that to have the best farro soup I should go to the nearby province of Lucca. '*Lì, si che la fanno buona.*' (That is where they make it well.) And why? Because that is where the best farro is grown.

But there are two vital factors that are present throughout all Italian cooking, in all regions. The first and foremost is the importance always given to using only top quality ingredients, which are respected and appreciated for what they are. What Italians want when they eat is for the flavour of the main ingredient to come through loud and clear. All the other ingredients are there to help this aim. In a soup, a risotto, a stew, a dish of vegetables or even a sauce for pasta, a basis of flavours supports and enhances the main ingredient.

The second factor, a direct consequence of the first, is the love Italians have for home cooking. There is no haute cuisine in Italy, only *cucina casalinga* (home cooking), and this obviously means *cucina regionale.* Even recipes developed by the greatest chefs can be traced back to home cooking. For instance, sauces are only used to dress staple foods such as pasta and polenta. They are not, as in the French cuisine, used as an addition to meat or fish. The precept of Italian cooking is that the ingredient must always be respected and appreciated in its own right.

This respect for the ingredients is common to most Mediterranean cooking. It is also ancient, as can be seen by reading the Sicilian cookery writer Archestratus, who lived in the fourth century BC, when Sicily was part of the Greek empire. He writes: 'Sauces of cheese or pickled herbs are added to inferior fish, but in general this cooking is not based on sauces, the preference being for the addition of oil and light herbs to the fish juices. Meats are prepared with equal simplicity. Ingredients are cooked with few flavourings.' Such flavouring as there is comes from the beginning of the cooking, often in the form of a *battuto* or a *soffritto*, which together form the point of departure of most dishes. Many dishes from these northern regions are 'slow food', cooked at length to suit the long cold evenings by the fire.

You might be surprised to see how very few pasta dishes there are in this book, but pasta – apart from the home-made egg pasta of Emilia-Romagna – is not part of the traditional cooking of most of these regions. No sun-dried tomatoes, no rocket or arugula, few aubergines [US eggplants] and even fewer mozzarella dishes. Here we are in the North where the palpable influences often come from beyond the Alps.

The book is divided into ten regions, of which seven are the real northern Italian regions. To these I have added three regions which geographically are part of central Italy; they are Tuscany, Umbria and Marche. These regions, plus Liguria, bring in the Mediterranean kind of food which is traditionally lacking in the northern regions. It is here that pasta and olive oil have prevailed over rice and butter, not only in the past 20 years of health-conscious eating, but for many centuries.

With the 160 recipes collected here I wanted to give an idea of the enormous variety of northern Italian cooking. All the recipes represent the cooking of the regions they belong to. Some are classic recipes, like the ossobuco alla milanese and the Genoese cappon magro, while others are less well known, given to me by local cooks and friends. I have also been careful to choose recipes that can be reproduced successfully in this country, bearing in mind the availability of ingredients and the fact that some dishes do not export as well as others. But mostly these are recipes for dishes I like, collected for this personal book. My remarks concerning the presentation of the dishes reflect the way dishes are served in an Italian family, each dish being brought to the table on a large platter for the diners to help themselves.

What I have also set out to do is to throw some light, through the food and the cooking of these northern regions, on the less obvious aspects of this part of Italy, which I understand so well and love so much.

Afterthoughts, Advice, Hints and Tips

My English friends have suggested that I should include some of the little points that crop up in my conversation with them and which, they say, are often unfamiliar to the non-professional cook. So I start by giving an explanation of some of the Italian culinary terms I use.

Battuto is a pounded mixture (the word comes from *battere* – to beat or pound). The battuto is the basis of most dishes, from a pasta sauce to a bean soup. In the old days, when people were blissfully unaware of cholesterol and the furring-up of arteries, a battuto always contained salted pork fat – *lardo* – which was pounded with onion, celery, carrot, parsley and other herbs, and sometimes garlic. Nowadays olive oil and butter is used instead of pork fat, with possibly a little pancetta (see below) or prosciutto. When I add pancetta or prosciutto I use a food processor, which does an excellent job in a whizz.

A battuto usually becomes a soffritto (see below), except when it is added *a crudo* (in the raw state) to a sauce or a soup.

Soffritto is the battuto which has been fried, or actually 'under-fried', which is what the word means. The battuto is sautéed in a saucepan or a frying pan over a gentle heat until the onion is soft. When using garlic, this should be added to the onion later, when the onion is nearly done, or the garlic will become too dark by the time the onion is soft. Only when the battuto contains pancetta or fatty prosciutto can the garlic be added at the same time.

A well-made soffritto is fundamental to the final taste of the dish.

Insaporire is to let the ingredients take up the flavour of the soffritto or of the sauce. This is a very important step in the making of a dish, and one to which the right amount of time should be devoted. In the making of a bolognese ragù, for instance, the minced meat added to the soffritto must be well *insaporito* on a lively heat, while turning it over and over, before the wine, stock or milk is added for the slow cooking that follows.

Now, here are some afterthoughts and tips, arranged in alphabetical order.

BUTTER

I always use unsalted butter because it has a more delicate flavour and it can be heated to a higher temperature. Salted butter contains impurities which turn black at a high temperature and give the dish a coarse taste. Salted butter is also totally unsuitable in pastry, cakes and desserts, and delicate sauces.

I never clarify butter, because it removes its character. When I need to heat butter to a higher temperature, I add some olive oil. The oil can be heated to a high temperature without burning.

CHILLI

In the northern regions of Italy chillies are used very little, if ever. They appear in Tuscany, Umbria and Marche. The kind used there are the small dried ones, reputedly among the hottest of them all. Even these vary, however, so I suggest that you experiment with what you buy, keeping in mind that Italian dishes are never very hot, the chilli being considered a flavouring to blend with others and not to provide an overriding fire.

DRIED PORCINI

I suggest that they should be soaked for about 1 hour. This may be longer than they need, but it depends on the porcini. If they are beautiful, large fresh-looking slices they will only need 20 minutes or so, but if they are small dried-up bits you must give them longer in the soaking water.

EGGS

To see whether your eggs are fresh, place them in a bowl of salted water. If they fall to the bottom and stay there, they are fresh and suitable to be used raw or with a minimum of cooking. If you keep your eggs in the fridge, remove them from it in good time and bring them back to room temperature before using them.

FISH

Wash any fish in a mixture of water and and wine vinegar to freshen it up. When you add boiling water or stock to a fish which is stewing, pour it gently into the side of the pan to avoid breaking the fish's skin

FLOUR

In all the recipes I suggest using Italian 00 flour, which is available in Italian specialist food shops and in some of the best supermarkets. It is a flour which is easier to knead when used for cakes, pastry, pasta-making etc. and it has a more fragrant flavour.

FORK VERSUS SPOON

Use a fork to stir sautéeing potatoes, carrots, courgettes etc. Spoons tend to break them.

GARLIC

To keep the garlic you brought back from Italy or France, peel it and put it in a jar. Cover with extra virgin olive oil and refrigerate. You can use the oil as well; it will be garlic-flavoured oil.

LEMON

Add a few drops of lemon juice to prevent the sugar from crystalising when you make caramel, and to egg whites to stabilise them before beating.

LEMONS AND ORANGES

In any recipe that calls for orange or lemon rind I strongly advise you to use unwaxed fruits. The wax sprayed on the fruit is toxic, and it does not wash off easily. If you cannot find unwaxed fruits, put your lemons or oranges in a sink of very hot water and scrub hard.

MEAT

Remove meat from the fridge in good time before cooking, so that it reaches room temperature.

OLIVE OIL

When you use olive oil as a base for a soffritto together with butter, you do not need to use an extra virgin olive oil. A plain olive oil will do, because it has less flavour and it is lighter.

Whenever necessary I have suggested which kind of extra virgin olive oil you should use in a recipe. Some of the Tuscan *fruttati* olive oils, for instance, are too strong to dress sea bass or a plate of seafood. These oils are also not suitable as cooking oils.

I use plain olive oil or groundnut oil [US peanut oil] for deep frying. These two oils can be heated to the high temperature needed for deep frying. I never re-use oil after frying, because with prolonged heating oil develops toxic substances.

ONIONS AND LEEKS

If your onions, spring onions or leeks are too strong, cut them in half and soak them for a couple of hours in salted water. Squeeze out, rinse and dry.

PANCETTA

Pancetta, from the belly of a pig, is a similar cut to streaky bacon, but is differently cured. In some supermarkets you can buy pancetta, smoked or unsmoked, already diced, in vacuum packs. This is ideal for a battuto. If you cannot find this, buy pancetta *stesa*, which is better for cooking than the sausage-shaped version called pancetta *arrotolata*. This latter is less fatty and can be eaten instead of salame or prosciutto.

PROSCIUTTO

If you have a friendly Italian shop-keeper, ask for the knuckle of a prosciutto, which you can usually get at half the price of the prosciutto itself. This end piece has the right proportion of lean meat to fat, necessary for battuti, sauce bases or for stuffing or larding. Ask the shop-keeper to cut all the rind off the knuckle (keep this for flavouring a pulse soup or a stew), and then you should cut the meat into chunks and keep them in the freezer.

For cooking I prefer to use prosciutto di San Daniele rather than prosciutto di Parma because it has a stronger flavour.

PULSES

Apart from lentils, all pulses need soaking overnight before cooking. Cook the pulses, covered with fresh water by at least 5cm/2in, on a very low heat or in a low oven. Add the salt at the end of the cooking because salt tends to crack the skin.

Chick-peas take longer to cook than any other pulses. Their skin is tougher, and in order to soften it I mix a paste made with 1 tablespoon of flour and 1 tablespoon of bicarbonate of soda [US baking soda] into the soaking water. Rinse thoroughly before cooking.

RISOTTO

With each recipe I have suggested the best kind of rice to use. Whatever the kind, however, it must be Italian because only Italian rice has the right combination of starches to allow the grain to absorb the liquid.

The amount of stock given in each risotto recipe is as close as possible to what you will need. But you might find that you have finished the stock before the risotto is ready. Do not despair – just add boiling water.

SALT

An unfashionable ingredient, alas, in spite of being essential in the diet of all animals. Salt is unfashionable because it is said to be bad for those with high blood pressure and heart disease.

Salt enhances the flavour of food. The right amount of salt – a personal choice – should be added at the beginning or during the cooking, in time for it to dissolve properly and flavour all the dish. If added at the table, not only is the result unsatisfactory, but also more salt usually has to be added to achieve the right seasoning. Always add salt to the water before you add pasta, rice or vegetables.

Good sea salt, such as Maldon, is best for cooking and for your health.

STOCK

Add the outside leaf of an onion to impart a lovely golden colour to your chicken stock.

STOCK OR BOUILLON CUBES

Italian cooks use stock cubes in quite a few dishes. This is not an aberration. Stock cubes in Italy are less strong than those sold in this country. However, some stock cubes are now available here that contain a minimum of monosodium glutamate or none at all, and they are really quite good. Remember that stock cubes are salty, so add less salt.

Having said that, I must stress that a good, traditional, well-flavoured home-made stock is invaluable, unsurpassable and totally necessary for clear soups and delicate risotti.

TOMATOES

Keep tomatoes out of the fridge, preferably on a sunny windowsill. They will become tastier and their all-too-often leathery skins will soften.

VEGETABLES

This is one of my hobby horses. When I came to England in the '50s the vegetables were cooked, and that meant boiled, to a mush. Then came the nouvelle cuisine revolution, and now the vegetables served in many restaurants are simply raw. For us Italians, crunchy French beans or al dente asparagus are anathema, and even worse are crunchy turnips, lentils or artichokes.

It is not possible to give a precise cooking time for vegetables, since it depends on their quality and freshness. It also depends on whether the vegetable has been grown in proper earth or in a hydroponic culture, in which case it will cook very quickly indeed. Also remember that the cooking time for stewing vegetables, in very little liquid, is longer than for boiling in plenty of water or for frying. Carrots, for instance, will be cooked in 20 minutes maximum in boiling water, but will take longer, even cut into sticks, if you cook them in oil and/or butter with a little stock or water added gradually.

VINEGAR

I am always surprised that so much has been written about the finer points of olive oils, and so little has been written about the importance of good wine vinegar. A salad dressed even with the best extra virgin olive oil can be ruined by a second-rate vinegar.

You will know a vinegar is good by its price – good vinegar is not cheap, because a good vinegar comes from a decent wine. The process of making the vinegar must not be accelerated by the addition of chemicals.

Wine vinegar is the only one traditionally used in Italy. Red and white wine vinegar differ mainly in colour, the flavour being similar.

WATER

Water plays an important part in Italian cooking. It is the added ingredient that allows a piece of meat or a dish of vegetables to cook for the right amount of time without burning, drying up or becoming too concentrated.

Water must be added very gradually so that it can be absorbed slowly, allowing the food to cook. Do not drown any ingredient in water, but use it to develop the flavour and to achieve the right point of 'doneness'.

WINE

I only suggest the use of a particular wine when that wine is crucial to the final taste of the dish. Otherwise I leave the choice to you. When you use red wine, use one with body but not too much tannin, as this would come out in the taste of the dish.

Use good wine. Any wine that is not good enough for drinking is not good enough for cooking. When you use poor wine you ruin the dish, something that is worse than when you are just drinking it.

Batteria di Cucina

I am always fascinated by what a cook – and by this I mean a person who likes cooking, not a professional – uses in his or her kitchen. Some people can produce a perfect dinner with only a few utensils and a minimum of space. These I admire. I need space, although I use few utensils, and even fewer gadgets, but I also need the right saucepan. Here are my suggestions for a *batteria di cucina* suitable for Italian cooking, to be added to a normal kitchen batterie.

The right saucepan is fundamental to the success of many dishes. First you will need one large saucepan with lid, for pasta, of at least 41/6pt [USA 4 qt] capacity, plus a large colander with feet. The saucepan does not need to be heavy. But you need a large heavy-based saucepan, or a flameproof casserole, for risotto, which can double up for making polenta. Two sauté pans with lids, a large and a medium, will come in handy for many dishes from meat to apples, as will an oval casserole for braising meat, and a heavy ridged cast-iron pan for grilling vegetables.

I also recommend two earthenware pots of the kind you can put directly on the heat – a large deep one for soups and pulses and a shallow one for stews and fish.

Now the gadgets. I could not cook without my *mezzaluna* (half-moon knife) for chopping, but maybe you can chop well and fast with a heavy, well-sharpened knife. Nor could I cook without my food mill, which I find essential for puréeing vegetables, sauces etc. I also use my food processor a lot, but not for puréeing. A flame diffuser and an electric carving knife are also invaluable.

That's all.

The Recipes

After an introduction to each region, the recipes are arranged in the order in which a meal is served in Italy: antipasti, primi (1st course), secondi (2nd course) and desserts, cakes and biscuits or cookies. But of course you can serve a traditional primo such as a risotto as a secondo, an antipasto as a primo or a secondo . . . and so on.

The recipes are usually for four persons. However, some recipes are for more because the dish can only be made successfully in larger quantities, for example a piece of braised meat, a cappon magro (page 138) or a cake. Do not try to reduce these. Prepare the lot and eat it in two or more sittings.

On the other hand you can always increase the quantities, and here is a rule to follow. You do not need to increase the quantity of the cooking fat in the same proportion as the other ingredients. Some of the fat, say 1 tablespoon of the oil or of the butter, is there 'for the pan'. This rule does not apply, of course, when for capacity reasons you have to use two saucepans.

Measures and Quantities

When you follow a recipe, use just one system of measures – metric, imperial or American cups – all through the recipe.

All spoons are meant to be level, and 1 tablespoon=15ml, 1 teaspoon=5ml. A set of measuring spoons is a great help to a cook. A set includes 5 spoons which measure from 'a pinch' to 1 tablespoon.

I have given specific egg sizes in some recipes. Where no size is specified you can use size 2 or 3 (US extra large or large), whichever is in your refrigerator.

It is important to pay attention to the proportions of the various ingredients used. This will teach you to achieve the 'Italian flavour', and having learnt that, you will no longer need to follow a recipe slavishly. However, I would also stress that good cooking requires precision, care and patience. Creativity comes later, just as in any other art or craft.

LOMBARDIA

Gastronomically speaking, I am convinced that Lombardy is the most interesting region of Italy. You might well think, 'She would say that, being Milanese,' but I have tried to dispel any feelings of chauvinism before coming to this conclusion. And, after all, 'interesting' does not necessarily mean 'best'.

There are nine provinces in Lombardy, and there are nine different cuisines. In the two years prior to finishing this book I have been all over Lombardy, visiting various towns, many food producers and, of course, eating my way from Valtellina in the North to the river Po in the South, and from the eastern bank of the Ticino river in the West to the western bank of Lake Garda in the East. The rustic *polenta taragna* from the mountains behind Bergamo in the North is miles away from the aristocratic elegance of the ravioli di zucca of Mantua, ravioli stuffed with pumpkin, amaretti and mostarda di Cremona and heightened by a splash of Grappa. The *bresaola* cured in the caves of Valtellina, with its clean taste of beef, redolent of the German heritage, is another example of the characteristics of that northern area, as is the smoked salame made from venison and beef.

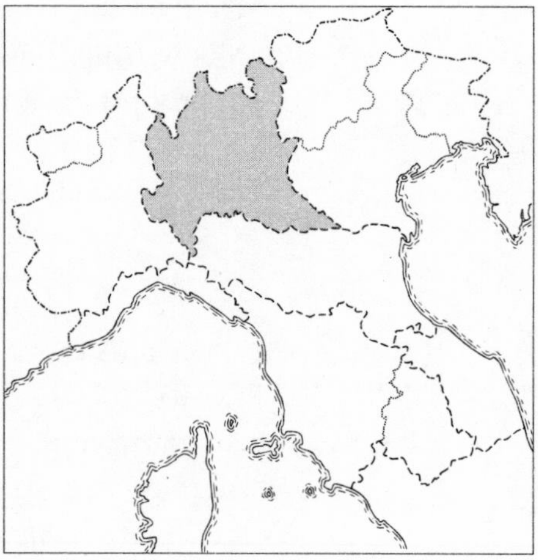

Valtellina is the longest Alpine valley, stretching eastwards from the northern shores of Lake Como to the Stelvio peak, 3500 metres high. This spectacular valley was loved by Leonardo da Vinci, who even mentioned the good *osterie* (inns) you can find along the route. As in other northern valleys the food is that of mountain people. The home-made pasta, pizzoccheri (see page 25), is made with buckwheat flour, a grain that grows strongly up to 800 metres. The pasta is layered with potatoes and cabbage, locally grown, and dressed with *bitto*, a local cheese, and the magnificent local butter.

Another local cheese used a lot in cooking is *casera*, a semi-hard cheese with that unmistakable flavour of the cow-shed. With it the locals prepare *sciatt*, a sort of fritter made with buckwheat and white flour to which shredded casera and Grappa are added. The best sciatt I ate were made at the delightful Hotel della Posta in Sondrio, the capital of Valtellina, where with Philippa Davenport I spent a gastronomic week as guests of the local Chamber of Commerce. The most enjoyable thing, after the sciatt, was the time spent with the owner of the hotel, Renato Sozzani, talking food and eating the splendid meals he provided. He is the author of a book on the food of the valley, a real connoisseur, the sort who muses with nostalgia over past meals such as the pizzoccheri eaten on, say the 6th November 1975, which were better than the ones he had on the 14th January 1984. The Italian author Prezzolini compares the gastronomic memories of the Italians to the theatrical memories of the British, who can compare the production of a 1959 *Hamlet* with that of 20 years later.

The dairy products of Valtellina are especially good because of the pasture on which the cows graze, and also because of the particular breed of cows. They are the least cow-like cows I know; they are small, strong, nervous and quick as they move uphill from the valleys, where they spend the winter, to the Alpeggi, the meadows high in the mountains where they stay from June to September.

In fact, all Lombardy is renowned for its dairy products. The list of local cheeses is long and varied, from a soft sweet *stracchino* (one of my favourite cheeses, especially when eaten with mostarda di Cremona) to the piquant gorgonzola di montagna, the old-fashioned gorgonzola beloved of cheese connoisseurs. The creamy mascarpone from south Lombardy has conquered the world under the ubiquitous guise of tiramisù. But the real mascarpone, and not the UHT long-life product that travels the world, bought in situ and available only during the winter, must be enjoyed neat, just as it is, in all its virgin purity. That was how I enjoyed the mascarpone and the ricotta piemontese that a woman brought to our flat in Milan every Tuesday during the autumn. She was dressed all in black, which contrasted sharply with the whiteness of her wares, wrapped in immaculate muslin on a large flat wicker basket. The mascarpone and ricotta we bought were weighed on her steelyard, placed on a plate and carried to the kitchen to be served and finished that same day.

The flavour of these cheeses lingers in my memory, as does that of the herbs and wild greens brought to the house during the spring by Lina. Lina came from nearby Segrate, now a spaghetti junction of motorways next to the asphalt jungle of Linate airport. Lina's baskets were overflowing with borage, sage, dandelions, nettles, sorrel, and masses and masses of parsley.

As the best basil comes from Liguria, so the best parsley comes from Lombardy. I can still remember the taste of the salsa verde made every Monday to go with the *lesso* (boiled beef). I hardly touched the beef, but gorged myself first on the deliciously tangy salsa verde and then went on to savour the sweet piquancy of the mostarda di Cremona, the other accompaniment to the lesso.

Up to last year I was sure that the best local dishes were all to be enjoyed in winter, probably because I have spent more time in Lombardy during the winter months. But then, in 1993, I was in Pavia, Mantua and the vicinity in

August and September, and I discovered a world I had forgotten. The beautiful large yellow sweet peppers of Voghera are served grilled in an antipasto or used to make one of the freshest and most colourful risotti. The river shrimps are also used in a risotto, or just boiled and eaten like that, with lemon juice. And the frogs, fried whole (headless of course), make the most succulent and crunchy antipasto I know. Alas, they are rapidly disappearing, along with the river shrimps, which survive only in some private estates.

I watched frog fishing one hot August afternoon, alongside the canals of the rice paddies in that flat country, geometrically divided by lines of Lombard plane trees that remind one of a Mondrian painting. It is a still, hazy countryside, silent apart from the continuous screeching of the cicadas and the buzzing of insects. Men with very long rods stood silently on the banks of these tiny canals, looking at me disapprovingly in fear that my presence would frighten away their prey. But the catch was small, hardly enough even for a risotto, one of the men told me disconsolately.

The fishermen fishing in the lakes usually have better luck. I was told that the lakes are less polluted now than they were a few years ago. At the trattorie beside the lakes perch and tench have come back, to be served in many ways, the traditional being *a cotoletta* – breaded and fried in butter. Butter, which Julius Caesar is said to have eaten for the first time in the Po valley on his return from the Gallic wars, is still the right cooking fat for traditional dishes. I felt very humbled when in Casteggio, near Voghera, at the Trattoria Da Lina I asked if their delicious risotto coi peperoni was made with olive oil. Lina, the attractive owner-chef, looked at me in bewilderment. 'Oil? Certainly not. This is an old local recipe.' I didn't dare to tell her that I, a Lombard, make an excellent risotto coi peperoni with oil.

Olive oil, up to the Second World War, was only used by well-to-do families to dress salad, instead of the more plebeian rape-seed oil or walnut oil, which was otherwise used to polish furniture. After this, the walnut trees of Lombardy were all felled to make enough furniture to replace that destroyed during the war. Because of this the Lombards began to use olive oil more extensively.

Another strong influence was given after the war by the Tuscan restaurateurs, who opened their trattorie, with the flask of Chianti on the table, just as they did in the '50s in London. Then, in the '60s, the southern labourers came north with their Mediterranean diet, and the Lombards began to eat and enjoy the food of southern Italy – healthier, yes, but less varied. Some took up aubergines [US eggplant] and rocket [US arugula] and forgot the sweet onions of Brianza, the deep-flavoured Savoy cabbages, the rich pumpkins of

Mantua and even the earthy-tasting potatoes that Alessandro Volta – he of voltage fame – had brought from France and grown first on his land in Brianza.

But these good things are not totally forgotten. Italians are too chauvinistic where food is concerned. Lombards still believe that the best salame is the salame of Varzi in southern Lombardy, and that the best luganega is made in and around Monza. Not long ago I visited an artisanal factory making pork sausages where the luganega was still flavoured with wine and Parmesan, as in the old days.

In Milan you can enjoy some of the best Lombard cooking. After years when the local cooking seemed to be swamped by the invasion of chefs from Tuscany, Naples, Bologna and Puglia, I find that now Milanese and Lombard cooking, with its rich *cassoeula* (page 40), its *polpette* (page 42) and its risotti, is triumphantly back on the menu.

My good friend and mentor, the octogenarian food historian Massimo Alberini, feels very encouraged by the turn taken by the cooking in restaurants. He is quite sure that there is a strong renaissance of traditional regional cooking which is going to stay. The lovely thing about Alberini is that in spite of his long memory of the food of the past, he has good words to say about the present state of affairs. He pointed out to me the wealth of exotic ingredients available now and on display in the Milanese food shops. Japanese-inspired dishes sit next to *calzoni* from Puglia, *gravad lax* from Sweden or *caponata* from Sicily.

Yet the bulk of the most popular dishes are from old Lombardy, very similar to the dishes that were sold in Zanocco, our local delicatessen, now defunct, whose prosciutto was reputed to be even better than that of Peck. I remember the ritual of the daily shopping with my mother, who unlike most of her contemporaries used to go herself *a fare la spesa.* She used to say that, '*un buon pranzo comincia nel negozio*' (a good dinner begins in the shop), and off we went to be fêted by the local shops. To me it was just like stepping on to a stage. First, Signora Bianchi in Via Montenapoleone (just opposite where we lived in Via Gesù) who presided, with her crinkly hair à la Queen Mother, over her bread, sweet breads, biscotti, focaccie and tortelli. Then Zanocco, where chubby Arturo always gave me a slice of prosciutto, and then to Pasini the grocer, my favourite stop. In those days, when food was not prepacked, a grocer's shop was the most intense experience for the sense of smell. The greengrocer in Via Borgospesso, on the other hand, was a delight to the eyes with its assortment of fruit and vegetables which quickly told you which month it was. And just further on at the corner of Via Spiga there was the man selling *calde arrosto* (roast chestnuts). I am sure I learnt how to shop from those early days. As the late Jane Grigson so aptly puts it in her *Fish Cookery*, 'Children are coloured indelibly by their mother's expertise – or lack of it. Conversations with butcher, baker, nurseryman, are picked up by a pair of ears at counter level and stored in the infant lumber room.'

Somehow my fondest memories of Milan are all autumnal, unlike those of Stendhal, who has described Lombardy mostly in the summer. Let me borrow some lines from Stendhal, who loved Lombardy, its food and its women, lines that are very evocative of the varied appeal of this region. 'We are at the top of the hill; to the right a splendid view: fertile planes and two or three lakes; to the left another splendid view, which in detail is the opposite of the other. . . This beautiful Lombardy, with all the luxurious appeal of its greenery, its riches and its endless horizons.'

PIZZOCCHERI Ⓥ

Buckwheat Pasta with Potato and Cabbage

Until 10 years ago pizzoccheri were only eaten in Valtellina, an Alpine valley running east from Lake Como. Although they were mainly eaten by the locals, pizzoccheri were also consumed by the hordes of skiers who, every weekend, go up the slopes and down again, thus burning up the energy derived from the huge quantities of pizzoccheri ingested at every meal. But now pizzoccheri appear at smart hostesses' dinners, on the menu in restaurants in Milan and further afield, and are even produced industrially.

Pizzoccheri are made from the only cereal, buckwheat, which can grow in mountainous regions. The acrid-smokey flavour of buckwheat, which used to be despised by our grandparents because of its association with poverty, has now become an emblem of the good earthy food appreciated by gourmets.

Centuries ago buckwheat was grown in all the Alpine regions and both pasta and polenta were made with it. Then maize arrived from the New World and supplanted the old staple. Soon polenta was being made with maize, and pasta, imported from further south, was made with white flour. Nowadays buckwheat is only grown in Valtellina and Carnia, in the eastern Alps.

Recently I saw pizzoccheri being made in the ideal setting and by the ideal maker. Laura, the pizzoccheri-maker in question, is a dark local Ceres, living in a house surrounded by fields where cats, dogs and horses roam happily around. On the way there we drove through some fields of buckwheat. It is an unimpressive plant, with heart-shaped leaves and a tall reddish stem carrying the dark seeds. Laura had just had a baby, so she seemed to knead and roll the dough with an even more gentle and loving movement.

In the local tradition the dinner consisted of a large platter of different local salami, and then an ever larger platter of pizzoccheri, followed by a crostata – a jam tart, the most usual country sweet. Perfect. We could gorge ourselves on pizzoccheri, which oddly enough are not over-filling; nourishing, yes, but you certainly do not feel blown up after two serious helpings. I had many excellent plates of pizzoccheri after that, but none so perfect as those made by Laura. And I was set to wondering how much the atmosphere can influence the palate.

THE RECIPE

The cheese traditionally used in this dish is *bitto*, a local cows' milk cheese which has a complex herby flavour and which melts very well. After a certain amount of trial and error I have decided that a good substitute is fontina. Fontina can be bought in specialist Italian shops or top supermarkets. If you cannot get it, buy a French St Paulin which has good melting properties and a not too dissimilar flavour.

Buckwheat flour is sold in most health-food shops, though I have noticed that it varies considerably from one brand to another. Some buckwheat flours are easier to knead than others, so you might have to vary the amount of white wheat flour. The pasta here is made with a dough enriched with egg and milk, whereas originally the flours were only blended with water.

Pizzoccheri are made with Savoy cabbage, Swiss chard or green beans, whichever are in season at the time. I have also successfully used Brussels sprout tops and spring greens, whose bitterness is a good match for the smokey earthiness of the pasta. You can also use a mixture of these vegetables.

SERVES 6

FOR THE PASTA

200g/7oz [US 2 cups] buckwheat flour
100g/3½oz [US scant 1 cup] flour, preferably Italian 00, approximate weight
1 tsp salt
1 size-2 egg [US extra-large egg]
120ml/4fl oz warm milk, approximately

FOR THE DRESSING

225g/8oz potato, cut into cubes
salt and freshly ground black pepper
300g/10oz Savoy cabbage, cut into 1cm/½in strips
75g/2½oz [US 5 tbsp] unsalted butter
1 small onion, very finely chopped
1 garlic clove, very finely chopped
6 fresh sage leaves, torn into pieces
150g/5oz fontina, cut into slivers
75g/2½oz [US ½ cup + 2 tbsp] freshly grated Parmesan

First make the dough. Mix together the two flours and the salt on the work surface. Make a well in the middle and break the egg into it. Using a fork, begin to bring in the flour from the wall, while slowly adding the milk. Do not add all the milk at once, since you may not need all of it. Or, depending on the absorbency of the flour and the humidity of the atmosphere, you may need to add a little warm water as well, or a couple of tablespoons of white flour. The dough should be soft and elastic, although it is much stickier and wetter than a dough made with only white flour and eggs. Knead for 5 minutes and then wrap the dough in a linen towel or cling film and let it rest for a minimum of 1 hour. I have sometimes made my dough the day before and kept it overnight in the fridge.

When the time comes to cook the dish, roll out the dough, either by hand to a thickness of about 2mm/1/12in, or using a hand-cranked pasta machine, pushing the strips through the rollers up to the last but two notches. You have to flour the strips quite often when rolling them out. Cut the rolled-out pasta into pappardelle-size noodles, about 2 × 10cm/¾ × 4in. Lay the strips out on clean cloths, not letting them touch each other. (You can prepare all this a day in advance. The next day the pizzoccheri will be dried, but just as good.)

Put a large saucepan containing about 41/7pt [US 4qt] of water on the heat. Add 1½ tablespoons of salt and the potato and bring to the boil. After 10 minutes or so, when the potato cubes begin to soften at the edges, throw in the cabbage and continue cooking for about 5 minutes, until the cabbage has lost its crunchiness. Now it is time to slide in the pizzoccheri. Mix well and cook for 5 minutes after the water has come back to the boil.

While all this preparation is going on, put the butter, onion, garlic and sage in a small heavy-based pan and cook gently, stirring very often and letting the onion became pale gold. Fish out the sage.

Heat the oven to 180°C/350°F/Gas Mark 4.

Butter a shallow oven dish. When the pizzoccheri are done, drain the whole mixture in a colander. Spoon a ladleful or two of the pasta mixture over the bottom of the dish and add a little of the two cheeses, a little of the onion-butter sauce and plenty of pepper. Add more pasta and dress it again in the same way until the whole lot is dressed. Toss thoroughly. Cover with foil and put in the oven for 5 minutes, so that the cheese will melt properly.

Serve with plenty of red wine from the Valtellina, such as a Sassella or a marvellous Inferno, if you can find them!

Risotto alla Milanese
Risotto with Saffron

In my previous books I have written at length about this favourite dish of mine, one of the pillars of Milanese cooking. So here I'll skip the preamble and go straight to the recipe.

Like all over-popular dishes, risotto alla milanese (known in its native city as risotto giallo, or yellow risotto) has been the subject of endless variations. This is my recipe, which has been in use in my family for generations, or at least for as long as my father (who would now be 104) could remember. He insisted that risotto giallo was made like this. The only liberty I am taking is to suggest the use of pancetta instead of bone-marrow, which is difficult to come by these days. It is not the same, but a nice fatty unsmoked pancetta is quite a good substitute. Prosciutto can also be used, but it must be fatty and not the fatless, and far less tasty, prosciutto one usually gets in this country. (See my tips on prosciutto on page 15.)

If you can, use Carnaroli rice. Otherwise use a good quality Arborio. The better the rice, the longer it takes to cook. In Italy we cook Carnaroli for 18 minutes from the time you begin to add the stock. Arborio will take 1 or 2 minutes less.

SERVES 4

1.2l/2pt [US 5 cups] home-made meat stock (page 230)
1 shallot or ½ small onion, very finely chopped
60g/2oz beef-marrow, unsmoked pancetta or fatty prosciutto, very finely chopped
75g/2½oz [US 5 tbsp] butter
350g/12oz [US 1¾ cups] Italian rice, preferably Carnaroli
120ml/4fl oz red wine
⅓ tsp powdered saffron of 1 tsp saffron strands
salt and freshly ground pepper
60g/2oz [US ½ cup] freshly grated Parmesan

Bring the stock to simmering point and keep it at a very low simmer.

Put the shallot, beef-marrow (or the substitutes) and 60g/2oz [US 4 tbsp] of the butter in a saucepan and sauté until the shallot is soft and translucent. Add the rice and stir until well coated with fat. Pour in the wine, boil for 2 minutes, stirring constantly, and then pour in 200ml/7fl oz of the simmering stock. Cook until nearly all the stock has been absorbed and then add another 150ml/5fl oz of stock. The risotto should cook at a steady lively simmer. Continue adding the stock in small quantities like this, waiting for one to be nearly all absorbed before adding the next.

About half-way through the cooking add the saffron dissolved in a little hot stock. When the rice is ready – it should be soft and creamy, not mushy or runny – taste and adjust the seasoning.

Draw off the heat and add the rest of the butter and 3 tablespoons of the Parmesan. Leave to rest for a minute or two and then give the risotto a good stir. This is what we call the ***mantecatura***, the final touch, to make the risotto even creamier. Serve immediately, with the rest of the cheese handed separately.

RISOTTO AL GORGONZOLA Ⓥ

Risotto with Gorgonzola

This old recipe from Lombardy is for the quintessential creamy risotto, yet the flavour is unexpectedly piquant. The cheese used must be real gorgonzola and not Dolcelatte, a new type of cheese created by Galbani for the British market, which does not have enough oomph. Parmesan is never served with this risotto.

SERVES 4 AS A FIRST COURSE OR 3 AS A MAIN COURSE

4 shallots, very finely chopped
60g/2oz [US 4 tbsp] unsalted butter
salt and freshly ground black pepper
1.2l/2pt [US 5 cups] vegetable or light meat stock (pages 230–1)
300g/10oz [US 1½ cups] Italian rice, preferably Carnaroli
150ml/5fl oz dry white wine
250g/9oz gorgonzola piccante or di montagna, cut into small pieces
a lovely bunch of fresh flat-leaf parsley, chopped

Put the shallots and the butter in a large, heavy-based saucepan. Add a pinch of salt to release the moisture in the shallots, thus preventing them from browning, and sauté gently for about 7 minutes or until soft and translucent, stirring frequently.

Meanwhile, heat the stock in a separate saucepan to simmering point. Keep it simmering all through the cooking of the rice.

Add the rice to the shallots and stir well, coating the grains in the butter. Sauté until the rice is partly translucent. Turn the heat up and pour over the wine. Let it bubble away, stirring constantly, and then begin to add the simmering stock little by little, in the usual way for a risotto.

After 15 minutes, mix in the Gorgonzola. Stir constantly until the cheese has melted and then continue cooking the rice, adding the rest of the simmering stock little by little. If you have used up all the stock use a little boiling water to finish the cooking.

When the rice is al dente, season with plenty of pepper. Taste and if necessary season also with salt, although the saltiness in the cheese and stock may be enough.

Transfer to a heated bowl and sprinkle with the parsley. Serve immediately.

TORTELLI DI CREMA Ⓥ

Ravioli from Crema

Crema, a small town in south-east Lombardy, boasts two things, and rightly so: a splendid square with the Duomo and a Renaissance arcade, and these tortelli. For years I had wanted to go to Crema, more for the tortelli, which are made nowhere else, than for the square, the likes of which are two a penny in provincial Italian towns. The best tortelli, I was told, were made by Maria Pia Triassi at her restaurant, the Cral Ferriera, in the outskirts of the town. And so that is precisely where I went, and I was certainly not disappointed.

The tortelli di Crema are typical of the best in the cooking of southern Lombardy, where the flavours of the Renaissance are still strongly discernible. People there seem to keep the gastronomic glories of the past in their repertoire more than anywhere else. The subtle taste resulting from the combination of sweet and savoury is very well defined in this dish.

Maria Pia uses a special kind of amaretti that contain a small amount of chocolate. Being a perfectionist she warned me against using other kinds of amaretti, but I liked the tortelli di Crema so much that I was prepared to experiment with other amaretti. And this is my adaptation of her recipe.

THE RECIPE

This is not a dish you can prepare in half an hour, nor is it a dish you can serve to anyone. It has an unusual flavour that some people might not appreciate.

I make small ravioli, which is the traditional way to make them. Nowadays most restaurants, especially in Britain, serve very large ravioli, 2 or 3 per person. This is to save labour, but the taste of the ravioli changes, often for the worse, due to the difference in proportion between stuffing and pasta.

The pasta for the tortelli di Crema is a 'poor man's' pasta, i.e. made with eggs and water. Because it is very soft it goes better with the stuffing. But if you are more familiar with the more common *pasta emiliana* containing only eggs, make this by all means. Use amaretti di Saronno; they have the right amount of bitter almonds for this dish.

MAKES ABOUT 60 RAVIOLI, ENOUGH FOR 5 TO 6 PEOPLE

FOR THE PASTA

400g/14oz [US 3½ cups] Italian 00 flour
1 tsp salt
2 size-2 eggs [US extra-large eggs]
1 tbsp oil

FOR THE STUFFING

1 tbsp sultanas [US golden raisins]
1 tbsp chopped candied citron
2 tbsp dry Marsala or dry sherry
100g/3½oz amaretti di Saronno
1 tsp grated dark chocolate
75g/2½oz [US ½ cup + 2 tbsp] freshly grated Parmesan
1 size-2 egg [US extra-large egg]
3 tbsp fine white breadcrumbs
4 tbsp mascarpone
salt and freshly ground black pepper

FOR THE DRESSING

75g/2½oz [US 5 tbsp] unsalted butter
1 fresh sage sprig
60g/2oz [US ½ cup] freshly grated Parmesan

First prepare the stuffing. Soak the sultanas and the citron in the Marsala for 20 minutes or so.

Put the amaretti in the food processor and process to fine crumbs. Turn into a bowl and add all the other ingredients. Mix very thoroughly – a job best done with your hands. Add also the sultanas, citron peel and Marsala. Season with salt and pepper to taste. Cover the bowl with cling film and put in the fridge to chill. (It is much easier to work on chilled stuffing.)

While the stuffing is chilling make the pasta. Put the flour and the salt on the work surface. Make a well and break the eggs into it. Add about 7 to 8 tablespoons of lukewarm water. Beat with a fork, gradually drawing the flour in from the walls of the well. When most of the flour is incorporated, begin to knead with your hands. (You can do all the foregoing in a food processor.) When you have properly kneaded the dough, wrap it in cling film and leave aside to rest for at least half an hour.

After a rest for the dough (and for you, perhaps) give the dough a good kneading, and cut off about one eighth to begin work on. Keep the rest of the dough well wrapped in cling film. Roll out a sheet of dough up to the last but one notch of the hand-cranked pasta machine, or, if you are making the pasta by hand, to a thickness of about ½mm/⅕0in.

Trim the dough to a strip 10cm/4in wide. Dot with generous teaspoons of stuffing, at intervals of 5cm/2in, all down the strip, setting the stuffing 2.5cm/1in back from one of the long edges in a line parallel to the edge. Fold the other long edge over the stuffing to join the first edge. Trim the joined edges with a fluted pastry wheel and then, with the same wheel, cut across between each mound of stuffing. Separate the squares, squeeze out any air and seal the ravioli all around. If necessary, moisten your fingers to seal the edges better. Spread the ravioli out on clean dry linen towels, making sure they do not touch, to prevent them sticking. Making ravioli sounds very difficult when you read the instructions, but it is quite easy once you are actually making them.

Proceed to work on the next eighth of the dough, and then the next, until you have no stuffing, or pasta, left. If you are not cooking the ravioli straight away, leave them to dry, turning them over two or three times so that they dry evenly.

Put a large, wide saucepan full of water on the heat. Bring to the boil and then add 1 tablespoon of oil and 1½ tablespoons of salt. Gently drop in the ravioli. Stir gently and bring the water back to the boil. Lower the heat so that the water does not boil too fiercely – otherwise the ravioli might break – and cook until al dente, about 2 to 5 minutes depending on the thickness of the dough and the dryness of the ravioli. The best way to tell if they are done is to cut a bit off the edge and taste it.

While the ravioli are cooking, melt the butter for the dressing with the sage in a small saucepan.

Lift the ravioli out of the water with a slotted spoon, pat dry gently with kitchen paper towel and transfer them to a heated shallow dish. Pour some melted butter and sprinkle some cheese on each ladleful of ravioli, so that they will all be well dressed. This is the only and the best dressing for these extraordinary tortelli.

Rotolo di Spinaci Ⓥ

Spinach Roll

There is a more usual rotolo di spinaci made in Emilia-Romagna with pasta dough. My mother used to make her rotolo with potato dough, which I think is much nicer, and here is her recipe.

You can also dress the rotolo with a good tomato sauce (see page 228), or with the fontina sauce on page 65, all perfect in their different ways.

SERVES 8

800g/1¾lb floury potatoes, such as King Edwards, as nearly the same size as possible
40g/1½oz shallots, finely chopped
150g/5oz [US 10 tbsp] unsalted butter
1.2kg/2½lb spinach, cooked, very thoroughly drained and chopped
180g/6oz [US ¾ cup] ricotta cheese
125g/4oz [US 1 cup] freshly grated Parmesan
a large pinch of grated nutmeg
1 size-2 egg plus 2 egg yolks [US extra-large eggs]
salt and freshly ground black pepper
1½ tsp baking powder
200g/7oz [US 1¾ cups] Italian 00 flour
1 tbsp coarsely chopped fresh sage leaves
2 garlic cloves, bruised

Scrub the potatoes and boil them in their skins in plenty of lightly salted water until tender, about 25 minutes.

While the potatoes are cooking, prepare the filling. Sauté the shallots in a third of the butter for 4 to 5 minutes, until soft. Add the spinach and cook for a further 2 minutes, stirring constantly. Transfer the spinach mixture to a bowl and add the ricotta, half the Parmesan, the nutmeg, one egg yolk, and some salt and pepper. Mix very thoroughly.

When the potatoes are cooked, drain them thoroughly. As soon as they are cool enough to handle, peel them and push through the small disc of a food mill, or a potato ricer, straight on to a work surface. (Do not use a blender or a food processor because these will not incorporate air into the purée, to make it light.) Make a well in the centre of the potato purée, drop in the whole egg and the second egg yolk and add a little salt, the baking powder and most of the flour. Knead for about 5 minutes, adding more flour if necessary: the dough should be soft, smooth and slightly sticky. Shape the dough into a ball.

Flour your work surface and roll out the potato dough into a rectangle about 35 × 30cm/14 × 12in. Spread the spinach filling over it evenly, leaving a 2cm/¾in border all around. Roll up the potato dough into a Swiss roll [US jelly roll] shape. Wrap the roll tightly in muslin or cheesecloth and tie at each end.

Fill a fish kettle or oval-shaped flameproof casserole three-quarters full of water and bring to the boil. Add salt, and gently lower the roll into the water. Return the water to the boil and simmer, partly covered, for 30 to 40 minutes. See that the water keeps a constant simmer. Remove the roll from the water, unwrap and leave to cool.

Heat the oven to 200°C/400°F/Gas Mark 6.

Cut the roll into 2cm/¾in slices and place them, slightly overlapping, in an ovenproof dish. Melt the remaining butter and add the chopped sage leaves and the garlic. When the butter begins to turn golden, draw the pan off the heat. Fish out and discard the garlic. Pour the butter mixture over the slices. Bake in the oven for 15 minutes. About 5 minutes before the reheating is finished, sprinkle with half of the remaining Parmesan.

Let the dish rest for a couple of minutes before serving, with the remainder of the cheese.

POLENTA TARAGNA Ⓥ

Buckwheat Polenta with Butter and Cheese

This is a speciality of the Valtellina and the other Alpine valleys that run between Bergamo in Lombardy and Merano in Alto Adige. A certain amount of buckwheat flour is substituted for maize (polenta) flour, thus producing a sweeter, nuttier polenta. Laced with cheese and butter, it makes a magnificent dish that is served by itself as a first course. The cheese used should ideally be a local soft cheese called scimud. I have also used Caerphilly, Wensleydale and Lancashire, all of which have a similar texture and just a little of that tangy flavour needed in a good polenta taragna.

I use two-thirds maize (polenta) flour to one-third buckwheat, but you could make it half and half for an earthier, nuttier flavour. As with the usual polenta, you must use a deep but wide saucepan.

SERVES 4 TO 5

250g/9oz maize (polenta) flour [US 2 cups coarse cornmeal]

125g/4oz [US 1¼ cups] buckwheat flour

2 tsp salt

100g/3½oz [US 7 tbsp] unsalted butter, cut into pieces

100g/3½oz cheese (see introduction), cut into slices

Heat the oven to 180°C/350°F/Gas Mark 4.

Heat 2l/3½pt [US 2qt] of water to just boiling point. (I find that the flours are less likely to form lumps if you add them when the water is not yet boiling.)

Meanwhile, mix the two flours and the salt together. When the water is nearly simmering – it will begin to form bubbles at the edge – draw the pan off the heat and add the flour, letting it fall between your closed fingers, fistful by fistful, while you beat the mixture in the pan hard with the other hand. When all the flour has been added, put the pan back on the heat and cook, beating constantly, until the mixture is bubbling hard like an erupting vulcano. Buckwheat polenta needs longer cooking than plain polenta, so I advise you to use the method for 'polenta made in the oven' described on page 234.

Butter an oven dish very well and pour the polenta mixture into it. Place a piece of buttered foil on the top and bake for at least 1½ hours.

When done, beat in the butter pieces and then the cheese. Continue to stir hard until the cheese and the butter have melted. Serve immediately in a heated large bowl.

Razza in Salsa d'Acciuga

Skate with Anchovy Sauce

All I know of the origins of this recipe is that it comes from my family, and my family comes – almost entirely – from northern Italy. Skate is mainly eaten in the north of Italy, and in fact the way this dish is cooked points to a French influence. Thus, the fish is poached in a French court-bouillon, and the sauce, which contains no tomatoes, is thickened with flour.

Skate is easy to find on the market and it is usually fresh and good. I was very pleased to read in Alastair Little's excellent book *Keep It Simple* that he, like me, finds that the ammonia smell, sometimes detectable in a piece of skate, remains through the cooking and ruins the taste of the fish. This is contrary to what some experts say, which is that this unpleasant smell is a sign of the freshness of the fish and will disappear when the fish is cooked. My advice is to smell your skate before you buy it!

SERVES 4

900g/2lb skate, cut into 4 portions by the fishmonger
1.2l/2pt [US 5 cups] fish stock (page 231)

FOR THE SAUCE

30g/1oz [US 2 tbsp] unsalted butter
2 tbsp olive oil
1 garlic clove, bruised
1 layer of sweet onion
60g/2oz canned anchovy fillets, drained and chopped
2 tsp flour
3 tbsp capers
2 tbsp chopped fresh flat-leaf parsley
1 tbsp lemon juice
freshly ground black pepper

Poach the fish in the simmering fish stock for 8 to 10 minutes. When the fish is done, drain it and keep warm. Reserve the cooking liquid.

To make the sauce, choose a sauté pan large enough to hold the fish later in a single layer. Heat the butter and the oil and throw in the garlic and the onion layer. When you begin to smell the aroma of the garlic and onion, fish them out and discard them. Turn the heat down and add the anchovies. Press them against the bottom of the pan to reduce them to a mash.

Mix in the flour and then add 150ml/5fl oz of the fish cooking liquid. Cook over gentle heat for about 5 minutes, stirring constantly and adding, if necessary, a little more fish liquid until you get a fluid sauce, like single cream [US light cream].

Rinse the capers and add to the pan together with the parsley, lemon juice and plenty of pepper. Taste and correct seasoning. Carefully transfer the fish to the pan and heat it up in the sauce, while you spoon the sauce over it. Five minutes should be enough.

Now that the dish is ready you can divide it among the individual plates. As fish is not easy to transfer, it may be an idea to do this in the calm of the kitchen with the right tool, rather than at the table with everybody watching. But if it is family, and your pan is attractive, bring this to the table. It is always more convivial and homely to serve food from a single large container.

COSTE AL GRATIN Ⓥ

Gratin of Swiss Chard Stalks

Although a gratin of vegetables might be considered a French dish, it is also a very familiar feature of Lombard cooking. Very often, during my youth in Milan, our dinner consisted of a soup, a gratin dish and fruit to finish. The gratin could be of fennel, spinach or courgettes [US zucchini], or – the best to my mind – of Swiss chard, as in this recipe.

The amount of Swiss chard you have to buy depends on the size of the stalks. As a guide, you should buy twice the weight you need for the recipe. The delicious leaves can be used in the same way as spinach, as a vegetable or in a filling, or to make the dish on page 135.

SERVES 3 TO 4

enough Swiss chard to yield about 700g/1½lb of stalks

salt and freshly ground black pepper

a béchamel sauce (page 228), made with 60g/2oz [US 4 tbsp] unsalted butter, 40g/1½oz [US ¼ cup] flour and 450ml/15fl oz full fat milk

4 tbsp freshly grated Parmesan

grated nutmeg

butter for the dish

1 tbsp dried breadcrumbs

15g/½oz [US 1 tbsp] unsalted butter

Wash the Swiss chard stalks thoroughly and cut into 5cm/2in pieces.

Make the béchamel as usual, and keep it cooking gently over a flame diffuser or in a bain-marie for about 30 minutes, stirring occasionally. Then mix in the Parmesan, plenty of pepper, and salt and nutmeg to taste.

While the béchamel is gently cooking, cook the Swiss chard stalks in plenty of salted boiling water for about 10 minutes, until they are soft. Drain and dry with kitchen paper towel.

Heat the oven to 180°C/350°F/Gas Mark 4.

Butter a shallow oven dish. Spread 2 tablespoons of the béchamel over the bottom. Cover with the Swiss chards and spread with the remaining béchamel. Sprinkle with the breadcrumbs and dot with the butter. Bake until golden on top, about 15 minutes.

Take the dish from the oven and allow to rest for 5 minutes before serving it.

CIPOLLE RIPIENE

Stuffed Onions

I think that every cook in northern Italy has his or her favourite way of stuffing onions. This is how onions were usually stuffed in my home in Milan. The sweetness and crunchiness of the onion cups are a pleasantly contrasting foil to the rich stuffing.

SERVES 4

4 Spanish onions, about 225g/8oz each
salt and freshly ground black pepper
60g/2oz [US 4 tbsp] unsalted butter
180g/6oz minced veal [US ground veal]
30g/1oz mortadella, finely chopped
4 tbsp freshly grated Parmesan
1 egg
2 tbsp Marsala
2 tbsp dried white breadcrumbs
120ml/4fl oz meat stock (page 230)

Wash the onions and plunge them into a large saucepan of salted boiling water. Boil for about 20 minutes, until you can easily pierce the onion with the point of a knife. Drain and leave to cool a little.

Peel the onions; you usually have to remove two or three layers of skin as well. Cut each onion in half around its 'equator' and remove the centre. Make 12 cups with the larger onion halves and arrange them side by side in a buttered oven dish.

Now prepare the stuffing. Chop the inside of the onions to the size of grains of rice. I suggest you do this by hand and not in a food processor, which would reduce the onion to a pulp and extract all the juices.

Heat half the butter in a smallish frying pan. Add the veal and sauté until the meat has lost its raw colour. Add 8 tablespoons of the chopped onion and stir well (keep the rest for another dish). Now mix in the mortadella, season with salt and pepper to taste and fry the lovely mixture for 2 minutes or so. Transfer the mixture to a bowl and add all the other ingredients, except the stock and remaining butter. Mix thoroughly and then taste to check if you need to add a little more salt and pepper.

Heat the oven to 200°C/400°F/Gas Mark 6.

Fill the onion cups with the mixture and place a nugget of the remaining butter on top of each onion. Pour the stock over and around the onions. Bake for 15 minutes, then turn the heat down to 180°C/350°F/Gas Mark 4. Baste the onions with the juices, cover the dish with foil and bake for a further 30 minutes or so. Serve warm or at room temperature.

FARAONE AL MASCARPONE

Guinea Fowl with Mascarpone

It is notable that in Italy even a town has its own style of cooking, and is proud of it. This recipe comes from a book called *La Cucina Lodigiana* (The Cooking of Lodi). Lodi is a town in southern Lombardy, the area where rich pastures nourish fat cows.

Mascarpone is a local cream cheese, which is now also available abroad in its UHT form. Although UHT mascarpone is not as good as the fresh product eaten in Lombardy, it is good enough to use in this excellent recipe. The mascarpone keeps the bird moist during the cooking, oozing out of the cavity and mixing with the cooking juices.

SERVES 3 OR 4

1 guinea fowl
salt and freshly ground pepper
2 tbsp mascarpone
60g/2oz [US 4 tbsp] unsalted butter
1 small onion, cut into pieces
1 carrot, cut into pieces
2 celery stalks, cut into pieces
3 or 4 cloves
a pinch of ground cinnamon
120ml/4fl oz dry white wine
2 tbsp white rum

Heat the oven to 200°C/400°F/Gas Mark 6.

Singe the guinea fowl and remove as many of the stubborn quills as you can. (As they are now plucked by machine, pheasants and guinea fowl need a lot of attention before being cooked.) Wash and dry it thoroughly inside and out. Season with salt and pepper and spoon the mascarpone into the cavity.

Choose an oval flameproof casserole in which the bird will sit snugly. Put the butter, onion, carrot, celery, cloves and cinnamon into it and sprinkle with salt. Place the guinea fowl on the vegetables and pour over the wine and the rum.

Place the casserole on the heat and bring the liquid slowly to the boil. Cover the pan and place in the oven. Cook for about 1 to 1¼ hours, until the bird is tender.

Cut the bird into small pieces. Place them on a dish and keep them warm, well covered with foil.

Remove and discard the cloves, then process the cooking vegetables and all the juices to a purée. Taste and adjust seasoning. Spoon some of the sauce over the pieces of guinea fowl and hand around the rest in a sauce boat.

CAPPONE RIPIENO DI NOCI

Poached Chicken Stuffed with Walnuts, Ricotta and Parmesan

Capon is the original Christmas bird of northern Italy. A capon is a cock that has been castrated at around 2 months. The bird grows larger than a cock and has a white, delicately tasty meat. All through the history of cooking, capon has been a favourite on court tables, and many old recipes are dedicated to this bird. In Italy you can still find capons raised in farms, ready for Christmas, and they are a very different bird from the mass-produced battery chicken. In this country capons do not exist any longer; they are illegal because the cocks were being 'caponized' with hormones.

In Italy capons are sometimes cooked on the spit, flavoured with black truffles – a method no longer so popular since 120g/4oz of truffles are needed for one bird – and sometimes boiled, particularly in Lombardy. Roasted capon is traditional in Tuscany, Umbria and Marche. In grand Christmas dinners or country feasts, boiled capons precede the roast, which nowadays is often turkey. The advantage over turkey is that capon makes the best meat stock, which is used to prepare the risotto giallo (saffron risotto), the traditional Christmas first course in Lombard homes.

The recipe I give here calls for the bird to be stuffed. The stuffing is quite delicious and unexpected with its nutty flavour and texture relieved by the delicate milky ricotta, while the Parmesan brings that wonderful flavour that no other cheese can give. The use of walnuts in the stuffing is definitely a Lombard tradition.

Up to the Second World War there were many walnut trees in Lombardy. The fruit was not as good as that from the walnut trees of southern Italy, being smaller and less sweet. So it was used in stuffings, while the *noci di Sorrento* (Sorrento walnuts) were, and still are, the most highly prized for eating at table. After the War most of the walnut trees in northern Italy were felled to be used for furniture. Walnut trees are now rare in Lombardy, but the traditional stuffing for capon, or walnut sauces for pasta as made in Liguria and Piedmont, are still very popular.

THE RECIPE

Here, in the absence of capons, I buy a large chicken from my excellent butcher. It cooks much quicker than a farmyard capon, but the texture of the meat and its flavour is quite good. Be careful not to overcook it or it will become dry.

Buy the very best walnut kernels or, better still, buy walnuts in their shells and crack them yourself.

SERVES 10

a fresh free-range chicken of about 2.5–3kg/6–7lb
salt and freshly ground black pepper
2l/3½pt [US 2qt] chicken stock
150ml/5fl oz dry white wine

FOR THE STUFFING

200g/7oz [US 2 cups] walnut kernels (see above)
a large bunch of fresh flat-leaf parsley
40g/1½oz celery leaves
2 eggs
100ml/3½fl oz double cream [US heavy cream]
150g/5oz [US ⅔ cup] ricotta
90g/3oz [US ¾ cup] freshly grated Parmesan
salt and freshly ground black pepper
grated nutmeg

FOR THE SAUCE

90g/3oz [US 6 tbsp] unsalted butter
100g/3½oz [US ⅔ cup] flour
1–1½ tbsp chopped fresh tarragon
4 tbsp double cream [US heavy cream]
salt and freshly ground pepper, white if available

First prepare the stuffing. Put the walnut pieces in a small saucepan of boiling water and boil for 20 seconds. Lift out a few pieces at a time and remove as much as you can of the bitter skin. This is quite a time-consuming job. The walnuts are undoubtedly sweeter and nicer without the skin; however, if you do not have the time, or the inclination, to spend something like 40 minutes doing this, forget it. Dry the walnuts if you have peeled them, and chop them in a food processor together with the parsley and the celery leaves. Put the mixture in a bowl and add all the other ingredients for the stuffing. Mix very thoroughly and set aside.

Wipe the chicken inside and out and season the inside with salt and pepper. Push the stuffing into the cavity of the chicken and sew up the hole with thick cotton thread.

Put the chicken on a wire rack in a large deep pan or a heavy roasting tin. Pour in enough stock to come level with the top of the chicken. Put the pan on the heat and bring to the boil.

Heat the wine in a small saucepan and as soon as it is bubbling pour it over the chicken. Taste the stock and add a little salt if necessary. Bring to the boil again. Cover the pan tightly with its lid or with a double sheet of foil and simmer very gently for about 1½ hours. Test if the bird is ready by inserting the point of a knife in the thickest part of the thigh. The knife should penetrate very easily.

Lift out the chicken and place on a dish. Cover with foil and keep warm in a cool oven. Strain the stock and measure about 1.2l/2pt [US 5 cups] for the sauce.

Melt the butter in a heavy-based saucepan. Mix in the flour and, as soon as the butter has absorbed it, begin to add the measured hot stock gradually, while whisking constantly. Return the saucepan to the heat and cook very gently, stirring constantly, until the sauce begins to bubble. Now put the sauce over a flame diffuser and continue cooking for about 10 minutes. Mix in the tarragon and the cream just before transferring the sauce to a heated sauceboat. Taste and add salt and pepper if needed.

Cut the chicken into pieces and lay them on a heated dish. Fish the stuffing out of the cavity with a metal spoon and place in blobs around the chicken. Pour over 3 or 4 tablespoons of the stock to keep the chicken and stuffing nicely moist and then coat the chicken pieces with a little of the sauce. Serve the rest of the sauce alongside in a heated sauceboat.

Ossobuco alla Milanese

Milanese Ossobuco

I get very annoyed when I read recipes for ossobuco alla milanese containing tomatoes. Oddly enough, even some of the Italian writers I respect, and who should know, include tomatoes in their recipes for ossobuco.

The traditional ossobuco alla milanese does not contain tomatoes. In fact, few Milanese dishes contain tomatoes or tomato sauce. As with Veneto or Piedmontese cooking, tomato hardly ever became part of the traditional repertoire. The reason is obvious – no tomatoes grow in these most northerly regions of Italy.

And then think of the traditional accompaniment to ossobuco alla milanese. It is risotto alla milanese – risotto with saffron (page 27). Saffron and rich tomato sauce do not go together, nor does tomato sauce go with the delicious *gremolada* added at the end of the cooking, the taste of which must come through loud and clear against the winey flavour of the meat, and nothing else.

I am afraid another reason for ossobuco alla milanese containing tomatoes is that it has been the habit of Italian restaurants outside Italy to put tomato sauce with everything. For them it has been the signature of traditional Italian cooking, no matter if the dish comes from Milan, Valle d'Aosta or Naples.

There is an ossobuco cooked in a tomato sauce, and this originated in Emilia-Romagna. It is not served with risotto and it is not finished off with the magical gremolada.

Let me finish this diatribe by quoting the 'Italian Mrs Beeton' Pellegrino Artusi, who includes tomatoes in his recipe for ossobuco, without specifying 'alla milanese', however. 'This is a dish to be made by the Milanese because it is a Lombard speciality. I only want to describe it, without any pretensions, in fear of being laughed at.'

THE RECIPE

Ossobuchi come from the hind leg of a calf, and ideally should be no more than 4cm/1½in thick. Buy ossobuchi all of the same size so that they take the same amount of time to cook.

SERVES 4

4 ossobuchi, about 250g/9oz each
2 tbsp olive oil
flour for dusting
salt and freshly ground pepper
40g/1½oz [US 3 tbsp] butter
1 small onion, finely chopped
½ celery stalk, finely chopped
150ml/5fl oz dry white wine
300ml/10fl oz meat stock (page 230)

FOR THE GREMOLADA

1 tsp grated rind from an unwaxed lemon
½ garlic clove, very finely chopped
2 tbsp chopped fresh flat-leaf parsley

Tie the ossobuchi around and across with string as you would a parcel. Choose a heavy sauté pan, with a tight-fitting lid, large enough to hold the ossobuchi in a single layer. Heat the oil, and meanwhile lightly coat the ossobuchi with some flour in which you have mixed a teaspoon of salt. Brown the ossobuchi on both sides and then remove to a side dish.

Add 30g/1oz [US 2 tbsp] of the butter to the sauté pan together with the onion and the celery. Sprinkle with a little salt, which will help the onion to release its liquid so that it gets soft without browning. When the vegetables are soft – after about 10 minutes – return the meat to the pan along with the juice that will have accumulated.

Heat the wine and pour over the meat. Turn the heat up and boil to reduce by half, while scraping the bottom of the pan with a metal spoon.

Heat the stock in the pan you used to heat the wine and pour about half over the ossobuchi. Turn the heat down to very low and cover the pan. Cook for 1½ to 2 hours, until the meat has begun to come away from the bone. Carefully turn the ossobuchi over every 20 minutes or so, taking care not to damage the marrow in the bone. If necessary, add more stock during the cooking, but very gradually – not more than 3 or 4 tablespoons at a time. If, by the time the meat is cooked, the sauce is too thin, remove the meat from the pan and reduce the liquid by boiling briskly.

Transfer the ossobuchi to a heated dish and remove the string. Keep warm in a cool oven.

Cut the remaining butter into 3 or 4 pieces and add gradually to the sauce. As soon as the butter has melted, remove from the heat, as the sauce should not boil. This addition of the butter will give the sauce a glossy shine and a delicate taste.

Mix the ingredients for the gremolada together, stir into the sauce and leave for a minute or two. After that, just spoon the sauce over the ossobuchi and serve immediately.

CAZZOEULA

Stewed Pork with Cabbage

'*L'ha de vess trachenta e minga sbrodolona e sbrodolenta*' (it must be thick and not watery and soupy). Thus goes the saying in Milanese dialect about this great Lombard dish. Its name obviously has the same etymological origin as the French cassoulet, and the two dishes are in fact similar. But it is thought that the dish was actually brought to Lombardy by the Spaniards who were lords of this region for several centuries.

Whatever its origin, cazzoeula is now one of the dishes mainly associated with Milan and the Brianza, the hilly area between the city and the lakes where, once upon a time, the Milanese aristocracy used to spend their summers.

When I was very young my family, too, spent the month of September in Brianza, staying with friends named Grossi, in Erba, a little town between Como and Lecco. I found this recipe in my mother's recipe book, with the note 'Nina's recipe – the local cook in the Grossi's house'. I remember nothing about Nina or the Grossi, who seem to have disappeared from my mother's life long ago. But I do know that my mother's cazzoeula was delectable. She was often asked to prepare cazzoeula for my younger brother and all his friends on All Souls' Day, 2nd November, a day when this dish was traditionally eaten in most Milanese homes.

THE RECIPE

Cazzoeula is one of the recipes that can be produced in this country without searching too far for ingredients. Luganega is the only ingredient that is not available everywhere, although a good Toulouse, or coarse ground pork sausage with 100% meat content and no flavouring, would do.

Cazzoeula can be served with polenta, or just with lots of bread.

SERVES 6

2 pig's trotters, split into quarters
250g/9oz pork rind
2 tbsp olive oil
30g/1oz [US 2 tbsp] butter
2 large onions, chopped
700g/1½lb meaty pork spare ribs, cut into 2- or 3-rib pieces
2 large carrots, chopped
2 celery stalks, chopped
1.3kg/3lb Savoy cabbage, shredded into 2.5cm/1in pieces
450g/1lb luganega, or other coarse ground pure pork sausage, cut into 5cm/2in pieces
salt and freshly ground black pepper

Cover the trotters and the pork rind with 1l/ 1¾pt [US 1qt] of water, bring to the boil and cook for 45 minutes. Remove the trotters and the rind, cut off the excess fat and chop the rind into 5cm/2in squares; set aside. Allow the stock to cool, then refrigerate; when the fat has solidified on the surface, remove it and discard. (I have found that removing the fat makes the dish lighter, but if you haven't got time, you can omit this step and proceed.)

Put the oil, butter and onions in a large 4l/7pt [US 4qt] heavy-based saucepan or stockpot and fry for 5 to 10 minutes, until the onion is soft but not brown. Add the trotters and the rind and sauté for 30 seconds. Add the spare ribs and cook for 10 minutes, stirring frequently. Add the carrots and celery and sauté for a further 2 minutes, then cover with the stock from the trotters.

Cook, covered, over a very low heat for 3 hours, stirring every now and then and adding some hot water if the stew gets too dry.

Blanch the cabbage for 2 minutes and drain very well. Add it and the luganega to the saucepan, mix well and cook for a further 30 minutes. Taste and adjust the seasonings before serving straight from the heat, preferably in the stockpot.

FRICANDO
Rich Braised Beef

'Fricandeau' is the subject of an entry in *Larousse Gastronomique*. It is very similar to the Italian fricandò. So was it originally French or Italian? Here, as often elsewhere in the gastronomic arena, France and Italy compete. Many historians maintain that the dish originated in Italy and went to France, as did many other sophisticated dishes during the Renaissance when Italy was the leader in culinary matters. It then came back to Milan with Napoleon or, more precisely, with his Egyptian chef, who, when Napoleon's fortunes turned sour, stayed on in Milan to open a restaurant.

I feel sure that the dish was made in both countries, being a typical method of braising a piece of meat, but in Italy in the 19th century, it took the French name when it became fashionable to eat 'a la française'. The Italian version, however, has assumed the characteristic trademarks of its country. Thus it is larded with prosciutto, and celery is usually one of the braising vegetables.

THE RECIPE

The original fricandò is made with *noix de veau*. Because veal is unpopular and/or not easily available in this country, I suggest replacing it with a young but well-hung piece of beef. A piece of chuck or the eye of the silverside are the best cuts. Topside is not suitable for braising. The piece should be about 10cm/4in in diameter. Ask your butcher to tie it in a neat roll, so that it will keep its shape while cooking. Remember to remove the meat from the fridge at least 2 hours before you begin to cook it.

The prosciutto should be thickly sliced – about 3mm/⅛in. I buy prosciutto from the end of the ham, as it has more fat. It is also much cheaper. Your Italian food shop will keep the knuckle for you and slice it thickly. I prefer San Daniele prosciutto for larding and stuffing because it has a stronger flavour than Parma.

The traditional accompaniment to fricandò is potato purée.

SERVES 8

200g/7oz fatty prosciutto, thickly sliced

a 1.3–1.5kg/3–3½lb piece of beef (see above), securely tied in a roll

salt and freshly ground pepper

60g/2oz [US 4 tbsp] unsalted butter

2 tbsp olive oil

100g/3½oz Italian or Spanish onion

4 cloves

30g/1oz fresh flat-leaf parsley, leaves only

60g/2oz carrot, cut into chunks

30g/1oz celery, preferably the leaves of a stalk

150ml/5fl oz meat stock (page 230)

Cut the prosciutto roughly into large pieces. Put the pieces in a food processor and whizz for a few seconds until it is very coarsely chopped. Scoop it out on to a board.

Take the meat and stand it on one of its extremities. With a sharp, pointed knife – I use a boning knife which is long and narrow – make a deep incision in the roll of meat, along the grain, i.e. along the length of the roll. Take a lump of minced prosciutto between your fingers and push it into the cut. Push it down to the bottom of the cut, using a round chopstick or a round pencil. Make 4 or 5 incisions and then turn the meat over and repeat the operation. If your incisions are deep enough you will be able to lard half the meat from one end and the other half from the other end.

Put 1 tablespoon or so of salt on the board and mix it with plenty of freshly ground pepper. Roll the meat in the mixture and pat the seasoning hard into the meat. Pat in also any bits of leftover prosciutto.

Choose a heavy flameproof casserole in which the meat will fit fairly tightly. Heat the butter and oil and, when the foam of the butter begins to subside, lower the meat into the pan. Brown the meat on all sides on a lively heat. Let one side get lovely and brown before you turn the meat over. This operation is very important for the final result: caramelizing the outside of the meat gives the dish the right flavour. To do it properly takes about 10 minutes.

Heat the oven to 150°C/300°F/Gas Mark 2.

Cut the onion in half, or into quarters, depending on its size, and stick it with the cloves. Throw it into the casserole together with the parsley, carrot and celery. Give the vegetables a good stir and then pour in the stock. Put the lid on and place the casserole in the oven. Cook for 3 to 3½ hours. Keep an eye on it and turn the meat over every 20 minutes or so.

When the meat is tender, i.e. when the prongs of a fork can penetrate it easily, lift it out, loosely cover it with foil and set it aside. Let the juices rest for a couple of minutes and then skim as much fat as you can from the top. (Do not throw this fat away; it's mainly butter. Put it into a bowl and keep it in the fridge to be used for braising potatoes or cabbage or for meat sauces and ragù.) Transfer the juices to a food processor or a blender and blend until smooth.

Carve the meat into fairly thick slices – about 1cm/⅜in. If you were to carve it any thinner it would crumble. You need a very sharp knife or, an invaluable tool, an electric carving knife. Carve as many slices as you think you will need. Place the unsliced end piece at one end of a heated oval dish and lay the slices all the way down the dish, slightly overlapping.

Reheat the sauce and spoon a little over the carved meat. Pour the rest into a heated sauce-boat to hand round separately.

Note: You can cook the meat and prepare the sauce in advance. Put everything back in the casserole to be reheated in a moderate oven when the time comes.

POLPETTE
Meat Rissoles

'Polpette are the quintessential Italian food, or rather I should say, a particularly Lombard food. The real motherland of polpette is Milan, where a great many are eaten, and where I remember years ago having heard an old aristocrat saying "If one could gather all the polpette that I have eaten during my life, one could pave the city from Piazza del Duomo to Porta Orientale"' . . . which is 1½ kilometres. I have translated that passage from *L'Arte di Convitare* by Giovanni Raiberti, published in 1939.

Polpette, however, are very much older than 1939. Cristoforo Messisbugo's book *Libro Novo* was published in 1557, and in it he has three different kinds of polpette. Although he was the chef of the wealthy Don Hippolito d'Este, polpette were mainly food of the poor. And the northern regions of Italy were indeed poor up to the end of the last century.

Old-fashioned polpette are made mainly with left-over meat – any meat, whether chicken, beef or veal – which could have been boiled, braised or roasted. But in the old days that was never enough for another meal, so bread, cheese, mortadella or other pork products were added to make the meat go further. Nowadays, when meat is everyday food for anyone who wants it, polpette are usually made with raw meat.

'Polpette', writes Elizabeth David in her *Italian Food*, 'are not at all dull; in fact they make a most excellent little luncheon dish.' Well, I think they make an ideal family dish for lunch or dinner.

THE RECIPE

These are the polpette of my childhood, as made by our cook Maria. Maria came from Friuli, a region that had the reputation of supplying the best cooks for private houses. The poverty of Friuli sharpened the wits of its inhabitants, who learned to embellish the most humble ingredients – just what family cooks need to do. A case in point is to be found in these polpette. During the autumn Maria used to put a little morsel of truffle in each polpetta, a small gem to be discovered within the unpretentiousness of minced meat.

The ricotta adds lightness to the meat, which could otherwise be heavy and stodgy. I prefer to buy good braising meat rather than meat already minced; then I know what's there. Ask your butcher to cut off the fat before mincing the meat.

SERVES 4

450g/1lb lean minced beef [US ground round]
125g/4oz [US ½ cup] fresh ricotta
1 egg
a small bunch of parsley sprigs, leaves only, chopped
1 garlic clove, very finely chopped
3 tbsp freshly grated Parmesan
salt and freshly ground pepper
about 2 tbsp flour
1 tbsp olive oil
15g/½oz [US 1 tbsp] butter

Put the meat in a bowl and mix in the ricotta. Lightly beat the egg and then incorporate it into the meat mixture together with the parsley, garlic and Parmesan. Now season with salt and pepper according to your taste. But do remember that salt brings out the flavour of the ingredients; be wise, but not mean. Mix everything together very thoroughly. I use my hands because I find them the best tool for breaking up the nuggets of meat.

Pull away some of the mixture the size of a golf ball. Roll it in your hands quickly and without squeezing too hard. (It is easier if you moisten your hands.) Flatten the balls at opposite poles to shape the polpette, which ideally should be about 2cm/¾in thick. Continue making polpette until you have used up all the meat. If you have time, place the polpette in the fridge for at least 30 minutes, to firm them up.

When you are ready to cook, put the flour on a plate and lightly coat each polpetta with flour. Heat the oil and butter in a frying pan. When the fat is golden, slide in the polpette and cook them for 2 minutes. Turn them over and cook the other side. How long you cook them depends on how you like your meat. I prefer polpette like these to be pink inside, and that takes about 5 to 7 minutes over lively heat. A sign to look out for is when the reddish juices begin to trickle through to the surface. If you like your polpette cooked through, turn the heat down a little and let them cook for a few more minutes.

This is the basic recipe. Now you can vary your polpette by transferring them, without the cooking juices, into another frying pan containing a good tomato sauce. Let them *insaporire* – take up the flavour of – the sauce for about 15 minutes, turning them over once, and then serve. Another excellent way to finish polpette comes from Artusi's book, *La Scienza in Cucina e l'Arte di Mangiar Bene.* He suggests adding at the end a little mixture of egg yolk and lemon juice.

UCCELLI SCAPPATI

Pork Bundles with Pancetta and Herbs

The name of this recipe means 'birds that have flown away'. The explanation of this curious name is that the pork bundles are cooked in the same way as little birds. Small birds, eaten with polenta, are a traditional dish of northern Lombardy and many other regions. In his *Voyages dans la Brianza*, Stendhal wrote that Milanese ladies were very fond of this peasant dish, as he was too: 'In the evening the delights and joy of the dinner with the uccelletti, polenta and the general gaiety.'

The prepared pork escalopes sold in good supermarkets are ideal for this recipe. They are thin, and all more or less of the same neat shape. This is one of the few cuts of meat which I prefer to buy in a supermarket. If you go to a butcher, buy thin slices of loin of pork and ask the butcher to trim them to a neat rectangle and to beat them thin.

It is a very simple, quick and easy dish that I am sure you will like.

SERVES 4

12 thin pork escalopes, about 450g/1lb total weight
salt and freshly ground pepper
12 slices of unsmoked pancetta, about 150g/5oz total weight
3 fresh rosemary sprigs
2 dozen fresh sage leaves
40g/1½oz [US 3 tbsp] unsalted butter
1 layer of onion
4 tbsp dry white wine

Put the escalopes on a board and season them with salt and pepper on both sides. Cover each of them with a slice of pancetta, cut a little smaller than the escalope. Scatter a few rosemary needles over and then roll up the escalopes from a long side. Thread one sage leaf, one bundle, one sage leaf, one bundle, then another sage leaf and the last bundle plus the last sage leaf on to a short metal skewer. Repeat with three more skewers. Thus you have three bundles on each skewer, each enough for one person.

When all the skewers are ready, heat the butter with the onion layer in a large frying pan. When the foam begins to subside and the butter begins to take on a lovely hazelnut colour, place the skewers in the pan. Sauté at a lively heat for 2 or 3 minutes, then turn the skewers over and sauté the other side of the bundles for about 2 minutes.

Pour over the wine and cook at a lively heat for 2 more minutes, then turn the heat down and finish cooking for a couple of minutes. Taste and adjust seasonings. Draw the pan off the heat and let the meat rest for 5 minutes before serving. During this time the meat juices will be released and mix in with the winey liquid. Uccelli scappati should not have much cooking liquid; just about 1 tablespoon per serving.

POLLO BRUSCO DI ANNAMARIA

Poached Chicken in a Vinegary Sauce

Annamaria de'Pedrini is a fine cook and a generous friend. She gave me the recipe for this excellent dish, which has been served at Christmas in the de'Pedrini household in Lombardy for generations. The chicken forms part of the antipasti, together with lobster, prawns, pâté de foie gras and *affettato* – mixed cured meats.

You can often see a similar dish in the windows of the best Milanese *salumerie* (delicatessens). It is an easy dish, ideal for a buffet party or for a dinner in the summer.

SERVES 4 TO 6

1 carrot
1 onion, stuck with 2 cloves
1 celery stalk
2 meat bouillon cubes
2 black peppercorns
2 bay leaves
a few parsley stalks
300ml/10fl oz dry white wine
salt and freshly ground pepper
a free-range chicken of about 1.5kg/3½lb

FOR THE SAUCE

150ml/5fl oz extra virgin olive oil
150ml/5fl oz white wine vinegar
2 tbsp capers, rinsed and dried
4 garlic cloves
60g/2oz anchovy fillets
2 tbsp flour
180g/6oz porcini under oil, drained
150g/5oz artichokes under oil, drained

Put the carrot, onion, celery, bouillon cubes, peppercorns, bay leaves, parsley stalks, wine and a little salt in a stockpot. Add the chicken and fill with cold water up to the level of the chicken. Now remove the chicken from the pan and set aside. Bring the water to the boil and then put the chicken back in the pot. When the water has come back to the boil, turn the heat down so that the water just trembles, but does not really boil. The secret of successful poaching lies in keeping the water just under the simmering point. The temperature of the water should be maintained so that only an occasional bubble breaks slowly to the surface. Cook until the chicken is done, about 1¼ hours. Leave in the stock while you prepare the sauce.

Put the oil and vinegar in a small saucepan. Chop together the capers, garlic and anchovies and add to the pan. Heat the mixture and, when bubbles begin to appear at the edges, throw in all the flour while you whisk hard with a small wire balloon whisk. Cook gently for 2 or 3 minutes and then add 6 tablespoons of the chicken stock. Continue cooking for a further 2 or 3 minutes, whisking constantly. Draw off the heat.

If the porcini pieces are large, cut them into about 2.5cm/1in pieces; cut the artichokes in half. Mix into the sauce, which should be quite thick. Taste, add salt and pepper and set aside.

Skin the chicken and cut into small portions: 2 pieces from each breast cut across, 2 drumsticks and 2 thighs. Put into a container and coat each piece with a little of the sauce, keeping some back for the final coating. Cover the container and refrigerate for 2 or 3 days. Also refrigerate the sauce that has been set aside.

Transfer the chicken pieces to a serving dish and spoon the remaining sauce over them to give them a fresh and glossy look.

La Terrina di Pollo della Trattoria all'Antica

Chicken Terrine

When I am in Milan, my home town, I rarely go out to dine in restaurants. I am either asked by friends and relations to their homes, or, when staying with my brother, I like to cook and try out recipes, so that I can compare different foods and ingredients with what I can get in England. But on one of my last visits I decided I must reconfirm my old dictum that you eat better in Milan than in any other Italian city. So I asked Marco, my brother, to book a table at a very typical Milanese restaurant, and the Trattoria all'Antica, in one of the oldest parts of the city, could not have been a better choice.

We were welcomed by the elegant Maria, and by an enchanting Chinese waitress speaking perfect Italian. A large figure in white with his chef's hat poised at a rakish angle was hovering in the background. He came to meet us at the table and simply said that the food would arrive soon. No menu, and that was that. It was a perfect meal, redolent of the aromas and flavours of the Milanese cooking of my youth, with no concession to sun-dried tomatoes or any other southern Italian intrusions.

I was torn between asking for the recipe for the superb crespelle with cheese or this terrine, but then I opted for the terrine because I realized that the crespelle could be made in this country only in London, and in Edinburgh thanks to Valvona & Crolla, and only by hunting around in search of the right cheeses.

THE RECIPE

Domenico Passera, he of the chef's hat, suggests serving the terrine on a bed of *insalatina*. This could be mâche, frisée or watercress, but not rocket [US arugula] which would jar with the delicate flavour of the terrine and would not be in keeping with Lombard traditions, having been unknown there until the '60s.

I buy chicken thighs with the bone in because the bone adds a lot of flavour to the meat.

SERVES 8

800g/1¾lb fresh chicken thighs
3 tbsp olive oil
2 garlic cloves, bruised
salt and freshly ground pepper
1 fresh rosemary sprig
200g/7oz chicken livers
200g/7oz [US 14 tbsp] unsalted butter
100g/3½oz [US ½ cup] very finely chopped onion
1 bay leaf
6 tbsp brandy

Heat the oven to 200°C/400°F/Gas Mark 6.

Skin the chicken thighs, remove and discard the fat attached to them, and place in a roasting tin.

In a bowl mix together the oil, garlic, 2 teaspoons of salt and a good grinding of pepper. Brush the thighs all over with the seasoned oil using the rosemary sprig. Throw the rosemary, the garlic and any left-over oil into the tin and place the tin in the oven. After 5 minutes remove and discard the garlic. Cook, basting once or twice, for about 20 minutes. The chicken should no longer be bloody though still undercooked. Leave to cool while you cook the chicken liver. Leave the oven on.

Trim the fat and gristle off the chicken livers and cut the livers into pieces. Heat 60g/2oz [US 4 tbsp] of the butter, the onion, bay leaf and 1 teaspoon of salt in a frying pan and cook to soften the onion. As soon as the onion is soft add the chicken livers. Fry for 5 minutes, then splash with the brandy. Finally, cook rapidly for 2 or 3 minutes.

Go back to the chicken thighs. Remove the bone and cut the meat into pieces. Put the meat, the chicken livers with all the cooking juices, and the remaining butter cut into pieces in a food processor and give it a whizz for 2 or 3 seconds. Add salt and pepper. (I add 1 teaspoon of salt and ½ teaspoon of ground pepper, because any pâté or terrine that is served chilled needs a lot of seasoning.) Whizz again to a very coarse texture – not a smooth pâté-like consistency. Taste and check seasoning.

Line a 1l/1¾pt [US 1qt] loaf tin with foil and spoon the mixture into it, pushing it down and banging the tin hard on the work surface to eliminate any air pockets. Cover with cling film.

Now you must cook the terrine in a bain-marie in the oven. To do that, place the terrine in a roasting tin and pour some boiling water into the tin to come half to three-quarters of the way up the side of the tin. Bake for 20 minutes.

When the terrine is cold, refrigerate for at least 3 hours.

You can serve the whole terrine in a dish, surrounding it with a little salad, drizzled with a few drops of extra virgin olive oil, or you can slice the terrine and put it on individual plates on a bed of lightly dressed salad.

Animelle
Sweetbreads

All kinds of offal [US variety meats] are popular in Italy, but I am including only sweetbreads, for the simple reason that they are the offal I like best. They are delicate in flavour and texture and can be cooked in many interesting ways.

First let me tell you what sweetbreads are, in case you don't know. They are the thymus glands in the upper chest of a young animal, and they disappear as soon as it becomes adult. A sweetbread is formed of two parts attached to each other, called the heart, and the throat. The heart is large, lean and regular in shape, while the throat consists of little pieces, because the inedible bits have been removed from around the edible ones. These latter sweetbreads are particularly suited for going into stuffings, while the heart is used for proper sweetbread dishes.

Both calf's sweetbreads and lamb's sweetbreads are available in most butchers, or can be ordered. The calf's are much larger and sweeter and are more highly regarded. But lamb's sweetbreads are good too and should not be underestimated. They are also much cheaper and more easily available.

THE RECIPES

All sweetbreads need some preparation before you proceed to follow a recipe. First you must soak them in cold water for about 2 hours to let the blood run out. After that, bring to the boil a saucepan of water containing a slice of onion and a small stalk of celery. Add 1 tablespoon of wine vinegar and some salt. When the water is boiling throw in the sweetbreads and simmer gently for 5 minutes if calf's heart sweetbreads, but only for 2 minutes if they are the throat ones or if they are lamb's sweetbreads. Having blanched them in this way, drain and rinse them, then peel off the membrane and remove any bits of fat or hardened blood.

And now you can proceed to cook them in your favourite way. These are mine.

Animelle a Cotoletta

Breaded Calf Sweetbreads

In Lombardy this is a traditional way of cooking a number of different ingredients, such as veal escalopes, cèpe caps, brains and fish fillets, as well as these sweetbreads.

This recipe should be made with the heart part of a calf's sweetbread, which you can cut into neat slices. Having said that, I have also made it with lamb's sweetbread, which has the characteristic stronger flavour of lamb's meat.

Instead of using clarified butter, I replace some of the butter with olive oil, which allows the butter to heat to a higher temperature without burning.

SERVES 4

600g/1¼lb calf's sweetbreads
2 eggs
salt and freshly ground pepper
about 100g/3½oz [US 1 cup] dried white breadcrumbs, spread on a board
75g/2½oz [US 5 tbsp] unsalted butter
1 tbsp olive oil
lemon wedges

Prepare the sweetbreads as described in the introduction and then cut them into neat pieces.

Lightly beat the eggs in a soup plate and season with salt and pepper.

Coat both sides of the sweetbread pieces in the eggs and then let the excess egg flow back into the plate. Now coat the pieces with the breadcrumbs, patting firmly with your hands.

Heat the butter and the oil in a frying pan, which must be large enough to contain the sweetbreads without crowding them. When the butter foam begins to subside, slip in the sweetbreads and cook for 3 minutes, then flip them over and cook for 2 minutes, until deeply gilded. Make sure you keep the heat high enough to cook the sweetbreads, but not so hot as to burn the butter.

Transfer to a heated dish and serve straight away, surrounded by lemon wedges.

Animelle in Frittura Piccata

Sautéed Sweetbreads with Lemon and Parsley

This is another way of cooking veal that is also used for cooking sweetbreads. You can use calf's throat sweetbreads, or lamb's sweetbreads which I find very suitable for this preparation. Use a pan that you can bring to the table, if you have one.

SERVES 4

700g/1½lb sweetbreads

60g/2oz [US 4 tbsp] unsalted butter

1 garlic clove, bruised

100g/3½oz [US ⅔ cup] flour

about 5 tbsp meat stock (page 230)

salt and freshly ground pepper

the juice of 1 lemon

3 tbsp chopped fresh flat-leaf parsley

Prepare the sweetbreads as described in the introduction.

Heat the butter and the garlic in a frying pan.

Quickly flour the sweetbreads and throw them into the pan as soon as the butter foam begins to subside. Sauté for 2 minutes over moderate heat, shaking the pan frequently but not constantly, so that the sweetbreads can brown. Add the stock and cook for a further minute or so. Season with salt and pepper, pour over the lemon juice and sprinkle with the parsley. Mix quickly and serve at once.

La Torta Paradiso

Paradise Cake

After considering various alternatives for the English name of this cake (Heavenly Cake?) I decided that only a literal translation of the Italian does it justice. Torta paradiso is synonymous with Pavia, a city to the south of Milan, where it was created by Enrico Vigoni at the end of the last century. Pavia is a delightful city which boasts a noble past and one of the oldest universities in Europe. It is a city where the sleepy habits of the surrounding misty countryside mingle with the lively entrepreneurial spirit of the Lombards.

As my son Guy lives there, I am often in Pavia and I love it. One of the treats when I'm there is to go to the Pasticceria Vigoni in the Strada Nuova, to have an espresso or a cappuccino with one of their exquisite *paste* (small cakes) and buy a piece of torta paradiso to take home.

When I was preparing this book I went to talk to the manager of Vigoni, Pietro Grecchi. I immediately told him that I was not there to ask for the recipe of the torta paradiso, since I knew it was a well-guarded secret. But Grecchi refuted this by saying that the only secret lies in the quality of the ingredients. The flour is the best flour produced specifically for cakes and biscuits [US cookies] the eggs are supplied by local breeders who give their hens plenty of space and feed them with the best food, while the butter is made by the old churning method, using the whole cream and not the whey of the cream used for cheese-making. Sadly, this butter cannot be bought in shops in Italy.

Grecchi told me that, to the Pavesi, torta paradiso means their city. At Christmas he sends thousands of the cakes to the Pavesi dotted around the world, accompanied by a bottle of Santa Maria della Versa, a spumante Brut produced with local grapes. Grecchi also assured me that torta paradiso is a most nourishing food, so much so, in fact, that he runs the Milan-Pavia race (32 kilometres) on nothing more than 50g of torta paradiso and a glass of milk!

Well, a lot of fascinating information, but I came out of the beautiful art nouveau shop without the recipe. However, a few days later I was given a very similar and excellent recipe by a kind lady who has a pasta shop in a small town near by. And this is her recipe, which I call La Torta Paradiso di Wilma Magagnato. Apart from being utterly delicious, the cake has the added benefit of being suitable for people who are allergic to wheat flour. Serve it, as in Pavia, with sparkling wine at the end of a dinner, although it is also good as an accompaniment to poached fruit, or taken at tea time . . . coffee time . . . any time.

THE RECIPE

Potato flour is available in good supermarkets, specialist food shops and health-food shops.

SERVES 10 TO 12

325g/11oz [US 3 sticks less 2 tbsp] best unsalted butter, at room temperature

325g/11oz caster sugar [US 1½ cups granulated sugar]

3 size-2 very fresh eggs [US extra-large eggs]

325g/11oz [US 2⅓ cups] potato flour

3g/a generous ½ tsp cream of tartar

3g/a generous ½ tsp bicarbonate of soda [US baking soda]

3g/a generous ½ tsp salt

1 unwaxed lemon

butter and dried breadcrumbs for the tin

icing sugar [US confectioners' sugar], to finish

Heat the oven to 170°C/350°F/Gas Mark 3.

Cut the butter into small pieces and put them in a bowl. Add the sugar and mix together until wholly blended. (I use my hands, because it's easier and quicker than a spoon.) Add one egg at a time to the butter-sugar cream, while beating constantly. For this operation I use a hand-held electric mixer. Do not add a second egg until the previous one is totally incorporated.

Sift the potato flour with the cream of tartar, bicarbonate of soda and salt, and sprinkle large spoonfuls over the surface of the butter-cream. Incorporate each spoonful of flour with a large metal spoon and a high movement to incorporate some air as well.

Wash and dry the lemon and, using a zester or a small grater, grate the rind – only the yellow part – into the mixture. Mix well.

Prepare a 25cm/10in spring-clip tin by buttering the inside very generously and sprinkling the surface with dried breadcrumbs. Turn the tin upside-down and tap out all excess crumbs. Spoon the cake mixture into the tin, give the tin a jerk or two to settle the mixture and bake for 45 minutes or thereabouts, until the cake is dry inside and has shrunk from the edge.

Unmould the cake and leave on a wire rack to cool. Use great care when you transfer this very fragile cake. Before serving, sprinkle the top with a thick layer of icing sugar.

You can keep the cake, well wrapped in foil, for . . . how long? You may well ask. I'm afraid I don't know because in my house a torta paradiso is likely to be polished off in 2 or 3 days. But you can keep it for a week or so, although it will lose its fragrance.

Fettine di Mele all'Antica

Sautéed Sliced Apples

La Cucina Mantovana is a very informative book on the cooking of Mantua. Cia Eramo, its author, claims that the recipe on which the following is based is by the great Bartolomeo Stefani (although I could not find it in his book). Stefani was chef to Ottavio Gonzaga and wrote *L'Arte di Ben Cucinare*, published in 1662. He was the first chef to reject the over-elaborate cooking of the Renaissance, and to approach food and cooking in a more workaday fashion. His recipes are never extravagant and his influence is still felt to this day.

The liqueurs suggested in Eramo's book are Calvados and Grand Marnier. I prefer to use only Calvados. I have tried the dish with and without cream and I am sure it is better on its own, as in its original version. Eramo concludes her recipe by writing, 'A dessert which is a genuine delicacy'.

SERVES 4

4 crisp dessert apples
45g/1¾oz [US 3 tbsp] unsalted butter
150–180g/5–6oz caster sugar [US ¾–1 cup granulated sugar], depending on the sweetness of the apples
2 unwaxed lemons
4 tbsp fresh orange juice
4 tbsp Calvados

Peel the apples and remove the core, leaving the apples whole. Cut them across into slices about 1cm/½in thick.

Choose a large frying pan into which the apple slices will fit in a single layer. If you don't have a large enough pan use two frying pans, increasing the amount of butter to 30g/1oz [US 2 tbsp] per pan. Melt the butter and add 4 or 5 tablespoons of the sugar. Let it caramelize a little and then add the apple slices. Sauté on one side over a lively heat until golden, then gently turn the slices over and add another 2 or 3 tablespoons of sugar.

Wash one of the lemons, grate the rind and add to the pan. Squeeze both lemons and add 6 tablespoons of the juice to the pan together with the orange juice. Continue cooking, while gradually adding the remaining sugar, until the apple slices can be easily pierced by the point of a small knife.

Now heat the Calvados in a metal ladle. Pour it into the pan while you put a match to it. Let the flame die down, then transfer the apples to a heated dish and spoon over that delicious buttery syrup. Serve at once.

You can prepare the dish in advance and reheat it in the oven. Flame it just before serving.

Il Gelato di Limone
Lemon Ice-cream

Charles, my English son-in-law, came back to this country recently after living in Italy for a year. The other day, while eating this ice-cream approvingly, he asked me if I could explain why ice-creams are always so much better in Italy. 'Easy,' I said, 'the fruit ripens in the hot Italian sun and it's only picked when it's properly ripe.' But then he pointed out that all ice-creams are better, not only the fruit ones. And my answer to that was that in Italy ice-creams are made with eggs as well as cream or milk, not only with cream. It is the egg yolk that gives the ice-cream that silky smooth texture and delicate yet positive flavour.

I wonder if this lemon ice-cream is the one that Stendhal refers to in his diary for 4th October 1816. After an evening at La Scala in Milan, he writes, 'Half way through the evening it is the normal duty of the escorting gallant to regale his mistress with ices, which are served in the box. These sorbets are divine; they may be of three kinds: gelati, crepé and pezzi duri, and no one should fail to make so rewarding an acquaintance. I am still undecided which of the three species is the most exquisite; and so, every evening, I resort to experiment.'

THE RECIPE

If you use waxed lemons you should scrub them very hard under hot water. You will feel a greasy substance coming off the lemon. Not very pleasant. So try to get unwaxed lemons, which you must wash and dry.

SERVES 4 OR 5

3 unwaxed lemons
150g/5oz [US ¾ cup] sugar
2 size-2 egg yolks [US extra-large egg yolks]
150ml/5fl oz double cream [US heavy cream]

Remove the zest from 2 of the lemons with a vegetable peeler, leaving the white pith behind as this would give the ice-cream a bitter flavour. Put the zest in a small saucepan and add 150ml/5fl oz of water and the sugar.

Squeeze all the 3 lemons and pour the juice into the saucepan. Bring the mixture very slowly to the boil and simmer for 5 minutes, stirring the whole time to help the sugar to dissolve. Strain the syrup.

Beat the egg yolks in another saucepan, which should have a heavy base. Pour in the syrup while you beat. I use a hand-held electric mixer for this. The mixture will become very light and bubbly. Put the saucepan on a very low heat and heat until the mixture begins to thicken. Stir constantly with a wooden spoon, no longer with the electric mixer. Draw off the heat and put the pan in a sink of cold water. Continue to stir for a couple of minutes until the saucepan has cooled down, otherwise the custard might still curdle at the bottom. Stir in the cream.

When the mixture is cold, pour it into an ice-cream maker and freeze, following the manufacturer's instructions.

If you have kept the ice-cream in the freezer, don't forget to transfer it to the fridge about 30 to 40 minutes before you want to serve it. Ice-cream is nicer a little sloppy rather than solid.

Pan con l'Uva
Bread with Raisins

Nothing brings back my early schooldays more vividly than pan con l'uva. Opposite the entrance to our primary school in Milan's Via della Spiga there was a tiny baker's shop, and all the way down the narrow street one could smell the most delicious breads being baked. Before gathering in the school hall for assembly we all queued for our favourite bread – pan con l'uva. A piece, about

5cm/2in long, just out of the oven at the back of the shop, was handed to us wrapped in thick yellow absorbent paper. We used to put this *merenda* in our desk, which meant that the classroom was pervaded by the best smell in the world, that of freshly baked bread plus the sweet smell of the *zibibbo* – large fat dried grapes. The zibibbo come from Sicily or Pantelleria. They are reconstituted in water before baking and, when hot, they exude the exhilarating smell of fresh grapes.

When my children started school in London and came back with descriptions of what they could buy in the tuck shop, I thought how lucky I had been to have had in my desk something I looked forward to so much that even the most boring lesson was part of the treat.

In her fascinating book *La Lombardia in Cucina*, Ottorina Perna Bozzi writes that the first pan con l'uga (its name in dialect) appeared in 1876 on a stall at Porta Venezia. This was at the terminus of the first tram line, the Milano–Monza, which had just been built. The bread was apparently made in Monza and brought to Milan by a clever entrepreneur. Eventually a baker opened a shop in Milan where the Milanese flocked to buy their beloved pan con l'uva before catching the tram. Ottorina Perna Bozzi goes on to say that this bread soon established itself as the favourite snack for children to take to school, as it certainly was up to my time.

THE RECIPE

The best dried grapes to use are the dried Muscatel, which you can find in a few specialist shops. They have a flavour and juiciness that is similar to the zibibbo. Other than those, I prefer raisins to sultanas [US golden raisins] because they have a more pronounced and slightly less sweet flavour.

This bread is best eaten when still warm. If you have made it in advance, reheat it in a low oven for 10 minutes or so.

SERVES 6–8

200g/7oz [US 1⅓ cups] dried Muscatels or raisins
225g/8oz [US 2 cups] white flour, preferably Italian 00
15g/½oz easy-blend dried yeast [US 2pkg rapid-rise yeast]
a pinch of salt
100ml/3½fl oz semi-skimmed milk [US low-fat milk]
40g/1½oz [US 3 tbsp] unsalted butter, melted
2–3 tbsp lukewarm water
2 tbsp dark Muscovado sugar

If you are using Muscatels, remove the grapes from the stalk. Soak the Muscatels or raisins in hot water for about 4 hours. Drain them and pat them dry with kitchen paper towel. Set aside.

Mix the dry ingredients together in a bowl and then add the milk and the butter. Knead, adding enough water to form an elastic, silky and smooth dough. Knead for about 5 minutes, then place the dough in an oiled bowl. Roll the dough to coat with oil all over, to prevent the surface becoming dry and crusty. Cover with a thick linen towel and let the dough rise in a warm place until it has doubled in volume, about 2 to 2½ hours.

Place the dough on a lightly floured work surface and pat or roll it into an oval shape, about 1cm/½in thick. This dough will be a little sticky.

Sprinkle about one-third of the raisins over the dough and pat them into the dough. Now do the same with another batch of raisins, and then again until all the raisins are embedded in the dough. Pat the raisins down with the palm of your hands and sprinkle with the brown sugar. Roll the dough up, Swiss-roll [US jelly-roll] fashion, tapering at each end. Tuck the ends of the dough roll under, and place the bread on a floured baking tray. Place the tray in a warm corner of the kitchen, cover with a linen towel and leave it for a second rising, until the dough has doubled, about 1 hour.

Heat the oven to 200°C/400°F/Gas Mark 6.

Place the bread in the oven and bake for 15 minutes. Turn the heat down to 180°C/350°F/Gas Mark 4 and bake for a further 30 minutes. Transfer the bread to a wire rack and allow to cool a little before serving. It is nicest when warm but can also be eaten cold.

Il Sandwich di Panettone
Panettone Sandwich

I am not giving a recipe for panettone, first because it is very difficult to make successfully, and secondly because the panettone you can buy in shops is better than any home-made panettone I have ever tasted.

Nowadays panettone comes in three versions, the plain old-fashioned one, one with chocolate chips, and a panettone stuffed with zabaione or with tiramisù. Some brands of panettone are better than others. A good one is made by Scarpato. It contains no additives, and the panettone is hand-made in the traditional way with good creamy butter and the right amount of dried fruit; it has a beautiful light texture. It is a plain panettone in the old-fashioned squat dome shape, and all these points commend it to an old-fashioned Milanese like me.

Panettone, which to me means a Milanese Christmas, has recently become the Christmas cake par excellence all over Italy. And now it is marching on to conquer the world. It is available all year round from Italian food shops, and it is always welcome, whether eaten with a cup of coffee for breakfast, with a cup of tea at tea-time, with a glass of Vinsanto at the end of a meal or just on its own at any time.

The origins of panettone go back to the Middle Ages, when a large loaf of bread, sometimes enriched with various ingredients – called *pan grande* – was made in every home; on the top the master of the house would mark a cross. Its name has probably come about through adding an affectionate diminutive (denoting sweetness) to *pane*, hence panetto, and then the suffix *-one*, which always indicates largeness.

THE RECIPE

In recent years panettone has been used in this country to make a kind of bread and butter pudding. Being light it lends itself to this treatment, and many chefs have created their own version. I find this one the best. It is a recipe by Vincenzo Bergonzoli of the Ristorante San Vicenzo in London, where I have always eaten well. Vincenzo serves the pudding on its own, in the real Italian tradition, but it also goes well with a jug of hot zabaione.

SERVES 8

450g/1lb panettone
1 unwaxed orange
1 unwaxed lemon
3 size-2 eggs [US extra-large eggs]
450g/1lb mascarpone
6 drops of vanilla extract
2 pinches of ground cinnamon
3 tbsp caster sugar [US granulated sugar]
40g/1½oz [US 3 tbsp] unsalted butter
4 tbsp sweet white vermouth
icing sugar [US confectioners' sugar], to finish

Cut half the panettone into slices just over 1cm/½in thick, and the other half into slightly thinner slices. Keep them separate. Leave the panettone to dry uncovered for 24 hours or so.

Wash the orange and the lemon and dry them. Grate the rind and then squeeze the juice. Strain the juice.

Heat the oven to 170°C/325°F/Gas Mark 3.

Beat the eggs in a large bowl. Add the mascarpone and beat until the eggs have been incorporated. Now beat in the vanilla, cinnamon, lemon and orange rind and juice, and sugar. (I use a hand-held electric mixer for the final whisking.) The mixture should be quite thick. Melt half the butter and add to the mixture.

Take a shallow oven dish in which the panettone will fit in two layers. (I use a rectangular metal dish measuring 22 × 17cm/9 × 7in.) Grease the dish with a little of the remaining butter and line with greaseproof paper [US wax paper]. Grease the paper too. Lay the thicker slices of panettone over the bottom, plugging any holes with pieces of panettone. Moisten with some vermouth using a pastry brush. Spread over the mascarpone cream and then cover with the thinner slices of panettone, moistening these slices also with the remaining vermouth. Dot with the rest of the butter and bake for half an hour.

Cut the pudding into slices or squares, depending on the shape of your oven dish. Release the pieces all around the edge with the help of a thin knife and transfer them to individual plates. Sprinkle with icing sugar just before serving.

Pan di Miglio

Polenta and Elderflower Cake

In Lombardy this cake is eaten on St George's day, St George being regarded (for reasons that are totally obscure) as the patron saint of dairy farmers. I still remember the joy, as a child, of pouring rich Lombard cream into a soup plate and placing in the middle a small round of pan di miglio. The pan di miglio just softens in the cream and you get mouthfuls of a simple bready sweetness mellowed in the cream.

This traditional sweet bread used to be made with millet flour (*miglio*) before the arrival of maize from the New World, which has replaced it.

Pick the elderflowers when in full bloom, from bushes growing in full sunshine; they have more flavour. Pick the little white elderflowers off the stalks, trying to remove as many of the tiny stalks as you can.

You can make about 8 small (5cm/2in) buns, which will then spread and grow to about twice that size. Or you can put the dough in a 20–22cm/8–9in shallow tin, which I find easier and better.

SERVES 6

100g/3½oz [US 7 tbsp] unsalted butter
200g/7oz coarse-ground maize (polenta) flour [US 1¾ cups coarse cornmeal]
125g/4oz [US 1 cup] white flour, preferably Italian 00
1½ tsp baking powder
a pinch of salt
125g/4oz caster sugar [US ½ cup+2 tbsp granulated sugar]
1 egg
2 tbsp milk
6 level tbsp elderflowers
butter for the tin

Heat the oven to 180°C/350°F/Gas Mark 4.

Melt the butter very slowly in a small saucepan.

Mix the dry ingredients together in a bowl. Add the egg, melted butter and milk and mix well. Now mix in the elderflowers.

Generously butter a 20cm/8in tart tin and fill with the mixture. Spread it and level it with your hands. Bake for about 40 minutes or until the point of a sharp knife inserted in the middle of the pan di miglio comes out dry. Serve with thick pouring cream, or eat it as it is with tea, coffee or a glass of sweet wine.

Valle d'Aosta & Piemonte

When my children were young we used to drive to Italy for our summer holidays, rather than fly. We enjoyed the journey across France, the changing face of nature as we travelled south and the warming of the climate. But most of all we enjoyed the thought of getting closer to Italy. And then, at last, the crossing of the frontier; this was the exciting moment, France behind us, then no-man's-land and then l'Italia! I shall always remember once after parking near the Gran San Bernardo frontier post, looking behind me as we walked towards our first espresso and seeing my elder son, Paul, kneeling down and kissing the concrete of the petrol station.

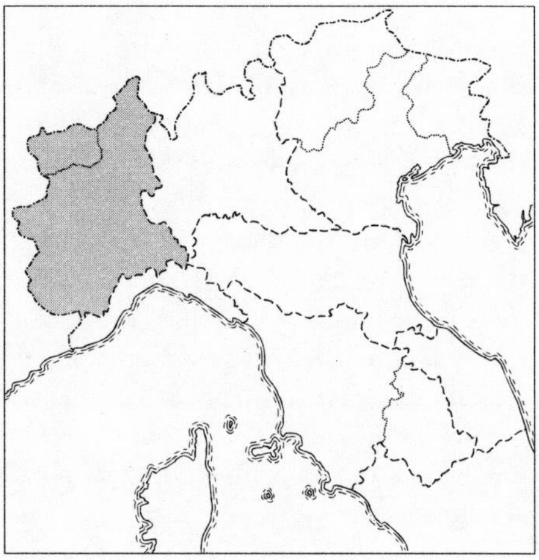

The Mont Blanc tunnel was a favourite of ours. You got into the tunnel in France and, after 10 dark minutes, you came out in Italy, whose sun was usually there to greet us. But what my young children noticed with disappointment year after year was that, although we were in Italy, we seemed to be still in France. The language heard in the bars sounded like French, the names of the villages were French, the coins used were still French francs. Only when we eventually got to Aosta, the capital of the region, did we begin to feel safely home.

One thing, however, was a clear indication of where we were: the food. In the bars, pizze and focaccie were lined up next to croissants and brioches; Baci Perugina and Pocket Coffee were there next to the cashier and, best of all, coffee was a proper espresso.

The food and cooking of Valle d'Aosta, while nominally Italian, is more northern European than Mediterranean, with its emphasis on dairy products and its lack of vegetables. No pasta, no olive oil, no tomatoes. There are nourishing soups based on bread, as well as sausages, rice and polenta and chestnuts dressed with butter and cream – a Teutonic type of cooking. The reason for this, of course, is the Germanic influence. Germanic peoples descended through Switzerland into the lateral valleys of Valle d'Aosta in the 13th century, and there they remained, isolated, speaking their language and keeping their traditions.

Years ago in Gressoney I met an old lady, Signora Martini, who could hardly speak Italian. She spoke a sort of German patois. Her cooking was the most valdostano I have ever tasted. In her cellar hung a *mocetta*, a local salame which was then made from the thigh of a wild goat, but now is usually made with domestic goat meat. Beautiful Reinette apples and Martin Sech pears were lined up next to jars containing all kinds of fungi under oil and even preserved meat, which this old woman was still making. Meat was preserved in salt and herbs for the winter months and used then to make carbonata, a direct descendant of the Flemish carbonade, the difference being that the beer is replaced by wine.

Signora Martini asked us to dinner the next day. We started with a glistening white mountain of *gnocchi alla bava* – potato gnocchi dressed with fontina, the best local cheese, now also available here, albeit in a mass-produced form that does not do justice to the flowery, herby and nutty flavour of the real product. After a magnificently generous bowl of carbonata, the meal was rounded off with caffé valdostano. This is coffee mixed with Grappa, red wine, sugar and lemon rind, and it is served in the *grolla*, a large earthenware container with six or eight spouts from which the coffee is drunk by the various guests while the grolla is handed around.

I am afraid that night was the scene of one of the more embarrassing episodes of my life. My son Guy, then aged six, wanted to have a sip too, in spite of my warnings that the drink contained spirits, which he hated. But the Martinis loved children and were ready to spoil him. '*Ma glielo lasci assaggiare!*' (but let him try it). And so Guy sipped, and the next moment the sip came out of his mouth in a perfect spray, spattering the previously immaculate white tablecloth with black spots. Guy was in tears, I was nearly in tears, but the Martinis seemed to enjoy the happening and laughed heartily. To be honest, I didn't like that coffee either and wished I could do the same as Guy, instead of having to swallow that nasty black concoction. The drinking of coffee in this way is a symbol of comradeship and hospitality, and Italians, I know, are touchy on that subject.

In Aosta the cooking begins to take a different shape. It becomes more complex and sophisticated, with vegetables to the fore, heralding the wealth of vegetables in Piedmont. Piedmontese cooking seems to me to be divided according to its topography. The lowland area next to Lombardy is mainly devoted to rice culture, the Alpine zone shares the characteristics of the cooking of Valle d'Aosta, and the rich hilly area is a mecca for the gourmet with its arrays of excellent dishes and famous produce. The prize of this area is the white truffle. And what a prize it is, one of which the locals are hugely proud, and rightly so.

I have been in or around Alba quite a few times during the truffle season. The last time was at the truffle fair in Moncalvo, an attractive town north of

Asti, to which I was invited by the great gastronome and author, Giovanni Goria. The square was packed with people and with stalls selling pumpkins, cheeses, honey, mushrooms and all sorts of those horrid ethnic knick-knacks that have become a fixture at any fair anywhere in the western world. The stalls with truffles, being the most important, were under the *loggiato* (arches), with the mayor and the judges standing at the central stall. The names of the winners were called out over a loudspeaker, to great applause from the bystanders, as up to the mayor went each winning *cavatore* (truffle hunter) leading his dog. These dogs are usually a cross between a mongrel and a hound. The hound provides the nose, while the less aristocratic parent contributes the intelligence! I was completely won over by Diana, a smallish sort of grey pointer. She was named 'best truffle dog of the year', but she was afflicted with stage-fright and kept hiding between her master's legs, trembling at the flashes from all the surrounding cameras. Her owner told me, however, that once free on the field, Diana became a different dog, courageous, adventurous and unyielding.

After the ceremony we all went to eat at the social club, which sounds awful, and I dare say was not Claridges, and yet the meal I had there was one of the best ever. The truffles, alas, appeared only, and with parsimony, in the risotto and in the *tajarin* – the local tagliatelle, which were simply dressed with melted butter, flavoured with garlic, herbs and plenty of grated Parmesan. But the nine courses were so good that one forgave the minimal appearance of the truffles. The meal ended with *la coppa di Seiràss* and lots of local biscuits such as brutti ma buoni (page 75) and melting-in-the-mouth soft amaretti. La coppa di Seiràss is a creamy pudding made with the magical ricotta piemontese, a softer richer ricotta than the romana, which is the sort you can buy here in Italian food shops. Ricotta piemontese is a by-product of cheeses made with cow's milk, while ricotta romana is a by-product of pecorino.

There are many other remarkable cheeses from Piedmont, the best being the toma and tomini, which can be eaten young, when still fresh, milky and soft, or aged, when they became robust and charmingly aggressive. Fresh tome are used a lot in antipasti, the range of which, in Piedmont, is infinite. Any decent Piedmontese meal will kick off with a minimum of five antipasti, the cold ones placed on the table and the hot brought in from the kitchen in quick succession. In these Lucullan antipasti the pride of place is given to the magnificent vegetables from the hilly areas: the asparagus of Santena, the small onions of Ivrea, the sweet peppers and leeks of the Valle del Tanaro, to mention but a few.

Equally rich and diverse is the last course. *Torte* (cakes), *cioccolatini*, *biscotti* and *budini* (puddings) are a feast to the eye and, of course, the palate. Turin, the capital, is the best place to enjoy all this. For the chocoholic, the Pasticceria Peyrano is the must of all musts. Even I, not a chocoholic and not even very keen on chocolate, cannot resist buying a tray of this and a tray of that whenever I set foot in the shop. My favourite *pasticceria*, however, is the Forneria Polo in Corso Dante, where the charming Sandra produces excellent breads and all sorts of cakes, biscuits and cookies, with her husband helping in the back of the kitchen by baking, rolling, stirring and filling. I used to go to Turin often when my older brother lived there. Now that he has retired to the country I think back with nostalgia to these two shops, the like of which it would be difficult to find anywhere in the world.

My appreciation of Piedmontese sweets is reflected in the fact that I have included more recipes for desserts and cakes from Piedmont than from any other region.

MINESTRA DI RISO E CASTAGNE Ⓥ

Rice and Chestnut Soup

A chestnut soup of one kind or another is made in nearly all Alpine towns. This one can be made with milk instead of stock, but I find that too thick and heavy and prefer the lighter touch of a good vegetable stock.

A word of warning about chestnuts. Buy good large, shining nuts. Peeling them is a bit of a bother, but however hard I have tried, I have not been able to find any simpler or quicker way. For this recipe you don't have to peel a great many chestnuts, so it is not too bad.

SERVES 4

450g/1lb chestnuts
1.2l/2pt [US 5 cups] vegetable stock (page 231)
125g/4oz [US ½ cup] Italian rice, preferably Vialone Nano
salt
20g/¾oz [US 1½ tbsp] unsalted butter
2 tbsp chopped fresh flat-leaf parsley

First rinse the chestnuts in cold water. Then, using a small pointed knife, slit the shell of each chestnut across the whole of the rounded side, being careful not to cut too deep and dig into the actual nut. Put the chestnuts in a saucepan, cover with cold water and bring to the boil. Boil for 15 to 20 minutes. The chestnuts will still be slightly undercooked, but do not worry; they will finish cooking later in the stock.

Now the boring job of peeling them, which means that you must remove not only the outer shell, which is easy enough, but also the brownish inner skin with its unpleasant bitter taste. You will need a small pointed knife. To peel, lift a few chestnuts from the water, leaving the rest in the hot water (warm chestnuts are easier to peel). Throw away any bad nuts – you will notice them by the acrid smell they give off as soon as you begin to peel them.

Cut the chestnuts coarsely into pieces and put them in a clean saucepan. Cover with the stock and bring to the boil. Simmer gently, with the lid on, for 30 minutes. Mix in the rice and cook until al dente. Taste and check salt. No pepper should be added to this slightly sweet soup. Draw the pan off the heat and stir in the butter and the parsley. Ladle the soup as soon as the butter has melted.

MINESTRA DI RISO E SEDANO Ⓥ

Rice and Celery Soup

The best rice soups are from the more northerly regions of Piedmont, Lombardy and Veneto. This recipe is from the valley of the River Tanaro, which rises on the other side of the Alps from San Remo and runs North into the Po, crossing all the southern part of Piedmont. The valley is very fertile and produces some of the best vegetables in Italy.

Use green celery whenever in season as it has a stronger flavour than white celery.

SERVES 4 TO 5

450g/1lb celery, preferably green celery
125g/4oz floury potato
2.2l/4pt [US 2¼qt] vegetable stock (page 231)
4 tbsp extra virgin olive oil
30g/1oz [US 2 tbsp] unsalted butter
2 tbsp finely chopped onion
125g/4oz [US ½ cup] Italian rice, preferably Vialone Nano
freshly grated Parmesan

Remove the inside leaves from the celery. Wash and dry them and then chop them. Set them aside for the final touch.

Remove the strings from the outer celery stalks with a potato peeler. Wash the stalks and cut half of them into pieces.

Peel the potato and cut into similar pieces. Put both chopped vegetables in a heavy pot with half the stock and half the oil. Bring to the boil and simmer gently until the vegetables are cooked. Now pour the contents of the pan into the bowl of a food processor and whizz until smooth, or put it through a food mill fitted with the small-hole disc. This second method might be slower but it certainly gives the best result, since the purée is more homogeneous.

Wash the saucepan and finish the soup. Put the remaining oil, the butter and onion into the pan and sauté the onion for about 10 minutes. Cut the remaining celery into thin sticks, about 2.5cm/1in long, and throw into the pan. Stir it around to *insàporire* – pick up the flavour – for 5 to 6 minutes.

Add the celery and potato purée to the pot. Mix well and then pour in the remaining stock gradually, while stirring with the other hand to incorporate the purée into the stock. Bring to the boil.

Now you must add the rice. Give a good stir and let it cook until tender, about 10 minutes.

Ladle the soup into soup bowls, sprinkle with the reserved celery leaves and serve with grated Parmesan. Some people will love to add it.

Zuppa di Ceci Astigiana

Chick-pea and Vegetable Soup

I recently bought an excellent book by one of the greatest Italian gastronomes, Giovanni Goria, who is the expert on Piedmontese cooking. The book gives a recipe for this soup, and I was fascinated to read in its introduction about the connection between chick-peas and All Souls' Day.

It reminded me of a superstition I was told as a child by our cook from Friuli. At her home, every year on the night of 1st November, her mother used to put two bowls of chick-peas on the kitchen table. One of the two was for them to eat the next day, while the other was *per i morti* – for those who had died, who were supposed to be allowed to come down (definitely not up!) to earth to eat them. The chick-peas always remained untouched, and to explain this, Maria would say, 'Well, I expect the good Lord needed them up there for something special.' Goria writes about this story though with slight variations, so it is evidently part of the common lore of peasant superstitions.

Chick-peas are humble, unpretentious food, but I cannot see why they should be food for the dead. Perhaps it is because they are so good that one hopes to be able to eat them in the next life!

THE RECIPE

Chick-peas are eaten all over northern Italy on All Saints' or All Souls' Day. The recipes differ quite considerably, the only constant ingredient being, of course, the chick-peas. This recipe is for a thick, nourishing soup from Asti in south-eastern Piedmont. It is a soup that I only discovered in 1993, when I went there for a truffle fair.

My recipe is based on that included in *La Cucina del Piemonte* by Giovanni Goria. The soup can also be ladled over slices of lightly toasted white country bread, such as Pugliese, that has been rubbed with garlic. It then becomes the ideal meal for a cold winter night. Buy chick-peas from a reliable shop with a quick turnover. If they have been stored for too long, chick-peas never become tender no matter how long you cook them. And there is nothing more unpleasant than undercooked pulses.

SERVES 8

500g/1lb 2oz [US 2½ cups] best dried chick-peas
1 tbsp flour
1 tsp bicarbonate of soda [US baking soda]
1 tsp salt
1 onion, cut into pieces
a fresh bouquet garni, containing parsley, rosemary, sage and bay leaf
2 garlic cloves
150g/5oz fresh pork rind
1 leek, both white and green part, cut into matchsticks
2 carrots, cut into matchsticks
2 medium potatoes, cut into matchsticks
1 celery heart with its yellow leaves, cut into matchsticks
2 or 3 outside leaves of cabbage, cut into strips
salt and freshly ground pepper

FOR THE SOFFRITTO

15g/½oz dried porcini
90g/3oz pancetta
2 garlic cloves
the needles of 1 fresh rosemary sprig
the leaves of 1 fresh sage sprig
2 tbsp extra virgin olive oil

The day before, put the chick-peas in a large bowl and cover with lukewarm water. If you live in a part of the country where the water is very hard, use filtered water or, better still, rain water. Make a paste with the flour, bicarbonate of soda, salt and some water and mix it into the bowl. Leave to soak for 24 hours or so.

The next day, drain the chick-peas and rinse them quickly under cold water. Put them in a large stockpot. I use an earthenware pot for pulses and soups, earthenware being the best material because it heats slowly and diffuses the heat all over the container. It is, therefore, ideal for slow cooking. Cover with 4.5–5l/8–9pt [US 4½–5qt] of cold water and add the onion, bouquet garni and peeled garlic cloves. Bring to a simmer and cook for about 2 to 3 hours, setting the lid slightly askew over the pot. This cooking, as for all pulses, must be very gentle indeed.

While the chick-peas are cooking, blanch the pork rind for 15 minutes in boiling water to rid it of some of the fat. After that, cut it in 5mm/¼in strips and throw it into the stockpot to cook with the chick-peas.

To prepare the *soffritto* soak the dried porcini for about 1 hour in hot water. I have found that the recommended 30 minutes is often not long enough, especially when the porcini are not very good and have been dried too quickly to a leathery texture. After the hour, or less if you have beautiful slices of dried porcini, lift them out. If gritty, rinse them under cold water. Chop them finely. Filter the liquid through a sieve lined with muslin, cheesecloth or kitchen paper towel.

Add all the cut-up vegetables to the pot to cook with the chick-peas for a further hour. During this long slow cooking you might have to add some water. Always add boiling water.

Chop finely the pancetta, garlic, rosemary and sage and put in a small frying pan with the olive oil. Sauté gently for 2 minutes and then add the chopped porcini and a pinch of salt. Continue cooking for about 10 minutes, keeping the heat very low so that the whole mixture will sauté gently and not fry. Add a couple of tablespoons of the porcini liquid if you see it getting too dry.

About 10 minutes before the soup is ready, scrape in the soffritto. Mix well and then taste. Check salt and add plenty of pepper.

When the soup is ready ladle it into individual bowls. Pass round a bottle of your best oil at the table for your family or guests to pour some into their soup.

Riso in Cagnone alla Piemontese Ⓥ

Rice Dressed with Fontina and Butter

'Everyone talked of the excellent table I kept . . . My macaroni al sughillo, my rice sometimes as pilau, sometimes in cagnone, my olla podridas were the talk of the town.' Thus wrote Casanova in his *Memorie.*

I wonder if his riso in cagnone was Lombard or Piedmontese, since there are two versions. The rice in the Lombard version is dressed with butter flavoured with sage leaves and garlic, a very traditional dressing for rice or pasta. This is the Piedmontese version, made with local fontina, a cheese from Valle d'Aosta, which is available in specialist cheese shops or Italian food shops.

THE RECIPE

If you cannot find Italian fontina, use raclette, a similar cheese from Switzerland.

SERVES 4 AS A FIRST COURSE OR 3 AS A MAIN COURSE

350g/12oz [US 1¾ cups] Italian rice (Carnaroli or Arborio)

salt

125g/4oz fontina

60g/2oz [US 4 tbsp] unsalted butter

Cook the rice in plenty of boiling salted water.

Meanwhile, cut the cheese into tiny cubes and put half in a serving bowl. Put the bowl in a low oven.

Melt the butter and let it become the deep golden colour of hazelnuts. Add half to the bowl in the oven.

When the rice is done, drain it, but leave it quite wet, and transfer it to the bowl with the cheese and butter. Mix thoroughly and then add the remaining cheese. Toss again very well until the cheese has melted completely. Pour over the rest of the melted butter and serve immediately.

Note: traditionally no pepper is added.

GNOCCHI DI PATATE Ⓥ

Potato Gnocchi

Whenever I make gnocchi in my kitchen in Barnes I am suddenly transported back to our family kitchen in Via Gesù in Milan, and I can still see my little fingers flipping gnocchi over a white linen napkin, while my beloved Maria, our cook, was saying, 'Brava, you make them even better than I do.' Flick, flip, first into the flour then down the prongs of the fork. I used to love making them, though I cannot remember if I was equally keen on eating them.

Now, 'forty years on', I love eating gnocchi, but I find the flipping rather boring. So I am looking forward to the day when my little granddaughter will sit with me in the kitchen and flip gnocchi.

Gnocchi can be made with or without eggs. Broadly speaking, gnocchi with eggs are made in Veneto, while in Piedmont not only do they not use eggs but the best gnocchi makers manage to add only 100g of flour to 1kg of potatoes!

THE RECIPE

Potato gnocchi, like many traditional basic dishes, are not as easy to make as it seems. You have to know the right potatoes to use, to add just enough flour to hold the gnocchi together but not to make them heavy, and to boil them on the right heat, just enough for the flour to cook. Gnocchi containing eggs are easier to cook because they do not present the problem that '. . . faced the lady, who as soon as she had immersed the spoon in the saucepan to stir them around, found nothing in it; the gnocchi had disappeared.' This extract is from Artusi's book *La Scienza in Cucina e l'Arte di Mangiar Bene*. Artusi puts the blame on the lady not adding enough flour. But I have had it happen to me, when I've used the wrong sort of potatoes. So I advise you to start by cooking only 2 or 3 gnocchi. If they disintegrate, or stick to each other in a gluey mess, add an egg and a little flour to the dough.

Once you find a variety of potato that makes good gnocchi, stick to it. I make egg-less gnocchi with waxy potatoes, Desirée or Estima, while I add an egg to the floury varieties. The flavour of gnocchi with egg or without is, of course, different. Those without egg are softer and lighter in the mouth and the potato flavour is more pronounced. Gnocchi with eggs have more 'spirit' and more body. I prefer gnocchi without eggs, simply dressed with butter and cheese, or with a fontina or a gorgonzola sauce, plus a shaving of truffle if I am in luck. The sturdier gnocchi with eggs I like dressed with a tomato sauce (page 228) or with a pesto alla genovese (page 131).

GNOCCHI WITHOUT EGGS

SERVES 4

900g/2lb waxy potatoes

1½ tsp salt

150–180g/5–6oz [US 1¼–1½ cups] flour, preferably Italian 00

Boil the potatoes in their skins. When the point of a small knife can easily be pushed through to the middle, the potatoes are ready. Drain and peel them as soon as you can handle them. Purée them through the smaller disc of a food mill, or a potato ricer, straight on to your work surface. Spread the purée around to cool it and then add the salt and some of the flour. Do not add all the flour at once. Stop as soon as you can knead the mixture into a dough, which should be soft, smooth and still slightly sticky. Shape the dough into sausages about 2.5cm/1in in diameter, and cut the sausages into 2cm/¾in chunks.

Now you have to put the grooves into the gnocchi, a more complicated operation. The grooves, by the way, are there for a reason, not just for beauty – they thin out the middle of the gnocchi, so that they will cook more evenly and, when cooked, will trap more sauce. Keeping your

CLOCKWISE FROM TOP LEFT:
BUCKWHEAT POLENTA WITH
BUTTER AND CHEESE (PAGE 32)
STEWED VENISON (PAGE 84)
AND FUNGI STEW (PAGE 80)

POACHED CHICKEN
IN A VINEGARY SAUCE
(PAGE 45)

POTATO RAVIOLI, LEFT (PAGE 117); BUCKWHEAT PASTA WITH POTATO AND CABBAGE (PAGE 25)

PARADISE CAKE, LEFT (PAGE 49)
BUCKWHEAT CAKE (PAGE 86)

KNOBBLY NUTTY BISCUITS (PAGE 75);
BISCUITS WITH FENNEL (PAGE 121);
LITTLE RING BISCUITS (PAGE 227)

hands, the fork and any surface lightly floured, flip each dumpling against the prongs of the fork, without dragging it, letting it drop on to a clean linen towel. Some cooks flip the dumpling towards the handle; others, like me, go from the handle to the point of the prongs. You will find your favourite way.

When all the gnocchi are grooved, bring a large saucepan of salted water to the boil. Cook the gnocchi in 3 or 4 batches, not all at once. The gnocchi will first sink to the bottom of the pan, when you must give them a very gentle stir, and then very shortly after they will float up to the surface. Count to 10 and then retrieve them with a slotted spoon. Pat them dry quickly with a piece of kitchen paper towel and transfer them to a heated dish. Dress each batch with a little of whichever sauce you have chosen. When all the gnocchi are cooked, pour over all the remaining sauce and serve at once.

GNOCCHI WITH EGG

Add 1 egg to the potato purée and then add the flour. With the egg you might have to add a little more flour, up to 200g/7oz [US 1¾ cups].

GNOCCHI ALLA BAVA

This is the fontina dressing made in Piedmont. It is hardly a sauce. Each batch of drained gnocchi is layered with fresh butter and very thinly sliced fontina cheese. For 4 people you will need 60g/2oz [US 4 tbsp] of unsalted butter and 125g/4oz of fontina. Leave the dish in a preheated very hot oven for 5 minutes, enough for the cheese to melt. They are quite delicious.

TROTELLE AL VINO ROSSO

Trout Baked in Red Wine

Red wine is combined with fish in quite a few Italian dishes. Being more robust, red wine, rather than white, goes into squid, inkfish and octopus stews, as well as into fish soups. This recipe, however, is different in that it combines red wine with trout, a more delicate fish. The reason is surely that red wine is the Piedmontese wine par excellence, white wine being limited to far fewer zones. And this is a Piedmontese recipe.

As the sauce is robust, the addition of a little anchovy paste is needed to enhance the fish flavour, lacking in our new breed of farmed trout.

SERVES 4

4 trout, about 225g/8oz each
salt and freshly ground black pepper
1 small carrot
2 shallots
1 small celery stalk
1 garlic clove
2 bay leaves
a small bunch of parsley
4 fresh sage leaves
the leaves of 4 fresh thyme sprigs
2 tbsp olive oil
500ml/16fl oz red wine
30g/1oz [US 2 tbsp] butter
1 tbsp flour
6 anchovy fillets, drained and chopped

Wash and dry the trout and then season them inside and out with salt and pepper. Lightly oil a roasting tin and lay the trout in it.

Heat the oven to 200°C/400°F/Gas Mark 6.

Chop together finely the carrot, shallots, celery, garlic and herbs and put into a saucepan with the oil, 2 tablespoons of water and 1 teaspoon of salt. Cook gently for 5 minutes, stirring occasionally. Add the wine, bring to the boil and simmer for 10 minutes.

While the sauce is cooking, put the fish in the oven and bake for 5 minutes. Now spoon the sauce around the fish and bake for a further 10 minutes. The trout should be just right after this time. Lift them out of the tin and place them on individual plates. Keep them warm in the turned-off oven while you finish the sauce.

Pound together the butter, flour and anchovy fillets.

Strain the cooking juices into a small saucepan and, when it is just beginning to boil, add the anchovy butter a little at a time, while you whisk constantly with a small balloon whisk. Taste and check seasoning. Spoon a little sauce around each fish and serve at once.

Torta di Peperoni

Sausage and Peppers Pie

The best sweet peppers in Italy come from an area that stretches from Voghera in southern Lombardy to Asti in the fertile valley of the Tanaro, a tributary of the Po in southern Piedmont. And in a way that happens so often in Italy, the best dishes with peppers are from the region where the best peppers grow.

The local pastry is made with water, flour and olive oil, and stretched very thin – not an easy task. I suggest using filo pastry, which is similar to the original.

Buy plain pork sausages with at least 90% meat content. They should have no flavourings, since that might clash with the flavour of the peppers.

SERVES 6 TO 8

225g/8oz Spanish onions
120ml/4fl oz extra virgin olive oil
salt and freshly ground black pepper
1 tsp brown sugar
120ml/4fl oz semi-skimmed milk [US low-fat milk]
700g/1½lb red and yellow sweet peppers
200g/7oz pure pork sausages
3 size–2 eggs [US extra-large eggs]
4 tbsp freshly grated Parmesan
1 packet filo pastry, about 225g/8oz, defrosted if frozen

Slice the onions very thinly and put them into a sauté pan with 2 or 3 tablespoons of the oil, a good pinch of salt and the sugar. Cook for about 5 minutes and then add 3 or 4 tablespoons of the milk. Mix and continue cooking, at the lowest heat, until the onions are very soft indeed, about 40 minutes. If the heat is a bit too high you might have to add a little more milk. Keep a watch on the pan.

Meanwhile, wash and dry the peppers. Quarter them and remove core, ribs and seeds. Once they are clean, cut them into very small pieces, about 1cm/½in. Add to the onion and cook at a higher heat for about 10 minutes.

Skin the sausages and crumble them or chop them, whichever you find easier. Add them to the pan too and sauté until the meat looks properly cooked, another 10 minutes or so. Stir often. Add seasonings to taste, remembering that this pie is served cold. (Food served cold needs a little more seasoning than when served hot.) When this is done, scoop the whole thing into a large bowl.

Beat the eggs together lightly and slide into the bowl. Add the cheese and mix very well. Set aside.

Heat the oven to 180°C/350°F/Gas Mark 4.

Take a 20cm/8in spring-clip tin and brush the inside with some of the remaining oil. Line it with a sheet of filo pastry, letting the surplus hang over the rim. Brush the filo with oil and then add a further 3 sheets of filo, placing each sheet at a slightly different angle and brushing each sheet thoroughly with oil. Spoon the peppers and sausage mixture into the tin. Turn the hanging pastry sheets over the top, laying them loosely, all lovely and wavy, and oiling each layer well. If the folded-over pastry sheets are not long enough to cover the top, place another sheet or two, still loosely, as this makes the pie look very pretty when baked. Don't forget to brush these with oil as well.

Place the tin in the oven and bake for 30 minutes. Turn the heat up to 220°C/425°F/Gas Mark 7 and bake at this higher temperature for 10 minutes to give the pie a rich brown colour.

Cool it in the tin and then unclip and unmould it. Serve tepid or at room temperature.

Pollo ai Funghi e alla Panna

Chicken with Cream and Mushrooms

Quick and easy, this dish is always a success. There is little in it to go wrong, provided you buy a good fresh chicken, which nowadays is not a tall order, and follow my instructions.

SERVES 4 OR 5

a free-range chicken of about 1.5kg/3¼lb
1 lemon
20g/¾oz dried porcini
2 tbsp olive oil
salt and freshly ground black pepper
30g/1oz [US 2 tbsp] unsalted butter
1 small onion, finely chopped
200g/7oz brown mushrooms, coarsely chopped
300ml/10fl oz double cream [US heavy cream]

Ask the butcher to cut the chicken into 8 pieces. When you are back home, skin the chicken pieces and then wash and dry them. Cut the lemon in half and rub each piece well with the cut lemon.

Put the dried porcini in a bowl and pour over about 300ml/10fl oz of boiling water. Leave them to reconstitute for about 1 hour (see page 13).

Heat the oil in a frying pan large enough to hold all the chicken pieces in a single layer. When very hot, add the chicken pieces and brown well first on one side and then on the other. Now season all the pieces with salt and pepper and transfer them to a casserole.

Heat the oven to 180°C/350°F/Gas Mark 4.

Heat the butter in a smallish frying pan or sauté pan and, when the butter foam starts to diminish, add the onion. Season with 1 teaspoon of salt and sauté until pale gold.

Meanwhile, fish the porcini out of the water and rinse them in cold water, being careful to remove any bits of soil embedded in their folds. Pat them dry and cut them into small pieces. Now go back to the liquid and filter it through a sieve lined with muslin or cheesecloth.

Throw the porcini pieces into the onion pan and, after 5 minutes, throw in the cultivated mushrooms as well. Cook for 5 more minutes, stirring frequently. Then add the cream, 4 or 5 tablespoons of the porcini liquid and salt and pepper to taste. Simmer for a further minute, then turn the whole thing over the chicken.

Place the casserole in the oven and cook until the chicken is done, about 30 to 40 minutes. Turn the chicken pieces over once or twice during the cooking, and taste the sauce to correct seasoning.

If the sauce has dried up too much, transfer the chicken to a serving dish and add a couple of tablespoons of water to the sauce. Boil for 1 minute and then spoon over and around the chicken.

PETTI DI POLLO ALL'EBRAICA

Chicken Breasts Jewish-Style

I was given this excellent recipe by a Jewish friend in Milan, whose family originally came from Piedmont. Recently I was looking through the best book on Piedmontese cooking, *La Cucina del Piemonte* by G. Goria, and there I found a very similar recipe, but the poultry used was a turkey breast. Goria writes that the dish originates from the Jewish community of Moncalvo, a lovely town in southern Piedmont. This community fitted happily into the local traditions, as did most Jewish communities in Italy up to the War. And many of their dishes had much in common with the local dishes. The Jewish community was dispersed during the persecutions of 1943 to 1945, but the dishes at least remain as witness to the Jewish culinary tradition.

Goria writes that the turkey was served with a sweet-and-sour relish, which is indeed very Middle Eastern. In my friend's recipe the chicken breasts were served by themselves. I cannot decide whether they are better with or without the relish. So I am giving you the recipe for the relish, and I leave it to you to decide. Maybe you prefer to serve it as an antipasto, as I do.

THE RECIPE

You can use the breast of a small turkey instead, although that is not too easy to find. The onions must be sweet, so use Spanish or red onions.

SERVES 4

4 chicken breasts [US breast halves]
salt and freshly ground pepper
1 tbsp chopped fresh sage
2 tbsp olive oil
900/2lb onions, very finely sliced

Heat the oven to 240°C/430°F/Gas Mark 8.

Rub the chicken breasts all over with salt and pepper and the sage. Grease a small roasting tin or shallow oven dish with half the oil. Lay the seasoned breasts in the dish and cover with the onion. Sprinkle with salt and pepper and pour over the remaining oil. Bake for half an hour or until the juices coming out of the thickest part of the breasts are pale and clear. The onion should be just tender – crisp on the top and juicy underneath. Serve immediately. A very easy dish indeed.

THE VEGETABLE RELISH

1 yellow sweet pepper of about 150g/5oz
125g/4oz aubergine [US eggplant]
100g/3½oz celery stalks
200ml/7fl oz red wine vinegar
salt and freshly ground pepper
4 tbsp extra virgin olive oil
1 tbsp concentrated tomato paste
3 tbsp sugar

Cut the vegetables into small pieces, about 1cm/½in. Put them in a saucepan with the vinegar and pour in 200ml/7fl oz of water. The liquid should be level with the vegetables. Add 1 teaspoon of salt and bring to the boil. Simmer for 10 minutes and then drain.

Heat the oil in a frying pan and stir in the tomato paste and the sugar. Cook for 5 minutes or so to caramelize the sugar a little, while stirring constantly. Now add the vegetables and turn them over and over to coat them in the caramelized oil. Turn the heat down and cook for a further 15 minutes. You must stir very frequently because there is very little liquid and you do not want the vegetables to catch. The vegetables should be just crisp at the end of the cooking. Season with plenty of pepper and check the salt.

Serve hot with the chicken; or warm or at room temperature as an antipasto.

PESCHE FARCITE ALLA PIEMONTESE

Stuffed Peaches

Piedmontese peaches are of the yellow kind, large and smooth, with beautiful gradations of colour from pale yellow to deep red. In this dish they are combined with two other ingredients loved by the Piedmontese, almonds and rum. The Piedmontese have a longstanding love affair with rum (see page 72). And the almond biscuits called amaretti were traditional in southern Piedmont long before Davide Lazzaroni started his very successful biscuit industry in Lombardy in the late 19th century, producing the best known amaretti – the amaretti di Saronno – a pair of crisp sugar-studded biscuits wrapped in the special paper.

Any respectable cookery book on northern Italian cooking must contain a recipe for pesche ripiene. My recipe is not really 'mine', but an adaptation of the recipe titled 'Pesche Farcite alla Borghese' which appears in the 19th-century book *Trattato di Cucina-Pasticceria Moderna* by Giovanni Vialardi. Vialardi was the chef-pâtissier to Carlo Alberto of Savoy, and to his son Victor Emanuel II, the first king of Italy. The book is a large collection of Italian and foreign recipes, but its value lies mainly in its recording of the many traditional Piedmontese recipes such as this one.

THE RECIPE

The peaches must be ripe yet firm, and of the freestone variety. Add a few drops of pure almond extract, not essence, which will give the stuffing a bitter almond flavour.

You are bound to have some filling left over. What I do is to pour it into 1 or 2 buttered ramekins and place these in the oven to bake alongside the peaches. It is my *bonne bouche* the next day when I eat it cold, with a drop of yogurt to counterbalance the unavoidable sweetness of the filling.

SERVES 6

6 yellow peaches
4 tbsp caster sugar [US granulated sugar]
100ml/3½fl oz white wine
30g/1oz [US 2 tbsp] unsalted butter
3 tbsp Marsala
125g/4oz amaretti
a few drops of pure almond extract
2 egg yolks plus 1 egg white
2 tbsp dark rum
2 pinches of ground cinnamon

Wash and dry the peaches. Cut them in half, and open them by twisting the two halves in opposite directions. Remove the stones.

Heat the oven to 170°C/325°F/Gas Mark 3.

Put 2 tablespoons of the sugar and the wine in a small saucepan and bring gently to the boil. When the sugar has dissolved pour the syrup into a shallow oven dish large enough to hold the peach halves.

Now with a sharp teaspoon, a small knife or, better still, a curved grapefruit knife, scoop some of the pulp out of each half peach, leaving about 1cm/½in of pulp all around. Set the pulp aside and place the peach halves in the dish, cut sides up. Place a tiny blob of butter in each half. Bake for 15 minutes – just enough to soften the fruit. Remove the peaches, then turn the oven up to 190°C/375°F/Gas Mark 5.

Put the rest of the butter and the remaining sugar in a small frying pan. Add the scooped-out peach pulp and sauté for a couple of minutes, then pour in the Marsala. Continue cooking gently for 10 minutes.

Now you can make the filling. Spoon the peach pulp and all the juices into a food processor. Add the amaretti and the almond extract and process until smooth. Transfer to a bowl and mix in the egg yolks, rum and cinnamon. Whisk the egg white until stiff and fold gently into the mixture.

Fill each peach half with some of the mixture and then bake for 20 minutes or thereabouts until the top is set to the touch. Serve hot.

PERE AL BAROLO

Pears Baked in Red Wine

The pears used in the traditional recipe are the Martin Sech, a fairly small, rust-coloured pear which grows in Valle d'Aosta. Nowadays this variety is practically unavailable outside this region. Conference pears have a similar grainy texture as Martin Sech, but I find English Conference unreliable because they are often picked too early, before the flavour has developed. William's, Bartlett or Rocha are good substitutes and, on the whole, are more reliable pears.

Barolo, the wine in which the pears are poached, is one of the great wines from Piedmont made from Nebbiolo grapes. It is full-bodied and rich, ideal to counterbalance the sweetness of the fruit.

SERVES 6

375ml/13fl oz (½ bottle) Barolo or other full-bodied red wine
the pared rind and juice of 1 unwaxed lemon
the pared rind and juice of ½ unwaxed orange
2 cloves
½ cinnamon stick
4 peppercorns
1 bay leaf
180g/6oz caster sugar [US ¾ cup + 2 tbsp granulated sugar]
6 pears, ripe but firm

Heat the oven to 150°C/300°F/Gas Mark 2.

Put all the ingredients except the pears in a saucepan. Add 150ml/5 fl oz of water and bring slowly to the boil, stirring constantly to dissolve the sugar. Boil for about 15 minutes, stirring occasionally.

Wash the pears, leaving the skin and the stalk on. Choose an oven dish into which the pears will fit snugly standing up. Pour the wine syrup around the pears in the dish and bake uncovered for about 1¼ to 1½ hours, until the pears can easily be pierced through by the point of a small knife.

Stand a pear on each plate and spoon the syrup around it. They look very pretty.

These pears can be served warm or cold, but not straight from the oven or chilled. If you like you can hand around a bowl of whipped cream or crème fraîche.

You could also hand around a mascarpone and cream mixture. For this you will need 200ml/7fl oz of whipping cream and the same quantity of mascarpone. Whip the cream until stiff and then add the mascarpone, first breaking it up with a fork and then folding it in thoroughly with a spoon. The cream and mascarpone mixture is tastier than plain whipping cream and sweeter than crème fraîche.

Torta di Noci

Walnut Pie

I was in two minds about whether to place this pie in Emilia instead of here, in Piedmont. In Emilia there is a cake called La Bonissima which is very similar. But when I recently discovered this Piedmontese version, I found it more successful. The fresh breadcrumbs, which do not appear in La Bonissima, make a filling more substantial and yet more subtle. Also, because of the baking powder, the pastry is not genuine pastry; it is half way between a sponge and a pâte sucrée. Being bready rather than biscuity it makes the ideal container for the nutty filling.

Walnuts are one of my hobby horses. It is extremely difficult in this country to get shelled walnuts that are fresh. Walnuts, in fact, have a very short shelf-life. They might appear to be still all right, with their sell-by date as much as 6 months ahead, but good they are not. The wonderful flavour of the walnut has evaporated, to be replaced by the beginnings of rancidity. My advice is to buy a good supply of walnuts in their shells at Christmas. After you have had as many as you want just like that, put the rest in this pudding.

The honey used in Piedmont is the very scented and sweet acacia honey. You can serve the pie at tea-time, or any time. As a dessert it is excellent with pouring cream.

SERVES 6 TO 8

FOR THE PASTRY

150g/5oz [US 1¼ cups] flour, preferably Italian 00
1 tsp baking powder
a pinch of salt
75g/2½oz caster sugar [US 6 tbsp granulated sugar]
75g/2½oz [US 5 tbsp] unsalted butter, cut into small pieces
the grated rind of 1 unwaxed lemon
1 size-2 egg [US extra-large egg], lightly beaten
butter for the tin

FOR THE FILLING

150g/5oz [US 1 heaped cup] walnut kernels
60g/2oz good country-type white bread, crust removed
150g/5oz [US ½ cup] honey
2 tbsp dark rum
1 tbsp lemon juice
icing sugar [US confectioners' sugar], to finish

First make the pastry. Sift the flour, baking powder and salt on to a working surface. Mix in the sugar and then rub in the butter, using the tips of your fingers. Add the lemon rind and the egg. Work the mixture quickly together to form a ball. Wrap the dough in cling film and refrigerate for at least half an hour. (You can make the pastry in a food processor by simply putting all the ingredients in the bowl and processing until it forms a ball.)

While the pastry is chilling, put the walnuts, and the bread cut into 3 or 4 large pieces, into the food processor and process to coarse crumbs. If you do not have a food processor, chop the mixture by hand.

Heat the honey in a small saucepan, add the walnut and bread mixture and cook gently until it is all nicely coated. Draw the pan off the heat and add the rum and the lemon juice. Mix very well and leave to cool.

Heat the oven to 180°C/350°F/Gas Mark 4.

Generously butter a 20cm/8in tart tin or a pie plate.

Bring the pastry back on to the work surface, and divide it in half. This pastry is quite difficult to roll out. I find it much easier to roll it out between two sheets of well-floured greaseproof or parchment paper. When you have rolled out half the dough, lift away the top piece of paper and turn the bottom paper over so that the dough falls into the tin. Press it down properly, and up the edge. Spoon the walnut mixture into the tin. Proceed to roll out the top in the same way and flip this over the filling. Seal the edges tightly, pressing them together.

Make a few holes in the top of the pie with the point of a knife and bake for about 30 to 40 minutes, until the pastry is golden brown. Let the pie cool in the tin before you turn it over on to a dish for bringing to the table.

Sprinkle a lot of sifted icing sugar over the top before serving.

BONET

Amaretti Pudding

A *bönet* is a soft cap in Piedmontese dialect, the word clearly coming from the French *bonnet*. The name describes the shape of this pudding, which is rather like a mob-cap.

Bönet is characteristic of Piedmontese cooking in its almondy flavour, laced with Marsala and rum. Rum appears in many Piedmontese dishes. Giovanni Goria, my mentor in these matters, gives an explanation of the love affair between Piedmont and rum. The Duke of Savoia, during the second half of the 16th century, established a Piedmontese navy based in the port of Villefranche, which was Savoyard territory. Its sailors were the first to bring this spirit, made from the Caribbean sugar cane, to Piedmont, and it soon found favour with the locals.

Bönet is a very popular pudding, and the variations are endless. There is, for instance, a *bönet giallo* – a yellow bönet, in which the coffee and cocoa are eliminated and the flavouring is vanilla.

The original version is made with milk rather than cream, not much of which is used in Piedmontese cooking. But milk as it used to be, especially if it was country milk, was a different thing from our pasteurized milk. So I decided to replace some of the milk with cream, and it works well. The other 'liberty' taken is that I have replaced part of the amaretti with some Savoiardi because I find that the flavour of amaretti can be slightly overpowering. The Savoiardi bring a lighter touch and a softer texture, and they are totally in keeping with the origins of the bönet.

THE RECIPE

The flavour of light Muscovado sugar is perfect in a bönet; I use the delicious Billington sugar. Good Savoiardi and amaretti are now available in most large supermarkets and in Italian food shops. I use the espresso powder in sachets, which is perfect for this purpose, but not good enough for a proper cup of coffee.

For the traditional bönet shape you need a 1.5l/2½pt [US 1½qt] dome-shaped metal bowl. However, you can use a soufflé dish, little individual ramekins or popover moulds.

SERVES 6

450ml/15fl oz full fat milk

300ml/10fl oz double cream [US heavy cream]

4 size-2 eggs [US extra-large eggs]

50g/1¾oz [US ¼ cup] sugar, preferably light Muscovado

2½ tbsp unsweetened cocoa powder

1 sachet (2 tsp) instant espresso coffee

2 tbsp dark rum

1 tbsp Marsala

125g/4oz amaretti

50g/1¾oz Savoiardi

FOR THE CARAMEL

125g/4oz caster sugar [US ½ cup + 2 tbsp granulated sugar]

1 tsp lemon juice

First prepare the caramel. Start by heating the mould (see introduction) for the bönet in a low oven. I find that if the mould is cold, the caramel hardens before it can cover all the surface of the mould smoothly.

Put the sugar, 2 tablespoons of water and the lemon juice in a small heavy saucepan. Heat over very gentle heat, stirring until the sugar has completely dissolved. Now remove the spoon, turn the heat up and let the syrup caramelize. Do not stir any more, but stand there and be patient, ready to withdraw the pan. The syrup will become blond first, and then quickly turn into a beautiful dark colour. Swirl the saucepan occasionally while the syrup is becoming caramelized.

Take the mould out of the oven and pour the caramel into it. Swirl the caramel around to cover all the surface nicely. And now that the mould is ready, prepare the pudding.

Heat the oven to 180°C/350°F/Gas Mark 4.

Bring the milk and cream to a simmer. While this mixture is heating beat the eggs with the sugar. Add the milk mixture in a thin stream, letting it fall from a height so that the egg mixture will not be affected by too high a heat.

Add the cocoa powder, letting it fall into the egg and milk mixture through a sieve. Add also the espresso powder, rum and Marsala. Mix thoroughly.

Crumble the amaretti and Savoiardi with a rolling pin. You can also do this in a food processor, but do not over-process. Spoon the crumbled biscuits into the egg and milk mixture and fold everything together well.

Pour the mixture into the prepared mould. Put the mould in a roasting tin and pour boiling water into the tin to come three-quarters of the way up the side of the mould. Now place the roasting tin with the mould in the oven and cook until the bönet is set – at least 1 hour. The time can differ depending on whether the mould is metal or ceramic, large or individual. When ready, the blade of a small knife inserted into the middle of the pudding should come out clean.

Unmould while still hot on to a round dish that is deep enough to hold the lovely caramel sauce as well. When cold, put in the refrigerator to chill.

In Piedmont, bönet is served on its own, but you can decorate it with some piped whipped cream and serve some more cream in a bowl on the side. It goes very well.

Le Tazzine di Maddalena

Chocolate and Hazelnut Truffle Cups

Maddalena Bonino is the chef at the Bertorelli Restaurant in London. As a true Piedmontese she has developed quite a few interesting dishes based on the flavours of her native region. This recipe is one such; it comes from her lovely book *Fast and Fresh Entertaining*.

The flavour of the tazzine is strongly reminiscent of the delicious Gianduiotti, the Torinese chocolates, traditionally wrapped in gold paper, made with a mixture of hazelnuts and chocolate.

SERVES 4

180g/6oz dark chocolate

2–3 tbsp rum or brandy

125g/4oz [US ¾ cup] hazelnuts, toasted, skins removed and roughly chopped

2 egg whites

2 tbsp caster sugar [US granulated sugar]

300ml/10fl oz double cream [US heavy cream]

Melt the chocolate with the rum or brandy and the hazelnuts in a bowl over a pan of simmering water. When melted, remove from the heat and cool, stirring occasionally, until lukewarm.

Whisk the egg whites until they hold their shape, then add the sugar and whisk until stiff. Set aside.

Whip the cream until thick.

Fold the egg whites into the chocolate mixture, mixing evenly, then fold in the cream. Spoon into serving cups, chill for 10 minutes and serve.

Panna Cotta al Caffé

Coffee-flavoured Cream Pudding

Some dishes catch people's imagination more than others. Panna cotta is one of them. This dessert, which has existed in Piedmont for centuries, has now become popular, first all over Italy and then abroad, in the space of just a few years. This new-found popularity is perhaps due to the fact that panna cotta has a clean taste and looks very attractive in the way it is served nowadays – brilliantly white, surrounded by a red fruit coulis. But in the past, panna cotta was always served by itself, so that one could appreciate the excellence of good cream.

Although I am a purist and a traditionalist, I too have succumbed to fashion in this case. I do not very much like panna cotta with fruit, but I find the coffee-flavoured version even better than the plain panna cotta of the old days.

THE RECIPE

The secret of a good panna cotta is to add the minimum of gelatine, just enough for the dish to be unmoulded. It should be wobbling and trembly, never firm. I always use gelatine leaves, which dissolve much more evenly than powdered gelatine and have no flavour at all. They vary in size, so I give the weight of the gelatine needed, which can also apply to the powder.

SERVES 6

10g/⅓oz gelatine leaves or 2 tsp unflavoured gelatine powder

450ml/15fl oz double cream [US heavy cream]

150ml/5fl oz full fat milk

125g/4oz caster sugar [US ½ cup + 2 tbsp granulated sugar]

2 tsp instant espresso coffee powder

½ tsp pure vanilla extract

4 tbsp dark rum

FOR DECORATION

125g/4oz chocolate-coated coffee beans

If you are using gelatine leaves, put them in a bowl and fill the bowl with water. As soon as the leaves soften, bend them so that they are totally submerged in water. Leave to soak for 15 to 20 minutes. Squeeze the leaves out and put them in a saucepan with 4 tablespoons of water. Dissolve over very low heat while stirring constantly.

If you are using powdered gelatine, put 4 tablespoons of water in a small saucepan and sprinkle over the gelatine. Leave to sponge for 10 minutes or so and then heat the mixture gently until the gelatine has dissolved completely. Do not let the liquid come to the boil.

Mix the cream and milk together in a saucepan. Add the sugar and heat slowly to dissolve. Stir in the coffee powder and the vanilla and bring to the boil. Draw off the heat and add the rum and the gelatine. Mix very thoroughly.

Brush six 150ml/5fl oz ramekins with a little flavourless oil. Pour the panna cotta into the ramekins. Allow to cool, then cover with cling film and chill until set, at least 3 hours.

To unmould, place the ramekins in a sink of hot water for about 30 seconds. Run a thin knife around the sides of the ramekins, put a dessert plate over the top and turn the plate and the ramekin over. Give a knock or two to the base of the ramekin and then lift it away. It should come away easily, but if the pudding is still stuck, put the ramekin back in hot water for a few more seconds. Put the unmoulded puddings back into the fridge.

Before serving, sprinkle some of the chocolate-coated coffee beans here and there around the panna cotta. They look pretty and their flavour is an ideal match to the delicacy of the pudding.

Brutti ma Buoni

Knobbly Nutty Biscuits

The name of this recipe means 'ugly but good'. I certainly think they are good, but I don't find them ugly, perhaps because I like them so much. These hard, knobbly biscuits, or cookies, are a speciality of northern Piedmont. In Tuscany similar biscuits, called brutti *e* buoni, are made with almonds instead of hazelnuts. The recipe is more or less the same, so you can use either of the nuts, or a mixture of the two.

I specify the quantity of egg whites by weight because it is important to have just the right amount. Eggs differ in size, but the weight is constant and precise.

MAKES ABOUT 70

400g/14oz [US 3 cups] shelled hazelnuts

180g/6oz [US ⅔ cup] egg whites

350g/12oz caster sugar [US 1¾ cups superfine sugar]

a pinch of ground cinnamon

10 drops of vanilla extract

butter for the oven trays

Heat the oven to 180°C/350°F/Gas Mark 4.

Spread the hazelnuts out on baking trays and toast them in the oven for about 10 minutes, until the aroma rises and they begin to get brown. Now get rid of some of the skin by putting them in a Turkish or other rough towel and rubbing them against each other. There is no need to take all the skin off, which would be a difficult task in any case, as you need some of the skin still on. Put all the nuts in a food processor and process until the nuts are evenly ground.

Whisk the egg whites until stiff. This should be done by hand with a large balloon whisk because it incorporates more air than an electric mixer. When the whites are really stiff, gradually fold in the sugar. Mix well and then fold in the ground hazelnuts, cinnamon and vanilla. Mix very thoroughly, but lightly, and then transfer the mixture to a very heavy-based saucepan. Put the saucepan on a very low heat – I use a flame diffuser – and let the mixture cook very very slowly, so that it dries a little, for 20 minutes or so, while you stir very frequently with a metal spoon.

Heat the oven to 150°C/300°F/Gas Mark 2.

Prepare the oven trays by buttering them quite generously. When the hazelnut mixture has cooled a little, place small mounds of it on the trays. These meringues do not grow, so you can put them quite close. Bake them for about 30 minutes, until hard.

Brutti ma buoni are delicious with zabaglione, vanilla or chocolate ice-cream, or any other cream or custard-based pudding. They are also good just like that, on their own.

TRENTINO-ALTO ADIGE

Although considered as one region, I find Trentino and Alto Adige very different in most respects. When you are in Trentino you are still definitely in Italy: everyone speaks Italian, there are no road-signs in German and the food is predominantly Italian. Admittedly you do begin to detect some 'Mitteleuropean' influence, making a cuisine that is not easy to define. In Alto Adige, however, the cooking – and everything else – is Austrian, even if there is a slight Italian influence.

There is one element that sets Trentino apart and makes it the Mecca for gourmets: the fungi. In Trento there is an extraordinary open market for fungi where up to 250 different species can be found. The market takes place from May through to the autumn when it is in its full glory. As the famous chef Gualtiero Marchesi writes in his *La Cucina Regionale Italiana* (a very valid book): 'Fungi are not, thank goodness, a vegetable, so they can be repeated within a menu.'

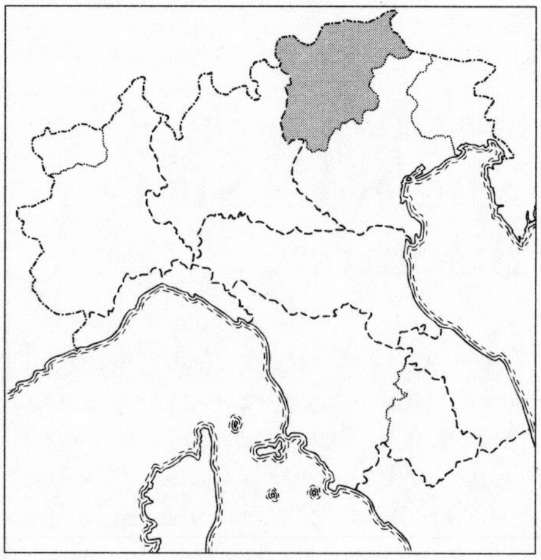

And that is what I chose to do at the trattoria Il Crucolo, high in the mountains above Trento. What a lunch that was! It was a cold, wet Sunday in June. My husband, in the typical English way, wanted to book a table. I, in typical Italian fashion, laughed the suggestion off. With such appalling weather who would drive up to 800 metres amongst the clouds for lunch? Up and up we drove – more rain, stronger wind, thicker clouds, until suddenly we were confronted by a sea of parked cars. All Italy and his wife had come to eat at Crucolo. Cars with a Modena number plate were parked next to the MI of Milan and the VE of Venezia. After one hour of waiting, which I spent happily with Signora Purini in the kitchen, where 200 meals were prepared that day, we sat down to an antipasto of traditional *salumi*, mostly smoked, demonstrating the Austrian influence, and preserved porcini, followed by a superb zupa de brise – mushroom soup (page 78), followed by *cotechino* with sauerkraut and funghi trifolati – sautéed porcini. The dessert was a torta saracena, made with buckwheat flour and again reminding me of our proximity to South Tyrol where buckwheat flour is very popular. This cake, incidentally, is the *pièce de resistance* of the elegant pasticceria König in Merano (page 86).

Another item of food that sets Trentino apart from any other region is the apple. Trentino is a luscious orchard full of every kind of apple. Whether juicy, dry, sweet, tart, red, green or yellow, they are eaten raw, poached, baked, fried, encased in pastry as in the strudel, decorating a tart or used in a budino (page 85).

Driving north towards the Dolomites the apple orchards give way to vineyards, salads disappear from traditional menus, cream is piled up next to puddings, and Italian becomes a foreign language. The gastronomic attractions are the smoked cured meats and the bread. Bread comes in endless shapes, flavours and colours, cheering the shop windows and scenting the nearby air. I saw more different kinds of bread in South Tyrol in a week than I would see in a year in the rest of Italy.

While I was staying in Merano I went to Lana to see Frau Heidi Schmidt (her real name!) whose bakery is well known thereabouts and whose knowledge of breadmaking is profound. She showed me rye bread, buckwheat bread, white bread and brown bread, dressed with cumin, aniseeds, linseeds, fennel seeds, coriander and even a special variety of clover that grows high in the mountains. These dressed breads are mostly eaten at breakfast with cheeses and cured meats as in Germany. *Speck*, the local speciality, is always on the breakfast table, and what a treat it is to start the day with the mild and subtle smoked flavour of a slice of speck. Speck is the flank of a pig, first cured in a spiced brine and then smoked gently and gradually for a few hours a day and aged for at least six months. That is the genuine speck; what passes for speck in some places is another matter. Speck is also added to *knödel*, or bread gnocchi, which by tradition are served with meat. But I like them, and serve them, by themselves, with plenty of cheese inside, dressed with butter and a green snow of snipped chives, in a rather Italian way, as I had them at an inn (and it was definitely an Austrian inn, not an Italian *osteria*) in Cortaccia near Lake Caldaro, with a bottle of *eccellente Marzemino*, like Don Giovanni at his last supper.

I can see why the Germans have chosen Alto Adige as their stamping ground, apart, that is, from the fact that everyone speaks their language. The food is good, the pâtisserie is delicious, the wines are superb, the prices at hotels and restaurants are low, and the scenery is breathtakingly beautiful.

SCHWAMMERSUPPE Ⓥ

Mushroom Soup

I have recently discovered a book that is new to me, although it was first published in Germany in 1822, three years before the well-known *Physiology of Taste* by Brillat-Savarin. The book in question is *The Essence of Cooking* by Karl Freiherr von Rumohr, published by Prospect Books in an excellent translation. Comparing it to the Brillat-Savarin classic, Alan Davidson writes: 'In some ways it is a better book, meatier and less pretentious.' I would go even further and say it is better in most ways. Rumohr's advice is more valid, sounder and more adaptable to modern cooking. Maybe I am biased towards Rumohr because of his great love and understanding of Italian cooking. However, I do recommend this book to anybody interested in food and cooking, and, particularly, in food and cooking as an aspect of national characters and cultures. For instance: 'The art of cooking is closely linked to national character and to the intellectual development of separate races . . .' and, further on, 'The Italians wholeheartedly applied their love of art and their sense of beauty to the table.'

But to return to the Schwammersuppe and its connection to Rumohr, he writes at length about the browning of flour. Here are three extracts. 'The cook should be very careful when browning flour because, if this process is rushed, small particles will become burnt and will then impart a bitter harsh flavour instead of the requisite full, roasted flavour.' 'It is not true that if flour is burnt its nutritional value is destroyed.' 'Moreover a well browned flour has a very beneficial effect on the stomach.'

THE RECIPE

Just as the name of this soup is not Italian, nor is the use of sour cream. Yet the soup shows a strong Italian influence, that of sautéing the mushrooms separately with garlic and parsley. As in many dishes from South Tyrol and Friuli, the butter and flour roux is cooked to a hazelnut colour before the stock is added. This gives the dish a characteristic and pleasant, slightly burnt taste.

In South Tyrol this soup is made with wild wood mushrooms, usually an assortment just as they are picked, as in this recipe. And, of course, these are the best mushrooms to use. But I find that you can successfully use cultivated mushrooms, as long as you add a handful of dried porcini and their soaking liquid.

This soup is usually served with croûtons, sautéed in butter. Oil is not a cooking fat of the region.

SERVES 4

75g/2½oz [US 5 tbsp] unsalted butter
100g/3½oz [US ½ cup] onion, finely chopped
1 garlic clove, finely chopped
15g/½oz fresh flat-leaf parsley, chopped
225g/8oz selection of wild mushrooms: boletes, chanterelles, saffron milk caps, honey fungi etc.
4 tbsp milk
salt and freshly ground black pepper
grated nutmeg
1.2l [US 5 cups] vegetable stock (page 231) or chicken stock
40g/1½oz [US ¼ cup] flour
4 tbsp sour cream

Heat half the butter with the onion, garlic and parsley in a sauté pan and sauté for 5 minutes, stirring frequently.

Cut the fresh mushrooms into small dice and then throw them into the sauté pan. Sauté them for 5 minutes, until they have absorbed all the butter. Pour in the milk and season with salt and nutmeg. Cook for a further few minutes.

Heat the stock to simmering point.

In another saucepan melt the remaining butter until the foam begins to subside. Draw the pan off the heat and beat in the flour. Return the pan to the heat and cook over low heat until the mixture becomes first pale gold and then deeper in colour. Draw the pan off the heat once more and begin to add the stock gradually, by the ladleful. Stir constantly to avoid lumps forming. Return the pan to a low heat. When all the stock has been added, add the mushrooms and all their rich cooking juices. Bring the whole thing to the boil and simmer for 20 minutes. Add pepper, and taste to check the salt.

Ladle the soup into individual bowls and then spoon a tablespoon of sour cream into the middle of each bowl.

POLENTA PASTICCIATA Ⓥ

Baked Polenta with Mushrooms and Cheese

Pasticciata means 'messed about', but there is no messing about in this well-constructed and balanced dish. Polenta can be 'pasticciata' in many ways, according to local traditions, to the cook's preference and the ingredients available. The most common way to prepare the dish is by layering the slices of polenta with a good meat ragù, such as you would do with lasagne. Another excellent polenta pasticciata is made with three or four different cheeses and béchamel. My recipe here adds mushrooms to the cheeses, typical of mountain regions.

If you can find wild cèpes and chanterelles, use these, omitting the dried porcini.

SERVES 6

polenta made with 300g/10oz maize (polenta) flour [US 2½ cups coarse cornmeal]
20g/¾oz dried porcini
a béchamel sauce (page 228), made with 60g/2oz [US 4 tbsp] unsalted butter, 40g/1½oz [US ¼ cup] flour, 450ml/15fl oz full fat milk
30g/1oz [US 2 tbsp] unsalted butter
1 garlic clove, bruished
150g/5oz mixed cultivated mushrooms: brown mushrooms, field mushrooms, oyster mushrooms, sliced
salt and freshly ground pepper
5 tbsp milk
40g/1½oz fontina or gruyère
40g/1½oz young pecorino [US romano]
40g/1½oz taleggio
6 tbsp freshly grated Parmesan
grated nutmeg
butter for the dish

Make the polenta at least 3 hours in advance to give it time to cool completely. You can even make it 1 or 2 days in advance. The baked method on page 234 is ideal for this recipe. When you remove it from the oven, cover the top with a clean sheet of buttered foil to prevent a hard crust from forming.

An hour or so before you start cooking, put the dried porcini in a bowl and cover with boiling water. Leave to soak for about 1 hour (see page 13) and then lift them out of the liquid. Check that there is no grit trapped in the folds of the porcini. If you see any, rinse under a cold tap. Dry thoroughly and chop the porcini.

Filter the porcini liquid through a sieve lined with muslin or cheesecloth and set aside.

Now make the béchamel. While the béchamel is gently bubbling away, heat the butter with the garlic in a frying pan. When the aroma of the garlic begins to rise, fish the garlic out and discard it. Add the porcini and sauté for 5 minutes. Now add the fresh mushrooms and sauté for 2 or 3 minutes, turning them over frequently. Season with salt and pepper. When the mushrooms begin to release their liquid, turn the heat up to evaporate it, cooking for 2 or 3 minutes. Pour in the milk, stir well and continue cooking for a further 10 minutes. If the milk evaporates too quickly, add a couple of tablespoons of the mushroom liquid. Taste and check seasoning.

Cut the polenta into 1cm/½in slices. Slice the cheeses thinly.

Heat the oven to 180°C/350°F/Gas Mark 4.

Now you can assemble the dish. Choose an ovenproof dish in which you can make 3 layers of polenta. I use a 20 × 16cm/8 × 6in dish. Butter the dish generously and then spread a couple of tablespoons of béchamel over the bottom. Lay about one-third of the polenta slices over the sauce and cover with half the mushrooms, half the sliced cheeses, 2 tablespoons of the Parmesan and a couple of tablespoons of béchamel. Now place another layer of polenta slices in the dish and cover with the same layers of ingredients. The top layer is polenta, well covered with the remaining béchamel and sprinkled with the remaining 2 tablespoons of Parmesan.

Place the dish in the oven to bake for 30 minutes, until the polenta is hot through. To test it, push the blade of a small knife into the middle of the dish and then touch it gently against your lip. It should feel burning hot. If it doesn't, place the dish back in the oven for a few more minutes. Let the dish rest for about 6 to 7 minutes outside the oven for the flavours to blend and then bring it to the table.

FUNGHI IN UMIDO Ⓥ

Fungi Stew

This dish is at its best when made with a selection of wild fungi. This is easy to do in Trento where, between the months of May and November, there is a large fungi market. At the peak time 250 different species are on sale there, all checked by mycologist inspectors who look, smell, sniff and even taste all the specimens brought by the pickers in their baskets. As in other parts of Italy, porcini – *boletus edulis* – are the favourites, but the woods of the nearby Dolomites provide a host of other species.

For this recipe, if you cannot use wild fungi, use a selection of cultivated mushrooms plus 30g/1oz of dried porcini, which you must soak in hot water for about an hour (see page 13).

A note on health. Wild fungi are very difficult to digest because they contain toxic substances. I know that to be so from my own experience, and I always advise people to eat them sparingly.

SERVES 4 TO 6

700g/1½lb mixed wild fungi or cultivated mushrooms
a bunch of fresh flat-leaf parsley, chopped
2 garlic cloves, very finely chopped
2 tbsp olive oil
40g/1½oz [US 3 tbsp] unsalted butter
salt and freshly ground black pepper
8 tbsp full fat milk

Scrape off any grit from the stalks of the wild fungi and wipe them all over very carefully with dampened kitchen paper towel. Cut the caps into 5mm/¼in slices and the stalks lengthwise into similar slices. If you are using cultivated mushrooms, wipe them with kitchen paper towel and slice in a similar manner.

Put half the parsley, the garlic, oil and butter in a large sauté pan and cook until the fat sizzles and the aroma of the *soffritto* (frying mixture) rises.

If you are using dried porcini, add them to the pan 5 minutes before you add the fresh mushrooms. Now throw in the fungi or mushrooms, turn them over and over so that they all get a chance of absorbing some of the fat, and cook at a lively heat. Season with salt and pepper and continue cooking until the liquid that has at first come out of the fungi has evaporated. (Different species of mushrooms contain different amounts of water.) After that lower the heat and add the milk. Cook gently, stirring occasionally, for half an hour if you are using wild fungi, or for 15 minutes for the cultivated species. Taste and check seasoning.

These stewed fungi or mushrooms are a perfect accompaniment to the venison on page 84, to the shin of pork on page 83 or to a mountain of golden polenta for a vegetarian meal.

Manzo alla Trentina

Beef Braised in Vinegar and Cream

The best cut for this recipe is a piece of chuck steak, or brisket or silverside. The meat should not be too fresh and should have a little fat around. It should also be neatly rolled into a not-too-large piece, ideally of about 10cm/4in diameter.

I prefer to cook any braised or stewed meat a day in advance so that I can easily remove the solidified fat from the top.

I like to serve this beef with polenta made with a mixture of maize (polenta) flour and buckwheat flour because it has a nutty and 'dark' flavour that is a perfect foil to the oniony sauce. The recipe for this polenta is on page 233. Prepare the recipe without the addition of the butter and cheese.

SERVES 4

450g/1lb small white onions or pickling onions
75g/2½oz smoked pancetta
the needles from 2 fresh rosemary sprigs, each about 20cm/8in long
salt and freshly ground black pepper
a 1.5kg/3¼lb piece of boneless beef
60g/2oz [US 4 tbsp] unsalted butter
1 tbsp olive oil
150ml/5fl oz wine vinegar
300ml/10fl oz single cream [US light cream]

First peel the onions. If you want to do this the easy way, and without shedding too many tears, put them in a bowl and cover them with boiling water. When you peel them, leave the root on the onion so that it can keep the onion whole. If you are using small white sweet onions, you can now set them apart, ready to be added to the meat. But if you use pickling onions, put them back in the bowl and cover with boiling water again so that you get rid of some of their too strong oniony flavour. Leave them to soak for 15 minutes before draining.

Chop the pancetta and the rosemary needles together very finely. (I find that the quickest and best way to make this type of *battuto*, or pounded mixture, containing pancetta is to use a food processor. The mixture becomes a real *battuto* in a split second.) Season this mixture with salt and pepper.

Make deep incisions in the meat along the grain and push into it some of the *battuto*, pushing it well in with a chopstick. When you have done one end, turn the meat over and lard from the other end, so that the whole length of the piece will be larded. Pat the meat with salt and pepper all over and with any left-over *battuto*.

Heat the oven to 170°C/325°F/Gas Mark 3.

Heat the butter and oil in a flameproof casserole. When the butter foam begins to subside add the meat and brown on all sides. Add the onions and sauté for 5 minutes, then pour over the vinegar and boil briskly for a further 3 or 4 minutes.

Meanwhile, heat the cream. When it is nearly boiling, add it to the casserole with some salt and pepper. Cover the casserole tightly and place it in the oven. Cook for 1 hour, then turn the heat down to 150°C/300°F/Gas Mark 2 and continue cooking for another 2½ to 3 hours, until the meat is very tender indeed.

Transfer the beef to a carving board and cut it into thickish slices with a very sharp knife. (I find an electric knife invaluable for slicing this type of meat.) Lay the slices, slightly overlapping, on a heated dish. Check the seasoning of the sauce before spooning 2 or 3 tablespoons over the meat. Ladle the rest of the sauce and the little onions into a terrine and serve with polenta, as they do in Trentino.

Spezzatino di Maiale alla Bolzanese

Pork Stew with Paprika

I have been making this dish for as long as I can remember. It is an old favourite which I always thought was from Bolzano in Alto Adige. Recently, however, I saw an almost identical recipe in a book on the cooking of Venezia Giulia. The dish was called gulash alla triestina.

The two different sources of the same dish bear witness to the influence of the Austro-Hungarian empire on the cooking of all eastern Italy, an area that had been dominated by that empire for centuries. Almost the only difference is that whereas this, the Alto-Adige recipe, contains wine, the Triestina version has no wine but includes marjoram and rosemary. Still, this squares with the well-known fact that the people of Trentino and Alto-Adige are among the heaviest consumers of wine in Italy.

This dish is usually accompanied by polenta (page 233).

SERVES 4 OR 5

800g/1¾lb pork steaks
30g/1oz [US 2 tbsp] butter
125g/4oz smoked pancetta, cut into cubes
225g/8oz sweet onions, sliced
salt
1 tbsp paprika, approximately – depending on its strength
1 tbsp flour
200ml/7fl oz dry white wine
300ml/10fl oz tomato passata
1 dozen fresh sage leaves, snipped
2 bay leaves

Remove the sinews and gristle from the pork but leave the fat. Cut the meat into neat chunks of about 2.5cm/1in.

Heat the butter with the pancetta in your stewing pan. Sauté for 5 minutes, until the fat of the pancetta has melted. Add the onion and 2 pinches of salt and cook for 20 minutes or so, stirring frequently.

Throw the meat into the pan and fry on all sides for 10 minutes, then mix in the paprika and the flour. Cook for 1 minute. Splash with the wine and bring to the boil. Cook for a couple of minutes, then add the passata, sage and bay leaves. Season with salt, stir well and cook gently uncovered for 1½ to 2 hours, adding a couple of tablespoons of boiling water whenever the sauce gets too dry.

Fish out the bay leaves and discard. Taste and check seasoning before bringing the dish to the table with a mound of smoking golden polenta.

Stinco di Maiale alla Tirolese

Pot-roasted Shin of Pork

The cooking of South Tyrol contains elements of Italian, Austrian and Middle European cooking. I find this dish, however, distinctly Italian both in the way it is prepared and in its flavour.

Any self-respecting butcher can supply you with pork shins (not trotters), which weigh about 700g/1½lb each. One shin is enough for 2 to 3 portions. Remember to take any meat out of the fridge about 2 hours before cooking, if you can.

Choose a casserole into which the shins will fit snugly, though not so tight that you cannot turn them over.

If you prefer a smoother sauce, purée the cooking juices into a small pan. Work together 15g/½oz [US 1 tbsp] of butter with 2 tsp of flour with a fork and drop this mixture (*beurre manié*) little by little into the simmering puréed cooking juices, adding a little more stock if necessary.

SERVES 4 TO 6

2 pork shins [US fresh ham hocks]
salt and freshly ground pepper
2 tbsp olive oil
1 celery stalk
½ onion, chopped
1 small carrot
1 garlic clove
5 fresh sage leaves
the needles from a rosemary sprig about 5cm/2in long
150ml/5fl oz dry white wine
3 tbsp Grappa or eau-de-vie
2 juniper berries, bruised
150ml/5fl oz meat stock (page 230)

Heat the oven to 200°C/400°F/Gas Mark 6.

Burn any stubborn hairs off the rind of the shins. Wash and dry them. Season with salt and pepper all over.

Put the oil in a flameproof casserole and brown the shins well on all sides. Lift them out and put them on a side dish.

While the meat is browning, chop the celery, onion, carrot, garlic, sage and rosemary very finely. When the meat is out of the pan, throw this mixture into the pan with ½ teaspoon of salt and sauté gently for 5 minutes. Place the shins on top of the mixture and turn the heat up. Pour over the wine and Grappa and let them bubble rapidly for a minute or so, turning the meat over once. After that throw in the juniper berries and add half the stock.

Cover the casserole and place it in the oven. Cook for about 1½ hours, turning the shins over twice and adding a little more stock if the cooking juices are too dry. The meat is ready when it is tender. Remove the rind, which is quite good, and cut into strips for the people who like it. Cut the meat into chunks and spoon the cooking juices over and around it, unless you prefer to make the smooth sauce described in the introduction.

CAPRIOLO ALLA ALTO ATESINA

Stewed Venison

In Alto Adige fur game is still eaten a lot during the shooting season, the most prized being chamois, a small deer with beautiful hooked horns, which live high up in the Alps and the Appennines. The chamois venison found on the market is often from farmed animals whose meat has less flavour, but needs to be hung for a shorter period. In this country I have made the dish with venison, which usually is the meat of red deer. Sour cream is used a lot in this region, whose cooking is redolent of the Austro-Hungarian empire.

SERVES 6

1.3kg/3lb boneless venison
4 tbsp olive oil
2 tbsp flour
60g/2oz smoked pancetta, diced
60g/2oz pure lard
1 Spanish onion, about 225g/8oz, very thinly sliced
salt and freshly ground pepper
¼ tsp ground cinnamon
¼ tsp ground cloves
300ml/10fl oz sour cream

FOR THE MARINADE

1 carrot, cut into pieces
1½ onions, coarsely sliced
1 celery stalk, cut into pieces
1 tbsp coarse sea salt
1 dozen juniper berries, crushed
8 peppercorns, bruised
3 cloves
1 fresh rosemary sprig
2–3 fresh thyme sprigs
1 fresh sage sprig
3 tbsp olive oil
3 bay leaves
3 garlic cloves
1 bottle good full-bodied red wine (750ml)

Heat all the ingredients for the marinade until just boiling.

Cut the venison into pieces about 5cm/2in thick. Put these in a bowl and add the marinade. Cover the bowl and leave for 2 days, preferably in a cool larder rather than in the fridge.

Lift the meat from the marinade and pat dry with kitchen paper towel. Drain the marinade, saving only the liquid.

Heat the oven to 170°C/325°F/Gas 3.

Heat 2 tablespoons of the oil in a large cast-iron frying pan. Add the meat and brown very thoroughly on each side. Fry in two batches rather than crowding the meat together, when it wouldn't brown properly. Transfer the meat to a side plate.

Add the flour to the frying pan and cook until brown, stirring and scraping the bottom of the pan with a metal spoon. Add about half the marinade liquid. Bring to the boil, stirring constantly and breaking down any lumps of flour with the back of the spoon.

Put the rest of the oil, the pancetta and lard in a flameproof casserole and cook for 5 minutes. Add the onion and a pinch of salt and continue cooking until the onion is really soft, about 15 minutes. Add a couple of tablespoons of hot water to prevent the onion from burning.

Now add the meat with all the juice that has leaked out, the roux from the frying pan and about 150ml/5fl oz of the remaining marinade liquid. Season with salt and pepper and with the spices and bring slowly to the boil. Cover the casserole and place in the oven. Cook for about 1 hour, or until the meat is very tender, adding a little more marinade liquid twice during the cooking.

Add the sour cream to the casserole. Return the pot to the oven and cook for a further half an hour or until the meat is very tender. It is difficult to say how long the cooking takes since it depends on the quality and age of the animal.

Serve with polenta and with a dish of stewed mushrooms.

Budino di Mele
Apple Pudding

This recipe is like an apple charlotte, but it tastes different, the bread having been mixed into the apples in the form of dried breadcrumbs. It combines two popular local foods, apples and bread.

The breadcrumbs must be made from the best bread, which could be white or wholemeal, but it must be good. For the apples I have successfully used Bramleys and also windfalls, as long as they are tasty. What you must do is correct the sugar according to the acidity of the apples.

SERVES 4 TO 6

60g/2oz [US 7 tbsp] raisins
450g/1lb cooking apples
about 100ml/3½fl oz dry white wine
about 90g/3oz caster sugar [US ½ cup granulated sugar]
30g/1oz [US 2 tbsp] unsalted butter
the grated rind of ½ unwaxed lemon
¼ tsp ground cinnamon
5 tbsp fine dried breadcrumbs
2 egg yolks plus 3 egg whites
butter and breadcrumbs for the tin
300ml/10fl oz whipping cream, whipped, to serve

Puff up the raisins in hot water for about half an hour. When you are ready to start the pudding, drain and dry them.

Peel and core the apples and slice them finely. Pour enough wine into a fairly large sauté pan to cover the bottom. Add the apples and cook, covered, until the apples have become a soft purée. Beat them up, add nearly all the sugar and put the pan back on the heat to dry the purée. Do this on a lively heat, stirring constantly.

When the purée is nice and dry, draw the pan off the heat and add the butter, lemon rind, cinnamon, raisins and breadcrumbs. Mix very thoroughly and then drop in the egg yolks, incorporating one yolk at a time. Now taste the purée and check the sugar. You may want to add a little more; it all depends on your taste and the acidity of the apples.

Heat the oven to 180°C/350°F/Gas Mark 4.

Whisk the egg whites until stiff and fold gently into the apple purée.

Butter very generously a metal tin of 1l/1¾pt [US 1qt] capacity. A charlotte tin is the traditional one to use, but you can use a cake tin or an oval bread tin. Fill the prepared tin with the apple mixture and bake the pudding for about 40 minutes, until it is spongy to the touch and has shrunk away from the side of the tin. Allow to cool a little in the tin and then unmould it. Serve hot with whipped cream.

Torta di Grano Saraceno
Buckwheat Cake

Buckwheat, which will grow at altitudes as high as 800m/2600ft, is used in a few dishes from South Tyrol and various of the Alpine valleys. Buckwheat is not a *graminacea*, a cereal, but belongs to the family of the *poligonacee*. It is treated as a cereal because it presents the same nutritional properties as the cereals, being rich in proteins, vitamins, iron and mineral salts.

While buckwheat used to be the grain of the poor in these valleys, now it is the grain of the rich because only a few mills have the right machines to deal with it. Buckwheat flour is dark in colour and, once cooked, has a very pleasing bitter taste and a rather sticky consistency. It is more perishable than wheat flour and I advise you to keep it in the freezer.

THE RECIPE

The delightful town of Merano is brimming with elegant shops, and smart cafés where the locals and the tourists sit around to have a rest after their shopping spree. The oldest and best known café is the Pasticceria König, founded in 1893 and still the property of the fifth generation of the family.

Margherita König, who is in charge of this elegant meeting place, was kind enough to give me the König recipe for one of the traditional cakes of South Tyrol. La Torta di Grano Saraceno is a cake to be enjoyed at any time of the day, which is what everybody seems to do at the Pasticceria König. I have halved Signora König's quantities to make a cake more suitable for a family. An ideal cake for gluten-free diets.

SERVES 8

125g/4oz [US ¾ cup] shelled almonds
125g/4oz caster sugar [US ½ cup + 2 tbsp granulated sugar]
125g/4oz [US 1 stick] butter, softened
3 size-3 eggs [US extra-large eggs], separated
125g/4oz [US 1¼ cups] fine buckwheat flour
2 tsp baking powder
a pinch of salt
1 tsp grated rind from an unwaxed lemon
2 pinches of ground cinnamon
butter for the tin
about 350g/12oz [US 1 cup] best blackcurrant jam
icing sugar [US confectioners' sugar], to finish

Heat the oven to 180°C/350°F/Gas Mark 4.

Blanch the almonds in boiling water for 30 seconds. Drain and skin them by squeezing out the almond between your thumb and index finger. The fresher the almonds, the easier it is to remove the skin. Spread them out on an oven tray and pop the tray in the oven to toast for 10 minutes. (Almonds release more flavour when toasted.) When cold, transfer them to a food processor and grind them finely.

Measure out 75g/2½oz [US 6 tbsp] of the sugar and put it in a bowl. Add the softened butter and beat together until creamy.

Incorporate the egg yolks thoroughly into the butter-cream and then add the buckwheat flour, baking powder, salt, lemon rind, almonds and ground cinnamon. Mix very thoroughly.

Whisk the egg whites until soft peaks form. Whisk in half the remaining sugar by the tablespoon and finally fold in the rest of the sugar. Now fold the meringue into the buckwheat mixture, using a large metal spoon and a gentle but deep movement.

Butter a 20cm/8in spring-clip tin and line the bottom with a disc of parchment paper. Lightly butter the paper too. Spoon the cake mixture into the tin and bake for about 30 to 40 minutes, until a wooden toothpick pushed into the middle of the cake comes out dry. Unmould the cake on to a wire rack. (Be very careful because this is a fragile cake.) Leave it to cool. Peel off the parchment paper.

Using a serrated knife, cut the cake in half horizontally to form two flat rounds. Spread the jam over the bottom half and place the other half on top. Sprinkle lavishly with icing sugar before serving.

VENETO

Whenever I think of Veneto, one place comes to my mind, obliterating all else. That unique place is, of course, Venezia, where I spent many blissful months, shopping at the Rialto market, gazing at palazzi and churches, and walking about in the leisurely way that is only possible in car-less Venice.

The food is as interesting as everything else connected with that magical city. Unfortunately very few of the local restaurants do justice to its cuisine, which stands slightly apart from that of all the rest of Italy. The Venetians have assimilated the flavours of their former dominions more than any other maritime republic. They assimilated and adapted them to their own cooking, ignoring, even in more recent years, the flavours of southern Italy that have conquered the North. Tomato rarely appears in Venetian cooking or, for that matter, in the cooking of all Veneto, while curry, for instance, used nowhere else in Italy, comes into a few Venetian dishes.

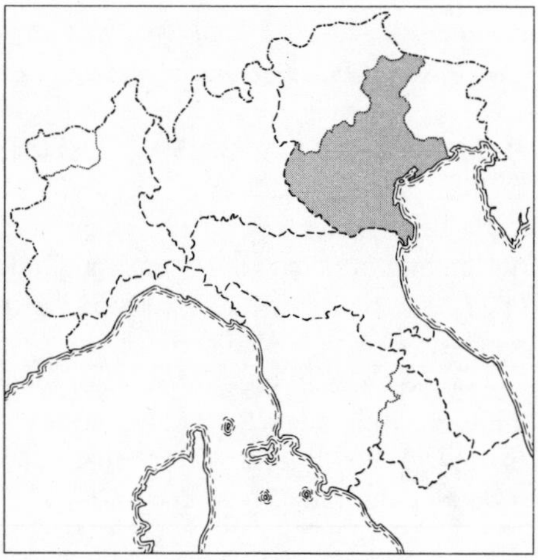

The most vivid example of this marriage of flavours from East and West is a dish of sfogi in saor. *Sfogi* is sole in Venetian dialect, and *saor* is sauce. The sole, a characteristic fish of the Adriatic, is first fried and then marinated in a vinegary sauce containing many spices, sultanas and pine nuts. It is the dish eaten for the Festa del Redentore, the third Sunday in July, when the whole of Venice and the surrounding *terraferma* (hinterland) gathers on and around the laguna and the Giudecca, where the splendid Palladian church of the Redentore stands, built as an 'ex voto' for the end of the plague in 1576. I have been in Venice for the Feast of the Redentore on three occasions, eating sfogi, anara rosta – roast duck – and then juicy iced watermelon, while sitting on the quay of the Giudecca and watching the display of fireworks which set the bacino di San Marco aglow. One of those memories that make life worth living.

Due to its topography, traditions die harder in Venice than in any other part of Italy and this applies also to gastronomic traditions. On St Mark's Day, 25th April, every Venetian man arrives home with a *bocolo* (a red rose bud) for his *innamorata*, ready to eat a voluptuous dish of risi e bisi (page 96) – rice with peas. The peas are the first to arrive at the Rialto market from the rich vegetable gardens on the islands of the lagoon. Even my English husband used to come home with the bocolo during the years we had a flat in Venice. But often, instead of risi e bisi at home, we used to go to the local *bacaro* – a Venetian snack bar – called La Vedova, for a *cicchetto* and an *ombra* – a snack and a glass of wine. The snacks were 'drowned' octopus, sardines 'in saor', Lamon beans, creamy garlicky stockfish or, best of all, seafood, simply boiled and dressed with a drizzle of the delicate oil from Lake Garda.

No meat here on the counter of a bacaro, just vegetables and fish. And from La Vedova, if you take the ferry at Santa Sofia, to be transported across the Canal Grande while doing a balancing act standing in the gondola, and arrive at the Rialto market, the first glance around will give you an idea of the abundance and variety of Venetian vegetables and fish. Shellfish of every kind, crustaceans and cephalopods of every size, blue fish, red fish, silver fish from the tiny whitebait to the beautiful sea bass, they all contend for the attention of the choosy and thrifty Venetian housewife.

There are two supreme seafood specialities in Venice, beloved also in the terraferma: *moleche* and *grancevole* – soft shell crab or shore crab, and spider crab. Moleche have been cultivated in the lagoon since the 18th century and they are now a large industry. The male crabs are kept in large baskets called *vieri*, immersed in the water, and, just at the moment of changing their shells in the spring and autumn, when the shells become soft, they are taken out and sold. I still remember the pleasure as a child, when we spent an Easter holiday at the Lido, of digging my young teeth into a tender fried moleca. I still wonder whether it was a plain moleca or a *moleca col pien* (stuffed). This dish is one of the great Venetian gourmandises. The live soft crabs are put in a bowl containing beaten egg yolks and Parmesan and are left there for two to three hours. The moleche fill up with the mixture and die happy. They are then floured and fried in olive oil.

This, and the grancevola (granceola in Venetian) are the only crabs I like – yet another instance that makes me wonder how much the like or dislike of a particular food derives from memories of previous experiences, and the surrounding atmosphere. Memories of Venice can make any dish taste a thousand times better!

Vegetables are another important element in the cooking of Veneto, creating a mellow and gentle cuisine, never aggressive yet always positive and well defined.

If you want to taste real Veneto cooking, a trattoria in one of the smaller towns – Padua, Treviso or Bassano – would be the ideal place. There you would eat traditional food prepared for the locals who, just like all other Italians, go to a restaurant in the expectation of eating a better edition of their favourite dish. They go to Treviso to have a *sopa coâda* – 'broody' soup – made with pigeon and lots of vegetables, a soup which was ennobled in Verona to become a zuppa alla scaligera, said to have been served at the court of the Della Scala, the lords of Verona. The original recipe has recently been rediscovered and published by the great Veronese gastronome, Giorgio Gioco, of the famous restaurant I Dodici Apostoli in Verona.

One of the best meals I ever had was at Alla Riviera in charming Bassano. The restaurant is next to the beautiful wooden bridge across the Brenta river, where the Bassanesi, and the tourists, take their *passeggiata* before going home, or to Alla Riviera, for lunch. I was there not long ago on a cold and wet Saturday, but my spirits were soon restored when I started my lunch with *nervetti caldi* – hot brawn. This was a surprise, since I always connected nervetti with Milan, where they are served cold with onions and other *sottaceti*. After the nervetti I had one of the best pasta e fagioli ever, and a perfect baccalà alla vicentina – stockfish, not salt cod, in Veneto – cooked in milk with anchovy fillets, parsley and a good deal of olive oil from Lake Garda. The fagioli were borlotti beans from Lamon. These are in a different class from normal borlotti: silky, velvety and large, they fill your mouth and exquisitely and slowly melt in it. The local asparagus, my favourite asparagus, were not, alas, in season. Large, white and incredibly tasty, they are served hot with a sauce of pounded hard-boiled eggs and olive oil.

Another vegetable I must mention is radicchio, of which there are three traditional varieties: Treviso, Verona and Castelfranco. Now there is also the modern radicchio di Chioggia, the one we see in shops outside Italy and, alas, the least interesting of them all, with its coarse cabbagey texture and flavour.

The risotto made in Treviso with the local radicchio is the one that best expresses the creativity of the Veneti for making the most delectable vegetable risotti. They combine rice with all the seasonal vegetables. Even I, a Milanese, have to grant the Veneti supremacy in this field. In Milan we might have created the best known risotto, that with saffron (page 27), but in Veneto they can boast an infinite variety of risotti, mostly with vegetables and fish. There are said to be 365 different risotti in Veneto, one for each day of the year. The rice for these risotti is Vialone Nano, a chubby semifino rice, a highly important produce of the province of Verona. Giovanni Capsnit, vice-president of the Accademia della Cucina Italiana, writes in his erudite book *La Cucina Veronese* that contemporary documents confirm that in the 16th century, buildings, yards and stores were built for the handling and storage of rice, which was even then an important industry. Still now, rice is the first course of a meal in the Veneto, not only in the form of a risotto but also in one of an infinite variety of rice soups.

These rice dishes are mainly based on a *soffritto* made with olive oil. The oil is the local oil of Lake Garda, which is sweet and has nothing of the pepperiness of the *fruttato* oils. It is similar to the Ligurian oil, though even sweeter. This rare oil is made from olive trees that grow at this most northern latitude, thanks to the very temperate climate that exists around the lake.

The other popular first course is potato gnocchi (page 64), which here are usually made with eggs and dressed with a lovely tomato sauce (page 228), or with the juices of a roast.

With this wealth of first courses, who wants pasta? After all, there is only one local pasta, *bigoli*, a thick spaghetti made with a blend of wholewheat flour and white flour and traditionally dressed with a piquant anchovy sauce or with the juices of the roast duck that follows, accompanied by salsa peverada (page 104).

There are plenty of dolci. In Venice some show an oriental influence, while in other parts there is an Austrian flavour, as in tortion (page 110) which is very similar to strudel. Finally, I must mention that tiramisù comes originally from Treviso. It is a relatively modern dish that, like all dishes that achieve universal success, has been subjected to endless variations. I have not included a recipe in this book because I think tiramisù has been done to death, and should be left to rest in peace.

Linguine e Capesante alla Veneziana

Linguine and Scallops Venetian Style

The scallops from the Adriatic are amongst the tastiest in the world, and the Venetians know how to make the best of them. The texture of the breadcrumbs is in sharp contrast to the softness of the pasta and the seafood, while their flavours are in complete harmony.

The sauce takes less time to prepare than the pasta takes to cook. The secret of this sauce lies in correct timing, both for the scallops and for the pasta; neither should be overcooked.

The use of curry powder in Italy is found only in the Venetian cuisine. The reason is simple – Venice, in the past, always looked towards the sea, and her main trade was with the East. Just think of Marco Polo, a Venetian after all.

SERVES 4

350g/12oz linguine or spaghetti
120ml/4fl oz extra virgin olive oil
60g/2oz [US heaping ½ cup] dried white breadcrumbs
2 tbsp chopped fresh parsley, preferably flat-leaf
4 garlic cloves, bruised
2 tsp best curry powder
350g/12oz shelled scallops [US sea scallops]
salt and freshly ground pepper

Put a large pot of water on the heat and cook the linguine in the usual way.

Meanwhile, put half the oil in a small frying pan. When the oil is hot add the breadcrumbs and stir-fry until golden. Set aside.

Clean the scallops and rinse them quickly under cold water. Pat dry with kitchen paper towel. Detach the little coral tongues and set aside. Cut the white part into very small pieces.

Choose a large frying pan and heat the remaining oil with the parsley, garlic and curry powder. When you can smell the garlic aroma, fish the garlic out of the oil and discard it.

When the linguine are very nearly cooked, add the white part of the scallops to the frying pan containing the parsley. Stir-fry for no longer than 30 seconds, until the scallops begin to become opaque.

Drain the pasta and turn it immediately into the frying pan. Add the coral tongues and stir rapidly, lifting the linguine up high so that each strand is coated with the oil. Do this for a minute or so, then transfer to a heated bowl and top with the fried breadcrumbs. Serve immediately.

Pasticcio di Tagliatelle e Pesce

Fish and Tagliatelle Pie

There are many versions of this dish from Venice and the islands of the lagoon. One of the best versions comes from San Pietro in Volta on the island of Pellestrina, south of Venice, and the other from Burano, an island to the north of Venice, close to Torcello.

I have chosen the Burano recipe simply because I find Burano so enchanting that I like anything remotely connected with it, from the *tombolo* (local lace) to the little houses gaily painted in ice-cream colours all along the wide canals. I like, too, the *panetterie* (bakers' shops), brimming with *zaleti*, polenta biscuits, and *baicoli*, which are crisp biscuits [US cookies] to be dunked in wine from Cyprus or in large cups of steaming hot chocolate, sitting at a café on the laguna.

Back to my pie. It is a rather elaborate dish that calls for first class ingredients and care. I would advise you to make your own tagliatelle. Short of that, buy good fresh pasta. Some supermarkets make good fresh pasta with imported Italian flour and eggs, while others import dried egg pasta from Italy such as that made by Spinosi or Cipriani, two of the best producers.

SERVES 6

tagliatelle made with 3 eggs and 300g/10oz [US 2½ cups] Italian 00 flour; or 500g/1lb 2oz fresh tagliatelle; or 300g/10oz best dried tagliatelle
200ml/7fl oz dry white wine
½ small onion
2 bay leaves
salt and freshly ground pepper, preferably white
450g/1lb sole fillets, skinned
225g/8oz raw king or tiger prawns in shell [US large raw shrimp]
600ml/1pt [US 2½ cups] full fat milk
125g/4oz [US 1 stick] unsalted butter
3 tbsp flour
4 tbsp chopped fresh flat-leaf parsley
60g/2oz [US ½ cup] freshly grated Parmesan

If you are making your own pasta, start by doing this, following the instructions on page 232.

Put the wine in a large sauté pan. Add the onion, bay leaves and salt and bring to the boil. Add the fish and the prawns. When the wine has come back to the boil turn the heat down and simmer for 5 minutes. Strain the liquid into another pan and add the milk. Put the pan on the heat and bring to simmering point.

Peel the prawns and cut into pieces. Cut the sole into strips. Set aside.

Melt half the butter in a heavy-based saucepan. Mix in the flour and cook for half a minute, stirring constantly. Remove from the heat and gradually add the milk and fish liquid, whisking the whole time. (If you do this off the heat you are less likely to finish with a lumpy white sauce. But if this should happen, don't worry – just turn the whole thing into a food processor and give it a whizz. This is easier than trying to remove the lumps by squashing them one by one against the side of the pan.) Return the pan to a low heat and bring to the boil. To make a velvety sauce you should cook it for about 15 to 20 minutes, either in a bain-marie (setting the pan in a larger pan half full of simmering water) or using a flame diffuser – an invaluable tool easily available in most kitchen shops. Mix in the parsley, salt and pepper to taste, and the Parmesan.

Cook the pasta in plenty of boiling salted water. Drain, but be careful not to overdrain, and return the pasta to the saucepan. Dress it with one-third of the sauce.

Heat the oven to 190°C/375°F/Gas Mark 5.

Butter a shallow oven dish with a little of the remaining butter. Cover with half the pasta. Spoon the fish over it and pour over a couple of tablespoons of the sauce. Cover with the rest of the pasta and spread the remaining sauce all over the top. Melt the remaining butter and pour over the surface.

Bake for 20 minutes. Do not serve straight away after taking the pasticcio out of the oven. Let it rest and cool down for 5 minutes or so for the flavours to blend.

PANCOTTO VENEZIANO

Venetian Bread Soup

It always surprises me that, in this country, the best-known Italian dishes are from Tuscany. I quite see that a lot of British people spend their holidays there, but I am sure it's not only that. I feel it is the ability of the Tuscans who, unlike the rest of the Italians, are good at selling their region and its products.

Look at olive oil, for instance. There are excellent estate oils from most other regions – totally unknown – but the Tuscan oil reigns supreme. Or bread soups, which are made in most regions. Why has only pappa col pomodoro from Tuscany (see page 180) become famous? It certainly is good, but so are others. It all depends on the recipe and what you put in the dish.

So I give here another bread soup, which is from Veneto and totally different from pappa col pomodoro. No tomatoes here, as with many Veneto dishes, but a touch of the Orient instead in the form of the spices and pine nuts, the characteristic Venetian flavours. This is a warming and nourishing soup.

THE RECIPE

I do not recommend using the normal sandwich loaf; when soaked its texture becomes gluey and quite horrid. You can of course make your own bread, with unbleached stone-ground flour, or you can buy a Pugliese loaf or a French country bread. Try to use only good home-made meat stock.

SERVES 6

150g/5oz country-type white bread
1.35l/2¼pt [US 5½ cups] meat stock (page 230)
60g/2oz [US 4 tbsp] unsalted butter
1 garlic clove, very finely sliced
1 bay leaf
2 tbsp pine nuts
salt and freshly ground black pepper
3 eggs
6 tbsp freshly grated Parmesan
½ tsp grated nutmeg
a pinch of ground cinnamon

Heat the oven to 150°C/300°F/Gas Mark 2.

Break the bread into pieces and spread it on a baking tray. Bake for about 30 minutes, until toasted. Now put it into a saucepan.

Keep aside 200ml/7fl oz of the stock and pour the rest over the bread. Leave to soak for about 15 minutes. When the bread has absorbed the stock, add the butter, garlic and bay leaf and put the pan on a low heat.

Chop the pine nuts by hand or in a food processor and mix into the bread mixture. Stir in the reserved stock and season to taste. (Be careful with the salt because at the end you will be adding a fair amount of Parmesan, which is salty.) Bring the mixture slowly to the boil, stirring constantly, and then let it simmer gently for half an hour while you beat it with a wire whisk as often as you can. It should be beaten constantly, but I find that I can do a few other things around the kitchen in between one good whisking and the next.

Lightly beat the eggs with the cheese and the spices in a small bowl.

When the soup is done, remove from the heat. Let it rest for 5 minutes, then whisk in the egg mixture. Ladle the soup into individual bowls and serve.

Risotto Nero

Cuttlefish Risotto

This recipe from Venice uses cuttlefish, a favourite seafood of the Venetians. The cuttlefish ink is used too, not just to give a black 'designer' look to the risotto, but also – and most importantly – for the stronger fish flavour.

Cuttlefish are sometimes available in good fishmongers in this country. They are often caught in British waters, mainly during the early spring. Local cuttlefish are usually large, about 450g/1lb each, and they are more suitable for slow cooking, as in this recipe, than for grilling and frying.

You can use squid, which are more easily available, instead of cuttlefish. They cook more quickly, and the flavour is similar to cuttlefish although less strong.

Ask your fishmonger to clean your cuttlefish and to give you the little ink sac or sacs intact. You might find it easier to buy cuttlefish ink already prepared in little sachets. These come from France or Spain, and are good. For this recipe you would need 2 sachets of ink. Squeeze them into a cupful of hot water and pour a little water into the sachet to rinse out all the ink.

The rice used in Venice is Vialone Nano, a *semifino* variety available in good Italian food shops. However, the more common Arborio will do perfectly well.

You can cook the cuttlefish in advance, even the day before, and keep it refrigerated. Heat before you add it to the rice.

SERVES 4 TO 5 AS A MAIN COURSE

900g/2lb cuttlefish, or 600g/1¼lb cleaned weight
1 onion, finely chopped
2 garlic cloves, very finely chopped
3 tbsp olive oil
salt and freshly ground black pepper
300ml/10fl oz dry white wine
1.5l/2½pt [US 1½qt] vegetable stock (page 231) or light fish stock (page 231)
75g/2½oz [US 5 tbsp] butter
450g/1lb [US 2¼ cups] Italian rice, preferably Vialone Nano
2 tbsp brandy
2 tbsp freshly grated Parmesan

Wash the cuttlefish, and slice the body into thin short strips and the tentacles into morsels. If you are using them, keep the ink sacs separate and do not lose them!

Put the onion, garlic, oil and 1 teaspoon of salt in a heavy-based saucepan and cook gently until the onion is soft and translucent.

Throw in the cuttlefish and sauté gently for 10 minutes or so, stirring frequently. Add half the wine and cover the pan. Now the cuttlefish must cook until tender on the lowest heat, which will take at least 45 minutes. Keep a watch on the pan. Stir every now and then and check that the cuttlefish is always cooking in some liquid. If necessary, add a little boiling water.

Heat the stock and keep it gently simmering all through the preparation of the risotto. In another large, heavy-based saucepan heat half the butter until just sizzling and add the rice. 'Toast' the rice (as we say in Italian) over a lively heat for about 1 to 1½ minutes and then pour over the rest of the wine. Stir and cook for 1 minute to reduce the alcohol content of the wine.

Now you begin to make the risotto proper by adding the simmering stock by the ladleful. Halfway through the cooking – Vialone Nano takes about 15 minutes to cook, Arborio a couple of minutes longer – scoop in the cuttlefish and all the juices. Squeeze in the ink from the sacs, or add the water with the ink sachets dissolved in it (see introduction). Mix well and continue the cooking of the risotto until the rice is done.

A few minutes before you think the rice is ready, stir in the brandy. Draw the pan from the heat and add the remaining butter, plenty of pepper and the Parmesan. Leave covered for a minute or two, then give the risotto a good stir and transfer it to your warm serving dish. Risotto does not like waiting: serve it immediately.

RISI E BISI Ⓥ

Rice and Peas

This dish is a good example of the excellence of Venetian home cooking. Homely and even humble it may be, but it is one of very few dishes that can boast the patronage of the Doges.

Risi e bisi was served to the Doge on St Mark's Day, the 25th April, when the first peas arrive at the Rialto market. The Doge had first claim on the *primizie* – early crops – from the islands on the lagoon, and particularly the peas from the island of Sant' Erasmo. As Dino Boscorato, owner of the well-known Trattoria Dall' Amelia, put it, the Doge had '*ius primi bisi*' – the right, not of the first night, but of the first peas. When I went to his restaurant in Mestre not long ago I had a remarkable meal as well as an interesting talk. He was very dismissive of some new versions of risi e bisi which add cream at the end of the cooking or where, instead of the stock being made with the pea pods to accentuate its sweet flavour, it is made with meat, chicken or vegetable stock.

THE RECIPE

This recipe derives from the risi e bisi I ate at Dall' Amelia. It is like a very thick soup – half-way between a risotto and a soup – and should be eaten with a spoon. The Venetian peas are just like small petits pois, not easy to find in this country. But nowadays you can buy sugar snap peas, which are often large but can still be eaten whole, pod and all. I find them suitable for this recipe because the pods, which go in the soup, are sweet and fleshy, and not stringy. If the sugar snap peas are very fresh and small, you can liquidize and process the cooked pods and add the purée directly to the stock. If they are older and bigger, I advise you first to process the pods and then push them through a food mill to rid them of the strings.

An old Venetian recipe adds a few fennel seeds, a very imaginative and successful addition.

SERVES 4

900g/2lb young fresh petits pois or sugar snap peas
salt and freshly ground black pepper
30g/1oz [US 2 tbsp] unsalted butter
2 tbsp extra virgin olive oil of a delicate flavour, e.g. an oil from Liguria or Lake Garda
1 small onion, very finely chopped
3 tbsp chopped fresh flat-leaf parsley
225g/8oz [US 1 cup + 2 tbsp] Italian rice, preferably Vialone Nano
½-1 tbsp fennel seeds, according to taste, crushed
45g/1¾oz [US ¼ cup] freshly ground Parmesan

Top and tail and pod the peas, keeping the pods and peas separate. Discard any blemished pods and wash the others. Put them in a pan and add 1.5l/2½pt [US 1½qt] of water and 2 teaspoons of salt. Boil until the pods are very tender. Drain, reserving the liquid, and process the pods. If stringy, and I find that they usually are, work them through the small hole disc of a food mill or through a metal sieve. Measure 1l/1¾pt [US 1qt] of the liquid and add to the purée. Put the mixture in a saucepan and bring slowly to the boil.

Meanwhile, put the butter, oil, onion and 1 tablespoon of the parsley in a stockpot. Sauté very gently for 5 minutes or so and then throw in the podded peas. Cook, stirring them constantly, for 2 minutes.

Add the rice and stir to coat the grains in the butter and oil. Pour over the simmering pod stock containing the pod purée. Mix well and bring to the boil. Now add the fennel seeds and some freshly ground pepper and boil, covered, until the rice is cooked – about 15 to 20 minutes depending on the quality of the rice. Turn off the heat and mix in the Parmesan and the remaining parsley. Ladle the soup into individual soup bowls and serve immediately. Alternatively, transfer the soup to a soup terrine and bring the terrine to the table, this being the way it is done in Venetian homes.

Asparagi in Salsina d'Uovo e Limone Ⓥ

Asparagus with Egg and Lemon Sauce

Asparagus should be properly cooked, which means that they should be not crunchy but just resistant to the bite, and bend graciously when you pick them up to lower them into your mouth. I shall long remember the horror in the eyes of an Italian friend, eating in a very well-known restaurant, when she picked up an asparagus spear that stayed as rigid as a stick. '*Ma questi sono crudi!*' (but these are raw) she exclaimed, and left them without even trying one. It is difficult to specify the time it takes to cook asparagus. When thin and fresh they can take as little as 5 minutes, but when thick and not so fresh I find that 15 minutes is the minimum.

The accompanying sauce is similar to mayonnaise, but much lighter and kinder on the stomach. It is a sauce from Veneto, where some of the best asparagus – those of Bassano – grow.

SERVES 4 TO 5

1.3kg/3lb asparagus

3 eggs

the juice of 1 lemon, or more or less according to taste

salt and freshly ground black pepper

6 tbsp olive oil

First slice off about 2.5cm/1in of the end of each asparagus spear. Next pare, if necessary, or just scrape the stalks. Wash the asparagus thoroughly in plenty of cold water.

If you haven't got an asparagus boiler, use a large sauté or frying pan in which the asparagus can lie flat. Fill with water, bring to the boil and add salt in the proportion of 1 tablespoon per 450g/1lb of asparagus. When the water boils, slide in the asparagus, cover the pan so as to bring the water back to the boil as quickly as possible, and then cook, uncovered, until they are done.

When the asparagus are cooked lift them out of the water and place them on kitchen paper towel to drain properly before you transfer them on to an oval dish.

To make the sauce put the eggs, lemon juice, salt and a generous grinding of pepper in a heat-proof bowl and whisk until pale. Slowly add the oil while beating with a small balloon whisk to emulsify the sauce. Set the bowl over a saucepan of just simmering water and cook, whisking constantly, until the sauce begins to thicken. Do not let the water in the pan boil or the eggs will curdle. Serve warm.

Asparagus should always be served warm or at room temperature, never piping hot, nor chilled.

Verze Sofegae

Stewed Savoy Cabbage

Vegetables are one of the main ingredients of the cuisine of Veneto, and slow cooking is a typical way of preparing them. The literal translation of this recipe's Venetian name is 'smothered Savoy cabbage'. By the end of the cooking this humble vegetable is transformed into a dish that can be enjoyed on its own, just with some lovely bread.

I use an earthenware pot of the sort you can put directly on the heat, this being the ideal for long, slow cooking. I have also cooked a Primo cabbage in this way. Primo cabbage has a less strong flavour but it works quite well too.

SERVES 4

1 medium Savoy cabbage
125g/4oz unsmoked pancetta or unsmoked streaky bacon
1 onion
1 tbsp fresh rosemary needles
1 garlic clove, peeled
2 tbsp olive oil
salt and freshly ground pepper
180ml/6fl oz dry white wine

Remove and discard the outer dark green leaves of the cabbage. Cut into quarters, cut off and discard the hard core and cut the cabbage into 1cm/½in strips. Put in a sink of cold water to wash and then drain in a colander.

Finely chop together the pancetta, onion, rosemary and garlic (you can do this very well and very quickly in a food processor). Heat with the oil in a heavy saucepan. Cook slowly for 10 minutes and then add the cabbage. The cabbage will wilt as it begins to cook. Turn it over and over to coat in the *soffritto* (the fried mixture). Season with salt and pepper and add the wine. Bring to the boil, cover the saucepan and cook very gently for 1½ hours.

Zucca e Zucchine in Saor Ⓥ

Squash and Courgettes in a Sweet and Sour Sauce

I never use what I call Hallowe'en pumpkin for cooking. It tastes of nothing and it is so watery that it creates problems. But butternut squash or onion squash are good, and there are plenty of them in the shops between October and February.

This recipe is a classic of old Venetian cooking, where many ingredients are prepared *in saor* – a Venetian contraction of the word *sapore*. Sapore means flavour, and in the old days the word was used for a sauce, such as this one, that was particularly rich in flavour.

The balsamic vinegar (not a Venetian ingredient) is my addition because I find that it rounds out the flavours of the wine vinegar and the wine. Use good – in other words, expensive – vinegars, since they are the only ones made from good wine and free from chemical additives.

SERVES 6

450g/1lb butternut or onion squash
350g/12oz courgettes [US zucchini]
salt and freshly ground black pepper
30g/1oz [US 3 tbsp] raisins
oil for frying
3 tbsp extra virgin olive oil
1 large Spanish onion, or 2 red onions, about 225g/8oz, very finely sliced
15g/½oz [US 2½ tbsp] pine nuts
2 cloves
a pinch of ground cinnamon
1 tsp grated rind from an unwaxed lemon
100ml/3½fl oz good red wine vinegar
4 tbsp balsamic vinegar
150ml/5fl oz dry white wine

Cut the squash in half, skin it and scoop out any seeds and filaments. Cut each half into 5mm/¼in slices.

Wash and dry the courgettes and cut them into slices of the same thickness. Put the courgette and squash slices in two bowls and sprinkle with salt. Leave for 1 hour to disgorge some of the water, then drain and pat dry.

Soak the raisins in some boiling water for about 15 minutes to plump them up, then drain them.

Heat a wok or a frying pan. Add your frying oil and when it is very hot slide in about half of the squash. Fry until the slices begin to turn gold at the edge. Turn them over and fry for a further 2 or 3 minutes. Retrieve the slices with a fish slice or a slotted spoon. Let the oil drip back into the pan and then transfer the squash slices to a dish lined with kitchen paper towel to absorb the excess oil.

Next, do the same with the rest of the squash and then with the courgettes. Remember to put plenty of kitchen paper towel between each batch of fried vegetables.

Now prepare the *saor*. Put the olive oil and the onion in a frying or sauté pan and sauté until soft. Do this on a low heat, turning the onion very often and mixing in small additions of hot water, so that the onion stews rather than fries. After about 20 minutes add the drained raisins, the pine nuts and cloves and season with cinnamon, lemon rind, salt and pepper. Cook, stirring, for 2 minutes.

Add the two vinegars and the wine and boil for 5 minutes. Do not boil too fast or too much will evaporate. Pour this hot marinade over the vegetables. (Do not forget to remove the layers of kitchen paper towel from the vegetable dish before you pour over the wine mixture!)

Leave to cool, then cover with cling film and keep in the fridge for 48 hours before eating – you can actually keep it for up to 4 days. Do not serve the dish chilled: let it come back to room temperature, which takes about 2 to 3 hours.

RADICCHIO CON LA PURÉ DI BORLOTTI Ⓥ

Red Radicchio with Borlotti Bean Purée

Red radicchio and borlotti are a classic combination in the Veneto cuisine. The mealy nuttiness of the borlotti is the perfect foil to the bitterness of the radicchio, which ideally should be the real radicchio of Treviso. One of the typical regional dishes is a superb soup of borlotti finished off with radicchio. Here is another classic.

In the spring, the radicchio is the wild species just picked from the fields, at the same time as the borlotti are fresh on the market. For obvious reasons I have had to adapt the traditional recipe to the radicchio and the dried borlotti available here. And I decided to purée half the beans instead of leaving them whole, because this gives a total combination of the two flavours with each spoonful. It works very well, and is a most attractive dish in its subtle hues of red.

After many trials I have come to the conclusion that I prefer to cook pulses in the oven. If you want to do them on top of the stove you must cook them over the lowest possible heat, so that the surface of the liquid is just broken by the occasional bubble. You might also have to add a little boiling water. That is why I find the oven method safer and more reliable.

SERVES 4

180g/6oz [US 1 cup] dried borlotti beans
6 garlic cloves
1 bay leaf
salt and freshly ground black pepper
vegetable stock (page 231)
250g/9oz red radicchio
6 tbsp extra virgin olive oil
1 tbsp wine vinegar

The day before you want to serve this salad, put the borlotti in a bowl and cover with cold water. If you live in an area where the water is very hard, you should use filtered water. Leave to soak overnight.

Heat the oven to 150°C/300°F/ Gas Mark 2.

Drain and rinse the beans and transfer to a heavy-based saucepan with an ovenproof handle and lid, or to an earthenware pot that you can put directly on the heat. Cover with water by about 4cm/1½in and add the garlic, bay leaf and 1 teaspoon of salt. Bring to the boil, then put the lid on the pan and place it in the oven. Let the beans cook gently until very soft, which will take at least 1½ hours.

When the beans are very tender fish out and discard the bay leaf. Then scoop out half of the beans and the garlic cloves, and transfer to a food processor, a blender or a food mill. Add some of the cooking liquid and process to a purée, adding a little more liquid to help with the operation.

Transfer the purée to a bowl and add enough of the beans' cooking liquid to make a runny purée. If you do not have enough cooking liquid, you must add some vegetable stock. Please do not ask how much. It is impossible for me to say without seeing, but the purée must be half-way between a vegetable cream soup and puréed potatoes. Season with plenty of pepper and then taste and adjust the salt.

Wash and dry the radicchio. Cut it into very thin strips and dress it with half the oil, the vinegar, salt and pepper. Toss well and transfer to the middle of a round dish.

Mix the whole beans into the purée and spoon the lot around the radicchio. Drizzle the remaining oil all over.

Serve at room temperature, taking care that the radicchio is also at room temperature and not straight from the fridge.

Sogliole Ripiene

Stuffed Sole in Saffron Sauce

Saffron was used a lot in old Venetian cooking, as a sign of wealth and to give food the coveted colour of real gold, instead of using gold leaf. Buy good saffron – it is very expensive – and use it in moderation. Saffron adds a deliciously complex and exotic flavour to a dish, but it can also ruin it if used with too generous a hand.

The addition of pine nuts and sultanas is characteristic of Venetian cooking, which has been strongly influenced by the cooking of the Middle East. After all, Venice dominated part of the Near and Middle East for centuries, and there was a considerable exchange of cultures.

SERVES 6

2 tbsp sultanas [US golden raisins]
3 Dover soles, filleted
salt and freshly ground pepper
125g/4oz young spinach
2 tbsp pine nuts
about 25 saffron strands
½ tsp sugar
120ml/4fl oz Prosecco wine
40g/1½ oz [US 3 tbsp] unsalted butter, cut into small pieces

FOR THE FISH FUMET

the heads and bones of the soles
1 onion, unpeeled, stuck with 1 clove
1 carrot
1 celery stalk
1 bay leaf
6 peppercorns
1 tsp salt
250ml/9fl oz dry white wine

First make the fumet. Put all the ingredients in a pot. Add 1l/1¾pt [US 1 qt] of water and bring to the boil. Boil fast for 30 minutes, until reduced and tasty, then strain the liquid into a large sauté pan. You should have about 600ml/1pt [US 2½ cups] of liquid.

Cover the sultanas with hot water and leave them to plump up. Then drain them and pat dry with kitchen paper towel.

Season the sole fillets lightly with salt and pepper on both sides. Lay some spinach leaves over the fillets and place a few sultanas and a few pine nuts on each fillet. Roll up the fillets and tie them with string, or pin with a wooden toothpick.

Bring the fumet to the boil. Turn the heat down, then add the fish bundles and poach gently, covered, for 6 minutes.

Meanwhile, put the saffron strands with the sugar in a small mortar and pound until crushed. Add a tablespoon or two of the hot fish liquid to dissolve the mixture.

Take the sole bundles out of the liquid and keep hot.

Pour the saffron mixture and the Prosecco into the liquid and boil to reduce by half over high heat, until full of flavour. Mix in the cold butter bit by bit. When all the butter has been absorbed, taste and check seasoning. Spoon the sauce around the fish bundles and serve.

BACCALÀ MANTECATO

Creamed Salt Cod with Garlic and Parsley

Dried cod, whether in the form of salt cod or stockfish (air-dried, not salted) is the most popular type of fish all over Italy. I find it quite fascinating that a foreign food should have so entirely conquered Italian kitchens because Italians are very suspicious of foreign food. Up to the Second World War they used, more or less, to eat only the food they actually saw growing or being produced. Pasta was ignored in the North as rice was in the South. And here is a food coming from Norway (there is no cod in the Mediterranean), which has become part of the cooking repertoire of nearly every region, such an intrinsic part that in any regional cookery book there are more recipes for salt cod or stockfish than for any other sort of fish!

Perhaps salt cod and stockfish have been in Italy for so long that they have by now been totally assimilated into the national cuisine. After all, dried cod arrived in Italy centuries ago, brought there by the Normans. The Italians, ever appreciative of good food, made it their own and developed innumerable recipes for it. They even wrote poems, such as this one in Venetian dialect: '*Chixe che ga inventà/polenta e baccalà?/Disèmelo creature/sto nome'sto portento che toga le misure/per farghe un monumento.*' (Tell me who invented polenta and baccalà, and I will take his name and measurements so that I can make a monument to him.)

In this recipe from Venice the fish used is stockfish, which the Veneti call *baccalà*. In proper Italian, of course, stockfish is – as you would expect – *stoccafisso*, and salt cod is baccalà. To confuse matters further, I have to admit that I am suggesting the use of salt cod in a recipe that calls for stockfish. This is simply because stockfish is virtually unavailable in Britain, and even if you found a supplier the chances are that the stockfish would be woody, and woolly, no matter how long you cooked it.

THE RECIPE

There is plenty of salt cod in Portuguese, Spanish and Italian food shops and in the best fishmongers, such as my supplier, Jarvis in Kingston. So I suggest you buy a good piece of salt cod, at least 3cm/1¼in thick.

Because I love this dish so much I have made it with Finnan smoked haddock when I could not find salt cod. It is not the same, and it is not quite as good, but Finnan haddock is available in most fishmongers and this is a new and healthy way to prepare it.

Baccalà mantecato makes a lovely antipasto, or a supper dish served with grilled polenta or boiled potatoes. You must remember to buy the fish at least 2 days before you want to cook it. Once soaked, baccalà must be cooked straight away. If possible use a sweet olive oil, such as a Ligurian one.

SERVES 3 TO 4

450g/1lb salt cod
½ dozen black peppercorns
1 bay leaf
2 cloves
600ml/1pt semi-skimmed milk [US 2½ cups low-fat milk]
4 garlic cloves
120ml/4fl oz extra virgin olive oil
freshly ground black pepper
2 tbsp chopped fresh flat-leaf parsley

Ask the fishmonger to cut the salt cod into chunks. When you arrive home, put the salt cod in a bowl and leave it under running water for 48 hours, or leave it to soak for the same length of time, changing the water at least four times a day.

Do not cut down on the 2 days' soaking, as some recipes suggest; you'd have a tough, dried and unpleasantly salty piece of fish.

Put the soaked baccalà, skin side up, in a sauté pan with the peppercorns, bay leaf and cloves. Cover with the milk and bring slowly to the boil. Simmer for 15 minutes, until soft through the thickest part, then lift the fish out on to a board to cool enough for you to handle it.

Meanwhile, pour about 120ml/4fl oz of the cooking milk into a small saucepan. Add the garlic and simmer for 15 minutes.

Remove the skin and any bones from the fish pieces and transfer them to a large mortar or a heavy bowl. Add the cooked garlic, and the milk in which it has cooked, to the fish and pound with a pestle to break the fibres of the fish. Beat and pound until the baccalà is broken up, if necessary adding a couple of tablespoons more of the cooking milk. Now gradually add the oil in a thin stream, as you would for a mayonnaise. Season with pepper and mix in the parsley. The mixture should be quite thick, like mashed – rather than puréed – potatoes. Taste and check the seasoning, and serve. It is very good.

I have tried to do this pounding of the fish in a food processor, but I'm afraid the result is different and less satisfactory, because the fish is cut and puréed, not broken and beaten. Still . . . it is a far easier and quicker way!

Sarde Ripiene
Stuffed Sardines

Sardines are stuffed in many different ways all up and down the Italian coast. In Veneto rosemary is added, and I think rosemary combines perfectly with baked blue fish.

Unfortunately sardines in Britain are often not as fresh as they should be. In that case I prefer to buy frozen sardines, or fresh herrings or sprats, less strong in flavour, maybe, but usually much fresher. Both herrings and sprats belong to the same family, *culpidae*, as sardines.

SERVES 4

800g/1¾lb fresh sardines
4 tbsp dried breadcrumbs
4 tbsp freshly grated Parmesan
1 tbsp chopped fresh rosemary
1 tbsp chopped fresh flat-leaf parsley
2 garlic cloves, finely chopped
salt and freshly ground black pepper
6 tbsp extra virgin olive oil
the juice of 1 lemon

Ask your fishmonger to fillet your sardines, keeping them in one piece at the back. If you buy frozen sardines you will have to do this yourself once they have thawed. And this is how you should do it. Give a good pull to the head and remove it. Using your fingers, open up the belly all the way down to the tail. Now place the sardine, open-side down, on a board and press down along the spine. The fish will flatten out and you can then easily remove the backbone.

Wash all the fish and dry them thoroughly.

Heat the oven to 200°C/400°F/ Gas Mark 6.

For the stuffing, put the breadcrumbs, Parmesan, rosemary, parsley, garlic, salt and pepper in a bowl and mix them all up with a fork. Pour in 4 tablespoons of the oil and blend everything together. Place a little stuffing on each open sardine and close it up so that it resumes its original shape, although headless. Choose a roasting tin in which the sardines will fit very tightly but in a single layer and brush it with oil. Arrange the sardines in the tin and sprinkle with salt and pepper. Drizzle with the remaining oil and with the lemon juice.

Bake for 10 to 15 minutes, until the flesh is white, opaque and compact. Serve warm, or at room temperature, as a delicious but simple first course.

Salsa Peverada per gli Arrosti da Penne

Peppery Sauce for Roast Fowl

The Veneti are very fond of fowl of any sort and, as so often happens in such a case, they have created the best recipes for these birds. They have them stuffed, roasted, boiled, braised . . . in lots of ways, all of them good.

When they serve roast guinea fowl, roast pheasant or even roast chicken they like to put this sauce on the table. It is a strong, rich sauce with a touch of acidity, and I have tasted, and tested, many versions of it. This is my favourite one and it comes from a book, *Antica Cucina Veneziana*, written by two people I admire a lot – the food historian Massimo Alberini and the teacher and writer Romana Bosco. Alberini wrote the fascinating introduction and chose the recipes; Romana wrote and tested them. The ideal combination of talents.

Romana's peverada contains vinegar instead of the more usual wine, and the result is more of a sweet-and-sour type of sauce. I like it very much and hope you will too.

SERVES 4

2 tbsp olive oil

1 garlic clove, finely chopped

1 small onion, finely chopped

salt and freshly ground black pepper

100g/3½oz luganega or other mild, coarse-ground, pure pork sausage, skinned and crumbled

1 fresh sage leaf, chopped

1 tbsp chopped fresh flat-leaf parsley

100g/3½oz chicken livers, cleaned and chopped

a small pinch of ground cinnamon

4 tbsp red wine vinegar

1 tbsp sugar

Heat the oil in a sauté pan with the garlic, onion, 1 teaspoon of salt and a couple of tablespoons of hot water. Let the mixture stew gently for 15 minutes or so and then add the luganega, sage and half the parsley. Sauté for a couple of minutes, then add the chicken livers and season with the cinnamon and plenty of pepper. Let the sauce cook for 10 to 15 minutes while giving it an occasional stir.

Meanwhile, put the vinegar in a small pan. Add the sugar and simmer over gentle heat until the sugar has dissolved. Mix the vinegar into the chicken liver mixture together with the remaining parsley. Taste and adjust seasoning before spooning the sauce into a bowl and bringing it to the table with the roast bird.

IL BRASATO DELLA NONNA CATERINA

My Grandmother's Braised Beef

Although many of my colleagues say they were taught to cook by their grandmothers, this is a claim I cannot make. One of my grandmothers died when I was a baby and the other when I was seven. But I do remember this second one, Nonna Caterina, and two things about her cooking. One is that she made the only *caffè e latte* (coffee and milk) that I would drink for my *merenda*; the other being the most delicious cooking smell that I loved to sniff along the long corridor leading to the kitchen of her flat in Milan. Later on I learnt that the heavenly smell came from her brasato. My mother, of course, made it too, with the identical recipe, but to me it wasn't the same.

I have always found smells the most evocative of all senses. It may be that I loved her brasato because I loved her and her house. Nonna Caterina came from Venice, and her brasato might have been a Venetian version, although it contains what are known as 'the four Lombard spices': pepper, cinnamon, nutmeg and cloves. Brasati or stufati are in fact made everywhere from Valle d'Aosta to Trieste. It is a typical northern Italian dish, always prepared with one piece of beef, which should be from a young animal. Served with polenta, it is the Italian answer to the English roast beef and Yorkshire pudding, to be prepared on Sundays or for important feasts.

THE RECIPE

A piece of chuck, of top rump or round, or the eye of the silverside are all suitable cuts. But make sure that the beef is not too fresh or it will be tough however long you cook it.

SERVES 6 TO 8

a 1.6kg/3½lb boneless piece of beef, tied up in a neat roll
1 large onion, cut into chunks
2 carrots, cut into chunks
1 or 2 celery stalks, depending on size, cut into pieces
2 bay leaves
75g/2½oz [US 5 tbsp] unsalted butter
2 tbsp olive oil
grated nutmeg
2 pinches of ground cloves
½ tsp ground cinnamon
salt and freshly ground pepper
150ml/5fl oz dry Marsala
about 150ml/5fl oz meat stock (page 230)

FOR THE MARINADE

300ml/10fl oz red wine
½ onion, cut into pieces
1 celery stalk, cut into pieces
1 carrot, cut into pieces
6 peppercorns, bruised
1 tbsp sea salt

Put the meat in a bowl and add all the ingredients for the marinade. Leave it, covered, for 6 to 8 hours out of the fridge. (All marinating should be done out of the fridge unless the weather is very hot.) Turn the meat over as often as you can remember. When the meat is ready for cooking, take it out of the marinade and dry it thoroughly. Discard the marinade.

Heat the oven to 170°C/325°F/Gas Mark 3.

Put the onion, carrots, celery, bay leaves, half the butter and the oil in an oval flameproof casserole just large enough for the meat to fit snugly. Now set the meat on the vegetables and cook the whole thing for about 10 minutes, turning the meat over a few times. Season with the spices and salt and add the Marsala. Raise the heat and boil briskly for a couple of minutes to evaporate the alcohol. Now add half the stock, cover the casserole and place in the oven to cook for 3 to 3½ hours. Turn the meat over and baste every 20 to 30 minutes.

If your meat is good and does not contain water, all the liquid in the casserole might have evaporated before the meat is done. If this should happen, add the remaining stock and some water if necessary. If, however, there is more than about 200ml/7fl oz of liquid when the meat is ready (it should be very tender when prodded with a fork) take the meat out of the pot, keep it warm covered with foil, turn the heat up to high and boil the liquid briskly to reduce. Remove and discard the bay leaves.

Now you must pour the contents of the pot – but not the meat! – into a food processor to be puréed. Or, better still for a smoother sauce, you should purée it through a food mill. Pour the sauce into a small saucepan and add the rest of the butter. Cook gently until the butter has melted, then have a last tasting of the sauce to check the salt.

Place the beef on a carving board and slice it rather thickly. Arrange the slices on a heated dish, pour over the sauce and bring to the table.

Torta Carotina

Carrot Cake

When my 93-year-old mother was in a home near Pavia, in southern Lombardy, I used to go and see her as often as I could. Sitting there with my knitting I got to know a lot of local people and, of course, all the nurses, the cook and the various helpers. They were fascinated with my profession of cookery writer, all giving me tips, recipes, asking about food in England, the English and, of course, 'Diana e Carlo', about whom they knew far more than I did!

In the course of my visits I learned a lot about the locality and, more importantly, about its cooking. The food at the old peoples' home was very good, always prepared with the utmost care. The lovely cook, Giovanna, helped by her sister, used to say, 'The poor old things, they have nothing to look forward to except what I bring up from the kitchen.' And those poor old things were very fussy indeed! A favourite dish of theirs, and mine too, was a veal stew cooked on a bed of onions and covered with bay leaves.

One of the helpers, Wilma Magagnato, had a pasta shop in the village, run by her daughter. Wilma prepared the pasta and cakes in the morning before starting work in the home. Her cakes were quite delicious; they had the sophisticated simplicity of home-made cakes, made, of course, to perfection. One of her jewels, and she was very proud of it, is this carrot cake. I was amazed, never having come across a carrot cake in Italy. I thought it must be yet another American import, like hamburgers and Coke. 'Ma no, signora,' Wilma replied, 'my father used to make it for us when we were little. And as we didn't have an oven at home, he used to take it to the baker to be baked in the bread oven.' Wilma's father came from near Belluno in Veneto. Apparently carrot cake is popular in that area, although this is something I haven't yet had a chance to verify.

THE RECIPE

This is a very good cake, the fragrant freshness of the almond acquiring a deeper side through the darker flavour of the carrot and the rum. It is also an ideal cake for people who are allergic to dairy products and/or gluten, since it contains neither.

Buy almonds in their skin. They are usually fresher than the skinned ones. Potato flour is available in speciality food shops and good supermarkets. When making this cake I have used Billington's golden granulated sugar, which is so good, and ideal in this recipe. It is available in most good grocers and supermarkets. As with most country cakes, the finishing touch is simply a thick layer of icing sugar.

150g/5oz [US 1 cup] shelled almonds
3 eggs, separated
125g/4oz [US ½ cup + 2 tbsp] sugar
60g/2oz [US ½ cup] potato flour
salt
1½ tsp baking powder
150g/5oz [US 1⅓ cups] carrots, grated
2 tbsp rum
butter and dried breadcrumbs for the tin
icing sugar [US confectioners' sugar], to finish

Heat the oven to 180°C/350°F/Gas Mark 4.

Slide the almonds into a saucepan of boiling water. Boil for 20 seconds, then drain and skin them. The fresher they are, the easier it is to skin them by squeezing them between thumb and forefinger. Put the skinned almonds on a baking tray and dry them in the oven for 7 to 10 minutes. (Keep the oven on for baking the cake.) After that, chop them finely in a food processor or by hand. They should be chopped very fine, but not as fine as ground almonds.

Beat the egg yolks with the sugar until they have doubled their volume.

Sift the potato flour with the salt and baking powder and add with a large metal spoon to the egg and sugar mixture. Fold well and then add the carrots and the rum. Mix thoroughly.

Whisk the egg whites until standing in firm peaks. Fold them into the carrot mixture by the spoonful, gradually and carefully.

Butter an 18cm/7in spring-clip tin. Line the bottom with a disc of parchment paper and butter the paper. Sprinkle about 2 tablespoons of dried breadcrumbs over the bottom and side of the tin and then shake out any excess crumbs.

Spoon the cake mixture into the prepared tin and bake for 40 to 45 minutes, until the cake is lovely and golden brown. It will have shrunk from the side of the tin, and a wooden toothpick inserted into the middle of the cake should come out dry.

Remove the cake from the tin and turn it over on to a wire rack. Peel off the paper and let the cake cool. Serve covered with icing sugar.

Sorbetto di Sgropin

A Venetian Sorbet

Sgropin is a chilled drink which, as its name in dialect indicates, is drunk at the end of a good meal to clean the palate and stomach. I have transformed the drink into a sorbet, first because I like it better this way, and secondly because I shall never forget a glass of sgropin cascading down the chest of the man sitting next to me at a dinner I organized for Venice in Peril. The sgropin was solid at the top but liquid underneath, and when the top broke the rest came out in a flood.

SERVES 4 OR 5

4 unwaxed lemons

1 unwaxed orange

200g/7oz caster sugar [US 1 cup granulated sugar]

100ml/3½fl oz Grappa

Thinly peel the rind from the lemons and the orange, leaving the white pith on the fruit. Put the rind in a frying pan. Add the sugar and 300ml/10fl oz of water. Bring slowly to the boil to dissolve the sugar, then turn the heat up and boil for 5 minutes. Add the Grappa and set aside to cool.

Squeeze the fruit. Mix the juice with the cold syrup, then strain the whole mixture. Pour into an ice-cream maker and freeze according to the manufacturer's instructions.

Because of the high alcohol content the mixture does not freeze hard. Spoon it into chilled flute glasses for serving.

Amor Polenta

Polenta Cake

I was amazed when, a few years ago, I first set eyes on the name of this cake in bakers' shops in Venice. It was obviously the old-fashioned polenta cake, but it had been baked in a new shape of tin, cylindrical and wavy. Why 'Amor Polenta'? The name is catchy, I agree, but does a good old-fashioned cake need a new name?

The excellence of this simple cake depends totally on the almonds. Buy the best almonds you can find, or bring back a supply from Italy or France and keep them in the freezer. They must have a fresh, plump appearance, without any wrinkles.

Serve your polenta cake for tea or with a glass of wine. A white Albana from Romagna or the more easily available Vinsanto would be the best.

100g/3½oz [US ⅔ cup] shelled almonds

75g/2½oz [US ½ cup+2 tbsp] Italian 00 flour

2 tsp baking powder

a pinch of salt

125g/4oz [US 1 stick] unsalted butter, softened

125g/4oz caster sugar [US ½ cup + 2 tbsp granulated sugar]

2 size-2 eggs plus 2 egg yolks [US extra-large eggs]

100g/3½oz maize (polenta) flour [US ¾ cup + 2 tbsp coarse cornmeal]

butter and fine dried breadcrumbs for the tin

Heat the oven to 180°C/350°F/Gas Mark 4.

Blanch the almonds for 20 seconds in boiling water. Drain and squeeze the almonds out of their skins – an easy job, especially if they are fresh, as indeed they should be. Put the skinned almonds on a baking tray and toast them in the oven for 10 minutes or so, until they begin to get brown. Remove from the oven, but leave the oven on.

Sift the white flour with the baking powder and the salt.

Put the butter and sugar in a bowl and beat well until smooth. (I cream them together first with a fork or, better still, with my hands, which being warm amalgamate the butter faster. Then I use a hand-held electric mixer at low speed, to prevent splattering the mixture everywhere.)

Lightly beat the eggs and egg yolks together and add to the butter-cream by the spoonful alternately with spoonfuls of the sifted flour mixture.

Grind the almonds in a food processor together with a couple of tablespoons of the maize flour, which will absorb the almond oil. Grind into grains, not to a coarse powder, and then add to the cake mixture together with the remaining maize flour. Mix thoroughly.

Butter a loaf tin that measures 17 × 5cm/ 7 × 2in. Sprinkle in a couple of tablespoons of breadcrumbs to coat all over and then shake out the excess. Spoon the cake mixture into the tin and bake for about 45 minutes, until the cake is cooked. Test by inserting a wooden toothpick in the middle – it should come out dry. The cake will be springy and have shrunk from the sides of the tin.

Loosen the cake all around the tin with a thin knife and turn it on to a wire rack to cool. Wrap it in foil if you do not want to eat it straight away; it keeps well for 3 or 4 days. It is pretty covered with sifted icing sugar [US confectioners' sugar].

Gnocchi Dolci di Latte

Sweet Milk Gnocchi

I had forgotten all about this pudding until the other day, when I saw it on the menu at Riva, our local Italian restaurant in Barnes. As soon as I tasted it I was taken back many many years to our cousins' villa on Lake Como, where their nanny made the best gnocchi di latte ever. Later on, I used to make them for my children when they were young, but I never succeeded in recapturing the flavour of Balia Teresa's gnocchi. Then here I was in Barnes, of all places, eating the gnocchi of my childhood. I wonder whether it is that Francesco, the talented young chef at Riva, comes from Pordenone in Veneto, as Balia Teresa did.

At Riva, of course, they are served in a grown-up honeyed rum sauce, while ours were either plain or with a blob of jam or honey on each gnocco. The shape is also different; our gnocchi were just rounds, while Francesco makes very pretty crescents which he surrounds with a few crescents of apple in a very attractive presentation.

THE RECIPE

Gnocchi di latte are made in Lombardy, Veneto and Emilia-Romagna, the regions famous for their dairy products. And then they are found again in Marche, a region further south which prides itself on an excellent breed of cow, where traditionally 2 tablespoons of Parmesan are added to the mixture. There are, however, some variations from one place to another. This is the gnocchi di latte served at Riva.

SERVES 4

4 size-2 egg yolks [US extra-large egg yolks]
200g/7oz [US 1 cup] sugar
60g/2oz cornflour [US ½ cup cornstarch]
½ tsp pure vanilla extract
a pinch of salt
500ml/16fl oz full fat milk

FOR THE SAUCE AND GARNISH

1 apple, unpeeled, sliced into very thin segments
100g/3½oz [US ⅓ cup] honey
200ml/7fl oz dark rum
45g/1¾oz [US 3½ tbsp] unsalted butter, cut into small cubes

In a bowl beat the egg yolks and sugar until creamy. Add the cornflour gradually, while beating constantly, until it has all been incorporated. Add the vanilla extract and the pinch of salt.

Slowly pour in the milk, mixing the whole time. Transfer the mixture to a saucepan and cook on medium heat, stirring constantly with a wooden spoon. When the mixture has thickened whisk it briefly to eliminate any possible lumps. Cook for a further couple of minutes, stirring constantly.

Moisten a baking tray or a large shallow dish with cold water and then pour the egg mixture into it. Spread it out to a thickness of about 1cm/½in. Cool it a little and then cover the tray or dish and put it in the fridge.

When cold, cut into shapes with a crescent-shaped biscuit cutter and place in an ovenproof dish.

Arrange the slices of apple around the gnocchi.

In a bowl blend together the honey and rum. Pour the mixture into the dish and add the butter here and there. Place in a hot oven, or under a preheated grill [US broiler], for about 10 minutes or until golden, and serve hot.

Francesco rightly suggests that these gnocchi can be prepared a day in advance and heated up just before serving them.

Tortion

A Venetian Strudel

In these Eastern regions there are many different kinds of strudel, going under different names and existing in different versions, although all have their origins in the Austrian or Slav cuisines. The tortion is the Venetian version, its name meaning 'curved' in Venetian dialect. And curved it is, since it is in the shape of a ring, sometimes totally closed, sometimes with the two ends not quite meeting.

I use filo pastry because the pastry for a strudel such as this should be rolled out very thin, which calls for considerable expertise. Filo pastry is there in the shop, all ready for you. But remember to be quite generous in brushing each layer with plenty of melted butter.

Buy the candied peel in segments; the kind that is already chopped is not good enough.

SERVES 6 TO 8

2 tbsp sultanas [US golden raisins]
2 tbsp dark rum
2 tart dessert apples
1 tbsp candied citron and/or lemon, cut into tiny cubes
1 tbsp pine nuts
2 pinches of ground cinnamon
4 Savoiardi, crushed into fine crumbs
100g/3½oz [US 7 tbsp] unsalted butter
225g/8oz filo pastry, approximate weight, defrosted if frozen

Soak the sultanas in the rum for 15 to 20 minutes.

Peel, core and quarter the apples and then cut them across into thin slices. Put them in a bowl and add the candied peel, sultanas and rum, pine nuts, cinnamon and Savoiardi.

Melt the butter in a small saucepan and add 2 tablespoons to the fruit mixture. Mix thoroughly.

Heat the oven to 180°C/350°F/Gas Mark 4.

Line an oven tray with a piece of foil and brush the foil with a little melted butter. Unwrap the filo pastry and lay a sheet of about 30 × 20cm/12 × 8in on the foil. If the filo sheets are not big enough, patch them up, overlapping a little, to form a rectangle of more or less this size. Brush the sheet with plenty of butter and then place another sheet over it. If you are patching it, make sure the joins come in different places for each sheet. Lay 4 sheets in all in this manner, remembering the melted butter.

Spread the filling evenly over the pastry and then roll up the pastry to form a large sausage. Curve it around to form a fat ring. As mentioned in the introduction, the ring should have a gap between the two extremities.

Brush with all the remaining butter and bake for 20 minutes.

Serve hot or warm.

Mostarda di Venezia

Quince and Mustard Preserve

While I have never been successful in producing good mostarda di Cremona, I have made excellent mostarda di Venezia.

There is another reason why I have never persevered with mostarda di Cremona, while I have with the Venetian counterpart. Mostarda di Cremona is on sale in most Italian food shops and it is excellent. I have never met anyone in Italy who makes their own. Mostarda di Venezia, however, is very difficult to find in shops but is very easy to make. This recipe is based on the one published in *The Compleat Mustard*, a book by Robin Weir and Rosamond Man, and on a recipe given to me by my good and generous friend Maria Deana. Maria is the daughter of the famous Arturo Deana, the original owner of the Ristorante La Colomba in Venice. The late Arturo Deana used to serve traditional Venetian food to the international élite before Harry's Bar came on the scene. Good food was not Deana's only passion, as he also loved good paintings, some of which used to hang in his restaurant. His collection started with the inevitable gift of a painter who couldn't pay his bill; by the end of his life Deana's collection included a number of paintings by De Chirico, Chagall and Kokoschka.

At La Colomba, the mostarda di Venezia was served with a sweetened mascarpone cream laced with a small glass of rum. The little pastry biscuits to accompany this delightful ensemble were shaped like a *colomba* (dove). Maria said to me, 'In this way, cheese, pudding and fruit were all supplied in a single dish.' Try it, it's a winner.

THE RECIPE

Buy proper candied peel sold in large segments and not the chopped up kind.

1.8kg/4lb quinces
1 bottle of dry white wine (750ml)
the grated rind and juice of 1 unwaxed lemon
sugar
5 tablespoons mustard powder
salt
150g/5oz candied peel, cut into small cubes

Peel and core the quinces and cut into pieces. Put them in a pan and cover them with the wine. Add the lemon rind and juice. Cook until soft, about 40 minutes.

Purée the mixture and then add the same weight in sugar. Return to the pan. Dissolve the mustard powder in a little hot water and add to the purée with 1 teaspoon of salt and the candied peel. Cook gently until the liquid is reduced and the mostarda becomes dense, about 20–30 minutes.

Sterilize some jars and fill with the mostarda. When it is cool, cover, seal and store away. Keep for about 1 month before you use it.

Friuli-Venezia Giulia

My love for this small region tucked away in the north-eastern corner of northern Italy began with my fondness for particular Friulani. First I must mention our cook Maria, to whom I was devoted, and two other maids who stayed in the family for years ('All the best servants come from Friuli' was a dictum I heard in Milan ages ago and which has always stuck in my mind.) But Friulani do not only make the best servants, they also make the best friends, thanks to their generosity, their cheerfulness and their warmth of character. Unfortunately my visits to that least touristy part of Italy have been far too sporadic and always too brief. There are plenty of good hotels and even better restaurants and *osterie* in the rolling hills covered with vines . . . and no tourists. I feel I really should not be broadcasting this secret!

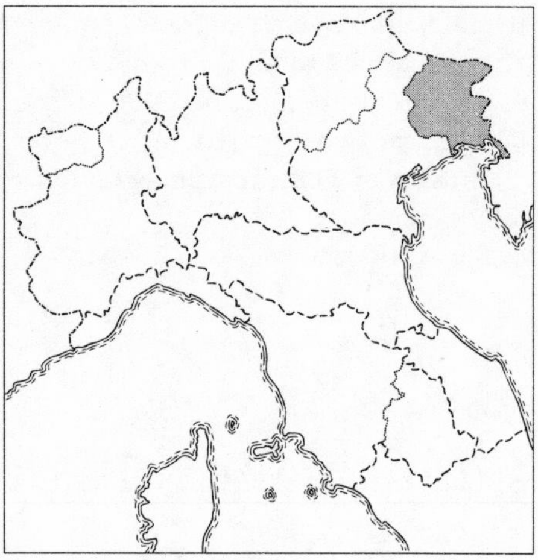

Friuli – the name is a contraction of *Forum Juli* – has been occupied by many different tribes and peoples, from the Celts to the Austrians. All of them have left their mark. But the people whom the modern Friulani consider their ancestors are the Longobards – meaning long-bearded – a Germanic tribe that descended upon Italy in the 6th century and went as far as Pavia and Milan. Hence the name Lombardy. Maybe it is our shared ancestry that makes me feel so close to the Friulani.

As in Lombardy, the cooking excels in winter dishes: soups of every kind, vegetable stews (page 119), rich sausages and, of course, prosciutti and prosciutti and yet more prosciutti. This speciality of prosciutto-making benefits from a balance between the warm breezes coming from the Adriatic and the cold air from the mountains to the North, the right degree of humidity and, of course, the ability of the locals, who are excellent craftsmen in everything they touch. San Daniele is the prosciutto that springs to mind, but there are others. I also love the prosciutto of Sauris, with its very porky flavour and a touch of smoke. But the outstanding treat I had was a prosciutto made by a man called Gigi d'Osvaldo, who apparently hangs them up in his bedroom! He lives near Cormons, actually in Venezia Giulia, where there is one of the best restaurants in Italy, called La Subida.

You can spend a few blissful days at La Subida – it has rooms – while tasting such local specialities as potato ravioli (page 117), roast shin of veal and perfect venison with blueberry sauce – shades of Austria here – to finish with a rich *gubana*, a sort of strudel filled with dried fruit and nuts moistened with the superb Piccolit wine and then shaped round and round like a snail's shell. Very pretty, but I must confess I have never managed to achieve that lovely snail effect.

The region's cooking is fundamentally cucina very *povera*, with a glorious choice of soups, gnocchi, game (plenty of roebucks, deer and chamois in the mountains), sausages and cheeses. There is one cheese that I particularly like, and I loved the way it was served at the trattoria Blasut in Lavariano. Blasut is the sort of place that very cleverly manages to be elegant and rustic at the same time. A half cheese, *montasio* being the cheese in question, was brought to the table, a half of about 30cm/12in in diameter. The cheese was scooped out and cut into little cubes that you just picked up and popped into your mouth with great ease. Montasio is a DOC cheese (i.e. carries the stamp of origin) made with semi-skimmed cow's milk. It has a delicate milky flavour when young and used as a table cheese, getting sapid and deliciously tangy when mature, being then used mostly for making *frico*. This is a dish you would never have anywhere else, even though it could be done with other semi-soft mountain cheeses. To make frico the montasio is very thinly sliced and fried in butter, oil or lard, with a little onion. The cheese will melt at first and then solidify, at which point it is time to turn it over like a pancake. Frico can accompany fried eggs or prosciutto, but I liked it best with very soft scrambled eggs made with red wine vinegar, a recipe by Gianna Modotti.

Gianna, who has a cookery school in the elegant town of Udine, has a deep knowledge of the cooking of the region. She told me that there is just one traditional pasta dish, cialzons, which is first mentioned in a 14th-century document. There are endless variations of this type of ravioli, but there are only two basic types: the cialzons made in the low land around Udine and the cialzons of the mountain regions. The former contain meat and are served *in brodo* – in a meat stock, as a soup. There is a recipe for these meat cialzons, written by the Mother Superior of the Convento delle Dimesse in Udine, which contains roast chicken, brain and other delicacies, demonstrating yet again the culinary expertise of the nuns and their great appreciation of good food. The cialzons made in the mountains 'never contain meat, ricotta being the base', Gianna Modotti explained. Ricotta plus dried fruits, fresh fruits such as pears, quinces, apples, plums, and then cocoa, potatoes, cinnamon and similar ingredients. The filling is always flavoured with marjoram, and the cialzons are dressed with brown butter which is a trademark of this cuisine.

This same brown butter, plus a sprinkling of sugar, was the dressing of the lasagne al papavero – with poppy seeds, which I had in Trieste at the Hostaria Voliga, up near the splendid church of San Giusto. Lasagne with poppy seeds is the most successful marriage between Italian and Hungarian ingredients. Hungarian influences are also noticeable in the abundance of different gulasch, always less fierce in Venezia Giulia than the original Hungarian one.

In Venezia Giulia we have left behind the cooking of the mountains to embrace the cooking of the sea, with its superb seafood risotti, fish soups, *capelonghe* (razor clams) which are cooked in Trieste in a delicate *soffritto* of parsley and garlic and served hot, and *grancevole* (spider crabs), which remind you of the proximity to Venice. But Trieste is proud of a very personal type of cooking based on Austrian, Hungarian and Slav traditions, intermingled with oriental and Jewish influences. The Jewish settlement in Trieste was very strong.

A modern dish I recently came across in that part of Italy is orzotto, which is risotto made with *orzo* (pearl barley) instead of rice. Pearl barley appears quite often in Friulano cooking. The first time I had orzotto was at a very smart wedding in the country near Udine. The head caterer told me that they prefer to do this instead of risotto for parties, because pearl barley does not become *scotto* (overcooked) like rice does. The orzotto at the wedding was the porcini and truffle edition of the similar risotto, but I had an orzotto a few days later at a friend's house made with wonderful beans from Carnia, which are a highly prized variety of borlotti.

Finally, a view of Friuli from outside. In the small town of Crema in Lombardy, the patronne of the restaurant Cral, who gave me her recipe for her superb and unusual ravioli (page 28), was Friulana. When I pressed her about recipes of her own Friuli, she said, 'Eh no, it is too difficult, the cooking of Friuli does not export well. You must eat it in one of those large, dark country kitchens dominated by the *fogolar*.' And she is quite right. You need a fogolar, the raised open fireplace, to properly enjoy bean and barley soup (opposite), polenta and frico, *musetto* (a pork sausage made with the snout of the pig) and *brovada* – turnip fermented with the dregs of pressed grapes; an acquired taste, I dare say. All this would be washed down by the *tajut*, the glass of white wine which is a part of a ritual gregarious drinking. To finish you off you will be offered a *resentin*, a coffee *corretto* with an ample shot of Grappa.

MINESTRA DI FAGIOLI E ORZO
Bean and Barley Soup

Barley is only eaten in the Alpine regions of Italy, and most of the dishes it appears in are of foreign origin.

The recipe for this soup was given to me by Gianna Modotti of Udine, a most generous friend and an accomplished cook.

In some supermarkets you can find pancetta already cut into small cubes, which is ideal for this recipe.

SERVES 6

150g/5oz [US ¾ cup] dried borlotti beans
1 medium potato
1 medium onion
1 celery stalk
1 small carrot
1 fresh bay leaf
2 fresh sage leaves
1 fresh rosemary sprig
3 or 4 fresh flat-leaf parsley sprigs
1 garlic clove
salt and freshly ground black pepper
125g/4oz [US heaping ½ cup] pearl barley
125g/4oz smoked pancetta, chopped
2–3 tbsp extra virgin olive oil

Soak the beans in water for at least 8 hours. If you live in an area where the water is hard, use filtered water.

Drain and rinse the beans and put them in your stockpot or in an earthenware soup pot, earthenware being the best material for slow cooking. Add all the vegetables, cut into chunks, all the herbs and the garlic. Cover with 1l/1¾pt [US 1qt] of water and season with 1 teaspoon of salt. Bring to the boil and cook, covered, for at least 2 hours at the lowest simmer. 'The lowest simmer' are the crucial words here: the surface of the water should just be broken by the occasional bubble. I have left the beans cooking away (because I forgot them) for 3 or 4 hours and they were better than ever – whole and soft, and they had time to develop all their sweet chestnutty flavour. The amount of water is enough if you boil the beans really slowly; otherwise you might have to add some boiling water during the cooking.

Rinse the barley under cold water, throw it into a large pan and add the pancetta, 1 teaspoon of salt and plenty of pepper. Cover with 1l/1¾pt [US 1qt] of water and cook until the barley is very tender, about 1 hour.

Now discard the bay leaf and rosemary stalk, then purée half the beans and all the cooking vegetables through a food mill. If you do not have this invaluable tool, purée in a food processor, although the result will not be as perfect because the skin of the beans, even though minutely cut up, will be in the soup.

Add the bean purée and the whole beans with all the liquid to the barley and mix well. Taste and adjust seasoning, then bring the whole thing to the boil. Simmer for 10 minutes. Although this is a thick soup, you may have to add a little hot water or stock because of the evaporation during the lengthy boiling.

Ladle the soup into individual bowls and drizzle a little olive oil into each bowl. Alternatively, put a bottle of your best olive oil on the table for everyone to add their own.

RISOTTO DI GAMBERI

Risotto with Prawns

Rice is fashionable, prawns are fashionable, hence risotto with prawns is one of the most fashionable of all risotti. But along the coast from Trieste to Venice this risotto is no new fad; it has been popular there for centuries.

This recipe is my interpretation of one of the best fish risotti I have ever had. It comes from Harry's Grill at the Hotel Duchi d'Aosta in Trieste. While I had this, my husband had an excellent risotto al nero – with squid ink. A delicious start to a good dinner, spoiled only by the local *bora*, the wind blowing down on Trieste from the north-east, which prevented us having our meal outside on that very elegant piazza.

SERVES 3 TO 4

450g/1lb raw king or tiger prawns in shell [US large raw shrimp]
2 tbsp extra virgin olive oil
60g/2oz [US 4 tbsp] unsalted butter
1 small onion, finely chopped
a bunch of fresh flat-leaf parsley
1 garlic clove
1.2l/2pt [US 5 cups] fish stock, preferably home-made (page 231)
2 ripe plum tomatoes
350g/12oz [US 1¾ cups] Italian rice, preferably Vialone Nano
2 pinches of chilli powder
150ml/5fl oz Prosecco wine, or other good sparkling wine
2 tbsp brandy
4–5 tbsp freshly grated Parmesan
salt

Peel the prawns and remove the dark veins. Wash them and dry them thoroughly with kitchen paper towel. Cut them into 1cm/½in pieces.

Heat the oil, 40g/1½oz [US 3 tbsp] of the butter and the onion in a heavy saucepan and sauté for 10 minutes or so.

Meanwhile, discard the stalks of the parsley. Chop the leaves with the garlic and then add to the onion. Continue cooking for 2 minutes.

Bring the fish stock to the simmer and keep it simmering gently, close to where you are cooking the risotto.

Peel the tomatoes, either by plunging them into boiling water for 30 seconds or, a quicker method, by holding them, speared on the prongs of a fork, over a gas flame until the skin cracks. When they are peeled, chop them coarsely and throw them into the pan. Let them cook briskly for 5 minutes, then mix in the rice.

Cook to 'toast' the rice for half a minute, while stirring it quickly. Sprinkle with the chilli powder and splash with the wine. Let it bubble away for a minute, then begin to add the fish stock, one ladleful at a time, while you stir the rice constantly. When all the liquid has been absorbed, add another ladleful, stirring and making sure to scrape the bottom and sides of the pan. Continue in this way for about 15 minutes. Now taste the rice; it is done when it is tender but still firm to the bite. Near the end of the cooking reduce the quantity of stock you add each time or you may have too much liquid when the rice is ready. By the end of the cooking the risotto should be moist but not runny.

When the rice is nearly ready, mix in the prawns and the brandy and cook, stirring, for the last 2 or 3 minutes.

Now draw the pan from the heat, and add the rest of the butter and the cheese. Leave to rest for a minute and then stir thoroughly. Taste and correct salt.

Ravioli di Patate
Potato Ravioli

In the eastern corner of Friuli, practically in Slovenia, there is a town called Cormòns, where there is a restaurant called La Subida, where there is a chef called Stefano. Recently Stefano flew to London to promote the food and the wines of that unknown pocket of Italy, and the lucky Londoners enjoyed a week of Friulano cooking at Sandrini in Knightsbridge. Now although Knightsbridge and Friuli are many miles apart, the dinners I had in Knightsbridge were more representative of traditional Friulano cooking than any meal I have had in Friuli. There, many restaurateurs are only too willing to defer to the tastes of their clients and serve fashionably healthy – yet so boring – *grigliate* (grills) of meat or fish.

Stefano's dinner in London consisted of seven courses. I cannot, here, describe them all, so after much heart-searching I chose these ravioli because they are so characteristic of the ability of the Friulani to produce interesting dishes out of everyday food.

These potato ravioli are a very unusual shape, unlike any stuffed pasta I have ever eaten, a sort of square parcel with pinched ends, like a wrapped toffee. I went down to the kitchen to see how they were made, but when I asked Stefano how I could possibly describe how to make that shape, his only answer was, 'That's your problem'! So I decided to forget the toffee shape and give you the instructions for lovely large, ravioli-shaped ravioli.

THE RECIPE

Traditionally, the potato ravioli are dressed in a juice of roast veal. If you happen to have this in the fridge, or if you are cooking a roast as a second course, well and good. If not, melted butter and a touch of cinnamon or poppy seeds is perfect. The butter must be more than melted, it must begin to colour, as they like it in Friuli. The use of cinnamon and poppy seeds in savoury dishes is typical of the region.

This is Stefano's recipe, which was absolutely perfect in the exactness of the quantities.

SERVES 6

700g/1½lb floury potatoes
30g/1oz onion
60g/2oz smoked pancetta
4 tbsp olive oil
salt and freshly ground black pepper
1 egg yolk
1 tbsp chopped fresh chives
2 tbsp chopped fresh marjoram
1 tbsp freshly grated Parmesan

FOR THE PASTA

300g/10oz [US 2½ cups] Italian 00 flour
3 eggs

FOR THE DRESSING

60g/2oz [US 4 tbsp] unsalted butter
1 tsp ground cinnamon or 2 tbsp poppy seeds
30g/1oz Parmesan shavings

First make the dough for the pasta, following the instructions on page 232. Wrap it in cling film and put aside to rest while you prepare the stuffing.

Boil the potatoes in their skins. When cooked, peel them (if you wear rubber gloves you can do this when they are still hot, which is quicker) and purée them through a food mill, or potato ricer, into a bowl.

Chop the onion and the pancetta very thoroughly. (When there is pancetta or prosciutto in a mixture to be chopped I find that the food processor does a very good job. It takes only a minute and the result is very much like a well-made *battuto*, which would take much longer.) Heat the oil in a large frying pan, add the battuto and sauté for 5 minutes. Mix in the potato purée and add salt to taste and a good grinding of pepper. Transfer the mixture back into the bowl and mix in the egg yolk, chives, marjoram and grated Parmesan. Mix very well and set aside to cool.

Unwrap the dough and place on a floured work surface. Roll out the dough, which should not be stretched too thin – about 1mm/1⁄25in is the ideal thickness. Work one sheet of dough at a time, keeping the rest covered to stop it drying up. Cut the rolled-out sheets into 8cm/just over 3in squares. Place a mound of stuffing the size of a walnut on one square and cover with another square. Seal the dough all around with dampened fingers, making sure that no air has been trapped in the dough. Place each raviolo on clean linen towels.

When all the ravioli are made, bring a large saucepan of water to the boil. Add 1½ tablespoons of salt and then gently slide in half the ravioli. Cook until done, from 3 to 8 minutes depending on whether the dough was still fresh, and then retrieve the ravioli with a slotted spoon and transfer, well drained, to a heated large and shallow dish. Cook the second batch and keep warm.

Melt the butter and cook until it begins to become brown. Pour over the ravioli, mix gently around and cover with a gentle spray of one or other of the spices.

To make Parmesan shavings, use a swivel-blade vegetable peeler, shaving a piece of Parmesan until you have prepared a nice little mound. Sprinkle the shavings over the ravioli and serve immediately.

FRITE DI ORT Ⓥ

A Dish of Mixed Garden Vegetables

'To make *Frite di Ort* you go into the vegetable garden (*ort* in local dialect) and pick what is ready. Just as three or four months earlier you would go into the fields and pick what was growing. And with whatever you picked you would be able to make the *Frite di Camp* (field).' These were the words of Gianna Modotti, who runs a cookery school in Udine and is the expert on the cooking of Friuli. She was explaining this recipe to me, and pointing out how it is typical of Friuli cooking, combining simplicity with quality. 'Simple ingredients, cooked so as to produce a good dish.'

I thought of myself, and most of my readers, going into the garden in Britain, and I realized that we could find nearly all the vegetables she was mentioning: spinach, Swiss chard, broccoli, leeks, celery; they all grow or could grow in this northern climate. And how nice to mix them together in a sort of northern ratatouille well suited to an autumnal supper in a cold climate. Sweet peppers, tomato and aubergine or eggplant can strike a discordant note in a northern setting. Food, after all, like clothes, has a time and a place.

THE RECIPE

Use a mild oil from Liguria or Lake Garda. A plain, good olive oil, rather than an extra virgin, is also suitable, since you do not want the flavour of a strong oil to come through.

SERVES 6

900g/2lb mixed vegetables: spinach, Swiss chard, broccoli, leek, celery, greens

60g/2oz [US 4 tbsp] unsalted butter

1 tbsp olive oil

2 garlic cloves, sliced

1 tbsp flour

salt and freshly ground black pepper

Wash the vegetables and cut them into large pieces. Keep them separate. Now blanch them separately. I heat 3 saucepans of salted water to the boil, and I blanch the vegetables in turn in these 3 pans. Blanch the vegetables briefly to keep them crunchy.

Lift the vegetables out of the pans with a slotted spoon or metal sieve and put them all together in a bowl; keep some of the liquid in one of the pans. Now take them out of the bowl, leaving the liquid behind, and place them on a board. Chop them coarsely and return them to the bowl.

Heat the butter, oil and garlic in a large sauté pan and sauté until the garlic begins to release its aroma. Mix in the flour and cook it for about 2 minutes, stirring constantly. The flour should begin to colour. Mix in a couple of tablespoons of the vegetable liquid and then spoon all the vegetables and the liquid in the bowl into the pan. Add salt and pepper to taste and cook, stirring frequently, for about 10 minutes, until the vegetables are tender. You might have to add a couple more tablespoons of the reserved liquid during the cooking. The vegetables, when ready to be brought to the table, should be just wet, but the dish should not be a soup.

Transfer to a heated dish. Use an earthenware dish if you have one as this keeps the vegetables hotter than any other type of dish. Frite is one of the few Italian dishes that is traditionally eaten 'piping hot'.

Agnello al Cren

Lamb in Horseradish Sauce

Horseradish is hardly known in Italy except in some pockets of the north-eastern regions, whose cooking has been influenced either by Central Europe or by the Slav countries, or both.

This recipe comes originally from Venezia Giulia, which lies on the border with ex-Yugoslavia. But it has been in my repertoire for so many years that I cannot remember how it came there in the first place. The only thing I know is that it is a very good recipe.

SERVES 4 TO 6

a 1.8kg/4lb shoulder of lamb (weight with bone)
60g/2oz [US 4 tbsp] unsalted butter
2 tbsp olive oil
1 onion, sliced
1 fresh thyme sprig
3 bay leaves
6 tbsp good wine vinegar
180ml/6fl oz meat stock (page 230)
salt and freshly ground pepper
3 tbsp horseradish sauce (not the creamed kind)
4 tbsp chopped fresh flat-leaf parsley

Ask your butcher to bone the meat for you. Then, at home, remove and discard most of the fat and all the gristle and cut the meat into 2.5cm/1in cubes.

Put half the butter, the oil, onion, thyme, bay leaves, vinegar, stock, salt and pepper into a heavy flameproof casserole (ideally an earthenware pot that you can put directly on the heat) and bring slowly to the boil. Add the meat and cook, covered, for about 1 hour. By this time the meat should be very tender; if not, let it cook away for a further 20 minutes or so.

When the meat is ready there should be very little liquid in the pan. If there is a lot of liquid, fish out the meat with a slotted spoon, keep it warm and boil the liquid to reduce over high heat. Return the meat to the pot.

Melt the remaining butter in a small saucepan and mix in the horseradish and the parsley. Cook, stirring constantly, for 1 minute. Pour the horseradish sauce over the meat and mix thoroughly to coat the meat with the sauce. Taste and check seasoning before you bring the pot to the table.

PANDOLOS CUL FENOLI Ⓥ

Biscuits with Fennel

Pandolo is the biscuit [US cookie] of Friuli. In local dialect the word means a tall person, good for nothing. (What the connection is between the two, nobody could explain!) Pandoli are oval, about 6 × 3cm/2½ × 1¼in. They are eaten at the end of a meal, or at other times of day, with the Verduzzo di Ramandolo, a wine made from the Friuli verduzzo grape. Ramandolo has a honeyed, fruity bouquet, very distinctive and interesting, and a lovely straw colour with gold flashes.

MAKES ABOUT 40

150g/5oz [US 1¼ cups] white flour, preferably Italian 00

1 size-2 egg [US extra-large egg]

30g/1oz [US 2 tbsp] unsalted butter, cut into small pieces, at room temperature

75g/2½oz caster sugar [US 6½ tbsp granulated sugar]

a pinch of salt

1½ tsp baking powder

½ tsp fennel seeds

butter for the tray

Put the flour on the work top, make a well and break the egg into it. Mix with a little flour and then add the butter, sugar, salt and baking powder to the well.

Pound the fennel seeds in a mortar or under the blade of a large knife and add to the mixture. Mix and knead quickly to form a ball of dough. (The dough can also be made in a food processor.) Wrap the dough in cling film and refrigerate for at least half an hour.

Heat the oven to 180°C/350°F/Gas Mark 4.

Dust the work top with flour and roll out the dough to a thickness of about 3mm/⅛in. Stamp out the biscuits with an oval cutter. Butter an oven tray, lay the biscuits on it and bake for 10–15 minutes, until golden.

LIGURIA

If I were to be told that I could eat dishes from only one of Italy's 20 regions, I would unhesitatingly choose Liguria. I would find in them the kind of food that most appeals to me: aromatic, delicate, with few spices but with many herbs. The dishes are complex, with different flavours that always combine well and never clash. The cooking is usually slow, to bring the best out of the ingredients, which are humble, and such as can be found everywhere – but always of the best quality.

Liguria is a boomerang-shaped strip of land, only about 10 kilometres deep, stretching from the French frontier to the Gulf of Spezia, some 270 kilometres. This strip is very mountainous, with many narrow and precipitous valleys running down to the sea – no flat meadows or gentle hills. *Un terreno da capra* (a land for goats), which makes the growing of any crop difficult and laborious. The sides of the mountains are so steep that they have to be terraced. Olive trees, fruit trees, vines, vegetable gardens are all crammed on to these small terraces, kept up by dry stone walls, now, as since time immemorial. No machine here to pick grapes, olives or tomatoes – a great advantage this, for the quality of the produce. And in every garden, patio and window box herbs are grown, mingled with geraniums, nasturtiums and marigolds.

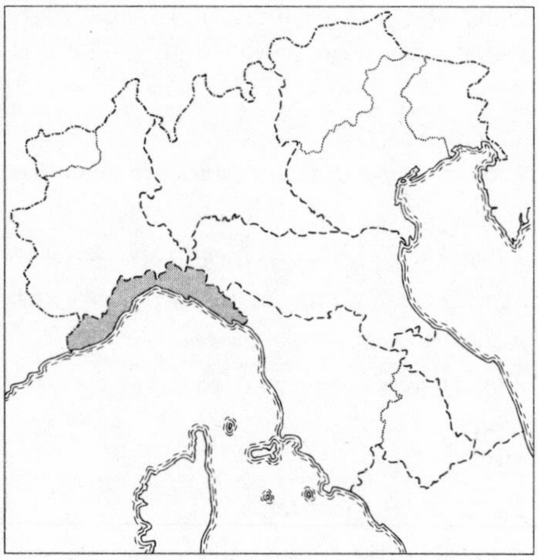

The cooking of Liguria has been totally conditioned by these geographical factors. Yet, although making anything grow is a hard task, the Ligurians have created in this narrow strip of land one of the most luscious vegetable gardens in Europe. In this they have been helped by a temperate climate and the beneficial effect of the sea air. The result is to be seen in the abundance of wild salads and aromatic herbs carpeting the Ligurian mountains. This produce of the land goes to provide the favourite ingredients of the local cooks, but they are used differently, and differently combined, according to whether you are in the western or eastern part of the region.

I was recently in Bordighera, a delightful town only 6 kilometres from the French border, where the smart English set used to winter in the 19th century before they moved westwards to Nice and the Côte d'Azur. Bordighera has a very mild microclimate that allows date palms to grow to impressive heights. A curiosity I came across there is that it is the privilege of Bordighera to supply the young palm shoots – *i palmorelli* – to the Vatican on Palm Sunday. But I was more interested in the food than in the palm trees. And I noticed that nearly all the restaurants that were recommended were away from the coast. That was because the coast and its food was given over to the tourists and what they want to eat, and the truly Ligurian fare receded to the hinterland.

The 'truly Ligurian' cooking of the western Riviera, especially in places near the French border, is more similar to the cooking of Provence than to that of any other part of Italy. Then, when you drive towards Genoa and past, the cooking changes, being influenced first by Piedmont and then, at the tip of the opposite corner of the boomerang, by Tuscany and Emilia-Romagna. The dish that exemplifies these changes most is a torta di verdura – vegetable pie or tourte. These *torte* are one of the hallmarks of all Ligurian cooking, though with endless variations. However, in the western end of the western Riviera, close to France, they are made without ricotta or other soft cheeses, much in the manner of French tourtes.

All dishes are liberally doused with the local olive oil. I found that the same oil is used all over Liguria. Even close to Tuscany, in the province of La Spezia, the oil used to douse their *mesciua* – the poorest yet most delicious soup made with beans, lentils and wheat germ – is the Ligurian oil, a delicate sweet oil with very little peppery aftertaste, produced in the western Riviera, in the province of Imperia.

I went to see two producers of excellent extra virgin olive oil, Roy in Valle Argentina and Crespi in Valle Armea. I was with a business colleague who pointedly commented that I seemed to do my research only in the most beautiful spots. There is a great difference between these two valleys: the Argentina precipitous and narrow with dramatic gorges, the Val Armea wide and serene, almost arcadian. Both are surrounded by hills carpeted with silver olive trees, small vines and beautifully kept vegetable gardens, all fighting for room on the narrow terraces.

The olive trees grown there are one of the most highly prized species. It is the Taggiasca which produces very small olives, similar to those of Provence, with a high concentration of oil in the small amount of pulp. The olives themselves are the favourite of most connoisseurs. The locals use these olives in their cooking, for example to flavour pot-roasted rabbit, or to add to pasta sauces such as I had at the Ristorante del Ponte in Badalucco, where the rubicund Bastianina serves a magnificent dish of crêpes cut into ribbons, dressed with pesto, tomatoes and olives.

This Ligurian oil is the only oil that should be used for pesto, its fruitiness being delicate enough not to interfere with the flavour of the basil, another great product of Liguria. It is interesting that almost the only Ligurian dish that has travelled beyond the borders of Liguria is pesto, when in fact it is the one that most needs the local oil and basil. Of course you can buy Genoese basil everywhere – and at the time of writing it is growing on my window sill in London – but alas you cannot buy the two essentials for an aromatic yet sweet basil, the Ligurian sun and the Mediterranean breezes.

Another herb used a lot in the local cooking is marjoram, which is often mixed with parsley in basic sauces or vegetable dishes. The other trademark of Ligurian cooking is the use of mushrooms, and especially porcini, whether eaten by themselves or as a flavouring for most things from vegetables to fish and especially for chicken and rabbit.

Herbs and vegetables in abundance, therefore, but beef, lamb and even pork – the meat of peasants – seldom appear on Ligurian tables. Rabbit is a favourite local meat; being a delicate meat it goes well with the various herbs. But the other meats, when they do appear, are masquerading in elaborate stuffings, for no better reason than that meat was scarce and expensive. A little meat is made to go a long way by adding cheese, egg, bread, offal and mushrooms.

Oddly enough, the cooking of a region with such a long coastline contains few recipes for fish. The Ligurian sea yields a poor harvest, and the Ligurian people, thrifty and hard working as they are, have to make the best of what there is. They have created delicious, simple dishes from humble fish, such as mackerel with peas, or seppie in zimino (page 142). Their ciuppin and brodino (pages 128 and 129) again use everyday fish. But fish of higher quality, such as sea bass, turbot and daurade, are treated simply, out of respect for their intrinsic flavour. They are roasted, poached or boiled, and served with no sauce but with a generous dribbling of golden olive oil.

The fish, however, that – as in most other regions – brings the creativity of the locals to the fore is stockfish or salt cod. (This used to be the fish of the poor people, but now costs so much as to have become the fish of the rich.) I can demonstrate its importance by reference to the best book on Ligurian cooking, *Cuciniera Genovese* by G B & Giovanni Ratto. Out of 37 recipes for fish, the book has 12 recipes for stockfish or salt cod, all cooked in the most inventive ways such as salt cod stuffed with porcini, pine nuts, whitebait and Parmesan.

The scarcity of recipes for fresh fish makes sense when one looks at the region's history. Genoa was one of the great maritime republics. Her sailors were at sea for months at a time, and the food they had was all preserved. The endless proximity to the sea and its smell must have made anything to do with it pall on their senses. The ship reeked of the sea and of the spices that were being brought back, spices that never touched the sailors' food. When eventually they arrived home all they wanted was fresh food, especially the lovely vegetables and herbs of their beloved hills. The meal to welcome the sailors home was remarkably elaborate, with pansôti – ravioli stuffed with wild herbs and dressed with walnut sauce – stuffed breast of veal, many vegetable pies, and triumphantly in the middle of the table, in all its glory, a beautiful cappon magro (page 138). These dishes, all of which are still strong in the Ligurian repertoire, must all have cost the women hours of labour. There can surely be few greater proofs of love and devotion than such an array of time-consuming dishes.

I have been unable to discover what sweets were prepared for the welcoming party. There would probably have been masses of fresh and candied fruit, together with bowls of confectionery.

Genoa is the motherland of the best candied fruit. The Genoese, and of course the Venetians, were the first to import cane sugar from Egypt, and they discovered how much better a sweetener it was than honey. They soon learned from Arabian traders how to preserve fruit and flower petals by coating them with sugar. They became great experts, and the candied fruit industry was the first industry established in Genoa at the end of the 18th century. European royal houses, the Mountbattens included (or Battenburgs, as they were called then), were clients of the famous Confetteria Romanengo, founded in the 1780s and still flourishing. Even Giuseppe Verdi, not known as a gourmet, dropped into Romanengo's whenever he went to Genoa. In 1881 he wrote to the Maestro Arrivabene: '. . . I had never noticed that at Romanengo they are able to candy any kind of fruit in such an exquisite manner.'

The few Ligurian cakes are typical of northern Italy – more like sweet bread than cakes – and, of these, the *pandolce* is the best known. It is similar to the Milanese panettone but has a more compact texture, is richer in candied and dried fruit, and is flavoured with fennel seeds and orange water, a flavouring reminiscent of the aromas of Arabia. The biscuits [US cookies] too, are dry and simple. Like most of the region's cooking, its sweets reflect the complex character of its inhabitants: brusque yet gentle, thrifty but never mean, honest and direct, and always surprising you with hidden wit.

Focaccia ⓥ

Focaccia is a popular dish everywhere now. Its motherland is Liguria, where the version made with cheese is probably the most popular. Here is the basic recipe for plain focaccia. You can add chopped fresh rosemary (or sage) and garlic to the dough, or olives. Alternatively you can top the focaccia with chopped peeled tomatoes, or very finely sliced sweet onion. The important thing is to be able to make a good basic focaccia, soft and tasty.

I prefer to use easy-blend dried yeast, first because it does blend more easily than fresh or ordinary dried yeast, and secondly because I can always have some to hand when I want to make focaccia or bread.

MAKES 1 LARGE SHAPE

500g/1lb 2oz [US 4½ cups] Italian 00 flour

1½ tsp easy-blend dried yeast [US rapid-rise dry yeast]

1 heaped tsp fine salt

6 tbsp extra virgin olive oil

1 tsp coarse sea salt

Put the flour in a bowl. Sprinkle with the yeast and the fine salt and pour in about 4 tablespoons of the oil. Mix very quickly and then gradually add about 300–350ml/10–12fl oz of water. Mix again quickly and stop as soon as the dough is blended. Put the dough on the floured work surface and knead quickly for 1 to 2 minutes. This dough is very damp. Wash the bowl and dry it, then oil it lightly. Return the dough and cover the bowl with a damp cloth, folded over. Leave in a warm corner of the kitchen until doubled in size, about 2 hours.

Punch the dough down. Turn it over and over, punching it all over. Put it into a 30 × 23cm/12 × 9in baking tray and press out in an even layer. Cover and leave in a warm place for a further hour or so, until the dough is soft and light.

Heat the oven to 240°C/475°F/Gas Mark 9.

Mix the remaining oil with a little water. Dip your fingers into this mixture and press down into the focaccia to form hollows. Sprinkle with the coarse sea salt and brush the top with the remaining oil and water mixture. (The water, mixed with the oil, keeps the surface soft during the baking.)

Turn the heat down to 220°C/425°F/Gas Mark 7 and bake the focaccia until golden, about 20 minutes. Turn the focaccia out on to a wire rack and eat while still warm. Otherwise, reheat it in a low oven before eating.

FARINATA Ⓥ

Chick-pea Flour Pancake

Farinata is made from Ventimiglia (where it is also called *soca*, as in Nice) to Livorno, all around the boomerang coast of Liguria and down the straight Tuscan coast. In Versiglia, the coastal strip that stretches from the border of Liguria to Livorno, farinata changes its name and becomes *calda-calda* – hot-hot.

Farinata is mainly eaten there and then, in the street outside the shop, or near the stall, where it is made in a huge round copper pan.

You can use chick-pea flour or gram flour, which is the flour of a variety of chick-pea called chana dahl. This is available in Indian and oriental shops. Doves Farm produces an excellent gram flour, perfect for farinata. I like to serve farinata with pre-prandial drinks – with plenty of paper napkins for wiping oily fingers!

SERVES ABOUT 6 AS AN APPETIZER

150g/5oz [US 1¼ cups] chick-pea flour
400ml/14fl oz lukewarm water
½ tsp salt
the needles of a fresh rosemary sprig about 25cm/10in long
4 tbsp extra virgin olive oil
freshly ground pepper

Put the chick-pea flour in a large bowl. Add the water gradually while beating hard. (I use a hand-held electric mixer.) Season with salt and continue beating for a further minute. Set aside for 4 to 6 hours.

Heat the oven to 240°C/475°F/Gas Mark 9.

Skim off the froth from the surface of the chick-pea mixture using a slotted spoon. Whisk again briefly and then add the rosemary. Pour the oil into a 30cm/12in shallow tin or a 22 × 32cm/ 8½ × 13in oven tray. Stir the chick-pea mixture and then pour into the tin.

Place the tin in the oven. Turn the heat down to 220°C/425°C/Gas Mark 7 and bake for about 20 minutes, until the mixture has set. Grind a lot of pepper all over the top of the farinata. Leave out of the oven for 10 minutes before serving. Farinata is best served hot, but it is also good at room temperature.

IL CIUPPIN DI SESTRI LEVANTE E IL BRODINO DI LERICI

Two Ligurian Fish Soups

Although based on the same ingredients and similar cooking methods, these two soups are surprisingly dissimilar, being finished off differently.

I had Il Ciuppin at the Ristorante Angiolina in Sestri Levante, an old-fashioned resort half-way down the eastern Riviera. There it is a speciality of the house, as it certainly deserves to be. The fish was in neat chunks, only the head being removed, but the chunks of fish were complete with their bones and other bits and pieces, something that the southern Europeans, like the Orientals, do not mind, but that annoys the British. Here the diners have to do the work at the table, while in the other soup – the Brodino di Lerici – it is the cook who does the work.

For both soups you must use only white fish, no oily blue fish or salmon.

IL CIUPPIN

Chunky Fish Soup

SERVES 8

900g/2lb assorted fish, such as hake, grouper, dogfish, whiting, John Dory, haddock
1 large onion, chopped
1 celery stalk, chopped
1 carrot, chopped
1 garlic clove, chopped, plus a few peeled garlic cloves
120ml/4fl oz olive oil
150ml/5fl oz dry white wine
225g/8oz [US 1 cup] canned plum tomatoes, with their juice, chopped
salt and freshly ground black pepper
slices of country-type white bread, such as Pugliese
3 tbsp chopped fresh parsley

Clean and wash the fish and cut into large chunks. Discard the head and tail.

In a large saucepan, fry all the vegetables and the chopped garlic gently in 90ml/3fl oz of the oil for 10 minutes, stirring frequently. Add the fish, mix thoroughly and fry gently for 5 minutes, turning it over frequently. Pour over the wine and boil rapidly to reduce by half.

Pour over 2l/3½pt [US 2qt] of boiling water and add the tomatoes and seasoning. Return the soup to the boil and simmer for 20 minutes. Taste and check seasoning.

Toast the bread for 10 minutes in a hot oven. Rub with peeled garlic cloves split in half and then place a piece or two of bread in individual soup bowls. Ladle the soup over the bread. Drizzle with the remaining oil, sprinkle over the parsley and serve.

POT-ROASTED SHIN OF PORK (PAGE 83);
CANNELLINI BEANS WITH GARLIC,
SAGE AND OIL (PAGE 184)

FENNEL AND PRAWNS
IN A WINEY SAUCE, LEFT (PAGE 218);
RED RADICCHIO WITH BORLOTTI BEAN
PURÉE (PAGE 100)

GENOESE FISH AND VEGETABLE SALAD
(PAGE 138)

CLOCKWISE FROM TOP:
MELON WITH BALSAMIC VINEGAR (PAGE 169); COFFEE-FLAVOURED CREAM PUDDING (PAGE 74); STRAWBERRIES WITH BALSAMIC VINEGAR (PAGE 169)

CUTTLEFISH RISOTTO
(PAGE 95)

Il Brodino
Smooth Fish Soup

Lerici is a delightful little town in the so-called Golfo dei Poeti – the Gulf of La Spezia – at the southernmost end of the Ligurian arc. It is here that Byron showed his mettle by swimming across the Gulf from Lerici to Portovenere, some 5 kilometres, and it is from here that Shelley embarked on his last, and fatal, sea journey.

Somehow Lerici has managed to keep some of the atmosphere that must have captivated these men. A kind of gentle and genteel adagio breathes through the palm trees along the promenade, while pensioners and young mothers with their babies enjoy the sun, sitting on the benches in the municipal *giardinetti*, cheered by the ubiquitous snap-dragons, tagetis and petunias in their clashing colours.

The fish market suitably reflects this atmosphere. It is a small, family affair: three fishwives with their stalls and the most beautiful grey-striped cat, who struck me as the happiest-looking cat I had ever seen. I soon discovered why. When I offered him a sardine, he turned and walked slowly away in dignified disgust. '*Ah, ma lui mangia solo le triglie*' (he only eats red mullet), explained one of the women, and they had to be *di scoglio* (rock red mullet) she added, laughing. I had forgotten that in Italy even the animals have discerning palates.

The three women are the wives of the fishermen who, weather permitting, go out every day at 4 a.m., and come back at about 9 a.m. with their catch. For all the hard work they do, the catch is poor. The Ligurian sea has been depleted by pollution and overfishing. Now the situation is a little better, because of the cleaning of the sea and the ban on fishing during one or two months of the year. But I saw with my own eyes during the week I recently spent there that the fishermen bring home very little. Only once did I see a splended sea bass of about 4kg/8¾lb, such a difference from the omnipresent sea bass offered in restaurants, each weighing precisely 250g/9oz, all coming from the nearby fish farms.

The rest of the catch while I was there was cuttlefish, a few silvery anchovies, red mullet, slim mackerel, one or two turbot and a handful of sole. There were a few other fish that I did not know, so different were they from those here in England or those caught in the Adriatic with which I am more familiar.

One of these odd species were the Sparli, a fish of the large Sparidae family which includes all the breams. I asked one of the women how she cooked them. And, as always in Italy, the recipe came out with all the vague 'two fingers of this' and 'a little of that', plus the comments and corrections of the other fishwives and of the few shoppers standing around.

THE RECIPE

This is my interpretation of the recipe given to me by Caterina Padulo and Giovanna Simeone of the Lerici market. Brodino means little stock, but it is hardly that, since it consists of a fairly thick liquid with pasta floating in it. The addition of the pasta gives the soup a different texture and tones down the fishiness of the liquid. The fact that it is puréed makes the soup very easy to eat at the table.

In Lerici they use only fish of one kind when they make Il Brodino.

Ideally this soup should be made in an earthenware pot of the kind that you can put straight on the heat. If you don't have one, use a heavy-based saucepan.

SERVES 6

6 tbsp olive oil
125g/4oz onion, cut into chunks
100g/3½oz celery, cut into chunks
60g/2oz carrot, cut into chunks
2 garlic cloves, chopped
15g/½oz fresh flat-leaf parsley, chopped
½ dried hot chilli pepper, crumbled
salt and freshly ground pepper
150g/5oz potato, cubed
2 tomatoes, peeled and chopped
700g/1½lb sea bream, hake, gurnard or whiting
90g/3oz small pasta, such as ditalini or conchigliette

Heat the oil in the pot with the onion, celery, carrot, garlic, parsley, chilli and 1 teaspoon of salt and cook very gently for 10 minutes, stirring occasionally. Now add the potato and the tomatoes and cook for a further 15 minutes or so.

While this is going on, wash the cleaned fish and cut it into chunks. Throw it into the pot – heads, tails, the lot – and sauté in the *soffritto* for 5 minutes, turning the pieces over and over. (The head is cooked in the soup because it has a delicious strong flavour.) Pour over 1.8l/3pt [US 7½ cups] of boiling water and simmer for 20 minutes, uncovered.

Lift the chunks of fish out on to a plate and leave aside to cool a little, then remove and discard the head, backbones and fins. Strain the liquid into a clean saucepan. Pick out the pieces of vegetable and any pieces of fish left in the strainer. Remove any bone you can see and discard. Add the vegetables and the rest to the cleaned fish. Look again and feel with your hands (the best tool) for any bones you might have missed.

Spoon this lot into a food processor, add a ladleful or two of the liquid and process to a coarse purée. Pour this purée into the rest of the liquid in the saucepan and bring to the boil.

Before you add the pasta, add a little boiling water if the soup is too thick. Check salt and pepper. Cook the pasta gently, not at a roaring boil, as you would when making *pasta asciutta* (pasta cooked the normal way).

Pesto ⓥ

> And what is this scent of Alpine herbs that mixes so strangely with the smell of the rocks, pervading the air of all the Riviera from Lerici to Turbia? All the region is enveloped by it as from the surf of the sea. It is a lively and exciting scent. . . It is the scent of pesto, the condiment made with basil, pecorino, garlic, pine nuts, beaten in a mortar and diluted with olive oil. Is that all? Yes, that is all, and a unique thing is created. There are condiments that appear in many regions, but this is solely Ligurian; it speaks the Ligurian dialect.

Thus wrote Paolo Monelli in his best seller *Il Ghiottone Errante*, a gastronomic tour of Italy published in 1935.

I was in Liguria in July 1994 to visit an artisanal factory, Crespi in Cernaia, which produces what I rate as the best bottled pesto. As soon as I got out of the car the pungent scent of basil reminded me of that piece by Monelli. It was an unpleasantly hot day, but the scent revived me and reminded me of endless meals under a canopy of vines in the silvery-green hills of Liguria. There, pesto would be dressing a dish of *trenette* – Ligurian tagliatelle, *picagge* – narrow local lasagne, or deliciously thick *trofiette*, which look like tiny spinning tops and which, as children, we tried to spin. All home-made Ligurian pasta is 'poor man's' pasta, i.e. containing a higher proportion of water to egg. But for me, the best use of pesto is on a dish of feather-light potato gnocchi.

THE RECIPE

There are two things that I ask people to observe when making pesto. One is the use of the right oil, the other the use of fresh pine nuts. By 'fresh' I mean pine nuts that have been shelled within the year. You may well ask how you can tell the age of a pine nut. In fact, if you look carefully at the nuts they will tell you. They must be large and smooth, of a creamy ivory colour, and without any darker patches. Although Chinese pine nuts are more easily available than Italian ones, the Italian pine nuts have a better flavour.

The right oil is a Ligurian oil, i.e. a *dolce* (sweet oil) and not a *fruttato* (peppery oil), such as a Tuscan oil. There are some good Ligurian oils on the market that you can keep for your pesto, for salsa verde or for dressing steamed fish or vegetables when a fruttato would be too aggressive.

The purists make pesto by hand, pounding the basil leaves in the mortar with a pestle. They point out that making pesto in a food processor or a blender is risky because the oil might 'cook' the basil as a result of the heat produced by the machine. If you want to use the food processor or the blender, switch the machine on and off very often so that the blade does not heat up.

Old-fashioned pesto consisted only of basil leaves, garlic and olive oil. This is the pesto that is mixed into a minestrone alla genovese (page 132), when the cheese is added at the table.

FOR 4 PORTIONS OF PASTA OR GNOCCHI

PESTO MADE IN THE MORTAR

20g/¾oz [US 3½ tbsp] pine nuts
60g/2oz fresh basil leaves
1 garlic clove
a pinch of coarse sea salt
4 tbsp freshly grated Parmesan
2 tbsp freshly grated aged pecorino [US romano] (If you cannot get pecorino, replace the pecorino with additional Parmesan)
120ml/4fl oz extra virgin olive oil, preferably Ligurian

Heat the oven to 180°C/350°F/Gas Mark 4. Spread the pine nuts on a baking tray and put the tray in the oven for 3 to 4 minutes. I do this because toasting releases the aroma in nuts.

Put the basil leaves, the garlic, pine nuts and

salt in a mortar and grind against the sides of the mortar with the pestle, crushing all the ingredients, until the mixture has become a paste.

Mix in the grated cheeses and pour over the oil very gradually, beating with a wooden spoon.

PESTO MADE IN A FOOD PROCESSOR OR A BLENDER

Heat the oven to 180°C/350°F/Gas Mark 4. Spread the pine nuts on a baking tray and put the tray in the oven for 3 to 4 minutes.

Put all the ingredients, except the cheeses, in the bowl of the food processor or blender. Process at high speed, and when evenly blended transfer to a bowl.

Mix in the cheeses.

Pesto freezes very well. Omit the garlic and the cheeses, and add them just before you are going to use the sauce.

PASTA WITH PESTO

Put the pesto in the serving bowl and place this in a very low oven to heat up a little. Now cook the pasta.

The suitable shapes of pasta are: tagliatelle, fettuccine, linguine and spaghetti. In western Liguria a potato cut into cubes and a handful of French or other fine green beans, cut into small pieces, are thrown into the pasta water. When they are nearly cooked, and by this I mean soft and not crunchy, is the time to slide in the pasta. When the pasta is ready, retrieve a mugful of the pasta water and stir 2 or 3 tablespoons of it into the pesto. This is absolutely necessary to give the pasta the right fluidity. Drain the pasta (plus the potato and beans) and transfer to the bowl with the pesto. Here I do something that is not accepted by the purists – I add a piece of unsalted butter to sweeten the pesto and to make the pasta more creamy. Toss well and serve at once.

MINESTRONE COL PESTO Ⓥ

Minestrone with Pesto

Of all the different minestroni, the Genoese, when properly made, has the cleanest and the freshest flavour. G B & Giovanni Ratto write as follows in their cookery book, which is considered to be the best on Ligurian cooking: 'This soup, very characteristic of the Genoese, has the most exquisite taste when well made. It is usually made during the season in which there are more and better vegetables on the market. . . It can be eaten hot or cold.'

This is Ratto's recipe with very slight alterations. The best green beans to use are the large flat ones.

SERVES 6

150g/5oz aubergine [US eggplant], cut into 1cm/½in cubes
150g/5oz green beans, topped and tailed and broken into short pieces
400g/14oz cooked or canned borlotti beans
200g/7oz potatoes, cut into 1cm/½in cubes
200g/7oz cabbage, very coarsely shredded
250g/9oz sweet onion, thickly sliced
150g/5oz courgette [US zucchini], cut into 1cm/½in cubes
2 celery stalks, cut into small pieces
100g/3½oz flat mushrooms, cut into small pieces
4 ripe tomatoes, peeled and coarsely chopped
salt and freshly ground pepper
150g/5oz small tubular pasta, such as ditalini
4 tbsp pesto (page 131)
freshly grated Parmesan for the table

Fill your stockpot with 2l/3½pt [US 2qt] of water. Add 1 tablespoon of salt, and bring to the boil. Add all the vegetables and simmer very gently, covered, for about 2½ to 3 hours. The longer you cook a minestrone, the better it will be. The vegetables do not break or become a mush during the cooking; they keep their shape perfectly.

The last thing is to throw in the pasta, but before you do that, check that there is enough liquid. If not, add a ladleful or two of boiling water. Remember, however, that this is a very thick soup. The pasta should cook gently, contrary to the way of cooking pasta when served *asciutta* (drained).

When the pasta is ready, taste and check salt and then add a good grinding of pepper and the pesto. Mix well and serve with plenty of cheese on the side. In the summer, when you can get the best vegetables, I recommend serving the minestrone at room temperature. It is excellent this way.

Due Polpettoni di Verdure

Two Vegetable Tourtes

In Liguria, and only there, polpettone means a baked dish of vegetables. Anywhere else in Italy it means a meat loaf.

There are several vegetable polpettoni, but these two are the most popular. The polpettone di fagiolini comes from the province of Genoa, while the Swiss chard polpettone is a traditional dish from the valley of the river Magra, the border between Liguria and Tuscany. Tarragon, a herb used mainly in Tuscany, begins here to make its appearance.

Polpettoni used to be the dish that people took for a *scampagnata* (a picnic), when 'going for a picnic' meant to walk just outside the walls of the town and sit there on the field admiring the view. I bet that each polpettone at each picnic would have been different, albeit based on the two main ingredients, vegetables and eggs. My two following recipes exemplify just this.

POLPETTONE DI FAGIOLINI Ⓥ

Green Bean Tourte

The cheese traditionally used in many vegetable polpettoni is *quagliata*, which is known only in Liguria. It is a very soft creamy cheese, half-way between cream cheese and sour cream. After some trial and error I decided that a mixture of sour cream and ricotta makes a good substitute.

SERVES 6

20g/¾oz dried porcini
450g/1lb green beans
salt and freshly ground pepper
60g/2oz crustless white country-type bread
100ml/3½fl oz milk
5 tbsp extra virgin olive oil
2 garlic cloves, very finely chopped
1 tbsp chopped fresh marjoram
3 eggs
30g/1oz [US 2 tbsp] ricotta
4 tbsp sour cream
60g/2oz [US ½ cup] freshly grated Parmesan
40g/1½oz [US ½ cup] dried white breadcrumbs plus more for the tin

Soak the dried porcini in hot water for about an hour (see page 13). If they are still gritty when you lift them out of the water, rinse them under cold water. Dry them with kitchen paper towel and chop them coarsely.

Top and tail the beans and wash them. Plunge them into plenty of boiling salted water and cook them for just over 5 minutes. (Remember that the water in which beans are cooked needs more salt than is needed for any other vegetable.) Drain, refresh them under cold water and drain thoroughly. Now you have to chop them up coarsely, either by hand or in the food processor, being careful to stop the machine before the beans become a purée.

While the beans are cooking put the bread in a bowl, add the milk and leave it to soak.

Heat the oven to 180°C/350°F/Gas Mark 4.

Heat half the oil, the garlic and the marjoram in a frying pan. Throw in the dried porcini and the chopped beans and sauté gently for 2 or 3 minutes.

Squeeze the excess milk out of the bread and add the bread to the bean mixture, crumbling it through your fingers. Continue to fry for a further 5 minutes, turning the whole thing over and over to take up the flavours.

Beat the eggs together lightly in a large bowl. Crumble the ricotta and add to the eggs together with the sour cream, Parmesan, dried breadcrumbs and a generous grinding of pepper. Mix well and then scoop in all the contents of the frying pan. Mix thoroughly. Taste and check seasoning.

Grease a 20cm/8in spring-clip tin with a little of the remaining oil. Sprinkle with enough breadcrumbs to cover all the surface, but be sure to tip out any excess crumbs.

Spoon the bean mixture into the prepared tin and pour over the remaining oil in a thin stream. Bake for about 40 minutes, until a thin skewer or a wooden toothpick pushed into the middle of the tourte comes out dry. Let the tourte cool in the tin for 5 minutes and then unmould it on to a round dish.

Serve hot or warm, or even at room temperature as when part of a picnic.

POLPETTONE DI BIETOLE

Swiss Chard Tourte

Swiss chard polpettoni can be plain or can contain sausage, wild mushrooms or tuna. I think the tuna version is the most successful, as long, of course, as you buy proper tuna canned under olive oil and not skipjack tuna.

SERVES 4 TO 5

300g/10oz potatoes
salt and freshly ground black pepper
7 tbsp extra virgin olive oil
1kg/2¼lb Swiss chard
1 small onion, very finely chopped
1 garlic clove, very finely chopped
½ tbsp chopped fresh tarragon
2 tbsp chopped fresh parsley
2 eggs plus 1 egg yolk
4 tbsp freshly grated Parmesan
125g/4oz best Spanish or Italian canned tuna, drained
2 anchovy fillets, chopped
dried breadcrumbs for the tin

Cook the potatoes in their skins in boiling salted water until soft. Drain and peel them. Purée them into a large bowl through the small hole disc of a food mill or a potato ricer. Dress the purée with 2 tablespoons of the oil.

Remove the green leaf part from the white stalks of the Swiss chard. Set the white stalks aside for another dish, as for instance that on page 34. Wash the green leaves and put them in a pot with only the water that clings to them and 1 teaspoon of salt. Cook over a lively heat until tender. Drain and, as soon as it is cool enough, squeeze out all the moisture with your hands. Chop coarsely.

Sweat the onion in 3 tablespoons of the oil for 7 minutes or so. Add the garlic, tarragon and parsley. Sauté for 5 minutes and then mix in the Swiss chard. Sauté for 5 to 7 minutes, turning it over frequently. Transfer the whole contents of the pan to the bowl containing the potatoes.

Heat the oven to 190°C/375°F/Gas Mark 5.

Add the eggs and egg yolk, Parmesan and pepper to the vegetable mixture and mix very thoroughly. Flake the tuna into small shreds and add that too, together with the anchovy fillets. Mix very thoroughly – hands are best. Taste and check seasoning.

Brush an 18cm/7in spring-clip tin with some of the remaining oil. Line with greaseproof paper [US wax paper] and brush with a little more oil. Sprinkle with the dried breadcrumbs and then shake out excess crumbs.

Spoon the Swiss chard mixture into the prepared tin and dribble the remaining oil over the top. Bake for 40 to 50 minutes, until set.

Allow to cool a little in the tin and then turn it over on to a round dish. Serve warm or at room temperature.

TORTA DI ZUCCHINE Ⓥ

Courgette Tourte

One of the glories of Ligurian cooking is its wealth of vegetable dishes. Vegetables are served stuffed, braised or fried, but the best to my mind are the vegetable tourtes.

The eggless pastry made there, and the way it is stretched, is very similar to filo, and I wonder whether the Genoese sailors did not bring the know-how back from their journeys to the eastern Mediterranean where they must have encountered filo pastry.

This pastry is used here to envelope a filling made with courgettes and rice. The rice is used raw, but it then sits in the rest of the filling for 2 hours, thus becoming soft. An interesting way to treat rice.

SERVES 4

325g/11oz courgettes [US zucchini]
1 white onion or ½ small Spanish onion
125g/4oz [US ½ cup + 2 tbsp] Italian rice, preferably Arborio
8 tbsp extra virgin olive oil
3 tbsp freshly grated Parmesan
1 tbsp finely chopped fresh marjoram, or 1 tsp dried marjoram or oregano
salt and freshly ground black pepper
2 size-2 eggs [US extra-large eggs]
125–150g/4–5oz filo pastry, defrosted if frozen

Put the courgettes in a sink full of cold water and scrub them gently, then rinse and dry them. Cut off and discard the ends of the courgettes, then slice them very finely indeed. (I use the fine disc slicer of the food processor.) Put the courgettes in a bowl.

Peel the onion and slice it paper-thin. Add to the courgettes together with the rice, 5 tablespoons of the oil, the Parmesan, marjoram, salt and a good grinding of pepper.

Beat the eggs lightly and add to the bowl. Mix the whole thing very thoroughly. (I find the best tool for this is a pair of clean hands.) Cover the bowl and set aside for a couple of hours. Mix again and again whenever you remember during this time, because the liquid sinks to the bottom and you want the rice and the courgette to sit in it equally.

Heat the oven to 180°C/350°F/Gas Mark 4.

Pour the remaining oil into a small bowl. Use a little of it to oil a 20cm/8in spring-clip tin.

Unfold the filo pastry leaves carefully, one at a time. Keep the rest covered while you work on each leaf because filo pastry dries out and cracks very quickly. Lay one leaf of pastry over the bottom and up the sides of the tin, allowing the ends to hang over the outside of the tin. Using a pastry brush, brush the pastry with a little of the oil, then lay another leaf of filo across the previous one so as to cover the sides of the tin completely. Brush with oil, and cover with 2 more leaves, brushing each leaf as before. You will then have 4 layers of filo pastry.

Stir the courgette mixture thoroughly and spoon it into the prepared case. Fold the overhanging pieces of pastry over the top, one at a time, brushing with oil in between each leaf. If necessary, patch up with pieces of filo so that the filling is totally covered. Trim the edges and fold them down into the sides of the tin.

Place the tin in the oven and bake for about 30 minutes. Turn the heat up to 200°C/400°F/Gas Mark 6 to crisp the top until it becomes a lovely golden brown colour.

Let the tourte cool slightly in the tin, then unmould and transfer to a round serving dish and serve warm or at room temperature. To cut, use a very sharp knife or the pastry will crumble.

TORTINO DI POMODORI Ⓥ

Tomato Crumble

I have two 19th-century cookery books on Genoese cooking. One, *Cuciniera Genovese* by G B & Giovanni Ratto, is the definitive book on the subject, and in the recipe for this dish the tomatoes are baked between two layers of breadcrumb mixture. The other book, *L'Antica Cuciniera Genovese*, has a similar recipe called Pomodori all'Inferno (why 'in hell'?) where the ingredients are the same, but the tomato halves are placed directly on the tin and the breadcrumb mixture is spread over the top. I prefer the first version; it makes a delicious thick tomato crumble.

As is often the case with old, and very simple, recipes, no quantities are given. So the quantities are mine, as also is the addition of a little vegetable stock which I find necessary to keep the crumb mixture moist during the baking. The stock replaces the delicious juices that the Ligurian tomatoes would produce.

THE RECIPE

Buy seasonal tomatoes, ripe but firm, and all of the same size. I find that the best way to deal with the new species of hard-skinned tomato is to keep them for 4 or 5 days on a sunny windowsill before using them. The skin gets softer and they manage to develop a little more flavour. The breadcrumbs must be made from good-quality white bread, but not olive or tomato bread or any other dressed bread.

SERVES 4

8 tomatoes

60g/2oz [US ⅔ cup] dried breadcrumbs

4 tbsp freshly grated Parmesan

4 tbsp chopped fresh flat-leaf parsley

3 tbsp chopped fresh oregano

2 tbsp capers, rinsed and dried (optional)

2 garlic cloves, finely chopped

salt and freshly ground black pepper

4 or 5 tbsp vegetable stock (page 231)

120ml/4fl oz extra virgin olive oil

Wash and dry the tomatoes. Cut them in half across the 'equator', and not across the two 'poles'. This is because you can discard many more seeds when you cut the tomatoes in this way. Squeeze out some of the seeds.

Mix the breadcrumbs, cheese, herbs, optional capers, garlic, salt and a generous grinding of pepper. Moisten with the stock and with half the olive oil.

Heat the oven to 180°C/350°F/Gas Mark 4.

Grease a large oven tin with 1 tablespoon of the remaining oil. Spread about half the crumb mixture over the bottom and place the tomatoes, cut side up, on it. Sprinkle with the rest of the crumb mixture and pour over the remaining oil. Bake for about 40 minutes, until the tomatoes are soft and the crumbs at the top are toasted.

Serve warm or at room temperature, but neither straight from the oven nor straight from the fridge. In fact, this dish should never see the inside of the fridge. You can certainly make it a day in advance, but you must keep it outside the fridge.

CAPPON MAGRO

Genoese Fish and Vegetable Salad

The name of this dish means 'capon for a meatless day'. This seems a nonsense until one realizes that since capon was considered the most delicious of all meats, this dish, made with fish and vegetables, is comparable to capon because it is equally delicious. It is the elaborate dish originally made for Genoese sailors, to celebrate their homecoming after months at sea. There are many versions of the recipe even in Genoa, and successful variations can be created by using whichever are the best fish and vegetables available. All the ingredients are piled up in layers to make a cupola.

In the 19th-century book *Cuciniera Genovese*, which is considered the bible of Ligurian cooking, the authors G B and Giovanni Ratto write: 'As ravioli are the queen of all first courses, so Cappon Magro, when properly made, is the best of all known salads.'

THE RECIPE

I used to make this dish with crackers until I read Philippa Davenport, in the *Financial Times*, suggesting the use of baked bread. As usual, she was absolutely right. The bread baked at length becomes similar to the ships' biscuits used by the Genoese.

You can enrich cappon magro by placing oysters around the dish, or a small lobster on the top. Alternatively, you can cut out the Dublin Bay prawns and increase the quantity of cheaper prawns. But this would be a pity as cappon magro is a festive dish and needs a certain flourish. It is a lovely party piece.

SERVES 6 TO 8

1 large (round) Pugliese loaf or French country-type loaf
salt
½ onion
1 bay leaf
6 peppercorns
2 tbsp wine vinegar
700g/1½lb hake, haddock, bream or any good-quality firm white fish, filleted
150g/5oz French or other green beans, topped and tailed
225g/8oz new potatoes
125g/4oz carrots
150g/5oz cauliflower florets
120ml/4fl oz extra virgin olive oil, preferably Ligurian
the juice of ½ lemon
5 raw Dublin Bay prawns in shell
1 garlic clove
225g/8oz cooked peeled prawns [US cooked peeled small shrimp]

FOR THE SAUCE

30g/1oz crustless country-type bread
4 or 5 tbsp wine vinegar, depending on strength
30g/1oz fresh flat-leaf parsley, leaves only
1 garlic clove
2 tbsp capers
30g/1oz canned anchovy fillets, drained, or salted anchovies, cleaned and rinsed
4 tbsp pine nuts
the yolks of 2 hard-boiled eggs
6 green olives, pitted
150ml/5fl oz extra virgin olive oil
salt and freshly ground black pepper

FOR DECORATION

2 hard-boiled eggs
1 dozen black olives

Heat the oven to 150°C/300°F/Gas Mark 2.

Remove the crust from the base of the round loaf and then cut a 1cm/½in thick slice across the loaf. If your loaf is not a large one, i.e. about 20cm/8in, cut 2 slices. Remove the crust all around this disc, or discs, and then put the disc(s) in the oven. Bake for about ¾ to 1 hour, until very crisp.

Meanwhile, heat a pan of salted water with the onion half, bay leaf, peppercorns and 1 tablespoon of the vinegar to boiling. Add the fish and poach for about 2 to 5 minutes, depending on the thickness of the fillets. Remove from the heat, leaving the fish in the liquid.

Cook the French beans, unpeeled potatoes, carrots and cauliflower separately in boiling salted water until done. Drain thoroughly. Peel the potatoes and slice them and the carrots; cut the beans into short pieces. Keeping them separate, dress each vegetable with 1 tablespoon of the oil. Mix gently but thoroughly and set aside in separate bowls.

Remove the fish fillets from the cooking liquid and break into morsels, discarding any bones and skin. Dress with the lemon juice and 2 tablespoons of the oil. Mix and set aside.

Boil the Dublin Bay prawns for about 2 minutes in the fish liquid. Drain and set aside 3 prawns; peel and devein the other 2 prawns, cut them into pieces and mix into the fish.

Now make the sauce. Break the crustless bread into small pieces. Place these in the bowl of a food processor and pour over 4 tablespoons of the vinegar. Leave for 5 minutes to soak and then add the parsley, garlic, capers, anchovies, pine nuts, egg yolks and the olives. Whizz, while adding the oil through the funnel, until dense and creamy. Scoop the sauce out into a bowl, taste and add plenty of pepper and salt, if necessary. Also check the vinegar and add a little more to taste. The sauce should be very piquant.

Now everything is ready to assemble the dish. Rub the toasted disc or discs of bread on both sides with the garlic and place on a round dish. If you have 2 discs, cut off a small piece from each one, lay the slices one next to the other and then add the cut-off pieces at the top and bottom of the adjoining slices, so as to make a larger circle, however imperfect.

Mix the remaining 1 tablespoon of vinegar and 2 tablespoons of oil together and pour evenly over the bread. This is the base of the cappon magro. Spread a thin layer of sauce over the bread and then cover with a layer of beans, a couple of tablespoons of fish and prawn morsels, a layer of potatoes and then again some fish and prawn morsels, a layer of cauliflower and so on, and on, until you have piled everything up, making a sort of dome shape.

Spread the rest of the sauce all over the mound and scatter with the peeled cooked prawns. Place the three unshelled Dublin Bay prawns on top. Garnish the base of the cappon magro with the hard-boiled eggs, cut into wedges, and the black olives. Cover with cling film and chill until needed, but remove from the fridge at least 1 hour before serving.

PATATE ALL'ALBINA Ⓥ

Braised Potatoes

A friend of mine in Santa Margherita has a lovely cook by the name of Albina, and it was Albina who gave me this recipe. Albina lives up the hill, behind Paraggi, in a small house surrounded by olive trees and vines, as well as mandarin, apricot and plum trees. Scrabbling chickens and munching rabbits complete the pastoral scene. The house overlooks the Golfo del Tigullio, the large bay that lies between Portofino and Sestri Levante. Albina was born in that house, and I sometimes wonder how much she takes the splendour of her surroundings for granted. It is one of the most beautiful spots I have seen, and it is still totally unspoilt. That part of the Portofino peninsula belongs to landowners who have been wise and sensitive enough to limit the building explosion, even during the prodigal spending of the '60s and '70s.

THE RECIPE

Use waxy potatoes of a kind that do not break while cooking. To the potatoes you can add some herbs, in keeping with the rest of the meal. Parsley is always suitable, while dried oregano or marjoram are better where the potatoes are accompanying a more robust kind of meat. If you serve the potatoes with fish, a teaspoon or two of crushed fennel seeds are ideal. Alternatively, you can forget the herbs, in which case the accent will be on the good olive oil and the lovely potatoes flavoured only with garlic.

SERVES 4

800g/1¾lb waxy potatoes
3 tbsp extra virgin olive oil, preferably Ligurian
4 garlic cloves, peeled
salt and freshly ground pepper

Peel and wash the potatoes. Cut them into wedges and throw them into a sauté pan in which they will fit in roughly 2 layers. Add the oil and garlic and enough boiling water to come level with the potatoes, not to submerge them. Season with salt and bring back to the boil. Put the lid on the pan, lower the heat and cook until the potatoes are tender, about 20 to 25 minutes.

Shake the pan and turn the potatoes over occasionally during the cooking. Use a fork to turn them over, not a spoon which would be more likely to break them. Check that they do not cook dry; if they do, add a little boiling water.

When the potatoes are tender, all the liquid should have been absorbed. If not, transfer the potatoes to a serving bowl with a slotted spoon and reduce the liquid over high heat until only a couple of tablespoons are left. Pour over the potatoes. Taste to check the salt, and add pepper, if wanted.

Lacerti coi Piselli

Mackerel with Peas

A characteristic trait of Ligurian cooking is to make dishes worthy of grand tables out of the poorest of fish. This is one such dish. It achieves its success through the way the sweetness of the peas relieves the oiliness of the fish. The dish should be made in the spring, when the young peas have just arrived and the mackerel are still plentiful: mackerel are less common in the summer months.

Mackerel must be fresh, i.e. their eyes should be bright, the gills red and the flesh firm. Mackerel that are past their 'sell-by date', as they are far too often in British fishmongers, have an unpleasant flavour and are highly indigestible.

This recipe can, of course, be made with frozen peas, but frozen peas do not have the mealy flavour that is necessary to counterbalance the fish oil. 'The frozen pea caricatures the real thing, but so closely that it spoils it,' wrote Jane Grigson in her admirable *Vegetable Book*. How well she puts it and how right she is! Of course it all depends on how much time you can spare to pod fresh peas. I only hope that, like me, you will find the operation 'restful and relaxing, like saying a rosary', as the food historian Massimo Alberini wrote.

SERVES 4

900g/2lb fresh garden peas

4 tbsp extra virgin olive oil

4 tbsp chopped fresh flat-leaf parsley

1 tbsp chopped fresh marjoram

1 garlic clove, finely chopped

salt and freshly ground pepper

4 small mackerel, about 200g/7oz each, or 2 larger ones

4 tbsp tomato passata

Pod the peas. Choose a large sauté pan that can later contain the fish and add the oil, half the parsley, the marjoram and garlic. Let them sauté for about 1 minute and then add the peas and 4 or 5 tablespoons of hot water. Season with salt and pepper. Cover the pan and cook gently for 5 to 10 minutes, depending on the size of the peas.

Meanwhile, wash and dry the fish and sprinkle some salt and pepper inside them.

Stir the passata into the peas and then lay the fish on top. Cover the pan firmly and cook for about 10 to 13 minutes or until, by lifting one side of the fish with a flat knife, you can see that the flesh is white and opaque next to the bone from which it comes easily away. Then, and only then, the fish is ready. You might have to add a couple more tablespoons of hot water during the cooking. Just keep a watch on the pan, but remember that there should be the minimum of liquid, so as to concentrate the flavour.

Transfer the fish to an oval dish and surround them with the peas. Scatter the remaining parsley all over and serve.

TONNO IN PADELLA

Tuna Fish with Dried Porcini and Anchovies

This delicious dish brings together the various flavours I most associate with Ligurian fish dishes.

The cooking of a steak of fresh tuna is critical as to its timing; undercooked and it is unpleasantly bloody, overcooked and it becomes dry and stringy. It is difficult to say how long the cooking time should be, since it depends on the thickness of the steak and the heat under the pan. I prefer my tuna steaks no thicker than 1.5cm/⅝in, and I cook them for about 2 minutes each side.

SERVES 4

15g/½oz dried porcini
2 garlic cloves
a lovely bunch of fresh flat-leaf parsley
a few fresh marjoram sprigs
3 salted anchovies, rinsed and cleaned, or 6 canned anchovy fillets, drained
1 tbsp capers, rinsed
6 tbsp extra virgin olive oil
1 tbsp flour
150ml/5fl oz dry white wine
salt and freshly ground black pepper
4 fresh tuna steaks, about 600g/1¼lb in total
the juice of ½ lemon

Soak the dried porcini in hot water for about an hour (see page 13). If gritty, rinse them under cold water. Dry them with kitchen paper towel and put them on a board. Add the garlic, parsley, marjoram, anchovies and capers and chop the whole lot together. (To save time this can be done in the food processor, but be careful not to grind the mixture too fine.)

Heat the oil and the parsley mixture in a large sauté or frying pan and sauté for 2 minutes, stirring frequently. Blend in the flour, cook for about 1 minute and then pour in the wine. Boil for 3 or 4 minutes, stirring the whole time. If the sauce seems too thick, pour in 4 or 5 tablespoons of boiling water. Add salt and plenty of pepper.

If still on, remove the skin from the tuna steaks. Rinse and dry them with kitchen paper towel and lay them in the pan in a single layer. Cook for 2 or 3 minutes, depending on their thickness, and then turn the steaks over and continue to cook until no blood comes to the surface. Push a small pointed knife into the middle of one of the steaks to see if it is cooked; if there is still some blood, cook a little longer.

Taste the sauce and adjust seasoning. Transfer the steaks to a heated serving dish or individual plates and spoon the sauce around them. Drizzle with the lemon juice and serve at once.

SEPPIE IN ZIMINO

Cuttlefish with Spinach

Cuttlefish is the traditional seafood for this dish from Liguria and Versilia, the Tuscan coast north of Livorno. But cuttlefish is difficult to find in this country. This is in spite of its being fairly common off the south coast of England, as Alan Davidson writes in his *Mediterranean Seafood* (my bible on the subject). I wonder where cuttlefish go after they are caught.

I have often used squid, which are easy to find on the market and good. I buy squid caught in British waters because they are fresh and full of flavour. They are also large, which is what you need for this dish that needs a long slow cooking.

I have given here the quantity of cooked spinach you need, because the waste varies according to the kind of spinach. If you buy young, pre-packed supermarket spinach there is much less waste than with large bunchy spinach.

To give an idea, you need from 700g to 900g/ 1½lb to 2lb of fresh spinach to get 450g/1lb of cooked spinach.

Nowadays most fishmongers will clean the cuttlefish or squid for you. If yours does not, find a more obliging fishmonger, or follow my instructions below.

If you have a good-looking pot, such as an earthenware one that you can put directly on the heat, use it for cooking this dish, and you can bring it straight to the table. Seppie in zimino is a peasant dish and should be treated as such.

SERVES 6 TO 8

1.8kg/4lb cuttlefish or squid

150g/5oz onion

150g/5oz celery

2 garlic cloves

1 dried hot chilli pepper

30g/1oz fresh flat-leaf parsley

75ml/2½fl oz olive oil

150g/5oz [US ¾ cup] chopped tomato

6 tbsp red wine

salt and freshly ground pepper

enough spinach to yield 450g/1lb when cooked

To clean the squid or the cuttlefish, hold the body in one hand and pull off the tentacles, which will come away with the inside. Cut the tentacles across above the eyes and discard everything from the eyes down. Squeeze off the small beak at the base of the tentacles. Remove the bone from the body and peel off the outer translucent skin. Wash the bodies and tentacles thoroughly. Drain and pat dry. Cut open the bodies and then slice them into 1cm/½in strips. Cut the tentacles into small pieces.

Chop together the onion, celery, garlic, chilli and parsley and put this *battuto* (beaten mixture) in a heavy-based saucepan together with the oil. Sauté gently for about 10 minutes, stirring frequently, and then mix in the tomato and cook for a further 5 minutes or so.

Now that the base is ready, you can slide in the fish. Turn them over and over for the first 2 or 3 minutes for them to take up the flavour. When the squid or cuttlefish turn opaque, splash with the wine and let it bubble away for a couple of minutes. Season with salt and pepper. Cover the pan and leave to cook very gently for about 45 minutes.

Meanwhile, wash the spinach thoroughly and put it in a large saucepan with no water – the water clinging to the leaves is enough. Add 2 teaspoons of salt and cook until just tender. Drain and, when cool, squeeze out any remaining liquid with your hands. Cut the spinach into strips more or less the same size as the squid bodies.

Add the spinach to the fish, mix well and continue to stew gently for 15 to 20 minutes, until the squid are tender. (Squid and cuttlefish must either cook very quickly in boiling oil or very slowly for at least 40 minutes, so as to lose their unpleasant rubbery texture.) Taste and adjust seasoning before you bring the dish to the table.

Some slices of grilled polenta go very well with this dish.

Agnello e Carciofi in Fricassea

Fricassee of Artichokes and Lamb

The word *fricassea* is the Italianization of the French *fricassée*. Fricassea first appeared in Italian recipe books in the middle of the 18th century, about a hundred years after it was first mentioned in *Le Cuisinier François* by La Varenne. Crossing the Alps fricassée abandoned the northern cream to adopt the Mediterranean lemon as one of its ingredients. Fricassea became a favourite method of cooking rabbit, lamb and also vegetables, both in Liguria and in Tuscany.

THE RECIPE

Although the meat and artichokes are cooked together in this recipe, they manage to retain their individual flavours. I like to serve potatoes all'Albina (page 140) with this dish, to produce a nourishing Ligurian course.

For the preparation of the artichokes turn to page 186. If you do not have marjoram, increase the quantity of chopped parsley. Ask your butcher to bone the leg of lamb and to chop the bone into 2 or 3 pieces for you to use in the cooking.

SERVES 6

2 Bréton globe artichokes
900g/2lb boneless leg of lamb
4 tbsp extra virgin olive oil
2 tbsp chopped fresh flat-leaf parsley
2 tbsp chopped fresh marjoram
2 garlic cloves, sliced
150ml/5fl oz dry white wine
salt and freshly ground black pepper
1 egg yolk
the juice of 1 lemon

When you have trimmed all the tough leaves off the artichokes, cut the artichokes into quarters and remove the fuzzy chokes and the prickly purple leaves at the base. Put the cleaned quarters back into the acidulated water. Now go back to the stalks and peel off all the outside part of them, so that you have only the tender marrow left. Cut this into rounds and throw into the acidulated water.

To prepare the lamb, remove fat and gristle from the outside of the leg and any nugget of fat lurking inside. Cut into 2.5cm/1in chunks.

Now that you have prepared the two basic ingredients, you can at last start cooking, which will not take long. Heat the oven to 150°C/300°F/Gas Mark 2. Heat the oil with the herbs and garlic in a flameproof casserole and sauté until the aroma of the *soffritto* (fried mixture) rises. Throw in the lamb, and the pieces of bone for flavour. Brown the meat carefully on all sides. Splash with the wine and boil for a minute or two.

Drain the artichoke pieces and add to the casserole. Let them *insaporire* (take up the flavour) for about 5 minutes, turning them over frequently. Season with salt and pepper. Cover the casserole and cook in the oven for about 1 hour. Keep a watch on the cooking, and add a little hot water if there is no liquid left.

Remove the pieces of bone from the casserole. Let the dish cool for 5 minutes or so, while you beat together the egg yolk and the lemon juice. Pour this over the meat and stir well. Check seasoning and then serve.

SCIUMETTE

Soft Meringues with Cinnamon and Pistachio

In the summer of 1993 I went to Recco in Liguria to eat at one of the restaurants of my youth, Manuelina. Old Signora Manuelina, now dead, started a lorry drivers' eating place straight after the Second World War. By the early '50s all of us from Milan and Genoa went to Manuelina to eat her splendid Focaccia di Recco and other local specialities. The restaurant and small hotel next door are now run by her granddaughters, who were taught by Manuelina herself. The restaurant has the smart casualness of a well-known place. And the food is typically local, traditional and excellent.

My lunch started with a small tasting of a superb cappon magro (page 138), followed by seppie in zimino. My recipe on page 142 uses calamari, because seppie – cuttlefish – are difficult to find in Britain. But what really excited me were the delicate sciumette. Sciumette are the traditional Christmas pudding of the Ligurians. They also appear on the table during Carnival week, together with the festive sweet ravioli – fried ravioli stuffed with candied pumpkin and candied citrus fruit.

THE RECIPE

Sciumette means little sponges in Genoese dialect. And this is what they look like. They are very similar to the French Oeufs à la Neige, delicate white blobs floating in a sea of yellow custard, speckled with the bright green of the pistachio and veiled with the dusky brown of ground cinnamon.

SERVES 6 TO 8

1.2l/2 pt [US 5 cups] full fat milk

the pared rind of 1 unwaxed lemon

250g/9oz caster sugar [US 1¼ cups + 2 tbsp granulated sugar]

4 whites from size-2 eggs [US extra-large eggs]

1 tsp lemon juice

2 pinches of ground cinnamon plus 1 tsp ground cinnamon to finish

5 yolks from size-2 eggs [US extra-large eggs]

2 tbsp pistachio nuts, blanched, peeled and chopped

Bring the milk very slowly to a boil in a large sauté pan. Add the lemon rind and 2 tablespoons of the sugar and stir gently. Keep an eye on the milk.

Meanwhile, whisk the egg whites until they begin to form soft peaks. Add the lemon juice, 125g/4oz [US ½ cup + 2 tbsp] of the sugar and the cinnamon. Whisk until the mixture is very firm.

When the milk starts to boil, adjust the heat so that the milk is just simmering. Scoop out a few heaped dessertspoons of the meringue and slide gently into the simmering milk. Put in only a few spoonfuls at a time, as the meringues swell and each mound must be kept separate. Poach for about 1½ minutes on each side, flipping them over very carefully. Use two forks, not spoons which tend to break the meringues. Remove the sciumette from the milk and transfer them to a large tray lined with kitchen paper towel. Repeat this operation until you have used up all the whisked egg white. Re-whisk the whites every time before you poach another batch of sciumette. Make sure that the milk never comes to a proper boil.

Strain the milk and, if necessary, add some extra milk to come up to 700ml/1¼pt [US 3 cups].

Beat the egg yolks in a heavy-based saucepan. Add the remaining sugar and beat very thoroughly until pale and forming ribbons.

Add the milk gradually to the egg yolks while beating constantly with a wooden spoon. Cook until the custard thickens, but do not let the custard come to the boil or it will curdle. If that should happen, pour the contents of the pan into the food processor and whizz for 30 seconds until the custard is smooth. Put the pan in a bowl of cold water to cool. Stir occasionally.

Pour the cooled custard into a large deep dish or a large bowl and carefully arrange the sciumette on top. Scatter the chopped pistachios over the top and dust lightly with cinnamon.

EMILIA-ROMAGNA

Whenever I return from Emilia-Romagna my taste buds tingle with the memory of superb culinary experiences. Each time I am reminded that this region is indeed a paradise for gourmets.

From among several great meals I had on a recent visit I must mention a dinner at Fini in Modena, one of the very few Michelin-starred restaurants in Italy able to combine local traditions with *grande cucina*. This dinner was a perfect example of that combination. Having cautiously declared myself not very hungry, I was cajoled into starting with 'just a taste of our *culatello*'. Culatello is made from the rump of a boned pig's thigh. It comes from Zibello, which lies in the flat lands between Parma and the Po and enjoys the damp, warm breezes that are just right for the air-drying of the culatello. This is in marked contrast to the cool, dry winds of the foothills of the Apennines needed for the curing of prosciutto. This difference arises because the large, egg-shaped culatello is very lean, while prosciutto is covered by a layer of fat. Culatello connoisseurs keep it moist before slicing by wrapping it in a cloth moistened with white wine.

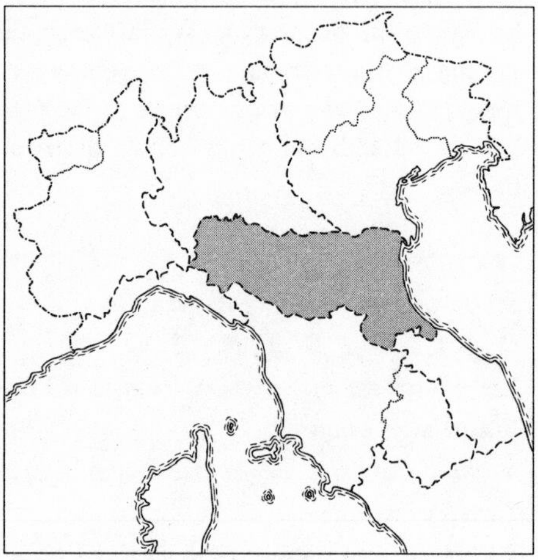

After the culatello I chose soup, knowing that nowhere else could I have such perfect tortellini in brodo. In a lake of pale clear stock there were a dozen tortellini, as tiny as if twisted round a child's fingers. The stuffing was rich in flavour and yet incredibly delicate in its mixture of prosciutto, mortadella, pork and turkey, bound by egg and bone-marrow and seasoned with parmigiano-reggiano.

Next, a bollito misto was wheeled in on the traditional drum trolley: chicken, turkey, veal, beef, tongue, cotechino and calf's head, all hot and moist. It was served with four different sauces – salsa verde, a raw vegetable sauce, a tomato and carrot sauce spiked with a dash of balsamic vinegar, and mostarda di Cremona.

The other traditional dish I wanted to try, because it is now served only in old-fashioned restaurants, was the fritto misto. After the luxuriant richness of the bollito, the fritto misto was monastic in its simplicity. A mound of golden courgette [zucchini] sticks was surrounded by fried custard, fried apple rings, tiny lamb chops, sticks of prosciutto and béchamel, and ricotta and spinach fritters. No sauces or dips, just the purity of beautiful fried foods as light as air.

I finished with a slice of *ciambella* (sweet bread) and a sip of Nocino, the local walnut *digestivo* – such an ugly word for such a good drink. All in all, a perfect meal, although in retrospect the tortellini soup of the nearby Villa Gaidello (see recipe for Bensone on page 171) was every bit as good. But the pasticcio di tortellini in crosta dolce (see page 155), which one of my companions had, was unforgettable in its perfection of balance between the sweetness of the pastry and the bold meatiness of the tortellini.

When you start comparing a dish of pasta, stuffed or not, eaten, for instance, in Piacenza, with another tasted in Bologna, you become embroiled in a web of hedonistic pleasures of such complexity that it becomes an intellectual game. Cooking changes subtly but noticeably from one town to the next. Let's just take a piece of stuffed pasta – now universally known as a raviolo – and trace it from the north-west extremity of Emilia to the eastern Adriatic coast of Romagna. In Piacenza the pasta parcels are called anolini and come in a half-moon shape. They contain chopped braised beef (stracotto – see page 163) plus the usual ingredients of any pasta filling. Fifty kilometres down the Via Emilia (the Roman road that bisects Emilia-Romagna horizontally), in Parma, the anolini are still called anolini but they are usually round, and braised meat is represented in the filling only in the bread soaked in its rich juices, produced by cooking the meat for at least 16 hours and then pressing it down. Both these anolini are traditionally served *in brodo* (in clear stock) as are the more famous tortellini of Modena and Bologna, further down the Via Emilia.

Here we meet the authentic square ravioli which nowadays are usually *di magro* (meatless). The part of Romagna that used to be the dukedom of the Este family is the motherland of all cappelletti and cappellacci, made respectively with meat and cheese, and with pumpkin – my favourite. Cappelletti are also the traditional filled pasta of Reggio Emilia, but with a different stuffing, influenced by the Lombard cooking of Mantova.

Squashed between the gastronomically and artistically more fascinating Parma and Modena, Reggio Emilia tends to be forgotten. But not by me, thanks to some dear friends who have lavished on me some of their culinary jewels. After all, Reggio Emilia shares with Parma and Modena the glory of producing two of the greatest jewels: Parmigiano-reggiano and balsamic vinegar. I am often struck by how restrained the use of these two products is in the very places where they originate.

Balsamic vinegar has been made in the provinces of Modena and Reggio Emilia since the Middle Ages. Authentic balsamic vinegar, known officially as 'Traditional', must age for at least 12 years. It cannot contain ordinary vinegar or caramel, and its flavour is very complex and luscious, more comparable to a vintage port than to a normal vinegar. This balsamic vinegar is very expensive, but it lasts a long time. I still have a small bottle given to me by a producer in 1988. It is so precious that I hardly dare use it! Every now and then I have a little tasting, on its own, or I sprinkle a few drops – as if it were holy water – on a dish of warm grilled chicory. Then there is the balsamic vinegar that everybody knows and uses, called *'Industriale'* in Italy. It is rather acidic and it certainly does not taste like old port. Yet the well-made brands have the right balance of sweetness and tartness and add an interesting and pleasant flavour to sauces and roasts. It is for this, and not as part of a vinaigrette dressing for salad, that balsamic vinegar is mainly used in its places of origin. It is added to a roasting bird, to game or to braised vegetables, as well as being used to preserve the vegetables that are to be eaten later in an antipasto. Preserved in balsamic vinegar, the vegetables do not acquire that jarring flavour usually associated with industrial *verdure sott'aceto*.

Parmigiano-reggiano is a great cheese. It was respected by Boccaccio, Molière, Samuel Pepys and the 19th-century writer Giovanni Raiberti, who wrote, 'Parmesan is to all other cheeses what Jupiter is to the rabble of the minor deities.' A chunky sliver of Parmigiano-reggiano is the ideal starter to a meal and an even larger sliver is the perfect finale. This nourishing and very digestible cheese seems to me to embody what the taste buds desire most as an *amuse-gueule*, as well as a *digestivo*. Yet its use must be discreet. Most risotti and pasta dishes, especially egg pasta, benefit from an abundant snowfall of Parmesan, as do cooked vegetables – fennel and leeks being those that come first to mind. It is equally good flaked over some raw salads such as a warm chicory and radicchio salad, a young ceps salad and on freshly grilled vegetables.

The border between Emilia and Romagna is elusive; even the locals are not sure where Emilia ends and Romagna begins. One saying has it that going east from Bologna, Romagna begins at the first farm where, when you ask for a drink, you are offered wine rather than water. The food of Romagna is simpler and more unified than that of Emilia; it is strongly reminiscent of the cooking of Marche. There are historical reasons for this. At the capitulation of the Roman empire Emilia was divided among local lords, while Romagna was dominated by the Byzantine empire, the Este and ultimately by the Vatican, who ruled over the whole of central Italy.

Romagna has a serene arcadian beauty which is hardly known outside the region. The locals are very chauvinistic and dismiss most things from further afield. They certainly dismiss the cooking. I was highly amused when, in the small town of Gatteo Mare, a lovely round Romagnola lady (the women of Romagna are considered among the most attractive in Italy) rebuked me for thinking that the *garganelli* – home-made penne – with prosciutto she was serving at dinner were from a local recipe. 'It is my family's recipe', she declared, 'and I come from Gatteo di Sopra' – a village all of five kilometres up the road.

Romagna is the fruit orchard of Italy, and one of the most luscious in Europe. The best peaches, cherries, pears, and now even the best kiwis, are grown there. Artichokes, broad beans, courgettes and pumpkins are just as excellent and are treated in the simplest way – just grilled. Also melons and watermelons, of which the Romagnoli are inordinately fond. The pasta of Emilia gives way here to a poorer kind of pasta, containing fewer eggs. Romagnolo cooking is marked by a freedom and spontaneity that reflects the character of the people, who are fun-loving, humorous and humane.

The dressed bread dough, which in Emilia is fried in circles or squares to make the exquisite crescentine of Bologna and the gnocco fritto of Modena and Reggio, in Romagna is simply cooked on a hot stone (*piadina*) and then stuffed with the magical *squacquerone*. I came across this melt-in-the-mouth cheese for the first time only a few years ago. Squacquerone is practically unknown outside Romagna – incredible, since it is one of the most lovely fresh cheeses I have ever tasted. Spread on a hot piadina, it melts a little inside, while the rest melts in your mouth. Sometimes the piadina also contains prosciutto, but I prefer to enjoy the taste of the cheese on its own.

The other local product is, of course, fish. The long coastline of Romagna and the richness of the Adriatic waters see to that. It was in search of a Romagnolo fishing port that I had a very interesting experience. It started at the street market in Cento, a typical Po valley town between Modena and Ferrara. The impressive 14th-century castle was the background to the market stalls and barrows, among which I was strolling, looking and smelling. I was attracted by the large stall (actually, like so many others, a converted van) of a fishmonger, where the fish were very fresh and the choice was vast considering the size of Cento. Fish was the passion of this particular fishmonger, who began to extol the importance of buying fish straight from the fishermen.

'You must go to Goro, and be there by four in the afternoon when the auction begins,' he told me. It was midday, just time to have lunch and drive to Goro, a port on the Po delta little known except to those involved with catching and selling fish. Goro's large harbour is home to a huge fleet of fishing boats, and next to the harbour is a vast hangar where the auction takes place.

Small knots of people were standing around piles of boxes and baskets teeming with fish. Coils of large and small eels were undulating gently, octopus and squids were stroking each other with their prehensile tentacles, while a few scampi had managed to crawl lazily, thus upsetting the symmetry in which they were lined up in the box. I looked at a box of small pink crabs and thought of the time I had them last in Cesenatico, just down the coast, cut in half and sautéed in oil with parsley and garlic.

The auction was starting, I was told, and silence fell in the hangar. No shouting, no raising of hands, only a whisper in the ear of the auctioneer. He then knocked the crate of fish down to the person who had whispered the highest offer, an offer nobody else heard. This strange procedure has been adopted because it is much faster, as indeed it was, since all the fish has to be auctioned in two hours so that it can be transported to – in many cases – distant cities and be in the shops by the next day. An attractive girl, the only woman bidder there, had been the most successful bidder that day. 'You have to be tough,' she told me. 'They don't like you.' She was driving to Milan with her crates in time for the 4 a.m. opening of the market. Thanks partly to her efforts, Milan is one of the best supplied fish markets in Europe.

Another landmark of my visits to Emilia-Romagna was a baker's shop in Ferrara. Ferrara is famous for its bread, but of all the bakeries there the Panificio Orsatti was the one I was urged to go and see. They sell 38 different kinds of bread, from the classic *coppia*, which is also called *manina*, to the delicate *farfalle*. Most breads are made with *pasta dura*, a very compact yet soft dough, some dressed with oil or, as in the old days, with pork fat. The Orsatti also sell an array of piadine, pizze, spianate, focacce etc., some local, some from further afield, as well as interesting cakes. Their torta di taglierini, the traditional cake served on special occasions, derives directly from the Renaissance when it was served at the beginning of a dinner. It is a tart filled with an almond mixture over which a few strands of home-made taglierini (very thin tagliatelle) are thrown. These taglierini bake to a crunchy, airy texture which lightens the almond filling.

My favourite Emilian dolci are those of Parma, where the Grand Duchess Marie Louise, the Hapsburg princess who became Napoleon's second wife, reigned supreme for over 30 years. Her legacies are the candied violets, the delicate Parma yellow which makes the palazzi so characteristic, and delicious cakes and desserts. Maria Luigia, as she is called in Parma, brought her pâtissiers from Vienna, but it is thanks to her last chef, Vincenzo Agnoletti, that we know a great deal about the cuisine of the time. Some of Agnoletti's recipes are collected in his book *Manuale del Cuoco e del Pasticcere.* His recipe for zuppa inglese brings this everyday pudding to new heights, and another triumph is a recipe for a kind of half-moon shaped biscuits [US cookie], which has been rewritten by Ugo Falavigna, a famous Parmigiano pâtissier of today. The pastry crescents are stuffed with a mixture containing spinach and almonds. A similar spinach mixture is the ingredient of a Lombard sweet and savoury cake and of a sweet tart from Lucca, where the Swiss chard is sitting on crème pâtissière and topped with pine nuts and bits of chocolate.

But that is Tuscany, and I am in Emilia-Romagna, closing this introduction with the hope that for once you might leave Tuscany and head for this region, where the warm hospitality of its lovable inhabitants renders the delights of its table even more delightful.

BISCOTTI ALLA CIPOLLA Ⓥ

Onion Biscuits

Margherita and Valeria Simili are cookery teachers in Italy. They are twins, but not identical, only '*simili*' – similar – as they say their name explains! They have a school in Bologna and, although they teach most things, their particular speciality is the making of bread, focacce, pizze, biscuits and various doughs, all of which call for different techniques. I was very interested when I heard Margherita saying that each kind of bread must be made with different movements of the hands and body. Quite fascinating.

One of the days I was there, the sisters were concentrating on *stuzzichini* (amuse-gueules). *Stuzzicare*, in fact, means to tickle. And they tickled my fancy so much that when I finished tasting them I had no room for anything else! There were lovely breads stuffed with fresh grapes, in the shape of bunches of grapes, cigars of pasta dough wrapped around anchovy fillets, little savoury chilli knots, deliciously hot and garlicky, and nutty gruyère biscuits. But my favourites were these onion squares, which incorporate the traditional flavours of rich Bolognese cooking.

THE RECIPE

This is a translation – with the necessary adaptations – of the recipe given to me by Margherita and Valeria Simili. The biscuits [US crackers] are ideal to go with a pre-prandial drink or as an accompaniment to a lovely dish of grilled vegetables or ratatouille.

MAKES ABOUT 40

250g/9oz sweet onion
2 tbsp extra virgin olive oil
salt
250g/9oz [US 2 cups] Italian 00 flour
1½ tsp baking powder
45g/1¾oz [US 3½ tbsp] unsalted butter
1 egg
4 tbsp semi-skimmed milk [US low-fat milk]
butter for the trays

Slice the onion very finely and then chop the slices coarsely. Put the oil and the onion in a heavy-based frying pan and sauté gently, adding a pinch of salt to prevent the onion catching. The onions should not brown, only cook gently for 30 minutes or so. Allow to cool.

Put the flour in a bowl with 1 teaspoon of salt and the baking powder. Cut the cold butter into small pieces and add to the flour mixture. Work with your fingers until the mixture becomes like breadcrumbs, and then work in the onion with its juices.

Lightly beat together the egg with the milk and add gradually to the dough. Work quickly, and as soon as you can gather the mixture into a ball, stop working. Wrap the ball of dough in cling film and refrigerate for at least 30 minutes.

Heat the oven to 190°C/375°F/ Gas Mark 5.

Lightly butter 2 oven trays.

Flour the work surface and roll out the dough with a floured rolling pin to a thickness of about 1cm/½in. Cut into 5cm/2in squares and transfer these to the buttered trays. Bake for 15 to 20 minutes, until lovely and golden.

I prefer the biscuits hot, or warm, but they are also good cold.

PASTICCIO DI PENNE E VERDURE AL FORNO Ⓥ

Baked Penne and Roast Vegetables

In 1993 I was invited by the Mulino Spadoni, producers of some of the very best flours, to visit their factory. I was driven from the hotel by Mario and, as always happens when I am in Italy, we talked about food, with me trying to extract as many recipes as possible. One of the recipes Mario told me was this one. 'My wife makes the best pasticcio I have ever eaten,' he said. Oddly enough the dish didn't sound particularly Romagnolo to me. But then back in London I read a very similar recipe in *The Splendid Table of Emilia-Romagna* by Lynne Rossetto Kasper. The book is equally splendid and very reliable. In her introduction the author writes: 'Originally the vegetables were prepared by Adriatic fishermen's wives to eat with the day's catch. Many cooks transform them into a first course by tossing the vegetables with maccheroni.' So it is obviously a traditional local recipe.

THE RECIPE

In Romagna the cheese used is a very soft cheese called *squaccherone*, which is unavailable outside Romagna. Lynne Rossetto Kasper suggests a young pecorino and I agree with her. However, when I can find it I prefer to use *crescenza* because it is much closer in taste and texture to squaccherone. Crescenza is sold in Italian food shops, but being highly perishable only a few will stock it.

SERVES 6

1 aubergine [US eggplant], about 250g/9oz

2 medium courgettes [US zucchini], about 250g/9oz in total

2 sweet peppers, about 350g/12oz in total

6 large ripe tomatoes, about 600g/1¼lb in total, skinned

3 sweet red onions, about 350g/12oz in total

8 tbsp extra virgin olive oil

salt and freshly ground black pepper

3 garlic cloves

30g/1oz fresh flat-leaf parsley, leaves only

1 dozen fresh basil leaves

4 anchovy fillets

1 tbsp capers, rinsed

4 tbsp dried white breadcrumbs

350g/12oz penne

225g/8oz crescenza or mild young pecorino [US romano]

Heat the oven to 200°C/400°F/Gas Mark 6.

Wash and dry the aubergine, courgettes, peppers and tomatoes. Cut the aubergine and courgettes across in half, or into 3 chunks, depending on size, and then lengthwise into 5mm/¼in thick slices. Slice the tomatoes into similar thickish slices. Cut the peppers into quarters, remove seeds, core and ribs, and then cut each quarter in half again. Slice the onions into rings of about the same thickness as the other vegetables.

Grease 2 large oven trays with a little oil and place the sliced vegetables on them, keeping them separate. Brush them with a couple of tablespoons of the oil and season with salt and plenty of pepper. Bake until the vegetables are soft and beginning to brown at the edges, about 45 minutes.

Chop together the garlic, parsley, basil, anchovies and capers. Heat 2 tablespoons of the oil in a large frying pan. When the oil is very hot add the breadcrumbs and fry until lovely and golden. Now mix in the chopped mixture and sauté for a minute or so over gentle heat. After that, draw the pan from the heat while you cook the penne.

When the pasta is still just slightly undercooked, drain it and tip it into the frying pan. Stir-fry for a minute or two. Taste and check seasoning.

Choose a deep oven dish and grease it with a little oil. Heat the oven to 180°C/350°F/Gas Mark 4.

Slice or crumble the crescenza (not an easy job because crescenza is a very soft cheese) or thinly slice the pecorino.

Now you are ready to assemble the dish. Spread a thin layer of pasta in the oven dish, cover with the courgettes and a few onion rings and add a little cheese. Put in another layer of pasta, then the peppers and some onion rings, more cheese, pasta again, then the aubergine, the rest of the onion rings, a little more cheese and the remaining pasta. On the top place the tomato slices and the remaining cheese. Drizzle with the remaining oil and bake for 15 minutes or so, until the cheese has melted.

Do not serve straight from the oven, but let the dish rest outside for about 5 minutes before you bring it to the table.

RAGÙ
Bolognese Sauce

Ragù is the perfect example of Bolognese cooking: rich yet well balanced, lavish and yet restrained, meaty and yet fresh. There are hundreds of versions of ragù, but the classic one, the one that everybody identifies with its place of origin, is the bolognese.

Nowadays ragù is out of fashion – too rich, unhealthy, bad for the heart, bad for everything, but certainly not bad for the palate. This recipe is not too rich, I think. It follows closely the precepts of a classic ragù, but it is lighter on fat.

Remember that it is very important to chop the vegetables very finely, so that they are the size of grains of rice.

MAKES ENOUGH SAUCE FOR 6 HELPINGS OF PASTA

60g/2oz [US 4 tbsp] butter
2 tbsp extra virgin olive oil
60g/2oz unsmoked pancetta, finely chopped
1 small onion, finely chopped
1 carrot, finely chopped
1 celery stalk, finely chopped
1 garlic clove, finely chopped
1 bay leaf
400g/14oz lean chuck or braising beef, coarsely minced [US ground]
2 tbsp concentrated tomato paste
150ml/5fl oz red wine, such as a Sangiovese or a Barbera
2 pinches of grated nutmeg
salt and freshly ground pepper
150ml/5fl oz meat stock (page 230)
150ml/5fl oz full fat milk

Heat the butter and oil in a heavy-based saucepan and cook the pancetta for 5 minutes, stirring frequently.

Add the onion, and when it has begun to soften add the carrot, celery, garlic and bay leaf. Cook for a further 10 minutes, stirring frequently.

Put in the minced beef and cook until it is medium brown in colour and nearly crisp, crumbling it in the pot with a fork. Do this over high heat so that the meat browns rather than stews, but be careful not to let the mince become too brown and hard.

Add the tomato paste and continue to cook over high heat for a further 2 minutes. Still over high heat, add the wine, nutmeg, salt and pepper, and the stock. Bring to the boil and then turn the heat down to very low so that the mixture will reduce very slowly. This slow lengthy reduction is of paramount importance. Set the lid askew over the pan and cook for about 2 hours, adding a couple of tablespoons of the milk from time to time. By the end of this time all the milk should have been added and absorbed, and the ragù should be rich and thick, like a thick soup.

Taste and adjust seasoning. The ragù is now ready to dress a dish of home-made tagliatelle, thus producing one of the greatest dishes of Emilia.

Pasticcio di Maccheroni in Crosta Dolce

Macaroni Pie in a Sweet Pastry Case

In his book *Emiliani e Romagnoli a Tavola*, Massimo Alberini, the great octogenarian food historian, describes this dish as follows: 'A recipe whose Renaissance roots can be seen in the marriage of sweet and salty flavours. A covering of sweet pastry is filled with a meat sauce and a rum-flavoured custard.'

The dish can be traced back to Cristoforo da Messisbugo, steward to Don Ippolito d'Este of Ferrara. Messibugo wrote a fascinating book, *Libro Novo*, published in Venice in 1557, which contains many recipes for *torte*. These consisted of a sweet pastry case filled with various savoury ingredients – Swiss chard, pigeons, capons, almonds, etc.

Messisbugo does not mention rum in any of his dishes – it was probably unknown at the time. This addition must have come later when rum became popular. Pellegrino Artusi, writing in the 19th century, also has no mention of rum in his pasticcio, and has replaced the custard with béchamel to be more in keeping with the new tastes. My recipe is based on Artusi's.

Still today, as in Artusi's time, this pasticcio is the great dish eaten during Carnival week in Romagna.

A similar pasticcio is made in Emilia, using tortellini for the filling instead of macaroni. It is an even grander dish, but because of having to make the tortellini it is more complicated. So I have opted for the Romagnola recipe.

THE RECIPE

This is an elaborate dish, the making of which calls for some experience, and time. However, if you follow my instructions carefully you should be able to make it very successfully.

Allow the various elements of the pie to cool before you put them in the tin lined with the dough.

SERVES 8

20g/¾oz dried porcini
125g/4oz lamb's sweetbreads
125g/4oz fresh chicken livers
40g/1½oz [US 3 tbsp] unsalted butter
4 or 5 fresh sage leaves, snipped
salt and freshly ground black pepper
4 tbsp dry white wine
30g/1oz unsmoked pancetta, preferably in a slab
30g/1oz fatty prosciutto
75g/2½oz small onion
60g/2oz celery
60g/2oz carrot
a bunch of fresh flat-leaf parsley, leaves only
1 tbsp olive oil
2 pinches of ground cinnamon
a pinch of ground cloves
4 tbsp full fat milk
250g/9oz macaroni or penne
a béchamel sauce (page 228) made with 30g/1oz [US 2 tbsp] unsalted butter, 30g/1oz [US 3 tbsp] flour, 500ml/16fl oz full fat milk and 3 pinches of grated nutmeg
1 tbsp dried white breadcrumbs
60g/2oz [US ½ cup] freshly grated Parmesan

FOR THE PASTRY

350g/12oz [US 3 cups] flour, preferably Italian 00
180g/6oz [US 1½ sticks] unsalted butter, cut into small pieces
125g/4oz caster sugar [US ½ cup + 2 tbsp granulated sugar]
a pinch of salt
1 size-2 egg plus 2 egg yolks [US extra-large egg]
butter for the tin

FOR THE GLAZE

1 egg yolk
a pinch of salt
2 tbsp milk

First make the pastry, which is the Italian equivalent of the French pâte sucrée. I make it in a food processor, putting everything in except the egg and egg yolks, which I add through the feed tube while the machine is running. If you do not have a food processor, put the flour on the work surface, make a well in the centre and add the egg, egg yolks, sugar and salt. Mix lightly and then add the butter. Blend quickly together. If the dough is too dry, add a little cold water; if too moist, mix in a little more flour. It is difficult to be precise about quantities because it depends on the flour you are using and even on the humidity of your kitchen. Gather the dough up into a soft ball, wrap it in cling film and put it into the fridge.

Now you must prepare the filling. Soak the dried porcini in boiling water. I have come to the conclusion that some porcini need a lot longer than the 30 minutes usually suggested, so I now prefer to soak any dried porcini for 1 hour. After that lift the porcini out of the liquid, rinse them if necessary and dry them carefully with kitchen paper towel. Chop them and set them aside. Filter the liquid through a strainer lined with a piece of muslin or cheesecloth.

Remove any bits of fat from the sweetbreads. Rinse them and pat them dry with kitchen paper towel. Cut off and discard the gristle and any green spots from the chicken livers. Rinse quickly and pat them dry very well.

Heat the butter in a smallish frying pan. Throw in the sage leaves and, when they begin to sizzle, add the sweetbreads. Sauté at medium heat for 2 minutes and then add the chicken livers. Sauté for a further couple of minutes, turning the mixture over and over to soak up the butter. Season with salt and pepper. Splash with the wine and let it cook for a few more minutes. Draw the pan off the heat. Lift the offal out of the pan with a slotted spoon on to a chopping board and chop it coarsely. Return it to the pan and set aside.

Now prepare the prosciutto sauce, which in Italian is called *il sugo finto di carne* (the mock meat sauce). Chop the pancetta, prosciutto, onion, celery, carrot and parsley to a granular paste. (I find a food processor ideal for the job. It makes a real *battuto* – pounded mixture – in 1 minute, just as you would have done by chopping by hand for a long time.) Put the battuto in a clean frying pan together with the oil and ½ teaspoon of salt. Sauté over very low heat for 5 minutes, and then add the chopped porcini. Sauté for a further 5 minutes, stirring very frequently. The mixture should not fry, just gently cook. Stir in the spices and a couple of tablespoons of hot water and continue cooking gently. After 10 minutes or so mix in the milk and a couple of tablespoons of porcini liquid. Continue cooking for a further 30 minutes, adding a little porcini liquid and hot water now and then, mixing and making sure that the mixture does not catch.

While you are watching over the sauce, cook the pasta in plenty of boiling salted water. Drain thoroughly when still slightly undercooked (6 minutes should be enough) and dress immediately with the prosciutto sauce. Mix well and set aside.

Remove the pastry from the fridge to let it warm up a little, so that you can handle it.

Make the béchamel and mix into the pasta very thoroughly. If you are not sure how to make a good béchamel, turn to page 228 for my version. Don't forget to taste and adjust the seasoning.

Heat the oven to 220°C/425°F/Gas Mark 7.

Now that you have prepared the various elements of the pasticcio it is time to assemble it. Prepare a 20cm/8in spring-clip tin by greasing it with a little butter. Roll out about a quarter of the dough on a piece of floured greaseproof paper [US wax paper]. Turn the dough over on to the bottom of the tin and peel off the paper. (This pastry dough is difficult to handle. If you roll it out on a piece of greaseproof paper you will find it much easier to transfer.) Roll out another quarter or so of the dough into strips to line the sides of the tin.

Mix the tablespoon of breadcrumbs with 1 tablespoon of grated Parmesan and sprinkle this mixture over the dough covering the bottom of the tin. Lay about one-third of the pasta at the bottom, cover with half the sweetbread and chicken liver mixture, and sprinkle with some Parmesan. Next add another layer of pasta, the remaining sweetbread and chicken liver mixture and more Parmesan. Finish with a topping of pasta and the remaining Parmesan.

Roll out a round of dough to cover the pie and seal the edges well. Make a small flat strip or a thin roll with some of the remaining dough and place it all around the top edge of the pie. Press down with the prongs of a floured fork to seal. With the left-over dough make your favourite pie decorations. The traditional decoration for this pie is a bow. Make a few holes in the dough here and there with a fork to let the steam escape.

Lightly beat together the egg yolk, salt and milk for the glaze. Brush this mixture all over the pie using a pastry brush.

At last, the pie is ready for baking! Bake it at the high temperature for the first 5 minutes, then turn the oven down to 180°C/350°F/Gas Mark 4 and continue baking for 20 to 30 minutes, until the pastry is beautifully golden all over. Leave the pie in the tin to cool down for 10 minutes before you unmould it. Place the unmoulded pie on a lovely round dish and bring it to the table.

RISOTTO COI FUNGHI DELL'ARTUSI

Mushroom Risotto

Dotted around this book you will find a good handful of recipes by Artusi. Pellegrino Artusi wrote his *La Scienza in Cucina e l'Arte di Mangiar Bene* in the second half of the last century. The book is deservedly still a best-seller.

Artusi was the first cookery writer to unify Italy gastronomically, although his recipes tend to be from the northern Italian tradition, as the author himself was born in Romagna and lived in Florence. And it is specifically in the cooking of these two regions that Artusi found the inspiration for the book.

The book is a large collection of 790 recipes, most of them valid to this day, always enlivened by anecdotes, pleasantries and delightful personal comments. Artusi was very keen on the health-giving properties of good food, although the abundant use of butter might make some modern health gurus shudder.

THE RECIPE

There are as many risotti coi funghi in northern Italy as there are cooks. Having tried a few from my family, friends and restaurants, I have decided that the Artusi one is a version particularly suited to being made in this country because it can be totally based on dried porcini, which are always available. When you buy dried porcini, buy large pieces sold in clear cellophane bags, so that you can see what you are buying. Do not buy dried porcini that look like dried-up brown crumbs with no mushroom shape left. Dried porcini are expensive, but they can lift a dish from banality to excellence.

SERVES 4 AS A FIRST COURSE

30g/1oz dried porcini
2 tbsp olive oil
½ onion, very finely chopped
1 celery stalk, very finely chopped
1 small carrot, very finely chopped
1 garlic clove, very finely chopped
6 parsley sprigs, very finely chopped
1 tbsp concentrated tomato paste
100ml/3½fl oz milk
salt and freshly ground black pepper
1.2l/2pt [US 5 cups] vegetable stock (page 231), or light chicken or meat stock (page 230)
60g/2oz [US 4 tbsp] unsalted butter
300g/10oz [US 1½ cups] Italian rice, preferably Carnaroli
100ml/3½fl oz dry white wine
freshly grated Parmesan

Put the dried porcini in a bowl and cover with boiling water. Leave to reconstitute for about an hour (see page 13).

Heat the oil with the onion in a frying pan for 2 or 3 minutes. Add the celery, carrot, garlic and parsley and sauté gently until the vegetables are soft, stirring very frequently.

Stir in the tomato paste and fry for a minute, then pour in half the milk. Continue cooking for about 7 minutes.

Fish the dried porcini out of the liquid. Rinse them under cold water and dry them well.

Chop the dried porcini to the size of rice grains and add to the vegetable mixture together with the rest of the milk. Season with salt and pepper and cook for about 10 minutes on very low heat.

Heat the stock for the risotto and keep it just simmering all through the cooking of the rice.

Melt the butter in a heavy-based saucepan. Add the rice and 'toast' it for a minute or so, stirring constantly. Splash with the wine and let it evaporate while you continue stirring.

Now begin to add the simmering stock, a ladleful at a time, letting each addition be absorbed by the rice before you add the next. About 15 minutes after you have begun to add the stock, spoon in the mushroom mixture with all its juices. Continue cooking and gradually adding the remaining stock until the rice is ready – about 18 minutes.

Transfer the risotto to a shallow bowl or a deep dish and serve with the grated Parmesan on the side.

Risotto col Pesce

Risotto with Fish

All along the Adriatic coast risotto with fish is very popular. This is a risotto I had at the Titon restaurant in Cesenatico, a delightful port in Romagna, a port which has the distinction of having been planned by Leonardo da Vinci. The fish used there was John Dory, but I have also used monkfish, which is more easily available. The cleaned fish should be the same weight as the rice, so that when the risotto is done the predominant ingredient is the rice, since rice increases its volume by about three times during the cooking.

SERVES 4 AS A MAIN COURSE

1.2l/2pt [US 5 cups] fish stock (page 231)
2 tbsp chopped onion
1 tbsp chopped celery
1 garlic clove, chopped
30g/1oz [US 2 tbsp] butter
2 tbsp extra virgin olive oil
2 fresh tomatoes, peeled and coarsely chopped
350g/12oz [US 1¾ cups] Italian rice, preferably Vialone Nano
200ml/7fl oz dry white wine
salt and freshly ground pepper
225g/8oz firm white fish, cleaned weight
4 shelled scallops [US sea scallops]
2 tbsp chopped fresh flat-leaf parsley

Heat the stock in a saucepan and bring slowly to the boil. Keep it simmering very gently all through the cooking.

Put the onion, celery, garlic, butter and oil in a heavy-based wide saucepan and sauté for about 10 minutes, until the vegetables are soft. Do this very gently and stir very frequently. Add the tomatoes and continue cooking for 5 minutes.

Mix in the rice and cook for 2 minutes, stirring constantly. Turn the heat up, pour over the wine and let it bubble away.

Now start adding the simmering stock by the ladleful, letting one ladleful be absorbed before you add the next. Add salt, unless the stock is already salted.

Cut the fish into neat morsels, removing any skin if necessary, and add to the rice after about 9 minutes from the moment you began to add the stock.

Cut the white part of the scallops into morsels of the same size as the fish and throw them into the pan when the rice is nearly done. Cut the coral in half and add to the risotto with the parsley and pepper. Cook for a further minute and then draw off the heat. Taste to check seasoning and transfer to a bowl. Serve immediately.

Bomba di Risotto alla Piacentina

Risotto and Pigeon Timbale

Piacenza is a city on the borders of Lombardy and Emilia-Romagna. Its cooking is also delicately poised between the cooking of the two regions. Some dishes originate in southern Lombardy, while others share the characteristics of the fully-fledged rich Emilian cuisine.

There are two traditional local dishes based on pigeon. One is a pasta pie, which is similar to the deliciously rich pasta pies of Bologna, and the other is this risotto timbale, which has strong leanings towards Lombard cooking. The latter was traditionally prepared for the feast of the Assumption of the Virgin on 15th August.

I am not very keen on the pigeons available here; they always seem so tough to me. But they are perfect for this dish. I only use the breast of the pigeons, because I find it is the only part worth eating. Make a gamey stock with the rest. The delicate risotto successfully balances the slightly bitter flavour of the pigeons. Do not overcook the risotto or the pigeons; both receive a second cooking in the oven.

SERVES 6

FOR THE PIGEONS

20g/¾oz dried porcini

the boneless breasts of 2 pigeons

30g/1oz onion

20g/¾oz celery

30g/1oz carrot

a small bunch of fresh flat-leaf parsley, leaves only

6 fresh sage leaves

40g/1½oz [US 3 tbsp] unsalted butter

salt and freshly ground pepper

150ml/5fl oz red wine

FOR THE RISOTTO

1.5l/2½pt [US 1½qt] meat stock (page 230)
60g/2oz [US 4 tbsp] unsalted butter
30g/1oz shallot, finely chopped
salt
375g/13oz [US 2 cups] Italian rice (Carnaroli or Arborio)
5 tbsp white wine
2 tbsp freshly grated Parmesan
2 tbsp dried breadcrumbs plus extra for the dish

Put the dried porcini in a small bowl and cover with 200ml/7fl oz boiling water. Leave for about 1 hour (see page 13) and then rinse them. Filter the liquid through a sieve lined with muslin [US cheesecloth].

Chop very finely the onion, celery, carrot, parsley and sage and put them into a sauté pan with the butter and 2 pinches of salt. Let the *soffritto* sauté nicely for 10 minutes or so. The heat must be very gentle and you must stir the soffritto quite often or it will catch.

Wash the pigeon breasts and pat them dry with kitchen paper towel. Season them with plenty of salt and pepper. Place them in the pan and brown them on both sides. Chop the dried porcini and add to the pan. Splash with the wine and bring to the boil. Add the dried porcini liquid. Cover the pan and cook for 5 to 8 minutes, turning the pigeon breasts twice during the cooking.

While the pigeon breasts are cooking, start to prepare the risotto. Put the stock on the heat and bring to a gentle simmer. Keep it simmering all through the cooking of the risotto. Melt half the butter in a heavy-based saucepan and add the shallot and a pinch of salt. Let the shallot cook gently for 5 or 6 minutes, then throw in the rice and sauté it over moderate heat for about 2 minutes, stirring constantly. Splash with the wine and let it bubble away.

Now begin to add the simmering stock one ladleful at a time while you stir very frequently, if not constantly. Let each ladleful be absorbed before adding the next. Remove the saucepan from the heat when the rice is just a little underdone. Mix in half the remaining butter and the Parmesan. Set aside.

Heat the oven to 220°C/425°F/Gas Mark 7.

Cut the pigeon breasts into strips. Taste the juices and correct any seasoning. If you find the juices not rich enough in flavour, boil to reduce them over high heat (something, however, I have never found necessary).

Generously butter a soufflé dish or deep oven dish of 2l/3½pt [US 2qt] capacity and sprinkle with breadcrumbs to cover all the surface. Shake out excess crumbs.

Cover the bottom of the dish and up the sides with some risotto. Place the pigeon strips in the hole in the middle and pour most of the juices over them. Cover with the remaining risotto so as to make a box. Drizzle with the rest of the juices, sprinkle with the 2 tablespoons of breadcrumbs and dot with the little bit of butter left over.

Place the dish in the oven to bake for 20 minutes or so, until a lovely golden crust has formed on the top. Wait 5 minutes before you bring the dish to the table – let it rest and cool down a little so that the flavours can blend better.

A lighter version of this dish is made by boiling the rice instead of making a risotto. Then the rice is dressed with butter, Parmesan and the juices of the pigeon before being moulded around the inside of the dish and filled with the pigeon meat.

Pesce al Forno alla Romagnola

White Fish Baked in Tomato Sauce

This recipe came originally from a family friend from Cesena in Romagna. However, it has been in my family, both in Milan and in London, for so long that I do not know how many alterations the recipe has gone through, and whether it should, by adoption, be in the Lombardy section.

I use any good fresh white fish, but not one like sea bass or turbot, whose flavour is too good to be submerged in a tomato sauce. Sea bream, whiting (a very underrated fish in this country), hake, grey mullet or a fillet of haddock are all suitable. If you use fillet you should cook it a little less.

SERVES 4

a white fish of about 1.3kg/3lb, cleaned but with the head on
5 tbsp extra virgin olive oil
1 small onion, finely chopped
1 small celery stalk, finely chopped
1 garlic clove, finely chopped
1 tbsp chopped parsley
4 fresh tomatoes, peeled, or canned tomatoes, coarsely chopped
150ml/5fl oz dry white wine
salt and freshly ground black pepper

Heat the oven to 200°C/400°F/Gas Mark 6.

Put 4 tablespoons of the oil, the onion, celery, garlic and parsley into a saucepan and sauté until the vegetables are soft. Add the tomatoes and the wine and cook for 10 minutes or so over a lively heat. Season with salt and pepper and draw off the heat.

Wash and pat dry the fish. Season with salt inside and out. Grease a roasting tin with the remaining oil and place the fish in the tin. Spoon the sauce over the fish and around it and cover with foil. Bake for about 30 minutes, until the fish is cooked. To test, insert a knife into the thickest part of the body, lift out a little of one side and have a peep. The flesh should be opaque but still moist, and it should easily come clean off the bone.

Transfer the fish very carefully to an oval dish and spoon the sauce around it. Alternatively, place the portions directly on individual plates, with a good tablespoon of the sauce on the side – an easier operation.

STRACOTTO DI SAN NICOLÒ
Braised Beef

Not long ago I spent a most interesting morning in Piacenza with a charming lady, Magda Lucchini. She let me into her flat, at the top of a 19th-century house that was typical of northern Italy. Large rooms, lovely mosaic or parquet floors covered with Persian rugs, the walls covered with paintings, and every corner of any flat surface filled with knick-knacks and photographs, some very valuable, some of no distinction, but all expressing the personality of the charming owner.

Magda Lucchini is the Presidentessa dell'Associazione del Fornello, a *fornello* being a kitchen range. The members of this association are up-market ladies who dine together every 2 months. But eating, however deliciously, is not the main object of this group. The members, who are all excellent cooks, want to keep alive and hand down the tradition of a good table around which the family gathers, not only to eat excellent food, but also to express opinions and exchange ideas. They in fact want to foster the family atmosphere, of which the mother is the focal point and her cooking the welcome tie that keeps the family together. The recipe for a piece of beef, slowly braised, is one of Magda Lucchini's favourite dishes from her home town, Piacenza. It is the dish she likes to serve on St Nicholas' Day, the 6th of December.

THE RECIPE

This stracotto is cooked in an interesting way that was new to me. The result is very tender meat with a delicate flavour of wine that is just detectable. The meat is cooked in a pot, preferably earthenware, with another pot, or a deep dish, placed on top so as to seal it. This second dish *must* be earthenware to allow the vapour from the wine, with which it is full, to go through.

The meat must be suitable for braising rather than roasting. I use chuck steak, and make the dish a day in advance so that I can remove the fat easily once it is cold. (I keep the fat to make stewed potatoes.)

The best accompaniment is polenta or boiled potatoes.

SERVES 8 TO 10

a 2kg/4½lb boneless piece of beef
350g/12oz Spanish onions, finely chopped
250g/9oz carrots, finely chopped
225g/8oz celery, finely chopped
3 garlic cloves, chopped
a handful of flat-leaf parsley leaves, finely chopped
the needles from a 5cm/2in fresh rosemary sprig, finely chopped
1 fresh sage sprig, finely chopped
6 fresh thyme sprigs, finely chopped
100g/3½oz [US 7 tbsp] unsalted butter
salt and freshly ground pepper
1 tbsp olive oil
600ml/1pt [US 2½ cups] good red wine
3 cloves
a pinch of ground cinnamon
6 peppercorns
2 bay leaves

Tie the piece of beef neatly in a roll.

Put all the chopped vegetables, garlic, herbs and butter in a pot (see introduction) and sauté for 5 minutes. Season with salt and pepper and sauté for a further 10 minutes or so, stirring frequently.

Heat the oven to 150°C/300°F/Gas Mark 2.

While the vegetables are cooking, heat the oil in a frying pan and, when hot, brown the meat on all sides – also at the two extremities by standing the roll on end. When it is a lovely deep brown colour, season with salt and pepper and place it on top of the vegetables.

Fill the top dish with the wine (see introduction). Add the cloves, cinnamon, peppercorns and bay leaves and set the dish on top of the pot so as to cover it tightly. Cover the top dish with a tight-fitting lid and place this construction of pots in the oven. Cook for 8 hours. Because it is cooked so slowly I find no need to add any liquid to the meat, but should the meat become dry, add a couple of tablespoons of that water.

Remove the meat to one side and skim off as much of the fat as you can. Allow the meat to cool a little and then carve it in thickish slices (an electric knife makes the job much easier). Place the slices on a dish and spoon over a little of the vegetable sauce. Place the rest around the meat, and serve.

POLPETTONE ALLA ROMAGNOLA

Baked Meat Roll

During one of my visits to sunny Romagna I met a chef who was very kind and informative. He took me around the fish market of Cesenatico, and we exchanged recipes and discussed food. Sadly enough I didn't make a note of his name, so I cannot credit him for this very good recipe.

Meat roll in England always seems to me to have undertones of patched-up food made with left-over meat and whatever else is in the fridge. In Italy a polpettone, although '*cucina povera*', is thought of as a very valid and excellent dish – as long as it is well made. In fact a good polpettone can demonstrate the expertise of the cook, who must be able to season and adjust the flavour so as to achieve a well-balanced dish.

THE RECIPE

While most polpettoni are cooked in a sauté pan, this one has the advantage of being cooked in the oven, so that it can be partly ignored without fear of it getting burnt. The use of three different meats gives the dish a more complex flavour. The seasoning must be assertive, with the right amount of salt and pepper.

If you have any left-over polpettone, serve it cold, but not chilled, dressed with a little sauce of chopped parsley, cornichons and capers floating in extra virgin olive oil and sharpened by a few drops of lemon juice (see salsa verde on page 229).

SERVES 6 TO 7

60g/2oz good white country-type bread, crustless
about 120ml/4fl oz milk
250g/9oz lean beef, minced [US ground]
250g/9oz lean pork, minced [US ground]
250g/9oz boned chicken breast, minced [US ground]
2 eggs
60g/2oz [US ½ cup] freshly grated Parmesan
15g/½oz fresh flat-leaf parsley, leaves only
15g/½oz mixed fresh thyme, rosemary needles and sage
1 tbsp chopped sweet onion
grated nutmeg
salt and freshly ground black pepper
300ml/10fl oz dry white wine
300ml/10fl oz rich meat stock (page 230)
30g/1oz [US 2 tbsp] unsalted butter
20g/¾oz [US 2 tbsp] flour

Break the bread into pieces, put it in a bowl and cover with milk. Leave to soak up some of the milk and then squeeze the excess milk out and crumble the bread with a fork. Put it in a large bowl.

Heat the oven to 200°C/400°F/Gas Mark 6.

Add the three meats to the bowl, also the eggs, cheese, herbs and onion and mix very thoroughly. I do this with my hands – definitely the best way. Season with nutmeg, salt and pepper. I recommend adding at least 1½ teaspoons of salt, because salt is fundamental to the final result, especially in a dish like this where you cannot satisfactorily add it at the end. Mix and pound again.

Now cut a 30cm/12in square sheet of foil and place it on the work surface. Brush it all over with oil and then transfer the meat mixture on to it. Shape the mixture into a fat salame and pat it together to eliminate any air bubbles and empty spaces. Then roll it up in the foil and pat again. Close the ends firmly, transfer the package to a roasting tin and bake for 30 minutes, until the polpettone is firm to the touch.

Cut the foil open and pour 4 or 5 tablespoons of the wine over the meat. Place the tin back in the oven. After 10 minutes pour over a little more wine, then repeat the operation once more after a further 10 minutes. Now the polpettone will have cooked for about 1 hour and it should be done. Remove it from the oven and transfer it, without the foil, to a carving board. (Use great care in transferring the polpettone, because it might break in the middle; however if this does happen, don't worry – you have to slice it up in any case!) Keep warm, covered with a clean piece of foil. Be careful to retain the cooking juices in the foil.

Pour the cooking juices collected in the foil and in the tin into a saucepan and bring to the boil. Add the remaining wine and the stock and reduce over high heat by about one-third, until syrupy, rich and full of flavour.

Blend the butter and flour together with the prongs of a fork. Turn the heat down and add the flour mixture (*beurre manié*, to give it its culinary name) little by little to the simmering sauce. When all has been added, taste the sauce and adjust seasoning.

Carve the polpettone into 1cm/½in slices. If you do not have an electric knife – an invaluable tool for this type of dish, as well as for braised meat or roulades – use a very sharp, straight-bladed knife. Transfer the slices to a heated oval plate, overlapping them slightly. Spoon around a few tablespoons of the sauce and serve at once, with the rest of the sauce handed separately in a sauce-boat.

Serve the polpettone with a buttery potato purée and/or with spinach or sautéed courgettes [US zucchini], according to the season.

COTOLETTE ALLA BOLOGNESE

Bolognese Veal Steaks

Bolognese cotolette are thicker (about 1cm/½in) than Wienerschnitzel. I sometimes use loin of pork steaks, or I use turkey breast steaks which are just the right thickness.

This is a dish that typifies the exuberance of the local cuisine. To the meat, which has been coated in egg, breaded and fried in butter, is added the delicate prosciutto di Parma, plus the other glory of the region, Parmigiano-Reggiano and, to finish the dish off, a little tomato sauce. When in season, a truffle can be slivered over the meat at the very end. In the past, the truffle used to be put on the meat before it was coated and breaded, a sophisticated touch of the kind that fascinates even the most experienced gourmet. Personally, I find truffles and tomato sauce an unhappy match.

This dish is particularly suitable when you do not want to be in the kitchen at the last minute. You can prepare it totally beforehand and heat it up gently, for a little longer, just before serving it. It is a good dish, when properly made, even if it has been overly exploited by second-rate Italian restaurants. The addition of a little olive oil to the butter is to prevent the butter from burning. An alternative is to use clarified butter.

SERVES 4

a piece of Parmesan
4 veal or loin of pork steaks, about 450g/1lb in total
1 egg
salt
8 tbsp fine dried white breadcrumbs
60g/2oz [US 4 tbsp] unsalted butter
1 tbsp olive oil
60g/2oz prosciutto di Parma, thinly sliced

FOR THE TOMATO SAUCE

15g/½oz [US 1 tbsp] unsalted butter
1 tbsp very finely chopped onion
salt and freshly ground pepper
6 tbsp tomato passata
4 tbsp meat stock (page 230)

First make the tomato sauce. The onion must be chopped really fine, like grains of rice. Put the butter, the onion and a pinch of salt in a small saucepan. Sauté gently for 5 minutes or so and then add the passata. Cook for 10 minutes over gentle heat. Add the stock and bring to the simmer. Taste and adjust seasoning.

Using a potato peeler, sliver 40g/1½oz of shavings from your piece of Parmesan and set aside.

See that the steaks are all of a good shape, and of the right thickness. Also cut off any fat that might be on the edge of the steaks.

In a soup plate beat the egg lightly with 1 teaspoon of salt. Spread the breadcrumbs on a plate next to the egg. Coat the meat on both sides in the egg, let the excess egg fall back into the plate, and then transfer the steaks to the plate of crumbs. Coat each side, pressing the crumbs into the meat with your hands to form a thickish layer.

Now, if you have time, place the steaks in the fridge to chill. It will be easier to fry them properly when chilled.

Choose a frying pan or a sauté pan large enough to hold the steaks one next to the other. Put the butter and the oil into it and heat until the foam has subsided. Put the meat in the fat and fry on a lively heat until the underside is of a golden colour. Turn the steaks over and fry the other side. Be careful not to burn the butter, or the meat will be speckled with black spots instead of being lovely and golden. Turn the heat down if necessary.

Divide the prosciutto into 4 portions and place one over each steak. Do the same with the cheese shavings, placing them over the prosciutto. Spoon the tomato sauce around the meat. Cover the pan with a lid and cook, over low heat, for 7 to 10 minutes. Transfer to a heated dish and serve at once.

Sciarlotta di Pere
Pear Charlotte

In 1988 I went to Parma to receive the Gran Duchessa Maria Luigia prize for my book *Gastronomy of Italy.* After the prize-giving ceremony there was a fantastic banquet in a beautiful palazzo, a banquet in the manner of the Duchess herself. Marie Louise, a Hapsburg princess, was the wife, and later widow, of Napoleon. The Parmigiani adored her and still consider her their only true sovereign. She certainly must have been a fascinating lady who enjoyed life to the full, which is why she decided that rather than join Napoleon in far-flung Elba, she would stay put in delightful little Parma with her dashing Austrian general, Adam Albert Neipperg.

Maria Luigia, as she was called in Parma, loved a good table, and for that she employed one of the best chefs of the time, Vincenzo Agnoletti. She also imported from Vienna many talented pâtissiers, who taught the Parmigiani the art of cake-making, as well as cake-loving.

Parma is still renowned for its pâtissieries, and when I was there the most famous was the Pasticceria Torino. At the banquet I met the man who is the inspiration behind the delicious dolci (sweet things) sold at the Torino, Ugo Falavigna. He was responsible for all the cakes, puddings, friandises and chocolates served at the banquet, which were presented on beautifully moulded chocolate plates (which we soon demolished).

Falavigna gave me a copy of his delightful book, *Arte della Pasticceria a Parma*, which contains the basis of the following recipe for a pear charlotte.

THE RECIPE

If you cannot find Savoiardi, try to make your own sponge fingers, which are called ladyfingers in the US. Bought sponge fingers can be used too. They are sweeter than Savoiardi, so you must make a less sweet syrup. They are also less absorbent, but the result is quite satisfactory.

SERVES 6

1½ unwaxed lemons
800g/1¾lb ripe but firm pears
150ml/5fl oz white wine
180g/6oz caster sugar [US ¾ cup + 2 tbsp granulated sugar]
⅛ tsp ground cinnamon
⅛ tsp ground cloves
2 tbsp Poire William's eau-de-vie or Grappa
approximately 16–17 Savoiardi

Wash and dry the lemon. Using a potato peeler, peel off 3 strips of rind and set aside. Squeeze the lemons and pour the juice into a bowl.

Peel the pears, quarter and core them, and slice them very thinly. Put these slices in the bowl and mix them so that they get coated with lemon juice. This has the double function of preventing the pears from discolouring as well as giving them a lovely flavour. Leave to macerate for 1 hour.

Put the wine and the same amount of water in a large sauté pan. Add the sugar, spices and the strips of lemon rind and heat over low heat until the sugar has dissolved. Stir the syrup constantly. Simmer gently for 5 minutes and then slide in the pears with their juices. Turn them over a few times for the first 2 or 3 minutes or so and then leave to cook over very low heat until they are tender. This will only take a few minutes if you have sliced the pears thinly. Taste and add a little sugar if necessary. It is difficult to give the exact amount of sugar since it depends on the quality of the pears.

Lift the pears out of the pan with a slotted spoon and set them aside. Discard the lemon rind. Turn the heat up and reduce the juices until they are heavy with syrup and rich with flavour. Mix in the liqueur.

Line a 1.2l/2pt [US 5 cup] pudding basin or other dome-shaped mould with cling film. Soak the Savoiardi in the lovely syrup, just enough to soften them, and then line the basin with them. Spoon the pears and their juices into the basin and cover with more Savoiardi soaked in syrup. Pour over any remaining syrup. Cover with cling film and chill for at least 6 hours.

To unmould the charlotte, remove the cover of film and place a pretty round dish over the top of the basin. Turn dish and basin over and lift the basin off. Peel off the film lining.

I decorate the charlotte with some whipped cream and serve some more cream in a bowl at the table. Alternatively I make a mixture of cream and mascarpone in the proportion of 2 to 1, and sweeten it with 2 tablespoons of sifted icing sugar [US confectioners' sugar].

FRUTTA FRESCA ALL'ACETO BALSAMICO

Fresh Fruit and Balsamic Vinegar

In the following two recipes you will find aceto balsamico used to flavour fruit: strawberries and melon. Both recipes are from the provinces of Modena and Reggio Emilia, where aceto balsamico is made. They are extremely simple to make, but, as with all the simplest recipes, you must use a very good aceto balsamico and, of course, top-quality fruit. The balsamic vinegar brings out the flavour of the fruit without imparting any vinegary taste to the fruit.

I have put these two ideas (I can hardly call them recipes) together, but I would never serve them together. Strawberries and melon are definitely not a match. Another fruit that is suited to this treatment is mango – hardly Italian! – and this would be a perfect companion to strawberries.

FRAGOLE ALL'ACETO BALSAMICO
Strawberries with Balsamic Vinegar

SERVES 4

700g/1½lb strawberries

2–3 tbsp sugar

2 tbsp best-quality balsamic vinegar

Cut the larger strawberries in half, or even into quarters. Put them all in a bowl.

About 2 hours before serving sprinkle over the sugar and toss gently but thoroughly. Half an hour before serving sprinkle with the balsamic vinegar and toss again gently and with care. Serve chilled.

MELONE ALL'ACETO BALSAMICO
Melon with Balsamic Vinegar

The most popular melon in Italy is the cantaloupe, but any melon is delicious served in this way, as long as it is ripe.

SERVES 6 TO 8

1 medium melon

1 tbsp caster sugar [US granulated sugar]

2 tbsp best-quality balsamic vinegar

Cut the melon into thin wedges. Peel them and scrape out all the seeds. Place in a lovely glass bowl.

Sprinkle with the sugar and with the balsamic vinegar half an hour before serving. Serve chilled.

SEMIFREDDO SEMPLICE
Plain Semifreddo

'Now I shall let you into a secret; the secret of the Italian meringue.' This is what Signora Cantoni said to me in Bologna when I met her at the cookery school run by the Simili sisters, one of the most renowned cookery schools in Italy. Signora Cantoni is the granddaughter of a famous Bolognese ice-cream maker. So I was delighted that she was happy to pass on to me one of her secrets. She told me that by using Italian meringue one can make delicious semifreddi which, served with different sauces, can take on many different guises. It is one of the gelati she always makes for her grandchildren – lucky them!

THE RECIPE

A semifreddo, as the name tells us, is a half-frozen concoction, very similar to a frozen mousse. It often contains layers of sponge cake, but it can also be made just with a mousse-type mixture.

Italian meringue is a more stable mixture than the usual Swiss meringue, since the egg whites are heated by the hot syrup poured over them.

This semifreddo is made with Italian meringue that is simply flavoured with lemon rind. I find it quite delicious by itself, but a sauce does add to the pleasure. My favourite sauce is a raspberry coulis (see following recipe) flavoured with geranium leaves, a delightfully sensual gastronomic pleasure. A coffee-flavoured chocolate sauce is an excellent alternative, in which case I would substitute a few drops of pure vanilla extract and a pinch or two of ground cinnamon for the lemon rind. When you make the sauce, keep in mind that the semifreddo itself is very sweet.

I prefer to give the amount of egg whites in weight rather than number, because egg sizes differ so much.

The temperature of the sugar syrup is critical, so I feel you do need a jam thermometer.

SERVES 6 TO 8

125g/4oz [US ½ cup + 2 tbsp] sugar

100ml/3½fl oz water

1 tbsp lemon juice

150g/5oz [US ⅔ cup] egg whites

the grated rind of 1 unwaxed lemon

Put the sugar, water and lemon juice in a small saucepan. Heat, slowly at first, and faster when the syrup is clear, until a jam thermometer registers 110°C/225°F. Brush down the sides of the pan frequently with a wet pastry brush.

Now you must begin to whisk the egg whites with the lemon rind. I use a copper bowl and a hand-held electric mixer. Whisk until the whites are stiff but still moist. The snow should remain in position when you turn the bowl upside-down (if you dare to do this!). When the syrup reaches 130°C/250°F, pour it in a steady stream into the bowl, letting it fall into the middle of the egg snow. Do not stop whisking; go on and on until the mixture is cool. (Feel it by pushing a finger down to the bottom of the bowl. It should be no warmer than room temperature.) Line a 1.2l/2pt [US 5 cup] loaf tin with cling film and spoon the meringue into it. Smooth it down, cover with more film and freeze.

When you want to serve the semifreddo, transfer it to a board, remove the film and cut into thickish slices. Place on individual dessert plates surrounded by a pool of the chosen sauce.

This semifreddo can be eaten as soon as it comes out of the freezer.

SUGO DI LAMPONE

A Raspberry Coulis

SERVES 6

450g/1lb fresh raspberries

150g/5oz icing sugar [US 1¼ cups confectioners' sugar], sifted

the juice of 1 lemon

3 or 4 young sweet geranium leaves, torn into small pieces (optional)

Blend together the raspberries, sugar, lemon juice and the optional sweet geranium leaves in a food processor or blender. Taste and add more sugar and/or lemon juice, according to taste. If you want a smooth sauce, strain it through a fine sieve, pushing the purée with a spoon.

SALSA DI CIOCCOLATO

A Chocolate Sauce

SERVES 6

200g/7oz bitter chocolate with a high cocoa butter and cocoa solids content

120ml/4fl oz strong espresso coffee

6 tbsp caster sugar [US granulated sugar]

120ml/4fl oz double cream [US heavy cream]

Break the chocolate into small pieces and place in a heavy-based pan. Add the coffee and the sugar and dissolve over very gentle heat, stirring constantly. Mix in the cream and keep on the heat until the sauce is smoking. Pour into a sauce-boat and serve immediately.

BENSONE DI VILLA GAIDELLO
Sweet Focaccia

Villa Gaidello is a charming guest-farm near Modena, owned by Paola Bini. Paola was born there and has inherited the farm from her grandmother. To make it possible for her to keep it, she has refurbished the barn, the house and outhouses into a sort of hotel *cum* restaurant. The surrounding countryside has the placid serenity of the Po valley, at first sight seemingly a little dull although appreciation of it grows with time. Appreciation of Villa Gaidello's food, however, is immediate.

Paola has a brigade of local women who, following her guidance, cook for her. She decides on the menu according to what is best in the shops or in the vegetable gardens. The menu is fixed. You sit in the large conservatory-like dining room (it used to be the barn) with a pile of six white plates in front of you. After each of the six courses a waitress comes round with a large basket into which she whisks the dirty top plate in readiness for the next course on the clean plate beneath. I thought it was the best local food I had ever had, comparable to the marvellous meals I have enjoyed at the homes of my many friends in Reggio Emilia and Parma. The soup, a stock in which a few perfect tortellini were gently floating, was particularly memorable – an unforgettable delight.

Traditionally, bensone is an S-shaped cake, often eaten warm with chilled sweet Lambrusco. You break your piece of bensone into the glass of Lambrusco and you eat it with a spoon. Paola Bini's bensone, although a little different, is also excellent for dunking; when dunked it softens and absorbs the flavour of the liquid, but without disintegrating.

THE RECIPE

At the Villa Gaidello the bensone was shaped in individual rounds and served with fruits preserved under spirit. I suggest you serve it, as I do, with a lovely eggy crème anglaise. If you prefer to serve it with wine – still a perfect way to enjoy it – I suggest a Moscato d'Asti or a heavenly Albana from Romagna, although only Lambrusco has that slightly sharp fizzy flavour that makes it the ideal accompaniment. But alas, *good* sweet Lambrusco is not easily found outside Italy, or even outside Emilia-Romagna.

MAKES 8

300g/10oz [US 2½ cups] white flour, preferably Italian 00

150g/5oz caster sugar [US ¾ cup granulated sugar]

2 tsp baking powder

a pinch of salt

150g/5oz [US 10 tbsp] unsalted butter, melted

1 size-2 egg [US extra-large egg]

the grated rind of ½ unwaxed lemon

Heat the oven to 180°C/350°F/Gas Mark 4.

Mix together the flour, sugar, baking powder and salt on the working surface. Make a well and add the butter, the egg and the lemon rind. Stir them with a fork to blend, gradually adding the dry ingredients that form the well. Knead quickly into a ball, avoiding beating or overworking the dough as this would toughen it.

Wipe the work surface clean and then lightly flour it. Divide the dough into 8 portions. Roll out or pat each portion into a round.

Lightly butter two baking trays and place the rounds on them, spacing them out as they will spread when baking. Place the trays in the oven and bake for 15 to 20 minutes, until pale gold. Transfer to a wire rack and let them cool for about 10 minutes before serving.

Toscana

The Tuscan contadini are sober; their meals are healthy and varied; the bread, the best of nourishment, is excellent, of pure wheat, grey yes, but free of husk . . . One must remember that the Tuscan contadino makes his own oil not only for lighting his lamps, but also to dress the vegetables on which he feeds, thus making them more tasty and nourishing.' This passage comes from a book, *Delle Condizione degli Agricoltori in Toscana*, written in 1860 by G Sismondi. Apart from the lighting of lamps, this passage could have been written yesterday.

The well-known sobriety of the Tuscans has at times been confused with avarice, as the journalist Indro Montanelli has pointed out. 'The Tuscan countryside is bare, lean, disdainful of trivialities and the superfluous. The cooking, too, is lean, made of three or four essentials. And their parsimony is leanness, which should never be confused with meanness, because it is a mental attitude rather than a financial calculation.' Once again, and maybe more obviously than in most other regions, the cooking reflects the character of the people.

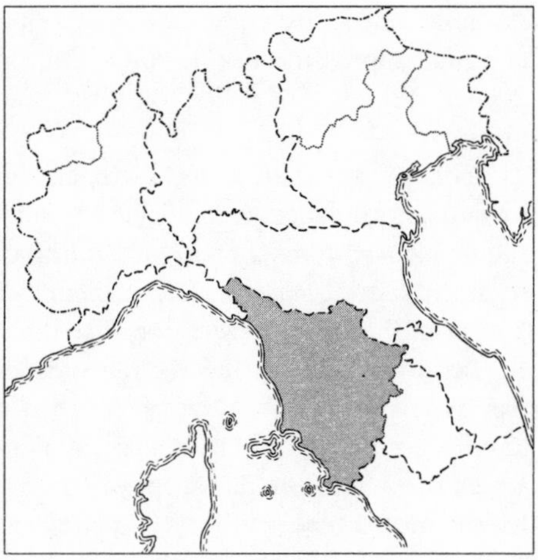

Another factor that underlines this sobriety is that Tuscany is not as fertile as most people imagine. Only a small part of this large region is lowland; other parts are hilly, but most is mountainous. The soil is poor, yet nature here seems to make up in quality what is lacking in quantity. With this sort of quality it is no wonder that only the minimum is necessary to dress it up. This minimum usually consists of the olive oil, which, on the table, is the symbol of Tuscan cooking, as the olive tree is that of the countryside. Olive oil is the only condiment used in Tuscany, and perhaps this is why traditional Tuscan cooking has no risotti and very few pasta dishes in its repertoire.

But let me take you around Tuscany, the way I recently went, from the Ligurian border to the southern Maremma. The cooking of northern Tuscany and that of Liguria have very strong links. The best place to appreciate this is at the Trattoria Bussè in Pontremoli, where Antonietta Bartocchi reigns in the kitchen and her brother Luciano entertains the guests with his remarkable knowledge of local food.

It is there that I was first introduced to *testaroli*. Testaroli are made of a water-based batter poured into flat, round, cast-iron or earthenware moulds which have been heated to a very high temperature by being placed between hot embers. The embers should contain dried chestnut leaves for their aroma. The fire is lit in a room next to the house, called the *gradile*, a room where bread is made too. The testaroli, which are about 40cm/17in in diameter, are kept there. When they are to be served they are cut into squares and thrown into boiling salted water, just like lasagne, and then dressed with a light pesto – the Ligurian influence.

As an alternative, the torta di bietole – Swiss chard tourte (for a similar dish see page 135) – is more Ligurian than Tuscan, the pastry being the poor man's pastry of flour, oil and water characteristic of Liguria.

The *involtini di vitello* which follow at Bussè again show great similarity with the Ligurian *tomaxelle*, slices of veal wrapped around a delicate mixture of sweetbread and minced veal. Antonietta cooks her involtini in a beautiful shallow earthenware dish for at least two hours. While I was enjoying them I remembered a passage from one of the autobiographies I enjoyed most in recent years, *A Tuscan Childhood*. The author, Kinta Beevor, grew up before the Second World War in the Fortezza della Brunella in nearby Aulla. When Kinta tried to reproduce in England the Tuscan involtini of her childhood, to keep them rolled up she used toothpicks bought from a chemist, which turned out to be medicated!

But involtini are the food of the wealthy, while Lunigiana and the adjacent valley of Garfagnana are rich only in their wealth of peasant dishes. The flour from the superb local chestnuts is used to prepare castagnaccio (page 197), nowadays mostly eaten in the street straight from the baker, or polenta, which with its sweetish flavour matches perfectly the pork or sausages that traditionally accompany it.

The new wave of restaurateurs now make pappardelle with chestnut flour, and delicious they are indeed, especially when dressed with stewed hare or a ragù of wild boar. Pappardelle are one of the only two traditional Tuscan pastas, the other being *pici*, a sort of thick hand-made spaghetti. Pici, which near Montalcino are called *pinci*, are made with a poor man's dough, just water and plain flour, and are traditionally dressed with a ragù of wild mushrooms.

The subject of mushrooms brings me back to my journey through Tuscany, where the next stop is in Chianti. We had a house there for a long time, but decided to sell it after I counted no less than seven British cars parked in our local village of Gaiole. Chianti had become Chiantishire! I used to go mushroom hunting with the locals, who disdained all fungi other than boletes, a preference I fully endorse. Later on, when a friend and I ran a cookery school in Chianti, we used the different species we found for a risotto (as on page

158), but the fungi which gave the best flavour to the dish were undoubtedly the boletes which shot up overnight in the woods to welcome the bright autumn sun.

In Chianti as in Lucchesia the choice for a first course should be soup. A ribollita (page 181) made with black cabbage, a pappa col pomodoro, and a zuppa di farro (page 179) are three examples of superb soups in which bread or beans stand in for pasta or rice. Hot, warm or even cold in the summer, soup brings together two of the strongest elements of Tuscan cooking: bread and vegetables. The vegetables, more than anything else, confirm the fact that quality is of paramount importance. The small broad beans eaten raw with young pecorino (which 'should never be peppery but only sapid' as the gastronome Giovanni Righi Parenti writes), the noble cardoons (called *gobbi* – hunchbacks – in Tuscany because of the way they are grown there), the small succulent artichokes of Caterina de'Medici fame (the old tyrant ate so many that she was sick for days), the fat garlic with which the Senesi prepare the delicious fried garlic on St John's Day, 24th June, and of course the beans . . . and the beans . . . and more beans. Not for nothing are the Tuscans called *mangia fagioli* (bean eaters).

But the Tuscans also eat wonderful meat and even better chicken and game. The best way to appreciate the quality of the meat and chicken is to have it in a *grigliata* – mixed grill, which usually includes fegatelli – slices of pig's liver wrapped in 'crépine' and flavoured with wild fennel seeds.

Oh, the herbs of Tuscany! You go for a walk and you pass through mist after mist of different scents, according to what you are treading on or brushing against. *Nepitella*, a kind of wild mint; *finocchietto*, wild fennel; *ramerino*, rosemary – the constant partner to roast meat; *pepolino*, wild thyme, for the rabbit; and even *dragoncello*, tarragon, which is hardly used in other regions. The best foil for the herbs are the delicious schiacciate (see page 177) – Tuscan focacce – scented with herbs and moistened, though never dripping, with the green olive oil of this perfect country.

Going south you arrive in the Maremma, a land of biblical beauty in its wide green valleys and steep dramatic hills topped by old crenellated towns. The vineyards and the olive groves have given way to fields of tomatoes, sunflowers and cereals, but the lines of cypresses, the landmark of the Tuscan countryside, are still there. And the food is still similar, with its accent on simplicity and quality: vegetables and bean soups again, such as *acquacotta*, literally 'cooked water', the Cinderella of all soups.

Acquacotta is made with whatever vegetables are ready, wild or cultivated, plus the beans, of course, and water, which should be *di fonte* (spring water). 'I cook the eggs gently in a little of the soup stock and put them on top of the soup; that's easier than the more usual method of breaking the eggs over the soup and putting the stockpot in the oven for the eggs to cook.' This is what I was told by Lorenzo Seghi, chef of the Taverna del Borgo Vecchio in Massa Marittima, a town well worth a detour also for its incredible beauty.

Acquacotta is also popular in Arezzo and its surrounding villages, but there it does not contain eggs and the soup is ladled on to bread. 'Acquacotta is made with natural ingredients and this is why the Italians love it.' This short passage precedes the recipe written by a six-year-old girl who, in typical Tuscan fashion, confuses Tuscany with Italy! The recipe appears in a book edited by Guido Gianni, the delegate of the Accademia Italiana della Cucina in Arezzo. All the recipes were written by primary school pupils in the province of Arezzo. They are recipes the children have learnt from mothers and grandmothers, and they are an interesting social comment on the local food. I was fascinated by the book and its charming drawings; but, alas, I only had it on loan.

After much thought I decided not to include a recipe for acquacotta because, more than any other soup, it needs vegetables grown in earthy soil and ripened by the sun, and not pale imitations of vegetables grown in water and ripened in air-conditioned greenhouses. I feel an acquacotta made in Britain would taste just like its name implies: 'cooked water'.

A word about the fish that are caught and cooked all down the coast, from the river Magra to Orbetello. Simplicity, again, in the grilling or roasting of the fish, or in the boiling of prawns and langoustines. These are dressed with local olive oil, and sometimes combined with cannellini beans, in one of the most creative fish salads ever, known as *i ricchi e i poveri* (the rich and the poor). Only *cacciucco* – fish soup – and *triglie alla livornese* (page 187) demand a complicated treatment and the skill of the cook. Of all Italian fish soups, cacciucco (of which it is said that the soup should contain five different fish, one for each c in its name) is the most similar to bouillabaisse. As with bouillabaisse one of the fish must be rascasse rouge – scorpion fish – for the flavour. Cacciucco, however, does not contain saffron, and the piquancy is given by *zenzero*, as they call chilli in Tuscany (in Italian zenzero is ginger, and chilli is peperoncino; so do not be fooled when you are told that cacciucco contains ginger!).

Another Tuscan speciality are *cee*, a Tuscan contraction of *cieche*, meaning blind, elvers. The incredible story of the elvers swimming to Europe from the Sargasso Sea fascinated me so much when I first heard it as a child that I sat motionless and speechless in front of a dish of the most exquisite *cee alla salvia* in Viareggio, unable to touch them. What also disturbed me deeply was that these tiny translucent fish, blind as I was told they are, are alive until thrown into the boiling oil, so alive that when they touch the hot oil, they regain their full strength to such an extent that the cook must quickly cover the frying pan with a lid and keep it firmly on. Now I can eat cee with delight, but it is a rare treat indeed since they are astronomically expensive. This, I have been told, is due to the fact that the government has prohibited the catching of elvers because they are in danger of extinction. But, inevitably, they are still caught – in the middle of the night – to be served in expensive restaurants.

And how do you finish your meal in Tuscany? Like the Tuscans, with pecorino and pears, when they are in season, or with an almondy cantuccio di Prato dipped in Vinsanto. As for me, I love their country tarts, where the soft shell of sweet pastry is brought alive by its contrast with the sharp home-made jam (page 199). A real treat in a repertoire that abounds with good, simple things.

SCHIACCIATA CON LE NOCI Ⓥ

Flat Bread with Walnuts

Schiacciata is to Tuscany what focaccia is to Liguria, a kind of dressed flat bread. The traditional schiacciata is made with flour, yeast, water and rendered pork fat instead of the oil used in the Ligurian focaccia. Nowadays oil usually replaces the pork fat for the benefit of health, but to the detriment of the flavour. There are many different schiacciate, most of them slightly sweet, such as the schiacciata fiorentina which is eaten in Florence during Carnival.

Schiacciata means squashed flat, but quite a few shiacciate are deliciously light and puffy. Paolo Petroni, in his excellent book *La Cucina Fiorentina*, suggests that the name might derive from the meaning of *shiacciare* in relation to the eggs, i.e. to break the eggs, since schiacciate were also made at Easter time. After Lent, when the eating of eggs was forbidden, every larder was bursting with eggs. An arguable theory, to which I cannot subscribe since quite a few schiacciate are made without eggs, as, for instance, this one. I think that the name simply comes from the shape. The dough is rolled out to about 2cm/¾in thick and is baked in a rectangular oven tray. The result is a bread usually no thicker than 2–3cm/ 1–1½in.

THE RECIPE

Of the several different schiacciate I have tried, this is the one I like best. The recipe, which contains maize (polenta) flour, appears in the fascinating book *Italy in Small Bites* by the American food writer Carol Field. I adapted my previous recipe because I found that the added maize flour in Carol Field's recipe gives the schiacciata a sweet flavour and a gritty texture that is particularly appealing.

I use easy-blend yeast because I find it easier. It does not need dissolving and it mixes better.

SERVES 8 AS AN APPETIZER

60g/1oz [US ½ cup] walnut kernels

150g/5oz [US 1¼ cups] white flour, preferably Italian 00

60g/2oz coarse-ground maize (polenta) flour [US ½ cup coarse cornmeal]

1 tsp fine sea salt

1 tsp easy-blend dried yeast [US rapid-rise dry yeast]

2 tbsp extra virgin olive oil

½ tbsp chopped fresh rosemary (optional)

coarse sea salt

Heat the oven to 180°C/350°F/Gas Mark 4.

Spread the walnuts on a baking tray and, when the oven is hot, place them in the oven to toast for about 10 minutes. You will know when they are ready because of the lovely smell that will pervade your kitchen.

Put the walnuts on a chopping board and chop them very coarsely. I do not like to use a food processor for this recipe because the walnuts will either become ground, if you process for too long, or if you process for only a few seconds some kernels will be ground and others will be whole.

Mix the two flours, fine sea salt and yeast together on the working surface. Make a well and pour into it 1 tablespoon of the oil. Gradually add 150ml/5fl oz of lukewarm water while gathering the dry mixture from the inside walls of the well. When all the water has been added, begin to knead as usual for about 4 or 5 minutes. Knead in the chopped walnuts. (If you do not like kneading you can make the dough in a food processor, but transfer the dough to a working surface to knead in the walnuts quickly.)

Place the dough in a bowl that has been lightly greased with olive oil and cover with a damp linen towel. Put the bowl in a warm corner of the kitchen, out of any draught. Leave for about 1 hour.

Roll out or stretch the dough to fit a 30 × 25cm/ 12 × 10in baking tray. Cover again with the towel and leave to rise for another 50 minutes or so.

Turn on the oven to 200°C/400°F/Gas Mark 6 half an hour before baking.

Mix the remaining oil with 1 tablespoon of water. Just before you put the dough in the oven, moisten your fingers in the oil mixture and make dimples in the top of the dough. Sprinkle with the optional rosemary and some coarse sea salt and bake until golden, about 20 to 25 minutes.

Schiacciata is excellent hot or at room temperature. If you are eating it at room temperature, transfer it to a wire rack after baking.

SALVIATA Ⓥ

Sage Omelette

There are two traditional Tuscan omelettes, one with mint and the other with sage, both characteristic of the freshness and simplicity of Tuscan cooking.

To make the dish more complete you can present salviata as they do at the prestigious Enoteca Pinchiorri in Florence. The salviata is cut into thin strips and dressed with a fresh tomato sauce. This is, in fact, an old Roman dish called Uova in Trippa, which is traditionally made with a cheese omelette.

SERVES 4

6 size-3 free-range eggs [US large eggs]
1 tbsp flour
2 tbsp milk
1 tbsp chopped fresh sage
1 small garlic clove, very finely chopped
6 tbsp freshly grated Parmesan
½ tsp salt
freshly ground black pepper
2 tbsp olive oil

Lightly beat the eggs with a fork. Mix together the flour and the milk and then beat into the eggs. Add the sage, garlic, Parmesan, salt and pepper.

Heat the oil in a large non-stick frying pan – I use a 25cm/10in frying pan – and when hot pour in the egg mixture. Turn the heat down immediately and let the mixture cook very gently. When the omelette is nearly all set, but still shows a pool of uncooked eggs at the top, place it under a low grill [US broiler] until the top is set too.

Serve hot, warm or cold; it is equally good.

ZUPPA DI FARRO DELLA VECCHIA OSTERIA DI PONTE A BOZZONE Ⓥ

Emmer and Pulses Soup

Farro – emmer wheat – is the ancestor of present-day durum wheat. It was the food on which the Roman soldiers won their empire. I can see why they were such great conquerors: they fought hard so as to survive for their next dish of farro. At that time farro was mainly milled into flour – *farina* in Italian – and eaten mixed with water in a porridge-like mixture called *puls*, the predecessor of maize polenta.

The origins of emmer wheat are shrouded in mystery. Elizabeth David, in her book *English Bread and Yeast Cookery*, writes '. . . in the Mediterranean world wheat exported from Alexandria was much prized for the good bread it made. It is thought to have been this variety, later known to us as emmer wheat, which was the ancestor of our European grain.' However, emmer is a species of durum wheat, not of the soft wheat that is usually the one used in this country to make bread.

For centuries farro was the food of the poor Lucchesi and other Tuscans. But in the last 10 years it has become one of the foods of discerning gourmets, and zuppa di farro is now the most chic soup ever, served even at the three-Michelin-star restaurant, the Enoteca Pinchiorri in Florence.

Like the best olive oil, its natural companion, zuppa di farro originally comes from Lucchesia, and it is in that zone that the recipes abound. However, my recipe is from Siena. I had this soup for the first time some years ago when we were looking for good, and not too expensive, restaurants where we could take the pupils of our cookery school in Tuscany. One of our chosen restaurants was the Vecchia Osteria, just north of Siena, where Cinzia presides over the kitchen and Gianfranco looks after his impressive cellar. This *simpatico* couple is outstandingly knowledgeable, each in their own field. Cinzia knows all about the history and traditions of Tuscan cooking, which she follows carefully while adding light personal touches of her own. And here is Cinzia's recipe.

THE RECIPE

You can now buy farro in a few specialist Italian foodshops. However, if you cannot find it, whole wheat grain or pearl barley are good substitutes. If you use whole wheat grain you must soak it overnight; pearl barley does not need soaking. The soup is thick and of a consistency that fills your mouth with the earthy flavours of the pulses and the gluey sweet texture of the farro.

SERVES 6 TO 8

225g/8oz [US 1 cup] farro
150g/5oz [US scant 1 cup] dried cannellini beans
100g/3½oz [US ½ cup] dried chick-peas
1 dried chilli
4 garlic cloves
4 tbsp extra virgin olive oil
3 small fresh rosemary sprigs
300g/10oz [US 1½ cups] canned peeled tomatoes, chopped, with their juice
600ml/1pt [US 2½ cups] vegetable stock (page 231)
salt and freshly ground black pepper
extra virgin olive oil for the table

The evening before you want to cook the soup, put the farro, the beans and the chick-peas in 3 separate bowls. Cover with water and soak overnight. I usually add a flour paste, for which you will find the instructions on page 15, to the water for the chick-peas. The next day drain the lot and rinse under cold water.

Put the beans, chick-peas and farro in 3 saucepans and cover with cold water by no less than 5cm/2in. Bring slowly to the boil and simmer, covered, at the lowest heat, until very tender. The times can vary, but as a guide I can say that the chick-peas will take 2 to 2½ hours and the cannellini 1 to 1½, while the farro will cook quite quickly – in about 20 minutes. Whatever you do, please do not undercook them. The contemporary mania among smart restaurateurs to serve pulses that are like bullets is totally deplorable. Anyhow, for this recipe you must cook the pulses thoroughly, since you have to purée them later. Drain and keep the liquid.

Process the cannellini beans with half the chick-peas until smooth. If you want a more homogenized purée, without any bits of skin, you must pass the mixture through a food mill set with the small hole disc.

Chop the chilli and 2 of the garlic cloves; bruise the other 2 with the side of a broad-bladed knife. In your stockpot make a little *soffritto* (frying mixture) with the oil, the chopped and bruised garlic, rosemary and chilli and fry gently until the garlic begins to turn gold. Mix in the tomatoes and cook for 15 minutes. Fish out the bruised garlic cloves and discard them. Mix in the farro and the whole chick-peas and stir them around to *insaporire* (take up the flavour) for a couple of minutes. Add the purée of pulses and enough vegetable stock for the soup to be the right consistency. You will probably need about 300ml/10fl oz of the stock, but it depends on how much liquid was left in the pan after the pulses and the farro were cooked. Bring gently to the boil. Season with salt and pepper and then taste the soup and correct the seasoning. Fish out the rosemary sprigs. Cook for a further 15 minutes and then ladle the soup into individual bowls.

Pass around a bottle of your best extra virgin olive oil so that everyone can 'christen' the soup with it.

Pappa col Pomodoro Ⓥ

Bread and Tomato Soup

As its name implies, this soup is like a pap you give to babies. The taste, however, is worthy of the most discerning palate.

Like minestrone, or any other peasant soup, pappa col pomodoro can be made in countless different ways. But two ingredients that are always present are the best-quality extra virgin olive oil and good, properly baked bread. I use a Pugliese loaf, which you can buy in most supermarkets.

This is a soup to be made during the summer, when you can get really good tomatoes. ('Grown for their flavour', as they are so absurdly advertised in supermarkets. Whatever else does one grow tomatoes for?) If you cannot find good tomatoes, use best-quality Italian canned tomatoes.

You can now find good bouillon cubes on the market that contain no monosodium glutamate, or only a small amount which is neither dangerous to health nor predominant in the flavour.

SERVES 6 TO 8

150ml/5fl oz extra virgin olive oil
1 sweet onion, very finely chopped
3 garlic cloves, very finely chopped
1 small leek, very finely chopped
1–2 dried chillies, according to strength and taste, very finely chopped
salt
1kg/2¼lb fresh ripe tomatoes, or best-quality canned peeled tomatoes with their juice
500ml/16fl oz vegetable stock (page 231) or 2 vegetable bouillon cubes dissolved in the same amount of water
300g/10oz country-type bread, such as Pugliese, 2 or 3 days old
extra virgin olive oil for serving

Put the oil, onion, garlic, leek and chilli in a heavy stockpot. (I use my earthenware soup pot which goes directly on the heat because it is ideal for slow cooking.) Sprinkle with salt and sauté for 10 minutes over low heat, stirring very often.

Meanwhile, purée the tomatoes through a food mill set with the small hole disc.

Add the tomato purée to the *soffritto* (frying mixture). Let it come slowly to the boil and then add the stock. Bring the liquid back to the boil again.

Break the bread into small pieces, or slice it thinly, and throw it into the pot. Break it up with a fork and bring to a simmer. Cook very gently for about 1 hour, mixing occasionally. By the end of the cooking the soup should be quite thick, like a porridge. If it is too thick, add a little boiling water; if too thin let it boil on higher heat a little longer. Taste and check salt. Add pepper if you wish.

Ladle the soup into individual bowls and let it sit until it has cooled a little. This soup is also delicious served at room temperature. Whatever you choose, do not serve it either piping hot or chilled.

At the table hand around a bottle of your best olive oil for everyone to give the soup the necessary *battesimo* (christening) by dribbling a little oil into their soup.

LA RIBOLLITA Ⓥ

Tuscan Bean Soup

'Ribollita' means 'boiled again', and boiled again this soup should be since it is traditionally made the day before it's eaten. La Ribollita contains two of the most characteristic ingredients of Tuscan cooking: cannellini beans and *cavolo nero*. This is a kind of cabbage that has a less cabbagey flavour than a common cabbage and it is now available in a few specialized greengrocers. Spring greens are a good substitute.

This peasant soup is very thick, and it makes a good meal on its own. It can be served hot, warm or at room temperature.

SERVES 6 TO 8

225g/8oz [US 1¼ cups] dried cannellini beans
100ml/3½fl oz extra virgin olive oil
1 Spanish onion, sliced
1 or 2 dried chillies, seeded and chopped
2 ripe tomatoes, peeled, seeded and coarsely chopped
1 tbsp concentrated tomato paste
3 medium potatoes, cut into small cubes
2 medium carrots, cut into small cubes
1 small leek, both white and green part, cut into small pieces
3 celery stalks, cut into small pieces
350g/12oz greens, cut into thin strips
2 garlic cloves, sliced
3 or 4 fresh thyme sprigs
salt and freshly ground pepper

FOR COOKING THE BEANS

1 medium onion, cut into quarters

1 small celery stalk

fresh sage, rosemary and parsley sprigs

3 garlic cloves

salt

FOR THE REHEATING

1 or 2 Spanish onions

6–8 slices of country-type bread, such as Pugliese

2 garlic cloves, cut in half

Soak the beans overnight in cold water. The next day, drain and rinse them and put them in a heavy pot with all of the ingredients for cooking the beans. Cover with cold water by about 5cm/2in and bring slowly to the boil. Add 2 teaspoons of salt, cover the pan and cook very gently until the beans are well done, about 1½ to 2 hours. Lift all the beans out of the liquid and purée three-quarters of them into a bowl using a food mill with the large hole disc fitted. (If you do not have a food mill – a most valuable tool – you can purée the beans in a food processor, but you will get a very coarse purée with unpleasant bits of skin in it.) Leave the remaining beans whole. Transfer the cooking liquid to another bowl.

Put three-quarters of the oil, the onion and the chillies in the pot in which you cooked the beans. Sprinkle with a pinch of salt and sauté for 10 minutes or so. Add the tomatoes and the tomato paste, cook for 2 or 3 minutes and then mix in the bean purée. Let it take up the flavour for a couple of minutes while you stir it around, and then add all the other vegetables, the garlic and the thyme.

Measure the bean liquid and add enough water to make it up to about 1.5l/2½pt [US 1½qt]. Add to the pot and bring to the boil. Cook over the lowest heat for about 2 hours. Check seasoning and leave until the next day.

The next day, mix in the whole beans. Heat the oven to 180°C/350°F/Gas Mark 4. Slice very finely enough onion to make a nice thin layer all over the surface of the soup. Put the pot in the oven and cook until the onion is tender, about 1 hour.

Rub the bread with the garlic cloves, then toast under the grill [US broiler]. Put the bread into individual soup bowls and ladle the soup over it. Dribble the remaining oil over each bowl.

RISOLATA Ⓥ

Risotto with Cos Lettuce

The odd name of this recipe comes from the elision of two words, *riso* and *insalata* – rice and salad. But when you eat the dish there is nothing that would remind you of a salad. It is a soft risotto with a slightly bitter flavour – a soft, creamy dish that brings comfort and health.

I am quite sure this is a modern recipe, but I feel no qualms about including it because it is well within the traditions of Tuscan cooking. The dish is one of the delights of the restaurant La Baraonda in Florence. Duccio, its owner, is a real Florentine: quick, witty and extremely good at promoting his fare, which is certainly worth promoting. We used to take the students at our cookery school to eat there, and that was after thorough research into the best value for money.

THE RECIPE

You should use only the green outside leaves of a cos lettuce, which has a stronger flavour than any other.

You can add a little chopped parsley at the end, but I prefer it without.

SERVES 4 AS A MAIN COURSE, OR 5 TO 6 AS A FIRST COURSE

350g/12oz cos lettuce [US romaine], the green outside leaves only
2 shallots, very finely chopped
1 garlic clove, very finely chopped
1 tbsp very finely chopped celery leaves
2 tbsp extra virgin olive oil
40g/1½oz [US 3 tbsp] unsalted butter
salt and freshly ground black pepper
1½ tsp concentrated tomato paste
1.5l/2½pt [US 1½qt] vegetable stock (page 231)
350g/12oz [US 2 cups] Arborio rice
6 tbsp freshly grated Parmesan plus more Parmesan for the table

Wash the lettuce leaves and cut them across into 1cm/½in strips.

Choose a heavy-based saucepan that is large and deep; the rice in a risotto increases its volume by nearly three times. Heat the shallots, garlic, celery leaves, oil and half the butter in the pan, adding 2 pinches of salt to help the onion and garlic to cook without browning. Stir frequently, and after about 5 minutes mix in the tomato paste. Cook for 1 minute.

While the onion is cooking, bring the stock to simmering point. As with all risottos, the stock must be gently simmering all the time the rice is cooking because it must be boiling when added to the rice or the rice will cook unevenly.

Slide the rice into the pan with the vegetables and 'toast' it, as we say in Italy (meaning that the outside of the grain should be exposed to a lively heat) for a couple of minutes. Then throw the lettuce into the pan and sauté for 1 minute, stirring the whole time.

Now you must begin to add the simmering stock by the ladleful. Wait until one ladleful is absorbed before you add the next one. And add even less stock when the rice is nearly done, or there will be too much liquid in the pan when the rice is ready.

When the risotto is ready, remove from the heat. Check seasoning and add the remaining small bit of butter and the Parmesan. Put the lid on the saucepan and leave for a minute or two. This allows the butter and the Parmesan to melt. Now give the risotto a good stir and transfer it to a heated dish. Bring to the table, with more grated cheese on the side if you wish.

FAGIOLI ALL'UCCELLETTO Ⓥ

Cannellini Beans with Garlic, Sage and Oil

'Uccelletto' means little bird. But why this dish of beans is called all'uccelletto is anybody's guess. I, along with other cookery writers, think the dish has acquired its name because it is the traditional accompaniment to uccelletti, of which the Tuscans are inordinately fond. The writer Paolo Petroni suggests that the name probably derives from the fact that the dish contains sage, a herb always included in the cooking of birds.

Fagioli all'uccelletto are the accompaniment de rigueur to the arista. The beans are served warm, while the meat is usually served cold.

THE RECIPE

In Tuscany the dish is made with fresh cannellini, which are not available in Britain. I make it with dried beans.

There are two versions of the recipe, one with tomatoes and one without. I give you the option of either in the recipe below, since the method is fundamentally the same.

SERVES 4 AS AN ACCOMPANIMENT

225g/8oz [US 1¼ cups] dried cannellini beans, soaked overnight, or 700g/1½lb canned cannellini beans

a flavouring of garlic, rosemary, sage and onion, if using dried beans

3 tbsp extra virgin olive oil plus more for serving

1 beautiful fresh sage sprig

2 garlic cloves, bruised

3 fresh tomatoes, peeled and chopped, or 3 canned tomatoes, chopped (optional)

salt and freshly ground black pepper

If you are using dried cannellini, cook them with the usual flavouring of garlic, rosemary, sage and a piece of onion until tender; rinse and drain canned cannellini. Put the olive oil in a sauté pan with the sprig of fresh sage and bruised garlic cloves. Sauté until the sage begins to sizzle and the garlic aroma rises. At that point remove and discard the garlic. If you want your fagioli to be red, add the tomatoes. Stir for a minute or so, then add the beans and flavour them in the cooking juices. Pour in enough water or stock just to cover the bottom of the pan, about 4 to 6 tablespoons. Season with a little salt and a lot of pepper and cook until most of the liquid has been absorbed. Now you can remove and discard the sage, although I leave it because I like to eat it.

Transfer the beans to a dish or bowl and let them cool: they should be eaten just warm. Pour over a couple of tablespoons of extra virgin olive oil before serving – this is the touch that makes all the difference!

Zucchine in Umido o al Funghetto Ⓥ
Braised Courgettes

This is a recipe from a cookery book I discovered recently, and which has now become one of my favourites. It is *La Cucina di Casa Mia* by Zenone Benini, written in the 1950s. In Benini's recipes quantities are sometimes approximate, since he assumes that his readers are familiar with the basics of cooking. The style is chatty, not didactic, which I find much more appealing, and the book is full of useful suggestions. I give her a literal translation so as to convey the flavour of the original. The comments in square brackets are mine.

'I am not here to talk to you about boiled courgettes, because everyone knows how to do them. You put them in salted boiling water and they are cooked in 20 minutes. [Note the length of time needed to cook courgettes grown out-of-doors and not in greenhouses or in water as are most of the courgettes we buy these days. Besides, al dente vegetables are an altogether non-Italian concept.] They are usually served cold. Nor is there much to say about fried courgettes. They are cut into sticks, floured and fried in boiling oil, a few at a time.

'I'd like to linger a little on courgettes cooked in a sauté pan. They can be cooked in two ways, "al funghetto" and "in umido". To tell you the truth the difference between these two methods is not great. It consists of a modest addition of tomato at the beginning of the cooking of the courgettes in umido. Therefore, take 1kg (2lb) of medium size courgettes. Brush them, wash them and cut them in four lengthwise. Then cut them into pieces of about 2cm (¾in). Put them in a sauté pan with 6 tablespoons of olive oil [extra virgin] over moderate heat together with a small clove of fresh garlic and a sprig of ***nepitella*** (a kind of mint with small leaves and a more delicate flavour, popular in Tuscany and Rome). No water: they make enough themselves. Let them boil, covered, for 20 minutes or so, stirring every now and then.

'As I said before, to cook them in umido add, right at the beginning, a little fresh or canned tomato or concentrated tomato paste. And if you can't find nepitella, do without it and use a few leaves of mint, its close relation.'

When I make this recipe with 900g/2lb of courgettes [US zucchini], I add 300g/10oz of good fresh tomatoes, peeled, or, rather than not so good fresh tomatoes, the same quantity of canned peeled tomatoes without the juice. If you want to use concentrated tomato paste, 1 tablespoon is the right amount to be added, diluted with 120ml/4fl oz of hot water. This recipe is enough for 6 people.

CARCIOFI IN TEGAME Ⓥ

Artichokes Stewed in Milk

In Italy, artichokes are one of the most popular vegetables. From January to April there are mountains of different kinds of artichoke displayed in every street market, in every town. The thin and thorny Spinoso Sardo and the fatter Spinoso of Palermo are the first to appear, followed by the round and plump Romanesco, very reminiscent of the Bréton. The Violetto of Tuscany, with its beautiful mauvy shades appears shy and sombre in comparison with the acid green of the Precoce di Chioggia. None, however, is as pretty or as delicious as the small Castraura of the Venetian lagoon, which makes Easter in Venice an even more glorious occasion.

Artichokes were first grown in southern Italy, where they arrived from North Africa with the Arab name of *Al-kharsuff.* Once carciofi became established in Italy, they soon became known north of the Alps and won the approval of the French, who took to them and began to develop local species, of which the Bréton we buy in this country is the most popular.

But undoubtedly it is in Italian cooking that these beautiful sculptural vegetables find their best fulfilment. The recipes for artichokes are numerous. They can be stewed, stuffed or eaten raw. They can be fried and used to make delicious risotti or vegetable pies or timbales or stuffing for fish and chicken. In every recipe they are superb; very seldom are they just boiled, as they are in France and Britain.

Having said all that, I must mention the one snag, which is that they are difficult to prepare. In what follows I explain how to go about it.

HOW TO PREPARE ARTICHOKES

Buy fresh-looking artichokes without blemish or brown parts. If they have leaves these should be silvery-green and alive-looking.

Before you start, rub your hands with half a lemon to protect them from the artichoke juice, which would otherwise make them black. Cut off the artichokes at the base and rub the cut parts with the lemon. Hold the artichoke in one hand and with the other break off the tough outer leaves. It is hard to say how many layers of these tough leaves must be discarded, since it depends on the age and quality of the artichoke. Next snap off the green part of each leaf by bending it back with a sharp movement. This leaves the tender part attached to the bottom. Continue snapping off the tough tops until you get to the central cone of paler leaves.

With a very sharp knife cut off about 2.5cm/1in straight across the top of the cone. What is left is the edible part of the artichoke, without the stringy parts that will remain uneatable however long you cook them. Every time you cut this edible part, rub immediately with the lemon, and, finally, drop into a bowl of cold water to which you have added the juice of ½ lemon.

THE RECIPE

This recipe, the one used in my home in Milan, is actually from Tuscany, but carciofi in tegame are made all over northern Italy, every cook having his or her own recipe. My mother's contains milk instead of the more common water or vegetable stock. Artichokes cooked in this way are excellent by themselves or as an accompaniment to roast meat or roast or grilled fish.

If you have any carciofi left over, make a frittata di carciofi, one of the best frittate ever. See page 143 for the frittata recipe.

SERVES 6

10 globe artichokes
4 tbsp olive oil
4 tbsp chopped fresh flat-leaf parsley
½ garlic clove, finely chopped
2 tsp flour
salt and freshly ground black pepper
a cupful of milk

Prepare the artichokes as described above, removing all the tough leaves, which would be woody and uneatable however long you cook them.

Cut each artichoke into quarters lengthwise and remove the fuzzy chokes and the prickly purple leaves at the bottom. Put them back into the acidulated water until you are ready to cook them.

Heat the oil in a sauté pan. Drain and roughly dry the artichokes. Slide them into the pan and sauté nicely for 5 or 6 minutes. Add the parsley and garlic and cook for a further minute. Sprinkle with the flour and let it cook for a minute or so, stirring constantly.

Season with salt and pepper and then, when the artichokes begin to release their liquid, add a little of the milk – about 6 or 7 tablespoons. Cover the pan tightly and let the artichokes stew gently until tender. The cooking time varies a lot according to the kind and freshness of the artichokes. To test whether they are done, pierce the core with a fork, or taste an outside leaf. If they are not ready and there's no liquid in the pan, add a couple more tablespoons of milk. When tender, check salt and pepper before serving them.

Triglie alla Livornese

Red Mullet in a Piquant Tomato Sauce

Red mullet is one of the most highly prized Mediterranean fish. Unfortunately it has quite a few bones, and I expect this is one of the reasons why it is unpopular in this country. This may also explain why, oddly enough, it is always served filleted in restaurants. To do this is odd because, as any connoisseur knows, red mullet must be cooked whole so that the liver, which is the best part, remains in place. It is for this reason that red mullet is sometimes known as the woodcock of the sea. Besides, it is such an attractive fish that it seems a pity not to enjoy its full beauty on the plate.

Red mullet is always cooked very simply, with the minimum of flavourings, so as not to distract from the delicate taste of its meat. There are innumerable versions of triglie alla livornese. Some people flour the fish before frying it; others cook it straightaway in the tomato sauce. Onion is sometimes added to the *soffritto* (frying mixture); chilli is sometimes left out. Whatever you choose, use a very light hand when you add any flavouring.

SERVES 4

4 fresh red mullet, about 225g/8oz each
salt and freshly ground pepper
4 tbsp extra virgin olive oil
½ garlic clove, very finely chopped
3 tbsp chopped parsley
1 small celery stalk, preferably with its leaves, very finely chopped
1 dried chilli , very finely chopped
225g/8oz [US 1 cup] best-quality canned tomatoes, coarsely chopped

Whether or not you have cleaned them, wash and dry the red mullet. Sprinkle with salt and pepper inside and out.

Heat 2 tablespoons of the oil in a small frying pan with the garlic, half the parsley, the celery and chilli for about 2 minutes and then pour in the tomatoes. Cook for 10 minutes or so at a lively simmer to concentrate the flavour.

While the tomato sauce is cooking, heat the rest of the oil in a large frying pan in which the fish can fit in a single layer. When the oil is very hot, slide in the fish. Cook for 3 minutes and then turn them over very gently and cook for a further 2 minutes.

Spoon the tomato sauce over the fish, and cook the fish for a further 10 minutes. Taste and check seasoning.

Sprinkle the rest of the parsley over the top and serve at once. Triglie alla livornese are traditionally served in the pan in which they cook.

Polpi alla Versigliese

Stewed Octopus from Versiglia

I hesitated before including this excellent recipe. Octopus are not popular in Britain and not easily available. Yet we Italians love octopus and eat them a lot. So I decided that a serious book on Italian cooking should contain at least one octopus recipe.

I also hope to popularize this underrated, although unalluring, cephalopod. After all, squid – no prettier – were hardly known in Britain 10 years ago and now they appear on the shelves of most fishmongers and good supermarkets. Perhaps octopus will be next.

In northern Italy octopus are usually just boiled and eaten as an antipasto, dressed with a light extra virgin olive oil and lemon juice. This recipe from the coast north of Livorno is typical of the way the Tuscans of that area cook their fish: in oil flavoured with garlic, parsley and a soupçon of *zenzero* – dried chilli in Tuscan parlance, but ginger in proper Italian, something that always causes confusion.

THE RECIPE

Octopus are quite plentiful during the summer around the coasts of southern England, where they come after spending the winter in deep waters. Your fishmonger will clean the octopus, but he might not skin it or beat it. So when you get home you must remove the skin from the body and the thicker part of the tentacles, an easy job, and then beat it with a meat pounder to tenderize it. Some cooks swear that a cork placed in the pot with the octopus will make it tender. Frankly, I've tried cooking half an octopus with the cork and the other half without, and found no difference!

The best octopus are the *veraci*, which have two rows of suckers on each tentacle. Small octopus are better than large ones for this recipe.

Squid can be cooked in the same way; they are more tender than octopus, but to my mind less tasty.

SERVES 4

1.3kg/3lb octopus

a lovely bunch of fresh flat-leaf parsley

4 garlic cloves

1 or 2 dried chillies, according to strength and taste

100ml/3½fl oz extra virgin olive oil

salt

100ml/3½fl oz dry white wine

Beat the octopus (see above), skin it and wash it thoroughly, taking care to squeeze out the specks of dirt from the suckers. Cut the body into short strips and the tentacles into morsels.

If you have one, use an earthenware pot of the sort you can put straight on the heat, otherwise use a heavy flameproof casserole. Chop together the parsley, garlic and chilli and put them in the pot with the oil and 1 teaspoon of salt. Let this sizzle for a minute and then throw in the octopus. Cook for 5 minutes or so, turning the pieces over and over. Add the wine and bring to the boil.

Now turn down the heat so that the liquid is bubbling gently. Cook, uncovered, for about 30 minutes and then cover the pot and continue cooking until tender. The cooking can take from under 1 hour to 2 hours, depending on the size of the octopus.

At the end of the cooking, taste and adjust seasoning. If the liquid is a bit watery, turn the heat up and boil rapidly in the uncovered pot to reduce.

In the summer I prefer to serve this dish warm or even at room temperature, never hot.

Pollo alla Diavola

Grilled Devilled Chicken

Why this dish is called devilled chicken I cannot make out. Pellegrino Artusi, the great 19th-century writer, called it 'Pollo al Diavolo' and gave this amusing explanation. 'It is so called because it should be dressed with a lot of cayenne pepper and served with a very piquant sauce, so that whoever eats it, when his mouth is on fire, would like to send the chicken and the cook to hell.' Marcella Hazan is also of the opinion that it is so called because of 'the diabolical quantity of black pepper'. Whatever the name, the recipe is quick and easy, and the result excellent.

Here is the Tuscan version, which uses chilli instead of black pepper as in Rome.

I prefer to buy a poussin for this dish. Being small, they are easier to handle and they cook more quickly without becoming too dry.

SERVES 2

a fresh poussin [US squab chicken] of about 700g/1½lb

4 tbsp extra virgin olive oil

3 tbsp lemon juice

2 good pinches of chilli powder, or more according to strength

salt

2 garlic cloves, bruised

Ask your butcher to split the chicken open from the back and pound it flat. If you are doing this yourself, place the poussin on a work counter, breast-side down. Split it open along the back-bone with a large chopping knife or a cleaver. Crack the breast bone and open the chicken up flat, using the palm of your hands. Now pound the poussin as flat as you can, using a meat pounder.

Mix together with a fork the oil and 2 tablespoons of lemon juice to form an emulsion. Add the chilli powder and salt and mix again.

Lay the chicken on a dish, pour over the oil mixture and then add the garlic. Leave to marinate for about 2 hours. Turn the chicken over and baste it from time to time.

Preheat a cast-iron frying pan until very hot. Place the poussin in it, skin side down, and cook over high heat until brown, not just golden, pressing it down against the bottom of the pan with a fish slice. Now turn the bird over and brown the underside.

Choose a lid that is smaller then the pan so that it drops inside the pan and sits on the bird. Turn the heat down. Add the marinade, cover with the lid and place a weight on the lid. Cook for about 15 minutes. Turn the bird over and continue cooking, covered, until done, another 10 minutes or thereabouts. When the chicken is ready dribble over a few drops of fresh lemon juice and serve.

If you prefer to cook over charcoal, light the fire in good time and, once browned, turn the bird frequently until it is cooked, basting it with the marinade, or, if you have run out of marinade before the chicken is cooked, with a little extra virgin olive oil.

Coniglio in Dolceforte

Rabbit in Sweet-and-Sour Sauce

The cooking of food in a sweet-and-sour sauce is characteristic of Venice, Tuscany and Sicily. Each region tends to specialize in one type of ingredient. Venice offers recipes for various different fish in a sweet-and-sour sauce, while Sicily is more concerned with vegetables. In Tuscany it is meat – hare and wild boar, which are cooked most successfully in this way, and rabbit too. In the past it would have been a wild rabbit, but nowadays most rabbits eaten in Italy are domestic ones. I have come to the conclusion that these are the only rabbits worth cooking, and the same applies in this country. The wild ones are too unreliable: often too tough and sometimes with an unpleasant flavour.

Please, use good vinegar, remembering that cheap vinegar is made from ultra-cheap wine and the flavour of your dish will be affected.

This dish is even better made a day in advance. If you have some left over, remove all the meat from the bone and cut into small pieces, then use the sauce to dress some pappardelle or tagliatelle. But add a tablespoon of butter to the sauce before you reheat it. The pasta needs the sweetness of the butter. This sauce is particularly good with chestnut pasta, and you will find the basic proportions for that at the end of this recipe.

SERVES 4

a rabbit of about 1.3–1.5kg/3–3¼lb, cut into pieces
30g/1oz sultanas [US 3 tbsp golden raisins]
1 carrot
2 celery stalks
1 garlic clove
a handful of fresh flat-leaf parsley
1 tbsp fresh rosemary needles
60g/2oz prosciutto
5 tbsp olive oil
1 tbsp flour
salt and freshly ground black pepper
300ml/10fl oz meat or chicken stock (page 230)
120ml/4fl oz good red wine vinegar
20g/¾oz candied peel, cut into tiny pieces
30g/1oz bitter chocolate, broken into small pieces
30g/1oz [US ⅓ cup] pine nuts
1½ tbsp brown sugar, preferably Muscovado

Wash and dry the rabbit pieces.

Soak the sultanas in a cupful of hot water to plump them up.

Make a *battuto* (chopped mixture) with the carrot, celery, garlic, parsley, rosemary and prosciutto.

In a heavy flameproof casserole sauté the rabbit in the oil together with the battuto. Turn the rabbit pieces so that they brown well all over. After this sprinkle with the flour and with salt and pepper. Add the stock and cook, covered, for about 1 hour.

Meanwhile, prepare the *dolceforte*. Drain and dry the sultanas, and put them in a small saucepan with the vinegar, candied peel, chocolate, pine nuts and sugar. Cook gently, stirring constantly, until the chocolate and the sugar have melted, then pour the whole mixture over the rabbit. Turn the pieces over and over, and cook for a further 30 minutes or so, stirring and turning the pieces over occasionally.

Serve from the casserole, with polenta or with chestnut pasta.

For chestnut tagliatelle, you need 100g/3½oz [US scant 1 cup] chestnut flour, 125g/4oz [US 1 cup] Italian 00 flour and 2 size-2 eggs [US extra-large eggs]. Do not roll out this dough as thinly as you would a traditional pasta dough.

Fagiano alla Maremmana

Pheasant Stewed in Vinegar and Oil

Cooked this way, the pheasant has a fresh, lively flavour – a welcome change from the usual roast pheasant.

SERVES 3

a hen pheasant
150ml/5fl oz olive oil
4 tbsp white wine vinegar
salt
1 small onion
1 carrot
2 celery stalks
1 garlic clove, peeled
2 bay leaves
1 small fresh sage sprig
1 small fresh rosemary sprig
a handful of parsley, preferably flat-leaf
6 fresh basil leaves
4 or 5 fresh thyme sprigs
a pinch of ground cinnamon
4 juniper berries, bruised
6 black peppercorns, bruised

Skin the pheasant and remove the yellow fat. Cut the pheasant up into 6 pieces: 2 drumsticks, 2 thighs and 2 breasts. The pieces are small, which is what you want. Use the wings and the back to make a rich game stock, adding all the flavouring vegetables, spices and herbs that you like.

Mix together 4 tablespoons of the oil and 1 tablespoon of the vinegar. Add ½ teaspoon of salt and coat each piece of pheasant in this mixture. Put all the pieces in a bowl and pour over any left-over oil and vinegar mixture. Leave to marinate outside the fridge for 4 or 5 hours.

Cut the onion, carrot and celery into small pieces and throw them into a flameproof casserole with all the other ingredients in the list. Season with 1 teaspoon of salt. Bury the pheasant pieces in this mixture and pour over the remaining oil and vinegar, plus 5 tablespoons of water. Put the casserole on a low heat and cook for about 45 minutes, until the pheasant is done. Remove the pieces to a heated deep dish and keep warm.

For the sauce, pick out and discard the bay leaves and all the woody stems of the herbs. Pass the vegetables and the juices through a food mill set with the small disc. You are bound to throw away some of the vegetables after all the juices have been pressed through into the sauce. Return the sauce to the casserole. Thin the sauce to the desired consistency with some game stock (keep the rest of the stock for a soup). Taste and check seasoning. Heat the sauce, then spoon over the pheasant. You may prefer to coat the pheasant with a little of the sauce and serve the rest separately in a sauce-boat.

Il Lesso
Boiled Beef

'The food of the gods and of all true people.' This is how the Tuscan Zenone Benini describes this dish in his invaluable book *La Cucina di Casa Mia*. While bollito misto is traditionally one of the great meat dishes of Piedmont, Lombardy and Emilia-Romagna, lesso is more popular in Tuscany, although in my Milanese home, for instance, lesso was prepared more commonly than bollito misto. And this is for a very good reason: lesso is made with two or three cuts of beef rather than with the beef, veal, tongue, cotechino and chicken that go to make an ideal bollito misto. Lesso is, therefore, much more suitable for an average family, being either finished at one sitting or leaving enough left over for a meal of polpette or of 'lesso rifatto' – re-made lesso (see recipe following).

The suitable cuts for lesso are of beef, and the meat should be that of a young ox or a heifer. This might be a tall order for the modern cook who often buys meat cut and wrapped and ready at supermarkets (a habit of which I disapprove). You should see that the meat is not too fresh, i.e. the colour should not be bright red, but verging on a browny-red, and the fat, which should be there, should be the colour of butter and not white. The best cuts are brisket, silverside, chuck, shank and shin, all in one piece. I also put in some bones, but only a few or the broth, which I use for soups, will take on an unpleasant flavour.

In my home lesso was made every Monday for lunch, so that there was always some stock handy for the week. It was served with boiled vegetables, salsa verde and mostarda di Cremona. In Tuscany it is served with *peperonata* – peppers stewed in tomato sauce – stewed cannellini, vegetables under vinegar or oil, radishes and spinach, everything dressed in plain olive oil and that's all. Still, what more does one want?

MACARONI PIE IN A SWEET PASTRY CASE
(PAGE 155)

CLOCKWISE FROM LEFT:
FLAT BREAD WITH WALNUTS (PAGE 177);
CHEESE BREAD (PAGE 205)
CHICK-PEA FLOUR PANCAKE (PAGE 127)

BEAN AND BARLEY SOUP
(PAGE 115)

FLORENTINE ROAST PORK (PAGE 194),
SERVED ON STEWED SAVOY CABBAGE
(PAGE 98)

SLOW-ROASTED SQUABS
(PAGE 224)

SERVES 7 OR 8

1 large onion, stuck with 2 cloves
2 carrots
2 celery stalks
1.8kg/4lb different cuts of beef (see introduction)
2 ripe tomatoes
a few flat-leaf parsley stalks
6 peppercorns
2 bay leaves
salt

In your stockpot, or other large heavy pot, put the onion, carrots and celery. Add about 5l/9pt [US 5qt] of water and bring to the boil. Slowly immerse the meat in the boiling water and bring back to the boil. Adjust the heat so that the liquid is just simmering. Remove the scum that comes to the surface during the first few minutes.

Now add the tomatoes, parsley, peppercorns, bay leaves and salt. Cover the pan and continue cooking at the lowest simmer for at least 4 hours, although 5 would be better. The secret of a good lesso is very long cooking at the lowest possible simmer.

When the meat is tender – you should be able to cut lesso with a fork – slice it and arrange it on a dish. Do not slice more meat than you think will be eaten at one sitting. Keep the rest of the lesso in the stock and slice more if necessary.

LESSO RIFATTO ALLA SENESE
Left-over Boiled Beef

This is the best and simplest use of left-over lesso.

SERVES 4

450g/1lb left-over lesso
700g/1½lb sweet onions, very finely sliced
5 tbsp extra virgin olive oil
450g/1lb ripe tomatoes
½ dried chilli, crumbled
salt

Cut the meat into thick slices and set aside. Sauté the onions in the oil for about 10 minutes, then add the remaining ingredients and cook for 20 minutes or thereabouts.

Mix in the meat and let it slowly absorb the lovely flavour of the tomato sauce for 15 minutes. Turn the slices over gently every now and then.

BISTECCA ALLA FIORENTINA
Grilled Steak

The steak used in Florence for this famous dish comes from the Chiana breed of cattle, a breed that produces very tasty meat in ample quantities, even from an animal no more than 2 years old. Buy the best Scottish meat, and you will eat something similar to the original steak from Florence.

La Fiorentina is always cooked on a charcoal or wood fire.

SERVES 2 OR 3

a T-bone steak of about 600g/1¼lb, at least 2.5cm/1in thick

salt and freshly ground black pepper

olive oil or lemon juice

Season the steak with pepper on both sides, rubbing it into the meat.

Grill the steak over a charcoal or wood fire. When one side is done (the steak must be served rare), sprinkle the cooked side with salt, turn the steak over and grill the other side. Each side takes about 3 to 4 minutes to cook.

Some cooks dribble 1 tablespoon of extra virgin olive oil over the meat just before serving, while others prefer a light squeeze of lemon juice.

ARISTA ALLA FIORENTINA
Florentine Roast Pork

The origin of the name 'arista' has always been a matter of dispute. Does it relate to the comment made by one of the Byzantine patriarchs at the Ecumenical Council held in Florence in 1439? While he was tasting the meat he is supposed to have said '*Aristos!*', meaning 'the best' in Greek. A nice little story, but not true, since arista is referred to in a short story by Franco Sacchetti written before that, in the 14th century. Another possibility, as Paolo Petroni writes in *Il Libro della Vera Cucina Fiorentina*, is that *arista* does indeed come from the Greek: quite a few Greek merchants had lived in Florence since the 13th century and might have christened the Florentine roast they enjoyed eating.

But I have another theory. Arista is the Latin for the beard on an ear of corn, thus the word was also used to mean 'harvest'. Perhaps, then, this roast pork was the food served as part of a harvest feast. After all, arista is usually eaten cold in Tuscany, and it could easily be a July dish (harvest time in Italy), served with the fagioli all'uccelletto – stewed beans – which are just ready in July.

Whatever the origin of its name, I recommend arista heartily. Not only is it excellent, but it seems to be particularly well suited to a good English loin of pork.

THE RECIPE

Ask the butcher to remove the bones, keeping the loin bone in one piece. Ask him also to remove the rind. Bring the bone and the rind home.

SERVES 6

4 garlic cloves, finely sliced

the needles of 3 fresh rosemary sprigs, each about 10cm/4in long

salt and freshly ground black pepper

a 1.6kg/3½lb loin of pork (weight with bone)

2 cloves

3 tbsp olive oil

Chop together the garlic and the rosemary, add ½ tablespoon of salt and plenty of pepper, and mix well. Make small incisions in the pork and push a little of the mixture into the meat. Stick the meat with the cloves and rub with half the oil.

Pour the rest of the oil into a roasting tin. Place the bone in it and spread over half the remaining rosemary mixture. Now place the meat on the bone, spread the rest of the rosemary mixture over the meat and cover with the rind. Marinade for a few hours, preferably outside the fridge, unless the weather is very hot.

Heat the oven to 180°C/350°F/Gas Mark 4.

Place the tin in the oven and roast for about 2 hours, basting and turning the pork every 20 minutes or so. The meat is ready when it is quite tender. Lift the piece of rind and remove it. Turn the oven up to 220°C/425°F/Gas Mark 7 and brown the meat for about 10 minutes, then transfer to a wooden board.

Remove as much fat from the cooking liquid as you can. Add 4 tablespoons of hot water to the pan and boil briskly while loosening the delicious bits at the bottom of the tin.

Carve the meat into 1cm/½in slices, spoon over the cooking juices and serve.

You can serve the roast cold; it is equally succulent and delicious.

Buglione dell'Albergo Guastini

Lamb Stewed in Wine

Buglione is a very odd name. In his *La Cucina Maremmana*, Aldo Santini writes that it is an ancient word meaning *brodo* (stock), of the same etymology as bouillon. The name certainly describes the dish, a very liquid stew, which in the Maremma is served in a wide soup bowl and eaten with a spoon. However, it only appears there in a few restaurants, being the sort of dish that has gone out of fashion, partly because it is 'slow food'.

But I wave the flag for slow food. After all, you can prepare it all one or two days in advance. Besides, slow food is only slow in cooking, which it does by itself without you having to watch over it. It is the ideal food to serve for a group of friends, when you don't want to be banished to the kitchen to cook last-minute 'fast food'.

Buglione is made with red wine in Grosseto and in the northern Maremma, while in the southern part it is made with white wine. The reason is simple: the wine of southern Maremma is predominantly white, the best known being the Bianco di Pitigliano.

It is indeed Pitigliano that this recipe comes from. (If you want to know more about this beautiful town, turn to page 197.) There I met a charming young-looking grandmother, Signora Loreta Guastini, the owner of the hotel of the same name, which stands on the town bastion made of *tufo*, the local volcanic rock. After a perfect traditional lunch, starting with bread gnocchi dressed with wild boar, and finishing with a homely plum tart, Signora Loreta sat at our table and with great generosity gave me her recipe, which I now pass on to you.

THE RECIPE

I prefer to make buglione with lamb neck fillets, which become beautifully tender by the end of the cooking, as indeed the meat was in Pitigliano. There, however, the leg was used, but the lambs in Tuscany are killed when they are much younger.

SERVES 6

2 or 3 dried chillies, depending on size and strength
1.25–1.3kg/2¾–3lb lamb neck fillets
3 tbsp extra virgin olive oil
4 garlic cloves, peeled
salt
500ml/16fl oz dry white wine
2 garlic heads, unpeeled
1 tbsp chopped fresh rosemary
2 tbsp concentrated tomato paste

Put the chillies in a small bowl and cover with hot water. Leave them in the water until you need them.

Remove most of the fat from the lamb fillets and cut into smallish chunks.

Heat the oil with the peeled garlic cloves in a large sauté pan. When the garlic aroma rises, take out the cloves and discard them. Now brown the meat on all sides without crowding it or it will stew instead of browning. If your sauté pan is not large enough, fry the meat in two batches. When you see drops of blood seeping to the surface, the meat is ready to be seasoned with salt and covered with the wine.

Divide the garlic heads into cloves and remove only the outer layer of skin. Throw the unpeeled cloves into the pan together with the soaked chillies, which should be broken up into tiny pieces. Bring to the boil and simmer, covered, for half an hour.

After that mix in the rosemary and the concentrated tomato paste, turning the meat over. Continue cooking gently, with the lid still on, for a further hour. The meat should cook in plenty of liquid and still have quite a lot of juices at the end of the cooking, so you must pour in small additions of boiling water whenever necessary. It is impossible to state how much water to add, since it depends on the heat, the quality of the meat (nowadays meat often contains a lot of water that comes out during the cooking) and how well the lid fits on the pan. The meat should be very tender indeed. Don't forget to taste and check the seasoning before you bring the stew to the table.

If you are serving the buglione in the traditional way, place one or two slices of toasted bread in each bowl. Otherwise, serve buglione with polenta. The polenta should be freshly made, not grilled, so as to absorb the sauce better.

CASTAGNACCIO

Chestnut Flour Cake

An original speciality of Lucchesia, the province of which Lucca is the capital. Slices of castagnaccio are sold in bakers' shops and often eaten in the streets.

You can buy chestnut flour in the best Italian food shops. As chestnut flour does not keep long, it should be stored in the freezer and used within 6 months.

The original recipe does not contain sugar, but I find that the chestnut flour we can buy here does not have the same depth of flavour as the flour one can get in Tuscany. A little sugar brings out the flavour.

SERVES 6

75g/2½oz sultanas [US ½ cup golden raisins]
300g/10oz [US 2½ cups] chestnut flour
a pinch of salt
2 tbsp caster sugar [US granulated sugar]
3 tbsp extra virgin olive oil
40g/1½oz [US ½ cup] pine nuts
1 tbsp fresh rosemary needles

Soak the sultanas in warm water for 20 minutes, then drain them.

Heat the oven to 200°C/400°F/Gas Mark 6.

Sift the chestnut flour into a bowl. Add the salt and sugar and about 400ml/14fl oz of cold water to make a smooth soft batter. Add 2 tablespoons of the oil and the sultanas and stir well.

Grease a metal tin with oil. The tin, which traditionally should be rectangular, must be large enough to allow the mixture to spread to a thickness of about 2cm/¾in. Pour in the chestnut batter and sprinkle the top with the pine nuts and rosemary needles. Dribble the rest of the oil over and bake until the top is crisp and cracked and a lovely deep brown in colour, about 35 to 40 minutes.

SFRATTI

Honey and Walnut Sweets

It is difficult to describe sfratti in one word since they are neither sweets nor biscuits. They look like sticks and, in fact, they take their name from the stick used to evict (*sfrattare*) the *contadini* who could not pay their rent.

Sfratti are the best known of the dolci made by the Jews who used to live in the Tuscan Maremma. However, some food historians claim that sfratti precede the Jewish settlement and were a speciality of the Etruscans who first civilized this area. Whichever is the case, they have been around for a long time.

The principal place where sfratti are made is Pitigliano, a town in southern Tuscany which has all the characteristics of an Etruscan town. Pitigliano, sometimes called the little Jerusalem, became a Jewish settlement at the beginning of the 14th century, and remained a flourishing town with a strong and well-integrated Jewish population up to 1940, when Mussolini joined the Nazis in their persecution of the Jews.

Pitigliano is a beautiful town, built on a high ridge of *tufo* – the local volcanic rock – with a magnificent 16th-century aqueduct and an impressive castle. But these architectural splendours, however stunning, are quite common in Italy, and especially in Tuscany. What sets Pitigliano apart from other beautiful towns is its Jewish ghetto, a fascinating network of tiny dark alleys, through which, every now and then, comes a shaft of bright sunshine and a glimpse of the dramatic surrounding countryside. There is also a beautiful small synagogue, the inside of which unfortunately I have never been able to see. Edda Servi Machlin, in her fascinating book *The Classic Cuisine of the Italian Jews*, vividly describes the life of this small Jewish community, of which her father was the rabbi.

While wandering idly through this maze of alleys I was suddenly assailed by the delicious scent of freshly baked bread. Following my nose, I finished in a tiny shop, under an archway, where a delightful girl was behind the counter selling hot bread to her customers. Catia Franci showed me the specialities, but sadly 'No,' she did not know how the various breads were made, and mother and father weren't there. But her sweet face lit up when I asked about the sfratti. 'Ah,' she said triumphantly, 'I make those myself,' and she gave me the recipe. And here it is.

THE RECIPE
Make this dessert for Christmas when you are sure to find good fresh walnuts in the shops. I like to serve sfratti with a good dessert wine.

MAKES 3 SFRATTI, CUT INTO 36 SLICES

FOR THE PASTRY

250g/9oz [US 2 cups] Italian 00 flour
90g/3oz caster sugar [US ½ cup granulated sugar]
a pinch of salt
30g/1oz [US 2 tbsp] unsalted butter, just melted
6 tbsp dry white wine
½ tbsp brandy
5 drops of pure vanilla extract

FOR THE FILLING

250g/9oz [US ¾ cup] honey
250g/9oz [US 2 cups] walnut kernels, coarsely chopped
grated nutmeg
a pinch of ground cloves
¼ tsp ground cinnamon

Put the flour, sugar and salt on the work surface and mix lightly. Make a well in the centre and put in the butter and wine. Gradually mix with a fork, incorporating the flour around the well. Add the brandy and the vanilla and enough cold water (about 3 or 4 tablespoons) to form a ball of dough. (You can make the dough in a food processor.) Knead for a few minutes, then wrap the dough in cling film and refrigerate.

Now make the filling. Heat the honey in a 20cm/8in sauté or frying pan. Bring it to a vigorous boil and then boil fast for 3 minutes or until a jam thermometer registers 130°C/250°F – the soft ball stage. Now add all the other ingredients and cook for 5 minutes exactly. Place the pan in a sink of shallow cold water to cool the mixture. Stir it constantly or the mixture at the bottom of the pan will solidify while the top is still hot.

As soon as the mixture is cool enough to handle, divide it into 3 portions and make a 30cm/12in long sausage out of each portion. Now leave to cool completely.

Heat the oven to 190°C/375°F/ Gas Mark 5.

Take the pastry dough out of the fridge and divide this too into 3 portions. On a floured board, and with a floured rolling pin, roll out each piece of dough into a 10 × 33cm/4 × 13in strip. Place one of the sticks of filling over each strip of dough and roll the dough around it, without overlapping it too much. Pinch the ends tightly together and place on a well-floured baking tray, with the pastry seam down. Bake for 35 to 40 minutes, until golden. When cold cut each sfratto into about 12 slices.

To store, keep the sfratti whole, wrapped in foil, and cut just before you want to serve them.

Crostata di Marmellata

Jam Tart

Although *crostata* is the Italian for a tart, this crostata is in fact very different from an English tart. It is more like a compact and buttery sponge cake. The mixture contains a small amount of baking powder and a higher proportion of egg than would be used for pastry. When the crostata comes out of the oven it has jam on top in the middle, surrounded by a wide circle of puffy sponge.

This type of crostata is very popular in Tuscany, although it can also be found in Emilia Romagna and in Marche. It is served at the very end of a meal, always with a glass of Vinsanto or other dessert wine. It is definitely a country cake, often made to use up the home-made jam.

SERVES 8

75g/2½oz [US 5 tbsp] butter, at room temperature
150g/5oz caster sugar [US ¾ cup granulated sugar]
2 eggs
200g/7oz [US 1¾ cups] flour, preferably Italian 00
a pinch of salt
1 tsp baking powder
the grated rind of 1 unwaxed lemon
200g/7oz [US 1 heaped cup] plum or apricot jam

Heat the oven to 180°C/350°F/Gas Mark 4.

Beat the butter and sugar together in a bowl – use a fork first to start amalgamating them and then, if you have one, a hand-held electric mixer. When the butter and sugar have properly amalgamated, drop in the eggs one at a time and continue beating until the volume has increased.

Sift the flour, salt and baking powder together and gradually fold into the egg-butter mixture. Also mix in the lemon rind.

Butter a 22cm/9in tart tin and spoon the mixture into the tin. Spread it out, leaving a thicker edge of about 2.5cm/1in all around. Spoon the jam into the centre, leaving the edge clear. Bake for 35 to 45 minutes. Let the crostata cool in the tin, then gently unmould and transfer to a serving dish.

UMBRIA

If I had to choose one word to describe Umbria, it would be 'magical'. Magical in the hazy blue colour of its landscape, magical in its towns built on gnarled and jagged hills girded with silvery olive trees, magical in its romantic valleys, in its sunny aquamarine lakes and in its warm, welcoming people who produce magically good food out of the humble ingredients that grow there in abundance.

Umbria is a small region of central Italy, straddling the Appennines between Tuscany to the west, Marche to the east and Lazio to the south. Although it shares a lot with its neighbours, artistically, culturally and gastronomically, the distinctive Umbrian mark is always there.

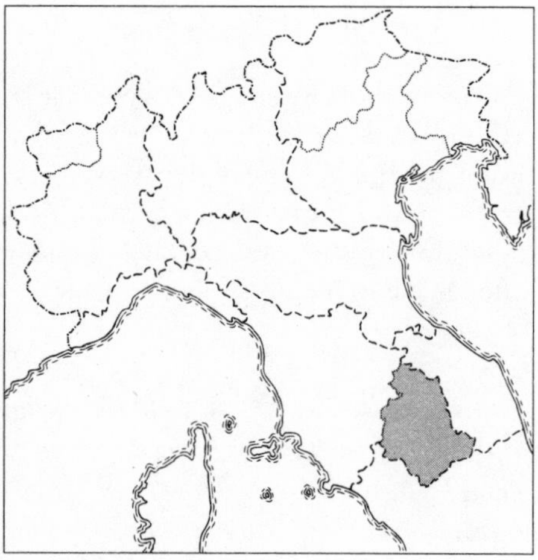

I drove into Umbria from Le Marche during June recently, crossing the Appennines at one of the range's highest points. I was heading for Todi in southern Umbria via Castelluccio, where I wanted to see the fields of lentils. I knew that Castelluccio lentils were among the best in the world, but what I was not prepared for was the magic of the plain on which they grow, the Piano Grande. It is a wide, flat expanse, chequered with pale greeny-blue fields of lentils, while all around the mountain tops rise up to enclose it. In the middle of the plain, perched on a little hill, sits the small town of Castelluccio. The fields of lentils were broken here and there by others, crowded with the red, blue and white of poppies, cornflowers and marguerites. For a while I forgot that I was there for the lentils as I walked among the myriad wild flowers.

I did justice to the lentils, however, at lunch time. They were cooked very simply, as in the recipe on page 206. I also had ricotta salata – salted ricotta – another speciality of Castelluccio, and a rich assortment of the local *salumi*, cured pork meats.

These salumi, in fact, would not be considered local in Italy, since they came from Norcia, which is all of 30 kilometres away. The pork butchers of Umbria, and in particular those of Norcia, are master salumi makers, so much so that a *norcino* is the butcher who, after the killing of the pig, is there in his important role of maker of all the many pork products. Among the best known of these salumi are *capocollo*, salame made with the upper part of the pig's neck (as its name implies) and flavoured with pepper and garlic; *finocchiella*, salame flavoured with wild fennel; and *coppa di testa*, a succulent kind of pig's brawn, [US head cheese], flavoured with orange and lemon peel (page 211).

Norcia is well worth a detour, and not only for the salumi. Leaving its handsome square behind me I went straight to the Salumeria Ansuini which, as I approached, proclaimed its speciality by means of three large stuffed boars' heads gazing at me soulfully from outside the shop. Once inside, one of the Ansuini brothers showed me all the different salami they make, from pig, from wild boar and from a mixture of the two. From wild boar they also make prosciutti. These are thinner than the usual prosciutti, dark red, strong and full of gamey flavour. In one of the windows a large wooden bowl was piled high with a rising spiral of small, fat sausages, all strung together in a long coil. And in between these mouthwatering specialities, stuffed baby boars looked mutely on in their striped fur coats, supervising their future!

As it was June I missed another of Norcia's famous products, the black truffle, *tuber melanosporum*, identical to the better known truffe de Périgord. The tartufo nero, unlike the Piedmontese white truffle, requires slight heating to express its pungent aroma and subtle richness. Its best use is in a sauce for spaghetti consisting of grated truffles and chopped anchovy fillets, or in a humble dish of scrambled eggs.

My voyage through Umbria eventually took me to my destination, a restaurant on Lake Corbara, near Todi, where I was going to eat and to talk to the owner, Gianfranco Vissani. I found Lake Corbara rather gloomy, but Vissani's food amply compensated for the lack of natural beauty. His restaurant is famous all over Italy, and people drive up from Rome, something like 1½ hours away, just to eat there. Vissani is a local man who has been able to bring the simplicity of Umbrian cooking to the level of *grande cucina*, 'grande' here denoting excellence rather than sophistication.

As an example, I had a dish of pasta dressed with a sauce of young white onions and marinated fresh anchovies. Perfection! The sauce has its origin, Vissani told me, in a local dish, a frittata made with young onions served with a sauce of marinated fresh anchovies. The original combination of ingredients was therefore still there, albeit in a different guise. The pasta was an egg pasta, which Vissani makes with only the yolks of the eggs, thus accentuating the egginess. Neither butter, nor cream, nor *fonds de cuisson* enter into Vissani's kitchen, yet his sauces, made with the best local oil and stock, are rich and full of flavours. These flavours usually include lemon rind and chilli, a traditional Umbrian combination that is also very popular in nearby Marche.

Another dish that Umbria shares with Marche is made with squabs (see recipe on page 224). These, locally called *palombacci*, are destined for the pot before they can fly, that is, when their cotton wool coat begins to turn into feathers. Vissani, following the old custom, does not clean his squabs. 'I starve them for two days before I put them on the spit, insides and all, and I tell you that the inside is my favourite bit.'

I had another great dish during that trip, in the town of Montefalco. It was a plate of tagliatelle dressed with field mushrooms and chilli, the mushrooms very finely chopped. The point of interest was that the tagliatelle were made with flour, egg and Sagrantino. This is a wine made only around Montefalco from local black grapes. Victor Hazan, in his excellent book *Italian Wine*, writes, 'A dark, strong red made near Perugia in the Montefalco appellation zone. The small black grape was originally thought to have been brought to Umbria by one of St Francis of Assisi's followers, but it is now believed to have existed all along. The grapes are partly shrivelled before crushing. . . It is high in alcohol and slightly bitter in taste.' It certainly gave an unexpected and undefinable flavour to the large tagliatelle, and cut perfectly into the heavy sweetness of the mushroom sauce.

In the true country tradition, Umbria excels in vegetable dishes. Vegetables are seldom served as an accompaniment to meat or fish; they are a dish in their own right, and Umbrian vegetables certainly deserve to be treated as such. The cardoons are exceptional – often prepared 'alla parmigiana', parboiled, fried and then layered with tomato and cheese – as are the tiny peas from Bettona. The tender broad beans are cooked with pancetta and Swiss chard in a dish called scafata (page 207), while the cheerful and patriotic la bandiera – flag – is so called because of the red of the tomato, the white of the onion and the green of the excellent local sweet peppers (page 208).

La bandiera is ideal as an accompaniment to porchetta, the most famous of all central Italian dishes. A lean young pig weighing about 40–50 kilos is boned and stuffed with wild fennel, garlic, salt and pepper. It is stuck through with a spit and traditionally cooked in the bread oven. A long-handled container called a *leccarda* is placed under it to collect the rich juices. The cooked porchetta, golden brown and glistening, is one of the most appetizing sights at village feasts or on market stalls. Juicy pieces of the meat, sandwiched between slices of thick country bread, make the perfect 'elevenses'.

Meats are cooked either in wood-fired ovens, on the spit or under the grill, the three oldest methods of cooking. Olive, myrtle, rosemary and other scented woods fuel the fire and impart a hint of their aroma to the meat through the ointment of the local oil. The green Umbrian oil is regarded as one of the best in Italy; it has the right balance of fats and a pronounced flavour, without being too pungent. In the old days fresh pork fat was used but nowadays, for health reasons, oil is the predominant cooking fat. This change produces a lighter touch in the finished dish, but a lack of that sensual porky flavour so necessary in some dishes.

In recent years I have had endless discussions with local people and chefs about the use of pork fat. It is mainly restaurateurs who prefer to use only oil. In homes I have found pork fat still in use, in moderation perhaps, but still there to give the desired touch to a dish of spaghetti, to a soup of rice and lentils, or to a coniglio in porchetta – rabbit cooked in the manner of a porchetta. This dish results from the locals' love for their porchetta, which is so great that they have created a version that can be made at home, using a small homely rabbit instead of a large festive pig.

In my rambles through Umbria so far I have rather neglected the beginning and the end of the meal. Umbria is rich in paste, pizze, savoury *torte*, minestre and polenta dishes. There are quite a few home-made paste peculiar to the region. These include *umbrici* or *ciriole*, thick spaghetti traditionally dressed with *sugo finto*, imitation meat sauce and pecorino; *fiocchetti*, bow-ties made with an egg dough flavoured with lemon rind and nutmeg and dressed with tomato sauce and Parmesan; and *stringozzi*, so called because they look like shoe laces (*stringhe*). They are dressed with an incredibly delicious wild asparagus sauce.

The pizze are not what is generally meant by that term. They are the predecessors of the Neapolitan pizza, which is of a more recent date. The original pizze, usually called pizze rustiche, are nothing more than pies. The dough can vary, being made with butter or oil or pork fat, with eggs or with water and no eggs, and sometimes with sugar. Yes, sugar in savoury pies, a relic of Renaissance cooking when sweet and savoury intermingled in very successful combinations. Some of these pizze are no more than savoury bread; sometimes they contain a rich filling of cheese and salumi. Tomato hardly ever appears in the pizza rustica – after all, tomato is a newcomer.

As in every country where the cooking is still fundamentally *casalinga* (homely) soups take an important place. There is a soup the name of which alone makes me want to eat it: blò blò. This name describes the noise the soup makes while gently boiling! It consists of very thin fettuccine made with an eggless dough cooked in a broth based on lard, fresh marjoram and garlic, reddened by home-made tomato passata.

At the end of my meal in Montefalco, at the charming Coccorone restaurant, I was served the traditional local finale, *torzetti* dipped in a glass of chilled Sagrantino. Torzetti are very hard almond biscuits [US cookies] which you have to dunk before you can take a bite. The resulting flavour in your mouth is that of very tipsy almond crumble. All Umbrian dolci are of this kind: homely and rustic, more like sweet breads than cakes. These breads are often studded with dried fruits and nuts, in the manner of the best-known spiced breads, the panforte of Siena and the *spongata* of Emilia-Romagna. Sweets of this type are the oldest in Italy. It is a testimony to the cultural traditions of Umbria that anything from the past survives more strongly there than in any other region.

There are also some biscuits made in the shape of shin bones. These are called *stinchetti* (*stinco* is the Italian for a shin bone) or *ossa di morto* – dead man's bones. They contain marzipan flavoured with cocoa. We, as children, found the idea of eating dead man's bones fascinating, a passion not shared by Paul Valéry, who wrote in his *L'Italie Confortable*: '*Cet horrible bonbon, qui a sa moëlle comme les ossements humains, rappelle, par sa forme et son nom, l'ancienne réputation de férocité des habitants, heureusement fort adoucie!*' Valéry clearly did not know the superstition which said that eating bone-shaped biscuits would strengthen one's bones.

Finally, mention must be made of the most famous Umbrian sweet, the *Bacio* – kiss. It was introduced in 1922 by Perugina, who still produce some of the country's best factory-made chocolates.

Although most people will find Umbria magical because of the works of Raphael and Pintoricchio, I hope I have demonstrated that there is something quite out of the ordinary in Umbrian cooking as it still is to this day.

PIZZA AL FORMAGGIO Ⓥ
Cheese Bread

'Pizza' means savoury bread. There are many different kinds of pizza, of which the Neapolitan is the only one known around the world. This pizza al formaggio predates the Neapolitan one by quite a few centuries.

In Umbria and in Marche this pizza is eaten at Easter with the new salame, which is just ready by then. I had it in Marche on an occasion when four beautiful pizze had the place of honour in the most magnificent display of antipasti I had seen in a long while.

Provolone is not easily available; if you cannot find it you can use a good farmhouse Cheddar instead.

SERVES 8 TO 10 AS AN ACCOMPANIMENT TO AN ANTIPASTO

30g/1oz fresh yeast

350g/12oz [US 3 cups] white flour, preferably Italian 00

2 size-2 eggs [US extra-large eggs]

45g/1½oz [US 6 tbsp] freshly grated Parmesan

45g/1½oz freshly grated pecorino [US 6 tbsp freshly grated romano]

2 tbsp extra virgin olive oil

1 tsp salt

freshly ground black pepper (optional)

60g/2oz provolone, cut into 1cm/½in cubes

40g/1½oz gruyère, cut into 1cm/½in cubes

Put the yeast in a bowl and add 3 tablespoons of warm water. Leave it for 10 minutes and then mix it until creamy.

Measure 100g/3½oz [US just under 1 cup] of the flour and place it in a mound on the work surface. Make a well, pour in the yeast and knead to make a ball of dough. Place the dough in a bowl, cover with a heavy linen towel and leave in a warm corner of the kitchen. In about 1 hour the dough will have doubled in size.

Break the eggs into a bowl and mix in the grated cheeses.

Put the remaining flour on the work surface, make a well and pour the oil into it. Add the salt, optional pepper and the risen dough ball. Knead to incorporate, while adding the egg and cheese mixture. Add enough warm water (about 3 to 4 tablespoons) until you can form a ball. The dough should be soft. Incorporate the little cubes of cheese. (You can use a food processor for all of this.) Now knead for about 10 minutes – if you can! Shape the dough into a neat ball.

Brush an 18cm/7in cake tin with olive oil and place the dough in it. Cover with the towel and leave for 2 hours in the warm.

Heat the oven to 200°C/400°F/Gas Mark 6. Bake the bread for 20 minutes, then turn the oven down to 180°C/350°F/Gas Mark 4 and bake for a further 20 minutes, until the bread sounds hollow when you tap it on the base. Place on a wire rack to cool a little before serving.

LENTICCHIE IN UMIDO COME A CASTELLUCCIO Ⓥ

Stewed Lentils

Castelluccio is a small town in Umbria, high up in the Appennines, built on a hilltop that rises out of the Piano Grande, a plateau equally famous for its lentils and its wild flowers. The view of the Piano Grande, when it comes into sight after turning the last hairpin, is breathtakingly beautiful. A wide expanse of brilliantly coloured wild flowers spreads out in front of you, and it is among these that the lentils grow in symbiosis. The lentil plant is small and its flower pale blue, as humble a plant as is its fruit.

Castelluccio lentils are very small, similar in size to the equally good Puy lentils, and, like those, they do not need soaking. They keep their shape while cooking and, unlike most other continental lentils, they do not have that unpleasant papery skin that sticks between your teeth. Unfortunately they are rather difficult to find.

THE RECIPE

This is my interpretation of a splendid dish of lentils I had for lunch at the Ristorante Sibilla in Castelluccio. If you cannot find Castelluccio lentils, I suggest you buy Puy lentils, which are similar.

Actually this is hardly a recipe. In all its simplicity it is utterly delicious, as long as you use top-quality lentils, good country bread and the best extra virgin olive oil from Umbria or Tuscany. It should be a rich fruity oil with a well-balanced peppery flavour and a full after-taste.

SERVES 4 AS A FIRST COURSE

400g/14oz [US 2 cups] lentils (or 100g/3½oz per person)

1 celery stalk, cut into pieces

4 garlic cloves plus halved cloves to rub the bread

salt and freshly ground black pepper

4 or 8 thick slices of good country-type bread

extra virgin olive oil, preferably Tuscan or Umbrian

Rinse the lentils under cold water carefully, picking out any pieces of grit or husk lurking among them. Put them in a saucepan. (I always use earthenware pots to cook my pulses, the type of earthenware you can place directly on the heat, because earthenware is the ideal material for slow cooking.) Add the celery, whole garlic cloves, 1 teaspoon of salt and a generous grinding of pepper. Add enough cold water to come level with the lentils and bring to the boil.

Cook, uncovered, over a very low heat until the lentils are tender. It is difficult to state exactly how long they take; you must taste them. But please let them cook until they are really tender. Forget the undercooked lentils served in some fashionable pseudo-Italian restaurants in this country. Add a little boiling water whenever the lentils are cooking without any liquid, but add it gradually and never drown the lentils. By the time the lentils are cooked there should be hardly any liquid in the pot.

Meanwhile, gently toast the slices of bread under the grill [US broiler] so that the outside becomes just crusty. Rub them with a cut clove or two of garlic and place them in soup bowls. Dribble ½ tablespoon of olive oil over the bread and then, when the lentils are lovely and tender, ladle them over the bread. Now you must perform the christening of the dish by pouring another tablespoon or so of oil in each bowl.

SCAFATA

Broad Beans and Swiss Chard Stewed in Tomato and Wine

While touring Umbria in search of good food, good recipes and kind people to probe, I went to see Alastair Little at his summer cooking school near Orvieto. The school is in a most beautiful spot even by the standards of that most beautiful part of Italy. The school is held in a farmhouse which is part of an *azienda agrituristica* – a farming plus tourism enterprise – owned by Avvocato Belcapo and his wife Clara, who cooks for the guests in her villa. Over a cup of coffee she very kindly gave me her recipe for this local broad bean dish.

THE RECIPE

I have tried this recipe with fresh broad beans and frozen ones. Of course, small fresh broad beans – which is how they should be – are better because their skin is tender. But if you cook large, or frozen, broad beans long enough, as in fact this recipe demands, you will find that the skin will soften and the final dish will be good.

SERVES 6

1.8kg/4lb fresh broad beans [US fava beans] or 700g/1½lb frozen broad beans [US fava or lima beans]
1 or 2 dried chillies, according to taste and strength
100g/3½oz unsmoked pancetta, cut into pieces
1 small carrot
1 onion
1 celery stalk
1 fresh rosemary sprig
2 tbsp extra virgin olive oil
150ml/5fl oz dry white wine
225g/8oz [US 1 cup] tomato passata
salt
450g/1lb Swiss chard

Pod the fresh broad beans or thaw the frozen ones.

If you have an earthenware dish that you can put directly on the heat, use this; otherwise use a heavy-based saucepan.

Put the chillies in a bowl and cover with hot water to soften.

Now make the *battuto* (chopped mixture) by hand or in the food processor, which I find makes a wonderful job when the battuto contains pancetta. Chop or process the pancetta, carrot, onion, celery, rosemary needles and drained chilli. If you do this by hand, chop to a very fine consistency.

Put the mixture in the pan with the oil and sauté gently for about 10 minutes. Throw in the broad beans, stir them around for a couple of minutes to take up the flavour of the *soffritto*, and then pour over the wine. Bring to the boil and boil for 5 minutes. Now add the passata and salt, keeping in mind that broad beans, like French beans, need more salt than other vegetables. Cover the pan and cook very gently for 1½ hours. Check the pan every 20 minutes or so and add a little boiling water if the dish gets too dry.

Wash the Swiss chard and remove the green leaves from the white stalks (keep the stalks for another dish such as the one on page 34). Cut the green leaves into 1cm/½in strips. Pack them into the pan and as soon as they have wilted turn them over and over to mingle with the broad beans. When the mixture is back to the boil, cover the pan again and cook for about half an hour longer, stirring occasionally and adding a little boiling water whenever necessary. Taste and check salt. Serve hot.

Scafata is a lovely vegetable dish in its own right, just as it is good as an accompaniment to a roast, or some grilled chops.

LA BANDIERA DI VERA Ⓥ
Roasted Vegetables

This bandiera (meaning flag) does not look like the traditional dish of the same name, because it is made with more vegetables. The original bandiera contains only green peppers, tomatoes and onion, thus combining the three colours of the Italian flag.

My Umbrian friend Vera Collingwood has given me the recipe for her bandiera, which I think is much nicer. It contains more vegetables, but the cooking and the presentation are similar to the traditional dish.

SERVES 3 TO 4

1–1½ red sweet peppers
200g/7oz aubergine [US eggplant]
150g/5oz courgettes [US zucchini]
200g/7oz large waxy potato
5 tbsp extra virgin olive oil
225g/8oz sweet onion, very finely sliced
225g/8oz [US 1 cup] tomato passata
salt and freshly ground pepper
1 tbsp chopped fresh mint
1 tbsp fresh rosemary needles
½ tbsp dried oregano
2 tbsp chopped fresh flat-leaf parsley
2 garlic cloves, finely sliced

First prepare the vegetables. Wash and dry the peppers and cut in half. Remove seeds, core and ribs, and cut into quarters. Wash and dry the aubergine and cut it in half. Cut each half lengthwise into thickish slices – about 5mm/¼in. Do the same with the courgettes and with the potato, peeled, of course. See that the slices are more or less the same size.

Heat the oven to 180°C/350°F/ Gas Mark 4.

Oil a rectangular oven dish, about 30 × 20cm/ 12 × 8in. Spread the onion over the bottom and drop on 2 or 3 blobs of passata. Season with salt and a generous grinding of freshly milled pepper, and add about 5 to 6 tablespoons of water. Place the pepper quarters down the length of the dish in a tidy overlapping strip. Do the same with all the other vegetables, so that at the end you have an attractive looking dish of four parallel strips of vegetables.

Sprinkle the mint over the courgette strip, the rosemary over the potato, the oregano over the peppers and the parsley over the aubergine. Season with the garlic, salt and pepper. Spoon the remaining passata here and there over the vegetables and drizzle with all the remaining oil.

Bake until the vegetables are soft, about 1½ hours, basting occasionally. You will find that the strange thing is that the courgette will take just as long to cook as the potatoes. Don't worry if the aubergine cooks first; it will be even nicer soft, and rich with the juices.

Serve hot, warm or even at room temperature – it is equally good.

IMPASTOIATA Ⓥ

Polenta and Cannellini Beans

The name of this dish is descriptive; *impastare* means to knead and impastoiata is a mixture similar to a dough. It is one of the more esoteric polenta dishes, since the dressing of stewed beans is added to the polenta while it is still cooking, for a final cooking all together. It is a lovely earthy dish, and very healthy too.

I derived this recipe from one of my favourite books, *Un Secolo di Cucina Umbra* (A Century of Umbrian Cooking) by Guglielma Corsi. In the original recipe the polenta is made with water, but I find stock gives more flavour to the dish.

SERVES 5 TO 6

2 tbsp olive oil
1 small onion, finely chopped
1 garlic clove, finely chopped
4 fresh sage leaves, chopped
the needles of a 10cm/4in fresh rosemary sprig
salt and freshly ground pepper
400g/14oz canned tomatoes, coarsely chopped, with their juice
1.5l/2½pt [US 1½qt] vegetable stock (page 231) or 2 vegetable bouillon cubes dissolved in the same amount of water
225g/8oz maize (polenta) flour [US 2 cups coarse cornmeal]
300g/10oz cooked or canned cannellini beans

First make the sauce. Put the oil, onion, garlic, sage, rosemary, 1 teaspoon of salt and plenty of pepper in a saucepan and cook for 10 minutes over low heat. Add the tomatoes and cook until the sauce has thickened and the oil comes to the surface, about 20 to 25 minutes.

While the sauce is cooking, make the polenta. Heat the vegetable stock. When it begins just to show bubbles at the side, add the maize flour in a very thin stream, while beating hard with a large balloon whisk or a wooden spoon. Cook, stirring constantly at the beginning, and then very frequently, for about half an hour.

Now throw the cannellini into the tomato sauce, mix well and let them cook for 10 minutes or so.

When the polenta has cooked for half an hour mix the cannellini stew into it and cook the whole thing together for a further 10 minutes. Taste and check seasoning, and then spoon this nourishing and tasty mixture into individual soup bowls. Pass around a bottle of your best extra virgin olive oil for everybody to drizzle a little over the impastoiata.

Il Coniglio della Zia Lidoria

Old-fashioned Rabbit (or Chicken) from Umbria

Zia Lidoria is a cousin of a great friend of mine. She lives near Orvieto in Umbria. I have never met the lady, but judging by some of the dishes of hers I have had at her cousin's house, she must be a great cook.

I have also made this recipe with chicken, maybe a less tasty meat than good rabbit, but just as suitable. I've discovered that the best rabbits here are French – expensive but as good as the Umbrian ones. Wild rabbits are too unreliable, sometimes perfectly all right, sometimes having an unpleasant wild flavour, and at other times so tough that no length of cooking can make them eatable. I shall always remember once in the country at a friend's house when the leg of a lovely bunny shot across the table as one of the guests tried in vain to cut into it.

SERVES 4

a domestic rabbit of about 1.6kg/3½lb, cut into small pieces
12 fresh sage leaves
3 garlic cloves
6 tbsp extra virgin olive oil
150ml/5fl oz white wine vinegar
salt and freshly ground pepper
60g/2oz [US ⅓ cup] capers
1 unwaxed lemon
4 canned anchovy fillets, drained, or 2 salted anchovies, rinsed and cleaned
½ tbsp potato flour

Wash and dry the rabbit pieces.

Make a little *battuto* (chopped mixture) with the sage and the garlic. Heat the oil in a large sauté pan, add the battuto and cook for 1 minute or so. Add as many of the rabbit pieces as will fit in a single layer and sauté them until dark golden and slightly caramelized. If your pan is not large enough, do this in two batches. This is a very important step in the recipe since you need the meat to be really deep golden to get that particular flavour out of it. When you have finished browning all the pieces, put them all back in the pan together. Pour over the vinegar mixed with the same quantity of boiling water. Season with salt and pepper and cook gently, with a lid on, for 40 minutes.

Test if the rabbit is done by pushing the point of a small knife into the thick part of the leg. The knife should penetrate easily. Take the rabbit pieces out of the pan, place them on the serving dish and keep warm, covered with foil. Taste the cooking juices and boil to reduce, if necessary, until rich and full of flavour.

Rinse and dry the capers. Wash the lemon and pare off a thin layer of rind from half the fruit. Chop finely the capers, anchovy fillets and lemon rind and put this mixture in a small bowl. Add the potato flour and dilute with 2 or 3 tablespoons of the rabbit juices. Beat well with a fork and then pour this mixture into the pan with the rabbit juices. Bring to the boil and cook for 1 minute. Spoon the sauce over the rabbit and serve with boiled new potatoes (skin removed) or potato purée to mop up the delicious juices.

Coppa di Testina di Maiale
Pig's Head Brawn

Although this recipe is not to everyone's taste, I decided to include it because it is very representative of the cooking of Umbria and Marche. This is an Umbrian recipe, although the Marche one would be very similar.

The brawn is full of the flavour of the herbs, spices and orange.

SERVES 8

half a pig's head
3 tbsp coarse salt
3 bay leaves
a few parsley stalks
1 onion, unpeeled, stuck with 2 cloves
1 large celery stalk
1 carrot
3 juniper berries, bruised
1cm/½in cinnamon stick
7 peppercorns
a generous grating of nutmeg
2 cloves
a small piece of dried chilli
½ tbsp fennel seeds
1 garlic clove
1 tsp sugar
4 tbsp red wine vinegar, preferably aceto balsamico
salt
the rind of 1 unwaxed orange and 1 unwaxed lemon, without any of the white pith
30g/1oz [US ⅓ cup] pine nuts
30g/1oz [US 3 tbsp] pistachio nuts, blanched and peeled

Ask the butcher to chop the half head into 2 or 3 chunks. Burn away all the hairs from the pig's head and scrape the rind thoroughly. Rub the coarse salt all over the pieces of meat and then put them in a bowl with 2 of the bay leaves and the parsley stalks. Leave for 24 hours.

Rinse the meat chunks, put them in a stockpot and cover with cold water. Bring to the boil and boil for 5 minutes. Drain and put the head back in the stockpot with the onion, celery, carrot, juniper berries and remaining bay leaf. Cover with cold water, bring to the boil and simmer steadily for about 4 to 4½ hours, until the meat comes away easily from the bones. Allow to cool a little.

As soon as you can touch the meat, remove all the meat pieces and set aside. Strain the liquid, reserve and cool. Remove the bones from the pieces of meat, cut the meat into bite-size pieces and transfer to a bowl.

Pound together in a mortar the cinnamon, peppercorns, nutmeg, cloves, chilli, fennel seeds, garlic and sugar, moistening the mixture with the vinegar. Stir into the meat pieces and add salt in generous quantity, remembering that when cold the flavourings will become much milder. Cut the orange and lemon rind into tiny pieces and add to the bowl together with the pine nuts and the pistachios. Add the reserved cooking liquid. Mix very thoroughly with your hands. Taste and adjust seasoning.

Lay a clean linen towel on the work surface and transfer the meat mixture on to it. Roll the meat up tight like a Swiss roll, with the help of the cloth. Tie both ends with string and put the meat roll on a wooden board. Place another board and a weight on it and leave until cold. When it is cold, put the coppa in the fridge to chill well.

To serve, unwrap the coppa and cut it into thin slices. Serve covered with a thin salsa verde (page 229), or simply with a little vinaigrette sauce.

MARCHE

Up to a few years ago Marche was an uncharted territory for me. Of course, I knew Urbino with its incredible ducal palace and its soft surrounding hills. I had been to Ancona, a sad city destroyed by the bombardments of the Second World War, and to the extraordinary sanctuary of Loreto, built by five of the greatest Renaissance architects around the Holy House of Mary, which had been miraculously transported there from Nazareth by a host of angels. But I did not know the fascination of Marche's hinterland, nor the warmth and hospitality of its inhabitants, nor indeed the pleasures of its cooking.

This new knowledge has come to me recently, since my daughter Julia and her husband bought Faveto No. 65. Why 65 is a mystery, since Faveto is a tiny hamlet of 10 or 12 houses, dotted around three different roads, in the southern province of Ascoli Piceno, judged by André Gide 'the most beautiful town in Italy'. Faveto sits in the foothills of the Appennines, which rise steeply to Monte Vettore, the most beautifully shaped mountain I know, especially when seen in the morning lit by the rising sun. The hills are gentle and green, and speak of all the food they provide. The older generation still works these fields that are divided between different crops and dotted with fruit trees. The pattern of their lives is set by ancestral rhythms which keep them sane and serene.

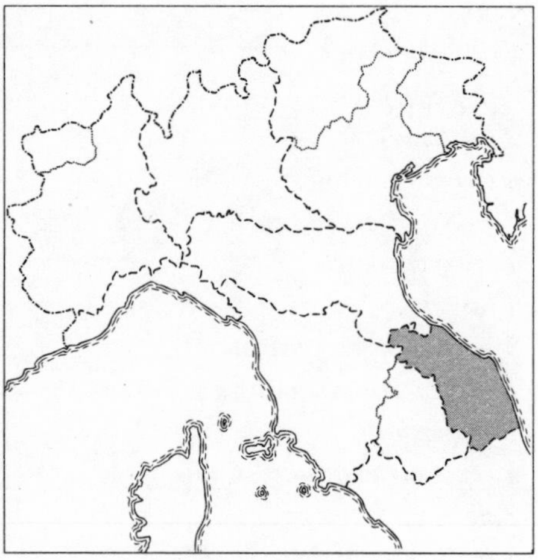

Last time I was there it was June. The cherries were ready and we spent hours dealing with them. Some were preserved under alcohol or wine, others went for jam. I was so overwhelmed by the quantity of cherries that I shared a lot with Magda, Matilda and Maud, Julia's three Livornese hens, and the six beautiful but nameless white ducks. Every day one of the neighbours arrived with a gift: a quarter of pecorino or a bowl of freshly made ricotta, a home-made salamino, half a pizza dolce (rich fruit cake), a young rabbit, a pot of *strutto* – melted pork fat for us to sauté the potatoes that were just beginning to be dug up. But best of all was the gift of *olive ascolane.* These are giant local green olives that are pitted and stuffed with minced veal and pork and then breadcrumbed and fried in oil.

Olive ascolane are the characteristic centrepiece of any antipasto all over the region, as I noticed when I went to the medieval town of Staffolo, near Ancona, in September 1994. That occasion was for me unforgettable, not only because

I was awarded the Verdicchio d'Oro prize, but also for the many excellent things that I managed to eat in two days. The banquet after the prize-giving ceremony took place at a restaurant called La Ciminiera, and I was assured by the many knowledgeable members of the Accademia Italiana della Cucina who surrounded me that the food was typical of the best Marchigiano cooking. In recounting what we ate I can give you a good idea of the cooking of Marche.

The alfresco lunch started with an immense spread of antipasti. The small pieces of fried food were breadcrumbed, as is traditional in the region, rather than the more usual coating in batter. The most interesting was the *crema fritta* – fried squares of crème pâtissière which are served as part of an antipasto. Their sweetness is a very pleasant and welcome contrast to the richness of the salame di Fabriano or the prosciutto di Carpegna, two outstanding local pork products. Sage leaves were gently fried, and they served as a palate cleanser. Three or four pizze al formaggio (page 205) were lined up as centrepieces instead of bread or focaccia. Pizza al formaggio is very different from Neapolitan pizza. It is a panettone-shaped bread of a feathery-light consistency, studded with morsels of mild young pecorino.

After two excellent *primi*, the *secondi* brought the climax of the meal, with a succulent porchetta and a coniglio in porchetta. That select group of people judged the coniglio in porchetta to be the best dish. It is rabbit cooked in the manner of a porchetta, the melt-in-the-mouth suckling pig that is the best known traditional dish of Tuscany, Umbria, Marche and Lazio. The rabbit in question was just as melting in the mouth, with that incredible sweet and yet assertive flavour of wild fennel.

It reminded me of the previous time I had eaten coniglio in porchetta at my daughter's house. The rabbit had been given, ready for the oven, by a much older Giulia, a Faveto neighbour, and I went to see how she prepared it. She had made two *battuti* (pounded mixtures); one was more like a paste with a good amount of *strutto* – fat from her last year's pig – mixed with lemon rind, lemon juice, garlic, wild fennel, rosemary, vinegar and *vincotto* – a kind of syrup made with new must from sweet grapes. The other battuto was a herb one, containing a stock cube (see page 16) which she pushed into small cuts in the thighs and placed in the inside of the rabbit, which was already thickly lined with home-made prosciutto. And what amazed me was the amount of salt she put in the battuto: 'it needs it, or the dish will be *sciocco*' (insipid). I was fascinated by the care and tenderness with which Giulia proceeded to pat the first battuto all over the rabbit's body. Not a single scrap of meat was left uncovered: pat, pat, pat in every nook and cranny. Then she put the rabbit in the roasting dish and gave it to me, just as she would have handed me her first-born baby.

It was a triumph, and we sucked every little bone, and scraped every little crust attached to the tin. It was so good that I forgot to keep a little for Giulia for her to taste the next day and have proof of her triumph. I have her recipe, but when I made it here it wasn't what I expected. The rabbit was not good, the lard was different, vincotto is not to be had here, nor is wild fennel. So rather than write a patched-up recipe, I prefer to leave it and just keep the memory of a coniglio in porchetta of supreme perfection. There are other recipes for rabbit in this book which can be made here without loss.

With its long coastline, Marche enjoys a rich harvest of fish, supplying 10 per cent of the national catch. The ports of San Benedetto del Tronto, Fano, Porto San Giorgio and Civitanova Marche are packed with fishing boats which disgorge on the quay grey mullet and hake, sole and turbot, squid and cuttlefish, anchovies and mackerel, prawns and mussels, red mullet and gurnard and even lobster. No *brodetto* (local fish shop) is worthy of its name unless it contains 13 different species of fish.

At Pedaso one day, before going to the beach, I discovered a large firm specializing in the purification of mussels. The mussels are 'planted' in the wild, not in farms, and are then purified by keeping them for 24 hours in tanks of sea water pumped from the sea 600 metres out from the coast. This sea water is highly oxygenated by ozone to achieve the right balance. The mussels are then packed into plastic bags marked with a 'sell-by' date set at five days after leaving the firm as well as the name of the technician responsible for the cleansing. A very impressive operation. But what surprised me most was that there was no fishy smell in the factory.

An even more interesting visit was the one I made to a buffalo farm near Faveto. The breeder, Francesco Tofoni, started his farm four years ago with 82 buffaloes imported from Battipaglia, the original buffalo breeding area in Campania. Tofoni has very cleverly increased the production by keeping some Marchigiane cows as well, for suckling the buffalo calves, thus keeping all the buffalo milk for delicious mozzarella made by the local dairy. The buffaloes, slim, active and inquisitive, with their large eyes half hidden by their centre-parted brown locks, don't seem to mind having to give up their new-born calves to placid white cows, who indeed looked better suited to their role of wet nurse.

I could go on writing about the food of Marche for ever, but my editor would cut it out! So I'd better round off this introduction with a mention of the dolci. The Marchigiani have a very sweet tooth, nearly as much so as the Sicilians. Ugo Bellesi, a local gastronome, writes that in the province of Pesaro alone some 70 recipes for different dolci have been discovered. The variations are slight, but they exist. There are two reasons for the abundance of Marchigiani sweets. Firstly, there – more than in most other regions – dolci are closely linked to the feast days of the calendar or celebrations of special occasions; and secondly because in Marche the dolci from northern Italy and those from the South are both present. Thus there are the bready and cakey dolci of the North and the dolci based on candied fruits and nuts of the South; and even the two mixed together, which call to mind similar dolci from Sardinia.

Another reason for the abundance of dolci could be that the sugar beet of Jesi has the reputation of being the best in Italy. As a sweetener it superseded honey earlier than in most other regions, although old recipes for dolci made with honey are still in use. These latter dolci often contain soft pecorino.

As with all other dishes, they are dolci made with the produce of the region, and this is one of the glories of Marchigiano cooking – a natural, traditional cooking still based on local produce. It has not been spoiled by tourism, either from the big cities or from abroad. No spaghetti bolognese or sauerkraut there, nor beer, but tons of sausages and gallons of Verdicchio.

FETTUCCINE COL SUGO ALL'ASCOLANA

Fettuccine with Sausage, Mushroom and Green Olive Sauce

In his dish from Ascoli Piceno, the sauce is used to dress home-made fettuccine. If you do not have the time or inclination to make your own pasta, buy some fresh tagliatelle from an Italian food shop or from a good supermarket, or a good-quality dried pasta (Spinosi and Cipriani are the best brands). The sauce combines sausage, mushrooms, green olives and lemon rind, a very popular local flavouring. The local olives, fat and meaty with their exciting and lively flavour, are a perfect foil to the sensuality of a rich pork sausage, while the whole dish is enlivened by the pleasing bitterness of the lemon rind. It is a superb sauce.

SERVES 4

home-made fettuccine (page 232) made with 3 eggs and 300g/10oz [US 2½ cups] Italian 00 flour, or 450g/1lb best fresh tagliatelle, or 300g/10oz dried egg tagliatelle

20g/¾oz dried porcini

225g/8oz coarse-grained pure pork sausage, Italian or French

1 tbsp olive oil

60g/2oz [US 4 tbsp] unsalted butter

90g/3oz cultivated brown mushrooms, thinly sliced

salt and freshly ground pepper

2 tbsp chopped parsley

1 tsp grated rind from an unwaxed lemon

1 garlic clove, very finely chopped

12–18 green olives, large and sweet, pitted and cut into strips

2 tbsp extra virgin olive oil

If you are making your own pasta, do this first. My instructions are on page 232.

Cover the porcini with boiling water and leave to soak for about an hour (see page 13). Drain, rinse under cold water and dry them. Chop them coarsely and set aside.

Cut the sausage into thin rounds and put in a frying pan with the oil. Fry for 10 minutes, stirring frequently.

Choose another frying pan large enough to hold the cooked pasta later. Heat the butter and add the mushrooms and the dried porcini. Sauté for 5 minutes over a lively heat. Season with salt and pepper and stir in the parsley, lemon rind and garlic. Cook for 1 to 2 minutes and then add the sausage. Turn the heat down and continue cooking for a further 5 minutes, stirring very frequently.

Add the olives and cook for 1 minute. Taste and check seasoning.

Meanwhile, cook the fettuccine in plenty of salted boiling water. Drain, but do not overdrain, and reserve a cupful of the pasta water. Turn the pasta into the large frying pan and pour over the extra virgin olive oil and a couple of tablespoons of the reserved pasta water. Cook for 1 minute while tossing constantly and lifting the strands up high so that they are all glistening. Serve immediately, preferably from the pan.

VINCISGRASSI

Lasagne with Ceps and Parma Ham

The name of this dish from Macerata is odd to an Italian, and I, together with many other cookery writers, had previously attributed its etymology to the name of the Austrian general, Windisch Graetz, who was stationed in Ancona in 1799, and in whose honour this dish was said to have been created. However romantically alluring that may sound, the facts point to something quite different. In Antonio Nebbia's book *Il Cuoco Maceratese*, published in 1784, a similar dish had already appeared, called Princisgrass.

THE RECIPE

I have made and written recipes for vincisgrassi, and been quite happy. But then I tasted Franco Taruschio's dish at his restaurant, The Walnut Tree, near Abergavenny in Wales, and it was even better. This is his recipe.

I would like to suggest just one alteration to Franco's recipe. The pasta for vincisgrassi should contain Vinsanto or dry Marsala. So substitute about 3 tablespoons of the wine for 1 egg. This makes a pasta with a more positive flavour to balance the taste of the porcini.

If you can't find fresh porcini, use the same quantity of cultivated mushrooms plus 30g/1oz dried porcini, which you must soak (see page 13).

SERVES 6

FOR THE PASTA

500g/1lb 2oz [US 4½ cups] Italian 00 flour or strong plain bread flour

2 whole eggs plus 4 egg yolks

1 tsp salt

FOR THE SAUCE

150g/5oz [US 10 tbsp] butter
60g/2oz [US 6 tbsp] flour
1.2l/2pt [US 5 cups] milk
400g/14oz fresh ceps, sliced
4 tbsp extra virgin olive oil
200g/7oz Parma ham, cut into julienne
200ml/7fl oz single cream [US light cream]
3 tbsp finely chopped parsley
salt and freshly ground black pepper
150g/5oz [US 1¼ cups] freshly grated Parmesan
truffle oil, or if possible a little shaved white truffle

Make a dough from the pasta ingredients (see page 232). Knead well and roll through a pasta machine as you would for lasagne. Cut the pasta lengths into 12.5cm/5in squares. Cook the squares in plenty of boiling salted water, a few at a time. Place on linen towels to drain.

For the sauce, melt 60g/2oz [US 4 tbsp] of the butter, add the flour and blend in well. Add the milk, which has been previously heated, a little at a time, beating well with a balloon whisk. Cook the porcini in the olive oil and add to the béchamel. Stir in the Parma ham. Add the cream and parsley, season and bring to the boil. Remove from the heat.

Heat the oven to 220°C/425°F/Gas Mark 7.

To assemble the vincisgrassi, butter a gratin dish and cover the bottom with a layer of pasta. Then spread over a layer of béchamel, dot with butter and sprinkle with some Parmesan cheese. Continue the process, making layer after layer, finishing with a béchamel layer and a sprinkling of Parmesan cheese. Bake for 20 minutes.

Serve with a little truffle oil splashed on top or, better still, with shavings of white truffle, and a little Parmesan cheese.

Finocchi e Gamberi in Salsa di Vino

Fennel and Prawns in a Winey Sauce

This is definitely not a traditional recipe. It is an excellent modern one that could come from anywhere up and down the coast of northern Italy. But since I had the inspiration from a similar dish I ate at the Ristorante Davide, in Porto San Giorgio, I have decided to place the dish in the Marche region.

SERVES 4

450g/1lb bulb fennel
200ml/7fl oz dry white wine
1 layer of onion
1 garlic clove
½ celery stalk
1 bay leaf
6 peppercorns
salt
350g/12oz raw king or tiger prawns in shell [US raw large shrimp]
4 tbsp sweet extra virgin olive oil, such as Ligurian

If necessary remove the bruised part of the fennel as well as the stalks and the fronds. Wash and dry the fronds and set aside for decoration. Cut the fennel lengthwise into quarters and then into thin segments, being careful that each segment is attached to the central core so that it will keep whole during the cooking. Wash them well and drain.

Pour the wine into a sauté pan. Add the fennel, onion, garlic, celery, bay leaf, peppercorns and 1 teaspoon of salt. Add enough water to cover the fennel. Bring to the boil and cook, uncovered, until the fennel is tender but still crunchy. Turn it over every so often during the cooking. Lift it out of the liquid with a slotted spoon into a deep serving dish.

Throw the prawns into the liquid and cook for 2 minutes. Fish them out, peel them and remove the black veins. Put about half a dozen of the best looking prawns in the fridge in a covered container. Cut the rest into 1cm/½in pieces. Mix these pieces into the fennel.

Now you must boil the cooking liquid over high heat to reduce it until its flavour is concentrated and rich. When you think it is just right, add a little more salt if needed. Pour this lovely juice and half the oil over the fennel and prawn mixture and toss lightly. When the dish is cold, cover with cling film and refrigerate.

About 2 hours before you want to sit at table, take the dish and the whole prawns out of the fridge. They must have time to come back to room temperature before you serve them.

The last thing to do is to scatter the whole prawns over the top. Pour the remaining oil all over the dish to give a lovely fresh sheen. Snip the fennel fronds with your kitchen scissors directly here and there over the dish.

I Piselli di Tarsilia

Drunken Peas

Tarsilia is one of my daughter's neighbours at Faveto, the remote hamlet in the foothills of the Marchigiane mountains where she has a house. The day after we arrived on our last visit we were, as always, immediately asked for lunch. I make a point of writing down all we eat in these people's houses, and one of these days I'm going to write a book on the subject which will contain every dish Tarsilia cooked for us. But here I can only include her 'drunken peas', which are an interesting alternative to the usual boiled peas with mint and butter. The colour won't be as pretty, but the flavour will be a hundred times more interesting.

Do use a good wine (a good Verdicchio di Jesi was what Tarsilia used) and, please, cook the peas properly and not al dente.

SERVES 4

1.3kg/3lb fresh young peas
4 tbsp extra virgin olive oil
100g/3½oz unsmoked pancetta, very finely chopped
1 tbsp chopped onion
salt and freshly ground black pepper
dry white wine

Pod the peas.

Heat the oil and the pancetta in a large sauté pan. Add the onion and sauté for 5 minutes or so, stirring frequently. When the onion is beginning to get soft throw in all the peas. Turn them over and over for a couple of minutes and season with salt and pepper.

Pour enough wine into the pan to come level with the peas. Cook, uncovered and over gentle heat, for 15 to 20 minutes, until the peas are tender, stirring occasionally. Vegetables cooked in this way take longer to be ready than if boiled or steamed. The wine will have partly evaporated and partly been absorbed by the peas. But if there is too much liquid in the pan once the peas are ready, transfer the peas to a heated bowl with a slotted spoon and boil the liquid rapidly to reduce. Pour the reduced liquid over the peas and serve. On the other hand, if the peas are not cooked when all the liquid has gone, add a couple of tablespoons of boiling water.

Cavolfiore Stracinato di Teresa Ⓥ

Stewed Cauliflower

Teresa Cesaritti is a charming lady who was my hostess in Jesi, near Ancona, when I was invited there to receive the Verdicchio d'Oro prize.

Teresa, in her warm and spontaneous manner, gave me this recipe: 'It is so simple and so delicious that I must pass it on to you.'

SERVES 4

a cauliflower head of about 600–700g/1¼–1½lb
5 tbsp extra virgin olive oil
2 garlic cloves, bruised
½ or 1 dried chilli, according to size and strength
3 tbsp chopped fresh flat-leaf parsley
salt
100ml/3½fl oz dry white wine

Remove the end stalk and the outside leaves of the cauliflower, leaving only the young and tender leaves surrounding the head itself. Divide the head into very small florets and cut the stalks and the tender leaves into neat small pieces. Wash and drain the lot.

Heat the oil with the garlic in a sauté pan. When the garlic begins to brown at the edge, fish it out and discard it. (If you like garlic flavour you can leave it in and search for it at the end of the cooking. To make this task easier, pierce the garlic cloves with a wooden toothpick. Alternatively, you can chop the garlic, add it and forget about it.) Add the chilli, 2 tablespoons of the parsley and the cauliflower florets and sauté gently for 5 minutes to *insaporire* – take up the flavour. Now add enough water to come about half-way up the cauliflower. Season with salt and bring to the boil. Half cover the pan and cook for 5 minutes or so.

Pour in the wine and cook until the cauliflower is tender. Taste a piece of thick stalk as these take longer to cook. It should be *tender*, not crunchy.

It is not possible to say how long a cauliflower takes to cook. If it is grown in the old-fashioned way it takes twice as long as a cauliflower grown with the hydroponic method, which also releases a lot of water during the cooking. The liquid should have nearly all evaporated. If there is still too much liquid when the cauliflower is ready, transfer the cauliflower to a bowl and boil to reduce the juices briskly until full of flavour.

Pour the juices over the cauliflower and sprinkle with the remaining parsley before serving. Check the salt before you remove the cauliflower from the pan.

Pesce Arrosto alla Marchigiana

Baked Fish with Herbs and Black Olives

When I was staying at my daughter's house in the foothills of the Appennines I realized that I was very close to Campofilone, a small town I knew of only because my favourite egg pasta, Spinosi, is made there. So I rang the Spinosi and they immediately asked me to lunch and to visit their pasta and ravioli factory, of which Sandro Spinosi is rightly very proud.

Campofilone is a pretty little town about 3 kilometres from the coast, 3 kilometres up rather than along, on a hill that dominates the surrounding countryside. Lunch at the Spinosi's was based on fish, as is quite usual near the sea. First course was a huge seafood salad, perfect in its simplicity – many different kinds of seafood dressed with excellent olive oil and lemon juice. The main course was a baked sea bass, another simple triumph, and here is Paola's recipe, which she told me she uses also for salmon.

THE RECIPE

You can use any large fish. On different occasions I have used codling (how sad that it is so difficult to find), hake and grey mullet, and they were all good. A sea bass, of course, would be better than a grey mullet or a codling. But the most important thing is that the fish should be fresh.

It was in Marche that I learnt to soak the dried chilli for certain dishes. The chilli becomes soft and easy to de-seed and chop; it also becomes just a little less hot.

SERVES 4

1 dried chilli

a fish of about 1.2kg/2½lb, head and tail on

a bunch of fresh flat-leaf parsley, leaves only

the needles of 2 fresh rosemary sprigs, each about 10cm/4in long

1 garlic clove

salt and freshly ground black pepper

1 unwaxed lemon

6 tbsp extra virgin olive oil

4 tbsp dried white breadcrumbs

1 dozen plain black olives

8 tbsp dry white wine

Soak the chilli for 10 minutes in hot water and then de-seed it.

Heat the oven to 200°C/400°F/ Gas Mark 6.

Wash the fish and wipe the cavity clean with kitchen paper towel. Dry the whole thing. Chop the herbs, garlic and chilli. Season with salt and put this mixture into the cavity of the fish. Stitch up the opening of the cavity with one or two wooden toothpicks.

Scrub the lemon under cold water and then dry it. Grate the rind from one half into a bowl. Squeeze the whole lemon and pour the juice into a small jug to bring to the table. Add half the oil, the breadcrumbs, salt and pepper to the lemon rind and mix well. Pat this mixture all over the body of the fish and then place the fish in a roasting tin together with the olives. Pour the rest of the oil, the wine and 4 tablespoons of water around the fish, but not over it or you will wash away the crumb mixture. Bake for about 20 minutes, basting two or three times with the cooking juices during the cooking. The fish is ready when the flesh near the backbone can easily be detached. To find out, just push a small knife into the thickest part of the body and peer down.

Now you can either transfer the fish carefully to a heated oval dish to bring to the table, or you can 'plate' the fish in the kitchen, which is easier as you don't risk breaking the fish in two when you transfer it. Spoon the delicious juices around the fish and place a few olives on each plate.

Put a bottle of your best olive oil on the table, as well as the little jug with the lemon juice. Someone may like to add a drizzle of one or the other, or even both.

POLLO IN POTACCHIO

Chicken with Tomato and Rosemary Sauce

Potacchio is the odd name of a sauce that is added to chicken or rabbit for a final cooking. It has the characteristic aroma of the cooking of Marche: garlic, chilli and lemon rind, joined here by abundant rosemary.

Do remember that rosemary, just like any other herb, is sweeter in the spring, with its new shoots, and it gets stronger later in the year. So use this knowledge and your discretion when you add the rosemary – or any other herb, for that matter.

SERVES 4 TO 6

a free-range chicken of about 1.5kg/3¼lb, cut into pieces
½ lemon
2 tbsp olive oil
60g/2oz [US 4 tbsp] unsalted butter
150ml/5fl oz dry white wine
1 onion, finely chopped
2 garlic cloves, finely chopped
salt and freshly ground pepper

FOR THE POTACCHIO SAUCE

1 small onion or 3 shallots
2 or 3 fresh rosemary sprigs, each 12cm/5in long
the rind of 1 unwaxed lemon
½ to 1 dried chilli, according to strength
3 tbsp extra virgin olive oil
450g/1lb fresh tomatoes, peeled and coarsely chopped, or 400g/14oz canned plum tomatoes, drained and coarsely chopped

Wash and dry the chicken pieces. Rub each piece with the half lemon. Heat the oil and the butter in a large sauté pan. When the butter foam begins to subside put in the chicken pieces and fry on all sides until they are nicely browned. Add the wine, bring to the boil and boil for 1 minute. Turn the heat down and throw in the onion and the garlic. Season with salt and pepper, then cover the pan and cook for 20 minutes.

While the chicken is cooking, prepare the sauce. Chop very finely together the onion or shallots, rosemary needles, the rind of the lemon and the chilli. Put the oil in a frying pan and when it is hot add the chopped ingredients. Sauté gently for 5 minutes or so and then add the tomatoes and a little salt. Cook over lively heat for about 15 minutes, stirring frequently.

Now that the potacchio is done, scoop it into the sauté pan with the chicken and mix it with all the lovely cooking juices at the bottom of the pan. Let the whole thing cook together for another quarter of an hour so that the chicken will *insaporire* – take the flavour of the sauce.

Test the chicken for doneness by pricking the thigh with the point of a small knife or a thin skewer. The juices that run out should be clear. Correct the seasoning before bringing the dish to the table.

PICCIONCINI DI MAFALDA

Slow-roasted Squabs

In Umbria, Tuscany and Marche, squabs are still raised with loving care just for the pleasure of eventually eating them. Mafalda is one of my daughter's septuagenarian neighbours in the remote and hilly countryside of Marche. Having abandoned their old house, Mafalda and her husband Beppe now live in their modernized upstairs flat, complete with plastic flowers, above the store-rooms where oil, wine, ham, pulses, salami, liqueurs and preserved vegetables are all, in their turn, stored away through the year, to last until the next supply is made.

It was June when we had squabs for lunch, so the store-rooms were fairly empty, although there was still plenty of oil and salame and, of course, wine, which is always plentiful. Wine, after all, is the only commodity that does not have to be finished within the year. The rest, as any good *massaia* (housewife) knows, must be used up before the new crop comes in.

We were asked to go round on the previous day to 'choose' the squabs. My Italian origins and my interest in food helped me to overcome the acquired British attitude of not wanting to connect the lovable living creature with the appetizing dish on my plate. I feel that either you become a vegetarian or you must be prepared to accept the link. The squabs, 10 in all, were chirping away in the cage. '*Guarda come son belli*,' Beppe said, '*bisogna proprio mangiarli*.' (Look how lovely they are, they are just ready for the pot – squabs must be eaten while still fledglings.) They were lovely indeed in their, by now, nearly full plumage of different tender browns, greys and whites. Mafalda touched, pinched, caressed, fondled all the birds in turn and then pointed out the chosen six to her husband.

Next day we arrived and, after the obligatory salami and tagliatelle, the piccioncini were brought to the table, surrounded by *patatine*, in a beautiful old copper *teglia* (roasting tin). This must have been one of the few of its kind to have escaped the Fascist net when every bit of copper had to be given to the State to try to counteract the consequences of the sanctions imposed on Italy at the time of the Abyssinian war.

The squabs were just magical. My dish, when I made it here in London was, inevitably, not quite up to the same standard. After all, I don't rear squabs in my back garden, nor grow olives to press in my local *frantoio* in Barnes.

THE RECIPE

Squabs are milk-fed domestic pigeons, ready for the pot before they begin to fly. They have a gamey flavour and a darkish skin, but they are very tender, unlike pigeon, of which I find only the breast is edible. Until recently they were imported from France, but now there are some squabs reared in Britain which are equally good, and cheaper. They can be bought, or ordered, from the best butchers.

This recipe can also be used for poussins. In either case you will need one bird per person, but remember that poussins take less time to cook. If you have time, prepare the stuffing a few hours in advance so the flavours can mix and blend.

The squabs are cooked slowly and for what you might think is too long. The timing is correct. 'They must be cooked for a long time', Mafalda explains, 'and not . . . *bom, bam, bin in due minuti come é di moda adesso*' (and not in 2 minutes as is the fashion these days).

SERVES 4

4 squabs
salt and freshly ground black pepper
2 tbsp olive oil
4 tbsp extra virgin olive oil
the juice of 1 lemon
2 tbsp good red wine vinegar

FOR THE STUFFING

125g/4oz fatty prosciutto, very finely chopped
150g/5oz minced pork [US ground pork]
6 tbsp freshly grated Parmesan
2 tbsp chopped fresh flat-leaf parsley
the grated rind of 1 unwaxed lemon
1 tbsp chopped fresh rosemary
2 garlic cloves, very finely chopped
½ tsp salt
2 pinches of freshly ground black pepper
2 eggs, size 3

To prepare the stuffing, put the prosciutto and minced meat in a bowl and add all the other ingredients except the eggs. Mix very well – hands are the best tool – and then drop in one egg. Mix the egg in, which will take some time to incorporate. Do the same with the second egg. Once the mixture is perfectly well blended, but not before, cover the bowl with cling film and refrigerate until you need it.

Squabs often have livers and hearts left in the cavity. Take these out, chop them and mix into the stuffing. Wash the birds and dry them thoroughly.

Heat the oven to 180°C/350°F/ Gas Mark 4.

Divide the stuffing roughly into 4 portions and stuff a portion into each cavity. 'A bird should never be over-stuffed or it will burst, and the stuffing will appear too uniform when the bird is carved.' These are the instructions given by Baron von Rumohr in his invaluable book *The Essence of Cookery*, first published in 1822. Sew up the opening or stitch with two wooden toothpicks. Rub salt and pepper all over the birds.

Now you must brown the birds in the hot olive oil. I use a cast-iron frying pan and turn them over to brown on all sides.

Transfer the birds to a roasting tin and pour the extra virgin olive oil into it. Add enough hot water just to cover the bottom of the tin and then roast for 15 minutes.

Take the tin out of the oven and pour half the lemon juice over the squabs. Turn the birds on to their breasts, return the tin to the oven and roast for 15 minutes. Pour over the vinegar. After a further 15 minutes of roasting, add the remaining lemon juice. Now turn the birds on to their backs and let them cook for at least a further 45 minutes to 1 hour, basting them every 15 minutes or so. Squabs must, as this recipe demands, be cooked slowly and at length.

Place a squab on each heated plate, surrounded by the cooking juices.

If you want to serve some potatoes with the birds, parboil them in their skins for 10–15 minutes. Then peel and cut them into cubes and put them around the squabs for the last 30 to 40 minutes. Be gentle when you turn the potatoes over or they might break. Use a waxy, rather than a starchy, variety of potato.

Costolettine di Agnello con le Olive Nere

Lamb Cutlets with Black Olives

The culinary imprint of Marche consists of lemon rind, chilli and garlic. This mixture goes into many dishes, especially in southern Marche which is affected by its proximity to the southern cooking of Abruzzi, where chilli and garlic reign supreme.

The olives must be plain, not dressed with other superfluous ingredients. I always buy olives with the stone still in, for the simple reason that they are better.

SERVES 4

12 best end lamb cutlets [US lamb rib chops]
6 tbsp extra virgin olive oil
3 garlic cloves, thickly sliced
1–2 dried chillies
the grated rind of 1 unwaxed lemon
1 tsp dried oregano
salt
2 tbsp lemon juice
about 15 large black olives, or 20 small ones, pitted and sliced

Remove all fat from around the cutlets and flatten them down gently. Place them in a large dish. Pour over 4 tablespoons of the oil and add the garlic, chillies, lemon rind and oregano. Season with salt on both sides and leave to marinate for about 1 hour. Do *not* refrigerate. Meat to be cooked must be at room temperature.

Heat a very large frying pan – or two pans – until hot. Add the remaining oil. If you are using two pans you must add an extra ½ tablespoon of oil. When the oil is hot, add the cutlets and cook them for about 2 minutes on one side, shaking the pan occasionally so that they do not stick. Turn them over and cook for 1 minute. Now scoop in all the bits of the marinade from the dish, and add the lemon juice and the olives.

Cook for about 5 minutes for rare cutlets, or a little longer if you prefer lamb well cooked. The timing also depends on the thickness of the cutlets. A sign to look for is when blood rises to the surface of the meat; this means that the meat is no longer bloody inside.

While the cutlets are cooking, add a couple of tablespoons of hot water, so that the meat cooks in a little liquid. When you think the lamb is done the way you like it, transfer to a serving dish and keep warm.

Remove and discard the chillies. If the cooking juices are too syrupy and thick add a little hot water and boil, stirring, for a minute. Taste and adjust seasoning, then spoon the juices around the lamb.

CIAMBELLINE MARCHIGIANE
Little Ring Biscuits

You see trays of ciambelline in almost every baker's shop in Marche. They can be flavoured with fennel seeds, with orange rind or with pine nuts; the recipe is the same. The recipe I give here is for ciambelline with pine nuts, which are the more difficult to make. For the other two versions you simply add the crushed fennel seeds or the grated orange rind to the egg mixture.

The preliminary blanching of the biscuits, or cookies, helps keep them soft inside, while it hardens the outside during the baking, as with American bagels.

MAKES ABOUT 60

600g/1¼lb [US 5 cups] flour, preferably Italian 00
salt
3 size-2 eggs [US extra-large eggs]
180g/6oz caster sugar [US 1 cup granulated sugar]
the grated rind of 1 large unwaxed lemon
a pinch of ground cinnamon
100g/3½oz [US 7 tbsp] unsalted butter
6 tbsp milk
butter for the trays
30g/1oz [US ⅓ cup] pine nuts

Sift the flour with 2 pinches of salt on to your work surface and make a well.

Whisk 2 of the eggs and the white of the third one with the sugar until the mixture thickens. This will take quite a time unless you have a hand-held electric mixer. Add the lemon rind and the cinnamon.

Now melt the butter over very low heat. Just melt it; do not let it sizzle. Pour gradually into the well of flour. Keep pouring, alternately, the egg mixture and butter, while with the other hand you begin to incorporate the flour from the inside wall of the well. When you have poured in all the butter, heat nearly all the milk in the same small saucepan and pour this into the flour too. When the egg mixture, butter and milk have all been incorporated into the flour, knead the dough for 5 minutes or so, until lovely and smooth. Wrap the ball of dough in cling film and chill for half an hour to harden, so that it becomes easier to shape.

Pinch some dough off the ball – about the size of a walnut – and roll it out with floured hands into a little sausage, about 7.5cm/3in long and 1cm/½in across. Bend the little sausage around to form a ring and seal the two ends very thoroughly. Continue taking dough from the ball and making rings until you have used all the dough.

While you are shaping the biscuits, bring some water to the boil in a large sauté pan. When it is boiling gently lower just enough little rings in to cover the bottom of the pan, where they will sink. After about 3 minutes of simmering they will begin to float to the surface. Lift them out of the water with a slotted spoon and place them on kitchen paper towel to dry well. Blanch all the rings in this way, and dry them.

Heat the oven to 190°C/375°F/Gas Mark 5.

Place the rings on well-buttered baking trays. Lightly beat the remaining egg yolk with the little milk you left aside. With a small pastry brush, glaze the little rings all over. Place 5 or 6 pine nuts on each ring and press them in gently to prevent them falling off. Now the rings are ready to be baked in the preheated oven for about 20 minutes, until golden.

Cool on a wire rack and then store in an airtight tin.

Rustic and simple they may be, but ciambelline are very good.

Basics

Sugo di Pomodoro
Tomato Sauce

I use good fresh tomatoes when they are in season. When they are not I prefer to use good canned tomatoes rather than out-of-season fresh tomatoes, which do not taste like tomatoes and have an unpleasantly thick and woolly pulp. Unless the tomatoes are really good I like to add 1 teaspoon of concentrated tomato paste to give depth to the sauce. I should point out that northern Italian tomato sauces have a richer flavour compared with the freshness beloved by the Southerners.

MAKES ABOUT 600ML/1PT [US 2½ CUPS]

2 tbsp extra virgin olive oil
30g/1oz [US 2 tbsp] unsalted butter
150g/5oz Spanish onion, sliced
1 celery stalk, cut into pieces
1 carrot, cut into pieces
1 garlic clove, peeled
1 tsp concentrated tomato paste
a handful of fresh flat-leaf parsley
6 fresh basil leaves
200g/2lb fresh ripe tomatoes, cut into quarters, or canned plum tomatoes with their juices
salt and freshly ground pepper

Heat the oil and the butter in a saucepan. Add the onion, celery, carrot and garlic and sauté for 10 minutes. Mix in the concentrated tomato paste, if you are using it, and cook for 1 minute, stirring constantly. Then add the herbs, the tomatoes, salt and pepper and cook at a moderate heat for 30 minutes.

Pass the sauce through a food mill or a sieve. If you want to use a food processor you must first peel the fresh tomatoes and squeeze out some of the seeds.

Salsa Besciamella
Béchamel Sauce

Béchamel is not an Italian sauce and it did not appear in Italian recipes as such until the 19th century. It came from France, where it was allegedly created in the seventeenth century by Louis de Béchamel, steward to Louis XIV. However, a similar sauce, based on such everyday ingredients as milk, butter and flour, must have already existed both in France and northern Italy. After all, béchamel is the ideal partner to home-made pasta and it is inconceivable that the creative Emiliani would not have 'discovered' this combination earlier.

Béchamel is an easy sauce to make. Its density can vary according to its use. I prefer to make a thin sauce when I use the béchamel in combination with pasta and a thicker sauce whenever I use it as a binder. The sauce here is a medium thickness.

I like to flavour my béchamel differently according to the dish in which it is used. If it is for a pasta dish I add some grated nutmeg, or I infuse one or two garlic cloves or a layer of onion in the milk. If the béchamel is to be added to fish or meat I like the milk to be flavoured with a bay leaf and maybe with a light grating of nutmeg too.

MAKES ABOUT 450ML/15FL OZ

600ml/1pt [US 2½ cups] milk
60g/2oz [US 4 tbsp] unsalted butter
45g/1½oz [US ¼ cup] flour, preferably Italian 00
salt

Heat the milk until it just begins to bubble at the edge.

Meanwhile, melt the butter in a heavy-based saucepan over low heat. Blend in the flour, stirring vigorously. Remove the pan from the heat and add the hot milk, a few tablespoons at a time.

You must let the flour mixture absorb each addition thoroughly before adding more.

When all the milk has been absorbed and the sauce is lovely and smooth, return the pan to the heat. Add salt to taste and bring to the boil. Cook over the gentlest heat for at least 10 minutes, stirring frequently. I use a flame diffuser, or else I put the saucepan in a larger saucepan containing 5cm/2in or so of simmering water, so that I do not need to stir the whole time.

This lengthy cooking is not really necessary, but it does give the sauce a more delicate flavour.

SALSA VERDE

Green Sauce

In Lombardy and Piedmont this is the traditional accompaniment to bollito misto, lesso (page 192) and boiled calf's head; it is also used on hard-boiled eggs. The oil should be a sweet oil from Liguria or Lake Garda, not a *fruttato* (peppery one).

MAKES 150ML/5FL OZ

15g/½oz [US ⅓ cup] fresh white breadcrumbs
1 tbsp red wine vinegar
1 garlic clove
about 15g/½oz fresh flat-leaf parsley
2 tbsp capers
½ dozen cornichons (very small gherkins – if unobtainable use 1 extra tbsp capers)
1 hard-boiled egg, shelled
4 anchovy fillets, or 2 salted anchovies, boned and rinsed
2 tsp Dijon mustard
120ml/4fl oz extra virgin olive oil
salt and freshly ground black pepper

Put the breadcrumbs in a bowl and pour the vinegar over them. Set aside.

Peel the garlic clove, cut it in half and remove the hard central core, if necessary. This is the part that has a pungent flavour instead of a sweet flavour.

Squeeze out excess vinegar from the bread and put in a food processor. Add all the other ingredients except the oil, salt and pepper. Process while you add the oil slowly through the funnel. Stop often to scoop the mixture down from the sides of the bowl. At the end add salt and pepper to taste.

BRODO DI CARNE
Italian Meat Stock

Il brodo is typical of Italian cooking, delicate yet full of well balanced and harmonizing flavours, flavours that would never be too assertive. For this reason, none of the ingredients is ever sautéed in butter or oil beforehand.

A good stock depends entirely on the quality of the ingredients. 'A stock that is made with garbage will taste of garbage,' wrote Alice Waters of Chez Panisse fame. The classic brodo di carne is made with three different kinds of meat: veal, beef and chicken – never lamb or pork, which make too strong a stock. Meat must be present as well as bones, to give the stock the right flavour. Too many bones and the stock will have an unpleasant sweetish flavour. The same applies to chicken carcasses. If possible use half, or a quarter, of a boiling chicken, which a good butcher will have or will get for you.

I prefer to add a minimum of salt and then season the stock at the end. This is to avoid producing a stock that is too salty after the reduction.

MAKES 1.5–2L/2½–3½PT [US 1½–2QT]

1.5kg/3¼lb assorted meat, in large pieces
1 onion, cut in half and stuck with 3 cloves
1 or 2 carrots, cut into pieces
2 celery stalks, cut into pieces
1 leek, cut into pieces
a handful of mushroom peelings or stalks
½ dozen parsley stalks
1 bay leaf
2 garlic cloves, unpeeled
1 ripe tomato, cut into quarters
1 tsp salt

Put all the ingredients in a stockpot. Add about 3l/5pt [US 3qt] of cold water, or enough to cover, and bring to the boil. The water must be cold to start with, so that the meat and the vegetables can slowly release their juices. Set the lid very slightly askew so that the steam can escape. Turn the heat down to the minimum for the stock to simmer. The best stock is made from liquid that cooks at a temperature of 80°C/175°F, rather than 100°C/220°F, the boiling point. Using a slotted spoon, or – better still – a skimmer, skim off the scum that comes to the surface during the first quarter of an hour of cooking. Cook for about 3 hours.

Strain the stock through a large strainer lined with muslin or cheesecloth into a large bowl. Leave to cool and then put in the refrigerator.

Remove the fat that will have solidified on the surface. At the end of the operation, when it is hard to remove a few specks of fat, heat the stock a little, then lay a piece of kitchen paper towel on the top of the stock and drag it gently across the surface. Most of the fat 'eyes' will stick to the paper.

Taste and, if you think it is a bit too mild, reduce over high heat, remembering, however, that the stock may taste mild because it contains a minimal amount of salt. Cover with cling film and keep in the fridge for up to 3 days or in the freezer for up to 3 months.

If you want to use the stock for sauces, boil to reduce over high heat until the flavour is very concentrated. Cool, then pour it into ice-cube trays and freeze. When the stock is frozen, unmould the cubes and place them in 2 or 3 plastic bags. Seal tightly and place back in the freezer. These cubes are very handy to use for stewing vegetables, for sauces etc. – whenever only a little stock is needed.

BRODO DI PESCE

Fish Stock

MAKES ABOUT 1.25L/2PT [US 5 CUPS]

1.3kg/3lb heads and bones of white fish, such as turbot, brill, sole, haddock etc.
1 large onion
1 carrot
1 celery stalk
3 or 4 parsley stalks
a handful of bulb fennel tops, if available
2 tomatoes
3 garlic cloves, peeled
1 dozen peppercorns
1 tsp salt
2 bay leaves
300ml/10fl oz dry white wine

If still there, cut off and discard the gills in the heads of the fish, as they would give the stock a bitter taste. Wash the heads and bones and put them in a stockpot. Cut the vegetables into chunks and add them to the pot together with all the other ingredients except the wine. Add 2l/3½pt [US 2qt] of water. Bring to the boil and simmer for 15 minutes, then add the wine and simmer for another 15 minutes.

Strain the stock through a large fine sieve into a clean saucepan. Now you must boil to reduce this stock by about half, over high heat.

BRODO VEGETALE

Vegetable Stock

A good vegetable stock is just as useful a standby in the kitchen as a meat stock. It can be used for many vegetable risottos, for stewing vegetables and for adding to soups and sauces.

MAKES ABOUT 1.5L/2½PT [US 1½QT]

3 celery stalks
4 carrots
2 leeks, both white and green part
2 tomatoes
1 courgette [US zucchini] (optional)
a bunch of greens, such as beet spinach or lettuce leaves but not spring [US collard] greens (optional)
1 onion, stuck with 1 clove
2 garlic cloves, peeled
a large bunch of parsley, leaves and stalks
2 bay leaves
6 peppercorns
1 tsp salt

Cut the vegetables into pieces. Put them in a stockpot with the herbs and the peppercorns. Cover with 2.5l/4¼pt [US 2½qt] cold water, add the salt and bring to the boil. Simmer gently for about 2 hours. Strain and leave to cool, then refrigerate in a covered container.

Stock keeps in the refrigerator for about 3 days, after which it must be brought back to the boil and boiled for at least 5 minutes. Or it can be frozen.

If you want a stronger flavoured stock, boil to reduce the stock over high heat until the flavour is more concentrated. This stronger stock is best for adding in small quantities to vegetable stews or sauces. Pour the stock into ice-cube trays and freeze. One cube is equal to about 1 tablespoon.

Home-made Pasta

This is the recipe for home-made pasta as it is made in Emilia. In other regions an egg is often replaced by water or, as in the case of vincisgrassi (page 217), by Vinsanto. The mixture in this recipe makes a good pasta with a delicate flavour and a nice bite. I make pasta with an old-fashioned hand-cranked machine, which is cheap, noiseless and easy to work. It makes very good pasta and it is easy to use and to clean.

I recommend the use of Italian grade 00 flour for making pasta because it absorbs the eggs more evenly, is easier to knead and roll out and, above all, makes pasta with a more fragrant flavour and a more delicate texture. You can buy 00 flour in most Italian food shops and good supermarkets.

MAKES ABOUT 350G/12OZ PASTA, ENOUGH FOR 4 PEOPLE AS A FIRST COURSE OR 3 AS A MAIN COURSE

2 size-2 free-range eggs [US extra-large eggs]

approximately 225g/8oz [US 2 cups] Italian 00 flour or stone-ground plain flour

semolina for dusting

Put most of the flour on the work-top and make a well in the centre; place the rest of the flour to one side. Break the eggs into the well. Beat them lightly with a fork, drawing the flour in gradually from the inner wall of the well. Now use your hands to mix and then knead for 5 minutes or so. The dough should be elastic and soft, but not moist. If necessary add more flour. Wrap in cling film and leave to rest for at least half an hour. This resting is very important because it allows the gluten in the flour to relax.

Knead the dough for 1 or 2 minutes, then divide it into 4 equal portions. Take one piece of dough and re-wrap the other pieces in cling film.

Set the rollers of the pasta machine to the widest opening. Flatten the piece of dough slightly, so that it is nearly as wide as the rollers. Run it through the machine 5 or 6 times, folding the sheet over and giving it a 180° turn each time. Now run the sheet, unfolded and without turning it, through all the settings, closing the rollers one notch at a time, until you achieve the desired thickness. You may have to dust the dough with flour every now and then. Pasta made in the hand-cranked machine needs more flour than that made by hand.

For tonnarelli (like spaghetti but square in section) stop the rolling out at the second from last setting. For tagliatelle, fettuccine or pappardelle stop at the last but one. For lasagne, ravioli or cannelloni stop at the last setting.

When you make long pasta you must allow the pasta sheets to dry until no longer damp, but not yet leathery, before you cut them, or the strands will stick together. For stuffed pasta, lasagne and cannelloni proceed immediately to the next operation.

Sprinkle semolina in between strands or sheets of fresh pasta to prevent sticking.

If you are making pasta without the help of a machine, you must knead the dough for much longer – no less than 5 minutes. Give it a rest, well wrapped in cling film, and then proceed to roll out. If you do not possess a long Italian rolling pin, divide the dough into 4 portions and work on one at a time, keeping the rest well wrapped. Roll out the piece of dough as thin as you can, especially if you are making lasagne or ravioli.

Polenta

The first people to make polenta with maize flour are said to have been the Friulani, although I am sure that many people who started to grow maize after it first arrived from the New World must have tried using its flour in the way they had always used buckwheat, chick-pea or other kinds of flour. The advantage of maize was that it grew in areas where no other crop would easily grow, so it was soon intensively cultivated in the marshlands and elsewhere in northern Italy. Thus polenta soon became a staple, taking its place alongside rice, which grew further south in the Po valley.

The polenta of Friuli and Veneto is softer than that of Lombardy or Trentino. There it is made not only with a smaller proportion of water to flour, but also with a finer maize flour. In Veneto it is often made with a kind of white maize, *polentina bianca*, which makes a deliciously delicate polenta.

Polenta is traditionally made in a *paiolo*, a large bucket-shaped pan made of unlined copper, which conducts the heat very rapidly all over the surface. The tool used for stirring is a long wooden stick-like implement, a *bastone*. Failing these, use a large, deep saucepan and stir with a long wooden spoon so that the polenta can boil fast without danger to your hand.

The making of polenta is a task taken very seriously by polenta devotees. I sometimes prefer to cut a few corners, depending on how my polenta is going to be used. However, the corner I refuse to cut is that involving the use of pre-cooked polenta flour, which I find is not good enough. But when I am short of time, or especially when I am making polenta for grilling or for a baked dish, I make polenta either in a pressure cooker or in the oven (see recipes below).

When I cook polenta in the traditional way I follow the instructions given to me by a friend who is a seriously good cook, Rosanna Lockhart. She has devised a method for making a very light polenta, which she finds much preferred in this country. And I totally agree with her. My English husband never really liked plain polenta, until I learnt Rosanna's method. The only drawback to this method is that it needs constant presence and a strong wrist because instead of a spoon you use a balloon whisk.

I use a good brand of polenta flour, like Spadoni polenta bramata, which is available in good supermarkets and in most Italian food shops.

THESE QUANTITIES MAKE ENOUGH POLENTA FOR ABOUT 6 PEOPLE

ROSANNA'S POLENTA

Bring to the simmer – not the boil – 1.8l/3pt [US 7½ cups] of water. Add 2 teaspoons of salt and then add 250g/9oz of maize (polenta) flour [US 2 cups coarse cornmeal], letting the flour fall into the water through the fingers of a clenched fist while with the other hand you beat the mixture in the pan with a large metal balloon whisk. When all the flour has been added, cook at a lively boil for 40 minutes, whisking constantly at first and then as often as you can between one short rest and the next. This whisking aerates the mixture, making it much lighter in texture and more delicate in flavour than polenta stirred with the wooden stick.

Polenta is traditionally served on a wooden board lined with a linen napkin to absorb the excess moisture. But Rosanna's polenta is a bit too floppy, and I prefer to serve it in a deep bowl, preferably earthenware for absorbing the moisture.

POLENTA MADE IN THE PRESSURE COOKER

Put 1.8l/3pt [US 7½ cups] of water and 2 teaspoons of salt in the pressure cooker and bring to the simmer. Draw the pan from the heat and add 400g/14oz of maize (polenta) flour [US 3½ cups coarse cornmeal] in a very thin stream, letting it run through the fingers of your clenched fist, while with the other hand you stir the mixture in the pan rapidly with a long wooden spoon, always in the same direction. When you have added all the flour, return the pan to the heat and bring to the boil, stirring constantly. Fit the lid on the pressure cooker and bring up to pressure. Put the weight in position and cook for 20 minutes. The polenta is now ready.

POLENTA SENZA BASTONE (POLENTA MADE IN THE OVEN)

Bring 1.8l/3pt [US 7½ cups] of water to the simmering point. Remove the pan from the heat and add 2 teaspoons of salt, then gradually add 350g/12oz of maize (polenta) flour [US 3 cups coarse cornmeal], letting it fall through your fingers while you stir rapidly with a long wooden spoon. Return the pan to the heat and bring slowly to the boil, stirring constantly in the same direction. Boil for 5 minutes, still stirring. Now transfer the polenta to a buttered oven dish. Cover with buttered foil and cook in a preheated oven (190°C/375°F/Gas Mark 5) for 1 hour.

A revolutionary note. Lately, and after much tasting and testing, I have come to the conclusion that – as pointed out to me by Lynda Brown, a friend and colleague – adding the maize (polenta) flour to cold water is much easier than adding the flour to boiling water. You can add the flour all in one go, because, the water being cold, there is no risk of lumps forming, and the final result is just as good.

In Italy maize (polenta) flour is always added to boiling water simply because nobody dared to flout the age-old tradition. In the country kitchens of the 16th century the water was always boiling in the *paiolo* hanging over the open fire, ready for the maize to be added. When the open fire was replaced by gas or electricity, the ritual of polenta making was too deeply ingrained for anyone to dream of suggesting that there might be an easier way.

FRITTATA
Italian Flat Omelette

Although this is not a basic recipe, it belongs to so many regions of northern Italy that there seemed nowhere else to put it. In Tuscany you would add sage or mint, in Lombardy onion, in Umbria a black truffle, in Liguria porcini and in Piedmont sweet peppers. You can add other vegetables, such as left-over sautéed courgettes [US zucchini] or stewed fennel, or even left-over spaghetti or tagliatelle. They all go to make a delicious frittata.

A good frittata should be set and moist, never dry and stiff.

Here is the recipe for cheese frittata. If you are adding vegetables, use only 5 eggs and less Parmesan.

SERVES 4

7 size-2 eggs [US extra-large eggs]
40g/1½oz [US 6 tbsp] freshly grated Parmesan
salt and freshly ground black pepper
30g/1oz [US 2 tbsp] unsalted butter

Break the eggs into a bowl and beat lightly until blended. Add the Parmesan, salt and pepper, remembering not to add too much salt because the cheese is salty. Beat again.

Melt the butter in a heavy-based 30cm/12in frying pan and, as soon as the butter has melted, pour in the egg mixture. Turn the heat down to very low. When the eggs have set and only the top surface is still runny, pass the pan under a preheated grill [US broiler], just for 30 seconds, enough to set the top.

Loosen the frittata with a spatula and cut into lovely wedges. Transfer to a serving dish or individual plates.

Frittata is a perfect dish for picnics or, cut into small pieces, for snacks with a drink.

MARMELLATA DI CIPOLLE

Onion Jam

When you find some sweet onions in the shops, and you have a little spare time, buy a kilo and prepare this jam to keep in the fridge. It is a good starter for stew, sauces and soups. Instead of having to sauté the onion gently for, say, half an hour, you just add 1 tablespoon or so of this jam.

MAKES ABOUT 450G/1LB

900g/2lb onions

15g/½oz [US 1 tbsp] butter

2 tbsp olive oil

1 tsp salt

Slice the onions very finely and put them in a large sauté pan with all the other ingredients. Add 150ml/5fl oz of hot water and cook at the lowest simmer (I use a flame diffuser), with the lid firmly on, for about 1 hour, stirring occasionally. At the end the onion will be very soft but there will probably still be too much liquid. Take the lid off the pan and cook very rapidly to reduce. The jam should be thick and have a lovely golden colour.

Spoon the jam into a jar or a plastic container and keep in the fridge. It will come in useful many a time . . . if you manage to make it last! It is so good that I have also served it around some meat, made a frittata with it, and eaten it on a crostino.

INDEX

A

Alberini, Massimo 23, 104, 141, 155
almonds
  Carrot cake 106–7
  Polenta cake 108–9
Alto Adige 76–87
amaretti biscuits 69
  Amaretti pudding 72–3
anchovies
  Skate with anchovy sauce 33
  Tuna fish with dried porcini and anchovies 142
Aosta 56, 57
apples 76–7
  Apple pudding 86–5
  Sautéed sliced apples 51
Arezzo 175
artichokes 186
  Artichokes stewed in milk 186–7
  Fricassee of artichokes and lamb 143–4
Artusi, Pellegrino 155, 158, 189
asparagus 90
  Asparagus with egg and lemon sauce 97–8

B

baccalà see salt cod
balsamic vinegar 99, 147–8
  Melon with balsamic vinegar 169
  Strawberries with balsamic vinegar 169
basil, pesto 123–4, 131–2
Bassano 90
battuto (pounded mixture) 12
beans *see* borlotti beans; broad beans; cannellini beans; green beans
Béchamel sauce 228–9
beef
  Beef braised in vinegar and cream 81–2
  Boiled beef 192–3
  Bolognese sauce 154–5
  Braised beef 163–4
  Grilled steak 194
  Left-over boiled beef 193
  Meat rissoles 42–3
  My grandmother's braised beef 105–6
  Rich braised beef 41–2
Benini, Zenone 185, 192
biscuits 125, 151, 203–4, 204
  amaretti 69, 72–3
  Biscuits with fennel 121
  Honey and walnut sweets 197–8
  Knobbly nutty biscuits 75
  Little ring biscuits 227
  Onion biscuits 152
bitto cheese 20, 25
Bolognese sauce 154–5
Bordighera 122–3
borlotti beans 90
  Bean and barley soup 115
  Red radicchio with borlotti bean purée 100
brawn, Pig's head 211
breads 77, 149, 150, 204, 213
  Bread with raisins 52–4
  Bread and tomato soup 180–1
  Cheese bread 205
  Flat bread with walnuts 177–8
  Focaccia 126
  Panettone sandwich 54–5
  Venetian bread soup 94
Broad beans and swiss chard stewed in tomato and wine 207–8
buckwheat 25, 76, 86
  Buckwheat cake 86–7
  Buckwheat pasta with potato and cabbage 25–6
  Buckwheat polenta with butter and cheese 32
Burano 92
butter 9, 12–13, 22, 113–14
  Buckwheat polenta with butter and cheese 32
  Rice dressed with fontina and butter 63

C

cabbage
  Buckwheat pasta with potato and cabbage 25–6
  Stewed pork with cabbage 40
  Stewed savoy cabbage 98
  Tuscan bean soup 181–2
cakes 125
  Buckwheat cake 86–7
  Carrot cake 106–7
  Chestnut flour cake 197
  Jam tart 199
  Paradise cake 49–50
  Polenta cake 108–9
  Polenta and elderflower cake 55
  Sweet focaccia 171
  see also desserts
Campofilone 221
cannellini beans
  Cannellini beans with garlic, sage and oil 184
  Polenta and cannellini beans 209
  Tuscan bean soup 181–2
capons, Poached chicken stuffed with walnuts, ricotta and parmesan 36–8
Carrot cake 106–7
casera cheese 20
Casteggio 22
Castelluccio 200, 206
cauliflower, Stewed 220–1
celery, Rice and celery soup 60–1
Cento 149
Cesenatico 159
cheeses 58
  Baked polenta with mushrooms and cheese 79–80
  bitto 20, 25
  Buckwheat polenta with butter and cheese 32
  casera 20
  montasio 113
  squacquerone 149, 153
  see also fontina; gorgonzola; mascarpone; parmesan; ricotta
chestnuts 60
  Chestnut flour cake 197
  Rice and chestnut soup 60
Chianti 173–4
chick-peas 15, 61
  Chick-pea flour pancake 127
  Chick-pea and vegetable soup 61–3
chicken 174
  Chicken breasts Jewish-style 68
  Chicken with cream and mushrooms 67
  Chicken terrine 46–7
  Chicken with tomato and rosemary sauce 223
  Grilled devilled chicken 189–90
  Old-fashioned chicken from Umbria 210
  Poached chicken stuffed with walnuts, ricotta and parmesan 36–8
  Poached chicken in a vinegary sauce 45
chillies 13
chocolate
  Chocolate and hazelnut truffle cups 73–4
  Chocolate sauce 170
cinnamon, Soft meringues with cinnamon and pistachio 144–5
cod *see* salt cod; stockfish
coffee 57
  Coffee-flavoured cream pudding 74–5
Cormòns 117
courgettes
  Braised courgettes 185
  Courgette tourte 136
  Squash and courgettes in a sweet and sour sauce 99
crabs 89
cream
  Beef braised in vinegar and cream 81–2
  Chicken with cream and mushrooms 67
  Coffee-flavoured cream pudding 74–5
  mascarpone and cream mixture 70
Crema 28, 114
culatello 146
cuttlefish
  Cuttlefish risotto 95–6
  Cuttlefish with spinach 142–3

D

desserts 59
  A Venetian sorbet 108
  A Venetian strudel 110–11
  Amaretti pudding 72–3
  Apple pudding 85–6
  Chocolate and hazelnut truffle cups 73–4

Coffee-flavoured cream pudding 74–5
Fresh fruit and balsamic vinegar 168–9
Lemon ice-cream 52
Panettone sandwich 54–5
Pear charlotte 167–8
Pears baked in red wine 70–1
Plain semifreddo 169–70
Sautéed sliced apples 51
Soft meringues with cinnamon and pistachio 144–5
Stuffed peaches 69–70
Sweet milk gnocchi 109–10
Walnut pie 71–2
see also cakes

E

eggs 13
Asparagus with egg and lemon sauce 97–8
Italian flat omelette 234
Sage omelette 178
elder flowers, Polenta and elderflower cake 55
Emilia-Romagna 146–71
emmer wheat (farro) 9, 179
Emmer and pulses soup 179–80

F

Faveto 212
fennel
Biscuits with fennel 121
Fennel and prawns in a winey sauce 218–19
Ferrara 150
Fettuccine with sausage, mushroom and green olive sauce 216–17
filo pastry
A Venetian strudel 110–11
Courgette tourte 136
Sausage and peppers pie 66
fish 13, 89, 124, 129, 149–50, 175–6, 214
Baked fish with herbs and black olives 221–2
Chunky fish soup 128
Fish stock 231
Fish and tagliatelle pie 92–3
Geonese fish and vegetable salad 138–9
Risotto with fish 159–60
Smooth fish soup 129–30
White fish baked in tomato sauce 162
see also anchovies; mackerel; octopus; red mullet; salt cod; sardines; skate; sole; stockfish; trout; tuna
Florence 194
flour 13
fontina cheese
Buckwheat pasta with potato and cabbage 25–6
fontina dressing 65
Rice dressed with fontina and butter 63
Friuli-Venezia Guilia 112–21
frogs 22
fruit 149
candied 125
see also apples; lemons; melon; olives; oranges; peaches; pears; quinces; raspberries; strawberries
fungi 76
Fungi stew 80–1
see also mushrooms; porcini; truffles

G

game 174
Peppery sauce for roast fowl 104
see also guinea fowl; pheasant; pigeon; rabbit; venison
garlic 12, 14
Cannellini beans with garlic, sage and oil 184
Genoa 124, 125, 138
gnocchi 91
Potato gnocchi 64–5
Sweet milk gnocchi 109–10
gorganzola cheese 21, Risotto with gorgonzola 28
Goria, Giovanni 61, 68, 72
Goro 149–50
Grecchi, Pietro 49–50
Green bean tourte 134
Guinea fowl with mascarpone 35–6

H

hazelnuts
Chocolate and hazelnut truffle cups 73–4
Knobbly nutty biscuits 75
Honey and walnut sweets 197–8
horseradish, Lamb in horseradish sauce 120

I

ice-cream, Lemon 52
insaporire (take up the flavour) 12

J

Jam tart 199

L

lamb
Fricassee of artichokes and lamb 143–4
Lamb cutlets with black olives 226
Lamb in horseradish sauce 120
Lamb stewed in wine 195–6
Lasagne with porcini and parma ham 217–18
leeks 15
lemons 14
A Venetian sorbet 108
Asparagus with egg and lemon sauce 97–8
Lemon ice-cream 52
Sautéed sweetbreads with lemon and parsley 49
lentils 200, 206
Stewed lentils 206
Lerici 129
lettuce, Risotto with cos 182–3
Liguria 122–45
Linguine and scallops Venetian sytle 92
Lodi 35
Lombardy 20–55, 112
luganega 23, 40

M

Macaroni pie in a sweet pastry case 155–7
Mackerel with peas 141
maize *see* polenta
Marche 212–27
marjoram 124
mascarpone cheese 21
Guinea fowl with mascarpone 35–6
mascarpone and cream mixture 70
meat 14, 124, 174, 202
Italian meat stock 230
Meat rissoles 42–3
Meat roll 164–5
see also beef; chicken; game; lamb; offal; pork; sausages; veal
Melon with balsamic vinegar 169
Merano 77, 86
meringues
Plain semifreddo 169–70
Soft meringues with cinnamon and pistachio 144–5
mezzaluna (half-moon knife) 18
Milan 23–4, 35, 38, 40, 42
milk
Artichokes stewed in milk 186–7
Sweet milk gnocchi 109–10
Modena 146, 147
Modotti, Gianna 113, 119
Moncalvo 68
montasio cheese 113
Monte Falco 202
mushrooms 124, 173–4
Baked polenta with mushrooms and cheese 79–80
Chicken with cream and mushrooms 67
Fettuccine with sausage, mushroom and green olive sauce 216–17
Mushroom soup 78–9
see also fungi; porcini
mussels 214
mustard, Quince and mustard preserve 111

N

Norcia 200–1

nuts *see* almonds; chestnuts; hazelnuts; pistachio; walnuts

O

octopus 188
Stewed octopus from Versiglia 188–9
offal
Macaroni pie in a sweet pastry case 155–7
see also sweetbreads
oils 9, 14
olive oil 14, 22, 91, 119, 123
Cannellini beans with garlic, sage and oil 184
pesto 123, 131–2
Pheasant stewed in vinegar and oil 191–2
olives 212
Baked fish with herbs and black olives 221–2
Fettuccine with sausage, mushroom and green olive sauce 216–17
Lamb cutlets with black olives 226
onions 12, 15
Chicken breasts Jewish-style 68
Left-over boiled beef 193
Onion biscuits 152
Onion jam 235
Stuffed onions 35
oranges 14
A Venetian sorbet 108

P

pancetta 15
Bean and barley soup 115
Pork bundles with pancetta and herbs 44
Risotto with saffron 27
paprika, Pork stew with 82
Parma 147, 150, 167
parma ham, Lasagne with porcini and 217–18
parmesan cheese (parmigiano-reggiano) 148, 153, 166
Poached chicken stuffed with walnuts, ricotta and parmesan 36–8
parsley 21
Sautéed sweetbreads with lemon and parsley 49
pasta 10, 91, 113, 147, 173, 202, 203
Baked penne and roast vegetables 153–4
Buckwheat pasta with potato and cabbage 25–6
Fettuccine with sausage, mushroom and green olive sauce 216–17
Fish and tagliatelle pie 92–3
Home-made pasta 232
Lasagne with porcini and parma ham 217–18
Linguine and scallops Venetian style 92
Macaroni pie in a sweet pastry case 155–7
with pesto 131, 132
Potato ravioli 117–18
Ravioli from Crema 28–30
pastry
Macaroni pie in a sweet pastry case 155–7
see also filo pastry
Pavia 49
peaches, Stuffed 69–70
pearl barley 114
Bean and barley soup 115
pears
Pear charlotte 167–8
Pears baked in red wine 70
peas
Drunken peas 219–20
Mackerel with peas 141
Rice and peas 96–7
penne and roast vegetables, Baked 153–4
peppers 22
Sausage and peppers pie 66–7
pesto 123–4, 131–2
Minestrone with pesto 132–3
Pheasant stewed in vinegar and oil 191–2
Piacenza 147, 163
Piemonte 57–75
pigeons
Risotto and pigeon timbale 160–1
Slow-roasted squabs 224–5
pine nuts 131
pistachio nuts, Soft meringues with cinnamon and 144–5
Pitigliano 196, 197
pizzas 203, 213
Cheese bread 205
polenta 9, 233–4
Baked polenta with mushrooms and cheese 79–80
Buckwheat polenta with butter and cheese 32
Polenta cake 108–9
Polenta and cannellini beans 209
Polenta and elderflower cake 55
Pontremoli 172
porcini 13, 124
Lasagne with porcini and parma ham 217–18
Mushroom risotto 158–9
Tuna fish with dried porcini and anchovies 142
see also mushrooms
pork 77, 200, 202
Florentine roast pork 194–5
Pig's head brawn 211
Pork bundles with pancetta and herbs 44
Pork stew with paprika 82
Pot-roasted shin of pork 83
Sausage and peppers pie 66–7
Stewed pork with cabbage 40
potatoes
Braised potatoes 140
Buckwheat pasta with potato and cabbage 25–6
Potato gnocchi 64–5
Potato ravioli 117–18
Spinach roll 31
poultry
Peppery sauce for roast fowl 104
see also chicken
prawns
Fennel and prawns in a winey sauce 218–19
Risotto with prawns 116
preserves
Onion jam 235
Quince and mustard preserve 111
prosciutto 12, 15, 27, 112, 201
prosciutto sauce 156
Rich braised beef 41–2
puddings *see* desserts
pulses 15, 100
Emmer and pulses soup 179–80
see also borlotti beans; cannellini beans; chick-peas; lentils

Q

Quince and mustard preserve 111

R

rabbit 213–14
Old-fashioned rabbit from Umbria 210
Rabbit in sweet-and-sour sauce 190–1
radicchio 90
Red radicchio with borlotti bean purée 100
ragù 154–5
raisins, Bread with 52–4
Raspberry coulis 170
ravioli 113, 147
Potato ravioli 117–18
Ravioli from Crema 28–30
Red mullet in a piquant tomato sauce 187–8
rice 9
Cuttlefish risotto 95–6
Mushroom risotto 158–9
Rice and celery soup 60–1
Rice and chestnut soup 60
Rice dressed with fontina and butter 63
Rice and peas 96–7
risotto 9, 15, 90–1, 114
Risotto with cos lettuce 182–3
Risotto with fish 159–60
Risotto with gorgonzola 28
Risotto and pigeon timbale 160–1
Risotto with prawns 116
Risotto with saffron 27
ricotta cheese 21, 58
Meat rissoles 42–3
Poached chicken stuffed with walnuts, ricotta and parmesan 36–8
Romagna 148–71
rosemary, Chicken with tomato and

rosemary sauce 223
Rumohr, Karl Freiherr von 78

S
saffron
Risotto with saffron 27
Stuffed sole in saffron sauce 101
sage
Cannellini beans with garlic, sage and oil 184
Sage omelette 178
salt 16
salt cod (*baccalà*) 8–9, 102, 124
Creamed salt cod with garlic and parsley 102–3
sardines, Stuffed 103–4
saucepans 18
sauces
Béchamel sauce 228–9
Bolognese sauce 154–5
Chocolate sauce 170
Green sauce 229
Peppery sauce for roast fowl 104
Potacchio sauce 223
Raspberry coulis 170
Tomato sauce 228
sausages 23
Fettuccine with sausage, mushroom and green olive sauce 216–17
Sausage and peppers pie 66–7
scallops, Linguine and scallops Venetian style 92
shellfish *see* crabs; cuttlefish; mussels; prawns; scallops; shrimps
shrimps 22
Simili, Margherita and Valeria 152
Skate with anchovy sauce 33
soffritto (under-fried) 12
sole 88
Stuffed sole in saffron sauce 101
Sondrio 20
soups 89–90, 174, 174–5, 203
Bean and barley soup 115
Bread and tomato soup 180–1
Chick-pea and vegetable soup 61–3
Chunky fish soup 128
Emmer and pulses soup 179–80
Minestrone with pesto 132–3
Mushroom soup 78–9
Rice and celery soup 60–1
Rice and chestnut soup 60
Smooth fish soup 129–30
Tuscan bean soup 181–2
Venetian bread soup 94
Sozzari, Renato 20–1
speck (flank of pork) 77
spinach
Cuttlefish with spinach 142–3
Spinach roll 31
squabs 201–2, 224
Slow-roasted squabs 224–5
squacquerone cheese 149, 153
Squash and courgettes in a sweet and sour sauce 99
Staffolo 212–13
Stefani, Bartolomeo 51
stockfish (air-dried cod *stoccafisso*) 8–9, 102, 124
stocks 16
Fish stock 231
Italian meat stock 230
Vegetable stock 231
Strawberries with balsamic vinegar 169
sweetbreads 47–8
Breaded calf sweetbreads 48
Sautéed sweetbreads with lemon and parsley 49
sweets 125, 204, 215
Honey and walnut sweets 197–8
swiss chard
Broad beans and swiss chard stewed in tomato and wine 207–8
Gratin of swiss chard stalks 34
Swiss chard tourte 135

T
tagliatelle 202
Fish and tagliatelle pie 92–3
Todi 201
tomatoes 16, 38
Bolognese veal steaks 166–7
Bread and tomato soup 180–1
Broad beans and swiss chard stewed in tomato and wine 207–8
Chicken with tomato and rosemary sauce 223
Red mullet in a piquant tomato sauce 187–8
Tomato crumble 137
Tomato sauce 228
White fish baked in tomato sauce 162
tourte 123
Courgette tourte 136
Green bean tourte 134
Swiss chard tourte 135
Trentino 76–87
Trento 76, 80
Treviso 89, 90
Trieste 114, 116
Trout baked in red wine 65–6
truffles 36, 57–8, 166, 201
tuna
Swiss chard tourte 135
Tuna fish with dried porcini and anchovies 142
Turin 59
Tuscany (Toscana) 172–99

U
Umbria 200–11

V
Valle D'Aosta 56–7, 60–75
Valtellina valley 20–1, 25, 32
veal
Bolognese veal steaks 166–7
Milanese Ossobuco 38–9
Stuffed onions 35
vegetables 16–17, 89, 174, 202
A dish of mixed garden vegetables 119
Baked penne and roast vegetables 153–4
Chick-pea and vegetable soup 61–3
Genoese fish and vegetable salad 138–9
Roasted vegetables 208–9
Vegetable relish 68
Vegetable stock 231
see also artichokes; asparagus; broad beans; cabbage; carrots; cauliflower; celery; courgettes; fennel; fungi; green beans; leeks; lettuce; onions; peas; peppers; potatoes; pulses; radicchio; spinach; squash; swiss chard; tomatoes
Veneto 9, 88–111
Venice (Venezia) 88–9
venison, Stewed 84–5
vinegar 17
Beef braised in vinegar and cream 81–2
Pheasant stewed in vinegar and oil 191–2
Poached chicken in a vinegary sauce 45
see also balsamic vinegar
Vissani, Gianfranco 201
Voghera 22

W
walnuts 36–7, 71
Flat bread with walnuts 177–8
Honey and walnut sweets 197–8
Poached chicken stuffed with walnuts, ricotta and parmesan 36–8
walnut oil 22
Walnut pie 71–2
water 17
wine 17
Broad beans and swiss chard stewed in tomato and wine 207–8
Drunken peas 219–20
Fennel and prawns in a winey sauce 218–19
Lamb stewed in wine 195–6
Pears baked in red wine 70
Trout baked in red wine 65–6
wine vinegar 17

ACKNOWLEDGEMENTS

I am deeply grateful to many friends and acquaintances who so generously gave me ideas and recipes. My particular thanks go to members of the Accademia Italiana della Cucina: firstly to Massimo Alberini, the Honorary Vice-President, a dear friend who has helped me all through my writing career, and then to Giovanni Capsit, the Vice-President, to Ugo and Teresa Cesaritti, Giovanni Goria, Giuseppe Moraglia and Barth Pallanca.

I am indebted to Romana Bosco, Gianna Modotti and Margherita and Valeria Simili who run cookery schools in Turin, Udine and Bologna respectively.

The following are some of the people in Italy to whom I want to send special thanks:

Dina Alberghini of La Buca di San Petronio in Bologna
Claudio Aliani, chef of Grand Hotel del Mare in Bordighera
Ezio and Maria Anghinetti of the Trattoria La Maesta near Parma
The Ansuini brothers, sausage makers in Umbria
Luigi Aquilante, Mayor of Staffolo in Marche
Pio Bartolini, sausage maker in Marche
Clara Belcapo
Capineta Nodio Benini
Antonietta and Luciano Bertocchi of the Trattoria Da Bussè in Pontremoli
Mariateresa Bestetti
Francesca Bianchi
Luigi Bianchi of the Grand Hotel del Mare in Bordighera
Paola Bini of the Villa Gaidello Club near Modena
Baldo Arno and Ferdinando Anegg of the Albergo Rosa in Alto Adige
Andrea Bordignan and Dante Bernardi of Blasut in Montegliano, Friuli
Dino Boscorato of the Trattoria dall'Amelia in Mestre
Leopoldo e Costanza Budini Gattai
Giovanni Cabani of Miranda in Tellaro near La Spezia
Lina and Giuseppe Campioni of Da Lina in Casteggio near Pavia
Sorelle Carboni of Manuelina in Recco near Genoa
Cinzia Certosini of Vecchia Osteria del Ponte a Bozzone near Siena
Giovanni Colombo, cheese producer near Pavia
Livio Crespi, oil producer in Liguria
Maria Deana
Guido and Bianca Del Conte
Marco Del Conte
Gastone Delio of Gastone in Dolceacqua near Ventimiglia
Antonio Farinella
Giorgio Fini of the eponymous restaurant in Modena
Catia Franci, bread maker in Pitigliano
Ferdinanda Galletti di San Cataldo
Grazia Gay
Marco Ghezzi
Pietro Grecchi of the pasticceria Vigoni in Pavia
Loreta Guastini of Albergo Guastini in Pitigliano
Margherita König of the pasticceria König in Merano
Magda Lucchini
Wilma Magagnato
Tarsilia Mancini
Signor Martinotti, rice producer in Piedmont
Mariella Massola
Elsa Mazzolini
Giulia Mercuri
Geltrude Mitterman of Hotel Bella Vista in Mendola, Alto Adige
Lalla Morassutti
Mara Mori of the Leone in Pomponesco, near Mantua
Giuseppe e Mariadele Muzio of Angiolina in Sestri Levante
Domenico Passero of Trattoria all'Antica in Milan
Annamaria de'Pedrini
Joan Peregalli
Sandra Polo, baker in Turin
Angelina Purin of Crucolo near Trento
Fritz Rabauser, butcher in Alto Adige
Franco Roi, oil producer in Liguria
Giovanna Rosti
Paolo Scarpellini
Heidi Schmidt, baker in Lana, Alto Adige
Lorenzo Secchi of Taverna del Vecchio Borgo in Massa Marittima
Signor Seibstock, salumiere in Merano
Renato Sozzani of Hotel della Posta in Sondrio
Sandro and Paola Spinosi, pasta producers in Marche
Antonio Stoppani of Peck in Milan
Artemio Strazzi
Carla Toffoloni
Francesco Tofoni, buffalo breeder in Marche
Maria Pia and Domenico Triassi of Cral Ferrera in Crema
Alberto Varisco of the Leon d'Oro in La Spezia
Gianfranco Vissani of the Ristorante Vissani near Todi
Guy Waley

In Britain I have special thanks for the following who helped me generously, one way or another, with their expertise:

Anthony Beevor
Vincenzo and Anne Bergonzoli of Al San Vicenzo in London
Mauro Bregoli of The Old Manor House in Romsey
Charles and Julia Cardozo
Gianfranco Carraro
Philippa Davenport
Willi Elsener and Paolo Sari of the Dorchester
Geraldine Gartrell
Albino and Anna Gorini of Salumeria Estense in London
Therèse Ingram
Gioacchino La Franca
Rosanna Lockheart
George and Betsy Newell
Pietro Pesce
Eve Pollekoff
Andrea Riva and Francesco Zanchetta of Riva in London
Antonello Tagliabue of Bice in London
Ann and Franco Taruschio of The Walnut Tree near Abergavenny
Carla Tomasi
Claudia Wolfers Vasquez
Paul Waley
Lyn Williamson

My deepest gratitude goes to my husband Oliver, who had to go without food, or eat four meals a day, during the long gestation of this book. He has been my adviser, support, constant help and – as always – my word processor.

Finally, I thank everyone at Pavilion who has been involved in producing this book, and particularly the cookery editors Gillian Young, John Midgley and Rachel King. Thanks also to Norma MacMillan, who has been the most thorough yet unassuming copy editor, and to Caroline Liddell for preparing the dishes so beautifully for photography. And, as ever, I owe a great deal to Vivien Green, my agent, who was always at the other end of the telephone to support me and cheer me up.

Some Important Organic Functional Groups

	Functional Group*	Example	IUPAC Name		Functional Group*	Example	IUPAC Name
Acid anhydride	$-\overset{\ddot{O}}{\overset{\|}{C}}-\ddot{O}-\overset{\ddot{O}}{\overset{\|}{C}}-$	$CH_3\overset{O}{\overset{\|}{C}}O\overset{O}{\overset{\|}{C}}CH_3$	Ethanoic anhydride (Acetic anhydride)	Amine, tertiary	$-\ddot{N}-$ (with third bond down)	$(CH_3CH_2)_3N$	Triethylamine
Acid chloride	$-\overset{\ddot{O}}{\overset{\|}{C}}-\ddot{Cl}:$	$CH_3\overset{O}{\overset{\|}{C}}Cl$	Ethanoyl chloride (Acetyl chloride)	Arene	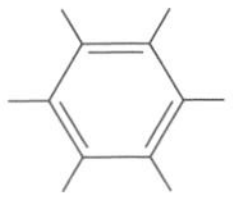		Benzene
Alcohol	$-\ddot{O}H$	CH_3CH_2OH	Ethanol (Ethyl alcohol)	Carboxylic acid	$-\overset{\ddot{O}}{\overset{\|}{C}}-\ddot{O}-H$	$CH_3\overset{O}{\overset{\|}{C}}OH$	Ethanoic acid (Acetic acid)
Aldehyde	$-\overset{\ddot{O}}{\overset{\|}{C}}-H$	$CH_3\overset{O}{\overset{\|}{C}}H$	Ethanal (Acetaldehyde)	Disulfide	$-\ddot{S}-\ddot{S}-$	CH_3SSCH_3	Dimethyl disulfide
Alkane	--------	CH_3CH_3	Ethane	Ester	$-\overset{\ddot{O}}{\overset{\|}{C}}-\ddot{O}-\overset{\|}{\underset{\|}{C}}-$	$CH_3\overset{O}{\overset{\|}{C}}OCH_3$	Methyl ethanoate (Methyl acetate)
Alkene	$>C=C<$	$CH_2=CH_2$	Ethene (Ethylene)	Haloalkane	$-\ddot{X}:$ $X = F, Cl, Br, I$	CH_3CH_2Cl	Chloroethane (Ethyl chloride)
Alkyne	$-C\equiv C-$	$HC\equiv CH$	Ethyne (Acetylene)	Ketone	$-\overset{\ddot{O}}{\overset{\|}{C}}-$	$CH_3\overset{O}{\overset{\|}{C}}CH_3$	Propanone (Acetone)
Amide	$-\overset{\ddot{O}}{\overset{\|}{C}}-\ddot{N}-$ (with third bond down)	$CH_3\overset{O}{\overset{\|}{C}}NH_2$	Ethanamide (Acetamide)	Phenol	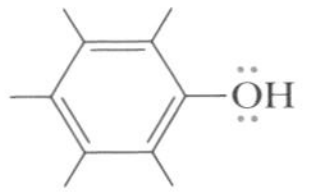	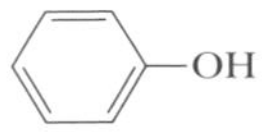	Phenol
Amine, primary	$-\ddot{N}H_2$	$CH_3CH_2NH_2$	Ethylamine	Sulfide	$-\ddot{S}-$	CH_3SCH_3	Dimethyl sulfide
Amine, secondary	$-\ddot{N}H-$	$(CH_3CH_2)_2NH$	Diethylamine	Thiol	$-\ddot{S}-H$	CH_3CH_2SH	Ethanethiol (Ethyl mercaptan)

* Where bonds to an atom are not specified, the atom is assumed to be bonded to one or more carbon or hydrogen atoms in the rest of the molecule.

Introduction to
Organic Chemistry

FIFTH EDITION

Introduction to
Organic Chemistry

FIFTH EDITION

WILLIAM H. BROWN
Beloit College

THOMAS POON
Claremont McKenna College
Scripps College
Pitzer College

WILEY
JOHN WILEY & SONS, INC.

VP & Publisher: Kaye Pace
Associate Publisher & Acquisition Editor: Petra Recter
Senior Project Editor: Jennifer Yee
Marketing Manager: Kristine Ruff
Production Manager: Juanita Thompson
Senior Production Editor: Sandra Dumas
Designer: Wendy Lai
Senior Product Designer: Bonnie Roth
Media Specialist: Lana Barskaya
Editorial Assistant: Ashley Gayle
Photo Department Manager: Hilary Newman
Photo Editor: Lisa Gee
Production Management Services: cMPreparé/Francesca Monaco

This book was typeset in 10/12 New Baskerville at cMPreparé and printed and bound by Courier/Kendallville. The cover was printed by Courier/Kendallville.

The paper in this book was manufactured by a mill whose forest management programs include sustained yield harvesting of its timberlands. Sustained yield harvesting principles ensure that the number of trees cut each year does not exceed the amount of new growth.

This book is printed on acid-free paper.

ISBN 13 978-1118-083383
ISBN 13 978-1118-152188

Printed in the United States of America.

10 9 8 7 6 5 4 3 2 1

To Carolyn,
with whom life is a joy

Bill Brown

To Sophia,
sky, fish, fireworks

Thomas Poon

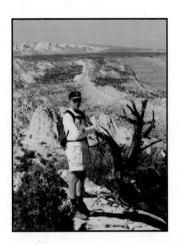

WILLIAM H. BROWN is Professor Emeritus at Beloit College, where he was twice named Teacher of the Year. He is also the author of two other college textbooks: *Organic Chemistry* 5/e, coauthored with Chris Foote, Brent Iverson, and Eric Anslyn, published in 2009, and *General, Organic, and Biochemistry* 9/e, coauthored with Fred Bettelheim, Mary Campbell, and Shawn Farrell, published in 2010. He received his Ph.D. from Columbia University under the direction of Gilbert Stork and did postdoctoral work at California Institute of Technology and the University of Arizona. Twice he was Director of a Beloit College World Affairs Center seminar at the University of Glasgow, Scotland. In 1999, he retired from Beloit College to devote more time to writing and development of educational materials. Although officially retired, he continues to teach Special Topics in Organic Synthesis on a yearly basis.

Bill and his wife Carolyn enjoy hiking in the canyon country of the Southwest. In addition, they both enjoy quilting and quilts.

THOMAS POON is Professor of Chemistry in the W.M. Keck Science Department of Claremont McKenna, Pitzer, and Scripps Colleges, three of the five undergraduate institutions that make up the Claremont Colleges in Claremont, California. He received his B.S. degree from Fairfield University (CT) and his Ph.D. from the University of California, Los Angeles under the direction of Christopher S. Foote. Poon was a Camille and Henry Dreyfus Postdoctoral Fellow under Bradford P. Mundy at Colby College (ME) before joining the faculty at Randolph-Macon College (VA) where he received the Thomas Branch Award for Excellence in Teaching in 1999. He was a visiting scholar at Columbia University (NY) in 2002 (and again in 2004) where he worked on projects in both research and education with his friend and mentor, Nicholas J. Turro. He has taught organic chemistry, forensic chemistry, upper-level courses in advanced laboratory techniques, and a first-year seminar class titled *Science of Identity*. His favorite activity is working alongside undergraduates in the laboratory on research problems involving the investigation of synthetic methodology in zeolites, zeolite photochemistry, natural products isolation, and reactions of singlet oxygen.

When not in the lab, he likes to play guitar and sing chemistry songs to his daughter Sophie.

CONTENTS OVERVIEW

01 Covalent Bonding and Shapes of Molecules 1

02 Acids and Bases 41

03 Alkanes and Cycloalkanes 63

04 Alkenes and Alkynes 108

05 Reactions of Alkenes and Alkynes 129

06 Chirality: The Handedness of Molecules 167

07 Haloalkanes 200

08 Alcohols, Ethers, and Thiols 239

09 Benzene and Its Derivatives 282

10 Amines 331

11 Spectroscopy 361

12 Aldehydes and Ketones 416

13 Carboxylic Acids 457

14 Functional Derivatives of Carboxylic Acids 488

15 Enolate Anions 526

16 Organic Polymer Chemistry 564

17 Carbohydrates 586

18 Amino Acids and Proteins 619

19 Lipids 649

20 Nucleic Acids (Online Chapter) **674**

21 The Organic Chemistry of Metabolism (Online Chapter) **700**

CONTENTS

01 Covalent Bonding and Shapes of Molecules 1

1.1 How Do We Describe the Electronic Structure of Atoms? **2**
1.2 What Is the Lewis Model of Bonding? **5**
1.3 How Do We Predict Bond Angles and the Shapes of Molecules? **14**
1.4 How Do We Predict If a Molecule Is Polar or Nonpolar? **18**
1.5 What Is Resonance? **19**
1.6 What Is the Orbital Overlap Model of Covalent Bonding? **22**
1.7 What Are Functional Groups? **28**
Summary of Key Questions **32**
Quick Quiz **34**
Problems **35**
Looking Ahead **40**
Group Learning Activities **40**

CHEMICAL CONNECTIONS

1A Buckyball: A New Form of Carbon **17**

02 Acids and Bases 41

2.1 What Are Arrhenius Acids and Bases? **42**
2.2 What Are Brønsted–Lowry Acids and Bases? **43**
2.3 How Do We Measure the Strength of an Acid or Base? **46**
2.4 How Do We Determine the Position of Equilibrium in an Acid–Base Reaction? **48**
2.5 What Are the Relationships between Acidity and Molecular Structure? **50**
2.6 What Are Lewis Acids and Bases? **54**
Summary of Key Questions **57**
Quick Quiz **58**
Key Reactions **59**
Problems **59**
Looking Ahead **62**
Group Learning Activities **62**

03 Alkanes and Cycloalkanes 63

3.1 What Are Alkanes? **64**
3.2 What Is Constitutional Isomerism in Alkanes? **66**
3.3 How Do We Name Alkanes? **69**
3.4 What Are Cycloalkanes? **73**
3.5 What Is the IUPAC System of Nomenclature? **75**
3.6 What Are the Conformations of Alkanes and Cycloalkanes? **76**
3.7 What Is *Cis–Trans* Isomerism in Cycloalkanes? **83**
3.8 What Are the Physical Properties of Alkanes and Cycloalkanes? **87**
3.9 What Are the Characteristic Reactions of Alkanes? **91**
3.10 What Are the Sources of Alkanes? **91**
Summary of Key Questions **94**
Quick Quiz **96**
Key Reactions **97**
Problems **97**
Looking Ahead **102**
Group Learning Activities **104**
Putting It Together **104**

CHEMICAL CONNECTIONS

3A The Poisonous Puffer Fish **84**
3B Octane Rating: What Those Numbers at the Pump Mean **94**

04 Alkenes and Alkynes 108

4.1 What Are the Structures and Shapes of Alkenes and Alkynes? **110**
4.2 How Do We Name Alkenes and Alkynes? **112**
4.3 What Are the Physical Properties of Alkenes and Alkynes? **120**
4.4 Why Are 1-Alkynes (Terminal Alkynes) Weak Acids? **122**
Summary of Key Questions **123**
Quick Quiz **124**
Problems **124**
Looking Ahead **128**
Group Learning Activities **128**

CHEMICAL CONNECTIONS
4A Ethylene, a Plant Growth Regulator **109**
4B *Cis–Trans* Isomerism in Vision **111**
4C Why Plants Emit Isoprene **121**

05 Reactions of Alkenes and Alkynes 129

5.1 What Are the Characteristic Reactions of Alkenes? **130**
5.2 What Is a Reaction Mechanism? **130**
5.3 What Are the Mechanisms of Electrophilic Additions to Alkenes? **136**
5.4 What Are Carbocation Rearrangements? **147**
5.5 What Is Hydroboration–Oxidation of an Alkene? **150**
5.6 How Can an Alkene Be Reduced to an Alkane? **153**
5.7 How Can an Acetylide Anion Be Used to Create a New Carbon–Carbon Bond? **155**
5.8 How Can Alkynes Be Reduced to Alkenes and Alkanes? **157**
Summary of Key Questions **158**
Quick Quiz **159**
Key Reactions **160**
Problems **161**
Looking Ahead **165**
Group Learning Activities **166**

CHEMICAL CONNECTIONS
5A Catalytic Cracking and the Importance of Alkenes **133**

06 Chirality: The Handedness of Molecules 167

6.1 What Are Stereoisomers? **168**
6.2 What Are Enantiomers? **169**
6.3 How Do We Designate the Configuration of a Stereocenter? **173**
6.4 What Is the 2^n Rule? **176**
6.5 How Do We Describe the Chirality of Cyclic Molecules with Two Stereocenters? **180**
6.6 How Do We Describe the Chirality of Molecules with Three or More Stereocenters? **182**
6.7 What Are the Properties of Stereoisomers? **183**
6.8 How Is Chirality Detected in the Laboratory? **184**
6.9 What Is the Significance of Chirality in the Biological World? **185**
6.10 How Can Enantiomers Be Resolved? **186**
Summary of Key Questions **189**
Quick Quiz **190**
Problems **191**
Chemical Transformations **195**
Looking Ahead **196**
Group Learning Activities **196**
Putting It Together **196**

CHEMICAL CONNECTIONS
6A Chiral Drugs **187**

07 Haloalkanes 200

7.1 How Are Haloalkanes Named? **201**
7.2 What Are the Characteristic Reactions of Haloalkanes? **203**

7.3 What Are the Products of Nucleophilic Aliphatic Substitution Reactions? **206**

7.4 What Are the S_N2 and S_N1 Mechanisms for Nucleophilic Substitution? **208**

7.5 What Determines Whether S_N1 or S_N2 Predominates? **211**

7.6 How Can S_N1 and S_N2 Be Predicted Based on Experimental Conditions? **217**

7.7 What Are the Products of β-Elimination? **219**

7.8 What Are the E1 and E2 Mechanisms for β-Elimination? **222**

7.9 When Do Nucleophilic Substitution and β-Elimination Compete? **225**

Summary of Key Questions **229**

Quick Quiz **230**

Key Reactions **231**

Problems **231**

Chemical Transformations **236**

Looking Ahead **237**

Group Learning Activities **238**

CHEMICAL CONNECTIONS

7A The Environmental Impact of Chlorofluorocarbons **204**

7B The Effect of Chlorofluorocarbon Legislation on Asthma Sufferers **228**

08 Alcohols, Ethers, and Thiols 239

8.1 What Are Alcohols? **240**

8.2 What Are the Characteristic Reactions of Alcohols? **246**

8.3 What Are Ethers? **260**

8.4 What Are Epoxides? **264**

8.5 What Are Thiols? **268**

8.6 What Are the Characteristic Reactions of Thiols? **271**

Summary of Key Questions **272**

Quick Quiz **274**

Key Reactions **274**

Problems **275**

Chemical Transformations **279**

Looking Ahead **280**

Group Learning Activities **281**

CHEMICAL CONNECTIONS

8A Nitroglycerin: An Explosive and a Drug **243**

8B Blood Alcohol Screening **260**

8C Ethylene Oxide: A Chemical Sterilant **268**

09 Benzene and Its Derivatives 282

9.1 What Is the Structure of Benzene? **283**

9.2 What Is Aromaticity? **286**

9.3 How Are Benzene Compounds Named, and What Are Their Physical Properties? **289**

9.4 What Is the Benzylic Position, and How Does It Contribute to Benzene Reactivity? **292**

9.5 What Is Electrophilic Aromatic Substitution? **295**

9.6 What Is the Mechanism of Electrophilic Aromatic Substitution? **296**

9.7 How Do Existing Substituents on Benzene Affect Electrophilic Aromatic Substitution? **305**

9.8 What Are Phenols? **314**

Summary of Key Questions **321**

Quick Quiz **322**

Key Reactions **322**

Problems **324**

Chemical Transformations **329**

Looking Ahead **330**

Group Learning Activities **330**

CHEMICAL CONNECTIONS

9A Carcinogenic Polynuclear Aromatics and Cancer **293**

9B Capsaicin, for Those Who Like It Hot **318**

10 Amines 331

10.1 What Are Amines? **333**

10.2 How Are Amines Named? **334**

10.3 What Are the Characteristic Physical Properties of Amines? **337**

10.4 What Are the Acid–Base Properties of Amines? **340**

10.5 What Are the Reactions of Amines with Acids? **344**
10.6 How Are Arylamines Synthesized? **346**
10.7 How Do Amines Act as Nucleophiles? **347**
Summary of Key Questions **349**
Quick Quiz **350**
Key Reactions **350**
Problems **351**
Chemical Transformations **356**
Looking Ahead **357**
Group Learning Activities **357**
Putting It Together **357**

CHEMICAL CONNECTIONS
10A Morphine as a Clue in the Design and Discovery of Drugs **332**
10B The Poison Dart Frogs of South America: Lethal Amines **338**

11 **Spectroscopy** 361

11.1 What Is Electromagnetic Radiation? **362**
11.2 What Is Molecular Spectroscopy? **364**
11.3 What Is Infrared Spectroscopy? **364**
11.4 How Do We Interpret Infrared Spectra? **367**
11.5 What Is Nuclear Magnetic Resonance? **378**
11.6 What Is Shielding? **380**
11.7 What Is an NMR Spectrum? **380**
11.8 How Many Resonance Signals Will a Compound Yield in Its NMR Spectrum? **382**
11.9 What Is Signal Integration? **385**
11.10 What Is Chemical Shift? **386**
11.11 What Is Signal Splitting? **388**
11.12 What Is ^{13}C-NMR Spectroscopy, and How Does It Differ from ^{1}H-NMR Spectroscopy? **391**
11.13 How Do We Solve an NMR Problem? **394**
Summary of Key Questions **398**
Quick Quiz **400**
Problems **401**
Looking Ahead **414**
Group Learning Activities **415**

CHEMICAL CONNECTIONS
11A Infrared Spectroscopy: A Window on Brain Activity **368**
11B Magnetic Resonance Imaging **391**

12 **Aldehydes and Ketones** 416

12.1 What Are Aldehydes and Ketones? **417**
12.2 How Are Aldehydes and Ketones Named? **417**
12.3 What Are the Physical Properties of Aldehydes and Ketones? **421**
12.4 What Is the Most Common Reaction Theme of Aldehydes and Ketones? **422**
12.5 What Are Grignard Reagents, and How Do They React with Aldehydes and Ketones? **423**
12.6 What Are Hemiacetals and Acetals? **427**
12.7 How Do Aldehydes and Ketones React with Ammonia and Amines? **434**
12.8 What Is Keto–Enol Tautomerism? **437**
12.9 How Are Aldehydes and Ketones Oxidized? **441**
12.10 How Are Aldehydes and Ketones Reduced? **443**
Summary of Key Questions **445**
Quick Quiz **447**
Key Reactions **447**
Problems **448**
Chemical Transformations **454**
Spectroscopy **455**
Looking Ahead **456**
Group Learning Activities **456**

CHEMICAL CONNECTIONS
12A A Green Synthesis of Adipic Acid **442**

13 **Carboxylic Acids** 457

13.1 What Are Carboxylic Acids? **458**
13.2 How Are Carboxylic Acids Named? **458**
13.3 What Are the Physical Properties of Carboxylic Acids? **461**

13.4 What Are the Acid–Base Properties of Carboxylic Acids? **462**
13.5 How Are Carboxyl Groups Reduced? **466**
13.6 What Is Fischer Esterification? **470**
13.7 What Are Acid Chlorides? **473**
13.8 What Is Decarboxylation? **475**
Summary of Key Questions **479**
Quick Quiz **480**
Key Reactions **480**
Problems **481**
Chemical Transformations **486**
Looking Ahead **487**
Group Learning Activities **487**

CHEMICAL CONNECTIONS
13A From Willow Bark to Aspirin and Beyond **466**
13B Esters as Flavoring Agents **472**
13C Ketone Bodies and Diabetes **476**

14 Functional Derivatives of Carboxylic Acids 488

14.1 What Are Some Derivatives of Carboxylic Acids, and How Are They Named? **489**
14.2 What Are the Characteristic Reactions of Carboxylic Acid Derivatives? **495**
14.3 What Is Hydrolysis? **496**
14.4 How Do Carboxylic Acid Derivatives React with Alcohols? **501**
14.5 How Do Carboxylic Acid Derivatives React with Ammonia and Amines? **503**
14.6 How Can Functional Derivatives of Carboxylic Acids Be Interconverted? **505**
14.7 How Do Esters React with Grignard Reagents? **507**
14.8 How Are Derivatives of Carboxylic Acids Reduced? **509**
Summary of Key Questions **513**
Quick Quiz **514**
Key Reactions **515**
Problems **516**
Chemical Transformations **522**
Looking Ahead **523**
Group Learning Activities **523**
Putting It Together **523**

CHEMICAL CONNECTIONS
14A Ultraviolet Sunscreens and Sunblocks **490**
14B From Moldy Clover to a Blood Thinner **491**
14C The Penicillins and Cephalosporins: β-Lactam Antibiotics **492**
14D The Pyrethrins: Natural Insecticides of Plant Origin **503**
14E Systematic Acquired Resistance in Plants **506**

15 Enolate Anions 526

15.1 What Are Enolate Anions, and How Are They Formed? **527**
15.2 What Is the Aldol Reaction? **530**
15.3 What Are the Claisen and Dieckmann Condensations? **537**
15.4 How Are Aldol Reactions and Claisen Condensations Involved in Biological Processes? **545**
15.5 What Is the Michael Reaction? **547**
Summary of Key Questions **554**
Quick Quiz **554**
Key Reactions **555**
Problems **556**
Chemical Transformations **561**
Looking Ahead **562**
Group Learning Activities **563**

CHEMICAL CONNECTIONS
15A Drugs That Lower Plasma Levels of Cholesterol **546**
15B Antitumor Compounds: The Michael Reaction in Nature **553**

16 Organic Polymer Chemistry 564

16.1 What Is the Architecture of Polymers? **565**
16.2 How Do We Name and Show the Structure of a Polymer? **565**
16.3 What Is Polymer Morphology? Crystalline versus Amorphous Materials **567**
16.4 What Is Step-Growth Polymerization? **568**

16.5 What Are Chain-Growth Polymers? **573**
16.6 What Plastics Are Currently Recycled in Large Quantities? **579**
Summary of Key Questions **580**
Quick Quiz **581**
Key Reactions **582**
Problems **582**
Looking Ahead **584**
Group Learning Activities **585**

CHEMICAL CONNECTIONS
16A Stitches That Dissolve **573**
16B Paper or Plastic? **575**

17 **Carbohydrates** 586

17.1 What Are Carbohydrates? **586**
17.2 What Are Monosaccharides? **587**
17.3 What Are the Cyclic Structures of Monosaccharides? **591**
17.4 What Are the Characteristic Reactions of Monosaccharides? **596**
17.5 What Are Disaccharides and Oligosaccharides? **601**
17.6 What Are Polysaccharides? **604**
Summary of Key Questions **606**
Quick Quiz **608**
Key Reactions **608**
Problems **609**
Looking Ahead **614**
Group Learning Activities **614**
Putting It Together **615**

CHEMICAL CONNECTIONS
17A Relative Sweetness of Carbohydrate and Artificial Sweeteners **602**
17B A, B, AB, and O Blood-Group Substances **603**

18 **Amino Acids and Proteins** 619

18.1 What Are the Many Functions of Proteins? **620**
18.2 What Are Amino Acids? **620**
18.3 What Are the Acid–Base Properties of Amino Acids? **623**
18.4 What Are Polypeptides and Proteins? **630**
18.5 What Is the Primary Structure of a Polypeptide or Protein? **631**
18.6 What Are the Three-Dimensional Shapes of Polypeptides and Proteins? **635**
Summary of Key Questions **642**
Quick Quiz **643**
Key Reactions **644**
Problems **645**
Looking Ahead **648**
Group Learning Activities **648**

CHEMICAL CONNECTIONS
18A Spider Silk: A Chemical and Engineering Wonder of Nature **640**

19 **Lipids** 649

19.1 What Are Triglycerides? **650**
19.2 What Are Soaps and Detergents? **653**
19.3 What Are Phospholipids? **655**
19.4 What Are Steroids? **657**
19.5 What Are Prostaglandins? **662**
19.6 What Are Fat-Soluble Vitamins? **665**
Summary of Key Questions **668**
Quick Quiz **669**
Problems **669**
Looking Ahead **672**
Group Learning Activities **673**

CHEMICAL CONNECTIONS
19A Snake Venom Phospholipases **657**
19B Nonsteroidal Estrogen Antagonists **661**

20 **Nucleic Acids (Online Chapter)** **674**

20.1 What Are Nucleosides and Nucleotides? **675**
20.2 What Is the Structure of DNA? **678**
20.3 What Are Ribonucleic Acids (RNA)? **685**

20.4 What Is the Genetic Code? **687**
20.5 How Is DNA Sequenced? **689**
Summary of Key Questions **694**
Quick Quiz **696**
Problems **696**
Group Learning Activities **699**

CHEMICAL CONNECTIONS
20A The Search for Antiviral Drugs **677**
20B DNA Fingerprinting **694**

21 The Organic Chemistry of Metabolism (Online Chapter) **700**

21.1 What Are the Key Participants in Glycolysis, the β-Oxidation of Fatty Acids, and the Citric Acid Cycle? **701**
21.2 What Is Glycolysis? **706**
21.3 What Are the Ten Reactions of Glycolysis? **707**
21.4 What Are the Fates of Pyruvate? **711**
21.5 What Are the Reactions of the β-Oxidation of Fatty Acids? **713**
21.6 What Are the Reactions of the Citric Acid Cycle? **717**
Summary of Key Questions **720**
Quick Quiz **721**
Key Reactions **722**
Problems **722**
Group Learning Activities **724**

Appendix 1 **Acid Ionization Constants for the Major Classes of Organic Acids A.1**
Appendix 2 **Characteristic ^{1}H-NMR Chemical Shifts A.2**
Appendix 3 **Characteristic ^{13}C-NMR Chemical Shifts A.3**
Appendix 4 **Characteristic Infrared Absorption Frequencies A.4**
Glossary G.1
Answers Section Ans.1
Index I.1

Goals of This Text

This text is designed for an introductory course in organic chemistry and assumes, as background, a prior course of general chemistry. Both its form and content have been shaped by our experiences in the classroom and by our assessment of the present and future direction of the brief organic course.

A brief course in organic chemistry must achieve several goals. First, most students who elect this course are oriented toward careers in science, but few if any intend to become professional chemists; rather, they are preparing for careers in areas that require a grounding in the essentials of organic chemistry. Here is the place to examine the structure, properties, and reactions of rather simple molecules. Students can then build on this knowledge in later course work and professional life.

Second, an introductory course must portray something of the scope and content of organic chemistry as well as its tremendous impact on the ways we live and work. To do this, we have included specific examples of pharmaceuticals, plastics, soaps and detergents, natural and synthetic textile fibers, petroleum refining, petrochemicals, pesticides, artificial flavoring agents, chemical ecology, and so on at appropriate points in the text.

Third, a brief course must convince students that organic chemistry is more than just a catalog of names and reactions. There are certain organizing themes or principles, which not only make the discipline easier to understand, but also provide a way to analyze new chemistry. The relationship between molecular structure and chemical reactivity is one such theme. Electronic theory of organic chemistry, including Lewis structures, atomic orbitals, the hybridization of atomic orbitals, and the theory of resonance are presented in Chapter 1. Chapter 2 explores the relationship between molecular structure and one chemical property, namely, acidity and basicity. Variations in acidity and basicity among organic compounds are correlated using the concepts of electronegativity, the inductive effect, and resonance. These same concepts are used throughout the text in discussions of molecular structure and chemical reactivity. Stereochemistry is a second theme that recurs throughout the text. The concept and importance of the spatial arrangement of atoms is introduced in Chapter 3 with the concept of conformations in alkanes and cycloalkane, followed by *cis/trans* isomerism in Chapters 3 (in cycloalkanes) and 4 (in alkenes). Molecular symmetry and asymmetry, enantiomers and absolute configuration, and the significance of asymmetry in the biological world are discussed in Chapter 6. The concept of a mechanistic understanding of the reactions of organic substances is a third major theme. Reaction mechanisms are first presented in Chapter 5; they not only help to minimize memory work but also provide a satisfaction that comes from an understanding of the molecular logic that governs how and why organic reactions occur as they do. In this chapter we present a set of five fundamental patterns that are foundational to the molecular logic of organic reactions. An understanding and application of these patterns will not only help to minimize memory work but also provide a satisfaction that comes from an understanding of how and why organic reactions occur as they do.

The Audience

This book provides an introduction to organic chemistry for students who intend to pursue careers in the sciences and who require a grounding in organic chemistry. For this reason, we make a special effort throughout to show the interrelation between organic chemistry and other areas of science, particularly the biological and health sciences. While studying with this book, we hope that students will see that organic chemistry is a tool for these many disciplines, and that organic compounds, both natural and synthetic, are all around them—in pharmaceuticals, plastics, fibers, agrochemicals, surface coatings, toiletry preparations and cosmetics, food additives, adhesives, and elastomers. Furthermore, we hope that students will recognize that organic chemistry is a dynamic and ever-expanding area of science waiting openly for those who are prepared, both by training and an inquisitive nature, to ask questions and explore.

New to This Edition

- "**Mechanism**" boxes have been added for each mechanism in the book. These Mechanism boxes serve as road maps and are a new way of presenting mechanisms using basic steps and recurring themes that are common to most organic reaction mechanisms. This approach allows students to see that reactions have many steps in common, and it makes the reactions easier to understand and remember. By graphically highlighting the mechanisms in the text, we emphasize the importance of mechanisms for learning organic chemsitry, and mechanisms are easier for the students to locate quickly.

Mechanism

Electrophilic Addition of HCl to 2-Butene

STEP 1: **Add a proton.** The reaction begins with the transfer of a proton from HCl to 2-butene, as shown by the two curved arrows on the left side of Step 1:

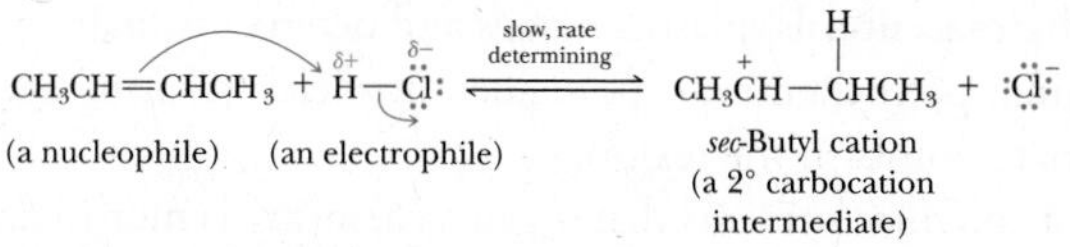

The first curved arrow shows the breaking of the pi bond of the alkene and its electron pair now forming a new covalent bond with the hydrogen atom of HCl. In this step, the carbon–carbon double bond of the alkene is the nucleophile (the electron-rich, nucleus-seeking species) and HCl is the electrophile (the electron-poor, electron-seeking species). The second curved arrow shows the breaking of the polar covalent bond in HCl and this electron pair being given entirely to chlorine, forming chloride ion. Step 1 in this mechanism results in the formation of an organic cation and chloride ion.

STEP 2: **Reaction of an electrophile and a nucleophile to form a new covalent bond.** The reaction of the *sec*-butyl cation (an electrophile and a Lewis acid) with chloride ion (a nucleophile and a Lewis base) completes the valence shell of carbon and gives 2-chlorobutane:

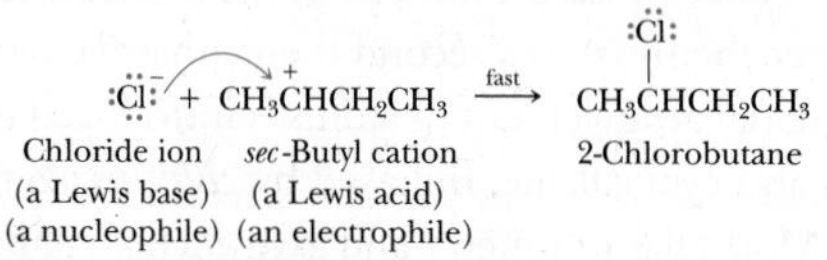

- New "**Group Learning Activities**" appear with the end-of-chapter problems, and provide students with the opportunity to learn organic chemistry collaboratively. This will encourage students to work in groups and foster more active learning in their studying.

GROUP LEARNING ACTIVITIES

5.55 Take turns quizzing each other on the reactions presented in this chapter in the following ways:

(a) Say the name of a reaction and ask each other to come up with the reagents and products of that reaction. For example, if you say "catalytic hydrogenation of an alkene" the answer should be "H_2/Pt reacts to give an alkane."

(b) Describe a set of reagents and ask each other what functional group(s) the reagents react with. For example, if you say "H_2/Pt," the answer should be "alkenes" and "alkynes."

(c) Name a functional group or class of compound as a product of a reaction and ask what functional group or class of compound could be used to synthesize that product. For example, if you say "alkene," the answer should be "alkyne."

5.56 Using a piece of paper or, preferably, a whiteboard or chalkboard, take turns drawing the mechanisms of each reaction in this chapter from memory. If you forget a step or make a mistake, another member of the group should step in and finish it.

5.57 With the exception of ethylene to ethanol, the acid-catalyzed hydration of alkenes cannot be used for the synthesis of primary alcohols. Explain why this is so.

- Due to overwhelming demand, we have combined the chapters on organic spectroscopic techniques into one chapter, Chapter 11, while still providing a sound conceptual treatise on organic spectroscopy. In combining the chapters, students are shown that the absorption of electromagnetic radiation and transitions between energy states are common themes to both infrared spectroscopy and NMR spectroscopy.
- "**Key Terms and Concepts**" now appear within the "Summary of Key Questions." In doing so, we shift the emphasis from simply memorizing a list of terms to seeing the terms (highlighted in bold) in the context of important conceptual questions.
- We have reduced the length of the text. Using reviewer input and feedback from instructors who have used the text, we removed material that we identified as being less important to our audience's learning of organic chemistry. We also moved some chapters online, to the text website and to *WileyPLUS*. The result is a manageable amount of material that still provides a thorough introduction to organic chemistry. Chapter 20, Nucleic Acids, and Chapter 21, The Organic Chemistry of Metabolism, will be available in *WileyPLUS* and at the text website: www.wiley.com/college/brown.

Special Features

"How To" Boxes: Have your students ever wished for an easy-to-follow, step-by-step guide to understanding a problem or concept? We have identified topics in nearly every chapter that often give students a difficult time and created step-by-step *How To* guides for approaching them.

HOW TO 5.1

Draw Mechanisms

Mechanisms show how bonds are broken and formed. Although individual atoms may change positions in a reaction, the curved arrows used in a mechanism are only for the purpose of showing electron movement. Therefore, it is important to remember that curved arrow notation always shows the arrow originating from a bond or from an unshared electron pair (not the other way around).

Correct use of curved arrows...

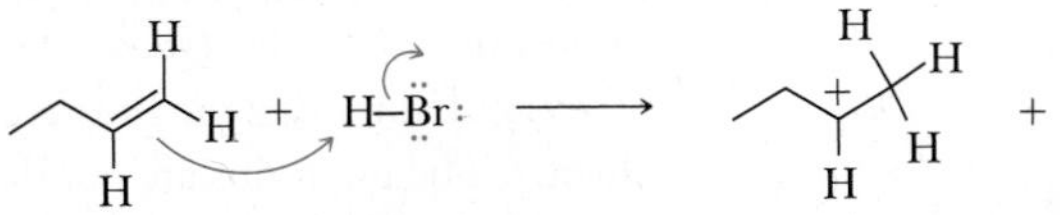

Incorrect use of curved arrows...

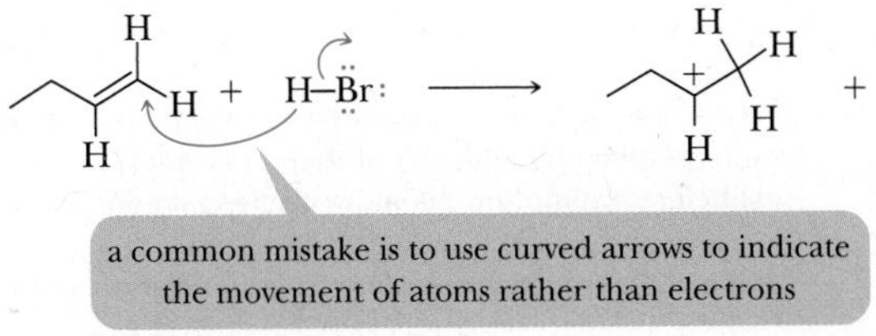
a common mistake is to use curved arrows to indicate the movement of atoms rather than electrons

Chemical Connection Boxes include **applications of organic chemistry to the world around us, particularly to the biochemical, health, and biological sciences**. The topics covered in these boxes represent real-world applications of organic chemistry and highlight the relevance between organic chemistry and the students' future careers.

"Putting It Together" Cumulative Review Questions: In this text, end-of-chapter problems are organized by section, allowing students to easily refer back to the chapter if difficulties arise. This way of organizing practice problems is very useful for learning new material. Wouldn't it be helpful for students to know whether they could do a problem that wasn't categorized for them (i.e., to know whether they could recognize that problem in a different context, such as an exam setting)? To help students in this regard, we have added a section called *Putting It Together* (PIT) at the end of Chapters 3, 6, 10, 14, and 17. Each PIT section is structured much like an exam would be organized, with questions of varying type (multiple choice, short answer, naming, mechanism problems, predict the products, synthesis problems, etc.) and difficulty (often requiring knowledge of concepts from two or more previous chapters). Students' performance on the PIT questions will aid them in assessing their knowledge of the concepts from these groupings of chapters. The solutions to the Putting It Together questions appear in the Student Solutions Manual.

Problem-Solving Strategies: One of the greatest difficulties students often encounter when attempting to solve problems is knowing where to begin. To help students overcome this challenge, we include a *Strategy* step for every worked example in the text. The strategy step will help students to determine the starting point for each of the example problems. Once students are familiar with the strategy, they can apply it to all problems of that type.

EXAMPLE 5.5

Draw a structural formula for the product of the acid-catalyzed hydration of 1-methylcyclohexene.

STRATEGY

Use Markovnikov's rule, which states that the H adds to the carbon of the carbon–carbon double bond bearing the greater number of hydrogens and that OH adds to the carbon bearing the lesser number of hydrogens.

SOLUTION

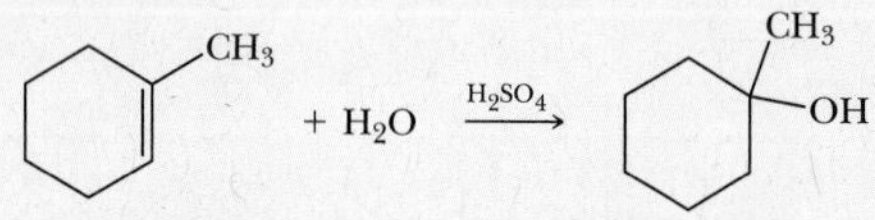

1-Methylcyclohexene 1-Methylcyclohexanol

See problems 5.19, 5.20, 5.28, 5.32

Quick Quizzes: Research on reading comprehension has shown that good readers self-monitor their understanding of what they have just read. We have provided a tool that will allow students to do this, called the *Quick Quiz*. Quick quizzes are a set of true or false questions at the end of every chapter designed to test students' understanding of the basic concepts presented in the chapter. The questions are not designed to be an indicator of their readiness for an exam. Rather, they are provided for students to assess whether they have the bare minimum of knowledge needed

QUICK QUIZ

Answer true or false to the following questions to assess your general knowledge of the concepts in this chapter. If you have difficulty with any of them, you should review the appropriate section in the chapter (shown in parentheses) before attempting the more challenging end-of-chapter problems.

1. Catalytic reduction of an alkene is syn stereoselective. (5.6)
2. Borane, BH_3, is a Lewis acid. (5.5)
3. All electrophiles are positively charged. (5.3)
4. Catalytic hydrogenation of cyclohexene gives hexane. (5.6)
5. A rearrangement will occur in the reaction of 2-methyl-2-pentene with HBr. (5.4)
6. All nucleophiles are negatively charged. (5.3)
7. In hydroboration, BH_3 behaves as an electrophile. (5.5)
8. In catalytic hydrogenation of an alkene, the reducing agent is the transition metal catalyst. (5.6)
9. Alkene addition reactions involve breaking a pi bond and forming two new sigma bonds in its place. (5.3)
10. The foundation for Markovnikov's rule is the relative stability of carbocation intermediates. (5.3)
11. Acid-catalyzed hydration of an alkene is regioselective. (5.3)
12. The mechanism for addition of HBr to an alkene involves one transition state and two reactive intermediates. (5.3)
13. Hydroboration of an alkene is regioselective and stereoselective. (5.5)
14. According to the mechanism given in the text for acid-catalyzed hydration of an alkene, the —H and —OH groups added to the double bond both arise from the same molecule of H_2O. (5.3)
15. Acid-catalyzed addition of H_2O to an alkene is called *hydration.* (5.3)
16. If a compound fails to react with Br_2, it is unlikely that the compound contains a carbon–carbon double bond. (5.3)
17. Addition of Br_2 and Cl_2 to cyclohexene is anti-stereoselective. (5.3)
18. A carbocation is a carbon that has four bonds to it and bears a positive charge. (5.3)
19. The geometry about the positively charged carbon of a carbocation is best described as trigonal planar. (5.3)
20. The carbocation derived by proton transfer to ethylene is $CH_3CH_2^+$. (5.3)
21. Alkyl carbocations are stabilized by the electron-withdrawing inductive effect of the positively charged carbon of the carbocation. (5.3)

to begin approaching the end-of-chapter problems. The answers to the quizzes are provided at the bottom of the page, so that students can quickly check their progress, and if necessary, return to the appropriate section in the chapter to review the material.

More Practice Problems: It is widely agreed that one of the best ways to learn the material in organic chemistry is to have students do as many of the practice problems available as possible. We have increased the number of practice problems in the text by 15%, providing students with even more opportunities to learn the material. For example, we've included a section called *Chemical Transformations* in nearly every chapter, which will help students to familiarize themselves with the reactions covered both in that chapter and in previous chapters. These problems provide a constructivist approach to learning organic chemistry. That is, they illustrate how concepts constantly build on each other throughout the course.

Organic Synthesis: In this text, we treat organic synthesis and all of the challenges it presents as a teaching tool. We recognize that the majority of students taking this course are intending to pursue careers in the health and biological sciences, and that very few intend to become synthetic organic chemists. We also recognize that what organic chemists do best is to synthesize new compounds; that is, they make things. Furthermore, we recognize that one of the keys to mastering organic chemistry is extensive problem solving. To this end, we have developed a large number of synthetic problems in which the target molecule is one with an applied, real-world use. Our purpose in this regard is to provide drills in recognizing and using particular reactions within the context of real syntheses. It is not our intent, for example, that students be able to propose a synthesis for procaine (Novocaine), but rather that when they are given an outline of the steps by which it can be made, they can supply necessary reagents.

Greater Attention to Visual Learning: Research in knowledge and cognition has shown that visualization and organization can greatly enhance learning. We have increased the number of callouts (short dialog bubbles) to highlight important features of many of the illustrations throughout the text. This places most of the important information in one location. When students try to recall a concept or attempt to solve a problem, we hope that they will try to visualize the relevant illustration from the text. They may be pleasantly surprised to find that the visual cues provided by the callouts help them to remember the content as well as the context of the illustration.

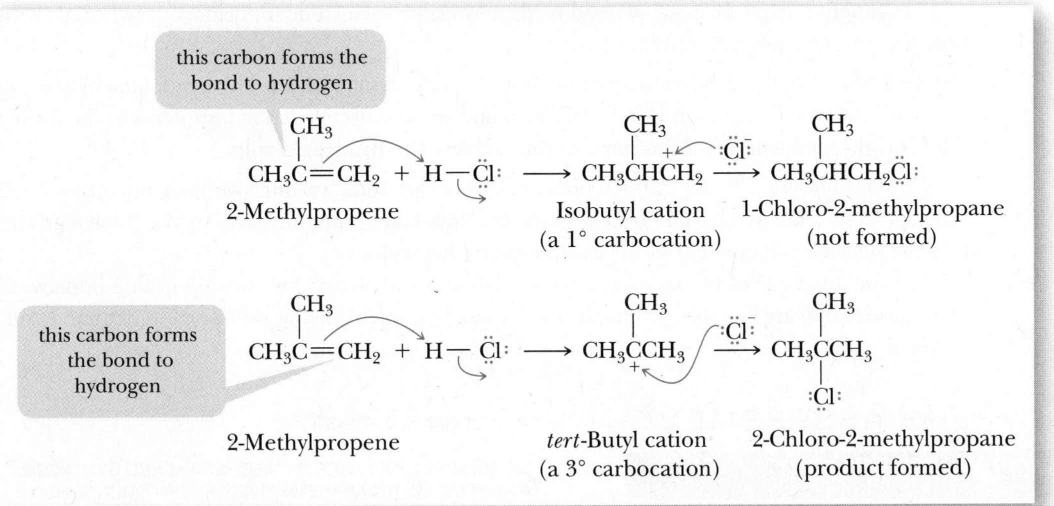

Organization: An Overview

Chapters 1–10 begin a study of organic compounds by first reviewing the fundamentals of covalent bonding, the shapes of molecules, and acid–base chemistry. The structures and typical reactions of several important classes of organic compounds are then discussed: alkanes, alkenes and alkynes, haloalkanes, alcohols and ethers, benzene and its derivatives, and amines, aldehydes, and ketones, and finally carboxylic acids and their derivatives.

Chapter 11 introduces IR spectroscopy, and ^{1}H-NMR and ^{13}C-NMR spectroscopy. Discussion of spectroscopy requires no more background than what students receive in general chemistry. The chapter is freestanding and can be taken up in any order appropriate to a particular course.

Chapters 12–16 continue the study of organic compounds, including aldehydes and ketones, carboxylic acids, and finally carboxylic acids and their derivatives. Chapter 15 concludes with an introduction to the aldol, Claisen, and Michael reactions, all three of which are important means for the formation of new carbon–carbon bonds. Chapter 16 provides a brief introduction to organic polymer chemistry.

Chapters 17–20 present an introduction to the organic chemistry of carbohydrates, amino acids and proteins, nucleic acids, and lipids. Chapter 21, The Organic Chemistry of Metabolism, demonstrates how the chemistry developed to this point can be applied to an understanding of three major metabolic pathways—glycolysis, the β-oxidation of fatty acids, and the citric acid cycle.

WILEY PLUS *WileyPLUS* for Organic Chemistry—A Powerful Teaching and Learning Solution

Wiley*PLUS* is an innovative, research-based online environment for effective teaching and learning.

Wiley*PLUS builds students' confidence because it takes the guesswork out of studying by providing students with a clear road map: what they should do, how they should do it, and if they did it right.* This interactive approach focuses on:

CONFIDENCE: Research shows that students experience a great deal of anxiety over studying. That's why we provide a structured learning environment that helps students focus on **what to do**, along with the support of immediate resources.

MOTIVATION: To increase and sustain motivation throughout the semester, *WileyPLUS* helps students learn **how to do it** at a pace that's right for them. Our integrated resources—available 24/7—function like a personal tutor, directly addressing each student's demonstrated needs with specific problem-solving techniques.

SUCCESS: *WileyPLUS* helps to ensure that each study session has a positive outcome by putting students in control. Through instant feedback and study objective reports, students know **if they did it right,** and where to focus next, so they achieve the strongest results.

With *WileyPLUS*, our efficacy research shows that students improve their outcomes by as much as one letter grade. *WileyPLUS* helps students take more initiative, so you'll have greater impact on their achievement in the classroom and beyond.

Four unique silos of assessment are available to instructors for creating online homework and quizzes and are designed to enable and support problem-solving skill development and conceptual understanding:

WILEYPLUS ASSESSMENT	FOR ORGANIC CHEMISTRY
REACTION EXPLORER	MEANINGFUL PRACTICE OF MECHANISM AND SYNTHESIS PROBLEMS (A DATABASE OF OVER 100,000 QUESTIONS)
IN CHAPTER/EOC ASSESSMENT	90-100% OF REVIEW PROBLEMS AND END-OF-CHAPTER QUESTIONS ARE CODED FOR ON LINE ASSESSMENT
CONCEPT MASTERY	PREBUILT CONCEPT MASTERY ASSIGNMENTS (FROM DATABASE OF OVER 25,000 QUESTIONS)
TEST BANK	RICH TESTBANK CONSISTING OF OVER 3,000 QUESTIONS

Reaction Explorer—Students' ability to understand mechanisms and predict synthesis reactions greatly impacts their level of success in the course. **Reaction Explorer** is an interactive system for **learning and practicing reactions**, **syntheses**, and **mechanisms** in organic chemistry with advanced support for the automatic generation of random problems and curved arrow mechanism diagrams.

Mechanism Explorer provides valuable practice of reactions and mechanisms:

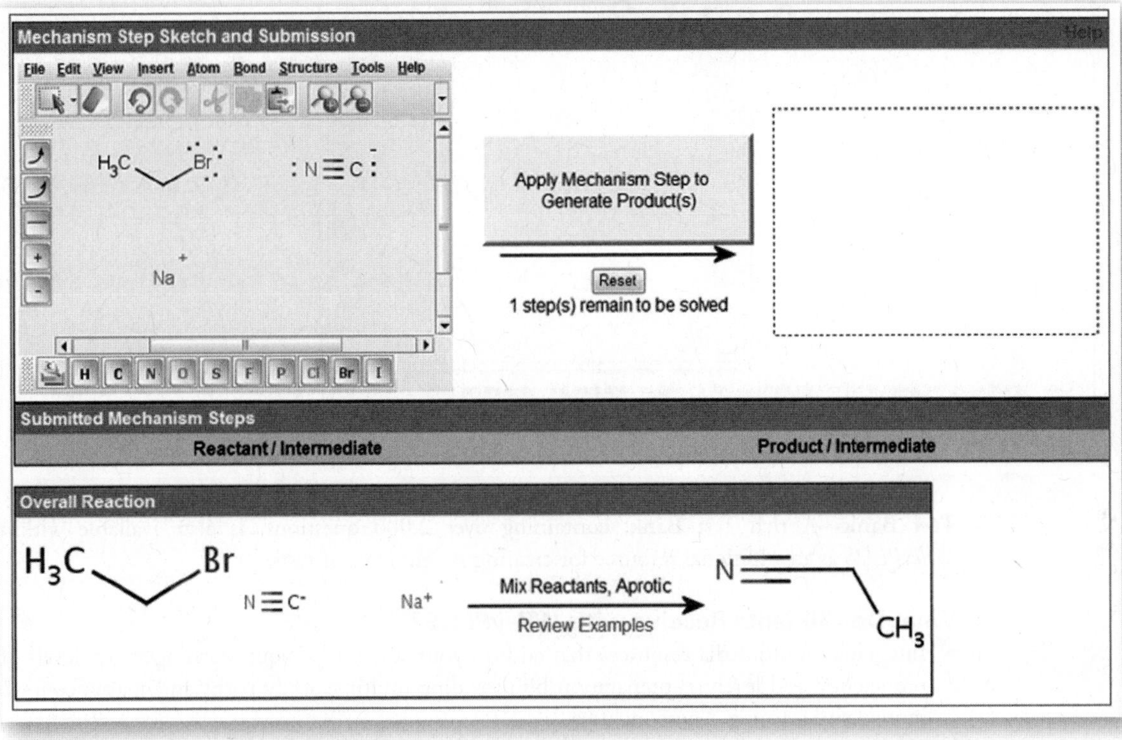

Synthesis Explorer provides meaningful practice of single and multistep synthesis:

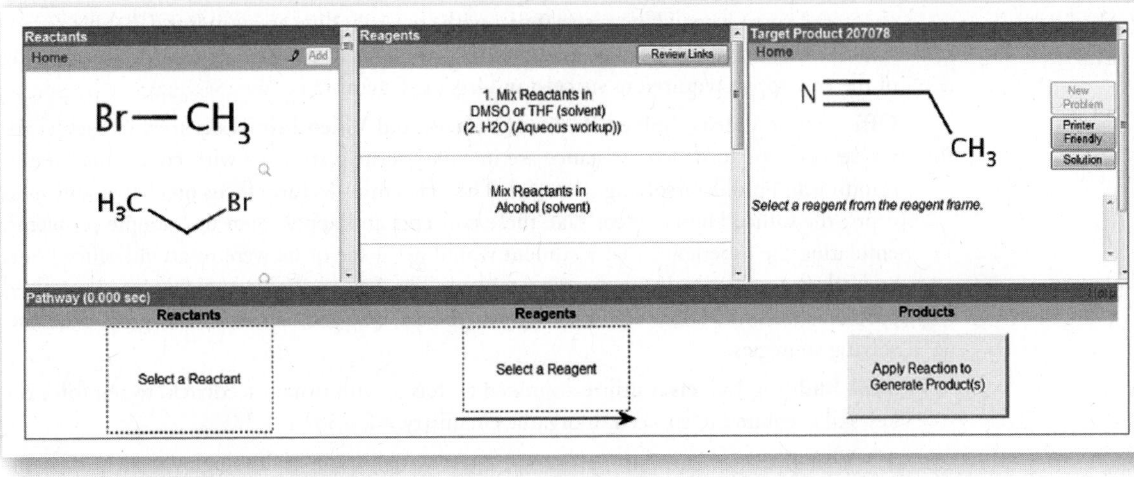

End-of-Chapter Problems—A subset of the end-of-chapter problems is included for use in *WileyPLUS*. Many of the problems are algorithmic and feature structure drawing/assessment functionality using MarvinSketch, with immediate answer feedback.

Prebuilt Concept Mastery Assignments—Students must continuously practice and work organic chemistry problems in order to master the concepts and skills presented in the course. **Prebuilt concept mastery assignments** offer students ample opportunities for practice in each chapter. Each assignment is organized by topic and features **feedback for incorrect answers.** These assignments pull from a unique database of over 25,000 questions, over half of which require students to draw a structure using MarvinSketch.

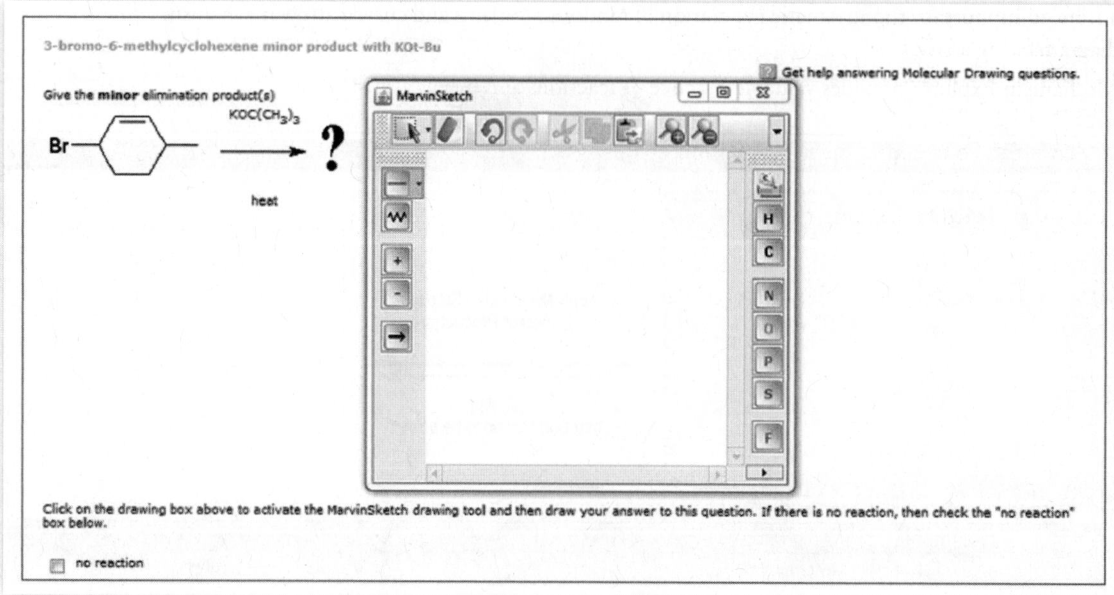

Test Bank—A rich Test Bank, containing over 2,000 questions, is also available within *WileyPLUS* as an additional resource for creating assignments or tests.

What Do Students Receive with *WileyPLUS*?

- Integrated, multimedia resources that address your students' unique learning styles, levels of proficiency, and levels of preparation by providing multiple study paths and that encourage more active learning. These include:
  - **New* Chapter Zero: General Chemistry Refresher.** To ensure that students have mastered the necessary prerequisite content from General Chemistry, and to eliminate the burden on instructors to review this material in lecture, *WileyPLUS* now includes a complete chapter of core General Chemistry topics with corresponding assignments. Chapter Zero is available to students and can be assigned in *WileyPLUS* to ensure and gauge understanding of the core topics required to succeed in Organic Chemistry.
  - **Office Hour Videos, Solved Problem Videos, and Video Mini-Lectures.** In each chapter, several types of video assistance are included to help students with conceptual understanding and problem-solving strategies. The video mini-lectures focus on challenging concepts; the Office Hours videos take these concepts and apply them to example problems, emulating the experience that a student would get if she or he were to attend office hours and ask for assistance in working a problem. The Solved Problem videos use the solved problems from the book, audio, and a whiteboard. The goal is to illustrate good problem-solving strategies.
  - **Skill-Building Exercises** utilize animated exercises, with instant feedback, to reinforce the key skills required to succeed in organic chemistry.
  - **3D Visualization Animations** use the latest visualization technologies to help students visualize concepts with audio. Instructors can assign quizzes based on these visualizations in *WileyPLUS*.
- The complete digital textbook, saving students up to 60% off the cost of a printed text.
- Question assistance, including links to relevant sections in the online digital textbook.
- Immediate feedback and proof of progress, 24/7.

What Do Instructors Receive with *WileyPLUS*?

- Four unique silos of assessment for creating online homework and quizzes.
- **Reliable resources** that reinforce course goals inside and outside of the classroom.

- The ability to easily identify those students who are falling behind by tracking their progress and offering assistance early, even before they come to office hours. *WileyPLUS* simplifies and automates such tasks as student performance assessment, creating assignments, scoring student work, keeping grades, and more.
- Media-rich course materials and assessment content that allow you to customize your classroom presentation with a wealth of resources and functionality from PowerPoint slides to a database of rich visuals. You can even add your own materials to your *WileyPLUS* course.

Support Package for Students

Student Solutions Manual: Authored by Felix Lee, of The University of Western Ontario. The Student Study Guide contains detailed solutions to all problems, including the Quick Quiz questions and the Putting It Together questions.

Support Package for Instructors

All Instructor Resources are available within *WileyPLUS* or they can be accessed by contacting your local Wiley Sales Representative.

PowerPoint Presentations: Authored by William Brown, the PPT lecture slides provide a prebuilt set of approximately 700 slides corresponding to every chapter in the text. The slides include examples and illustrations that help reinforce and test students' grasp of organic chemistry concepts. An additional set of PPT slides, featuring the illustrations, figures, and tables from the text, are also available. All PPT slide presentations are customizable to fit your course.

Test Bank: Authored by Stefan Bossmann of Kansas State University, the Test Bank for this edition has been revised and updated to include over 2,000 short-answer, multiple-choice, and true-false questions. It is available in both printed and computerized versions.

Digital Image Library: Images from the text are available online in JPEG format. Instructors may use these to customize their presentations and to provide additional visual support for quizzes and exams.

Customization and Flexible Options to Meet Your Needs

Wiley Custom Select allows you to create a textbook with precisely the content you want, in a simple, three-step online process that brings your students a cost-efficient alternative to a traditional textbook. Select from an extensive collection of content at http://customselect.wiley.com, upload your own materials as well, and select from multiple delivery formats—full color or black and white print with a variety of binding options, or eBook. Preview the full text online, get an instant price quote, and submit your order; we'll take it from there.

WileyFLEX offers content in flexible and cost-saving options to students. Our goal is to deliver our learning materials to our customers in the formats that work best for them, whether traditional text, eTextbook, *WileyPLUS*, loose-leaf binder editions, or customized content through Wiley Custom Select.

Acknowledgments

While one or a few persons are listed as "authors" of any textbook, the book is in fact the product of collaboration of many individuals, some obvious and some not so obvious. It is with gratitude that we acknowledge the contributions of the many. We begin with our senior project editor, Jennifer Yee, who ably guided this major revision from beginning to end and did so with grace and professionalism. We thank Felix Lee for his keen eye and attention to detail while working on the solutions to problems in the text. We thank Petra Recter, Associate Publisher; Donna Mulder, Proof Reader; Betty Pessagno, Copy Editor; and Francesca Monaco, Project Manager, for their creative and stylistic contributions to the text. We also thank Ashley Gayle, Editorial Assistant; Sandra Dumas, Senior Production Editor; Bonnie Roth, Product Designer; Lana Barskaya, Media Specialist; Kristine Ruff, Marketing Manager; Lisa Gee, Photo Editor; and Andrew Ginsberg, Marketing Assistant. We thank Sophia Brown for a student's eye view of the PowerPoint Lecture series. Finally, we thank all our students, both past and present, for their many positive interactions over the years that have guided us in creating this textbook.

List of Reviewers

The authors gratefully acknowledge the following reviewers for their valuable critiques of this book in its many stages as we were developing the Fifth Edition:

Stefan Bossmann, *Kansas State University*
Richard Bretz, *Miami University*
Jared Butcher, *Ohio University*
Dana Chatellier, *University of Delaware*
Steven Chung, *Bowling Green State University*
Mary Cloninger, *Montana State University—Bozeman*
Wendi David, *Texas State University—San Marcos*
Jordan Fantini, *Denison University*
Maria Gallardo-Williams, *North Carolina State University*
Amanda Henry, *Fresno City College*
James Hershberger, *Miami University*
Steven Holmgren, *Montana State University*
Roger House, *Harper College*
Felix Lee, *University of Western Ontario*
David Madar, *Arizona State University Polytechnic*
Jacob Magolan, *University of Idaho*
Gagik Melikyan, *California State University—Northridge*
James Miranda, *California State University—Sacramento*
Katie Mitchell-Koch, *University of Kansas*
Christine Pruis, *Arizona State University*
Toni Rice, *Grand Valley State University*
David Rotella, *Montclair State University*
Mary Setzer, *University of Alabama*
Alline Somlai, *Delta State University*
Eduardo Veliz, *Nova Southeastern University*
Kjirsten Wayman, *Humboldt State University*

We are also grateful to the many people who provided reviews that guided preparation of the earlier editions of our book:

Jennifer Batten, *Grand Rapids Community College*
Debbie Beard, *Mississippi State University*
Patricia Chernovitz, *Grantham University*
Sushama Dandekar, *University of North Texas*
Joseph Gandler, *California State University—Fresno*
Michel Gravel, *University of Saskatchewan*
John Grutzner, *Purdue University*
Ben Gung, *Miami University*
Peter Hamlet, *Pittsburgh State University*
Bettina Heinz, *Palomar College*
John F. Helling, *University of Florida—Gainesville*
Klaus Himmeldirk, *Ohio University—Athens*
Richard P. Johnson, *University of New Hampshire*
Dennis Neil Kevill, *Northern Illinois University*
Dalila G. Kovacs, *Michigan State University—East Lansing*
Spencer Knapp, *Rutgers University*
Douglas Linebarrier, *University of North Carolina at Greensboro*
Brian A. Logue, *South Dakota State University*
Brian Love, *East Carolina University*
Tom Munson, *Concordia University*
Robert H. Paine, *Rochester Institute of Technology*
Jeff Piquette, *University of Southern Colorado—Pueblo*
Any Pollock, *Michigan State University*
Ginger Powe-McNair, *Louisiana State University*
Michael Rathke, *Michigan State University*
Christian Ray, *University of Illinois at Urbana—Champaign*
Michelle Richards-Babb, *West Virginia University*
Joe Saunders, *Pennsylvania State University*
K. Barbara Schowen, *University of Kansas—Lawrence*
Jason Serin, *Glendale Community College*
Robert P. Smart, *Grand Valley State University*
Joshua R. Smith, *Humboldt State University*
Richard T. Taylor, *Miami University—Oxford*
Eric Trump, *Emporia State University*

Introduction to
Organic Chemistry

FIFTH EDITION

01

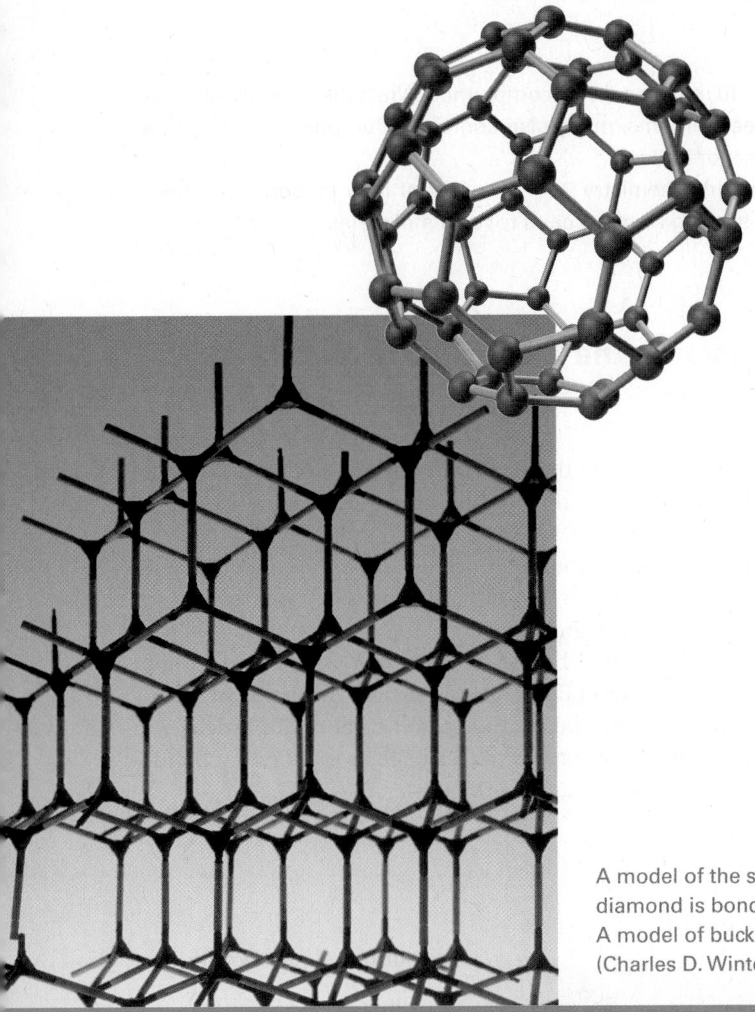

Covalent Bonding and Shapes of Molecules

A model of the structure of diamond, one form of pure carbon. Each carbon atom in diamond is bonded to four other carbon atoms at the corners of a tetrahedron. Inset: A model of buckyball, a form of carbon with a molecular formula of C_{60}. (Charles D. Winters)

KEY QUESTIONS

1.1 **How Do We Describe the Electronic Structure of Atoms?**

1.2 **What Is the Lewis Model of Bonding?**

1.3 **How Do We Predict Bond Angles and the Shapes of Molecules?**

1.4 **How Do We Predict If a Molecule Is Polar or Nonpolar?**

1.5 **What Is Resonance?**

1.6 **What Is the Orbital Overlap Model of Covalent Bonding?**

1.7 **What Are Functional Groups?**

HOW TO

1.1 **How to Draw Lewis Structures for Molecules and Ions**

CHEMICAL CONNECTIONS

1A **Buckyball: A New Form of Carbon**

ACCORDING TO the simplest definition, **organic chemistry** is the study of the compounds of carbon. As you study this text, you will realize that organic compounds are everywhere around us—in our foods, flavors, and fragrances; in our medicines, toiletries, and cosmetics; in our plastics, films, fibers, and resins; in our paints and varnishes; in our glues and adhesives; and, of course, in our bodies and in all living things.

Perhaps the most remarkable feature of organic chemistry is that it is the chemistry of carbon and only a few other elements—chiefly hydrogen, oxygen, and nitrogen. Chemists have discovered or made well over 10 million organic compounds. While the majority of them contain carbon and just those three elements, many also contain sulfur, phosphorus, and a halogen (fluorine, chlorine, bromine, or iodine).

Let us begin our study of organic chemistry with a review of how carbon, hydrogen, oxygen, and nitrogen combine by sharing electron pairs to form molecules.

Shell A region of space around a nucleus where electrons are found.

Orbital A region of space where an electron or pair of electrons spends 90 to 95% of its time.

1.1 How Do We Describe the Electronic Structure of Atoms?

You are already familiar with the fundamentals of the electronic structure of atoms from a previous study of chemistry. Briefly, an atom contains a small, dense nucleus made of neutrons and positively charged protons (Figure 1.1a).

Electrons do not move freely in the space around a nucleus, but rather are confined to regions of space called **principal energy levels** or, more simply, **shells**. We number these shells 1, 2, 3, and so forth from the inside out (Figure 1.1b).

Shells are divided into subshells designated by the letters *s*, *p*, *d*, and *f*, and within these subshells, electrons are grouped in orbitals (Table 1.1). An **orbital** is a region of space that can hold 2 electrons. In this course, we focus on compounds of carbon with hydrogen, oxygen, and nitrogen, all of which use only electrons in *s* and *p* orbitals for covalent bonding. Therefore, we are concerned primarily with *s* and *p* orbitals.

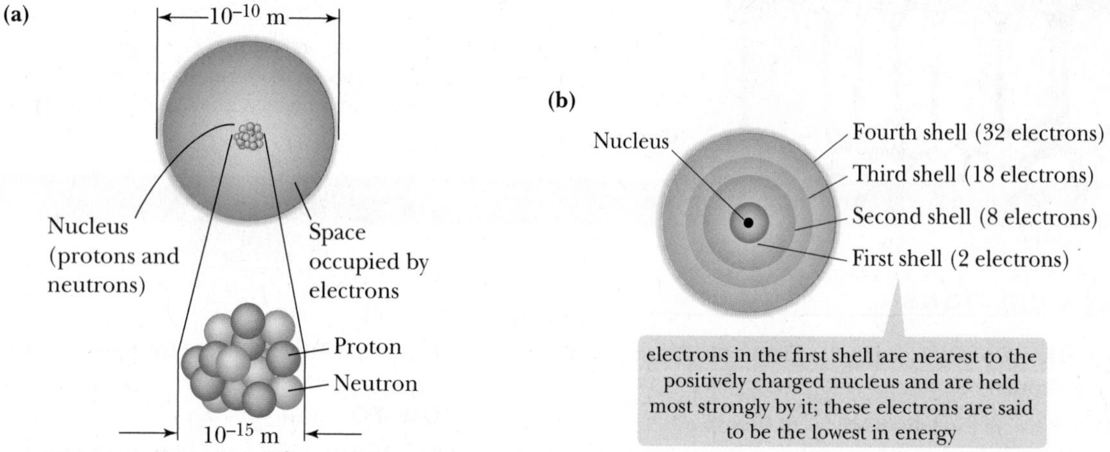

FIGURE 1.1
A schematic view of an atom. (a) Most of the mass of an atom is concentrated in its small, dense nucleus, which has a diameter of 10^{-14} to 10^{-15} meter (m). (b) Each shell can contain up to $2n^2$ electrons, where n is the number of the shell. Thus, the first shell can hold 2 electrons, the second 8 electrons, the third 18, the fourth 32, and so on. (Table 1.1).

the first shell contains a single orbital called a 1*s* orbital. The second shell contains one 2*s* orbital and three 2*p* orbitals. All *p* orbitals come in sets of three and can hold up to 6 electrons. The third shell contains one 3*s* orbital, three 3*p* orbitals, and five 3*d* orbitals. All *d* orbitals come in sets of five and can hold up to 10 electrons. All *f* orbitals come in sets of seven and can hold up to 14 electrons

TABLE 1.1 Distribution of Orbitals within Shells

Shell	Orbitals Contained in Each Shell	Maximum Number of Electrons Shell Can Hold	Relative Energies of Electrons in Each Shell
4	One 4*s*, three 4*p*, five 4*d*, and seven 4*f* orbitals	2 + 6 + 10 + 14 = 32	Higher
3	One 3*s*, three 3*p*, and five 3*d* orbitals	2 + 6 + 10 = 18	
2	One 2*s* and three 2*p* orbitals	2 + 6 = 8	
1	One 1*s* orbital	2	Lower

TABLE 1.2 Ground-State Electron Configurations for Elements 1–18*

First Period	H	1	$1s^1$	
	He	2	$1s^2$	
Second Period	Li	3	$1s^2s^1$	[He] $2s^1$
	Be	4	$1s^22s^2$	[He] $2s^2$
	B	5	$1s^22s^22p_x^1$	[He] $2s^22p_x^1$
	C	6	$1s^22s^22p_x^12p_y^1$	[He] $2s^22p_x^12p_y^1$
	N	7	$1s^22s^22p_x^12p_y^12p_z^1$	[He] $2s^22p_x^12p_y^12p_z^1$
	O	8	$1s^22s^22p_x^22p_y^12p_z^1$	[He] $2s^22p_x^22p_y^12p_z^1$
	F	9	$1s^22s^22p_x^22p_y^22p_z^1$	[He] $2s^22p_x^22p_y^22p_z^1$
	Ne	10	$1s^22s^22p_x^22p_y^22p_z^2$	[He] $2s^22p_x^22p_y^22p_z^2$
Third Period	Na	11	$1s^22s^22p_x^22p_y^22p_z^23s^1$	[Ne] $3s^1$
	Mg	12	$1s^22s^22p_x^22p_y^22p_z^23s^2$	[Ne] $3s^2$
	Al	13	$1s^22s^22p_x^22p_y^22p_z^23s^23p_x^1$	[Ne] $3s^23p_x^1$
	Si	14	$1s^22s^22p_x^22p_y^22p_z^23s^23p_x^13p_y^1$	[Ne] $3s^23p_x^13p_y^1$
	P	15	$1s^22s^22p_x^22p_y^22p_z^23s^23p_x^13p_y^13p_z^1$	[Ne] $3s^23p_x^13p_y^13p_z^1$
	S	16	$1s^22s^22p_x^22p_y^22p_z^23s^23p_x^23p_y^13p_z^1$	[Ne] $3s^23p_x^23p_y^13p_z^1$
	Cl	17	$1s^22s^22p_x^22p_y^22p_z^23s^33p_x^23p_y^33p_z^1$	[Ne] $3s^23p_x^23p_y^23p_z^1$
	Ar	18	$1s^22s^22p_x^22p_y^22p_z^23s^23p_x^23p_y^23p_z^2$	[Ne] $3s^23p_x^23p_y^23p_z^2$

*Elements are listed by symbol, atomic number, ground-state electron configuration, and shorthand notation for the ground-state electron configuration, in that order.

Rule 1. Orbitals in these elements fill in the order $1s$, $2s$, $2p$, $3s$, and $3p$.

Rule 2. Notice that each orbital contains a maximum of two electrons. In neon. there are six additional electrons after the $1s$ and $2s$ orbitals are filled. These are written as $2p_x^22p_y^22p_z^2$. Alternatively, we can group the three filled $2p$ orbitals and write them in a condensed form as $2p^6$.

Rule 3. Because the p_x, p_y, and p_z orbitals are equal in energy, we fill each with one electron before adding a second electron. That is, only after each $3p$ orbital contains one electron do we add a second electron to the $3p_x$ orbital.

A. Electron Configuration of Atoms

The electron configuration of an atom is a description of the orbitals the electrons in the atom occupy. Every atom has an infinite number of possible electron configurations. At this stage, we are concerned only with the **ground-state electron configuration**—the electron configuration of lowest energy. Table 1.2 shows ground-state electron configurations for the first 18 elements of the Periodic Table. We determine the ground-state electron configuration of an atom with the use of the following three rules:

Ground-state electron configuration The electron configuration of lowest energy for an atom, molecule, or ion.

Rule 1. *Orbitals fill in order of increasing energy from lowest to highest* (Figure 1.2).

Rule 2. *Each orbital can hold up to two electrons with their spins paired. Spin pairing* means that each electron spins in a direction opposite that of its partner (Figure 1.3). We show this pairing by writing two arrows, one with its head up and the other with its head down.

Rule 3. *When orbitals of equivalent energy are available, but there are not enough electrons to fill them completely, then we add one electron to each equivalent orbital before we add a second electron to any one of them.*

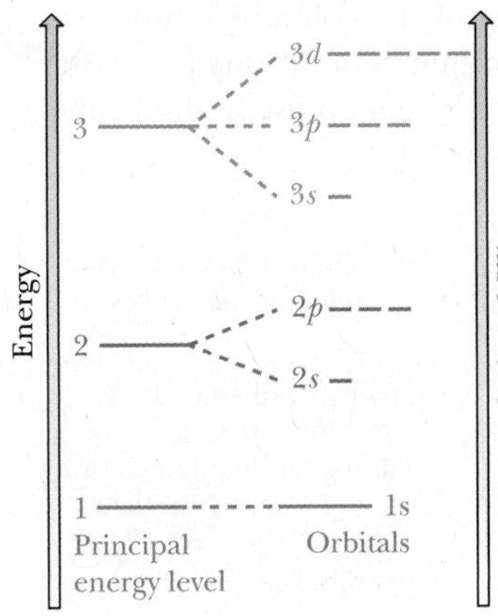

FIGURE 1.2 Relative energies and order of filling of orbitals through the 3*d* orbitals.

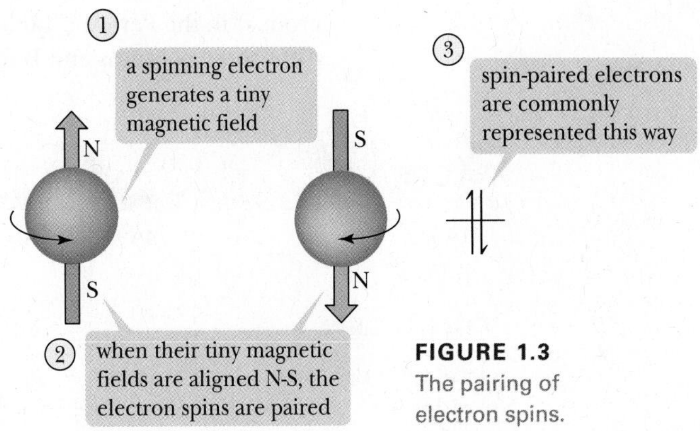

FIGURE 1.3 The pairing of electron spins.

EXAMPLE 1.1

Write ground-state electron configurations for these elements:
(a) Lithium (b) Oxygen (c) Chlorine

STRATEGY

Locate each atom in the Periodic Table and determine its atomic number. The order of filling of orbitals is $1s$, $2s$, $2p_x$, $2p_y$, $2p_z$, and so on.

SOLUTION

(a) Lithium (atomic number 3): $1s^22s^1$. Alternatively, we can write the ground-state electron configuration as [He] $2s^1$.

(b) Oxygen (atomic number 8): $1s^22s^22p_x^{\,2}2p_y^{\,1}2p_z^{\,1}$. Alternatively, we can group the four electrons of the $2p$ orbitals together and write the ground-state electron configuration as $1s^22s^22p^4$. We can also write it as [He] $2s^22p^4$.

(c) Chlorine (atomic number 17): $1s^22s^22p^63s^23p^5$. Alternatively, we can write it as [Ne] $3s^23p^5$.

See problems 1.17–1.20

PROBLEM 1.1

Write and compare the ground-state electron configurations for the elements in each set. What can be said about the outermost shell of orbitals for each pair of elements?

(a) Carbon and silicon
(b) Oxygen and sulfur
(c) Nitrogen and phosphorus

B. Lewis Structures

Valence electrons Electrons in the valence (outermost) shell of an atom.

Valence shell The outermost electron shell of an atom.

Lewis structure of an atom The symbol of an element surrounded by a number of dots equal to the number of electrons in the valence shell of the atom.

In discussing the physical and chemical properties of an element, chemists often focus on the outermost shell of its atoms, because electrons in this shell are the ones involved in the formation of chemical bonds and in chemical reactions. We call outer-shell electrons **valence electrons**, and we call the energy level in which they are found the **valence shell**. Carbon, for example, with a ground-state electron configuration of $1s^22s^22p^2$, has four valence (outer-shell) electrons.

To show the outermost electrons of an atom, we commonly use a representation called a **Lewis structure**, after the American chemist Gilbert N. Lewis (1875–1946), who devised this notation. A Lewis structure shows the symbol of the element, surrounded by a number of dots equal to the number of electrons in the outer shell of an atom of that element. In Lewis structures, the atomic symbol represents the nucleus and all filled inner shells. Table 1.3 shows Lewis structures for the first 18 elements of the Periodic Table. As you study the entries in the table, note that, with the exception of helium, the number of valence electrons of the element corresponds to the group number of the element in the Periodic Table; for example, oxygen, with six valence electrons, is in Group 6A.

At this point, we must say a word about the numbering of the columns (families or groups) in the Periodic Table. Dmitri Mendeleev gave them numerals and added the letter A for some columns and B for others. This pattern remains in common use in the United

TABLE 1.3 Lewis Structures for Elements 1–18 of the Periodic Table

1A	2A	3A	4A	5A	6A	7A	8A
H·							He:
Li·	Be:	B:	·C:	·N:	:O:	:F:	:Ne:
Na·	Mg:	Al:	·Si:	·P:	:S:	:Cl:	:Ar:

helium and neon have filled valence shells

neon and argon have in common an electron configuration in which the *s* and *p* orbitals of their valence shells are filled with eight electrons

States today. In 1985, however, the International Union of Pure and Applied Chemistry (IUPAC) recommended an alternative system in which the columns are numbered 1 to 18 beginning on the left and without added letters. Although we use the original Mendeleev system in this text, the Periodic Table on the inside back cover of the text shows both.

Notice from Table 1.3 that, for C, N, O, and F in period 2 of the Periodic Table, the valence electrons belong to the second shell. It requires 8 electrons to fill this shell. For Si, P, S, and Cl in period 3 of the Periodic Table, the valence electrons belong to the third shell. With 8 electrons, this shell is only partially filled: The $3s$ and $3p$ orbitals are fully occupied, but the five $3d$ orbitals can accommodate an additional 10 valence electrons. Because of the differences in number and kind of valence shell orbitals available to elements of the second and third periods, significant differences exist in the covalent bonding of oxygen and sulfur and of nitrogen and phosphorus. For example, although oxygen and nitrogen can accommodate no more than 8 electrons in their valence shells, many phosphorus-containing compounds have 10 electrons in the valence shell of phosphorus, and many sulfur-containing compounds have 10 and even 12 electrons in the valence shell of sulfur.

UPI/TMCorbis

Gilbert N. Lewis (1875–1946) introduced the theory of the electron pair that extended our understanding of covalent bonding and of the concept of acids and bases. It is in his honor that we often refer to an "electron dot" structure as a Lewis structure.

1.2 What Is the Lewis Model of Bonding?

A. Formation of Ions

In 1916, Lewis devised a beautifully simple model that unified many of the observations about chemical bonding and reactions of the elements. He pointed out that the chemical inertness of the noble gases (Group 8A) indicates a high degree of stability of the electron configurations of these elements: helium with a valence shell of two electrons ($1s^2$), neon with a valence shell of eight electrons ($2s^22p^6$), argon with a valence shell of eight electrons ($3s^23p^6$), and so forth.

Noble Gas	Noble Gas Notation
He	$1s^2$
Ne	[He] $2s^22p^6$
Ar	[Ne] $3s^23p^6$
Kr	[Ar] $4s^24p^63d^{10}$
Xe	[Kr] $5s^25p^64d^{10}$

The tendency of atoms to react in ways that achieve an outer shell of eight valence electrons is particularly common among elements of Groups 1A–7A (the main-group elements). We give this tendency the special name, the **octet rule**. An atom with almost eight valence electrons tends to gain the needed electrons to have eight electrons in its valence shell and an electron configuration like that of the noble gas nearest it in atomic number. In gaining electrons, the atom becomes a negatively charged ion called an **anion**. An atom with only one or two valence electrons tends to lose the number of electrons required to have the same electron configuration as the noble gas nearest it in atomic number. In losing one or more electrons, the atom becomes a positively charged ion called a **cation**.

Octet rule The tendency among atoms of Group 1A–7A elements to react in ways that achieve an outer shell of eight valence electrons.

Anion An atom or group of atoms bearing a negative charge.

Cation An atom or group of atoms bearing a positive charge.

EXAMPLE 1.2

Show how the loss of one electron from a sodium atom to form a sodium ion leads to a stable octet:

Na	$\longrightarrow$	Na^+	+	e^-
A sodium atom		A sodium ion		An electron

STRATEGY

To see how this chemical change leads to a stable octet, write the condensed ground-state electron configuration for a sodium atom and for a sodium ion, and then compare the two to that of neon, the noble gas nearest to sodium in atomic number.

SOLUTION

A sodium atom has one electron in its valence shell. The loss of this one valence electron changes the sodium atom to a sodium ion, Na^+, which has a complete octet of electrons in its valence shell and the same electron configuration as neon, the noble gas nearest to it in atomic number.

Na (11 electrons): $1s^22s^22p^63s^1$

Na^+ (10 electrons): $1s^22s^22p^6$

Ne (10 electrons): $1s^22s^22p^6$

See problems 1.22, 1.23

PROBLEM 1.2

Show how the gain of two electrons by a sulfur atom to form a sulfide ion leads to a stable octet:

$$S + 2e^- \longrightarrow S^{2-}$$

B. Formation of Chemical Bonds

According to the Lewis model of bonding, atoms interact with each other in such a way that each atom participating in a chemical bond acquires a valence-shell electron configuration the same as that of the noble gas closest to it in atomic number. Atoms acquire completed valence shells in two ways:

Ionic bond A chemical bond resulting from the electrostatic attraction of an anion and a cation.

1. An atom may lose or gain enough electrons to acquire a filled valence shell. An atom that gains electrons becomes an anion, and an atom that loses electrons becomes a cation. A chemical bond between an anion and a cation is called an **ionic bond**.

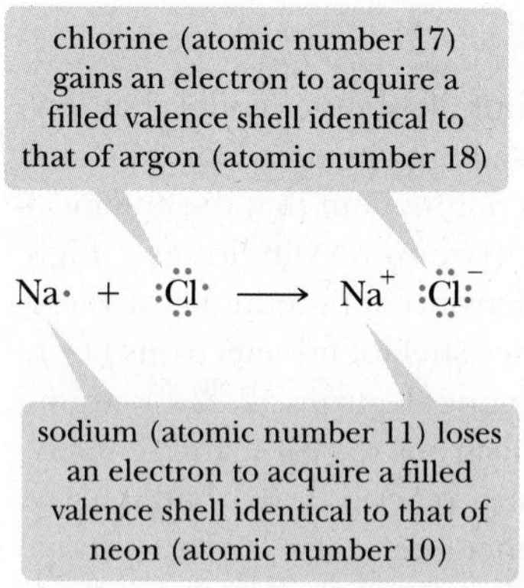
chlorine (atomic number 17) gains an electron to acquire a filled valence shell identical to that of argon (atomic number 18)
Na· + :Cl· ⟶ Na+ :Cl:−
sodium (atomic number 11) loses an electron to acquire a filled valence shell identical to that of neon (atomic number 10)

Covalent bond A chemical bond resulting from the sharing of one or more pairs of electrons.

2. An atom may share electrons with one or more other atoms to acquire a filled valence shell. A chemical bond formed by sharing electrons is called a **covalent bond**.

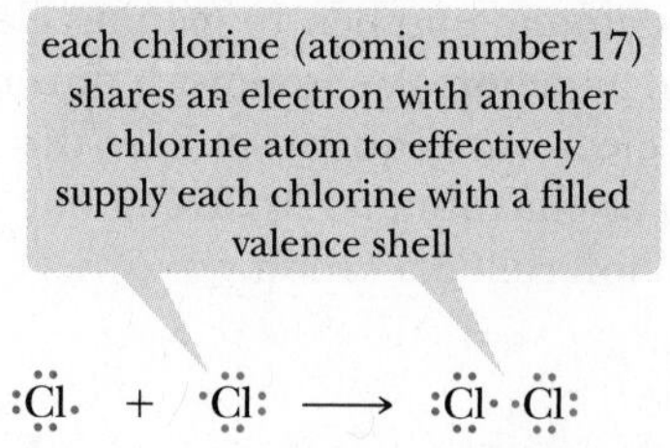
each chlorine (atomic number 17) shares an electron with another chlorine atom to effectively supply each chlorine with a filled valence shell
:Cl· + ·Cl: ⟶ :Cl··Cl:

Electronegativity A measure of the force of an atom's attraction for electrons it shares in a chemical bond with another atom.

We now ask how we can find out whether two atoms in a compound are joined by an ionic bond or a covalent bond. One way to answer this question is to consider the relative positions of the two atoms in the Periodic Table. Ionic bonds usually form between a metal and a nonmetal. An example of an ionic bond is that formed between the metal sodium and the nonmetal chlorine in the compound sodium chloride, Na^+Cl^-. By contrast, when two nonmetals or a metalloid and a nonmetal combine, the bond between them is usually covalent. Examples of compounds containing covalent bonds between nonmetals include Cl_2, H_2O, CH_4, and NH_3. Examples of compounds containing covalent bonds between a metalloid and a nonmetal include BF_3, $SiCl_4$, and AsH_4.

Another way to identify the type of bond is to compare the electronegativities of the atoms involved, which is the subject of the next subsection.

C. Electronegativity and Chemical Bonds

Electronegativity is a measure of the force of an atom's attraction for electrons that it shares in a chemical bond with another atom. The most widely used scale of electronegativities (Table 1.4) was devised by Linus Pauling in the 1930s. On the Pauling scale, fluorine, the most electronegative element, is assigned an electronegativity of 4.0, and all other elements are assigned values in relation to fluorine.

As you study the electronegativity values in this table, note that they generally increase from left to right within a period of the Periodic Table and generally increase from bottom to top within a group. Values increase from left to right because of the increasing positive charge on the nucleus, which leads to a stronger attraction for electrons in the valence shell. Values increase going up a column because of the decreasing distance of the valence electrons from the nucleus, which leads to stronger attraction between a nucleus and its valence electrons.

Note that the values given in Table 1.4 are only approximate. The electronegativity of a particular element depends not only on its position in the Periodic Table, but also on its oxidation state. The electronegativity of Cu(I) in Cu_2O, for example, is 1.8, whereas the electronegativity of Cu(II) in CuO is 2.0. In spite of these variations, electronegativity is still a useful guide to the distribution of electrons in a chemical bond.

UPI/TMCorbis

Linus Pauling (1901–1994) was the first person ever to receive two unshared Nobel Prizes. He received the Nobel Prize for Chemistry in 1954 for his contributions to the nature of chemical bonding. He received the Nobel Prize for Peace in 1962 for his efforts on behalf of international control of nuclear weapons and against nuclear testing.

TABLE 1.4 Electronegativity Values for Some Atoms (Pauling Scale)

1A	2A	3B	4B	5B	6B	7B	8B	8B	8B	1B	2B	3A	4A	5A	6A	7A
								H 2.1								
Li 1.0	Be 1.5											B 2.0	C 2.5	N 3.0	O 3.5	F 4.0
Na 0.9	Mg 1.2											Al 1.5	Si 1.8	P 2.1	S 2.5	Cl 3.0
K 0.8	Ca 1.0	Sc 1.3	Ti 1.5	V 1.6	Cr 1.6	Mn 1.5	Fe 1.8	Co 1.8	Ni 1.8	Cu 1.9	Zn 1.6	Ga 1.6	Ge 1.8	As 2.0	Se 2.4	Br 2.8
Rb 0.8	Sr 1.0	Y 1.2	Zr 1.4	Nb 1.6	Mo 1.8	Tc 1.9	Ru 2.2	Rh 2.2	Pd 2.2	Ag 1.9	Cd 1.7	In 1.7	Sn 1.8	Sb 1.9	Te 2.1	I 2.5
Cs 0.7	Ba 0.9	La 1.1	Hf 1.3	Ta 1.5	W 1.7	Re 1.9	Os 2.2	Ir 2.2	Pt 2.2	Au 2.4	Hg 1.9	Tl 1.8	Pb 1.8	Bi 1.9	Po 2.0	At 2.2

<1.0   1.0 – 1.4   1.5 – 1.9   2.0 – 2.4   2.5 – 2.9   3.0 – 4.0

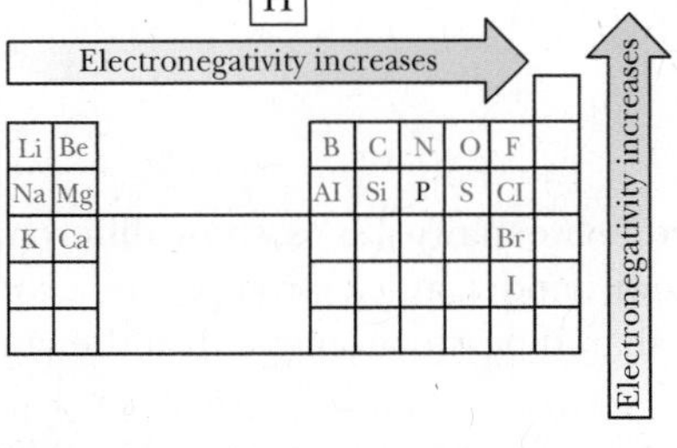

Partial Periodic Table showing commonly encountered elements in organic chemistry. Electronegativity generally increases from left to right within a period and from bottom to top within a group. Hydrogen is less electronegative than the elements in red and more electronegative than those in blue. Hydrogen and phosphorus have the same electronegativity on the Pauling scale.

Ionic Bonds

An ionic bond forms by the transfer of electrons from the valence shell of an atom of lower electronegativity to the valence shell of an atom of higher electronegativity. The more electronegative atom gains one or more valence electrons and becomes an anion; the less electronegative atom loses one or more valence electrons and becomes a cation.

EXAMPLE 1.3

Judging from their relative positions in the Periodic Table, which element in each pair has the larger electronegativity?

(a) Lithium or carbon (b) Nitrogen or oxygen
(c) Carbon or oxygen

STRATEGY

Determine whether the pair resides in the same period (row) or group (column) of the Periodic Table. For those in the same period, electronegativity increases from left to right. For those in the same group, electronegativity increases from bottom to top.

SOLUTION

The elements in these pairs are all in the second period of the Periodic Table. Electronegativity in this period increases from left to right.

(a) C > Li (b) O > N (c) O > C

See problem 1.24

PROBLEM 1.3

Judging from their relative positions in the Periodic Table, which element in each pair has the larger electronegativity?

(a) Lithium or potassium
(b) Nitrogen or phosphorus
(c) Carbon or silicon

As a guideline, we say that this type of electron transfer to form an ionic compound is most likely to occur if the difference in electronegativity between two atoms is approximately 1.9 or greater. A bond is more likely to be covalent if this difference is less than 1.9. Note that the value 1.9 is somewhat arbitrary: Some chemists prefer a slightly larger value, others a slightly smaller value. The essential point is that the value 1.9 gives us a guidepost against which to decide whether a bond is more likely to be ionic or more likely to be covalent.

An example of an ionic bond is that formed between sodium (electronegativity 0.9) and fluorine (electronegativity 4.0). The difference in electronegativity between these two elements is 3.1. In forming Na^+F^-, the single 3*s* valence electron of sodium is transferred to the partially filled valence shell of fluorine:

$$Na(1s^2\,2s^2\,2p^6\,3s^1) + F(1s^2\,2s^2\,2p^5) \longrightarrow Na^+(1s^2 2s^2 2p^6) + F^-(1s^2 2s^2\,2p^6)$$

As a result of this transfer of one electron, both sodium and fluorine form ions that have the same electron configuration as neon, the noble gas closest to each in atomic number. In the following equation, we use a single-headed curved arrow to show the transfer of one electron from sodium to fluorine:

Covalent Bonds

A covalent bond forms when electron pairs are shared between two atoms whose difference in electronegativity is 1.9 or less. According to the Lewis model, an electron pair in a covalent bond functions in two ways simultaneously: It is shared by two atoms, and, at the same time, it fills the valence shell of each atom.

The simplest example of a covalent bond is that in a hydrogen molecule, H_2. When two hydrogen atoms bond, the single electrons from each atom combine to form an electron pair with the release of energy. A bond formed by sharing a pair of electrons is called a *single bond* and is represented by a single line between the two atoms. The electron pair shared between the two hydrogen atoms in H_2 completes the valence shell of each hydrogen. Thus, in H_2, each hydrogen has two electrons in its valence shell and an electron configuration like that of helium, the noble gas nearest to it in atomic number:

$$H\cdot + \cdot H \longrightarrow H{-}H \qquad \Delta H^0 = -435\ kJ/mol\ (-104\ kcal/mol)$$

The Lewis model accounts for the stability of covalently bonded atoms in the following way: In forming a covalent bond, an electron pair occupies the region between two nuclei and serves to shield one positively charged nucleus from the repulsive force of the other positively charged nucleus. At the same time, an electron pair attracts both nuclei. In other words, an electron pair in the space between two nuclei bonds them together and fixes the internuclear distance to within very narrow limits. The distance between nuclei participating in a chemical bond is called a **bond length**. Every covalent bond has a definite bond length. In H—H, it is 74 pm, where 1 pm $= 10^{-12}$ m.

Although all covalent bonds involve the sharing of electrons, they differ widely in the degree of sharing. We classify covalent bonds into two categories—nonpolar covalent and polar covalent—depending on the difference in electronegativity between the bonded atoms. In a **nonpolar covalent bond**, electrons are shared equally. In a **polar covalent bond**, they are shared unequally. It is important to realize that no sharp line divides these two categories, nor, for that matter, does a sharp line divide polar covalent bonds and ionic bonds. Nonetheless, the rule-of-thumb guidelines in Table 1.5 will help you decide whether a given bond is more likely to be nonpolar covalent, polar covalent, or ionic.

Nonpolar covalent bond A covalent bond between atoms whose difference in electronegativity is less than approximately 0.5.

Polar covalent bond A covalent bond between atoms whose difference in electronegativity is between approximately 0.5 and 1.9.

A covalent bond between carbon and hydrogen, for example, is classified as nonpolar covalent because the difference in electronegativity between these two atoms is $2.5 - 2.1 = 0.4$ unit. An example of a polar covalent bond is that of H—Cl. The difference in electronegativity between chlorine and hydrogen is $3.0 - 2.1 = 0.9$ unit.

TABLE 1.5 Classification of Chemical Bonds

Difference in Electronegativity between Bonded Atoms	Type of Bond	Most Likely Formed Between
Less than 0.5	Nonpolar covalent	Two nonmetals or a nonmetal and a metalloid
0.5 to 1.9	Polar covalent	Two nonmetals or a nonmetal and a metalloid
Greater than 1.9	Ionic	A metal and a nonmetal

EXAMPLE 1.4

Classify each bond as nonpolar covalent, polar covalent, or ionic:

(a) O—H
(b) N—H
(c) Na—F
(d) C—Mg

STRATEGY

Use the difference in electronegativity between the two atoms and compare this value with the range of values given in Table 1.5.

SOLUTION

On the basis of differences in electronegativity between the bonded atoms, three of these bonds are polar covalent and one is ionic:

Bond	Difference in Electronegativity	Type of Bond
(a) O—H	$3.5 - 2.1 = 1.4$	polar covalent
(b) N—H	$3.0 - 2.1 = 0.9$	polar covalent
(c) Na—F	$4.0 - 0.9 = 3.1$	ionic
(d) C—Mg	$2.5 - 1.2 = 1.3$	polar covalent

See problem 1.25

PROBLEM 1.4

Classify each bond as nonpolar covalent, polar covalent, or ionic:

(a) S—H (b) P—H (c) C—F (d) C—Cl

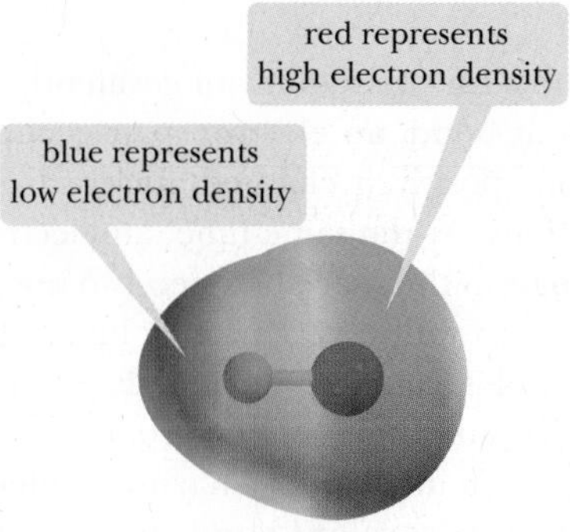

$\overset{\delta+\ \delta-}{\text{H—Cl}}$ (dipole arrow $\longmapsto$ pointing toward Cl)

FIGURE 1.4
An electron density model of HCl. Red indicates a region of high electron density, and blue indicates a region of low electron density.

An important consequence of the unequal sharing of electrons in a polar covalent bond is that the more electronegative atom gains a greater fraction of the shared electrons and acquires a partial negative charge, which we indicate by the symbol $\delta-$ (read "delta minus"). The less electronegative atom has a lesser fraction of the shared electrons and acquires a partial positive charge, which we indicate by the symbol $\delta+$ (read "delta plus"). This separation of charge produces a **dipole** (two poles). We can also show the presence of a bond dipole by an arrow, with the head of the arrow near the negative end of the dipole and a cross on the tail of the arrow near the positive end (Figure 1.4).

We can display the polarity of a covalent bond by a type of molecular model called an *electron density model.* In this type of model, a blue color shows the presence of a $\delta+$ charge, and a red color shows the presence of a $\delta-$ charge. Figure 1.4 shows an electron density model of HCl. The ball-and-stick model in the center shows the orientation of the two atoms in space. The transparent surface surrounding the ball-and-stick model shows the relative sizes of the atoms (equivalent to the size shown by a space-filling model). Colors on the surface show the distribution of electron density. We see by the blue color that hydrogen bears a $\delta+$ charge and by the red color that chlorine bears a $\delta-$ charge.

EXAMPLE 1.5

Using a bond dipole arrow and the symbols $\delta-$ and $\delta+$, indicate the direction of polarity in these polar covalent bonds:

(a) C—O (b) N—H (c) C—Mg

STRATEGY

To determine the polarity of a covalent bond and the direction of the polarity, compare the electronegativities of the bonded atoms. Remember that a bond dipole arrow always points toward the more electronegative atom.

SOLUTION

For (a), carbon and oxygen are both in period 2 of the Periodic Table. Because oxygen is farther to the right than carbon, it is more electronegative. For (b), nitrogen is more electronegative than hydrogen. For (c), magnesium is a metal located at the far left of the Periodic Table, and carbon is a nonmetal located at the right. All nonmetals, including hydrogen, have a greater electronegativity than do the metals in columns 1A and 2A. The electronegativity of each element is given below the symbol of the element:

(a) $\overset{\delta+\ \ \delta-}{\text{C—O}}$ 2.5 3.5 (b) $\overset{\delta-\ \ \delta+}{\text{N—H}}$ 3.0 2.1 (c) $\overset{\delta-\ \ \delta+}{\text{C—Mg}}$ 2.5 1.2

See problems 1.26, 1.38, 1.40

PROBLEM 1.5

Using a bond dipole arrow and the symbols $\delta-$ and $\delta+$, indicate the direction of polarity in these polar covalent bonds:

(a) C—N (b) N—O (c) C—Cl

In summary, the twin concepts of electronegativity and the polarity of covalent bonds will be very helpful in organic chemistry as a guide to locating centers of chemical reactions. In many of the reactions we will study, reaction is initiated by the attraction between a center of partial positive charge and a center of partial negative charge.

Draw Lewis Structures of Molecules and Ions

HOW TO 1.1

The ability to draw Lewis structures for molecules and ions is a fundamental skill in the study of organic chemistry. The following steps will help you to do this (as you study these steps look at the examples in Table 1.6). As an example, let us draw a Lewis structure of acetic acid, molecular formula $C_2H_4O_2$. Its structural formula, CH_3COOH, gives a hint of the connectivity.

STEP 1: **Determine the number of valence electrons in the molecule or ion.** To do so, add the number of valence electrons contributed by each atom. For ions, add one electron for each negative charge on the ion, and subtract one electron for each positive charge on the ion. For example, the Lewis structure of the water molecule, H_2O, must show eight valence electrons: one from each hydrogen and six from oxygen. The Lewis structure for the hydroxide ion, OH^-, must also show eight valence electrons: one from hydrogen, six from oxygen, plus one for the negative charge on the ion. For acetic acid the molecular formula is $C_2H_4O_2$. The Lewis structure must show 8(2 carbons) + 4(4 hydrogens) + 12(2 oxygens) = 24 valence electrons.

STEP 2: **Determine the arrangement of atoms in the molecule or ion.** This step is the most difficult part of drawing a Lewis structure. Fortunately, the structural formula of a compound can provide valuable information about connectivity. The order in which the atoms are listed in a structural formula is a guide. For example, the CH_3 part of the structural formula of acetic acid tells you that three hydrogen atoms are bonded to the carbon written on the left, and the COOH part tells you that both oxygens are bonded to the same carbon and a hydrogen is bonded to one of the oxygens.

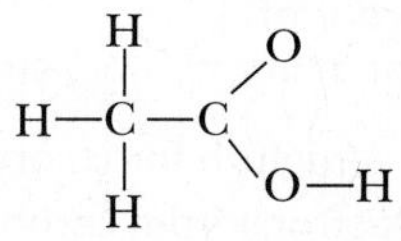

Except for the simplest molecules and ions, the connectivity must be determined experimentally. For some molecules and ions we give as examples, we ask you to propose a connectivity of the atoms. For most, however, we give you the experimentally determined arrangement.

STEP 3: **Arrange the remaining electrons in pairs so that each atom in the molecule or ion has a complete outer shell. Show a pair of *bonding electrons* as a single line between the bonded atoms; show a pair of *nonbonding electrons* as a pair of Lewis dots.** To accomplish this, connect the atoms with single bonds. Then arrange the remaining electrons in pairs so that each atom in the molecule or ion has a complete outer shell. Each hydrogen atom must be surrounded by two electrons. Each atom of carbon, oxygen, and nitrogen, as well as each halogen, must be surrounded by eight electrons (per the octet rule). Recall that each neutral carbon atom has four valence electrons and each neutral oxygen atom has six valence electrons. The structure here shows the required 24 valence electrons. The left carbon has four single bonds and a complete valence shell. Each hydrogen also has a complete valence shell. The lower oxygen has two single bonds and two unshared pairs of electrons and, therefore, has a complete valence shell. The original six valence electrons of the upper oxygen are accounted for, but it does not yet have a filled valence shell. Similarly, the original four valence electrons of the right carbon atom are accounted for but it still does not have a complete valence shell.

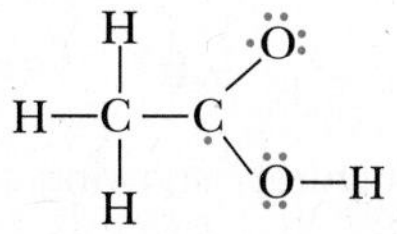

Notice that in the structure so far, we have accounted for all valence electrons, but two atoms do not yet have completed valence shells. Furthermore, one carbon atom and one oxygen atom each have a single unpaired electron.

STEP 4: **Use multiple bonds where necessary to eliminate unpaired electrons.** In a **single bond**, two atoms share one pair of electrons. It is sometimes necessary for atoms to share more than one pair of electrons. In a **double bond**, they share two pairs of electrons; we show a double bond by drawing two parallel lines between the bonded atoms. In a **triple bond**, two atoms share three pairs of electrons; we show a triple bond by three parallel lines between the bonded atoms. The following structure combines the unpaired electrons on carbon and oxygen and creates a double bond (C=O) between these two atoms. The Lewis structure is now complete.

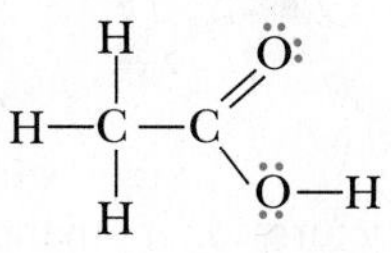

TABLE 1.6 Lewis Structures for Several Compounds. The number of valence electrons in each molecule is given in parentheses after the molecule's molecular formula.

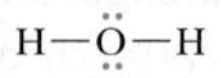	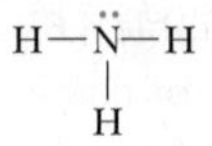	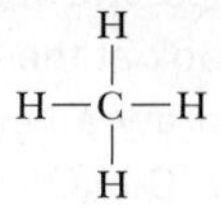	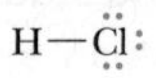
H_2O (8) Water	NH_3 (8) Ammonia	CH_4 (8) Methane	HCl (8) Hydrogen chloride
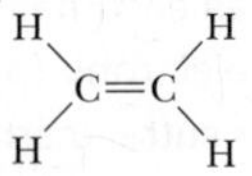	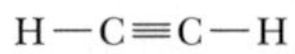	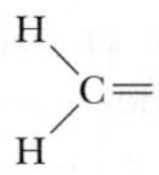	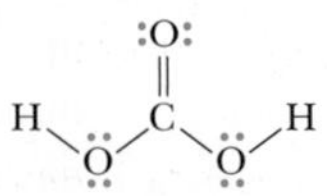
C_2H_4 (12) Ethylene	C_2H_2 (10) Acetylene	CH_2O (12) Formaldehyde	H_2CO_3 (24) Carbonic acid

Bonding electrons Valence electrons shared in a covalent bond.

Nonbonding electrons Valence electrons not involved in forming covalent bonds, that is, unshared electrons.

From the study of the compounds in Table 1.6 and other organic compounds, we can make the following generalizations: In neutral (uncharged) organic compounds,

- H has one bond.
- C has four bonds.
- N has three bonds and one unshared pair of electrons.
- O has two bonds and two unshared pair of electrons.
- F, Cl, Br, and I have one bond and three unshared pairs of electrons.

EXAMPLE 1.6

Draw Lewis structures, showing all valence electrons, for these molecules:

(a) H_2O_2 **(b)** CH_3OH **(c)** CH_3Cl

STRATEGY

Determine the number of valence electrons and the connectivity of the atoms in each molecule. Connect the bonded atoms by single bonds and then arrange the remaining valence electrons so that each atom has a filled valence shell.

SOLUTION

(a) A Lewis structure for hydrogen peroxide, H_2O_2, must show 6 valence electrons from each oxygen and 1 from each hydrogen, for a total of 12 + 2 = 14 valence electrons. We know that hydrogen forms only one covalent bond, so the connectivity of the atoms must be as follows:

H—O—O—H

The three single bonds account for 6 valence electrons. We place the remaining 8 valence electrons on the oxygen atoms to give each a complete octet:

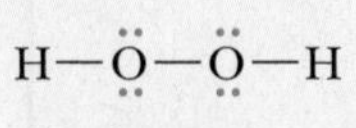

Lewis structure

Ball-and-stick models show only nuclei and covalent bonds; they do not show unshared pairs of electrons

(b) A Lewis structure for methanol, CH_3OH, must show 4 valence electrons from carbon, 1 from each hydrogen, and 6 from oxygen, for a total of 4 + 4 + 6 = 14 valence electrons. The connectivity of the atoms in methanol is given on the left. The five single bonds in this partial structure account for 10 valence electrons. We place the remaining 4 valence electrons on oxygen as two Lewis dot pairs to give it a complete octet.

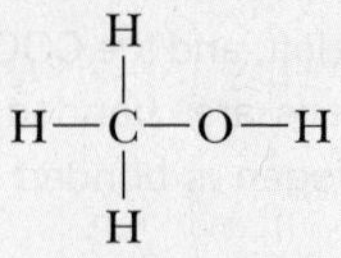

The order of attachment of atoms

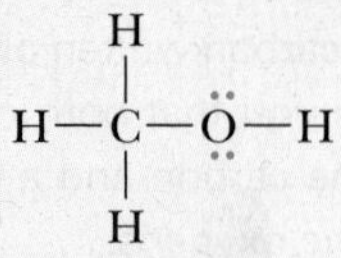

Lewis structure

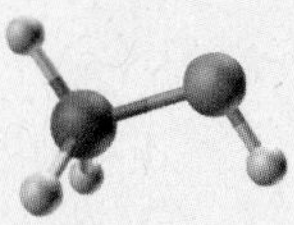

(c) A Lewis structure for chloromethane, CH_3Cl, must show 4 valence electrons from carbon, 1 from each hydrogen, and 7 from chlorine, for a total of 4 + 3 + 7 = 14. Carbon has four bonds, one to each of the hydrogens and one to chlorine. We place the remaining 6 valence electrons on chlorine as three Lewis dot pairs to complete its octet.

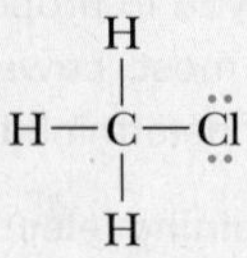

Lewis structure

See problems 1.27, 1.28

PROBLEM 1.6

Draw Lewis structures, showing all valence electrons, for these molecules:
(a) C_2H_6 (b) CS_2 (c) HCN

E. Formal Charge

Throughout this course, we deal not only with molecules, but also with polyatomic cations and polyatomic anions. Examples of polyatomic cations are the hydronium ion, H_3O^+, and the ammonium ion, NH_4^+. An example of a polyatomic anion is the bicarbonate ion, HCO_3^-. It is important that you be able to determine which atom or atoms in a molecule or polyatomic ion bear the positive or negative charge. The charge on an atom in a molecule or polyatomic ion is called its **formal charge**. To derive a formal charge,

Formal charge The charge on an atom in a molecule or polyatomic ion.

Step 1: *Write a correct Lewis structure for the molecule or ion.*

Step 2: *Assign to each atom all its unshared (nonbonding) electrons and one-half its shared (bonding) electrons.*

Step 3: *Compare the number arrived at in Step 2 with the number of valence electrons in the neutral, unbonded atom.* If the number of electrons assigned to a bonded atom is less than that assigned to the unbonded atom, then more positive charges are in the nucleus than counterbalancing negative charges, and the atom has a positive formal charge. Conversely, if the number of electrons assigned to a bonded atom is greater than that assigned to the unbonded atom, then the atom has a negative formal charge.

$$\text{Formal charge} = \begin{array}{c}\text{Number of valence}\\ \text{electrons in neutral}\\ \text{unbonded atom}\end{array} - \left(\begin{array}{c}\text{All unshared}\\ \text{electrons}\end{array} + \begin{array}{c}\text{One-half of all}\\ \text{shared electrons}\end{array}\right)$$

EXAMPLE 1.7

Draw Lewis structures for these ions, and show which atom in each bears the formal charge:
(a) H_3O^+ (b) CH_3O^-

STRATEGY

Draw a correct Lewis structure molecule showing all valence electrons on each atom. Then determine the location of the formal charge.

SOLUTION

(a) The Lewis structure for the hydronium ion must show 8 valence electrons: 3 from the three hydrogens, 6 from oxygen, minus 1 for the single positive charge. A neutral, unbonded oxygen atom has 6 valence electrons. To the oxygen atom in H_3O^+, we assign two unshared electrons and one from each shared pair of electrons, giving it a formal charge of 6 − (2 + 3) = +1.

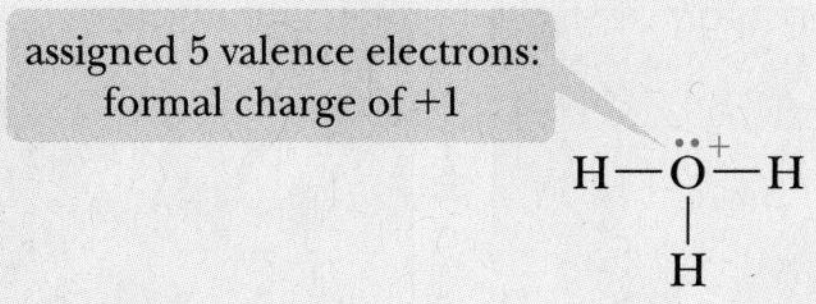

(b) The Lewis structure for the methoxide ion, CH_3O^-, must show 14 valence electrons: 4 from carbon, 6 from oxygen, 3 from the hydrogens, plus 1 for the single negative charge. To carbon, we assign 1 electron from each shared pair, giving it a formal charge of 4 − 4 = 0. To oxygen, we assign 7 valence electrons, giving it a formal charge of 6 − 7 = −1.

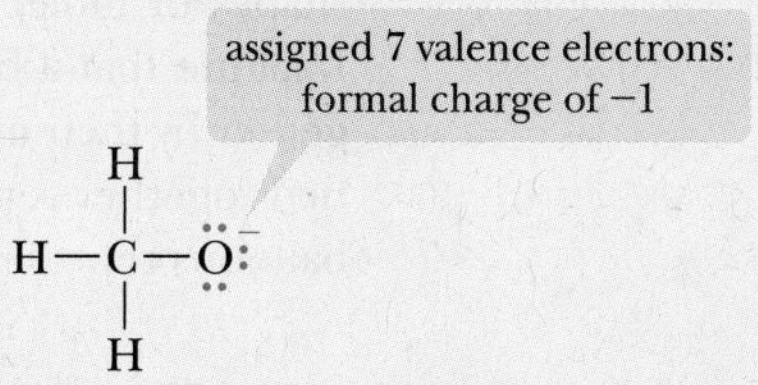

See problems 1.30–1.32, 1.34

PROBLEM 1.7

Draw Lewis structures for these ions, and show which atom in each bears the formal charge(s):
(a) $CH_3NH_3^+$ (b) CH_3^+

In writing Lewis structures for molecules and ions, you must remember that elements of the second period, including carbon, nitrogen, and oxygen, can accommodate no more than eight electrons in the four orbitals ($2s$, $2p_x$, $2p_y$, and $2p_z$) of their valence shells. Following are two Lewis structures for nitric acid, HNO_3, each with the correct number of valence electrons, namely, 24; one structure is acceptable and the other is not:

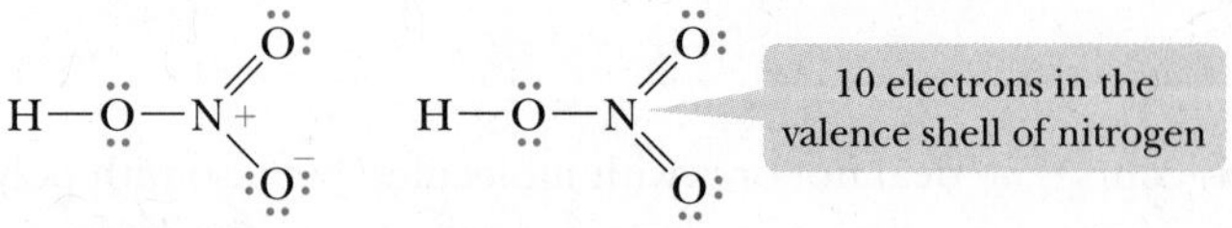

An acceptable Lewis structure   Not an acceptable Lewis structure

The structure on the left is an acceptable Lewis structure. It shows the required 24 valence electrons, and each oxygen and nitrogen has a completed valence shell of 8 electrons. Further, the structure on the left shows a positive formal charge on nitrogen and a negative formal charge on one of the oxygens. An acceptable Lewis structure must show these formal charges. The structure on the right is *not* an acceptable Lewis structure. Although it shows the correct number of valence electrons, it places 10 electrons in the valence shell of nitrogen, yet the four orbitals of the second shell ($2s$, $2p_x$, $2p_y$, and $2p_z$) can hold no more than 8 valence electrons!

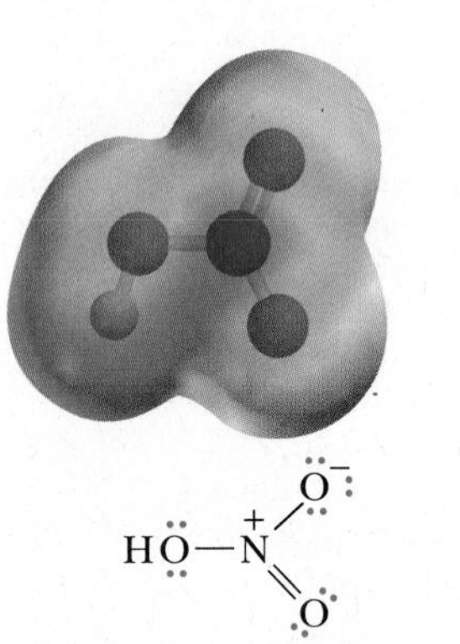

The Lewis structure of HNO_3 shows the negative formal charge localized on one of the oxygen atoms. The electron density model, on the other hand, shows that the negative charge is distributed equally over the two oxygen atoms on the right. The concept of resonance can explain this phenomenon and will be discussed in Section 1.6. Notice also the intense blue color on nitrogen, which is due to its positive formal charge.

1.3 How Do We Predict Bond Angles and the Shapes of Molecules?

In Section 1.2, we used a shared pair of electrons as the fundamental unit of a covalent bond and drew Lewis structures for several small molecules containing various combinations of single, double, and triple bonds. (See, for example, Table 1.6.) We can predict bond angles in these and other molecules in a very straightforward way by using the concept of **valence-shell electron-pair repulsion (VSEPR)**. According to this concept, the valence electrons of an atom may be involved in the formation of single, double, or triple bonds, or they may be unshared. Each combination creates a region of electron density that, because it is occupied by electrons, is negatively charged. Because like charges repel each other, the various regions of electron density around an atom spread so that each is as far away from the others as possible.

Recall from your prior studies in chemistry that VSEPR can be used to predict the shapes of molecules. This can be demonstrated in a very simple way by using balloons. Imagine that a balloon represents a region of electron density. If you tie two balloons together by their ends, they assume the shapes shown in Figure 1.5. The point where they are tied together represents the atom about which you want to predict a bond angle, and the balloons represent regions of electron density about that atom.

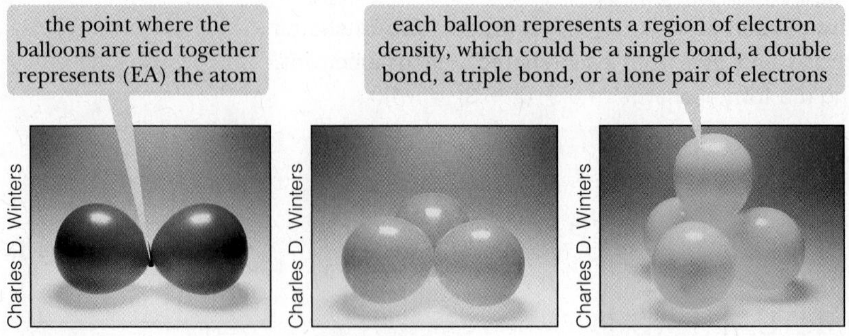

Linear (a)   Trigonal planar (b)   Tetrahedral (c)

FIGURE 1.5
Balloon models used to predict bond angles. (a) Two balloons assume a linear shape with a bond angle of 180° about the tie point. (b) Three balloons assume a trigonal planar shape with bond angles of 120° about the tie point. (c) Four balloons assume a tetrahedral shape with bond angles of 109.5° about the tie point.

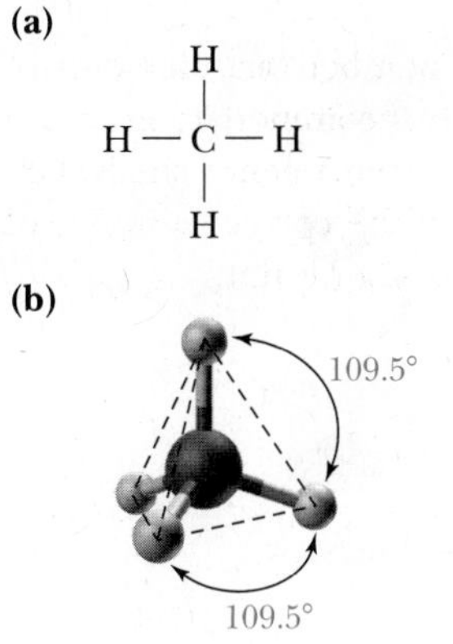

FIGURE 1.6
The shape of a methane molecule, CH_4. (a) Lewis structure and (b) ball-and-stick model. The single bonds occupy four regions of electron density, causing the molecule to be **tetrahedral**. The hydrogens occupy the four corners of a regular tetrahedron, and all H—C—H bond angles are 109.5°.

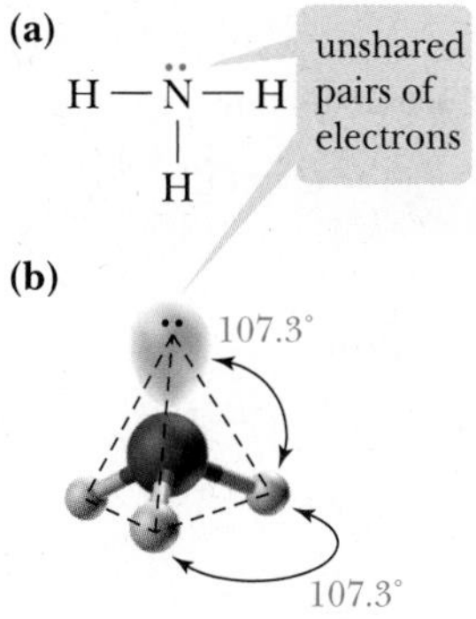

FIGURE 1.7
The shape of an ammonia molecule, NH_3. (a) Lewis structure and (b) ball-and-stick model. The three single bonds and one lone pair of electrons create four regions of electron density. This allows the lone pair and the three hydrogens to occupy the four corners of a tetrahedron. However, we do not take lone pairs of electrons into account when describing the shape of the molecule. For this reason, we describe the geometry of an ammonia molecule as **pyramidal**; that is, the molecule has a shape like a triangular-based pyramid with the three hydrogens at the base and nitrogen at the apex. The observed bond angles are 107.3°. We account for this small difference between the predicted and observed angles by proposing that the unshared pair of electrons on nitrogen repels adjacent electron pairs more strongly than bonding pairs repel each other.

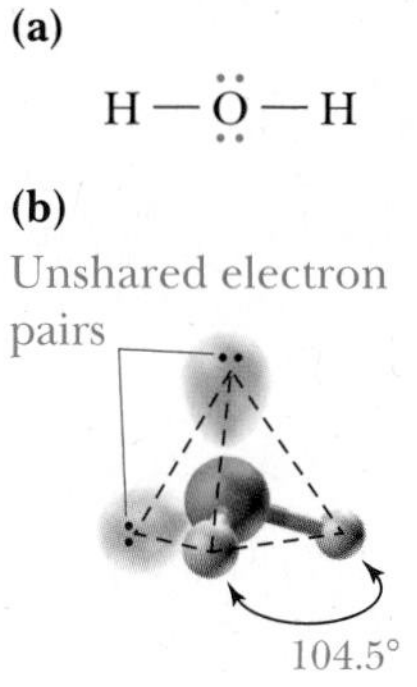

FIGURE 1.8
The shape of a water molecule, H_2O. (a) A Lewis structure and (b) a ball-and-stick model. Using VSEPR, we predict that the four regions of electron density around oxygen are arranged in a tetrahedral manner and that the H–O–H bond angle is 109.5°. Experimental measurements show that the actual H–O–H bond angle is 104.5°, a value smaller than that predicted. We explain this difference between the predicted and observed bond angle by proposing, as we did for NH_3, that unshared pairs of electrons repel adjacent pairs more strongly than do bonding pairs. Note that the distortion from 109.5° is greater in H_2O, which has two unshared pairs of electrons, than it is in NH_3, which has only one unshared pair. We describe the shape of water as **bent**.

We can use the example of the balloons to model the shapes that methane (CH_4), ammonia (NH_3), and water (H_2O) assume. As you look at each of these molecules in Figures 1.6–1.8, take note of (1) the number of regions of electron density shown by the Lewis structure, (2) the geometry that is required to maximize the separation of these regions of electron density, and (3) the names of the shapes that result from this treatment using VSEPR.

A general prediction emerges from this discussion of the shapes of CH_4, NH_3, and H_2O molecules. If a Lewis structure shows four regions of electron density around an atom, then VSEPR predicts a tetrahedral distribution of electron density and bond angles of approximately 109.5°.

In many of the molecules we encounter, an atom is surrounded by three regions of electron density. Figure 1.9 shows Lewis structures for formaldehyde (CH_2O) and ethylene

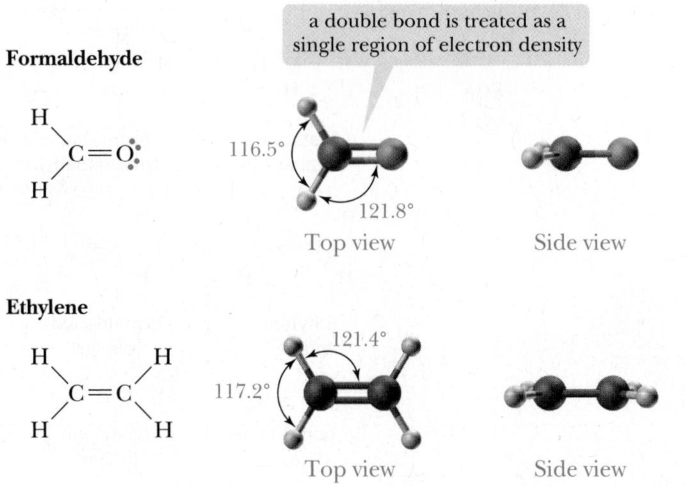

FIGURE 1.9
Shapes of formaldehyde (CH_2O) and ethylene (C_2H_4). In each molecule, the carbons are surrounded by three regions of electron density. Three regions of electron density about an atom are farthest apart when they lie in a plane and make angles of 120° with each other. We describe the geometry about each carbon atom as **trigonal planar**.

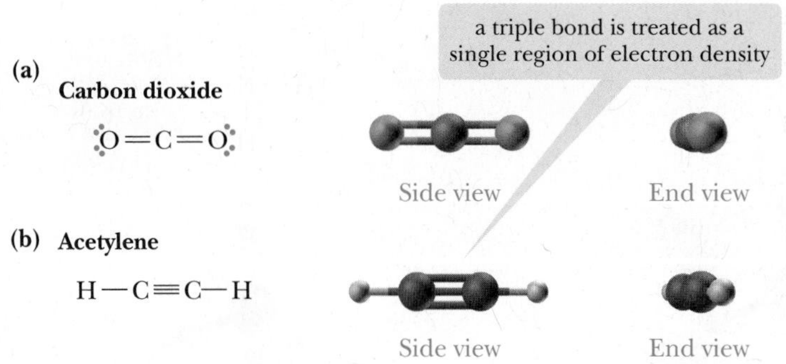

FIGURE 1.10
Shapes of (a) carbon dioxide (CO_2) and (b) acetylene (C_2H_2). In each case, the two regions of electron density are farthest apart if they form a straight line through the central atom and create an angle of 180°. Both carbon dioxide and acetylene are referred to as **linear** molecules.

(C_2H_4). As you look at these two molecules, take note of (1) the number of regions of electron density shown by the Lewis structure, (2) the geometry that is required to maximize the separation of these regions of electron density, and (3) the names of the shapes that result from this treatment using VSEPR. Also notice that using VSEPR, we treat a double bond as a single region of electron density.

In still other types of molecules, a central atom is surrounded by only two regions of electron density. Figure 1.10 shows Lewis structures and ball-and-stick models of carbon dioxide (CO_2) and acetylene (C_2H_2). As with double bonds, VSEPR treats triple bonds as one region of electron density.

Table 1.7 summarizes the predictions of VSEPR.

TABLE 1.7 Predicted Molecular Shapes (VSEPR)

Regions of Electron Density around Central Atom	Predicted Distribution of Electron Density about the Central Atom	Predicted Bond Angles	Examples (Shape of the Molecule)
4	Tetrahedral	109.5°	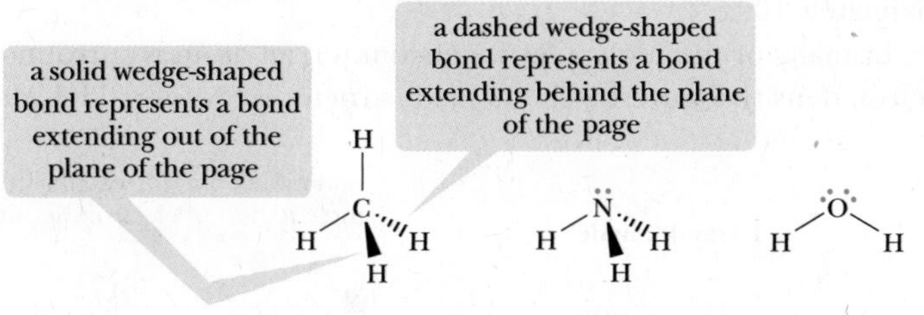 Methane (tetrahedral); Ammonia (pyramidal); Water (bent)
3	Trigonal planar	120°	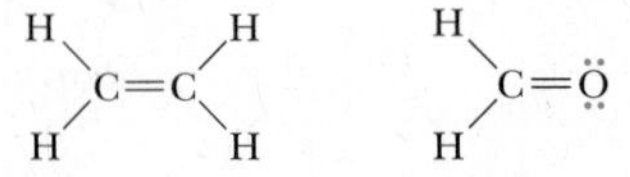 Ethylene (planar); Formaldehyde (planar)
2	Linear	180°	$O=C=O$ Carbon dioxide (linear); H—C≡C—H Acetylene (linear)

EXAMPLE 1.8

Predict all bond angles in these molecules:

(a) CH_3Cl **(b)** $CH_2{=}CHCl$

STRATEGY

To predict bond angles, first draw a correct Lewis structure for the molecule. Be certain to show all unpaired electrons. Then determine the number of regions of electron density (either 2, 3, or 4) around each atom and use that number to predict bond angles (either 180°, 120°, or 109.5°).

SOLUTION

(a) The Lewis structure for CH_3Cl shows carbon surrounded by four regions of electron density. Therefore, we predict that the distribution of electron pairs about carbon is tetrahedral, that all bond angles are 109.5°, and that the shape of CH_3Cl is tetrahedral:

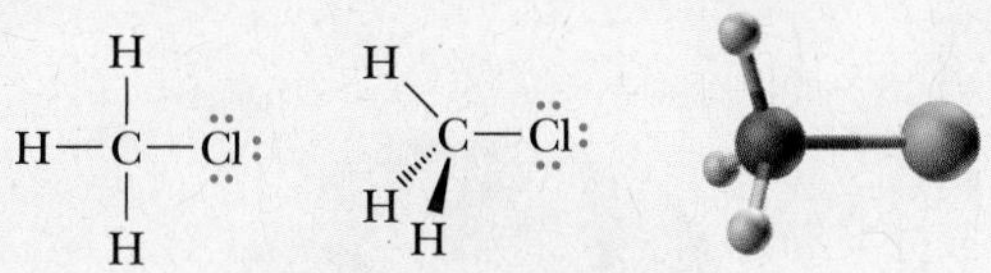

(b) The Lewis structure for $CH_2{=}CHCl$ shows each carbon surrounded by three regions of electron density. Therefore, we predict that all bond angles are 120°.

(Top view) (Viewed along the C=C bond)

See problems 1.41–1.43

PROBLEM 1.8

Predict all bond angles for these molecules:

(a) CH_3OH **(b)** CH_2Cl_2 **(c)** H_2CO_3 (carbonic acid)

Chemical Connections 1A

BUCKYBALL: A NEW FORM OF CARBON

Many elements in the pure state can exist in different forms. We are all familiar with the fact that pure carbon is found in two forms: graphite and diamond. These forms have been known for centuries, and it was generally believed that they were the only forms of carbon having extended networks of C atoms in well-defined structures.

But that is not so! The scientific world was startled in 1985 when Richard Smalley of Rice University and Harry W. Kroto of the University of Sussex, England, and their coworkers announced that they had detected a new form of carbon with a molecular formula C_{60}. They suggested that the molecule has a structure resembling a soccer ball: 12 five-membered rings and 20 six-membered rings arranged such that each five-membered ring is surrounded by six-membered rings. This structure reminded its discoverers of a geodesic dome, a structure invented by the innovative American engineer and philosopher R. Buckminster Fuller. Therefore, the official name of the new allotrope of carbon has become fullerene. Kroto, Smalley, and Robert F. Curl were awarded the Nobel Prize for Chemistry in 1996 for their work with fullerenes. Many higher fullerenes, such as C_{70} and C_{84}, have also been isolated and studied.

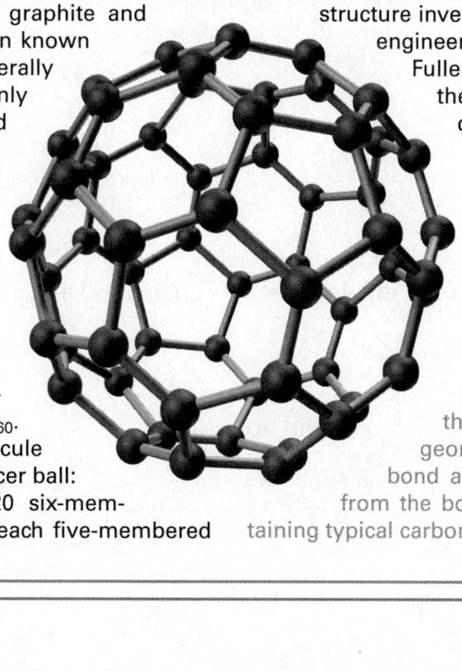

Question

Predict the bond angles about the carbon atoms in C_{60}. What geometric feature distinguishes the bond angles about each carbon in C_{60} from the bond angles of a compound containing typical carbon–carbon bonds?

1.4 How Do We Predict If a Molecule Is Polar or Nonpolar?

In Section 1.2C, we used the terms *polar* and *dipole* to describe a covalent bond in which one atom bears a partial positive charge and the other bears a partial negative charge. We also saw that we can use the difference in electronegativity between bonded atoms to determine the polarity of a covalent bond and the direction of its polarity. We can now combine our understanding of bond polarity and molecular geometry (Section 1.3) to predict the polarity of molecules.

A molecule will be polar if (1) it has polar bonds and (2) the vector sum of its bond dipoles is zero (i.e., the bond dipoles cancel each other). Consider first carbon dioxide, CO_2, a molecule with two polar carbon–oxygen double bonds. Because carbon dioxide is a linear molecule, the vector sum of its two bond dipoles is zero; therefore, this molecule is nonpolar.

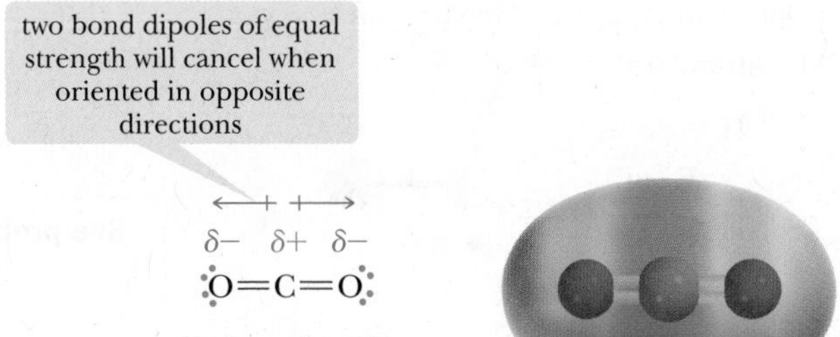

Carbon dioxide
(a nonpolar molecule)

In a water molecule, each O—H bond is polar, with oxygen, the more electronegative atom, bearing a partial negative charge and each hydrogen bearing a partial positive charge. Because water is a bent molecule, the center of its partial positive charge is between the two hydrogen atoms, and the center of its partial negative charge is on oxygen. Thus, water has polar bonds and, because of its geometry, it is a polar molecule.

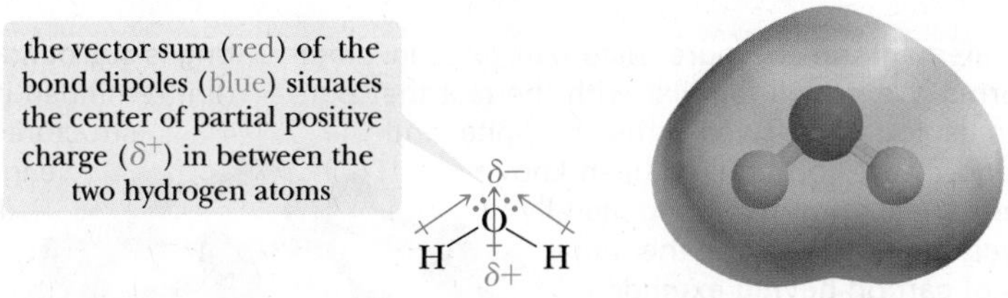

Water
(a polar molecule)

Ammonia has three polar N—H bonds, and because of its geometry, the vector sum of their bond dipoles does not equal zero. Thus, ammonia is a polar molecule.

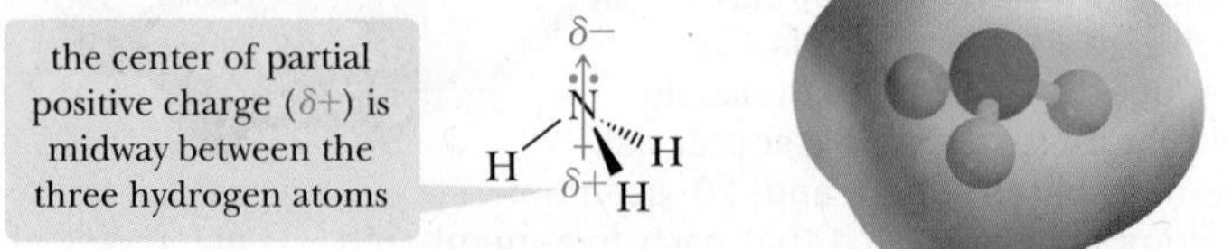

Ammonia
(a polar molecule)

EXAMPLE 1.9

Which of these molecules are polar? For each that is polar, specify the direction of its polarity.

(a) CH_3Cl (b) CH_2O (c) C_2H_2

STRATEGY

To determine whether a molecule is polar, first determine if it has polar bonds, and if it does, determine whether the vector sum of the bond dipoles is zero. If the vector sum of the bond dipoles is not zero, the molecule is polar.

SOLUTION

Both chloromethane (CH_3Cl) and formaldehyde (CH_2O) have polar bonds and, because of their geometry, are polar molecules. Because acetylene (C_2H_2) is linear, and each of its C—H bonds is nonpolar covalent, the molecule is nonpolar.

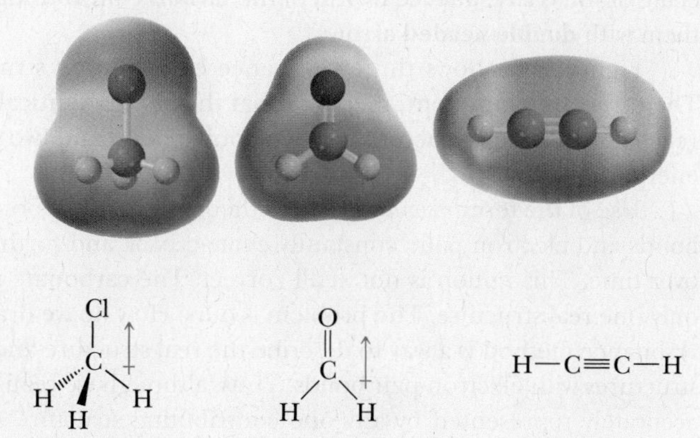

Chloromethane (polar) Formaldehyde (polar) Acetylene (nonpolar)

See problems 1.44, 1.46

PROBLEM 1.9

Both carbon dioxide (CO_2) and sulfur dioxide (SO_2) are triatomic molecules. Account for the fact that carbon dioxide is a nonpolar molecule, whereas sulfur dioxide is a polar molecule.

1.5 What Is Resonance?

As chemists developed a better understanding of covalent bonding in organic compounds, it became obvious that, for a great many molecules and ions, no single Lewis structure provides a truly accurate representation. For example, Figure 1.11 shows three Lewis structures for the carbonate ion, CO_3^{2-}, each of which shows carbon bonded to three oxygen atoms by a combination of one double bond and two single bonds. Each Lewis structure implies that one carbon–oxygen bond is different from the other two. This, however, is not the case; it has been shown that all three carbon–oxygen bonds are identical.

To describe the carbonate ion, as well as other molecules and ions for which no single Lewis structure is adequate, we turn to the theory of resonance.

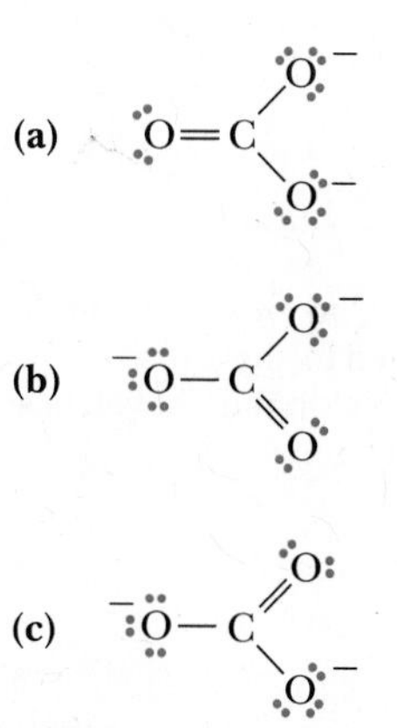

FIGURE 1.11 Three Lewis structures for the carbonate ion.

A. The Theory of Resonance

The theory of resonance was developed by Linus Pauling in the 1930s. According to this theory, many molecules and ions are best described by writing two or more Lewis structures and considering the real molecule or ion to be a composite of these structures. We call

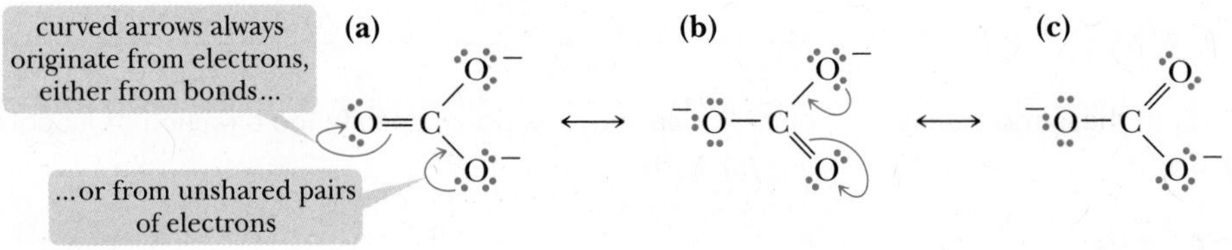

FIGURE 1.12
The carbonate ion represented as a hybrid of three equivalent contributing structures. Curved arrows show the redistribution of valence electrons between one contributing structure and the next.

Resonance contributing structures Representations of a molecule or ion that differ only in the distribution of valence electrons.

Resonance hybrid A molecule or ion that is best described as a composite of a number of contributing structures.

Double-headed arrow A symbol used to connect contributing structures.

individual Lewis structures **resonance contributing structures**. We show that the real molecule or ion is a **resonance hybrid** of the various contributing structures by interconnecting them with **double-headed arrows**.

Figure 1.12 shows three resonance contributing structures for the carbonate ion. The three are equivalent, meaning that they have identical patterns of covalent bonding (each contributing structure has one double bond and two single bonds) and are of equal energy.

Use of the term *resonance* for this theory of covalent bonding might suggest to you that bonds and electron pairs constantly change back and forth from one position to another over time. This notion is not at all correct. The carbonate ion, for example, has one and only one real structure. The problem is ours: How do we draw that one real structure? The resonance method is a way to describe the real structure and at the same time retain Lewis structures with electron-pair bonds. Thus, although we realize that the carbonate ion is not accurately represented by any one contributing structure shown in Figure 1.12, we continue to represent it as one of these for convenience. We understand, of course, that what is intended is the resonance hybrid.

A final note. Do not confuse resonance contributing structures with equilibration among different species. A molecule described as a resonance hybrid is not equilibrating among individual electron configurations. Rather, the molecule has only one structure, which is best described as a hybrid of its various contributing structures. The colors of the color wheel provide a good analogy. Green is not a primary color; the colors yellow and blue are mixed to make green. You can think of molecules represented by resonance hybrids as being green. Green is not sometimes yellow and sometimes blue. Green is green! In an analogous way, a molecule described as a resonance hybrid is not sometimes one contributing structure and sometimes another. It is a single structure all of the time—the resonance hybrid.

B. Curved Arrows and Electron Pushing

Curved arrow A symbol used to show the redistribution of valence electrons.

Notice in Figure 1.12 that the only change from resonance contributing structure (a) to (b) and then from (b) to (c) is a redistribution of valence electrons. To show how this redistribution of valence electrons occurs, chemists use a symbol called a **curved arrow**, which shows the repositioning of an electron pair from its origin (the tail of the arrow) to its destination (the head of the arrow). The repositioning may be from an atom to an adjacent bond or from a bond to an adjacent atom.

A curved arrow is nothing more than a bookkeeping symbol for keeping track of electron pairs or, as some call it, **electron pushing**. Do not be misled by its simplicity. Electron pushing will help you see the relationship between contributing structures. Furthermore, it will help you follow bond-breaking and bond-forming steps in organic reactions. Understanding this type of electron pushing is a survival skill in organic chemistry; your success in this course depends on it.

C. Rules for Writing Acceptable Resonance Contributing Structures

You must follow these four rules in writing acceptable resonance contributing structures:

1. All contributing structures must have the same number of valence electrons.
2. All contributing structures must obey the rules of covalent bonding; thus, no contributing structure may have more than 2 electrons in the valence shell of hydrogen or more than 8 electrons in the valence shell of a second-period element. Third-period elements, such as sulfur and phosphorus, may have up to 12 electrons in their valence shells.
3. The positions of all nuclei must be the same; that is, contributing structures differ only in the distribution of valence electrons.
4. All contributing structures must have the same total number of paired and unpaired electrons.

EXAMPLE 1.10

Which sets are pairs of acceptable resonance contributing structures?

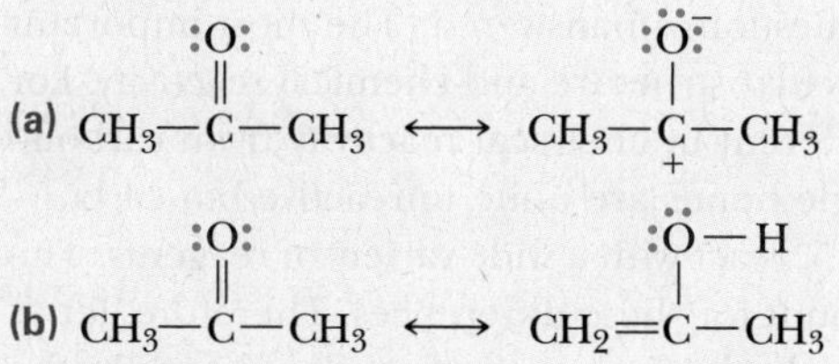

STRATEGY

The concept being examined here is that resonance involves the redistribution of valence electrons; the connectivity of atoms does not change.

SOLUTION

(a) A pair of resonance contributing structures. They differ only in the distribution of valence electrons.

(b) Not a pair of resonance contributing structures. They differ in the arrangement of their atoms. Oxygen is bonded to a hydrogen atom in the Lewis structure on the right, but the other structure contains no such bond.

See problem 1.47

PROBLEM 1.10

Which sets are pairs of resonance contributing structures?

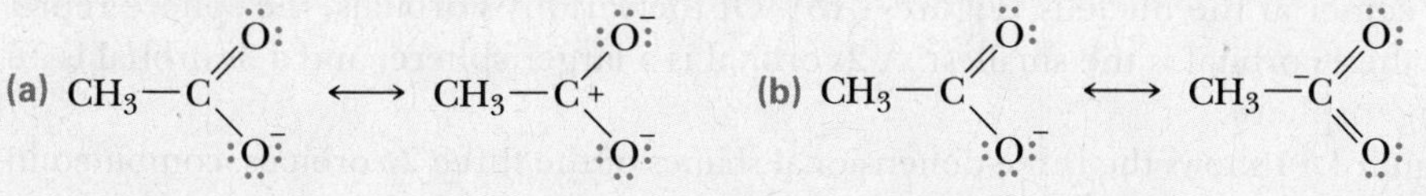

EXAMPLE 1.11

Draw the resonance contributing structure indicated by the curved arrows. Be certain to show all valence electrons and all formal charges.

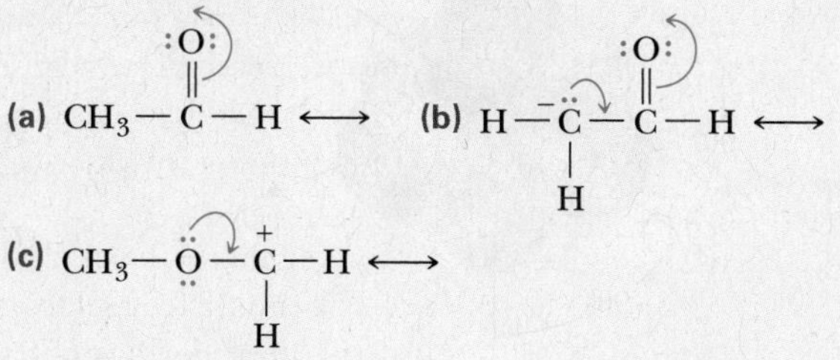

STRATEGY

Any curved arrow that points to an atom will generate a lone pair of electrons. Any curved arrow that points to a bond will result in an additional bond on top of the original bond. That is, a single bond will become a double bond and a double bond will become a triple bond.

SOLUTION

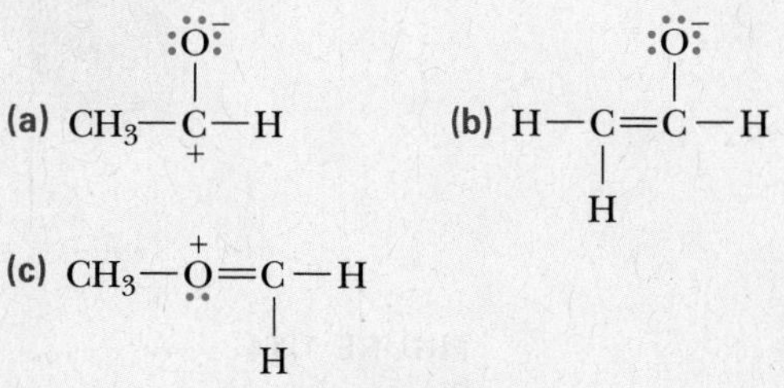

See problems 1.48, 1.50

PROBLEM 1.11

Use curved arrows to show the redistribution of valence electrons in converting resonance contributing structure (a) to (b) and then (b) to (c). Also show, using curved arrows, how (a) can be converted to (c) without going through (b).

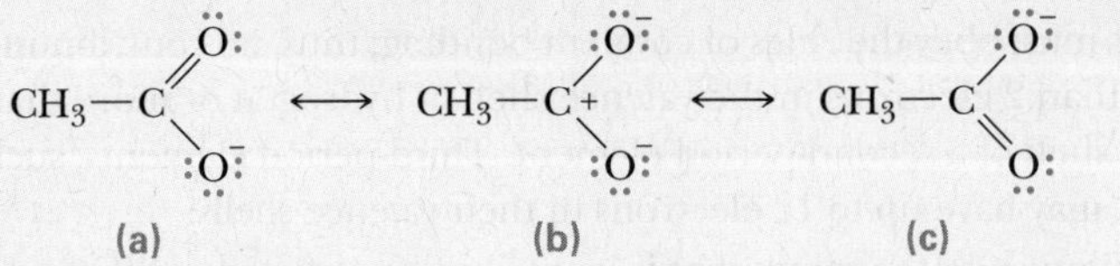

1.6 What Is the Orbital Overlap Model of Covalent Bonding?

As much as the Lewis and VSEPR models help us to understand covalent bonding and the geometry of molecules, they leave many questions unanswered. The most important of these questions is the relation between molecular structure and chemical reactivity. For example, carbon–carbon double bonds are different in chemical reactivity from carbon–carbon single bonds. Most carbon–carbon single bonds are quite unreactive but carbon–carbon double bonds, as we will see in Chapter 5, react with a wide variety of reagents. The Lewis model and VSEPR give us no way to account for these differences. Therefore, let us turn to a newer model of covalent bonding, namely, the formation of covalent bonds by the overlap of atomic orbitals.

A. Shapes of Atomic Orbitals

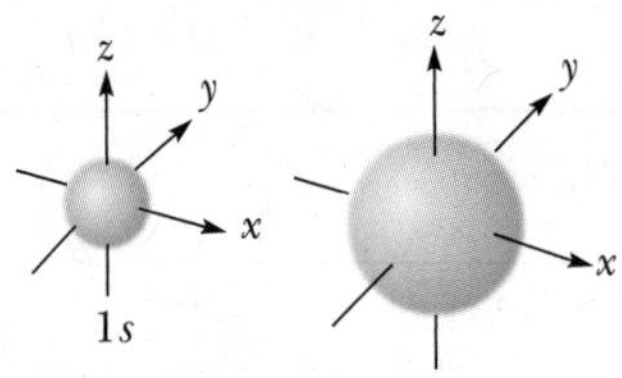

FIGURE 1.13
Shapes of 1*s* and 2*s* atomic orbitals.

One way to visualize the electron density associated with a particular orbital is to draw a boundary surface around the region of space that encompasses some arbitrary percentage of the negative charge associated with that orbital. Most commonly, we draw the boundary surface at 95%. Drawn in this manner, all *s* orbitals have the shape of a sphere with its center at the nucleus (Figure 1.13). Of the various *s* orbitals, the sphere representing the 1*s* orbital is the smallest. A 2*s* orbital is a larger sphere, and a 3*s* orbital is an even larger sphere.

Figure 1.14 shows the three-dimensional shapes of the three 2*p* orbitals, combined in one diagram to illustrate their relative orientations in space. Each 2*p* orbital consists of two

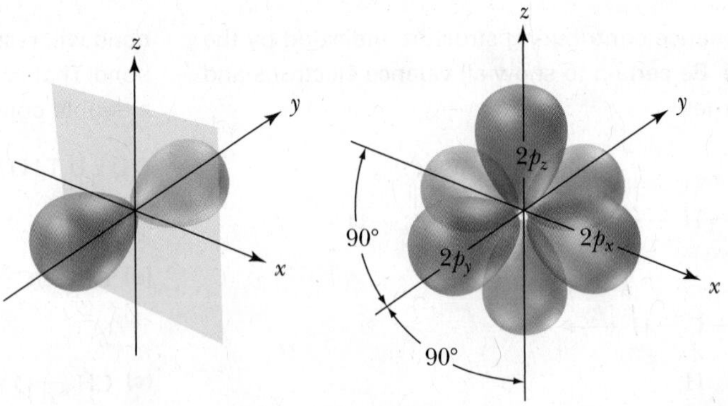

FIGURE 1.14
Shapes of $2p_x$, $2p_y$, and $2p_z$ atomic orbitals. The three 2*p* orbitals are mutually perpendicular. One lobe of each orbital is shown in red, the other in blue.

lobes arranged in a straight line with the nucleus in the middle. The three $2p$ orbitals are mutually perpendicular and are designated $2p_x$, $2p_y$, and $2p_z$.

B. Formation of a Covalent Bond by the Overlap of Atomic Orbitals

According to the orbital overlap model, a covalent bond is formed when a portion of an atomic orbital of one atom overlaps a portion of an atomic orbital of another atom. In forming the covalent bond in H_2, for example, two hydrogens approach each other so that their $1s$ atomic orbitals overlap to form a sigma covalent bond (Figure 1.15). A **sigma (σ) bond** is a covalent bond in which orbitals overlap along the axis joining the two nuclei.

Sigma (σ) bond A covalent bond in which the overlap of atomic orbitals is concentrated along the bond axis.

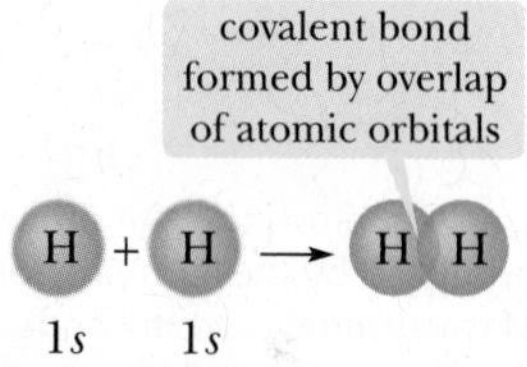

FIGURE 1.15 Formation of the covalent bond in H_2 by the overlap of the $1s$ atomic orbitals of each hydrogen.

C. Hybridization of Atomic Orbitals

The formation of a covalent bond between two hydrogen atoms is straightforward. The formation of covalent bonds with second-period elements, however, presents the following problem: In forming covalent bonds, atoms of carbon, nitrogen, and oxygen (all second-period elements) use $2s$ and $2p$ atomic orbitals. The three $2p$ atomic orbitals are at angles of 90° to one another (Figure 1.14), and if atoms of second-period elements used these orbitals to form covalent bonds, the bond angles around each would be approximately 90°. Bond angles of 90°, however, are rarely observed in organic molecules. What we find, instead, are bond angles of approximately 109.5° in molecules with only single bonds, 120° in molecules with double bonds, and 180° in molecules with triple bonds:

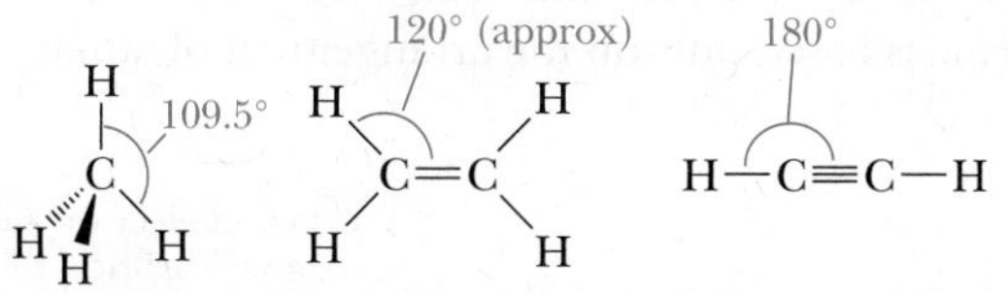

To account for these observed bond angles, Pauling proposed that atomic orbitals combine to form new orbitals, called **hybrid orbitals.** In your introductory chemistry course, you learned about several types of hybrid orbitals made up from *s*, *p*, and even *d* atomic orbitals. In organic chemistry, because we deal almost exclusively with elements of the first and second periods of the Periodic Table, we are mostly concerned with the hybrid orbitals that result from the combination of *s* and *p* atomic orbitals. These are aptly named the *sp*-type hybrid orbitals, of which there are three types. The type and number of hybrid orbitals formed are equal to the number of atomic orbitals combined. Elements of the second period form these three types of hybrid orbitals, designated sp^3, sp^2, and sp, each of which can contain up to two electrons. We review these hybrid orbitals for you here. Keep in mind that superscripts in the designation of hybrid orbitals tell you how many atomic orbitals have been combined to form the hybrid orbitals. The designation sp^3, for example, tells you that *one s* atomic orbital and *three p* atomic orbitals are combined in forming the hybrid orbital. Do not confuse this use of superscripts with how we use superscripts in writing a ground-state electron configuration—for example, $1s^2 2s^2 2p^5$ for fluorine. In the case of an electron configuration, superscripts tell you the number of electrons in each orbital or set of orbitals.

Hybrid orbital An orbital produced from the combination of two or more atomic orbitals.

As you review each type of hybrid orbital in the following subsections, take note of (1) the number and types of atomic orbitals that were combined to make the hybrid orbitals, (2) the number of *p* orbitals that remain uncombined, and (3) the three-dimensional arrangement in space of the hybrid orbitals and any uncombined *p* orbitals. In particular, you will find that these three-dimensional arrangements will retain the names (tetrahedral, trigonal planar, linear) and bond angles (109.5°, 120°, and 180°) used to describe the shapes of molecules in our section on VSEPR (Section 1.3).

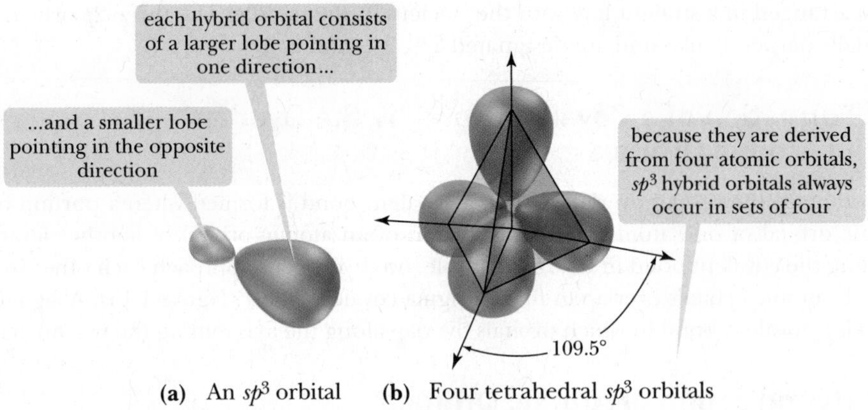

FIGURE 1.16
sp^3 Hybrid orbitals. (a) Representation of a single sp^3 hybrid orbital showing two lobes of unequal size. (b) Three-dimensional representation of four sp^3 hybrid orbitals, which point toward the corners of a regular tetrahedron. The smaller lobes of each sp^3 hybrid orbital are hidden behind the larger lobes.

D. sp^3 Hybrid Orbitals: Bond Angles of Approximately 109.5°

***sp^3* Hybrid orbital** An orbital produced by the combination of one *s* atomic orbital and three *p* atomic orbitals.

The combination of one 2*s* atomic orbital and three 2*p* atomic orbitals forms four equivalent ***sp^3* hybrid orbitals** (Figure 1.16).

In Section 1.2, we described the covalent bonding in CH_4, NH_3, and H_2O in terms of the Lewis model, and in Section 1.3 we used VSEPR to predict bond angles of approximately 109.5° in each molecule. Figure 1.17 shows the bonding in these molecules in terms of the overlap of orbitals. Notice that the central atom in each compound uses four sp^3 hybrid orbitals to either form a sigma (σ) bond with a hydrogen atom or to hold unshared pairs of electrons. In each case, the orbitals are arranged tetrahedrally, while the shape that describes each molecule is based only on the arrangement of atoms.

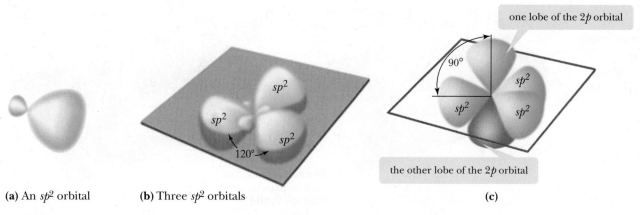

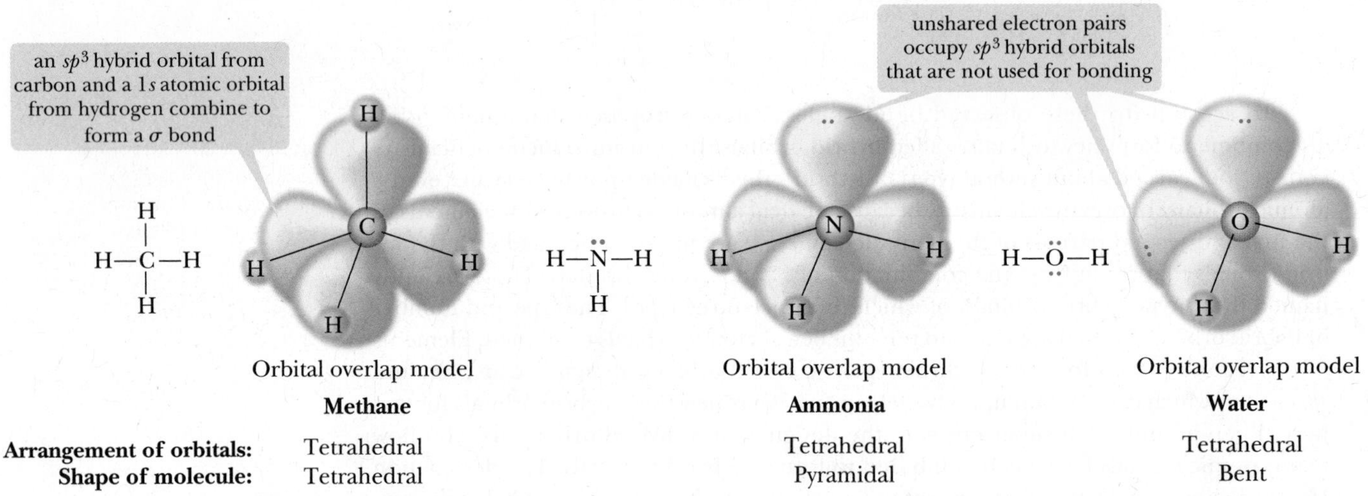

FIGURE 1.17
Orbital overlap models of methane, ammonia, and water.

E. sp^2 Hybrid Orbitals: Bond Angles of Approximately 120°

***sp^2* Hybrid orbital** An orbital produced by the combination of one *s* atomic orbital and two *p* atomic orbitals.

The combination of one 2*s* atomic orbital and two 2*p* atomic orbitals forms three equivalent ***sp^2* hybrid orbitals** (Figure 1.18). Because they are derived from three atomic orbitals, sp^2 hybrid orbitals always occur in sets of three. The third 2*p* atomic orbital (remember $2p_x$, $2p_y$, and $2p_z$) is not involved in hybridization and consists of two lobes lying perpendicular to the plane of the hybrid orbitals [Figure 1.18(c)].

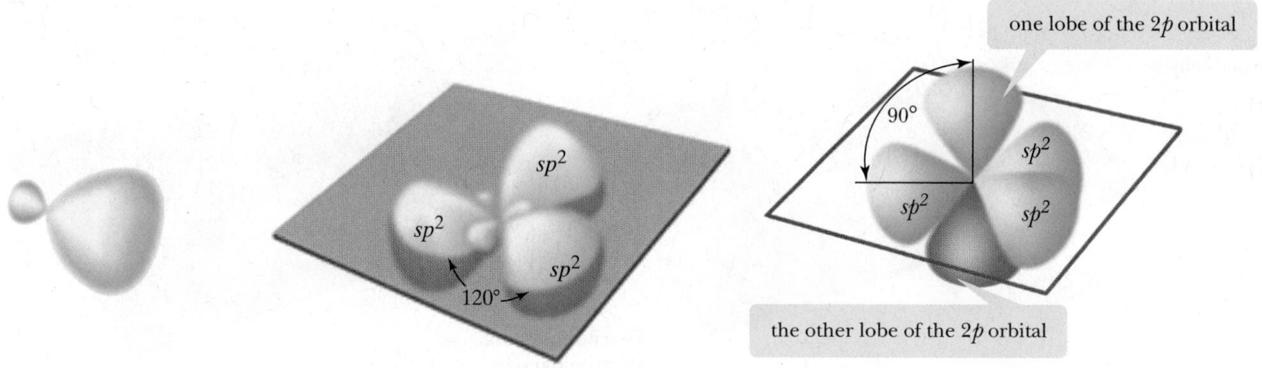

(a) An sp^2 orbital **(b)** Three sp^2 orbitals **(c)**

FIGURE 1.18
sp^2 Hybrid orbitals. (a) A single sp^2 hybrid orbital showing two lobes of unequal size. (b) The three sp^2 hybrid orbitals with their axes in a plane at angles of 120°. (c) The unhybridized $2p$ atomic orbital perpendicular to the plane created by the three sp^2 hybrid orbitals.

Second-period elements use sp^2 hybrid orbitals to form double bonds. Figure 1.19(a) shows a Lewis structure for ethylene, C_2H_4. A sigma bond between the carbons in ethylene forms by the overlap of sp^2 hybrid orbitals along a common axis [Figure 1.19(b)]. Each carbon also forms sigma bonds to two hydrogens. The remaining $2p$ orbitals on adjacent carbon atoms lie parallel to each other and overlap to form a pi bond [Figure 1.19(c)]. A **pi (π) bond** is a covalent bond formed by the overlap of parallel p orbitals. Because of the lesser degree of overlap of orbitals forming pi bonds compared with those forming sigma bonds, pi bonds are generally weaker than sigma bonds.

Pi (π) bond A covalent bond formed by the overlap of parallel p orbitals.

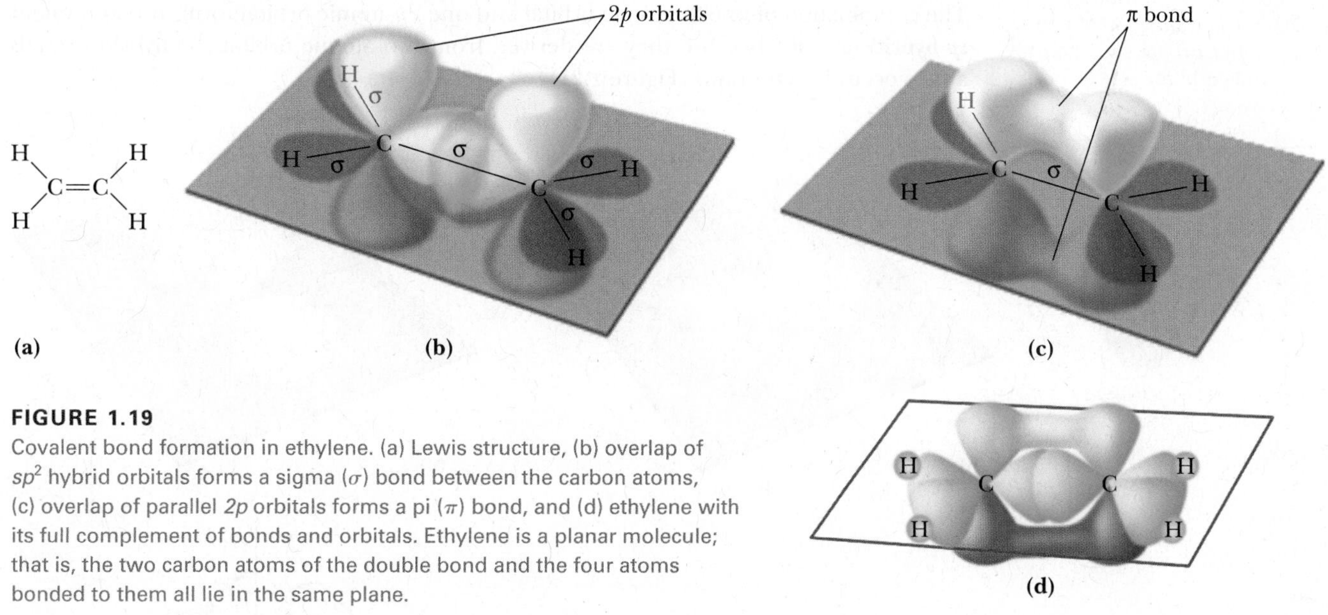

(a) **(b)** **(c)** **(d)**

FIGURE 1.19
Covalent bond formation in ethylene. (a) Lewis structure, (b) overlap of sp^2 hybrid orbitals forms a sigma (σ) bond between the carbon atoms, (c) overlap of parallel $2p$ orbitals forms a pi (π) bond, and (d) ethylene with its full complement of bonds and orbitals. Ethylene is a planar molecule; that is, the two carbon atoms of the double bond and the four atoms bonded to them all lie in the same plane.

The orbital overlap model describes all double bonds in the same way that we have described a carbon–carbon double bond. In formaldehyde, CH_2O, the simplest organic molecule containing a carbon–oxygen double bond, carbon forms sigma bonds to two hydrogens by the overlap of an sp^2 hybrid orbital of carbon and the $1s$ atomic orbital of

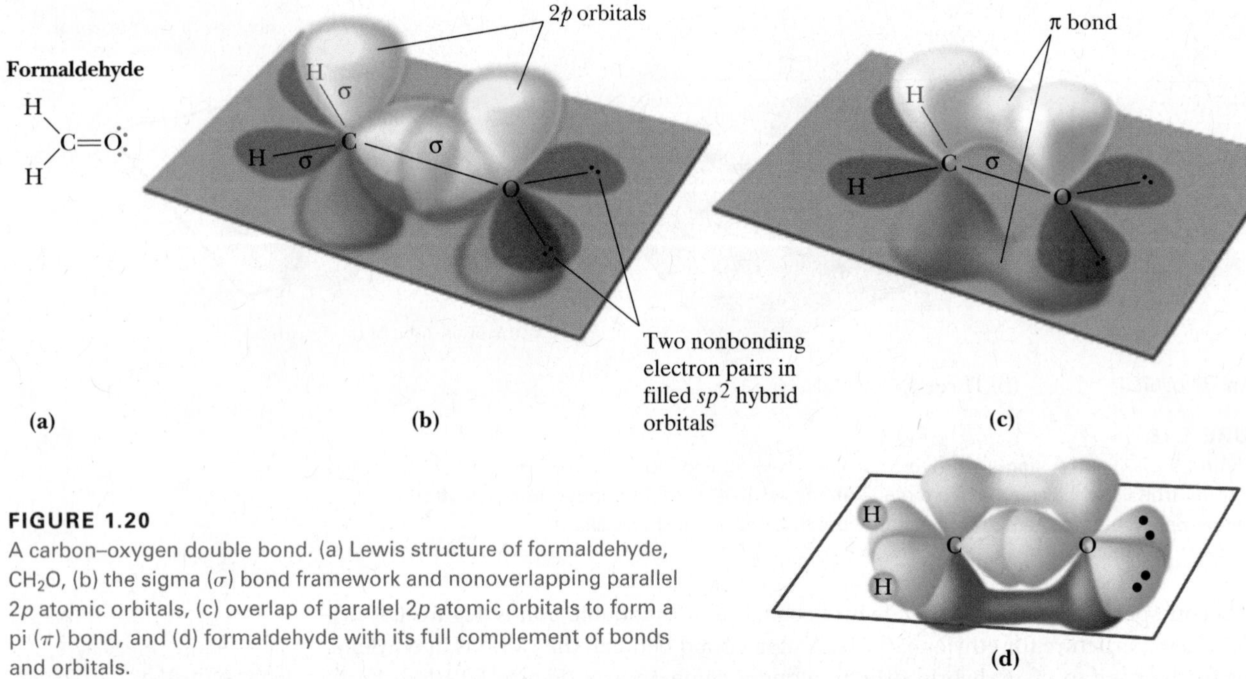

FIGURE 1.20
A carbon–oxygen double bond. (a) Lewis structure of formaldehyde, CH_2O, (b) the sigma (σ) bond framework and nonoverlapping parallel 2*p* atomic orbitals, (c) overlap of parallel 2*p* atomic orbitals to form a pi (π) bond, and (d) formaldehyde with its full complement of bonds and orbitals.

each hydrogen. Carbon and oxygen are joined by a sigma bond formed by the overlap of sp^2 hybrid orbitals and a pi bond formed by the overlap of unhybridized 2*p* atomic orbitals (Figure 1.20).

F. *sp* Hybrid Orbitals: Bond Angles of Approximately 180°

***sp* Hybrid orbital** A hybrid atomic orbital produced by the combination of one *s* atomic orbital and one *p* atomic orbital.

The combination of one 2*s* atomic orbital and one 2*p* atomic orbital forms two equivalent ***sp* hybrid orbitals**. Because they are derived from two atomic orbitals, *sp* hybrid orbitals always occur in sets of two (Figure 1.21).

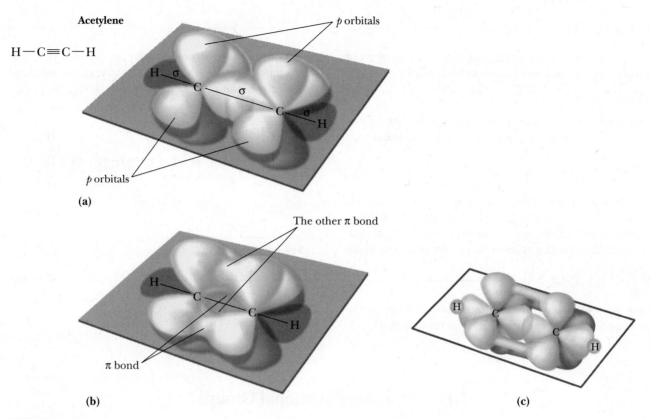

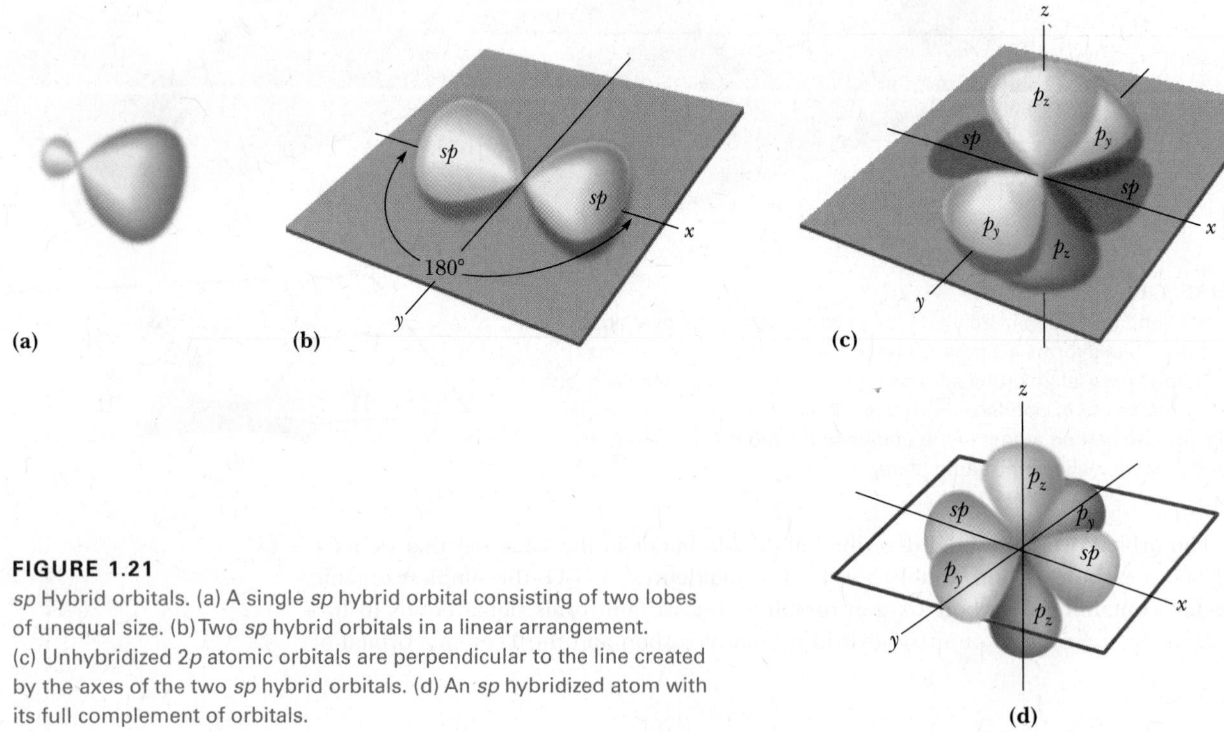

FIGURE 1.21
sp Hybrid orbitals. (a) A single *sp* hybrid orbital consisting of two lobes of unequal size. (b) Two *sp* hybrid orbitals in a linear arrangement. (c) Unhybridized 2*p* atomic orbitals are perpendicular to the line created by the axes of the two *sp* hybrid orbitals. (d) An *sp* hybridized atom with its full complement of orbitals.

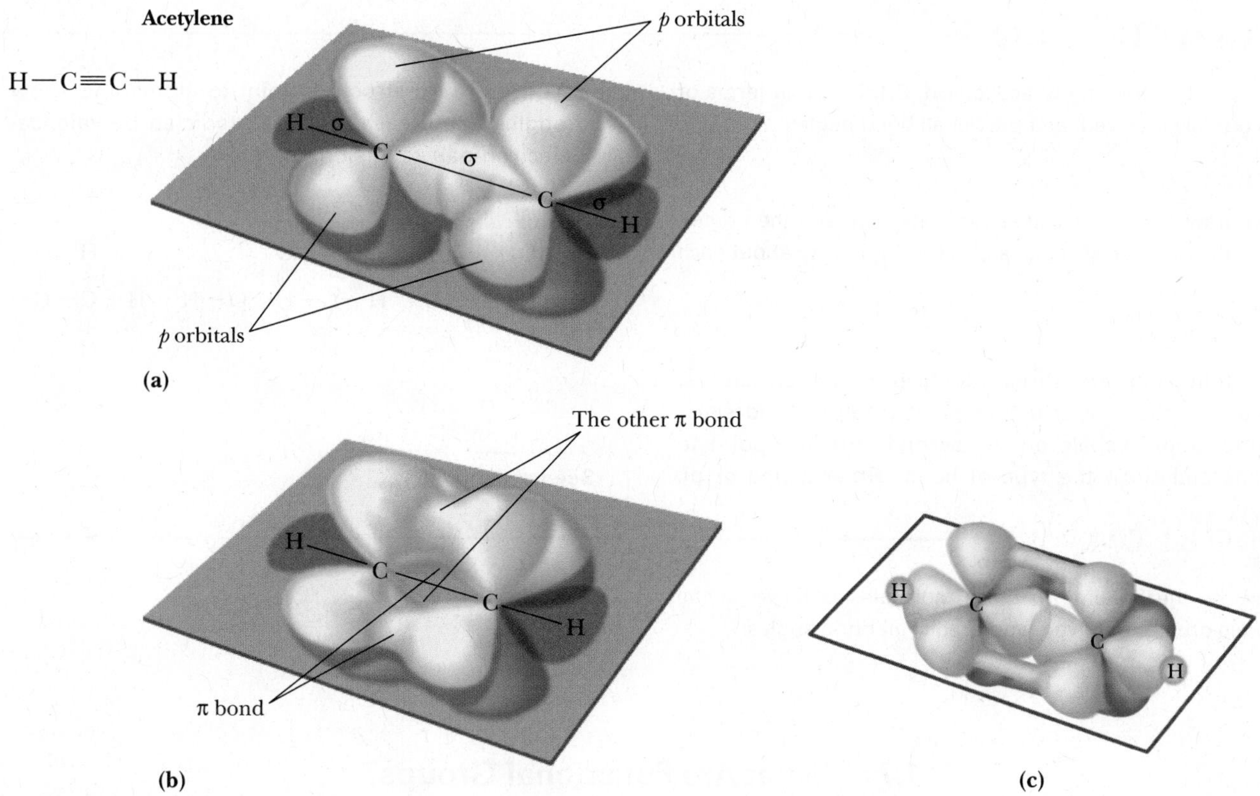

FIGURE 1.22
Covalent bonding in acetylene. (a) The sigma bond framework shown along with nonoverlapping 2*p* atomic orbitals. (b) Formation of two pi bonds by overlap of two sets of parallel 2*p* atomic orbitals. (c) Acetylene with its full complement of bonds and orbitals.

Figure 1.22 shows a Lewis structure and an orbital overlap diagram for acetylene, C_2H_2. A carbon–carbon triple bond consists of one sigma bond and two pi bonds. The sigma bond is formed by the overlap of *sp* hybrid orbitals. One pi bond is formed by the overlap of a pair of parallel 2*p* atomic orbitals. The second pi bond is formed by the overlap of a second pair of parallel 2*p* atomic orbitals.

Table 1.8 summarizes the relationship among the number of groups bonded to carbon, orbital hybridization, and the types of bonds involved.

TABLE 1.8 Covalent Bonding of Carbon

Groups Bonded to Carbon	Orbital Hybridization	Predicted Bond Angles	Types of Bonds to Carbon	Example	Name
4	sp^3	109.5°	four sigma bonds	H H H—C—C—H H H	ethane
3	sp^2	120°	three sigma bonds and one pi bond	H H C=C H H	ethylene
2	*sp*	180°	two sigma bonds and two pi bonds	H—C≡C—H	acetylene

EXAMPLE 1.12

Describe the bonding in acetic acid, CH_3COOH, in terms of the orbitals involved, and predict all bond angles.

STRATEGY

First draw a Lewis structure for acetic acid and then determine the number of regions of electron density about each atom.

SOLUTION

The following are three identical Lewis structures. Labels on the first structure point to atoms and show hybridization. Labels on the second structure point to bonds and show the type of bond, either sigma or pi. Labels on the third structure point to atoms and show bond angles about each atom as predicted by valence-shell electron-pair repulsion.

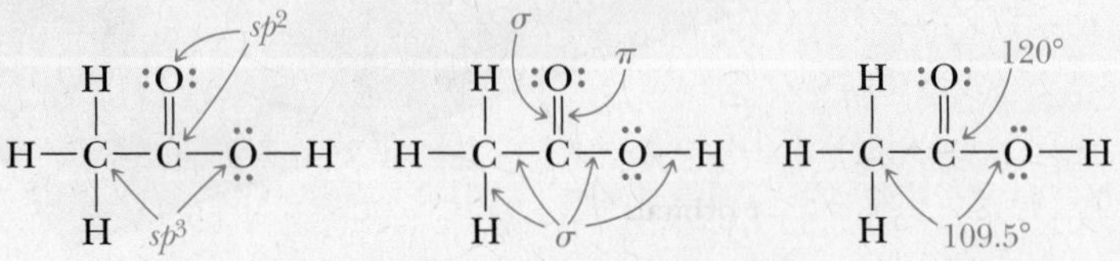

See problem 1.51

PROBLEM 1.12

Describe the bonding in these molecules in terms of the atomic orbitals involved, and predict all bond angles:

(a) $CH_3CH{=}CH_2$
(b) CH_3NH_2

1.7 What Are Functional Groups?

Functional group An atom or a group of atoms within a molecule that shows a characteristic set of physical and chemical properties.

Over 10 million organic compounds have been discovered or made by organic chemists! Surely it would seem to be an almost impossible task to learn the physical and chemical properties of this many compounds. Fortunately, the study of organic compounds is not as formidable a task as you might think. While organic compounds can undergo a wide variety of chemical reactions, only certain portions of their structure are changed in any particular reaction. The part of an organic molecule that undergoes chemical reactions is called a **functional group**, and, as we will see, the same functional group, in whatever organic molecule we find it, undergoes the same types of chemical reactions. Therefore, you do not have to study the chemical reactions of even a fraction of the 10 million known organic compounds. Instead you need only to identify a few characteristic types of functional groups and then study the chemical reactions that each undergoes.

Functional groups are also important because they are the units by which we divide organic compounds into families of compounds. For example, we group those compounds which contain an —OH (hydroxyl) group bonded to a tetrahedral carbon into a family called alcohols, and compounds containing a —COOH (carboxyl) group into a family called carboxylic acids. In Table 1.9, we introduce five of the most common functional groups. A complete list of all functional groups we will study is on the inside front cover of the text.

At this point, our concern is only pattern recognition—that is, how to recognize these five functional groups when you see them and how to draw structural formulas of molecules containing them.

Finally, functional groups serve as the basis for naming organic compounds. Ideally, each of the 10 million or more organic compounds must have a name that is different from every other compound.

To summarize, functional groups

- are sites of chemical reaction; a particular functional group, in whatever compound we find it, undergoes the same types of chemical reactions.
- determine, in large measure, the physical properties of a compound.
- are the units by which we divide organic compounds into families.
- serve as a basis for naming organic compounds.

TABLE 1.9 Five Common Functional Groups

Functional Group	Name of Group	Present In	Example	Name of Example
$-OH$	hydroxyl	alcohols	CH_3CH_2OH	Ethanol
$-NH_2$	amino	amines	$CH_3CH_2NH_2$	Ethanamine
$-\overset{\overset{O}{\|}}{C}-H$	carbonyl	aldehydes	$CH_3\overset{\overset{O}{\|}}{C}H$	Ethanal
$-\overset{\overset{O}{\|}}{C}-$	carbonyl	ketones	$CH_3\overset{\overset{O}{\|}}{C}CH_3$	Acetone
$-\overset{\overset{O}{\|}}{C}-OH$	carboxyl	carboxylic acids	$CH_3\overset{\overset{O}{\|}}{C}OH$	Acetic acid

A. Alcohols

The functional group of an **alcohol** is an **—OH (hydroxyl)** group bonded to a tetrahedral (*sp^3* hybridized) carbon atom. In the general formula that follows, we use the symbol R to indicate either a hydrogen or another carbon group. The important point in the general structure is that the —OH group is bonded to a tetrahedral carbon atom:

Hydroxyl group An —OH group.

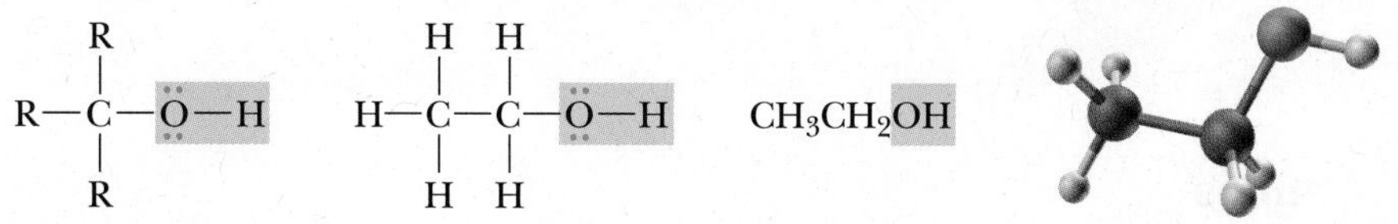

Functional group (R=H or carbon group) — Structural formula — Condensed structural formula

The rightmost representation of this alcohol is a **condensed structural formula**, CH_3CH_2OH. In a condensed structural formula, CH_3 indicates a carbon bonded to three hydrogens, CH_2 indicates a carbon bonded to two hydrogens, and CH indicates a carbon bonded to one hydrogen. We generally do not show unshared pairs of electrons in a condensed structural formula.

Alcohols are classified as **primary (1°)**, **secondary (2°)**, or **tertiary (3°)**, depending on the number of carbon atoms bonded to the carbon bearing the —OH group:

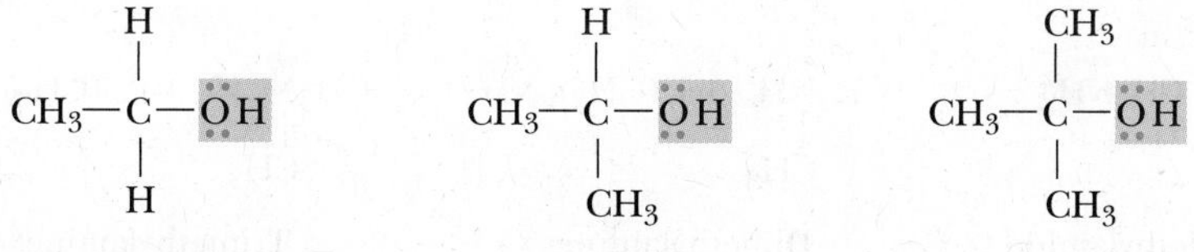

A 1° alcohol — A 2° alcohol — A 3° alcohol

EXAMPLE 1.13

Write condensed structural formulas for the two alcohols with the molecular formula C_3H_8O. Classify each as primary, secondary, or tertiary.

STRATEGY

First, bond the three carbon atoms in a chain with the —OH (hydroxyl) group bonded to either an end carbon or the middle carbon of the chain. Then, to complete each structural formula, add seven hydrogens so that each carbon has four bonds to it.

SOLUTION

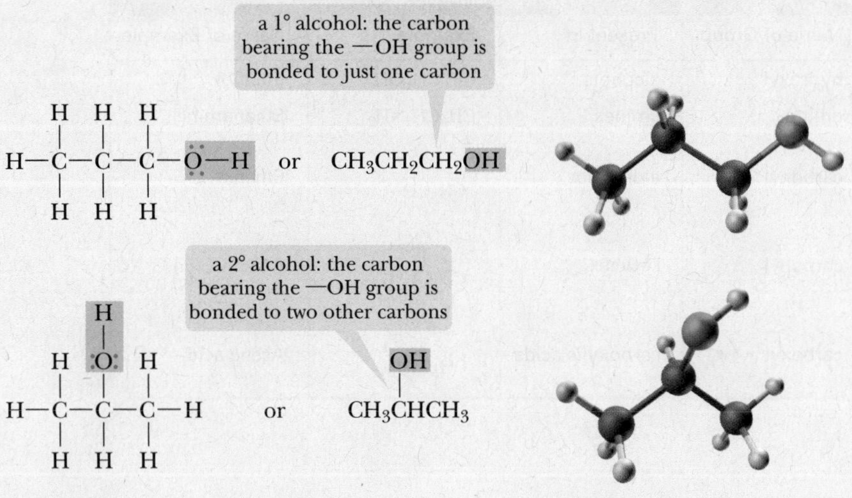

See problems 1.53–1.56, 1.58, 1.59

PROBLEM 1.13

Write condensed structural formulas for the four alcohols with the molecular formula $C_4H_{10}O$. Classify each as primary, secondary, or tertiary.

B. Amines

Amino group An sp^3 hybridized nitrogen atom bonded to one, two, or three carbon groups.

The functional group of an amine is an **amino group**—a nitrogen atom bonded to one, two, or three carbon atoms. In a **primary (1°) amine**, nitrogen is bonded to one carbon atom. In a **secondary (2°) amine**, it is bonded to two carbon atoms, and in a **tertiary (3°) amine**, it is bonded to three carbon atoms. The second and third structural formulas below can be written in a more abbreviated form by collecting the CH_3 groups and writing them as $(CH_3)_2NH$ and $(CH_3)_3N$, respectively.

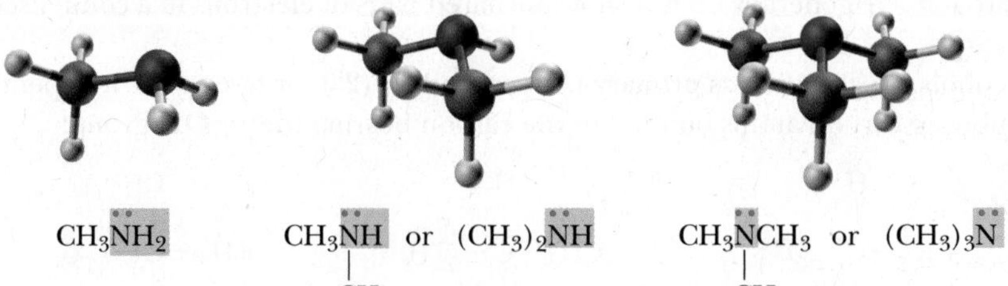

Methylamine (a 1° amine) | Dimethylamine (a 2° amine) | Trimethylamine (a 3° amine)

EXAMPLE 1.14

Write condensed structural formulas for the two primary (1°) amines with the molecular formula C_3H_9N.

STRATEGY

For a primary amine, draw a nitrogen atom bonded to two hydrogens and one carbon. The nitrogen may be bonded to the three-carbon chain in two different ways. Then add the seven hydrogens to give each carbon four bonds and give the correct molecular formula.

SOLUTION

$CH_3CH_2CH_2NH_2$

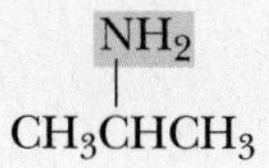

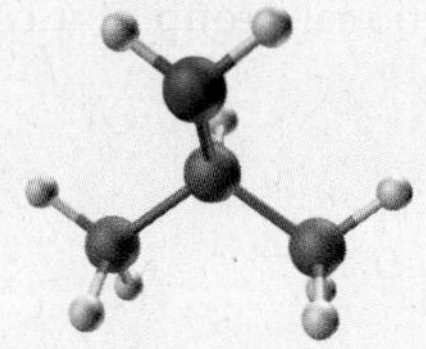

See problems 1.53–1.56, 1.58, 1.59

PROBLEM 1.14

Write condensed structural formulas for the three secondary amines with molecular formula $C_4H_{11}N$.

C. Aldehydes and Ketones

Both aldehydes and ketones contain a **C=O (carbonyl)** group. The **aldehyde** functional group contains a carbonyl group bonded to a hydrogen. In formaldehyde, CH_2O, the simplest aldehyde, the carbonyl carbon is bonded to two hydrogen atoms. In a condensed structural formula, the aldehyde group may be written showing the carbon–oxygen double bond as CH=O, or, alternatively, it may be written —CHO. The functional group of a **ketone** is a carbonyl group bonded to two carbon atoms.

Carbonyl group A C=O group.

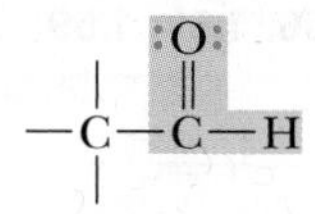

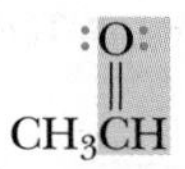

Functional group — An aldehyde

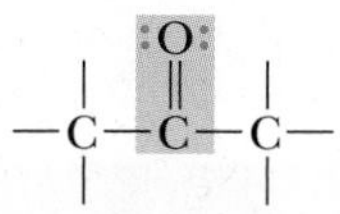

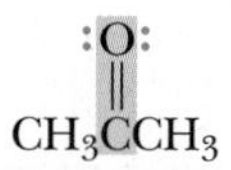

Functional group — A ketone

EXAMPLE 1.15

Write condensed structural formulas for the two aldehydes with the molecular formula C_4H_8O.

STRATEGY

First, draw the functional group of an aldehyde and add the remaining carbons, which in this case may be bonded in two different ways. Then, add seven hydrogens to complete the four bonds of each carbon and give the correct molecular formula: Note that the aldehyde group may be written showing the carbon–oxygen double bond as C=O, or, alternatively, it may be written —CHO.

See problems 1.53–1.56, 1.58, 1.59

SOLUTION

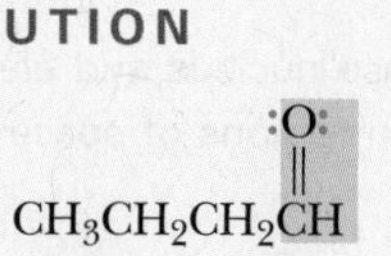

or

$CH_3CH_2CH_2CHO$

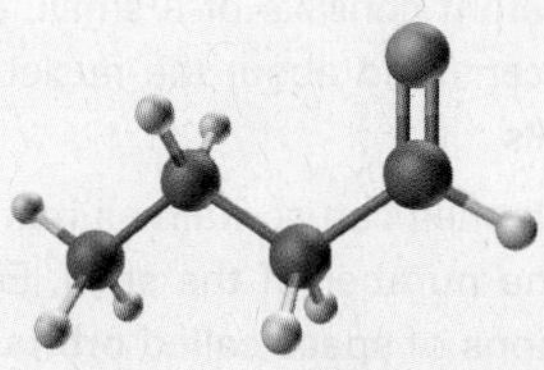

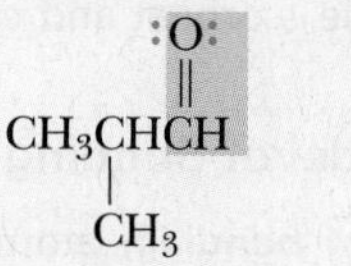

or

$(CH_3)_2CHCHO$

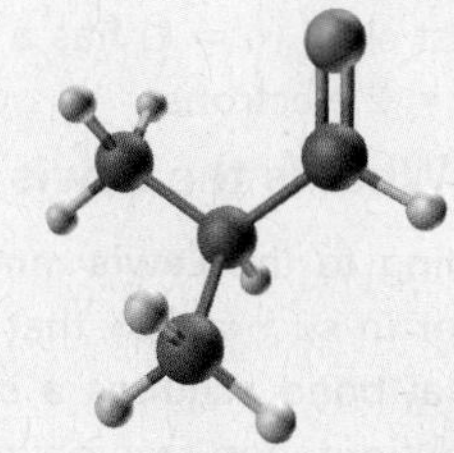

PROBLEM 1.15

Write condensed structural formulas for the three ketones with the molecular formula $C_5H_{10}O$.

D. Carboxylic Acids

Carboxyl group A —COOH group.

The functional group of a carboxylic acid is a **—COOH** (**carboxyl:** *carb*onyl + hydr*oxyl*) group:

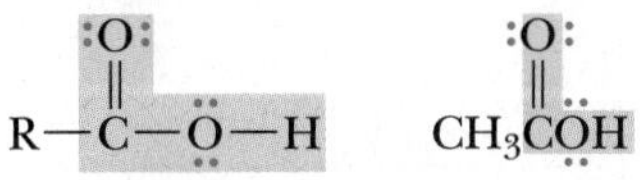

Functional group Acetic acid

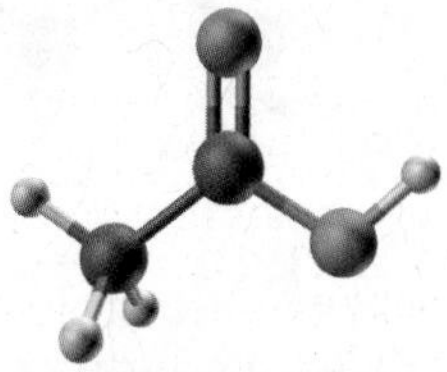

EXAMPLE 1.16

Write a condensed structural formula for the single carboxylic acid with the molecular formula $C_3H_6O_2$.

STRATEGY

First draw the carboxyl group and add the two remaining carbons. Finally, add the five remaining hydrogens in such a way that each carbon in the molecule has four bonds to it.

SOLUTION

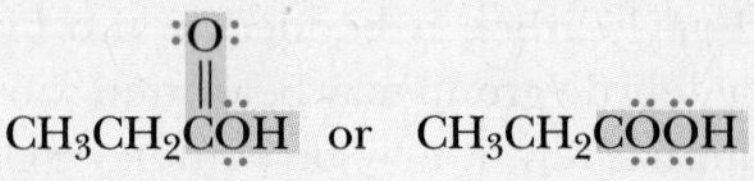

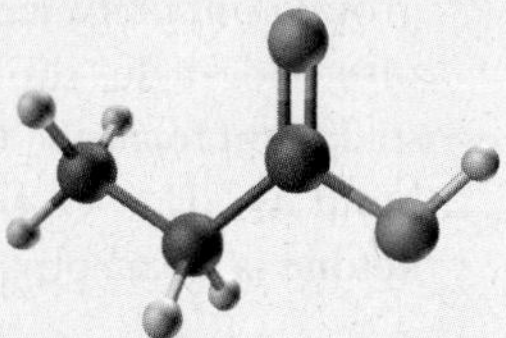

See problems 1.53–1.56, 1.58, 1.59

PROBLEM 1.16

Write condensed structural formulas for the two carboxylic acids with the molecular formula $C_4H_8O_2$.

SUMMARY OF KEY QUESTIONS

1.1 How Do We Describe the Electronic Structure of Atoms?

- An atom consists of a small, dense nucleus and electrons concentrated about the nucleus in regions of space called **shells**.
- Each shell can contain as many as $2n^2$ electrons, where n is the number of the shell. Each shell is subdivided into regions of space called **orbitals**.
- The first shell ($n = 1$) has a single *s* orbital and can hold $2 \times 1^2 = 2$ electrons.
- The second shell ($n = 2$) has one *s* orbital and three *p* orbitals and can hold $2 \times 2^2 = 8$ electrons.
- The **Lewis structure** of an element shows the symbol of the element surrounded by a number of dots equal to the number of electrons in its **valence shell**.

1.2 What Is the Lewis Model of Bonding?

- According to the **Lewis model of bonding**, atoms bond together in such a way that each atom participating in a chemical bond acquires a completed valence-shell electron configuration resembling that of the noble gas nearest it in atomic number.
- Atoms that lose sufficient electrons to acquire a completed valence shell become **cations**; atoms that gain sufficient electrons to acquire a completed valence shell become **anions**.
- An **ionic bond** is a chemical bond formed by the attractive force between an anion and a cation.
- A **covalent bond** is a chemical bond formed by the sharing of electron pairs between atoms.
- The tendency of main-group elements (those of Groups 1A–7A) to achieve an outer shell of eight **valence electrons** is called the **octet rule**.

- **Electronegativity** is a measure of the force of attraction by an atom for electrons it shares in a chemical bond with another atom. Electronegativity increases from left to right and from bottom to top in the Periodic Table.
- A **Lewis structure** for a molecule or an ion must show (1) the correct arrangement of atoms, (2) the correct number of valence electrons, (3) no more than two electrons in the outer shell of hydrogen, (4) no more than eight electrons in the outer shell of any second-period element, and (5) all formal charges.
- **Formal charge** is the charge on an atom in a molecule or polyatomic ion.

1.3 How Do We Predict Bond Angles and the Shapes of Molecules?

- **Valence-shell electron pair repulsion (VSEPR)** predicts bond angles of 109.5° about atoms surrounded by four regions of electron density, bond angles of 120° about atoms surrounded by three regions of electron density, and bond angles of 180° about atoms surrounded by two regions of electron density.
- The common shapes of small molecules include **tetrahedral, pyramidal, linear**, and **bent**.

1.4 How Do We Predict If a Molecule Is Polar or Nonpolar?

- As a rough guideline, we say that a **nonpolar covalent bond** is a covalent bond in which the difference in electronegativity between the bonded atoms is less than 0.5 unit.
- A **polar covalent bond** is a covalent bond in which the difference in electronegativity between the bonded atoms is between 0.5 and 1.9 units. In a polar covalent bond, the more electronegative atom bears a partial negative charge ($\delta-$) and the less electronegative atom bears a partial positive charge ($\delta+$).
- A molecule is polar if the vector sum of its bond **dipoles** equals zero.

1.5 What Is Resonance?

- According to the **theory of resonance**, a molecule or ion for which no single Lewis structure is adequate is best described by writing two or more **resonance contributing structures** and considering the real molecule or ion to be a **hybrid** of the various contributing structures.
- Resonance contributing structures are interconnected by **double-headed arrows.**
- We show how valence electrons are redistributed from one contributing structure to the next by **curved arrows.** A curved arrow extends from where the electrons are initially shown (on an atom or in a covalent bond) to their new location (an adjacent atom or an adjacent covalent bond).
- The use of curved arrows in this way is commonly referred to as **electron pushing.**

1.6 What Is the Orbital Overlap Model of Covalent Bonding?

- According to the **orbital overlap model**, the formation of a covalent bond results from the overlap of **atomic orbitals**.
- The greater the overlap, the stronger is the resulting covalent bond.
- The combination of atomic orbitals is called **hybridization**, and the resulting orbitals are called **hybrid orbitals**.
- The combination of one 2*s* atomic orbital and three 2*p* atomic orbitals produces four equivalent ***sp*^{3} hybrid orbitals**, each pointing toward a corner of a regular tetrahedron at angles of 109.5°.
- The combination of one 2*s* atomic orbital and two 2*p* atomic orbitals produces three equivalent ***sp*^{2} hybrid orbitals**, the axes of which lie in a plane at angles of 120°.

Most C=C, C=O, and C=N **double bonds** are a combination of one **sigma (σ) bond** formed by the overlap of ***sp*^{2} hybrid orbitals** and one **pi (π) bond** formed by the overlap of parallel 2*p* atomic orbitals.

- The combination of one 2*s* atomic orbital and one 2*p* atomic orbital produces two equivalent ***sp* hybrid orbitals**, the axes of which lie in a plane at an angle of 180°.
- All C≡C triple bonds are a combination of one sigma bond formed by the overlap of *sp* hybrid orbitals and two pi bonds formed by the overlap of two pairs of parallel 2*p* atomic orbitals.
- Hybrid orbitals can be arranged in tetrahedral, **trigonal planar**, and linear geometries.

1.7 What Are Functional Groups?

- **Functional groups** are characteristic structural units by which we divide organic compounds into classes and that serve as a basis for nomenclature. They are also sites of chemical reactivity; a particular functional group, in whatever compound we find it, undergoes the same types of reactions.
- Important functional groups for us at this stage in the course are
    - the **hydroxyl group** of **1°, 2°**, and **3° alcohols**
    - the **amino group** of **1°, 2°**, and **3° amines**
    - the **carbonyl group** of **aldehydes** and **ketones**
    - the **carboxyl group** of **carboxylic acids**

QUICK QUIZ

Answer true or false to the following questions to assess your general knowledge of the concepts in this chapter. If you have difficulty with any of them, you should review the appropriate section in the chapter (shown in parentheses) before attempting the more challenging end-of-chapter problems.

1. These bonds are arranged in order of increasing polarity C—H < N—H < O—H. (1.2)
2. All atoms in a contributing structure must have complete valence shells. (1.5)
3. An electron in a 1*s* orbital is held closer to the nucleus than an electron in a 2*s* orbital. (1.1)
4. A sigma bond and a pi bond have in common that each can result from the overlap of atomic orbitals. (1.6)
5. The molecular formula of the smallest aldehyde is C_3H_6O, and that of the smallest ketone is also C_3H_6O. (1.7)
6. To predict whether a covalent molecule is polar or nonpolar, you must know both the polarity of each covalent bond and the geometry (shape) of the molecule. (1.4)
7. An orbital is a region of space that can hold two electrons. (1.1)
8. In the ground-state electron configuration of an atom, only the lowest-energy orbitals are occupied. (1.1)
9. Electronegativity generally increases with atomic number. (1.2)
10. Paired electron spins means that the two electrons are aligned with their spins North Pole to North Pole and South Pole to South Pole. (1.1)
11. According to the Lewis model of bonding, atoms bond together in such a way that each atom participating in the bond acquires an outer-shell electron configuration matching that of the noble gas nearest it in atomic number. (1.2)
12. A primary amine contains one N—H bond, a secondary amine contains two N—H bonds, and a tertiary amine contains three N—H bonds. (1.7)
13. All bond angles in sets of resonance contributing structures must be the same. (1.5)
14. Electronegativity is a measure of an atom's attraction for electrons it shares in a chemical bond with another atom. (1.2)
15. An orbital can hold a maximum of two electrons with their spins paired. (1.1)
16. Fluorine in the upper right corner of the Periodic Table is the most electronegative element; hydrogen, in the upper left corner, is the least electronegative element. (1.2)
17. A primary alcohol has one —OH group, a secondary alcohol has two —OH groups, and a tertiary alcohol has three —OH groups. (1.7)
18. H_2O and NH_3 are polar molecules, but CH_4 is nonpolar. (1.4)
19. Electronegativity generally increases from top to bottom in a column of the Periodic Table. (1.2)
20. All contributing structures must have the same number of valence electrons. (1.5)
21. A carbon–carbon double bond is formed by the overlap of sp^2 hybrid orbitals, and a triple bond is formed by the overlap of sp^3 hybrid orbitals. (1.6)
22. A covalent bond formed by sharing two electrons is called a double bond. (1.2)
23. The functional groups of an alcohol, an aldehyde, and a ketone have in common the fact that each contains a single oxygen atom. (1.7)
24. Electrons in atoms are confined to regions of space called principal energy levels. (1.1)
25. In a single bond, two atoms share one pair of electrons; in a double bond, they share two pairs of electrons; and in a triple bond, they share three pairs of electrons. (1.2)
26. The Lewis structure for ethene, C_2H_4, must show eight valence electrons. (1.2)
27. The Lewis structure for formaldehyde, CH_2O, must show eight valence electrons. (1.2)
28. The letters VSEPR stand for valence-shell electron pair repulsion. (1.3)
29. In predicting bond angles about a central atom in a covalent bond, VSEPR considers only shared pairs (pairs of electrons involved in forming covalent bonds). (1.3)
30. An *sp* hybrid orbital may contain a maximum of four electrons, an sp^2 hybrid orbital may contain a maximum of six valence electrons, and an sp^3 hybrid orbital may contain a maximum of eight electrons. (1.6)
31. For a central atom surrounded by three regions of electron density, VSEPR predicts bond angles of $360°/3 = 120°$. (1.3)
32. The three 2*p* orbitals are aligned parallel to each other. (1.1)
33. All molecules with polar bonds are polar. (1.4)
34. Electronegativity generally increases from left to right across a period of the Periodic Table. (1.2)
35. A compound with the molecular formula C_3H_6O may be an aldehyde, a ketone, or a carboxylic acid. (1.7)
36. Dichloromethane, CH_2Cl_2 is polar, but tetrachloromethane, CCl_4, is nonpolar. (1.4)
37. A covalent bond is formed between atoms whose difference in electronegativity is less than 1.9. (1.2)
38. Each principal energy level can hold two electrons. (1.1)
39. Atoms that share electrons to achieve filled valence shells form covalent bonds. (1.2)
40. Contributing structures differ only in the distribution of valence electrons. (1.5)
41. In creating hybrid orbitals (*sp*, sp^2, and sp^3), the number of hybrid orbitals created is equal to the number of atomic orbitals hybridized. (1.6)
42. VSEPR treats the two electron pairs of a double bond and the three electron pairs of a triple bond as one region of electron density. (1.3)

43. If the difference in electronegativity between two atoms is zero (they have identical electronegativities), then the two atoms will not form a covalent bond. (1.2)

44. A carbon–carbon triple bond is a combination of one sigma bond and two pi bonds. (1.6)

45. A carbon–carbon double bond is a combination of two sigma bonds. (1.6)

46. An *s* orbital has the shape of a sphere with the center of the sphere at the nucleus. (1.1)

47. A functional group is a group of atoms in an organic molecule that undergoes a predictable set of chemical reactions. (1.7)

48. In a polar covalent bond, the more electronegative atom has a partial negative charge ($\delta-$) and the less electronegative atom has a partial positive charge ($\delta+$). (1.2)

49. Electronegativity depends on both the nuclear charge and the distance of the valence electrons from the nucleus. (1.2)

50. There are two alcohols with the molecular formula C_3H_8O. (1.7)

51. In methanol, CH_3OH, the O—H bond is more polar than the C—O bond. (1.4)

52. The molecular formula of the smallest carboxylic acid is $C_2H_6O_2$. (1.7)

53. Each 2*p* orbital has the shape of a dumbbell with the nucleus at the midpoint of the dumbbell. (1.1)

54. Atoms that lose electrons to achieve a filled valence shell become cations and form ionic bonds with anions. (1.1)

55. There are three amines with the molecular formula C_3H_9N. (1.7)

Detailed explanations for many of these answers can be found in the accompanying Solutions Manual.

Answers: (1) T (2) F (3) T (4) T (5) F (6) T (7) T (8) T (9) F (10) F (11) T (12) F (13) F (14) T (15) T (16) F (17) F (18) T (19) F (20) T (21) F (22) F (23) T (24) T (25) T (26) F (27) F (28) T (29) F (30) F (31) T (32) F (33) F (34) T (35) F (36) T (37) T (38) F (39) T (40) T (41) T (42) T (43) F (44) T (45) F (46) T (47) T (48) T (49) F (50) T (51) T (52) F (53) T (54) T (55) F

PROBLEMS

A problem marked with an asterisk indicates an applied "real-world" problem. Answers to problems whose numbers are printed in blue are given in Appendix D.

Section 1.1 Electronic Structure of Atoms

1.17 Write the ground-state electron configuration for each element: **(See Example 1.1)**

(a) Sodium
(b) Magnesium
(c) Oxygen
(d) Nitrogen
(e) Potassium
(f) Aluminum
(g) Phosphorus
(h) Argon

1.18 Write the ground-state electron configuration for each ion: **(See Example 1.1)**

(a) Na^+
(b) Cl^-
(c) Mg^{2+}
(d) H^+
(e) H^-
(f) K^+
(g) Br^+
(h) Li^+

1.19 Which element has the ground-state electron configuration **(See Example 1.1)**

(a) $1s^22s^22p^63s^23p^4$
(b) $1s^22s^22p^4$

1.20 Which element or ion does not have the ground-state electron configuration $1s^22s^22p^63s^23p^6$? **(See Example 1.1)**

(a) S^{2-} (b) Cl^- (c) Ar
(d) Ca^{2+} (e) K

1.21 Define *valence shell* and *valence electron*. Why are valence electrons more important to bonding than other types of electrons?

1.22 How many electrons are in the valence shell of each element? **(See Example 1.2)**

(a) Carbon (b) Nitrogen (c) Chlorine
(d) Aluminum (e) Oxygen

1.23 How many electrons are in the valence shell of each ion? **(See Example 1.2)**

(a) H^+ (b) H^- (c) F^- (d) Cl^+

Section 1.2 Lewis Structures

1.24 Judging from their relative positions in the Periodic Table, which element in each set is more electronegative? **(See Example 1.3)**

(a) Carbon or nitrogen (b) Chlorine or bromine
(c) Oxygen or sulfur (d) Oxygen or phosphorus

1.25 Which compounds have nonpolar covalent bonds, which have polar covalent bonds, and which have ionic bonds? **(See Example 1.4)**

(a) LiF (b) CH_3F (c) $MgCl_2$ (d) HCl

1.26 Using the symbols $\delta-$ and $\delta+$, indicate the direction of polarity, if any, in each covalent bond: **(See Example 1.5)**

(a) C—Cl (b) S—H (c) C—S (d) P—H

1.27 Write Lewis structures for each of the following compounds, showing all valence electrons (none of the compounds contains a ring of atoms): **(See Example 1.6)**

(a) Hydrogen peroxide, H_2O_2
(b) Hydrazine, N_2H_4
(c) Methanol, CH_3OH
(d) Methanethiol, CH_3SH
(e) Methanamine, CH_3NH_2
(f) Chloromethane, CH_3Cl
(g) Dimethyl ether, CH_3OCH_3
(h) Ethane, C_2H_6
(i) Ethylene, C_2H_4
(j) Acetylene, C_2H_2
(k) Carbon dioxide, CO_2
(l) Formaldehyde, CH_2O
(m) Acetone, CH_3COCH_3
(n) Carbonic acid, H_2CO_3
(o) Acetic acid, CH_3COOH

1.28 Write Lewis structures for these ions: **(See Example 1.6)**

(a) Bicarbonate ion, HCO_3^-
(b) Carbonate ion, CO_3^{2-}
(c) Acetate ion, CH_3COO^-
(d) Chloride ion, Cl^-

1.29 Why are the following molecular formulas impossible?

(a) CH_5 (b) C_2H_7 (c) H_2^{2+}

1.30 Following the rule that each atom of carbon, oxygen, and nitrogen reacts to achieve a complete outer shell of eight valence electrons, add unshared pairs of electrons as necessary to complete the valence shell of each atom in the following ions. Then, assign formal charges as appropriate: **(See Example 1.7)**

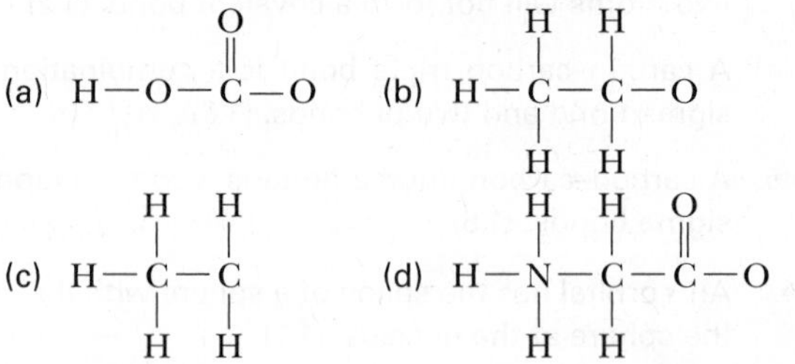

1.31 The following Lewis structures show all valence electrons. Assign formal charges in each structure as appropriate. **(See Example 1.7)**

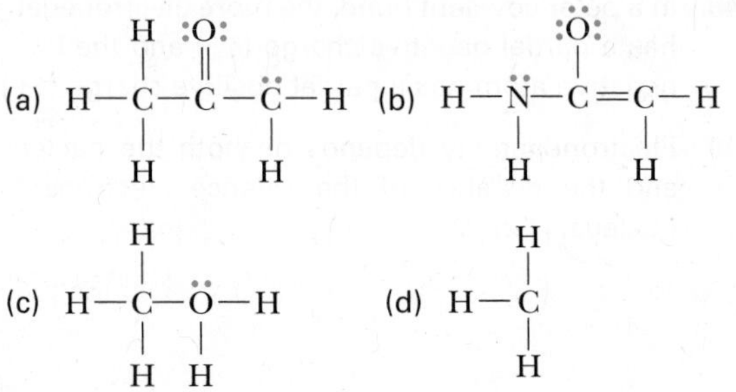

1.32 Each compound contains both ionic and covalent bonds. Draw a Lewis structure for each, and show by charges which bonds are ionic and by dashes which bonds are covalent. **(See Example 1.7)**

(a) NaOH (b) $NaHCO_3$ (c) NH_4Cl
(d) CH_3COONa (e) CH_3ONa

1.33 Silver and oxygen can form a stable compound. Predict the formula of this compound, and state whether the compound consists of ionic or covalent bonds.

1.34 Draw Lewis structures for the following molecule and ions: **(See Example 1.7)**

(a) NH_3 (b) NH_4^+ (c) NH_2^-

Section 1.2 Polarity of Covalent Bonds

1.35 Which statement is true about electronegativity?

(a) Electronegativity increases from left to right in a period of the Periodic Table.
(b) Electronegativity increases from top to bottom in a column of the Periodic Table.
(c) Hydrogen, the element with the lowest atomic number, has the smallest electronegativity.
(d) The higher the atomic number of an element, the greater is its electronegativity.

1.36 Why does fluorine, the element in the upper right corner of the Periodic Table, have the largest electronegativity of any element?

1.37 Arrange the single covalent bonds within each set in order of increasing polarity:

(a) C—H, O—H, N—H
(b) C—H, C—Cl, C—I
(c) C—C, C—O, C—N
(d) C—Li, C—Hg, C—Mg

1.38 Using the values of electronegativity given in Table 1.4, predict which indicated bond in each set is more polar and, using the symbols $\delta+$ and $\delta-$, show the direction of its polarity: **(See Example 1.5)**

(a) CH_3—OH or CH_3O—H
(b) H—NH_2 or CH_3—NH_2

(c) CH_3—SH or CH_3S—H
(d) CH_3—F or H—F
(e) H_2C=NH or H_2C=O
(f) H_2B—H or F_2B—F
(g) H_2C=O or H_2C=S
(h) CH_3—MgBr or CH_3—Li

1.39 Identify the most polar bond in each molecule:

(a) $HSCH_2CH_2OH$
(b) $CHCl_2F$
(c) $HOCH_2CH_2NH_2$

1.40 Predict whether the carbon–metal bond in each of these organometallic compounds is nonpolar covalent, polar covalent, or ionic. For each polar covalent bond, show its direction of polarity using the symbols δ+ and δ−. **(See Example 1.5)**

(a) 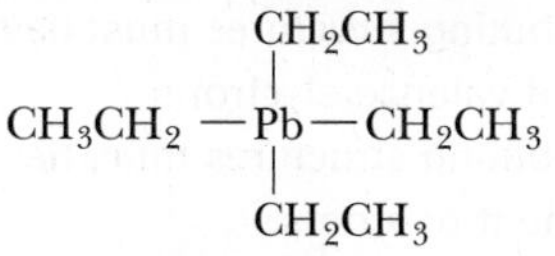

Tetraethyllead

(b) CH_3—Mg—Cl
Methylmagnesium chloride

(c) CH_3—Hg—CH_3
Dimethylmercury

Section 1.3 Bond Angles and Shapes of Molecules

1.41 Using VSEPR, predict bond angles about each highlighted atom: **(See Example 1.8)**

(a) 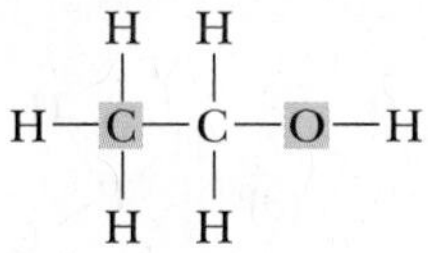

(b) 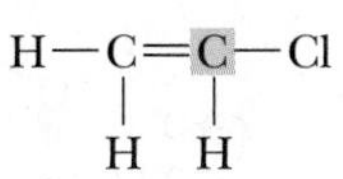

(c) 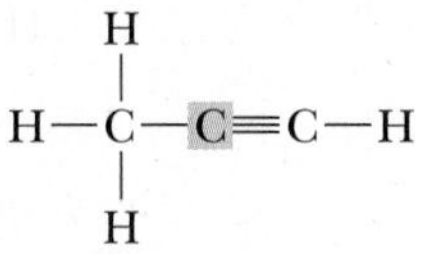 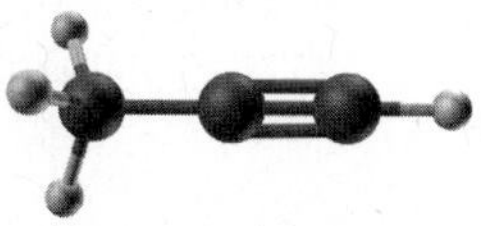

(d) 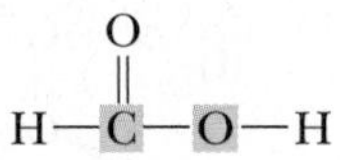

(e) 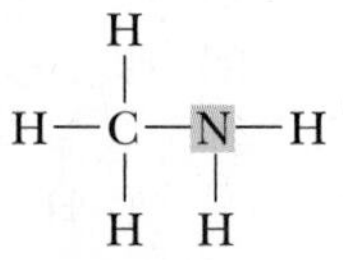

(f) H—O—N=O 

1.42 Using VSEPR, predict bond angles about each atom of carbon, nitrogen, and oxygen in these molecules. (*Hint*: First add unshared pairs of electrons as necessary to complete the valence shell of each atom, and then make your predictions of bond angles.) **(See Example 1.8)**

(a) CH_3—CH_2—CH_2—OH

(b) 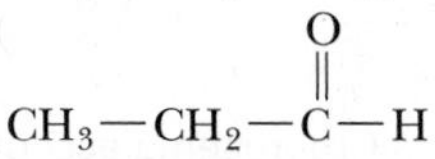

(c) CH_3—CH=CH_2

(d) CH_3—C≡C—CH_3

(e) 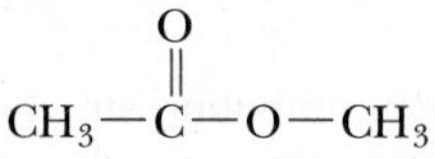

(f) 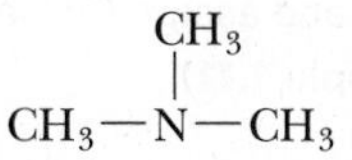

1.43 Silicon is immediately below carbon in the Periodic Table. Predict the C—Si—C bond angle in tetramethylsilane, $(CH_3)_4Si$. **(See Example 1.8)**

Section 1.4 Polar and Nonpolar Molecules

1.44 Draw a three-dimensional representation for each molecule. Indicate which molecules are polar and the direction of their polarity: **(See Example 1.9)**

(a) CH_3F	(b) CH_2Cl_2	(c) $CHCl_3$
(d) CCl_4	(e) CH_2=CCl_2	(f) CH_2=CHCl
(g) CH_3C≡N	(h) $(CH_3)_2C$=O	(i) $N(CH_3)_3$

***1.45** Tetrafluoroethylene, C_2F_4, is the starting material for the synthesis of the polymer poly(tetrafluoroethylene), commonly known as Teflon. Molecules of tetrafluoroethylene are nonpolar. Propose a structural formula for this compound.

***1.46** Until several years ago, the two chlorofluorocarbons (CFCs) most widely used as heat-transfer media for refrigeration systems were Freon-11 (trichlorofluoromethane, CCl_3F) and Freon-12 (dichlorodifluoromethane, CCl_2F_2). Draw a three-dimensional representation of each molecule, and indicate the direction of its polarity. **(See Example 1.9)**

Section 1.5 Resonance Contributing Structures

1.47 Which of these statements are true about resonance contributing structures? **(See Example 1.10)**

(a) All contributing structures must have the same number of valence electrons.

(b) All contributing structures must have the same arrangement of atoms.

(c) All atoms in a contributing structure must have complete valence shells.

(d) All bond angles in sets of contributing structures must be the same.

(e) The following pair represents acceptable resonance contributing structures:

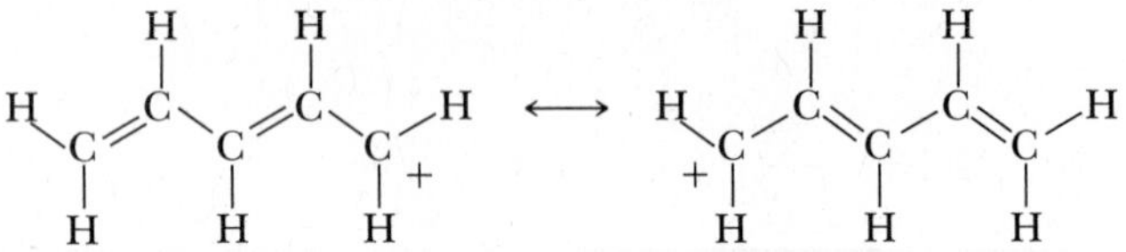

(f) The following pair represents acceptable resonance contributing structures:

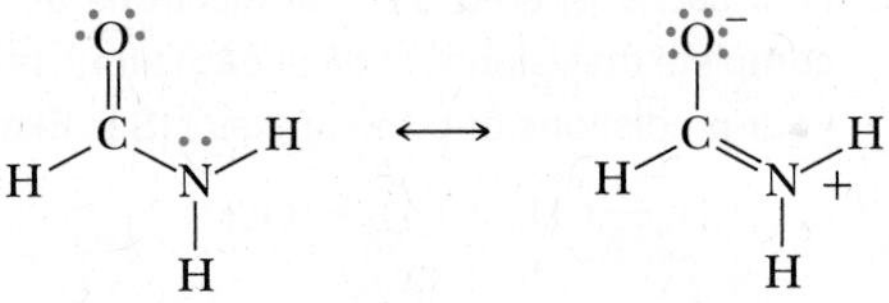

(g) The following pair represents acceptable resonance contributing structures:

$\ddot{O}=C=\ddot{N}H \longleftrightarrow :\overset{-}{\ddot{O}}-C\equiv\overset{+}{N}H$

1.48 Draw the resonance contributing structure indicated by the curved arrow(s), and assign formal charges as appropriate: **(See Example 1.11)**

(a) 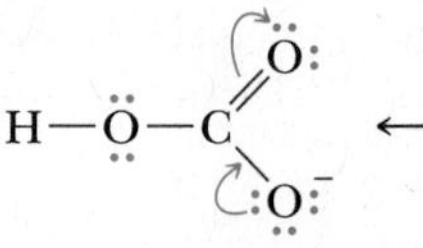

(b) 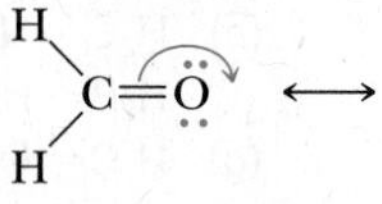

(c) 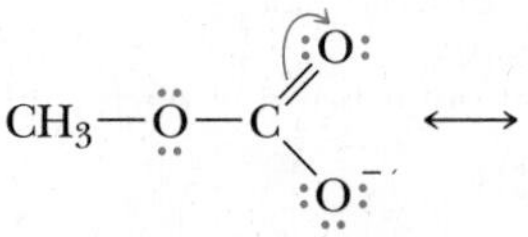

1.49 Using VSEPR, predict the bond angles about the carbon atom in each pair of contributing structures in Problem 1.48. In what way do the bond angles change from one contributing structure to the other?

1.50 Draw acceptable resonance contributing structure(s) for each of the compounds shown. **(See Example 1.11)**

(a) 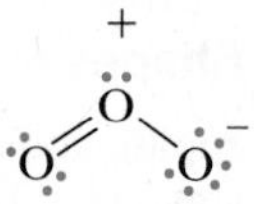

(b) $H-\overset{+}{N}\equiv C-\overset{-}{\ddot{N}}-H$

(c) 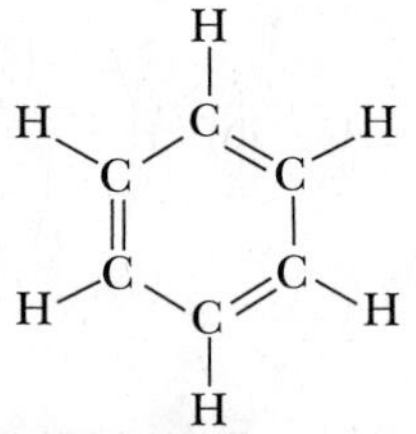

(d) 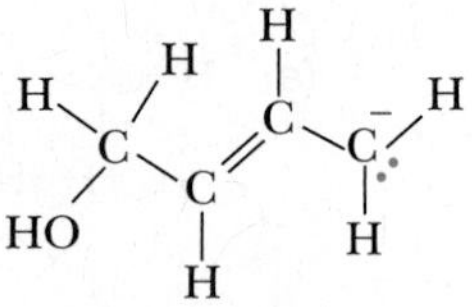

(e) 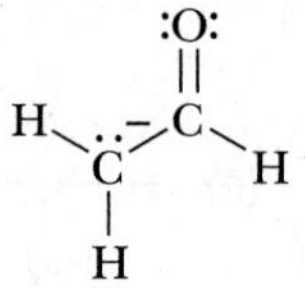

(f) 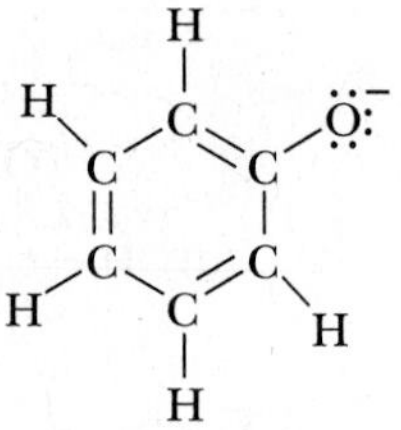

Section 1.6 Hybridization of Atomic Orbitals

1.51 State the hybridization of each highlighted atom:

(a) 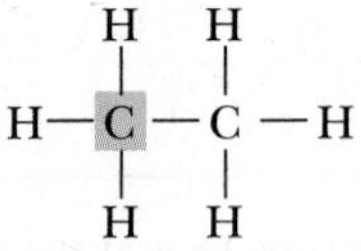

(b) 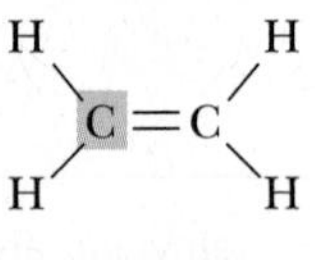

(c) 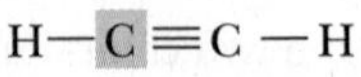 $H-C\equiv C-H$

(d) 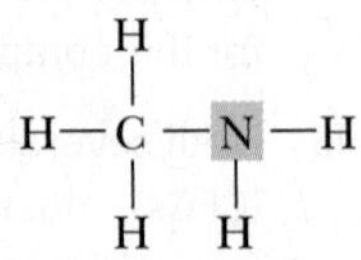

(e) 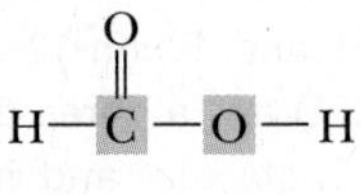

(f) 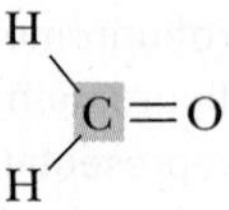

1.52 Describe each highlighted bond by indicating the type of bond(s) and the hybridization of the highlighted atoms: **(See Example 1.12)**

(a) 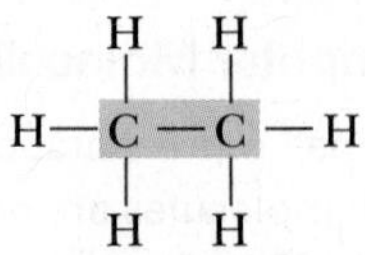

(b) 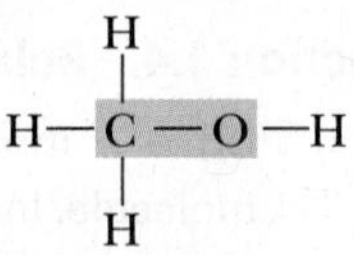

(c) 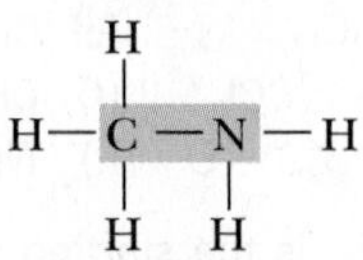

(d) 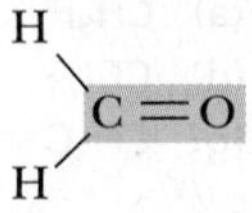

(e) 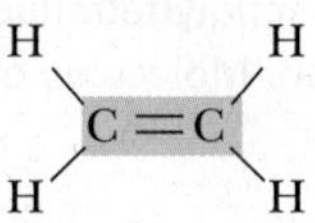

(f) 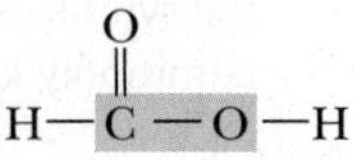

Section 1.7 Functional Groups

1.53 Draw Lewis structures for these functional groups. Be certain to show all valence electrons on each: **(See Examples 1.13–1.16)**

(a) Carbonyl group (b) Carboxyl group
(c) Hydroxyl group (d) Primary amino group

1.54 Draw the structure for a compound with the molecular formula **(See Examples 1.13–1.16)**

(a) C_2H_6O that is an alcohol.
(b) C_3H_6O that is an aldehyde.
(c) C_3H_6O that is a ketone.
(d) $C_3H_6O_2$ that is a carboxylic acid.
(e) $C_4H_{11}N$ that is a tertiary amine.

1.55 Draw condensed structural formulas for all compounds with the molecular formula C_4H_8O that contain **(See Examples 1.13–1.16)**

(a) a carbonyl group. (There are two aldehydes and one ketone.)
(b) a carbon–carbon double bond and a hydroxyl group. (There are eight.)

1.56 Draw structural formulas for **(See Examples 1.13–1.16)**

(a) the eight alcohols with the molecular formula $C_5H_{12}O$.
(b) the eight aldehydes with the molecular formula $C_6H_{12}O$.
(c) the six ketones with the molecular formula $C_6H_{12}O$.
(d) the eight carboxylic acids with the molecular formula $C_6H_{12}O_2$.
(e) the three tertiary amines with the molecular formula $C_5H_{13}N$.

*1.57 Identify the functional groups in each compound (we study each compound in more detail in the indicated section):

(a) 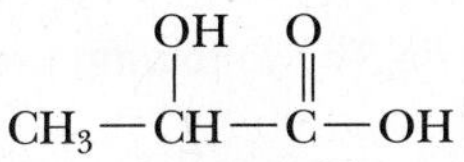
Lactic acid
(Section 21.4A)

(b) $HO—CH_2—CH_2—OH$
Ethylene glycol
(Section 8.1B)

(c) 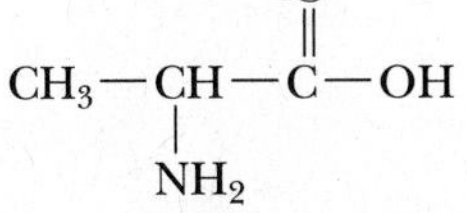
Alanine
(Section 18.2B)

(d) 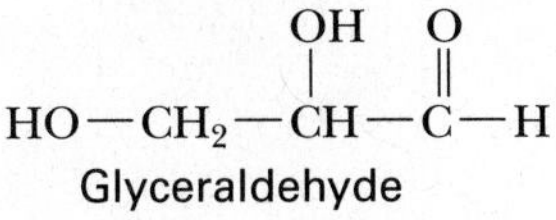
Glyceraldehyde
(Section 17.2A)

(e) 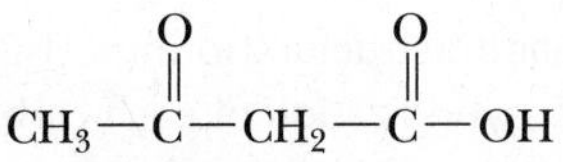
Acetoacetic acid
(Section 13.2B)

(f) $H_2NCH_2CH_2CH_2CH_2CH_2CH_2NH_2$
1,6-Hexanediamine
(Section 16.4A)

*1.58 Dihydroxyacetone, $C_3H_6O_3$, the active ingredient in many sunless tanning lotions, contains two 1° hydroxyl groups, each on a different carbon, and one ketone group. Draw a structural formula for dihydroxyacetone. **(See Examples 1.13–1.16)**

*1.59 Propylene glycol, $C_3H_8O_2$, commonly used in airplane deicers, contains a 1° alcohol and a 2° alcohol. Draw a structural formula for propylene glycol. **(See Examples 1.13–1.16)**

*1.60 Ephedrine is a molecule found in the dietary supplement ephedra, which has been linked to adverse health reactions such as heart attacks, strokes, and heart palpitations. The use of ephedra in dietary supplements is now banned by the FDA.

(a) Identify at least two functional groups in ephedrine.
(b) Would you predict ephedrine to be polar or nonpolar?

Ephedrine 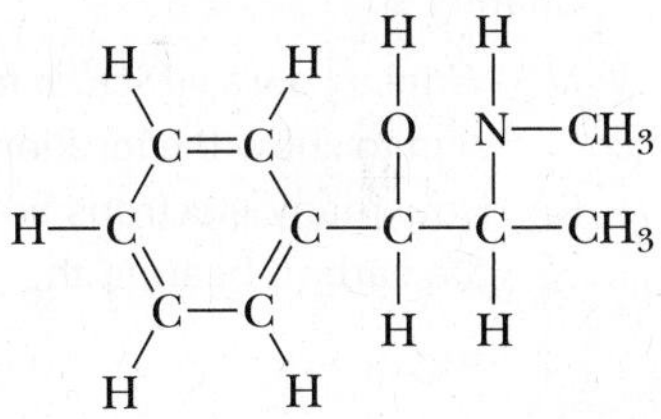

*1.61 Ozone (O_3) and carbon dioxide (CO_2) are both known as greenhouse gases. Compare and contrast their shapes, and indicate the hybridization of each atom in the two molecules.

*1.62 In the lower atmosphere that is also contaminated with unburned hydrocarbons, NO_2 participates in a series of reactions. One product of these reactions is peroxyacetyl nitrate (PAN). The connectivity of the atoms in PAN appears below.

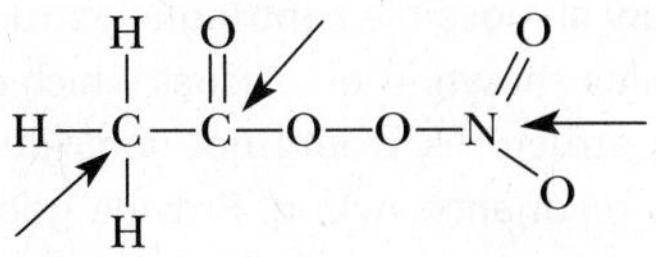

(a) Determine the number of valence electrons in this molecule, and then complete its Lewis structure.
(b) Give the approximate values of the bond angles around each atom indicated with an arrow.

LOOKING AHEAD

1.63 Allene, C_3H_4, has the structural formula $H_2C{=}C{=}CH_2$. Determine the hybridization of each carbon in allene and predict the shape of the molecule.

1.64 Dimethylsulfoxide, $(CH_3)_2SO$, is a common solvent used in organic chemistry.

(a) Write a Lewis structure for dimethylsulfoxide.
(b) Predict the hybridization of the sulfur atom in the molecule.
(c) Predict the geometry of dimethylsulfoxide.
(d) Is dimethylsulfoxide a polar or a nonpolar molecule?

1.65 In Chapter 5, we study a group of organic cations called carbocations. Following is the structure of one such carbocation, the *tert*-butyl cation:

tert-Butyl cation

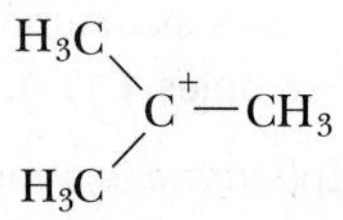

(a) How many electrons are in the valence shell of the carbon bearing the positive charge?
(b) Predict the bond angles about this carbon.
(c) Given the bond angles you predicted in (b), what hybridization do you predict for this carbon?

1.66 We also study the isopropyl cation, $(CH_3)_2CH^+$, in Chapter 5.

(a) Write a Lewis structure for this cation. Use a plus sign to show the location of the positive charge.
(b) How many electrons are in the valence shell of the carbon bearing the positive charge?
(c) Use VSEPR to predict all bond angles about the carbon bearing the positive charge.
(d) Describe the hybridization of each carbon in this cation.

1.67 In Chapter 9, we study benzene, C_6H_6, and its derivatives.

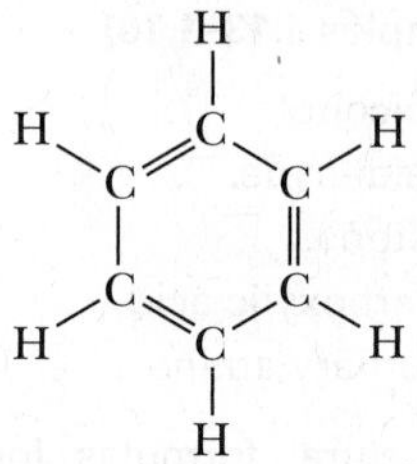

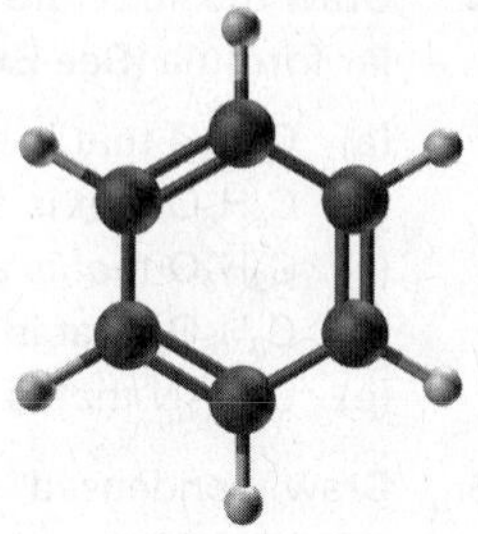

(a) Predict each H—C—C and each C—C—C bond angle on benzene.
(b) State the hybridization of each carbon in benzene.
(c) Predict the shape of a benzene molecule.

1.68 Explain why all the carbon–carbon bonds in benzene are equal in length.

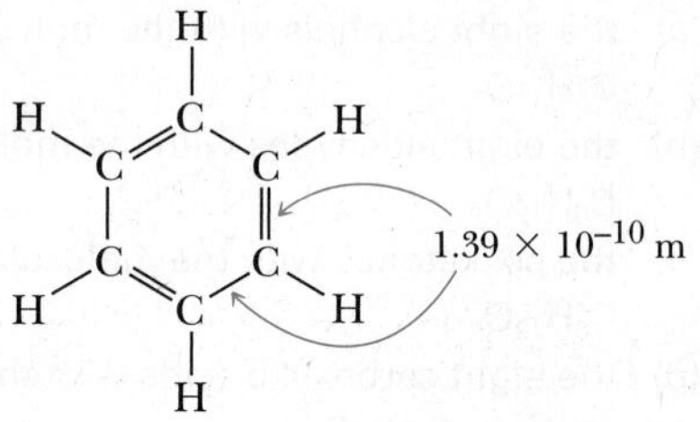

GROUP LEARNING ACTIVITIES

Studies have shown that working in groups enhances learning and fosters camaraderie. The following problems represent activities that you can do in groups of two or more.

1.69 Take turns by naming a functional group and challenging each other to draw an organic molecule with at least three carbon atoms that contains that functional group.

1.70 Draw all possible contributing structures for the molecules shown. Then discuss which of these contributing structures would not contribute significantly to the resonance hybrid. Provide good reasons for the structures you eliminate.

(a)

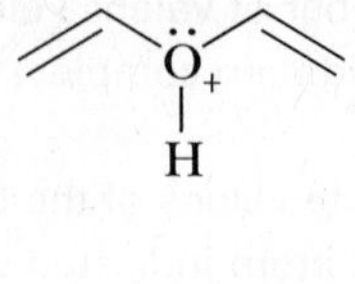

(b)

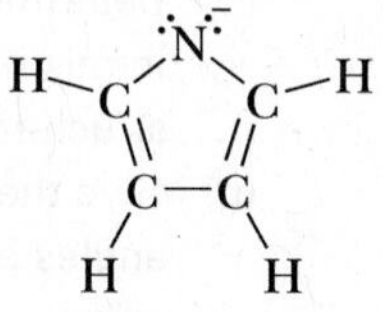

1.71 Refer to the list of functional groups on the inside front cover of this text. Take turns choosing one of the examples in the list and indicate the hybridization of each C, O, N, or S atom in the example.

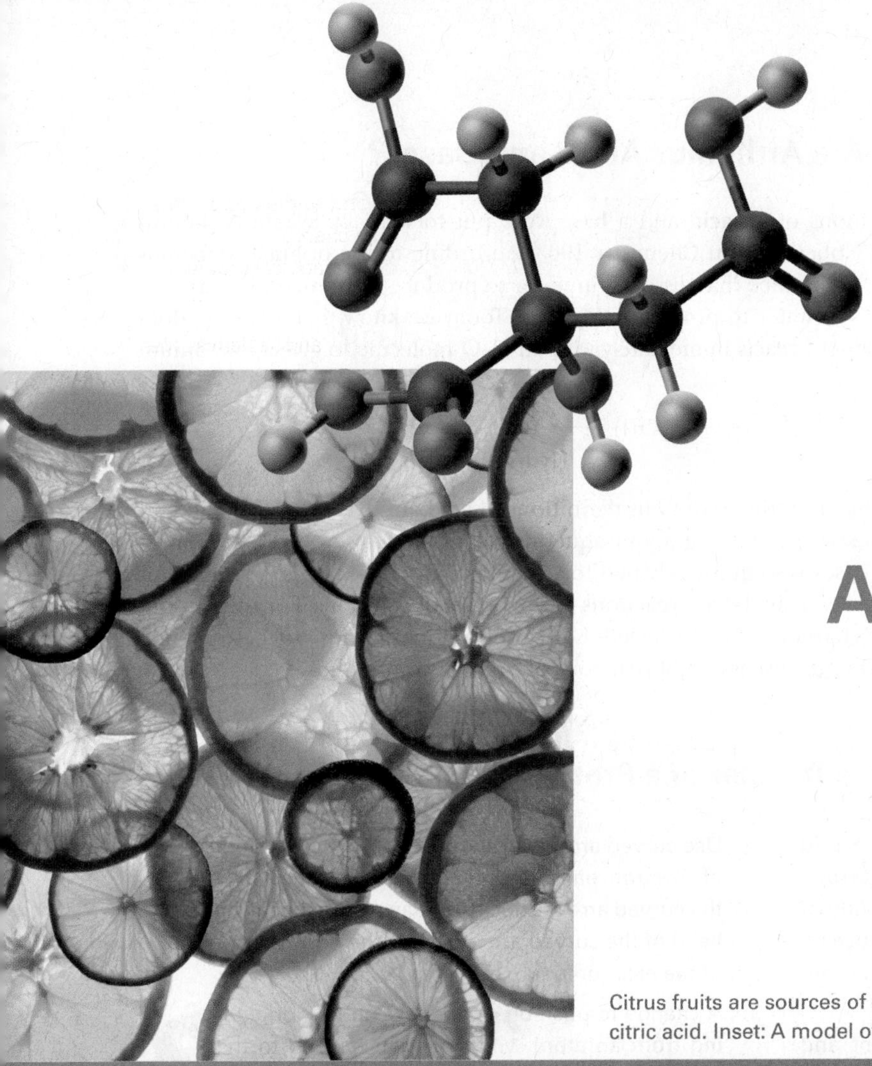

02 Acids and Bases

Citrus fruits are sources of citric acid. Lemon juice, for example, contains 5–8% citric acid. Inset: A model of citric acid. (© Rickard Blommengren/iStockphoto)

KEY QUESTIONS

2.1 What Are Arrhenius Acids and Bases?

2.2 What Are Brønsted–Lowry Acids and Bases?

2.3 How Do We Measure the Strength of an Acid or Base?

2.4 How Do We Determine the Position of Equilibrium in an Acid–Base Reaction?

2.5 What Are the Relationships between Acidity and Molecular Structure?

2.6 What Are Lewis Acids and Bases?

HOW TO

2.1 How to Use Curved Arrows to Show the Transfer of a Proton from an Acid to a Base

2.2 How to Determine the Position of Equilibrium in an Acid–Base Reaction

A GREAT MANY ORGANIC reactions are acid–base reactions. In this and later chapters, we will study the acid–base properties of the major classes of organic compounds, including alcohols, phenols, carboxylic acids, carbonyl compounds containing α-hydrogens, amines, amino acids, proteins, and, finally, nucleic acids. Furthermore, many organic reactions are catalyzed by proton-donating acids, such as H_3O^+ and $CH_3OH_2^+$. Others are catalyzed by Lewis acids, such as $AlCl_3$. It is essential, therefore, that you have a good grasp of the fundamentals of acid–base chemistry.

2.1 What Are Arrhenius Acids and Bases?

Arrhenius acid A substance that dissolves in water to produce H^+ ions.

Arrhenius base A substance that dissolves in water to produce OH^- ions.

The first useful definitions of an **acid** and a **base** were put forward by Svante Arrhenius (1859–1927) in 1884; Nobel Prize in Chemistry 1903. According to the original Arrhenius definitions, an acid is a substance that dissolves in water to produce H^+ ions, and a base is a substance that dissolves in water to produce OH^- ions. Today we know that a H^+ ion does not exist in water because it reacts immediately with an H_2O molecule to give a hydronium ion, H_3O^+:

$$H^+(aq) + H_2O(l) \longrightarrow \underset{\text{Hydronium ion}}{H_3O^+(aq)}$$

Apart from this modification, the Arrhenius definitions of acid and base are still valid and useful today, as long as we are talking about aqueous solutions. However, the Arrhenius concept of acids and bases is so intimately tied to reactions that take place in water that it has no good way to deal with acid–base reactions in nonaqueous solutions. For this reason, we concentrate in this chapter on the Brønsted–Lowry definitions of acids and bases, which are more useful to us in our discussion of reactions of organic compounds.

HOW TO 2.1 Use Curved Arrows to Show the Transfer of a Proton from an Acid to a Base

We can show the transfer of a proton from an acid to a base by using a symbol called a **curved arrow**. Curved arrows will be used throughout your study of organic chemistry to describe how reactions proceed. Therefore, it is very important that you become proficient in their use.

1. Write the Lewis structure of each reactant and product, showing all valence electrons on reacting atoms.
2. Use curved arrows to show the change in position of electron pairs during the reaction. The tail of the curved arrow is located at an electron pair. The head of the curved arrow shows the new position of the electron pair.
3. A change in position of an electron pair originating from an atom will form a new bond to that atom, while a change in position of an electron pair originating from a bond will result in breaking that bond.

EXAMPLE 1

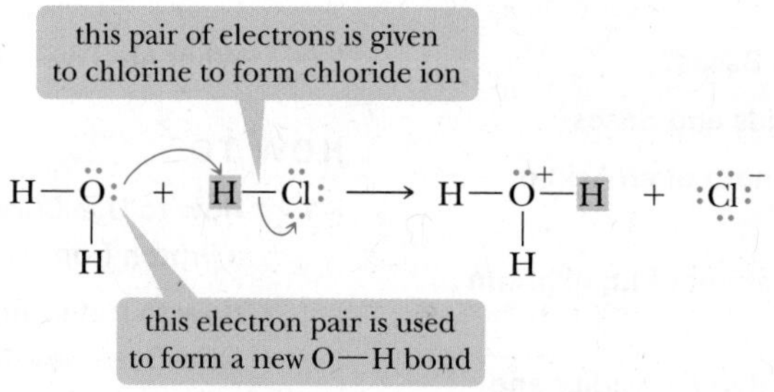
this pair of electrons is given to chlorine to form chloride ion
this electron pair is used to form a new O—H bond

EXAMPLE 2

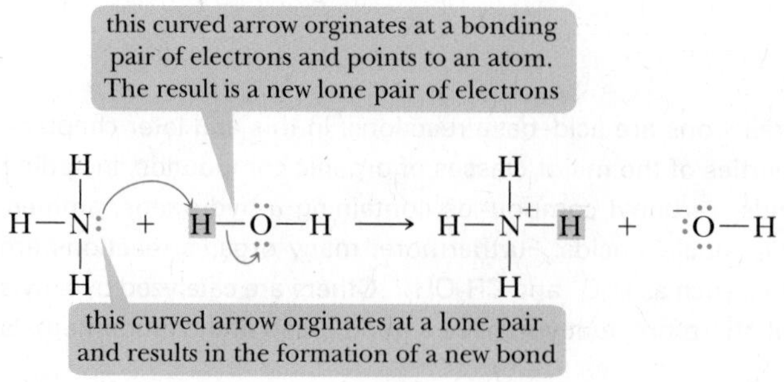
this curved arrow orginates at a bonding pair of electrons and points to an atom. The result is a new lone pair of electrons
this curved arrow orginates at a lone pair and results in the formation of a new bond

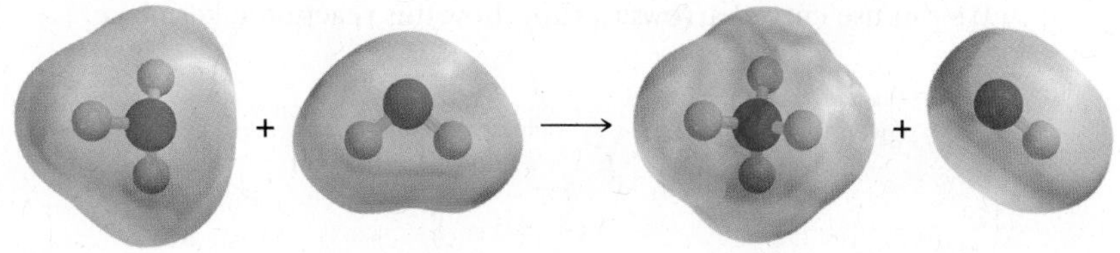

Notice the increase in charge distribution upon protonation of NH_2 and deprotonation of H_2O. The nitrogen of NH_4^+ shows a more intense blue than the nitrogen of NH_2, and the oxygen of OH^- shows a more intense red than the oxygen of H_2O.

2.2 What Are Brønsted–Lowry Acids and Bases?

In 1923, the Danish chemist Johannes Brønsted and the English chemist Thomas Lowry independently proposed the following definitions: An **acid** is a **proton donor**, a **base** is a **proton acceptor**, and an acid–base reaction is a **proton-transfer reaction**. Furthermore, according to the Brønsted–Lowry definitions, any pair of molecules or ions that can be interconverted by the transfer of a proton is called a **conjugate acid–base pair**. When an acid transfers a proton to a base, the acid is converted to its **conjugate base**. When a base accepts a proton, the base is converted to its **conjugate acid**.

Brønsted–Lowry acid A proton donor.

Brønsted–Lowry base A proton acceptor.

Conjugate base The species formed when an acid donates a proton.

Conjugate acid The species formed when a base accepts a proton.

We can illustrate these relationships by examining the reaction of hydrogen chloride with water to form chloride ion and hydronium ion:

conjugate acid–base pair (HCl / Cl^-)
conjugate acid–base pair (H_2O / H_3O^+)

$$HCl(aq) + H_2O(l) \longrightarrow Cl^-(aq) + H_3O^+(aq)$$

HCl(aq)	H_2O(l)	Cl^-(aq)	H_3O^+(aq)
Hydrogen chloride (Acid)	Water (Base)	Chloride ion (Conjugate base of HCl)	Hydronium ion (Conjugate acid of water)

In this reaction, the acid HCl donates a proton and is converted to its conjugate base, Cl^-. The base H_2O accepts a proton and is converted to its conjugate acid, H_3O^+.

We have illustrated the application of the Brønsted–Lowry definitions with water as a reactant. These definitions, however, do not require water as a reactant. Consider the following reaction between acetic acid and ammonia:

conjugate acid–base pair (CH_3COOH / CH_3COO^-)
conjugate acid–base pair (NH_3 / NH_4^+)

$$CH_3COOH + NH_3 \rightleftharpoons CH_3COO^- + NH_4^+$$

CH_3COOH	NH_3	CH_3COO^-	NH_4^+
Acetic acid (Acid)	Ammonia (Base)	Acetate ion (Conjugate base of acetic acid)	Ammonium ion (Conjugate acid of ammonia)

We can use curved arrows to show how this reaction takes place:

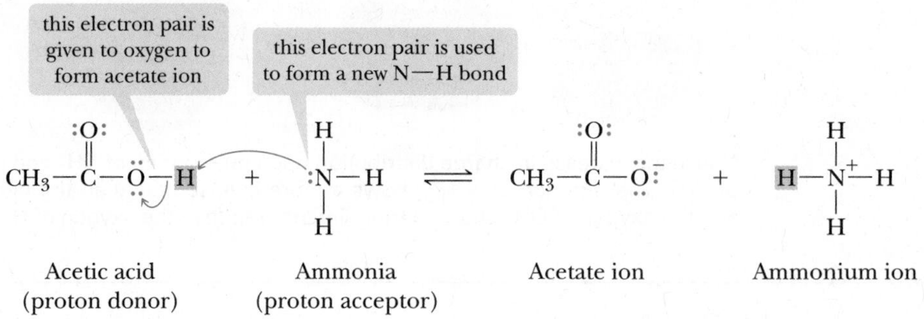

The rightmost curved arrow shows that the unshared pair of electrons on nitrogen becomes shared between N and H to form a new H—N bond. At the same time that the H—N bond forms, the O—H bond breaks, and the electron pair of the O—H bond moves entirely to oxygen to form the —O$^-$ of the acetate ion. The result of these two electron-pair shifts is the transfer of a proton from an acetic acid molecule to an ammonia molecule. Table 2.1 gives examples of common acids and their conjugate bases. As you study the examples of conjugate acid–base pairs in the table, note the following points:

1. An acid can be positively charged, neutral, or negatively charged. Examples of these charge types are H_3O^+, H_2CO_3, and $H_2PO_4^-$.
2. A base can be negatively charged or neutral. Examples of these charge types are Cl^- and NH_3.
3. Acids are classified as monoprotic, diprotic, or triprotic, depending on the number of protons each may give up. Examples of **monoprotic acids** include HCl, HNO_3, and CH_3COOH. Examples of **diprotic acids** include H_2SO_4 and H_2CO_3. An example of a

TABLE 2.1 Some Acids and Their Conjugate Bases

	Acid	Name	Conjugate Base	Name	
	HI	hydroiodic acid	I^-	iodide ion	
Strong Acids ↑	HCl	hydrochloric acid	Cl^-	chloride ion	Weak Bases ↓
	H_2SO_4	sulfuric acid	HSO_4^-	hydrogen sulfate ion	
	HNO_3	nitric acid	NO_3^-	nitrate ion	
	H_3O^+	hydronium ion	H_2O	water	
	HSO_4^-	hydrogen sulfate ion	SO_4^{2-}	sulfate ion	
	H_3PO_4	phosphoric acid	$H_2PO_4^-$	dihydrogen phosphate ion	
	CH_3COOH	acetic acid	CH_3COO^-	acetate ion	
	H_2CO_3	carbonic acid	HCO_3^-	bicarbonate ion	
	H_2S	hydrogen sulfide	HS^-	hydrogen sulfide ion	
	$H_2PO_4^-$	dihydrogen phosphate ion	HPO_4^{2-}	hydrogen phosphate ion	
	NH_4^+	ammonium ion	NH_3	ammonia	
	HCN	hydrocyanic acid	CN^-	cyanide ion	
	C_6H_5OH	phenol	$C_6H_5O^-$	phenoxide ion	
	HCO_3^-	bicarbonate ion	CO_3^{2-}	carbonate ion	
	HPO_4^{2-}	hydrogen phosphate ion	PO_4^{3-}	phosphate ion	
Weak Acids	H_2O	water	OH^-	hydroxide ion	Strong Bases
	C_2H_5OH	ethanol	$C_2H_5O^-$	ethoxide ion	

triprotic acid is H_3PO_4. Carbonic acid, for example, loses one proton to become bicarbonate ion and then a second proton to become carbonate ion:

$$\underset{\text{Carbonic acid}}{H_2CO_3} + H_2O \rightleftharpoons \underset{\text{Bicarbonate ion}}{HCO_3^-} + H_3O^+$$

$$\underset{\text{Bicarbonate ion}}{HCO_3^-} + H_2O \rightleftharpoons \underset{\text{Carbonate ion}}{CO_3^{2-}} + H_3O^+$$

4. Several molecules and ions appear in both the acid and conjugate base columns; that is, each can function as either an acid or a base. The bicarbonate ion, HCO_3^-, for example, can give up a proton to become CO_3^{2-} (in which case it is an acid) or it can accept a proton to become H_2CO_3 (in which case it is a base).
5. There is an inverse relationship between the strength of an acid and the strength of its conjugate base. **The stronger the acid, the weaker is its conjugate base.** HI, for example, is the strongest acid listed in Table 2.1, and I^-, its conjugate base, is the weakest base. As another example, CH_3COOH (acetic acid) is a stronger acid than H_2CO_3 (carbonic acid); conversely, CH_3COO^- (acetate ion) is a weaker base than HCO_3^- (bicarbonate ion).

EXAMPLE 2.1

Write the following acid–base reaction as a proton-transfer reaction. Label which reactant is the acid and which the base, as well as which product is the conjugate base of the original acid and which is the conjugate acid of the original base. Use curved arrows to show the flow of electrons in the reaction.

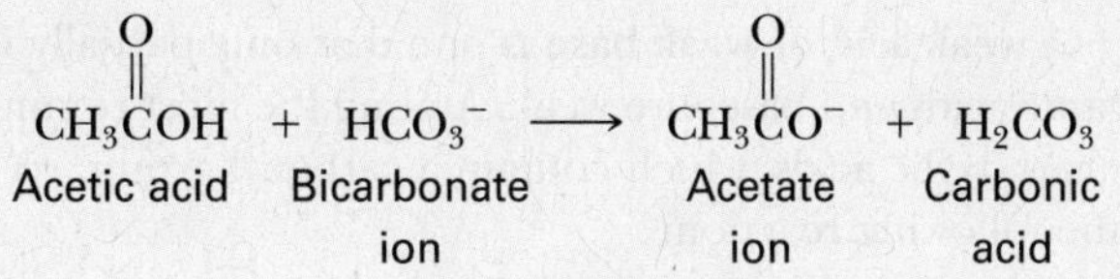

STRATEGY

First, write a Lewis structure for each reactant by showing all valence electrons on the reacting atoms: Acetic acid is the acid (proton donor), and bicarbonate ion is the base (proton acceptor). The members of a conjugate acid–base pair differ only by a proton, with the acid having the greater number of protons. To find the formula of the conjugate base, we remove one proton from the acid.

SOLUTION

From Table 2.1, we see that acetic acid is a stronger acid and, therefore, is the proton donor in this reaction.

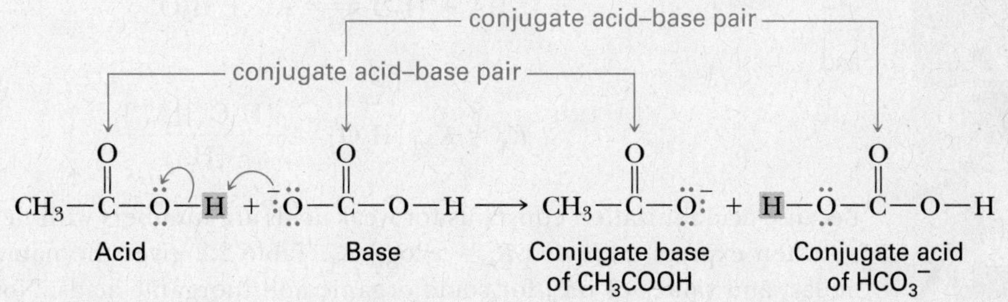

See problems 2.7, 2.8

PROBLEM 2.1

Write each acid–base reaction as a proton-transfer reaction. Label which reactant is the acid and which product is the base, as well as which product is the conjugate base of the original acid and which is the conjugate acid of the original base. Use curved arrows to show the flow of electrons in each reaction.

(a) $CH_3SH + OH^- \longrightarrow CH_3S^- + H_2O$ (b) $CH_3OH + NH_2^- \longrightarrow CH_3O^- + NH_3$

2.3 How Do We Measure the Strength of an Acid or Base?

Strong acid An acid that is completely ionized in aqueous solution.

Strong base A base that is completely ionized in aqueous solution.

A **strong acid** or **strong base** is one that ionizes completely in aqueous solution. When HCl is dissolved in water, a proton is transferred completely from HCl to H_2O to form Cl^- and H_3O^+. There is no tendency for the reverse reaction to occur—for the transfer of a proton from H_3O^+ to Cl^- to form HCl and H_2O. Therefore, when we compare the relative acidities of HCl and H_3O^+, we conclude that HCl is the stronger acid and H_3O^+ is the weaker acid. Similarly, H_2O is the stronger base and Cl^- is the weaker base.

Examples of strong acids in aqueous solution are HCl, HBr, HI, HNO_3, $HClO_4$, and H_2SO_4. Examples of strong bases in aqueous solution are LiOH, NaOH, KOH, $Ca(OH)_2$, and $Ba(OH)_2$.

Weak acid An acid that only partially ionizes in aqueous solution.

Weak base A base that only partially ionizes in aqueous solution.

A **weak acid** or **weak base** is one that only partially ionizes in aqueous solution. Most organic acids and bases are weak. Among the most common organic acids we deal with are the carboxylic acids, which contain a carboxyl group, —COOH (Section 1.7D), as shown in the following reaction:

$$CH_3\overset{\overset{\large O}{\|}}{C}OH + H_2O \rightleftharpoons CH_3\overset{\overset{\large O}{\|}}{C}O^- + H_3O^+$$

Acid (weaker acid)	Base (weaker base)	Conjugate base of CH_3COOH (stronger base)	Conjugate acid of H_2O (stronger acid)

The equation for the ionization of a weak acid, HA, in water and the acid ionization constant K_a for this equilibrium are, respectively,

$$HA + H_2O \rightleftharpoons A^- + H_3O^+$$

and

$$K_a = K_{eq}[H_2O] = \frac{[H_3O^+][A^-]}{[HA]}$$

Because acid ionization constants for weak acids are numbers with negative exponents, we often express them as $\mathbf{p}K_a = -\log_{10} K_a$. Table 2.2 gives the names, molecular formulas, and values of pK_a for some organic and inorganic acids. Note that the larger the value of pK_a, the weaker is the acid. Also note the inverse relationship between the strengths of the conjugate acid–base pairs; the stronger the acid, the weaker is its conjugate base.

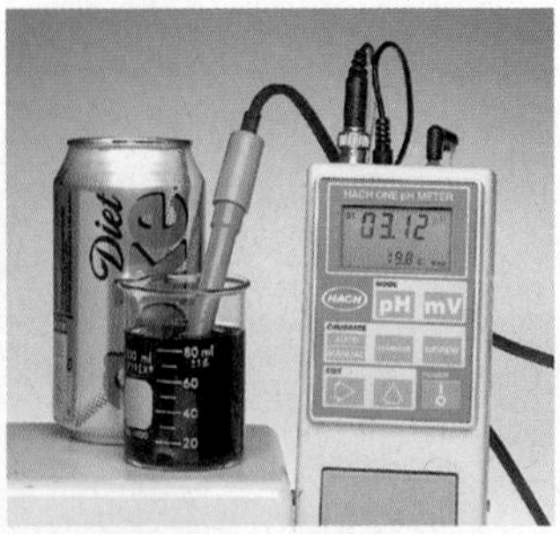

Charles D. Winters

The pH of this soft drink is 3.12. Soft drinks are often quite acidic.

EXAMPLE 2.2

For each value of pK_a, calculate the corresponding value of K_a. Which compound is the stronger acid?

(a) Ethanol, $pK_a = 15.9$

(b) Carbonic acid, $pK_a = 6.36$

STRATEGY

The stronger acid has the smaller value of pK_a (the larger value of K_a).

SOLUTION

(a) For ethanol, $K_a = 1.3 \times 10^{-16}$

(b) For carbonic acid, $K_a = 4.4 \times 10^{-7}$

Because the value of pK_a for carbonic acid is smaller than that for ethanol, carbonic acid is the stronger acid and ethanol is the weaker acid.

See problem 2.16

PROBLEM 2.2

For each value of K_a, calculate the corresponding value of pK_a. Which compound is the stronger acid?

(a) Acetic acid, $K_a = 1.74 \times 10^{-5}$

(b) Water, $K_a = 2.00 \times 10^{-16}$

Caution: In exercises such as Example 2.2 and Problem 2.2, we ask you to select the stronger acid. You must remember that these and all other acids with ionization constants considerably less than 1.00 are *weak* acids. Thus, although acetic acid is a considerably stronger acid than water, it still is only slightly ionized in water. The ionization of acetic acid in a 0.1 M solution, for example, is only about 1.3%; the major form of this weak acid that is present in a 0.1 M solution is the unionized acid!

"stronger acid" is used as a relative term. Keep in mind that acids with K_a values less than 1 ($pK_a \geq 0$) are considered weak acids

Forms present in 0.1 M acetic acid

$$\underset{98.7\%}{CH_3\overset{O}{\overset{\|}{C}}OH} + H_2O \rightleftharpoons \underset{1.3\%}{CH_3\overset{O}{\overset{\|}{C}}O^-} + H_3O^+$$

TABLE 2.2 pK_a Values for Some Organic and Inorganic Acids

	Acid	Formula	pK_a	Conjugate Base	
Weaker acid	ethane	CH_3CH_3	51	$CH_3CH_2^-$	Stronger base
	ammonia	NH_3	38	NH_2^-	
	ethanol	CH_3CH_2OH	15.9	$CH_3CH_2O^-$	
	water	H_2O	15.7	HO^-	
	methylammonium ion	$CH_3NH_3^+$	10.64	CH_3NH_2	
	bicarbonate ion	HCO_3^-	10.33	CO_3^{2-}	
	phenol	C_6H_5OH	9.95	$C_6H_5O^-$	
	ammonium ion	NH_4^+	9.24	NH_3	
	carbonic acid	H_2CO_3	6.36	HCO_3^-	
	acetic acid	CH_3COOH	4.76	CH_3COO^-	
	benzoic acid	C_6H_5COOH	4.19	$C_6H_5COO^-$	
	phosphoric acid	H_3PO_4	2.1	$H_2PO_4^-$	
	hydronium ion	H_3O^+	−1.74	H_2O	
	sulfuric acid	H_2SO_4	−5.2	HSO_4^-	
	hydrogen chloride	HCl	−7	Cl^-	
Stronger acid	hydrogen bromide	HBr	−8	Br^-	Weaker base
	hydrogen iodide	HI	−9	I^-	

the weaker the acid, the stronger is its conjugate base

the stronger the acid, the weaker is its conjugate base

2.4 How Do We Determine the Position of Equilibrium in an Acid–Base Reaction?

We know that HCl reacts with H_2O according to the following equilibrium:

$$HCl + H_2O \longrightarrow Cl^- + H_3O^+$$

We also know that HCl is a strong acid, which means that the position of this equilibrium lies very far to the right.

As we have seen, acetic acid reacts with H_2O according to the following equilibrium:

$$\underset{\text{Acetic acid}}{CH_3COOH} + H_2O \rightleftharpoons \underset{\text{Acetate ion}}{CH_3COO^-} + H_3O^+$$

Acetic acid is a weak acid. Only a few acetic acid molecules react with water to give acetate ions and hydronium ions, and the major species present at equilibrium in aqueous solution is CH_3COOH. The position of this equilibrium, therefore, lies very far to the left.

In the preceding two acid–base reactions, water was the base (proton acceptor). But what if we have a base other than water as the proton acceptor? How can we determine which are the major species present at equilibrium? That is, how can we determine whether the position of equilibrium lies toward the left or toward the right?

As an example, let us examine the acid–base reaction between acetic acid and ammonia to form acetate ion and ammonium ion:

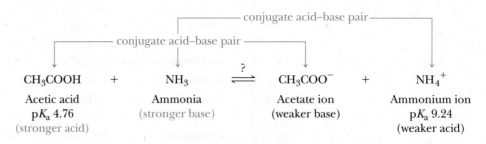

Charles D. Winters

Vinegar (which contains acetic acid) and baking soda (sodium bicarbonate) react to produce sodium acetate, carbon dioxide, and water. The carbon dioxide inflates the balloon.

$$\underset{\substack{\text{Acetic acid}\\\text{(Acid)}}}{CH_3COOH} + \underset{\substack{\text{Ammonia}\\\text{(Base)}}}{NH_3} \overset{?}{\rightleftharpoons} \underset{\substack{\text{Acetate ion}\\\text{(Conjugate base}\\\text{of } CH_3COOH)}}{CH_3COO^-} + \underset{\substack{\text{Ammonium}\\\text{ion (Conjugate}\\\text{acid of } NH_3)}}{NH_4^+}$$

As indicated by the question mark over the equilibrium arrow, we want to determine whether the position of this equilibrium lies toward the left or toward the right. There are two acids present: acetic acid and ammonium ion. There are also two bases present: ammonia and acetate ion. From Table 2.2, we see that CH_3COOH (pK_a 4.76) is the stronger acid, which means that CH_3COO^- is the weaker conjugate base. Conversely, NH_4^+ (pK_a 9.24) is the weaker acid, which means that NH_3 is the stronger conjugate base. We can now label the relative strengths of each acid and base in the equilibrium:

conjugate acid–base pair (NH_3 / NH_4^+)

conjugate acid–base pair (CH_3COOH / CH_3COO^-)

$$\underset{\substack{\text{Acetic acid}\\pK_a\ 4.76\\\text{(stronger acid)}}}{CH_3COOH} + \underset{\substack{\text{Ammonia}\\\text{(stronger base)}}}{NH_3} \overset{?}{\rightleftharpoons} \underset{\substack{\text{Acetate ion}\\\text{(weaker base)}}}{CH_3COO^-} + \underset{\substack{\text{Ammonium ion}\\pK_a\ 9.24\\\text{(weaker acid)}}}{NH_4^+}$$

In an acid–base reaction, the position of equilibrium always favors reaction of the stronger acid and stronger base to form the weaker acid and weaker base. Thus, at equilibrium, the major species present are the weaker acid and weaker base. In the reaction between acetic acid and ammonia, therefore, the equilibrium lies to the right, and the major species present are acetate ion and ammonium ion:

$$\underset{\substack{\text{Acetic acid}\\\text{(stronger acid)}}}{CH_3COOH} + \underset{\substack{\text{Ammonia}\\\text{(stronger base)}}}{NH_3} \rightleftharpoons \underset{\substack{\text{Acetate ion}\\\text{(weaker base)}}}{CH_3COO^-} + \underset{\substack{\text{Ammonium ion}\\\text{(weaker acid)}}}{NH_4^+}$$

HOW TO 2.2

Determine the Position of Equilibrium in an Acid–Base Reaction

1. Identify the two acids in the equilibrium; one is on the left side of the equilibrium, the other on the right side.
2. Using the information in Table 2.2, determine which acid is the stronger and which the weaker. In the absence of pK_a data, use the concepts presented in Section 2.5 to determine the stronger and weaker acid.
3. Identify the stronger base and weaker base in each equilibrium. Remember that the stronger acid gives the weaker conjugate base and the weaker acid gives the stronger conjugate base.
4. The stronger acid and stronger base react to give the weaker acid and weaker base, and the position of equilibrium lies on the side of the weaker acid and weaker base.

EXAMPLE 2.3

For each acid–base equilibrium, label the stronger acid, the stronger base, the weaker acid, and the weaker base. Then predict whether the position of equilibrium lies toward the right or toward the left.

(a) $H_2CO_3 + OH^- \rightleftharpoons HCO_3^- + H_2O$

Carbonic acid; Bicarbonate ion

(b) $C_6H_5OH + HCO_3^- \rightleftharpoons C_6H_5O^- + H_2CO_3$

Phenol; Bicarbonate ion; Phenoxide ion; Carbonic acid

STRATEGY

Identify the two acids in the equilibrium and their relative strengths and the two bases and their relative strengths. The position of the equilibrium lies toward the weaker acid and the weaker base.

SOLUTION

Arrows over each equilibrium show the conjugate acid–base pairs. The position of equilibrium in (a) lies toward the right. In (b) it lies toward the left.

(conjugate acid–base pair: H_2CO_3 / HCO_3^-; conjugate acid–base pair: OH^- / H_2O)

(a) $H_2CO_3 + OH^- \rightleftharpoons HCO_3^- + H_2O$

H_2CO_3	OH^-	HCO_3^-	H_2O
Carbonic acid pK_a 6.36 (stronger acid)	(stronger base)	Bicarbonate ion (weaker base)	Water pK_a 15.7 (weaker acid)

(conjugate acid–base pair: C_6H_5OH / $C_6H_5O^-$; conjugate acid–base pair: HCO_3^- / H_2CO_3)

(b) $C_6H_5OH + HCO_3^- \rightleftharpoons C_6H_5O^- + H_2CO_3$

C_6H_5OH	HCO_3^-	$C_6H_5O^-$	H_2CO_3
Phenol pK_a 9.95 (weaker acid)	Bicarbonate ion (weaker base)	Phenoxide ion (stronger base)	Carbonic acid pK_a 6.36 (stronger acid)

See problems 2.11, 2.12, 2.17, 2.25

PROBLEM 2.3

For each acid–base equilibrium, label the stronger acid, the stronger base, the weaker acid, and the weaker base. Then predict whether the position of equilibrium lies toward the right or the left.

(a) $CH_3NH_2 + CH_3COOH \rightleftharpoons CH_3NH_3^+ + CH_3COO^-$

Methylamine	Acetic acid	Methylammonium ion	Acetate ion

(b) $CH_3CH_2O^- + NH_3 \rightleftharpoons CH_3CH_2OH + NH_2^-$

Ethoxide ion	Ammonia	Ethanol	Amide ion

2.5 What Are the Relationships between Acidity and Molecular Structure?

Now let us examine the relationship between the acidity of organic compounds and their molecular structure. The most important factor in determining the relative acidities of organic acids is the relative stability of the anion, A^-, formed when the acid, HA, transfers a proton to a base. We can understand the relationship involved by considering (A) the electronegativity of the atom bonded to H, (B) resonance, (C) the inductive effect, and (D) the size and delocalization of charge on A^-. We will look at each of these factors briefly in this chapter. We will study them more fully in later chapters when we deal with particular functional groups.

A. Electronegativity: Acidity of HA within a Period of the Periodic Table

Recall that electronegativity is a measure of an atom's attraction for electrons it shares in a covalent bond with another atom. The more electronegative an atom is, the greater its ability to sustain electron density around itself. The relative acidity of the hydrogen acids within a period of the Periodic Table is determined by the stability of A^-, that is, by the stability of the anion that forms when a proton is transferred from HA to a base. Thus, the greater the electronegativity of A, the greater the stability of the anion A^-, and the stronger the acid HA. For example, carbon and oxygen are in the same period of the Periodic Table. Because oxygen is more electronegative than carbon, oxygen is better able to sustain the added electron density incurred when it is negatively charged than is carbon when it is negatively charged.

when comparing negatively charged *atoms in the same period* of the Periodic Table, **the more electronegative the atom, the better it is at sustaining the negative charge**

	$H_3C{-}H$	$H_2N{-}H$	$HO{-}H$	$F{-}H$
pK_a	51	38	15.7	3.5
Electronegativity of A in A–H	2.5	3.0	3.5	4.0

Increasing acid strength →

Caution: Electronegativity is the major factor when comparing the stability of negatively charged atoms in the same period of the Periodic Table. Other factors, which we will discuss in Section 2.5D and in future chapters, will become significant when comparing atoms in the same group (vertical column) of the Periodic Table.

B. Resonance Effect: Delocalization of the Charge in A^-

Carboxylic acids are weak acids: Values of pK_a for most unsubstituted carboxylic acids fall within the range from 4 to 5. The value of pK_a for acetic acid, for example, is 4.76:

$$\underset{\text{A carboxylic acid}}{CH_3COOH} + H_2O \rightleftharpoons \underset{\text{A carboxylate anion}}{CH_3COO^-} + H_3O^+ \quad pK_a = 4.76$$

Values of pK_a for most alcohols, compounds that also contain an —OH group, fall within the range from 15 to 18; the value of pK_a for ethanol, for example, is 15.9:

$$\underset{\text{An alcohol}}{CH_3CH_2O{-}H} + H_2O \rightleftharpoons \underset{\text{An alkoxide ion}}{CH_3CH_2O^-} + H_3O^+ \quad pK_a = 15.9$$

Thus, alcohols are slightly weaker acids than water ($pK_a = 15.7$) and are much weaker acids than carboxylic acids.

We account for the greater acidity of carboxylic acids compared with alcohols in part by using the resonance model and looking at the relative stabilities of the alkoxide ion and the carboxylate ion. Our guideline is this: The more stable the anion, the farther the position of equilibrium is shifted toward the right and the more acidic is the compound.

There is no resonance stabilization in an alkoxide anion. The ionization of a carboxylic acid, however, gives an anion for which we can write two equivalent contributing structures in which the negative charge of the anion is delocalized; that is, it is spread evenly over the two oxygen atoms:

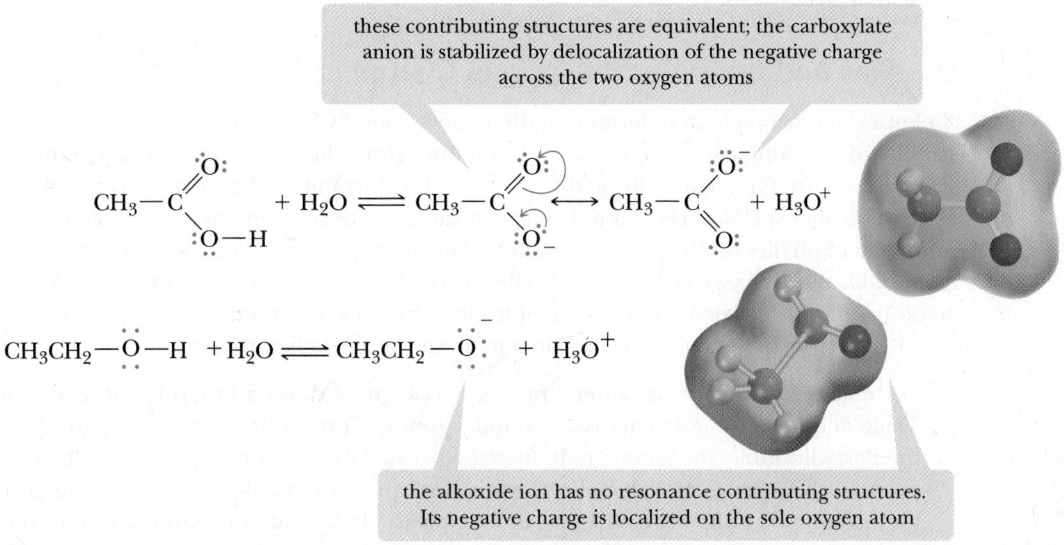

these contributing structures are equivalent; the carboxylate anion is stabilized by delocalization of the negative charge across the two oxygen atoms
the alkoxide ion has no resonance contributing structures. Its negative charge is localized on the sole oxygen atom

Because of the delocalization of its charge, a carboxylate anion is significantly more stable than an alkoxide anion. Therefore, the equilibrium for the ionization of a carboxylic acid is shifted to the right relative to that for the ionization of an alcohol, and a carboxylic acid is a stronger acid than an alcohol.

a resonance effect that delocalizes the charge of an ion will have the effect of stabilizing that ion

C. The Inductive Effect: Withdrawal of Electron Density from the HA Bond

The **inductive effect** is the polarization of electron density transmitted through covalent bonds by a nearby atom of higher electronegativity. We see the operation of the inductive effect when we compare the acidities of acetic acid (pK_a 4.76) and trifluoroacetic acid (pK_a 0.23). Fluorine is more electronegative than carbon and polarizes the electrons of the C—F bond, creating a partial positive charge on the carbon of the $-CF_3$ group. The

Inductive effect The polarization of electron density transmitted through covalent bonds caused by a nearby atom of higher electronegativity.

partial positive charge, in turn, withdraws electron density from the negatively charged $-CO_2^-$ group. The withdrawal of electron density delocalizes the negative charge and makes the conjugate base of trifluoroacetic acid more stable than the conjugate base of acetic acid. The delocalizing effect is apparent when the electron density map of each conjugate base is compared.

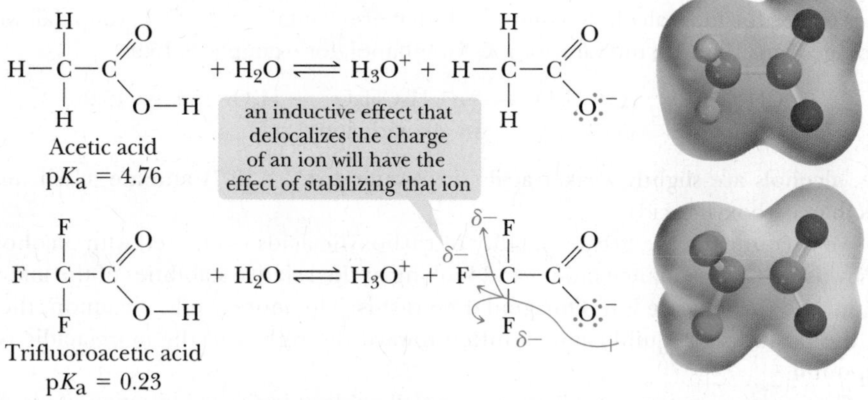
Acetic acid
pKa = 4.76
an inductive effect that delocalizes the charge of an ion will have the effect of stabilizing that ion
Trifluoroacetic acid
pKa = 0.23

Notice that the oxygen atoms on the trifluoroacetate ion are less negative (represented by a lighter shade of red). Thus, the equilibrium for ionization of trifluoroacetic acid is shifted more to the right relative to the ionization of acetic acid, making trifluoroacetic acid more acidic than acetic acid.

D. Size and the Delocalization of Charge in A^-

An important principle in determining the relative stability of unionized acids, HA, is the stability of the conjugate base anion, A^-, resulting from the loss of a proton. The more stable the anion, the greater the acidity of the acid. For example, the relative acidity of the hydrogen halides, HX, is related to the size of the atom bearing the negative charge. The principles of physics teach us that a system bearing a charge (either negative or positive) is more stable if the charge is delocalized. The larger the volume over which the charge of an anion (or cation) is delocalized, the greater the stability of the anion.

Recall from general chemistry that atomic size is a periodic property.

when comparing negatively charged *atoms in the same group* of the Periodic Table, **the larger the atom bearing the negative charge, the better it is at sustaining the charge**

1. **For main group elements, atomic radii increase going down a group in the Periodic Table and increase going across a period.** From the top to the bottom of a group in the Periodic Table, the atomic radii increase because electrons occupy orbitals that are successively larger as the value of *n*, the principal quantum number, increases. Thus, for the halogens (Group 8A elements), iodine has the largest atomic radius and fluorine has the smallest (I > Br > Cl > F).

2. **Anions are always larger than the atoms from which they are derived.** For anions, the nuclear charge is unchanged, but the added electron(s) introduce new repulsions and electron clouds swell. Among the halide ions, I^- has the largest atomic radius and F^- has the smallest ($I^- > Br^- > Cl^- > F^-$).

Thus, when considering the relative acidities of the hydrogen halide acids, we need to consider the relative stabilities of the resulting halide ions formed by ionization of the acid. We know that HI is the strongest acid and that HF is the weakest. We account for this trend by the fact that the negative charge on iodide ion is delocalized over a larger area than is the negative charge on bromide ion. The negative charge on bromide ion in turn is delocalized over a larger area than is the negative charge on chloride ion, and so forth. Thus, HI is the strongest acid in the series because iodide ion is the most stable anion, and HF is the weakest acid because fluoride ion is the least stable ion.

We should note here that a result of resonance (Section 2.5B) is also the delocalization of charge density. Through resonance, the negative charge associated with a carboxylate ion, for example, is more delocalized than is the negative charge associated with an alkoxide ion. Thus a carboxylate ion is more stable than is an alkoxide ion and, therefore, a carboxylic acid is a stronger acid than an alcohol.

EXAMPLE 2.4

(a) Arrange the following compounds in the order from most acidic to least acidic.

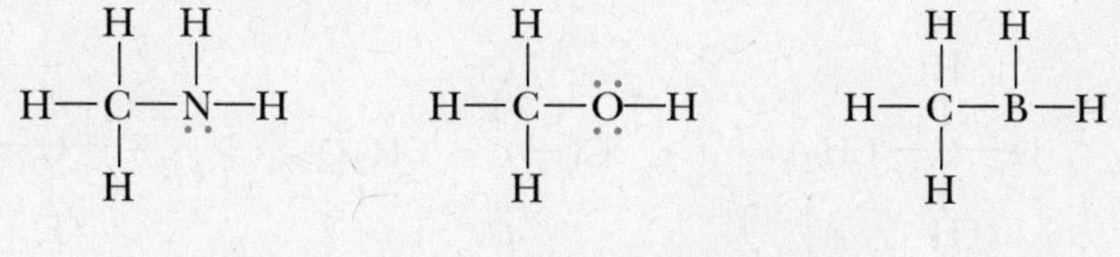

(b) Arrange the following compounds in order from most basic to least basic.

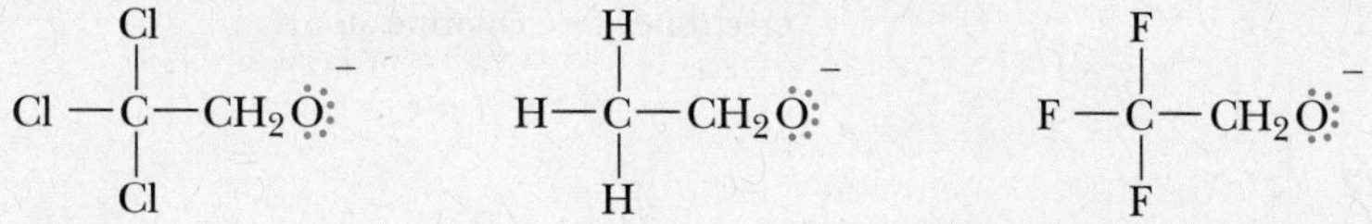

STRATEGY

When determining acidity, assess the stability of the conjugate base—the compound formed after the acid has transferred its proton to a base. Any feature (e.g., electronegativity, resonance, inductive effect, or anion size) that helps to stabilize the conjugate base will make the original acid more acidic. When determining the basicity of a negatively charged species, assess the stability of the base. Any feature (e.g., electronegativity, resonance, or inductive effect) that helps to stabilize the base will make it less basic. That is, a more stable base will be less reactive.

SOLUTION

Because the elements compared in this example (B, C, and O) are all in the same period of the Periodic Table, the stability of the conjugate bases can be compared based on the electronegativity of the element bearing the negative charge. Oxygen, the most electronegative element, is most able to bear the electron density and negative charge. Boron, the least electronegative element, is least able to bear the electron density and negative charge.

(a)

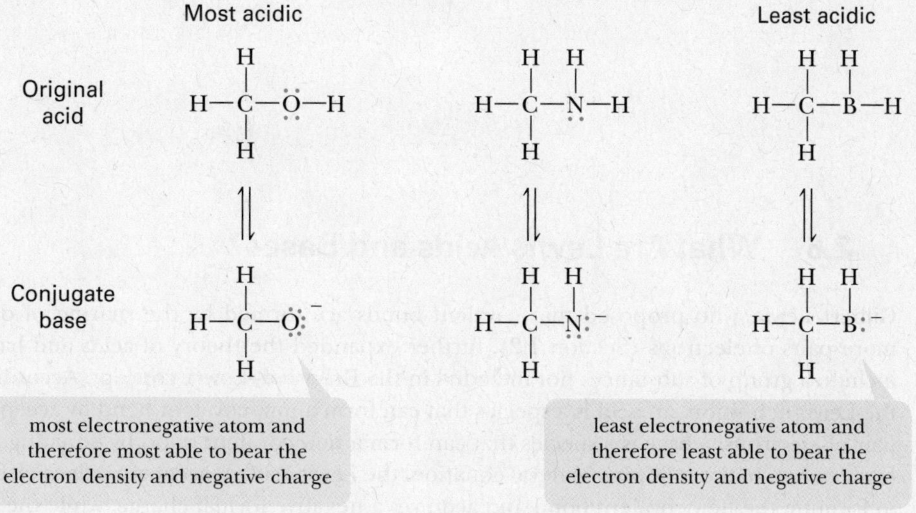

(b) The stability of bases can be compared based on the extent of an inductive effect within each compound. Fluorine, the most electronegative element, will exert a strong inductive effect on the negatively charged oxygen, thereby delocalizing the negative charge to some extent. This delocalization of negative charge makes the $F_3CCH_2O^-$ ion more stable than either of the other two. Chlorine can also exert an inductive effect on the negatively charged oxygen. Chlorine, however, is less electronegative than fluorine, so the stabilizing effect is less.

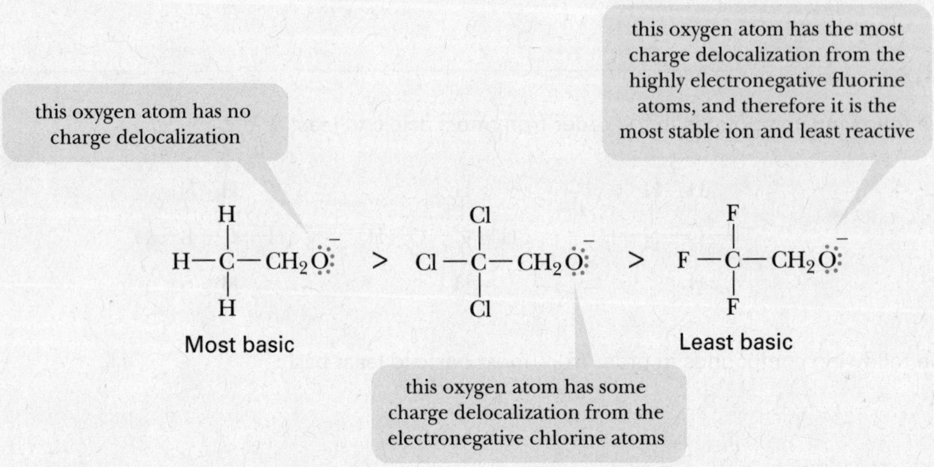
this oxygen atom has no charge delocalization
this oxygen atom has the most charge delocalization from the highly electronegative fluorine atoms, and therefore it is the most stable ion and least reactive
Most basic
Least basic
this oxygen atom has some charge delocalization from the electronegative chlorine atoms

See problems 2.20–2.22

PROBLEM 2.4

(a) Arrange the following compounds in the order from most acidic to least acidic.

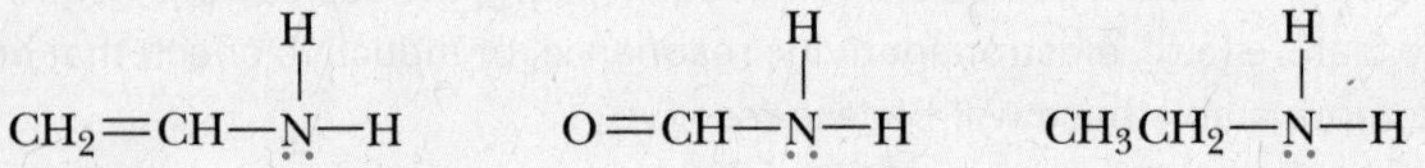

(b) Arrange the following compounds in the order from most basic to least basic.

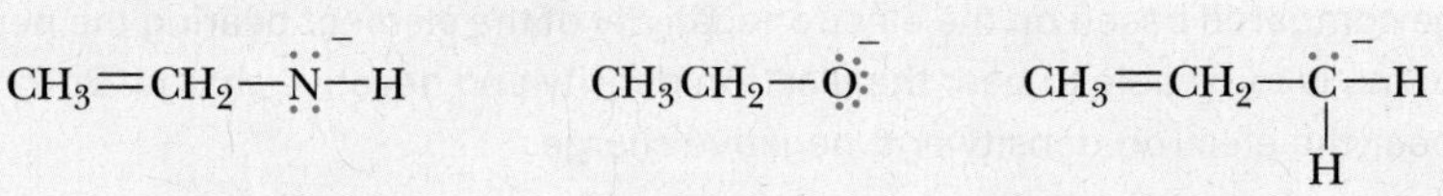

2.6 What Are Lewis Acids and Bases?

Lewis acid Any molecule or ion that can form a new covalent bond by accepting a pair of electrons.

Lewis base Any molecule or ion that can form a new covalent bond by donating a pair of electrons.

Gilbert Lewis, who proposed that covalent bonds are formed by the sharing of one or more pairs of electrons (Section 1.2), further expanded the theory of acids and bases to include a group of substances not included in the Brønsted–Lowry concept. According to the Lewis definition, an **acid** is a species that can form a new covalent bond by accepting a pair of electrons; a **base** is a species that can form a new covalent bond by donating a pair of electrons. In the following general equation, the Lewis acid, A, accepts a pair of electrons in forming the new covalent bond and acquires a negative formal charge, while the Lewis base, :B, donates the pair of electrons in forming the new covalent bond and acquires a positive formal charge:

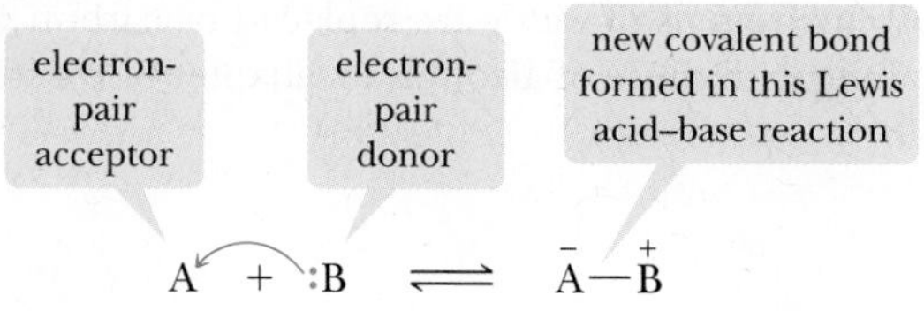

Lewis acid Lewis base

Note that, although we speak of a Lewis base as "donating" a pair of electrons, the term is not fully accurate. "Donating" in this case does not imply that the electron pair under consideration is removed completely from the valence shell of the base. Rather, "donating" means that the electron pair is shared with another atom to form a covalent bond.

As we will see in the chapters that follow, a great many organic reactions can be interpreted as Lewis acid–base reactions. Perhaps the most important (but not the only) Lewis acid is the proton. Isolated protons, of course, do not exist in solution; rather, a proton attaches itself to the strongest available Lewis base. When HCl is dissolved in water, for example, the strongest available Lewis base is an H_2O molecule, and the following proton-transfer reaction takes place:

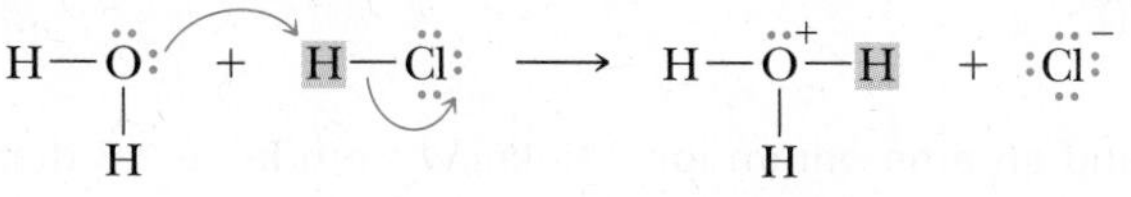

Hydronium ion

When HCl is dissolved in methanol, the strongest available Lewis base is a CH_3OH molecule, and the following proton-transfer reaction takes place. An **oxonium** ion is an ion that contains an oxygen atom with three bonds and bears a positive charge.

Oxonium ion An ion that contains an oxygen atom that bears a positive charge and with three bonds to oxygen.

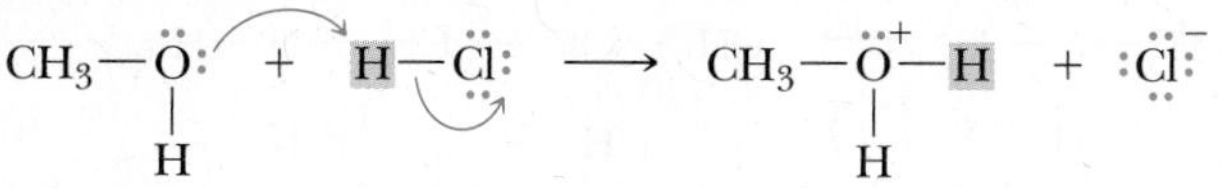

Methanol (a Lewis base) An oxonium ion

Table 2.3 gives examples of the most important types of Lewis bases we will encounter in this text arranged in order of their increasing strength in proton-transfer

TABLE 2.3 Some Organic Lewis Bases and Their Relative Strengths in Proton-Transfer Reactions

Halide Ions	Water, Alcohols, and Ethers	Ammonia and Amines	Hydroxide Ion and Alkoxide Ions	Amide Ions
$:\ddot{Cl}:^-$	$H-\ddot{O}-H$	$H-\ddot{N}(H)-H$	$H-\ddot{O}:^-$	$H-\ddot{N}(H):^-$
$:\ddot{Br}:^-$	$CH_3-\ddot{O}-H$	$CH_3-\ddot{N}(H)-H$	$CH_3-\ddot{O}:^-$	$CH_3-\ddot{N}(H):^-$
$:\ddot{I}:^-$	$CH_3-\ddot{O}-CH_3$	$CH_3-\ddot{N}(CH_3)-H$		$CH_3-\ddot{N}(CH_3):^-$
		$CH_3-\ddot{N}(CH_3)-CH_3$		
Very weak	Weak	Strong	Stronger	Very strong

reactions. Note that each of the Lewis bases has at least one atom with an unshared pair of electrons. It is this atom that functions as the Lewis base. Ethers are organic derivatives of water in which both hydrogens of water are replaced by carbon groups. We study the properties of ethers along with those of alcohols in Chapter 8. We study the properties of amines in Chapter 10.

EXAMPLE 2.5

Complete this acid–base reaction. Use curved arrows to show the redistribution of electrons in the reaction. In addition, predict whether the position of this equilibrium lies toward the left or the right.

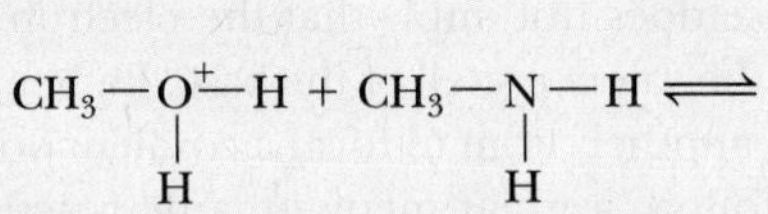

STRATEGY

First, add unshared pairs of electrons on the reacting atoms to give each a complete octet. Then identify the Lewis base (the electron-pair donor) and the Lewis acid (the electron-pair acceptor). The position of equilibrium lies on the side of the weaker acid and weaker base.

SOLUTION

Proton transfer takes place to form an alcohol and an ammonium ion. We know from Table 2.3 that amines are stronger bases than alcohols. We also know that the weaker the base, the stronger its conjugate acid, and vice versa. From this analysis, we conclude that the position of this equilibrium lies to the right, on the side of the weaker acid and the weaker base.

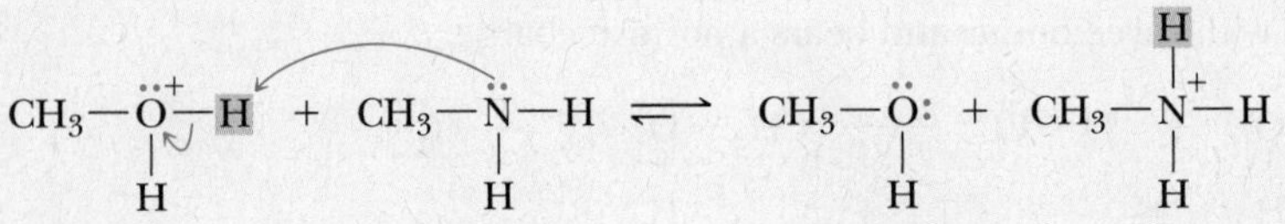

See problems 2.7, 2.8, 2.11, 2.26–2.32

PROBLEM 2.5

Complete this acid–base reaction. First add unshared pairs of electrons on the reacting atoms to give each atom a complete octet. Use curved arrows to show the redistribution of electrons in the reaction. In addition, predict whether the position of the equilibrium lies toward the left or the right.

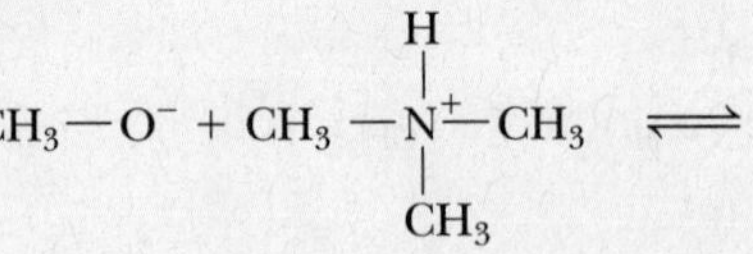

Another type of Lewis acid we will encounter in later chapters is an organic cation in which a carbon is bonded to only three atoms and bears a positive formal charge. Such carbon cations are called carbocations. Consider the reaction that occurs when the following organic cation reacts with a bromide ion:

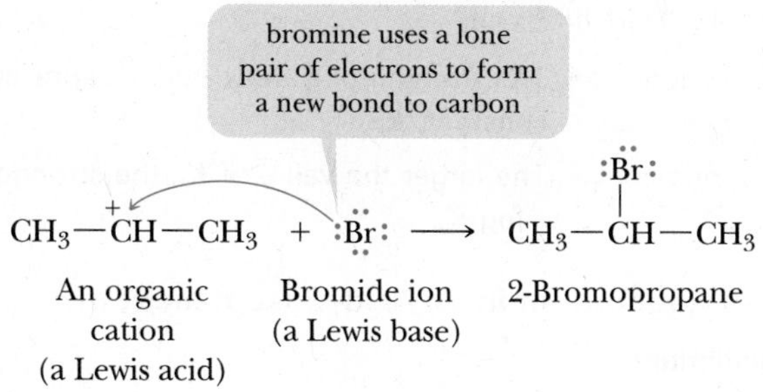

In this reaction, the organic cation is the electron-pair acceptor (the Lewis acid), and bromide ion is the electron-pair donor (the Lewis base).

EXAMPLE 2.6

Complete the following Lewis acid–base reaction. Show all electron pairs on the reacting atoms and use curved arrows to show the flow of electrons in the reaction:

$$CH_3-\overset{+}{C}H-CH_3 + H_2O \longrightarrow$$

STRATEGY

Determine which compound will be the electron-pair donor and which will be the electron-pair acceptor. *Hint:* Compounds with empty orbitals in their valence shell usually act as Lewis acids.

SOLUTION

The trivalent carbon atom in the organic cation has an empty orbital in its valence shell and, therefore, is the Lewis acid. Water is the Lewis base.

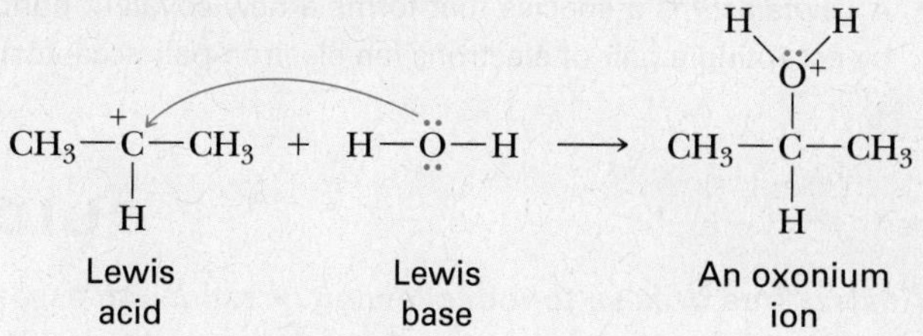

See problems 2.30–2.32

PROBLEM 2.6

Write an equation for the reaction between each Lewis acid–base pair, showing electron flow by means of curved arrows. (*Hint:* Aluminum is in Group 3A of the Periodic Table, just under boron. Aluminum in $AlCl_3$ has only six electrons in its valence shell and thus has an incomplete octet.)

(a) $Cl^- + AlCl_3 \longrightarrow$ **(b)** $CH_3Cl + AlCl_3 \longrightarrow$

SUMMARY OF KEY QUESTIONS

2.1 What Are Arrhenius Acids and Bases?

- An **Arrhenius acid** is a substance that dissolves in aqueous solution to produce H_3O^+ ions.
- An **Arrhenius base** is a substance that dissolves in aqueous solution to produce OH^- ions.

2.2 What Are Brønsted–Lowry Acids and Bases?

- A **Brønsted–Lowry acid** is a proton donor.
- A **Brønsted–Lowry base** is a proton acceptor.
- Neutralization of an acid by a base is a **proton-transfer reaction** in which the acid is transformed into its **conjugate base**, and the base is transformed into its **conjugate acid**.

2.3 How Do We Measure the Strength of an Acid or Base?

- A **strong acid** or **strong base** is one that completely ionizes in water.
- A **weak acid** or **weak base** is one that only partially ionizes in water.
- The strength of a weak acid is expressed by its **ionization constant, K_a**.
- The larger the value of K_a, the stronger the acid, $pK_a = -\log K_a$.

2.4 How Do We Determine the Position of Equilibrium in an Acid–Base Reaction?

- In an acid–base reaction, the **position of equilibrium** favors the reaction of the stronger acid and the stronger base to form the weaker acid and the weaker base.

2.5 What Are the Relationships between Acidity and Molecular Structure?

The relative acidities of the organic acids, HA, are determined by

- the electronegativity of A.
- the **resonance stabilization** of the conjugate base, A^-.
- the electron-withdrawing **inductive effect**, which also stabilizes the conjugate base.
- the size of the atom with the negative charge on the conjugate base.

2.6 What Are Lewis Acids and Bases?

- A **Lewis acid** is a species that forms a new covalent bond by accepting a pair of electrons (an electron-pair acceptor).
- A **Lewis base** is a species that forms a new covalent bond by donating a pair of electrons (an electron-pair donor).

QUICK QUIZ

Answer true or false to the following questions to assess your general knowledge of the concepts in this chapter. If you have difficulty with any of them, you should review the appropriate section in the chapter (shown in parentheses) before attempting the more challenging end-of-chapter problems.

1. If NH_3 were to behave as an acid, its conjugate base would be NH_2^-. (2.2)
2. Delocalization of electron density is a stabilizing factor. (2.5)
3. Amide ion, NH_2^-, is a Lewis base. (2.6)
4. H_3O^+ is a stronger acid than NH_4^+ and, therefore, NH_3 is a stronger base than H_2O. (2.3)
5. Inductive effects can be used to describe electron delocalization. (2.5)
6. The direction of equilibrium in an acid–base reaction favors the side containing the stronger acid and stronger base. (2.4)
7. The conjugate base of CH_3CH_2OH is $CH_3CH_2O^-$. (2.2)
8. CH_3^+ and NH_4^+ are Lewis acids. (2.6)
9. When an acid, HA, dissolves in water, the solution becomes acidic because of the presence of H^+ ions. (2.1)
10. Between a strong acid and a weak acid, the weak acid will give rise to the stronger conjugate base. (2.4)
11. H_2O can function as an acid (proton donor) and as a base (proton acceptor). (2.2)
12. The strongest base that can exist in aqueous solution is OH^-. (2.4)
13. A strong acid is one that completely ionizes in aqueous solution. (2.3)
14. NH_3 is a Lewis base. (2.6)
15. A Brønsted–Lowry acid is a proton donor. (2.2)
16. When comparing the relative strength of acids, the stronger acid has the smaller value of pK_a. (2.3)
17. When comparing the relative strengths of acids, the stronger acid has the smaller value of K_a. (2.3)
18. The formulas of a conjugate acid–base pair differ only by a proton. (2.2)
19. A Lewis base is an electron pair donor. (2.6)
20. Acetic acid, CH_3COOH, is a stronger acid than carbonic acid, H_2CO_3, and, therefore, acetate ion, CH_3COO^-, is a stronger base than bicarbonate ion, HCO_3^-. (2.2)
21. The strongest acid that can exist in aqueous solution is H_3O^+. (2.4)
22. A Lewis acid–base reaction results in the formation of a new covalent bond between the Lewis acid and the Lewis base. (2.6)
23. When a base accepts a proton in an acid–base reaction, it is converted into its conjugate base. (2.2)

24. When a metal hydroxide, MOH, dissolves in water, the solution becomes basic because of the presence of hydroxide ions, OH^-. (2.1)

25. A Lewis acid is a proton acceptor. (2.6)

26. If NH_3 were to behave as a base, its conjugate acid would be NH_4^+. (2.2)

27. Resonance effects can be used to describe electron delocalization. (2.5)

28. All Lewis acid–base reactions involve transfer of a proton from the acid to the base.

29. BF_3 is a Lewis acid. (2.6)

30. When HCl dissolves in water, the major ions present are H^+ and Cl^-. (2.3)

31. According to the Arrhenius definitions, acids and bases are limited substances that dissolve in water. (2.1)

32. Acid–base reactions take place only in aqueous solution. (2.6)

33. The conjugate acid of HCO_3^- is H_2CO_3. (2.2)

Detailed explanations for many of these answers can be found in the accompanying Solutions Manual.

Answers: (1) T (2) T (3) T (4) T (5) T (6) F (7) T (8) F (9) F (10) T (11) T (12) T (13) T (14) T (15) T (16) T (17) F (18) T (19) T (20) F (21) T (22) T (23) F (24) T (25) F (26) T (27) T (28) F (29) T (30) F (31) T (32) F (33) T

KEY REACTIONS

1. **Proton-Transfer Reaction (Section 2.2)**

   This reaction involves the transfer of a proton from a proton donor (a Brønsted–Lowry acid) to a proton acceptor (a Brønsted–Lowry base):

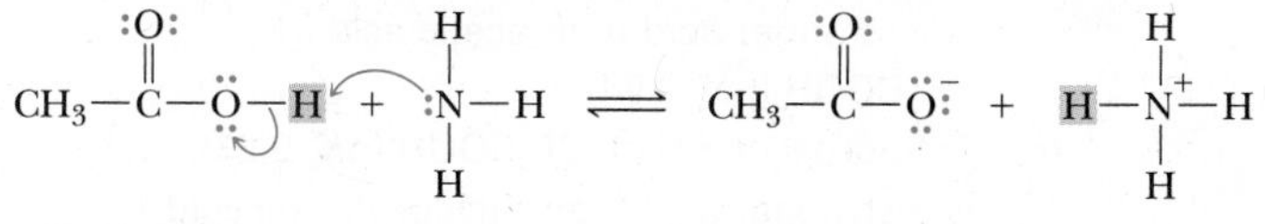

Acetic acid (proton donor)	Ammonia (proton acceptor)	Acetate ion	Ammonium ion

2. **Position of Equilibrium in an Acid–Base Reaction (Section 2.4)**

   Equilibrium favors reaction of the stronger acid with the stronger base to give the weaker acid and the weaker base:

$$CH_3COOH + NH_3 \rightleftharpoons CH_3COO^- + NH_4^+$$

Acetic acid pK_a 4.76 (stronger acid)	(stronger base)	(weaker base)	Ammonium ion pK_a 9.24 (weaker acid)

3. **Lewis Acid–Base Reaction (Section 2.6)**

   A Lewis acid–base reaction involves sharing an electron pair between an electron-pair donor (a Lewis base) and an electron-pair acceptor (a Lewis acid):

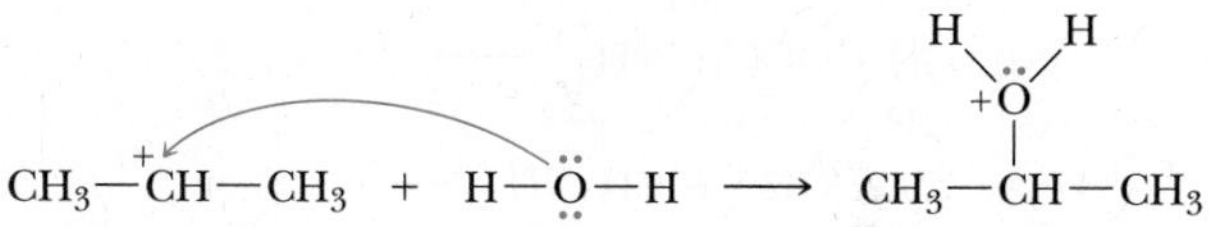

A Lewis acid	A Lewis base	An oxonium ion

PROBLEMS

A problem marked with an asterisk indicates an applied "real-world" problem. Answers to problems whose numbers are printed in blue are given in Appendix D.

Section 2.1 Arrhenius Acids and Bases

2.7 Complete the net ionic equation for each acid placed in water. Use curved arrows to show the flow of electron pairs in each reaction. Also, for each reaction, determine the direction of equilibrium, using Table 2.2 as a reference for the pK_a values of proton acids. **(See Examples 2.1, 2.5)**

(a) $NH_4^+ + H_2O \rightleftharpoons$

(b) $HCO_3^- + H_2O \rightleftharpoons$

(c) $CH_3-\overset{\overset{\displaystyle O}{\|}}{C}-OH + H_2O \rightleftharpoons$

(d) $CH_3CH_2O^- + H_2O \rightleftharpoons$

2.8 Complete the net ionic equation for each base placed in water. Use curved arrows to show the flow of electron pairs in each reaction. Also, for each reaction, determine the direction of equilibrium, using Table 2.2 as a reference for the pK_a values of proton acids formed. **(See Examples 2.1, 2.5)**

(a) $CH_3NH_2 + H_2O \rightleftharpoons$

(b) $HSO_4^- + H_2O \rightleftharpoons$

(c) $Br^- + H_2O \rightleftharpoons$

(d) $CO_3^{2-} + H_2O \rightleftharpoons$

Section 2.2 Brønsted–Lowry Acids and Bases

2.9 How are the formulas of the members of a conjugate acid–base pair related to each other? Within a pair, how can you tell which is the acid?

2.10 Write the structural formula for the conjugate acids of the following structures.

(a) $CH_3—CH_2—\ddot{N}(H)—H$

(b) $H—\ddot{N}(H)—CH_2—CH_2—\ddot{O}H$

(c) 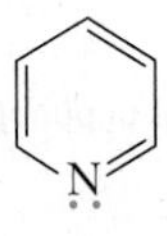

(d) $CH_3CH_2\ddot{C}H_2^-$

2.11 Complete a net ionic equation for each proton-transfer reaction, using curved arrows to show the flow of electron pairs in each reaction. In addition, write Lewis structures for all starting materials and products. Label the original acid and its conjugate base; label the original base and its conjugate acid. If you are uncertain about which substance in each equation is the proton donor, refer to Table 2.2 for the pK_a values of proton acids. **(See Examples 2.3, 2.5)**

(a) $NH_3 + HCl \longrightarrow$
(b) $CH_3CH_2O^- + HCl \longrightarrow$
(c) $HCO_3^- + OH^- \longrightarrow$
(d) $CH_3COO^- + NH_4^+ \longrightarrow$
(e) $NH_4^+ + OH^- \longrightarrow$
(f) $CH_3COO^- + CH_3NH_3^+ \longrightarrow$
(g) $CH_3CH_2O^- + NH_4^+ \longrightarrow$
(h) $CH_3NH_3^+ + OH^- \longrightarrow$

***2.12** One kind of baking powder contains sodium bicarbonate and calcium dihydrogen phosphate: When water is added, the following reaction occurs. **(See Example 2.3)**

$$HCO_3^-(aq) + H_2PO_4^-(aq) \longrightarrow H_2CO_3(aq) + HPO_4^{2-}(aq)$$

Identify the two acids and the two bases in this reaction. (The H_2CO_3 decomposes to release CO_2, which causes the cake to rise.)

2.13 Each of these molecules and ions can function as a base. Complete the Lewis structure of each base, and write the structural formula of the conjugate acid formed by its reaction with HCl.

(a) CH_3CH_2OH (b) $HC(=O)H$
(c) $(CH_3)_2NH$ (d) HCO_3^-

2.14 Offer an explanation for the following observations:

(a) H_3O^+ is a stronger acid than NH_4^+.
(b) Nitric acid, HNO_3, is a stronger acid than nitrous acid, HNO_2 (pK_a 3.7).
(c) Ethanol, CH_3CH_2OH, and water have approximately the same acidity.
(d) Trichloroacetic acid, CCl_3COOH (pK_a 0.64), is a stronger acid than acetic acid, CH_3COOH (pK_a 4.74).
(e) Trifluoroacetic acid, CF_3COOH (pK_a 0.23), is a stronger acid than trichloroacetic acid, CCl_3COOH (pK_a 0.64).

2.15 Select the most acidic proton in the following compounds:

(a) $CH_3—C(=O)—CH_2—C(=O)—CH_3$

(b) $H_2N—C(=NH_2^+)—NH_2$

Section 2.3 Quantitative Measure of Acid Strength

2.16 Which has the larger numerical value? **(See Example 2.2)**

(a) The pK_a of a strong acid or the pK_a of a weak acid?
(b) The K_a of a strong acid or the K_a of a weak acid?

***2.17** In each pair, select the stronger acid: **(See Example 2.3)**

(a) Pyruvic acid (pK_a 2.49) or lactic acid (pK_a 3.85)
(b) Citric acid (pK_{a1} 3.08) or phosphoric acid (pK_{a1} 2.10)
(c) Nicotinic acid (niacin, K_a 1.4×10^{-5}) or acetylsalicylic acid (aspirin, K_a 3.3×10^{-4})
(d) Phenol (K_a 1.12×10^{-10}) or acetic acid (K_a 1.74×10^{-5})

2.18 Arrange the compounds in each set in order of increasing acid strength. Consult Table 2.2 for pK_a values of each acid.

(a) CH_3CH_2OH (Ethanol) | $HOC(=O)O^-$ (Bicarbonate ion) | $C_6H_5C(=O)OH$ (Benzoic acid)

(b) $HOC(=O)OH$ (Carbonic acid) | $CH_3C(=O)OH$ (Acetic acid) | HCl (Hydrogen chloride)

2.19 Arrange the compounds in each set in order of increasing base strength. Consult Table 2.2 for pK_a values of the conjugate acid of each base. (*Hint:* The stronger the acid, the weaker is its conjugate base, and vice versa.)

(a) NH_3 | $HOC(=O)O^-$ | $CH_3CH_2O^-$

(b) OH^- | $HOC(=O)O^-$ | $CH_3C(=O)O^-$

(c) H_2O NH_3 $CH_3\overset{O}{\overset{\|}{C}}O^-$

(d) NH_2^- $CH_3\overset{O}{\overset{\|}{C}}O^-$ OH^-

2.20 Using only the Periodic Table, choose the stronger acid of each pair. **(See Example 2.4)**

(a) H_2Se or HBr (b) H_2Se or H_2Te
(c) CH_3OH or CH_3SH

2.21 Explain why H_2S is a stronger acid than H_2O. **(See Example 2.4)**

2.22 Which is the stronger Brønsted–Lowry base, $CH_3CH_2O^-$ or $CH_3CH_2S^-$? What is the basis for your selection? **(See Example 2.4)**

Section 2.4 Position of Equilibrium in Acid–Base Reactions

2.23 Unless under pressure, carbonic acid in aqueous solution breaks down into carbon dioxide and water, and carbon dioxide is evolved as bubbles of gas. Write an equation for the conversion of carbonic acid to carbon dioxide and water.

2.24 For each of the following compounds, will carbon dioxide be evolved when sodium bicarbonate is added to an aqueous solution of the compound?

(a) H_2SO_4 (b) CH_3CH_2OH (c) NH_4Cl

2.25 Acetic acid, CH_3COOH, is a weak organic acid, pK_a 4.76. Write equations for the equilibrium reactions of acetic acid with each base. Which equilibria lie considerably toward the left? Which lie considerably toward the right? **(See Example 2.3)**

(a) $NaHCO_3$ (b) NH_3 (c) H_2O (d) NaOH

2.26 The amide ion, NH_2^-, is a very strong base; it is even stronger than OH^-. Write an equation for the reaction that occurs when amide ion is placed in water. Use this equation to show why the amide ion cannot exist in aqueous solution. **(See Example 2.5)**

2.27 For an acid–base reaction, one way to indicate the predominant species at equilibrium is to say that the reaction arrow points to the acid with the higher value of pK_a. For example **(See Example 2.5)**

$$\underset{pK_a\ 9.24}{NH_4^+} + H_2O \longleftarrow NH_3 + \underset{pK_a\ -1.74}{H_3O^+}$$

$$\underset{pK_a\ 9.24}{NH_4^+} + OH^- \longrightarrow NH_3 + \underset{pK_a\ 15.7}{H_2O}$$

Explain why this rule works.

Section 2.5 Relationship between Acidity and Basicity and Molecular Structure

2.28 For each pair of compounds, determine the stronger acid without using Table 2.2 and provide a rationale for your answer choice. **(See Example 2.5)**

(a) $CF_3CH_2CH_2OH$ versus $CBr_3CH_2CH_2OH$
(b) $H_2C{=}CHOH$ versus CH_3CH_2OH
(c) HBr versus HCl
(d) $H{-}\overset{O}{\overset{\|}{C}}{-}H$ versus $H{-}\overset{O}{\overset{\|}{C}}{-}OH$
(e) CH_3OCH_2OH versus CH_3SCH_2OH
(f) $H{-}\overset{O}{\overset{\|}{C}}{-}NH_2$ versus $H{-}\overset{O}{\overset{\|}{C}}{-}OH$
(g) CH_3NH_2 versus FCH_2NH_2

2.29 For each compound, determine the more basic of the atoms highlighted in yellow and provide a rationale for your answer. **(See Example 2.5)**

(a) $CH_3{-}\overset{O}{\overset{\|}{C}}{-}OH$ (b) $CH_3{-}\overset{NH}{\overset{\|}{C}}{-}OH$
(c) $\ddot{C}H^-{=}CH\ddot{C}H_2^-$ (d) $HOCH_2CH_2NH_2$

Section 2.6 Lewis Acids and Bases

2.30 Complete the following acid–base reactions, using curved arrow notation to show the flow of electron pairs. In solving these problems, it is essential that you show all valence electrons for the atoms participating directly in each reaction. **(See Examples 2.5, 2.6)**

(a) BF_3 + 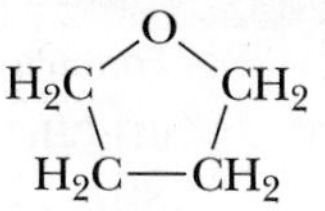 $\longrightarrow$

(b) $(CH_3)_3C{-}Cl + AlCl_3 \longrightarrow$

2.31 Complete equations for these reactions between Lewis acid–Lewis base pairs. Label which starting material is the Lewis acid and which is the Lewis base, and use a curved arrow to show the flow of the electron pair in each reaction. In solving these problems, it is essential that you show all valence electrons for the atoms participating directly in each reaction. **(See Examples 2.5, 2.6)**

(a) $CH_3{-}\overset{+}{C}H{-}CH_3 + CH_3{-}O{-}H \longrightarrow$
(b) $CH_3{-}\overset{+}{C}H{-}CH_3 + Br^- \longrightarrow$
(c) $(CH_3)_3C^+ + H{-}O{-}H \longrightarrow$

2.32 Use curved arrow notation to show the flow of electron pairs in each Lewis acid–base reaction. Be certain to show all valence electron pairs on each atom participating in the reaction. **(See Examples 2.5, 2.6)**

(a) 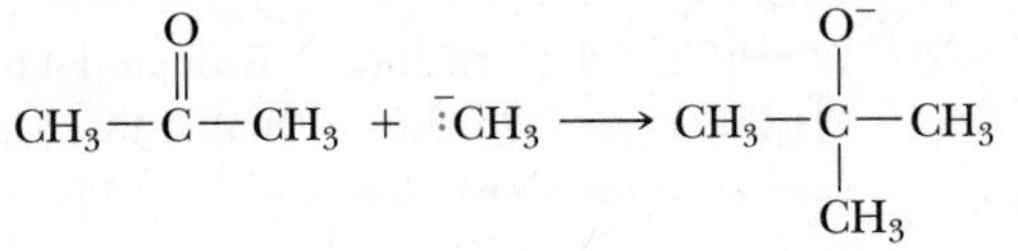

(b) 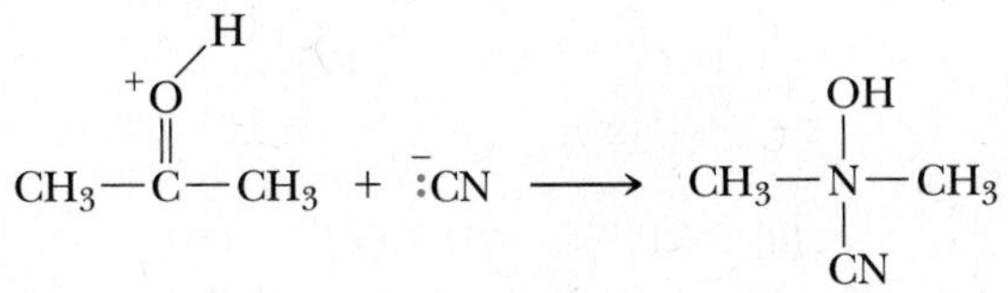

(c) $CH_3O^- + CH_3{-}Br \longrightarrow CH_3{-}O{-}CH_3 + Br^-$

LOOKING AHEAD

2.33 Alcohols (Chapter 8) are weak organic acids, pK_a 15–18. The pK_a of ethanol, CH_3CH_2OH, is 15.9. Write equations for the equilibrium reactions of ethanol with each base. Which equilibria lie considerably toward the right? Which lie considerably toward the left?

(a) $NaHCO_3$ (b) NaOH (c) $NaNH_2$ (d) NH_3

2.34 Phenols (Chapter 9) are weak acids, and most are insoluble in water. Phenol, C_6H_5OH (pK_a 9.95), for example, is only slightly soluble in water, but its sodium salt, $C_6H_5O^-Na^+$, is quite soluble in water. In which of these solutions will phenol dissolve?

(a) Aqueous NaOH (b) Aqueous $NaHCO_3$
(c) Aqueous Na_2CO_3

2.35 Carboxylic acids (Chapter 13) of six or more carbons are insoluble in water, but their sodium salts are very soluble in water. Benzoic acid, C_6H_5COOH (pK_a 4.19), for example, is insoluble in water, but its sodium salt, $C_6H_5COO^-Na^+$, is quite soluble in water. In which of these solutions will benzoic acid dissolve?

(a) Aqueous NaOH (b) Aqueous $NaHCO_3$
(c) Aqueous Na_2CO_3

2.36 As we shall see in Chapter 15, hydrogens on a carbon adjacent to a carbonyl group are far more acidic than those not adjacent to a carbonyl group. The highlighted H in propanone, for example, is more acidic than the highlighted H in ethane:

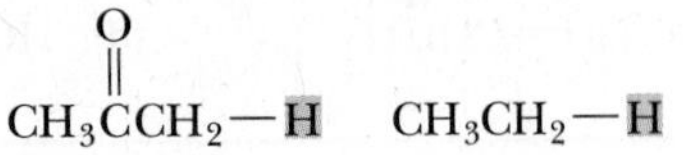

Propanone pK_a = 22 Ethane pK_a = 51

Account for the greater acidity of propanone in terms of (a) the inductive effect and (b) the resonance effect.

2.37 Explain why the protons in dimethyl ether, $CH_3{-}O{-}CH_3$, are not very acidic.

2.38 Predict whether sodium hydride, NaH, will act as a base or an acid, and provide a rationale for your decision.

***2.39** Alanine is one of the 20 amino acids (it contains both an amino and a carboxyl group) found in proteins (Chapter 18). Is alanine better represented by the structural formula A or B? Explain.

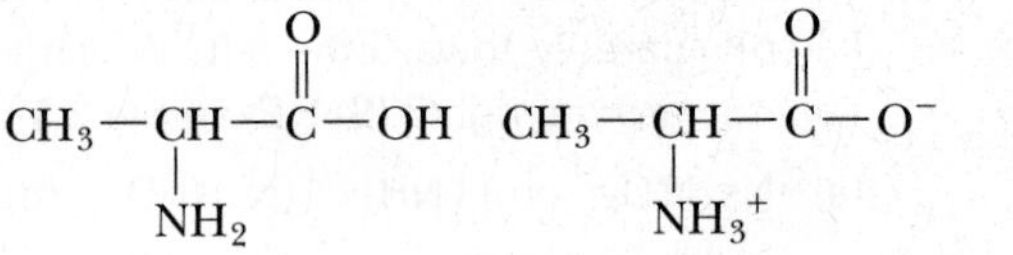

A B

***2.40** Glutamic acid is another of the amino acids found in proteins (Chapter 18):

Glutamic acid 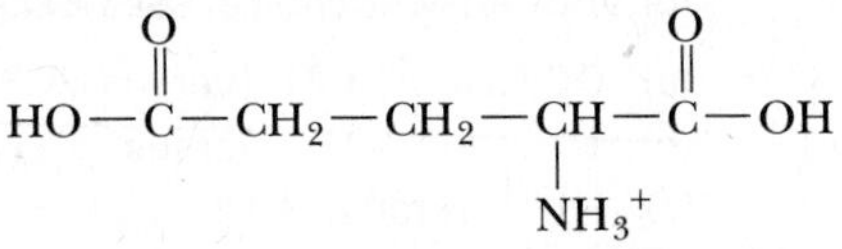

Glutamic acid has two carboxyl groups, one with pK_a 2.10, the other with pK_a 4.07.

(a) Which carboxyl group has which pK_a?
(b) Account for the fact that one carboxyl group is a considerably stronger acid than the other.

GROUP LEARNING ACTIVITIES

2.41 Take turns naming one of the functional groups presented in Section 1.7. Discuss and show how each functional group can act as an acid, a base, or both.

2.42 Starting at the top of the following table, take turns explaining why each acid is less acidic than the acid directly below it. Which factor in Section 2.5 plays the most dominant role in your explanation?

pK_a Values for Representative Acids

Acid	Formula	pK_a
ethane	CH_3CH_3	51
ammonia	NH_3	38
ethanol	CH_3CH_2OH	15.9
ethanethiol	CH_3CH_2SH	10.6
phenol	C_6H_5OH	9.95
acetic acid	CH_3CO_2H	4.76
trifluoroacetic acid	CF_3CO_2H	0.23

03

Alkanes and Cycloalkanes

The burners of gas grills are fueled by liquefied petroleum gas (LPG). LPG contains mostly propane, which is how their containers became known as "propane tanks," but LPG also contains small amounts of ethane, propene, and butane. Inset: A model of propane. (© Lauri Patterson/iStockphoto)

KEY QUESTIONS

3.1 What Are Alkanes?

3.2 What Is Constitutional Isomerism in Alkanes?

3.3 How Do We Name Alkanes?

3.4 What Are Cycloalkanes?

3.5 What Is the IUPAC System of Nomenclature?

3.6 What Are the Conformations of Alkanes and Cycloalkanes?

3.7 What Is *Cis–Trans* Isomerism in Cycloalkanes?

3.8 What Are the Physical Properties of Alkanes and Cycloalkanes?

3.9 What Are the Characteristic Reactions of Alkanes?

3.10 What Are the Sources of Alkanes?

HOW TO

3.1 How to Interpret Line-Angle Formulas

3.2 How to Visualize and Draw a Newman Projection

3.3 How to Draw Alternative Chair Conformations of Cyclohexane

CHEMICAL CONNECTIONS

3A The Poisonous Puffer Fish

3B Octane Rating: What Those Numbers at the Pump Mean

IN THIS CHAPTER, we begin our study of organic compounds with the physical and chemical properties of alkanes, the simplest types of organic compounds. Actually, alkanes are members of a larger class of organic compounds called **hydrocarbons.** A hydrocarbon is a compound composed of only carbon and hydrogen. Figure 3.1 shows the four classes of hydrocarbons, along with the characteristic type of bonding between carbon atoms in each.

Hydrocarbon A compound that contains only carbon atoms and hydrogen atoms.

FIGURE 3.1
The four classes of hydrocarbons.

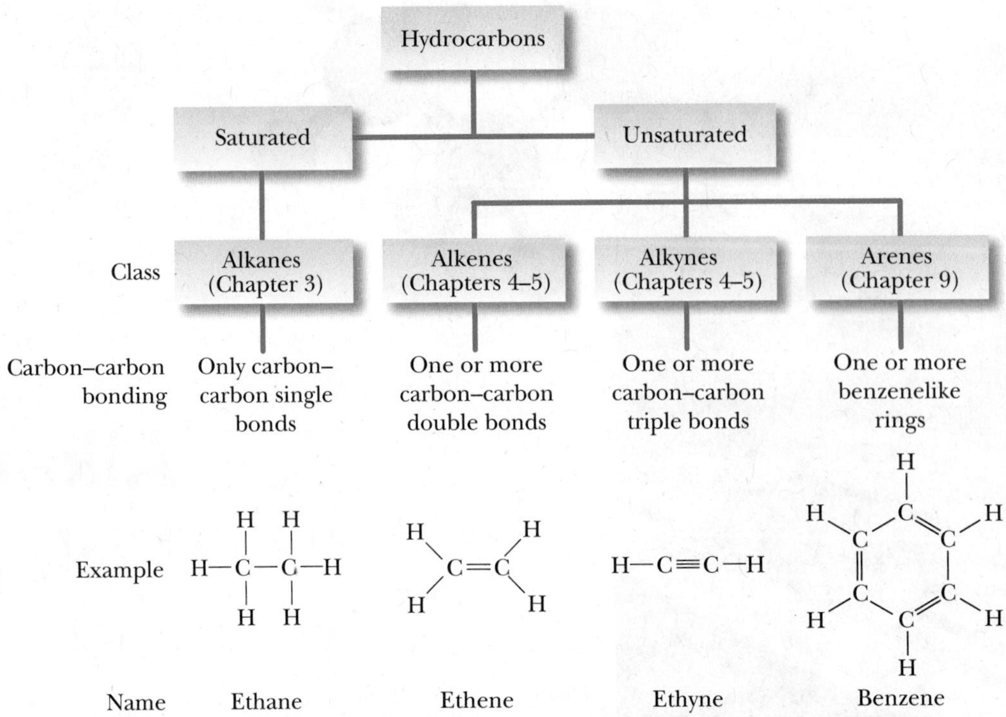

Alkane A saturated hydrocarbon whose carbon atoms are arranged in an open chain.

Saturated hydrocarbon A hydrocarbon containing only carbon–carbon single bonds.

Aliphatic hydrocarbon An alternative term to describe an alkane.

Alkanes are **saturated hydrocarbons;** that is, they contain only carbon–carbon single bonds. In this context, "saturated" means that each carbon has the maximum number of hydrogens bonded to it. We often refer to alkanes as **aliphatic hydrocarbons,** because the physical properties of the higher members of this class resemble those of the long carbon-chain molecules we find in animal fats and plant oils (Greek: *aleiphar,* fat or oil).

A hydrocarbon that contains one or more carbon–carbon double bonds, triple bonds, or benzene rings is classified as an **unsaturated hydrocarbon.** We study alkanes (saturated hydrocarbons) in this chapter. We study alkenes and alkynes (both unsaturated hydrocarbons) in Chapters 4 and 5, and arenes (also unsaturated hydrocarbons) in Chapter 9.

Charles D. Winters

Butane is the fuel in this lighter. Butane molecules are present in the liquid and gaseous states in the lighter.

3.1 What Are Alkanes?

Methane (CH_4) and ethane (C_2H_6) are the first two members of the alkane family. Figure 3.2 shows molecular formulas, Lewis structures, and ball-and-stick models for these molecules. The shape of methane is tetrahedral, and all H—C—H bond angles are 109.5°. Each carbon atom in ethane is also tetrahedral, and all bond angles are approximately 109.5°.

Although the three-dimensional shapes of larger alkanes are more complex than those of methane and ethane, the four bonds about each carbon atom are still arranged in a tetrahedral manner, and all bond angles are still approximately 109.5°.

The next members of the alkane family are propane, butane, and pentane. In the representations that follow, these hydrocarbons are drawn first as condensed structural formulas that show all carbons and hydrogens. They are then drawn in an even more

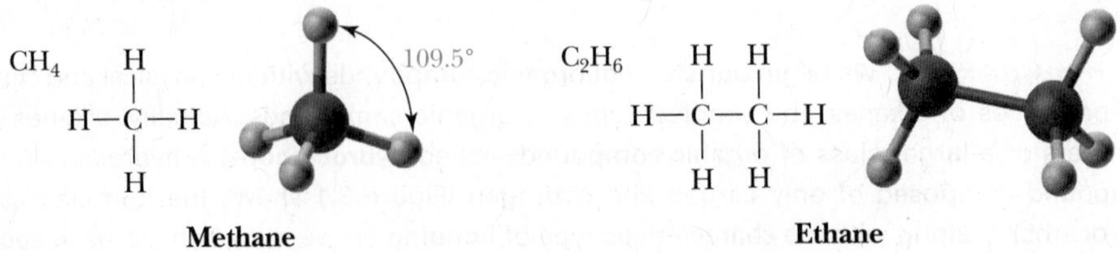

FIGURE 3.2
Methane and ethane.

abbreviated form called a **line-angle formula.** In this type of representation, a line represents a carbon–carbon bond, and an angle represents a carbon atom. A line ending represents a —CH_3 group. Although hydrogen atoms are not shown in line-angle formulas, they are assumed to be there in sufficient numbers to give each carbon four bonds.

Line-angle formula An abbreviated way to draw structural formulas in which each vertex and each line ending represents a carbon atom and a line represents a bond.

Ball-and-stick model

Line-angle formula

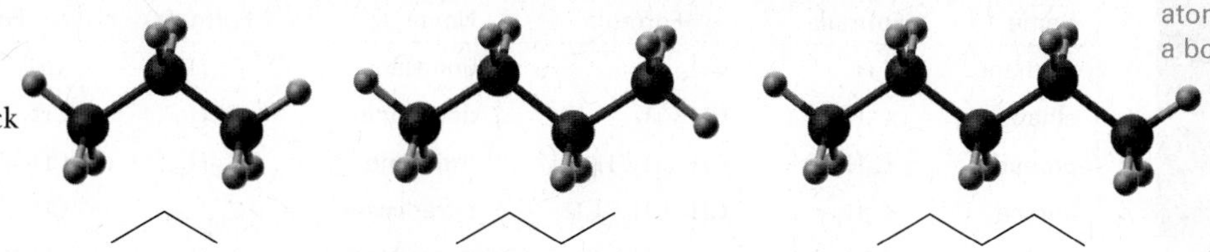

Condensed structural formula

$CH_3CH_2CH_3$	$CH_3CH_2CH_2CH_3$	$CH_3CH_2CH_2CH_2CH_3$
Propane	Butane	Pentane

We can write structural formulas for alkanes in still another abbreviated form. The structural formula of pentane, for example, contains three CH_2 (methylene) groups in the middle of the chain. We can collect these groups together and write the structural formula as $CH_3(CH_2)_3CH_3$. Table 3.1 gives the names and molecular formulas of the first 20 alkanes. Note that the names of all these alkanes end in *-ane.* We will have more to say about naming alkanes in Section 3.3.

HOW TO 3.1

Interpret Line-Angle Formulas

Use the mnemonic "a carbon at every *bend* and at every *end*. . ."

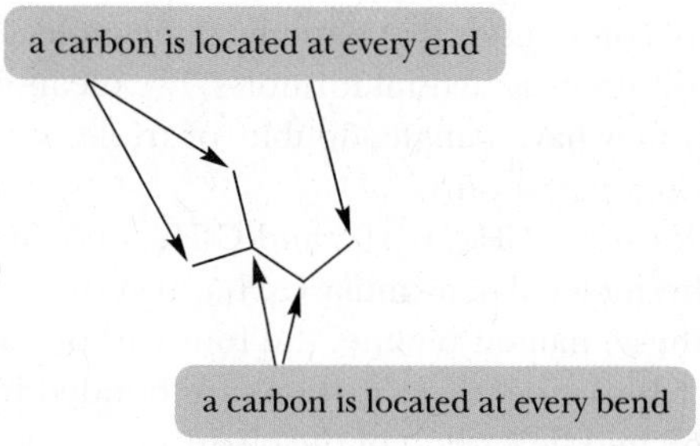

Because carbon requires four bonds to satisfy its valency, count the number of visible bonds to each carbon and then subtract this number from 4 to determine the number of hydrogens also bonded to that carbon (but not shown).

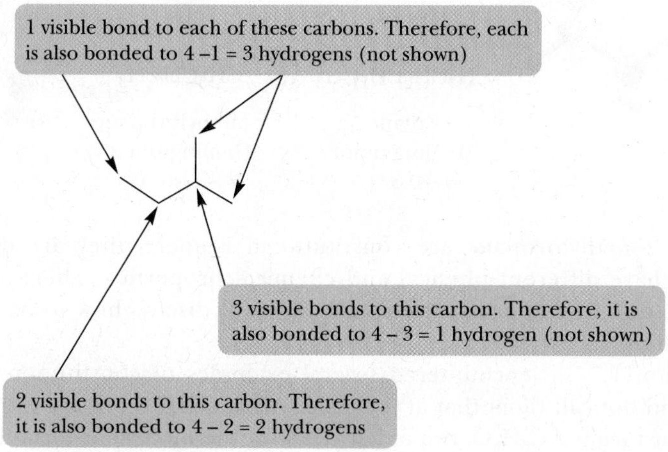

Media Bakery

A tank for propane fuel.

TABLE 3.1 Names, Molecular Formulas, and Condensed Structural Formulas for the First 20 Alkanes with Unbranched Chains

Name	Molecular Formula	Condensed Structural Formula	Name	Molecular Formula	Condensed Structural Formula
methane	CH_4	CH_4	undecane	$C_{11}H_{24}$	$CH_3(CH_2)_9CH_3$
ethane	C_2H_6	CH_3CH_3	dodecane	$C_{12}H_{26}$	$CH_3(CH_2)_{10}CH_3$
propane	C_3H_8	$CH_3CH_2CH_3$	tridecane	$C_{13}H_{28}$	$CH_3(CH_2)_{11}CH_3$
butane	C_4H_{10}	$CH_3(CH_2)_2CH_3$	tetradecane	$C_{14}H_{30}$	$CH_3(CH_2)_{12}CH_3$
pentane	C_5H_{12}	$CH_3(CH_2)_3CH_3$	pentadecane	$C_{15}H_{32}$	$CH_3(CH_2)_{13}CH_3$
hexane	C_6H_{14}	$CH_3(CH_2)_4CH_3$	hexadecane	$C_{16}H_{34}$	$CH_3(CH_2)_{14}CH_3$
heptane	C_7H_{16}	$CH_3(CH_2)_5CH_3$	heptadecane	$C_{17}H_{36}$	$CH_3(CH_2)_{15}CH_3$
octane	C_8H_{18}	$CH_3(CH_2)_6CH_3$	octadecane	$C_{18}H_{38}$	$CH_3(CH_2)_{16}CH_3$
nonane	C_9H_{20}	$CH_3(CH_2)_7CH_3$	nonadecane	$C_{19}H_{40}$	$CH_3(CH_2)_{17}CH_3$
decane	$C_{10}H_{22}$	$CH_3(CH_2)_8CH_3$	eicosane	$C_{20}H_{42}$	$CH_3(CH_2)_{18}CH_3$

Alkanes have the general molecular formula C_nH_{2n+2}. Thus, given the number of carbon atoms in an alkane, it is easy to determine the number of hydrogens in the molecule and also its molecular formula. For example, decane, with 10 carbon atoms, must have $(2 \times 10) + 2 = 22$ hydrogens and the molecular formula $C_{10}H_{22}$.

3.2 What Is Constitutional Isomerism in Alkanes?

Constitutional isomers Compounds with the same molecular formula, but a different order of attachment of their atoms.

Constitutional isomers are compounds that have the same molecular formula, but different structural formulas. By "different structural formulas," we mean that these compounds differ in the kinds of bonds they have (single, double, or triple) or in their connectivity (the order of attachment among their atoms).

For the molecular formulas CH_4, C_2H_6, and C_3H_8, only one order of attachment of atoms is possible. For the molecular formula C_4H_{10}, two orders of attachment of atoms are possible. In one of these, named butane, the four carbons are bonded in a chain; in the other, named 2-methylpropane, three carbons are bonded in a chain, with the fourth carbon as a branch on the middle carbon of the chain.

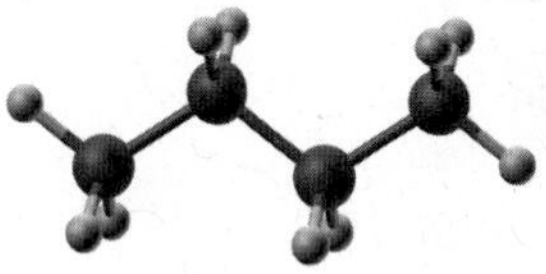

$CH_3CH_2CH_2CH_3$

Butane (boiling point = −0.5 °C)

CH_3
CH_3CHCH_3

2-Methylpropane (boiling point = −11.6 °C)

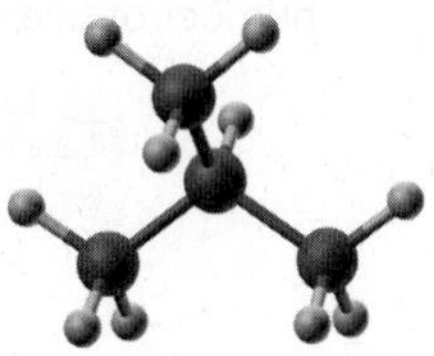

Butane and 2-methylpropane are constitutional isomers; they are different compounds and have different physical and chemical properties. Their boiling points, for example, differ by approximately 11°C. We will discuss how to name alkanes in the next section.

In Section 1.7, we encountered several examples of constitutional isomers, although we did not call them that at the time. We saw that there are two alcohols with the molecular formula C_3H_8O, two aldehydes with the molecular formula C_4H_8O, and two carboxylic acids with the molecular formula $C_4H_8O_2$.

To find out whether two or more structural formulas represent constitutional isomers, write the molecular formula of each and then compare them. All compounds that have the same molecular formula, but different structural formulas, are constitutional isomers.

EXAMPLE 3.1

Do the structural formulas in each pair represent the same compound or constitutional isomers?

(a) $CH_3CH_2CH_2CH_2CH_2CH_3$ and 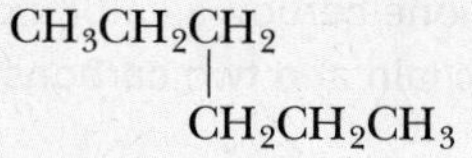 (each is C_6H_{14})

(b) 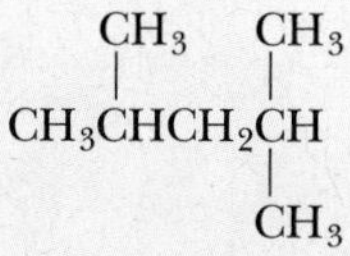 and 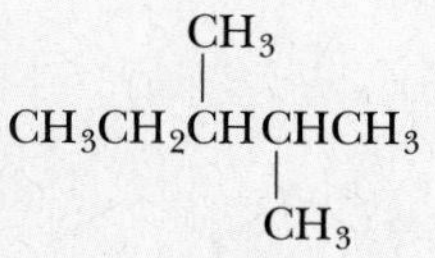 (each is C_7H_{16})

STRATEGY

To determine whether these structural formulas represent the same compound or constitutional isomers, first find the longest chain of carbon atoms in each. Note that it makes no difference whether the chain is drawn straight or bent. Second, number the longest chain from the end nearest the first branch. Third, compare the lengths of each chain and the sizes and locations of any branches. Structural formulas that have the same connectivity of atoms represent the same compound; those that have a different connectivity of atoms represent constitutional isomers.

SOLUTION

(a) Each structural formula has an unbranched chain of six carbons. The two structures are identical and represent the same compound:

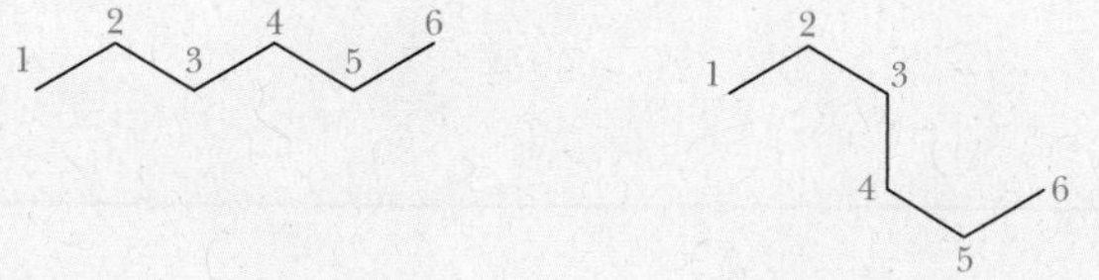

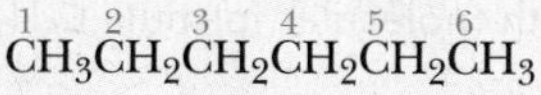 and 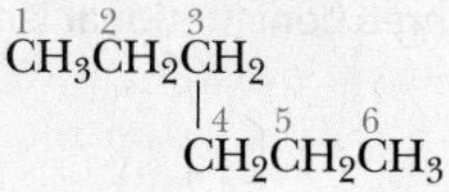

(b) Each structural formula has a chain of five carbons with two CH_3 branches. Although the branches are identical, they are at different locations on the chains. Therefore, these structural formulas represent constitutional isomers:

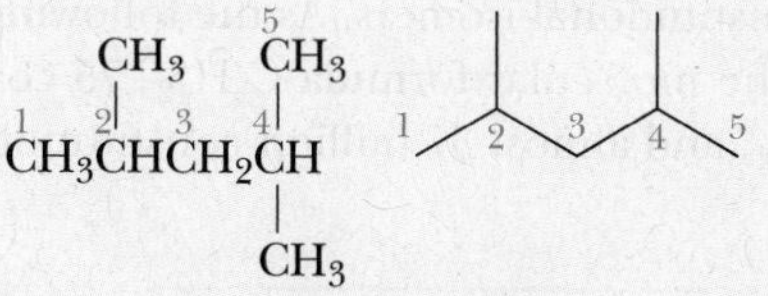 and 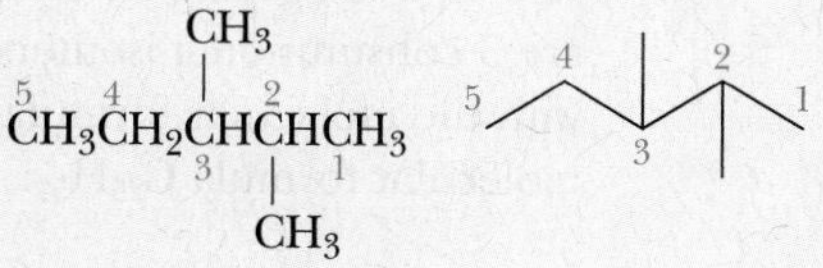

See problems 3.17–3.20, 3.22

PROBLEM 3.1

Do the structural formulas in each pair represent the same compound or constitutional isomers?

(a) 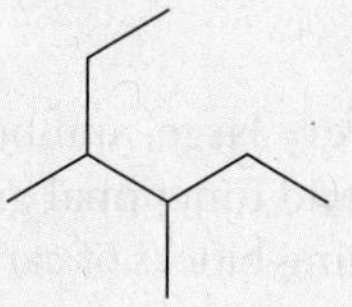 and 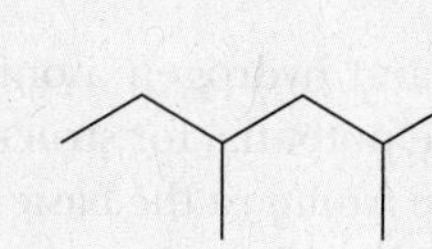 (b) 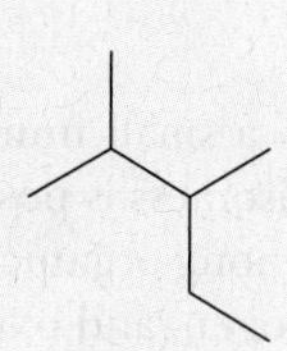 and 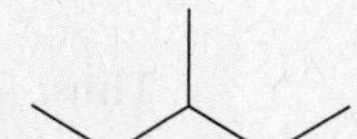

EXAMPLE 3.2

Draw structural formulas for the five constitutional isomers with the molecular formula C_6H_{14}.

STRATEGY

In solving problems of this type, you should devise a strategy and then follow it. Here is one such strategy: First, draw a line-angle formula for the constitutional isomer with all six carbons in an unbranched chain. Then, draw line-angle formulas for all constitutional isomers with five carbons in a chain and one carbon as a branch on the chain. Finally, draw line-angle formulas for all constitutional isomers with four carbons in a chain and two carbons as branches.

SOLUTION

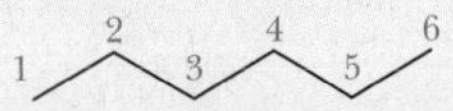

Six carbons in an unbranched chain

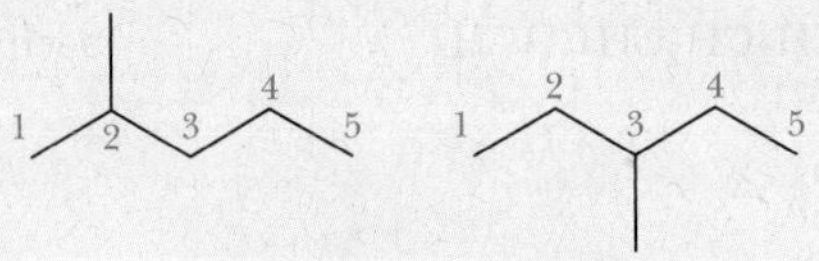

Five carbons in a chain; one carbon as a branch

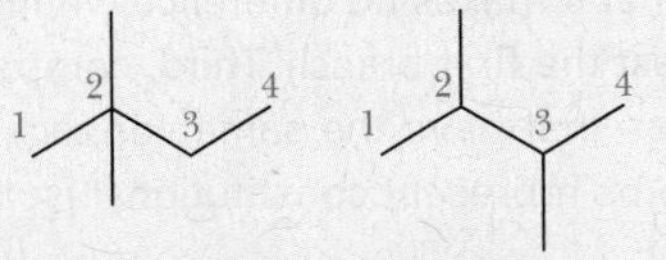

Four carbons in a chain; two carbons as branches

No constitutional isomers with only three carbons in the longest chain are possible for C_6H_{14}.

See problems 3.21, 3.23

PROBLEM 3.2

Draw structural formulas for the three constitutional isomers with molecular formula C_5H_{12}.

The ability of carbon atoms to form strong, stable bonds with other carbon atoms results in a staggering number of constitutional isomers. As the following table shows, there are 3 constitutional isomers with the molecular formula C_5H_{12}, 75 constitutional isomers with the molecular formula $C_{10}H_{22}$, and almost 37 million constitutional isomers with the molecular formula $C_{25}H_{52}$:

Carbon Atoms	Constitutional Isomers
1	0
5	3
10	75
15	4,347
25	36,797,588

Thus, for even a small number of carbon and hydrogen atoms, a very large number of constitutional isomers is possible. In fact, the potential for structural and functional group individuality among organic molecules made from just the basic building blocks of carbon, hydrogen, nitrogen, and oxygen is practically limitless.

3.3 How Do We Name Alkanes?

A. The IUPAC System

Ideally, every organic compound should have a name from which its structural formula can be drawn. For this purpose, chemists have adopted a set of rules established by an organization called the International Union of Pure and Applied Chemistry (IUPAC).

The IUPAC name of an alkane with an unbranched chain of carbon atoms consists of two parts: (1) a prefix that indicates the number of carbon atoms in the chain and (2) the ending **-ane** to show that the compound is a saturated hydrocarbon. Table 3.2 gives the prefixes used to show the presence of 1 to 20 carbon atoms.

The first four prefixes listed in Table 3.2 were chosen by the IUPAC because they were well established in the language of organic chemistry. In fact, they were well established even before there were hints of the structural theory underlying the discipline. For example, the prefix *but-* appears in the name *butyric acid,* a compound of four carbon atoms formed by the air oxidation of butter fat (Latin: *butyrum,* butter). Prefixes to show five or more carbons are derived from Greek or Latin numbers. (See Table 3.1 for the names, molecular formulas, and condensed structural formulas for the first 20 alkanes with unbranched chains.)

The IUPAC name of an alkane with a branched chain consists of a **parent name** that indicates the longest chain of carbon atoms in the compound and substituent names that indicate the groups bonded to the parent chain.

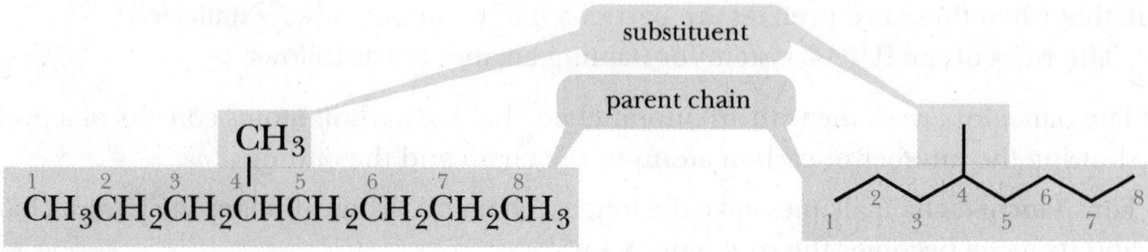

4-Methyloctane

A substituent group derived from an alkane by the removal of a hydrogen atom is called an **alkyl group** and is commonly represented by the symbol **R-**. We name alkyl groups by dropping the *-ane* from the name of the parent alkane and adding the suffix *-yl.* Table 3.3 gives the names and structural formulas for eight of the most common alkyl groups. The prefix *sec-* is an abbreviation for secondary, meaning a carbon bonded to two other carbons. The

Alkyl group A group derived by removing a hydrogen from an alkane; given the symbol R-.

R- A symbol used to represent an alkyl group.

TABLE 3.2 Prefixes Used in the IUPAC System to Show the Presence of 1 to 20 Carbons in an Unbranched Chain

Prefix	Number of Carbon Atoms	Prefix	Number of Carbon Atoms
meth-	1	undec-	11
eth-	2	dodec-	12
prop-	3	tridec-	13
but-	4	tetradec-	14
pent-	5	pentadec-	15
hex-	6	hexadec-	16
hept-	7	heptadec-	17
oct-	8	octadec-	18
non-	9	nonadec-	19
dec-	10	eicos-	20

TABLE 3.3 Names of the Most Common Alkyl Groups

Name	Condensed Structural Formula	Name	Condensed Structural Formula
methyl	$-CH_3$	isobutyl	$-CH_2CHCH_3$ $\quad\;\;\,|$ $\quad\;\;CH_3$
ethyl	$-CH_2CH_3$	*sec*-butyl abbreviation for "secondary"	$-CHCH_2CH_3$ $\;\;|$ $\;\;CH_3$
propyl	$-CH_2CH_2CH_3$	*tert*-butyl abbreviation for "tertiary"	$\;\;CH_3$ $\;\;|$ $-CCH_3$ $\;\;|$ $\;\;CH_3$
isopropyl	$-CHCH_3$ $\;\;|$ $\;\;CH_3$		
butyl	$-CH_2CH_2CH_2CH_3$		

prefix *tert-* is an abbreviation for tertiary, meaning a carbon bonded to three other carbons. Note that when these two prefixes are part of a name, they are always italicized.

The rules of the IUPAC system for naming alkanes are as follows:

1. The name for an alkane with an unbranched chain of carbon atoms consists of a prefix showing the number of carbon atoms in the chain and the ending *-ane.*
2. For branched-chain alkanes, take the longest chain of carbon atoms as the parent chain, and its name becomes the root name.
3. Give each substituent on the parent chain a name and a number. The number shows the carbon atom of the parent chain to which the substituent is bonded. Use a hyphen to connect the number to the name:

$$\begin{array}{c} \quad CH_3 \\ \quad | \\ CH_3CHCH_3 \end{array}$$

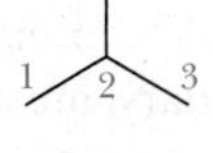

2-Methylpropane

4. If there is one substituent, number the parent chain from the end that gives it the lower number:

$$\begin{array}{r} CH_3\quad\;\, \\ |\qquad\;\; \\ CH_3CH_2CH_2CHCH_3 \end{array}$$

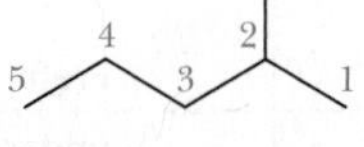

2-Methylpentane

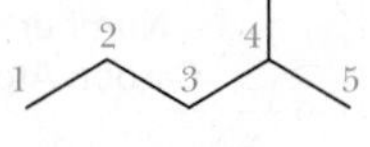

(not 4-methylpentane)

5. If there are two or more identical substituents, number the parent chain from the end that gives the lower number to the substituent encountered first. The number of times the substituent occurs is indicated by the prefix *di-*, *tri-*, *tetra-*, *penta-*, *hexa-*, and so on. A comma is used to separate position numbers:

$$\begin{array}{l} \qquad\quad CH_3 \quad\; CH_3 \\ \qquad\quad | \qquad\quad\; | \\ CH_3CH_2CHCH_2CHCH_3 \end{array}$$

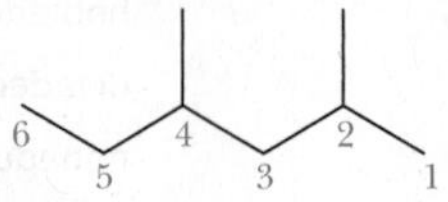

2,4-Dimethylhexane

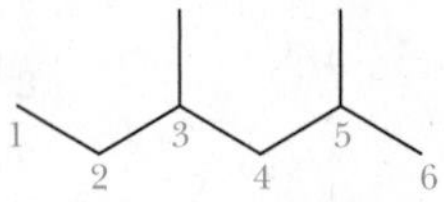

(not 3,5-dimethylhexane)

6. If there are two or more different substituents, list them in alphabetical order, and number the chain from the end that gives the lower number to the substituent encountered first. If there are different substituents in equivalent positions on opposite ends of the parent chain, the substituent of lower alphabetical order is given the lower number:

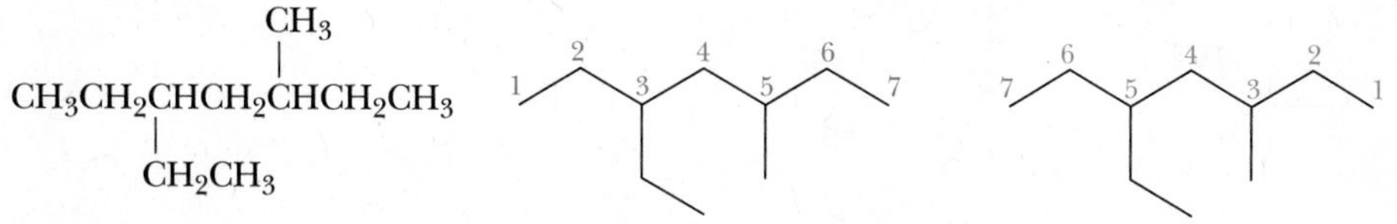

3-Ethyl-5-methylheptane (not 3-methyl-5-ethylheptane)

7. The prefixes *di-*, *tri-*, *tetra-*, and so on are not included in alphabetizing. Neither are the hyphenated prefixes *sec-* and *tert-*. "Iso," as in isopropyl, is included in alphabetizing. Alphabetize the names of the substituents first, and then insert the prefix. In the following example, the alphabetizing parts are ethyl and methyl, not ethyl and dimethyl:

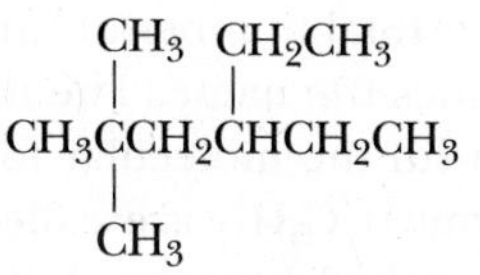

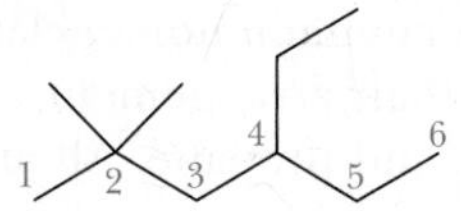

4-Ethyl-2,2-dimethylhexane
(not 2,2-dimethyl-4-ethylhexane)

EXAMPLE 3.3

Write IUPAC names for these alkanes:

(a) 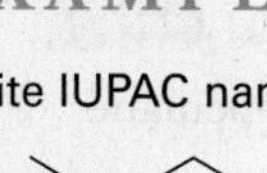

(b) 

(c) 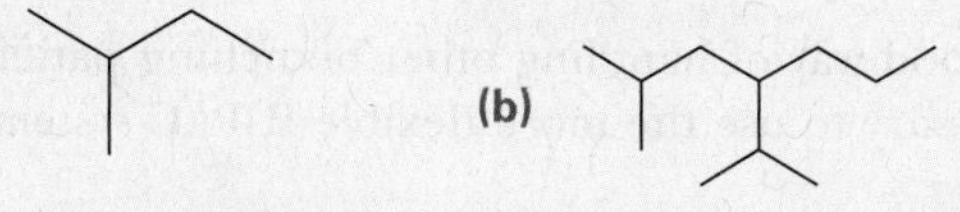

(d) 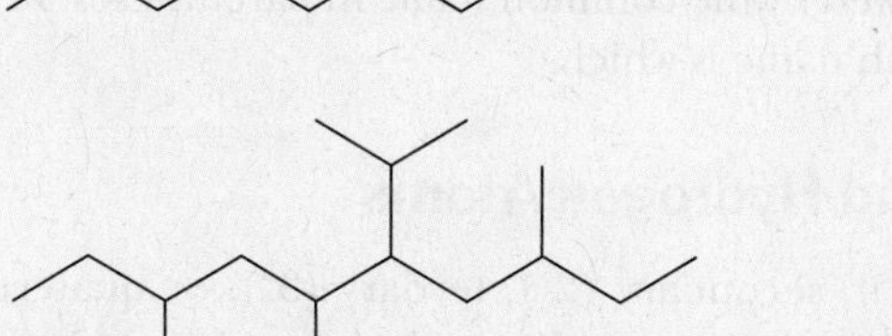

STRATEGY

First determine the root name of the alkane. Then name the substituents and place them in alphabetical order. Number the parent chain so as to give the lower number to the substituents encountered first. If substituents have equivalent positions, the lower number is assigned to the substituents with the lower alphabetical order.

See problems 3.24, 3.25, 3.28

SOLUTION

(a) 

2-Methylbutane

(b) 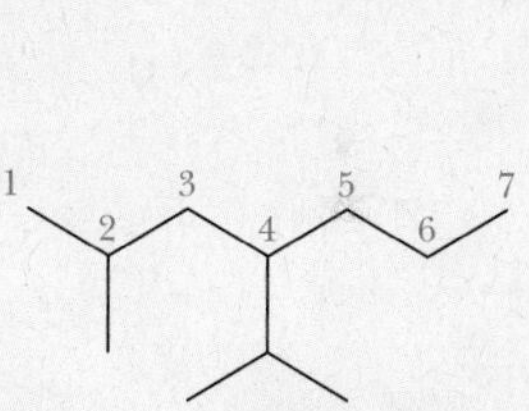

4-Isopropyl-2-methylheptane

(c) 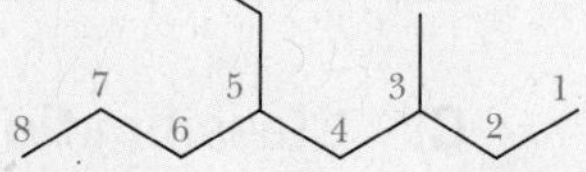

5-Ethyl-3-methyloctane

(d) 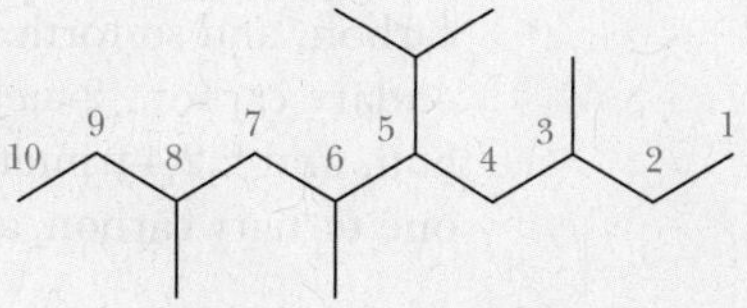

5-Isopropyl-3,6,8-trimethyldecane
(not 6-isopropyl-3,5,8-trimethyldecane)

PROBLEM 3.3

Write IUPAC names for these alkanes:

(a)

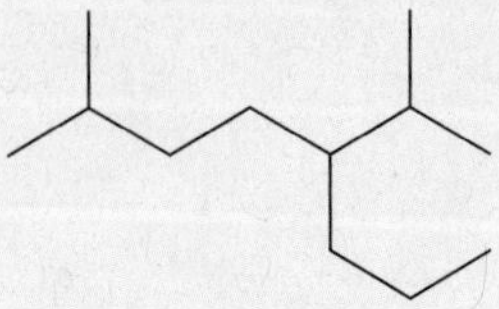

(b)

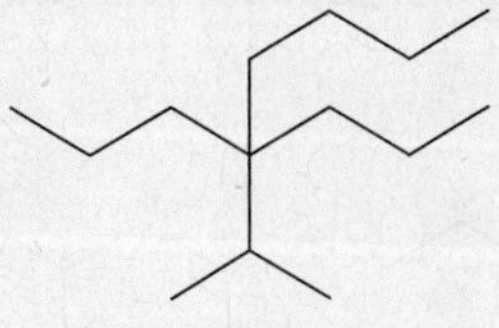

(c)

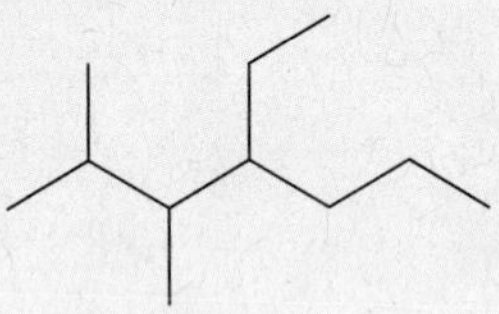

(d)

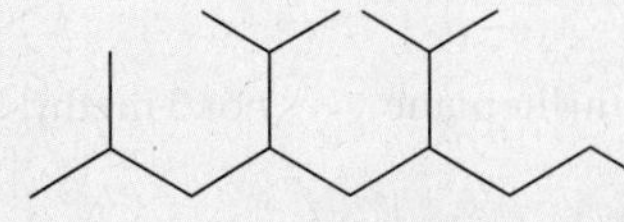

B. Common Names

In the older system of common nomenclature, the total number of carbon atoms in an alkane, regardless of their arrangement, determines the name. The first three alkanes are methane, ethane, and propane. All alkanes with the molecular formula C_4H_{10} are called butanes, all those with the molecular formula C_5H_{12} are called pentanes, and all those with the molecular formula C_6H_{14} are called hexanes. For alkanes beyond propane, *iso* indicates that one end of an otherwise unbranched chain terminates in a $(CH_3)_2CH-$group. Following are examples of common names:

$CH_3CH_2CH_2CH_3$	$CH_3CH(CH_3)CH_3$	$CH_3CH_2CH_2CH_2CH_3$	$CH_3CH_2CH(CH_3)CH_3$
Butane	Isobutane	Pentane	Isopentane

This system of common names has no good way of handling other branching patterns, so, for more complex alkanes, it is necessary to use the more flexible IUPAC system of nomenclature.

In this text, we concentrate on IUPAC names. However, we also use common names, especially when the common name is used almost exclusively in the everyday discussions of chemists and biochemists. When both IUPAC and common names are given in the text, we always give the IUPAC name first, followed by the common name in parentheses. In this way, you should have no doubt about which name is which.

C. Classification of Carbon and Hydrogen Atoms

We classify a carbon atom as primary (1°), secondary (2°), tertiary (3°), or quaternary (4°), depending on the number of carbon atoms bonded to it. A carbon bonded to one carbon atom is a primary carbon; a carbon bonded to two carbon atoms is a secondary carbon, and so forth. For example, propane contains two primary carbons and one secondary carbon, 2-methylpropane contains three primary carbons and one tertiary carbon, and 2,2,4-trimethylpentane contains five primary carbons, one secondary carbon, one tertiary carbon, and one quaternary carbon:

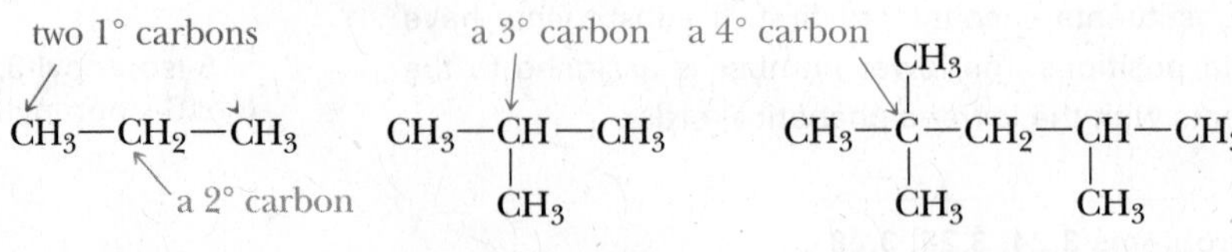

Propane   2-Methylpropane   2,2,4-Trimethylpentane

Similarly, hydrogens are also classified as primary, secondary, or tertiary, depending on the type of carbon to which each is bonded. Those bonded to a primary carbon are classified as primary hydrogens, those on a secondary carbon are secondary hydrogens, and those on a tertiary carbon are tertiary hydrogens.

EXAMPLE 3.4

Classify each carbon atom in the following compounds as 1°, 2°, 3°, or 4°.

(a) 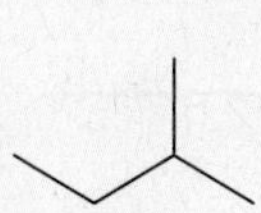

(b) 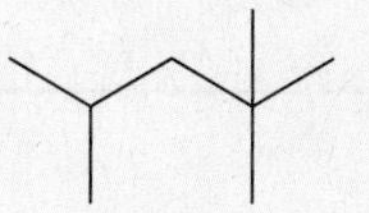

STRATEGY

To classify carbons, determine whether each is bonded to 1 carbon (1°), 2 carbons (2°), 3 carbons (3°), or 4 carbons (4°).

SOLUTION

(a) 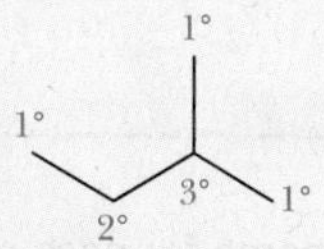

(b) 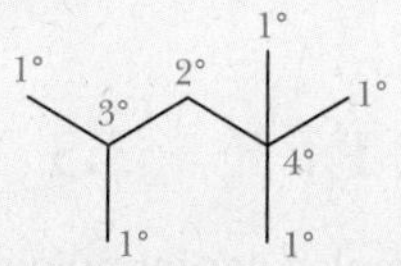

See problems 3.26, 3.27

PROBLEM 3.4

Classify each hydrogen atom in the following compounds as 1°, 2°, or 3°.

(a) 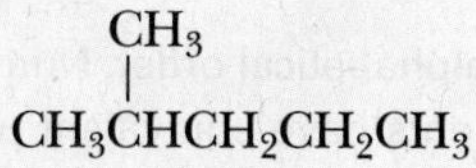

(b) 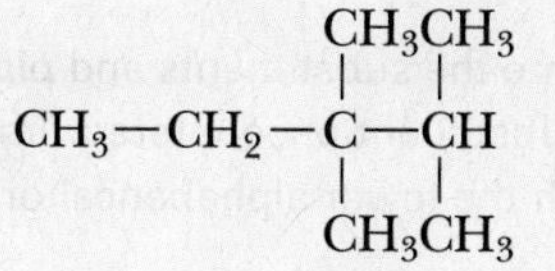

3.4 What Are Cycloalkanes?

A hydrocarbon that contains carbon atoms joined to form a ring is called a *cyclic hydrocarbon.* When all carbons of the ring are saturated, we call the hydrocarbon a **cycloalkane.** Cycloalkanes of ring sizes ranging from 3 to over 30 abound in nature, and, in principle, there is no limit to ring size. Five-membered (cyclopentane) and six-membered (cyclohexane) rings are especially abundant in nature and have received special attention.

Cycloalkane A saturated hydrocarbon that contains carbon atoms joined to form a ring.

Figure 3.3 shows the structural formulas of cyclobutane, cyclopentane, and cyclohexane. When writing structural formulas for cycloalkanes, chemists rarely show all carbons and hydrogens. Rather, they use line-angle formulas to represent cycloalkane rings. Each ring is represented by a regular polygon having the same number of sides as there are carbon atoms in the ring. For example, chemists represent cyclobutane by a square, cyclopentane by a pentagon, and cyclohexane by a hexagon.

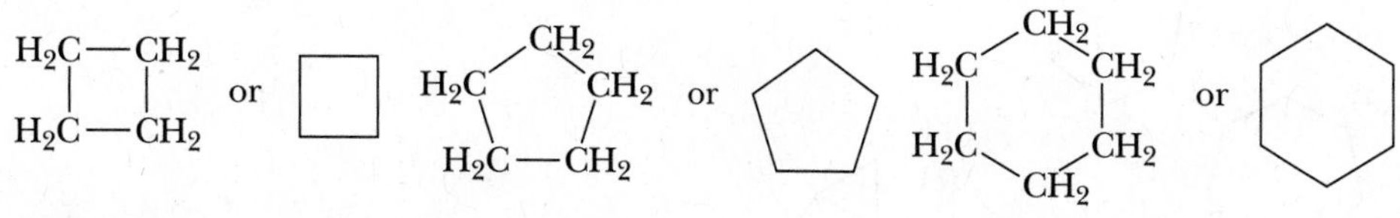

Cyclobutane　Cyclopentane　Cyclohexane

FIGURE 3.3 Examples of cycloalkanes.

Cycloalkanes contain two fewer hydrogen atoms than an alkane with the same number of carbon atoms. For instance, compare the molecular formulas of cyclohexane (C_6H_{12}) and hexane (C_6H_{14}). The general formula of a cycloalkane is C_nH_{2n}.

To name a cycloalkane, prefix the name of the corresponding open-chain hydrocarbon with *cyclo-*, and name each substituent on the ring. If there is only one substituent, there is no need to give it a number. If there are two substituents, number the ring by beginning with the substituent of lower alphabetical order. If there are three or more substituents, number the ring so as to give them the lowest set of numbers, and then list the substituents in alphabetical order.

EXAMPLE 3.5

Write the molecular formula and IUPAC name for each cycloalkane.

(a) 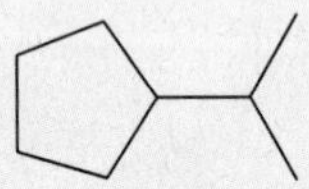 (b) 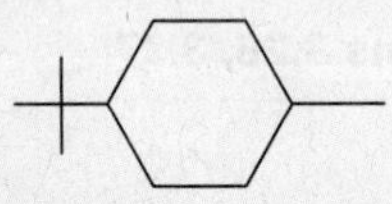 (c) 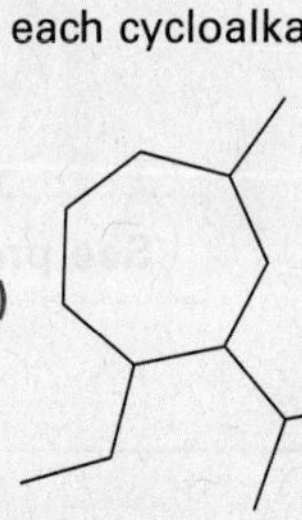 (d) 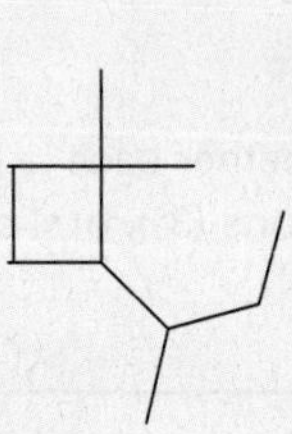

STRATEGY

First determine the root name of the cycloalkane. Then name the substituents and place them in alphabetical order. Number the parent chain so as to give the lower number to the substituent encountered first. If substituents have equivalent positions, the lower number is assigned to the substituent with the lower alphabetical order.

SOLUTION

(a) The molecular formula of this cycloalkane is C_8H_{16}. Because there is only one substituent on the ring, there is no need to number the atoms of the ring. The IUPAC name of this compound is isopropylcyclopentane.

(b) Number the atoms of the cyclohexane ring by beginning with *tert*-butyl, the substituent of lower alphabetical order. The compound's name is 1-*tert*-butyl-4-methylcyclohexane, and its molecular formula is $C_{11}H_{22}$.

recall that *tert* is not considered when alphabetizing substituents

(c) The molecular formula of this cycloalkane is $C_{13}H_{26}$. The compound's name is 1-ethyl-2-isopropyl-4-methylcycloheptane. The ethyl group is numbered 1 because this allows the isopropyl group to be encountered sooner than if the methyl group were numbered 1.

recall that "iso" is considered when alphabetizing substituents. The numbering pattern 1,2,4 is preferred over 1,3,4 or 1,5,7

(d) The molecular formula of this cycloalkane is $C_{10}H_{20}$. The compound's name is 2-*sec*-butyl-1,1-dimethylcyclobutane. This example illustrates that "*sec*" and "di" are not used in alphabetizing for nomenclature.

See problems 3.24, 3.25, 3.28

PROBLEM 3.5

Write the molecular formula and IUPAC name for each cycloalkane:

(a) 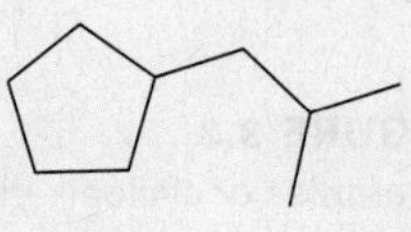 (b) 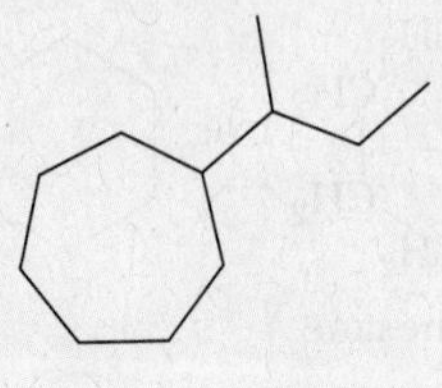 (c) 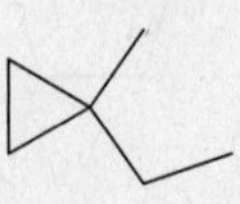

3.5 What Is the IUPAC System of Nomenclature?

The naming of alkanes and cycloalkanes in Sections 3.3 and 3.4 illustrates the application of the IUPAC system of nomenclature to these two specific classes of organic compounds. Now let us describe the general approach of the IUPAC system. The name we give to any compound with a chain of carbon atoms consists of three parts: a prefix, an infix (a modifying element inserted into a word), and a suffix. Each part provides specific information about the structural formula of the compound.

1. The prefix shows the number of carbon atoms in the parent chain. Prefixes that show the presence of 1 to 20 carbon atoms in a chain were given in Table 3.2.
2. The infix shows the nature of the carbon–carbon bonds in the parent chain:

Infix	Nature of Carbon–Carbon Bonds in the Parent Chain
-an-	all single bonds
-en-	one or more double bonds
-yn-	one or more triple bonds

keep in mind that the infix refers to the nature of the *C–C bonds in the parent chain*

3. The suffix shows the class of compound to which the substance belongs:

Suffix	Class of Compound
-e	hydrocarbon
-ol	alcohol
-al	aldehyde
-one	ketone
-oic acid	carboxylic acid

we will learn suffixes for other classes of compounds in later chapters

EXAMPLE 3.6

Following are IUPAC names and structural formulas for four compounds:

(a) $CH_2{=}CHCH_3$ Propene

(b) CH_3CH_2OH Ethanol

(c) $CH_3CH_2CH_2CH_2\overset{O}{\overset{\|}{C}}OH$ Pentanoic acid

(d) $HC{\equiv}CH$ Ethyne

Divide each name into a prefix, an infix, and a suffix, and specify the information about the structural formula that is contained in each part of the name.

STRATEGY

First look at the first few letters of the name (meth, eth, prop, but, etc.). This is the prefix that tells the number of carbons in the parent chain. Next look at "an," "en," or "yn." These infixes indicate the nature of the carbon–carbon bonds in the parent chain. The letters that follow the infix are part of the suffix, which determines the class of compound to which the molecule belongs.

SOLUTION

(a) propene
- "en": a carbon–carbon double bond
- "e": a hydrocarbon
- "prop": three carbon atoms

(b) ethanol
- "an": only carbon–carbon single bonds
- "ol": an alcohol
- "eth": two carbon atoms

only carbon–carbon single bonds

(c) pentanoic acid

a carboxylic acid

five carbon atoms

a carbon–carbon triple bond

(d) ethyne

a hydrocarbon

two carbon atoms

See problems 3.29, 3.30

PROBLEM 3.6

Combine the proper prefix, infix, and suffix, and write the IUPAC name for each compound:

(a) 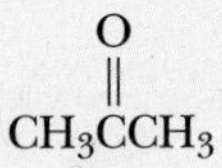 **(b)** 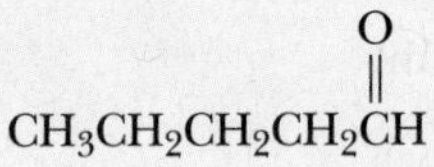 **(c)** 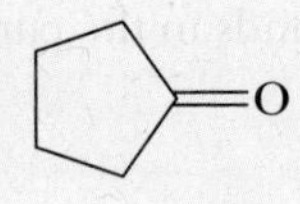 **(d)** 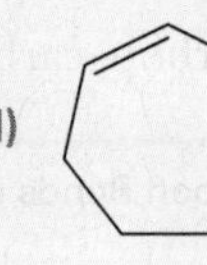

3.6 What Are the Conformations of Alkanes and Cycloalkanes?

Even though structural formulas are useful for showing the order of attachment of atoms, they do not show three-dimensional shapes. As chemists try to understand more and more about the relationships between structure and the chemical and physical properties of molecules, it becomes increasingly important to know more about the three-dimensional shapes of molecules.

In this section, we concentrate on ways to visualize molecules as three-dimensional objects and to visualize not only bond angles within molecules, but also distances between various atoms and groups of atoms not bonded to each other. We also describe strain, which we divide into three types: torsional strain, angle strain, and steric strain. We urge you to build models and to study and manipulate them. Organic molecules are three-dimensional objects, and it is essential that you become comfortable in dealing with them as such.

Conformation Any three-dimensional arrangement of atoms in a molecule that results by rotation about a single bond.

Staggered conformation A conformation about a carbon–carbon single bond in which the atoms on one carbon are as far apart as possible from the atoms on the adjacent carbon.

A. Alkanes

Alkanes with two or more carbons can be twisted into a number of different three-dimensional arrangements of their atoms by rotating about one or more carbon–carbon bonds. Any three-dimensional arrangement of atoms that results from rotation about a single bond is called a **conformation**. Figure 3.4(a) shows a ball-and-stick model of a **staggered conformation**

Newman projection A way to view a molecule by looking along a carbon–carbon bond.

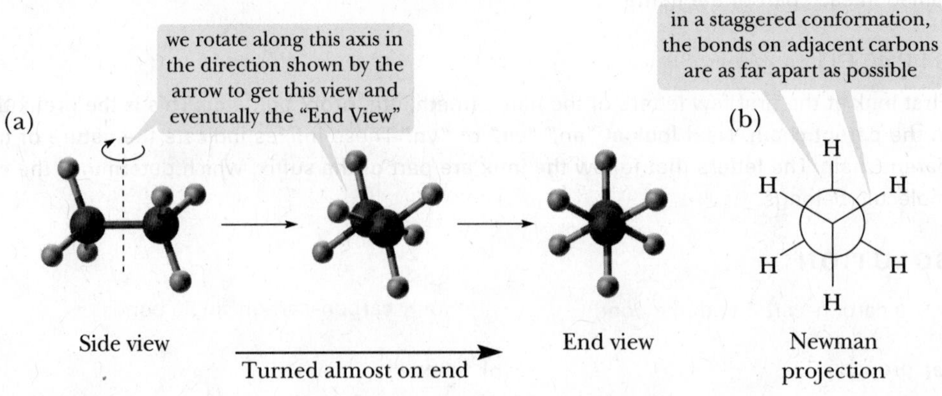

FIGURE 3.4
A staggered conformation of ethane. (a) Ball-and-stick model and (b) Newman projection.

of ethane. In this conformation, the three C—H bonds on one carbon are as far apart as possible from the three C—H bonds on the adjacent carbon. Figure 3.4(b), called a **Newman projection**, is a shorthand way of representing the staggered conformation of ethane. In a Newman projection, we view a molecule along the axis of a C—C bond. The three atoms or groups of atoms nearer your eye appear on lines extending from the center of the circle at angles of 120°. The three atoms or groups of atoms on the carbon farther from your eye appear on lines extending from the circumference of the circle at angles of 120°. Remember that bond angles about each carbon in ethane are approximately 109.5° and not 120°, as this Newman projection might suggest.

HOW TO 3.2

Visualize and Draw a Newman Projection

A Newman projection is a two-dimensional drawing of a three-dimensional molecule viewed down a carbon–carbon bond. Here are some steps you can apply when drawing Newman projections of molecules:

1. **Select the C–C bond you wish to look down.** Using butane as an example, let's select the C_2–C_3 bond.

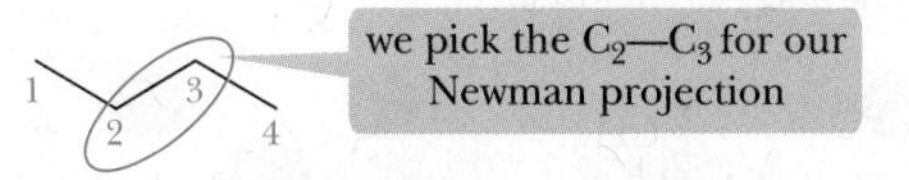

2. **Draw in the hydrogens** using dashed wedges to show bonds going behind the plane of the paper and solid wedges to show bonds coming out of the plane of the paper. Hydrogens and groups that are not attached to the bond we are looking down can be shown as condensed formulas.

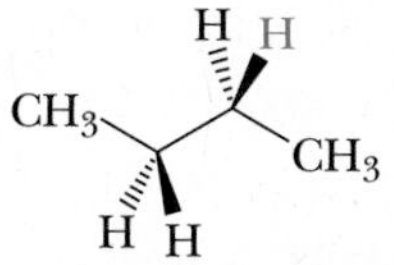

3. **Decide which direction to view the bond from.** Here we view the bond from right to left. The hydrogen closest to the right and coming out of the plane of the page is shown in red as a reference point.

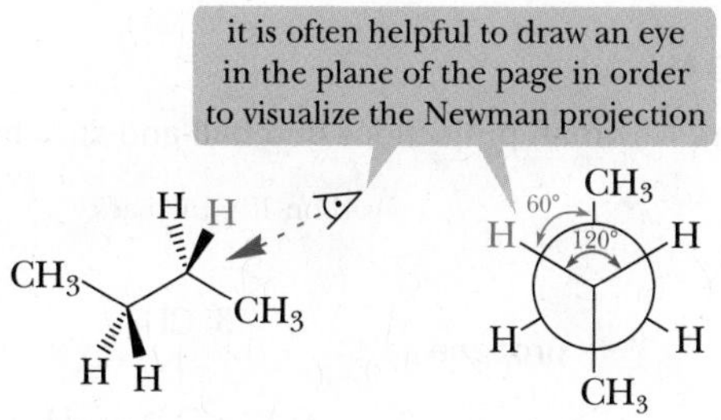

4. Place the atoms and groups in your Newman projection. You can reference the groups to the eye that you drew. Here, the red hydrogen is to the left of the eye and pointing diagonally upward and thus ends up on the bond pointing left and diagonally upward in the Newman projection. The rightmost methyl group is pointing down relative to the eye that we drew and is therefore drawn on the vertical bond in the Newman projection. In this way, you can accurately draw in the remaining atoms and groups. This molecule turns out to be in a staggered conformation.

Figure 3.5 shows a ball-and-stick model and a Newman projection of an **eclipsed conformation** of ethane. In this conformation, the three C—H bonds on one carbon are as close as possible to the three C—H bonds on the adjacent carbon. In other words, hydrogen atoms on the back carbon are eclipsed by the hydrogen atoms on the front carbon.

Eclipsed conformation A conformation about a carbon–carbon single bond in which the atoms on one carbon are as close as possible to the atoms on the adjacent carbon.

For a long time, chemists believed that rotation about the C—C single bond in ethane was completely free. Studies of ethane and other molecules, however, have shown that a potential energy difference exists between its staggered and eclipsed conformations and that rotation

FIGURE 3.5 An eclipsed conformation of ethane. (a, b) Ball-and-stick models and (c) Newman projection.

Torsional strain (also called eclipsed interaction strain) Strain that arises when atoms separated by three bonds are forced from a staggered conformation to an eclipsed conformation.

is not completely free. In ethane, the potential energy of the eclipsed conformation is a maximum and that of the staggered conformation is a minimum. The difference in potential energy between these two conformations is approximately 12.6 kJ/mol (3.0 kcal/mol).

The strain induced in the eclipsed conformation of ethane is an example of torsional strain. **Torsional strain** (also called eclipsed interaction strain) is strain that arises when nonbonded atoms separated by three bonds are forced from a staggered conformation to an eclipsed conformation.

EXAMPLE 3.7

Draw Newman projections for one staggered conformation and one eclipsed conformation of propane.

STRATEGY

Draw the line-angle formula of propane and choose a bond along which to view for the Newman projection. Keep track of the carbons in the line-angle formula and in the Newman projection (numbering them helps). Draw the staggered and eclipsed Newman projections and complete them by adding in the carbons and hydrogens.

SOLUTION

Following are Newman projections and ball-and-stick models of these conformations:

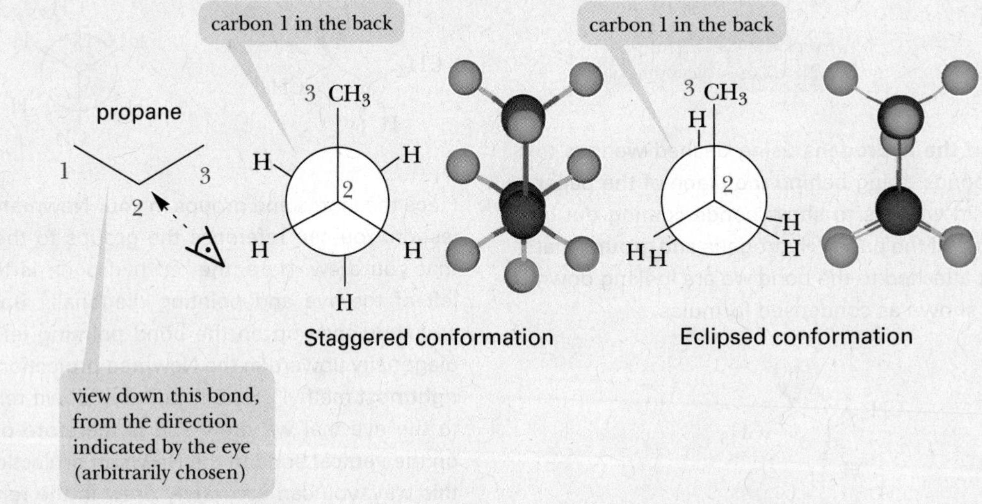

Staggered conformation

Eclipsed conformation

See problems 3.32, 3.37

PROBLEM · 3.7

Draw Newman projections for two staggered and two eclipsed conformations of 1,2-dichloroethane.

B. Cycloalkanes

We limit our discussion to the conformations of cyclopentanes and cyclohexanes because these are the most common carbon rings in the molecules of nature.

Cyclopentane

We can draw cyclopentane [Figure 3.6(a)] as a planar conformation with all C—C—C bond angles equal to 108° [Figure 3.6(b)]. This angle differs only slightly from the tetrahedral

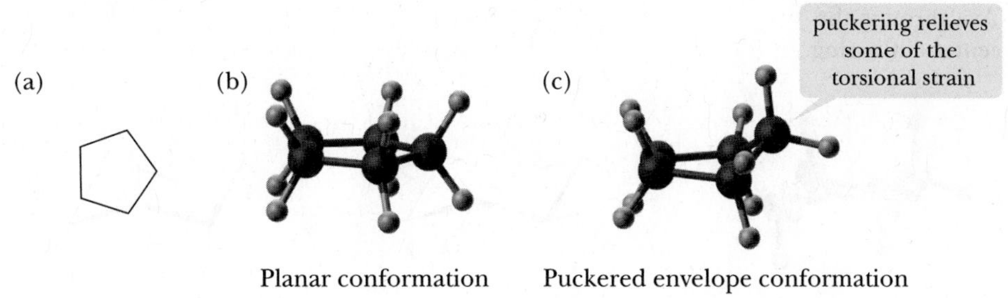

FIGURE 3.6 Cyclopentane. (a) Structural formula. (b) In the planar conformation, there are 10 pairs of eclipsed C—H interactions. (c) The most stable conformation is a puckered "envelope" conformation.

angle of 109.5°; consequently, there is little angle strain in the planar conformation of cyclopentane. **Angle strain** results when a bond angle in a molecule is either expanded or compressed compared with its optimal values. There are 10 fully eclipsed C—H bonds creating a torsional strain of approximately 42 kJ/mol (10 kcal/mol). To relieve at least a part of this strain, the atoms of the ring twist into the "envelope" conformation [Figure 3.6(c)]. In this conformation, four carbon atoms are in a plane, and the fifth is bent out of the plane, rather like an envelope with its flap bent upward.

Angle strain The strain that arises when a bond angle is either compressed or expanded compared with its optimal value.

In the envelope conformation, the number of eclipsed hydrogen interactions is reduced, thereby decreasing torsional strain. The C—C—C bond angles, however, are also reduced, which increases angle strain. The observed C—C—C bond angles in cyclopentane are 105°, indicating that, in its conformation of lowest energy, cyclopentane is slightly puckered. The strain energy in cyclopentane is approximately 23.4 kJ/mol (5.6 kcal/mol).

Cyclohexane

Cyclohexane adopts a number of puckered conformations, the most stable of which is a **chair conformation**. In this conformation (Figure 3.7), all C—C—C bond angles are 109.5° (minimizing angle strain), and hydrogens on adjacent carbons are staggered with respect to one another (minimizing torsional strain). Thus, there is very little strain in a chair conformation of cyclohexane.

In a chair conformation, the C—H bonds are arranged in two different orientations. Six C—H bonds are called **equatorial bonds**, and the other six are called **axial bonds**. One way to visualize the difference between these two types of bonds is to imagine an axis through the center of the chair, perpendicular to the floor [Figure 3.8(a)]. Equatorial bonds are approximately perpendicular to our imaginary axis and alternate first slightly up and then slightly down as you move from one carbon of the ring to the next. Axial bonds are parallel to the imaginary axis. Three axial bonds point up; the other three point down. Notice that axial bonds alternate also, first up and then down as you move from one carbon of the ring to the next. Notice further that if the axial bond on a carbon points upward, then the equatorial bond on that carbon points slightly downward. Conversely, if the axial bond on a particular carbon points downward, then the equatorial bond on that carbon points slightly upward.

Chair conformation The most stable puckered conformation of a cyclohexane ring; all bond angles are approximately 109.5°, and bonds to all adjacent carbons are staggered.

Equatorial bond A bond on a chair conformation of a cyclohexane ring that extends from the ring roughly perpendicular to the imaginary axis of the ring.

Axial bond A bond on a chair conformation of a cyclohexane ring that extends from the ring parallel to the imaginary axis of the ring.

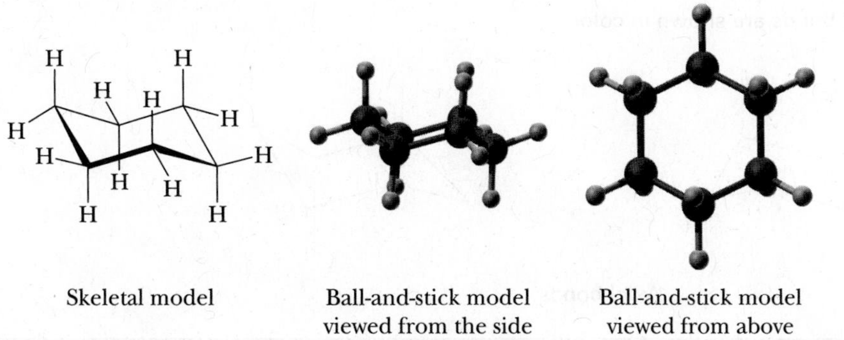

FIGURE 3.7 Cyclohexane. The most stable conformation is the puckered "chair" conformation.

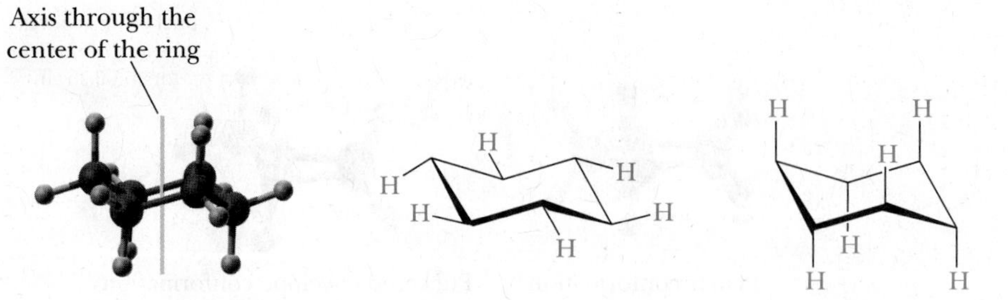

(a) Ball-and-stick model showing all 12 hydrogens (b) The six equatorial C—H bonds shown in red (c) The six axial C—H bonds shown in blue

FIGURE 3.8
Chair conformation of cyclohexane, showing axial and equatorial C—H bonds.

HOW TO 3.3 Draw Alternative Chair Conformations of Cyclohexane

You will be asked frequently to draw three-dimensional representations of chair conformations of cyclohexane and to show spatial relationships among atoms and groups of atoms bonded to the ring. Here are four steps that will help you to draw them. With a little practice you will find them easy to draw.

STEP 1: Draw two sets of parallel lines, one line in each set offset from the other in the set as shown.

STEP 2: Complete the chair by drawing the head and foot pieces, one up and the other down.

STEP 3: Draw the equatorial bonds using ring bonds as a guide. Remember that each equatorial bond is parallel to two ring bonds, and that equatorial bonds on opposite carbons of the ring are parallel to one another. Sets of parallel equatorial and ring bonds are shown here in color.

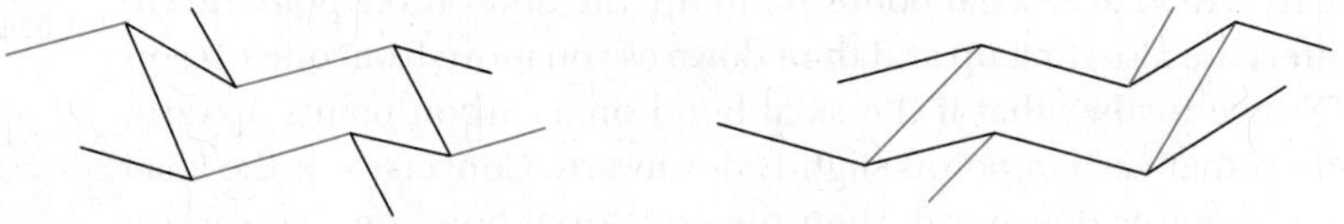

Equatorial bonds

STEP 4: Draw the six axial bonds, as vertical lines. Remember that all axial bonds are parallel to each other. Sets of parallel axial bonds are shown in color.

Axial bonds

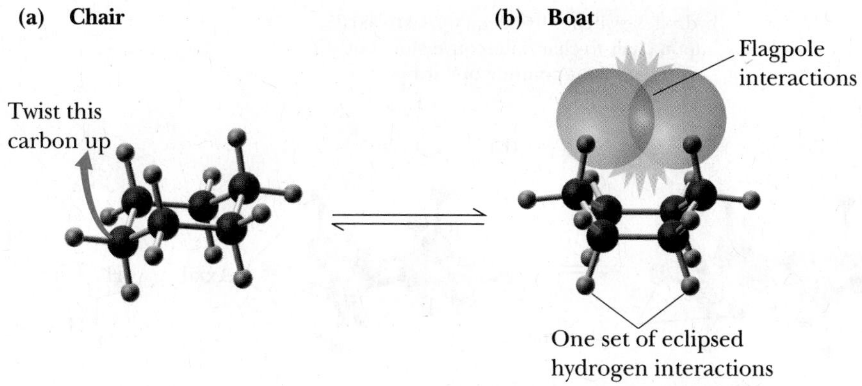

FIGURE 3.9 Conversion of (a) a chair conformation to (b) a boat conformation. In the boat conformation, there is torsional strain due to the four sets of eclipsed hydrogen interactions and steric strain due to the one set of flagpole interactions. A chair conformation is more stable than a boat conformation.

There are many other nonplanar conformations of cyclohexane, one of which is the **boat conformation**. You can visualize the interconversion of a chair conformation to a boat conformation by twisting the ring as illustrated in Figure 3.9. A boat conformation is considerably less stable than a chair conformation. In a boat conformation, torsional strain is created by four sets of eclipsed hydrogen interactions, and steric strain is created by the one set of flagpole interactions. **Steric strain** (also called nonbonded interaction strain) results when nonbonded atoms separated by four or more bonds are forced abnormally close to each other—that is, when they are forced closer than their atomic (contact) radii allow. The difference in potential energy between chair and boat conformations is approximately 27 kJ/mol (6.5 kcal/mol), which means that, at room temperature, approximately 99.99% of all cyclohexane molecules are in the chair conformation.

Boat conformation A puckered conformation of a cyclohexane ring in which carbons 1 and 4 of the ring are bent toward each other.

Steric strain The strain that arises when atoms separated by four or more bonds are forced abnormally close to one another.

EXAMPLE 3.8

Following is a chair conformation of cyclohexane showing a methyl group and one hydrogen:

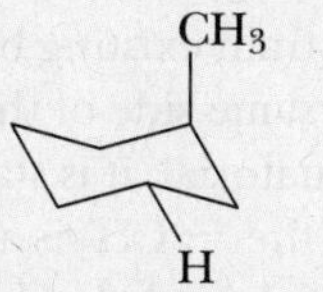

(a) Indicate by a label whether each group is equatorial or axial.

(b) Draw the other chair conformation, and again label each group as equatorial or axial.

STRATEGY

A chair-to-chair interconversion is most often done by changing the orientation of the rightmost and leftmost carbons in the chair conformation of cyclohexane. Remember that after such an interconversion, all prior axial substituents become equatorial and all prior equatorial substituents become axial.

SOLUTION

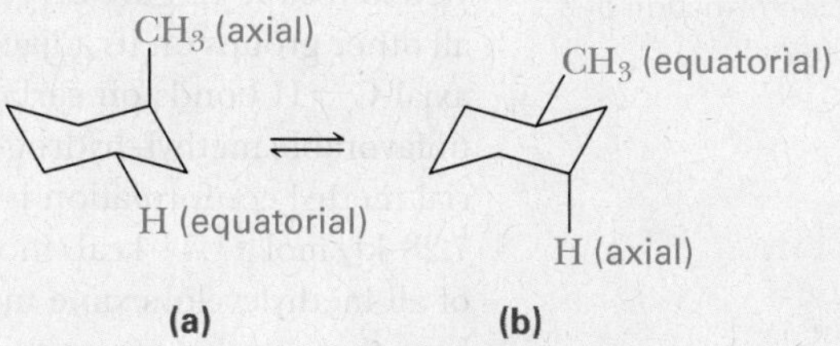

See problems 3.38, 3.47

PROBLEM 3.8

Following is a chair conformation of cyclohexane with carbon atoms numbered 1 through 6:

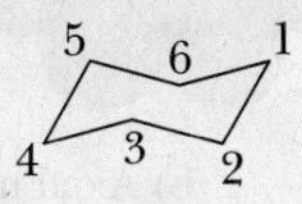

(a) Draw hydrogen atoms that are above the plane of the ring on carbons 1 and 2 and below the plane of the ring on carbon 4.

(b) Which of these hydrogens are equatorial? Which are axial?

(c) Draw the other chair conformation. Now which hydrogens are equatorial? Which are axial? Which are above the plane of the ring, and which are below it?

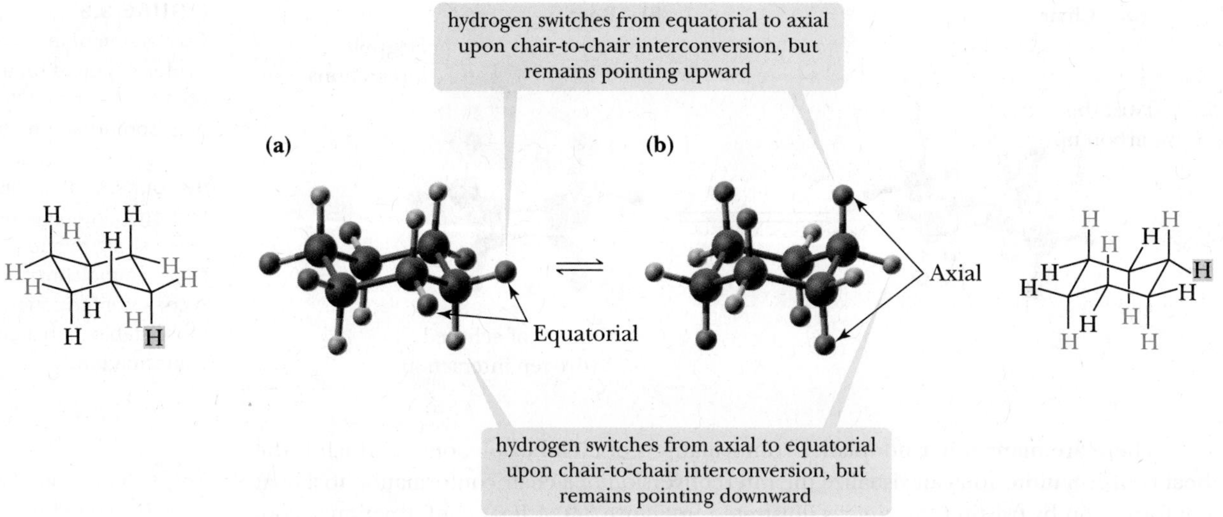

FIGURE 3.10
Interconversion of chair cyclohexanes. All C—H bonds that are equatorial in one chair are axial in the alternative chair, and vice versa.

For cyclohexane, the two equivalent chair conformations can interconvert by one chair twisting first into a boat and then into the other chair. When one chair is converted to the other, a change occurs in the relative orientations in space of the hydrogen atoms bonded to each carbon: All hydrogen atoms equatorial in one chair become axial in the other, and vice versa (Figure 3.10). The interconversion of one chair conformation of cyclohexane to the other occurs rapidly at room temperature.

If we replace a hydrogen atom of cyclohexane by an alkyl group, the group occupies an equatorial position in one chair and an axial position in the other chair. This means that the two chairs are no longer equivalent and no longer of equal stability.

Diaxial interactions Interactions between groups in parallel axial positions on the same side of a chair conformation of a cyclohexane ring.

A convenient way to describe the relative stabilities of chair conformations with equatorial or axial substituents is in terms of a type of steric strain called **axial–axial (diaxial) interaction.** *Axial–axial interaction* refers to the steric strain existing between an axial substituent and an axial hydrogen (or other group) on the same side of the ring. Consider methylcyclohexane (Figure 3.11). When the $—CH_3$ is equatorial, it is staggered with respect to all other groups on its adjacent carbon atoms. When the $—CH_3$ is axial, it is parallel to the axial C—H bonds on carbons 3 and 5. Thus, for axial methylcyclohexane, there are two unfavorable methyl–hydrogen axial–axial interactions. For methylcyclohexane, the equatorial methyl conformation is favored over the axial methyl conformation by approximately 7.28 kJ/mol (1.74 kcal/mol). At equilibrium at room temperature, approximately 95% of all methylcyclohexane molecules have their methyl group equatorial, and less than 5% have their methyl group axial.

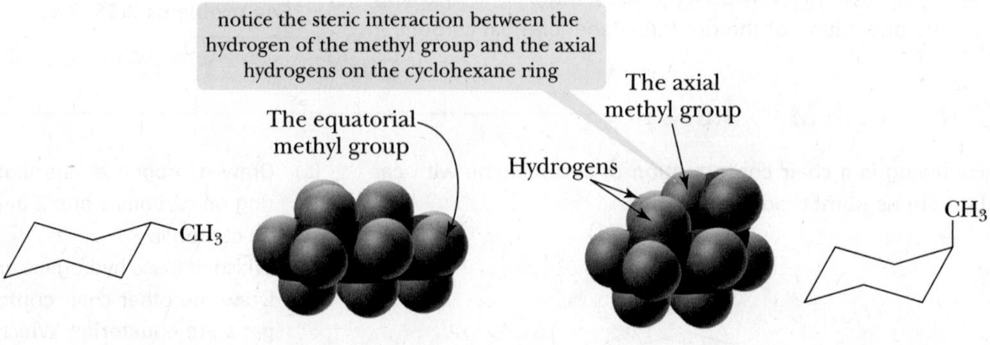

FIGURE 3.11
Two chair conformations of methylcyclohexane. The two axial–axial interactions (steric strain) make conformation (b) less stable than conformation (a) by approximately 7.28 kJ/mol (1.74 kcal/mol).

As the size of the substituent increases, the relative amount of the conformation with the group equatorial increases. When the group is as large as *tert*-butyl, the equatorial conformation is approximately 4,000 times more abundant at room temperature than the axial conformation, and, in effect, the ring is "locked" into a chair conformation with the *tert*-butyl group equatorial.

EXAMPLE 3.9

Label all axial–axial interactions in the following chair conformation:

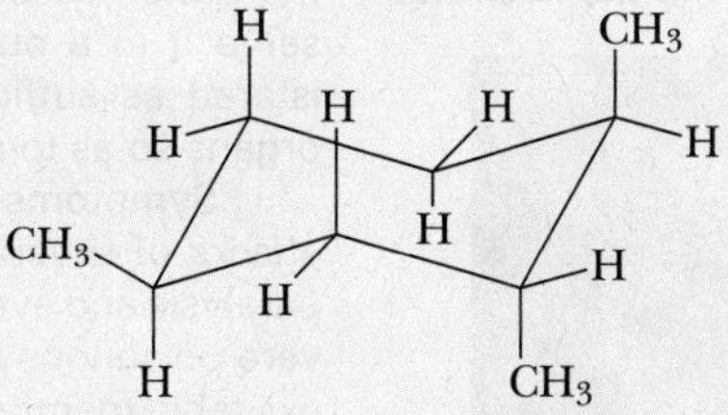

STRATEGY

Find each axial group. Those on the same side of the chair conformation (either above or below the ring) will participate in axial–axial interactions. Remember that the equatorial substituents do not participate in axial–axial interactions.

SOLUTION

There are four axial–axial interactions: Each axial methyl group has two sets of axial–axial interactions with parallel hydrogen atoms on the same side of the ring. The equatorial methyl group has no axial–axial interactions.

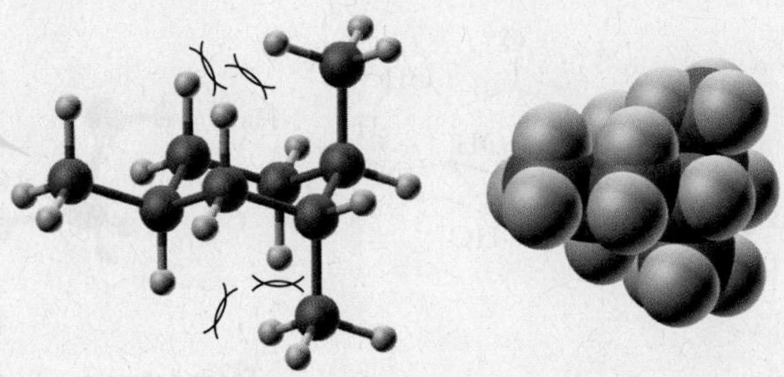

because equatorial groups do not have axial–axial interactions, it is energetically more favorable for a group to be equatorial rather than axial

See problem 3.38

PROBLEM 3.9

The conformational equilibria for methyl-, ethyl-, and isopropylcyclohexane are all about 95% in favor of the equatorial conformation, but the conformational equilibrium for *tert*-butylcyclohexane is almost completely on the equatorial side. Explain why the conformational equilibria for the first three compounds are comparable, but that for *tert*-butylcyclohexane lies considerably farther toward the equatorial conformation.

3.7 What Is *Cis–Trans* Isomerism in Cycloalkanes?

Cycloalkanes with substituents on two or more carbons of the ring show a type of isomerism called ***cis–trans* isomerism**. *Cis–trans* isomers have (1) the same molecular formula, (2) the same order of attachment of atoms, and (3) an arrangement of atoms that cannot be interchanged by rotation about sigma bonds under ordinary conditions. By way of comparison,

***Cis–trans* isomers** Isomers that have the same order of attachment of their atoms, but a different arrangement of their atoms in space, due to the presence of either a ring or a carbon–carbon double bond.

Chemical Connections 3A

THE POISONOUS PUFFER FISH

Nature is by no means limited to carbon in six-membered rings. Tetrodotoxin, one of the most potent toxins known, is composed of a set of interconnected six-membered rings, each in a chair conformation. All but one of these rings have atoms other than carbon in them. Tetrodotoxin is produced in the liver and ovaries of many species of *Tetraodontidae*, especially the puffer fish, so called because it inflates itself to an almost spherical spiny ball when alarmed. The puffer is evidently a species that is highly preoccupied with defense, but the Japanese are not put off. They regard the puffer, called *fugu* in Japanese, as a delicacy. To serve it in a public restaurant, a chef must be registered as sufficiently skilled in removing the toxic organs so as to make the flesh safe to eat.

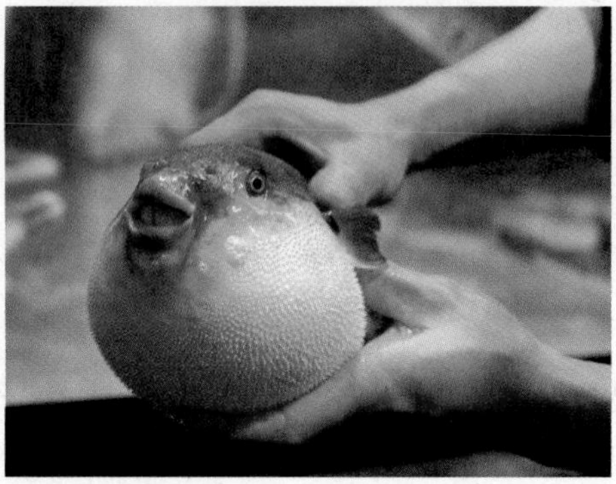

A puffer fish inflated.

Symptoms of tetrodotoxin poisoning begin with attacks of severe weakness, progressing to complete paralysis and eventual death. Tetrodotoxin exerts its severe poisonous effect by blocking Na^+ ion channels in excitable membranes. The $=NH_2^+$ end of tetrodotoxin lodges in the mouth of a Na^+ ion channel, thus blocking further transport of Na^+ ions through the channel.

Questions

How many chair conformations are present in tetrodotoxin? Which substituents in tetrodotoxin are involved in axial–axial interactions?

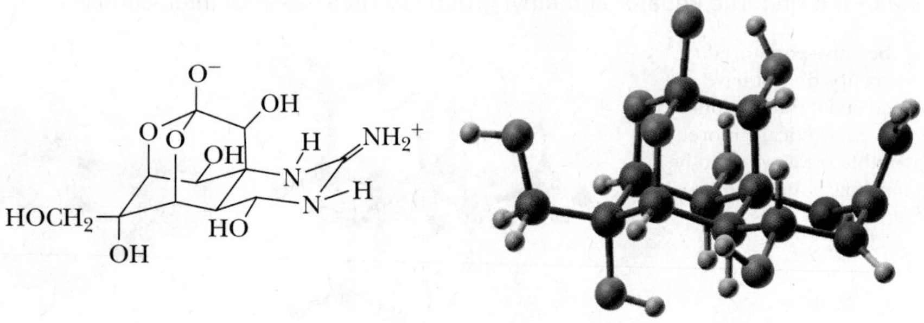

Tetrodotoxin

the potential energy difference between conformations is so small that they can be interconverted easily at or near room temperature by rotation about single bonds, while *cis–trans* isomers can only be interconverted at extremely high temperatures or not at all.

Cis A prefix meaning "on the same side."

Trans A prefix meaning "across from."

We can illustrate *cis–trans* isomerism in cycloalkanes using 1,2-dimethylcyclopentane as an example. In the following structural formula, the cyclopentane ring is drawn as a planar pentagon viewed edge on (in determining the number of *cis–trans* isomers in a substituted cycloalkane, it is adequate to draw the cycloalkane ring as a planar polygon):

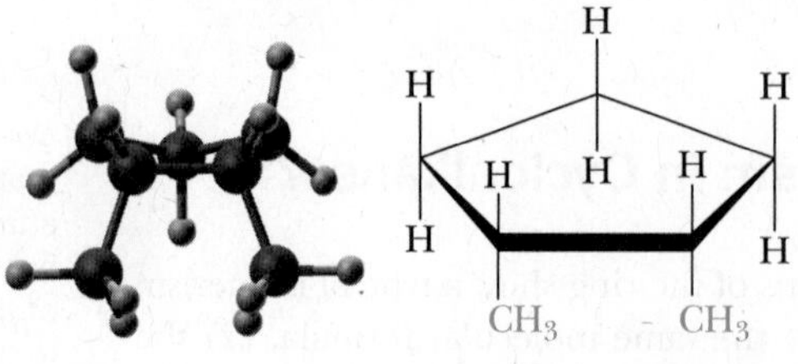

cis-1,2-Dimethylcyclopentane

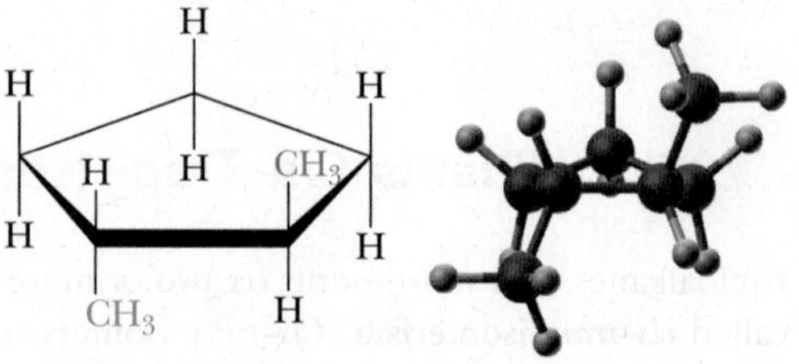

trans-1,2-Dimethylcyclopentane

Carbon–carbon bonds of the ring that project forward are shown as heavy lines. When viewed from this perspective, substituents bonded to the cyclopentane ring project above and below the plane of the ring. In one isomer of 1,2-dimethylcyclopentane, the methyl groups are on the same side of the ring (either both above or both below the plane of the ring); in the other isomer, they are on opposite sides of the ring (one above and one below the plane of the ring).

Alternatively, the cyclopentane ring can be viewed from above, with the ring in the plane of the paper. Substituents on the ring then either project toward you (that is, they project up above the page) and are shown by solid wedges, or they project away from you (they project down below the page) and are shown by broken wedges. In the following structural formulas, only the two methyl groups are shown (hydrogen atoms of the ring are not shown):

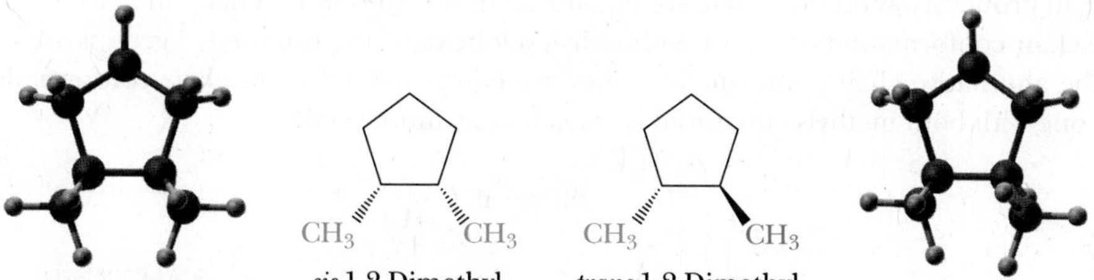

cis-1,2-Dimethylcyclopentane   *trans*-1,2-Dimethylcyclopentane

EXAMPLE 3.10

Which cycloalkanes show *cis–trans* isomerism? For each that does, draw both isomers.

(a) Methylcyclopentane (b) 1,1-Dimethylcyclobutane (c) 1,3-Dimethylcyclobutane

STRATEGY

In order to exhibit *cis–trans* isomerism, a cyclic compound must have at least two substituents on the ring and there must be two possible arrangements (*cis* and *trans*) for any pair of substituents.

SOLUTION

(a) Methylcyclopentane does not show *cis–trans* isomerism: It has only one substituent on the ring.

(b) 1,1-Dimethylcyclobutane does not show *cis–trans* isomerism: Only one arrangement is possible for the two methyl groups on the ring, and they must be *trans*.

(c) 1,3-Dimethylcyclobutane shows *cis–trans* isomerism. Note that, in these structural formulas, we show only the hydrogens on carbons bearing the methyl groups.

cis-1,3-Dimethylcyclobutane   *trans*-1,3-Dimethylcyclobutane

See problems 3.41–3.44, 3.46

PROBLEM 3.10

Which cycloalkanes show *cis–trans* isomerism? For each that does, draw both isomers.

(a) 1,3-Dimethylcyclopentane (b) Ethylcyclopentane (c) 1-Ethyl-2-methylcyclobutane

Two *cis–trans* isomers exist for 1,4-dimethylcyclohexane. For the purposes of determining the number of *cis–trans* isomers in substituted cycloalkanes, it is adequate to draw the cycloalkane ring as a planar polygon, as is done in the following disubstituted cyclohexanes:

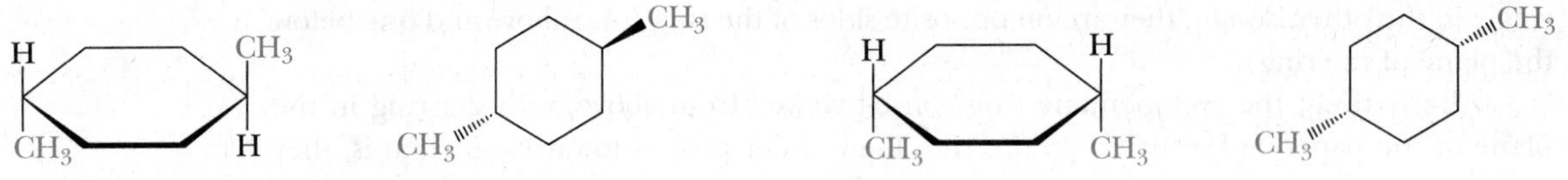

trans-1,4-Dimethylcyclohexane　　　*cis*-1,4-Dimethylcyclohexane

We can also draw the *cis* and *trans* isomers of 1,4-dimethylcyclohexane as nonplanar chair conformations. In working with alternative chair conformations, it is helpful to remember that all groups axial on one chair are equatorial in the alternative chair, and vice versa. In one chair conformation of *trans*-1,4-dimethylcyclohexane, the two methyl groups are axial; in the alternative chair conformation, they are equatorial. Of these chair conformations, the one with both methyls equatorial is considerably more stable.

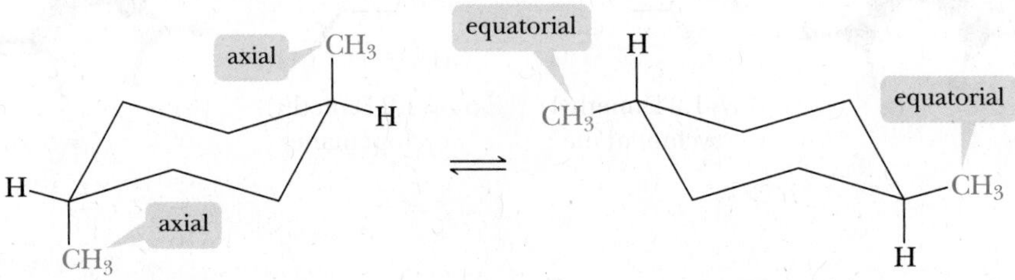

(less stable)　　　(more stable)

trans-1,4-Dimethylcyclohexane

The alternative chair conformations of *cis*-1,4-dimethylcyclohexane are of equal energy. In each chair conformation, one methyl group is equatorial and the other is axial.

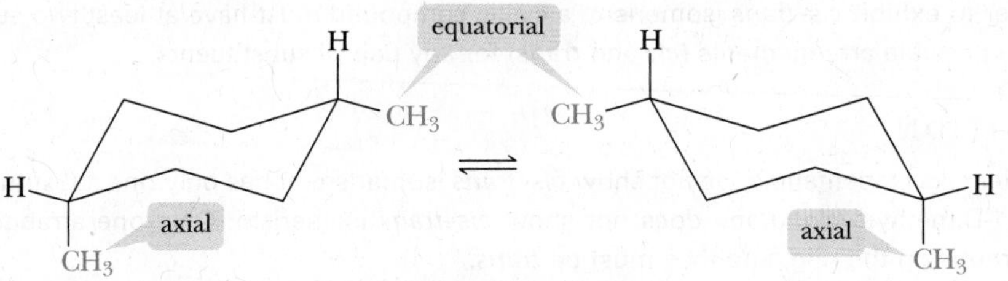

cis-1,4-Dimethylcyclohexane
(these conformations are of equal stability)

EXAMPLE 3.11

Following is a chair conformation of 1,3-dimethylcyclohexane:

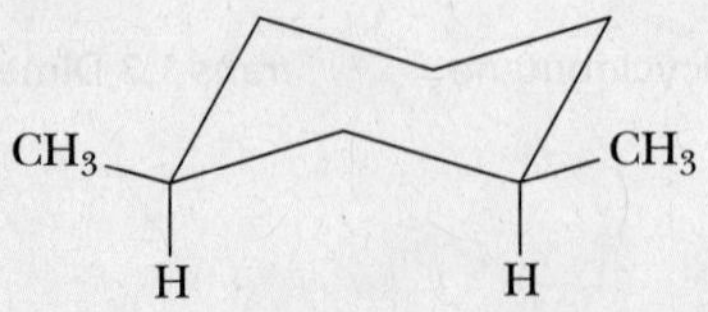

(a) Is this a chair conformation of *cis*-1,3-dimethylcyclohexane or of *trans*-1,3-dimethylcyclohexane?

(b) Draw the alternative chair conformation. Of the two chair conformations, which is the more stable?

(c) Draw a planar hexagon representation of the isomer shown in this example.

STRATEGY

Determine whether substituents are on the same or different sides of the ring to determine *cis* or *trans*. To perform a chair-to-chair interconversion, change the orientation of the rightmost and leftmost carbons in the chair conformation of cyclohexane. Remember that after such an interconversion, all prior axial substituents become equatorial and all prior equatorial substituents become axial. When converting to planar representations of cyclohexane, show substituents above the ring as coming out of the page (wedges) and those below the ring as going behind the page (dashes).

SOLUTION

(a) The isomer shown is *cis*-1,3-dimethylcyclohexane; the two methyl groups are on the same side of the ring.

(b)

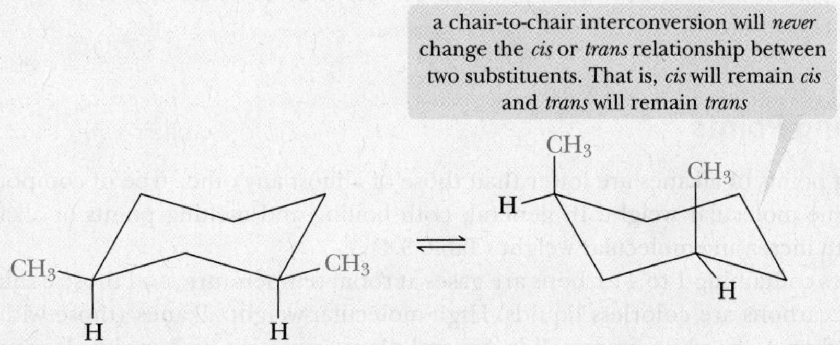
a chair-to-chair interconversion will *never* change the *cis* or *trans* relationship between two substituents. That is, *cis* will remain *cis* and *trans* will remain *trans*
CH3
CH3
H
CH3
CH3
H
H
H

(more stable) (less stable)

(c)

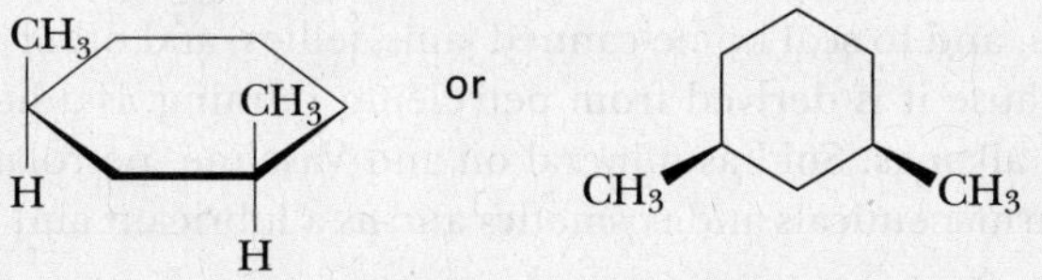
CH3
CH3
H
H
or
CH3
CH3

See problems 3.41–3.44, 3.46, 3.47

PROBLEM 3.11

Following is a planar hexagon representation of one isomer of 1,2,4-trimethylcyclohexane. Draw the alternative chair conformations of this compound, and state which is the more stable.

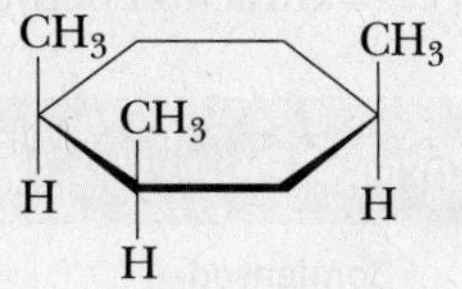
CH3
CH3
CH3
H
H
H

3.8 What Are the Physical Properties of Alkanes and Cycloalkanes?

The most important property of alkanes and cycloalkanes is their almost complete lack of polarity. As we saw in Section 1.2C, the difference in electronegativity between carbon and hydrogen is 2.5 − 2.1 = 0.4 on the Pauling scale, and given this small difference, we classify a C—H bond as nonpolar covalent. Therefore, alkanes are nonpolar compounds, and there are only weak interactions between their molecules.

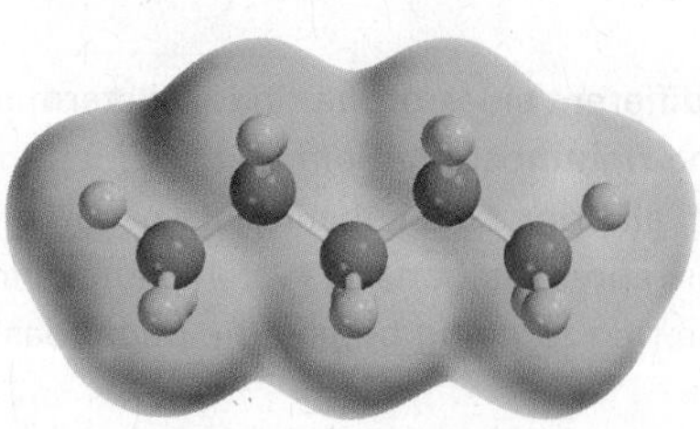

Pentane

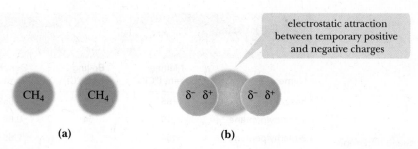

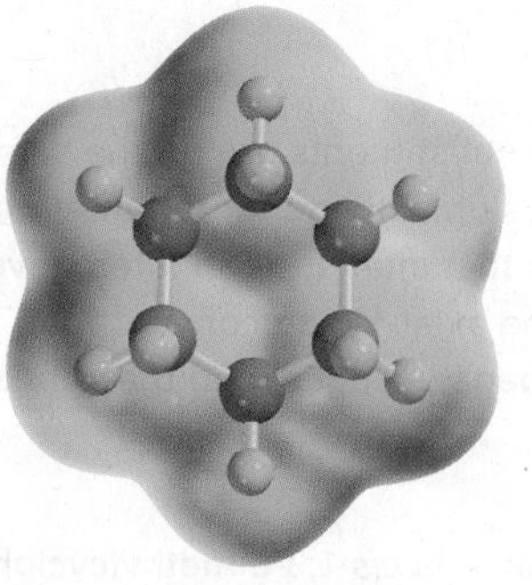
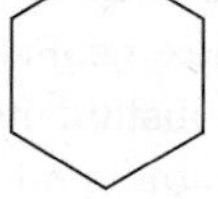

Cyclohexane

Pentane and cyclohexane. The electron density models show no evidence of any polarity in alkanes and cycloalkanes.

A. Boiling Points

The boiling points of alkanes are lower than those of almost any other type of compound with the same molecular weight. In general, both boiling and melting points of alkanes increase with increasing molecular weight (Table 3.4).

Alkanes containing 1 to 4 carbons are gases at room temperature, and those containing 5 to 17 carbons are colorless liquids. High-molecular-weight alkanes (those with 18 or more carbons) are white, waxy solids. Several plant waxes are high-molecular-weight alkanes. The wax found in apple skins, for example, is an unbranched alkane with the molecular formula $C_{27}H_{56}$. Paraffin wax, a mixture of high-molecular-weight alkanes, is used for wax candles, in lubricants, and to seal home-canned jams, jellies, and other preserves. Petrolatum, so named because it is derived from petroleum refining, is a liquid mixture of high-molecular-weight alkanes. Sold as mineral oil and Vaseline, petrolatum is used as an ointment base in pharmaceuticals and cosmetics and as a lubricant and rust preventative.

B. Dispersion Forces and Interactions between Alkane Molecules

Methane is a gas at room temperature and atmospheric pressure. It can be converted to a liquid if cooled to −164 °C and to a solid if further cooled to −182 °C. The fact that methane (or any other compound, for that matter) can exist as a liquid or a solid depends on the existence of forces of attraction between particles of the pure compound. Although the

TABLE 3.4 Physical Properties of Some Unbranched Alkanes

Name	Condensed Structural Formula	Melting Point (°C)	Boiling Point (°C)	*Density of Liquid (g/mL at 0 °C)
methane	CH_4	−182	−164	(a gas)
ethane	CH_3CH_3	−183	−88	(a gas)
propane	$CH_3CH_2CH_3$	−190	−42	(a gas)
butane	$CH_3(CH_2)_2CH_3$	−138	0	(a gas)
pentane	$CH_3(CH_2)_3CH_3$	−130	36	0.626
hexane	$CH_3(CH_2)_4CH_3$	−95	69	0.659
heptane	$CH_3(CH_2)_5CH_3$	−90	98	0.684
octane	$CH_3(CH_2)_6CH_3$	−57	126	0.703
nonane	$CH_3(CH_2)_7CH_3$	−51	151	0.718
decane	$CH_3(CH_2)_8CH_3$	−30	174	0.730

*For comparison, the density of H_2O is 1 g/mL at 4 °C.

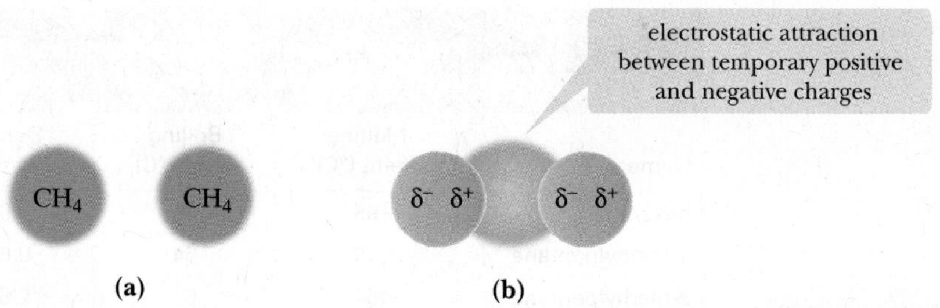

FIGURE 3.12
Dispersion forces. (a) The average distribution of electron density in a methane molecule is symmetrical, and there is no polarity. (b) Temporary polarization of one molecule induces temporary polarization in an adjacent molecule. Electrostatic attractions between temporary partial positive and partial negative charges are called *dispersion forces.*

forces of attraction between particles are all electrostatic in nature, they vary widely in their relative strengths. The strongest attractive forces are between ions—for example, between Na^+ and Cl^- in NaCl (787 kJ/mol, 188 kcal/mol). Hydrogen bonding is a weaker attractive force (8–42 kJ/mol, 2–10 kcal/mol). We will have more to say about hydrogen bonding in Chapter 8 when we discuss the physical properties of alcohols—compounds containing polar O—H groups.

Dispersion forces (0.08–8 kJ/mol, 0.02–2 kcal/mol) are the weakest intermolecular attractive forces. It is the existence of dispersion forces that accounts for the fact that low-molecular-weight, nonpolar substances such as methane can be liquefied. When we convert methane from a liquid to a gas at −164 °C, for example, the process of separating its molecules requires only enough energy to overcome the very weak dispersion forces.

To visualize the origin of dispersion forces, it is necessary to think in terms of instantaneous distributions of electron density rather than average distributions. Over time, the distribution of electron density in a methane molecule is symmetrical [Figure 3.12(a)], and there is no separation of charge. However, at any instant, there is a nonzero probability that the electron density is polarized (shifted) more toward one part of a methane molecule than toward another. This temporary polarization creates temporary partial positive and partial negative charges, which in turn induce temporary partial positive and negative charges in adjacent methane molecules [Figure 3.12(b)]. **Dispersion forces** are weak electrostatic attractive forces that occur between temporary partial positive and partial negative charges in adjacent atoms or molecules.

Dispersion forces Very weak intermolecular forces of attraction resulting from the interaction of temporary induced dipoles.

Because interactions between alkane molecules consist only of these very weak dispersion forces, the boiling points of alkanes are lower than those of almost any other type of compound with the same molecular weight. As the number of atoms and the molecular weight of an alkane increase, the strength of the dispersion forces among alkane molecules increases, and consequently, boiling points increase.

C. Melting Point and Density

The melting points of alkanes increase with increasing molecular weight. The increase, however, is not as regular as that observed for boiling points, because the ability of molecules to pack into ordered patterns of solids changes as the molecular size and shape change.

The average density of the alkanes listed in Table 3.4 is about 0.7 g/mL; that of higher-molecular-weight alkanes is about 0.8 g/mL. All liquid and solid alkanes are less dense than water (1.0 g/mL); therefore, they float on water.

D. Constitutional Isomers Have Different Physical Properties

Alkanes that are constitutional isomers are different compounds and have different physical properties. Table 3.5 lists the boiling points, melting points, and densities of the five constitutional isomers with the molecular formula C_6H_{14}. The boiling point of

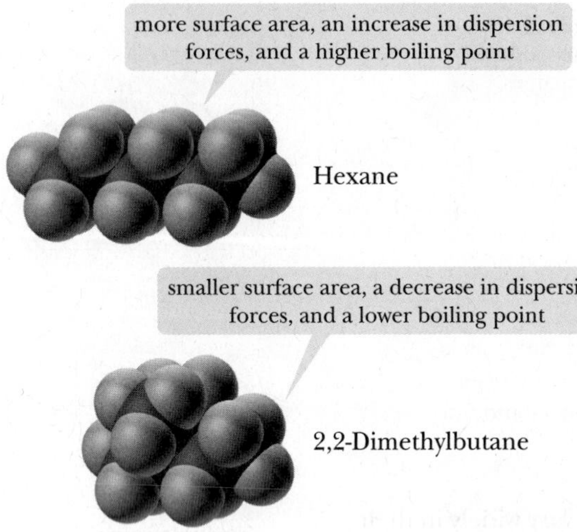
more surface area, an increase in dispersion forces, and a higher boiling point
Hexane
smaller surface area, a decrease in dispersion forces, and a lower boiling point
2,2-Dimethylbutane

TABLE 3.5 Physical Properties of the Isomeric Alkanes with the Molecular Formula C_6H_{14}

Name	Melting Point (°C)	Boiling Point (°C)	Density (g/mL)
hexane	−95	69	0.659
3-methylpentane	−118	64	0.664
2-methylpentane	−154	62	0.653
2,3-dimethylbutane	−129	58	0.662
2,2-dimethylbutane	−100	50	0.649

each of its branched-chain isomers is lower than that of hexane itself, and the more branching there is, the lower is the boiling point. These differences in boiling points are related to molecular shape in the following way: The only forces of attraction between alkane molecules are dispersion forces. As branching increases, the shape of an alkane molecule becomes more compact, and its surface area decreases. As the surface area decreases, the strength of the dispersion forces decreases, and boiling points decrease. Thus, for any group of alkane constitutional isomers, it is usually observed that the least-branched isomer has the highest boiling point and the most-branched isomer has the lowest boiling point. The trend in melting points is less obvious, but as previously mentioned, it correlates with a molecule's ability to pack into ordered patterns of solids.

EXAMPLE 3.12

Arrange the alkanes in each set in order of increasing boiling point:

(a) Butane, decane, and hexane **(b)** 2-Methylheptane, octane, and 2,2,4-trimethylpentane

STRATEGY

When determining relative boiling points, remember that as the number of carbon atoms in the chain increases, the dispersion forces among molecules increase and the boiling points increase. Boiling point is also dependent on the degree of branching. For constitutional isomers, the most highly branched isomer has the smallest surface area and the lowest boiling point.

SOLUTION

(a) All of the compounds are unbranched alkanes. As the number of carbon atoms in the chain increases, the dispersion forces among molecules increase, and the boiling points increase. Decane has the highest boiling point, butane the lowest:

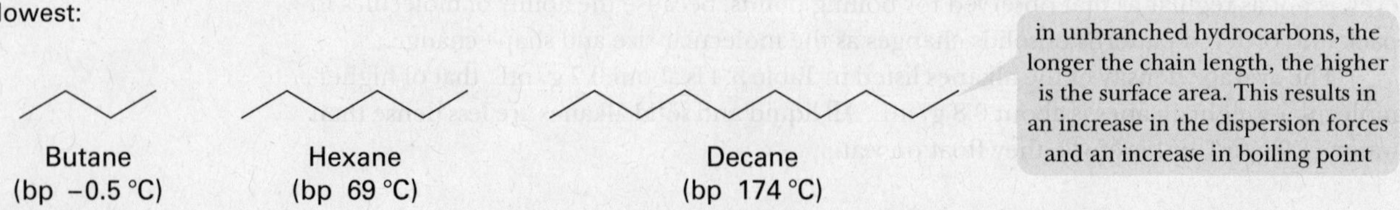
in unbranched hydrocarbons, the longer the chain length, the higher is the surface area. This results in an increase in the dispersion forces and an increase in boiling point
Butane
(bp −0.5 °C)
Hexane
(bp 69 °C)
Decane
(bp 174 °C)

(b) These three alkanes are constitutional isomers with the molecular formula C_8H_{18}. Their relative boiling points depend on the degree of branching. 2,2,4-Trimethylpentane, the most highly branched isomer, has the smallest surface area and the lowest boiling point. Octane, the unbranched isomer, has the largest surface area and the highest boiling point.

the greater the branching, the lower is the surface area, causing a decrease in the dispersion forces and a decrease in boiling point

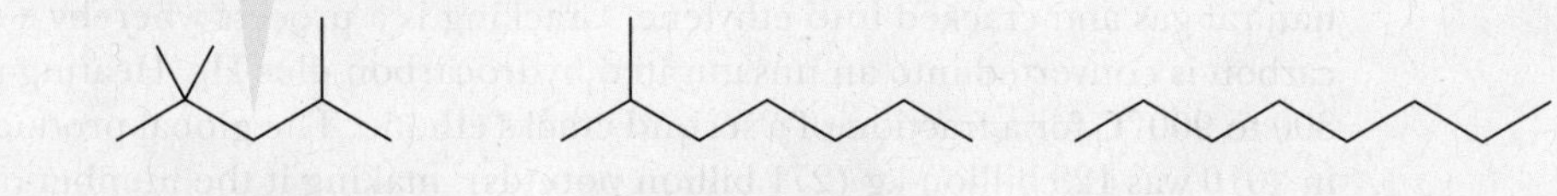

2,2,4-Trimethylpentane (bp 99 °C) | 2-Methylheptane (bp 118 °C) | Octane (bp 125 °C)

See problem 3.49

PROBLEM 3.12

Arrange the alkanes in each set in order of increasing boiling point:

(a) 2-Methylbutane, 2,2-dimethylpropane, and pentane **(b)** 3,3-Dimethylheptane, 2,2,4-trimethylhexane, and nonane

3.9 What Are the Characteristic Reactions of Alkanes?

The most important chemical property of alkanes and cycloalkanes is their inertness. They are quite unreactive toward most reagents, a behavior consistent with the fact that they are nonpolar compounds containing only strong sigma bonds. Under certain conditions, however, alkanes and cycloalkanes do react, with oxygen, O_2. By far their most important reaction with oxygen is oxidation (combustion) to form carbon dioxide and water. The oxidation of saturated hydrocarbons is the basis for their use as energy sources for heat [natural gas, liquefied petroleum gas (LPG), and fuel oil] and power (gasoline, diesel fuel, and aviation fuel). Following are balanced equations for the complete combustion of methane, the major component of natural gas, and for propane, the major component of LPG:

when balancing equations for combustion reactions of hydrocarbons, first balance the number of carbons, next balance the number of hydrogens, then balance the number of oxygens. If the equation is still not balanced, consider doubling all coefficients on each side of the equation arrow

$$\underset{\text{Methane}}{CH_4} + 2O_2 \longrightarrow CO_2 + 2H_2O \quad \Delta H° = -886\ \text{kJ/mol}(-212\ \text{kcal/mol})$$

$$\underset{\text{Propane}}{CH_3CH_2CH_3} + 5O_2 \longrightarrow 3CO_2 + 4H_2O \quad \Delta H° = -2{,}220\ \text{kJ/mol}(-530\ \text{kcal/mol})$$

3.10 What Are the Sources of Alkanes?

The three major sources of alkanes throughout the world are the fossil fuels: natural gas, petroleum, and coal. Fossil fuels account for approximately 90% of the total energy consumed in the United States. Nuclear electric power and hydroelectric power make up most of the remaining 10%. In addition, fossil fuels provide the bulk of the raw material for the organic chemicals consumed worldwide.

A. Natural Gas

Natural gas consists of approximately 90–95% methane, 5–10% ethane, and a mixture of other relatively low-boiling alkanes—chiefly propane, butane, and 2-methylpropane. The current widespread use of ethylene as the organic chemical industry's most important building block is largely the result of the ease with which ethane can be separated from natural gas and cracked into ethylene. Cracking is a process whereby a saturated hydrocarbon is converted into an unsaturated hydrocarbon plus H_2. Heating it in a furnace at 800 to 900 °C for a fraction of a second cracks ethane. The global production of ethylene in 2010 was 123 billion kg (271 billion pounds), making it the number-one organic compound produced, on a weight basis. The bulk of the ethylene produced is used to create organic polymers, as described in Chapter 16.

$$\underset{\text{Ethane}}{CH_3CH_3} \xrightarrow[\text{(thermal cracking)}]{800\text{–}900\,°C} \underset{\text{Ethylene}}{CH_2{=}CH_2} + H_2$$

B. Petroleum

© George Clerk/iStockphoto

A petroleum refinery.

Petroleum is a thick, viscous liquid mixture of literally thousands of compounds, most of them hydrocarbons, formed from the decomposition of marine plants and animals. Petroleum and petroleum-derived products fuel automobiles, aircraft, and trains. They provide most of the greases and lubricants required for the machinery of our highly industrialized society. Furthermore, petroleum, along with natural gas, provides close to 90% of the organic raw materials used in the synthesis and manufacture of synthetic fibers, plastics, detergents, drugs, dyes, and a multitude of other products.

It is the task of a petroleum refinery to produce usable products, with a minimum of waste, from the thousands of different hydrocarbons in this liquid mixture. The various physical and chemical processes for this purpose fall into two broad categories: separation processes, which separate the complex mixture into various fractions, and re-forming processes, which alter the molecular structure of the hydrocarbon components themselves.

The fundamental separation process utilized in refining petroleum is fractional distillation (Figure 3.13). Practically all crude oil that enters a refinery goes to distillation units,

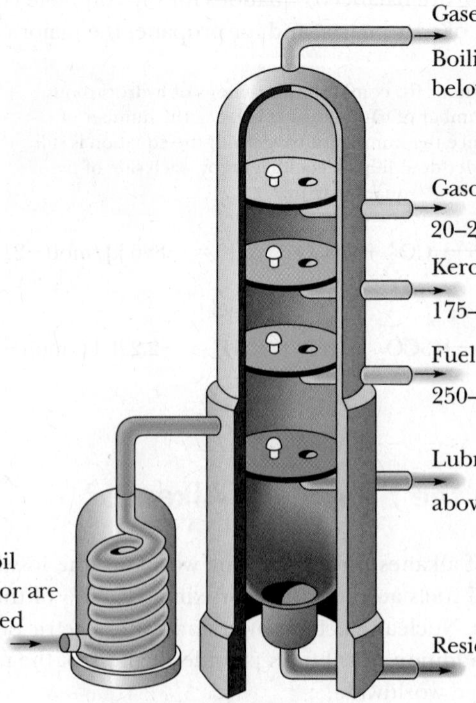

FIGURE 3.13 Fractional distillation of petroleum. The lighter, more volatile fractions are removed from higher up the column and the heavier, less volatile fractions from lower down.

where it is heated to temperatures as high as 370 to 425 °C and separated into fractions. Each fraction contains a mixture of hydrocarbons that boils within a particular range:

1. Gases boiling below 20 °C are taken off at the top of the distillation column. This fraction is a mixture of low-molecular-weight hydrocarbons, predominantly propane, butane, and 2-methylpropane, substances that can be liquefied under pressure at room temperature. The liquefied mixture, known as liquefied petroleum gas (LPG), can be stored and shipped in metal tanks and is a convenient source of gaseous fuel for home heating and cooking.
2. Naphthas, bp 20 to 200 °C, are a mixture of C_5 to C_{12} alkanes and cycloalkanes. Naphthas also contain small amounts of benzene, toluene, xylene, and other aromatic hydrocarbons (Chapter 9). The light naphtha fraction, bp 20 to 150 °C, is the source of straight-run gasoline and averages approximately 25% of crude petroleum. In a sense, naphthas are the most valuable distillation fractions, because they are useful not only as fuel, but also as sources of raw materials for the organic chemical industry.
3. Kerosene, bp 175 to 275 °C, is a mixture of C_9 to C_{15} hydrocarbons.
4. Fuel oil, bp 250 to 400 °C, is a mixture of C_{15} to C_{18} hydrocarbons. Diesel fuel is obtained from this fraction.
5. Lubricating oil and heavy fuel oil distill from the column at temperatures above 350 °C.
6. Asphalt is the black, tarry residue remaining after the removal of the other volatile fractions.

The two most common re-forming processes are cracking, illustrated by the thermal conversion of ethane to ethylene (Section 3.10A), and catalytic re-forming, illustrated by the conversion of hexane first to cyclohexane and then to benzene:

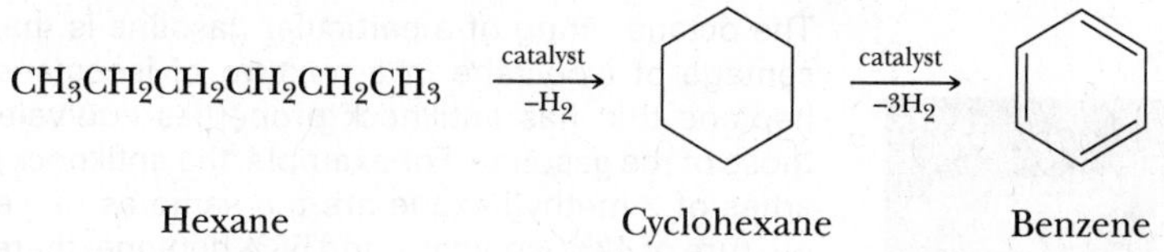

C. Coal

To understand how coal can be used as a raw material for the production of organic compounds, it is necessary to discuss synthesis gas. Synthesis gas is a mixture of carbon monoxide and hydrogen in varying proportions, depending on the means by which it is manufactured. Synthesis gas is prepared by passing steam over coal. It is also prepared by the partial oxidation of methane by oxygen.

$$\underset{\text{Coal}}{C} + H_2O \xrightarrow{\text{heat}} CO + H_2$$

$$\underset{\text{Methane}}{CH_4} + \frac{1}{2}O_2 \xrightarrow{\text{catalyst}} CO + 2H_2$$

Two important organic compounds produced today almost exclusively from carbon monoxide and hydrogen are methanol and acetic acid. In the production of methanol, the ratio of carbon monoxide to hydrogen is adjusted to 1:2, and the mixture is passed over a catalyst at elevated temperature and pressure:

$$CO + 2H_2 \xrightarrow{\text{catalyst}} \underset{\text{Methanol}}{CH_3OH}$$

The treatment of methanol, in turn, with carbon monoxide over a different catalyst gives acetic acid:

$$\underset{\text{Methanol}}{CH_3OH} + CO \xrightarrow{\text{catalyst}} \underset{\text{Acetic acid}}{CH_3\overset{\overset{\large O}{\|}}{C}OH}$$

Because the processes for making methanol and acetic acid directly from carbon monoxide are commercially proven, it is likely that the decades ahead will see the development of routes to other organic chemicals from coal via methanol.

Chemical Connections 3B

OCTANE RATING: WHAT THOSE NUMBERS AT THE PUMP MEAN

Gasoline is a complex mixture of C_6 to C_{12} hydrocarbons. The quality of gasoline as a fuel for internal combustion engines is expressed in terms of an *octane rating.* Engine knocking occurs when a portion of the air–fuel mixture explodes prematurely (usually as a result of heat developed during compression) and independently of ignition by the spark plug. Two compounds were selected as reference fuels. One of these, 2,2,4-trimethylpentane (isooctane), has very good antiknock properties (the fuel–air mixture burns smoothly in the combustion chamber) and was assigned an octane rating of 100. (The name *isooctane* is a trivial name; its only relation to the name 2,2,4-trimethylpentane is that both names show eight carbon atoms.) Heptane, the other reference compound, has poor antiknock properties and was assigned an octane rating of 0.

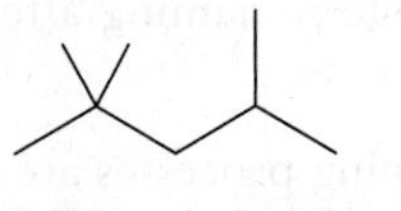

2,2,4-Trimethylpentane (octane rating 100)

Heptane (octane rating 0)

The octane rating of a particular gasoline is that percentage of isooctane in a mixture of isooctane and heptane that has antiknock properties equivalent to those of the gasoline. For example, the antiknock properties of 2-methylhexane are the same as those of a mixture of 42% isooctane and 58% heptane; therefore, the octane rating of 2-methylhexane is 42. Octane itself has an octane rating of −20, which means that it produces even more engine knocking than heptane. Ethanol, the additive to gasohol, has an octane rating of 105. Benzene and toluene have octane ratings of 106 and 120, respectively.

Typical octane ratings of commonly available gasolines.

Question

Which would you expect to have a higher boiling point, octane or isooctane (2,2,4-trimethylpentane)?

SUMMARY OF KEY QUESTIONS

3.1 What Are Alkanes?

- A **hydrocarbon** is a compound that contains only carbon and hydrogen. An alkane is a **saturated hydrocarbon** and contains only single bonds. **Alkanes** have the general formula C_nH_{2n+2}.

3.2 What Is Constitutional Isomerism in Alkanes?

- **Constitutional isomers** have the same molecular formula but a different connectivity (a different order of attachment) of their atoms.

3.3 How Do We Name Alkanes?

- Alkanes are named according to a set of rules developed by the **International Union of Pure and Applied Chemistry (IUPAC)**.
- A carbon atom is classified as **primary (1°)**, **secondary (2°)**, **tertiary (3°)**, or **quaternary (4°)**, depending on the number of carbon atoms bonded to it.
- A hydrogen atom is classified as **primary (1°)**, **secondary (2°)**, or **tertiary (3°)**, depending on the type of carbon to which it is bonded.

3.4 What Are Cycloalkanes?

- A **cycloalkane** is an alkane that contains carbon atoms bonded to form a ring.
- To name a cycloalkane, prefix the name of the open-chain hydrocarbon with "cyclo."
- Five-membered rings (cyclopentanes) and six-membered rings (cyclohexanes) are especially abundant in the biological world.

3.5 What Is the IUPAC System of Nomenclature?

- The IUPAC system is a general system of **nomenclature**. The IUPAC name of a compound consists of three parts:
  (1) A **prefix** that indicates the number of carbon atoms in the **parent chain**,
  (2) An **infix** that indicates the nature of the carbon–carbon bonds in the parent chain, and
  (3) A **suffix** that indicates the class to which the compound belongs.
- **Substituents** derived from alkanes by the removal of a hydrogen atom are called **alkyl groups** and are given the symbol **R**. The name of an alkyl group is formed by dropping the suffix -ane from the name of the parent alkane and adding -yl in its place.

3.6 What Are the Conformations of Alkanes and Cycloalkanes?

- A **conformation** is any three-dimensional arrangement of the atoms of a molecule that results from rotation about a single bond.
- One convention for showing conformations is the **Newman projection. Staggered conformations** are lower in energy (more stable) than **eclipsed conformations.**
- There are three types of **molecular strain:**

  Torsional strain (also called **eclipsed interaction strain**) that results when nonbonded atoms separated by three bonds are forced from a staggered conformation to an eclipsed conformation

  Angle strain that results when a bond angle in a molecule is either expanded or compressed compared with its optimal values, and

  Steric strain (also called **nonbonded interaction strain**) that results when nonbonded atoms separated by four or more bonds are forced abnormally close to each other—that is, when they are forced closer than their **atomic (contact) radii** would otherwise allow.
- Cyclopentanes, cyclohexanes, and all larger cycloalkanes exist in dynamic equilibrium between a set of **puckered conformations.** The lowest energy conformation of cyclopentane is an **envelope conformation.** The lowest energy conformations of cyclohexane are two interconvertible **chair conformations.** In a chair conformation, six bonds are **axial** and six are **equatorial.** Bonds axial in one chair are equatorial in the alternative chair, and vice versa. A **boat conformation** is higher in energy than chair conformations. The more stable conformation of a substituted cyclohexane is the one that minimizes **axial–axial interactions.**

3.7 What Is *Cis–Trans* Isomerism in Cycloalkanes?

- ***Cis–trans* isomers** have the same molecular formula and the same order of attachment of atoms, but arrangements of atoms in space that cannot be interconverted by rotation about single bonds. ***Cis*** means that substituents are on the same side of the ring; ***trans*** means that they are on opposite sides of the ring. Most cycloalkanes with substituents on two or more carbons of the ring show *cis–trans* isomerism.

3.8 What Are the Physical Properties of Alkanes and Cycloalkanes?

- Alkanes are **nonpolar compounds**, and the only forces of attraction between their molecules are **dispersion forces**, which are weak electrostatic interactions between temporary partial positive and negative charges of atoms or molecules. Low-molecular-weight alkanes, such as methane, ethane, and propane, are gases at room temperature and atmospheric pressure.
- Higher-molecular-weight alkanes, such as those in gasoline and **kerosene**, are liquids.
- Very high-molecular-weight alkanes, such as those in **paraffin wax**, are solids.
- Among a set of alkane constitutional isomers, the least branched isomer generally has the highest boiling point; the most branched isomer generally has the lowest boiling point.

3.9 What Are the Characteristic Reactions of Alkanes?

- The most important chemical property of alkanes and cycloalkanes is their inertness. Because they are nonpolar compounds containing only strong sigma bonds, they are quite unreactive toward most reagents.
- By far, their most important reaction is **combustion** to form carbon dioxide and water. The oxidation of saturated hydrocarbons is the basis for their use as energy sources for heat and power.

3.10 What Are the Sources of Alkanes?

- **Natural gas** consists of 90–95% methane with lesser amounts of ethane and other lower-molecular-weight hydrocarbons.
- **Petroleum** is a liquid mixture of literally thousands of different hydrocarbons.
- **Synthesis gas**, a mixture of carbon monoxide and hydrogen, can be derived from natural gas and coal.

QUICK QUIZ

Answer true or false to the following questions to assess your general knowledge of the concepts in this chapter. If you have difficulty with any of them, you should review the appropriate section in the chapter (shown in parentheses) before attempting the more challenging end-of-chapter problems.

1. Combustion of alkanes is an endothermic process. (3.9)
2. All alkanes that are liquid at room temperature are more dense than water. (3.8)
3. The two main sources of alkanes the world over are petroleum and natural gas. (3.10)
4. There are four alkyl groups with the molecular formula C_4H_9. (3.3)
5. Sets of constitutional isomers have the same molecular formula and the same physical properties. (3.2)
6. A hydrocarbon is composed of only carbon and hydrogen. (3.1)
7. Cycloalkanes are saturated hydrocarbons. (3.4)
8. The products of complete combustion of an alkane are carbon dioxide and water. (3.9)
9. Alkanes and cycloalkanes show *cis–trans* isomerism. (3.6)
10. Alkenes and alkynes are unsaturated hydrocarbons. (3.1)
11. There are two constitutional isomers with the molecular formula C_4H_{10}. (3.2)
12. Hexane and cyclohexane are constitutional isomers. (3.4)
13. The propyl and isopropyl groups are constitutional isomers. (3.3)
14. There are five constitutional isomers with the molecular formula C_5H_{12}. (3.2)
15. Boiling points among alkanes with unbranched carbon chains increase as the number of carbons in the chain increases. (3.8)
16. In a cyclohexane ring, if an axial bond is above the plane of the ring on a particular carbon atom, axial bonds on the two adjacent carbons are below the plane of the ring. (3.5)
17. Fractional distillation of petroleum separates hydrocarbons based on their melting points (3.10)
18. Among alkane constitutional isomers, the least branched isomer generally has the lowest boiling point. (3.8)
19. The parent name of a cycloalkane is the name of the unbranched alkane with the same number of carbon atoms as are in the cycloalkane ring. (3.4)
20. Octane and 2,2,4-trimethylpentane are constitutional isomers and have the same octane number. (3.10)
21. Liquid alkanes and cycloalkanes are soluble in each other. (3.8)
22. Alkanes and cycloalkanes are insoluble in water. (3.8)
23. The more stable chair conformation of a substituted cyclohexane has the greater number of substituents in equatorial positions. (3.5)

24. The parent name of an alkane is the name of the longest chain of carbon atoms. (3.3)
25. Alkanes are saturated hydrocarbons. (3.1)
26. The general formula of an alkane is C_nH_{2n}, where n is the number of carbon atoms in the alkane. (3.1)
27. The octane number of a particular gasoline is the number of grams of octane per liter. (3.10)
28. *Cis* and *trans* isomers have the same molecular formula, the same connectivity, and the same physical properties. (3.8)
29. A *cis* isomer of a disubstituted cycloalkane can be converted to a *trans* isomer by rotation about an appropriate carbon–carbon single bond. (3.6)
30. All cycloalkanes with two substituents on the ring show *cis–trans* isomerism. (3.6)
31. In all conformations of ethane, propane, butane, and higher alkanes, all C—C—C and C—C—H bond angles are approximately 109.5°. (3.5)
32. Conformations have the same molecular formula and the same connectivity, but differ in the three-dimensional arrangement of their atoms in space. (3.5)
33. Constitutional isomers have the same molecular formula and the same connectivity of their atoms. (3.2)

Answers: (1) F (2) F (3) T (4) T (5) F (6) T (7) T (8) T (9) F (10) T (11) T (12) F (13) T (14) F (15) T (16) T (17) F (18) F (19) T (20) F (21) T (22) T (23) T (24) T (25) T (26) F (27) F (28) F (29) F (30) F (31) T (32) T (33) F

Detailed explanations for many of these answers can be found in the accompanying Solutions Manual.

KEY REACTIONS

1. Oxidation of Alkanes (Section 3.9)

The oxidation of alkanes to carbon dioxide and water is the basis for their use as energy sources of heat and power:

$$CH_3CH_2CH_3 + 5O_2 \longrightarrow 3CO_2 + 4H_2O + \text{energy}$$

PROBLEMS

A problem marked with an asterisk indicates an applied "real-world" problem. Answers to problems whose numbers are printed in blue are given in Appendix D.

Section 3.1 Structure of Alkanes

3.13 For each condensed structural formula, write a line-angle formula:

(a)
CH_2CH_3 CH_3
$CH_3CH_2CHCHCH_2CHCH_3$
$CH(CH_3)_2$

(b)
CH_3
CH_3CCH_3
CH_3

(c) $(CH_3)_2CHCH(CH_3)_2$

(d)
CH_2CH_3
$CH_3CH_2CCH_2CH_3$
CH_2CH_3

(e) $(CH_3)_3CH$

(f) $CH_3(CH_2)_3CH(CH_3)_2$

3.14 Write a condensed structural formula and the molecular formula of each alkane:

(a) 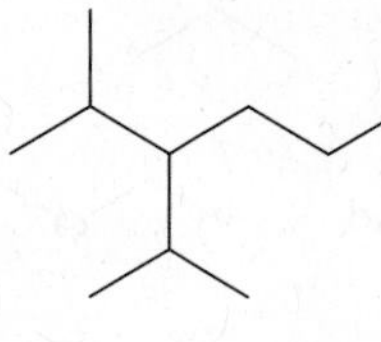

(b) 

(c) 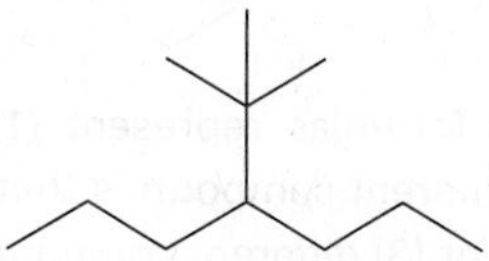

(d) 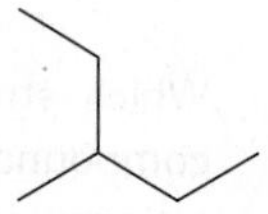

3.15 For each of the following condensed structural formulas, provide an even more abbreviated formula, using parentheses and subscripts:

(a)
CH_3
$CH_3CH_2CH_2CH_2CH_2CHCH_3$

(b)
$CH_2CH_2CH_3$
$HCCH_2CH_2CH_3$
$CH_2CH_2CH_3$

(c)
$CH_2CH_2CH_3$
$CH_3CCH_2CH_2CH_2CH_2CH_3$
$CH_2CH_2CH_3$

Section 3.2 Constitutional Isomerism

3.16 Which statements are true about constitutional isomers?

(a) They have the same molecular formula.
(b) They have the same molecular weight.
(c) They have the same order of attachment of atoms.
(d) They have the same physical properties.
(e) Conformations are not constitutional isomers.

3.17 Each member of the following set of compounds is an alcohol; that is, each contains an —OH (hydroxyl group, Section 1.7A): **(See Example 3.1)**

(a) 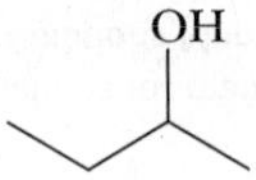
(b) 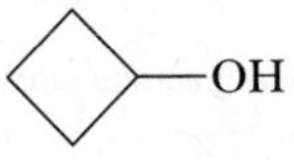
(c) 
(d) 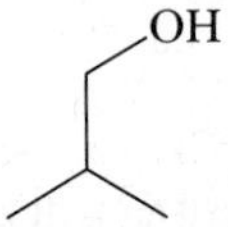
(e) 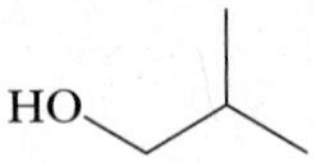
(f) 
(g) 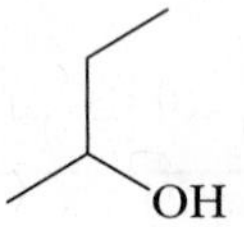
(h) 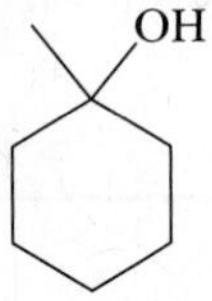

Which structural formulas represent (1) the same compound, (2) different compounds that are constitutional isomers, or (3) different compounds that are not constitutional isomers?

3.18 Each member of the following set of compounds is an amine; that is, each contains a nitrogen atom bonded to one, two, or three carbon groups (Section 1.7B): **(See Example 3.1)**

(a) 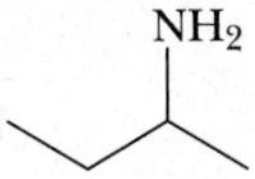
(b) 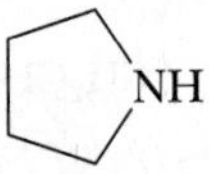
(c) 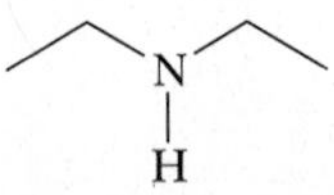
(d) 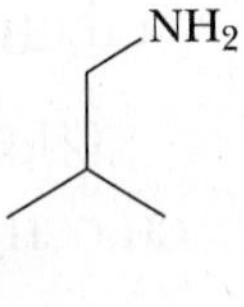
(e) 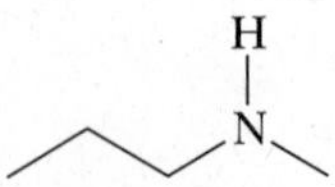
(f) 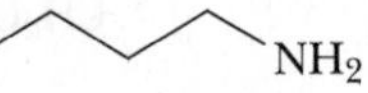
(g) 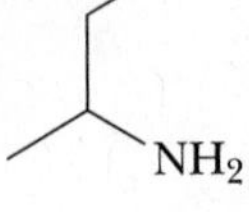
(h) 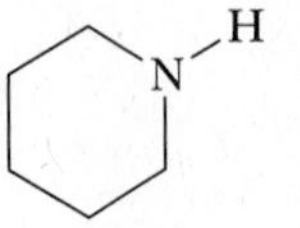

Which structural formulas represent (1) the same compound, (2) different compounds that are constitutional isomers, or (3) different compounds that are not constitutional isomers?

3.19 Each member of the following set of compounds is either an aldehyde or a ketone (Section 1.7C): **(See Example 3.1)**

(a) 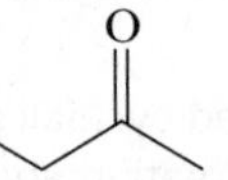
(b) 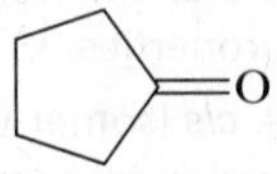
(c) 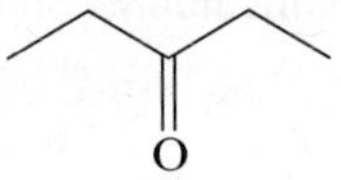
(d) 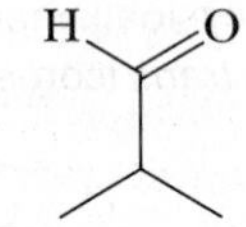
(e) 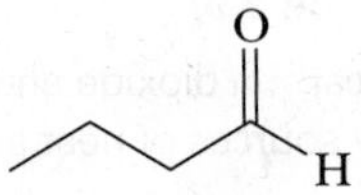
(f) 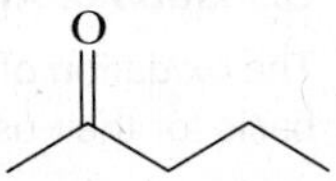
(g) 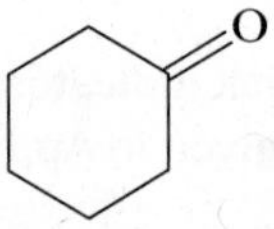
(h) 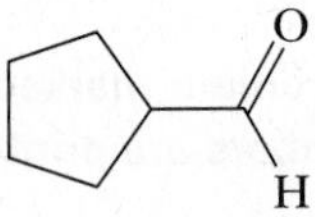

Which structural formulas represent (1) the same compound, (2) different compounds that are constitutional isomers, or (3) different compounds that are not constitutional isomers?

3.20 For each pair of compounds, tell whether the structural formulas shown represent **(See Example 3.1)**

(1) the same compound,
(2) different compounds that are constitutional isomers, or
(3) different compounds that are not constitutional isomers:

(a)  and 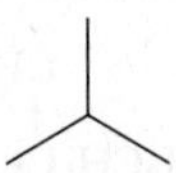

(b) 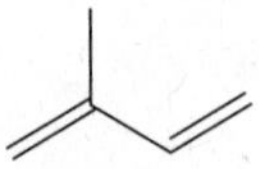 and 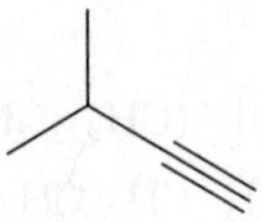

(c)  and 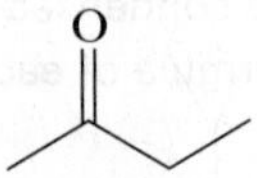

(d)  and 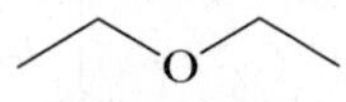

(e) 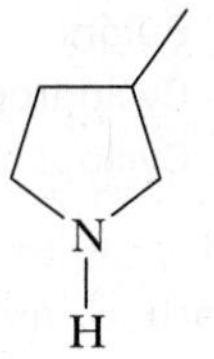 and 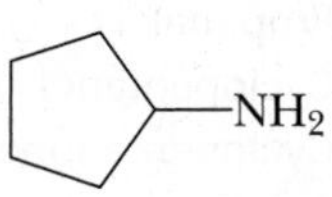

(f)  and 

3.21 Name and draw line-angle formulas for the nine constitutional isomers with the molecular formula C_7H_{16}. **(See Example 3.2)**

3.22 Tell whether the compounds in each set are constitutional isomers: **(See Example 3.1)**

(a) CH_3CH_2OH and CH_3OCH_3

(b) $CH_3\overset{O}{\overset{\|}{C}}CH_3$ and $CH_3CH_2\overset{O}{\overset{\|}{C}}H$

(c) $CH_3\overset{O}{\overset{\|}{C}}OCH_3$ and $CH_3CH_2\overset{O}{\overset{\|}{C}}OH$

(d) $CH_3\overset{OH}{\overset{|}{C}}HCH_2CH_3$ and $CH_3\overset{O}{\overset{\|}{C}}CH_2CH_3$

(e) 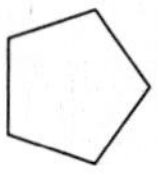 and $CH_3CH_2CH_2CH_2CH_3$

(f) 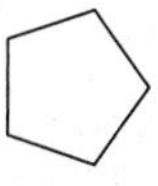 and $CH_2{=}CHCH_2CH_2CH_3$

3.23 Draw line-angle formulas for **(See Example 3.2)**

(a) The four alcohols with the molecular formula $C_4H_{10}O$.

(b) The two aldehydes with the molecular formula C_4H_8O.

(c) The one ketone with the molecular formula C_4H_8O.

(d) The three ketones with the molecular formula $C_5H_{10}O$.

(e) The four carboxylic acids with the molecular formula $C_5H_{10}O_2$.

Sections 3.3 – 3.5 Nomenclature of Alkanes and Cycloalkanes

3.24 Write IUPAC names for these alkanes and cycloalkanes: **(See Examples 3.3, 3.5)**

(a) $CH_3\underset{CH_3}{\underset{|}{C}}HCH_2CH_2CH_3$

(b) $CH_3\underset{CH_3}{\underset{|}{C}}HCH_2CH_2\underset{CH_3}{\underset{|}{C}}HCH_3$

(c) $CH_3(CH_2)_4\underset{CH_2CH_3}{\underset{|}{C}}HCH_2CH_3$

(d) 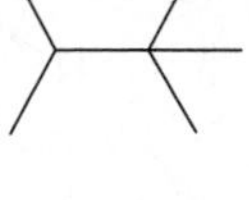

(e) 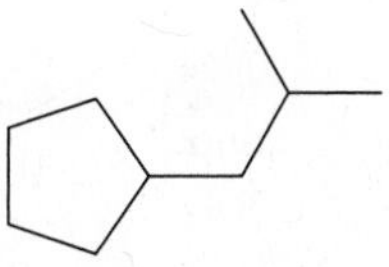

(f) 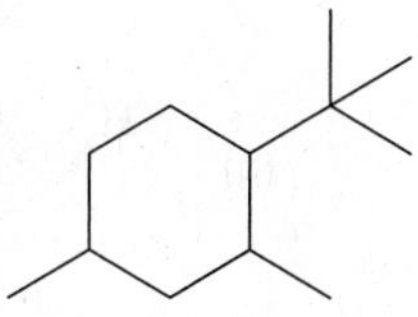

3.25 Write line-angle formulas for these alkanes: **(See Examples 3.3, 3.5)**

(a) 2,2,4-Trimethylhexane
(b) 2,2-Dimethylpropane
(c) 3-Ethyl-2,4,5-trimethyloctane
(d) 5-Butyl-2,2-dimethylnonane
(e) 4-Isopropyloctane
(f) 3,3-Dimethylpentane
(g) *trans*-1,3-Dimethylcyclopentane
(h) *cis*-1,2-Diethylcyclobutane

***3.26** Following is the structure of limonene, the chemical component of oranges that is partly responsible for their citrus scent. Draw the hydrogens present in limonene and classify those bonded to sp^3 hybridized carbons as 1°, 2°, or 3°. **(See Example 3.4)**

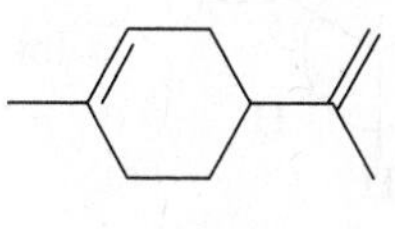

Limonene

***3.27** Following is the structure of Germacrene A, a hydrocarbon synthesized in plants and studied for its insecticidal properties. Classify each of the sp^3 hybridized carbons on Germacrene A as 1°, 2°, 3°, or 4°. **(See Example 3.4)**

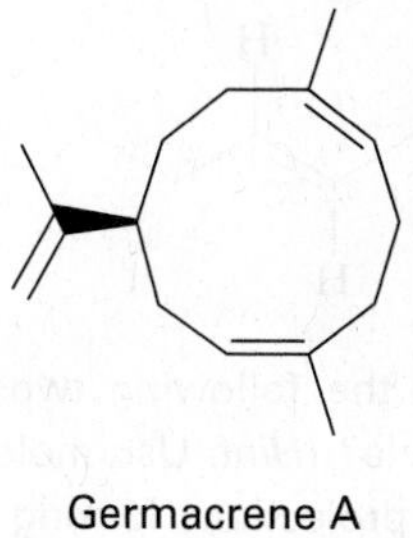

Germacrene A

3.28 Explain why each of the following names is an incorrect IUPAC name and write the correct IUPAC name for the intended compound: **(See Examples 3.3, 3.5)**

(a) 1,3-Dimethylbutane
(b) 4-Methylpentane
(c) 2,2-Diethylbutane
(d) 2-Ethyl-3-methylpentane
(e) 2-Propylpentane
(f) 2,2-Diethylheptane
(g) 2,2-Dimethylcyclopropane
(h) 1-Ethyl-5-methylcyclohexane

3.29 Draw a structural formula for each compound: **(See Example 3.6)**

(a) Ethanol (b) Ethanal
(c) Ethanoic acid (d) Butanone
(e) Butanal (f) Butanoic acid
(g) Propanal (h) Cyclopropanol
(i) Cyclopentanol (j) Cyclopentene
(k) Cyclopentanone

3.30 Write the IUPAC name for each compound: **(See Example 3.6)**

(a) $CH_3\overset{O}{\overset{\|}{C}}CH_3$ (b) $CH_3(CH_2)_3\overset{O}{\overset{\|}{C}}H$

(c) $CH_3(CH_2)_8\overset{O}{\overset{\|}{C}}OH$ (d) 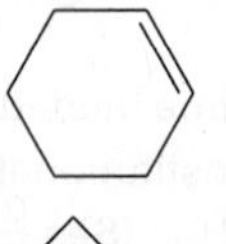

(e) 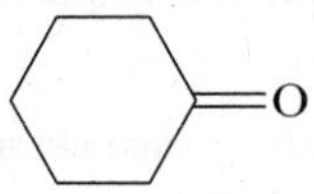 (f) 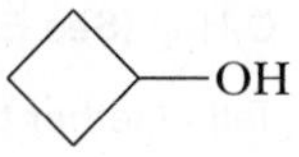

Section 3.6 Conformations of Alkanes and Cycloalkanes

3.31 How many *different* staggered conformations are there for 2-methylpropane? How many *different* eclipsed conformations are there?

3.32 Looking along the bond between carbons 2 and 3 of butane, there are two different staggered conformations and two different eclipsed conformations. Draw Newman projections of each, and arrange them in order from the most stable conformation to the least stable conformation. **(See Example 3.7)**

3.33 Explain why each of the following Newman projections might not represent the most stable conformation of that molecule:

(a) 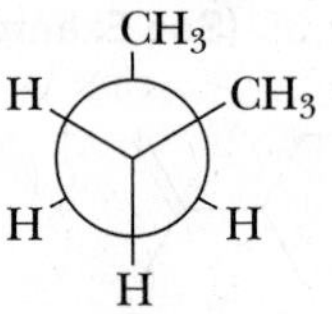

(b) 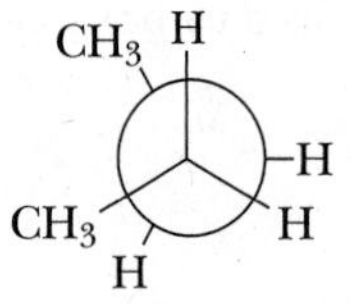

(c) 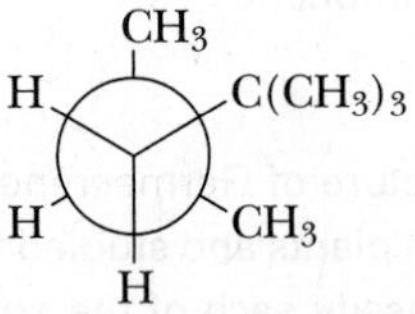

(d) 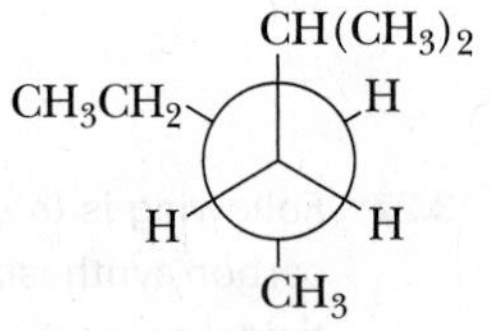

3.34 Explain why the following are not different conformations of 3-hexene:

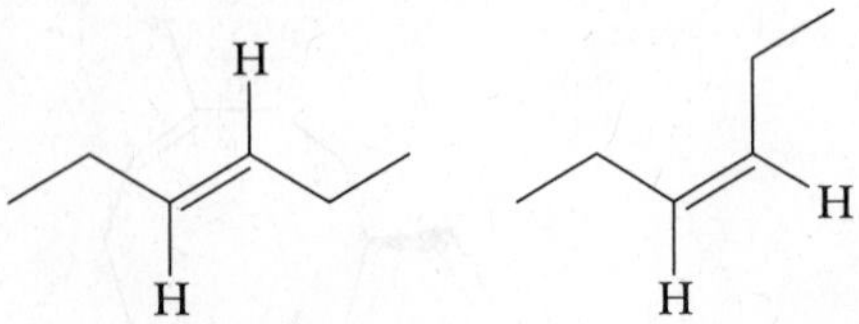

3.35 Which of the following two conformations is the more stable? (*Hint:* Use molecular models or draw Newman projections looking down the bond being rotated to compare structures):

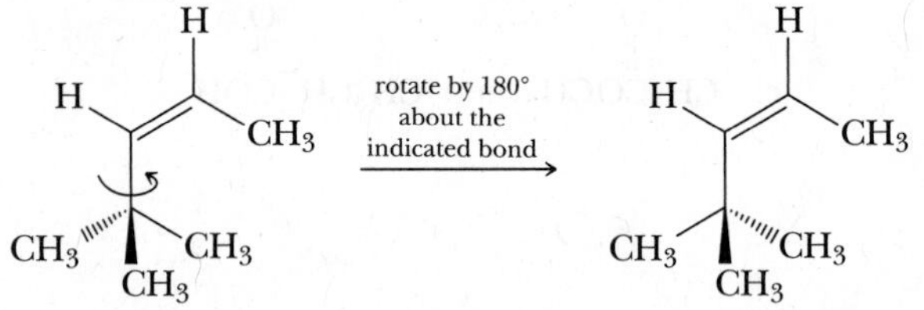

(a) (b)

3.36 Determine whether the following pairs of structures in each set represent the same molecule or constitutional isomers, and if they are the same molecule, determine whether they are in the same or different conformations:

(a) 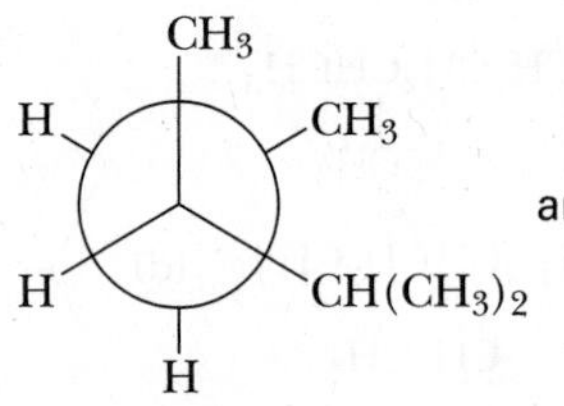

and 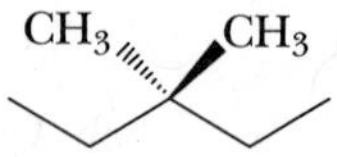

(b) 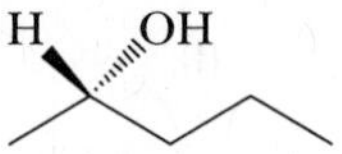

and 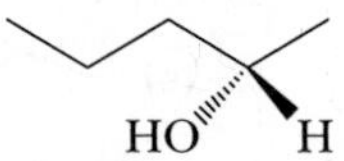

(c) 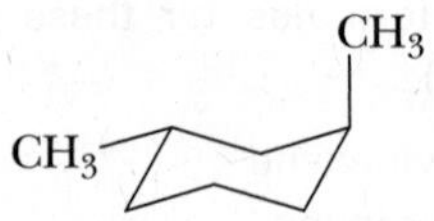

and 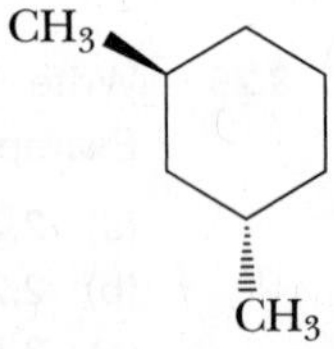

(d) 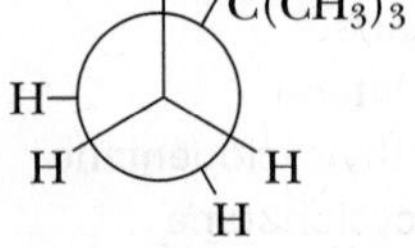

and 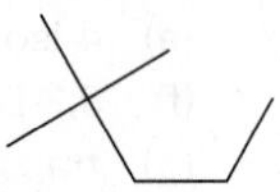

3.37 Draw Newman projections for the most stable conformation of each of the following compounds looking down the indicated bond. **(See Example 3.7)**

(a) 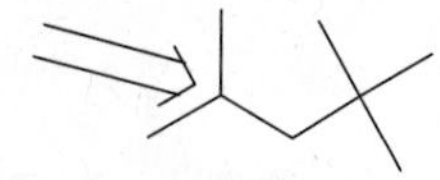

(b) 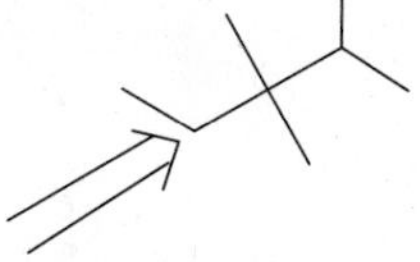

(c) 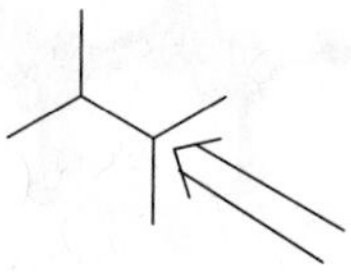

(d) 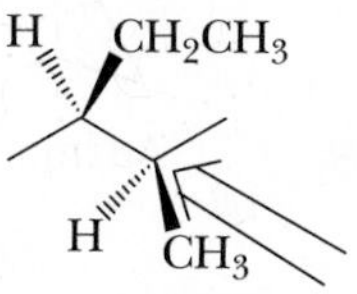

3.38 Draw both chair forms of each of the following compounds and indicate the more stable conformation. **(See Examples 3.8, 3.9)**

(a) 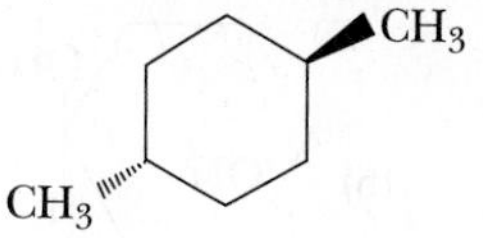

(b) 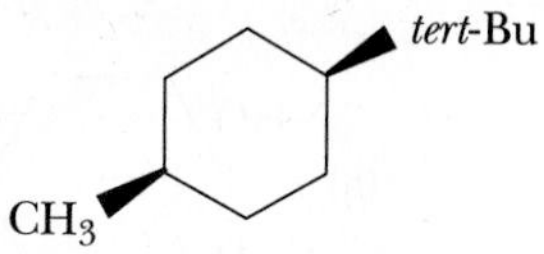

(c) 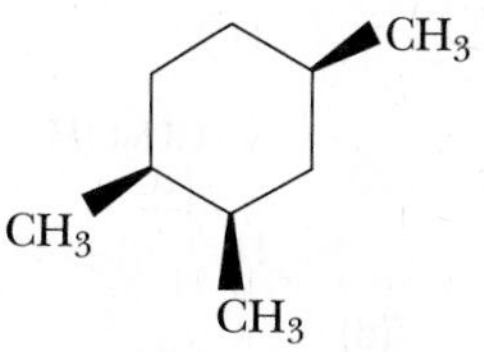

(d) 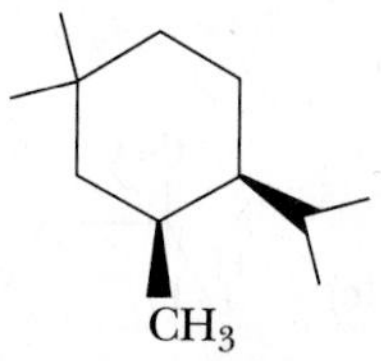

Section 3.7 *Cis–Trans* Isomerism in Cycloalkanes

3.39 What structural feature of cycloalkanes makes *cis–trans* isomerism in them possible?

3.40 Is *cis–trans* isomerism possible in alkanes?

3.41 Name and draw structural formulas for the *cis* and *trans* isomers of 1,2 dimethylcyclopropane. **(See Examples 3.10, 3.11)**

3.42 Name and draw structural formulas for all cycloalkanes with the molecular formula C_5H_{10}. Be certain to include *cis–trans* isomers, as well as constitutional isomers. **(See Examples 3.10, 3.11)**

3.43 Using a planar pentagon representation for the cyclopentane ring, draw structural formulas for the *cis* and *trans* isomers of **(See Examples 3.10, 3.11)**

(a) 1,2-Dimethylcyclopentane
(b) 1,3-Dimethylcyclopentane

3.44 Draw the alternative chair conformations for the *cis* and *trans* isomers of 1,2-dimethylcyclohexane, 1,3-dimethylcyclohexane, and 1,4-dimethylcyclohexane. **(See Examples 3.10, 3.11)**

(a) Indicate by a label whether each methyl group is axial or equatorial.
(b) For which isomer(s) are the alternative chair conformations of equal stability?
(c) For which isomer(s) is one chair conformation more stable than the other?

3.45 Use your answers from Problem 3.44 to complete the following table, showing correlations between *cis, trans* isomers and axial, equatorial positions for disubstituted derivatives of cyclohexane:

Position of Substitution	*cis*	*trans*
1,4-	a,e or e,a	e,e or a,a
1,3-	___ or ___	___ or ___
1,2-	___ or ___	___ or ___

***3.46** There are four *cis–trans* isomers of 2-isopropyl-5-methylcyclohexanol: **(See Examples 3.10, 3.11)**

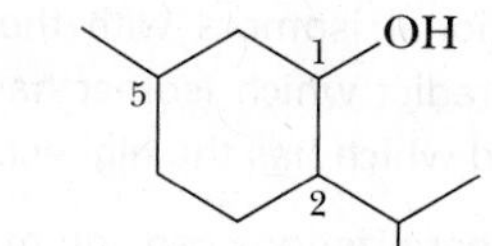

2-Isopropyl-5-methylcyclohexanol

(a) Using a planar hexagon representation for the cyclohexane ring, draw structural formulas for these four isomers.
(b) Draw the more stable chair conformation for each of your answers in part (a).
(c) Of the four *cis–trans* isomers, which is the most stable? If you answered this part correctly, you picked the isomer found in nature and given the name menthol.

© Jose Antonio Santiso Fernández/iStockphoto

Peppermint plant (*Mentha piperita*), a source of menthol, is a perennial herb with aromatic qualities used in candies, gums, hot and cold beverages, and garnish for punch and fruit.

3.47 Draw alternative chair conformations for each substituted cyclohexane, and state which chair is the more stable: **(See Examples 3.8, 3.11)**

(a) 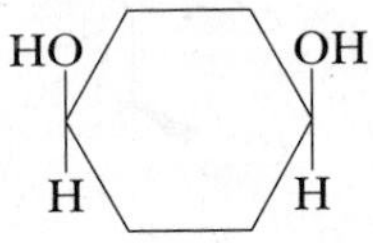

(b) 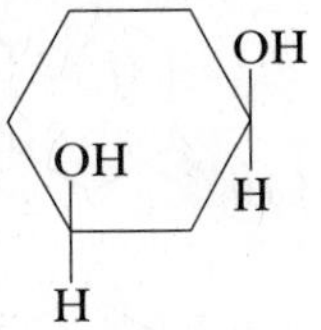

(c) 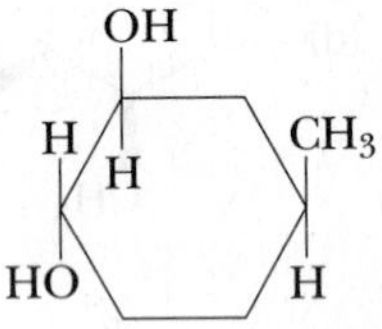

(d) 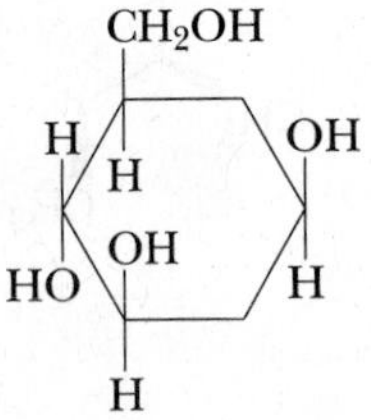

3.48 How many six-membered rings exist in adamantane? What kinds of conformations do the six-membered rings exhibit in adamantane? (*Hint:* Build a molecular model of the compound.)

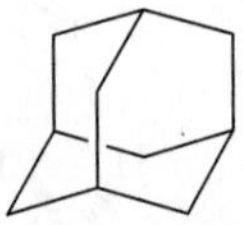

Adamantane

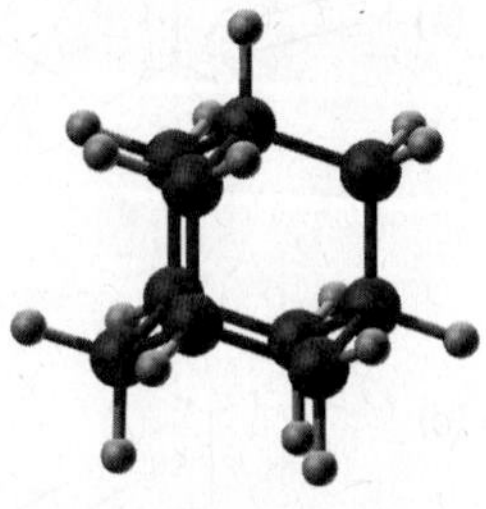

Section 3.8 Physical Properties of Alkanes and Cycloalkanes

3.49 In Problem 3.21, you drew structural formulas for all constitutional isomers with the molecular formula C_7H_{16}. Predict which isomer has the lowest boiling point and which has the highest. **(See Example 3.12)**

3.50 What generalizations can you make about the densities of alkanes relative to that of water?

3.51 What unbranched alkane has about the same boiling point as water? (See Table 3.4.) Calculate the molecular weight of this alkane, and compare it with that of water. Explain why water, which is lower in mass than the alkane, boils at the same temperature.

3.52 As you can see from Table 3.4, each CH_2 group added to the carbon chain of an alkane increases the boiling point of the alkane. The increase is greater going from CH_4 to C_2H_6 and from C_2H_6 to C_3H_8 than it is from C_8H_{18} to C_9H_{20} or from C_9H_{20} to $C_{10}H_{22}$. What do you think is the reason for this trend?

3.53 Dodecane, $C_{12}H_{26}$, is an unbranched alkane. Predict the following:

(a) Will it dissolve in water?
(b) Will it dissolve in hexane?
(c) Will it burn when ignited?
(d) Is it a liquid, solid, or gas at room temperature and atmospheric pressure?
(e) Is it more or less dense than water?

***3.54** As stated in Section 3.8A, the wax found in apple skins is an unbranched alkane with the molecular formula $C_{27}H_{56}$. Explain how the presence of this alkane prevents the loss of moisture from within an apple.

Section 3.9 Reactions of Alkanes

3.55 Write balanced equations for the combustion of each hydrocarbon. Assume that each is converted completely to carbon dioxide and water.

(a) Hexane (b) Cyclohexane (c) 2-Methylpentane

***3.56** Following are heats of combustion of methane and propane:

Hydrocarbon	Component of	ΔH° [kJ/mol (kcal/mol)]
CH_4	natural gas	−886 (−212)
$CH_3CH_2CH_3$	LPG	−2220 (−530)

On a gram-for-gram basis, which of these hydrocarbons is the better source of heat energy?

***3.57** When ethanol is added to gasoline to produce gasohol, the ethanol promotes more complete combustion of the gasoline and is an octane booster (Section 3.10 B). Compare the heats of combustion of 2,2,4-trimethylpentane 5460 kJ/mol (1304 kcal/mol) and ethanol 1369 kJ/mol (327 kcal/mol). Which has the higher heat of combustion in kJ/mol? in kJ/g?

LOOKING AHEAD

3.58 Explain why 1,2-dimethylcyclohexane can exist as *cis–trans* isomers, while 1,2-dimethylcyclododecane cannot.

***3.59** Following is a representation of the glucose molecule (we discuss the structure and chemistry of glucose in Chapter 17):

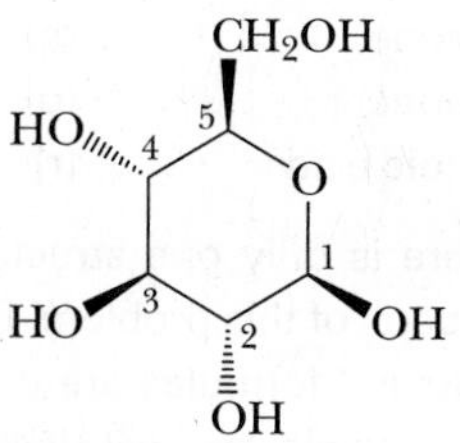

Glucose

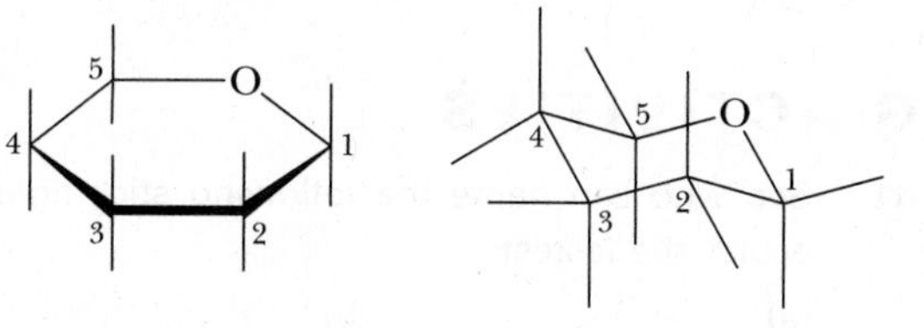

(a) (b)

(a) Convert this representation to a planar hexagon representation.
(b) Convert this representation to a chair conformation. Which substituent groups in the chair conformation are equatorial? Which are axial?

*3.60 Following is the structural formula of cholic acid (Section 19.4A), a component of human bile whose function is to aid in the absorption and digestion of dietary fats:

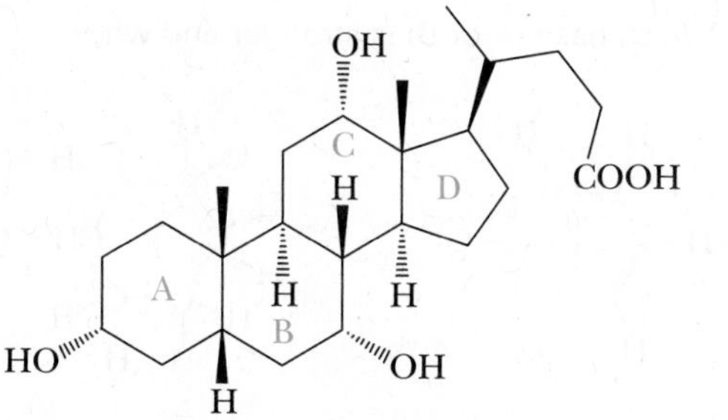

Cholic acid

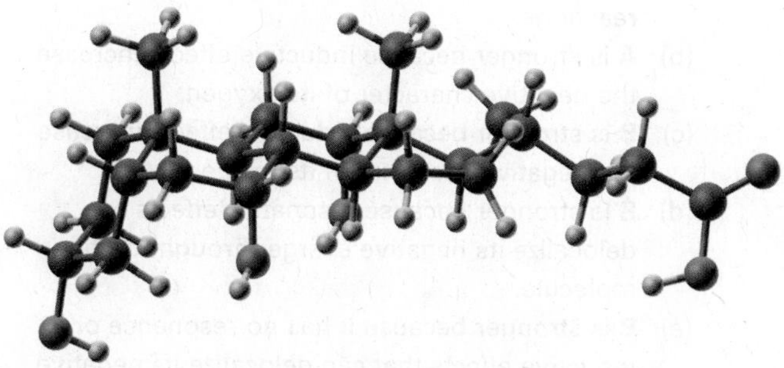

(a) What are the conformations of rings A, B, C, and D?
(b) There are hydroxyl groups on rings A, B, and C. Tell whether each is axial or equatorial.
(c) Is the methyl group at the junction of rings A and B axial or equatorial to ring A? Is it axial or equatorial to ring B?
(d) Is the methyl group at the junction of rings C and D axial or equatorial to ring C?

*3.61 Following is the structural formula and ball-and-stick model of cholestanol:

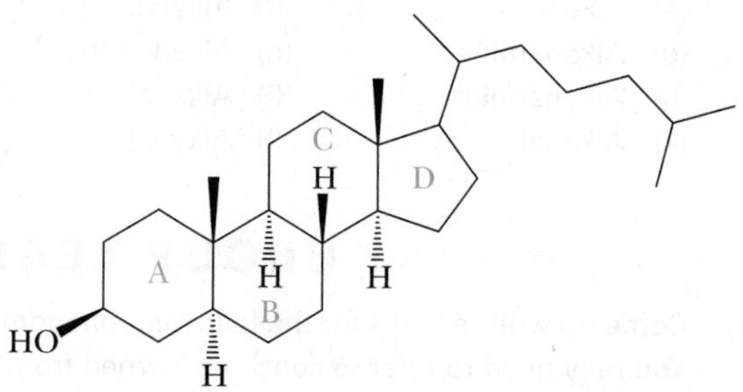

Cholestanol

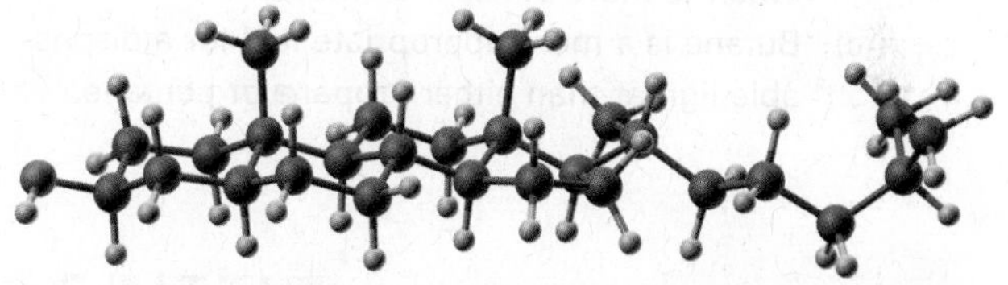

The only difference between this compound and cholesterol (Section 19.4A) is that cholesterol has a carbon–carbon double bond in ring B.

(a) Describe the conformation of rings A, B, C, and D in cholestanol.
(b) Is the hydroxyl group on ring A axial or equatorial?
(c) Consider the methyl group at the junction of rings A and B. Is it axial or equatorial to ring A? Is it axial or equatorial to ring B?
(d) Is the methyl group at the junction of rings C and D axial or equatorial to ring C?

3.62 As we have seen in Section 3.4, the IUPAC system divides the name of a compound into a prefix (showing the number of carbon atoms), an infix (showing the presence of carbon–carbon single, double, or triple bonds), and a suffix (showing the presence of an alcohol, amine, aldehyde, ketone, or carboxylic acid). Assume for the purposes of this problem that, to be alcohol (-ol) or amine (-amine), the hydroxyl or amino group must be bonded to a tetrahedral (sp^3 hybridized) carbon atom.

number of carbon atoms	en / yn	ol / amine / al / one / oic acid
↘	↓	↙

alk-an-e

Given this information, write the structural formula of a compound with an unbranched chain of four carbon atoms that is an:

(a) Alkane (b) Alkene
(c) Alkyne (d) Alkanol
(e) Alkenol (f) Alkynol
(g) Alkanamine (h) Alkenamine
(i) Alkynamine (j) Alkanal
(k) Alkenal (l) Alkynal
(m) Alkanone (n) Alkenone
(o) Alkynone (p) Alkanoic acid
(q) Alkenoic acid (r) Alkynoic acid

(*Note:* There is only one structural formula possible for some parts of this problem. For other parts, two or more structural formulas are possible. Where two or more are possible, we will deal with how the IUPAC system distinguishes among them when we come to the chapters on those particular functional groups.)

GROUP LEARNING ACTIVITIES

***3.63** Come up with reasons for the following phenomena. You may need to refer to concepts learned from previous chapters or from general chemistry.

(a) Gasoline is cool to the touch when spilled on bare skin.
(b) Water is more dense than methane.
(c) Butane is a more appropriate fuel for a disposable lighter than either propane or pentane.

3.64 See who can name the following stick figure molecules the fastest:

(a)

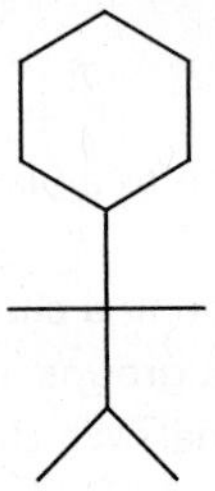

(b)

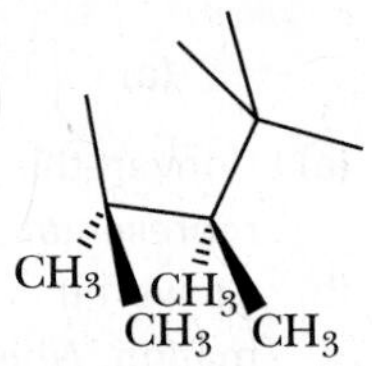

PUTTING IT TOGETHER

The following problems bring together concepts and material from Chapters 1–3.

Choose the best answer for each of the following questions.

1. Which of the following molecules has a net charge of +1?
(a) CH_2CHCH_3 (b) CH_3CHCH_3
(c) $CHCCH_3$ (d) $(CH_3)_3CH$
(e) CH_2CH_2

2. Which of the following statements is true concerning the following compound?

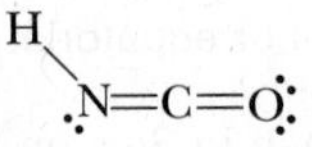

(a) The central carbon is sp^2 hybridized, and the molecule is planar in geometry.
(b) The central carbon is sp^2 hybridized, and the molecule is nonplanar in geometry.
(c) The central carbon is *sp* hybridized, and the molecule is planar in geometry.
(d) The central carbon is *sp* hybridized, and the molecule is nonplanar in geometry.
(e) None of these statements is true.

3. Which of the following statements is false concerning *p* orbitals?
(a) They consist of two equivalent lobes.
(b) They are absent from the first shell of atomic orbitals.
(c) They can form π bonds.
(d) They only participate in bonding on carbon atoms.
(e) They can hold a maximum of two electrons.

4. Which base (A or B) is stronger and why?

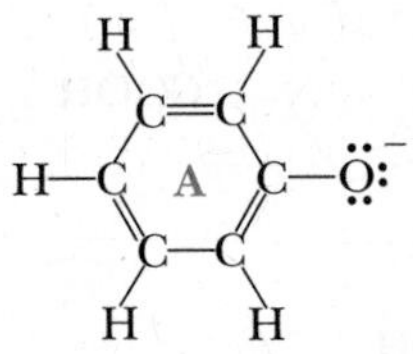

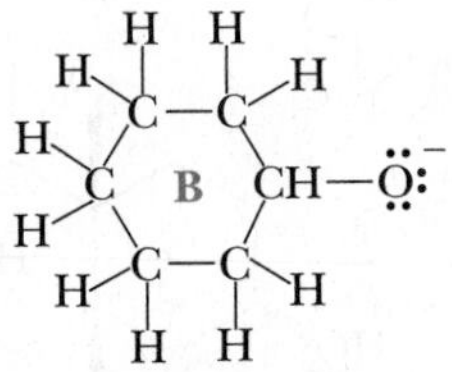

(a) **A** is stronger because it has fewer protons for the acid to compete with in acid–base reactions.
(b) **A** is stronger because inductive effects increase the negative character of its oxygen.
(c) **B** is stronger because inductive effects increase the negative character of its oxygen.
(d) **B** is stronger because resonance effects can delocalize its negative charge throughout the molecule.
(e) **B** is stronger because it has no resonance or inductive effects that can delocalize its negative charge throughout the molecule.

5. Which of the following is the initial product of the reaction between $(CH_3)_3C^+$ and CH_3OH?

(a) 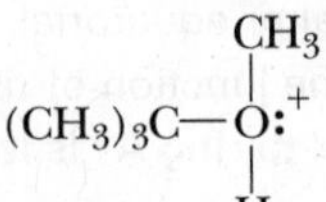

(b) 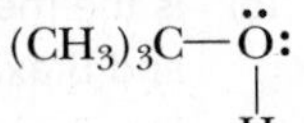

(c) $(CH_3)_3C—\ddot{\underset{..}{O}}{:}^- + H_2$ (d) $(CH_3)_3C—CH_2^- + H_2\ddot{O}{:}$

(e) $(CH_3)_3C—H + CH_3—\ddot{\underset{..}{O}}{:}^-$

6. Select the statement that is false concerning the following acid–base reaction.

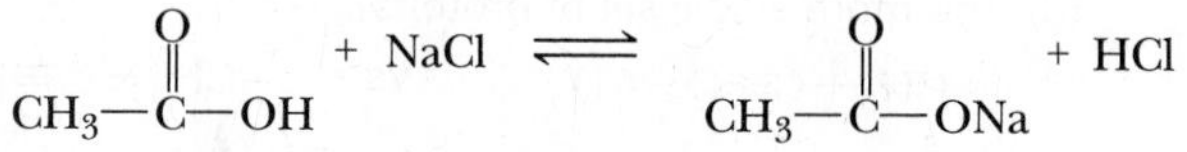

(a) The equilibrium lies on the product side of the reaction.
(b) The carboxylic acid does not possess a positive charge.
(c) The chloride ion acts as a Lewis base.
(d) The chloride ion acts as a Brønsted–Lowry base.
(e) The carboxylic acid is a weaker acid than HCl.

7. Which of the following statements is false?
(a) Nonbonded interaction (steric) strain contributes to the energy of butane in the eclipsed conformation.
(b) All staggered conformations possess zero strain.
(c) A Newman projection is the picture of a molecule viewed down at least one of its bonds.
(d) Bonds represented by Newman projections do not freely rotate because they must overcome an energy barrier to rotation.
(e) Ring strain contributes to the instability of cyclopropane.

8. Which of the following statements is true concerning the isomers *cis*-1,2-dimethylcyclohexane and *cis*-1,3-dimethylcyclohexane?
(a) They are not constitutional isomers.
(b) They are conformers.
(c) The favored conformer of the 1,3-isomer is more stable than that of the 1,2-isomer.
(d) The favored conformer of the 1,3-isomer and that of the 1,2-isomer are equal in energy.
(e) The relative stability of the two molecules cannot be predicted.

9. Select the correct order of stability (least stable → most stable) for the following conformations.

(a)

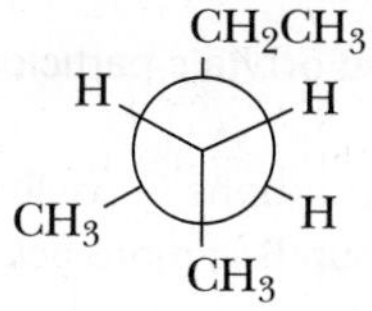

(b)

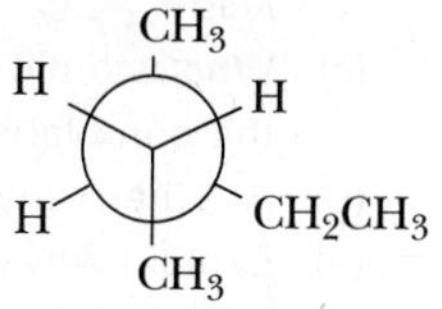

(c)

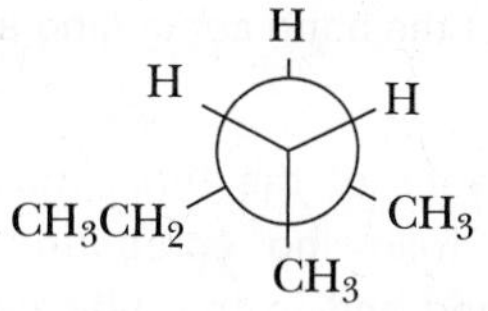

(a) a, b, c   (b) a, c, b   (c) b, a, c
(d) c, a, b   (e) c, b, a

10. Select the most stable conformation of those shown for 1-*tert*-butyl-3,5-dimethylcyclohexane.

(a)

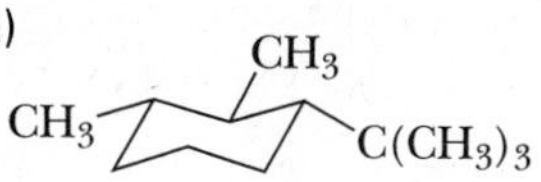

(b)

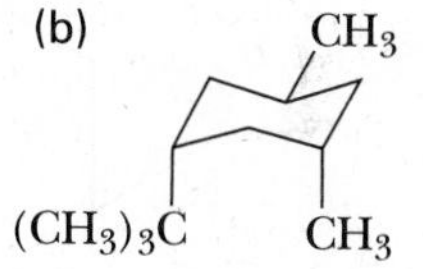

(c)

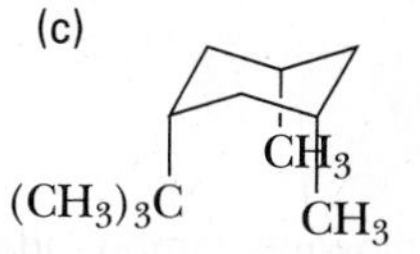

(d)

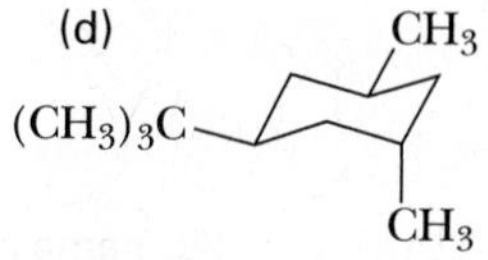

(e)

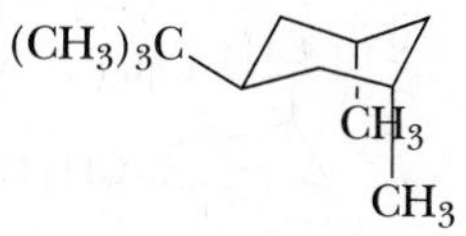

11. Answer the questions that follow regarding the structure of paclitaxel (trade name Taxol®), a compound first isolated from the Pacific Yew tree, which is now used to treat ovarian, breast, and non–small cell lung cancer.
(a) Identify all the hydroxy groups and classify them as 1°, 2°, or 3°.

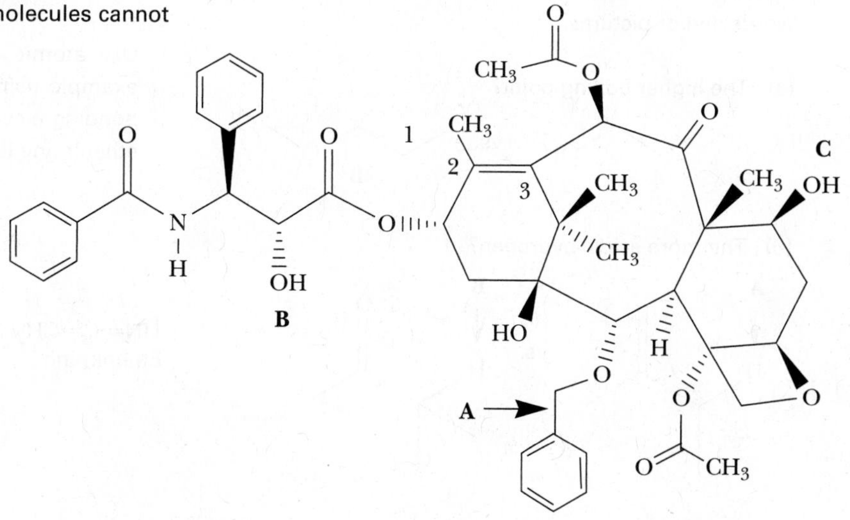

(b) Identify all the carbonyl groups. Are any of them part of an aldehyde, a ketone, or a carboxylic acid?
(c) What atomic or hybridized orbitals participate in the bond labeled **A**?
(d) Are there any quaternary carbons in paclitaxel?
(e) Explain why hydroxyl group **B** is more acidic than hydroxyl group **C**.
(f) What is the angle of the bond containing atoms 1–2–3?

12. Draw Newman projections of the three most stable conformations of the following compound viewed down the indicated bond and in the indicated direction. Indicate the most favorable conformation. You should be able to briefly describe or illustrate why your choice is the most favorable conformation.

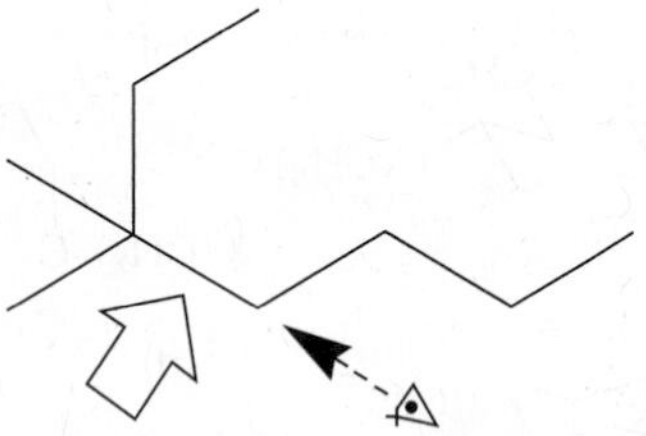

13. Provide IUPAC names for the following compounds.

(a)

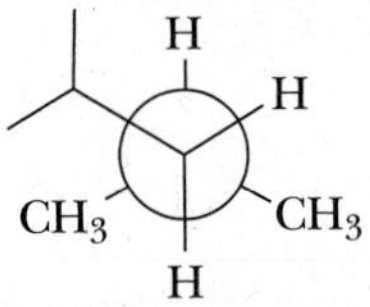

(b)

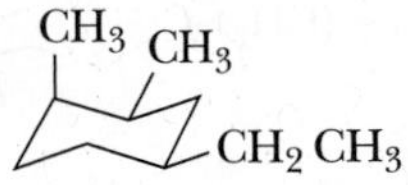

(c) $CH_3CH_2CH(CH_3)CH(CH_2CH_3)CH_2CH(CH_3)_2$

14. For each pair of molecules, select the one that best fits the accompanying description. Provide a concise but thorough rationale for each of your decisions using words and/or pictures.

(a) The higher boiling point?

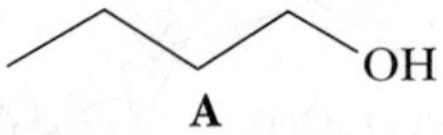

vs.

A **B**

(b) The more acidic hydrogen?

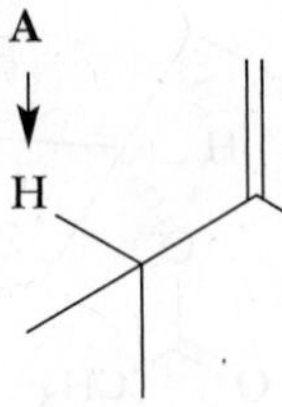

vs.

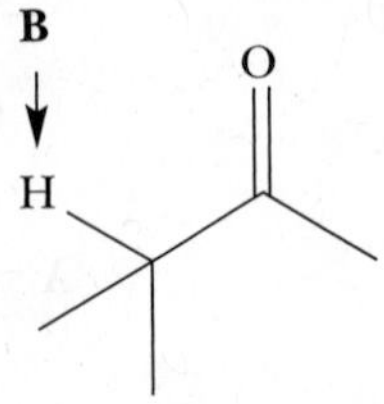

(c) The more basic atom?

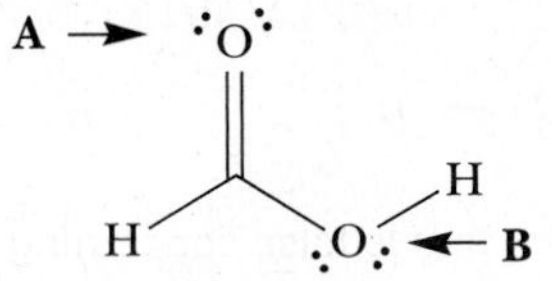

(d) The more acidic set of protons?

$CH_3-C\equiv C-CH_3$ vs. $CH_3-C\equiv N:$

A **B**

(e) The stronger base?

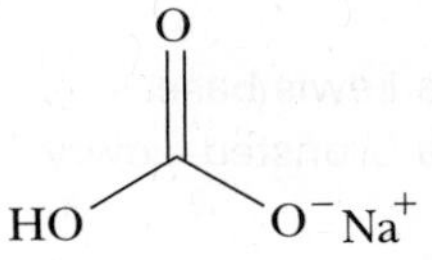

vs.

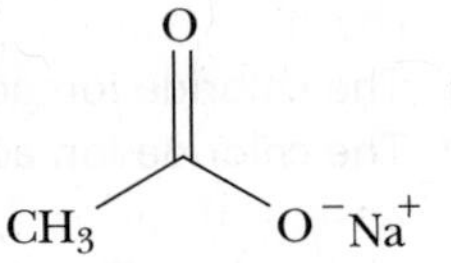

A **B**

(f) Possesses the least nonbonding interaction (steric) strain?

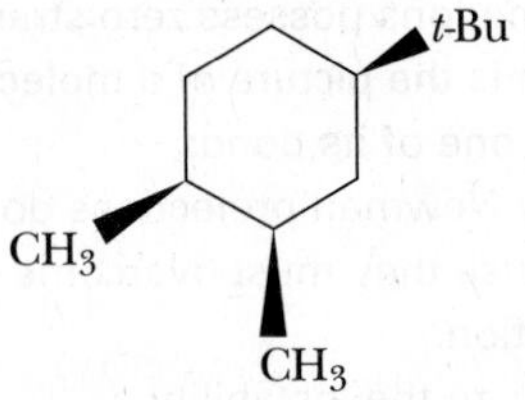

vs.

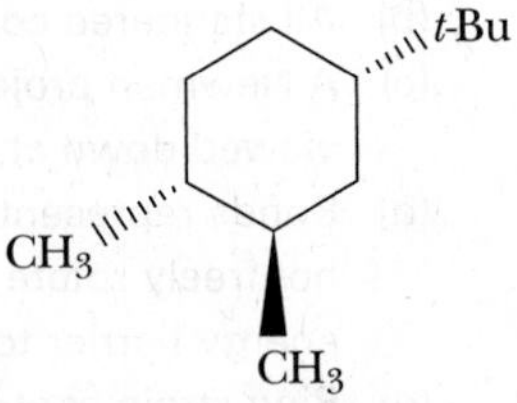

15. Glutamic acid is one of the common amino acids found in nature. Draw the predominant structure of glutamic acid when placed in a solution of p$H = 3.2$ and indicate its overall charge.

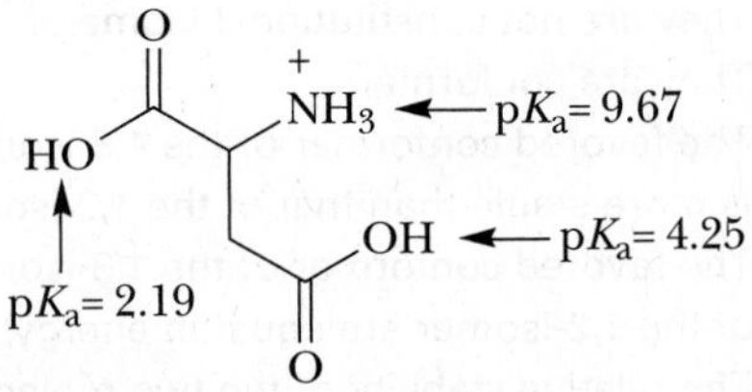

16. Use atomic and hybridized orbitals to illustrate (see example using H_2O) the location of bonding and nonbonding electrons in ethenimine. Do all of the atoms in ethenimine lie in the same plane?

$HN=C=CH_2$
Ethenimine

Example orbital illustration for H_2O

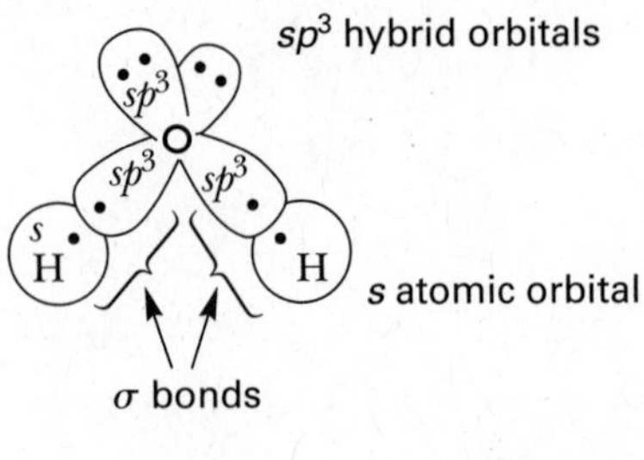

17. The following values have been determined for the amount of energy it takes to place a substituent in the axial position. As shown in the table, going from H to CH_3 causes a drastic increase in free energy (7.28 kJ/mol). However, increasing the size of the R group results in only a minor change in ΔG even when the R group is isopropyl (this only increases ΔG by 1.72 kJ/mol over methyl). *Using perspective (dash-wedge) drawings,* illustrate and explain why the increase in ΔG is only gradual up to isopropyl but increases drastically when the R group is *t*-butyl.

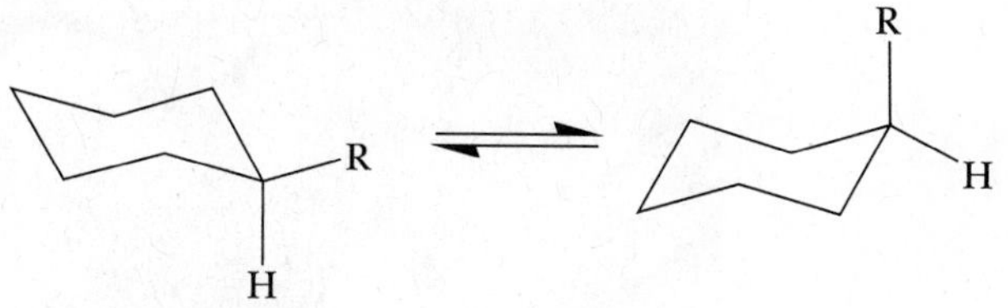

R	ΔG kJ/mol (kcal/mol)
H	0
CH_3	7.28 (1.74)
CH_2CH_3	7.32 (1.75)
$CH(CH_3)_2$	9.00 (2.15)
$C(CH_3)_3$	20.92 (5.00)

18. (a) Draw the two possible products that can form from the Lewis acid–base reaction between methyl formate and BF_3. Indicate the major product and use curved arrow notation to illustrate its formation. Show all charges and nonbonded electrons *in your products.* (b) Use pictures and words to explain why the product you indicated is favored over the other product.

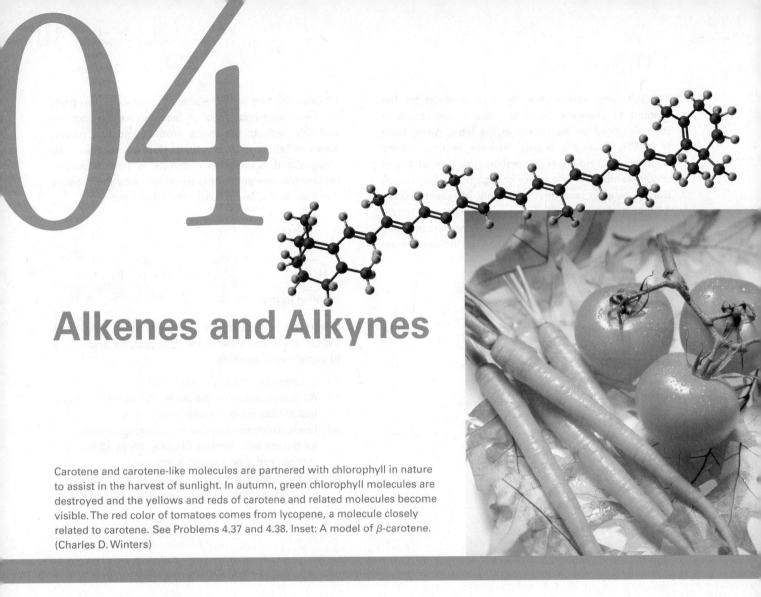

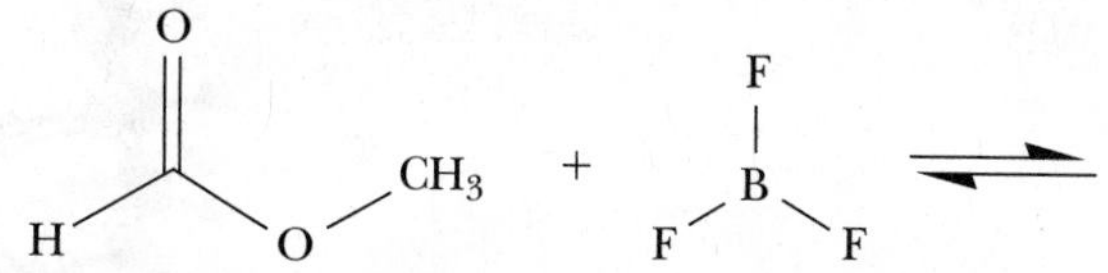

Methyl formate

19. Use resonance theory to predict whether $[CNO]^-$ or $[NCO]^-$ is the more stable ion. Use pictures *and* words to explain your decision.

20. Provide structures as indicated:
    (a) All compounds with the molecular formula C_5H_{10} that exhibit *cis–trans* isomerism.
    (b) Lewis structures and any resonance structures for the ion with formula CH_2NO_2. Show all formal charges and lone pairs of electrons.
    (c) All compounds that upon combustion with 6 mol of O_2 would yield 4 mol of CO_2 and 4 mol of H_2O.

04

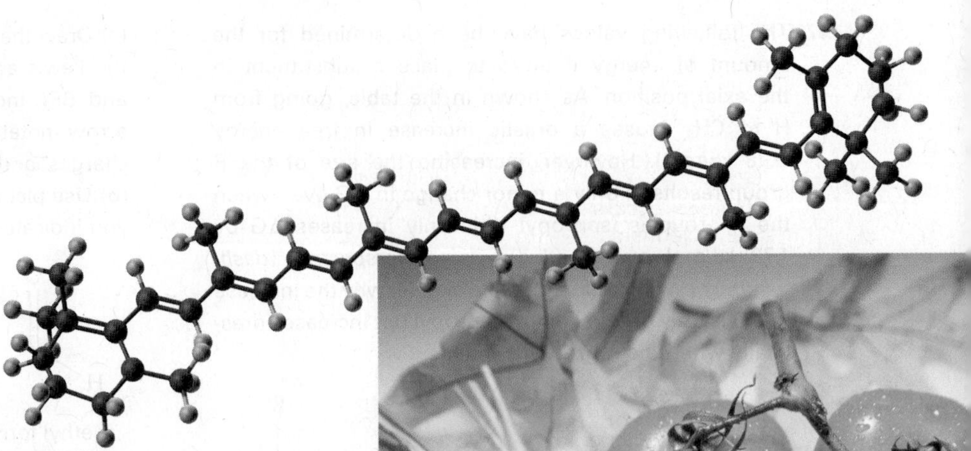

Alkenes and Alkynes

Carotene and carotene-like molecules are partnered with chlorophyll in nature to assist in the harvest of sunlight. In autumn, green chlorophyll molecules are destroyed and the yellows and reds of carotene and related molecules become visible. The red color of tomatoes comes from lycopene, a molecule closely related to carotene. See Problems 4.37 and 4.38. Inset: A model of β-carotene. (Charles D. Winters)

KEY QUESTIONS

HOW TO

CHEMICAL CONNECTIONS

IN THIS CHAPTER, we begin our study of unsaturated hydrocarbons. An unsaturated hydrocarbon is a hydrocarbon that has fewer hydrogens bonded to carbon than an alkane has. There are three classes of unsaturated hydrocarbons: alkenes, alkynes, and arenes. **Alkenes** contain one or more carbon–carbon double bonds, and **alkynes** contain one or more carbon–carbon triple bonds. Ethene (ethylene) is the simplest alkene, and ethyne (acetylene) is the simplest alkyne:

Alkene An unsaturated hydrocarbon that contains a carbon–carbon double bond.

Alkyne An unsaturated hydrocarbon that contains a carbon–carbon triple bond.

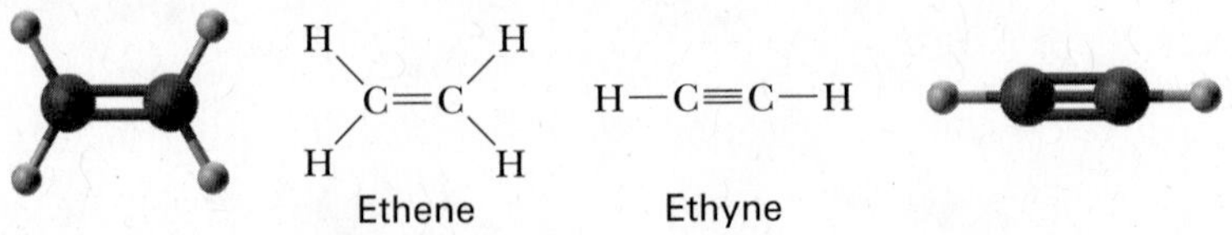

Ethene (an alkene) Ethyne (an alkyne)

Chemical Connections 4A

ETHYLENE, A PLANT GROWTH REGULATOR

Ethylene occurs only in trace amounts in nature. Still, scientists have discovered that this small molecule is a natural ripening agent for fruits. Thanks to this knowledge, fruit growers can pick fruit while it is green and less susceptible to bruising. Then, when they are ready to pack the fruit for shipment, the growers can treat it with ethylene gas to induce ripening. Alternatively, the fruit can be treated with ethephon (Ethrel), which slowly releases ethylene and initiates ripening.

Ethephon $Cl{-}CH_2{-}CH_2{-}P(=O)(OH){-}OH$

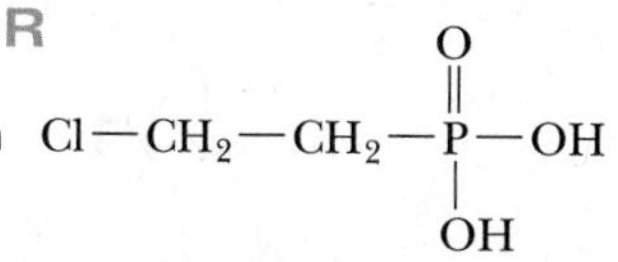

The next time you see ripe bananas in the market, you might wonder when they were picked and whether their ripening was artificially induced.

Question

Explain the basis for the saying "A rotten apple can spoil the barrel."

Arenes are the third class of unsaturated hydrocarbons. The characteristic structural feature of an arene is the presence of one or more benzene rings. The simplest arene is benzene:

Arene A compound containing one or more benzene rings.

although benzene and other arenes contain C–C double bonds, we must remember that their double bonds are not reactive in the ways we will describe in Chapters 5–8 (i.e., we will leave them unreacted in reactions that we cover in these chapters)

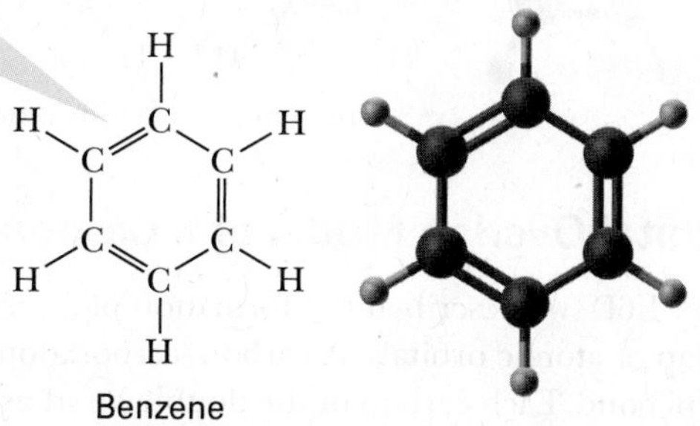

Benzene
(an arene)

The chemistry of benzene and its derivatives is quite different from that of alkenes and alkynes. Even though we do not study the chemistry of arenes until Chapter 9, we will show structural formulas of compounds containing benzene rings in earlier chapters. What you need to remember at this point is that a benzene ring is not chemically reactive under any of the conditions we describe in Chapters 4–8.

Compounds containing carbon–carbon double bonds are especially widespread in nature. Furthermore, several low-molecular-weight alkenes, including ethylene and propene, have enormous commercial importance in our modern, industrialized society. The organic chemical industry produces more pounds of ethylene worldwide than any other chemical. Annual production in the United States alone exceeds 20 billion kg (45 billion pounds).

What is unusual about ethylene is that it occurs only in trace amounts in nature. The enormous amounts of it required to meet the needs of the chemical industry are derived the world over by thermal cracking of hydrocarbons. In the United States and other areas of the world with vast reserves of natural gas, the major process for the production of ethylene is thermal cracking of the small quantities of ethane extracted from natural gas. In **thermal cracking**, a saturated hydrocarbon is converted to an unsaturated hydrocarbon plus H_2. Heating ethane in a furnace to 800–900°C for a fraction of a second cracks it to ethylene and hydrogen.

$$\underset{\text{Ethane}}{CH_3CH_3} \xrightarrow[\text{(thermal cracking)}]{800\text{–}900\,°C} \underset{\text{Ethylene}}{CH_2{=}CH_2} + H_2$$

Europe, Japan, and other areas of the world with limited supplies of natural gas depend almost entirely on thermal cracking of petroleum for their ethylene.

The crucial point to recognize is that ethylene and all of the commercial and industrial products made from it are derived from either natural gas or petroleum—both nonrenewable natural resources!

4.1 What Are the Structures and Shapes of Alkenes and Alkynes?

A. Shapes of Alkenes

Using valence-shell electron-pair repulsion (VSEPR; Section 1.3), we predict a value of 120° for the bond angles about each carbon in a double bond. The observed H—C—C bond angle in ethylene is 121.7°, a value close to that predicted by VSEPR. In other alkenes, deviations from the predicted angle of 120° may be somewhat larger as a result of strain between groups bonded to one or both carbons of the double bond. The C—C—C bond angle in propene, for example, is 124.7°.

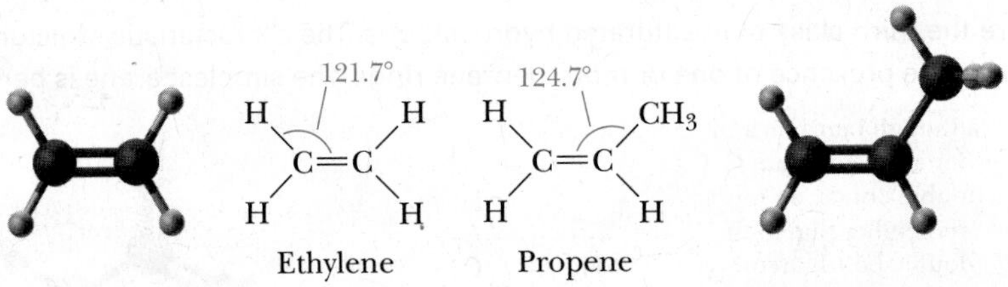

B. Orbital Overlap Model of a Carbon–Carbon Double Bond

In Section 1.6D, we described the formation of a carbon–carbon double bond in terms of the overlap of atomic orbitals. A carbon–carbon double bond consists of one sigma bond and one pi bond. Each carbon of the double bond uses its three sp^2 hybrid orbitals to form sigma bonds to three atoms. The unhybridized $2p$ atomic orbitals, which lie perpendicular to the plane created by the axes of the three sp^2 hybrid orbitals, combine to form the pi bond of the carbon–carbon double bond.

It takes approximately 264 kJ/mol (63 kcal/mol) to break the pi bond in ethylene—that is, to rotate one carbon by 90° with respect to the other so that no overlap occurs between $2p$ orbitals on adjacent carbons (Figure 4.1). This energy is considerably greater than

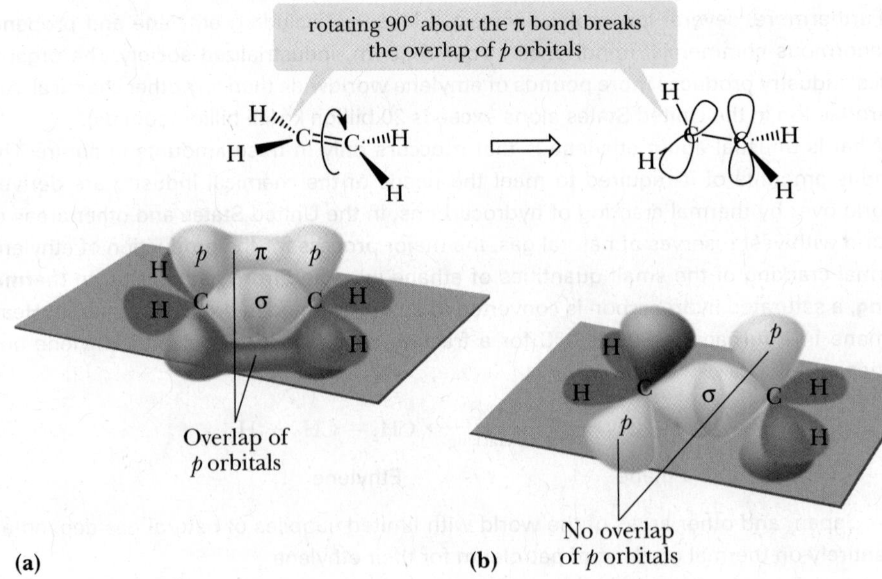

FIGURE 4.1 Restricted rotation about the carbon–carbon double bond in ethylene. (a) Orbital overlap model showing the pi bond. (b) The pi bond is broken by rotating the plane of one H—C—H group by 90° with respect to the plane of the other H—C—H group.

the thermal energy available at room temperature, and, as a consequence, rotation about a carbon–carbon double bond is severely restricted. You might compare rotation about a carbon–carbon double bond, such as the bond in ethylene, with that about a carbon–carbon single bond, such as the bond in ethane (Section 3.6A). Whereas rotation about the carbon–carbon single bond in ethane is relatively free (the energy barrier is approximately 13 kJ/mol), rotation about the carbon–carbon double bond in ethylene is restricted (the energy barrier is approximately 264 kJ/mol).

C. *Cis–Trans* Isomerism in Alkenes

Cis–trans isomerism Isomers that have the same order of attachment of their atoms, but a different arrangement of their atoms in space due to the presence of either a ring (Chapter 3) or a carbon–carbon double bond (Chapter 4).

Because of restricted rotation about a carbon–carbon double bond, an alkene in which each carbon of the double bond has two different groups bonded to it shows *cis–trans* isomerism.

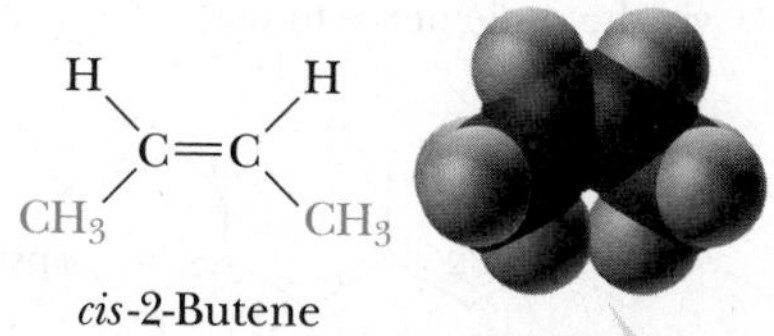

cis-2-Butene
mp −139 °C, bp 4 °C

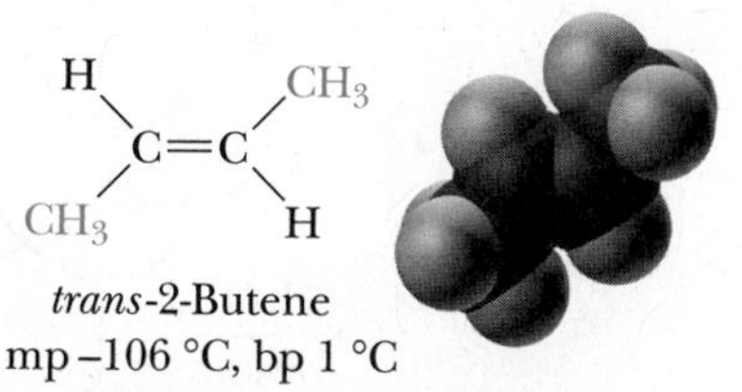

trans-2-Butene
mp −106 °C, bp 1 °C

nonbonded interaction (steric) strain makes *cis*-2-butene less stable than *trans*-2-butene

Consider, for example, 2-butene: In *cis*-2-butene, the two methyl groups are on the same side of the double bond; in *trans*-2-butene, the two methyl groups are on opposite sides of the double bond. These two compounds cannot be converted into one another at room temperature because of the restricted rotation about the double bond; they are different compounds, with different physical and chemical properties.

It takes approximately 264 kJ (63 kcal/mol) to break the π bond of ethylene—that is, to rotate one carbon by 90° with respect to the other where there is zero overlap between the 2*p* orbitals of adjacent carbons (Figure 4.1). This energy is considerably greater than the thermal energy available at room temperature; consequently, rotation about a carbon–carbon double bond does not occur under normal conditions.

Cis alkenes are less stable than their *trans* isomers because of nonbonded interaction strain between alkyl substituents on the same side of the double bond in the *cis* isomer, as can be seen in space-filling models of the *cis* and *trans* isomers of 2-butene. This is the same type of steric strain that results in the preference for equatorial methylcyclohexane over axial methylcyclohexane (Section 3.6B).

Charles D. Winters

The combustion of acetylene yields energy that produces the very hot temperatures of an oxyacetylene torch.

Chemical Connections 4B

CIS–TRANS ISOMERISM IN VISION

The retina—the light-detecting layer in the back of our eyes—contains reddish compounds called *visual pigments*. Their name, *rhodopsin*, is derived from the Greek word meaning "rose colored." Each rhodopsin molecule is a combination of one molecule of a protein called opsin and one molecule of 11-*cis*-retinal, a derivative of vitamin A in which the CH_2OH group of the vitamin is converted to an aldehyde group, —CHO, and the double bond between carbons 11 and 12 of the side chain is in the less stable *cis* configuration. When rhodopsin absorbs light energy, the less stable 11-*cis* double bond is converted to the more stable 11-*trans* double bond. This isomerization changes the shape of the rhodopsin molecule, which in turn causes the neurons of the optic nerve to fire and produce a visual image.

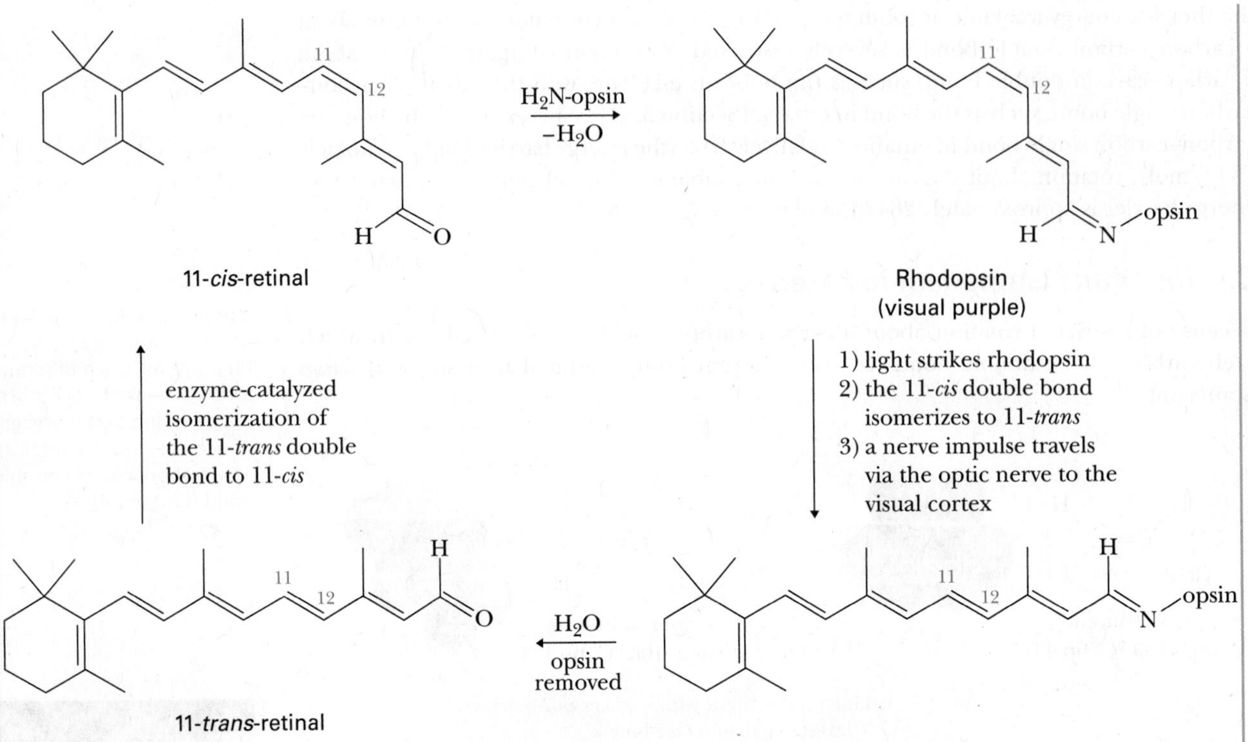

The retina of vertebrates has two kinds of cells that contain rhodopsin: rods and cones. Cones function in bright light and are used for color vision; they are concentrated in the central portion of the retina, called the *macula*, and are responsible for the greatest visual acuity. The remaining area of the retina consists mostly of rods, which are used for peripheral and night vision. 11-*cis*-Retinal is present in both cones and rods. Rods have one kind of opsin, whereas cones have three kinds—one for blue, one for green, and one for red color vision.

Question

The four *trans* double bonds in the side chain of retinal are labeled a–d. Double bond c (between carbons 11 and 12) is isomerized to its *cis* isomer by an enzyme in the body. Which of the other three double bonds in the side chain of retinal would yield the least stable isomer of *cis* retinal if it were to be isomerized? (*Hint:* Think steric strain.)

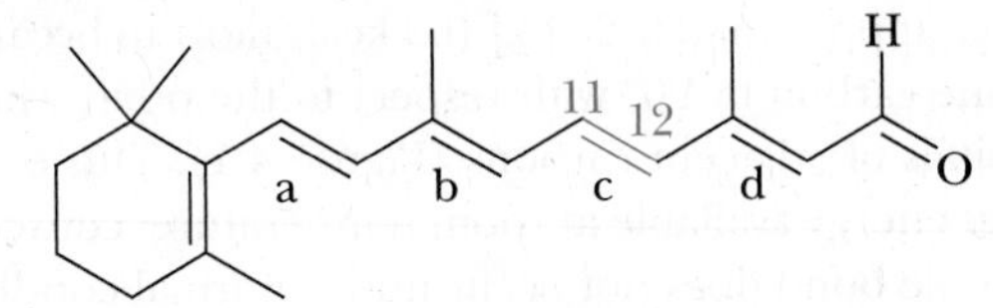

11-*trans*-retinal

D. Structure of Alkynes

The functional group of an alkyne is a **carbon–carbon triple bond**. The simplest alkyne is ethyne, C_2H_2. Ethyne is a linear molecule; all of its bond angles are 180° (Figure 1.10).

According to the orbital overlap model (Section 1.6F), a triple bond is described in terms of the overlap of *sp* hybrid orbitals of adjacent carbons to form a sigma bond, the overlap of parallel $2p_y$ orbitals to form one pi bond, and the overlap of parallel $2p_z$ orbitals to form the second pi bond. In ethyne, each carbon forms a bond to a hydrogen by the overlap of an *sp* hybrid orbital of carbon with a 1*s* atomic orbital of hydrogen.

4.2 How Do We Name Alkenes and Alkynes?

Alkenes are named using the IUPAC system, but, as we shall see, some are still referred to by their common names.

A. IUPAC Names

We form IUPAC names of alkenes by changing the **-an-** infix of the parent alkane to **-en-** (Section 3.5). Hence, $CH_2{=}CH_2$ is named ethene, and $CH_3CH{=}CH_2$ is named propene. In higher alkenes, where isomers exist that differ in the location of the double bond, we use a numbering system. We number the longest carbon chain that contains the double bond in the direction that gives the carbon atoms of the double bond the lower set of numbers. We then use the number of the first carbon of the double bond to show its location. We name branched or substituted alkenes in a manner similar to the way we name alkanes (Section 3.3). We number the carbon atoms, locate the double bond, locate and name substituent groups, and name the main (parent) chain.

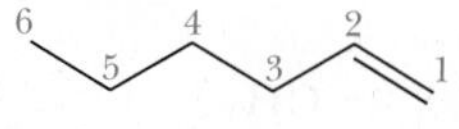

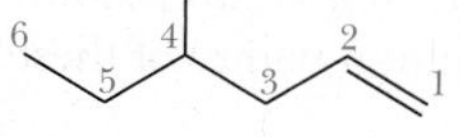

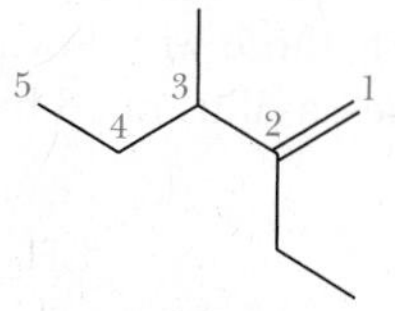

in naming alkenes, the parent chain is the longest chain containing the entire C=C bond, even if a different chain that doesn't contain the C=C bond is longer

$\overset{6}{C}H_3\overset{5}{C}H_2\overset{4}{C}H_2\overset{3}{C}H_2\overset{2}{C}H{=}\overset{1}{C}H_2$ — 1-Hexene

$\overset{6}{C}H_3\overset{5}{C}H_2\overset{4}{C}H(CH_3)\overset{3}{C}H_2\overset{2}{C}H{=}\overset{1}{C}H_2$ — 4-Methyl-1-hexene

$\overset{5}{C}H_3\overset{4}{C}H_2\overset{3}{C}H(CH_3)\overset{2}{C}(CH_2CH_3){=}\overset{1}{C}H_2$ — 2-Ethyl-3-methyl-1-pentene

Note that there is a six-carbon chain in 2-ethyl-3-methyl-1-pentene. However, because the longest chain that contains the carbon–carbon double bond has only five carbons, the parent hydrocarbon is pentane, and we name the molecule as a disubstituted 1-pentene.

We form IUPAC names of alkynes by changing the **-an-** infix of the parent alkane to **-yn-** (Section 3.5). Thus, $HC{\equiv}CH$ is named ethyne, and $CH_3C{\equiv}CH$ is named propyne. The IUPAC system retains the name *acetylene*; therefore, there are two acceptable names for $HC{\equiv}CH$: *ethyne* and *acetylene*. Of these two names, *acetylene* is used much more frequently. For larger molecules, we number the longest carbon chain that contains the triple bond from the end that gives the triply bonded carbons the lower set of numbers. We indicate the location of the triple bond by the number of the first carbon of the triple bond.

$\overset{4}{C}H_3\overset{3}{C}H(CH_3)\overset{2}{C}{\equiv}\overset{1}{C}H$

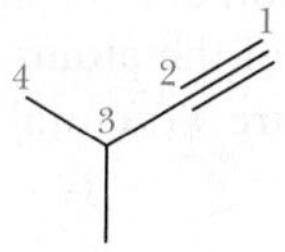

3-Methyl-1-butyne

$\overset{1}{C}H_3\overset{2}{C}H_2\overset{3}{C}{\equiv}\overset{4}{C}\overset{5}{C}H_2\overset{6}{C}(CH_3)_2\overset{7}{C}H_3$

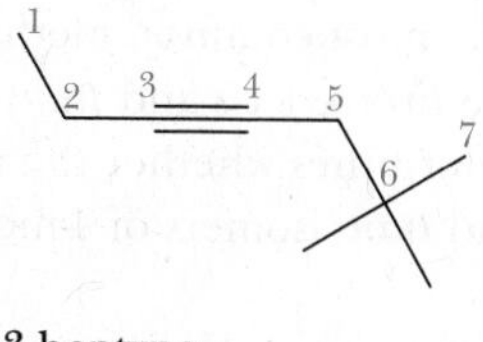

6,6-Dimethyl-3-heptyne

EXAMPLE 4.1

Write the IUPAC name of each unsaturated hydrocarbon:

(a) $CH_2{=}CH(CH_2)_5CH_3$ **(b)** 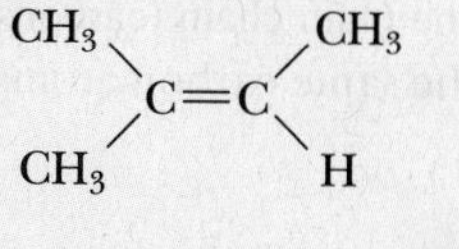 **(c)** $CH_3(CH_2)_2C{\equiv}CCH_3$

STRATEGY

First look for the longest carbon chain that contains the multiple bond. This chain determines the root name. Number the carbon chain to give the placement of the multiple bond the lowest possible set of numbers. Then identify substituents and give each a name and a number. Locate the position of the multiple bond by the number of its first carbon.

SOLUTION

(a) 1-Octene **(b)** 2-Methyl-2-butene **(c)** 2-Hexyne

See problems 4.15–4.20

PROBLEM 4.1

Write the IUPAC name of each unsaturated hydrocarbon:

(a)  (b) 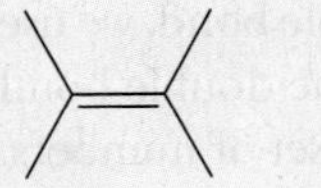 (c) 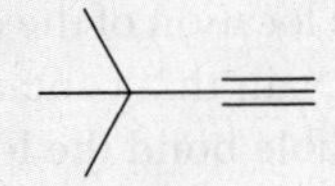

B. Common Names

Despite the precision and universal acceptance of IUPAC nomenclature, some alkenes, particularly those with low molecular weight, are known almost exclusively by their common names, as illustrated by the common names of these alkenes:

	$CH_2{=}CH_2$	$CH_3CH{=}CH_2$	$CH_3C(CH_3){=}CH_2$
IUPAC name:	Ethene	Propene	2-Methylpropene
Common name:	Ethylene	Propylene	Isobutylene

Furthermore, the common names **methylene** (a CH_2 group), **vinyl**, and **allyl** are often used to show the presence of the following alkenyl groups.

Alkenyl Group	Common Name	Example	Common Name
$CH_2{=}CH{-}$	Vinyl	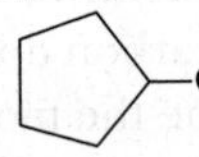 $-CH{=}CH_2$	Vinylcyclopentane
$CH_2{=}CHCH_2{-}$	Allyl	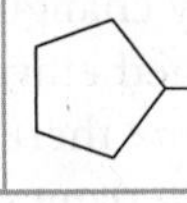 $-CH_2CH{=}CH_2$	Allylcyclopentane

C. Systems for Designating Configuration in Alkenes

The *Cis–Trans* System

The most common method for specifying the configuration of a disubstituted alkene uses the prefixes *cis* and *trans.* In this system, the orientation of the atoms of the parent chain determines whether the alkene is *cis* or *trans.* Following are structural formulas for the *cis* and *trans* isomers of 4-methyl-2-pentene:

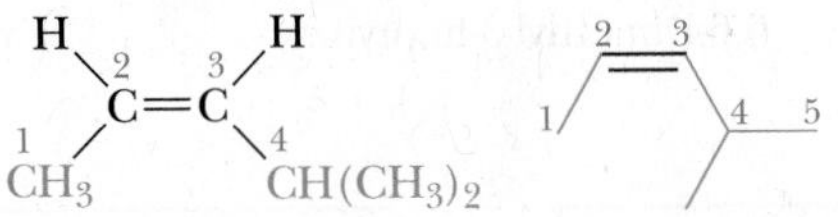

cis-4-Methyl-2-pentene

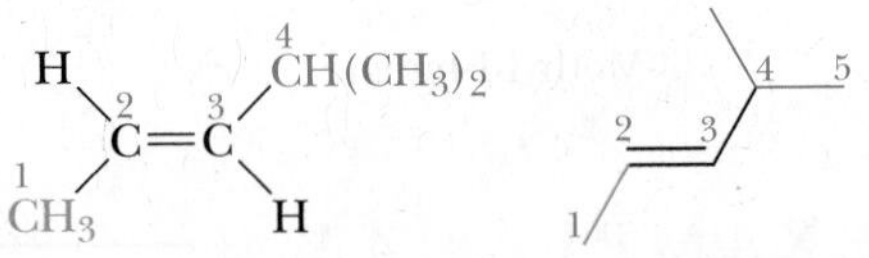

trans-4-Methyl-2-pentene

In the *cis* example, carbon atoms of the main chain (carbons 1 and 4) are on the same side of the double bond. In the *trans* example, the same carbon atoms of the main chain are on opposite sides of the double bond.

EXAMPLE 4.2

Name each alkene, and, using the *cis–trans* system, show the configuration about each double bond:

(a) 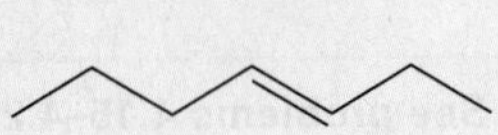 (b) 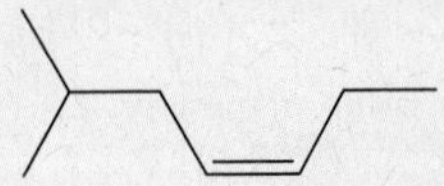

STRATEGY

Locate the longest carbon chain that contains the multiple bond and number it from the end that gives the lower set of numbers to the carbon atoms of the multiple bond. Indicate the location of the multiple bond by the number of its first carbon atom. Configuration of a carbon–carbon double bond (*cis* or *trans*) in a common name is determined by the orientation of the carbon atoms of the parent chain relative to each other. If you are having difficulty discerning the orientation of the carbon atoms, draw in the hydrogen atoms on the C=C bond and determine their orientation relative to each other.

SOLUTION

(a) The chain contains seven carbon atoms and is numbered from the end that gives the lower number to the first carbon of the double bond. The carbon atoms of the parent chain are on opposite sides of the double bond. The compound's name is *trans*-3-heptene.

(b) The longest chain contains seven carbon atoms and is numbered from the right, so that the first carbon of the double bond is carbon 3 of the chain. The carbon atoms of the parent chain are on the same side of the double bond. The compound's name is *cis*-6-methyl-3-heptene.

See problems 4.21, 4.22

PROBLEM 4.2

Name each alkene, and, using the *cis–trans* system, specify its configuration:

(a) 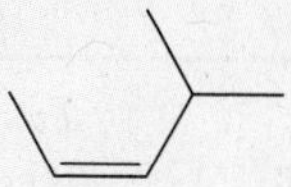

(b) 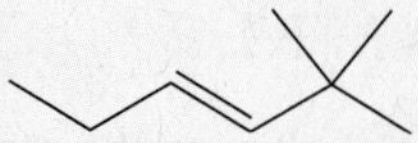

The E,Z System

The **E,Z system** must be used for tri- and tetrasubstituted alkenes. This system uses a set of rules to assign priorities to the substituents on each carbon of a double bond. If the groups of higher priority are on the same side of the double bond, the configuration of the alkene is **Z** (German: *zusammen*, together). If the groups of higher priority are on opposite sides of the double bond, the configuration is **E** (German: *entgegen*, opposite).

Z (*zusammen*) **E** (*entgegen*)

E,Z system A system used to specify the configuration of groups about a carbon–carbon double bond.

Z From the German *zusammen*, meaning together; specifies that groups of higher priority on the carbons of a double bond are on the same side.

E From the German *entgegen*, meaning opposite; specifies that groups of higher priority on the carbons of a double bond are on opposite sides.

The first step in assigning an E or a Z configuration to a double bond is to label the two groups bonded to each carbon in order of priority.

Priority Rules

1. Priority is based on atomic number: The higher the atomic number, the higher is the priority. Following are several substituents arranged in order of increasing priority (the atomic number of the atom determining priority is shown in parentheses):

$$\underset{(1)}{-H},\ \underset{(6)}{-CH_3},\ \underset{(7)}{-NH_2},\ \underset{(8)}{-OH},\ \underset{(16)}{-SH},\ \underset{(17)}{-Cl},\ \underset{(35)}{-Br},\ \underset{(53)}{-I}$$

Increasing priority →

2. If priority cannot be assigned on the basis of the atoms that are bonded directly to the double bond, look at the next set of atoms, and continue until a priority can be assigned. Priority is assigned at the first point of difference. Following is a series of groups, arranged in order of increasing priority (again, numbers in parentheses give the atomic number of the atom on which the assignment of priority is based):

$$\underset{(1)}{-CH_2-H}\quad \underset{(6)}{-CH_2-CH_3}\quad \underset{(7)}{-CH_2-NH_2}\quad \underset{(8)}{-CH_2-OH}\quad \underset{(17)}{-CH_2-Cl}$$

Increasing priority →

3. In order to compare carbons that are not sp^3 hybridized, the carbons must be manipulated in a way that allows us to maximize the number of groups bonded to them. Thus, we treat atoms participating in a double or triple bond as if they are bonded to an equivalent number of similar atoms by single bonds; that is, atoms of a double bond are replicated. Accordingly,

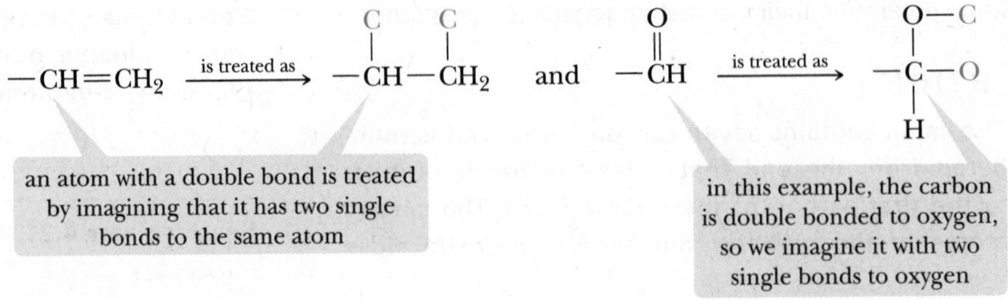
is treated as
and
is treated as
an atom with a double bond is treated by imagining that it has two single bonds to the same atom
in this example, the carbon is double bonded to oxygen, so we imagine it with two single bonds to oxygen

EXAMPLE 4.3

Assign priorities to the groups in each set:

(a)
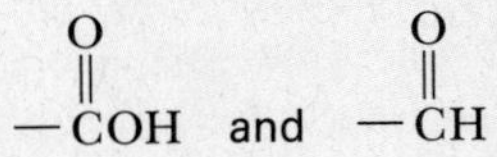

(b)
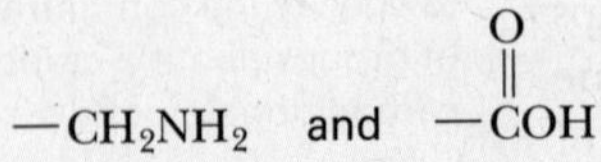

STRATEGY

Priority is based on atomic number; the higher the atomic number, the higher the priority. If priority cannot be determined on the basis of the atoms bonded directly to the carbon–carbon double bond, continue to the next set of atoms and continue in this manner until a priority can be assigned.

See problems 4.23, 4.27, 4.28, 4.32

SOLUTION

(a) The first point of difference is the O of the —OH in the carboxyl group, compared with the —H in the aldehyde group. The carboxyl group is higher in priority:

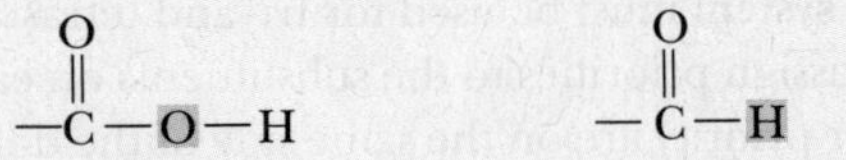

Carboxyl group (higher priority) | Aldehyde group (lower priority)

(b) Oxygen has a higher priority (higher atomic number) than nitrogen. Therefore, the carboxyl group has a higher priority than the primary amino group:

lower priority | higher priority

EXAMPLE 4.4

Name each alkene and specify its configuration by the E,Z system:

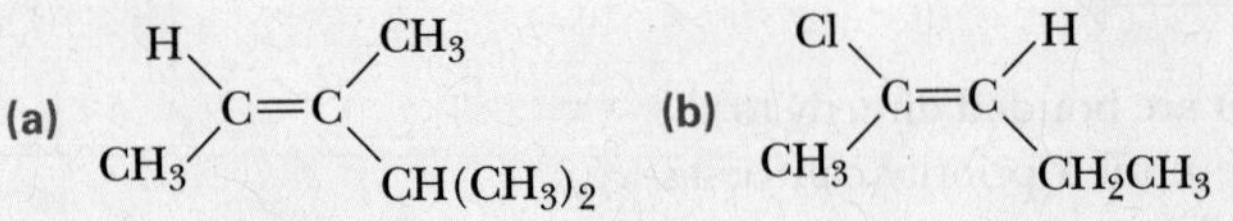

STRATEGY

Assign a priority to each atom or group of atoms on the carbon–carbon double bond. If the groups of higher priority are on the same side of the double bond, the alkene has the Z configuration; if they are on opposite sides, the alkene has the E configuration.

SOLUTION

(a) The group of higher priority on carbon 2 is methyl; that of higher priority on carbon 3 is isopropyl. Because the groups of higher priority are on the same side of the carbon–carbon double bond, the alkene has the Z configuration. Its name is (*Z*)-3,4-dimethyl-2-pentene.

(b) Groups of higher priority on carbons 2 and 3 are —Cl and $—CH_2CH_3$. Because these groups are on opposite sides of the double bond, the configuration of this alkene is E, and its name is (*E*)-2-chloro-2-pentene.

See problems 4.23, 4.27, 4.28, 4.32

PROBLEM 4.3

Name each alkene and specify its configuration by the E,Z system:

(a) 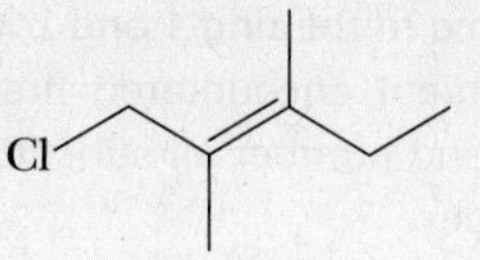

(b) 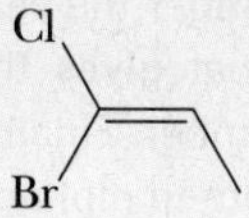

(c) 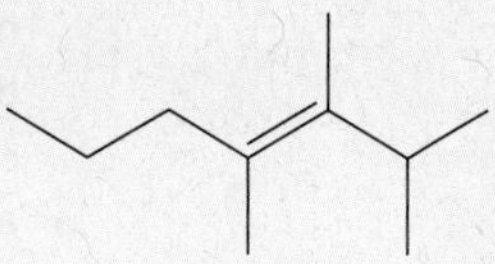

HOW TO 4.1

Name an Alkene

As an example of how to name an alkene, consider the following alkene, drawn here as a line-angle formula.

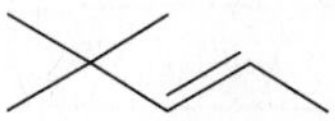

1. *Determine the parent chain, that is, the longest chain of carbon atoms that contains the functional group.*

   In this example, the parent chain is five carbon atoms, making the compound a disubstituted pentene.

2. *Number the parent chain from the end that gives the carbon atoms of the double bond the lower set of numbers.*

   In this example, the parent chain is a disubstituted 2-pentene.

   when numbering an alkene, give the C=C bond priority over any alkyl substituents

   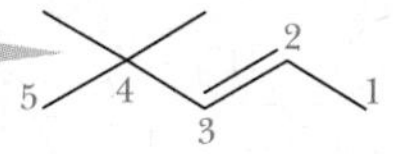

   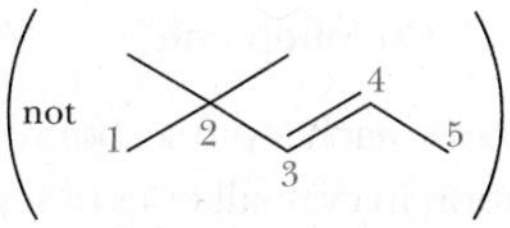

3. *Name and locate the substituents on the parent chain.*

   There are two methyl substituents on carbon 4 of the parent chain, and they are named 4,4-dimethyl-. The name to this point is 4,4-dimethyl-2-pentene.

4. *Determine whether the molecule shows* cis–trans *isomerism. If it does, use either the cis–trans or the E,Z system to specify the configuration.*

   In this example, the molecule shows *cis–trans* isomerism, and the double bond has the *trans* configuration. Therefore, the IUPAC name is *trans*-4,4-dimethyl-2-pentene.

   Note that the double bond locator may be placed either before the parent name, as in the name just given, or immediately before the infix specifying the double bond to give the name *trans*-4,4-dimethylpent-2-ene.

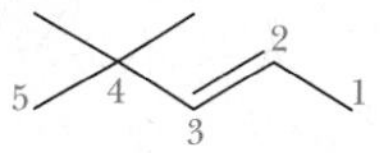

***trans*-4,4-Dimethyl-2-pentene**
or
***trans*-4,4-Dimethylpent-2-ene**
or
(*E*)-4,4-Dimethyl-2-pentene

D. Naming Cycloalkenes

In naming **cycloalkenes**, we number the carbon atoms of the ring double bond 1 and 2 in the direction that gives the substituent encountered first the smaller number. We name and locate substituents and list them in alphabetical order, as in the following compounds:

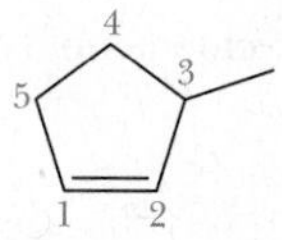

3-Methylcyclopentene
(not 5-methylcyclopentene)

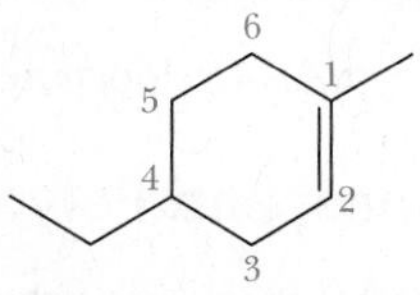

4-Ethyl-1-methylcyclohexene
(not 5-ethyl-2-methylcyclohexene)

EXAMPLE 4.5

Write the IUPAC name for each cycloalkene:

(a) 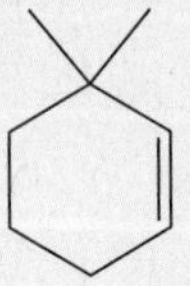

(b) 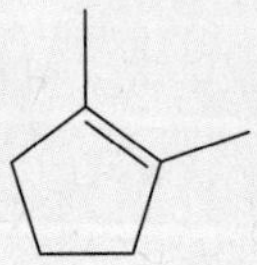

(c) 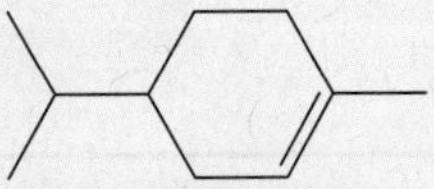

STRATEGY

The parent name of a cycloalkene is derived from the name of the alkene with the same number of carbon atoms (e.g., for a 6-carbon cycloalkene, use "cyclohexene" as the parent name). Number the carbon atoms of the ring 1 and 2 in the direction that gives the substituent encountered first the smaller number. Finally, name and number all substituents and list them in alphabetical order.

SOLUTION

(a) 3,3-Dimethylcyclohexene
(b) 1,2-Dimethylcyclopentene
(c) 4-Isopropyl-1-methylcyclohexene

See problems 4.15–4.20

PROBLEM 4.4

Write the IUPAC name for each cycloalkene:

(a) 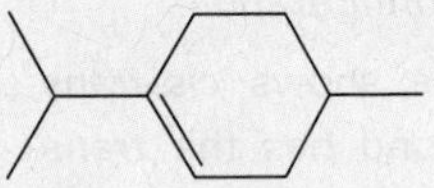

(b) 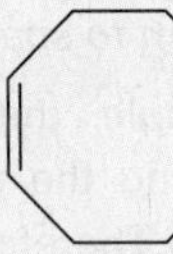

(c) 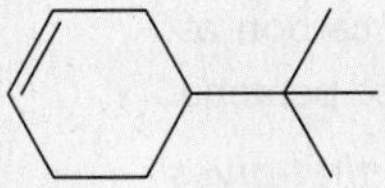

E. *Cis–Trans* Isomerism in Cycloalkenes

Following are structural formulas for four cycloalkenes:

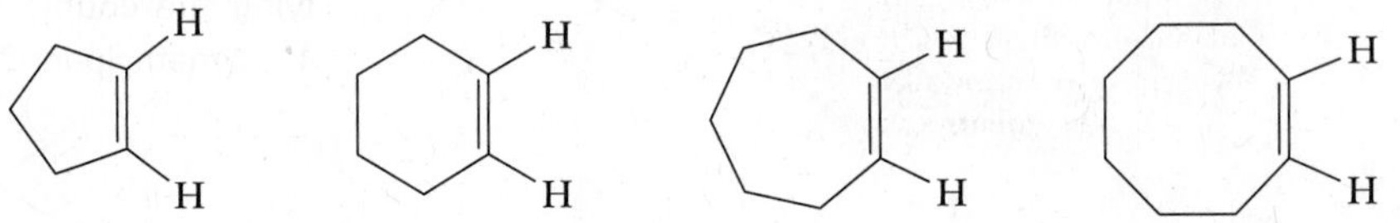

Cyclopentene   Cyclohexene   Cycloheptene   Cyclooctene

In these representations, the configuration about each double bond is *cis*. Because of angle strain, it is not possible to have a *trans* configuration in cycloalkenes of seven or fewer carbons. To date, *trans*-cyclooctene is the smallest *trans*-cycloalkene that has been prepared in pure form and is stable at room temperature. Yet, even in this *trans*-cycloalkene, there is considerable intramolecular strain. *cis*-Cyclooctene is more stable than its *trans* isomer by 38 kJ/mol (9.1 kcal/mol).

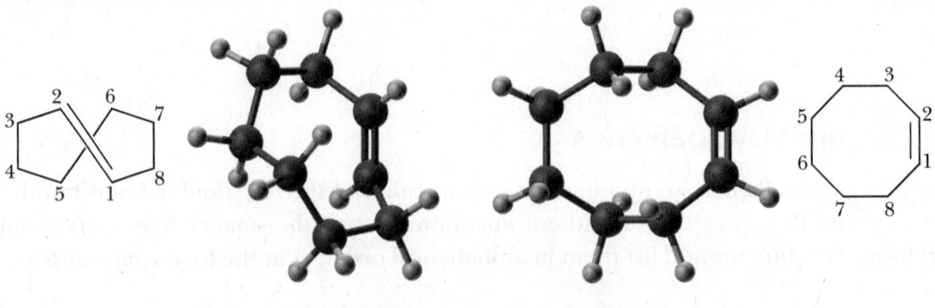

trans-Cyclooctene   *cis*-Cyclooctene

F. Dienes, Trienes, and Polyenes

We name alkenes that contain more than one double bond as alkadienes, alkatrienes, and so forth. We refer to those that contain several double bonds more generally as polyenes (Greek: *poly*, many). Following are three examples of dienes:

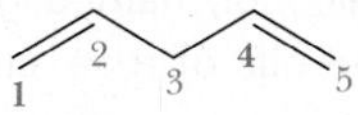

$CH_2{=}CHCH_2CH{=}CH_2$

1,4-Pentadiene

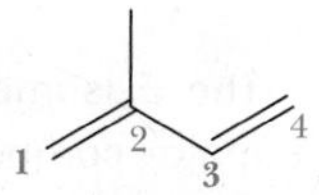

$CH_2{=}C(CH_3)CH{=}CH_2$

2-Methyl-1,3-butadiene (Isoprene)

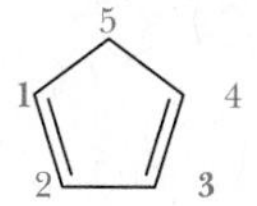

1,3-Cyclopentadiene

G. *Cis–Trans* Isomerism in Dienes, Trienes, and Polyenes

Thus far, we have considered *cis–trans* isomerism in alkenes containing only one carbon–carbon double bond. For an alkene with one carbon–carbon double bond that can show *cis–trans* isomerism, two *cis–trans* isomers are possible. For an alkene with ***n*** carbon–carbon double bonds, each of which can show *cis–trans* isomerism, $\mathbf{2^n}$ *cis–trans* isomers are possible.

EXAMPLE 4.6

How many *cis–trans* isomers are possible for 2,4-heptadiene?

STRATEGY

Determine which of the carbon–carbon double bonds can show *cis–trans* isomerism. The number of *cis–trans* isomers possible is 2^n. *n* is the number of double bonds that may exhibit this type of isomerism.

SOLUTION

This molecule has two carbon–carbon double bonds, each of which exhibits *cis–trans* isomerism. As the following table shows, $2^2 = 4$ *cis–trans* isomers are possible (below the table are line-angle formulas for two of these isomers):

Double bond	
$C_2{-}C_3$	$C_4{-}C_5$
trans	*trans*
trans	*cis*
cis	*trans*
cis	*cis*

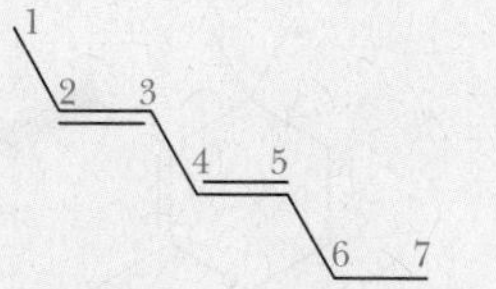

trans,trans-2,4-Heptadiene

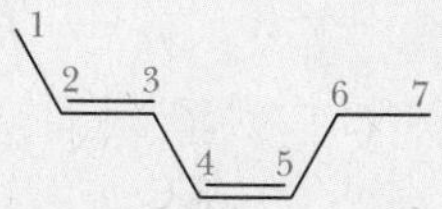

trans,cis-2,4-Heptadiene

See problem 4.36

PROBLEM 4.5

Draw structural formulas for the other two *cis–trans* isomers of 2,4-heptadiene.

EXAMPLE 4.7

Draw all possible *cis–trans* isomers for the following unsaturated alcohol:

$CH_3C(CH_3){=}CHCH_2CH_2C(CH_3){=}CHCH_2OH$

STRATEGY

Identify the number of C–C double bonds, *n*, that exhibit *cis–trans* isomerism. The number of possible *cis–trans* isomers will then be equal to 2^n. Alkene carbons that are bonded to two identical groups do not exhibit *cis–trans* isomerism.

SOLUTION

Cis–trans isomerism is possible only for the double bond between carbons 2 and 3 of the chain. It is not possible for the other double bond because carbon 7 has two identical groups on it. Thus, $2^1 = 2$ *cis–trans* isomers are possible. Each isomer may be named by the *cis–trans* system, but as noted earlier, for structures containing a tri- or tetrasubstituted double bond, it is preferable to use the E,Z system.

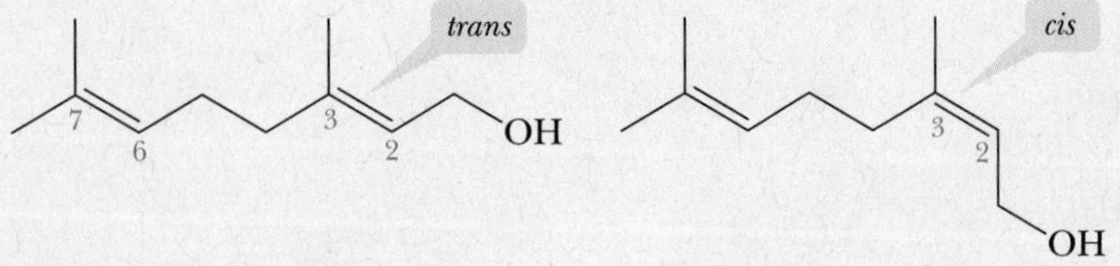

The *E* isomer (The *trans* isomer)

The *Z* isomer (The *cis* isomer)

The *E* isomer of this alcohol, named geraniol, is a major component of the oils of rose, citronella, and lemongrass.

See problem 4.36

PROBLEM 4.6

How many *cis–trans* isomers are possible for the following unsaturated alcohol?

$$CH_3\overset{\overset{\displaystyle CH_3}{|}}{C}{=}CHCH_2CH_2\overset{\overset{\displaystyle CH_3}{|}}{C}{=}CHCH_2CH_2\overset{\overset{\displaystyle CH_3}{|}}{C}{=}CHCH_2OH$$

Vitamin A is an example of a biologically important compound for which a number of *cis–trans* isomers are possible. There are four carbon–carbon double bonds in the chain of carbon atoms bonded to the substituted cyclohexene ring, and each has the potential for *cis–trans* isomerism. Thus, $2^4 = 16$ *cis–trans* isomers are possible for this structural formula. Vitamin A is the all *trans* isomer. The enzyme-catalyzed oxidation of vitamin A converts the primary hydroxyl group to a carbonyl group of an aldehyde to give retinal, the biologically active form of the vitamin:

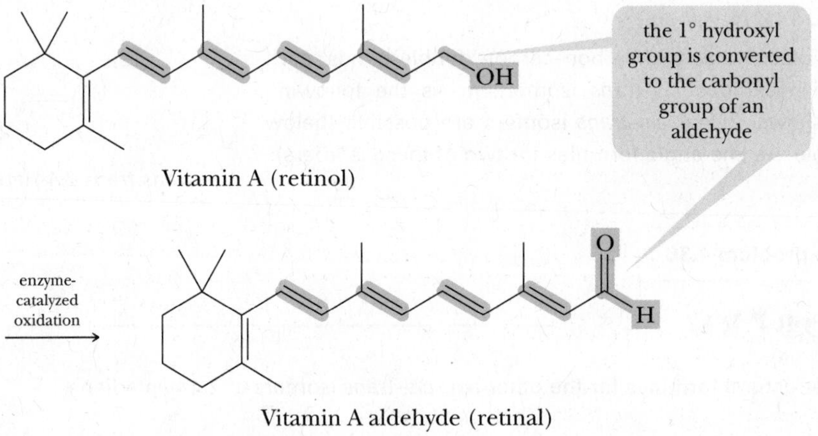

Vitamin A aldehyde (retinal)

4.3 What Are the Physical Properties of Alkenes and Alkynes?

Alkenes and alkynes are nonpolar compounds, and the only attractive forces between their molecules are dispersion forces (Section 3.8B). Therefore, their physical properties are similar to those of alkanes (Section 3.8) with the same carbon skeletons. Alkenes and alkynes that are liquid at room temperature have densities less than 1.0 g/mL. Thus, they are less dense than water. Like alkanes, alkenes and alkynes are nonpolar and are soluble in each other. Because of their contrasting polarity with water, they do not dissolve in water. Instead, they form two layers when mixed with water or another polar organic liquid such as ethanol.

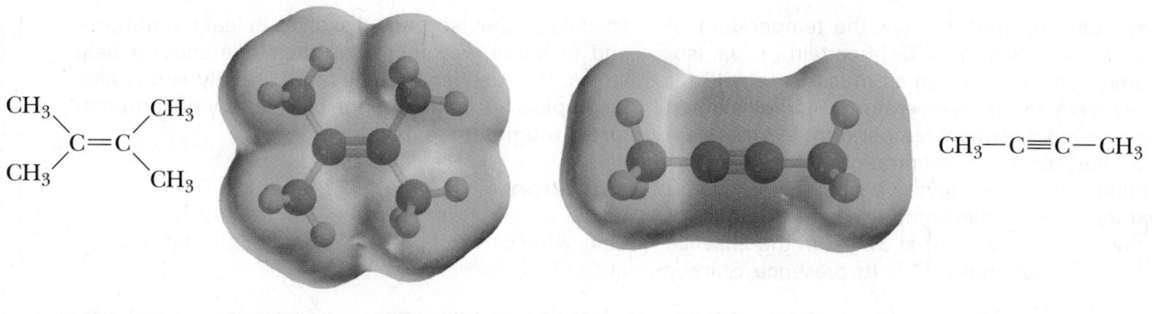

Tetramethylethylene and dimethylacetylene. Both a carbon–carbon double bond and a carbon–carbon triple bond are sites of high electron density and, therefore, sites of chemical reactivity.

EXAMPLE 4.8

Describe what will happen when 1-nonene is added to the following compounds:

(a) Water

(b) 8-Methyl-1-nonyne

STRATEGY

First determine the polarity of the solvent and the solute. Then apply the generalization, "like dissolves like."

SOLUTION

(a) 1-Nonene is an alkene and, therefore, nonpolar. It will not dissolve in a polar solvent such as water. Water and 1-nonene will form two layers; water, which has the higher density, will be the lower layer, and 1-nonene will be the upper layer.

(b) Because alkenes and alkynes are both nonpolar, they will dissolve in one another.

Chemical Connections 4C

WHY PLANTS EMIT ISOPRENE

Names like Virginia's *Blue Ridge*, Jamaica's *Blue Mountain Peak*, and Australia's *Blue Mountains* remind us of the bluish haze that hangs over wooded hills in the summertime. In the 1950s, it was discovered that this haze is rich in isoprene, which means that isoprene is far more abundant in the atmosphere than anyone thought. The haze is caused by the scattering of light from an aerosol produced by the photooxidation of isoprene and other hydrocarbons. Scientists now estimate that the global emission of isoprene by plants is 3×10^{11} kg/yr (3.3×10^{8} ton/yr), which represents approximately 2% of all carbon fixed by photosynthesis.

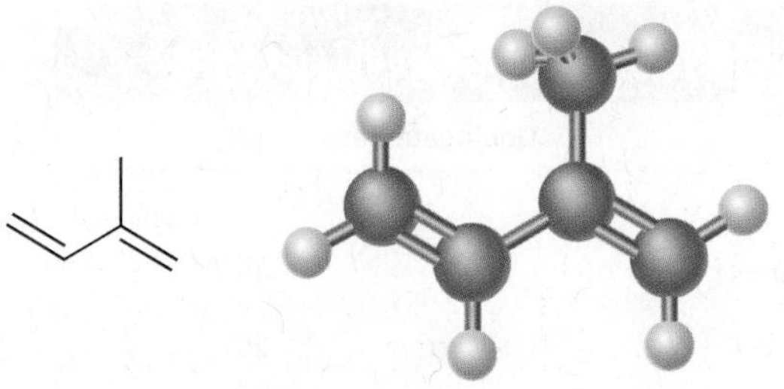

Isoprene

A recent study of hydrocarbon emissions in the Atlanta area revealed that plants are by far the largest emitters of hydrocarbons, with plant-derived isoprene accounting for almost 60% of the total.

Why do plants emit so much isoprene into the atmosphere rather than use it for the synthesis of terpenes and other natural products? Tom Starkey, a University of Wisconsin plant physiologist, found that the emission of isoprene is extremely sensitive to temperature. Plants grown at 20 °C do not emit isoprene,

Digital Vision

The haze of the Smoky Mountains is caused by light-scattering from the aerosol produced by the photooxidation of isoprene and other hydrocarbons.

but they begin to emit it when the temperature of their leaves increases to 30 °C. In certain plants, isoprene emission can increase as much as tenfold for a 10 °C increase in leaf temperature. Starkey studied the relationship between temperature-induced leaf damage and isoprene concentration in leaves of the kudzu plant, a nonnative invasive vine. He discovered that leaf damage, as measured by the destruction of chlorophyll, begins to occur at 37.5 °C in the absence of isoprene, but not until 45 °C in its presence. Starkey speculates that isoprene dissolves in leaf membranes and in some way increases their tolerance to heat stress. Because isoprene is made rapidly and is also lost rapidly, its concentration correlates with temperature throughout the day.

Question

Based on the information in this Chemical Connections what can you deduce about the physical properties of leaf cell membranes?

4.4 Why Are 1-Alkynes (Terminal Alkynes) Weak Acids?

One of the major differences between the chemistry of alkynes and that of alkenes and alkanes is that a hydrogen bonded to a carbon atom of a terminal alkyne is sufficiently acidic (pK_a 25) that it can be removed by a strong base, such as sodium amide, $NaNH_2$, to give an acetylide anion.

$$H{-}C{\equiv}C{-}H + {:}\ddot{N}H_2^- \rightleftharpoons H{-}C{\equiv}C{:}^- + \ddot{N}H_3 \qquad K_{eq} = 10^{13}$$

Acetylene	Amide anion	Acetylide anion	Ammonia
pK_a 25			pK_a 38
(stronger acid)	(stronger base)	(weaker base)	(weaker acid)

In this equilibrium, acetylene is the stronger acid and sodium amide is the stronger base, and the position of equilibrium lies considerably toward the right and favors formation of the acetylide anion and ammonia (Section 2.4). Table 4.1 gives pK_a values for an alkane, alkene, and an alkyne hydrogen. Also given for comparison is the value for water.

Because water (pK_a 15.7) is a stronger acid than acetylene (pK_a 25), the hydroxide ion is not a strong enough base to convert a terminal alkyne to an alkyne anion. The position of equilibrium for this acid–base reaction lies toward the left.

$$H{-}C{\equiv}C{-}H + {:}\ddot{O}H^- \rightleftharpoons H{-}C{\equiv}C{:}^- + H{-}\ddot{O}H$$

pK_a 25			pK_a 15.7
(weaker acid)	(weaker base)	(stronger base)	(stronger acid)

The pK_a values for alkene hydrogens (pK_a approximately 44) and alkane hydrogens (pK_a approximately 51) are so large (they are so weakly acidic) that neither the commonly used alkali metal hydroxides nor sodium amide are strong enough bases to remove a proton from an alkene or an alkane.

TABLE 4.1 Acidity of Alkanes, Alkenes, and Alkynes

Weak Acid		Conjugate Base	pK_a	
Water	$HO{-}H$	HO^-	15.7	Increasing acidity ↑
Alkyne	$HC{\equiv}C{-}H$	$HC{\equiv}C$	25	
Alkene	$CH_2{=}CH{-}H$	$CH_2{=}CH^-$	44	
Alkane	$CH_3CH_2{-}H$	$CH_3CH_2^-$	51	

Why is the acidity of a hydrogen bonded to a triple-bonded carbon so much more acidic than one bonded to a double-bonded carbon of an alkene or to an alkane? We explain these relative acidities in the following way. The lone pair of electrons on a carbon anion lies in a hybrid orbital: an sp^3 hybrid orbital for an alkane, an sp^2 hybrid orbital for an alkene, and an *sp* hybrid orbital for an alkyne. An *sp* hybrid orbital has 50% *s* character, an sp^2 hybrid orbital has 33% *s* character, and an sp^3 hybrid orbital has 25% *s* character. Recall from your course in general chemistry and from Chapter 1 of this text that a 2*s* orbital is lower in energy than a 2*p* orbital. Consequently, electrons in a 2*s* orbital are held more tightly to the nucleus than those in a 2*p* orbital. The more *s* character in a hybrid orbital of carbon, the more electronegative the carbon atom will be, resulting in a greater stability of the anion and thus a more acidic hydrogen. Of the three types of organic compounds in the series alkyne, alkene, and alkane, the carbon in an alkyne (*sp* hybridized with 50% *s* character) is the most electronegative. Therefore, an alkyne anion is the most stable of the series, and an alkyne is the strongest acid of the series. By similar reasoning, the alkane carbon (sp^3 hybridized and 25% *s* character) is the least electronegative, and an alkane is the weakest acid of the series. An alkene, with 33% *s* character, is intermediate. Finally, it is only the hydrogen of a 1-alkyne that shows this type of acidity. No other hydogens of an alkyne have comparable acidity, and no other hydrogens are removed by $NaNH_2$.

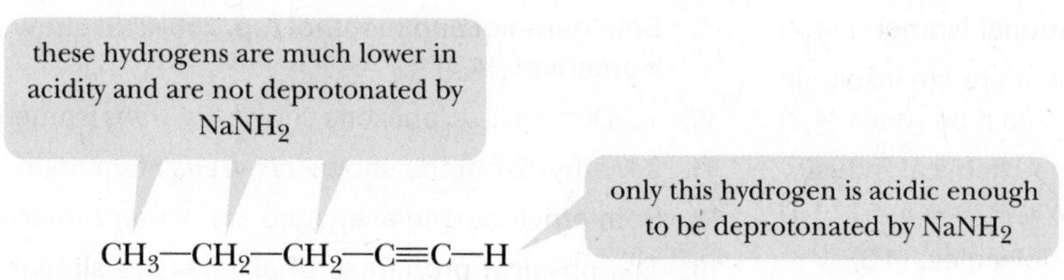
these hydrogens are much lower in acidity and are not deprotonated by NaNH2
only this hydrogen is acidic enough to be deprotonated by NaNH2
CH3—CH2—CH2—C≡C—H

SUMMARY OF KEY QUESTIONS

4.1 What Are the Structures and Shapes of Alkenes and Alkynes?

- An **alkene** is an **unsaturated hydrocarbon** that contains a carbon–carbon double bond.
- Alkenes have the general formula C_nH_{2n}.
- An **alkyne** is an unsaturated hydrocarbon that contains a carbon–carbon triple bond.
- Alkynes have the general formula C_nH_{2n-2}.
- According to the **orbital overlap model**, a carbon–carbon double bond consists of one sigma bond formed by the overlap of sp^2 hybrid orbitals and one pi bond formed by the overlap of parallel 2*p* atomic orbitals. It takes approximately 264 kJ/mol (63 kcal/mol) to break the pi bond in ethylene.
- A carbon–carbon triple bond consists of one sigma bond formed by the overlap of *sp* hybrid orbitals and two pi bonds formed by the overlap of pairs of parallel 2*p* orbitals.
- The structural feature that makes ***cis–trans*** **isomerism** possible in alkenes is restricted rotation about the two carbons of the double bond.
- To date, *trans*-cyclooctene is the smallest *trans*-cycloalkene that has been prepared in pure form and is stable at room temperature.

4.2 How Do We Name Alkenes and Alkynes?

- According to the IUPAC system, we show the presence of a **carbon–carbon double bond** by changing the infix of the parent hydrocarbon from **-an-** to **-en-**.
- The names *vinyl* and *allyl* are commonly used to show the presence of $—CH{=}CH_2$ and $—CH_2CH{=}CH_2$ groups.
- We show the presence of a **carbon–carbon triple bond** by changing the infix of the parent alkane from **-an-** to **-yn-**.
- The orientation of the carbon atoms of the parent chain about the double bond determines whether an alkene is *cis* or *trans*. If atoms of the parent are on the same side of the double bond, the configuration of the alkene is *cis*; if they are on opposite sides, the configuration is *trans*.
- Using a set of priority rules, we can also specify the configuration of a carbon–carbon double bond by the **E,Z system**.

- If the two groups of higher priority are on the same side of the double bond, the configuration of the alkene is **Z** (German: *zusammen*, together); if they are on opposite sides, the configuration is **E** (German: *entgegen*, opposite).
- To name an alkene containing two or more double bonds, we change the infix to -adien-, -atrien-, and so forth. Compounds containing several double bonds are called polyenes.

4.3 What Are the Physical Properties of Alkenes and Alkynes?

- Alkenes and alkynes are nonpolar compounds, and the only interactions between their molecules are **dispersion forces**.
- The physical properties of alkenes and alkynes are similar to those of alkanes.

4.4 Why Are 1-Alkynes (Terminal Alkynes) Weak Acids?

- Terminal alkynes are weakly acidic (pK_a 25) and can be converted to alkyne anions by strong bases such as sodium amide, $NaNH_2$.

QUICK QUIZ

Answer true or false to the following questions to assess your general knowledge of the concepts in this chapter. If you have difficulty with any of them, you should review the appropriate section in the chapter (shown in parentheses) before attempting the more challenging end-of-chapter problems.

1. Ethylene and acetylene are constitutional isomers. (4.2)
2. Alkanes that are liquid at room temperature are insoluble in water and when added to water will float on water. (4.3)
3. The bulk of the ethylene used by the chemical industry worldwide is obtained from nonrenewable resources. (4.1)
4. Alkenes and alkynes are nonpolar molecules. (4.3)
5. The IUPAC name of $CH_3CH{=}CHCH_3$ is 1,2-dimethylethylene. (4.2)
6. Cyclohexane and 1-hexene are constitutional isomers. (4.1)
7. The IUPAC name of an alkene is derived from the name of the longest chain of carbon atoms that contains the double bond. (4.2)
8. There are two classes of unsaturated hydrocarbons, alkenes and alkynes. (4.1)
9. Both geraniol and menthol (pp. 258–259) show *cis–trans* isomerism. (4.4)
10. 1,2-Dimethylcyclohexene shows *cis–trans* isomerism. (4.2)
11. 2-Methyl-2-butene shows *cis–trans* isomerism. (4.2)
12. Both ethylene and acetylene are planar molecules. (4.1)
13. The physical properties of alkenes are similar to those of alkanes with the same carbon skeletons. (4.3)
14. Isoprene is the common name for 2-methyl-1,3-butadiene. (4.4)

Answers: (1) F (2) T (3) T (4) T (5) F (6) T (7) T (8) F (9) T (10) F (11) F (12) T (13) T (14) T

Detailed explanations for many of these answers can be found in the accompanying Solutions Manual.

PROBLEMS

A problem marked with an asterisk indicates an applied "real-world" problem. Answers to problems whose numbers are printed in blue are given in Appendix D.

Section 4.1 Structure of Alkenes and Alkynes

4.7 Describe what will happen when *trans*-3-heptene is added to the following compounds:

(a) Cyclohexane (b) Ammonia (*l*)

4.8 Each carbon atom in ethane and in ethylene is surrounded by eight valence electrons and has four bonds to it. Explain how VSEPR (Section 1.3) predicts a bond angle of 109.5° about each carbon in ethane, but an angle of 120° about each carbon in ethylene.

4.9 Explain the difference between saturated and unsaturated.

4.10 Use valence-shell electron-pair repulsion (VSEPR) to predict all bond angles about each of the following highlighted carbon atoms.

(a) 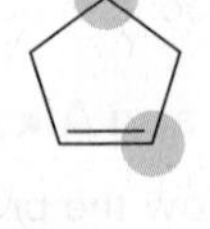

(b) 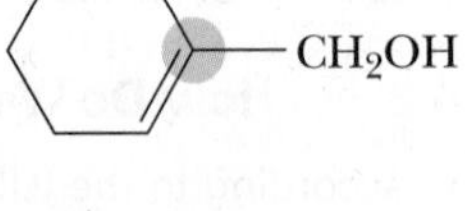

(c) $HC{\equiv}C{-}CH{=}CH_2$

(d) 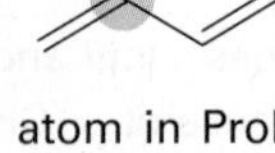

4.11 For each highlighted carbon atom in Problem 4.10, identify which orbitals are used to form each sigma bond and which are used to form each pi bond.

4.12 Predict all bond angles about each highlighted carbon atom:

(a) 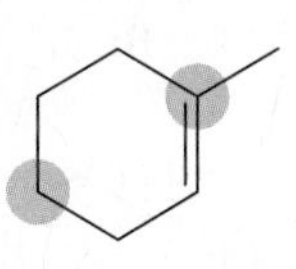

(b) 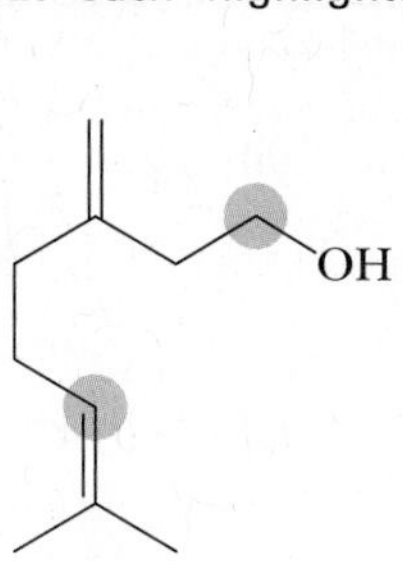

(c) 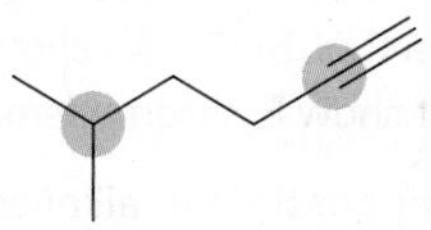

(d) 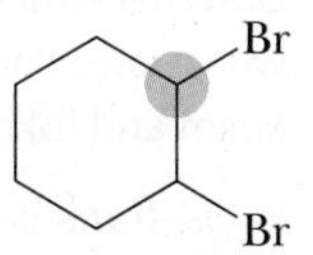

4.13 For each highlighted carbon atom in Problem 4.12, identify which orbitals are used to form each sigma bond and which are used to form each pi bond.

4.14 Following is the structure of 1,2-propadiene (allene). In it, the plane created by H—C—H of carbon 1 is perpendicular to that created by H—C—H of carbon 3.

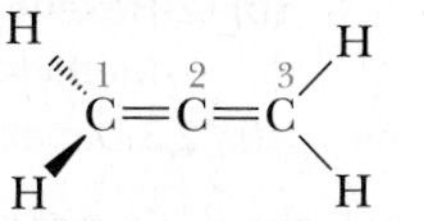

1,2-Propadiene (Allene)

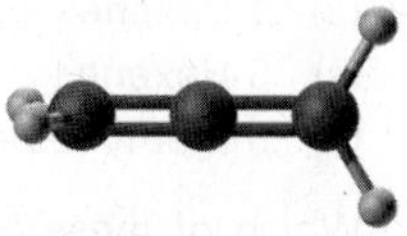

Ball-and-stick model

(a) State the orbital hybridization of each carbon in allene.
(b) Account for the molecular geometry of allene in terms of the orbital overlap model. Specifically, explain why all four hydrogen atoms are not in the same plane.

Section 4.2 Nomenclature of Alkenes and Alkynes

4.15 Draw a structural formula for each compound: **(See Examples 4.1, 4.5)**

(a) *trans*-2-Methyl-3-hexene
(b) 2-Methyl-3-hexyne
(c) 2-Methyl-1-butene
(d) 3-Ethyl-3-methyl-1-pentyne
(e) 2,3-Dimethyl-2-butene
(f) *cis*-2-Pentene
(g) (*Z*)-1-Chloropropene
(h) 3-Methylcyclohexene

4.16 Draw a structural formula for each compound: **(See Examples 4.1, 4.5)**

(a) 1-Isopropyl-4-methylcyclohexene
(b) (6*E*)-2,6-Dimethyl-2,6-octadiene
(c) *trans*-1,2-Diisopropylcyclopropane
(d) 2-Methyl-3-hexyne
(e) 2-Chloropropene
(f) Tetrachloroethylene

4.17 Write the IUPAC name for each compound: **(See Examples 4.1, 4.5)**

(a) 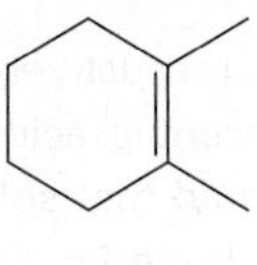

(b) 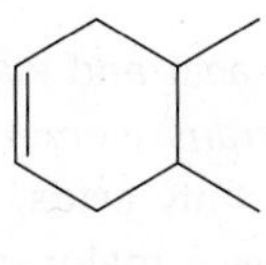

(c) 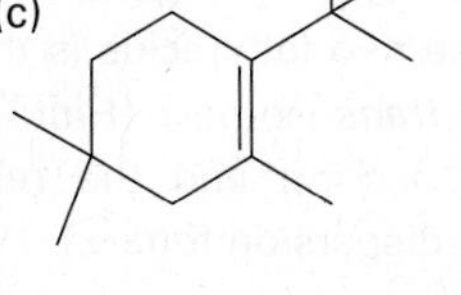

(d) 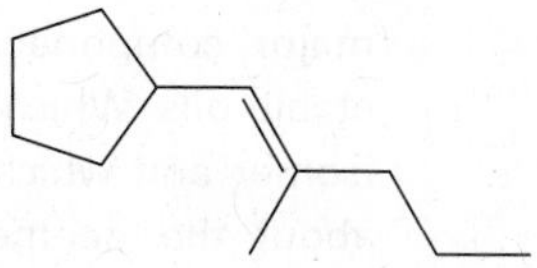

4.18 Write the IUPAC name for each compound: **(See Examples 4.1, 4.5)**

(a) 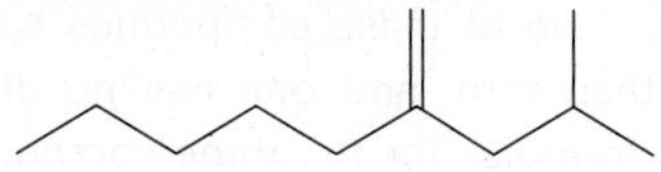

(b) 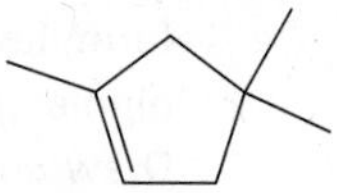

(c) 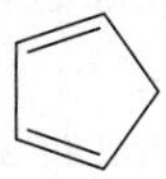

(d) 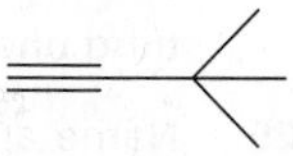

(e) 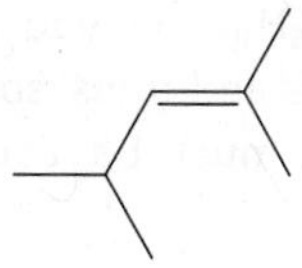

(f) 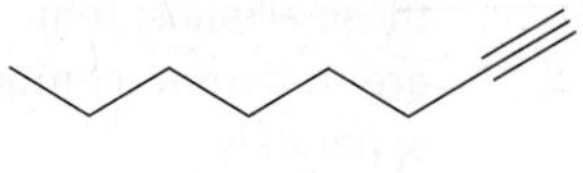

(g) 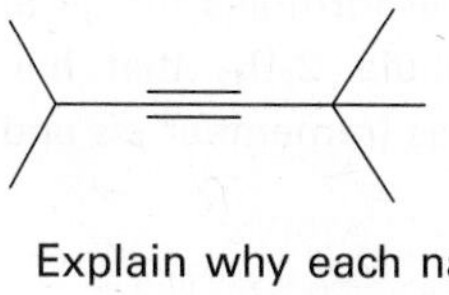

(h) 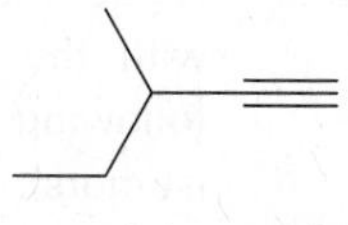

4.19 Explain why each name is incorrect, and then write a correct name for the intended compound: **(See Examples 4.1, 4.5)**

(a) 1-Methylpropene
(b) 3-Pentene
(c) 2-Methylcyclohexene
(d) 3,3-Dimethylpentene
(e) 4-Hexyne
(f) 2-Isopropyl-2-butene

4.20 Explain why each name is incorrect, and then write a correct name for the intended compound: **(See Examples 4.1, 4.5)**

(a) 2-Ethyl-1-propene
(b) 5-Isopropylcyclohexene
(c) 4-Methyl-4-hexene
(d) 2-*sec*-Butyl-1-butene
(e) 6,6-Dimethylcyclohexene
(f) 2-Ethyl-2-hexene

Sections 4.2 and 4.3 *Cis–Trans* (E/Z) Isomerism in Alkenes and Cycloalkenes

4.21 Which of these alkenes show *cis–trans* isomerism? For each that does, draw structural formulas for both isomers. **(See Example 4.2)**

(a) 1-Hexene (b) 2-Hexene
(c) 3-Hexene (d) 2-Methyl-2-hexene
(e) 3-Methyl-2-hexene (f) 2,3-Dimethyl-2-hexene

4.22 Which of these alkenes show *cis–trans* isomerism? For each that does, draw structural formulas for both isomers. **(See Example 4.2)**

(a) 1-Pentene
(b) 2-Pentene
(c) 3-Ethyl-2-pentene
(d) 2,3-Dimethyl-2-pentene
(e) 2-Methyl-2-pentene
(f) 2,4-Dimethyl-2-pentene

4.23 Which alkenes can exist as pairs of E/Z isomers? For each alkene that does, draw both isomers. **(See Examples 4.3, 4.4)**

(a) $CH_2{=}CHBr$ (b) $CH_3CH{=}CHBr$
(c) $(CH_3)_2C{=}CHCH_3$ (d) $(CH_3)_2CHCH{=}CHCH_3$

4.24 There are three compounds with the molecular formula $C_2H_2Br_2$. Two of these compounds have a dipole greater than zero, and one has no dipole. Draw structural formulas for the three compounds, and explain why two have dipole moments but the third one has none.

4.25 Name and draw structural formulas for all alkenes with the molecular formula C_5H_{10}. As you draw these alkenes, remember that *cis* and *trans* isomers are different compounds and must be counted separately.

4.26 Name and draw structural formulas for all alkenes with the molecular formula C_6H_{12} that have the following carbon skeletons (remember *cis* and *trans* isomers):

(a) 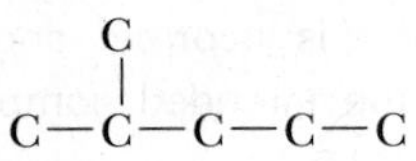 (b) 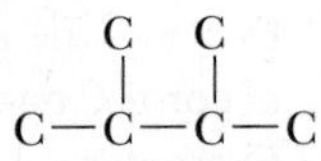

(c) 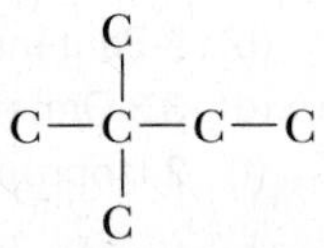 (d) 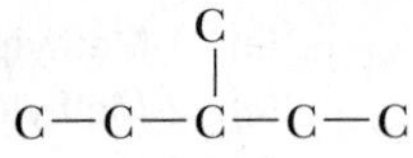

4.27 Arrange the groups in each set in order of increasing priority: **(See Examples 4.3, 4.4)**

(a) $-CH_3, -Br, -CH_2CH_3$
(b) $-OCH_3, -CH(CH_3)_2, -CH_2CH_2NH_2$
(c) $-CH_2OH, -COOH, -OH$
(d) $-CH{=}CH_2, -CH{=}O, -CH(CH_3)_2$

4.28 Name each alkene and specify its configuration using the E,Z system. **(See Examples 4.3, 4.4)**

(a) 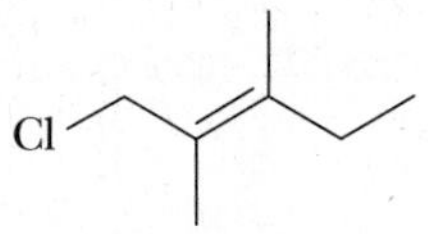

(b) 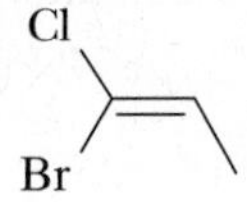

(c) 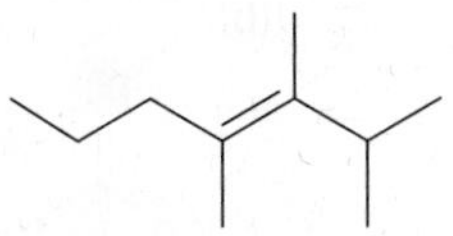 (d) 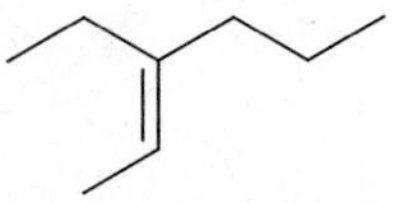

4.29 Draw the structural formula for at least one bromoalkene with molecular formula C_5H_9Br that **(a)** shows E,Z isomerism and **(b)** does not show E,Z isomerism.

4.30 Is *cis–trans* isomerism possible in alkanes? Is it possible in alkynes? Explain.

4.31 For each molecule that shows *cis–trans* isomerism, draw the *cis* isomer:

(a) 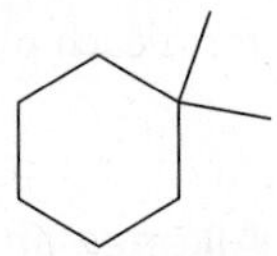 (b) 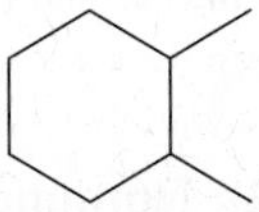

(c) 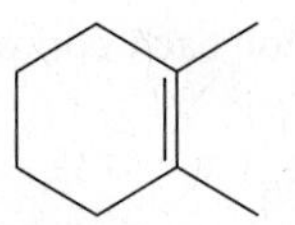 (d) 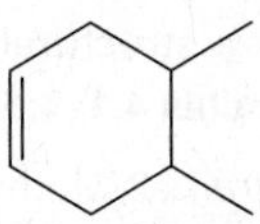

4.32 Explain why each name is incorrect or incomplete, and then write a correct name: **(See Examples 4.3, 4.4)**

(a) (*Z*)-2-Methyl-1-pentene
(b) (*E*)-3,4-Diethyl-3-hexene
(c) *trans*-2,3-Dimethyl-2-hexene
(d) (1*Z*,3*Z*)-2,3-Dimethyl-1,3-butadiene

4.33 Draw structural formulas for all compounds with the molecular formula C_5H_{10} that are

(a) Alkenes that do not show *cis–trans* isomerism.
(b) Alkenes that do show *cis–trans* isomerism.
(c) Cycloalkanes that do not show *cis–trans* isomerism.
(d) Cycloalkanes that do show *cis–trans* isomerism.

***4.34** *β*-Ocimene, a triene found in the fragrance of cotton blossoms and several essential oils, has the IUPAC name (3*Z*)-3,7-dimethyl-1,3,6-octatriene. Draw a structural formula for *β*-ocimene.

***4.35** Oleic acid and elaidic acid are, respectively, the *cis* and *trans* isomers of 9-octadecenoic acid. One of these fatty acids, a colorless liquid that solidifies at 4 °C, is a major component of butterfat. The other, a white solid with a melting point of 44–45 °C, is a major component of partially hydrogenated vegetable oils. Which of these two fatty acids is the *cis* isomer and which is the *trans* isomer? (*Hint*: Think about the geometry of packing and the relative strengths of the resulting dispersion forces.)

4.36 Determine whether the structures in each set represent the same molecule, *cis–trans* isomers, or constitutional isomers. If they are the same molecule, determine whether they are in the same or different conformations as a result of rotation about a carbon–carbon single bond. **(See Examples 4.6, 4.7)**

(a) 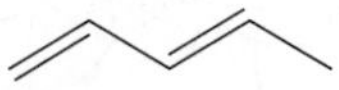 and 

(b) 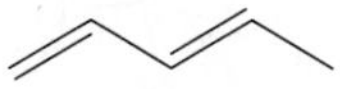 and 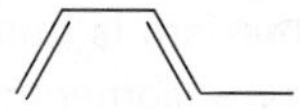

(c) 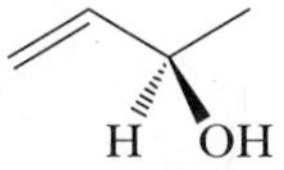 and 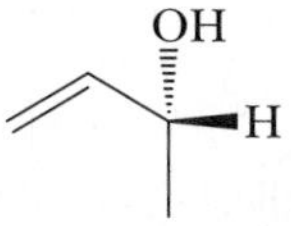

(d)  and 

***4.37** Following is the structural formula of lycopene, a deep-red compound that is partially responsible for the red color of ripe fruits, especially tomatoes:

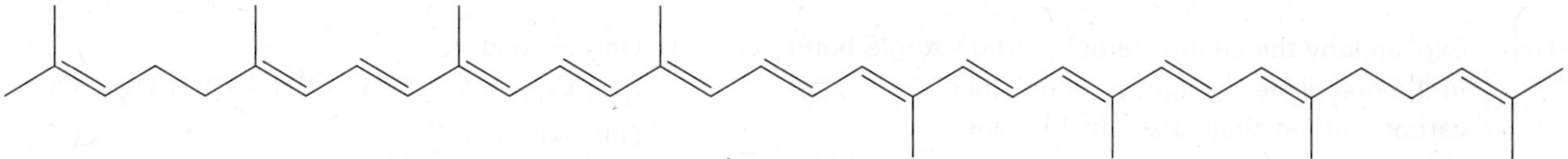

Lycopene

Approximately 20 mg of lycopene can be isolated from 1 kg of fresh, ripe tomatoes. How many of the carbon–carbon double bonds in lycopene have the possibility for *cis–trans* isomerism? Use the E,Z system to assign the configuration of all applicable double bonds.

***4.38** As you might suspect, β-carotene, a precursor of vitamin A, was first isolated from carrots. Dilute solutions of β-carotene are yellow—hence its use as a food coloring. In plants, it is almost always present in combination with chlorophyll to assist in harvesting the energy of sunlight. As tree leaves die in the fall, the green of their chlorophyll molecules is replaced by the yellows and reds of carotene and carotene-related molecules.

(a) Compare the carbon skeletons of β-carotene and lycopene. What are the similarities? What are the differences?

(b) Use the E,Z system to assign the configuration of all applicable double bonds.

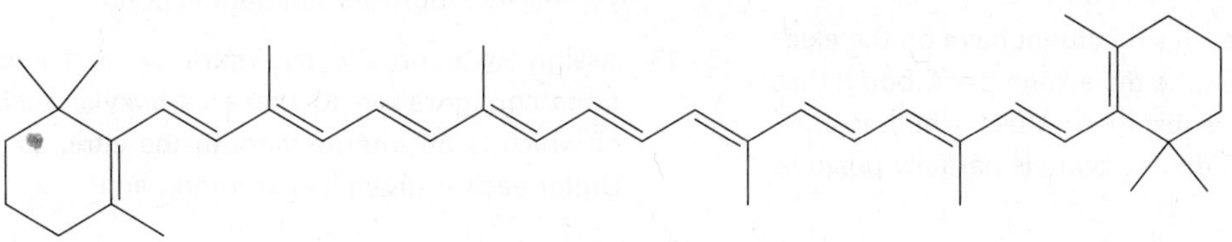

β-Carotene

***4.39** In many parts of South America, extracts of the leaves and twigs of *Montanoa tomentosa* are used as a contraceptive, to stimulate menstruation, to facilitate labor, and as an abortifacient. The compound responsible for these effects is zoapatanol:

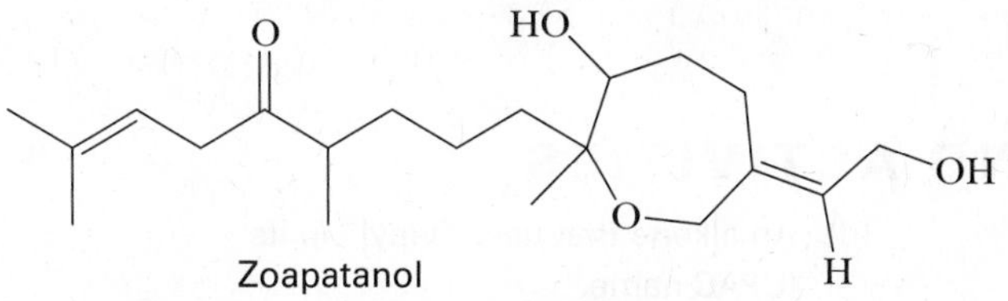

Zoapatanol

(a) Specify the configuration about the carbon–carbon double bond to the seven-membered ring, according to the E,Z system.

(b) How many *cis–trans* isomers are possible for zoapatanol? Consider the possibilities for *cis–trans* isomerism in cyclic compounds and about carbon–carbon double bonds.

***4.40** Pyrethrin II and pyrethrosin are natural products isolated from plants of the chrysanthemum family:

Chrysanthemum blossoms.

Pyrethrin II is a natural insecticide and is marketed as such.

(a) Label all carbon–carbon double bonds in each about which *cis–trans* isomerism is possible.

(b) Why are *cis–trans* isomers possible about the three-membered ring in pyrethrin II, but not about its five-membered ring?

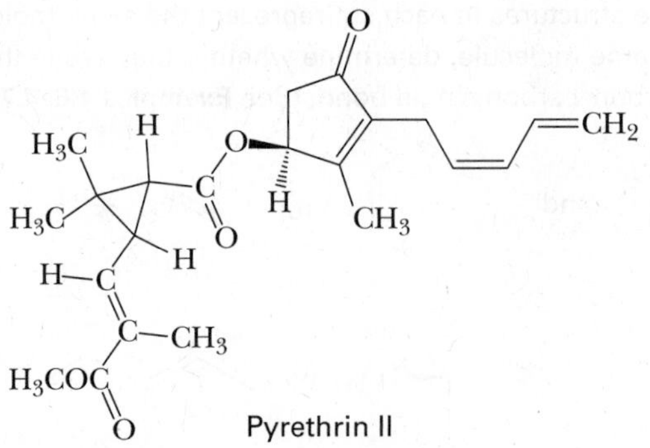

Pyrethrin II

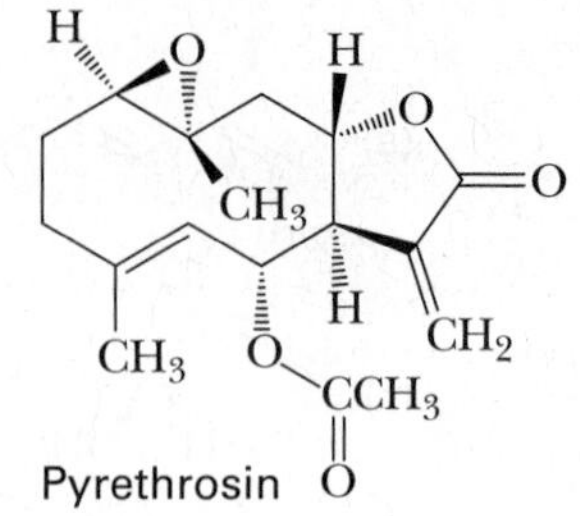

Pyrethrosin

LOOKING AHEAD

4.41 Explain why the central carbon–carbon single bond in 1,3-butadiene is slightly shorter than the central carbon–carbon single bond in 1-butene:

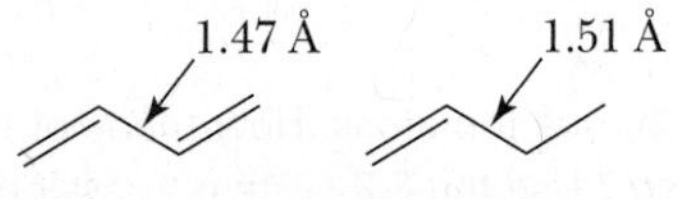

1,3-Butadiene 1-Butene

4.42 What effect might the ring size in the following cycloalkenes have on the reactivity of the C=C double bond in each?

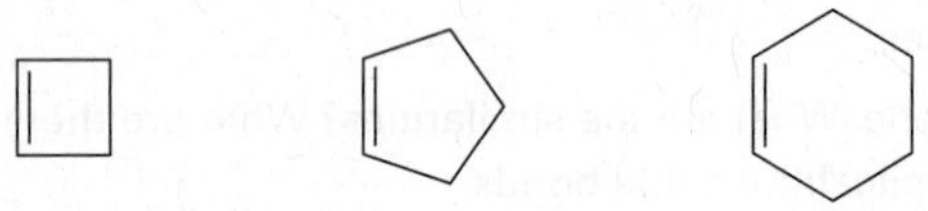

4.43 What effect might each substituent have on the electron density surrounding the alkene C=C bond; that is, how does each substituent affect whether each carbon of the C—C double bond is partially positive or partially negative?

(a) 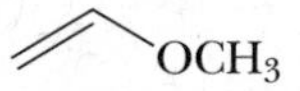

(b) 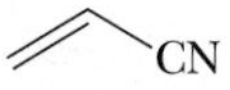

(c) 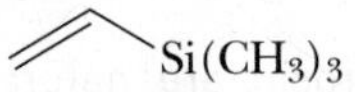

***4.44** In Section 19.1 on the biochemistry of fatty acids, we will study the following three long-chain unsaturated carboxylic acids:

Oleic acid

$CH_3(CH_2)_7CH{=}CH(CH_2)_7COOH$

Linoleic acid

$CH_3(CH_2)_4CH{=}CHCH_2CH{=}CH(CH_2)_7COOH$

Linolenic acid

$CH_3CH_2CH{=}CHCH_2CH{=}CHCH_2CH{=}CH(CH_2)_7COOH$

Each has 18 carbons and is a component of animal fats, vegetable oils, and biological membranes. Because of their presence in animal fats, they are called fatty acids.

(a) How many *cis–trans* isomers are possible for each fatty acid?

(b) These three fatty acids occur in biological membranes almost exclusively in the *cis* configuration. Draw line-angle formulas for each fatty acid, showing the *cis* configuration about each carbon–carbon double bond.

***4.45** Assign an E or a Z configuration and a *cis* or a *trans* configuration to these carboxylic acids, each of which is an intermediate in the citric acid cycle. Under each is given its common name.

(a) 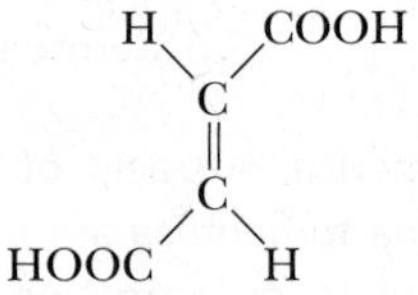

Fumaric acid

(b) 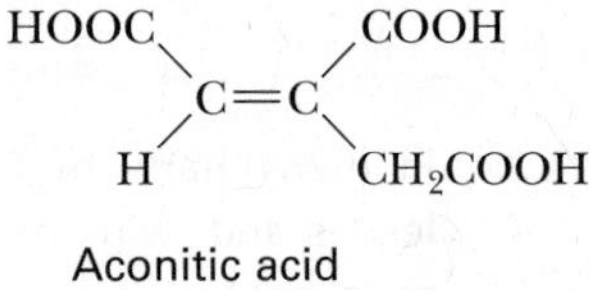

Aconitic acid

GROUP LEARNING ACTIVITIES

4.46 Take turns coming up with structures that fit the following criteria. For each structure you come up with, explain to the group why your answer is correct.

(a) An alkene with the formula C_6H_{12} that cannot be named using *cis–trans* or E,Z.

(b) A compound with the formula C_7H_{12} that does not contain a pi bond.

(c) A compound with the formula C_6H_{10} that does not contain a methylene group.

(d) An alkene that uses "vinyl" in its IUPAC name.

(e) A compound that can be named with the E,Z system but not with the *cis–trans* system.

(f) A compound that can be named with the *cis–trans* system but not with the E,Z system.

(g) A *trans*-cycloalkene that has no ring or angle strain. (*Hint*: You may need to use a model kit to explain.)

05

Reactions of Alkenes and Alkynes

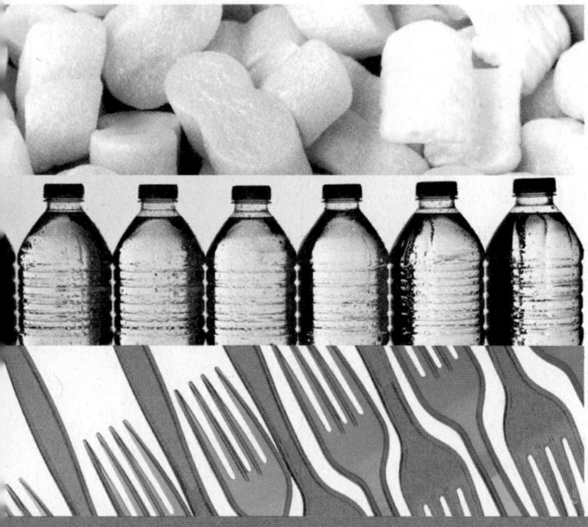

Polyethylene is the most widely used plastic, making up items such as packing foam, plastic bottles, and plastic utensils (top: © Jon Larson/iStockphoto; middle: GNL Media/Digital Vision/Getty Images, Inc.; bottom: © Lakhesis/iStockphoto). Inset: A model of ethylene.

KEY QUESTIONS

5.1 What Are the Characteristic Reactions of Alkenes?

5.2 What Is a Reaction Mechanism?

5.3 What Are the Mechanisms of Electrophilic Additions to Alkenes?

5.4 What Are Carbocation Rearrangements?

5.5 What Is Hydroboration–Oxidation of an Alkene?

5.6 How Can an Alkene Be Reduced to an Alkane?

5.7 How Can an Acetylide Anion Be Used to Create a New Carbon–Carbon Bond?

5.8 How Can Alkynes Be Reduced to Alkenes and Alkanes?

HOW TO

5.1 How to Draw Mechanisms

CHEMICAL CONNECTIONS

5A Catalytic Cracking and the Importance of Alkenes

IN THIS CHAPTER, we begin our systematic study of organic reactions and their mechanisms. Reaction mechanisms are step-by-step descriptions of how reactions proceed and are one of the most important unifying concepts in organic chemistry. We use the reactions of alkenes as the vehicle to introduce this concept.

5.1 What Are the Characteristic Reactions of Alkenes?

The most characteristic reaction of alkenes is **addition to the carbon–carbon double bond** in such a way that the pi bond is broken and, in its place, sigma bonds are formed to two new atoms or groups of atoms. Several examples of reactions at the carbon–carbon double bond are shown in Table 5.1, along with the descriptive name(s) associated with each.

TABLE 5.1 Characteristic Reactions of Alkenes

Reaction	Descriptive Name(s)
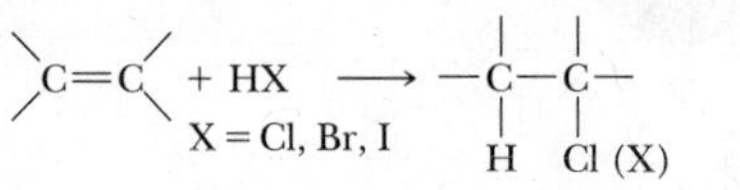	Hydrochlorination (hydrohalogenation)
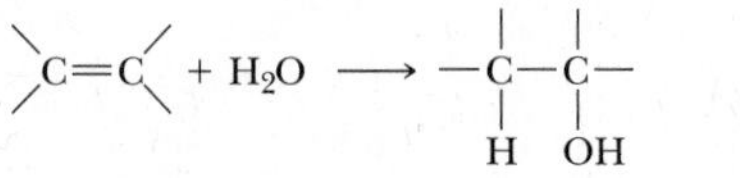	Hydration
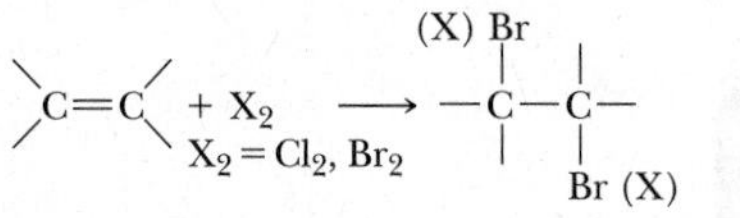	Bromination (halogenation)
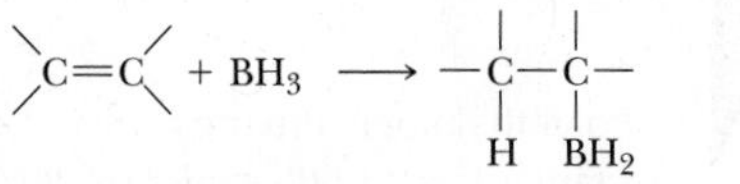	Hydroboration
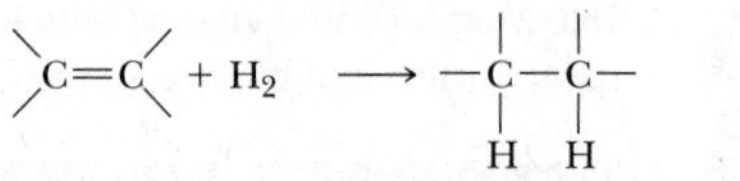	Hydrogenation (reduction)

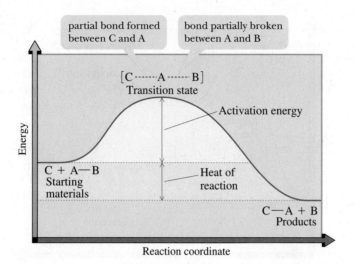

From the perspective of the chemical industry, the single most important reaction of ethylene and other low-molecular-weight alkenes is the production of **chain-growth polymers** (Greek: *poly*, many, and *meros*, part). In the presence of certain catalysts called *initiators*, many alkenes form polymers by the addition of **monomers** (Greek: *mono*, one, and *meros*, part) to a growing polymer chain, as illustrated by the formation of polyethylene from ethylene:

$$n\text{CH}_2 = \text{CH}_2 \xrightarrow{\text{initiator}} \leftarrow \text{CH}_2\text{CH}_2 \rightarrow_n$$

In alkene polymers of industrial and commercial importance, n is a large number, typically several thousand. We discuss this alkene reaction in Chapter 16.

5.2 What Is a Reaction Mechanism?

Reaction mechanism A step-by-step description of how a chemical reaction occurs.

A **reaction mechanism** describes in detail how a chemical reaction occurs. It describes which bonds break and which new ones form, as well as the order and relative rates of the various bond-breaking and bond-forming steps. If the reaction takes place in solution, the reaction mechanism describes the role of the solvent; if the reaction involves a catalyst, the reaction mechanism describes the role of the catalyst.

A. Energy Diagrams and Transition States

To understand the relationship between a chemical reaction and energy, think of a chemical bond as a spring. As a spring is stretched from its resting position, its energy increases. As

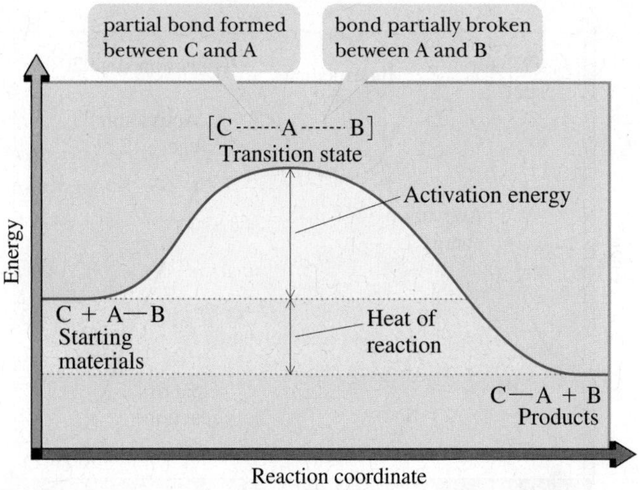

FIGURE 5.1 An energy diagram for a one-step reaction between C and A—B. The dashed lines in the transition state indicate that the new C—A bond is partially formed and the A—B bond is partially broken. The energy of the reactants is higher than that of the products—the reaction is exothermic.

it returns to its resting position, its energy decreases. Similarly, during a chemical reaction, bond breaking corresponds to an increase in energy, and bond forming corresponds to a decrease in energy. We use an **energy diagram** to show the changes in energy that occur in going from reactants to products. Energy is measured along the vertical axis, and the change in position of the atoms during a reaction is measured on the horizontal axis, called the **reaction coordinate**. The reaction coordinate indicates how far the reaction has progressed, from no reaction to a completed reaction.

Energy diagram A graph showing the changes in energy that occur during a chemical reaction; energy is plotted on the *y*-axis, and the progress of the reaction is plotted on the *x*-axis.

Reaction coordinate A measure of the progress of a reaction, plotted on the *x*-axis in an energy diagram.

Figure 5.1 shows an energy diagram for the reaction of C + A—B to form C—A + B. This reaction occurs in one step, meaning that bond breaking in reactants and bond forming in products occur simultaneously.

The difference in energy between the reactants and products is called the **heat of reaction**, ΔH. If the energy of the products is lower than that of the reactants, heat is released and the reaction is called **exothermic**. If the energy of the products is higher than that of the reactants, heat is absorbed and the reaction is called **endothermic**. The one-step reaction shown in Figure 5.1 is exothermic.

Heat of reaction The difference in energy between reactants and products.

Exothermic reaction A reaction in which the energy of the products is lower than the energy of the reactants; a reaction in which heat is liberated.

Endothermic reaction A reaction in which the energy of the products is higher than the energy of the reactants; a reaction in which heat is absorbed.

A **transition state** is the point on the reaction coordinate at which the energy is at a maximum. At the transition state, sufficient energy has become concentrated in the proper bonds so that bonds in the reactants break. As they break, energy is redistributed and new bonds form, giving products. Once the transition state is reached, the reaction proceeds to give products, with the release of energy.

A transition state has a definite geometry, a definite arrangement of bonding and nonbonding electrons, and a definite distribution of electron density and charge. Because a transition state is at an energy maximum on an energy diagram, we cannot isolate it and we cannot determine its structure experimentally. Its lifetime is on the order of a picosecond (the duration of a single bond vibration). As we will see, however, even though we cannot observe a transition state directly by any experimental means, we can often infer a great deal about its probable structure from other experimental observations.

Transition state An unstable species of maximum energy formed during the course of a reaction; a maximum on an energy diagram.

For the reaction shown in Figure 5.1, we use dashed lines to show the partial bonding in the transition state. At the same time, as C begins to form a new covalent bond with A, the covalent bond between A and B begins to break. Upon completion of the reaction, the A—B bond is fully broken and the C—A bond is fully formed.

The difference in energy between the reactants and the transition state is called the **activation energy**. The activation energy is the minimum energy required for a reaction to occur; it can be considered an energy barrier for the reaction. The activation energy determines the rate of a reaction—that is, how fast the reaction occurs. If the activation energy is large, a very few molecular collisions occur with sufficient energy to reach the transition state, and the reaction is slow. If the activation energy is small, many collisions generate sufficient energy to reach the transition state and the reaction is fast.

Activation energy The difference in energy between reactants and the transition state.

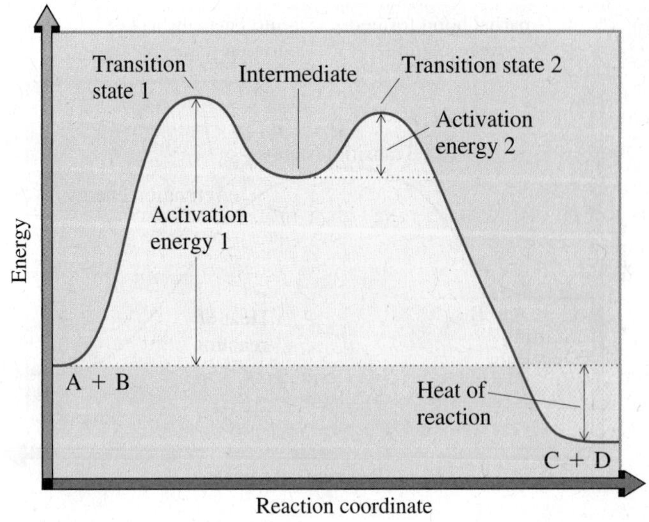

FIGURE 5.2 Energy diagram for a two-step reaction involving the formation of an intermediate. The energy of the reactants is higher than that of the products, and energy is released in the conversion of A + B to C + D.

Reaction intermediate An unstable species that lies in an energy minimum between two transition states.

Rate-determining step The step in a reaction sequence that crosses the highest energy barrier; the slowest step in a multistep reaction.

In a reaction that occurs in two or more steps, each step has its own transition state and activation energy. Shown in Figure 5.2 is an energy diagram for the conversion of reactants to products in two steps. A **reaction intermediate** corresponds to an energy minimum between two transition states, in this case an intermediate between transition states 1 and 2. Note that because the energies of the reaction intermediates we describe are higher than the energies of either the reactants or the products, these intermediates are highly reactive, and rarely, if ever, can one be isolated.

The slowest step in a multistep reaction, called the **rate-determining step**, is the step that crosses the highest energy barrier. In the two-step reaction shown in Figure 5.2, Step 1 crosses the higher energy barrier and is, therefore, the rate-determining step.

EXAMPLE 5.1

Draw an energy diagram for a two-step exothermic reaction in which the second step is rate determining.

STRATEGY

A two-step reaction involves the formation of an intermediate. In order for the reaction to be exothermic, the products must be lower in energy than the reactants. In order for the second step to be rate determining, it must cross the higher energy barrier.

SOLUTION

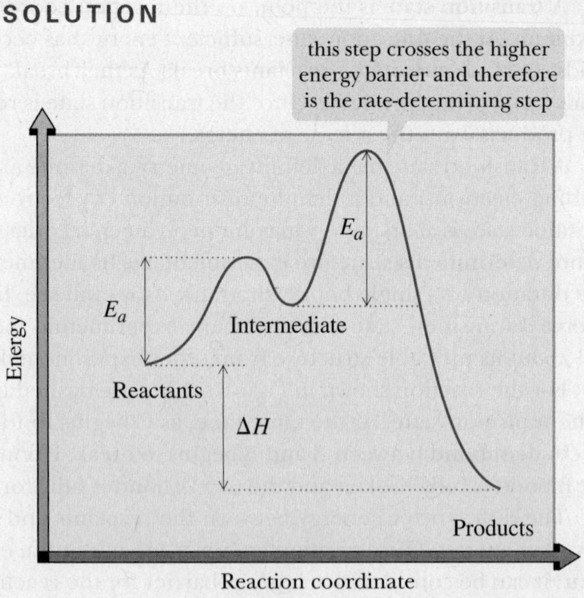

See problems 5.12, 5.13

PROBLEM 5.1

In what way would the energy diagram drawn in Example 5.1 change if the reaction were endothermic?

Chemical Connections 5A

CATALYTIC CRACKING AND THE IMPORTANCE OF ALKENES

By far, the largest source of hydrocarbons is crude oil, which contains mostly alkanes. This is unfortunate because, as we learned in Chapter 3, alkanes are relatively inert and would not be very useful as starting materials for organic reactions to produce the myriad of compounds used in society today.

Fortunately, crude oil is readily converted to alkenes, compounds with a reactive functional group (the C—C double bond), through the process of catalytic cracking. In catalytic cracking, the hydrocarbon feedstocks of crude oil are mixed with solid catalysts and heated to temperatures above 500 °C. These conditions allow C—C single bonds to be broken, forming reactive intermediates that eventually react to form smaller alkanes and alkenes.

$$CH_3CH_2CH_2CH_2CH_2CH_3 \xrightarrow[\text{catalyst}]{\text{heat}} CH_3CH_2CH_2CH_3 + \underset{\text{ethylene}}{CH_2{=}CH_2}$$

The smaller hydrocarbons formed in the initial reactions react again to form even smaller hydrocarbons. After several cracking cycles, the major alkene product formed is ethylene, the smallest possible alkene.

$$CH_3CH_2CH_2CH_3 \xrightarrow[\text{catalyst}]{\text{heat}} CH_3CH_3 + \underset{\text{ethylene}}{CH_2{=}CH_2}$$

$$CH_3CH_3 \xrightarrow[\text{catalyst}]{\text{heat}} H_2 + \underset{\text{ethylene}}{CH_2{=}CH_2}$$

The ethylene is then collected and subjected to other reactions, such as hydration to give ethanol.

$$CH_2{=}CH_2 \xrightarrow{\text{hydration}} \underset{\text{ethanol}}{CH_3CH_2OH}$$

Through this process, crude oil is converted to functionalized organic compounds which can, in turn, be used for many of the organic reactions presented in this text.

Question

Would you predict the catalytic cracking reactions to be exothermic or endothermic?

B. Developing a Reaction Mechanism

To develop a reaction mechanism, chemists begin by designing experiments that will reveal details of a particular chemical reaction. Next, through a combination of experience and intuition, they propose one or more sets of steps or mechanisms, each of which might account for the overall chemical transformation. Finally, they test each proposed mechanism against the experimental observations to exclude those mechanisms that are not consistent with the facts.

A mechanism becomes generally established by excluding reasonable alternatives and by showing that it is consistent with every test that can be devised. This, of course, does not mean that a generally accepted mechanism is a completely accurate description of the chemical events, but only that it is the best chemists have been able to devise. It is important to keep in mind that, as new experimental evidence is obtained, it may be necessary to modify a generally accepted mechanism or possibly even discard it and start all over again.

Before we go on to consider reactions and reaction mechanisms, we might ask why it is worth the trouble to establish them and your time to learn about them. One reason is very practical. Mechanisms provide a theoretical framework within which to organize a great deal of descriptive chemistry. For example, with insight into how reagents add to particular alkenes, it is possible to make generalizations and then predict how the same reagents might add to other alkenes. A second reason lies in the intellectual satisfaction derived from constructing models that accurately reflect the behavior of chemical systems. Finally, to a creative scientist, a mechanism is a tool to be used in the search for new knowledge and new understanding. A mechanism consistent with all that is known about a reaction can be used to make predictions about chemical interactions as yet unexplored, and experiments can be designed to test these predictions. Thus, reaction mechanisms provide a way not only to organize knowledge, but also to extend it.

C. Some Common Patterns in Reaction Mechanisms

At this point, let us stop for a moment and analyze several of the common reaction mechanism patterns to be seen in the mechanisms we will present in this and following chapters. You may notice that some of these mechanisms are similar to each other. It is the result of the reaction and the mechanistic steps involved that are being highlighted because of their prevalence in organic chemistry.

Pattern 1: Add a proton. In Section 2.2, we learned that an acid is a proton donor, a base is a proton acceptor, and an acid–base reaction is a proton-transfer reaction. In addition, we saw that we can use curved arrows to show how a proton-transfer reaction takes place, as for example, in the acid–base reaction between acetic acid and ammonia to form acetate ion and ammonium ion. This is an example of a *nonbonded pair of electrons being used to add a proton* to a compound.

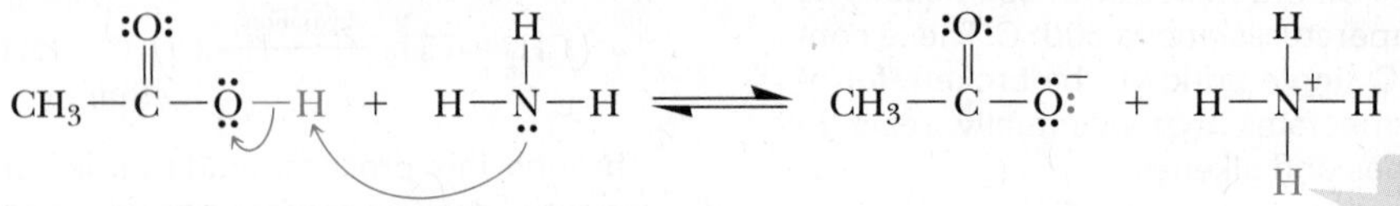

we have **added a proton** to the nitrogen atom as a result of its nonbonded pair of electrons abstracting the proton from the acid

Following is another example of **adding a proton**. Here, the *proton is added* across the pi bond of the C—C double bond. The compounds below are labeled as "proton donor" and "proton acceptor," terms used to describe Brønsted acids and bases. They can also be labeled according to Lewis acid–base theory as "electrophile" and "nucleophile."

the electrons in this single bond were once part of the pi bond that abstracted the proton from hydronium

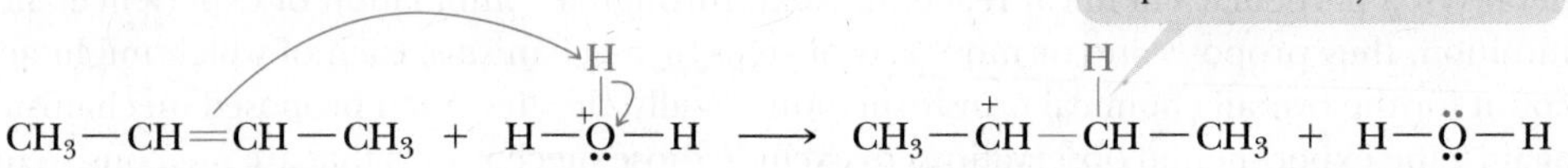

An alkene (proton acceptor or nucleophile) | **Hydronium ion (proton donor or electrophile)** | **A carbocation**

This pattern is typical in all reactions in which the reaction is catalyzed by an acid. Remember that in a carbon–carbon double bond, two pairs of electrons are shared between the two carbon atoms. An acid–base reaction in which a double bond provides the pair of electrons for the hydrogen transfer creates a carbocation. And remember that, as shown in Section 2.2, a proton, H^+, does not exist as such in aqueous solution. Instead it immediately combines with a water molecule to form the hydronium ion, H_3O^+.

While the above equation is the most accurate way to write the proton transfer in aqueous solution, we will simplify the equation to show just the proton and formation of the new covalent bond.

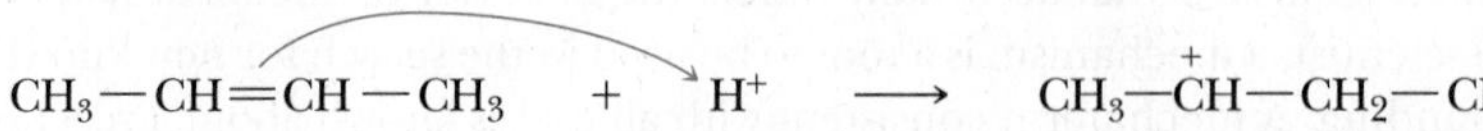

An alkene (proton acceptor or nucleophile) | **A proton (proton donor or electrophile)** | **A carbocation**

Pattern 2: Take a proton away. If we run the "add a proton" reaction in reverse, then it corresponds to "take a proton away" from the ammonium ion and transfer it to the acetate ion. We can also use curved arrows to show the flow of electron pairs in this type of reaction as well. The mechanism for taking a proton away is similar to adding a proton, only we focus our attention on the compound that loses the proton.

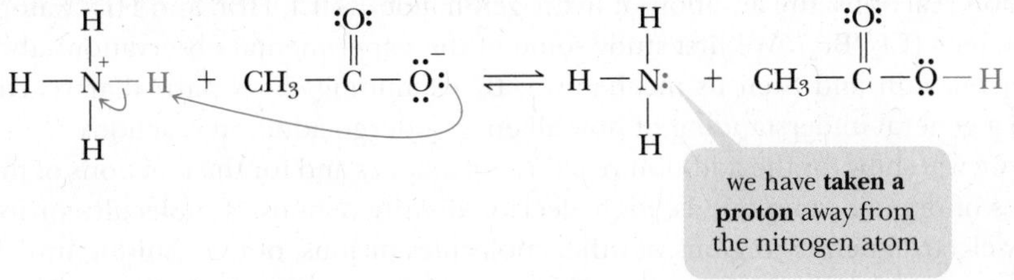
we have taken a proton away from the nitrogen atom

Pattern 3: Reaction of an electrophile and a nucleophile to form a new covalent bond. Another characteristic pattern is the reaction between an **electrophile** (an electron-poor species that can accept a pair of electrons to form a new covalent bond) and a **nucleophile** (an electron-rich species that can donate a pair of electrons to form a new covalent bond). An example of this type of reaction is that between a carbocation and halide ion. The driving force behind this reaction is the strong attraction between the positive and negative charges of the reacting species and the energy released when the new covalent bond forms. The following equation shows the flow of electron pairs in this type of reaction.

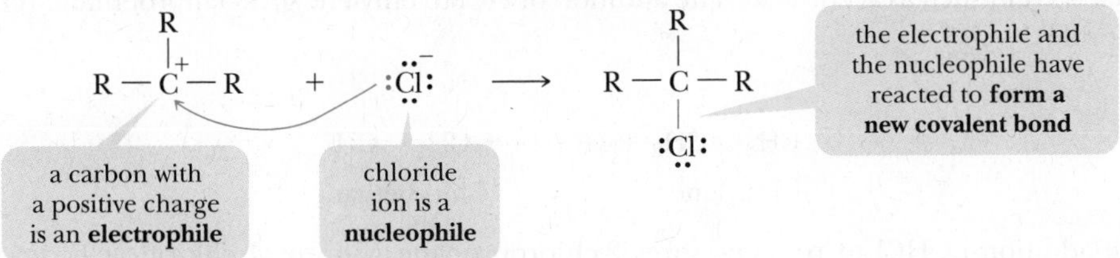
the electrophile and the nucleophile have reacted to form a new covalent bond
a carbon with a positive charge is an electrophile
chloride ion is a nucleophile

Pattern 4: Rearrangement of a bond. A common reaction that occurs in carbocations is the shift of a hydrogen or an alkyl group to place the positive charge at a more stable position. A rearrangement occurs when the electrons in a sigma bond break their bond from one carbon atom to form a new bond to another carbon atom as shown. The driving force for this process is the greater stability of the newly formed carbocation over the original. We will have more to say about rearrangements in Section 5.4.

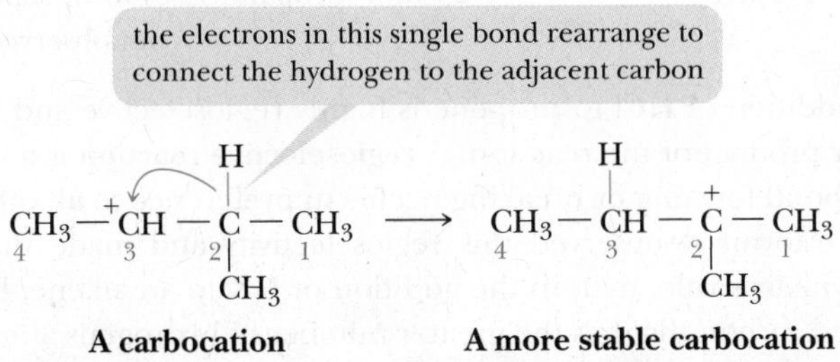
the electrons in this single bond rearrange to connect the hydrogen to the adjacent carbon
A carbocation
A more stable carbocation

Pattern 5: Break a bond to form a stable ion or molecule. A carbocation can also be formed when a chemical species breaks off from a molecule, taking the electrons from the former single bond with it. The chemical species that broke off is called a leaving group, and the bond breaks because it forms one or more stable ions or molecules. We will have more to say about leaving groups in Section 7.5C.

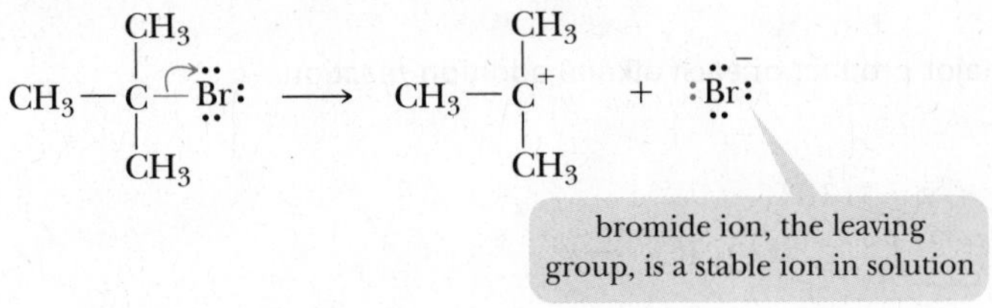
bromide ion, the leaving group, is a stable ion in solution

5.3 What Are the Mechanisms of Electrophilic Additions to Alkenes?

We begin our introduction to the chemistry of alkenes with an examination of three types of addition reactions: the addition of hydrogen halides (HCl, HBr, and HI), water (H_2O), and halogens (Cl_2, Br_2). We first study some of the experimental observations about each addition reaction and then its mechanism. By examining these particular reactions, we develop a general understanding of how alkenes undergo addition reactions.

As we will show for the addition reactions of alkenes and for the reactions of many other classes of organic compounds, high-electron-density regions of molecules or ions react with low-electron-density regions of other molecules or ions, often resulting in the formation of a new covalent bond. We call an electron-rich species a **nucleophile** (nucleus loving), meaning that it seeks a region of low electron density. We call a low-electron-density species an **electrophile** (electron loving), meaning that it seeks a region of high electron density. Note that nucleophiles are Lewis bases and electrophiles are Lewis acids (Section 2.6).

Electrophile An electron-poor species that can accept a pair of electrons to form a new covalent bond; alternatively, a Lewis acid (Section 2.6).

A. Addition of Hydrogen Halides

The hydrogen halides HCl, HBr, and HI add to alkenes to give haloalkanes (alkyl halides). These additions may be carried out either with the pure reagents or in the presence of a polar solvent such as acetic acid. The addition of HCl to ethylene gives chloroethane (ethyl chloride):

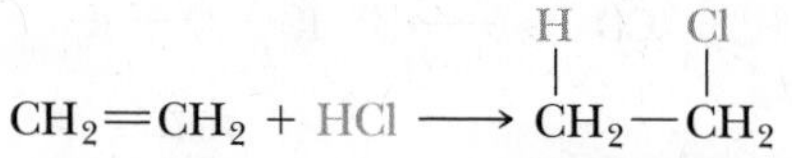

Ethylene Chloroethane

The addition of HCl to propene gives 2-chloropropane (isopropyl chloride); hydrogen adds to carbon 1 of propene and chlorine adds to carbon 2. If the orientation of addition were reversed, 1-chloropropane (propyl chloride) would be formed. The observed result is that 2-chloropropane is formed to the virtual exclusion of 1-chloropropane:

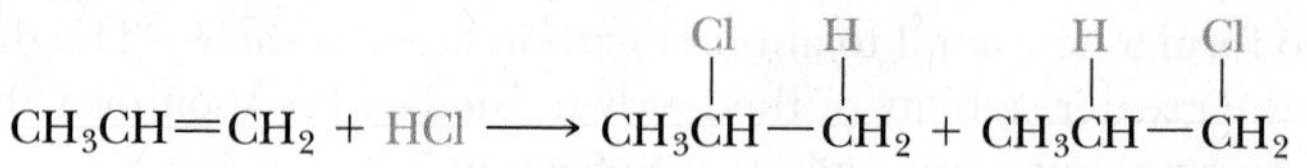

Propene 2-Chloropropane 1-Chloropropane (not observed)

Regioselective reaction A reaction in which one direction of bond forming or bond breaking occurs in preference to all other directions.

Markovnikov's rule In the addition of HX or H_2O to an alkene, hydrogen adds to the carbon of the double bond having the greater number of hydrogens.

We say that the addition of HCl to propene is highly regioselective and that 2-chloropropane is the major product of the reaction. A **regioselective reaction** is a reaction in which one direction of bond forming or breaking occurs in preference to all other directions.

Vladimir Markovnikov observed this regioselectivity and made the generalization, known as **Markovnikov's rule**, that, in the addition of HX to an alkene, hydrogen adds to the doubly bonded carbon that has the greater number of hydrogens already bonded to it. Although Markovnikov's rule provides a way to predict the product of many alkene addition reactions, it does not explain why one product predominates over other possible products.

EXAMPLE 5.2

Name and draw a structural formula for the major product of each alkene addition reaction:

(a) 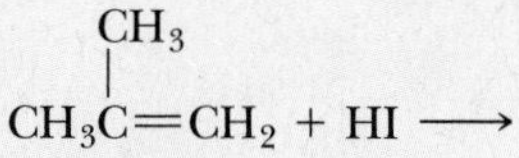

(b) 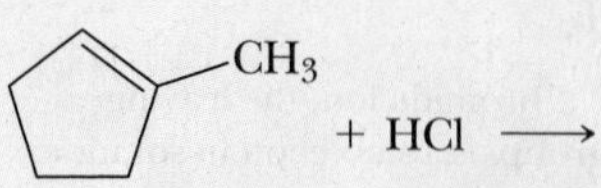

STRATEGY

Use Markovnikov's rule, which predicts that H adds to the least substituted carbon of the double bond and halogen adds to the more substituted carbon.

SOLUTION

(a)

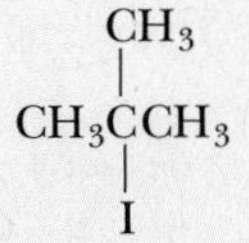

2-Iodo-2-methylpropane

(b)

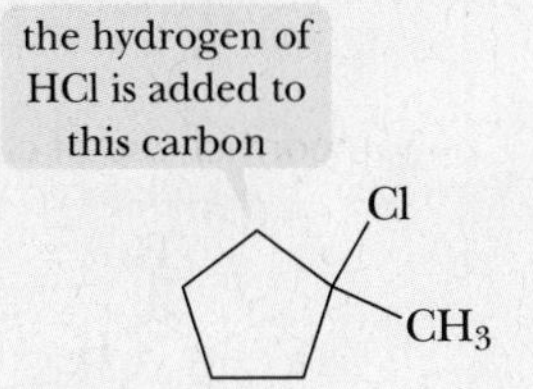

1-Chloro-1-methylcyclopentane

See problems 5.17–5.20, 5.28

PROBLEM 5.2

Name and draw a structural formula for the major product of each alkene addition reaction:

(a) $CH_3CH{=}CH_2 + HI \longrightarrow$

(b)

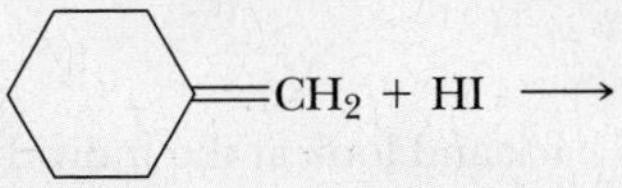

Chemists account for the addition of HX to an alkene by a two-step mechanism, which we illustrate by the reaction of 2-butene with hydrogen chloride to give 2-chlorobutane. Let us first look at this two-step mechanism in general and then go back and study each step in detail.

Mechanism

Electrophilic Addition of HCl to 2-Butene

STEP 1: Add a proton. The reaction begins with the transfer of a proton from HCl to 2-butene, as shown by the two curved arrows on the left side of Step 1:

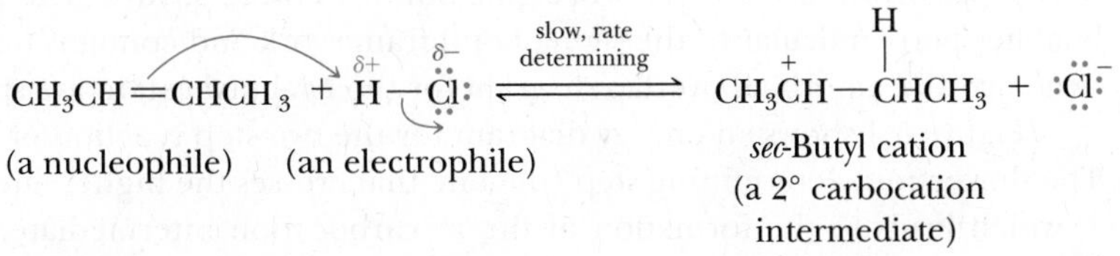

The first curved arrow shows the breaking of the pi bond of the alkene and its electron pair now forming a new covalent bond with the hydrogen atom of HCl. In this step, the carbon–carbon double bond of the alkene is the nucleophile (the electron-rich, nucleus-seeking species) and HCl is the electrophile (the electron-poor, electron-seeking species). The second curved arrow shows the breaking of the polar covalent bond in HCl and this electron pair being given entirely to chlorine, forming chloride ion. Step 1 in this mechanism results in the formation of an organic cation and chloride ion.

STEP 2: Reaction of an electrophile and a nucleophile to form a new covalent bond. The reaction of the *sec*-butyl cation (an electrophile and a Lewis acid) with chloride ion (a nucleophile and a Lewis base) completes the valence shell of carbon and gives 2-chlorobutane:

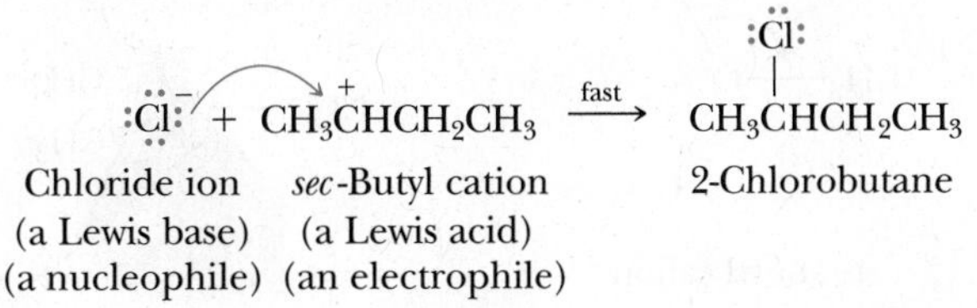

HOW TO 5.1

Draw Mechanisms

Mechanisms show how bonds are broken and formed. Although individual atoms may change positions in a reaction, the curved arrows used in a mechanism are only for the purpose of showing electron movement. Therefore, it is important to remember that curved arrow notation always shows the arrow originating from a bond or from an unshared electron pair (not the other way around).

Correct use of curved arrows...

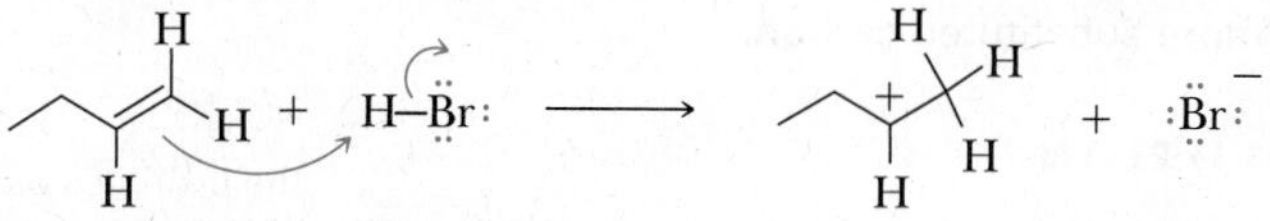

Incorrect use of curved arrows...

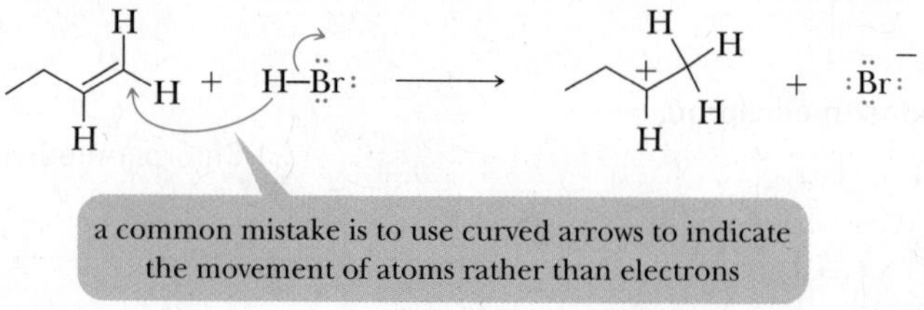

Now let us go back and look at the individual steps in more detail. There is a great deal of important organic chemistry embedded in these two steps, and it is crucial that you understand it now.

Step 1 results in the formation of an organic cation. One carbon atom in this cation has only six electrons in its valence shell and carries a charge of +1. A species containing a positively charged carbon atom is called a **carbocation** (*carbon* + *cation*). Carbocations are classified as primary (1°), secondary (2°), or tertiary (3°), depending on the number of carbon atoms bonded directly to the carbon bearing the positive charge. All carbocations are Lewis acids (Section 2.6) and electrophiles.

Carbocation A species containing a carbon atom with only three bonds to it and bearing a positive charge.

In a carbocation, the carbon bearing the positive charge is bonded to three other atoms, and, as predicted by valence-shell electron-pair repulsion (VSEPR), the three bonds about that carbon are coplanar and form bond angles of approximately 120°. According to the orbital overlap model of bonding, the electron-deficient carbon of a carbocation uses its sp^2 hybrid orbitals to form sigma bonds to three groups. The unhybridized $2p$ orbital lies perpendicular to the sigma bond framework and contains no electrons. A Lewis structure and an orbital overlap diagram for the *tert*-butyl cation are shown in Figure 5.3.

Figure 5.4 shows an energy diagram for the two-step reaction of 2-butene with HCl. The slower, rate-determining step (the one that crosses the higher energy barrier) is Step 1, which leads to the formation of the 2° carbocation intermediate. This intermediate lies in an energy minimum between the transition states for Steps 1 and 2. As soon as the carbocation intermediate (a Lewis acid) forms, it reacts with chloride ion (a Lewis base) in a Lewis acid–base reaction to give 2-chlorobutane. Note that the energy level for 2-chlorobutane (the product) is lower than the energy level for 2-butene and HCl (the reactants). Thus, in this alkene addition reaction, heat is released; the reaction is, accordingly, exothermic.

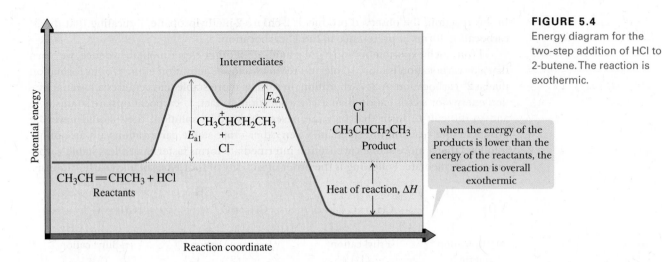

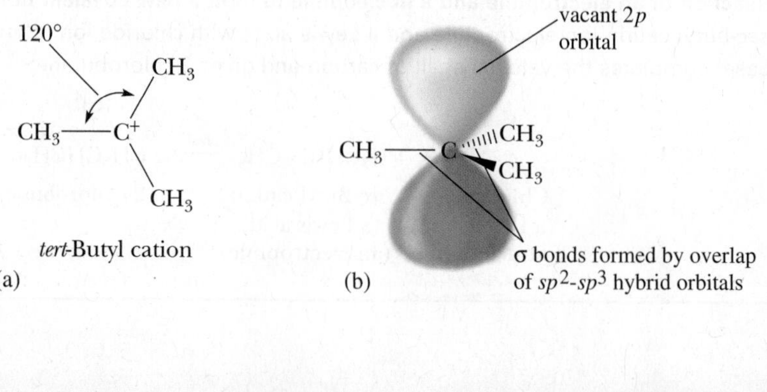

FIGURE 5.3 The structure of the *tert*-butyl cation. (a) Lewis structure and (b) an orbital picture.

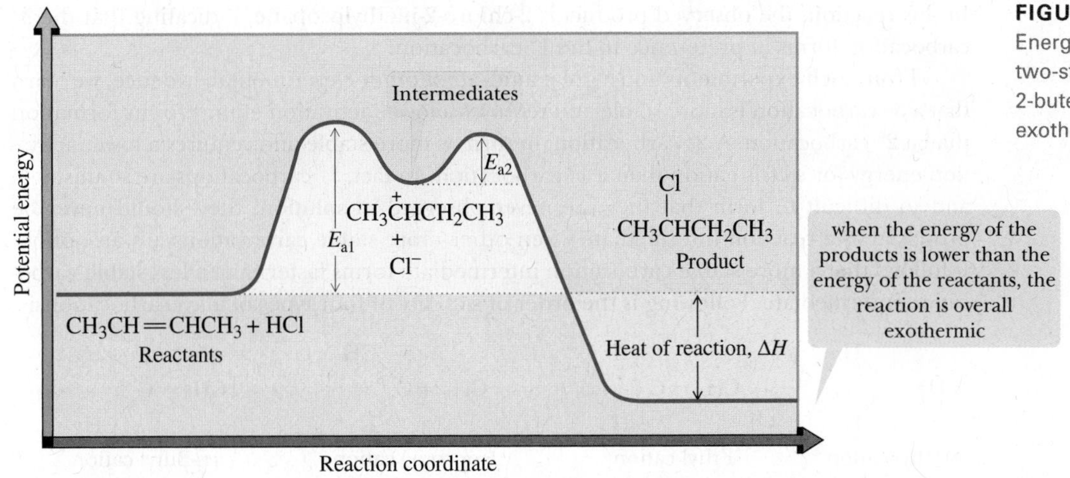

FIGURE 5.4 Energy diagram for the two-step addition of HCl to 2-butene. The reaction is exothermic.

Relative Stabilities of Carbocations: Regioselectivity and Markovnikov's Rule

The reaction of HX and an alkene can, at least in principle, give two different carbocation intermediates, depending on which of the doubly bonded carbon atoms forms a bond with H^+, as illustrated by the reaction of HCl with propene:

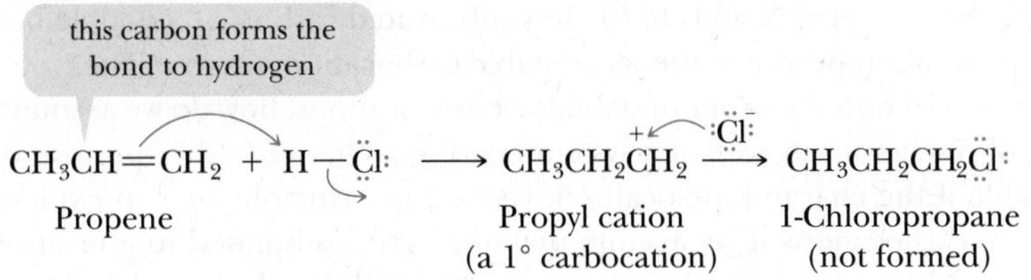

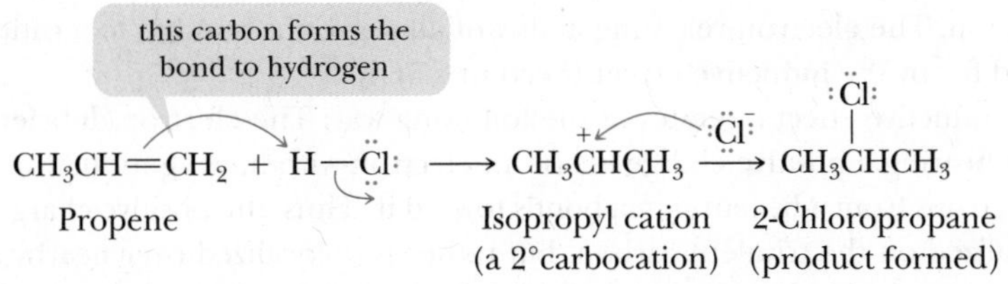

The observed product is 2-chloropropane. Because carbocations react very quickly with chloride ions, the absence of 1-chloropropane as a product tells us that the 2° carbocation is formed in preference to the 1° carbocation.

Similarly, in the reaction of HCl with 2-methylpropene, the transfer of a proton to the carbon–carbon double bond might form either the isobutyl cation (a 1° carbocation) or the *tert*-butyl cation (a 3° carbocation):

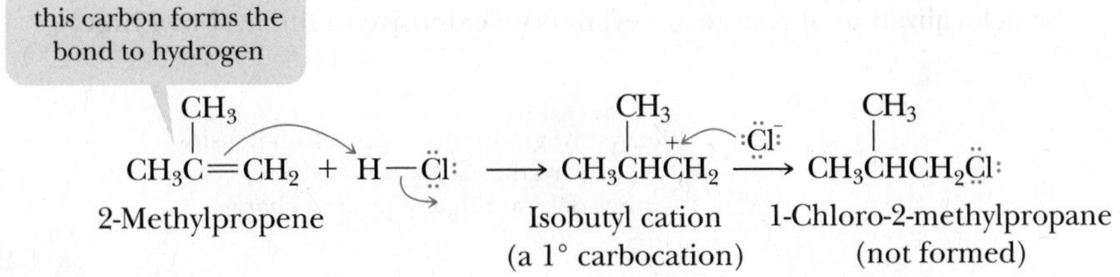

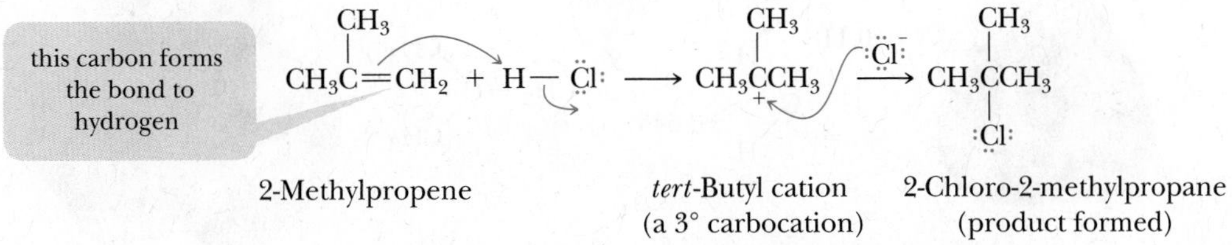

In this reaction, the observed product is 2-chloro-2-methylpropane, indicating that the 3° carbocation forms in preference to the 1° carbocation.

From such experiments and a great amount of other experimental evidence, we learn that a 3° carbocation is more stable and requires a lower activation energy for its formation than a 2° carbocation. A 2° carbocation, in turn, is more stable and requires a lower activation energy for its formation than a 1° carbocation. In fact, 1° carbocations are so unstable and so difficult to form that they are never observed in solution; they should never be proposed as a reaction intermediate when other more stable carbocations are an option. It follows that a more stable carbocation intermediate forms faster than a less stable carbocation intermediate. Following is the order of stability of four types of alkyl carbocations:

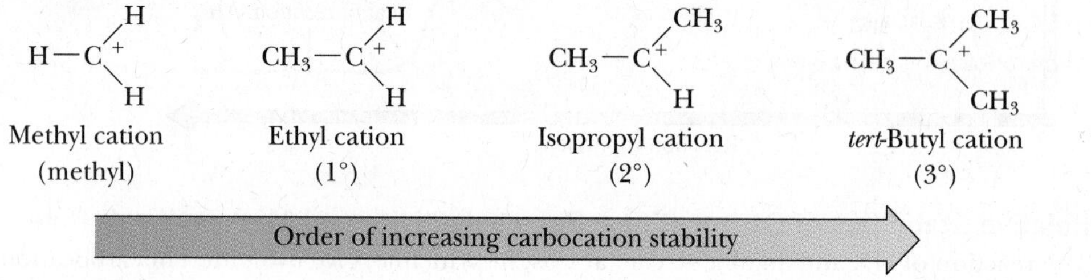

Although the concept of the relative stabilities of carbocations had not been developed in Markovnikov's time, their relative stabilities are the underlying basis for his rule; that is, the proton of H—X adds to the less substituted carbon of a double bond because this mode of addition produces the more stable carbocation intermediate.

Now that we know the order of stability of carbocations, how do we account for it? The principles of physics teach us that a system bearing a charge (either positive or negative) is more stable if the charge is delocalized. Using this principle, we can explain the order of stability of carbocations if we assume that alkyl groups bonded to a positively charged carbon release electrons toward the cationic carbon and thereby help delocalize the charge on the cation. The electron-releasing ability of alkyl groups bonded to a cationic carbon is accounted for by the **inductive effect** (Section 2.5C).

The inductive effect operates in the following way: The electron deficiency of the carbon atom bearing a positive charge exerts an electron-withdrawing inductive effect that polarizes electrons from adjacent sigma bonds toward it. Thus, the positive charge of the cation is not localized on the trivalent carbon, but rather is delocalized over nearby atoms as well. The larger the volume over which the positive charge is delocalized, the greater is the stability of the cation. Thus, as the number of alkyl groups bonded to the cationic carbon increases, the stability of the cation increases as well. Figure 5.5 illustrates the electron-withdrawing inductive effect of the positively charged carbon and the resulting delocalization of charge. According to quantum mechanical calculations, the charge on carbon in the methyl cation is approximately +0.645, and the charge on each of the hydrogen atoms is +0.118. Thus, even in the methyl cation, the positive charge is not localized on carbon. Rather, it is delocalized over the volume of space occupied by the entire ion. The polarization of electron density and the delocalization of charge are even more extensive in the *tert*-butyl cation.

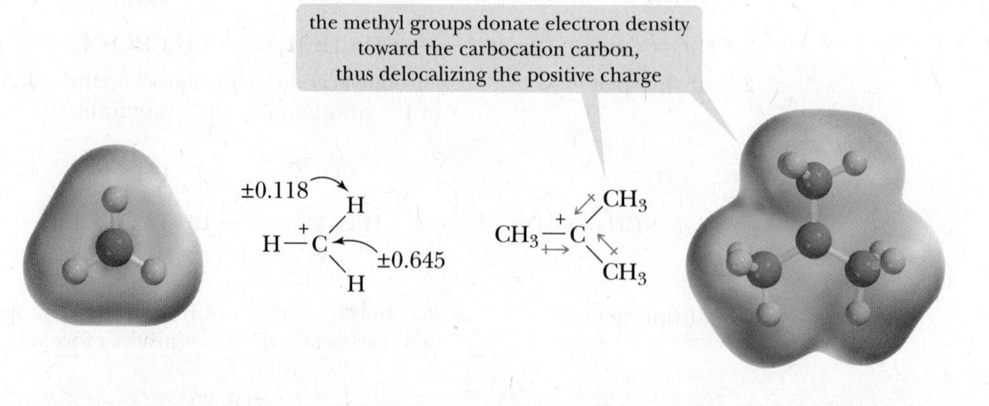

FIGURE 5.5
Methyl and *tert*-butyl cations. Delocalization of positive charge by the electron-withdrawing inductive effect of the trivalent, positively charged carbon according to molecular orbital calculations.

EXAMPLE 5.3

Arrange these carbocations in order of increasing stability:

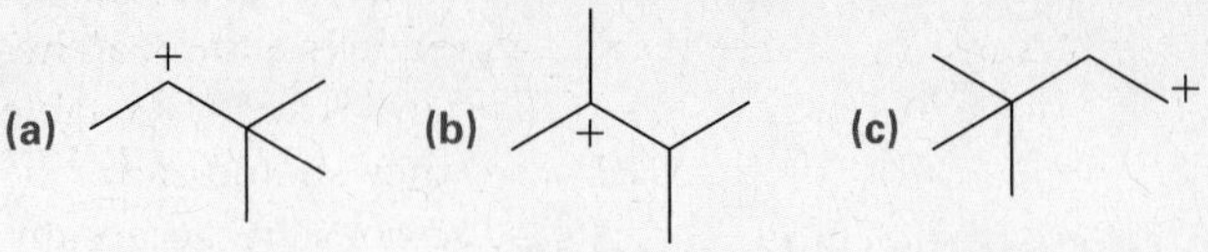

STRATEGY

Determine the degree of substitution of the positively charged carbon and then consider the order of decreasing stability of alkyl carbocations is 3° > 2° > 1°.

SOLUTION

Carbocation (a) is secondary, (b) is tertiary, and (c) is primary. In order of increasing stability, they are $c < a < b$.

See problems 5.15, 5.16

PROBLEM 5.3

Arrange these carbocations in order of increasing stability:

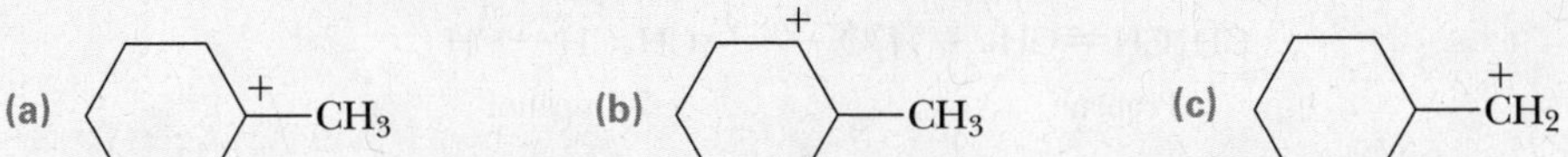

EXAMPLE 5.4

Propose a mechanism for the addition of HI to methylenecyclohexane to give 1-iodo-1-methylcyclohexane:

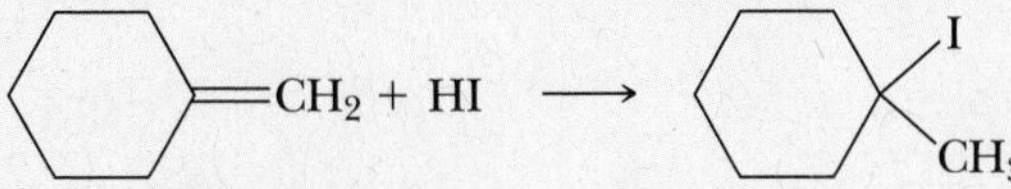

Methylenecyclohexane 1-Iodo-1-methylcyclohexane

Which step in your mechanism is rate determining?

STRATEGY

Propose a two-step mechanism similar to that proposed for the addition of HCl to propene. Formation of the carbocation intermediate is rate determining.

SOLUTION

STEP 1: Add a proton. A rate-determining proton transfer from HI to the carbon–carbon double bond gives a 3° carbocation intermediate:

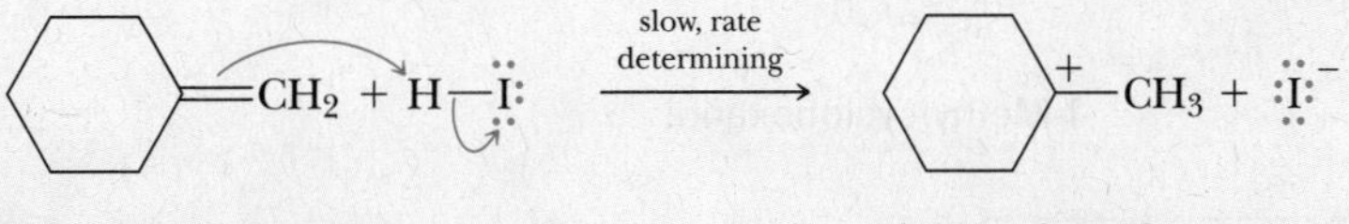

Methylenecyclohexane A 3° carbocation intermediate

STEP 2: Reaction of a nucleophile and an electrophile to form a new covalent bond. Reaction of the 3° carbocation intermediate (a Lewis acid) with iodide ion (a Lewis base) completes the valence shell of carbon and gives the product:

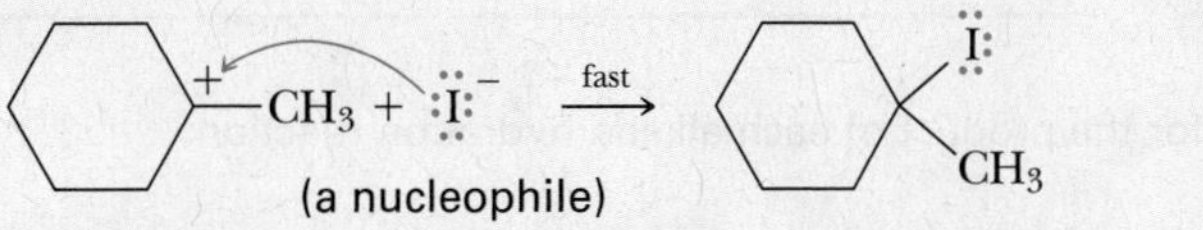

(a nucleophile)

(an electrophile) 1-Iodo-1-methylcyclohexane

See problem 5.29

PROBLEM 5.4

Propose a mechanism for the addition of HI to 1-methylcyclohexene to give 1-iodo-1-methylcyclohexane. Which step in your mechanism is rate determining?

B. Addition of Water: Acid-Catalyzed Hydration

Hydration Addition of water.

In the presence of an acid catalyst—most commonly, concentrated sulfuric acid—water adds to the carbon-carbon double bond of an alkene to give an alcohol. The addition of water is called hydration. In the case of simple alkenes, H adds to the carbon of the double bond with the greater number of hydrogens and OH adds to the carbon with the lesser number of hydrogens. Thus, H-OH adds to alkenes in accordance with Markovnikov's rule:

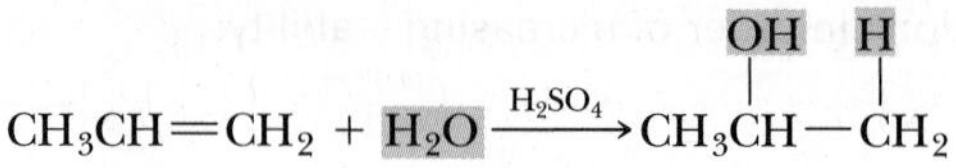

$$\begin{array}{c} \text{OH} \quad \text{H} \\ \text{CH}_3\text{CH} = \text{CH}_2 + \text{H}_2\text{O} \xrightarrow{\text{H}_2\text{SO}_4} \text{CH}_3\text{CH} - \text{CH}_2 \\ \text{Propene} \qquad \qquad 2\text{-Propanol} \\ \\ \text{CH}_3 \\ \text{CH}_3\text{C} = \text{CH}_2 + \text{H}_2\text{O} \xrightarrow{\text{H}_2\text{SO}_4} \text{CH}_3\text{C} - \text{CH}_2 \\ \text{2-Methylpropene} \\ \end{array}$$

2-Methyl-2-propanol

EXAMPLE 5.5

Draw a structural formula for the product of the acid-catalyzed hydration of 1-methylcyclohexene.

STRATEGY

Use Markovnikov's rule, which states that the H adds to the carbon of the carbon-carbon double bond bearing the greater number of hydrogens and that OH adds to the carbon bearing the lesser number of hydrogens.

SOLUTION

$$CH_3$$
 $+ H_2O$ $\xrightarrow{H_2SO_4}$ CH_3 OH

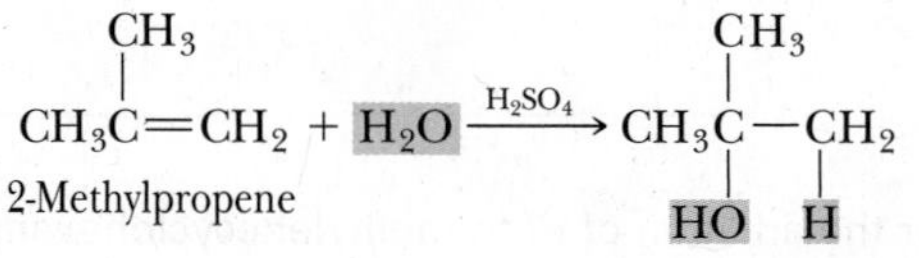

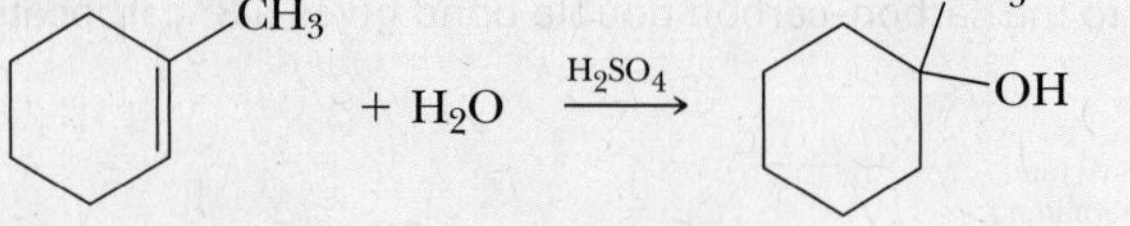

1-Methylcyclohexene

1-Methylcyclohexanol

See problems 5.19, 5.20, 5.28, 5.32

PROBLEM 5.5

Draw a structural formula for the product of each alkene hydration reaction:

(a)
$$+ H_2O \xrightarrow{H_2SO_4}$$
 (b) $+ H_2O \xrightarrow{H_2SO_4}$

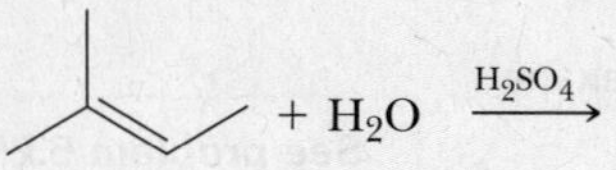

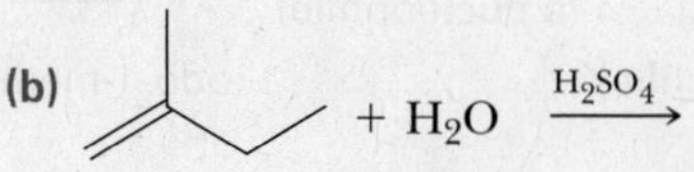

The mechanism for the acid-catalyzed hydration of alkenes is quite similar to what we have already proposed for the addition of HCl, HBr, and HI to alkenes and is illustrated by the hydration of propene to 2-propanol. This mechanism is consistent with the fact that acid is a catalyst. An H_3O^+ is consumed in Step 1, but another is generated in Step 3.

Mechanism

Acid-Catalyzed Hydration of Propene

STEP 1: Add a proton. Proton transfer from the acid catalyst, in this case, the hydronium ion, to propene gives a 2° carbocation intermediate (a Lewis acid):

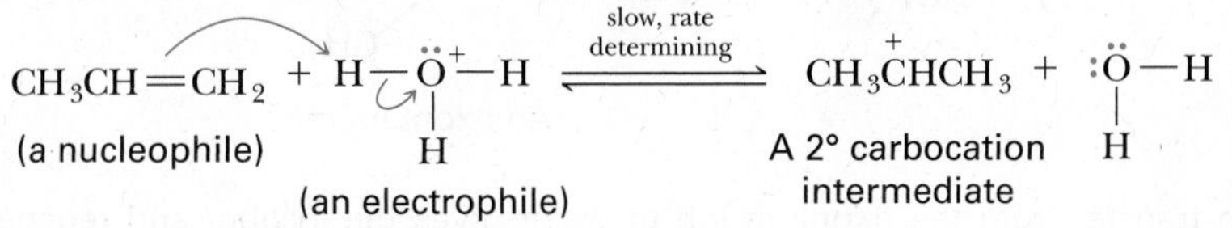

In this step, the carbon–carbon double bond of the alkene functions as a nucleophile and the hydronium ion functions as an electrophile.

STEP 2: Reaction of a nucleophile and an electrophile to form a new covalent bond. Reaction of the carbocation intermediate (a Lewis acid) with water (a Lewis base) completes the valence shell of carbon and gives an **oxonium ion:**

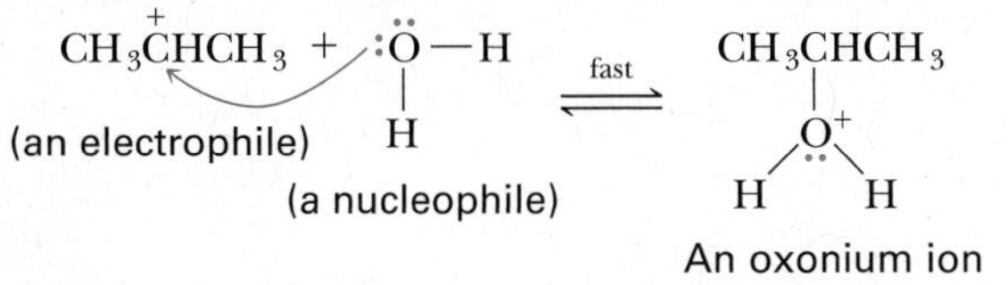

Oxonium ion An ion that contains an oxygen atom that bears a positive charge and with three bonds to oxygen.

STEP 3: Take a proton away. Proton transfer from the oxonium ion to water gives the alcohol and generates a new molecule of the catalyst:

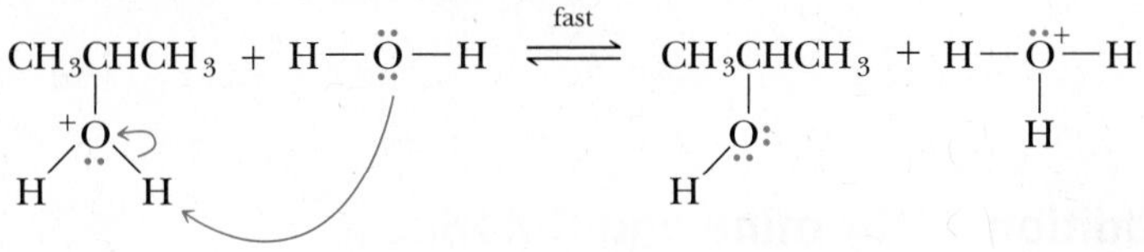

EXAMPLE 5.6

Propose a mechanism for the acid-catalyzed hydration of methylenecyclohexane to give 1-methylcyclohexanol. Which step in your mechanism is rate determining?

STRATEGY

Propose a three-step mechanism similar to that for the acid-catalyzed hydration of propene.

SOLUTION

The formation of the 3° carbocation intermediate in Step 1 is rate determining.

STEP 1: Add a proton. Proton transfer from the acid catalyst to the alkene gives a 3° carbocation intermediate (a Lewis acid):

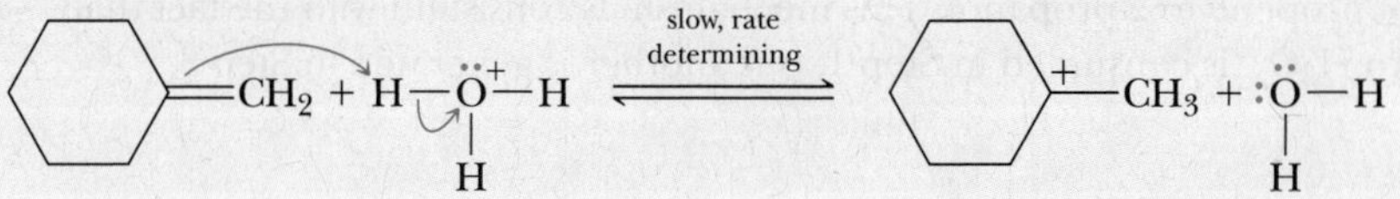

A 3° carbocation intermediate

STEP 2: Reaction of a nucleophile and an electrophile to form a new covalent bond. Reaction of the carbocation intermediate (a Lewis acid) with water (a Lewis base) completes the valence shell of carbon and gives an oxonium ion:

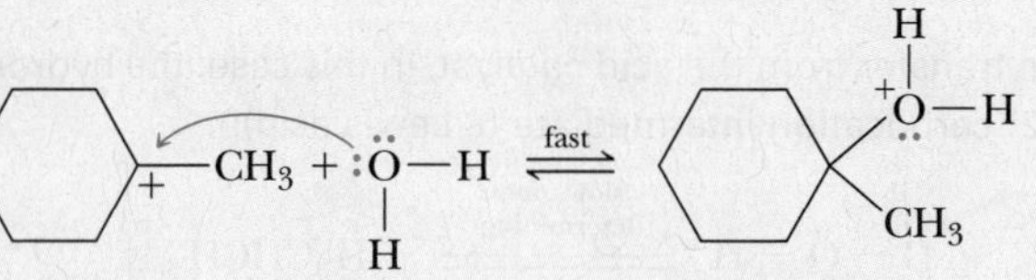
fast

An oxonium ion

STEP 3: Take a proton away. Proton transfer from the oxonium ion to water gives the alcohol and regenerates the acid catalyst:

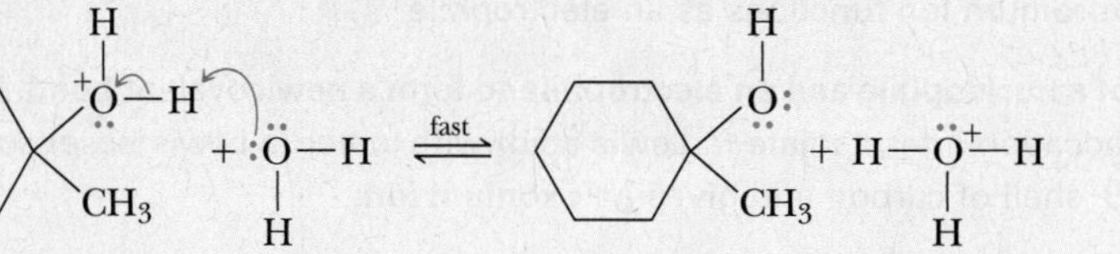

See problems 5.29–5.31, 5.38

PROBLEM 5.6

Propose a mechanism for the acid-catalyzed hydration of 1-methylcyclohexene to give 1-methylcyclohexanol. Which step in your mechanism is rate determining?

C. Addition of Bromine and Chlorine

Chlorine (Cl_2) and bromine (Br_2) react with alkenes at room temperature by the addition of halogen atoms to the two carbon atoms of the double bond, forming two new carbon–halogen bonds:

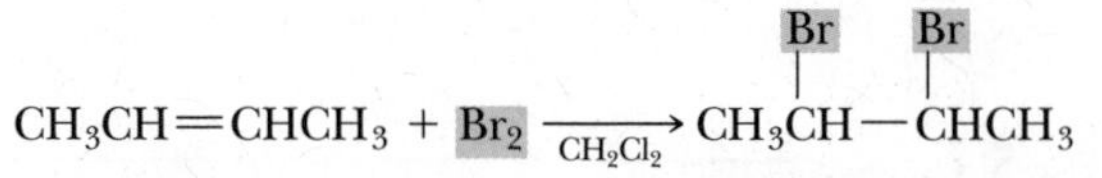
Br
Br
$CH_3CH{=}CHCH_3 + Br_2 \xrightarrow{CH_2Cl_2} CH_3CH{-}CHCH_3$

2-Butene 2,3-Dibromobutane

Stereoselective reaction A reaction in which one stereoisomer is formed or destroyed in preference to all others that might be formed or destroyed.

Anti stereoselectivity Addition of atoms or groups of atoms from opposite sides or faces of a carbon–carbon double bond.

Fluorine, F_2, also adds to alkenes, but because its reactions are very fast and difficult to control, addition of fluorine is not a useful laboratory reaction. Iodine, I_2, also adds, but the reaction is not preparatively useful.

The addition of bromine and chlorine to a cycloalkene gives a *trans* dihalocycloalkane. For example, the addition of bromine to cyclohexene gives *trans*-1,2-dibromocyclohexane; the *cis* isomer is not formed. Thus, the addition of a halogen to a cycloalkene is stereoselective. A **stereoselective reaction** is a reaction in which one stereoisomer is formed or destroyed in preference to all others that might be formed or destroyed. We say that addition of bromine to an alkene occurs with **anti stereoselectivity**.

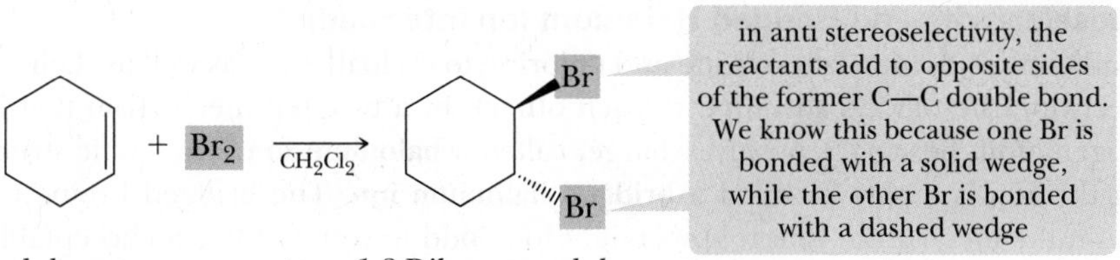

+ Br$_2$
CH$_2$Cl$_2$
Br
Br
in anti stereoselectivity, the reactants add to opposite sides of the former C—C double bond. We know this because one Br is bonded with a solid wedge, while the other Br is bonded with a dashed wedge

Cyclohexene *trans*-1,2-Dibromocyclohexane

The reaction of bromine with an alkene is a particularly useful qualitative test for the presence of a carbon–carbon double bond. If we dissolve bromine in dichloromethane, the solution turns red. Both alkenes and dibromoalkanes are colorless. If we now mix a few drops of the bromine solution with an alkene, a dibromoalkane is formed, and the solution becomes colorless.

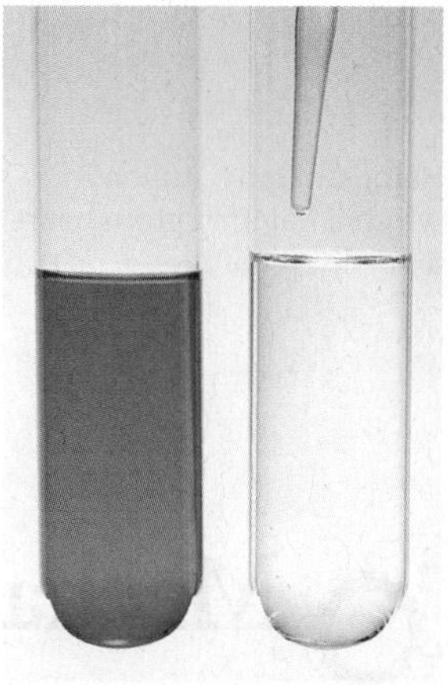

Charles D. Winters

A solution of bromine in dichloromethane is red. Add a few drops of an alkene and the red color disappears.

EXAMPLE 5.7

Complete these reactions, showing the stereochemistry of each product:

(a) 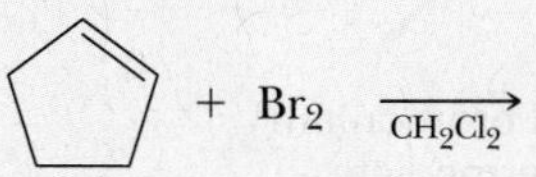

(b) 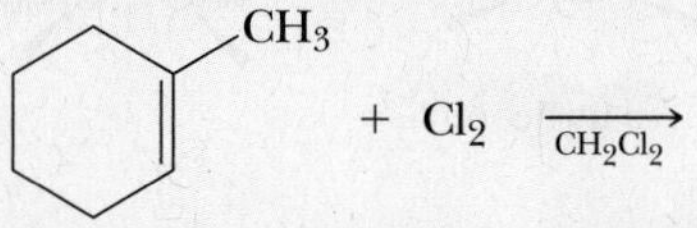

STRATEGY

The addition of both Br_2 and Cl_2 to cycloalkenes occurs with anti stereoselectivity; the two halogen atoms are *trans* to each other in the product.

SOLUTION

(a) 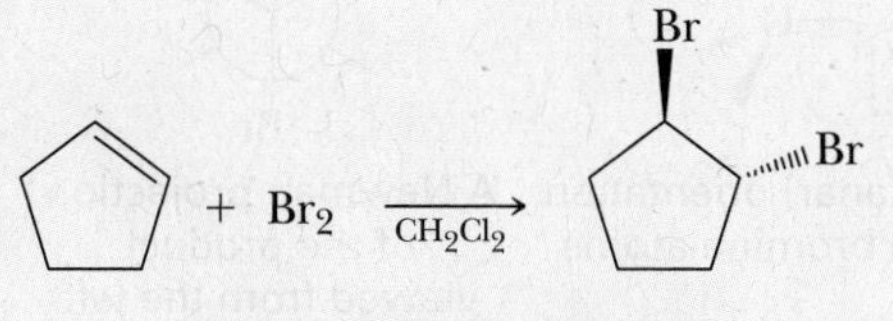

(b) 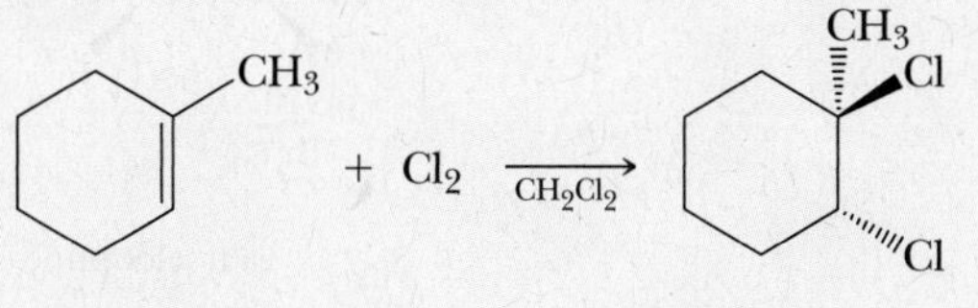

See problem 5.21

PROBLEM 5.7

Complete these reactions:

(a) 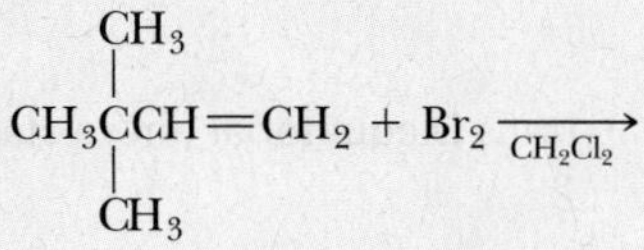

(b) 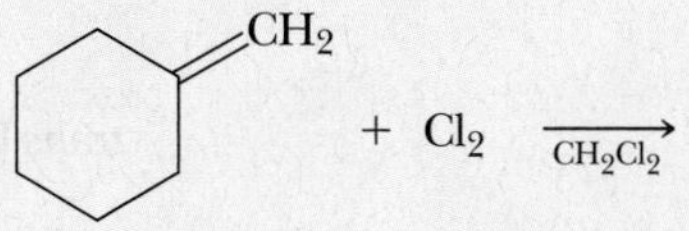

Stereoselectivity and Bridged Halonium Ion Intermediates

Halonium ion An ion in which a halogen atom bears a positive charge.

We explain the addition of bromine and chlorine to cycloalkenes, as well as their anti stereoselectivity (they always add *trans* to each other), by a two-step mechanism that involves a halogen atom bearing a positive charge, called a **halonium ion**. The cyclic structure of which this ion is a part is called a **bridged halonium ion**. The bridged bromonium ion shown in the mechanism that follows might look odd to you, but it is an acceptable Lewis structure. A calculation of formal charge places a positive charge on bromine. Then, in Step 2, a bromide ion reacts with the bridged intermediate from the side opposite that occupied by the bromine atom, giving the dibromoalkane. Thus, bromine atoms add from opposite faces of the carbon–carbon double bond.

Mechanism

Addition of Bromine with Anti Selectivity

STEP 1: Reaction of a nucleophile and an electrophile to form a new covalent bond. Reaction of the pi electrons of the carbon–carbon double bond (a nucleophile) with bromine (an electrophile) forms a bridged bromonium ion intermediate in which bromine bears a positive formal charge:

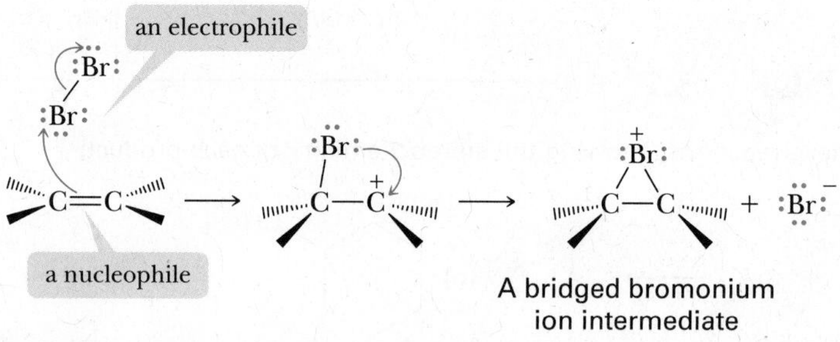

STEP 2: Reaction of a nucleophile and an electrophile to form a new covalent bond. A bromide ion (a nucleophile and a Lewis base) attacks carbon (an electrophile and a Lewis acid) from the side opposite the bridged bromonium ion, opening the three-membered ring:

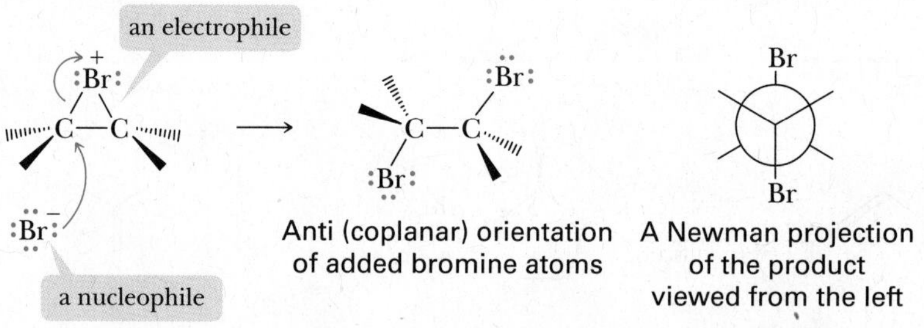

The addition of chlorine or bromine to cyclohexene and its derivatives gives a *trans* diaxial product because only axial positions on adjacent atoms of a cyclohexane ring are anti and coplanar. The initial *trans* diaxial conformation of the product is in equilibrium with the *trans* diequatorial conformation, and, in simple derivatives of cyclohexane, the latter is the more stable conformation and predominates.

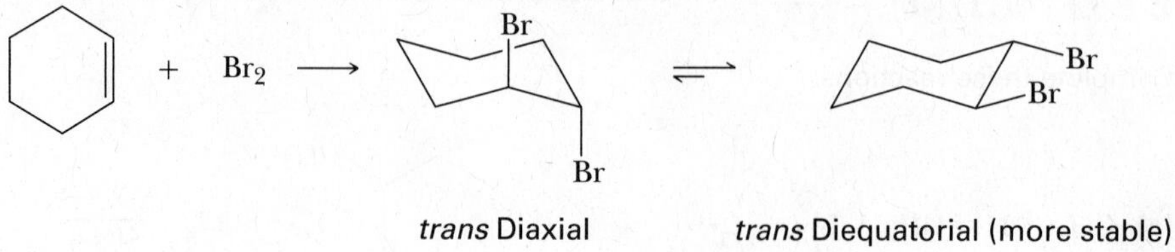

5.4 What Are Carbocation Rearrangements?

As we have seen in the preceding discussion, the expected product of electrophilic addition to a carbon–carbon double bond involves rupture of the π bond and formation of two new σ bonds in its place. In the addition of HCl to 3,3-dimethyl-1-butene, however, only 17% of 2-chloro-3, 3-dimethylbutane, the expected product, is formed. The major product is 2-chloro-2,3-dimethylbutane, a compound with a different connectivity of its carbon atoms than that in the starting material. We say that the formation of 2-chloro-2,3-dimethylbutane involves a **rearrangement**. Typically, either an alkyl group or a hydrogen atom migrates, with its bonding pair of electrons, from an adjacent atom to an electron-deficient atom. In the rearrangements we examine in this chapter, migration is to an adjacent electron-deficient carbon atom bearing a positive charge. In other words, rearrangement is to the positively charged carbon of a carbocation.

Rearrangement A reaction in which a carbon or hydrogen atom has shifted its connectivity to another atom within the molecule.

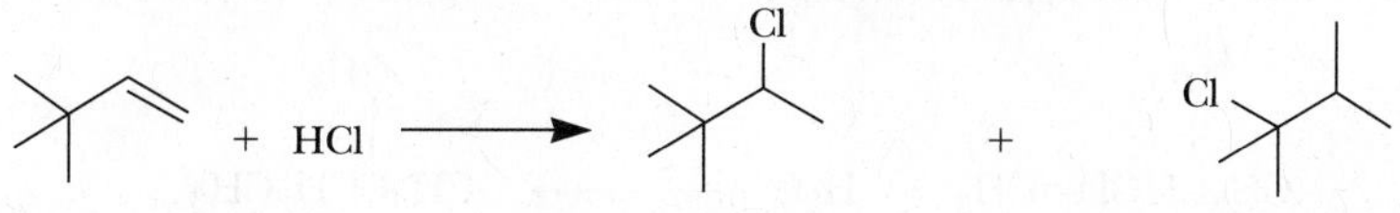

3,3-Dimethyl-1-butene | 2-Chloro-3,3-dimethylbutane (the expected product 17%) | 2-Chloro-2,3-dimethylbutane (the major product 83%)

Formation of the rearranged product in this reaction can be accounted for by the following mechanism, the key step of which is a type of rearrangement called a **1,2-shift**. In the rearrangement shown in Step 2, the migrating group is a methyl group with its pair of bonding electrons.

Mechanism

Rearrangement by a 1,2-Shift

STEP 1: Add a proton. Proton transfer from the HCl (an electrophile) to the alkene (a nucleophile) gives a 2° carbocation intermediate.

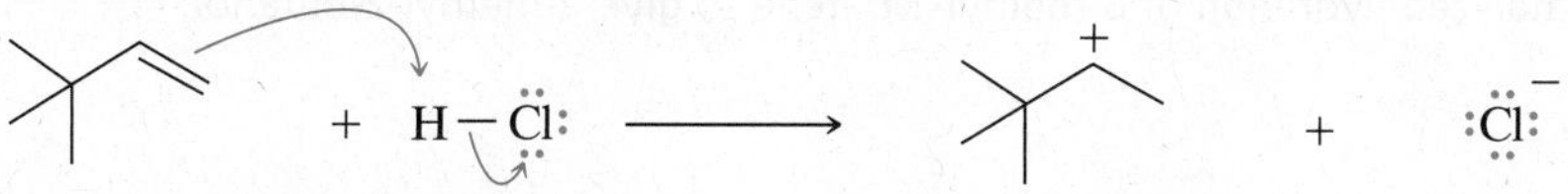

(an electrophile)

3,3-Dimethyl-1-butene (a nucleophile)

A 2° carbocation intermediate

STEP 2: Rearrangement of a bond. Migration of a methyl group with its bonding electrons from an adjacent carbon gives a more stable 3° carbocation intermediate. The major movement is that of the bonding electron pair with the methyl group following.

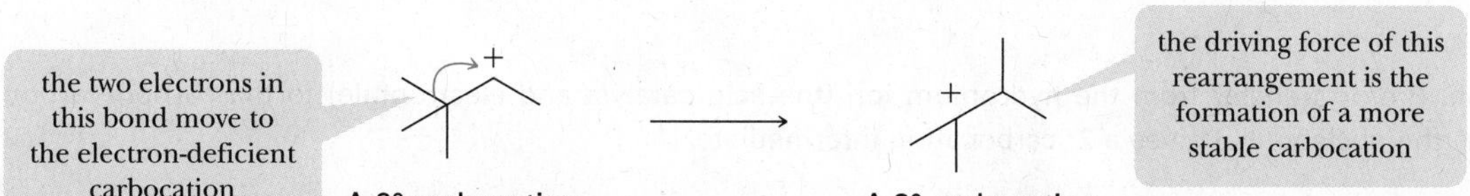

the two electrons in this bond move to the electron-deficient carbocation
+
+
the driving force of this rearrangement is the formation of a more stable carbocation

A 2° carbocation intermediate

A 3° carbocation intermediate

STEP 3: Reaction of a nucleophile and an electrophile to form a new covalent bond. Reaction of the 3° carbocation intermediate (an electrophile and a Lewis acid) with chloride ion (a nucleophile and a Lewis base) gives the rearranged product.

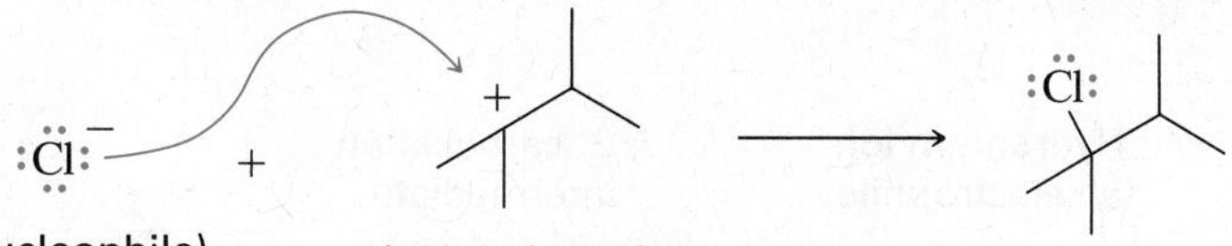

(a nucleophile)

A 3° carbocation intermediate (an electrophile)

The driving force for this rearrangement is the fact that the less stable 2° carbocation is converted to a more stable 3° carbocation. From the study of this and other carbocation rearrangements, we find that 2° carbocations rearrange to 3° carbocations. 1° Carbocations are never observed for reactions taking place in solution and should not be proposed as reaction intermediates.

Rearrangements also occur in the acid-catalyzed hydration of alkenes, especially when a carbocation formed in the first step can rearrange to a more stable carbocation. For example, the acid-catalyzed hydration of 3-methyl-1-butene gives 2-methyl-2-butanol. In this example, the group that migrates is a hydrogen with its bonding pair of electrons, in effect, a hydride ion H:⁻.

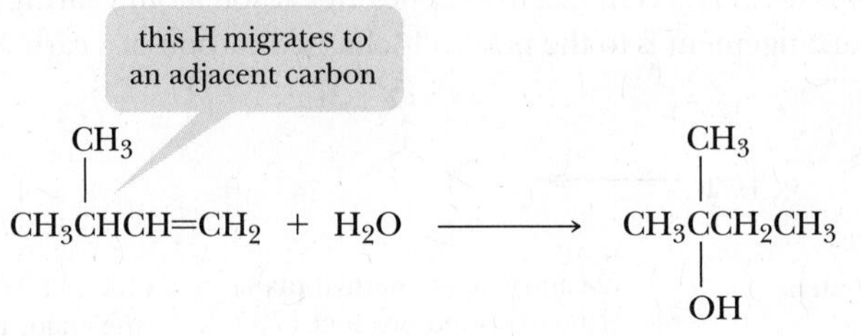
this H migrates to an adjacent carbon

3-Methyl-1-butene → 2-Methyl-2-butanol

In summary, a rearrangement is likely to occur when a secondary carbocation forms and can rearrange by a 1,2-shift to a more stable tertiary carbocation.

EXAMPLE 5.8

Propose a mechanism for the acid-catalyzed hydration of 3-methyl-1-butene to give 2-methyl-2-butanol.

STRATEGY

Propose a mechanism similar to that proposed for the acid-catalyzed hydration of an alkene involving proton transfer from the acid catalyst to form a carbocation intermediate, rearrangement of the carbocation intermediate to a more stable intermediate, reaction of the more stable carbocation with water to form an oxonium ion, and finally proton transfer from the oxonium ion to water to give the product and regenerate the acid catalyst. Lest you be tempted to use H^+ to initiate the reaction, remember that ionization of a strong acid in water generates a hydronium ion and an anion. Hydronium ion and not H^+ is the true catalyst in this reaction.

SOLUTION

STEP 1: Add a proton. Proton transfer from the hydronium ion (the acid catalyst and electrophile) to the carbon–carbon double bond (the nucleophile) gives a 2° carbocation intermediate.

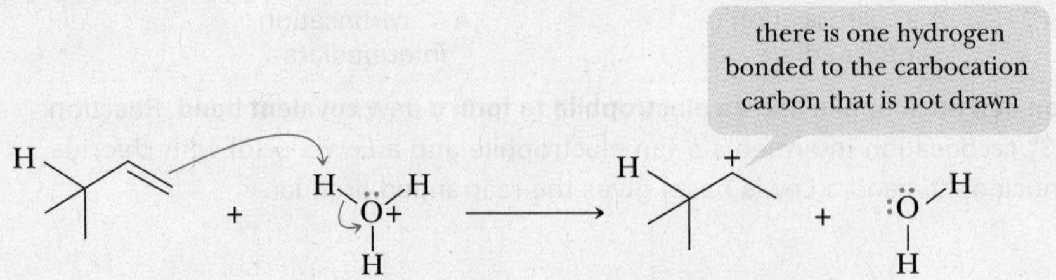
there is one hydrogen bonded to the carbocation carbon that is not drawn

3-Methyl-1-butene (a nucleophile) | Hydronium ion (an electrophile) | A 2° carbocation intermediate

STEP 2: Rearrangement of a bond. A 1,2-shift of a hydrogen from an adjacent carbon with its bonding pair of electrons to the positively charged carbon gives a more stable 3° carbocation intermediate.

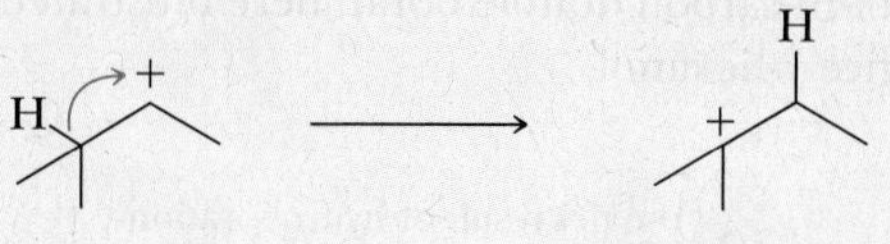

A 2° carbocation intermediate — A 3° carbocation intermediate

STEP 3: Reaction of a nucleophile and an electrophile to form a new covalent bond. Reaction of the 3° carbocation (an electrophile and a Lewis acid) with a water molecule (a nucleophile and a Lewis base) completes the valence shell of carbon and gives an oxonium ion.

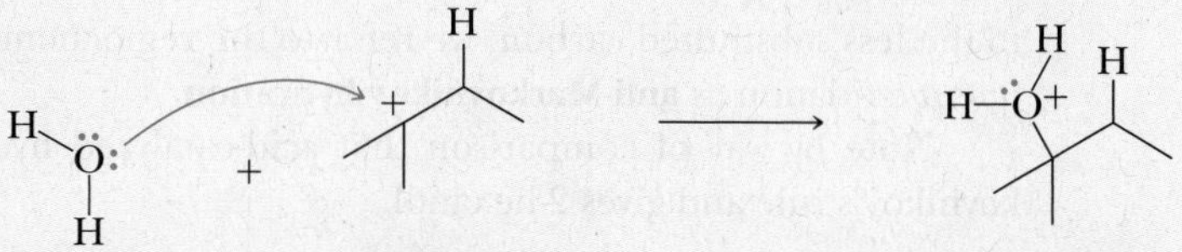

(a nucleophile) — A 2° carbocation intermediate (an electrophile) — An oxonium ion

STEP 4: Take a proton away. Proton transfer from the oxonium ion to water gives the alcohol and regenerates the acid catalyst.

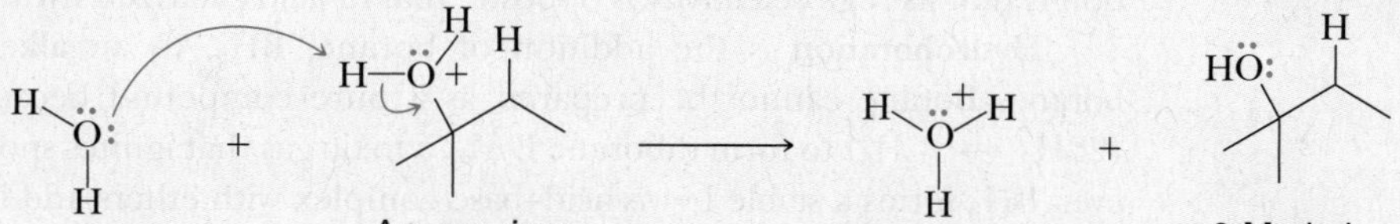

An oxonium ion — Hydronium ion — 2-Methyl-2-butanol

See problems 5.29–5.31, 5.38

PROBLEM 5.8

The acid-catalyzed hydration of 3,3-dimethyl-1-butene gives 2,3-dimethyl-2-butanol as the major product. Propose a mechanism for the formation of this alcohol.

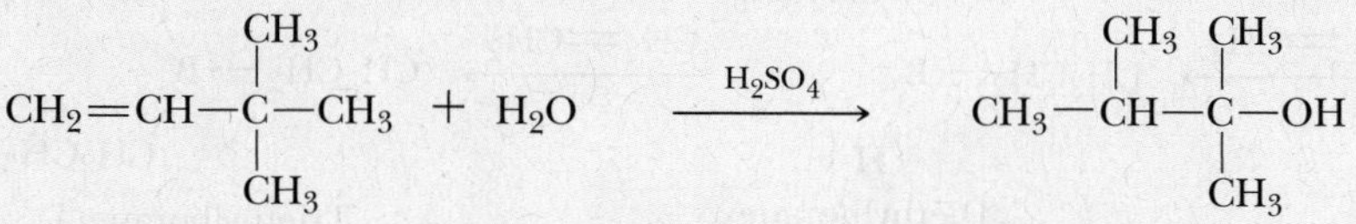

3,3-Dimethyl-1-butene — 2,3-Dimethyl-2-butanol

5.5 What Is Hydroboration–Oxidation of an Alkene?

The result of hydroboration and subsequent oxidation of an alkene is hydration of the carbon–carbon double bond, here illustrated by the hydroboration–oxidation of 1-hexene to give 1-hexanol.

the net result of hydroboration–oxidation is the addition of H and OH across the C—C double bond

contrary to Markovnikov's rule, the hydrogen has added to the former double-bond carbon with the fewer hydrogens

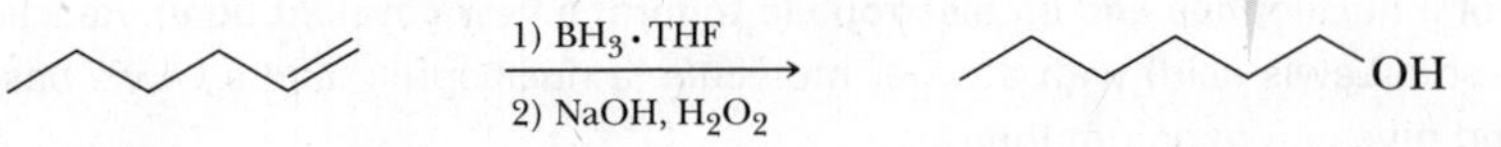

Because hydrogen is added to the more substituted carbon of the double bond and —OH to the less substituted carbon, we refer to the regiochemistry of hydroboration and subsequent oxidation as **anti-Markovnikov hydration**.

Note by way of comparison that acid-catalyzed hydration of 1-hexene follows Markovnikov's rule and gives 2-hexanol.

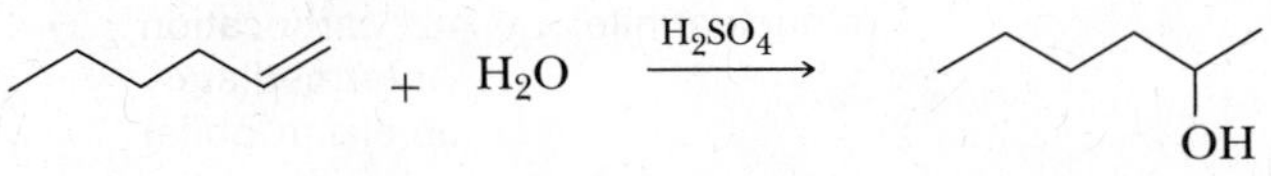

1-Hexene 2-Hexanol

The special value of hydration of an alkene by the combination of hydroboration–oxidation is that its regioselectivity is opposite that of acid-catalyzed hydration.

Hydroboration is the addition of borane, BH_3, to an alkene to form a trialkylborane. Borane cannot be prepared as a pure compound because it reacts with itself ($2BH_3 \rightarrow B_2H_6$) to form diborane B_2H_6, a toxic gas that ignites spontaneously in air. However, BH_3 forms a stable Lewis acid–base complex with ethers and is most commonly used as a commercially available solution of BH_3 in tetrahydrofuran (THF).

Tetrahydrofuran (THF) $BH_3 \cdot THF$

The overall reaction of BH_3 with a C—C double bond occurs in three steps. Borane reacts first with one molecule of the alkene to form an alkylborane, then with a second molecule of alkene to form a dialkylborane, and finally with a third molecule of alkene to form a trialkylborane. Although borane reacts with three equivalents of alkene to form the trialkylborane, we will focus on just the reaction of the first equivalent of C═C to explain the selectivities of the reaction.

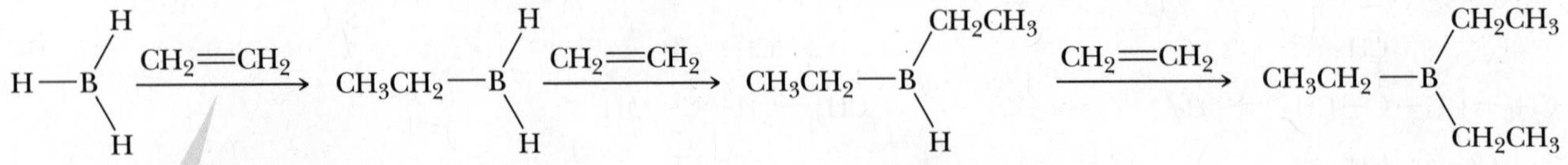

Borane Ethylborane (an alkylborane) Diethylborane (a dialkylborane) Triethylborane (a trialkylborane)

we will focus on just this first reaction to explain the selectivities of the hydroboration reaction

Boron, atomic number 5, has three electrons in its valence shell. To bond with three other atoms, boron uses sp^2 hybrid orbitals. Study the orbital model of BH_3 and take note of its types of orbitals and their geometrical arrangement. Because of the vacant $2p$ orbital in the valence shell of boron, BH_3, BF_3, and other tricovalent compounds of boron are electrophiles and closely resemble carbocations, except that they are electrically neutral.

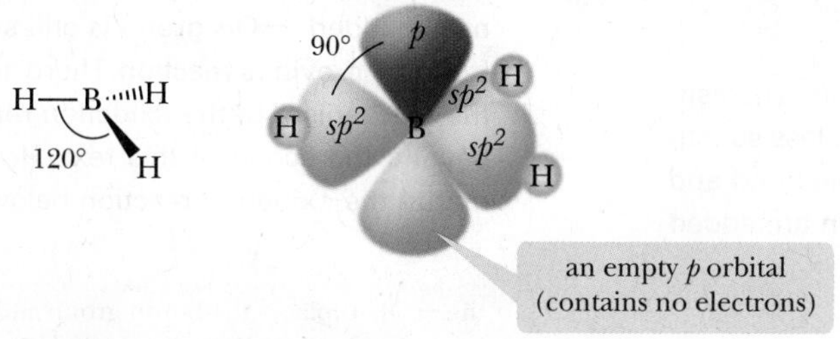

Addition of borane to alkenes is regioselective and stereoselective in the following ways:

- Regioselective: In the addition of borane to an unsymmetrical alkene, boron becomes bonded predominantly to the less substituted carbon of the double bond.
- Stereoselective: Hydrogen and boron add from the same face of the double bond; that is, the reaction is **syn** (from the same side) **stereoselective**.

Both the regioselectivity and syn stereoselectivity are illustrated by hydroboration of 1-methylcyclopentene.

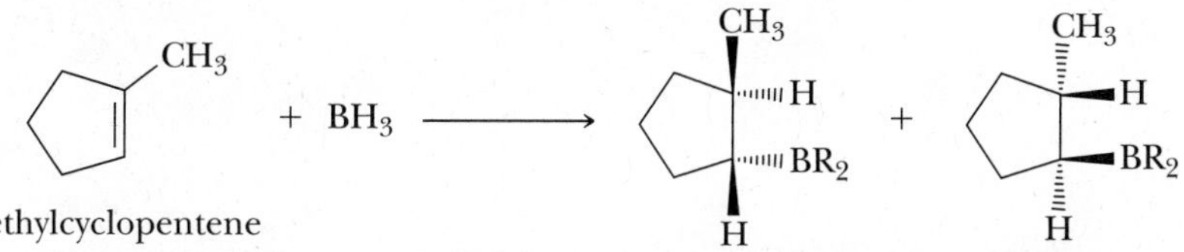

Mechanism

Hydroboration of an Alkene

STEP 1. Reaction of a nucleophile and an electrophile to form a new covalent bond. The addition of borane to an alkene is initiated by coordination of the vacant $2p$ orbital of boron (an electrophile) with the electron pair of the pi bond (a nucleophile). Chemists account for the stereoselectivity of hydroboration by proposing the formation of a cyclic, four-center transition state. Boron and hydrogen add simultaneously and from the same face of the double bond, with boron adding to the less substituted carbon atom of the double bond. This accounts for the syn stereoselectivity of the reaction. As shown in the mechanism, there is a slight polarity (about 5%) to the B—H bond because hydrogen (2.1) is slightly more electronegative than boron (2.0).

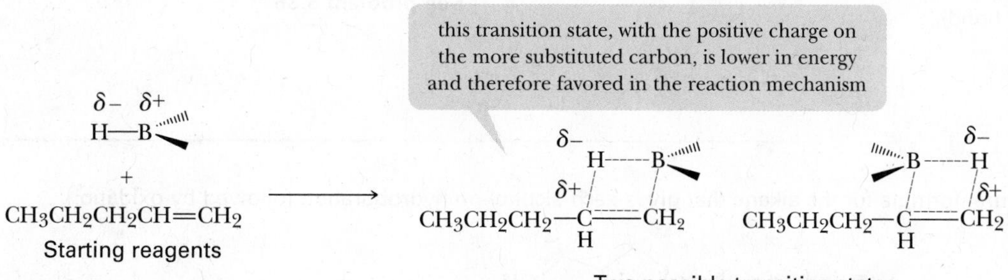

We account for the regioselectivity by steric factors. Boron, the larger part of the reagent, adds selectively to the less hindered carbon of the double bond, and hydrogen, the smaller part of the reagent, adds to the more hindered carbon. It is believed that the observed regioselectivity is due largely to steric effects.

Step 2 and beyond. Step 1 in this mechanism explains why the proton ends up on the less substituted carbon of the former C-C double bond and why the newly added boron and proton are added

syn. The boranes that are formed in the hydroboration reaction are typically oxidized using hydrogen peroxide under basic conditions. Oxidation by hydrogen peroxide results in the replacement of the boron group with an -OH group. In fact, the hydroxyl group replaces the boron such that the newly added — OH group is still syn to the proton from the previous reaction. There are many steps in the mechanism of the oxidation reaction which are beyond the scope of this text. However, we summarize the oxidation reaction below:

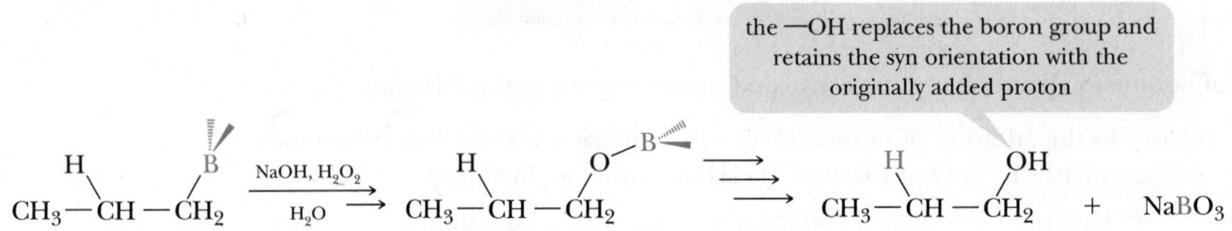

the -OH replaces the boron group and retains the syn orientation with the originally added proton

EXAMPLE 5.9

Draw structural formulas for the alcohol formed by hydroboration-oxidation of each alkene.

$$CH_3$$
|
(a) $CH_3C = CHCH_3$

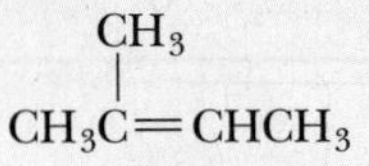

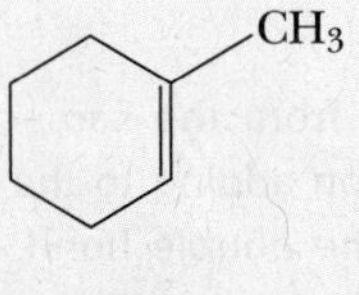

STRATEGY

Hydroboration-oxidation is regioselective (-OH adds to the more substituted carbon of the carbon-carbon double bond, and -H adds to the more substituted carbon). It is also stereoselective (-H and -OH add to the same face of the double bond).

SOLUTION

3-Methyl-2-butanol

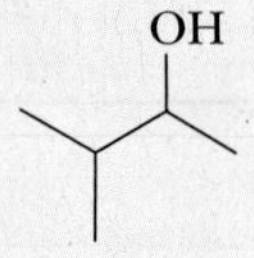

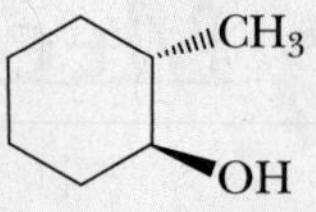

trans-2-Methylcylohexanol

See problem 5.36

PROBLEM 5.9

Draw a structural formula for the alkene that gives each alcohol on hydroboration followed by oxidation.

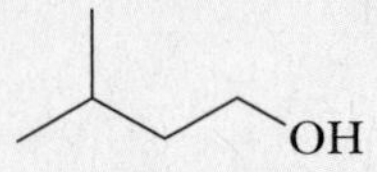

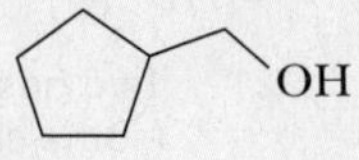

5.6 How Can an Alkene Be Reduced to an Alkane?

Most alkenes react quantitatively with molecular hydrogen, H_2 in the presence of a transition metal catalyst to give alkanes. Commonly used transition metal catalysts include platinum, palladium, ruthenium, and nickel. Yields are usually quantitative or nearly so. Because the conversion of an alkene to an alkane involves reduction by hydrogen in the presence of a catalyst, the process is called **catalytic reduction** or, alternatively, **catalytic hydrogenation**.

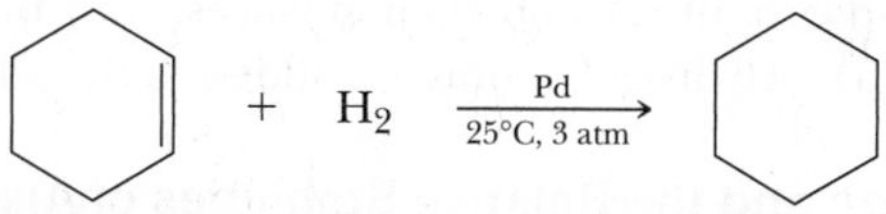

Cyclohexene Cyclohexane

The metal catalyst is used as a finely powdered solid, which may be supported on some inert material such as powdered charcoal or alumina. The reaction is carried out by dissolving the alkene in ethanol or another nonreacting organic solvent, adding the solid catalyst, and exposing the mixture to hydrogen gas at pressures from 1 to 100 atm. Alternatively, the metal may be chelated with certain organic molecules and used in the form of a soluble complex.

Catalytic reduction is stereoselective, the most common pattern being the **syn addition** of hydrogens to the carbon–carbon double bond. The catalytic reduction of 1,2-dimethylcyclohexene, for example, yields *cis*-1,2-dimethylcyclohexane along with lesser amounts of *trans*-1,2-dimethylcyclohexane.

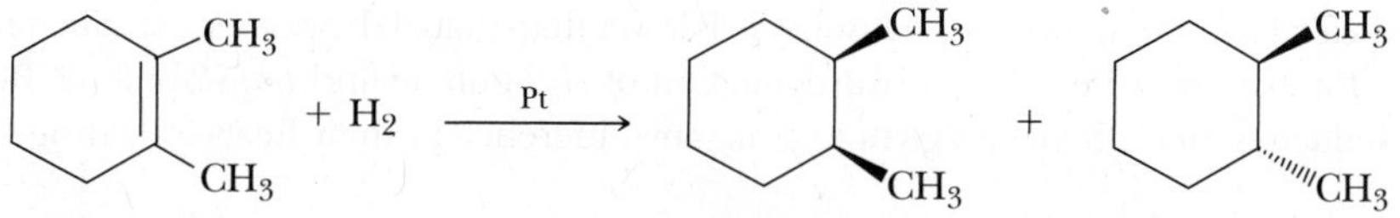

1,2-Dimethyl-cyclohexene — 70% to 85% *cis*-1,2-Dimethyl-cyclohexane — 30% to 15% *trans*-1,2-Dimethyl-cyclohexane

The transition metals used in catalytic reduction are able to adsorb large quantities of hydrogen onto their surfaces, probably by forming metal–hydrogen sigma bonds. Similarly,

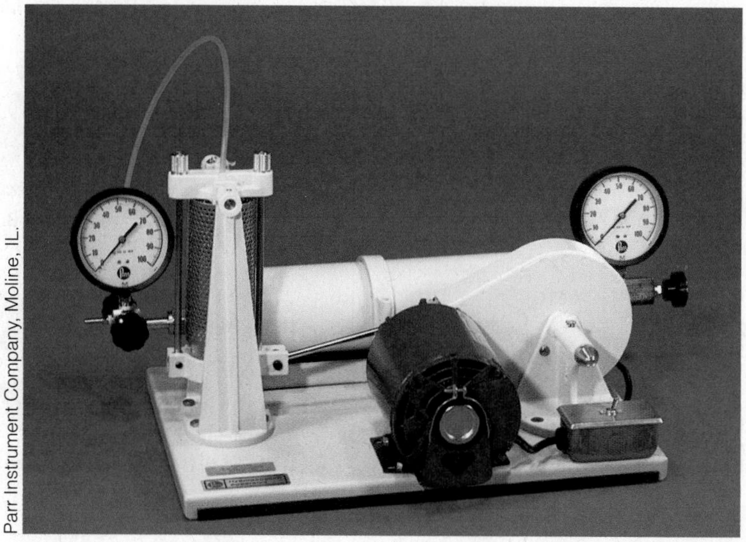

A Parr shaker-type hydrogenation apparatus.

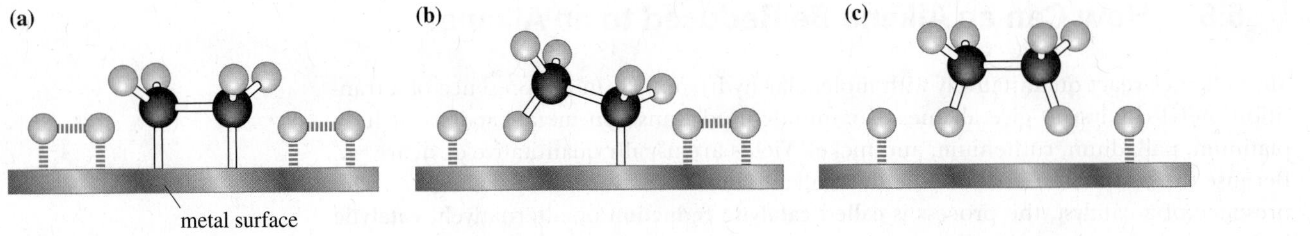

FIGURE 5.6
Syn addition of hydrogen to an alkene involving a transition metal catalyst. (a) Hydrogen and alkene are adsorbed on the metal surface, and (b) one hydrogen atom is transferred to the alkene, forming a new C—H bond. The other carbon remains adsorbed on the metal surface. (c) A second C—H bond forms, and the alkane is desorbed.

these transition metals adsorb alkenes on their surfaces, with the formation of carbon–metal bonds [Figure 5.6(a)]. Hydrogen atoms are added to the alkene in two steps.

Heats of Hydrogenation and the Relative Stabilities of Alkenes

The **heat of hydrogenation** of an alkene is defined as its heat of reaction, $\Delta H°$, with hydrogen, to form an alkane. Table 5.2 lists the heats of hydrogenation of several alkenes.

Three important points follow from the information given in the table.

1. The reduction of an alkene to an alkane is an exothermic process. This observation is consistent with the fact that, during hydrogenation, there is net conversion of a weaker pi bond to a stronger sigma bond; that is, one sigma bond (H—H) and one pi bond (C=C) are broken, and two new sigma bonds (C—H) are formed.
2. The heat of hydrogenation depends on the degree of substitution of the carbon–carbon double bond: The greater the substitution, the lower is the heat of hydrogenation. Compare, for example, the heats of hydrogenation of ethylene (no substituents), propene (one substituent), 1-butene (one substituent), and the *cis* and *trans* isomers of 2-butene (two substituents each).
3. The heat of hydrogenation of a *trans* alkene is lower than that of the isomeric *cis* alkene. Compare, for example, the heats of hydrogenation of *cis*-2-butene and *trans*-2-butene. Because the reduction of each alkene gives butane, any difference in their heats of hydrogenation

TABLE 5.2 Heats of Hydrogenation of Several Alkenes

Name	Structural Formula	ΔH [kJ (kcal/mol)]	
Ethylene	$CH_2{=}CH_2$	−137 (−32.8)	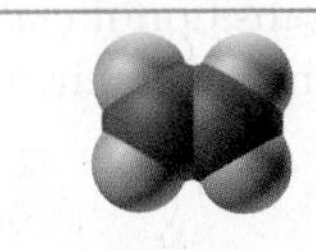 Ethylene
Propene	$CH_3CH{=}CH_2$	−126 (−30.1)	
1-Butene	$CH_3CH_2CH{=}CH_2$	−127 (−30.3)	
cis-2-Butene	CH_3 CH_3 C=C H H	−120 (−28.6)	
trans-2-Butene	CH_3 H C=C H CH_3	−115 (−27.6)	 *trans*-2-Butene
2-Methyl-2-butene	CH_3 CH_3 C=C CH_3 H	−113 (−26.9)	
2,3-Dimethyl-2-butene	CH_3 CH_3 C=C CH_3 CH_3	−111 (−26.6)	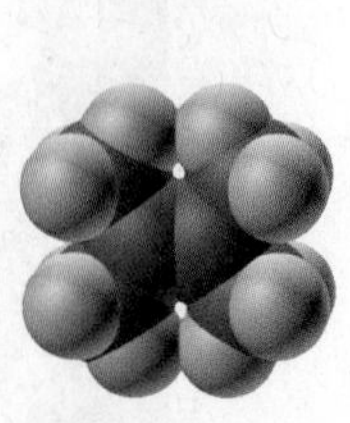 2,3-Dimethyl-2-butene

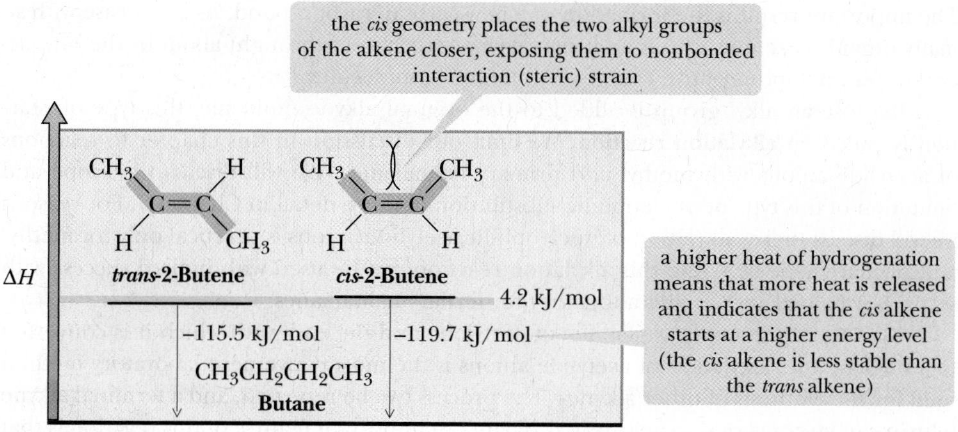
the *cis* geometry places the two alkyl groups of the alkene closer, exposing them to nonbonded interaction (steric) strain
ΔH
trans-2-Butene
cis-2-Butene
4.2 kJ/mol
-115.5 kJ/mol
-119.7 kJ/mol
CH3CH2CH2CH3
Butane
a higher heat of hydrogenation means that more heat is released and indicates that the *cis* alkene starts at a higher energy level (the *cis* alkene is less stable than the *trans* alkene)

FIGURE 5.7 Heats of hydrogenation of *cis*-2-butene and *trans*-2-butene. *trans*-2-Butene is more stable than *cis*-2-butene by 4.2 kJ/mol (1.0 kcal/mol).

must be due to a difference in relative energy between the two alkenes (Figure 5.7). The alkene with the lower (less negative) value of $\Delta H°$ is the more stable alkene.

These features of a hydrogenation reaction allow us to compare the stabilities and reactivities of any two alkenes that would yield the same product upon hydrogenation. Thus we explain the greater stability of *trans* alkenes relative to *cis* alkenes in terms of nonbonded interaction strain. In *cis*-2-butene, the two $-CH_3$ groups are sufficiently close to each other that there is repulsion between their electron clouds. This repulsion is reflected in the larger heat of hydrogenation (decreased stability) of *cis*-2-butene compared with that of *trans*-2-butene (approximately 4.2 kJ/mol).

5.7 How Can an Acetylide Anion Be Used to Create a New Carbon–Carbon Bond?

In this section, we cover one of two very important reactions of alkynes for organic synthesis. As we have seen (Section 4.4) an acetylide anion is a strong base. It is also a nucleophile—it has an unshared pair of electrons that it can donate to an electrophilic carbon atom to form a new carbon–carbon bond.

To see how the use of an acetylide anion can lead to the formation of a new carbon–carbon bond, consider chloromethane, CH_3Cl. The C—Cl bond of chloromethane is polar covalent, with carbon bearing a partial positive charge because of the difference in electronegativity between carbon and chlorine.

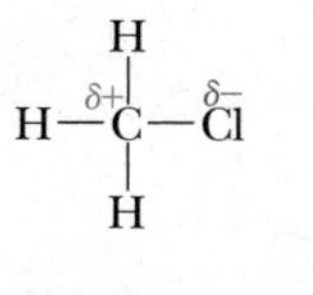

In this instance, an acetylide anion donates its unshared pair of electrons to the carbon of chloromethane and in so doing displaces the halogen atom. Notice that this mechanism follows one of our common patterns, **the reaction of a nucleophile with an electrophile to form a new covalent bond**:

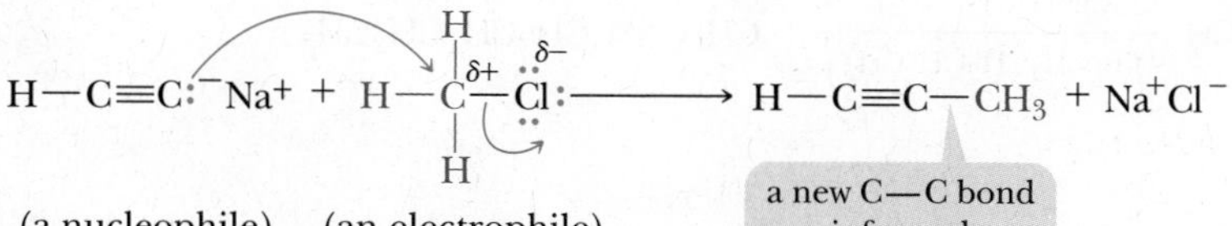
(a nucleophile)
(an electrophile)
a new C—C bond is formed

The important result is the formation of a new carbon–carbon bond. As is the case with so many organic reactions, this is an instance where reaction is brought about by the interaction of positive and negative charges of interacting molecules.

Because an alkyl group is added to the original alkyne molecule, this type of reaction is called an **alkylation reaction**. We limit our discussion in this chapter to reactions of acetylide anions with methyl and primary haloalkanes. We will discuss the scope and limitation of this type of nucleophilic substitution in more detail in Chapter 7. For reasons we will discuss there, alkylation of nucleophilic acetylide anions is practical only for methyl and primary halides. While this alkylation reaction can be used with limited success with secondary haloalkanes, it fails altogether for tertiary haloalkanes.

Because of the ready availability of acetylene and the ease with which it is converted to a nucleophile, alkylation of acetylide anions is the most convenient laboratory method used for the synthesis of other alkynes. The process can be repeated, and a terminal alkyne in turn can be converted to an internal alkyne. An important feature of this reaction is that a new carbon–carbon skeleton can be made, allowing for the construction of larger carbon skeletons from smaller ones. In the following scheme, the carbon skeleton of 3-heptyne is constructed from acetylene and two lower-molecular-weight haloalkanes.

$$\underset{\text{Acetylene}}{HC{\equiv}CH} \xrightarrow[\text{2) } CH_3CH_2Br]{\text{1) } NaNH_2} \underset{\text{1-Butyne}}{CH_3CH_2C{\equiv}CH} \xrightarrow[\text{4) } CH_3CH_2CH_2Br]{\text{3) } NaNH_2} \underset{\text{3-Heptyne}}{CH_3CH_2C{\equiv}CCH_2CH_2CH_3}$$

EXAMPLE 5.10

Propose a synthesis for each alkyne starting with acetylene and any necessary organic and inorganic reagents.

(a) 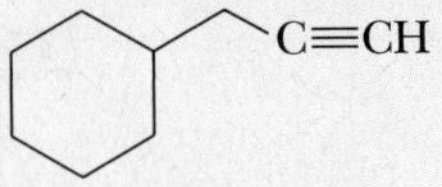

(b) $CH_3C{\equiv}CCH_2CH(CH_3)CH_3$ (c) $CH_3C{\equiv}CCH_2CH_2CH_2CH_3$

STRATEGY

Each alkyne can be synthesized by alkylation of an appropriate alkyne anion. First decide which new carbon–carbon bond or bonds must be formed by alkylation and which alkyne anion nucleophile and haloalkane pair is required to give the desired product. Synthesis of a terminal alkyne from acetylene requires only one nucleophilic substitution, and synthesis of an internal alkyne from acetylene requires two nucleophilic substitutions.

SOLUTION

(a) 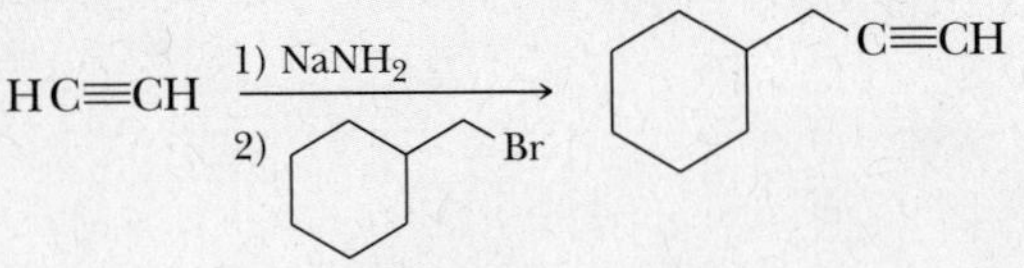

(b) $$HC{\equiv}CH \xrightarrow[\text{2) } BrCH_3]{\text{1) } NaNH_2} CH_3C{\equiv}CH \xrightarrow[\text{4) } BrCH_2CH(CH_3)CH_3]{\text{3) } NaNH_2} CH_3C{\equiv}CCH_2CH(CH_3)CH_3$$

(c) $$HC{\equiv}CH \xrightarrow[\text{2) } BrCH_3]{\text{1) } NaNH_2} CH_3C{\equiv}CH \xrightarrow[\text{4) } BrCH_2CH_2CH_2CH_3]{\text{3) } NaNH_2} CH_3C{\equiv}CCH_2CH_2CH_2CH_3$$

See problem 5.50

PROBLEM 5.10

Propose a synthesis for each alkyne starting with acetylene and any necessary organic and inorganic reagents.

(a) 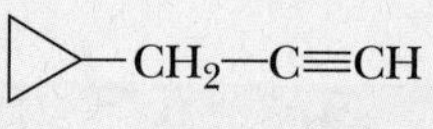 (b) 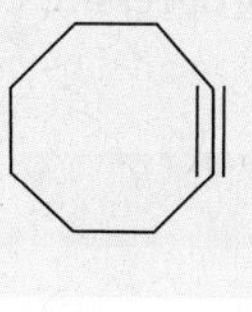

5.8 How Can Alkynes Be Reduced to Alkenes and Alkanes?

In the previous section, we saw how terminal alkynes can be used to form C—C bonds and synthesize larger alkynes. In this section, we will learn how alkynes can be reduced to alkanes and alkenes. Because of the rich number of reactions available to alkenes, we can now use these two reactions in tandem to synthesize a large variety of compounds:

$$R{-}C{\equiv}C{-}H \xrightarrow{NaNH_2} R{-}C{\equiv}C{:}^{-}\,Na^{+} \xrightarrow{R{-}X} R{-}C{\equiv}C{-}R \xrightarrow{\text{reduce}} R{-}C{=}C{-}R \xrightarrow[\text{reactions}]{\text{various}} \text{alcohols, haloalkanes, dihaloalkanes, alkanes, and others}$$

Treatment of an alkyne with H_2 in the presence of a transition metal catalyst, most commonly Pd, Pt, or Ni, results in the addition of two moles of H_2 to the alkyne and its conversion to an alkane. Catalytic reduction of an alkyne can be brought about at or slightly above room temperature and with moderate pressures of hydrogen gas.

$$\underset{\text{2-Butyne}}{CH_3C{\equiv}CCH_3} + 2H_2 \xrightarrow[\text{3 atm}]{\text{Pd, Pt, or Ni}} \underset{\text{Butane}}{CH_3CH_2CH_2CH_3}$$

Reduction of an alkyne occurs in two stages: first, addition of one mole of H_2 to form an alkene and then addition of the second mole of H_2 to the alkene to form the alkane. In most cases, it is not possible to stop the reaction at the alkene stage. However, by careful choice of catalyst, it is possible to stop the reaction at the addition of one mole of hydrogen. The catalyst most commonly used for this purpose consists of finely powdered palladium metal deposited on solid calcium carbonate that has been specially modified with lead salts. This combination is known as the **Lindlar catalyst**. Reduction (hydrogenation) of alkynes over a Lindlar catalyst is stereoselective: **syn addition** of two hydrogen atoms to the carbon–carbon triple bond gives a *cis* alkene:

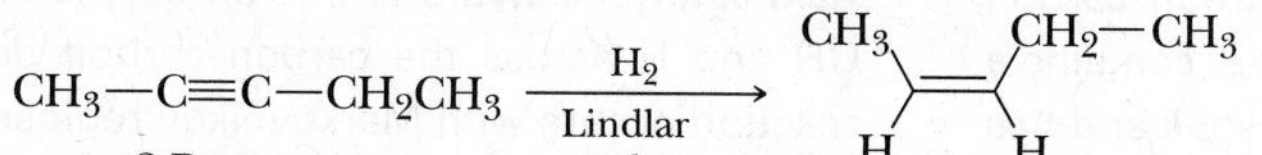

2-Pentyne → *cis*-2-Pentene

Because addition of hydrogen in the presence of the Lindlar catalyst is stereoselective for syn addition, it has been proposed that reduction proceeds by simultaneous or nearly simultaneous transfer of two hydrogen atoms from the surface of the metal catalyst to the alkyne. Earlier we presented a similar mechanism for the catalytic reduction of an alkene to an alkane (Section 5.6).

Organic chemistry is the foundation for the synthesis of new compounds such as medicines, agrochemicals, and plastics, to name just a few. In order to make these compounds, organic chemists must rely on a vast collection of reactions. The reactions presented in this chapter will already allow you to achieve the synthesis of complex molecules that may require multiple steps to make. As you continue your studies of organic chemistry, new reactions will be presented, the same reactions that have allowed for the creation of the millions of compounds that have contributed to the progress of civilization.

SUMMARY OF KEY QUESTIONS

5.1 What Are the Characteristic Reactions of Alkenes?

- A characteristic reaction of alkenes is **addition**, during which a pi bond is broken and sigma bonds are formed to two new atoms or groups of atoms. Alkene addition reactions include addition of halogen acids, H—Cl, acid-catalyzed addition of H_2O to form an alcohol, addition of halogens, X_2, hydroboration followed by oxidation to give an alcohol, and transition metal-catalyzed addition of H_2 to form an alkane.

5.2 What Is a Reaction Mechanism?

- A **reaction mechanism** is a description of (1) how and why a chemical reaction occurs, (2) which bonds break and which new ones form, (3) the order and relative rates in which the various bond-breaking and bond-forming steps take place, and (4) the role of the catalyst if the reaction involves a catalyst.
- **Transition state theory** provides a model for understanding the relationships among reaction rates, molecular structure, and energetics.
- A key postulate of transition state theory is that a **transition state** is formed in all reactions.
- The difference in energy between reactants and the transition state is called the **activation energy**.
- An **intermediate** is an energy minimum between two transition states.
- The slowest step in a multistep reaction, called the **rate-determining step**, is the one that crosses the highest energy barrier.
- There are many patterns that occur frequently in organic reaction mechanisms. These include **adding a proton, taking a proton away**, the **reaction of a nucleophile and electrophile to form a new bond**, and **rearrangement of a bond**.

5.3 What Are the Mechanisms of Electrophilic Additions to Alkenes?

- An **electrophile** is any molecule or ion that can accept a pair of electrons to form a new covalent bond. All electrophiles are Lewis acids.
- A **nucleophile** is an electron-rich species that can donate a pair of electrons to form a new covalent bond. All nucleophiles are Lewis bases.
- The rate-determining step in **electrophilic addition** to an alkene is reaction of an electrophile with a carbon–carbon double bond to form a **carbocation**, an ion that contains a carbon with only six electrons in its valence shell and has a positive charge.
- Carbocations are planar with bond angles of 120° about the positive carbon.
- The order of stability of carbocations is 3° > 2° > 1° > methyl. Primary carbocations, however, are so unstable and have such a high energy of activation for their formation that they are never formed in solution.
- **Electrophilic addition of a hydrogen halide** to an alkene is the addition of a halogen (Cl, Br, or I) and H across the carbon–carbon double bond. The reaction occurs with **Markovnikov regioselectivity** with the H adding to the carbon with the greater number of hydrogens.
- **Acid-catalyzed hydration** of an alkene is the addition of OH and H across the carbon–carbon double bond. The reaction occurs with Markovnikov regioselectivity.
- **Addition of bromine and chlorine** to an alkene is the addition of two halogens across the carbon–carbon double bond. The mechanism involves a **bridged halonium ion** as an intermediate and is an **anti stereoselective**.

5.4 What Are Carbocation Rearrangements?

- The driving force for a **carbocation rearrangement** is conversion of an initially formed carbocation to a more stable 2° or 3° carbocation.
- Rearrangement is by a **1,2-shift** in which an atom or group of atoms with its bonding electrons moves from an adjacent carbon to an electron-deficient carbon.

5.5 What Is Hydroboration–Oxidation of an Alkene?

- **Hydroboration** of an alkene is the addition of BH_2 and H across a C—C double bond.
- Hydroboration occurs with **anti-Markovnikov** regioselectivity with the H adding to the carbon with the fewer number of hydrogens.
- **Oxidation** of the hydroboration product results in the replacement of the boron group with an —OH group.
- **Hydroboration–oxidation** is **syn stereoselective.**

5.6 How Can an Alkene Be Reduced to an Alkane?

- The reaction of an alkene with H_2 in the presence of a transition metal catalyst converts all C—C double bonds in the alkene to C—C single bonds via the syn stereoselective addition of a hydrogen to each carbon of the former double bond.
- The **heats of reaction,** ΔH, of **hydrogenation reactions** can be used to compare the relative stabilities of alkenes.

5.7 How Can an Acetylide Anion Be Used to Create a New Carbon–Carbon Bond?

- **Acetylide anions** are both strong bases and nucleophiles. As nucleophiles, they can be alkylated by treatment with a methyl, primary, or secondary haloalkane. In this way, acetylene serves as a two-carbon building block for the synthesis of larger carbon skeletons.

5.8 How Can Alkynes Be Reduced to Alkenes and Alkanes?

- Treatment of alkyne with H_2 in the presence of a transition metal catalyst, most commonly Pd, Pt, or Ni, results in the addition of two moles of H_2 to the alkyne and its conversion to an alkane.
- Reduction of an alkyne using the **Lindlar catalyst** results in syn-stereoselective addition of one mole of H_2 to an alkyne. With this reagent, a disubstituted alkyne can be reduced to a *cis*-alkene.

QUICK QUIZ

Answer true or false to the following questions to assess your general knowledge of the concepts in this chapter. If you have difficulty with any of them, you should review the appropriate section in the chapter (shown in parentheses) before attempting the more challenging end-of-chapter problems.

1. Catalytic reduction of an alkene is syn stereoselective. (5.6)
2. Borane, BH_3, is a Lewis acid. (5.5)
3. All electrophiles are positively charged. (5.3)
4. Catalytic hydrogenation of cyclohexene gives hexane. (5.6)
5. A rearrangement will occur in the reaction of 2-methyl-2-pentene with HBr. (5.4)
6. All nucleophiles are negatively charged. (5.3)
7. In hydroboration, BH_3 behaves as an electrophile. (5.5)
8. In catalytic hydrogenation of an alkene, the reducing agent is the transition metal catalyst. (5.6)
9. Alkene addition reactions involve breaking a pi bond and forming two new sigma bonds in its place. (5.3)
10. The foundation for Markovnikov's rule is the relative stability of carbocation intermediates. (5.3)
11. Acid-catalyzed hydration of an alkene is regioselective. (5.3)
12. The mechanism for addition of HBr to an alkene involves one transition state and two reactive intermediates. (5.3)
13. Hydroboration of an alkene is regioselective and stereoselective. (5.5)
14. According to the mechanism given in the text for acid-catalyzed hydration of an alkene, the —H and —OH groups added to the double bond both arise from the same molecule of H_2O. (5.3)
15. Acid-catalyzed addition of H_2O to an alkene is called *hydration.* (5.3)
16. If a compound fails to react with Br_2, it is unlikely that the compound contains a carbon–carbon double bond. (5.3)
17. Addition of Br_2 and Cl_2 to cyclohexene is anti-stereoselective. (5.3)
18. A carbocation is a carbon that has four bonds to it and bears a positive charge. (5.3)
19. The geometry about the positively charged carbon of a carbocation is best described as trigonal planar. (5.3)
20. The carbocation derived by proton transfer to ethylene is $CH_3CH_2^+$. (5.3)
21. Alkyl carbocations are stabilized by the electron-withdrawing inductive effect of the positively charged carbon of the carbocation. (5.3)

22. The oxygen atom of an oxonium ion obeys the octet rule. (5.3)
23. Markovnikov's rule refers to the regioselectivity of addition reactions to carbon–carbon double bonds. (5.3)
24. A rearrangement, in which a hydride ion shifts, will occur in the reaction of 3-methyl-1-pentene with HCl. (5.4)
25. Acid-catalyzed hydration of 1-butene gives 1-butanol, and acid-catalyzed hydration of 2-butene gives 2-butanol. (5.3)
26. Alkenes are good starting materials for reactions in which it is necessary to form a C—C bond. (5.7)
27. Alkynes can be reduced to *cis* alkenes. (5.8)

Detailed explanations for many of these answers can be found in the accompanying Solutions Manual.

(1) T (2) T (3) F (4) F (5) F (6) F (7) T (8) F (9) T (10) T (11) T (12) F
(13) T (14) F (15) T (16) T (17) T (18) F (19) T (20) T (21) T (22) T
(23) T (24) T (25) F (26) F (27) F

KEY REACTIONS

1. Addition of H—X to an Alkene (Section 5.3A)

The addition of H—X is regioselective and follows Markovnikov's rule. Reaction occurs in two steps and involves the formation of a carbocation intermediate:

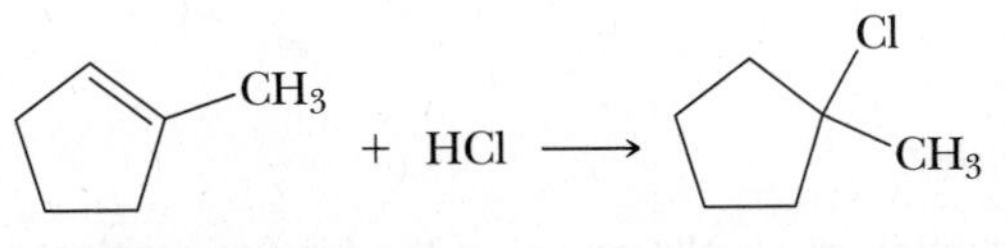

2. Acid-Catalyzed Hydration of an Alkene (Section 5.3B)

Hydration of an alkene is regioselective and follows Markovnikov's rule. Reaction occurs in two steps and involves the formation of a carbocation intermediate:

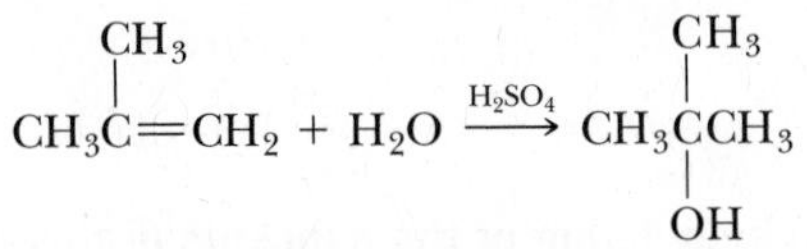

3. Addition of Bromine and Chlorine to an Alkene (Section 5.3C)

Addition of halogen occurs in two steps and involves anti-stereoselective addition by way of a bridged bromonium or chloronium ion intermediate:

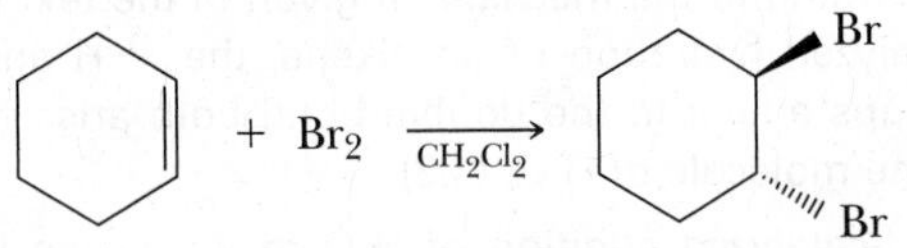

4. Carbocation Rearrangements (Section 5.4)

Rearrangement is from a less stable carbocation intermediate to a more stable one by a 1,2-shift. Rearrangements often occur during the hydrochlorination and acid-catalyzed hydration of alkenes.

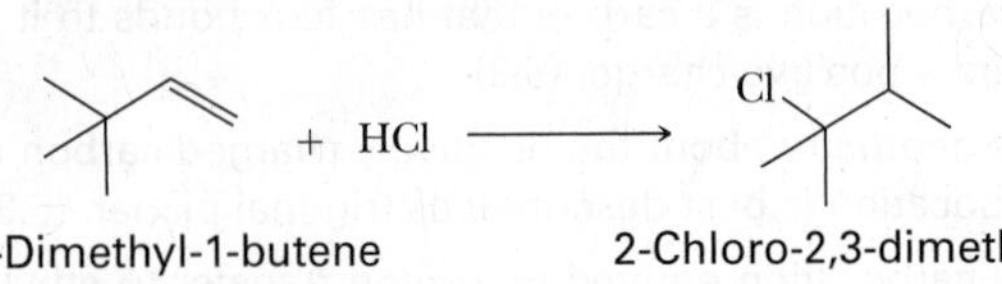

3,3-Dimethyl-1-butene 2-Chloro-2,3-dimethylbutane

5. Hydroboration–Oxidation of an Alkene (Section 5.5)

Addition of BH_3 to an alkene is syn-stereoselective and regioselective: boron adds to the less substituted carbon of the double bond, and hydrogen adds to the more substituted carbon. Hydroboration–oxidation results in anti-Markovnikov hydration of the alkene.

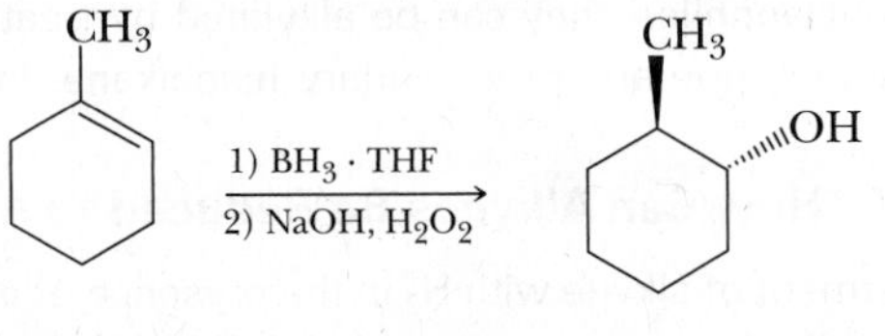

6. Reduction of an Alkene: Formation of Alkanes (Section 5.6)

Catalytic reduction involves predominantly the syn-stereoselective addition of hydrogen:

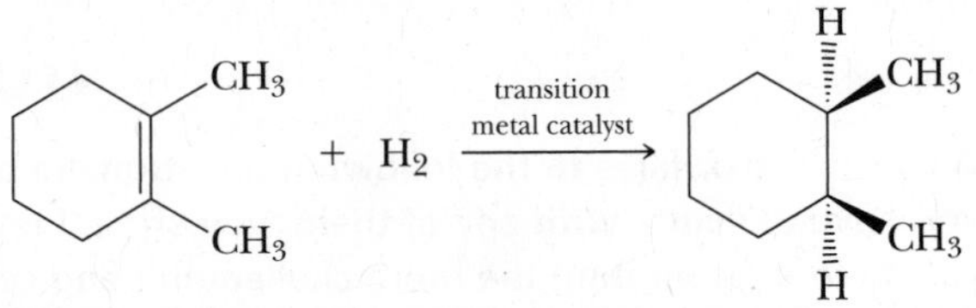

7. Alkylation on an Acetylide Anion (Section 5.7)

Acetylide anions are nucleophiles and displace halogen from methyl and 1° haloalkanes. Alkylation of acetylide anions is a valuable way to assemble a larger carbon skeleton.

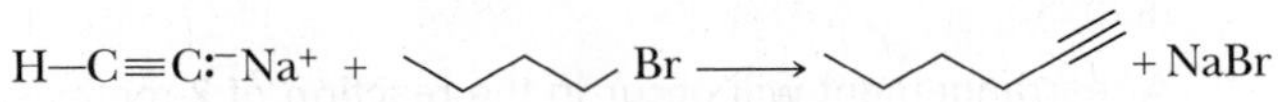

8. Reduction of an Alkyne (Section 5.8)

Several different reagents reduce alkynes. Catalytic reduction using a transition metal catalyst gives an alkane. Catalytic reduction using a specially prepared catalyst called the Lindlar catalyst gives a *cis* alkene.

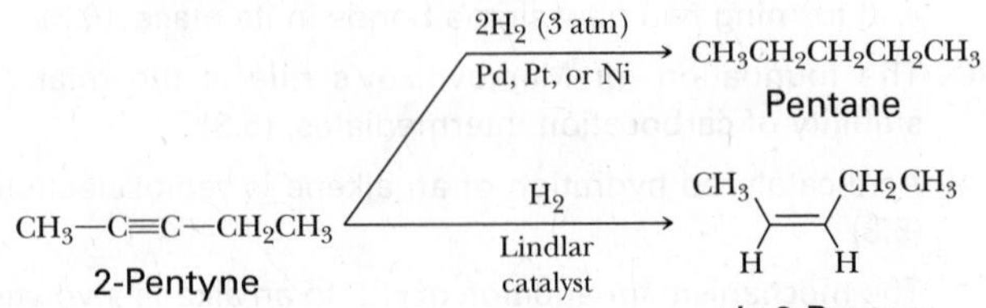

PROBLEMS

A problem marked with an asterisk indicates an applied "real-world" problem. Answers to problems whose numbers are printed in blue are given in Appendix D.

Section 5.2 Energy Diagrams

5.11 Describe the differences between a transition state and a reaction intermediate.

5.12 Sketch an energy diagram for a one-step reaction that is very slow and only slightly exothermic. How many transition states are present in this reaction? How many intermediates are present? **(See Example 5.1)**

5.13 Sketch an energy diagram for a two-step reaction that is endothermic in the first step, exothermic in the second step, and exothermic overall. How many transition states are present in this two-step reaction? How many intermediates are present? **(See Example 5.1)**

5.14 Determine whether each of the following statements is true or false, and provide a rationale for your decision:

(a) A transition state can never be lower in energy than the reactants from which it was formed.

(b) An endothermic reaction cannot have more than one intermediate.

(c) An exothermic reaction cannot have more than one intermediate.

Sections 5.3–5.5 Electrophilic Additions to Alkenes, Rearrangements, and Hydroboration–Oxidation

5.15 From each pair, select the more stable carbocation: **(See Example 5.3)**

(a) $CH_3CH_2CH_2^+$ or $CH_3\overset{+}{C}HCH_3$

(b) $CH_3\overset{CH_3}{\overset{|}{C}}H\underset{+}{C}HCH_3$ or $CH_3\underset{+}{\overset{CH_3}{\overset{|}{C}}}CH_2CH_3$

5.16 From each pair, select the more stable carbocation: **(See Example 5.3)**

(a) 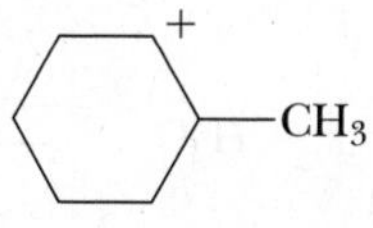

or 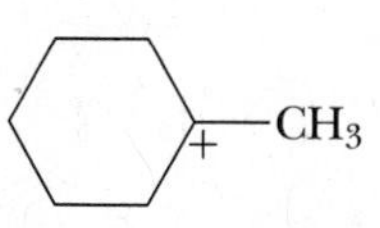

(b) 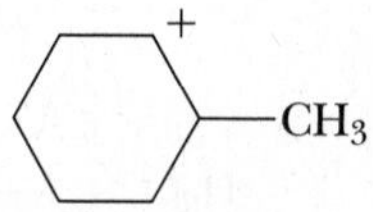

or 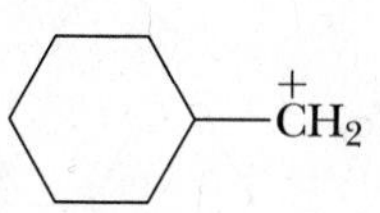

5.17 Draw structural formulas for the isomeric carbocation intermediates formed by the reaction of each alkene with HCl. Label each carbocation as primary, secondary, or tertiary, and state which, if either, of the isomeric carbocations is formed more readily. **(See Example 5.2)**

(a) 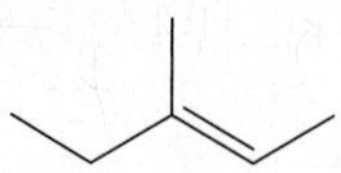

(b) 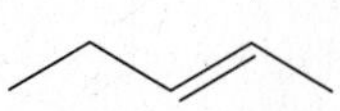

(c) 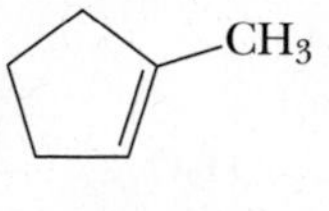

(d) 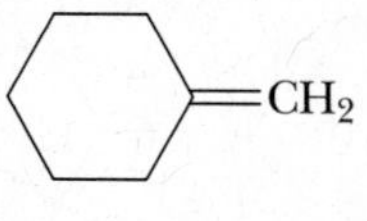

5.18 From each pair of compounds, select the one that reacts more rapidly with HI, draw the structural formula of the major product formed in each case, and explain the basis for your ranking: **(See Example 5.2)**

(a) 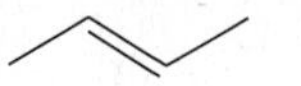 and 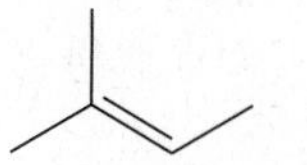

(b) 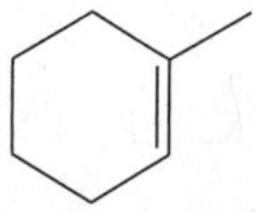 and 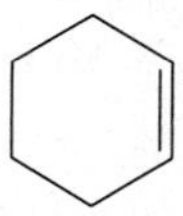

5.19 Complete these equations by predicting the major product formed in each reaction: **(See Examples 5.2, 5.5)**

(a) 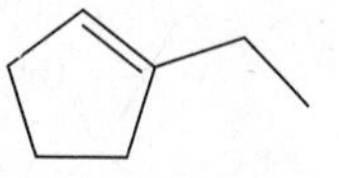 $+ \ HCl \longrightarrow$

(b) 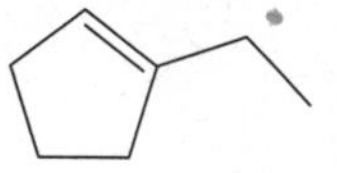 $+ \ H_2O \xrightarrow{H_2SO_4}$

(c) 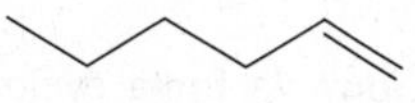 $+ \ HI \longrightarrow$

(d) 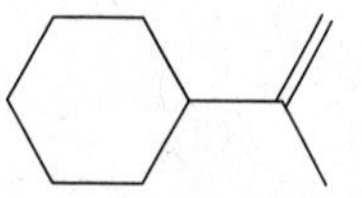 $+ \ HCl \longrightarrow$

(e) 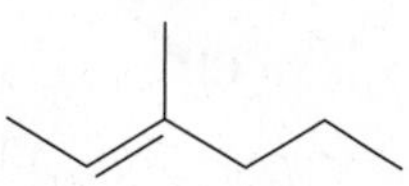 $+ \ H_2O \xrightarrow{H_2SO_4}$

(f)  $+ \ H_2O \xrightarrow{H_2SO_4}$

5.20 The reaction of 2-methyl-2-pentene with each reagent is regioselective. Draw a structural formula for the product of each reaction, and account for the observed regioselectivity. **(See Examples 5.2, 5.5, 5.9)**

(a) HI

(b) H_2O in the presence of H_2SO_4

(c) BH_3 followed by H_2O_2, NaOH

5.21 The addition of bromine and chlorine to cycloalkenes is stereoselective. Predict the stereochemistry of the product formed in each reaction: **(See Example 5.7)**

(a) 1-Methylcyclohexene + Br_2

(b) 1,2-Dimethylcyclopentene + Cl_2

5.22 Draw a structural formula for an alkene with the indicated molecular formula that gives the compound shown as the major product. Note that more than one alkene may give the same compound as the major product.

(a) $C_5H_{10} + H_2O \xrightarrow{H_2SO_4}$ 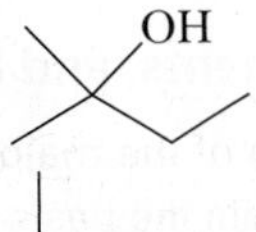

(b) $C_5H_{10} + Br_2 \longrightarrow$ 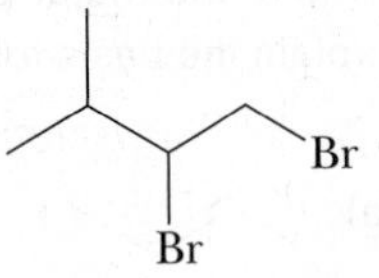

(c) C_7H_{12} + HCl $\longrightarrow$ 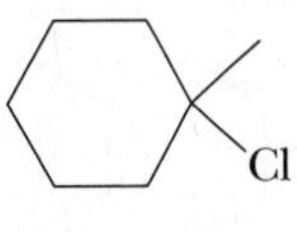

5.23 Draw the structural formula for an alkene with the molecular formula C_5H_{10} that reacts with Br_2 to give each product:

(a) 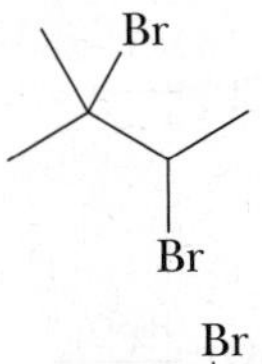

(b) 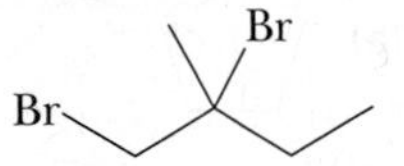

(c) 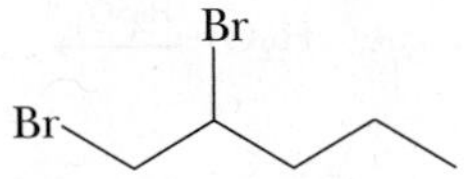

5.24 Draw the structural formula for a cycloalkene with the molecular formula C_6H_{10} that reacts with Cl_2 to give each compound:

(a) 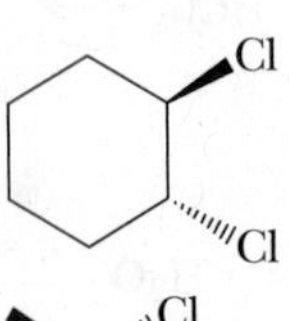

(b) 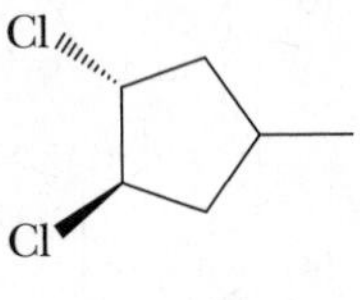

(c) 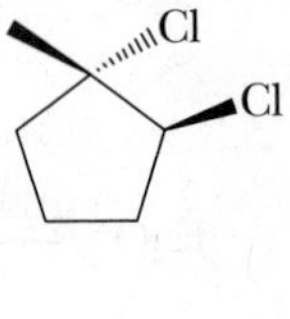

(d) 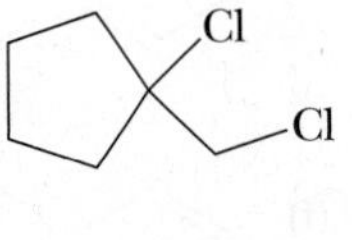

5.25 Draw the structural formula for an alkene with the molecular formula C_5H_{10} that reacts with HCl to give the indicated chloroalkane as the major product:

(a) 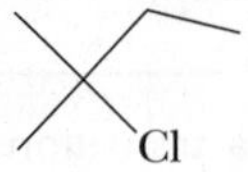

(b) 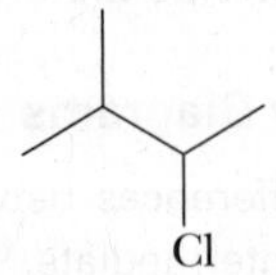

(c) 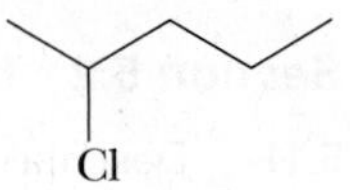

5.26 Draw the structural formula of an alkene that undergoes acid-catalyzed hydration to give the indicated alcohol as the major product. More than one alkene may give each compound as the major product.

(a) 3-Hexanol (b) 1-Methylcyclobutanol

(c) 2-Methyl-2-butanol (d) 2-Propanol

5.27 Draw the structural formula of an alkene that undergoes acid-catalyzed hydration to give each alcohol as the major product. More than one alkene may give each compound as the major product.

(a) Cyclohexanol

(b) 1,2-Dimethylcyclopentanol

(c) 1-Methylcyclohexanol

(d) 1-Isopropyl-4-methylcyclohexanol

5.28 Complete these equations by predicting the major product formed in each reaction. Note that certain of these reactions involve rearrangements. **(See Examples 5.2, 5.5)**

(a) 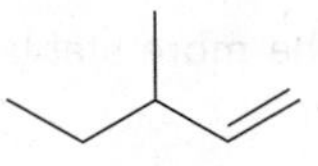 + HBr $\longrightarrow$

(b) 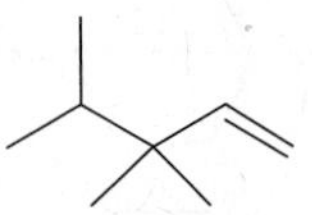 + $H_2O \xrightarrow{H_2SO_4}$

(c) 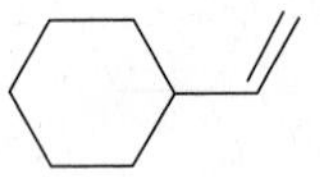 + $H_2O \xrightarrow{H_2SO_4}$

(d) 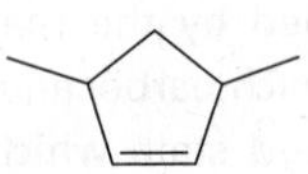 + HI $\longrightarrow$

(e) 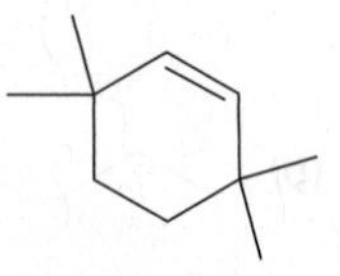 + HCl $\longrightarrow$

(f) 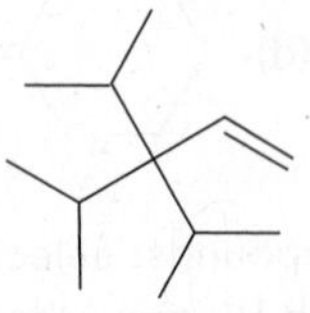 + $H_2O \xrightarrow{H_2SO_4}$

5.29 Propose a mechanism for each reaction in Problem 5.28. **(See Examples 5.4, 5.6, 5.8)**

5.30 Propose a mechanism for the following acid-catalyzed dehydration. **(See Examples 5.6, 5.8)**

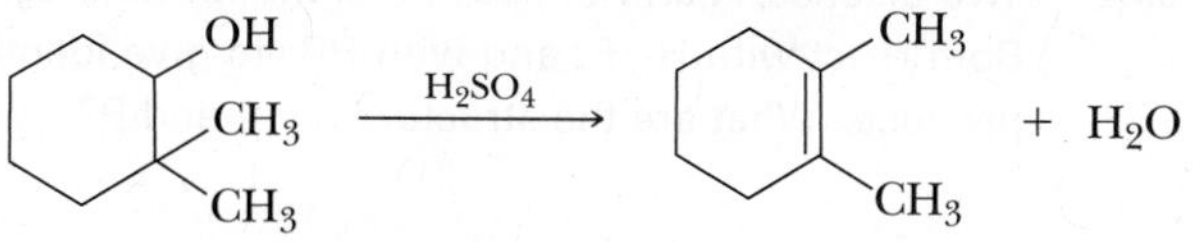

5.31 Propose a mechanism for each of the following transformations. **(See Examples 5.4, 5.6, 5.8)**

(a)

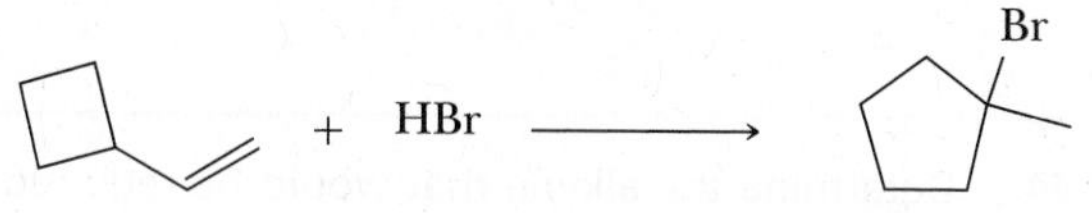

(b)

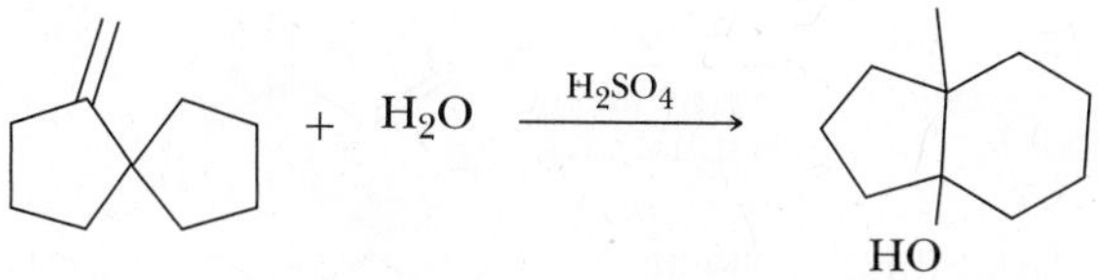

5.32 Terpin is prepared commercially by the acid-catalyzed hydration of limonene: **(See Example 5.5)**

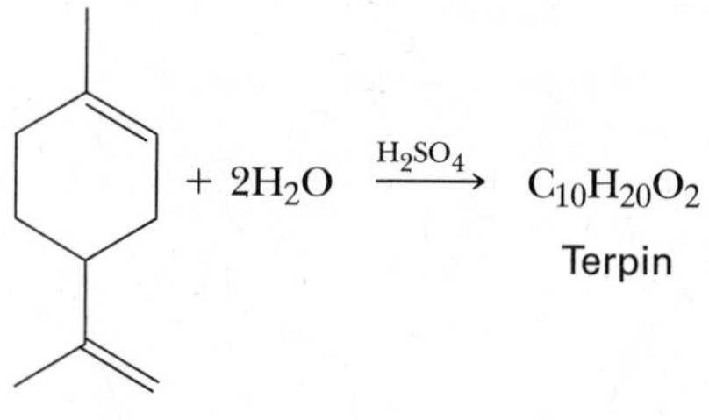

Limonene

Terpin

(a) Propose a structural formula for terpin and a mechanism for its formation.

(b) How many *cis–trans* isomers are possible for the structural formula you propose?

(c) Terpin hydrate, the isomer in terpin in which the one-carbon and three-carbon substituents are *cis* to each other, is used as an expectorant in cough medicines. Draw the alternative chair conformations for terpin hydrate, and state which of the two is the more stable.

5.33 Propose a mechanism for this reaction and account for its regioselectivity.

$$CH_3-\underset{}{\overset{CH_3}{\overset{|}{C}}}=CH_2 + ICl \longrightarrow CH_3-\underset{\underset{Cl}{|}}{\overset{CH_3}{\overset{|}{C}}}-CH_2I$$

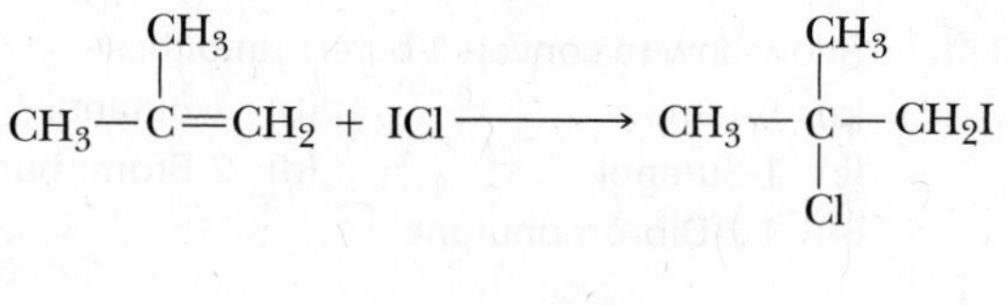

5.34 The treatment of 2-methylpropene with methanol in the presence of a sulfuric acid catalyst gives *tert*-butyl methyl ether:

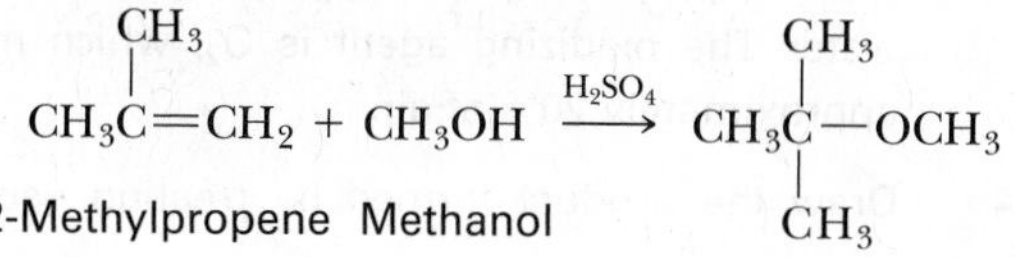

2-Methylpropene Methanol *tert*-Butyl methyl ether

Propose a mechanism for the formation of this ether.

5.35 Treating cyclohexene with HBr in the presence of acetic acid gives a mixture of bromocyclohexane and cyclohexyl acetate.

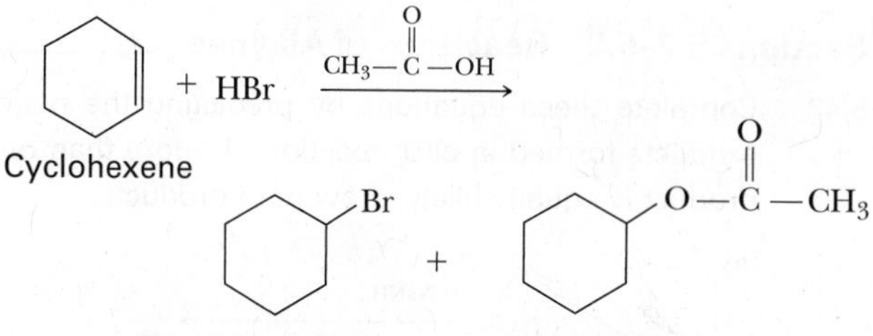

Bromocyclohexane (85%) Cyclohexyl acetate (15%)

Account for the formation of each product but do not be concerned with the relative percentages of each.

5.36 Draw a structural formula for the alcohol formed by treating each alkene with borane in tetrahydrofuran (THF), followed by hydrogen peroxide in aqueous sodium hydroxide, and specify the stereochemistry where appropriate. **(See Example 5.9)**

(a)

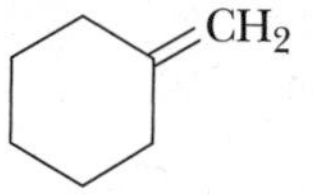

(b)

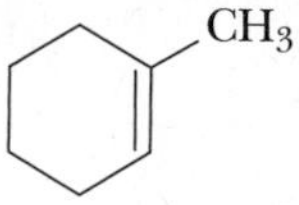

(c)

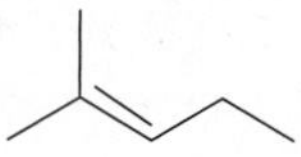

(d)

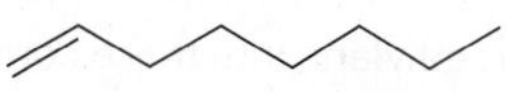

(e)

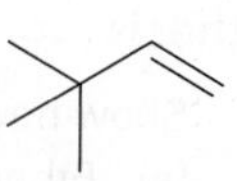

5.37 Treatment of 1-methylcyclohexene with methanol in the presence of a sulfuric acid catalyst gives a compound with the molecular formula $C_8H_{16}O$. Propose a structural formula for this compound and a mechanism for its formation.

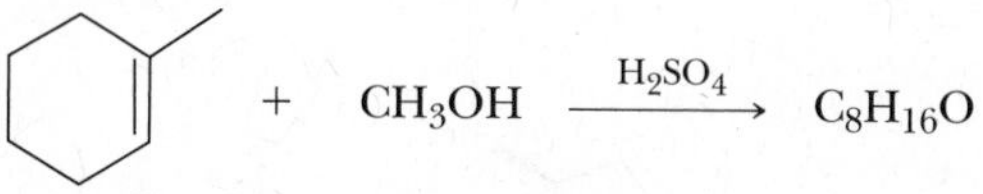

1-Methylcyclohexene Methanol

5.38 *cis*-3-Hexene and *trans*-3-hexene are different compounds and have different physical and chemical properties. Yet, when treated with H_2O/H_2SO_4, each gives the same alcohol. What is the alcohol, and how do you account for the fact that each alkene gives the same one? **(See Examples 5.6, 5.8)**

Section 5.6 Oxidation–Reduction

5.39 Write a balanced equation for the combustion of 2-methylpropene in air to give carbon dioxide and water. The oxidizing agent is O_2, which makes up approximately 20% of air.

5.40 Draw the product formed by treating each alkene with H_2/Ni:

(a)  (b) 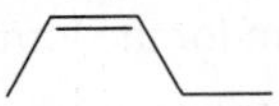 (c) 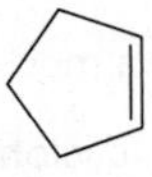 (d) 

5.41 Hydrocarbon A, C_5H_8, reacts with 2 moles of Br_2 to give 1,2,3,4-tetrabromo-2-methylbutane. What is the structure of hydrocarbon A?

5.42 Two alkenes, A and B, each have the formula C_5H_{10}. Both react with H_2/Pt and with HBr to give identical products. What are the structures of A and B?

Sections 5.7–5.8 Reactions of Alkynes

5.43 Complete these equations by predicting the major products formed in each reaction. If more than one product is equally likely, draw both products.

(a)

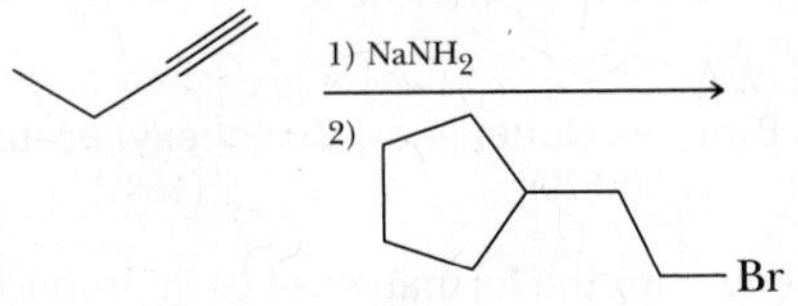

(b)

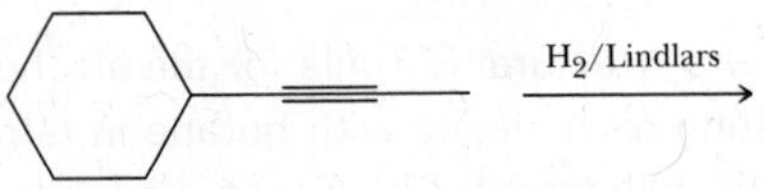

(c) $(CH_3)_2CH_2CCH \xrightarrow[\substack{2)\ CH_3(CH_2)_4Br \\ 3)\ H_2/Pd \cdot C}]{1)\ NaNH_2}$

5.44 Determine the alkyne that would be required in the following sequences of reactions.

(a)

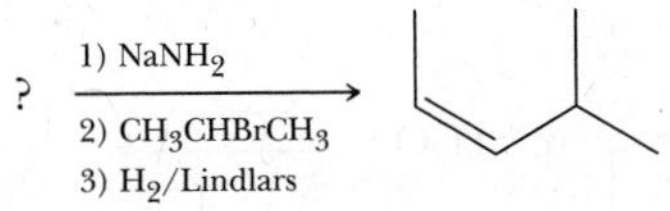

(b)

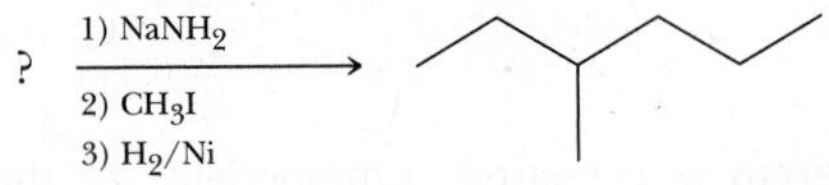

Synthesis

5.45 Show how to convert ethylene into these compounds:

(a) Ethane (b) Ethanol
(c) Bromoethane (d) 1,2-Dibromoethane
(e) Chloroethane

5.46 Show how to convert cyclopentene into these compounds:

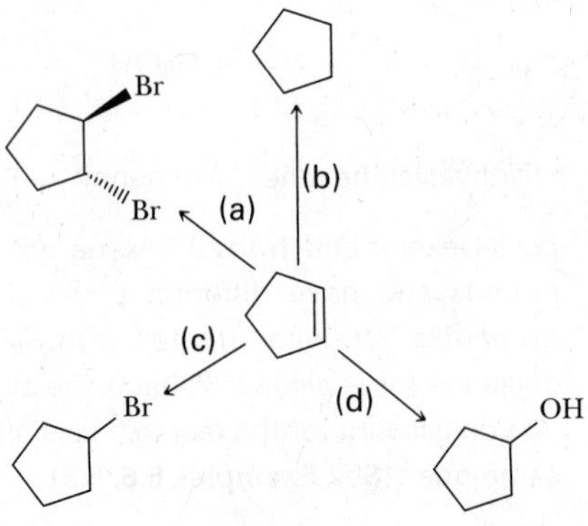

5.47 Show how to convert methylenecyclohexane into each of these compounds.

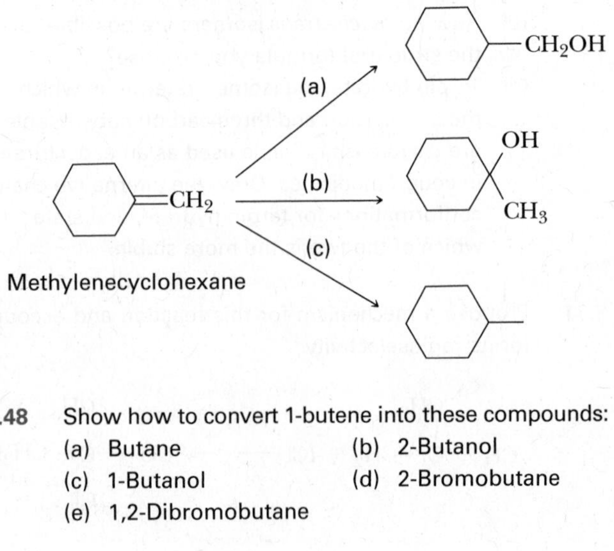

5.48 Show how to convert 1-butene into these compounds:

(a) Butane (b) 2-Butanol
(c) 1-Butanol (d) 2-Bromobutane
(e) 1,2-Dibromobutane

5.49 Show how the following compounds can be synthesized in good yields from an alkene:

(a) 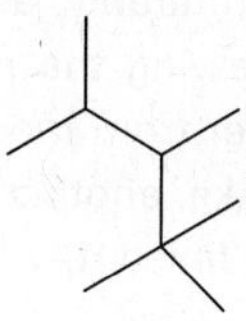

(b) 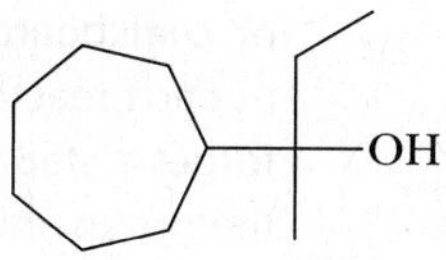

(c) 

(d) 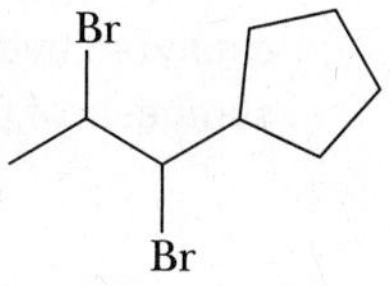

5.50 How would you prepare *cis*-3-hexene using only acetylene as the source of carbon atoms, and using any necessary inorganic regents? **(See Example 5.10)**

5.51 Test your cumulative knowledge of the reactions learned thus far by completing the following chemical transformations. Note that some will require more than one step.

(a) 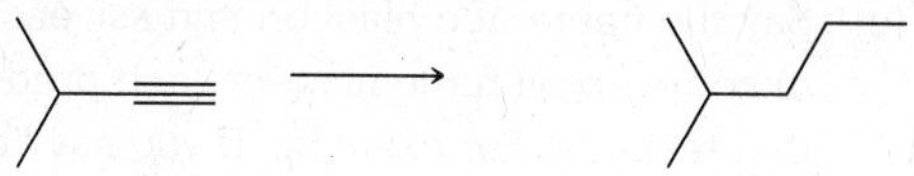

(b) 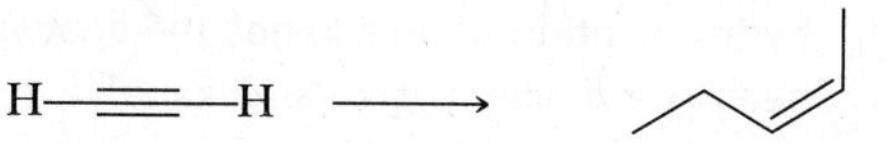

(c) 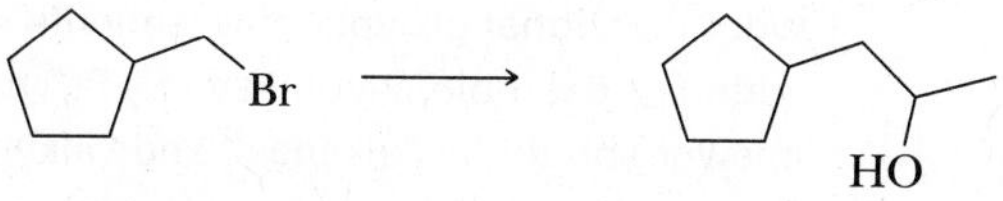

(d) 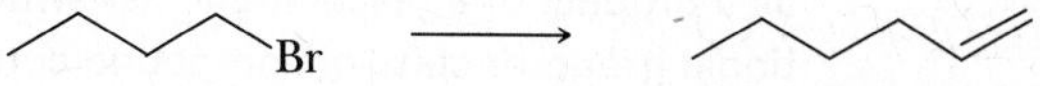

(e) 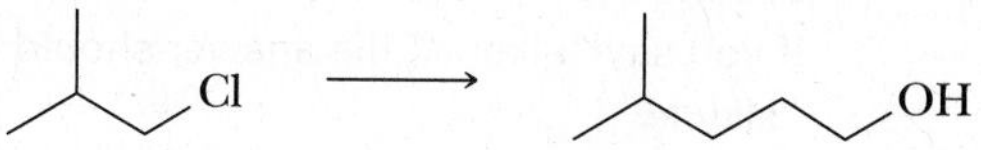

(f) 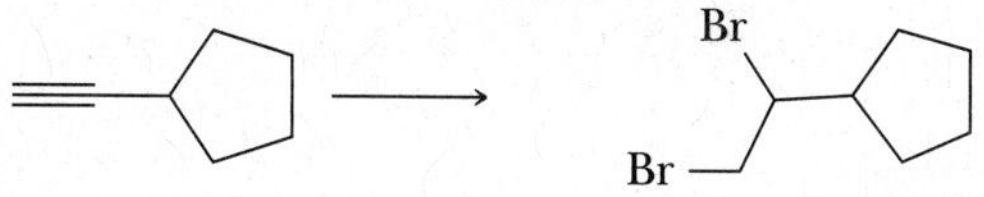

LOOKING AHEAD

5.52 Each of the following 2° carbocations is more stable than the tertiary-butyl carbocation shown:

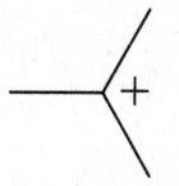

a tertiary carbocation

(a) 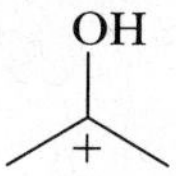

(b) 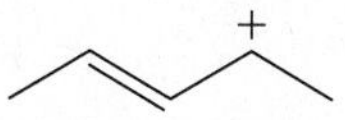

(c) 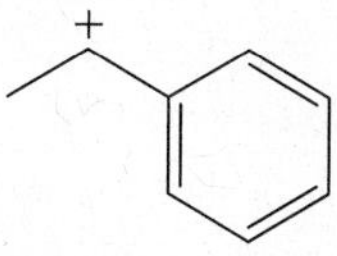

Provide an explanation for each cation's enhanced stability.

5.53 Recall that an alkene possesses a π cloud of electrons above and below the plane of the C=C bond. Any reagent can therefore react with either face of the double bond. Determine whether the reaction of each of the given reagents with the top face of *cis*-2-butene will produce the same product as the reaction of the same reagent with the bottom face. (*Hint*: Build molecular models of the products and compare them.)

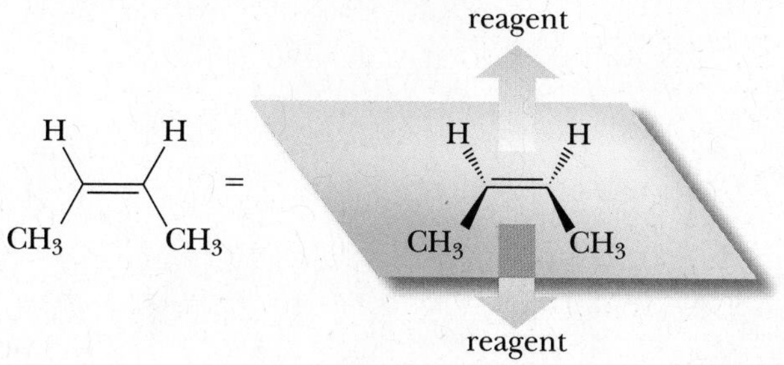

(a) H_2/Pt

(b) $\frac{\text{1) } BH_3 \cdot THF}{\text{2) NaOH, HOOH}}$

(c) Br_2/CH_2Cl_2

5.54 This reaction yields two products in differing amounts:

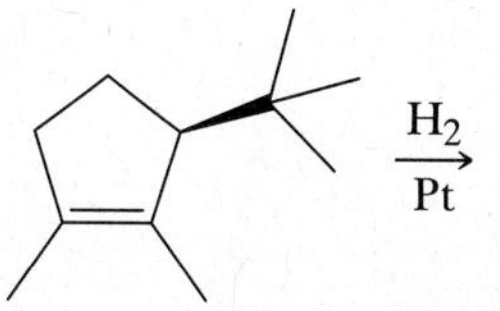

Draw the two products and predict which product is favored.

GROUP LEARNING ACTIVITIES

5.55 Take turns quizzing each other on the reactions presented in this chapter in the following ways:

(a) Say the name of a reaction and ask each other to come up with the reagents and products of that reaction. For example, if you say "catalytic hydrogenation of an alkene" the answer should be "H_2/Pt reacts to give an alkane."

(b) Describe a set of reagents and ask each other what functional group(s) the reagents react with. For example, if you say "H_2/Pt," the answer should be "alkenes" and "alkynes."

(c) Name a functional group or class of compound as a product of a reaction and ask what functional group or class of compound could be used to synthesize that product. For example, if you say "alkene," the answer should be "alkyne."

5.56 Using a piece of paper or, preferably, a whiteboard or chalkboard, take turns drawing the mechanisms of each reaction in this chapter from memory. If you forget a step or make a mistake, another member of the group should step in and finish it.

5.57 With the exception of ethylene to ethanol, the acid-catalyzed hydration of alkenes cannot be used for the synthesis of primary alcohols. Explain why this is so.

06

Chirality: The Handedness of Molecules

Tartaric acid is found in grapes and other fruits, both free and as its salts (see Section 6.4B). Inset: A model of tartaric acid.
(© fatihhoca/iStockphoto)

KEY QUESTIONS

6.1 What Are Stereoisomers?

6.2 What Are Enantiomers?

6.3 How Do We Designate the Configuration of a Stereocenter?

6.4 What Is the 2^n Rule?

6.5 How Do We Describe the Chirality of Cyclic Molecules with Two Stereocenters?

6.6 How Do We Describe the Chirality of Molecules with Three or More Stereocenters?

6.7 What Are the Properties of Stereoisomers?

6.8 How Is Chirality Detected in the Laboratory?

6.9 What Is the Significance of Chirality in the Biological World?

6.10 How Can Enantiomers Be Resolved?

HOW TO

6.1 How to Draw Enantiomers

6.2 How to Determine the R & S Configuration without Rotating the Molecule

6.3 How to Determine Whether Two Compounds Are the Same, Enantiomers, or Diastereomers without the Need to Spatially Manipulate the Molecule

CHEMICAL CONNECTIONS

6A Chiral Drugs

IN THIS CHAPTER, we will explore the relationships between three-dimensional objects and their mirror images. When you look in a mirror, you see a reflection, or **mirror image**, of yourself. Now, suppose your mirror image becomes a three-dimensional object.

Mirror image The reflection of an object in a mirror.

William H. Brown

The horns of this African gazelle show chirality and are mirror images of each other.

We could then ask, "What is the relationship between you and your mirror image?" By relationship, we mean "Can your reflection be superposed on the original 'you' in such a way that every detail of the reflection corresponds exactly to the original?" The answer is that you and your mirror image are not superposable. If you have a ring on the little finger of your right hand, for example, your mirror image has the ring on the little finger of its left hand. If you part your hair on your right side, the part will be on the left side in your mirror image. Simply stated, you and your reflection are different objects. You cannot superpose one on the other.

An understanding of relationships of this type is fundamental to an understanding of organic chemistry and biochemistry. In fact, the ability to visualize molecules as three-dimensional objects is a survival skill in organic chemistry and biochemistry. We suggest that you purchase a set of molecular models. Alternatively you may have access to a computer lab with a modeling program. We urge you to use molecular models frequently as an aid to visualizing the spatial concepts in this and later chapters.

6.1 What Are Stereoisomers?

Stereoisomers Isomers that have the same molecular formula and the same connectivity, but different orientations of their atoms in space.

Stereoisomers have the same molecular formula and the same connectivity of atoms in their molecules, but different three-dimensional orientations of their atoms in space. The one example of stereoisomers we have seen thus far is that of *cis–trans* isomers in cycloalkanes (Section 3.7) and alkenes (Section 4.1C):

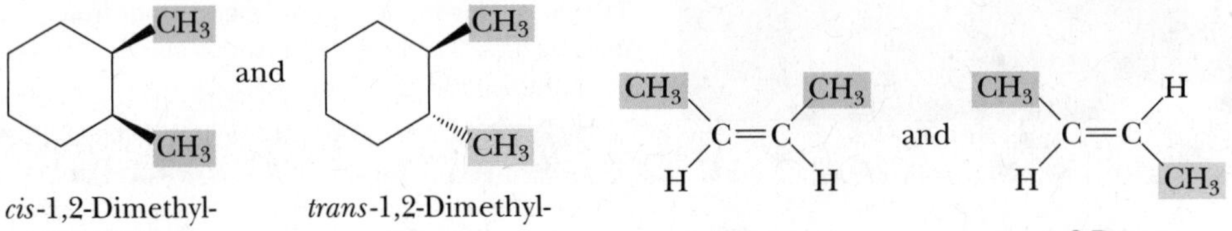

cis-1,2-Dimethylcyclohexane   *trans*-1,2-Dimethylcyclohexane   *cis*-2-Butene   *trans*-2-Butene

In this chapter, we study enantiomers and diastereomers (Figure 6.1).

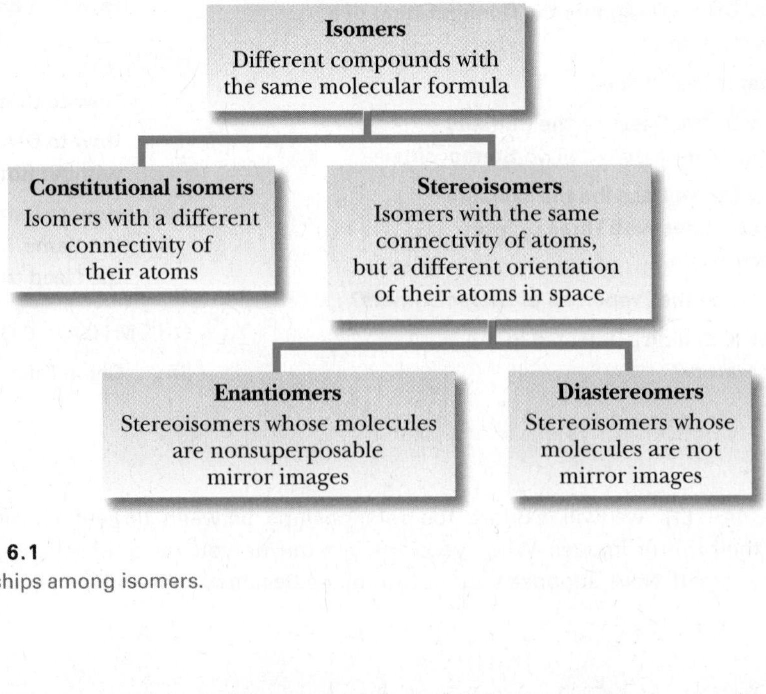

FIGURE 6.1
Relationships among isomers.

6.2 What Are Enantiomers?

Enantiomers Stereoisomers that are nonsuperposable mirror images; the term refers to a relationship between pairs of objects.

Enantiomers are stereoisomers that are nonsuperposable mirror images. The significance of enantiomerism is that, except for inorganic and a few simple organic compounds, the vast majority of molecules in the biological world show this type of isomerism, including carbohydrates (Chapter 17), lipids (Chapter 19), amino acids and proteins (Chapter 18), and nucleic acids (DNA and RNA, Chapter 20). Further, approximately one-half of the medications used in human medicine also show this type of isomerism.

As an example of a molecule that exhibits enantiomerism, let us consider 2-butanol. As we go through the discussion of this molecule, we focus on carbon 2, the carbon bearing the —OH group. What makes this carbon of interest is that it has four different groups bonded to it. The most common cause of enantiomerism among organic molecules is a carbon bonded to four different groups.

the four different "groups" bonded to this carbon are —H, —OH, $—CH_3$, and $—CH_2CH_3$

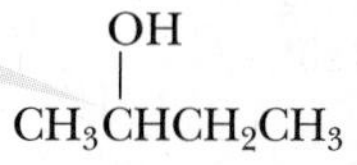

2-Butanol

The structural formula we have just drawn does not show the shape of 2-butanol or the orientation of its atoms in space. To do this, we must consider the molecule as a three-dimensional object. On the left are a ball-and-stick model of 2-butanol and a perspective drawing of what we will call the "original" molecule. In this drawing, the —OH and $—CH_3$ groups on carbon-2 are in the plane of the paper; the —H is behind the plane and the $—CH_2CH_3$ group is in front of the plane.

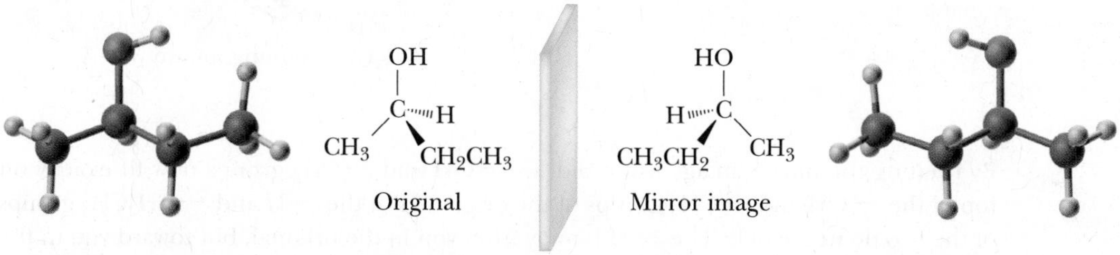

To the right in the preceding diagram is the mirror image of the original molecule. Every molecule and, in fact, every object in the world around us, has a mirror image. The question we now need to ask is "What is the relationship between the original of 2-butanol and its mirror image?" To answer this question, you need to imagine that you can pick up the mirror image and move it in space in any way you wish. If you can move the mirror image in space and find that it fits over the original so that every bond, atom, and detail of the mirror image exactly matches the bonds, atoms, and details of the original, then the two are **superposable**. In this case, the mirror image and the original represent the same molecule; they are only oriented differently in space. If, however, no matter how you turn the mirror image in space, it will not fit exactly on the original with every detail matching, then the two are **nonsuperposable**; they are different molecules.

The key point here is that either an object is superposable on its mirror image or it isn't. Now let us look at 2-butanol and its mirror image and ask, "Are they or are they not superposable?"

The following drawings illustrate one way to see that the mirror image of 2-butanol is not superposable on the original molecule:

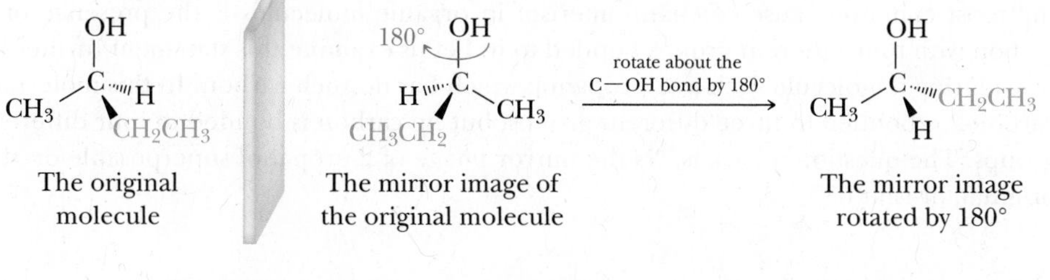

Imagine that you hold the mirror image by the C—OH bond and rotate the bottom part of the molecule by 180° about this bond. The —OH group retains its position in space, but the $-CH_3$ group, which was to the right and in the plane of the paper, is still in the plane of the paper, but now to the left. Similarly, the $-CH_2CH_3$ group, which was in front of the plane of the paper and to the left, is now behind the plane and to the right.

Now move the rotated mirror image in space, and try to fit it on the original so that all bonds and atoms match:

Charles D. Winters

Left- and right-handed sea shells. If you cup a right-handed shell in your right hand with your thumb pointing from the narrow end to the wide end, the opening will be on your right.

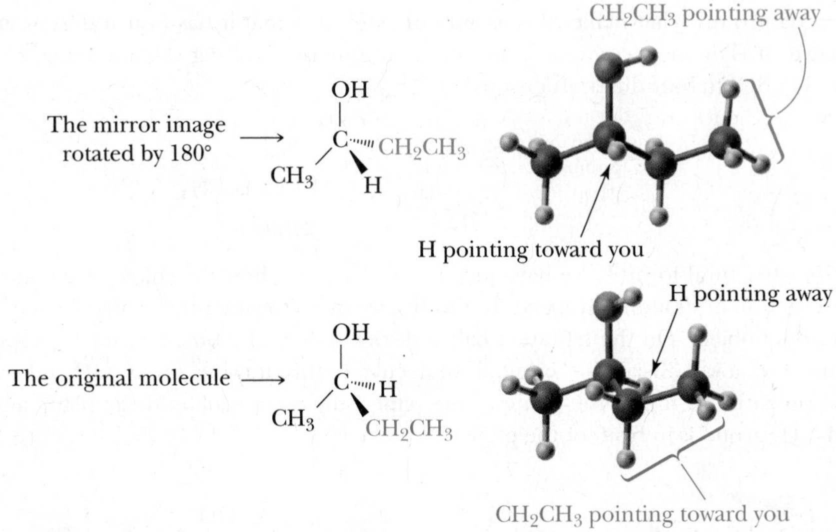

By rotating the mirror image as we did, its —OH and $-CH_3$ groups now fit exactly on top of the —OH and $-CH_3$ groups of the original. But the —H and $-CH_2CH_3$ groups of the two do not match: The —H is away from you in the original, but toward you in the mirror image; the $-CH_2CH_3$ group is toward you in the original, but away from you in the mirror image. We conclude that the original of 2-butanol and its mirror image are nonsuperposable and, therefore, are different compounds.

To summarize, we can rotate the mirror image of 2-butanol in space in any way we want, but as long as no bonds are broken or rearranged, only two of the four groups bonded to carbon-2 of the mirror image can be made to coincide with those on the original. Because 2-butanol and its mirror image are not superposable, they are enantiomers. Like gloves, enantiomers always occur in pairs.

Chiral From the Greek *cheir,* meaning hand; objects that are not superposable on their mirror images.

Objects that are not superposable on their mirror images are said to be **chiral** (pronounced ki′-ral, rhymes with spiral; from the Greek: *cheir,* hand); that is, they show handedness. Chirality is encountered in three-dimensional objects of all sorts. Your left hand is chiral, and so is your right hand. A spiral binding on a notebook is chiral. A machine screw with a right-handed twist is chiral. A ship's propeller is chiral. As you examine the objects in the world around you, you will undoubtedly conclude that the vast majority of them are chiral.

As we said before we examined the original and the mirror image of 2-butanol, the most common cause of enantiomerism in organic molecules is the presence of a carbon with four different groups bonded to it. Let us examine this statement further by considering a molecule such as 2-propanol, which has no such carbon. In this molecule, carbon-2 is bonded to three different groups, but no carbon is bonded to four different groups. The question we ask is, "Is the mirror image of 2-propanol superposable on the original, or isn't it?"

In the following diagram, on the left is a three-dimensional representation of 2-propanol, and on the right is its mirror image:

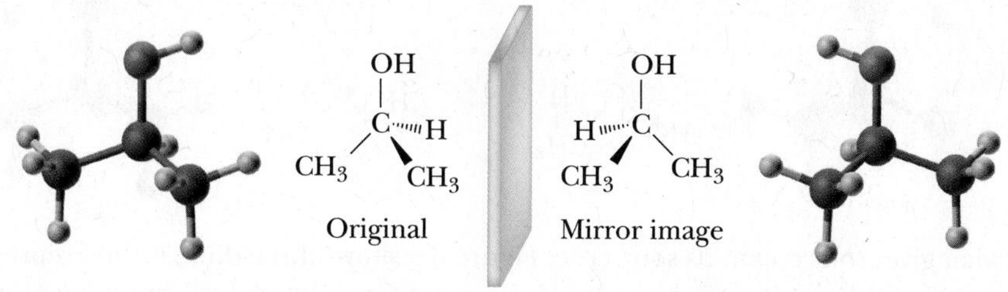

The question we now ask is "What is the relationship of the mirror image to the original?" This time, let us rotate the mirror image by 120° about the C—OH bond and then compare it with the original. When we do this rotation, we see that all atoms and bonds of the mirror image fit exactly on the original. This means that the structures we first drew for the original and its mirror image are, in fact, the same molecule viewed from different perspectives:

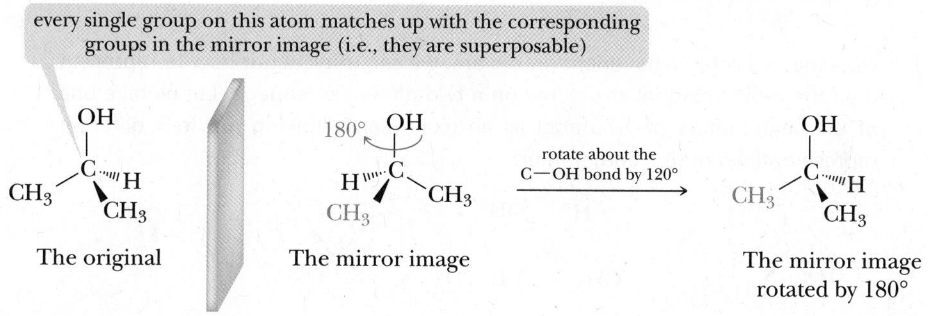

If an object and its mirror image are superposable, then the object and its mirror image are identical, and there is no possibility of enantiomerism. We say that such an object is **achiral** (without chirality).

An achiral object has at least one plane of symmetry. A **plane of symmetry** (also called a *mirror plane*) is an imaginary plane passing through an object and dividing it so that one-half of the object is the reflection of the other half. The beaker shown in Figure 6.2 has a single plane of symmetry, whereas a cube has several planes of symmetry. 2-Propanol also has a single plane of symmetry.

To repeat, the most common cause of chirality in organic molecules is a tetrahedral carbon atom with four different groups bonded to it. We call such a carbon atom a **chiral center**. Chiral centers are one type of **stereocenter**, which describes an atom at which the interchange of two atoms or groups of atoms bonded to it produces a different stereoisomer. 2-Butanol has one stereocenter; 2-propanol has none.

As another example of a molecule with a stereocenter, consider 2-hydroxypropanoic acid, more commonly named lactic acid. Lactic acid is a product of anaerobic glycolysis

Achiral An object that lacks chirality; an object that has no handedness and is superposable on its mirror image.

Plane of symmetry An imaginary plane passing through an object and dividing it such that one half is the mirror image of the other half.

Chiral center An atom, such as carbon, with four different groups bonded to it.

Stereocenter An atom at which the interchange of two atoms or groups of atoms bonded to it produces a different stereoisomer.

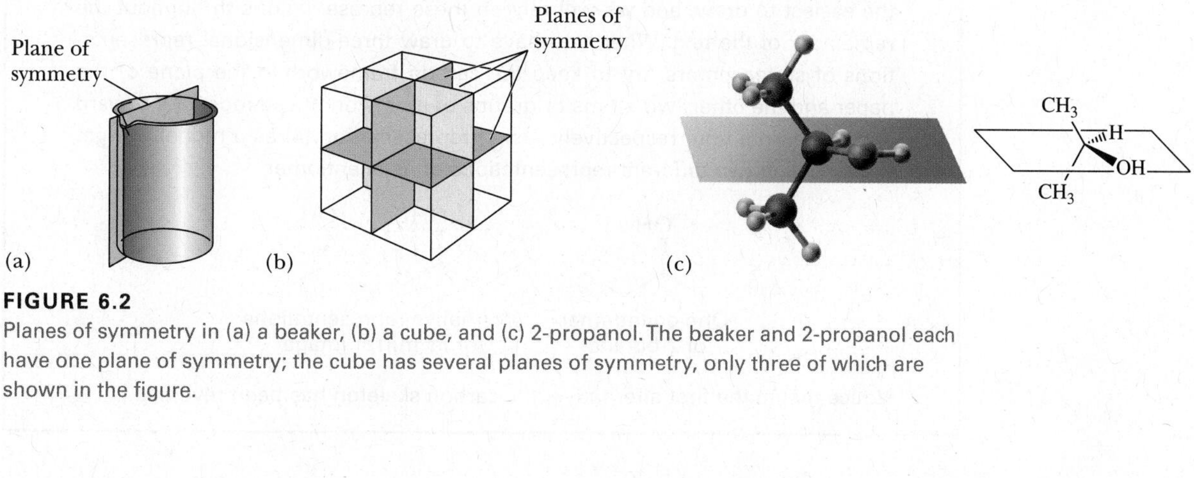

FIGURE 6.2
Planes of symmetry in (a) a beaker, (b) a cube, and (c) 2-propanol. The beaker and 2-propanol each have one plane of symmetry; the cube has several planes of symmetry, only three of which are shown in the figure.

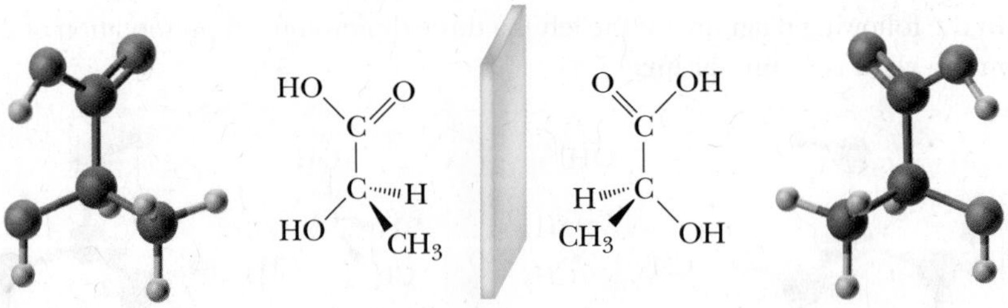

FIGURE 6.3 Three-dimensional representations of lactic acid and its mirror image.

and is what gives sour cream its sour taste. Figure 6.3 shows three-dimensional representations of lactic acid and its mirror image. In these representations, all bond angles about the central carbon atom are approximately 109.5°, and the four bonds projecting from it are directed toward the corners of a regular tetrahedron. Lactic acid shows enantiomerism; that is, it and its mirror image are not superposable, but rather are different molecules.

HOW TO 6.1

Draw Enantiomers

Now that we know what enantiomers are, we can think about how to represent their three-dimensional structures on a two-dimensional page. Let us take one of the enantiomers of 2-butanol as an example. Following are four different representations of this enantiomer:

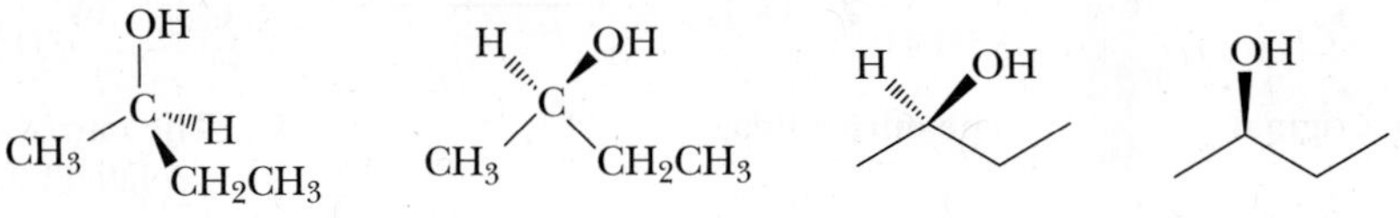

(1) (2) (3) (4)

In our initial discussions of 2-butanol, we used (1) to show the tetrahedral geometry of the stereocenter; in it, two groups are in the plane of the paper, a third is coming out of the plane toward us, and the fourth is behind the plane, away from us. We can turn (1) slightly in space and tip it a bit to place the carbon framework in the plane of the paper. Doing so gives us representation (2), in which we still have two groups in the plane of the paper, one coming toward us and one going away from us. For an even more abbreviated representation of this enantiomer of 2-butanol, we can turn (2) into the line-angle formula (3). Although we don't normally show hydrogens in a line-angle formula, we do so in (3) just to remind ourselves that the fourth group on this stereocenter is really there and that it is H. Finally, we can carry the abbreviation a step further and write 2-butanol as (4). Here, we omit the H on the stereocenter, but we know that it must be there (carbon needs four bonds), and we know that it must be behind the plane of the paper. Clearly, the abbreviated formulas (3) and (4) are the easiest to draw, and we will rely on these representations throughout the remainder of the text. When you have to draw three-dimensional representations of stereocenters, try to keep the carbon framework in the plane of the paper and the other two atoms or groups of atoms on the stereocenter toward and away from you, respectively. Using representation (4) as a model, we get the following two different representations of its enantiomer:

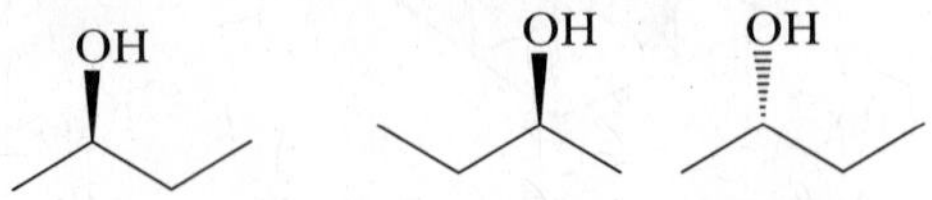

One enantiomer of 2-butanol — Alternative representations for its mirror image

Notice that in the first alternative, the carbon skeleton has been reversed.

EXAMPLE 6.1

Each of the following molecules has one stereocenter:

(a) $CH_3\overset{\displaystyle Cl}{\overset{|}{C}}HCH_2CH_3$ (b) 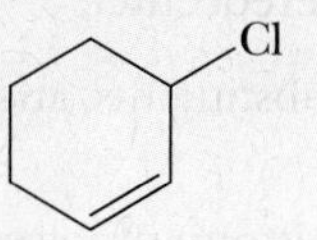

Identify the stereocenter in each and draw stereorepresentations of the enantiomers of each.

STRATEGY

When locating stereocenters, it is often helpful to draw in the hydrogens in line-angle drawings. Carbon atoms with only one or two lines extending from them, as well as sp^2 and sp hybridized carbons, can be excluded from consideration. Once the stereocenters are identified, use dashed and solid wedges to show the bonds to substituents.

SOLUTION

You will find it helpful to study models of each pair of enantiomers and to view them from different perspectives. As you work with these models, notice that each enantiomer has a carbon atom bonded to four different groups, which makes the molecule chiral. Translate what you see in each model by using perspective drawings. The hydrogen at the stereocenter is shown in (a) but not in (b).

(a) 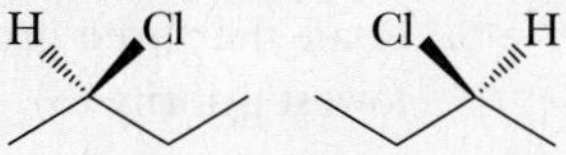

(b) 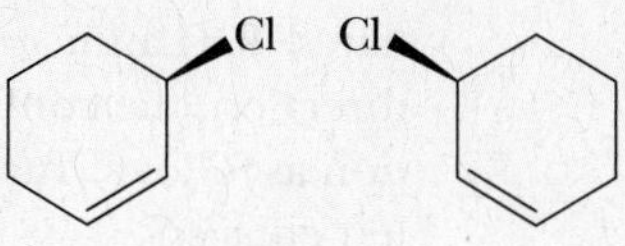

See problems 6.15, 6.19–6.22

PROBLEM 6.1

Each of the following molecules has one stereocenter:

(a) 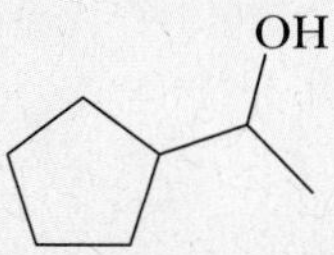

(b) 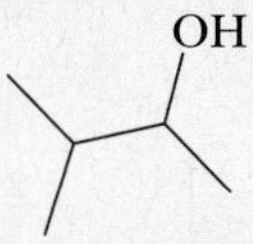

(c) 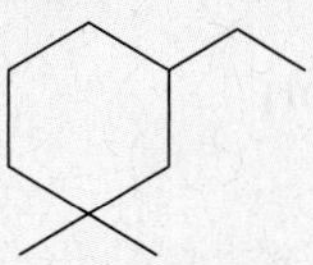

Identify the stereocenter in each and draw stereorepresentations of the enantiomers of each.

6.3 How Do We Designate the Configuration of a Stereocenter?

Because enantiomers are different compounds, each must have a different name. The over-the-counter drug ibuprofen, for example, shows enantiomerism and can exist as the pair of enantiomers shown here:

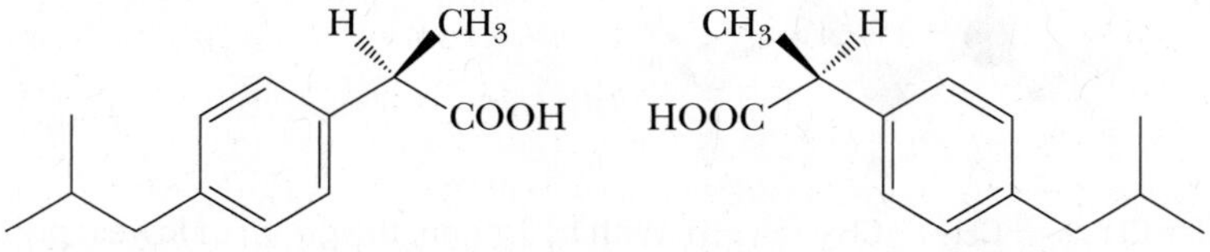

The inactive enantiomer of ibuprofen The active enantiomer

Only one enantiomer of ibuprofen is biologically active. This enantiomer reaches therapeutic concentrations in the human body in approximately 12 minutes. However, in this case, the inactive enantiomer is not wasted. The body converts it to the active enantiomer, but that takes time.

What we need is a way to name each enantiomer of ibuprofen (or any other pair of enantiomers for that matter) so that we can refer to them in conversation or in writing. To do so, chemists have developed the **R,S system**. The first step in assigning an R or S

R,S system A set of rules for specifying the configuration about a stereocenter.

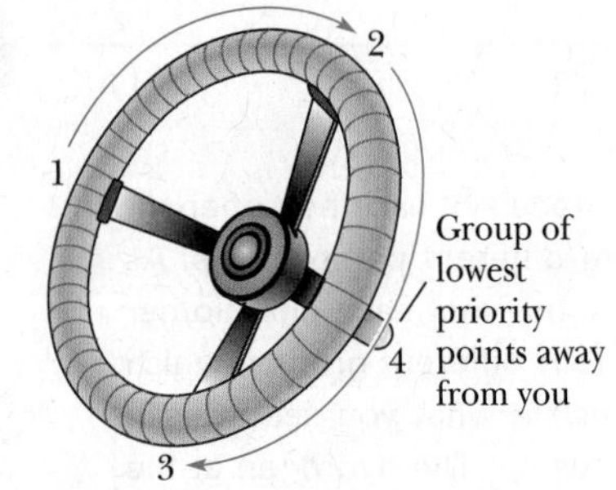

R From the Latin *rectus*, meaning right; used in the R,S system to show that the order of priority of groups on a stereocenter is clockwise.

S From the Latin *sinister*, meaning left; used in the R,S system to show that the order of priority of groups on a stereocenter is counterclockwise.

configuration to a stereocenter is to arrange the groups bonded to it in order of priority. For this, we use the same set of **priority rules** we used in Section 4.2C to assign an E,Z configuration to an alkene.

To assign an R or S configuration to a stereocenter,

1. Locate the stereocenter, identify its four substituents, and assign a priority from 1 (highest) to 4 (lowest) to each substituent.
2. Orient the molecule in space so that the group of lowest priority (4) is directed away from you, as would be, for instance, the steering column of a car. The three groups of higher priority (1–3) then project toward you, as would the spokes of a steering wheel.
3. Read the three groups projecting toward you in order, from highest priority (1) to lowest priority (3).
4. If reading the groups proceeds in a clockwise direction, the configuration is designated **R** (Latin: *rectus*, straight, correct); if reading proceeds in a counterclockwise direction, the configuration is **S** (Latin: *sinister*, left). You can also visualize this situation as follows: Turning the steering wheel to the right equals R, and turning it to the left equals S.

EXAMPLE 6.2

Assign an R or S configuration to each stereocenter:

(a) 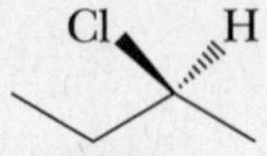

(b) 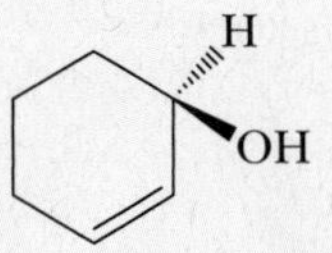

STRATEGY

First determine the priorities of the groups bonded to the stereocenter. If necessary reorient the molecule so that the group of lowest priority is away from you. Then read the R/S configuration by going from highest to lowest priority.

SOLUTION

View each molecule through the stereocenter and along the bond from the stereocenter toward the group of lowest priority.

(a) The order of priority is $-Cl > -CH_2CH_3 > -CH_3 > -H$. The group of lowest priority, H, points away from you. Reading the groups in the order 1, 2, 3 occurs in the counterclockwise direction, so the configuration is S.

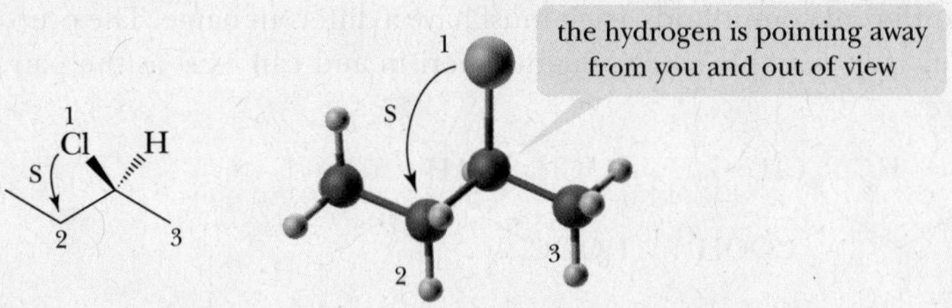

(b) The order of priority is $-OH > -CH{=}CH > -CH_2-CH_2 > -H$. With hydrogen, the group of lowest priority, pointing away from you, reading the groups in the order 1, 2, 3 occurs in the clockwise direction, so the configuration is R.

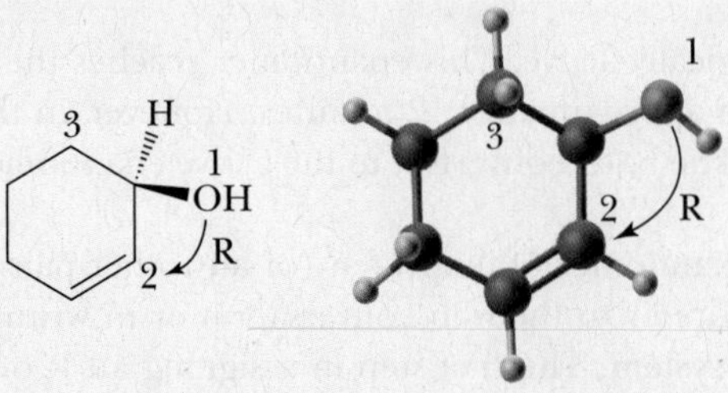

See problems 6.24–6.27, 6.29, 6.39

PROBLEM 6.2

Assign an R or S configuration to each stereocenter:

(a) 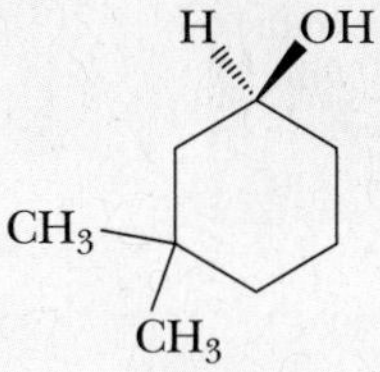

(b) 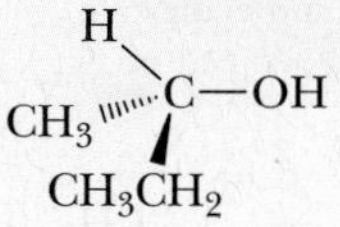

(c) 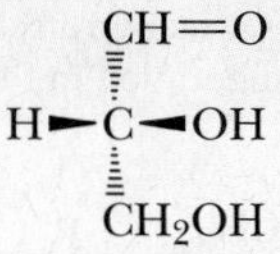

Now let us return to our three-dimensional drawing of the enantiomers of ibuprofen and assign each an R or S configuration. In order of decreasing priority, the groups bonded to the stereocenter are $-COOH > -C_6H_4 > -CH_3 > H$. In the enantiomer on the left, reading the groups on the stereocenter in order of priority occurs clockwise. Therefore, this enantiomer is (*R*)-ibuprofen, and its mirror image is (*S*)-ibuprofen:

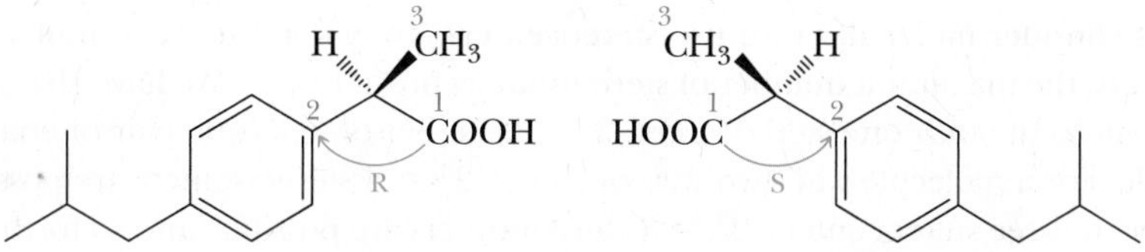

(*R*)-Ibuprofen (the inactive enantiomer) | (*S*)-Ibuprofen (the active enantiomer)

HOW TO 6.2

Determine the R & S Configuration without Rotating the Molecule

If you are having difficulty visualizing the spatial rotation of perspective drawings, the following techniques may be of use.

SCENARIO 1: **The lowest priority group is already directed away from you.** If the perspective drawing contains the lowest priority group on a dashed bond, it is a simple matter of reading the other three groups from highest to lowest priority.

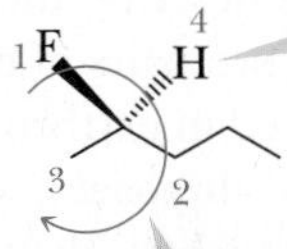

the lowest priority group is already pointed away from you

(*R*)-2-Fluoropentane

the R/S configuration is read without the need for any spatial manipulation

SCENARIO 2: **The lowest priority group is directed toward you.** If the perspective drawing contains the lowest priority group on a wedged bond, read the priority of the other three groups, but assign a configuration that is opposite to what is actually read.

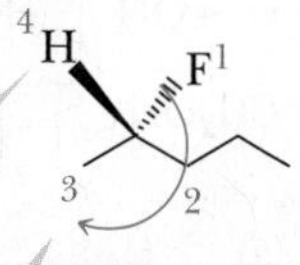

the lowest priority group is pointed toward you

(*S*)-2-Fluoropentane

the R/S configuration is read, but then the opposite configuration is chosen. In this example, the priority reading appears to be *R*, but we switch it to *S* because the lowest priority group is pointed toward you

SCENARIO 3: **The lowest priority group is in the plane of the page.** If the perspective drawing contains the lowest priority group in the plane of the page, view down the bond connecting the group to the stereocenter and draw a Newman projection (Section 3.6A).

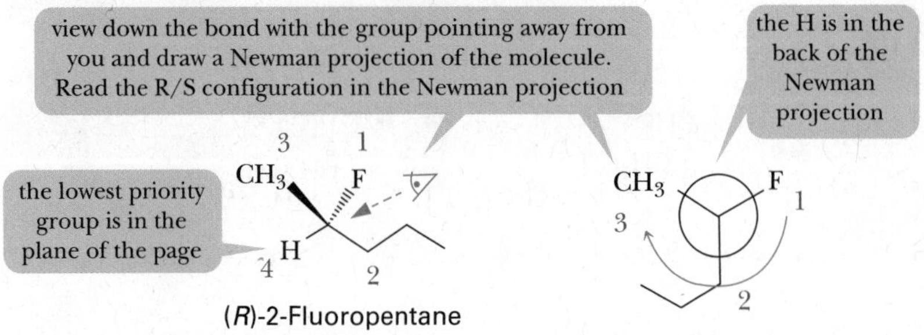

(*R*)-2-Fluoropentane

6.4 What Is the 2^n Rule?

Now let us consider molecules with two stereocenters. To generalize, for a molecule with ***n*** stereocenters, the maximum number of stereoisomers possible is $\mathbf{2^n}$. We have already verified that, for a molecule with one stereocenter, $2^1 = 2$ stereoisomers (one pair of enantiomers) are possible. For a molecule with two stereocenters, $2^2 = 4$ stereoisomers are possible; for a molecule with three stereocenters, $2^3 = 8$ stereoisomers are possible, and so forth.

A. Enantiomers and Diastereomers

We begin our study of molecules with two stereocenters by considering 2,3,4-trihydroxybutanal. Its two stereocenters are marked with asterisks:

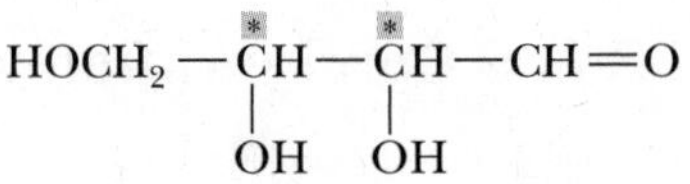

2,3,4-Trihydroxybutanal

The maximum number of stereoisomers possible for this molecule is $2^2 = 4$, each of which is drawn in Figure 6.4.

Stereoisomers (a) and (b) are nonsuperposable mirror images and are, therefore, a pair of enantiomers. Stereoisomers (c) and (d) are also nonsuperposable mirror images and are a second pair of enantiomers. We describe the four stereoisomers of 2,3,4-trihydroxybutanal by saying that they consist of two pairs of enantiomers. Enantiomers (a) and (b) are named **erythrose**, which is synthesized in erythrocytes (red blood cells)—hence the name. Enantiomers (c) and (d) are named **threose**. Erythrose and threose belong to the class of compounds called carbohydrates, which we discuss in Chapter 17.

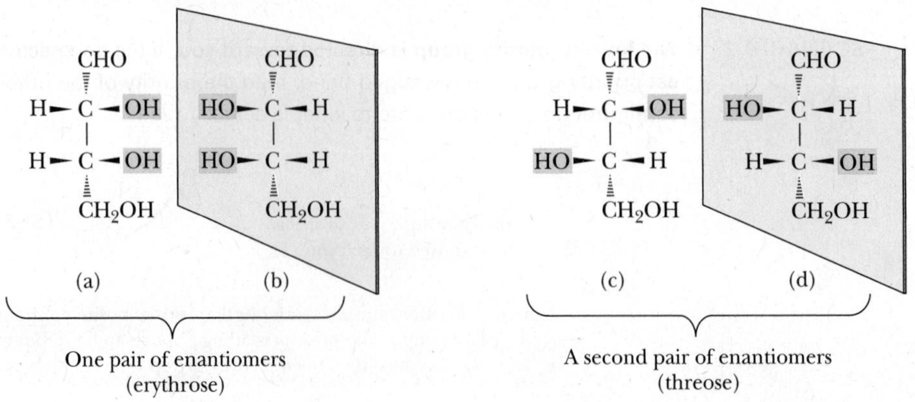

FIGURE 6.4
The four stereoisomers of 2,3,4-trihydroxybutanal, a compound with two stereocenters. Configurations (a) and (b) are (2*R*,3*R*) and (2*S*,3*S*), respectively. Configurations (c) and (d) are (2*R*,3*S*) and (2*S*,3*R*), respectively.

We have specified the relationship between (a) and (b) and between (c) and (d). What is the relationship between (a) and (c), between (a) and (d), between (b) and (c), and between (b) and (d)? The answer is that they are diastereomers. **Diastereomers** are stereoisomers that are not enantiomers; that is, they are stereoisomers that are not mirror images of each other.

Diastereomers Stereoisomers that are not mirror images of each other; the term refers to relationships among objects.

HOW TO 6.3

Determine Whether Two Compounds Are the Same, Enantiomers, or Diastereomers without the Need to Spatially Manipulate the Molecule

If you are having difficulty visualizing the spatial rotation of perspective drawings, the following technique may be of use.

STEP 1: Verify that the compounds are stereoisomers. Make sure that the two compounds in question have the same molecular formula and the same connectivity of atoms.

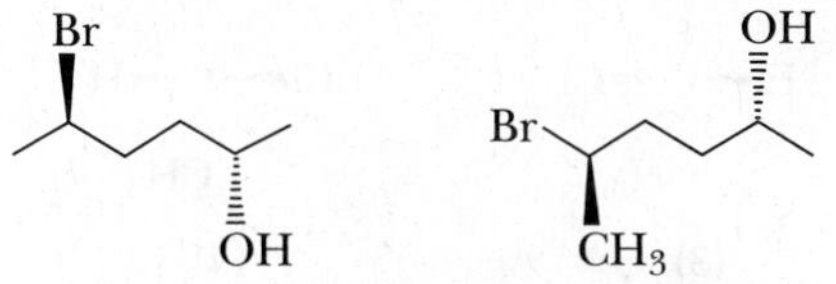

Chemical Formula for both: $C_6H_{13}BrO$
Both have a 6-carbon chain with Br at the 5 position and OH at the 2 position

STEP 2: Assign R/S configurations to each stereocenter in both compounds. See How To 6.2 for instructions.

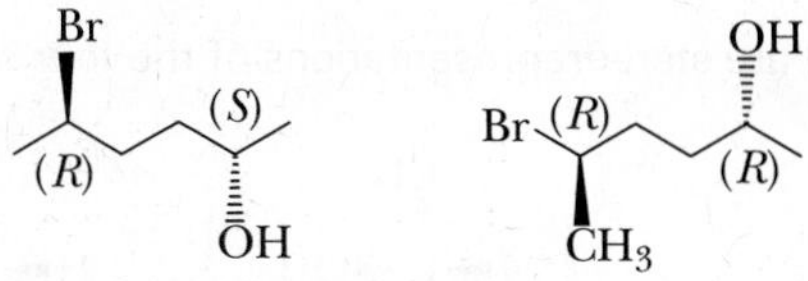

STEP 3: Compare the configuration at corresponding stereocenters. If the configurations match, the compounds are identical. If the configurations are opposite at each corresponding stereocenter, the compounds are enantiomers. Any other scenario indicates that the compounds are diastereomers.

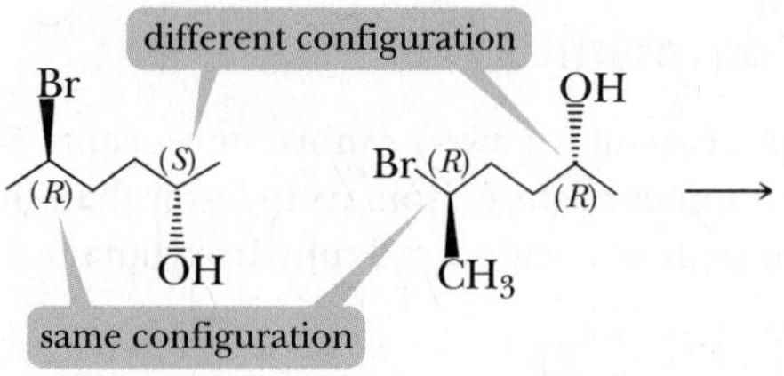

Possible Scenario	Relationship
all configurations the same	identical compounds
all configurations opposite	enantiomers
any other scenario	diastereomers

EXAMPLE 6.3

Following are stereorepresentations of the four stereoisomers of 1,2,3-butanetriol:

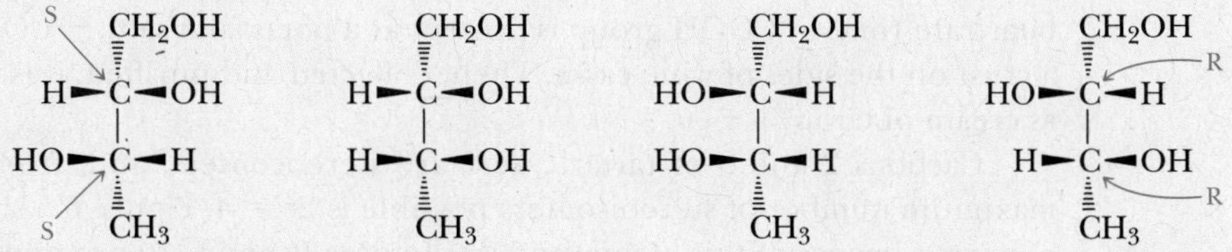

(1) (2) (3) (4)

Configurations are given for the stereocenters in (1) and (4).
(a) Which compounds are enantiomers? **(b)** Which compounds are diastereomers?

STRATEGY

Determine the R/S configuration of the stereocenters in each compound and compare corresponding stereocenters to determine their relationship (see How To 6.3).

SOLUTION

(a) Compounds (1) and (4) are one pair of enantiomers, and compounds (2) and (3) are a second pair of enantiomers. Note that the configurations of the stereocenters in (1) are the opposite of those in (4), its enantiomer.

(b) Compounds (1) and (2), (1) and (3), (2) and (4), and (3) and (4) are diastereomers.

See problem 6.23

PROBLEM 6.3

Following are stereorepresentations of the four stereoisomers of 3-chloro-2-butanol:

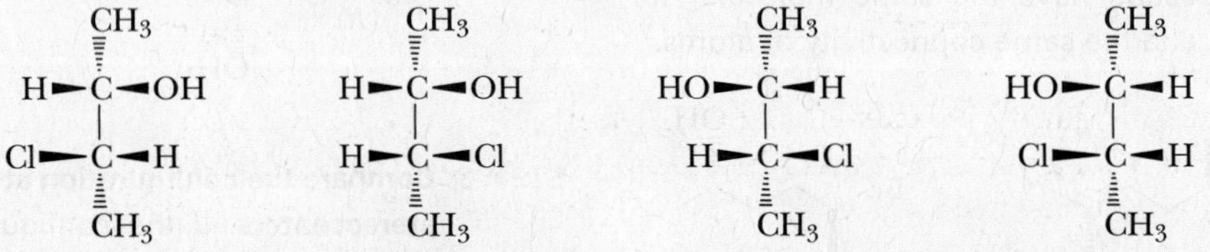

(1) (2) (3) (4)

(a) Which compounds are enantiomers? **(b)** Which compounds are diastereomers?

B. Meso Compounds

Certain molecules containing two or more stereocenters have special symmetry properties that reduce the number of stereoisomers to fewer than the maximum number predicted by the 2^n rule. One such molecule is 2,3-dihydroxybutanedioic acid, more commonly named tartaric acid:

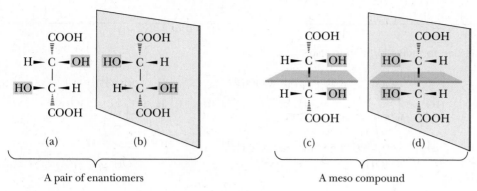

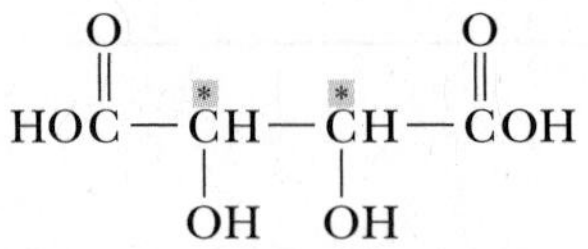

2,3-Dihydroxybutanedioic acid (tartaric acid)

Tartaric acid is a colorless, crystalline compound occurring largely in the vegetable kingdom, especially in grapes. During the fermentation of grape juice, potassium bitartrate (one —COOH group is present as a potassium salt, $—COO^- K^+$) deposits as a crust on the sides of wine casks. Then, collected and purified, it is sold commercially as cream of tartar.

Carbons 2 and 3 of tartaric acid are stereocenters, and, from the 2^n rule, the maximum number of stereoisomers possible is $2^2 = 4$. Figure 6.5 shows the two pairs of mirror images of this compound. Structures (a) and (b) are nonsuperposable mirror images and, therefore, are a pair of enantiomers. Structures (c) and (d) are also mirror images, but they are superposable. To see this, imagine that you rotate (d) by 180° in the plane of the paper, lift it out of the plane of the paper, and place it on top of (c). If you do this mental manipulation correctly, you will find that (d) is

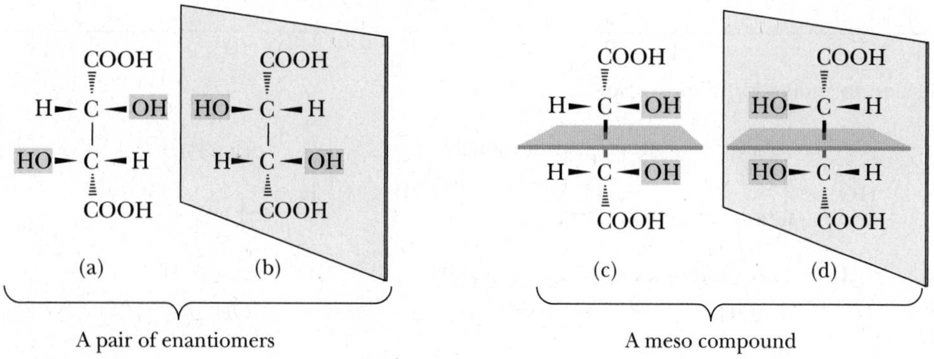

FIGURE 6.5
Stereoisomers of tartaric acid. One pair of enantiomers and one meso compound. The presence of an internal plane of symmetry indicates that the molecule is achiral.

superposable on (c). Therefore, (c) and (d) are *not* different molecules; they are the same molecule, just oriented differently. Because (c) and its mirror image are superposable, (c) is achiral.

Another way to verify that (c) is achiral is to see that it has a plane of symmetry that bisects the molecule in such a way that the top half is the reflection of the bottom half. Thus, even though (c) has two stereocenters, it is achiral. The stereoisomer of tartaric acid represented by (c) or (d) is called a **meso compound**, defined as an achiral compound that contains two or more stereocenters.

Meso compound An achiral compound possessing two or more stereocenters.

We can now return to the original question: How many stereoisomers are there of tartaric acid? The answer is three: one meso compound and one pair of enantiomers. Note that the meso compound is a diastereomer of each of the other stereoisomers.

EXAMPLE 6.4

Following are stereorepresentations of the three stereoisomers of 2,3-butanediol:

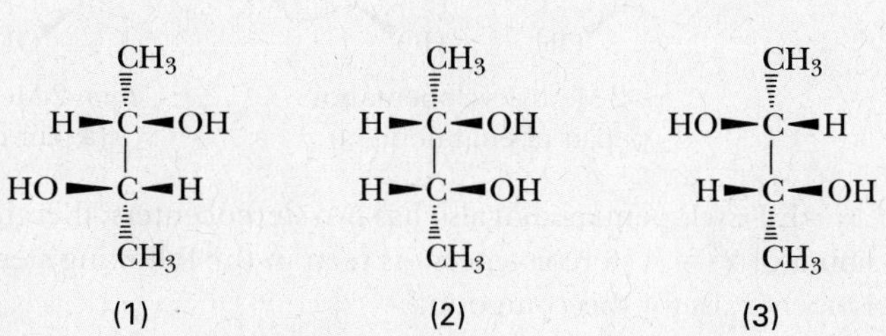

(a) Which are enantiomers? **(b)** Which is the meso compound?

STRATEGY

Enantiomers are nonsuperposable mirror images. A meso compound is an achiral compound with two or more stereocenters, that is, a compound with two or more stereocenters that has a superposable mirror image.

SOLUTION

(a) Compounds (1) and (3) are enantiomers.
(b) Compound (2) has an internal plane of symmetry and, therefore, is a meso compound.

See problems 6.23, 6.36, 6.38

PROBLEM 6.4

Following are four Newman projection formulas for tartaric acid:

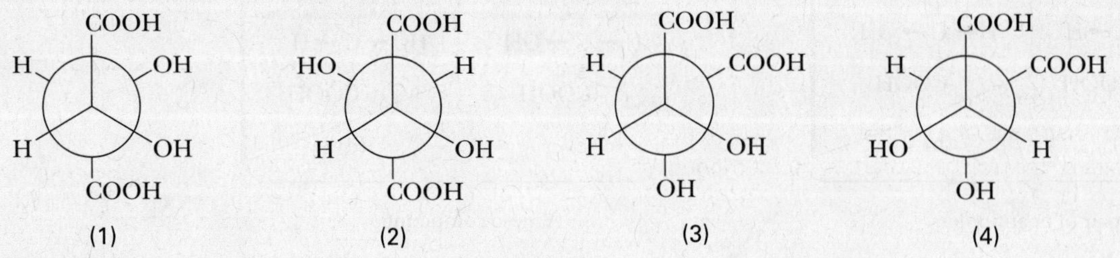

(a) Which represent the same compound? (b) Which represent enantiomers? (c) Which represent(s) meso tartaric acid?

6.5 How Do We Describe the Chirality of Cyclic Molecules with Two Stereocenters?

In this section, we concentrate on derivatives of cyclopentane and cyclohexane that contain two stereocenters. We can analyze chirality in these cyclic compounds in the same way we analyzed it in acyclic compounds.

A. Disubstituted Derivatives of Cyclopentane

Let us start with 2-methylcyclopentanol, a compound with two stereocenters. Using the 2^n rule, we predict a maximum of $2^2 = 4$ stereoisomers. Both the *cis* isomer and the *trans* isomer are chiral. The *cis* isomer exists as one pair of enantiomers, and the *trans* isomer exists as a second pair:

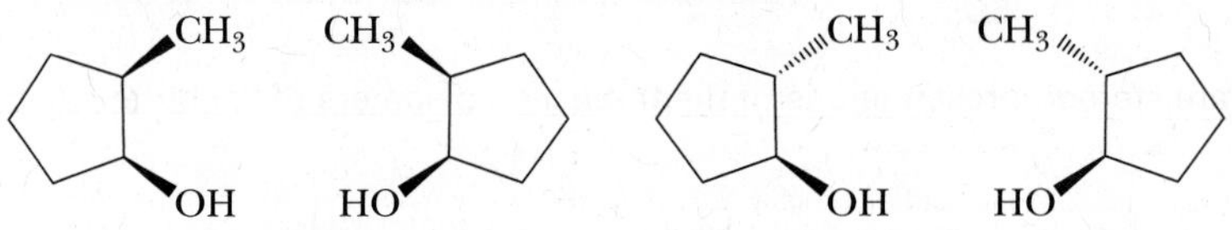

cis-2-Methylcyclopentanol (a pair of enantiomers)

trans-2-Methylcyclopentanol (a pair of enantiomers)

1,2-Cyclopentanediol also has two stereocenters; therefore, the 2^n rule predicts a maximum of $2^2 = 4$ stereoisomers. As seen in the following stereodrawings, only three stereoisomers exist for this compound:

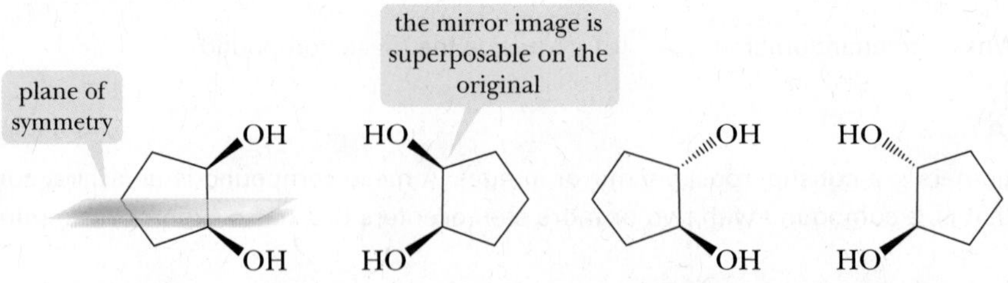

cis-1,2-Cyclopentanediol (a meso compound)

trans-1,2-Cyclopentanediol (a pair of enantiomers)

The *cis* isomer is achiral (meso) because it and its mirror image are superposable. Alternatively, the *cis* isomer is achiral because it possesses a plane of symmetry that bisects the molecule into two mirror-image halves. The *trans* isomer is chiral and exists as a pair of enantiomers.

EXAMPLE 6.5

How many stereoisomers are possible for 3-methylcyclopentanol?

STRATEGY

First identify all possible stereocenters, draw all possible pairs of stereoisomers, and determine which, if any, of the possible pairs of stereoisomers are meso compounds.

SOLUTION

There are two stereocenters in this compound and, therefore, four stereoisomers of 3-methylcyclopentanol. The *cis* isomer exists as one pair of enantiomers and the *trans* isomer as a second pair:

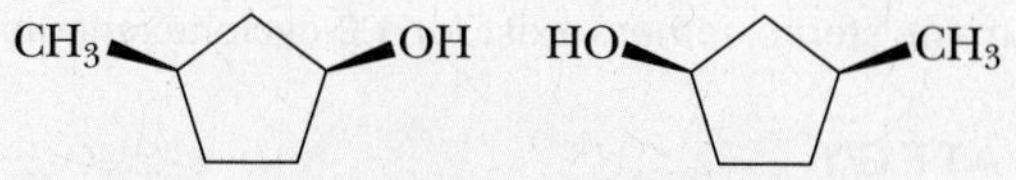

cis-3-Methylcyclopentanol
(a pair of enantiomers)

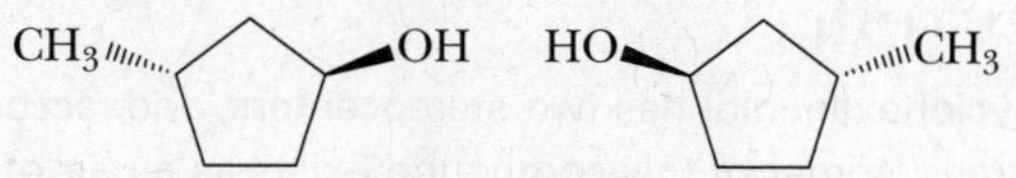

trans-3-Methylcyclopentanol
(a pair of enantiomers)

See problems 6.31, 6.33–6.35, 6.38, 6.39

PROBLEM 6.5

How many stereoisomers are possible for 1,3-cyclopentanediol?

B. Disubstituted Derivatives of Cyclohexane

As an example of a disubstituted cyclohexane, let us consider the methylcyclohexanols. 4-Methylcyclohexanol can exist as two stereoisomers—a pair of *cis–trans* isomers:

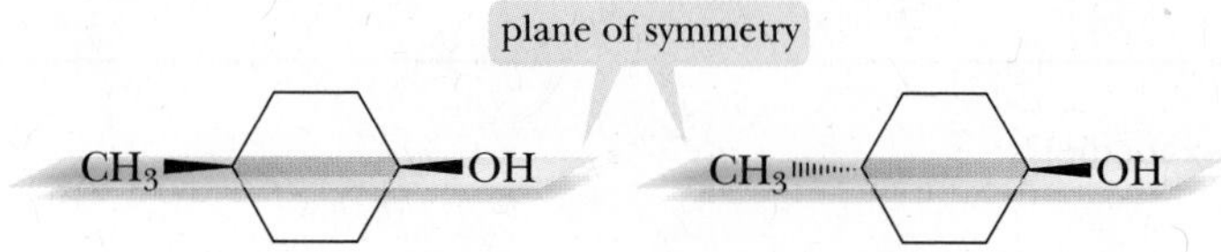

cis-4-Methylcyclohexanol *trans*-4-Methylcyclohexanol

Both the *cis* and the *trans* isomers are achiral. In each, a plane of symmetry runs through the CH_3 and OH groups and the two attached carbons.

3-Methylcyclohexanol has two stereocenters and exists as $2^2 = 4$ stereoisomers, with the *cis* isomer existing as one pair of enantiomers and the *trans* isomer as a second pair:

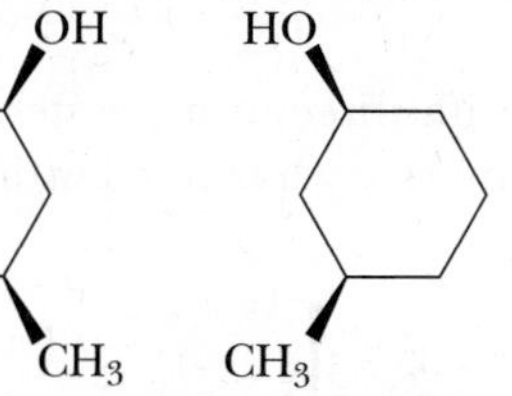

cis-3-Methylcyclohexanol
(a pair of enantiomers)

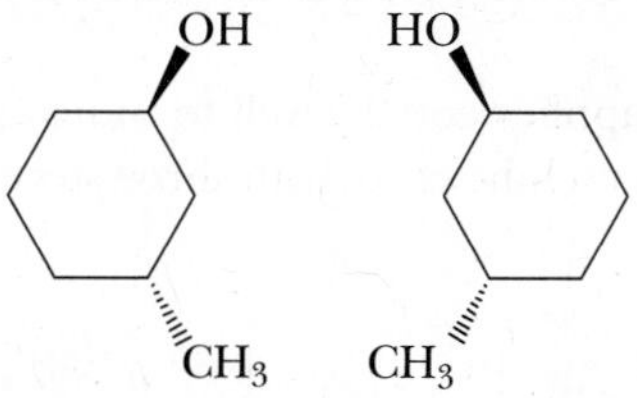

trans-3-Methylcyclohexanol
(a pair of enantiomers)

Similarly, 2-methylcyclohexanol has two stereocenters and exists as $2^2 = 4$ stereoisomers, with the *cis* isomer existing as one pair of enantiomers and the *trans* isomer as a second pair:

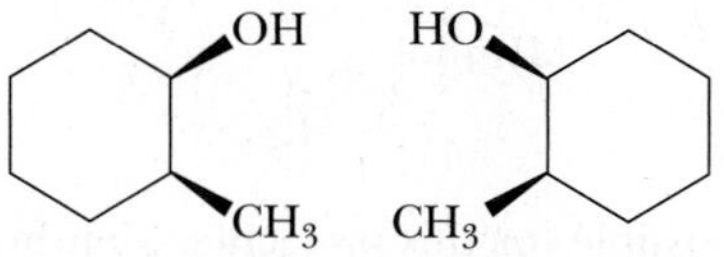

cis-2-Methylcyclohexanol
(a pair of enantiomers)

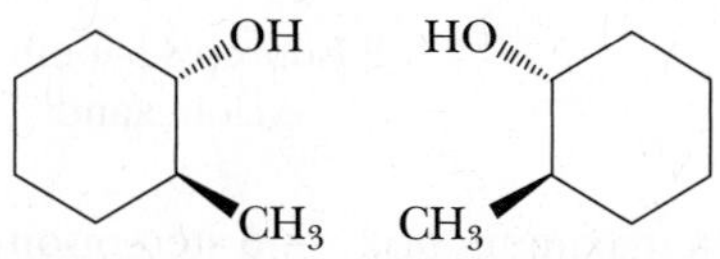

trans-2-Methylcyclohexanol
(a pair of enantiomers)

EXAMPLE 6.6

How many stereoisomers exist for 1,3-cyclohexanediol?

STRATEGY

Locate all stereocenters and use the 2^n rule to determine the maximum number of stereoisomers possible. Determine which, if any, of the possible stereoisomers are meso compounds.

SOLUTION

1,3-Cyclohexanediol has two stereocenters, and, according to the 2^n rule, a maximum of $2^2 = 4$ stereoisomers is possible. The *trans* isomer of this compound exists as a pair of enantiomers. The *cis* isomer has a plane of symmetry and is a meso compound. Therefore, although the 2^n rule predicts a maximum of four stereoisomers for 1,3-cyclohexanediol, only three exist—one pair of enantiomers and one meso compound:

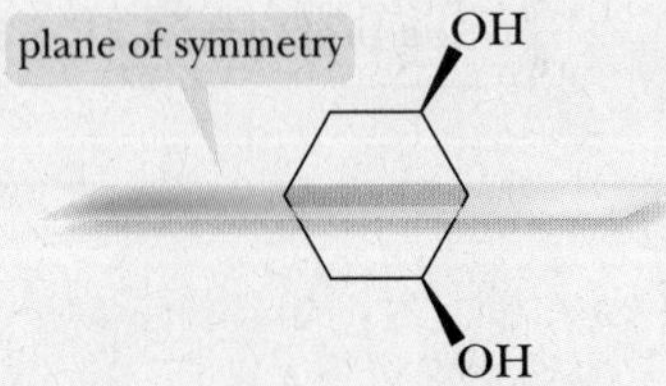

cis-1,3-Cyclohexanediol
(a meso compound)

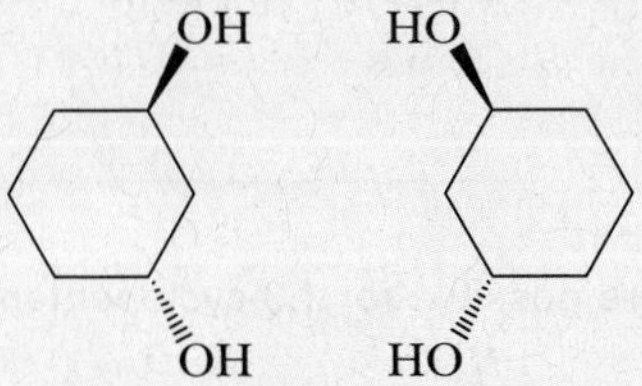

trans-1,3-Cyclohexanediol
(a pair of enantiomers)

See problems 6.31, 6.33–6.35, 6.38, 6.39

PROBLEM 6.6

How many stereoisomers exist for 1,4-cyclohexanediol?

6.6 How Do We Describe the Chirality of Molecules with Three or More Stereocenters?

The 2^n rule applies equally well to molecules with three or more stereocenters. Here is a disubstituted cyclohexanol with three stereocenters, each marked with an asterisk:

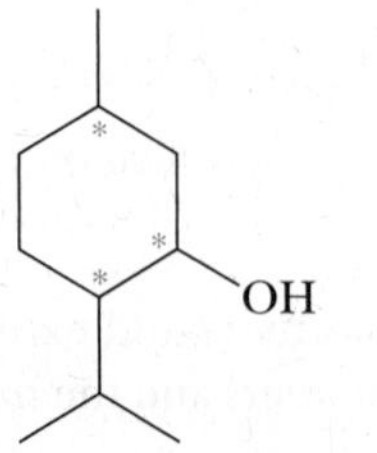

2-Isopropyl-5-methyl-
cyclohexanol

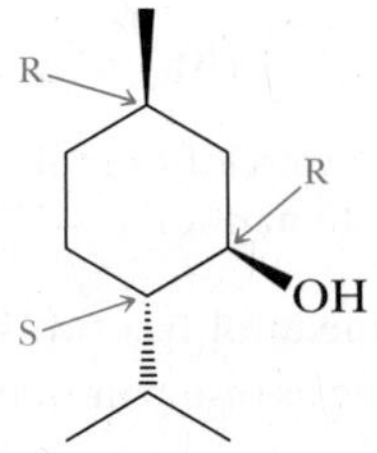

Menthol

There is a maximum of $2^3 = 8$ stereoisomers possible for this molecule. Menthol, one of the eight, has the configuration shown on the right. The configuration at each stereocenter is indicated. Menthol is present in peppermint and other mint oils.

Cholesterol, a more complicated molecule, has eight stereocenters:

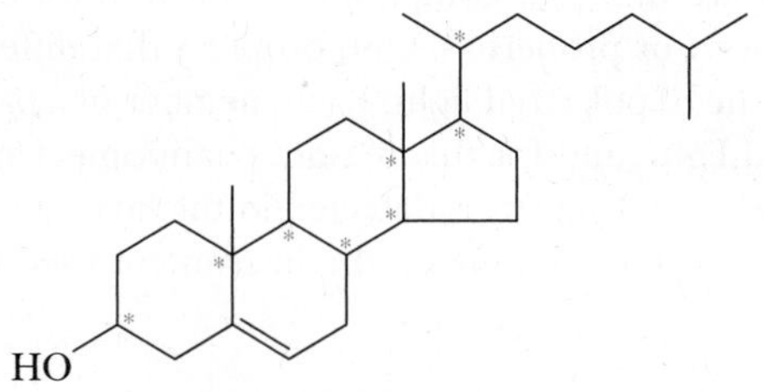

Cholesterol has 8 stereocenters; 256 stereoisomers are possible

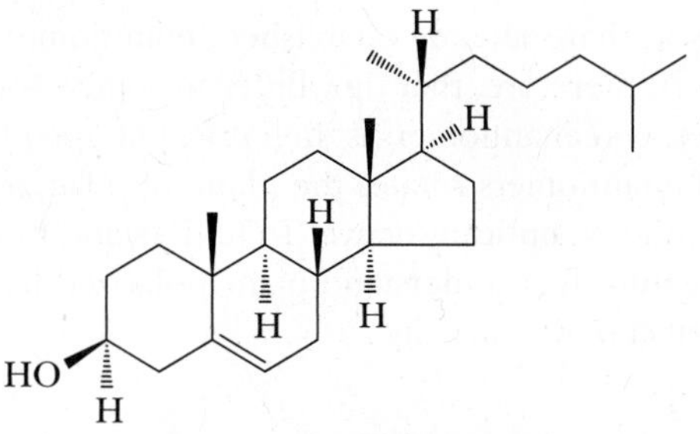

This is the stereoisomer found in human metabolism

To identify the stereocenters, remember to add an appropriate number of hydrogens to complete the tetravalence of each carbon you think might be a stereocenter.

6.7 What Are the Properties of Stereoisomers?

Enantiomers have identical physical and chemical properties in achiral environments. The enantiomers of tartaric acid (Table 6.1), for example, have the same melting point, the same boiling point, the same solubilities in water and other common solvents, and the same values of pK_a (the acid ionization constant), and they all undergo the same acid–base reactions. The enantiomers of tartaric acid do, however, differ in optical activity (the ability to rotate the plane of polarized light), a property that is discussed in the next section.

Diastereomers have different physical and chemical properties, even in achiral environments. Meso-tartaric acid has different physical properties from those of the enantiomers.

TABLE 6.1 Some Physical Properties of the Stereoisomers of Tartaric Acid

	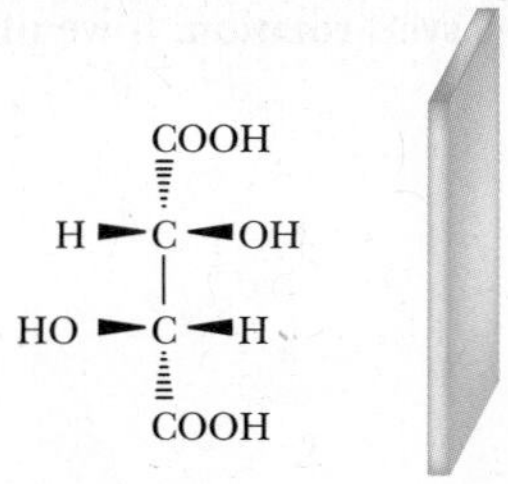	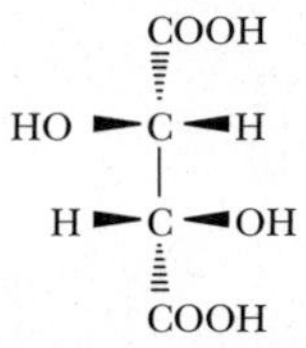	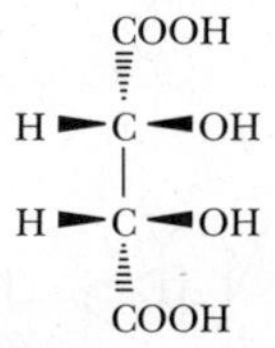
	(*R,R*)-Tartaric acid	(*S,S*)-Tartaric acid	Meso-tartaric acid
Specific rotation*	+12.7	−12.7	0
Melting point (°C)	171–174	171–174	146–148
Density at 20 °C (g/cm^3)	1.7598	1.7598	1.660
Solubility in water at 20 °C (g/100 mL)	139	139	125
pK_1 (25 °C)	2.98	2.98	3.23
pK_2 (25 °C)	4.34	4.34	4.82

*Specific rotation is discussed in the next section.

6.8 How Is Chirality Detected in the Laboratory?

As we have already established, enantiomers are different compounds, and we must expect, therefore, that they differ in some property or properties. One property that differs between enantiomers is their effect on the plane of polarized light. Each member of a pair of enantiomers rotates the plane of polarized light, and for this reason, enantiomers are said to be **optically active**. To understand how optical activity is detected in the laboratory, we must first understand plane-polarized light and a polarimeter, the instrument used to detect optical activity.

Optically active Showing that a compound rotates the plane of polarized light.

A. Plane-Polarized Light

Ordinary light consists of waves vibrating in all planes perpendicular to its direction of propagation (Figure 6.6). Certain materials, such as calcite and Polaroid™ sheet (a plastic film containing properly oriented crystals of an organic substance embedded in it), selectively transmit light waves vibrating in parallel planes. Electromagnetic radiation vibrating in only parallel planes is said to be **plane polarized**.

Plane-polarized light Light vibrating only in parallel planes.

Richard Megna, 1992/ Fundamental Photographs

A polarimeter is used to measure the rotation of plane-polarized light as it passes through a sample.

B. A Polarimeter

A **polarimeter** consists of a light source, a polarizing filter and an analyzing filter (each made of calcite or Polaroid™ film), and a sample tube (Figure 6.6). If the sample tube is empty, the intensity of light reaching the detector (in this case, your eye) is at its maximum when the polarizing axes of the two filters are parallel. If the analyzing filter is turned either clockwise or counterclockwise, less light is transmitted. When the axis of the analyzing filter is at right angles to the axis of the polarizing filter, the field of view is dark. This position of the analyzing filter is taken to be 0° on the optical scale.

The ability of molecules to **rotate the plane of polarized light** can be observed with the use of a polarimeter in the following way: First, a sample tube filled with solvent is placed in the polarimeter, and the analyzing filter is adjusted so that no light passes through to the observer; that is, the filter is set to 0°. Then we place a solution of an optically active compound in the sample tube. When we do so, we find that a certain amount of light now passes through the analyzing filter. We also find that the plane of polarized light from the polarizing filter has been rotated so that it is no longer at an angle of 90° to the analyzing filter. Consequently, we rotate the analyzing filter to restore darkness in the field of view. The number of degrees, α, through which we must rotate the analyzing filter to restore darkness to the field of view is called the **observed rotation**. If we must turn the analyzing

Polarimeter An instrument for measuring the ability of a compound to rotate the plane of polarized light.

Observed rotation The number of degrees through which a compound rotates the plane of polarized light.

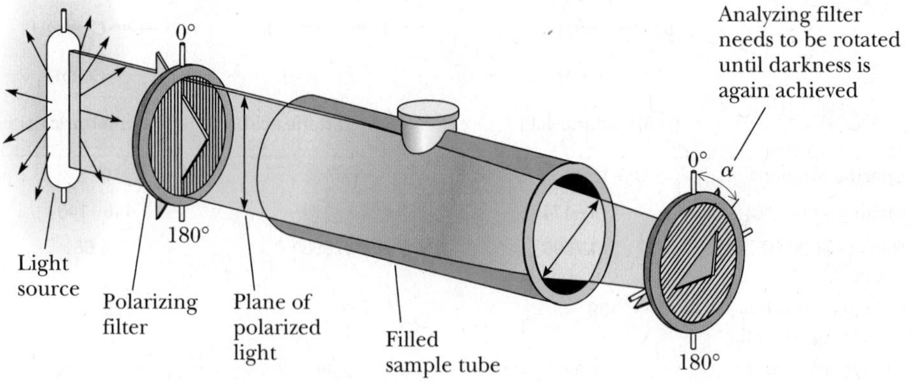

FIGURE 6.6
Schematic diagram of a polarimeter with its sample tube containing a solution of an optically active compound. The analyzing filter has been turned clockwise by α degrees to restore the dark field.

filter to the right (clockwise) to restore the dark field, we say that the compound is **dextrorotatory** (Latin: *dexter*, on the right side); if we must turn it to the left (counterclockwise), we say that the compound is **levorotatory** (Latin: *laevus*, on the left side).

Dextrorotatory Rotating the plane of polarized light in a polarimeter to the right.

Levorotatory Rotating the plane of polarized light in a polarimeter to the left.

The magnitude of the observed rotation for a particular compound depends on its concentration, the length of the sample tube, the temperature, the solvent, and the wavelength of the light used. The **specific rotation**, $[\alpha]$, is defined as the observed rotation at a specific cell length and sample concentration expressed in grams per milliliter.

Specific rotation Observed rotation of the plane of polarized light when a sample is placed in a tube 1.0 dm long at a concentration of 1.0 g/mL.

$$\text{Specific rotation} = [\alpha]_{\lambda}^{T} = \frac{\text{Observed rotation (degrees)}}{\text{Length (dm)} \times \text{Concentration}}$$

The standard cell length is 1 decimeter (1 dm $= 0.1$ m). For a pure liquid sample, the concentration is expressed in grams per milliliter (g/mL; density). The temperature (T, in degrees centigrade) and wavelength (λ, in nanometers) of light are designated, respectively, as superscripts and subscripts. The light source most commonly used in polarimetry is the sodium D line ($\lambda = 589$ nm), the same line responsible for the yellow color of sodium-vapor lamps.

In reporting either observed or specific rotation, it is common to indicate a dextrorotatory compound with a plus sign in parentheses, (+), and a levorotatory compound with a minus sign in parentheses, (−). For any pair of enantiomers, one enantiomer is dextrorotatory and the other is levorotatory. For each member, the value of the specific rotation is exactly the same, but the sign is opposite. Following are the specific rotations of the enantiomers of 2-butanol at 25 °C, observed with the D line of sodium:

(*S*)-(+)-2-Butanol $[\alpha]_{D}^{25}$ + 13.52°

(*R*)-(−)-2-Butanol $[\alpha]_{D}^{25}$ −13.52°

C. Racemic Mixtures

An equimolar mixture of two enantiomers is called a **racemic mixture**, a term derived from the name "racemic acid" (Latin: *racemus*, a cluster of grapes), originally given to an equimolar mixture of the enantiomers of tartaric acid (Table 6.1). Because a racemic mixture contains equal numbers of the dextrorotatory and the levorotatory molecules, its specific rotation is zero. Alternatively, we say that a racemic mixture is **optically inactive**. A racemic mixture is indicated by adding the prefix (±) to the name of the compound.

Racemic mixture A mixture of equal amounts of two enantiomers.

Optically inactive Showing that a compound or mixture of compounds does not rotate the plane of polarized light.

6.9 What Is the Significance of Chirality in the Biological World?

Except for inorganic salts and a relatively few low-molecular-weight organic substances, the molecules in living systems, both plant and animal, are chiral. Although these molecules can exist as a number of stereoisomers, almost invariably only one stereoisomer is found in nature. Of course, instances do occur in which more than one stereoisomer is found, but these rarely exist together in the same biological system.

A. Chirality in Biomolecules

Perhaps the most conspicuous examples of chirality among biological molecules are the enzymes, all of which have many stereocenters. An example is chymotrypsin, an enzyme found in the intestines of animals. This enzyme catalyzes the digestion of proteins (Section 19.5). Chymotrypsin has 251 stereocenters. The maximum number of stereoisomers possible is

FIGURE 6.7 A schematic diagram of an enzyme surface capable of interacting with (*R*)-(+)-glyceraldehyde at three binding sites, but with (*S*)-(−)-glyceraldehyde at only two of these sites.

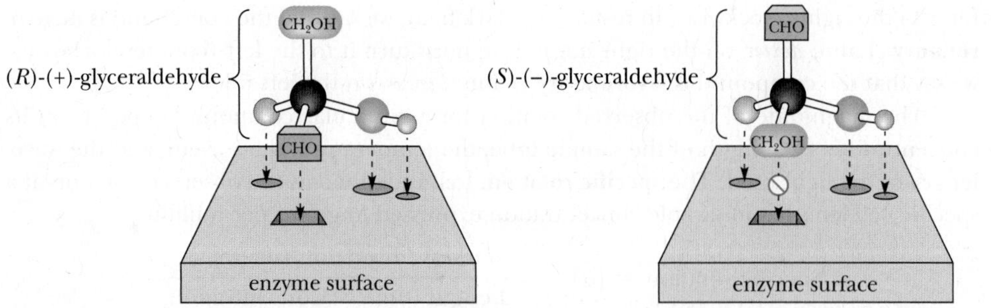

This enantiomer of glyceraldehyde fits the three specific binding sites on the enzyme surface

This enantiomer of glyceraldehyde does not fit the same binding sites

thus 2^{251}, a staggeringly large number, almost beyond comprehension. Fortunately, nature does not squander its precious energy and resources unnecessarily: Only one of these stereoisomers is produced and used by any given organism.

Because enzymes are chiral substances, most either produce or react with only substances that match their stereochemical requirements.

B. How an Enzyme Distinguishes between a Molecule and Its Enantiomer

An enzyme catalyzes a biological reaction of a molecule by first positioning it at a **binding site** on the enzyme's surface. An enzyme with binding sites specific for three of the four groups on a stereocenter can distinguish between a molecule and its enantiomer or one of its diastereomers. Assume, for example, that an enzyme involved in catalyzing a reaction of glyceraldehyde has on its surface a binding site specific for —H, a second specific for —OH, and a third specific for —CHO. Assume further that the three sites are arranged on the enzyme surface as shown in Figure 6.7. The enzyme can distinguish (*R*)-(+)-glyceraldehyde (the natural, or biologically active, form) from its enantiomer because the natural enantiomer can be absorbed, with three groups interacting with their appropriate binding sites; for the S enantiomer, at best only two groups can interact with these binding sites.

Because interactions between molecules in living systems take place in a chiral environment, it should come as no surprise that a molecule and its enantiomer or one of its diastereomers elicit different physiological responses. As we have already seen, (*S*)-ibuprofen is active as a pain and fever reliever, whereas its R enantiomer is inactive. The S enantiomer of the closely related analgesic naproxen is also the active pain reliever of this compound, but its R enantiomer is a liver toxin!

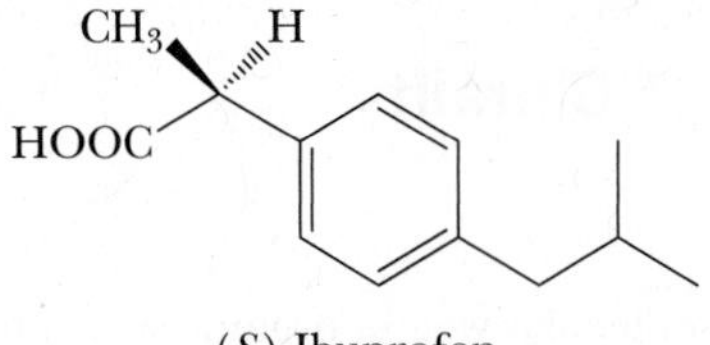

(*S*)-Ibuprofen

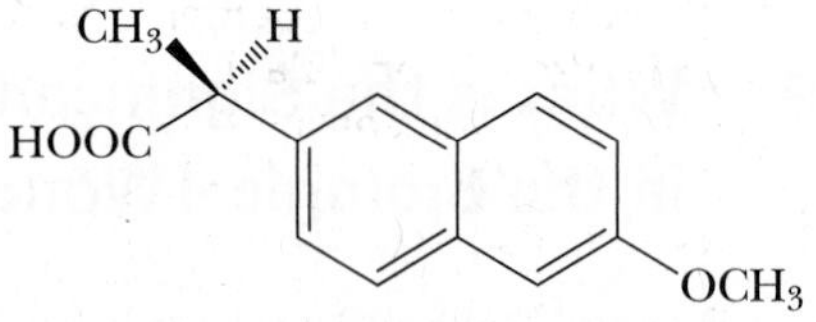

(*S*)-Naproxen

6.10 How Can Enantiomers Be Resolved?

Resolution Separation of a racemic mixture into its enantiomers.

Resolution is the separation of a racemic mixture into its enantiomers. Because two enantiomers have the same physical properties, separating them, in general, is difficult, but scientists have developed a number of ways to do it. In this section, we illustrate just two of the several laboratory methods for resolution: the use of enzymes as chiral catalysts and the use of solid chiral materials to differentiate between enantiomers made to come in contact with these materials.

Chemical Connections 6A

CHIRAL DRUGS

Some of the common drugs used in human medicine (for example, aspirin, Section 14.4B) are achiral. Others are chiral and are sold as single enantiomers. The penicillin and erythromycin classes of antibiotics and the drug Captopril are all chiral drugs. Captopril, which is highly effective for the treatment of high blood pressure and congestive heart failure, was developed in a research program designed to discover effective inhibitors of angiotensin-converting enzyme (ACE). Captopril is manufactured and sold as the (*S,S*)-stereoisomer. A large number of chiral drugs, however, are sold as racemic mixtures. The popular analgesic ibuprofen (the active ingredient in Motrin®, Advil®, and many other nonaspirin analgesics) is an example. Only the S enantiomer of the pain reliever ibuprofen is biologically active.

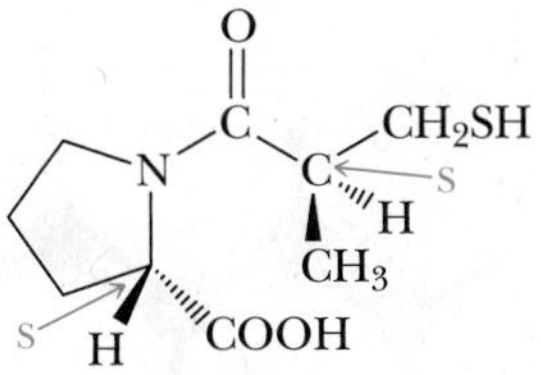

Captopril

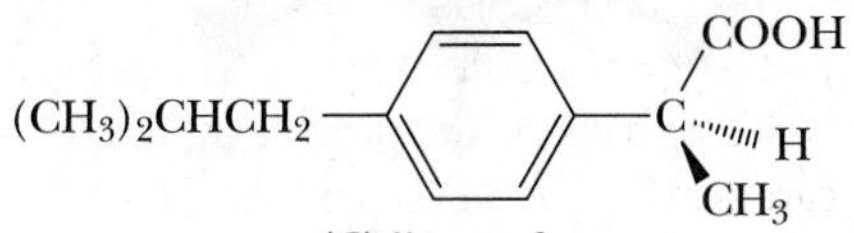

(*S*)-Ibuprofen

For racemic drugs, most often only one enantiomer exerts the beneficial effect, whereas the other enantiomer either has no effect or may exert a detrimental effect. Thus, enantiomerically pure drugs should, more often than not, be more effective than their racemic counterparts. A case in point is 3,4-dihydroxyphenylalanine, which is used in the treatment of Parkinson's disease. The active drug is dopamine. Unfortunately, this compound does not cross the blood–brain barrier to the required site of action in the brain. Consequently, what is administered instead is the prodrug, a compound that is not active by itself, but is converted in the body to an active drug. 3,4-Dihydroxyphenylalanine is such a prodrug; it crosses the blood–brain barrier and then undergoes decarboxylation, catalyzed by the enzyme dopamine decarboxylase, to give dopamine. Decarboxylation is the loss of carbon dioxide from a carboxyl group ($R{-}CO_2H$).

$$R{-}CO_2H \xrightarrow{\text{decarboxylation}} R{-}H + CO_2$$

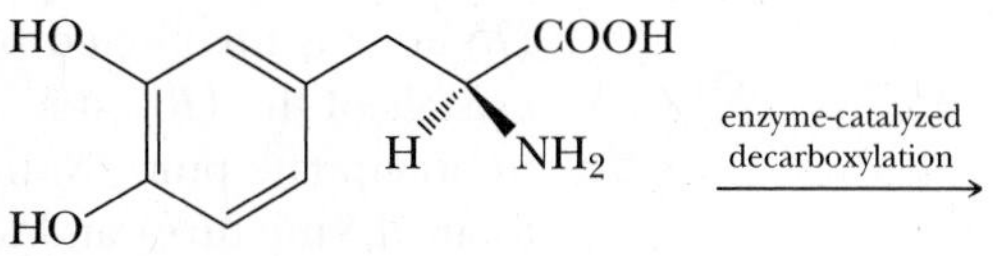

(*S*)-(−)-3,4-Dihydroxyphenylalanine
(L-DOPA)
$[\alpha]_D^{13}$ −13.1°

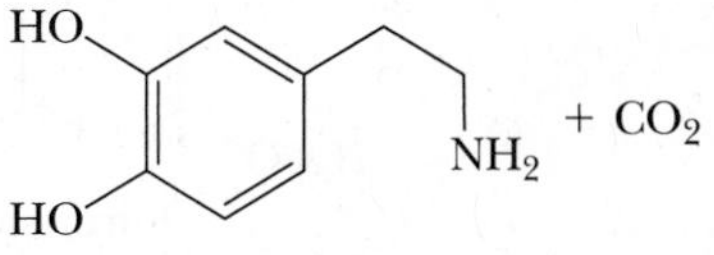

Dopamine

Dopamine decarboxylase is specific for the S enantiomer, which is commonly known as L-DOPA. It is essential, therefore, to administer the enantiomerically pure prodrug. Were the prodrug to be administered in a racemic form, there could be a dangerous buildup of the R enantiomer, which cannot be metabolized by the enzymes present in the brain.

Question

Following are structural formulas for three other angiotensin-converting enzyme (ACE) inhibitors, all members of the *"pril"* family. Which are chiral? For each that is chiral, determine the number of stereoisomers possible for it. List the similarities in structure among each of these four drugs.

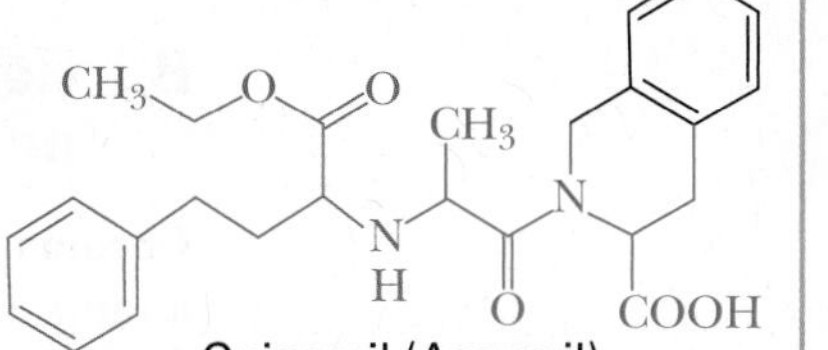

Quinapril (Accupril)

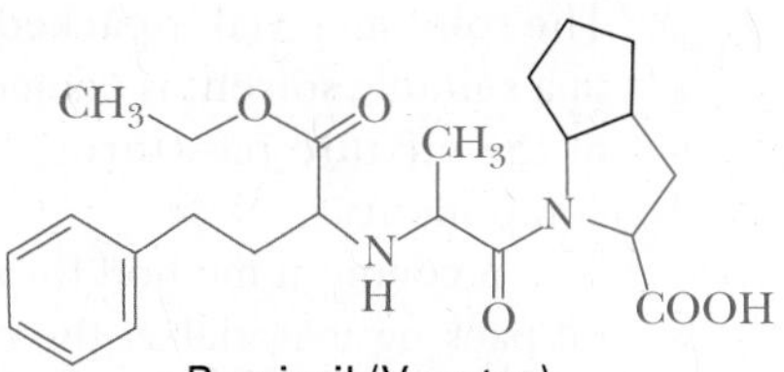

Ramipril (Vasotec)

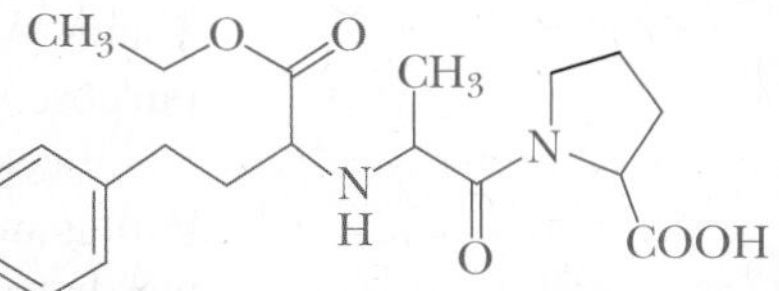

Enalapril (Altace)

A. Enzymes as Resolving Agents

One class of enzymes that has received particular attention in this regard is the esterases, which catalyze the hydrolysis of esters (Section 14.1C) to give an alcohol and a carboxylic acid. We illustrate this method by describing the resolution of (*R*,*S*)-naproxen. The ethyl esters of both (*R*)- and (*S*)-naproxen are solids with very low solubilities in water. Chemists then use an esterase in alkaline solution to selectively hydrolyze the (*S*)-ester, which goes into the aqueous solution as the sodium salt of the (*S*)-carboxylic acid. The (*R*)-ester is unaffected by these conditions. Filtering the alkaline solution recovers the crystals of the (*R*)-ester. After the crystals are removed, the alkaline solution is acidified to precipitate pure (*S*)-naproxen. The recovered (*R*)-ester can be racemized (converted to an *R*,*S*-mixture) and again treated with the esterase. Thus, by recycling the (*R*)-ester, all the racemic ester is converted to (*S*)-naproxen.

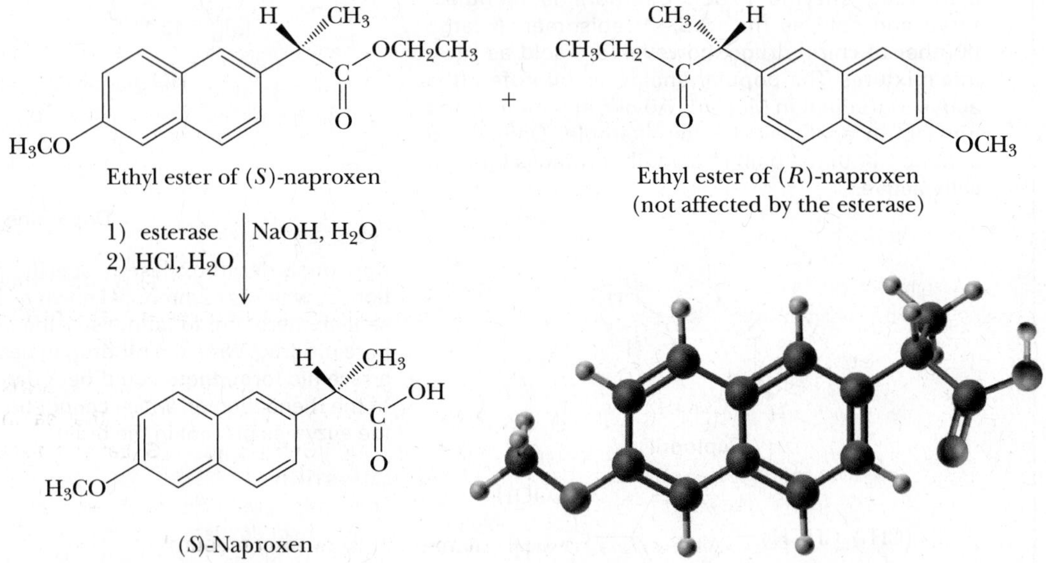

The sodium salt of (*S*)-naproxen is the active ingredient in Aleve® and a score of other over-the-counter nonsteroidal anti-inflammatory preparations.

B. Resolution by Means of Chromatography on a Chiral Substrate

Chromatography is a term used to describe the purification of substances in which a sample to be purified interacts with a solid material, and different components of the sample separate based on differences in their interactions with the solid material. The solid material is packed into a column, and a solution of the substance dissolved in a suitable solvent is passed down the column. The more weakly bound components of the mixture pass through the column more quickly than the more tightly bound components.

A common method for resolving enantiomers today is chromatography using a chiral packing material in the column. Each enantiomer in principle interacts differently with the chiral packing material, and the elution time will be different for each enantiomer. A wide variety of chiral column packing materials have been developed for this purpose.

Recently, the U.S. Food and Drug Administration established new guidelines for the testing and marketing of chiral drugs. After reviewing these guidelines, many drug companies have decided to develop only single enantiomers of new chiral drugs. In addition to regulatory pressure, there are patent considerations: If a company has patents on a racemic drug, a new patent can often be taken out on one of its enantiomers.

SUMMARY OF KEY QUESTIONS

6.1 What Are Stereoisomers?

- **Stereoisomers** have the same connectivity of their atoms, but a different three-dimensional orientation of their atoms in space.
- A **mirror image** is the reflection of an object in a mirror.

6.2 What Are Enantiomers?

- **Enantiomers** are a pair of stereoisomers that are nonsuperposable mirror images. A molecule that is not superposable on its mirror image is said to be **chiral**.
- Chirality is a property of an object as a whole, not of a particular atom.
- An **achiral** object possesses a **plane of symmetry**—an imaginary plane passing through the object and dividing it such that one half is the reflection of the other half.
- A **stereocenter** is an atom at which the interchange of two atoms or groups of atoms bonded to it produces a different stereoisomer.
- The most common type of stereocenter among organic compounds is a **chiral center**, a tetrahedral carbon atom with four different groups bonded to it.

6.3 How Do We Designate the Configuration of a Stereocenter?

- The **configuration** at a stereocenter can be specified by the **R,S convention**.
- To apply this convention, (1) each atom or group of atoms bonded to the stereocenter is assigned a priority and numbered from highest priority to lowest priority, (2) the molecule is oriented in space so that the group of lowest priority is directed away from the observer, and (3) the remaining three groups are read in order, from highest priority to lowest priority.
- If the reading of groups is clockwise, the configuration is **R** (Latin: *rectus*, right). If the reading is counterclockwise, the configuration is **S** (Latin: *sinister*, left).

6.4 What Is the 2^n Rule?

- For a molecule with ***n*** stereocenters, the maximum number of stereoisomers possible is $\mathbf{2^n}$.
- **Diastereomers** are stereoisomers that are not mirror images.
- Certain molecules have special symmetry properties that reduce the number of stereoisomers to fewer than that predicted by the **2^n rule**.
- A **meso** compound contains two or more stereocenters assembled in such a way that its molecules are achiral.
- Enantiomers have identical physical and chemical properties in achiral environments.
- Diastereomers have different physical and chemical properties.

6.5 How Do We Describe the Chirality of Cyclic Molecules with Two Stereocenters?

- When evaluating the symmetry of cyclic structures, such as derivatives of cyclohexane and cyclopentane, it is helpful to evaluate planar representations.

6.6 How Do We Describe the Chirality of Molecules with Three or More Stereocenters?

- For a molecule with *n* stereocenters, the maximum number of stereoisomers possible is 2^n.

6.7 What Are the Properties of Stereoisomers?

- Enantiomers have identical physical and chemical properties in achiral environments.
- Diastereomers have different physical and chemical properties.

6.8 How Is Chirality Detected in the Laboratory?

- Light that vibrates in only parallel planes is said to be **plane polarized**.
- A **polarimeter** is an instrument used to detect and measure the magnitude of optical activity. **Observed rotation** is the number of degrees the plane of polarized light is rotated.

- **Specific rotation** is the observed rotation measured with a cell 1 dm long and a solution with a concentration of 1.00 g/mL.
- If the analyzing filter must be turned clockwise to restore the zero point, the compound is **dextrorotatory**. If the analyzing filter must be turned counterclockwise to restore the zero point, the compound is **levorotatory**.
- A compound is said to be **optically active** if it rotates the plane of polarized light. Each member of a pair of enantiomers rotates the plane of polarized light an equal number of degrees, but opposite in direction.
- A **racemic mixture** is a mixture of equal amounts of two enantiomers and has a specific rotation of zero.
- A **meso** compound is optically inactive.

6.9 What Is the Significance of Chirality in the Biological World?

- An enzyme catalyzes the biological reactions of molecules by first positioning them at a binding site on its surface. An enzyme with a binding site specific for three of the four groups on a stereocenter can distinguish between a molecule and its enantiomer or its diastereomers.

6.10 How Can Enantiomers Be Resolved?

- **Resolution** is the experimental process of separating a mixture of enantiomers into two pure enantiomers.
- One means of resolution is to treat the racemic mixture with an enzyme that catalyzes a specific reaction of one enantiomer, but not the other.
- A common method for resolving enantiomers is chromatography using a chiral packing material in the column. Each enantiomer in principle interacts differently with the chiral packing material and the elution time will be different for each enantiomer.

QUICK QUIZ

Answer true or false to the following questions to assess your general knowledge of the concepts in this chapter. If you have difficulty with any of them, you should review the appropriate section in the chapter (shown in parentheses) before attempting the more challenging end-of-chapter problems.

1. Enantiomers are always chiral. (6.2)
2. An unmarked cube is chiral. (6.1)
3. Stereocenters can be designated using E and Z. (6.3)
4. A chiral molecule will always have a diastereomer. (6.2)
5. Every object in nature has a mirror image. (6.1)
6. A molecule that possesses an internal plane of symmetry can never be chiral. (6.2)
7. Pairs of enantiomers have the same connectivity. (6.1)
8. Enantiomers, like gloves, occur in pairs. (6.2)
9. A cyclic molecule with two stereocenters will always have only three stereoisomers. (6.5)
10. An achiral molecule will always have a diastereomer. (6.2)
11. The *cis* and *trans* isomers of 2-butene are chiral. (6.1)
12. A human foot is chiral. (6.1)
13. A compound with n stereocenters will always have 2^n stereoisomers. (6.4)
14. A molecule with three or more stereocenters cannot be meso. (6.6)
15. A molecule with three or more stereocenters must be chiral. (6.6)
16. Each member of a pair of enantiomers will have the same boiling point. (6.7)
17. If a molecule is not superposable on its mirror image, it is chiral. (6.1)
18. For a molecule with two tetrahedral stereocenters, four stereoisomers are possible. (6.2)
19. Constitutional isomers have the same connectivity. (6.1)
20. Enantiomers can be separated by interacting them with the same chiral environment or chemical agent. (6.10)
21. Enzymes are achiral molecules that can differentiate chiral molecules. (6.9)
22. *Cis* and *trans* stereoisomers of a cyclic compound can be classified as diastereomers. (6.5)
23. 3-Pentanol is the mirror image of 2-pentanol. (6.2)
24. Diastereomers do not have a mirror image. (6.2)
25. The most common cause of chirality in organic molecules is the presence of a tetrahedral carbon atom with four different groups bonded to it. (6.1)
26. Each member of a pair of enantiomers will have the same density. (6.7)
27. The carbonyl carbon of an aldehyde or a ketone cannot be a stereocenter. (6.1)
28. For a molecule with three stereocenters, $3^2 = 9$ stereoisomers are possible. (6.2)
29. Diastereomers can be resolved using traditional methods such as distillation. (6.10)
30. A racemic mixture is optically inactive. (6.8)
31. 2-Pentanol and 3-pentanol are chiral and show enantiomerism. (6.2)
32. A diastereomer of a chiral molecule must also be chiral. (6.2)
33. In order to designate the configuration of a stereocenter, the priority of groups must be read in a clockwise or

counterclockwise fashion after the lowest priority group is placed facing toward the viewer. (6.3)

34. A compound with *n* stereocenters will always be one of the 2^n stereoisomers of that compound. (6.4)

35. Each member of a pair of enantiomers could react differently in a chiral environment. (6.7)

36. A chiral molecule will always have an enantiomer. (6.2)

37. Each member of a pair of diastereomers will have the same melting point. (6.7)

38. If a chiral compound is dextrorotatory, its enantiomer is levorotatory by the same number of degrees. (6.8)

39. All stereoisomers are optically active. (6.8)

40. There are usually equal amounts of each enantiomer of a chiral biological molecule in a living organism. (6.9)

Answers: (1) T (2) F (3) F (4) F (5) T (6) T (7) T (8) T (9) F (10) F (11) F (12) T (13) F (14) F (15) F (16) T (17) T (18) T (19) F (20) T (21) F (22) T (23) F (24) F (25) T (26) T (27) T (28) F (29) T (30) T (31) F (32) F (33) F (34) T (35) T (36) T (37) F (38) T (39) F (40) F

Detailed explanations for many of these answers can be found in the accompanying Solutions Manual.

PROBLEMS

A problem marked with an asterisk indicates an applied "real-world" problem. Answers to problems whose numbers are printed in blue are given in Appendix D.

Section 6.1 Chirality

6.7 Define the term *stereoisomer*. Name four types of stereoisomers.

6.8 In what way are constitutional isomers different from stereoisomers? In what way are they the same?

6.9 Compare and contrast the meaning of the terms *conformation* and *configuration*.

***6.10** Which of these objects are chiral (assume that there is no label or other identifying mark)?

(a) A pair of scissors (b) A tennis ball
(c) A paper clip (d) A beaker
(e) The swirl created in water as it drains out of a sink or bathtub

***6.11** Think about the helical coil of a telephone cord or the spiral binding on a notebook, and suppose that you view the spiral from one end and find that it has a left-handed twist. If you view the same spiral from the other end, does it have a right-handed twist or a left-handed twist from that end as well?

***6.12** Next time you have the opportunity to view a collection of augers or other seashells that have a helical twist, study the chirality of their twists. Do you find an equal number of left-handed and right-handed augers, or, for example, do they all have the same handedness? What about the handedness of augers compared with that of other spiral shells?

Kaz Chiba/Getty Images, Inc.

Median cross section through the shell of a chambered nautilus found in the deep waters of the Pacific Ocean. The shell shows handedness; this cross section is a right-handed spiral.

***6.13** Next time you have an opportunity to examine any of the seemingly endless varieties of spiral pasta (rotini, fusilli, radiatori, tortiglioni), examine their twist. Do the twists of any one kind all have a right-handed twist, do they all have a left-handed twist, or are they a racemic mixture?

6.14 One reason we can be sure that sp^3-hybridized carbon atoms are tetrahedral is the number of stereoisomers that can exist for different organic compounds.

(a) How many stereoisomers are possible for $CHCl_3$, CH_2Cl_2, and CHBrClF if the four bonds to carbon have a tetrahedral geometry?
(b) How many stereoisomers are possible for each of the compounds if the four bonds to the carbon have a square planar geometry?

Section 6.2 Enantiomers

6.15 Which compounds contain stereocenters? **(See Example 6.1)**

(a) 2-Chloropentane
(b) 3-Chloropentane
(c) 3-Chloro-1-pentene
(d) 1,2-Dichloropropane

6.16 Using only C, H, and O, write a structural formula for the lowest-molecular-weight chiral molecule of each of the following compounds:

(a) Alkane (b) Alcohol
(c) Aldehyde (d) Ketone
(e) Carboxylic acid

6.17 Which alcohols with the molecular formula $C_5H_{12}O$ are chiral?

6.18 Which carboxylic acids with the molecular formula $C_6H_{12}O_2$ are chiral?

6.19 Draw the enantiomer for each molecule: **(See Example 6.1)**

(a) 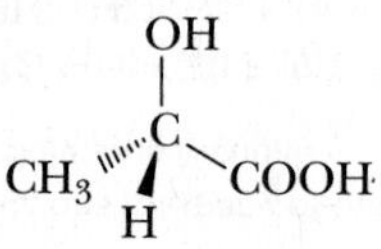

(b) 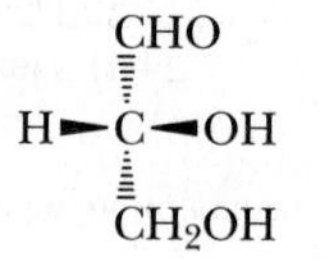

(c) 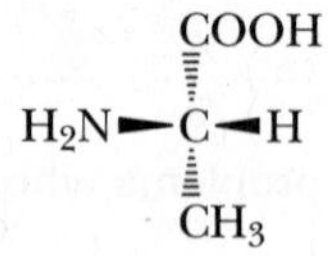

(d) 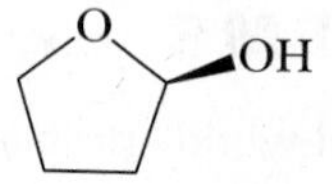

(e) 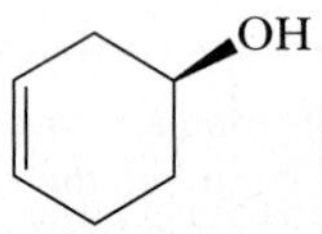

(f) 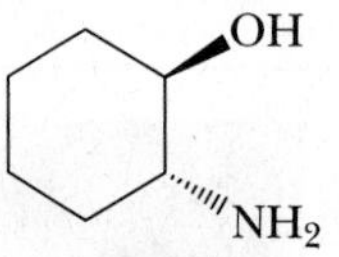

(g) 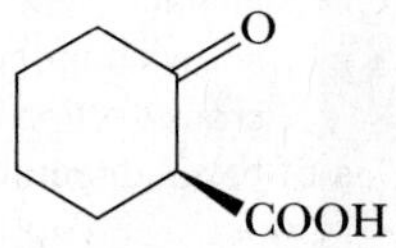

(h) 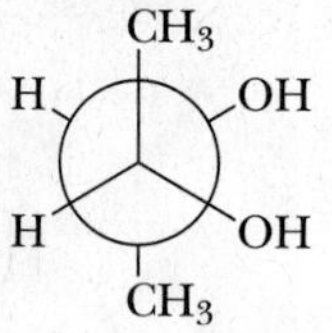

(i) 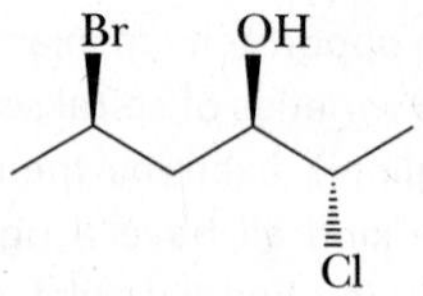

(j) 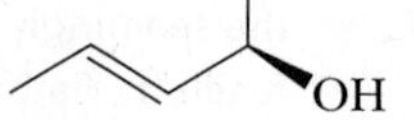

(k) 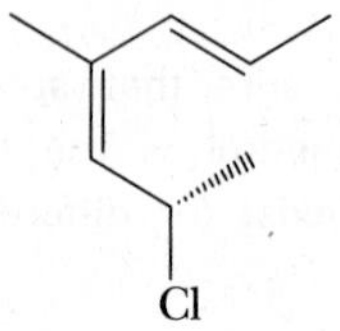

(l) 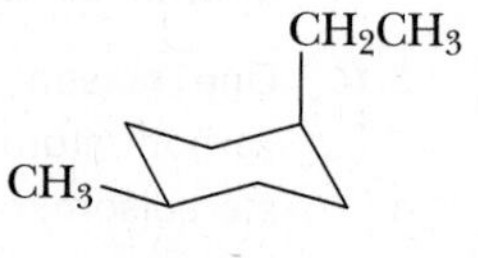

6.20 Mark each stereocenter in these molecules with an asterisk (note that not all contain stereocenters): **(See Example 6.1)**

(a) 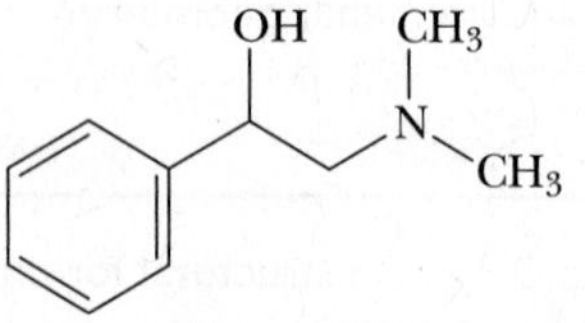

(b) 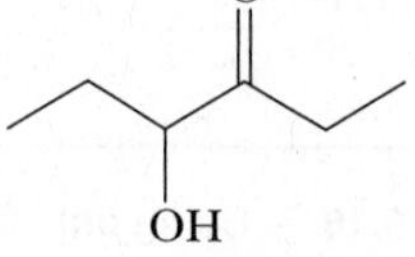

(c) 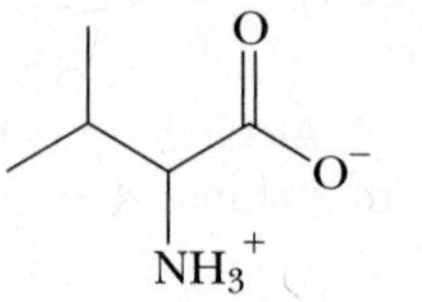

(d) 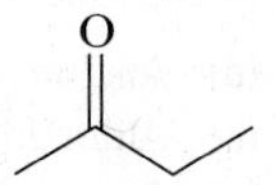

6.21 Mark each stereocenter in these molecules with an asterisk (note that not all contain stereocenters): **(See Example 6.1)**

(a) 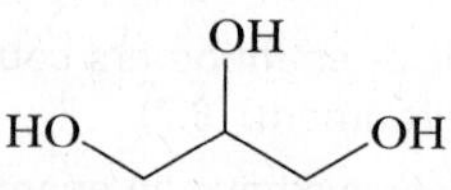

(b) 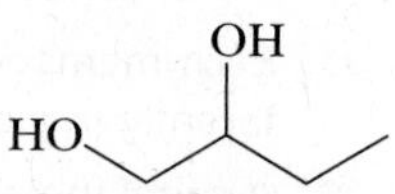

(c) 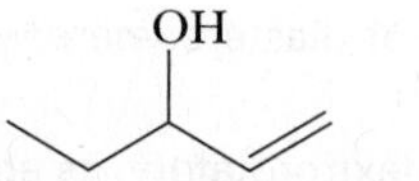

(d) 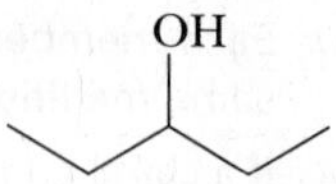

6.22 Mark each stereocenter in these molecules with an asterisk (note that not all contain stereocenters): **(See Example 6.1)**

(a) 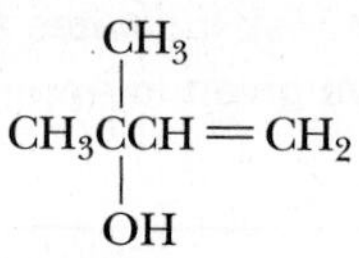

(b) 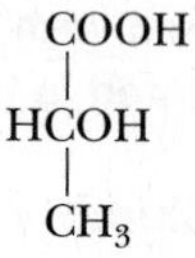

(c) 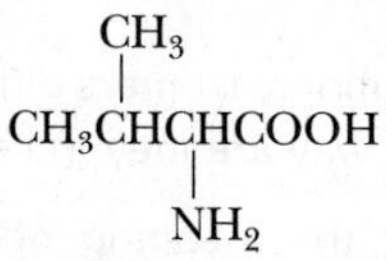

(d) 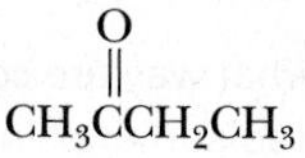

(e) 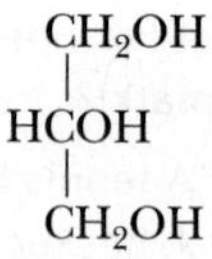

(f) 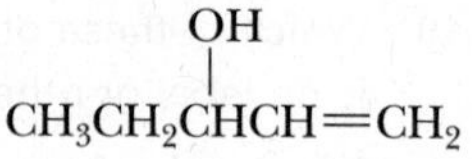

(g) 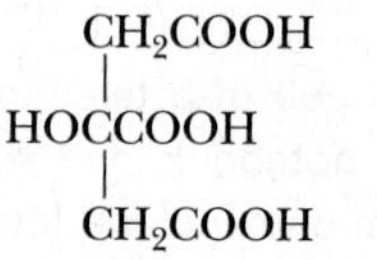

(h) $(CH_3)_3CCH_2CH(OH)CH_3$

6.23 Following are eight stereorepresentations of lactic acid: **(See Examples 6.3, 6.4)**

(a) 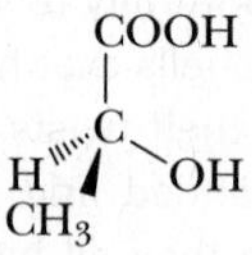

(b) 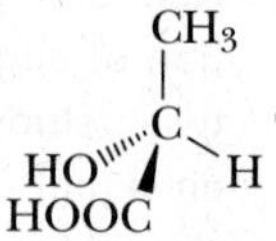

(c) 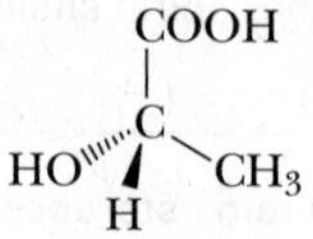

(d) 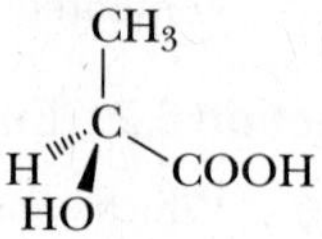

(e) 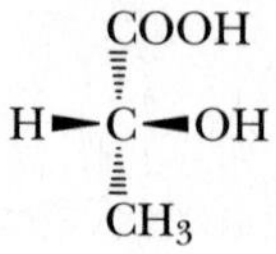

(f) 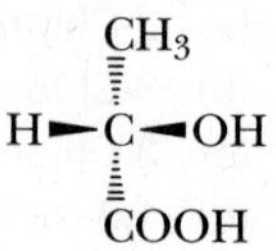

(g) 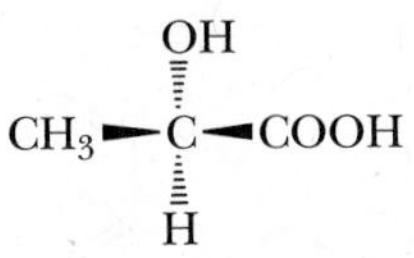 (h) 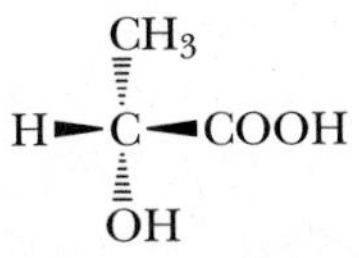

Take (a) as a reference structure. Which stereorepresentations are identical with (a) and which are mirror images of (a)?

Section 6.3 Designation of Configuration: The R,S Convention

6.24 Assign priorities to the groups in each set: **(See Example 6.2)**

(a) $-H \quad -CH_3 \quad -OH \quad -CH_2OH$

(b) $-CH_2CH{=}CH_2 \quad -CH{=}CH_2 \quad -CH_3 \quad -CH_2COOH$

(c) $-CH_3 \quad -H \quad -COO^- \quad -NH_3^+$

(d) $-CH_3 \quad -CH_2SH \quad -NH_3^+ \quad -COO^-$

(e) $-CH(CH_3)_2 \quad -CH{=}CH_2 \quad -C(CH_3)_3 \quad -C{\equiv}CH$

6.25 Which molecules have R configurations? **(See Example 6.2)**

(a) 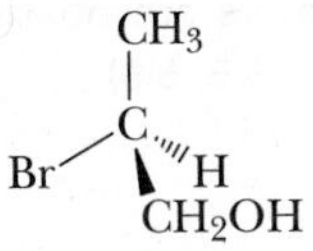 (b) 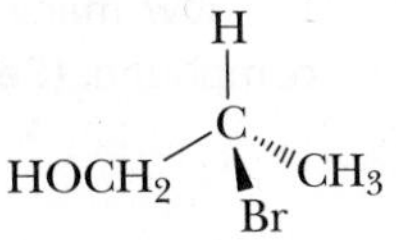

(c) 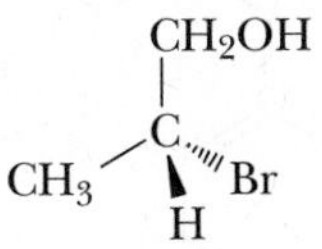 (d) 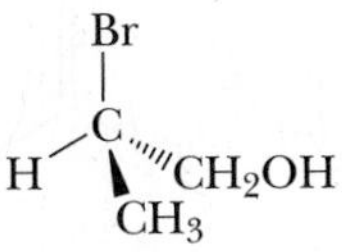

***6.26** Following are structural formulas for the enantiomers of carvone: **(See Example 6.2)**

(−)-Carvone (Spearmint oil)

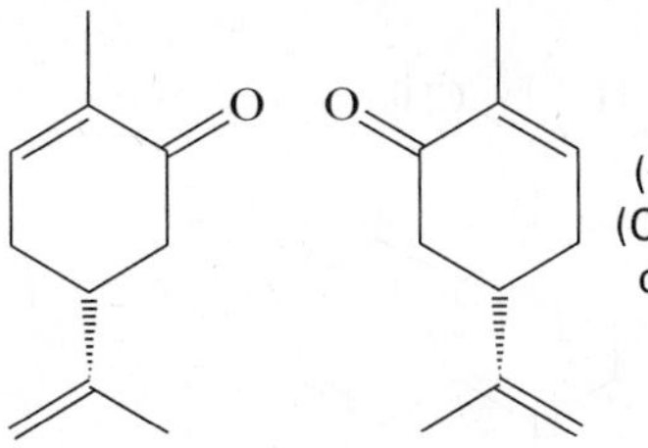

(+)-Carvone (Caraway and dillseed oil)

Each enantiomer has a distinctive odor characteristic of the source from which it can be isolated. Assign an R or S configuration to the stereocenter in each. How can they have such different properties when they are so similar in structure?

6.27 Following is a staggered conformation of one of the stereoisomers of 2-butanol: **(See Example 6.2)**

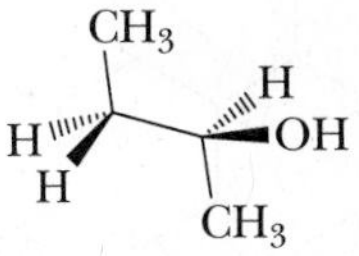

(a) Is this (*R*)-2-butanol or (*S*)-2-butanol?

(b) Draw a Newman projection for this staggered conformation, viewed along the bond between carbons 2 and 3.

(c) Draw a Newman projection for one more staggered conformations of this molecule. Which of your conformations is the more stable? Assume that $-OH$ and $-CH_3$ are comparable in size.

Sections 6.5 and 6.6 Molecules with Two or More Stereocenters

6.28 Write the structural formula of an alcohol with molecular formula $C_6H_{14}O$ that contains two stereocenters.

***6.29** For centuries, Chinese herbal medicine has used extracts of *Ephedra sinica* to treat asthma. Investigation of this plant resulted in the isolation of ephedrine, a potent dilator of the air passages of the lungs. The naturally occurring stereoisomer is levorotatory and has the following structure: **(See Example 6.2)**

Ephedrine

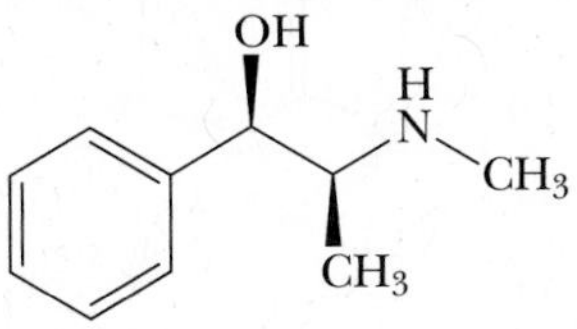

Assign an R or S configuration to each stereocenter.

Ephedra sinica, a source of ephedrine, a potent bronchodilator.

***6.30** The specific rotation of naturally occurring ephedrine, shown in Problem 6.29, is −41°. What is the specific rotation of its enantiomer?

6.31 Label each stereocenter in these molecules with an asterisk and tell how many stereoisomers exist for each. **(See Examples 6.5, 6.6)**

(a) 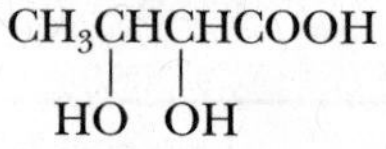

(b) 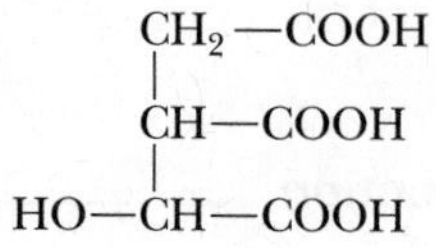

(c) 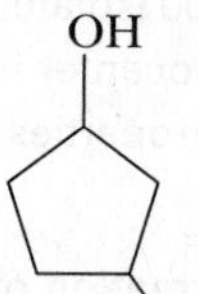

(d) 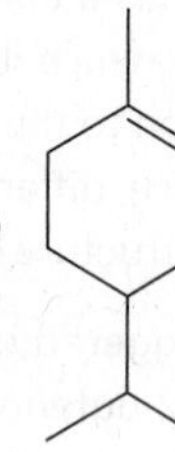

(e) 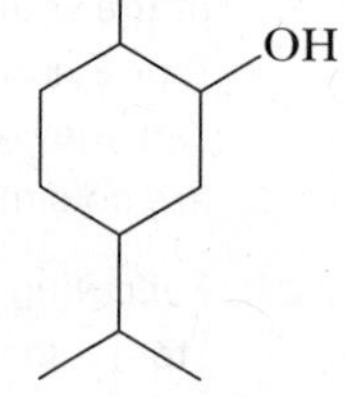

(f) 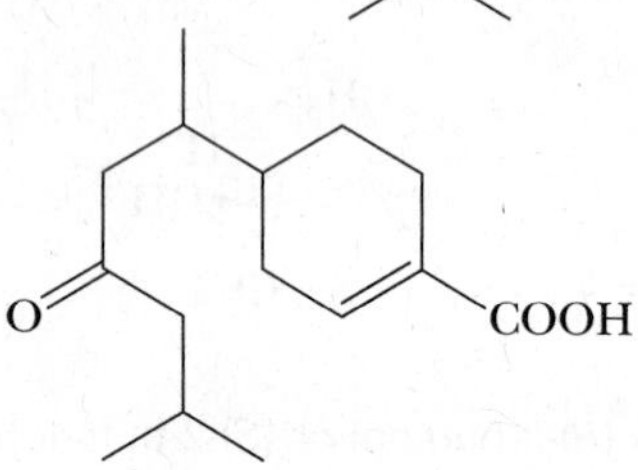

(g) 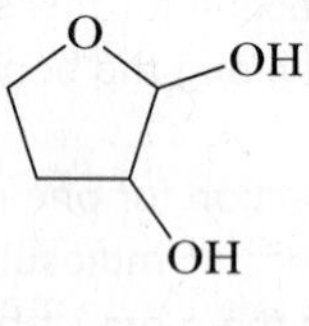

(h) 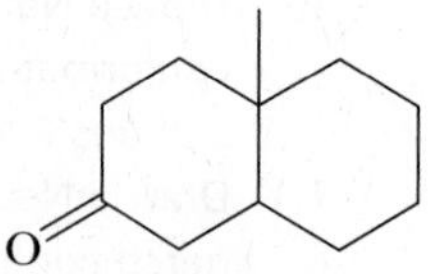

How many stereoisomers are possible for each molecule?

***6.32** Label the four stereocenters in amoxicillin, which belongs to the family of semisynthetic penicillins:

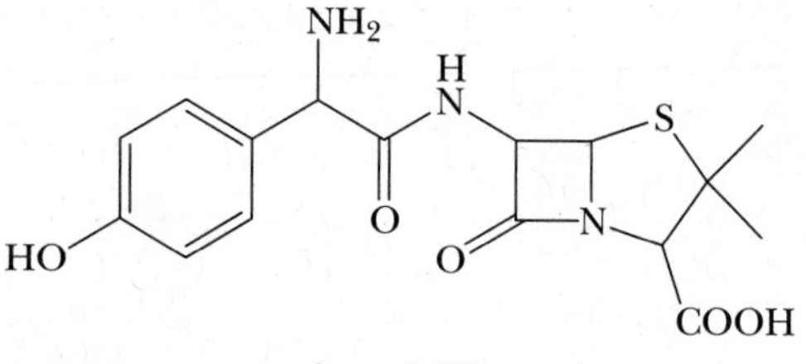

Amoxicillin

***6.33** Label all stereocenters in loratadine (Claritin®) and fexofenadine (Allegra®), now the top-selling antihistamines in the United States. Tell how many stereoisomers are possible for each. **(See Examples 6.5, 6.6)**

(a) 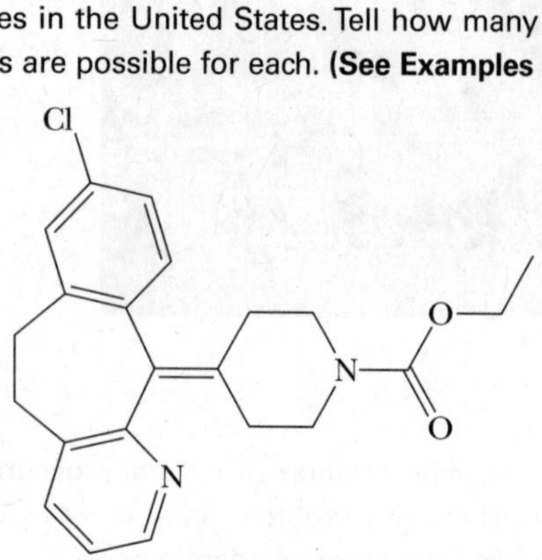

Loratadine
(Claritin)

(b) 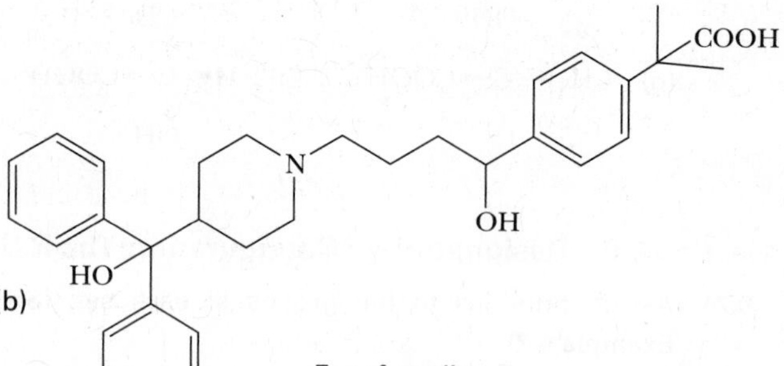

Fexofenadine
(Allegra)

How many stereoisomers are possible for each compound?

***6.34** Following are structural formulas for three of the most widely prescribed drugs used to treat depression. Label all stereocenters in each compound and tell how many stereoisomers are possible for each compound. **(See Examples 6.5, 6.6)**

(a) 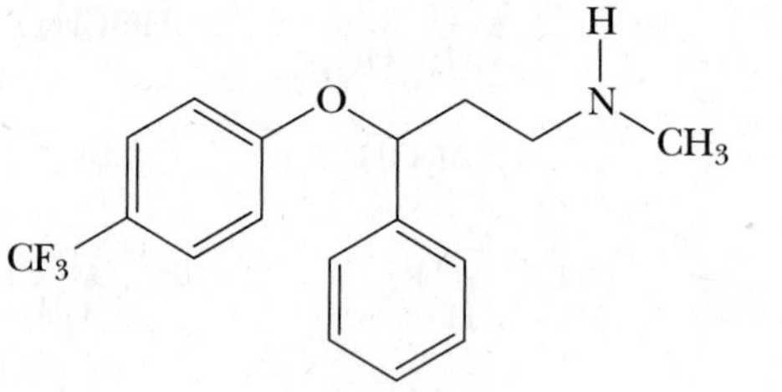

Fluoxetine
(Prozac®)

(b) 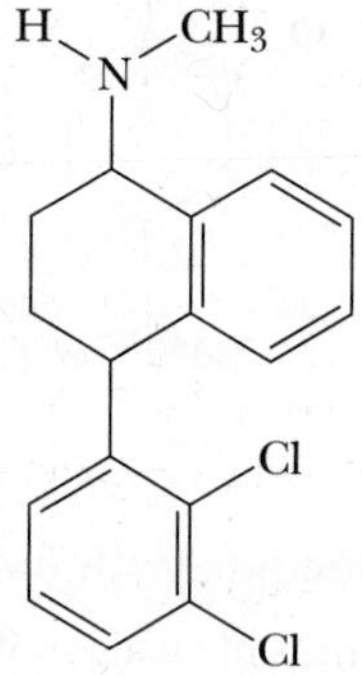

Sertraline
(Zoloft®)

(c) 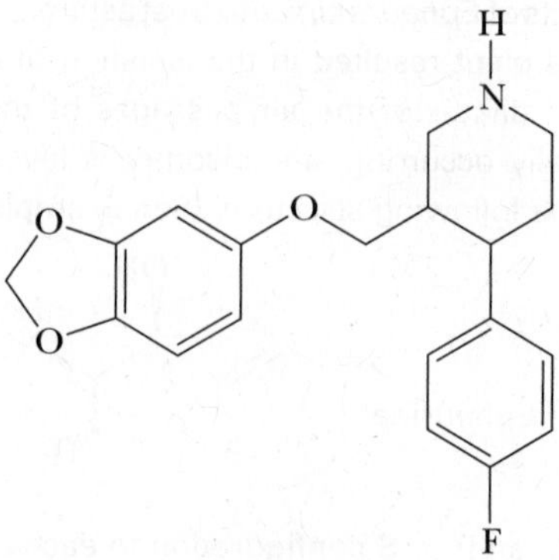

Paroxetine
(Paxil®)

***6.35** Triamcinolone acetonide, the active ingredient in Azmacort® Inhalation Aerosol, is a steroid used to treat bronchial asthma: **(See Examples 6.5, 6.6)**

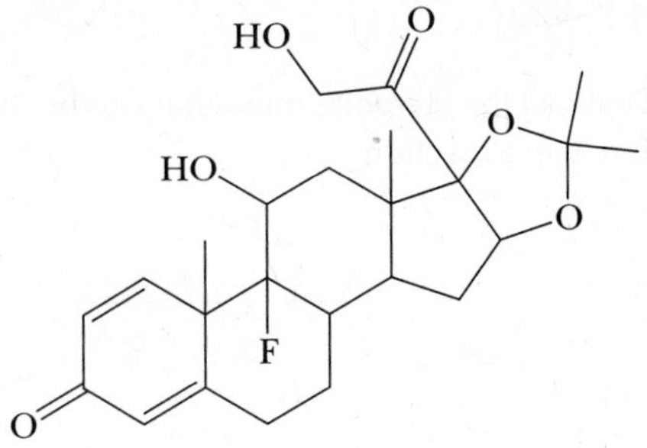

Triamcinolone acetonide

(a) Label the eight stereocenters in this molecule.
(b) How many stereoisomers are possible for the molecule? (Of this number, only one is the active ingredient in Azmacort.)

6.36 Which of these structural formulas represent meso compounds? **(See Example 6.4)**

(a) 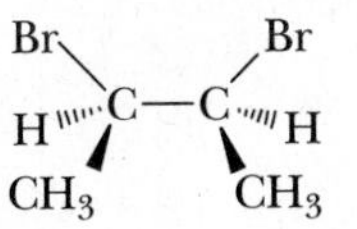

(b) 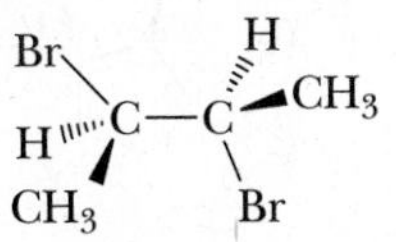

(c) 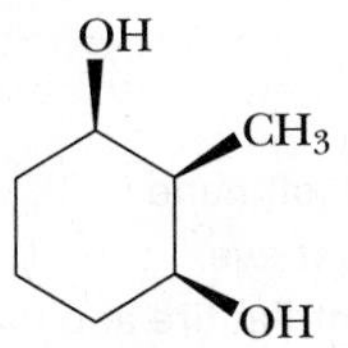

(d) 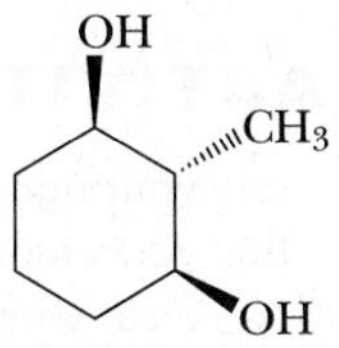

(e) 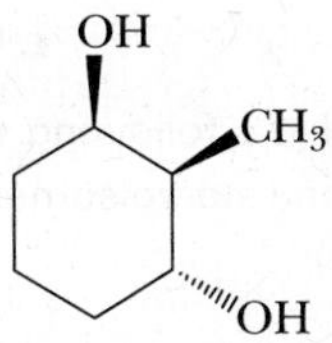

(f) 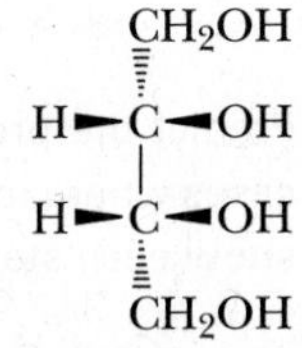

6.37 Draw a Newman projection, viewed along the bond between carbons 2 and 3, for both the most stable and the least stable conformations of meso-tartaric acid:

$$HOOC{-}\overset{\displaystyle OH}{\overset{|}{C}H}{-}\overset{\displaystyle OH}{\overset{|}{C}H}{-}COOH$$

6.38 How many stereoisomers are possible for 1,3-dimethylcyclopentane? Which are pairs of enantiomers? Which are meso compounds? **(See Examples 6.4–6.6)**

6.39 In Problem 3.59, you were asked to draw the more stable chair conformation of glucose, a molecule in which all groups on the six-membered ring are equatorial: **(See Examples 6.2, 6.5, 6.6)**

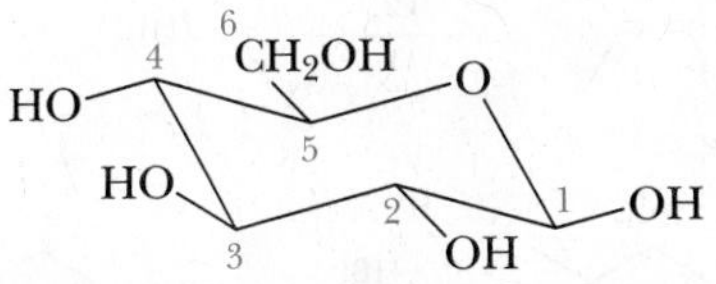

(a) Identify all stereocenters in this molecule.
(b) How many stereoisomers are possible?
(c) How many pairs of enantiomers are possible?
(d) What is the configuration (*R* or *S*) at carbons 1 and 5 in the stereoisomer shown?

6.40 What is a racemic mixture? Is a racemic mixture optically active? That is, will it rotate the plane of polarized light?

CHEMICAL TRANSFORMATIONS

6.41 Test your cumulative knowledge of the reactions learned so far by completing the following chemical transformations. Pay particular attention to the stereochemistry in the product. Where more than one stereoisomer is possible, show each stereoisomer. *Note that some transformations will require more than one step.*

(a) 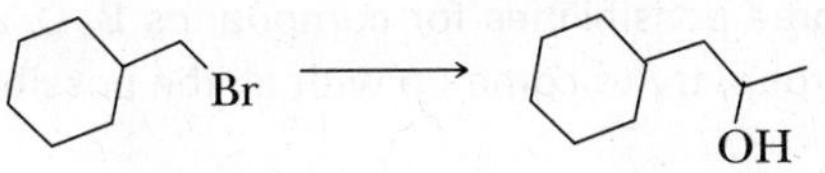

(b) 

(c) 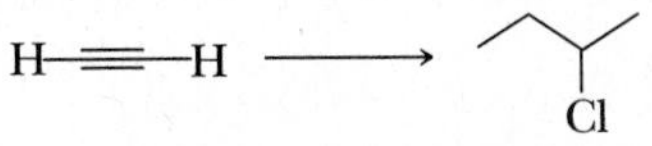

(d) 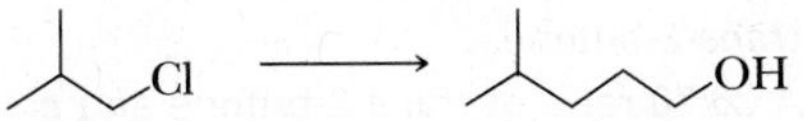

(e) 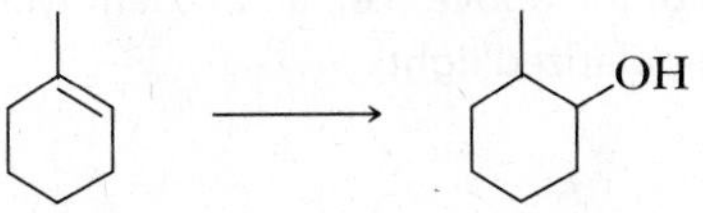

(f) 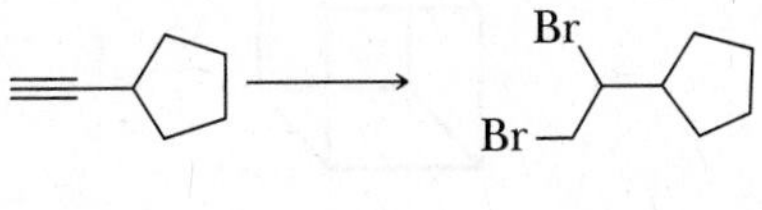

(g) 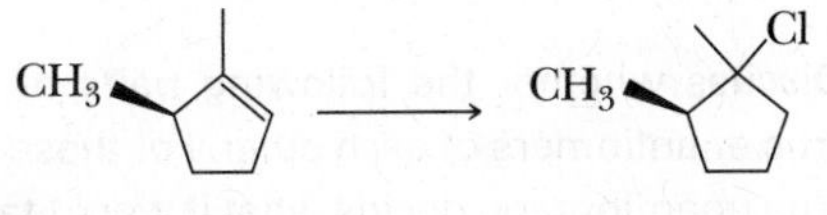

(h) 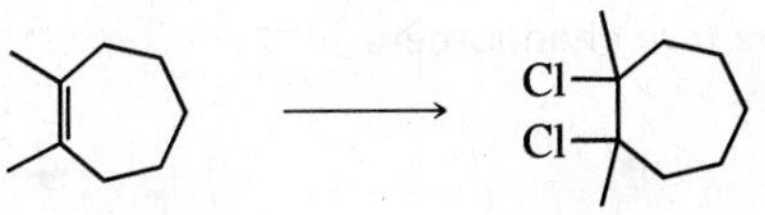

(i) 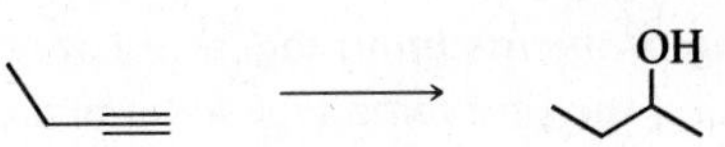

(j) 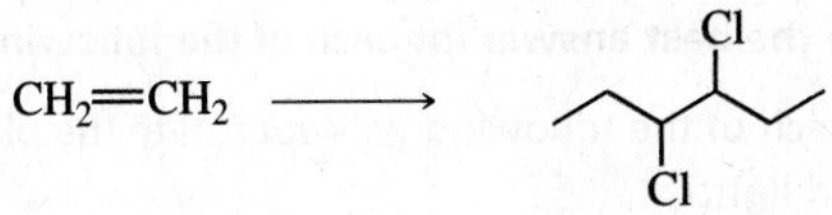

LOOKING AHEAD

6.42 Predict the product(s) of the following reactions (in cases where more than one stereoisomer is possible, show each stereoisomer):

(a) 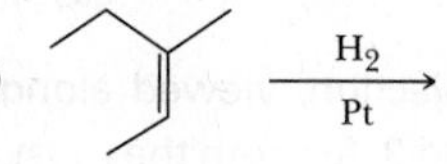

(b) 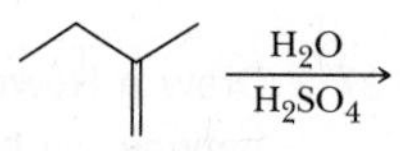

(e) 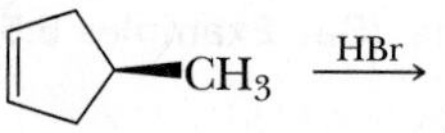

(f) 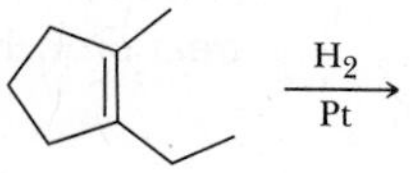

6.43 What alkene, when treated with H_2/Pd, will ensure a 100% yield of the stereoisomer shown?

(a) 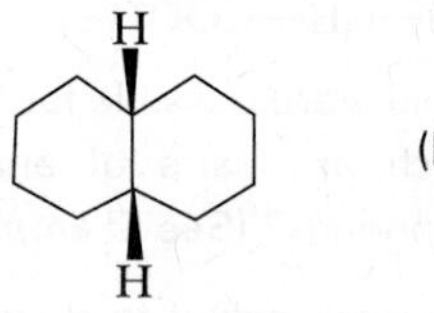

(b) 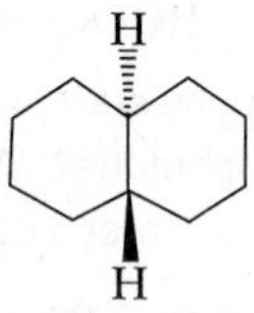

6.44 Which of the following reactions will yield a racemic mixture of products?

(a) 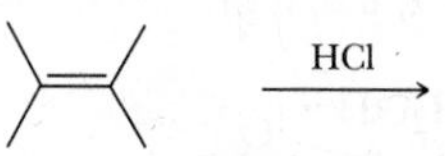

(b) 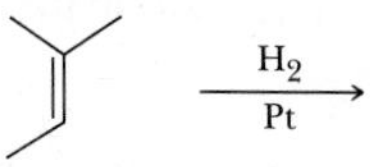

(c) 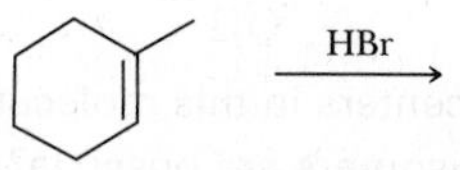

(d) 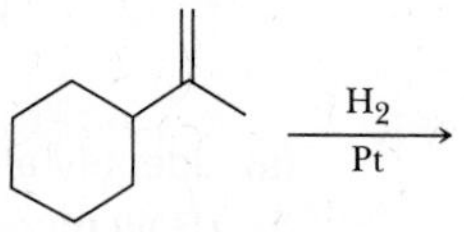

6.45 Draw all the stereoisomers that can be formed in the following reaction:

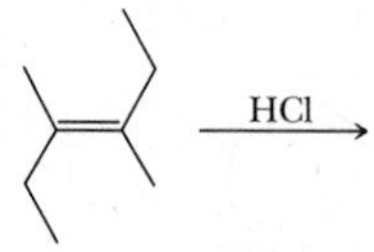

Comment on the utility of this particular reaction as a synthetic method.

6.46 Explain why the product of the following reaction does not rotate the plane of polarized light:

(a) 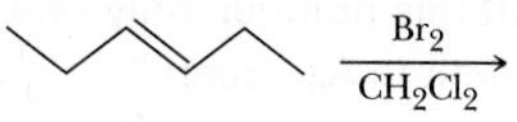

(b) 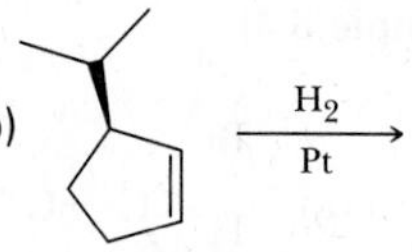

GROUP LEARNING ACTIVITIES

***6.47** Identify objects in your surroundings and take turns deciding if each object is chiral or achiral.

6.48 Take turns identifying the planes of symmetry in cubane (note: the hydrogen atoms are not shown).

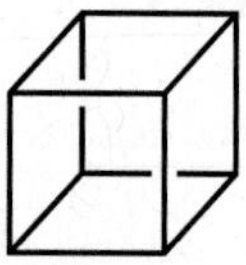

Cubane

6.49 Discuss whether the following pairs of objects are true enantiomers of each other. For those that are not true enantiomers, decide what it would take for them to be true enantiomers.

(a) your right hand and left hand
(b) your right eye and left eye
(c) a car with a left, front flat tire and the same car with a right, front flat tire

6.50 Compound **A** (C_5H_8) is not optically active and cannot be resolved. It reacts with Br_2 in CCl_4 to give compound **B** ($C_5H_8Br_2$). When compound **A** is treated with H_2/Pt, it is converted to compound **C** (C_5H_{10}). When treated with HBr, compound **A** is converted to compound **D** (C_5H_9Br). Given this information, propose structural formulas for **A**, **B**, **C**, and **D**. There are at least three possibilities for compound **A** and, in turn, three possibilities for compounds **B**, **C**, and **D**. As a group, try to come up with all the possibilities.

PUTTING IT TOGETHER

The following problems bring together concepts and material from Chapters 4–6. Although the focus may be on these chapters, the problems will also build on concepts discussed thus far.

Choose the best answer for each of the following questions.

1. Which of the following will *not* rotate the plane of polarized light?

(a) A 50:50 ratio of (*R*)-2-butanol and *cis*-2-butene.
(b) A 70:20 ratio of (*R*)-2-butanol and *S*-2-butanol.
(c) A 50:25:25 ratio of (*S*)-2-butanol, *cis*-2-butene, and *trans*-2-butene.
(d) A 20:70 ratio of *trans*-2-butene and *cis*-2-butene.
(e) None of the above (i.e., all of them will rotate plane-polarized light)

2. Which of the following *cis* isomers of dimethylcyclohexane is *not* meso?
   (a) *cis*-1,4-dimethylcyclohexane
   (b) *cis*-1,3-dimethylcyclohexane
   (c) *cis*-1,2-dimethylcyclohexane
   (d) All of the above (i.e., none of them is meso)
   (e) None of the above (i.e., all of them are meso)

3. How many products are possible in the following Lewis acid–base reaction?

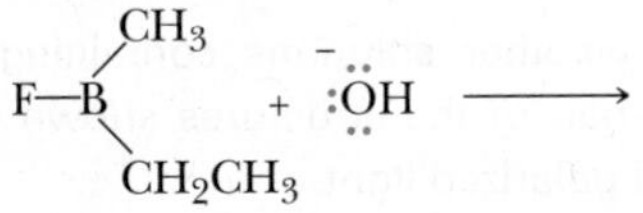

   (a) One (b) Two (c) Three (d) Four
   (e) None (no reaction will take place)

4. What is the relationship between the following two molecules?

A 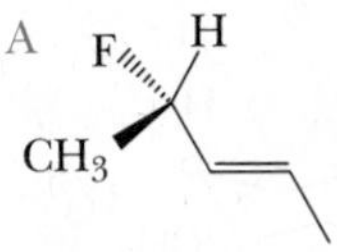 B 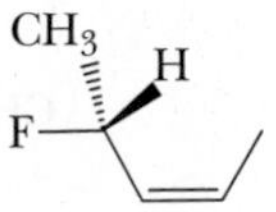

   (a) They are identical.
   (b) They are enantiomers.
   (c) They are diastereomers.
   (d) They are constitutional isomers.
   (e) They are nonisomers.

5. Which stereoisomer of 2,4-hexadiene is the *least* stable?
   (a) *Z,Z*-2,4-hexadiene
   (b) *Z,E*-2,4-hexadiene
   (c) *E,Z*-2,4-hexadiene
   (d) *E,E*-2,4-hexadiene
   (e) All are equal in stability.

6. Select the shortest C—C single bond in the following molecule.

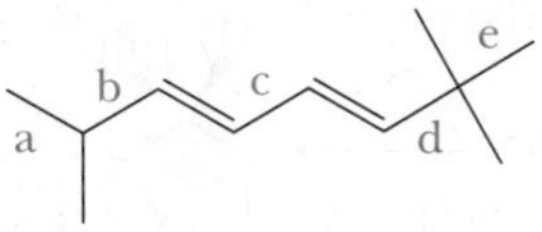

   (a) a (b) b (c) c (d) d (e) e

7. Which of the following statements is true of β-bisabolol?

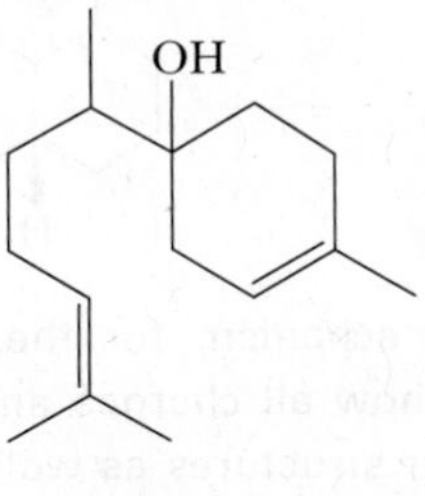

β-Bisabolol

   (a) There are 6 stereoisomers of β-bisabolol.
   (b) β-Bisabolol is soluble in water.
   (c) β-Bisabolol is achiral.
   (d) β-Bisabolol has a meso stereoisomer.
   (e) None of the above.

8. How many products are formed in the following reaction?

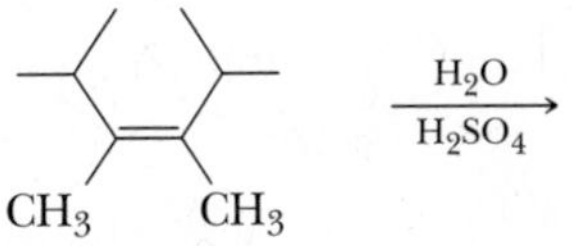

   (a) 1 (b) 2 (c) 3 (d) 4 (e) 5

9. Which of the following is *true* when two isomeric alkenes are treated with H_2/Pt?
   (a) The alkene that releases more energy in the reaction is the more stable alkene.
   (b) The alkene with the lower melting point will release less energy in the reaction.
   (c) The alkene with the lower boiling point will release less energy in the reaction.
   (d) Both alkenes will release equal amounts of energy in the reaction.
   (e) None of these statements is true.

10. An unknown compound reacts with two equivalents of H_2 catalyzed by Ni. The unknown also yields 5 CO_2 and 4 H_2O upon combustion. Which of the following could be the unknown compound?

   (a) 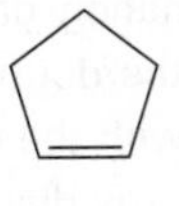 (b) 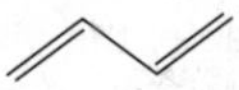

   (c) 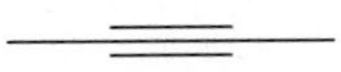 (d) 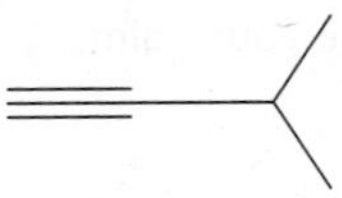

   (e) 

11. Provide structures for all possible compounds of formula C_5H_6 that would react quantitatively with $NaNH_2$.

12. Answer the questions that follow regarding the following compound, which has been found in herbal preparations of *Echinacea*, the genus name for a variety of plants marketed for their immunostimulant properties.

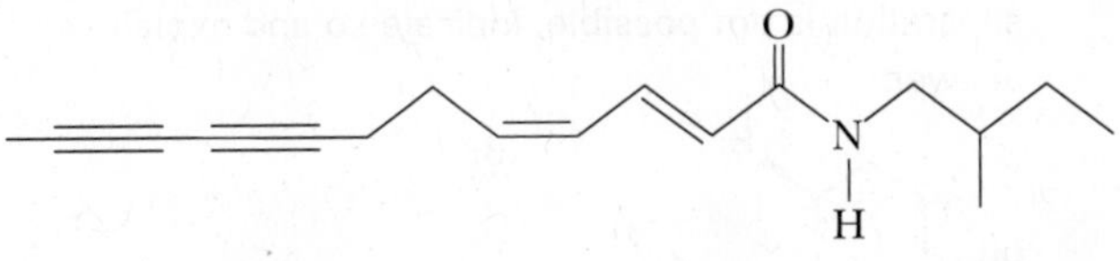

   (a) How many stereoisomers exist for the compound shown?

(b) Would you expect the compound to be soluble in water?

(c) Is the molecule chiral?

(d) What would be the product formed in the reaction of this compound with an excess amount of H_2/Pt?

13. Provide IUPAC names for the following compounds.

(a) 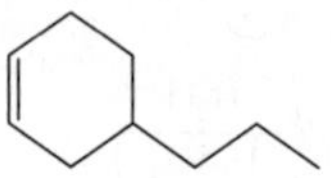

(b) 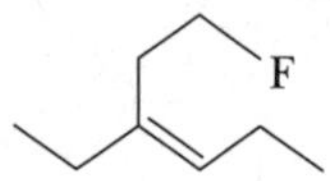

(c) 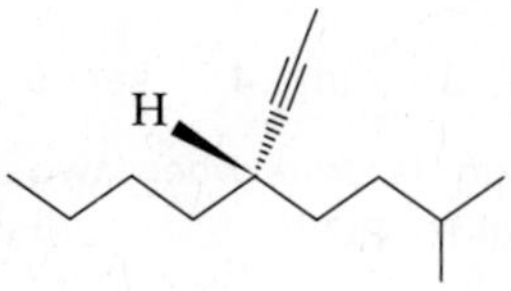

14. Compound **A** is an optically inactive compound with a molecular formula of C_5H_8. Catalytic hydrogenation of **A** gives an optically inactive compound, **B** (C_5H_{10}), as the sole product. Furthermore, reaction of **A** with HBr results in a single compound, **C**, with a molecular formula of C_5H_9Br. Provide structures for **A**, **B**, and **C**.

15. An optically active compound, **A**, has a molecular formula of C_6H_{12}. Hydroboration–oxidation of **A** yields an optically active product, **B**, with a molecular formula of $C_6H_{14}O$. Catalytic hydrogenation of **A** yields an optically inactive product, **C**, with a molecular formula of C_6H_{14}. Propose structures for **A**, **B**, and **C**.

16. Based on the following hydrogenation data, which is more stable, the alkene **(A)** with the double bond outside of the ring or the alkene **(B)** with the double bond inside the ring? Use a reaction energy diagram to illustrate your point.

$\Delta H = -23.84$ kcal/mol

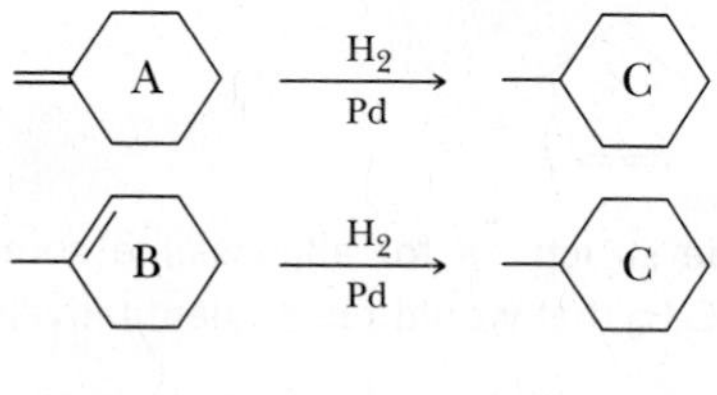

$\Delta H = -20.69$ kcal/mol

17. Explain whether the following pairs of compounds could be separated by resolution of enantiomers. If such separation is not possible, indicate so and explain your answer.

(a) 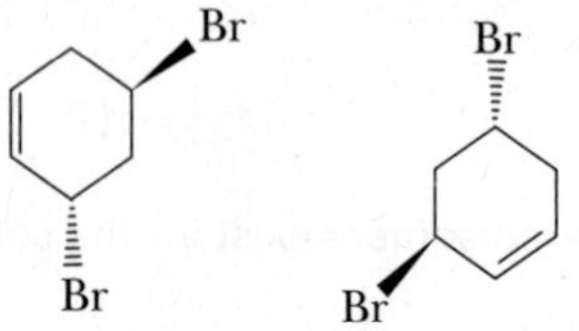

(b) 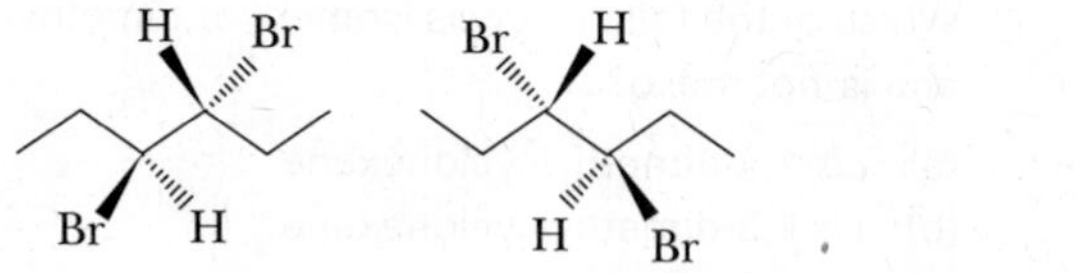

(c) 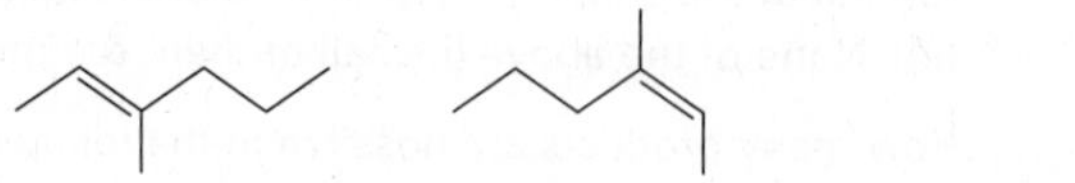

18. Predict whether solutions containing equal amounts of each pair of the structures shown would rotate the plane of polarized light.

(a) 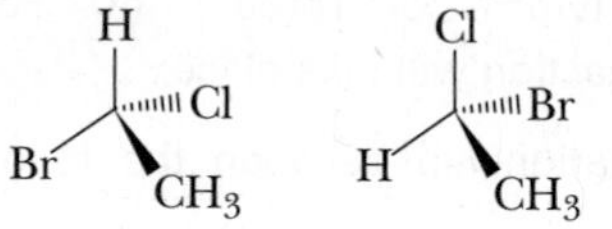

(b) 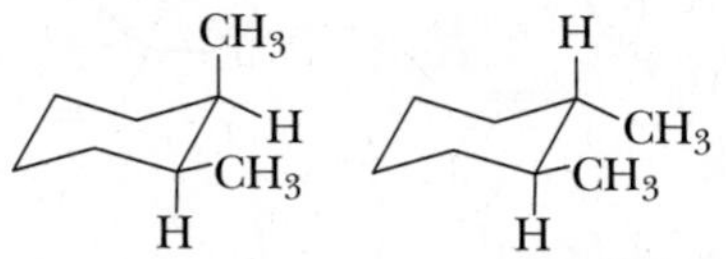

(c) 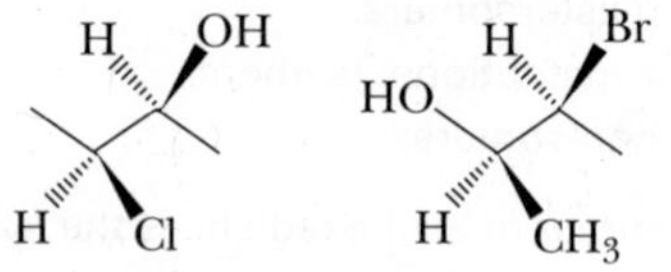

19. Complete the following chemical transformations.

(a) 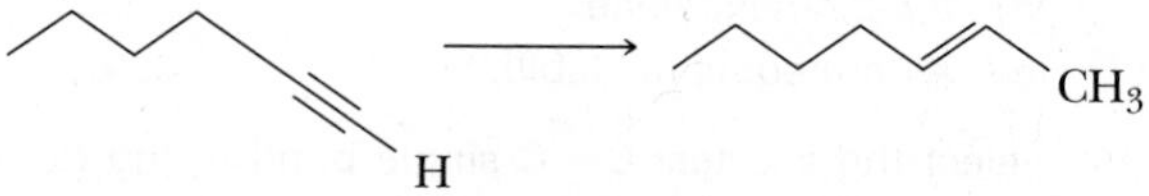

(b) 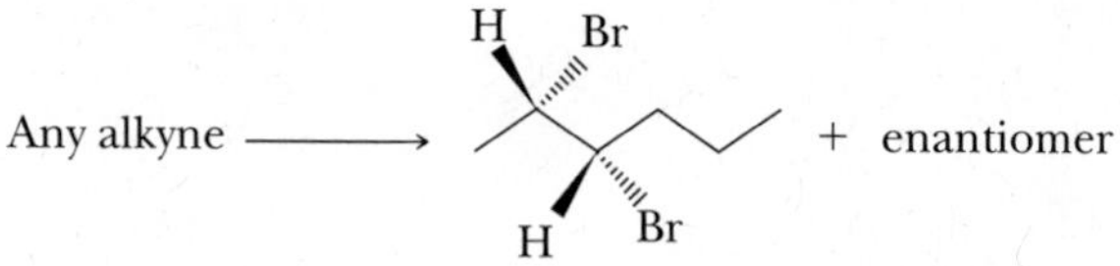
Any alkyne
H
Br
H
Br
+ enantiomer

(c) 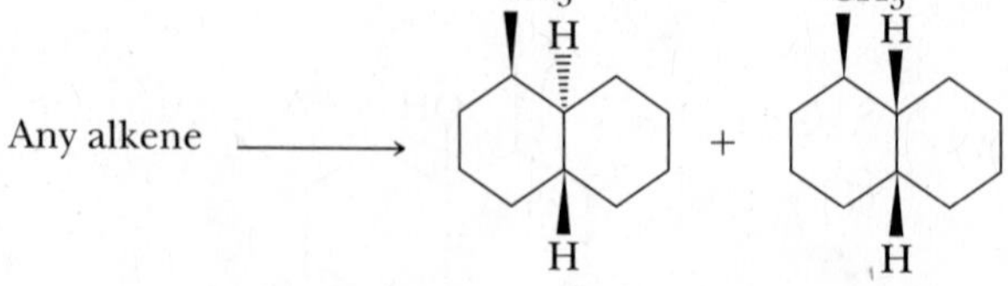

20. Provide a mechanism for the following series of reactions. Show all charges and lone pairs of electrons in your structures as well as the structures of all intermediates.

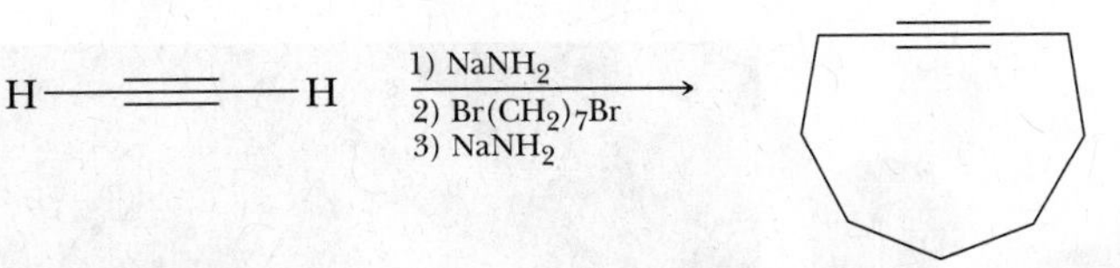

21. Predict the major product or products of each of the following reactions. Be sure to consider stereochemistry in your answers.

(a) 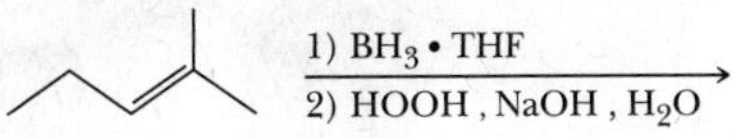

(b) 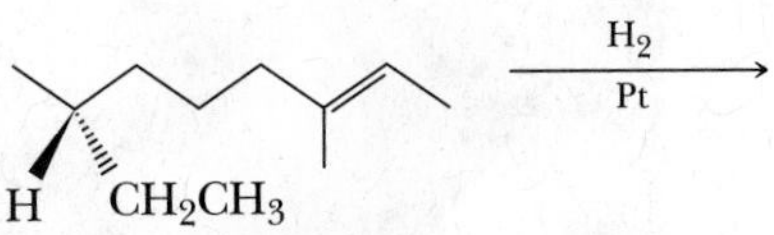

(c) 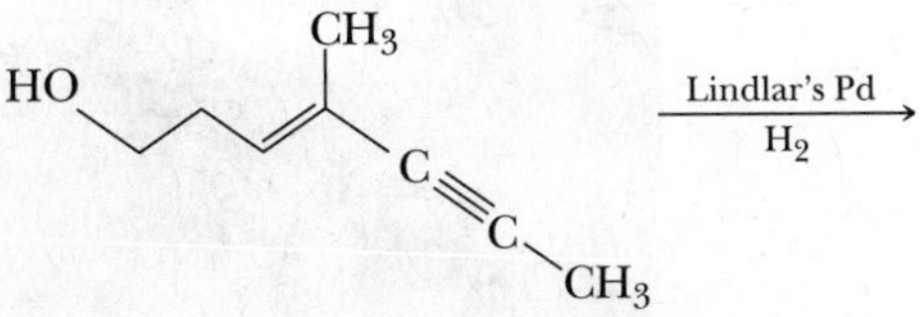

(d) 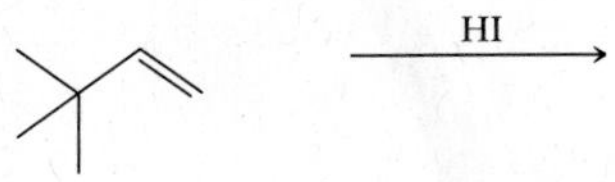

(e) 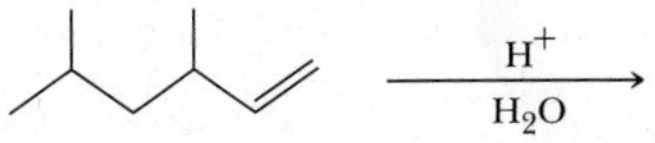

(f) 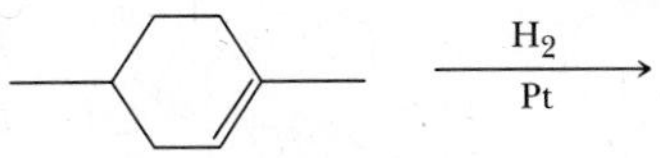

22. Provide a mechanism for the following reaction. Show all charges and lone pairs of electrons in your structures as well as the structures of all intermediates.

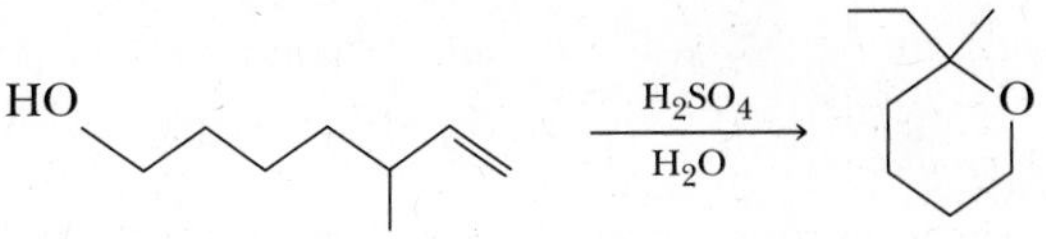

07

Haloalkanes

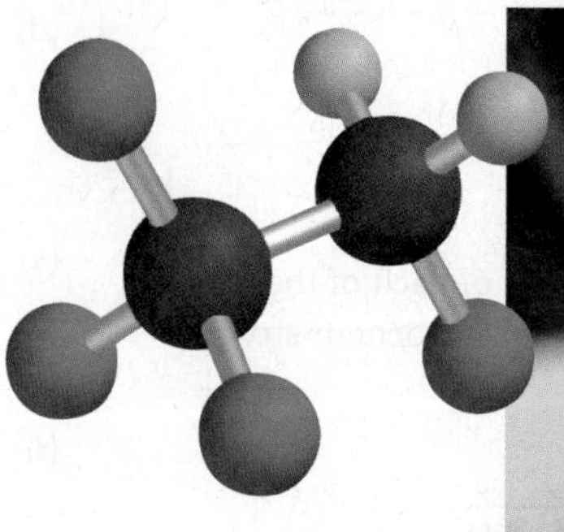

Asthma patient using a metered-dose inhaler to deliver the drug albuterol. The drug is propelled by haloalkanes such as 1,1,1,2-tetrafluoroethane. Inset: A molecule of 1,1,1,2-tetrafluoroethane (HFA-134a). (Carolyn A. McKeone/Photo Researchers, Inc.)

KEY QUESTIONS

- 7.1 How Are Haloalkanes Named?
- 7.2 What Are the Characteristic Reactions of Haloalkanes?
- 7.3 What Are the Products of Nucleophilic Aliphatic Substitution Reactions?
- 7.4 What Are the S_N2 and S_N1 Mechanisms for Nucleophilic Substitution?
- 7.5 What Determines Whether S_N1 or S_N2 Predominates?
- 7.6 How Can S_N1 and S_N2 Be Predicted Based on Experimental Conditions?
- 7.7 What Are the Products of β-Elimination?
- 7.8 What Are the E1 and E2 Mechanisms for β-Elimination?
- 7.9 When Do Nucleophilic Substitution and β-Elimination Compete?

HOW TO

- 7.1 How to Name Cyclic Haloalkanes
- 7.2 How to Recognize Substitution and β-Elimination Reactions
- 7.3 How to Complete a Substitution Reaction
- 7.4 How to Predict the Type of Substitution Reaction a Haloalkane Will Undergo
- 7.5 How to Complete an Elimination Reaction
- 7.6 How to Draw Mechanisms
- 7.7 How to Predict the Type of β-Elimination Reaction a Haloalkane Will Undergo

CHEMICAL CONNECTIONS

- 7A The Environmental Impact of Chlorofluorocarbons
- 7B The Effect of Chlorofluorocarbon Legislation on Asthma Sufferers

COMPOUNDS CONTAINING a halogen atom covalently bonded to an sp^3 hybridized carbon atom are named **haloalkanes** or, in the common system of nomenclature, *alkyl halides*. The general symbol for an **alkyl halide** is R—X, where X may be F, Cl, Br, or I:

Alkyl halide A compound containing a halogen atom covalently bonded to an sp^3 hybridized carbon atom; given the symbol RX.

R—$\ddot{\text{X}}$:

A haloalkane (An alkyl halide)

In this chapter, we study two characteristic reactions of haloalkanes: nucleophilic substitution and β-elimination. Haloalkanes are useful molecules because they can be converted to alcohols, ethers, thiols, amines, and alkenes and are thus versatile molecules. Indeed, haloalkanes are often used as starting materials for the synthesis of many useful compounds encountered in medicine, food chemistry, and agriculture (to name a few).

7.1 How Are Haloalkanes Named?

A. IUPAC Names

IUPAC names for haloalkanes are derived by naming the parent alkane according to the rules given in Section 3.3A:

- Locate and number the parent chain from the direction that gives the substituent encountered first the lower number.
- Show halogen substituents by the prefixes *fluoro-*, *chloro-*, *bromo-*, and *iodo-*, and list them in alphabetical order along with other substituents.
- Use a number preceding the name of the halogen to locate each halogen on the parent chain.
- In haloalkenes, the location of the double bond determines the numbering of the parent hydrocarbon. In molecules containing functional groups designated by a suffix (for example, *-ol*, *-al*, *-one*, *-oic acid*), the location of the functional group indicated by the suffix determines the numbering:

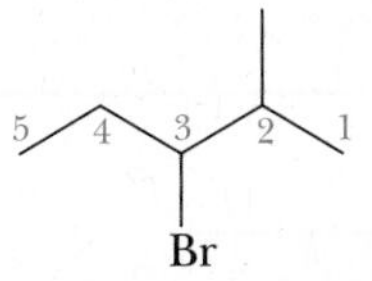

3-Bromo-2-methylpentane

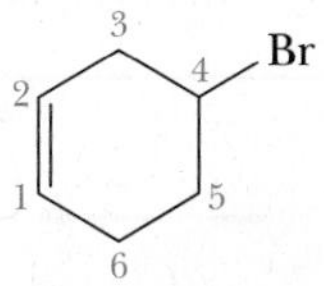

4-Bromocyclohexene

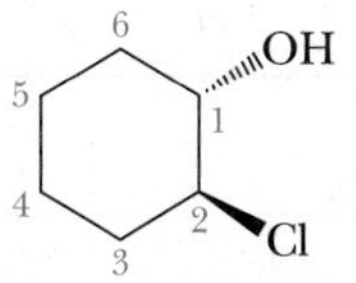

(1*S*,2*S*)-2-Chlorocyclohexanol
or
trans-2-Chlorocyclohexanol

B. Common Names

Common names of haloalkanes consist of the common name of the alkyl group, followed by the name of the halide as a separate word. Hence, the name **alkyl halide** is a common name for this class of compounds. In the following examples, the IUPAC name of the compound is given first, followed by its common name, in parentheses:

$CH_3CH(F)CH_2CH_3$	$CH_2{=}CHCl$
2-Fluorobutane	Chloroethene
(*sec*-Butyl fluoride)	(Vinyl chloride)

Several of the polyhalomethanes are common solvents and are generally referred to by their common, or trivial, names. Dichloromethane (methylene chloride) is the most widely used haloalkane solvent. Compounds of the type CHX_3 are called **haloforms**. The common name for $CHCl_3$, for example, is *chloroform*. The common name for CH_3CCl_3 is *methyl chloroform*. Methyl chloroform and trichloroethylene are solvents for commercial dry cleaning.

CH_2Cl_2	$CHCl_3$	CH_3CCl_3	$CCl_2{=}CHCl$
Dichloromethane (Methylene chloride)	Trichloromethane (Chloroform)	1,1,1-Trichloroethane (Methyl chloroform)	Trichloroethylene (Trichlor)

HOW TO 7.1 Name Cyclic Haloalkanes

(a) First, determine the root name of the cycloalkane.

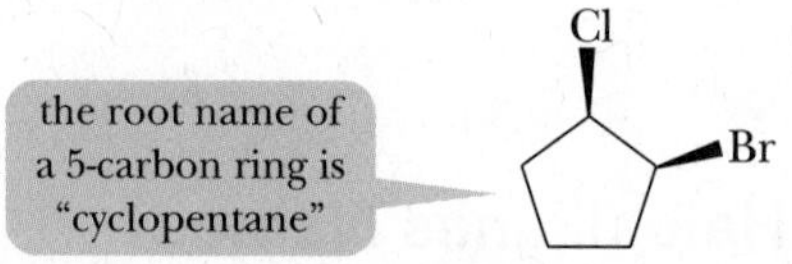

Cyclopentane

(b) Name and number the halogen substituents.

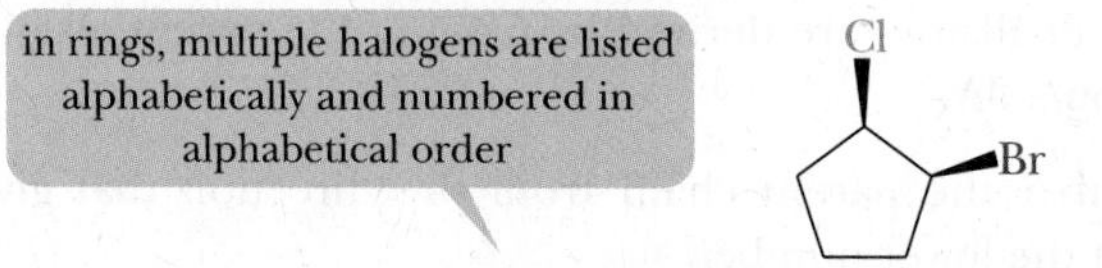

1 -Bromo-2-chlorocyclopentane

(c) Don't forget to indicate stereochemistry.

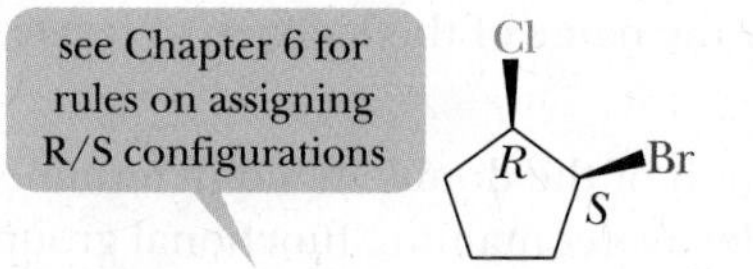

(1*S*,2*R*)-1-Bromo-2-chlorocyclopentane
or
cis -1-Bromo-2-chlorocyclopentane

EXAMPLE 7.1

Write the IUPAC name for each compound:

(a) 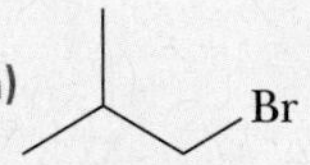

(b) 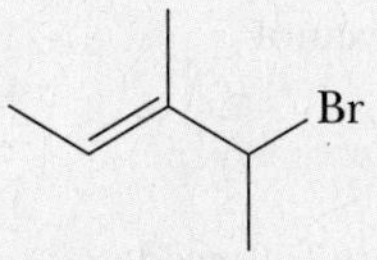

(c) 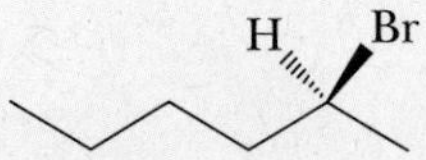

(d) 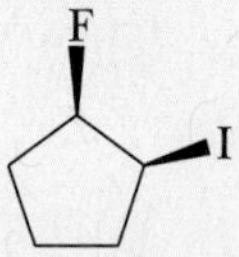

STRATEGY

First look for the longest chain of carbons. This will allow you to determine the root name. Then identify the atoms or groups of atoms that are not part of that chain of carbons. These are your substituents. Remember to include stereochemical configurations, *E*/*Z* or *R*/*S*, where applicable.

SOLUTION

(a) 1-Bromo-2-methylpropane. Its common name is isobutyl bromide.
(b) (*E*)-4-Bromo-3-methyl-2-pentene.
(c) (*S*)-2-Bromohexane.
(d) (1*R*,2*S*)-1-Fluoro-2-iodocyclopentane or *cis*-1-fluoro-2-iodocyclopentane.

See problems 7.9–7.12

PROBLEM 7.1

Write the IUPAC name for each compound:

(a) 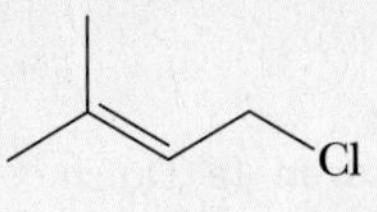

(b) 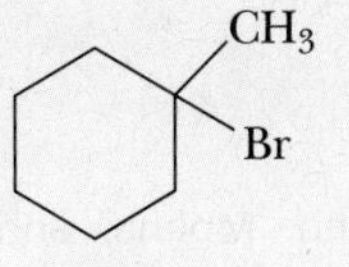

(c) $CH_3\overset{Cl}{\overset{|}{C}}HCH_2Cl$

(d) 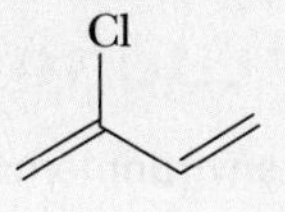

Of all the haloalkanes, the **chlorofluorocarbons (CFCs)** manufactured under the trade name Freon® are the most widely known. CFCs are nontoxic, nonflammable, odorless, and noncorrosive. Originally, they seemed to be ideal replacements for the hazardous compounds such as ammonia and sulfur dioxide formerly used as heat-transfer agents in refrigeration systems. Among the CFCs most widely used for this purpose were trichlorofluoromethane (CCl_3F, Freon-11) and dichlorodifluoromethane (CCl_2F_2, Freon-12). The CFCs also found wide use as industrial cleaning solvents to prepare surfaces for coatings, to remove cutting oils and waxes from millings, and to remove protective coatings. In addition, they were employed as propellants in aerosol sprays. They are now, however, banned from use in most developed countries (see Chemical Connections 7A).

7.2 What Are the Characteristic Reactions of Haloalkanes?

A **nucleophile** (nucleus-loving reagent) is any reagent that donates an unshared pair of electrons to form a new covalent bond. **Nucleophilic substitution** is any reaction in which one nucleophile is substituted for another. In the following general equations, $Nu:^-$ is the nucleophile, X is the leaving group, and substitution takes place on an sp^3 hybridized carbon atom:

Nucleophile An atom or a group of atoms that donates a pair of electrons to another atom or group of atoms to form a new covalent bond.

Nucleophilic substitution A reaction in which one nucleophile is substituted for another.

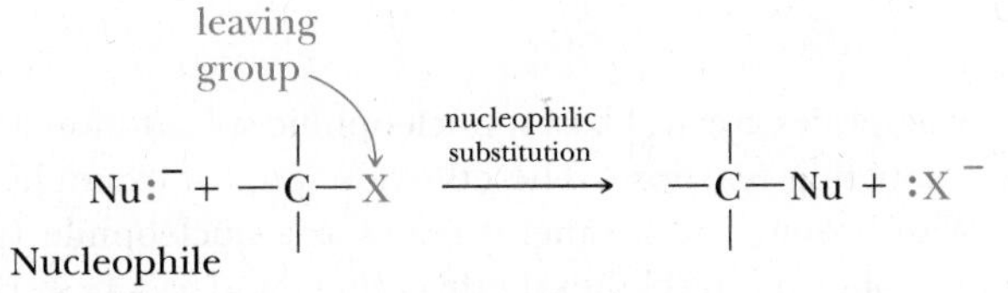
leaving group
nucleophilic substitution
Nu:⁻ + —C—X → —C—Nu + :X⁻
Nucleophile

Halide ions are among the best and most important leaving groups. Recall from Section 5.7 that nucleophilic substitution occurs in the alkylation of an acetylide ion:

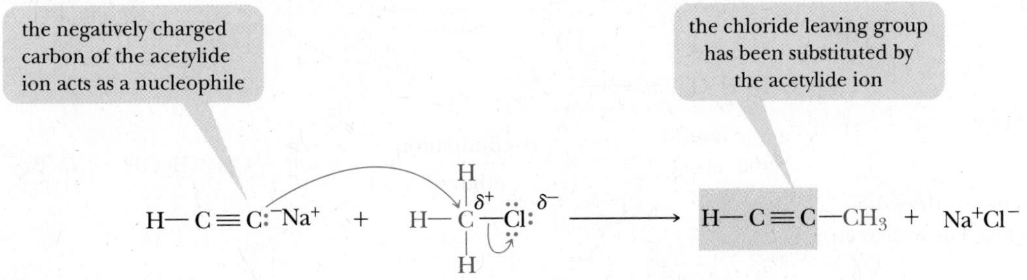
the negatively charged carbon of the acetylide ion acts as a nucleophile
the chloride leaving group has been substituted by the acetylide ion
H—C≡C:⁻Na⁺ + H—C—Cl: → H—C≡C—CH₃ + Na⁺Cl⁻

Chemical Connections 7A

THE ENVIRONMENTAL IMPACT OF CHLOROFLUOROCARBONS

Concern about the environmental impact of CFCs arose in the 1970s when researchers found that more than 4.5×10^5 kg/yr of these compounds were being emitted into the atmosphere. In 1974, Sherwood Rowland and Mario Molina announced their theory, which has since been amply confirmed, that CFCs catalyze the destruction of the stratospheric ozone layer. When released into the air, CFCs escape to the lower atmosphere. Because of their inertness, however, they do not decompose there. Slowly, they find their way to the stratosphere, where they absorb ultraviolet radiation from the sun and then decompose. As they do so, they set up a chemical reaction that leads to the destruction of the stratospheric ozone layer, which shields the Earth against short-wavelength ultraviolet radiation from the sun. An increase in short-wavelength ultraviolet radiation reaching the Earth is believed to promote the destruction of certain crops and agricultural species and even to increase the incidence of skin cancer in light-skinned individuals.

The concern about CFCs prompted two conventions, one in Vienna in 1985 and one in Montreal in 1987, held by the United Nations Environmental Program. The 1987 meeting produced the Montreal Protocol, which set limits on the production and use of ozone-depleting CFCs and urged the complete phase-out of their production by the year 1996. Only two members of the UN have failed to ratify the protocol in its original form.

Rowland, Molina, and Paul Crutzen (a Dutch chemist at the Max Planck Institute for Chemistry in Germany) were awarded the 1995 Nobel Prize for chemistry. As the Royal Swedish Academy of Sciences noted in awarding the prize, "By explaining the chemical mechanisms that affect the thickness of the ozone layer, these three researchers have contributed to our salvation from a global environmental problem that could have catastrophic consequences."

The chemical industry responded to the crisis by developing replacement refrigerants that have a much lower ozone-depleting potential. The most prominent replacements are the hydrofluorocarbons (HFCs) and hydrochlorofluorocarbons (HCFCs), such as the following:

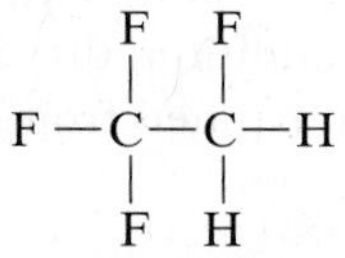

HFC-134a

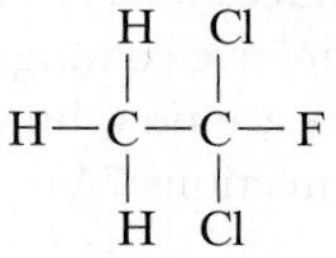

HCFC-141b

These compounds are much more chemically reactive in the atmosphere than the Freons are and are destroyed before they reach the stratosphere. However, they cannot be used in air conditioners in 1994 and earlier model cars.

Question

Provide IUPAC names for HFC-134a and HCFC-141b.

***β*-Elimination reaction** The removal of atoms or groups of atoms from two adjacent carbon atoms, as for example, the removal of H and X from an alkyl halide or H and OH from an alcohol to form a carbon–carbon double bond.

Because all nucleophiles are also bases, nucleophilic substitution and base-promoted ***β*-elimination** are competing reactions. The ethoxide ion, for example, is both a nucleophile and a base. With bromocyclohexane, it reacts as a nucleophile (pathway shown in red) to give ethoxycyclohexane (cyclohexyl ethyl ether) and as a base (pathway shown in blue) to give cyclohexene and ethanol:

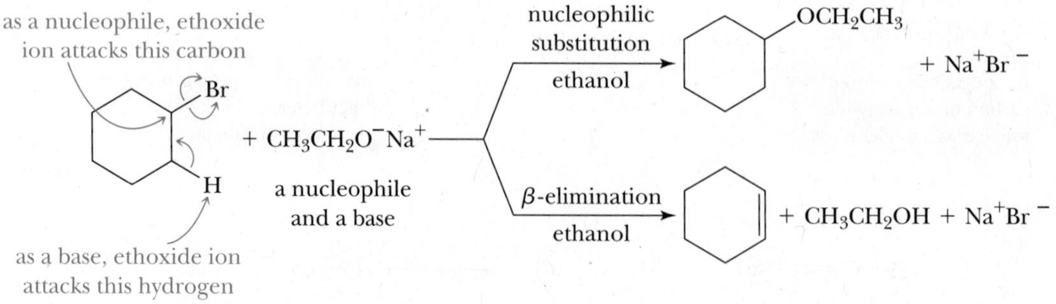

HOW TO 7.2

Recognize Substitution and β-Elimination Reactions

(a) Substitution reactions always result in the replacement of one atom or group of atoms in a reactant with another atom or group of atoms.

(b) β-Elimination reactions always result in the removal of a hydrogen and an atom or group of atoms on adjacent carbon atoms and in the formation of a C—C double bond.

In this chapter, we study both of these organic reactions. Using them, we can convert haloalkanes to compounds with other functional groups including alcohols, ethers, thiols, sulfides, amines, nitriles, alkenes, and alkynes. Thus, an understanding of nucleophilic substitution and β-elimination opens entirely new areas of organic chemistry.

EXAMPLE 7.2

Determine whether the following haloalkanes underwent substitution, elimination, or both substitution and elimination:

(a)
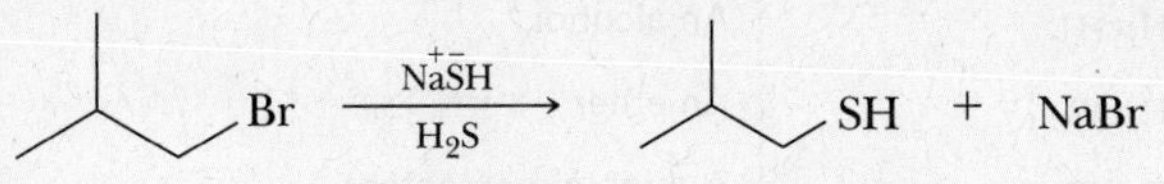

(b)
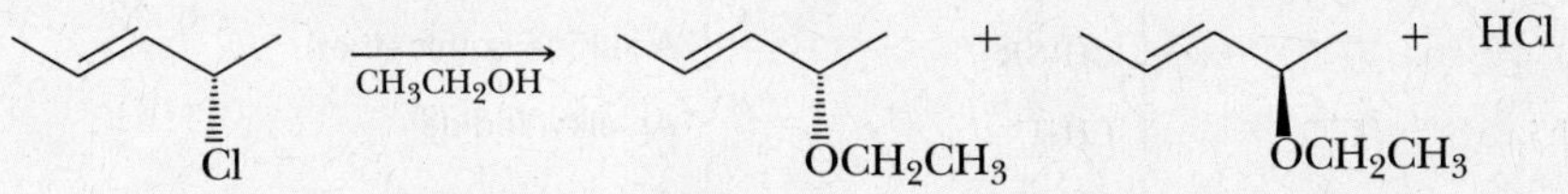

(c)
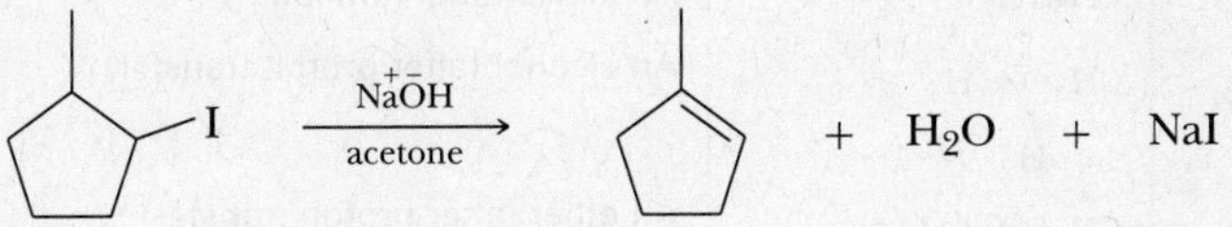

STRATEGY

Look for the halogen in the reactant. Has it been replaced by a different atom or group of atoms in the product(s)? If so, the reaction was a substitution reaction. If the carbon that was once bonded to the halogen is now part of a C—C double bond in the product(s), an elimination reaction has occurred.

SOLUTION

(a) Substitution; the bromine was replaced by a thiol group.
(b) Substitution; in both products, an ethoxyl group replaces chlorine.
(c) β-Elimination; a hydrogen atom and an iodo group have been removed, and an alkene forms as a result.

PROBLEM 7.2

Determine whether the following haloalkanes underwent substitution, elimination, or both substitution and elimination:

(a)
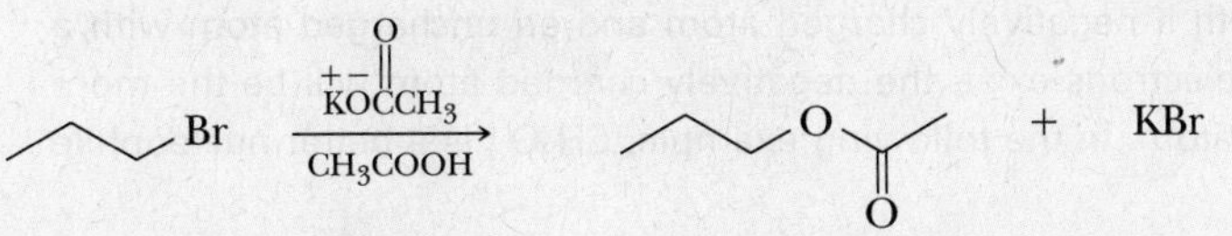

(b)
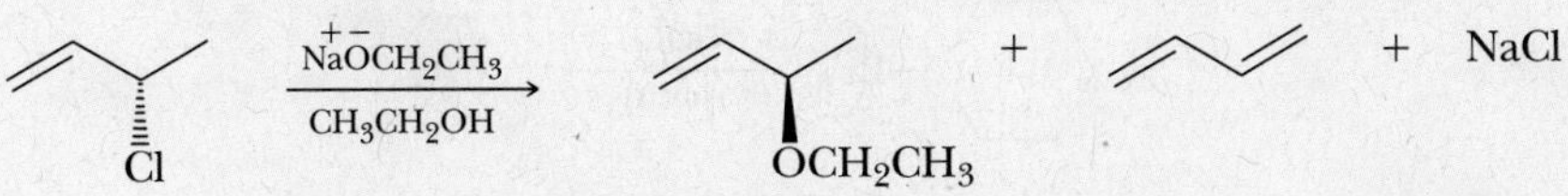

7.3 What Are the Products of Nucleophilic Aliphatic Substitution Reactions?

Nucleophilic substitution is one of the most important reactions of haloalkanes and can lead to a wide variety of new functional groups, several of which are illustrated in Table 7.1. As you study the entries in this table, note the following points:

1. If the nucleophile is negatively charged, as, for example, OH^- and RS^-, then the atom donating the pair of electrons in the substitution reaction becomes neutral in the product.
2. If the nucleophile is uncharged, as, for example, NH_3 and CH_3OH, then the atom donating the pair of electrons in the substitution reaction becomes positively charged in the product. The products then often undergo a second step involving proton transfer to yield a neutral substitution product.

TABLE 7.1 Some Nucleophilic Substitution Reactions

Reaction: $Nu:^- + CH_3X \longrightarrow CH_3Nu + :X^-$

Nucleophile		Product	Class of Compound Formed
$HO:^-$	⟶	CH_3OH	An alcohol
$RO:^-$	⟶	CH_3OR	An ether
$HS:^-$	⟶	CH_3SH	A thiol (a mercaptan)
$RS:^-$	⟶	CH_3SR	A sulfide (a thioether)
$:I:^-$	⟶	$CH_3I:$	An alkyl iodide
$:NH_3$	⟶	$CH_3NH_3^+$	An alkylammonium ion
HOH	⟶	$CH_3O^+(H)—H$	An alcohol (after proton transfer)
CH_3OH	⟶	$CH_3O^+(H)—CH_3$	An ether (after proton transfer)

notice that a nucleophile does not need to be negatively charged

HOW TO 7.3

Complete a Substitution Reaction

(a) Identify the leaving group.

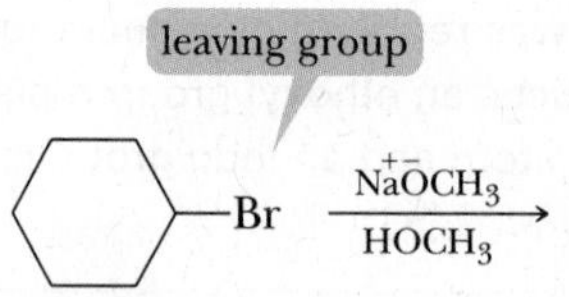

(b) Identify the nucleophile and its nucleophilic atom. The nucleophilic atom will be the negatively charged atom or the atom with a lone pair of electrons to donate. If both a negatively charged atom and an uncharged atom with a lone pair of electrons exist, the negatively charged atom will be the more nucleophilic atom. In the following example, CH_3O^- is a better nucleophile than $HOCH_3$.

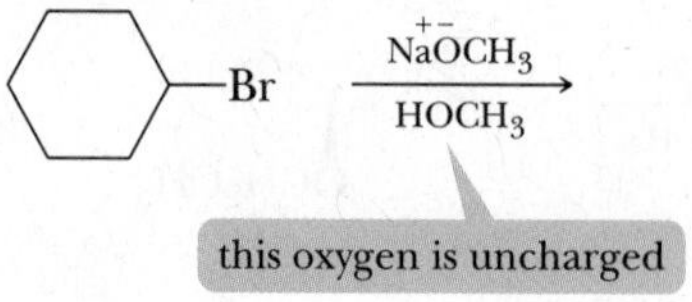

(c) Replace the leaving group in the reactant with the nucleophilic atom or group. Any groups connected to the nucleophilic atom through covalent bonds will remain bonded to that atom in the product.

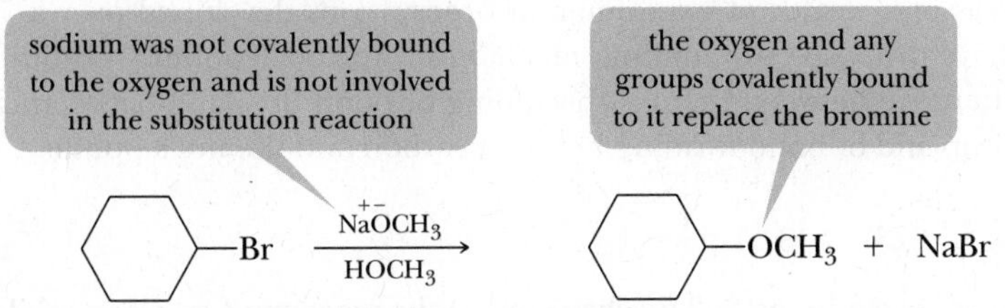

(d) Spectator ions will usually be shown as part of an ion pair with the negatively charged leaving group.

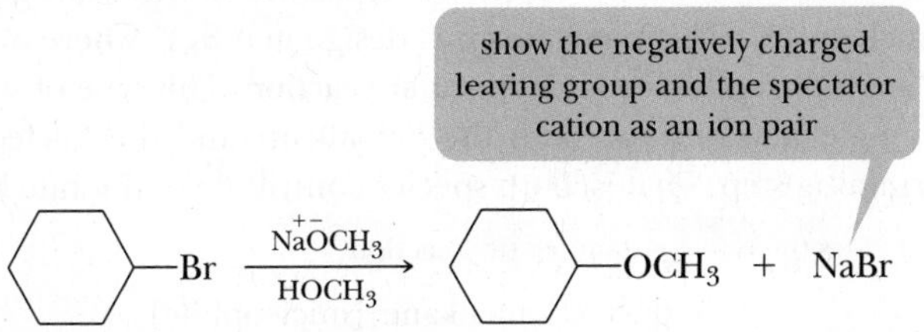

EXAMPLE 7.3

Complete these nucleophilic substitution reactions:

(a)  **(b)** 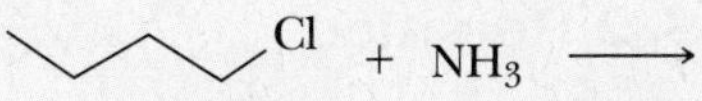

STRATEGY

First identify the nucleophile. Then break the bond between the halogen and the carbon it is bonded to and create a new bond from that same carbon to the nucleophile.

SOLUTION

(a) Hydroxide ion is the nucleophile, and bromine is the leaving group:

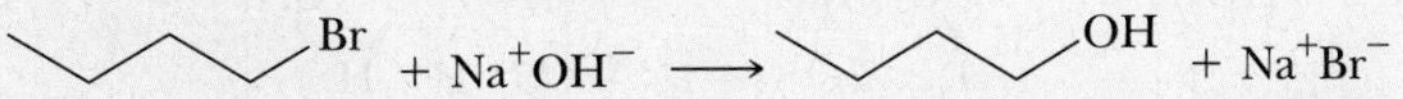

1-Bromobutane | Sodium hydroxide | 1-Butanol | Sodium bromide

(b) Ammonia is the nucleophile, and chlorine is the leaving group:

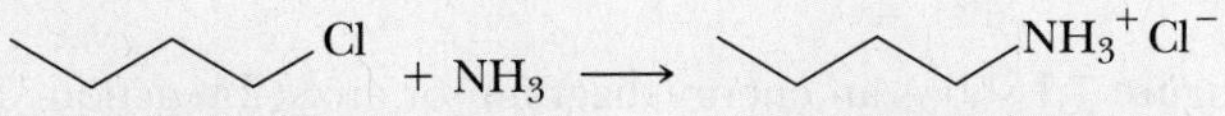

1-Chlorobutane | Ammonia | Butylammonium chloride

See problems 7.21, 7.22, 7.26

PROBLEM 7.3

Complete these nucleophilic substitution reactions:

(a) 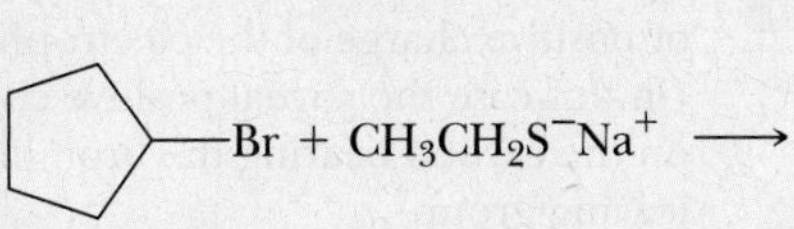 **(b)** 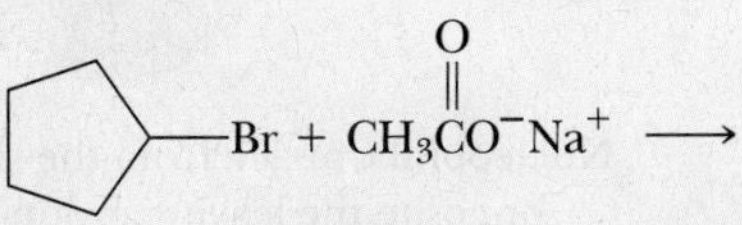

7.4 What Are the S_N2 and S_N1 Mechanisms for Nucleophilic Substitution?

On the basis of a wealth of experimental observations developed over a 70-year period, chemists have proposed two limiting mechanisms for nucleophilic substitutions. A fundamental difference between them is the timing of bond breaking between carbon and the leaving group and of bond forming between carbon and the nucleophile.

A. S_N2 Mechanism

Two processes occur in the S_N2 mechanism: (1) the reaction of an electrophile and a nucleophile to form a new covalent bond and (2) the breaking of a bond to form a stable ion or molecule. At one extreme, the two processes are *concerted*, meaning that bond breaking and bond forming occur simultaneously. Thus, the departure of the leaving group is assisted by the incoming nucleophile. This mechanism is designated **S_N2**, where *S* stands for *S*ubstitution, *N* for *N*ucleophilic, and 2 for a ***bi*molecular reaction**. This type of substitution reaction is classified as bimolecular because both the haloalkane and the nucleophile are involved in the rate-determining step. That is, both species contribute to the rate law of the reaction:

Bimolecular reaction A reaction in which two species are involved in the reaction leading to the transition state of the rate-determining step.

k is the rate constant for the reaction

$$\text{Rate} = k[\text{haloalkane}][\text{nucleophile}]$$

Following is an S_N2 mechanism for the reaction of hydroxide ion and bromomethane to form methanol and bromide ion:

Mechanism

An S_N2 Reaction

The nucleophile attacks the reactive center from the side opposite the leaving group; that is, an S_N2 reaction involves a backside attack by the nucleophile. **(1) The reaction of an electrophile and a nucleophile to form a new covalent bond and (2) the breaking of a bond to form a stable ion or molecule** occur simultaneously.

Inversion of configuration The reversal of the arrangement of atoms or groups of atoms about a reaction center in an S_N2 reaction.

note inversion of the reactive center

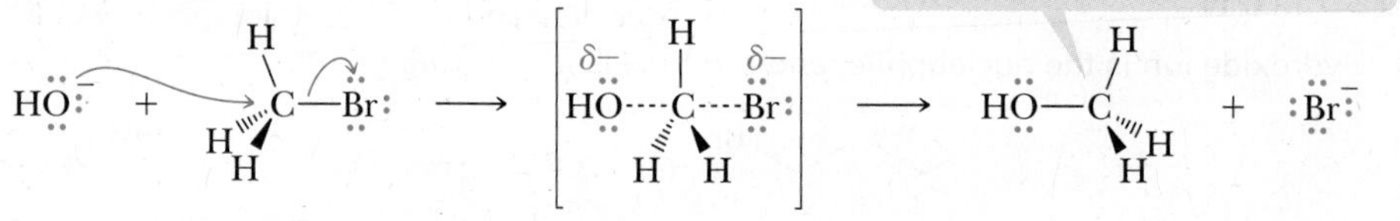

Reactants | Transition state with simultaneous bond breaking and bond forming | Products

Figure 7.1 shows an energy diagram for an S_N2 reaction. There is a single transition state and no reactive intermediate.

the negatively charged (red) oxygen atom is attracted to the electropositive (blue) carbon atom

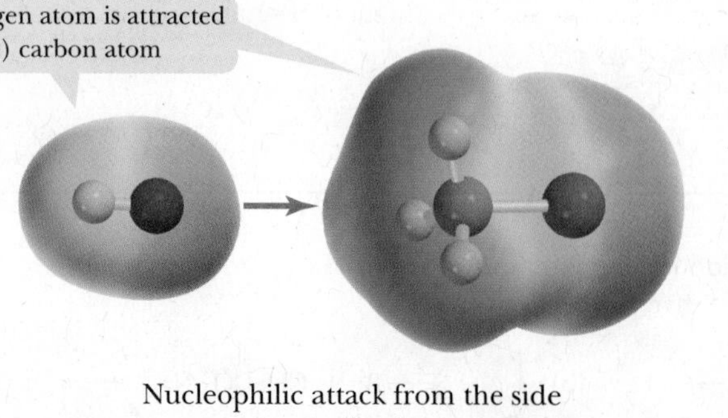

Nucleophilic attack from the side opposite the leaving group

An S_N2 reaction is driven by the attraction between the negative charge of the nucleophile (in this case the negatively charged oxygen of the hydroxide ion) and the center of positive charge of the electrophile (in this case the partial positive charge on the carbon bearing the bromine leaving group).

FIGURE 7.1
An energy diagram for an S_N2 reaction. There is one transition state and no reactive intermediate.

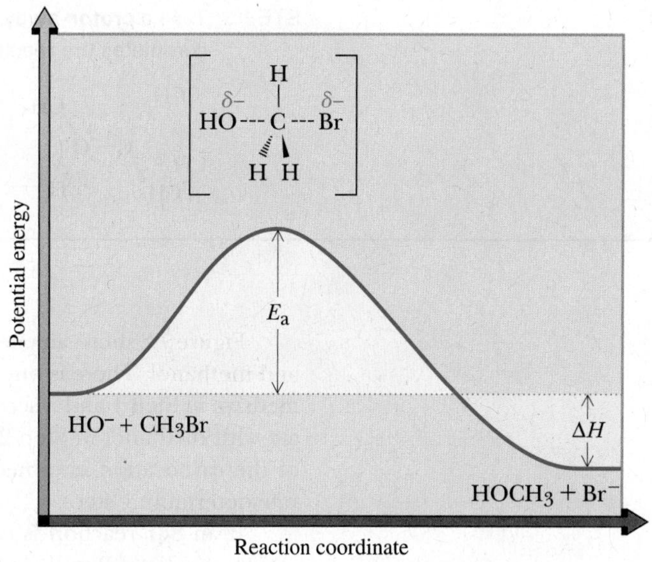

B. S_N1 Mechanism

In the other limiting mechanism, called S_N1, bond breaking between carbon and the leaving group is completed before bond forming with the nucleophile begins. In the designation S_N1, *S* stands for *S*ubstitution, *N* stands for *N*ucleophilic, and *1* stands for a ***unimolecular reaction***. This type of substitution is classified as unimolecular because only the haloalkane is involved in the rate-determining step; that is, only the haloalkane contributes to the rate law governing the rate-determining step:

$$\text{Rate} = k[\text{haloalkane}]$$

An S_N1 reaction is illustrated by the **solvolysis** reaction of 2-bromo-2-methylpropane (*tert*-butyl bromide) in methanol to form 2-methoxy-2-methylpropane (*tert*-butyl methyl ether). You may notice that the second step of the mechanism is identical to the second step of the mechanism for the addition of hydrogen halides (H—X) to alkenes (Section 5.3A) and the acid-catalyzed hydration of alkenes (Section 5.3B).

Unimolecular reaction A reaction in which only one species is involved in the reaction leading to the transition state of the rate-determining step.

Solvolysis A nucleophilic substitution reaction in which the solvent is the nucleophile.

Mechanism

An S_N1 Reaction

STEP 1: Break a bond to form a more stable ion or molecule. The ionization of a C—X bond forms a 3° carbocation intermediate:

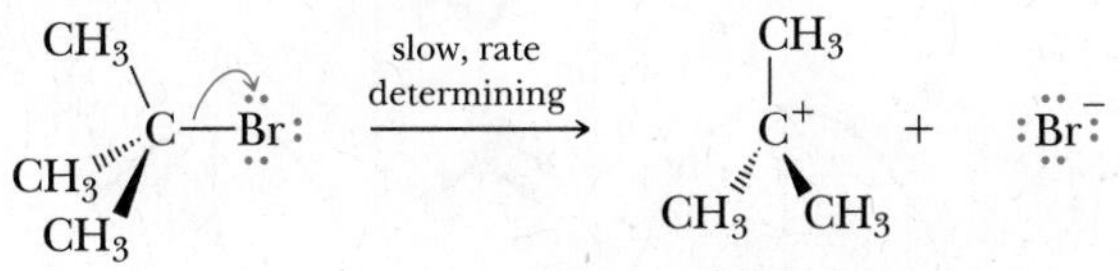

A carbocation intermediate; carbon is trigonal planar

STEP 2: Reaction of a nucleophile and an electrophile to form a new covalent bond. Reaction of the carbocation intermediate (an electrophile) with methanol (a nucleophile) gives an oxonium ion. Attack by the nucleophile occurs with equal probability from either face of the planar carbocation intermediate.

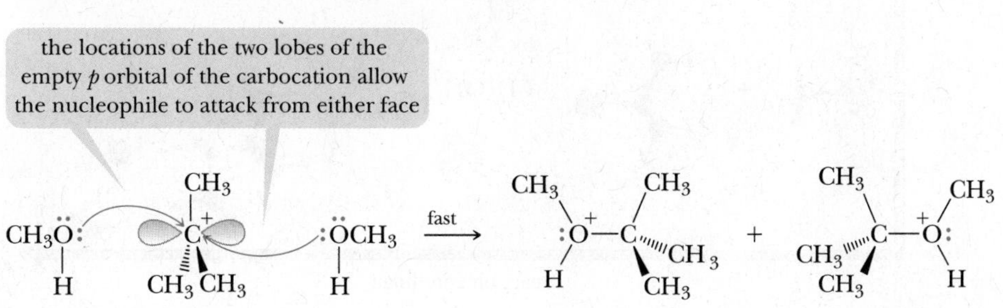

STEP 3: Take a proton away. Proton transfer from the oxonium ion to methanol (the solvent) completes the reaction and gives *tert*-butyl methyl ether:

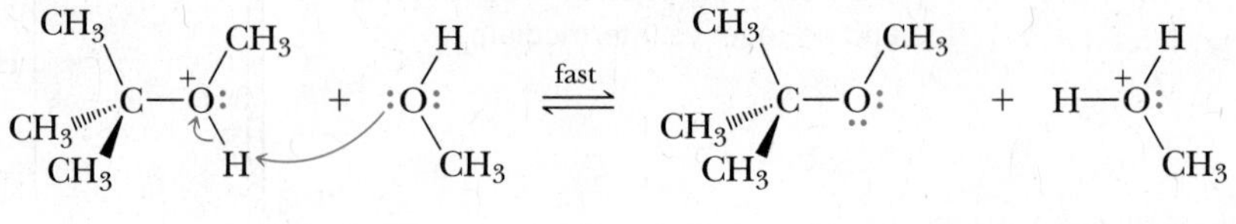

Figure 7.2 shows an energy diagram for the S_N1 reaction of 2-bromo-2-methyl propane and methanol. There is one transition state leading to formation of the carbocation intermediate in Step 1 and a second transition state for reaction of the carbocation intermediate with methanol in Step 2 to give the oxonium ion. The reaction leading to formation of the carbocation intermediate crosses the higher energy barrier and is, therefore, the rate-determining step.

If an S_N1 reaction is carried out on a 2° haloalkane, a 2° carbocation is formed as an intermediate. Recall from Section 5.4 that a 2° carbocation can undergo a rearrangement to form a more stable 3° carbocation. This is illustrated in the solvolysis reaction of 2-bromo-3,3-dimethylbutane in ethanol.

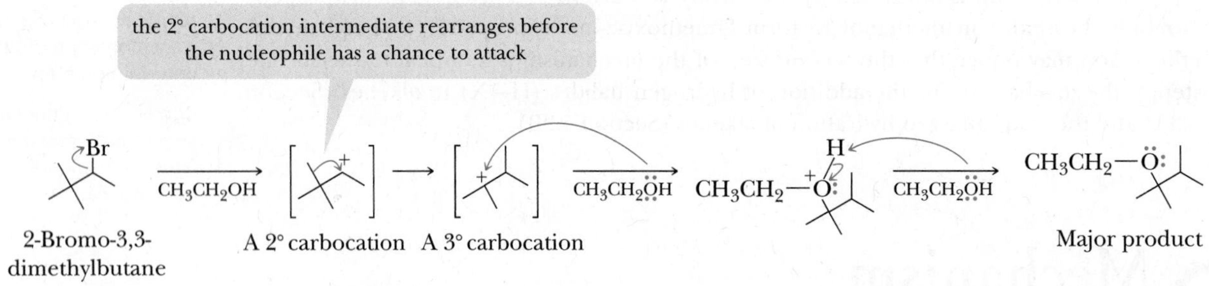

If an S_N1 reaction is carried out at a tetrahedral stereocenter, the major product is a racemic mixture. We can illustrate this result with the following example: Upon ionization,

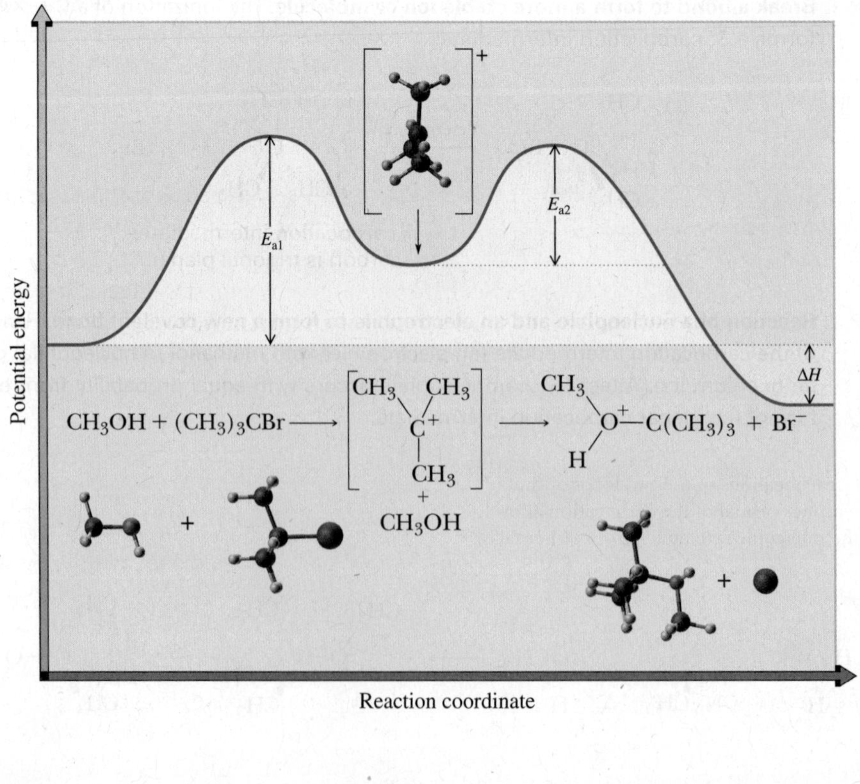

FIGURE 7.2 An energy diagram for the S_N1 reaction of 2-bromo-2-methylpropane and methanol. There is one transition state leading to formation of the carbocation intermediate in Step 1 and a second transition state for the reaction of the carbocation intermediate with methanol in Step 2. Step 1 crosses the higher energy barrier and is, therefore, rate determining.

the R enantiomer forms an achiral carbocation intermediate. Attack by the nucleophile from the left face of the carbocation intermediate gives the S enantiomer; attack from the right face gives the R enantiomer. Because attack by the nucleophile occurs with equal probability from either face of the planar carbocation intermediate, the R and S enantiomers are formed in equal amounts, and the product is a racemic mixture.

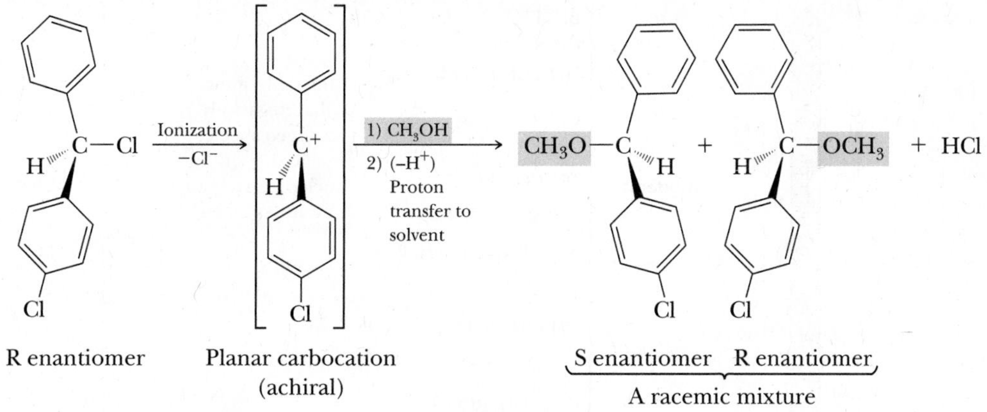

7.5 What Determines Whether S_N1 or S_N2 Predominates?

Let us now examine some of the experimental evidence on which these two contrasting mechanisms are based. As we do so, we consider the following questions:

1. What effect does the structure of the nucleophile have on the rate of reaction?
2. What effect does the structure of the haloalkane have on the rate of reaction?
3. What effect does the structure of the leaving group have on the rate of reaction?
4. What is the role of the solvent?

A. Structure of the Nucleophile

Nucleophilicity is a kinetic property, which we measure by relative rates of reaction. We can establish the relative nucleophilicities for a series of nucleophiles by measuring the rate at which each displaces a leaving group from a haloalkane—for example, the rate at which each displaces bromide ion from bromoethane in ethanol at 25 °C:

$$CH_3CH_2Br + NH_3 \longrightarrow CH_3CH_2NH_3^+ + Br^-$$

From these studies, we can then make correlations between the structure of the nucleophile and its **relative nucleophilicity**. Table 7.2 lists the types of nucleophiles we deal with most commonly in this text.

Relative nucleophilicity The relative rates at which a nucleophile reacts in a reference nucleophilic substitution reaction.

Because the nucleophile participates in the rate-determining step in an S_N2 reaction, the better the nucleophile, the more likely it is that the reaction will occur by that mechanism. The nucleophile does not participate in the rate-determining step for an S_N1 reaction. Thus, an S_N1 reaction can, in principle, occur at approximately the same rate with any of the common nucleophiles, regardless of their relative nucleophilicities.

B. Structure of the Haloalkane

S_N1 reactions are governed mainly by **electronic factors**, namely, the relative stabilities of carbocation intermediates. S_N2 reactions, by contrast, are governed mainly by **steric factors**, and their transition states are particularly sensitive to crowding about the site of reaction. The distinction is as follows:

Steric hindrance The ability of groups, because of their size, to hinder access to a reaction site within a molecule.

1. *Relative stabilities of carbocations.* As we learned in Section 5.3A, 3° carbocations are the most stable carbocations, requiring the lowest activation energy for their formation,

TABLE 7.2 Examples of Common Nucleophiles and Their Relative Effectiveness

Effectiveness as a Nucleophile	Nucleophile
good	Br^-, I^- CH_3S^-, RS^- HO^-, CH_3O^-, RO^-
moderate	Cl^-, F^- $CH_3C(=O)O^-$, $RC(=O)O^-$ CH_3SH, RSH, R_2S NH_3, RNH_2, R_2NH, R_3N
poor	H_2O CH_3OH, ROH $CH_3C(=O)OH$, $RC(=O)OH$

Increasing nucleophilicity (from poor to good)

the table shows that negatively charged species are better nucleophiles than neutral species

whereas 1° carbocations are the least stable, requiring the highest activation energy for their formation. In fact, 1° carbocations are so unstable that they have never been observed in solution. Therefore, 3° haloalkanes are most likely to react by carbocation formation; 2° haloalkanes are less likely to react in this manner, and methyl and 1° haloalkanes never react in that manner.

2. *Steric hindrance.* To complete a substitution reaction, the nucleophile must approach the substitution center and begin to form a new covalent bond to it. If we compare the ease of approach by the nucleophile to the substitution center of a 1° haloalkane with that of a 3° haloalkane, we see that the approach is considerably easier in the case of the 1° haloalkane. Two hydrogen atoms and one alkyl group screen the backside of the substitution center of a 1° haloalkane. In contrast, three alkyl groups screen the backside of the substitution center of a 3° haloalkane. This center in bromoethane is easily accessible to a nucleophile, while there is extreme crowding around the substitution center in 2-bromo-2-methylpropane:

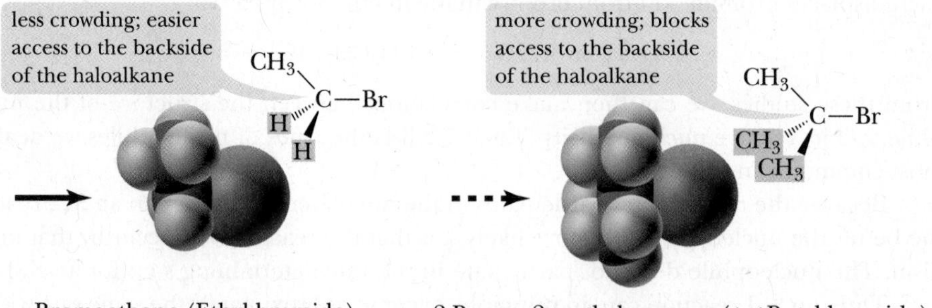

Bromoethane (Ethyl bromide) 2-Bromo-2-methylpropane (*tert*-Butyl bromide)

Given the competition between electronic and steric factors, we find that 3° haloalkanes react by an S_N1 mechanism because 3° carbocation intermediates are particularly stable and because the backside approach of a nucleophile to the substitution center in a 3° haloalkane is hindered by the three groups surrounding it; 3° haloalkanes never react by an S_N2 mechanism. Halomethanes and 1° haloalkanes have little crowding around the substitution center and react by an S_N2 mechanism; they never react by an S_N1 mechanism, because methyl and primary carbocations are so unstable.

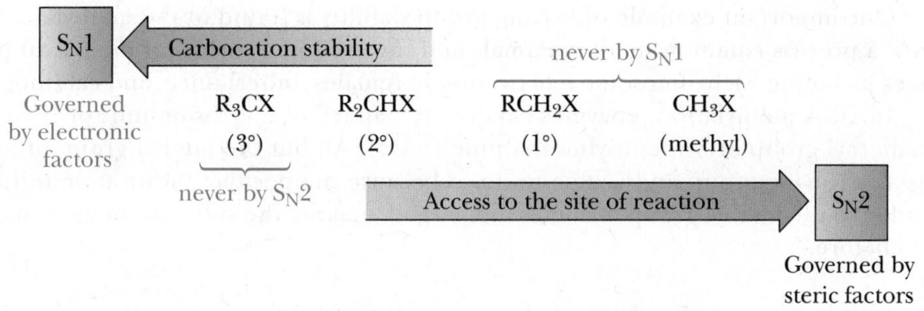

FIGURE 7.3 Effect of electronic and steric factors in competition between S_N1 and S_N2 reactions of haloalkanes.

Secondary haloalkanes may react by either an S_N1 or an S_N2 mechanism, depending on the nucleophile and solvent. The competition between electronic and steric factors and their effects on relative rates of nucleophilic substitution reactions of haloalkanes are summarized in Figure 7.3.

C. The Leaving Group

In the transition state for nucleophilic substitution on a haloalkane, the halogen leaving group develops a partial negative charge in both S_N1 and S_N2 reactions. The halogens Cl^-, Br^-, and I^- make good leaving groups because their size and electronegativity help to stabilize the resulting negative charge. Thus, the ability of a group to function as a leaving group is related to how stable it is as an anion. The most stable anions and the best leaving groups are the conjugate bases of strong acids. We can use the information on the relative strengths of organic and inorganic acids in Table 2.1 to determine which anions are the best leaving groups:

Greater ability to act as leaving group (←)

Rarely act as leaving groups in nucleophilic substitution and β-elimination reactions

$$I^- > Br^- > Cl^- > H_2O \gg CH_3CO^-\ (\text{C}{=}\text{O}) > HO^- > CH_3O^- > NH_2^-$$

Greater stability of anion; greater strength of conjugate acid (←)

The best leaving groups in this series are the halogens I^-, Br^-, and Cl^-. Hydroxide ion (OH^-), methoxide ion (CH_3O^-), and amide ion (NH_2^-) are such poor leaving groups that they rarely, if ever, are displaced in nucleophilic aliphatic substitution reactions. H_2O can act as a leaving group if an —OH group of an alcohol is first protonated by an acid.

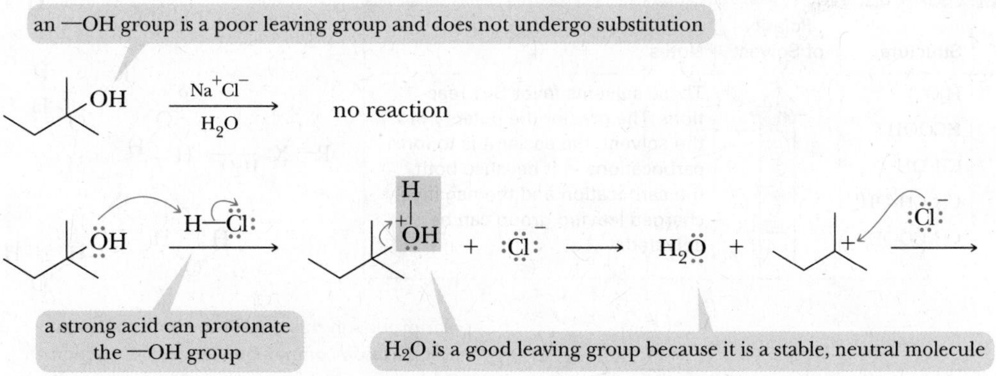

One important example of leaving group stability is found in the methylation of DNA, a process common in all mammals and involved in a variety of biological processes including X-chromosome inactivation in females, inheritance, and carcinogenesis. In DNA methylation, enzymes catalyze the attack of a cytosine unit of DNA on the methyl group of *S*-adenosylmethionine (SAM). All but the methyl group of SAM acts as a leaving group and is able to do so because the positive sulfur atom initially bonded to the methyl group becomes uncharged, making the sulfur atom more stable than before.

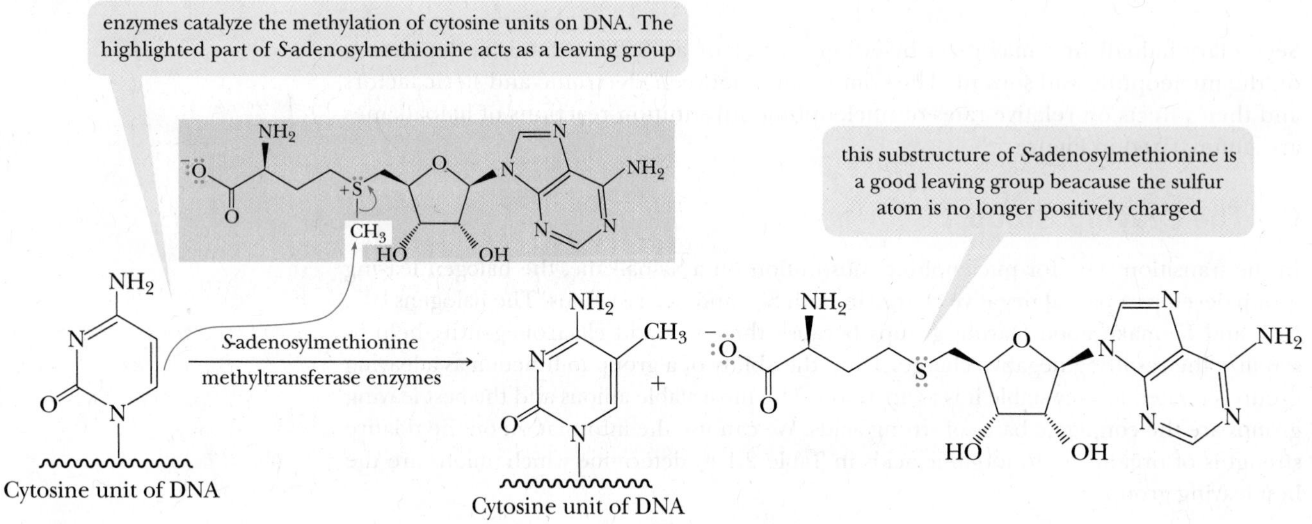
enzymes catalyze the methylation of cytosine units on DNA. The highlighted part of S-adenosylmethionine acts as a leaving group
this substructure of S-adenosylmethionine is a good leaving group beacause the sulfur atom is no longer positively charged
S-adenosylmethionine
methyltransferase enzymes
Cytosine unit of DNA
Cytosine unit of DNA

We will have more to say about leaving groups other than the halides in subsequent chapters.

D. The Solvent

Protic solvent A hydrogen bond donor solvent as, for example, water, ethanol, and acetic acid. We define hydrogen bond donors as compounds containing hydrogens that can participate in H-bonding.

Solvents provide the medium in which reactants are dissolved and in which nucleophilic substitution reactions take place. Common solvents for these reactions are divided into two groups: **protic** and **aprotic**.

Protic solvents contain —OH groups and are hydrogen-bond donors. Common protic solvents for nucleophilic substitution reactions are water, low-molecular-weight alcohols, and low-molecular-weight carboxylic acids (Table 7.3). Each is able to solvate both the

TABLE 7.3 Common Protic Solvents

Protic Solvent	Structure	Polarity of Solvent	Notes
Water	H_2O	Increasing (↑)	These solvents favor S_N1 reactions. The greater the polarity of the solvent, the easier it is to form carbocations in it because both the carbocation and the negatively charged leaving group can be solvated.
Formic acid	$HCOOH$		
Methanol	CH_3OH		
Ethanol	CH_3CH_2OH		
Acetic acid	CH_3COOH		

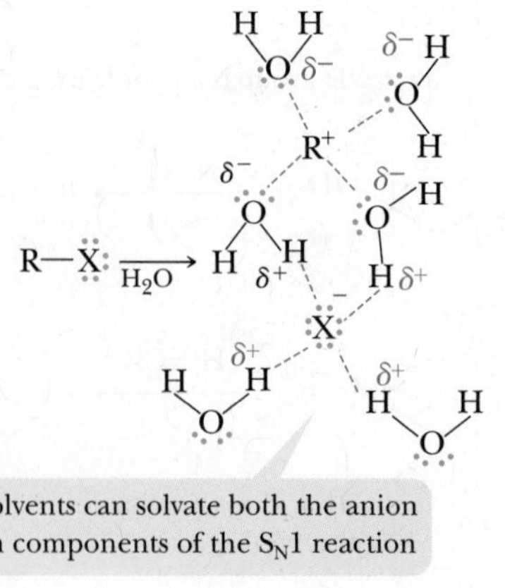
polar protic solvents can solvate both the anion and the cation components of the S_N1 reaction

TABLE 7.4 Common Aprotic Solvents

Aprotic Solvent	Structure	Polarity of Solvent	Notes
Dimethyl sulfoxide (DMSO)	$CH_3S(=O)CH_3$	Increasing (top = most polar)	These solvents favor S_N2 reactions. Although solvents at the top of this list are polar, the formation of carbocations in them is far more difficult than in protic solvents because the anionic leaving group cannot be solvated by these solvents.
Acetone	$CH_3C(=O)CH_3$		
Dichloromethane	CH_2Cl_2		
Diethyl ether	$(CH_3CH_2)_2O$		

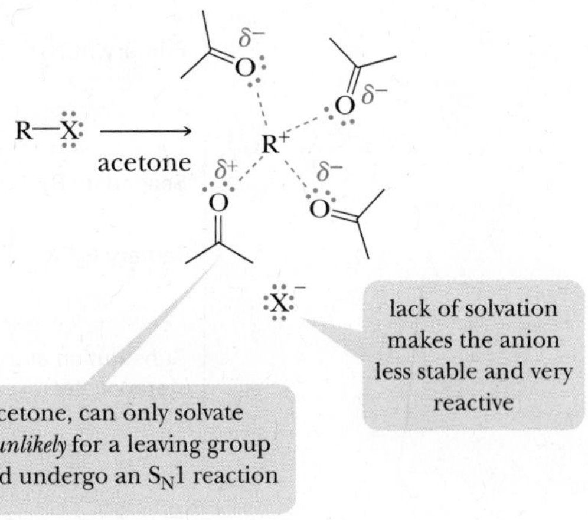

anionic and cationic components of ionic compounds by electrostatic interaction between its partially negatively charged oxygen(s) and the cation and between its partially positively charged hydrogen(s) and the anion. These same properties aid in the ionization of C—X bonds to give an X^- anion and a carbocation; thus, protic solvents are good solvents in which to carry out S_N1 reactions.

Aprotic solvents do not contain —OH groups and cannot function as hydrogen-bond donors. They are unable to promote the formation of a carbocation because the leaving group would be unsolvated. Therefore aprotic solvents cannot be used in S_N1 reactions. Table 7.4 lists the aprotic solvents most commonly used for nucleophilic substitution reactions. Dimethyl sulfoxide and acetone are polar aprotic solvents; dichloromethane and diethyl ether are less polar aprotic solvents. The aprotic solvents listed in the table are particularly good ones in which to carry out S_N2 reactions. Because polar aprotic solvents are able to solvate only cations and not anions, they allow for "naked" and highly reactive anions as nucleophiles when used with ionic nucleophiles such as Na^+CN^-, Na^+OH^-, and so on.

Aprotic solvent A solvent that cannot serve as a hydrogen bond donor as, for example, acetone, diethyl ether, and dichloromethane.

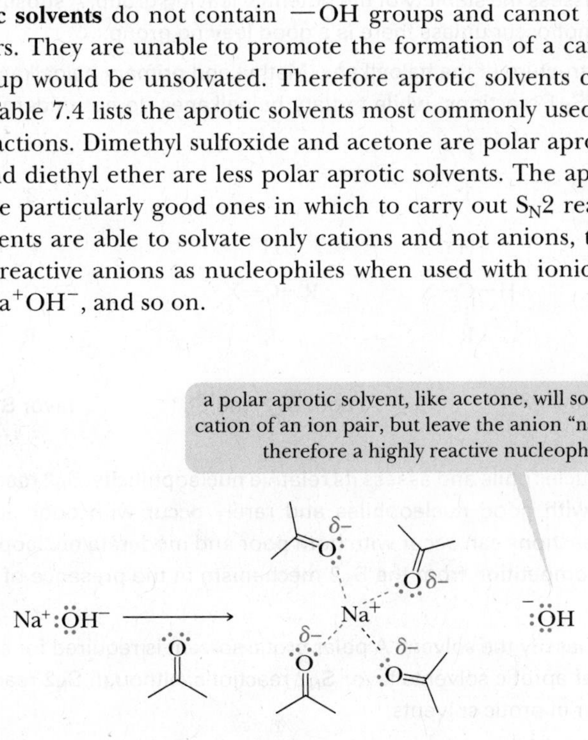

Table 7.5 summarizes the factors favoring S_N1 or S_N2 reactions; it also shows the change in configuration when nucleophilic substitution takes place at a stereocenter.

TABLE 7.5 Summary of S_N1 versus S_N2 Reactions of Haloalkanes

Type of Haloalkane	S_N2	S_N1
Methyl CH_3X	**S_N2 is favored.**	**S_N1 does not occur.** The methyl cation is so unstable that it is never observed in solution.
Primary RCH_2X	**S_N2 is favored.**	**S_N1 does not occur.** Primary carbocations are so unstable that they are not observed in solution.
Secondary R_2CHX	**S_N2 is favored** in aprotic solvents with good nucleophiles.	**S_N1 is favored** in protic solvents with poor nucleophiles.
Tertiary R_3CX	**S_N2 does not occur,** because of steric hindrance around the substitution center.	**S_N1 is favored** because of the ease of formation of tertiary carbocations.
Substitution at a stereocenter	**Inversion of configuration.** The nucleophile attacks the stereocenter from the side opposite the leaving group.	**Racemization.** The carbocation intermediate is planar, and attack by the nucleophile occurs with equal probability from either side.

HOW TO 7.4

Predict the Type of Substitution Reaction a Haloalkane Will Undergo

(a) Identify and assess the stability of the potential leaving group. A substitution reaction will not occur unless there is a good leaving group.

(b) Classify the structure of the haloalkane. Methyl and primary haloalkanes do not undergo S_N1 reactions, while tertiary haloalkanes do not undergo S_N2 reactions.

methyl 1° 2° 3°

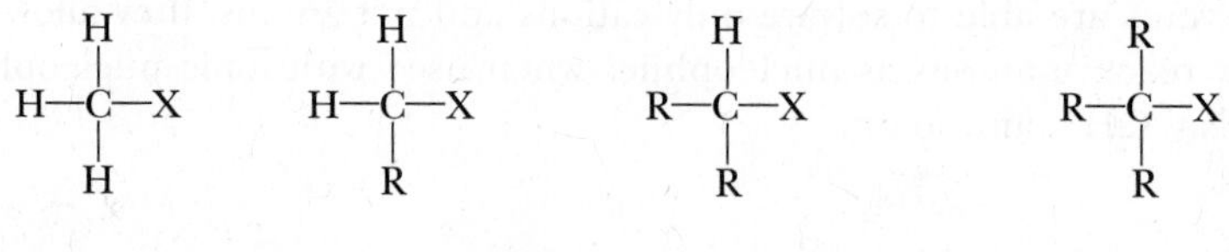

favor S_N2 both S_N2 and S_N1 favor S_N1

(c) Identify the nucleophile and assess its relative nucleophilicity. S_N2 reactions are favored with good nucleophiles and rarely occur with poor nucleophiles. S_N1 reactions can occur with both poor and moderate nucleophiles, but receive competition from the S_N2 mechanism in the presence of good nucleophiles.

(d) Identify and classify the solvent. A polar protic solvent is required for an S_N1 reaction. Polar aprotic solvents favor S_N2 reactions, although S_N2 reactions can also occur in protic solvents.

(e) If no single factor eliminates or mandates either substitution mechanism, try to determine whether these factors collectively favor the predominance of one mechanism over the other.

EXAMPLE 7.4

Answer the following questions:

(a) The rate of a substitution reaction of a haloalkane is unchanged when the nucleophile is switched from hydroxide to ammonia. What type of substitution reaction does this haloalkane likely undergo?

(b) When (*R*)-2-bromobutane is reacted with diethylamine, $(CH_3CH_2)_2NH$, the reaction solution gradually loses optical activity. What type of substitution mechanism is in operation in this reaction?

STRATEGY

It is important to remember the details that go along with each of the two substitution mechanisms. In an S_N1 reaction, look for (1) the rate of the reaction to be unaffected by the type or the concentration of the nucleophile or (2) the formation of two products (often enantiomers if stereochemistry exists at the reacting carbon). In an S_N2 reaction, look for (1) the rate of the reaction to be dependent on the type or the concentration of the nucleophile or (2) the formation of only one product.

SOLUTION

(a) S_N1. Hydroxide ion is a better nucleophile than ammonia. S_N1 reactions are unaffected by the effectiveness of the nucleophile. If the reaction were to occur by an S_N2 mechanism, we would expect reaction with the better nucleophile to result in a faster reaction.

(b) S_N1. Diethylamine is a moderate nucleophile and likely favors the S_N1 mechanism. This is confirmed by the stereochemical data, because an S_N2 reaction would yield only the S enantiomer because of the required backside attack. The loss of optical activity most likely indicates that a carbocation intermediate is formed, followed by the attack of the nucleophile to form equal amounts of the enantiomers shown.

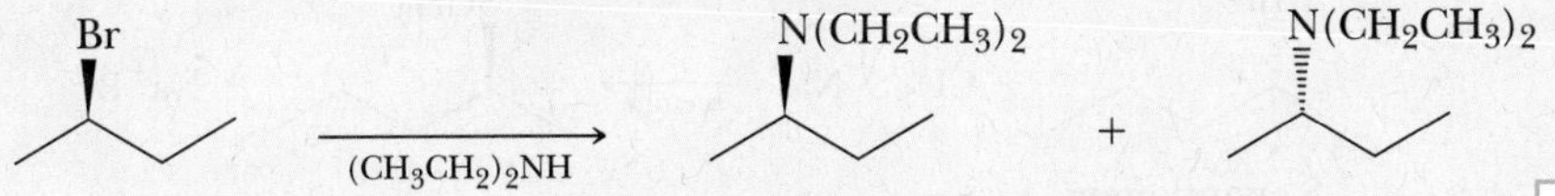

(*R*)-2-bromobutane (*R*) (*S*)

See problems 7.20, 7.23, 7.27

PROBLEM 7.4

Answer the following questions:

(a) Potassium cyanide, KCN, reacts faster than trimethylamine, $(CH_3)_3N$, with 1-chloropentane. What type of substitution mechanism does this haloalkane likely undergo?

(b) Compound A reacts faster with dimethylamine, $(CH_3)_2NH$, than compound B. What does this reveal about the relative ability of each haloalkane to undergo S_N2? S_N1?

A

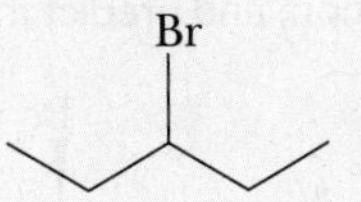

B

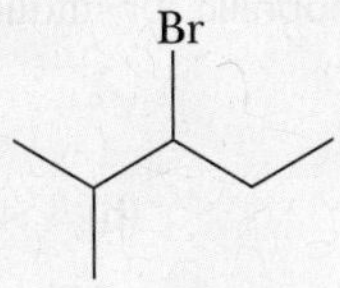

7.6 How Can S_N1 and S_N2 Be Predicted Based on Experimental Conditions?

Predictions about the mechanism for a particular nucleophilic substitution reaction must be based on considerations of the structure of the haloalkane, the nucleophile, and the solvent. Following are analyses of three such reactions:

Nucleophilic Substitution Example 1

before continuing, try to predict whether these reactions proceed by an S_N1 or S_N2 mechanism

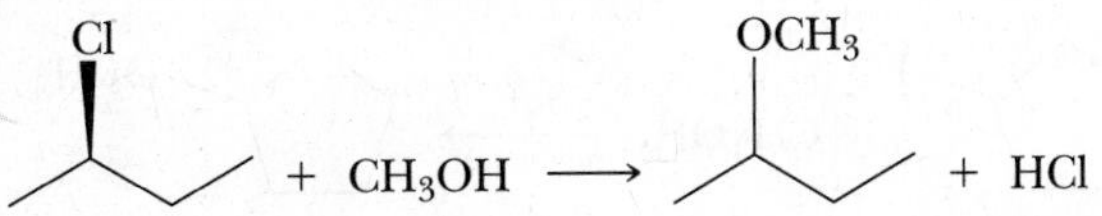

R enantiomer

Methanol is a polar protic solvent and a good one in which to form carbocations. 2-Chlorobutane ionizes in methanol to form a 2° carbocation intermediate. Methanol is a weak nucleophile. From this analysis, we predict that reaction is by an S_N1 mechanism. The 2° carbocation intermediate (an electrophile) then reacts with methanol (a nucleophile) followed by proton transfer to give the observed product. The product is formed as a 50:50 mixture of R and S configurations; that is, it is formed as a racemic mixture.

Nucleophilic Substitution Example 2

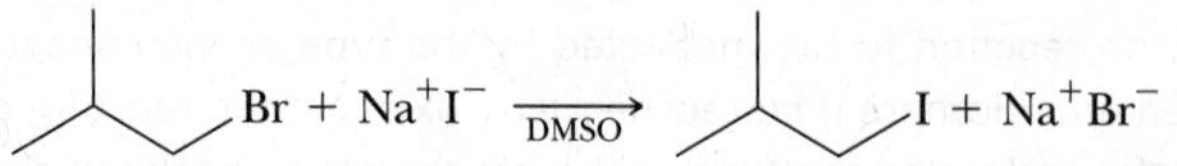

Br + Na⁺I⁻
DMSO
I + Na⁺Br⁻

This is a 1° bromoalkane in the presence of iodide ion, a good nucleophile. Because 1° carbocations are so unstable, they never form in solution, and an S_N1 reaction is not possible. Dimethyl sulfoxide (DMSO), a polar aprotic solvent, is a good solvent in which to carry out S_N2 reactions. From this analysis, we predict that reaction is by an S_N2 mechanism.

Nucleophilic Substitution Example 3

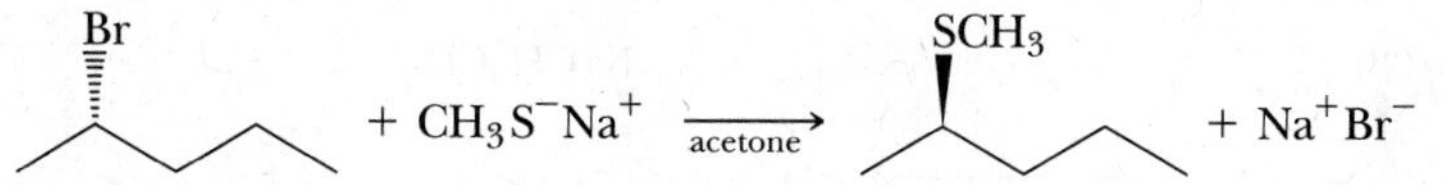

S enantiomer

Bromine ion is a good leaving group on a 2° carbon. The methylsulfide ion is a good nucleophile. Acetone, a polar aprotic solvent, is a good medium in which to carry out S_N2 reactions, but a poor medium in which to carry out S_N1 reactions. We predict that reaction is by an S_N2 mechanism and that the product formed has the R configuration.

EXAMPLE 7.5

Write the expected product for each nucleophilic substitution reaction, and predict the mechanism by which the product is formed:

(a)

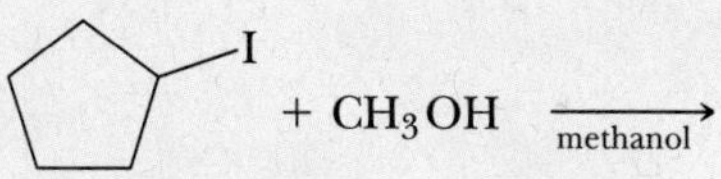

(b)

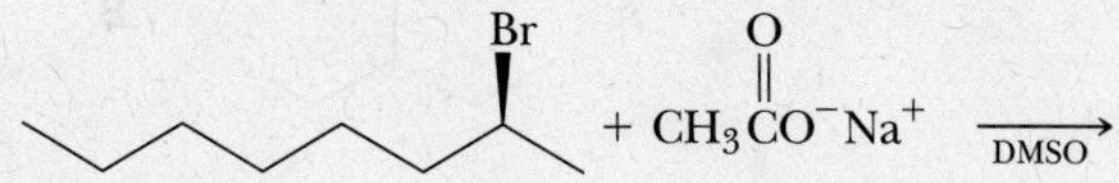

STRATEGY

Determine whether the electrophile's reaction center is 1°, 2°, or 3°. Then assess the nucleophilicity of the nucleophile. If it is poor, then the reaction will most likely proceed by an S_N1 mechanism, provided that there exists a polar protic solvent and the reaction center is 2° or 3°. If there is a good nucleophile, then the reaction will most likely proceed by an S_N2 mechanism, provided that the reaction center is 1° or 2°. If the nucleophile is moderate, focus on the solvent polarity and reaction center of the electrophile. Remember that S_N1 mechanisms only occur in polar protic solvents.

SOLUTION

(a) Methanol is a poor nucleophile. It is also a polar protic solvent that is able to solvate carbocations. Ionization of the carbon–iodine bond forms a 2° carbocation intermediate. We predict an S_N1 mechanism:

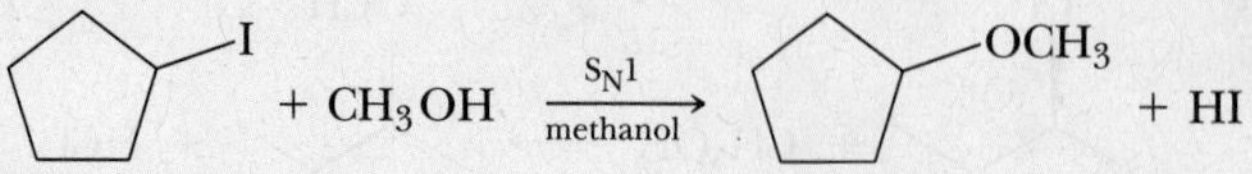

(b) Bromide is a good leaving group on a 2° carbon. Acetate ion is a moderate nucleophile. DMSO is a particularly good solvent for S_N2 reactions. We predict substitution by an S_N2 mechanism with inversion of configuration at the stereocenter:

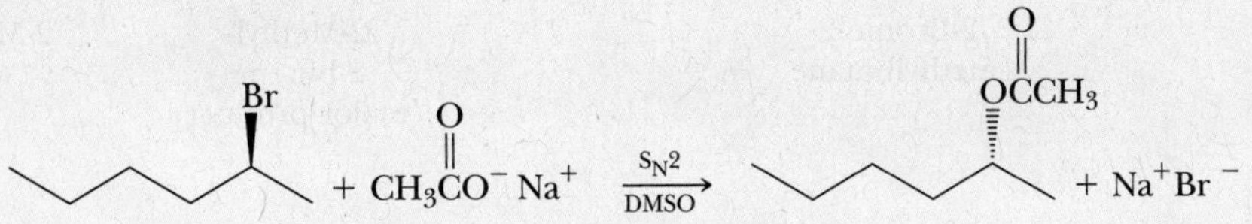

See problems 7.23, 7.25–7.28, 7.34, 7.35

PROBLEM 7.5

Write the expected product for each nucleophilic substitution reaction, and predict the mechanism by which the product is formed:

(a) 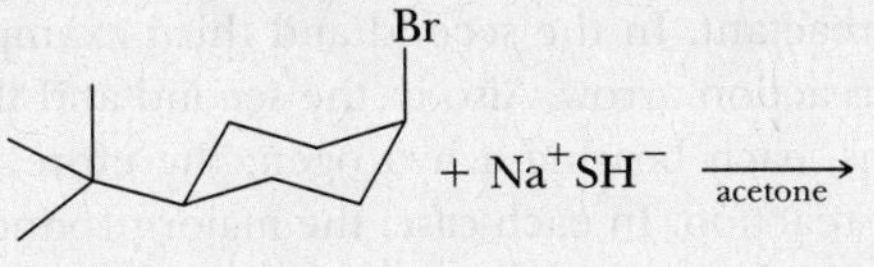

(b) $CH_3CHClCH_2CH_3$ (R) + $HCOOH$ $\xrightarrow{\text{formic acid}}$

7.7 What Are the Products of β-Elimination?

In this section, we study a type of β-elimination called **dehydrohalogenation.** In the presence of a strong base, such as hydroxide ion or ethoxide ion, halogen can be removed from one carbon of a haloalkane and hydrogen from an adjacent carbon to form a carbon–carbon double bond:

Dehydrohalogenation Removal of —H and —X from adjacent carbons; a type of β-elimination.

A haloalkane — Base — An alkene

As the equation shows, we call the carbon bearing the halogen the *α-carbon* and the adjacent carbon the *β-carbon.*

Because most nucleophiles can also act as bases and vice versa, it is important to keep in mind that β-elimination and nucleophilic substitution are competing reactions. In this section, we concentrate on β-elimination. In Section 7.9, we examine the results of competition between the two.

Common strong bases used for β-elimination are OH^-, OR^-, and NH_2^-. Following are three examples of base-promoted β-elimination reactions:

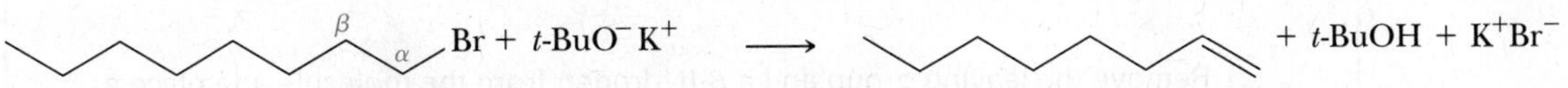

1-Bromooctane — Potassium *tert*-butoxide — 1-Octene

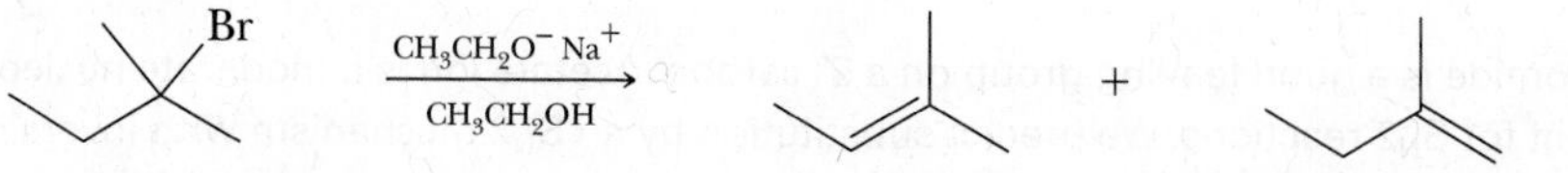

2-Bromo-2-methylbutane — 2-Methyl-2-butene (major product) — 2-Methyl-1-butene

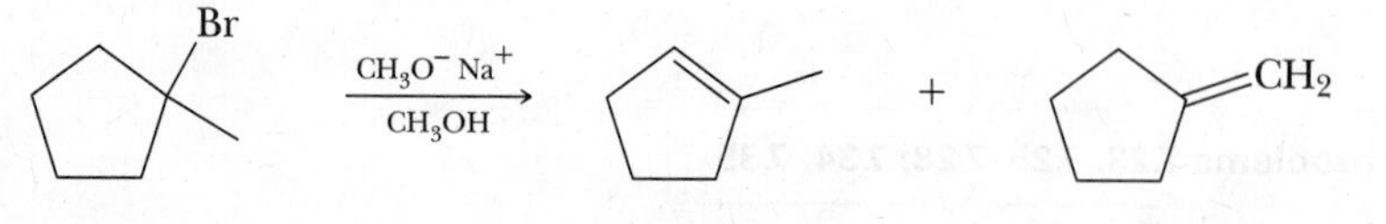

1-Bromo-1-methylcyclopentane — 1-Methylcyclopentene (major product) — Methylenecyclopentane

Zaitsev's rule A rule stating that the major product from a β-elimination reaction is the most stable alkene; that is, the major product is the alkene with the greatest number of substituents on the carbon–carbon double bond.

In the first example, the base is shown as a reactant. In the second and third examples, the base is a reactant, but is shown over the reaction arrow. Also in the second and third examples, there are nonequivalent β-carbons, each bearing a hydrogen; therefore, two alkenes are possible from each β-elimination reaction. In each case, the major product of these and most other β-elimination reactions is the more substituted (and therefore the more stable—see Section 5.6) alkene. We say that each reaction follows **Zaitsev's rule** or, alternatively, that each undergoes Zaitsev elimination, to honor the chemist who first made this generalization.

HOW TO 7.5

Complete an Elimination Reaction

(a) Identify and assess the leaving group. An elimination reaction will not occur unless there is a good leaving group.

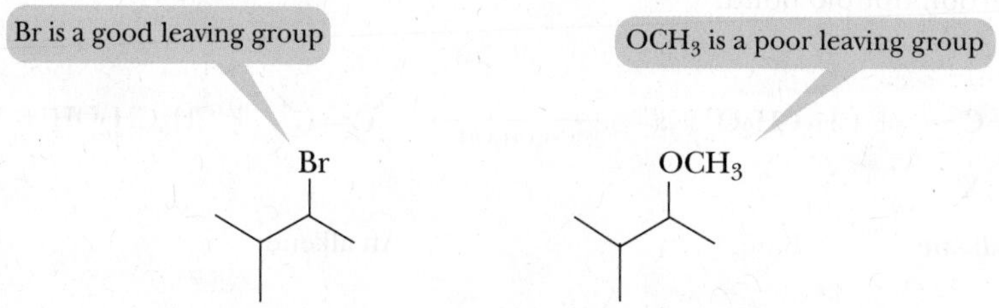

(b) Label the carbon bonded to the leaving group as "α" (alpha).

(c) Label any carbon bonded to the α-carbon as "β" (beta). *Note:* Only do so if the β-carbon is bonded to a hydrogen atom.

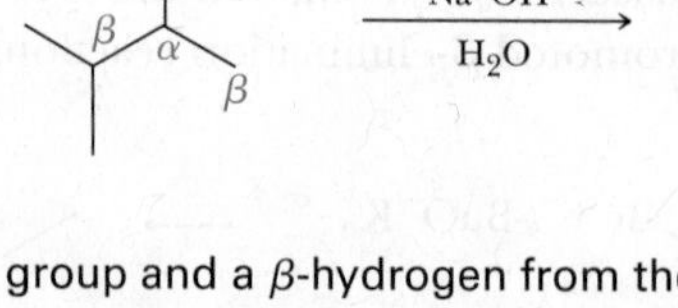

(d) Remove the leaving group and a β-hydrogen from the molecule and place a new double bond between the α and β carbons. This forms a β-elimination product.

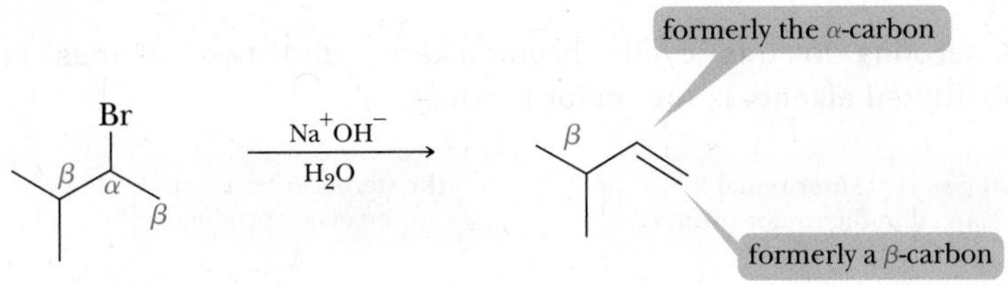

(e) Repeat Step (d) above for any other β-carbons to form a different β-elimination product.

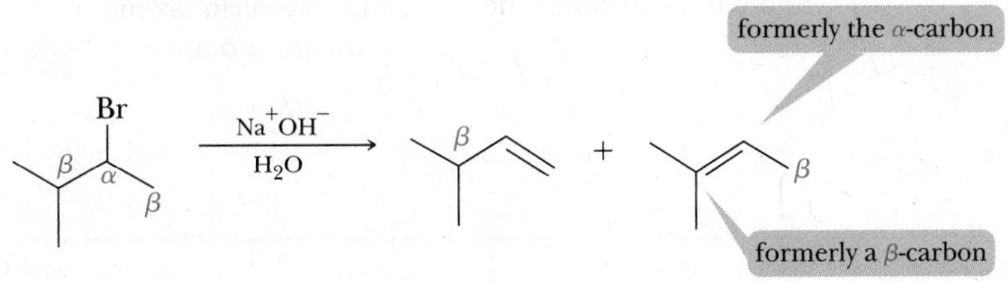

EXAMPLE 7.6

Predict the β-elimination product(s) formed when each bromoalkane is treated with sodium ethoxide in ethanol (if two might be formed, predict which is the major product):

(a) 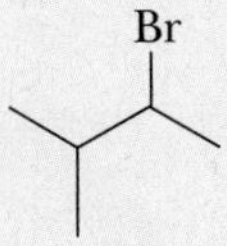

(b) 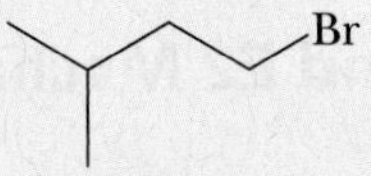

(c) 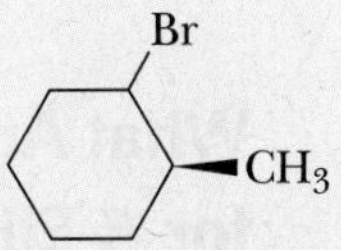

STRATEGY

Label the carbon bonded to the halogen as α. Then label any carbons next to the α-carbon as β. If the β-carbon is bonded to at least one hydrogen, remove that hydrogen and the halogen and draw a C—C double bond between the α- and β-carbons. Start over and repeat this process for any other β-carbons that meet this criteria. Each time you are able to do this will result in an elimination product.

SOLUTION

(a) There are two nonequivalent β-carbons in this bromoalkane, and two alkenes are possible. 2-Methyl-2-butene, the more substituted alkene, is the major product:

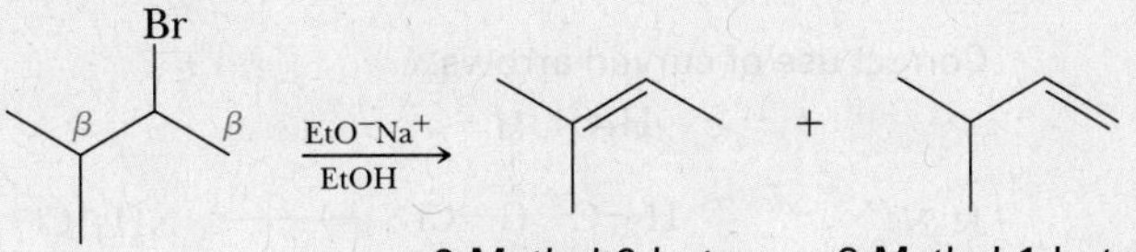

2-Methyl-2-butene (major product)   3-Methyl-1-butene

(b) There is only one β-carbon in this bromoalkane, and only one alkene is possible.

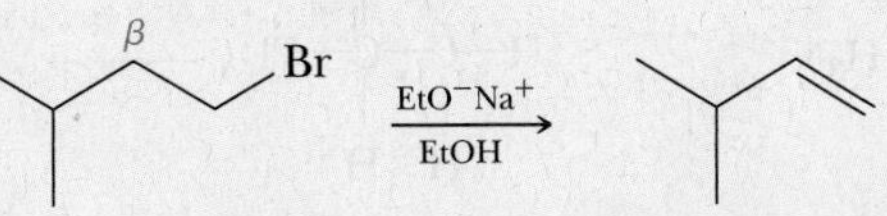

3-Methyl-1-butene

(c) There are two nonequivalent β-carbons in this cyclic bromoalkane, and two alkenes are possible. 1-Methylcyclohexene, the more substituted alkene, is the major product:

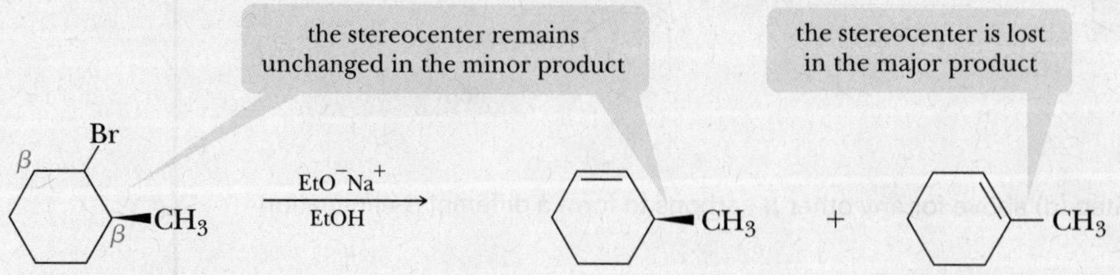

(*S*)-3-Methylcyclohexene   1-Methylcyclohexene (major product)

See problems 7.36–7.38

PROBLEM 7.6

Predict the β-elimination products formed when each chloroalkane is treated with sodium ethoxide in ethanol (if two products might be formed, predict which is the major product):

(a) 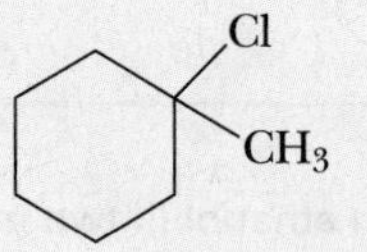 **(b)** 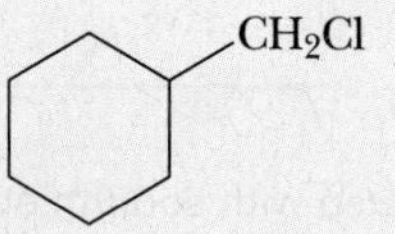 **(c)** 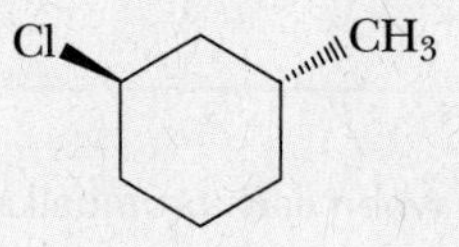

7.8 What Are the E1 and E2 Mechanisms for β-Elimination?

There are two limiting mechanisms of β-elimination reactions. A fundamental difference between them is the timing of the bond-breaking and bond-forming steps. Recall that we made this same statement about the two limiting mechanisms for nucleophilic substitution reactions in Section 7.4.

HOW TO 7.6 Draw Mechanisms

Remember that curved arrow notation always shows the arrow originating from a bond or from a lone pair of electrons.

Correct use of curved arrows...

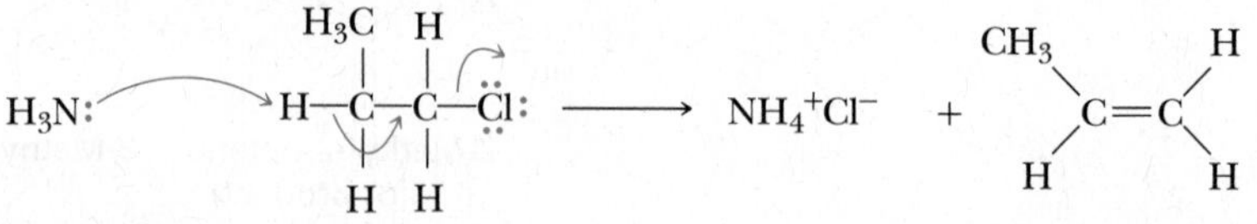

Incorrect use of curved arrows...

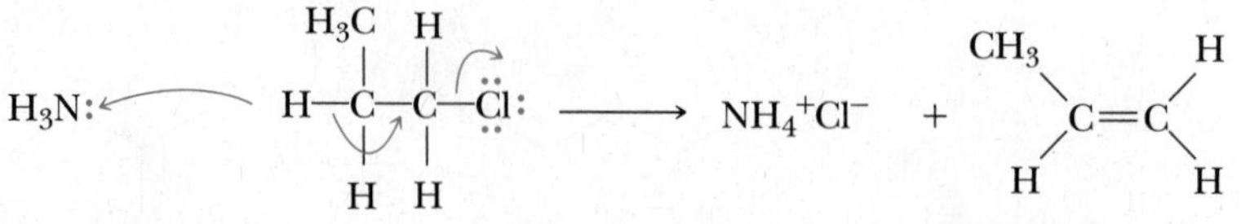

A. E1 Mechanism

At one extreme, breaking of the C—X bond is complete before any reaction occurs with base to lose a hydrogen and before the carbon–carbon double bond is formed. This mechanism is designated **E1**, where *E* stands for *e*limination and *1* stands for a *uni*molecular reaction; only *one* species, in this case the haloalkane, is involved in the rate-determining step. The rate law for an E1 reaction has the same form as that for an S_N1 reaction:

$$\text{Rate} = k[\text{haloalkane}]$$

The mechanism for an E1 reaction is illustrated by the reaction of 2-bromo-2-methylpropane to form 2-methylpropene. In this two-step mechanism, the rate-determining step is the ionization of the carbon–halogen bond to form a carbocation intermediate (just as it is in an S_N1 mechanism).

Mechanism

E1 Reaction of 2-Bromo-2-methylpropane

STEP 1: Break a bond. Rate-determining ionization of the C—Br bond gives a carbocation intermediate:

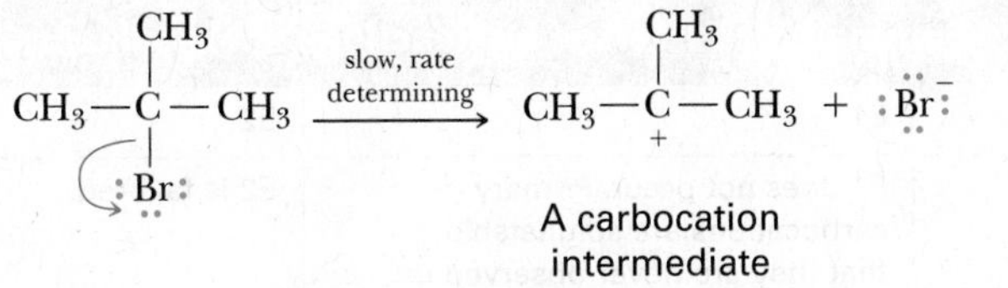

STEP 2: Take away a proton. Proton transfer from the carbocation intermediate to methanol (which in this instance is both the solvent and a reactant) gives the alkene:

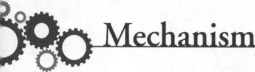

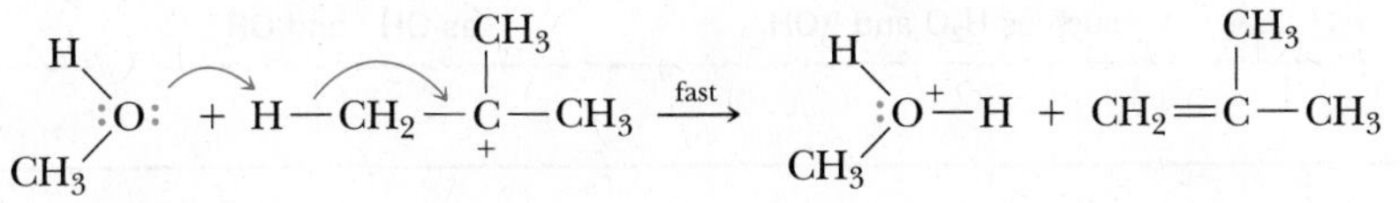

B. E2 Mechanism

At the other extreme is a concerted process. In an **E2** reaction, *E* stands for *e*limination, and *2* stands for *bi*molecular. Because the base removes a β-hydrogen at the same time the C—X bond is broken to form a halide ion, the rate law for the rate-determining step is dependent on both the haloalkane and the base:

$$\text{Rate} = k[\text{haloalkane}][\text{base}]$$

The stronger the base, the more likely it is that the E2 mechanism will be in operation. We illustrate an E2 mechanism by the reaction of 1-bromopropane with sodium ethoxide.

Mechanism

E2 Reaction of 1-Bromopropane

In the E2 mechanism we (1) take away a proton and (2) break a bond to form a stable ion or molecule. Proton transfer to the base, formation of the carbon–carbon double bond, and the ejection of bromide ion occur simultaneously; that is, all bond-forming and bond-breaking steps occur at the same time.

the E2 mechanism is concerted

$$CH_3CH_2\ddot{O}:^- + H-\underset{}{\overset{CH_3}{CH}}-CH_2-\ddot{Br}: \longrightarrow CH_3CH_2\ddot{O}-H + CH_3CH{=}CH_2 + :\ddot{Br}:^-$$

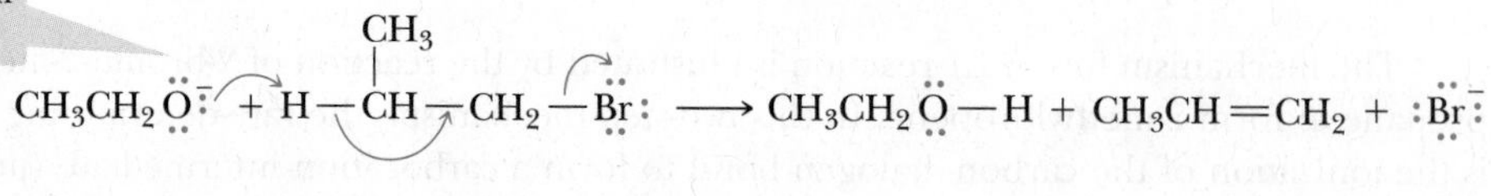

For both E1 and E2 reactions, the major product is that formed in accordance with Zaitsev's rule (Section 7.7) as illustrated by this E2 reaction:

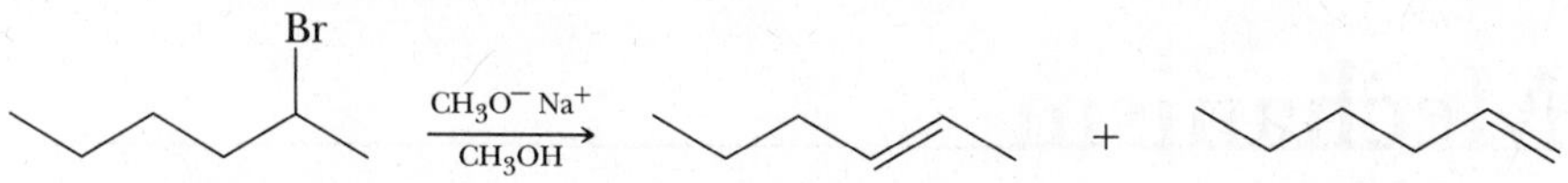

2-Bromohexane — *trans*-2-Hexene (74%) — 1-Hexene (26%)

Table 7.6 summarizes these generalizations about β-elimination reactions of haloalkanes.

TABLE 7.6 Summary of E1 versus E2 Reactions of Haloalkanes

Haloalkane	E1	E2
Primary RCH_2X	E1 does not occur. Primary carbocations are so unstable that they are never observed in solution.	E2 is favored.
Secondary R_2CHX	Main reaction with weak bases such as H_2O and ROH.	Main reaction with strong bases such as OH^- and OR^-.
Tertiary R_3CX	Main reaction with weak bases such as H_2O and ROH.	Main reaction with strong bases such as OH^- and OR^-.

HOW TO 7.7

Predict the Type of β-Elimination Reaction a Haloalkane Will Undergo

(a) Classify the structure of the haloalkane. Primary haloalkanes will not undergo E1 reactions. Secondary and tertiary haloalkanes will undergo both E1 and E2 reactions.

(b) Identify and assess the base. E2 reactions are favored with strong bases and rarely occur with weak bases. E2 reactions can occur in any solvent. E1 reactions can occur with both weak and strong bases, but require polar protic solvents to stabilize the carbocation formed in the first step of the reaction.

EXAMPLE 7.7

Predict whether each β -elimination reaction proceeds predominantly by an E1 or E2 mechanism, and write a structural formula for the major organic product:

(a)
$$CH_3$$
 CH_3 $CH_$

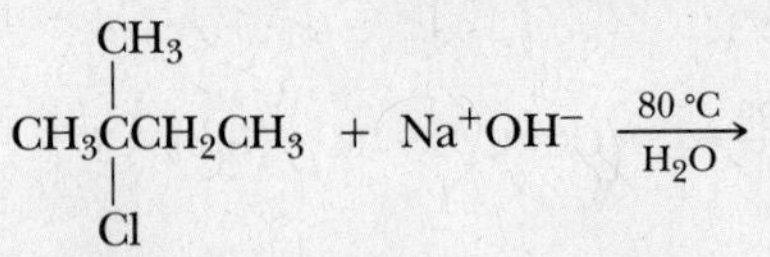

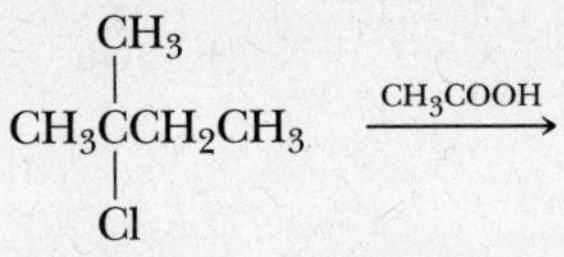

STRATEGY

Identify the solvent and the base. If the base is strong, an E2 mechanism is favored to occur. If the base is weak and the solvent is polar protic, then an E1 mechanism is favored to occur.

SOLUTION

(a) A 3° chloroalkane is heated with NaOH, a strong base. Elimination by an E2 reaction predominates, giving 2-methyl-2-butene as the major product:

$$\begin{array}{c} \text{CH}_3 \\ \mid \\ \text{CH}_3\text{CCH}_2\text{CH}_3 + \text{Na}^+\text{OH}^- \xrightarrow{80 \text{ °C}} \text{CH}_3\text{C} = \text{CHCH}_3 + \text{NaCl} + \text{H}_2\text{O} \\ \mid \\ \text{Cl} \end{array}$$

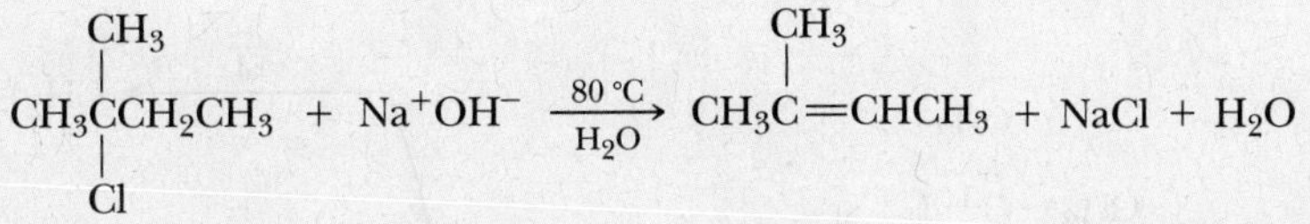

(b) A 3° chloroalkane dissolved in acetic acid, a solvent that promotes the formation of carbocations, forms a 3° carbocation that then loses a proton to give 2-methyl-2-butene as the major product. The reaction is by an E1 mechanism:

acetic acid acts as the solvent and as a week base
$$\begin{array}{ccc} CH_3 & CH_3 \\ & & CH_3 \\ CH_3CCH_2CH_3 & \xrightarrow{CH_3COOH} & CH_3C = CHCH_3 + CH_3COOH_2^+Cl^- \\ & & CI \end{array}$$

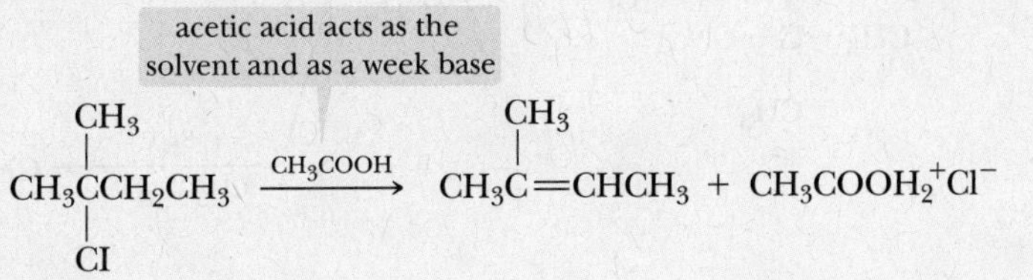

See problems 7.36-7.38

PROBLEM 7.7

Predict whether each elimination reaction proceeds predominantly by an E1 or E2 mechanism, and write a structural formula for the major organic product:

(a)
$$+ CH_3O^-Na^+ \xrightarrow{\text{methanol}}$$
 (b) $+ Na^+OH^- \xrightarrow{\text{acetone}}$

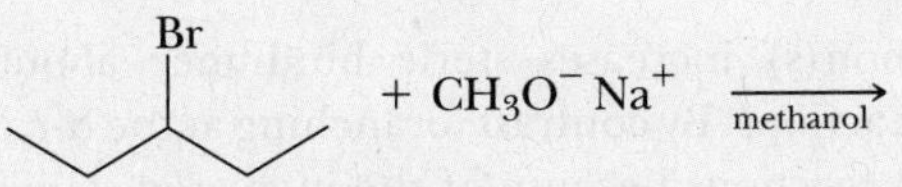

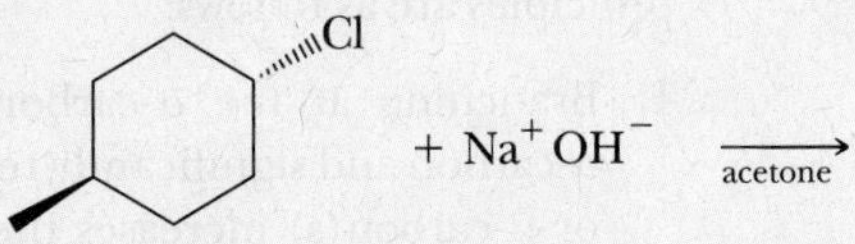

7.9 When Do Nucleophilic Substitution and β -Elimination Compete?

Thus far, we have considered two types of reactions of haloalkanes: nucleophilic substitution and β -elimination. Many of the nucleophiles we have examined—for example, hydroxide ion and alkoxide ions—are also strong bases. Accordingly, nucleophilic substitution and β-elimination often compete with each other, and the ratio of products formed by these reactions depends on the relative rates of the two reactions:

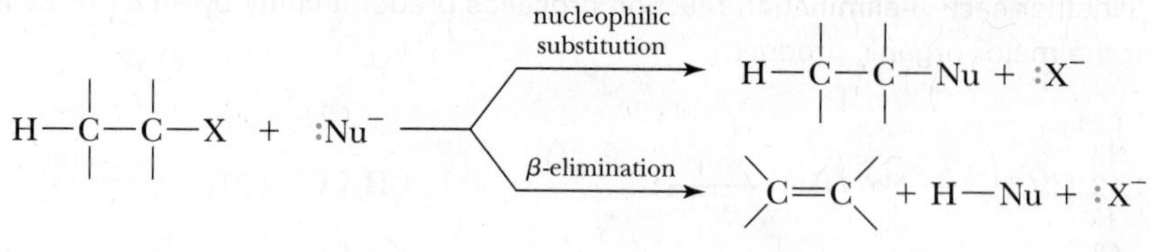
nucleophilic
substitution
β-elimination
H—C—C—X + :Nu⁻
H—C—C—Nu + :X⁻
C=C + H—Nu + :X⁻

A. S_N1-versus-E1 Reactions

Reactions of secondary and tertiary haloalkanes in polar protic solvents give mixtures of substitution and elimination products. In both reactions, Step 1 is the formation of a carbocation intermediate. This step is then followed by either (1) the loss of a hydrogen to give an alkene (E1) or (2) reaction with solvent to give a substitution product (S_N1). In polar protic solvents, the products formed depend only on the structure of the particular carbocation. For example, *tert*-butyl chloride and *tert*-butyl iodide in 80% aqueous ethanol both react with solvent, giving the same mixture of substitution and elimination products:

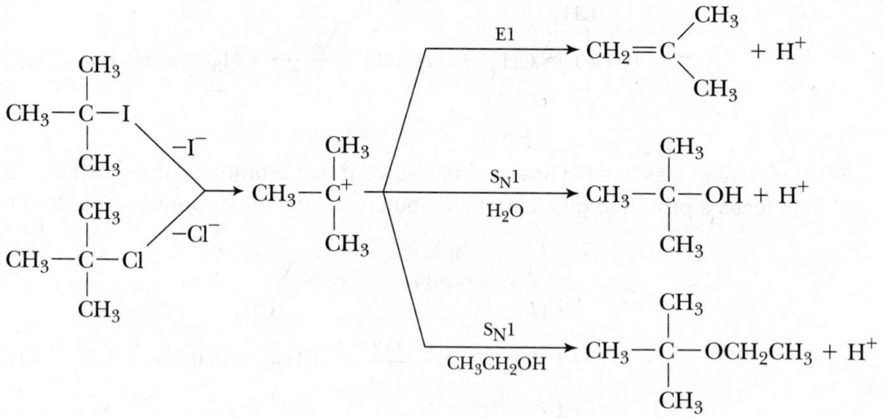
E1
S_N1
H_2O
S_N1
CH_3CH_2OH
$-I^-$
$-Cl^-$

Because iodide ion is a better leaving group than chloride ion, *tert*-butyl iodide reacts over 100 times faster than *tert*-butyl chloride. Yet the ratio of products is the same.

B. S_N2-versus-E2 Reactions

It is considerably easier to predict the ratio of substitution to elimination products for reactions of haloalkanes with reagents that act as both nucleophiles and bases. The guiding principles are as follows:

1. Branching at the α-carbon or β-carbon(s) increases steric hindrance about the α-carbon and significantly retards S_N2 reactions. By contrast, branching at the α-carbon or β-carbon(s) increases the rate of E2 reactions because of the increased stability of the alkene product.
2. The greater the nucleophilicity of the attacking reagent, the greater is the S_N2-to-E2 ratio. Conversely, the greater the basicity of the attacking reagent, the greater is the E2-to-S_N2 ratio.

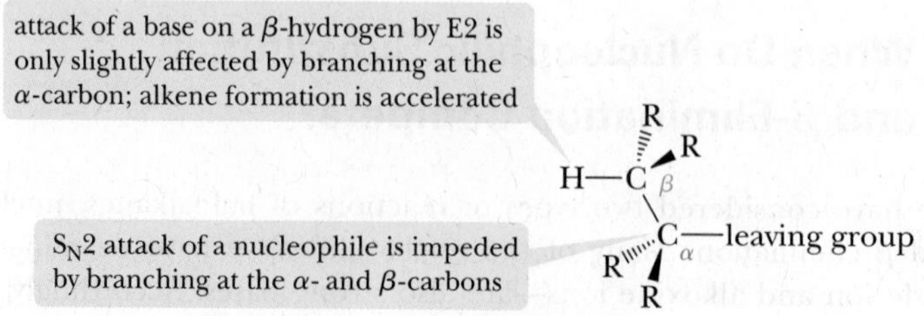
attack of a base on a β-hydrogen by E2 is only slightly affected by branching at the α-carbon; alkene formation is accelerated
S_N2 attack of a nucleophile is impeded by branching at the α- and β-carbons
leaving group

TABLE 7.7 Summary of Substitution versus Elimination Reactions of Haloalkanes

Halide	Reaction	Comments
Methyl	S_N2	The only substitution reactions observed.
CH_3X	~~S_N1~~	S_N1 reactions of methyl halides are never observed. The methyl cation is so unstable that it is never formed in solution.
Primary RCH_2X	S_N2	The main reaction with strong bases such as OH^- and EtO^-. Also, the main reaction with good nucleophiles/weak bases, such as I^- and CH_3COO^-.
	E2	The main reaction with strong, bulky bases, such as potassium *tert*-butoxide.
	~~S_N1/E1~~	Primary cations are never formed in solution; therefore, S_N1 and E1 reactions of primary halides are never observed.
Secondary R_2CHX	S_N2	The main reaction with weak bases/good nucleophiles, such as I^- and CH_3COO^-.
	E2	The main reaction with strong bases/good nucleophiles, such as OH^- and $CH_3CH_2O^-$.
	S_N1/E1	Common in reactions with weak nucleophiles in polar protic solvents, such as water, methanol, and ethanol.
Tertiary R_3CX	~~S_N2~~	S_N2 reactions of tertiary halides are never observed because of the extreme crowding around the 3° carbon.
	E2	Main reaction with strong bases, such as HO^- and RO^-.
	S_N1/E1	Main reactions with poor nucleophiles/weak bases.

Primary halides react with bases/nucleophiles to give predominantly substitution products. With strong bases, such as hydroxide ion and ethoxide ion, a percentage of the product is formed by an E2 reaction, but it is generally small compared with that formed by an S_N2 reaction. With strong, bulky bases, such as *tert*-butoxide ion, the E2 product becomes the major product. Tertiary halides react with all strong bases/good nucleophiles to give only elimination products.

Secondary halides are borderline, and substitution or elimination may be favored, depending on the particular base/nucleophile, solvent, and temperature at which the reaction is carried out. Elimination is favored with strong bases/good nucleophiles—for example, hydroxide ion and ethoxide ion. Substitution is favored with weak bases/poor nucleophiles—for example, acetate ion. Table 7.7 summarizes these generalizations about substitution versus elimination reactions of haloalkanes.

EXAMPLE 7.8

Predict whether each reaction proceeds predominantly by substitution (S_N1 or S_N2) or elimination (E1 or E2) or whether the two compete, and write structural formulas for the major organic product(s):

(a) 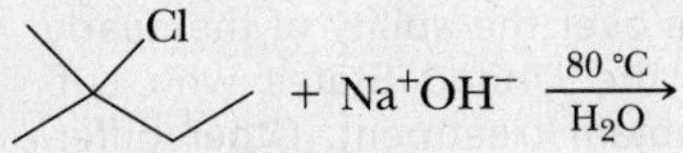

(b) 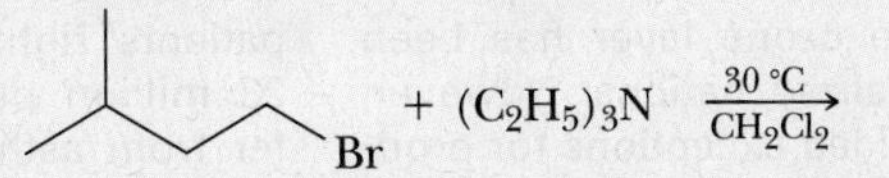

STRATEGY

First, determine whether the reagent acts predominantly as a base or a nucleophile. If it is a weak base but a good nucleophile, substitution is more likely to occur. If the reagent is a strong base but a poor nucleophile, elimination is more likely to occur. When the reagent can act equally as both a base and a nucleophile, use other factors to decide whether substitution or elimination predominates. These include the degree of substitution about the reacting center (1° haloalkanes will not undergo E1 or S_N1 reactions, 3° haloalkanes will not undergo S_N2 reactions) or type of solvent (E1 and S_N1 reactions require polar protic solvents).

SOLUTION

(a) A 3° halide is heated with a strong base/good nucleophile. Elimination by an E2 reaction predominates to give 2-methyl-2-butene as the major product:

a strong base/good nucleophile favors E2/S_N2. However, 3° halides cannot undergo S_N2 reactions

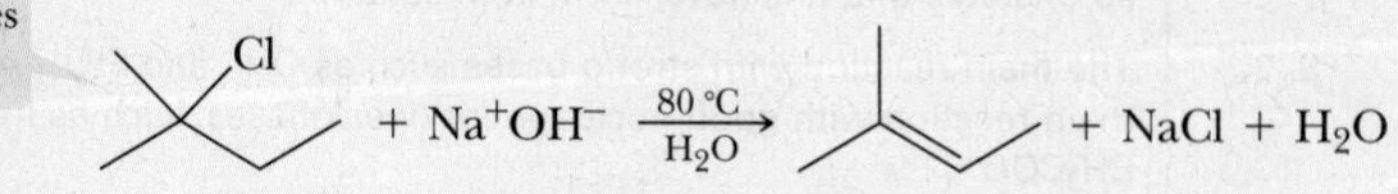

(b) Reaction of a 1° halide with triethylamine, a moderate nucleophile/weak base, gives substitution by an S_N2 reaction:

1° halides cannot undergo E1/S_N1 reactions. The base is not strong enough to undergo an E2 reaction

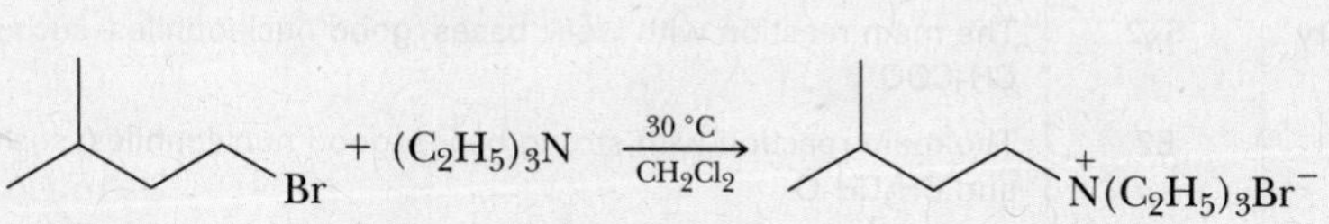

See problem 7.43

PROBLEM 7.8

Predict whether each reaction proceeds predominantly by substitution (S_N1 or S_N2) or elimination (E1 or E2) or whether the two compete, and write structural formulas for the major organic product(s):

(a) 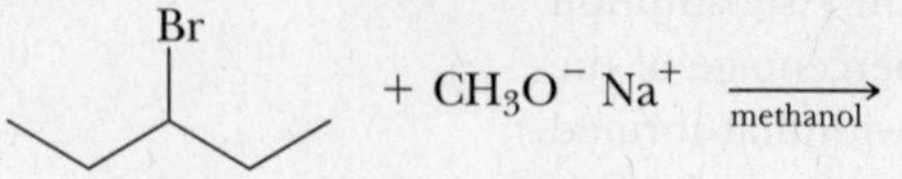

(b) 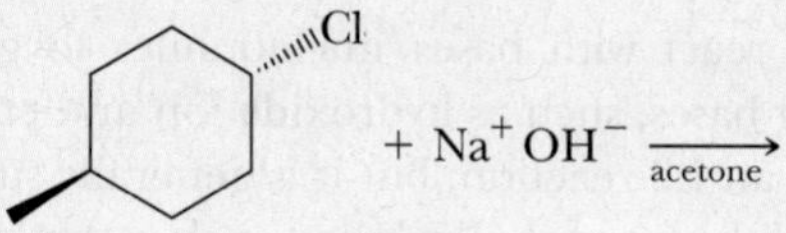

Chemical Connections 7B

THE EFFECT OF CHLOROFLUOROCARBON LEGISLATION ON ASTHMA SUFFERERS

The Montreal Protocol on Substances That Deplete the Ozone Layer was proposed in 1987 and enacted in 1989. As a result of this treaty, and its many revisions, the phaseout of CFCs and many other substances harmful to the ozone layer has been achieved in many industrialized nations. However, the Montreal Protocol provided exceptions for products in which the use of CFCs was essential because no viable alternatives existed. One such product was albuterol metered-dose inhalers, which use CFCs as propellants to deliver the drug and are used by asthma patients worldwide. In the United States, this exemption from the Montreal Protocol expired in December 2008, thanks to the Clean Air Act and the availability of another type of propellant known as hydrofluoroalkanes (HFAs). One drawback of HFA-equipped inhalers is that of cost; HFA inhalers cost three to six times as much as CFC-enabled inhalers because generic versions do not yet exist. This has sparked concerns from patients, physicians, and patients' rights groups over the ability of the nearly 23 million people in the United States who suffer from asthma to obtain treatment. Other differences include taste, smell, temperature of inhalant upon ejection, and effectiveness in colder climates and higher altitudes (HFAs are more effective under these conditions than CFCs). These practical differences are a result of the absence of chlorine in HFAs versus in CFCs, and are an excellent example of how changes in chemical structure can affect the properties of molecules and their ultimate applications in society.

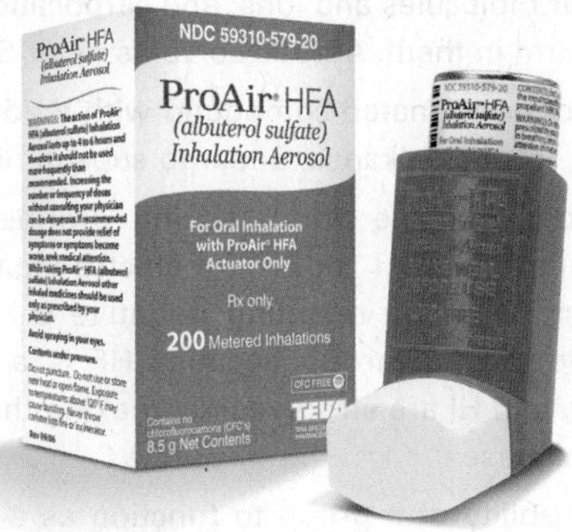

Courtesy Teva USA

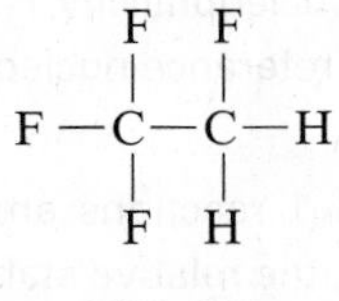

HFA-134a

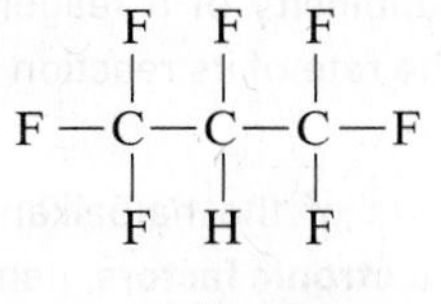

HFA-227

Hydrofluoroalkanes used in CFC-free medical inhalers

Question

Would you expect HFA-134a or HFA-227 to undergo an S_N1 reaction? An S_N2 reaction? Why or why not?

SUMMARY OF KEY QUESTIONS

7.1 How Are Haloalkanes Named?

- In the IUPAC system, halogen atoms are named as fluoro-, chloro-, bromo-, or iodo- substituents and are listed in alphabetical order with other substituents.
- In the common system, **haloalkanes** are named **alkyl halides**, where the name is derived by naming the alkyl group followed by the name of the halide as a separate word (e.g., methyl chloride).
- Compounds of the type CHX_3 are called **haloforms**.

7.2 What Are the Characteristic Reactions of Haloalkanes?

- Haloalkanes undergo **nucleophilic substitution** reactions and ***β*-elimination** reactions.
- In substitution reactions, the halogen is replaced by a reagent known as a **nucleophile**. A nucleophile is any molecule or ion with an unshared pair of electrons that can be donated to another atom or ion to form a new covalent bond; alternatively, a nucleophile is a Lewis base.
- In elimination reactions, the halogen and an adjacent hydrogen are removed to form an alkene.

7.3 What Are the Products of Nucleophilic Aliphatic Substitution Reactions?

- The product of a nucleophilic substitution reaction varies depending on the nucleophile used in the reaction. For example, when the nucleophile is hydroxide (HO^-), the product will be an alcohol (ROH).
- Nucleophilic substitution reactions can be used to transform haloalkanes into alcohols, ethers, thiols, sulfides, alkyl iodides, and alkyl ammonium ions, to name a few.

7.4 What Are the S_N2 and S_N1 Mechanisms for Nucleophilic Substitution?

- An **S_N2** reaction occurs in one step. The departure of the **leaving group** is assisted by the incoming nucleophile, and both nucleophile and leaving group are involved in the transition state. S_N2 reactions are stereoselective; reaction at a stereocenter proceeds with **inversion of configuration.**
- An **S_N1** reaction occurs in two steps. Step 1 is a slow, rate-determining ionization of the C—X bond to form a carbocation intermediate, followed in Step 2 by its rapid reaction with a nucleophile to complete the substitution. For S_N1 reactions taking place at a stereocenter, the major reaction occurs with **racemization.**

7.5 What Determines Whether S_N1 or S_N2 Predominates?

- The stability of the leaving group. The ability of a group to function as a leaving group is related to its stability as an anion. The most stable anions and the best leaving groups are the conjugate bases of strong acids.

- The **nucleophilicity** of a reagent. Nucleophilicity is measured by the rate of its reaction in a reference nucleophilic substitution.
- The structure of the haloalkane. S_N1 reactions are governed by **electronic factors**, namely, the relative stabilities of carbocation intermediates. S_N2 reactions are governed by **steric factors**, namely, the degree of crowding around the site of substitution.
- The nature of the solvent. **Protic solvents** contain —OH groups, interact strongly with polar molecules and ions, and are good solvents in which to form carbocations. Protic solvents favor S_N1 reactions. **Aprotic solvents** do not contain —OH groups. Common aprotic solvents are **dimethyl sulfoxide**, acetone, diethyl ether, and dichloromethane. Aprotic solvents do not interact as strongly with polar molecules and ions, and carbocations are less likely to form in them. Aprotic solvents favor S_N2 reactions.
- A nonhalogenated compound with a good leaving group can, like haloalkanes, undergo substitution reactions.
- Halogens make good leaving groups because either their size (as in I^- or Br^-) or electronegativity (Cl^-) helps to stabilize the resulting negative charge. F^- is not a good leaving group because HF is a weak acid. HCl, HBr, and HI are strong acids, making their halide anions weak bases.
- The ability of a group to function as a leaving group is related to how stable it is as an anion.
- The most stable anions and the best leaving groups are the conjugate bases of strong acids.

7.6 How Can S_N1 and S_N2 Be Predicted Based on Experimental Conditions?

- Predictions about the mechanism for a particular nucleophilic substitution reaction must be based on considerations of the structure of the haloalkane, the nucleophile, the leaving group, and the solvent.

7.7 What Are the Products of β-Elimination?

- **Dehydrohalogenation**, a type of β-elimination reaction, is the removal of H and X from adjacent carbon atoms, resulting in the formation of a carbon–carbon double bond.
- A β-elimination that gives the most highly substituted alkene is called **Zaitsev elimination**.

7.8 What Are the E1 and E2 Mechanisms for β-Elimination?

- An **E1** reaction occurs in two steps: breaking the C—X bond to form a carbocation intermediate, followed by the loss of an H^+ to form the alkene.
- An **E2** reaction occurs in one step: reaction with the base to remove an H^+, formation of the alkene, and departure of the leaving group, all occurring simultaneously.

7.9 When Do Nucleophilic Substitution and β-Elimination Compete?

- Many of the nucleophiles we have examined—for example, hydroxide ion and alkoxide ions—are also strong bases. As a result, nucleophilic substitution and β-elimination often compete with each other, and the ratio of products formed by these reactions depends on the relative rates of the two reactions.

QUICK QUIZ

Answer true or false to the following questions to assess your general knowledge of the concepts in this chapter. If you have difficulty with any of them, you should review the appropriate section in the chapter (shown in parentheses) before attempting the more challenging end-of-chapter problems.

1. An S_N1 reaction can result in two products that are stereoisomers. (7.4)
2. In naming halogenated compounds, "haloalkane" is the IUPAC form of the name while "alkyl halide" is the common form of the name. (7.1)
3. A substitution reaction results in the formation of an alkene. (7.3)
4. Ethoxide ion ($CH_3CH_2O^-$) can act as a base and as a nucleophile in its reaction with bromocyclohexane. (7.2)
5. The rate law of the E2 reaction is dependent on just the haloalkane concentration. (7.8)
6. The mechanism of the S_N1 reaction involves the formation of a carbocation intermediate. (7.4)
7. Polar protic solvents are required for E1 or S_N1 reactions to occur. (7.9)
8. OH^- is a better leaving group than Cl^-. (7.5)
9. When naming haloalkanes with more than one type of halogen, numbering priority is given to the halogen with the higher mass. (7.1)

10. S_N2 reactions prefer good nucleophiles, while S_N1 reactions proceed with most any nucleophile. (7.5)
11. The stronger the base, the better is the leaving group. (7.5)
12. S_N2 reactions are more likely to occur with 2° haloalkanes than with 1° haloalkanes. (7.9)
13. A solvolysis reaction is a reaction performed without solvent. (7.4)
14. The degree of substitution at the reaction center affects the rate of an S_N1 reaction but not an S_N2 reaction. (7.5)
15. A reagent must possess a negative charge to react as a nucleophile. (7.3)
16. Elimination reactions favor the formation of the more substituted alkene. (7.7)
17. The best leaving group is one that is unstable as an anion. (7.5)
18. In the S_N2 reaction, the nucleophile attacks the carbon from the side opposite that of the leaving group. (7.4)
19. Only haloalkanes can undergo substitution reactions. (7.5)
20. All of the following are polar aprotic solvents: acetone, DMSO, ethanol. (7.5)

Answers: (1) T (2) T (3) F (4) T (5) F (6) T (7) T (8) F (9) F (10) T (11) F (12) F (13) F (14) F (15) F (16) T (17) F (18) T (19) F (20) F

Detailed explanations for many of these answers can be found in the accompanying Solutions Manual.

KEY REACTIONS

1. Nucleophilic Aliphatic Substitution: S_N2 (Section 7.4A)

S_N2 reactions occur in one step, and both the nucleophile and the leaving group are involved in the transition state of the rate-determining step. The nucleophile may be negatively charged or neutral. S_N2 reactions result in an inversion of configuration at the reaction center. They are accelerated in polar aprotic solvents, compared with polar protic solvents. S_N2 reactions are governed by steric factors, namely, the degree of crowding around the site of reaction.

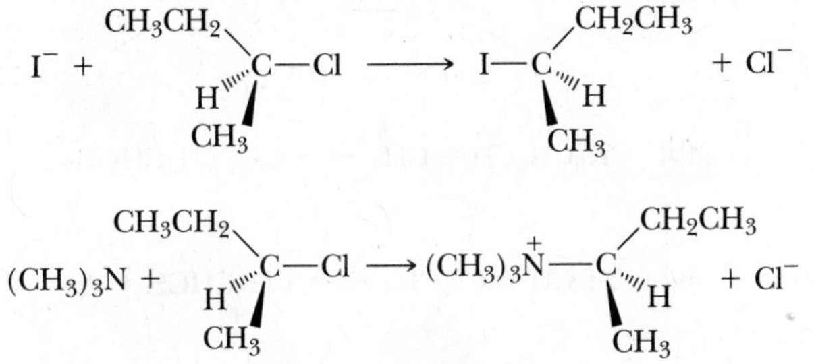

2. Nucleophilic Aliphatic Substitution: S_N1 (Section 7.4B)

An S_N1 reaction occurs in two steps. Step 1 is a slow, rate-determining ionization of the C—X bond to form a carbocation intermediate, followed in Step 2 by its rapid reaction with a nucleophile to complete the substitution. Reaction at a stereocenter gives a racemic product. S_N1 reactions are governed by electronic factors, namely, the relative stabilities of carbocation intermediates:

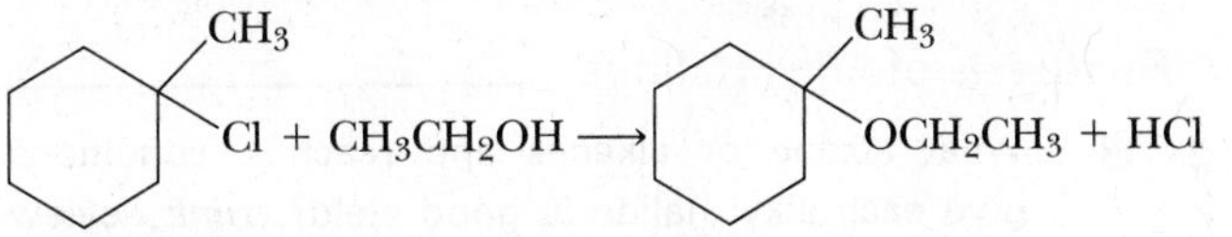

3. β-Elimination: E1 (Section 7.8A)

E1 reactions involve the elimination of atoms or groups of atoms from adjacent carbons. Reaction occurs in two steps and involves the formation of a carbocation intermediate:

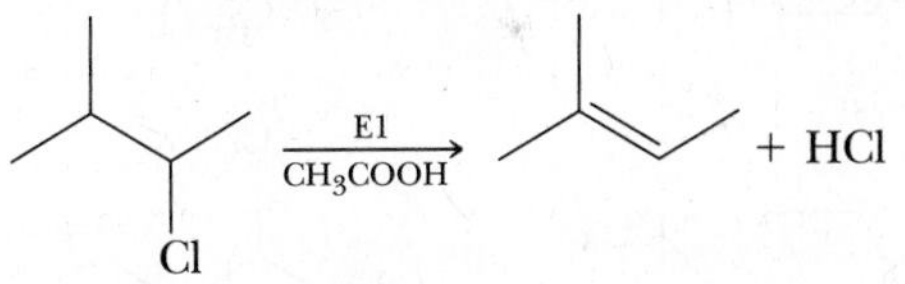

4. β-Elimination: E2 (Section 7.8B)

An E2 reaction occurs in one step: reaction with base to remove a hydrogen, formation of the alkene, and departure of the leaving group, all occurring simultaneously:

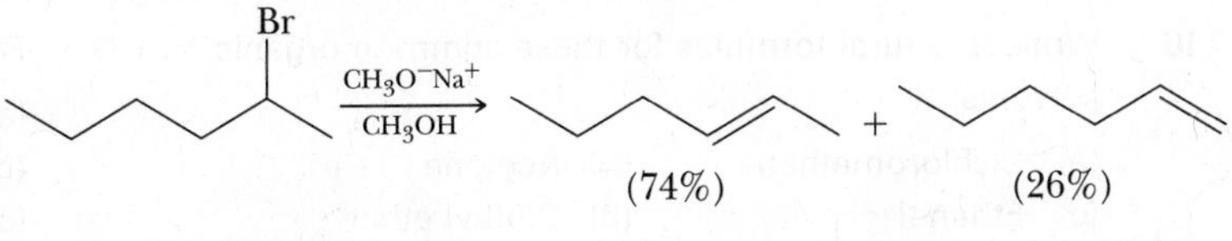

PROBLEMS

A problem marked with an asterisk indicates an applied "real-world" problem. Answers to problems whose numbers are printed in blue are given in Appendix D.

Section 7.1 Nomenclature

7.9 Write the IUPAC name for each compound: **(See Example 7.1)**

(a) $CH_2{=}CF_2$

(b) 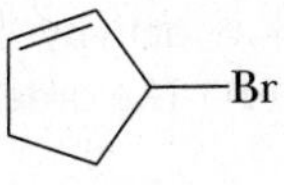

(c) 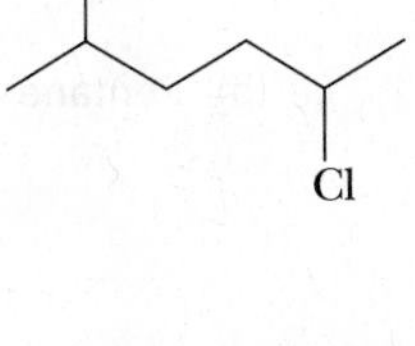

(d) $Cl(CH_2)_6Cl$

(e) CF_2Cl_2

(f) 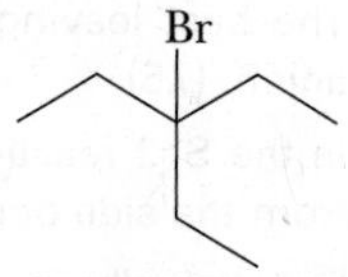

7.10 Write the IUPAC name for each compound (be certain to include a designation of configuration, where appropriate, in your answer): **(See Example 7.1)**

(a) 

(b) 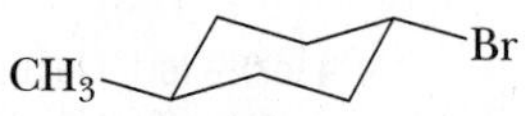

(c) 

(d) 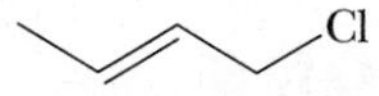

(e) 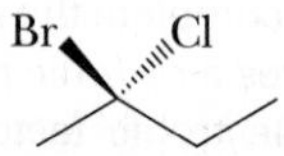

(f) 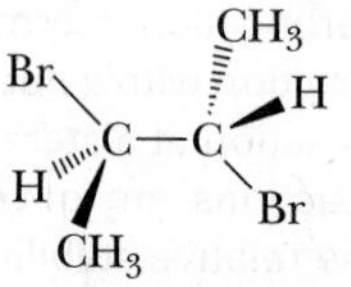

7.11 Draw a structural formula for each compound (given are IUPAC names): **(See Example 7.1)**

(a) 3-Bromopropene
(b) (*R*)-2-Chloropentane
(c) meso-3,4-Dibromohexane
(d) *trans*-1-Bromo-3-isopropylcyclohexane
(e) 1,2-Dichloroethane
(f) Bromocyclobutane

7.12 Draw a structural formula for each compound (given are common names): **(See Example 7.1)**

(a) Isopropyl chloride
(b) *sec*-Butyl bromide
(c) Allyl iodide
(d) Methylene chloride
(e) Chloroform
(f) *tert*-Butyl chloride
(g) Isobutyl chloride

7.13 Which compounds are 2° alkyl halides?

(a) Isobutyl chloride
(b) 2-Iodooctane
(c) *trans*-1-Chloro-4-methylcyclohexane

Synthesis of Alkyl Halides

7.14 What alkene or alkenes and reaction conditions give each alkyl halide in good yield? (*Hint*: Review Chapter 5.) **(See Example 5.2)**

(a) 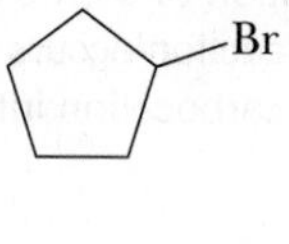

(b) CH_3
$CH_3CCH_2CH_2CH_3$
Br

(c) 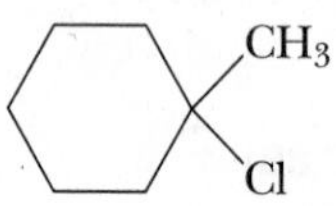

(d) 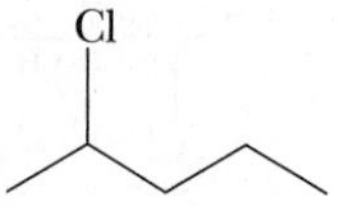
racemic

7.15 Show reagents and conditions that bring about these conversions: **(See Example 5.2)**

(a) 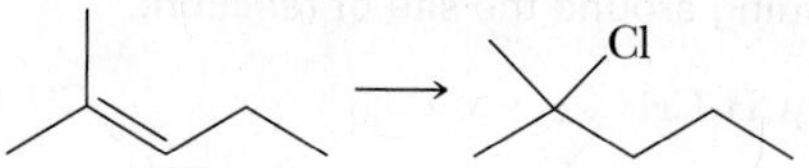

(b) $CH_3CH_2CH{=}CH_2 \longrightarrow CH_3CH_2CHICH_3$ (I on C-2)

(c) $CH_3CH{=}CHCH_3 \longrightarrow CH_3CHClCH_2CH_3$ (Cl on C-2)

(d) 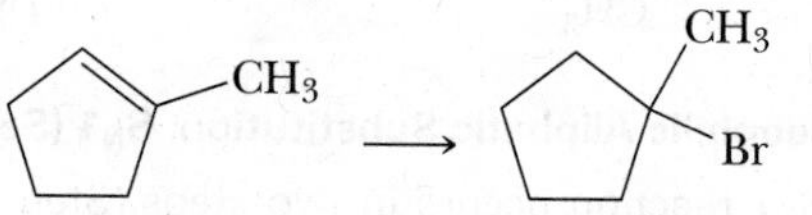

Sections 7.2–7.6 Nucleophilic Aliphatic Substitution

7.16 Write structural formulas for these common organic solvents:

(a) Dichloromethane
(b) Acetone
(c) Ethanol
(d) Diethyl ether
(e) Dimethyl sulfoxide
(f) *tert*-Butyl alcohol

7.17 Arrange these protic solvents in order of increasing polarity:

(a) H_2O
(b) CH_3CH_2OH
(c) CH_3OH

7.18 Arrange these aprotic solvents in order of increasing polarity:

(a) Acetone
(b) Pentane
(c) Diethyl ether

7.19 From each pair, select the better nucleophile:

(a) H_2O or OH^-
(b) CH_3COO^- or OH^-
(c) CH_3SH or CH_3S^-

7.20 Which statements are true for S_N2 reactions of haloalkanes? **(See Example 7.4)**

(a) Both the haloalkane and the nucleophile are involved in the transition state.
(b) The reaction proceeds with inversion of configuration at the substitution center.
(c) The reaction proceeds with retention of optical activity.
(d) The order of reactivity is 3° > 2° > 1° > methyl.

(e) The nucleophile must have an unshared pair of electrons and bear a negative charge.

(f) The greater the nucleophilicity of the nucleophile, the greater is the rate of reaction.

7.21 Complete these S_N2 reactions: **(See Examples 7.3, 7.5)**

(a) $Na^+I^- + CH_3CH_2CH_2Cl \xrightarrow{\text{acetone}}$

(b) 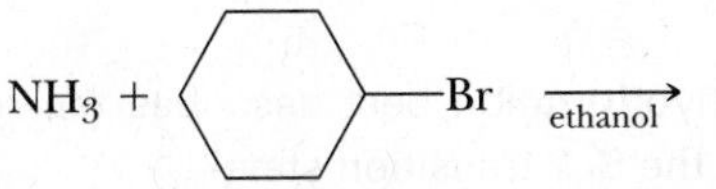

(c) $CH_3CH_2O^-Na^+ + CH_2{=}CHCH_2Cl \xrightarrow{\text{ethanol}}$

7.22 Complete these S_N2 reactions: **(See Examples 7.3, 7.5)**

(a) 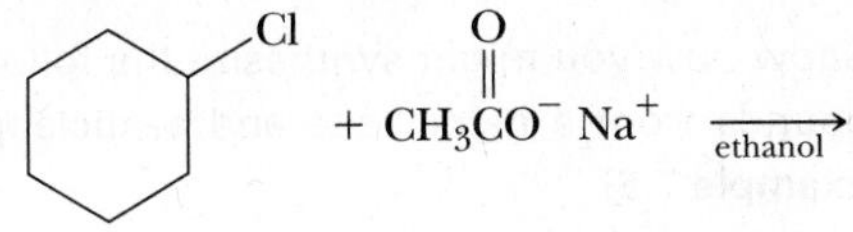

(b) $CH_3\overset{\displaystyle I}{\overset{|}{C}}HCH_2CH_3 + CH_3CH_2S^-Na^+ \xrightarrow{\text{acetone}}$

(c) $CH_3\overset{\displaystyle CH_3}{\overset{|}{C}}HCH_2CH_2Br + Na^+I^- \xrightarrow{\text{acetone}}$

(d) $(CH_3)_3N + CH_3I \xrightarrow{\text{acetone}}$

(e) 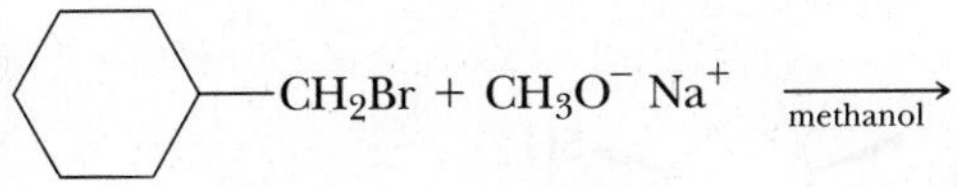

(f) 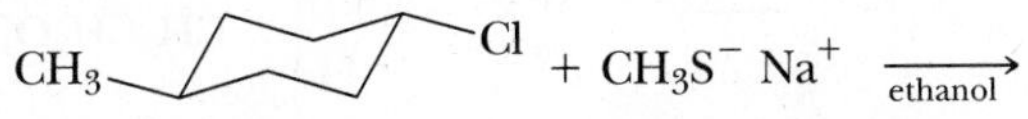

(g) 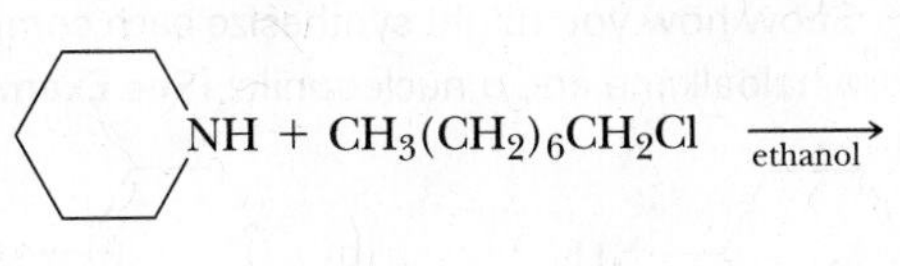

(h) 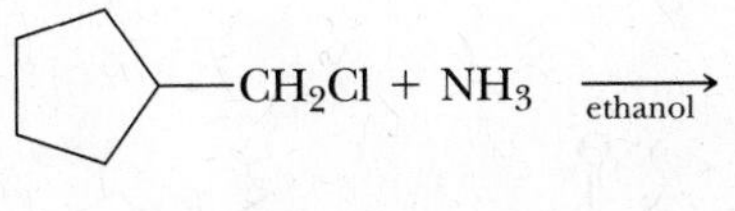

7.23 You were told that each reaction in Problem 7.22 proceeds by an S_N2 mechanism. Suppose you were not told the mechanism. Describe how you could conclude, from the structure of the haloalkane, the nucleophile, and the solvent, that each reaction is in fact an S_N2 reaction. **(See Examples 7.4, 7.5)**

7.24 In the following reactions, a haloalkane is treated with a compound that has two nucleophilic sites. Select the more nucleophilic site in each part, and show the product of each S_N2 reaction:

(a) $HOCH_2CH_2NH_2 + CH_3I \xrightarrow{\text{ethanol}}$

(b) 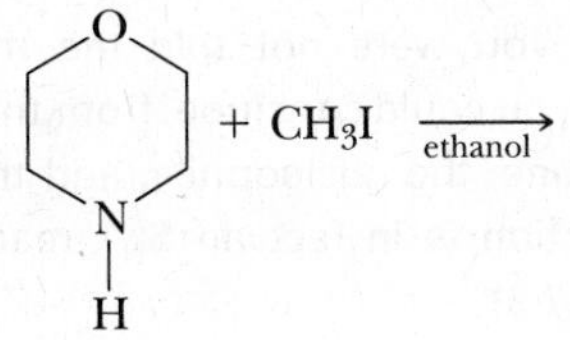

(c) $HOCH_2CH_2SH + CH_3I \xrightarrow{\text{ethanol}}$

7.25 Which statements are true for S_N1 reactions of haloalkanes? **(See Example 7.5)**

(a) Both the haloalkane and the nucleophile are involved in the transition state of the rate-determining step.

(b) The reaction at a stereocenter proceeds with retention of configuration.

(c) The reaction at a stereocenter proceeds with loss of optical activity.

(d) The order of reactivity is 3° > 2° > 1° > methyl.

(e) The greater the steric crowding around the reactive center, the lower is the rate of reaction.

(f) The rate of reaction is greater with good nucleophiles compared with poor nucleophiles.

7.26 Draw a structural formula for the product of each S_N1 reaction: **(See Examples 7.3, 7.5)**

(a) $CH_3\overset{\displaystyle Cl}{\overset{|}{C}}HCH_2CH_3 + CH_3CH_2OH \xrightarrow{\text{ethanol}}$
S enantiomer

(b) 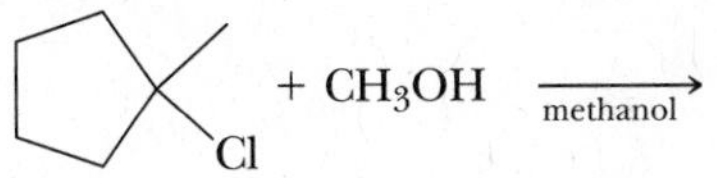

(c) $CH_3\underset{\displaystyle CH_3}{\overset{\displaystyle CH_3}{CCl}} + CH_3\overset{\displaystyle O}{\overset{\|}{C}}OH \xrightarrow{\text{acetic acid}}$

(d) 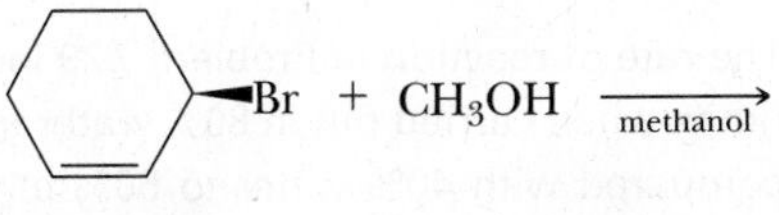

(e) 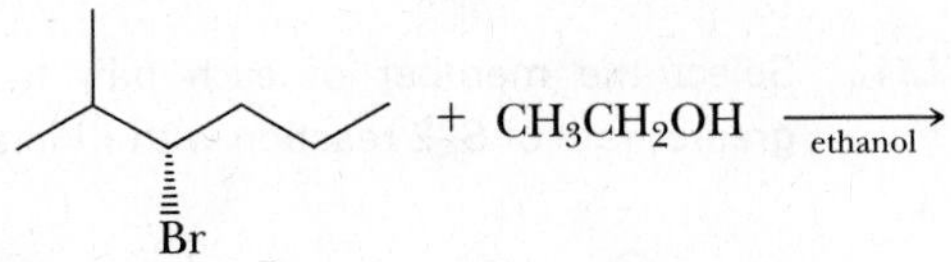

(f) 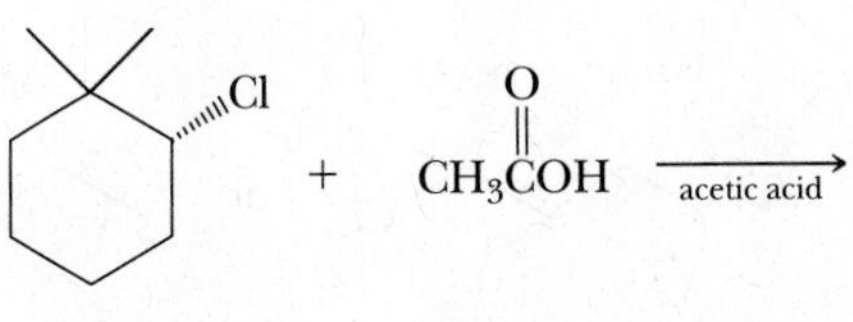

7.27 You were told that each substitution reaction in Problem 7.26 proceeds by an S_N1 mechanism. Suppose that you were not told the mechanism. Describe how you could conclude, from the structure of the haloalkane, the nucleophile, and the solvent, that each reaction is in fact an S_N1 reaction. **(See Examples 7.4, 7.5)**

7.28 Select the member of each pair that undergoes nucleophilic substitution in aqueous ethanol more rapidly: **(See Example 7.5)**

(a) 

or 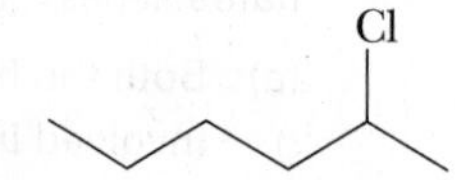

(b) 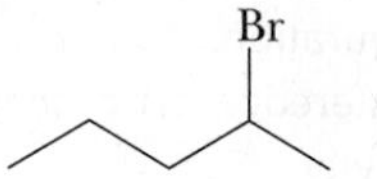

or 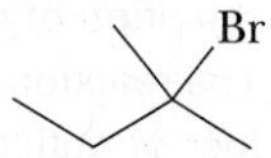

(c) 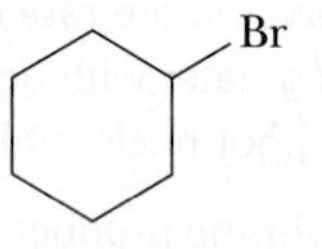

or 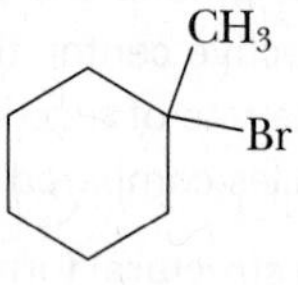

7.29 Propose a mechanism for the formation of the products (but not their relative percentages) in this reaction:

$$\mathrm{CH_3\overset{CH_3}{\underset{CH_3}{C}}Cl} \xrightarrow[25\ ^\circ C]{20\%H_2O,\ 80\%CH_3CH_2OH}$$

$$\underbrace{\mathrm{CH_3\overset{CH_3}{\underset{CH_3}{C}}OCH_2CH_3} + \mathrm{CH_3\overset{CH_3}{\underset{CH_3}{C}}OH}}_{85\%} + \underset{15\%}{\mathrm{CH_3\overset{CH_3}{C}{=}CH_2}} + HCl$$

7.30 The rate of reaction in Problem 7.29 increases by 140 times when carried out in 80% water to 20% ethanol, compared with 40% water to 60% ethanol. Account for this difference.

7.31 Select the member of each pair that shows the greater rate of S_N2 reaction with KI in acetone:

(a) 

or 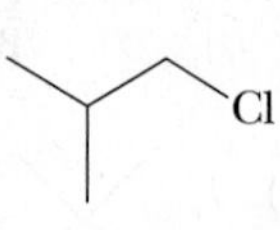

(b) 

or 

(c) 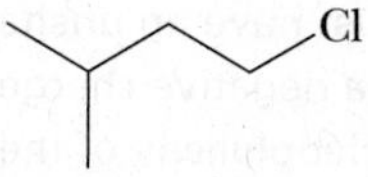

or 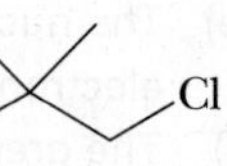

(d) 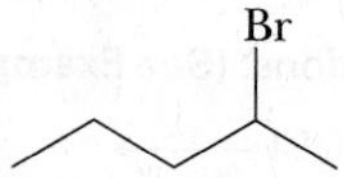

or 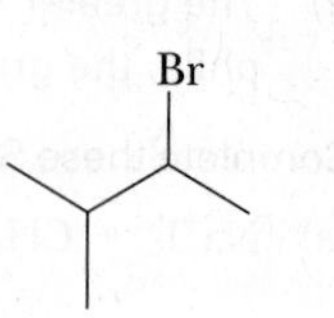

7.32 What hybridization best describes the reacting carbon in the S_N2 transition state?

7.33 Haloalkenes such as vinyl bromide, $CH_2{=}CHBr$, undergo neither S_N1 nor S_N2 reactions. What factors account for this lack of reactivity?

7.34 Show how you might synthesize the following compounds from a haloalkane and a nucleophile: **(See Example 7.5)**

(a) 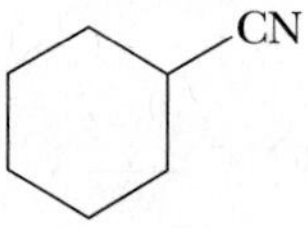

(b) 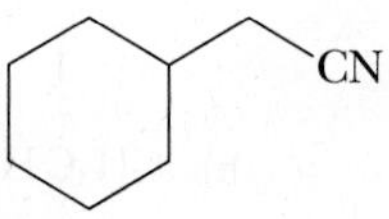

(c) 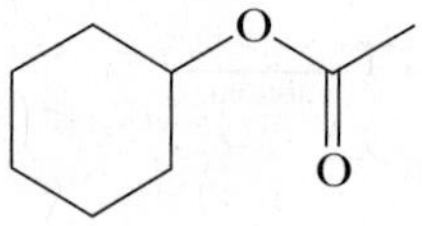

(d) 

(e) 

(f) 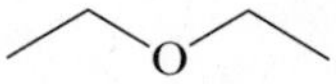

(g) 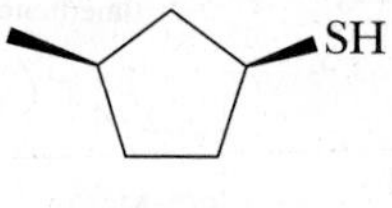

(h) 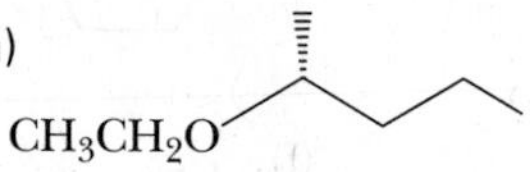

7.35 Show how you might synthesize each compound from a haloalkane and a nucleophile: **(See Example 7.5)**

(a) 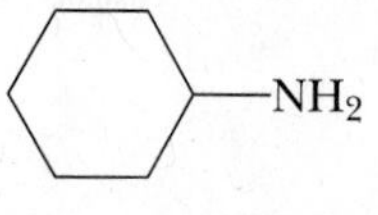

(b) 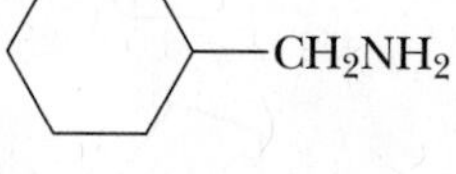

(c) 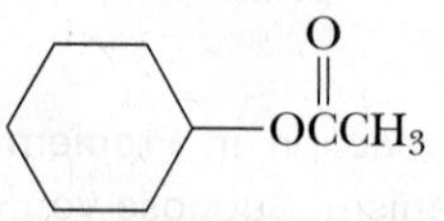

(d) 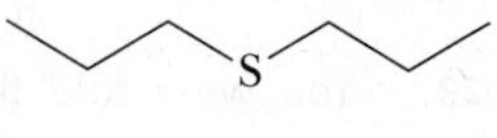

(e) 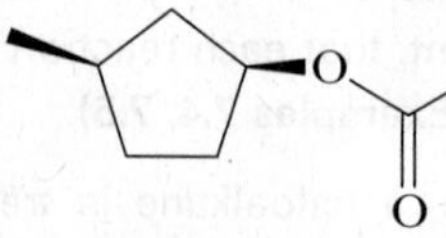

(f) $(CH_3CH_2CH_2CH_2)_2O$

Sections 7.7–7.8 β-Eliminations

7.36 Draw structural formulas for the alkene(s) formed by treating each of the following haloalkanes with sodium ethoxide in ethanol. Assume that elimination is by an E2 mechanism. Where two alkenes are possible, use Zaitsev's rule to predict which alkene is the major product: **(See Examples 7.6, 7.7)**

(a) 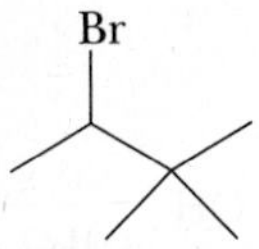

(b) 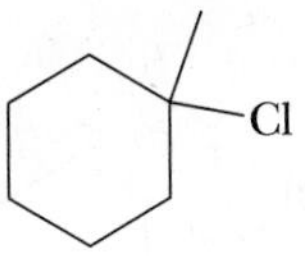

(c) 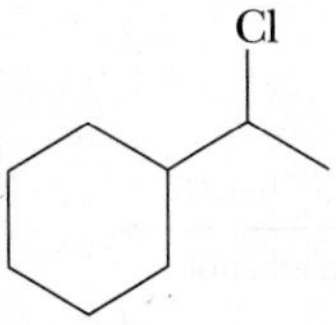

(d) 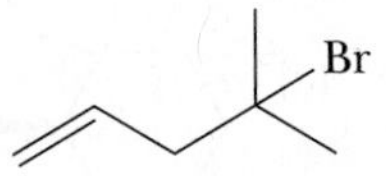

7.37 Which of the following haloalkanes undergo dehydrohalogenation to give alkenes that do not show *cis–trans* isomerism? **(See Examples 7.6, 7.7)**

(a) 2-Chloropentane (b) 2-Chlorobutane
(c) Chlorocyclohexane (d) Isobutyl chloride

7.38 How many isomers, including *cis–trans* isomers, are possible for the major product of dehydrohalogenation of each of the following haloalkanes? **(See Examples 7.6, 7.7)**

(a) 3-Chloro-3-methylhexane
(b) 3-Bromohexane

7.39 What haloalkane might you use as a starting material to produce each of the following alkenes in high yield and uncontaminated by isomeric alkenes?

(a) 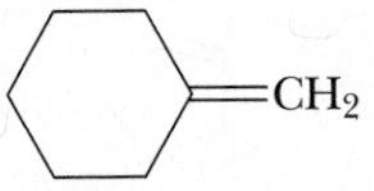

(b) $CH_3\overset{CH_3}{\overset{|}{C}}HCH_2CH{=}CH_2$

7.40 For each of the following alkenes, draw structural formulas of all chloroalkanes that undergo dehydrohalogenation when treated with KOH to give that alkene as the major product (for some parts, only one chloroalkane gives the desired alkene as the major product; for other parts, two chloroalkanes may work):

(a) 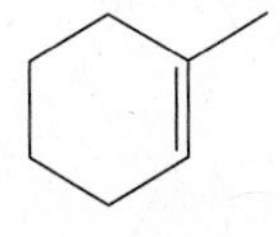

(b) 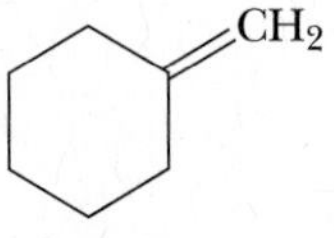

(c) 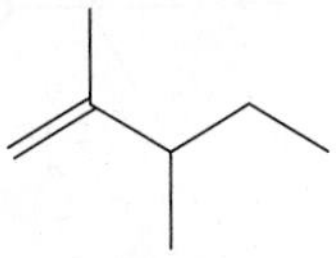

(d) 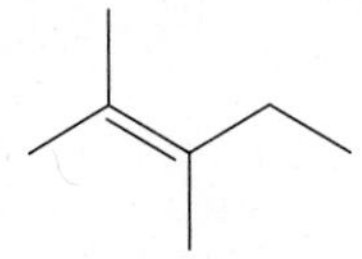

(e) 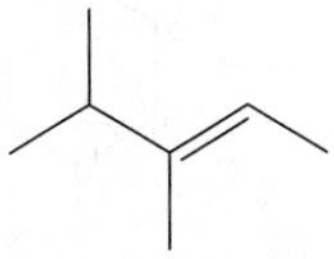

(f) 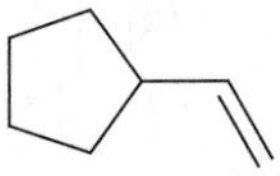

7.41 When *cis*-4-chlorocyclohexanol is treated with sodium hydroxide in ethanol, it gives only the substitution product *trans*-1,4-cyclohexanediol (1). Under the same experimental conditions, *trans*-4-chlorocyclohexanol gives 3-cyclohexenol (2) and product (3):

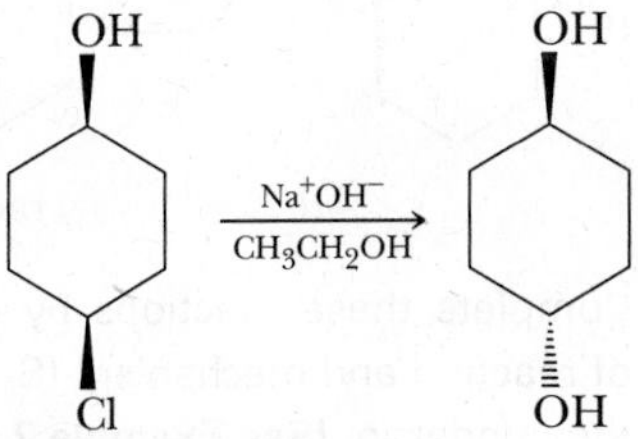

cis-4-Chloro-cyclohexanol (1)

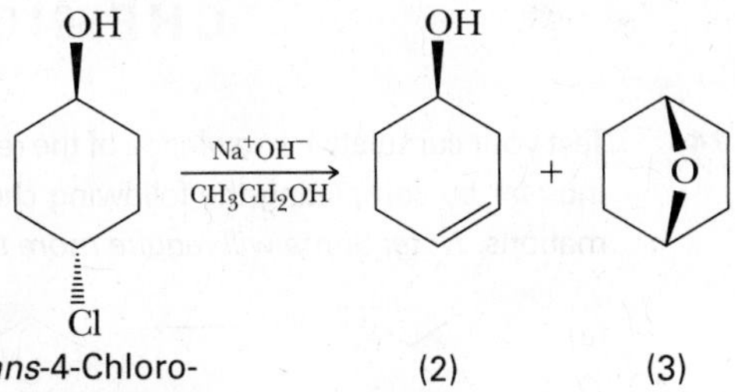

trans-4-Chloro-cyclohexanol (2) (3)

(a) Propose a mechanism for the formation of product (1), and account for its configuration.

(b) Propose a mechanism for the formation of product (2).

(c) Account for the fact that the product (3) is formed from the *trans* isomer, but not from the *cis* isomer.

Section 7.9 Synthesis and Predict the Product

7.42 Show how to convert the given starting material into the desired product (note that some syntheses require only one step, whereas others require two or more steps):

(a)

(b) 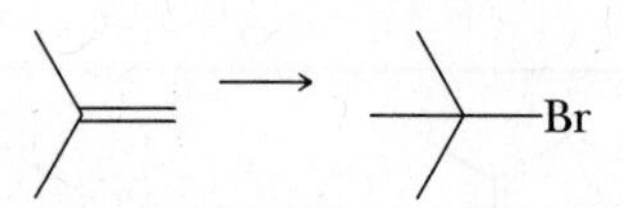

(c) 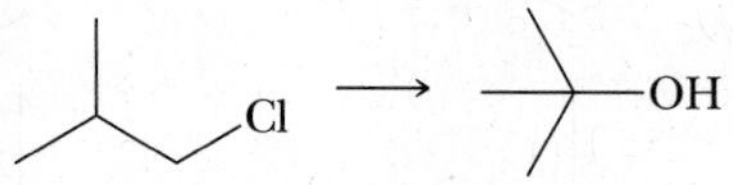

(d) 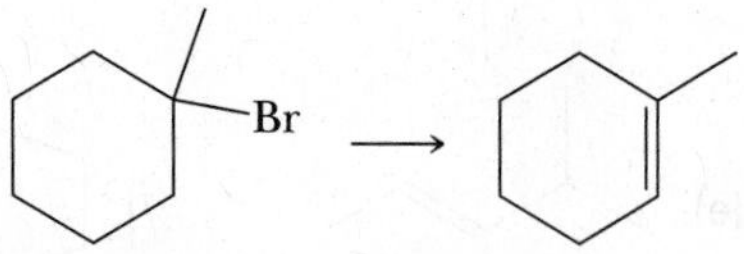

(e) 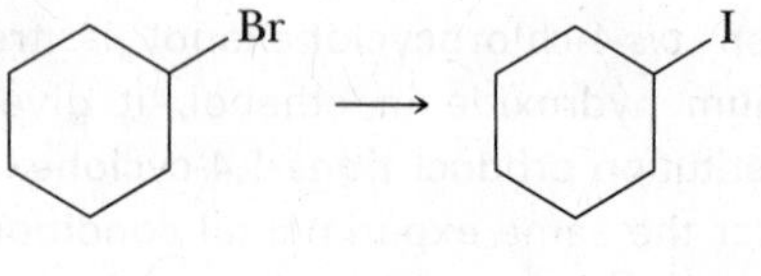

(f) 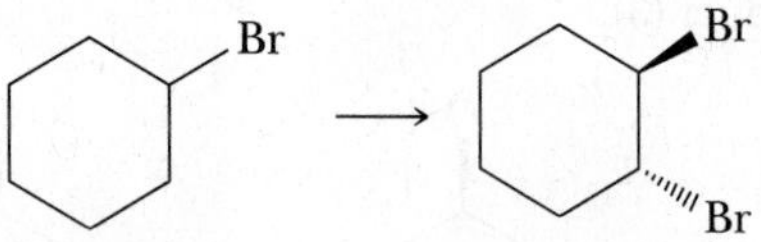

racemic

7.43 Complete these reactions by determining the type of reaction and mechanism (S_N1, S_N2, E1, or E2) that they undergo. **(See Example 7.8)**

(a) 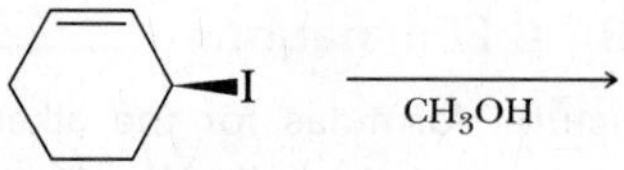

(b) 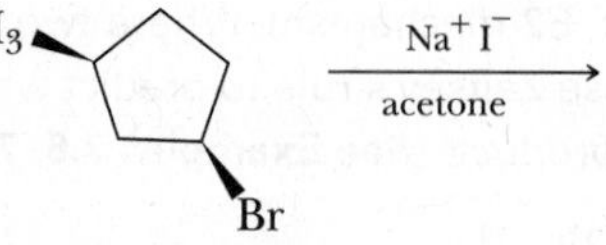

(c) 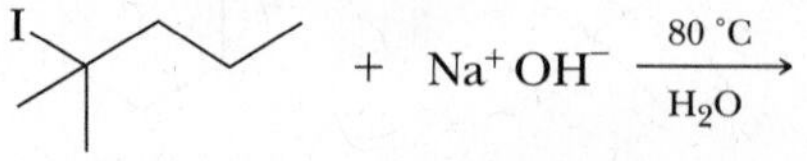

(d) 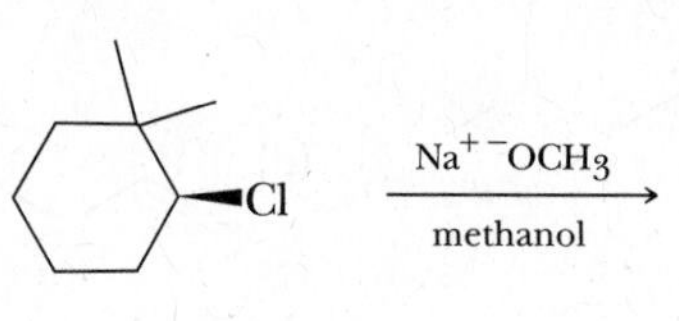

(e) 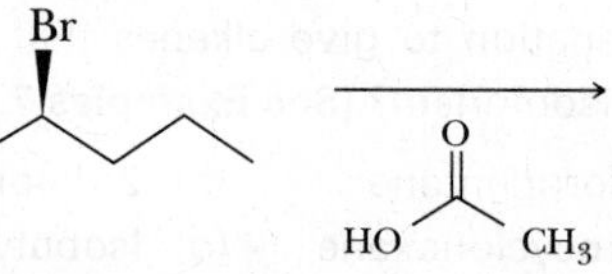

(acetic acid)

(f) 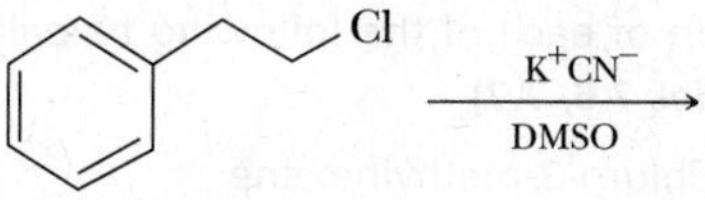

CHEMICAL TRANSFORMATIONS

7.44 Test your cumulative knowledge of the reactions learned thus far by completing the following chemical transformations. *Note: Some will require more than one step.*

(a) 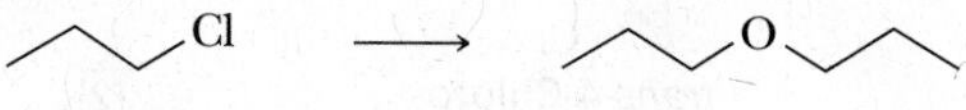

(b) 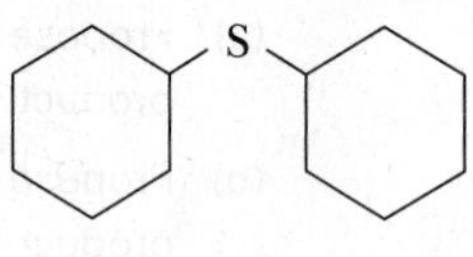

(c) 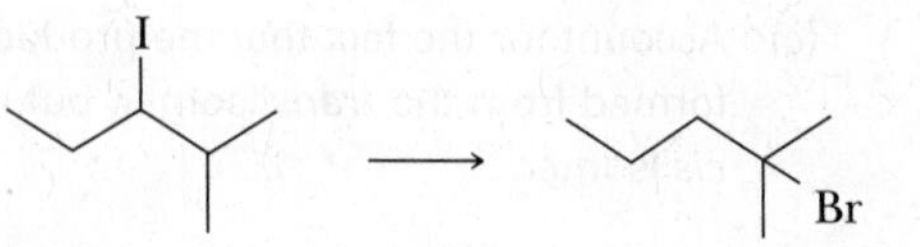

(d) 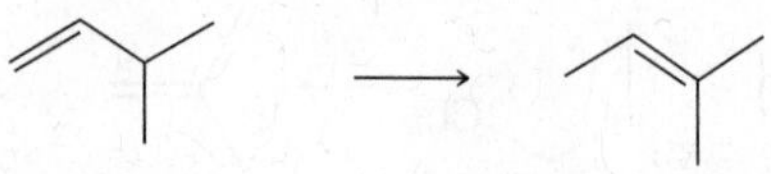

(e) 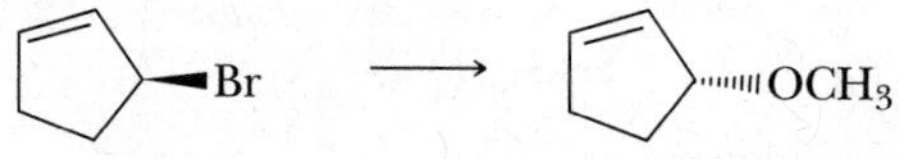

(f) 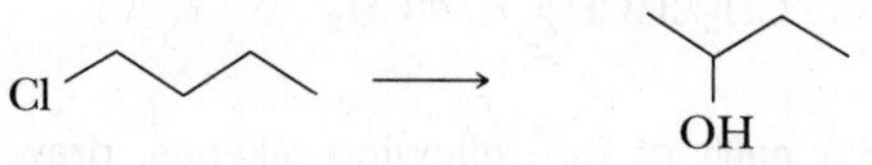

racemic

(g) 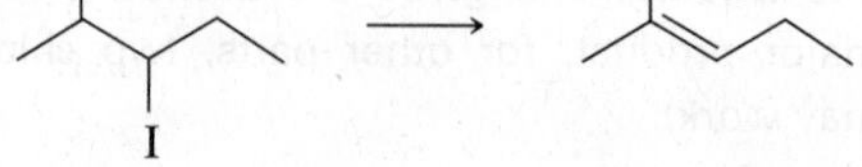

(h) 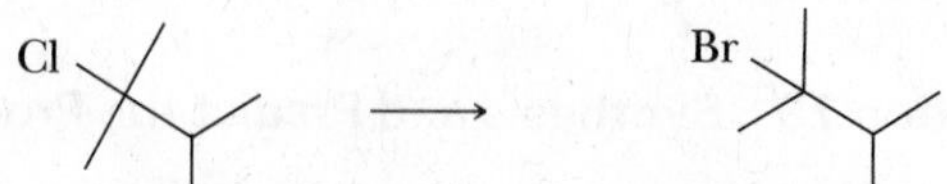

(i) 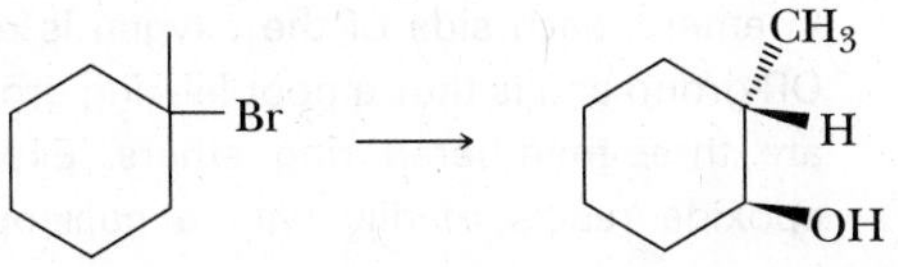
racemic

(j) 

(k) 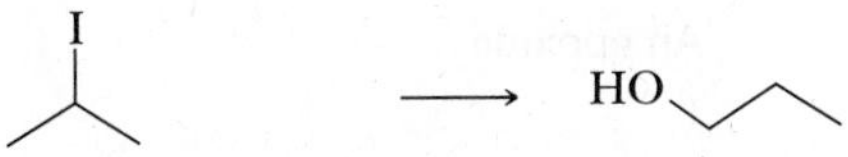

(l) 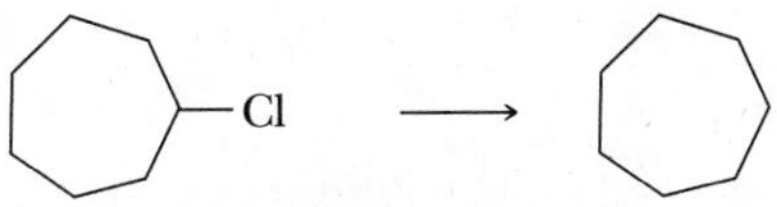

(m) 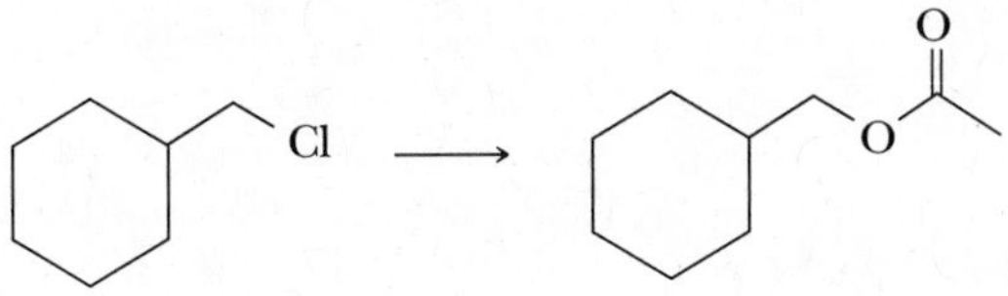

(n) 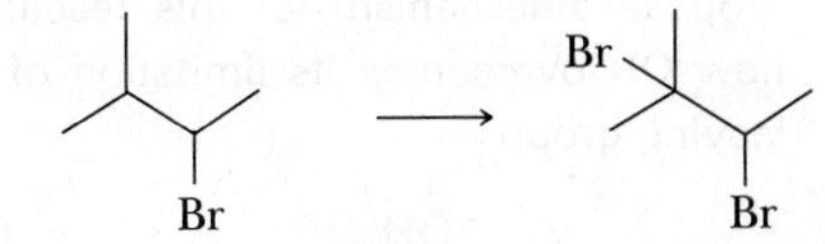
racemic

(o) 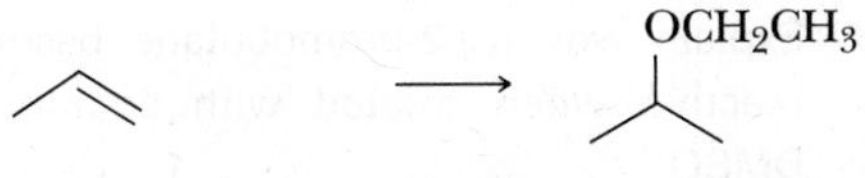

(p) 

(q) 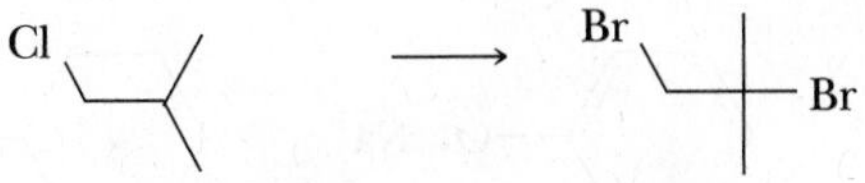

(r) 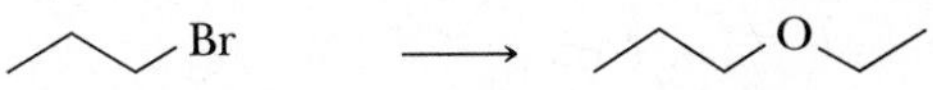

LOOKING AHEAD

7.45 The Williamson ether synthesis involves treating a haloalkane with a metal alkoxide. Following are two reactions intended to give benzyl *tert*-butyl ether. One reaction gives the ether in good yield, the other does not. Which reaction gives the ether? What is the product of the other reaction, and how do you account for its formation?

(a) 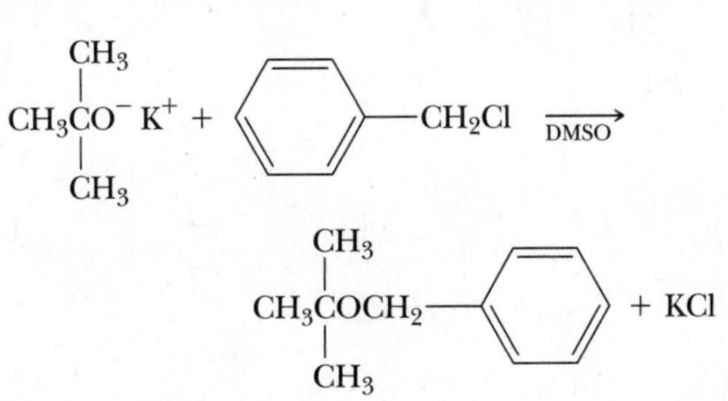

(b) 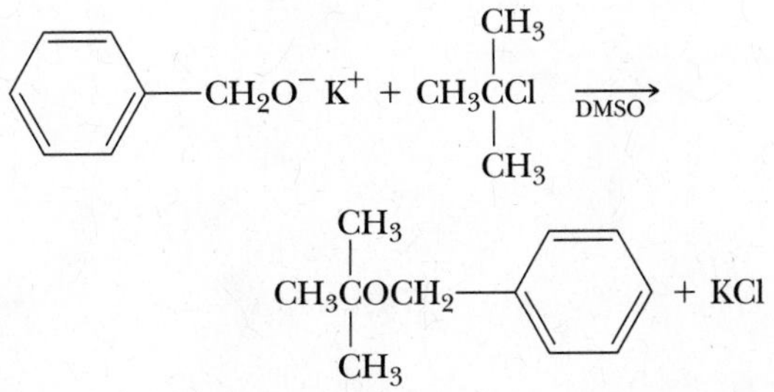

7.46 The following ethers can, in principle, be synthesized by two different combinations of haloalkane or halocycloalkane and metal alkoxide. Show one combination that forms ether bond (1) and another that forms ether bond (2). Which combination gives the higher yield of ether?

(a) 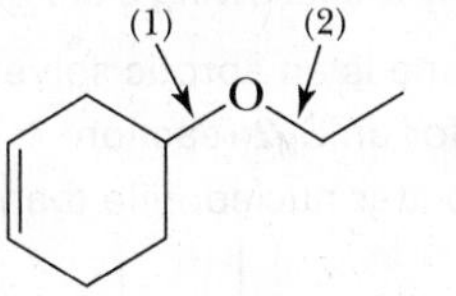

(b) 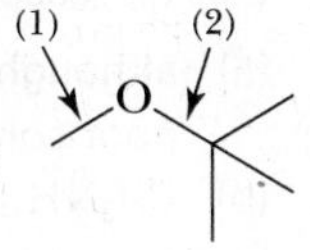

(c) 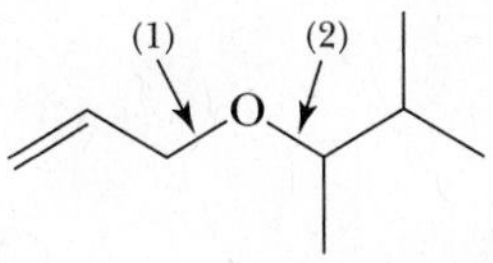

7.47 Propose a mechanism for this reaction:

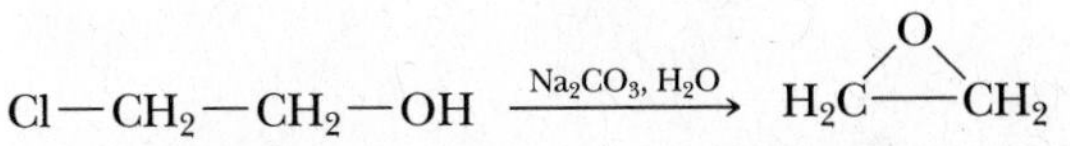

2-Chloroethanol Ethylene oxide

7.48 An OH group is a poor leaving group, and yet substitution occurs readily in the following reaction.

Propose amechanism for this reaction that shows how OH overcomes its limitation of being a poor leaving group.

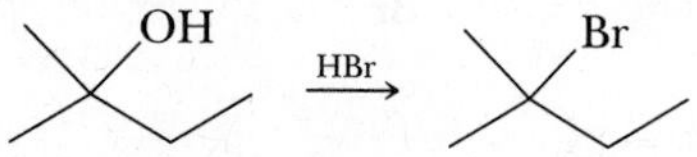

7.49 Explain why (*S*)-2-bromobutane becomes optically inactive when treated with sodium bromide in DMSO:

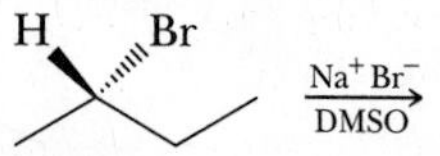

optically inactive

optically active

7.50 Explain why phenoxide is a much poorer nucleophile and weaker base than cyclohexoxide:

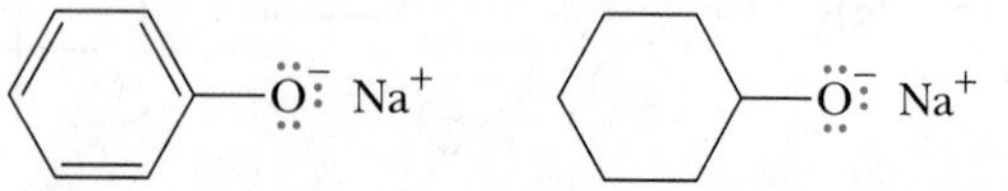

Sodium phenoxide Sodium cyclohexoxide

7.51 In ethers, each side of the oxygen is essentially an OR group and is thus a poor leaving group. Epoxides are three-membered ring ethers. Explain why an epoxide reacts readily with a nucleophile despite being an ether.

$$R{-}O{-}R \; + \; :Nu^- \longrightarrow \text{no reaction}$$

An ether

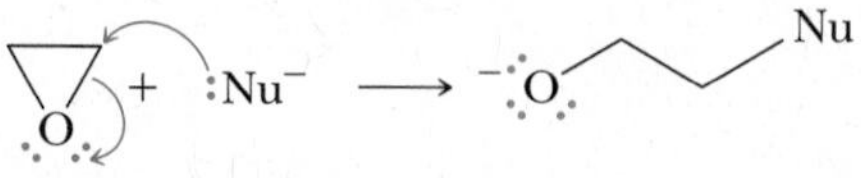

An epoxide

GROUP LEARNING ACTIVITIES

7.52 Discuss and come up with examples of the following:

(a) a negatively charged reagent that is a weak base
(b) a negatively charged reagent that is a poor nucleophile
(c) aside from chloride, bromide, or iodide, a negatively charged reagent that is a good leaving group

7.53 Discuss reasons why the following statements are true:

(a) although hexane is an aprotic solvent, it is a poor solvent for an S_N2 reaction
(b) $CH_3\ddot{N}H$, is a better nucleophile than $CH_3\ddot{O}:^-$, but

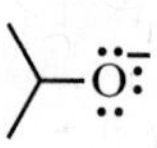 is better than 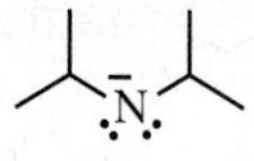

7.54 Discuss ways that you could speed up the following reactions without changing the products formed.

(a)

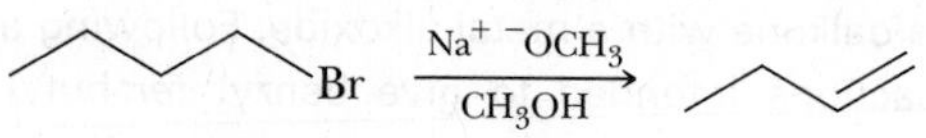

(b)

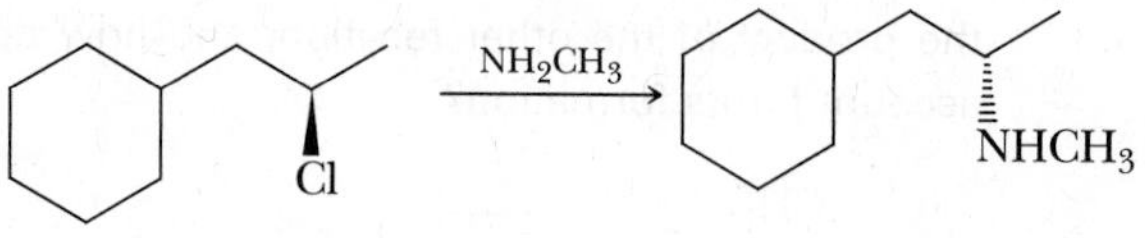

08

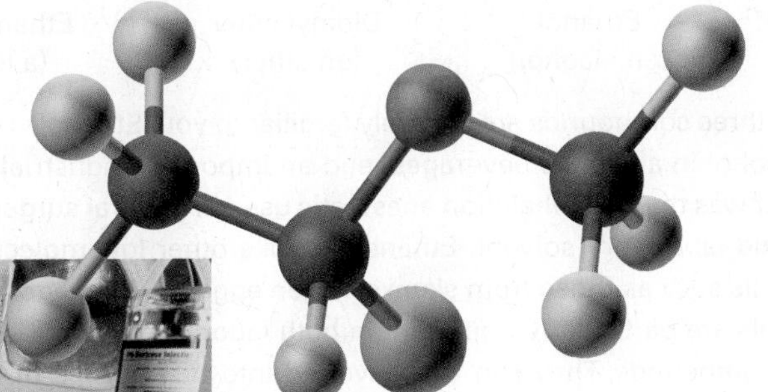

Alcohols, Ethers, and Thiols

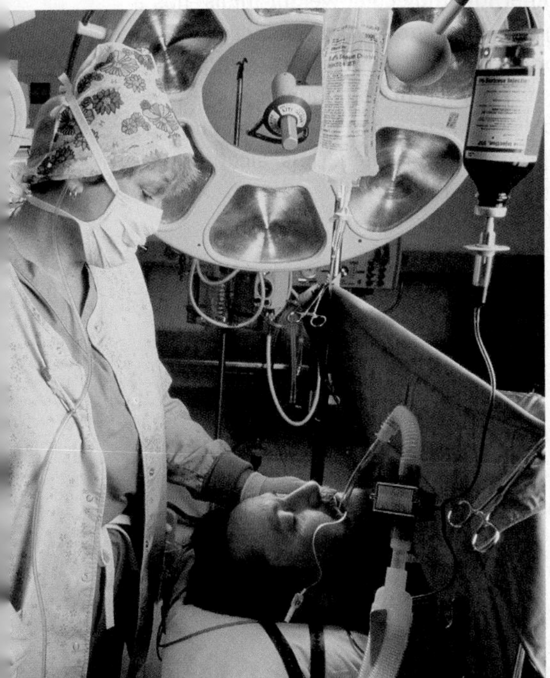

An anesthesiologist administers isoflurane to a patient before surgery. The discovery that inhaling ethers could make a patient insensitive to pain revolutionized the practice of medicine. Inset: A model of isoflurane, $CF_3CHClOCHF_2$, a halogenated ether widely used as an inhalation anesthetic in both human and veterinary medicine. (Alan Levenson/Stone/Getty Images)

KEY QUESTIONS

8.1 What Are Alcohols?

8.2 What Are the Characteristic Reactions of Alcohols?

8.3 What Are Ethers?

8.4 What Are Epoxides?

8.5 What Are Thiols?

8.6 What Are the Characteristic Reactions of Thiols?

HOW TO

8.1 How to Name Cyclic Alcohols

8.2 How to Predict Relative Boiling Points of Compounds of Similar Molecular Weight

8.3 How to Predict the Position of Equilibrium of an Acid–Base Reaction

8.4 How to Complete a Dehydration Reaction

8.5 How to Predict the Product of an Epoxidation Reaction

CHEMICAL CONNECTIONS

8A Nitroglycerin: An Explosive and a Drug

8B Blood Alcohol Screening

8C Ethylene Oxide: A Chemical Sterilant

IN THIS CHAPTER, we study the physical and chemical properties of alcohols and ethers, two classes of oxygen-containing compounds we have seen as products of chemical reactions (Sections 5.3B and 7.4). We also study thiols, a class of sulfur-containing compounds. Thiols are like alcohols in structure, except that they contain an —SH group rather than an —OH group.

CH_3CH_2OH	$CH_3CH_2OCH_2CH_3$	CH_3CH_2SH
Ethanol (an alcohol)	Diethyl ether (an ether)	Ethanethiol (a thiol)

These three compounds are certainly familiar to you. Ethanol is the fuel additive in gasoline, the alcohol in alcoholic beverages, and an important industrial and laboratory solvent. Diethyl ether was the first inhalation anesthetic used in general surgery. It is also an important industrial and laboratory solvent. Ethanethiol, like other low-molecular-weight thiols, has a stench. Smells such as those from skunks, rotten eggs, and sewage are caused by thiols.

Alcohols are particularly important in both laboratory and biochemical transformations of organic compounds. They can be converted into other types of compounds, such as alkenes, haloalkanes, aldehydes, ketones, carboxylic acids, and esters. Not only can alcohols be converted to these compounds, but they also can be prepared from them. Thus, alcohols play a central role in the interconversion of organic functional groups.

8.1 What Are Alcohols?

A. Structure

Alcohol A compound containing an —OH (hydroxyl) group bonded to an sp^3 hybridized carbon.

The functional group of an **alcohol** is an **—OH (hydroxyl) group** bonded to an sp^3 hybridized carbon atom (Section 1.7A). The oxygen atom of an alcohol is also sp^3 hybridized. Two sp^3 hybrid orbitals of oxygen form sigma bonds to atoms of carbon and hydrogen. The other two sp^3 hybrid orbitals of oxygen each contain an unshared pair of electrons. Figure 8.1 shows a Lewis structure and ball-and-stick model of methanol, CH_3OH, the simplest alcohol.

(a)

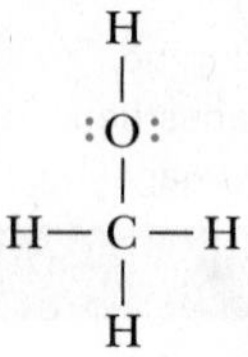

(b)

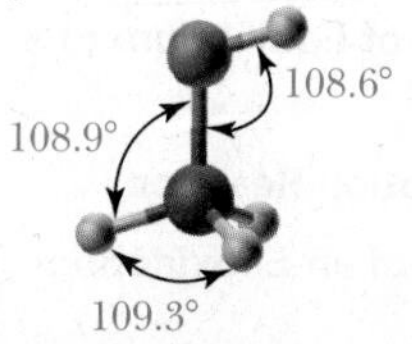

FIGURE 8.1 Methanol, CH_3OH. (a) Lewis structure and (b) ball-and-stick model. The measured H—O—C bond angle in methanol is 108.6°, very close to the tetrahedral angle of 109.5°.

B. Nomenclature

We derive the IUPAC names for alcohols in the same manner as those for alkanes, with the exception that the ending of the parent alkane is changed from *-e* to *-ol.* The ending *-ol* tells us that the compound is an alcohol.

1. Select, as the parent alkane, the longest chain of carbon atoms that contains the —OH, and number that chain from the end closer to the —OH group. In numbering the parent chain, the location of the —OH group takes precedence over alkyl groups and halogens.
2. Change the suffix of the parent alkane from *-e* to *-ol* (Section 3.5), and use a number to show the location of the —OH group. For cyclic alcohols, numbering begins at the carbon bearing the —OH group.
3. Name and number substituents and list them in alphabetical order.

To derive common names for alcohols, we name the alkyl group bonded to —OH and then add the word *alcohol.* Following are the IUPAC names and, in parentheses, the common names of eight low-molecular-weight alcohols:

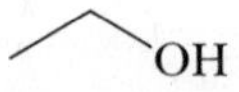

Ethanol (Ethyl alcohol)

1-Propanol (Propyl alcohol)

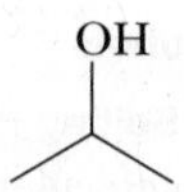

2-Propanol (Isopropyl alcohol)

1-Butanol (Butyl alcohol)

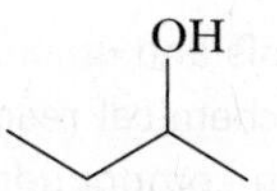

2-Butanol (*sec*-Butyl alcohol)

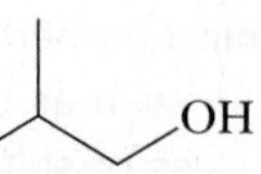

2-Methyl-1-propanol (Isobutyl alcohol)

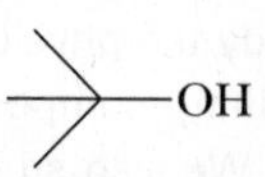

2-Methyl-2-propanol (*tert*-Butyl alcohol)

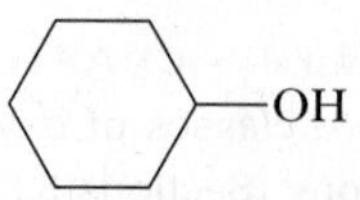

Cyclohexanol (Cyclohexyl alcohol)

HOW TO 8.1

Name Cyclic Alcohols

(a) First, determine the root name of the cycloalkane, and replace the suffix *-e* with *-ol*.

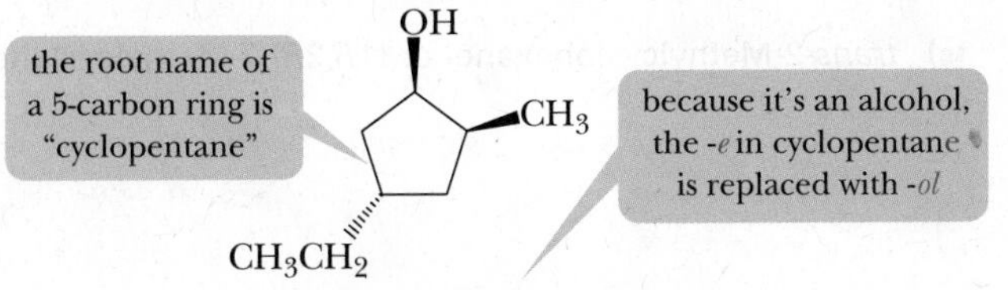

Cyclopentanol

(b) Name and number the substituents. Numbering begins at the carbon bearing the —OH group and proceeds in the direction that gives the lowest *total* for all substituents.

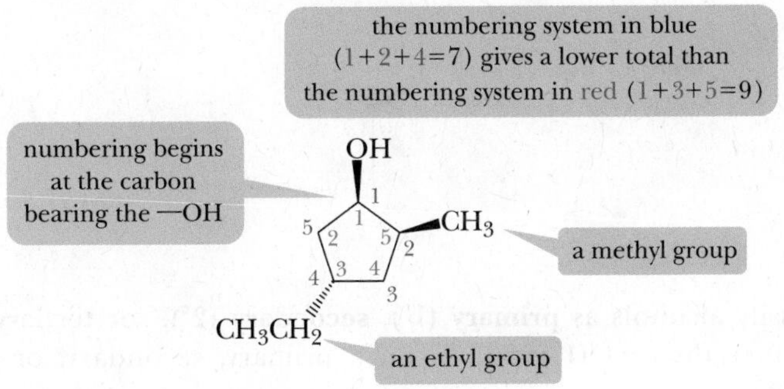

(c) Place substituents in alphabetical order preceded by its position on the ring. Position 1 for the —OH group is assumed.

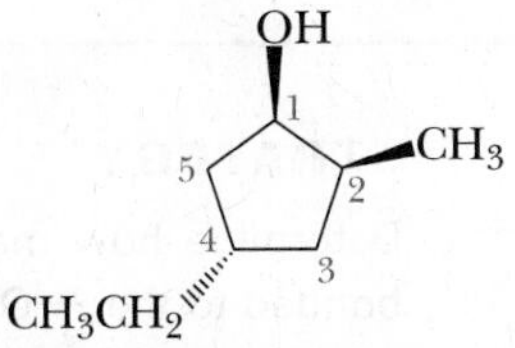

4-Ethyl-2-methylcyclopentanol

(d) Don't forget to indicate stereochemistry.

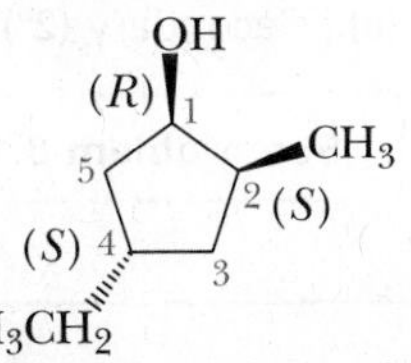

(1*R*,2*S*,4*S*)-4-Ethyl-2-methylcyclopentanol

EXAMPLE 8.1

Write the IUPAC name for each alcohol:

(a) $CH_3(CH_2)_6CH_2OH$ (b)  (c) 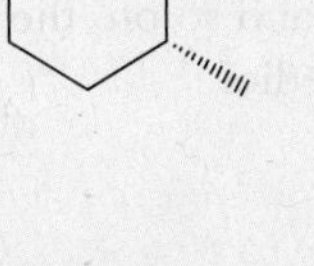

STRATEGY

First look for the longest chain of carbons that contains the —OH group. This will allow you to determine the root name. Then identify the atoms or groups of atoms that are not part of that chain of carbons. These are your substituents.

SOLUTION

(a) 1-Octanol (b) 4-Methyl-2-pentanol (c) *trans*-2-Methylcyclohexanol or (1*R*,2*R*)-2-Methylcyclohexanol

See problems 8.14, 8.15, 8.17

PROBLEM 8.1

Write the IUPAC name for each alcohol:

(a) 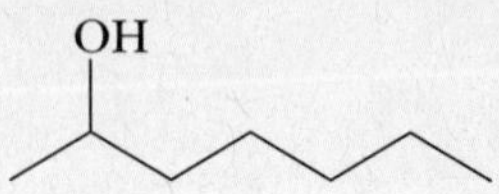
(b) 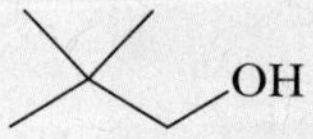
(c) 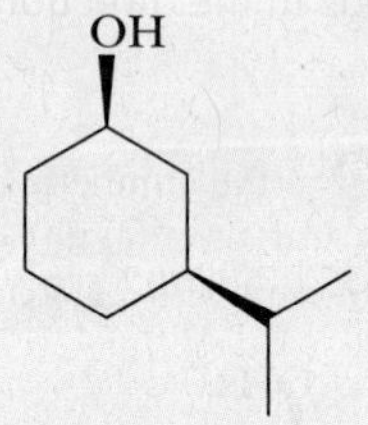

We classify alcohols as **primary (1°)**, **secondary (2°)**, or **tertiary (3°)**, depending on whether the —OH group is on a primary, secondary, or tertiary carbon (Section 1.7A).

EXAMPLE 8.2

Classify each alcohol as primary, secondary, or tertiary:

(a) 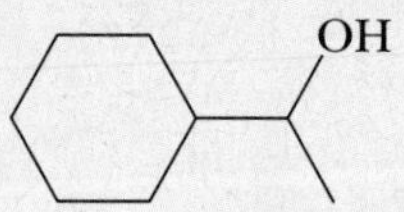

(b) CH_3 / CH_3COH / CH_3 (central C bearing two CH_3 groups, drawn above and below)

(c) 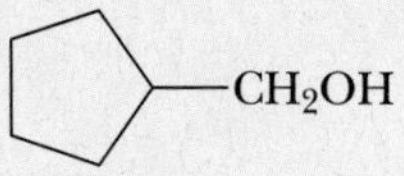

STRATEGY

Determine how many carbons are bonded to the carbon bonded to the —OH group (1 carbon = 1°, 2 carbons = 2°, and 3 carbons = 3°).

SOLUTION

(a) Secondary (2°) (b) Tertiary (3°) (c) Primary (1°)

See problem 8.13

PROBLEM 8.2

Classify each alcohol as primary, secondary, or tertiary:

(a) 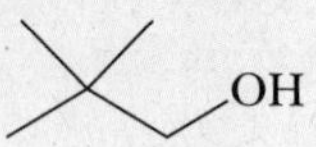
(b) 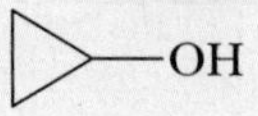
(c) $CH_2{=}CHCH_2OH$
(d) 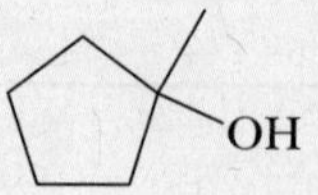

In the IUPAC system, a compound containing two hydroxyl groups is named as a **diol**, one containing three hydroxyl groups is named as a **triol**, and so on. In IUPAC names for diols, triols, and so on, the final *-e* of the parent alkane name is retained, as for example, in 1,2-ethanediol.

As with many organic compounds, common names for certain diols and triols have persisted. Compounds containing two hydroxyl groups on different carbons are often referred to as **glycols**. Ethylene glycol and propylene glycol are synthesized from ethylene and propylene, respectively—hence their common names:

Glycol A compound with two hydroxyl (—OH) groups on different carbons.

CH_2CH_2 with OH on each carbon ($HOCH_2CH_2OH$)

1,2-Ethanediol
(Ethylene glycol)

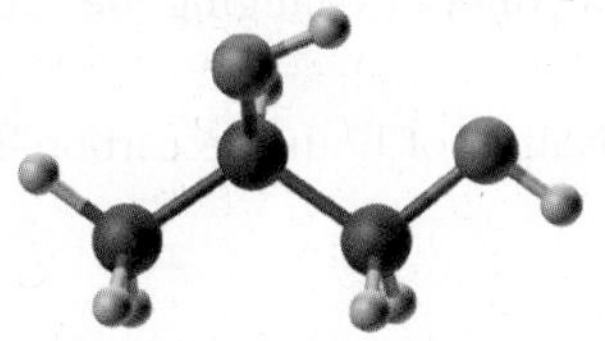

CH_3CHCH_2 with HO and OH on C-2 and C-1 ($CH_3CH(OH)CH_2OH$)

1,2-Propanediol
(Propylene glycol)

CH_2CHCH_2 with HO, HO, OH on each carbon ($HOCH_2CH(OH)CH_2OH$)

1,2,3-Propanetriol
(Glycerol, Glycerin)

Charles D. Winters

Ethylene glycol is a polar molecule and dissolves readily in water, a polar solvent.

Chemical Connections 8A

NITROGLYCERIN: AN EXPLOSIVE AND A DRUG

In 1847, Ascanio Sobrero (1812–1888) discovered that 1,2,3-propanetriol, more commonly named glycerin, reacts with nitric acid in the presence of sulfuric acid to give a pale yellow, oily liquid called nitroglycerin:

$$\begin{array}{l}CH_2-OH\\ |\\ CH-OH\\ |\\ CH_2-OH\end{array} + 3HNO_3 \xrightarrow{H_2SO_4} \begin{array}{l}CH_2-ONO_2\\ |\\ CH-ONO_2\\ |\\ CH_2-ONO_2\end{array} + 3H_2O$$

1,2,3-Propanetriol (Glycerol, Glycerin) → 1,2,3-Propanetriol trinitrate (Nitroglycerin)

Sobrero also discovered the explosive properties of the compound: When he heated a small quantity of it, it exploded! Soon, nitroglycerin became widely used for blasting in the construction of canals, tunnels, roads, and mines and, of course, for warfare.

One problem with the use of nitroglycerin was soon recognized: It was difficult to handle safely, and accidental explosions occurred frequently. The Swedish chemist Alfred Nobel (1833–1896) solved the problem: He discovered that a claylike substance called diatomaceous earth absorbs nitroglycerin so that it will not explode without a fuse. He gave the name *dynamite* to this mixture of nitroglycerin, diatomaceous earth, and sodium carbonate.

Surprising as it may seem, nitroglycerin is used in medicine to treat angina pectoris, the symptoms of which are sharp chest pains caused by a reduced flow of blood in the coronary artery. Nitroglycerin, which is available in liquid (diluted with alcohol to render it nonexplosive), tablet, or paste form, relaxes the smooth muscles of blood vessels, causing dilation of the coronary artery. This dilation, in turn, allows more blood to reach the heart.

When Nobel became ill with heart disease, his physicians advised him to take nitroglycerin to relieve his chest pains. He refused, saying he could not understand how the explosive could relieve chest pains. It took science more than 100 years to find the answer. We now know that it is nitric oxide, NO, derived from the nitro groups of nitroglycerin, that relieves the pain.

© Bettmann/Corbis

The fortune of Alfred Nobel, 1833–1896, built on the manufacture of dynamite, now funds the Nobel Prizes.

Question

Classify each hydroxyl group in glycerol as either 1°, 2°, or 3°.

We often refer to compounds containing —OH and C=C groups as unsaturated alcohols. To name an unsaturated alcohol,

1. Number the parent alkane so as to give the —OH group the lowest possible number.
2. Show the double bond by changing the infix of the parent alkane from *-an-* to *-en-* (Section 3.5), and show the alcohol by changing the suffix of the parent alkane from *-e* to *-ol.*
3. Use numbers to show the location of both the carbon–carbon double bond and the hydroxyl group.

EXAMPLE 8.3

Write the IUPAC name for each alcohol:

(a) $CH_2{=}CHCH_2OH$

(b) 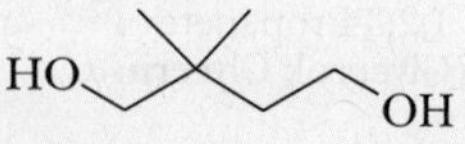

(c) 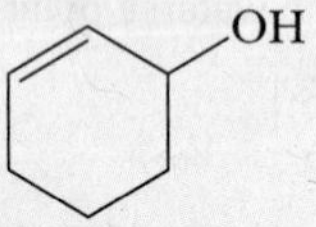

(d) 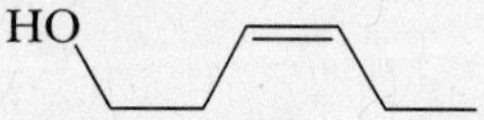

STRATEGY

First look for the longest chain of carbons. This will allow you to determine the root name. If the alcohol is unsaturated, the name will follow the general form #-alken-#-ol. If there are two —OH groups, name the compound as an #,#-alkanediol if it is saturated or as an #-alken-#,#-diol if it is unsaturated.

SOLUTION

(a) 2-Propen-1-ol. Its common name is allyl alcohol.
(b) 2,2-Dimethyl-1,4-butanediol.
(c) 2-Cyclohexenol.
(d) *cis*-3-Hexen-1-ol. This unsaturated alcohol is sometimes called leaf alcohol because of its occurrence in leaves of fragrant plants, including trees and shrubs.

in this cyclic alcohol, the location of the —OH group is assumed to be at C-1

See problems 8.14, 8.15, 8.17

PROBLEM 8.3

Write the IUPAC name for each alcohol:

(a) 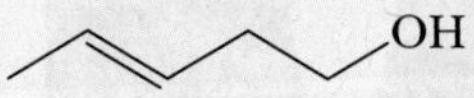

(b) 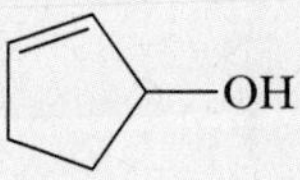

(c) 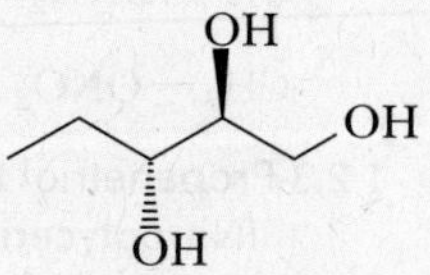

(d) 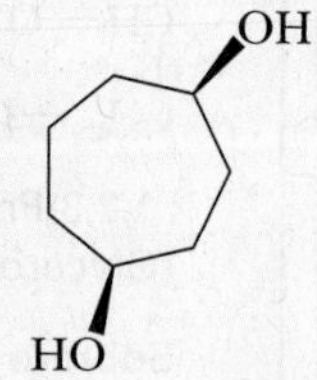

C. Physical Properties

The most important physical property of alcohols is the polarity of their —OH groups. Because of the large difference in electronegativity (Table 1.5) between oxygen and carbon (3.5 − 2.5 = 1.0) and between oxygen and hydrogen (3.5 − 2.1 = 1.4), both the C—O and O—H bonds of an alcohol are polar covalent, and alcohols are polar molecules, as illustrated in Figure 8.2 for methanol.

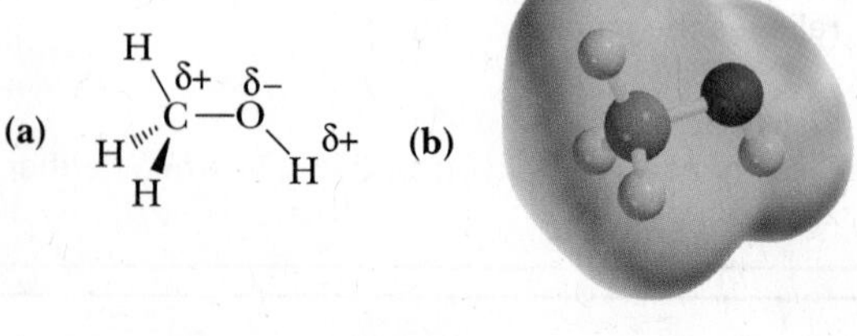

FIGURE 8.2
Polarity of the C—O—H bond in methanol. (a) There are partial positive charges on carbon and hydrogen and a partial negative charge on oxygen. (b) An electron density map showing the partial negative charge (in red) around oxygen and a partial positive charge (in blue) around hydrogen of the —OH group.

TABLE 8.1 Boiling Points and Solubilities in Water of Five Groups of Alcohols and Alkanes of Similar Molecular Weight

Structural Formula	Name	Molecular Weight	Boiling Point (°C)	Solubility in Water
CH_3OH	methanol	32	65	infinite
CH_3CH_3	ethane	30	−89	insoluble
CH_3CH_2OH	ethanol	46	78	infinite
$CH_3CH_2CH_3$	propane	44	−42	insoluble
$CH_3CH_2CH_2OH$	1-propanol	60	97	infinite
$CH_3CH_2CH_2CH_3$	butane	58	0	insoluble
$CH_3CH_2CH_2CH_2OH$	1-butanol	74	117	8 g/100 g
$CH_3CH_2CH_2CH_2CH_3$	pentane	72	36	insoluble
$CH_3CH_2CH_2CH_2CH_2OH$	1-pentanol	88	138	2.3 g/100 g
$HOCH_2CH_2CH_2CH_2OH$	1,4-butanediol	90	230	infinite
$CH_3CH_2CH_2CH_2CH_2CH_3$	hexane	86	69	insoluble

Table 8.1 lists the boiling points and solubilities in water for five groups of alcohols and alkanes of similar molecular weight. Notice that, of the compounds compared in each group, the alcohol has the higher boiling point and is the more soluble in water.

Alcohols have higher boiling points than alkanes of similar molecular weight, because alcohols are polar molecules and can associate in the liquid state by a type of dipole–dipole intermolecular attraction called **hydrogen bonding** (Figure 8.3). The strength of hydrogen bonding between alcohol molecules is approximately 8.4 to 21 kJ/mol (2 to 5 kcal/mol). For comparison, the strength of the O—H covalent bond in an alcohol molecule is approximately 460 kJ/mol (110 kcal/mol). As we see by comparing these numbers, an O----H hydrogen bond is considerably weaker than an O—H covalent bond. Nonetheless, it is sufficient to have a dramatic effect on the physical properties of alcohols.

Hydrogen bonding The attractive force between a partial positive charge on hydrogen and partial negative charge on a nearby oxygen, nitrogen, or fluorine atom.

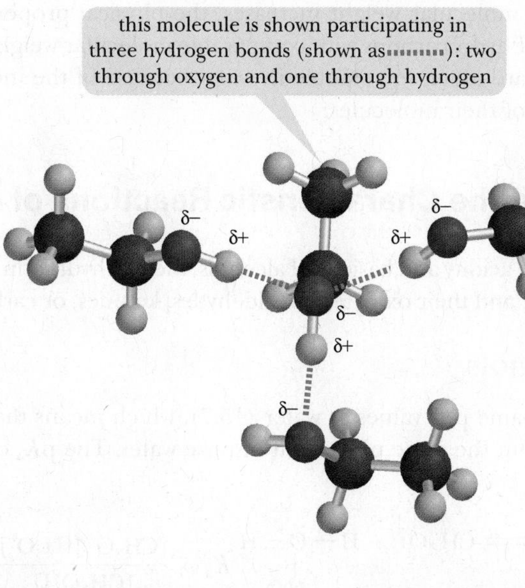

FIGURE 8.3
The association of ethanol molecules in the liquid state. Each O—H can participate in up to three hydrogen bonds (one through hydrogen and two through oxygen).

HOW TO 8.2

Predict Relative Boiling Points of Compounds of Similar Molecular Weight

(a) Look for features that make a compound's boiling point higher than another's such as greater polarity, the ability to form hydrogen bonds with that compound's molecules (true for compounds containing N—H or O—H bonds), and greater surface area.

(b) Boiling will typically follow the trend:

Higher Boiling | **Examples**

polar compounds that are **both** hydrogen bond donors and acceptors

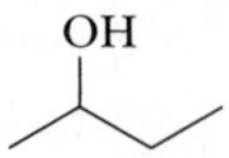

bp = 98 °C

polar compounds incapable of hydrogen bonding or only capable of being a hydrogen bond donor *or* a hydrogen bond acceptor, but not both

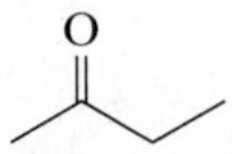

bp = 80 °C

nonpolar compounds

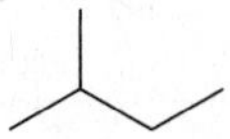

bp = 28 °C

Lower Boiling

Because of hydrogen bonding between alcohol molecules in the liquid state, extra energy is required to separate each hydrogen-bonded alcohol molecule from its neighbors—hence the relatively high boiling points of alcohols compared with those of alkanes. The presence of additional hydroxyl groups in a molecule further increases the extent of hydrogen bonding, as can be seen by comparing the boiling points of 1-pentanol (138 °C) and 1,4-butanediol (230 °C), both of which have approximately the same molecular weight.

Because of increased dispersion forces (Section 3.8B) between larger molecules, boiling points of all types of compounds, including alcohols, increase with increasing molecular weight. (Compare, for example, the boiling points of ethanol, 1-propanol, 1-butanol, and 1-pentanol.)

Alcohols are much more soluble in water than are alkanes, alkenes, and alkynes of comparable molecular weight. Their increased solubility is due to hydrogen bonding between alcohol molecules and water. Methanol, ethanol, and 1-propanol are soluble in water in all proportions. As molecular weight increases, the physical properties of alcohols become more like those of hydrocarbons with comparable molecular weight. Alcohols with higher molecular weight are much less soluble in water because of the increase in size of the hydrocarbon portion of their molecules.

8.2 What Are the Characteristic Reactions of Alcohols?

In this section, we study the acidity and basicity of alcohols, their dehydration to alkenes, their conversion to haloalkanes, and their oxidation to aldehydes, ketones, or carboxylic acids.

A. Acidity of Alcohols

Alcohols have about the same pK_a values as water (15.7), which means that aqueous solutions of alcohols have about the same pH as that of pure water. The pK_a of methanol, for example, is 15.5:

$$CH_3\ddot{O}{-}H + :\ddot{O}{-}H \rightleftharpoons CH_3\ddot{O}:^- + H{-}\ddot{O}^+{-}H \qquad K_a = \frac{[CH_3O^-][H_3O^+]}{[CH_3OH]} = 3.2 \times 10^{-16}$$

(with H below the O of water and H below the O of H_3O^+)

$$pK_a = 15.5$$

TABLE 8.2 pK_a Values for Selected Alcohols in Dilute Aqueous Solution*

Compound	Structural Formula	pK_a	
hydrogen chloride	HCl	−7	Stronger acid
acetic acid	CH_3COOH	4.8	↑
methanol	CH_3OH	15.5	
water	H_2O	15.7	
ethanol	CH_3CH_2OH	15.9	
2-propanol	$(CH_3)_2CHOH$	17	Weaker acid
2-methyl-2-propanol	$(CH_3)_3COH$	18	

*Also given for comparison are pK_a values for water, acetic acid, and hydrogen chloride.

Table 8.2 gives the acid ionization constants for several low-molecular-weight alcohols. Methanol and ethanol are about as acidic as water. Higher-molecular-weight, water-soluble alcohols are slightly weaker acids than water. Even though alcohols have some slight acidity, they are not strong enough acids to react with weak bases such as sodium bicarbonate or sodium carbonate. (At this point, it would be worthwhile to review Section 2.4 and the discussion of the position of equilibrium in acid–base reactions.) Note that, although acetic acid is a "weak acid" compared with acids such as HCl, it is still 10^{10} times stronger as an acid than alcohols are.

B. Basicity of Alcohols

In the presence of strong acids, the oxygen atom of an alcohol is a weak base and reacts with an acid by proton transfer to form an oxonium ion:

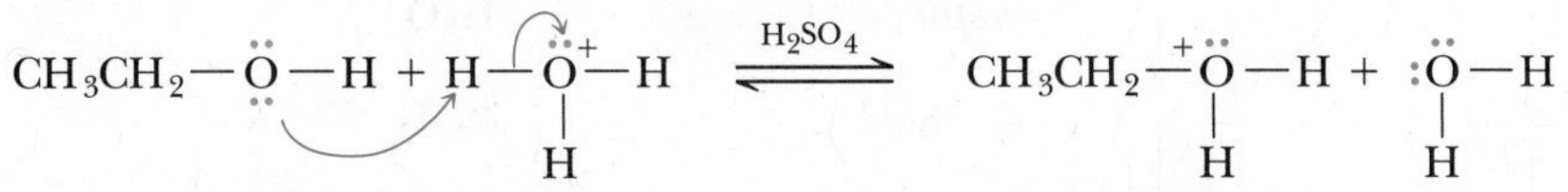

Ethanol — Hydronium ion (pK_a −1.7) — Ethyloxonium ion (pK_a −2.4)

Thus, alcohols can function as both weak acids and weak bases.

C. Reaction with Active Metals

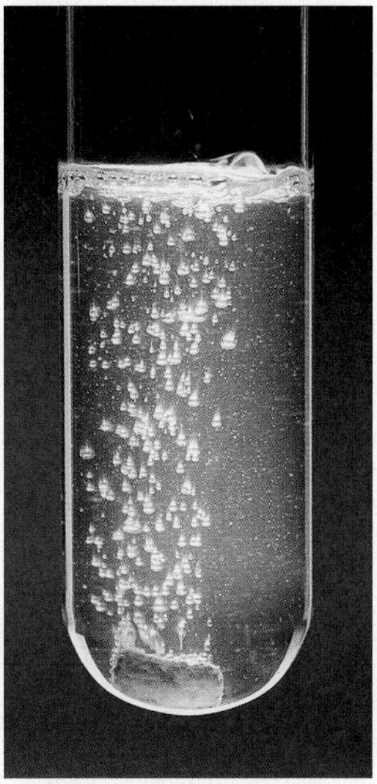
Charles D. Winters

Methanol reacts with sodium metal to give sodium methoxide along with the evolution of hydrogen gas.

Like water, alcohols react with Li, Na, K, Mg, and other active metals to liberate hydrogen and to form metal alkoxides. In the following oxidation–reduction reaction, Na is oxidized to Na^+ and H^+ is reduced to H_2:

$$2\,CH_3OH + 2\,Na \longrightarrow 2\,CH_3O^-\,Na^+ + H_2$$

Sodium methoxide

To name a metal alkoxide, name the cation first, followed by the name of the anion. The name of an alkoxide ion is derived from a prefix showing the number of carbon atoms and their arrangement (*meth-*, *eth-*, *isoprop-*, tert-*but-*, and so on) followed by the suffix *-oxide*.

Alkoxide ions are somewhat stronger bases than is the hydroxide ion. In addition to sodium methoxide, the following metal salts of alcohols are commonly used in organic reactions requiring a strong base in a nonaqueous solvent; sodium ethoxide in ethanol and potassium *tert*-butoxide in 2-methyl-2-propanol (*tert*-butyl alcohol):

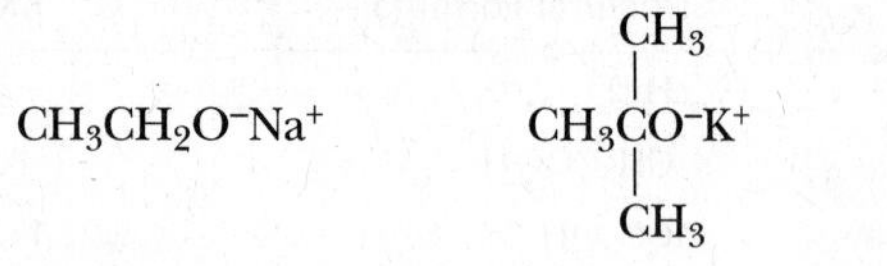

$$\underset{\text{Sodium ethoxide}}{CH_3CH_2O^-Na^+} \qquad \underset{\text{Potassium } \textit{tert}\text{-butoxide}}{CH_3\overset{\overset{CH_3}{|}}{\underset{\underset{CH_3}{|}}{C}}O^-K^+}$$

As we saw in Chapter 7, alkoxide ions can also be used as nucleophiles in substitution reactions.

HOW TO 8.3

Predict the Position of Equilibrium of an Acid–Base Reaction

(a) Identify the two acids and two bases in the equilibrium.

(b) The position of equilibrium lies on the side with the weaker acid and weaker base.

(c) Following are common types of compounds encountered in organic chemistry and their relative acidities.

		Example
Higher acidity ↑	mineral acids	HCl, H_2SO_4
	carboxylic acids	$RCOOH$
	phenols	
	water	H_2O
	alcohols	ROH
	alkynes (terminal)	$R-C\equiv C-H$
	ammonia and amines	NH_3, RNH_2, R_2NH
Lower acidity	alkenes and alkanes	$R_2C=CH_2$, RH

EXAMPLE 8.4

Write balanced equations for the following reactions. If the reaction is an acid–base reaction, predict its position of equilibrium.

(a) + Na ⟶

(b) $Na^+ NH_2^-$ + ⇌

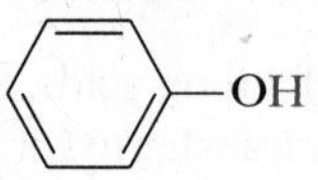

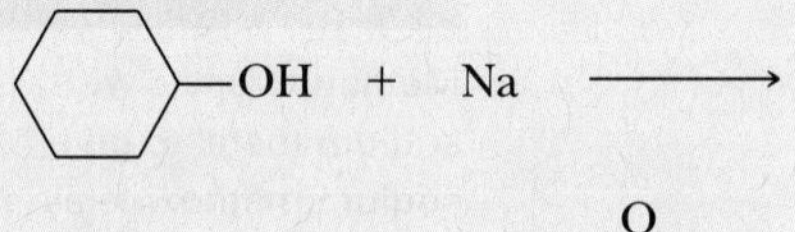

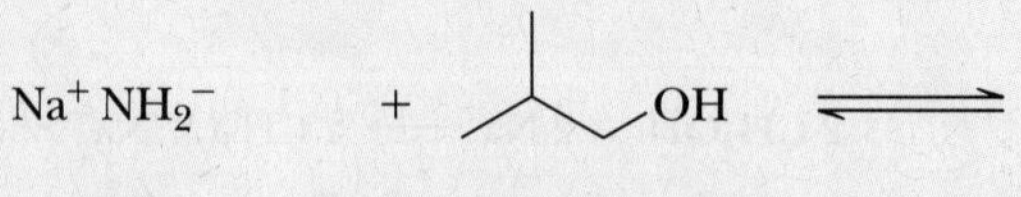

(c) $CH_3CH_2O^- Na^+ + CH_3-\overset{\overset{O}{\|}}{C}-OH \rightleftharpoons$

STRATEGY

First determine what type of reaction is occurring. When elemental sodium is used, an oxidation–reduction reaction takes place, producing a sodium alkoxide and hydrogen gas. In acid–base reactions, the position of the equilibrium resides on the side with the weaker acid and weaker base (i.e., the more stable species).

SOLUTION

(a)
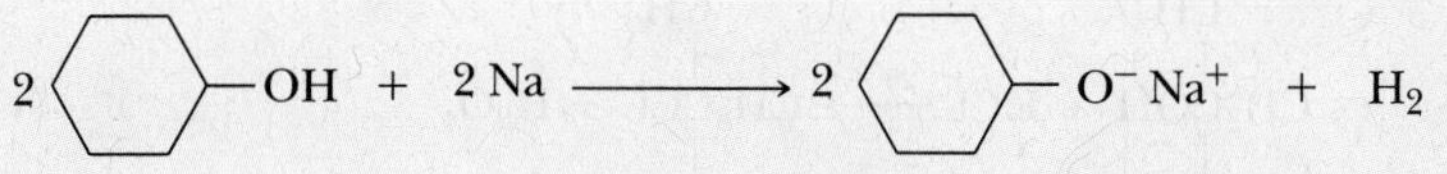

(b)
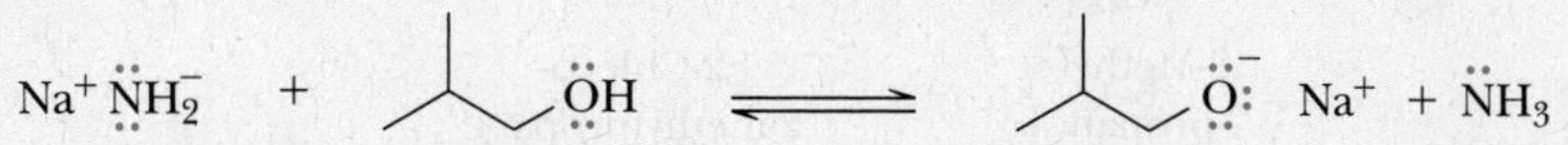

Stronger base	Stronger acid	Weaker base	Weaker acid
	$pK_a = 15.8$		$pK_a = 38$

the right side of the equation contains the more stable species, especially when comparing the alkoxide anion with NH_2^- because the oxygen in the alkoxide anion is more electronegative and better able to hold a negative charge than the nitrogen in NH_2^-

(c)
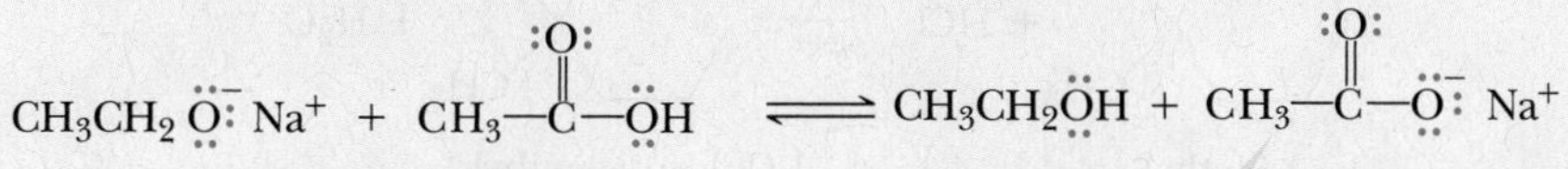

Stronger base	Stronger acid	Weaker acid	Weaker base
	$pK_a = 4.76$	$pK_a = 15.9$	

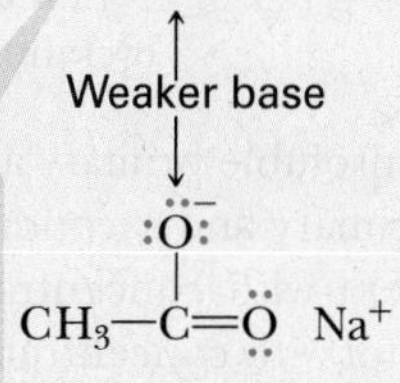

the right side of the equation contains the more stable species, especially when comparing the conjugate base of the carboxylic acid (known as a carboxylate anion) with the ethoxide anion because the negative charge in the carboxylate anion can be delocalized by resonance

See problems 8.28–8.32, 8.34, 8.35

PROBLEM 8.4

Write balanced equations for the following reactions. If the reaction is an acid–base reaction, predict its position of equilibrium.

(a)
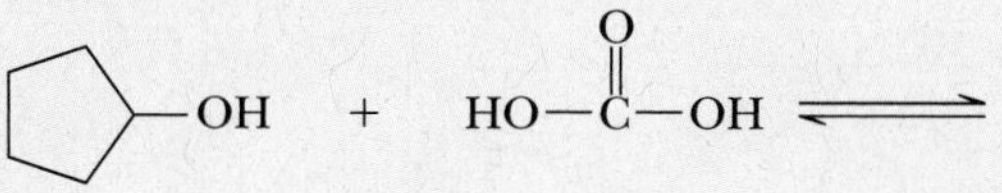

(b)

(c)
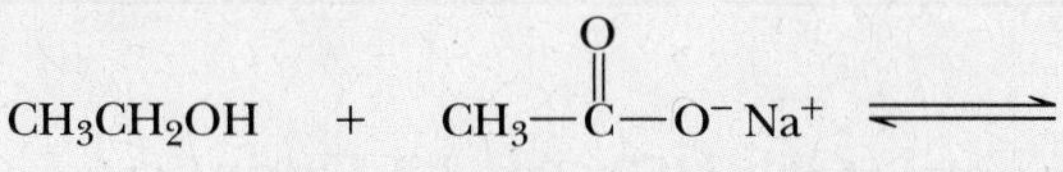

D. Conversion to Haloalkanes

The conversion of an alcohol to an alkyl halide involves substituting halogen for —OH at a saturated carbon. The most common reagents for this conversion are the halogen acids and $SOCl_2$.

Reaction with HCl, HBr, and HI

Water-soluble tertiary alcohols react very rapidly with HCl, HBr, and HI. Mixing a tertiary alcohol with concentrated hydrochloric acid for a few minutes at room temperature converts the alcohol to a water-insoluble chloroalkane that separates from the aqueous layer.

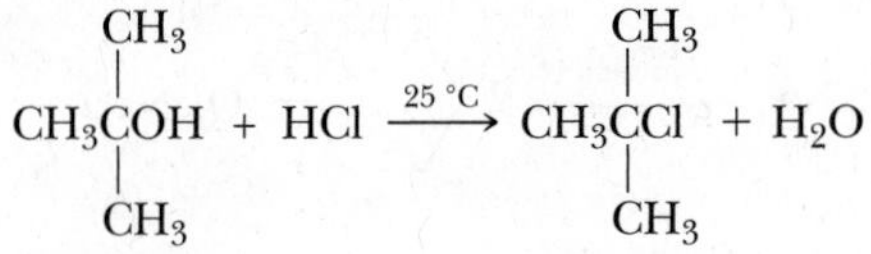

2-Methyl-2-propanol　　2-Chloro-2-methylpropane

Low-molecular-weight, water-soluble primary and secondary alcohols do not react under these conditions.

Water-insoluble tertiary alcohols are converted to tertiary halides by bubbling gaseous HX through a solution of the alcohol dissolved in diethyl ether or tetrahydrofuran (THF):

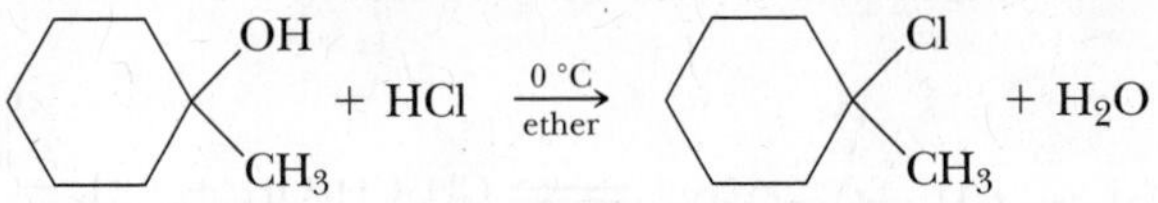

1-Methylcyclohexanol　　1-Chloro-1-methylcyclohexane

Water-insoluble primary and secondary alcohols react only slowly under these conditions.

Primary and secondary alcohols are converted to bromoalkanes and iodoalkanes by treatment with concentrated hydrobromic and hydroiodic acids. For example, heating 1-butanol with concentrated HBr gives 1-bromobutane:

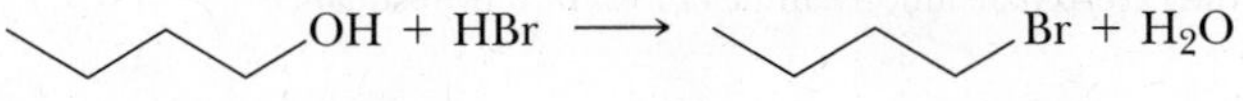

1-Butanol　　1-Bromobutane (Butyl bromide)

On the basis of observations of the relative ease of reaction of alcohols with HX (3° > 2° > 1°), it has been proposed that the conversion of tertiary and secondary alcohols to haloalkanes by concentrated HX occurs by an S_N1 mechanism (Section 7.4) and involves the formation of a carbocation intermediate. *Note:* Recall that secondary carbocations are subject to rearrangement to more stable tertiary carbocations (Section 5.4).

Mechanism

Reaction of a Tertiary Alcohol with HCl: An S_N1 Reaction

STEP 1: Add a proton. Rapid and reversible proton transfer from the acid to the OH group gives an oxonium ion. The result of this proton transfer is to convert the leaving group from OH^-, a poor leaving group, to H_2O, a better leaving group:

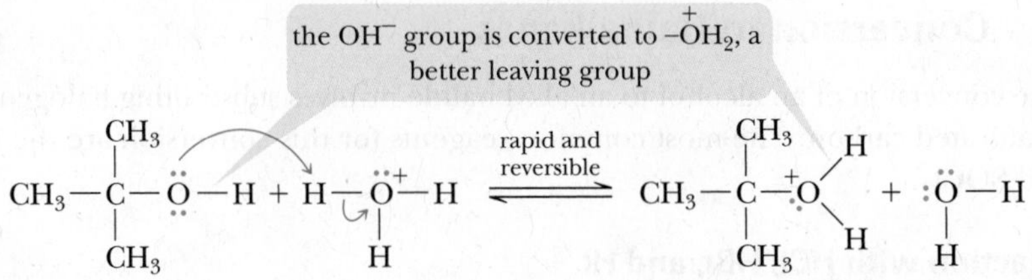

2-Methyl-2-propanol (*tert*-Butyl alcohol)　　An oxonium ion

STEP 2: Break a bond to form a stable molecule or ion. Loss of water from the oxonium ion gives a 3° carbocation intermediate:

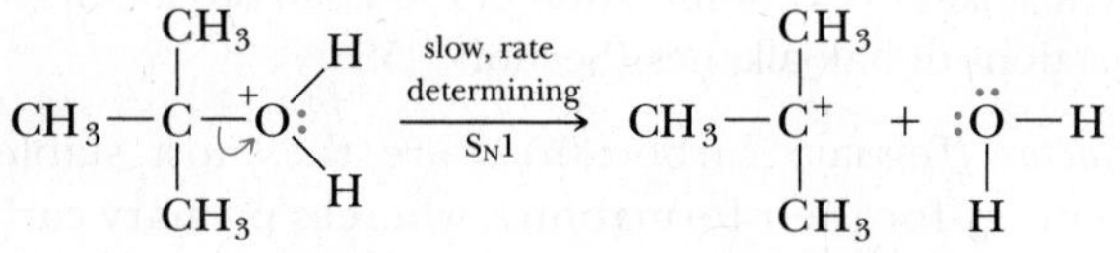

An oxonium ion

A 3° carbocation intermediate

STEP 3: Reaction of an electrophile and a nucleophile to form a new covalent bond. Reaction of the 3° carbocation intermediate (an electrophile) with chloride ion (a nucleophile) gives the product:

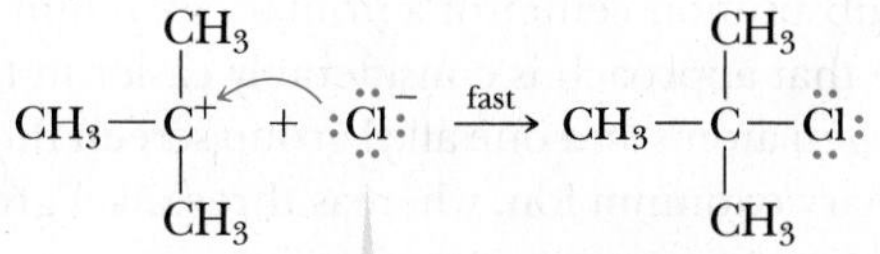

2-Chloro-2-methylpropane
(*tert*-Butyl chloride)

chloride ion is produced in the initial reaction of H_2O with HCl

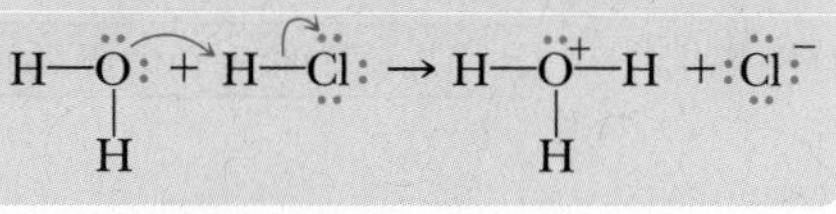

Primary alcohols react with HX by an S_N2 mechanism. In the rate-determining step, the halide ion displaces H_2O from the carbon bearing the oxonium ion. The displacement of H_2O and the formation of the C—X bond are simultaneous.

Mechanism

Reaction of a Primary Alcohol with HBr: An S_N2 Reaction

STEP 1: Add a proton. Rapid and reversible proton transfer to the OH group which converts the leaving group from OH^-, a poor leaving group, to H_2O, a better leaving group:

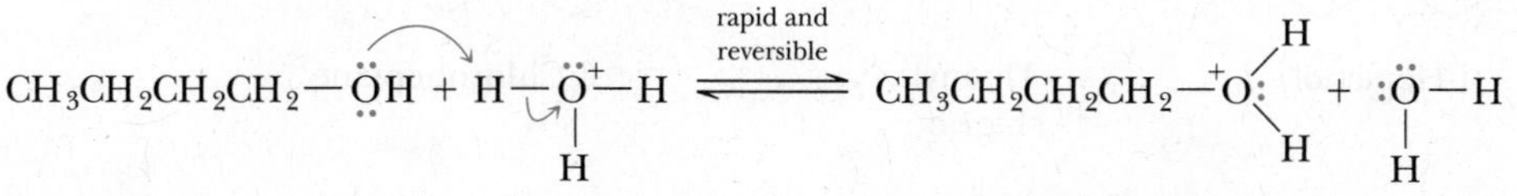

An oxonium ion

STEP 2: Reaction of an electrophile and a nucleophile to form a new covalent bond and break a bond to form a stable molecule or ion. The nucleophilic displacement of H_2O by Br^- gives the bromoalkane:

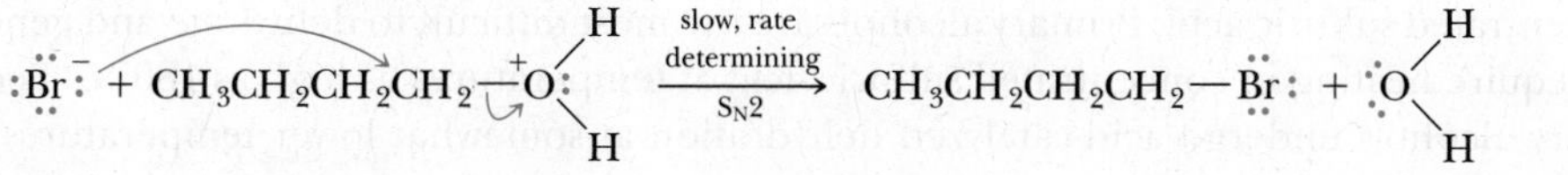

Why do tertiary alcohols react with HX by formation of carbocation intermediates, whereas primary alcohols react by direct displacement of —OH (more accurately, by displacement of $—OH_2^+$)? The answer is a combination of the same two factors involved in nucleophilic substitution reactions of haloalkanes (Section 7.5B):

1. *Electronic factors* Tertiary carbocations are the most stable (require the lowest activation energy for their formation), whereas primary carbocations are the least stable (require the highest activation energy for their formation). Therefore, tertiary alcohols are most likely to react by carbocation formation; secondary alcohols are intermediate, and primary alcohols rarely, if ever, react by carbocation formation.
2. *Steric factors* To form a new carbon–halogen bond, halide ion must approach the substitution center and begin to form a new covalent bond to it. If we compare the ease of approach to the substitution center of a primary oxonium ion with that of a tertiary oxonium ion, we see that approach is considerably easier in the case of a primary oxonium ion. Two hydrogen atoms and one alkyl group screen the back side of the substitution center of a primary oxonium ion, whereas three alkyl groups screen the back side of the substitution center of a tertiary oxonium ion.

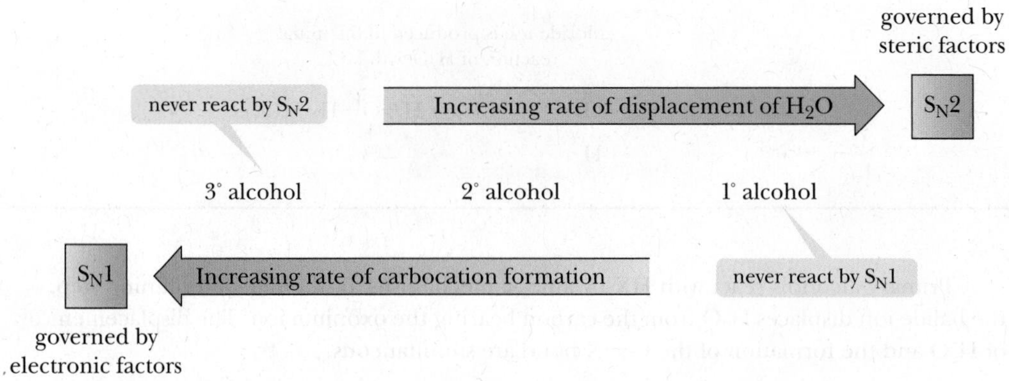

Reaction with Thionyl Chloride

The most widely used reagent for the conversion of primary and secondary alcohols to alkyl chlorides is thionyl chloride, $SOCl_2$. The by-products of this nucleophilic substitution reaction are HCl and SO_2, both given off as gases. Often, an organic base such as pyridine (Section 10.1) is added to react with and neutralize the HCl by-product:

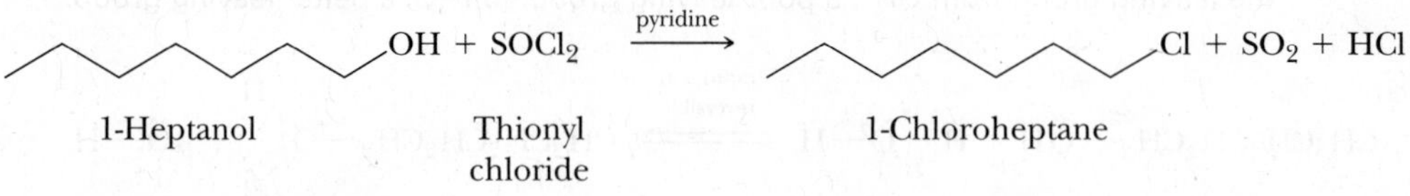

E. Acid-Catalyzed Dehydration to Alkenes

Dehydration Elimination of a molecule of water from a compound.

An alcohol can be converted to an alkene by **dehydration**—that is, by the elimination of a molecule of water from adjacent carbon atoms. In the laboratory, the dehydration of an alcohol is most often brought about by heating it with either 85% phosphoric acid or concentrated sulfuric acid. Primary alcohols are the most difficult to dehydrate and generally require heating in concentrated sulfuric acid at temperatures as high as 180 °C. Secondary alcohols undergo acid-catalyzed dehydration at somewhat lower temperatures. The acid-catalyzed dehydration of tertiary alcohols often requires temperatures only slightly above room temperature:

$$CH_3CH_2OH \xrightarrow[180\,°C]{H_2SO_4} CH_2{=}CH_2 + H_2O$$

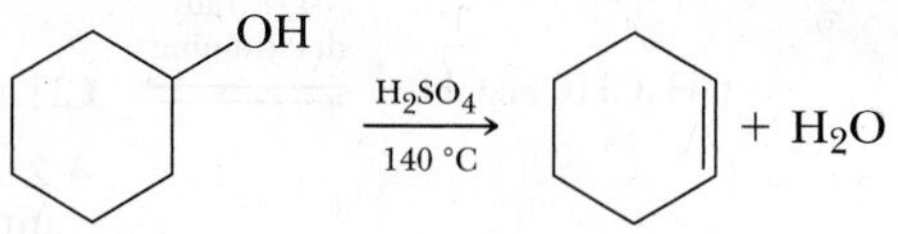

Cyclohexanol   Cyclohexene

$$CH_3\overset{\displaystyle CH_3}{\underset{\displaystyle CH_3}{C}}OH \xrightarrow[50\,°C]{H_2SO_4} CH_3\overset{\displaystyle CH_3}{C}{=}CH_2 + H_2O$$

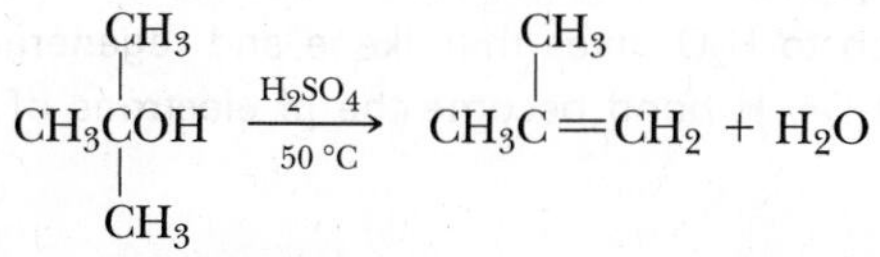

2-Methyl-2-propanol (*tert*-Butyl alcohol)   2-Methylpropene (Isobutylene)

Thus, the ease of acid-catalyzed dehydration of alcohols occurs in this order:

1° alcohol < 2° alcohol < 3° alcohol

Ease of dehydration of alcohols →

When isomeric alkenes are obtained in the acid-catalyzed dehydration of an alcohol, the more stable alkene (the one with the greater number of substituents on the double bond; see Section 5.3B) generally predominates; that is, the acid-catalyzed dehydration of alcohols follows Zaitsev's rule (Section 7.7):

$$CH_3CH_2\overset{\displaystyle OH}{C}HCH_3 \xrightarrow[heat]{85\%\ H_3PO_4} CH_3CH{=}CHCH_3 + CH_3CH_2CH{=}CH_2$$

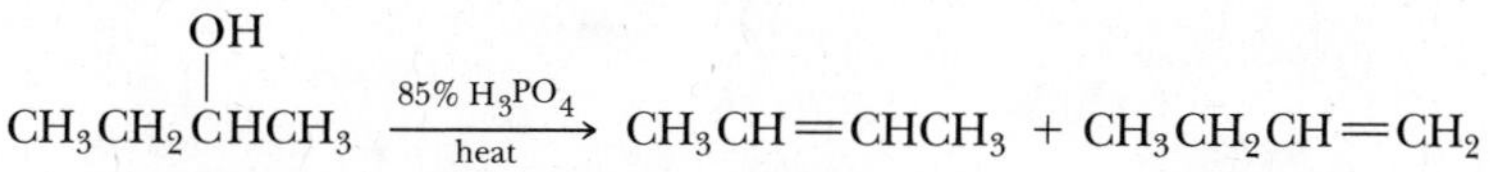

2-Butanol   2-Butene (80%)   1-Butene (20%)

On the basis of the relative ease of dehydration of alcohols (3° > 2° > 1°), chemists propose a three-step mechanism for the acid-catalyzed dehydration of secondary and tertiary alcohols. This mechanism involves the formation of a carbocation intermediate in the rate-determining step and therefore is an E1 mechanism.

Mechanism

Acid-Catalyzed Dehydration of 2-Butanol: An E1 Mechanism

STEP 1: Add a proton. Proton transfer from H_3O^+ to the OH group of the alcohol gives an oxonium ion. A result of this step is to convert OH^-, a poor leaving group, into H_2O, a better leaving group:

An oxonium ion

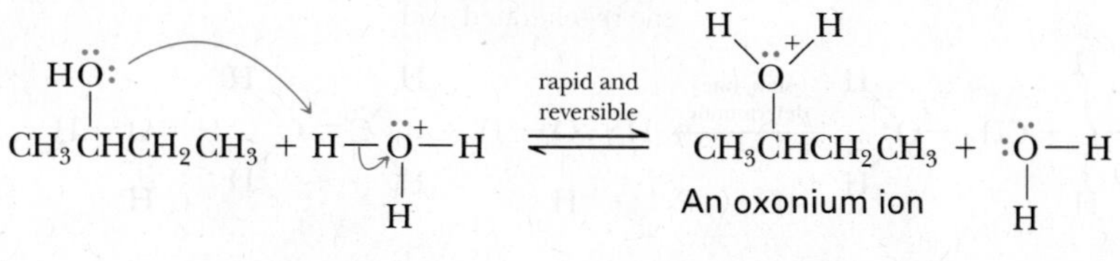

STEP 2: Break a bond to form a stable molecule or ion. Breaking of the C—O bond gives a 2° carbocation intermediate and H_2O:

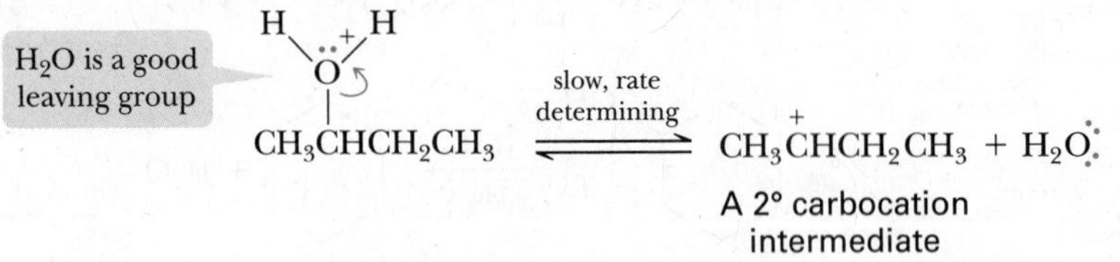

STEP 3: Take away a proton. Proton transfer from the carbon adjacent to the positively charged carbon to H_2O gives the alkene and regenerates the catalyst. The sigma electrons of a C—H bond become the pi electrons of the carbon–carbon double bond:

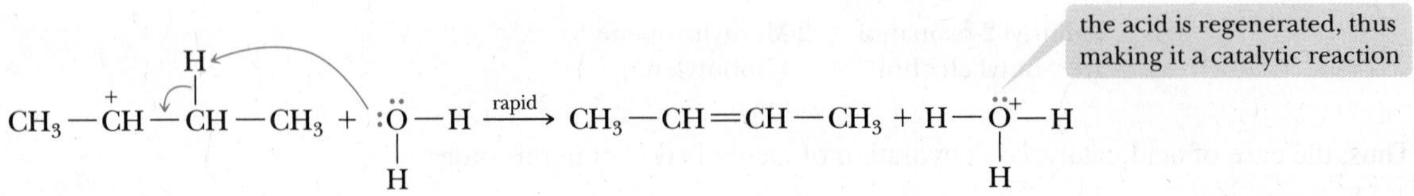

Because the rate-determining step in the acid-catalyzed dehydration of secondary and tertiary alcohols is the formation of a carbocation intermediate, the relative ease of dehydration of these alcohols parallels the ease of formation of carbocations.

Primary alcohols react by the following two-step mechanism, in which Step 2 is the rate-determining step.

Mechanism

Acid-Catalyzed Dehydration of a Primary Alcohol: An E2 Mechanism

STEP 1: Add a proton. Proton transfer from H_3O^+ to the OH group of the alcohol gives an oxonium ion:

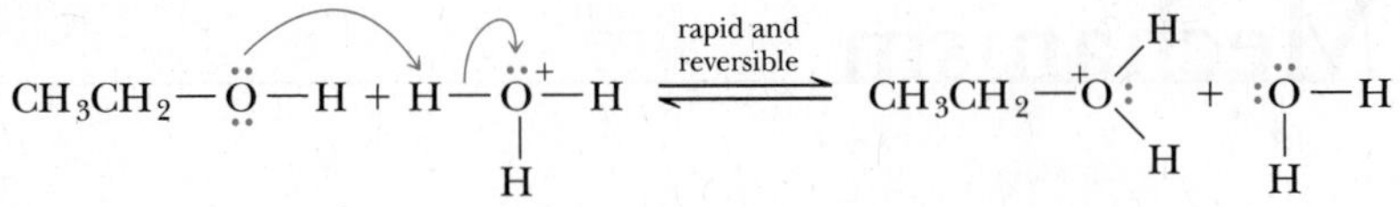

STEP 2: Take a proton away and break a bond to form a stable molecule or ion. Simultaneous proton transfer to solvent and loss of H_2O gives the alkene:

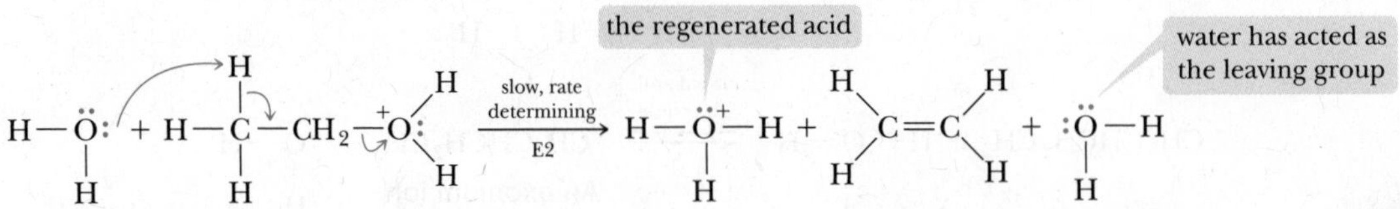

In Section 5.3B, we discussed the acid-catalyzed hydration of alkenes to give alcohols. In the current section, we discussed the acid-catalyzed dehydration of alcohols to give alkenes. In fact, hydration–dehydration reactions are reversible. Alkene hydration and alcohol dehydration are competing reactions, and the following equilibrium exists:

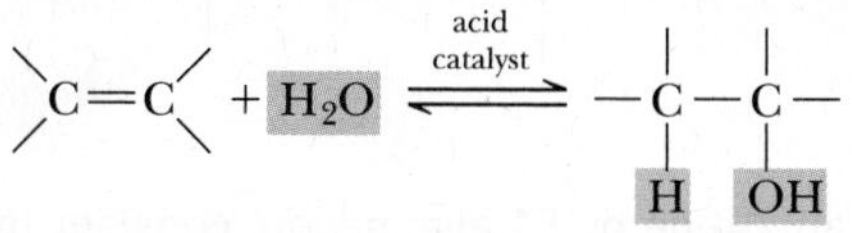

An alkene — An alcohol

How, then, do we control which product will predominate? Recall that LeChâtelier's principle states that a system in equilibrium will respond to a stress in the equilibrium by counteracting that stress. This response allows us to control these two reactions to give the desired product. Large amounts of water (achieved with the use of dilute aqueous acid) favor alcohol formation, whereas a scarcity of water (achieved with the use of concentrated acid) or experimental conditions by which water is removed (for example, heating the reaction mixture above 100 °C) favor alkene formation. Thus, depending on the experimental conditions, it is possible to use the hydration–dehydration equilibrium to prepare either alcohols or alkenes, each in high yields.

HOW TO 8.4

Complete a Dehydration Reaction

(a) A dehydration reaction is very similar to a dehydrohalogenation reaction (Section 7.7) except that the hydroxyl group must be protonated to generate a better leaving group.

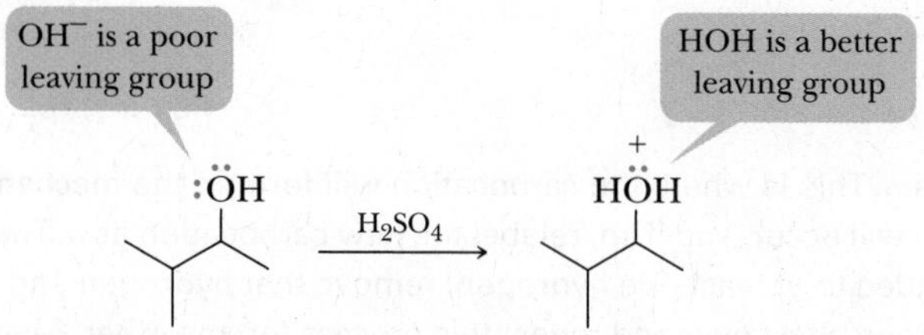

(b) Label the carbon bonded to the leaving group as "α" (alpha).

(c) Label any carbon bonded to the α-carbon as "β" (beta). *Note*: Only do so if the β-carbon is bonded to a hydrogen atom.

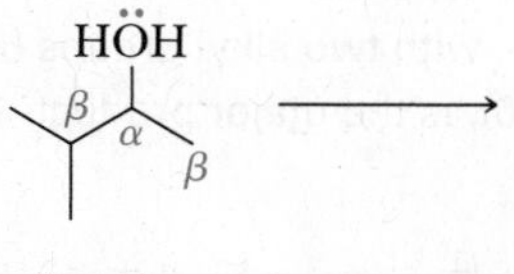

(d) Remove the leaving group (H_2O) and a β-hydrogen from the molecule and place a new double bond between the α and β carbons. This forms a dehydration product.

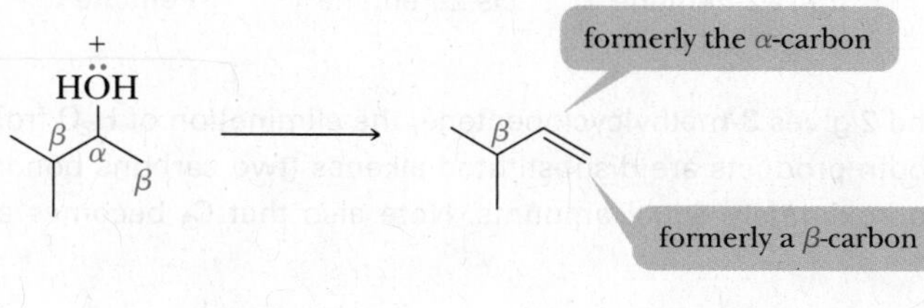

(e) Repeat step (d) above for any other β-carbons to form a different dehydration product.

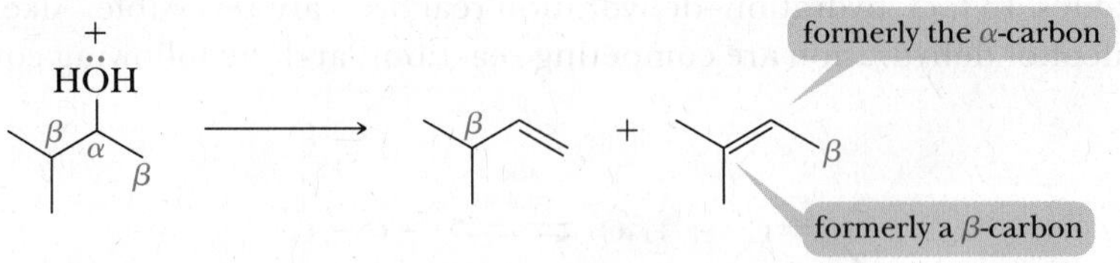

(f) When forming an alkene by E1 elimination, consider the fact that both *cis* and *trans* isomers of the alkene are possible.

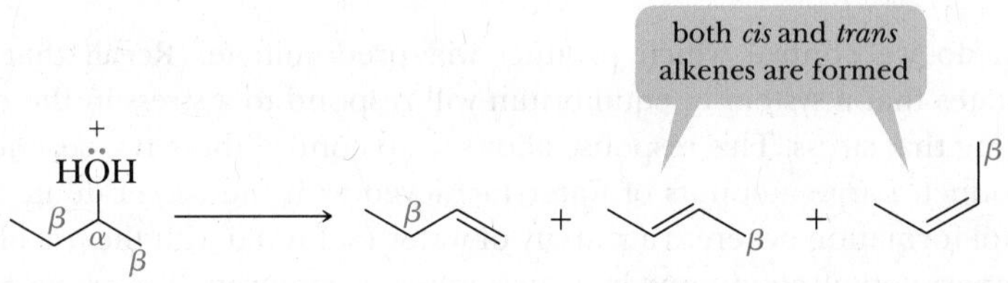

EXAMPLE 8.5

For each of the following alcohols, draw structural formulas for the alkenes that form upon acid-catalyzed dehydration, and predict which alkene is the major product from each alcohol. Be aware that rearrangements may occur because carbocations are formed in the reactions.

(a) 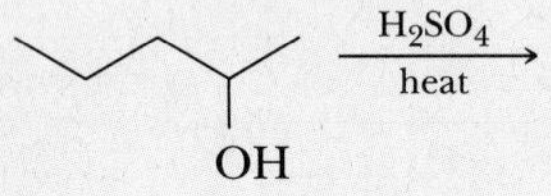

(b) 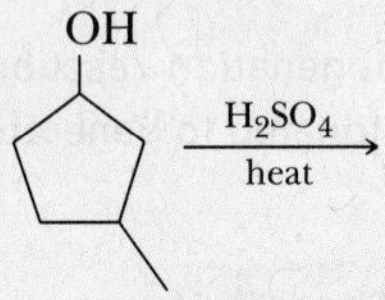

(c) 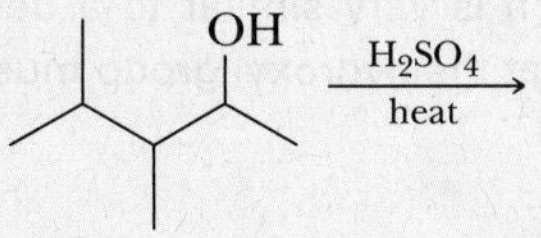

STRATEGY

Label the carbon bonded to the —OH group as α. This is where the carbocation will form in the mechanism of the reaction. Consider whether a rearrangement (Section 5.4) will occur, and if so, relabel the new carbocation as α. Then label any carbons next to the α-carbon as β. If the β-carbon is bonded to at least one hydrogen, remove that hydrogen and the —OH and draw a C—C double bond between the α- and β-carbons. Start over and repeat this process for any other β-carbons that meet this criteria. Each time you are able to do this will result in an elimination product.

SOLUTION

(a) The elimination of H_2O from carbons 2 and 3 gives 2-pentene, which can form as *cis–trans* isomers; the elimination of H_2O from carbons 1 and 2 gives 1-pentene. *trans*-2-Pentene, with two alkyl groups (an ethyl and a methyl) on the double bond and with *trans* being more stable than *cis* (Section 5.6), is the major product. 1-Pentene, with only one alkyl group (a propyl group) on the double bond, is a minor product:

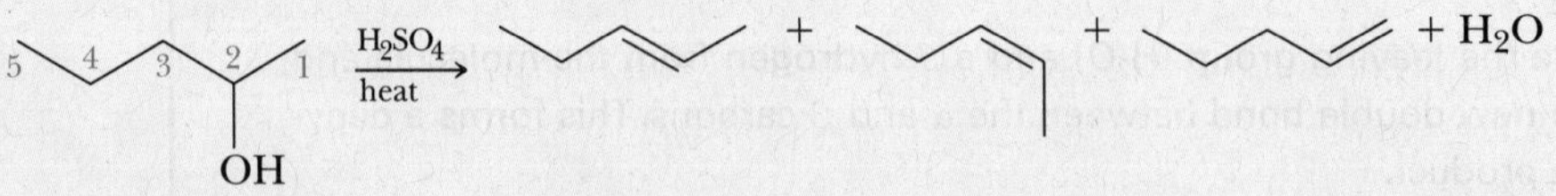

2-Pentanol — *trans*-2-Pentene (major product) — *cis*-2-Pentene — 1-Pentene

(b) The elimination of H_2O from carbons 1 and 2 gives 3-methylcyclopentene; the elimination of H_2O from carbons 1 and 5 gives 4-methylcyclopentene. Because both products are disubstituted alkenes (two carbons bonded to each C—C double bond), they will be formed in approximately equal amounts. Note also that C_3 becomes a stereocenter in 3-methylcyclopentene.

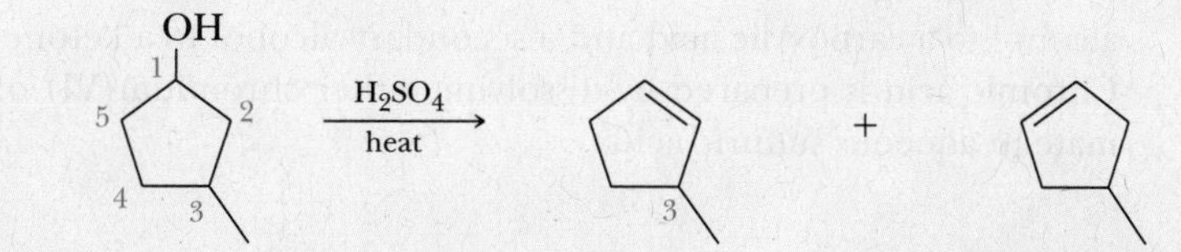

3-Methylcyclopentanol 3-Methylcyclopentene 4-Methylcyclopentene

(c) This reaction initially forms a 2° carbocation intermediate, which rearranges via a 1,2-hydride shift (Section 5.4) to form the more stable 3° carbocation. This new carbocation has three β hydrogens and a C—C double bond and can form in three places. 2,3-Dimethyl-2-pentene is the product with the more substituted double bond and is therefore the most stable and major product.

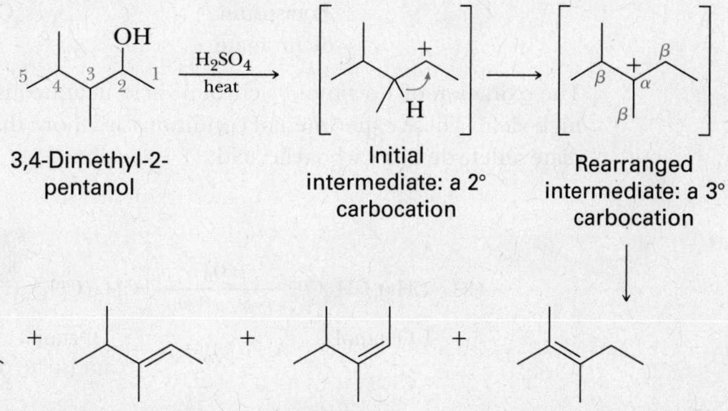

3,4-Dimethyl-2-pentanol; Initial intermediate: a 2° carbocation; Rearranged intermediate: a 3° carbocation

2-Ethyl-3-methyl-1-butene + (*E*)-3,4-Dimethyl-2-pentene + (*Z*)-3,4-Dimethyl-2-pentene + 2,3-Dimethyl-2-pentene (major product)

See problems 8.41–8.45

PROBLEM 8.5

For each of the following alcohols, draw structural formulas for the alkenes that form upon acid-catalyzed dehydration, and predict which alkene is the major product:

(a) 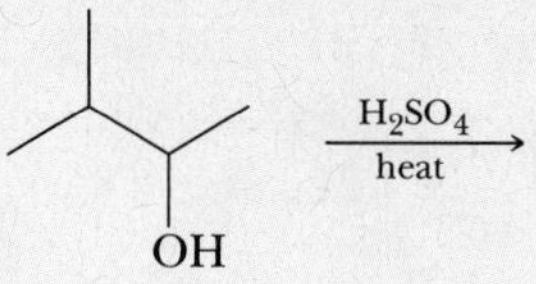

(b) 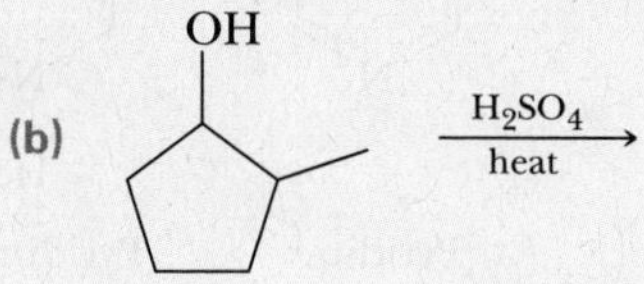

F. Oxidation of Primary and Secondary Alcohols

The oxidation of a primary alcohol gives an aldehyde or a carboxylic acid, depending on the experimental conditions. Secondary alcohols are oxidized to ketones. Tertiary alcohols are not oxidized. Following is a series of transformations in which a primary alcohol is oxidized first to an aldehyde and then to a carboxylic acid. The fact that each transformation involves oxidation is indicated by the symbol O in brackets over the reaction arrow:

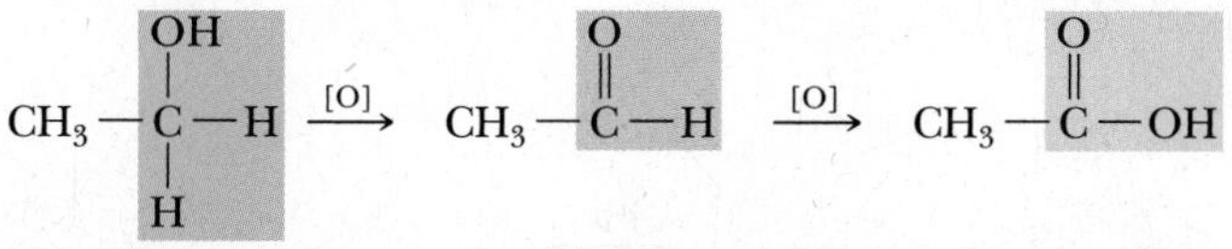

A primary alcohol An aldehyde A carboxylic acid

The reagent most commonly used in the laboratory for the oxidation of a primary alcohol to a carboxylic acid and a secondary alcohol to a ketone is chromic acid, H_2CrO_4. Chromic acid is prepared by dissolving either chromium(VI) oxide or potassium dichromate in aqueous sulfuric acid:

$$\underset{\text{Chromium(VI) oxide}}{CrO_3} + H_2O \xrightarrow{H_2SO_4} \underset{\text{Chromic acid}}{H_2CrO_4}$$

$$\underset{\text{Potassisum dichromate}}{K_2Cr_2O_7} \xrightarrow{H_2SO_4} H_2Cr_2O_7 \xrightarrow{H_2O} \underset{\text{Chromic acid}}{2\,H_2CrO_4}$$

The oxidation of 1-octanol by chromic acid in aqueous sulfuric acid gives octanoic acid in high yield. These experimental conditions are more than sufficient to oxidize the intermediate aldehyde to a carboxylic acid:

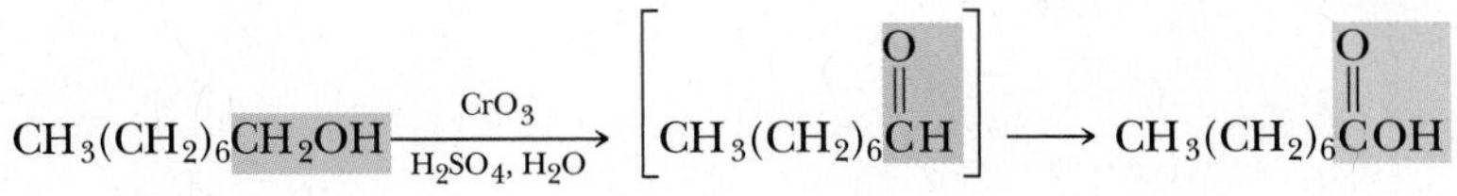

1-Octanol Octanal (not isolated) Octanoic acid

The form of Cr(VI) commonly used for the oxidation of a primary alcohol to an aldehyde is prepared by dissolving CrO_3 in aqueous HCl and adding pyridine to precipitate **pyridinium chlorochromate (PCC)** as a solid. PCC oxidations are carried out in aprotic solvents, most commonly dichloromethane, CH_2Cl_2:

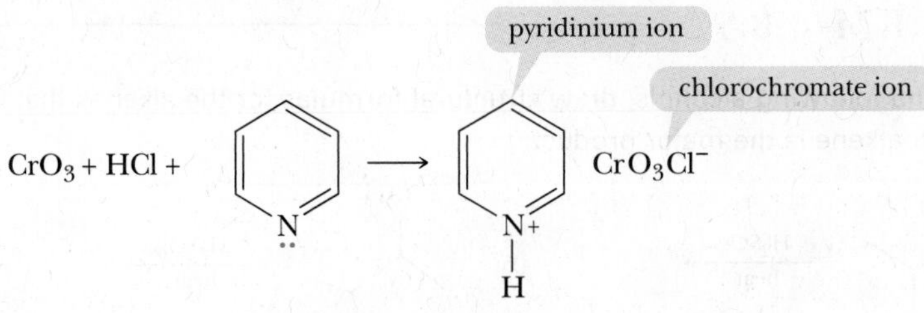

Pyridine Pyridinium chlorochromate (PCC)

PCC is selective for the oxidation of primary alcohols to aldehydes. It is less reactive than the previously discussed oxidation with chromic acid in aqueous sulfuric acid, and the reaction is run stoichiometrically so that no PCC remains once all the alcohol molecules have been converted to aldehyde. PCC also has little effect on carbon–carbon double bonds or other easily oxidized functional groups. In the following example, geraniol is oxidized to geranial without affecting either carbon–carbon double bond:

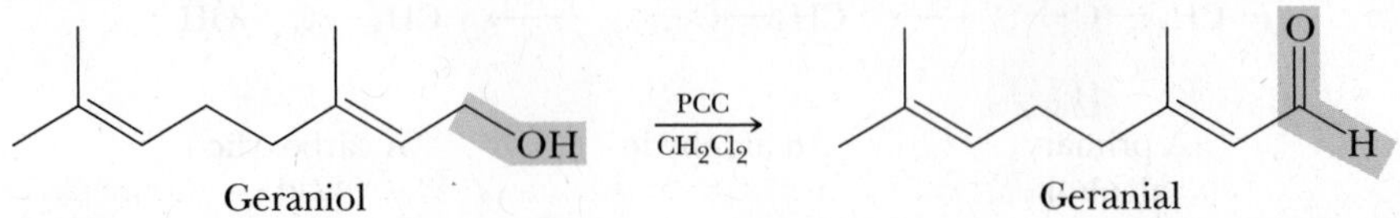

Geraniol Geranial

Secondary alcohols are oxidized to ketones by both chromic acid and PCC:

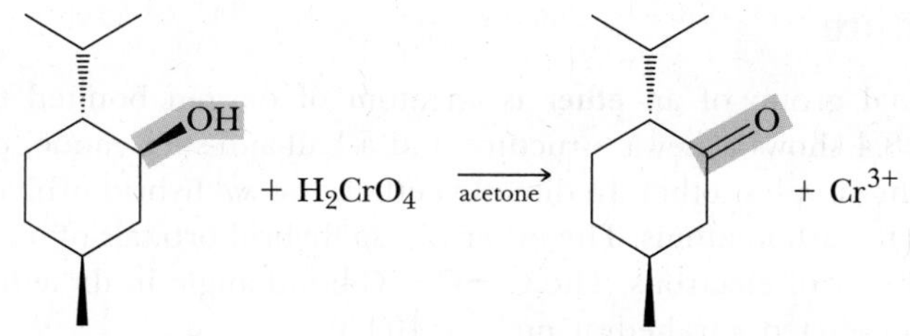

2-Isopropyl-5-methyl-cyclohexanol (Menthol) → 2-Isopropyl-5-methyl-cyclohexanone (Menthone)

Tertiary alcohols are resistant to oxidation, because the carbon bearing the —OH is bonded to three carbon atoms and therefore cannot form a carbon–oxygen double bond:

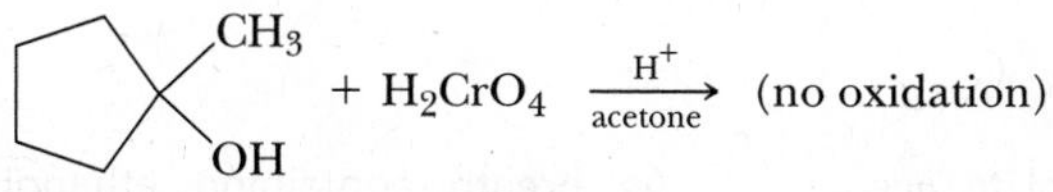

1-Methylcyclopentanol

Note that the essential feature of the oxidation of an alcohol is the presence of at least one hydrogen on the carbon bearing the OH group. Tertiary alcohols lack such a hydrogen; therefore, they are not oxidized.

EXAMPLE 8.6

Draw the product of the treatment of each of the following alcohols with PCC:
(a) 1-Hexanol (b) 2-Hexanol (c) Cyclohexanol

STRATEGY

In oxidation reactions of alcohols, identify the type of alcohol as 1°, 2°, or 3°. Tertiary alcohols remain unreactive. Secondary alcohols are oxidized to ketones. Primary alcohols are oxidized to aldehydes when PCC is used as the oxidizing agent, and to carboxylic acids when chromic acid is used as the oxidizing agent.

SOLUTION

1-Hexanol, a primary alcohol, is oxidized to hexanal. 2-Hexanol, a secondary alcohol, is oxidized to 2-hexanone. Cyclohexanol, a secondary alcohol, is oxidized to cyclohexanone.

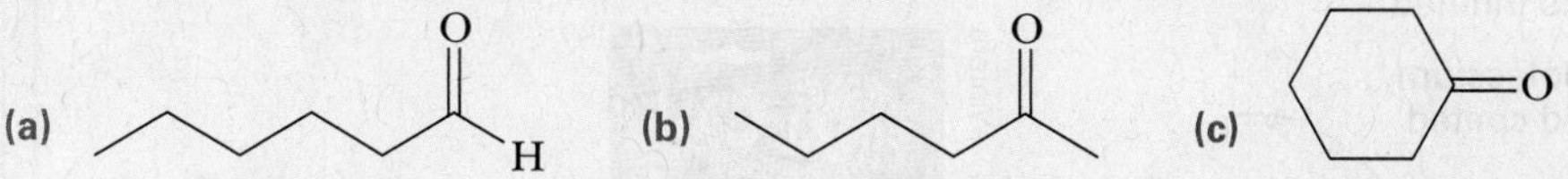

(a) Hexanal (b) 2-Hexanone (c) Cyclohexanone

See problems 8.34, 8.35, 8.38, 8.41–8.46

PROBLEM 8.6

Draw the product of the treatment of each alcohol in Example 8.6 with chromic acid.

8.3 What Are Ethers?

A. Structure

Ether A compound containing an oxygen atom bonded to two carbon atoms.

The functional group of an **ether** is an atom of oxygen bonded to two carbon atoms. Figure 8.4 shows a Lewis structure and a ball-and-stick model of dimethyl ether, CH_3OCH_3, the simplest ether. In dimethyl ether, two sp^3 hybrid orbitals of oxygen form sigma bonds to carbon atoms. The other two sp^3 hybrid orbitals of oxygen each contain an unshared pair of electrons. The C—O—C bond angle in dimethyl ether is 110.3°, close to the predicted tetrahedral angle of 109.5°.

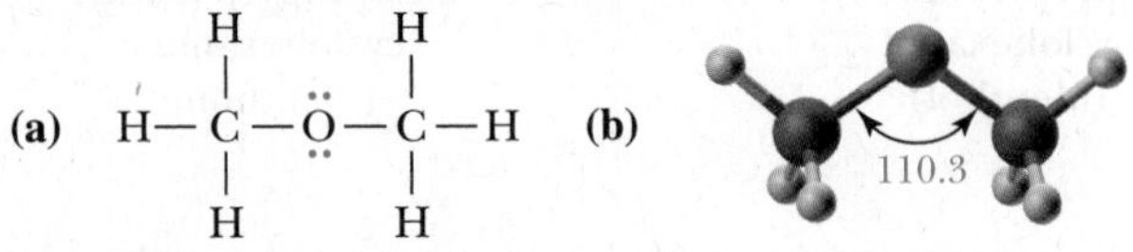

FIGURE 8.4 Dimethyl ether, CH_3OCH_3. (a) Lewis structure and (b) ball-and-stick model.

Chemical Connections 8B

BLOOD ALCOHOL SCREENING

Potassium dichromate oxidation of ethanol to acetic acid is the basis for the original breath alcohol screening test used by law enforcement agencies to determine a person's blood alcohol content. The test is based on the difference in color between the dichromate ion (reddish orange) in the reagent and the chromium(III) ion (green) in the product. Thus, color change can be used as a measure of the quantity of ethanol present in a breath sample:

$$\underset{\text{Ethanol}}{CH_3CH_2OH} + \underset{\text{Dichromate ion (reddish orange)}}{Cr_2O_7^{2-}} \xrightarrow[H_2O]{H_2SO_4} \underset{\text{Acetic acid}}{CH_3\overset{O}{\overset{\|}{C}}OH} + \underset{\text{Chromium(III) ion (green)}}{Cr^{3+}}$$

In its simplest form, a breath alcohol screening test consists of a sealed glass tube containing a potassium dichromate–sulfuric acid reagent impregnated on silica gel. To administer the test, the ends of the tube are broken off, a mouthpiece is fitted to one end, and the other end is inserted into the neck of a plastic bag. The person being tested then blows into the mouthpiece until the plastic bag is inflated.

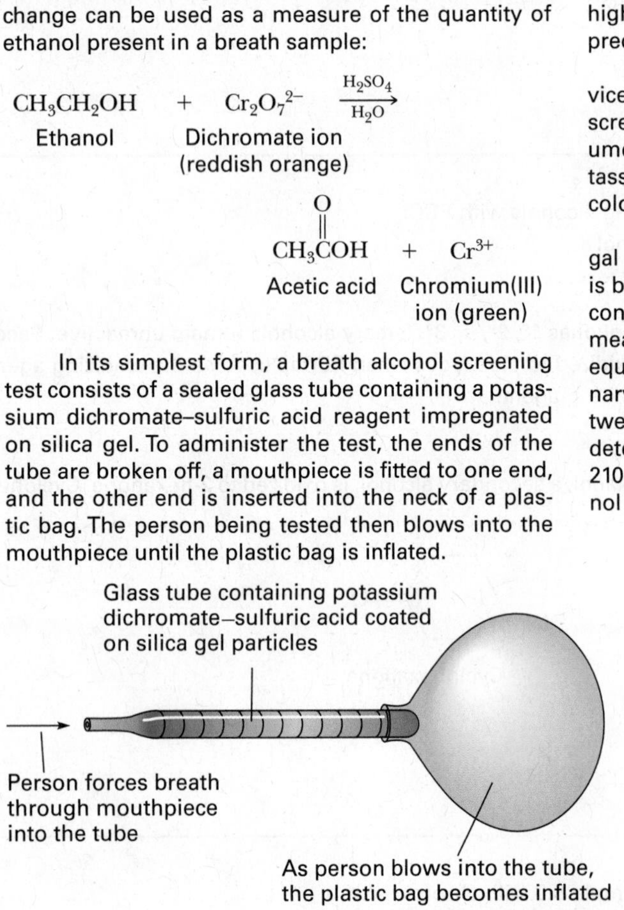

As breath containing ethanol vapor passes through the tube, reddish-orange dichromate ion is reduced to green chromium(III) ion. The concentration of ethanol in the breath is then estimated by measuring how far the green color extends along the length of the tube. When it extends beyond the halfway point, the person is judged as having a sufficiently high blood alcohol content to warrant further, more precise testing.

The Breathalyzer, a more precise testing device, operates on the same principle as the simplified screening test. In a Breathalyzer test, a measured volume of breath is bubbled through a solution of potassium dichromate in aqueous sulfuric acid, and the color change is measured spectrophotometrically.

Both tests measure alcohol in the breath. The legal definition of being under the influence of alcohol is based on *blood* alcohol content, not breath alcohol content. The chemical correlation between these two measurements is that air deep within the lungs is in equilibrium with blood passing through the pulmonary arteries, and an equilibrium is established between blood alcohol and breath alcohol. It has been determined by tests in persons drinking alcohol that 2100 mL of breath contains the same amount of ethanol as 1.00 mL of blood.

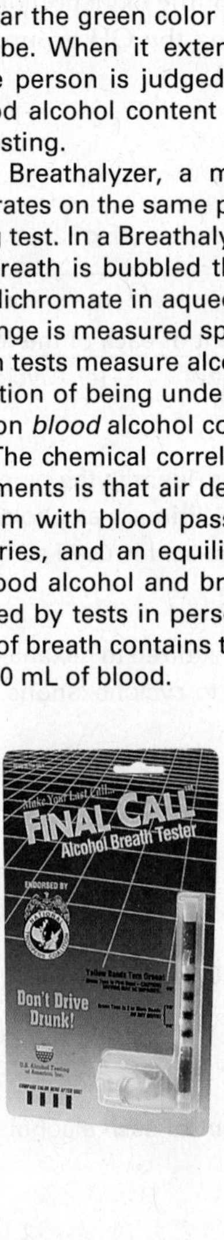

Charles D. Winters

A device for testing the breath for the presence of ethanol. When ethanol is oxidized by potassium dichromate, the reddish-orange color of dichromate ion turns to green as it is reduced to chromium(III) ion.

Questions

Although methanol* and isopropyl alcohol are much more toxic than ethanol and would rarely be found in one's breath, would these two compounds also give a positive alcohol screening test? If so, what would be the products of these reactions?

*Methanol is indeed much more toxic than ethanol, as many found out during Prohibition when they drank wood alcohol instead of ethanol. Methanol causes damage to the nerve sheaths, and one symptom of methanol poisoning is intense pain in response to light.

In ethyl vinyl ether, the ether oxygen is bonded to one sp^3 hybridized carbon and one sp^2 hybridized carbon:

$CH_3CH_2—O—CH{=}CH_2$

Ethyl vinyl ether

B. Nomenclature

In the IUPAC system, ethers are named by selecting the longest carbon chain as the parent alkane and naming the —OR group bonded to it as an **alkoxy** (*alkyl* + *oxygen*) **group**. Common names are derived by listing the alkyl groups bonded to oxygen in alphabetical order and adding the word *ether*.

$CH_3CH_2OCH_2CH_3$

Ethoxyethane (Diethyl ether)

$CH_3OC(CH_3)_2CH_3$ (drawn with CH₃ above and below the central C)

2-Methoxy-2-methylpropane (methyl *tert*-butyl ether, MTBE)

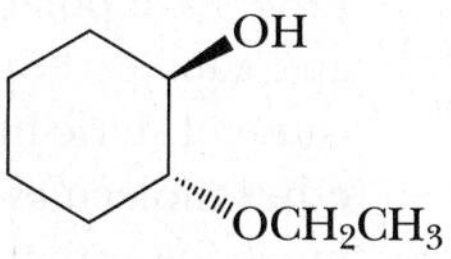

(1*R*,2*R*)-2-Ethoxycyclohexanol (*trans*-2-Ethoxycyclohexanol)

Chemists almost invariably use common names for low-molecular-weight ethers. For example, although ethoxyethane is the IUPAC name for $CH_3CH_2OCH_2CH_3$, it is rarely called that, but rather is called diethyl ether, ethyl ether, or, even more commonly, simply ether. The abbreviation for *tert*-butyl methyl ether, used at one time as an octane-improving additive to gasolines, is *MTBE*, after the common name of methyl *tert*-butyl ether.

Cyclic ethers are heterocyclic compounds in which the ether oxygen is one of the atoms in a ring. These ethers are generally known by their common names:

Ethylene oxide

Tetrahydrofuran (THF)

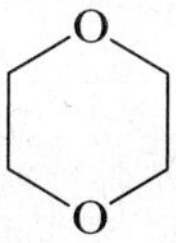

1,4-Dioxane

Boston Medical Library in the Francis A. Courtney Library of Medicine

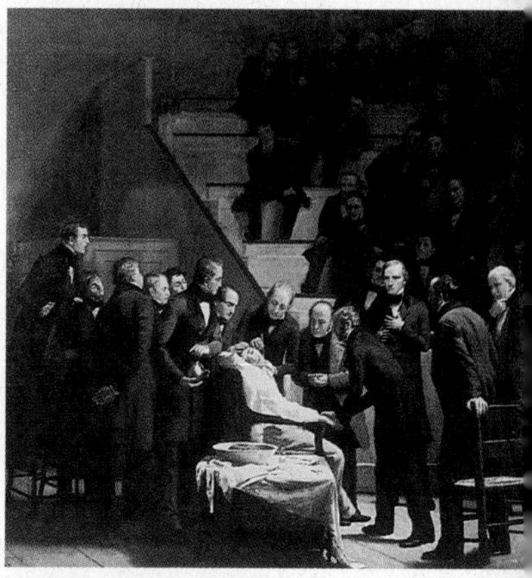

This painting by Robert Hinckley shows the first use of diethyl ether as an anesthetic in 1846. Dr. Robert John Collins was removing a tumor from the patient's neck, and the dentist W. T. G. Morton—who discovered its anesthetic properties—administered the ether.

Alkoxy group An —OR group, where R is an alkyl group.

Cyclic ether An ether in which the oxygen is one of the atoms of a ring.

EXAMPLE 8.7

Write the IUPAC and common names for each ether:

(a) $CH_3C(CH_3)_2OCH_2CH_3$ (drawn with CH₃ above and below the C)

(b)

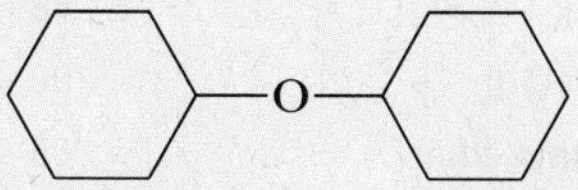

STRATEGY

As with all nomenclature problems, first determine the root name of the compound. In the IUPAC system, —OR groups are named as alkoxy groups. In the common nomenclature system, the alkyl groups bonded to oxygen are named in alphabetical order, followed by the word "ether."

SOLUTION

(a) 2-Ethoxy-2-methylpropane. Its common name is *tert*-butyl ethyl ether.
(b) Cyclohexoxycyclohexane. Its common name is dicyclohexyl ether.

See problem 8.16

PROBLEM 8.7

Write the IUPAC and common names for each ether:

(a) CH_3 (on the second carbon) $CH_3\overset{|}{C}HCH_2OCH_2CH_3$

(b) 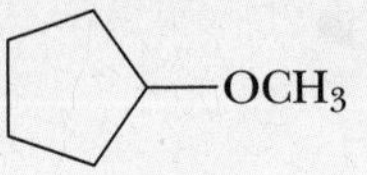

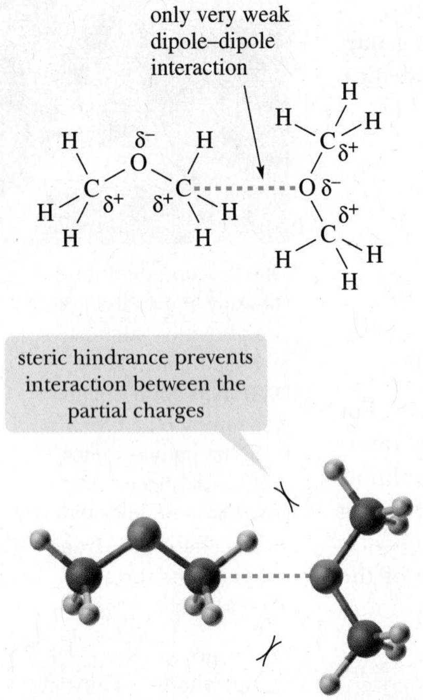

only very weak dipole–dipole interaction
δ−
δ+
δ+
δ−
δ+
δ+
steric hindrance prevents interaction between the partial charges

FIGURE 8.5
Ethers are polar molecules, but because of steric hindrance, only weak attractive interactions exist between their molecules in the pure liquid.

C. Physical Properties

Ethers are polar compounds in which oxygen bears a partial negative charge and each carbon bonded to it bears a partial positive charge (Figure 8.5). Because of steric hindrance, however, only weak forces of attraction exist between ether molecules in the pure liquid. Consequently, boiling points of ethers are much lower than those of alcohols of comparable molecular weight (Table 8.3). Boiling points of ethers are close to those of hydrocarbons of comparable molecular weight (compare Tables 3.4 and 8.3).

Because the oxygen atom of an ether carries a partial negative charge, ethers form hydrogen bonds with water (Figure 8.6) and are more soluble in water than are hydrocarbons of comparable molecular weight and shape (compare data in Tables 3.4 and 8.3).

The effect of hydrogen bonding is illustrated dramatically by comparing the boiling points of ethanol (78 °C) and its constitutional isomer dimethyl ether (−24 °C). The difference in boiling points between these two compounds is due to the polar O—H group in the alcohol, which is capable of forming

TABLE 8.3 Boiling Points and Solubilities in Water of Some Alcohols and Ethers of Comparable Molecular Weight

Structural Formula	Name	Molecular Weight	Boiling Point (°C)	Solubility in Water
CH_3CH_2OH	ethanol	46	78	infinite
CH_3OCH_3	dimethyl ether	46	−24	7.8 g/100 g
$CH_3CH_2CH_2CH_2OH$	1-butanol	74	117	7.4 g/100 g
$CH_3CH_2OCH_2CH_3$	diethyl ether	74	35	8 g/100 g
$CH_3CH_2CH_2CH_2CH_2OH$	1-pentanol	88	138	2.3 g/100 g
$HOCH_2CH_2CH_2CH_2OH$	1,4-butanediol	90	230	infinite
$CH_3CH_2CH_2CH_2OCH_3$	butyl methyl ether	88	71	slight
$CH_3OCH_2CH_2OCH_3$	ethylene glycol dimethyl ether	90	84	infinite

dimethyl ether in water. The partially negative oxygen of the ether is the hydrogen-bond acceptor, and a partially positive hydrogen of a water molecule is the hydrogen-bond donor

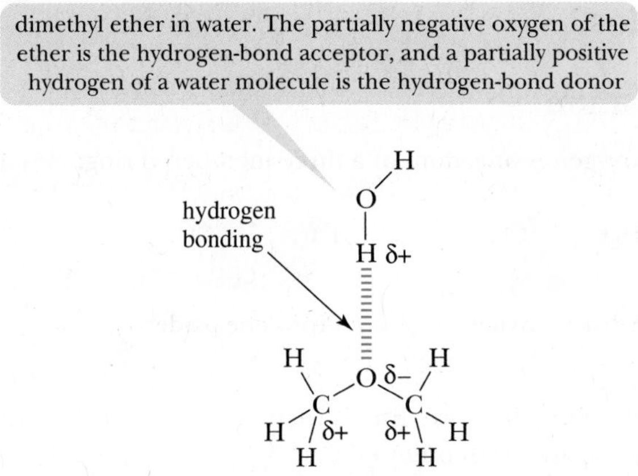

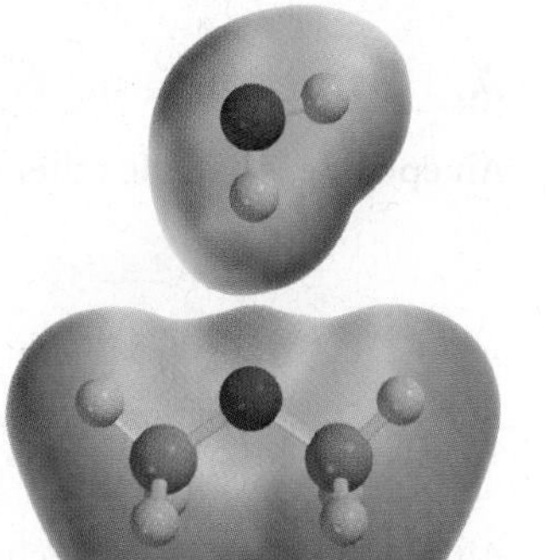

FIGURE 8.6 Ethers are hydrogen-bond acceptors only. They are not hydrogen-bond donors.

intermolecular hydrogen bonds. This hydrogen bonding increases the attractive force between molecules of ethanol; thus, ethanol has a higher boiling point than dimethyl ether:

 CH_3CH_2OH CH_3OCH_3 Ethanol Dimethyl ether bp 78 °C bp -24 °C

EXAMPLE 8.8

Arrange these compounds in order of increasing solubility in water:

CH₃OCH₂CH₂OCH₃

CH₃CH₂OCH₂CH₃

CH₃CH₂CH₂CH₂CH₂CH₃

Ethylene glycol dimethyl ether

Diethyl ether

Hexane

STRATEGY

Look for features that make organic compounds more soluble in water. These are, from most significant to least significant, (1) the ability to form hydrogen bonds with water, (2) polarity, and (3) low molecular weight.

SOLUTION

Water is a polar solvent. Hexane, a nonpolar hydrocarbon, has the lowest solubility in water. Both diethyl ether and ethylene glycol dimethyl ether are polar compounds, due to the presence of their polar C—O—C groups, and each interacts with water as a hydrogen-bond acceptor. Because ethylene glycol dimethyl ether has more sites within its molecules for hydrogen bonding, it is more soluble in water than diethyl ether:

CH₃CH₂CH₂CH₂CH₂CH₃

CH₃CH₂OCH₂CH₃

CH3OCH2CH2OCH3

Insoluble

8 g/100 g water

Soluble in all proportions

See problems 8.23-8.25

PROBLEM 8.8

Arrange these compounds in order of increasing boiling point:

CH₃OCH₂CH₂OCH₃

HOCH₂CH₂OH

CH₃OCH₂CH₂OH

D. Reactions of Ethers

Ethers, R—O—R, resemble hydrocarbons in their resistance to chemical reaction. They do not react with oxidizing agents, such as potassium dichromate or potassium permanganate. They are not affected by most acids or bases at moderate temperatures. Because of their good solvent properties and general inertness to chemical reaction, ethers are excellent solvents in which to carry out many organic reactions.

8.4 What Are Epoxides?

A. Structure and Nomenclature

Epoxide A cyclic ether in which oxygen is one atom of a three-membered ring.

An **epoxide** is a cyclic ether in which oxygen is one atom of a three-membered ring:

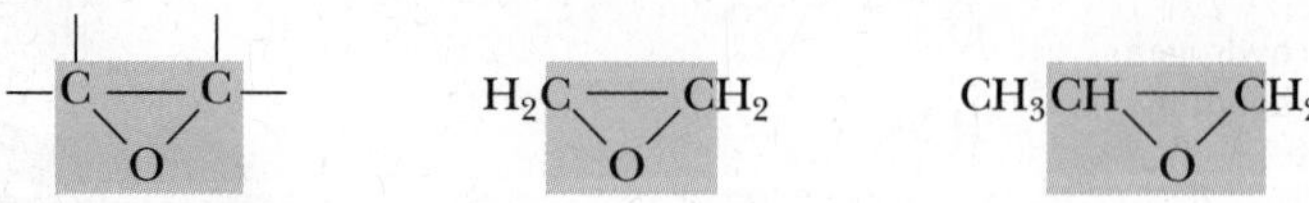

Functional group of an epoxide | Ethylene oxide | Propylene oxide

Although epoxides are technically classed as ethers, we discuss them separately because of their exceptional chemical reactivity compared with other ethers.

Common names for epoxides are derived by giving the common name of the alkene from which the epoxide might have been derived, followed by the word *oxide*; an example is ethylene oxide.

B. Synthesis from Alkenes

Ethylene oxide, one of the few epoxides manufactured on an industrial scale, is prepared by passing a mixture of ethylene and air (or oxygen) over a silver catalyst:

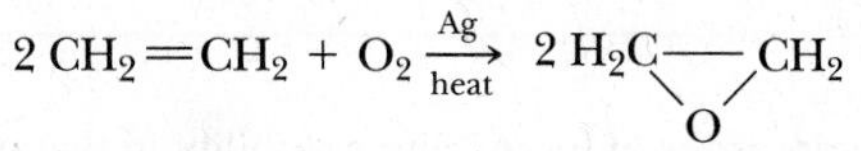

Ethylene | Ethylene oxide

In the United States, the annual production of ethylene oxide by this method is approximately 10^9 kg.

The most common laboratory method for the synthesis of epoxides from alkenes is oxidation with a peroxycarboxylic acid (a peracid), RCO_3H. One peracid used for this purpose is peroxyacetic acid:

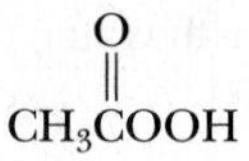

Peroxyacetic acid
(Peracetic acid)

Following is a balanced equation for the epoxidation of cyclohexene by a peroxycarboxylic acid. In the process, the peroxycarboxylic acid is reduced to a carboxylic acid:

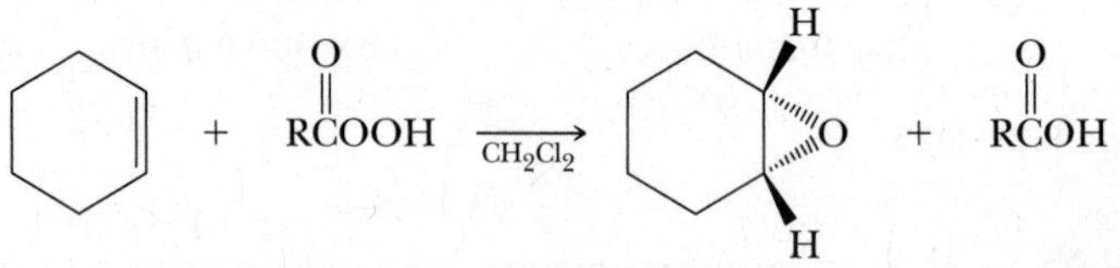

Cyclohexene | A peroxycarboxylic acid | 1,2-Epoxycyclohexane (Cyclohexene oxide) | A carboxylic acid

The epoxidation of an alkene is stereoselective. The epoxidation of *cis*-2-butene, for example, yields only *cis*-2-butene oxide:

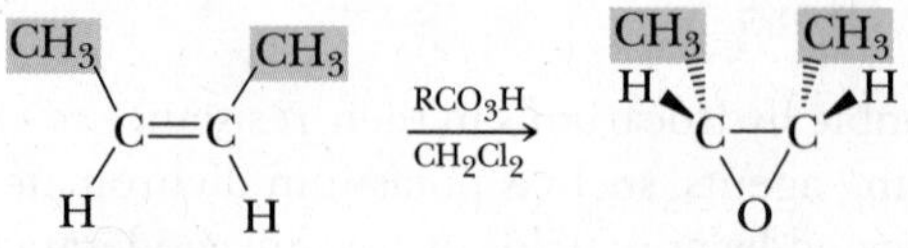

cis-2-Butene | *cis*-2-Butene oxide

HOW TO 8.5

Predict the Product of an Epoxidation Reaction

The key feature of an epoxidation reaction of an alkene and a peroxycarboxylic acid is the formation of an epoxide with retention of stereochemistry about the reacting C—C double bond. This means that the relative stereochemistry of all groups about the double bond must be the same in the product epoxide as shown in the acyclic and cyclic examples.

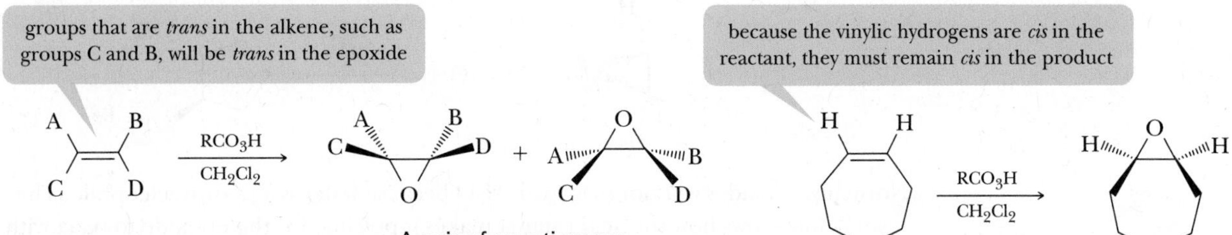

EXAMPLE 8.9

Draw a structural formula of the epoxide formed by treating *trans*-2-butene with a peroxycarboxylic acid.

STRATEGY

To predict the product of a peroxycarboxylic acid and an alkene, convert its C—C double bond to a C—C single bond in which both carbons are bonded to the same oxygen in a three-membered ring.

SOLUTION

The oxygen of the epoxide ring is added by forming both carbon–oxygen bonds from the same side of the carbon–carbon double bond:

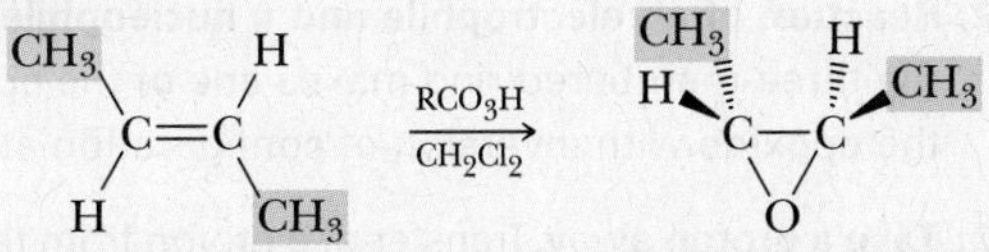

See problems 8.43–8.45, 8.47

PROBLEM 8.9

Draw the structural formula of the epoxide formed by treating 1,2-dimethylcyclopentene with a peroxycarboxylic acid.

C. Ring-Opening Reactions

Ethers are not normally susceptible to reaction with aqueous acid (Section 8.3D). Epoxides, however, are especially reactive because of the angle strain in the three-membered ring. The normal bond angle about an sp^3 hybridized carbon or oxygen atom is 109.5°. Because of the strain associated with the compression of bond angles in the three-membered epoxide ring from the normal 109.5° to 60°, epoxides undergo ring-opening reactions with a variety of nucleophilic reagents.

In the presence of an acid catalyst—most commonly, perchloric acid—epoxides are hydrolyzed to glycols. As an example, the acid-catalyzed hydrolysis of ethylene oxide gives 1,2-ethanediol:

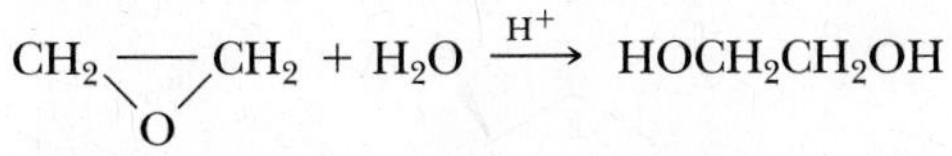

Ethylene oxide — 1,2-Ethanediol (Ethylene glycol)

Annual production of ethylene glycol in the United States is approximately 10^{10} kg. Two of its largest uses are in automotive antifreeze and as one of the two starting materials for the production of polyethylene terephthalate (PET), which is fabricated into such consumer products as Dacron® polyester, Mylar®, and packaging films (Section 17.4B).

The acid-catalyzed ring opening of epoxides shows a stereoselectivity typical of S_N2 reactions: The nucleophile attacks anti to the leaving hydroxyl group, and the —OH groups in the glycol thus formed are anti. As a result, the acid-catalyzed hydrolysis of an epoxycycloalkane yields a *trans*-1,2-cycloalkanediol:

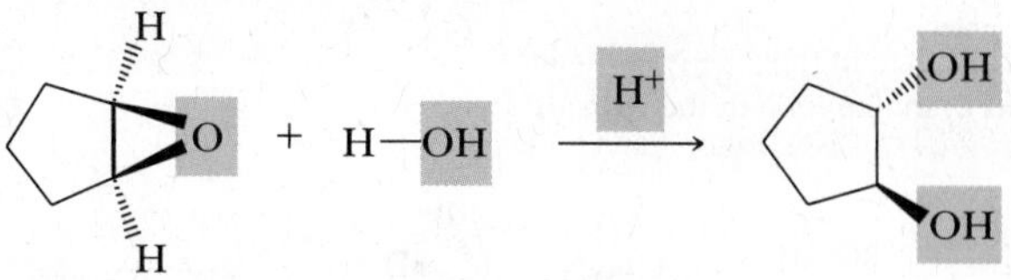

Normally, epoxides will not react with H_2O because water is a poor nucleophile. The mechanism below shows how the acid catalyst makes it possible for the epoxide to react with water.

Mechanism

Acid-Catalyzed Epoxide Ring Opening

STEP 1: Add a proton. The reaction is made possible because the acid catalyst protonates the epoxide oxygen, generating a highly reactive oxonium ion.

STEP 2: Reaction of an electrophile and a nucleophile to form a new covalent bond. The positive charge on the oxygen of the three-membered ring makes one of the epoxide carbons susceptible to nucleophilic attack by water. This opens the epoxide with inversion of configuration at the carbon that was attacked.

STEP 3: Take a proton away. Transfer of a proton from the resulting intermediate gives the *trans* glycol and regenerates the acid.

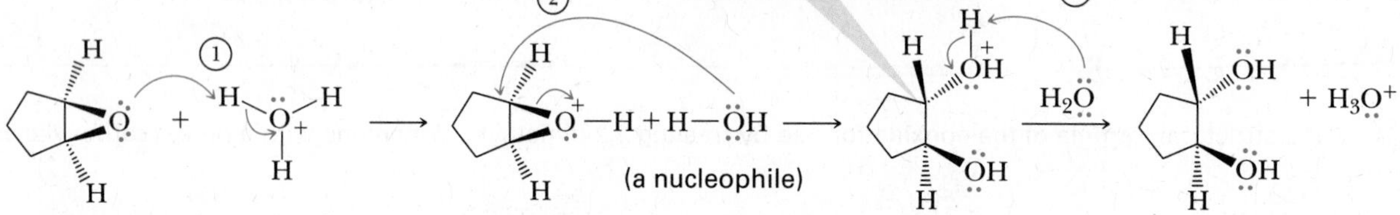

EXAMPLE 8.10

Draw the structural formula of the product formed by treating cyclohexene oxide with aqueous acid. Be certain to show the stereochemistry of the product.

STRATEGY

The acid-catalyzed ring opening of an epoxide always results in a *trans*-1,2,-diol, with the two carbons formerly part of the epoxide bonded to each of the two hydroxyl groups.

SOLUTION

The acid-catalyzed hydrolysis of the three-membered epoxide ring gives a *trans* glycol:

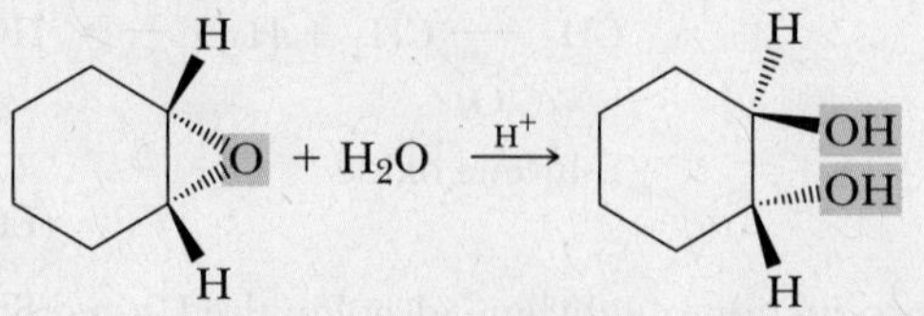

trans-1,2-Cyclohexanediol

See problems 8.26, 8.43–8.45

PROBLEM 8.10

Show how to convert 1,2-dimethylcyclohexene to *trans*-1,2-dimethylcyclohexane-1,2-diol.

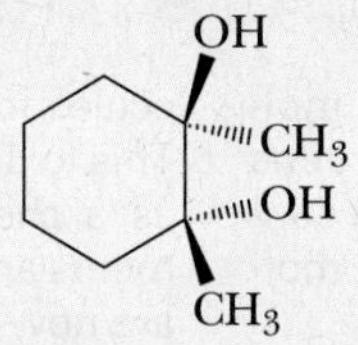

trans-1,2-Dimethylcyclohexane-1,2-diol

Just as ethers are not normally susceptible to reaction with electrophiles, neither are they normally susceptible to reaction with nucleophiles. Because of the strain associated with the three-membered ring, however, epoxides undergo ring-opening reactions with good nucleophiles such as ammonia and amines (Chapter 10), alkoxide ions, and thiols and their anions (Section 8.6). Good nucleophiles attack the ring by an S_N2 mechanism and show a stereoselectivity for attack of the nucleophile at the less hindered carbon of the three-membered ring. The result is an alcohol with the former nucleophile bonded to a carbon β to the newly formed hydroxyl group. An illustration is the reaction of 1-methylcyclohexene oxide with ammonia to give the stereoisomer of 2-amino-1-methylcyclohexanol in which the hydroxyl group and the amino group are *trans*:

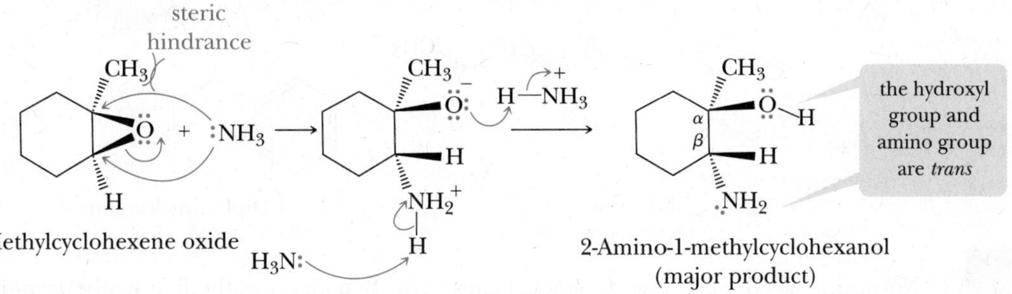

1-Methylcyclohexene oxide

2-Amino-1-methylcyclohexanol (major product)

The value of epoxides lies in the number of nucleophiles that bring about ring opening and the combinations of functional groups that can be prepared from them. The following chart summarizes the three most important of these nucleophilic ring-opening reactions (the characteristic structural feature of each ring-opening product is shown in color):

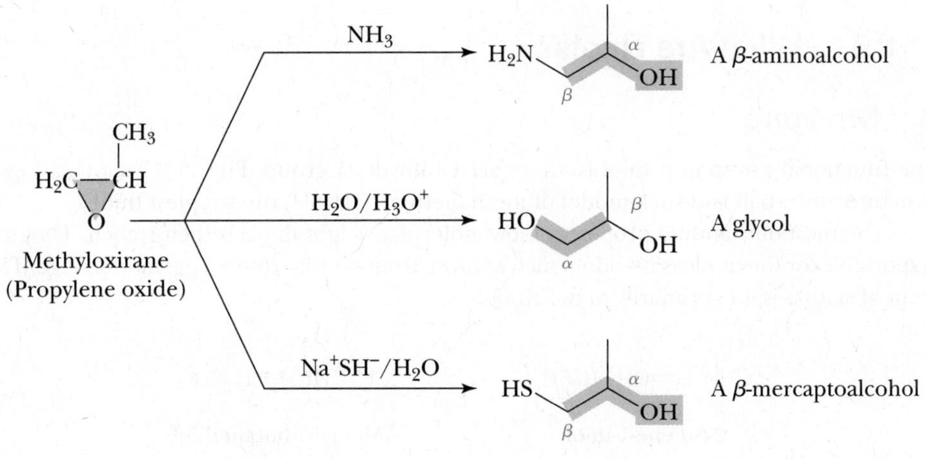

Chemical Connections 8C

ETHYLENE OXIDE: A CHEMICAL STERILANT

Because ethylene oxide is such a highly strained molecule, it reacts with the types of nucleophilic groups present in biological materials. At sufficiently high concentrations, ethylene oxide reacts with enough molecules in cells to cause the death of microorganisms. This toxic property is the basis for using ethylene oxide as a chemical sterilant. In hospitals, surgical instruments and other items that cannot be made disposable are now sterilized by exposure to ethylene oxide.

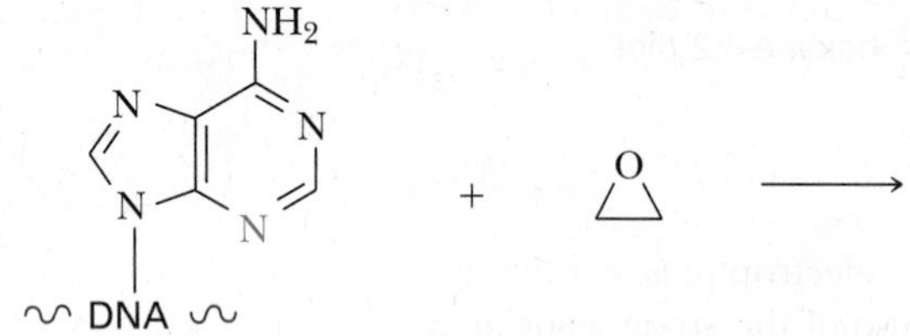

Question

One of the ways that ethylene oxide has been found to kill microorganisms is by reacting with the adenine components of their DNA at the atom indicated in red. Propose a mechanism and an initial product for this reaction. *Hint:* First draw in any lone pairs of electrons in adenine.

Ethylene oxide and substituted ethylene oxides are valuable building blocks for the synthesis of larger organic molecules. Following are structural formulas for two common drugs, each synthesized in part from ethylene oxide:

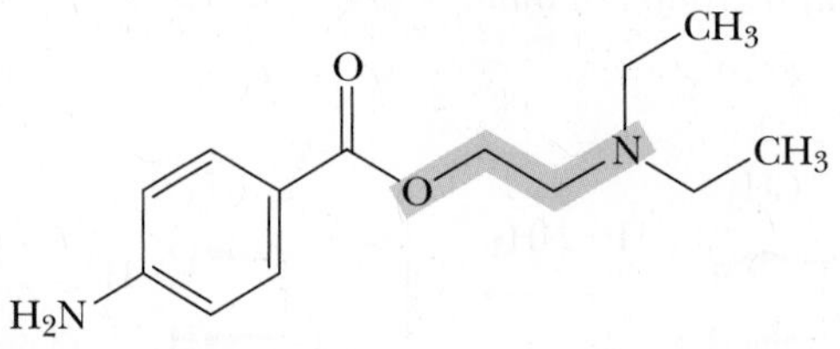

Procaine (Novocaine)

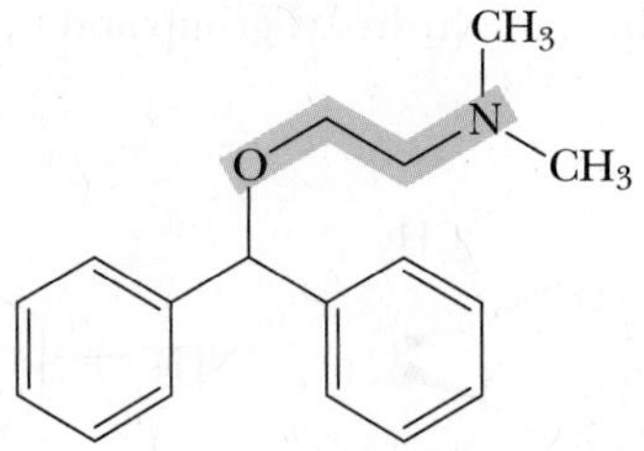

Diphenhydramine (Benadryl)

Stephen J. Krasemann/ Photo Researchers, Inc.

The scent of skunks is a mixture of two thiols, 3-methyl-1-butanethiol and 2-butene-1-thiol.

Novocaine was the first injectable local anesthetic. Benadryl was the first synthetic antihistamine. The portion of the carbon skeleton of each that is derived from the reaction of ethylene oxide with a nitrogen–nucleophile is shown in color.

In later chapters, after we have developed the chemistry of more functional groups, we will show how to synthesize Novocaine and Benadryl from readily available starting materials. For the moment, however, it is sufficient to recognize that the unit —O—C—C—Nu can be derived by nucleophilic opening of ethylene oxide or a substituted ethylene oxide.

8.5 What Are Thiols?

A. Structure

Thiol A compound containing an —SH (sulfhydryl) group.

The functional group of a **thiol** is an —SH (sulfhydryl) group. Figure 8.7 shows a Lewis structure and a ball-and-stick model of methanethiol, CH_3SH, the simplest thiol.

The most outstanding property of low-molecular-weight thiols is their stench. They are responsible for the unpleasant odors such as those from skunks, rotten eggs, and sewage. The scent of skunks is due primarily to two thiols:

$$CH_3CH{=}CHCH_2SH$$

2-Butene-1-thiol

$$CH_3\overset{\displaystyle CH_3\atop|}{C}HCH_2CH_2SH$$

3-Methyl-1-butanethiol

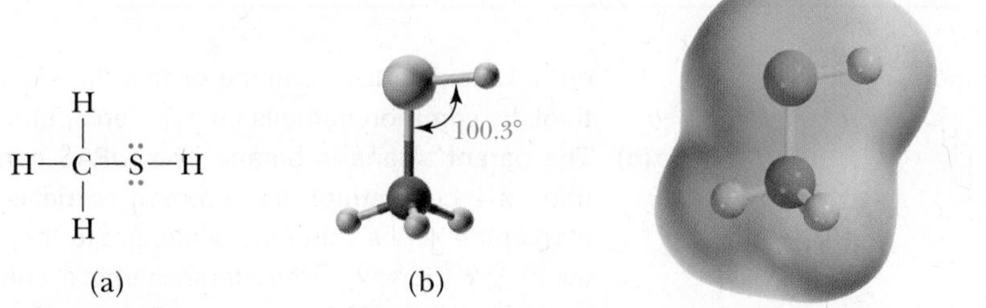

Methanethiol. The electronegativities of carbon and sulfur are virtually identical (2.5 each), while sulfur is slightly more electronegative than hydrogen (2.5 versus 2.1). The electron density model shows some slight partial positive charge on hydrogen of the S—H group and some slight partial negative charge on sulfur.

FIGURE 8.7 Methanethiol, CH_3SH. (a) Lewis structure and (b) ball-and-stick model. The C—S—H bond angle is 100.3°, somewhat smaller than the tetrahedral angle of 109.5°.

A blend of low-molecular-weight thiols is added to natural gas as an odorant. The most common of these odorants is 2-methyl-2-propanethiol (*tert*-butyl mercaptan), because it is the most resistant to oxidation and has the greatest soil penetration. 2-Propanethiol is also used for this purpose, usually as a blend with *tert*-butyl mercaptan.

Natural gas odorants:

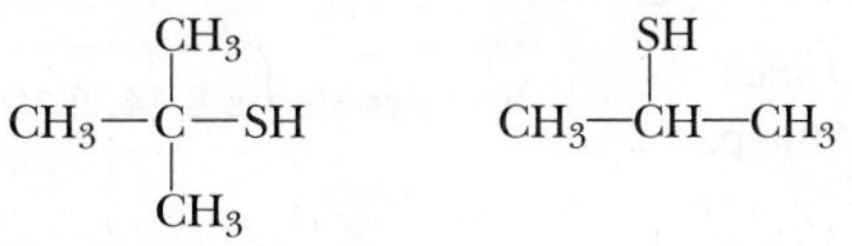

2-Methyl-2-propanethiol (*tert*-Butyl mercaptan) 2-Propanethiol (Isopropyl mercaptan)

B. Nomenclature

Mercaptan A common name for any molecule containing an —SH group.

The sulfur analog of an alcohol is called a thiol (thi- from the Greek: *theion*, sulfur) or, in the older literature, a **mercaptan**, which literally means "mercury capturing." Thiols react with Hg^{2+} in aqueous solution to give sulfide salts as insoluble precipitates. Thiophenol, C_6H_5SH, for example, gives $(C_6H_5S)_2Hg$.

In the IUPAC system, thiols are named by selecting as the parent alkane the longest chain of carbon atoms that contains the —SH group. To show that the compound is a thiol, we add *-thiol* to the name of the parent alkane and number the parent chain in the direction that gives the —SH group the lower number.

Common names for simple thiols are derived by naming the alkyl group bonded to —SH and adding the word *mercaptan*. In compounds containing other functional groups, the presence of an —SH group is indicated by the prefix **mercapto-**. According to the IUPAC system, —OH takes precedence over —SH in both numbering and naming:

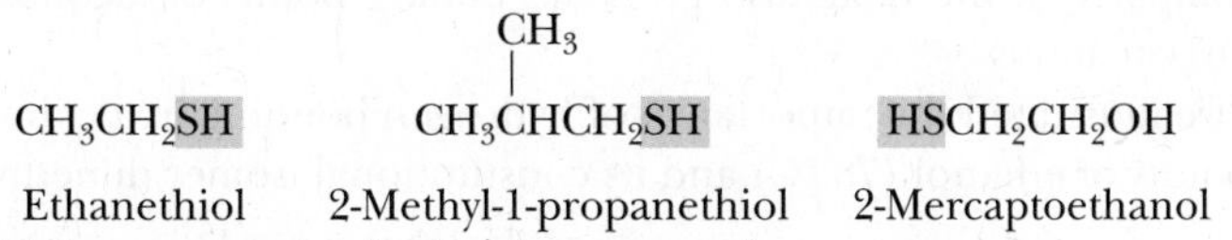

Ethanethiol (Ethyl mercaptan) 2-Methyl-1-propanethiol (Isobutyl mercaptan) 2-Mercaptoethanol

Sulfur analogs of ethers (thioethers) are named by using the word *sulfide* to show the presence of the —S— group. Following are common names of two sulfides:

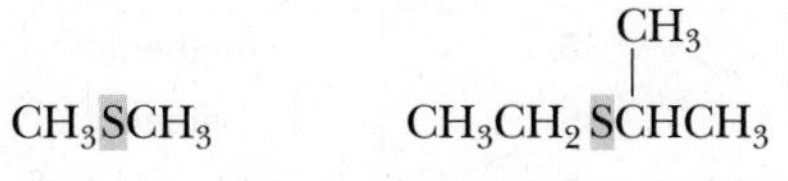

Dimethyl sulfide Ethyl isopropyl sulfide

Charles D. Winters

Mushrooms, onions, garlic, and coffee all contain sulfur compounds. One of these present in coffee is

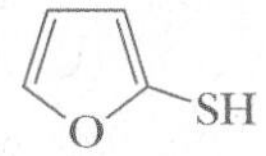

EXAMPLE 8.11

Write the IUPAC name for each compound:

(a) 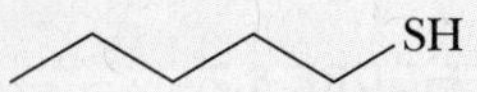 (b) 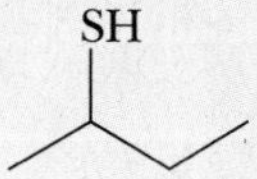

(c) 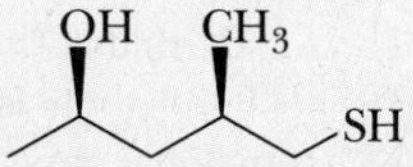

STRATEGY

Identify the root name of the compound. If the compound only contains an —SH group, name it as an alkanethiol. If the compound contains both an —OH group and an —SH group, name the compound as an alcohol with a mercapto substituent. Remember that priority for numbering is given to the —OH group.

SOLUTION

(a) The parent alkane is pentane. We show the presence of the —SH group by adding *thiol* to the name of the parent alkane. The IUPAC name of this thiol is 1-pentanethiol. Its common name is pentyl mercaptan.

(b) The parent alkane is butane. The IUPAC name of this thiol is 2-butanethiol. Its common name is *sec*-butyl mercaptan. It is a chiral molecule due to the stereocenter at C-2. However, the stereochemical configuration was not indicated here.

(c) The parent alkane is pentane. Because —OH receives priority over —SH, the compound is named as an alcohol, with the —OH group receiving priority for numbering as well.

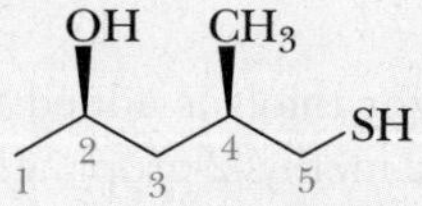 not 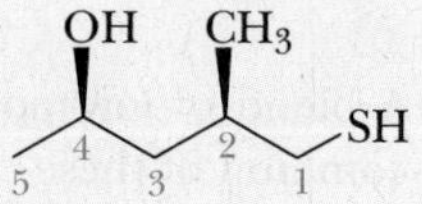

(2*R*,4*R*)-5-Mercapto-4-methylpentan-2-ol

See problems 8.14, 8.15

PROBLEM 8.11

Write the IUPAC name for each thiol:

(a) 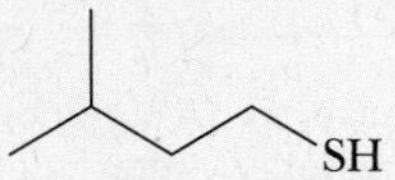 (b) 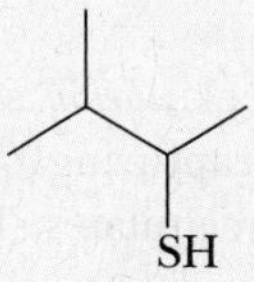

C. Physical Properties

Because of the small difference in electronegativity between sulfur and hydrogen (2.5 − 2.1 = 0.4), we classify the S—H bond as nonpolar covalent. Because of this lack of polarity, thiols show little association by hydrogen bonding. Consequently, they have lower boiling points and are less soluble in water and other polar solvents than are alcohols of similar molecular weight. Table 8.4 gives the boiling points of three low-molecular-weight thiols. For comparison, the table also gives the boiling points of alcohols with the same number of carbon atoms.

Earlier, we illustrated the importance of hydrogen bonding in alcohols by comparing the boiling points of ethanol (78 °C) and its constitutional isomer dimethyl ether (24 °C).

TABLE 8.4 Boiling Points of Three Thiols and Three Alcohols with the Same Number of Carbon Atoms

Thiol	Boiling Point (°C)	Alcohol	Boiling Point (°C)
methanethiol	6	methanol	65
ethanethiol	35	ethanol	78
1-butanethiol	98	1-butanol	117

By comparison, the boiling point of ethanethiol is 35 °C, and that of its constitutional isomer dimethyl sulfide is 37 °C:

CH_3CH_2SH	CH_3SCH_3
Ethanethiol	Dimethyl sulfide
bp 35 °C	bp 37 °C

The fact that the boiling points of these constitutional isomers are almost identical indicates that little or no association by hydrogen bonding occurs between thiol molecules.

8.6 What Are the Characteristic Reactions of Thiols?

In this section, we discuss the acidity of thiols and their reaction with strong bases, such as sodium hydroxide, and with molecular oxygen.

A. Acidity

Hydrogen sulfide is a stronger acid than water:

$$H_2O + H_2O \rightleftharpoons HO^- + H_3O^+ \qquad pK_a = 15.7$$

$$H_2S + H_2O \rightleftharpoons HS^- + H_3O^+ \qquad pK_a = 7.0$$

Similarly, thiols are stronger acids than alcohols. Compare, for example, the pK_a's of ethanol and ethanethiol in dilute aqueous solution:

$$CH_3CH_2OH + H_2O \rightleftharpoons CH_3CH_2O^- + H_3O^+ \qquad pK_a = 15.9$$

$$CH_3CH_2SH + H_2O \rightleftharpoons CH_3CH_2S^- + H_3O^+ \qquad pK_a = 8.5$$

thiols are more acidic than alcohols because sulfides are more stable conjugate bases than are alkoxides. There is more area to delocalize the valence electrons about the negative sulfur atom because sulfur is larger than oxygen.

Thiols are sufficiently strong acids that, when dissolved in aqueous sodium hydroxide, they are converted completely to alkylsulfide salts:

$$CH_3CH_2SH + Na^+OH^- \longrightarrow CH_3CH_2S^- Na^+ + H_2O$$

CH_3CH_2SH	Na^+OH^-	$CH_3CH_2S^- Na^+$	H_2O
pK_a 8.5			pK_a15.7
Stronger acid	Stronger base	Weaker base	Weaker acid

To name salts of thiols, give the name of the cation first, followed by the name of the alkyl group to which the suffix *-sulfide* is added. For example, the sodium salt derived from ethanethiol is named sodium ethylsulfide.

B. Oxidation to Disulfides

Many of the chemical properties of thiols stem from the fact that the sulfur atom of a thiol is oxidized easily to several higher oxidation states. The most common reaction of thiols in biological systems is their oxidation to disulfides, the functional group of which is a **disulfide** (—S—S—) bond. Thiols are readily oxidized to disulfides by molecular oxygen. In fact, they are so susceptible to oxidation that they must be protected from contact with air during storage. Disulfides, in turn, are easily reduced to thiols by several reagents. This easy interconversion between thiols and disulfides is very important in protein chemistry, as we will see in Chapter 18:

$$2\ HOCH_2CH_2SH \underset{\text{reduction}}{\overset{\text{oxidation}}{\rightleftharpoons}} HOCH_2CH_2S{-}SCH_2CH_2OH$$

A thiol — A disulfide

We derive common names of simple disulfides by listing the names of the groups bonded to sulfur and adding the word *disulfide*, as, for example, $CH_3S{-}SCH_3$, which is named dimethyldisulfide.

EXAMPLE 8.12

Predict the products of the following reactions. If the reaction is an acid–base reaction, predict its position of equilibrium.

(a) 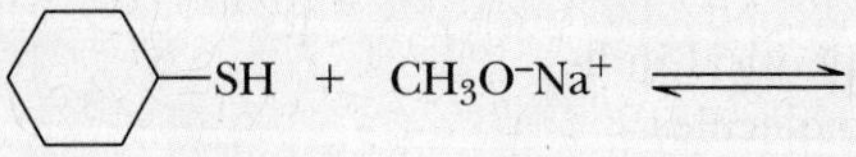

(b) 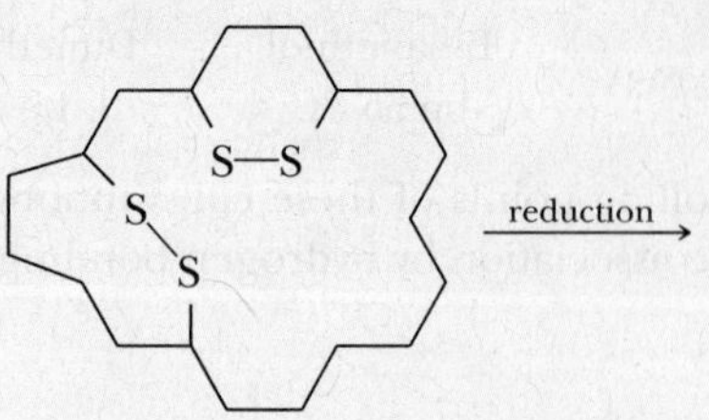

STRATEGY

First determine what type of reaction is occurring. An oxidation reaction of a thiol produces a disulfide bond (—S—S—). A reduction of a disulfide bond produces two mercapto groups. Thiols can also act as weak acids (although at a pK_a of 8.5, they are relatively strong for an organic acid).

SOLUTION

(a) 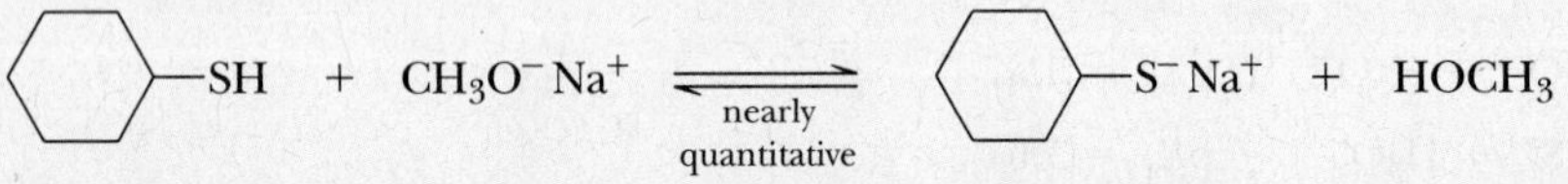

(b) 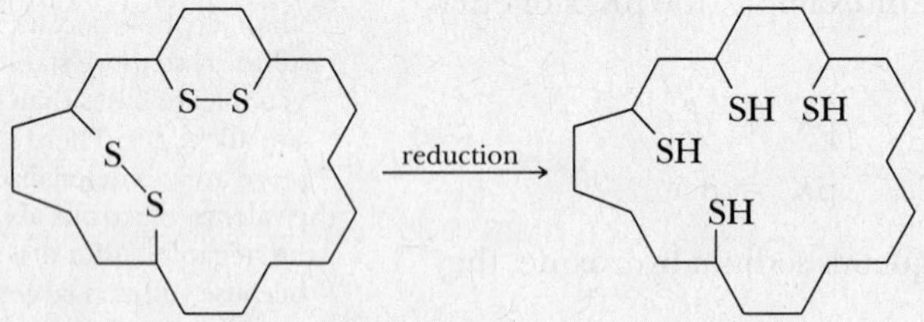

See problems 8.28–8.30, 8.32

PROBLEM 8.12

Predict the products of the following reactions. If the reaction is an acid–base reaction, predict its position of equilibrium.

(a) 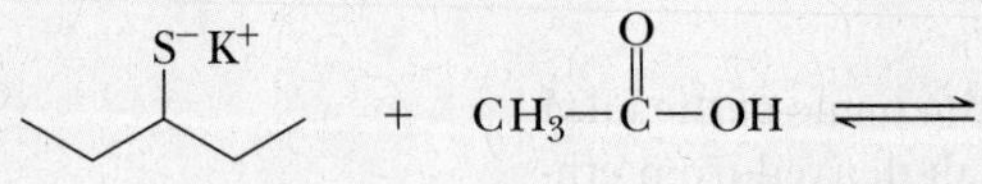

(b) 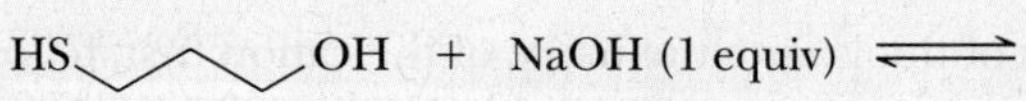

(c) 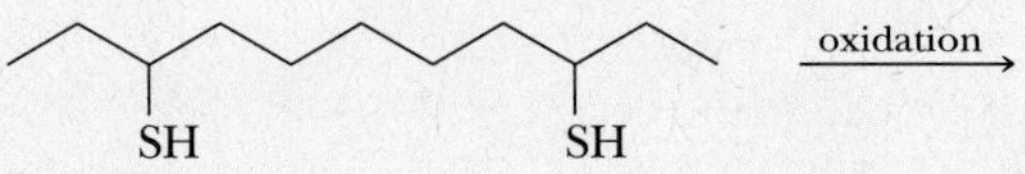

SUMMARY OF KEY QUESTIONS

8.1 What Are Alcohols?

- The functional group of an **alcohol** is an —OH **(hydroxyl) group** bonded to an sp^3 hybridized carbon.
- Alcohols are classified as 1°, 2°, or 3°, depending on whether the —OH group is bonded to a primary, secondary, or tertiary carbon.
- IUPAC names of alcohols are derived by changing the suffix of the parent alkane from *-e* to *-ol*. The chain is numbered to give the carbon bearing —OH the lower number.
- Common names for alcohols are derived by naming the alkyl group bonded to —OH and adding the word *alcohol*.

- Alcohols are polar compounds with oxygen bearing a partial negative charge and both the carbon and hydrogen bonded to it bearing partial positive charges.
- Because of intermolecular association by hydrogen bonding, the boiling points of alcohols are higher than those of hydrocarbons with comparable molecular weight.
- Because of increased dispersion forces, the boiling points of alcohols increase with increasing molecular weight.
- Alcohols interact with water by **hydrogen bonding** and therefore are more soluble in water than are hydrocarbons of comparable molecular weight.

8.2 What Are the Characteristic Reactions of Alcohols?

- Alcohols undergo acid–base reactions, acting both as weak acids and weak bases. The two smallest alcohols, methanol and ethanol, are comparable to water in acidity, while most 2° and 3° alcohols are less acidic than water.
- Alcohols react with **active metals** (e.g., Li, Na, K) to give **alkoxides**.
- Alcohols react with hydrogen halides (HCl, HBr, and HI) to give haloalkanes via substitution reactions. The mechanism of the reaction is either S_N1 or S_N2 depending on the classification (1°, 2°, or 3°) of the alcohol.
- Alcohols react with **thionyl chloride**, $SOCl_2$, to give chloroalkanes.
- Alcohols undergo **dehydration** in concentrated sulfuric or phosphoric acid. These elimination reactions follow Zaitsev's rule, yielding the more substituted alkene as the major product.
- Alcohols can be **oxidized** to ketones, aldehydes, and carboxylic acids. **Chromic acid** and **pyridinium chlorochromate** (PCC) both oxidize 2° alcohols to ketones. PCC oxidizes 1° alcohols to aldehydes, while chromic acid oxidizes 1° alcohols to carboxylic acids. 3°Alcohols are not oxidized.

8.3 What Are Ethers?

- The functional group of an **ether** is an atom of oxygen bonded to two carbon atoms. Ethers are used as solvents and in medicine as inhalation anesthetics.
- In the IUPAC name of an ether, the parent alkane is named, and then the —OR group is named as an alkoxy substituent. Common names are derived by naming the two groups bonded to oxygen followed by the word "ether". Ethers are weakly polar compounds. Their boiling points are close to those of hydrocarbons with comparable molecular weight. Because ethers are hydrogen-bond acceptors, they are more soluble in water than are hydrocarbons with comparable molecular weight.
- Ethers are relatively resistant to chemical transformation and, for this reason, are often employed as solvents in chemical reactions.

8.4 What Are Epoxides?

- An **epoxide** is a three-membered cyclic ether in which oxygen is one of the atoms of the three-membered ring.
- Epoxides can be synthesized from the reaction of an alkene with a **peroxycarboxylic acid** (RCO_3H). The reaction proceeds such that the relative stereochemistry about the C—C double bond is retained in the product epoxide.
- Epoxides undergo ring-opening reactions due to the strain of their three-membered rings. In acid-catalyzed hydrolysis, epoxides made from cyclic alkenes are transformed into *trans*-glycols. Good nucleophiles can also open the epoxide ring via nucleophilic attack at the least substituted carbon of the three-membered ring.

8.5 What Are Thiols?

- A **thiol** is the sulfur analog of an alcohol; it contains an —SH **(sulfhydryl) group** in place of an —OH group. Thiols are important compounds in several biological processes.
- Thiols are named in the same manner as alcohols, but the suffix *-e* is retained, and *-thiol* is added. Common names for thiols are derived by naming the alkyl group bonded to —SH and adding the word "**mercaptan**." In compounds containing functional groups of higher precedence, the presence of —SH is indicated by the prefix **mercapto-**. For thioethers, name the two groups bonded to sulfur, followed by the word **"sulfide."**
- The S—H bond is nonpolar covalent, and the physical properties of thiols are more like those of hydrocarbons with comparable molecular weight.

8.6 What Are the Characteristic Reactions of Thiols?

- Thiols ($pK_a \approx 8.5$) are stronger acids than alcohols and are quantitatively deprotonated by hydroxide.
- Thiols can be oxidized to give a **disulfide** (—S—S—) bond. This process is reversible through reduction.

QUICK QUIZ

Answer true or false to the following questions to assess your general knowledge of the concepts in this chapter. If you have difficulty with any of them, you should review the appropriate section in the chapter (shown in parentheses) before attempting the more challenging end-of-chapter problems.

1. Dehydration of an alcohol proceeds either by an E1 or an E2 mechanism. (8.2)
2. Epoxides are more reactive than acyclic ethers. (8.3, 8.4)
3. Attack of an electrophile on the carbon of an epoxide ring results in opening of the ring. (8.4)
4. A hydrogen bond is a form of dipole–dipole interaction. (8.1)
5. Alcohols have higher boiling points than thiols with the same molecular weight. (8.1, 8.5)
6. Thiols are more acidic than alcohols. (8.2, 8.5)
7. Alcohols can act as hydrogen-bond donors but not as hydrogen-bond acceptors. (8.1)
8. Alcohols can function as both acids and bases. (8.2)
9. Ethers can act as hydrogen-bond donors but not as hydrogen-bond acceptors. (8.3)
10. Reduction of a thiol produces a disulfide. (8.6)
11. Ethers are more reactive than alcohols. (8.2, 8.3)
12. $(CH_3CH_2)_2CHOH$ is classified as a 3° alcohol. (8.1)
13. PCC will oxidize a secondary alcohol to a ketone. (8.2)
14. PCC will oxidize a primary alcohol to a carboxylic acid. (8.2)
15. Alcohols have higher boiling points than ethers with the same molecular weight. (8.1, 8.3)
16. A dehydration reaction yields an epoxide as the product. (8.2)
17. Alcohols can be converted to alkenes. (8.2)
18. Alcohols can be converted to haloalkanes. (8.2)
19. In naming alcohols, "alkyl alcohol" is the IUPAC form of the name, while "alkanol" is the common form of the name. (8.1)
20. —OH is a poor leaving group. (8.2)
21. A glycol is any alcohol with at least two hydroxyl groups bonded to different carbons. (8.1)

Answers: (1) T (2) T (3) F (4) T (5) T (6) T (7) F (8) T (9) F (10) F
(11) F (12) F (13) T (14) F (15) T (16) F (17) T (18) T (19) F (20) T (21) T

Detailed explanations for many of these answers can be found in the accompanying Solutions Manual.

KEY REACTIONS

1. Acidity of Alcohols (Section 8.2A)

In dilute aqueous solution, methanol and ethanol are comparable in acidity to water. Secondary and tertiary alcohols are weaker acids than water.

$$CH_3OH + H_2O \rightleftharpoons CH_3O^- + H_3O^+ \qquad pK_a = 15.5$$

2. Reaction of Alcohols with Active Metals (Section 8.2C)

Alcohols react with Li, Na, K, and other active metals to form metal alkoxides, which are somewhat stronger bases than NaOH and KOH:

$$2\ CH_3CH_2OH + 2\ Na \longrightarrow 2\ CH_3CH_2O^-\ Na^+ + H_2$$

3. Reaction of Alcohols with HCl, HBr, and HI (Section 8.2D)

Primary alcohols react with HBr and HI by an S_N2 mechanism:

$$CH_3CH_2CH_2CH_2OH + HBr \longrightarrow CH_3CH_2CH_2CH_2Br + H_2O$$

Tertiary alcohols react with HCl, HBr, and HI by an S_N1 mechanism, with the formation of a carbocation intermediate:

$$(CH_3)_3COH + HCl \xrightarrow{25\ °C} (CH_3)_3CCl + H_2O$$

Secondary alcohols may react with HCl, HBr, and HI by an S_N2 or an S_N1 mechanism, depending on the alcohol and experimental conditions.

4. Reaction of Alcohols with $SOCl_2$ (Section 8.2D)

This is often the method of choice for converting an alcohol to an alkyl chloride:

$$CH_3(CH_2)_5OH + SOCl_2 \longrightarrow CH_3(CH_2)_5Cl + SO_2 + HCl$$

5. Acid-Catalyzed Dehydration of Alcohols (Section 8.2E)

When isomeric alkenes are possible, the major product is generally the more substituted alkene (Zaitsev's rule):

$$CH_3CH_2CH(OH)CH_3 \xrightarrow[heat]{H_3PO_4} CH_3CH{=}CHCH_3 + CH_3CH_2CH{=}CH_2 + H_2O$$

Major product

6. Oxidation of a Primary Alcohol to an Aldehyde (Section 8.2F)

This oxidation is most conveniently carried out by using pyridinium chlorochromate (PCC):

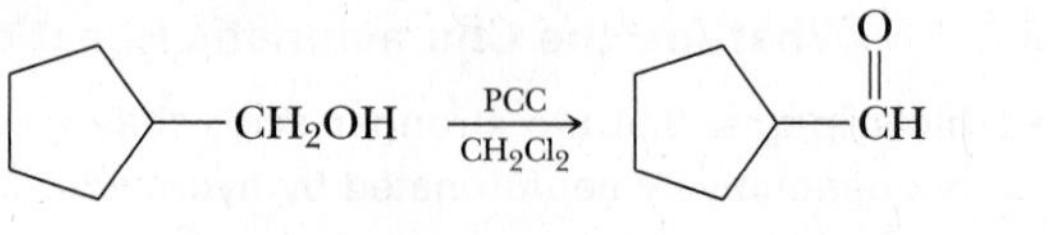

7. Oxidation of a Primary Alcohol to a Carboxylic Acid (Section 8.2F)

A primary alcohol is oxidized to a carboxylic acid by chromic acid:

$$CH_3(CH_2)_4CH_2OH + H_2CrO_4 \xrightarrow[\text{acetone}]{H_2O} CH_3(CH_2)_4\overset{\overset{O}{\|}}{C}OH + Cr^{3+}$$

8. Oxidation of a Secondary Alcohol to a Ketone (Section 8.2F)

A secondary alcohol is oxidized to a ketone by chromic acid and by PCC:

$$CH_3(CH_2)_4\overset{\overset{OH}{|}}{C}HCH_3 + H_2CrO_4 \longrightarrow CH_3(CH_2)_4\overset{\overset{O}{\|}}{C}CH_3 + Cr^{3+}$$

9. Oxidation of an Alkene to an Epoxide (Section 8.4B)

The most common method for the synthesis of an epoxide from an alkene is oxidation with a peroxycarboxylic acid, such as peroxyacetic acid:

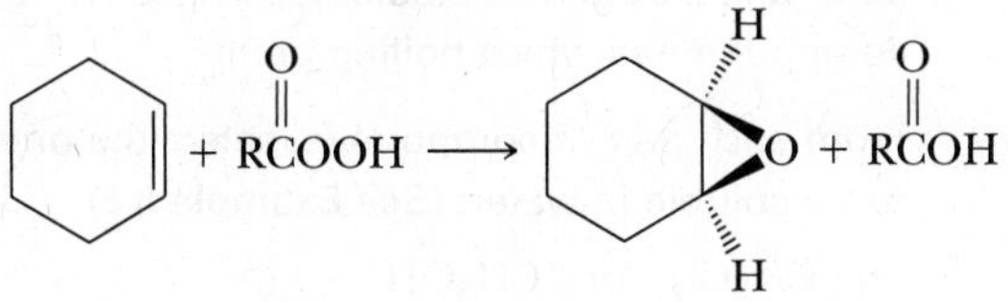

10. Acid-Catalyzed Hydrolysis of Epoxides (Section 8.4C)

Acid-catalyzed hydrolysis of an epoxide derived from a cycloalkene gives a *trans* glycol (hydrolysis of cycloalkene oxide is stereoselective, giving the *trans* glycol):

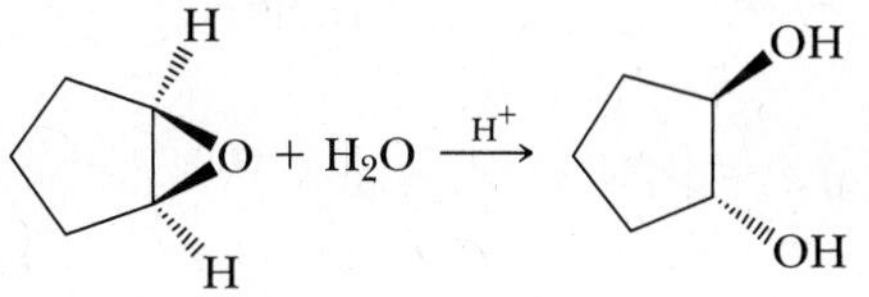

11. Nucleophilic Ring Opening of Epoxides (Section 8.4C)

Good nucleophiles, such as ammonia and amines, open the highly strained epoxide ring by an S_N2 mechanism and show a regioselectivity for attack of the nucleophile at the less hindered carbon of the three-membered ring. The reaction favors the stereoselective formation of the *trans* product:

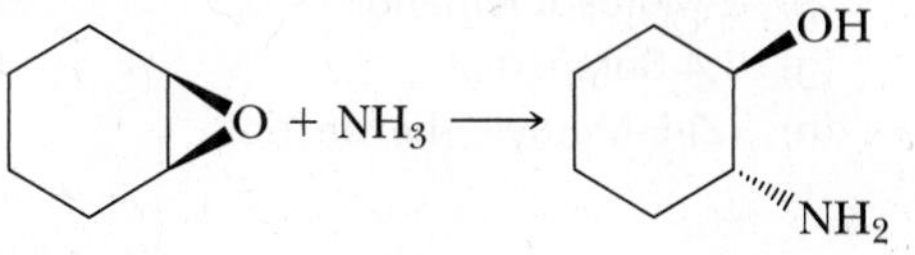

Cyclohexene oxide *trans*-2-Aminocyclohexanol

12. Acidity of Thiols (Section 8.6A)

Thiols are weak acids, pK_a 8–9, but are considerably stronger acids than alcohols, pK_a 16–18.

$$CH_3CH_2SH + H_2O \rightleftharpoons CH_3CH_2S^- + H_3O^+ \quad pK_a = 8.5$$

13. Oxidation to Disulfides (Section 8.6B)

Oxidation of a thiol by O_2 gives a disulfide:

$$2\,RSH + \tfrac{1}{2}O_2 \longrightarrow RS\text{-}SR + H_2O$$

PROBLEMS

A problem marked with an asterisk indicates an applied "real-world" problem. Answers to problems whose numbers are printed in blue are given in Appendix D.

Structure and Nomenclature

8.13 Classify the alcohols as primary, secondary, or tertiary. **(See Example 8.2)**

(a) 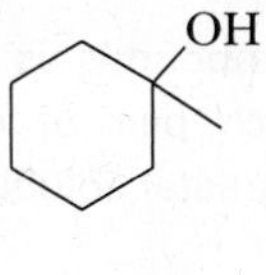

(b) $(CH_3)_3COH$

(c) 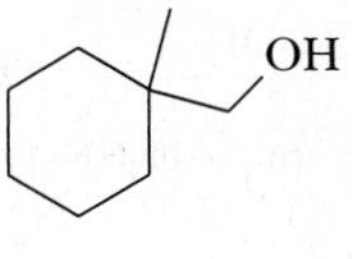

(d) 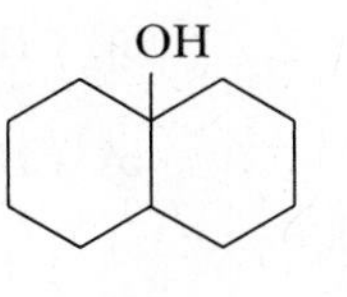

(e) 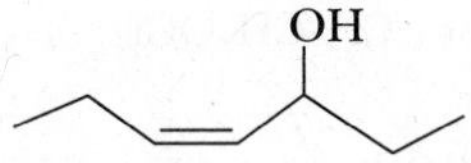

(f) 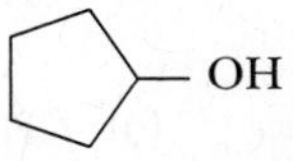

(g) 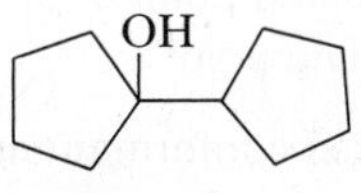

(h) 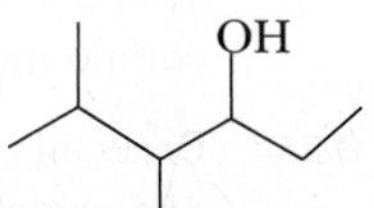

8.14 Provide an IUPAC or common name for these compounds: **(See Examples 8.1, 8.3, 8.11)**

(a) 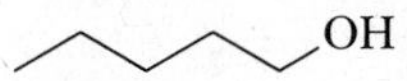

(b) 

(c) 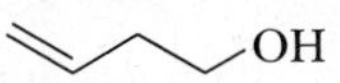

(d) 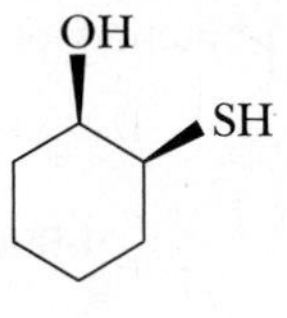

(e) 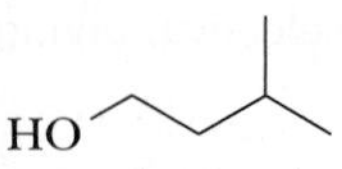 (f) 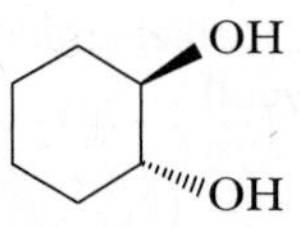

(g) 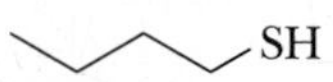 (h) 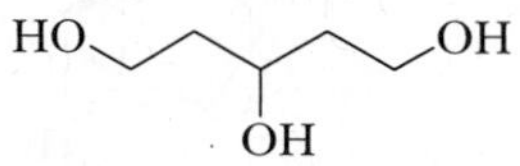

8.15 Draw a structural formula for each alcohol: **(See Examples 8.1, 8.3, 8.11)**

(a) Isopropyl alcohol
(b) Propylene glycol
(c) (*R*)-5-Methyl-2-hexanol
(d) 2-Methyl-2-propyl-1,3-propanediol
(e) 2,2-Dimethyl-1-propanol
(f) 2-Mercaptoethanol
(g) 1,4-Butanediol
(h) (*Z*)-5-Methyl-2-hexen-1-ol
(i) *cis*-3-Penten-1-ol
(j) *trans*-1,4-Cyclohexanediol

8.16 Write names for these ethers: **(See Example 8.7)**

(a) 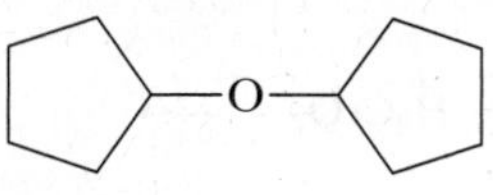

(b) 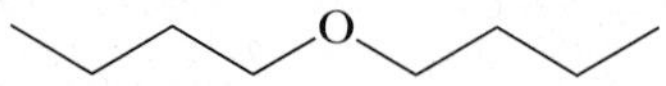

(c) 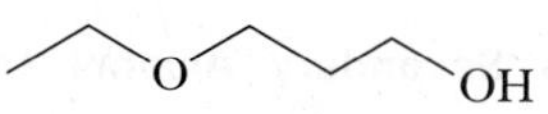

(d) 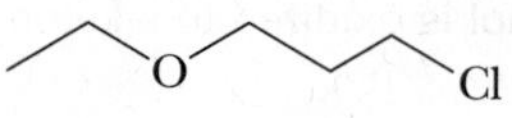

8.17 Name and draw structural formulas for the eight isomeric alcohols with molecular formula $C_5H_{12}O$. Which are chiral? **(See Examples 8.1, 8.3)**

Physical Properties

8.18 Arrange these compounds in order of increasing boiling point (values in °C are −42, 78, 117, and 198):

(a) $CH_3CH_2CH_2CH_2OH$ (b) CH_3CH_2OH
(c) $HOCH_2CH_2OH$ (d) $CH_3CH_2CH_3$

8.19 Arrange these compounds in order of increasing boiling point (values in °C are −42, −24, 78, and 118):

(a) CH_3CH_2OH (b) CH_3OCH_3
(c) $CH_3CH_2CH_3$ (d) CH_3COOH

8.20 Propanoic acid and methyl acetate are constitutional isomers, and both are liquids at room temperature:

$CH_3CH_2\overset{O}{\overset{\|}{C}}OH$ Propanoic acid

$CH_3\overset{O}{\overset{\|}{C}}OCH_3$ Methyl acetate

One of these compounds has a boiling point of 141 °C; the other has a boiling point of 57 °C. Which compound has which boiling point?

8.21 Draw all possible staggered conformations of ethylene glycol ($HOCH_2CH_2OH$). Can you explain why the conformation in which the —OH groups are closest to each other is more stable than the conformation in which the —OH groups are farthest apart by approximately 4.2 kJ/mol (1 kcal/mol)? **(See Example 3.7)**

8.22 Following are structural formulas for 1-butanol and 1-butanethiol:

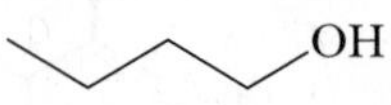
1-Butanol

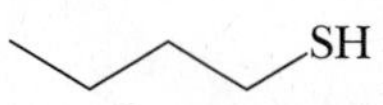
1-Butanethiol

One of these compounds has a boiling point of 98.5 °C; the other has a boiling point of 117 °C. Which compound has which boiling point?

8.23 From each pair of compounds, select the one that is more soluble in water: **(See Example 8.8)**

(a) CH_2Cl_2 or CH_3OH

(b) $CH_3\overset{O}{\overset{\|}{C}}CH_3$ or $CH_3\overset{CH_2}{\overset{\|}{C}}CH_3$

(c) CH_3CH_2Cl or $NaCl$

(d) $CH_3CH_2CH_2SH$ or $CH_3CH_2CH_2OH$

(e) $CH_3CH_2\overset{OH}{\overset{|}{C}}HCH_2CH_3$ or $CH_3CH_2\overset{O}{\overset{\|}{C}}CH_2CH_3$

8.24 Arrange the compounds in each set in order of decreasing solubility in water: **(See Example 8.8)**

(a) Ethanol; butane; diethyl ether
(b) 1-Hexanol; 1,2-hexanediol; hexane

8.25 Each of the following compounds is a common organic solvent. From each pair of compounds, select the solvent with the greater solubility in water. **(See Example 8.8)**

(a) CH_2Cl_2 or CH_3CH_2OH

(b) $CH_3CH_2OCH_2CH_3$ or CH_3CH_2OH

(c) $CH_3\overset{O}{\overset{\|}{C}}CH_3$ or $CH_3CH_2OCH_2CH_3$

(d) $CH_3CH_2OCH_2CH_3$ or $CH_3(CH_2)_3CH_3$

Synthesis of Alcohols

8.26 Give the structural formula of an alkene or alkenes from which each alcohol or glycol can be prepared: **(See Examples 5.5, 8.10)**

(a) 2-Butanol (b) 1-Methylcyclohexanol
(c) 3-Hexanol (d) 2-Methyl-2-pentanol
(e) Cyclopentanol (f) 1,2-Propanediol

8.27 The addition of bromine to cyclopentene and the acid-catalyzed hydrolysis of cyclopentene oxide are both stereoselective; each gives a *trans* product. Compare the mechanisms of these two reactions, and show how each mechanism accounts for the formation of the *trans* product.

Acidity of Alcohols and Thiols

8.28 From each pair, select the stronger acid, and, for each stronger acid, write a structural formula for its conjugate base: **(See Examples 8.4, 8.12)**

(a) H_2O or H_2CO_3
(b) CH_3OH or CH_3COOH
(c) CH_3COOH or CH_3CH_2SH

8.29 Arrange these compounds in order of increasing acidity (from weakest to strongest): **(See Examples 8.4, 8.12)**

$$CH_3CH_2CH_2OH \quad CH_3CH_2\overset{\overset{O}{\|}}{C}OH \quad CH_3CH_2CH_2SH$$

8.30 From each pair, select the stronger base, and, for each stronger base, write the structural formula of its conjugate acid: **(See Examples 8.4, 8.12)**

(a) OH^- or CH_3O^-
(b) $CH_3CH_2S^-$ or $CH_3CH_2O^-$
(c) $CH_3CH_2O^-$ or NH_2^-

8.31 Label the stronger acid, stronger base, weaker acid, and weaker base in each of the following equilibria, and then predict the position of each equilibrium (for pK_a values, see Table 2.1): **(See Example 8.4)**

(a) $CH_3CH_2O^- + HCl \rightleftharpoons CH_3CH_2OH + Cl^-$

(b) $CH_3\overset{\overset{O}{\|}}{C}OH + CH_3CH_2O^- \rightleftharpoons CH_3\overset{\overset{O}{\|}}{C}O^- + CH_3CH_2OH$

8.32 Predict the position of equilibrium for each acid–base reaction; that is, does each lie considerably to the left, does each lie considerably to the right, or are the concentrations evenly balanced? **(See Examples 8.4, 8.12)**

(a) $CH_3CH_2OH + Na^+OH^- \rightleftharpoons CH_3CH_2O^-Na^+ + H_2O$
(b) $CH_3CH_2SH + Na^+OH^- \rightleftharpoons CH_3CH_2S^-Na^+ + H_2O$
(c) $CH_3CH_2OH + CH_3CH_2S^-Na^+ \rightleftharpoons CH_3CH_2O^-Na^+ + CH_3CH_2SH$
(d) $CH_3CH_2S^-Na^+ + CH_3\overset{\overset{O}{\|}}{C}OH \rightleftharpoons CH_3CH_2SH + CH_3\overset{\overset{O}{\|}}{C}O^-Na^+$

Reactions of Alcohols

8.33 Show how to distinguish between cyclohexanol and cyclohexene by a simple chemical test. (*Hint:* Treat each with Br_2 in CCl_4 and watch what happens.)

8.34 Write equations for the reaction of 1-butanol, a primary alcohol, with these reagents: **(See Examples 8.4, 8.6)**

(a) Na metal
(b) HBr, heat
(c) $K_2Cr_2O_7$, H_2SO_4, heat
(d) $SOCl_2$
(e) Pyridinium chlorochromate (PCC)

8.35 Write equations for the reaction of 2-butanol, a secondary alcohol, with these reagents: **(See Examples 8.4, 8.6)**

(a) Na metal (b) H_2SO_4, heat
(c) HBr, heat (d) $K_2Cr_2O_7$, H_2SO_2, heat
(e) $SOCl_2$ (f) Pyridinium chlorochromate (PCC)

8.36 When (*R*)-2-butanol is left standing in aqueous acid, it slowly loses its optical activity. When the organic material is recovered from the aqueous solution, only 2-butanol is found. Account for the observed loss of optical activity.

8.37 What is the most likely mechanism of the following reaction?

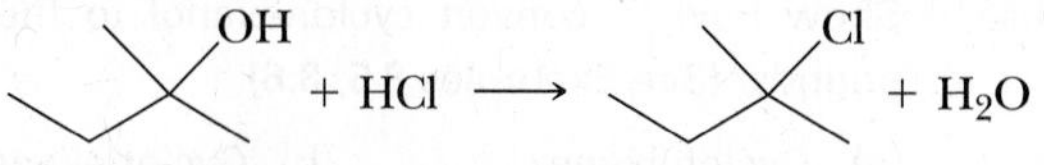

Draw a structural formula for the intermediate(s) formed during the reaction.

8.38 Complete the equations for these reactions: **(See Examples 8.6, 8.9)**

(a) 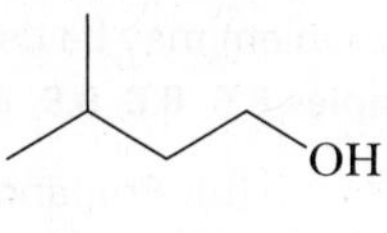

$+ H_2CrO_4 \longrightarrow$

(b) 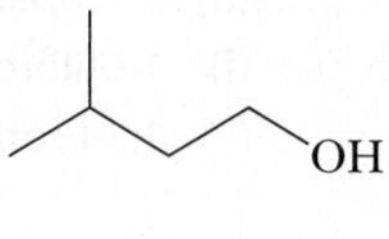

$+ SOCl_2 \longrightarrow$

(c) 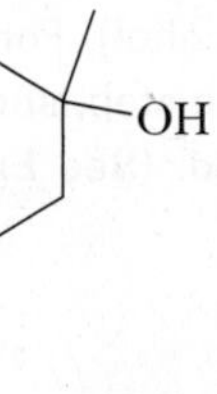

$+ HCl \longrightarrow$

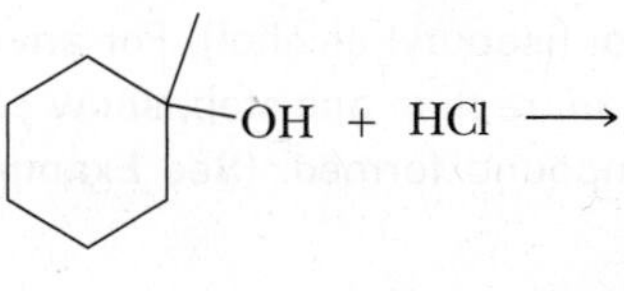

(d) (e) (f) ***8.39** In the commercial synthesis of methyl *tert*-butyl ether (MTBE), once used as an antiknock, octane-improving gasoline additive, 2-methylpropene and methanol are passed over an acid catalyst to give the ether. Propose a mechanism for this reaction. **(See Examples 5.5, 5.6)**

$$CH_3C(CH_3){=}CH_2 + CH_3OH \xrightarrow[\text{catalyst}]{\text{acid}} CH_3C(CH_3)_2OCH_3$$

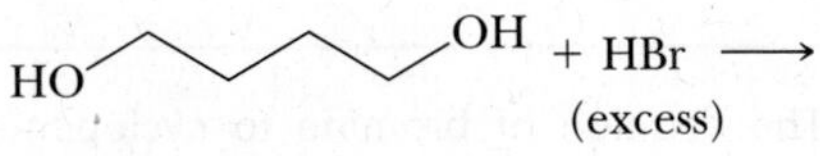

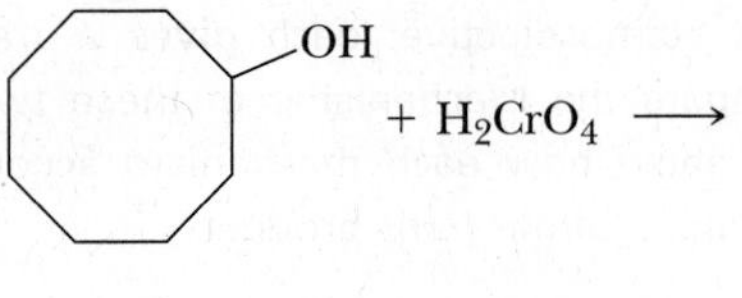

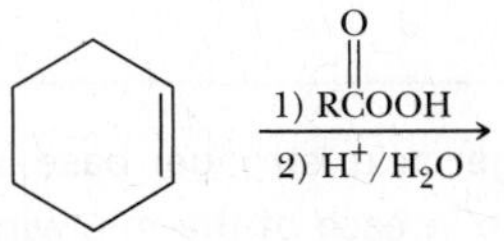

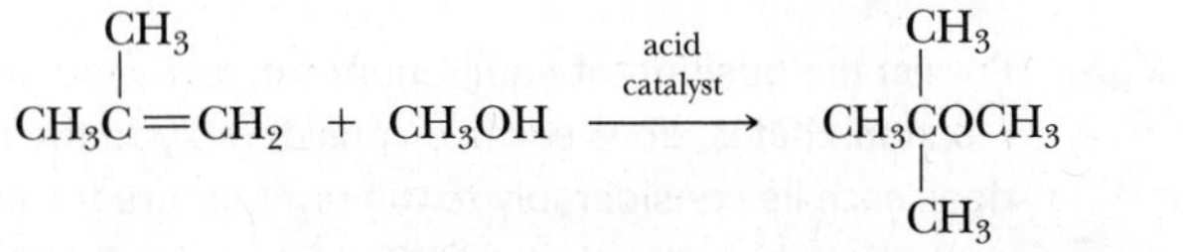

2-Methylpropene (Isobutylene) | Methanol | 2-Methoxy-2-methylpropane (Methyl tert-butyl ether, MTBE)

8.40 Cyclic bromoalcohols, upon treatment with base, can sometimes undergo intramolecular S_N2 reactions to form the ethers shown in reactions (a) and (b). Provide a mechanism for reactions (a) and (b). Indicate why equation (c) does not yield a similar reaction.

(a) (b) (c) no reaction

Syntheses

8.41 Show how to convert **(See Examples 8.5, 8.6, 8.10)**

(a) 1-Propanol to 2-propanol in two steps.
(b) Cyclohexene to cyclohexanone in two steps.
(c) Cyclohexanol to *trans*-1,2-cyclohexanediol in three steps.
(d) Propene to propanone (acetone) in two steps.

8.42 Show how to convert cyclohexanol to these compounds: **(See Examples 8.5, 8.6)**

(a) Cyclohexene (b) Cyclohexane
(c) Cyclohexanone (d) Cylohexene oxide

8.43 Show reagents and experimental conditions that can be used to synthesize these compounds from 1-propanol (any derivative of 1-propanol prepared in an earlier part of this problem may be used for a later synthesis): **(See Examples 8.5, 8.6, 8.9, 8.10)**

(a) Propanal (b) Propanoic acid
(c) Propene (d) 2-Propanol
(e) 2-Bromopropane (f) 1-Chloropropane
(g) Propanone (h) 1,2-Propanediol

8.44 Show how to prepare each compound from 2-methyl-1-propanol (isobutyl alcohol). For any preparation involving more than one step, show each intermediate compound formed. **(See Examples 8.5, 8.6, 8.9, 8.10)**

(a) $CH_3C(CH_3){=}CH_2$ (b) $CH_3C(CH_3)(OH)CH_3$

(c) $CH_3C(CH_3)(OH){-}CH_2OH$ (d) $CH_3CH(CH_3)COOH$

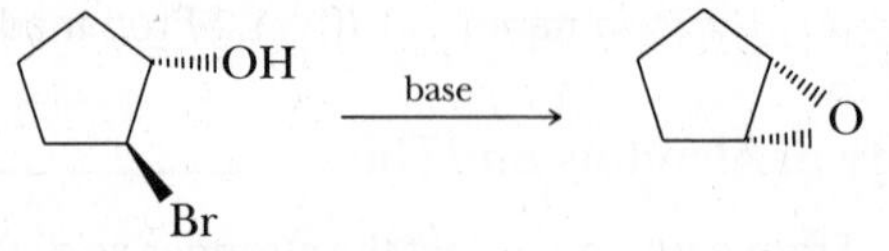

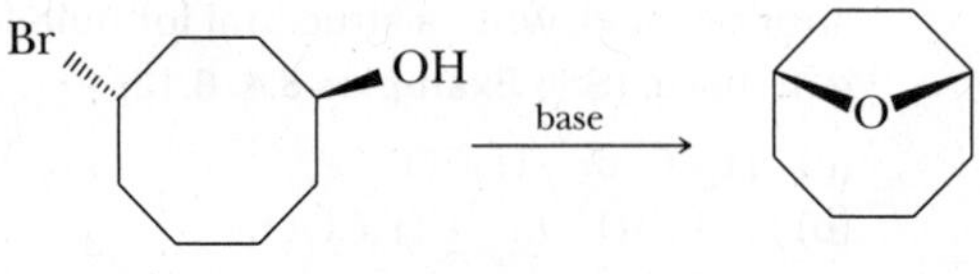

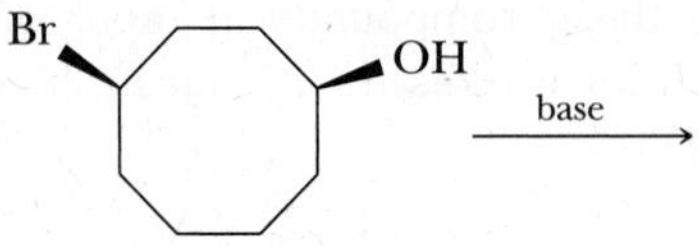

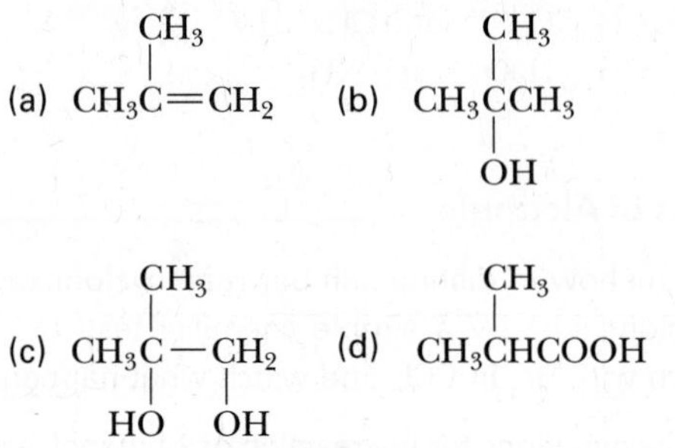

8.45 Show how to prepare each compound from 2-methylcyclohexanol: **(See Examples 8.5, 8.6, 8.9, 8.10)**

(a) (b) (c) (d) (e) (f) racemic

For any preparation involving more than one step, show each intermediate compound formed.

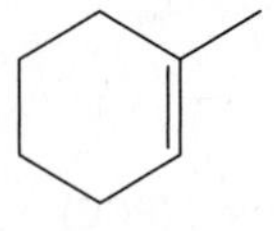

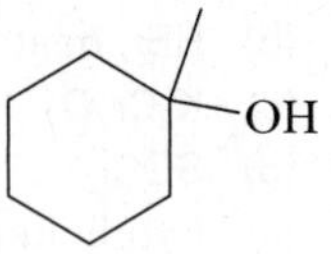

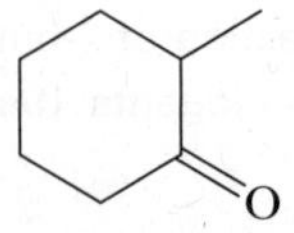

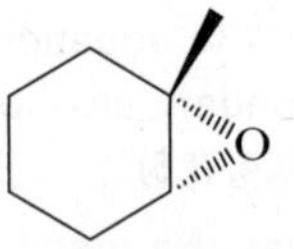

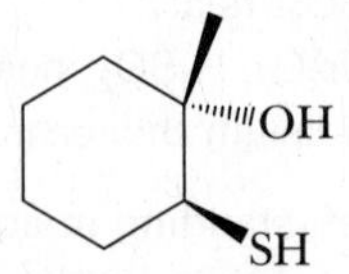

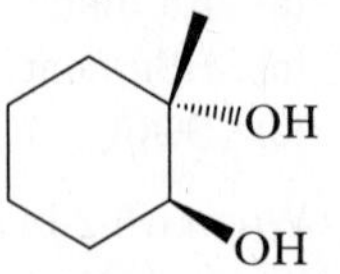

8.46 Show how to convert the alcohol on the left to compounds (a), (b), and (c). **(See Example 8.6)**

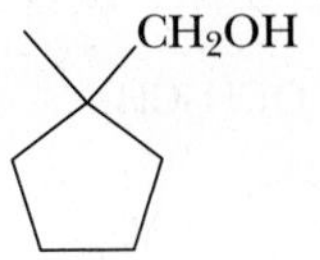

(a)

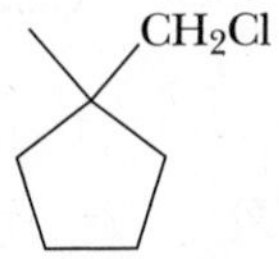

(b)

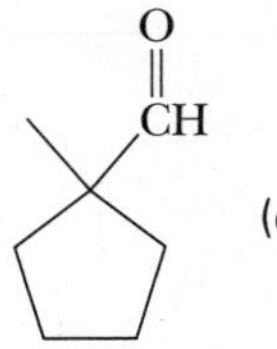

(c)

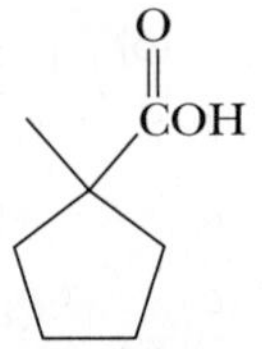

***8.47** Disparlure, a sex attractant of the gypsy moth (*Porthetria dispar*), has been synthesized in the laboratory from the following (*Z*)-alkene: **(See Example 8.9)**

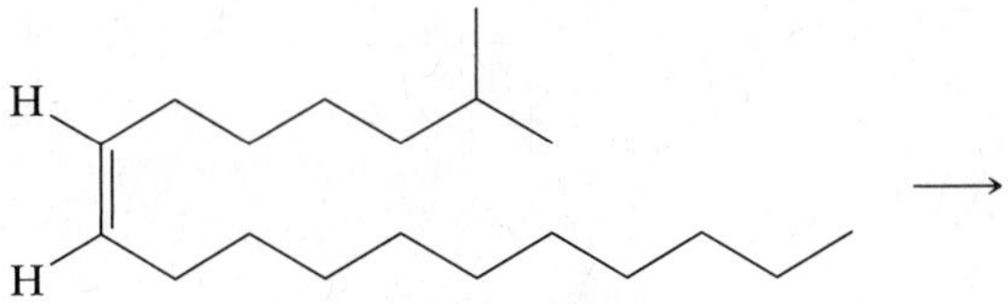

(*Z*)-2-Methyl-7-octadecene

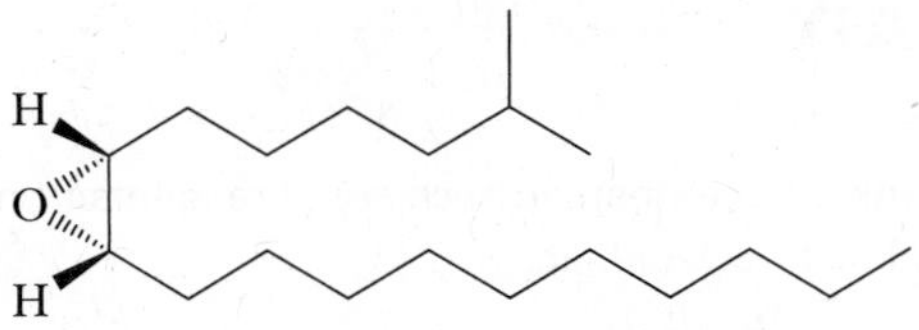

Disparlure

© Marek Swadzba/iStockphoto

Gypsy moth caterpillar.

(a) How might the (*Z*)-alkene be converted to disparlure?

(b) How many stereoisomers are possible for disparlure? How many are formed in the sequence you chose?

***8.48** The chemical name for bombykol, the sex pheromone secreted by the female silkworm moth to attract male silkworm moths, is *trans*-10-*cis*-12-hexadecadien-1-ol. (The compound has one hydroxyl group and two carbon–carbon double bonds in a 16-carbon chain.)

(a) Draw a structural formula for bombykol, showing the correct configuration about each carbon–carbon double bond.

(b) How many *cis–trans* isomers are possible for the structural formula you drew in part (a)? All possible *cis–trans* isomers have been synthesized in the laboratory, but only the one named bombykol is produced by the female silkworm moth, and only it attracts male silkworm moths.

CHEMICAL TRANSFORMATIONS

8.49 Test your cumulative knowledge of the reactions learned thus far by completing the following chemical transformations. *Note: Some will require more than one step.*

(a)

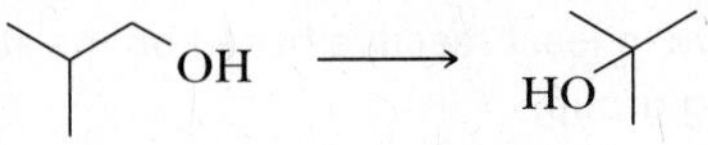

(b)

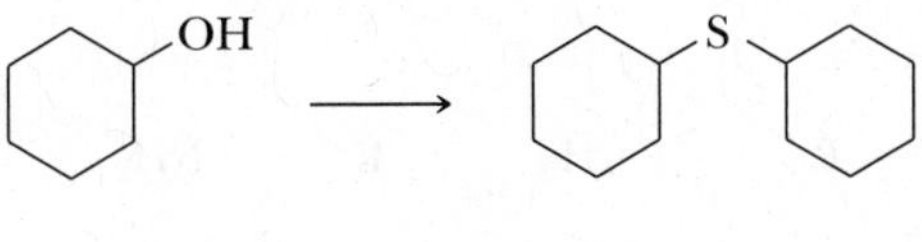

(c)

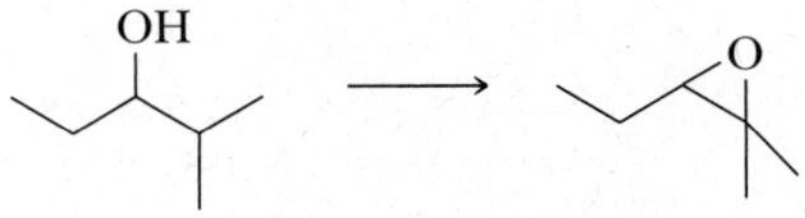

(d)

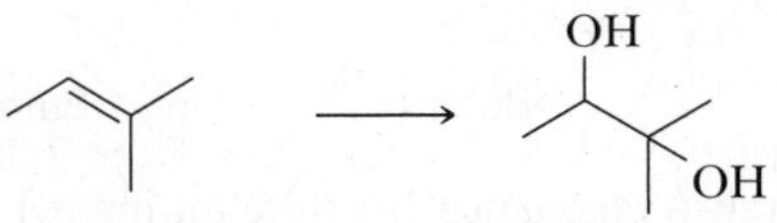

(e)

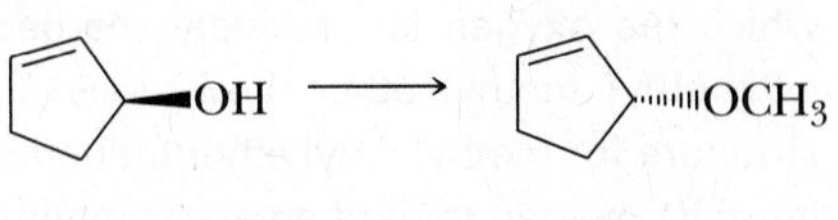

(f)

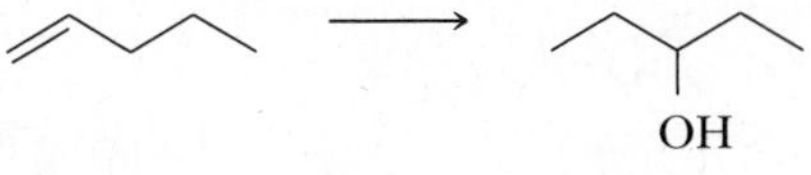

(g)

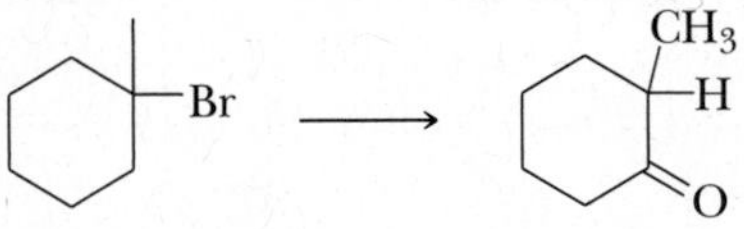

(h) 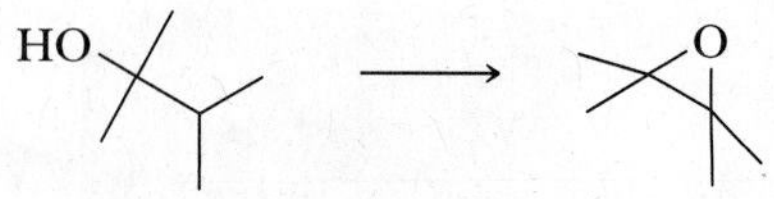

(i) 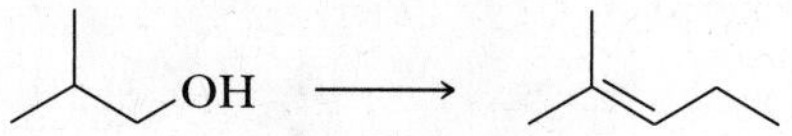

(j) 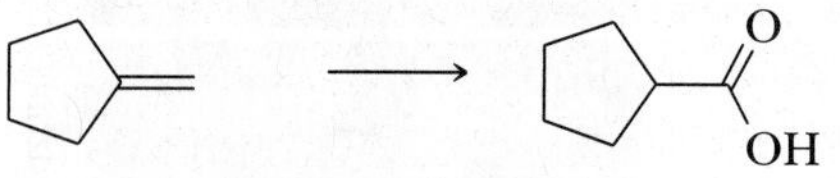

(k) 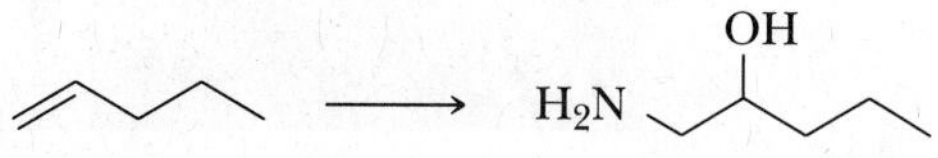

(l) 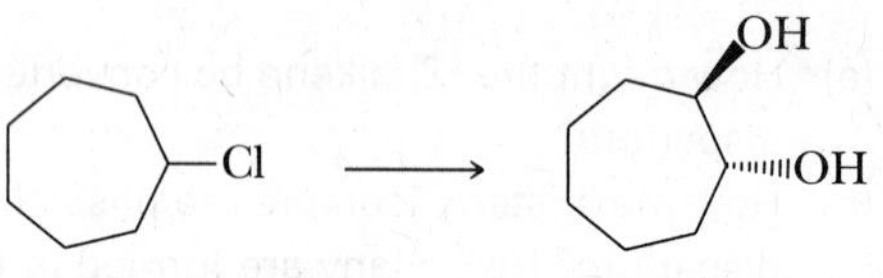

racemic

(m) 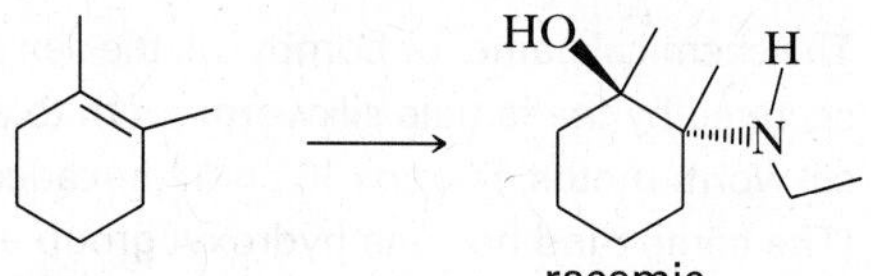

racemic

(n) 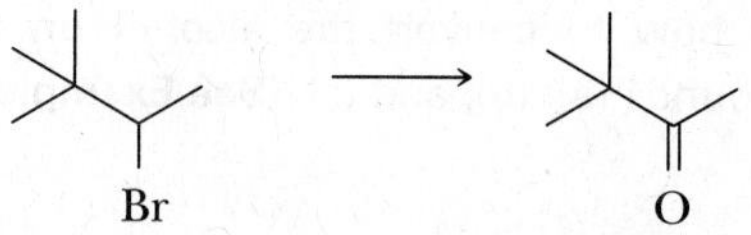

(o) 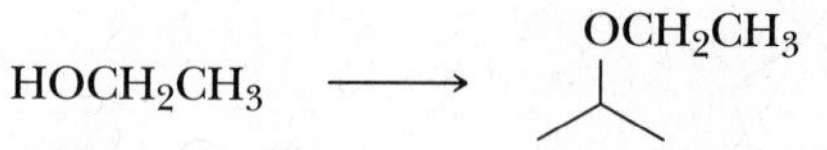

(p) 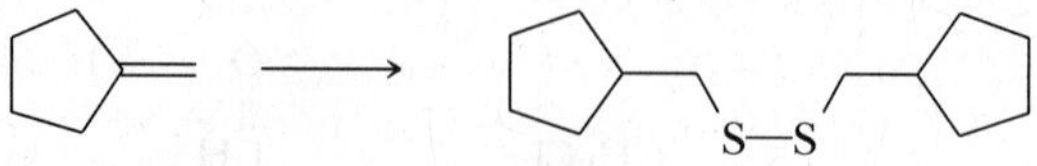

(q) 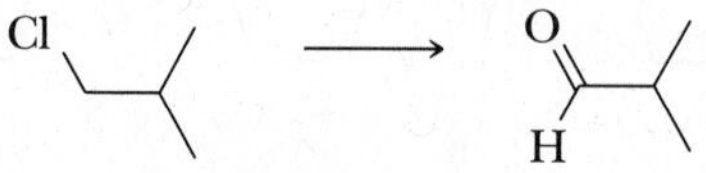

(r) 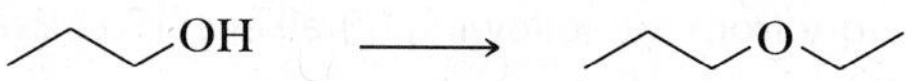

LOOKING AHEAD

8.50 Compounds that contain an N—H group associate by hydrogen bonding.

(a) Do you expect this association to be stronger or weaker than that between compounds containing an O—H group?

(b) Based on your answer to part (a), which would you predict to have the higher boiling point, 1-butanol or 1-butanamine?

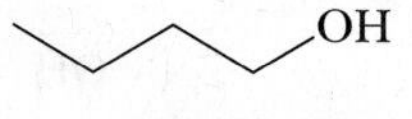

1-Butanol

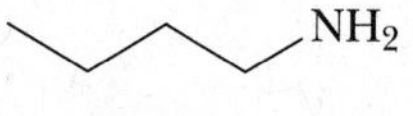

1-Butanamine

8.51 Draw a resonance structure for methyl vinyl ether in which the oxygen is positively charged. Compared with ethyl methyl ether, how does the resonance structure for methyl vinyl ether influence the reactivity of its oxygen toward an electrophile?

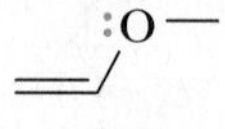

Methyl vinyl ether

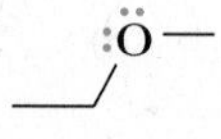

Ethyl methyl ether

8.52 Rank the members in each set of reagents from most to least nucleophilic:

(a) 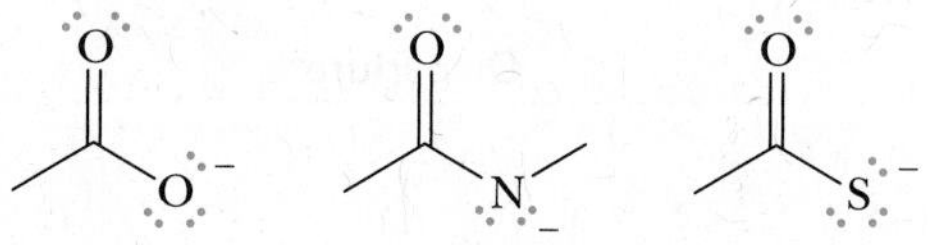

(b) $R—\ddot{O}:^-$ $R—\ddot{N}H^-$ $R—\ddot{C}H_2^-$

8.53 In Chapter 15 we will see that the reactivity of the following carbonyl compounds is directly proportional to the stability of the leaving group. Rank the order of reactivity of these carbonyl compounds from most reactive to least reactive based the stability of the leaving group.

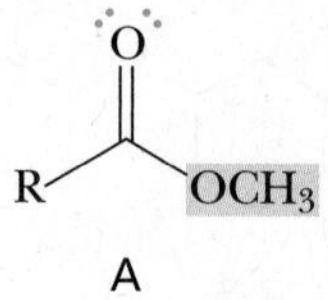

A

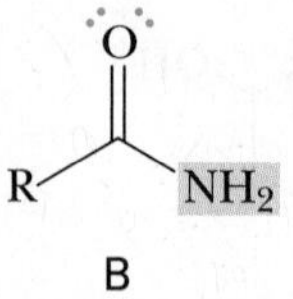

B

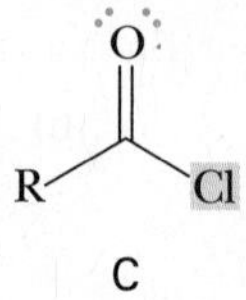

C

GROUP LEARNING ACTIVITIES

8.54 Discuss why primary alcohols (with the exception of ethanol) cannot be prepared by the acid-catalyzed hydration of alkenes. You'll want to discuss the mechanism of acid-catalyzed hydration and consider the reactive species involved.

8.55 Discuss why sodium hydroxide is not a good reagent for the synthesis of alkoxides from alcohols. Similarly, could sodium hydroxide be used to synthesize alkylsulfides from thiols? Why or why not? You'll want to discuss the type of reactions that would occur in both reactions as well as what makes a reaction synthetically useful.

8.56 One of the following alcohols is used to de-ice airplanes during extreme cold weather. As a group, decide which of the three alcohols would be most suitable for the job by discussing factors that one must consider for such an application.

CH_3OH	CH_3CH_2OH	$(CH_3)_3COH$
Methanol	Ethanol	*tert*-Butanol

09

Benzene and Its Derivatives

Peppers of the capsicum family. Hot peppers contain significant amounts of the chemical capsaicin, which is used for medicinal purposes as well as for tantalizing taste buds (see Chemical Connections, "Capsaicin, for Those Who Like It Hot"). Inset: A model of capsaicin. (Courtesy Douglas Brown)

KEY QUESTIONS

9.1 **What Is the Structure of Benzene?**

9.2 **What Is Aromaticity?**

9.3 **How Are Benzene Compounds Named, and What Are Their Physical Properties?**

9.4 **What Is the Benzylic Position, and How Does It Contribute to Benzene Reactivity?**

9.5 **What Is Electrophilic Aromatic Substitution?**

9.6 **What Is the Mechanism of Electrophilic Aromatic Substitution?**

9.7 **How Do Existing Substituents on Benzene Affect Electrophilic Aromatic Substitution?**

9.8 **What Are Phenols?**

HOW TO

9.1 **How to Determine Whether a Lone Pair of Electrons Is or Is Not Part of an Aromatic Pi System**

9.2 **How to Determine Whether a Substituent on Benzene Is Electron Withdrawing**

CHEMICAL CONNECTIONS

9A **Carcinogenic Polynuclear Aromatics and Cancer**

9B **Capsaicin, for Those Who Like It Hot**

BENZENE, A COLORLESS LIQUID, was first isolated by Michael Faraday in 1825 from the oily residue that collected in the illuminating gas lines of London. Benzene's molecular formula, C_6H_6, suggests a high degree of unsaturation. For comparison, an alkane with six carbons has a molecular formula of C_6H_{14}, and a cycloalkane with six carbons has a molecular formula of C_6H_{12}. Considering benzene's high degree of unsaturation, it might be expected to show many of the reactions characteristic of alkenes. Yet, benzene is remarkably *un*reactive! It does not undergo the addition, oxidation, and reduction reactions characteristic of alkenes. For example, benzene does not react with bromine, hydrogen chloride, or other reagents that usually add to carbon–carbon double bonds. Nor is benzene oxidized by peracids under conditions that readily oxidize alkenes. When benzene reacts, it does so by substitution in which a hydrogen atom is replaced by another atom or a group of atoms.

The term *aromatic* was originally used to classify benzene and its derivatives because many of them have distinctive odors. It became clear, however, that a sounder classification for these compounds would be one based on structure and chemical reactivity, not aroma. As it is now used, the term **aromatic** refers instead to the fact that benzene and its derivatives are highly unsaturated compounds that are unexpectedly stable toward reagents that react with alkenes.

We use the term **arene** to describe aromatic hydrocarbons, by analogy with alkane and alkene. Benzene is the parent arene. Just as we call a group derived by the removal of an H from an alkane an alkyl group and give it the symbol R—, we call a group derived by the removal of an H from an arene an **aryl group** and give it the symbol **Ar**—.

Aromatic compound A term used to classify benzene and its derivatives.

Arene An aromatic hydrocarbon.

Aryl group A group derived from an aromatic compound (an arene) by the removal of an H; given the symbol Ar—.

Ar— The symbol used for an aryl group, by analogy with R— for an alkyl group.

9.1 What Is the Structure of Benzene?

Let us imagine ourselves in the mid-nineteenth century and examine the evidence on which chemists attempted to build a model for the structure of benzene. First, because the molecular formula of benzene is C_6H_6, it seemed clear that the molecule must be highly unsaturated. Yet benzene does not show the chemical properties of alkenes, the only unsaturated hydrocarbons known at that time. Benzene does undergo chemical reactions, but its characteristic reaction is substitution rather than addition. When benzene is treated with bromine in the presence of ferric chloride as a catalyst, for example, only one compound with the molecular formula C_6H_5Br forms:

$$\underset{\text{Benzene}}{C_6H_6} + Br_2 \xrightarrow{FeCl_3} \underset{\text{Bromobenzene}}{C_6H_5Br} + HBr$$

Chemists concluded, therefore, that all six carbons and all six hydrogens of benzene must be equivalent. When bromobenzene is treated with bromine in the presence of ferric chloride, three isomeric dibromobenzenes are formed:

$$\underset{\text{Bromobenzene}}{C_6H_5Br} + Br_2 \xrightarrow{FeCl_3} \underset{\text{Dibromobenzene}}{C_6H_4Br_2} + HBr$$

(formed as a mixture of three constitutional isomers)

For chemists in the mid-nineteenth century, the problem was to incorporate these observations, along with the accepted tetravalence of carbon, into a structural formula for benzene. Before we examine their proposals, we should note that the problem of the structure of benzene and other aromatic hydrocarbons has occupied the efforts of chemists for over a century. It was not until the 1930s that chemists developed a general understanding of the unique structure and chemical properties of benzene and its derivatives.

A. Kekulé's Model of Benzene

The first structure for benzene, proposed by August Kekulé in 1872, consisted of a six-membered ring with alternating single and double bonds and with one hydrogen bonded to each carbon. Kekulé further proposed that the ring contains three double bonds that shift back and forth so rapidly that the two forms cannot be separated. Each structure has become known as a **Kekulé structure**.

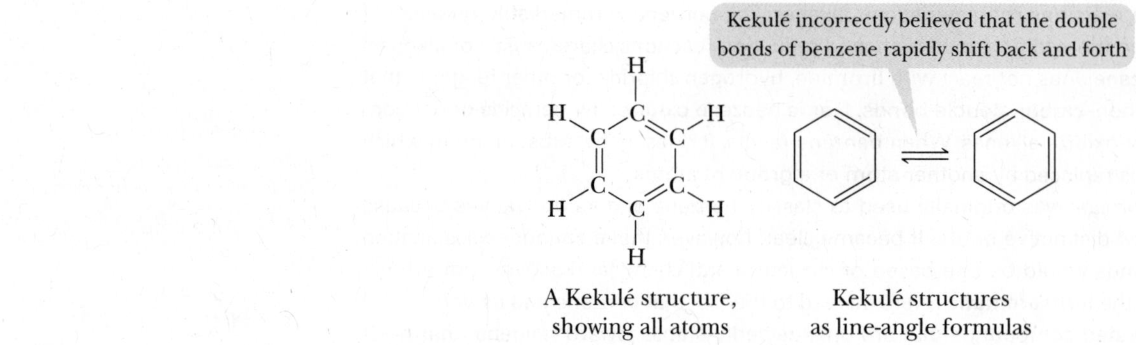
Kekulé incorrectly believed that the double bonds of benzene rapidly shift back and forth
A Kekulé structure, showing all atoms
Kekulé structures as line-angle formulas

Because all of the carbons and hydrogens of Kekulé's structure are equivalent, substituting bromine for any one of the hydrogens gives the same compound. Thus, Kekulé's proposed structure was consistent with the fact that treating benzene with bromine in the presence of ferric chloride gives only one compound with the molecular formula C_6H_5Br.

His proposal also accounted for the fact that the bromination of bromobenzene gives three (and only three) isomeric dibromobenzenes:

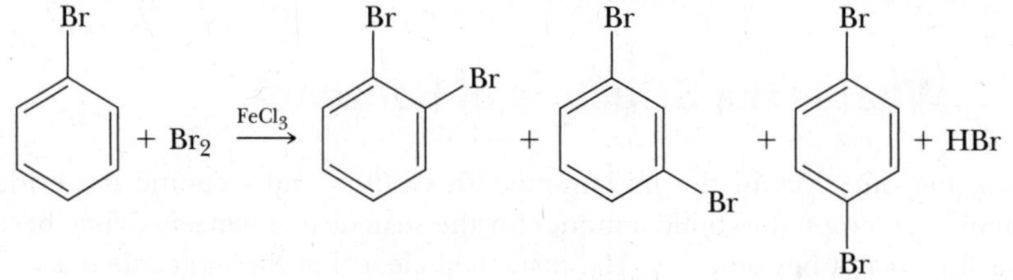

The three isomeric dibromobenzenes

Although Kekulé's proposal was consistent with many experimental observations, it was contested for years. The major objection was that it did not account for the unusual chemical behavior of benzene. If benzene contains three double bonds, why, his critics asked, doesn't it show the reactions typical of alkenes? Why doesn't it add three moles of bromine to form 1,2,3,4,5,6-hexabromocyclohexane? Why, instead, does benzene react by substitution rather than addition?

B. The Orbital Overlap Model of Benzene

The concepts of the **hybridization of atomic orbitals** and the **theory of resonance**, developed by Linus Pauling in the 1930s, provided the first adequate description of the structure of benzene. The carbon skeleton of benzene forms a regular hexagon with C—C—C and H—C—C bond angles of 120°. For this type of bonding, carbon uses sp^2 hybrid orbitals (Section 1.6E). Each carbon forms sigma bonds to two adjacent carbons by the overlap of sp^2–sp^2 hybrid orbitals and one sigma bond to hydrogen by the overlap of sp^2–1*s* orbitals. As determined experimentally, all carbon–carbon bonds in benzene are the same length, 1.39 Å, a value almost midway between the length of a single bond between sp^3 hybridized carbons (1.54 Å) and that of a double bond between sp^2 hybridized carbons (1.33 Å):

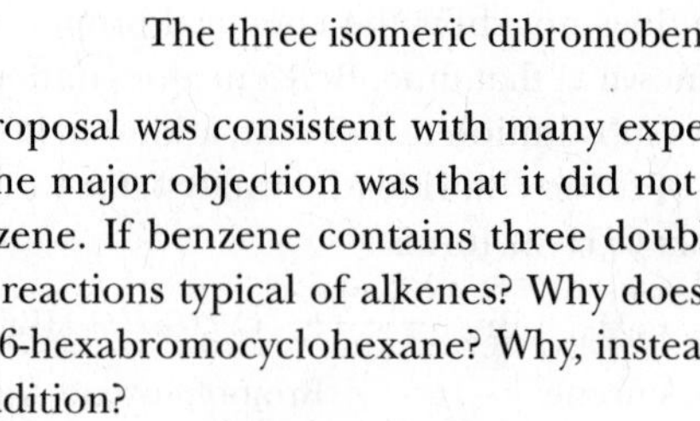

Each carbon also has a single unhybridized 2*p* orbital that contains one electron. These six 2*p* orbitals lie perpendicular to the plane of the ring and overlap to form a continuous pi cloud encompassing all six carbons. The electron density of the pi system of a benzene ring lies in one torus (a doughnut-shaped region) above the plane of the ring and a second torus below the plane (Figure 9.1).

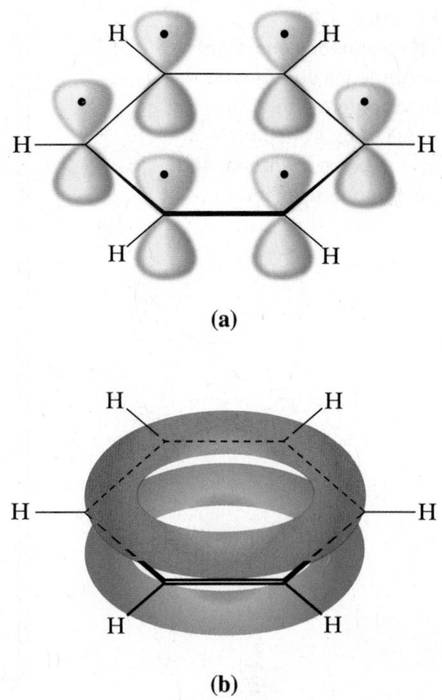

FIGURE 9.1 Orbital overlap model of the bonding in benzene. (a) The carbon, hydrogen framework. The six $2p$ orbitals, each with one electron, are shown uncombined. (b) The overlap of parallel $2p$ orbitals forms a continuous pi cloud, shown by one torus above the plane of the ring and a second below the plane of the ring.

C. The Resonance Model of Benzene

One of the postulates of resonance theory is that, if we can represent a molecule or ion by two or more contributing structures, then that molecule cannot be adequately represented by any single contributing structure. We represent benzene as a hybrid of two equivalent contributing structures, often referred to as *Kekulé structures*:

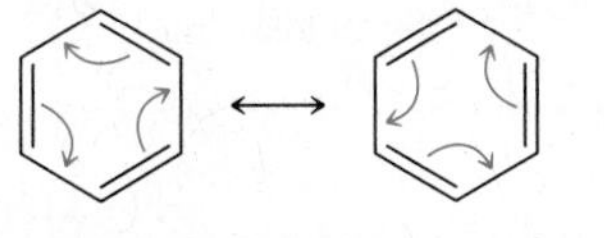

Benzene as a hybrid of two equivalent contributing structures

Each Kekulé structure makes an equal contribution to the hybrid; thus, the C—C bonds are neither single nor double bonds, but something intermediate. We recognize that neither of these contributing structures exists (they are merely alternative ways to pair $2p$ orbitals with no reason to prefer one over the other) and that the actual structure is a superposition of both. Nevertheless, chemists continue to use a single contributing structure to represent this molecule because it is as close as we can come to an accurate structure within the limitations of classical Lewis structures and the tetravalence of carbon.

D. The Resonance Energy of Benzene

Resonance energy is the difference in energy between a resonance hybrid and its most stable hypothetical contributing structure. One way to estimate the resonance energy of benzene is to compare the heats of hydrogenation of cyclohexene and benzene (benzene can be made to undergo hydrogenation under extreme conditions). In the presence of a transition metal catalyst, hydrogen readily reduces cyclohexene to cyclohexane (Section 5.6):

Resonance energy The difference in energy between a resonance hybrid and the most stable of its hypothetical contributing structures.

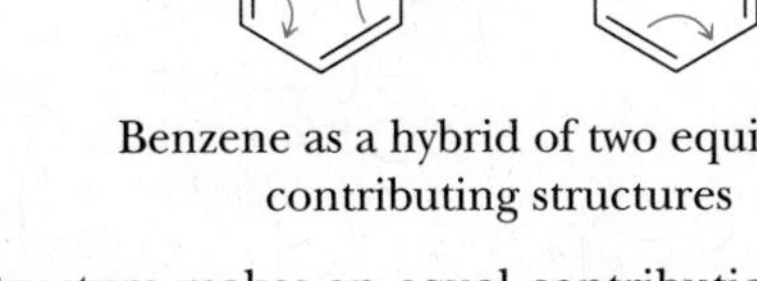

$\Delta H^0 = -120$ kJ/mol (−28.6 kcal/mol)

By contrast, benzene is reduced only very slowly to cyclohexane under these conditions. It is reduced more rapidly when heated and under a pressure of several hundred atmospheres of hydrogen:

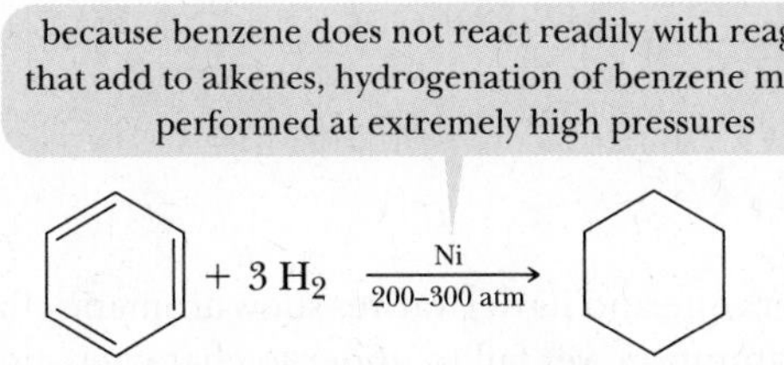

$\Delta H^0 = -209$ kJ/mol (−49.8 kcal/mol)

The catalytic reduction of an alkene is an exothermic reaction (Section 5.6B). The heat of hydrogenation per double bond varies somewhat with the degree of substitution of the double bond; for cyclohexene $\Delta H^0 = -120$ kJ/mol (−28.6 kcal/mol). If we imagine benzene in which the $2p$ electrons do not overlap outside of their original C—C double bonds, a hypothetical compound with alternating single and double bonds, we might expect its heat of hydrogenation to be $3 \times -120 = -359$ kJ/mol (−85.8 kcal/mol). Instead, the heat of hydrogenation of benzene is only −209 kJ/mol (−49.8 kcal/mol). The difference of 150 kJ/mol (35.8 kcal/mol) between the expected value and the experimentally observed value is the **resonance energy of benzene.** Figure 9.2 shows these experimental results in the form of a graph.

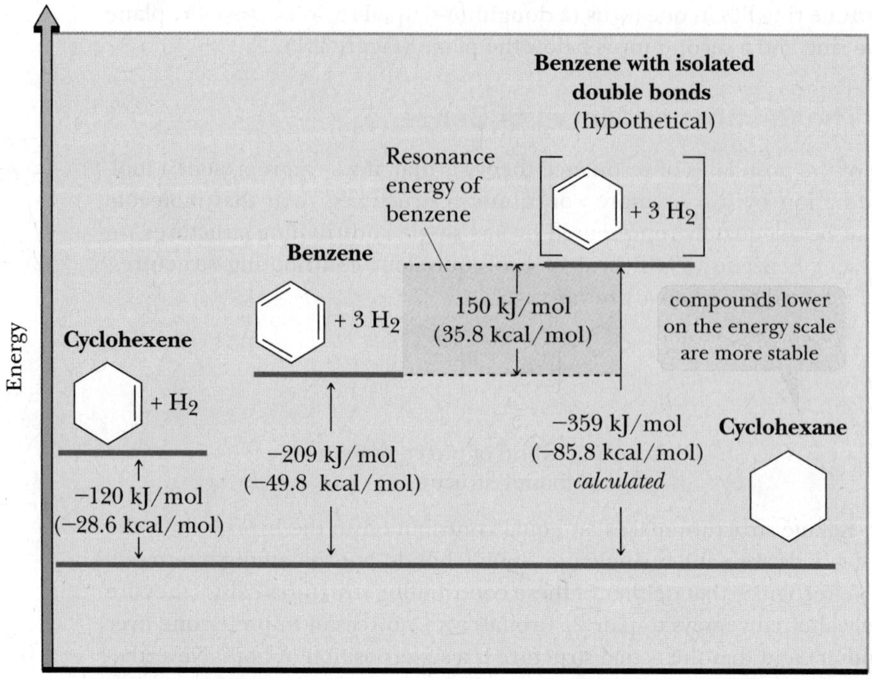

FIGURE 9.2
The resonance energy of benzene, as determined by a comparison of the heats of hydrogenation of cyclohexene, benzene, and the hypothetical benzene.

For comparison, the strength of a carbon–carbon single bond is approximately 333–418 kJ/mol (80–100 kcal/mol), and that of hydrogen bonding in water and low-molecular-weight alcohols is approximately 8.4–21 kJ/mol (2–5 kcal/mol). Thus, although the resonance energy of benzene is less than the strength of a carbon–carbon single bond, it is considerably greater than the strength of hydrogen bonding in water and alcohols. In Section 8.1C, we saw that hydrogen bonding has a dramatic effect on the physical properties of alcohols compared with those of alkanes. In this chapter, we see that the resonance energy of benzene and other aromatic hydrocarbons has a dramatic effect on their chemical reactivity.

Following are resonance energies for benzene and several other aromatic hydrocarbons:

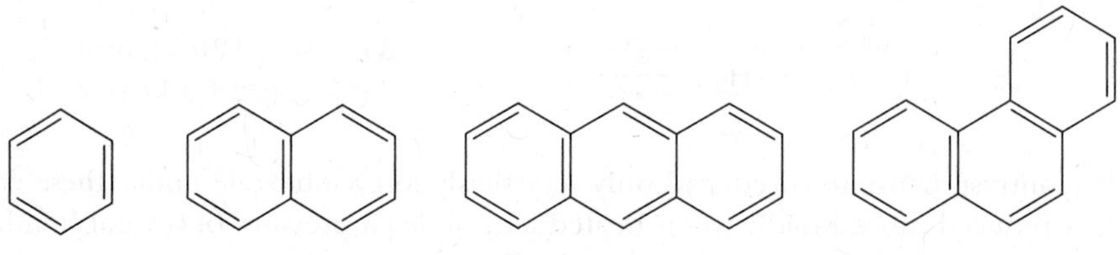

Resonance energy [kJ/mol (kcal/mol)]	Benzene	Naphthalene	Anthracene	Phenanthrene
	150 (35.8)	255 (60.9)	347 (82.9)	381 (91.0)

9.2 What Is Aromaticity?

Many other types of molecules besides benzene and its derivatives show aromatic character; that is, they contain high degrees of unsaturation, yet fail to undergo characteristic alkene addition and oxidation–reduction reactions. What chemists had long sought to understand were the principles underlying aromatic character. The German chemical physicist Erich Hückel solved this problem in the 1930s.

Hückel's criteria are summarized as follows. To be aromatic, a ring must

1. Have one $2p$ orbital on each of its atoms.
2. Be planar or nearly planar, so that there is continuous overlap or nearly continuous overlap of all $2p$ orbitals of the ring.
3. Have 2, 6, 10, 14, 18, and so forth pi electrons in the cyclic arrangement of $2p$ orbitals.

this criterion is also called the **$4n + 2$ rule** because the allowable numbers of pi electrons can be determined when n is substituted by any integer, including zero

Benzene meets these criteria. It is cyclic, planar, has one $2p$ orbital on each carbon atom of the ring, and has 6 pi electrons (an aromatic sextet) in the cyclic arrangement of its $2p$ orbitals.

Let us apply these criteria to several **heterocyclic compounds**, all of which are aromatic. Pyridine and pyrimidine are heterocyclic analogs of benzene. In pyridine, one CH group of benzene is replaced by a nitrogen atom, and in pyrimidine, two CH groups are replaced by nitrogen atoms:

Heterocyclic compound An organic compound that contains one or more atoms other than carbon in its ring.

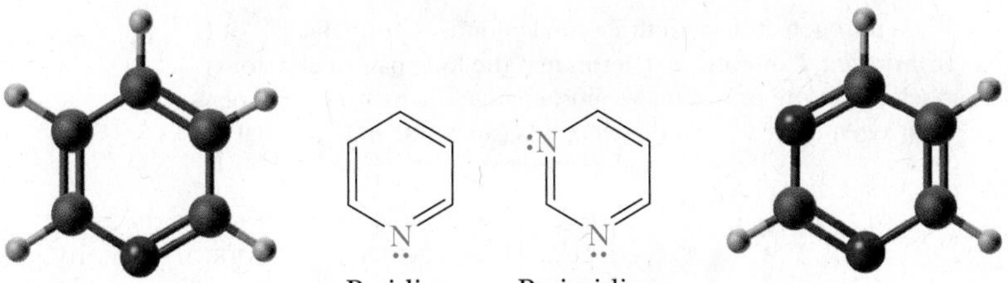

Pyridine Pyrimidine

Each molecule meets the Hückel criteria for aromaticity: Each is cyclic and planar, has one $2p$ orbital on each atom of the ring, and has six electrons in the pi system. In pyridine, nitrogen is sp^2 hybridized, and its unshared pair of electrons occupies an sp^2 orbital perpendicular to the $2p$ orbitals of the pi system and thus is not a part of the pi system. In pyrimidine, neither unshared pair of electrons of nitrogen is part of the pi system. The resonance energy of pyridine is 134 kJ/mol (32.0 kcal/mol), slightly less than that of benzene. The resonance energy of pyrimidine is 109 kJ/mol (26.0 kcal/mol).

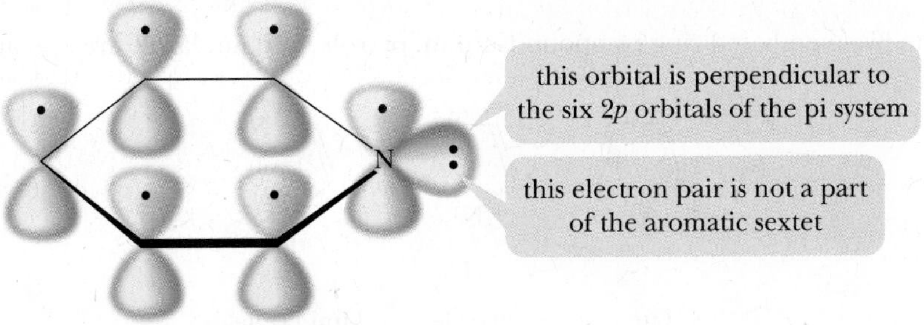

Pyridine

HOW TO 9.1

Determine Whether a Lone Pair of Electrons Is or Is Not Part of an Aromatic Pi System

(a) First, determine whether the atom containing the lone pair of electrons is part of a double bond. If it is part of a double bond, it is not possible for the lone pair to be part of the aromatic pi system.

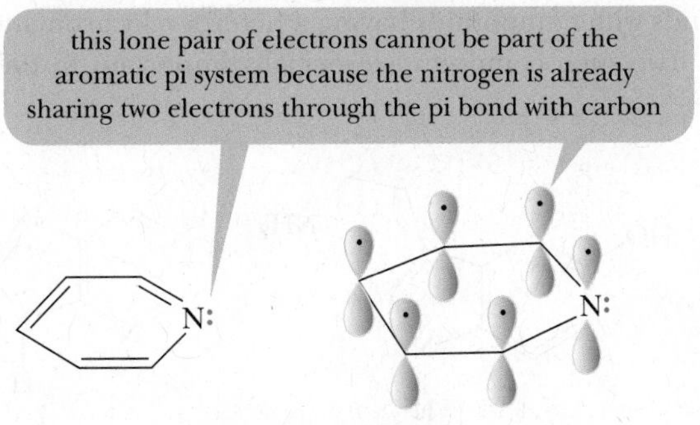

(b) If the atom containing the lone pair of electrons is not part of a double bond, it is possible for the lone pair of electrons to be part of the pi system.

Determine this by placing the atom in a hybridization state that places the lone pair of electrons in a *p* orbital. If this increases the number of aromatic pi electrons to either 2, 6, 10, 14, and so on, then the lone pair of electrons is part of the pi aromatic system. If placing the lone pair of electrons in the pi system changes the total number of pi electrons to any other number (e.g., 3–5, 7–9, etc.), the lone pair is not part of the aromatic pi system.

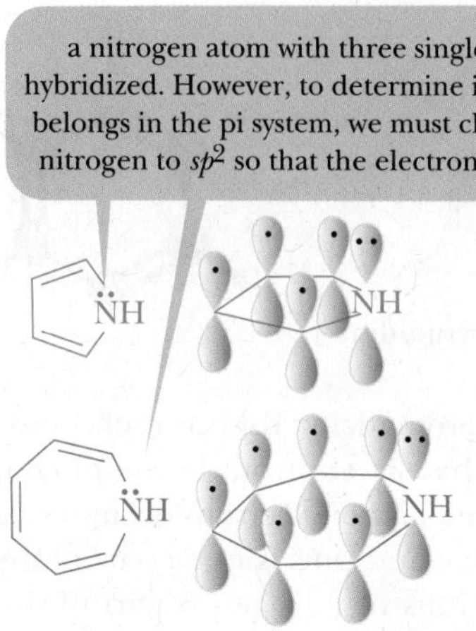
a nitrogen atom with three single bonds is normally sp^3 hybridized. However, to determine if the lone pair of electrons belongs in the pi system, we must change the hybridization of nitrogen to sp^2 so that the electrons can reside in a *p* orbital
NH
NH
NH
NH

The lone pair on nitrogen gives the pi system six electrons. Therefore, the nitrogen should be sp^2 hybridized.

The lone pair gives the pi system eight electrons. Therefore, the nitrogen should not be sp^2 hybridized.

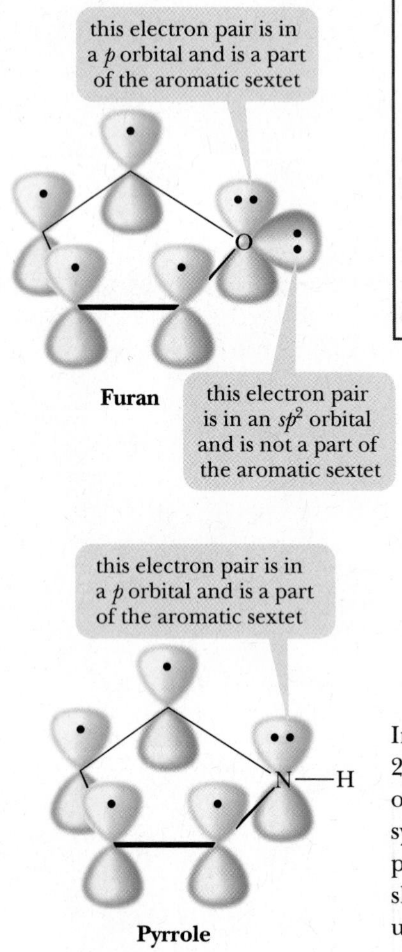
this electron pair is in a *p* orbital and is a part of the aromatic sextet
O
Furan
this electron pair is in an sp^2 orbital and is not a part of the aromatic sextet
this electron pair is in a *p* orbital and is a part of the aromatic sextet
N—H
Pyrrole

FIGURE 9.3
Origin of the six pi electrons (the aromatic sextet) in furan and pyrrole. The resonance energy of furan is 67 kJ/mol (16 kcal/mol); that of pyrrole is 88 kJ/mol (21 kcal/mol).

The five-membered-ring compounds furan, pyrrole, and imidazole are also aromatic:

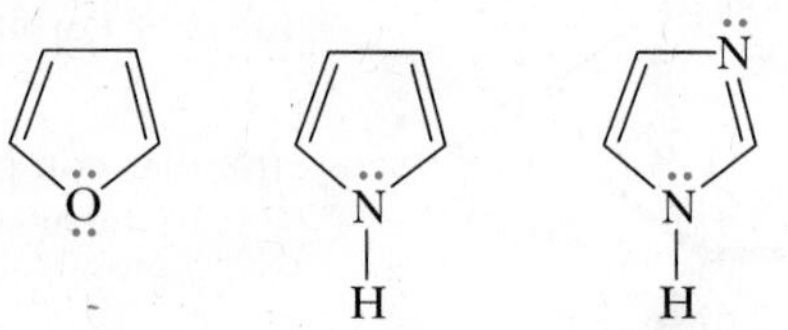
O
N
H
N
N
H

Furan Pyrrole Imidazole

In these planar compounds, each heteroatom is sp^2 hybridized, and its unhybridized $2p$ orbital is part of a continuous cycle of five $2p$ orbitals. In furan, one unshared pair of electrons of the heteroatom lies in the unhybridized $2p$ orbital and is a part of the pi system (Figure 9.3). The other unshared pair of electrons lies in an sp^2 hybrid orbital, perpendicular to the $2p$ orbitals, and is not a part of the pi system. In pyrrole, the unshared pair of electrons on nitrogen is part of the aromatic sextet. In imidazole, the unshared pair of electrons on one nitrogen is part of the aromatic sextet; the unshared pair on the other nitrogen is not.

Nature abounds with compounds having a heterocyclic aromatic ring fused to one or more other rings. Two such compounds especially important in the biological world are indole and purine:

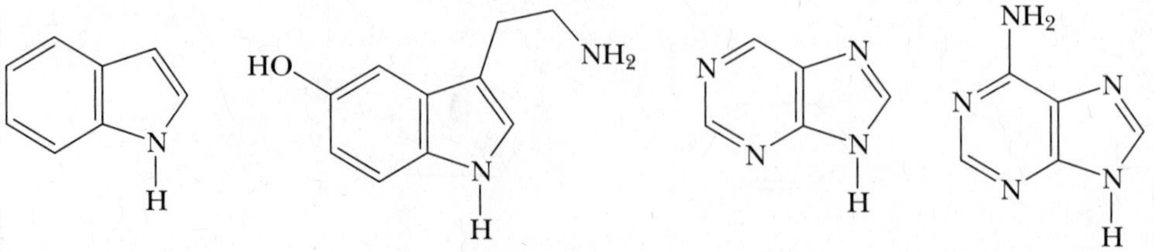
N
H
HO
NH2
N
H
N
N
N
N
H
NH2
N
N
N
N
H

Indole Serotonin (a neurotransmitter) Purine Adenine

Indole contains a pyrrole ring fused with a benzene ring. Compounds derived from indole include the amino acid L-tryptophan (Section 18.2C) and the neurotransmitter serotonin. Purine contains a six-membered pyrimidine ring fused with a five-membered imidazole ring. Adenine is one of the building blocks of deoxyribonucleic acids (DNA) and ribonucleic acids (RNA), as described in Chapter 20. It is also a component of the biological oxidizing agent nicotinamide adenine dinucleotide, abbreviated NAD^+ (Section 21.1B).

EXAMPLE 9.1

Which of the following compounds are aromatic?

(a) 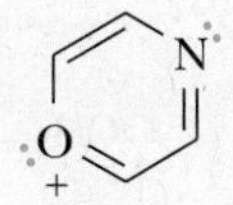 (b)  (c) 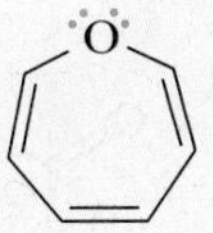

STRATEGY

Determine whether each atom of the ring contains a 2*p* orbital and whether the molecule is planar. If these criteria are met, determine the number of pi electrons. Those having 2, 6, 10, 14, and so on electrons are aromatic.

SOLUTION

(a) 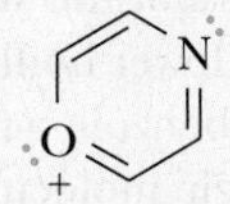 This molecule is planar, and each atom of the ring contains a 2*p* orbital. There is a total of 6 pi electrons. The molecule is aromatic.

(b) 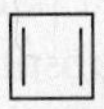 This molecule is planar, and each atom of the ring contains a 2*p* orbital. There is a total of 4 pi electrons. The molecule is not aromatic.

(c) 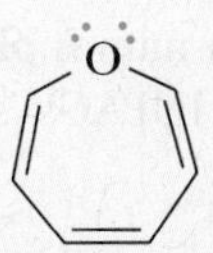 Treat the molecule as planar for the purposes of determining aromaticity. Also, treat each carbon atom in the ring as containing a 2*p* orbital. That is, treat the oxygen atom as sp^2 hybridized, so that one of its lone pairs of electrons will enter the pi electron system (if we do not do this, the molecule cannot be aromatic because an oxygen atom with two lone pairs of electrons and two single bonds is normally sp^3 hybridized). Despite these special considerations, the molecule ends up with a total of eight pi electrons, so the molecule is not aromatic. Because it is not aromatic, the oxygen has no driving force to be sp^2 hybridized and is, in fact, sp^3 hybridized. Also, the molecule has no driving force to be planar, and in fact, the molecule is nonplanar.

See problem 9.11

PROBLEM 9.1

Which of the following compounds are aromatic?

(a) 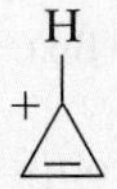 (b) 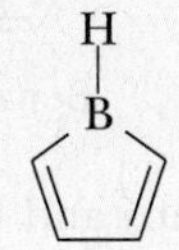 (c) 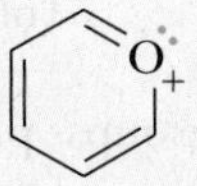

9.3 How Are Benzene Compounds Named, and What Are Their Physical Properties?

A. Monosubstituted Benzenes

Monosubstituted alkylbenzenes are named as derivatives of benzene; an example is ethylbenzene. The IUPAC system retains certain common names for several of the simpler monosubstituted alkylbenzenes. Examples are **toluene** (rather than methylbenzene) and

styrene (rather than phenylethylene):

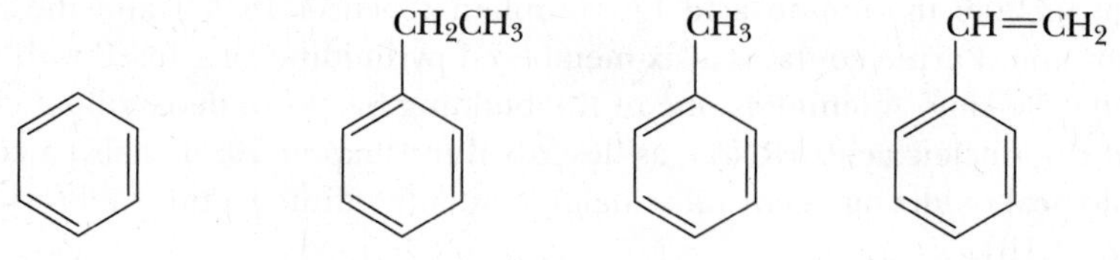

	Benzene	Ethylbenzene	Toluene	Styrene
mp (°C)	5.5	−95	−93	−31
bp (°C)	80	136	110	145

The common names **phenol**, **aniline**, **benzaldehyde**, **benzoic acid**, and **anisole** are also retained by the IUPAC system:

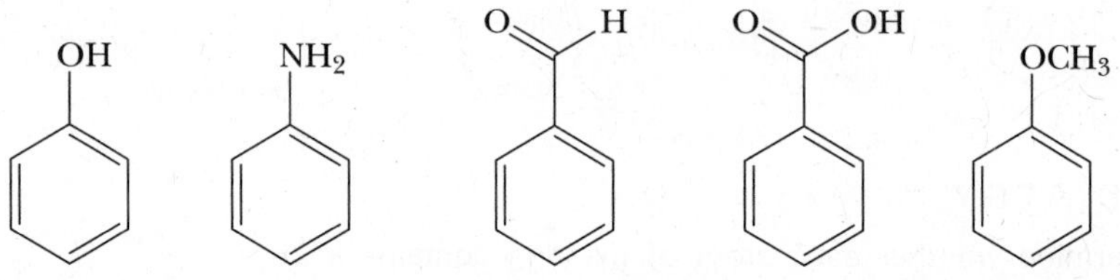

	Phenol	Aniline	Benzaldehyde	Benzoic acid	Anisole
mp (°C)	41	−6	−26	123	−37
bp (°C)	182	184	178	249	154

The physical properties of substituted benzenes vary depending on the nature of the substituent. Alkylbenzenes, like other hydrocarbons, are nonpolar and thus have lower boiling points than benzenes with polar substituents such as phenol, aniline, and benzoic acid. The melting points of substituted benzenes depend on whether or not their molecules can be packed close together. Benzene, which has no substituents and is flat, can pack its molecules very closely, giving it a considerably higher melting point than many substituted benzenes.

Phenyl group C_6H_5—, the aryl group derived by removing a hydrogen from benzene.

Benzyl group $C_6H_5CH_2$—, the alkyl group derived by removing a hydrogen from the methyl group of toluene.

As noted in the introduction to Chapter 5, the substituent group derived by the loss of an H from benzene is a **phenyl** group (Ph); that derived by the loss of an H from the methyl group of toluene is a **benzyl group** (Bn):

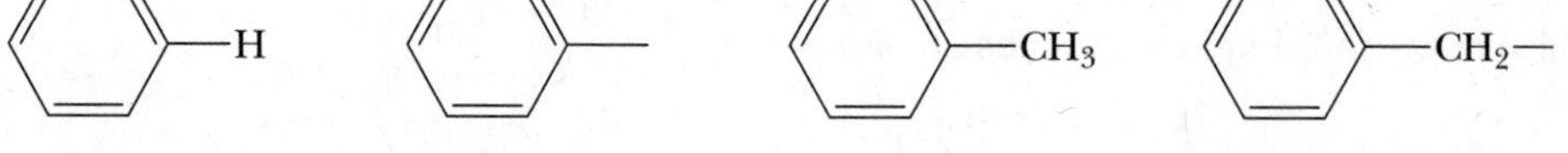

Benzene   Phenyl group (Ph)   Toluene   Benzyl group (Bn)

In molecules containing other functional groups, phenyl groups and benzyl groups are often named as substituents:

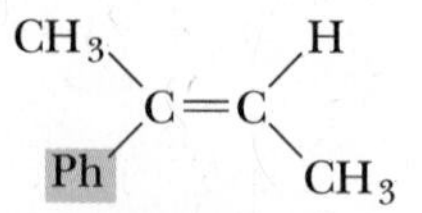

$PhCH_2CH_2OH$ $PhCH_2Cl$

(*Z*)-2-Phenyl-2-butene   2-Phenylethanol   Benzyl chloride

Ortho (*o*) Refers to groups occupying positions 1 and 2 on a benzene ring.

Meta (*m*) Refers to groups occupying positions 1 and 3 on a benzene ring.

Para (*p*) Refers to groups occupying positions 1 and 4 on a benzene ring.

B. Disubstituted Benzenes

When two substituents occur on a benzene ring, three constitutional isomers are possible. We locate substituents either by numbering the atoms of the ring or by using the locators **ortho**, **meta**, and **para**. The numbers 1,2- are equivalent to *ortho* (Greek: straight); 1,3- to *meta* (Greek: after); and 1,4- to *para* (Greek: beyond).

When one of the two substituents on the ring imparts a special name to the compound, as, for example, toluene, phenol, and aniline, then we name the compound as a derivative of that parent molecule. In this case, the special substituent occupies ring position number 1. The IUPAC system retains the common name **xylene** for the three isomeric dimethylbenzenes. When neither group imparts a special name, we locate the two substituents and list them in alphabetical order before the ending *-benzene.* The carbon of the benzene ring with the substituent of lower alphabetical ranking is numbered C-1.

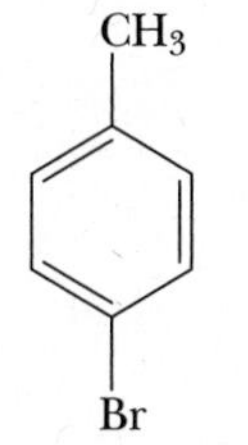

4-Bromotoluene
(*p*-Bromotoluene)

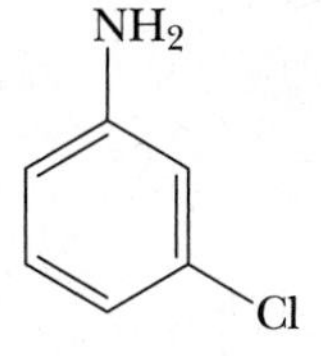

3-Chloroaniline
(*m*-Chloroaniline)

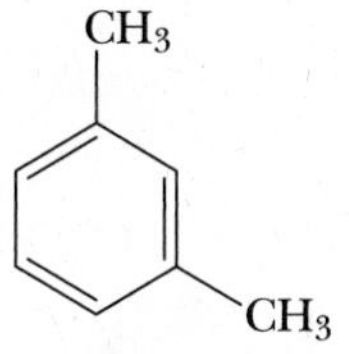

1,3-Dimethylbenzene
(*m*-Xylene)

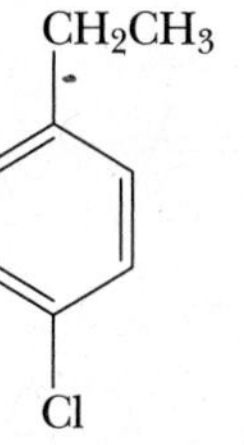

1-Chloro-4-ethylbenzene
(*p*-Chloroethylbenzene)

C. Polysubstituted Benzenes

When three or more substituents are present on a ring, we specify their locations by numbers. If one of the substituents imparts a special name, then the molecule is named as a derivative of that parent molecule. If none of the substituents imparts a special name, we number them to give the smallest set of numbers and list them in alphabetical order before the ending *-benzene.* In the following examples, the first compound is a derivative of toluene, and the second is a derivative of phenol. Because there is no special name for the third compound, we list its three substituents in alphabetical order, followed by the word *benzene.*

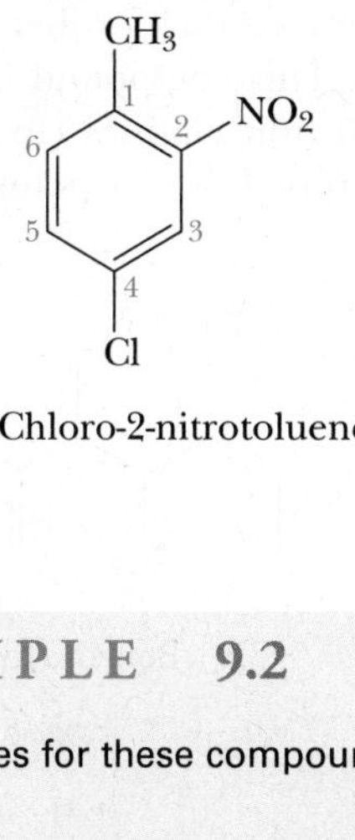

4-Chloro-2-nitrotoluene

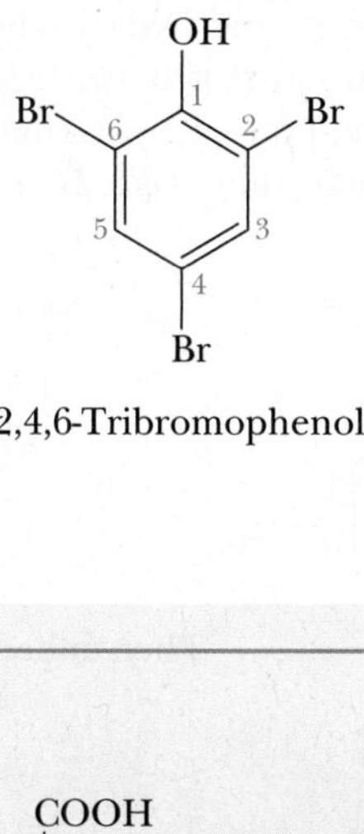

2,4,6-Tribromophenol

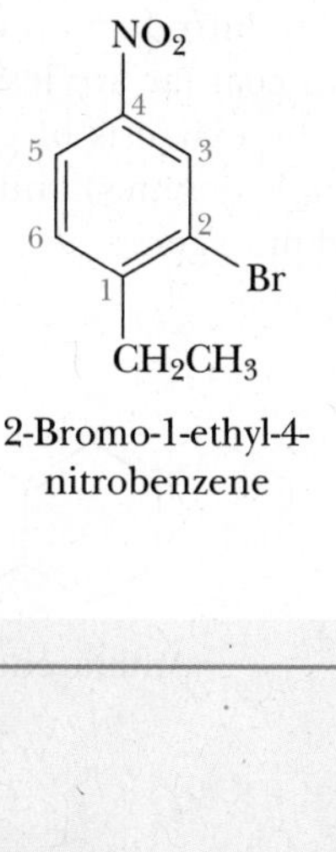

2-Bromo-1-ethyl-4-nitrobenzene

EXAMPLE 9.2

Write names for these compounds:

(a)

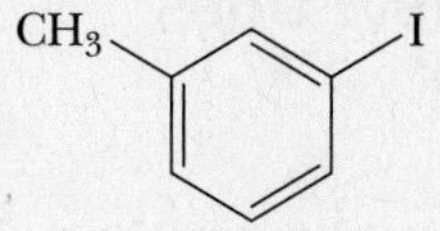

(b)

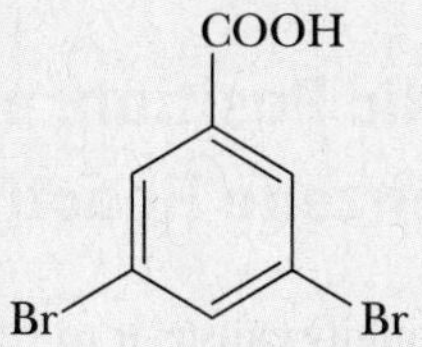

(c)

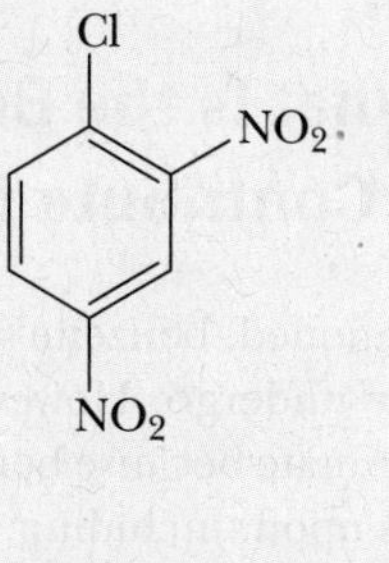

(d)

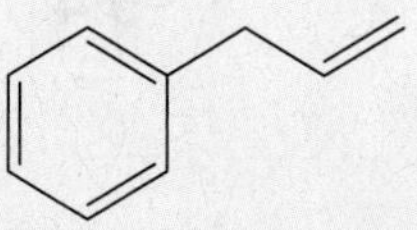

STRATEGY

First, determine whether one of the substituents imparts a special name to the benzene compound (e.g., toluene, phenol aniline). Identify all substituents and list them in alphabetical order. Use numbers to indicate relative position. The locato *ortho, meta,* or *para* can be used for disubstituted benzenes.

SOLUTION

(a) 3-Iodotoluene or *m*-iodotoluene (b) 3,5-Dibromobenzoic acid (c) 1-Chloro-2,4-dinitrobenzene (d) 3-Phenylpropene

See problems 9.13, 9.14

PROBLEM 9.2

Write names for these compounds:

(a) 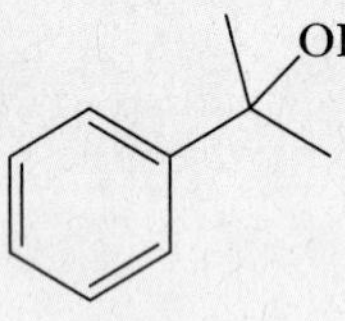

(b) 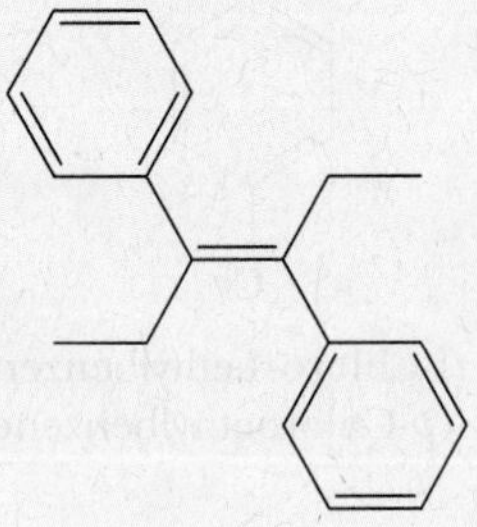

(c) 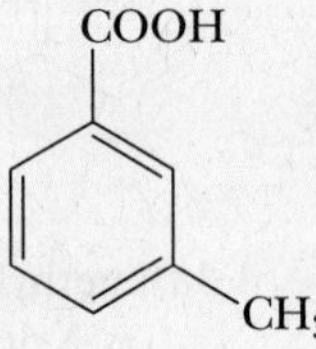

Polynuclear aromatic hydrocarbon A hydrocarbon containing two or more fused aromatic rings.

Polynuclear aromatic hydrocarbons (PAHs) contain two or more aromatic rings, each pair of which shares two ring carbon atoms. Naphthalene, anthracene, and phenanthrene, the most common PAHs, and substances derived from them are found in coal tar and high-boiling petroleum residues. At one time, naphthalene was used as a moth repellent and insecticide in protecting woolens and furs, but its use has decreased due to the introduction of chlorinated hydrocarbons such as *p*-dichlorobenzene. Also found in coal tar are lesser amounts of benzo[a]pyrene. This compound is found as well in the exhausts of gasoline-powered internal combustion engines (for example, automobile engines) and in cigarette smoke. Benzo[a]pyrene is a very potent carcinogen and mutagen.

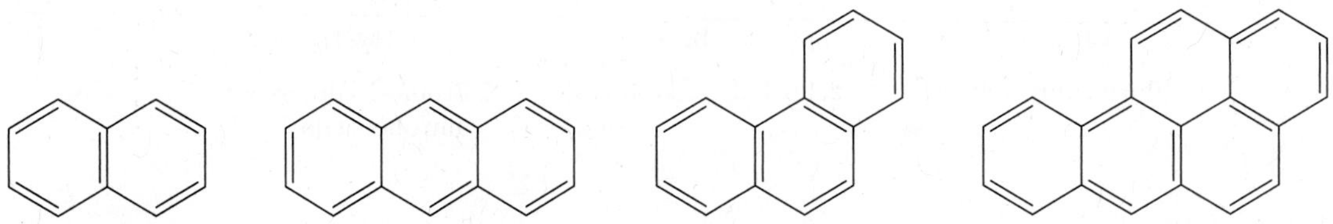

Naphthalene Anthracene Phenanthrene Benzo[a]pyrene

9.4 What Is the Benzylic Position, and How Does It Contribute to Benzene Reactivity?

As we have mentioned, benzene's aromaticity causes it to resist many of the reactions that alkenes typically undergo. However, chemists have been able to react benzene in other ways. This is fortunate because benzene rings are abundant in many of the compounds that society depends upon, including various medications, plastics, and preservatives for food. We begin our discussion of benzene reactions with processes that take place not on the ring itself, but at the carbon immediately bonded to the benzene ring. This carbon is known as a **benzylic carbon**.

Benzylic carbon An sp^3 hybridized carbon bonded to a benzene ring.

Benzene is unaffected by strong oxidizing agents, such as H_2CrO_4 and $KMnO_4$. When we treat toluene with these oxidizing agents under vigorous conditions, the side-chain methyl group is oxidized to a carboxyl group to give benzoic acid:

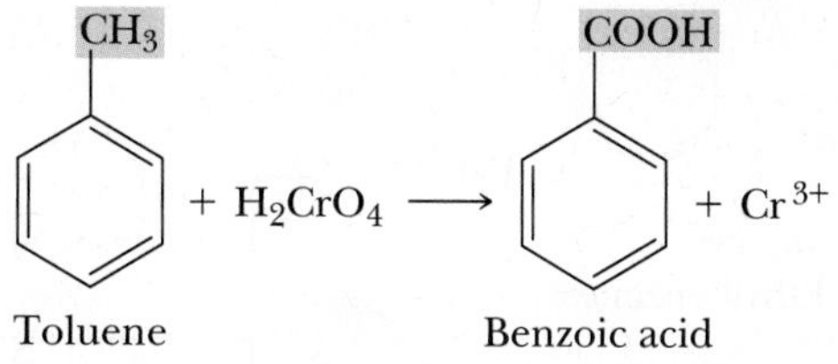

The fact that the side-chain methyl group is oxidized, but the aromatic ring is unchanged, illustrates the remarkable chemical stability of the aromatic ring. Halogen and nitro substituents on an aromatic ring are unaffected by these oxidations. For example, chromic acid oxidizes 2-chloro-4-nitrotoluene to 2-chloro-4-nitrobenzoic acid. Notice that in this oxidation, the nitro and chloro groups remain unaffected:

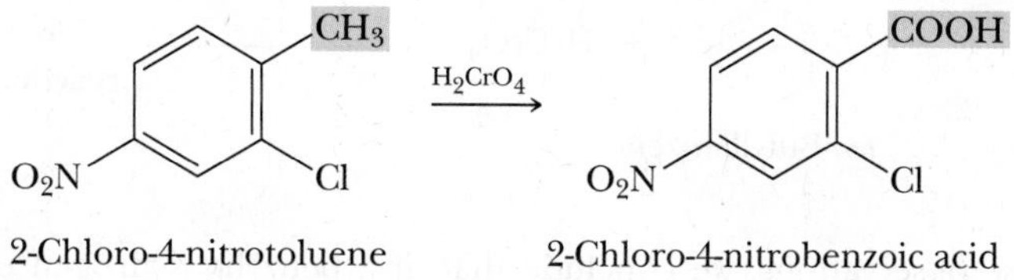

Chemical Connections 9A

CARCINOGENIC POLYNUCLEAR AROMATICS AND CANCER

A **carcinogen** is a compound that causes cancer. The first carcinogens to be identified were a group of polynuclear aromatic hydrocarbons, all of which have at least four aromatic rings. Among them is benzo[a] pyrene, one of the most carcinogenic of the aromatic hydrocarbons. It forms whenever there is incomplete combustion of organic compounds. Benzo[a]pyrene is found, for example, in cigarette smoke, automobile exhaust, and charcoal-broiled meats.

Benzo[a]pyrene causes cancer in the following way: Once it is absorbed or ingested, the body attempts to convert it into a more soluble compound that can be excreted easily. To this end, a series of enzyme-catalyzed reactions transforms benzo[a] pyrene into a **diol epoxide**, a compound that can bind to DNA by reacting with one of its amino groups, thereby altering the structure of DNA and producing a cancer-causing mutation:

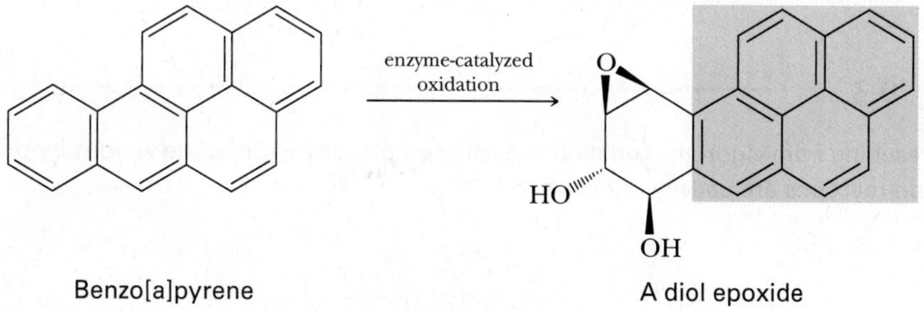

Question

Show how the outer perimeter of benzo[a]pyrene satisfies Hückel's criteria for aromaticity. Is the outer perimeter of the highlighted portion of the diol epoxide product of benzo[a]pyrene also aromatic?

Ethylbenzene and isopropylbenzene are also oxidized to benzoic acid under these conditions. The side chain of *tert*-butylbenzene, which has no benzylic hydrogen, is not affected by these oxidizing conditions.

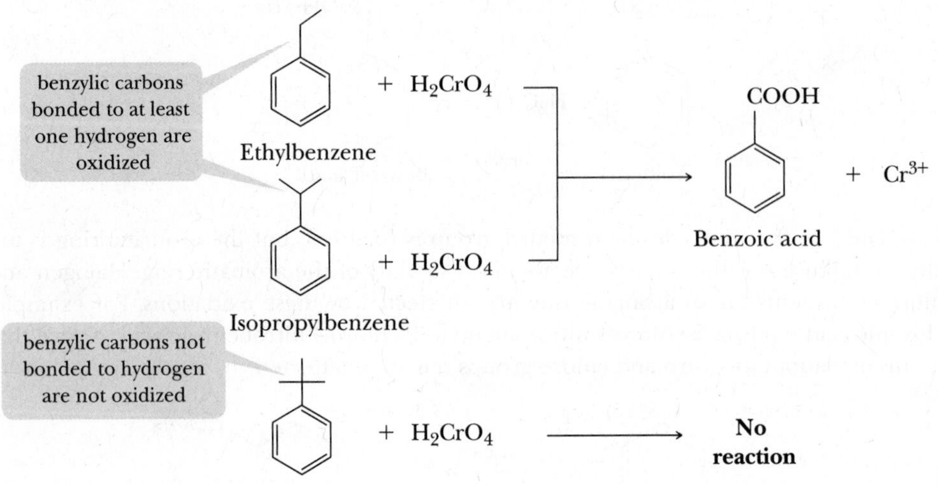

From these observations, we conclude that, if a benzylic hydrogen exists, then the benzylic carbon (Section 9.3A) is oxidized to a carboxyl group and all other carbons of the side chain are removed. If no benzylic hydrogen exists, as in the case of *tert*-butylbenzene, then the side chain is not oxidized.

If more than one alkyl side chain exists, each is oxidized to —COOH. Oxidation of *m*-xylene gives 1,3-benzenedicarboxylic acid, more commonly named isophthalic acid:

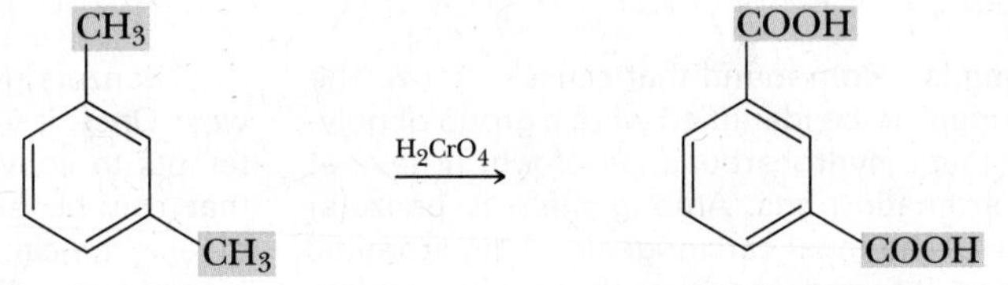

m-Xylene 1,3-Benzenedicarboxylic acid (Isophthalic acid)

EXAMPLE 9.3

Predict the products resulting from vigorous oxidation of each compound by H_2CrO_4. The various by-products that are formed from benzylic oxidation reactions are usually not specified.

(a) 1,4 -dimethylbenzene (*p*-xylene) (b)

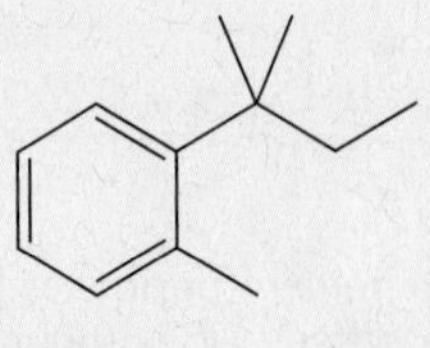

STRATEGY

Identify all the alkyl groups in the reactant. If a benzylic hydrogen exists on an alkyl group, chromic acid will oxidize it to a —COOH group.

SOLUTION

chromic acid oxidizes both alkyl groups to —COOH groups, and the product is terephthalic acid, one of two compounds required for the synthesis of Dacron polyester and Mylar (Section 17.4B)

(a)

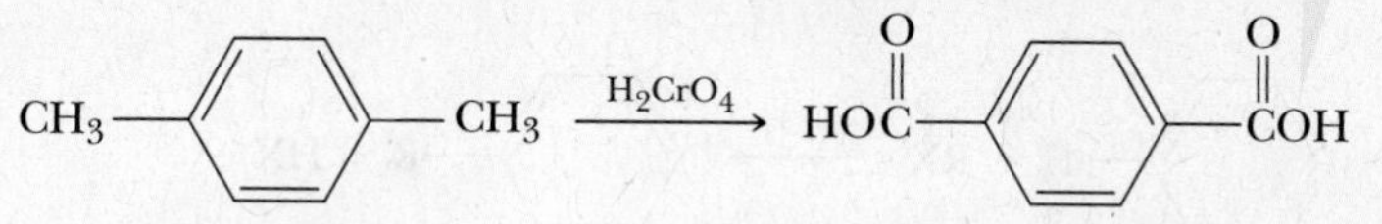

1,4-Dimethylbenzene (*p*-Xylene)

1,4-Benzenedicarboxylic acid (Terephthalic acid)

(b)

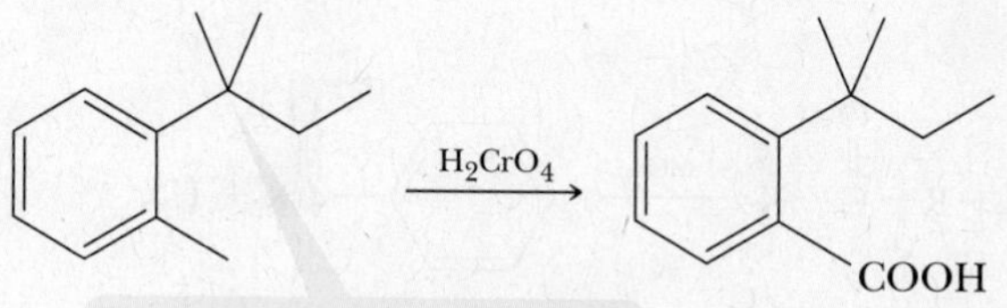

this alkyl group has no benzylic hydrogens and is not oxidized

See problem 9.30

PROBLEM 9.3

Predict the products resulting from vigorous oxidation of each compound by H_2CrO_4:

(a)

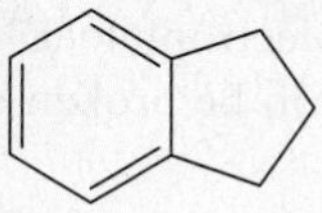

(b)

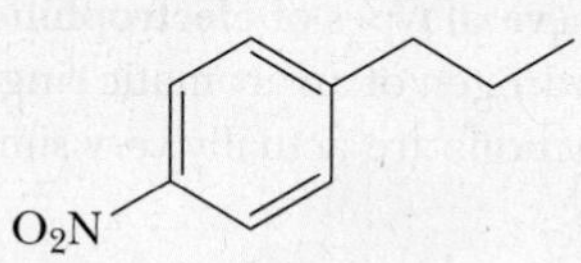

9.5 What Is Electrophilic Aromatic Substitution?

Although benzene is resistant to most of the reactions presented thus far for alkenes, it is not completely unreactive. By far the most characteristic reaction of aromatic compounds is substitution at a ring carbon. Some groups that can be introduced directly onto the ring are the halogens, the nitro ($—NO_2$) group, the sulfonic acid ($—SO_3H$) group, alkyl (—R) groups, and acyl (RCO—) groups.

Halogenation:

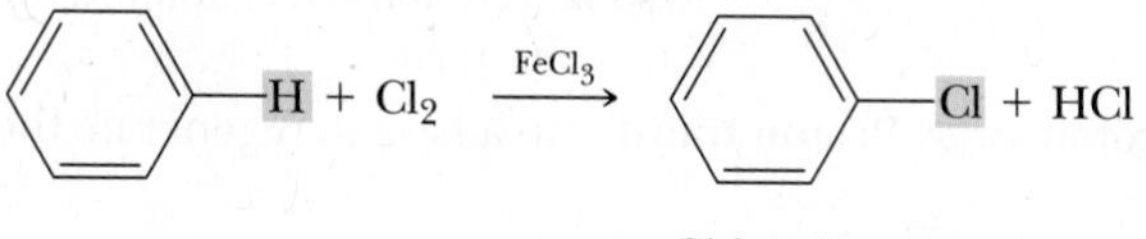

Chlorobenzene

Nitration:

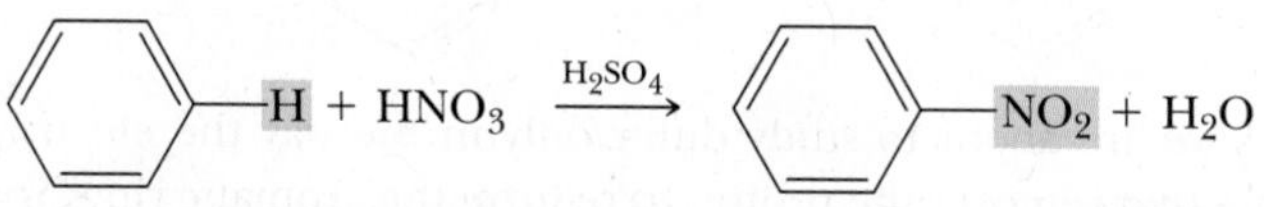

Nitrobenzene

Sulfonation:

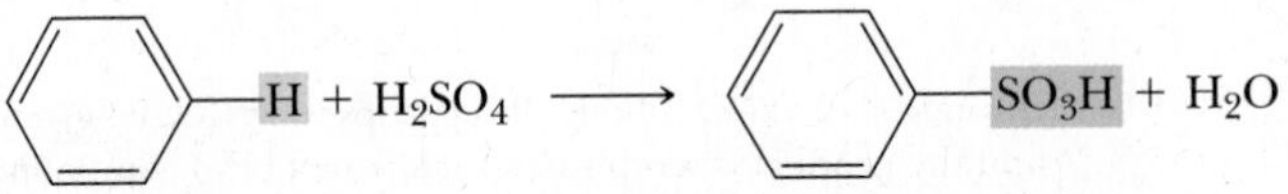

Benzenesulfonic acid

Alkylation:

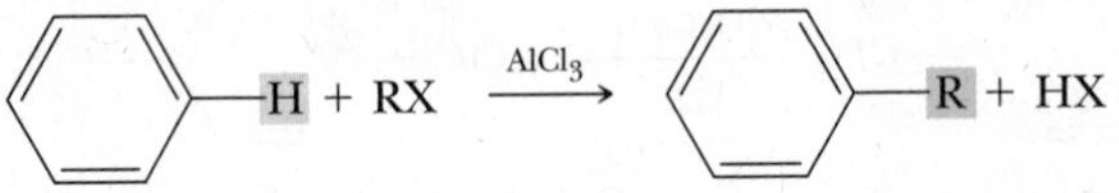

An alkylbenzene

Acylation:

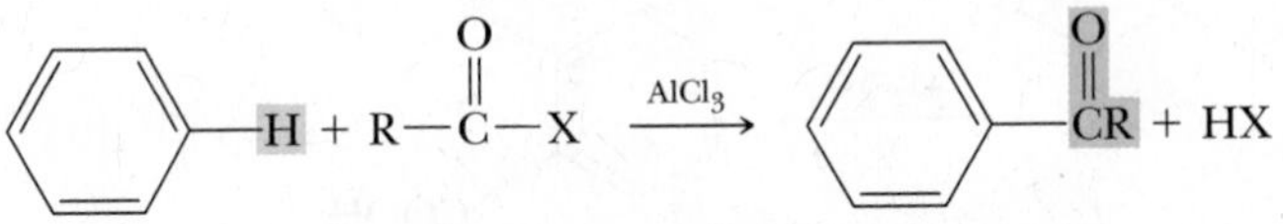

An acyl halide

An acylbenzene

9.6 What Is the Mechanism of Electrophilic Aromatic Substitution?

Electrophilic aromatic substitution A reaction in which an electrophile, E^+, substitutes for a hydrogen on an aromatic ring.

In this section, we study several types of **electrophilic aromatic substitution** reactions—that is, reactions in which a hydrogen of an aromatic ring is replaced by an electrophile, E^+. The mechanisms of these reactions are actually very similar. In fact, they can be broken down into three common steps:

Step 1: **Generation of the electrophile.** This is a reaction pattern specific to each particular electrophilic aromatic substitution reaction.

$$\text{Reagent(s)} \longrightarrow E^+$$

Step 2: **Reaction of a nucleophile and an electrophile to form a new covalent bond.** Attack of the electrophile on the aromatic ring to give a resonance-stabilized cation intermediate:

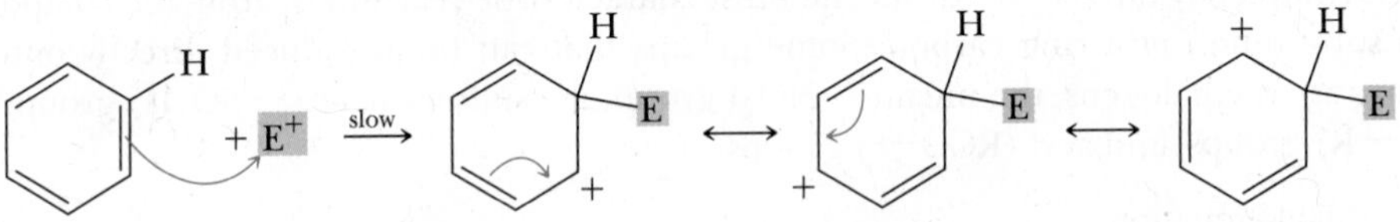

(the nucleophile)

Resonance-stabilized cation intermediate

Step 3: **Take a proton away.** Proton transfer to a base to regenerate the aromatic ring:

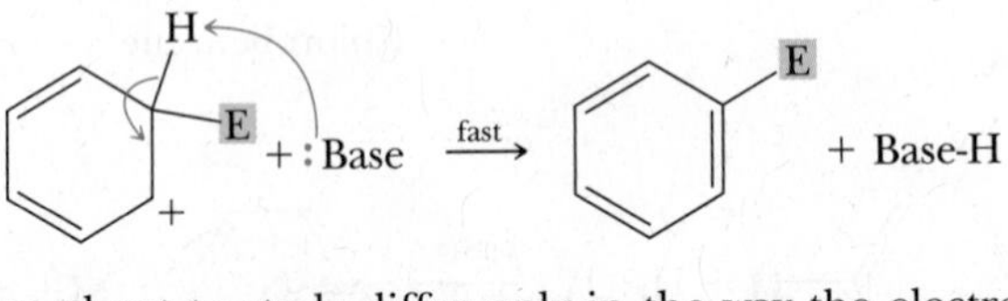

The reactions we are about to study differ only in the way the electrophile is generated and in the base that removes the proton to re-form the aromatic ring. You should keep this principle in mind as we explore the details of each reaction.

A. Chlorination and Bromination

Chlorine alone does not react with benzene, in contrast to its instantaneous addition to cyclohexene (Section 5.3C). However, in the presence of a Lewis acid catalyst, such as ferric chloride or aluminum chloride, chlorine reacts to give chlorobenzene and HCl. Chemists account for this type of electrophilic aromatic substitution by the following three-step mechanism:

Mechanism

Electrophilic Aromatic Substitution—Chlorination

STEP 1: Formation of the Electrophile. Reaction between chlorine (a Lewis base) and $FeCl_3$ (a Lewis acid) gives an ion pair containing a chloronium ion (an electrophile):

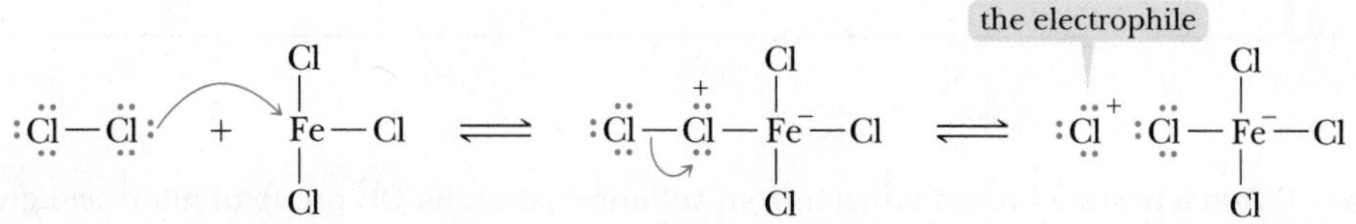

Chlorine (a Lewis base)	Ferric chloride (a Lewis acid)	A molecular complex with a positive charge on chlorine and a negative charge on iron	An ion pair containing a chloronium ion

STEP 2: Reaction of a nucleophile and an electrophile to form a new covalent bond. Reaction of the Cl_2–$FeCl_3$ ion pair with the pi electron cloud of the aromatic ring forms a resonance-stabilized cation intermediate, represented here as a hybrid of three contributing structures:

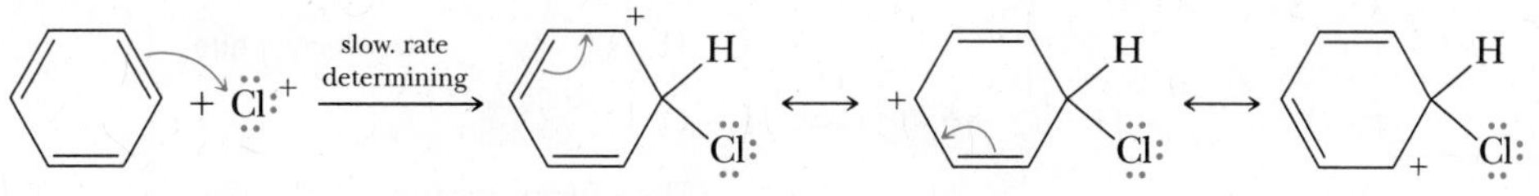

(the nucleophile) Resonance-stabilized cation intermediate

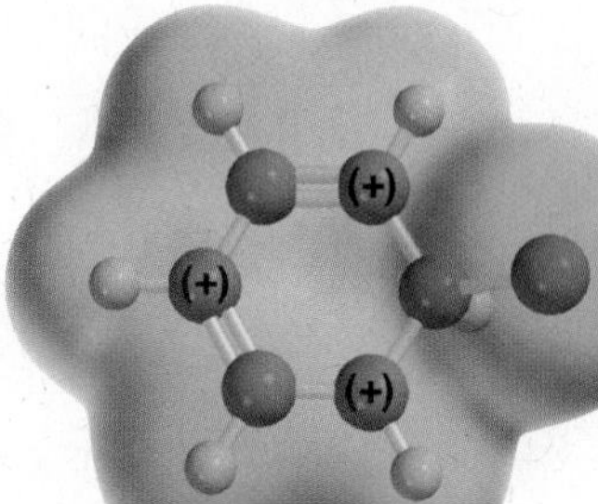

The positive charge on the resonance-stabilized intermediate is distributed approximately equally on the carbon atoms 2, 4, and 6 of the ring relative to the point of substitution.

STEP 3: Take a proton away. Proton transfer from the cation intermediate to $FeCl_4^-$ forms HCl, regenerates the Lewis acid catalyst, and gives chlorobenzene:

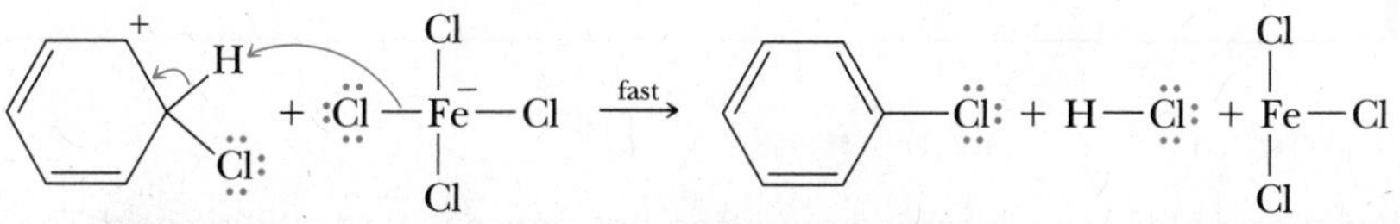

Cation intermediate Chlorobenzene

Treatment of benzene with bromine in the presence of ferric chloride or aluminum chloride gives bromobenzene and HBr. The mechanism for this reaction is the same as that for chlorination of benzene.

The major difference between the addition of halogen to an alkene and substitution by halogen on an aromatic ring is the fate of the cation intermediate formed after the halogen is added to the compound. Recall from Section 5.3C that the addition of chlorine to an alkene is a two-step process, the first and slower step of which is the formation of a bridged chloronium ion intermediate. This intermediate then reacts with chloride ion to complete the addition. With aromatic compounds, the cation intermediate loses H^+ to regenerate the aromatic ring and regain its large resonance stabilization. There is no such resonance stabilization to be regained in the case of an alkene.

B. Nitration and Sulfonation

The sequence of steps for the nitration and sulfonation of benzene is similar to that for chlorination and bromination. For nitration, the electrophile is the **nitronium ion**, NO_2^+, generated by the reaction of nitric acid with sulfuric acid. In the following equations nitric acid is written $HONO_2$ to show more clearly the origin of the nitronium ion.

Mechanism

Formation of the Nitronium Ion

STEP 1: Add a proton. Proton transfer from sulfuric acid to the OH group of nitric acid gives the conjugate acid of nitric acid:

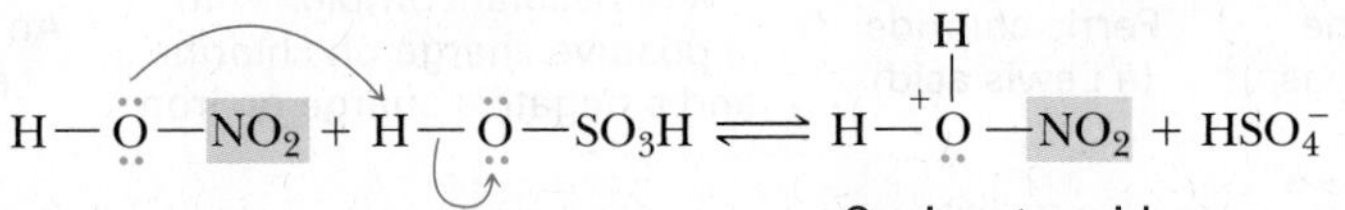

Nitric acid

Conjugate acid of nitric acid

STEP 2: Break a bond to form a stable ion or molecule. Loss of water from this conjugate acid gives the nitronium ion, NO_2^+:

the electrophile

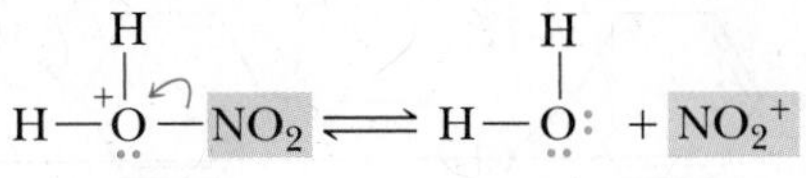

The nitronium ion

Mechanism

Formation of the Sulfonium Ion

The sulfonation of benzene is carried out using hot, concentrated sulfuric acid. The electrophile under these conditions is either SO_3 or HSO_3^+, depending on the experimental conditions. The HSO_3^+ electrophile is formed from sulfuric acid in the following way:

STEP 1: Add a proton. Proton transfer from one molecule of sulfuric acid to the OH group of another molecule of sulfuric acid gives the conjugate acid of sulfuric acid:

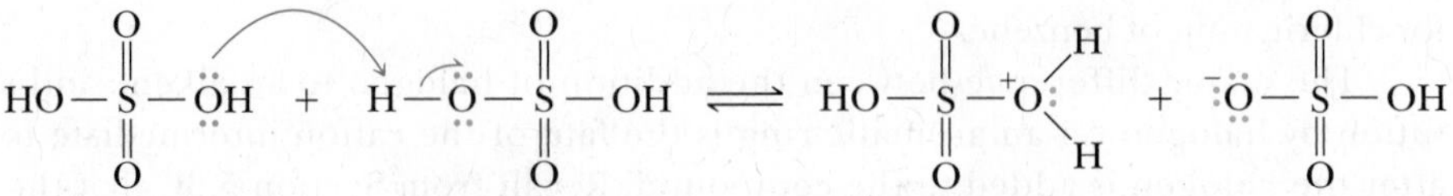

Sulfuric acid Sulfuric acid

STEP 2: Break a bond to form a more stable ion or molecule. Loss of water from this conjugate acid gives the sulfonium ion as the electrophile:

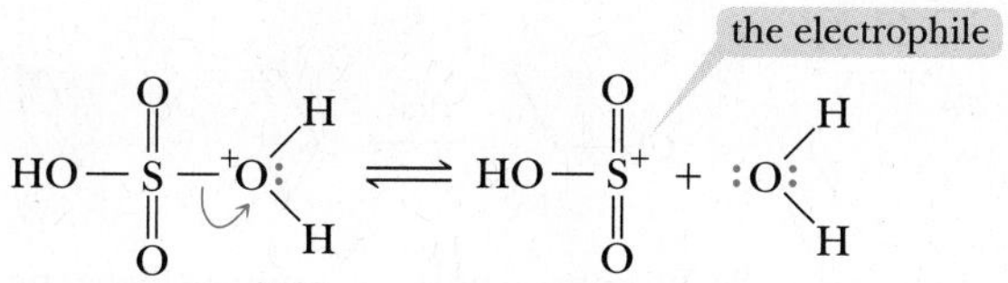

The sulfonium ion

EXAMPLE 9.4

Write a stepwise mechanism for the nitration of benzene.

STRATEGY

Keep in mind that the mechanisms of electrophilic aromatic substitution reactions are all very similar. After the formation of the electrophile, attack of the electrophile on the aromatic ring occurs to give a resonance-stabilized cation intermediate. The last step of the mechanism is proton transfer to a base to regenerate the aromatic ring. The base in nitration is water, which was generated in the formation of the electrophile.

SOLUTION

STEP 1: Reaction of a nucleophile and an electrophile to form a new covalent bond. Reaction of the nitronium ion (an electrophile) with the benzene ring (a nucleophile) gives a resonance-stabilized cation intermediate.

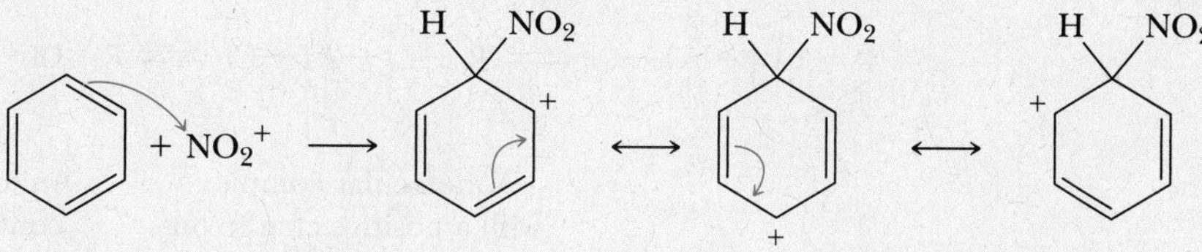

STEP 2: Take a proton away. Proton transfer from this intermediate to H_2O regenerates the aromatic ring and gives nitrobenzene:

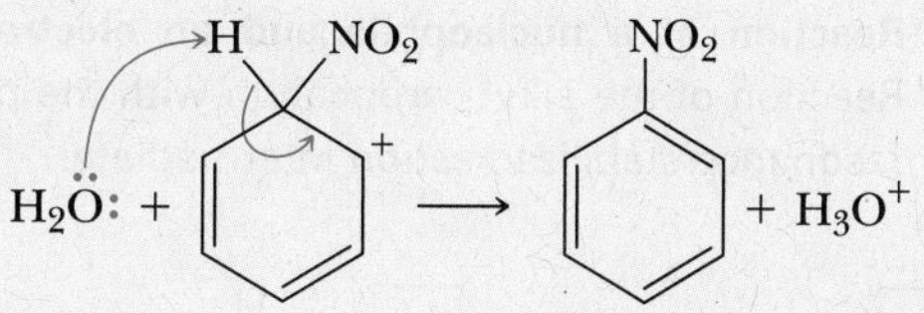

Nitrobenzene

See problems 9.21, 9.22

PROBLEM 9.4

Write a stepwise mechanism for the sulfonation of benzene. Use HSO_3^+ as the electrophile.

C. Friedel–Crafts Alkylation

Alkylation of aromatic hydrocarbons was discovered in 1877 by the French chemist Charles Friedel and a visiting American chemist, James Crafts. They discovered that mixing benzene, a haloalkane, and $AlCl_3$ results in the formation of an alkylbenzene and

HX. **Friedel–Crafts alkylation** forms a new carbon–carbon bond between benzene and an alkyl group, as illustrated by reaction of benzene with 2-chloropropane in the presence of aluminum chloride:

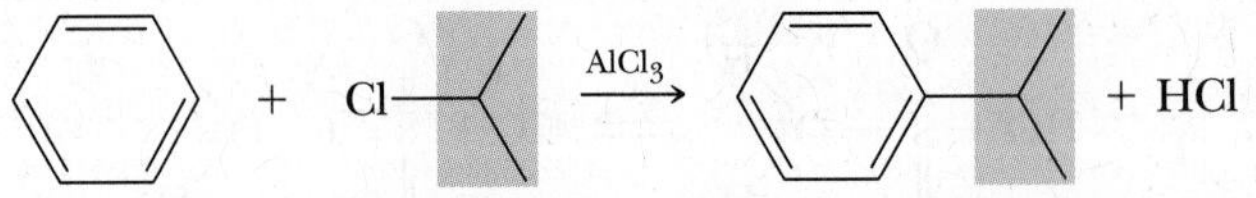

Benzene | 2-Chloropropane (Isopropyl chloride) | Isopropylbenzene (Cumene)

Friedel–Crafts alkylation is among the most important methods for forming new carbon–carbon bonds to aromatic rings.

Mechanism

Friedel–Crafts Alkylation

STEP 1: Formation of an electrophile. Reaction of a haloalkane (a Lewis base) with aluminum chloride (a Lewis acid) gives a molecular complex in which aluminum has a negative formal charge and the halogen of the haloalkane has a positive formal charge. Redistribution of electrons in this complex then gives an alkyl carbocation as part of an ion pair:

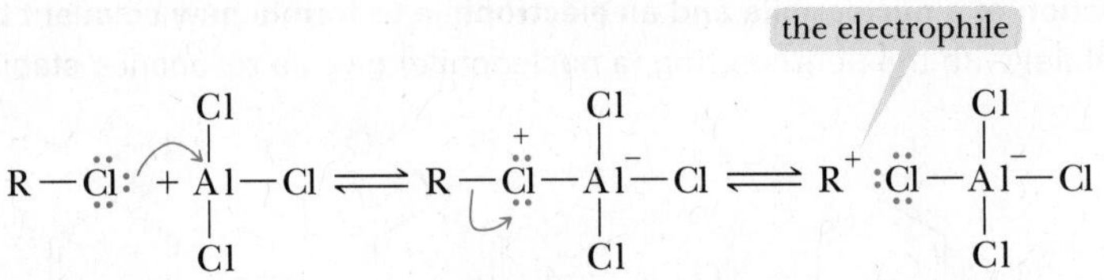

A molecular complex with a positive charge on chlorine and a negative charge on aluminum

An ion pair containing a carbocation

STEP 2: Reaction of a nucleophile and an electrophile to form a new covalent bond. Reaction of the alkyl carbocation with the pi electrons of the aromatic ring gives a resonance-stabilized cation intermediate:

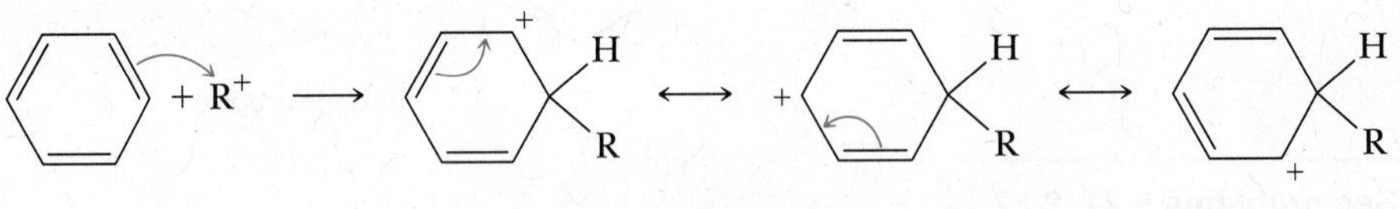

The positive charge is delocalized onto three atoms of the ring

STEP 3: Take a proton away. Proton transfer regenerates the aromatic character of the ring and the Lewis acid catalyst:

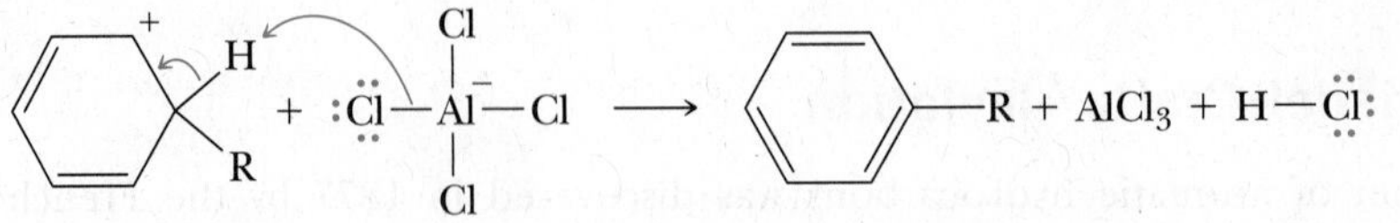

There are two major limitations on Friedel–Crafts alkylations. The first is that it is practical only with stable carbocations, such as 3° carbocations, resonance-stabilized carbocations, or 2° carbocations that cannot undergo rearrangement (Section 5.4). Primary carbocations will undergo rearrangement, resulting in multiple products as well as bonding of the benzene ring to unexpected carbons in the former haloalkane.

The second limitation on Friedel–Crafts alkylation is that it fails altogether on benzene rings bearing one or more strongly electron-withdrawing groups. The following table shows some of these groups:

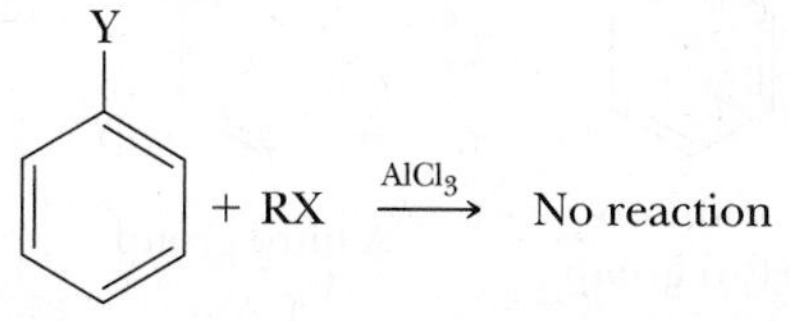

When Y Equals Any of These Groups, the Benzene Ring Does Not Undergo Friedel–Crafts Alkylation

$-\overset{O}{\overset{\|\|}{C}}H$	$-\overset{O}{\overset{\|\|}{C}}R$	$-\overset{O}{\overset{\|\|}{C}}OH$	$-\overset{O}{\overset{\|\|}{C}}OR$	$-\overset{O}{\overset{\|\|}{C}}NH_2$
$-SO_3H$	$-C{\equiv}N$	$-NO_2$	$-NR_3^{\ +}$	
$-CF_3$	$-CCl_3$			

HOW TO 9.2 Determine Whether a Substituent on Benzene Is Electron Withdrawing

Determine the charge or partial charge on the atom directly bonded to the benzene ring. If it is positive or partially positive, the substituent can be considered to be electron withdrawing. An atom will be partially positive if it is bonded to an atom more electronegative than itself.

the atom directly bonded to the benzene ring is partially positive in character due to inductive effects from electronegative atoms. The substituent acts as an electron-withdrawing group

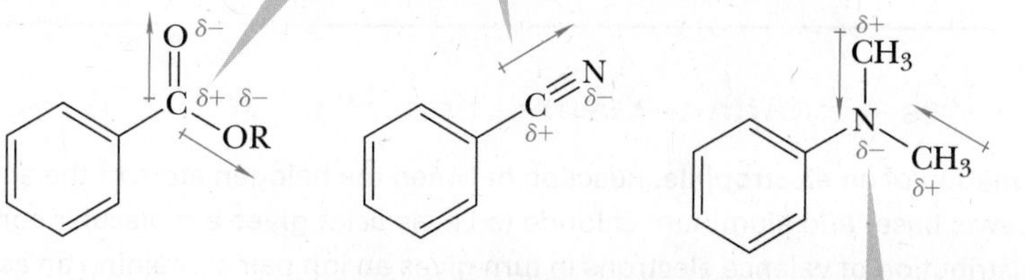

the atom (nitrogen) directly bonded to the benzene ring is partially negative in character because it is bonded to less electronegative atoms (carbons). The substituent *does not* act as an electron-withdrawing group

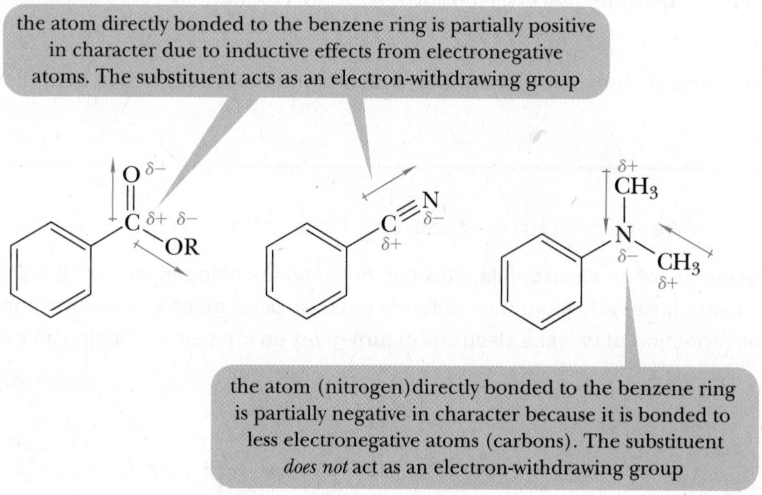

A common characteristic of the groups listed in the preceding table is that each has either a full or partial positive charge on the atom bonded to the benzene ring. For carbonyl-containing compounds, this partial positive charge arises because of the difference in electronegativity between the carbonyl oxygen and carbon. For $-CF_3$ and $-CCl_3$ groups, the partial positive charge on carbon arises because of the difference in electronegativity between carbon and the halogens bonded to it. In both the nitro group and the trialkylammonium group, there is a positive charge on nitrogen:

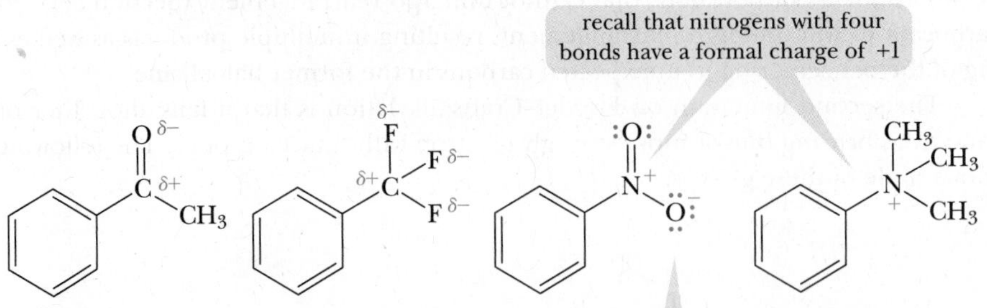
recall that nitrogens with four bonds have a formal charge of +1
recall that oxygens with only one bond and three lone pairs of electrons have a formal charge of −1

The carbonyl group of a ketone | A trifluoromethyl group | A nitro group | A trimethylammonium group

D. Friedel–Crafts Acylation

Acyl halide A derivative of a carboxylic acid in which the —OH of the carboxyl group is replaced by a halogen—most commonly, chlorine.

Friedel and Crafts also discovered that treating an aromatic hydrocarbon with an acyl halide in the presence of aluminum chloride gives a ketone. An **acyl halide** is a derivative of a carboxylic acid in which the —OH of the carboxyl group is replaced by a halogen, most commonly chlorine. Acyl halides are also referred to as acid halides. An RCO— group is known as an acyl group; hence, the reaction of an acyl halide with an aromatic hydrocarbon is known as **Friedel–Crafts acylation**, as illustrated by the reaction of benzene and acetyl chloride in the presence of aluminum chloride to give acetophenone:

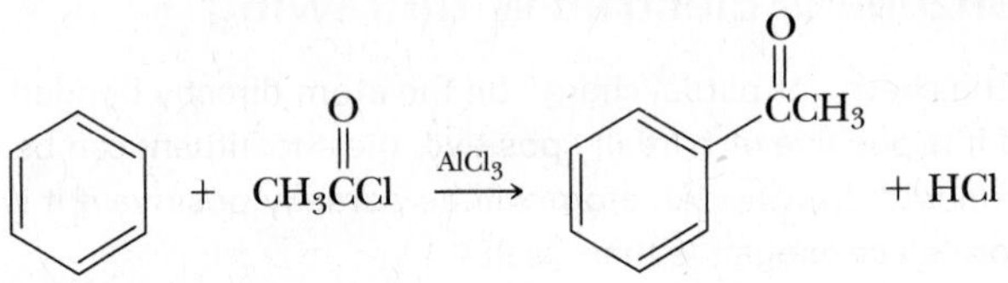

Benzene | Acetyl chloride (an acyl halide) | Acetophenone (a ketone)

In Friedel–Crafts acylations, the electrophile is an acylium ion, generated in the following way:

Mechanism

Friedel–Crafts Acylation—Generation of an Acylium Ion

STEP 1: Formation of an electrophile. Reaction between the halogen atom of the acyl chloride (a Lewis base) and aluminum chloride (a Lewis acid) gives a molecular complex. The redistribution of valence electrons in turn gives an ion pair containing an **acylium ion**:

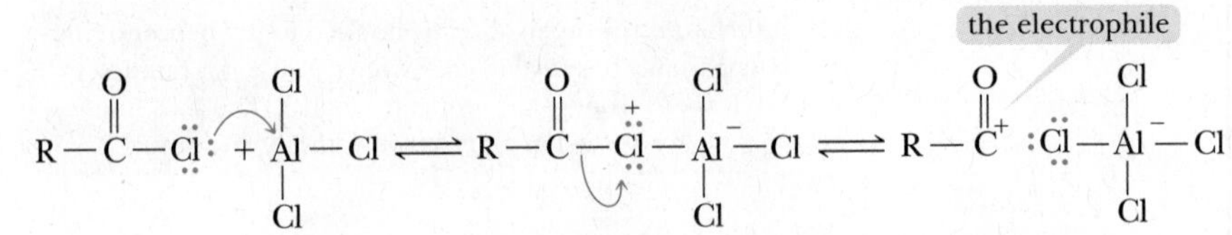
the electrophile

An acyl chloride (a Lewis acid) | Aluminum chloride (a Lewis acid) | A molecular complex with a positive charge on chlorine and a negative charge on aluminum | An ion pair containing an acylium ion

Steps 2 and 3 are identical to steps 2 and 3 of Friedel–Crafts alkylation (Section 9.6C).

EXAMPLE 9.5

Write a structural formula for the product formed by Friedel–Crafts alkylation or acylation of benzene with

(a) 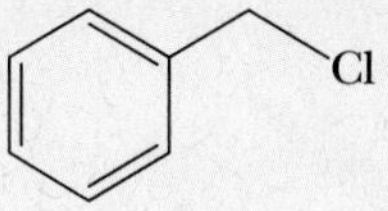 (b) 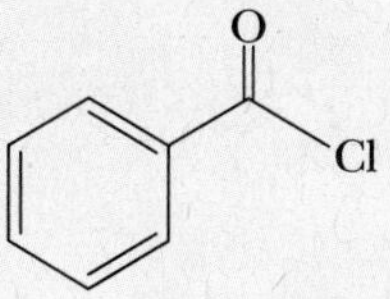 (c) 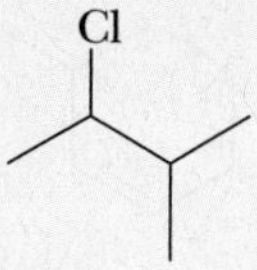

STRATEGY

Utilize the fact that the halogenated reagent in Friedel–Crafts reactions will normally form a bond with benzene at the carbon bonded to the halogen (Br or Cl). Therefore, to predict the product of a Friedel–Crafts reaction, replace the halogen in the haloalkane or acyl halide with the benzene ring. One thing to be wary of, however, is the possibility of rearrangement once the carbocation is formed.

SOLUTION

(a) Treatment of benzyl chloride with aluminum chloride gives the resonance-stabilized benzyl cation. Reaction of this cation (an electrophile) with benzene (a nucleophile), followed by loss of H^+, gives diphenylmethane:

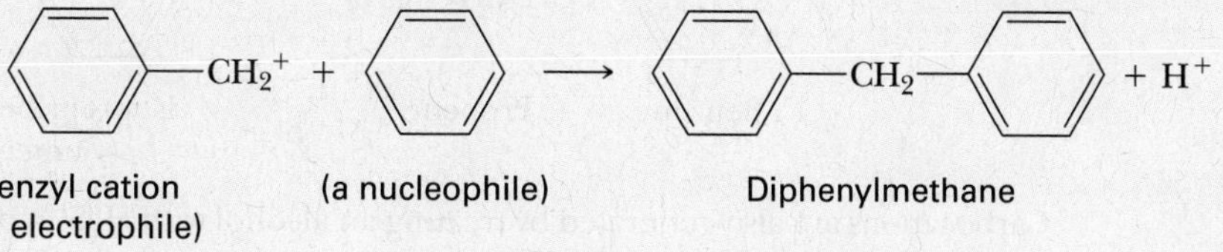

(b) Treatment of benzoyl chloride with aluminum chloride gives an acyl cation. Reaction of this cation with benzene, followed by loss of H^+, gives benzophenone:

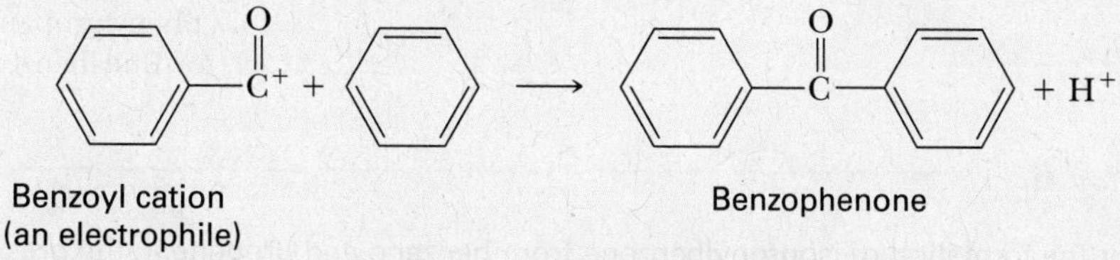

(c) Treatment of 2-chloro-3-methylbutane with aluminum chloride gives a 2° carbocation. Because there is an adjacent 3° hydrogen, a 1,2-hydride shift can occur to form the more stable 3° carbon. It is this carbon that reacts with benzene, followed by loss of H^+, to give 2-methyl-2-phenylbutane.

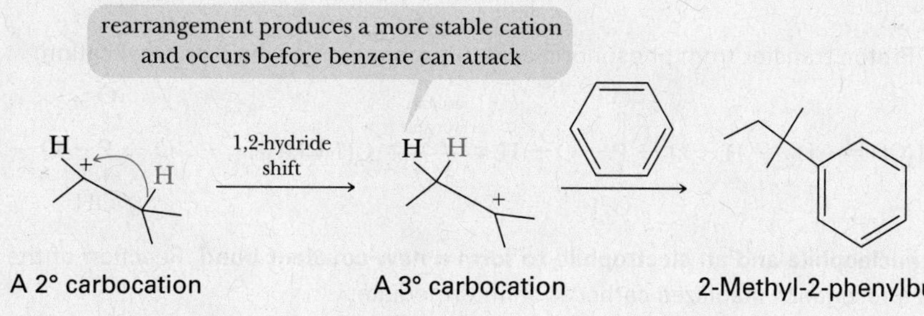

See problems 9.18, 9.19

PROBLEM 9.5

Write a structural formula for the product formed from Friedel–Crafts alkylation or acylation of benzene with

(a) 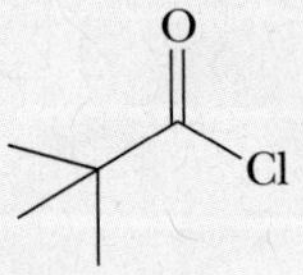

(b) 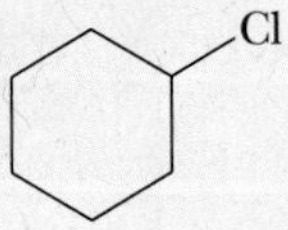

(c) 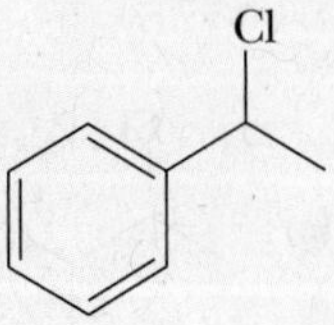

E. Other Electrophilic Aromatic Alkylations

Once it was discovered that Friedel–Crafts alkylations and acylations involve cationic intermediates, chemists realized that other combinations of reagents and catalysts could give the same intermediates. We study two of these reactions in this section: the generation of carbocations from alkenes and from alcohols.

As we saw in Section 5.3B, treatment of an alkene with a strong acid, most commonly H_2SO_4 or H_3PO_4, generates a carbocation. Isopropylbenzene is synthesized industrially by reacting benzene with propene in the presence of an acid catalyst:

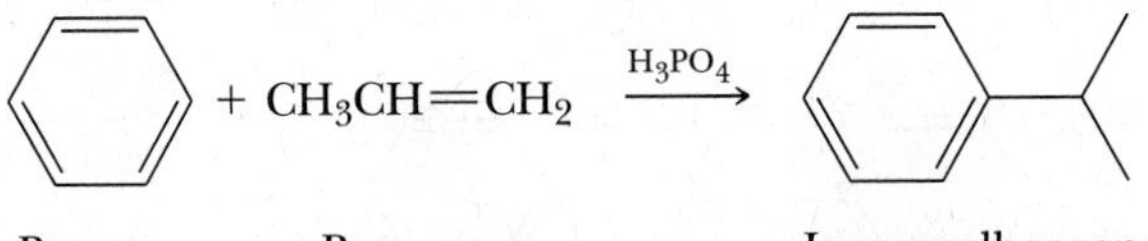

Benzene Propene Isopropylbenzene (Cumene)

Carbocations are also generated by treating an alcohol with H_2SO_4 or H_3PO_4 (Section 8.2E):

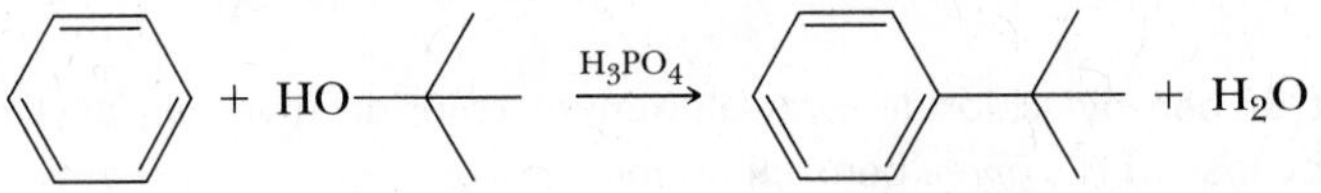

Benzene 2-Methyl-2-phenylpropane (*tert*-Butylbenzene)

EXAMPLE 9.6

Write a mechanism for the formation of isopropylbenzene from benzene and propene in the presence of phosphoric acid.

STRATEGY

Draw the mechanism for the formation of the carbocation. This step constitutes the generation of the electrophile. The remaining steps in the mechanism are the usual: attack of the electrophile on benzene and proton transfer to rearomatize the ring.

SOLUTION

STEP 1: Add a proton. Proton transfer from phosphoric acid to propene gives the isopropyl cation:

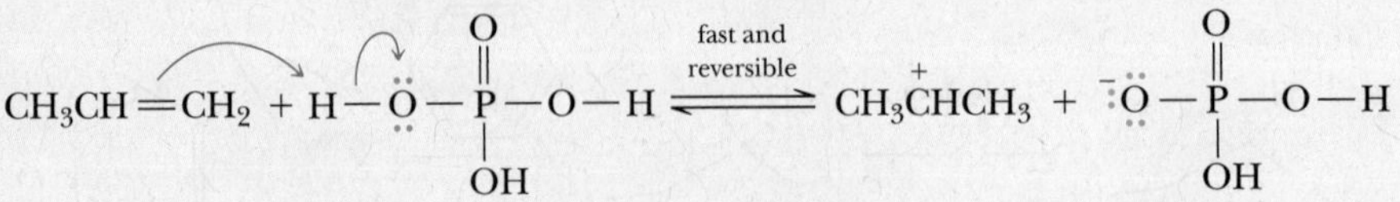

STEP 2: Reaction of a nucleophile and an electrophile to form a new covalent bond. Reaction of the isopropyl cation with benzene gives a resonance-stabilized carbocation intermediate:

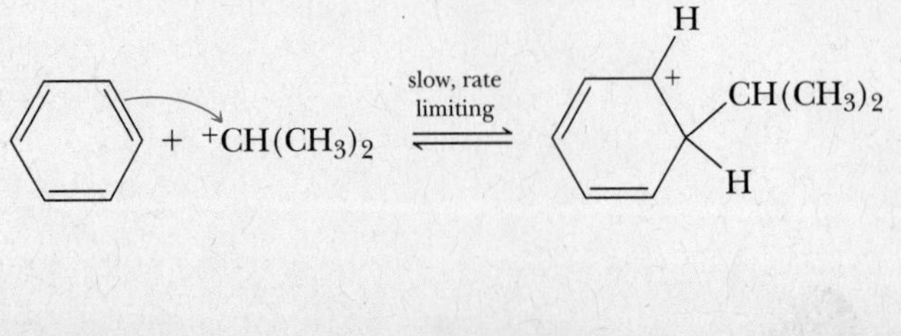

STEP 3: Take a proton away. Proton transfer from this intermediate to dihydrogen phosphate ion gives isopropylbenzene:

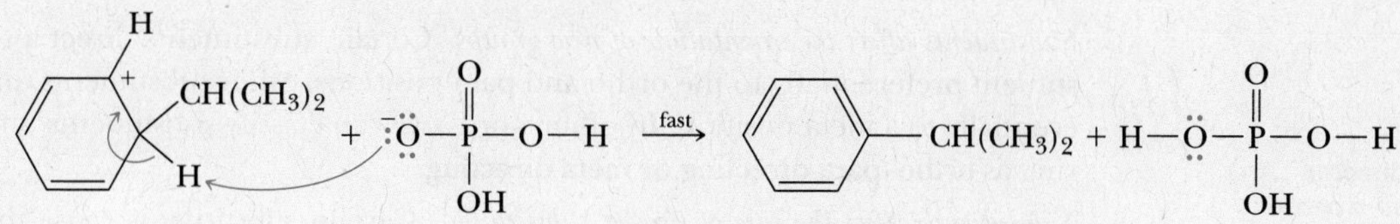

Isopropylbenzene

See problems 9.18, 9.19, 9.33, 9.34

PROBLEM 9.6

Write a mechanism for the formation of *tert*-butylbenzene from benzene and *tert*-butyl alcohol in the presence of phosphoric acid.

F. Comparison of Alkene Addition and Electrophilic Aromatic Substitution (EAS)

Electrophilic aromatic substitution represents the second instance in which we have encountered a C═C double bond attacking an electrophile. The first instance was in our discussion of alkene addition reactions in Section 5.3. Notice the similarities in the first step where a C═C double bond attacks an electrophilic atom (H^+ or E^+). In Step 2, however, alkene addition results in the attack of a nucleophile on the carbocation, while EAS results in abstraction of a hydrogen by base. In one reaction, the C═C double bond is destroyed, while in the other, the C═C double bond is regenerated.

Addition to an Alkene

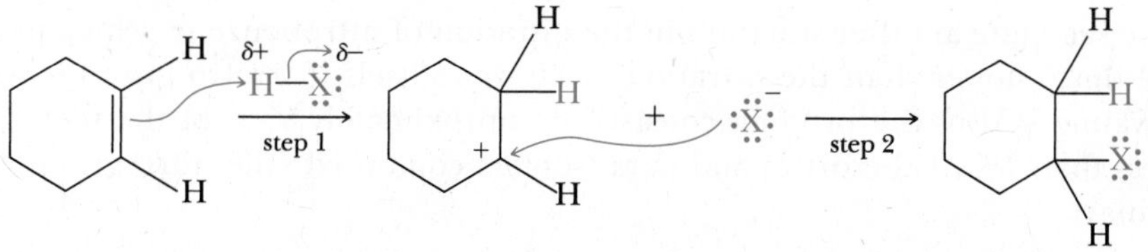

Electrophilic Aromatic Substitution

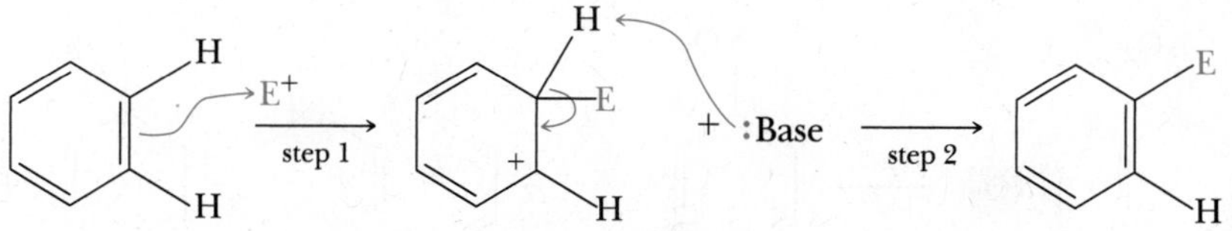

9.7 How Do Existing Substituents on Benzene Affect Electrophilic Aromatic Substitution?

A. Effects of a Substituent Group on Further Substitution

In the electrophilic aromatic substitution of a monosubstituted benzene, three isomeric products are possible: The new group may be oriented ortho, meta, or para to the existing group. On the basis of a wealth of experimental observations, chemists have made the

Ortho–para director Any substituent on a benzene ring that directs electrophilic aromatic substitution preferentially to ortho and para positions.

Meta director Any substituent on a benzene ring that directs electrophilic aromatic substitution preferentially to a meta position.

Activating group Any substituent on a benzene ring that causes the rate of electrophilic aromatic substitution to be greater than that for benzene.

Deactivating group Any substituent on a benzene ring that causes the rate of electrophilic aromatic substitution to be lower than that for benzene.

following generalizations about the manner in which an existing substituent influences further electrophilic aromatic substitution:

1. *Substituents affect the orientation of new groups.* Certain substituents direct a second substituent preferentially to the ortho and para positions; other substituents direct it preferentially to a meta position. In other words, we can classify substituents on a benzene ring as **ortho–para directing** or **meta directing**.
2. *Substituents affect the rate of further substitution.* Certain substituents cause the rate of a second substitution to be greater than that of benzene itself, whereas other substituents cause the rate of a second substitution to be lower than that of benzene. In other words, we can classify groups on a benzene ring as **activating** or **deactivating** toward further substitution.

To see the operation of these directing and activating–deactivating effects, compare, for example, the products and rates of bromination of anisole and nitrobenzene. Bromination of anisole proceeds at a rate 1.8×10^9 greater than that of bromination of benzene (the methoxy group is activating), and the product is a mixture of *o*-bromoanisole and *p*-bromoanisole (the methoxy group is ortho–para directing):

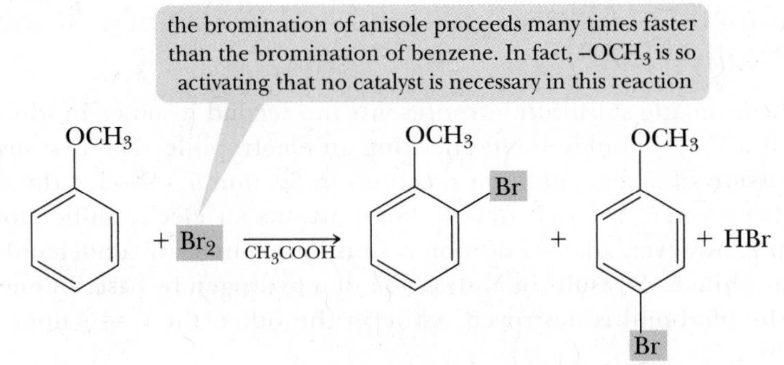

Anisole　　*o*-Bromoanisole (4%)　　*p*-Bromoanisole (96%)

We see quite another situation in the nitration of nitrobenzene, which proceeds 10,000 times slower than the nitration of benzene itself. (A nitro group is strongly deactivating.) Also, the product consists of approximately 93% of the meta isomer and less than 7% of the ortho and para isomers combined (the nitro group is meta directing):

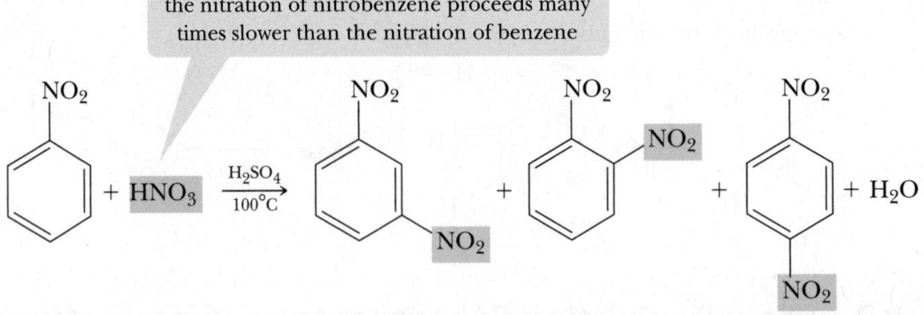

Nitrobenzene　　*m*-Dinitrobenzene (93%)　　*o*-Dinitrobenzene　　*p*-Dinitrobenzene

Less than 7% combined

Table 9.1 lists the directing and activating–deactivating effects for the major functional groups with which we are concerned in this text.

TABLE 9.1 Effects of Substituents on Further Electrophilic Aromatic Substitution

Ortho–Para Directing	strongly activating	$-\ddot{N}H_2$	$-\ddot{N}HR$	$-\ddot{N}R_2$	$-\ddot{O}H$	$-\ddot{O}R$	
	moderately activating	$-\ddot{N}H\overset{\overset{O}{\|}}{C}R$	$-\ddot{N}H\overset{\overset{O}{\|}}{C}Ar$	$-\ddot{O}\overset{\overset{O}{\|}}{C}R$	$-\ddot{O}\overset{\overset{O}{\|}}{C}Ar$		
	weakly activating	$-R$	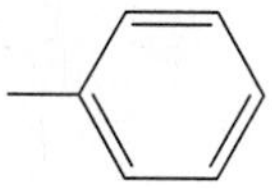				
	weakly deactivating	$-\ddot{F}:$	$-\ddot{Cl}:$	$-\ddot{Br}:$	$-\ddot{I}:$		
Meta Directing	moderately deactivating	$-\overset{\overset{O}{\|}}{C}H$	$-\overset{\overset{O}{\|}}{C}R$	$-\overset{\overset{O}{\|}}{C}OH$	$-\overset{\overset{O}{\|}}{C}OR$	$-\overset{\overset{O}{\|}}{C}NH_2$	$-\overset{\overset{O}{\|}}{\underset{\underset{O}{\|}}{S}}OH$
	strongly deactivating	$-NO_2$	$-NH_3^{\,+}$	$-CF_3$	$-CCl_3$		

Relative importance in directing further substitution (increasing reactivity relative to benzene ↑; decreasing reactivity relative to benzene ↓)

If we compare these ortho–para and meta directors for structural similarities and differences, we can make the following generalizations:

1. Alkyl groups, phenyl groups, and substituents in which the atom bonded to the ring has an unshared pair of electrons are ortho–para directing. All other substituents are meta directing.
2. Except for the halogens, all ortho–para directing groups are activating toward further substitution. The halogens are weakly deactivating.
3. All meta directing groups carry either a partial or full positive charge on the atom bonded to the ring.

We can illustrate the usefulness of these generalizations by considering the synthesis of two different disubstituted derivatives of benzene. Suppose we wish to prepare *m*-bromonitrobenzene from benzene. This conversion can be carried out in two steps: nitration and bromination. If the steps are carried out in just that order, the major product is indeed *m*-bromonitrobenzene. The nitro group is a meta director and directs bromination to a meta position:

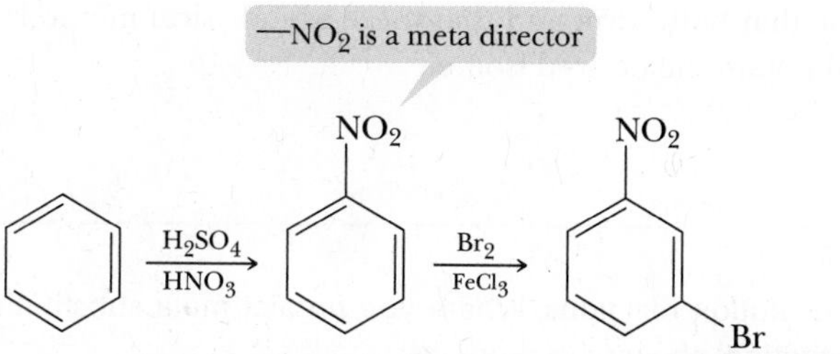

Nitrobenzene *m*-Bromonitrobenzene

If, however, we reverse the order of the steps and first form bromobenzene, we now have an ortho–para directing group on the ring. Nitration of bromobenzene then takes place preferentially at the ortho and para positions, with the para product predominating:

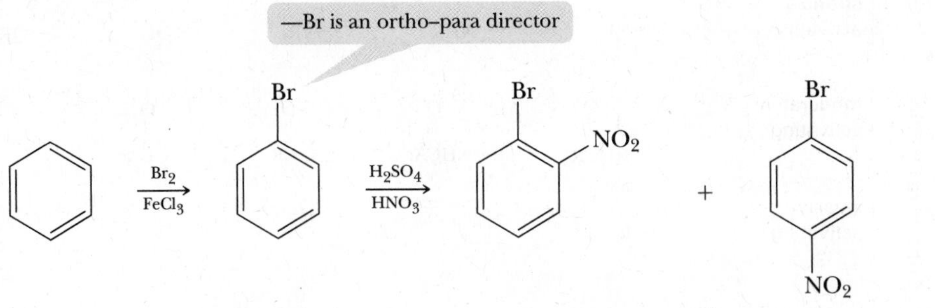

Bromobenzene *o*-Bromonitrobenzene *p*-Bromonitrobenzene

As another example of the importance of order in electrophilic aromatic substitutions, consider the conversion of toluene to nitrobenzoic acid. The nitro group can be introduced with a nitrating mixture of nitric and sulfuric acids. The carboxyl group can be produced by oxidation of the methyl group (Section 9.4).

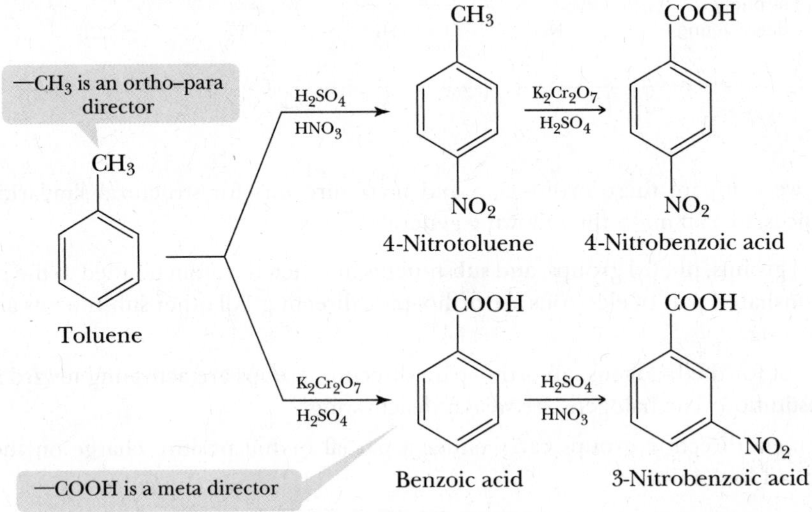

Nitration of toluene yields a product with the two substituents para to each other, whereas nitration of benzoic acid yields a product with the substituents meta to each other. Again, we see that the order in which the reactions are performed is critical.

Note that, in this last example, we show nitration of toluene producing only the para isomer. In practice, because methyl is an ortho–para directing group, both ortho and para isomers are formed. In problems in which we ask you to prepare one or the other of these isomers, we assume that both form and that there are physical methods by which you can separate them and obtain the desired isomer.

EXAMPLE 9.7

Complete the following electrophilic aromatic substitution reactions. Where you predict meta substitution, show only the meta product. Where you predict ortho–para substitution, show both products:

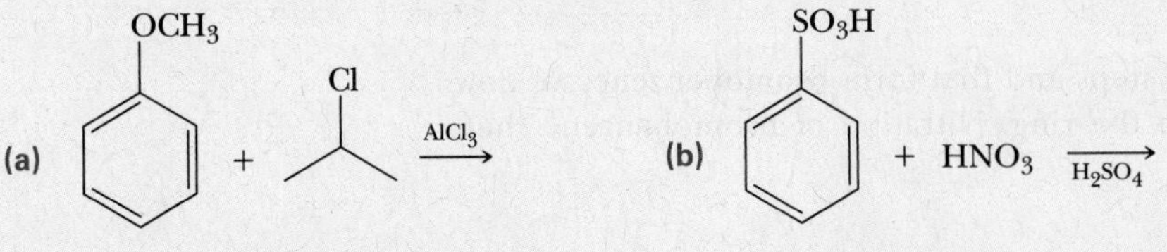

STRATEGY

Determine whether the existing substituent is ortho–para or meta directing prior to completing the reaction.

SOLUTION

The methoxyl group in (a) is ortho–para directing and strongly activating. The sulfonic acid group in (b) is meta directing and moderately deactivating.

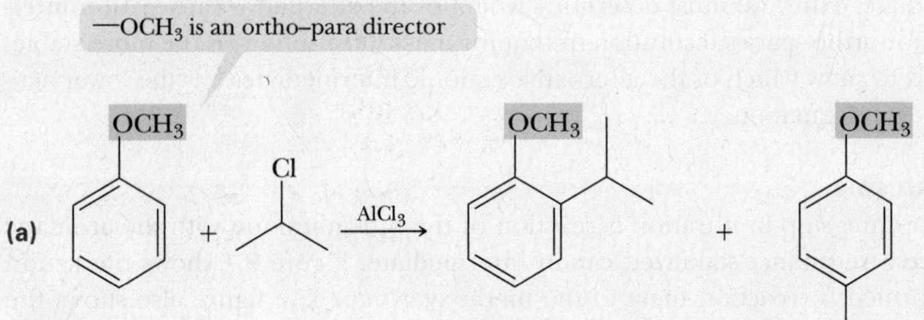

2-Isopropylanisole (ortho-isopropylanisole)

4-Isopropylanisole (para-isopropylanisole)

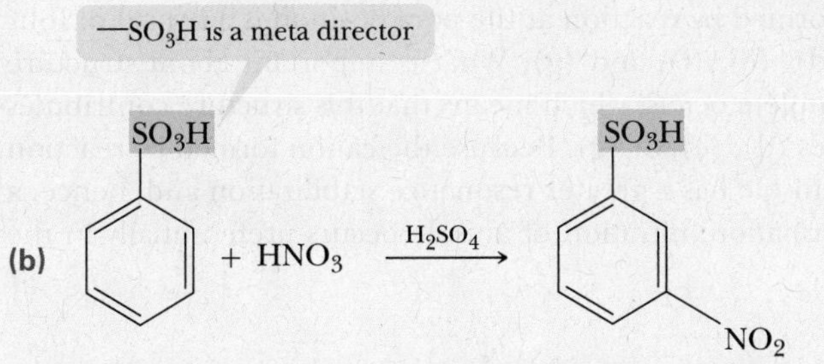

3-Nitrobenzenesulfonic acid (meta-nitrobenzenesulfonic acid)

See problems 9.24–9.26, 9.31, 9.32, 9.42–9.44, 9.46, 9.47

PROBLEM 9.7

Complete the following electrophilic aromatic substitution reactions. Where you predict meta substitution, show only the meta product. Where you predict ortho–para substitution, show both products:

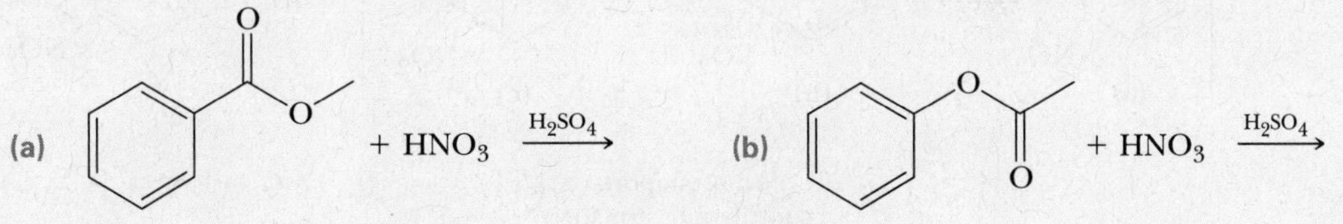

B. Theory of Directing Effects

As we have just seen, a group on an aromatic ring exerts a major effect on the patterns of further substitution. We can make these three generalizations:

1. If there is a lone pair of electrons on the atom bonded to the ring, the group is an ortho–para director.
2. If there is a full or partial positive charge on the atom bonded to the ring, the group is a meta director.
3. Alkyl groups are ortho–para directors.

We account for these patterns by means of the general mechanism for electrophilic aromatic substitution first presented in Section 9.5. Let us extend that mechanism to consider how a group already present on the ring might affect the relative stabilities of cation intermediates formed during a second substitution reaction.

We begin with the fact that the rate of electrophilic aromatic substitution is determined by the slowest step in the mechanism, which, in almost every reaction of an electrophile with the aromatic ring, is attack of the electrophile on the ring to give a resonance-stabilized cation intermediate. Thus, we must determine which of the alternative carbocation intermediates (that for ortho–para substitution or that for meta substitution) is the more stable. That is, we need to show which of the alternative cationic intermediates has the lower activation energy for its formation.

Nitration of Anisole

The rate-determining step in nitration is reaction of the nitronium ion with the aromatic ring to produce a resonance-stabilized cation intermediate. Figure 9.4 shows the cation intermediate formed by reaction meta to the methoxy group. The figure also shows the cationic intermediate formed by reaction para to the methoxy group. The intermediate formed by reaction at a meta position is a hybrid of three major contributing structures: (a), (b), and (c). These three are the only important contributing structures we can draw for reaction at a meta position.

The cationic intermediate formed by reaction at the para position is a hybrid of four major contributing structures: (d), (e), (f), and (g). What is important about structure (f) is that all atoms in it have complete octets, which means that this structure contributes more to the hybrid than structures (d), (e), or (g). Because the cation formed by reaction at an ortho or para position on anisole has a greater resonance stabilization and, hence, a lower activation energy for its formation, nitration of anisole occurs preferentially in the ortho and para positions.

Nitration of Nitrobenzene

Figure 9.5 shows the resonance-stabilized cation intermediates formed by reaction of the nitronium ion meta to the nitro group and also para to it.

Each cation in the figure is a hybrid of three contributing structures; no additional ones can be drawn. Now we must compare the relative resonance stabilizations of each

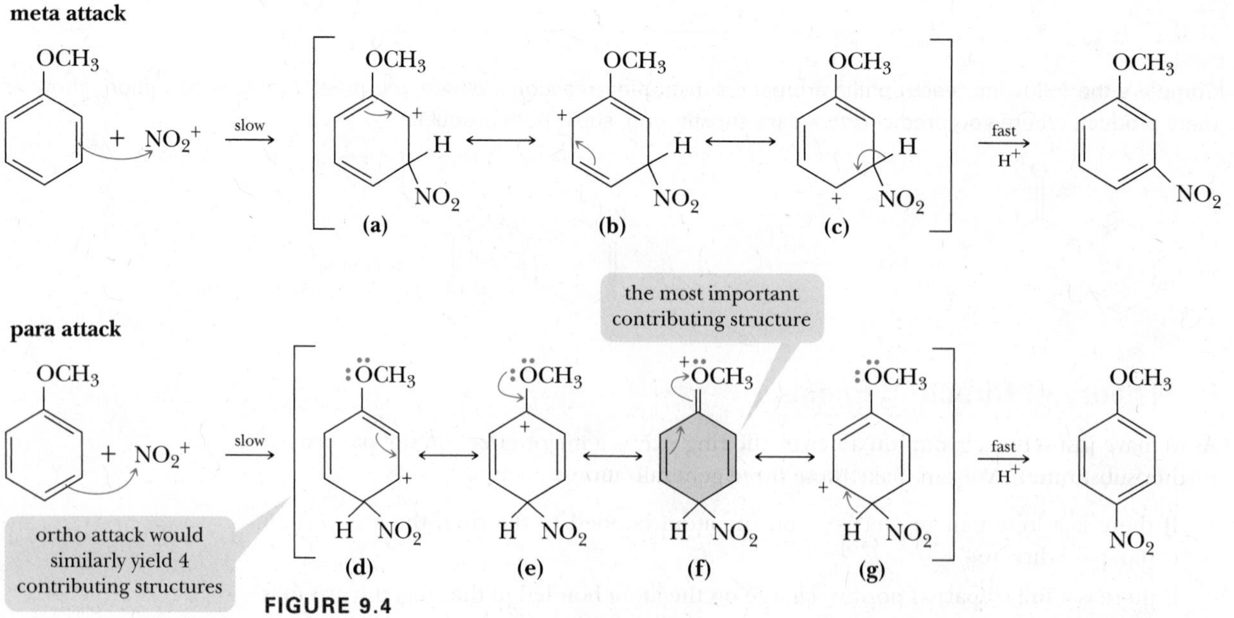

FIGURE 9.4
Nitration of anisole. Reaction of the electrophile meta and para to a methoxy group. Regeneration of the aromatic ring is shown from the rightmost contributing structure in each case.

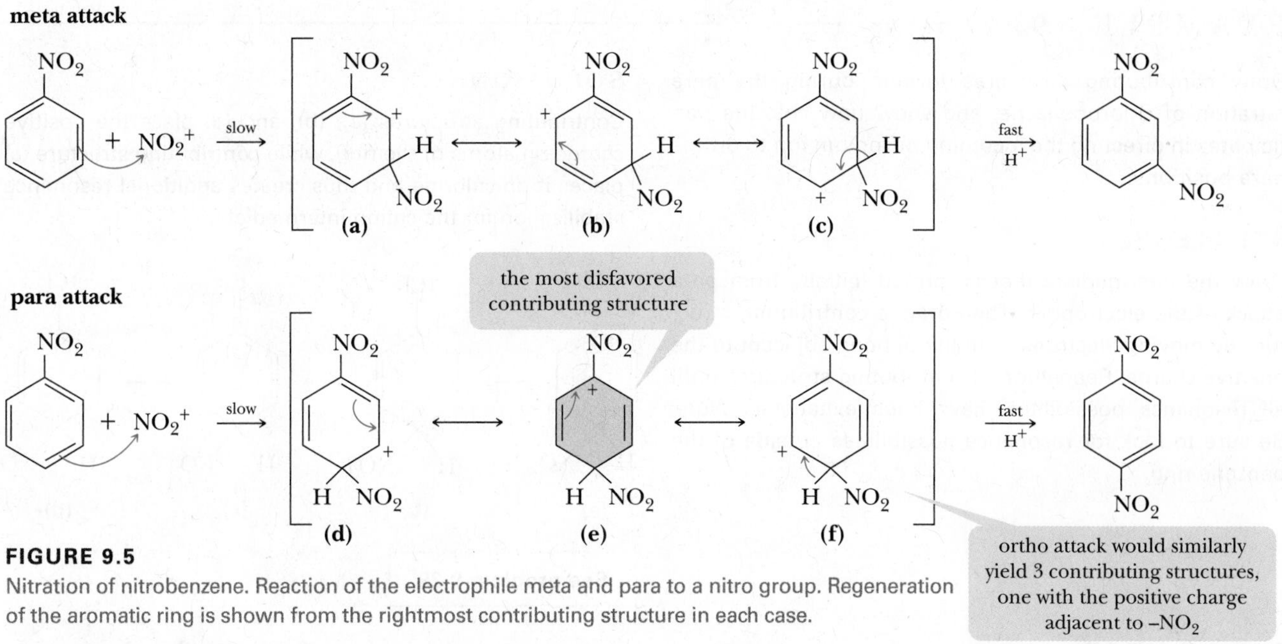

FIGURE 9.5
Nitration of nitrobenzene. Reaction of the electrophile meta and para to a nitro group. Regeneration of the aromatic ring is shown from the rightmost contributing structure in each case.

hybrid. If we draw a Lewis structure for the nitro group showing the positive formal charge on nitrogen, we see that contributing structure (e) places positive charges on adjacent atoms:

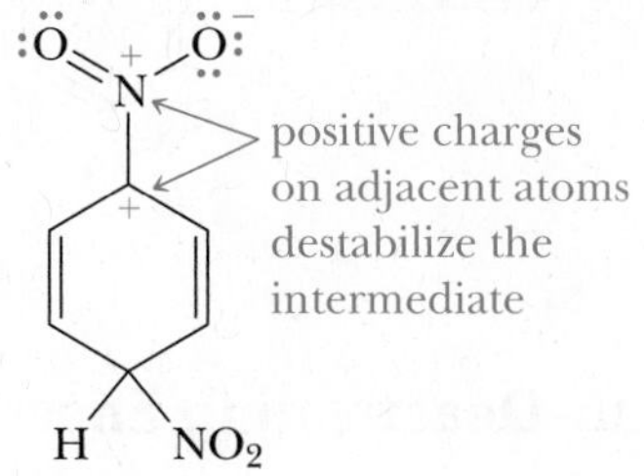

(e)

Because of the electrostatic repulsion thus generated, structure (e) makes only a negligible contribution to the hybrid. None of the contributing structures for reaction at a meta position places positive charges on adjacent atoms. As a consequence, resonance stabilization of the cation formed by reaction at a meta position is greater than that for the cation formed by reaction at a para (or ortho) position. Stated alternatively, the activation energy for reaction at a meta position is less than that for reaction at a para position.

A comparison of the entries in Table 9.1 shows that almost all ortho–para directing groups have an unshared pair of electrons on the atom bonded to the aromatic ring. Thus, the directing effect of most of these groups is due primarily to the ability of the atom bonded to the ring to delocalize further the positive charge on the cation intermediate.

The fact that alkyl groups are also ortho–para directing indicates that they, too, help to stabilize the cation intermediate. In Section 5.3A, we saw that alkyl groups stabilize carbocation intermediates and that the order of stability of carbocations is 3° > 2° > 1° > methyl. Just as alkyl groups stabilize the cation intermediates formed in reactions of alkenes, they also stabilize the carbocation intermediates formed in electrophilic aromatic substitutions.

To summarize, any substituent on an aromatic ring that further stabilizes the cation intermediate directs ortho–para, and any group that destabilizes the cation intermediate directs meta.

EXAMPLE 9.8

Draw contributing structures formed during the para nitration of chlorobenzene, and show how chlorine participates in directing the incoming nitronium ion to ortho–para positions.

STRATEGY

Draw the intermediate that is formed initially from para attack of the electrophile. Then draw a contributing structure by moving electrons from the pi bond adjacent to the positive charge. Repeat for all contributing structures until all resonance possibilities have been exhausted. *Note:* Be sure to look for resonance possibilities outside of the benzene ring.

SOLUTION

Contributing structures (a), (b), and (d) place the positive charge on atoms of the ring, while contributing structure (c) places it on chlorine and thus creates additional resonance stabilization for the cation intermediate:

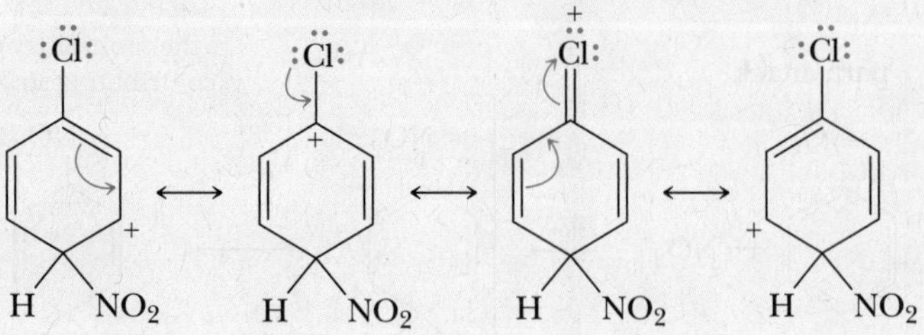

(a) (b) (c) (d)

See problem 9.29

PROBLEM 9.8

Because the electronegativity of oxygen is greater than that of carbon, the carbon of a carbonyl group bears a partial positive charge, and its oxygen bears a partial negative charge. Using this information, show that a carbonyl group is meta directing:

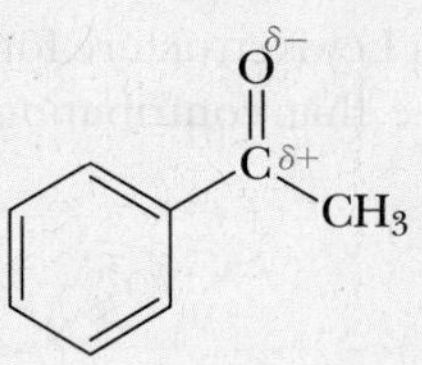

C. Theory of Activating–Deactivating Effects

We account for the activating–deactivating effects of substituent groups by a combination of resonance and inductive effects:

1. Any resonance effect, such as that of $-NH_2$, $-OH$, and $-OR$, which delocalizes the positive charge of the cation intermediate lowers the activation energy for its formation and is activating toward further electrophilic aromatic substitution. That is, these groups increase the rate of electrophilic aromatic substitution, compared with the rate at which benzene itself reacts.
2. Any resonance or inductive effect, such as that of $-NO_2$, $-C{=}O$, $-SO_3H$, $-NR_3^+$, $-CCl_3$, and $-CF_3$, which decreases electron density on the ring, deactivates the ring to further substitution. That is, these groups decrease the rate of further electrophilic aromatic substitution, compared with the rate at which benzene itself reacts.
3. Any inductive effect (such as that of $-CH_3$ or another alkyl group), which releases electron density toward the ring, activates the ring toward further substitution.

In the case of the halogens, the resonance and inductive effects operate in opposite directions. As Table 9.1 shows, the halogens are ortho–para directing, but, unlike other ortho–para directors listed in the table, the halogens are weakly deactivating. These observations can be accounted for in the following way.

1. *The inductive effect of halogens.* The halogens are more electronegative than carbon and have an electron-withdrawing inductive effect. Aryl halides, therefore, react more slowly in electrophilic aromatic substitution than benzene does.

2. *The resonance effect of halogens.* A halogen ortho or para to the site of electrophilic attack stabilizes the cation intermediate by delocalization of the positive charge:

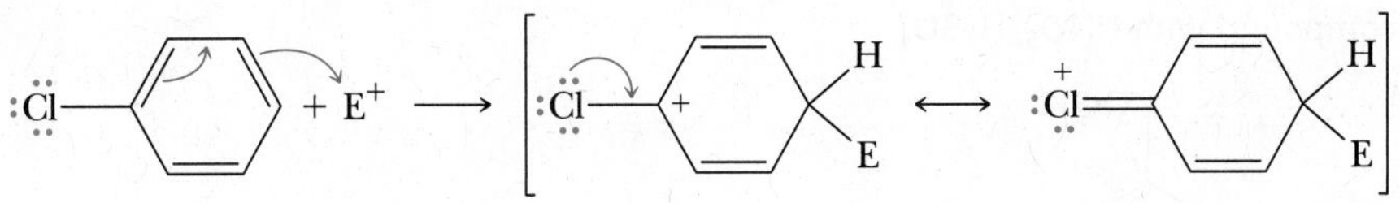

EXAMPLE 9.9

Predict the product of each electrophilic aromatic substitution.

(a) 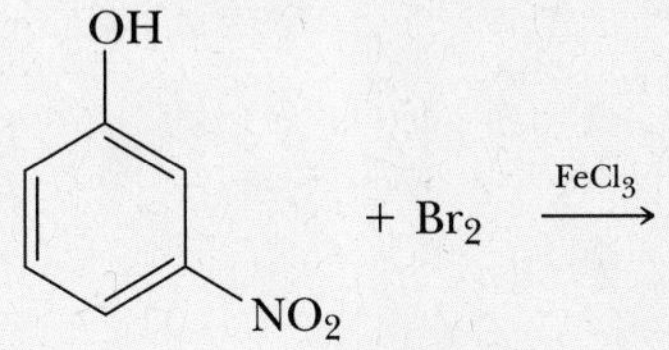

(b) 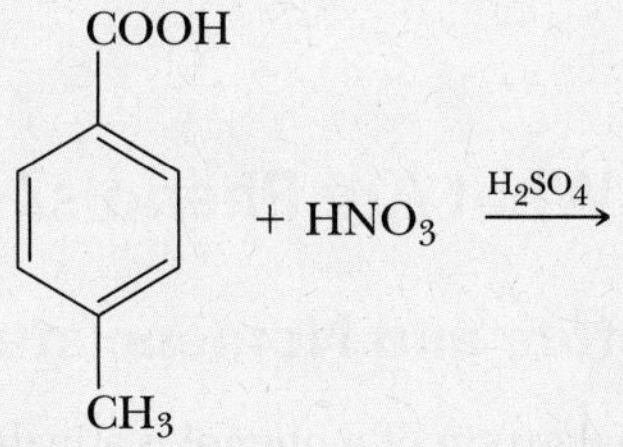

STRATEGY

Determine the activating and deactivating effect of each group. The key to predicting the orientation of further substitution on a disubstituted arene is that ortho–para directing groups are always better at activating the ring toward further substitution than meta directing groups (Table 9.1). This means that, when there is competition between ortho–para directing and meta directing groups, the ortho–para group wins.

SOLUTION

(a) The ortho–para directing and activating —OH group determines the position of bromination. Bromination between the —OH and —NO_2 groups is only a minor product because of steric hindrance to attack of bromine at this position:

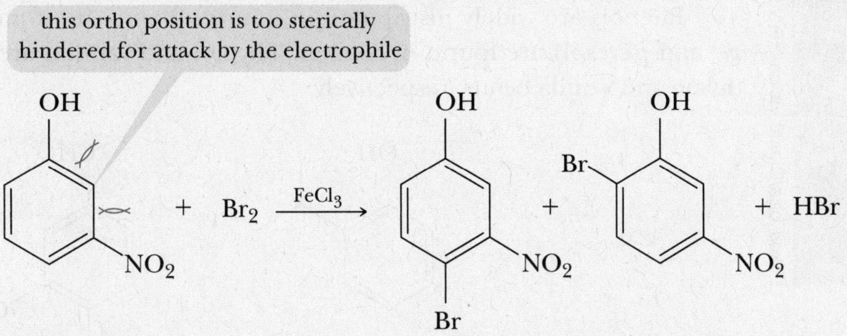

(b) The ortho–para directing and activating methyl group determines the position of nitration:

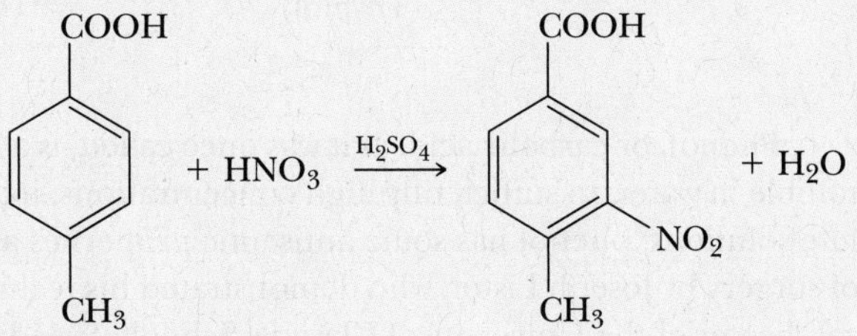

See problems 9.24–9.26, 9.31, 9.32, 9.42–9.44, 9.46, 9.47

PROBLEM 9.9

Predict the product of treating each compound with HNO_3/H_2SO_4:

(a) 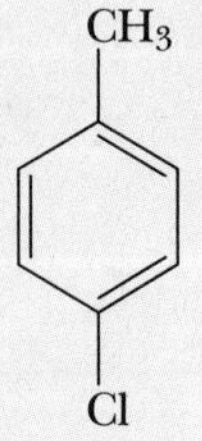

(b) 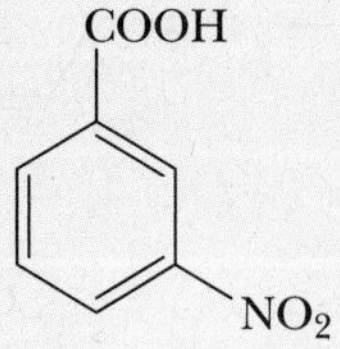

9.8 What Are Phenols?

A. Structure and Nomenclature

Phenol A compound that contains an —OH group bonded to a benzene ring.

Eriko Koga/Digital Vision/Getty Images, Inc

Thymol is a constituent of garden thyme, *Thymus vulgaris*.

The functional group of a **phenol** is a hydroxyl group bonded to a benzene ring. We name substituted phenols either as derivatives of phenol or by common names:

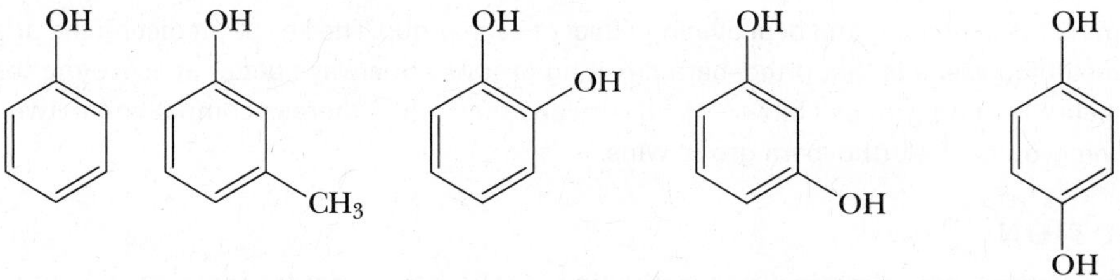

Phenol; 3-Methylphenol (*m*-Cresol); 1,2-Benzenediol (Catechol); 1,3-Benzenediol (Resorcinol); 1,4-Benzenediol (Hydroquinone)

Phenols are widely distributed in nature. Phenol itself and the isomeric cresols (*o*-, *m*-, and *p*-cresol) are found in coal tar. Thymol and vanillin are important constituents of thyme and vanilla beans, respectively:

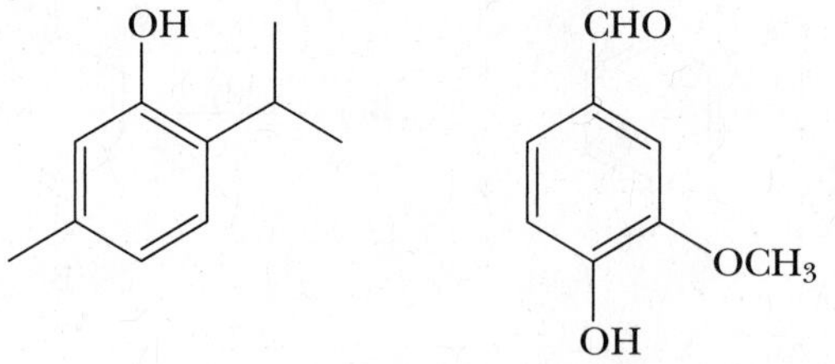

2-Isopropyl-5-methylphenol (Thymol); 4-Hydroxy-3-methoxybenzaldehyde (Vanillin)

Charles D. Winters

Poison ivy.

Phenol, or carbolic acid, as it was once called, is a low-melting solid that is only slightly soluble in water. In sufficiently high concentrations, it is corrosive to all kinds of cells. In dilute solutions, phenol has some antiseptic properties and was introduced into the practice of surgery by Joseph Lister, who demonstrated his technique of aseptic surgery in the surgical theater of the University of Glasgow School of Medicine in 1865. Nowadays, phenol has been replaced by antiseptics that are both more powerful and have fewer undesirable side effects. Among these is hexylresorcinol, which is widely used in nonprescription preparations as a mild antiseptic and disinfectant.

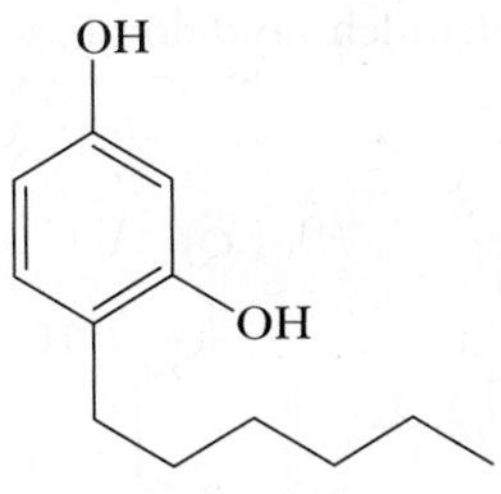

Hexylresorcinol

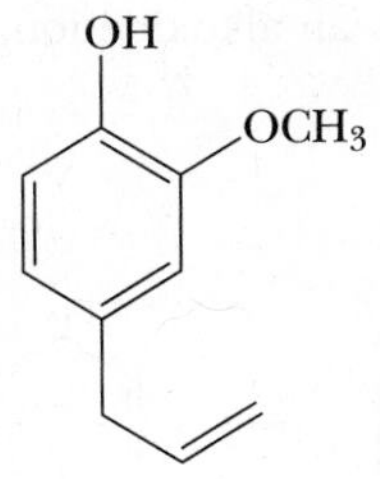

Eugenol

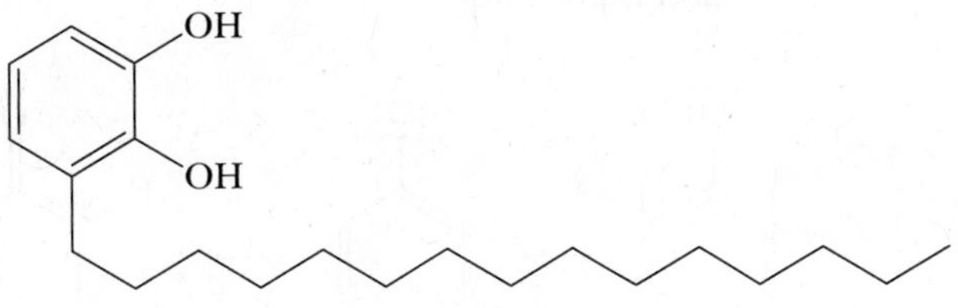

Urushiol

Eugenol, which can be isolated from the flower buds (cloves) of *Eugenia aromatica*, is used as a dental antiseptic and analgesic. Urushiol is the main component in the irritating oil of poison ivy.

B. Acidity of Phenols

Phenols and alcohols both contain an —OH group. We group phenols as a separate class of compounds, however, because their chemical properties are quite different from those of alcohols. One of the most important of these differences is that phenols are significantly more acidic than are alcohols. Indeed, the acid ionization constant for phenol is 10^6 times larger than that of ethanol!

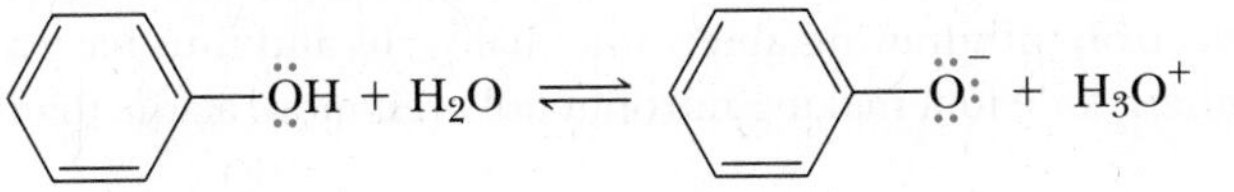

$K_a = 1.1 \times 10^{-10}$ $pK_a = 9.95$

Phenol Phenoxide ion

$$CH_3CH_2\ddot{O}H + H_2 \rightleftharpoons CH_3CH_2\ddot{O}{:}^- + H_3O^+ \qquad K_a = 1.3 \times 10^{-16} \quad pK_a = 15.9$$

Ethanol Ethoxide ion

Another way to compare the relative acid strengths of ethanol and phenol is to look at the hydrogen ion concentration and pH of a 0.1-M aqueous solution of each (Table 9.2). For comparison, the hydrogen ion concentration and pH of 0.1 M HCl are also included.

In aqueous solution, alcohols are neutral substances, and the hydrogen ion concentration of 0.1 M ethanol is the same as that of pure water. A 0.1-M solution of phenol is slightly acidic and has a pH of 5.4. By contrast, 0.1 M HCl, a strong acid (completely ionized in aqueous solution), has a pH of 1.0.

The greater acidity of phenols compared with alcohols results from the greater stability of the phenoxide ion compared with an alkoxide ion. The negative charge on the phenoxide ion is delocalized by resonance. The two contributing structures on the left for the phenoxide ion place the negative charge on oxygen, while the three on the right place the negative charge on the ortho and para positions of the ring. Thus, in the resonance hybrid, the negative charge of the phenoxide ion is delocalized over four atoms,

TABLE 9.2 Relative Acidities of 0.1-M Solutions of Ethanol, Phenol, and HCl

Acid Ionization Equation	$[H^+]$	pH
$CH_3CH_2OH + H_2O \rightleftharpoons CH_3CH_2O^- + H_3O^+$	1×10^{-7}	7.0
$C_6H_5OH + H_2O \rightleftharpoons C_6H_5O^- + H_3O^+$	3.3×10^{-6}	5.4
$HCl + H_2O \rightleftharpoons Cl^- + H_3O^+$	0.1	1.0

which stabilizes the phenoxide ion realtive to an alkoxide ion, for which no delocalization is possible:

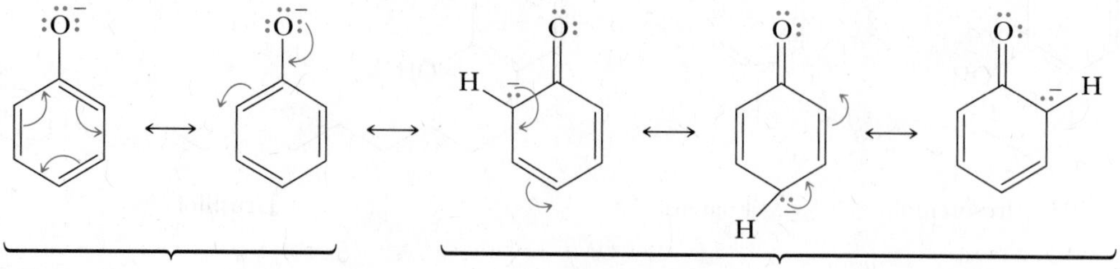

These two Kekulé structures are equivalent

These three contributing structures delocalize the negative charge onto carbon atoms of the ring

Note that, although the resonance model gives us a way of understanding why phenol is a stronger acid than ethanol, it does not provide us with any quantitative means of predicting just how much stronger an acid it might be. To find out how much stronger one acid is than another, we must determine their pK_a values experimentally and compare them.

Ring substituents, particularly halogen and nitro groups, have marked effects on the acidities of phenols through a combination of inductive and resonance effects. Because the halogens are more electronegative than carbon, they withdraw electron density from the negatively charged oxygen in the conjugate base, stabilizing the phenoxide ion. Nitro groups have greater electron-withdrawing ability than halogens and thus have a greater stabilizing effect on the phenoxide ion, making nitrophenol even more acidic than chlorophenol.

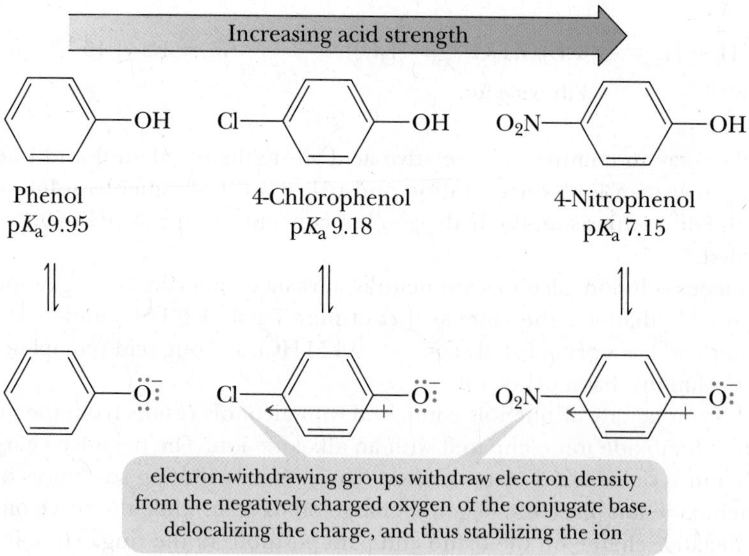

EXAMPLE 9.10

Arrange these compounds in order of increasing acidity: 2,4-dinitrophenol, phenol, and benzyl alcohol.

STRATEGY

Draw each conjugate base. Then determine which conjugate base is more stable using the principles of resonance and inductive effects. The more stable the conjugate base, the more acidic the acid from which it was generated.

SOLUTION

Benzyl alcohol, a primary alcohol, has a pK_a of approximately 16–18 (Section 8.2A). The pK_a of phenol is 9.95. Nitro groups are electron withdrawing and increase the acidity of the phenolic —OH group. In order of increasing acidity, these compounds are:

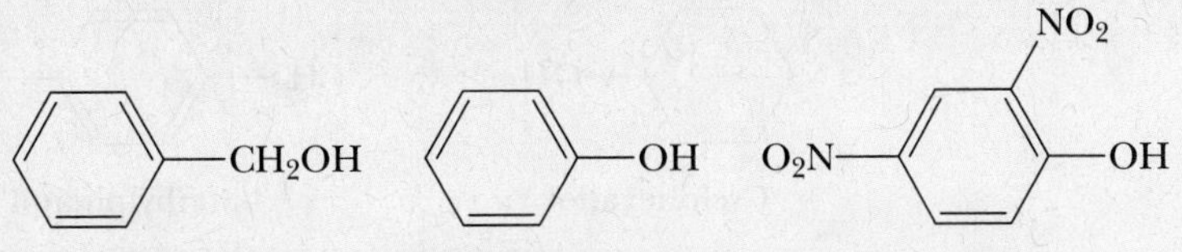

Benzyl alcohol	Phenol	2,4-Dinitrophenol
pK_a 16–18	pK_a 9.95	pK_a 3.96

See problems 9.36–9.38

PROBLEM 9.10

Arrange these compounds in order of increasing acidity: 2,4-dichlorophenol, phenol, cyclohexanol.

C. Acid–Base Reactions of Phenols

Phenols are weak acids and react with strong bases, such as NaOH, to form water-soluble salts:

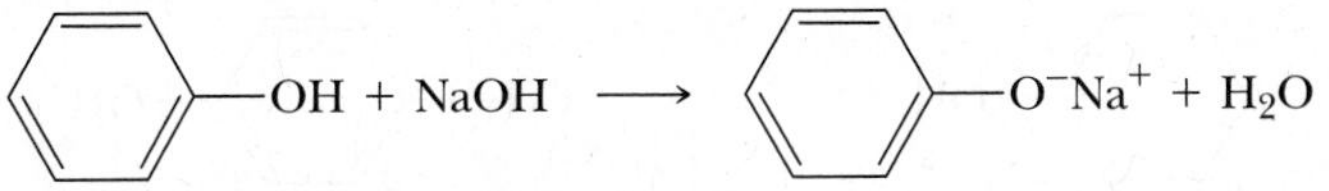

Phenol	Sodium	Sodium	Water
pK_a 9.95	hydroxide	phenoxide	pK_a 15.7
(stronger acid)	(stronger base)	(weaker base)	(weaker acid)

Most phenols do not react with weaker bases, such as sodium bicarbonate, and do not dissolve in aqueous sodium bicarbonate. Carbonic acid is a stronger acid than most phenols, and, consequently, the equilibrium for their reaction with bicarbonate ion lies far to the left (see Section 2.4):

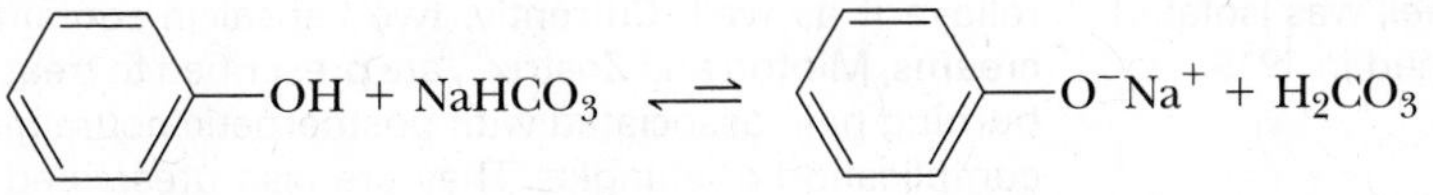

Phenol	Sodium	Sodium	Carbonic acid
pK_a 9.95	bicarbonate	phenoxide	pK_a 6.36
(weaker acid)	(weaker base)	(stronger base)	(stronger acid)

The fact that phenols are weakly acidic, whereas alcohols are neutral, provides a convenient way to separate phenols from water-insoluble alcohols. Suppose that we want to separate 4-methylphenol from cyclohexanol. Each is only slightly soluble in water; therefore, they cannot be separated on the basis of their water solubility. They can be separated, however, on the basis of their difference in acidity. First, the mixture of the two is dissolved in diethyl ether or some other water-immiscible solvent. Next, the ether solution is placed in a separatory funnel and shaken with dilute aqueous NaOH. Under these conditions, 4-methylphenol reacts with NaOH to give sodium 4-methylphenoxide, a water-soluble salt. The upper layer in the separatory funnel is now diethyl ether (density 0.74 g/cm^3), containing only dissolved cyclohexanol. The lower aqueous layer contains dissolved sodium 4-methylphenoxide. The layers are separated, and distillation of the ether (bp 35°C) leaves pure cyclohexanol (bp 161°C). Acidification of the aqueous phase with 0.1 M HCl or another strong acid converts sodium 4-methylphenoxide to 4-methylphenol, which is insoluble in water and can be extracted with ether and recovered in pure form. The following flowchart summarizes these experimental steps:

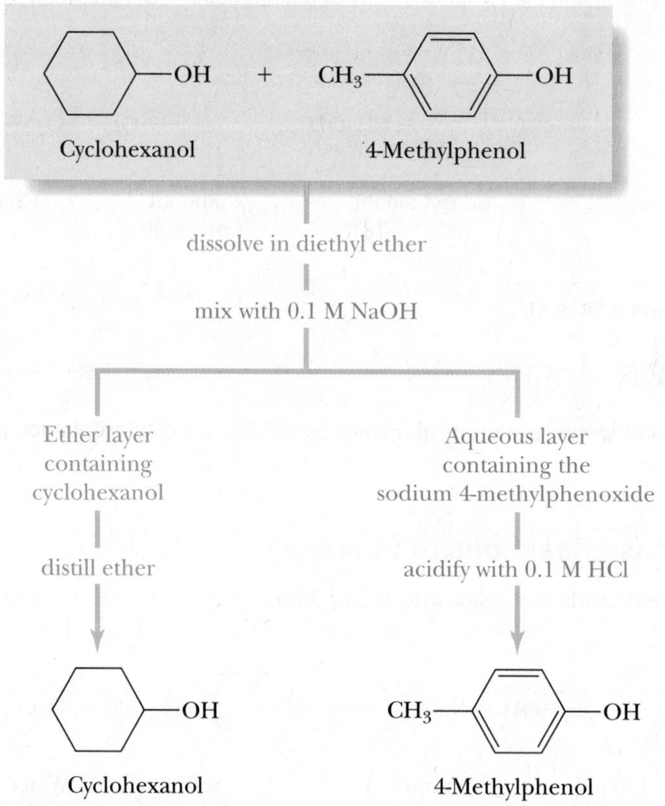

Chemical Connections 9B

CAPSAICIN, FOR THOSE WHO LIKE IT HOT

Capsaicin, the pungent principle from the fruit of various peppers (*Capsicum* and *Solanaceae*), was isolated in 1876, and its structure was determined in 1919:

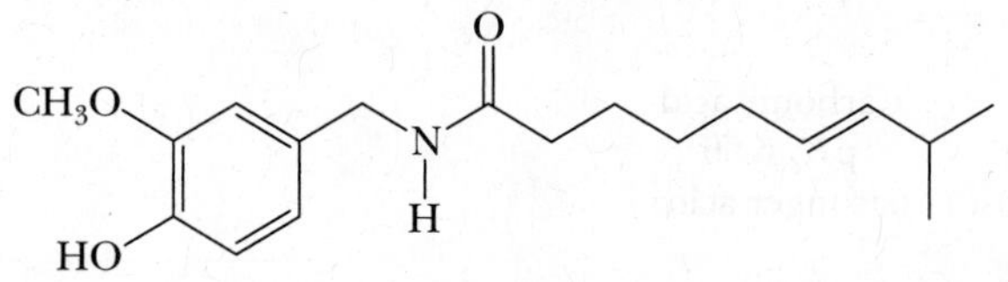

Capsaicin
(from various types of peppers)

The inflammatory properties of capsaicin are well known; the human tongue can detect as little as one drop of it in 5 L of water. Many of us are familiar with the burning sensation in the mouth and sudden tearing in the eyes caused by a good dose of hot chili peppers. Capsaicin-containing extracts from these flaming foods are also used in sprays to ward off dogs or other animals that might nip at your heels while you are running or cycling.

Ironically, capsaicin is able to cause pain and relieve it as well. Currently, two capsaicin-containing creams, Mioton and Zostrix®, are prescribed to treat the burning pain associated with postherpetic neuralgia, a complication of shingles. They are also prescribed for diabetics, to relieve persistent foot and leg pain.

The mechanism by which capsaicin relieves pain is not fully understood. It has been suggested that, after it is applied, the nerve endings in the area responsible for the transmission of pain remain temporarily numb. Capsaicin remains bound to specific receptor sites on these pain-transmitting neurons, blocking them from further action. Eventually, capsaicin is removed from the receptor sites, but in the meantime, its presence provides needed relief from pain.

Questions

Would you predict capsaicin to be more soluble in water or more soluble in 1-octanol?

Would your prediction remain the same if capsaicin were first treated with a molar equivalent of NaOH?

D. Phenols as Antioxidants

An important reaction in living systems, foods, and other materials that contain carbon–carbon double bonds is **autoxidation**—that is, oxidation requiring oxygen and no other reactant. If you open a bottle of cooking oil that has stood for a long time, you will notice a hiss of air entering the bottle. This sound occurs because the consumption of oxygen by autoxidation of the oil creates a negative pressure inside the bottle.

Cooking oils contain esters of polyunsaturated fatty acids. You need not worry now about what esters are; we will discuss them in Chapter 14. The important point here is that all vegetable oils contain fatty acids with long hydrocarbon chains, many of which have one or more carbon–carbon double bonds. (See Problem 4.44 for the structures of three of these fatty acids.) Autoxidation takes place at a carbon adjacent to a double bond—that is, at an **allylic carbon**.

Autoxidation is a radical chain process that converts an R—H group into an R—O—O—H group, called a *hydroperoxide.* The process begins when energy in the form of heat or light causes a molecule with a weak bond to form two **radicals**, atoms, or molecules with an unpaired electron. This step is known as **chain initiation**. In the laboratory, small amounts of compounds such as peroxides, ROOR, are used as initiators because they are easily converted to RO· radicals by light or heat. Scientists are still unsure precisely what compounds act as initiators in nature. Once a radical is generated, it reacts with a molecule by removing the hydrogen atom together with one of its electrons (H·) from an allylic carbon. The carbon losing the H· now has only seven electrons in its valence shell, one of which is unpaired.

Mechanism

Autoxidation

STEP 1: Chain Initiation—Formation of a Radical from a Nonradical Compound. The radical generated from the exposure of the initiator to light or heat causes the removal of a hydrogen atom (H·) adjacent to a C=C double bond to give an allylic radical:

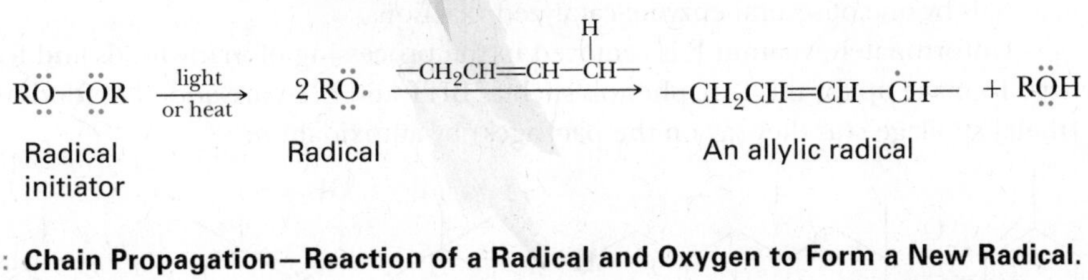

STEP 2a: Chain Propagation—Reaction of a Radical and Oxygen to Form a New Radical. The allylic radical reacts with oxygen, itself a diradical, to form a hydroperoxy radical. The new covalent bond of the hydroperoxy radical forms by the combination of one electron from the allylic radical and one electron from the oxygen diradical:

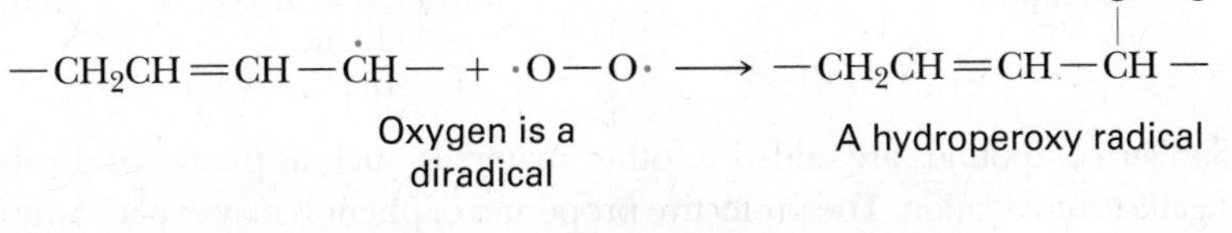

STEP 2b: Chain Propagation—Reaction of a Radical and a Molecule to Form a New Radical. The hydroperoxy radical removes an allylic hydrogen atom (H·) from a new fatty

Although we represent molecular oxygen with the Lewis structure shown in (a), oxygen has long been known to exist and behave as a diradical, as shown in (b).

acid hydrocarbon chain to complete the formation of a hydroperoxide and, at the same time, produce a new allylic radical:

$$\begin{array}{c} \text{O-O} \cdot \\ \mid \\ -\text{CH}_2\text{CH} = \text{CH} - \text{CH} - \\ + -\text{CH}_2\text{CH} = \text{CH} - \text{CH} - \\ \end{array} \longrightarrow \\ \begin{array}{c} \text{Section of a new fatty} \\ \text{acid hydrocarbon chain} \end{array}$$

$$O-O-H$$

$$-CH_2CH=CH-CH-CH_2-+-CH_2CH=CH-CH-$$
A hydroperoxide A new allylic radical

Butylated hydroxytoluene (BHT) is often used as an antioxidant in baked goods to "retard spoilage."

The most important point about the pair of chain propagation steps is that they form a continuous cycle of reactions. The new radical formed in Step 2b next reacts with another molecule of O_2 in Step 2a to give a new hydroperoxy radical, which then reacts with a new hydrocarbon chain to repeat Step 2b, and so forth. This cycle of propagation steps repeats over and over in a chain reaction. Thus, once a radical is generated in Step 1, the cycle of propagation steps may repeat many thousands of times, generating thousands and thousands of hydroperoxide molecules. The number of times the cycle of chain propagation steps repeats is called the **chain length**.

Hydroperoxides themselves are unstable and, under biological conditions, degrade to short-chain aldehydes and carboxylic acids with unpleasant "rancid" smells. These odors may be familiar to you if you have ever smelled old cooking oil or aged foods that contain polyunsaturated fats or oils. A similar formation of hydroperoxides in the low-density lipoproteins deposited on the walls of arteries leads to cardiovascular disease in humans. In addition, many effects of aging are thought to be the result of the formation and subsequent degradation of hydroperoxides.

Fortunately, nature has developed a series of defenses, including the phenol vitamin E, ascorbic acid (vitamin C), and glutathione, against the formation of destructive hydroperoxides. The compounds that defend against hydroperoxides are "nature's scavengers." Vitamin E, for example, inserts itself into either Step 2a or 2b, donates an H· from its phenolic —OH group to the allylic radical, and converts the radical to its original hydrocarbon chain. Because the vitamin E radical is stable, it breaks the cycle of chain propagation steps, thereby preventing the further formation of destructive hydroperoxides. While some hydroperoxides may form, their numbers are very small and they are easily decomposed to harmless materials by one of several enzyme-catalyzed reactions.

Unfortunately, vitamin E is removed in the processing of many foods and food products. To make up for this loss, phenols such as BHT and BHA are added to foods to "retard [their] spoilage" (as they say on the packages) by autoxidation:

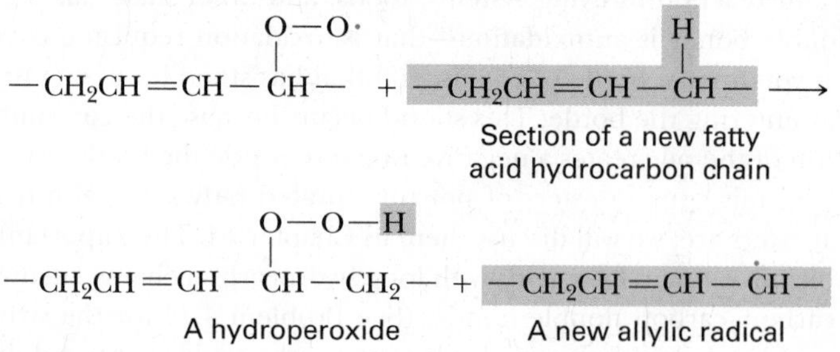

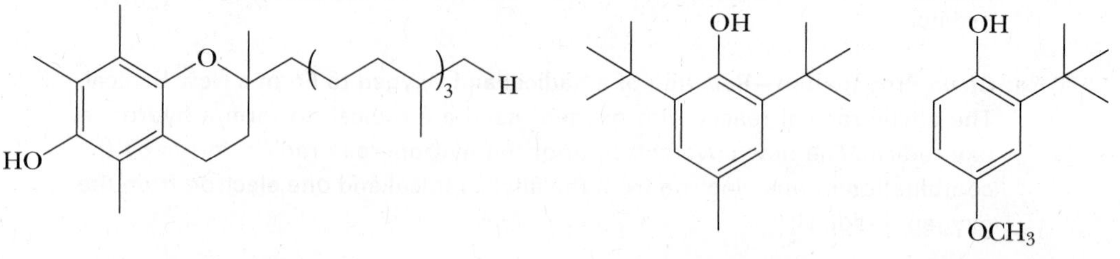

Similar compounds are added to other materials, such as plastics and rubber, to protect them against autoxidation. The protective properties of phenols may explain why the health benefits of foods such as green tea, wine, and blueberries (each of which contains large amounts of phenolic compounds) have been lauded by nutritionists and others in the medical community.

SUMMARY OF KEY QUESTIONS

9.1 What Is the Structure of Benzene?

- **Benzene** is a molecule with a high degree of unsaturation possessing the molecular formula C_6H_6. Each carbon has a single unhybridized 2*p* orbital that contains one electron. These six 2*p* orbitals lie perpendicular to the plane of the ring and overlap to form a continuous pi cloud encompassing all six carbons.
- Benzene and its alkyl derivatives are classified as **aromatic hydrocarbons,** or **arenes.**

9.2 What Is Aromaticity?

- According to the **Hückel criteria for aromaticity,** a cyclic compound is aromatic if it (1) has one 2*p* orbital on each atom of the ring, (2) is planar so that overlap of all *p* orbitals of the ring is continuous or nearly so, and (3) has 2, 6, 10, 14, and so on, pi electrons in the overlapping system of *p* orbitals (i.e., it has $4n + 2$ π electrons).
- A **heterocyclic aromatic compound** contains one or more atoms other than carbon in an aromatic ring.

9.3 How Are Benzene Compounds Named, and What Are Their Physical Properties?

- Aromatic compounds are named by the IUPAC system. The common names **toluene, xylene, styrene, phenol, aniline, benzaldehyde,** and **benzoic acid** are retained.
- The C_6H_5— group is named **phenyl,** and the $C_6H_5CH_2$— group is named **benzyl.**
- To locate two substituents on a benzene ring, either number the atoms of the ring or use the locators **ortho (*o*), meta (*m*),** and **para (*p*).**
- **Polynuclear aromatic hydrocarbons** contain two or more fused benzene rings.

9.4 What Is the Benzylic Position, and How Does It Contribute to Benzene Reactivity?

- The **benzylic position** is the carbon of an alkyl substituent immediately bonded to the benzene ring.
- The benzylic position of a benzene ring can be oxidized by chromic acid without affecting any of the benzene ring atoms.

9.5 What Is Electrophilic Aromatic Substitution?

- A characteristic reaction of aromatic compounds is **electrophilic aromatic substitution**, which involves the substitution of one of the ring hydrogens of benzene for an electrophilic reagent.
- The five types of electrophilic aromatic substitution discussed here are **nitration**, **halogenation**, **sulfonation**, **Friedel–Crafts alkylation**, and **Friedel–Crafts acylation**.

9.6 What Is the Mechanism of Electrophilic Aromatic Substitution?

- The mechanism of electrophilic aromatic substitution can be broken down into three common steps: (1) generation of the electrophile, (2) attack of the electrophile on the aromatic ring to give a resonance-stabilized cation intermediate, and (3) proton transfer to a base to regenerate the aromatic ring.
- The five electrophilic aromatic substitution reactions studied here differ in their mechanism of formation of the electrophile (Step 1) and the specific base used to effect the proton transfer to regenerate the aromatic ring (Step 3).

9.7 How Do Existing Substituents on Benzene Affect Electrophilic Aromatic Substitution?

- Substituents on an aromatic ring influence both the rate and site of further substitution.
- Substituent groups that direct an incoming group preferentially to the ortho and para positions are called **ortho–para directors.** Those that direct an incoming group preferentially to the meta positions are called **meta directors.**
- **Activating groups** cause the rate of further substitution to be faster than that for benzene; **deactivating groups** cause it to be slower than that for benzene.
- A mechanistic rationale for directing effects is based on the degree of resonance stabilization of the possible cation intermediates formed upon reaction of the aromatic ring and the electrophile.
- Groups that stabilize the cation intermediate are ortho–para directors; groups that destabilize it are deactivators and meta directors.

9.8 What Are Phenols?

- The functional group of a **phenol** is an —OH group bonded to a benzene ring.
- Phenol and its derivatives are weak acids, with pK_a approximately 10.0, but are considerably stronger acids than alcohols, with pK_a 16–18.
- Various phenols are used to prevent autoxidation, a radical chain process that converts an R—H group into an R—O—O—H (hydroperoxide) group and causes spoilage in foods.

QUICK QUIZ

Answer true or false to the following questions to assess your general knowledge of the concepts in this chapter. If you have difficulty with any of them, you should review the appropriate section in the chapter (shown in parentheses) before attempting the more challenging end-of-chapter problems.

1. The mechanism of electrophilic aromatic substitution involves three steps: generation of the electrophile, attack of the electrophile on the benzene ring, and proton transfer to regenerate the ring. (9.6)
2. The C—C double bonds in benzene do not undergo the same addition reactions that the C—C double bonds in alkenes undergo. (9.1)
3. Friedel–Crafts acylation is not subject to rearrangements. (9.5)
4. An aromatic compound is planar, possesses a 2*p* orbital on every atom of the ring, and contains either 4, 8, 12, 16, and so on, pi electrons. (9.2)
5. When naming disubstituted benzenes, the locators para, meta, and ortho refer to substituents that are 1,2, 1,3, and 1,4, respectively. (9.3)
6. The electrophile in the chlorination or bromination of benzene is an ion pair containing a chloronium or bromonium ion. (9.6)
7. An ammonium group ($-NH_3^+$) on a benzene ring will direct an attacking electrophile to a meta position. (9.7)
8. Reaction of chromic acid, H_2CrO_4, with a substituted benzene always oxidizes every alkyl group at the benzylic position to a carboxyl group. (9.4)
9. Benzene consists of two contributing structures that rapidly interconvert between each other. (9.1)
10. The electrophile in the nitration of benzene is the nitrate ion. (9.6)
11. A benzene ring with an —OH bonded to it is referred to as "phenyl." (9.3)
12. Friedel–Crafts alkylation of a primary haloalkane with benzene will always result in a new bond between benzene and the carbon that was bonded to the halogen. (9.5)
13. Resonance energy is the energy a ring contains due to the stability afforded it by its contributing structures. (9.1)
14. A phenol will react quantitatively with NaOH. (9.8)
15. The use of a haloalkane and $AlCl_3$ is the only way to synthesize an alkylbenzene. (9.6)
16. Phenols are more acidic than alcohols. (9.8)
17. Substituents of polysubstituted benzene rings can be numbered according to their distance from the substituent that imparts a special name to the compound. (9.3)
18. If a benzene ring contains both a weakly activating group and a strongly deactivating group, the strongly deactivating group will direct the attack of an electrophile. (9.7)
19. Oxygen, O_2, can be considered a diradical. (9.8)
20. The contributing structures for the attack of an electrophile to the ortho position of aniline are more stable than those for the attack at the meta position. (9.7)
21. A deactivating group will cause its benzene ring to react slower than benzene itself. (9.7)
22. Friedel–Crafts alkylation is promoted by the presence of electron-withdrawing groups. (9.5)
23. Autoxidation takes place at allylic carbons. (9.8)
24. The contributing structures for the attack of an electrophile to the meta position of nitrobenzene are more stable than those for the attack at the ortho or para position. (9.7)

Answers: (1) T (2) T (3) T (4) F (5) F (6) F (7) T (8) F (9) F (10) F (11) F (12) F (13) F (14) T (15) F (16) T (17) T (18) F (19) T (20) T (21) T (22) F (23) T (24) T

Detailed explanations for many of these answers can be found in the accompanying Solutions Manual.

KEY REACTIONS

1. Oxidation at a Benzylic Position (Section 9.4)

A benzylic carbon bonded to at least one hydrogen is oxidized to a carboxyl group:

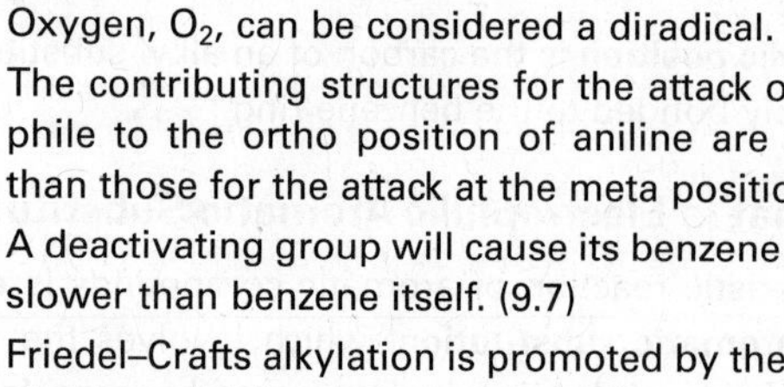

2. Chlorination and Bromination (Section 9.6A)

The electrophile is a halonium ion, Cl^+ or Br^+, formed by treating Cl_2 or Br_2 with $AlCl_3$ or $FeCl_3$:

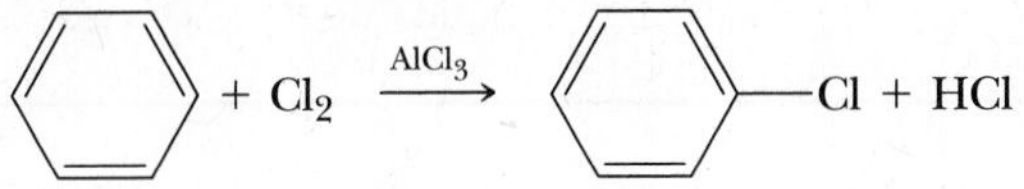

3. Nitration (Section 9.6B)

The electrophile is the nitronium ion, NO_2^+, formed by treating nitric acid with sulfuric acid:

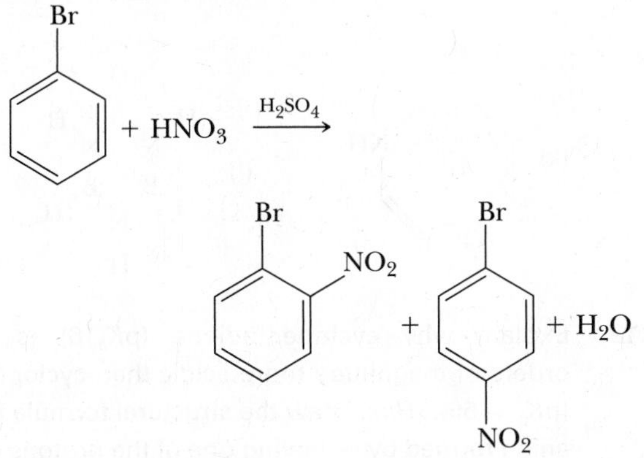

4. Sulfonation (Section 9.6B)

The electrophile is HSO_3^+:

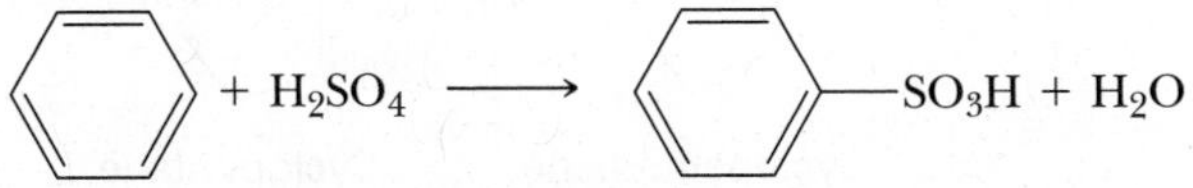

5. Friedel–Crafts Alkylation (Section 9.6C)

The electrophile is an alkyl carbocation formed by treating an alkyl halide with a Lewis acid:

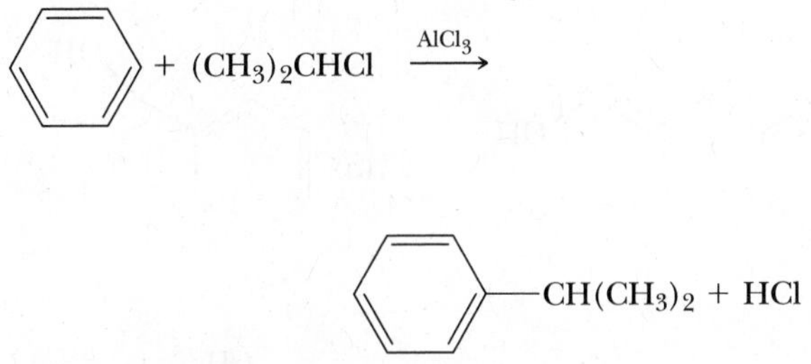

6. Friedel–Crafts Acylation (Section 9.6D)

The electrophile is an acyl cation formed by treating an acyl halide with a Lewis acid:

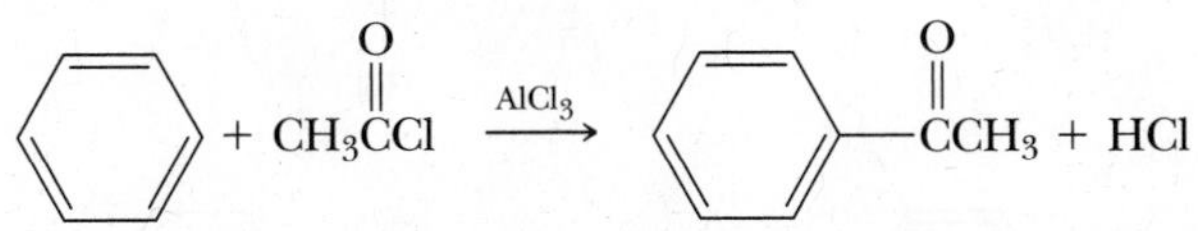

7. Alkylation Using an Alkene (Section 9.6E)

The electrophile is a carbocation formed by treating an alkene with H_2SO_4 or H_3PO_4:

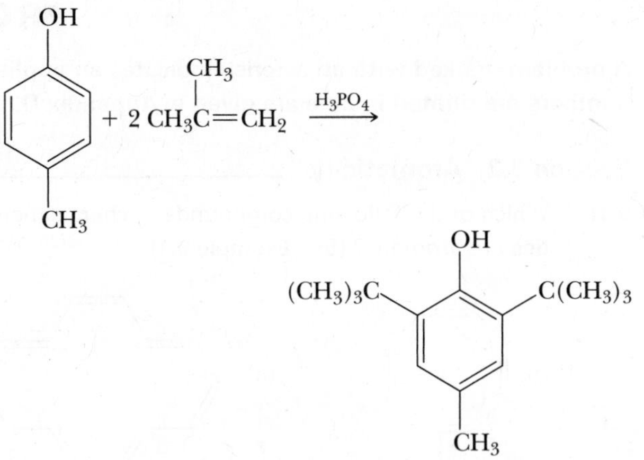

8. Alkylation Using an Alcohol (Section 9.6E)

The electrophile is a carbocation formed by treating an alcohol with H_2SO_4 or H_3PO_4:

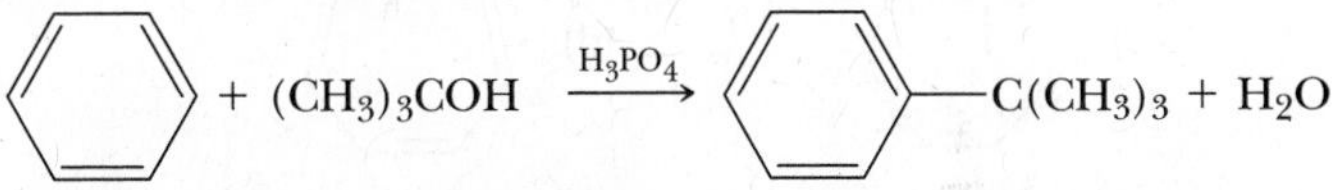

9. Acidity of Phenols (Section 9.8B)

Phenols are weak acids:

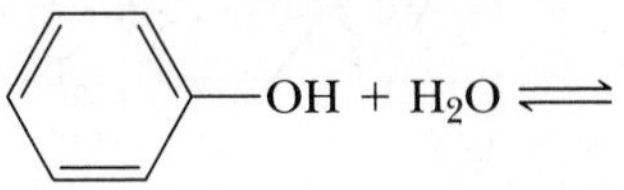

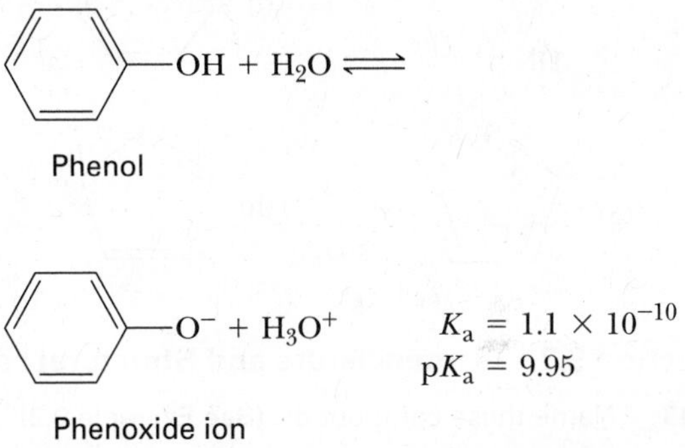

Phenol

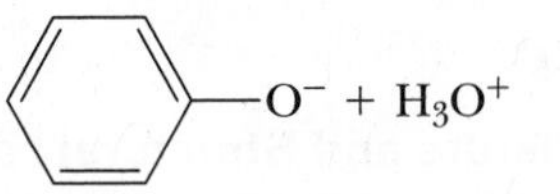

$K_a = 1.1 \times 10^{-10}$
$pK_a = 9.95$

Phenoxide ion

Substitution by electron-withdrawing groups, such as the halogens and the nitro group, increases the acidity of phenols.

10. Reaction of Phenols with Strong Bases (Section 9.8C)

Water-insoluble phenols react quantitatively with strong bases to form water-soluble salts:

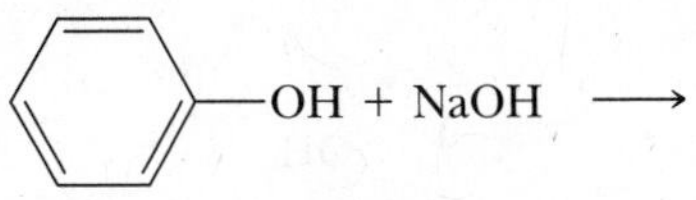

Phenol pK_a 9.95 (stronger acid) — Sodium hydroxide (stronger base)

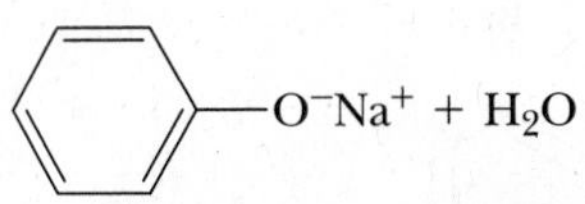

Sodium phenoxide (weaker base) — Water pK_a 15.7 (weaker acid)

PROBLEMS

A problem marked with an asterisk indicates an applied "real-world" problem. Answers to problems whose numbers are printed in blue are given in Appendix D.

Section 9.2 Aromaticity

9.11 Which of the following compounds or chemical entities are aromatic? **(See Example 9.1)**

(a) 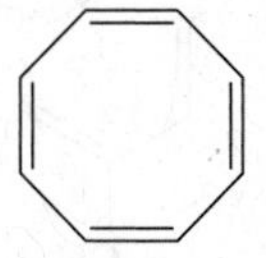

(b) 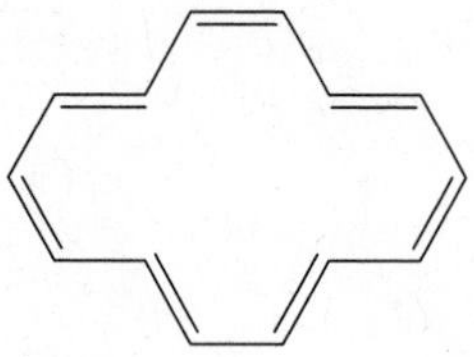

(c) 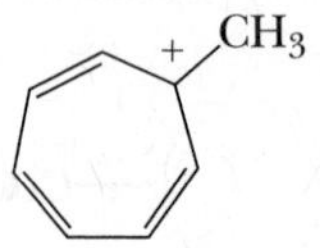

(d) 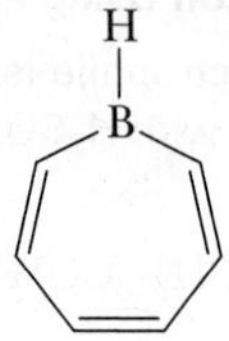

(e) 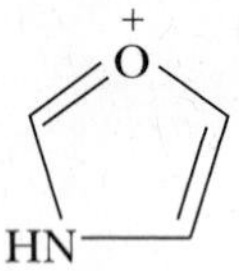

(f) 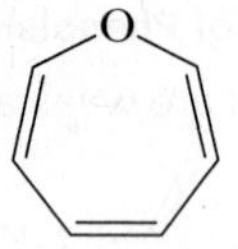

(g) 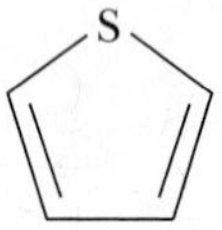

(h) 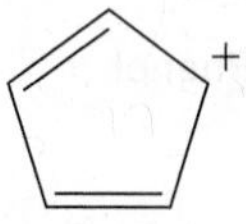

(i) 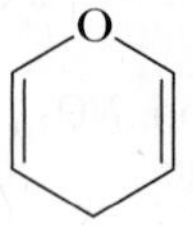

(j) 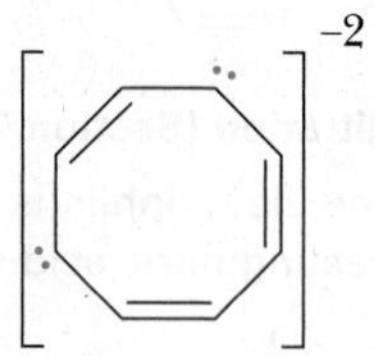

(k) 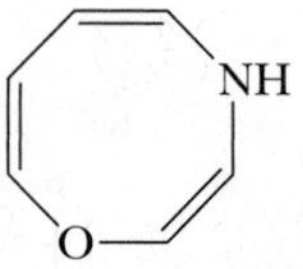

(l) 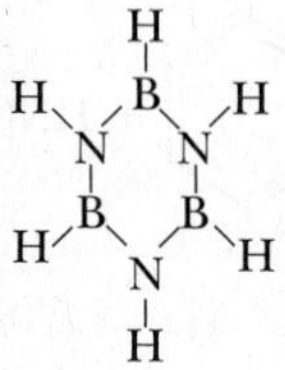

9.12 Explain why cyclopentadiene (pK_a 16) is many orders of magnitude more acidic than cyclopentane ($pK_a > 50$). (*Hint:* Draw the structural formula for the anion formed by removing one of the protons on the $-CH_2-$ group, and then apply the Hückel criteria for aromaticity.)

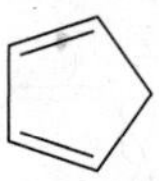

Cyclopentadiene

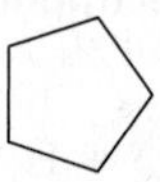

Cyclopentane

Section 9.3 Nomenclature and Structural Formulas

9.13 Name these compounds: **(See Example 9.2)**

(a) 

(b) 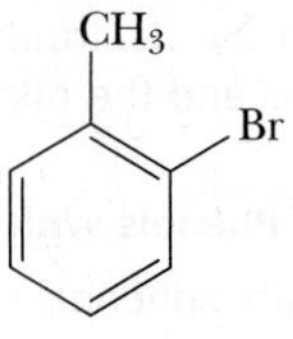

(c) 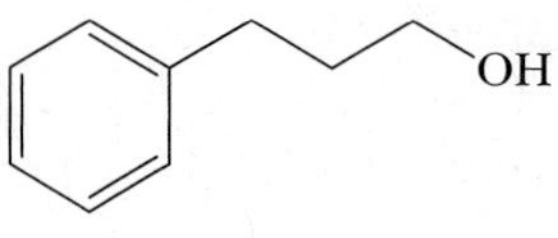

(d) 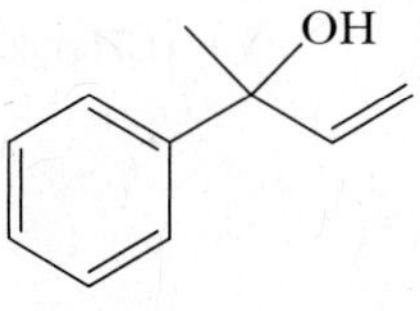

(e) 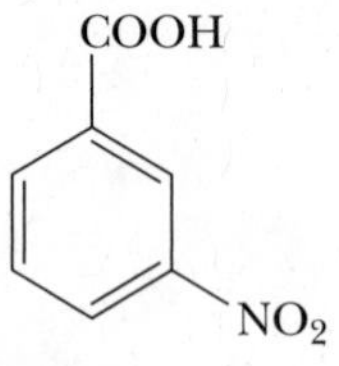

(f) 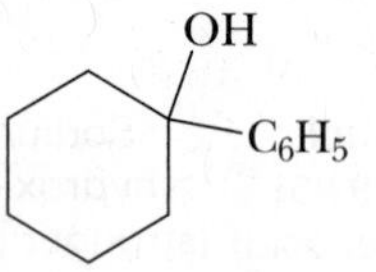

(g) 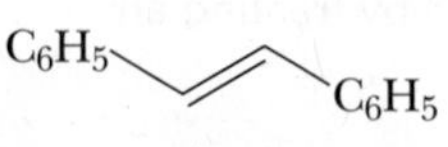

(h) 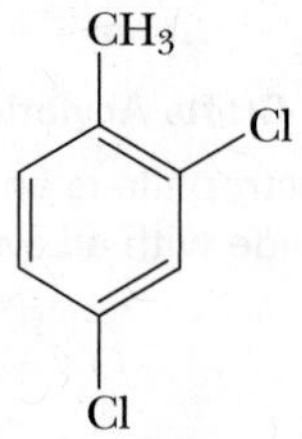

(i) 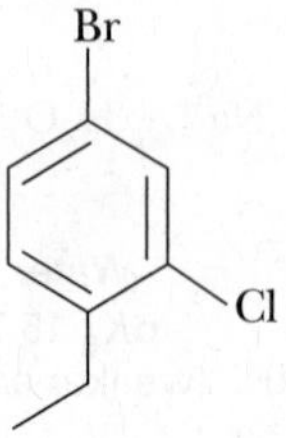

(j) 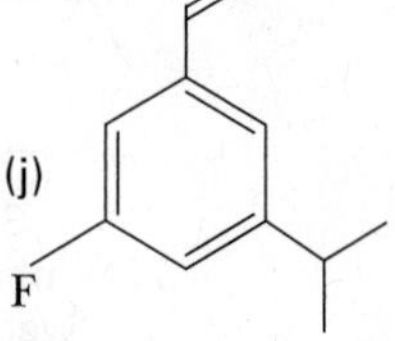

(k) 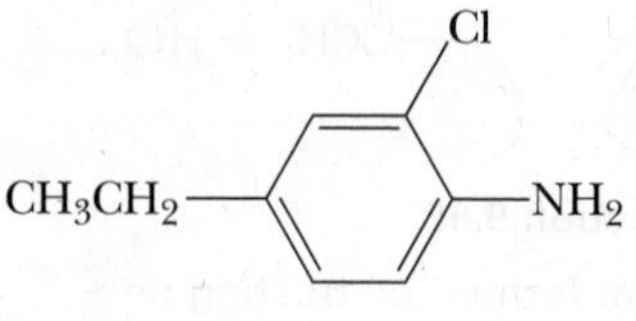

(l) 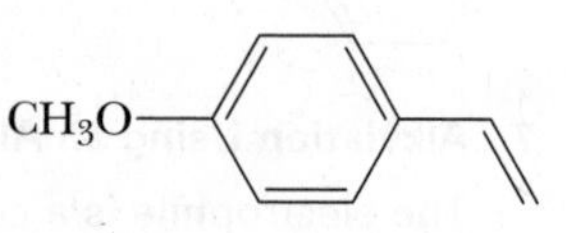

9.14 Draw structural formulas for these compounds: **(See Example 9.2)**

(a) 1-Bromo-2-chloro-4-ethylbenzene
(b) 4-Iodo-1,2-dimethylbenzene
(c) 2,4,6-Trinitrotoluene (TNT)
(d) 4-Phenyl-2-pentanol
(e) *p*-Cresol
(f) 2,4-Dichlorophenol
(g) 1-Phenylcyclopropanol
(h) Styrene (phenylethylene)
(i) *m*-Bromophenol
(j) 2,4-Dibromoaniline
(k) Isobutylbenzene
(l) *m*-Xylene
(m) 4-Bromo-1,2-dichlorobenzene
(n) 5-Fluoro-2-methylphenol
(o) 1-Cyclohexyl-3-ethylbenzene
(p) *m*-Phenylaniline
(q) 3-Methyl-2-vinylbenzoic acid
(r) 2,5-Dimethylanisole

9.15 Show that pyridine can be represented as a hybrid of two equivalent contributing structures.

9.16 Show that naphthalene can be represented as a hybrid of three contributing structures. Show also, by the use of curved arrows, how one contributing structure is converted to the next.

9.17 Draw four contributing structures for anthracene.

Section 9.5 Electrophilic Aromatic Substitution: Monosubstitution

9.18 Draw a structural formula for the compound formed by treating benzene with each of the following combinations of reagents: **(See Examples 9.5, 9.6)**

(a) $CH_3CH_2Cl/AlCl_3$ (b) $CH_2{=}CH_2/H_2SO_4$
(c) CH_3CH_2OH/H_2SO_4 (d) CH_3OCH_3/H_2SO_4

9.19 Show three different combinations of reagents you might use to convert benzene to isopropylbenzene. **(See Examples 9.5, 9.6)**

9.20 How many monochlorination products are possible when naphthalene is treated with $Cl_2/AlCl_3$?

9.21 Write a stepwise mechanism for the following reaction, using curved arrows to show the flow of electrons in each step: **(See Example 9.4)**

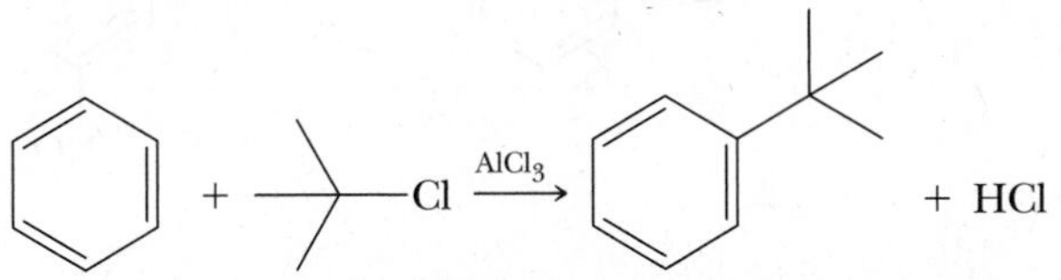

9.22 Write a stepwise mechanism for the preparation of diphenylmethane by treating benzene with dichloromethane in the presence of an aluminum chloride catalyst. **(See Example 9.4)**

9.23 The following alkylation reactions do not yield the compounds shown as the major product. Predict the major product for each reaction and provide a mechanism for their formation.

(a)

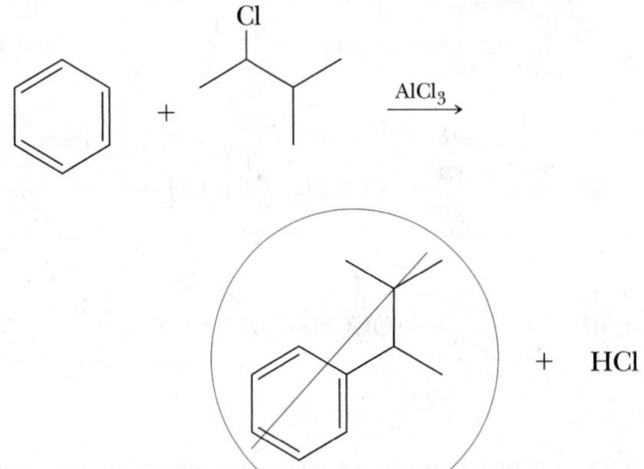

(b)

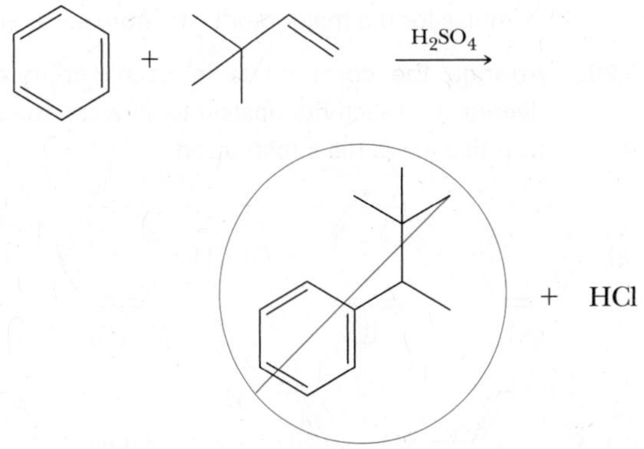

(c)

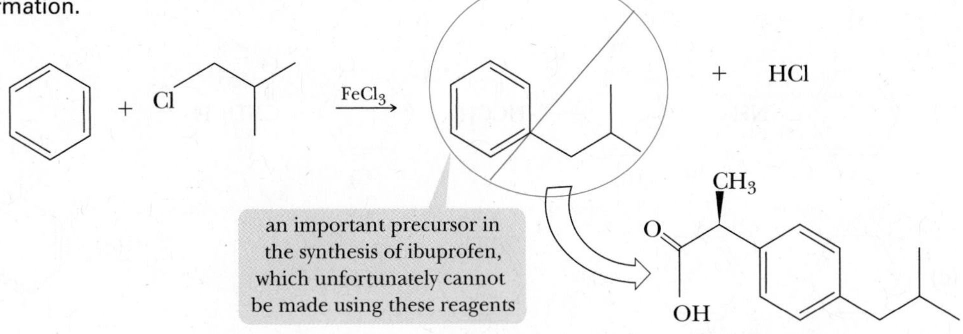

Ibuprofen

Section 9.7 Electrophilic Aromatic Substitution: Substitution Effects

9.24 When treated with $Cl_2/AlCl_3$, 1,2-dimethylbenzene (*o*-xylene) gives a mixture of two products. Draw structural formulas for these products. **(See Examples 9.7, 9.9)**

9.25 How many monosubstitution products are possible when 1,4-dimethylbenzene (*p*-xylene) is treated with $Cl_2/AlCl_3$? When *m*-xylene is treated with $Cl_2/AlCl_3$? **(See Examples 9.7, 9.9)**

9.26 Draw the structural formula for the major product formed upon treating each compound with $Cl_2/AlCl_3$: **(See Examples 9.7, 9.9)**

(a) Toluene (b) Nitrobenzene

(c) Chlorobenzene (d) *tert*-Butylbenzene

(e) 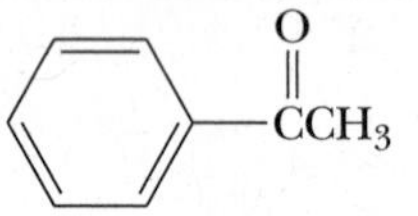 (f) 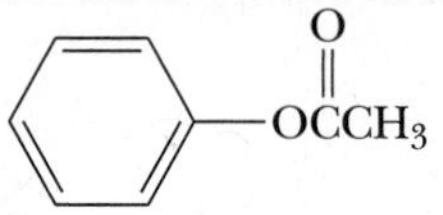

(g) 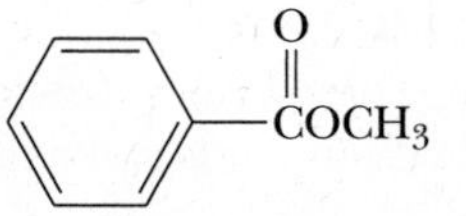 (h) 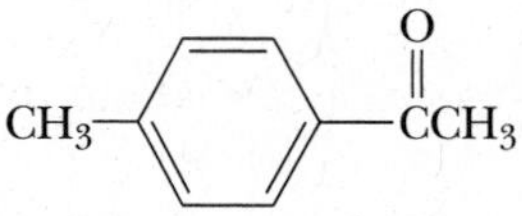

(i) 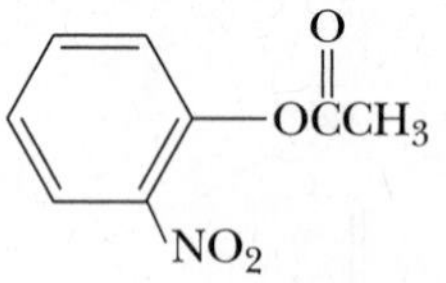 (j) 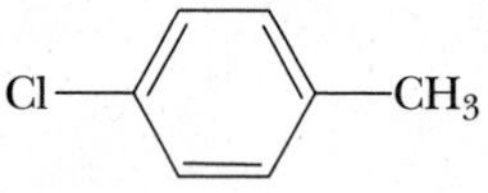

9.27 Which compound, chlorobenzene or toluene, undergoes electrophilic aromatic substitution more rapidly when treated with $Cl_2/AlCl_3$? Explain and draw structural formulas for the major product(s) from each reaction.

9.28 Arrange the compounds in each set in order of decreasing reactivity (fastest to slowest) toward electrophilic aromatic substitution:

(a)  (A) 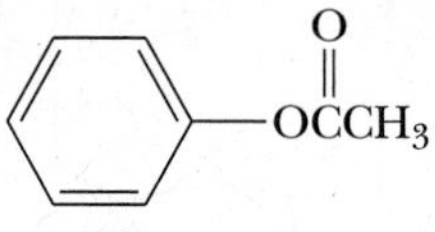 (B) 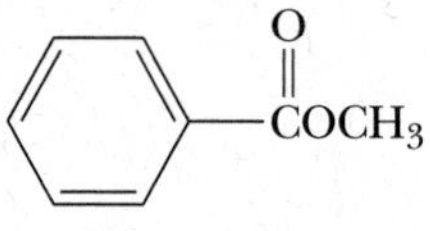 (C)

(b) 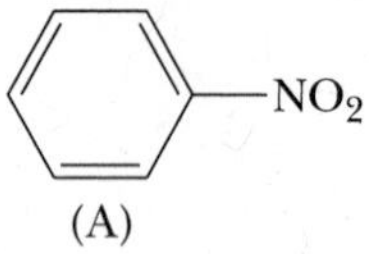 (A) 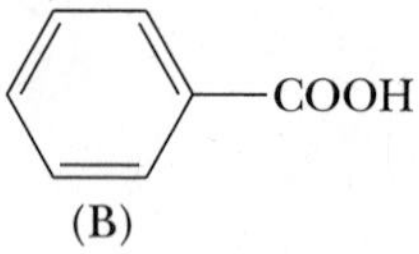 (B) 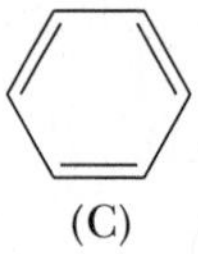 (C)

(c) 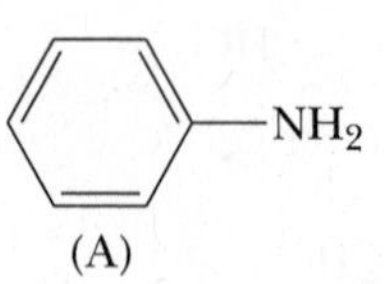 (A) 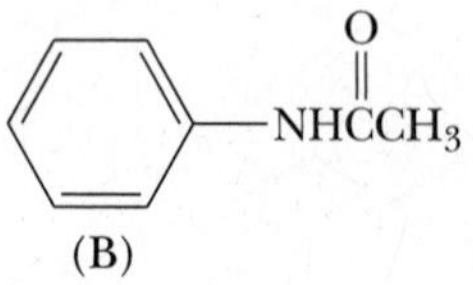 (B) 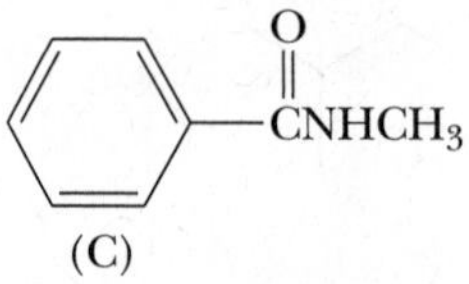 (C)

(d)  (A) 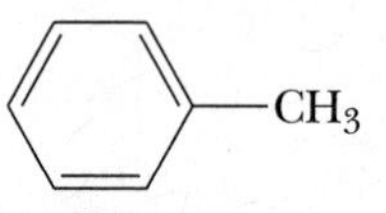 (B) 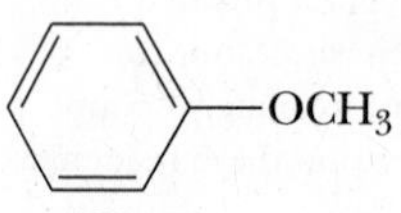 (C)

9.29 Account for the observation that the trifluoromethyl group is meta directing, as shown in the following example: **(See Example 9.8)**

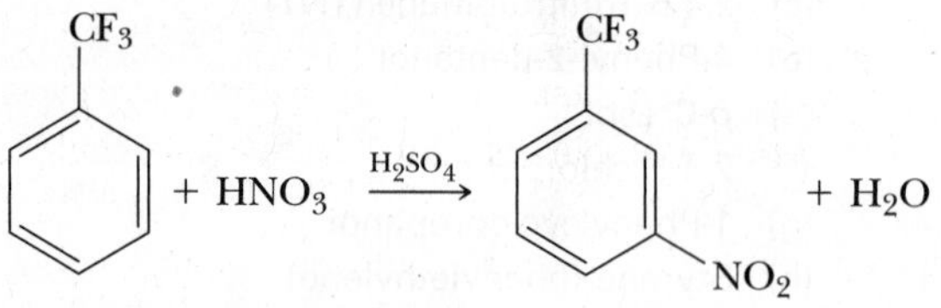

9.30 Show how to convert toluene to these carboxylic acids: **(See Example 9.3)**

(a) 4-Chlorobenzoic acid (b) 3-Chlorobenzoic acid

9.31 Show reagents and conditions that can be used to bring about these conversions: **(See Examples 9.7, 9.9)**

(a) 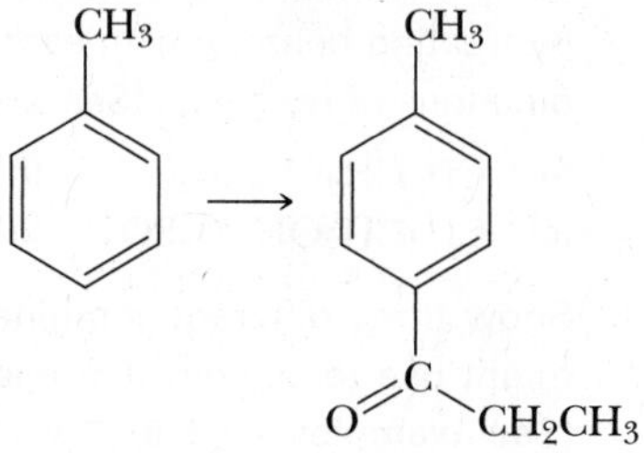

(b) 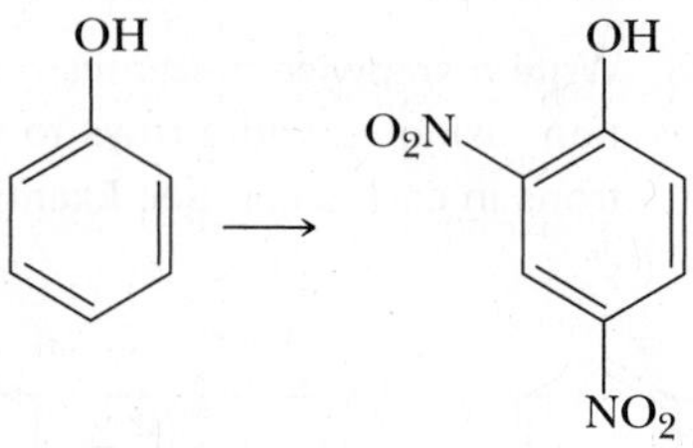

(c) 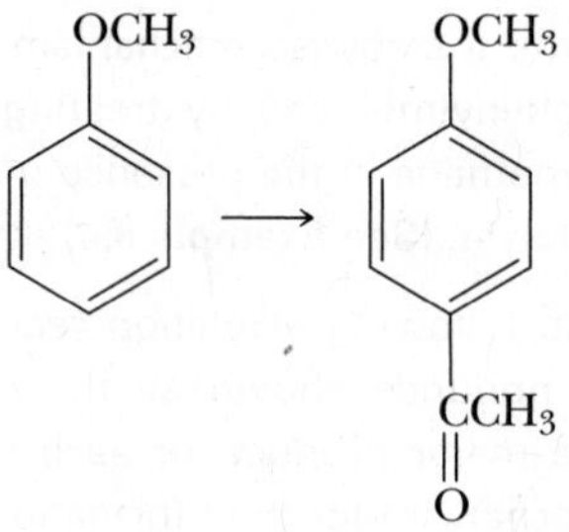

(d) 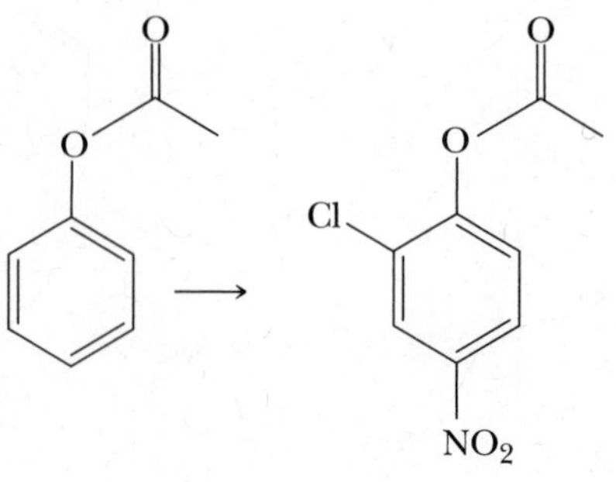

9.32 Propose a synthesis of triphenylmethane from benzene as the only source of aromatic rings. Use any other necessary reagents. **(See Examples 9.7, 9.9)**

***9.33** Reaction of phenol with acetone in the presence of an acid catalyst gives bisphenol A, a compound used in the production of polycarbonate and epoxy resins (Sections 16.4C and 16.4E): **(See Example 9.6)**

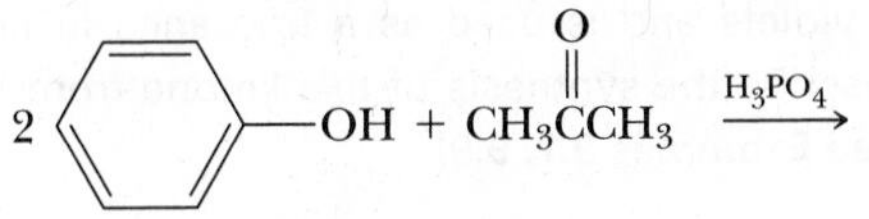

Acetone

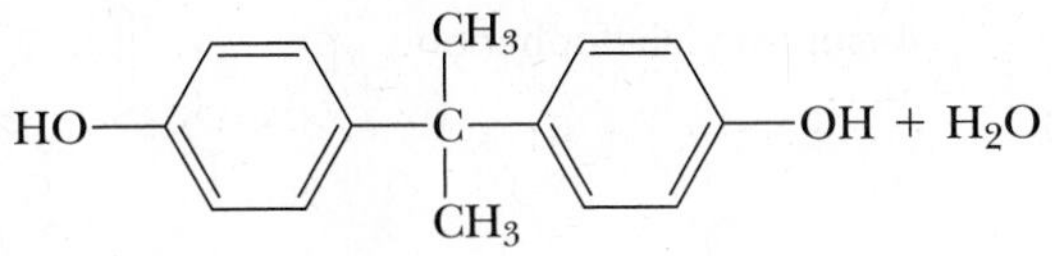

Bisphenol A

Propose a mechanism for the formation of bisphenol A. (*Hint:* The first step is a proton transfer from phosphoric acid to the oxygen of the carbonyl group of acetone.)

***9.34** 2,6-Di-*tert*-butyl-4-methylphenol, more commonly known as butylated hydroxytoluene, or BHT, is used as an antioxidant in foods to "retard spoilage." BHT is synthesized industrially from 4-methylphenol (*p*-cresol) by reaction with 2-methylpropene in the presence of phosphoric acid: **(See Example 9.6)**

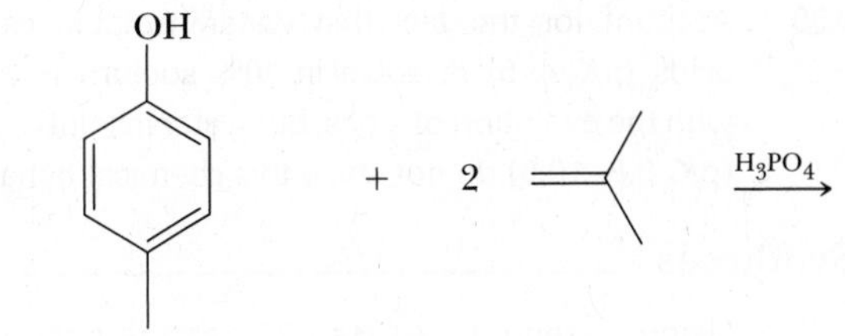

4-Methylphenol 2-Methylpropene

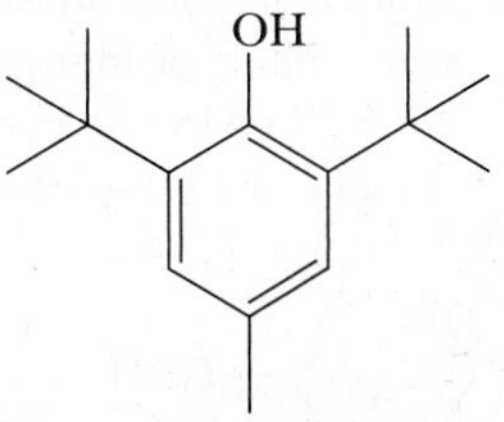

2,6-Di-*tert*-butyl-4-methylphenol
(Butylated hydroxytoluene, BHT)

Propose a mechanism for this reaction.

***9.35** The first herbicide widely used for controlling weeds was 2,4-dichlorophenoxyacetic acid (2,4-D). Show how this compound might be synthesized from 2,4-dichlorophenol and chloroacetic acid, $ClCH_2COOH$:

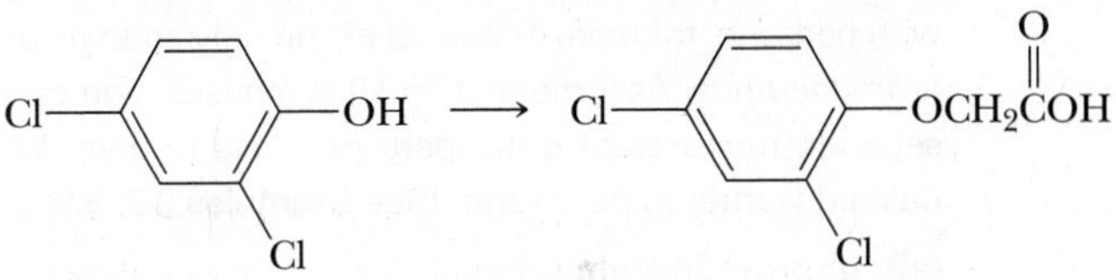

2,4-Dichlorophenol 2,4-Dichlorophenoxyacetic acid (2,4-D)

Section 9.8 Acidity of Phenols

9.36 Use resonance theory to account for the fact that phenol (pK_a 9.95) is a stronger acid than cyclohexanol (pK_a 18). **(See Example 9.10)**

9.37 Arrange the compounds in each set in order of increasing acidity (from least acidic to most acidic): **(See Example 9.10)**

(a) 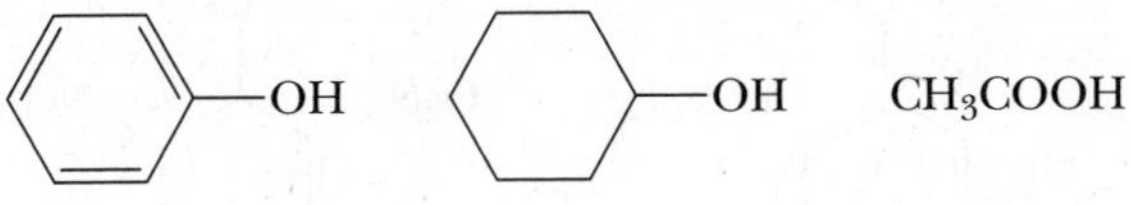

(b) 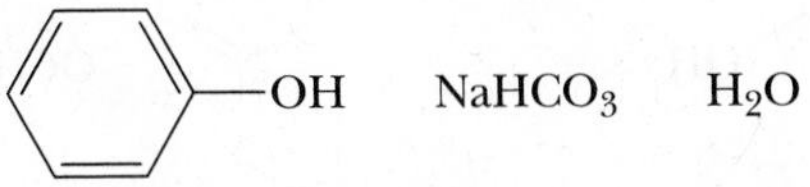

(c) 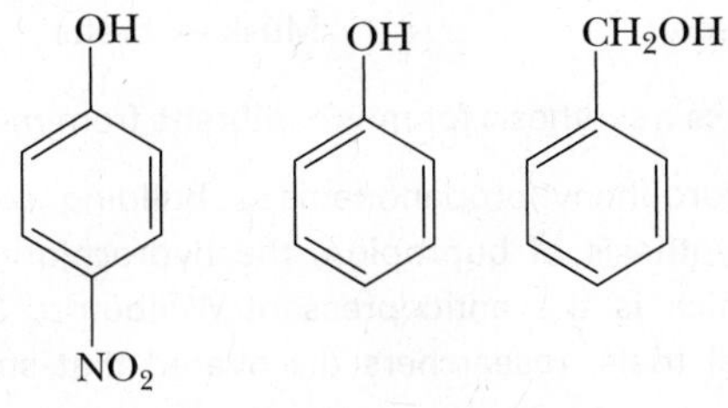

9.38 From each pair, select the stronger base: **(See Example 9.10)**

(a) 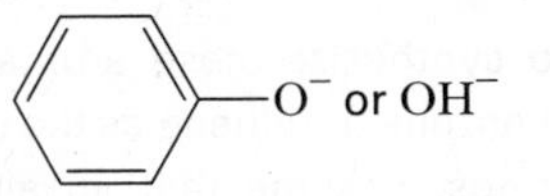

(b) 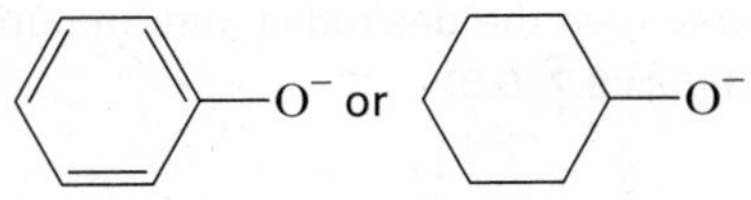

(c) 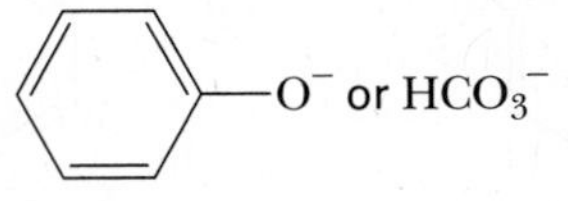

(d) 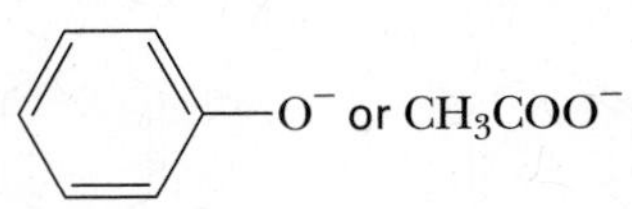

9.39 Account for the fact that water-insoluble carboxylic acids (pK_a 4–5) dissolve in 10% sodium bicarbonate with the evolution of a gas, but water-insoluble phenols (pK_a 9.5–10.5) do not show this chemical behavior.

9.40 Describe a procedure for separating a mixture of 1-hexanol and 2-methylphenol (*o*-cresol) and recovering each in pure form. Each is insoluble in water, but soluble in diethyl ether.

Syntheses

9.41 Using styrene, $C_6H_5CH{=}CH_2$, as the only aromatic starting material, show how to synthesize these compounds. In addition to styrene, use any other necessary organic or inorganic chemicals. Any compound synthesized in one part of this problem may be used to make any other compound in the problem:

(a) 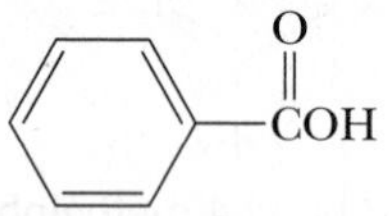
(b) 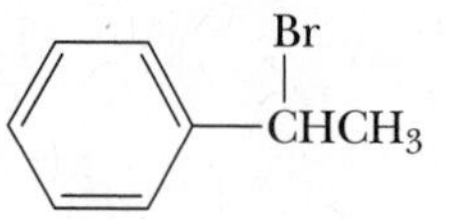
(c) 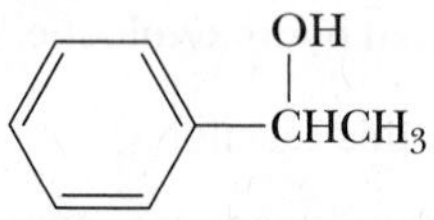
(d) 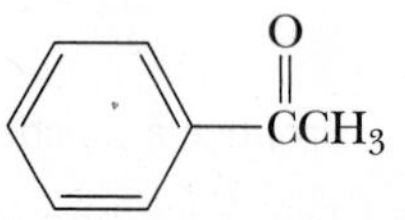
(e) 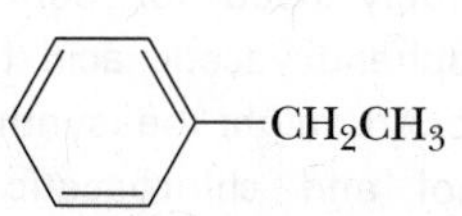
(f) 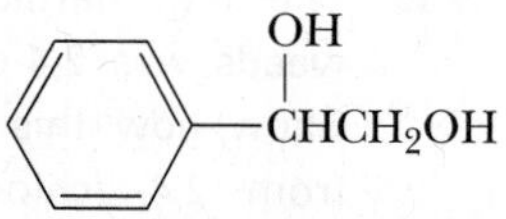

9.42 Show how to synthesize these compounds, starting with benzene, toluene, or phenol as the only sources of aromatic rings. Assume that, in all syntheses, you can separate mixtures of ortho–para products to give the desired isomer in pure form: **(See Examples 9.7, 9.9)**

(a) *m*-Bromonitrobenzene
(b) 1-Bromo-4-nitrobenzene
(c) 2,4,6-Trinitrotoluene (TNT)
(d) *m*-Bromobenzoic acid
(e) *p*-Bromobenzoic acid
(f) *p*-Dichlorobenzene
(g) *m*-Nitrobenzenesulfonic acid
(h) 1-Chloro-3-nitrobenzene

9.43 Show how to synthesize these aromatic ketones, starting with benzene or toluene as the only sources of aromatic rings. Assume that, in all syntheses, mixtures of ortho–para products can be separated to give the desired isomer in pure form: **(See Examples 9.7, 9.9)**

(a) 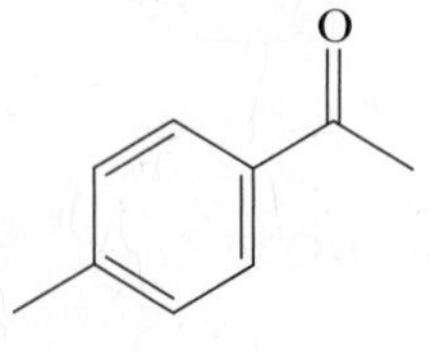
(b) 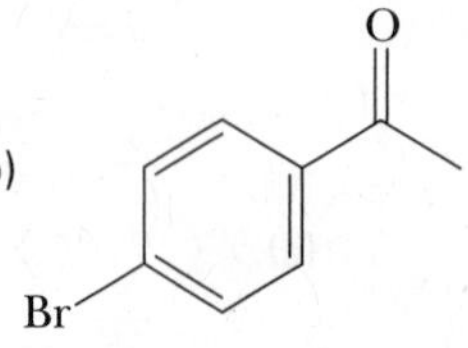
(c) 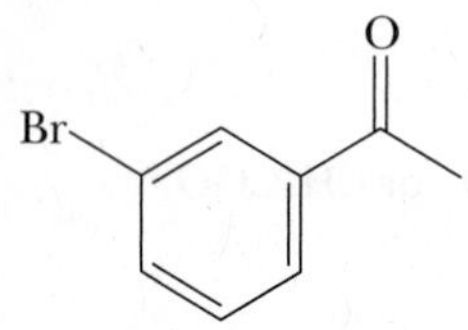
(d) 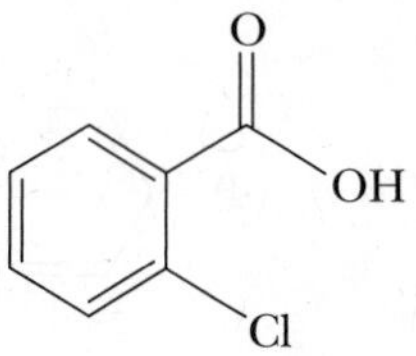

***9.44** The following ketone, isolated from the roots of several members of the iris family, has an odor like that of violets and is used as a fragrance in perfumes. Describe the synthesis of this ketone from benzene. **(See Examples 9.7, 9.9)**

4-Isopropylacetophenone 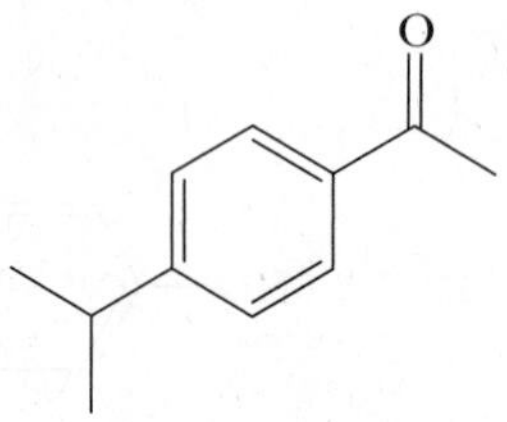

***9.45** The bombardier beetle generates *p*-quinone, an irritating chemical, by the enzyme-catalyzed oxidation of hydroquinone, using hydrogen peroxide as the oxidizing agent. Heat generated in this oxidation produces superheated steam, which is ejected, along with *p*-quinone, with explosive force.

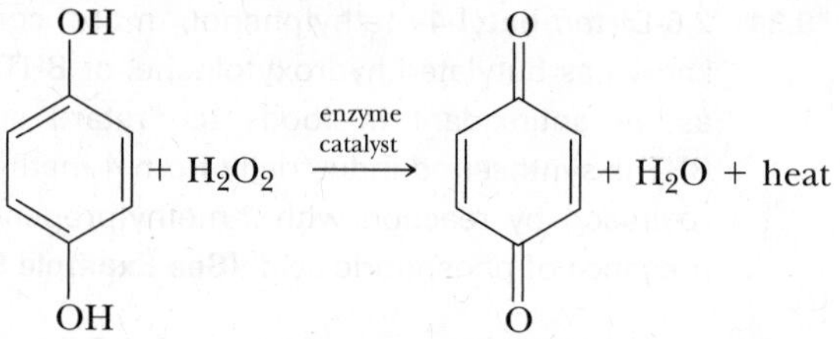

Hydroquinone — *p*-Quinone

(a) Balance the equation.
(b) Show that this reaction of hydroquinone is an oxidation.

***9.46** Following is a structural formula for musk ambrette, a synthetic musk used in perfumes to enhance and retain fragrance: **(See Examples 9.7, 9.9)**

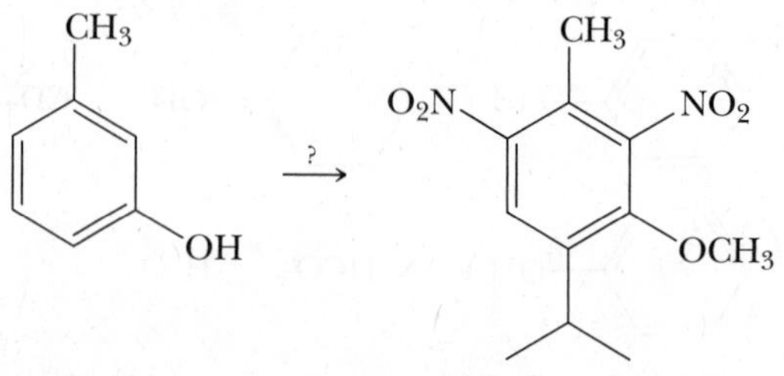

m-Cresol — Musk ambrette

Propose a synthesis for musk ambrette from *m*-cresol.

***9.47** (3-Chlorophenyl)propanone is a building block in the synthesis of bupropion, the hydrochloride salt of which is the antidepressant Wellbutrin. During clinical trials, researchers discovered that smokers reported a diminished craving for tobacco after one to two weeks on the drug. Further clinical trials confirmed this finding, and the drug is also marketed under the trade name Zyban® as an aid in smoking cessation. Propose a synthesis for this building block from benzene. (We will see in Section 12.8 how to complete the synthesis of bupropion.) **(See Examples 9.7, 9.9)**

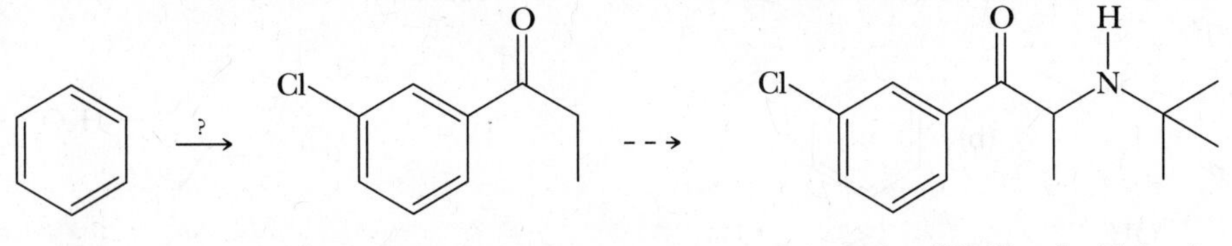

Benzene (3-Chlorophenyl)-1-propanone Bupropion (Wellbutrin, Zyban)

CHEMICAL TRANSFORMATIONS

9.48 Test your cumulative knowledge of the reactions learned thus far by completing the following chemical transformations. *Note: Some will require more than one step.*

(a) 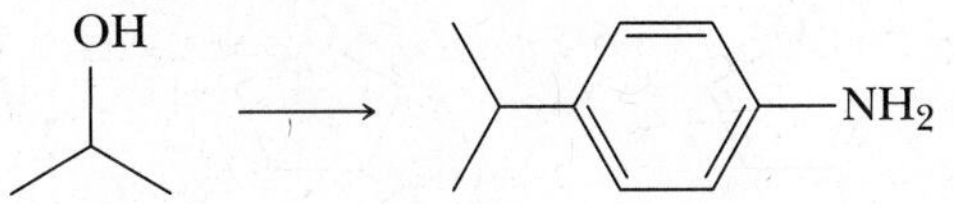

(b) 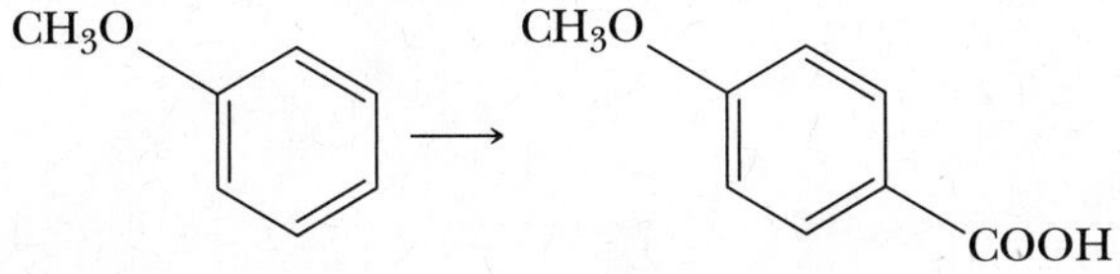

(c) 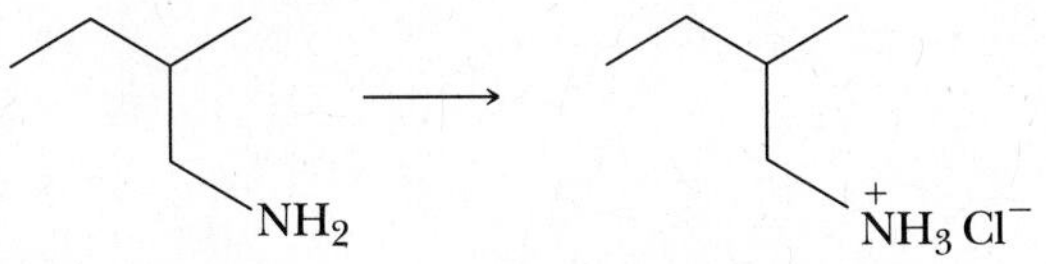

(d) 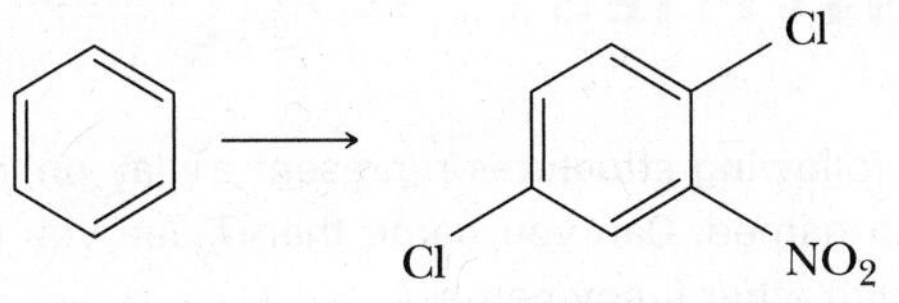

(e) 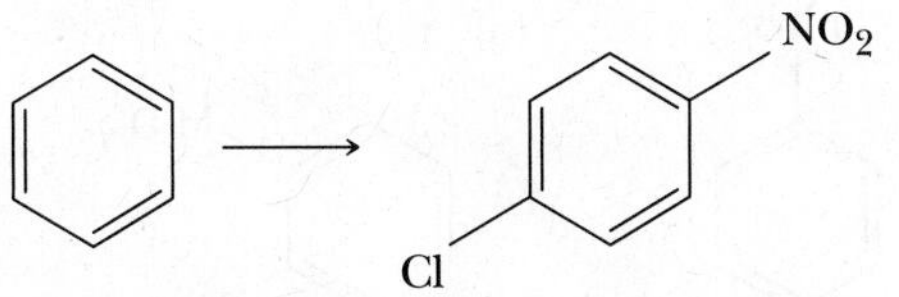

(f) 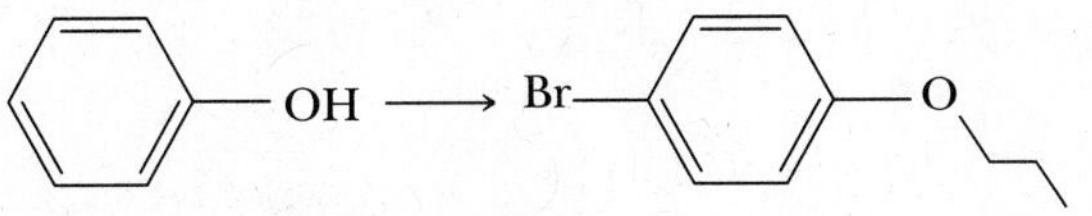

(g) 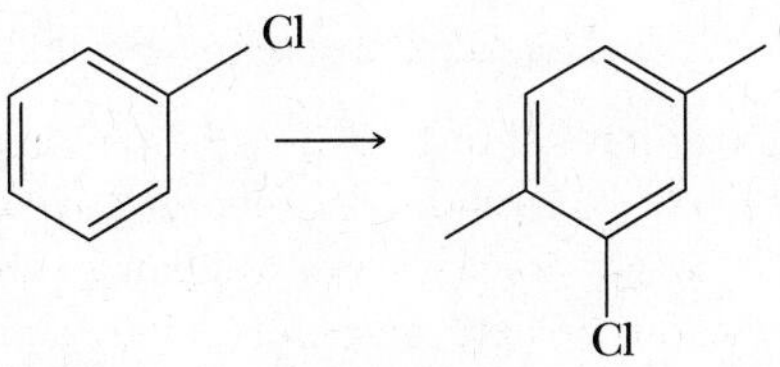

(h) 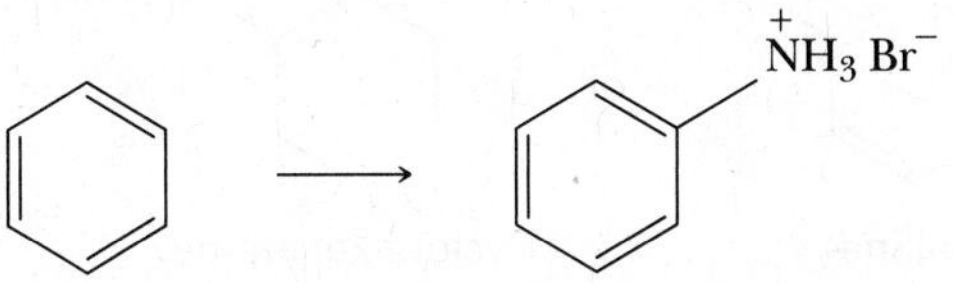

(i) 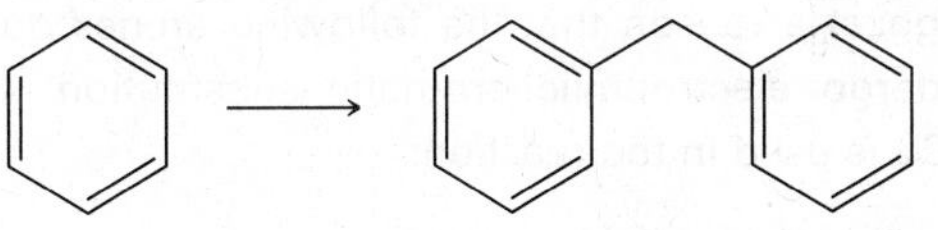

(j) 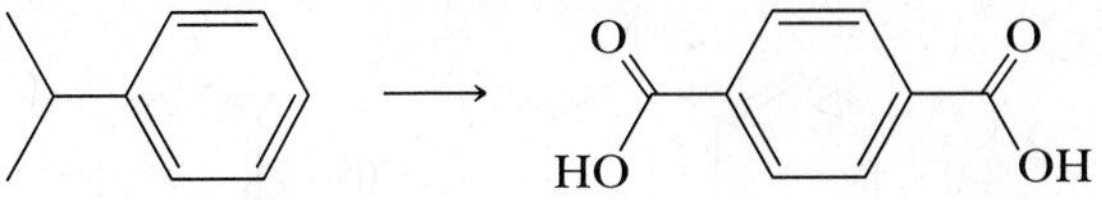

(k) 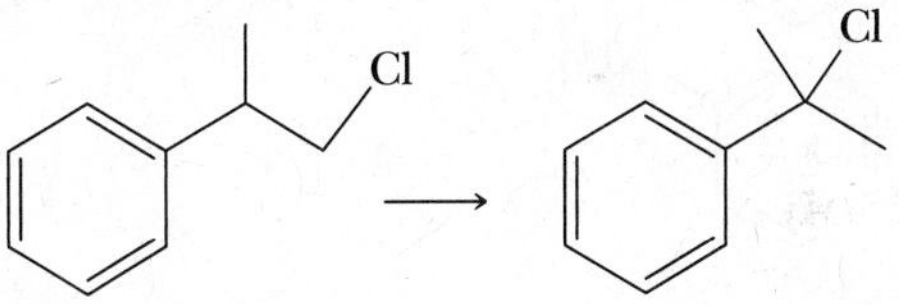

(l) 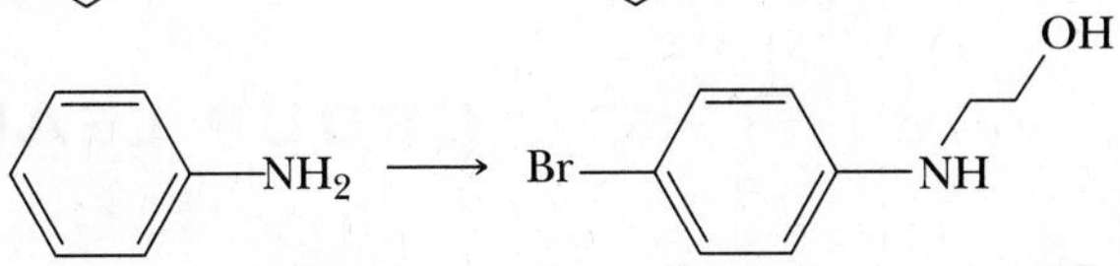

(m) 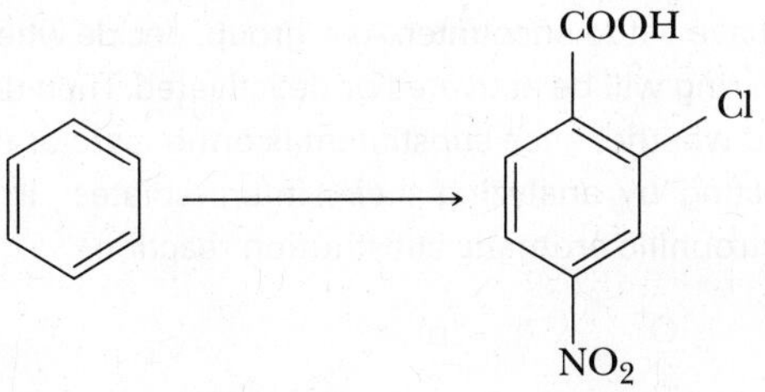

(n) 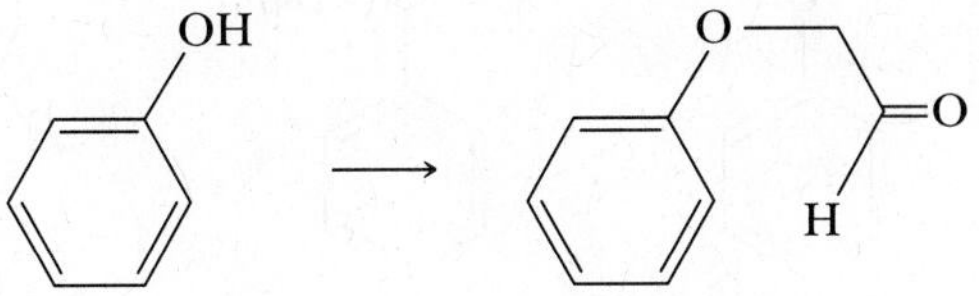

LOOKING AHEAD

9.49 Which of the following compounds can be made directly by using an electrophilic aromatic substitution reaction?

(a) 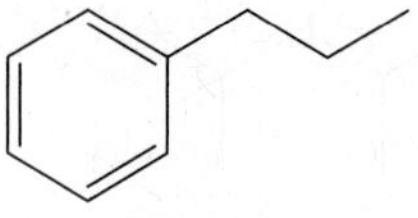 (b) 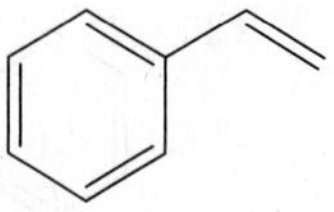

(c) 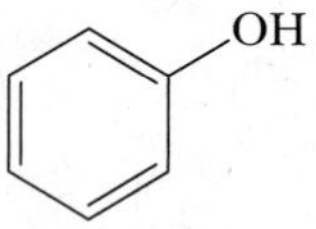 (d) 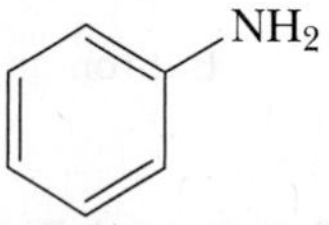

9.50 Which compound is a better nucleophile?

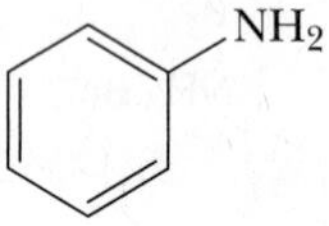 or 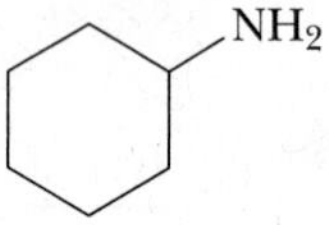

Aniline Cyclohexanamine

9.51 Suggest a reason that the following arenes do not undergo electrophilic aromatic substitution when $AlCl_3$ is used in the reaction:

(a) 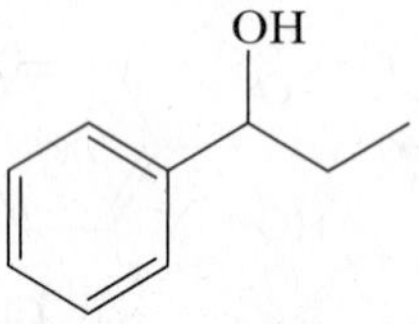 (b) 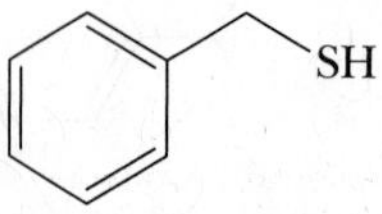

(c) 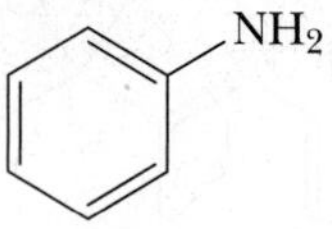

9.52 Predict the product of the following acid–base reaction:

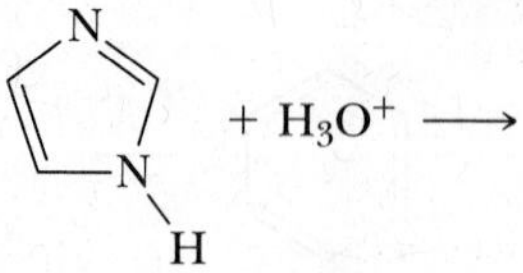

9.53 Which haloalkane reacts faster in an S_N1 reaction?

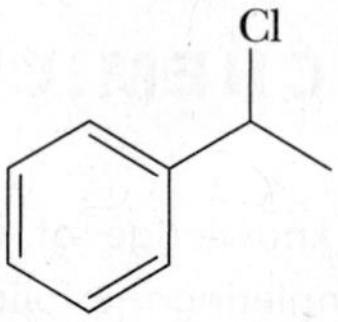 or 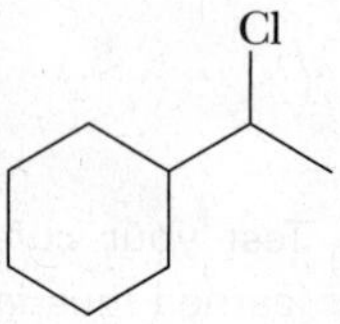

9.54 Which of the following compounds is more basic?

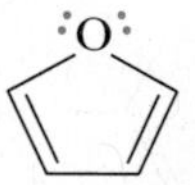 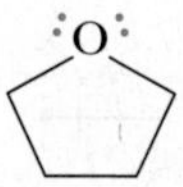

Furan or Tetrahydrofuran

GROUP LEARNING ACTIVITIES

9.55 Following are benzene compounds with substituents we have yet to encounter. As a group, decide whether each ring will be activated or deactivated. Then determine whether each substituent is ortho–para or meta directing by analyzing their intermediates in an electrophilic aromatic substitution reaction.

(a) 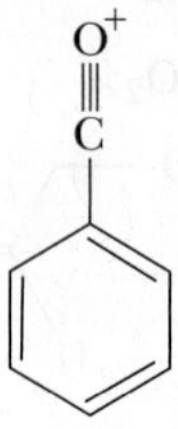 (b) 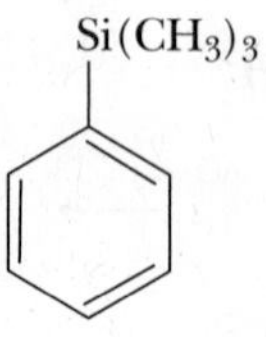

9.56 The following structures represent a play on words when named. Can you name them? Can you come up with other funny names?

(a) 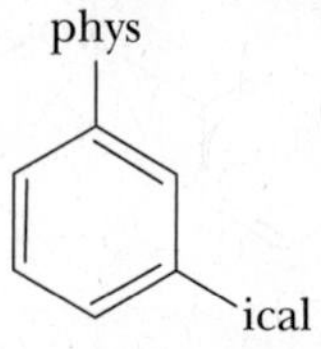

(b) 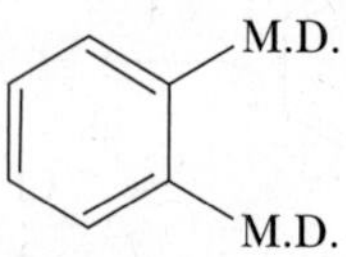

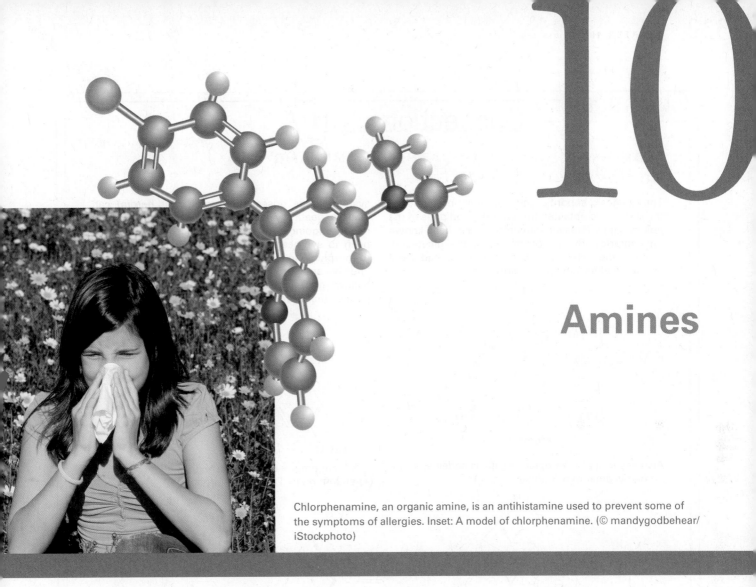

KEY QUESTIONS

- 10.1 What Are Amines?
- 10.2 How Are Amines Named?
- 10.3 What Are the Characteristic Physical Properties of Amines?
- 10.4 What Are the Acid-Base Properties of Amines?
- 10.5 What Are the Reactions of Amines with Acids?
- 10.6 How Are Arylamines Synthesized?
- 10.7 How Do Amines Act as Nucleophiles?

HOW TO

10.1 How to Predict the Relative Basicity of Amines

CHEMICAL CONNECTIONS

- 10A Morphine as a Clue in the Design and Discovery of Drugs
- 10B The Poison Dart Frogs of South America: Lethal Amines

CARBON, HYDROGEN, and oxygen are the three most common elements in organic compounds. Because of the wide distribution of amines in the biological world, nitrogen is the fourth most common element in organic compounds. The most important chemical properties of amines are their basicity and their nucleophilicity.

Chemical Connections 10A

MORPHINE AS A CLUE IN THE DESIGN AND DISCOVERY OF DRUGS

The analgesic, soporific, and euphoriant properties of the dried juice obtained from unripe seed pods of the opium poppy *Papaver somniferum* have been known for centuries. By the beginning of the nineteenth century, the active principal, morphine, had been isolated and its structure determined:

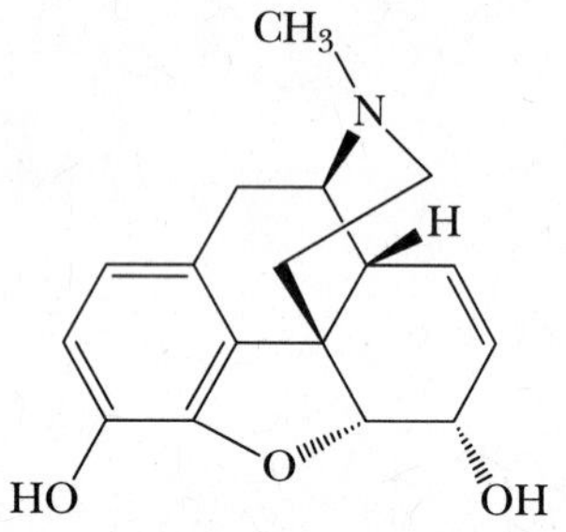

Morphine

Also occurring in the opium poppy is codeine, a monomethyl ether of morphine:

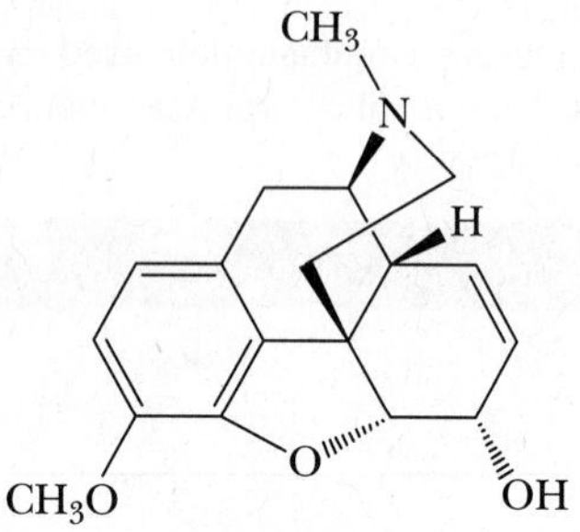

Codeine

Heroin is synthesized by treating morphine with two moles of acetic anhydride:

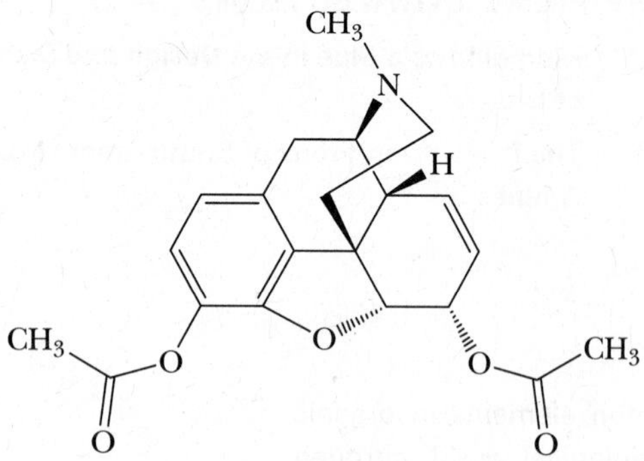

Heroin

Even though morphine is one of modern medicine's most effective painkillers, it has two serious side effects: It is addictive, and it depresses the respiratory control center of the central nervous system. Large doses of morphine (or heroin) can lead to death by respiratory failure. One strategy in the ongoing research to produce painkillers has been to synthesize compounds related in structure to morphine, in the hope that they would be equally effective analgesics, but with diminished side effects. Following are structural formulas for two such compounds that have proven to be clinically useful:

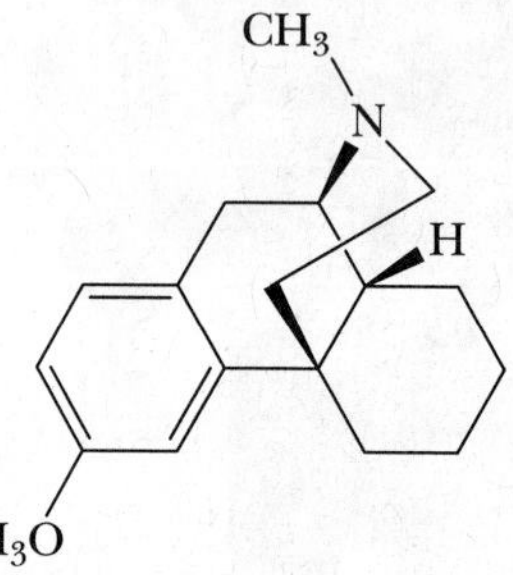

(−)-enantiomer = Levomethorphan
(+)-enantiomer = Dextromethorphan

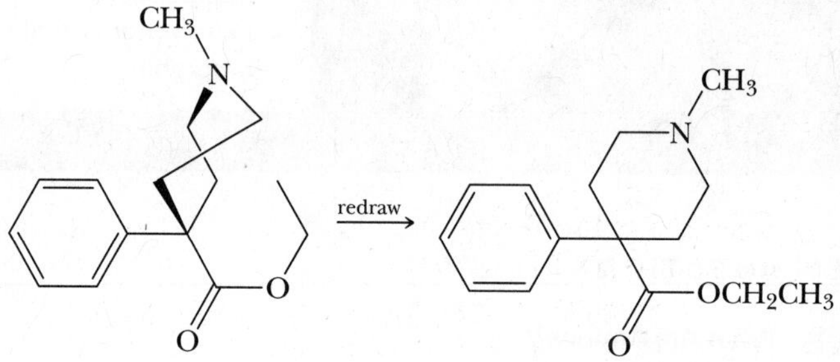

Meperidine
(Demerol)

Levomethorphan is a potent analgesic. Interestingly, its dextrorotatory enantiomer, dextromethorphan, has no analgesic activity. It does, however, show approximately the same cough-suppressing activity as morphine and is used extensively in cough remedies.

It has been discovered that there can be even further simplification in the structure of morphine-like analgesics. One such simplification is represented by meperidine, the hydrochloride salt of which is the widely used analgesic Demerol®.

It was hoped that meperidine and related synthetic drugs would be free of many of the morphine-like undesirable side effects. It is now clear, however, that they are not. Meperidine, for example, is definitely addictive. In spite of much determined research, there are as yet no agents as effective as morphine for the relief of severe pain that are absolutely free of the risk of addiction.

How and in what regions of the brain does morphine act? In 1979, scientists discovered that there are specific receptor sites for morphine and other opiates and that these sites are clustered in the brain's limbic system, the area involved in emotion and the perception of pain. Scientists then asked, "Why does the human brain have receptor sites specific for morphine?" Could it be that the brain produces its own opiates? In 1974, scientists discovered that opiate-like compounds are indeed present in the brain; in 1975, they isolated a brain opiate that was named *enkephalin*, meaning "in the brain." Unlike morphine and its derivatives, enkephalin possesses an entirely different structure consisting of a sequence of five amino acids (Section 18.4). Scientists have yet to understand the role of these natural brain opiates. Perhaps when we do understand their biochemistry, we may discover clues that will lead to the design and synthesis of more potent, but less addictive, analgesics.

Question

Identify the functional groups in morphine and meperidine. Classify the amino group in these opiates according to type (that is, primary, secondary, tertiary, heterocyclic, aliphatic, or aromatic).

10.1 What Are Amines?

Amines are derivatives of ammonia (NH_3) in which one or more hydrogens are replaced by alkyl or aryl groups. Amines are classified as primary (1°), secondary (2°), or tertiary (3°), depending on the number of hydrogen atoms of ammonia that are replaced by alkyl or aryl groups (Section 1.7B). As we saw with ammonia, the three atoms or groups bonded to the nitrogen in amines assume a trigonal pyramidal geometry:

:NH_3	$CH_3—\ddot{N}H_2$	$CH_3—\ddot{N}H—CH_3$	$CH_3—\ddot{N}(CH_3)—CH_3$
Ammonia	Methylamine (a 1° amine)	Dimethylamine (a 2° amine)	Trimethylamine (a 3° amine)

Amines are further divided into aliphatic amines and aromatic amines. In an **aliphatic amine**, all the carbons bonded directly to nitrogen are derived from alkyl groups; in an **aromatic amine**, one or more of the groups bonded directly to nitrogen are aryl groups:

Aliphatic amine An amine in which nitrogen is bonded only to alkyl groups.

Aromatic amine An amine in which nitrogen is bonded to one or more aryl groups.

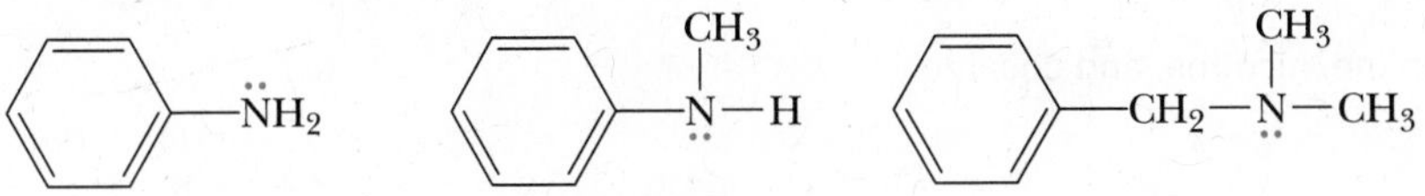

Aniline (a 1° aromatic amine) — *N*-Methylaniline (a 2° aromatic amine) — Benzyldimethylamine (a 3° aliphatic amine)

An amine in which the nitrogen atom is part of a ring is classified as a **heterocyclic amine**. When the nitrogen is part of an aromatic ring (Section 9.2), the amine is classified as a **heterocyclic aromatic amine**. Following are structural formulas for two heterocyclic aliphatic amines and two heterocyclic aromatic amines:

Heterocyclic amine An amine in which nitrogen is one of the atoms of a ring.

Heterocyclic aromatic amine An amine in which nitrogen is one of the atoms of an aromatic ring.

Pyrrolidine Piperidine (heterocyclic aliphatic amines) — Pyrrole Pyridine (heterocyclic aromatic amines)

EXAMPLE 10.1

Alkaloids are basic nitrogen-containing compounds of plant origin, many of which have physiological activity when administered to humans. The ingestion of coniine, present in water hemlock, can cause weakness, labored respiration, paralysis, and, eventually, death. Coniine was the toxic substance in "poison hemlock" that caused the death of Socrates. In small doses, nicotine is an addictive stimulant. In larger doses, it causes depression, nausea, and vomiting. In still larger doses, it is a deadly poison. Solutions of nicotine in water are used as insecticides. Cocaine is a central nervous system stimulant obtained from the leaves of the coca plant. Classify each amino group in these alkaloids according to type (that is, primary, secondary, tertiary, heterocyclic, aliphatic, or aromatic):

(a)

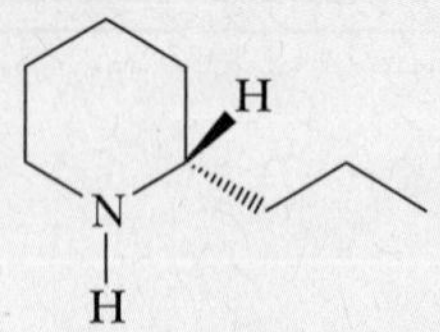

(S)-Coniine

(b)

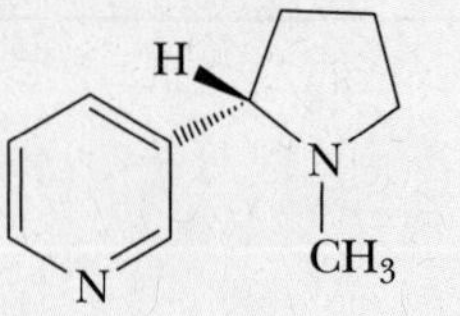

(S)-Nicotine

(c)

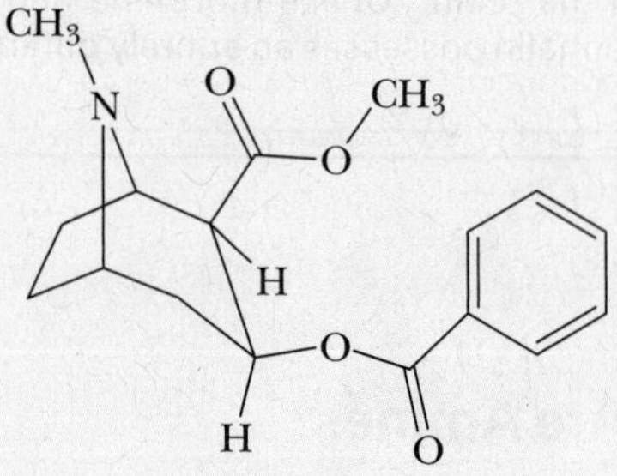

Cocaine

STRATEGY

Locate each nitrogen in each compound. If a nitrogen is part of a ring, the amine is heterocyclic. If that ring is aromatic, it is classified as a heterocyclic aromatic amine (1°, 2°, or 3° does not apply). If the ring is not aromatic, it is a heterocyclic aliphatic amine that should also be classified as 1°, 2°, or 3°. *Note*: The presence of more than one nitrogen can result in multiple classifications for the molecule, depending on the part of the compound being referred to.

SOLUTION

(a) A secondary (2°) heterocyclic aliphatic amine.
(b) One tertiary (3°) heterocyclic aliphatic amine and one heterocyclic aromatic amine.
(c) A tertiary (3°) heterocyclic aliphatic amine.

See problems 10.13–10.16

PROBLEM 10.1

Identify all carbon stereocenters in coniine, nicotine, and cocaine.

10.2 How Are Amines Named?

A. Systematic Names

Systematic names for aliphatic amines are derived just as they are for alcohols. The suffix *-e* of the parent alkane is dropped and is replaced by *-amine*; that is, they are named alkanamines:

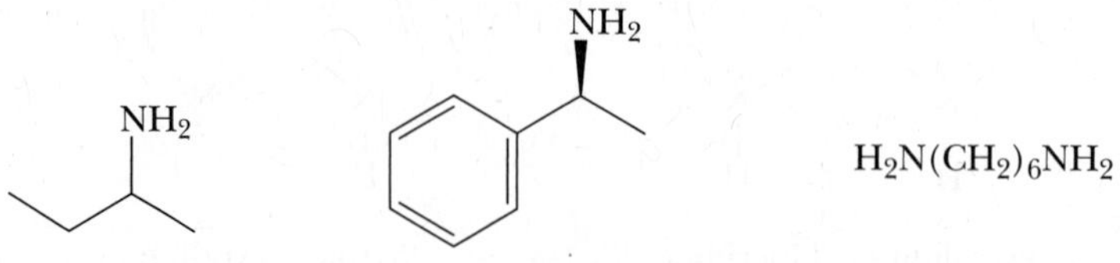

2-Butanamine (S)-1-Phenylethanamine 1,6-Hexanediamine

EXAMPLE 10.2

Write the IUPAC name or provide the structural formula for each amine:

(a) 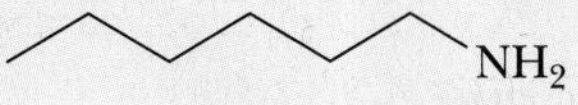

(b) 2-Methyl-1-propanamine

(c) 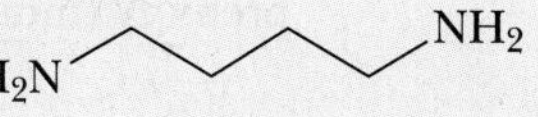

(d) *trans*-4-Methylcyclohexanamine

(e) 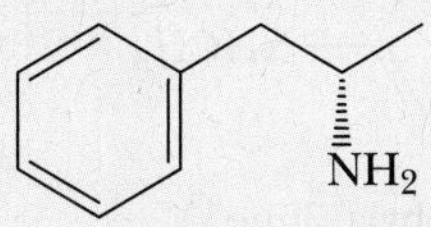

STRATEGY

When naming, look for the longest chain of carbons that contains the amino group. This will allow you to determine the root name. Then identify and name the substituents, the atoms or groups of atoms that are not part of that chain of carbons.

To translate a name to a structure, identify the carbon chain from the root name and add the substituents to the correct position on the chain.

SOLUTION

(a) 1-Hexanamine

(b) 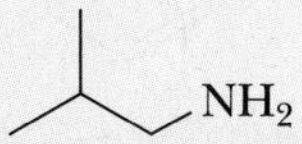

(c) 1,4-Butanediamine

(d) 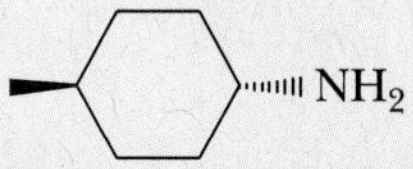

(e) The systematic name of this compound is (*S*)-1-phenyl-2-propanamine. Its common name is amphetamine. The dextrorotatory isomer of amphetamine (shown here) is a central nervous system stimulant and is manufactured and sold under several trade names. The salt with sulfuric acid is marketed as Dexedrine sulfate.

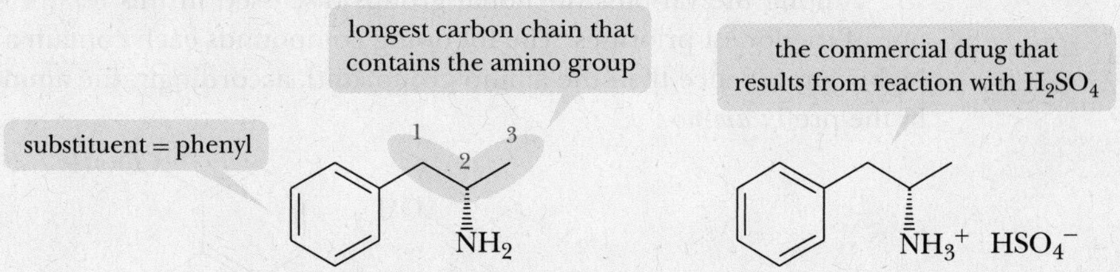

(*S*)-1-Phenyl-2-propanamine

Dexedrine sulfate

See problems 10.11, 10.12, 10.16

PROBLEM 10.2

Write a structural formula for each amine:

(a) 2-Methyl-1-propanamine (b) Cyclohexanamine (c) (*R*)-2-Butanamine

IUPAC nomenclature retains the common name **aniline** for $C_6H_5NH_2$, the simplest aromatic amine. Its simple derivatives are named with the prefixes *o*-, *m*-, and *p*-, or numbers to locate substituents. Several derivatives of aniline have common names that are still widely used. Among these are **toluidine**, for a methyl-substituted aniline, and **anisidine**, for a methoxy-substituted aniline:

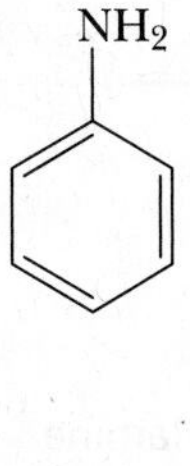

Aniline

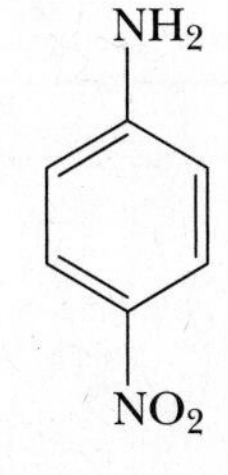

4-Nitroaniline
(*p*-Nitroaniline)

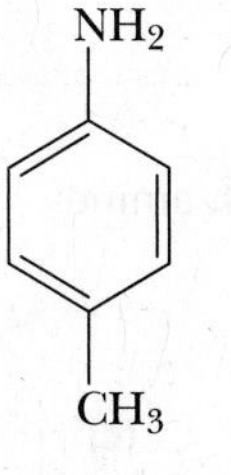

4-Methylaniline
(*p*-Toluidine)

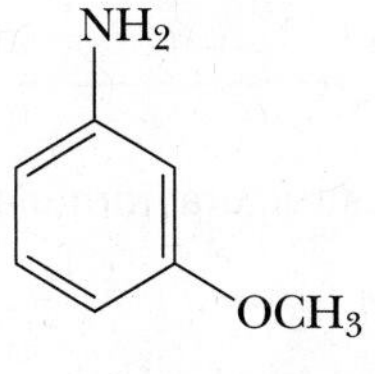

3-Methoxyaniline
(*m*-Anisidine)

Secondary and tertiary amines are commonly named as *N*-substituted primary amines. For unsymmetrical amines, the largest group is taken as the parent amine; then the smaller group or groups bonded to nitrogen are named, and their location is indicated by the prefix *N* (indicating that they are bonded to nitrogen):

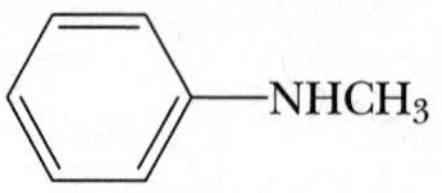

N-Methylaniline

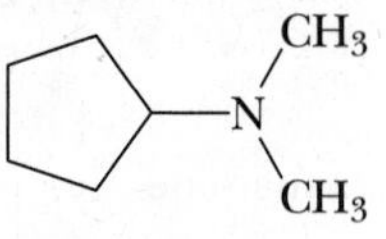

N,*N*-Dimethyl-cyclopentanamine

Following are names and structural formulas for four heterocyclic aromatic amines, the common names of which have been retained by the IUPAC:

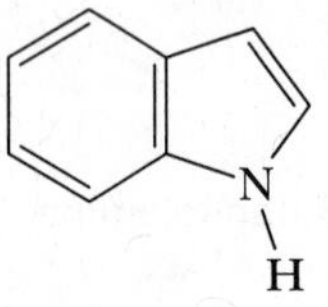

Indole

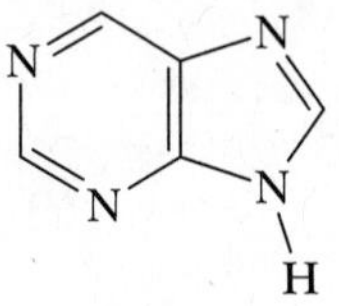

Purine

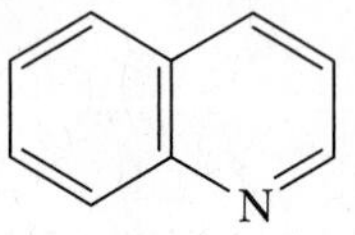

Quinoline

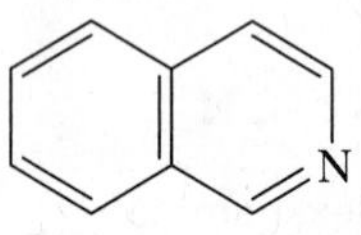

Isoquinoline

Among the various functional groups discussed in this text, the $-NH_2$ group has one of the lowest priorities. The following compounds each contain a functional group of higher precedence than the amino group, and, accordingly, the amino group is indicated by the prefix *amino-*:

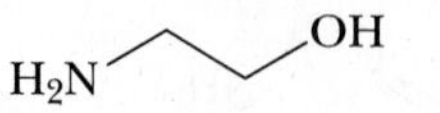

2-Aminoethanol
(Ethanolamine)

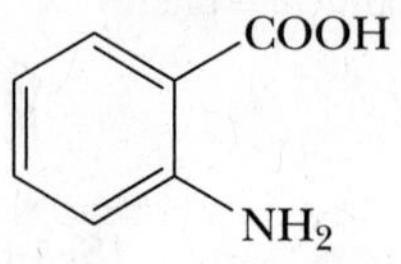

2-Aminobenzoic acid
(Anthranilic acid)

B. Common Names

Common names for most aliphatic amines are derived by listing the alkyl groups bonded to nitrogen in alphabetical order in one word ending in the suffix *-amine*; that is, they are named as **alkylamines**:

CH_3NH_2

Methylamine

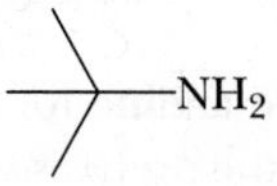

tert-Butylamine

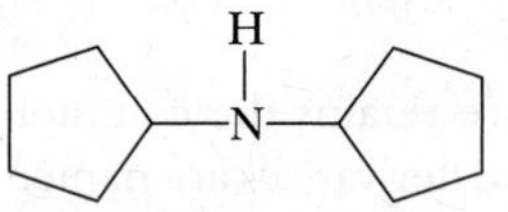

Dicyclopentylamine

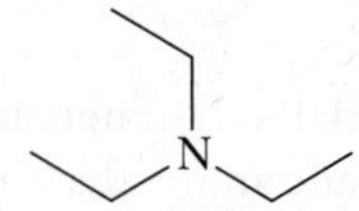

Triethylamine

EXAMPLE 10.3

Write the IUPAC name or provide the structural formula for each amine:

(a) 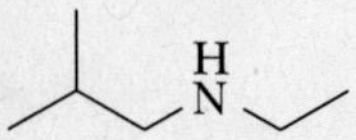

(b) Cyclohexylmethylamine

(c) 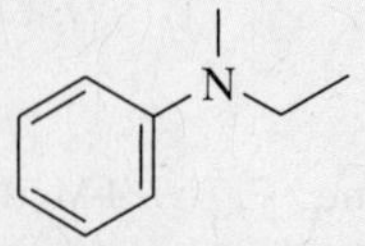

(d) Benzylamine

STRATEGY

When naming, look for the longest chain of carbons that contains the amino group. This will allow you to determine the root name. If the longest chain of carbons is a benzene ring, the amine may be named as an aniline derivative. When identifying the substituents, remember that substitutents bonded to a nitrogen are preceded by "*N*-."

To translate a name to a structure, identify the carbon chain from the root name and add the substituents to the correct position on the molecule.

SOLUTION

(a) *N*-ethyl-2-methyl-1-propanamine (b) 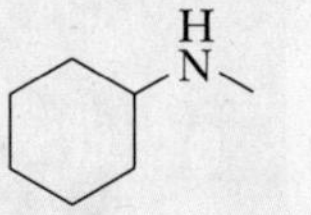

(c) *N*-ethyl-*N*-methylaniline (d) 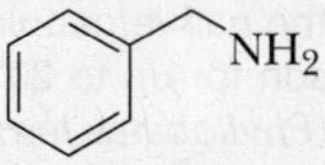

See problems 10.11, 10.12, 10.16

PROBLEM 10.3

Write a structural formula for each amine:

(a) Isobutylamine (b) Triphenylamine (c) Diisopropylamine

When four atoms or groups of atoms are bonded to a nitrogen atom, we name the compound as a salt of the corresponding amine. We replace the ending *-amine* (or aniline, pyridine, or the like) by *-ammonium* (or *anilinium, pyridinium,* or the like) and add the name of the anion (chloride, acetate, and so on). Compounds containing such ions have properties characteristic of salts, such as increased water solubility, high melting points, and high boiling points. Following are three examples (cetylpyridinium chloride is used as a topical antiseptic and disinfectant):

$(CH_3)_4N^+Cl^-$

Tetramethylammonium chloride

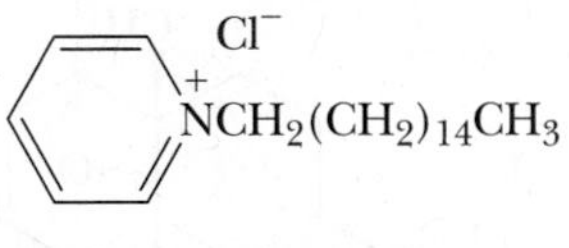

Hexadecylpyridinium chloride (Cetylpyridinium chloride)

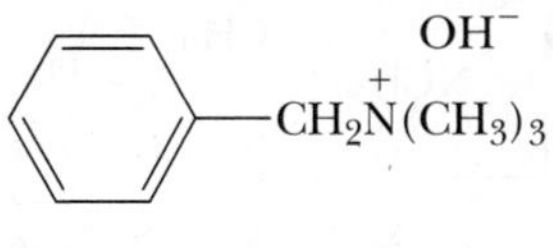

Benzyltrimethylammonium hydroxide

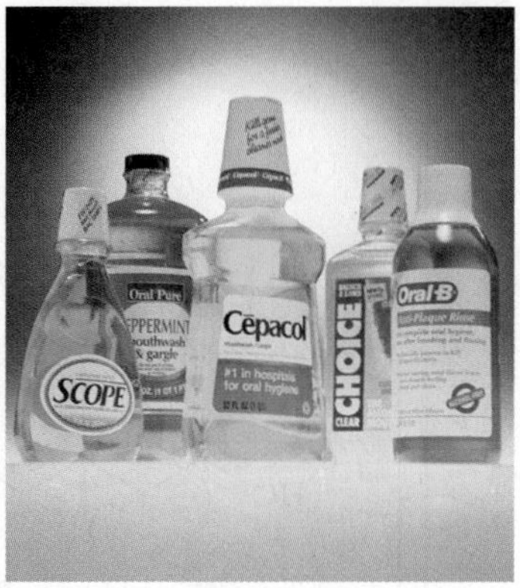

Charles D. Winters

Several over-the-counter mouthwashes contain *N*-alkylatedpyridinium chlorides as an antibacterial agent.

10.3 What Are the Characteristic Physical Properties of Amines?

Amines are polar compounds, and both primary and secondary amines form intermolecular hydrogen bonds (Figure 10.1).

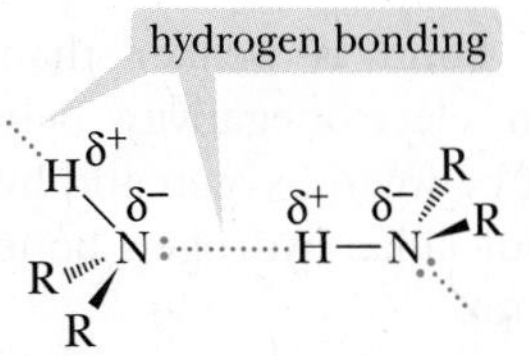

FIGURE 10.1
Intermolecular association of 1° and 2° amines by hydrogen bonding. Nitrogen is approximately tetrahedral in shape, with the axis of the hydrogen bond along the fourth position of the tetrahedron.

Chemical Connections 10B

THE POISON DART FROGS OF SOUTH AMERICA: LETHAL AMINES

The Noanamá and Embrá peoples of the jungles of western Colombia have used poison blow darts for centuries, perhaps millennia. The poisons are obtained from the skin secretions of several highly colored frogs of the genus *Phyllobates* (*neará* and *kokoi* in the language of the native peoples). A single frog contains enough poison for up to 20 darts. For the most poisonous species (*Phyllobates terribilis*), just rubbing a dart over the frog's back suffices to charge the dart with poison.

Scientists at the National Institutes of Health became interested in studying these poisons when it was discovered that they act on cellular ion channels, which would make them useful tools in basic research on mechanisms of ion transport. A field station was established in western Colombia to collect the relatively common poison dart frogs. From 5,000 frogs, 11 mg of batrachotoxin and batrachotoxinin A were isolated. These names are derived from *batrachos*, the Greek word for frog.

Batrachotoxin and batrachotoxinin A are among the most lethal poisons ever discovered:

Poison dart frog, *Phyllobates terribilis*.

The batrachotoxin story illustrates several common themes in the discovery of new drugs. First, information about the kinds of biologically active compounds and their sources are often obtained from the native peoples of a region. Second, tropical rain forests are a rich source of structurally complex, biologically active substances. Third, an entire ecosystem, not only the plants, is a potential source of fascinating organic molecules.

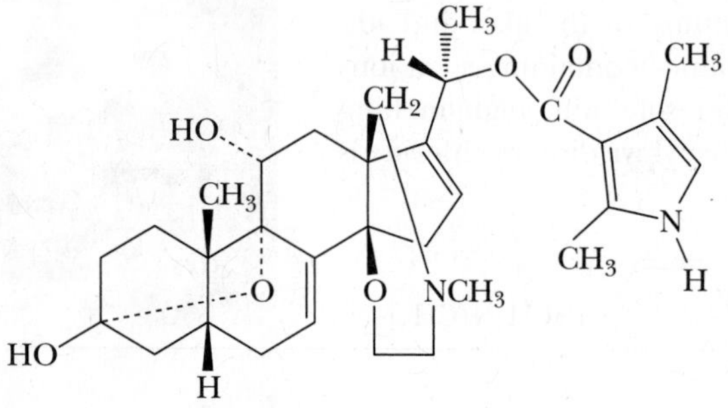

Batrachotoxin

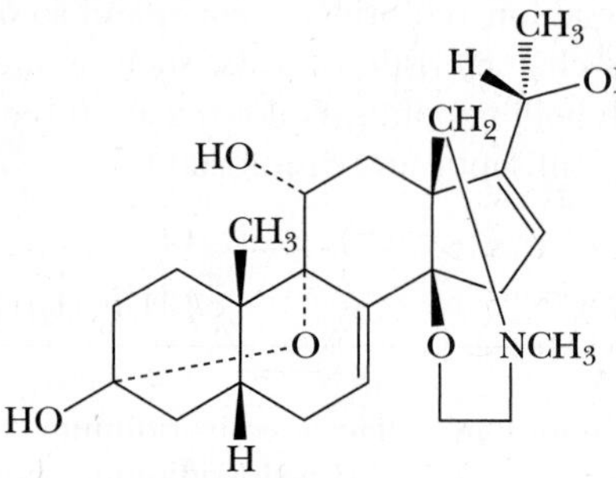

Batrachotoxinin A

It is estimated that as little as 200 μg of batrachotoxin is sufficient to induce irreversible cardiac arrest in a human being. It has been determined that they act by causing voltage-gated Na^+ channels in nerve and muscle cells to be blocked in the open position, which leads to a huge influx of Na^+ ions into the affected cell.

Questions

Would you expect batrachotoxin or batrachotoxinin A to be more soluble in water? Why?

Predict the product formed from the reaction of batrachotoxin with one equivalent of a weak acid such as acetic acid, CH_3COOH.

An N—H----N hydrogen bond is weaker than an O—H----O hydrogen bond, because the difference in electronegativity between nitrogen and hydrogen $(3.0 - 2.1 = 0.9)$ is less than that between oxygen and hydrogen $(3.5 - 2.1 = 1.4)$. We can illustrate the effect of intermolecular hydrogen bonding by comparing the boiling points of methylamine and methanol:

	CH_3NH_2	CH_3OH
molecular weight (g/mol)	31.1	32.0
boiling point (°C)	−6.3	65.0

TABLE 10.1 Physical Properties of Selected Amines

Name	Structural Formula	Melting Point (°C)	Boiling Point (°C)	Solubility in Water
Ammonia	NH_3	−78	−33	very soluble
Primary Amines				
methylamine	CH_3NH_2	−95	−6	very soluble
ethylamine	$CH_3CH_2NH_2$	−81	17	very soluble
propylamine	$CH_3CH_2CH_2NH_2$	−83	48	very soluble
butylamine	$CH_3(CH_2)_3NH_2$	−49	78	very soluble
benzylamine	$C_6H_5CH_2NH_2$	10	185	very soluble
cyclohexylamine	$C_6H_{11}NH_2$	−17	135	slightly soluble
Secondary Amines				
dimethylamine	$(CH_3)_2NH$	−93	7	very soluble
diethylamine	$(CH_3CH_2)_2NH$	−48	56	very soluble
Tertiary Amines				
trimethylamine	$(CH_3)_3N$	−117	3	very soluble
triethylamine	$(CH_3CH_2)_3N$	−114	89	slightly soluble
Aromatic Amines				
aniline	$C_6H_5NH_2$	−6	184	slightly soluble
Heterocyclic Aromatic Amines				
pyridine	C_5H_5N	−42	116	very soluble

Both compounds have polar molecules and interact in the pure liquid by hydrogen bonding. Methanol has the higher boiling point because hydrogen bonding between its molecules is stronger than that between molecules of methylamine.

All classes of amines form hydrogen bonds with water and are more soluble in water than are hydrocarbons of comparable molecular weight. Most low-molecular-weight amines are completely soluble in water (Table 10.1). Higher-molecular-weight amines are only moderately soluble or insoluble.

EXAMPLE 10.4

Account for the fact that butylamine has a higher boiling point than *t*-butylamine.

Butylamine
bp 78 °C

t-Butylamine
bp 46 °C

STRATEGY

Identify structural differences that might affect the intermolecular attractions between the molecules of each compound.

SOLUTION

Both molecules can participate in hydrogen bonding. However, the *t*-butyl group is larger and bulkier, making it more difficult for the molecules of *t*-butylamine to hydrogen bond to each other.

See problems 10.18–10.20

PROBLEM 10.4

Account for the fact that diethylamine has a higher boiling point than diethyl ether.

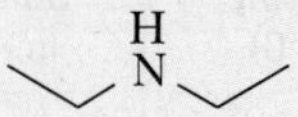

Diethylamine
bp 55 °C

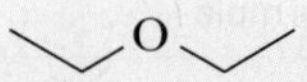

Diethyl ether
bp 34.6 °C

10.4 What Are the Acid–Base Properties of Amines?

Like ammonia, all amines are weak bases, and aqueous solutions of amines are basic. The following acid–base reaction between an amine and water is written using curved arrows to emphasize that, in this proton-transfer reaction, the unshared pair of electrons on nitrogen forms a new covalent bond with hydrogen and displaces hydroxide ion:

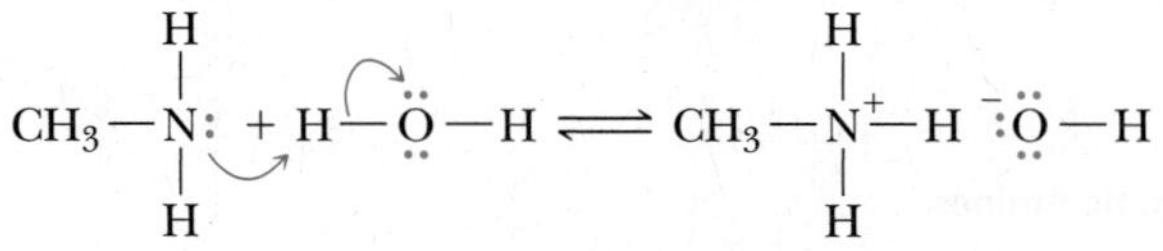

Methylamine

Methylammonium hydroxide

The equilibrium constant for the reaction of an amine with water, K_{eq}, has the following form, illustrated for the reaction of methylamine with water to give methylammonium hydroxide:

$$K_{eq} = \frac{[CH_3NH_3^+][OH^-]}{[CH_3NH_2][H_2O]}$$

Because the concentration of water in dilute solutions of methylamine in water is essentially a constant ($[H_2O] = 55.5$ mol/L), it is combined with K_{eq} in a new constant called a *base ionization constant*, K_b. The value of K_b for methylamine is 4.37×10^{-4} ($pK_b = 3.36$):

$$K_b = K_{eq}[H_2O] = \frac{[CH_3NH_3^+][OH^-]}{[CH_3NH_2]} = 4.37 \times 10^{-4} \quad pK_b = 3.36$$

It is also common to discuss the basicity of amines by referring to the acid ionization constant of the corresponding conjugate acid, as illustrated for the ionization of the methylammonium ion:

$$CH_3NH_3^+ + H_2O \rightleftharpoons CH_3NH_2 + H_3O^+$$

$$K_a = \frac{[CH_3NH_2][H_3O^+]}{[CH_3NH_3^+]} = 2.29 \times 10^{-11} \quad pK_a = 10.64$$

Values of pK_a and pK_b for any acid–conjugate base pair are related by the equation

$$pK_a + pK_b = 14.00$$

Values of pK_a and pK_b for selected amines are given in Table 10.2.

TABLE 10.2 Base Strengths (pK_b) of Selected Amines and Acid Strengths (pK_a) of Their Conjugate Acids*

Amine	Structure	pK_b	pK_a
Ammonia	NH_3	4.74	9.26
Primary Amines			
methylamine	CH_3NH_2	3.36	10.64
ethylamine	$CH_3CH_2NH_2$	3.19	10.81
cyclohexylamine	$C_6H_{11}NH_2$	3.34	10.66
Secondary Amines			
dimethylamine	$(CH_3)_2NH$	3.27	10.73
diethylamine	$(CH_3CH_2)_2NH$	3.02	10.98
Tertiary Amines			
trimethylamine	$(CH_3)_3N$	4.19	9.81
triethylamine	$(CH_3CH_2)_3N$	3.25	10.75
Aromatic Amines			
aniline	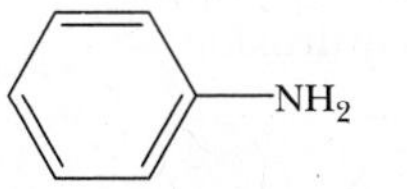	9.37	4.63
4-methylaniline (*p*-toluidine)	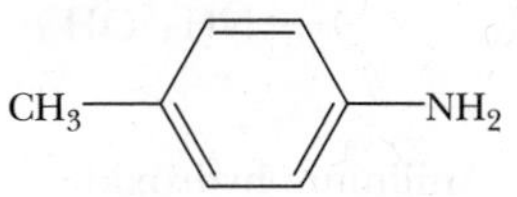	8.92	5.08
4-chloroaniline	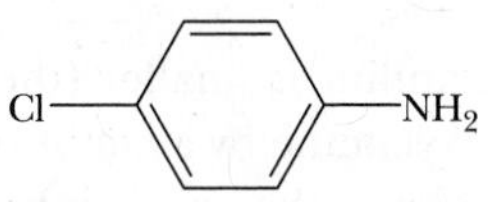	9.85	4.15
4-nitroaniline	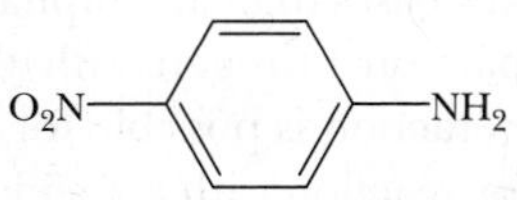	13.0	1.0
Heterocyclic Aromatic Amines			
pyridine	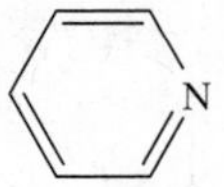	8.75	5.25
imidazole	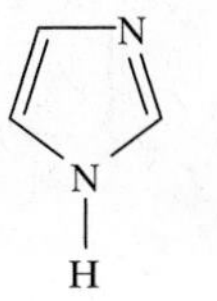	7.05	6.95

*For each amine, $pK_a + pK_b = 14.00$.

EXAMPLE 10.5

Predict the position of equilibrium for this acid–base reaction:

$$CH_3NH_2 + CH_3COOH \rightleftharpoons CH_3NH_3^+ + CH_3COO^-$$

STRATEGY

Use the approach we developed in Section 2.4 to predict the position of equilibrium in acid–base reactions. Equilibrium favors reaction of the stronger acid and stronger base to form the weaker acid and the weaker base. It is helpful to remember that even though ammonium ions are positively charged, they are much weaker acids than carboxylic acids.

SOLUTION

In this reaction, equilibrium favors the formation of methylammonium ion and acetate ion, which are the weaker acid and base, respectively:

$$CH_3NH_2 + CH_3COOH \rightleftharpoons CH_3NH_3^+ + CH_3COO^-$$

CH_3NH_2	CH_3COOH	$CH_3NH_3^+$	CH_3COO^-
	$pK_a = 4.76$	$pK_a = 10.64$	
Stronger base	Stronger acid	Weaker acid	Weaker base

See problem 10.25

PROBLEM 10.5

Predict the position of equilibrium for this acid–base reaction:

$$CH_3NH_3^+ + H_2O \rightleftharpoons CH_3NH_2 + H_3O^+$$

Given information such as that in Table 10.2, we can make the following generalizations about the acid–base properties of the various classes of amines:

1. All aliphatic amines have about the same base strength, pK_b 3.0–4.0, and are slightly stronger bases than ammonia.
2. Aromatic amines and heterocyclic aromatic amines are considerably weaker bases than are aliphatic amines. Compare, for example, values of pK_b for aniline and cyclohexylamine:

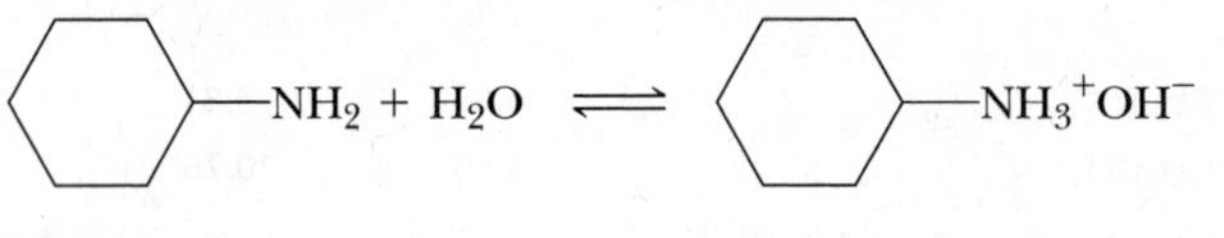

Cyclohexylamine — Cyclohexylammonium hydroxide

$pK_b = 3.34$
$K_b = 4.5 \times 10^{-4}$

the lower the value of pK_b, the stronger the base

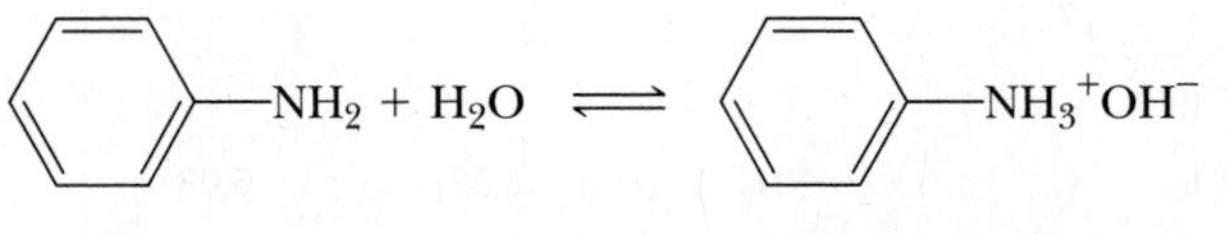

Aniline — Anilinium hydroxide

$pK_b = 9.37$
$K_b = 4.3 \times 10^{-10}$

The base ionization constant for aniline is smaller (the larger the value of pK_b, the weaker is the base) than that for cyclohexylamine by a factor of 10^6.

Aromatic amines are weaker bases than are aliphatic amines because of the resonance interaction of the unshared pair on nitrogen with the pi system of the aromatic ring. Because no such resonance interaction is possible for an alkylamine, the electron pair on its nitrogen is more available for reaction with an acid:

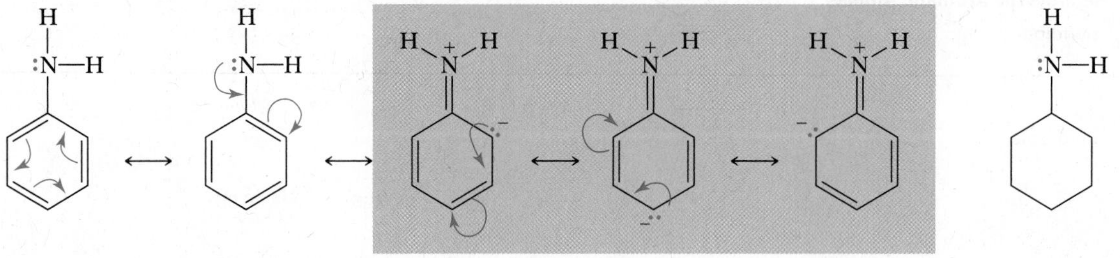

Two Kekulé structures

Interaction of the electron pair on nitrogen with the pi system of the aromatic ring reduces the availability of the electron pair to participate in a reaction with an acid

No resonance is possible with alkylamines

3. Electron-withdrawing groups such as halogen, nitro, and carbonyl decrease the basicity of substituted aromatic amines by decreasing the availability of the electron pair on nitrogen:

$-NO_2$ reduces the availability of the electron pair on nitrogen to participate in a reaction with an acid via both an inductive effect and a resonance effect

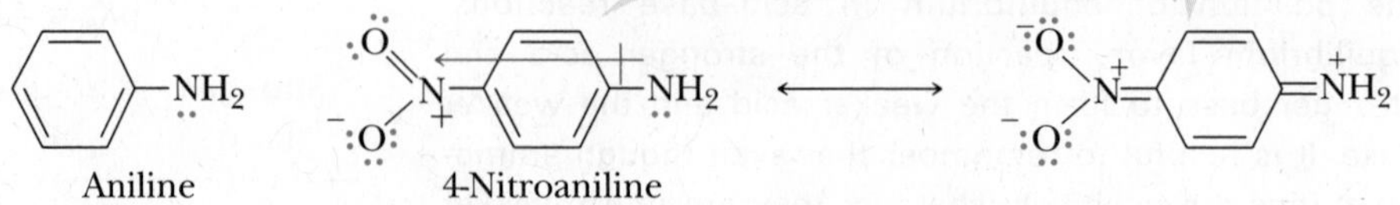

Aniline
pK_b 9.37

4-Nitroaniline
pK_b 13.0

Recall from Section 9.8B that these same substituents increase the acidity of phenols.

HOW TO 10.1

Predict the Relative Basicity of Amines

The basicity of an amine depends on the ability of its nitrogen atom to donate its lone pair of electrons in an acid–base reaction. When assessing an electron pair's availability, look for the following possibilities:

(a) Resonance contribution

this electron pair cannot participate in resonance and is therefore readily available to react with an acid

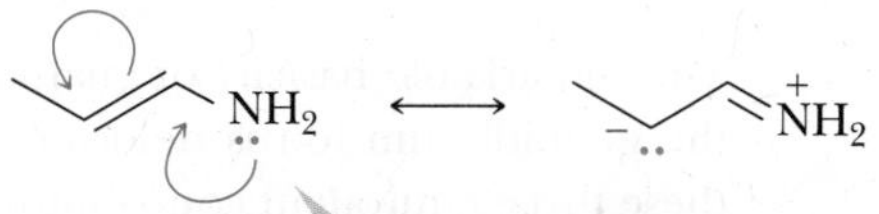

this electron pair is delocalized by resonance and is therefore less available to react with an acid. This feature of resonance delocalized amines makes them less basic

(b) Induction

this electron pair cannot participate in induction and is therefore readily available to react with an acid

this electron pair is delocalized by the inductive effect from the electronegative fluorine atom and is therefore less available to react with an acid. This results in reduced basicity

EXAMPLE 10.6

Select the stronger base in each pair of amines:

(a) 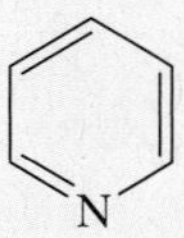 or 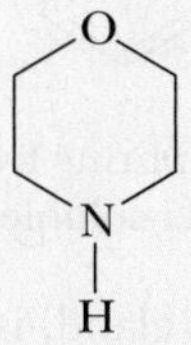

(A) (B)

(b) 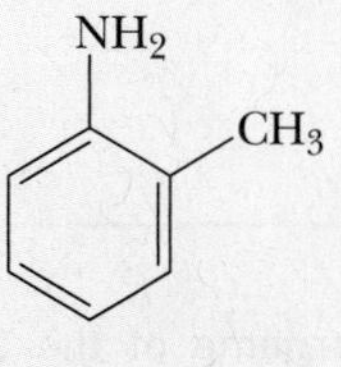 or 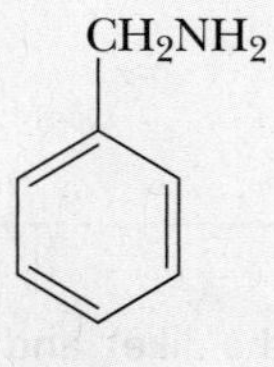

(C) (D)

STRATEGY

Use Table 10.2 to compare values of pK_b. Alternatively, look for resonance, inductive, or steric effects that might enhance or diminish the availability of a lone pair on the nitrogen of each molecule.

SOLUTION

(a) Morpholine (B) is the stronger base (pK_b 5.79). It has a basicity comparable to that of secondary aliphatic amines. Pyridine (A), a heterocyclic aromatic amine (pK_b 8.75), is considerably less basic than aliphatic amines.

(b) Benzylamine (D), a primary aliphatic amine, is the stronger base (pK_b 3–4). *o*-Toluidine (C), an aromatic amine, is the weaker base (pK_b 9–10). In the absence of Table 10.2, one can see that the electron pair on nitrogen in *o*-toluidine can participate in resonance with the benzene ring, while there are no resonance possibilities in benzylamine. This results in *o*-toluidine's electron pair being less available for reaction with an acid.

See problems 10.21–10.25, 10.29–10.31

PROBLEM 10.6

Select the stronger acid from each pair of ions:

(a) 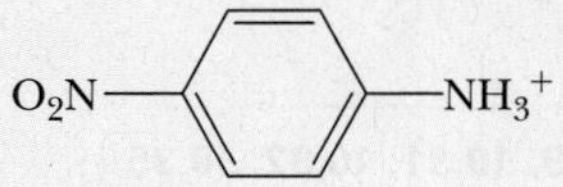 or 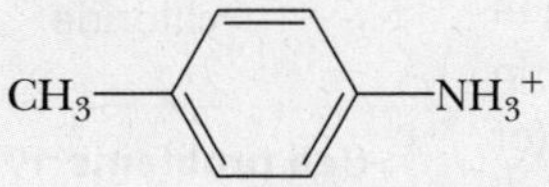 **(b)** 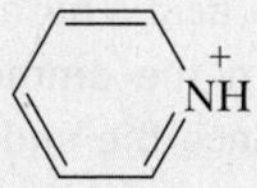 or 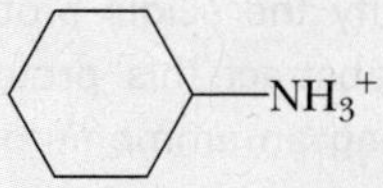

(A) (B) (C) (D)

Guanidine (pK_b 0.4) is the strongest base among neutral compounds:

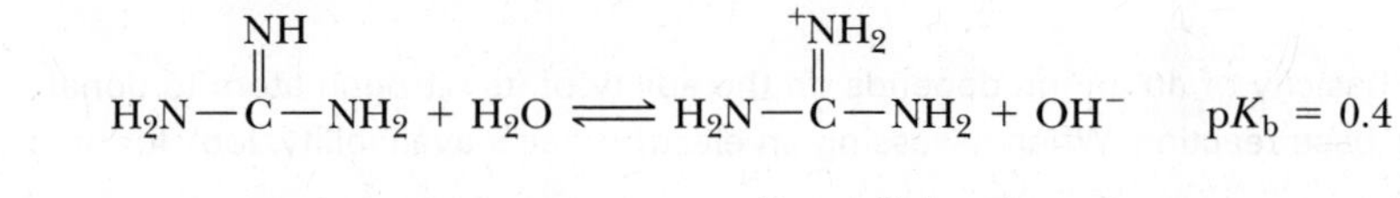

Guanidine Guanidinium ion

The remarkable basicity of guanidine is attributed to the fact that the positive charge on the guanidinium ion is delocalized equally over the three nitrogen atoms, as shown by these three equivalent contributing structures:

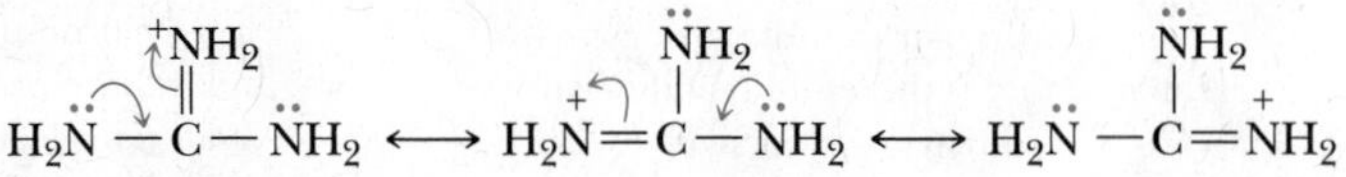

Three equivalent contributing structures

Hence, the guanidinium ion is a highly stable cation. The presence of a guanidine group on the side chain of the amino acid arginine accounts for the basicity of its side chain (Section 18.2A).

10.5 What Are the Reactions of Amines with Acids?

Amines, whether soluble or insoluble in water, react quantitatively with strong acids to form water-soluble salts, as illustrated by the reaction of (*R*)-norepinephrine (noradrenaline) with aqueous HCl to form a hydrochloride salt:

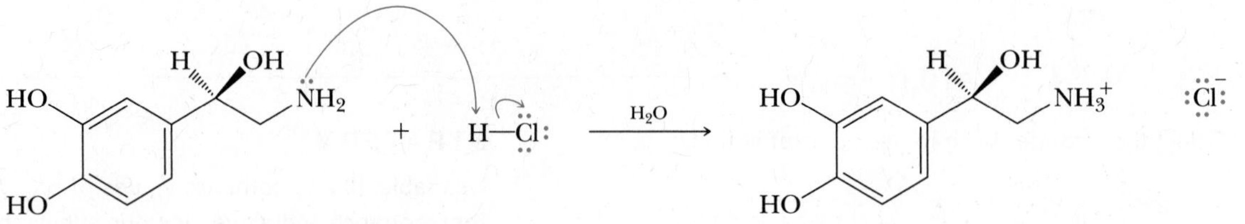

(*R*)-Norepinephrine (only slightly soluble in water)

(*R*)-Norepinephrine hydrochloride (a water-soluble salt)

Norepinephrine, secreted by the medulla of the adrenal gland, is a neurotransmitter. It has been suggested that it is a neurotransmitter in those areas of the brain that mediate emotional behavior.

EXAMPLE 10.7

Complete each acid–base reaction, and name the salt formed:

(a) $(CH_3CH_2)_2NH + HCl \longrightarrow$

(b)

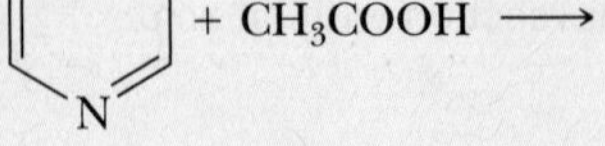

STRATEGY

Identify the acidic proton in the acid. The amine nitrogen will abstract this proton to form the ammonium salt. In naming an ammonium salt, replace the ending *-amine* (or aniline, pyridine, or the like) by *-ammonium* (or *anilinium*, *pyridinium*, or the like) and add the name of the anion (chloride, acetate, and so on).

SOLUTION

(a) $(CH_3CH_2)_2NH_2{}^+Cl^-$
Diethylammonium chloride

(b)

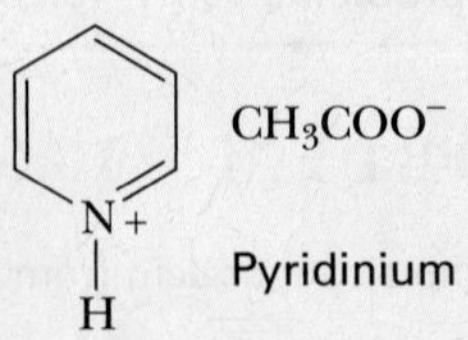

Pyridinium acetate

See problems 10.25, 10.29, 10.31, 10.32, 10.35

PROBLEM 10.7

Complete each acid–base reaction and name the salt formed:

(a) $(CH_3CH_2)_3N + HCl \longrightarrow$

(b) 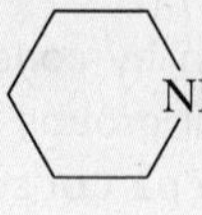 $NH + CH_3COOH \longrightarrow$

The basicity of amines and the solubility of amine salts in water can be used to separate amines from water-insoluble, nonbasic compounds. Shown in Figure 10.2 is a flowchart for the separation of aniline from anisole. Note that aniline is recovered from its salt by treatment with NaOH.

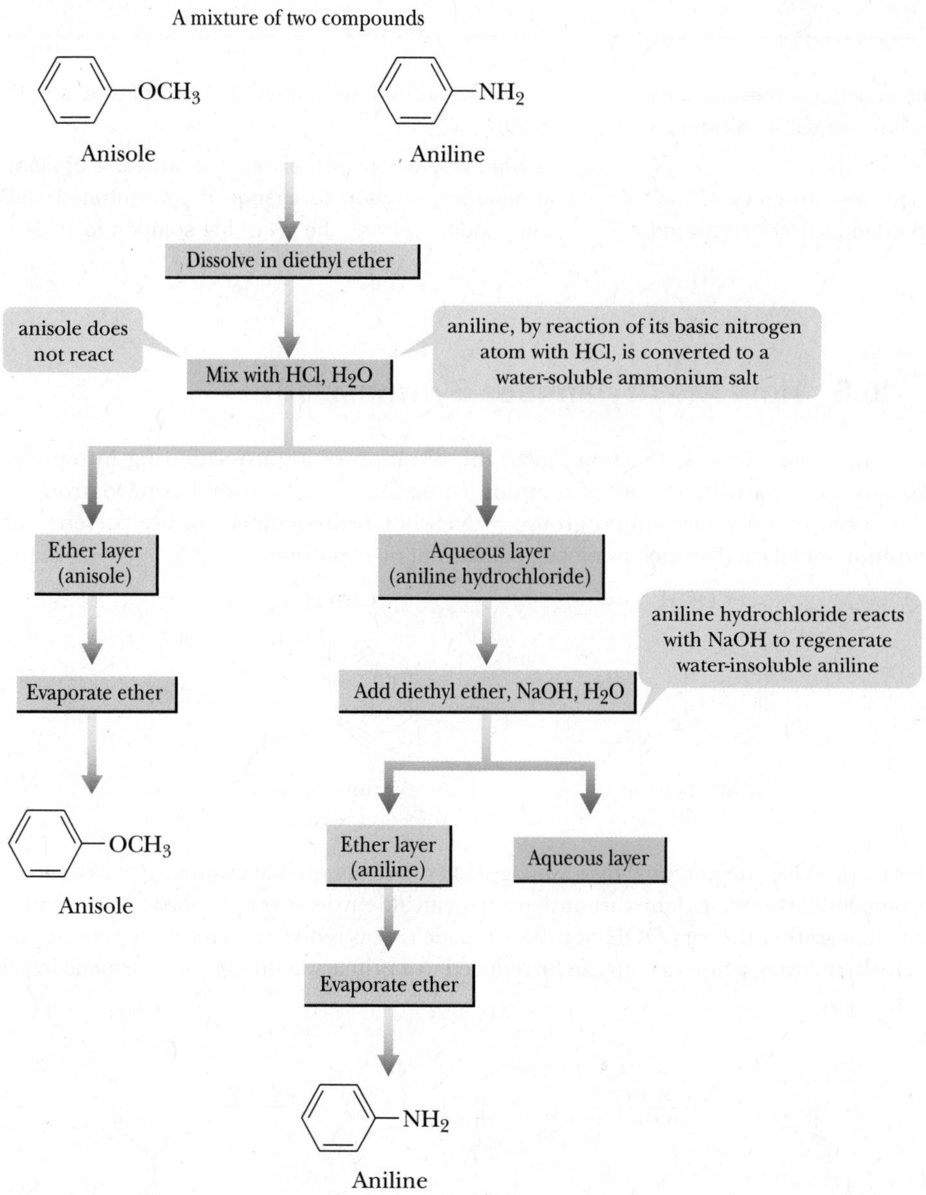

FIGURE 10.2
Separation and purification of an amine and a neutral compound.

EXAMPLE 10.8

Following are two structural formulas for alanine (2-aminopropanoic acid), one of the building blocks of proteins (Chapter 18):

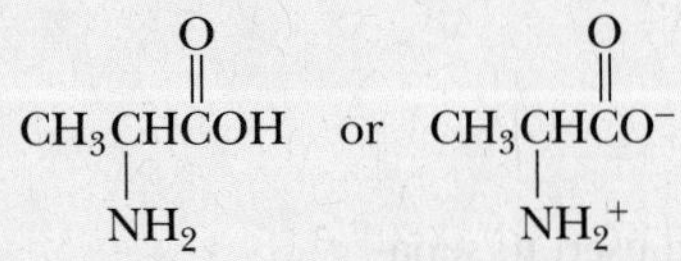

(A) (B)

Is alanine better represented by structural formula (A) or structural formula (B)?

STRATEGY

Begin by considering the acidity and basicity of the functional groups within alanine. How might they react if they were part of separate molecules?

SOLUTION

Structural formula (A) contains both an amino group (a base) and a carboxyl group (an acid). Proton transfer from the stronger acid (—COOH) to the stronger base (—NH_2) gives an internal salt; therefore, (B) is the better representation for alanine. Within the field of amino acid chemistry, the internal salt represented by (B) is called a **zwitterion** (Chapter 18).

PROBLEM 10.8

As shown in Example 10.8, alanine is better represented as an internal salt. Suppose that the internal salt is dissolved in water.

(a) In what way would you expect the structure of alanine in aqueous solution to change if concentrated HCl were added to adjust the pH of the solution to 2.0?

(b) In what way would you expect the structure of alanine in aqueous solution to change if concentrated NaOH were added to bring the pH of the solution to 12.0?

10.6 How Are Arylamines Synthesized?

As we have already seen (Section 9.6B), the nitration of an aromatic ring introduces a NO_2 group. A particular value of nitration is the fact that the resulting nitro group can be reduced to a primary amino group, —NH_2, by hydrogenation in the presence of a transition metal catalyst such as nickel, palladium, or platinum:

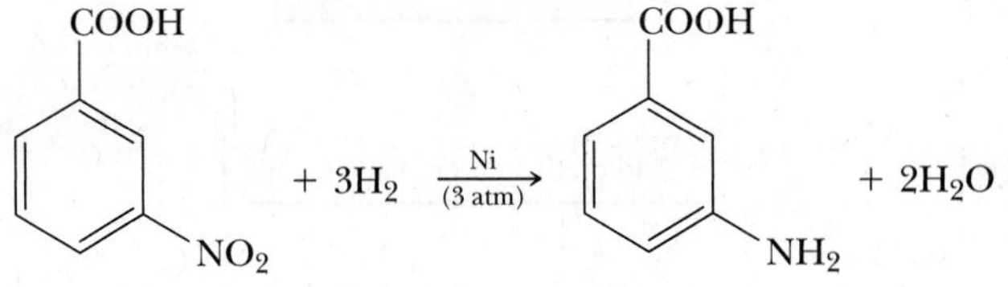

3-Nitrobenzoic acid — 3-Aminobenzoic acid

This method has the potential disadvantage that other susceptible groups, such as a carbon–carbon double bond, and the carbonyl group of an aldehyde or ketone, may also be reduced. Note that neither the —COOH nor the aromatic ring is reduced under these conditions.

Alternatively, a nitro group can be reduced to a primary amino group by a metal in acid:

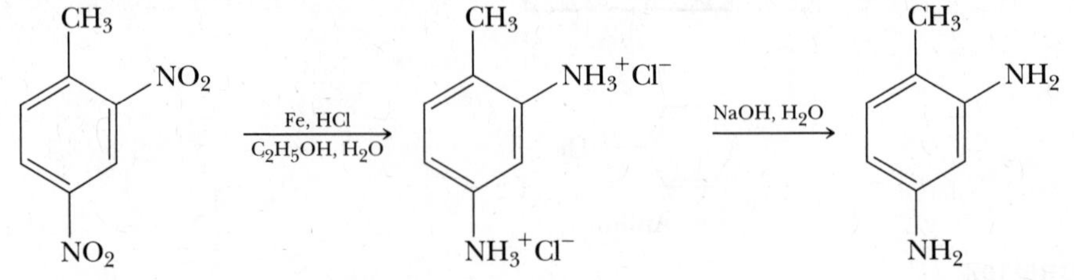

2,4-Dinitrotoluene — 2,4-Diaminotoluene

The most commonly used metal-reducing agents are iron, zinc, and tin in dilute HCl. When reduced by this method, the amine is obtained as a salt, which is then treated with a strong base to liberate the free amine.

EXAMPLE 10.9

Show the reagents that will bring about each step in this conversion of toluene to 4-aminobenzoic acid:

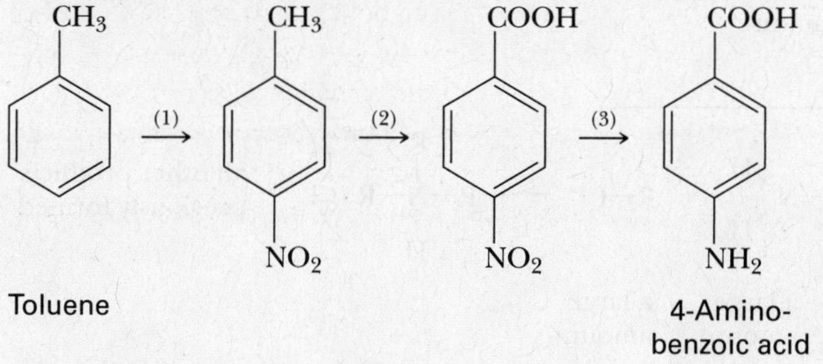

STRATEGY

Use a combination of reactions from this chapter and previous chapters. Remember to consider the regioselectivity of reactions.

SOLUTION

STEP 1: Nitration of toluene, using nitric acid/sulfuric acid (Section 9.6B), followed by separation of the ortho and para isomers.

STEP 2: Oxidation of the benzylic carbon, using chromic acid (Section 9.4).

STEP 3: Reduction of the nitro group, either using H_2 in the presence of a transition metal catalyst or using Fe, Sn, or Zn in the presence of aqueous HCl (Section 10.6).

See problems 10.36–10.44

PROBLEM 10.9

Show how you can use the same set of steps in Example 10.9, but in a different order, to convert toluene to 3-aminobenzoic acid.

10.7 How Do Amines Act as Nucleophiles?

In Chapter 7, we learned that amines are moderate nucleophiles (Table 7.2) due to the presence of a lone pair of electrons on the nitrogen atom. Therefore, they should undergo nucleophilic substitution reactions with haloalkanes and other compounds containing a good leaving group (Section 7.5).

Step 1: **Reaction of an electrophile and a nucleophile to form a new covalent bond.** The nitrogen atom of an amine displaces chlorine in a haloalkane to yield an ammonium chloride ion.

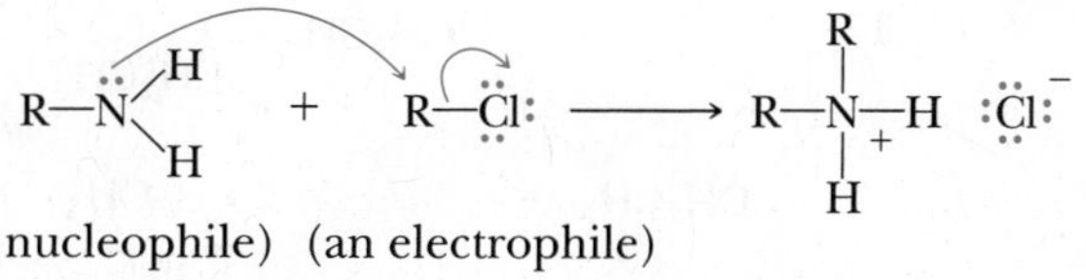

Step 2: **Take a proton away.** At the beginning of this reaction, when only a few product molecules are formed, plenty of amine starting material (a weak base) remains to react with the hydrogen of the ammonium salt to yield a secondary amine and another ammonium chloride ion.

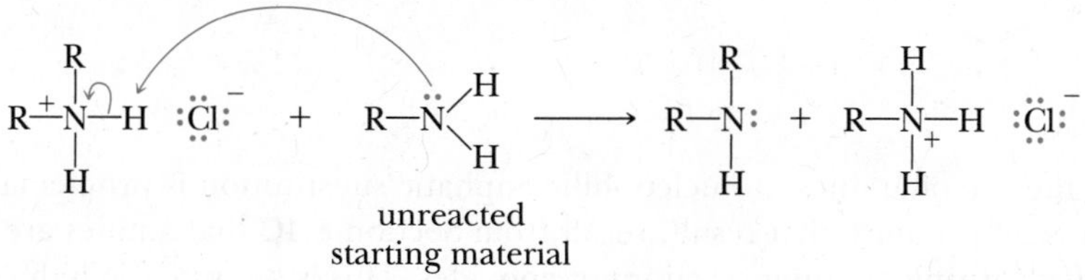

Remaining in the reaction mixture are some initial product, $R_2NH_2^+ \, Cl^-$, some of the secondary amine, R_2NH, and lots of unreacted starting material and haloalkane.

Step 3: Reaction of an electrophile and a nucleophile to form a new covalent bond. The secondary amine is also a nucleophile, and because only a few of the initial R—Cl molecules have reacted at this early stage of the reaction, there are plenty left to react with either amine now in the reaction mixture.

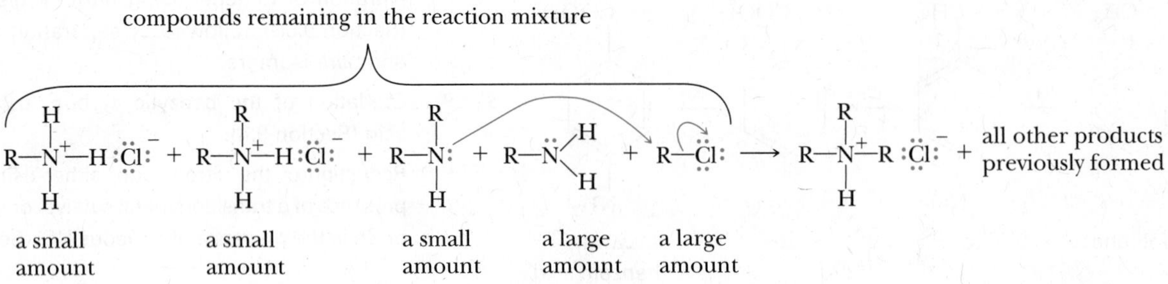

The process can continue to give one other nitrogen-based product, the quaternary ammonium salt. The final composition of the reaction will consist of varying ratios of RNH_2, R_2NH, R_3N, and $R_4N^+Cl^-$. Because the ratio of products is difficult to control or predict, we avoid using an amine (or ammonia) as a nucleophile in nucleophilic aliphatic substitution reactions.

EXAMPLE 10.10

Determine all possible nitrogen-based products that can be formed in the following reaction:

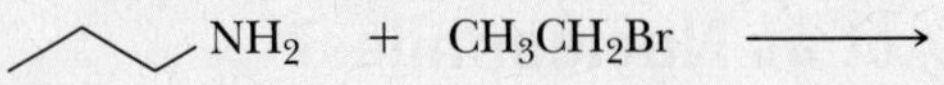

STRATEGY

Keep in mind that the reaction of amines with haloalkanes often results in multiple nitrogen-based products with one or more alkyl groups from the haloalkane forming a bond with the nitrogen atom of the original amine.

SOLUTION

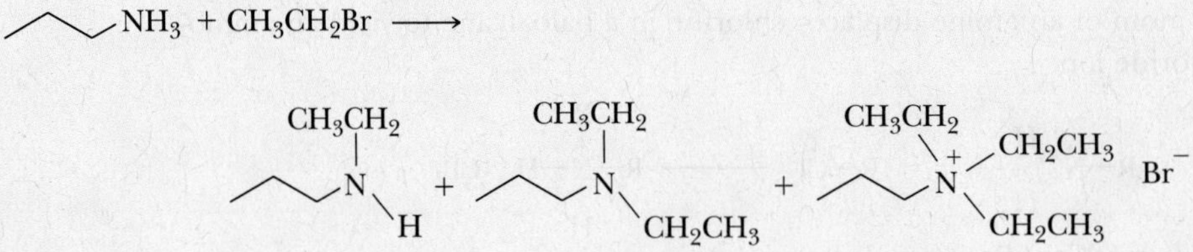

PROBLEM 10.10

Determine all possible nitrogen-based products that can be formed in the following reaction:

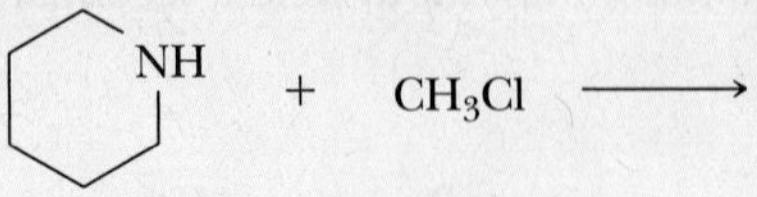

Although the use of amines in nucleophilic aliphatic substitution is problematic due to the mixtures of products that result, recall from Section 8.4C that amines are excellent nucleophiles for ring opening reactions of epoxides. This is because the inductive effect of the hydroxyl oxygen atom diminishes the nucleophilicity of the nitrogen atom in the product:

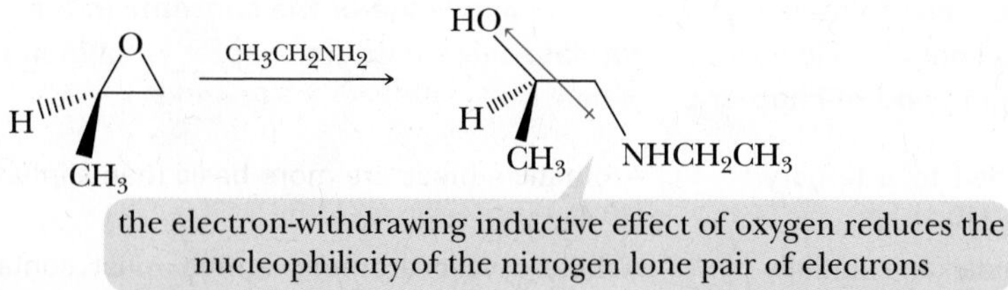

$CH_3CH_2NH_2$
HO
H
CH_3
$NHCH_2CH_3$
the electron-withdrawing inductive effect of oxygen reduces the nucleophilicity of the nitrogen lone pair of electrons

SUMMARY OF KEY QUESTIONS

10.1 What Are Amines?

- Amines are derivatives of ammonia (NH_3) in which one or more hydrogens are replaced by alkyl or aryl groups.
- Amines are classified as **primary**, **secondary**, or **tertiary**, depending on the number of hydrogen atoms of ammonia replaced by alkyl or aryl groups.
- In an **aliphatic amine**, all carbon atoms bonded to nitrogen are derived from alkyl groups.
- In an **aromatic amine**, one or more of the groups bonded to nitrogen are aryl groups.
- A **heterocyclic amine** is an amine in which the nitrogen atom is part of a ring.
- A **heterocyclic aromatic amine** is an amine in which the nitrogen atom is part of an aromatic ring.

10.2 How Are Amines Named?

- In systematic nomenclature, aliphatic amines are named **alkanamines**.
- In the common system of nomenclature, aliphatic amines are named **alkylamines**; the alkyl groups are listed in alphabetical order in one word ending in the suffix *-amine*.
- An ion containing nitrogen bonded to four alkyl or aryl groups is named as a **quaternary ammonium ion**.

10.3 What Are the Characteristic Physical Properties of Amines?

- Amines are polar compounds, and primary and secondary amines associate by intermolecular hydrogen bonding.
- Because an N—H----N hydrogen bond is weaker than an O—H----O hydrogen bond, amines have lower boiling points than alcohols of comparable molecular weight and structure.
- All classes of amines form hydrogen bonds with water and are more soluble in water than are hydrocarbons of comparable molecular weight.

10.4 What Are the Acid–Base Properties of Amines?

- Amines are weak bases, and aqueous solutions of amines are basic. The **base ionization constant** for an amine in water is given the symbol K_b.
- It is also common to discuss the acid–base properties of amines by reference to the **acid ionization constant**, K_a, for the conjugate acid of the amine.
- Acid and base ionization constants for an amine in water are related by the equation $pK_a + pK_b = 14.0$.

10.5 What Are the Reactions of Amines with Acids?

- Amines react quantitatively with strong acids to form water-soluble salts.
- The basicity of amines and the solubility of amine salts in water can be used to separate amines from water-insoluble, nonbasic compounds.

10.6 How Are Arylamines Synthesized?

- Arylamines can be made by reducing the nitro group on a benzene ring.

10.7 How Do Amines Act as Nucleophiles?

- Amines are moderate nucleophiles and can participate in **nucleophilic aliphatic substitution** reactions.
- Reaction of ammonia or amines with haloalkanes often results in multiple products in varying ratios.

QUICK QUIZ

Answer true or false to the following questions to assess your general knowledge of the concepts in this chapter. If you have difficulty with any of them, you should review the appropriate section in the chapter (shown in parentheses) before attempting the more challenging end-of-chapter problems.

1. An amine with an $-NH_2$ group bonded to a tertiary carbon is classified as a tertiary amine. (10.1)
2. The reaction of an amine with a haloalkane initially results in an ammonium halide salt. (10.7)
3. An efficient way to make diethylamine is to react ammonia with two equivalents of chloroethane. (10.7)
4. The IUPAC name of $CH_3CH_2CH_2CH_2NHCH_3$ is 2-pentanamine. (10.2)
5. An amino group can be directly added to a benzene ring via an electrophilic aromatic substitution reaction. (10.6)
6. A tertiary amine would be expected to be more water soluble than a secondary amine of the same molecular formula. (10.3)
7. The pK_b of an amine can be determined from the pK_a of its conjugate acid. (10.4)
8. The lower the value of pK_b, the stronger the base. (10.4)
9. The basicity of amines and the solubility of amine salts in water can be used to separate amines from water-insoluble, nonbasic compounds. (10.5)
10. Aromatic amines are more basic than aliphatic amines. (10.4)
11. A heterocyclic aromatic amine must contain one or more aryl groups directly bonded to nitrogen outside of the ring. (10.1)
12. Guanidine is a strong neutral base because its conjugate acid is resonance stabilized. (10.4)
13. Ammonia is a slightly weaker base than most aliphatic amines. (10.4)
14. An amino group forms stronger hydrogen bonds than a hydroxy group. (10.3)
15. A heterocyclic amine must contain a ring and a nitrogen atom as a member of the ring. (10.1)
16. An electron-withdrawing group in an amine decreases its basicity. (10.4)

Answers: (1) F (2) T (3) F (4) F (5) F (6) F (7) T (8) T (9) T (10) F (11) F (12) T (13) T (14) F (15) T (16) T

Detailed explanations for many of these answers can be found in the accompanying Solutions Manual.

KEY REACTIONS

1. Basicity of Aliphatic Amines (Section 10.4)

Most aliphatic amines have comparable basicities (pK_b 3.0–4.0) and are slightly stronger bases than ammonia:

$$CH_3NH_2 + H_2O \rightleftharpoons CH_3NH_3^+ + OH^- \qquad pK_b = 3.36$$

2. Basicity of Aromatic Amines (Section 10.4)

Aromatic amines (pK_b 9.0–10.0) are considerably weaker bases than are aliphatic amines. Resonance stabilization from interaction of the unshared electron pair on nitrogen with the pi system of the aromatic ring decreases the availability of that electron pair for reaction with an acid. Substitution on the ring by electron-withdrawing groups decreases the basicity of the $-NH_2$ group:

$pK_b = 9.37$

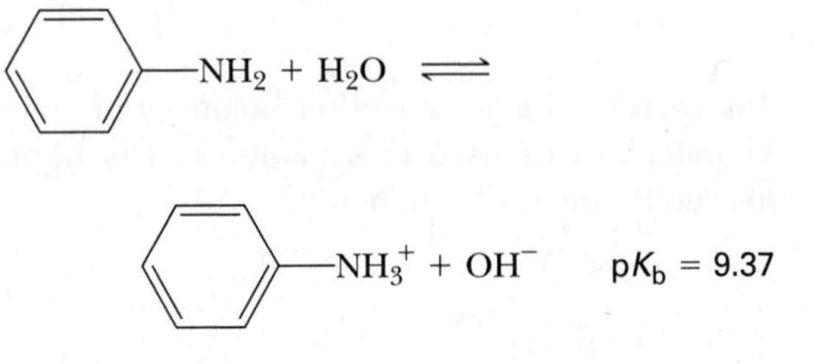

3. Reaction of Amines with Strong Acids (Section 10.5)

All amines react quantitatively with strong acids to form water-soluble salts:

Insoluble in water — A water-soluble salt

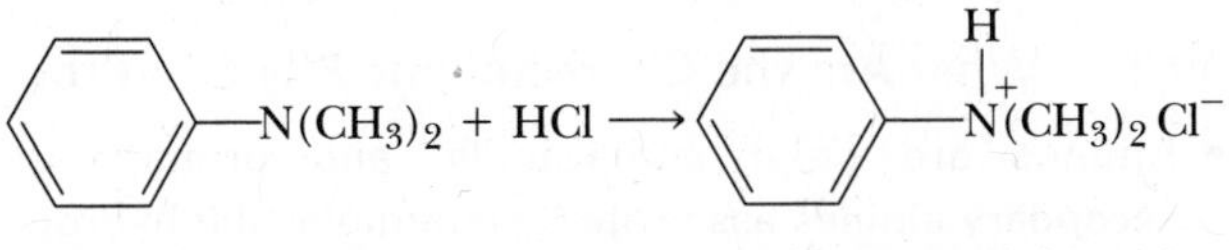

4. Reduction of an Aromatic NO_2 Group (Section 10.6)

An NO_2 group, for example on an aromatic ring, can be reduced to an amino group by catalytic hydrogenation or by treatment with a metal and hydrochloric acid, followed by a strong base to liberate the free amine:

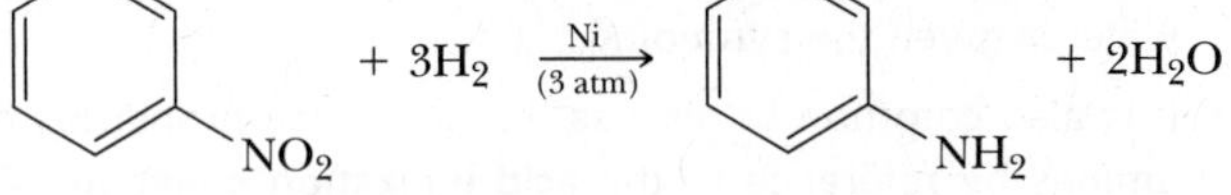

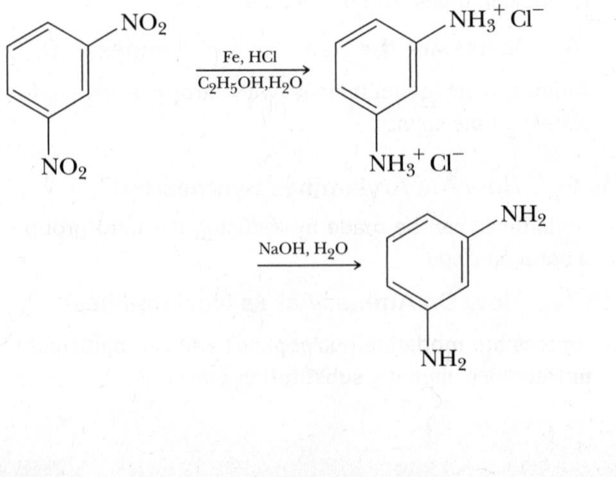

PROBLEMS

A problem marked with an asterisk indicates an applied "real-world" problem. Answers to problems whose numbers are printed in blue are given in Appendix D.

Structure and Nomenclature

10.11 Draw a structural formula for each amine: **(See Examples 10.2, 10.3)**

(a) (*R*)-2-Butanamine
(b) 1-Octanamine
(c) 2,2-Dimethyl-1-propanamine
(d) 1,5-Pentanediamine
(e) 2-Bromoaniline
(f) Tributylamine
(g) *N,N*-Dimethylaniline
(h) Benzylamine
(i) *tert*-Butylamine
(j) *N*-Ethylcyclohexanamine
(k) Diphenylamine
(l) Isobutylamine

10.12 Draw a structural formula for each amine: **(See Examples 10.2, 10.3)**

(a) 4-Aminobutanoic acid
(b) 2-Aminoethanol (ethanolamine)
(c) 2-Aminobenzoic acid
(d) (*S*)-2-Aminopropanoic acid (alanine)
(e) 4-Aminobutanal
(f) 4-Amino-2-butanone

10.13 Draw examples of 1°, 2°, and 3° amines that contain at least four sp^3 hybridized carbon atoms. Using the same criterion, provide examples of 1°, 2°, and 3° alcohols. How does the classification system differ between the two functional groups? **(See Example 10.1)**

***10.14** Classify each amino group as primary, secondary, or tertiary and as aliphatic or aromatic: **(See Example 10.1)**

(a)

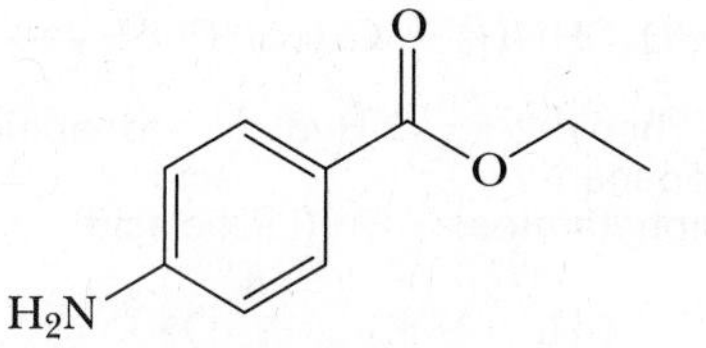

Benzocaine
(a topical anesthetic)

(b)

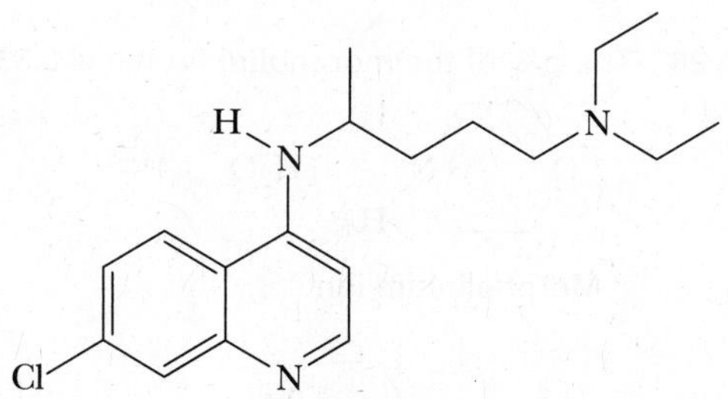

Chloroquine
(a drug for the treatment of malaria)

***10.15** Epinephrine is a hormone secreted by the adrenal medulla. Among epinephrine's actions, it is a bronchodilator. Albuterol, sold under several trade names, including Proventil® and Salbumol®, is one of the most effective and widely prescribed antiasthma drugs. The R enantiomer of albuterol is 68 times more effective in the treatment of asthma than the S enantiomer. **(See Example 10.1)**

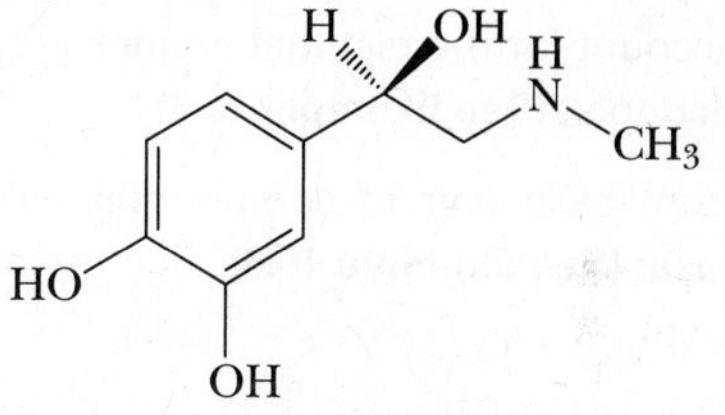

(*R*)-Epinephrine
(Adrenaline)

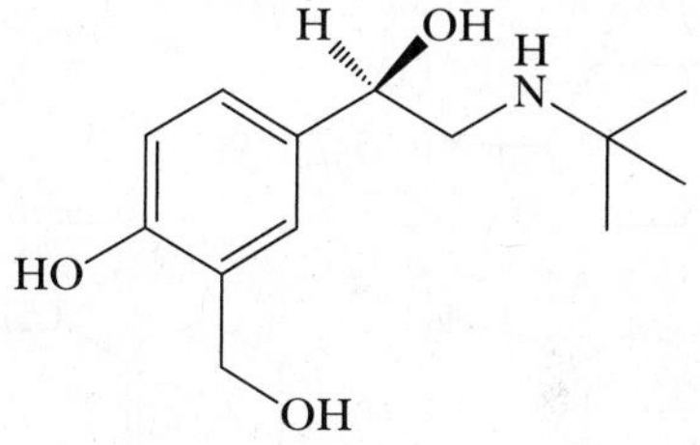

(*R*)-Albuterol

(a) Classify each amino group as primary, secondary, or tertiary.
(b) List the similarities and differences between the structural formulas of these compounds.

10.16 There are eight constitutional isomers with the molecular formula $C_4H_{11}N$. Name and draw structural formulas for each. Classify each amine as primary, secondary, or tertiary. **(See Examples 10.1–10.3)**

10.17 Draw a structural formula for each compound with the given molecular formula: **(See Example 10.3)**

(a) A 2° arylamine, C_7H_9N
(b) A 3° arylamine, $C_8H_{11}N$
(c) A 1° aliphatic amine, C_7H_9N
(d) A chiral 1° amine, $C_4H_{11}N$
(e) A 3° heterocyclic amine, $C_5H_{11}N$
(f) A trisubstituted 1° arylamine, $C_9H_{13}N$
(g) A chiral quaternary ammonium salt, $C_9H_{22}NCl$

Physical Properties

10.18 Propylamine, ethylmethylamine, and trimethylamine are constitutional isomers with the molecular formula C_3H_9N: **(See Example 10.4)**

$CH_3CH_2CH_2NH_2$	$CH_3CH_2NHCH_3$	$(CH_3)_3N$
bp 48 °C	bp 37 °C	bp 3 °C
Propylamine	Ethylmethylamine	Trimethylamine

Account for the fact that trimethylamine has the lowest boiling point of the three, and propylamine has the highest.

10.19 Account for the fact that 1-butanamine has a lower boiling point than 1-butanol: **(See Example 10.4)**

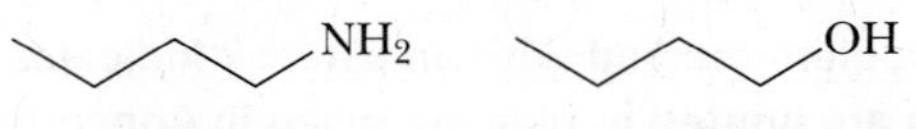

bp 78 °C
1-Butanamine

bp 117 °C
1-Butanol

***10.20** Account for the fact that putrescine, a foul-smelling compound produced by rotting flesh, ceases to smell upon treatment with two equivalents of HCl: **(See Example 10.4)**

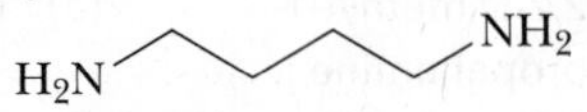

1,4-Butanediamine
(Putrescine)

Basicity of Amines

10.21 Account for the fact that amines are more basic than alcohols. **(See Example 10.6)**

10.22 From each pair of compounds, select the stronger base: **(See Example 10.6)**

(a) 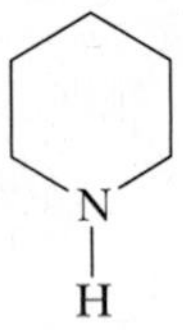 or 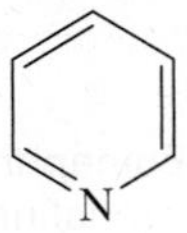

(b) 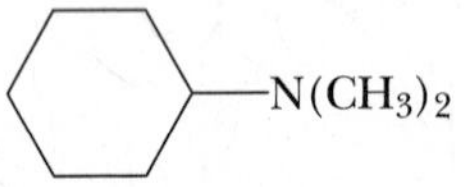 or 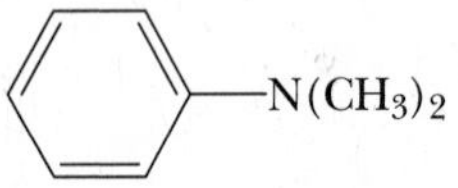

(c) 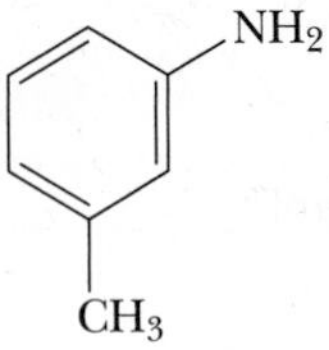 or 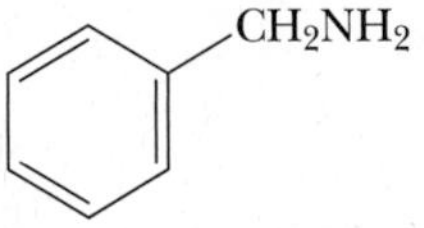

(d) 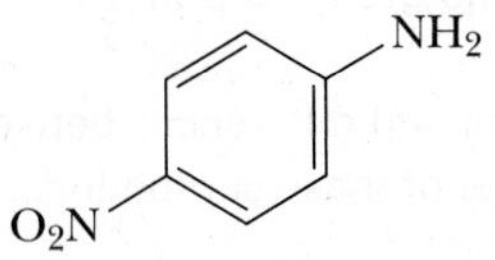 or 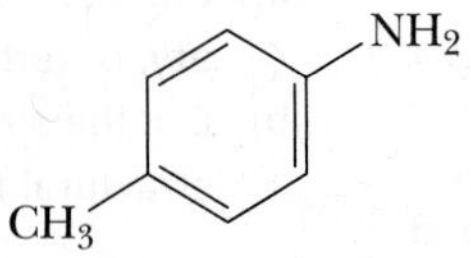

10.23 Account for the fact that substitution of a nitro group makes an aromatic amine a weaker base, but makes a phenol a stronger acid. For example, 4-nitroaniline is a weaker base than aniline, but 4-nitrophenol is a stronger acid than phenol. **(See Example 10.6)**

10.24 Select the stronger base in this pair of compounds: **(See Example 10.6)**

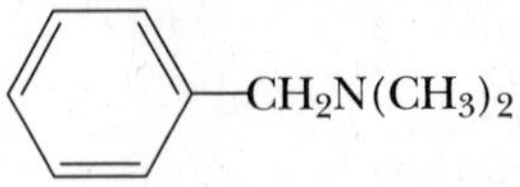 or 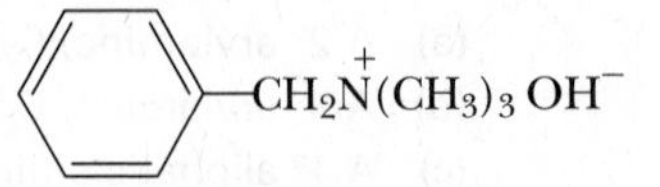

10.25 Complete the following acid–base reactions and predict the position of equilibrium for each. Justify your prediction by citing values of pK_a for the stronger and weaker acid in each equilibrium. For values of acid ionization constants, consult Table 2.2 (pK_a's of some inorganic and organic acids), Table 8.2 (pK_a's of alcohols), Section 9.8B (acidity of phenols), and Table 10.2 (base strengths of amines). Where no ionization constants are given, make the best estimate from aforementioned tables and section. **(See Examples 10.5–10.7)**

(a) CH_3COOH + 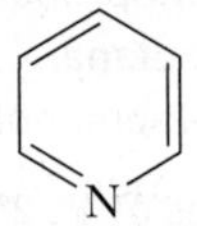 $\rightleftharpoons$

Acetic acid   Pyridine

(b) 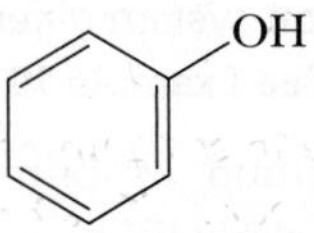 + $(CH_3CH_2)_3N$ $\rightleftharpoons$

Phenol   Triethylamine

(c) $PhCH_2CH(CH_3)NH_2 + CH_3CH(OH)COH(=O) \rightleftharpoons$

1-Phenyl-2-propanamine (Amphetamine)   2-Hydroxypropanoic acid (Lactic acid)

(d) $PhCH_2CH(CH_3)NHCH_3 + CH_3C(=O)OH \rightleftharpoons$

Methamphetamine   Acetic acid

10.26 The pK_a of the morpholinium ion is 8.33:

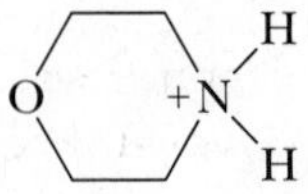 $+ H_2O \rightleftharpoons$

Morpholinium ion

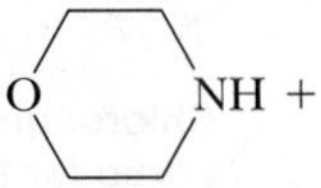 $+ H_3O^+$ pK_a=8.33

Morpholine

(a) Calculate the ratio of morpholine to morpholinium ion in aqueous solution at p*H* 7.0.
(b) At what p*H* are the concentrations of morpholine and morpholinium ion equal?

***10.27** The pK_b of amphetamine (Example 10.2e) is approximately 3.2. Calculate the ratio of amphetamine to its conjugate acid at p*H* 7.4, the p*H* of blood plasma.

10.28 Calculate the ratio of amphetamine to its conjugate acid at p*H* 1.0, such as might be present in stomach acid.

***10.29** Following is a structural formula of pyridoxamine, one form of vitamin B_6: **(See Examples 10.6, 10.7)**

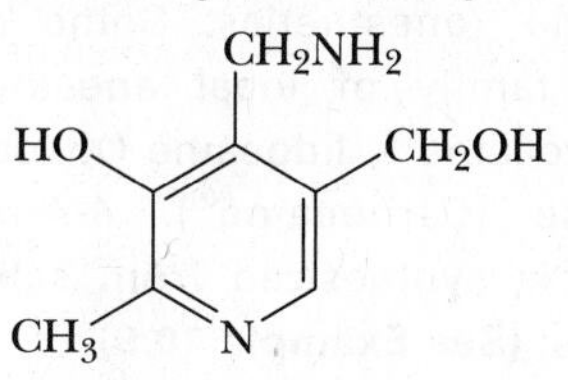

Pyridoxamine
(Vitamin B_6)

(a) Which nitrogen atom of pyridoxamine is the stronger base?
(b) Draw the structural formula of the hydrochloride salt formed when pyridoxamine is treated with one mole of HCl.

***10.30** Epibatidine, a colorless oil isolated from the skin of the Ecuadorian poison frog *Epipedobates tricolor*, has several times the analgesic potency of morphine. It is the first chlorine-containing, nonopioid (nonmorphine-like in structure) analgesic ever isolated from a natural source: **(See Example 10.6)**

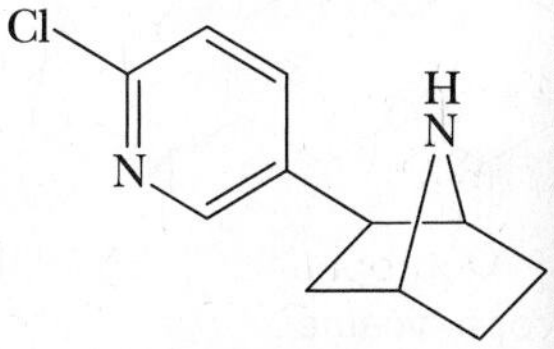

Epibatidine

Stephen J. Krasemann/Photo Researchers

Poison arrow frog.

(a) Which of the two nitrogen atoms of epibatidine is the more basic?
(b) Mark all stereocenters in this molecule.

***10.31** Procaine was one of the first local anesthetics for infiltration and regional anesthesia: **(See Examples 10.6, 10.7)**

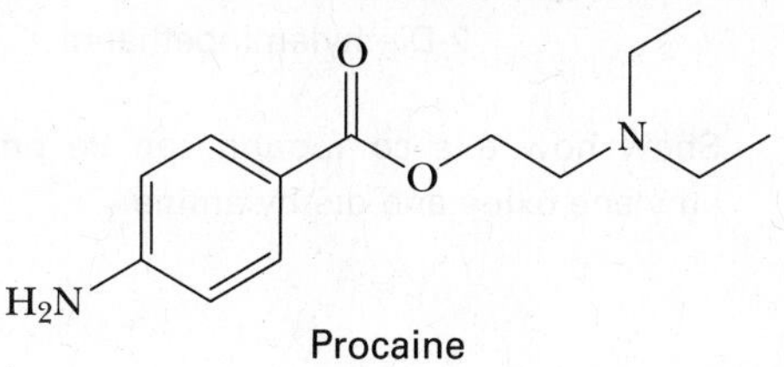

Procaine

The hydrochloride salt of procaine is marketed as Novocaine®.

(a) Which nitrogen atom of procaine is the stronger base?
(b) Draw the formula of the salt formed by treating procaine with one mole of HCl.
(c) Is procaine chiral? Would a solution of Novocaine in water be optically active or optically inactive?

***10.32** Treatment of trimethylamine with 2-chloroethyl acetate gives the neurotransmitter acetylcholine as its chloride salt: **(See Example 10.7)**

$$(CH_3)_3N + CH_3\overset{\overset{\displaystyle O}{\|}}{C}OCH_2CH_2Cl \longrightarrow C_7H_{16}ClNO_2$$

Acetylcholine chloride

Propose a structural formula for this quaternary ammonium salt and a mechanism for its formation.

10.33 Aniline is prepared by the catalytic reduction of nitrobenzene:

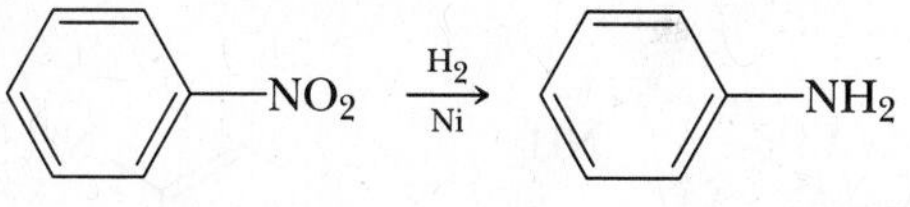

Devise a chemical procedure based on the basicity of aniline to separate it from any unreacted nitrobenzene.

10.34 Suppose that you have a mixture of the following three compounds:

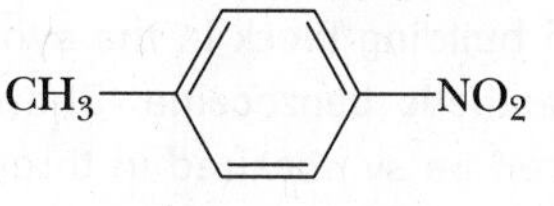

4-Nitrotoluene
(*p*-Nitrotoluene)

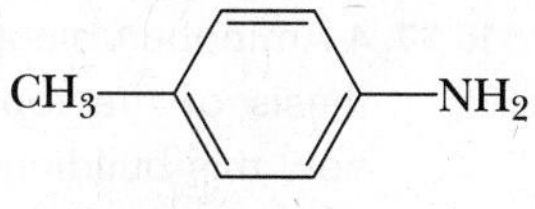

4-Methylaniline
(*p*-Toluidine)

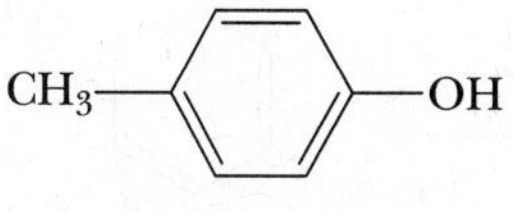

4-Methylphenol
(*p*-Cresol)

Devise a chemical procedure based on their relative acidity or basicity to separate and isolate each in pure form.

***10.35** Following is a structural formula for metformin, the hydrochloride salt of which is marketed as the antidiabetic Glucophage®: **(See Example 10.7)**

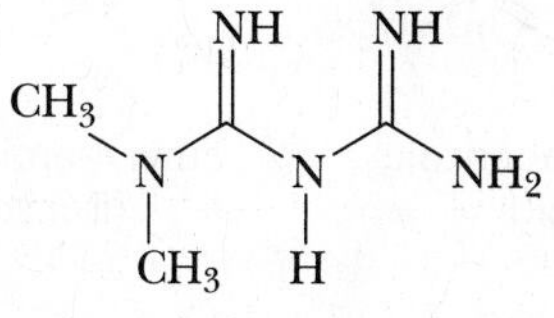

Metformin

Metformin was introduced into clinical medicine in the United States in 1995 for the treatment of type 2 diabetes. More than 25 million prescriptions for this drug were written in 2000, making it the most commonly prescribed brand-name diabetes medication in the nation.

(a) Draw the structural formula for Glucophage®.
(b) Would you predict Glucophage® to be soluble or insoluble in water? Soluble or insoluble in blood plasma? Would you predict it to be soluble or insoluble in diethyl ether? In dichloromethane? Explain your reasoning.

Synthesis

***10.36** 4-Aminophenol is a building block in the synthesis of the analgesic acetaminophen. Show how this building block can be synthesized in two steps from phenol (in Chapter 15, we will see how to complete the synthesis of acetaminophen): **(See Example 10.9)**

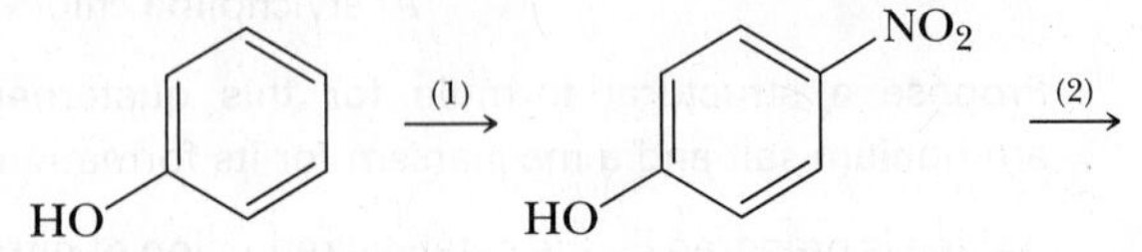

Phenol 4-Nitrophenol

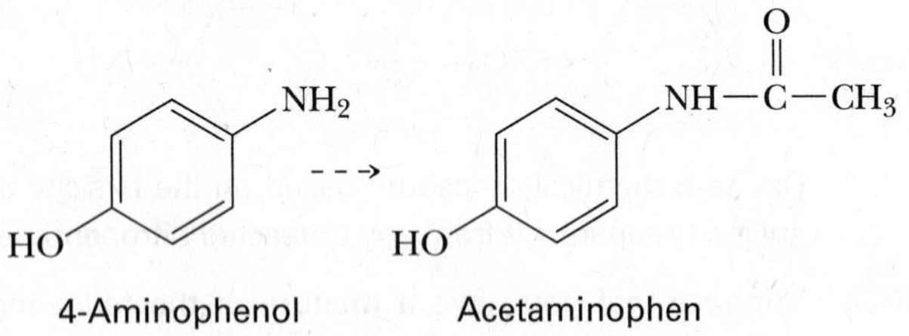

4-Aminophenol Acetaminophen

***10.37** 4-Aminobenzoic acid is a building block in the synthesis of the topical anesthetic benzocaine. Show how this building block can be synthesized in three steps from toluene (in Chapter 14, we will see how to complete the synthesis of benzocaine): **(See Example 10.9)**

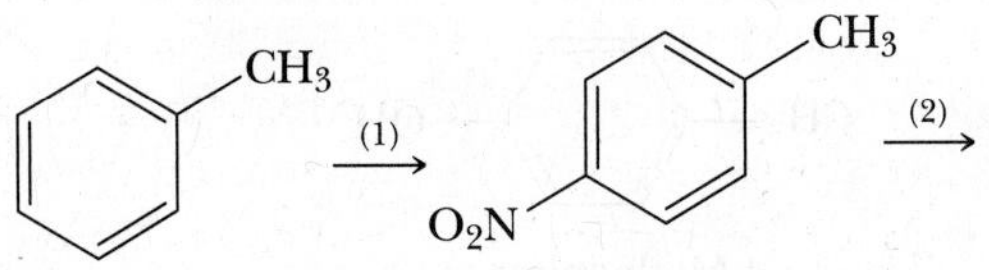

Toluene

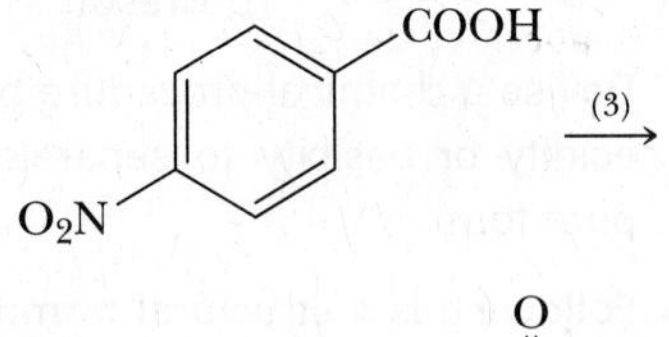

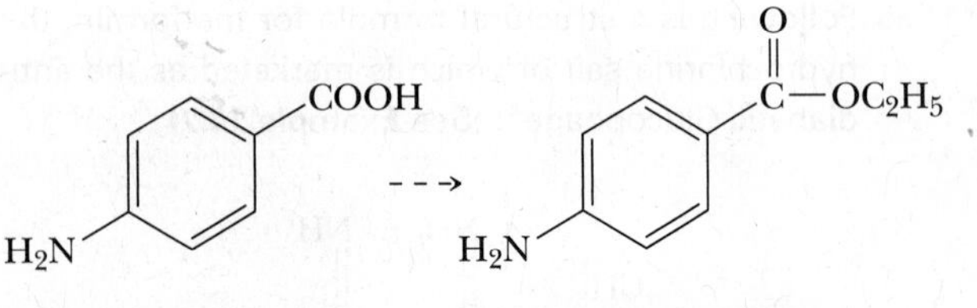

4-Aminobenzoic acid Ethyl 4-aminobenzoate (Benzocaine)

***10.38** The compound 4-amino-5-nitrosalicylic acid is one of the building blocks needed for the synthesis of propoxycaine, one of the family of "caine" anesthetics. Some other members of this family of local anesthetics are procaine (Novocaine®), lidocaine (Xylocaine®), and mepivicaine (Carbocaine®). 4-Amino-5-nitrosalicylic acid is synthesized from salicylic acid in three steps: **(See Example 10.9)**

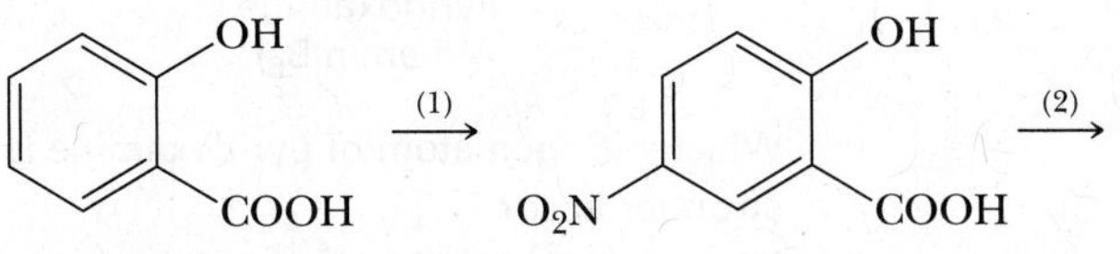

Salicylic acid

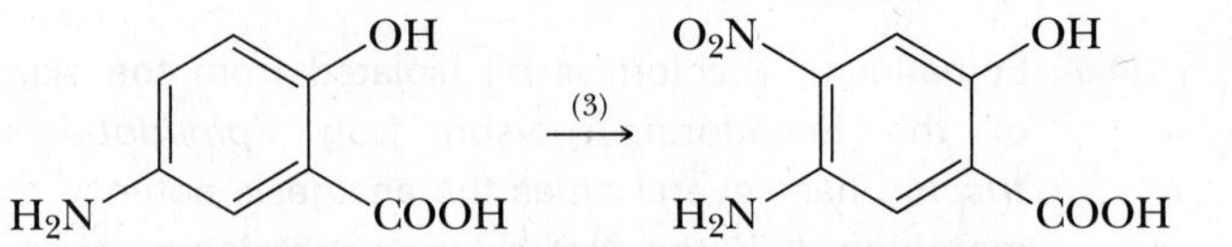

4-Amino-5-nitrosalicylic acid

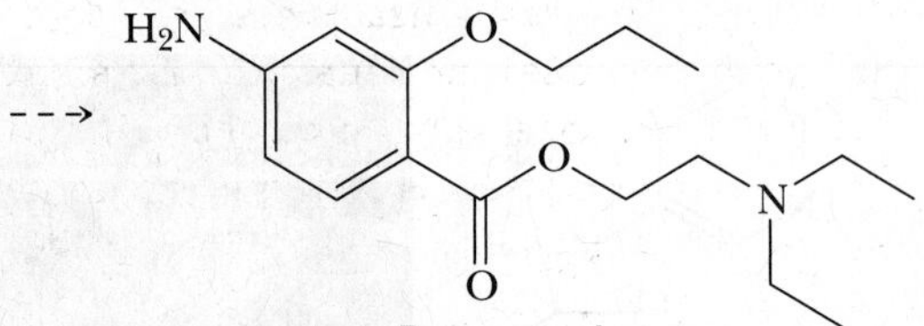

Propoxycaine

Show reagents that will bring about the synthesis of 4-amino-5-nitrosalicylic acid.

***10.39** A second building block for the synthesis of propoxycaine is 2-diethylaminoethanol: **(See Example 10.10)**

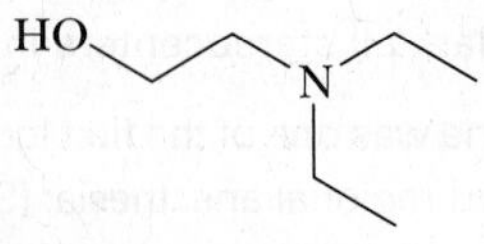

2-Diethylaminoethanol

Show how this compound can be prepared from ethylene oxide and diethylamine.

***10.40** Following is a two-step synthesis of the antihypertensive drug propranolol, a so-called beta blocker with vasodilating action: **(See Example 10.10)**

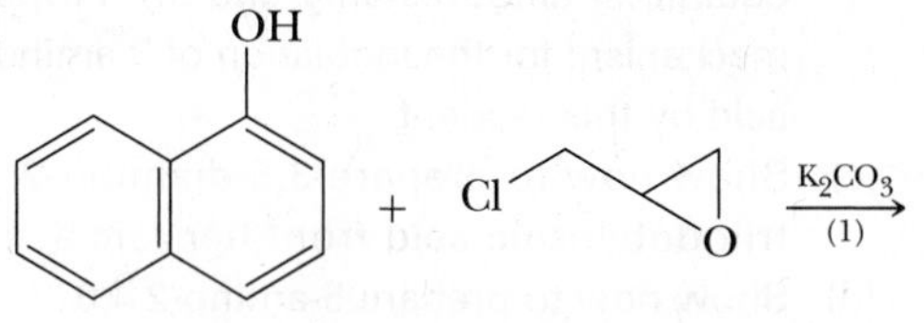

1-Naphthol Epichlorohydrin

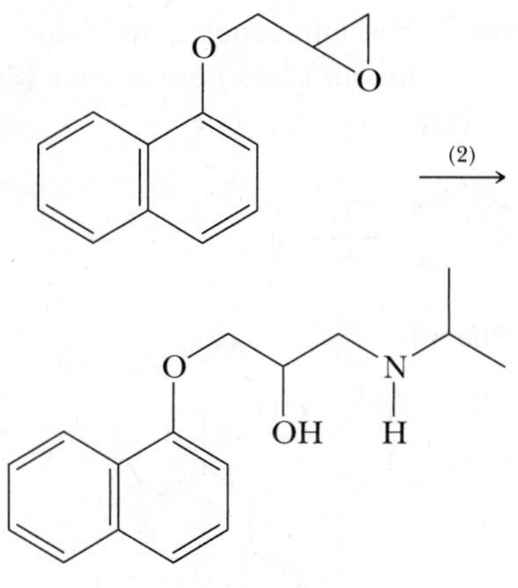

Propranolol
(Cardinol)

Propranolol and other beta blockers have received enormous clinical attention because of their effectiveness in treating hypertension (high blood pressure), migraine headaches, glaucoma, ischemic heart disease, and certain cardiac arrhythmias. The hydrochloride salt of propranolol has been marketed under at least 30 brand names, one of which is Cardinol®. (Note the "card-" part of the name, after *cardiac*.)

(a) What is the function of potassium carbonate, K_2CO_3, in Step 1? Propose a mechanism for the formation of the new oxygen–carbon bond in this step.

(b) Name the amine used to bring about Step 2, and propose a mechanism for this step.

(c) Is propranolol chiral? If so, how many stereoisomers are possible for it?

***10.41** The compound 4-ethoxyaniline, a building block of the over-the-counter analgesic phenacetin, is synthesized in three steps from phenol: **(See Example 10.9)**

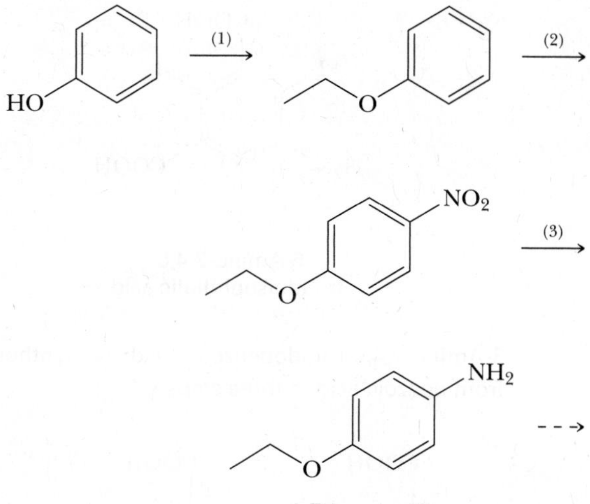

4-Ethoxyaniline

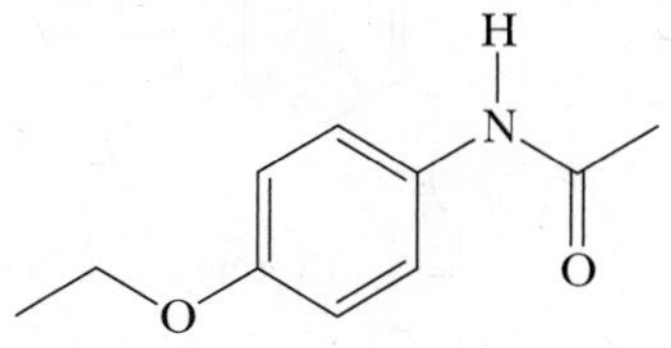

Phenacetin

Show reagents for each step of the synthesis of 4-ethoxyaniline. (In Chapter 14, we will see how to complete this synthesis.)

***10.42** Radiopaque imaging agents are substances administered either orally or intravenously that absorb X rays more strongly than body material does. One of the best known of these agents is barium sulfate, the key ingredient in the "barium cocktail" used for imaging of the gastrointestinal tract. Among other X-ray imaging agents are the so-called triiodoaromatics. You can get some idea of the kinds of imaging for which they are used from the following selection of trade names: Angiografin®, Gastrografin, Cardiografin, Cholografin, Renografin, and Urografin®. The most common of the triiodiaromatics are derivatives of these three triiodobenzenecarboxylic acids: **(See Example 10.9)**

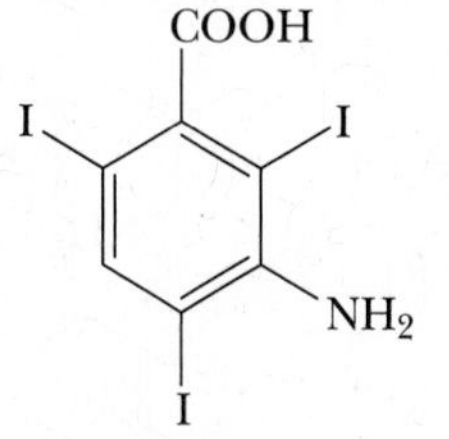

3-Amino-2,4,6-
triiodobenzoic acid

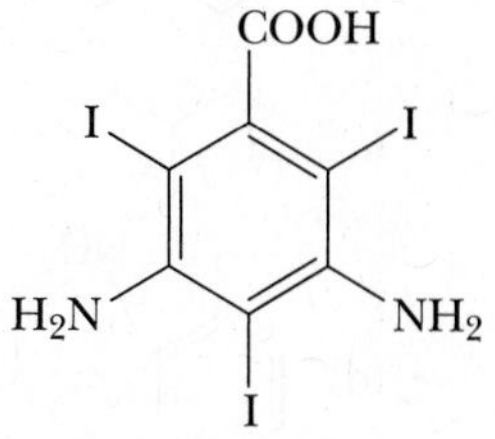

3,5-Diamino-2,4,6-
triiodobenzoic acid

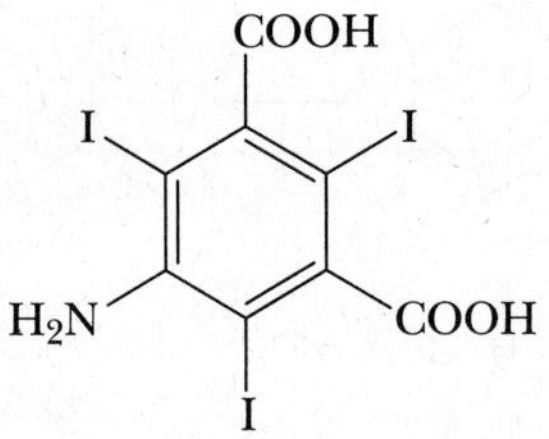

5-Amino-2,4,6-triiodoisophthalic acid

3-Amino-2,4,6-triiodobenzoic acid is synthesized from benzoic acid in three steps:

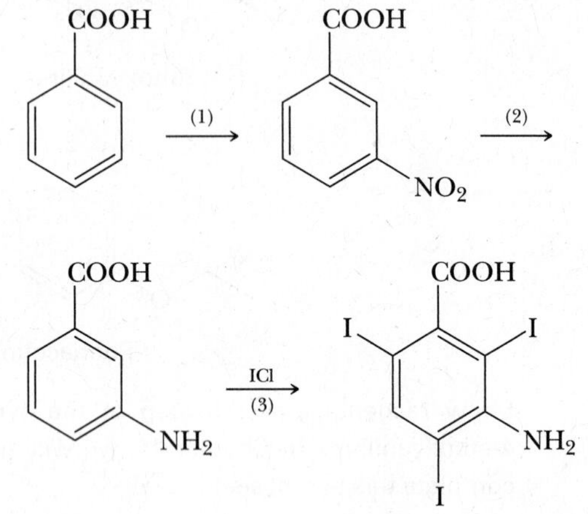

3-Amino-benzoic acid

3-Amino-2,4,6-triiodobenzoic acid

(a) Show reagents for Steps (1) and (2).
(b) Iodine monochloride, ICl, a black crystalline solid with a melting point of 27.2°C and a boiling point of 97°C, is prepared by mixing equimolar amounts of I_2 and Cl_2. Propose a mechanism for the iodination of 3-aminobenzoic acid by this reagent.
(c) Show how to prepare 3,5-diamino-2,4,6-triiodobenzoic acid from benzoic acid.
(d) Show how to prepare 5-amino-2,4,6-triiodoisophthalic acid from isophthalic acid (1,3-benzenedicarboxylic acid).

***10.43** The intravenous anesthetic propofol is synthesized in four steps from phenol: **(See Example 10.9)**

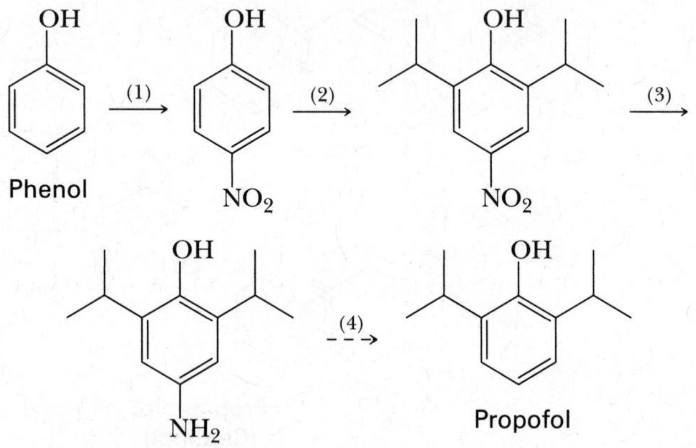

4-Amino-2,6-diisopropylphenol

Show reagents to bring about steps 1–3.

CHEMICAL TRANSFORMATIONS

10.44 Test your cumulative knowledge of the reactions learned thus far by completing the following chemical transformations. *Note: Some will require more than one step.* **(See Example 10.9)**

(a) 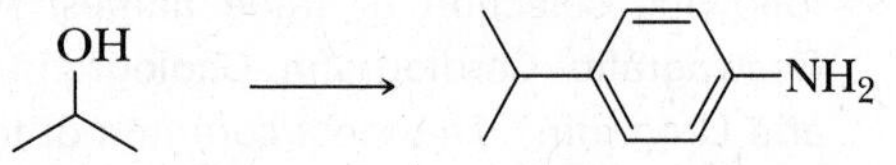

(b) 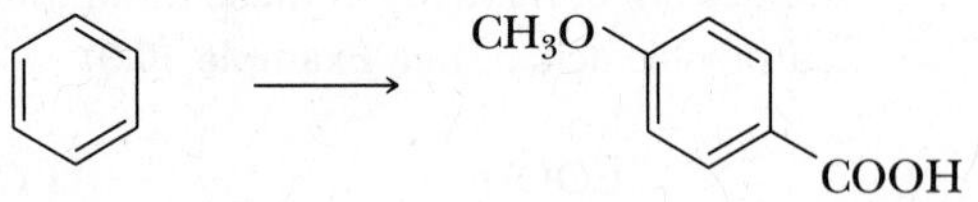

(c) 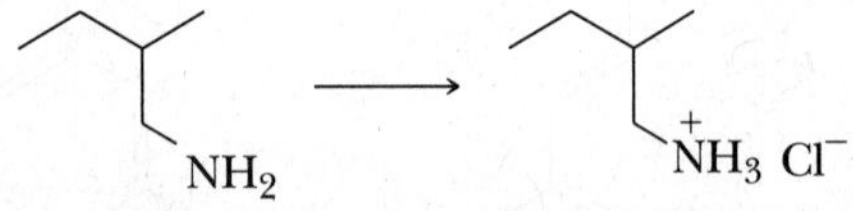

(d) 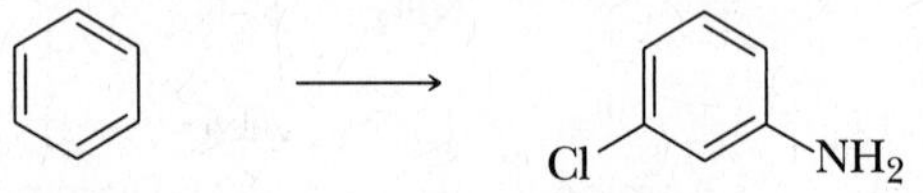

(e) 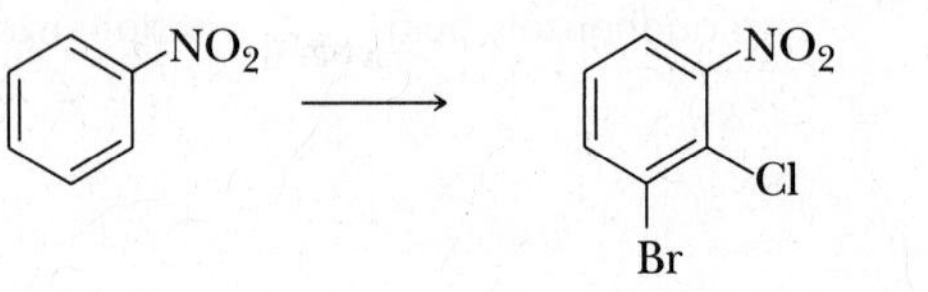

(f) 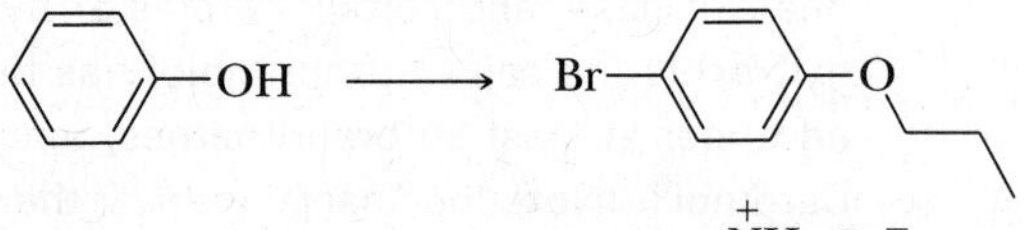

(g) 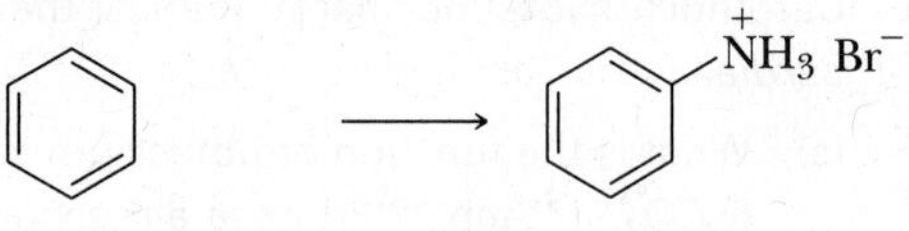

(h) 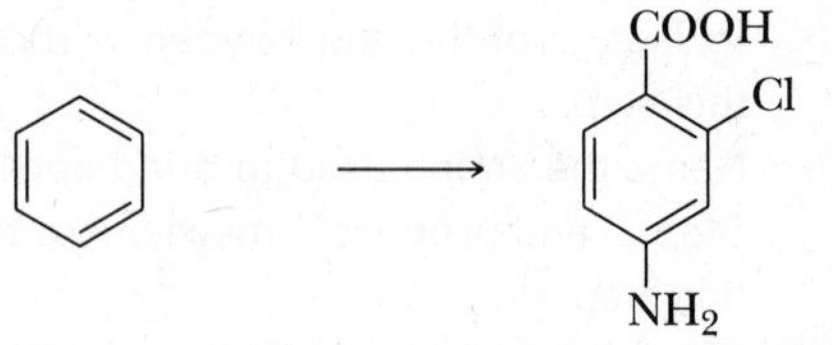

(i) 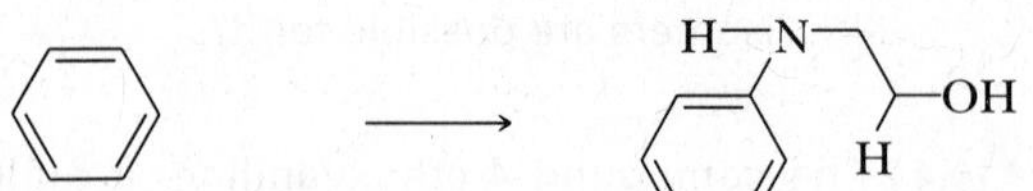

(j) 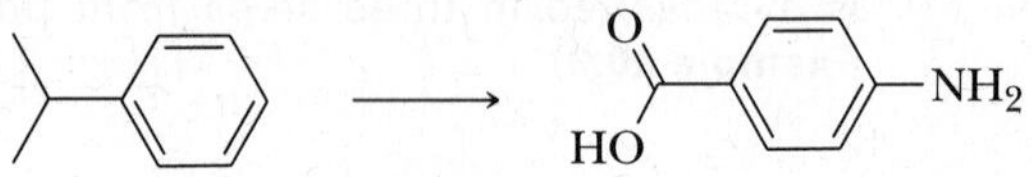

(k) 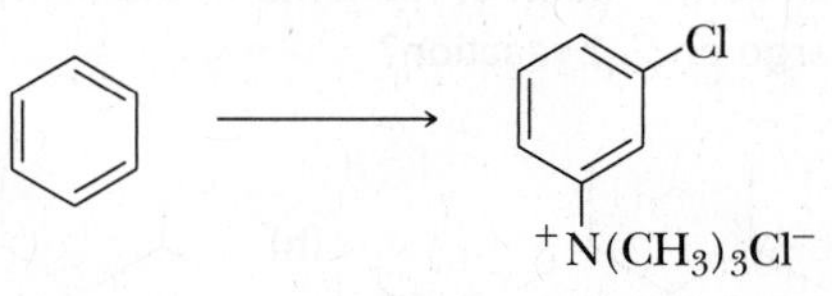

(l) 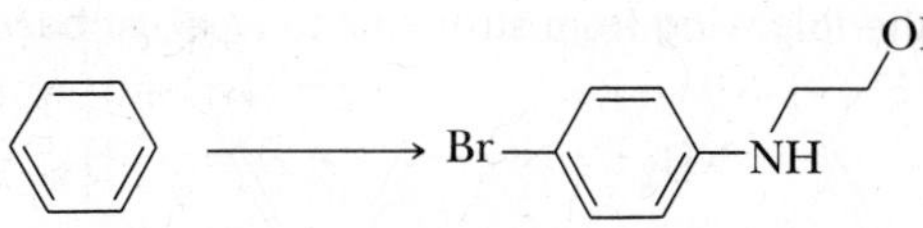

LOOKING AHEAD

10.45 State the hybridization of the nitrogen atom in each of the following compounds:

(a) 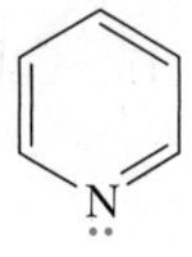

(b) 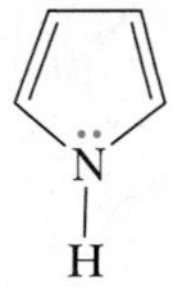

(c) 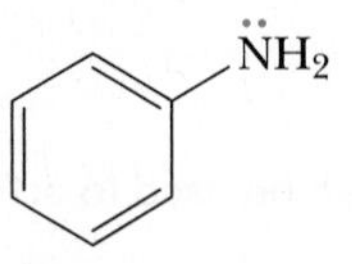

(d) 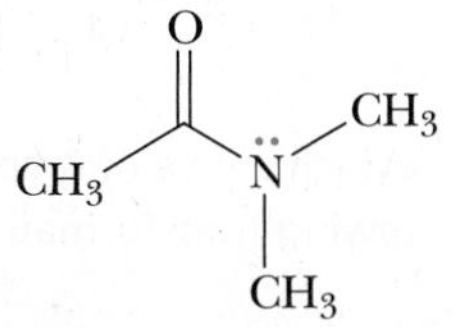

10.46 Amines can act as nucleophiles. For each of the following molecules, circle the most likely atom that would be attacked by the nitrogen of an amine:

(a) 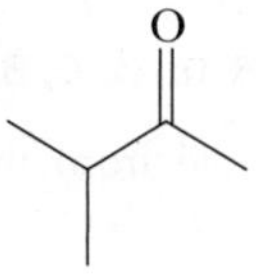

(b) 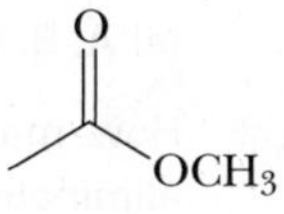

(c) 

10.47 Draw a Lewis structure for a molecule with the formula C_3H_7N that does not contain a ring or an alkene (a carbon–carbon double bond).

10.48 Rank the following leaving groups in order from best to worst:

$R-Cl$ $\quad R-O-C(=O)-R$ $\quad R-OCH_3$ $\quad R-N(CH_3)_2$

GROUP LEARNING ACTIVITIES

10.49 Discuss why $-NH_2$ is a stronger base than $-OH$. Are both bases strong enough to quantitatively (100%) abstract the hydrogen from a terminal alkyne? Why or why not?

10.50 Take turns listing all of the factors that affect the basicity of an atom in an organic molecule. Then do the same for acidity, nucleophilicity, and leaving group ability. Which factors are common to all four properties? Take turns providing molecules that are good or strong examples of each (e.g., a strong base, a good nucleophile, etc.). Then do the same for weak examples of each.

PUTTING IT TOGETHER

The following problems bring together concepts and material from Chapters 7–10. Although the focus may be on these chapters, the problems will also build on concepts discussed throughout the text thus far.

Choose the best answer for each of the following questions.

1. Arrange the following amines from lowest to highest boiling point.

A 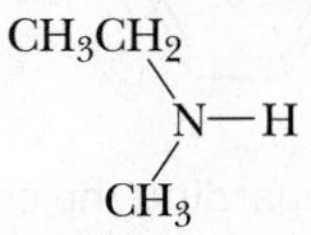
B $CH_3CH_2CH_2-NH_2$
C 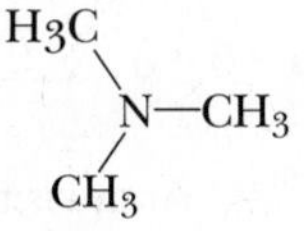

(a) **A, B, C** (b) **C, B, A** (c) **B, C, A**
(d) **B, A, C** (e) **C, A, B**

2. Which of the following statements is true regarding the following two molecules?

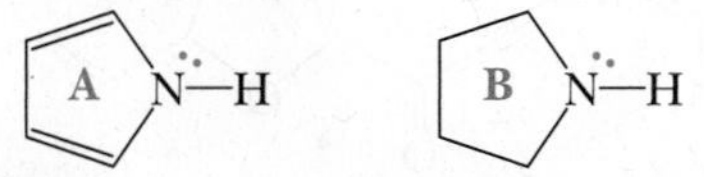

(a) Both **A** and **B** are aromatic.
(b) Both **A** and **B** are aliphatic amines.
(c) The nitrogen atoms in **A** and **B** are both sp^3 hybridized.
(d) **B** is more basic than **A**.
(e) Both **A** and **B** are planar molecules.

3. Which series of reagents can be used to achieve the following transformation?

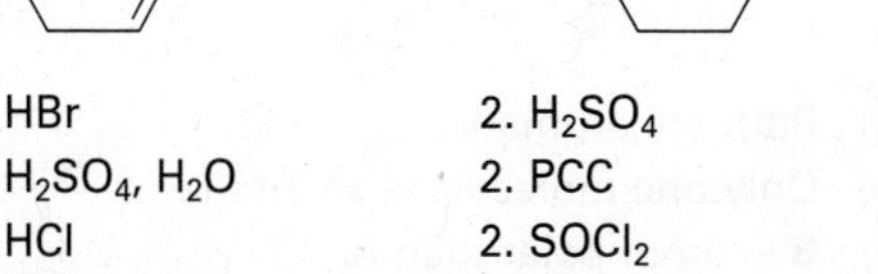

(a) 1. HBr 2. H_2SO_4
(b) 1. H_2SO_4, H_2O 2. PCC
(c) 1. HCl 2. $SOCl_2$
(d) 1. H_3PO_4, H_2O 2. H_2CrO_4
(e) More than one of these will achieve the transformation.

4. Arrange the following from strongest to weakest base.

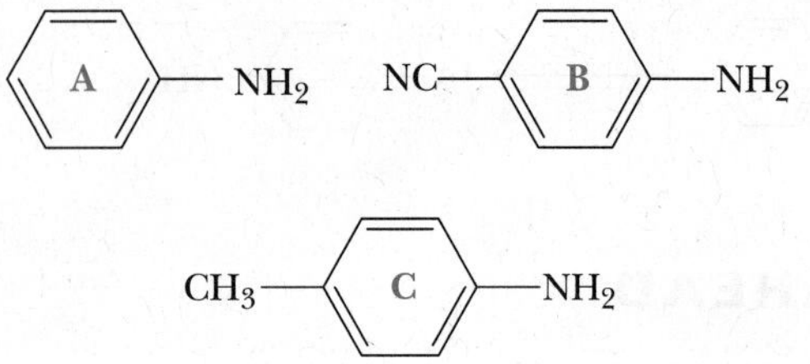

(a) **A, B, C** (b) **B, C, A** (c) **C, A, B** (d) **A, C, B** (e) **B, A, C**

5. How many products are possible from the following elimination reaction?

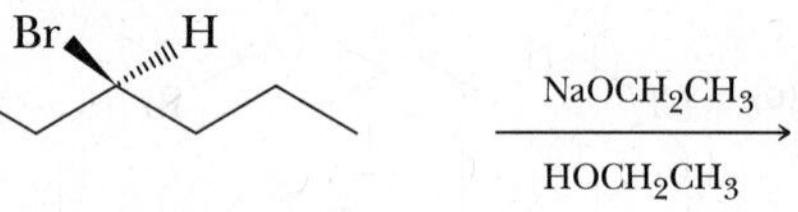

(a) one (b) two (c) three (d) four (e) six

6. Which series of reagents can be used to achieve the following transformation?

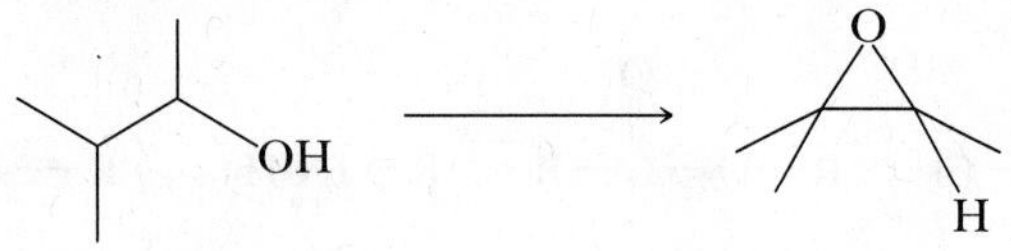

(a) 1) HCl 2) RCO_3H
(b) 1) $SOCl_2$ 2) RCO_3H
(c) 1) Na 2) RCO_3H
(d) 1) H_3PO_4 2) RCO_3H
(e) 1) H_2CrO_4 2) RCO_3H

7. Consider the following situation: An ether solution containing phenol and a neutral compound is extracted with 30% sodium bicarbonate. Next the ether solution is extracted with 30% NaOH. Finally, the ether solution is extracted with distilled water. Which solution contains the phenol?
(a) The 30% sodium bicarbonate solution.
(b) The 30% NaOH solution.
(c) The ether.
(d) The distilled water.
(e) Not enough information to determine.

8. Which of the following statements is true concerning the following two molecules?

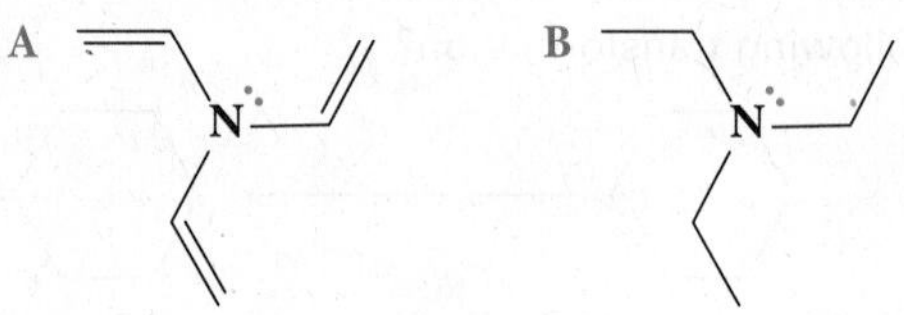

(a) Both are aromatic.
(b) Only one molecule is an amine.
(c) **B** is more polar than **A**.
(d) **A** is more basic than **B**.
(e) All of these statements are true.

9. Which combination of reagents would be most likely to undergo an S_N2 reaction?

(a) 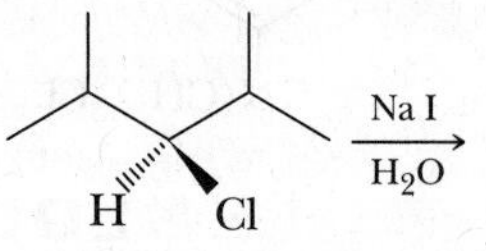
(b) 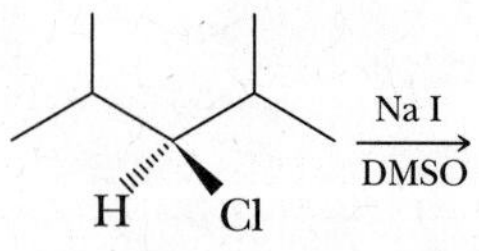
(c) 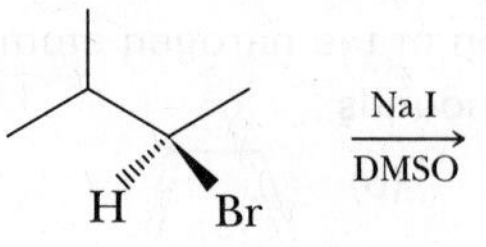
(d) 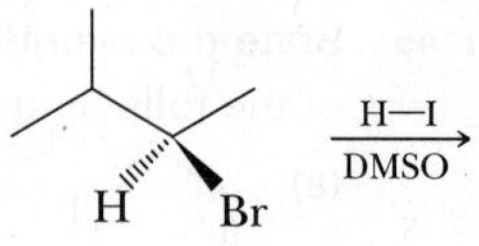
(e) 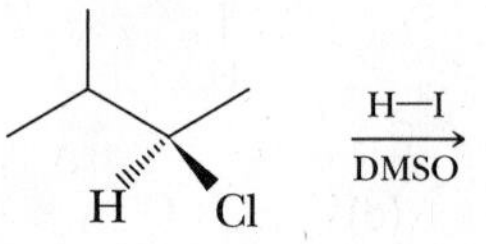

10. Which series of reagents can be used to achieve the following transformation?

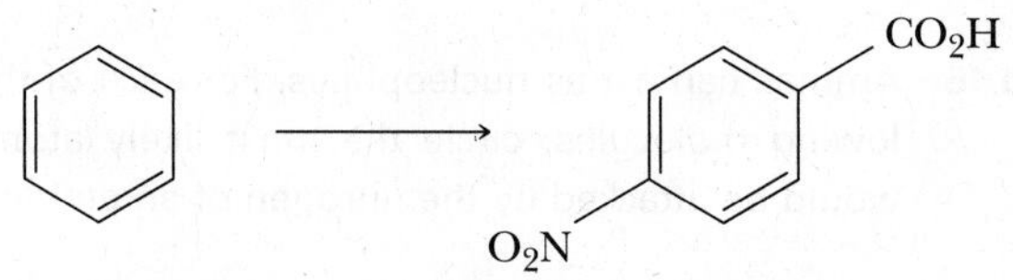

(a) 1) $CH_3Br/FeBr_3$
2) H_2SO_4/HNO_3
3) $H_2SO_4/K_2Cr_2O_4$
(b) 1) H_2SO_4/HNO_3
2) $H_2SO_4/K_2Cr_2O_4$
3) $CH_3Br/FeBr_3$
(c) 1) $H_2SO_4/K_2Cr_2O_4$
2) $CH_3Br/FeBr_3$
3) H_2SO_4/HNO_3
(d) 1) $CH_3Br/FeBr_3$
2) $H_2SO_4/K_2Cr_2O_4$
3) H_2SO_4/HNO_3
(e) 1) H_2SO_4/HNO_3
2) $CH_3Br/FeBr_3$
3) $H_2SO_4/K_2Cr_2O_4$

11. Determine which aryl amine (**A** or **B**) is more basic and provide a rationale for your determination.

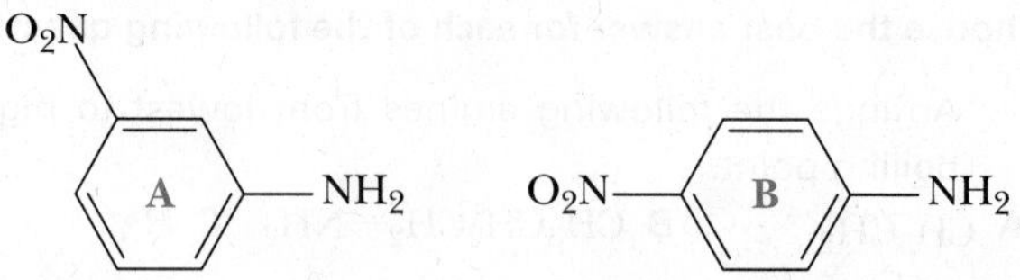

12. Answer the questions that follow regarding the compound Wyerone, which is obtained from fava beans (*Vicia faba*) and has been found to possess antifungal properties.

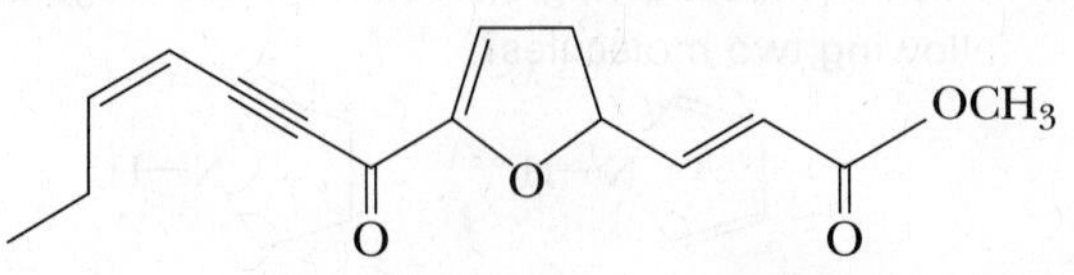

Wyerone

(a) Would you expect the compound to be soluble in water?
(b) How many stereoisomers exist for the compound shown?
(c) Is the molecule chiral?
(d) How many equivalents of Br_2 in CH_2Cl_2 would Wyerone be expected to react with?

13. Provide IUPAC names for the following compounds.

(a) 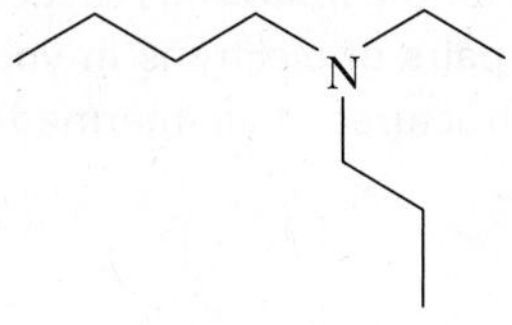

(b) 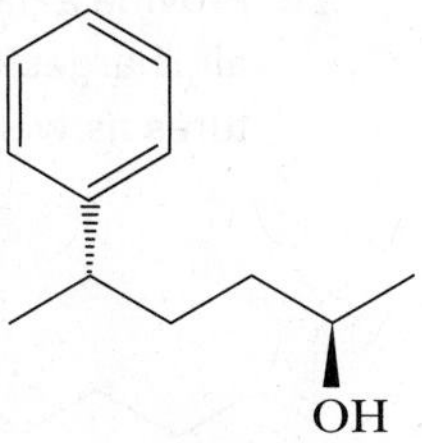

(c) 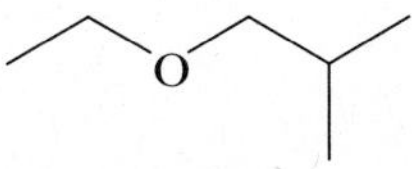

(d) 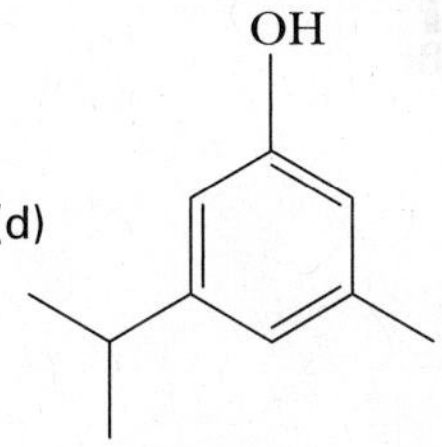

14. Determine whether highlighted proton **A** or **B** is more acidic and provide a rationale for your selection.

(a) 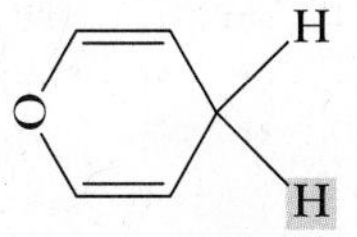

(b) 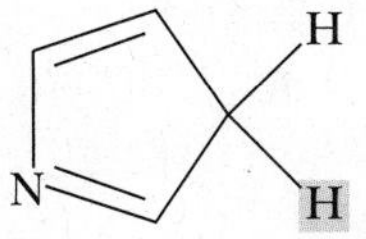

15. Select the answer that best fits each description and provide an explanation for your decision.

(a) The best nucleophile

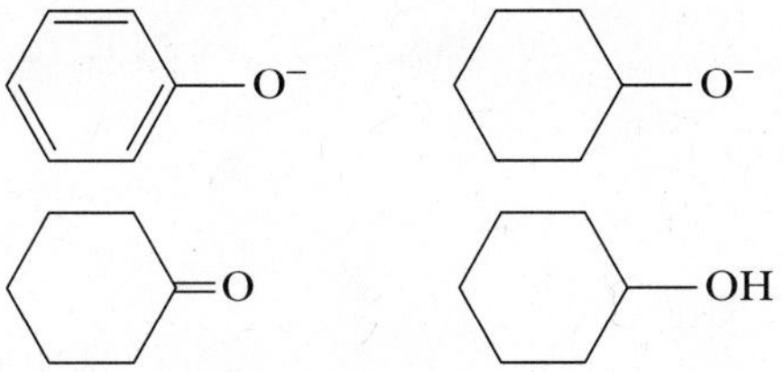

(b) The best leaving group

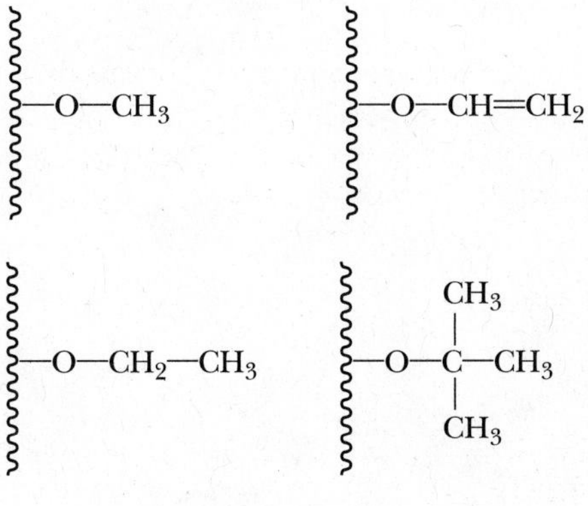

16. Provide a mechanism for the following reaction. Show all charges and lone pairs of electrons in your structures as well as the structures of all intermediates.

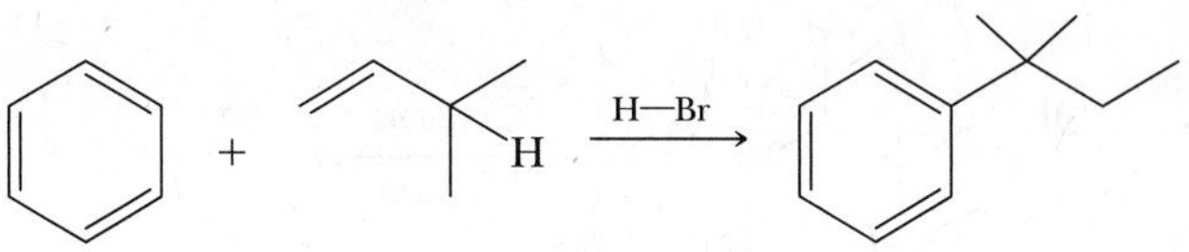

17. When the following nucleophilic substitution reaction was performed, the major product was found to possess the molecular formula $C_{13}H_{30}N$ rather than $C_5H_{13}N$, the formula of the desired product shown below. Provide the structure of the major product and explain why it is formed over the desired product.

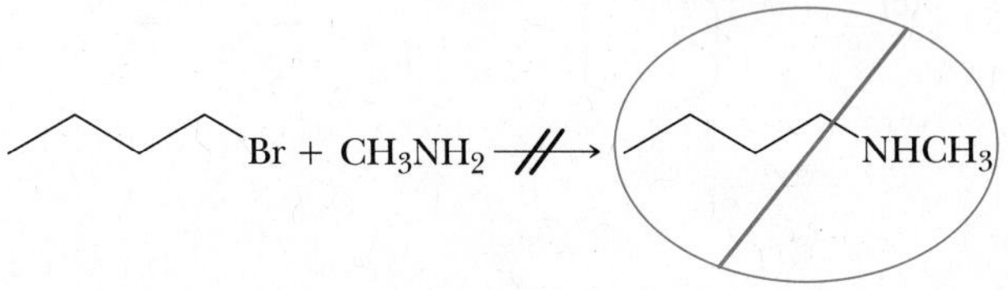

18. Complete the following chemical transformations.

(a) 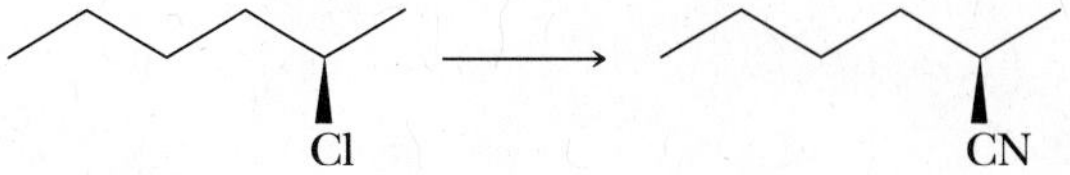

This enantiomer as the *only* product

(b) 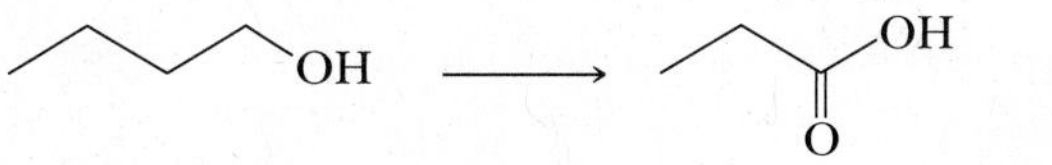

(c) 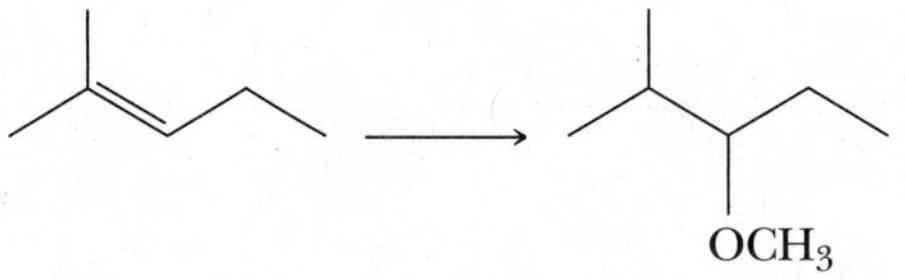

(racemic)

(d) 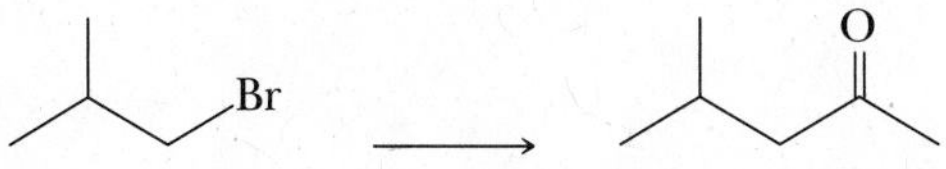

19. Provide a mechanism for the following reaction. Show all charges and lone pairs of electrons in your structures as well as the structures of all intermediates.

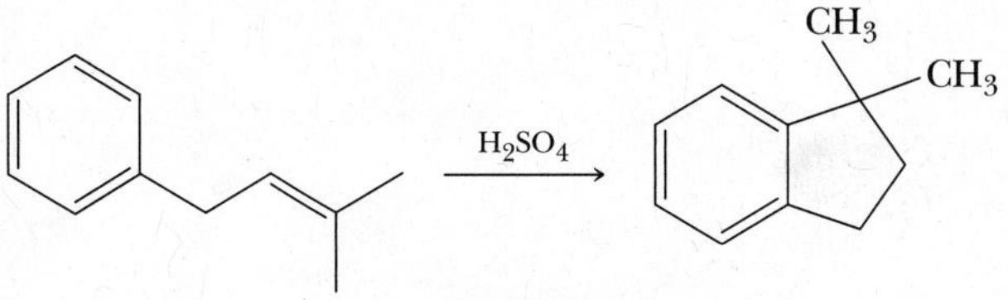

20. Predict the major product or products of each of the following reactions. Be sure to consider stereochemistry in your answers.

(a) 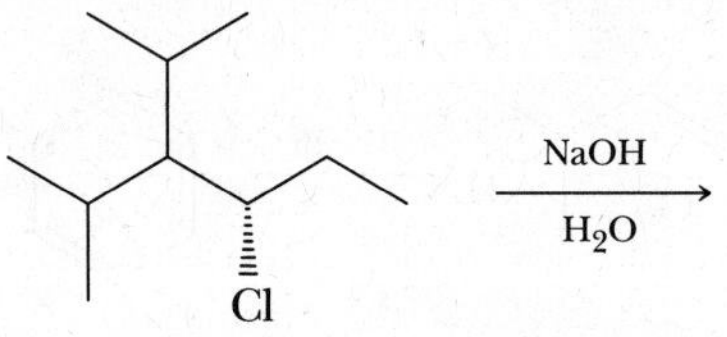

(b) 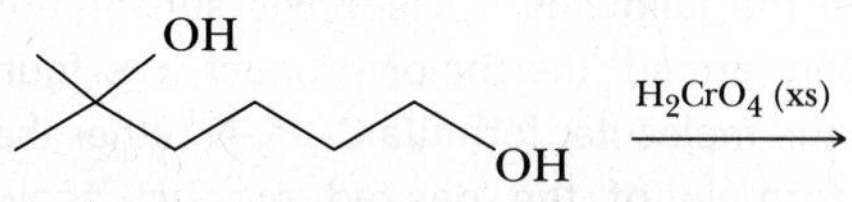

(c) 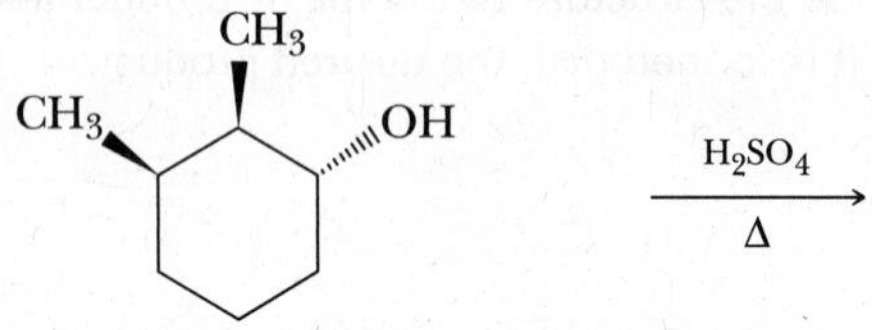

(d) 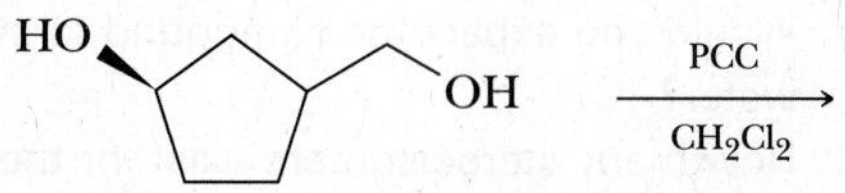

(e) 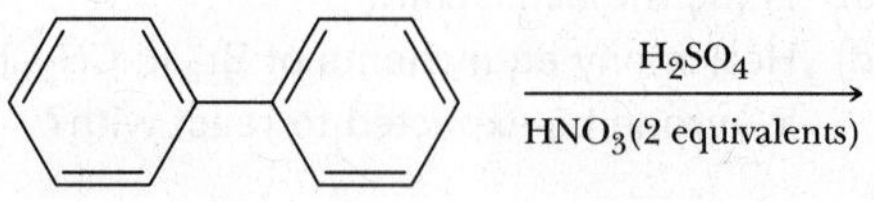

21. Provide a mechanism for the following reaction. Show all charges and lone pairs of electrons in your structures as well as the structures of all intermediates.

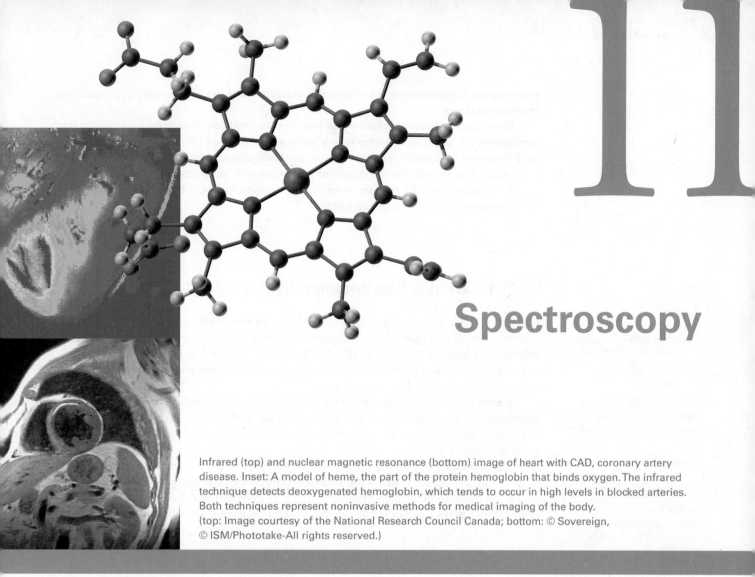

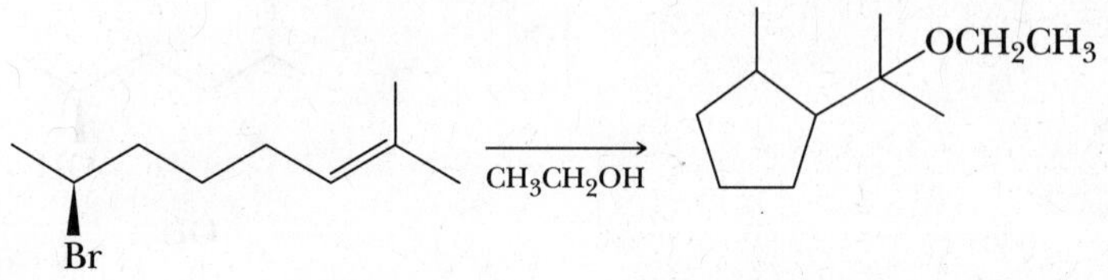

11

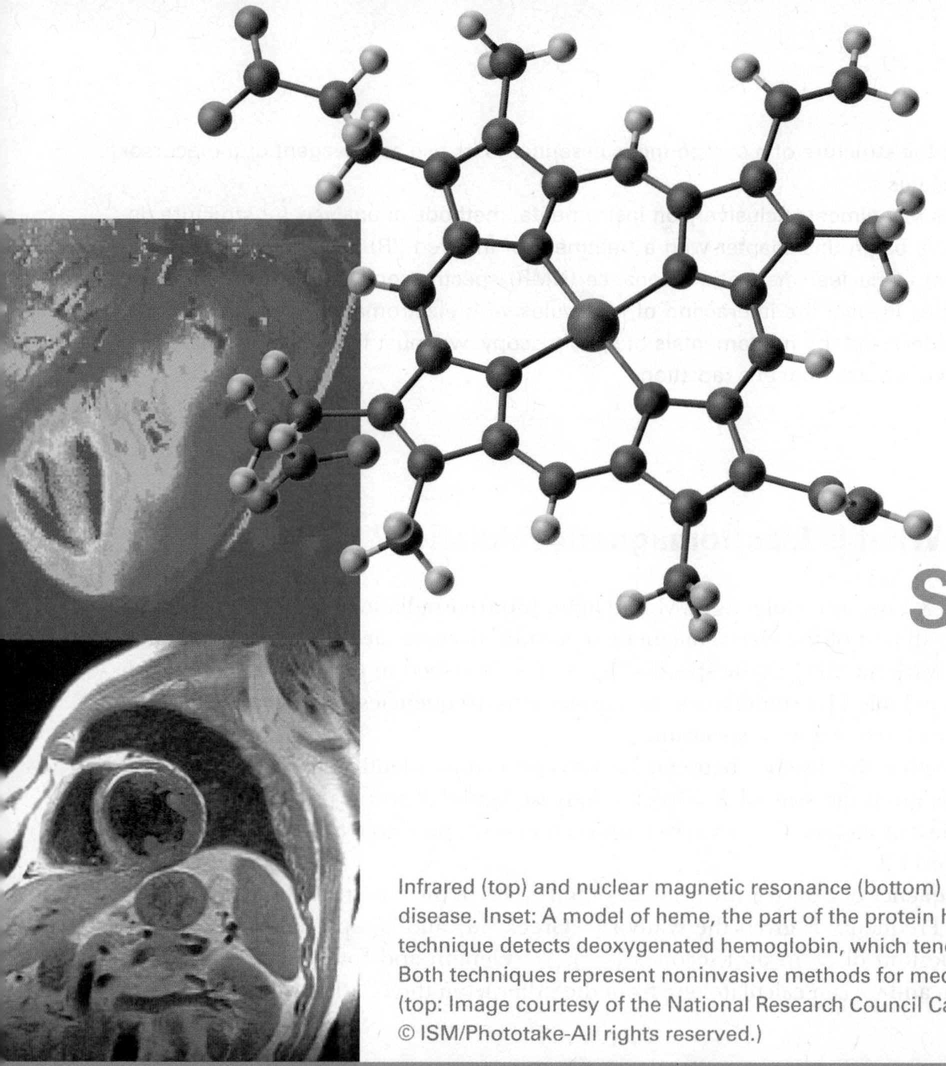

Spectroscopy

Infrared (top) and nuclear magnetic resonance (bottom) image of heart with CAD, coronary artery disease. Inset: A model of heme, the part of the protein hemoglobin that binds oxygen. The infrared technique detects deoxygenated hemoglobin, which tends to occur in high levels in blocked arteries. Both techniques represent noninvasive methods for medical imaging of the body. (top: Image courtesy of the National Research Council Canada; bottom: © Sovereign, © ISM/Phototake-All rights reserved.)

KEY QUESTIONS

11.1 What Is Electromagnetic Radiation?

11.2 What Is Molecular Spectroscopy?

11.3 What Is Infrared Spectroscopy?

11.4 How Do We Interpret Infrared Spectra?

11.5 What Is Nuclear Magnetic Resonance?

11.6 What Is Shielding?

11.7 What Is an NMR Spectrum?

11.8 How Many Resonance Signals Will a Compound Yield in Its NMR Spectrum?

11.9 What Is Signal Integration?

11.10 What Is Chemical Shift?

11.11 What Is Signal Splitting?

11.12 What Is ^{13}C-NMR Spectroscopy, and How Does It Differ from ^{1}H-NMR Spectroscopy?

11.13 How Do We Solve an NMR Problem?

HOW TO

11.1 How to Approach Infrared Spectroscopy Structure Determination Problems

11.2 How to Determine Whether an Atomic Nucleus Has a Spin (Behaves as If It Were a Tiny Bar Magnet)

CHEMICAL CONNECTIONS

DETERMINING THE MOLECULAR structure of a compound is a central theme in science. In medicine, for example, the structure of any drug must be known before the drug can be approved for use in patients. In the biotechnology and pharmaceutical industries, knowledge of a compound's structure can provide new leads to promising therapeutics. In organic chemistry, knowledge of the structure of a compound is essential to its use as a reagent or a precursor to other molecules.

Chemists rely almost exclusively on instrumental methods of analysis for structure determination. We begin this chapter with a treatment of infrared (IR) spectroscopy, followed by a treatment of nuclear magnetic resonance (NMR) spectroscopy. These two commonly used techniques involve the interaction of molecules with electromagnetic radiation. Thus, in order to understand the fundamentals of spectroscopy, we must first review some of the fundamentals of electromagnetic radiation.

11.1 What Is Electromagnetic Radiation?

Electromagnetic radiation Light and other forms of radiant energy.

Wavelength (λ) The distance between two consecutive identical points on a wave.

Frequency (ν) A number of full cycles of a wave that pass a point in a second.

Hertz (Hz) The unit in which wave frequency is reported; s^{-1} (read *per second*).

Gamma rays, X rays, ultraviolet light, visible light, infrared radiation, microwaves, and radio waves are all part of the electromagnetic spectrum. Because **electromagnetic radiation** behaves as a wave traveling at the speed of light, it is described in terms of its wavelength and frequency. Table 11.1 summarizes the wavelengths, frequencies, and energies of some regions of the electromagnetic spectrum.

Wavelength is the distance between any two consecutive identical points on the wave. Wavelength is given the symbol $\boldsymbol{\lambda}$ (Greek lowercase lambda) and is usually expressed in the SI base unit of meters. Other derived units commonly used to express wavelength are given in Table 11.2.

The **frequency** of a wave is the number of full cycles of the wave that pass a given point in a second. Frequency is given the symbol $\boldsymbol{\nu}$ (Greek nu) and is reported in **hertz** (Hz), which has the unit of reciprocal seconds (s^{-1}). Wavelength and frequency are inversely proportional, and we can calculate one from the other from the relationship

$$\nu\lambda = c$$

TABLE 11.1 Wavelength, Frequency, and Energy Relationships of Some Regions of the Electromagnetic Spectrum

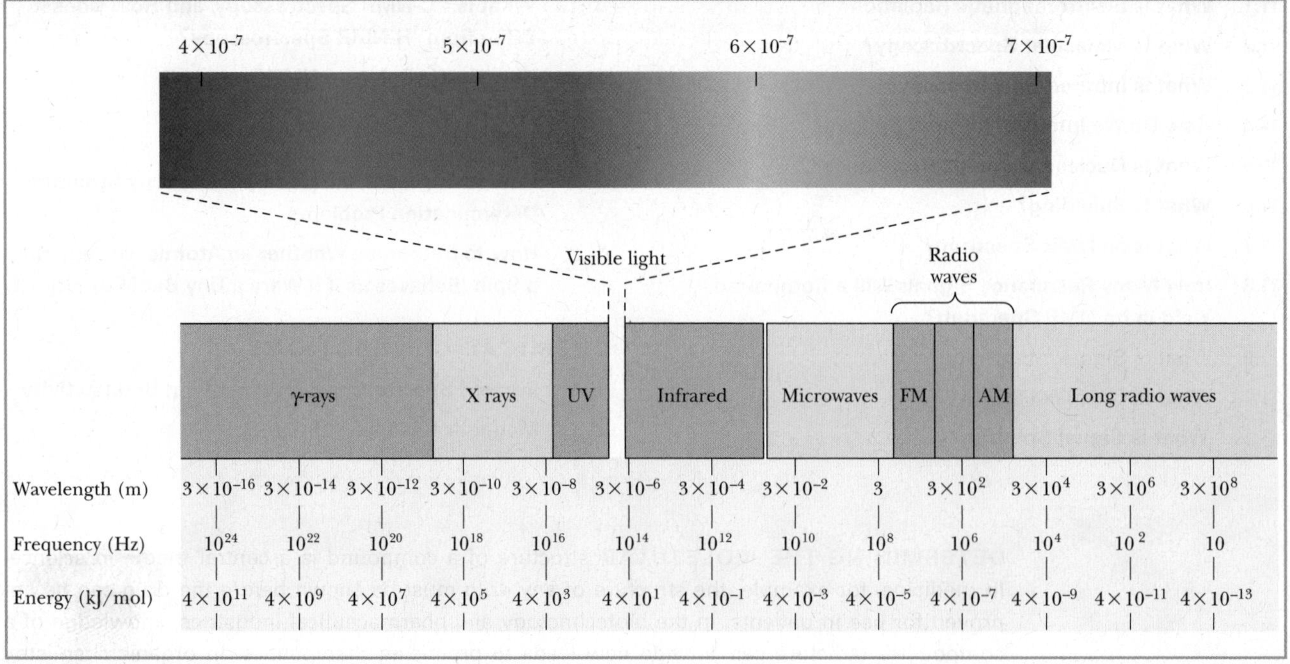

TABLE 11.2 Common Units Used to Express Wavelength (λ)

Unit	Relation to Meter
meter (m)	——
millimeter (mm)	1 mm = 10^{-3} m
micrometer (μm)	1 μm = 10^{-6} m
nanometer (nm)	1 nm = 10^{-9} m
Angstrom (Å)	1 Å = 10^{-10} m

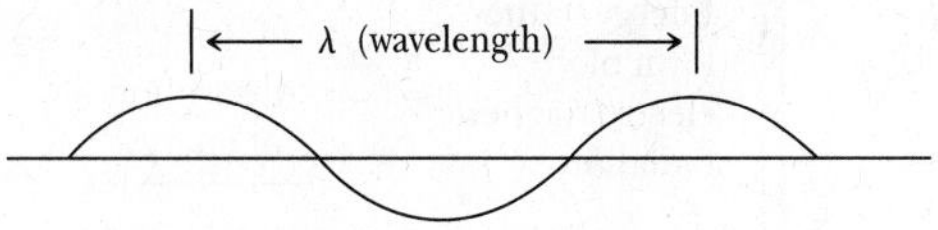

where ν is frequency in hertz, c is the velocity of light (3.00×10^8 m/s), and λ is the wavelength in meters. For example, consider infrared radiation—or heat radiation, as it is also called—with wavelength 1.5×10^{-5} m. The frequency of this radiation is

$$\nu = \frac{3.0 \times 10^8 \text{ m/s}}{1.5 \times 10^{-5} \text{ m}} = 2.0 \times 10^{13} \text{ Hz}$$

An alternative way to describe electromagnetic radiation is in terms of its properties as a stream of particles. We call these particles **photons**. The energy in a mole of photons and the frequency of radiation are related by the equation

$$E = h\nu = h\frac{c}{\lambda}$$

where E is the energy in kJ/mol and h is Planck's constant, 3.99×10^{-13} kJ·s·mol^{-1} (9.54×10^{-14} kcal·s·mol^{-1}). This equation tells us that high-energy radiation corresponds to short wavelengths, and vice versa. Thus, ultraviolet light (higher energy) has a shorter wavelength (approximately 10^{-7} m) than infrared radiation (lower energy), which has a wavelength of approximately 10^{-5} m.

EXAMPLE 11.1

Calculate the energy, in kiloJoules per mole of radiation, of a wave with wavelength 2.50 μm. What type of radiant energy is this? (Refer to Table 11.1.)

STRATEGY

Use the relationship $E = hc/\lambda$. Make certain that the dimensions for distance are consistent: If the dimension of wavelength is meters, then express the velocity of light in meters per second.

SOLUTION

First convert 2.50 μm to meters, using the relationship 1 μm = 10^{-6} m (Table 11.2):

$$2.50\ \mu\text{m} \times \frac{10^{-6}\text{ m}}{1\ \mu\text{m}} = 2.50 \times 10^{-6}\text{ m}$$

Now substitute this value into the equation $E = hc/\lambda$:

$$E = \frac{hc}{\lambda} = 3.99 \times 10^{-13}\frac{\text{kJ}\cdot\text{s}}{\text{mol}} \times 3.00 \times 10^{8}\frac{\text{m}}{\text{s}} \times \frac{1}{2.50 \times 10^{-6}\text{ m}}$$

$$= 47.7 \text{ kJ/mol } (11.4 \text{ kcal/mol})$$

Electromagnetic radiation with energy of 47.7 kJ/mol is radiation in the infrared region.

See problems 11.18–11.20

PROBLEM 11.1

Calculate the energy of red light (680 nm) in kilocalories per mole. Which form of radiation carries more energy, infrared radiation with wavelength 2.50 μm or red light with wavelength 680 nm?

FIGURE 11.1
Absorption of energy in the form of electromagnetic radiation excites an atom or a molecule in energy state E_1 to a higher energy state E_2.

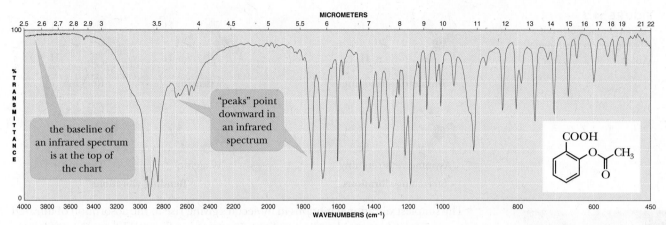

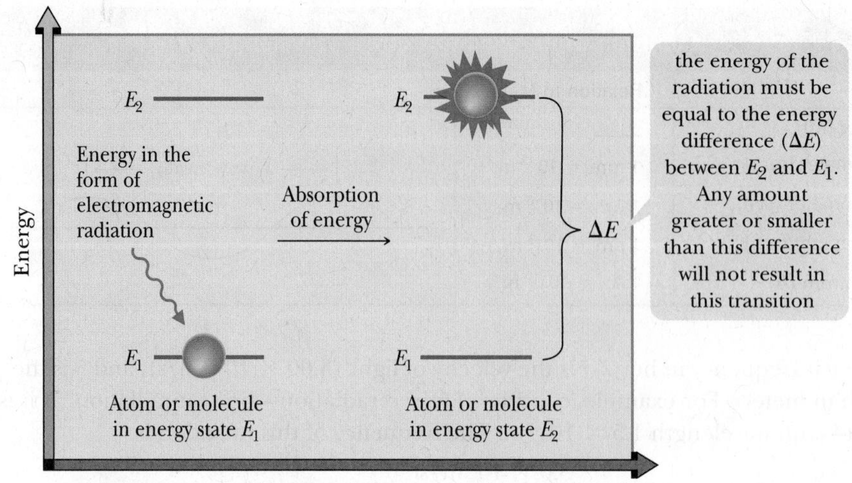

11.2 What Is Molecular Spectroscopy?

Organic molecules are flexible structures. They rotate in solution, their bonds stretch, bend, and rotate, and they contain electrons that can move from one electronic energy level to another. We know from experimental observations and from theories of molecular structure that all energy changes within a molecule are quantized; that is, they are subdivided into small, but well-defined, increments. For example, vibrations of bonds within molecules can undergo transitions only between allowed vibrational energy levels.

We can cause an atom or molecule to undergo a transition from energy state E_1 to a higher energy state E_2 by irradiating it with electromagnetic radiation corresponding to the energy difference between states E_1 and E_2, as illustrated schematically in Figure 11.1. When the atom or molecule returns to the ground state E_1, an equivalent amount of energy is emitted.

Molecular spectroscopy The study of the frequencies of electromagnetic radiation that are absorbed or emitted by substances and the correlation between these frequencies and specific types of molecular structure.

Molecular spectroscopy is the experimental process of measuring which frequencies of radiation a substance absorbs or emits and then correlating those frequencies with specific types of molecular structures. In **nuclear magnetic resonance (NMR) spectroscopy**, we irradiate a compound under the influence of a strong magnetic field with radio-frequency radiation, the absorption of which causes nuclei to be in a higher energy spin state. We will have more to say about NMR spectroscopy in Section 11.5. In **infrared (IR) spectroscopy**, we irradiate a compound with infrared radiation, the absorption of which causes covalent bonds to change from a lower vibrational energy level to a higher one. Because different functional groups have different bond strengths, the energy required to bring about these transitions will vary from one functional group to another. Thus, in infrared spectroscopy, we detect functional groups by the vibrations of their bonds.

11.3 What Is Infrared Spectroscopy?

A. The Vibrational Infrared Spectrum

Vibrational infrared The portion of the infrared region that extends from 4000 to 400 cm^{-1}.

Wavenumber ($\bar{\nu}$) A characteristic of electromagnetic radiation equal to the number of waves per centimeter.

In organic chemistry, we use a portion of the electromagnetic spectrum called the **vibrational infrared** region. This region extends from 2.5×10^{-6} to 25×10^{-6} m and corresponds to energies from 48–4.8 kJ/mol (11–1.2 kcal/mol). We commonly refer to radiation in the vibrational infrared region by its **wavenumber** ($\bar{\nu}$), the number of waves per centimeter:

$$\bar{\nu} = \frac{1}{\lambda\ (\text{cm})} = \frac{10^{-2}\ (\text{m} \cdot \text{cm}^{-1})}{\lambda\ (\text{m})}$$

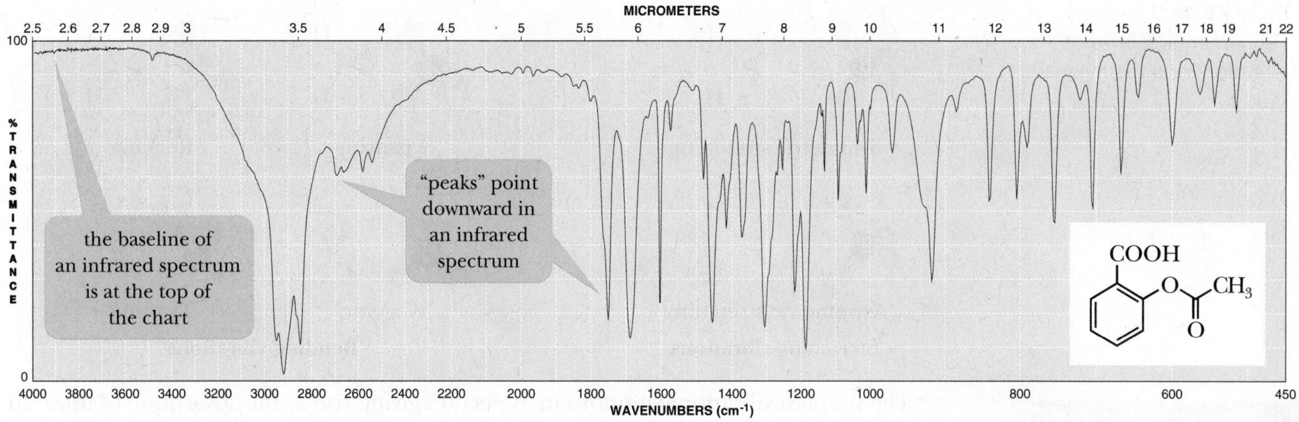

FIGURE 11.2
Infrared spectrum of aspirin.

Expressed in wavenumbers, the vibrational region of the infrared spectrum extends from 4000 to 400 cm^{-1} (the unit cm^{-1} is read "reciprocal centimeter"):

$$\bar{\nu} = \frac{10^{-2}\ \text{m} \cdot \text{cm}^{-1}}{2.5 \times 10^{-6}\ \text{m}} = 4000\ \text{cm}^{-1} \qquad \bar{\nu} = \frac{10^{-2}\ \text{m} \cdot \text{cm}^{-1}}{25 \times 10^{-6}\ \text{m}} = 400\ \text{cm}^{-1}$$

An advantage of using wavenumbers is that they are directly proportional to energy; the higher the wavenumber, the higher is the energy of radiation.

Figure 11.2 shows an infrared spectrum of aspirin. The horizontal axis at the bottom of the chart is calibrated in wavenumbers (cm^{-1}); that at the top is calibrated in wavelength (micrometers, μm). The wavenumber scale is often divided into two or more linear regions. For all spectra reproduced in this text, it is divided into three linear regions: 4000–2200 cm^{-1}, 2200–1000 cm^{-1}, and 1000–450 cm^{-1}. The vertical axis measures transmittance, with 100% transmittance at the top and 0% transmittance at the bottom. Thus, the baseline for an infrared spectrum (100% transmittance of radiation through the sample = 0% absorption) is at the top of the chart, and the absorption of radiation corresponds to a trough or valley. Strange as it may seem, we commonly refer to infrared absorptions as peaks, even though they are actually troughs.

B. Molecular Vibrations

For a molecule to absorb infrared radiation, the bond undergoing vibration must be polar, and its vibration must cause a periodic change in the bond dipole; the greater the polarity of the bond, the more intense is the absorption. Any vibration that meets this criterion is said to be **infrared active**. Covalent bonds in homonuclear diatomic molecules, such as H_2 and Br_2, and some carbon–carbon double bonds in symmetrical alkenes and alkynes do not absorb infrared radiation because they are not polar bonds. The multiple bonds in the following two molecules, for example, do not have a dipole moment and, therefore, are not infrared active:

Neither of the unsaturated bonds in these molecules is infrared active because the vibrational motions shown do not result in a change in bond dipole (due to the symmetry about these bonds).

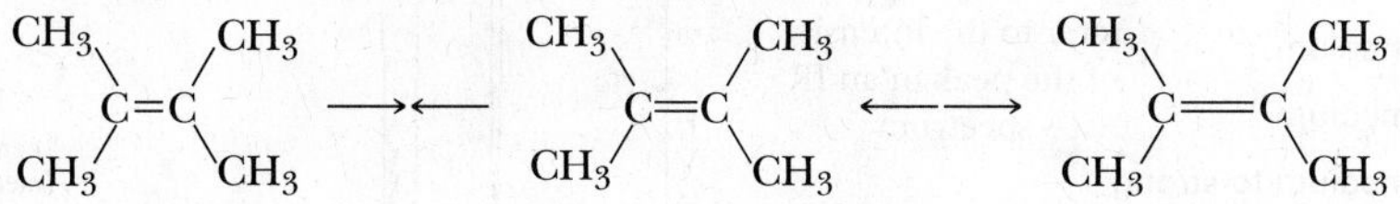

2,3-Dimethyl-2-butene

CH_3—C≡C—CH_3 ⟶⟵ CH_3—C≡C—CH_3 ⟵⟶ CH_3—C≡C—CH_3

2-Butyne

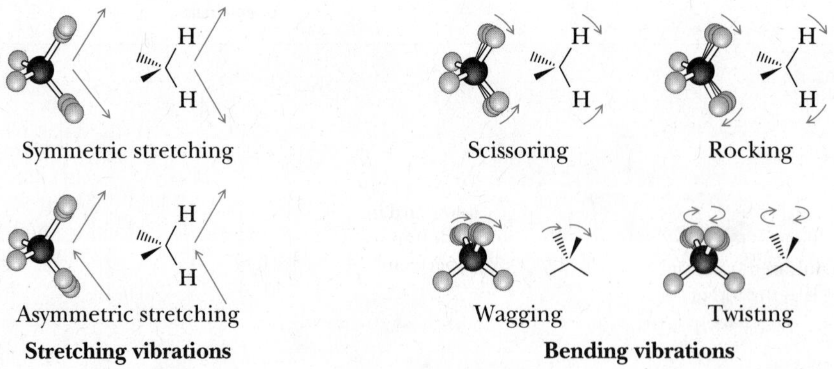

FIGURE 11.3 Fundamental modes of vibration for a methylene group.

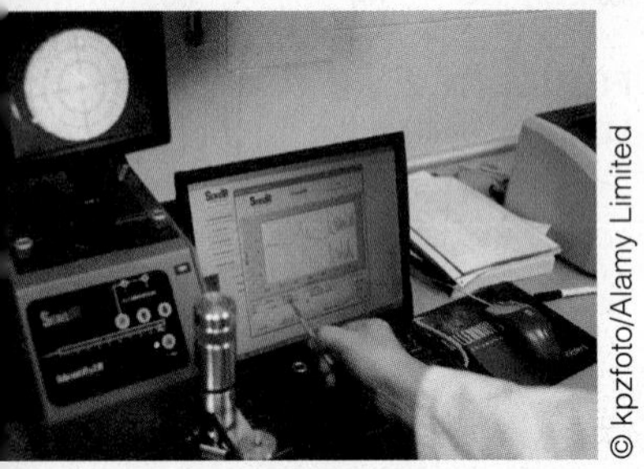

A Beckman Coulter DU 800 infrared spectrophotometer. Spectra are shown in the monitor.

The simplest vibrational motions in molecules giving rise to the absorption of infrared radiation are **stretching** and **bending** motions. Illustrated in Figure 11.3 are the fundamental stretching and bending vibrations for a methylene group.

To one skilled in the interpretation of infrared spectra, absorption patterns can yield an enormous amount of information about chemical structure. We, however, have neither the time nor the need to develop that level of competence. The value of infrared spectra for us is that we can use them to determine the presence or absence of particular functional groups. A carbonyl group, for example, typically shows strong absorption at approximately 1630–1800 cm^{-1}. The position of absorption for a particular carbonyl group depends on (1) whether it is that of an aldehyde, a ketone, a carboxylic acid, an ester, or an amide, and (2) if the carbonyl carbon is in a ring, the size of the ring.

C. Correlation Tables

Data on absorption patterns of selected functional groups are collected in tables called **correlation tables.** Table 11.3 gives the characteristic infrared absorptions for the types of bonds and functional groups we deal with most often. Appendix 4 contains a more comprehensive correlation table. In these tables, we refer to the intensity of a particular absorption as **strong (s)**, **medium (m)**, or **weak (w)**.

In general, we will pay most attention to the region from 3650 to 1000 cm^{-1} because the characteristic stretching vibrations for most functional groups are found in this region. Vibrations in the region from 1000 to 400 cm^{-1} are much more complex and far more difficult to analyze. It is often called the **fingerprint region** because even slight variations in molecular structure lead to differences in absorption patterns in this region. If two compounds have even slightly different structures, the differences in their infrared spectra are most clearly discernible in the fingerprint region.

Fingerprint region The portion of the vibrational infrared region that extends from 1000 to 400 cm^{-1} and that is unique to every compound.

TABLE 11.3 Characteristic IR Absorptions of Selected Functional Groups

Frequency range (cm^{-1})	Bond or functional group	Intensity
3500–3200	O—H alcohol	strong and broad
3400–2400	O—H carboxylic acid	strong and broad
3500–3100	N—H amine	medium
3330–3270	≡C—H alkyne	medium
3100–3000	=C—H alkene	medium
3000-2850	—C—H alkane	medium to strong
2260–2100	C≡C alkyne	weak
1800–1630	C=O carbonyl	strong
1680–1600	C=C alkene	weak
1250–1050	C—O ether	strong

these descriptors refer to the intensity of the peak in an IR spectrum

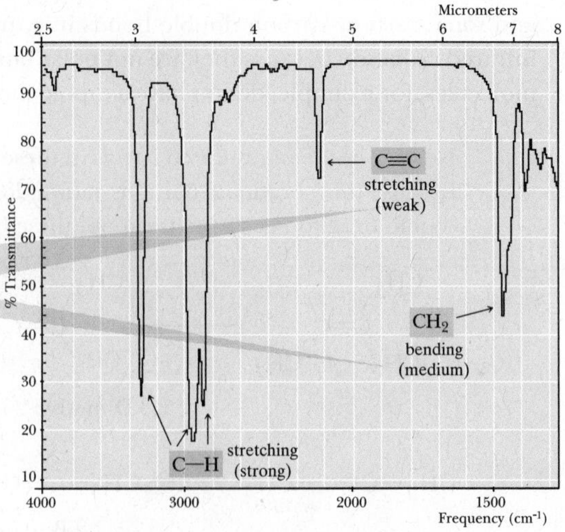

EXAMPLE 11.2

Determine the functional group that is most likely present if IR absorption appears at
(a) 1705 cm^{-1} (b) 2200 cm^{-1}

STRATEGY

Refer to correlation Table 11.3. Eventually, through the continual practice of problems in this chapter, many of these vibrational stretching frequencies and intensities will become familiar to you.

SOLUTION

(a) A C=O group (b) a C—C triple bond

See problems 11.29–11.31

PROBLEM 11.2

A compound shows strong, very broad IR absorption in the region from 3200 to 3500 cm^{-1} and strong absorption at 1715 cm^{-1}. What functional group accounts for both of these absorptions?

EXAMPLE 11.3

Propanone and 2-propen-1-ol are constitutional isomers. Show how to distinguish between these two isomers by IR spectroscopy.

$$CH_3-\overset{\overset{\displaystyle O}{\|}}{C}-CH_3 \qquad CH_2{=}CH-CH_2-OH$$

Propanone (Acetone) — 2-Propen-1-ol (Allyl alcohol)

STRATEGY

Because IR spectroscopy distinguishes between characteristic vibrational frequencies of differing *functional groups*, identify the *different* functional groups in the pair of molecules and predict (using correlation tables) the vibrational frequencies that these functional groups would exhibit in an IR spectrum.

SOLUTION

Only propanone shows strong absorption in the C=O stretching region, 1630–1800 cm^{-1}. Alternatively, only 2-propen-1-ol shows strong absorption in the O—H stretching region, 3200–3500 cm^{-1}.

See problems 11.29–11.31

PROBLEM 11.3

Propanoic acid and methyl ethanoate are constitutional isomers. Show how to distinguish between these two compounds by IR spectroscopy.

$$CH_3CH_2\overset{\overset{\displaystyle O}{\|}}{C}OH \qquad CH_3\overset{\overset{\displaystyle O}{\|}}{C}OCH_3$$

Propanoic acid — Methyl ethanoate (Methyl acetate)

11.4 How Do We Interpret Infrared Spectra?

Interpreting spectroscopic data is a skill that is easy to acquire through practice and exposure to examples. An IR spectrum will reveal not only the functional groups that are present in a sample, but also those that can be excluded from consideration. Often, we can determine the structure of a compound solely from the data in the spectrum of the compound and from information found in Table 11.3. Other times, we may need additional information, such as the molecular formula of the compound, or knowledge of the reactions used to synthesize the molecule. In this section, we will see specific examples of IR spectra for characteristic functional groups. Familiarizing yourself with them will help you to master the technique of spectral interpretation.

Chemical Connections 11A

INFRARED SPECTROSCOPY: A WINDOW ON BRAIN ACTIVITY

Some of the great advantages of infrared spectroscopy are the relatively low cost, sensitivity, and speed of its instrumentation. The medical and scientific community recognized these benefits, along with the fact that some frequencies of infrared light can harmlessly penetrate human tissue and bone, in creating a technique called functional Near Infrared Spectroscopy (fNIRS). In fNIRS, a patient is fitted with headgear containing many fiber optic cables that allow infrared light in the 700–1000 nm range to be shone through the skull and into the brain. Separate fiber optic cables in the headgear collect the light that reemerges from the brain and direct it to a spectrophotometer, which quantifies the intensity of the light. The instrument measures changes in the concentration of oxygenated and deoxygenated hemoglobin, which absorbs light in the 700–1000 nm range. Because an assortment of tasks that the brain may be asked to carry out results in varying blood flow and oxygenation levels in different parts of the brain, fNIRS can be used to determine how certain thoughts or actions affect brain activity.

Questions

Could fNIRS be used to detect free oxygen (O_2) levels in the lungs? Why or why not?

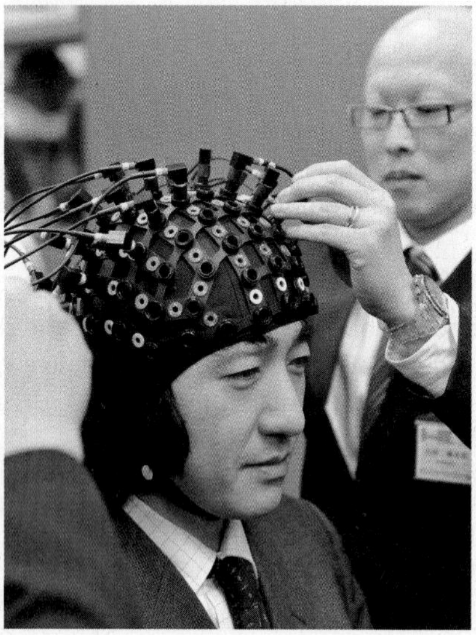

AFP/Getty Images, Inc.

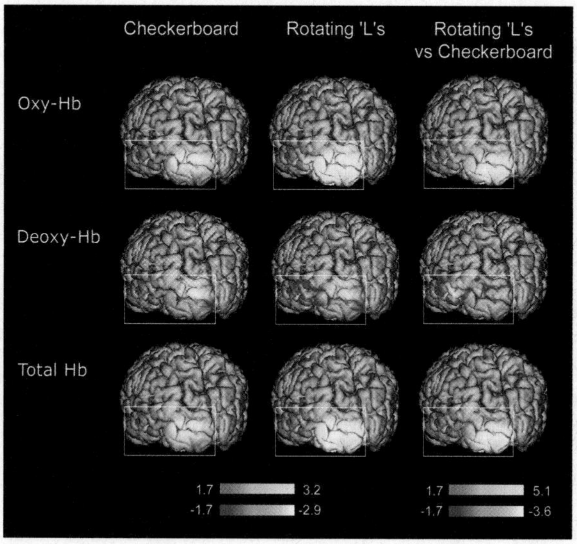

From Matthias L. Schroeter, NeuroImage 21: 284, Figure 2 (2004). Photo provided courtesy of M. Schroeter.

A research subject is asked to perform several mental tasks (left) while fNIRS analysis reveals varying levels of oxy- and deoxyhemoglobin in the blood flowing through the subject's brain.

A. Alkanes, Alkenes, and Alkynes

Figure 11.4 shows an infrared spectrum of decane. The strong peak with multiple splittings between 2850 and 3000 cm^{-1} is characteristic of alkane C—H stretching. The C—H peak is strong in this spectrum because there are so many C—H bonds and no other functional groups. Because alkane CH, CH_2, and CH_3 groups are present in many organic compounds, this peak is among the most commonly encountered in infrared spectroscopy.

Figure 11.5 shows the infrared spectrum of cyclopentene, which shows the easily recognized alkene stretching band slightly to the left of (at a greater wavenumber than) 3000 cm^{-1}. Also characteristic of alkenes is stretching at 1600 cm^{-1}. Notice that because cyclopentene has alkyl CH_2 groups, the characteristic alkane C—H stretching peak is also observed just below 3000 cm^{-1}.

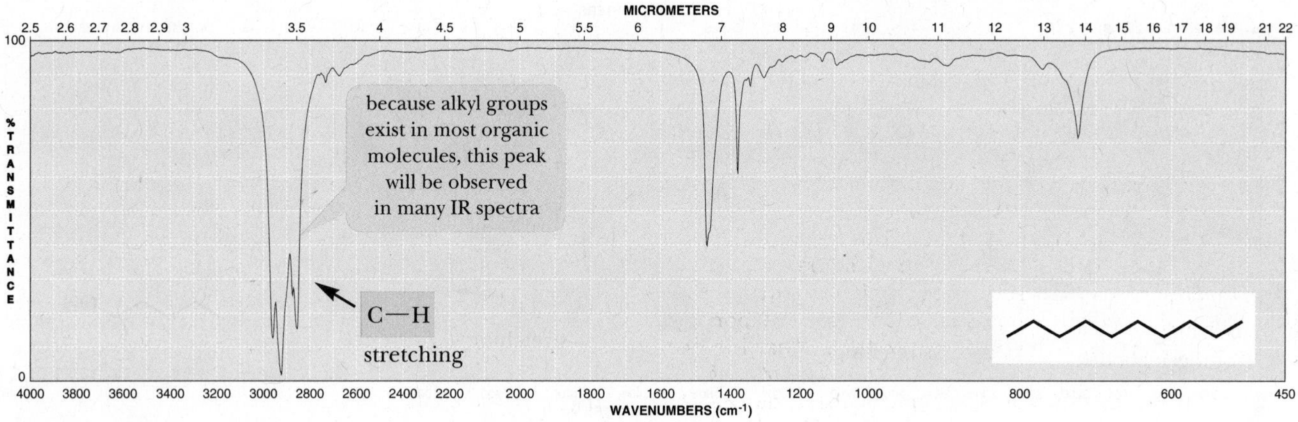

FIGURE 11.4
Infrared spectrum of decane.

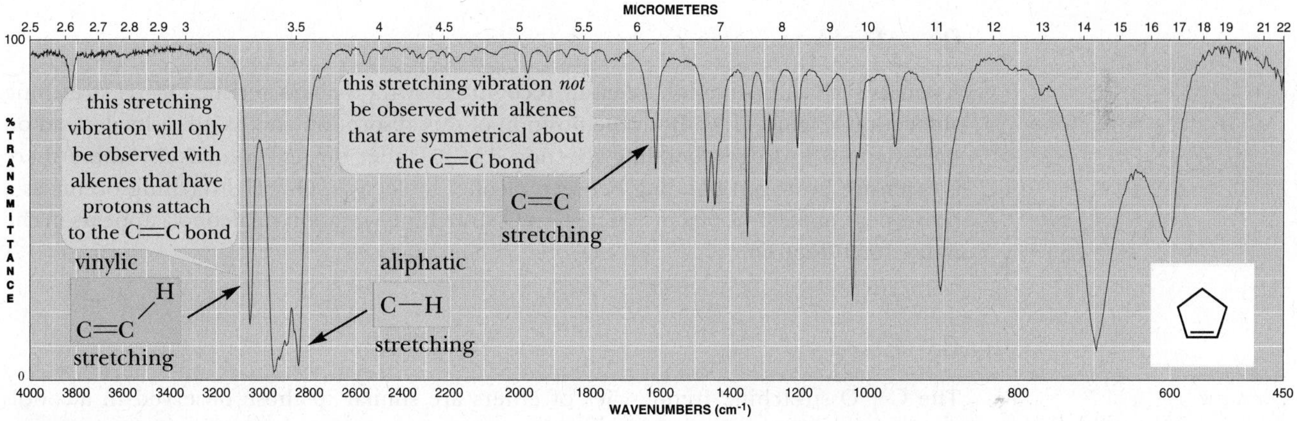

FIGURE 11.5
Infrared spectrum of cyclopentene.

Terminal alkynes exhibit C≡C—H stretching at 3300 cm^{-1}. This absorption band is absent in internal alkynes, because the triple bond is not bonded to a proton. All alkynes absorb weakly between 2100 and 2260 cm^{-1}, due to C≡C stretching. This stretching shows clearly in the spectrum of 1-octyne (Figure 11.6).

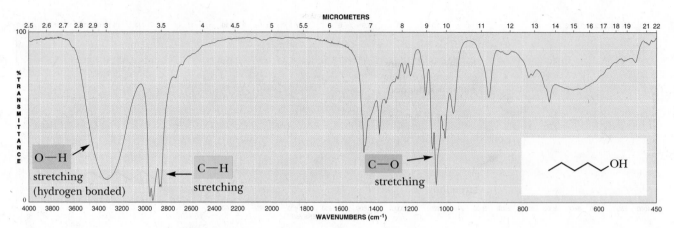

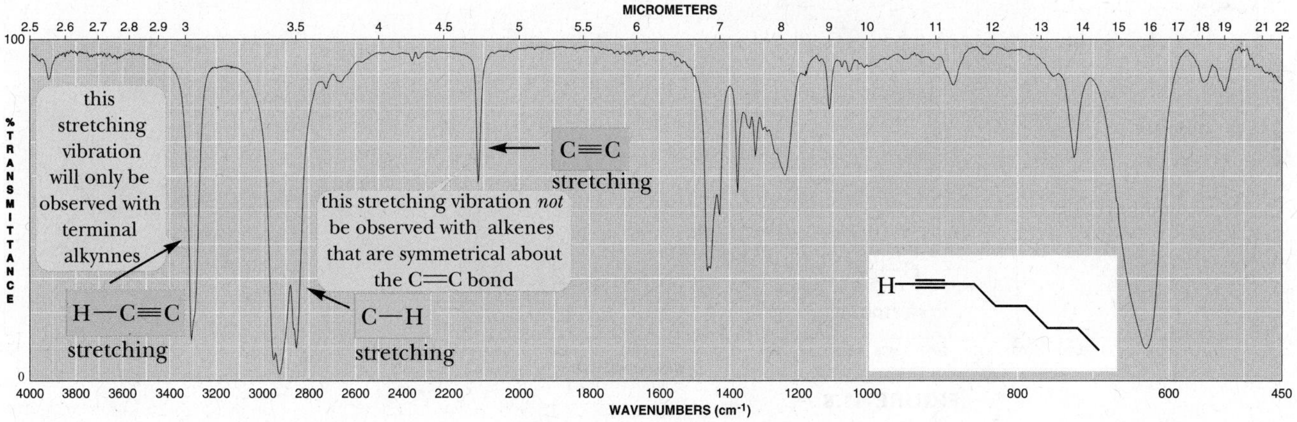

FIGURE 11.6
Infrared spectrum of 1-octyne.

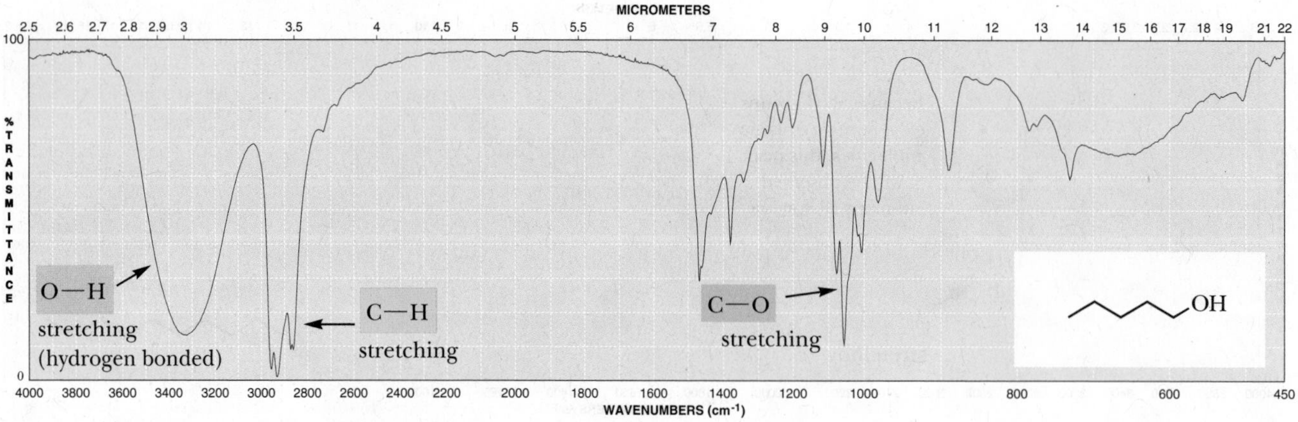

FIGURE 11.7
Infrared spectrum of 1-pentanol.

B. Alcohols

Alcohols such as 1-pentanol are easily recognized by their characteristic O—H stretching absorption (Figure 11.7). Both the position of this absorption and its intensity depend on the extent of hydrogen bonding (Section 8.1C). Under normal conditions, where there is extensive hydrogen bonding between alcohol molecules, O—H stretching occurs as a broad peak at 3200–3500 cm^{-1}. The C—O stretching vibration of alcohols appears in the range 1050–1250 cm^{-1}.

C. Ethers

The C—O stretching frequencies of ethers are similar to those observed in alcohols and esters (1070 and 1150 cm^{-1}). The presence or absence of O—H stretching at 3200–3500 cm^{-1} for a hydrogen-bonded O—H can be used to distinguish between an ether and an alcohol. The C—O stretching vibration is also present in esters. In this case, we can use the presence or absence of C=O stretching to distinguish between an ether and an ester. Figure 11.8 shows an infrared spectrum of diethyl ether. Notice the absence of O—H stretching.

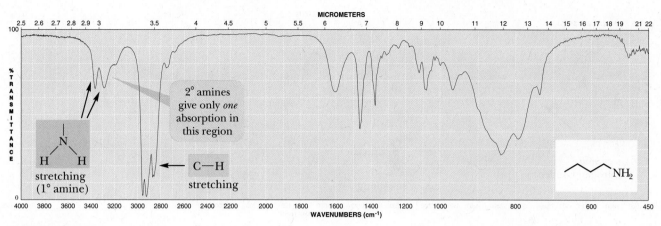

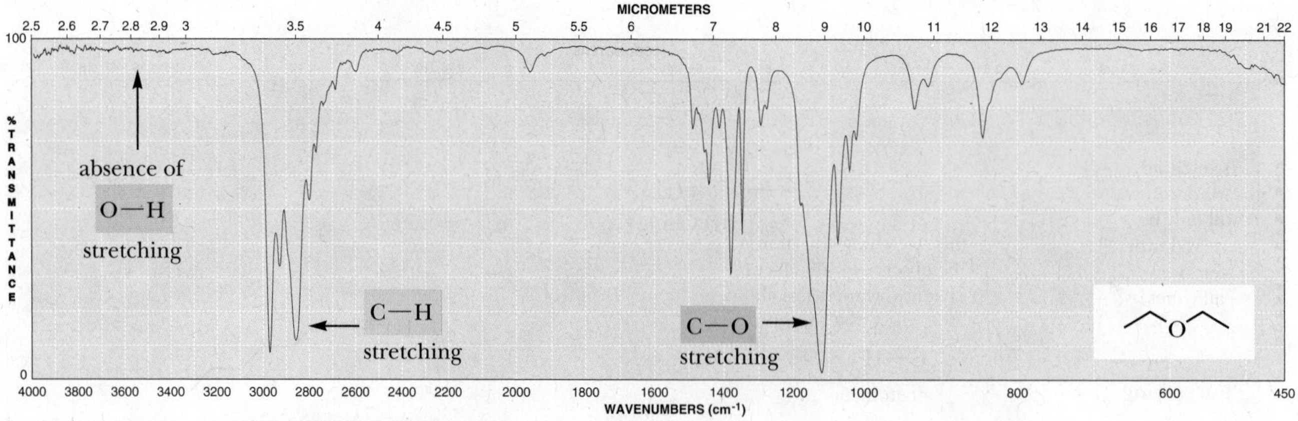

FIGURE 11.8
Infrared spectrum of diethyl ether.

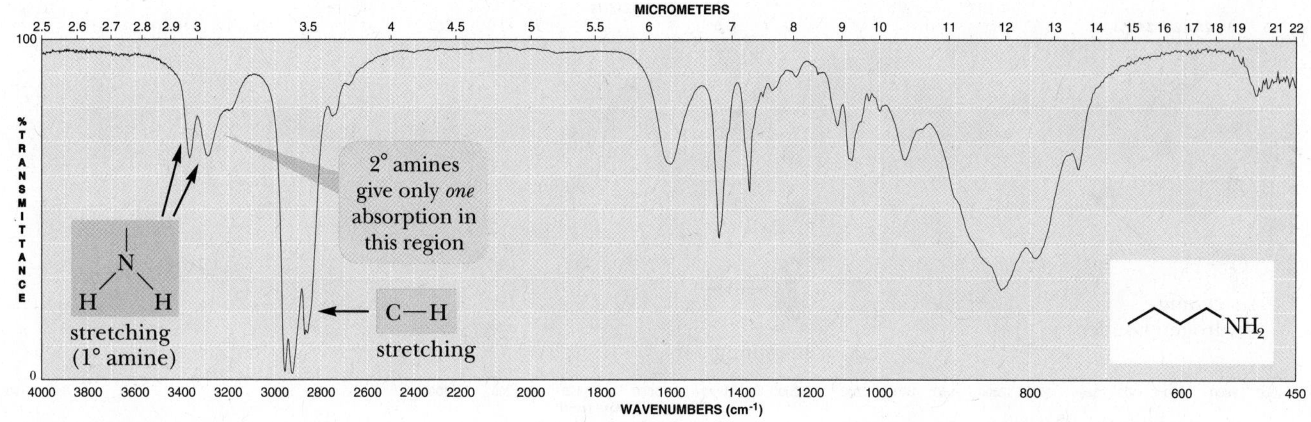

FIGURE 11.9
Infrared spectrum of butanamine, a primary amine.

D. Amines

The most important and readily observed infrared absorptions of primary and secondary amines are due to N—H stretching vibrations and appear in the region from 3100 to 3500 cm^{-1}. Primary amines have two peaks in this region, one caused by a symmetric stretching vibration and the other by asymmetric stretching. The two N—H stretching absorptions characteristic of a primary amine can be seen in the IR spectrum of butanamine (Figure 11.9). Secondary amines give only one absorption in this region. Tertiary amines have no N—H and therefore are transparent in this region of the infrared spectrum.

E. Aldehydes and Ketones

Aldehydes and ketones (Section 1.7C) show characteristic strong infrared absorption between 1705 and 1780 cm^{-1} associated with the stretching vibration of the carbon–oxygen double bond. The stretching vibration for the carbonyl group of menthone occurs at 1705 cm^{-1} (Figure 11.10).

Because several different functional groups contain a carbonyl group, it is often not possible to tell from absorption in this region alone whether the carbonyl-containing compound is an aldehyde, a ketone, a carboxylic acid, or an ester.

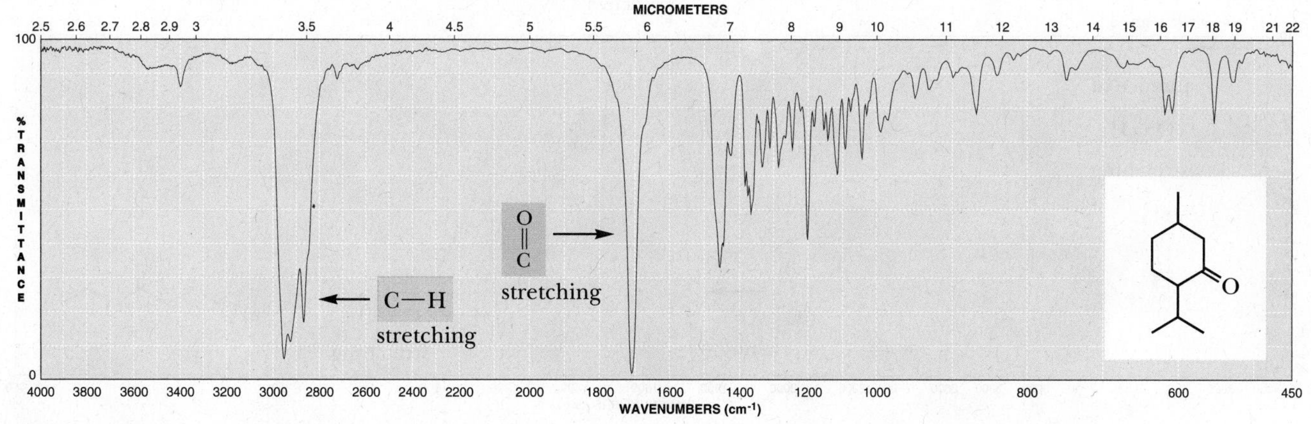

FIGURE 11.10
Infrared spectrum of menthone.

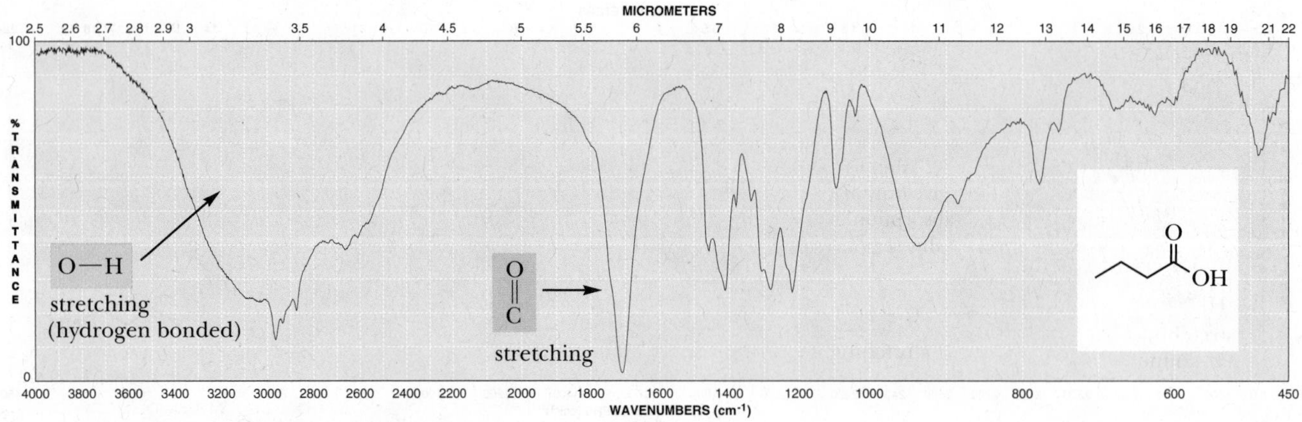

FIGURE 11.11
Infrared spectrum of butanoic acid.

F. Carboxylic Acids and Their Derivatives

The carboxyl group of a carboxylic acid gives rise to two characteristic absorptions in the infrared spectrum. One of these occurs in the region from 1700 to 1725 cm^{-1} and is associated with the stretching vibration of the carbonyl group. This region is essentially the same as that for the absorption of the carbonyl groups of aldehydes and ketones. The other infrared absorption characteristic of a carboxyl group is a peak between 2400 and 3400 cm^{-1} due to the stretching vibration of the O—H group. This peak, which often overlaps the C—H stretching absorptions, is generally very broad due to hydrogen bonding between molecules of the carboxylic acid. Both C=O and O—H stretchings can be seen in the infrared spectrum of butanoic acid, shown in Figure 11.11.

Esters display strong C=O stretching absorption in the region between 1735 and 1800 cm^{-1}. In addition, they display strong C—O stretching absorption in the region from 1000 to 1250 cm^{-1} (Figure 11.12).

The carbonyl stretching of amides occurs at 1630–1680 cm^{-1}, a lower series of wavenumbers than for other carbonyl compounds. Primary and secondary amides show N—H stretching in the region from 3200 to 3400 cm^{-1}; primary amides ($RCONH_2$) show two N—H absorptions, whereas secondary amides (RCONHR) show only a single N—H absorption. Tertiary amides, of course, do not show N—H stretching absorptions. See the three spectra in Figure 11.13.

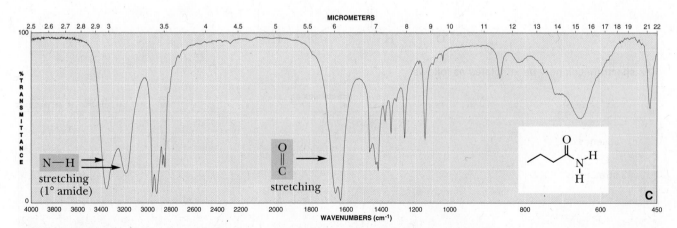

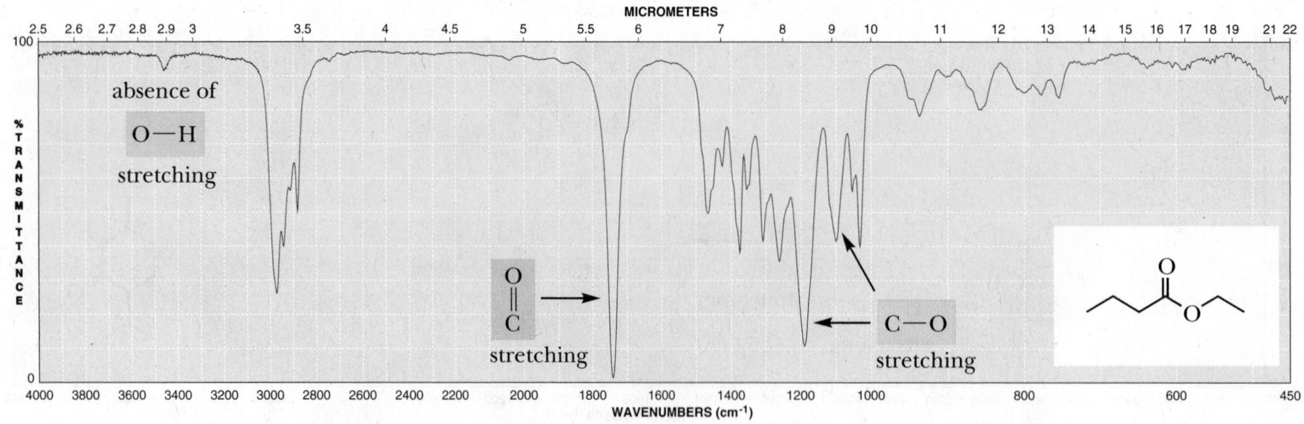

FIGURE 11.12
Infrared spectrum of ethyl butanoate.

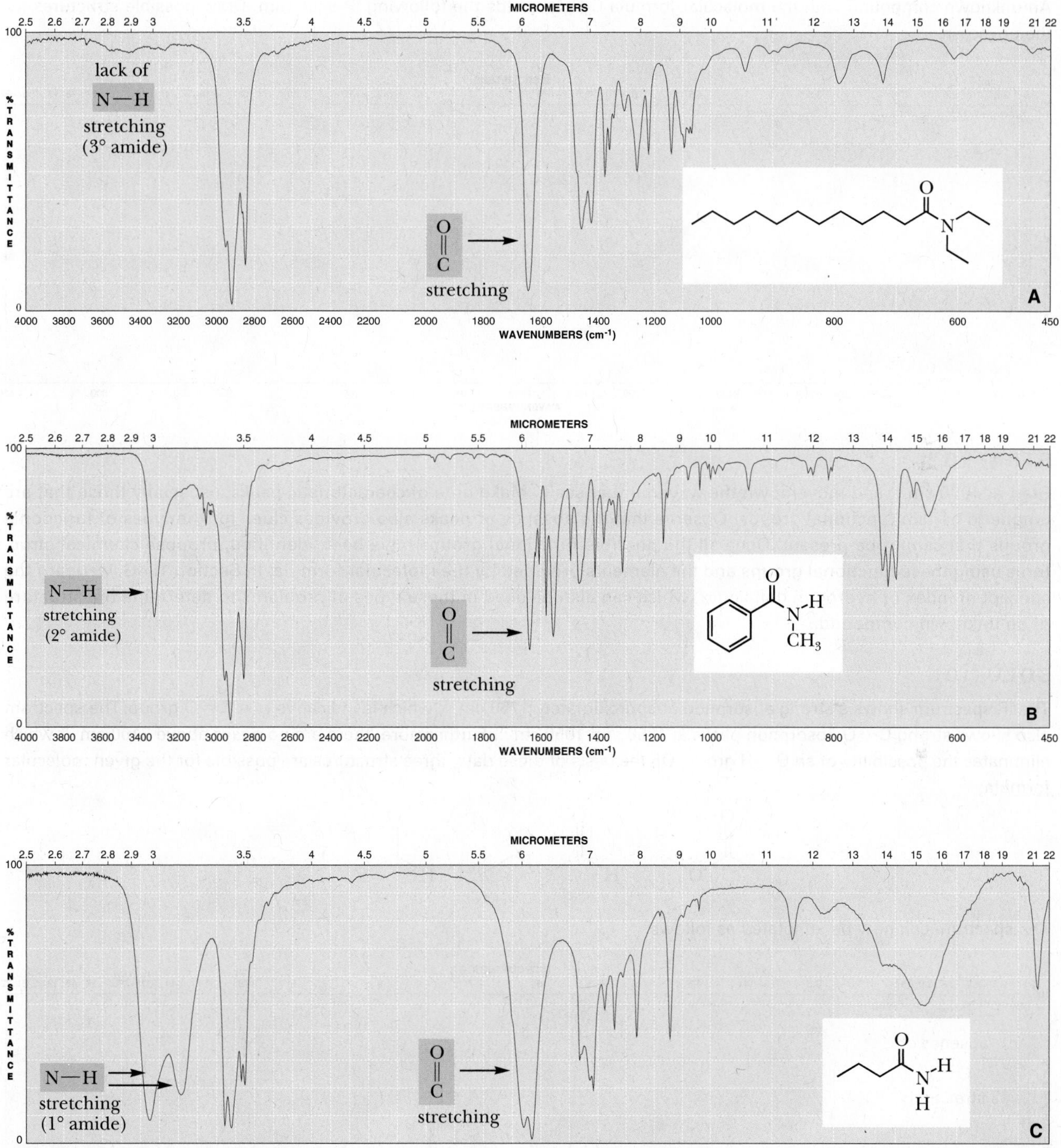

FIGURE 11.13
Infrared spectra of *N*,*N*-diethyldodecanamide (**A**, a tertiary amide), *N*-methylbenzamide (**B**, a secondary amide), butanamide (**C**, a primary amide).

EXAMPLE 11.4

An unknown compound with the molecular formula $C_3H_6O_2$ yields the following IR spectrum. Draw possible structures for the unknown.

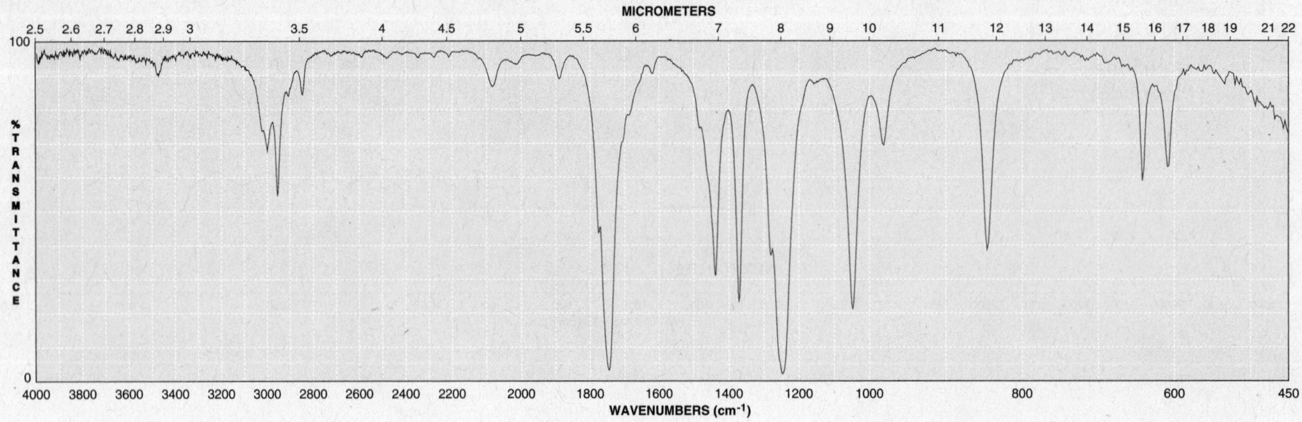

STRATEGY

Start at 4000 cm^{-1} and move down the wavenumber scale. Make note of characteristic peaks, especially those that are unique to certain functional groups. Observe that the absence of peaks also provides clues for the types of functional groups that cannot be present. Once all the possible functional groups have been identified, propose chemical structures using these functional groups and the elements provided by the molecular formula. In Section 11.4G, we learn the concept of index of hydrogen deficiency, which can also be used in these types of problems to determine the structure of an unknown compound.

SOLUTION

The IR spectrum shows a strong absorption at approximately 1750 cm^{-1}, which is indicative of a C=O group. The spectrum also shows strong C—O absorption peaks at 1250 and 1050 cm^{-1}. Furthermore, there are no peaks above 3100 cm^{-1}, which eliminates the possibility of an O—H group. On the basis of these data, three structures are possible for the given molecular formula:

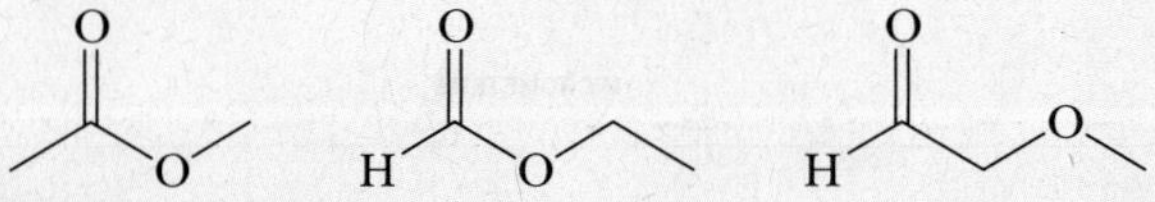

The spectrum can now be annotated as follows:

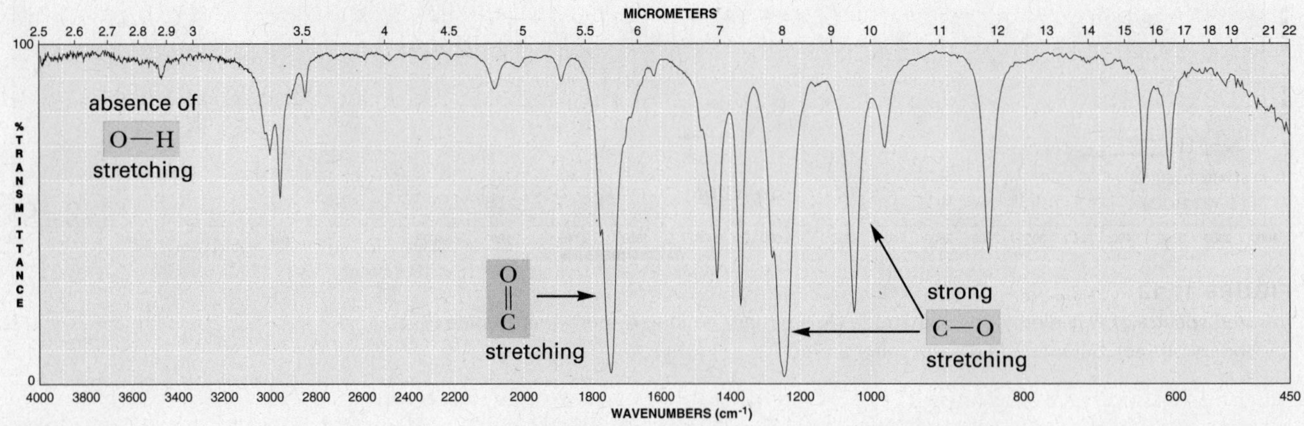

See problems 11.22–11.28

PROBLEM 11.4

What does the value of the wavenumber of the stretching frequency for a particular functional group indicate about the relative strength of the bond in that functional group?

G. Index of Hydrogen Deficiency

We can obtain valuable information about the structural formula of an unknown compound by inspecting its molecular formula. In addition to learning the number of atoms of carbon, hydrogen, oxygen, nitrogen, and so forth in a molecule of the compound, we can determine what is called its **index of hydrogen deficiency**, which is the sum of the number of rings and pi bonds in a molecule. We determine this quantity by comparing the number of hydrogens in the molecular formula of a compound of unknown structure with the number of hydrogens in a **reference compound** with the same number of carbon atoms and with no rings or pi bonds. The molecular formula of a reference hydrocarbon is C_nH_{2n+2} (Section 3.1).

Index of hydrogen deficiency The sum of the number of rings and pi bonds in a molecule.

$$\text{Index of hydrogen deficiency} = \frac{(H_{\text{reference}} - H_{\text{molecule}})}{2}$$

EXAMPLE 11.5

Calculate the index of hydrogen deficiency for 1-hexene, with the molecular formula C_6H_{12}, and account for this deficiency by reference to the structural formula of the compound.

STRATEGY

Determine the number of hydrogens in the reference compound; then use the formula

$$\text{Index of hydrogen deficiency} = \frac{(H_{\text{reference}} - H_{\text{molecule}})}{2}.$$

SOLUTION

The molecular formula of the reference hydrocarbon with six carbon atoms is C_6H_{14}. The index of hydrogen deficiency of 1-hexene is $(14 - 12)/2 = 1$ and is accounted for by the one pi bond in 1-hexene.

See problems 11.21–11.28

PROBLEM 11.5

Calculate the index of hydrogen deficiency of cyclohexene, C_6H_{10}, and account for this deficiency by reference to the structural formula of the compound.

To determine the molecular formula of a reference compound containing elements besides carbon and hydrogen, write the formula of the reference hydrocarbon, add to it other elements contained in the unknown compound, and make the following adjustments to the number of hydrogen atoms:

1. For each atom of a monovalent Group 7 element (F, Cl, Br, I) added to the reference hydrocarbon, subtract one hydrogen; halogen substitutes for hydrogen and reduces the number of hydrogens by one per halogen. The general formula of an acyclic monochloroalkane, for example, is $C_nH_{2n+1}Cl$.
2. No correction is necessary for the addition of atoms of Group 6 elements (O, S, Se) to the reference hydrocarbon. Inserting a divalent Group 6 element into a reference hydrocarbon does not change the number of hydrogens.
3. For each atom of a trivalent Group 5 element (N and P) added to the formula of the reference hydrocarbon, add one hydrogen. Inserting a trivalent Group 5 element adds one hydrogen to the molecular formula of the reference compound. The general molecular formula for an acyclic alkylamine, for example, is $C_nH_{2n+3}N$.

EXAMPLE 11.6

Isopentyl acetate, a compound with a bananalike odor, is a component of the alarm pheromone of honeybees. The molecular formula of isopentyl acetate is $C_7H_{14}O_2$. Calculate the index of hydrogen deficiency of this compound.

STRATEGY

Determine the number of hydrogens in the reference compound and then use the formula

$$\text{Index of hydrogen deficiency} = \frac{(H_{reference} - H_{molecule})}{2}$$

SOLUTION

The molecular formula of the reference hydrocarbon is C_7H_{16}. Adding oxygens to this formula does not require any correction in the number of hydrogens. The molecular formula of the reference compound is $C_7H_{16}O_2$, and the index of hydrogen deficiency is $(16 - 14)/2 = 1$, indicating either one ring or one pi bond. Following is the structural formula of isopentyl acetate, which contains one pi bond, in this case in the carbon–oxygen double bond:

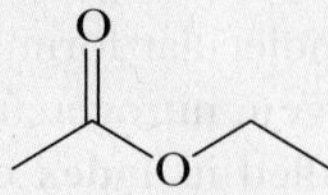

Isopentyl acetate

See problems 11.21–11.28

PROBLEM 11.6

The index of hydrogen deficiency of niacin is 5. Account for this value by reference to the structural formula of niacin.

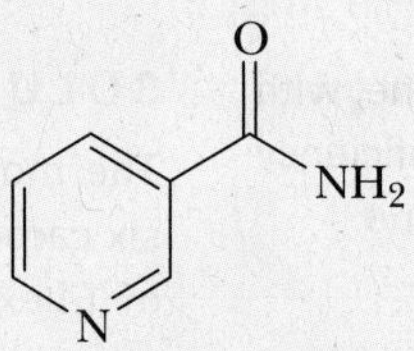

Nicotinamide
(Niacin)

HOW TO 11.1 Approach Infrared Spectroscopy Structure Determination Problems

It is useful to develop a systematic approach to problems that ask you to determine a structure given a molecular formula and an infrared spectrum. Following are some guidelines for tackling such problems.

(a) *Determine the index of hydrogen deficiency (IHD).* Knowing the potential number of rings, double bonds, or triple bonds in an unknown compound is of great assistance in solving the structure. For example, if IHD = 1, you know that the unknown can have either a ring or a double bond, but not both. It also cannot have a triple bond because that would require an IHD = 2.

(b) *Move from left to right to identify functional groups in the IR spectrum.* Because the types of transitions in an IR spectrum become less specific as absorptions approach and go lower than 1000 cm^{-1}, it is most useful to start on the left side of an IR spectrum. The shorter the bond, the higher in wavenumber its absorption. This is why O—H, N—H, and C—H bond vibrations occur above 3900 cm^{-1}. Proceeding to the right, we then encounter C—C triple bond stretching vibrations. C=O bonds are shorter than C=C bonds and therefore occur at higher wavenumbers (1800–1650 cm^{-1}) than C=C bonds (1680–1600 cm^{-1}).

(c) *Draw possible structures and verify your structures with the data.* Do not try to think of the answer entirely in your mind. Rather, jot down some structures on paper. Once you have one or more possible structures, verify that these possibilities work with the IHD value and the functional groups indicated by the IR spectrum. Usually, incorrect structures will obviously conflict with one or more of these data items.

EXAMPLE 11.7

Determine possible structures for a compound that yields the following IR spectrum and has a molecular formula of C_7H_8O:

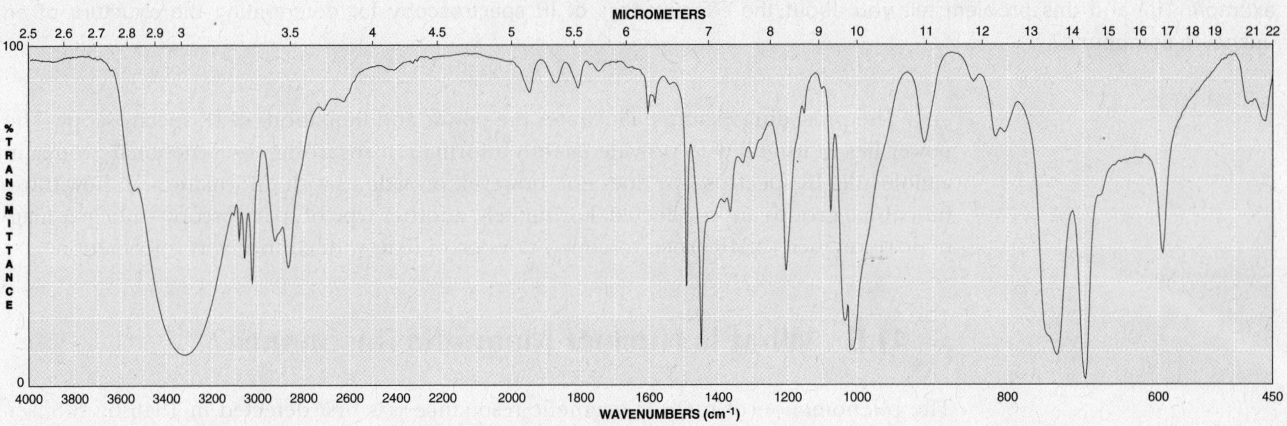

STRATEGY

Determine the index of hydrogen deficiency and use this value as a guide to the combination of rings, double bonds, or triple bonds possible in the unknown. Analyze the IR spectrum, starting at 4000 cm^{-1} and moving down the wavenumber scale. Make note of characteristic peaks, especially those that are unique to certain functional groups. Note that the absence of peaks also provides clues for the types of functional groups that cannot be present. Once all the possible functional groups have been identified, propose chemical structures using these functional groups and the elements provided by the molecular formula.

SOLUTION

The index of hydrogen deficiency for C_7H_8O is 4, based on the reference formula C_7H_{16}. We can exclude C—C triple bonds because of the absence of a peak from the triple bond C—C stretch (2100–2260 cm^{-1}) and the absence of a terminal alkyne C—H stretch (3300 cm^{-1}). We see C—C double bond C—H stretching peaks just above 3000 cm^{-1}. However, we don't see C—C double bond stretching between 1600 and 1680 cm^{-1}. Recall that aromatic hydrocarbons do not exhibit the same chemical properties as alkenes, so an arene ring remains a possibility. Benzene, with 3 double bonds and a ring, would have an index of hydrogen deficiency of 4 (this is a common functional group to keep in mind whenever we encounter an IHD of 4 or more). By considering a benzene ring as a possibility, the remaining structural possibilities are limited. Because there is no strong absorption between 1630 and 1800 cm^{-1}, a carbonyl group (C=O) can be excluded. The last piece of evidence is the strong, broad O—H stretching peak at approximately 3310 cm^{-1}. Because we must have an OH group, we cannot propose any structures with an OCH_3 (ether) group. Based on this interpretation of the spectrum, the following four structures are possible:

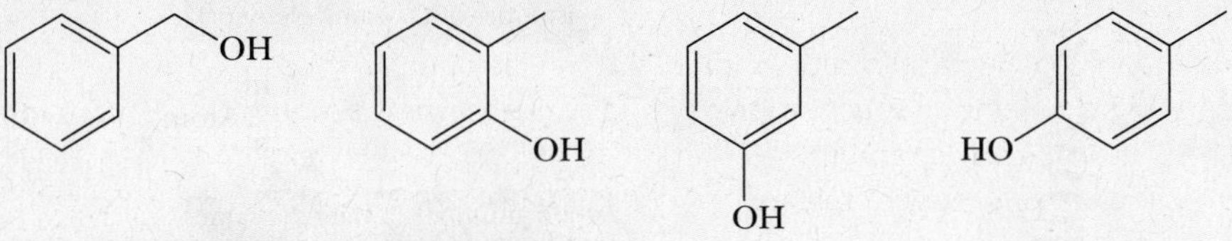

The given spectrum can now be annotated as follows:

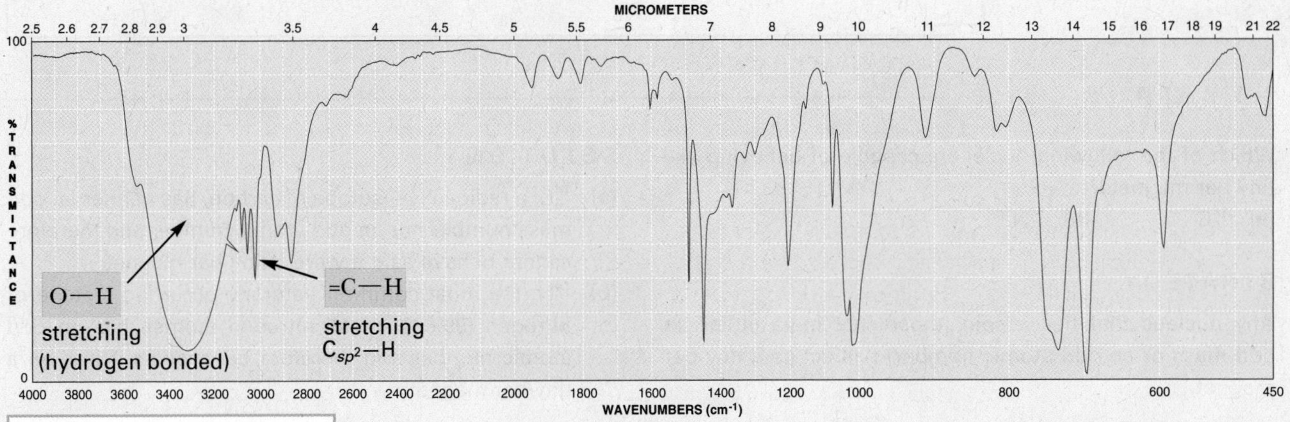

See problems 11.22–11.28

PROBLEM 11.7

Determine possible structures for the same spectrum (above) for a compound with molecular formula $C_8H_{10}O$. What does example 11.7 and this problem tell you about the effectiveness of IR spectroscopy for determining the structure of an unknown compound?

The preceding example illustrates the power and limitations of IR spectroscopy. The power lies in its ability to provide us with information regarding the functional groups in a molecule. IR spectroscopy does not, however, provide us with information on how those functional groups are connected. Fortunately, another type of spectroscopy—nuclear magnetic resonance (NMR) spectroscopy—does provide us with connectivity information.

11.5 What Is Nuclear Magnetic Resonance?

The phenomenon of nuclear magnetic resonance was first detected in 1946 by U.S. scientists Felix Bloch and Edward Purcell, who shared the 1952 Nobel Prize for Physics for their discoveries. The particular value of nuclear magnetic resonance (NMR) spectroscopy is that it gives us information about the number and types of atoms in a molecule, for example, about the number and types of hydrogens using **^{1}H-NMR spectroscopy**, and about the number and types of carbons using **^{13}C-NMR spectroscopy**.

From your study of general chemistry, you may already be familiar with the concept that an electron has a **spin** and that a spinning charge creates an associated magnetic field. In effect, an electron behaves as if it is a tiny bar magnet. An atomic nucleus that has an odd mass or an odd atomic number also has a spin and behaves as if it is a tiny bar magnet. Recall that when designating isotopes, a superscript represents the mass of the element.

HOW TO 11.2 Determine Whether an Atomic Nucleus Has a Spin (Behaves as If It Were a Tiny Bar Magnet)

Determine the mass and atomic number of the atom. If *either* is an odd number, the atom will have a spin and behave as a tiny bar magnet.

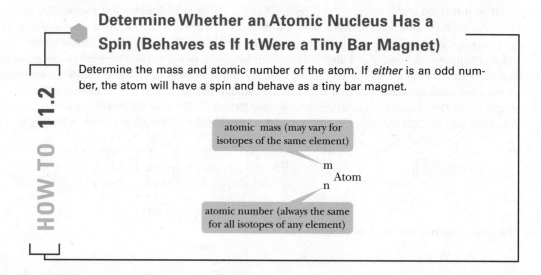

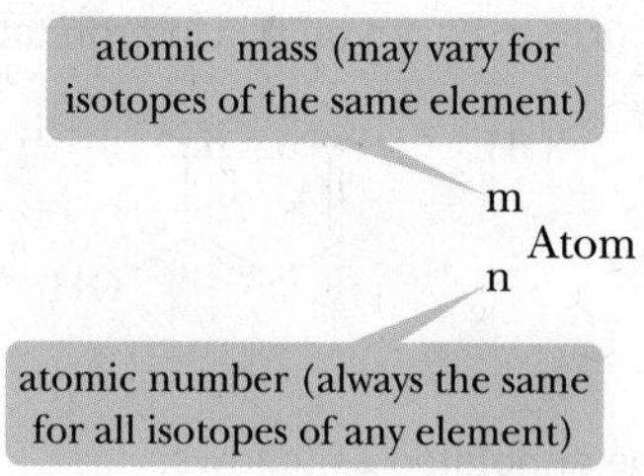

EXAMPLE 11.8

Which of the following nuclei are capable of behaving like tiny bar magnets?

(a) $^{14}_{6}C$ **(b)** $^{14}_{7}N$

STRATEGY

Any nucleus that has a spin (those that have either an odd mass or an odd atomic number) will act as a tiny bar magnet.

SOLUTION

(a) $^{14}_{6}C$, a radioactive isotope of carbon, has neither an odd mass number nor an odd atomic number and therefore cannot behave as if it were a tiny bar magnet.

(b) $^{14}_{7}N$, the most common naturally occurring isotope of nitrogen (99.63% of all nitrogen atoms), has an odd atomic number and therefore behaves as if it were a tiny bar magnet.

PROBLEM 11.8

Which of the following nuclei are capable of behaving like tiny bar magnets?
(a) $^{31}_{15}P$ (b) $^{195}_{78}Pt$

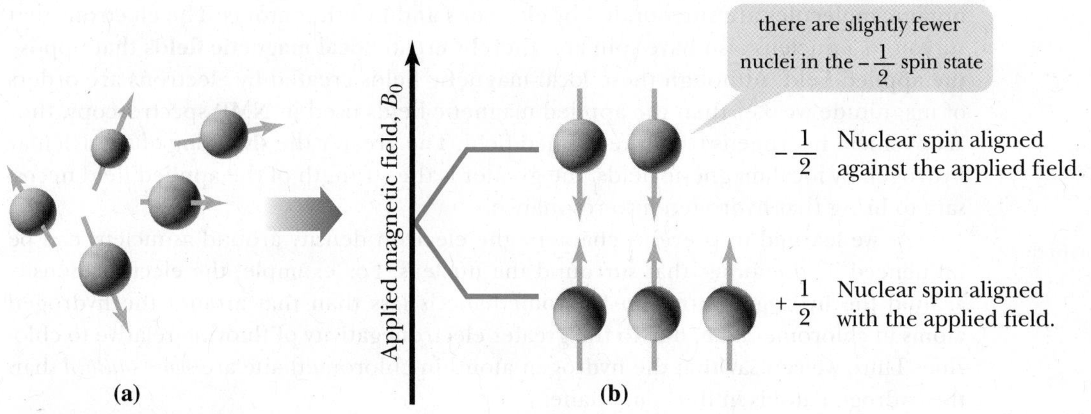

FIGURE 11.14
^1H and ^{13}C nuclei (a) in the absence of an applied magnetic field and (b) in the presence of an applied field. ^1H and ^{13}C nuclei with spin $+\frac{1}{2}$ are aligned with the applied magnetic field and are in the lower spin energy state; those with spin $-\frac{1}{2}$ are aligned against the applied magnetic field and are in the higher spin energy state.

Within a collection of ^1H and ^{13}C atoms, the spins of their tiny nuclear bar magnets are completely random in orientation. When we place them between the poles of a powerful magnet, however, interactions between their nuclear spins and the **applied magnetic field** are quantized, and only two orientations are allowed (Figure 11.14).

The difference in energy between these nuclear spin states for ^1H is 0.120 J/mol (0.0286 cal/mol), which corresponds to electromagnetic radiation of approximately 300 MHz (300,000,000 Hz). The difference in energy for the two spin states of ^{13}C is 0.035 J/mol (0.0072 cal/mol). Both of these values fall within the radio-frequency range of the electromagnetic spectrum, and irradiation of the nuclei in the lower energy spin state with radio-frequency radiation of the appropriate energy causes them to absorb energy and results in their nuclear spins flipping from the lower energy state to the higher energy state, as illustrated in Figure 11.15. In this context, **resonance** is defined as the absorption of electromagnetic radiation by a spinning nucleus and the resulting flip of its nuclear spin state. The instrument we use to detect this absorption and resulting flip of nuclear spin state records it as a **resonance signal**.

Resonance The absorption of electromagnetic radiation by a spinning nucleus and the resulting "flip" of its spin from a lower energy state to a higher energy state.

Resonance signal A recording of nuclear magnetic resonance in an NMR spectrum.

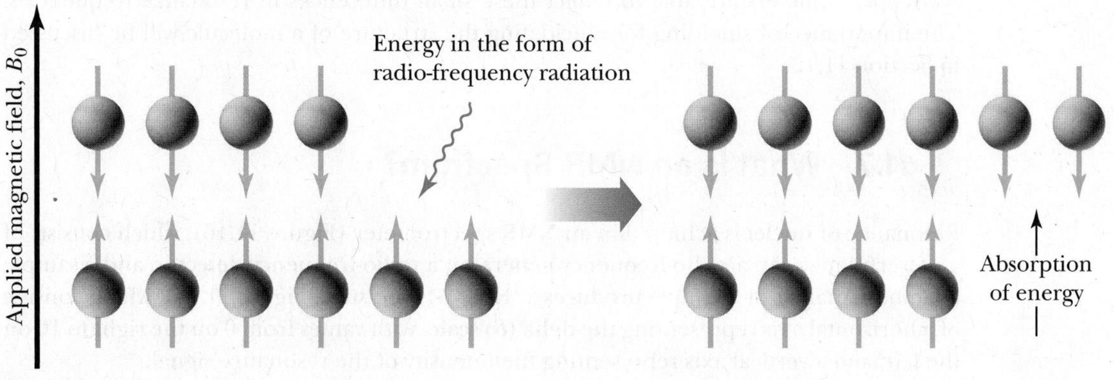

FIGURE 11.15
An example of resonance for nuclei of spin $\frac{1}{2}$.

11.6 What Is Shielding?

If all ^1H nuclei absorbed the same frequency of electromagnetic radiation (i.e., if they all resonated at the same frequency), all hydrogens in a compound would give rise to one and only one NMR signal, and NMR spectroscopy would be an ineffective technique for determining the structure of a molecule. Fortunately, hydrogens in most organic molecules are surrounded by electrons and by other atoms. The electrons that surround a nucleus also have spin and thereby create **local magnetic fields** that oppose the applied field. Although these local magnetic fields created by electrons are orders of magnitude weaker than the applied magnetic fields used in NMR spectroscopy, they act to shield hydrogens from the applied field. The greater the **shielding** of a particular hydrogen by local magnetic fields, the greater is the strength of the applied field necessary to bring that hydrogen into resonance.

Shielding In NMR spectroscopy, electrons around a nucleus create their own local magnetic fields and thereby shield the nucleus from the applied magnetic field.

As we learned in previous chapters, the electron density around a nucleus can be influenced by the atoms that surround the nucleus. For example, the electron density around the hydrogen atoms in fluoromethane is less than that around the hydrogen atoms in chloromethane, due to the greater electronegativity of fluorine relative to chlorine. Thus, we can say that the hydrogen atoms in chloromethane are *more shielded* than the hydrogen atoms in fluoromethane:

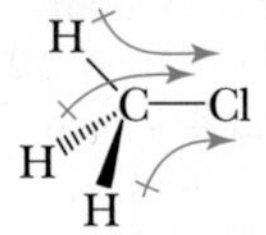

Chlorine is less electronegative than fluorine, resulting in a smaller inductive effect and thereby a greater electron density around each hydrogen. We say that the hydrogens in chloromethane are more **shielded** (by their local environment) than those in fluoromethane.

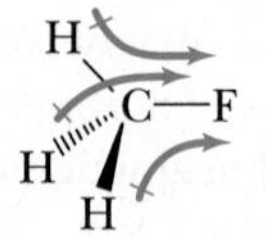

Fluorine's greater electronegativity produces a larger inductive effect and thereby reduces the electron density around each hydrogen. We say that these hydrogens are **deshielded**.

The differences in resonance frequencies among the various ^1H nuclei within a molecule caused by shielding are generally very small. The difference between the resonance frequencies of hydrogens in chloromethane compared with those in fluoromethane, for example, is only 360 Hz under an applied field of 7.05 tesla. Considering that the radio-frequency radiation used at this applied field is approximately 300 MHz (300×10^6 Hz), the difference in resonance frequencies between these two sets of hydrogens is only slightly greater than 1 **part per million** (1 ppm) compared with the irradiating frequency.

$$\frac{360 \text{ Hz}}{300 \times 10^6 \text{ Hz}} = \frac{1.2}{10^6} = 1.2 \text{ ppm}$$

NMR spectrometers are able to detect these small differences in resonance frequencies. The importance of shielding for elucidating the structure of a moleculc will be discussed in Section 11.10.

11.7 What Is an NMR Spectrum?

Resonance of nuclei is achieved in an NMR spectrometer (Figure 11.16), which consists of a powerful magnet, a radio-frequency generator, a radio-frequency detector, and a sample chamber. Analysis of a sample produces a ^1H-NMR spectrum (Figure 11.17), which consists of a horizontal axis representing the **delta (δ) scale**, with values from 0 on the right to 10 on the left, and a vertical axis representing the intensity of the resonance signal.

It is customary to measure the resonance frequencies of individual nuclei relative to the resonance frequency of the same nuclei in a reference compound. The

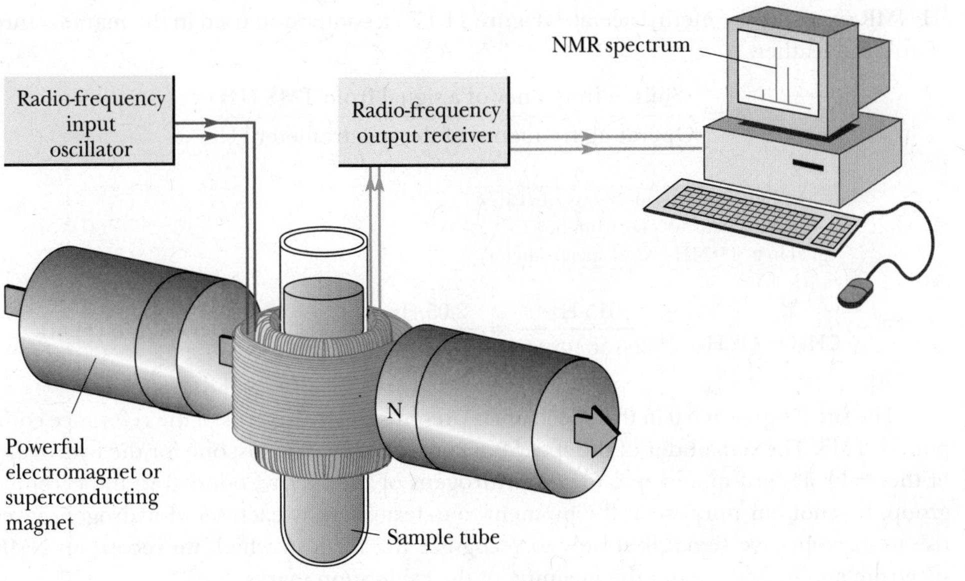

FIGURE 11.16
Schematic diagram of a nuclear magnetic resonance spectrometer.

reference compound now universally accepted for ^{1}H-NMR and ^{13}C-NMR spectroscopy is **tetramethylsilane (TMS)** because it is relatively unreactive and its hydrogen and carbon atoms are highly shielded due to the less electronegative silicon atom. The latter fact ensures that most other resonance signals will be less shielded than the signal for TMS.

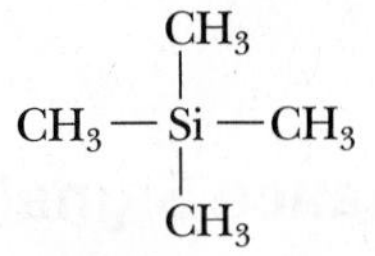

Tetramethylsilane (TMS)

When we determine a ^{1}H-NMR spectrum of a compound, we report how far the resonance signals of its hydrogens are shifted from the resonance signal of the hydrogens in TMS. When we determine a ^{13}C-NMR spectrum, we report how far the resonance signals of its carbons are shifted from the resonance signal of the four carbons in TMS.

To standardize reporting of NMR data, workers have adopted a quantity called the **chemical shift (δ)**. Chemical shift is calculated by dividing the shift in frequency of a signal (relative to that of TMS) by the operating frequency of the spectrometer. Because NMR spectrometers operate at MHz frequencies (i.e., millions of Hz), we express the chemical shift in parts per million. A sample calculation is provided for the signal at 2.05 ppm in the

Chemical shift, δ The position of a signal on an NMR spectrum relative to the signal of tetramethylsilane (TMS); expressed in delta (δ) units, where 1 δ equals 1 ppm.

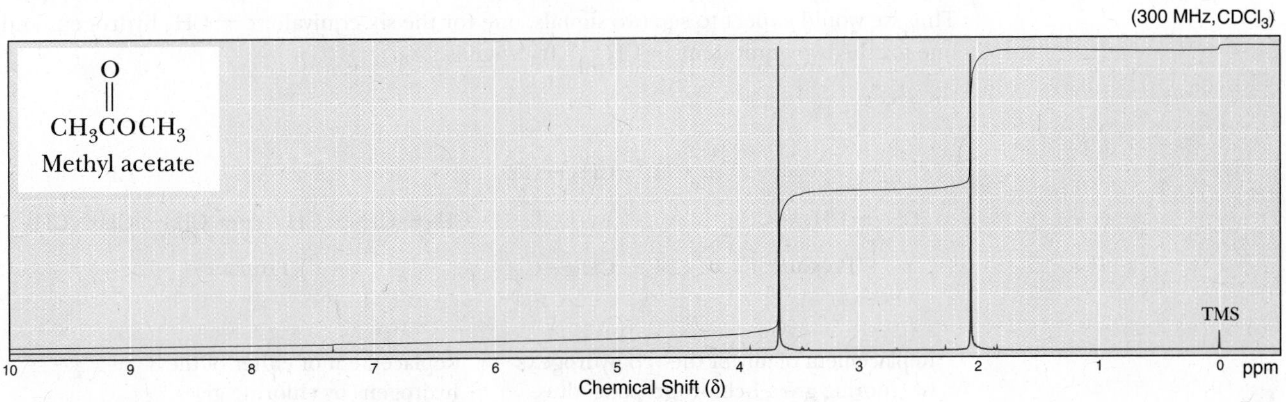

FIGURE 11.17
^{1}H-NMR spectrum of methyl acetate.

^{1}H-NMR spectrum for methyl acetate (Figure 11.17), a compound used in the manufacture of artificial leather.

$$\delta = \frac{\text{Shift in frequency of a signal from TMS (Hz)}}{\text{Operating frequency of the spectrometer (Hz)}}$$

the hydrogens on this methyl group cause a signal to occur 615 Hz from the TMS signal in a 300 MHz NMR spectrometer

$$\text{e.g.,}\quad CH_3\overset{O}{\overset{\|}{C}}{-}OCH_3 \qquad \frac{615\ \text{Hz}}{300 \times 10^6\ \text{Hz}} = \frac{2.05\ \text{Hz}}{\text{million Hz}} = 2.05 \text{ parts per million (ppm)}$$

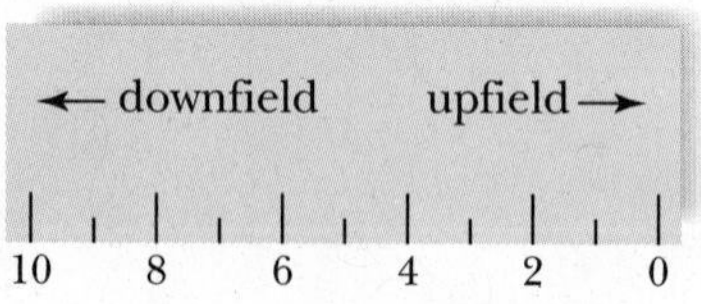

Downfield A term used to refer to the relative position of a signal on an NMR spectrum. Downfield indicates a peak to the left of the spectrum (a weaker applied field).

Upfield A term used to refer to the relative position of a signal on an NMR spectrum. Upfield indicates a peak to the right of the spectrum (a stronger applied field).

Equivalent hydrogens Hydrogens that have the same chemical environment.

The small signal at δ 0 in this spectrum represents the hydrogens of the reference compound, TMS. The remainder of the spectrum consists of two signals: one for the hydrogens of the $-OCH_3$ group and one for the hydrogens of the methyl bonded to the carbonyl group. It is not our purpose at the moment to determine why each set of hydrogens gives rise to its respective signal, but only to recognize the form in which we record an NMR spectrum and to understand the meaning of the calibration marks.

A note on terminology. If a signal is shifted toward the left on the chart paper, we say that it is shifted **downfield**, meaning that nuclei giving rise to that signal are less shielded and come into resonance at a weaker applied field. Conversely, if a signal is shifted toward the right of the spectrum, we say that it is shifted **upfield**, meaning that nuclei giving rise to that signal are more shielded and come into resonance at a stronger applied field.

11.8 How Many Resonance Signals Will a Compound Yield in Its NMR Spectrum?

Given the structural formula of a compound, how do we know how many signals to expect? The answer is that **equivalent hydrogens** give the same ^{1}H-NMR signal; conversely, nonequivalent hydrogens give different ^{1}H-NMR signals. A direct way to determine which hydrogens in a molecule are equivalent is to replace each in turn by a test atom, such as a halogen atom. Two hydrogens treated in this way are equivalent if their "substituted" versions are the same compound or if they are enantiomers of each other. If replacement gives compounds that are different and not enantiomers, the two hydrogens are nonequivalent.

Using this substitution test, we can show that propane contains two sets of equivalent hydrogens: a set of six equivalent 1° hydrogens and a set of two equivalent 2° hydrogens. Thus we would expect to see two signals, one for the six equivalent $-CH_3$ hydrogens and one for the two equivalent $-CH_2-$ hydrogens:

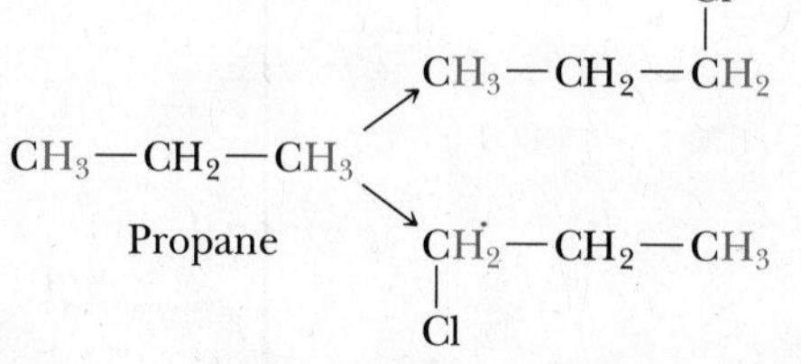

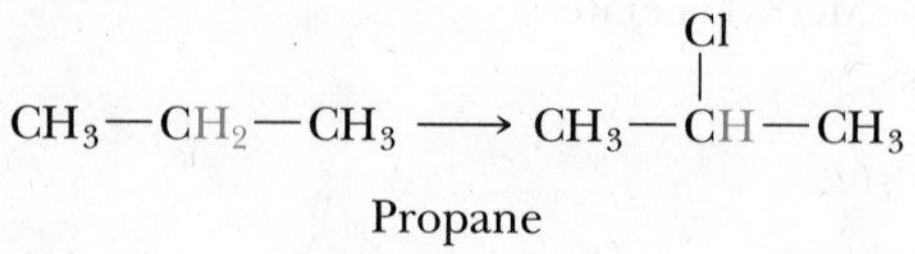

Replacement of any of the red hydrogens by chlorine gives 1-chloropropane; thus, all the red hydrogens are **equivalent**.

Replacement of either of the blue hydrogens by chlorine gives 2-chloropropane; thus, both of the blue hydrogens are **equivalent**.

EXAMPLE 11.9

State the number of sets of equivalent hydrogens in each compound and the number of hydrogens in each set:

(a) 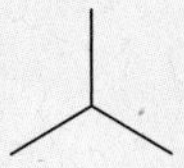

2-Methylpropane

(b) 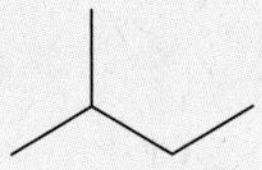

2-Methylbutane

(c) 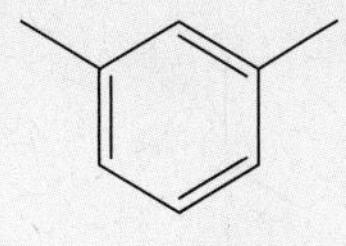

m-Xylene

STRATEGY

A reliable way to determine whether hydrogens are equivalent is to replace each with a halogen and name the resulting compound. Hydrogens are equivalent if the two molecules containing their replacements are the same compound or are enantiomers.

SOLUTION

(a) 2-Methylpropane contains two sets of equivalent hydrogens—a set of nine equivalent 1° hydrogens and one 3° hydrogen:

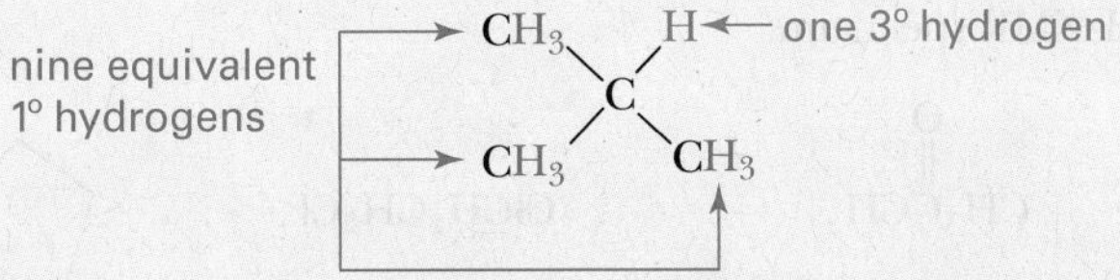

Replacing any one of the red hydrogens with a chlorine yields 1-chloro-2-methylpropane. Replacing the blue hydrogen with a chlorine yields 2-chloro-2-methylpropane.

(b) 2-Methylbutane contains four sets of equivalent hydrogens—two different sets of 1° hydrogens, one set of 2° hydrogens, and one 3° hydrogen:

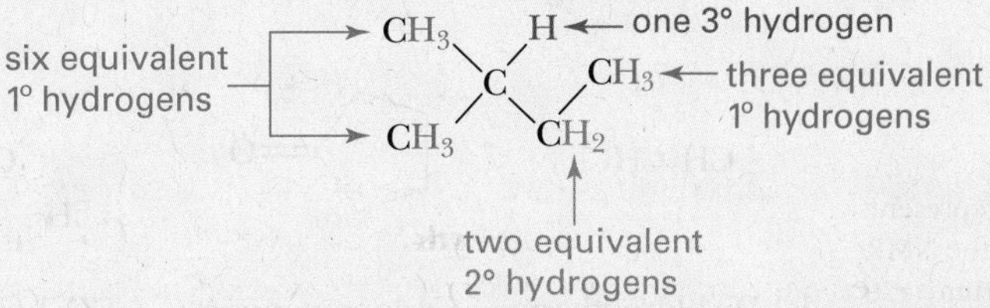

Replacing any one of the red hydrogens with a chlorine yields 1-chloro-2-methylbutane. Replacing the blue hydrogen with a chlorine yields 2-chloro-2-methylbutane. Replacing a purple hydrogen with a chlorine yields 2-chloro-3-methylbutane. Replacing a green hydrogen with chlorine yields 1-chloro-3-methylbutane.

(c) *m*-Xylene contains four sets of equivalent hydrogens—one set of methyl group hydrogens, one set of hydrogens on the benzene ring *ortho* to one methyl group, one hydrogen on the benzene ring *ortho* to both methyl groups, and one hydrogen on the benzene ring *meta* to both methyl groups. In this solution, symmetry is used to illustrate equivalency.

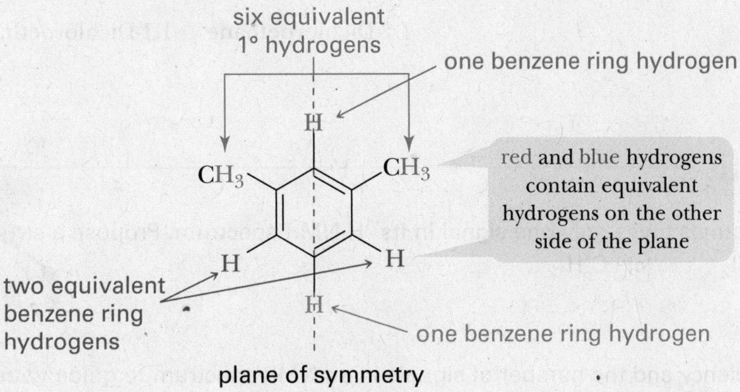

See problem 11.32

PROBLEM 11.9

State the number of sets of equivalent hydrogens in each compound and the number of hydrogens in each set:

(a) 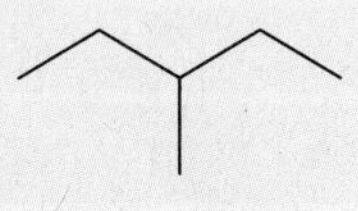

3-Methylpentane

(b) 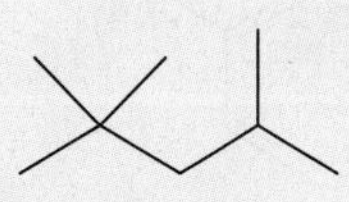

2,2,4-Trimethylpentane

(c) 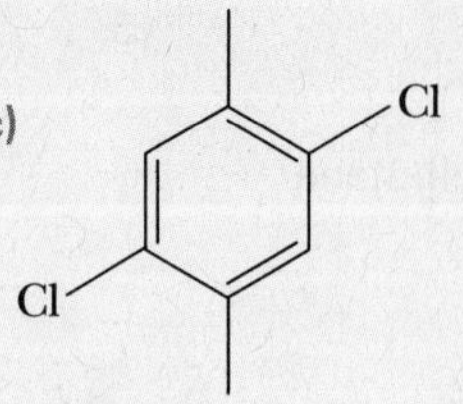

2,5-Dichloro-4-methyltoluene

Symmetrical compounds tend to contain a higher amount of equivalent hydrogens, and thus fewer resonance signals in their NMR spectra. Here are four symmetrical organic compounds, each of which has one set of equivalent hydrogens and gives one signal in its ^{1}H-NMR spectrum:

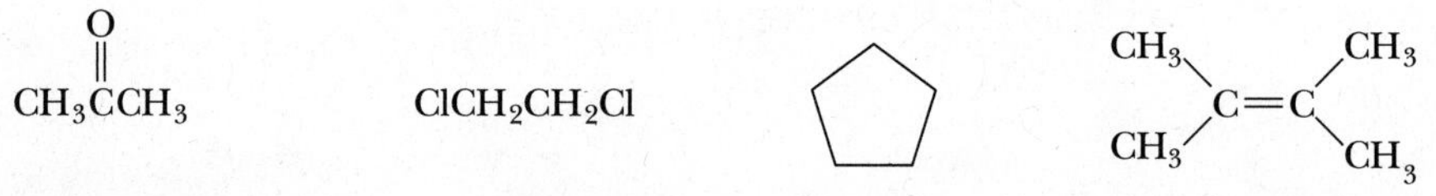

Propanone (Acetone) 1,2-Dichloroethane Cyclopentane 2,3-Dimethyl-2-butene

Molecules with two or more sets of equivalent hydrogens give rise to a different resonance signal for each set. 1,1-Dichloroethane, for example, has three equivalent 1° hydrogens (a) and one 2° hydrogen (b); there are two resonance signals in its ^{1}H-NMR spectrum.

each letter represents a signal in the NMR spectrum

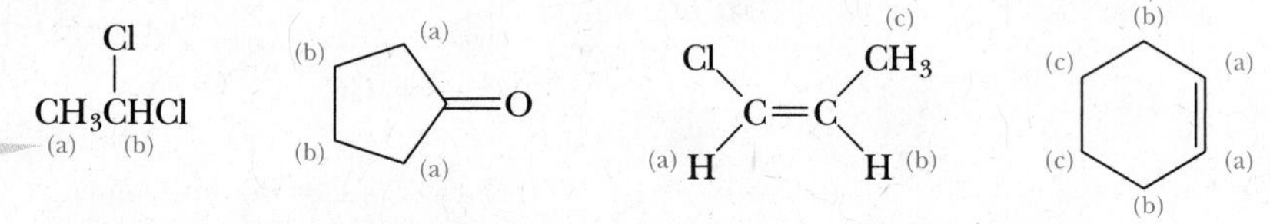

1,1-Dichloroethane (2 signals) Cyclopentanone (2 signals) (*Z*)-1-Chloropropene (3 signals) Cyclohexene (3 signals)

Notice how, by simply counting signals, you can distinguish between the constitutional isomers of 1,2-dichloroethane and 1,1-dichloroethane.

Isomers of $C_2H_4Cl_2$

an NMR spectrum of this isomer would show only one signal

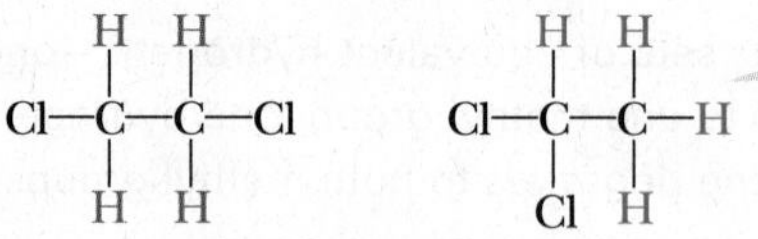

an NMR spectrum of this isomer would show two signals

1,2-Dichloroethane 1,1-Dichloroethane

EXAMPLE 11.10

Each of the following compounds gives only one signal in its ^{1}H-NMR spectrum. Propose a structural formula for each.

(a) C_2H_6O (b) $C_3H_6Cl_2$ (c) C_6H_{12}

STRATEGY

Use index of hydrogen deficiency and the number of signals in an NMR spectrum to guide your choice of structure. A compound that yields fewer signals than it has hydrogen atoms indicates symmetry in the molecule.

SOLUTION

Following are structural formulas for each of the given compounds. Notice that, for each structure, the replacement of any hydrogen with a chlorine will yield the same compound regardless of the hydrogen being replaced.

(a) CH_3OCH_3 (b) 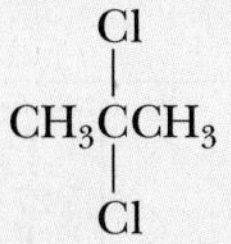 (c) 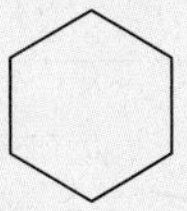 or 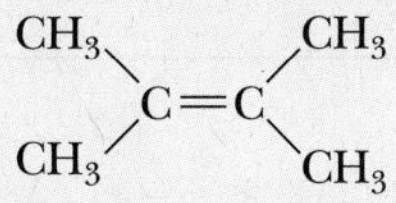

PROBLEM 11.10

Each of the following compounds gives only one signal in its ^{1}H-NMR spectrum. Propose a structural formula for each compound.

(a) C_3H_6O (b) C_5H_{10} (c) C_5H_{12} (d) $C_4H_6Cl_4$

11.9 What Is Signal Integration?

We have just seen that the number of signals in a ^{1}H-NMR spectrum gives us information about the number of sets of equivalent hydrogens. Signal areas in a ^{1}H-NMR spectrum can be measured by a mathematical technique called *integration.* In the spectra shown in this text, this information is displayed in the form of a **line of integration** superposed on the original spectrum. The vertical rise of the line of integration over each signal is proportional to the area under that signal, which, in turn, is proportional to the number of hydrogens giving rise to the signal.

Figure 11.18 shows an integrated ^{1}H-NMR spectrum of the gasoline additive *tert*-butyl acetate ($C_6H_{12}O_2$). The spectrum shows signals at δ 1.44 and 1.95. The integrated height of the upfield (to the right) signal is nearly three times as tall as the height of the downfield (to the left) signal (the heights can be accurately determined by assuming that the distance between horizontal grid lines is 10 units). This relationship corresponds to an **integration ratio** of 3 : 1. We know from the molecular formula that there is a total of 12 hydrogens in the molecule. The ratios obtained from the integration lines are consistent with the presence of one set of 9 equivalent hydrogens and one set of 3 equivalent hydrogens. We will often make use of shorthand notation in referring to an NMR spectrum of a molecule. The notation lists the chemical shift of each signal, beginning with the most deshielded signal and followed by the number of hydrogens that give rise to each signal (based on the integration). The shorthand notation describing the spectrum of *tert*-butyl acetate (Figure 11.18) would be δ 1.95 (3H) and δ 1.44 (9H).

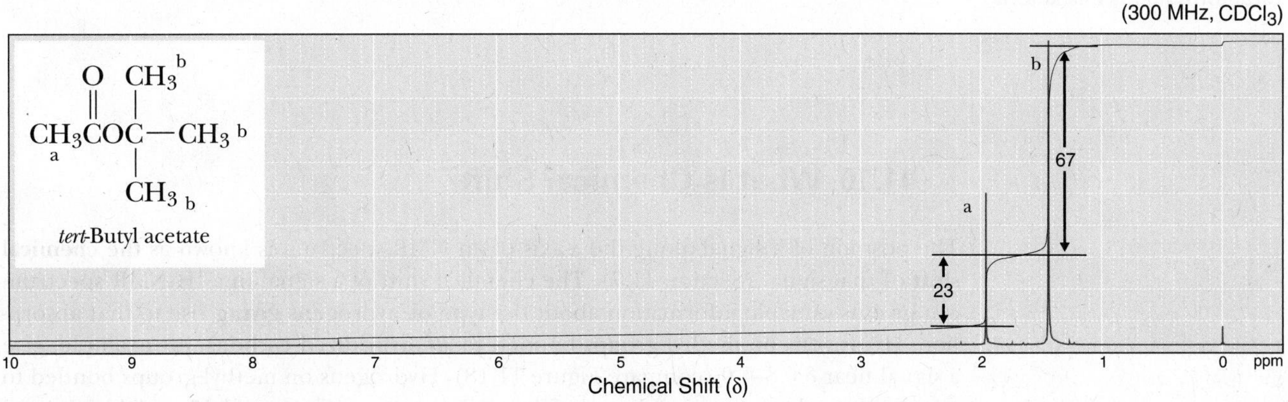

FIGURE 11.18
^{1}H-NMR spectrum of *tert*-butyl acetate, $C_6H_{12}O_2$, showing a line of integration. The ratio of signal heights for the two peaks is 3 : 1, which, for a molecule possessing 12 hydrogens, corresponds to 9 equivalent hydrogens of one set and 3 equivalent hydrogens of another set.

EXAMPLE 11.11

Following is a ¹H-NMR spectrum for a compound with the molecular formula $C_9H_{10}O_2$. From an analysis of the integration line, calculate the number of hydrogens giving rise to each signal.

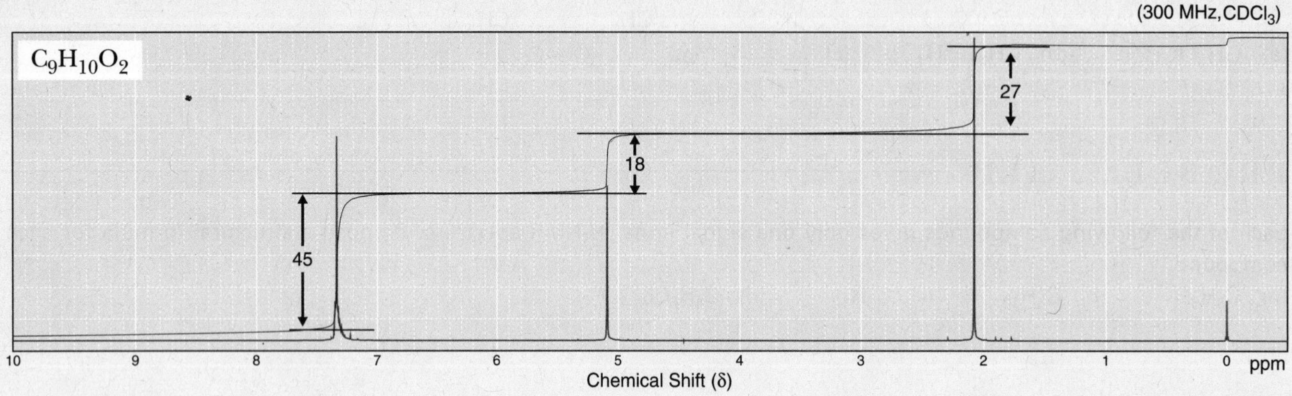

STRATEGY

Once the lengths of the integration lines are determined, divide all the numbers by the lowest value to obtain a minimized ratio. For example, if the lengths of the integration lines are 4 : 12 : 8, the minimized ratio becomes (4 : 12 : 8)/4 = 1 : 3 : 2. The minimized ratio values can be treated as the true number of hydrogens if the sum of these numbers is equal to the number of hydrogens from the molecular formula. If the molecular formula contains a greater number of hydrogens than the sum of the ratio values, the ratio values need to be multiplied by some factor to bring their sum to that of the total number of hydrogens. For example, if the minimized ratio is 1 : 3 : 2 and the total number of hydrogens is 12, the ratio must be adjusted by a factor of 2 to be 2 : 6 : 4.

SOLUTION

The ratio of the relative signal heights (obtained from the number of horizontal chart divisions) is 5:2:3 (from downfield to upfield). The molecular formula indicates that there are 10 hydrogens. Thus, the signal at δ 7.34 represents 5 hydrogens, the signal at δ 5.08 represents 2 hydrogens, and the signal at δ 2.06 represents 3 hydrogens. Consequently, the signals and the number of hydrogens each signal represents are δ 7.34 (5H), δ 5.08 (2H), and δ 2.06 (3H).

PROBLEM 11.11

The line of integration of the two signals in the ¹H-NMR spectrum of a ketone with the molecular formula $C_7H_{14}O$ shows a vertical rise of 62 and 10 chart divisions. Calculate the number of hydrogens giving rise to each signal, and propose a structural formula for this ketone.

11.10 What Is Chemical Shift?

The position of a signal along the *x*-axis of an NMR spectrum is known as the **chemical shift** of that signal (Section 11.7). The chemical shift of a signal in a ¹H-NMR spectrum can give us valuable information about the type of hydrogens giving rise to that absorption. Hydrogens on methyl groups bonded to sp^3 hybridized carbons, for example, give a signal near δ 0.8–1.0 (compare Figure 11.18). Hydrogens on methyl groups bonded to a carbonyl carbon give signals near δ 2.1–2.3 (compare Figures 11.17 and 11.18), and hydrogens on methyl groups bonded to oxygen give signals near δ 3.7–3.9 (compare Figure 11.17). Table 11.4 lists the average chemical shift for most of the types of hydrogens we deal with in this text.

TABLE 11.4 Average Values of Chemical Shifts of Representative Types of Hydrogens

Type of Hydrogen (R = alkyl, Ar = aryl)	Chemical Shift (δ)*	Type of Hydrogen (R = alkyl, Ar = aryl)	Chemical Shift (δ)*
$(CH_3)_4Si$	0 (by definition)	$R\overset{\overset{O}{\|}}{C}OCH_3$	3.7–3.9
RCH_3	0.8–1.0	$R\overset{\overset{O}{\|}}{C}OCH_2R$	4.1–4.7
RCH_2R	1.2–1.4	RCH_2I	3.1–3.3
R_3CH	1.4–1.7	RCH_2Br	3.4–3.6
$R_2C{=}CRCHR_2$	1.6–2.6	RCH_2Cl	3.6–3.8
$RC{\equiv}CH$	2.0–3.0	RCH_2F	4.4–4.5
$ArCH_3$	2.2–2.5	$ArOH$	4.5–4.7
$ArCH_2R$	2.3–2.8	$R_2C{=}CH_2$	4.6–5.0
ROH	0.5–6.0	$R_2C{=}CHR$	5.0–5.7
RCH_2OH	3.4–4.0	ArH	6.5–8.5
RCH_2OR	3.3–4.0	$R\overset{\overset{O}{\|}}{C}H$	9.5–10.1
R_2NH	0.5–5.0	$R\overset{\overset{O}{\|}}{C}OH$	10–13
$R\overset{\overset{O}{\|}}{C}CH_3$	2.1–2.3		
$R\overset{\overset{O}{\|}}{C}CH_2R$	2.2–2.6		

*Values are approximate. Other atoms within the molecule may cause the signal to appear outside these ranges.

Notice that most of the values shown fall within a rather narrow range from 0 to 13 δ units (ppm). In fact, although the table shows a variety of functional groups and hydrogens bonded to them, we can use the following rules of thumb to remember the chemical shifts of most types of hydrogen:

Chemical Shift (δ)	Type of Hydrogen
0–2	H bonded to an sp^3 carbon.
2–2.8	H bonded to an sp^3 carbon that is at an allylic or benzylic position (i.e., adjacent to a C—C double bond or a benzene ring).
2–4.5	H bonded to an sp^3 carbon that is close to an electronegative element such as N, O, or X. The more electronegative the element, the higher is the chemical shift. Also, the closer the electronegative atom, the higher is the chemical shift.
4.6–5.7	H bonded to an sp^2 carbon in an alkene.
6.5–8.5	H bonded to an sp^2 carbon in an aromatic compound.
9.5–10.1	H bonded to a C=O (an aldehyde hydrogen).
10–13	H of a carboxyl (COOH) group.

follow these rules of thumb for most ^{1}H-NMR spectra problems

EXAMPLE 11.12

Following are two constitutional isomers with the molecular formula $C_6H_{12}O_2$:

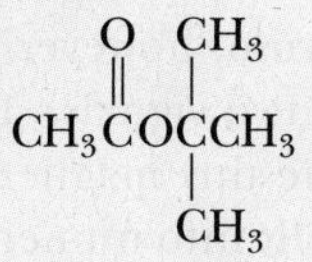

(1)

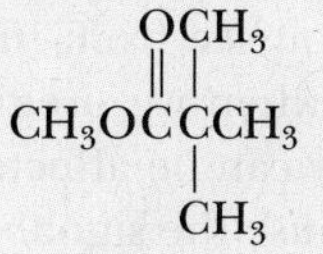

(2)

(a) Predict the number of signals in the ^{1}H-NMR spectrum of each isomer.

(b) Predict the ratio of areas of the signals in each spectrum.

(c) Show how to distinguish between these isomers on the basis of chemical shift.

STRATEGY

This example poses a series of steps that you will repeat often when asked to predict the ^{1}H-NMR spectrum of a compound. First, determine the number of signals by determining the number of equivalent hydrogens (Section 11.8). Then predict the ratio of areas of the signals by counting the number of hydrogens in each equivalent set (if the set of ratios can be reduced further, divide each number by a value that produces whole number ratios). Finally, predict the chemical shift of each set of equivalent hydrogens. If the rules of thumb for predicting chemical shift do not apply, refer to Table 11.4.

SOLUTION

(a) Each compound contains a set of nine equivalent methyl hydrogens and a set of three equivalent methyl hydrogens.

(b) The ^{1}H-NMR spectrum of each consists of two signals in the ratio 9:3, or 3:1.

(c) The two constitutional isomers can be distinguished by the chemical shift of the single $-CH_3$ group, or in other words, the signal that integrates to 3 (shown in red for each compound). Using our rules of thumb, we find that the hydrogens of CH_3O are less shielded (appear farther downfield) than the hydrogens of $CH_3C{=}O$. Table 11.4 gives approximate values for each chemical shift. Experimental values are as follows:

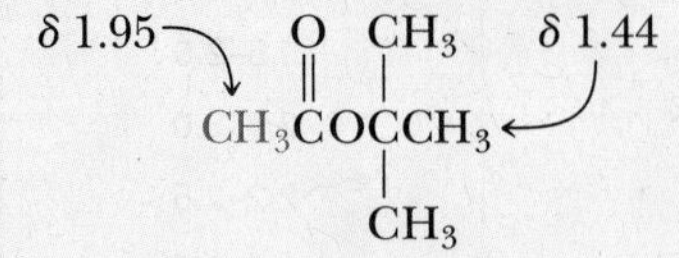

(1)

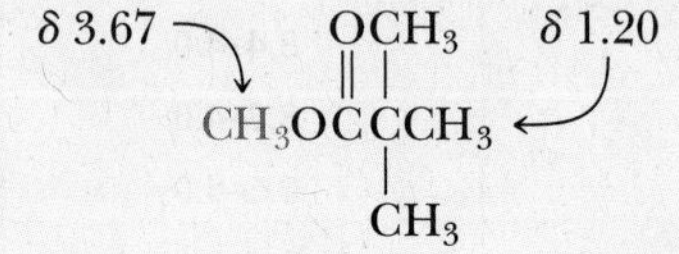

(2)

See problems 11.38, 11.42

PROBLEM 11.12

Following are two constitutional isomers with the molecular formula $C_4H_8O_2$:

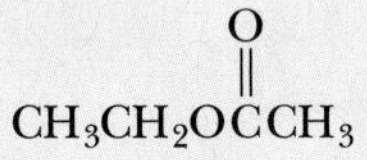

(1)

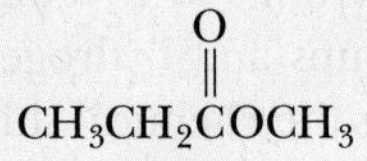

(2)

(a) Predict the number of signals in the ^{1}H-NMR spectrum of each isomer.

(b) Predict the ratio of areas of the signals in each spectrum.

(c) Show how to distinguish between these isomers on the basis of chemical shift.

11.11 What Is Signal Splitting?

We have now seen three kinds of information that can be derived from an examination of a ^{1}H-NMR spectrum:

1. From the number of signals, we can determine the number of sets of equivalent hydrogens.
2. By integrating over signal areas, we can determine the relative numbers of hydrogens giving rise to each signal.
3. From the chemical shift of each signal, we can derive information about the types of hydrogens in each set.

We can derive a fourth kind of information from the splitting pattern of each signal. Consider, for example, the ^{1}H-NMR spectrum of 1,1,2-trichloroethane (Figure 11.19), a solvent for waxes and natural resins. This molecule contains two 2° hydrogens and one 3° hydrogen, and, according to what we have learned so far, we predict two signals with relative areas 2:1, corresponding to the two hydrogens of the $-CH_2-$ group and the one hydrogen of the $-CHCl_2$ group. You see from the spectrum, however, that there are in fact five **peaks**. How can this be, when we predict only two signals? The answer is that a hydrogen's resonance frequency can be affected by the tiny magnetic fields of other hydrogens close by. Those fields cause the signal to be **split** into numerous peaks.

Peak (NMR) The units into which an NMR signal is split—two peaks in a doublet, three peaks in a triplet, and so on.

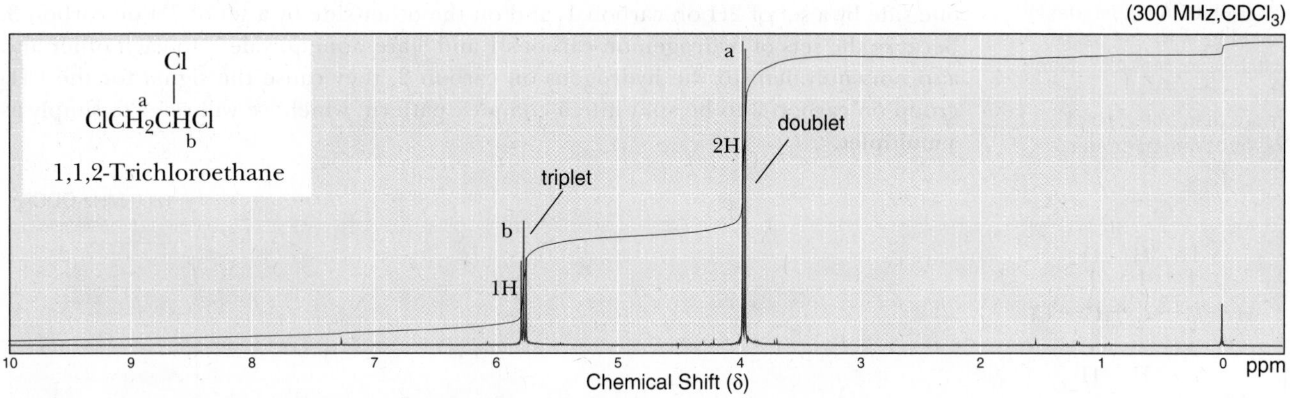

FIGURE 11.19
^{1}H-NMR spectrum of 1,1,2-trichloroethane.

Hydrogens split each other if they are separated by no more than three bonds—for example, H—C—C—H or H—C=C—H. (There are three bonds in each case.) If there are more than three bonds, as in H—C—C—C—H, then there is normally no splitting. A signal with just one peak is called a **singlet**. A signal that is split into two peaks is called a **doublet**. Signals that are split into three and four peaks are called **triplets** and **quartets**, respectively.

The grouping of two peaks at δ 3.96 in the ^{1}H-NMR spectrum of 1,1,2-trichloroethane is the signal for the hydrogens of the $—CH_2—$ group, and the grouping of three peaks at δ 5.77 is the signal for the single hydrogen of the $—CHCl_2$ group. We say that the CH_2 signal at δ 3.96 is split into a doublet and that the CH signal at δ 5.77 is split into a triplet. In this phenomenon, called **signal splitting**, the ^{1}H-NMR signal from one set of hydrogens is split by the influence of neighboring nonequivalent hydrogens.

The degree of signal splitting can be predicted on the basis of the **$(n + 1)$ rule**, according to which, if a hydrogen has n hydrogens nonequivalent to it, but equivalent among themselves, on the same or adjacent atom(s), then the ^{1}H-NMR signal of the hydrogen is split into $(n + 1)$ peaks.

Let us apply the $(n + 1)$ rule to the analysis of the spectrum of 1,1,2-trichloroethane. The two hydrogens of the $—CH_2—$ group have one nonequivalent neighboring hydrogen ($n = 1$); their signal is split into a doublet ($1 + 1 = 2$). The single hydrogen of the $—CHCl_2$ group has a set of two nonequivalent neighboring hydrogens ($n = 2$); its signal is split into a triplet ($2 + 1 = 3$).

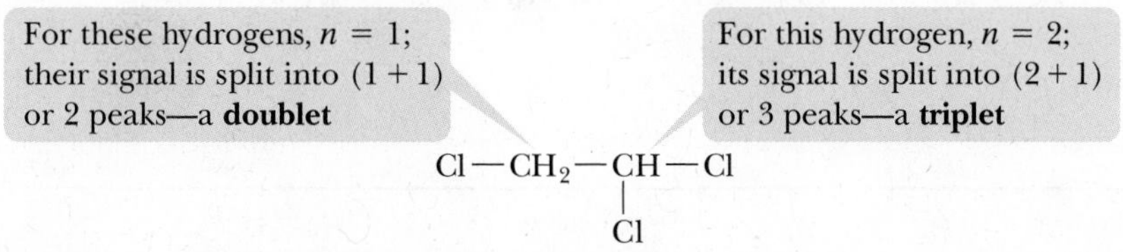

It is important to remember that the $(n + 1)$ rule of signal splitting applies only to hydrogens with *equivalent* neighboring hydrogens. When more than one set of neighboring hydrogens exists, the $(n + 1)$ rule no longer applies. An example of where the $(n + 1)$ rule no longer applies is illustrated in the ^{1}H-NMR spectrum of 1-chloropropane. The two hydrogens on carbon 2 (a CH_2 group) of 1-chloropropane are flanked on

Singlet A signal that consists of one peak; the hydrogens that give rise to the signal have no neighboring nonequivalent hydrogens.

Doublet A signal that is split into two peaks; the hydrogens that give rise to the signal have one neighboring nonequivalent hydrogen.

Triplet A signal that is split into three peaks; the hydrogens that give rise to the signal have two neighboring nonequivalent hydrogens that are equivalent to each other.

Quartet A signal that is split into four peaks; the hydrogens that give rise to the signal have three neighboring nonequivalent hydrogens that are equivalent to each other.

Signal splitting Splitting of an NMR signal into a set of peaks by the influence of neighboring nuclei.

$(n + 1)$ rule The ^{1}H-NMR signal of a hydrogen or set of equivalent hydrogens with n other hydrogens on neighboring carbons is split into $(n + 1)$ peaks.

Multiplet A signal that is split into multiple peaks, often of an irregular pattern, due to the presence of more than one type of neighboring hydrogens.

one side by a set of 2H on carbon 1, and on the other side by a set of 3H on carbon 3. Because the sets of hydrogen on carbons 1 and 3 are nonequivalent to each other and also nonequivalent to the hydrogens on carbon 2, they cause the signal for the CH_2 group on carbon 2 to be split into a complex pattern, which we will refer to simply as a **multiplet**.

(300 MHz,$CDCl_3$)

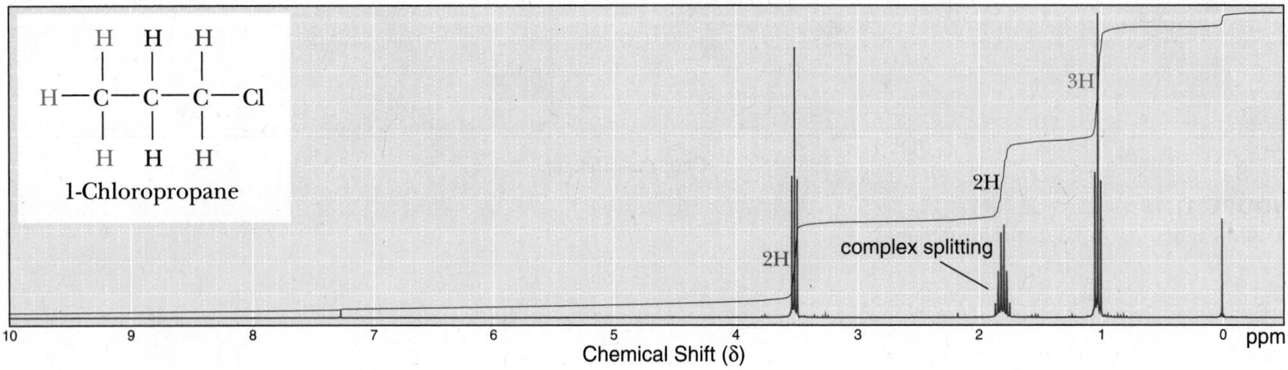

EXAMPLE 11.13

Predict the number of signals and the splitting pattern of each signal in the ¹H-NMR spectrum of each compound.

(a) $CH_3\overset{O}{\overset{\|}{C}}CH_2CH_3$ **(b)** $CH_3CH_2\overset{O}{\overset{\|}{C}}CH_2CH_3$ **(c)** $CH_3\overset{O}{\overset{\|}{C}}CH(CH_3)_2$

STRATEGY

Determine the number of signals by determining the number of equivalent hydrogens (Section 11.8). For each set of equivalent hydrogens, determine the number of equivalent neighbors (n) and apply the ($n + 1$) rule to determine the splitting pattern.

SOLUTION

The sets of equivalent hydrogens in each molecule are color coded. In molecule (a), the signal for the red methyl group is unsplit (a singlet) because the group is too far (>3 bonds) from any other hydrogens. The blue —CH_2— group has three neighboring hydrogens ($n = 3$) and thus shows a signal split into a quartet ($3 + 1 = 4$). The green methyl group has two neighboring hydrogens ($n = 2$), and its signal is split into a triplet. The integration ratios for these signals would be 3:2:3. Parts (b) and (c) can be analyzed in the same way. Thus, molecule (b) shows a triplet and a quartet in the ratio 3:2. Molecule (c) shows a singlet, a septet ($6 + 1 = 7$), and a doublet in the ratio 3:1:6.

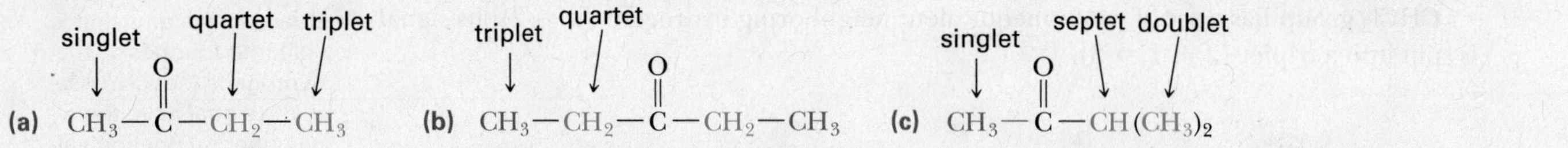

See problem 11.32

PROBLEM 11.13

Following are pairs of constitutional isomers. Predict the number of signals and the splitting pattern of each signal in the ¹H-NMR spectrum of each isomer.

(a) $CH_3OCH_2\overset{O}{\overset{\|}{C}}CH_3$ and $CH_3CH_2\overset{O}{\overset{\|}{C}}OCH_3$ **(b)** $CH_3\underset{Cl}{\overset{Cl}{C}}CH_3$ and $ClCH_2CH_2CH_2Cl$

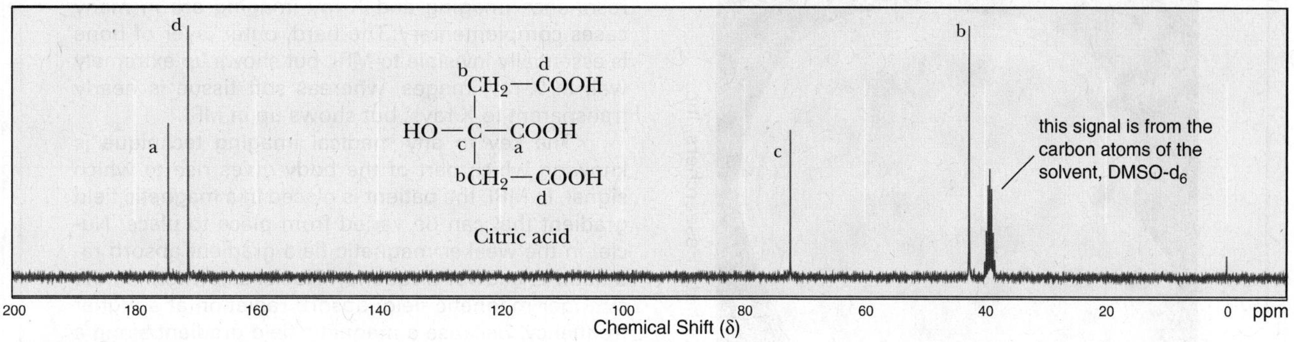

FIGURE 11.20
Hydrogen-decoupled ^{13}C-NMR spectrum of citric acid.

11.12 What Is ^{13}C-NMR Spectroscopy, and How Does It Differ from ^{1}H-NMR Spectroscopy?

Nuclei of carbon-12, the most abundant (98.89%) natural isotope of carbon, do not have nuclear spin and are not detected by NMR spectroscopy. Nuclei of carbon-13 (natural abundance 1.11%), however, do have nuclear spin and are detected by NMR spectroscopy in the same manner as hydrogens are detected. Thus, NMR can be used to obtain information about 1.11% of all the carbon atoms in a sample. Just as in ^{1}H-NMR spectroscopy, ^{13}C-NMR spectroscopy yields a signal for each set of equivalent carbons in a molecule.

Because both ^{13}C and ^{1}H have spinning nuclei and generate magnetic fields, ^{13}C couples with each ^{1}H bonded to it and gives a signal split according to the $(n + 1)$ rule. In the most common mode for recording a ^{13}C spectrum, this coupling is eliminated by instrumental techniques, so as to simplify the spectrum. In these **hydrogen-decoupled spectra**, all ^{13}C signals appear as singlets. The hydrogen-decoupled ^{13}C-NMR spectrum of citric acid (Figure 11.20), a compound used to increase the solubility of many pharmaceutical drugs in water, consists of four singlets. Again, notice that, as in ^{1}H-NMR, equivalent carbons generate only one signal.

Chemical Connections 11B

MAGNETIC RESONANCE IMAGING

Nuclear magnetic resonance was discovered and explained by physicists in the 1950s, and, by the 1960s, it had become an invaluable analytical tool for chemists. By the early 1970s, it was realized that the imaging of parts of the body via NMR could be a valuable addition to diagnostic medicine. Because the term *nuclear magnetic resonance* sounds to many people as if the technique might involve radioactive material, health care personnel call the technique *magnetic resonance imaging* (MRI).

The body contains several nuclei that, in principle, could be used for MRI. Of these, hydrogens, most of which come from water, triglycerides (fats), and membrane phospholipids, give the most useful signals. Phosphorus MRI is also used in diagnostic medicine.

Recall that, in NMR spectroscopy, energy in the form of radio-frequency radiation is absorbed by nuclei in the sample. The relaxation time is the characteristic time at which excited nuclei give up this energy and relax to their ground state.

In 1971, Raymond Damadian discovered that the relaxation of water in certain cancerous tumors takes much longer than the relaxation of water in normal cells. Thus, it was reasoned that if a relaxation image of the body could be obtained, it might be possible to identify tumors at an early stage. Subsequent work demonstrated that many tumors can be identified in this way.

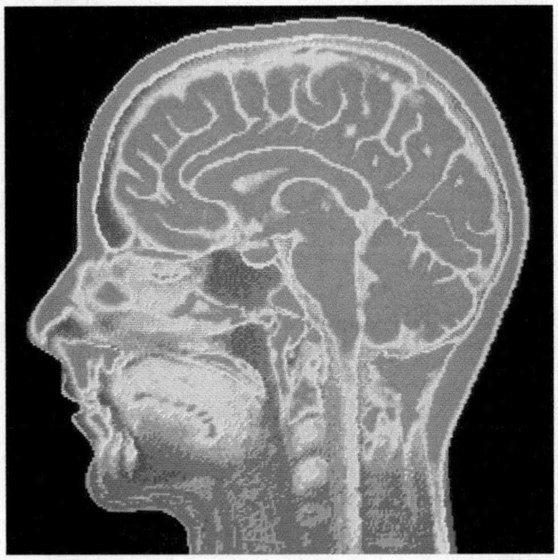

Computer-enhanced MRI scan of a normal human brain with pituitary gland highlighted

Another important application of MRI is in the examination of the brain and spinal cord. White and gray matter, the two different layers of the brain, are easily distinguished by MRI, which is useful in the study of such diseases as multiple sclerosis. Magnetic resonance imaging and X-ray imaging are in many cases complementary: The hard, outer layer of bone is essentially invisible to MRI, but shows up extremely well in X-ray images, whereas soft tissue is nearly transparent to X rays, but shows up in MRI.

The key to any medical imaging technique is knowing which part of the body gives rise to which signal. In MRI, the patient is placed in a magnetic field gradient that can be varied from place to place. Nuclei in the weaker magnetic field gradient absorb radiation at a lower frequency. Nuclei elsewhere, in the stronger magnetic field, absorb radiation at a higher frequency. Because a magnetic field gradient along a single axis images a plane, MRI techniques can create views of any part of the body in slicelike sections. In 2003, Paul Lauterbur and Sir Peter Mansfield were awarded the Nobel Prize in Physiology or Medicine for their discoveries that led to the development of these imaging techniques.

Question

In ^{1}H-NMR spectroscopy, the chemical sample is set spinning on its long axis to ensure that all parts of the sample experience a homogeneous applied field. Homogeneity is also required in MRI. Keeping in mind that the "sample" in MRI is a human being, how do you suppose this is achieved?

Table 11.5 shows approximate chemical shifts in ^{13}C-NMR spectroscopy. As with ^{1}H-NMR, we can use the following rules of thumb to remember the chemical shifts of various types of carbons:

follow these rules of thumb for most ^{13}C-NMR spectra problems

Chemical Shift (δ)	Type of Carbon
0–50	*sp*^{3} carbon (3° > 2° > 1°).
50–80	*sp*^{3} carbon bonded to an electronegative element such as N, O, or X. The more electronegative the element, the larger is the chemical shift.
100–160	*sp*^{2} carbon of an alkene or an aromatic compound.
160–180	carbonyl carbon of a carboxylic acid or carboxylic acid derivative (Chapters 13 and 14).
180–210	carbonyl carbon of a ketone or an aldehyde (Chapter 12).

Notice how much broader the range of chemical shifts is for ^{13}C-NMR spectroscopy (0–210 ppm) than for ^{1}H-NMR spectroscopy (0–12 ppm). Because of this expanded scale, it is very unusual to find any two nonequivalent carbons in the same molecule with identical chemical shifts. Most commonly, each different type of carbon within a molecule has a distinct signal that is clearly resolved (i.e., separated) from all other signals. Notice further that the chemical shift of carbonyl carbons is quite distinct from the chemical shifts of *sp*^{3} hybridized carbons and other types of *sp*^{2} hybridized carbons. The presence or absence of a carbonyl carbon is quite easy to recognize in a ^{13}C-NMR spectrum.

A great advantage of ^{13}C-NMR spectroscopy is that it is generally possible to count the number of different types of carbon atoms in a molecule. There is one caution here, however: Because of the particular manner in which spin-flipped ^{13}C nuclei return to their lower energy states, integrating signal areas is often unreliable, and it is generally not possible to determine the number of carbons of each type on the basis of the signal areas.

TABLE 11.5 ^{13}C-NMR Chemical Shifts

Type of Carbon	Chemical Shift (δ)	Type of Carbon	Chemical Shift (δ)
RCH_3	0–40	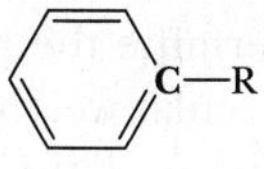	110–160
RCH_2R	15–55		
R_3CH	20–60		
RCH_2I	0–40	$R\overset{\overset{O}{\|}}{C}OR$	160–180
RCH_2Br	25–65		
RCH_2Cl	35–80	$R\overset{\overset{O}{\|}}{C}NR_2$	165–180
R_3COH	40–80		
R_3COR	40–80	$R\overset{\overset{O}{\|}}{C}OH$	175–185
$RC{\equiv}CR$	65–85		
$R_2C{=}CR_2$	100–150	$R\overset{\overset{O}{\|}}{C}H$, $R\overset{\overset{O}{\|}}{C}R$	180–210

EXAMPLE 11.14

Predict the number of signals in a proton-decoupled ^{13}C-NMR spectrum of each compound:

(a) $CH_3\overset{\overset{O}{\|}}{C}OCH_3$ **(b)** $CH_3CH_2CH_2\overset{\overset{O}{\|}}{C}CH_3$ **(c)** $CH_3CH_2\overset{\overset{O}{\|}}{C}CH_2CH_3$

STRATEGY

Because we cannot replace each carbon atom with a halogen (as we did to determine equivalency in ^{1}H-NMR), inasmuch as a halogen only has a valence of 1, we will need to use symmetry to determine equivalency.

SOLUTION

Here is the number of signals in each spectrum, along with the chemical shift of each, color coded to the carbon responsible for that signal. The chemical shifts of the carbonyl carbons are quite distinctive (Table 11.5) and occur at δ 171.37, 208.85, and 211.97 in these examples.

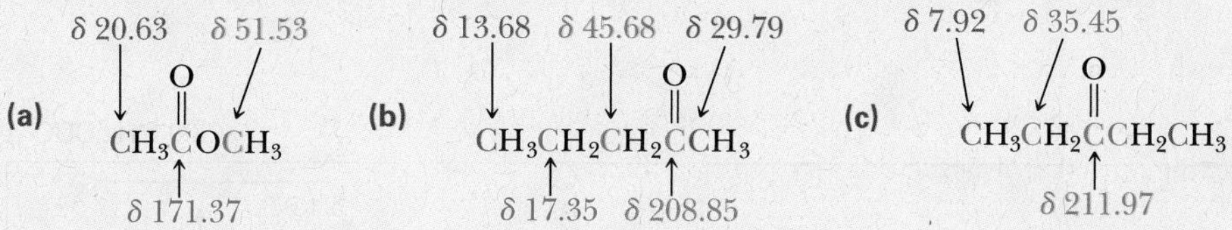

See problem 11.33

PROBLEM 11.14

Explain how to distinguish between the members of each pair of constitutional isomers, on the basis of the number of signals in the ^{13}C-NMR spectrum of each isomer:

(a) 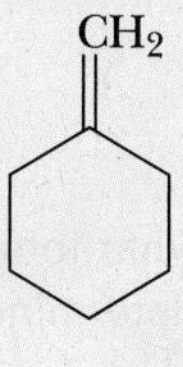

and 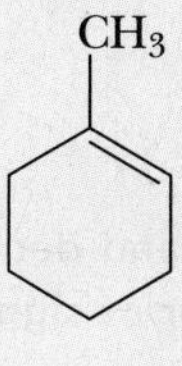

(b) 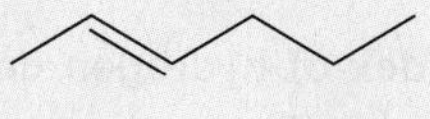 and 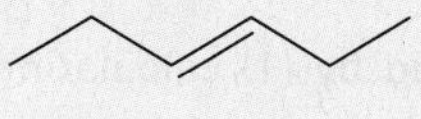

11.13 How Do We Solve an NMR Problem?

One of the first steps in determining the molecular structure of a compound is to establish the compound's molecular formula. In the past, this was most commonly done by elemental analysis, combustion to determine the percent composition, and so forth. More commonly today, we determine molecular weight and molecular formula by a technique known as *mass spectrometry* (an explanation of the technique is beyond the scope of this book). In the examples that follow, we assume that the molecular formula of any unknown compound has already been determined, and we proceed from there, using spectral analysis to determine a structural formula.

The following steps may prove helpful as a systematic approach to solving ^{1}H-NMR spectral problems:

Step 1: **Molecular formula and index of hydrogen deficiency.** Examine the molecular formula, calculate the index of hydrogen deficiency (Section 11.4G), and deduce what information you can about the presence or absence of rings or pi bonds.

Step 2: **Number of signals.** Count the number of signals to determine the minimum number of sets of equivalent hydrogens in the compound.

Step 3: **Integration.** Use signal integration and the molecular formula to determine the number of hydrogens in each set.

Step 4: **Pattern of chemical shifts.** Examine the NMR spectrum for signals characteristic of the most common types of equivalent hydrogens. (See the general rules of thumb for ^{1}H-NMR chemical shifts in Section 11.10.) Keep in mind that the ranges are broad and that hydrogens of each type may be shifted either farther upfield or farther downfield, depending on details of the molecular structure in question.

Step 5: **Splitting patterns.** Examine splitting patterns for information about the number of nonequivalent hydrogen neighbors.

Step 6: **Structural formula.** Write a structural formula consistent with the information learned in Steps 1–5.

EXAMPLE 11.15

Following is a ^{1}H-NMR spectrum for a compound that is a colorless liquid with the molecular formula $C_5H_{10}O$. Propose a structural formula for the compound.

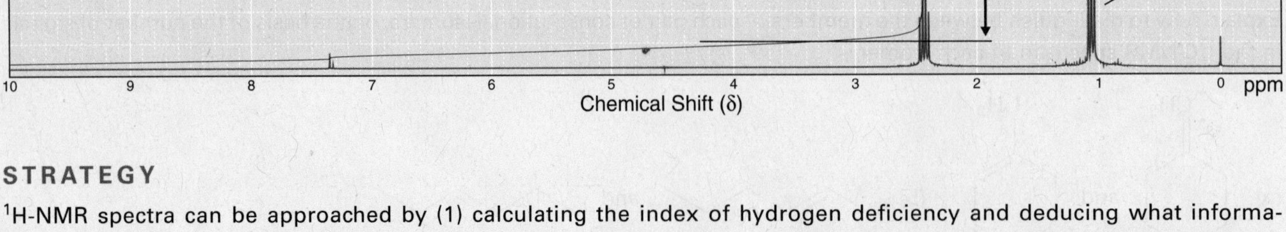

STRATEGY

^{1}H-NMR spectra can be approached by (1) calculating the index of hydrogen deficiency and deducing what information you can about the presence or absence of rings or pi bonds, (2) counting the number of signals to determine the minimum number of sets of equivalent hydrogens in the compound, (3) using signal integration and the molecular formula to determine the number of hydrogens in each set, (4) examining the NMR spectrum for signals characteristic of the most common types of equivalent hydrogens, (5) examining splitting patterns for information about the number of nonequivalent hydrogen neighbors, and (6) writing a structural formula consistent with the information learned in Steps 1–5.

SOLUTION

STEP 1: Molecular formula and index of hydrogen deficiency. The reference compound is $C_5H_{12}O$; therefore, the index of hydrogen deficiency is 1. The molecule thus contains either one ring or one pi bond.

STEP 2: Number of signals. There are two signals (a triplet and a quartet) and therefore two sets of equivalent hydrogens.

STEP 3: Integration. By signal integration, we calculate that the number of hydrogens giving rise to each signal is in the ratio 3:2. Because there are 10 hydrogens, we conclude that the signal assignments are δ 1.07 (6H) and δ 2.42 (4H).

STEP 4: Pattern of chemical shifts. The signal at δ 1.07 is in the alkyl region and, based on its chemical shift, most probably represents a methyl group. No signal occurs at δ 4.6 to 5.7; thus, there are no vinylic hydrogens. (If a carbon–carbon double bond is in the molecule, no hydrogens are on it; that is, it is tetrasubstituted.)

STEP 5: Splitting pattern. The methyl signal at δ 1.07 is split into a triplet (t); hence, it must have two neighboring hydrogens, indicating $-CH_2CH_3$. The signal at δ 2.42 is split into a quartet (q); thus, it must have three neighboring hydrogens, which is also consistent with $-CH_2CH_3$. Consequently, an ethyl group accounts for these two signals. No other signals occur in the spectrum; therefore, there are no other types of hydrogens in the molecule.

STEP 6: Structural formula. Put the information learned in the previous steps together to arrive at the following structural formula. Note that the chemical shift of the methylene group ($-CH_2-$) at δ 2.42 is consistent with an alkyl group adjacent to a carbonyl group.

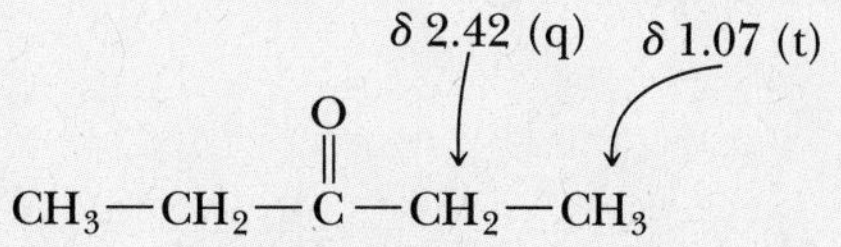

3-Pentanone

See problems 11.35–11.37, 11.39–11.41, 11.43–11.62

PROBLEM 11.15

Following is a ^{1}H-NMR spectrum for prenol, a compound that possesses a fruity odor and that is commonly used in perfumes. Prenol has the molecular formula $C_5H_{10}O$. Propose a structural formula for prenol.

(300 MHz, $CDCl_3$)

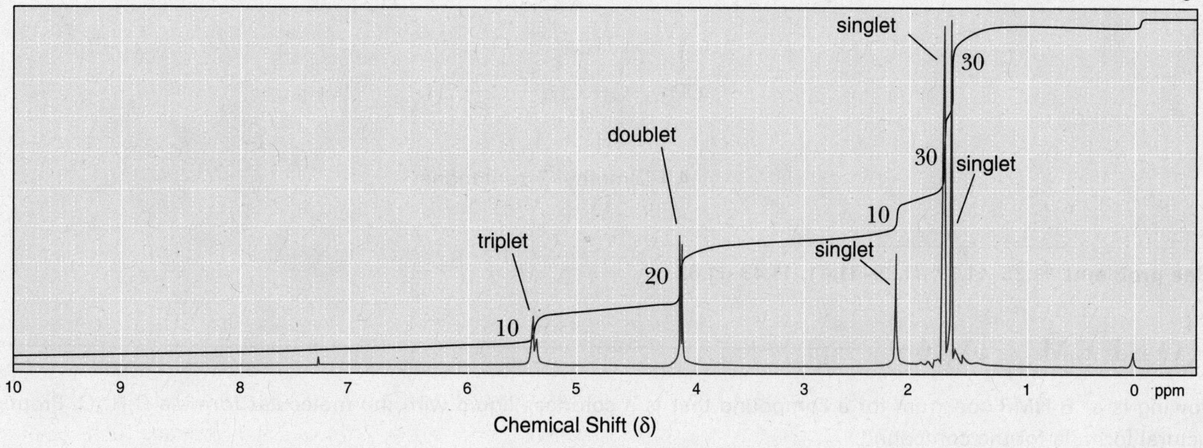

EXAMPLE 11.16

Following is a ¹H-NMR spectrum for a compound that is a colorless liquid with the molecular formula $C_7H_{14}O$. Propose a structural formula for the compound.

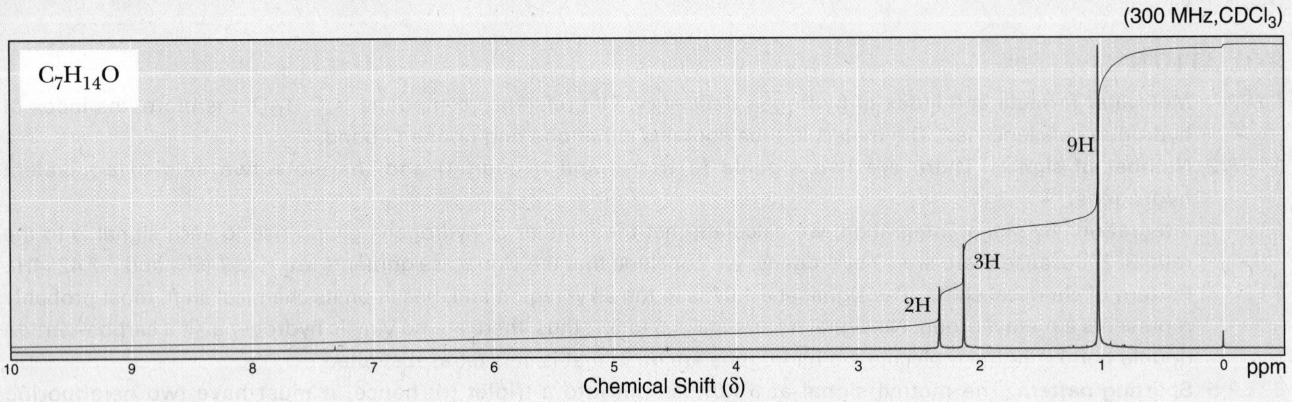

STRATEGY

¹H-NMR spectra can be approached by (1) calculating the index of hydrogen deficiency and deducing what information you can about the presence or absence of rings or pi bonds, (2) counting the number of signals to determine the minimum number of sets of equivalent hydrogens in the compound, (3) using signal integration and the molecular formula to determine the number of hydrogens in each set, (4) examining the NMR spectrum for signals characteristic of the most common types of equivalent hydrogens, (5) examining splitting patterns for information about the number of nonequivalent hydrogen neighbors, and (6) writing a structural formula consistent with the information learned in Steps 1–5.

SOLUTION

STEP 1: Molecular formula and index of hydrogen deficiency. The index of hydrogen deficiency is 1; thus, the compound contains one ring or one pi bond.

STEP 2: Number of signals. There are three signals and therefore three sets of equivalent hydrogens.

STEP 3: Integration. By signal integration, we calculate that the number of hydrogens giving rise to each signal is in the ratio 2:3:9, reading from left to right.

STEP 4: Pattern of chemical shifts. The singlet at δ 1.01 is characteristic of a methyl group adjacent to an sp^3 hybridized carbon. The singlets at δ 2.11 and 2.32 are characteristic of alkyl groups adjacent to a carbonyl group.

STEP 5: Splitting pattern. All signals are singlets (s), which means that none of the hydrogens are within three bonds of each other.

STEP 6: Structural formula. The compound is 4,4-dimethyl-2-pentanone:

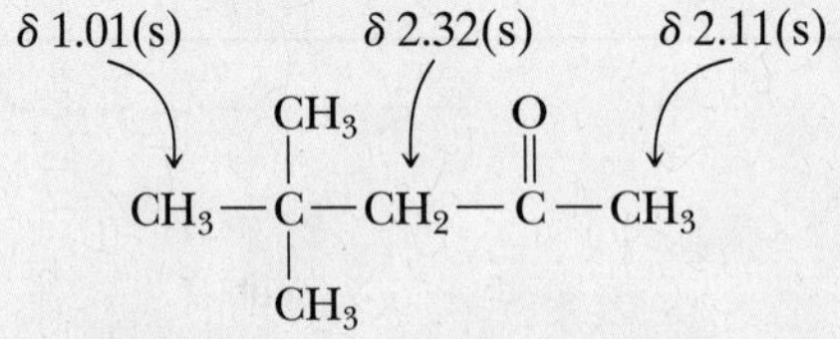

4,4-Dimethyl-2-pentanone

See problems 11.35–11.37, 11.39–11.41, 11.43–11.62

PROBLEM 11.16

Following is a ¹H-NMR spectrum for a compound that is a colorless liquid with the molecular formula $C_7H_{14}O$. Propose a structural formula for the compound.

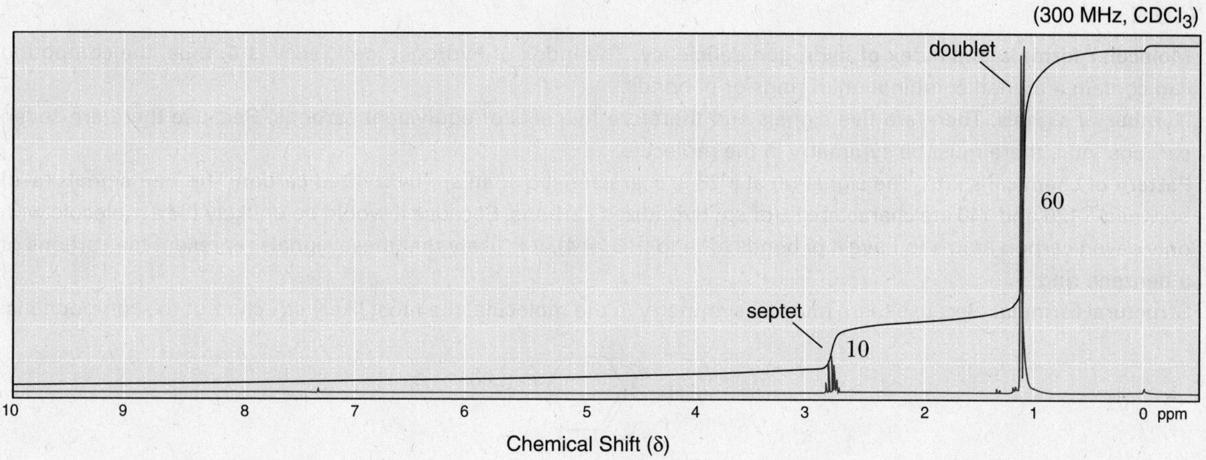

The following steps may prove helpful as a systematic approach to solving ^{13}C-NMR spectral problems:

Step 1: **Molecular formula and index of hydrogen deficiency**. Examine the molecular formula, calculate the index of hydrogen deficiency (Section 11.4G), and deduce what information you can about the presence or absence of rings or pi bonds.

Step 2: **Number of signals.** Count the number of signals to determine the minimum number of sets of equivalent carbons in the compound.

Step 3: **Pattern of chemical shifts.** Examine the NMR spectrum for signals characteristic of the most common types of equivalent carbons (see the general rules of thumb for ^{13}C-NMR chemical shifts in Section 11.12). Keep in mind that these ranges are broad and that carbons of each type may be shifted either farther upfield or farther downfield, depending on details of the molecular structure in question.

Step 4: **Structural formula.** Write a structural formula consistent with the information learned in Steps 1–3. *Note*: Because ^{13}C-NMR does not provide information about neighboring hydrogens, it may be more difficult to elucidate the structure of a compound based solely on ^{13}C-NMR data.

EXAMPLE 11.17

Following is a ^{13}C-NMR spectrum for a compound that is a colorless liquid with the molecular formula C_7H_7Cl. Propose a structural formula for the compound.

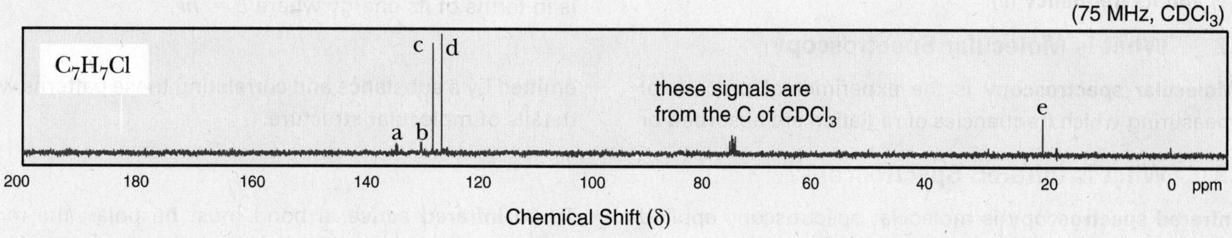

STRATEGY

^{13}C-NMR spectra can be approached by (1) calculating the index of hydrogen deficiency and deducing what information you can about the presence or absence of rings or pi bonds, (2) counting the number of signals to determine the minimum number of sets of equivalent carbons in the compound, (3) examining the NMR spectrum for signals characteristic of the most common types of equivalent carbons, and (4) writing a structural formula consistent with the information learned in Steps 1–3.

SOLUTION

STEP 1: **Molecular formula and index of hydrogen deficiency.** The index of hydrogen deficiency is 4; thus, the compound can contain a myriad combination of rings or pi bonds.

STEP 2: **Number of signals.** There are five signals and therefore five sets of equivalent carbons. Because there are seven carbons total, there must be symmetry in the molecule.

STEP 3: **Pattern of chemical shifts.** The signal (e) at δ 23 is characteristic of an sp^3 hybridized carbon. The four signals **(a–d)** between δ 120 and 140 are characteristic of sp^2 hybridized carbons. Because it would be unlikely for a molecule with only seven carbon atoms to have 4 pi bonds (due to IHD = 4), it is likely that these signals represent the carbons of a benzene ring.

STEP 4: **Structural formula.** Because there must be symmetry in the molecule, the most likely structure of the compound is:

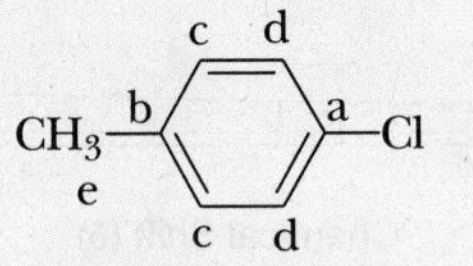

4-Chlorotoluene

See problems 11.34, 11.38, 11.39, 11.43, 11.44, 11.50–11.54

PROBLEM 11.17

Following is a ^{13}C-NMR spectrum for a compound that is a colorless liquid with the molecular formula $C_4H_8Br_2$. Propose a structural formula for the compound.

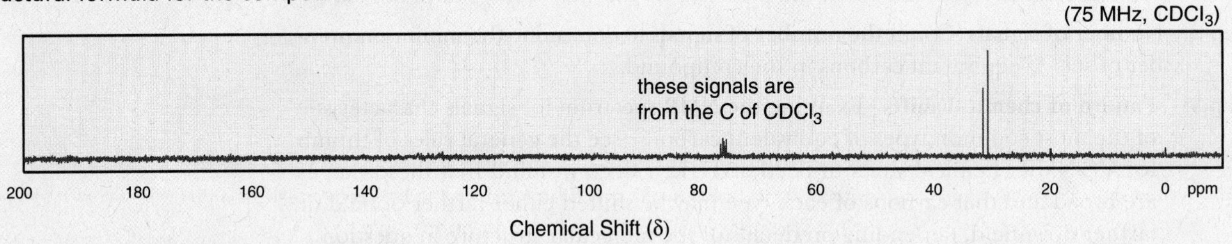

SUMMARY OF KEY QUESTIONS

11.1 What Is Electromagnetic Radiation?

- **Electromagnetic radiation** is a wave traveling at the speed of light that can be described in terms of its **wavelength** (λ) and its **frequency** (ν).
- Frequency is reported in **hertz (Hz)**.
- An alternative way to describe electromagnetic radiation is in terms of its energy where $E = h\nu$.

11.2 What Is Molecular Spectroscopy?

- **Molecular spectroscopy** is the experimental process of measuring which frequencies of radiation are absorbed or emitted by a substance and correlating these patterns with details of molecular structure.

11.3 What Is Infrared Spectroscopy?

- **Infrared spectroscopy** is molecular spectroscopy applied to frequencies of infrared radiation.
- Interactions of molecules with **infrared radiation** excite covalent bonds to higher vibrational energy levels.
- The **vibrational infrared** spectrum extends from 4000 to 400 cm^{-1}. Radiation in this region is referred to by its wavenumber ($\overline{\nu}$) in reciprocal centimeters (cm^{-1}).
- To be **infrared active**, a bond must be polar; the more polar it is, the stronger is its absorption of IR radiation.
- The simplest vibrations that give rise to the absorption of infrared radiation are **stretching** and **bending** vibrations.
- Stretching may be symmetrical or asymmetrical.

- A **correlation table** is a list of the absorption patterns of functional groups. The intensity of a peak is referred to as **strong (s)**, **medium (m)**, or **weak (w)**. Stretching vibrations for most functional groups appear in the region from 3400 to 1000 cm^{-1}.
- The region from 1000 to 400 cm^{-1} is referred to as the **fingerprint region**, so called because absorption bands in this region are unique to each compound.

11.4 How Do We Interpret Infrared Spectra?

- The **index of hydrogen deficiency** is the sum of the number of rings and pi bonds in a molecule. It can be determined by comparing the number of hydrogens in the molecular formula of a compound of unknown structure with the number of hydrogens in a reference compound with the same number of carbon atoms and with no rings or pi bonds.
- Using the index of hydrogen deficiency along with knowledge of characteristic IR absorptions for various functional groups, one can determine the possible structures for an unknown whose molecular formula is known.

11.5 What Is Nuclear Magnetic Resonance?

- An atomic nucleus that has an odd mass or an odd atomic number also has a **spin** and behaves as if it were a tiny bar magnet.
- When a collection of ^{1}H and ^{13}C atoms is placed between the poles of a powerful magnet, interactions between their nuclear spins and the applied magnetic field are quantized, and only two orientations are allowed.
- When placed between the poles of a powerful magnet, the nuclear spins of these elements become aligned either with the applied field or against it.
- Nuclear spins aligned with the applied field are in the lower energy state; those aligned against the applied field are in the higher energy state.
- **Resonance** is the absorption of electromagnetic radiation by a nucleus and the resulting "flip" of its nuclear spin from a lower energy spin state to a higher energy spin state.

11.6 What Is Shielding?

- The experimental conditions required to cause nuclei to resonate are affected by the local chemical and magnetic environment.
- Electrons around a hydrogen also have spin and create a local magnetic field that **shields** the hydrogen from the applied field.

11.7 What Is an NMR Spectrum?

- An **NMR spectrometer** records resonance as a signal, and the collection of all resonance signals for a sample is its **NMR spectrum**.

11.8 How Many Resonance Signals Will a Compound Yield in Its NMR Spectrum?

- **Equivalent hydrogens** within a molecule have identical chemical shifts.

11.9 What Is Signal Integration?

- The area of a ^{1}H-NMR signal is proportional to the number of equivalent hydrogens giving rise to that **signal**. Determination of these areas is termed **integration**.

11.10 What Is Chemical Shift?

- In a ^{1}H-NMR spectrum, a resonance signal is reported by how far it is shifted from the resonance signal of the 12 equivalent hydrogens in **tetramethylsilane (TMS)**.
- A resonance signal in a ^{13}C-NMR spectrum is reported by how far it is shifted from the resonance signal of the four equivalent carbons in TMS.
- A **chemical shift** (δ) is the frequency shift from TMS, divided by the operating frequency of the spectrometer.

11.11 What Is Signal Splitting?

- In **signal splitting**, the ^{1}H-NMR signal from one hydrogen or set of equivalent hydrogens is split by the influence of nonequivalent hydrogens on the same or adjacent carbon atoms.
- According to the **(n + 1) rule**, if a hydrogen has n hydrogens that are nonequivalent to it, but are equivalent among themselves, on the same or adjacent carbon atom(s), its ^{1}H-NMR signal is split into (n + 1) peaks.
- **Complex splitting** occurs when a hydrogen is flanked by two or more sets of hydrogens and those sets are nonequivalent.
- Splitting patterns are commonly referred to as **singlets, doublets, triplets, quartets, quintets,** and **multiplets.**

11.12 What Is ^{13}C-NMR Spectroscopy, and How Does It Differ from ^{1}H-NMR Spectroscopy?

- A ^{13}C-NMR spectrum normally spans the range δ 0–210 (versus δ 0–13 for ^{1}H-NMR).
- ^{13}C-NMR spectra are commonly recorded in a **hydrogen-decoupled** instrumental mode. In this mode, all ^{13}C signals appear as singlets.
- Integration is not normally performed in ^{13}C-NMR.

11.13 How Do We Solve an NMR Problem?

- ^{1}H-NMR spectra can be approached by (1) calculating the index of hydrogen deficiency and deducing what information you can about the presence or absence of rings or pi bonds, (2) counting the number of signals to determine the minimum number of sets of equivalent hydrogens in the compound, (3) using signal integration and the molecular formula to determine the number of hydrogens in each set, (4) examining the NMR spectrum for signals characteristic of the most common types of equivalent hydrogens, (5) examining splitting patterns for information about the number of nonequivalent hydrogen neighbors, and (6) writing a structural formula consistent with the information learned in Steps 1–5.
- ^{13}C-NMR spectra can be approached by (1) calculating the index of hydrogen deficiency and deducing what information you can about the presence or absence of rings or pi bonds, (2) counting the number of signals to determine the minimum number of sets of equivalent carbons in the compound, (3) examining the NMR spectrum for signals characteristic of the most common types of equivalent carbons, and (4) writing a structural formula consistent with the information learned in Steps 1–3.

QUICK QUIZ

Answer true or false to the following questions to assess your general knowledge of the concepts in this chapter. If you have difficulty with any of them, you should review the appropriate section in the chapter (shown in parentheses) before attempting the more challenging end-of-chapter problems.

1. A weak absorption band in an infrared spectrum can be attributed to, among other things, absorption of infrared light by a low polarity bond. (11.3)
2. Integration reveals the number of neighboring hydrogens in a ^{1}H-NMR spectrum. (11.11)
3. Wavelength and frequency are directly proportional. That is, as wavelength increases, frequency increases. (11.1)
4. An alkene (vinylic) hydrogen can be distinguished from a benzene ring hydrogen via ^{1}H-NMR spectroscopy. (11.10)
5. IR spectroscopy can be used to distinguish between a terminal alkyne and an internal alkyne. (11.4)
6. The NMR signal of a shielded nucleus appears more upfield than the signal for a deshielded nucleus. (11.7)
7. A transition between two energy states, E_1 and E_2, can be made to occur using light equal to or greater than the energy difference between E_1 and E_2. (11.2)
8. The chemical shift of a nucleus depends on its resonance frequency. (11.7)
9. A compound with the molecular formula $C_5H_{10}O$ could contain a C—C triple bond, two C=O bonds, or two rings. (11.4)
10. A ketone can be distinguished from an aldehyde via ^{13}C-NMR spectroscopy. (11.12)
11. A compound with the molecular formula $C_7H_{12}O$ has an index of hydrogen deficiency of 2. (11.4)
12. A ^{1}H-NMR spectrum with an integration ratio of 3:1:2 could represent a compound with the molecular formula C_5H_9O. (11.9)
13. Electromagnetic radiation can be described as a wave, as a particle, and in terms of energy. (11.1)
14. A set of hydrogens are equivalent if replacing each of them with a halogen results in compounds of the same name. (11.8)
15. The collection of absorption peaks in the 1000–400 cm^{-1} region of an IR spectrum is unique to a particular compound (i.e., no two compounds will yield the same spectrum in this region). (11.3)
16. The area under each peak in a ^{1}H-NMR spectrum can be determined using a technique known as integration. (11.9)
17. All atomic nuclei have a spin, which allows them to be analyzed by NMR spcctroscopy. (11.5)
18. C—H stretching vibrations occur at higher wavenumbers than C—C stretching vibrations. (11.4)
19. The resonance frequency of a nucleus depends on its amount of shielding. (11.6)

20. It is not possible to use IR spectroscopy to distinguish between a ketone and a carboxylic acid. (11.4)
21. A carboxylic acid can be distinguished from an aldehyde via ^{1}H-NMR spectroscopy. (11.10)
22. A wavenumber, $\bar{\nu}$, is directly proportional to frequency. (11.3)
23. Resonance is the excitation of a magnetic nucleus in one spin state to a higher spin state. (11.5)
24. IR spectroscopy cannot be used to distinguish between an alcohol and an ether. (11.4)
25. A compound with an index of hydrogen deficiency of 1 can contain either one ring, one double bond, or one triple bond. (11.4)
26. Infrared spectroscopy measures transitions between electronic energy levels. (11.2)
27. A set of hydrogens represented by a doublet indicates that there are two neighboring equivalent hydrogens. (11.11)
28. The index of hydrogen deficiency can reveal the possible number of rings, double bonds, or triple bonds in a compound based solely on its molecular formula. (11.4)
29. TMS, tetramethylsilane, is a type of solvent used in NMR spectroscopy. (11.7)
30. Light of wavelength 400 nm is higher in energy than light of wavelength 600 nm. (11.1)
31. The methyl carbon of 1-chlorobutane will yield a ^{1}H-NMR signal that appears as a triplet. (11.11)
32. A compound with the molecular formula $C_6H_{14}FN$ has an index of hydrogen deficiency of 1. (11.4)
33. IR spectroscopy can be used to distinguish between 1°, 2°, and 3° amines. (11.4)

Answers: (1) T (2) F (3) F (4) T (5) T (6) T (7) F (8) T (9) F (10) F (11) T (12) F (13) T (14) T (15) T (16) T (17) F (18) T (19) T (20) F (21) T (22) T (23) T (24) F (25) F (26) F (27) F (28) T (29) F (30) T (31) T (32) F (33) T

Detailed explanations for many of these answers can be found in the accompanying Solutions Manual.

PROBLEMS

A problem marked with an asterisk indicates an applied "real-world" problem. Answers to problems whose numbers are printed in blue are given in Appendix D.

Section 11.1 Electromagnetic Radiation

11.18 Which puts out light of higher energy, a green laser pointer or a red laser pointer? **(See Example 11.1)**

11.19 Calculate the energy, in kilocalories per mole of radiation, of a wave with wavelength 2 m. What type of radiant energy is this? **(See Example 11.1)**

11.20 A molecule possesses molecular orbitals that differ in energy by 82 kcal/mol. What wavelength of light would be required to cause a transition between these two energy levels? What region of the electromagnetic spectrum does this energy correspond to? **(See Example 11.1)**

Section 11.4 Interpreting Infrared Spectra

*11.21 Calculate the index of hydrogen deficiency of each compound: **(See Examples 11.5, 11.6)**

(a) Aspirin, $C_9H_8O_4$
(b) Ascorbic acid (vitamin C), $C_6H_8O_6$
(c) Pyridine, C_5H_5N
(d) Urea, CH_4N_2O
(e) Cholesterol, $C_{27}H_{46}O$
(f) Trichloroacetic acid, $C_2HCl_3O_2$

11.22 Compound A, with the molecular formula C_6H_{10}, reacts with H_2/Ni to give compound B, with the molecular formula C_6H_{12}. The IR spectrum of compound A is provided. From this information about compound A tell **(See Examples 11.4–11.7)**

(a) Its index of hydrogen deficiency.
(b) The number of rings or pi bonds (or both) in compound A.
(c) What structural feature(s) would account for compound A's index of hydrogen deficiency.

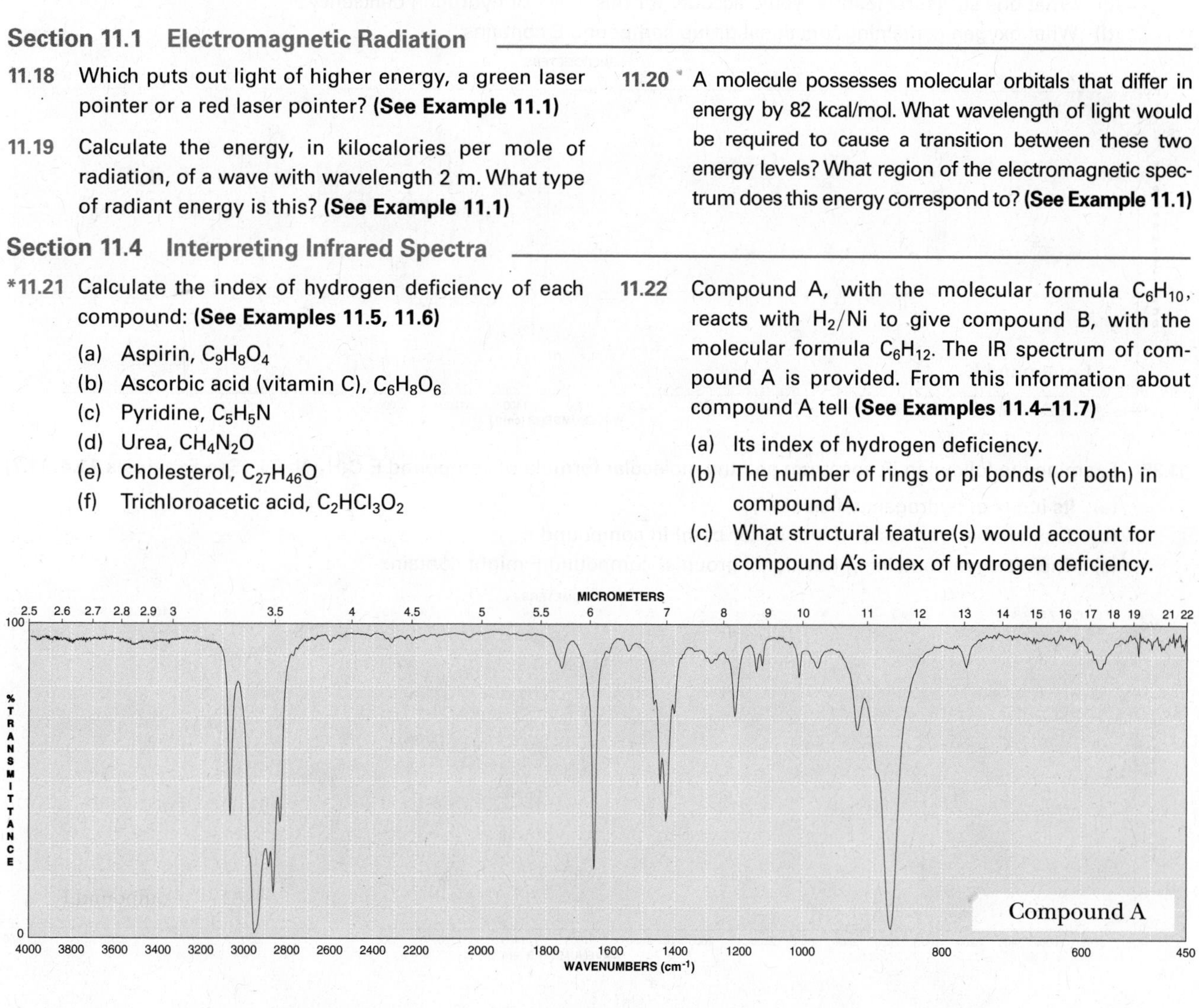

11.23 Compound C, with the molecular formula C_6H_{12}, reacts with H_2/Ni to give compound D, with the molecular formula C_6H_{14}. The IR spectrum of compound C is provided. From this information about compound C, tell **(See Examples 11.4–11.7)**

(a) Its index of hydrogen deficiency.
(b) The number of rings or pi bonds (or both) in compound C.
(c) What structural feature(s) would account for compound C's index of hydrogen deficiency.

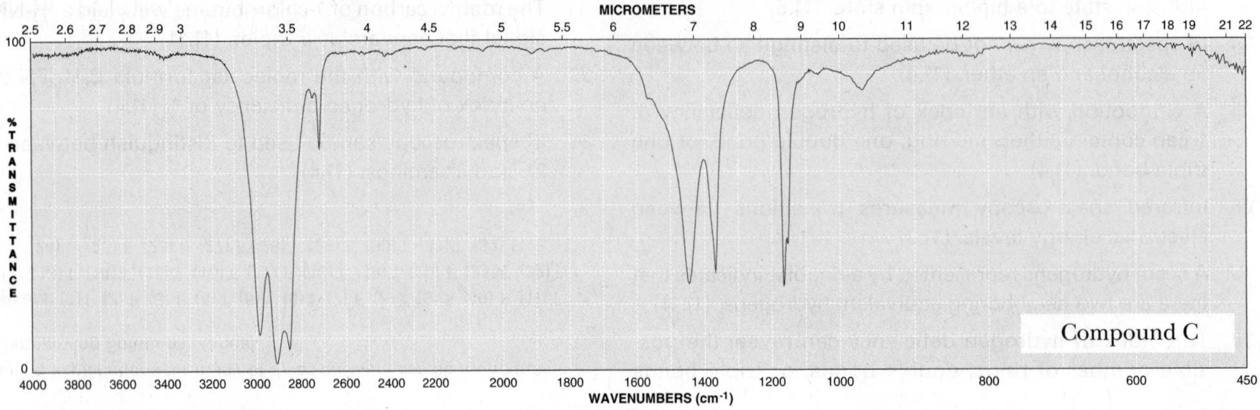

11.24 Examine the following IR spectrum and the molecular formula of compound E, $C_9H_{12}O$: Tell **(See Examples 11.4–11.7)**

(a) Its index of hydrogen deficiency.
(b) The number of rings or pi bonds (or both) in compound E.
(c) What one structural feature would account for this index of hydrogen deficiency.
(d) What oxygen-containing functional group compound E contains.

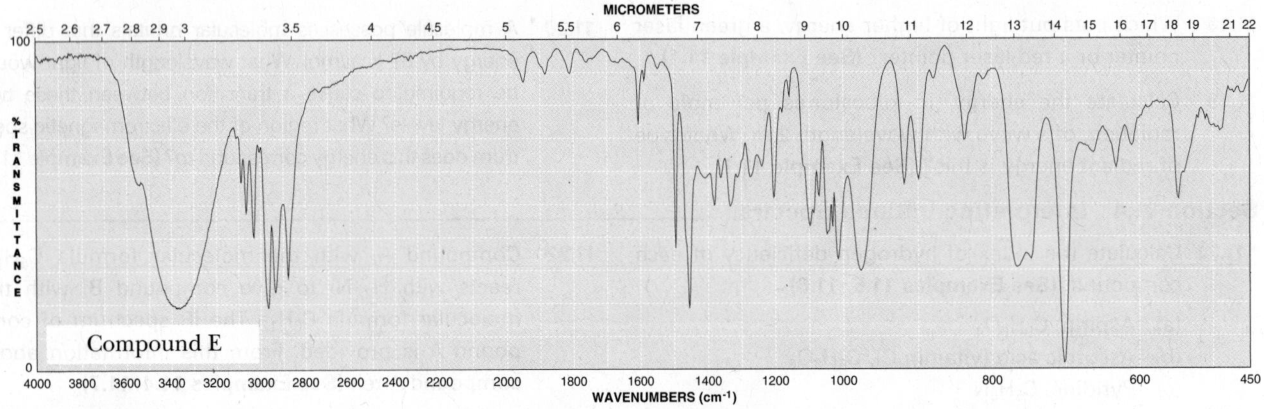

11.25 Examine the following IR spectrum and the molecular formula of compound F, $C_5H_{13}N$: Tell **(See Examples 11.4–11.7)**

(a) Its index of hydrogen deficiency.
(b) The number of rings or pi bonds (or both) in compound F.
(c) The nitrogen-containing functional group(s) compound F might contain.

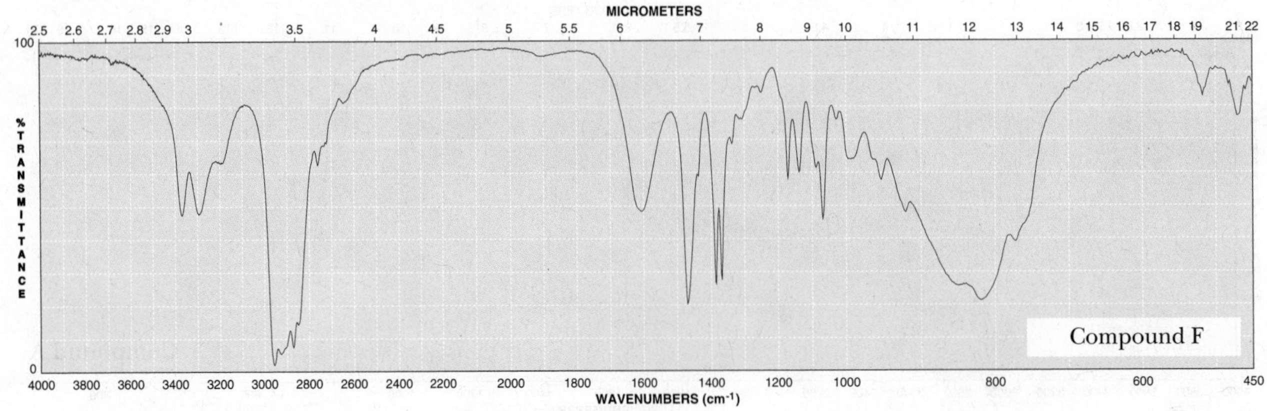

11.26 Examine the following IR spectrum and the molecular formula of compound G, $C_6H_{12}O$: Tell **(See Examples 11.4–11.7)**

(a) Its index of hydrogen deficiency.

(b) The number of rings or pi bonds (or both) in compound G.

(c) What structural features would account for this index of hydrogen deficiency.

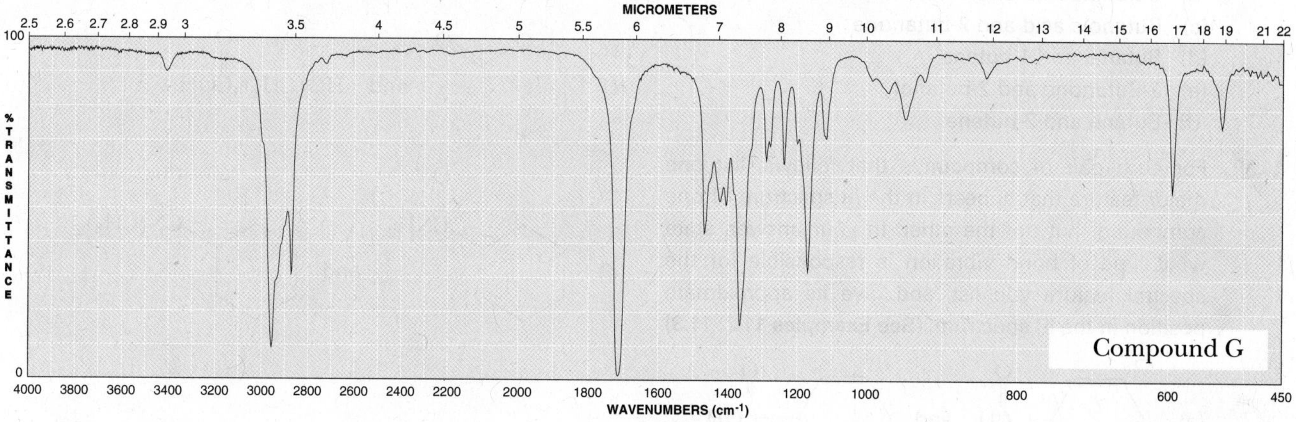

11.27 Examine the following IR spectrum and the molecular formula of compound H, $C_6H_{12}O_2$: Tell **(See Examples 11.4–11.7)**

(a) Its index of hydrogen deficiency.

(b) The number of rings or pi bonds (or both) in compound H.

(c) The oxygen-containing functional group(s) compound H might contain.

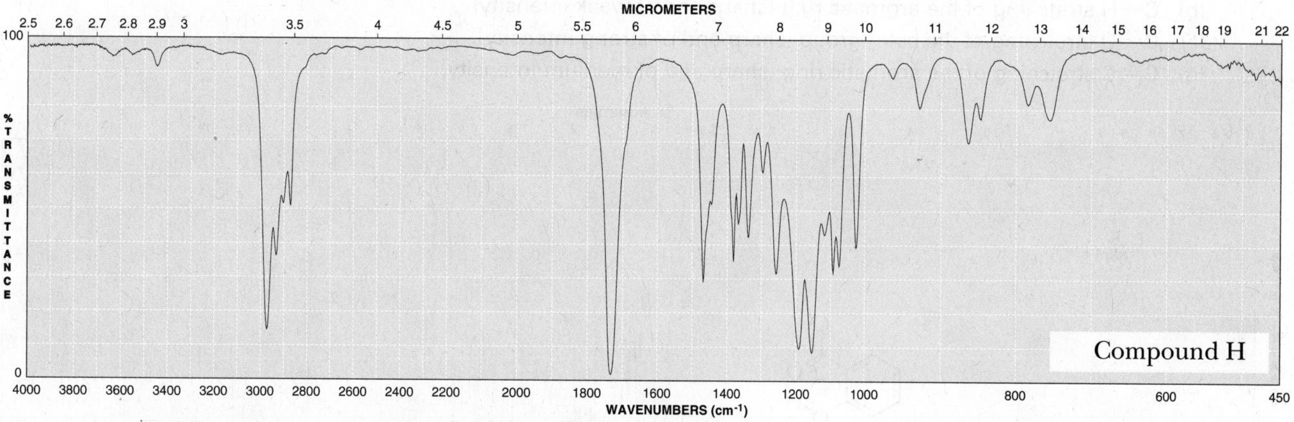

11.28 Examine the following IR spectrum and the molecular formula of compound I, C_3H_7NO: Tell **(See Examples 11.4–11.7)**

(a) Its index of hydrogen deficiency.

(b) The number of rings or pi bonds (or both) in compound I.

(c) The oxygen- and nitrogen-containing functional group(s) in compound I.

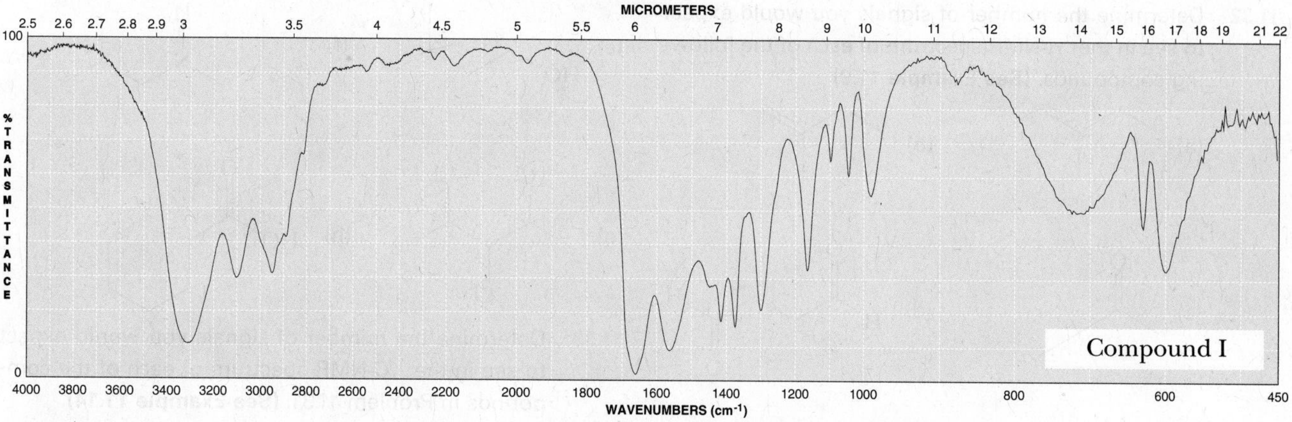

11.29 Show how IR spectroscopy can be used to distinguish between the compounds in each of the following pairs: **(See Examples 11.2, 11.3)**

(a) 1-Butanol and diethyl ether
(b) Butanoic acid and 1-butanol
(c) Butanoic acid and 2-butanone
(d) Butanal and 1-butene
(e) 2-Butanone and 2-butanol
(f) Butane and 2-butene

11.30 For each pair of compounds that follows, list one major feature that appears in the IR spectrum of one compound, but not the other. In your answer, state what type of bond vibration is responsible for the spectral feature you list, and give its approximate position in the IR spectrum. **(See Examples 11.2, 11.3)**

(a) 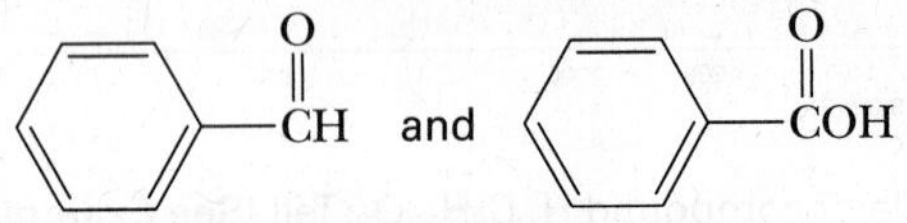

(b) 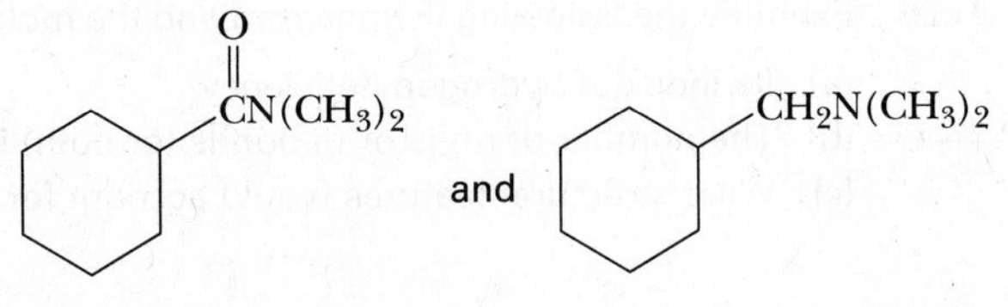

(c) 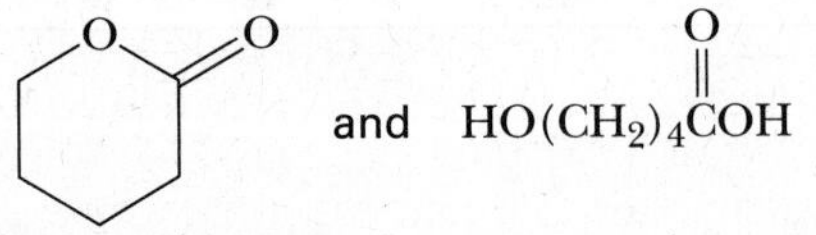

(d) 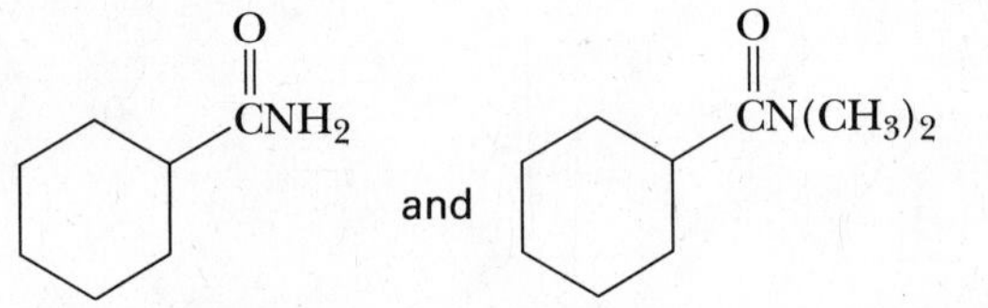

***11.31** Following are an infrared spectrum and a structural formula for methyl salicylate, the fragrant component of oil of wintergreen. On this spectrum, locate the absorption peak(s) due to **(See Examples 11.2, 11.3)**

(a) O—H stretching of the hydrogen-bonded —OH group (very broad and of medium intensity).
(b) C—H stretching of the aromatic ring (sharp and of weak intensity).
(c) C=O stretching of the ester group (sharp and of strong intensity).
(d) C=C stretching of the aromatic ring (sharp and of medium intensity).

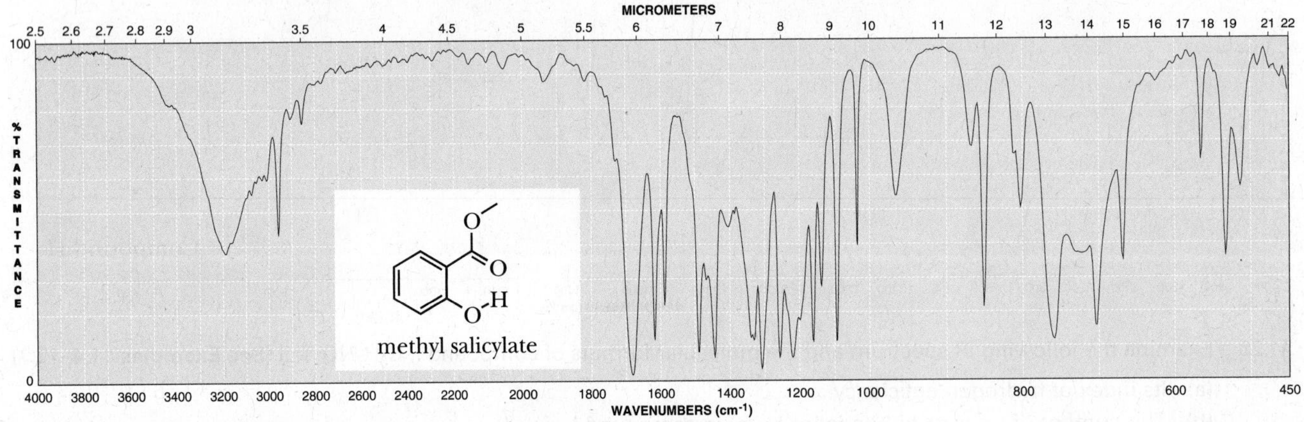

Section 11.8 Equivalency of Hydrogens and Carbons

11.32 Determine the number of signals you would expect to see in the ^{1}H-NMR spectrum of each of the following compounds. **(See Example 11.9)**

(a) 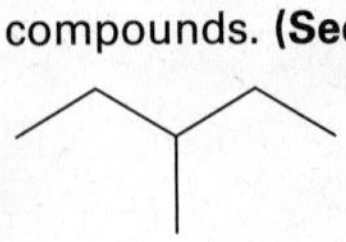

(b) 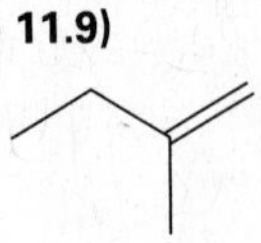

(c) 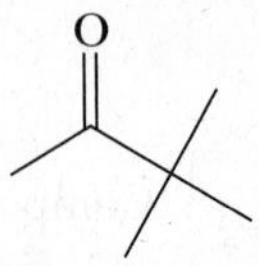

(d) 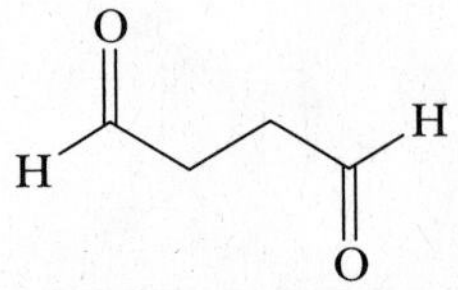

(e) 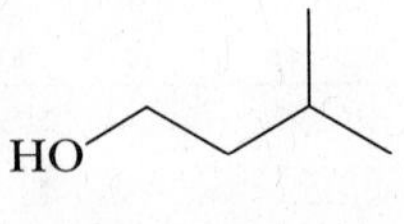

(f) 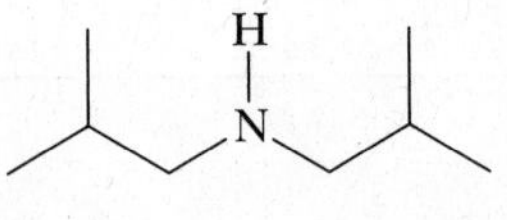

(g) 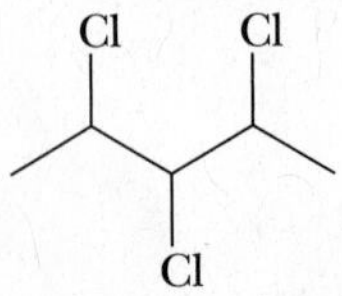

(h) 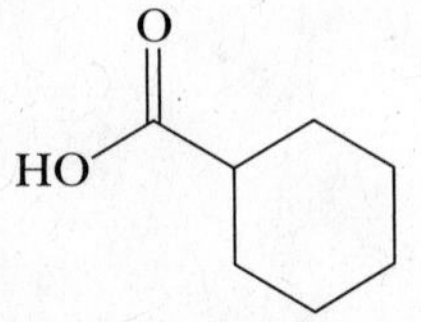

11.33 Determine the number of signals you would expect to see in the ^{13}C-NMR spectrum of each of the compounds in Problem 11.31. **(See Example 11.14)**

Section 11.13 Interpreting ^{1}H-NMR and ^{13}C-NMR Spectra

11.34 Following are structural formulas for the constitutional isomers of xylene and three sets of ^{13}C-NMR spectra. Assign each constitutional isomer its correct spectrum. **(See Example 11.17)**

(a)

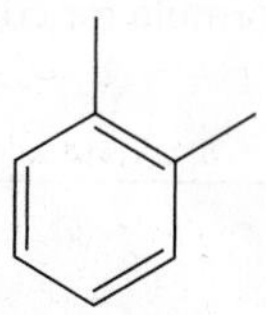

(b)

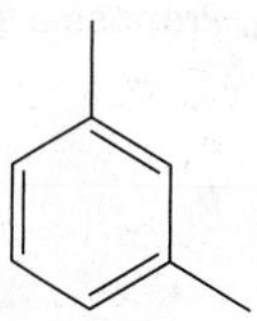

(c)

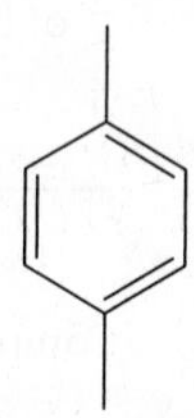

(75 MHz, $CDCl_3$)

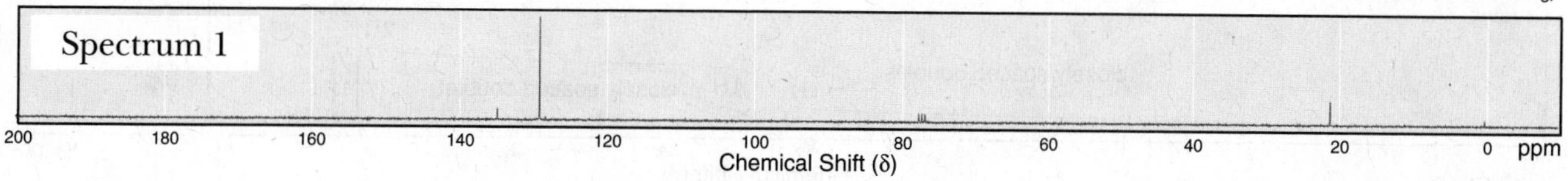

(75 MHz, $CDCl_3$)

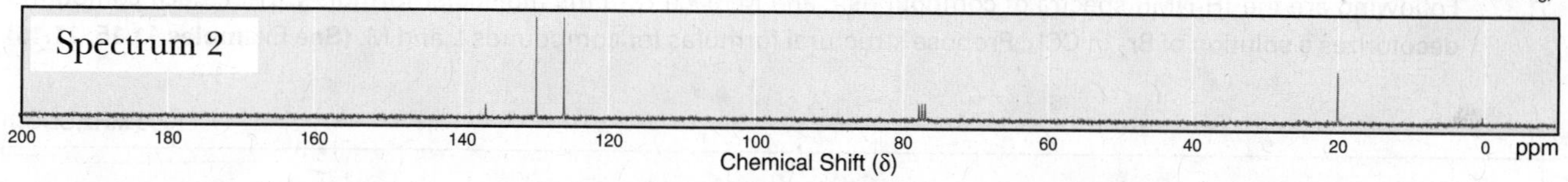

(75 MHz, $CDCl_3$)

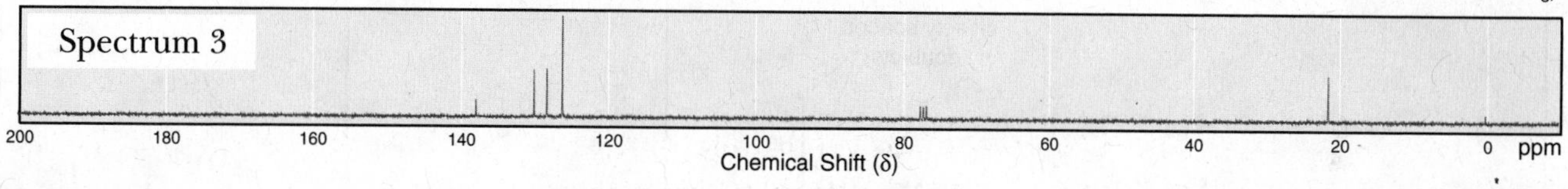

11.35 Following is a ^{1}H-NMR spectrum for compound J, with the molecular formula C_7H_{14}. Compound J decolorizes a solution of bromine in carbon tetrachloride. Propose a structural formula for compound J. **(See Examples 11.15, 11.16)**

(300 MHz, $CDCl_3$)

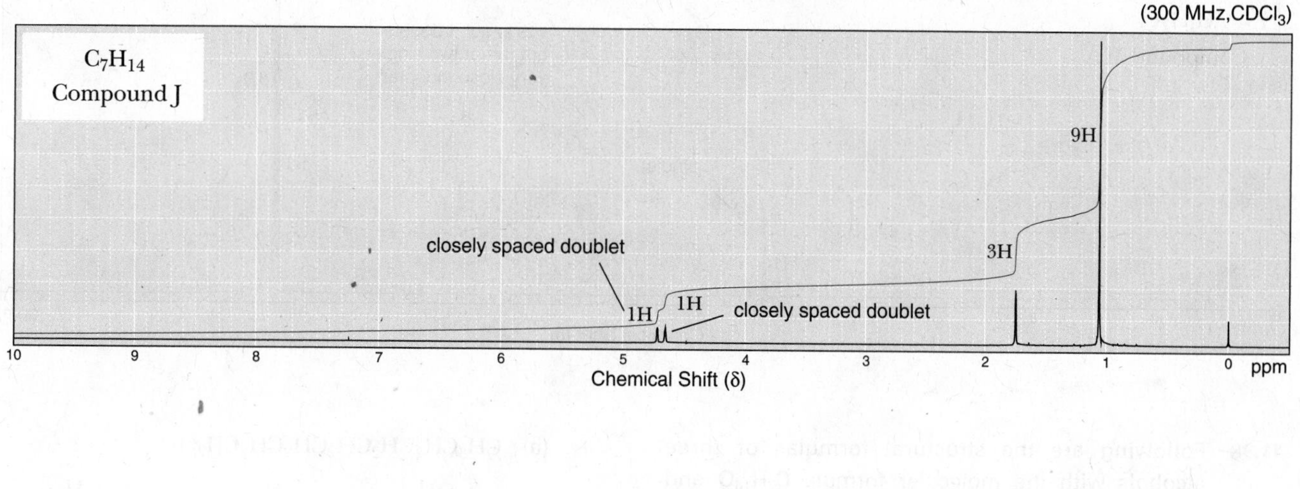

11.36 Following is a ^{1}H-NMR spectrum for compound K, with the molecular formula C_8H_{16}. Compound K decolorizes a solution of Br_2 in CCl_4. Propose a structural formula for compound K. **(See Examples 11.15, 11.16)**

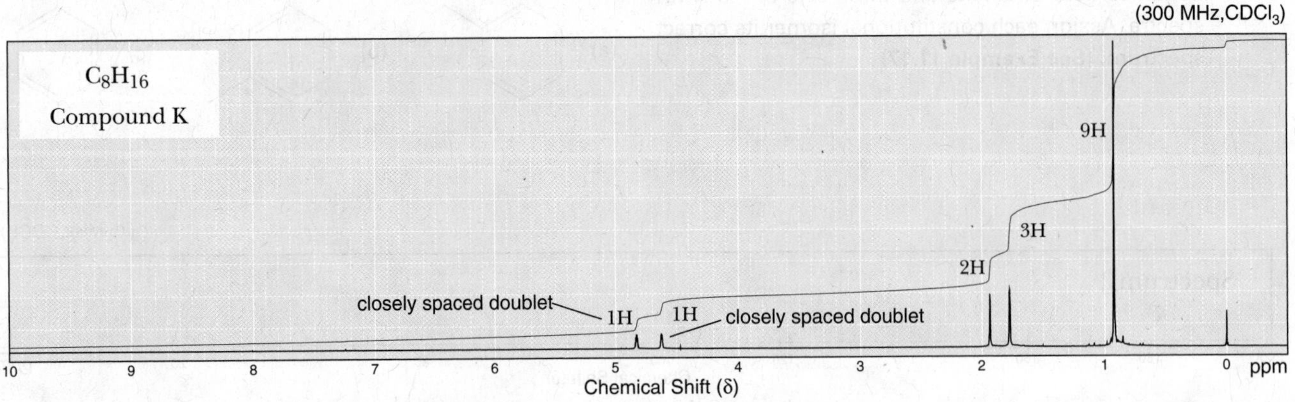

11.37 Following are the ^{1}H-NMR spectra of compounds L and M, each with the molecular formula C_4H_7Cl. Each compound decolorizes a solution of Br_2 in CCl_4. Propose structural formulas for compounds L and M. **(See Examples 11.15, 11.16)**

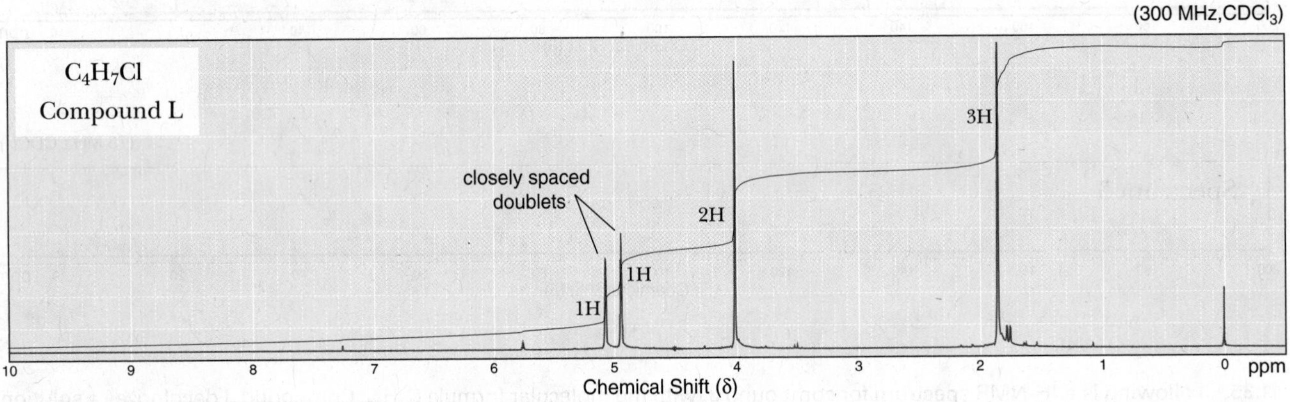

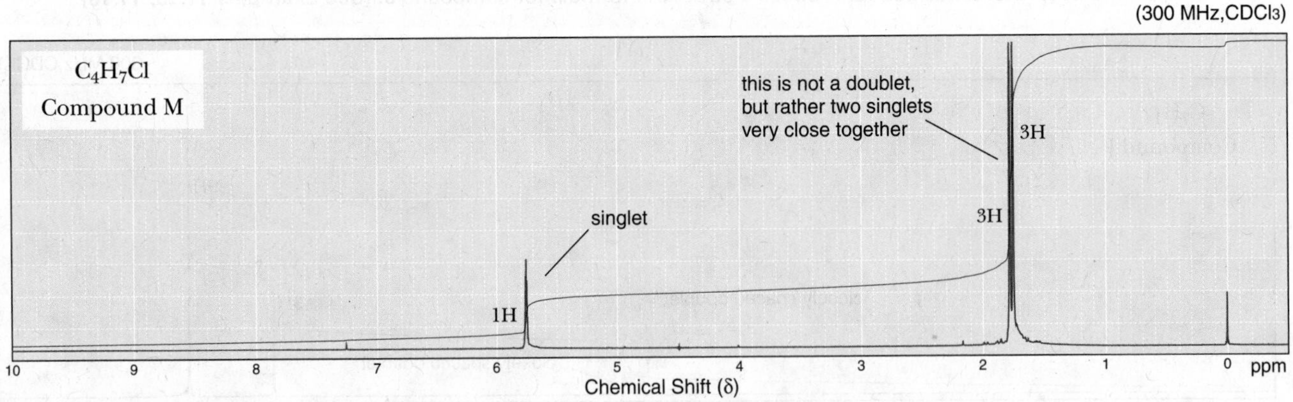

11.38 Following are the structural formulas of three alcohols with the molecular formula $C_7H_{16}O$ and three sets of ^{13}C-NMR spectral data. Assign each constitutional isomer to its correct spectral data. **(See Example 11.17)**

(a) $CH_3CH_2CH_2CH_2CH_2CH_2CH_2OH$

(b) $CH_3C(OH)(CH_3)CH_2CH_2CH_2CH_3$ (OH and CH_3 on C-2)

(c) $CH_3CH_2C(OH)(CH_2CH_3)CH_2CH_3$ (OH and CH_2CH_3 on C-3)

Spectrum 1	Spectrum 2	Spectrum 3
74.66	70.97	62.93
30.54	43.74	32.79
7.73	29.21	31.86
	26.60	29.14
	23.27	25.75
	14.09	22.63
		14.08

11.39 Alcohol N, with the molecular formula $C_6H_{14}O$, undergoes acid-catalyzed dehydration when it is warmed with phosphoric acid, giving compound O, with the molecular formula C_6H_{12}, as the major product. A ^{1}H-NMR spectrum of compound N shows peaks at δ 0.89 (t, 6H), 1.12 (s, 3H), 1.38 (s, 1H), and 1.48 (q, 4H). The ^{13}C-NMR spectrum of compound N shows peaks at δ 72.98, 33.72, 25.85, and 8.16. Propose structural formulas for compounds N and O. **(See Examples 11.15–11.17)**

11.40 Compound P, $C_6H_{14}O$, does not react with sodium metal and does not discharge the color of Br_2 in CCl_4. The ^{1}H-NMR spectrum of compound P consists of only two signals: a 12H doublet at δ 1.1 and a 2H septet at δ 3.6. Propose a structural formula for compound P. **(See Examples 11.15, 11.16)**

11.41 Propose a structural formula for each haloalkane: **(See Examples 11.15, 11.16)**

(a) $C_2H_4Br_2$ δ 2.5 (d, 3H) and 5.9 (q, 1H)
(b) $C_4H_8Cl_2$ δ 1.67 (d, 6H) and 2.15 (q, 2H)
(c) $C_5H_8Br_4$ δ 3.6 (s, 8H)
(d) C_4H_9Br δ 1.1 (d, 6H), 1.9 (m, 1H), and 3.4 (d, 2H)
(e) $C_5H_{11}Br$ δ 1.1 (s, 9H) and 3.2 (s, 2H)
(f) $C_7H_{15}Cl$ δ 1.1 (s, 9H) and 1.6 (s, 6H)

11.42 Following are structural formulas for esters (1), (2), and (3) and three ^{1}H-NMR spectra. Assign each compound its correct spectrum (Q, R, or S) and assign all signals to their corresponding hydrogens. **(See Examples 11.15, 11.16)**

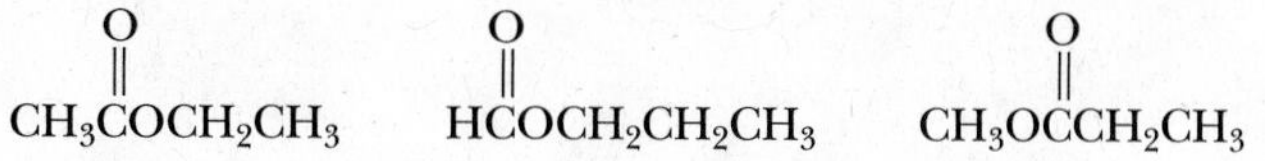

(1) (2) (3)

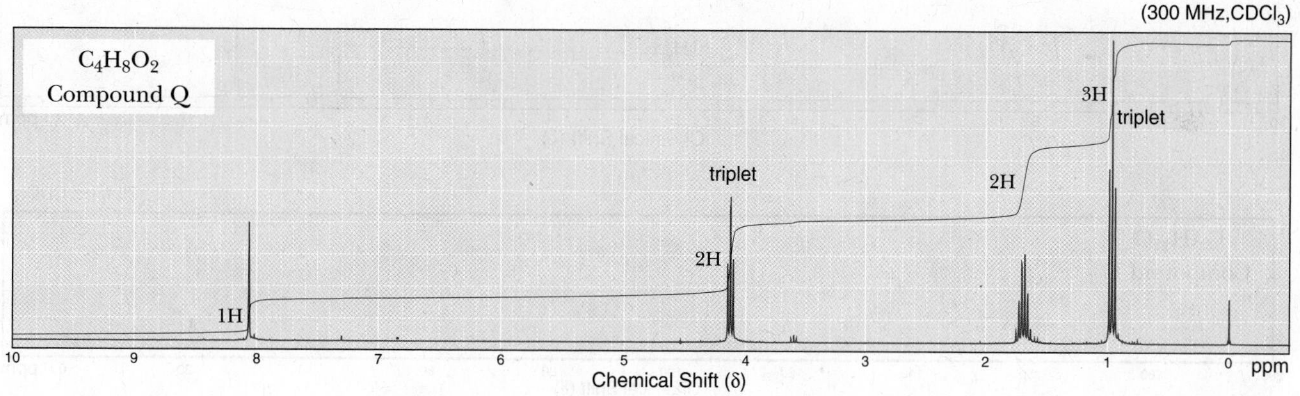

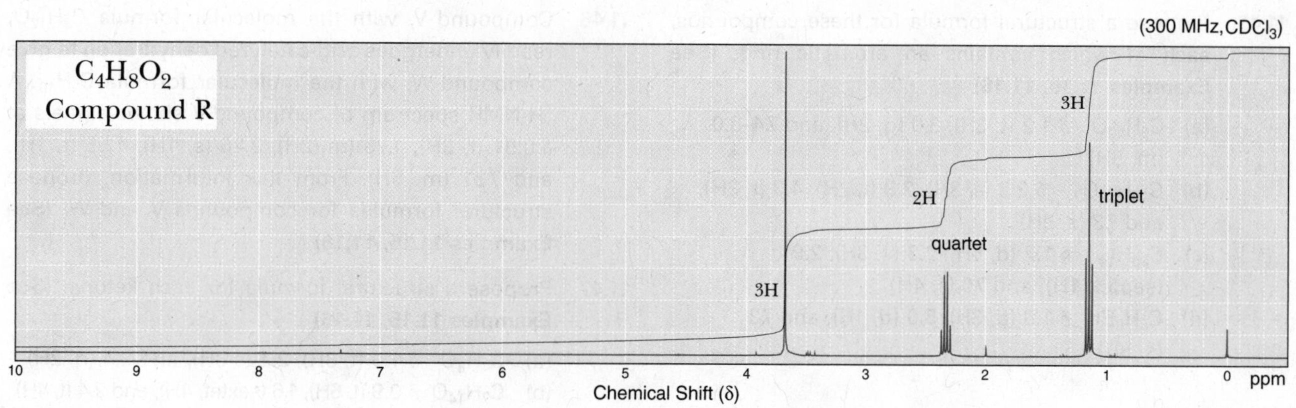

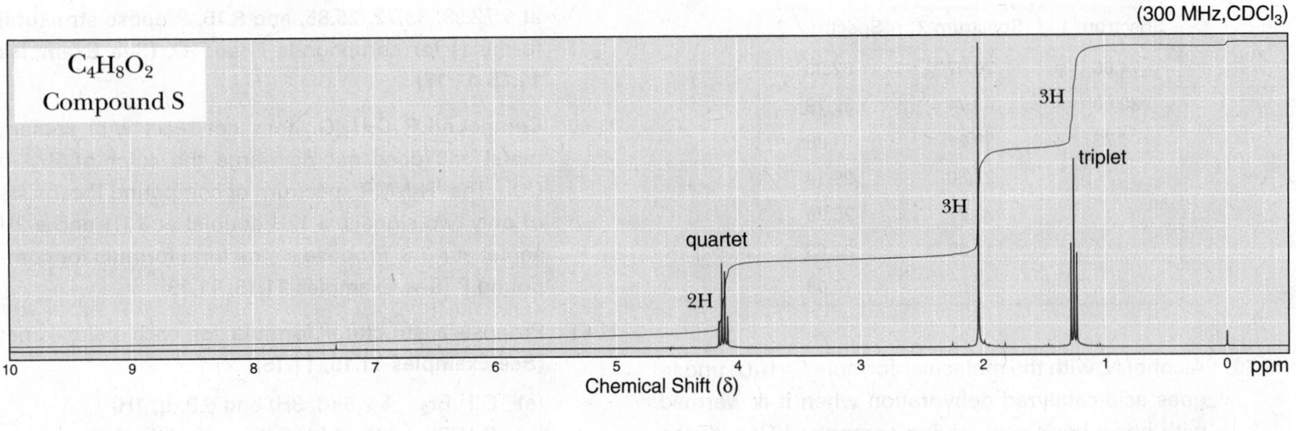

11.43 Compound T, $C_{10}H_{10}O_2$, is insoluble in water, 10% NaOH, and 10% HCl. A ^{1}H-NMR spectrum of compound T shows signals at δ 2.55 (s, 6H) and 7.97 (s, 4H). A ^{13}C-NMR spectrum of compound T shows four signals. From this information, propose a structural formula for T. **(See Examples 11.15–11.17)**

11.44 Compound U, $C_{15}H_{24}O$, is used as an antioxidant in many commercial food products, synthetic rubbers, and petroleum products. Propose a structural formula for compound U based on its ^{1}H-NMR and ^{13}C-NMR spectra. **(Sees Example 11.15–11.17)**

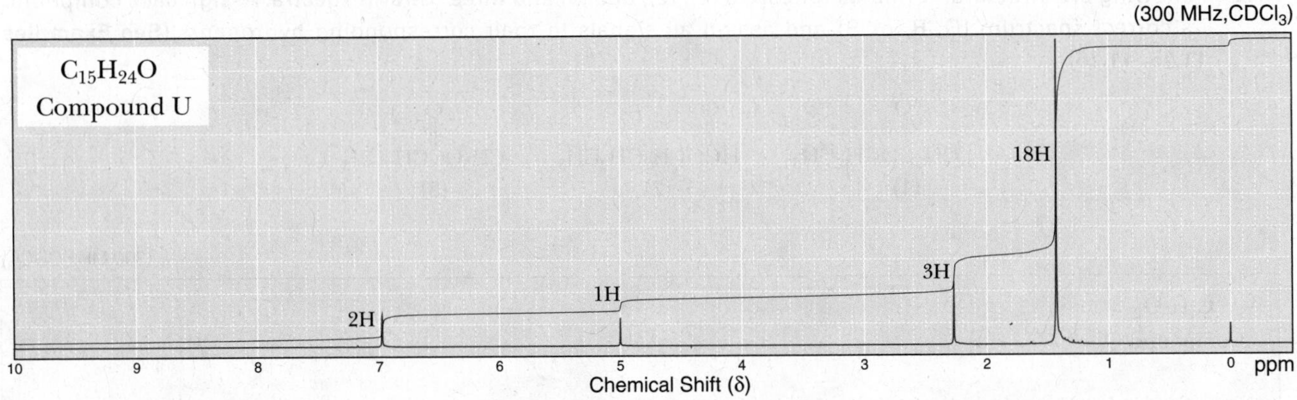

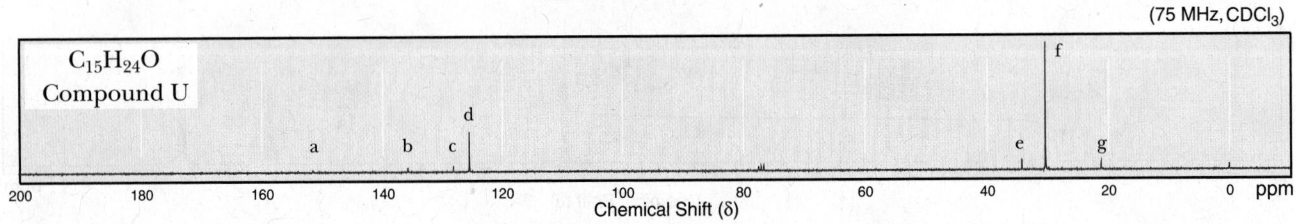

11.45 Propose a structural formula for these compounds, each of which contains an aromatic ring: **(See Examples 11.15, 11.16)**

(a) $C_9H_{10}O$ δ 1.2 (t, 3H), 3.0 (q, 2H), and 7.4–8.0 (m, 5H)

(b) $C_{10}H_{12}O_2$ δ 2.2 (s, 3H), 2.9 (t, 2H), 4.3 (t, 2H), and 7.3 (s, 5H)

(c) $C_{10}H_{14}$ δ 1.2 (d, 6H), 2.3 (s, 3H), 2.9 (septet, 1H), and 7.0 (s, 4H)

(d) C_8H_9Br δ 1.8 (d, 3H), 5.0 (q, 1H), and 7.3 (s, 5H)

11.46 Compound V, with the molecular formula $C_9H_{12}O$, readily undergoes acid-catalyzed dehydration to give compound W, with the molecular formula C_9H_{10}. A ^{1}H-NMR spectrum of compound V shows signals at δ 0.91 (t, 3H), 1.78 (m, 2H), 2.26 (s, 1H), 4.55 (t, 1H), and 7.31 (m, 5H). From this information, propose structural formulas for compounds V and W. **(See Examples 11.15, 11.16)**

11.47 Propose a structural formula for each ketone: **(See Examples 11.15, 11.16)**

(a) C_4H_8O δ 1.0 (t, 3H), 2.1 (s 3H), and 2.4 (q, 2H)

(b) $C_7H_{14}O$ δ 0.9 (t, 6H), 1.6 (sextet, 4H), and 2.4 (t, 4H)

11.48 Propose a structural formula for compound X, a ketone with the molecular formula $C_{10}H_{12}O$: **(See Examples 11.15, 11.16)**

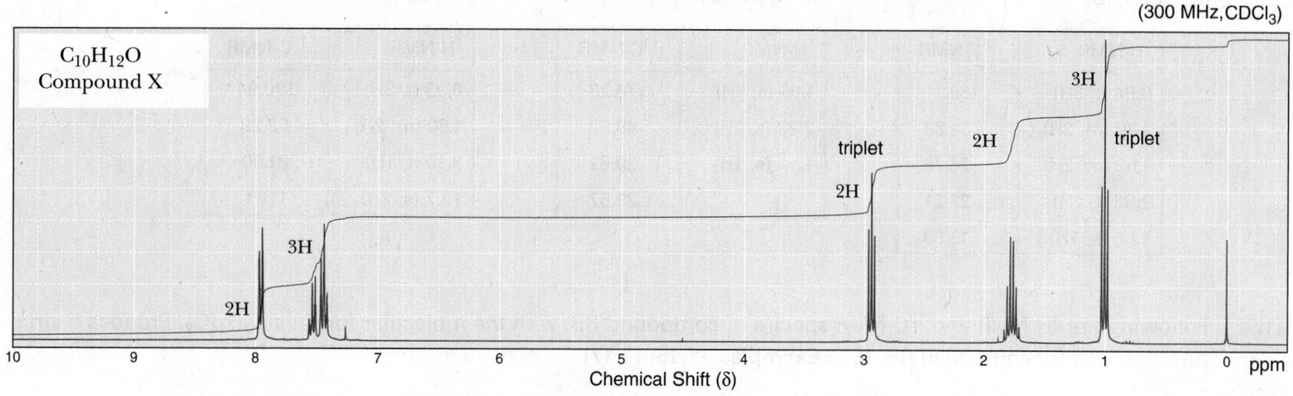

11.49 Following is a ¹H-NMR spectrum for compound Y, with the molecular formula $C_6H_{12}O_2$. Compound Y undergoes acid-catalyzed dehydration to give compound Z, $C_6H_{10}O$. Propose structural formulas for compounds Y and Z. **(See Examples 11.15, 11.16)**

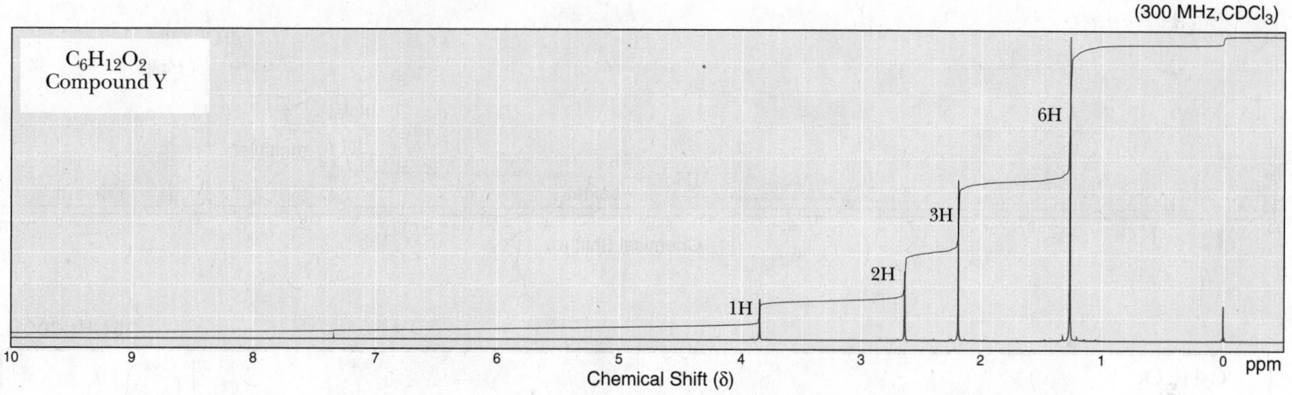

11.50 Propose a structural formula for compound AA, with the molecular formula $C_{12}H_{16}O$. Following are its ¹H-NMR and ¹³C-NMR spectra: **(See Examples 11.15–11.17)**

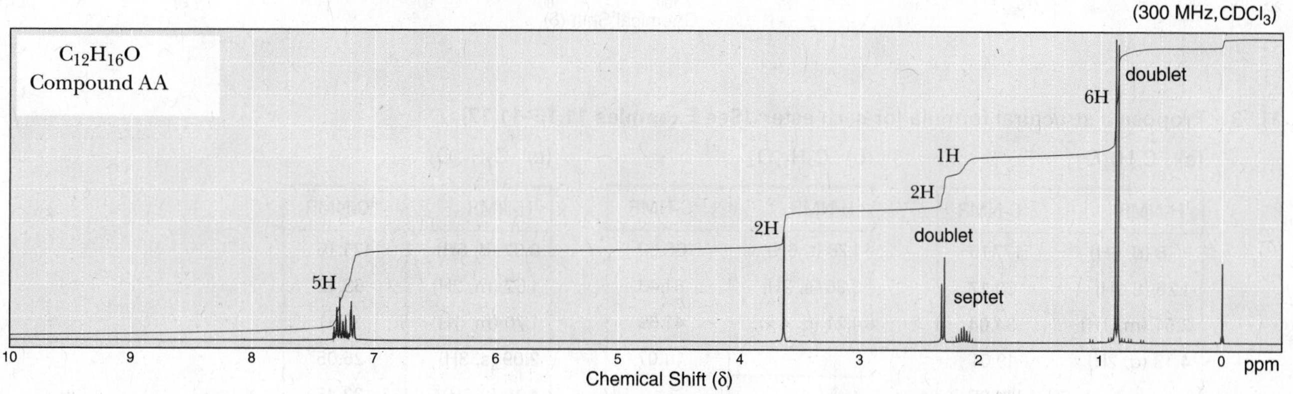

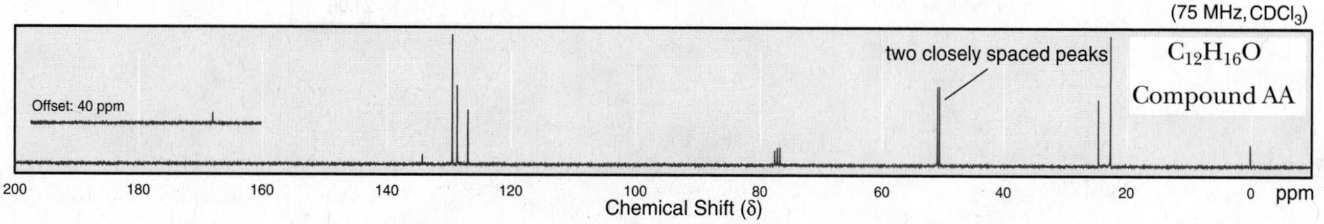

- 11.51 Propose a structural formula for each carboxylic acid: (See Examples 11.15–11.17)
 - (a) $C_5H_{10}O_2$

¹H-NMR ✓	¹³ C-NMR
0.94 (t, 3H)	180.7
1.39 (m, 2H)	33.89
1.62 (m, 2H)	26.76
2.35 (t, 2H)	22.21
12.0 (s, 1H)	13.69

(b) C₆H₁₂O₂

¹ H-NMR	¹³ C-NMR
1.08 (s, 9H)	179.29
2.23 (s, 2H)	46.82
12.1 (s, 1H)	30.62
	29.57

(c) C₅H₈O₄

¹ H-NMR	¹³ C-NMR
0.93 (t, 3H)	170.94
1.80 (m, 2H)	53.28
3.10 (t, 1H)	21.90
12.7 (s, 2H)	11.81

11.52 Following are ¹H-NMR and ¹³C-NMR spectra of compound BB, with the molecular formula C₇H₁₄O₂. Propose a structural formula for compound BB. (See Examples 11.15–11.17)

(300 MHz,CDCl₃)

(75 MHz, CDCl₃)

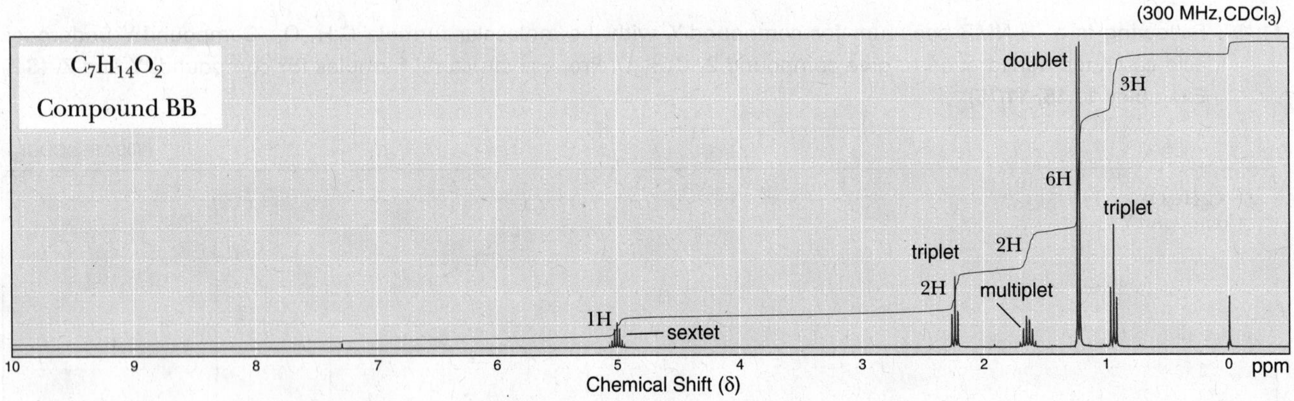

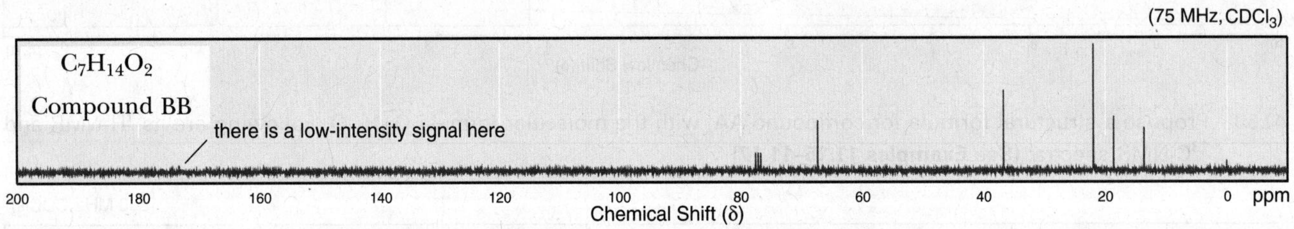

- 11.53 Propose a structural formula for each ester: (See Examples 11.15–11.17)
 - (a) $C_6H_{12}O_2$

¹ H-NMR	¹³ C-NMR
1.18 (d, 6H)	177.16
1.26 (t, 3H)	60.17
2.51 (m, 1H)	34.04
4.13 (q, 2H)	19.01
	14.25

(b) C₇H₁₂O₄

¹ H-NMR	¹³ C-NMR
1.28 (t, 6H)	166.52
3.36 (s, 2H)	61.43
4.21 (q, 4H)	41.69
	14.07

(c) C₇H₁₄O₂

¹ H-NMR	¹³ C-NMR
0.92 (d, 6H)	171.15
1.52 (m, 2H)	63.12
1.70 (m, 1H)	37.31
2.09 (s, 3H)	25.05
4.10 (t, 2H)	22.45
	21.06

11.54 Following are ^{1}H-NMR and ^{13}C-NMR spectra of compound CC, with the molecular formula $C_{10}H_{15}NO$. Propose a structural formula for this compound. **(See Examples 11.15–11.17)**

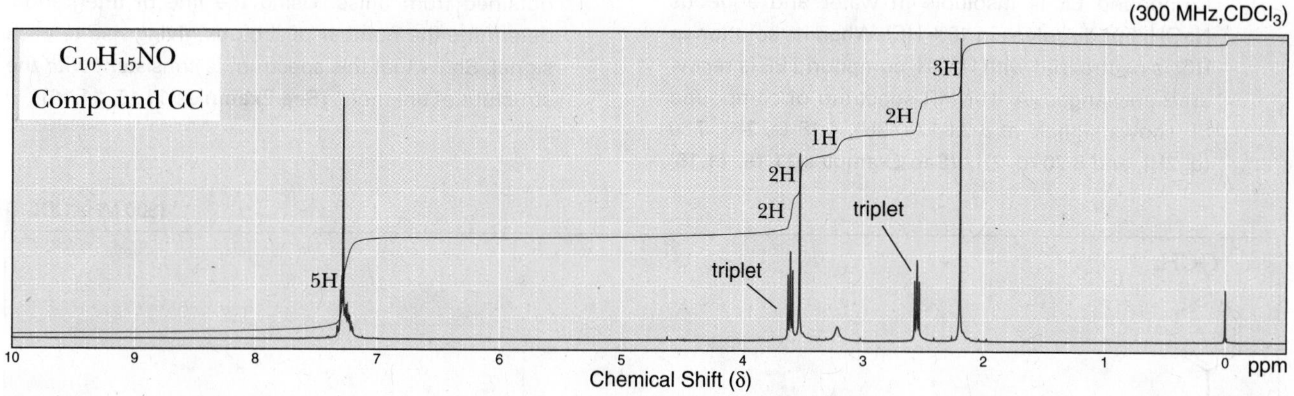

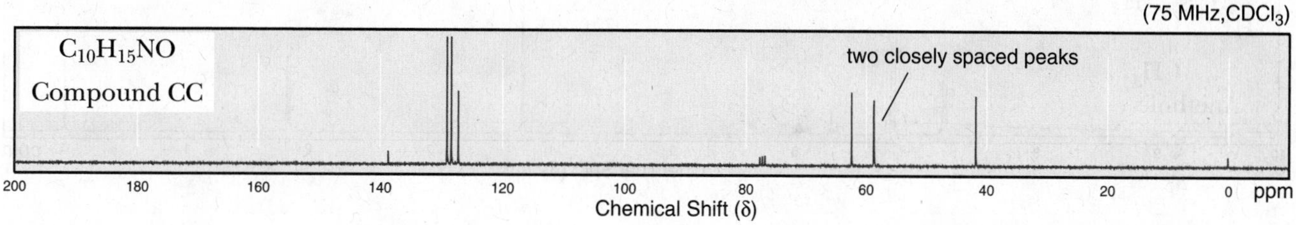

11.55 Propose a structural formula for amide DD, with the molecular formula $C_6H_{13}NO$: **(See Examples 11.15, 11.16)**

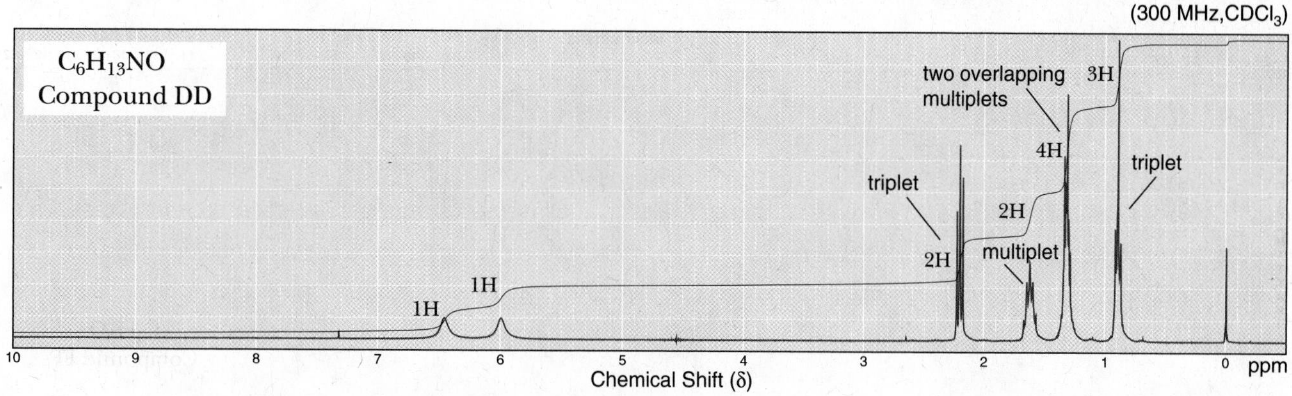

11.56 Propose a structural formula for the analgesic phenacetin, with molecular formula $C_{10}H_{13}NO_2$, based on its ^{1}H-NMR spectrum: **(See Examples 11.15, 11.16)**

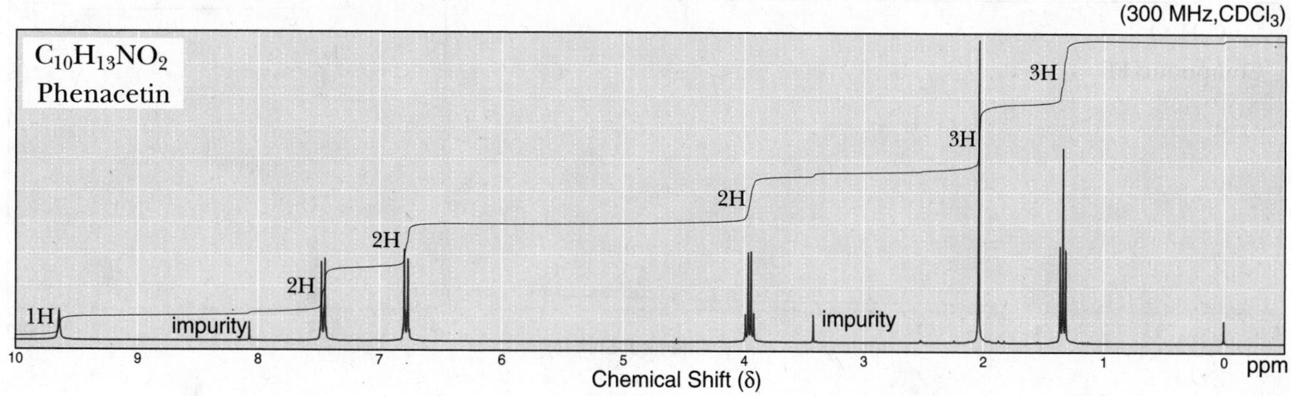

11.57 Propose a structural formula for compound EE, an oily liquid with the molecular formula $C_8H_9NO_2$. Compound EE is insoluble in water and aqueous NaOH, but dissolves in 10% HCl. When its solution in HCl is neutralized with NaOH, compound EE is recovered unchanged. A ^{1}H-NMR spectrum of compound EE shows signals at δ 3.84 (s, 3H), 4.18 (s, 2H), 7.60 (d, 2H), and 8.70 (d, 2H). **(See Examples 11.15, 11.16)**

11.58 Following is a ^{1}H-NMR spectrum and a structural formula for anethole, $C_{10}H_{12}O$, a fragrant natural product obtained from anise. Using the line of integration, determine the number of protons giving rise to each signal. Show that this spectrum is consistent with the structure of anethole. **(See Examples 11.15, 11.16)**

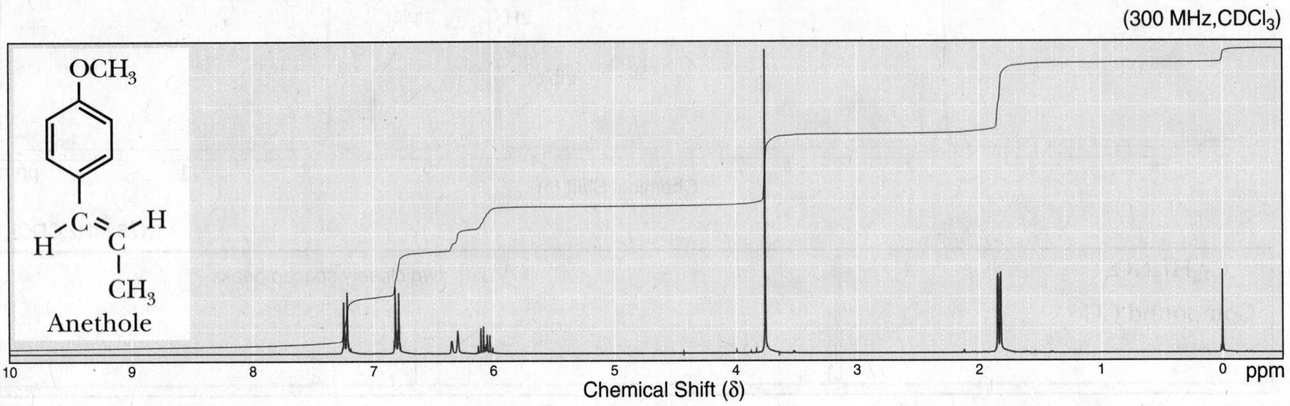

11.59 Propose a structural formula for compound FF, with the molecular formula C_4H_6O, based on the following IR and ^{1}H-NMR spectra: **(See Examples 11.15, 11.16)**

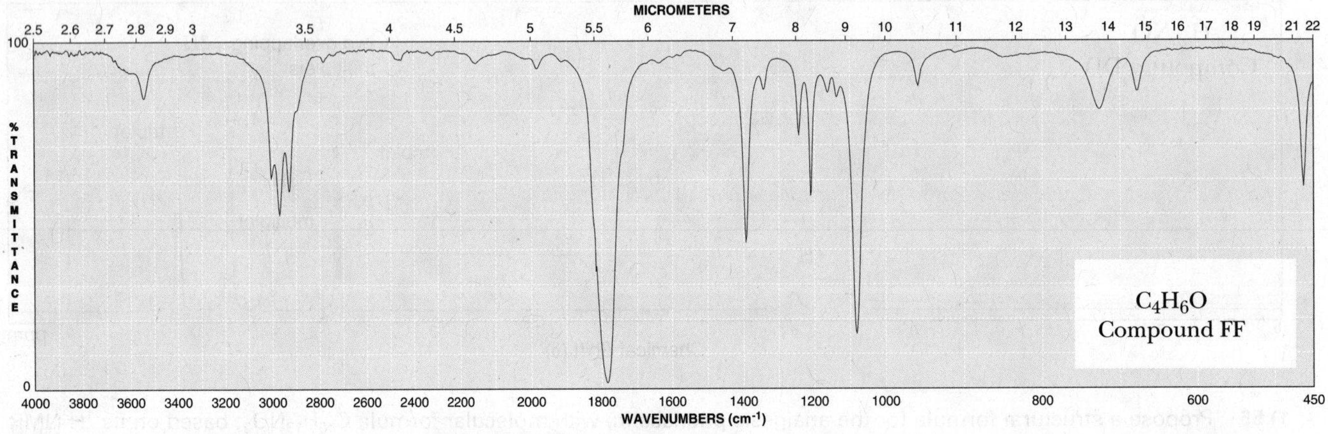

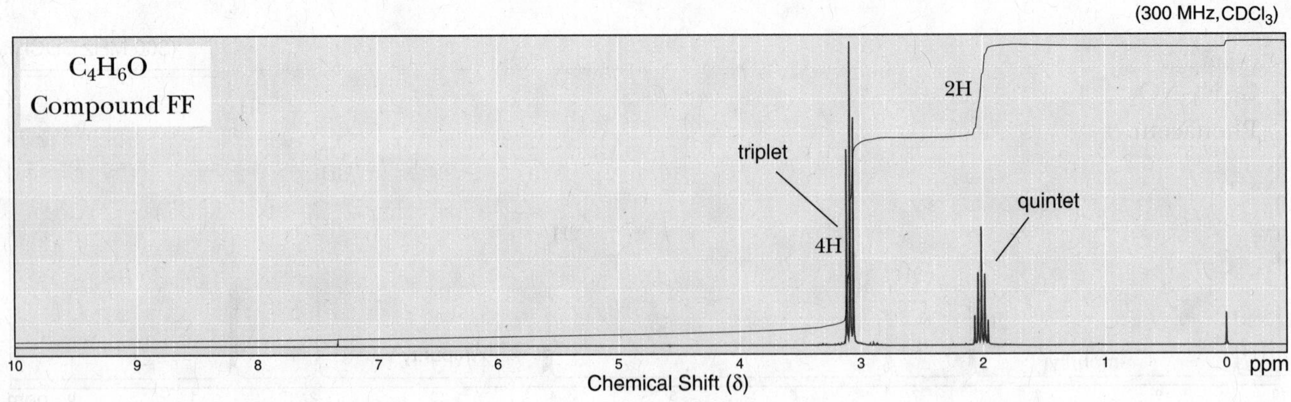

11.60 Propose a structural formula for compound GG, with the molecular formula $C_5H_{10}O_2$, based on the following IR and ^{1}H-NMR spectra: **(See Examples 11.15, 11.16)**

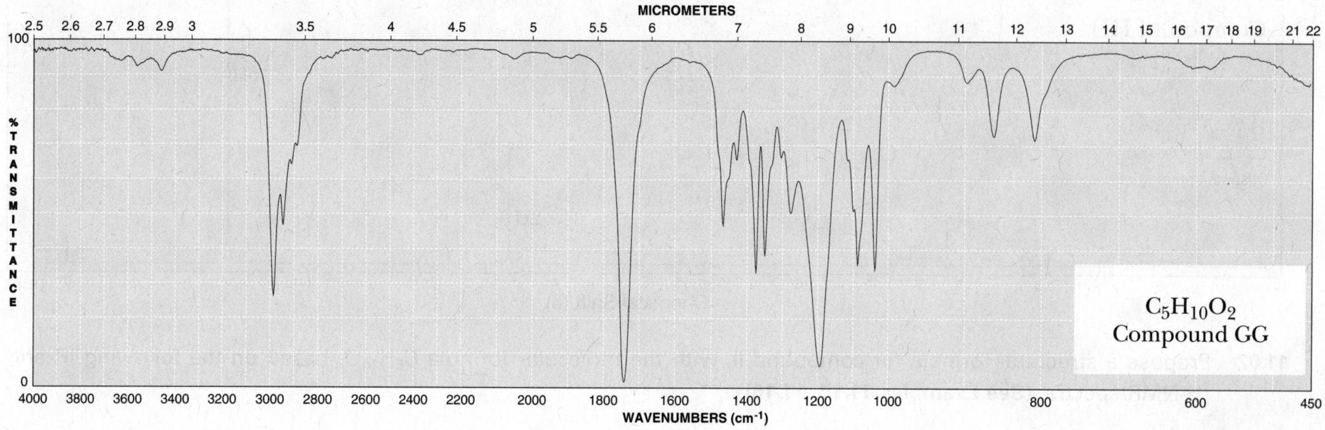

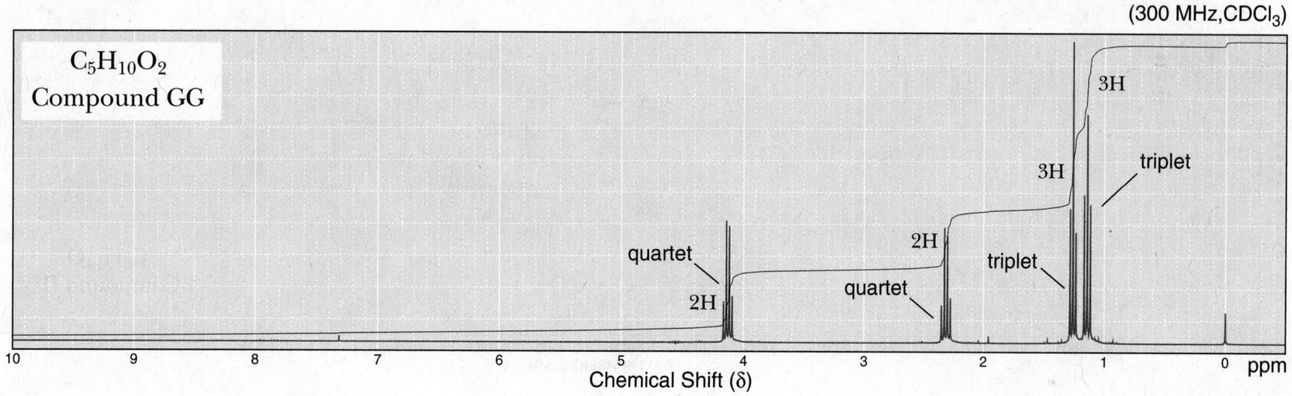

11.61 Propose a structural formula for compound HH, with the molecular formula $C_5H_9ClO_2$, based on the following IR and ^{1}H-NMR spectra: **(See Examples 11.15, 11.16)**

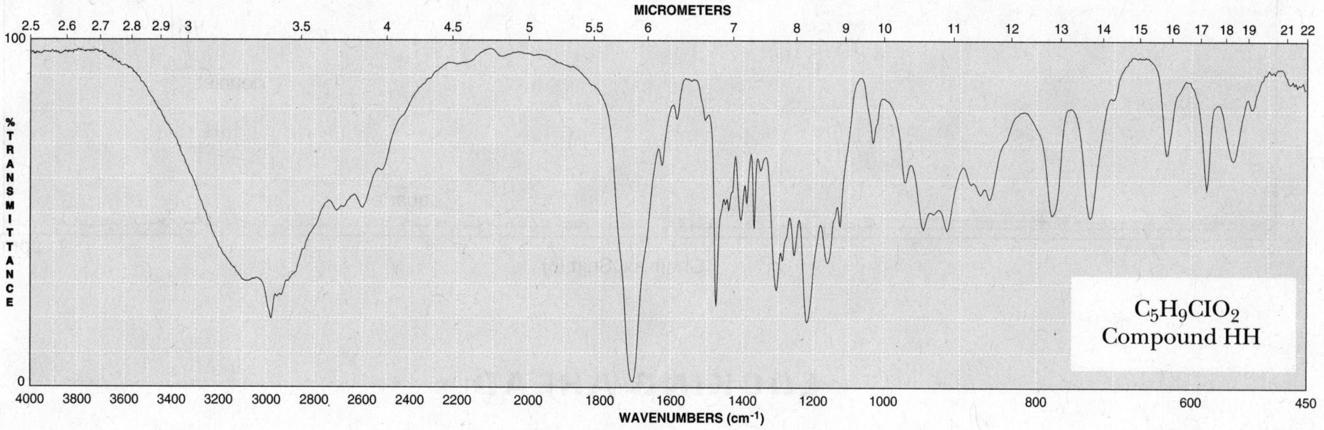

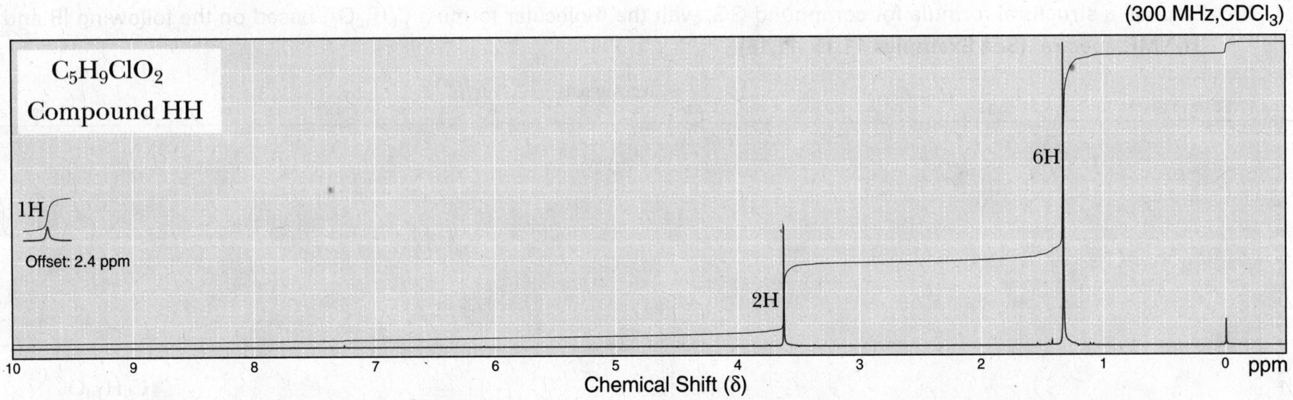

11.62 Propose a structural formula for compound II, with the molecular formula $C_6H_{14}O$, based on the following IR and ^{1}H-NMR spectra: **(See Examples 11.15, 11.16)**

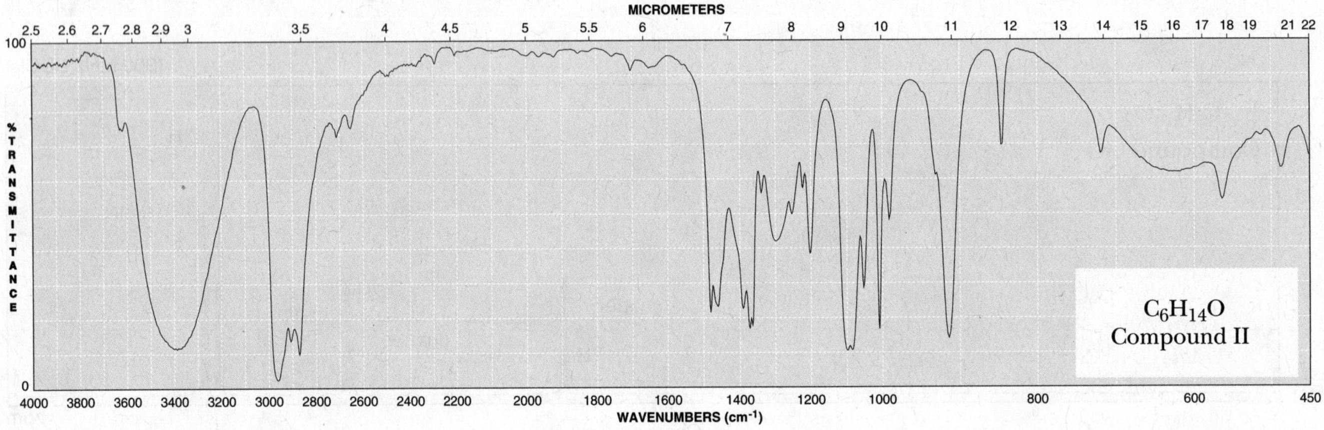

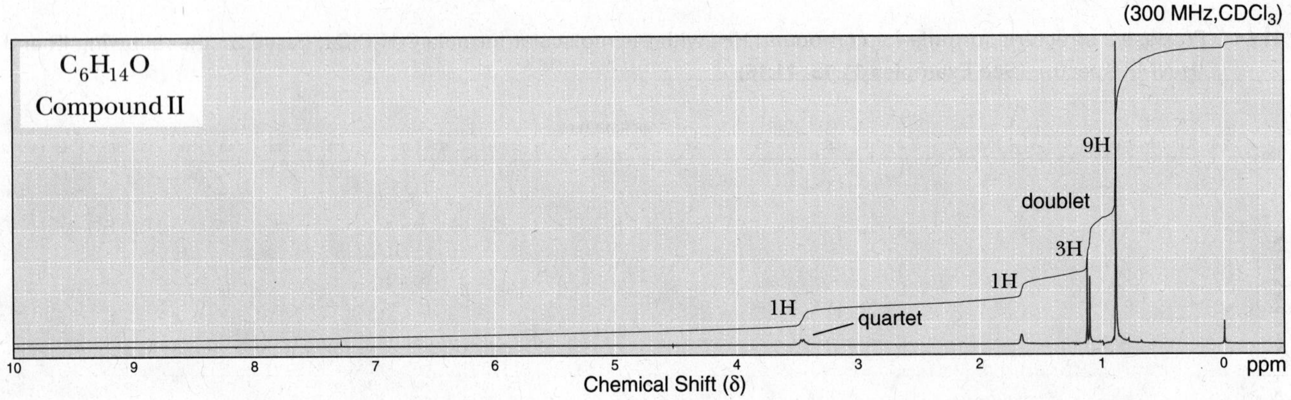

LOOKING AHEAD

11.63 Predict the position of the C=O stretching absorption in acetate ion relative to that in acetic acid:

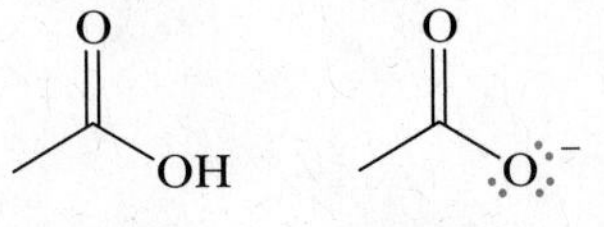

***11.64** Following is the IR spectrum of L-tryptophan, a naturally occurring amino acid that is abundant in foods such as turkey:

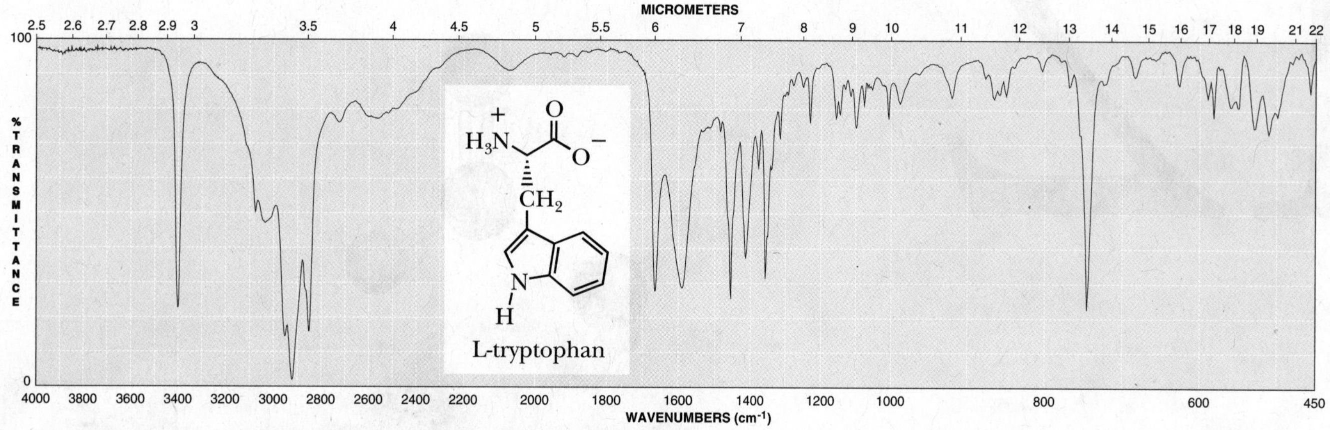

For many years, the L-tryptophan in turkey was believed to make people drowsy after Thanksgiving dinner. Scientists now know that consuming L-tryptophan makes one drowsy only if the compound is taken on an empty stomach. Therefore, it is unlikely that one's Thanksgiving Day turkey is the cause of drowsiness. Notice that L-tryptophan contains one stereocenter. Its enantiomer, D-tryptophan, does not occur in nature but can be synthesized in the laboratory. What would the IR spectrum of D-tryptophan look like?

GROUP LEARNING ACTIVITIES

11.65 Discuss whether IR or NMR spectroscopy could be used to distinguish between the following pairs of molecules. Be very specific in describing the spectral data that would allow you to identify each compound. Assume that you do not have the reference spectra of either molecule.

(a)  and 

(b) 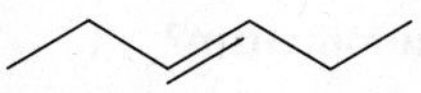 and 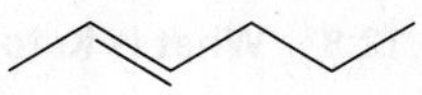

(c) 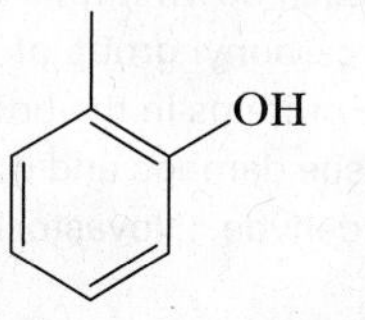 and 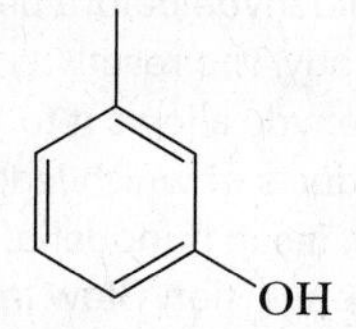

(d) 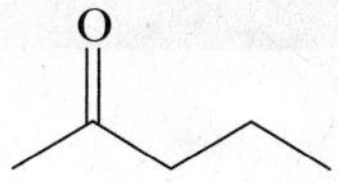 and 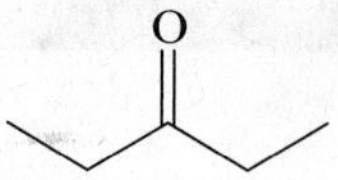

(e) 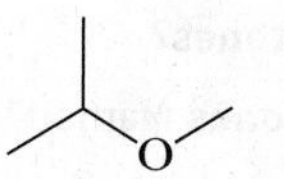 and 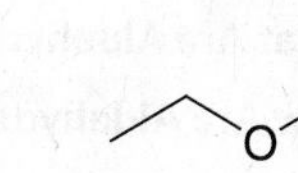

12

Aldehydes and Ketones

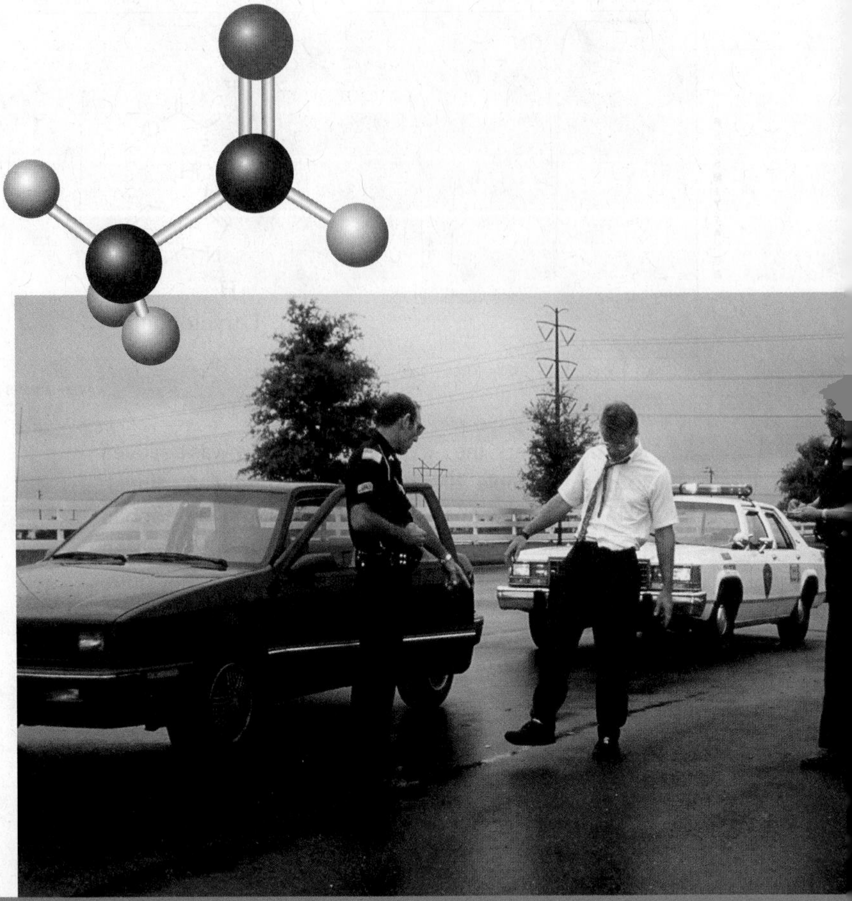

Ethanol from alcoholic beverages is first metabolized to acetaldehyde before being broken down further in the body. The reactivity of the carbonyl group of acetaldehyde allows it to bind to proteins in the body, the products of which lead to tissue damage and organ disease. Inset: A model of acetaldehyde. (Novastock/Stock Connection/Glow Images)

KEY QUESTIONS

- 12.1 What Are Aldehydes and Ketones?
- 12.2 How Are Aldehydes and Ketones Named?
- 12.3 What Are the Physical Properties of Aldehydes and Ketones?
- 12.4 What Is the Most Common Reaction Theme of Aldehydes and Ketones?
- 12.5 What Are Grignard Reagents, and How Do They React with Aldehydes and Ketones?
- 12.6 What Are Hemiacetals and Acetals?
- 12.7 How Do Aldehydes and Ketones React with Ammonia and Amines?
- 12.8 What Is Keto–Enol Tautomerism?
- 12.9 How Are Aldehydes and Ketones Oxidized?
- 12.10 How Are Aldehydes and Ketones Reduced?

HOW TO

- 12.1 How to Predict the Product of a Grignard Reaction
- 12.2 How to Determine the Reactants Used to Synthesize a Hemiacetal or Acetal

CHEMICAL CONNECTIONS

- 12A A Green Synthesis of Adipic Acid

IN THIS AND several of the following chapters, we study the physical and chemical properties of compounds containing the carbonyl group, C=O. Because this group is the functional group of aldehydes, ketones, and carboxylic acids and their derivatives, it is one of the most important functional groups in organic chemistry and in the chemistry of biological systems. The chemical properties of the carbonyl group are straightforward, and an understanding of its characteristic reaction themes leads very quickly to an understanding of a wide variety of organic reactions.

12.1 What Are Aldehydes and Ketones?

The functional group of an **aldehyde** is a carbonyl group bonded to a hydrogen atom (Section 1.7C). In methanal (common name: formaldehyde), the simplest aldehyde, the carbonyl group is bonded to two hydrogen atoms. In other aldehydes, it is bonded to one hydrogen atom and one carbon atom. The functional group of a **ketone** is a carbonyl group bonded to two carbon atoms (Section 1.7C). Following are Lewis structures for the aldehydes methanal and ethanal, and a Lewis structure for propanone, the simplest ketone. Under each in parentheses is its common name:

Aldehyde A compound containing a carbonyl group bonded to hydrogen (a CHO group).

Ketone A compound containing a carbonyl group bonded to two carbons.

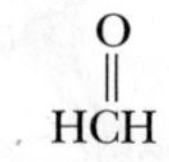
Methanal
(Formaldehyde)

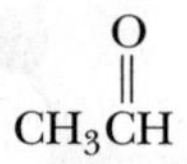
Ethanal
(Acetaldehyde)

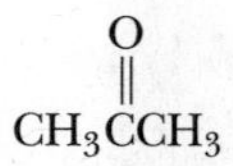
Propanone
(Acetone)

A carbon–oxygen double bond consists of one sigma bond formed by the overlap of sp^2 hybrid orbitals of carbon and oxygen and one pi bond formed by the overlap of parallel $2p$ orbitals. The two nonbonding pairs of electrons on oxygen lie in the two remaining sp^2 hybrid orbitals (Figure 1.20).

12.2 How Are Aldehydes and Ketones Named?

A. IUPAC Nomenclature

The IUPAC system of nomenclature for aldehydes and ketones follows the familiar pattern of selecting the longest chain of carbon atoms that contains the functional group as the parent alkane. We show the aldehyde group by changing the suffix *-e* of the parent alkane to *-al*, as in methanal (Section 3.5). Because the carbonyl group of an aldehyde can appear only at the end of a parent chain and numbering must start with that group as carbon-1, its position is unambiguous; there is no need to use a number to locate it.

For **unsaturated aldehydes**, the presence of a carbon–carbon double bond is indicated by the infix *-en-*. As with other molecules with both an infix and a suffix, the location of the suffix determines the numbering pattern.

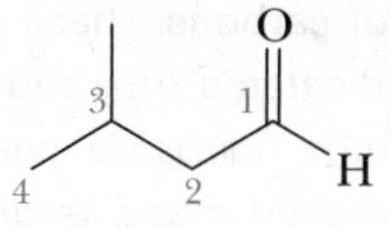
3-Methylbutanal

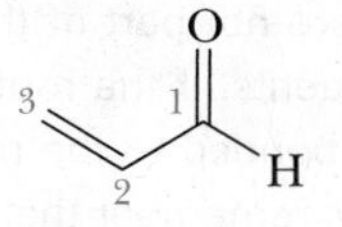
2-Propenal
(Acrolein)

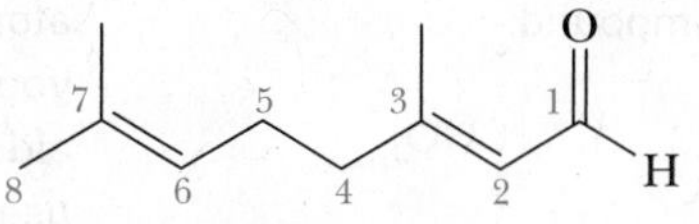
(2*E*)-3,7-Dimethyl-2,6-octadienal
(Geranial)

For cyclic molecules in which —CHO is bonded directly to the ring, we name the molecule by adding the suffix *-carbaldehyde* to the name of the ring. We number the atom of the ring bearing the aldehyde group as number 1:

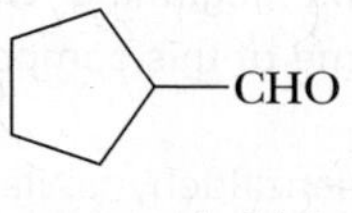
Cyclopentanecarbaldehyde

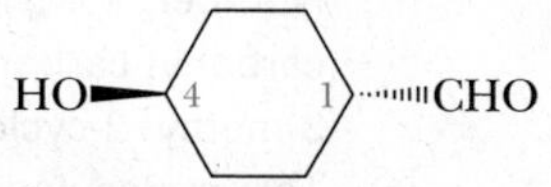
trans-4-Hydroxycyclohexanecarbaldehyde

Among the aldehydes for which the IUPAC system retains common names are benzaldehyde and cinnamaldehyde. Note here the alternative ways of writing the phenyl group.

Ken Karp for John WIley & Sons

Dihydroxyacetone is the active ingredient in several artificial tanning preparations.

In benzaldehyde it is written as a line-angle formula, and in cinnamaldehyde it is abbreviated C_6H_5—.

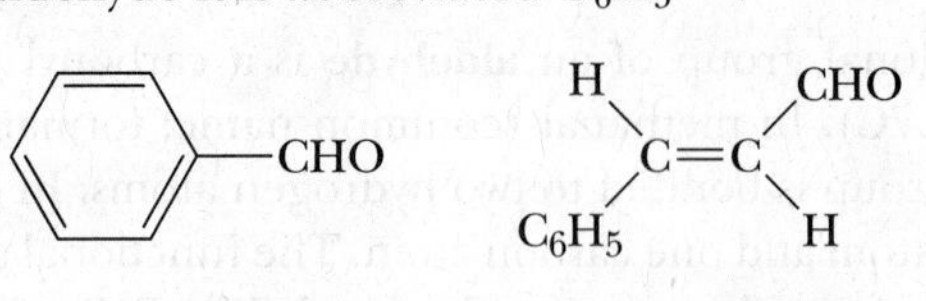

Benzaldehyde   *trans*-3-Phenyl-2-propenal (Cinnamaldehyde)

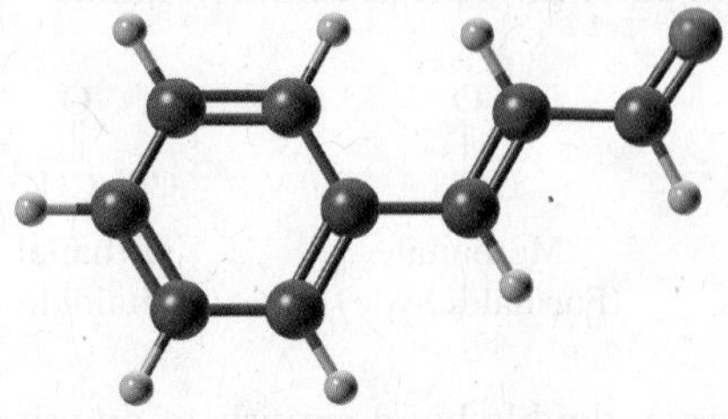

Two other aldehydes whose common names are retained in the IUPAC system are formaldehyde and acetaldehyde.

In the IUPAC system, we name ketones by selecting the longest chain that contains the carbonyl group and making that chain the parent alkane. We indicate the presence of the ketone by changing the suffix from *-e* to *-one* (Section 3.5). We number the parent chain from the direction that gives the carbonyl carbon the smaller number. The IUPAC system retains the common names acetophenone and benzophenone:

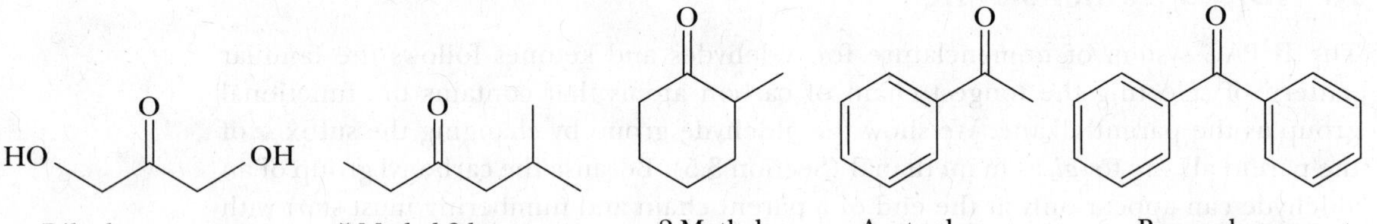

Dihydroxyacetone   5-Methyl-3-hexanone   2-Methylcyclohexanone   Acetophenone   Benzophenone

EXAMPLE 12.1

Write the IUPAC name for each compound:

(a) 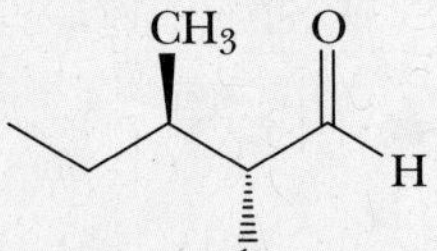

(c) 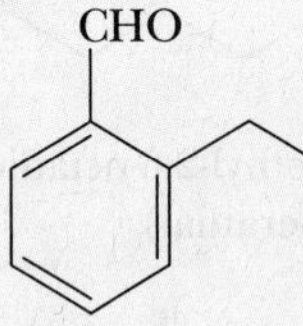

(b) 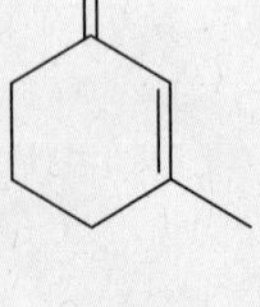

STRATEGY

First determine the root name from the longest chain of carbons that contains the carbonyl group. If the carbonyl is an aldehyde, the suffix will be *-al*. If the carbonyl is a ketone, the suffix will be *-one*. Then identify the atoms or groups of atoms that are not part of that chain of carbons. These are your substituents. If the root name indicates a ring and an aldehyde is bonded to the ring, the suffix *-carbaldehyde* is used. Finally, remember that certain aldehydes and ketones retain their common names in the IUPAC system.

SOLUTION

(a) The longest chain has six carbons, but the longest chain that contains the carbonyl group has five carbons. The IUPAC name of this compound is (2*R*,3*R*)-2-ethyl-3-methylpentanal.

(b) Number the six-membered ring beginning with the carbonyl carbon. The IUPAC name of this compound is 3-methyl-2-cyclohexenone.

(c) This molecule is derived from benzaldehyde. Its IUPAC name is 2-ethylbenzaldehyde.

See problems 12.17, 12.18

PROBLEM 12.1

Write the IUPAC name for each compound:

(a) 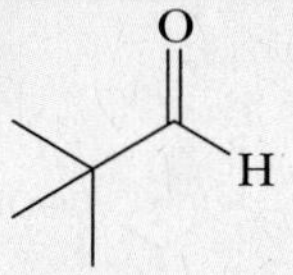 (b) 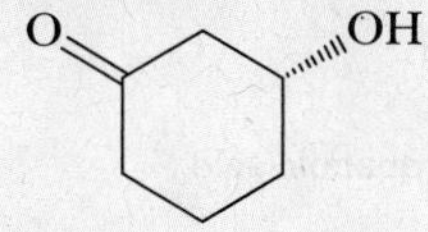 (c) 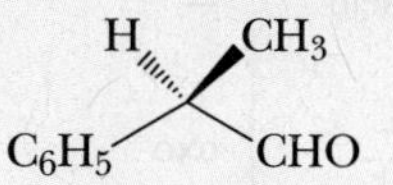

EXAMPLE 12.2

Write structural formulas for all ketones with the molecular formula $C_6H_{12}O$, and give each its IUPAC name. Which of these ketones are chiral?

STRATEGY

Start with an unbranched carbon skeleton. Place the carbonyl group, one at a time, at each position (except carbon-1). Next, consider branching possibilities, and repeat the process of placing the carbonyl at different positions. A ketone will be chiral if it has one stereocenter or if it has two or more stereocenters and is not superposable on its mirror image.

SOLUTION

Following are line-angle formulas and IUPAC names for the six ketones with the given molecular formula:

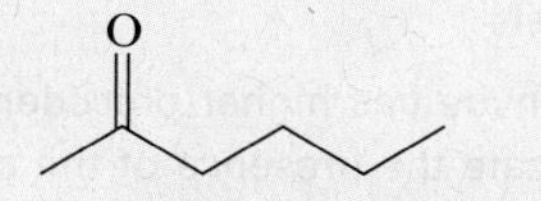
2-Hexanone

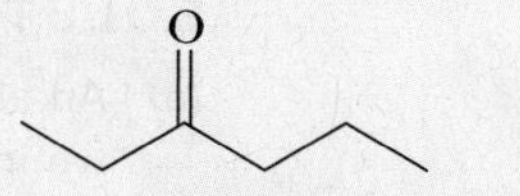
3-Hexanone

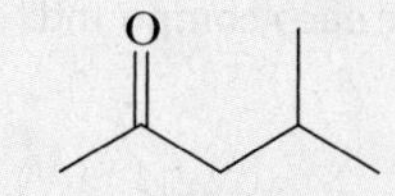
4-Methyl-2-pentanone

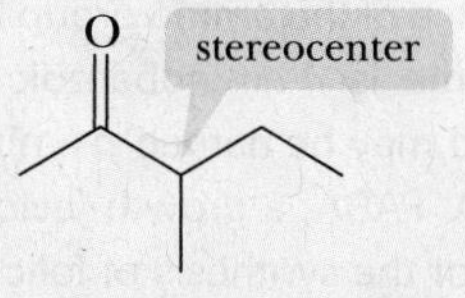

3-Methyl-2-pentanone

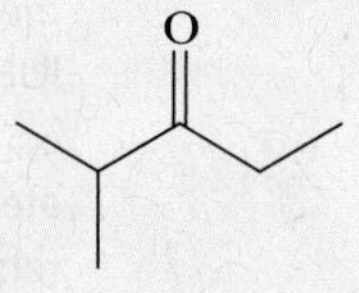
2-Methyl-3-pentanone

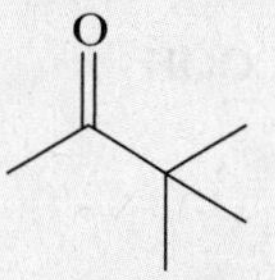
3,3-Dimethyl-2-butanone

Only 3-methyl-2-pentanone has a stereocenter and is chiral.

See problems 12.15, 12.16

PROBLEM 12.2

Write structural formulas for all aldehydes with molecular formula $C_6H_{12}O$, and give each its IUPAC name. Which of these aldehydes are chiral?

B. IUPAC Names for More Complex Aldehydes and Ketones

In naming compounds that contain more than one functional group, the IUPAC has established an **order of precedence of functional groups**. Table 12.1 gives the order of precedence for the functional groups we have studied so far.

Order of precedence of functional groups A system for ranking functional groups in order of priority for the purposes of IUPAC nomenclature.

TABLE 12.1 Increasing Order of Precedence of Six Functional Groups

Functional Group	Suffix	Prefix	Example of When the Functional Group Has Lower Priority	
Carboxyl	-oic acid	—		
Aldehyde	-al	oxo-	3-Oxopropanoic acid	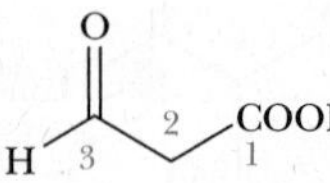
Ketone	-one	oxo-	3-Oxobutanal	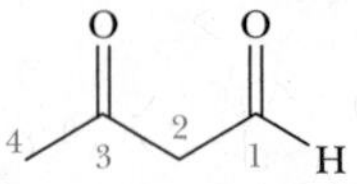
Alcohol	-ol	hydroxy-	4-Hydroxy-2-butanone	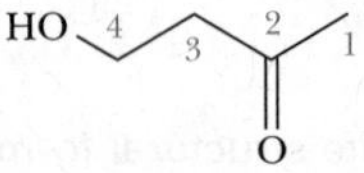
Amino	-amine	amino-	2-Amino-1-propanol	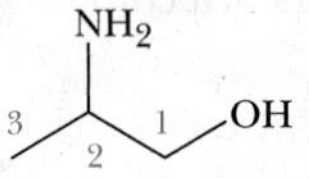
Sulfhydryl	-thiol	mercapto-	2-Mercaptoethanol	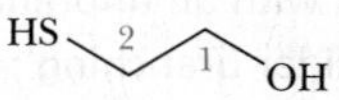

EXAMPLE 12.3

Write the IUPAC name for each compound:

(a) 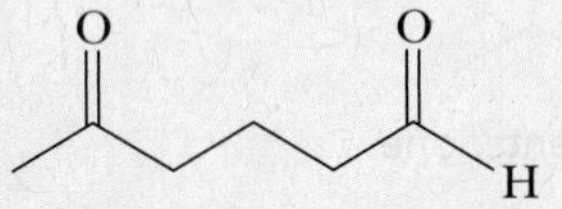

(b) 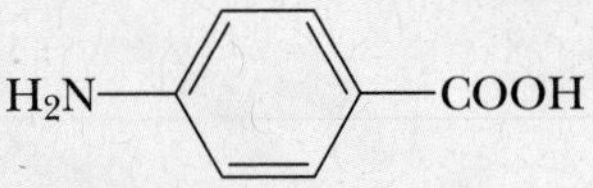

(c) 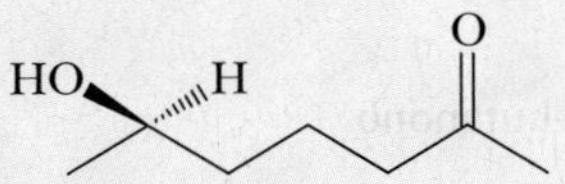

STRATEGY

First determine the root name from the longest chain of carbons that contains the carbonyl group. Use the priority rules in Table 12.1 to determine the suffix and prefix. For benzene ring compounds, remember to use any common names that have been retained in the IUPAC system.

SOLUTION

(a) An aldehyde has higher precedence than a ketone, so we indicate the presence of the carbonyl group of the ketone by the prefix *oxo-*. The IUPAC name of this compound is 5-oxohexanal.

(b) The carboxyl group has higher precedence, so we indicate the presence of the amino group by the prefix *amino-*. The IUPAC name is 4-aminobenzoic acid. Alternatively, the compound may be named *p*-aminobenzoic acid, abbreviated PABA. PABA, a growth factor of microorganisms, is required for the synthesis of folic acid.

(c) The C=O group has higher precedence than the —OH group, so we indicate the —OH group by the prefix *hydroxy-*. The IUPAC name of this compound is (*R*)-6-hydroxy-2-heptanone.

See problems 12.17, 12.18

PROBLEM 12.3

Write IUPAC names for these compounds, each of which is important in intermediary metabolism:

(a) 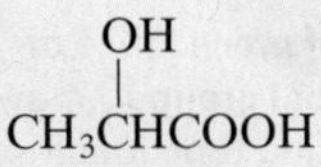
Lactic acid

(b) 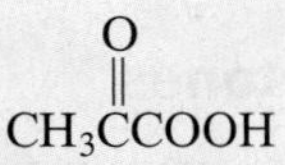
Pyruvic acid

(c) 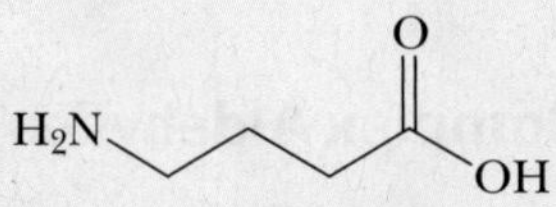
γ-Aminobutyric acid

The name shown is the one by which the compound is more commonly known in the biological sciences.

C. Common Names

The common name for an aldehyde is derived from the common name of the corresponding carboxylic acid by dropping the word *acid* and changing the suffix *-ic* or *-oic* to *-aldehyde.* Because we have not yet studied common names for carboxylic acids, we are not in a position to discuss common names for aldehydes. We can, however, illustrate how they are derived by reference to two common names of carboxylic acids with which you are familiar. The name formaldehyde is derived from formic acid, and the name acetaldehyde from acetic acid:

Formaldehyde

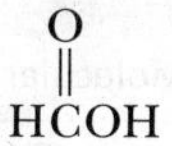
Formic acid

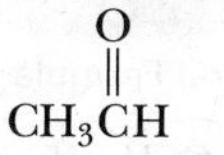
Acetaldehyde

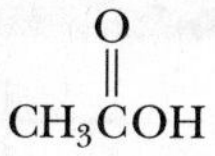
Acetic acid

Common names for ketones are derived by naming each alkyl or aryl group bonded to the carbonyl group as a separate word, followed by the word *ketone.* Groups are generally listed in order of increasing atomic weight. (Methyl ethyl ketone, abbreviated MEK, is a common solvent for varnishes and lacquers):

the lower-molecular-weight group bonded to the carbonyl comes first in the common name for a ketone

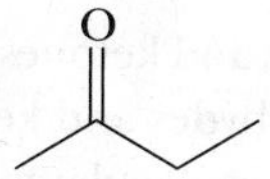
Methyl ethyl ketone (MEK)

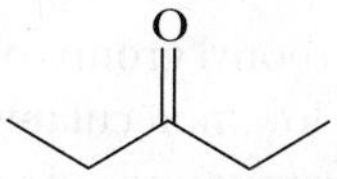
Diethyl ketone

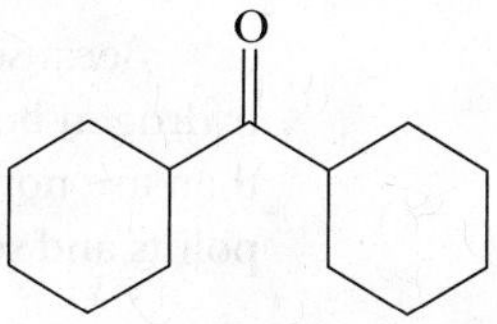
Dicyclohexyl ketone

12.3 What Are the Physical Properties of Aldehydes and Ketones?

Oxygen is more electronegative than carbon (3.5 compared with 2.5; Table 1.4); therefore, a carbon–oxygen double bond is polar, with oxygen bearing a partial negative charge and carbon bearing a partial positive charge:

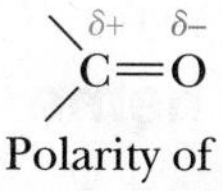
Polarity of a carbonyl group

the more important contributing structure

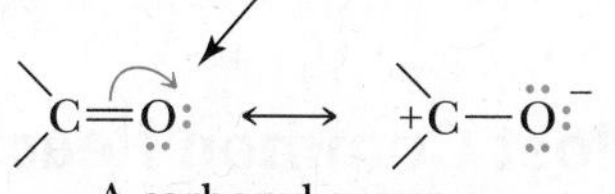
A carbonyl group as a resonance hybrid

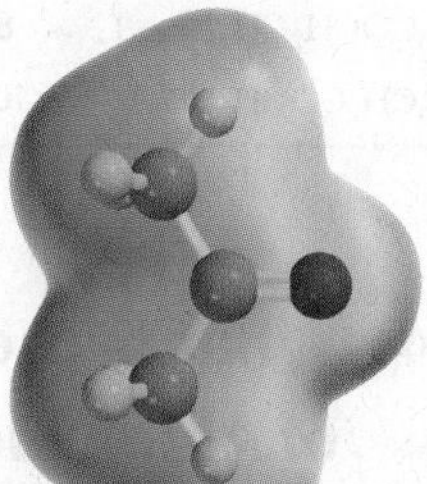

The electron density model shows that the partial positive charge on an acetone molecule is distributed both on the carbonyl carbon and on the two attached methyl groups as well.

In addition, the resonance structure on the right emphasizes that, in reactions of a carbonyl group, carbon acts as an electrophile and a Lewis acid. The carbonyl oxygen, by contrast, acts as a nucleophile and a Lewis base.

Because of the polarity of the carbonyl group, aldehydes and ketones are polar compounds and interact in the liquid state by dipole–dipole interactions. As a result, aldehydes and ketones have higher boiling points than those of nonpolar compounds with comparable molecular weight.

Table 12.2 lists the boiling points of six compounds of comparable molecular weight. Pentane and diethyl ether have the lowest boiling points of these six compounds. Both butanal and 2-butanone are polar compounds, and because of the intermolecular attraction between carbonyl groups, their boiling points are higher than those of pentane and diethyl ether. Alcohols (Section 8.1C) and carboxylic acids (Section 13.3) are polar compounds, and their molecules associate by hydrogen bonding; their boiling points are higher than those of butanal and 2-butanone, compounds whose molecules cannot associate in that manner.

TABLE 12.2 Boiling Points of Six Compounds of Comparable Molecular Weight

Name	Structural Formula	Molecular Weight	Boiling Point (°C)
Diethyl ether	$CH_3CH_2OCH_2CH_3$	74	34
Pentane	$CH_3CH_2CH_2CH_2CH_3$	72	36
Butanal	$CH_3CH_2CH_2CHO$	72	76
2-Butanone	$CH_3CH_2COCH_3$	72	80
1-Butanol	$CH_3CH_2CH_2CH_2OH$	74	117
Propanoic acid	CH_3CH_2COOH	72	141

Because the carbonyl groups of aldehydes and ketones interact with water molecules by hydrogen bonding, low-molecular-weight aldehydes and ketones are more soluble in water than are nonpolar compounds of comparable molecular weight. Table 12.3 lists the boiling points and solubilities in water of several low-molecular-weight aldehydes and ketones.

TABLE 12.3 Physical Properties of Selected Aldehydes and Ketones

IUPAC Name	Common Name	Structural Formula	Boiling Point (°C)	Solubility (g/100 g water)
Methanal	Formaldehyde	HCHO	−21	infinite
Ethanal	Acetaldehyde	CH_3CHO	20	infinite
Propanal	Propionaldehyde	CH_3CH_2CHO	49	16
Butanal	Butyraldehyde	$CH_3CH_2CH_2CHO$	76	7
Hexanal	Caproaldehyde	$CH_3(CH_2)_4CHO$	129	slight
Propanone	Acetone	CH_3COCH_3	56	infinite
2-Butanone	Methyl ethyl ketone	$CH_3COCH_2CH_3$	80	26
3-Pentanone	Diethyl ketone	$CH_3CH_2COCH_2CH_3$	101	5

although the "solubilities" of methanal and ethanal are reported as "infinite," it should be noted that 99% of initial methanal and 57% of initial ethanal are converted to compounds known as hydrates upon addition of water

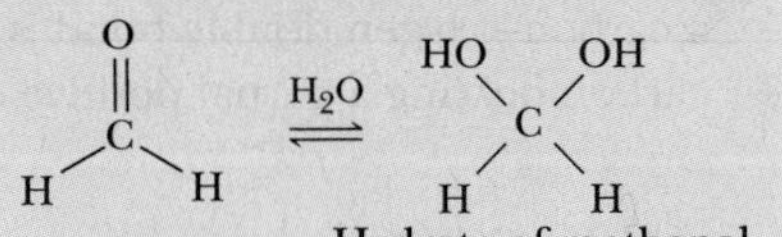

Hydrate of methanal

12.4 What Is the Most Common Reaction Theme of Aldehydes and Ketones?

The partially positive charge on the carbonyl carbon (Section 12.3) is the cause of the most common reaction theme of the carbonyl group, the addition of a nucleophile to form a **tetrahedral carbonyl addition intermediate**. In the following general reaction, the nucleophilic reagent is written as $Nu:^-$ to emphasize the presence of its unshared pair of electrons:

this is the common mechanism pattern: **Reaction of a nucleophile and an electrophile to form a covalent bond**

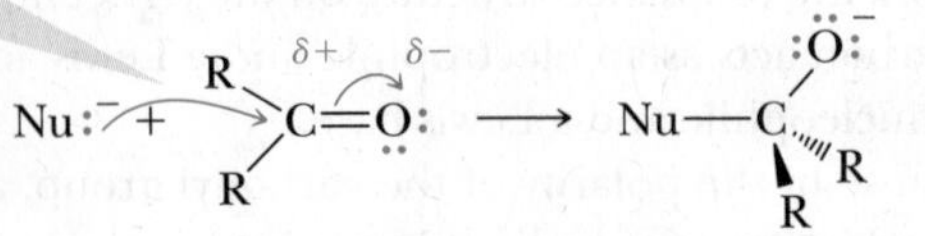

Tetrahedral carbonyl addition intermediate

12.5 What Are Grignard Reagents, and How Do They React with Aldehydes and Ketones?

From the perspective of the organic chemist, the addition of carbon nucleophiles is the most important type of nucleophilic addition to a carbonyl group because these reactions form new carbon–carbon bonds. In this section, we describe the preparation and reactions of Grignard reagents and their reaction with aldehydes and ketones.

A. Formation and Structure of Organomagnesium Compounds

Alkyl, aryl, and vinylic halides react with Group I, Group II, and certain other metals to form **organometallic compounds**. Within the range of organometallic compounds, organomagnesium compounds are among the most readily available, easily prepared, and easily handled. They are commonly named **Grignard reagents**, after Victor Grignard, who was awarded the 1912 Nobel Prize in Chemistry for their discovery and their application to organic synthesis.

Organometallic compound A compound containing a carbon–metal bond.

Grignard reagent An organomagnesium compound of the type RMgX or ArMgX.

Grignard reagents are typically prepared by the slow addition of a halide to a stirred suspension of magnesium metal in an ether solvent, most commonly diethyl ether or tetrahydrofuran (THF). Organoiodides and bromides generally react rapidly under these conditions, whereas chlorides react more slowly. Butylmagnesium bromide, for example, is prepared by adding 1-bromobutane to an ether suspension of magnesium metal. Aryl Grignards, such as phenylmagnesium bromide, are prepared in a similar manner:

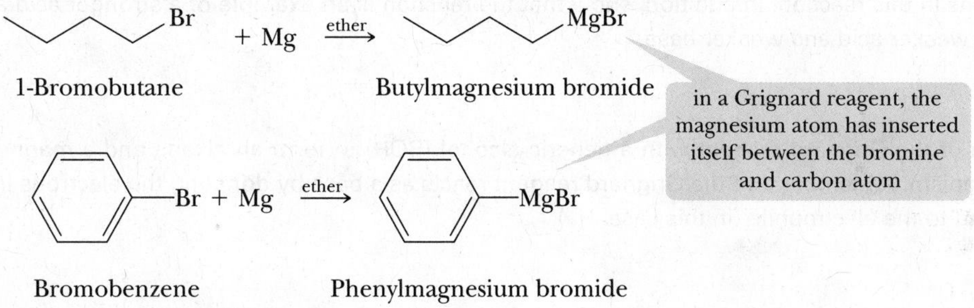

Given that the difference in electronegativity between carbon and magnesium is 1.3 units (2.5 − 1.2), the carbon–magnesium bond is best described as polar covalent, with carbon bearing a partial negative charge and magnesium bearing a partial positive charge. In the structural formula on the right, the carbon–magnesium bond is shown as ionic to emphasize its nucleophilic character. Note that although we can write a Grignard reagent as a **carbanion**, a more accurate representation shows it as a polar covalent compound:

Carbanion An anion in which carbon has an unshared pair of electrons and bears a negative charge.

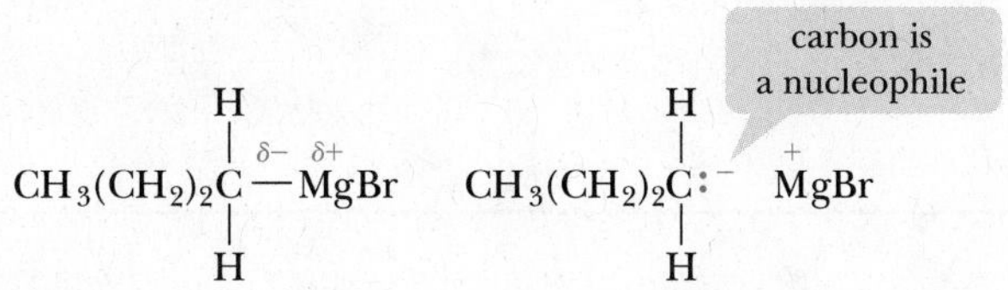

The feature that makes Grignard reagents so valuable in organic synthesis is that the carbon bearing the halogen is now transformed into a nucleophile.

B. Reaction with Protic Acids

Grignard reagents are very strong bases and react readily with a wide variety of acids (proton donors) to form alkanes. Ethylmagnesium bromide, for example, reacts instantly with water to give ethane and magnesium salts. This reaction is an example of a stronger acid and a stronger base reacting to give a weaker acid and a weaker base (Section 2.4):

$$\overset{\delta-}{CH_3CH_2}\text{—}\overset{\delta+}{MgBr} + H\text{—}OH \longrightarrow CH_3CH_2\text{—}H + Mg^{2+} + OH^- + Br^-$$

Stronger base	Stronger acid	Weaker acid	Weaker base
	pK_a 15.7	pK_a 51	

Any compound containing an O—H, N—H, and S—H group or a relatively acidic hydrogen will react with a Grignard reagent by proton transfer. Following are examples of compounds containing those functional groups:

HOH	ROH	ArOH	RCOOH	RNH_2	RSH	R—C≡C—H
Water	Alcohols	Phenols	Carboxylic acids	Amines	Thiols	Terminal alkynes

Because Grignard reagents react so rapidly with these proton acids, Grignard reagents cannot be made from any halogen-containing compounds that also contain them.

EXAMPLE 12.4

Write an equation for the acid–base reaction between ethylmagnesium iodide and an alcohol. Use curved arrows to show the flow of electrons in this reaction. In addition, show that the reaction is an example of a stronger acid and stronger base reacting to form a weaker acid and weaker base.

STRATEGY

Show the reaction of the Grignard reagent with a generic alcohol (ROH) to form an alkane and a magnesium alkoxide. In drawing the mechanism, remember that the Grignard reagent reacts as a base by donating the electrons in its C—Mg bond to form a new bond to the electrophile (in this case, H^+).

SOLUTION

The alcohol is the stronger acid, and ethyl carbanion is the stronger base:

$$CH_3CH_2\text{—}MgI + H\text{—}\ddot{O}R \longrightarrow CH_3CH_2\text{—}H + R\ddot{O}{:}^- Mg^{2+}\, I^-$$

Ethylmagnesium iodide	An alcohol pK_a 16–18	Ethane pK_a 51	A magnesium alkoxide
(stronger base)	(stronger acid)	(weaker acid)	(weaker base)

See problems 12.19, 12.21, 12.22

PROBLEM 12.4

Explain how these Grignard reagents react with molecules of their own kind to "self-destruct":

(a) 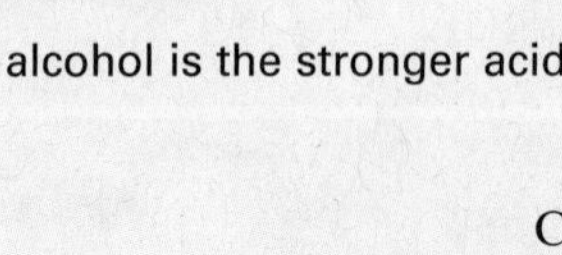

(b) 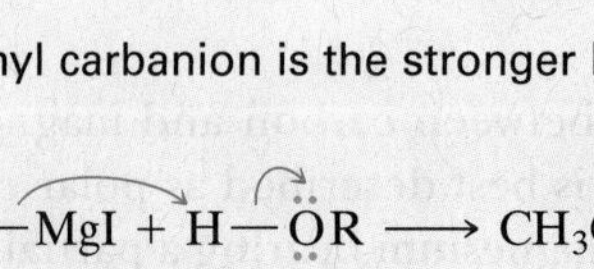

C. Addition of Grignard Reagents to Aldehydes and Ketones

The special value of Grignard reagents is that they provide excellent ways to form new carbon–carbon bonds. In their reactions, Grignard reagents behave as carbanions. A carbanion is a good nucleophile and adds to the carbonyl group of an aldehyde or a ketone to form a tetrahedral carbonyl addition intermediate. The driving force for these reactions is the attraction of the partial negative charge on the carbon of the organometallic compound to the partial positive charge of the carbonyl carbon. In the examples that follow, the magnesium–oxygen bond, which forms after the tetrahedral carbonyl addition intermediate is formed, is written $—O^{-}[MgBr]^{+}$ to emphasize its ionic character. The alkoxide ions formed in Grignard reactions are strong bases (Section 8.2C) and form alcohols when treated with an aqueous acid such as HCl or aqueous NH_4Cl during workup.

Addition to Formaldehyde Gives a 1° Alcohol

Treatment of a Grignard reagent with formaldehyde, followed by hydrolysis in aqueous acid, gives a primary alcohol:

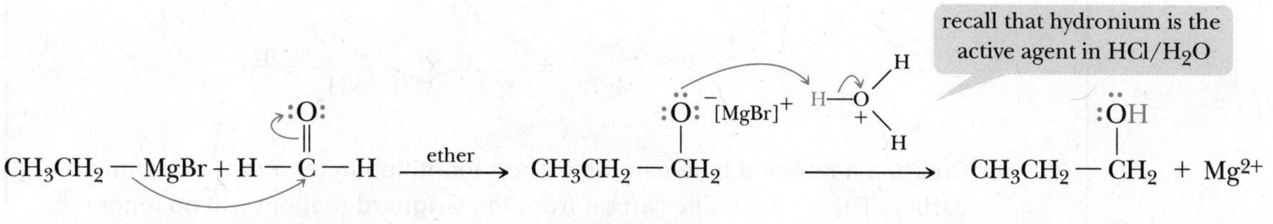

Formaldehyde — A magnasium alkoxide — 1-Propanol (a 1° alcohol)

Addition to an Aldehyde (Except Formaldehyde) Gives a 2° Alcohol

Treatment of a Grignard reagent with any aldehyde other than formaldehyde, followed by hydrolysis in aqueous acid, gives a secondary alcohol:

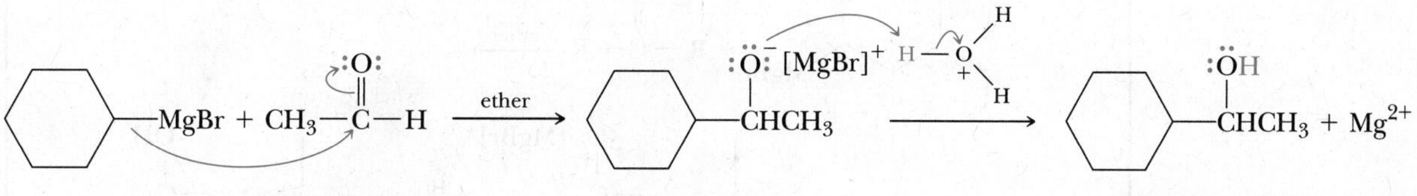

Acetaldehyde — A magnesium alkoxide — 1-Cyclohexylethanol (a 2° alcohol)

Addition to a Ketone Gives a 3° Alcohol

Treatment of a Grignard reagent with a ketone, followed by hydrolysis in aqueous acid, gives a tertiary alcohol:

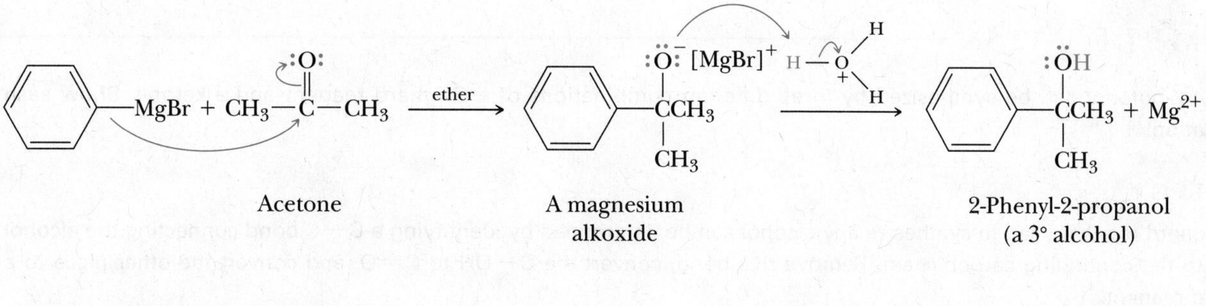

Acetone — A magnesium alkoxide — 2-Phenyl-2-propanol (a 3° alcohol)

HOW TO 12.1 Predict the Product of a Grignard Reaction

(a) Using the fact that a Grignard reaction involves the formation of a carbon–carbon bond, identify the nucleophilic carbon (i.e., the carbon bonded to the magnesium atom).

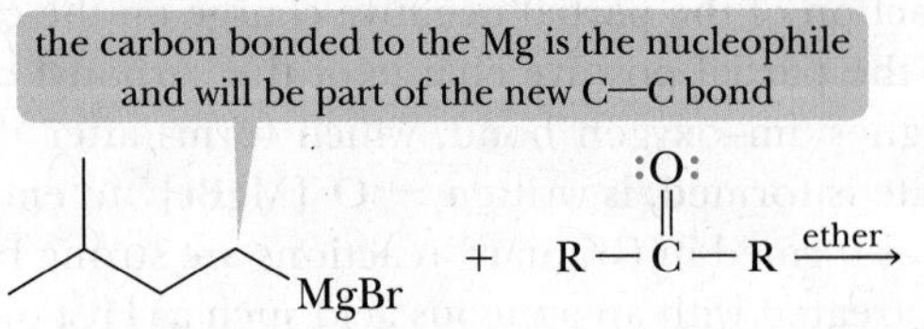
the carbon bonded to the Mg is the nucleophile and will be part of the new C—C bond
:O:
MgBr
+
R
C
R
ether

(b) Check to see that there are no O—H, N—H, or S—H groups in the reagents or solvent. These will undergo proton transfer with the Grignard reagent and prevent the reaction with the carbonyl from occurring.

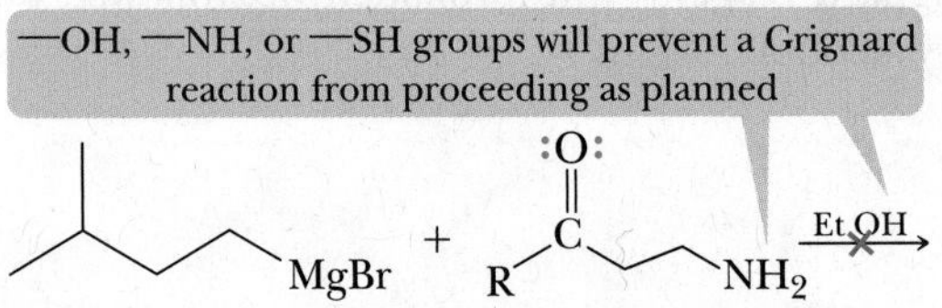
—OH, —NH, or —SH groups will prevent a Grignard reaction from proceeding as planned
:O:
MgBr
+
C
R
NH2
EtOH

(c) Create a new bond between the carbon identified in (a) and the carbonyl carbon. The nucleophilic carbon from the Grignard reagent will no longer be bonded to MgBr. Instead, the MgBr should be shown to be ionically coordinated with the negatively charged oxygen that was part of the carbonyl. If there is a workup step, the magnesium salt is converted to an alcohol.

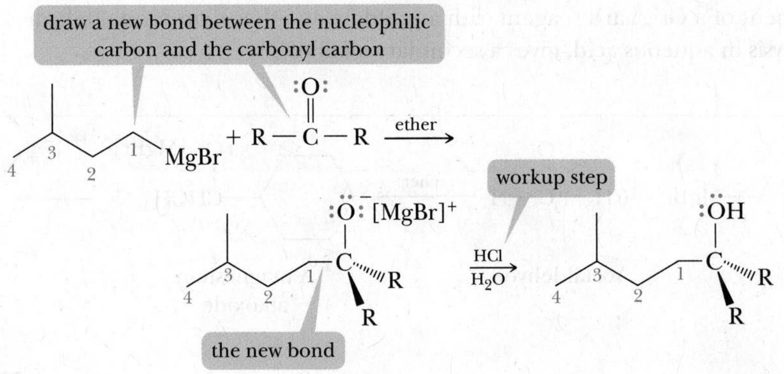
draw a new bond between the nucleophilic carbon and the carbonyl carbon
:O:
+ R—C—R
ether
MgBr
4
3
2
1
workup step
:O: [MgBr]+
C
R
R
HCl
H2O
:OH
the new bond

EXAMPLE 12.5

2-Phenyl-2-butanol can be synthesized by three different combinations of a Grignard reagent and a ketone. Show each combination.

STRATEGY

The Grignard reagent used to synthesize any alcohol can be determined by identifying a C—C bond connecting the alcohol carbon to the continuing carbon chain. Remove this bond, convert the C—OH to C=O, and convert the other piece to a Grignard reagent.

SOLUTION

Curved arrows in each solution show the formation of the new carbon–carbon bond and the alkoxide ion, and labels on the final product show which set of reagents forms each bond:

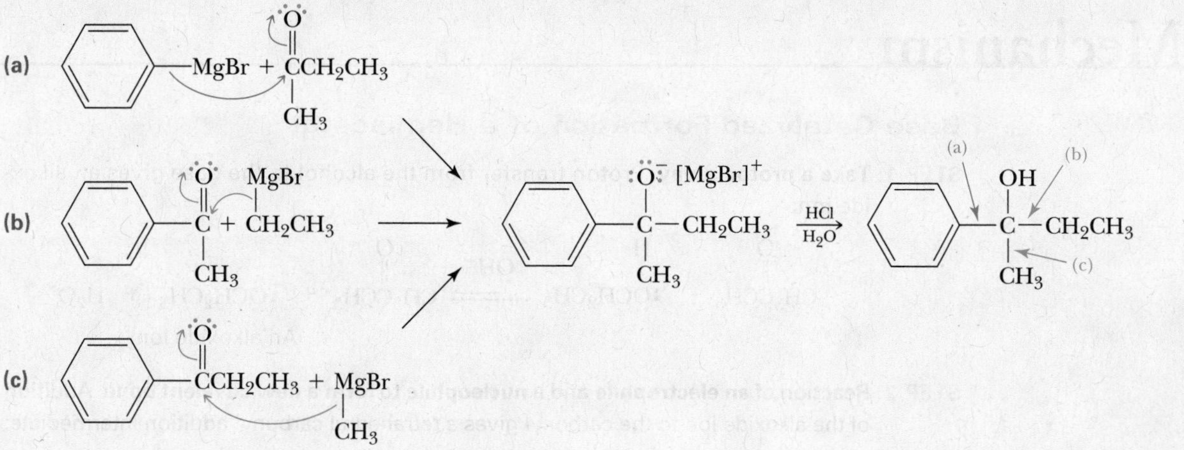

See problems 12.21, 12.22

PROBLEM 12.5

Show how these three compounds can be synthesized from the same Grignard reagent:

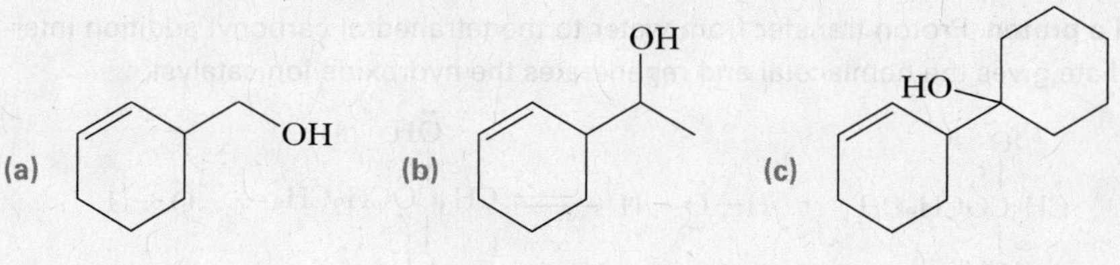

12.6 What Are Hemiacetals and Acetals?

A. Formation of Acetals

The addition of a molecule of alcohol to the carbonyl group of an aldehyde or a ketone forms a **hemiacetal** (a half-acetal). This reaction is catalyzed by both acid and base: Oxygen adds to the carbonyl carbon and hydrogen adds to the carbonyl oxygen:

Hemiacetal A molecule containing an —OH and an —OR or —OAr group bonded to the same carbon.

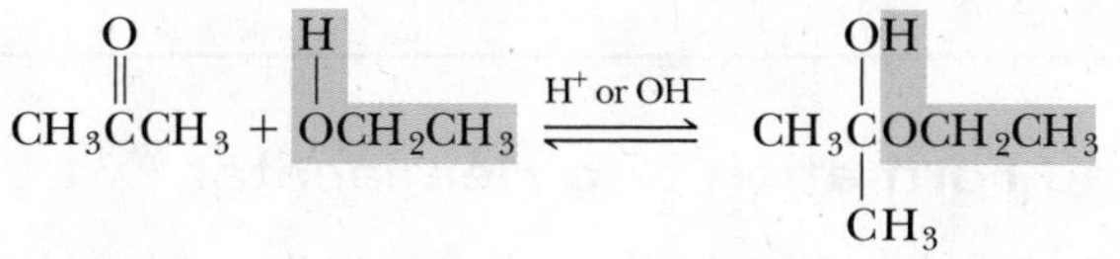

A hemiacetal

The functional group of a hemiacetal is a carbon bonded to an —OH group and an —OR or —OAr group:

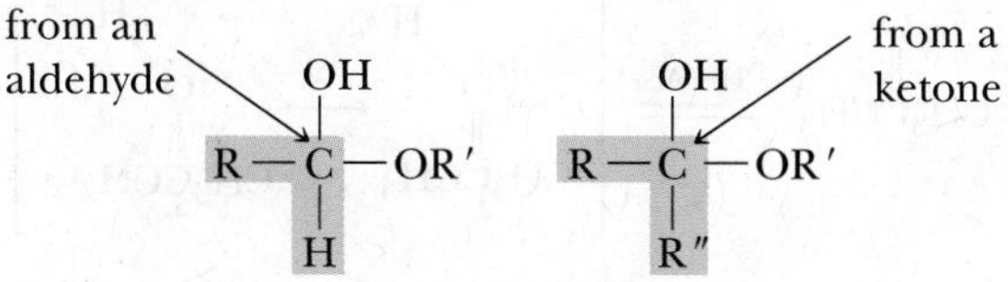

Hemiacetals

The mechanism for the base-catalyzed conversion of an aldehyde or a ketone to a hemiacetal can be divided into three steps. Note that the base OH^- is a true catalyst in this reaction; it is used in Step 1, but a replacement OH^- is generated in Step 3.

Mechanism

Base-Catalyzed Formation of a Hemiacetal

STEP 1: Take a proton away. Proton transfer from the alcohol to the base gives an alkoxide ion:

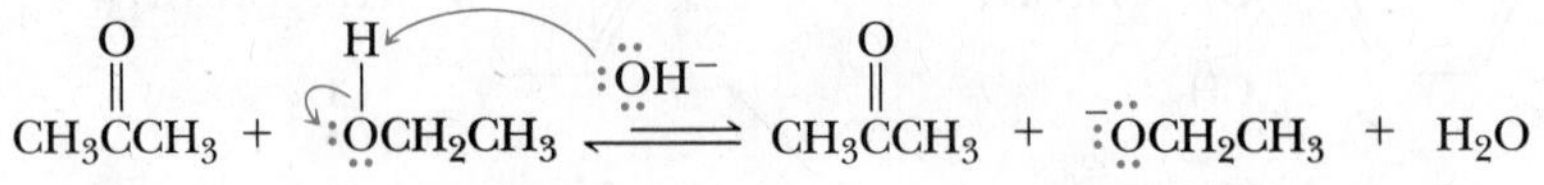

An alkoxide ion

STEP 2: Reaction of an electrophile and a nucleophile to form a new covalent bond. Addition of the alkoxide ion to the carbonyl gives a tetrahedral carbonyl addition intermediate:

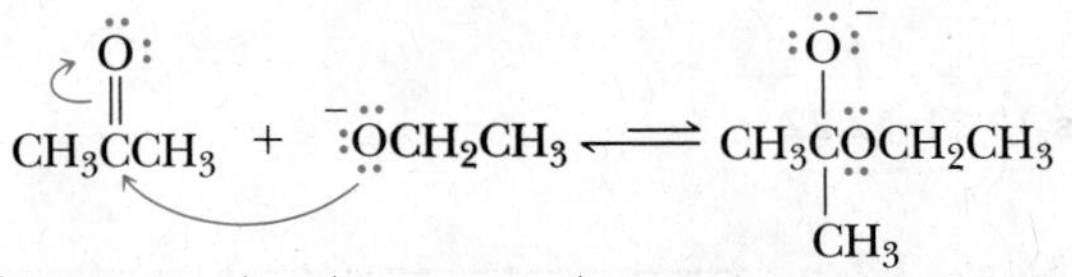

(an electrophile) (a nucleophile) Tetrahedral carbonyl addition intermediate

STEP 3: Add a proton. Proton transfer from water to the tetrahedral carbonyl addition intermediate gives the hemiacetal and regenerates the hydroxide ion catalyst:

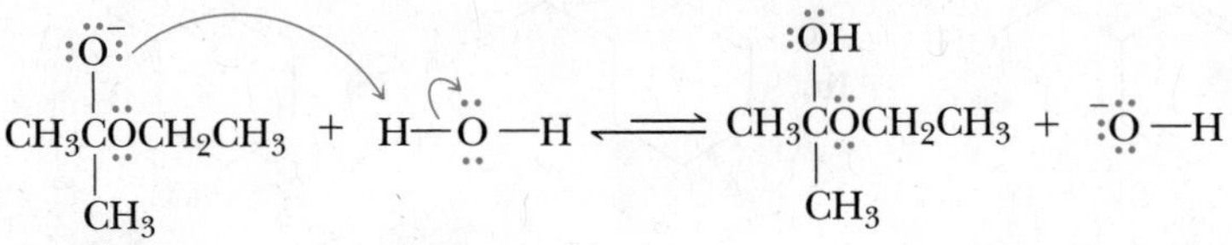

The mechanism for the acid-catalyzed conversion of an aldehyde or ketone to a hemiacetal can be divided into three steps. Note that the acid H—A is a true catalyst in this reaction; it is used in Step 1, but a replacement H—A is generated in Step 3.

Mechanism

Acid-Catalyzed Formation of a Hemiacetal

STEP 1: Add a proton. Proton transfer from H—A to the carbonyl gives a resonance-stabilized cation. The more significant resonance structure places the positive charge on the carbon:

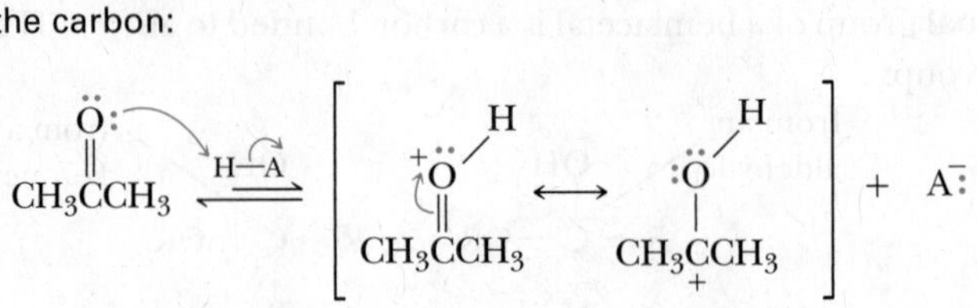

A resonance-stabilized cation

STEP 2: Reaction of an electrophile and a nucleophile to form a new covalent bond. Addition of the alcohol to the resonance-stabilized cation gives an oxonium ion. *Note*: The attack of the alcohol can be to either contributing structure:

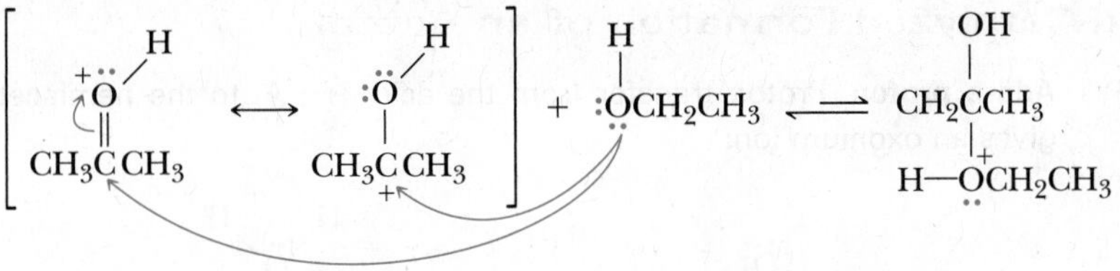

(an electrophile) (a nucleophile) An oxonium ion

STEP 3: Take a proton away. Proton transfer from the oxonium ion to A^- gives the hemiacetal and regenerates the acid catalyst:

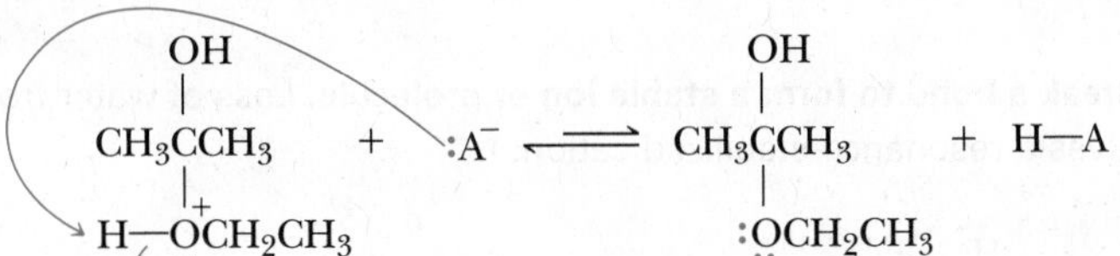

Hemiacetals are generally unstable and are only minor components of an equilibrium mixture, except in one very important type of molecule. When a hydroxyl group is part of the same molecule that contains the carbonyl group, and a five- or six-membered ring can form, the compound exists almost entirely in a cyclic hemiacetal form:

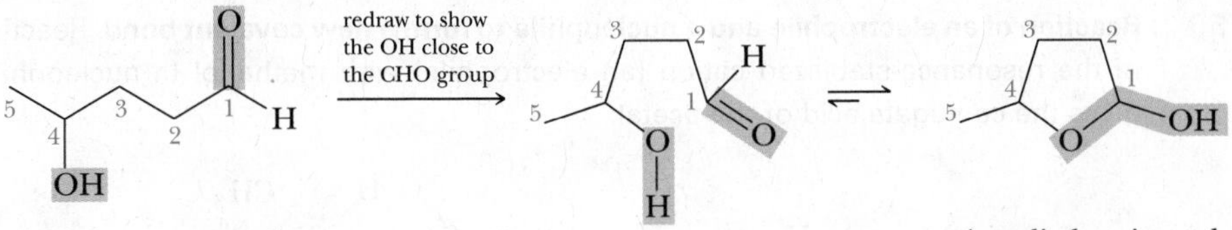

4-Hydroxypentanal

A cyclic hemiacetal (major form present at equilibrium)

We shall have much more to say about cyclic hemiacetals when we consider the chemistry of carbohydrates in Chapter 17.

Hemiacetals can react further with alcohols to form **acetals** plus a molecule of water. This reaction is acid catalyzed:

Acetal A molecule containing two —OR or —OAr groups bonded to the same carbon.

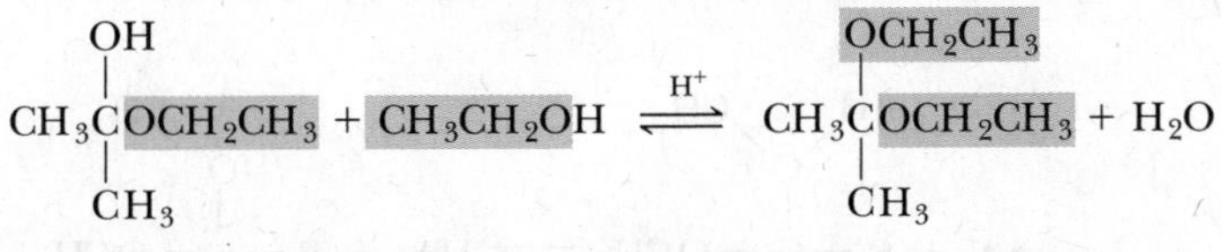

A hemiacetal A diethyl acetal

The functional group of an acetal is a carbon bonded to two —OR or —OAr groups:

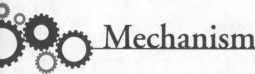

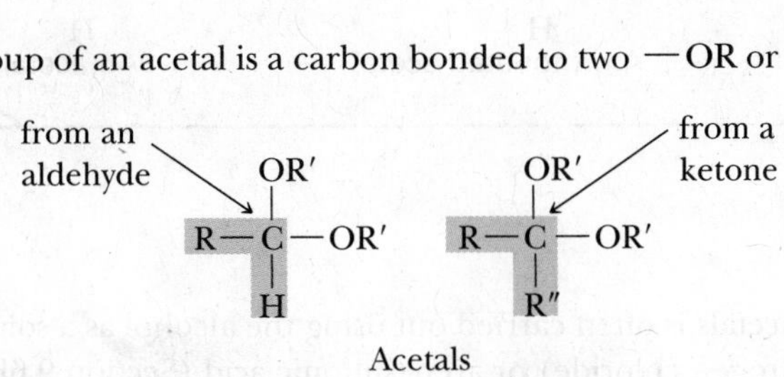

Acetals

The mechanism for the acid-catalyzed conversion of a hemiacetal to an acetal can be divided into four steps. Note that acid H—A is a true catalyst in this reaction; it is used in Step 1, but a replacement H—A is generated in Step 4.

Mechanism

Acid-Catalyzed Formation of an Acetal

STEP 1: Add a proton. Proton transfer from the acid, H—A, to the hemiacetal OH group gives an oxonium ion:

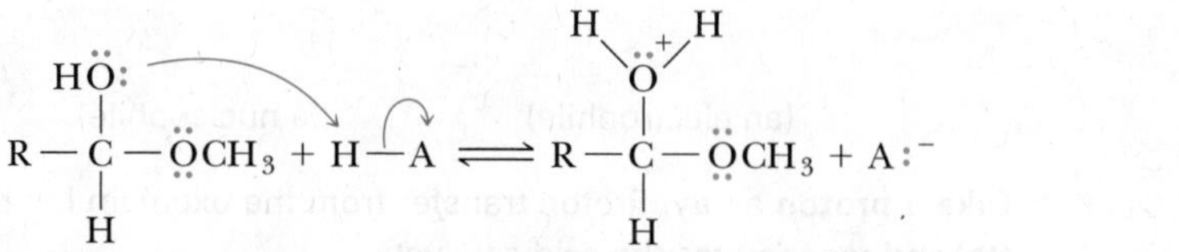

An oxonium ion

STEP 2: Break a bond to form a stable ion or molecule. Loss of water from the oxonium ion gives a resonance-stabilized cation:

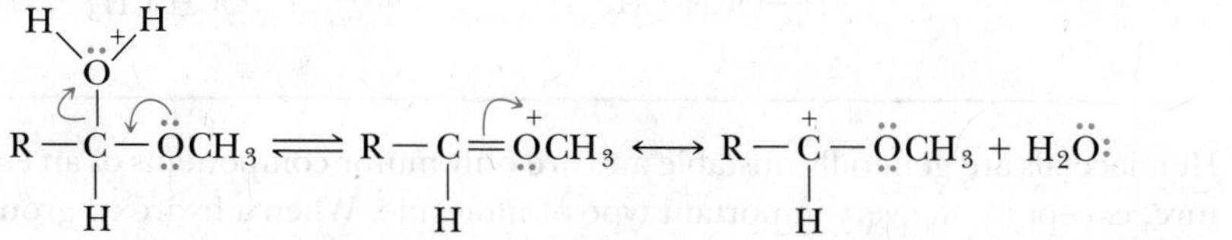

A resonance-stabilized cation

STEP 3: Reaction of an electrophile and a nucleophile to form a new covalent bond. Reaction of the resonance-stabilized cation (an electrophile) with methanol (a nucleophile) gives the conjugate acid of the acetal:

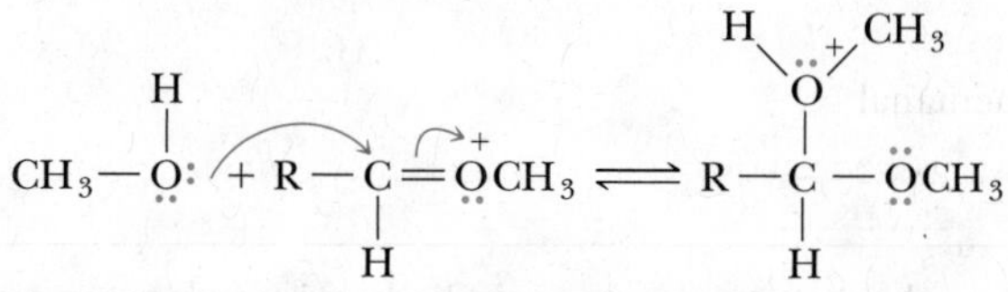

(a nucleophile) (an electrophile) A protonated acetal

STEP 4: Take a proton away. Proton transfer from the protonated acetal to A^- gives the acetal and generates a new molecule of H—A, the acid catalyst:

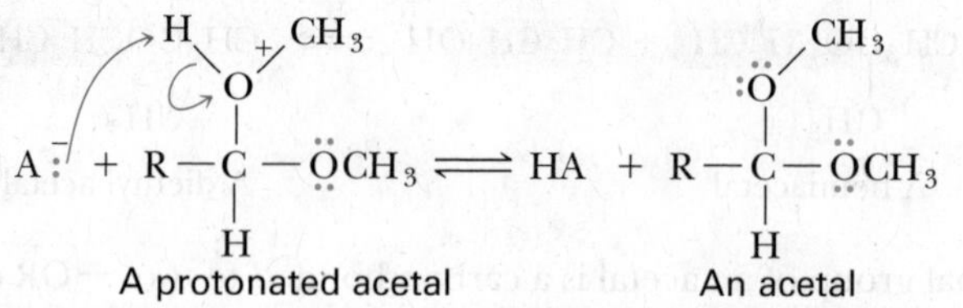

A protonated acetal An acetal

Formation of acetals is often carried out using the alcohol as a solvent and dissolving either dry HCl (hydrogen chloride) or arenesulfonic acid (Section 9.6B), $ArSO_3H$, in the alcohol. Because the alcohol is both a reactant and the solvent, it is present in large molar excess, which drives the reaction to the right and favors acetal formation. Alternatively, the reaction may be driven to the right by the removal of water as it is formed:

An excess of alcohol pushes the equilibrium toward acetal formation

Removal of water favors acetal formation

$$R-\overset{\overset{\displaystyle O}{\|}}{C}-R + 2CH_3CH_2OH \overset{H^+}{\rightleftharpoons} R-\underset{\underset{\displaystyle R}{|}}{\overset{\overset{\displaystyle OCH_2CH_3}{|}}{C}}-OCH_2CH_3 + H_2O$$

A diethyl acetal

HOW TO 12.2

Determine the Reactants Used to Synthesize a Hemiacetal or Acetal

(a) Identify the carbon atom that is bonded to two oxygen atoms. This carbon atom is the carbonyl carbon that was converted to the carbon of the acetal or hemiacetal group.

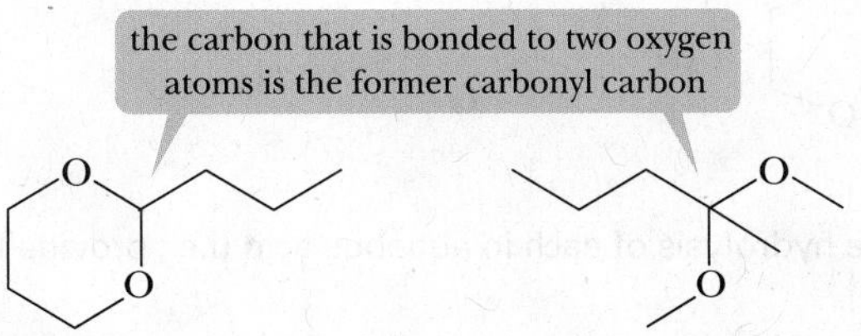

(b) Remove both C—O bonds and add back a hydrogen to each oxygen to obtain the alcohol reagent(s) used. Then convert the carbon identified in (a) to a carbonyl group.

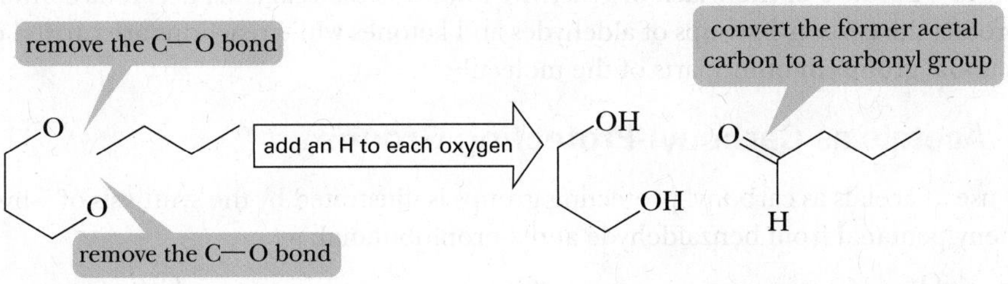

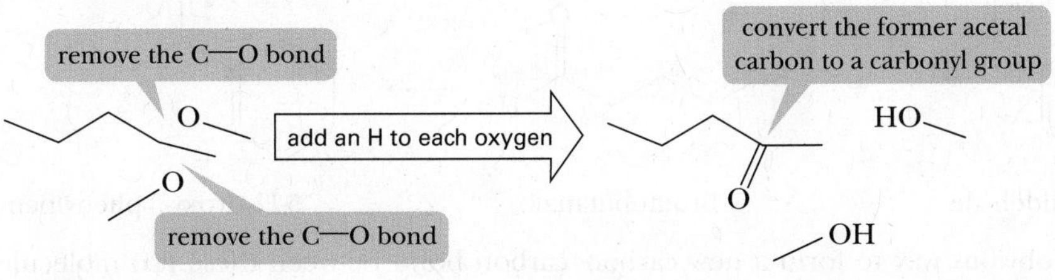

EXAMPLE 12.6

Show the reaction of the carbonyl group of each ketone with one molecule of alcohol to form a hemiacetal and then with a second molecule of alcohol to form an acetal (note that, in part (b), ethylene glycol is a diol, and one molecule of it provides both —OH groups):

(a) 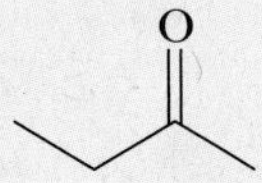 $+ 2\ CH_3CH_2OH \overset{H^+}{\rightleftharpoons}$

(b) 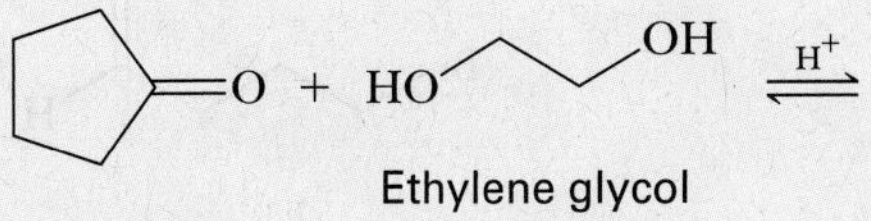

Ethylene glycol

STRATEGY

In forming the hemiacetal, one molecule of the alcohol is added to the carbonyl carbon, resulting in an OR group and an OH group bonded to the carbon that was previously part of the carbonyl. In forming an acetal, two molecules of the alcohol are added to the carbonyl carbon, resulting in two OR groups bonded to the carbon that was previously part of the carbonyl.

See problems 12.23–12.26

SOLUTION

Here are structural formulas of the hemiacetal and then the acetal:

(a)

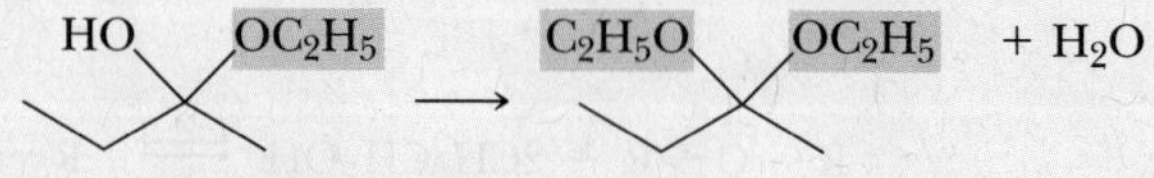

(b)

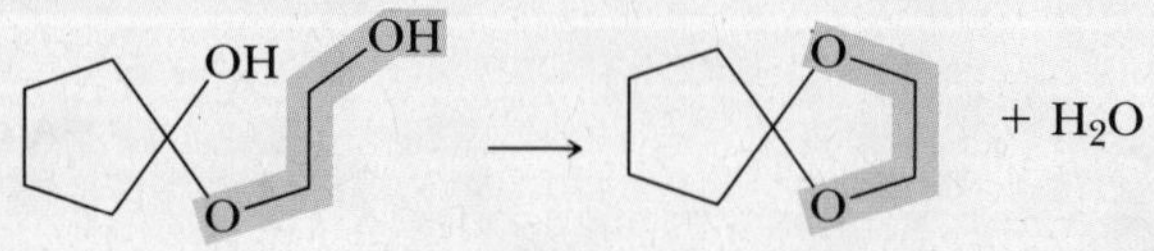

PROBLEM 12.6

The hydrolysis of an acetal forms an aldehyde or a ketone and two molecules of alcohol. Following are structural formulas for three acetals:

(a)

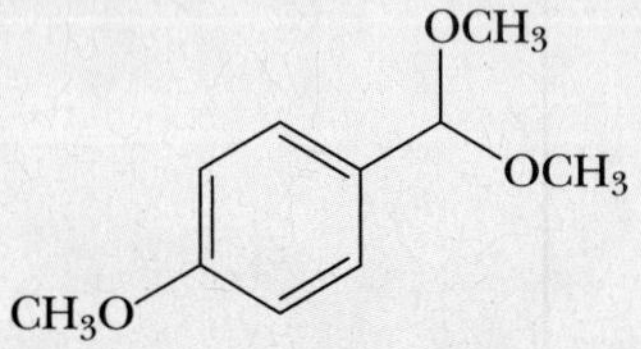

(b)

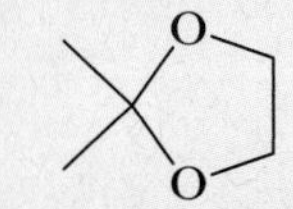

(c)

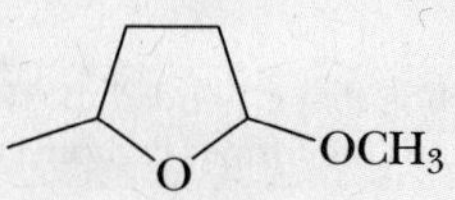

Draw the structural formulas for the products of the hydrolysis of each in aqueous acid (i.e., provide the carbonyl compound and alcohol(s) from which each acetal was derived).

Like ethers, acetals are unreactive to bases, to reducing agents such as H_2/M, to Grignard reagents, and to oxidizing agents (except, of course, those which involve aqueous acid). Because of their lack of reactivity toward these reagents, acetals are often used to protect the carbonyl groups of aldehydes and ketones while reactions are carried out on functional groups in other parts of the molecule.

B. Acetals as Carbonyl-Protecting Groups

The use of acetals as carbonyl-protecting groups is illustrated by the synthesis of 5-hydroxy-5-phenylpentanal from benzaldehyde and 4-bromobutanal:

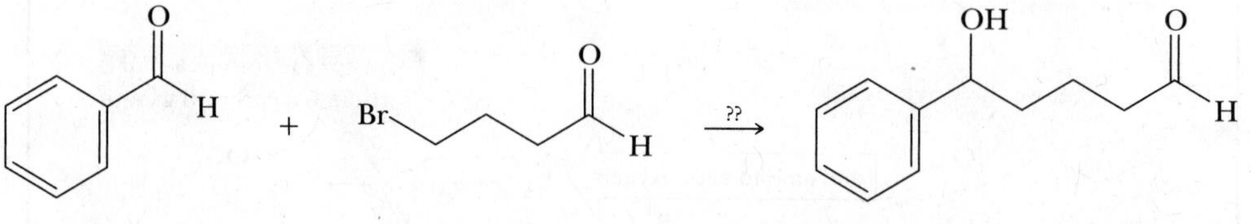

Benzaldehyde 4-Bromobutanal 5-Hydroxy-5-phenylpentanal

One obvious way to form a new carbon–carbon bond between these two molecules is to treat benzaldehyde with the Grignard reagent formed from 4-bromobutanal. This Grignard reagent, however, would react immediately with the carbonyl group of another molecule of 4-bromobutanal, causing it to self-destruct during preparation (Section 12.5B). A way to avoid this problem is to protect the carbonyl group of 4-bromobutanal by converting it to an acetal. Cyclic acetals are often used because they are particularly easy to prepare.

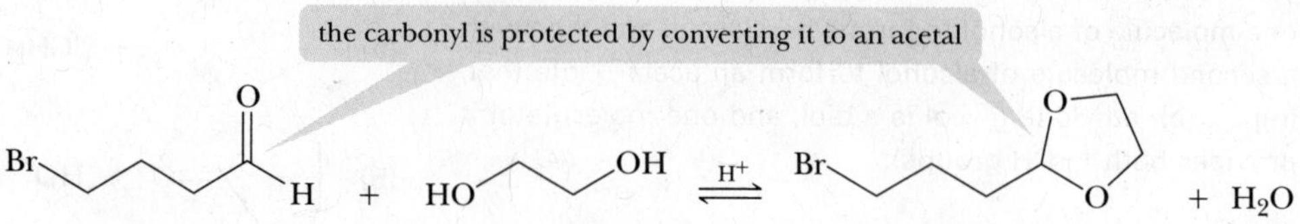

Ethylene glycol A cyclic acetal

Treatment of the protected bromoaldehyde with magnesium in diethyl ether, followed by the addition of benzaldehyde, gives a magnesium alkoxide:

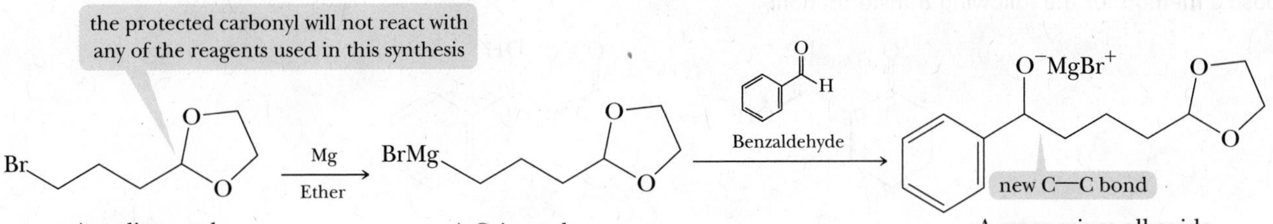

Treatment of the magnesium alkoxide with aqueous acid accomplishes two things. First, protonation of the alkoxide anion gives the desired hydroxyl group, and then, **hydrolysis** of the cyclic acetal regenerates the aldehyde group:

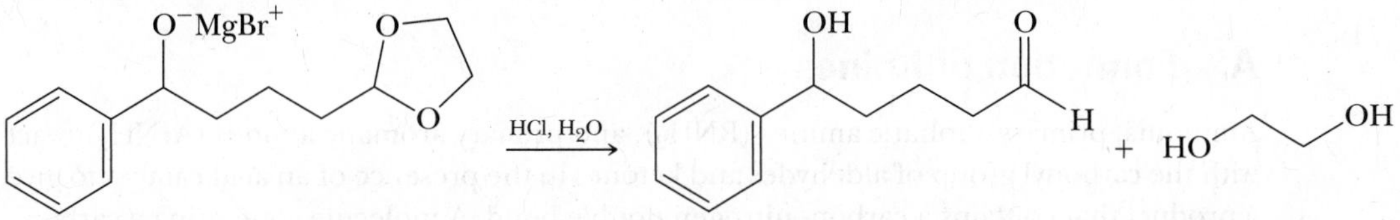

EXAMPLE 12.7

Propose a method for the following transformation. *Note*: Catalytic hydrogenation adds H_2 across C—O double bonds as well as across C—C double bonds.

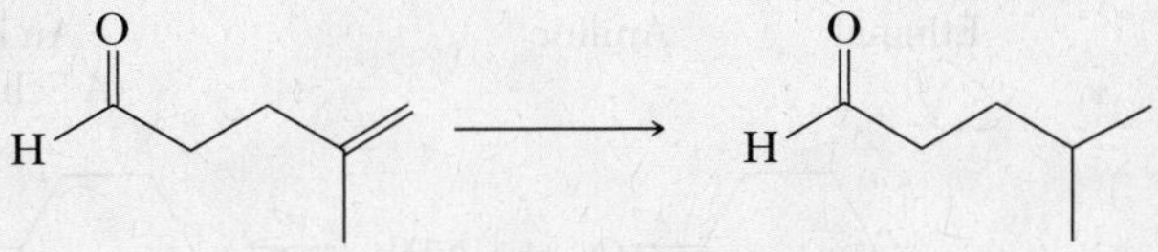

STRATEGY

Decide which reaction(s) are needed to achieve the interconversion of functional groups. Before applying any reaction to the targeted functional group, determine whether any other functional groups in the compound will react with the reagents proposed. If these other reactions are undesirable, determine whether the functional groups can be protected.

SOLUTION

It is important to protect the carbonyl group. Otherwise, it will be reduced to an alcohol by H_2/Pt:

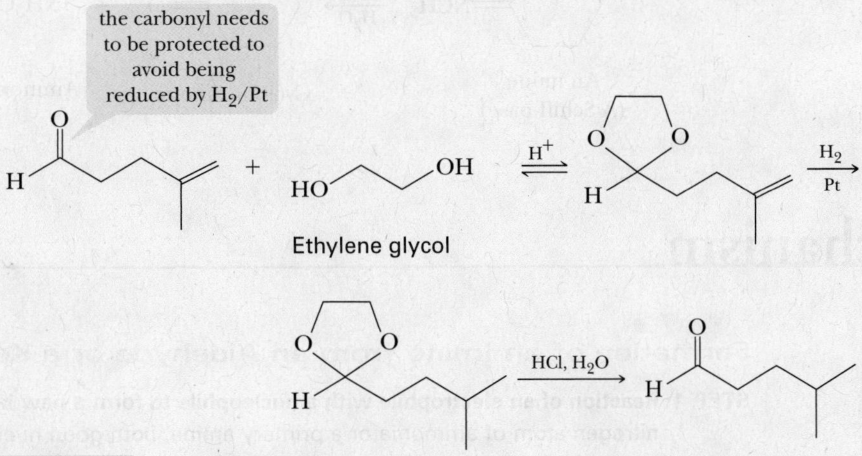

See problems 12.38–12.45

PROBLEM 12.7

Propose a method for the following transformation:

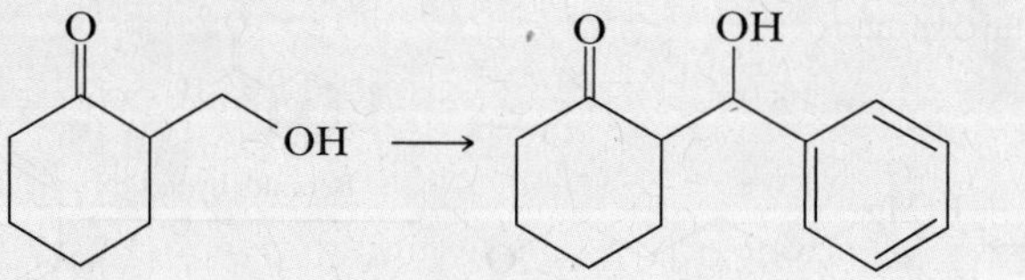

12.7 How Do Aldehydes and Ketones React with Ammonia and Amines?

A. Formation of Imines

Imine A compound containing a carbon–nitrogen double bond; also called a Schiff base.

Schiff base An alternative name for an imine.

Ammonia, primary aliphatic amines (RNH_2), and primary aromatic amines ($ArNH_2$) react with the carbonyl group of aldehydes and ketones in the presence of an acid catalyst to give a product that contains a carbon–nitrogen double bond. A molecule containing a carbon–nitrogen double bond is called an **imine** or, alternatively, a **Schiff base**:

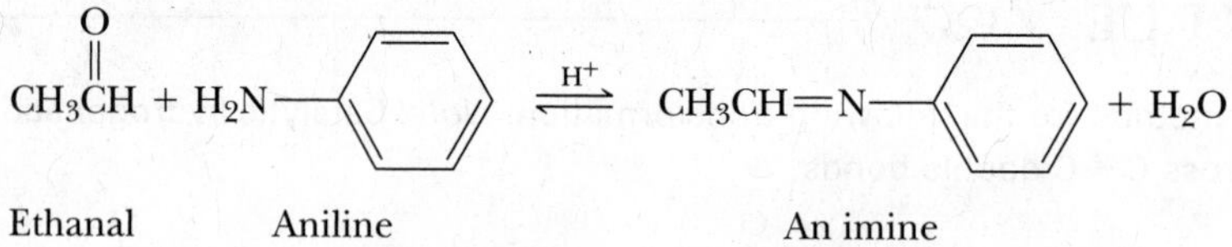

Ethanal Aniline An imine (A Schiff base)

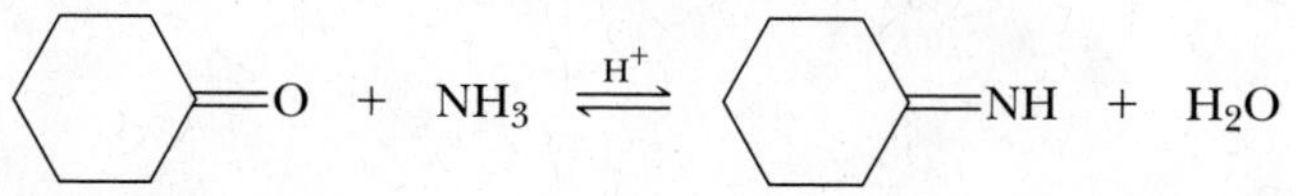

Cyclohexanone Ammonia An imine (A Schiff base)

As with hemiacetal- and acetal-forming reactions, imine formation is reversible; acid-catalyzed hydrolysis of an imine gives a 1° amine and an aldehyde or a ketone. When one equivalent of acid is used, the 1° amine, a weak base, is converted to an ammonium salt.

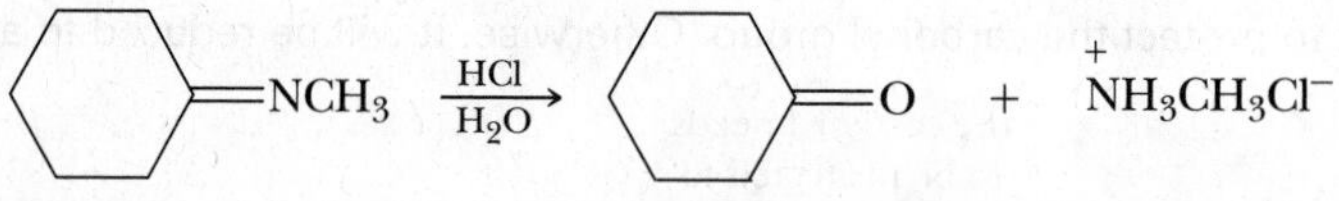

An imine (A Schiff base) Cyclohexanone Ammonium salt

Mechanism

Formation of an Imine from an Aldehyde or a Ketone

STEP 1: **Reaction of an electrophile with a nucleophile to form a new bond.** Addition of the nitrogen atom of ammonia or a primary amine, both good nucleophiles, to the carbonyl carbon, followed by a proton transfer, gives a tetrahedral carbonyl addition intermediate:

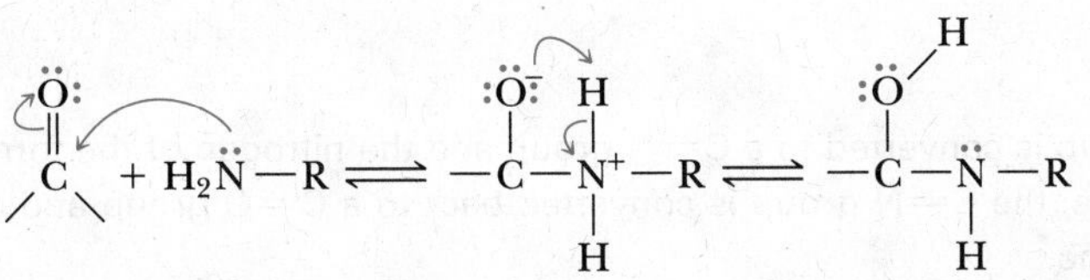

A tetrahedral carbonyl addition intermediate

STEP 2: Add a proton. Protonation of the OH group to form $-OH_2^+$, a good leaving group.

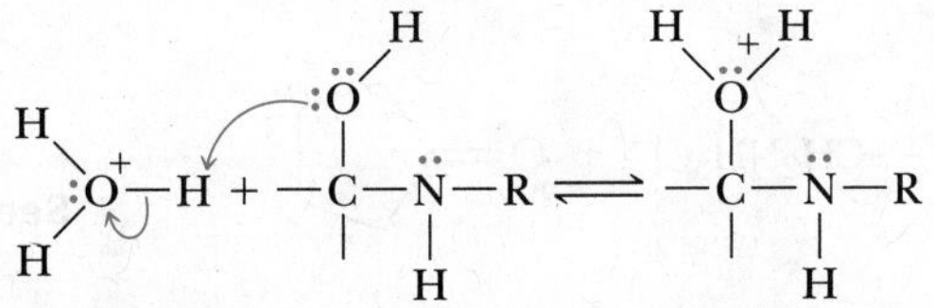

STEP 3: Take a proton away and break a bond to form a stable molecule. Loss of water and proton transfer to solvent gives the imine. Notice that the loss of water and the proton transfer have the characteristics of an E2 reaction. Three things happen simultaneously in this dehydration: a base (in this case a water molecule) removes a proton from N, the carbon–nitrogen double bond forms, and the leaving group (in this case, a water molecule) departs:

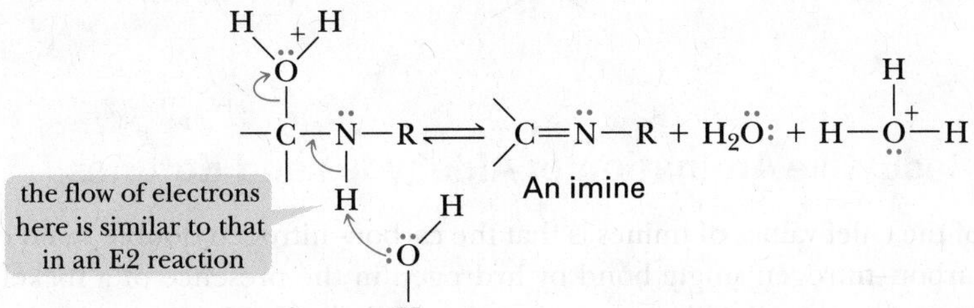
the flow of electrons here is similar to that in an E2 reaction
An imine

To give but one example of the importance of imines in biological systems, the active form of vitamin A aldehyde (retinal) is bound to the protein opsin in the human retina in the form of an imine called *rhodopsin* or *visual purple* (see Chemical Connections 4B). The amino acid lysine (see Table 18.1) provides the primary amino group for this reaction:

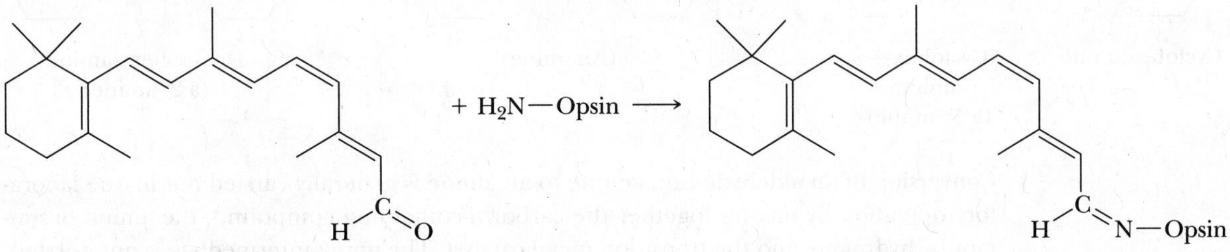

11-*cis*-Retinal

Rhodopsin (Visual purple)

EXAMPLE 12.8

Predict the products formed in each reaction:

(a) 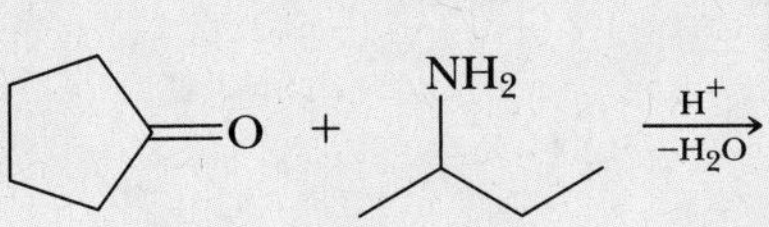

(b) 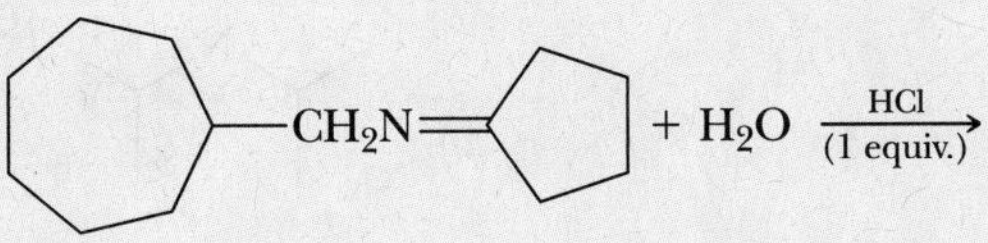

STRATEGY

In an imine-forming reaction, the C=O group is converted to a C=N group and the nitrogen of the former 1° amine loses both of its hydrogens. In the reverse process, the C=N group is converted back to a C=O group and two hydrogens are added back to the nitrogen to form a 1° amine.

SOLUTION

Reaction (a) is an imine-forming reaction, while reaction (b) is the acid-catalyzed hydrolysis of an imine to an ammonium salt and a ketone:

(a)
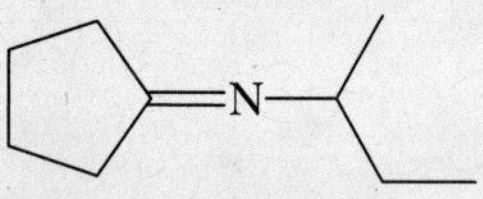

(b)
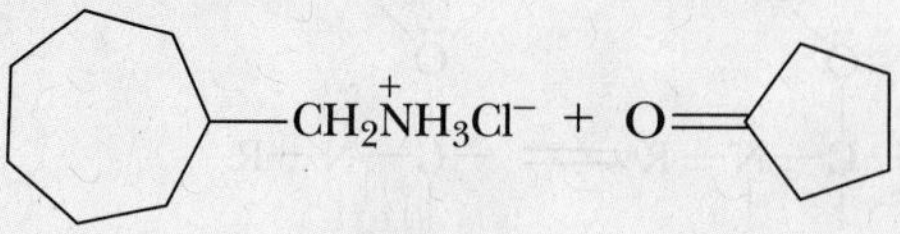

See problems 12.29–12.32

PROBLEM 12.8

Predict the products formed in each reaction. *Note*: Acid-catalyzed hydrolysis of an imine gives an amine and an aldehyde or a ketone. When one equivalent of acid is used, the amine is converted to its ammonium salt.

(a)
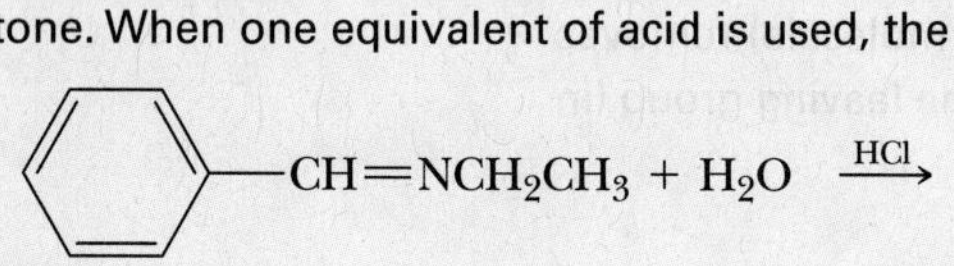
$-CH{=}NCH_2CH_3 + H_2O \xrightarrow{HCl}$

(b)
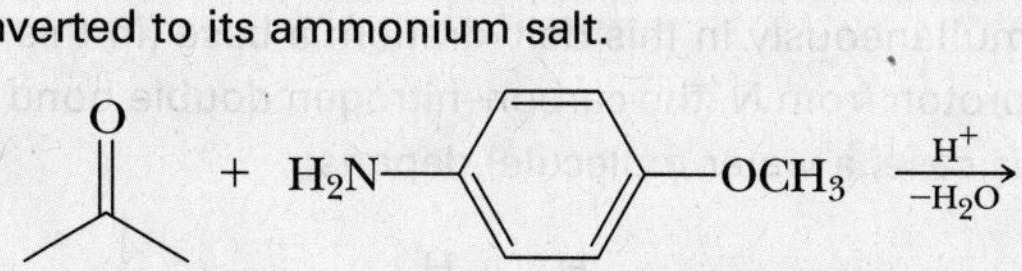
O
+ H_2N-
$-OCH_3 \xrightarrow[-H_2O]{H^+}$

B. Reductive Amination of Aldehydes and Ketones

Reductive amination The formation of an imine from an aldehyde or a ketone, followed by the reduction of the imine to an amine.

One of the chief values of imines is that the carbon–nitrogen double bond can be reduced to a carbon–nitrogen single bond by hydrogen in the presence of a nickel or other transition metal catalyst. By this two-step reaction, called **reductive amination**, a primary amine is converted to a secondary amine by way of an imine, as illustrated by the conversion of cyclohexylamine to dicyclohexylamine:

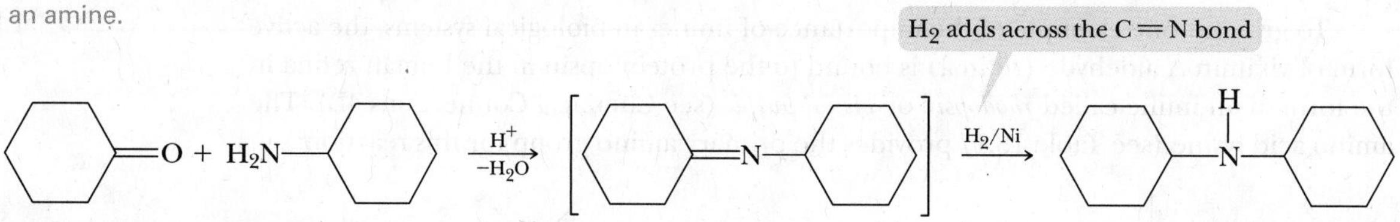

Cyclohexanone | Cyclohexyl-amine (a 1° amine) | (An imine) | Dicyclohexylamine (a 2° amine)

Conversion of an aldehyde or a ketone to an amine is generally carried out in one laboratory operation by mixing together the carbonyl-containing compound, the amine or ammonia, hydrogen, and the transition metal catalyst. The imine intermediate is not isolated.

EXAMPLE 12.9

Show how to synthesize each amine by a reductive amination:

(a)
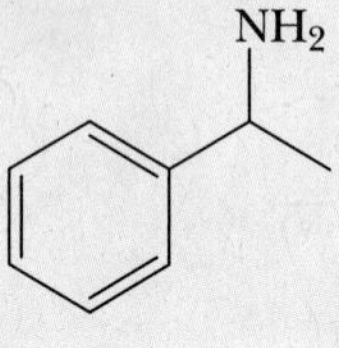
NH_2

(b)
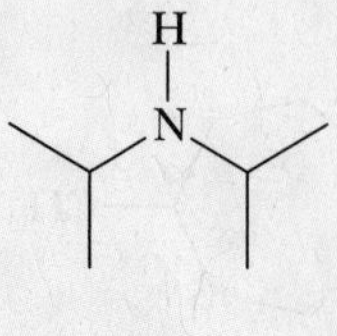

STRATEGY

Identify the C—N bond formed in the reductive amination. The carbon of the C—N bond is part of the carbonyl starting material, and the nitrogen is part of the 1° amine.

SOLUTION

Treat the appropriate compound, in each case a ketone, with ammonia or an amine in the presence of H_2/Ni:

(a) 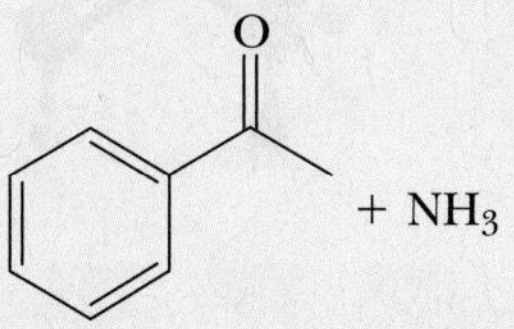

(b) 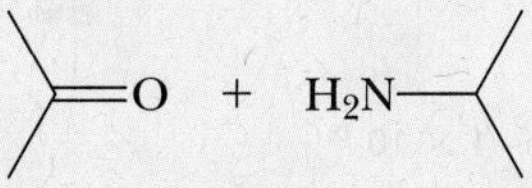

See problems 12.29–12.32

PROBLEM 12.9

Show how to prepare each amine by the reductive amination of an appropriate aldehyde or ketone:

(a) 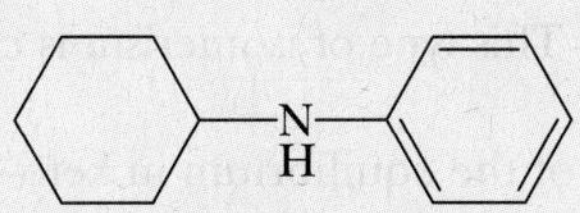

(b) 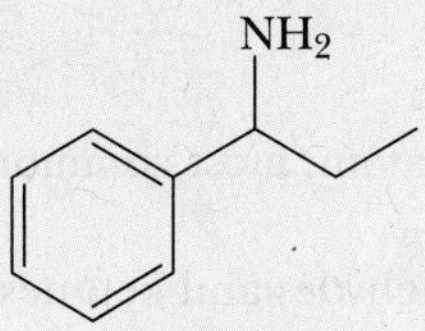

12.8 What Is Keto–Enol Tautomerism?

A. Keto and Enol Forms

A carbon atom adjacent to a carbonyl group is called an ***α*-carbon**, and any hydrogen atoms bonded to it are called ***α*-hydrogens:**

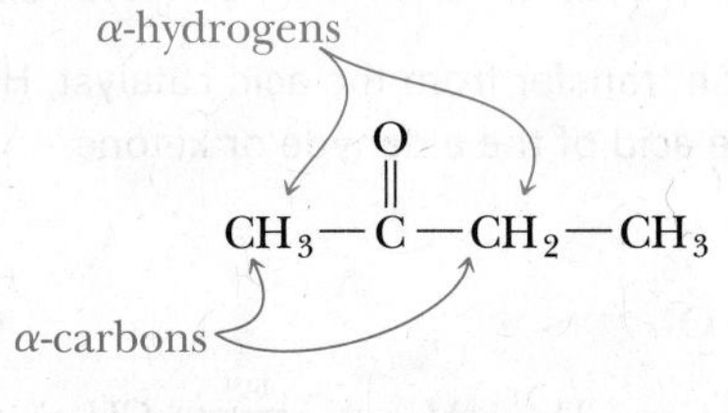

α-Carbon A carbon atom adjacent to a carbonyl group.

α-Hydrogen A hydrogen on an α-carbon.

An aldehyde or ketone that has at least one α-hydrogen is in equilibrium with a constitutional isomer called an **enol**. The name *enol* is derived from the IUPAC designation of it as both an alkene (*-en-*) and an alcohol (*-ol*):

Enol A molecule containing an —OH group bonded to a carbon of a carbon–carbon double bond.

$$\underset{\substack{\text{Acetone}\\ \text{(keto form)}}}{CH_3-\overset{\overset{\displaystyle O}{\|}}{C}-CH_3} \rightleftharpoons \underset{\substack{\text{Acetone}\\ \text{(enol form)}}}{CH_3-\overset{\overset{\displaystyle OH}{|}}{C}=CH_2}$$

Tautomers Constitutional isomers that differ in the location of hydrogen and a double bond relative to O, N, or S.

Keto and enol forms are examples of **tautomers**—constitutional isomers that are in equilibrium with each other and that differ in the location of a hydrogen atom and a double

TABLE 12.4 The Position of Keto–Enol Equilibrium for Four Aldehydes and Ketones*

Keto Form		Enol Form	% Enol at Equilibrium
$CH_3CH{=}O$ (O above C, double bond)	⇌	$CH_2{=}CH(OH)$	6×10^{-5}
$CH_3C(=O)CH_3$	⇌	$CH_3C(OH){=}CH_2$	6×10^{-7}
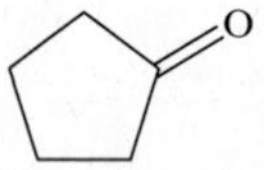	⇌	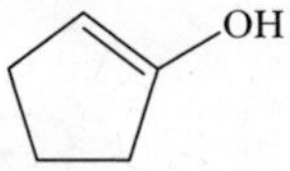	1×10^{-6}
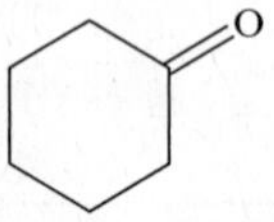	⇌	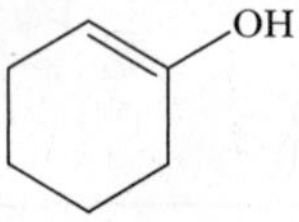	4×10^{-5}

*Data from J. March, *Advanced Organic Chemistry*, 4th ed. (New York, Wiley Interscience, 1992) p. 70.

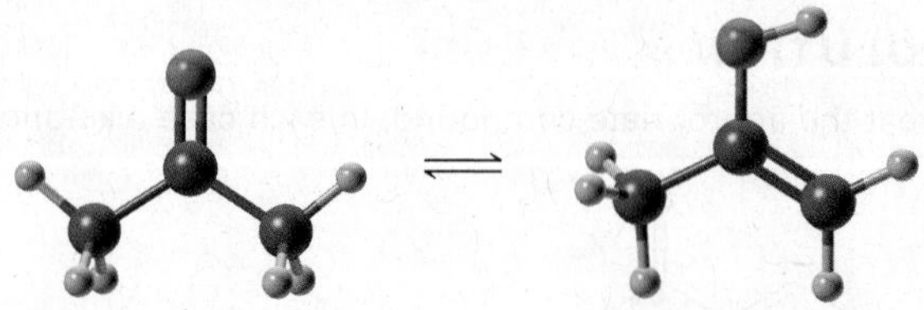

bond relative to a heteroatom, most commonly O, S, or N. This type of isomerism is called **tautomerism**.

For most simple aldehydes and ketones, the position of the equilibrium in keto–enol tautomerism lies far on the side of the keto form (Table 12.4), because a carbon–oxygen double bond is stronger than a carbon–carbon double bond.

The equilibration of keto and enol forms is catalyzed by acid, as shown in the following two-step mechanism (note that a molecule of H—A is consumed in Step 1, but another is generated in Step 2):

Mechanism

Acid-Catalyzed Equilibration of Keto and Enol Tautomers

STEP 1: Add a proton. Proton transfer from the acid catalyst, H—A, to the carbonyl oxygen forms the conjugate acid of the aldehyde or ketone:

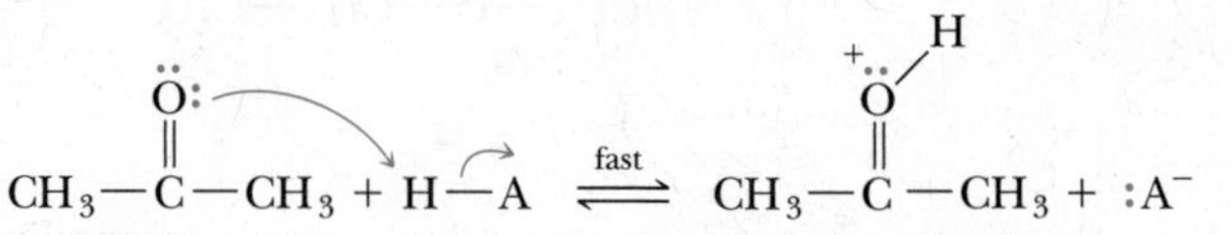

STEP 2: Take a proton away. Proton transfer from the α-carbon to the base, A^-, gives the enol and generates a new molecule of the acid catalyst, H—A:

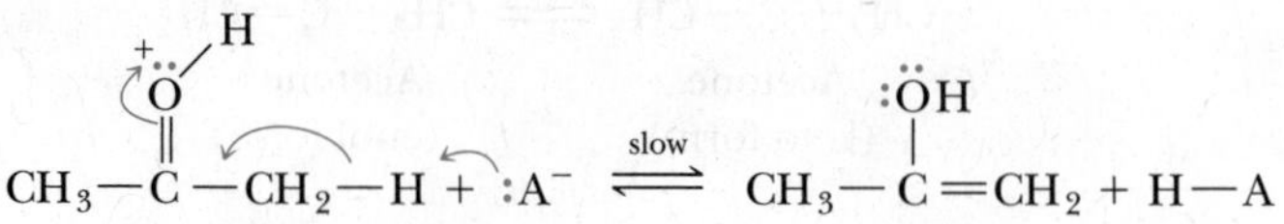

EXAMPLE 12.10

Write two enol forms for each compound, and state which enol of each predominates at equilibrium:

(a) 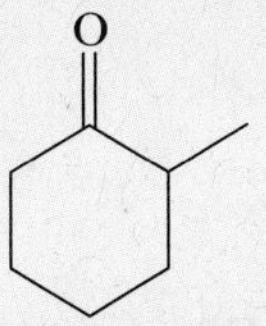 (b) 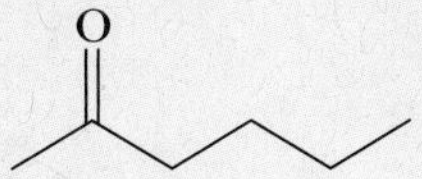

STRATEGY

An enol can form on either side of the carbonyl as long as there is an α-hydrogen to be abstracted in Step 2 of the mechanism. To decide which enol predominates, recall that the more substituted an alkene is, the more stable it is (see Section 5.7B).

SOLUTION

In each case, the major enol form has the more substituted (the more stable) carbon–carbon double bond:

(a) 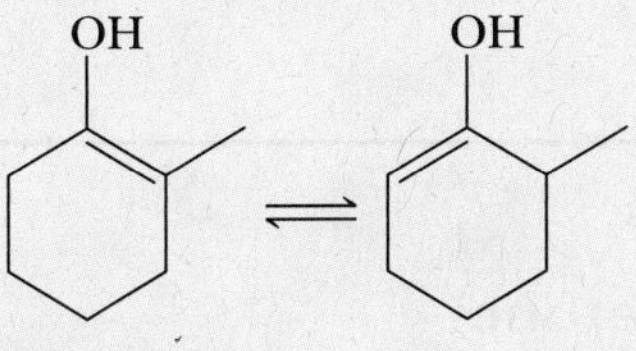

Major enol

(b) 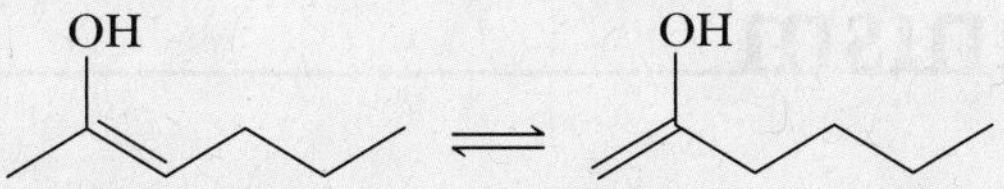

Major enol

See problem 12.34

PROBLEM 12.10

Draw the structural formula for the keto form of each enol:

(a) 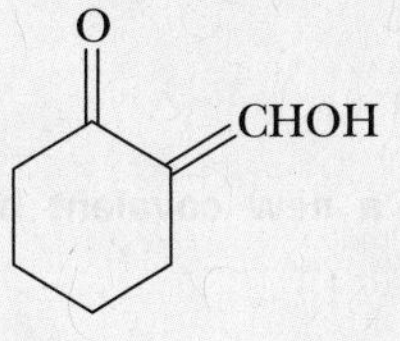 (b) 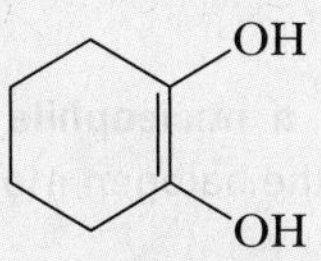 (c) 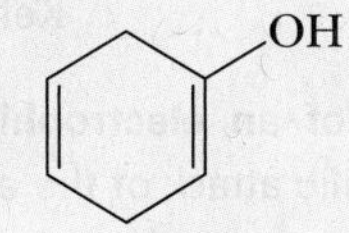

B. Racemization at an α-Carbon

When enantiomerically pure (either *R* or *S*) 3-phenyl-2-butanone is dissolved in ethanol, no change occurs in the optical activity of the solution over time. If, however, a trace of acid (for example, HCl) is added, the optical activity of the solution begins to decrease and gradually drops to zero. When 3-phenyl-2-butanone is isolated from this solution, it is found to be a racemic mixture (Section 6.8C). This observation can be explained by the acid-catalyzed formation of an achiral enol intermediate. Tautomerism of the achiral enol to the chiral keto form generates the *R* and *S* enantiomers with equal probability:

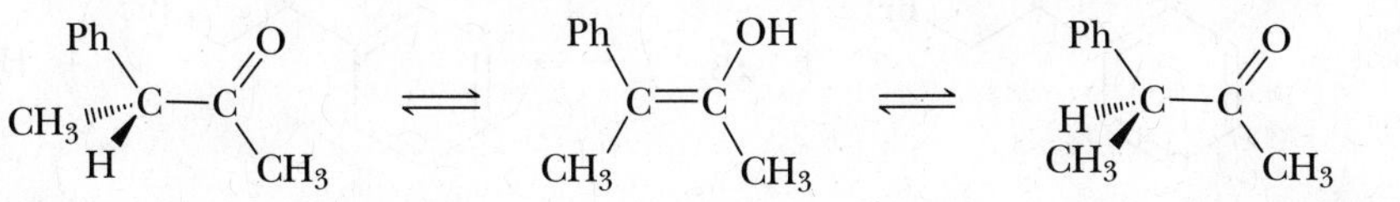

(*R*)-3-Phenyl-2-butanone — An achiral enol — (*S*)-3-Phenyl-2-butanone

Racemization by this mechanism occurs only at α-carbon stereocenters with at least one α-hydrogen. This process is usually an undesired side effect of acid impurities in a sample, because it is often, in medicine for example, important to have an enantiomerically pure form of a compound rather than a racemic mixture.

Racemization The conversion of a pure enantiomer into a racemic mixture.

C. α-Halogenation

Aldehydes and ketones with at least one α-hydrogen react with bromine and chlorine at the α-carbon to give an α-haloaldehyde or α-haloketone. Acetophenone, for example, reacts with bromine in acetic acid to give an α-bromoketone:

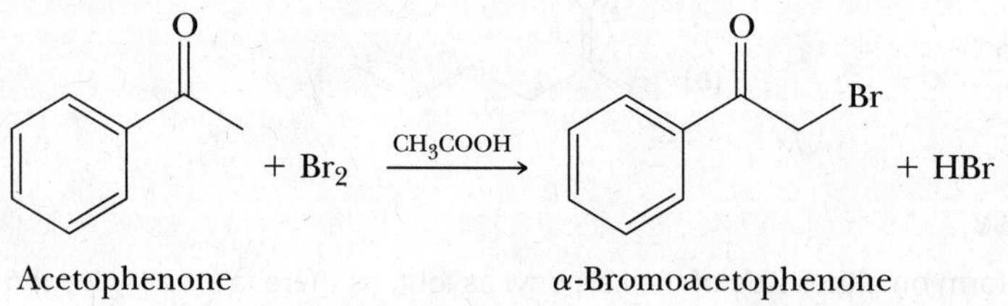

α-Halogenation is catalyzed by both acid and base. For acid-catalyzed halogenation, the HBr or HCl generated by the reaction catalyzes further reaction.

Mechanism

Acid-Catalyzed α-Halogenation of a Ketone

STEP 1: Keto–enol tautomerism (Section 12.8A). A small amount of enol is formed under acid-catalyzed conditions:

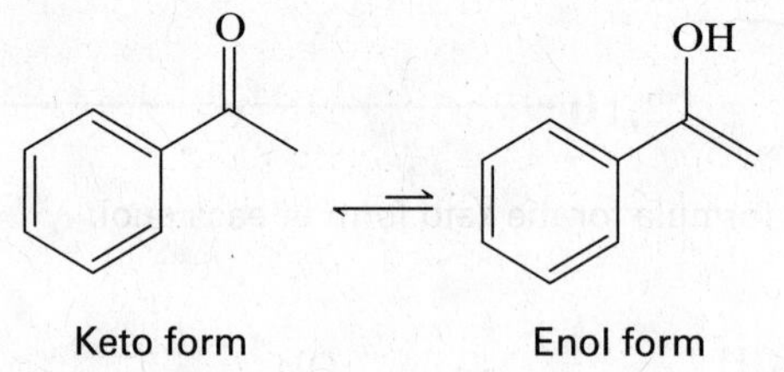

STEP 2: Reaction of an electrophile with a nucleophile to form a new covalent bond. Nucleophilic attack of the enol on the halogen molecule:

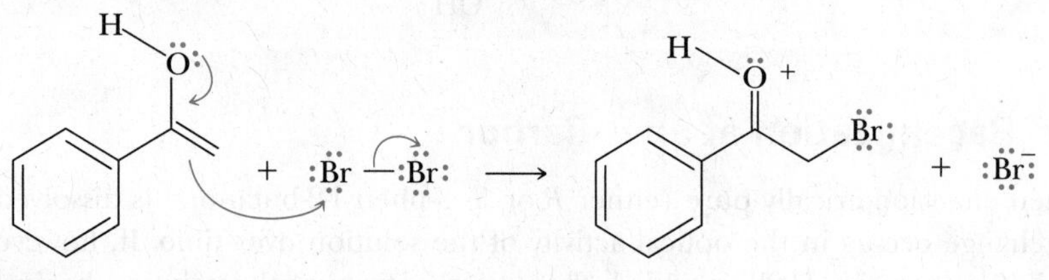

STEP 3: Take a proton away. Proton transfer generates HBr and gives the α-haloketone:

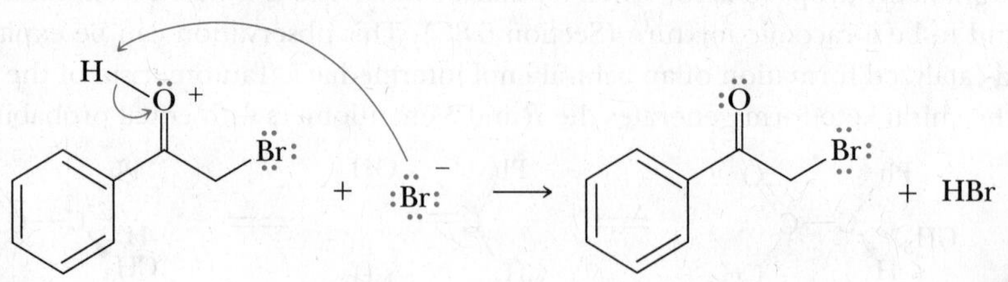

The value of α-halogenation is that it converts an α-carbon into a center that now has a good leaving group bonded to it and that is therefore susceptible to attack by a variety of good nucleophiles. In the following illustration, diethylamine (a nucleophile) reacts with the α-bromoketone to give an α-diethylaminoketone:

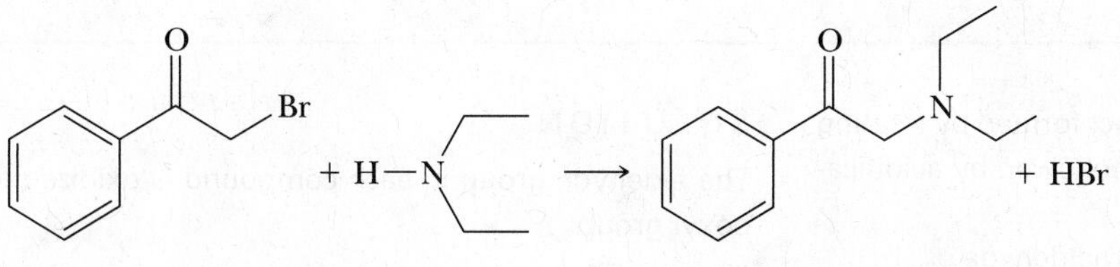

An α-bromoketone An α-diethylaminoketone

In practice, this type of nucleophilic substitution is generally carried out in the presence of a weak base such as potassium carbonate to neutralize the HX as it is formed.

12.9 How Are Aldehydes and Ketones Oxidized?

A. Oxidation of Aldehydes to Carboxylic Acids

Aldehydes are oxidized to carboxylic acids by a variety of common oxidizing agents, including chromic acid and molecular oxygen. In fact, aldehydes are one of the most easily oxidized of all functional groups. Oxidation by chromic acid (Section 8.2F) is illustrated by the conversion of hexanal to hexanoic acid:

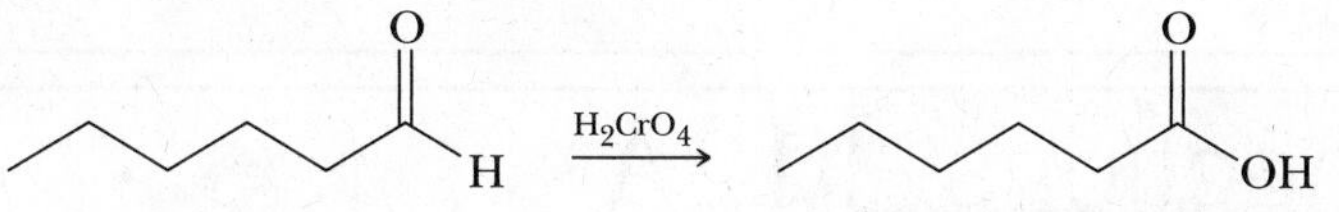

Hexanal Hexanoic acid

Aldehydes are also oxidized to carboxylic acids by silver ion. One common laboratory procedure uses **Tollens' reagent**, prepared by dissolving $AgNO_3$ in water, adding sodium hydroxide to precipitate silver ion as Ag_2O, and then adding aqueous ammonia to redissolve silver ion as the silver–ammonia complex ion:

$$Ag^{+}NO_3^{-} + 2NH_3 \xrightleftharpoons{NH_3,\ H_2O} Ag(NH_3)_2{}^{+}NO_3^{-}$$

When Tollens' reagent is added to an aldehyde, the aldehyde is oxidized to a carboxylic anion, and Ag^+ is reduced to metallic silver. If this reaction is carried out properly, silver precipitates as a smooth, mirrorlike deposit—hence the name **silver-mirror test**:

$$\overset{O}{\overset{\|}{RCH}} + 2Ag(NH_3)_2{}^{+} \xrightarrow{NH_3,\ H_2O} \overset{O}{\overset{\|}{RCO^{-}}} + \underset{\text{Precipitates as silver mirror}}{2Ag} + 4NH_3$$

Nowadays, Ag^+ is rarely used for the oxidation of aldehydes, because of the cost of silver and because other, more convenient methods exist for this oxidation. The reaction, however, is still used for silvering mirrors. In the process, formaldehyde or glucose is used as the aldehyde to reduce Ag^+.

Aldehydes are also oxidized to carboxylic acids by molecular oxygen and by hydrogen peroxide.

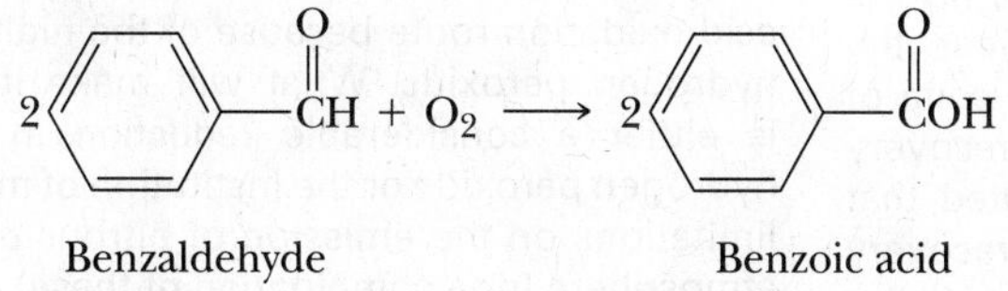

Benzaldehyde Benzoic acid

Molecular oxygen is the least expensive and most readily available of all oxidizing agents, and, on an industrial scale, air oxidation of organic molecules, including aldehydes, is common. Air oxidation of aldehydes can also be a problem: Aldehydes that are liquid at room temperature are so sensitive to oxidation by molecular oxygen that they must be protected from contact with air during storage. Often, this is done by sealing the aldehyde in a container under an atmosphere of nitrogen.

Charles D. Winters

A silver mirror has been deposited in the inside of this flask by the reaction of an aldehyde with Tollens' reagent.

EXAMPLE 12.11

Draw a structural formula for the product formed by treating each compound with Tollens' reagent, followed by acidification with aqueous HCl:

(a) Pentanal **(b)** Cyclopentanecarbaldehyde

STRATEGY

Aldehydes are oxidized to carboxylic acids by Tollens' reagent.

SOLUTION

The aldehyde group in each compound is oxidized to a carboxyl group:

(a)

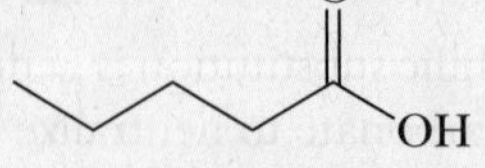

Pentanoic acid

(b)

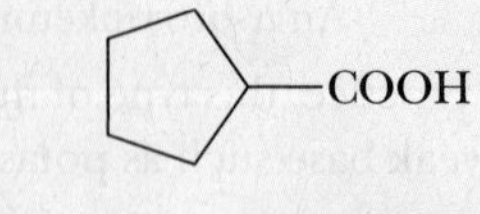

Cyclopentanecarboxylic acid

See problems 12.36, 12.37

PROBLEM 12.11

Complete these oxidations:

(a) 3-Oxobutanal + O_2 ⟶ **(b)** 3-Phenylpropanal + Tollens' reagent ⟶

Chemical Connections 12A

A GREEN SYNTHESIS OF ADIPIC ACID

The current industrial production of adipic acid relies on the oxidation of a mixture of cyclohexanol and cyclohexanone by nitric acid:

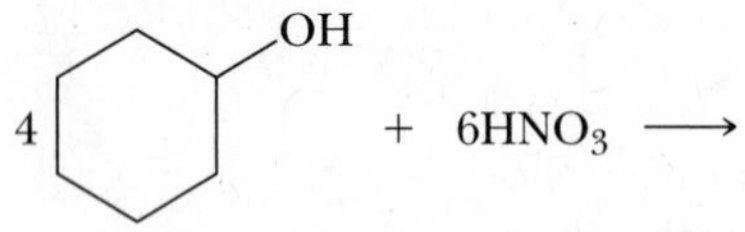

Cyclohexanol

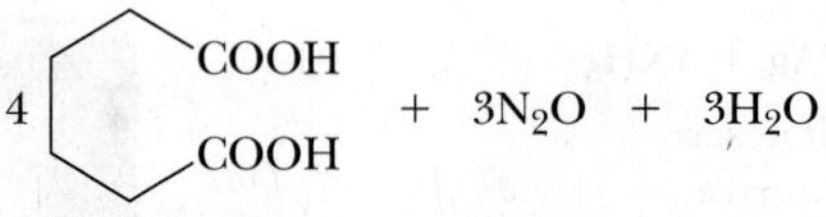

Hexanedioic acid (Adipic acid) Nitrous oxide

A by-product of this oxidation is nitrous oxide, a gas considered to play a role in global warming and the depletion of the ozone layer in the atmosphere, as well as contributing to acid rain and acid smog. Given the fact that worldwide production of adipic acid is approximately 2.2 billion metric tons per year, the production of nitrous oxide is enormous. In spite of technological advances that allow for the recovery and recycling of nitrous oxide, it is estimated that approximately 400,000 metric tons escapes recovery and is released into the atmosphere each year.

Recently, Ryoji Noyori (2001 Nobel Prize in Chemistry) and coworkers at Nagoya University in Japan developed a "green" route to adipic acid, one that involves the oxidation of cyclohexene by 30% hydrogen peroxide catalyzed by sodium tungstate, Na_2WO_4:

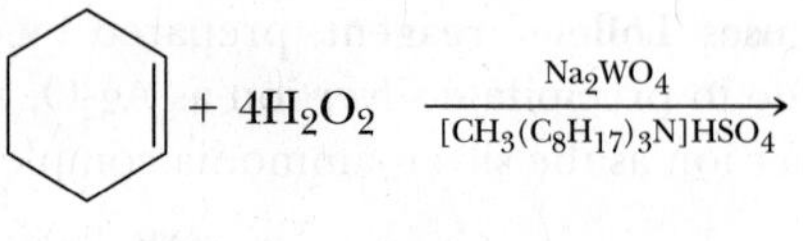

Cyclohexene

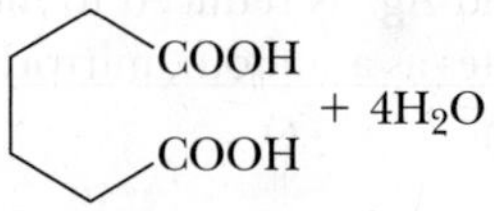

Hexanedioic acid (Adipic acid)

In this process, cyclohexene is mixed with aqueous 30% hydrogen peroxide, and sodium tungstate and methyltrioctylammonium hydrogen sulfate are added to the resulting two-phase system. (Cyclohexene is insoluble in water.) Under these conditions, cyclohexene is oxidized to adipic acid in approximately 90% yield.

While this route to adipic acid is environmentally friendly, it is not yet competitive with the nitric acid oxidation route because of the high cost of 30% hydrogen peroxide. What will make it competitive is either a considerable reduction in the cost of hydrogen peroxide or the institution of more stringent limitations on the emission of nitrous oxide into the atmosphere (or a combination of these).

Question

Using chemistry presented in this and previous chapters, propose a synthesis for adipic acid from cyclohexene.

B. Oxidation of Ketones to Carboxylic Acids

Ketones are much more resistant to oxidation than are aldehydes. For example, ketones are not normally oxidized by chromic acid or potassium permanganate. In fact, these reagents are used routinely to oxidize secondary alcohols to ketones in good yield (Section 8.2F).

Ketones undergo oxidative cleavage, via their enol form, by potassium dichromate and potassium permanganate at higher temperatures and by higher concentrations of nitric acid, HNO_3. The carbon–carbon double bond of the enol is cleaved to form two carboxyl or ketone groups, depending on the substitution pattern of the original ketone. An important industrial application of this reaction is the oxidation of cyclohexanone to hexanedioic acid (adipic acid), one of the two monomers required for the synthesis of the polymer nylon 66 (Section 16.4A):

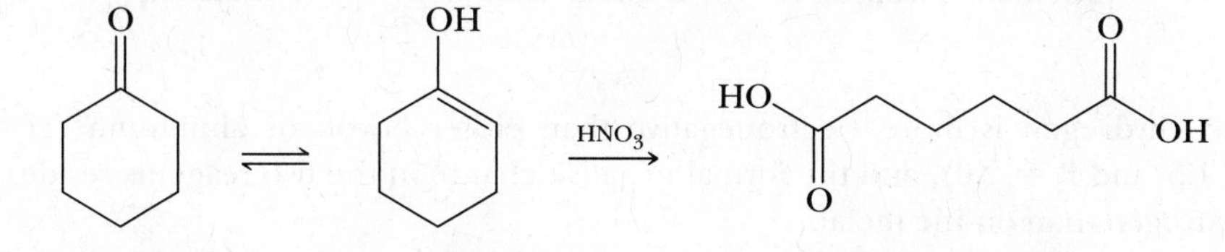

Cyclohexanone (keto form) | Cyclohexanone (enol form) | Hexanedioic acid (adipic acid)

12.10 How Are Aldehydes and Ketones Reduced?

Aldehydes are reduced to primary alcohols and ketones to secondary alcohols:

$$\underset{\text{An aldehyde}}{\overset{\displaystyle O}{\overset{\|}{R\text{C}H}}} \xrightarrow{\text{reduction}} \underset{\text{A primary alcohol}}{RCH_2OH} \qquad \underset{\text{A ketone}}{\overset{\displaystyle O}{\overset{\|}{R\text{C}R'}}} \xrightarrow{\text{reduction}} \underset{\text{A secondary alcohol}}{\overset{\displaystyle OH}{\overset{|}{R\text{C}HR'}}}$$

A. Catalytic Reduction

The carbonyl group of an aldehyde or a ketone is reduced to a hydroxyl group by hydrogen in the presence of a transition metal catalyst, most commonly finely divided palladium, platinum, nickel, or rhodium. Reductions are generally carried out at temperatures from 25 to 100 °C and at pressures of hydrogen from 1 to 5 atm. Under such conditions, cyclohexanone is reduced to cyclohexanol:

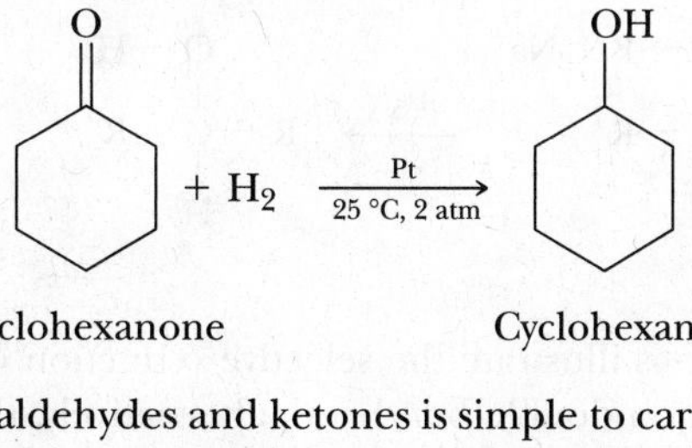

Cyclohexanone | Cyclohexanol

The catalytic reduction of aldehydes and ketones is simple to carry out, yields are generally very high, and isolation of the final product is very easy. A disadvantage is that some other functional groups (for example, carbon–carbon double bonds) are also reduced under these conditions.

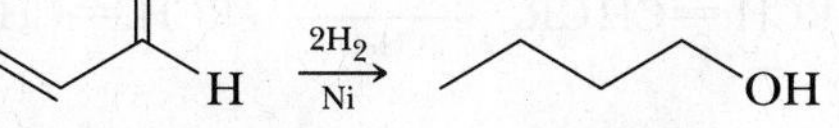

trans-2-Butenal (Crotonaldehyde) | 1-Butanol

B. Metal Hydride Reductions

Hydride ion A hydrogen atom with two electrons in its valence shell; H:⁻.

By far the most common laboratory reagents used to reduce the carbonyl group of an aldehyde or a ketone to a hydroxyl group are sodium borohydride and lithium aluminum hydride. Each of these compounds behaves as a source of **hydride ion**, a very strong nucleophile. The structural formulas drawn here for these reducing agents show formal negative charges on boron and aluminum:

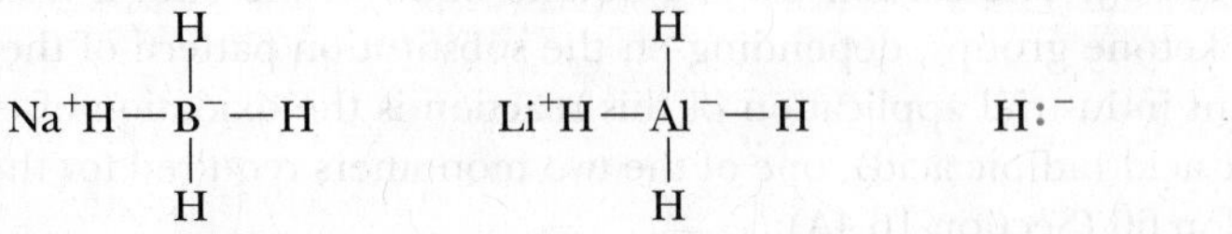

Sodium borohydride   Lithium aluminum hydride   Hydride ion

In fact, hydrogen is more electronegative than either boron or aluminum (H = 2.1, Al = 1.5, and B = 2.0), and the formal negative charge in the two reagents resides more on hydrogen than on the metal.

Lithium aluminum hydride is a very powerful reducing agent; it rapidly reduces not only the carbonyl groups of aldehydes and ketones, but also those of carboxylic acids (Section 13.5) and their functional derivatives (Section 14.8). Sodium borohydride is a much more selective reagent, reducing only aldehydes and ketones rapidly.

Reductions using sodium borohydride are most commonly carried out in aqueous methanol, in pure methanol, or in ethanol. The initial product of reduction is a tetraalkyl borate, which is converted to an alcohol and sodium borate salts upon treatment with water. One mole of sodium borohydride reduces 4 moles of aldehyde or ketone:

$$4RCH(=O) + NaBH_4 \xrightarrow{CH_3OH} \underset{\text{A tetraalkyl borate}}{(RCH_2O)_4B^-Na^+} \xrightarrow{H_2O} 4RCH_2OH + \text{borate salts}$$

The key step in the metal hydride reduction of an aldehyde or a ketone is the transfer of a hydride ion from the reducing agent to the carbonyl carbon to form a tetrahedral carbonyl addition intermediate. In the reduction of an aldehyde or a ketone to an alcohol, only the hydrogen atom attached to carbon comes from the hydride-reducing agent; the hydrogen atom bonded to oxygen comes from the water added to hydrolyze the metal alkoxide salt.

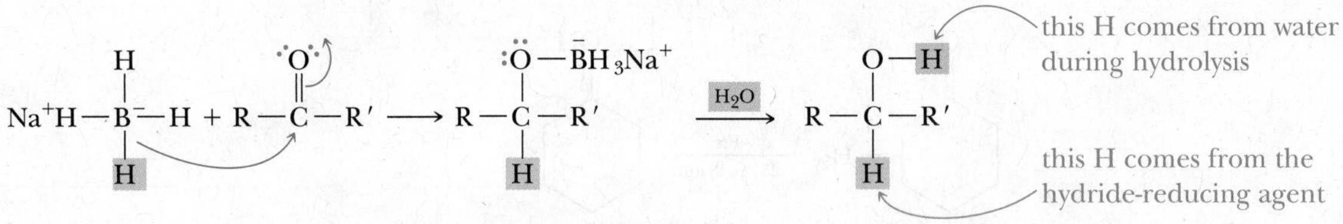

The next two equations illustrate the selective reduction of a carbonyl group in the presence of a carbon–carbon double bond and, alternatively, the selective reduction of a carbon–carbon double bond in the presence of a carbonyl group.

Selective reduction of a carbonyl group:

$$RCH{=}CHC(=O)R' \xrightarrow[2)\ H_2O]{1)\ NaBH_4} RCH{=}CHCH(OH)R'$$

A carbon–carbon double bond can be reduced selectively in the presence of a carbonyl group by first protecting the carbonyl group using an acetal.

Selective reduction of a carbon–carbon double bond using a protecting group:

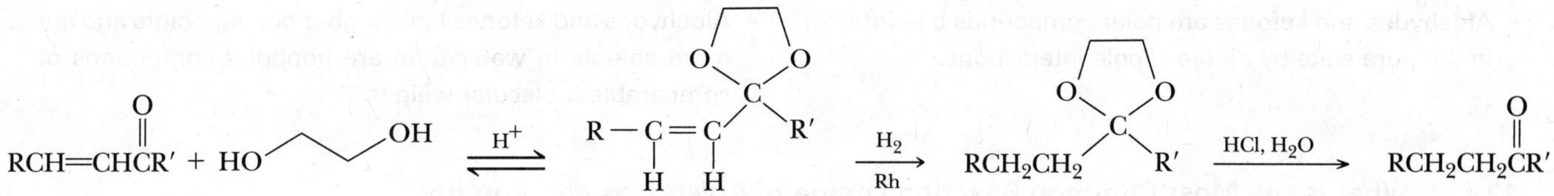

EXAMPLE 12.12

Complete these reductions:

(a) 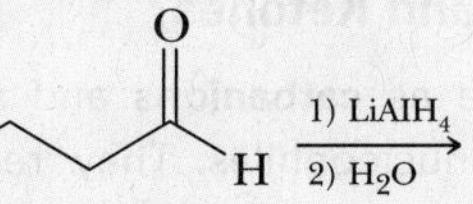

(b) 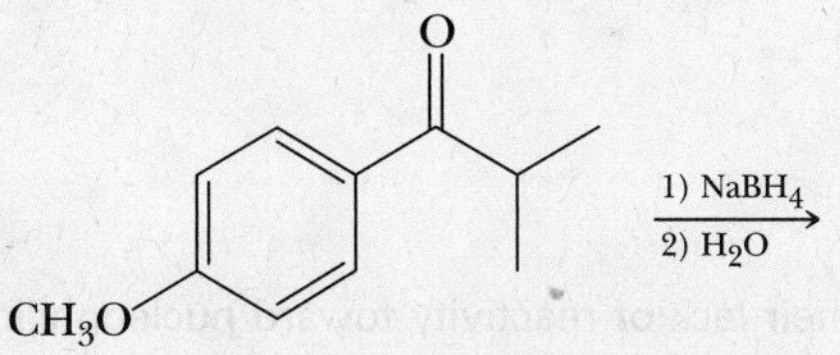

STRATEGY

Consider all the functional groups that can react with each reducing reagent. Alkenes, ketones, aldehydes, and imines are just some examples of functional groups that can be reduced.

SOLUTION

The carbonyl group of the aldehyde in (a) is reduced to a primary alcohol, and that of the ketone in (b) is reduced to a secondary alcohol:

(a) 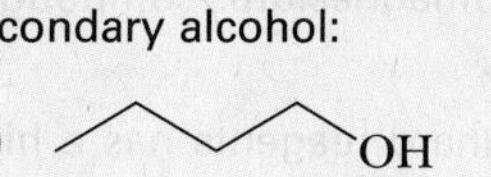

(b) 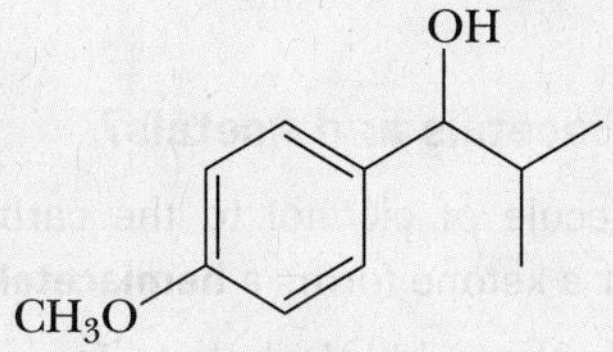

See problems 12.36, 12.37

PROBLEM 12.12

What aldehyde or ketone gives each alcohol upon reduction by $NaBH_4$?

(a) 

(b) 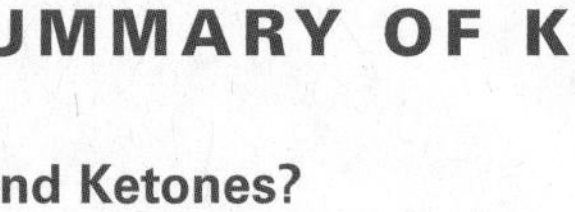

(c) 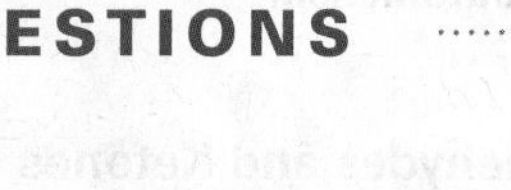

SUMMARY OF KEY QUESTIONS

12.1 What Are Aldehydes and Ketones?

- An **aldehyde** contains a carbonyl group bonded to a hydrogen atom and a carbon atom.
- A **ketone** contains a carbonyl group bonded to two carbons.

12.2 How Are Aldehydes and Ketones Named?

- An aldehyde is named by changing *-e* of the parent alkane to *-al.*
- A CHO group bonded to a ring is indicated by the suffix *-carbaldehyde.*
- A ketone is named by changing *-e* of the parent alkane to *-one* and using a number to locate the carbonyl group.
- In naming compounds that contain more than one functional group, the IUPAC system has established an **order of precedence of functional groups.** If the carbonyl group of an aldehyde or a ketone is lower in precedence than other functional groups in the molecule, it is indicated by the infix **-oxo-**.

12.3 What Are the Physical Properties of Aldehydes and Ketones?

- Aldehydes and ketones are polar compounds and interact in the pure state by dipole–dipole interactions.
- Aldehydes and ketones have higher boiling points and are more soluble in water than are nonpolar compounds of comparable molecular weight.

12.4 What Is the Most Common Reaction Theme of Aldehdyes and Ketones?

- The common reaction theme of the carbonyl group of aldehydes and ketones is the addition of a nucleophile to form a **tetrahedral carbonyl addition intermediate**.

12.5 What Are Grignard Reagents, and How Do They React with Aldehydes and Ketones?

- **Grignard reagents** are organomagnesium compounds with the generic formula RMgX.
- The carbon–metal bond in Grignard reagents has a high degree of partial ionic character.
- Grignard reagents behave as **carbanions** and are both strong bases and good nucleophiles. They react with aldehydes and ketones by adding to the carbonyl carbon.

12.6 What Are Hemiacetals and Acetals?

- The addition of a molecule of alcohol to the carbonyl group of an aldehyde or a ketone forms a **hemiacetal**.
- Hemiacetals can react further with alcohols to form **acetals** plus a molecule of water.
- Because of their lack of reactivity toward nucleophilic and basic reagents, acetals are often used to protect the carbonyl groups of aldehydes and ketones while reactions are carried out on functional groups in other parts of the molecule.

12.7 How Do Aldehydes and Ketones React with Ammonia and Amines?

- Ammonia, 1° aliphatic amines (RNH_2), and 1° aromatic amines ($ArNH_2$) react with the carbonyl group of aldehydes and ketones in the presence of an acid catalyst to give **imines**, compounds that contain a carbon–nitrogen double bond.

12.8 What Is Keto–Enol Tautomerism?

- A carbon atom adjacent to a carbonyl group is called an **α-carbon**, and any hydrogen atoms bonded to it are called **α-hydrogens**.
- An aldehyde or a ketone, which is said to be in its **keto** form, that has at least one α-hydrogen is in equilibrium with a constitutional isomer called an **enol**. This type of isomerism is called **tautomerism**.
- Tautomerism, catalyzed by trace amounts of acid or base, is the cause of **racemization** of chiral aldehydes and ketones when a stereocenter exists at an α-carbon.
- The enol form allows aldehydes and ketones to be halogenated at the α-position.

12.9 How Are Aldehydes and Ketones Oxidized?

- Aldehydes are oxidized to carboxylic acids by a variety of common oxidizing agents, including chromic acid, the Tollens' reagent, and molecular oxygen.
- Ketones are much more resistant to oxidation than are aldehydes. However, they undergo **oxidative cleavage**, via their enol form, by potassium dichromate and potassium permanganate at higher temperatures and by higher concentrations of HNO_3.

12.10 How Are Aldehydes and Ketones Reduced?

- Aldehydes are reduced to primary alcohols and ketones to secondary alcohols by catalytic hydrogenation or through the use of the metal hydrides $NaBH_4$ or $LiAlH_4$.

QUICK QUIZ

Answer true or false to the following questions to assess your general knowledge of the concepts in this chapter. If you have difficulty with any of them, you should review the appropriate section in the chapter (shown in parentheses) before attempting the more challenging end-of-chapter problems.

1. In a compound that contains both an aldehyde and a C—C double bond, each functional group can be reduced exclusive of the other. (12.10)
2. Nucleophiles react with aldehydes and ketones to form tetrahedral carbonyl addition intermediates. (12.4)
3. The carboxyl group (COOH) has a higher priority in naming than all other functional groups. (12.2)
4. A stereocenter at the α-carbon of an aldehyde or a ketone will undergo racemization over time in the presence of an acid or a base. (12.8)
5. Acetone is the lowest-molecular-weight ketone. (12.3)
6. Aldehydes can be oxidized to ketones and carboxylic acids. (12.9)
7. Ketones are less water soluble than alcohols with comparable molecular weight. (12.3)
8. A Grignard reagent cannot be formed in the presence of an NH, OH, or SH group. (12.5)
9. Ketones have higher boiling points than alkanes with comparable molecular weight. (12.3)
10. An aldehyde has a higher priority in naming than a ketone. (12.2)
11. A Grignard reagent is a good electrophile. (12.5)
12. Any reaction that oxidizes an aldehyde to a carboxylic acid will also oxidize a ketone to a carboxylic acid. (12.9)
13. Aldehydes are more water soluble than ethers with comparable molecular weight. (12.3)
14. Aldehydes react with Grignard reagents (followed by acid workup) to form 1° alcohols. (12.5)
15. An imine can be reduced to an amine through catalytic hydrogenation. (12.7)
16. Sodium borohydride, $NaBH_4$, is more reactive and less selective than lithium aluminum hydride, $LiAlH_4$. (12.10)
17. An acetal can only result from the base-catalyzed addition of an alcohol to a hemiacetal. (12.6)
18. A Grignard reagent is a strong base. (12.5)
19. Acetal formation is reversible. (12.6)
20. An imine is the result of the reaction of a 2° amine with an aldehyde or a ketone. (12.7)
21. Ketones react with Grignard reagents (followed by acid workup) to form 2° alcohols. (12.5)
22. Aldehydes and ketones can undergo tautomerism. (12.8)
23. Acetaldehyde is the lowest-molecular-weight aldehyde. (12.3)
24. A ketone that possesses an α-hydrogen can undergo α-halogenation. (12.8)
25. A carbonyl group is polarized such that the oxygen atom is partially positive and the carbon atom is partially negative. (12.3)
26. Acetals are stable to bases, nucleophiles, and reducing agents. (12.6)
27. A "carbaldehyde" is an aldehyde in which the carbonyl group is adjacent to a C—C double bond. (12.1)
28. A hemiacetal can result from the acid-catalyzed or base-catalyzed addition of an alcohol to an aldehyde or a ketone. (12.6)

Answers: (1)T (2)T (3)T (4)T (5)T (6)T (7)T (8)T (9)T (10)T (11) F (12) F (13)T (14) F (15)T (16) F (17) F (18)T (19)T (20) F (21) F (22)T (23) F (24)T (25) F (26)T (27) F (28)T

Detailed explanations for many of these answers can be found in the accompanying Solutions Manual.

KEY REACTIONS

1. Reaction with Grignard Reagents (Section 12.5C)

Treatment of formaldehyde with a Grignard reagent, followed by hydrolysis in aqueous acid, gives a primary alcohol. Similar treatment of any other aldehyde gives a secondary alcohol:

$$CH_3\overset{O}{\overset{\|}{C}}H \xrightarrow[2)\ HCl,\ H_2O]{1)\ C_6H_5MgBr} C_6H_5\overset{OH}{\overset{|}{C}}HCH_3$$

Treatment of a ketone with a Grignard reagent gives a tertiary alcohol:

$$CH_3\overset{O}{\overset{\|}{C}}CH_3 \xrightarrow[2)\ HCl,\ H_2O]{1)\ C_6H_5MgBr} C_6H_5\overset{OH}{\overset{|}{C}}(CH_3)_2$$

2. Addition of Alcohols to Form Hemiacetals (Section 12.6)

Hemiacetals are only minor components of an equilibrium mixture of aldehyde or ketone and alcohol, except where the —OH and C=O groups are parts of the same molecule and a five- or six-membered ring can form:

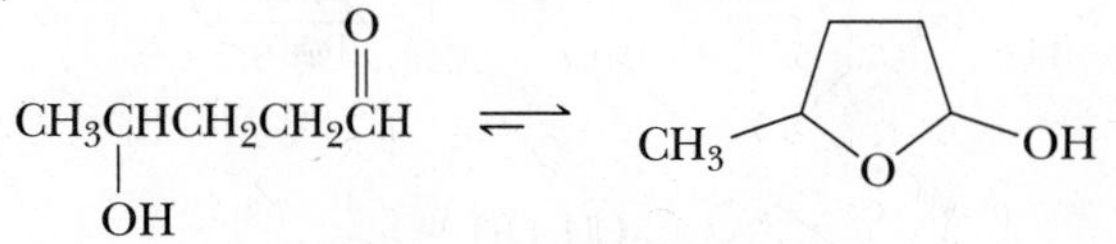

4-Hydroxypentanal A cyclic hemiacetal

3. Addition of Alcohols to Form Acetals (Section 12.6)

The formation of acetals is catalyzed by acid:

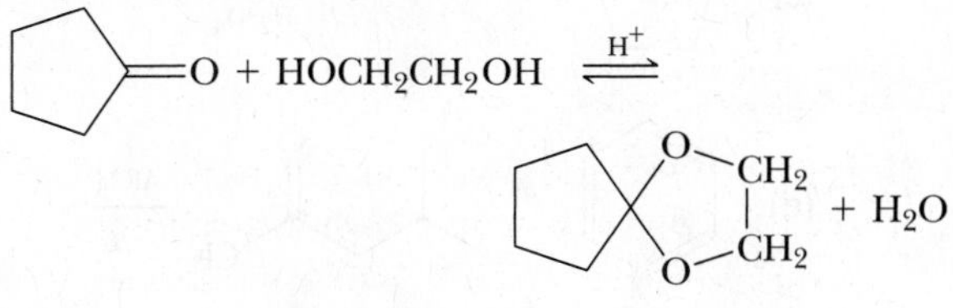

4. **Addition of Ammonia and Amines (Section 12.7)**

The addition of ammonia or a primary amine to the carbonyl group of an aldehyde or a ketone forms a tetrahedral carbonyl addition intermediate. Loss of water from this intermediate gives an imine (a Schiff base):

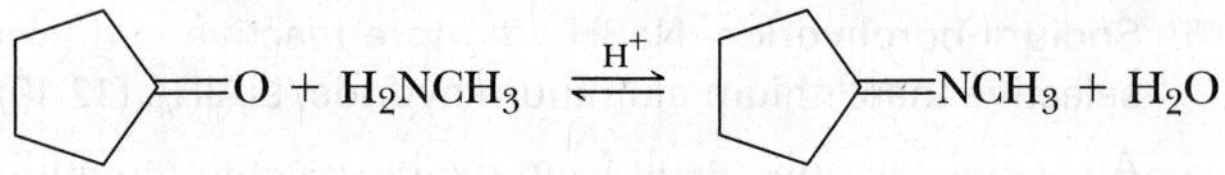

5. **Reductive Amination to Amines (Section 12.7B)**

The carbon–nitrogen double bond of an imine can be reduced by hydrogen in the presence of a transition metal catalyst to a carbon–nitrogen single bond:

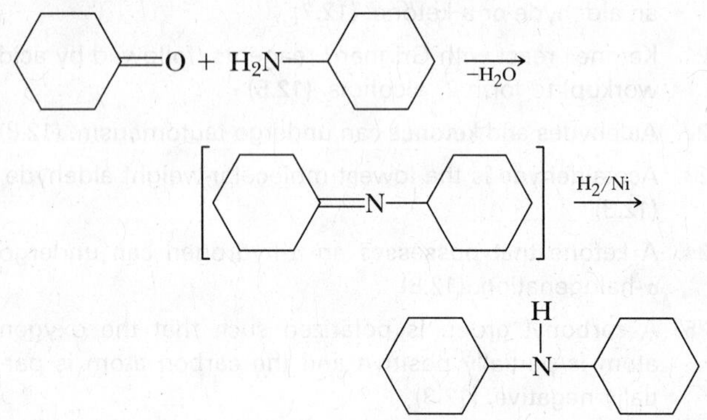

6. **Keto–Enol Tautomerism (Section 12.8A)**

The keto form generally predominates at equilibrium:

$$\underset{\text{Keto form (Approx 99.9\%)}}{CH_3\overset{O}{\overset{\|}{C}}CH_3} \rightleftharpoons \underset{\text{Enol form}}{CH_3\overset{OH}{\overset{|}{C}}=CH_2}$$

7. **Oxidation of an Aldehyde to a Carboxylic Acid (Section 12.9)**

The aldehyde group is among the most easily oxidized functional groups. Oxidizing agents include H_2CrO_4, Tollens' reagent, and O_2:

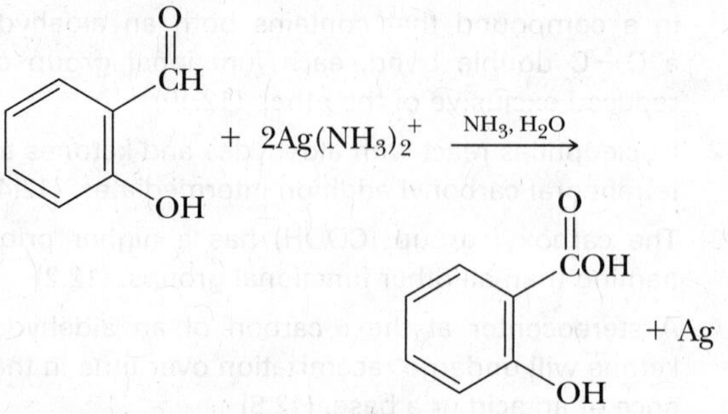

8. **Catalytic Reduction (Section 12.10A)**

Catalytic reduction of the carbonyl group of an aldehyde or a ketone to a hydroxyl group is simple to carry out, and yields of alcohols are high:

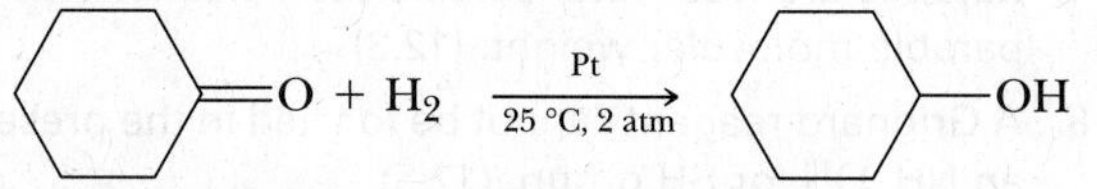

9. **Metal Hydride Reduction (Section 12.10B)**

Both $LiAlH_4$ and $NaBH_4$ reduce the carbonyl group of an aldehyde or a ketone to an hydroxyl group. They are selective in that neither reduces isolated carbon–carbon double bonds:

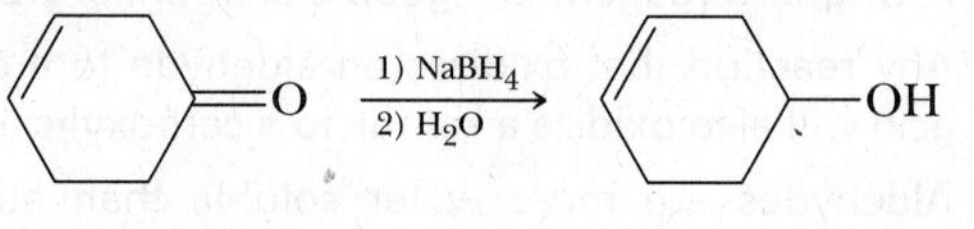

PROBLEMS

A problem marked with an asterisk indicates an applied "real-world" problem. Answers to problems whose numbers are printed in blue are given in Appendix D.

Preparation of Aldehydes and Ketones (see also Chapters 8 and 9)

12.13 Complete these reactions:

(a) 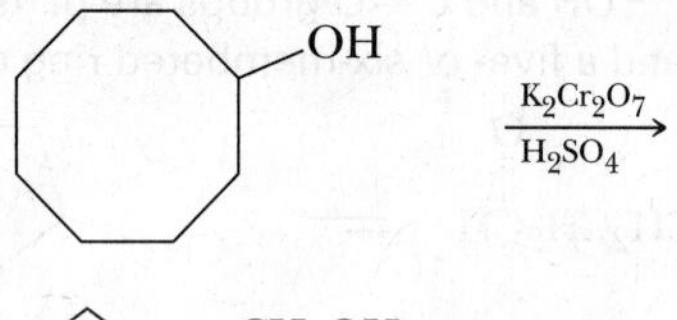

(b) 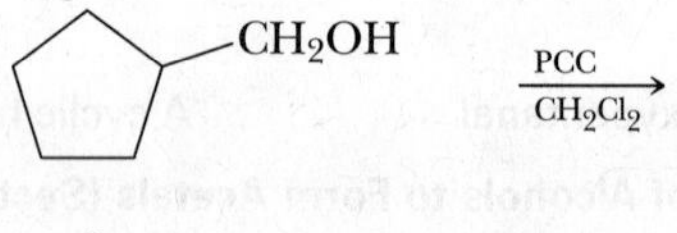

(c) 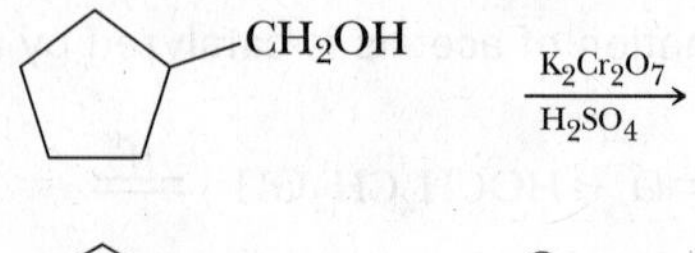

(d) 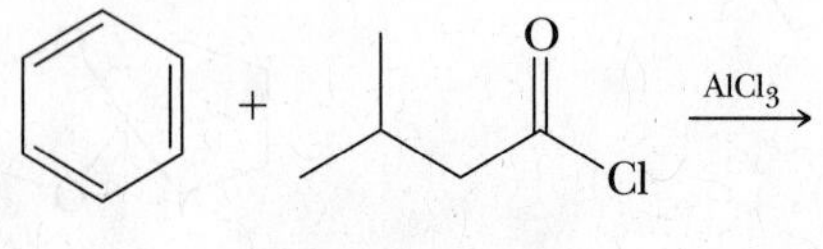

12.14 Show how you would bring about these conversions:

(a) 1-Pentanol to pentanal
(b) 1-Pentanol to pentanoic acid
(c) 2-Pentanol to 2-pentanone
(d) 1-Pentene to 2-pentanone
(e) Benzene to acetophenone
(f) Styrene to acetophenone
(g) Cyclohexanol to cyclohexanone
(h) Cyclohexene to cyclohexanone
(i) Benzene to 2-phenylethanal
(j) 1-Methylcyclohexene to (±)-2-methylcyclohexanone
(k) 1-Hexene to hexanal

Sections 12.1 and 12.2 Structure and Nomenclature

12.15 Draw a structural formula for the one ketone with molecular formula C_4H_8O and for the two aldehydes with molecular formula C_4H_8O. **(See Example 12.2)**

12.16 Draw structural formulas for the four aldehydes with molecular formula $C_5H_{10}O$. Which of these aldehydes are chiral? **(See Example 12.2)**

12.17 Name these compounds: **(See Examples 12.1, 12.3)**

(a) 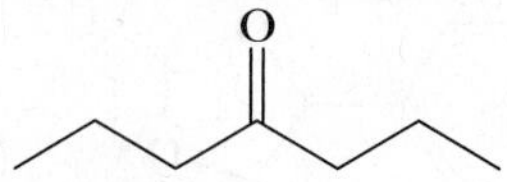

(b) 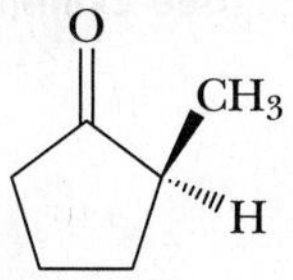

(c) 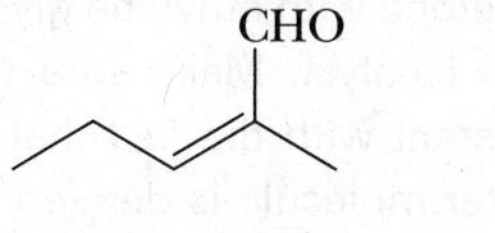

(d) 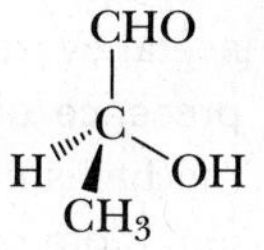

(e) 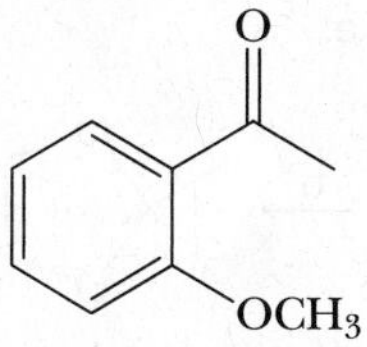

(f) 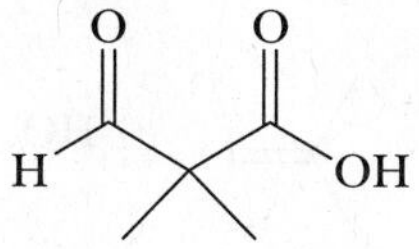

(g) 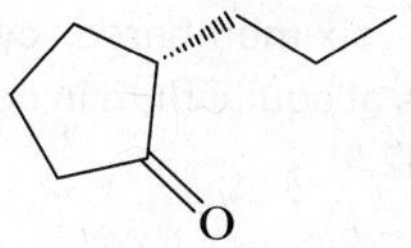

(h) 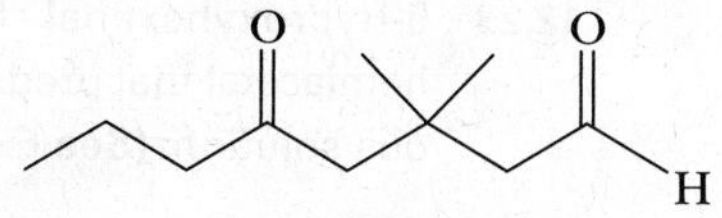

12.18 Draw structural formulas for these compounds: **(See Examples 12.1, 12.3)**

(a) 1-Chloro-2-propanone
(b) 3-Hydroxybutanal
(c) 4-Hydroxy-4-methyl-2-pentanone
(d) 3-Methyl-3-phenylbutanal
(e) *(S)*-3-bromocyclohexanone
(f) 3-Methyl-3-buten-2-one
(g) 5-Oxohexanal
(h) 2,2-Dimethylcyclohexanecarbaldehyde
(i) 3-Oxobutanoic acid
(j) 3-Phenylethanal
(k) *(R)*-2-Methylcyclohexanone
(l) 2,4-Pentanedione

Section 12.5 Addition of Carbon Nucleophiles

12.19 Write an equation for the acid–base reaction between phenylmagnesium iodide and a carboxylic acid. Use curved arrows to show the flow of electrons in this reaction. In addition, show that the reaction is an example of a stronger acid and stronger base reacting to form a weaker acid and weaker base. **(See Example 12.4)**

12.20 Diethyl ether is prepared on an industrial scale by the acid-catalyzed dehydration of ethanol:

$$2CH_3CH_2OH \xrightarrow[180\ ^\circ C]{H_2SO_4} CH_3CH_2OCH_2CH_3 + H_2O$$

Explain why diethyl ether used in the preparation of Grignard reagents must be carefully purified to remove all traces of ethanol and water.

12.21 Draw structural formulas for the product formed by treating each compound with propylmagnesium bromide, followed by hydrolysis in aqueous acid: **(See Examples 12.4, 12.5)**

(a) CH_2O

(b) 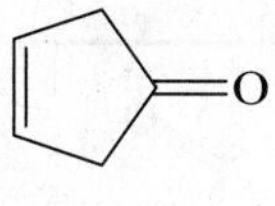

(c) 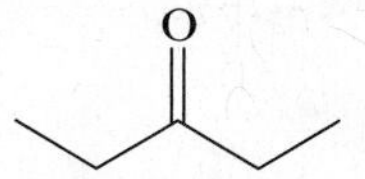

(d) 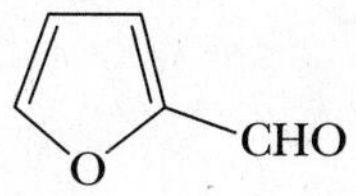

(e) 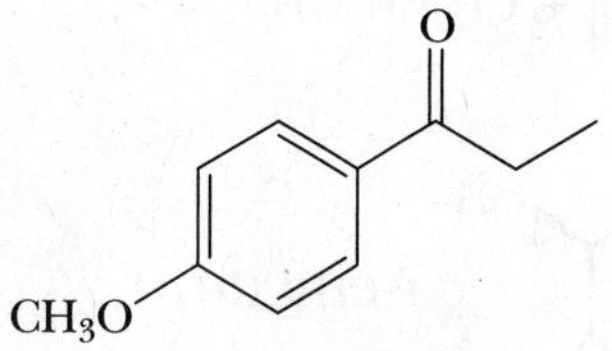

12.22 Suggest a synthesis for each alcohol, starting from an aldehyde or a ketone and an appropriate Grignard reagent (the number of combinations of Grignard reagent and aldehyde or ketone that might be used is shown in parentheses below each target molecule): **(See Examples 12.4, 12.5)**

(a) 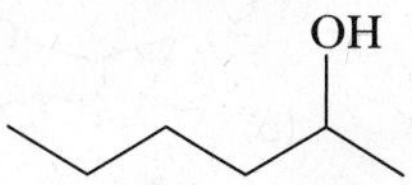

(Two combinations)

(b) 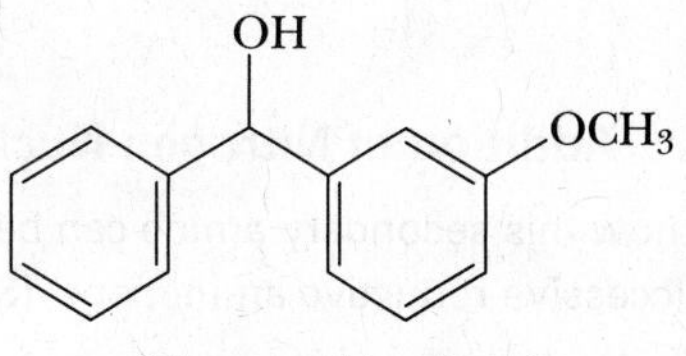

(Two combinations)

(c) 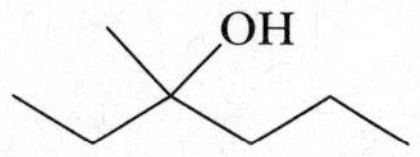

(Three combinations)

Section 12.6 Addition of Oxygen Nucleophiles

12.23 5-Hydroxyhexanal forms a six-membered cyclic hemiacetal that predominates at equilibrium in aqueous solution: **(See Example 12.6)**

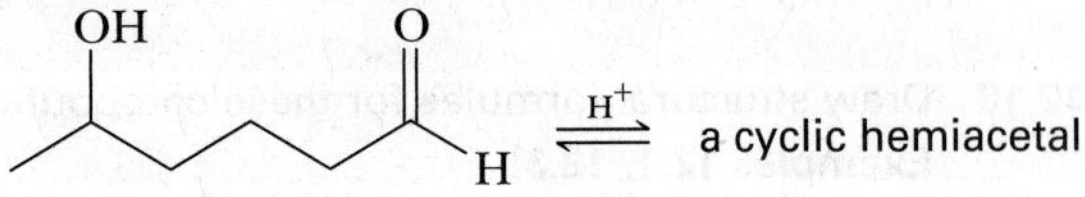

5-Hydroxyhexanal

(a) Draw a structural formula for this cyclic hemiacetal.
(b) How many stereoisomers are possible for 5-hydroxyhexanal?
(c) How many stereoisomers are possible for the cyclic hemiacetal?
(d) Draw alternative chair conformations for each stereoisomer.
(e) For each stereoisomer, which alternative chair conformation is the more stable?

12.24 Draw structural formulas for the hemiacetal and then the acetal formed from each pair of reactants in the presence of an acid catalyst: **(See Example 12.6)**

(a) 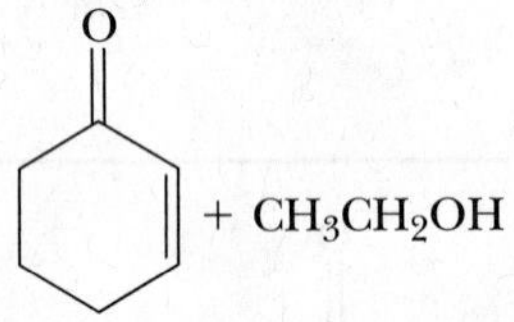

(b) 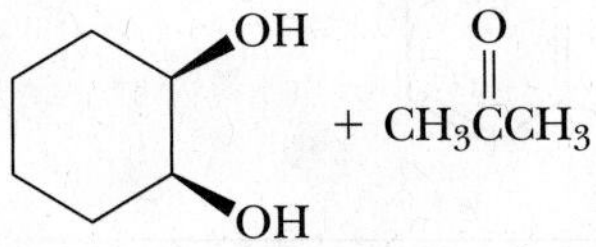

(c) 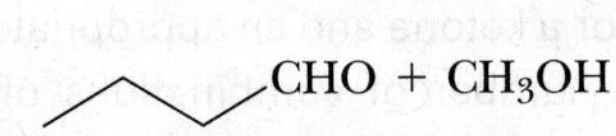

12.25 Draw structural formulas for the products of hydrolysis of each acetal in aqueous acid: **(See Example 12.6)**

(a) 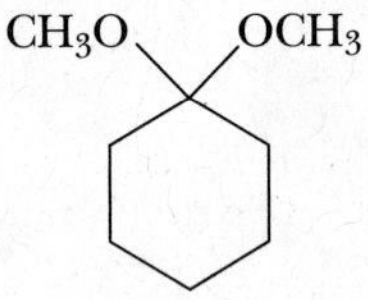

(b) 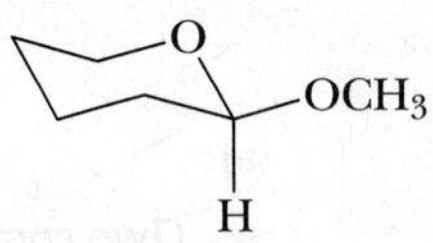

(c) 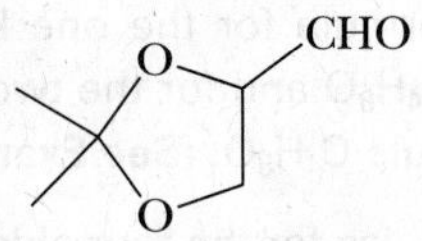

(d) 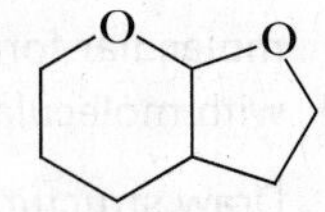

12.26 The following compound is a component of the fragrance of jasmine: From what carbonyl-containing compound and alcohol is the compound derived? **(See Example 12.6)**

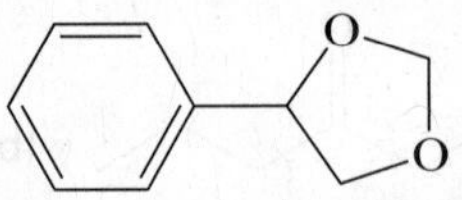

12.27 Propose a mechanism for the formation of the cyclic acetal by treating acetone with ethylene glycol in the presence of an acid catalyst. Make sure that your mechanism is consistent with the fact that the oxygen atom of the water molecule is derived from the carbonyl oxygen of acetone.

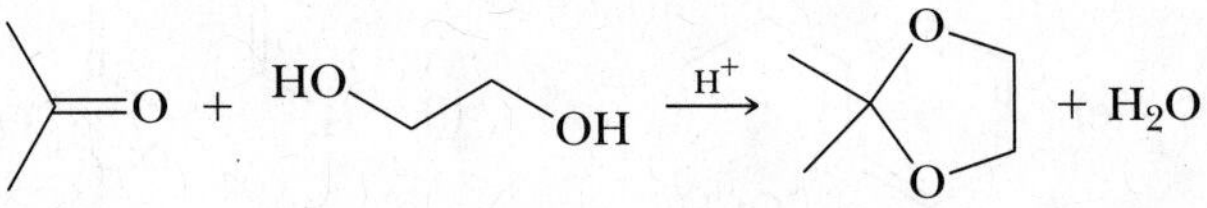

Acetone Ethylene glycol

12.28 Propose a mechanism for the formation of a cyclic acetal from 4-hydroxypentanal and one equivalent of methanol: If the carbonyl oxygen of 4-hydroxypentanal is enriched with oxygen-18, does your mechanism predict that the oxygen label appears in the cyclic acetal or in the water? Explain.

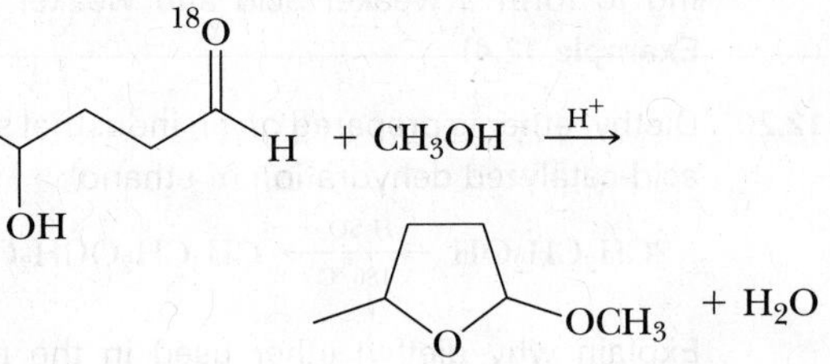

Section 12.7 Addition of Nitrogen Nucleophiles

12.29 Show how this secondary amine can be prepared by two successive reductive aminations: **(See Examples 12.8, 12.9)**

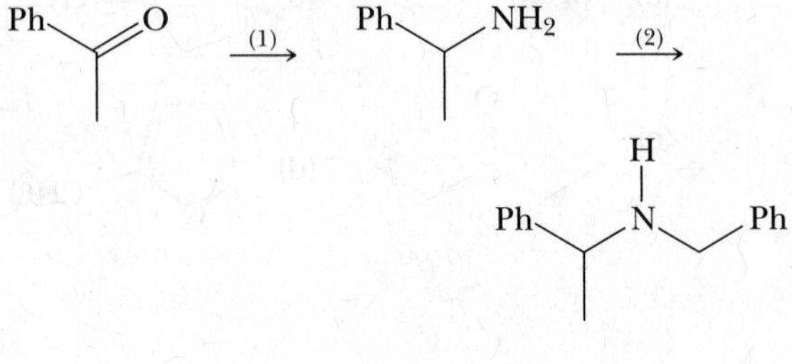

12.30 Show how to convert cyclohexanone to each of the following amines: **(See Examples 12.8, 12.9)**

(a) (b) (c) ***12.31** Following are structural formulas for amphetamine and methamphetamine: **(See Examples 12.8, 12.9)**

(a) Amphetamine

(b) Methamphetamine

The major central nervous system effects of amphetamine and amphetaminelike drugs are locomotor stimulation, euphoria and excitement, stereotyped behavior, and anorexia. Show how each drug can be synthesized by the reductive amination of an appropriate aldehyde or ketone.

***12.32** Rimantadine is effective in preventing infections caused by the influenza A virus and in treating established illness. The drug is thought to exert its antiviral effect by blocking a late stage in the assembly of the virus. Following is the final step in the synthesis of rimantadine: **(See Examples 12.8, 12.9)**

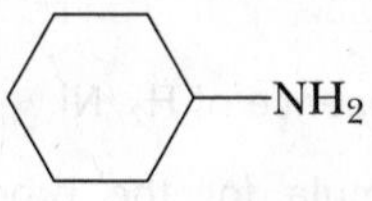

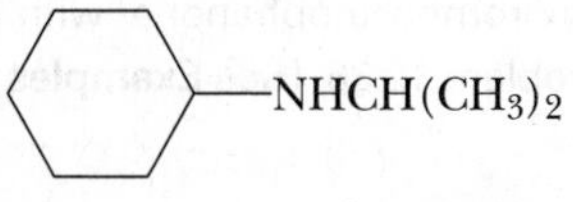

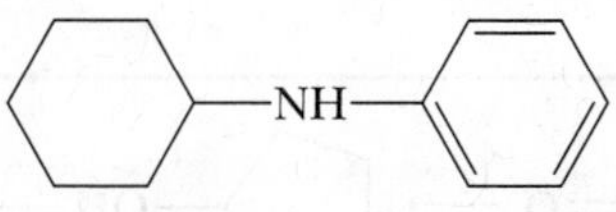

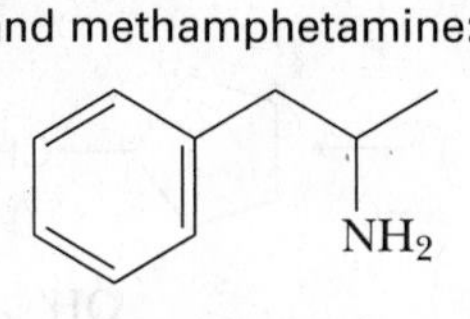

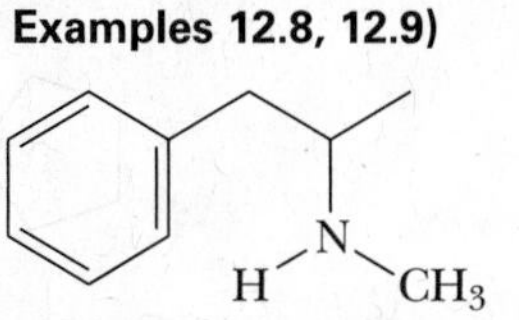

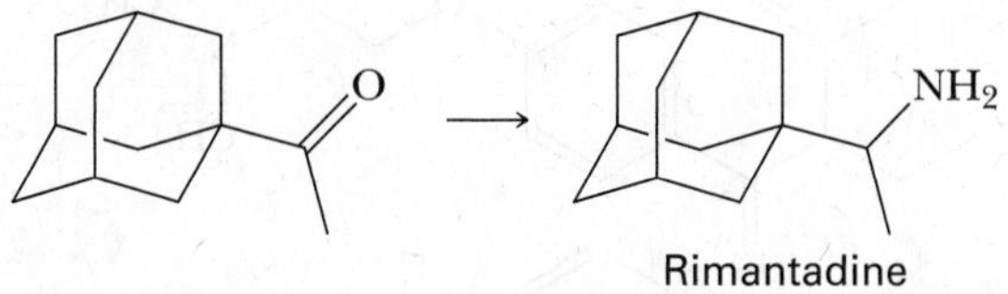

Rimantadine
(an antiviral agent)

(a) Describe experimental conditions to bring about this final step.
(b) Is rimantadine chiral?

***12.33** Methenamine, a product of the reaction of formaldehyde and ammonia, is a *prodrug*—a compound that is inactive by itself, but is converted to an active drug in the body by a biochemical transformation. The strategy behind the use of methenamine as a prodrug is that nearly all bacteria are sensitive to formaldehyde at concentrations of 20 mg/mL or higher. Formaldehyde cannot be used directly in medicine, however, because an effective concentration in plasma cannot be achieved with safe doses. Methenamine is stable at pH 7.4 (the pH of blood plasma), but undergoes acid-catalyzed hydrolysis to formaldehyde and ammonium ion under the acidic conditions of the kidneys and the urinary tract:

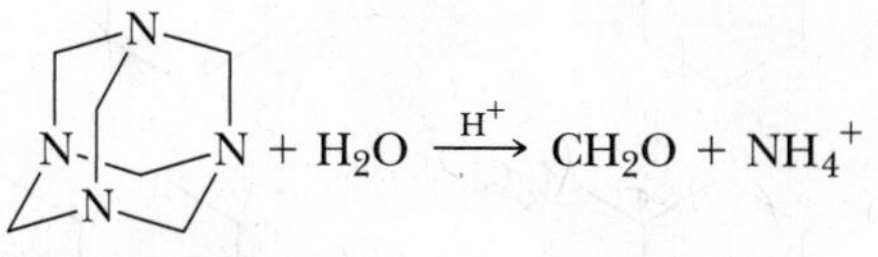

Methenamine

Thus, methenamine can be used as a site-specific drug to treat urinary infections.

(a) Balance the equation for the hydrolysis of methenamine to formaldehyde and ammonium ion.
(b) Does the pH of an aqueous solution of methenamine increase, remain the same, or decrease as a result of the hydrolysis of the compound? Explain.
(c) Explain the meaning of the following statement: The functional group in methenamine is the nitrogen analog of an acetal.
(d) Account for the observation that methenamine is stable in blood plasma, but undergoes hydrolysis in the urinary tract.

Section 12.8 Keto–Enol Tautomerism

12.34 The following molecule belongs to a class of compounds called enediols: Each carbon of the double bond carries an —OH group:

$$\alpha\text{-hydroxyaldehyde} \rightleftharpoons \begin{array}{c} HC-OH \\ \| \\ C-OH \\ | \\ CH_3 \end{array} \rightleftharpoons \alpha\text{-hydroxyketone}$$

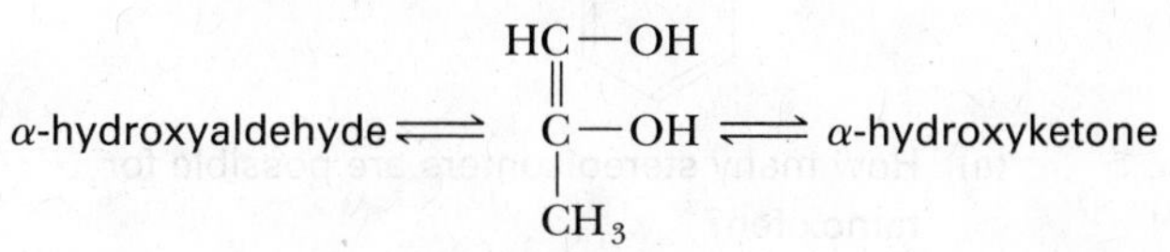

An enediol

Draw structural formulas for the α-hydroxyketone and the α-hydroxyaldehyde with which this enediol is in equilibrium. **(See Example 12.10)**

12.35 In dilute aqueous acid, (*R*)-glyceraldehyde is converted into an equilibrium mixture of (*R,S*)-glyceraldehyde and dihydroxyacetone:

$$\begin{array}{c} CHO \\ | \\ CHOH \\ | \\ CH_2OH \end{array} \xrightleftharpoons{H_2O,\ HCl} \begin{array}{c} CHO \\ | \\ CHOH \\ | \\ CH_2OH \end{array} + \begin{array}{c} CH_2OH \\ | \\ C=O \\ | \\ CH_2OH \end{array}$$

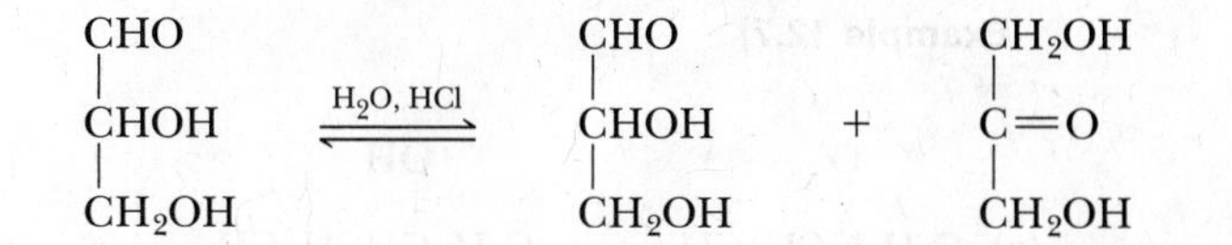

(*R*)-Glyceraldehyde; (*R,S*)-Glyceraldehyde; Dihydroxyacetone

Propose a mechanism for this isomerization.

Section 12.9 Oxidation/Reduction of Aldehydes and Ketones

12.36 Draw a structural formula for the product formed by treating butanal with each of the following sets of reagents: **(See Examples 12.11, 12.12)**

(a) $LiAlH_4$ followed by H_2O
(b) $NaBH_4$ in CH_3OH/H_2O
(c) H_2/Pt
(d) $Ag(NH_3)_2^+$ in NH_3/H_2O and then HCl/H_2O
(e) H_2CrO_4
(f) $C_6H_5NH_2$ in the presence of H_2/Ni

12.37 Draw a structural formula for the product of the reaction of *p*-bromoacetophenone with each set of reagents in Problem 12.36. **(See Examples 12.11, 12.12)**

Synthesis

12.38 Show the reagents and conditions that will bring about the conversion of cyclohexanol to cyclohexanecarbaldehyde: **(See Example 12.7)**

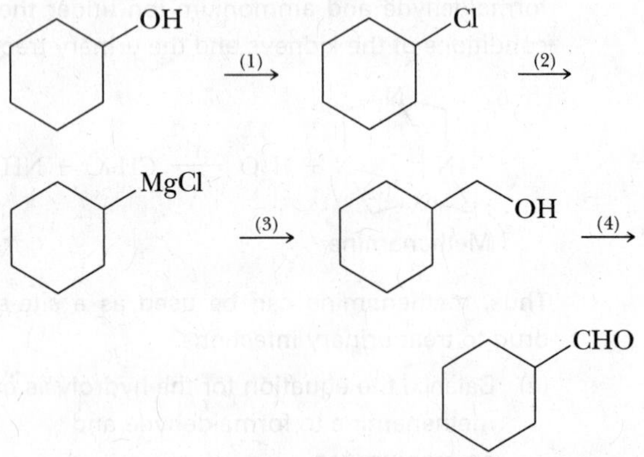

12.39 Starting with cyclohexanone, show how to prepare these compounds (in addition to the given starting material, use any other organic or inorganic reagents, as necessary): **(See Example 12.7)**

(a) Cyclohexanol
(b) Cyclohexene
(c) Bromocyclohexane
(d) 1-Methylcyclohexanol
(e) 1-Methylcyclohexene
(f) 1-Phenylcyclohexanol
(g) 1-Phenylcyclohexene
(h) Cyclohexene oxide
(i) *trans*-1,2-Cyclohexanediol

12.40 Show how to bring about these conversions (in addition to the given starting material, use any other organic or inorganic reagents, as necessary): **(See Example 12.7)**

(a) $C_6H_5\overset{O}{\overset{\|}{C}}CH_2CH_3 \longrightarrow C_6H_5\overset{OH}{\overset{|}{C}}HCH_2CH_3 \longrightarrow C_6H_5CH{=}CHCH_3$

(b)

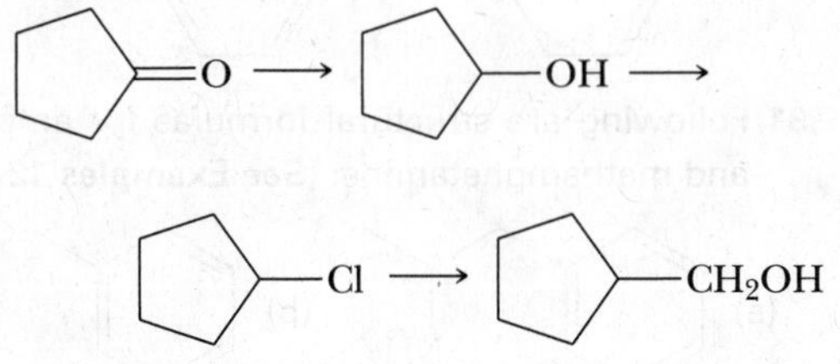

(c)

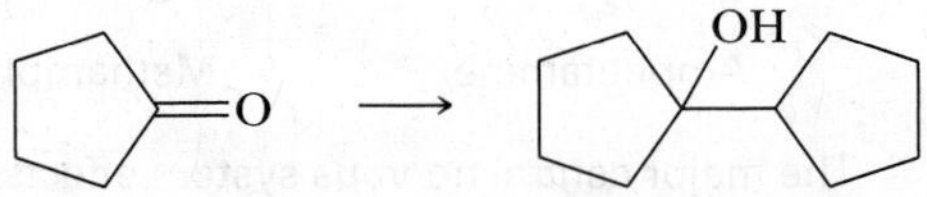

(d)

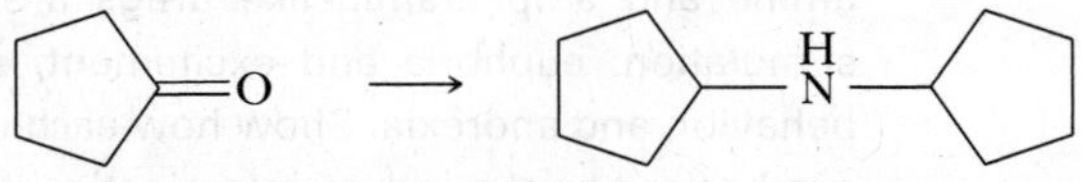

***12.41** Many tumors of the breast are estrogen dependent. Drugs that interfere with estrogen binding have antitumor activity and may even help prevent the occurrence of tumors. A widely used antiestrogen drug is tamoxifen: **(See Example 12.7)**

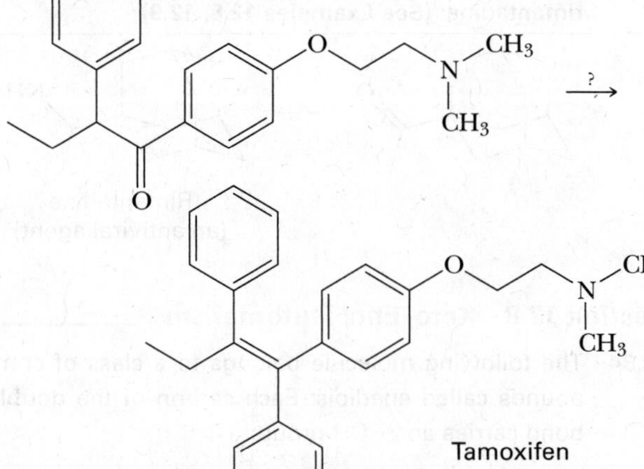

Tamoxifen

(a) How many stereoisomers are possible for tamoxifen?
(b) Specify the configuration of the stereoisomer shown here.
(c) Show how tamoxifen can be synthesized from the given ketone using a Grignard reaction, followed by dehydration.

***12.42** Following is a possible synthesis of the antidepressant bupropion (Wellbutrin®): **(See Example 12.7)**

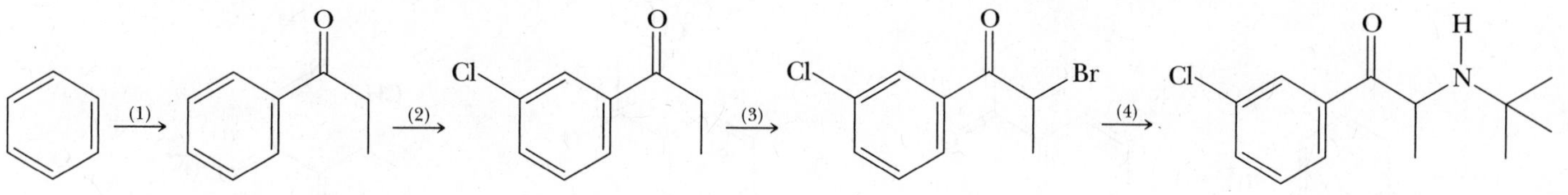

Bupropion (Wellbutrin®)

Show the reagents that will bring about each step in this synthesis.

***12.43** The synthesis of chlorpromazine in the 1950s and the discovery soon thereafter of the drug's antipsychotic activity opened the modern era of biochemical investigations into the pharmacology of the central nervous system. One of the compounds prepared in the search for more effective antipsychotics was amitriptyline. **(See Example 12.7)**

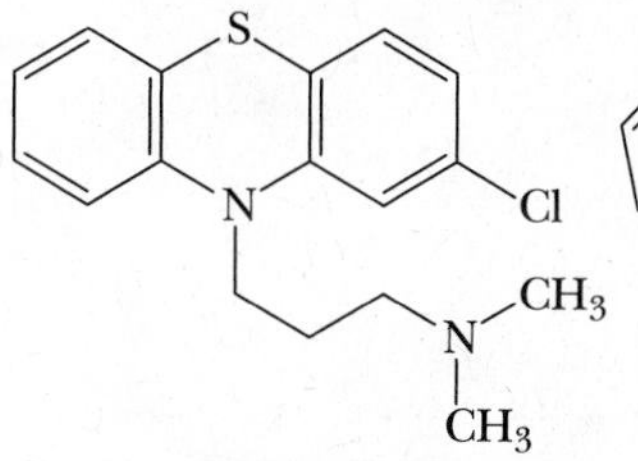

Chlorpromazine

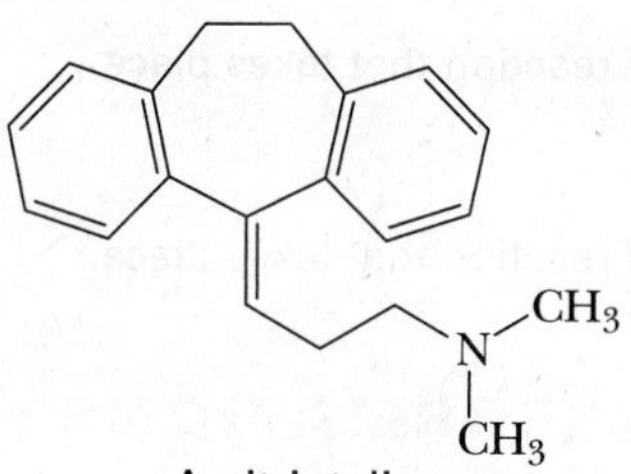

Amitriptyline

Surprisingly, amitriptyline shows antidepressant activity rather than antipsychotic activity. It is now known that amitriptyline inhibits the reuptake of norepinephrine and serotonin from the synaptic cleft. Because the reuptake of these neurotransmitters is inhibited, their effects are potentiated. That is, the two neurotransmitters remain available to interact with serotonin and norepinephrine receptor sites longer and continue to cause excitation of serotonin and norepinephrine-mediated neural pathways. The following is a synthesis for amitriptyline:

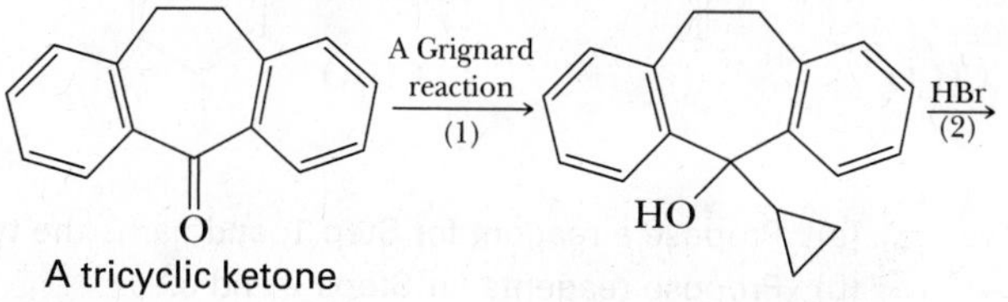

A tricyclic ketone

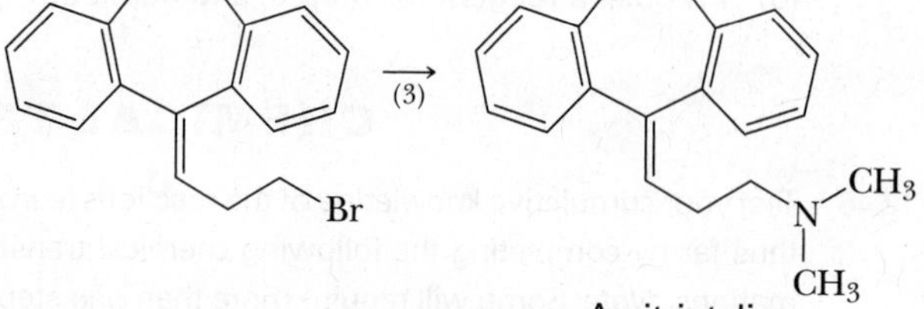

Amitriptyline

(a) Propose a reagent for Step 1.

(b) Propose a mechanism for Step 2. (*Note:* It is not acceptable to propose a primary carbocation as an intermediate.)

(c) Propose a reagent for Step 3.

***12.44** Following is a synthesis for diphenhydramine: **(See Example 12.7)**

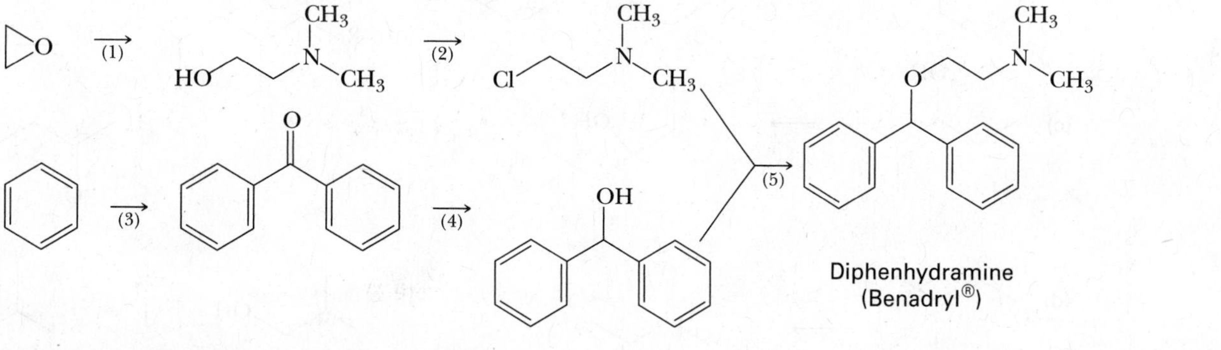

Diphenhydramine (Benadryl®)

The hydrochloride salt of this compound, best known by its trade name, Benadryl®, is an antihistamine.

(a) Propose reagents for Steps 1 and 2.

(b) Propose reagents for Steps 3 and 4.

(c) Show that Step 5 is an example of nucleophilic aliphatic substitution. What type of mechanism—S_N1 or S_N2—is more likely for this reaction? Explain.

*12.45 Following is a synthesis for the antidepressant venlafaxine: **(See Example 12.7)**

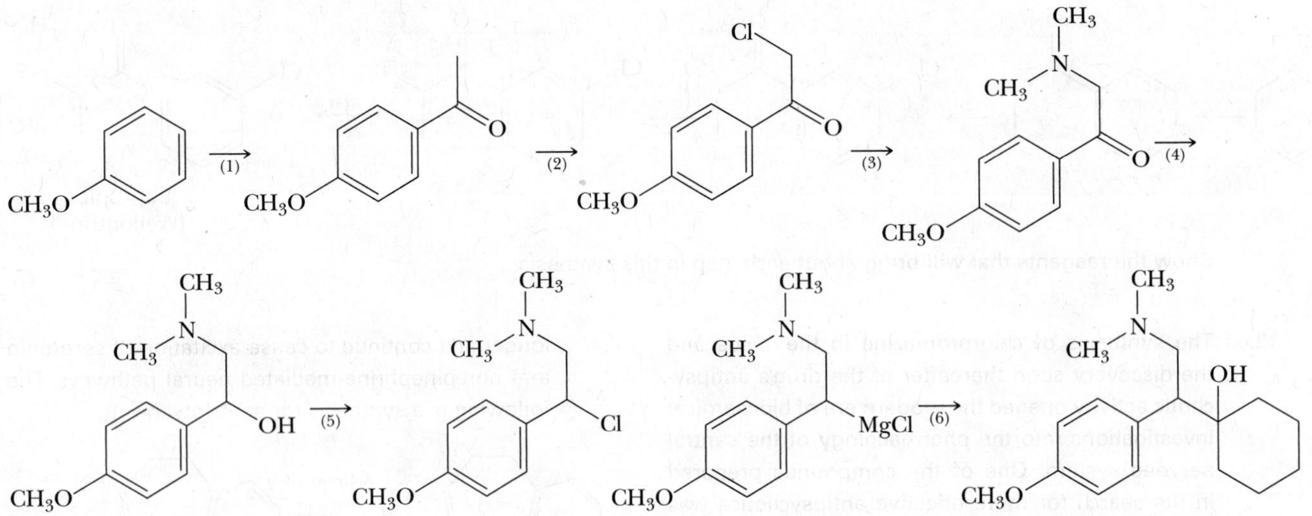

Venlafaxine

(a) Propose a reagent for Step 1, and name the type of reaction that takes place.
(b) Propose reagents for Steps 2 and 3.
(c) Propose reagents for Steps 4 and 5.
(d) Propose a reagent for Step 6, and name the type of reaction that takes place.

CHEMICAL TRANSFORMATIONS

12.46 Test your cumulative knowledge of the reactions learned thus far by completing the following chemical transformations. *Note*: Some will require more than one step.

(a)
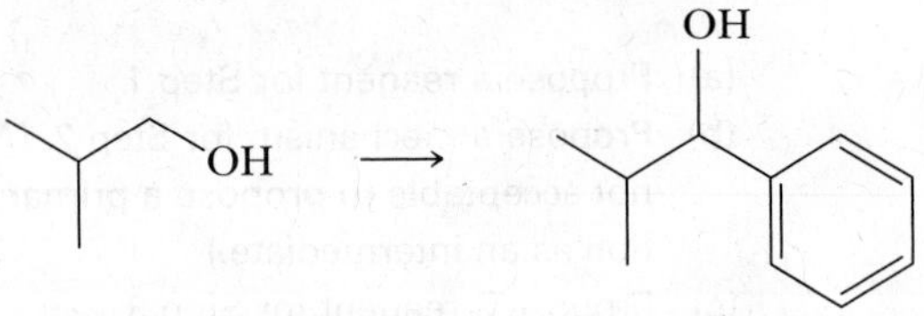

(b)
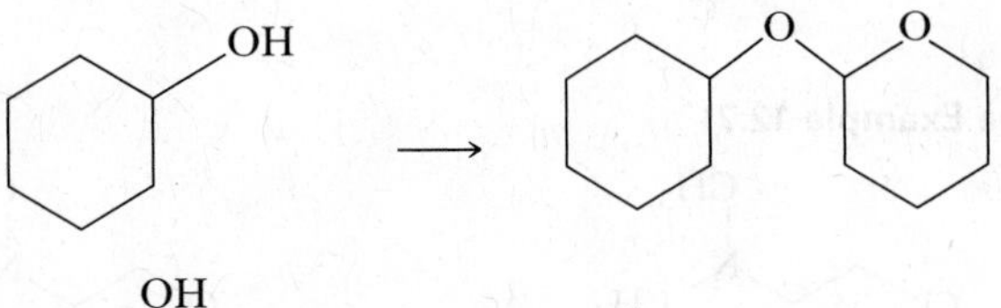

(c)
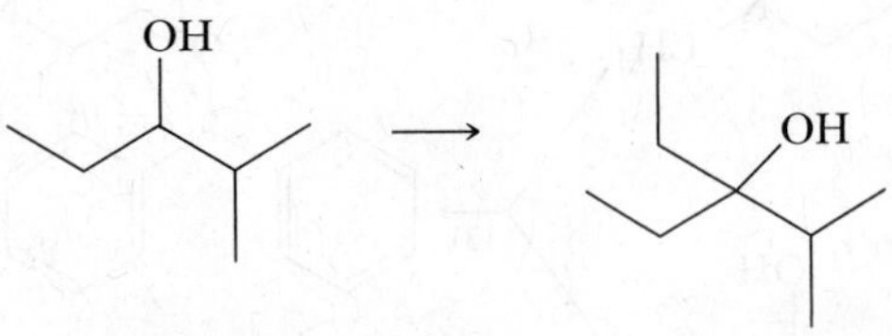

(d)
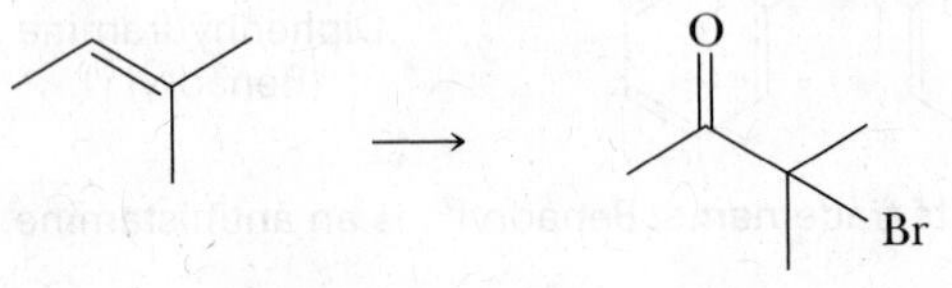

(e)
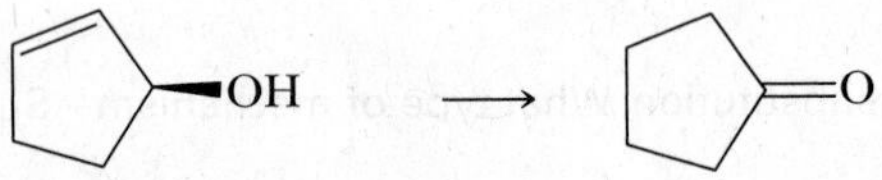

(f)
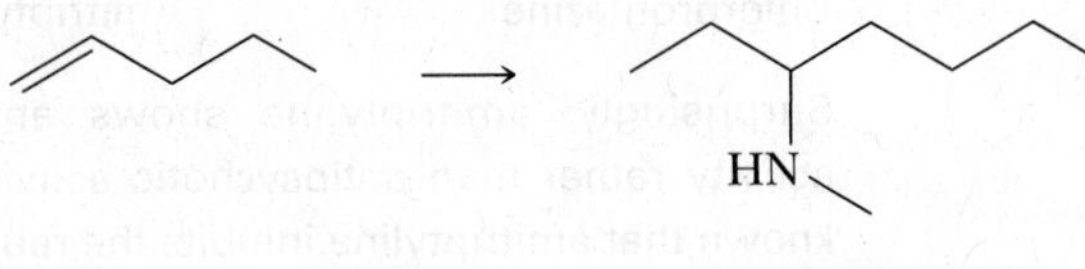

(g)
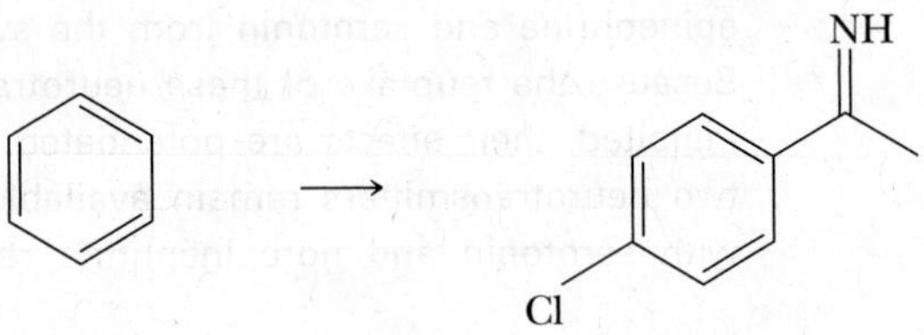

(h)
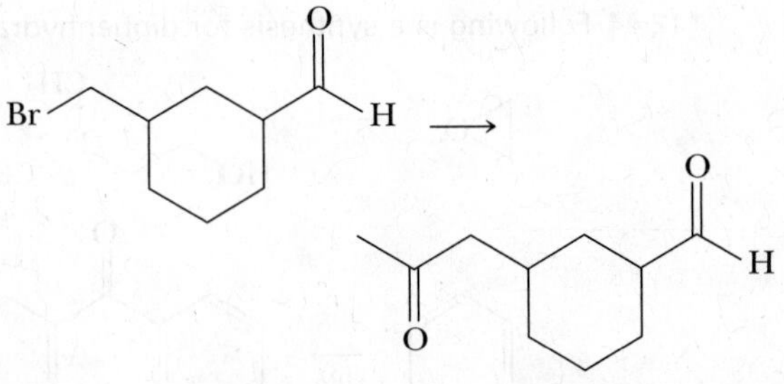

(i)

(j)
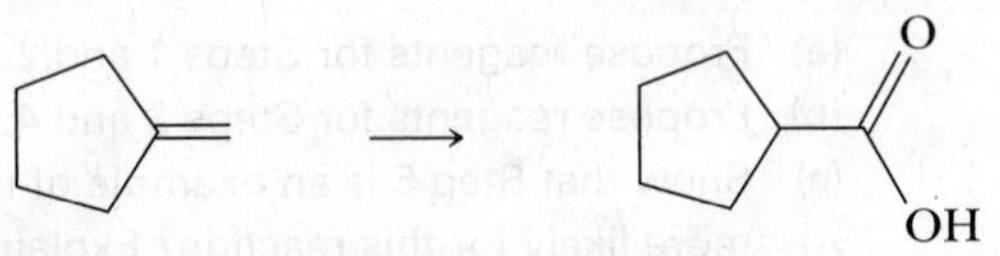

(k) 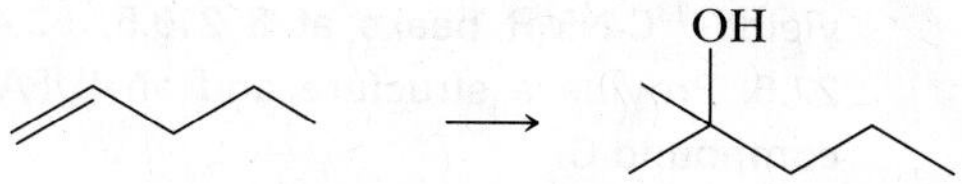

(o) 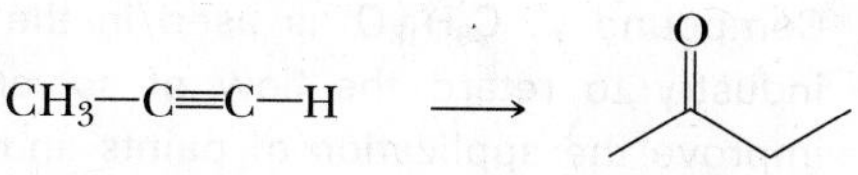

(l) 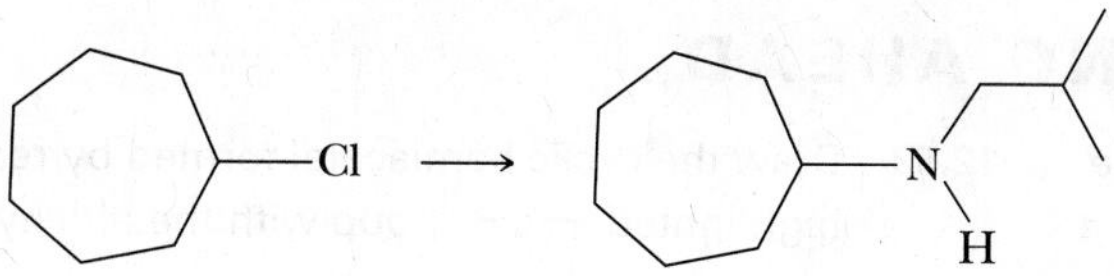

(p) 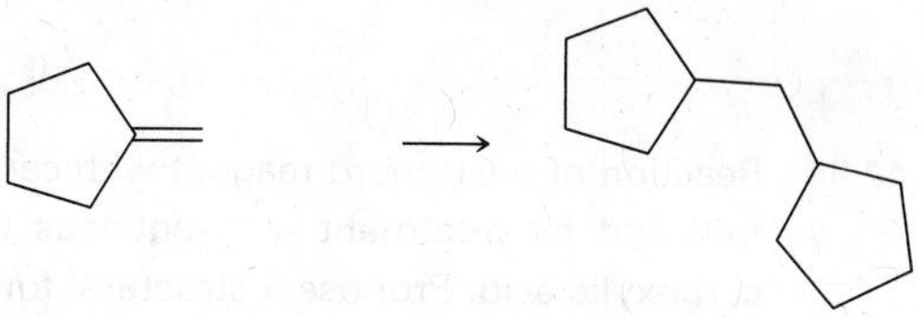

(m) 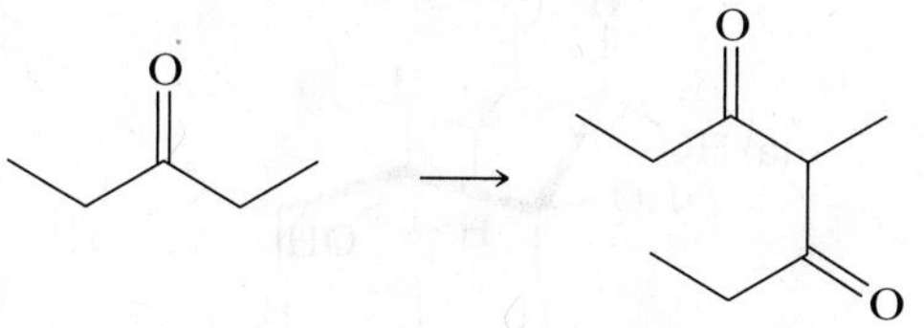

(q) 

(n) 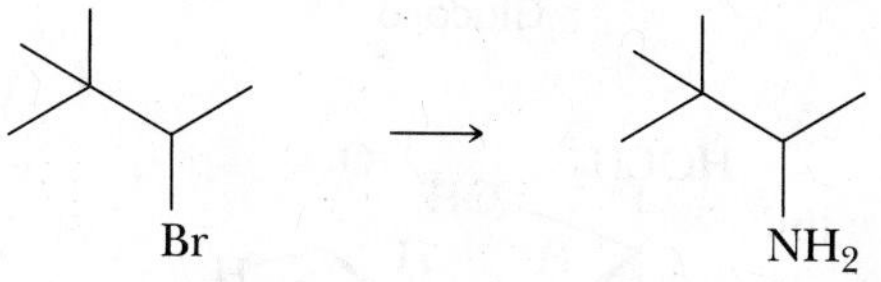

(r) 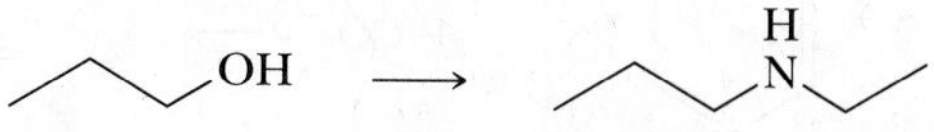

SPECTROSCOPY

12.47 Compound A, $C_5H_{10}O$, is used as a flavoring agent for many foods that possess a chocolate or peach flavor. Its common name is isovaleraldehyde, and it gives ^{13}C-NMR peaks at δ 202.7, 52.7, 23.6, and 22.6. Provide a structural formula for isovaleraldehyde and give its IUPAC name.

12.48 Following are ^1H-NMR and IR spectra of compound B, $C_6H_{12}O_2$:

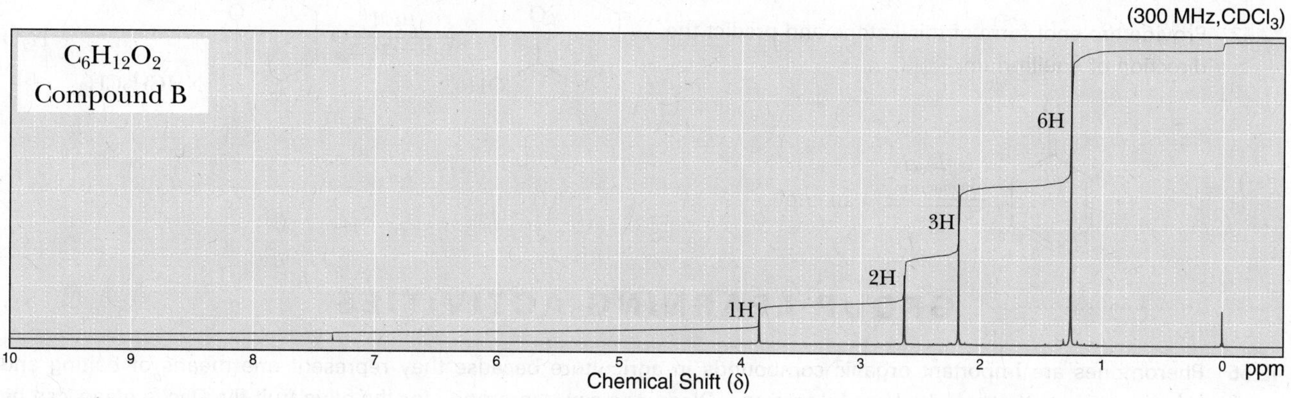

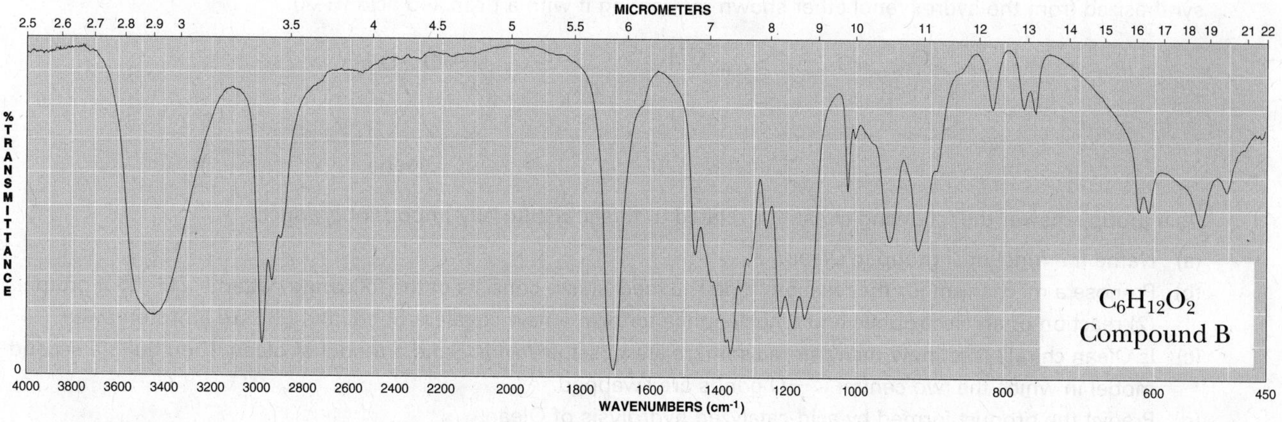

Propose a structural formula for compound B.

12.49 Compound C, $C_9H_{18}O$, is used in the automotive industry to retard the flow of solvent and thus improve the application of paints and coatings. It yields ^{13}C-NMR peaks at δ 210.5, 52.4, 24.5, and 22.6. Provide a structure and an IUPAC name for compound C.

LOOKING AHEAD

12.50 Reaction of a Grignard reagent with carbon dioxide, followed by treatment with aqueous HCl, gives a carboxylic acid. Propose a structural formula for the bracketed intermediate formed by the reaction of phenylmagnesium bromide with CO_2, and propose a mechanism for the formation of this intermediate:

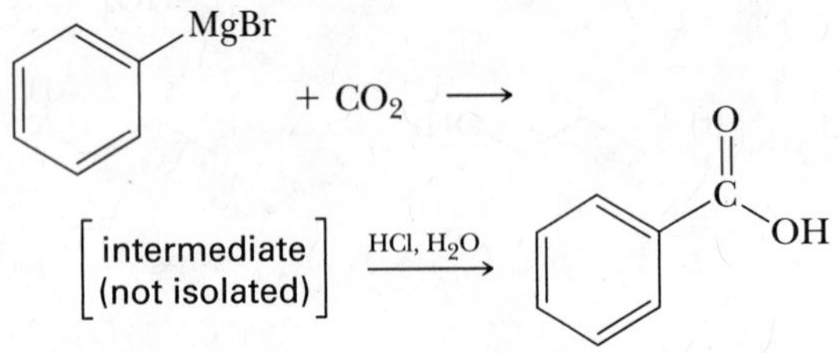

12.51 Rank the following carbonyls in order of increasing reactivity to nucleophilic attack, and explain your reasoning.

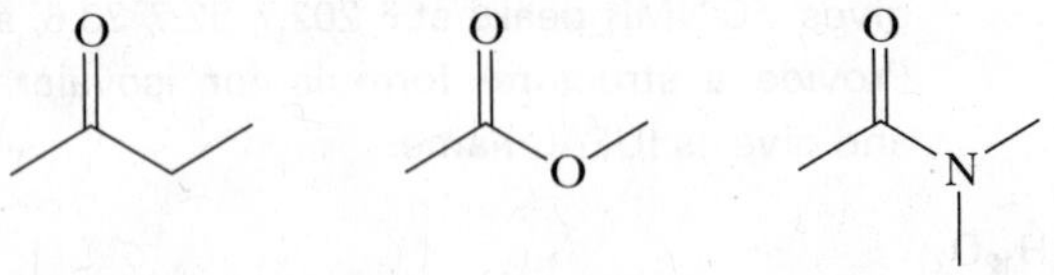

12.52 Provide the enol form of this ketone and predict the direction of equilibrium:

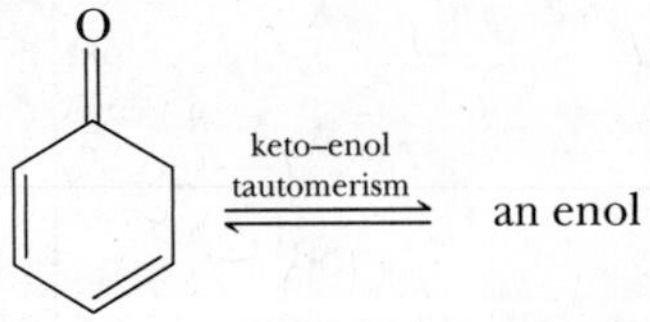

12.53 Draw the cyclic hemiacetal formed by reaction of the highlighted —OH group with the aldehyde group:

(a)
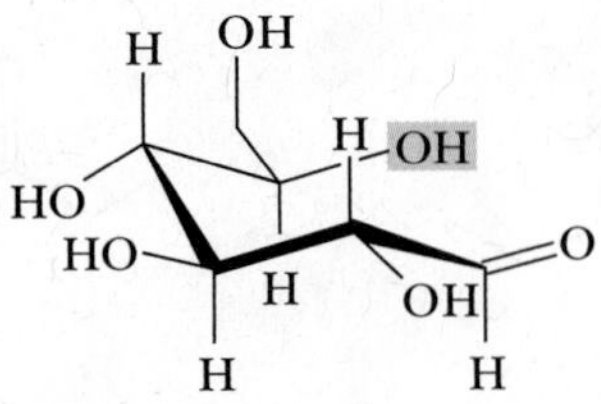

Glucose

(b)
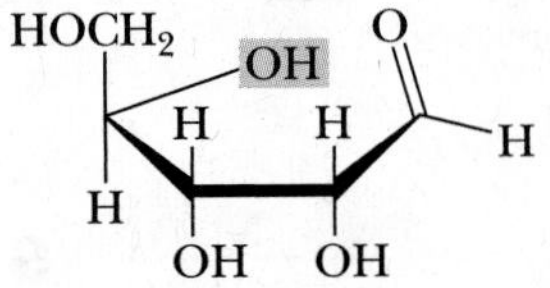

Ribose

12.54 Propose a mechanism for the acid-catalyzed reaction of the following hemiacetal, with an amine acting as a nucleophile:

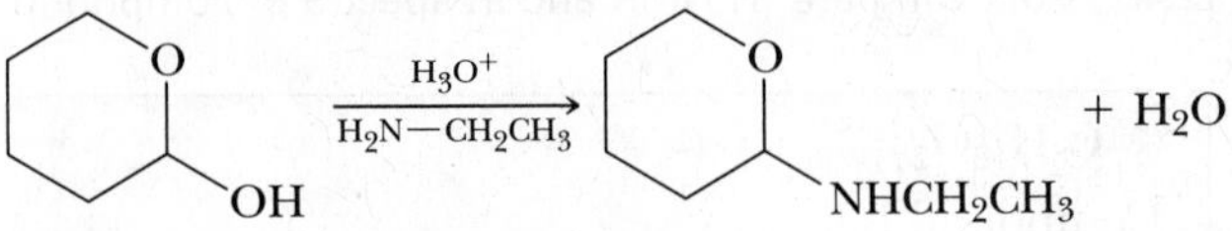

GROUP LEARNING ACTIVITIES

12.55 Pheromones are important organic compounds in agriculture because they represent one means of baiting and trapping insects that may be harmful to crops. Olean, the sex pheromone for the olive fruit fly, *Dacus oleae*, can be synthesized from the hydroxyenol ether shown by treating it with a Brønsted acid (H–A).

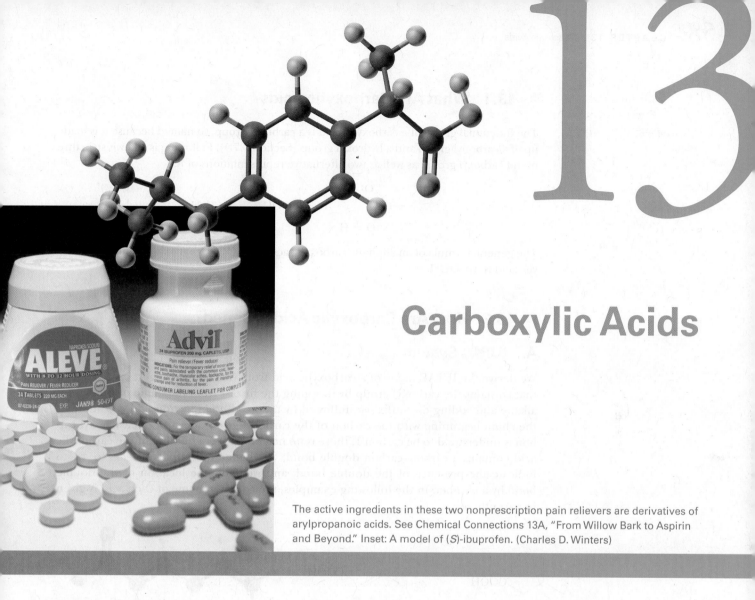

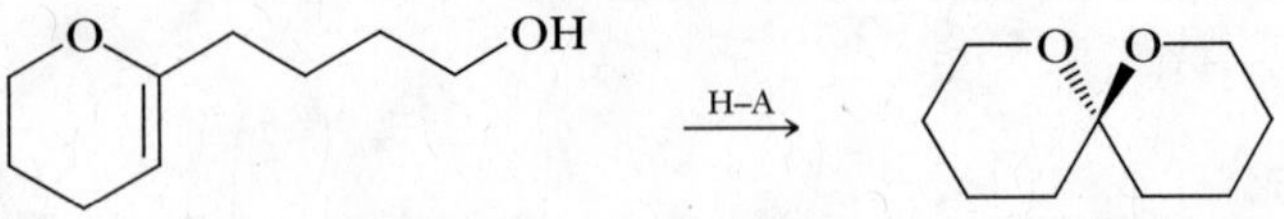

Olean

As a group, answer the following questions related to this agriculturally important product:

(a) Name the functional group in Olean.

(b) Propose a mechanism for the reaction. *Hint:* The mechanism consists of the following patterns: (1) add a proton, (2) reaction of an electrophile and a nucleophile to form a new covalent bond, and (3) take a proton away.

(c) Is Olean chiral? If so, how many stereoisomers are possible? *Hint:* Build a model of olean. Then build a second model in which the two central C—O bonds are swapped.

(d) Predict the product formed by acid-catalyzed hydrolysis of Olean.

13

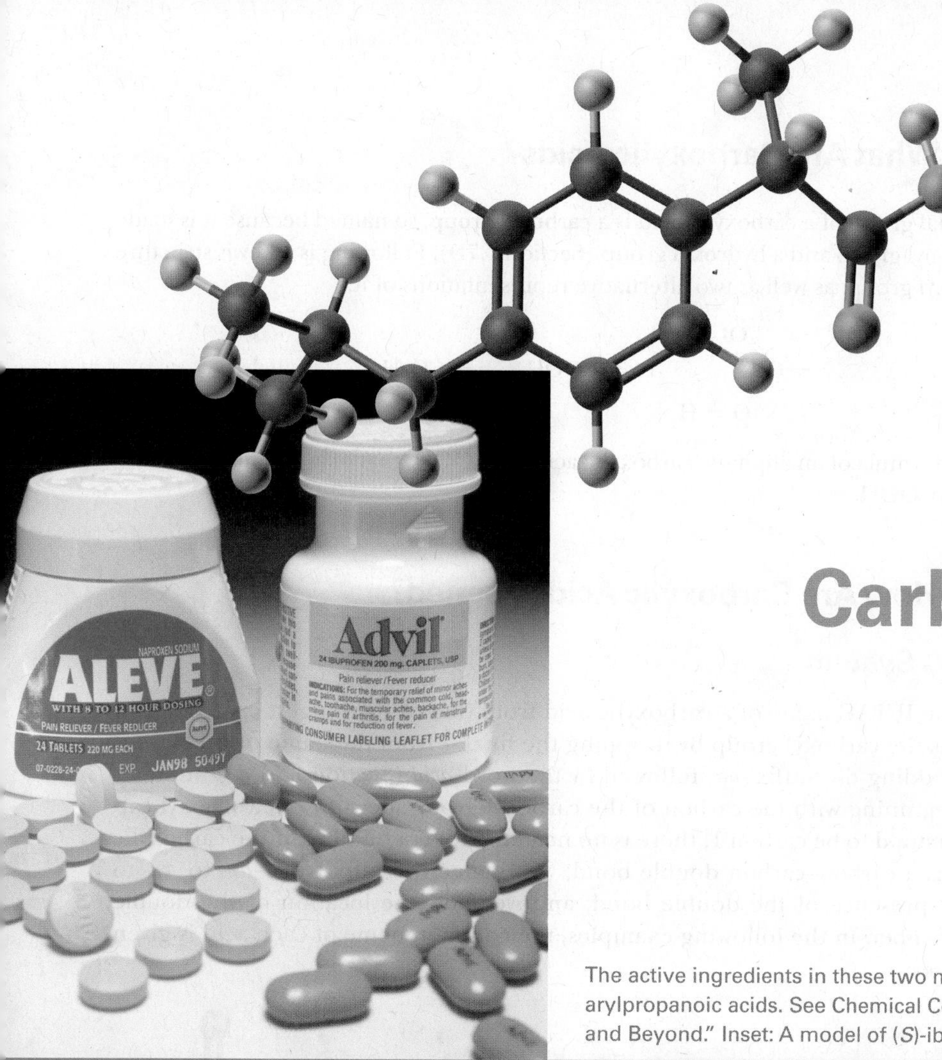

Carboxylic Acids

The active ingredients in these two nonprescription pain relievers are derivatives of arylpropanoic acids. See Chemical Connections 13A, "From Willow Bark to Aspirin and Beyond." Inset: A model of (*S*)-ibuprofen. (Charles D. Winters)

KEY QUESTIONS

- 13.1 What Are Carboxylic Acids?
- 13.2 How Are Carboxylic Acids Named?
- 13.3 What Are the Physical Properties of Carboxylic Acids?
- 13.4 What Are the Acid–Base Properties of Carboxylic Acids?
- 13.5 How Are Carboxyl Groups Reduced?
- 13.6 What Is Fischer Esterification?
- 13.7 What Are Acid Chlorides?
- 13.8 What Is Decarboxylation?

HOW TO

- 13.1 How to Predict the Product of a Fischer Esterification
- 13.2 How to Predict the Product of a β-Decarboxylation Reaction

CHEMICAL CONNECTIONS

- 13A From Willow Bark to Aspirin and Beyond
- 13B Esters as Flavoring Agents
- 13C Ketone Bodies and Diabetes

CARBOXYLIC ACIDS ARE another class of organic compounds containing the carbonyl group. Their occurrence in nature is widespread, and they are important components of foodstuffs such as vinegar, butter, and vegetable oils. The most important chemical property of carboxylic acids is their acidity. Furthermore, carboxylic acids form numerous important derivatives, including esters, amides, anhydrides, and acid halides. In this chapter, we study carboxylic acids themselves; in Chapters 14 and 15, we study their derivatives.

13.1 What Are Carboxylic Acids?

Carboxyl group A —COOH group.

The functional group of a carboxylic acid is a **carboxyl group**, so named because it is made up of a **carb**onyl group and a hydr**oxyl** group (Section 1.7D). Following is a Lewis structure of the carboxyl group, as well as two alternative representations of it:

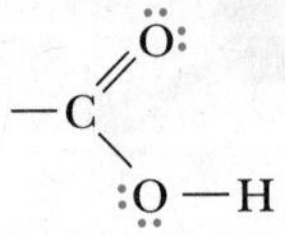

$-COOH$ $\quad$ $-CO_2H$

The general formula of an aliphatic carboxylic acid is RCOOH; that of an aromatic carboxylic acid is ArCOOH.

13.2 How Are Carboxylic Acids Named?

A. IUPAC System

We derive the IUPAC name of a carboxylic acid from that of the longest carbon chain that contains the carboxyl group by dropping the final *-e* from the name of the parent alkane and adding the suffix *-oic,* followed by the word *acid* (Section 3.5). We number the chain beginning with the carbon of the carboxyl group. Because the carboxyl carbon is understood to be carbon 1, there is no need to give it a number. If the carboxylic acid contains a carbon–carbon double bond, we change the infix from *-an-* to *-en-* to indicate the presence of the double bond, and we show the location of the double bond by a number. In the following examples, the common name of each acid is given in parentheses:

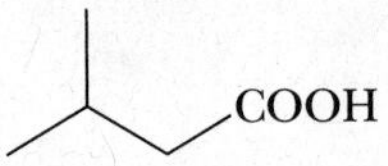

3-Methylbutanoic acid
(Isovaleric acid)

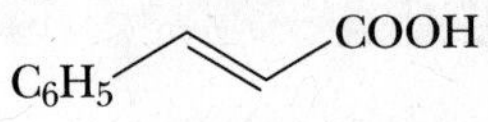

trans-3-Phenylpropenoic acid
(Cinnamic acid)

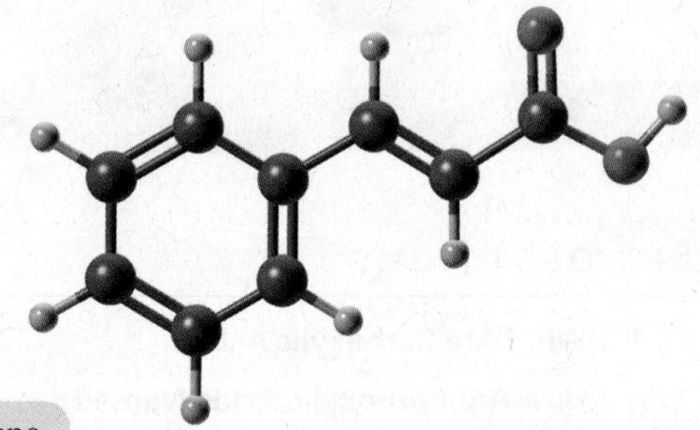

it is not necessary to indicate that the alkene occurs at position 2 because there is no other position where it can occur

In the IUPAC system, a carboxyl group takes precedence over most other functional groups (Table 12.1), including hydroxyl and amino groups, as well as the carbonyl groups of aldehydes and ketones. As illustrated in the following examples, an —OH group of an alcohol is indicated by the prefix *hydroxy-*, an $-NH_2$ group of an amine by *amino-*, and an =O group of an aldehyde or ketone by *oxo-*:

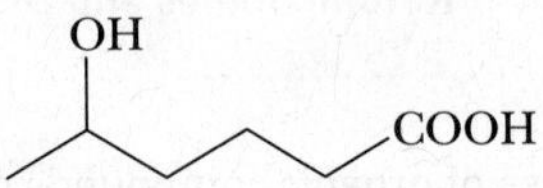

5-Hydroxyhexanoic acid

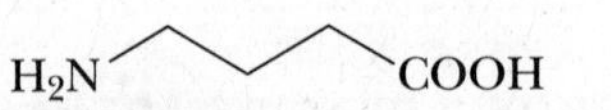

4-Aminobutanoic acid

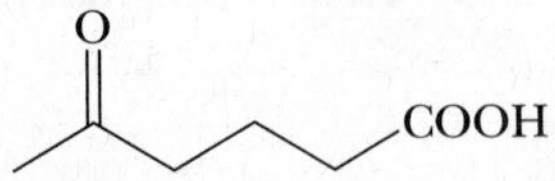

5-Oxohexanoic acid

Dicarboxylic acids are named by adding the suffix *-dioic,* followed by the word *acid,* to the name of the carbon chain that contains both carboxyl groups. Because the two carboxyl groups can be only at the ends of the parent chain, there is no need to number them. Following are IUPAC names and common names for several important aliphatic dicarboxylic acids:

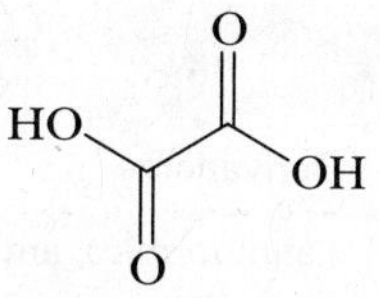

Ethanedioic acid
(Oxalic acid)

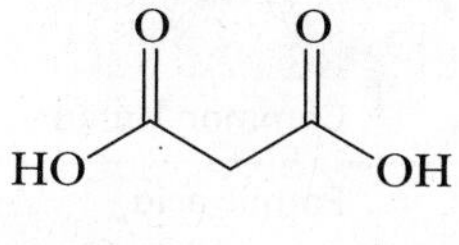

Propanedioic acid
(Malonic acid)

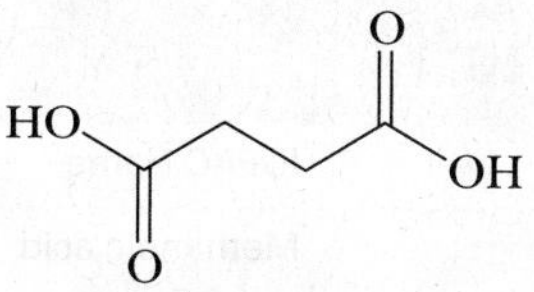

Butanedioic acid
(Succinic acid)

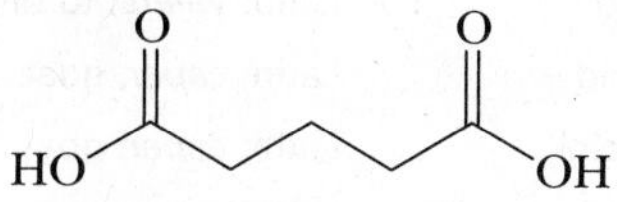

Pentanedioic acid
(Glutaric acid)

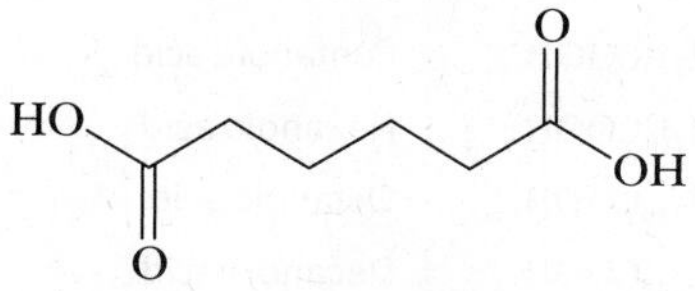

Hexanedioic acid
(Adipic acid)

The name *oxalic acid* is derived from one of its sources in the biological world, namely, plants of the genus *Oxalis,* one of which is rhubarb. Oxalic acid also occurs in human and animal urine, and calcium oxalate (the calcium salt of oxalic acid) is a major component of kidney stones. Adipic acid is one of the two monomers required for the synthesis of the polymer nylon 66. The U.S. chemical industry produces approximately 1.8 billion pounds of adipic acid annually, solely for the synthesis of nylon 66 (Section 16.4A).

Lisa Kyle Young/Getty Images, Inc.

Leaves of the rhubarb plant contain oxalic acid as its potassium and sodium salts.

A carboxylic acid containing a carboxyl group bonded to a cycloalkane ring is named by giving the name of the ring and adding the suffix *-carboxylic acid.* The atoms of the ring are numbered beginning with the carbon bearing the —COOH group:

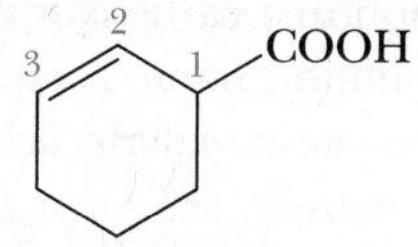

2-Cyclohexenecarboxylic acid

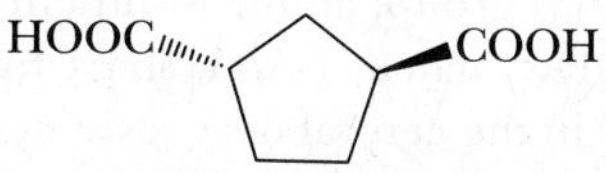

trans-1,3-Cyclopentanedicarboxylic acid

The simplest aromatic carboxylic acid is benzoic acid. Derivatives are named by using numbers and prefixes to show the presence and location of substituents relative to the carboxyl group. Certain aromatic carboxylic acids have common names by which they are more usually known. For example, 2-hydroxybenzoic acid is more often called salicylic acid, a name derived from the fact that this aromatic carboxylic acid was first obtained from the bark of the willow, a tree of the genus *Salix.* Aromatic dicarboxylic acids are named by adding the words *dicarboxylic acid* to *benzene.* Examples are 1,2-benzenedicarboxylic acid and 1,4-benzenedicarboxylic acid. Each is more usually known by its common name: phthalic acid and terephthalic acid, respectively. Terephthalic acid is one of the two organic components required for the synthesis of the textile fiber known as Dacron® polyester (Section 16.4B).

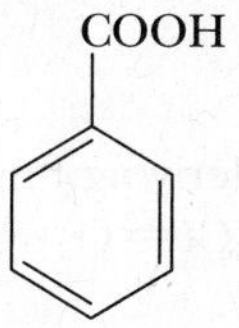

Benzoic acid

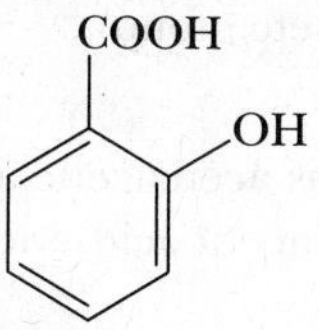

2-Hydroxybenzoic acid
(Salicylic acid)

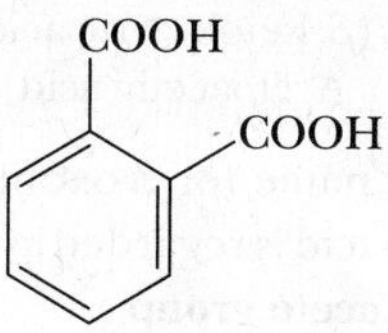

1,2-Benzenedicarboxylic acid
(Phthalic acid)

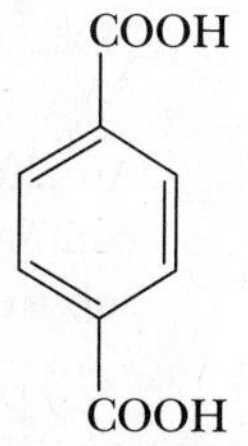

1,4-Benzenedicarboxylic acid
(Terephthalic acid)

B. Common Names

Aliphatic carboxylic acids, many of which were known long before the development of structural theory and IUPAC nomenclature, are named according to their source or for

Fotosearch RF/Getty Images, Inc.

Formic acid was first obtained in 1670 from the destructive distillation of ants, whose genus is *Formica*. It is one of the components of the venom of stinging ants.

TABLE 13.1 Several Aliphatic Carboxylic Acids and Their Common Names

Structure	IUPAC Name	Common Name	Derivation
$HCOOH$	Methanoic acid	Formic acid	Latin: *formica*, ant
CH_3COOH	Ethanoic acid	Acetic acid	Latin: *acetum*, vinegar
CH_3CH_2COOH	Propanoic acid	Propionic acid	Greek: *propion*, first fat
$CH_3(CH_2)_2COOH$	Butanoic acid	Butyric acid	Latin: *butyrum*, butter
$CH_3(CH_2)_3COOH$	Pentanoic acid	Valeric acid	Latin: *valere*, to be strong
$CH_3(CH_2)_4COOH$	Hexanoic acid	Caproic acid	Latin: *caper*, goat
$CH_3(CH_2)_6COOH$	Octanoic acid	Caprylic acid	Latin: *caper*, goat
$CH_3(CH_2)_8COOH$	Decanoic acid	Capric acid	Latin: *caper*, goat
$CH_3(CH_2)_{10}COOH$	Dodecanoic acid	Lauric acid	Latin: *laurus*, laurel
$CH_3(CH_2)_{12}COOH$	Tetradecanoic acid	Myristic acid	Greek: *myristikos*, fragrant
$CH_3(CH_2)_{14}COOH$	Hexadecanoic acid	Palmitic acid	Latin: *palma*, palm tree
$CH_3(CH_2)_{16}COOH$	Octadecanoic acid	Stearic acid	Greek: *stear*, solid fat
$CH_3(CH_2)_{18}COOH$	Icosanoic acid	Arachidic acid	Greek: *arachis*, peanut

some characteristic property. Table 13.1 lists several of the unbranched aliphatic carboxylic acids found in the biological world, along with the common name of each. Those with 16, 18, and 20 carbon atoms are particularly abundant in fats and oils (Section 19.1) and the phospholipid components of biological membranes (Section 19.3).

When common names are used, the Greek letters α, β, γ, δ, and so forth are often added as a prefix to locate substituents. The α-position in a carboxylic acid is the position next to the carboxyl group; an α-substituent in a common name is equivalent to a 2-substituent in an IUPAC name. *GABA*, short for gamma-*a*mino*b*utyric *a*cid, is an inhibitory neurotransmitter in the central nervous system of humans:

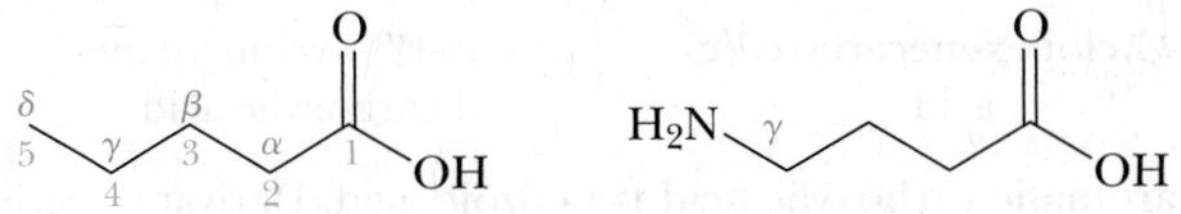

4-Aminobutanoic acid
(γ-Aminobutyric acid, GABA)

In common nomenclature, the prefix *keto-* indicates the presence of a ketone carbonyl in a substituted carboxylic acid (as illustrated by the common name β-ketobutyric acid):

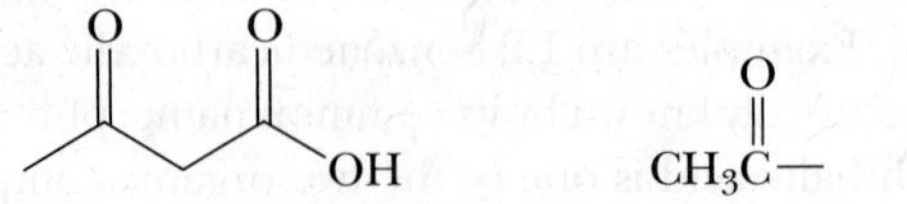

3-Oxobutanoic acid (β-Ketobutyric acid; Acetoacetic acid)

Acetyl group (Aceto group)

Aceto group A $CH_3C(=O)$ group.

An alternative common name for 3-oxobutanoic acid is acetoacetic acid. In deriving this common name, this ketoacid is regarded as a substituted acetic acid, and the $CH_3C(=O)-$ substituent is named an **aceto group**.

EXAMPLE 13.1

Write the IUPAC name for each carboxylic acid:

(a) 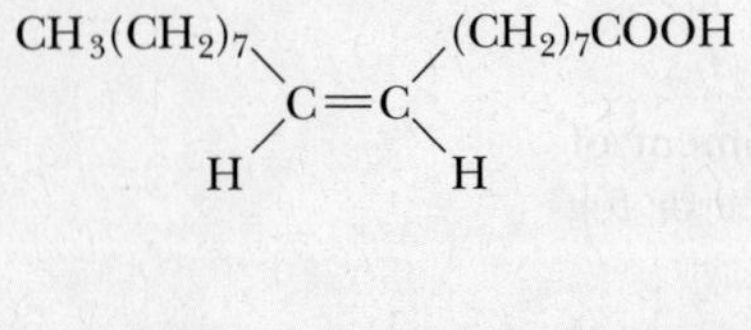

(b) 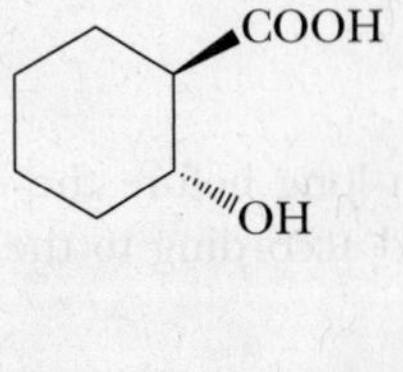

(c) 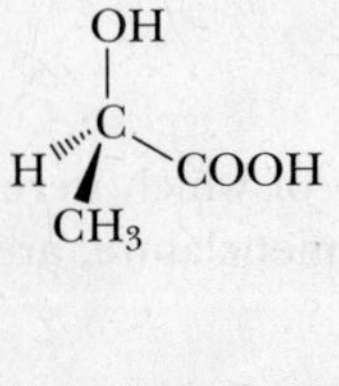

(d) $ClCH_2COOH$

STRATEGY

Identify the longest chain of carbon atoms that contains the carboxyl group to determine the root name. The suffix *-e* is then changed to *-anoic acid.* For cyclic carboxylic acids, *carboxylic acid* is appended to the name of the cycloalkane (without dropping the suffix *-e*). As usual, remember to note stereochemistry (*E/Z, cis/trans,* or *R/S*) where appropriate.

SOLUTION

(a) *cis*-9-Octadecenoic acid (oleic acid)

(b) *trans*-2-Hydroxycyclohexanecarboxylic acid

(c) (*R*)-2-Hydroxypropanoic acid [(*R*)-lactic acid]

(d) Chloroethanoic acid (chloroacetic acid)

See problems 13.9–13.12, 13.15

PROBLEM 13.1

Each of the following compounds has a well-recognized common name. A derivative of glyceric acid is an intermediate in glycolysis (Section 21.3). Maleic acid is an intermediate in the tricarboxylic acid (TCA) cycle. Mevalonic acid is an intermediate in the biosynthesis of steroids (Section 19.4B).

(a) 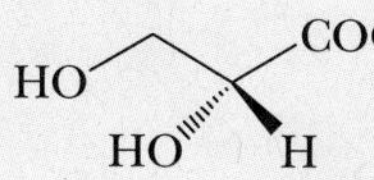

Glyceric acid

(b) 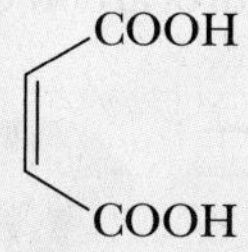

Maleic acid

(c) 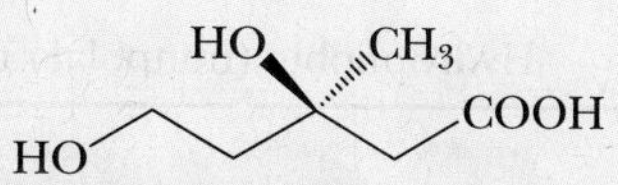

Mevalonic acid

Write the IUPAC name for each compound. Be certain to show the configuration of each.

13.3 What Are the Physical Properties of Carboxylic Acids?

In the liquid and solid states, carboxylic acids are associated by intermolecular hydrogen bonding into dimers, as shown for acetic acid:

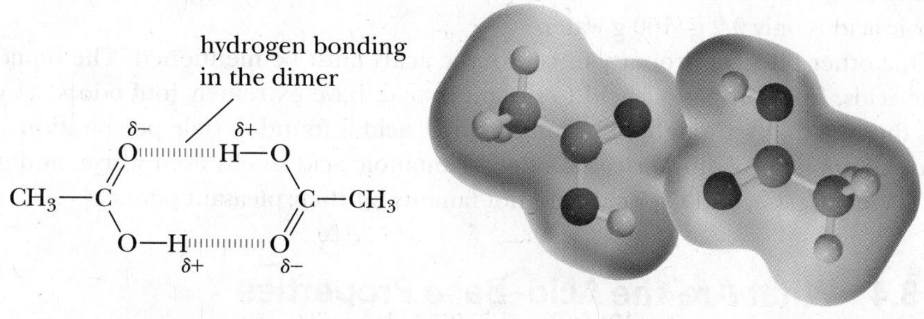

Carboxylic acids have significantly higher boiling points than other types of organic compounds of comparable molecular weight, such as alcohols, aldehydes, and ketones. For example, butanoic acid (Table 13.2) has a higher boiling point than either 1-pentanol or pentanal. The higher boiling points of carboxylic acids result from their polarity and from the fact that they form very strong intermolecular hydrogen bonds.

Carboxylic acids also interact with water molecules by hydrogen bonding through both their carbonyl and hydroxyl groups. Because of these hydrogen-bonding interactions, carboxylic acids are more soluble in water than are alcohols, ethers, aldehydes, and ketones with comparable molecular weight. The solubility of a carboxylic acid in water decreases as its molecular weight increases. We account for this trend in the following way: A carboxylic acid consists of two regions of different polarity—a polar hydrophilic carboxyl group and, except

TABLE 13.2 Boiling Points and Solubilities in Water of Selected Carboxylic Acids, Alcohols, and Aldehydes of Comparable Molecular Weight

Structure	Name	Molecular Weight	Boiling Point (°C)	Solubility (g/100 mL H_2O)
CH_3COOH	acetic acid	60.5	118	infinite
$CH_3CH_2CH_2OH$	1-propanol	60.1	97	infinite
CH_3CH_2CHO	propanal	58.1	48	16
$CH_3(CH_2)_2COOH$	butanoic acid	88.1	163	infinite
$CH_3(CH_2)_3CH_2OH$	1-pentanol	88.1	137	2.3
$CH_3(CH_2)_3CHO$	pentanal	86.1	103	slight
$CH_3(CH_2)_4COOH$	hexanoic acid	116.2	205	1.0
$CH_3(CH_2)_5CH_2OH$	1-heptanol	116.2	176	0.2
$CH_3(CH_2)_5CHO$	heptanal	114.1	153	0.1

Hydrophilic From the Greek, meaning "water loving."

Hydrophobic From the Greek, meaning "water hating."

for formic acid, a nonpolar hydrophobic hydrocarbon chain. The **hydrophilic** carboxyl group increases water solubility; the **hydrophobic** hydrocarbon chain decreases water solubility.

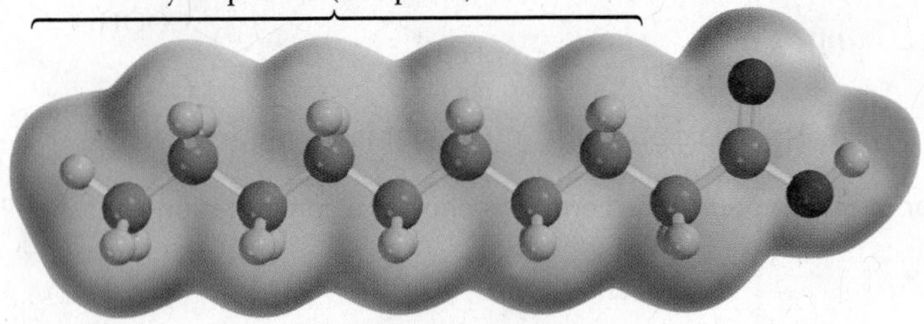

Decanoic acid
(0.2 g/100 mL H_2O)

The first four aliphatic carboxylic acids (formic, acetic, propanoic, and butanoic acids) are infinitely soluble in water because the hydrophilic character of the carboxyl group more than counterbalances the hydrophobic character of the hydrocarbon chain. As the size of the hydrocarbon chain increases relative to the size of the carboxyl group, water solubility decreases. The solubility of hexanoic acid in water is 1.0 g/100 g water; that of decanoic acid is only 0.2 g/100 g water.

One other physical property of carboxylic acids must be mentioned: The liquid carboxylic acids, from propanoic acid to decanoic acid, have extremely foul odors, about as bad as those of thiols, though different. Butanoic acid is found in stale perspiration and is a major component of "locker room odor." Pentanoic acid smells even worse, and goats, which secrete C_6, C_8, and C_{10} acids, are not famous for their pleasant odors.

13.4 What Are the Acid–Base Properties of Carboxylic Acids?

A. Acid Ionization Constants

Carboxylic acids are weak acids. Values of K_a for most unsubstituted aliphatic and aromatic carboxylic acids fall within the range from 10^{-4} to 10^{-5}. The value of K_a for acetic acid, for example, is 1.74×10^{-5}, and the pK_a of acetic acid is 4.76:

$$CH_3COOH + H_2O \rightleftharpoons CH_3COO^- + H_3O^+$$

$$K_a = \frac{[CH_3COO^-][H_3O^+]}{[CH_3COOH]} = 1.74 \times 10^{-5}$$

$$pK_a = 4.76$$

As we discussed in Section 2.5B, carboxylic acids (pK_a 4–5) are stronger acids than alcohols (pK_a 16–18) because resonance stabilizes the **carboxylate** anion by delocalizing its negative charge. No comparable resonance stabilization exists in alkoxide ions.

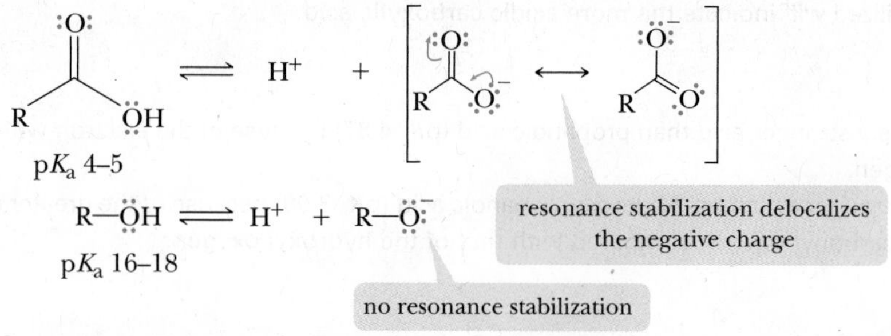

Substitution at the α-carbon of an atom or a group of atoms of higher electronegativity than carbon increases the acidity of carboxylic acids, often by several orders of magnitude (Section 2.5C). Compare, for example, the acidities of acetic acid (pK_a 4.76) and chloroacetic acid (pK_a 2.86). A single chlorine substituent on the α-carbon increases acid strength by nearly 100! Both dichloroacetic acid and trichloroacetic acid are stronger acids than phosphoric acid (pK_a 2.1):

the inductive effect of an electronegative atom delocalizes the negative charge and stabilizes the carboxylate ion

Formula:	CH_3COOH	$ClCH_2COOH$	$Cl_2CHCOOH$	Cl_3CCOOH
Name:	Acetic acid	Chloroacetic acid	Dichloroacetic acid	Trichloroacetic acid
pK_a:	4.76	2.86	1.48	0.70

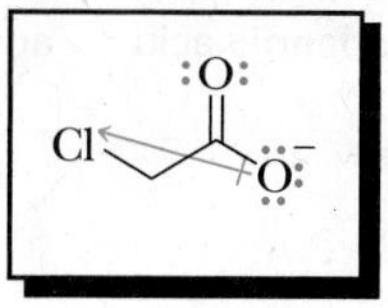

Increasing acid strength →

The acid-strengthening effect of halogen substitution falls off rather rapidly with increasing distance from the carboxyl group. Although the acid ionization constant for 2-chlorobutanoic acid (pK_a 2.83) is 100 times that for butanoic acid, the acid ionization constant for 4-chlorobutanoic acid (pK_a 4.52) is only about twice that for butanoic acid:

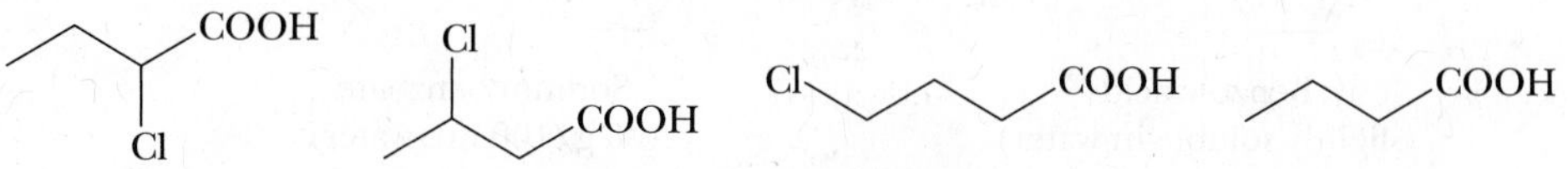

2-Chlorobutanoic acid (pK_a 2.83) | 3-Chlorobutanoic acid (pK_a 3.98) | 4-Chlorobutanoic acid (pK_a 4.52) | Butanoic acid (pK_a 4.82)

Decreasing acid strength →

EXAMPLE 13.2

Which acid in each set is the stronger?

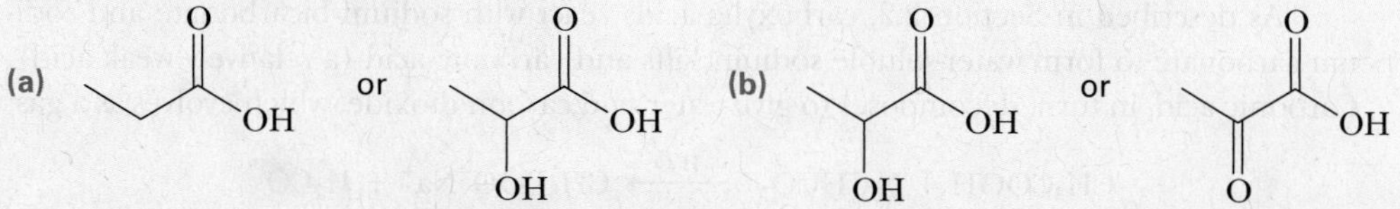

(a) Propanoic acid or 2-Hydroxypropanoic acid (Lactic acid)

(b) 2-Hydroxypropanoic acid (Lactic acid) or 2-Oxopropanoic acid (Pyruvic acid)

STRATEGY

Draw the conjugate base of each acid and look for possible stabilization of the ion via resonance or inductive effects. The conjugate base that is more greatly stabilized will indicate the more acidic carboxylic acid.

SOLUTION

(a) 2-Hydroxypropanoic acid (pK_a 3.85) is a stronger acid than propanoic acid (pK_a 4.87) because of the electron-withdrawing inductive effect of the hydroxyl oxygen.

(b) 2-Oxopropanoic acid (pK_a 2.06) is a stronger acid than 2-hydroxypropanoic acid (pK_a 3.08) because of the greater electron-withdrawing inductive effect of the carbonyl oxygen compared with that of the hydroxyl oxygen.

See problems 13.20–13.22, 13.48

PROBLEM 13.2

Match each compound with its appropriate pK_a value:

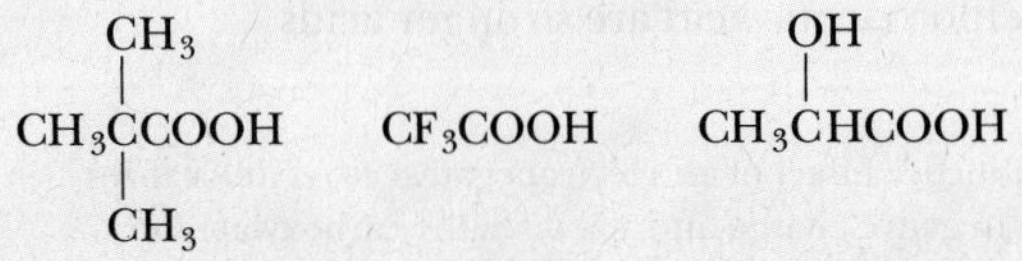

pK_a values= 5.03, 3.85, and 0.22.

2,2-Dimethylpropanoic acid — Trifluoroacetic acid — 2-Hydroxypropanoic acid (Lactic acid)

B. Reaction with Bases

All carboxylic acids, whether soluble or insoluble in water, react with NaOH, KOH, and other strong bases to form water-soluble salts:

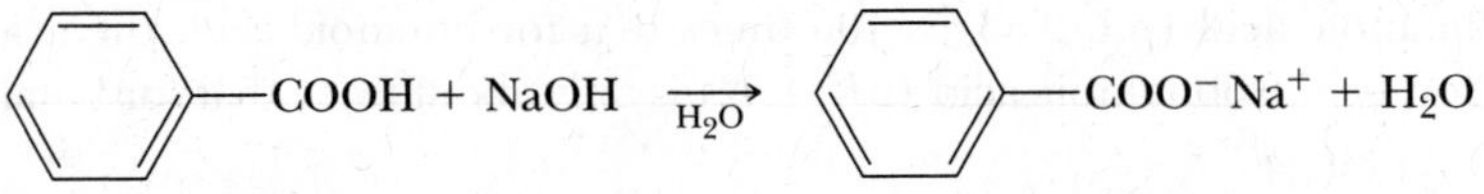

Benzoic acid (slightly soluble in water) — Sodium benzoate (60 g/100 mL water)

Sodium benzoate, a fungal growth inhibitor, is often added to baked goods "to retard spoilage." Calcium propanoate is used for the same purpose.

Carboxylic acids also form water-soluble salts with ammonia and amines:

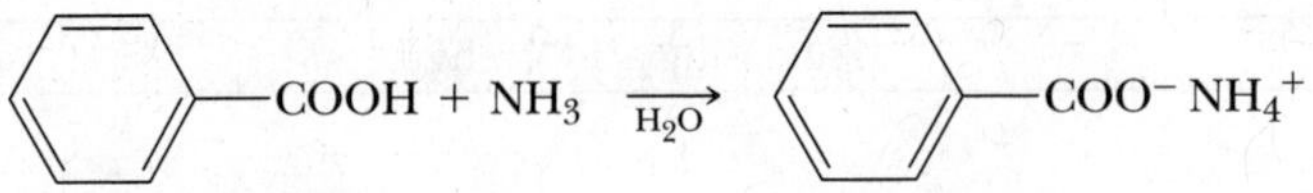

Benzoic acid (slightly soluble in water) — Ammonium benzoate (20 g/100 mL water)

As described in Section 2.2, carboxylic acids react with sodium bicarbonate and sodium carbonate to form water-soluble sodium salts and carbonic acid (a relatively weak acid). Carbonic acid, in turn, decomposes to give water and carbon dioxide, which evolves as a gas:

$$CH_3COOH + Na^+HCO_3^- \xrightarrow{H_2O} CH_3COO^-Na^+ + H_2CO_3$$

$$H_2CO_3 \longrightarrow CO_2 + H_2O$$

$$CH_3COOH + Na^+HCO_3^- \longrightarrow CH_3COO^-Na^+ + CO_2 + H_2O$$

Salts of carboxylic acids are named in the same manner as are salts of inorganic acids: Name the cation first and then the anion. Derive the name of the anion from the name of the carboxylic acid by dropping the suffix *-ic acid* and adding the suffix *-ate*. For example, the name of $CH_3CH_2COO^-Na^+$ is sodium propanoate, and that of $CH_3(CH_2)_{14}COO^-Na^+$ is sodium hexadecanoate (sodium palmitate).

EXAMPLE 13.3

Complete each acid–base reaction and name the salt formed:

(a)

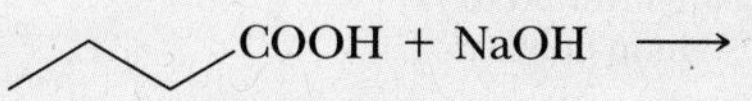
COOH + NaOH ⟶

(b)

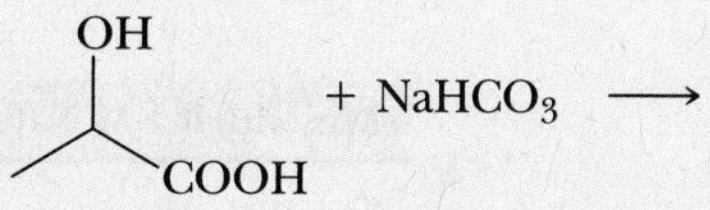
OH
+ NaHCO3 ⟶
COOH

STRATEGY

Identify the base and the most acidic hydrogen of the acid. Remember that sodium bicarbonate ($NaHCO_3$) typically reacts to yield carbonic acid, which subsequently decomposes to give CO_2 and H_2O.

SOLUTION

Each carboxylic acid is converted to its sodium salt. In (b), carbonic acid is formed (not shown) and decomposes to carbon dioxide and water:

(a)

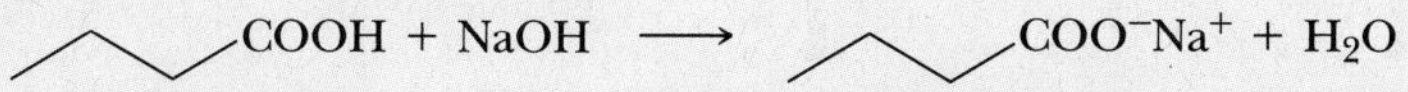
COOH + NaOH ⟶
COO⁻Na⁺ + H2O

Butanoic acid — Sodium butanoate

(b)

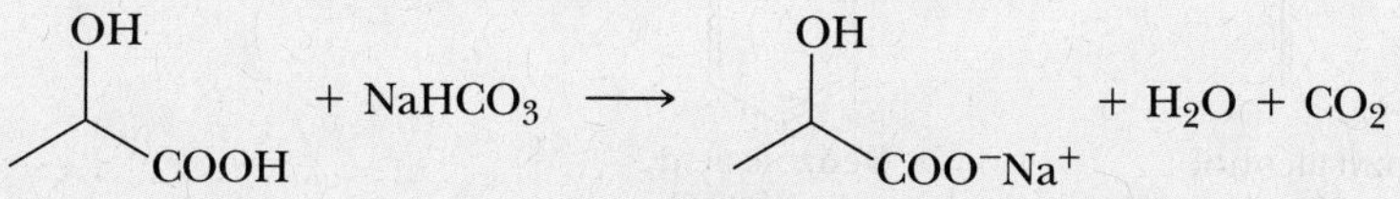

2-Hydroxypropanoic acid (Lactic acid) — Sodium 2-hydroxypropanoate (Sodium lactate)

See problems 13.23, 13.34

PROBLEM 13.3

Write an equation for the reaction of each acid in Example 13.3 with ammonia, and name the salt formed.

A consequence of the water solubility of carboxylic acid salts is that we can convert water-insoluble carboxylic acids to water-soluble alkali metal or ammonium salts and then extract them into aqueous solution. In turn, we can transform the salt into the free carboxylic acid by adding HCl, H_2SO_4, or some other strong acid. These reactions allow us to separate water-insoluble carboxylic acids from water-insoluble neutral compounds.

Figure 13.1 shows a flowchart for the separation of benzoic acid, a water-insoluble carboxylic acid, from benzyl alcohol, a water-insoluble nonacidic compound. First, we dissolve the mixture of benzoic acid and benzyl alcohol in diethyl ether. Next, we shake the ether solution with aqueous NaOH to convert benzoic acid to its water-soluble sodium salt. Then we separate the ether from the aqueous phase. Distillation of the ether solution yields first diethyl ether (bp 35 °C) and then benzyl alcohol (bp 205 °C). When we acidify the aqueous solution with HCl, benzoic acid precipitates as a water-insoluble solid (mp 122 °C) and is recovered by filtration. The ability to separate compounds based on their acid–base properties is very important in laboratory and industrial chemistry.

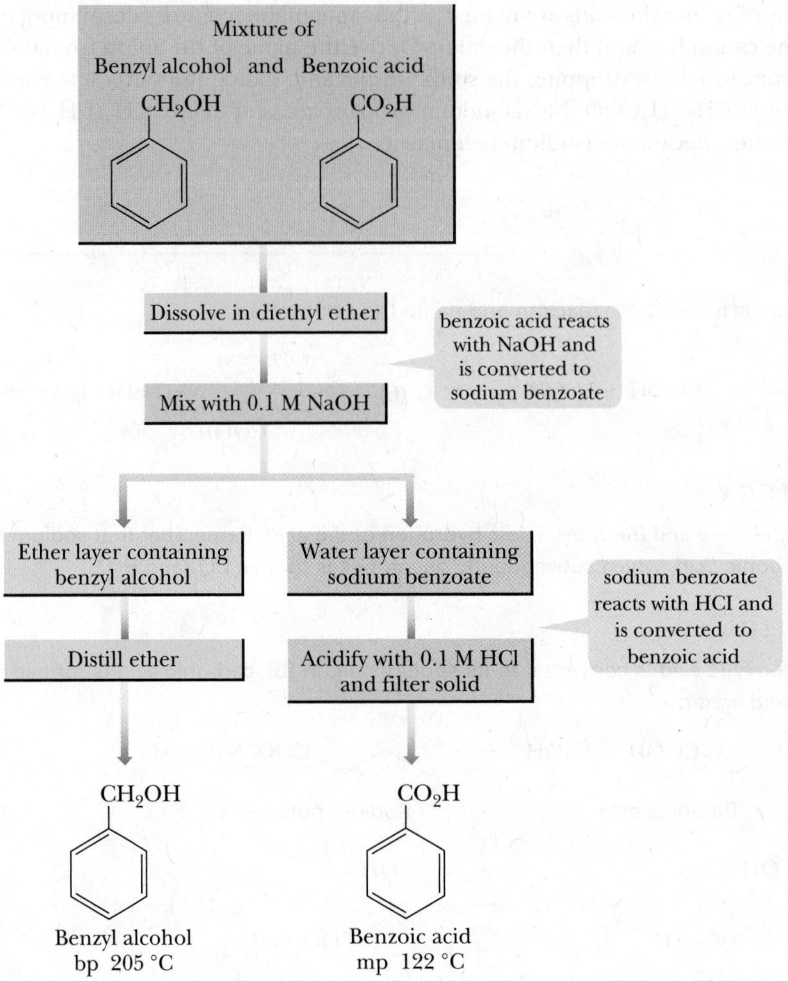

FIGURE 13.1 Flowchart for separation of benzoic acid from benzyl alcohol.

13.5 How Are Carboxyl Groups Reduced?

The carboxyl group is one of the organic functional groups that is most resistant to reduction. It is not affected by catalytic reduction (H_2/M) under conditions that easily reduce aldehydes and ketones to alcohols and that reduce alkenes to alkanes. The most common reagent for the reduction of a carboxylic acid to a primary alcohol is the very powerful reducing agent lithium aluminum hydride (Section 12.10).

Chemical Connections 13A

FROM WILLOW BARK TO ASPIRIN AND BEYOND

The first drug developed for widespread use was aspirin, today's most common pain reliever. Americans alone consume approximately 80 billion tablets of aspirin a year! The story of the development of this modern pain reliever goes back more than 2,000 years: In 400 B.C.E., the Greek physician Hippocrates recommended chewing bark of the willow tree to alleviate the pain of childbirth and to treat eye infections.

The active component of willow bark was found to be salicin, a compound composed of salicyl alcohol joined to a unit of β-D-glucose (Section 17.2). Hydrolysis of salicin in aqueous acid gives salicyl alcohol, which can then be oxidized to salicylic acid, an even more effective reliever of pain, fever, and inflammation than salicin and one without its extremely bitter taste:

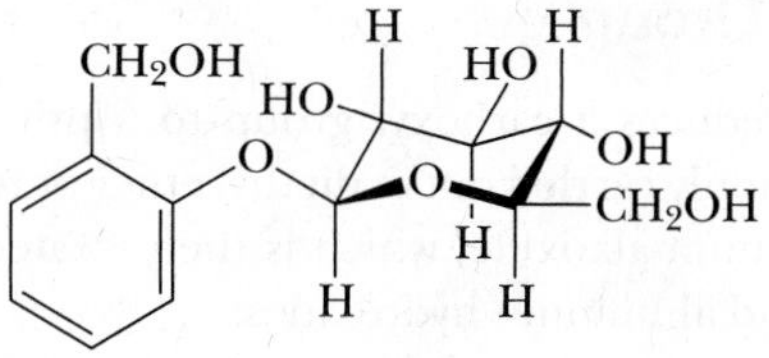

Salicin

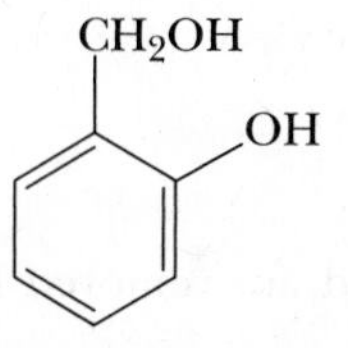

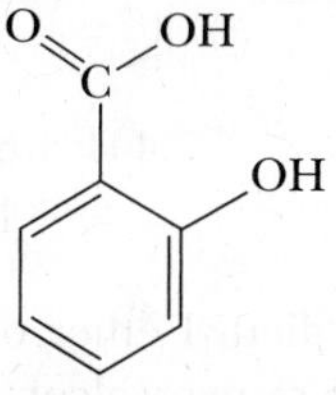

Salicyl alcohol Salicylic acid

Unfortunately, patients quickly recognized salicylic acid's major side effect: It causes severe irritation of the mucous membrane lining the stomach.

In the search for less irritating, but still effective, derivatives of salicylic acid, chemists at the Bayer division of I. G. Farben in Germany prepared acetylsalicylic acid in 1883 and gave it the name *aspirin*, a word derived from the German *spirsäure* (salicylic acid), with the initial *a* for the acetyl group:

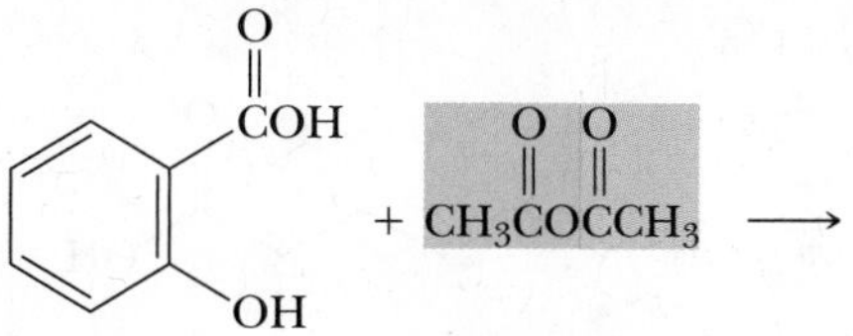

Salicylic acid Acetic anhydride

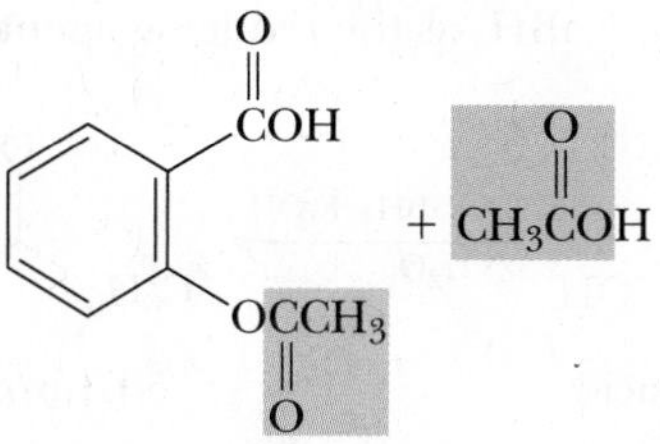

Acetyl salicylate (Aspirin)

Aspirin proved to be less irritating to the stomach than salicylic acid and also more effective in relieving the pain and inflammation of rheumatoid arthritis. Bayer began large-scale production of aspirin in 1899.

In the 1960s, in a search for even more effective and less irritating analgesics and anti-inflammatory drugs, the Boots Pure Drug Company in England studied compounds related in structure to salicylic acid. They discovered an even more potent compound, which they named ibuprofen, and soon thereafter, Syntex Corporation in the United States developed naproxen and Rhone–Poulenc in France developed ketoprofen:

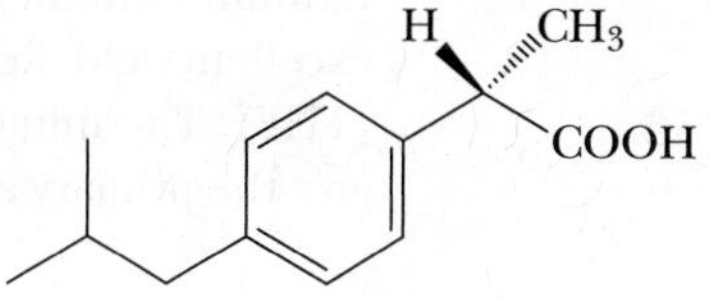

(*S*)-Ibuprofen

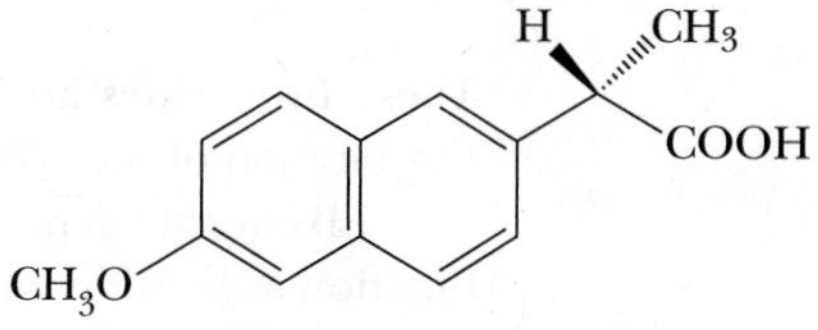

(*S*)-Naproxen

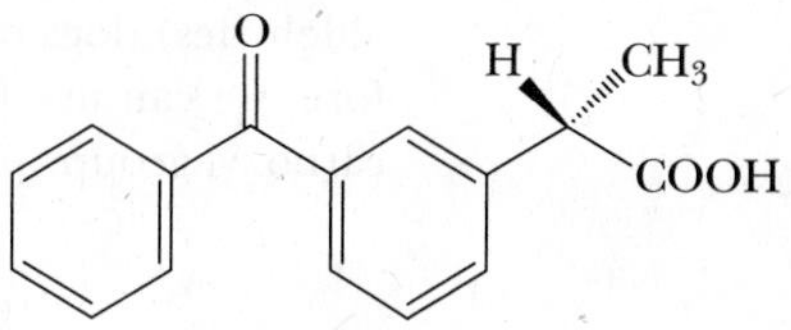

(*S*)-Ketoprofen

Notice that each compound has one stereocenter and can exist as a pair of enantiomers. For each drug, the physiologically active form is the *S* enantiomer. Even though the *R* enantiomer of ibuprofen has none of the analgesic or anti-inflammatory activity, it is converted in the body to the active *S* enantiomer.

In the 1960s, scientists discovered that aspirin acts by inhibiting cyclooxygenase (COX), a key enzyme in the conversion of arachidonic acid to prostaglandins (Section 19.5). With this discovery, it became clear why only one enantiomer of ibuprofen, naproxen, and ketoprofen is active: Only the *S* enantiomer of each has the correct handedness to bind to COX and inhibit its activity.

The discovery that these drugs owe their effectiveness to the inhibition of COX opened an entirely new avenue for drug research. If we know more about the structure and function of this key enzyme, might it be possible to design and discover even more effective nonsteroidal anti-inflammatory drugs for the treatment of rheumatoid arthritis and other inflammatory diseases?

And so continues the story that began with the discovery of the beneficial effects of chewing willow bark.

Question

Draw the product of the reaction of salicylic acid with (a) one equivalent of NaOH, (b) two equivalents of NaOH, and (c) two equivalents of $NaHCO_3$.

A. Reduction of a Carboxyl Group

Lithium aluminum hydride, $LiAlH_4$, reduces a carboxyl group to a primary alcohol in excellent yield. Reduction is most commonly carried out in diethyl ether or tetrahydrofuran (THF). The initial product is an aluminum alkoxide, which is then treated with water to give the primary alcohol and lithium and aluminum hydroxides:

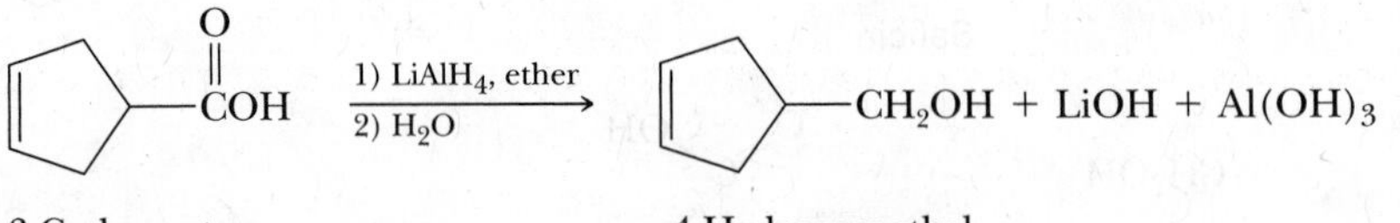

3-Cyclopentene-carboxylic acid

4-Hydroxymethyl-cyclopentene

These hydroxides are insoluble in diethyl ether or THF and are removed by filtration. Evaporation of the solvent yields the primary alcohol.

Alkenes are generally not affected by metal hydride-reducing reagents. These reagents function as hydride ion donors; that is, they function as nucleophiles, and alkenes are not normally attacked by nucleophiles.

B. Selective Reduction of Other Functional Groups

Catalytic hydrogenation (at least under the same conditions used to reduce ketones and aldehydes) does not reduce carboxyl groups, but does reduce alkenes to alkanes. Therefore, we can use H_2/M to reduce this functional group selectively in the presence of a carboxyl group:

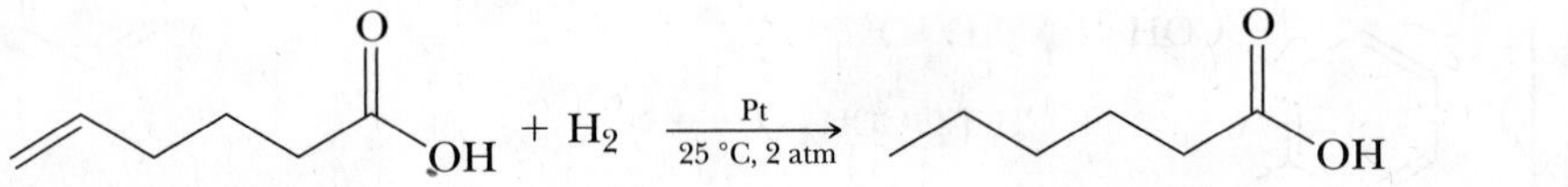

5-Hexenoic acid

Hexanoic acid

We saw in Section 12.10 that aldehydes and ketones are reduced to alcohols by both $LiAlH_4$ and $NaBH_4$. Only $LiAlH_4$, however, reduces carboxyl groups. Thus, it is possible to reduce an aldehyde or a ketone carbonyl group selectively in the presence of a carboxyl group by using the less reactive $NaBH_4$ as the reducing agent:

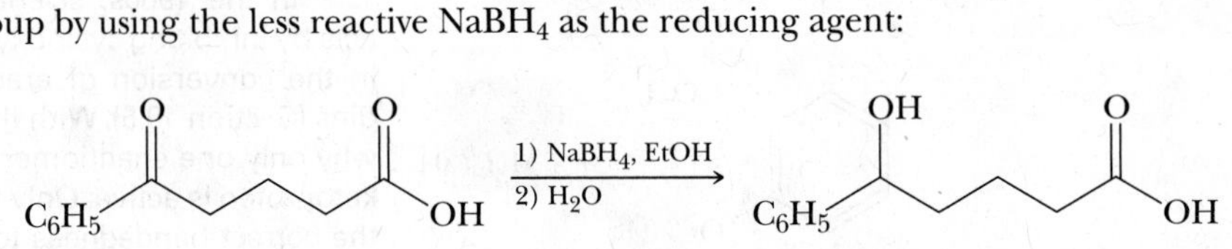

5-Oxo-5-phenylpentanoic acid

5-Hydroxy-5-phenylpentanoic acid

EXAMPLE 13.4

Provide the product formed when each of the following is treated with:

(i) H_2/Pd (ii) 1. $LiAlH_4$, ether 2. H_2O (iii) 1. $NaBH_4$, EtOH 2. H_2O

In each reaction, assume an excess of reagent is available for reaction.

(a)

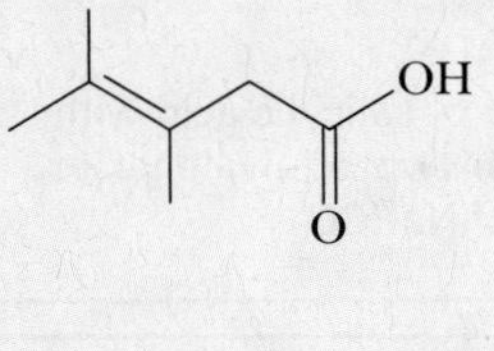

(b)

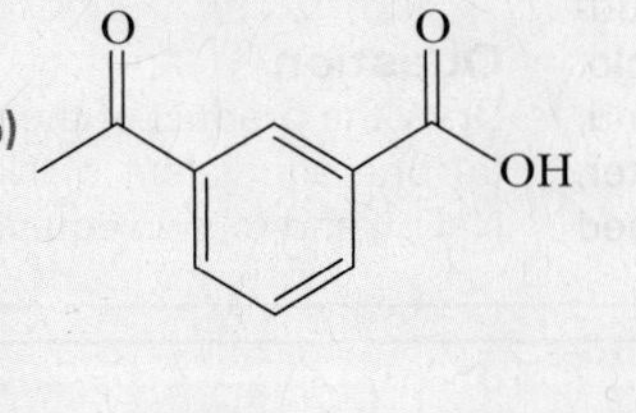

STRATEGY

Remember that carboxyl groups are only reduced by $LiAlH_4$, alkenes are only reduced by H_2/M, aldehydes and ketones are reduced by all metal hydride reducing agents, and benzene rings are resistant to each of these reducing reagents. Remember to consider stereochemistry in the outcome of each reaction.

SOLUTION

Here are structural formulas for the major product produced in each reaction:

(a)

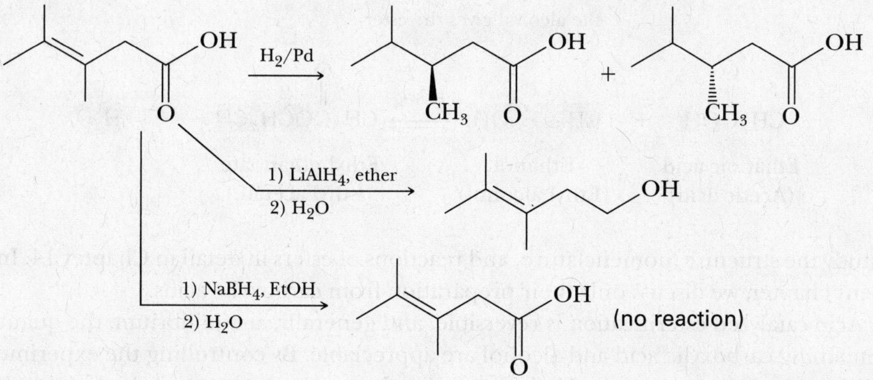

(b)

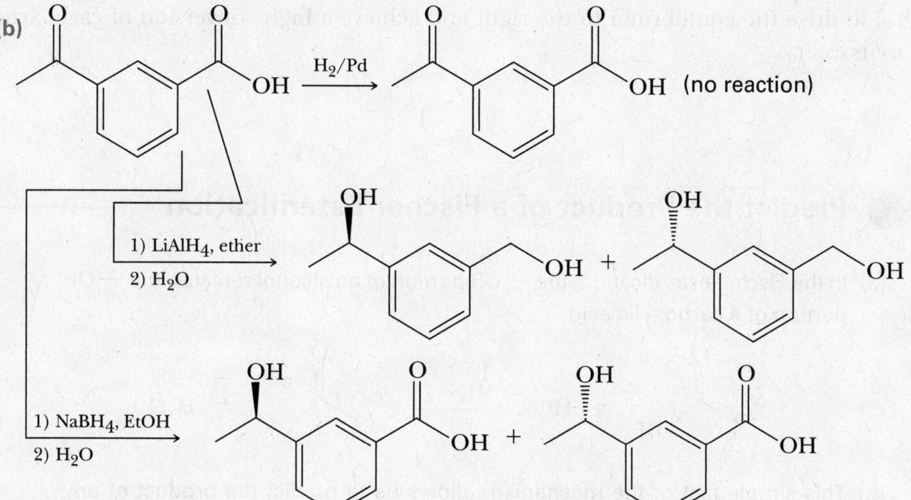

See problems 13.30–13.32, 13.47

PROBLEM 13.4

Provide the product formed when each of the following is treated with:

(i) H_2/Pd (ii) 1. $LiAlH_4$, ether 2. H_2O (iii) 1. $NaBH_4$, EtOH 2. H_2O

Presume that an excess of reagent is available for each reaction.

(a)

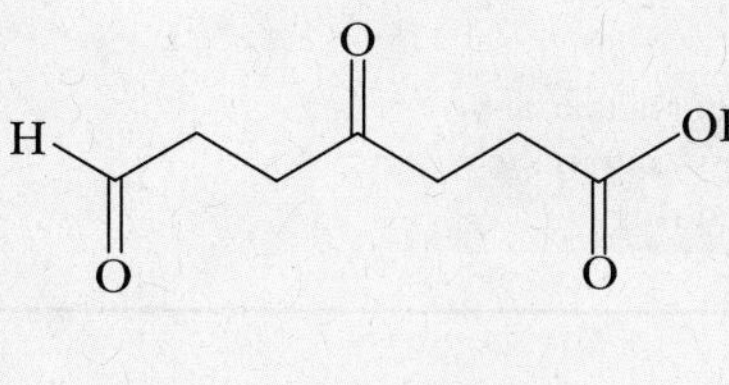

(b)

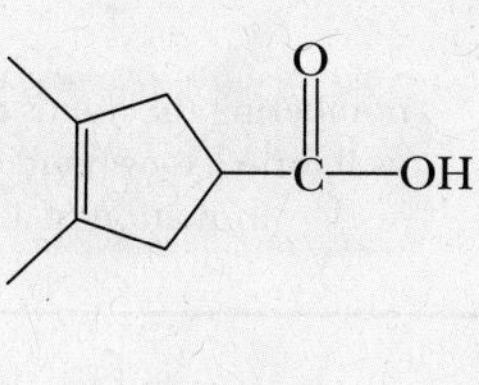

13.6 What Is Fischer Esterification?

Fischer esterification The process of forming an ester by refluxing a carboxylic acid and an alcohol in the presence of an acid catalyst, commonly sulfuric acid.

Treatment of a carboxylic acid with an alcohol in the presence of an acid catalyst—most commonly, concentrated sulfuric acid—gives an ester. This method of forming an ester is given the special name **Fischer esterification** after the German chemist Emil Fischer (1852–1919). As an example of Fischer esterification, treating acetic acid with ethanol in the presence of concentrated sulfuric acid gives ethyl acetate and water:

removal of OH from the acid and H from the alcohol gives the ester

$$\underset{\substack{\text{Ethanoic acid}\\ \text{(Acetic acid)}}}{CH_3\overset{O}{\overset{\|}{C}}OH} + \underset{\substack{\text{Ethanol}\\ \text{(Ethyl alcohol)}}}{CH_3CH_2OH} \xrightleftharpoons{H_2SO_4} \underset{\substack{\text{Ethyl ethanoate}\\ \text{(Ethyl acetate)}}}{CH_3\overset{O}{\overset{\|}{C}}OCH_2CH_3} + H_2O$$

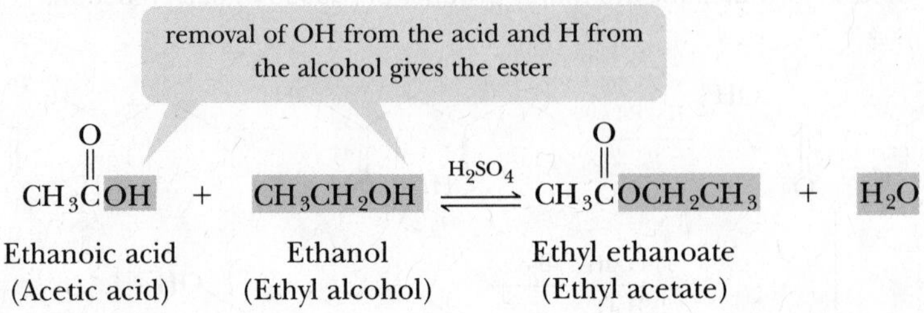

Ken Karp for John Wiley & Sons

These products all contain ethyl acetate as a solvent.

We study the structure, nomenclature, and reactions of esters in detail in Chapter 14. In the present chapter, we discuss only their preparation from carboxylic acids.

Acid-catalyzed esterification is reversible, and generally, at equilibrium, the quantities of remaining carboxylic acid and alcohol are appreciable. By controlling the experimental conditions, however, we can use Fischer esterification to prepare esters in high yields. If the alcohol is inexpensive compared with the carboxylic acid, we can use a large excess of the alcohol to drive the equilibrium to the right and achieve a high conversion of carboxylic acid to its ester.

HOW TO 13.1 Predict the Product of a Fischer Esterification

(a) In the Fischer esterification, the —OR portion of an alcohol replaces the —OH portion of a carboxylic acid.

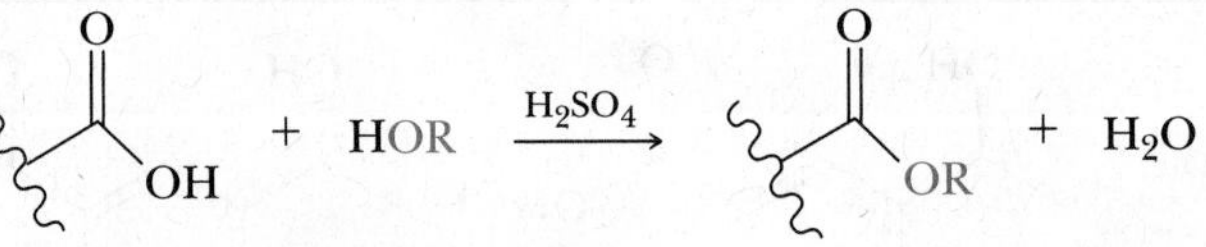

(b) This simple fact of the mechanism allows us to predict the product of any type of Fischer esterification. For example, in the following Fischer esterification, the alcohol is already a part of the molecule. In cases of intramolecular Fischer esterifications, it is often helpful to number the atoms in the molecule.

in this case, the R group is ultimately connected to the carboxyl group undergoing esterification

numbering the atoms allows us to see that atom-6 will form a new bond to atom-1, resulting in the formation of a six-membered ring

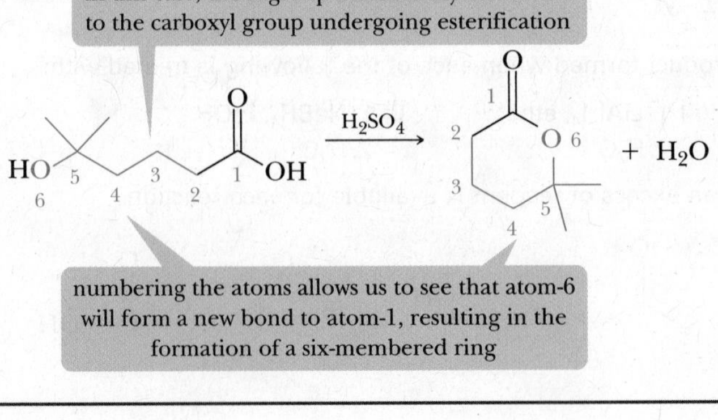

EXAMPLE 13.5

Complete these Fischer esterification reactions:

(a) 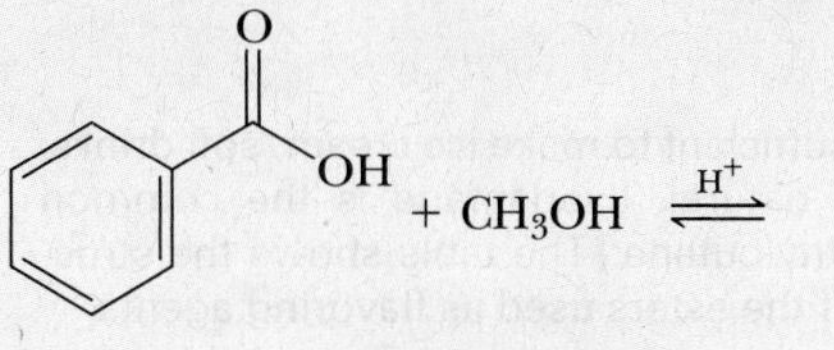

(b) 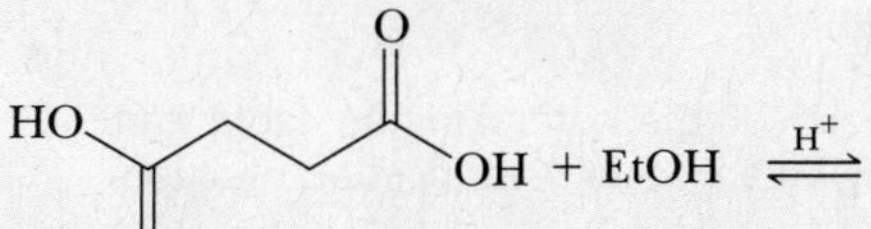

(excess)

STRATEGY

In a Fischer esterification, each carboxyl group is converted to an ester in which the —OR group originates from the alcohol reagent.

SOLUTION

Here is a structural formula for the ester produced in each reaction:

(a) 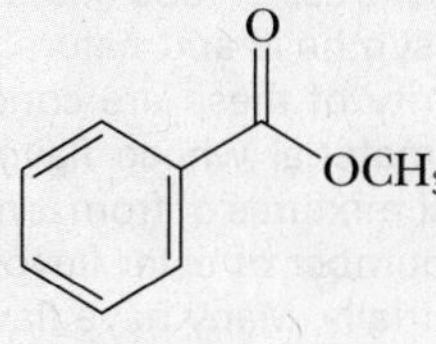

Methyl benzoate

(b) 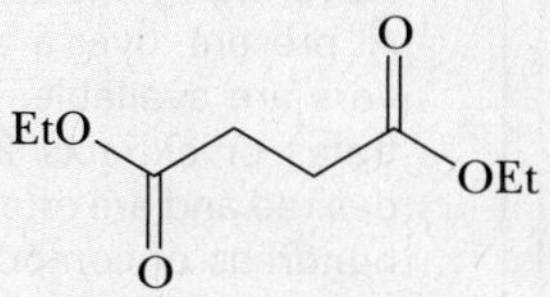

Diethyl butanedioate (Diethyl succinate)

See problems 13.30, 13.33, 13.39, 13.40, 13.47

PROBLEM 13.5

Complete these Fischer esterification reactions:

(a) 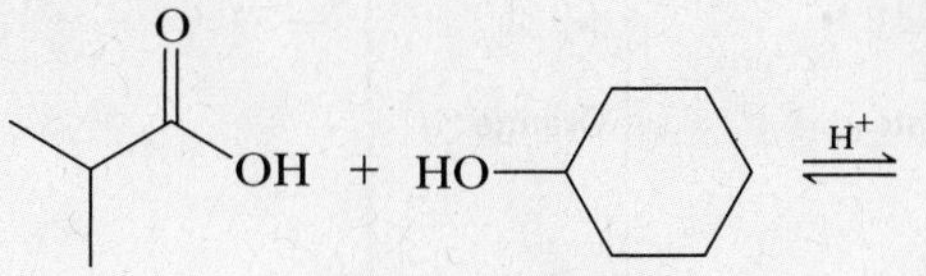

(b) 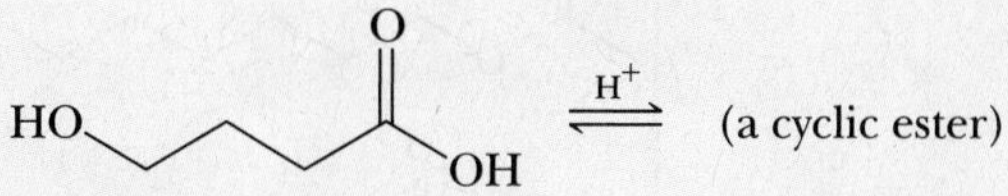

In Section 5.2C, we defined five common mechanistic patterns that we have subsequently seen in a variety of organic reactions. It is now time to define a sixth mechanistic pattern, one that we will encounter often in our study of carboxylic acids and functional derivatives of carboxylic acids (Chapter 14).

Pattern 6: Collapse of the tetrahedral carbonyl addition intermediate to eject a leaving group and regenerate the carbonyl group. After addition of a nucleophile (Nu) to a carbonyl, one possible mechanism is for the tetrahedral carbonyl intermediate to collapse back to a C=O while ejecting a leaving group (Lv). We will see, in this and the chapters to come, that both Nu and Lv can take many forms.

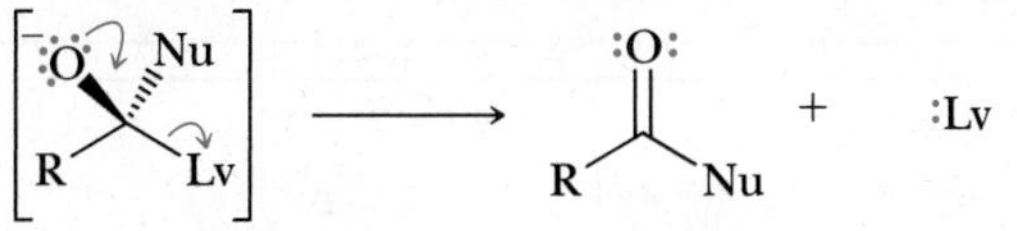

Tetrahedral carbonyl addition intermediate

Following is a mechanism for Fischer esterification, and we urge you to study it carefully. It is important that you understand this mechanism thoroughly because it is a model for many of the reactions of the functional derivatives of carboxylic acids presented in Chapter 14. Note that, although we show the acid catalyst as H_2SO_4 when we write Fisher esterification reactions, the actual proton-transfer acid that initiates the reaction is the oxonium formed by the transfer of a proton from H_2SO_4 (the stronger acid) to the alcohol (the stronger base) used in the esterification reaction:

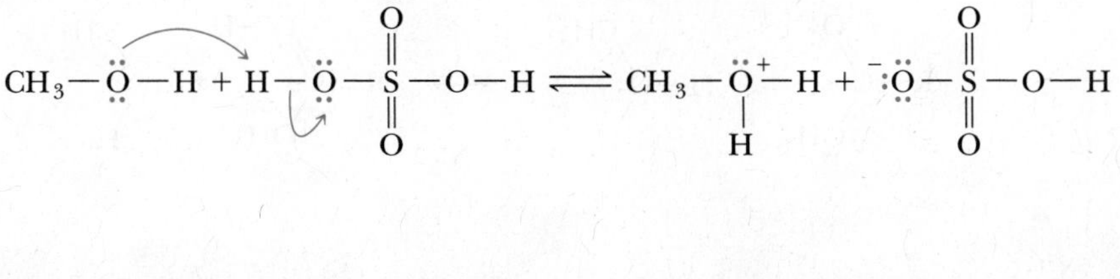

Chemical Connections 13B

ESTERS AS FLAVORING AGENTS

Flavoring agents are the largest class of food additives. At present, over a thousand synthetic and natural flavors are available. The majority of these are concentrates or extracts from the material whose flavor is desired and are often complex mixtures of from tens to hundreds of compounds. A number of ester flavoring agents are synthesized industrially. Many have flavors very close to the target flavor, and adding only one or a few of them is sufficient to make ice cream, soft drinks, or candy taste natural. (Isopentane is the common name for 2-methylbutane.) The table shows the structures of a few of the esters used as flavoring agents:

Question

Show how each of the esters in the table can be synthesized using a Fischer esterification reaction.

Structure	Name	Flavor
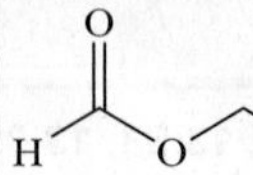	Ethyl formate	Rum
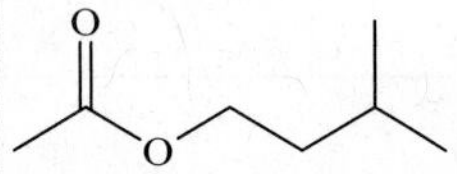	Isopentyl acetate	Banana
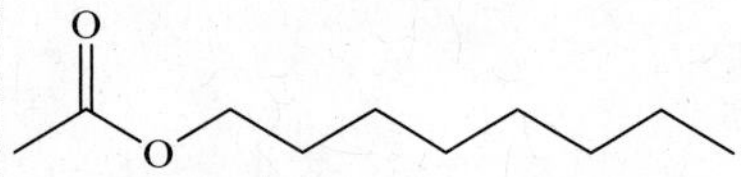	Octyl acetate	Orange
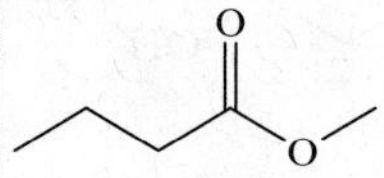	Methyl butanoate	Apple
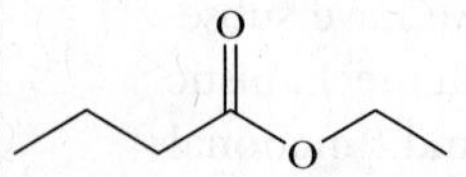	Ethyl butanoate	Pineapple
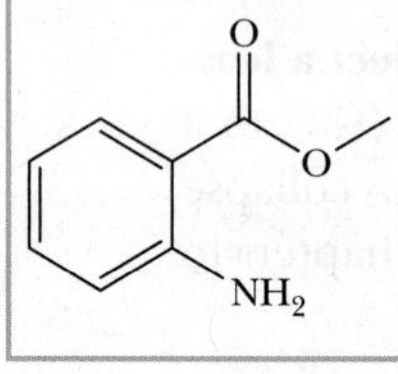	Methyl 2-aminobenzoate (Methyl anthranilate)	Grape

Mechanism

Fischer Esterification

STEP 1: Add a proton. Proton transfer from the acid catalyst to the carbonyl oxygen increases the electrophilicity of the carbonyl carbon:

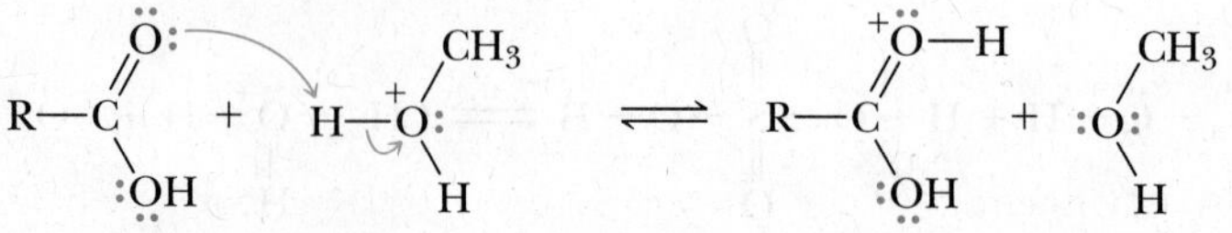

STEP 2: Reaction of a nucleophile and an electrophile to form a new covalent bond. The carbonyl carbon is then attacked by the nucleophilic oxygen atom of the alcohol to form an oxonium ion:

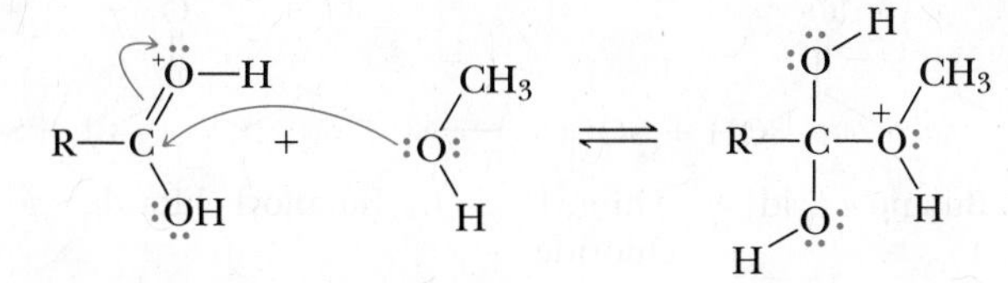

(an electrophile) (a nucleophile) (oxonium ion)

STEP 3: Take a proton away. Proton transfer from the oxonium ion to a second molecule of alcohol gives a tetrahedral carbonyl addition intermediate (TCAI):

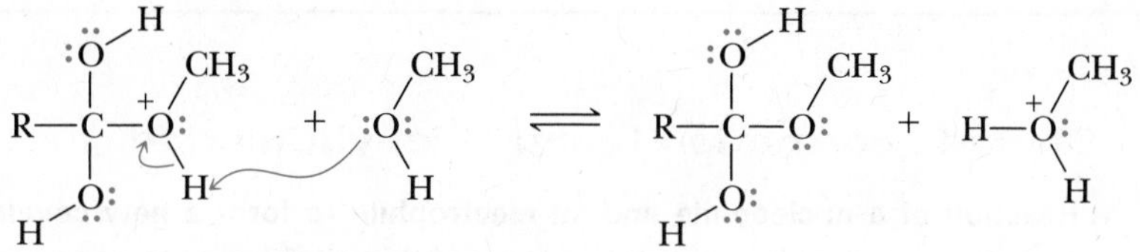

STEP 4: Add a proton. Proton transfer to one of the —OH groups of the TCAI gives a new oxonium ion:

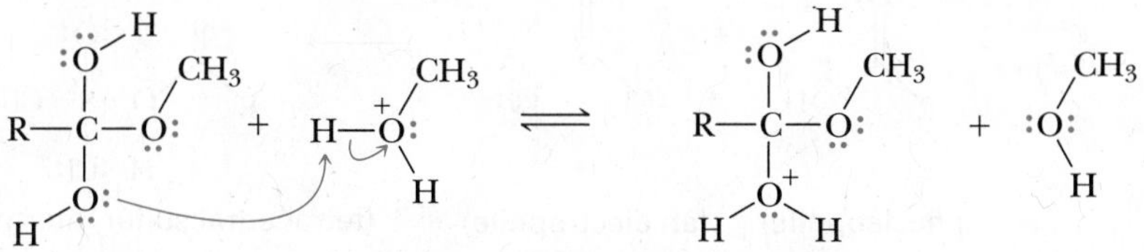

STEP 5: Collapse of the tetrahedral carbonyl addition intermediate to eject a leaving group and regenerate the carbonyl group. Loss of water from this oxonium ion gives the ester and regenerates the acid catalyst:

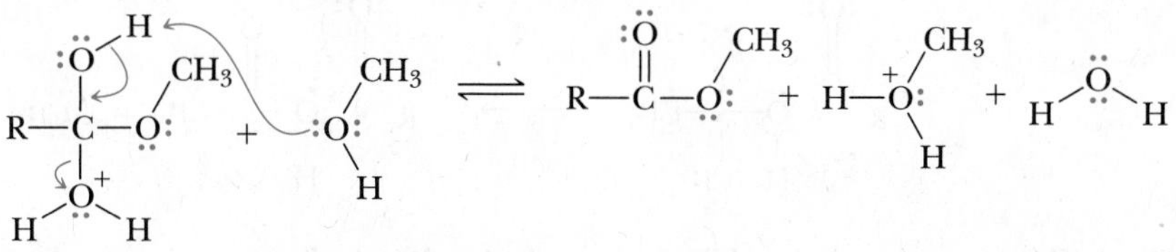

13.7 What Are Acid Chlorides?

The functional group of an acid halide is a carbonyl group bonded to a halogen atom. Among the acid halides, acid chlorides are the most frequently used in the laboratory and in industrial organic chemistry:

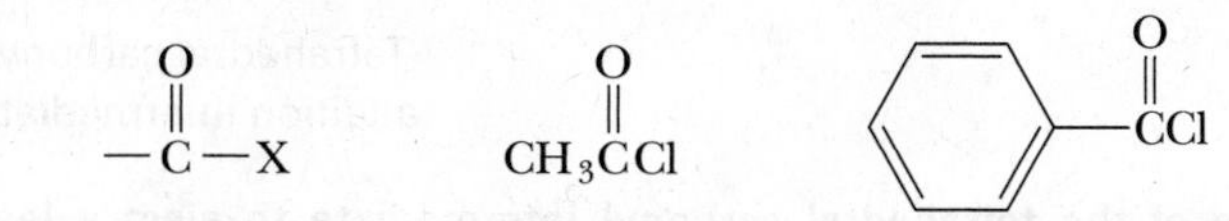

Functional group of an acid halide — Acetyl chloride — Benzoyl chloride

We study the nomenclature, structure, and characteristic reactions of acid halides in Chapter 14. In this chapter, our concern is only with their synthesis from carboxylic acids.

The most common way to prepare an acid chloride is to treat a carboxylic acid with thionyl chloride, the same reagent that converts an alcohol to a chloroalkane (Section 8.2D):

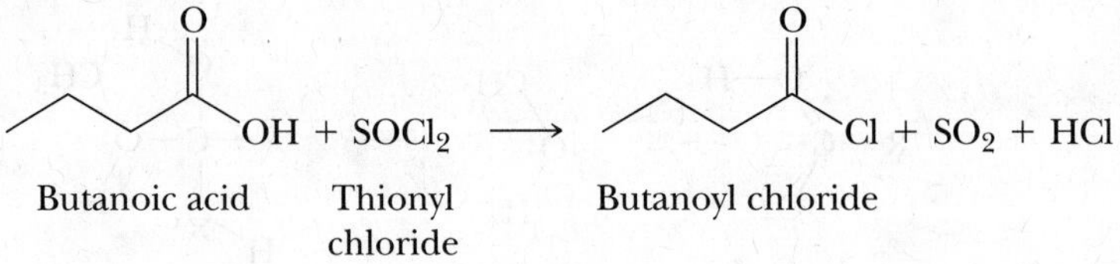

The mechanism of this reaction consists of four steps.

Mechanism

Acid Chloride Formation Using Thionyl Chloride

STEP 1: Reaction of a nucleophile and an electrophile to form a new covalent bond. The carboxyl group adds to the sulfur atom of thionyl chloride to generate a tetrahedral sulfur intermediate.

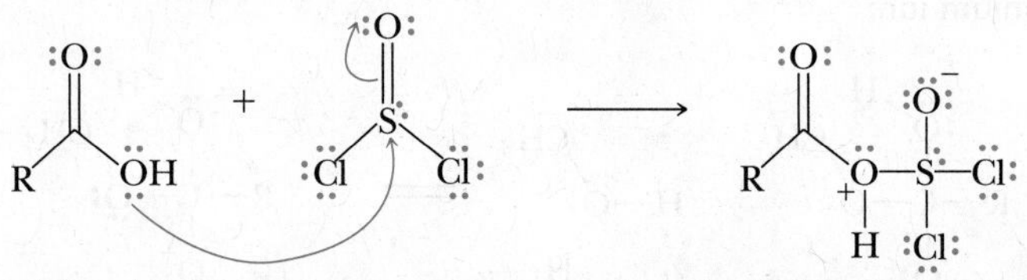

(a nucleophile) (an electrophile) (tetrahedral sulfur intermediate)

STEP 2: Collapse of the tetrahedral sulfur intermediate to eject a leaving group and regenerate the carbonyl group. Loss of chloride from the tetrahedral sulfur intermediate regenerates the sulfonyl group:

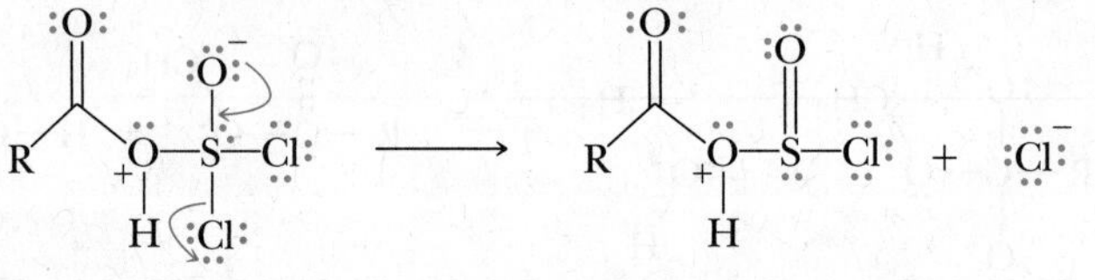

STEP 3: Reaction of a nucleophile and an electrophile to form a new covalent bond. The chloride ion attacks the carbonyl carbon, forming a tetrahedral carbonyl addition intermediate.

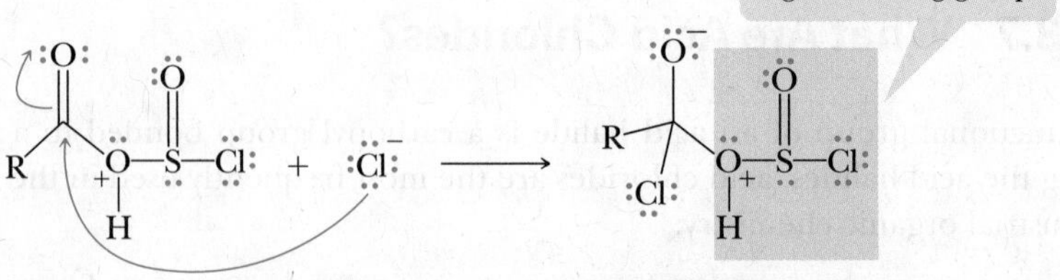

Tetrahedral carbonyl addition intermediate

STEP 4: Collapse of the tetrahedral carbonyl intermediate to eject a leaving group and regenerate the carbonyl group. The sulfonyl group highlighted in Step 3 is an excellent leaving group. This allows a lone pair of electrons to collapse back toward the bond to regenerate the carbonyl carbon while expelling the leaving group sulfochloridous acid. This sulfur-based acid is unstable and breaks down to yield sulfur dioxide and HCl. The mechanism shown below is a common mode of reactivity for functional derivatives of carboxylic acids (Chapter 14).

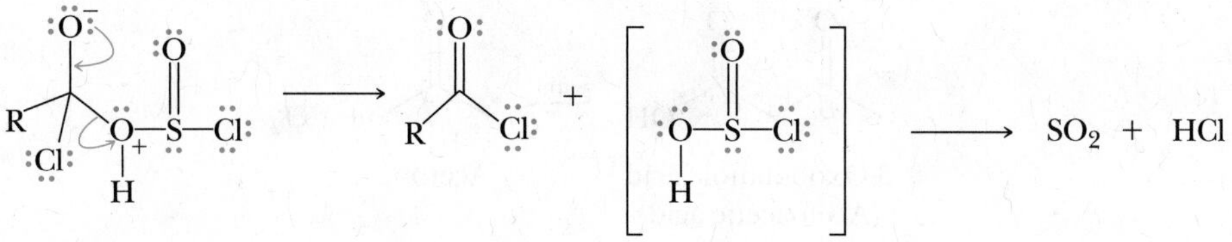

Sulfochloridous acid

EXAMPLE 13.6

Complete each equation:

(a)

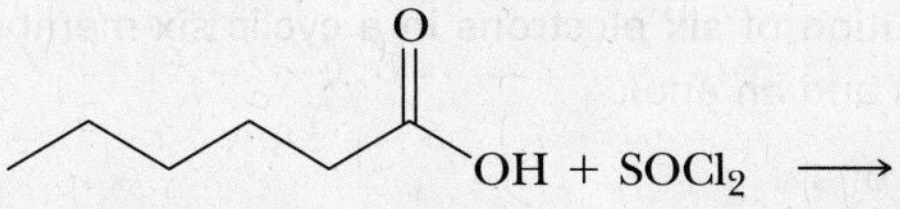

(b)

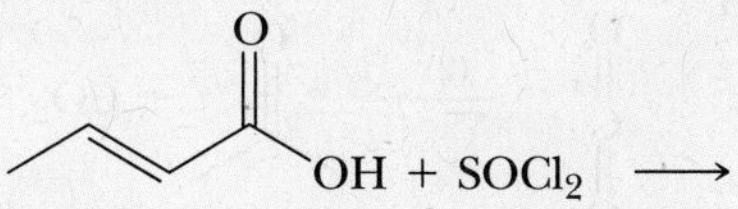

STRATEGY

Thionyl chloride effectively causes —OH groups (for example, those of alcohols and carboxylic acids) to be replaced by Cl. Don't forget to show the by-products of the reaction (SO_2 and HCl).

SOLUTION

Following are the products for each reaction:

(a)

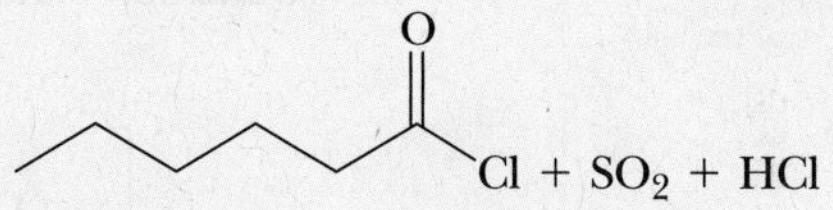

(b)

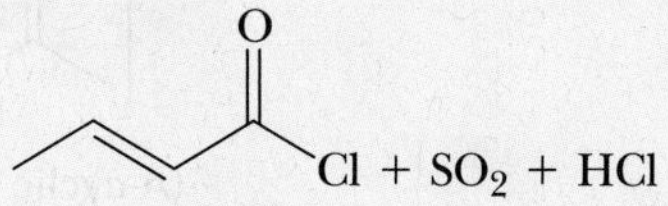

See problems 13.30, 13.47

PROBLEM 13.6

Complete each equation:

(a)

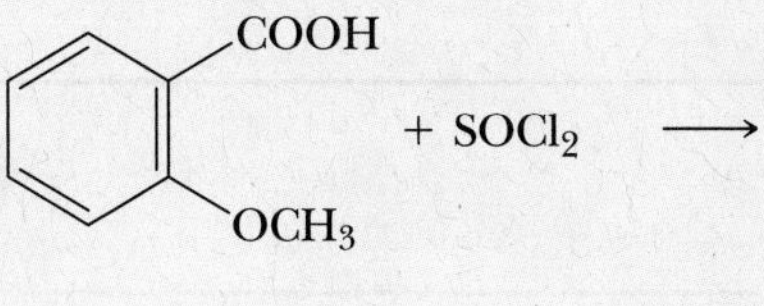

(b)

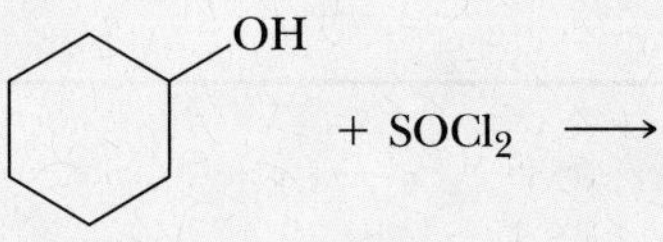

13.8 What Is Decarboxylation?

A. β-Ketoacids

Decarboxylation is the loss of CO_2 from a carboxyl group. Almost any carboxylic acid, heated to a very high temperature, undergoes decarboxylation:

Decarboxylation Loss of CO_2 from a carboxyl group.

$$RCOH\ (\text{C=O}) \xrightarrow[\text{(high temperature)}]{\text{decarboxylation}} RH + CO_2$$

Most carboxylic acids, however, are quite resistant to moderate heat and melt or even boil without decarboxylation. Exceptions are carboxylic acids that have a carbonyl group β to the carboxyl group. This type of carboxylic acid undergoes decarboxylation quite readily on mild heating. For example, when 3-oxobutanoic acid (acetoacetic acid) is heated moderately, it undergoes decarboxylation to give acetone and carbon dioxide:

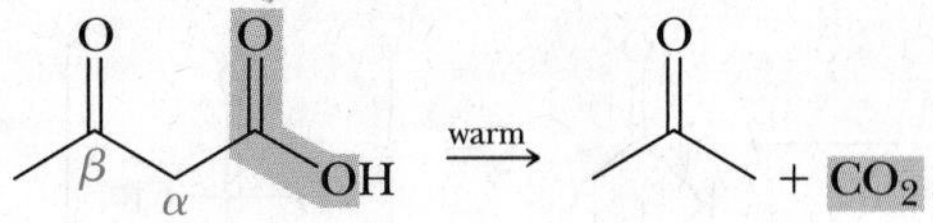

3-Oxobutanoic acid (Acetoacetic acid) — Acetone

Decarboxylation on moderate heating is a unique property of 3-oxocarboxylic acids (β-ketoacids) and is not observed with other classes of ketoacids.

Mechanism

Decarboxylation of a β-Ketocarboxylic Acid

STEP 1: Rearrangement of bonds. Redistribution of six electrons in a cyclic six-membered transition state gives carbon dioxide and an enol:

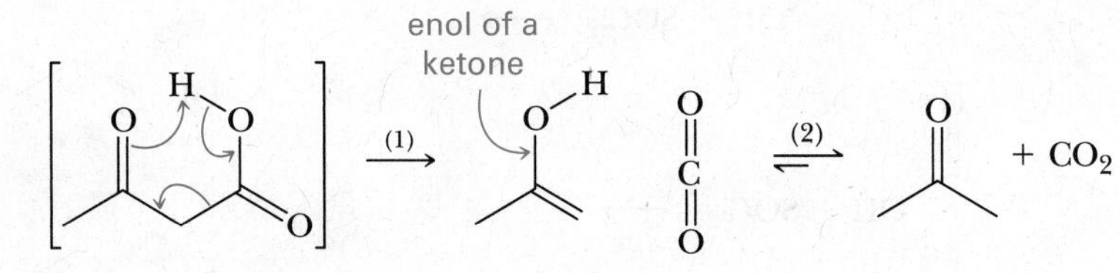

(A cyclic six-membered transition state)

STEP 2: Keto–enol tautomerism. Tautomerism (Section 12.8A) of the enol gives the more stable keto form of the product:

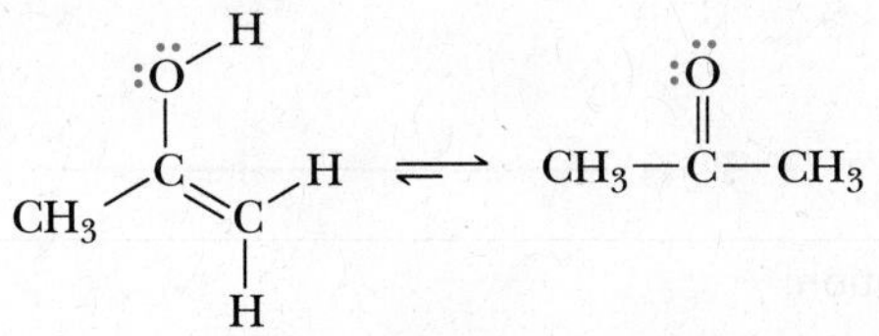

Chemical Connections 13C

KETONE BODIES AND DIABETES

3-Oxobutanoic acid (acetoacetic acid) and its reduction product, 3-hydroxybutanoic acid, are synthesized in the liver from acetyl-CoA, a product of the metabolism of fatty acids (Section 21.5C) and certain amino acids:

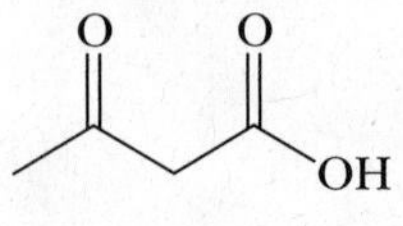

3-Oxobutanoic acid (Acetoacetic acid)

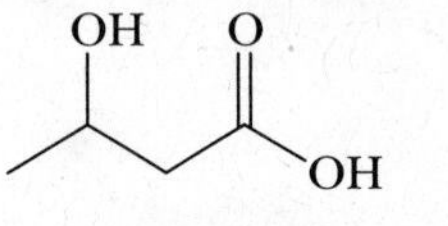

3-Hydroxybutanoic acid (β-Hydroxybutyric acid)

3-Hydroxybutanoic acid and 3-oxobutanoic acid are known collectively as ketone bodies.

The concentration of ketone bodies in the blood of healthy, well-fed humans is approximately 0.01 mM/L. However, in persons suffering from starvation or diabetes mellitus, the concentration of ketone bodies may increase to as much as 500 times normal. Under these conditions, the concentration of acetoacetic acid increases to the point where it undergoes spontaneous decarboxylation to form acetone and carbon dioxide. Acetone is not metabolized by humans and is excreted through the kidneys and the lungs. The odor of acetone is responsible for the characteristic "sweet smell" on the breath of severely diabetic patients.

Question

Show the mechanism for the decarboxylation of acetoacetic acid. Explain why 3-hydroxybutanoic acid cannot undergo decarboxylation.

HOW TO 13.2

Predict the Product of a β-Decarboxylation Reaction

(a) The most important criterion of a decarboxylation reaction is that the carbonyl group be at the β-position relative to a carboxyl group. Therefore, identify each carboxyl group in a molecule and determine whether a carbonyl is β to it.

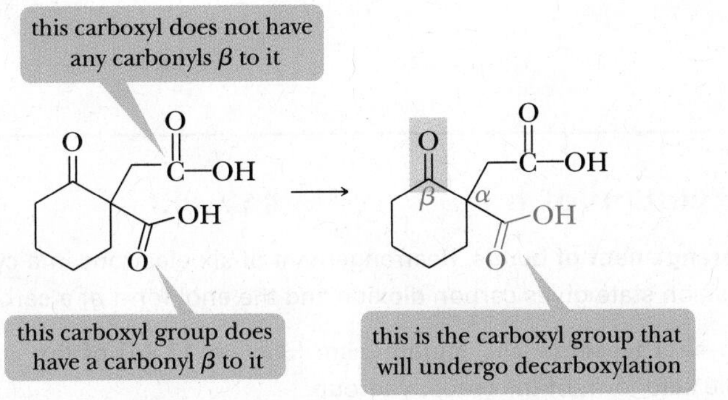

(b) Once all the carboxyl groups with β-carbonyls are identified, it is a simple matter of replacing the carboxyl groups with a hydrogen.

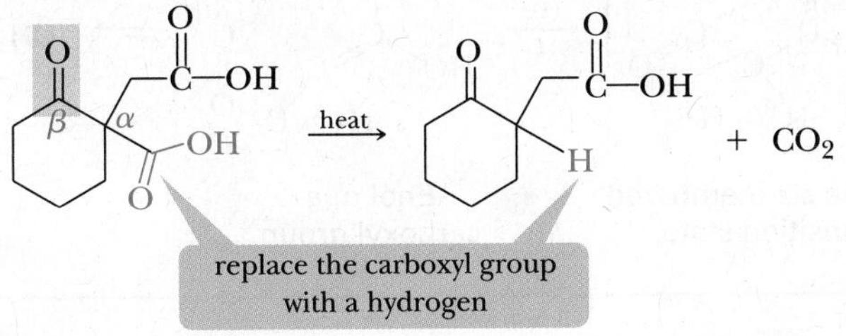

An important example of decarboxylation of a β-ketoacid in the biological world occurs during the oxidation of foodstuffs in the tricarboxylic acid (TCA) cycle. Oxalosuccinic acid, one of the intermediates in this cycle, undergoes spontaneous decarboxylation to produce α-ketoglutaric acid. Only one of the three carboxyl groups of oxalosuccinic acid has a carbonyl group in the position β to it, and it is this carboxyl group that is lost as CO_2:

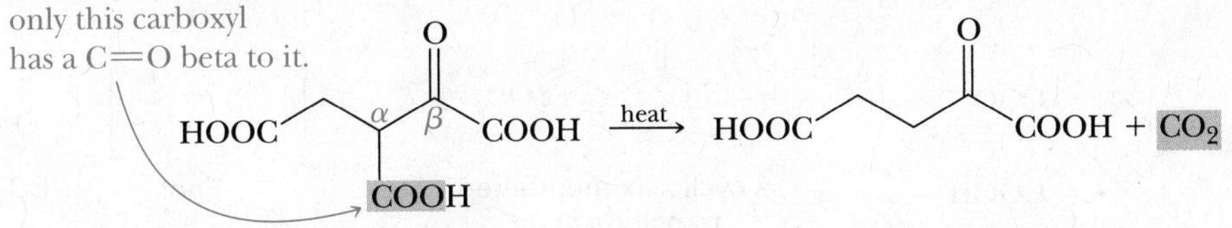

Oxalosuccinic acid — α-Ketoglutaric acid

B. Malonic Acid and Substituted Malonic Acids

The presence of a ketone or an aldehyde carbonyl group on the carbon β to the carboxyl group is sufficient to facilitate decarboxylation. In the more general reaction, decarboxylation is facilitated by the presence of any carbonyl group on the β carbon, including that of a carboxyl group or an ester. Malonic acid and substituted malonic acids, for example, undergo decarboxylation on heating, as illustrated by the decarboxylation of malonic acid when it is heated slightly above its melting point of 135–137 °C:

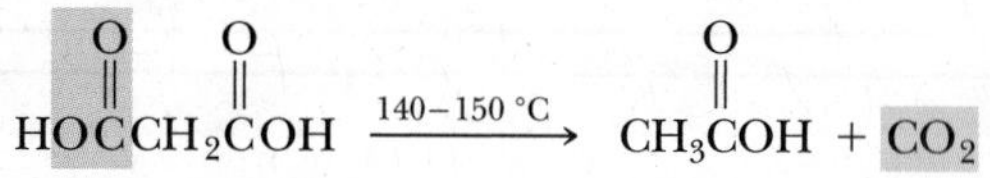

Propanedioic acid
(Malonic acid)

The mechanism for decarboxylation of malonic acids is similar to what we have just studied for the decarboxylation of β-ketoacids. The formation of a cyclic, six-membered transition state involving a redistribution of three electron pairs gives the enol form of a carboxylic acid, which, in turn, isomerizes to the carboxylic acid.

Mechanism

Decarboxylation of a β-Dicarboxylic Acid

STEP 1: Rearrangement of bonds. Rearrangement of six electrons in a cyclic six-membered transition state gives carbon dioxide and the enol form of a carboxyl group.

STEP 2: Keto–enol tautomerism. Tautomerism (Section 12.8A) of the enol gives the more stable keto form of the carboxyl group.

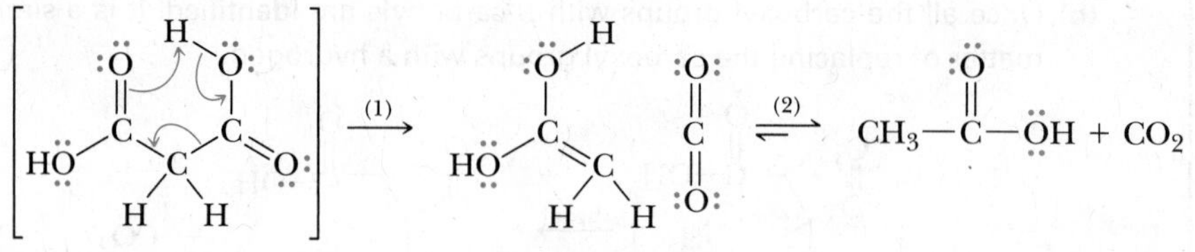

A cyclic six-membered transition state

Enol of a carboxyl group

EXAMPLE 13.7

Each of these carboxylic acids undergoes thermal decarboxylation:

(a)

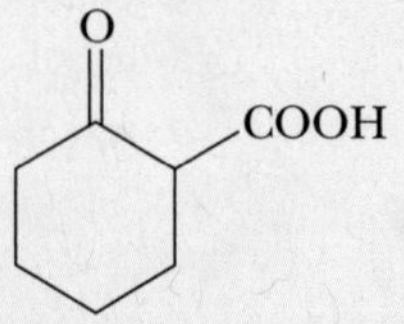

(b)

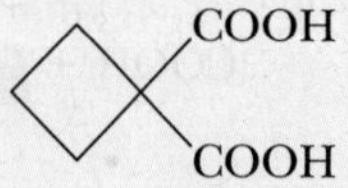

Draw a structural formula for the enol intermediate and final product formed in each reaction.

STRATEGY

It is often helpful to draw the full Lewis structure of the β-carboxyl group and to position it to allow a cyclic six-membered transition state:

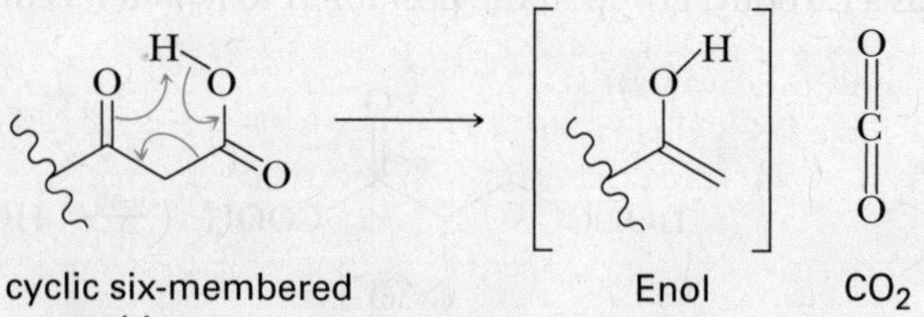

A cyclic six-membered transition state

Enol

CO_2

By carefully keeping track of the movement of electrons, the bonds made and the bonds broken, one can arrive at the enol intermediate. Predicting the final product is a simple matter of replacing the —COOH group that is β to a carbonyl in the molecule with a hydrogen atom.

SOLUTION

(a)

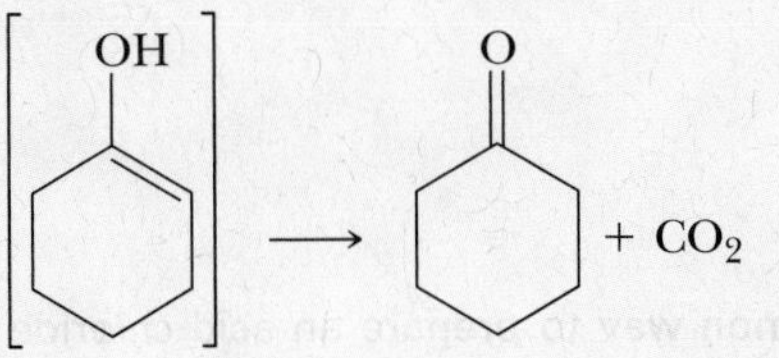

Enol intermediate

(b)

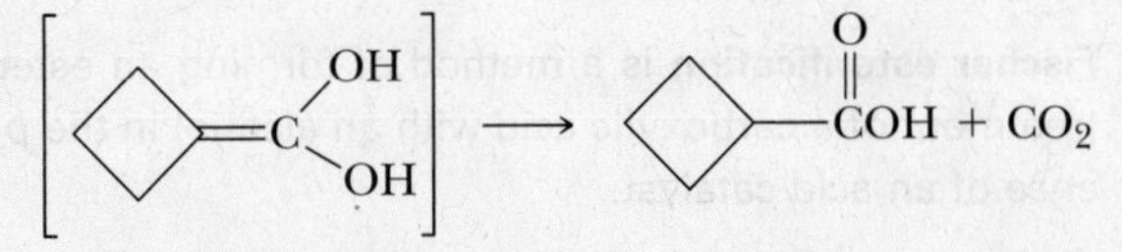

Enol intermediate

See problems 13.41, 13.47

PROBLEM 13.7

Draw the structural formula for the indicated β-ketoacid:

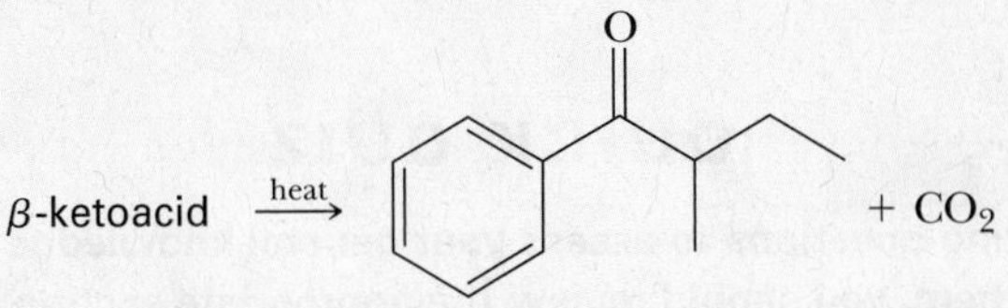

SUMMARY OF KEY QUESTIONS

13.1 What Are Carboxylic Acids?

- The functional group of a **carboxylic acid** is the **carboxyl group,** **—COOH.**

13.2 How Are Carboxylic Acids Named?

- IUPAC names of carboxylic acids are derived from the parent alkane by dropping the suffix *-e* and adding *-oic acid.*
- Dicarboxylic acids are named as *-dioic acids.*

13.3 What Are the Physical Properties of Carboxylic Acids?

- Carboxylic acids are polar compounds that associate by hydrogen bonding into **dimers** in the liquid and solid states.
- Carboxylic acids have higher boiling points and are more soluble in water than alcohols, aldehydes, ketones, and ethers of comparable molecular weight.
- A carboxylic acid consists of two regions of different polarity: a polar, **hydrophilic** carboxyl group, which increases solubility in water, and a nonpolar, **hydrophobic** hydrocarbon chain, which decreases solubility in water.
- The first four **aliphatic carboxylic acids** are infinitely soluble in water because the hydrophilic carboxyl group more than counterbalances the hydrophobic hydrocarbon chain.
- As the size of the carbon chain increases, the hydrophobic group becomes dominant, and solubility in water decreases.

13.4 What Are the Acid–Base Properties of Carboxylic Acids?

- Values of $\mathbf{p}K_a$ for aliphatic carboxylic acids are in the 4.0 to 5.0 range.
- Electron-withdrawing substituents near the carboxyl group increase acidity in both aliphatic and aromatic carboxylic acids.

13.5 How Are Carboxyl Groups Reduced?

- The carboxyl group is one of the organic functional groups that is most resistant to reduction. They do not react with H_2/M or $NaBH_4$.
- Lithium aluminum hydride, $LiAlH_4$, reduces a carboxyl group to a primary alcohol.

13.6 What Is Fischer Esterification?

- **Fischer esterification** is a method of forming an ester by treatment of a carboxylic acid with an alcohol in the presence of an acid catalyst.

13.7 What Are Acid Chlorides?

- The functional group of an **acid chloride** is a carbonyl group bonded to a chlorine atom.
- The most common way to prepare an acid chloride is to treat a carboxylic acid with **thionyl chloride**.

13.8 What Is Decarboxylation?

- **Decarboxylation** is the loss of CO_2 from a carboxyl group.
- Carboxylic acids that have a carbonyl group β to the carboxyl group readily undergo decarboxylation on mild heating.

QUICK QUIZ

Answer true or false to the following questions to assess your general knowledge of the concepts in this chapter. If you have difficulty with any of them, you should review the appropriate section in the chapter (shown in parentheses) before attempting the more challenging end-of-chapter problems.

1. In naming carboxylic acids, it is always necessary to indicate the position at which the carboxyl group occurs. (13.2)
2. 2-Propylpropanedioic acid can undergo decarboxylation at relatively moderate temperatures. (13.8)
3. Fischer esterification is reversible. (13.6)
4. The hydrophilic group of a carboxylic acid decreases water solubility. (13.3)
5. Both alcohols and carboxylic acids react with $SOCl_2$. (13.7)
6. Fischer esterification involves the reaction of a carboxylic acid with another carboxylic acid. (13.6)
7. An electronegative atom on a carboxylic acid can potentially increase the acid's acidity. (13.4)
8. A carboxyl group is reduced to a 1° alcohol by H_2/Pt. (13.5)
9. A carboxyl group is reduced to a 1° alcohol by $NaBH_4$. (13.5)
10. A carboxyl group that has been deprotonated is called a carboxylate group. (13.4)
11. A carboxyl group is reduced to a 1° alcohol by $LiAlH_4$. (13.5)
12. The conjugate base of a carboxylic acid is resonance-stabilized. (13.4)
13. Carboxylic acids possess both a region of polarity and a region of nonpolarity. (13.3)
14. Carboxylic acids are less acidic than phenols. (13.4)
15. 4-Oxopentanoic acid can undergo decarboxylation at relatively moderate temperatures. (13.8)
16. The γ position of a carboxylic acid refers to carbon-4 of the chain. (13.2)

Answers: (1) F (2) T (3) T (4) F (5) T (6) F (7) T (8) F (9) F (10) T (11) T (12) T (13) T (14) F (15) F (16) T

Detailed explanations for many of these answers can be found in the accompanying Solutions Manual.

KEY REACTIONS

1. Acidity of Carboxylic Acids (Section 13.4A)

Values of pK_a for most unsubstituted aliphatic and aromatic carboxylic acids are within the range from 4 to 5:

$$CH_3\overset{\overset{O}{\|}}{C}OH + H_2O \rightleftharpoons CH_3\overset{\overset{O}{\|}}{C}O^- + H_3O^+ \quad pK_a = 4.76$$

Substitution by electron-withdrawing groups decreases pK_a (increases acidity).

2. Reaction of Carboxylic Acids with Bases (Section 13.4B)

Carboxylic acids form water-soluble salts with alkali metal hydroxides, carbonates, and bicarbonates, as well as with ammonia and amines:

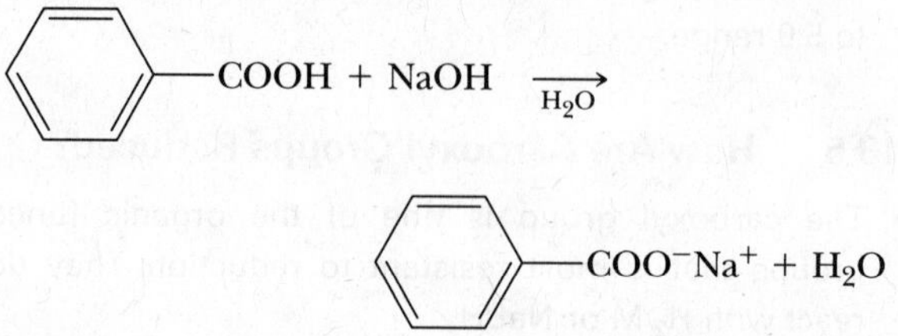

3. **Reduction by Lithium Aluminum Hydride (Section 13.5)**
   Lithium aluminum hydride reduces a carboxyl group to a primary alcohol:

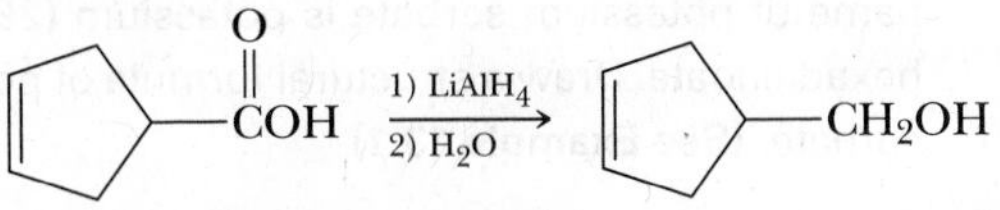

4. **Fischer Esterification (Section 13.6)**
   Fischer esterification is reversible:

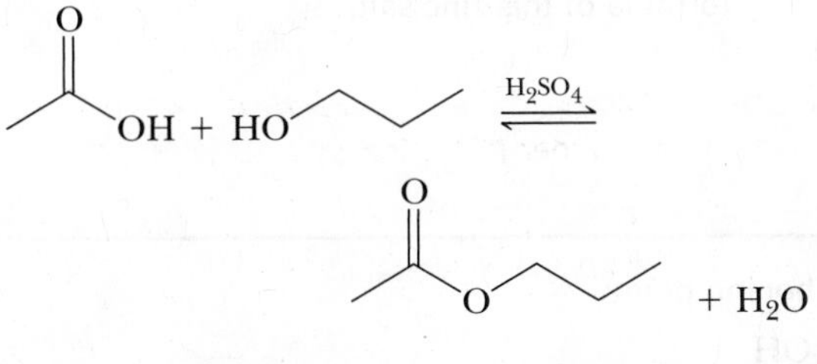

   One way to force the equilibrium to the right is to use an excess of the alcohol.

5. **Conversion to Acid Halides (Section 13.7)**
   Acid chlorides, the most common and widely used of the acid halides, are prepared by treating carboxylic acids with thionyl chloride:

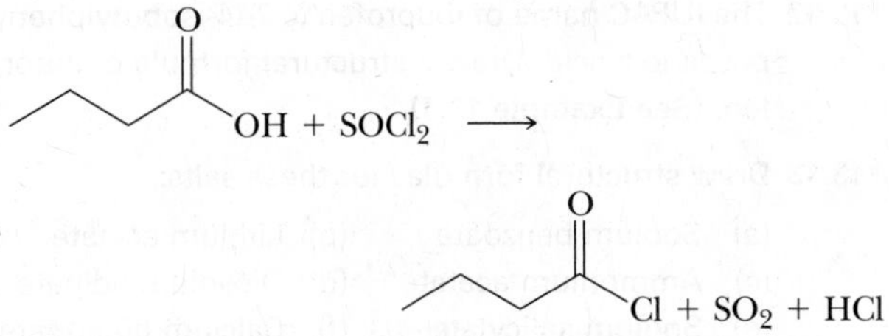

6. **Decarboxylation of β-Ketoacids (Section 13.8A)**
   The mechanism of decarboxylation involves the redistribution of bonding electrons in a cyclic, six-membered transition state:

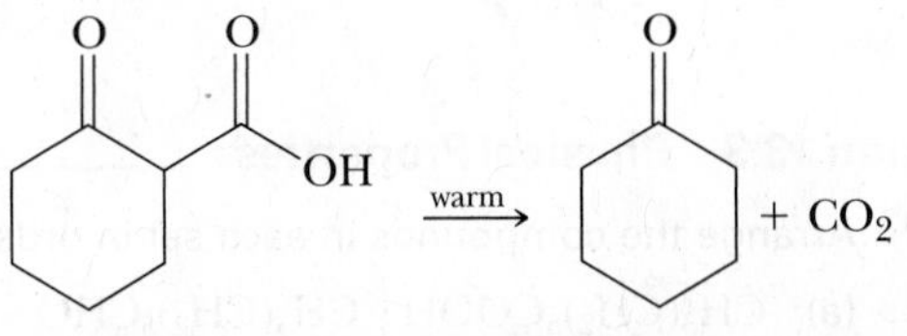

7. **Decarboxylation of β-Dicarboxylic Acids (Section 13.8B)**
   The mechanism of decarboxylation of a β-dicarboxylic acid is similar to that of decarboxylation of a β-ketoacid:

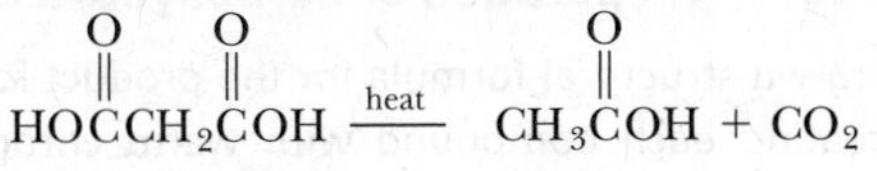

PROBLEMS

A problem marked with an asterisk indicates an applied "real-world" problem. Answers to problems whose numbers are printed in blue are given in Appendix D.

Section 13.2 Structure and Nomenclature

13.8 Name and draw structural formulas for the four carboxylic acids with molecular formula $C_5H_{10}O_2$. Which of these carboxylic acids is chiral?

13.9 Write the IUPAC name for each compound: **(See Example 13.1)**

(a) 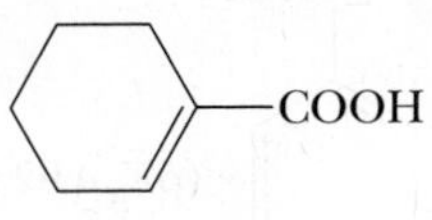

(b) 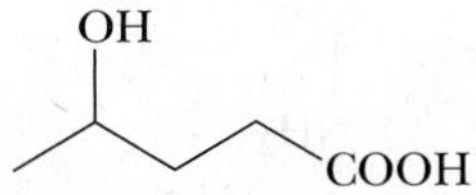

(c) 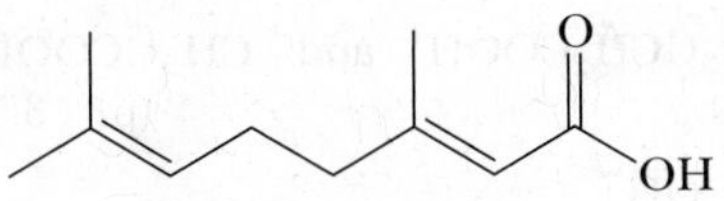

(d) 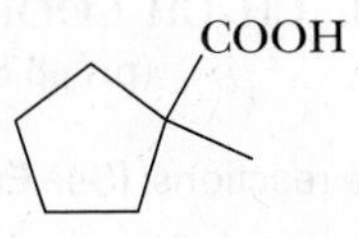

(e) 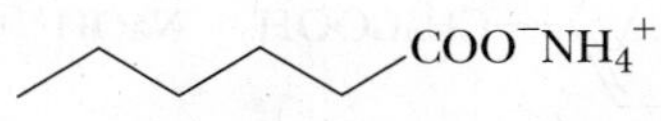

(f) 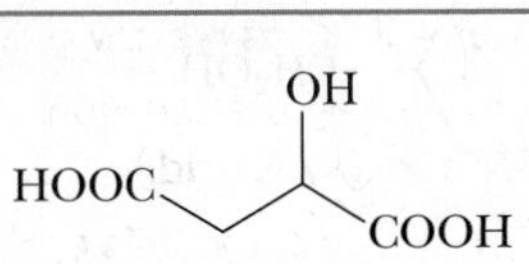

13.10 Draw a structural formula for each carboxylic acid: **(See Example 13.1)**

(a) 4-Nitrophenylacetic acid
(b) 4-Aminopentanoic acid
(c) 3-Chloro-4-phenylbutanoic acid
(d) *cis*-3-Hexenedioic acid
(e) 2,3-Dihydroxypropanoic acid
(f) 3-Oxohexanoic acid
(g) 2-Oxocyclohexanecarboxylic acid
(h) 2,2-Dimethylpropanoic acid

***13.11** Megatomoic acid, the sex attractant of the female black carpet beetle, has the structure **(See Example 13.1)**

$$CH_3(CH_2)_7CH{=}CHCH{=}CHCH_2COOH$$

Megatomoic acid

(a) What is the IUPAC name of megatomoic acid?
(b) State the number of stereoisomers possible for this compound.

*13.12 The IUPAC name of ibuprofen is 2-(4-isobutylphenyl) propanoic acid. Draw a structural formula of ibuprofen. **(See Example 13.1)**

*13.13 Draw structural formulas for these salts:

(a) Sodium benzoate (b) Lithium acetate
(c) Ammonium acetate (d) Disodium adipate
(e) Sodium salicylate (f) Calcium butanoate

*13.14 The monopotassium salt of oxalic acid is present in certain leafy vegetables, including rhubarb. Both oxalic acid and its salts are poisonous in high concentrations. Draw a structural formula of monopotassium oxalate.

*13.15 Potassium sorbate is added as a preservative to certain foods to prevent bacteria and molds from causing spoilage and to extend the foods' shelf life. The IUPAC name of potassium sorbate is potassium (2*E*,4*E*)-2,4-hexadienoate. Draw a structural formula of potassium sorbate. **(See Example 13.1)**

*13.16 Zinc 10-undecenoate, the zinc salt of 10-undecenoic acid, is used to treat certain fungal infections, particularly *tinea pedis* (athlete's foot). Draw a structural formula of this zinc salt.

Section 13.3 Physical Properties

13.17 Arrange the compounds in each set in order of increasing boiling point:

(a) $CH_3(CH_2)_5COOH$ $CH_3(CH_2)_6CHO$ $CH_3(CH_2)_6CH_2OH$
(b) CH_3CH_2COOH $CH_3CH_2CH_2CH_2OH$ $CH_3CH_2OCH_2CH_3$

Section 13.4 Preparation of Carboxylic Acids

13.18 Draw a structural formula for the product formed by treating each compound with warm chromic acid, H_2CrO_4:

(a) $CH_3(CH_2)_4CH_2OH$

(b) 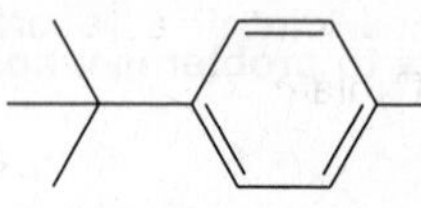

(c) 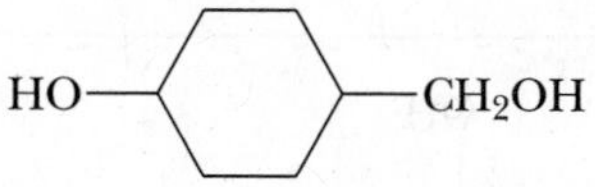

13.19 Draw a structural formula for a compound with the given molecular formula that, on oxidation by chromic acid, gives the carboxylic acid or dicarboxylic acid shown:

(a) $C_6H_{14}O \xrightarrow{\text{oxidation}}$ 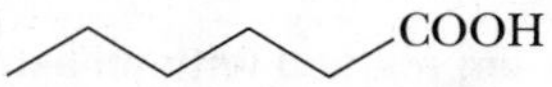

(b) $C_6H_{12}O \xrightarrow{\text{oxidation}}$ 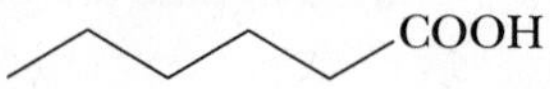

(c) $C_6H_{14}O_2 \xrightarrow{\text{oxidation}}$ 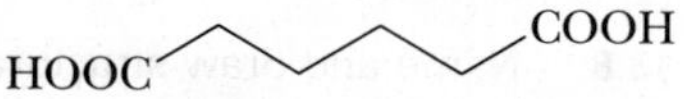

Acidity of Carboxylic Acids

13.20 Which is the stronger acid in each pair? **(See Example 13.2)**

(a) Phenol (pK_a 9.95) or benzoic acid (pK_a 4.17)
(b) Lactic acid (K_a 1.4×10^{-4}) or ascorbic acid (K_a 6.8×10^{-5})

13.21 Arrange these compounds in order of increasing acidity: benzoic acid, benzyl alcohol, and phenol. **(See Example 13.2)**

13.22 Assign the acid in each set its appropriate pK_a: **(See Example 13.2)**

(a) 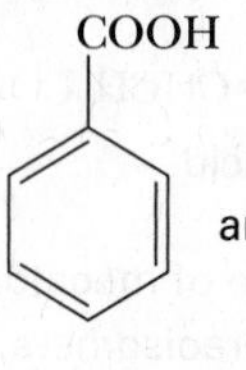 and 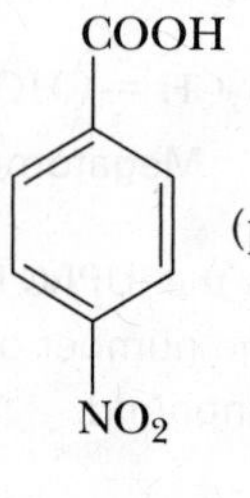 (pK_a 4.19 and 3.14)

(b) 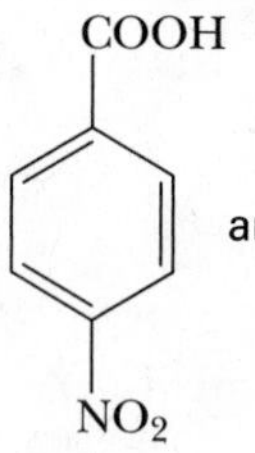 and 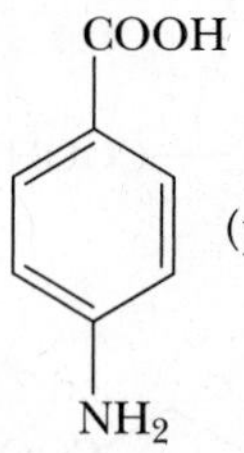 (pK_a 4.92 and 3.14)

(c) $CH_3\overset{O}{\overset{\|}{C}}CH_2COOH$ and $CH_3\overset{O}{\overset{\|}{C}}COOH$ (pK_a 3.58 and 2.49)

(d) $CH_3\overset{OH}{\overset{|}{C}}HCOOH$ and CH_3CH_2COOH (pK_a 3.85 and 4.78)

13.23 Complete these acid–base reactions: **(See Example 13.3)**

(a) 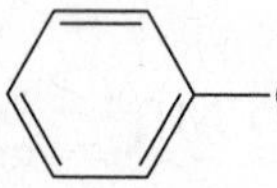 $-CH_2COOH + NaOH \longrightarrow$

(b) $CH_3CH{=}CHCH_2COOH + NaHCO_3 \longrightarrow$

(c) 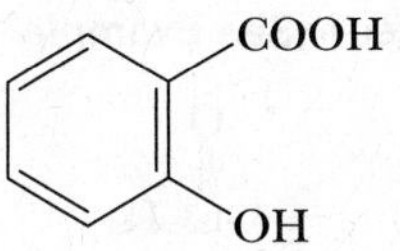 $+ NaHCO_3 \longrightarrow$

(d) $CH_3CH(OH)COOH + H_2NCH_2CH_2OH \longrightarrow$ (OH on C-2)

(e) $CH_3CH{=}CHCH_2COO^-Na^+ + HCl \longrightarrow$

*13.24 The normal pH range for blood plasma is 7.35–7.45. Under these conditions, would you expect the carboxyl group of lactic acid (pK_a 3.85) to exist primarily as a carboxyl group or as a carboxylate anion? Explain.

*13.25 The pK_a of salicylic acid (Section 13.2), is 2.97. Would you expect salicylic acid dissolved in blood plasma (pH 7.35–7.45) to exist primarily as salicylic acid or as salicylate anion? Explain.

*13.26 Vanillylmandelic acid (pK_a 3.42) is a metabolite found in urine, the pH of which is normally in the range from 4.8 to 8.4. Provide the structure of vanillylmandelic acid that you would expect to find in urine with pH 5.8?

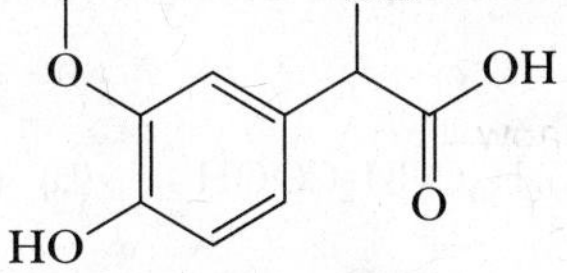

Vanillylmandelic acid

*13.27 The pH of human gastric juice is normally in the range from 1.0 to 3.0. What form of lactic acid (pK_a 3.85), lactic acid itself or its anion, would you expect to be present in the stomach?

*13.28 Following are two structural formulas for the amino acid alanine (Section 18.2):

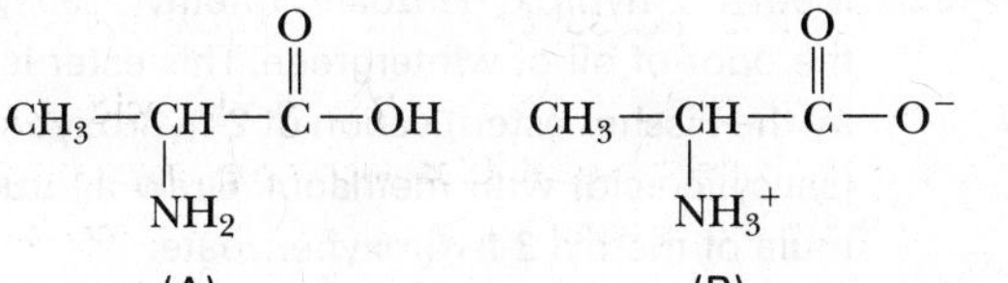

(A) (B)

Is alanine better represented by structural formula A or B? Explain.

*13.29 In Chapter 18, we discuss a class of compounds called amino acids, so named because they contain both an amino group and a carboxyl group. Following is a structural formula for the amino acid alanine in the form of an internal salt:

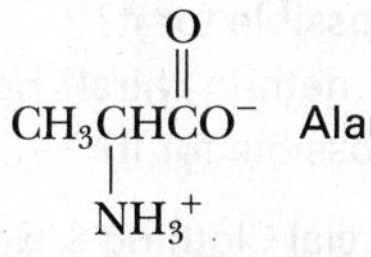 Alanine

What would you expect to be the major form of alanine present in aqueous solution at (a) pH 2.0, (b) pH 5–6, and (c) pH 11.0? Explain.

Sections 13.5–13.8 Reactions of Carboxylic Acids

13.30 Give the expected organic products formed when phenylacetic acid, $PhCH_2COOH$, is treated with each of the following reagents: **(See Examples 13.4–13.6)**

(a) $SOCl_2$
(b) $NaHCO_3$, H_2O
(c) NaOH, H_2O
(d) NH_3, H_2O
(e) $LiAlH_4$, followed by H_2O
(f) $NaBH_4$, followed by H_2O
(g) $CH_3OH + H_2SO_4$ (catalyst)
(h) H_2/Ni at 25 °C and 3 atm pressure

13.31 Show how to convert *trans*-3-phenyl-2-propenoic acid (cinnamic acid) to these compounds: **(See Example 13.4)**

(a) 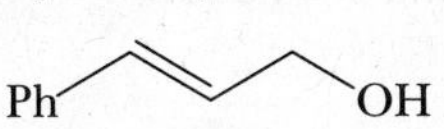

(b) 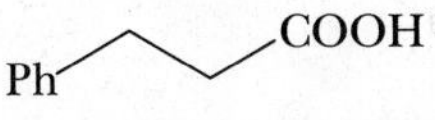

(c) 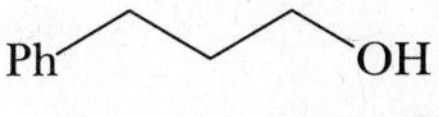

13.32 Show how to convert 3-oxobutanoic acid (acetoacetic acid) to these compounds: **(See Example 13.4)**

(a) $CH_3CH(OH)CH_2COOH$ (OH on C-3)

(b) $CH_3CH(OH)CH_2CH_2OH$ (OH on C-3)

(c) $CH_3CH{=}CHCOOH$

13.33 Complete these examples of Fischer esterification (assume an excess of the alcohol): **(See Example 13.5)**

(a) 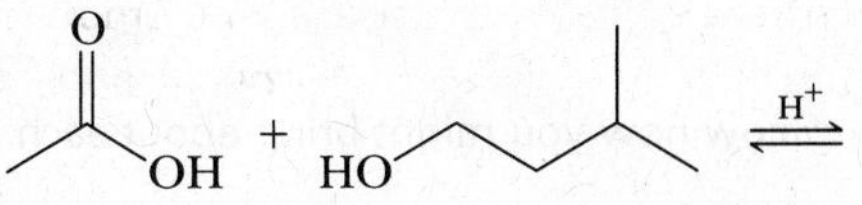

(b) 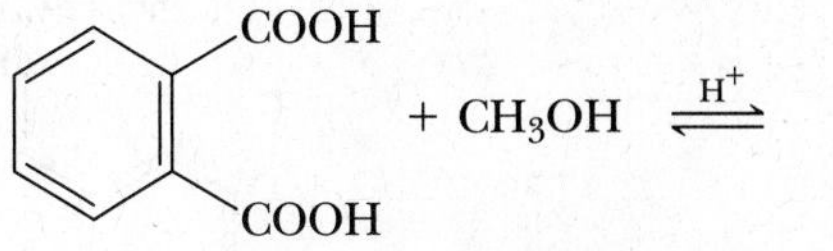

(c) 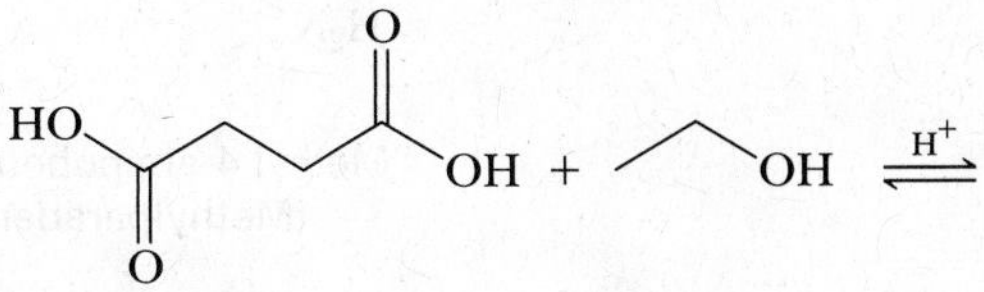

*13.34 Formic acid is one of the components responsible for the sting of biting ants and is injected under the skin by bees and wasps. A way to relieve the pain is to rub the area of the sting with a paste of baking soda ($NaHCO_3$) and water, which neutralizes the acid. Write an equation for this reaction. **(See Example 13.3)**

*13.35 Methyl 2-hydroxybenzoate (methyl salicylate) has the odor of oil of wintergreen. This ester is prepared by the Fischer esterification of 2-hydroxybenzoic acid (salicylic acid) with methanol. Draw a structural formula of methyl 2-hydroxybenzoate.

*13.36 Benzocaine, a topical anesthetic, is prepared by treating 4-aminobenzoic acid with ethanol in the presence of an acid catalyst, followed by neutralization. Draw a structural formula of benzocaine.

*13.37 Examine the structural formulas of pyrethrin and permethrin. (See Chemical Connections 14D.)

(a) Locate the ester groups in each compound.
(b) Is pyrethrin chiral? How many stereoisomers are possible for it?
(c) Is permethrin chiral? How many stereoisomers are possible for it?

*13.38 A commercial Clothing & Gear Insect Repellant gives the following information about permethrin, its active ingredient:

Cis/trans ratio: Minimum 35% (+/−) *cis* and maximum 65% (+/−) *trans*

(a) To what does the *cis/trans* ratio refer?
(b) To what does the designation "(+/−)" refer?

13.39 From what carboxylic acid and alcohol is each of the following esters derived? **(See Example 13.5)**

(a) 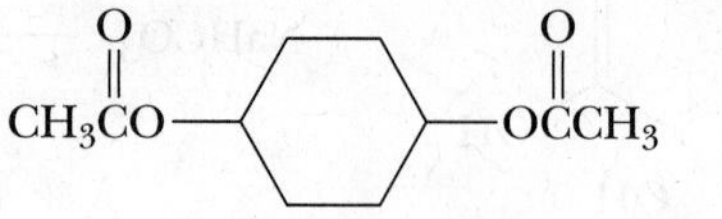

(b) $CH_3O\overset{O}{\overset{\|}{C}}CH_2CH_2\overset{O}{\overset{\|}{C}}OCH_3$

(c) 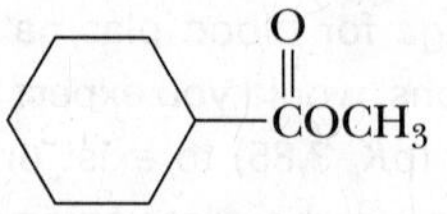

(d) $CH_3CH_2CH{=}CH\overset{O}{\overset{\|}{C}}OCH(CH_3)_2$

13.40 When treated with an acid catalyst, 4-hydroxybutanoic acid forms a cyclic ester (a lactone). Draw the structural formula of this lactone. **(See Example 13.5)**

13.41 Draw a structural formula for the product formed on thermal decarboxylation of each of the following compounds: **(See Example 13.7)**

(a) $C_6H_5\overset{O}{\overset{\|}{C}}CH_2COOH$

(b) $C_6H_5CH_2\overset{COOH}{\overset{|}{C}}HCOOH$

(c) 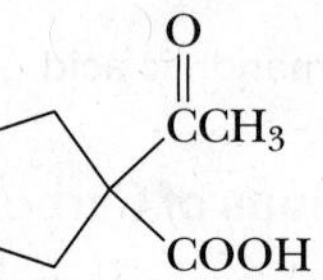

Synthesis

*13.42 Methyl 2-aminobenzoate, a flavoring agent with the taste of grapes (see Chemical Connections 13B), can be prepared from toluene by the following series of steps:

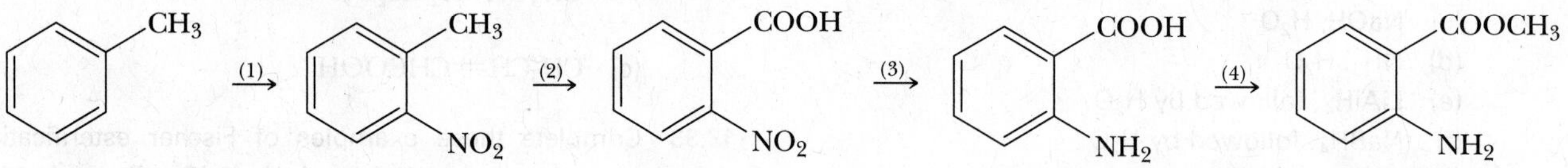

Toluene

Methyl 2-aminobenzoate

Show how you might bring about each step in this synthesis.

*13.43 Methylparaben and propylparaben are used as preservatives in foods, beverages, and cosmetics:

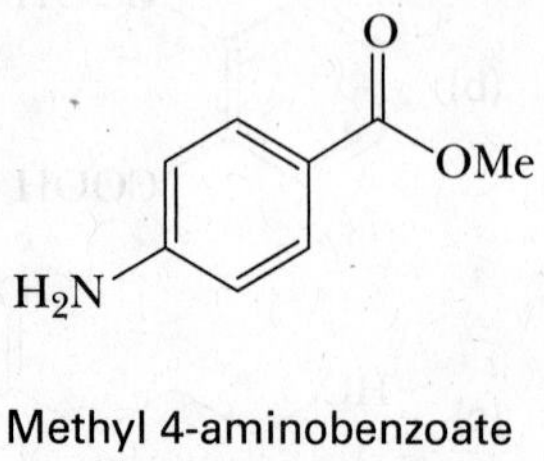

Methyl 4-aminobenzoate (Methylparaben)

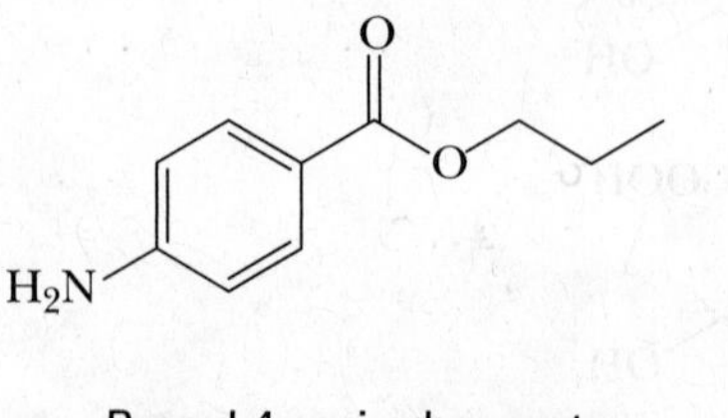

Propyl 4-aminobenzoate (Propylparaben)

Show how the synthetic scheme in Problem 13.42 can be modified to give each of these compounds.

***13.44** Procaine (its hydrochloride is marketed as Novocaine®) was one of the first local anesthetics developed for infiltration and regional anesthesia. It is synthesized by the following Fischer esterification:

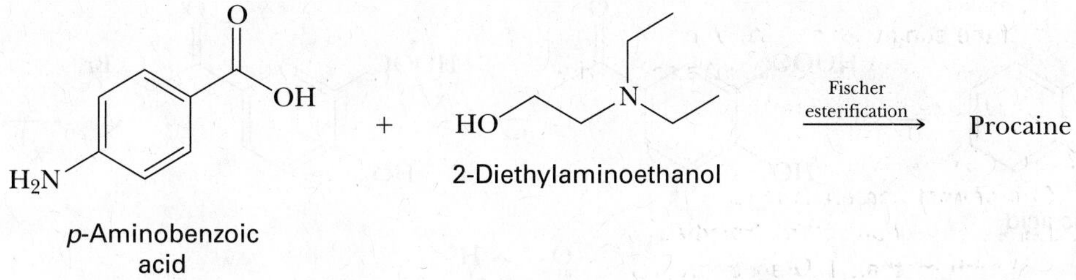

Draw a structural formula for procaine.

***13.45** Meclizine is an antiemetic: It helps prevent, or at least lessen, the vomiting associated with motion sickness, including seasickness. Among the names of the over-the-counter preparations of meclizine are Bonine®, Sea-Legs, Antivert®, and Navicalm®. Meclizine can be synthesized by the following series of steps:

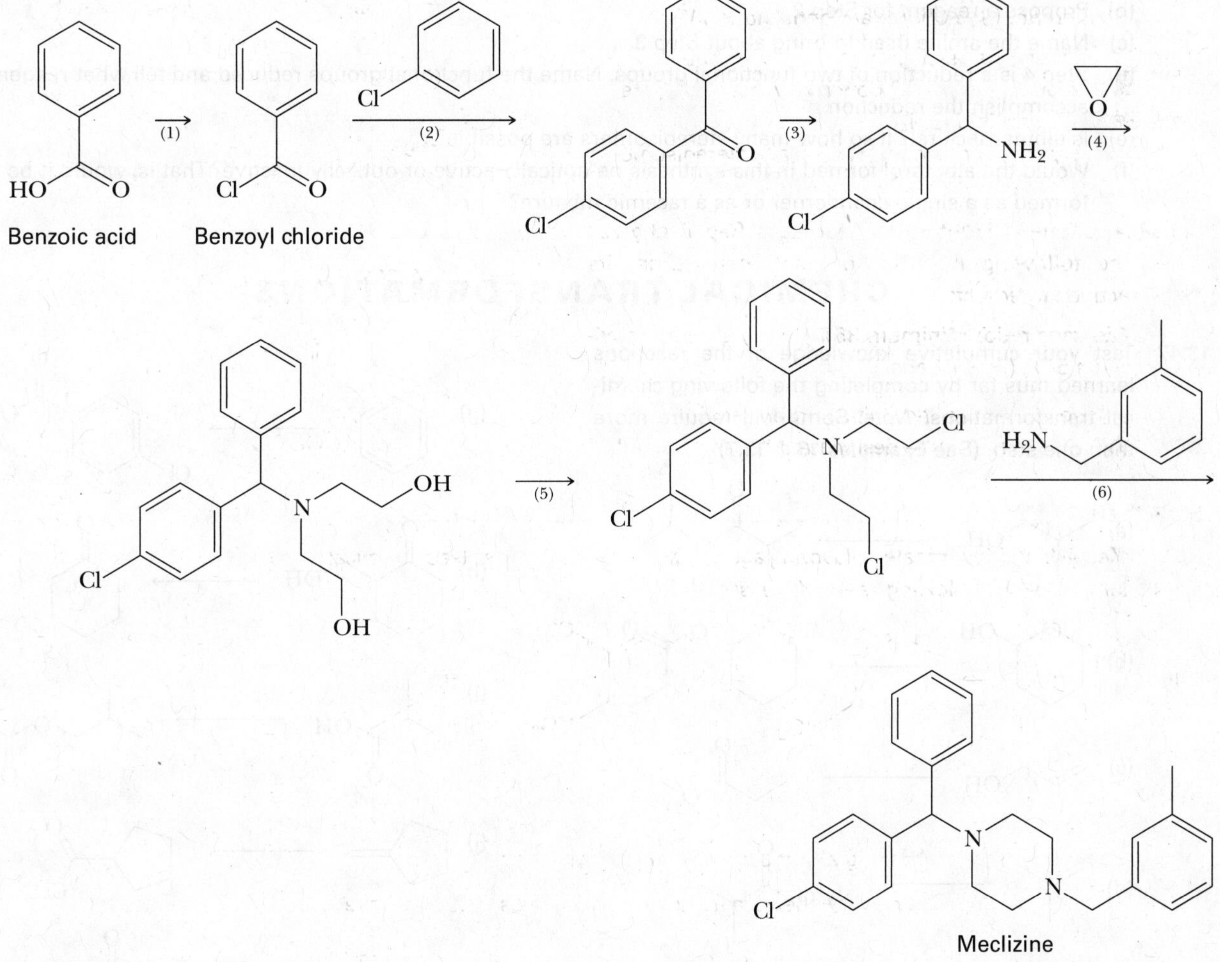

(a) Propose a reagent for Step 1.
(b) The catalyst for Step 2 is $AlCl_3$. Name the type of reaction that occurs in Step 2.
(c) Propose reagents for Step 3.
(d) Propose a mechanism for Step 4, and show that it is an example of nucleophilic aliphatic substitution.
(e) Propose a reagent for Step 5.
(f) Show that Step 6 is also an example of nucleophilic aliphatic substitution.

***13.46** Chemists have developed several syntheses for the antiasthmatic drug albuterol (Proventil). One of these syntheses starts with salicylic acid, the same acid that is the starting material for the synthesis of aspirin:

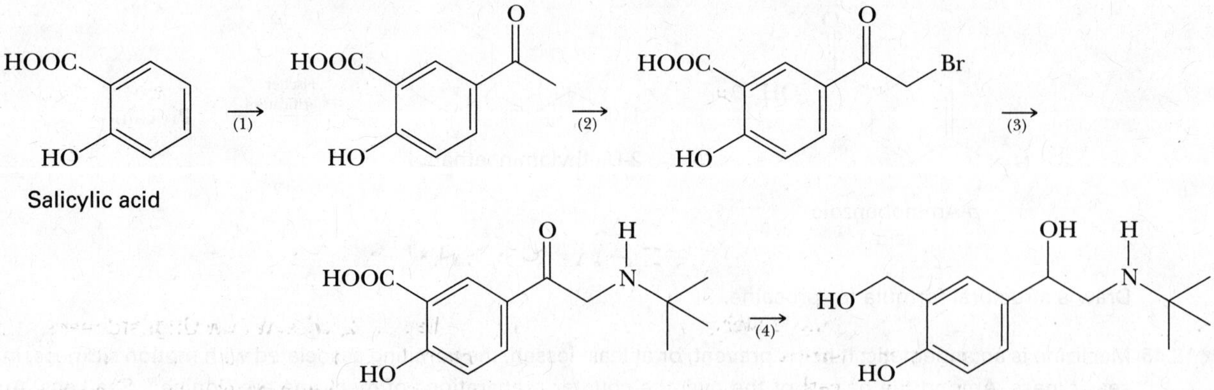

Salicylic acid

Albuterol

(a) Propose a reagent and a catalyst for Step 1. What name is given to this type of reaction?
(b) Propose a reagent for Step 2.
(c) Name the amine used to bring about Step 3.
(d) Step 4 is a reduction of two functional groups. Name the functional groups reduced and tell what reagent will accomplish the reduction.
(e) Is albuterol chiral? If so how many stereoisomers are possible?
(f) Would the albuterol formed in this synthesis be optically active or optically inactive? That is, would it be formed as a single enantiomer or as a racemic mixture?

CHEMICAL TRANSFORMATIONS

13.47 Test your cumulative knowledge of the reactions learned thus far by completing the following chemical transformations. *Note*: Some will require more than one step. **(See Examples 13.4–13.7)**

(a) 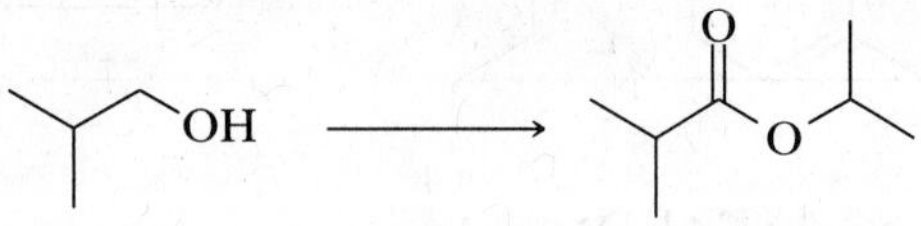

(b) 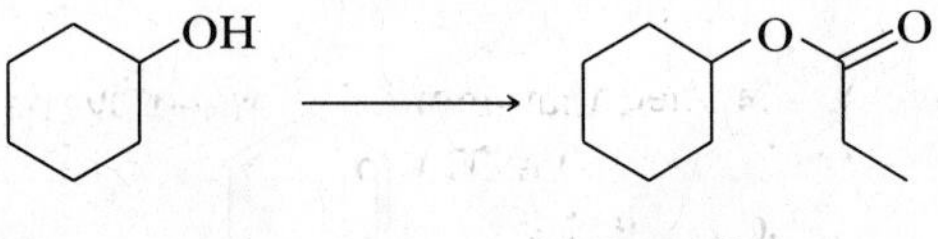

(c) 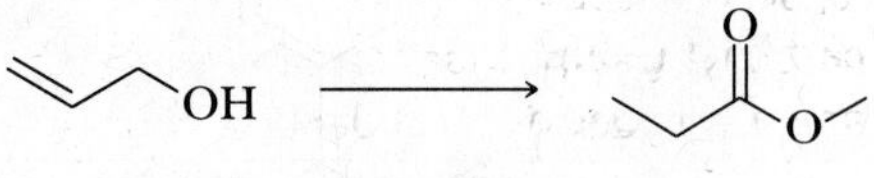

(d) 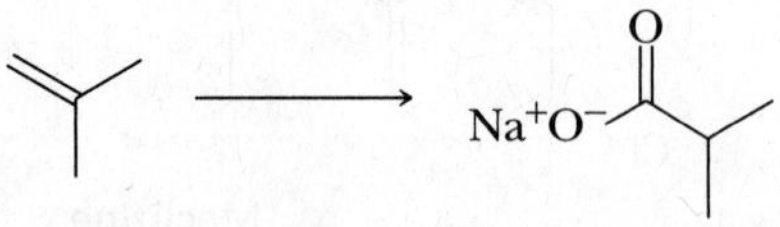

(e) 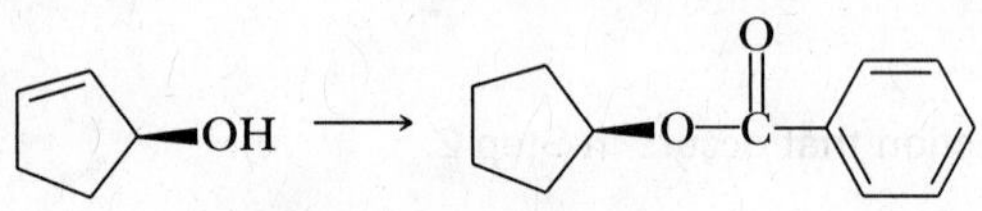

(f) 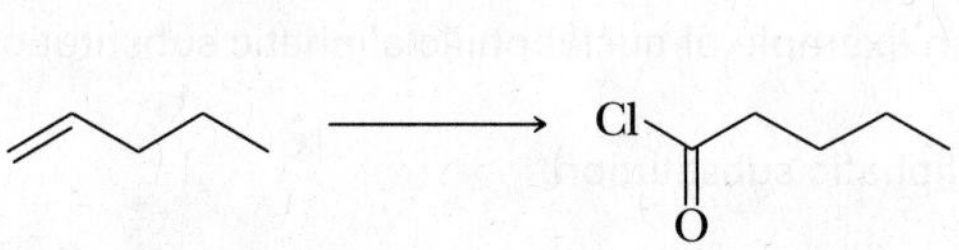

(g) 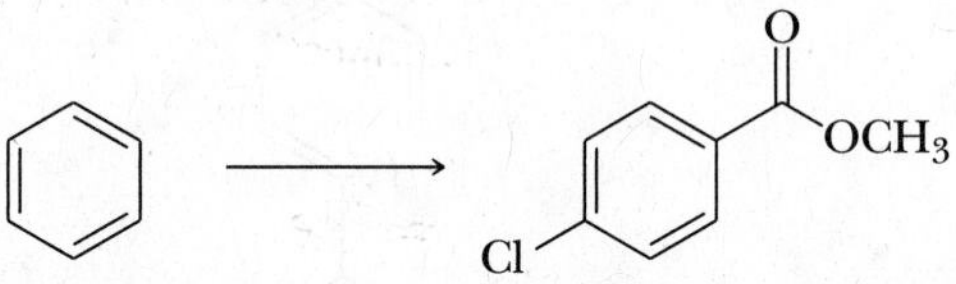

(h) 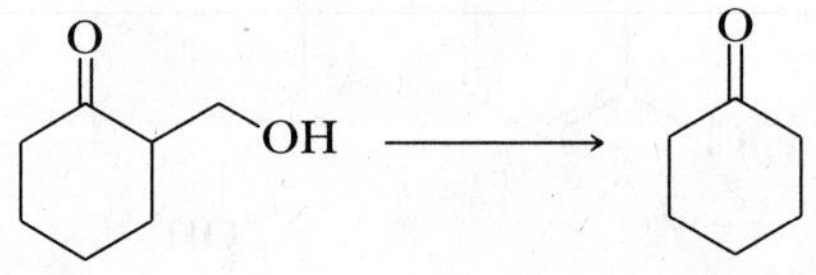

(i) 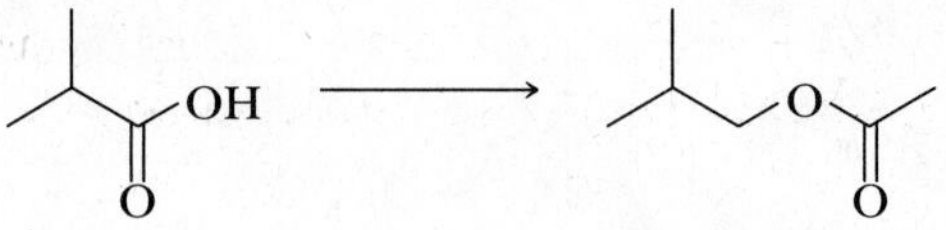

(j) 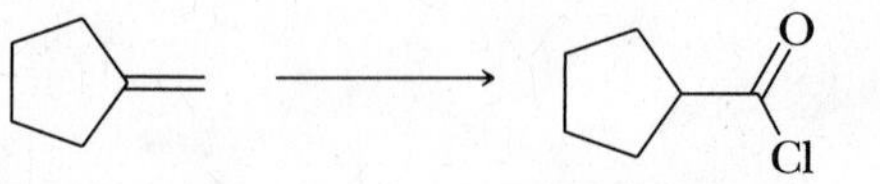

(k) 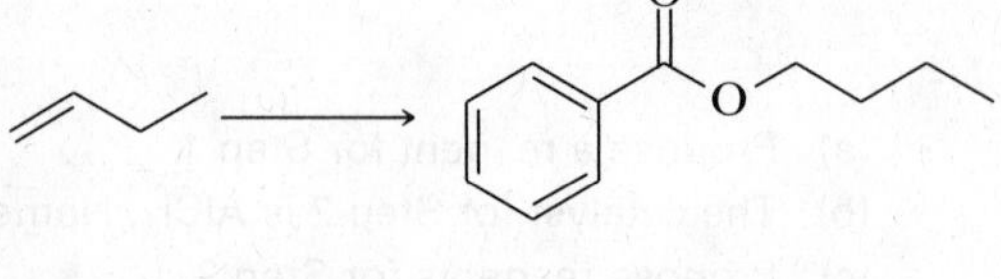

(l) 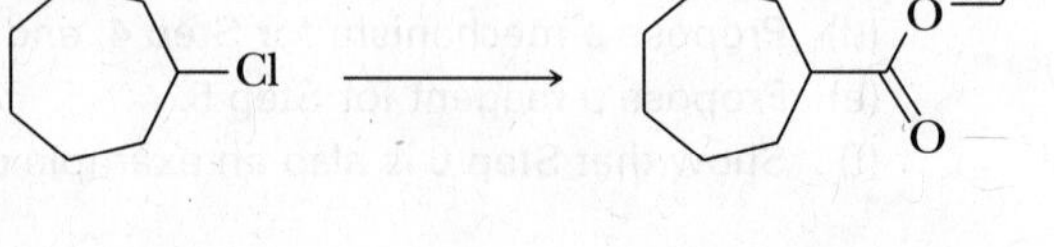

(m) 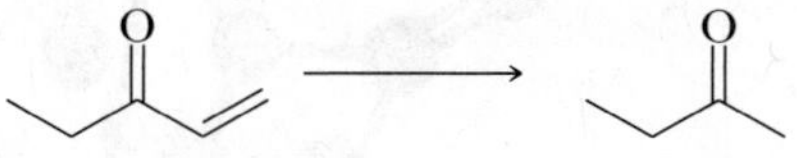

(n) 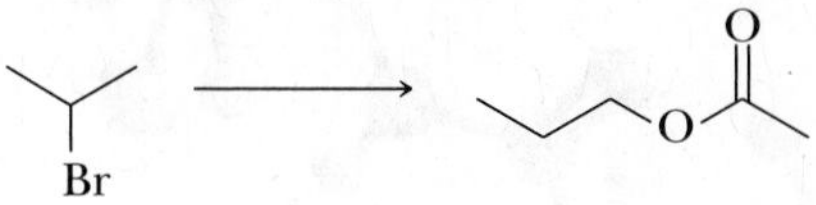

(o) 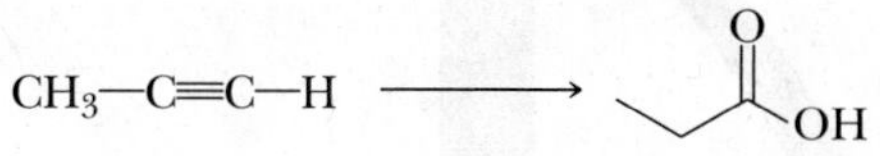

(p) 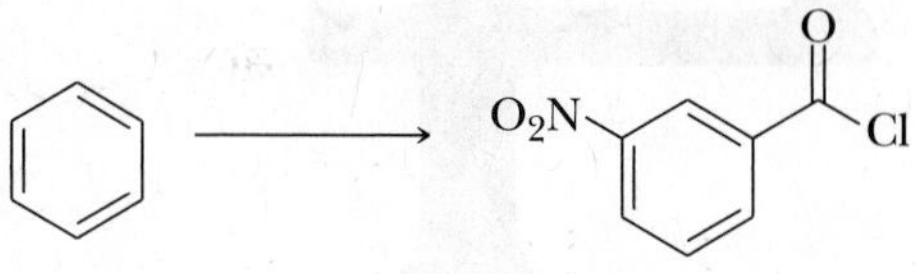

LOOKING AHEAD

13.48 Explain why α-amino acids, the building blocks of proteins (Chapter 18), are nearly a thousand times more acidic than aliphatic carboxylic acids: **(See Example 13.2)**

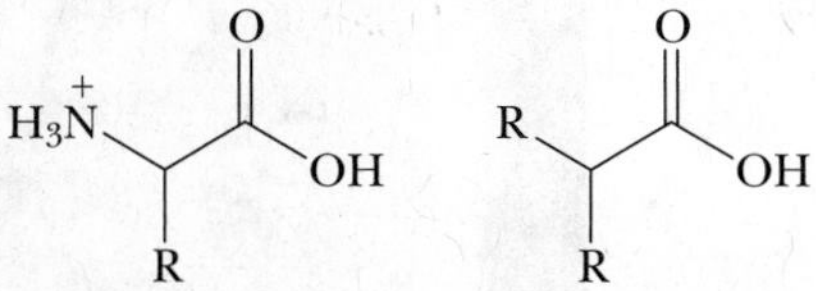

An α-amino acid p$K_a \approx 2$ An aliphatic acid p$K_a \approx 5$

13.49 Which is more difficult to reduce with $LiAlH_4$, a carboxylic acid or a carboxylate ion?

13.50 Show how an ester can react with H^+/H_2O to give a carboxylic acid and an alcohol (*Hint:* This is the reverse of Fischer esterification):

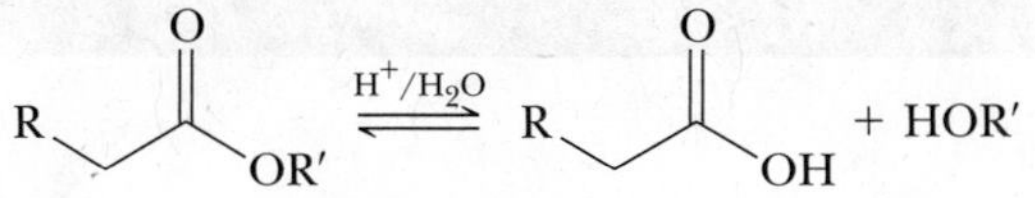

13.51 In Chapter 12, we saw how Grignard reagents readily attack the carbonyl carbon of ketones and aldehydes. Should the same process occur with Grignards and carboxylic acids? With esters?

13.52 In Section 13.6, it was suggested that the mechanism for the Fischer esterification of carboxylic acids would be a model for many of the reactions of the functional derivatives of carboxylic acids. One such reaction, the reaction of an acid halide with water, is the following:

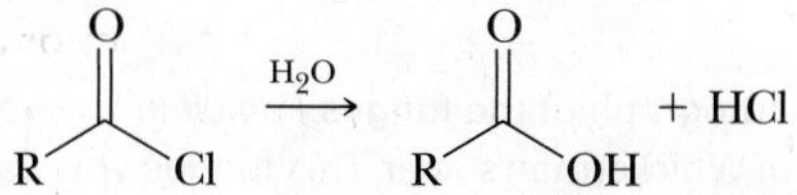

Suggest a mechanism for this reaction.

GROUP LEARNING ACTIVITIES

13.53 What acids are more acidic (lower pK_a) than carboxylic acids? What acids are less acidic (higher pK_a) than carboxylic acids? List and discuss any trends in this list of acids.

13.54 We learned that after it is formed by the attack of a nucleophile, the TCAI of a carboxylic acid can collapse to eject a leaving group and regenerate the carbonyl group. Discuss why the TCAIs of ketones and aldehydes don't undergo the same process.

14

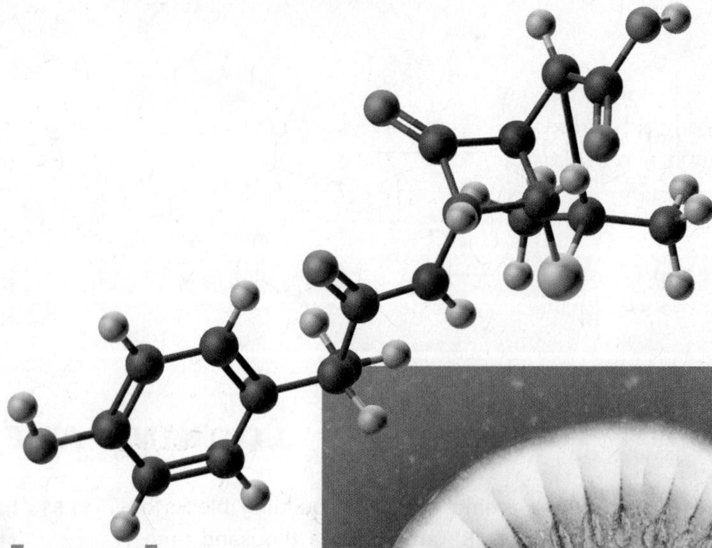

Functional Derivatives of Carboxylic Acids

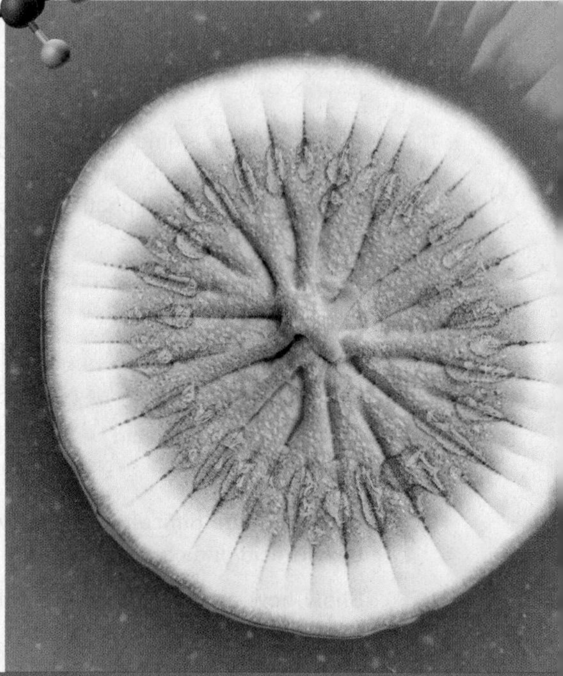

Macrophotograph of the fungus *Penicillium notatum* growing on a petri dish culture of Whickerman's agar. This fungus was used as an early source of the first penicillin antibiotic. Inset: A model of amoxicillin, a compound that contains two amide functional groups. Amides are functional derivatives of carboxylic acids. (Andrew McClenaghan/Photo Researchers, Inc.)

KEY QUESTIONS

- **14.1 What Are Some Derivatives of Carboxylic Acids, and How Are They Named?**
- **14.2 What Are the Characteristic Reactions of Carboxylic Acid Derivatives?**
- **14.3 What Is Hydrolysis?**
- **14.4 How Do Carboxylic Acid Derivatives React with Alcohols?**
- **14.5 How Do Carboxylic Acid Derivatives React with Ammonia and Amines?**
- **14.6 How Can Functional Derivatives of Carboxylic Acids Be Interconverted?**
- **14.7 How Do Esters React with Grignard Reagents?**
- **14.8 How Are Derivatives of Carboxylic Acids Reduced?**

HOW TO

- **14.1 How to Name Functional Derivatives of Carboxylic Acids**
- **14.2 How to Approach Multistep Synthesis Problems**

CHEMICAL CONNECTIONS

- **14A Ultraviolet Sunscreens and Sunblocks**
- **14B From Moldy Clover to a Blood Thinner**
- **14C The Penicillins and Cephalosporins: β-Lactam Antibiotics**
- **14D The Pyrethrins: Natural Insecticides of Plant Origin**
- **14E Systematic Acquired Resistance in Plants**

IN THIS CHAPTER, we study four classes of organic compounds, all derived from the carboxyl group: acid halides, acid anhydrides, esters, and amides. Under the general formula of each functional group is a drawing to help you see how the group is formally related to a carboxyl group. The loss of —OH from a carboxyl group and H— from H—Cl, for example, gives an acid chloride, and similarly, the loss of —OH from a carboxyl group and H— from ammonia gives an amide:

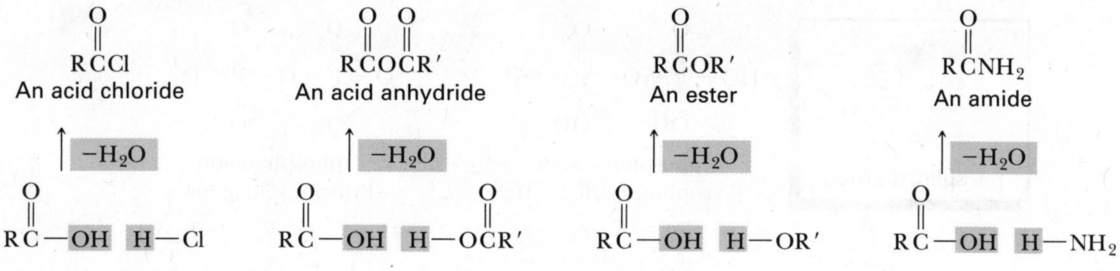

14.1 What Are Some Derivatives of Carboxylic Acids, and How Are They Named?

A. Acid Halides

The functional group of an **acid halide** (acyl halide) is an **acyl group (RCO—)** bonded to a halogen atom (Section 13.7). The most common acid halides are acid chlorides:

Acid halide A derivative of a carboxylic acid in which the —OH of the carboxyl group is replaced by a halogen—most commonly, chlorine.

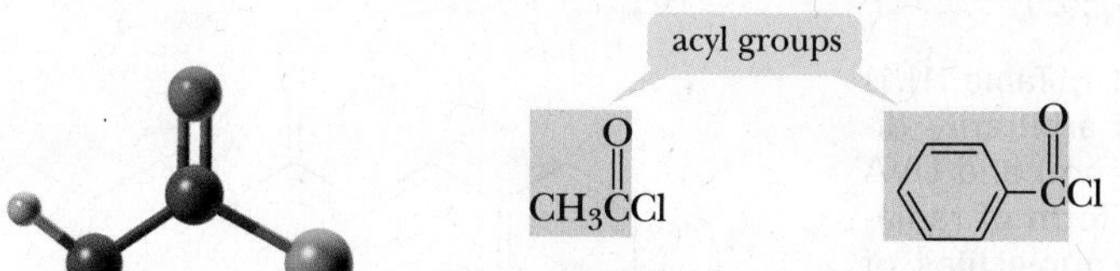

Ethanoyl chloride (Acetyl chloride)   Benzoyl chloride

Acid halides are named by changing the suffix *-ic acid* in the name of the parent carboxylic acid to *-yl halide.*

B. Acid Anhydrides

Carboxylic Anhydrides

The functional group of a **carboxylic anhydride** (commonly referred to simply as an anhydride) is two acyl groups bonded to an oxygen atom. The anhydride may be symmetrical (having two identical acyl groups), or it may be mixed (having two different acyl groups). Symmetrical anhydrides are named by changing the suffix *acid* in the name of the parent carboxylic acid to *anhydride.*

Carboxylic anhydride A compound in which two acyl groups are bonded to an oxygen.

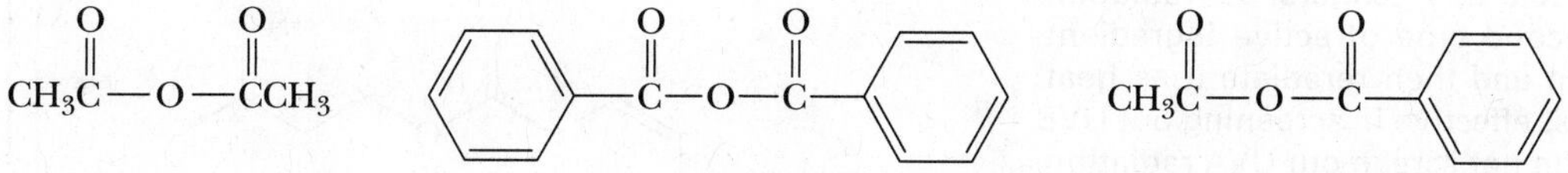

Acetic anhydride   Benzoic anhydride   Acetic benzoic anhydride (a mixed anhydride)

Mixed anhydrides are named by identifying the two parent carboxylic acids from both acyl groups and placing those names in succession, in alphabetical order, without the "acid" part of the name followed by the word *anhydride.*

Phosphoric Anhydrides

Because of the special importance of anhydrides of phosphoric acid in biochemical systems (Chapter 21), we include them here to show the similarity between them and the anhydrides of carboxylic acids. The functional group of a **phosphoric anhydride** is two phosphoryl groups bonded to an oxygen atom. Shown here are structural formulas for two anhydrides of phosphoric acid, H_3PO_4, and the ions derived by ionization of the acidic hydrogens of each:

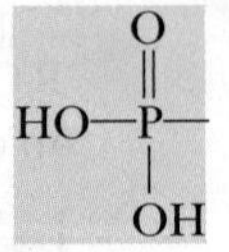

phosphoryl group

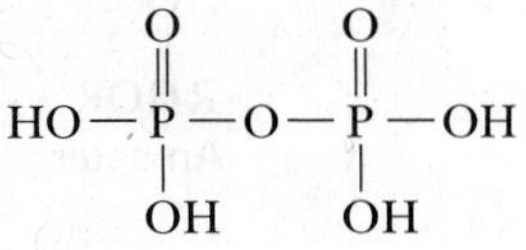

Diphosphoric acid
(Pyrophosphoric acid)

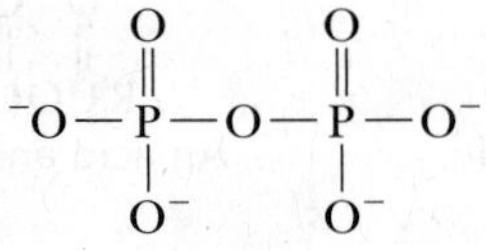

Diphosphate ion
(Pyrophosphate ion)

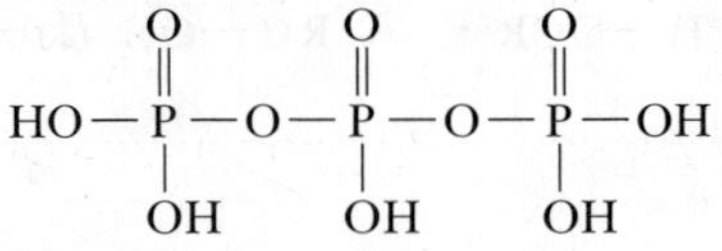

Triphosphoric acid

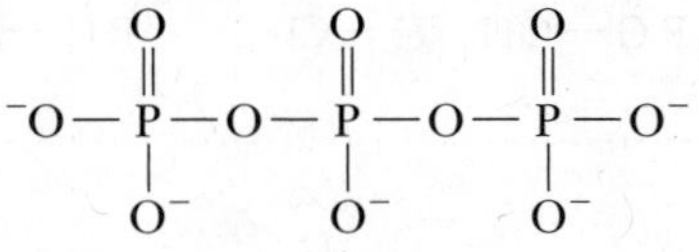

Triphosphate ion

Chemical Connections 14A

ULTRAVIOLET SUNSCREENS AND SUNBLOCKS

Ultraviolet (UV) radiation (Section 11.1, Table 11.1) penetrating the earth's ozone layer is arbitrarily divided into two regions: UVB (290–320 nm) and UVA (320–400 nm). UVB, a more energetic form of radiation than UVA, interacts directly with molecules of the skin and eyes, causing skin cancer, aging of the skin, eye damage leading to cataracts, and delayed sunburn that appears 12 to 24 hours after exposure. UVA radiation, by contrast, causes tanning. It also damages skin, albeit much less efficiently than UVB. The role of UVA in promoting skin cancer is less well understood.

Commercial sunscreen products are rated according to their sun protection factor (SPF), which is defined as the minimum effective dose of UV radiation that produces a delayed sunburn on protected skin compared with unprotected skin. Two types of active ingredients are found in commercial sunblocks and sunscreens. The most common sunblock agent is zinc oxide, ZnO, a white crystalline substance that reflects and scatters UV radiation. Sunscreens, the second type of active ingredient, absorb UV radiation and then reradiate it as heat. Sunscreens are most effective in screening out UVB radiation, but they do not screen out UVA radiation. Thus, they allow tanning, but prevent the UVB-associated damage. Given here are structural formulas for three common esters used as UVB-screening agents, along with the name by which each is most commonly listed in the "Active Ingredients" label on commercial products:

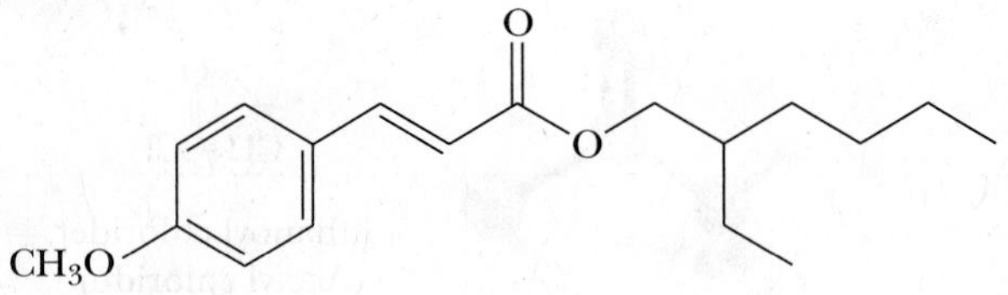

Octyl *p*-methoxycinnamate

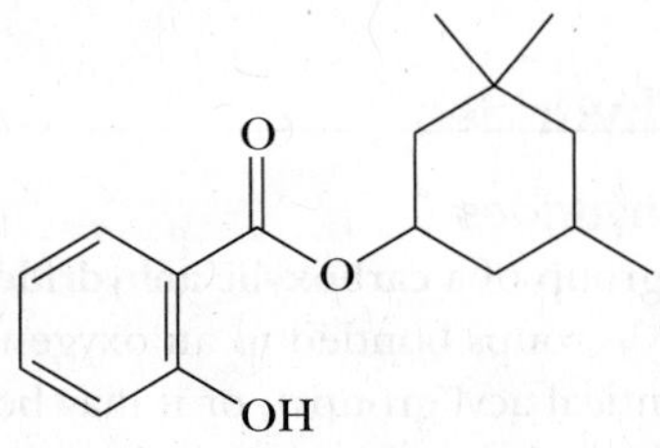

Homosalate

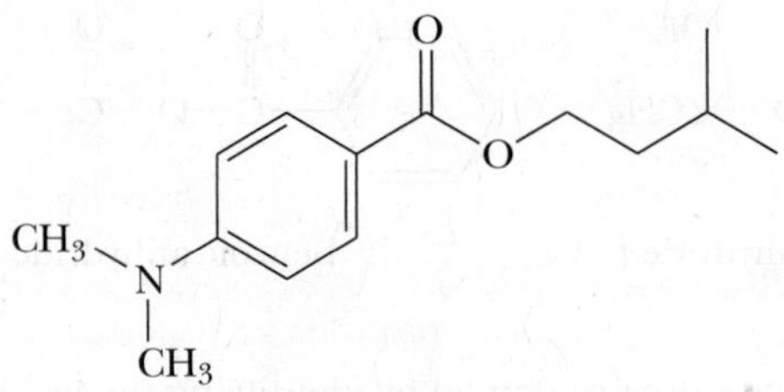

Padimate A

Question

Show how each sunscreen can be synthesized from a carboxylic acid and alcohol using the Fischer esterification reaction (Section 13.6).

C. Esters and Lactones

Esters of Carboxylic Acids

The functional group of a **carboxylic ester** (commonly referred to simply as an ester) is an acyl group bonded to —OR or —OAr. Both IUPAC and common names of esters are derived from the names of the parent carboxylic acids. The alkyl or aryl group bonded to oxygen is named first, followed by the name of the acid, in which the suffix *-ic acid* is replaced by the suffix *-ate*:

the name of the group bonded to the —O— comes first

$CH_3\overset{O}{\overset{\|}{C}}OCH_2CH_3$

Ethyl ethanoate
(Ethyl acetate)

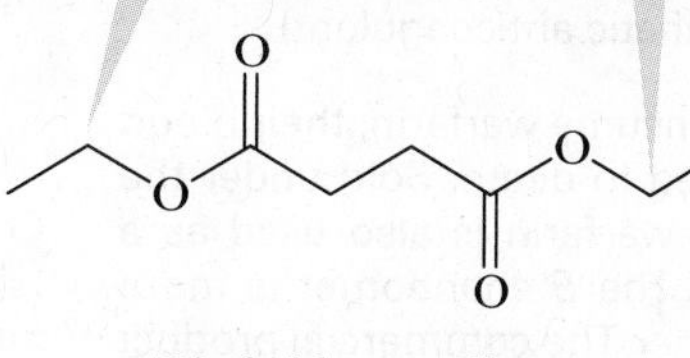

Diethyl butanedioate
(Diethyl succinate)

A cyclic ester is called a **lactone**. The IUPAC name of a lactone is formed by dropping the suffix *-oic acid* from the name of the parent carboxylic acid and adding the suffix *-olactone*. The common name is similarly derived. The location of the oxygen atom in the ring is indicated by a number if the IUPAC name of the acid is used and by a Greek letter α, β, γ, δ, ε, and so forth if the common name of the acid is used.

Lactone A cyclic ester.

4-Butanolactone
(A γ-lactone)

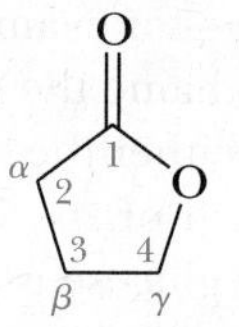

Chemical Connections 14B

FROM MOLDY CLOVER TO A BLOOD THINNER

In 1933, a disgruntled farmer delivered a pail of unclotted blood to the laboratory of Dr. Karl Link at the University of Wisconsin and told tales of cows bleeding to death from minor cuts. Over the next couple of years, Link and his collaborators discovered that when cows are fed moldy clover, their blood clotting is inhibited, and they bleed to death from minor cuts and scratches. From the moldy clover, Link isolated the anticoagulant dicoumarol, a substance that delays or prevents blood from clotting. Dicoumarol exerts its anticoagulation effect by interfering with vitamin K activity (Section 20.6D). Within a few years after its discovery, dicoumarol became widely used to treat victims of heart attack and others at risk for developing blood clots.

Dicoumarol is a derivative of coumarin, a cyclic ester that gives sweet clover its pleasant smell. Coumarin, which does not interfere with blood clotting and has been used as a flavoring agent, is converted to dicoumarol as sweet clover becomes moldy. Notice that coumarin is a lactone (cyclic ester), whereas dicoumarol is a dilactone:

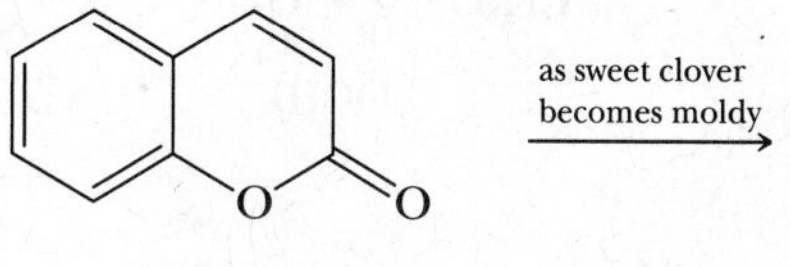

Coumarin
(from sweet clover)

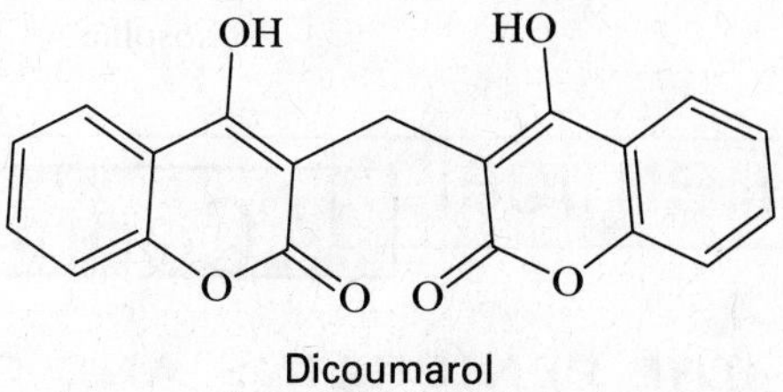

Dicoumarol
(an anticoagulant)

In a search for even more potent anticoagulants, Link developed warfarin (named after the Wisconsin Alumni Research Foundation), now used primarily as

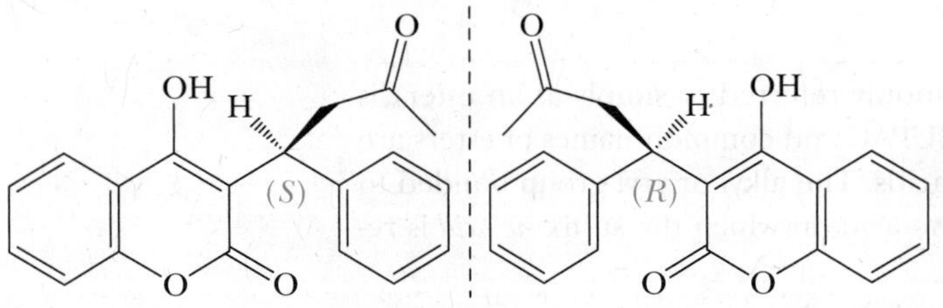

Warfarin
(a synthetic anticoagulant)

a rat poison: When rats consume warfarin, their blood fails to clot, and they bleed to death. Sold under the brand name Coumadin®, warfarin is also used as a blood thinner in humans. The *S* enantiomer is more active than the *R* enantiomer. The commercial product is a racemic mixture.

© Daniel MAR/iStockphoto

The powerful anticoagulant dicoumarol was first isolated from moldy clover.

Question

Identify warfarin as an α, β, γ, etc., lactone. Identify each part of warfarin that can undergo keto–enol tautomerization and show the tautomer at that position.

Charles D. Winters

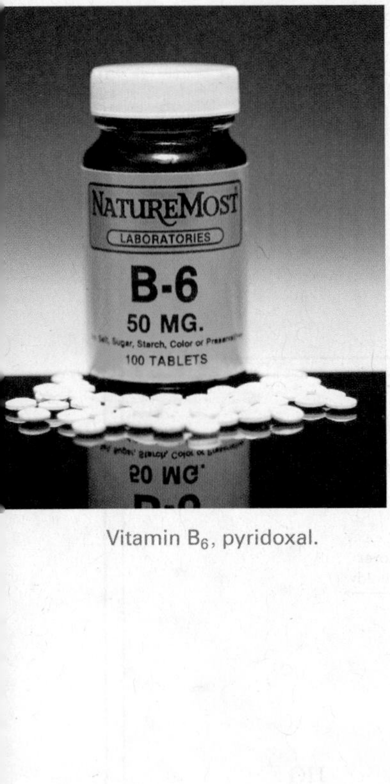

Vitamin B_6, pyridoxal.

Esters of Phosphoric Acid

Phosphoric acid has three —OH groups and forms mono-, di-, and triphosphoric esters, which are named by giving the name(s) of the alkyl or aryl group(s) bonded to oxygen, followed by the word *phosphate*—for example, dimethyl phosphate. In more complex phosphoric esters, it is common to name the organic molecule and then show the presence of the phosphoric ester by using either the word *phosphate* or the prefix *phospho-*. On the right are two phosphoric esters, each of special importance in the biological world. The first reaction in the metabolism of glucose is the formation of a phosphoric ester of D-glucose (Section 21.3), to give D-glucose 6-phosphate. Pyridoxal phosphate is one of the metabolically active forms of vitamin B_6. Each of these esters is shown as it is ionized at pH 7.4, the pH of blood plasma; the two hydrogens of each phosphate group are ionized, giving the phosphate group a charge of −2:

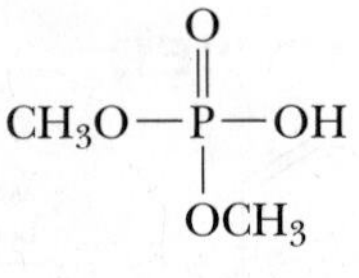

Dimethyl phosphate

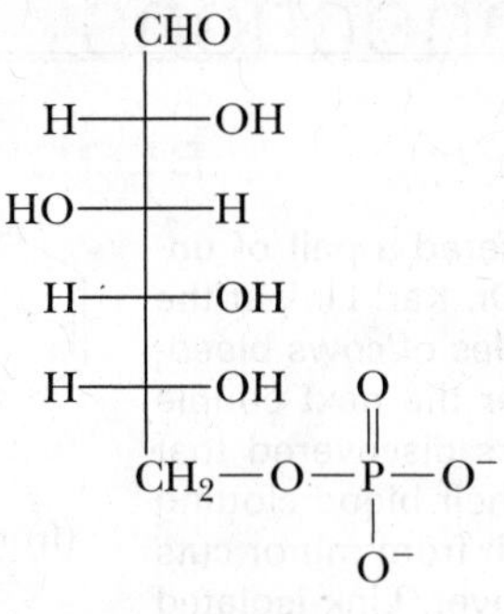

D-Glucose 6-phosphate

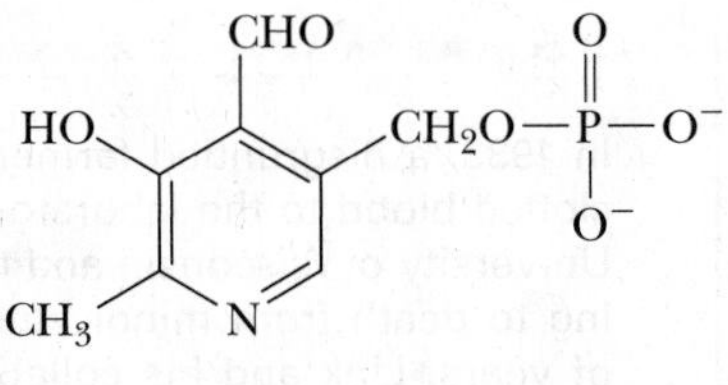

Pyridoxal phosphate

Chemical Connections 14C

THE PENICILLINS AND CEPHALOSPORINS: β-LACTAM ANTIBIOTICS

The **penicillins** were discovered in 1928 by the Scottish bacteriologist Sir Alexander Fleming. As a result of the brilliant experimental work of Sir Howard Florey, an Australian pathologist, and Ernst Chain, a German chemist who fled Nazi Germany, penicillin G was introduced into the practice of medicine in 1943. For their pioneering work in developing one of the most effective antibiotics of all time, Fleming, Florey, and Chain were awarded the Nobel Prize in Medicine or Physiology in 1945.

The mold from which Fleming discovered penicillin was *Penicillium notatum*, a strain that gives a relatively low yield of penicillin. Commercial production of the antibiotic uses *P. chrysogenum*, a strain cultured from a mold found growing on a grapefruit in a market in Peoria, Illinois. The penicillins owe their antibacterial activity to a common mechanism that inhibits the biosynthesis of a vital part of bacterial cell walls.

The structural feature common to all penicillins is a **β-lactam** ring fused to a five-membered ring containing one S atom and one N atom:

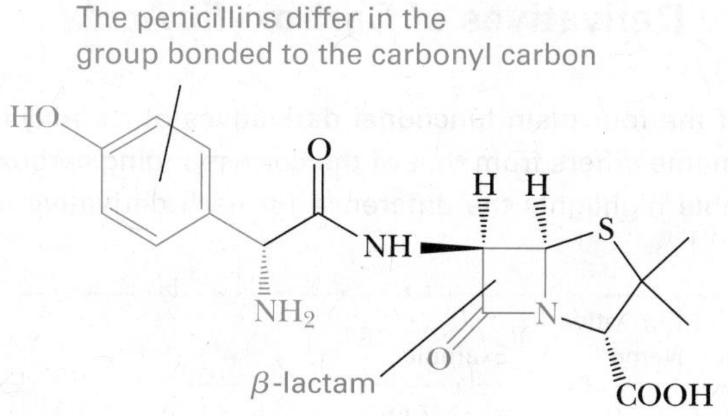

Amoxicillin
(a β-lactam antibiotic)

Soon after the penicillins were introduced into medical practice, penicillin-resistant strains of bacteria began to appear and have since proliferated. One approach to combating resistant strains is to synthesize newer, more effective penicillins. Among those that have been developed are ampicillin, methicillin, and amoxicillin. Another approach is to search for newer, more effective β-lactam antibiotics. The most effective of these discovered so far are the **cephalosporins**, the first of which was isolated from the fungus *Cephalosporium acremonium*. This class of β-lactam antibiotics has an even broader spectrum of antibacterial activity than the penicillins and is effective against many penicillin-resistant bacterial strains.

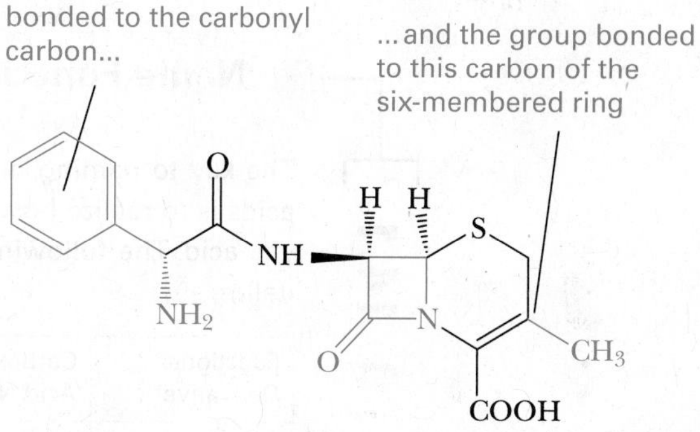

Keflex
(a β-lactam antibiotic)

Question

What would you except to be the major form of amoxicillin present in aqueous solution at (a) pH 2.0, (b) at pH 5–6, and (c) at pH 11.0? Explain.

D. Amides and Lactams

The functional group of an **amide** is an acyl group bonded to a trivalent nitrogen atom. Amides are named by dropping the suffix *-oic acid* from the IUPAC name of the parent acid, or *-ic acid* from its common name, and adding *-amide*. If the nitrogen atom of an amide is bonded to an alkyl or aryl group, the group is named and its location on nitrogen is indicated by *N*-. Two alkyl or aryl groups on nitrogen are indicated by *N,N*-di- if the groups are identical or by *N*-alkyl-*N*-alkyl if they are different:

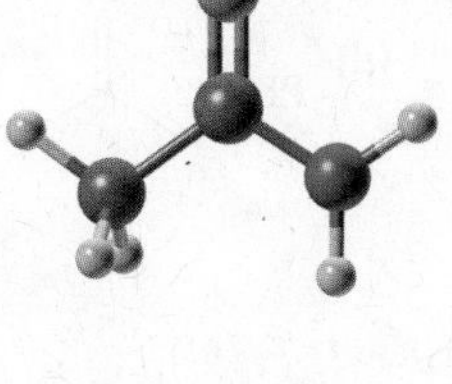

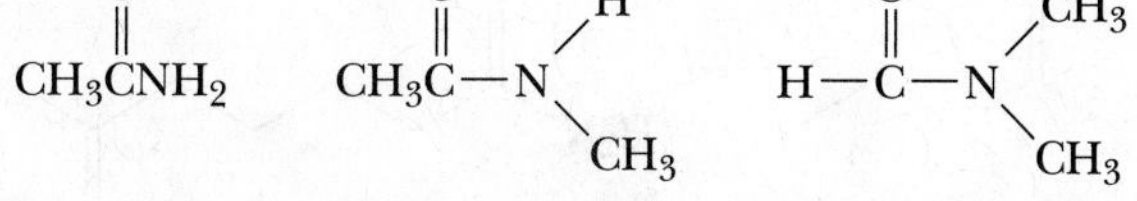

Acetamide (a 1° amide)

N-Methylacetamide (a 2° amide)

N,N-Dimethylformamide (DMF) (a 3° amide)

Amide bonds are the key structural feature that joins amino acids together to form polypeptides and proteins (Chapter 18).

Lactam A cyclic amide.

Cyclic amides are given the special name **lactam**. Their common names are derived in a manner similar to those of lactones, with the difference that the suffix *-olactone* is replaced by *-olactam:*

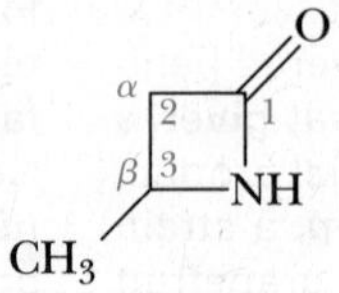

3-Butanolactam
(A β-lactam)

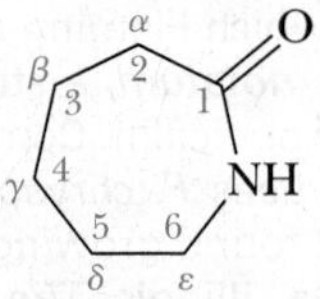

6-Hexanolactam
(An ε-lactam)

6-Hexanolactam is a key intermediate in the synthesis of nylon-6 (Section 16.4A).

HOW TO 14.1

Name Functional Derivatives of Carboxylic Acids

The key to naming one of the four main functional derivatives of carboxylic acids is to realize how its name differs from that of the corresponding carboxylic acid. The following table highlights the difference for each derivative in italics.

Functional Derivative	Carboxylic Acid Name	Derivative Name	Example	
acid halide	alkanoic *acid*	alkanoyl *halide*	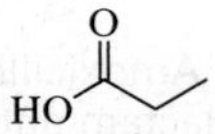 propanoic acid	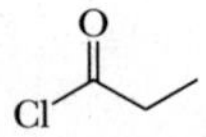 propanoyl chloride
acid anhydride	alkanoic *acid*	alkanoic *anhydride*	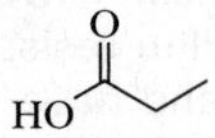 propanoic acid	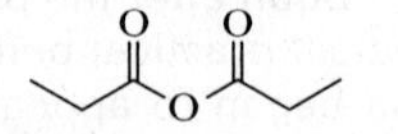 propanoic anhydride
ester	alkanoic *acid*	*alkyl* alkano*ate*	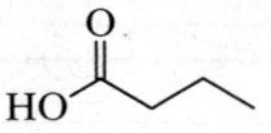 butanoic acid	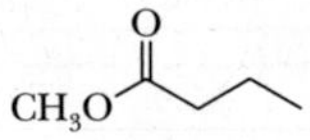 methyl butanoate
amide	alkanoic *acid*	alkan*amide*	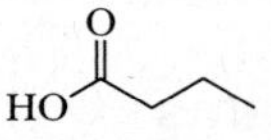 butanoic acid	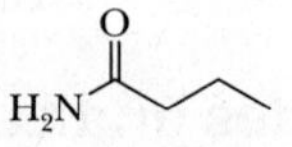 butanamide

EXAMPLE 14.1

Write the IUPAC name for each compound:

(a) 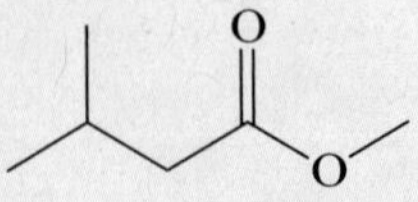

(b) 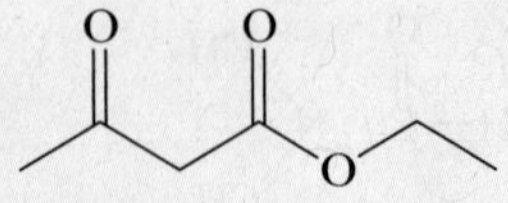

(c) 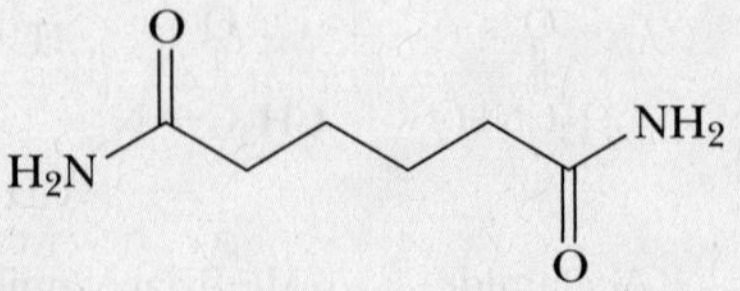

(d) 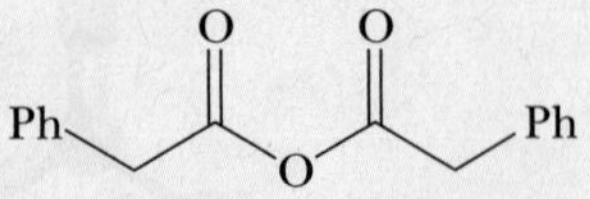

STRATEGY

Identify the longest chain containing the functional derivative to establish the root name. Treat the molecule as if each functional derivative group were a carboxyl group and name it as a carboxylic acid. Then change the suffix of the name to reflect the derivative. See How To 14.1 for examples.

SOLUTION

Given first are IUPAC names and then, in parentheses, common names:

(a) Methyl 3-methylbutanoate (methyl isovalerate, from isovaleric acid)
(b) Ethyl 3-oxobutanoate (ethyl β-ketobutyrate, from β-ketobutyric acid)
(c) Hexanediamide (adipamide, from adipic acid)
(d) Phenylethanoic anhydride (phenylacetic anhydride, from phenylacetic acid)

See problems 14.9–14.11

PROBLEM 14.1

Draw a structural formula for each compound:

(a) *N*-Cyclohexylacetamide
(b) *sec*-Butyl acetate
(c) Cyclobutyl butanoate
(d) *N*-(2-Octyl)benzamide
(e) Diethyl adipate
(f) Propanoic anhydride

14.2 What Are the Characteristic Reactions of Carboxylic Acid Derivatives?

The most common reaction theme of acid halides, anhydrides, esters, and amides is the addition of a nucleophile to the carbonyl carbon to form a tetrahedral carbonyl addition intermediate. To this extent, the reactions of these functional groups are similar to nucleophilic addition to the carbonyl groups in aldehydes and ketones (Section 12.4). The **tetrahedral carbonyl addition intermediate** (TCAI) formed from an aldehyde or a ketone then adds H^+. The result of this reaction is nucleophilic addition to a carbonyl group of an aldehyde or a ketone:

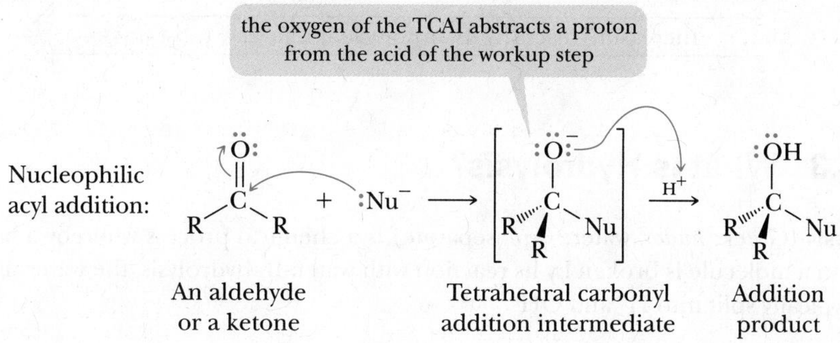
the oxygen of the TCAI abstracts a proton from the acid of the workup step
Nucleophilic acyl addition:
:Nu⁻
H⁺
An aldehyde or a ketone
Tetrahedral carbonyl addition intermediate
Addition product

For functional derivatives of carboxylic acids, the fate of the tetrahedral carbonyl addition intermediate is quite different from that of aldehydes and ketones. This intermediate collapses to expel the leaving group and regenerate the carbonyl group. The result of this addition–elimination sequence is **nucleophilic acyl substitution**:

Nucleophilic acyl substitution A reaction in which a nucleophile bonded to a carbonyl carbon is replaced by another nucleophile.

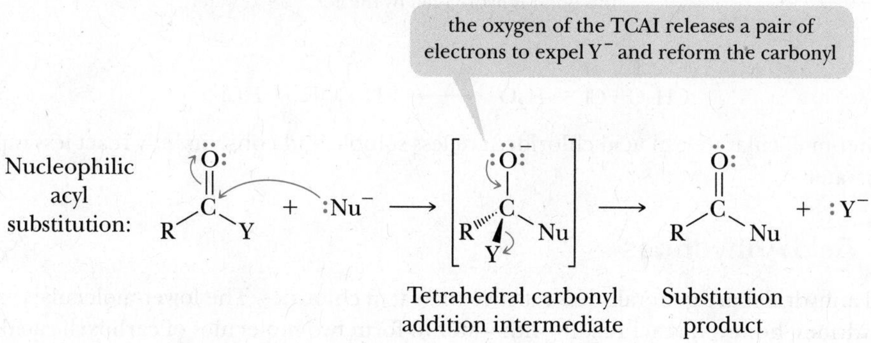
the oxygen of the TCAI releases a pair of electrons to expel Y⁻ and reform the carbonyl
Nucleophilic acyl substitution:
:Nu⁻
:Y⁻
Tetrahedral carbonyl addition intermediate
Substitution product

The major difference between these two types of carbonyl addition reactions is that aldehydes and ketones do not have a group, Y, that can leave as a stable anion. They undergo only nucleophilic acyl addition. The four carboxylic acid derivatives we study in this chapter do have a group, Y, that can leave as a stable anion; accordingly, they undergo nucleophilic acyl substitution.

In this general reaction, we show the nucleophile and the leaving group as anions. That need not be the case, however: Neutral molecules, such as water, alcohols, ammonia, and amines, may also serve as nucleophiles in the acid-catalyzed version of the reaction. We show the leaving groups here as anions to illustrate an important point about leaving groups, namely, that the weaker the base, the better is the leaving group (Section 7.5C):

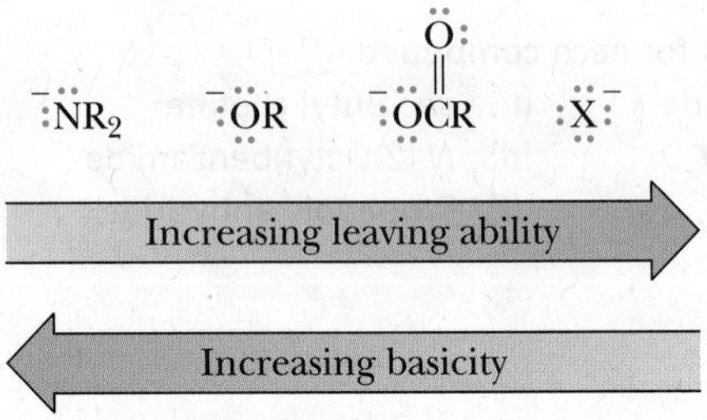

The weakest base in this series, and thus the best leaving group, is halide ion; acid halides are the most reactive toward nucleophilic acyl substitution. The strongest base, and hence the poorest leaving group, is amide ion; amides are the least reactive toward nucleophilic acyl substitution. Acid halides and acid anhydrides are so reactive that they are not found in nature. Esters and amides, however, are universally present.

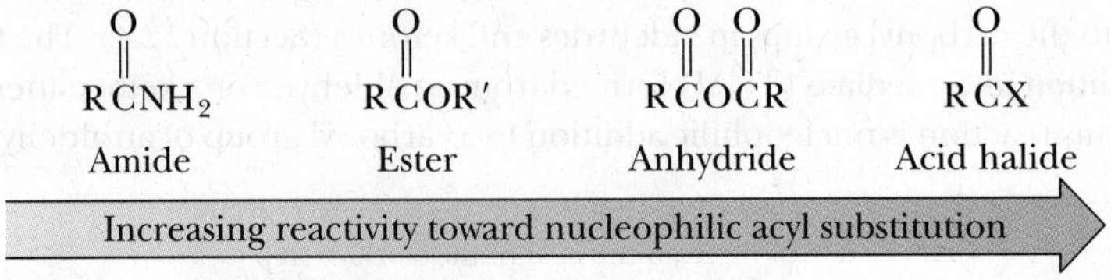

14.3 What Is Hydrolysis?

Hydrolysis (Greek: *hudor*, water; *lyein*, separate) is a chemical process whereby a bond (or bonds) in a molecule is broken by its reaction with water. In hydrolysis, the water molecule is also typically split into H^+ and OH^-.

A. Acid Chlorides

Low-molecular-weight acid chlorides react very rapidly with water to form carboxylic acids and HCl:

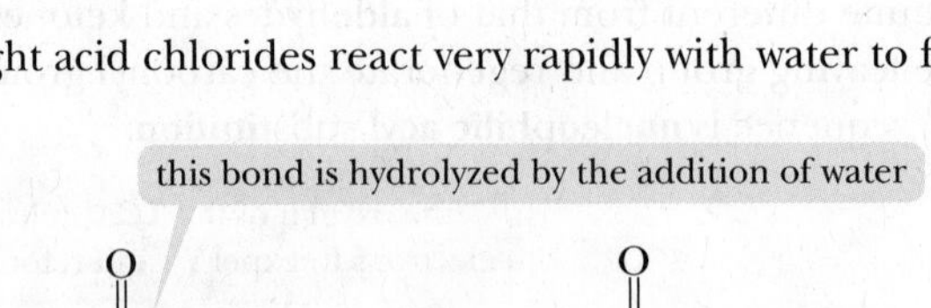

this bond is hydrolyzed by the addition of water

Higher-molecular-weight acid chlorides are less soluble and consequently react less rapidly with water.

B. Acid Anhydrides

Acid anhydrides are generally less reactive than acid chlorides. The lower-molecular-weight anhydrides, however, react readily with water to form two molecules of carboxylic acid:

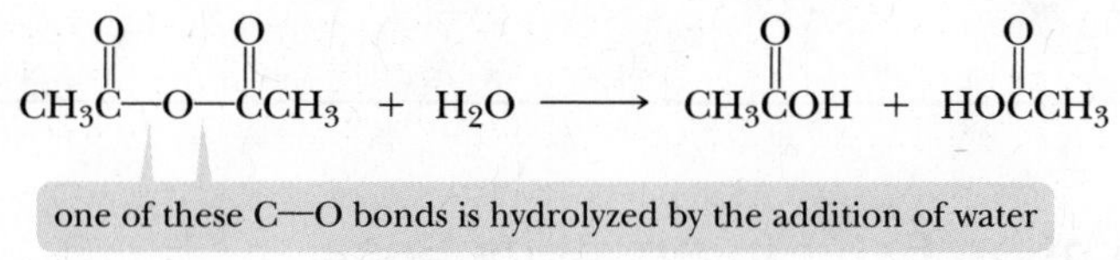
one of these C—O bonds is hydrolyzed by the addition of water

C. Esters

Esters are hydrolyzed only very slowly, even in boiling water. Hydrolysis becomes considerably more rapid, however, when esters are refluxed in aqueous acid or base. When we discussed acid-catalyzed (Fischer) esterification in Section 13.6, we pointed out that esterification is an equilibrium reaction. Hydrolysis of esters in aqueous acid is also an equilibrium reaction and proceeds by the same mechanism as esterification, except in reverse. The role of the acid catalyst is to protonate the carbonyl oxygen **(Step 1: Add a proton)**, thereby increasing the electrophilic character of the carbonyl carbon toward attack by water **(Step 2: Reaction of a nucleophile and an electrophile to form a new covalent bond)** to form a tetrahedral carbonyl addition intermediate. An internal proton transfer to the alkoxy group **(Step 3: Internal proton transfer)** makes that group a good leaving group and allows the collapse of this intermediate **(Step 4: Collapse of the tetrahedral carbonyl addition intermediate to eject a leaving group and regenerate the carbonyl group)** to give a carboxylic acid and an alcohol. In this reaction, acid is a catalyst; it is consumed in the first step, but another is generated at the end of the reaction:

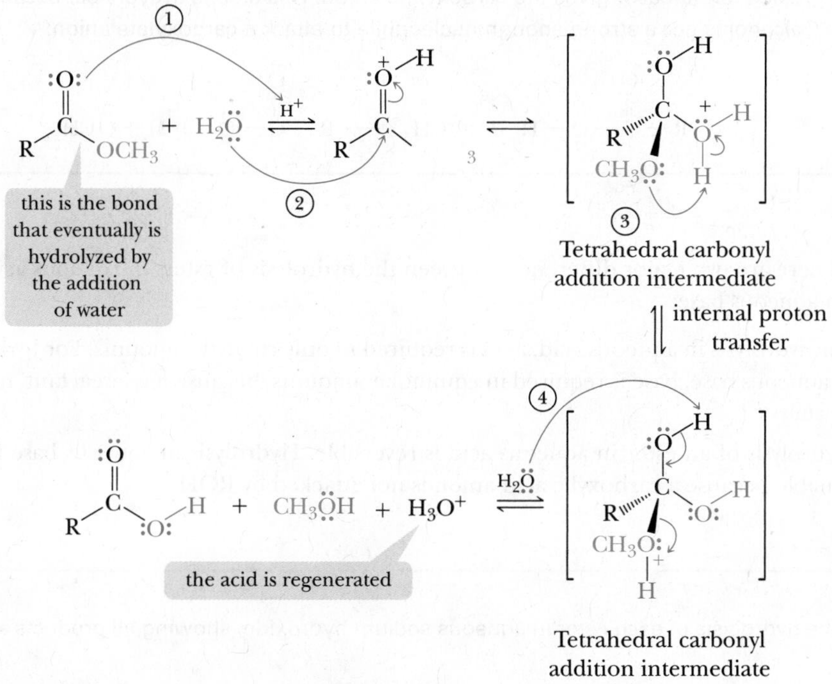
this is the bond that eventually is hydrolyzed by the addition of water
Tetrahedral carbonyl addition intermediate
internal proton transfer
the acid is regenerated
Tetrahedral carbonyl addition intermediate

Hydrolysis of esters may also be carried out with hot aqueous base, such as aqueous NaOH. Hydrolysis of esters in aqueous base is often called **saponification**, a reference to the use of this reaction in the manufacture of soaps (Section 19.2A). Each mole of ester hydrolyzed requires 1 mole of base, as shown in the following balanced equation:

Saponification Hydrolysis of an ester in aqueous NaOH or KOH to an alcohol and the sodium or potassium salt of a carboxylic acid.

$$\overset{O}{\overset{\|}{RC}}OCH_3 + NaOH \xrightarrow{H_2O} \overset{O}{\overset{\|}{RC}}O^-Na^+ + CH_3OH$$

Mechanism

Hydrolysis of an Ester in Aqueous Base

STEP 1: Reaction of a nucleophile and an electrophile to form a new covalent bond. Addition of hydroxide ion to the carbonyl carbon of the ester gives a tetrahedral carbonyl addition intermediate:

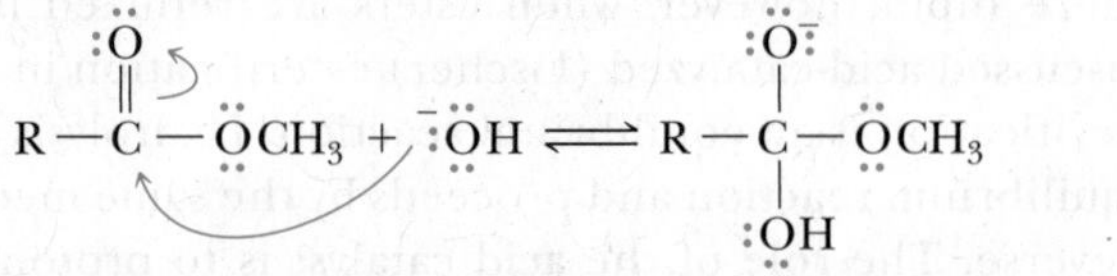

STEP 2: Collapse of the tetrahedral carbonyl addition intermediate to eject a leaving group and regenerate the carbonyl group. Collapse of this intermediate gives a carboxylic acid and an alkoxide ion:

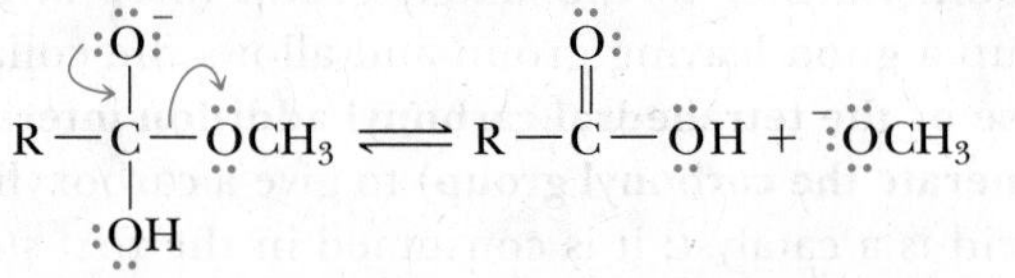

STEP 3: Take a proton away. Proton transfer from the carboxyl group (an acid) to the alkoxide ion (a base) gives the carboxylate anion. This step is irreversible because the alcohol is not a strong enough nucleophile to attack a carboxylate anion:

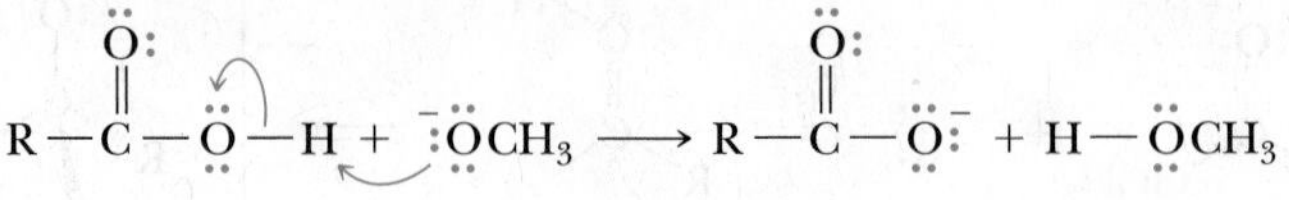

There are two major differences between the hydrolysis of esters in aqueous acid and that in aqueous base:

1. For hydrolysis in aqueous acid, acid is required in only catalytic amounts. For hydrolysis in aqueous base, base is required in equimolar amounts, because it is a reactant, not just a catalyst.
2. Hydrolysis of an ester in aqueous acid is reversible. Hydrolysis in aqueous base is irreversible because a carboxylic acid anion is not attacked by ROH.

EXAMPLE 14.2

Complete and balance equations for the hydrolysis of each ester in aqueous sodium hydroxide, showing all products as they are ionized in aqueous NaOH:

(a) 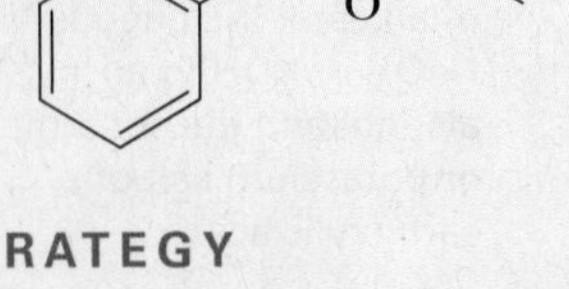 + NaOH $\xrightarrow{H_2O}$ **(b)** 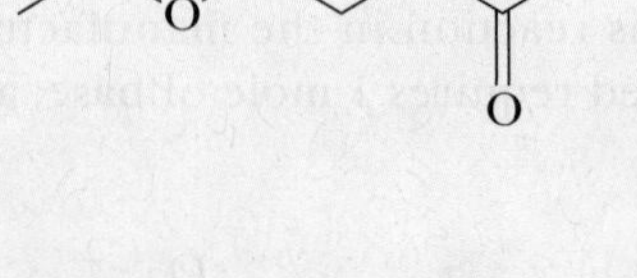 + NaOH $\xrightarrow{H_2O}$

STRATEGY

The hydrolysis of an ester results in a carboxyl group and an alcohol for every ester group in the molecule. In aqueous base, one mole of NaOH is consumed for every ester group in the molecule.

SOLUTION

The products of hydrolysis of (a) are benzoic acid and 2-propanol. In aqueous NaOH, benzoic acid is converted to its sodium salt. Therefore, 1 mole of NaOH is required for the hydrolysis of 1 mole of this ester. Compound (b) is a diester of ethylene glycol. Two moles of NaOH are required for its hydrolysis:

(a) 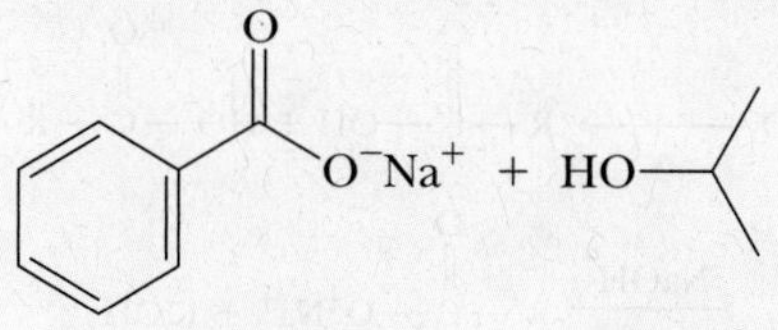

Sodium benzoate 2-Propanol (Isopropyl alcohol)

(b) $2\ CH_3\overset{O}{\overset{\|}{C}}O^-Na^+ + HOCH_2CH_2OH$

Sodium acetate 1,2-Ethanediol (Ethylene glycol)

See problems 14.19, 14.20, 14.31

PROBLEM 14.2

Complete and balance equations for the hydrolysis of each ester in aqueous solution, showing each product as it is ionized under the given experimental conditions:

(a) 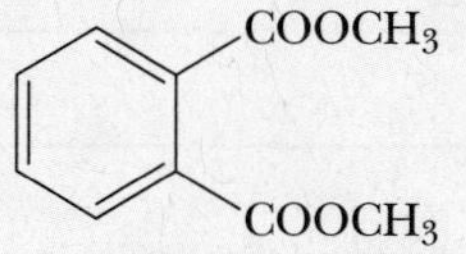 $+ \text{NaOH} \xrightarrow{H_2O}$ (excess)

(b) 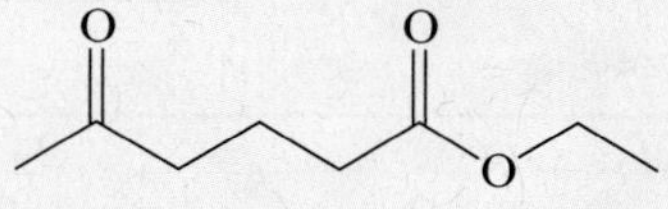 $+ H_2O \xrightarrow{HCl}$

D. Amides

Amides require considerably more vigorous conditions for hydrolysis in both acid and base than do esters. Amides undergo hydrolysis in hot aqueous acid to give a carboxylic acid and ammonia. Hydrolysis is driven to completion by the acid–base reaction between ammonia or the amine and acid to form an ammonium salt. One mole of acid is required per mole of amide:

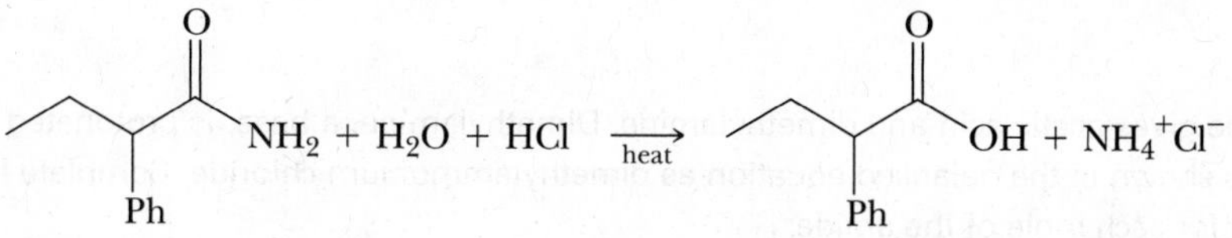

2-Phenylbutanamide 2-Phenylbutanoic acid

In aqueous base, the products of amide hydrolysis are a carboxylic acid and ammonia or an amine. Base-catalyzed hydrolysis is driven to completion by the acid–base reaction between the carboxylic acid and base to form a salt. One mole of base is required per mole of amide:

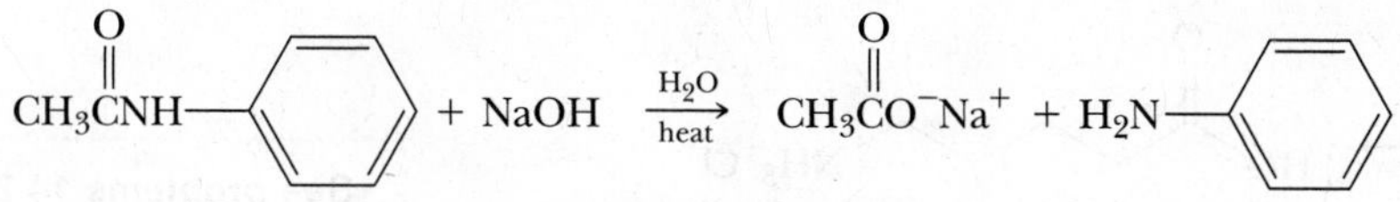

N-Phenylethanamide (*N*-Phenylacetamide, Acetanilide) Sodium acetate Aniline

The reactions of these functional groups with water are summarized in Table 14.1. Remember that, although all four functional groups react with water, there are large differences in the rates and experimental conditions under which they undergo hydrolysis.

TABLE 14.1 Summary of Reaction of Acid Chlorides, Anhydrides, Esters, and Amides with Water

$$R{-}\overset{\overset{\large O}{\|}}{C}{-}Cl + H_2O \longrightarrow R{-}\overset{\overset{\large O}{\|}}{C}{-}OH + HCl$$

$$R{-}\overset{\overset{\large O}{\|}}{C}{-}O{-}\overset{\overset{\large O}{\|}}{C}{-}R + H_2O \longrightarrow R{-}\overset{\overset{\large O}{\|}}{C}{-}OH + HO{-}\overset{\overset{\large O}{\|}}{C}{-}R$$

$$R{-}\overset{\overset{\large O}{\|}}{C}{-}OR' + H_2O \xrightarrow{NaOH} R{-}\overset{\overset{\large O}{\|}}{C}{-}O^-Na^+ + R'OH$$

$$R{-}\overset{\overset{\large O}{\|}}{C}{-}OR' + H_2O \xrightarrow{H_2SO_4} R{-}\overset{\overset{\large O}{\|}}{C}{-}OH + R'OH$$

$$R{-}\overset{\overset{\large O}{\|}}{C}{-}NH_2 + H_2O \xrightarrow{NaOH} R{-}\overset{\overset{\large O}{\|}}{C}{-}O^-Na^+ + NH_3$$

$$R{-}\overset{\overset{\large O}{\|}}{C}{-}NH_2 + H_2O \xrightarrow{HCl} R{-}\overset{\overset{\large O}{\|}}{C}{-}OH + NH_4^+Cl^-$$

esters and amides require acidic or basic conditions to be hydrolyzed

EXAMPLE 14.3

Write equations for the hydrolysis of these amides in concentrated aqueous HCl, showing all products as they exist in aqueous HCl and showing the number of moles of HCl required for the hydrolysis of each amide:

(a) $CH_3\overset{\overset{\large O}{\|}}{C}N(CH_3)_2$ **(b)** 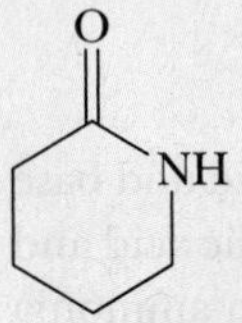

STRATEGY

The hydrolysis of an amide results in a carboxyl group and an ammonium chloride ion for every amide group in the molecule. Either 1 mole of NaOH (basic conditions) or 1 mole of HCl (acidic conditions) is consumed for every amide group in the molecule.

SOLUTION

(a) Hydrolysis of *N,N*-dimethylacetamide gives acetic acid and dimethylamine. Dimethylamine, a base, is protonated by HCl to form dimethylammonium ion and is shown in the balanced equation as dimethylammonium chloride. Complete hydrolysis of this amide requires 1 mole of HCl for each mole of the amide:

$$CH_3\overset{\overset{\large O}{\|}}{C}N(CH_3)_2 + H_2O + HCl \xrightarrow[heat]{} CH_3\overset{\overset{\large O}{\|}}{C}OH + (CH_3)_2NH_2^+Cl^-$$

(b) Hydrolysis of this δ-lactam gives the protonated form of 5-aminopentanoic acid. One mole of acid is required per mole of lactam:

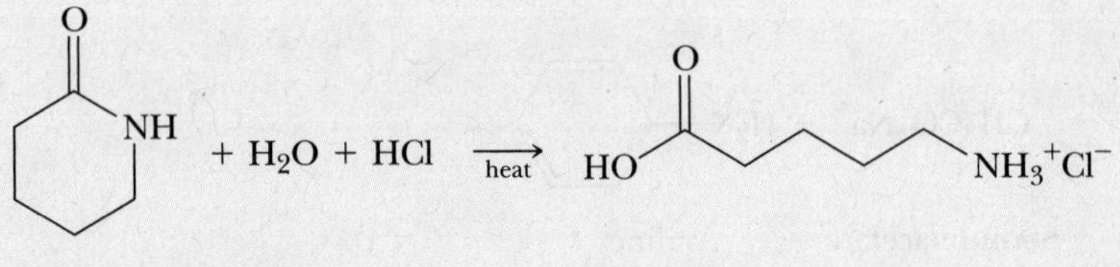

See problems 14.29, 14.32

PROBLEM 14.3

Complete equations for the hydrolysis of the amides in Example 14.3 in concentrated aqueous NaOH. Show all products as they exist in aqueous NaOH, and show the number of moles of NaOH required for the hydrolysis of each amide.

14.4 How Do Carboxylic Acid Derivatives React with Alcohols?

A. Acid Chlorides

Acid chlorides react with alcohols to give an ester and HCl:

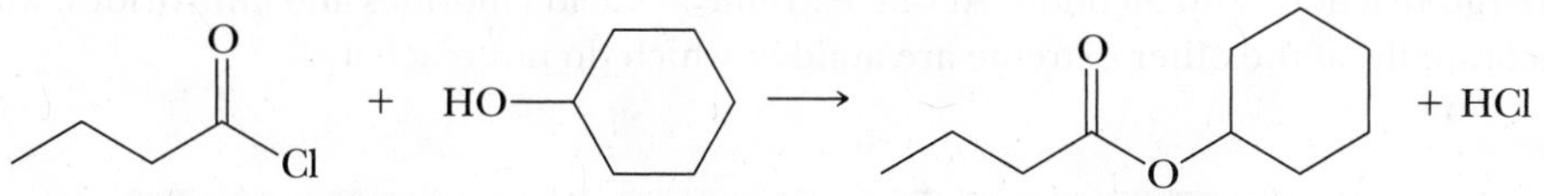

Butanoyl chloride — Cyclohexanol — Cyclohexyl butanoate

Because acid chlorides are so reactive toward even weak nucleophiles such as alcohols, no catalyst is necessary for these reactions. Phenol and substituted phenols also react with acid chlorides to give esters.

B. Acid Anhydrides

Acid anhydrides react with alcohols to give 1 mole of ester and 1 mole of a carboxylic acid.

$$\underset{\text{Acetic anhydride}}{CH_3\overset{O}{\overset{\|}{C}}O\overset{O}{\overset{\|}{C}}CH_3} + \underset{\text{Ethanol}}{HOCH_2CH_3} \longrightarrow \underset{\text{Ethyl acetate}}{CH_3\overset{O}{\overset{\|}{C}}OCH_2CH_3} + \underset{\text{Acetic acid}}{CH_3\overset{O}{\overset{\|}{C}}OH}$$

Thus, the reaction of an alcohol with an anhydride is a useful method for synthesizing esters. Aspirin is synthesized on an industrial scale by reacting acetic anhydride with salicylic acid:

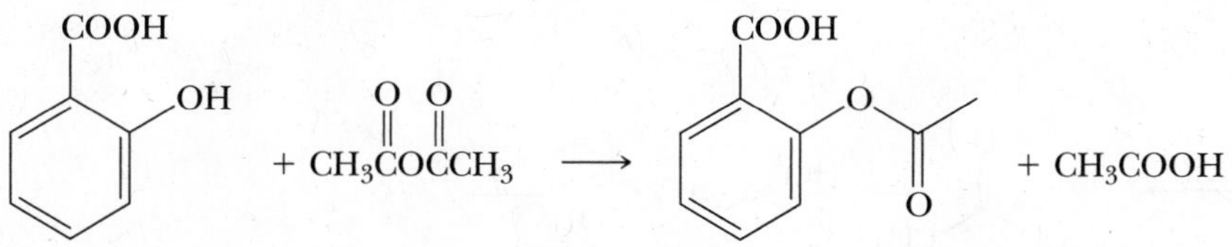

2-Hydroxybenzoic acid (Salicylic acid) — Acetic anhydride — Acetylsalicylic acid (Aspirin) — Acetic acid

C. Esters

When treated with an alcohol in the presence of an acid catalyst, esters undergo an exchange reaction called **transesterification**. In this reaction, the original —OR group of the ester is exchanged for a new —OR group. In the following example, the transesterification can be driven to completion by heating the reaction at a temperature above the boiling point of methanol (65 °C) so that methanol distills from the reaction mixture:

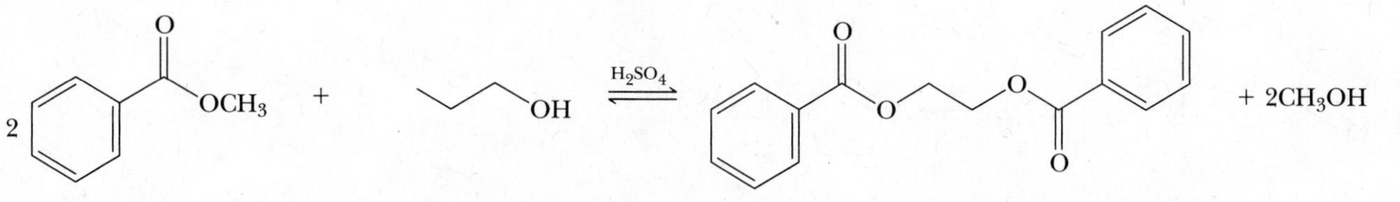

Methyl benzoate — 1,2-Ethanediol (Ethylene glycol) — (A diester of ethylene glycol)

D. Amides

Amides do not react with alcohols under any experimental conditions. Alcohols are not strong enough nucleophiles to attack the carbonyl group of an amide.

The reactions of the foregoing functional groups with alcohols are summarized in Table 14.2. As with reactions of these same functional groups with water (Section 14.3), there are large differences in the rates and experimental conditions under which they undergo reactions with alcohols. At one extreme are acid chlorides and anhydrides, which react rapidly; at the other extreme are amides, which do not react at all.

TABLE 14.2 Summary of Reaction of Acid Chlorides, Anhydrides, Esters, and Amides with Alcohols

$$R{-}\overset{O}{\overset{\|}{C}}{-}Cl + HOR'' \longrightarrow R{-}\overset{O}{\overset{\|}{C}}{-}OR'' + HCl$$

$$R{-}\overset{O}{\overset{\|}{C}}{-}O{-}\overset{O}{\overset{\|}{C}}{-}R + R''OH \longrightarrow R{-}\overset{O}{\overset{\|}{C}}{-}OR'' + HO{-}\overset{O}{\overset{\|}{C}}{-}R$$

$$R{-}\overset{O}{\overset{\|}{C}}{-}OR' + R''OH \xrightleftharpoons{H_2SO_4} R{-}\overset{O}{\overset{\|}{C}}{-}OR'' + R'OH$$

$$R{-}\overset{O}{\overset{\|}{C}}{-}NH_2 + R''OH \longrightarrow \text{No Reaction}$$

EXAMPLE 14.4

Complete these equations:

(a) 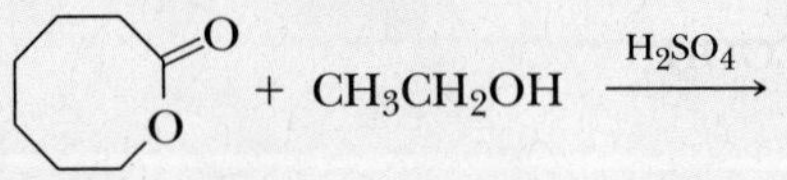

(b) 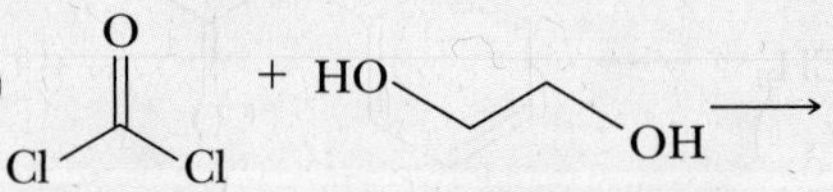

STRATEGY

Acid halides, anhydrides, and esters undergo nucleophilic acyl substitution with alcohols (HOR′), the net result being the replacement of each —X, —OC(O)R, or —OR group with the —OR′ group of the alcohol.

SOLUTION

(a) 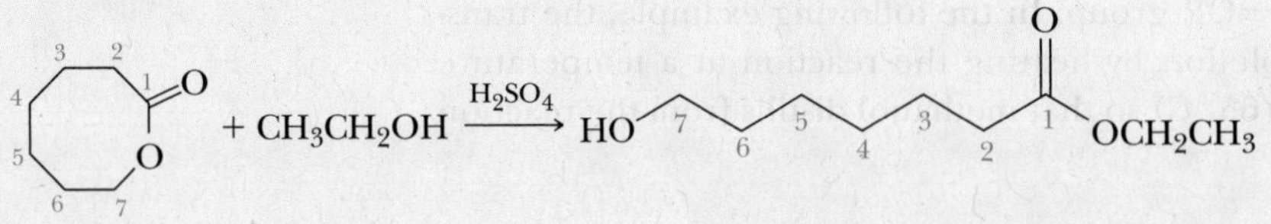

(b) 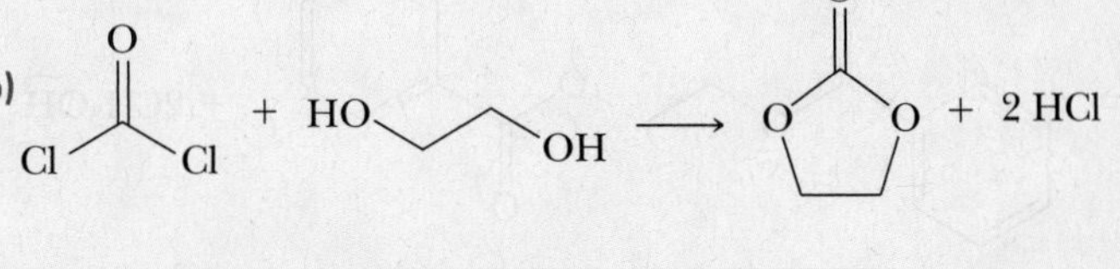

See problems 14.16, 14.17, 14.19–14.22, 14.28

PROBLEM 14.4

Complete these equations (the stoichiometry of each is given in the equation):

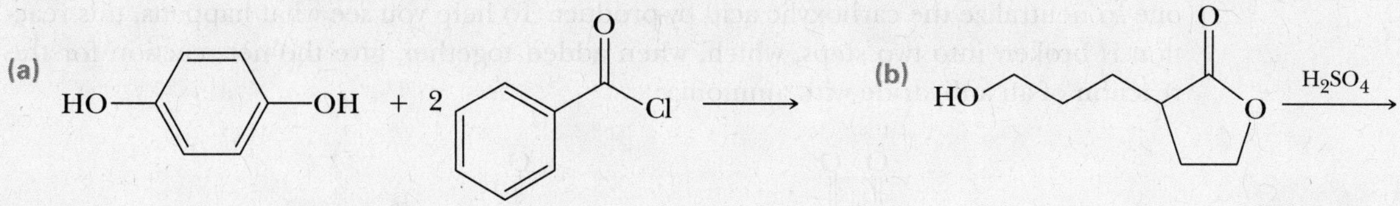

Chemical Connections 14D

THE PYRETHRINS: NATURAL INSECTICIDES OF PLANT ORIGIN

Pyrethrum is a natural insecticide obtained from the powdered flower heads of several species of *Chrysanthemum*, particularly *C. cinerariaefolium*. The active substances in pyrethrum, principally pyrethrins I and II, are contact poisons for insects and cold-blooded vertebrates. Because their concentrations in the pyrethrum powder used in chrysanthemum-based insecticides are nontoxic to plants and higher animals, pyrethrum powder is used in household and livestock sprays, as well as in dusts for edible plants. Natural pyrethrins are esters of chrysanthemic acid.

While pyrethrum powders are effective insecticides, the active substances in them are destroyed rapidly in the environment. In an effort to develop synthetic compounds as effective as these natural insecticides but with greater biostability, chemists have prepared a series of esters related in structure to chrysanthemic acid. Permethrin is one of the most commonly used synthetic pyrethrinlike compounds in household and agricultural products.

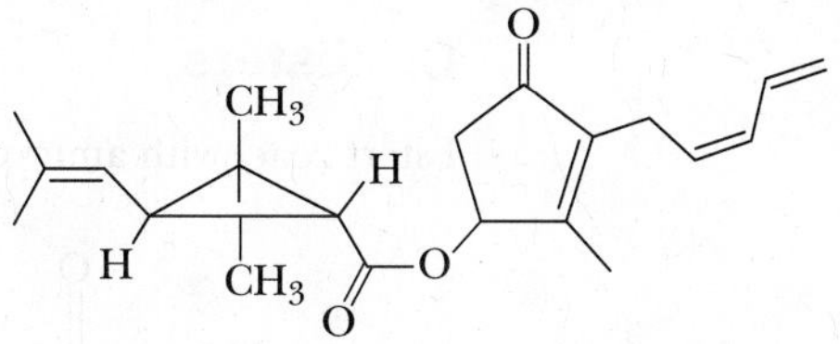

Pyrethrin I

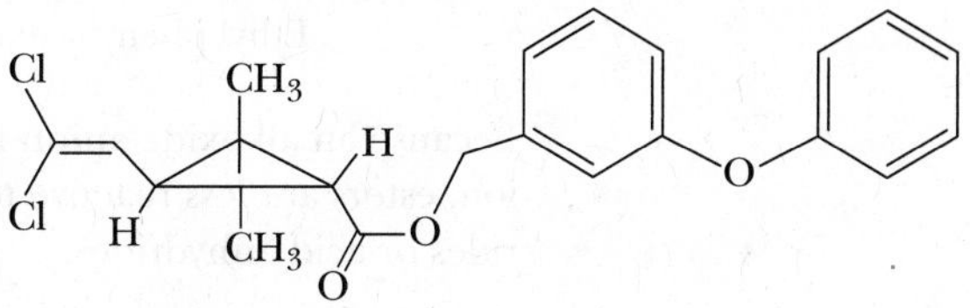

Permethrin

Question
Show the compounds that would result if pyrethrin I and permethrin were to undergo hydrolysis.

14.5 How Do Carboxylic Acid Derivatives React with Ammonia and Amines?

A. Acid Chlorides

Acid chlorides react readily with ammonia and with 1° and 2° amines to form amides. Complete conversion of an acid chloride to an amide requires 2 moles of ammonia or amine: one to form the amide and one to neutralize the hydrogen chloride formed:

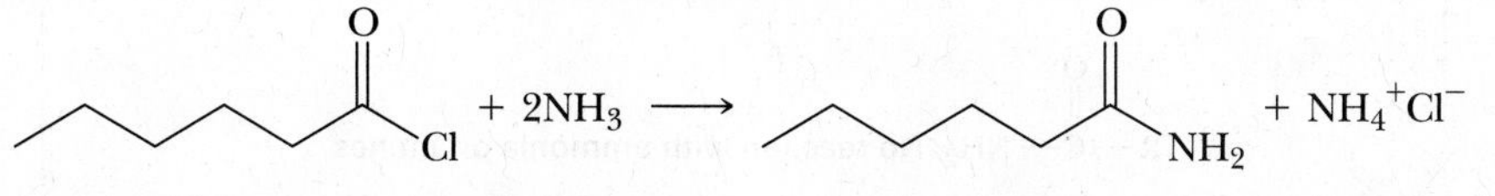

Hexanoyl chloride Ammonia Hexanamide Ammonium chloride

B. Acid Anhydrides

Acid anhydrides react with ammonia and with 1° and 2° amines to form amides. As with acid chlorides, 2 moles of ammonia or amine are required—one to form the amide and one to neutralize the carboxylic acid by-product. To help you see what happens, this reaction is broken into two steps, which, when added together, give the net reaction for the reaction of an anhydride with ammonia:

$$CH_3\overset{O}{\overset{\|}{C}}O\overset{O}{\overset{\|}{C}}CH_3 + NH_3 \longrightarrow CH_3\overset{O}{\overset{\|}{C}}NH_2 + CH_3\overset{O}{\overset{\|}{C}}OH$$

$$CH_3\overset{O}{\overset{\|}{C}}OH + NH_3 \longrightarrow CH_3\overset{O}{\overset{\|}{C}}O^-NH_4^+$$

$$CH_3\overset{O}{\overset{\|}{C}}O\overset{O}{\overset{\|}{C}}CH_3 + 2NH_3 \longrightarrow CH_3\overset{O}{\overset{\|}{C}}NH_3 + CH_3\overset{O}{\overset{\|}{C}}O^-NH_4^+$$

C. Esters

Esters react with ammonia and with 1° and 2° amines to form amides:

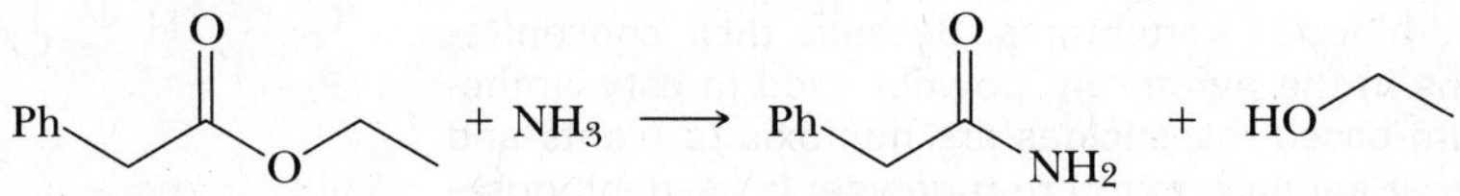

Ethyl phenylacetate Phenylacetamide Ethanol

Because an alkoxide anion is a poor leaving group compared with a halide or carboxylate ion, esters are less reactive toward ammonia, 1° amines, and 2° amines than are acid chlorides or acid anhydrides.

D. Amides

Amides do not react with ammonia or amines.

The reactions of the preceding four functional groups with ammonia and amines are summarized in Table 14.3.

TABLE 14.3 Summary of Reaction of Acid Chlorides, Anhydrides, Esters, and Amides with Ammonia and Amines

$$R-\overset{O}{\overset{\|}{C}}-Cl + 2NH_3 \longrightarrow R-\overset{O}{\overset{\|}{C}}-NH_2 + NH_4^+Cl^-$$

$$R-\overset{O}{\overset{\|}{C}}-O-\overset{O}{\overset{\|}{C}}-R + 2NH_3 \longrightarrow R-\overset{O}{\overset{\|}{C}}-NH_2 + R-\overset{O}{\overset{\|}{C}}-O^-NH_4^+$$

$$R-\overset{O}{\overset{\|}{C}}-OR' + NH_3 \rightleftharpoons R-\overset{O}{\overset{\|}{C}}-NH_2 + R'OH$$

$R-\overset{O}{\overset{\|}{C}}-NH_2$ No reaction with ammonia or amines

EXAMPLE 14.5

Complete these equations (the stoichiometry of each is given in the equation):

(a) 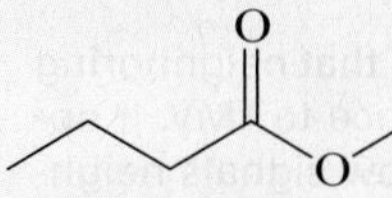 + NH_3 ⟶

Ethyl butanoate

(b) 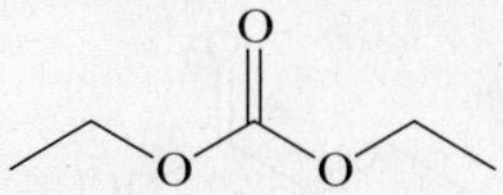 + $2NH_3$ ⟶

Diethyl carbonate

STRATEGY

Acid halides, anhydrides, and esters undergo nucleophilic acyl substitution with ammonia or amines, the net result being the replacement of each —X, —OC(O)R, or —OR group with the —NH_2 group of ammonia or the —NHR or —NR_2 group of the amine.

SOLUTION

(a) 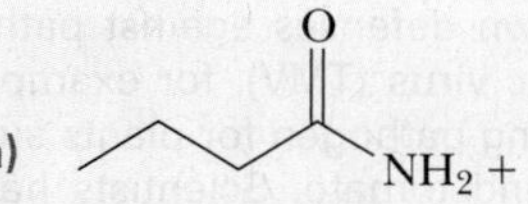 + CH_3CH_2OH

Butanamide

(b) 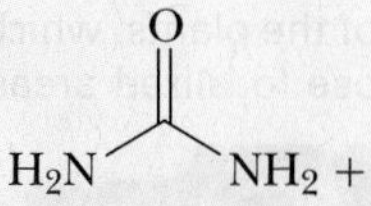 + $2CH_3CH_2OH$

Urea

See problems 14.18–14.22, 14.24–14.26, 14.31, 14.35

PROBLEM 14.5

Complete these equations (the stoichiometry of each is given in the equation):

(a) 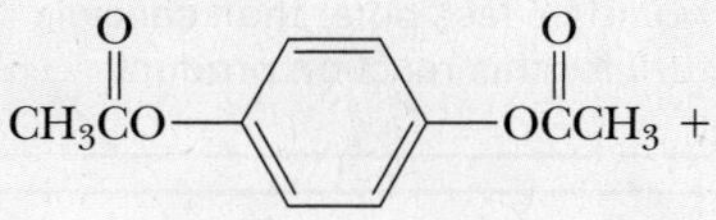 + $2NH_3$ ⟶ (b) 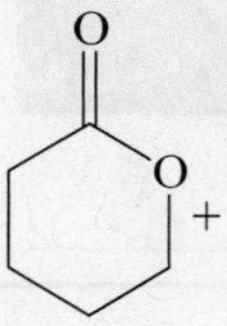 + NH_3 ⟶

14.6 How Can Functional Derivatives of Carboxylic Acids Be Interconverted?

In the last few sections, we have seen that acid chlorides are the most reactive carboxyl derivatives toward nucleophilic acyl substitution and that amides are the least reactive:

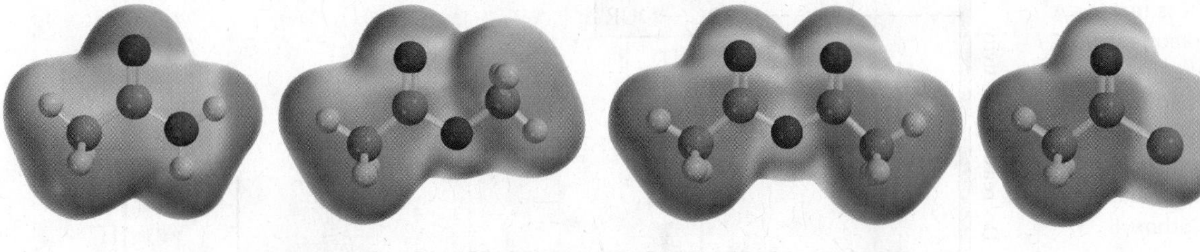

Amide < Ester < Acid anhydride < Acid halide

Increasing reactivity toward nucleophilic acyl substitution

Chemical Connections 14E

SYSTEMATIC ACQUIRED RESISTANCE IN PLANTS

The use of germicides to protect plants from harmful pathogens is common in farming. Recently, plant physiologists discovered that some plant species are able to generate their own defenses against pathogens. The tobacco mosaic virus (TMV), for example, is a particularly devastating pathogen for plants such as tobacco, cucumber, and tomato. Scientists have found that certain strains of these plants produce large amounts of salicylic acid upon being infected with TMV. Accompanying the infection is the appearance of lesions on the leaves of the plants, which help to contain the infection to those localized areas. Furthermore, scientists have discovered that neighboring plants tend to acquire some resistance to TMV. It appears that the infected plant somehow signals neighboring plants of the impending danger by converting salicylic acid to its ester, methyl salicylate:

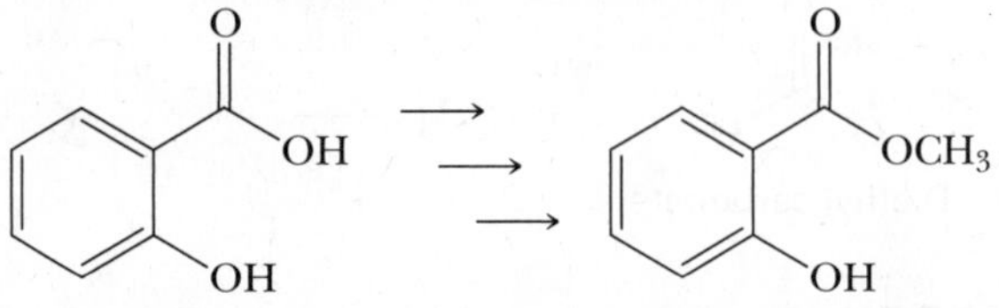

Salicylic acid   Methyl salicylate

With a lower boiling point and higher vapor pressure than salicylic acid has, the methyl salicylate diffuses into the air from the infected plant, and the surrounding plants use it as a signal to enhance their defenses against TMV.

© punyafamily/iStockphoto

The tobacco plant, *Nicotiana tobacum*.

Question

An early proposal in this research was that the tobacco plant could utilize two molecules of salicylic acid (molar mass 138.12 g/mol) in a nucleophilic acyl substitution reaction to yield a compound with a molar mass of 240.21 g/mol that would be less polar than salicylic acid. Propose a structure for this reaction product.

Another useful way to think about the relative reactivities of these four functional derivatives of carboxylic acids is summarized in Figure 14.1. Any functional group in this figure can be prepared from any functional group above it by treatment with an appropriate oxygen or nitrogen nucleophile. An acid chloride, for example, can be converted to an

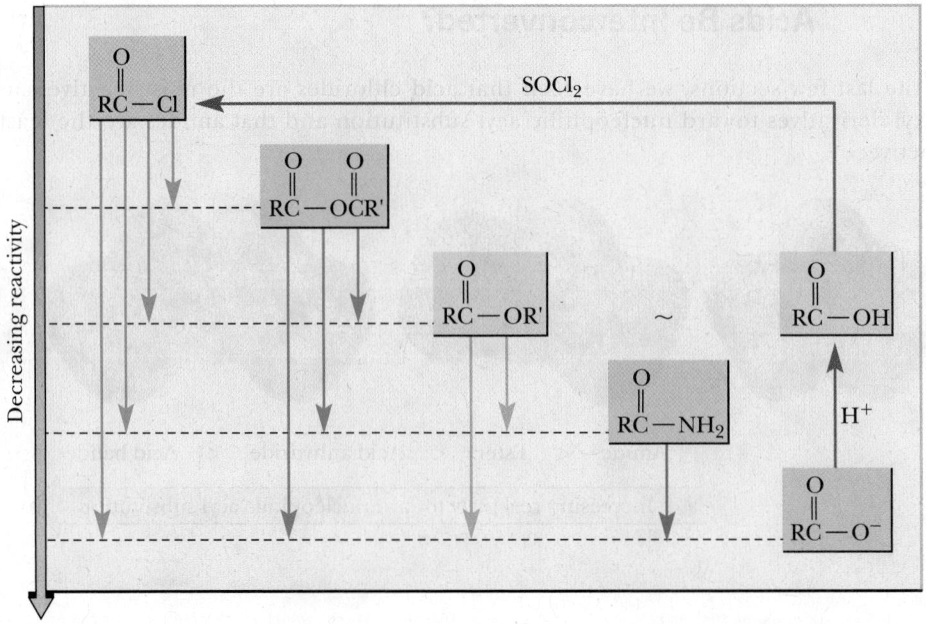

FIGURE 14.1 Relative reactivities of carboxylic acid derivatives toward nucleophilic acyl substitution. A more reactive derivative may be converted to a less reactive derivative by treatment with an appropriate reagent. Treatment of a carboxylic acid with thionyl chloride converts the carboxylic acid to the more reactive acid chloride. Carboxylic acids are about as reactive as esters under acidic conditions, but are converted to the unreactive carboxylate anions under basic conditions.

acid anhydride, an ester, an amide, or a carboxylic acid. An acid anhydride, ester, or amide, however, does not react with chloride ion to give an acid chloride.

Notice that all carboxylic acid derivatives can be converted to carboxylic acids, which in turn can be converted to acid chlorides. Thus, any acid derivative can be used to synthesize another, either directly or via a carboxylic acid.

14.7 How Do Esters React with Grignard Reagents?

Treating a formic ester with 2 moles of a Grignard reagent, followed by hydrolysis of the magnesium alkoxide salt in aqueous acid, gives a 2° alcohol, whereas treating an ester other than a formate with a Grignard reagent gives a 3° alcohol in which two of the groups bonded to the carbon bearing the —OH group are the same:

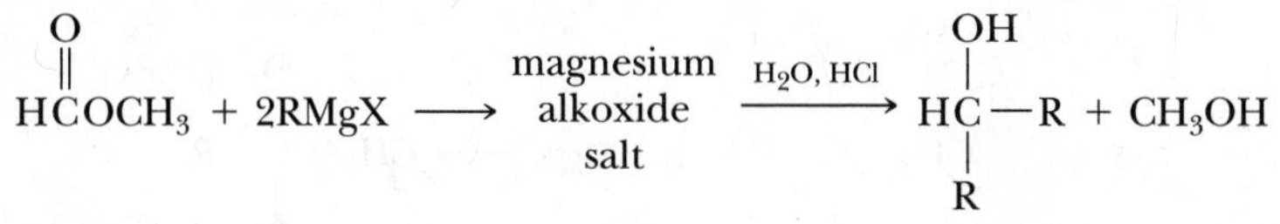

An ester of formic acid — A 2° alcohol

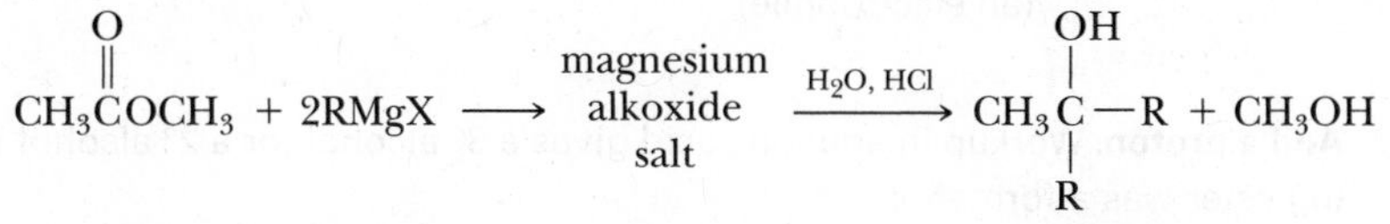

An ester other than formic acid — A 3° alcohol

Reaction of an ester with a Grignard reagent involves the formation of two successive tetrahedral carbonyl addition compounds. The first collapses to give a new carbonyl compound—an aldehyde from a formic ester, a ketone from all other esters. The second intermediate is stable and, when protonated, gives the final alcohol. It is important to realize that it is not possible to use RMgX and an ester to prepare an aldehyde or a ketone: The intermediate aldehyde or ketone is more reactive than the ester and reacts immediately with the Grignard reagent to give a tertiary alcohol.

Mechanism

Reaction of an Ester with a Grignard Reagent

STEP 1: Reaction of a nucleophile and an electrophile to form a new covalent bond. Reaction begins with the addition of 1 mole of Grignard reagent to the carbonyl carbon to form a tetrahedral carbonyl addition intermediate:

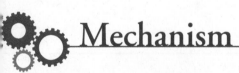

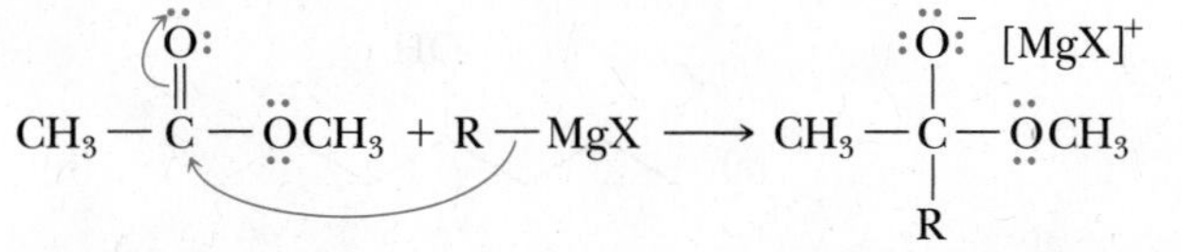

(an electrophile) (a nucleophile) — A magnesium salt (a tetrahedral carbonyl addition intermediate)

STEP 2: Collapse of the tetrahedral carbonyl addition intermediate to eject a leaving group and regenerate the carbonyl group. This intermediate then collapses to give a new carbonyl-containing compound and a magnesium alkoxide salt:

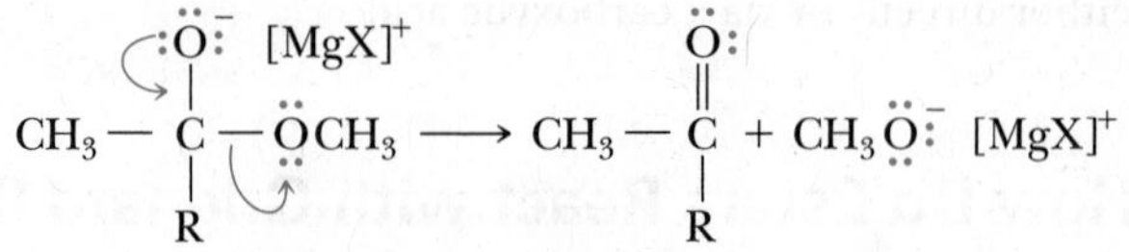

A ketone

STEP 3: Reaction of a nucleophile and an electrophile to form a new covalent bond. The new carbonyl-containing compound reacts with a second mole of Grignard reagent to form a second tetrahedral carbonyl addition compound:

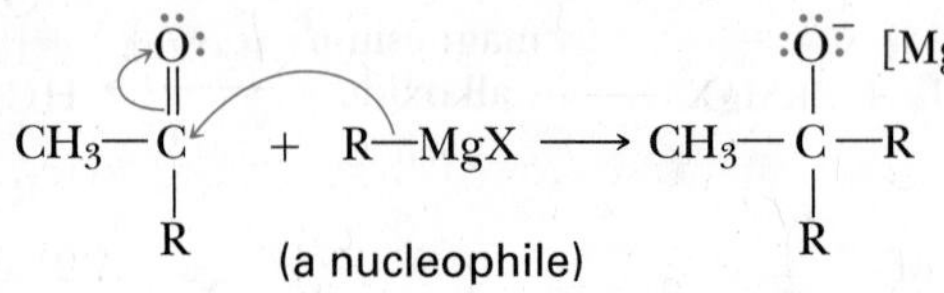

A ketone (an electrophile) (a nucleophile) Magnesium salt

STEP 4: Add a proton. Workup in aqueous acid gives a 3° alcohol (or a 2° alcohol if the starting ester was a formate):

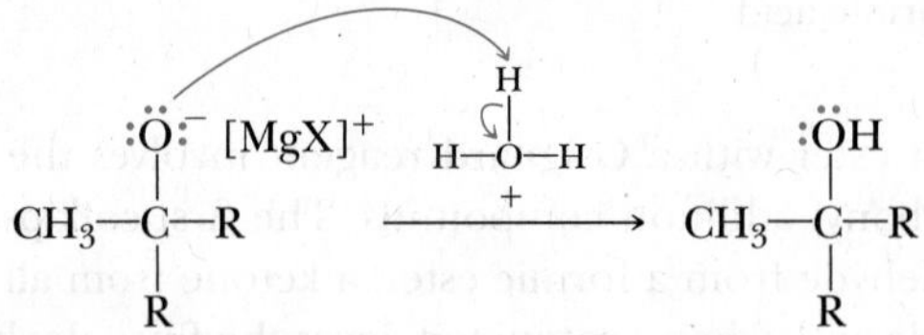

Magnesium salt A 3° alcohol

EXAMPLE 14.6

Complete each Grignard reaction:

(a) 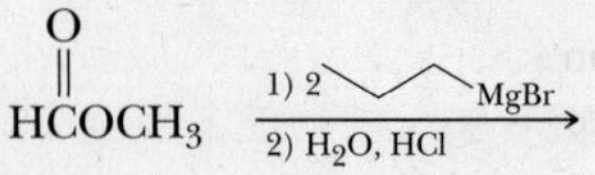

(b) 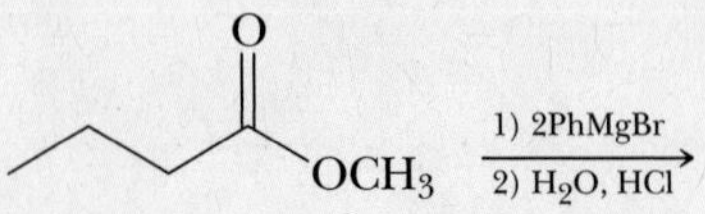

STRATEGY

Reaction of a Grignard reagent with an ester results in an alcohol containing two identical R groups (the R groups from the Grignard reagent) bonded to the former carbonyl carbon.

SOLUTION

Sequence (a) gives a 2° alcohol, and sequence (b) gives a 3° alcohol:

(a) 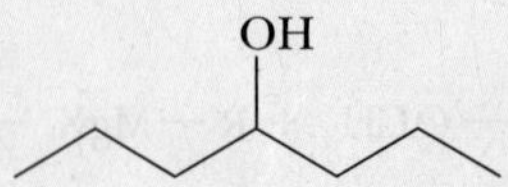

(b) 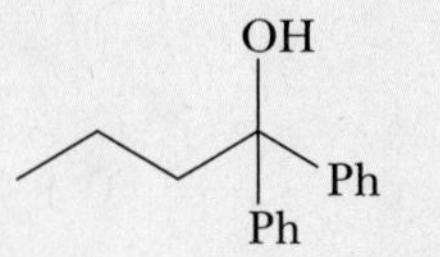

See problems 14.30, 14.33, 14.34

PROBLEM 14.6

Show how to prepare each alcohol by treating an ester with a Grignard reagent:

(a) 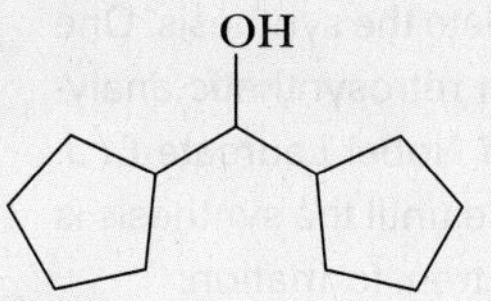

(b) 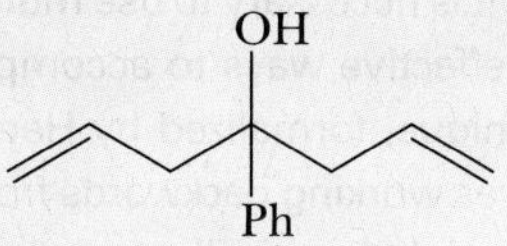

14.8 How Are Derivatives of Carboxylic Acids Reduced?

Most reductions of carbonyl compounds, including aldehydes and ketones, are now accomplished by transferring hydride ions from boron or aluminum hydrides. We have already seen the use of sodium borohydride to reduce the carbonyl groups of aldehydes and ketones to hydroxyl groups (Section 12.10B). We have also seen the use of lithium aluminum hydride to reduce not only the carbonyl groups of aldehydes and ketones, but also carboxyl groups (Section 13.5A), to hydroxyl groups.

A. Esters

An ester is reduced by lithium aluminum hydride to two alcohols. The alcohol derived from the acyl group is primary:

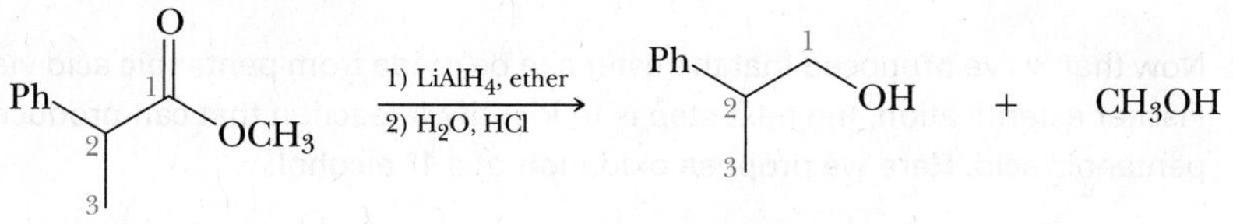

Methyl 2-phenylpropanoate — 2-Phenyl-1-propanol (a 1° alcohol) — Methanol

Sodium borohydride is not normally used to reduce esters because the reaction is very slow. Because of this lower reactivity of sodium borohydride toward esters, it is possible to reduce the carbonyl group of an aldehyde or a ketone to a hydroxyl group with this reagent without reducing an ester or a carboxyl group in the same molecule:

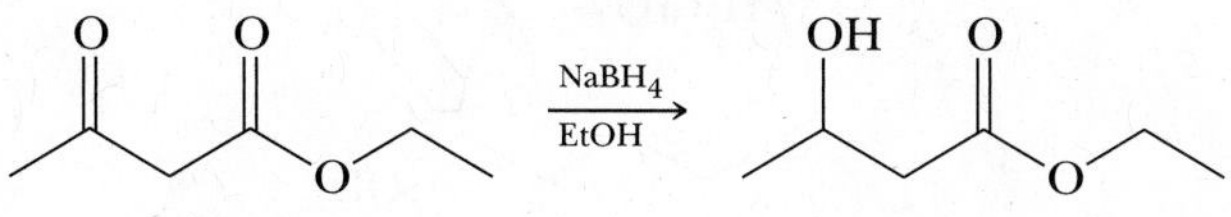

B. Amides

Reduction of amides by lithium aluminum hydride can be used to prepare 1°, 2°, or 3° amines, depending on the degree of substitution of the amide:

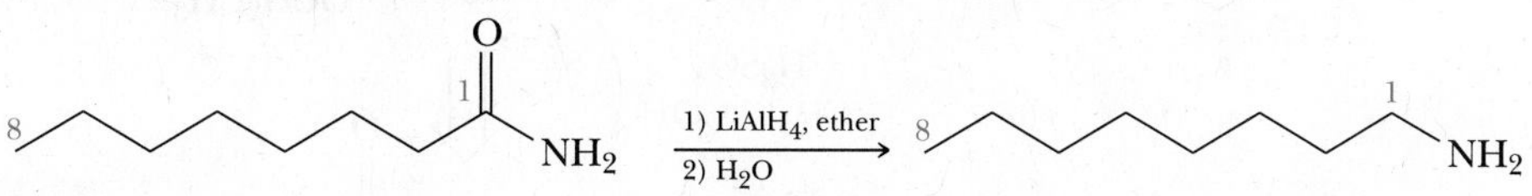

Octanamide — 1-Octanamine (a 1° amine)

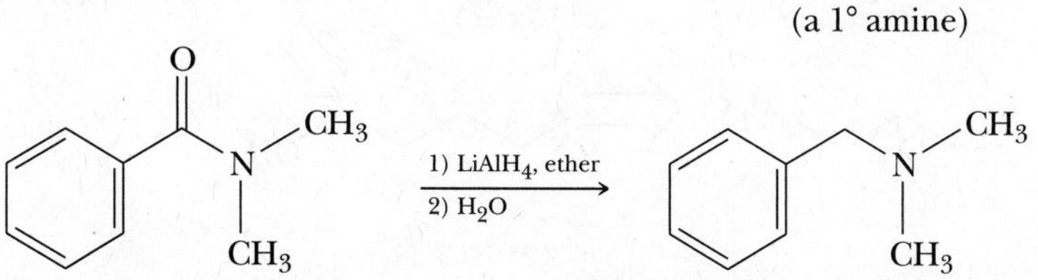

N,N-Dimethylbenzamide — *N,N*-Dimethylbenzylamine (a 3° amine)

HOW TO 14.2 Approach Multistep Synthesis Problems

(a) When a given chemical transformation cannot be achieved with a known chemical reaction, it is necessary to use multiple steps to complete the synthesis. One of the most effective ways to accomplish this is through retrosynthetic analysis. The technique, formalized by Harvard Professor and Nobel Laureate E. J. Corey, involves working backwards from a target molecule until the synthesis is achieved. The technique is illustrated using the following transformation:

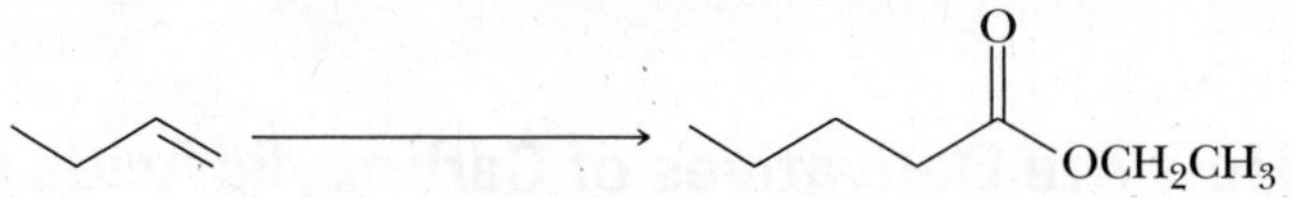

(b) Because there is no reaction that converts an alkene into an ester while also forming a new C—C bond, we work backwards from the ester. The goal is to identify a reaction (or reactions) that can synthesize esters. One such reaction is the Fischer esterification:

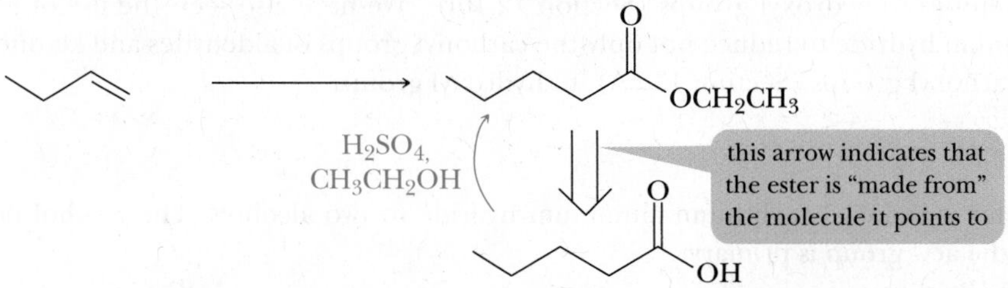

(c) Now that we've proposed that the ester can be made from pentanoic acid via Fischer esterification, the next step is to identify a reaction that can produce pentanoic acid. Here we propose oxidation of a 1° alcohol:

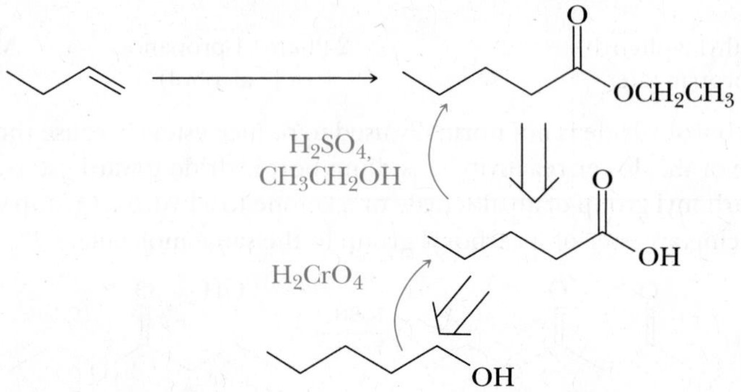

(d) The 1° alcohol, in turn, can be made from a Grignard reagent and formaldehyde:

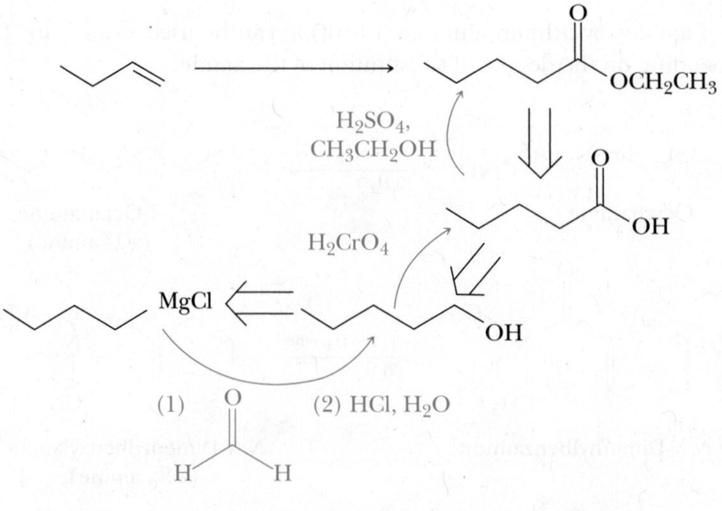

(e) In this manner, the alkene can be arrived at retrosynthetically:

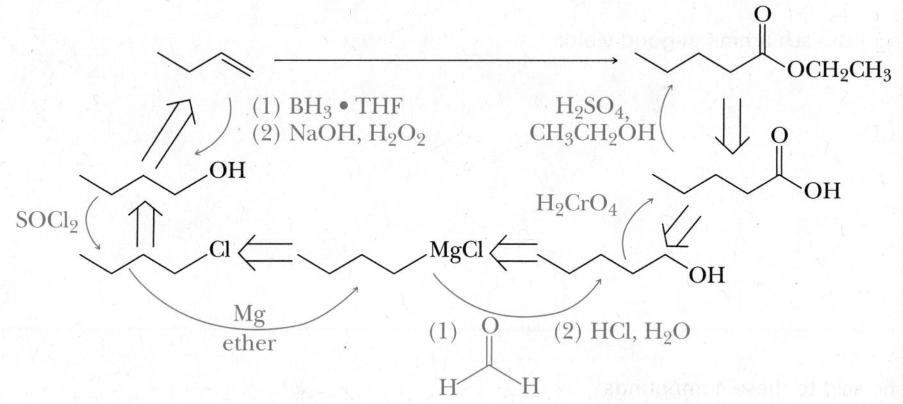

EXAMPLE 14.7

Show how to bring about each conversion:

(a) 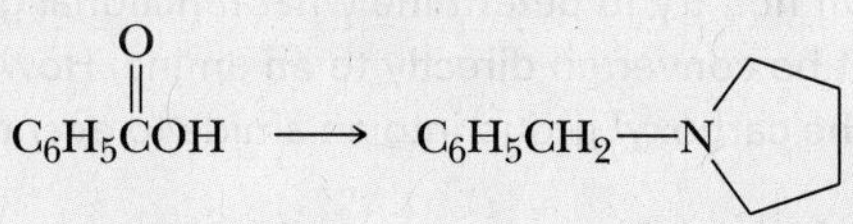

(b) 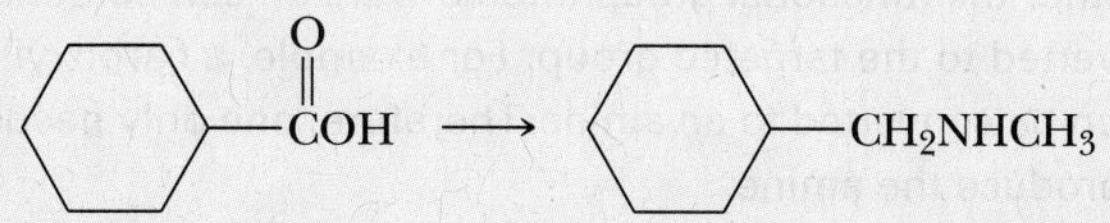

STRATEGY

The key in each part is to convert the carboxylic acid to an amide (Section 14.5D) and then reduce the amide with $LiAlH_4$ (Section 14.8B).

SOLUTION

Each amide can be prepared by treating the carboxylic acid with $SOCl_2$ to form the acid chloride (Section 13.7) and then treating the acid chloride with an amine (Section 14.5A). Alternatively, the carboxylic acid can be converted to an ester by Fischer esterification (Section 13.6) and the ester treated with an amine to give the amide. Solution (a) uses the acid chloride route, solution (b) the ester route:

(a) 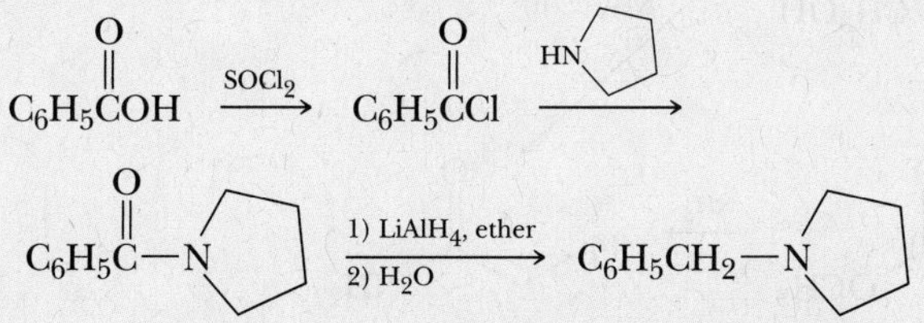

(b) 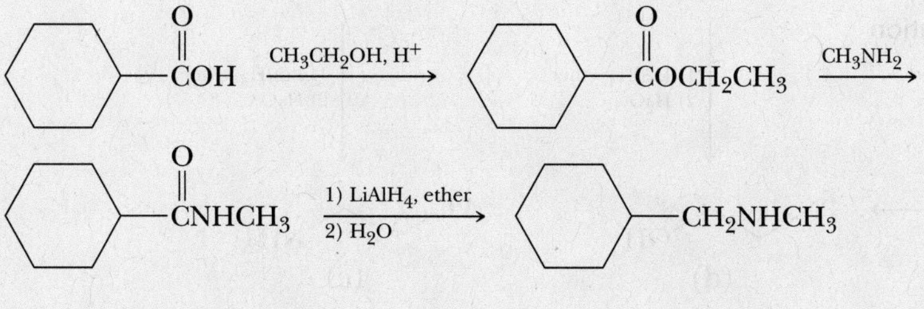

See problems 14.27, 14.29, 14.31, 14.32, 14.39, 14.46

PROBLEM 14.7

Show how to convert hexanoic acid to each amine in good yield:

(a) 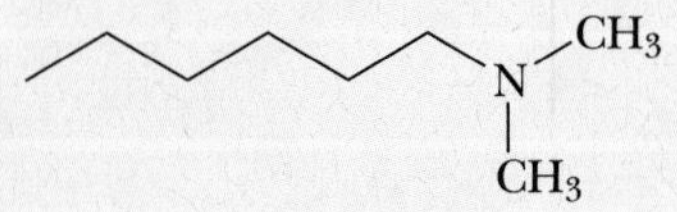

(b) 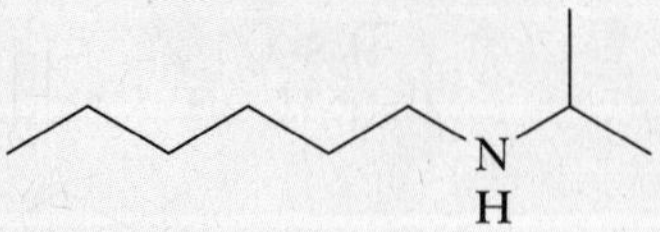

EXAMPLE 14.8

Show how to convert phenylacetic acid to these compounds:

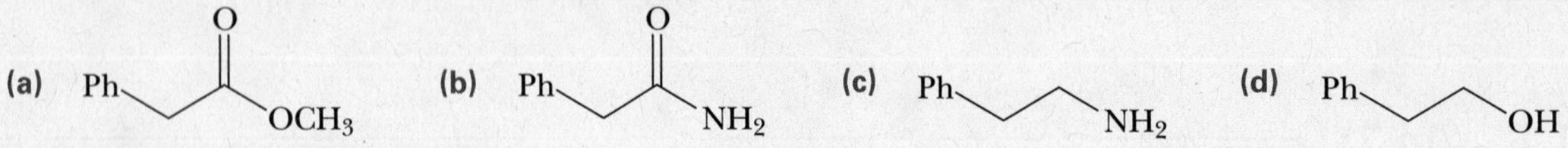

STRATEGY

Decide whether the functional group interconversion can be done in one step. If not, try to determine what functional group can be converted to the targeted group. For example, a carboxyl group cannot be converted directly to an amine. However, an amide can be converted to an amine. Therefore, one only needs to convert the carboxyl group into an amide to eventually be able to produce the amine.

SOLUTION

Prepare methyl ester (a) by Fischer esterification (Section 13.6) of phenylacetic acid with methanol. Then treat this ester with ammonia to prepare amide (b). Alternatively, treat phenylacetic acid with thionyl chloride (Section 13.7) to give an acid chloride, and then treat the acid chloride with two equivalents of ammonia to give amide (b). Reduction of amide (b) by $LiAlH_4$ gives the 1° amine (c). Similar reduction of either phenylacetic acid or ester (a) gives 1° alcohol (d):

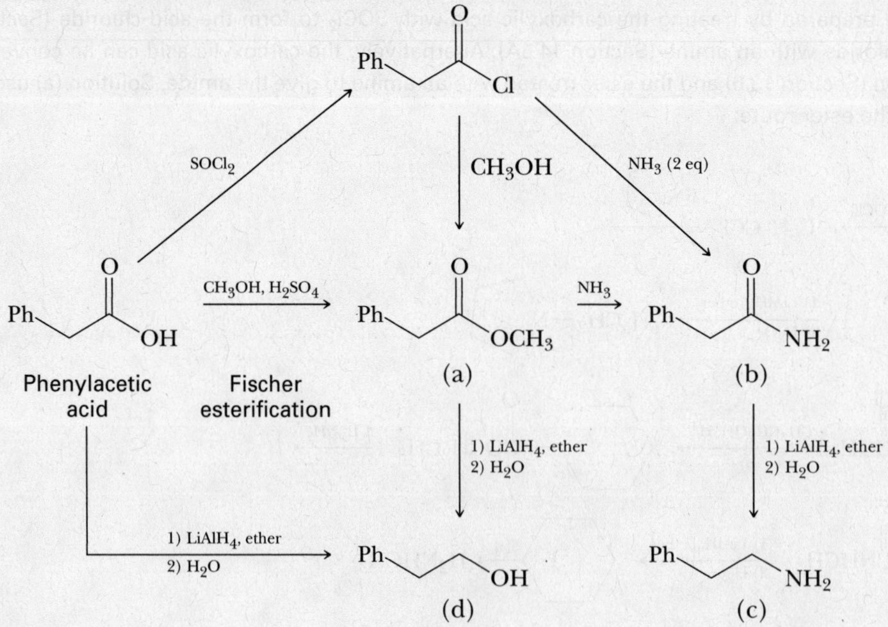

See problem 14.46

PROBLEM 14.8

Show how to convert (*R*)-2-phenylpropanoic acid to these compounds:

(a) 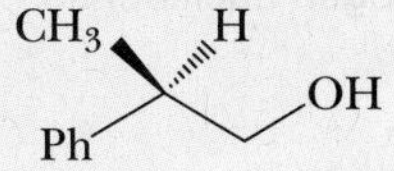

(*R*)-2-Phenyl-1-propanol

(b) 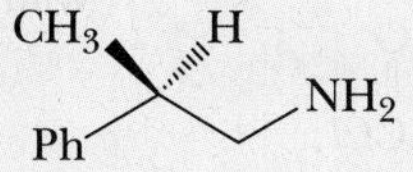

(*R*)-2-Phenyl-1-propanamine

SUMMARY OF KEY QUESTIONS

14.1 What Are Some Derivatives of Carboxylic Acids, and How Are They Named?

- The functional group of an **acid halide** is an acyl group bonded to a halogen.
- Acid halides are named by changing the suffix *-ic acid* in the name of the parent carboxylic acid to *-yl halide.*
- The functional group of a **carboxylic anhydride** is two acyl groups bonded to an oxygen.
- Symmetrical anhydrides are named by changing the suffix *acid* in the name of the parent carboxylic acid to *anhydride.*
- The functional group of a **carboxylic ester** is an acyl group bonded to —OR or —OAr.
- An ester is named by giving the name of the alkyl or aryl group bonded to oxygen first, followed by the name of the acid, in which the suffix *-ic acid* is replaced by the suffix *-ate.*
- A cyclic ester is given the name **lactone**.
- The functional group of an **amide** is an acyl group bonded to a trivalent nitrogen.
- Amides are named by dropping the suffix *-oic acid* from the IUPAC name of the parent acid, or *-ic acid* from its common name, and adding *-amide.*
- A cyclic amide is given the name **lactam**.

14.2 What Are the Characteristic Reactions of Carboxylic Acid Derivatives?

- A common reaction theme of functional derivatives of carboxylic acids is **nucleophilic acyl addition** to the carbonyl carbon to form a **tetrahedral carbonyl addition intermediate**, which then collapses to regenerate the carbonyl group. The result is **nucleophilic acyl substitution**.

14.3 What Is Hydrolysis?

- **Hydrolysis** is a chemical process whereby a bond (or bonds) in a molecule is broken by its reaction with water.
- Hydrolysis of a carboxylic acid derivative results in a carboxylic acid.

14.4 How Do Carboxylic Acid Derivatives React with Alcohols?

- Carboxylic acid derivatives (except for amides) react with alcohols to give esters.
- The reaction conditions required (i.e., neutral, acidic, or basic) depend on the type of derivative.

14.5 How Do Carboxylic Acid Derivatives React with Ammonia and Amines?

- Carboxylic acid derivatives (except for amides) react with ammonia and amines to give amides.

14.6 How Can Functional Derivatives of Carboxylic Acids Be Interconverted?

- Listed in order of increasing reactivity toward nucleophilic acyl substitution, these functional derivatives are:

$RC(=O)NH_2$	$RC(=O)OR'$	$RC(=O)OC(=O)R'$	$RC(=O)Cl$
Amide	Ester	Anhydride	Acid chloride

Reactivity toward nucleophilic acyl substitution →

Less reactive → More reactive

- Any more reactive functional derivative can be directly converted to any less reactive functional derivative by reaction with an appropriate oxygen or nitrogen nucleophile.

14.7 How Do Esters React with Grignard Reagents?

- Reaction of an ester with a Grignard reagent involves the formation of two successive tetrahedral carbonyl addition compounds. The result of the overall reaction is an alcohol containing the two identical alkyl groups from the Grignard reagent.

14.8 How Are Derivatives of Carboxylic Acids Reduced?

- Derivatives of carboxylic acids are resistant to reduction by $NaBH_4$. Therefore, ketones and aldehydes can be selectively reduced in the presence of a carboxylic acid derivative.
- Derivatives of carboxylic acids are resistant to catalytic hydrogenation by H_2/M. Therefore, C—C double and triple bonds can be selectively reduced in the presence of a carboxylic acid derivative.
- $LiAlH_4$ reduces the carboxyl group of acid halides, acid anhydrides, and esters to a 1° alcohol group.
- $LiAlH_4$ reduces amides to amines.

QUICK QUIZ

Answer true or false to the following questions to assess your general knowledge of the concepts in this chapter. If you have difficulty with any of them, you should review the appropriate section in the chapter (shown in parentheses) before attempting the more challenging end-of-chapter problems.

1. The stronger the base, the better the leaving group. (14.2)
2. Anhydrides can contain C—O double bonds or P—O double bonds. (14.1)
3. Acid anhydrides react with ammonia and amines without the need for acid or base. (14.5)
4. Derivatives of carboxylic acids are reduced by H_2/M. (14.8)
5. Aldehydes and ketones undergo nucleophilic acyl substitution reactions, while derivatives of carboxylic acids undergo nucleophilic addition reactions. (14.2)
6. Esters react with ammonia and amines without the need for acid or base. (14.5)
7. An acyl group is a carbonyl bonded to an alkyl (R) group. (14.1)
8. Hydrolysis is the loss of water from a molecule. (14.3)
9. Esters react with water without the need for acid or base. (14.4)
10. Acid anhydrides react with water without the need for acid or base. (14.3)
11. An acid halide can be converted to an amide in one step. (14.6)
12. An ester can be converted to an acid halide in one step. (14.6)
13. In the hydrolysis of an ester with base, hydroxide ion is a catalyst. (14.3)
14. Derivatives of carboxylic acids are reduced by $NaBH_4$. (14.8)
15. Acid anhydrides react with alcohols without the need for acid or base. (14.4)
16. Acid halides react with water without the need for acid or base. (14.3)
17. An ester of formic acid reacts with Grignard reagents to form a 3° alcohol. (14.7)
18. Acid halides react with ammonia and amines without the need for acid or base. (14.5)
19. A cyclic amide is called a lactone. (14.1)
20. The reactivity of a carboxylic acid derivative is dependent on the stability of its leaving group. (14.2)
21. Amides react with ammonia and amines without the need for acid or base. (14.5)
22. An amide can be converted to an ester in one step. (14.6)

23. Amides react with water without the need for acid or base. (14.3)
24. Esters react with alcohols without the need for acid or base. (14.3)
25. Amides react with alcohols under acidic or basic conditions. (14.4)
26. Esters other than formic acid esters react with Grignards to form ketones. (14.7)
27. Acid halides react with alcohols without the need for acid or base. (14.4)
28. An —OR group attached to a P—O double bond is known as an ester. (14.1)

Answers: (1) F (2) T (3) T (4) F (5) F (6) T (7) T (8) F (9) F (10) T (11) T (12) F (13) F (14) F (15) T (16) T (17) F (18) T (19) F (20) T (21) F (22) F (23) F (24) F (25) F (26) F (27) T (28) T

Detailed explanations for many of these answers can be found in the accompanying Solutions Manual.

KEY REACTIONS

1. Hydrolysis of an Acid Chloride (Section 14.3A)

Low-molecular-weight acid chlorides react vigorously with water; higher-molecular-weight acid chlorides react less rapidly:

$$CH_3\overset{O}{\overset{\|}{C}}Cl + H_2O \longrightarrow CH_3\overset{O}{\overset{\|}{C}}OH + HCl$$

2. Hydrolysis of an Acid Anhydride (Section 14.3B)

Low-molecular-weight acid anhydrides react readily with water; higher-molecular-weight acid anhydrides react less rapidly:

$$CH_3\overset{O}{\overset{\|}{C}}O\overset{O}{\overset{\|}{C}}CH_3 + H_2O \longrightarrow CH_3\overset{O}{\overset{\|}{C}}OH + HO\overset{O}{\overset{\|}{C}}CH_3$$

3. Hydrolysis of an Ester (Section 14.3C)

Esters are hydrolyzed only in the presence of base or acid; base is required in an equimolar amount, acid is a catalyst:

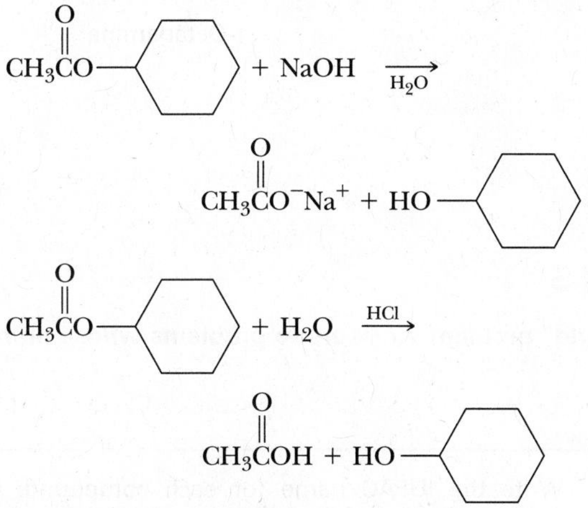

4. Hydrolysis of an Amide (Section 14.3D)

Either acid or base is required in an amount equivalent to that of the amide:

$$CH_3CH_2CH_2\overset{O}{\overset{\|}{C}}NH_2 + H_2O + HCl \xrightarrow[\text{Heat}]{H_2O} CH_3CH_2CH_2\overset{O}{\overset{\|}{C}}OH + NH_4{}^+Cl^-$$

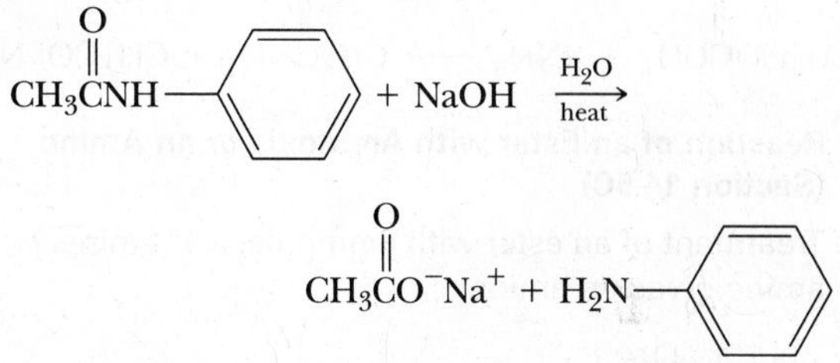

5. Reaction of an Acid Chloride with an Alcohol (Section 14.4A)

Treatment of an acid chloride with an alcohol gives an ester and HCl:

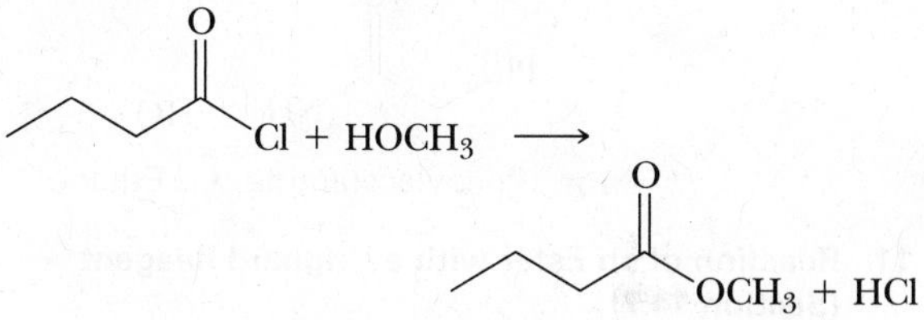

6. Reaction of an Acid Anhydride with an Alcohol (Section 14.4B)

Treatment of an acid anhydride with an alcohol gives an ester and a carboxylic acid:

$$CH_3\overset{O}{\overset{\|}{C}}O\overset{O}{\overset{\|}{C}}CH_3 + HOCH_2CH_3 \longrightarrow CH_3\overset{O}{\overset{\|}{C}}OCH_2CH_3 + CH_3\overset{O}{\overset{\|}{C}}OH$$

7. Reaction of an Ester with an Alcohol (Section 14.4C)

Treatment of an ester with an alcohol in the presence of an acid catalyst results in transesterification—that is, the replacement of one —OR group by a different —OR group:

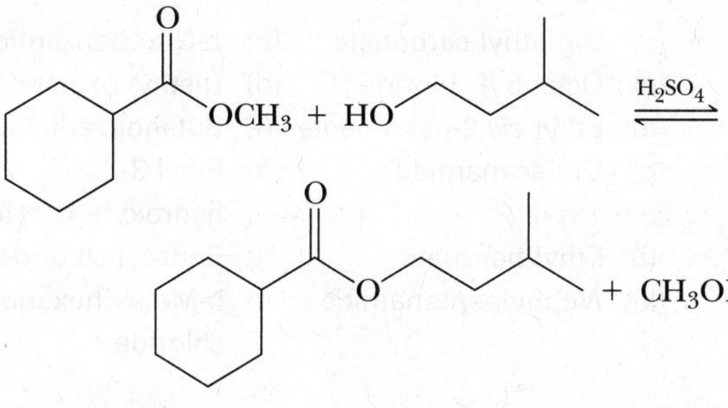

8. Reaction of an Acid Chloride with Ammonia or an Amine (Section 14.5A)

Reaction requires 2 moles of ammonia or amine—1 mole to form the amide and 1 mole to neutralize the HCl by-product:

$$CH_3\overset{O}{\overset{\|}{C}}Cl + 2NH_3 \longrightarrow CH_3\overset{O}{\overset{\|}{C}}NH_2 + NH_4{}^+Cl^-$$

9. Reaction of an Acid Anhydride with Ammonia or an Amine (Section 14.5B)

Reaction requires 2 moles of ammonia or amine—1 mole to form the amide and 1 mole to neutralize the carboxylic acid by-product:

$$CH_3\overset{O}{\overset{\|}{C}}O\overset{O}{\overset{\|}{C}}CH_3 + 2NH_3 \longrightarrow CH_3\overset{O}{\overset{\|}{C}}NH_2 + CH_3\overset{O}{\overset{\|}{C}}O^-NH_4{}^+$$

10. Reaction of an Ester with Ammonia or an Amine (Section 14.5C)

Treatment of an ester with ammonia, a 1° amine, or a 2° amine gives an amide:

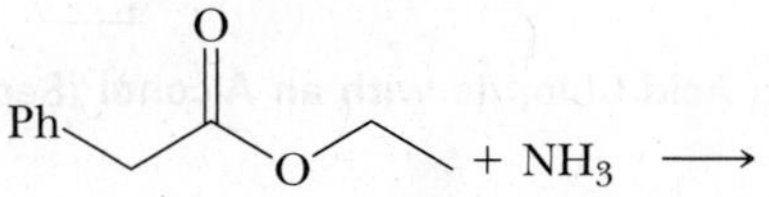

Ethyl phenylacetate

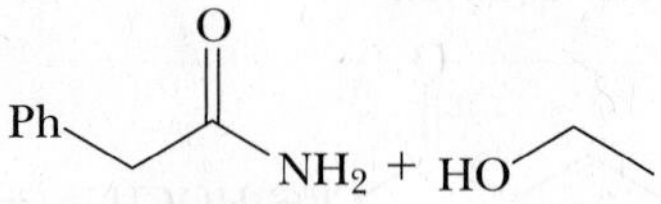

Phenylacetamide Ethanol

11. Reaction of an Ester with a Grignard Reagent (Section 14.7)

Treating a formic ester with a Grignard reagent, followed by hydrolysis, gives a 2° alcohol, whereas treating any other ester with a Grignard reagent gives a 3° alcohol:

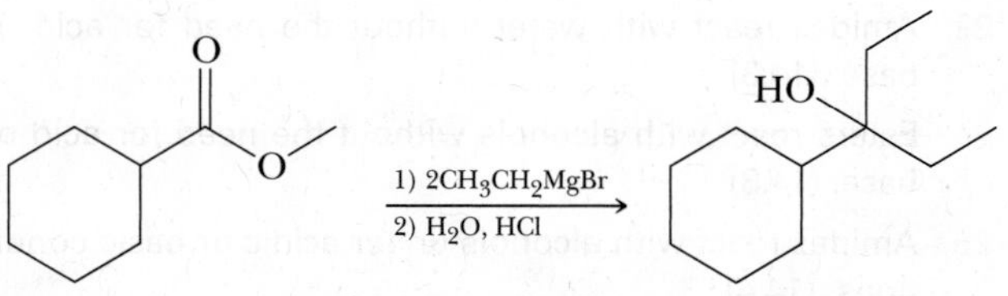

12. Reduction of an Ester (Section 14.8A)

Reduction by lithium aluminum hydride gives two alcohols:

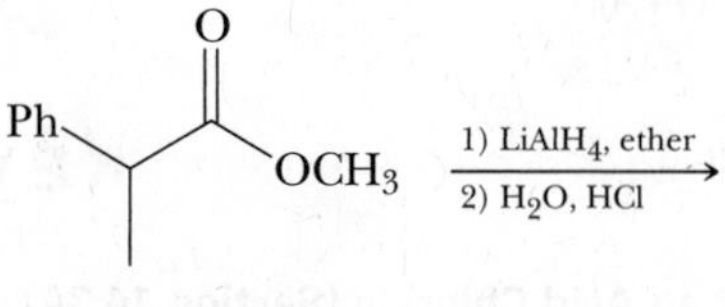

Methyl 2-phenyl-propanoate

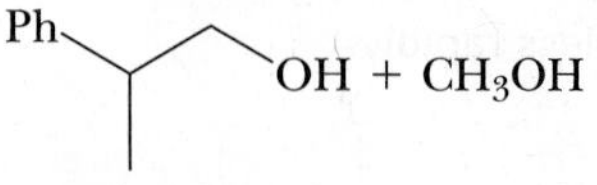

2-Phenyl-1-propanol Methanol

13. Reduction of an Amide (Section 14.8B)

Reduction by lithium aluminum hydride gives an amine:

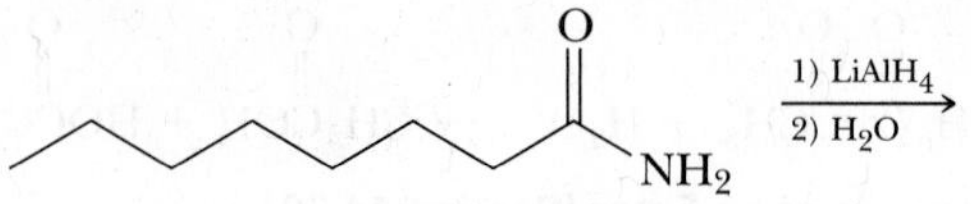

Octanamide

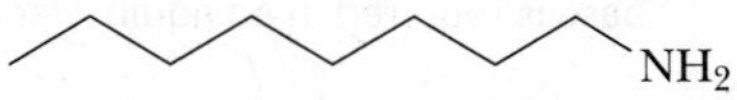

1-Octanamine

PROBLEMS

A problem marked with an asterisk indicates an applied "real-world" problem. Answers to problems whose numbers are printed in blue are given in Appendix D.

Section 14.1 Structure and Nomenclature

14.9 Draw a structural formula for each compound: **(See Example 14.1)**

(a) Dimethyl carbonate
(b) *p*-Nitrobenzamide
(c) Octanoyl chloride
(d) Diethyl oxalate
(e) Ethyl *cis*-2-pentenoate
(f) Butanoic anhydride
(g) Dodecanamide
(h) Ethyl 3-hydroxybutanoate
(i) Ethyl benzoate
(j) Benzoyl chloride
(k) *N*-Ethylpentanamide
(l) 5-Methylhexanoyl chloride

14.10 Write the IUPAC name for each compound: **(See Example 14.1)**

(a) 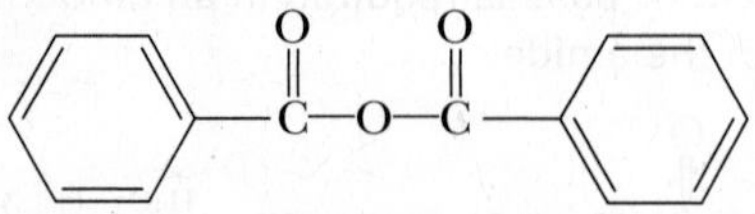

(b) $CH_3(CH_2)_{14}\overset{O}{\overset{\|}{C}}OCH_3$

(c) 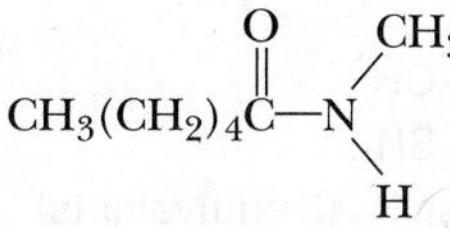

(d) 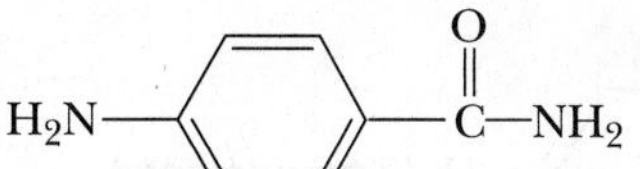

(e) 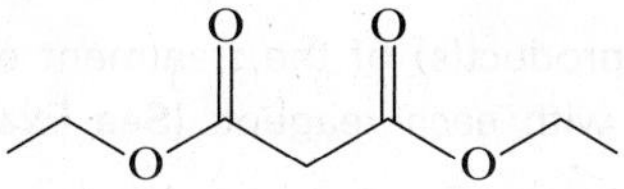

(f) 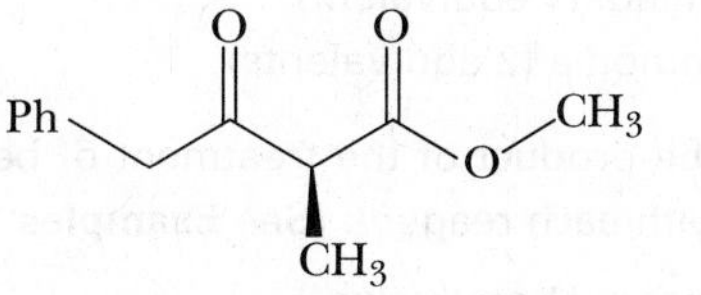

(g) 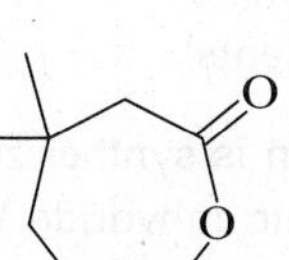

(h) 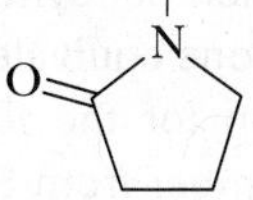

(i) 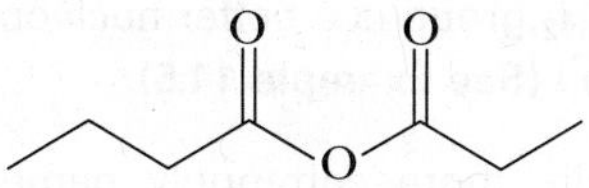

(j) 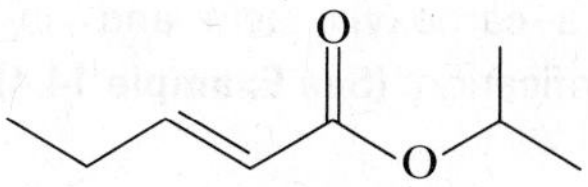

(k) 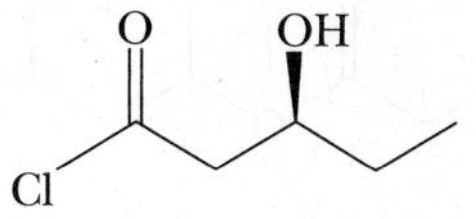

(l) 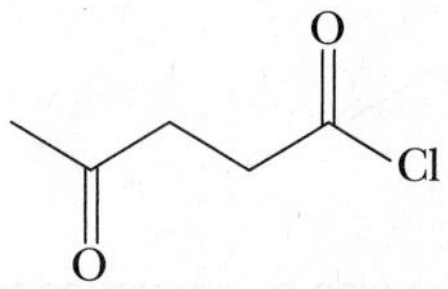

***14.11** When oil from the head of a sperm whale is cooled, spermaceti, a translucent wax with a white, pearly luster, crystallizes from the mixture. Spermaceti, which makes up 11% of whale oil, is composed mainly of hexadecyl hexadecanoate (cetyl palmitate). At one time, spermaceti was widely used in the making of cosmetics, fragrant soaps, and candles. Draw a structural formula of cetyl palmitate. **(See Example 14.1)**

Wolfgang Poelzer/Waterframe RM/ Getty Images, Inc.

Sperm whale, *Physterer macrocephalus*, diving, Kaikoura, NZ.

Physical Properties

14.12 Acetic acid and methyl formate are constitutional isomers. Both are liquids at room temperature, one with a boiling point of 32 °C, the other with a boiling point of 118 °C. Which of the two has the higher boiling point?

14.13 Butanoic acid (M. W. 88.11 g/mol) has a boiling point of 162 °C, whereas its propyl ester (M.W. 130.18 g/mol) has a boiling point of 142 °C. Account for the fact that the boiling point of butanoic acid is higher than that of its propyl ester, even though butanoic acid has a lower molecular weight.

14.14 The constitutional isomers pentanoic acid and methyl butanoate are both slightly soluble in water. One of these compounds has a solubility of 1.5 g/100 ml (25 °C), while the other has a solubility of 4.97 g/100 ml (25 °C). Assign the solubilities to each compound and account for the differences.

Sections 14.2–14.8 Reactions

14.15 Arrange these compounds in order of increasing reactivity toward nucleophilic acyl substitution:

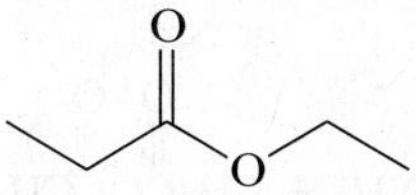

(1)

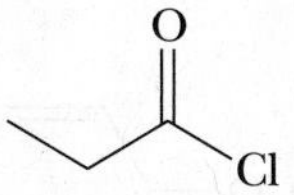

(2)

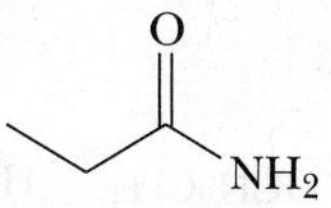

(3)

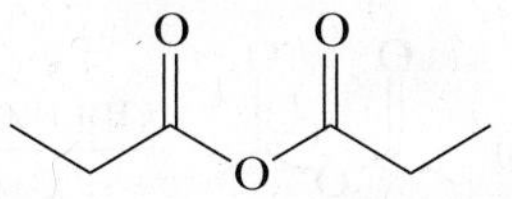

(4)

14.16 A carboxylic acid can be converted to an ester by Fischer esterification. Show how to synthesize each ester from a carboxylic acid and an alcohol by Fischer esterification: **(See Example 14.4)**

(a) 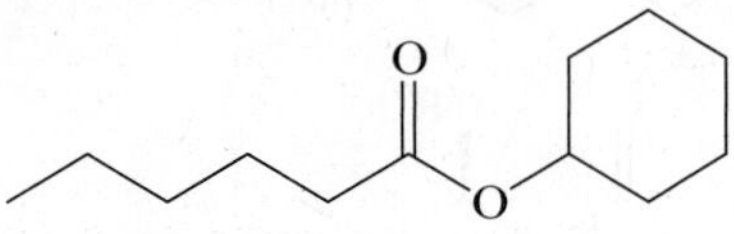

(b) 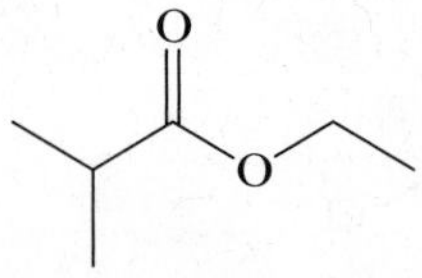

14.17 A carboxylic acid can also be converted to an ester in two reactions by first converting the carboxylic acid to its acid chloride and then treating the acid chloride with an alcohol. Show how to prepare each ester in Problem 14.16 from a carboxylic acid and an alcohol by this two-step scheme. **(See Example 14.4)**

14.18 Show how to prepare these amides by reaction of an acid chloride with ammonia or an amine: **(See Example 14.5)**

(a) 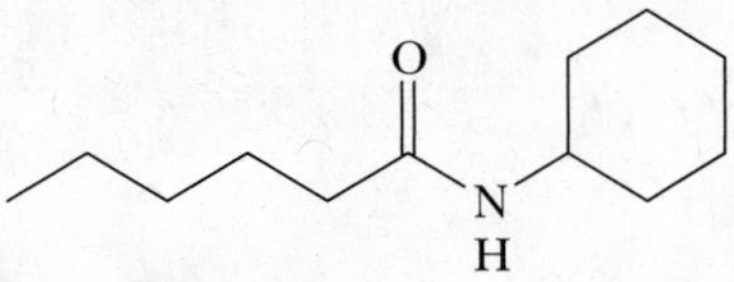

(b) 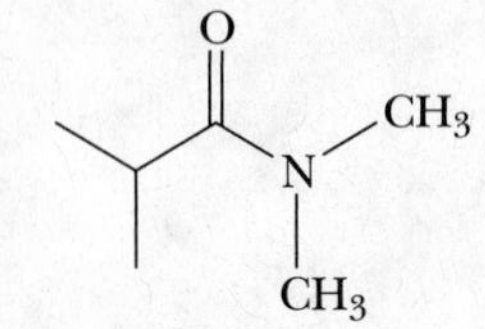

(c) 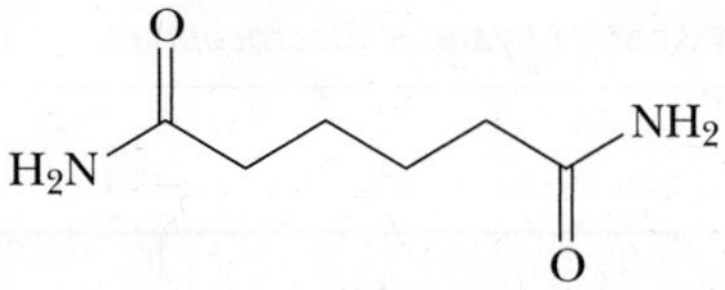

14.19 Balance and write a mechanism for each of the following reactions. **(See Examples 14.2, 14.4, 14.5)**

(a) 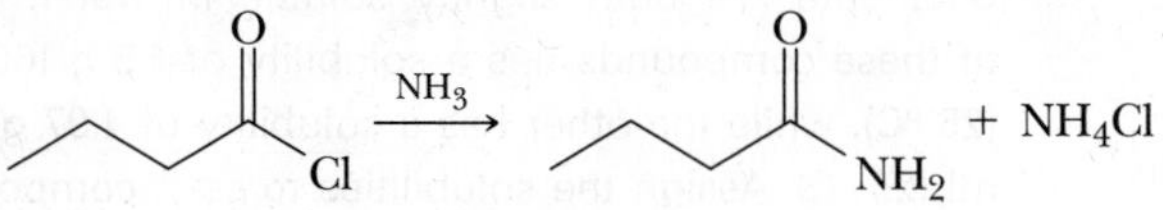

(b) 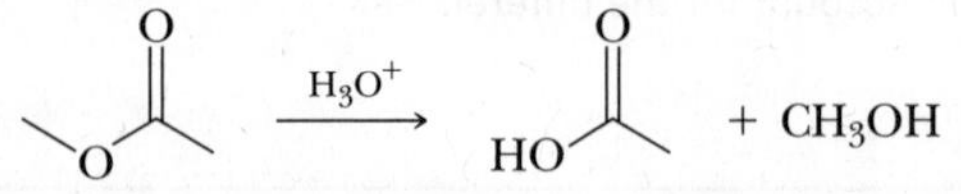

(c) 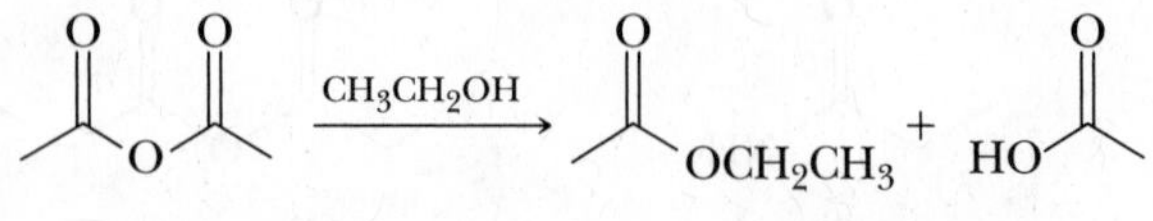

14.20 What product is formed when benzoyl chloride is treated with these reagents? **(See Examples 14.2, 14.4, 14.5)**

(a) C_6H_6, $AlCl_3$
(b) $CH_3CH_2CH_2CH_2OH$
(c) $CH_3CH_2CH_2CH_2SH$
(d) $CH_3CH_2CH_2CH_2NH_2$ (2 equivalents)
(e) H_2O
(f) 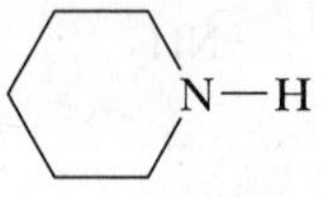 (2 equivalents)

14.21 Write the product(s) of the treatment of propanoic anhydride with each reagent: **(See Examples 14.4, 14.5)**

(a) Ethanol (1 equivalent)
(b) Ammonia (2 equivalents)

14.22 Write the product of the treatment of benzoic anhydride with each reagent: **(See Examples 14.4, 14.5)**

(a) Ethanol (1 equivalent)
(b) Ammonia (2 equivalents)

***14.23** The analgesic phenacetin is synthesized by treating 4-ethoxyaniline with acetic anhydride. Write an equation for the formation of phenacetin.

***14.24** The analgesic acetaminophen is synthesized by treating 4-aminophenol with one equivalent of acetic anhydride. Write an equation for the formation of acetaminophen. (*Hint*: Remember from Section 7.5A that an —NH_2 group is a better nucleophile than an —OH group.) **(See Example 14.5)**

***14.25** Nicotinic acid, more commonly named niacin, is one of the B vitamins. Show how nicotinic acid can be converted to ethyl nicotinate and then to nicotinamide: **(See Example 14.5)**

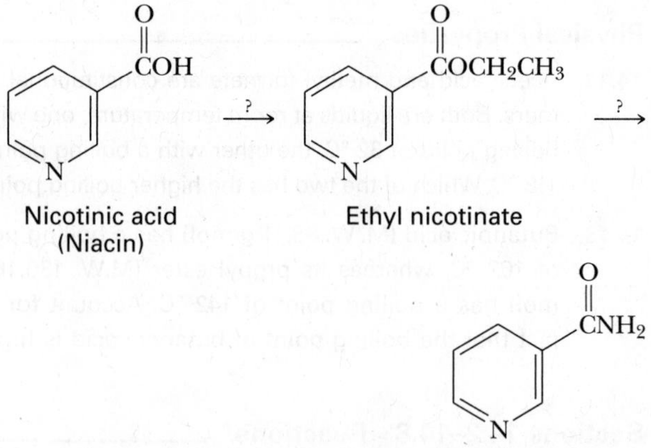

Nicotinic acid (Niacin) · Ethyl nicotinate · Nicotinamide

14.26 Complete these reactions: **(See Example 14.5)**

(a) 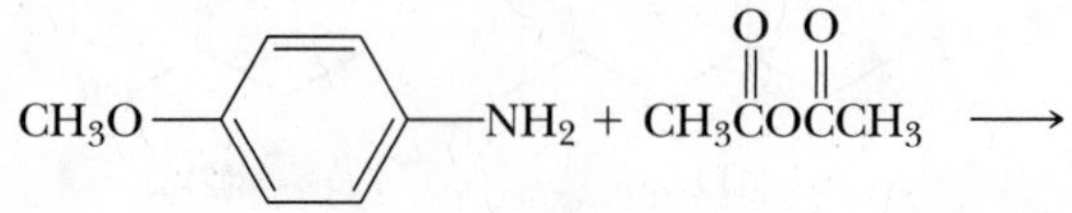

(b) 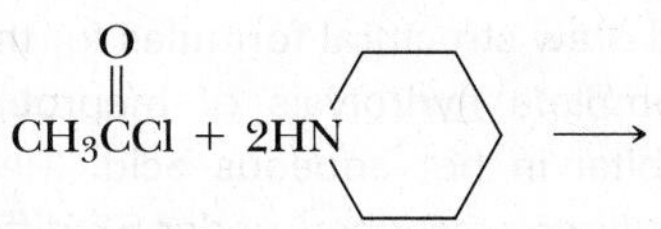

(c) 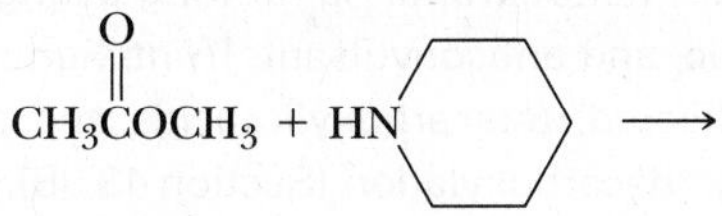

(d) 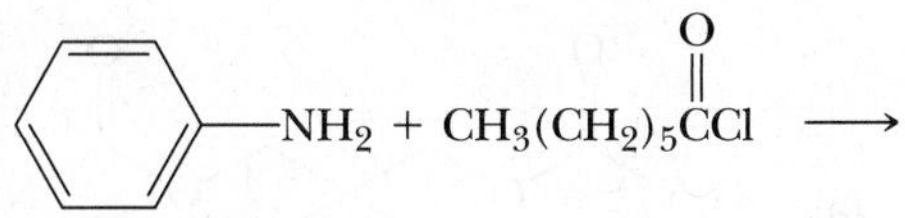

14.27 What product is formed when ethyl benzoate is treated with these reagents? **(See Example 14.7)**

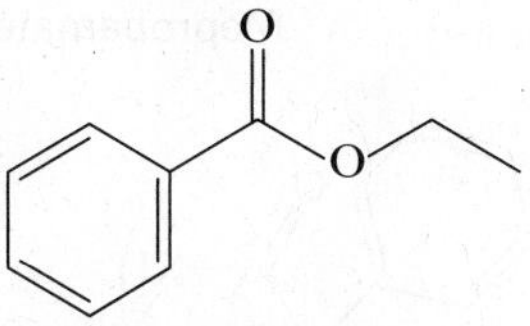

Ethyl benzoate

(a) H_2O, NaOH, heat
(b) $LiAlH_4$, then H_2O
(c) H_2O, H_2SO_4, heat
(d) $CH_3CH_2CH_2CH_2NH_2$
(e) C_6H_5MgBr (2 moles) and then H_2O/HCl

***14.28** Show how to convert 2-hydroxybenzoic acid (salicylic acid) to these compounds: **(See Example 14.4)**

(a) 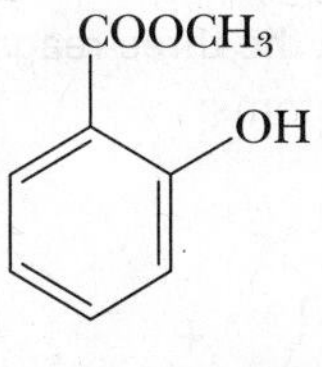

Methyl salicylate
(Oil of wintergreen)

(b) 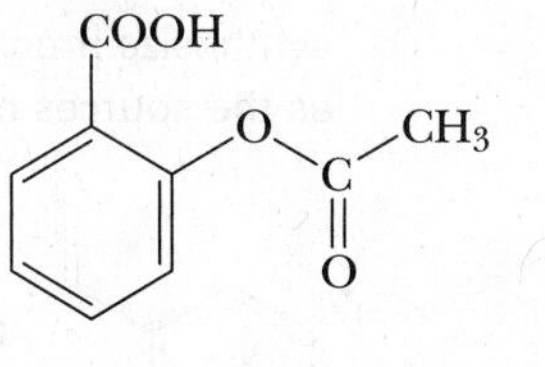

Acetyl salicylic acid
(Aspirin)

14.29 What product is formed when benzamide is treated with these reagents? **(See Examples 14.3, 14.7)**
(a) H_2O, HCl, heat
(b) NaOH, H_2O, heat
(c) $LiAlH_4$/ether, then H_2O

14.30 Treating γ-butyrolactone with two equivalents of methylmagnesium bromide, followed by hydrolysis in aqueous acid, gives a compound with the molecular formula $C_6H_{14}O_2$: **(See Example 14.6)**

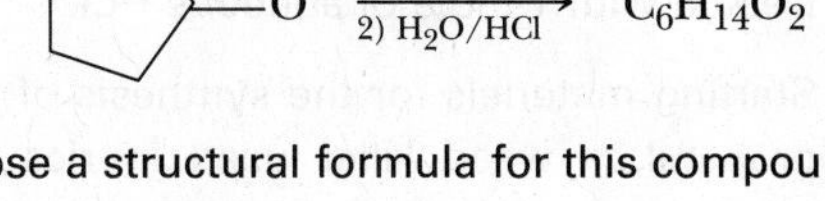

Propose a structural formula for this compound.

14.31 Show the product of treating γ-butyrolactone with each reagent: **(See Examples 14.2, 14.5, 14.7)**
(a) NH_3
(b) $LiAlH_4$/ether, then H_2O
(c) NaOH, H_2O, heat

14.32 Show the product of treating *N*-methyl-γ-butyrolactam with each reagent: **(See Examples 14.3, 14.7)**
(a) H_2O, HCl, heat
(b) NaOH, H_2O, heat
(c) $LiAlH_4$/ether, then H_2O

14.33 Complete these reactions: **(See Example 14.6)**

(a) 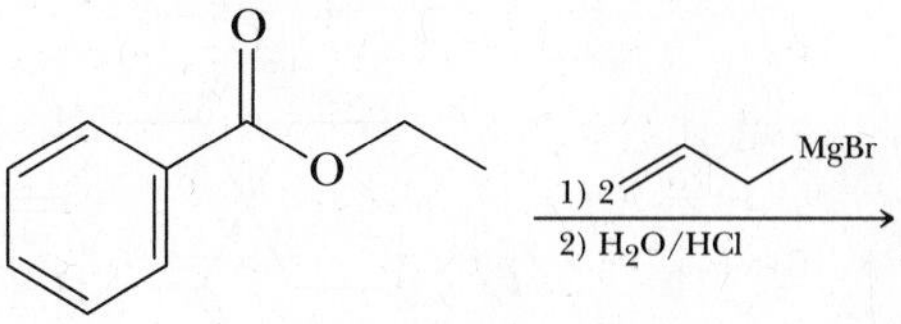

(b) 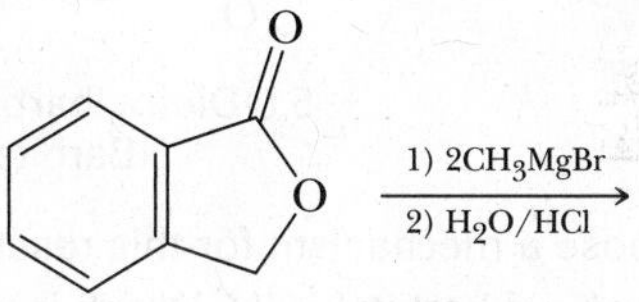

(c) 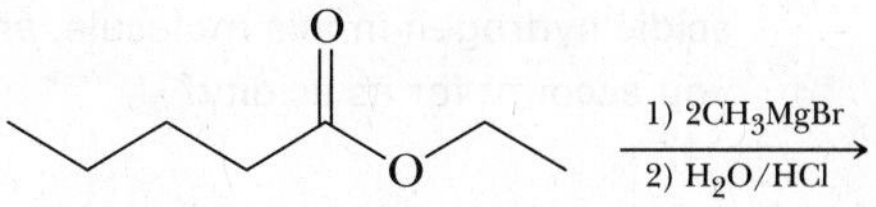

14.34 What combination of ester and Grignard reagent can be used to prepare each alcohol? **(See Example 14.6)**
(a) 2-Methyl-2-butanol
(b) 3-Phenyl-3-pentanol
(c) 1,1-Diphenylethanol

14.35 Reaction of a 1° or 2° amine with diethyl carbonate under controlled conditions gives a carbamic ester: **(See Example 14.5)**

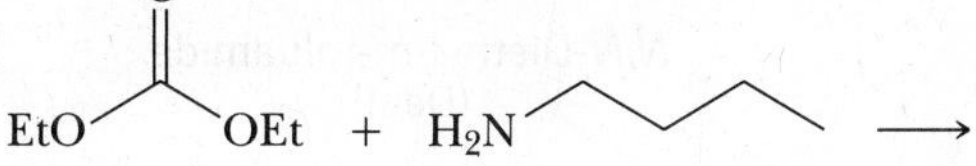

Diethyl carbonate   1-Butanamine (Butylamine)

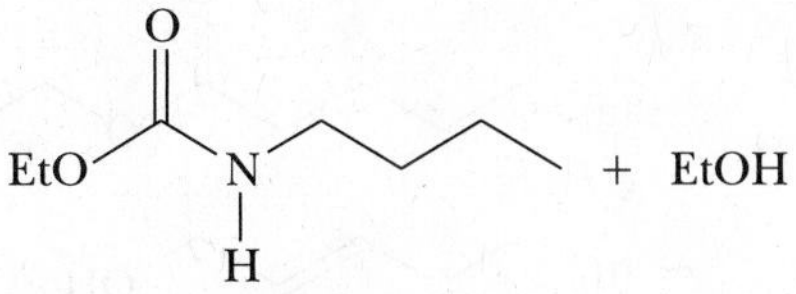

A carbamic ester

Propose a mechanism for this reaction.

14.36 Barbiturates are prepared by treating diethyl malonate or a derivative of diethyl malonate with urea in the presence of sodium ethoxide as a catalyst.

Following is an equation for the preparation of barbital from diethyl 2,2-diethylmalonate and urea (barbital, a long-duration hypnotic and sedative, is prescribed under a dozen or more trade names):

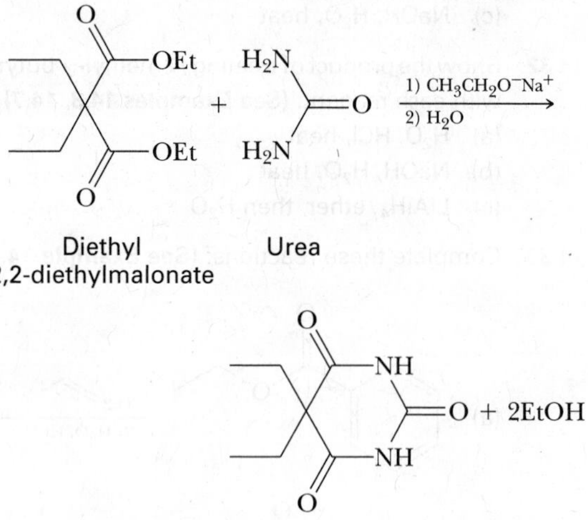

Diethyl 2,2-diethylmalonate

Urea

5,5-Diethylbarbituric acid (Barbital)

(a) Propose a mechanism for this reaction.
(b) The pK_a of barbital is 7.4. Which is the most acidic hydrogen in this molecule, and how do you account for its acidity?

*14.37 Name and draw structural formulas for the products of the complete hydrolysis of meprobamate and phenobarbital in hot aqueous acid. Meprobamate is a tranquilizer prescribed under 58 different trade names. Phenobarbital is a long-acting sedative, hypnotic, and anticonvulsant. [*Hint*: Remember that, when heated, β-dicarboxylic acids and β-ketoacids undergo decarboxylation (Section 13.8B).]

(a)

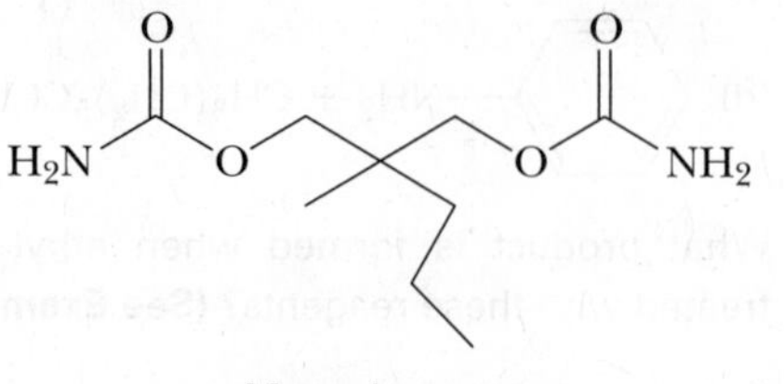

Meprobamate

(b)

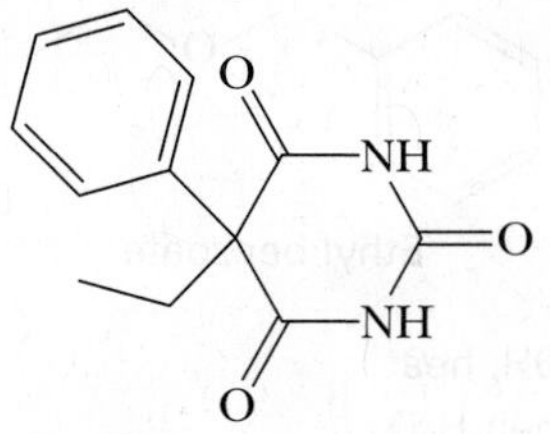

Phenobarbital

Synthesis

*14.38 The active ingredient in several common insect repellents *N,N*-Diethyl-*m*-toluamide (Deet) is synthesized from 3-methylbenzoic acid (*m*-toluic acid) and diethylamine:

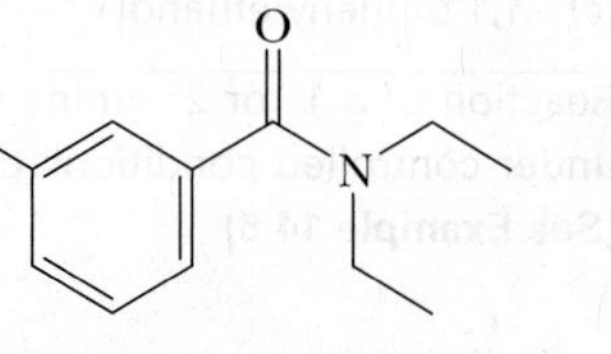

N,N-Diethyl-*m*-toluamide (Deet)

Show how this synthesis can be accomplished.

14.39 Show how to convert ethyl 2-pentenoate into these compounds: **(See Example 14.7)**

(a)

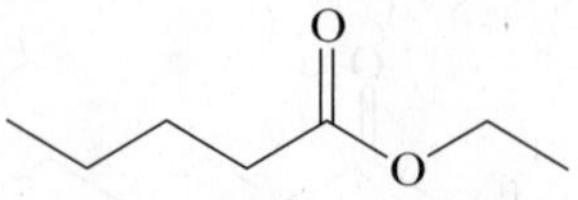

(b)

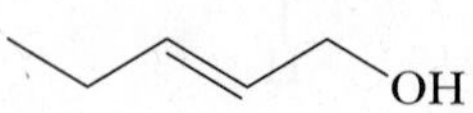

(c)

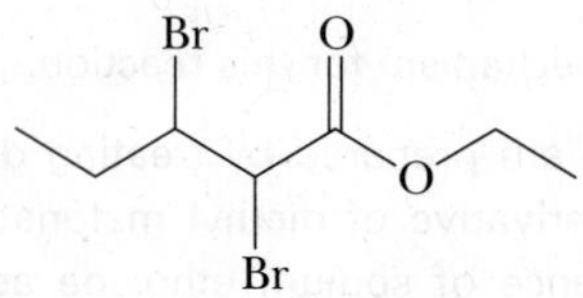

*14.40 Procaine (whose hydrochloride is marketed as Novocaine®) was one of the first local anesthetics for infiltration and regional anesthesia. Show how to synthesize procaine, using the three reagents shown as the sources of carbon atoms:

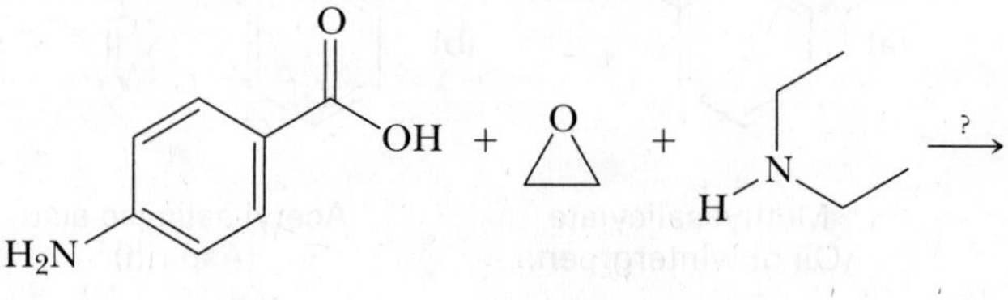

4-Aminobenzoic acid

Ethylene oxide

Diethylamine

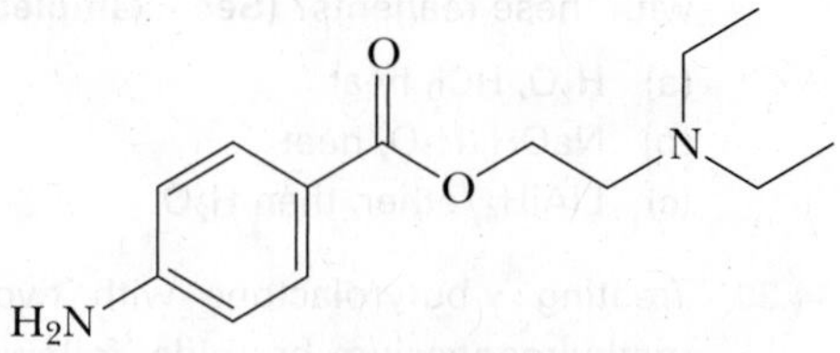

Procaine

*14.41 There are two nitrogen atoms in procaine. Which of the two is the stronger base? Draw the structural formula for the salt that is formed when procaine is treated with 1 mole of aqueous HCl.

*14.42 Starting materials for the synthesis of the herbicide propanil, a weed killer used in rice paddies, are benzene and propanoic acid. Show reagents to bring about this synthesis:

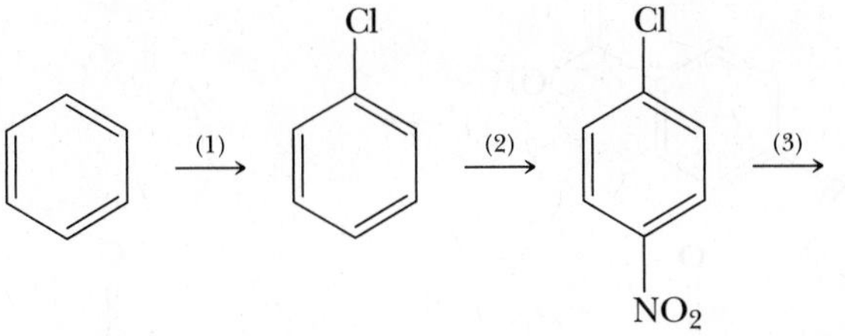

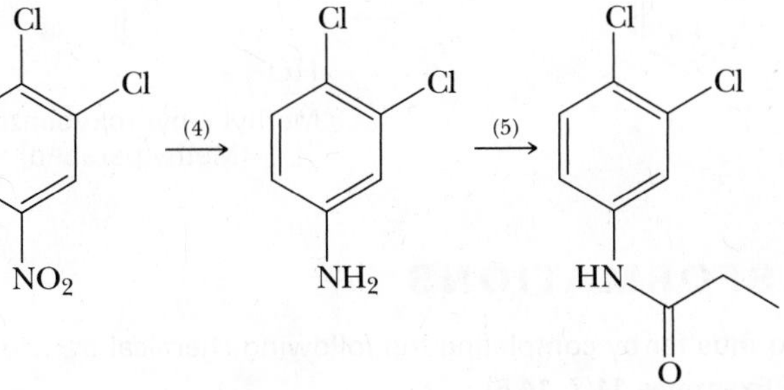

Propanil

***14.43** Following are structural formulas for three local anesthetics: Lidocaine was introduced in 1948 and is now the most widely used local anesthetic for infiltration and regional anesthesia. Its hydrochloride is marketed under the name Xylocaine®. Etidocaine (its hydrochloride is marketed as Duranest®) is comparable to lidocaine in onset, but its analgesic action lasts two to three times longer. Mepivacaine (its hydrochloride is marketed as Carbocaine®) is faster and somewhat longer in duration than lidocaine.

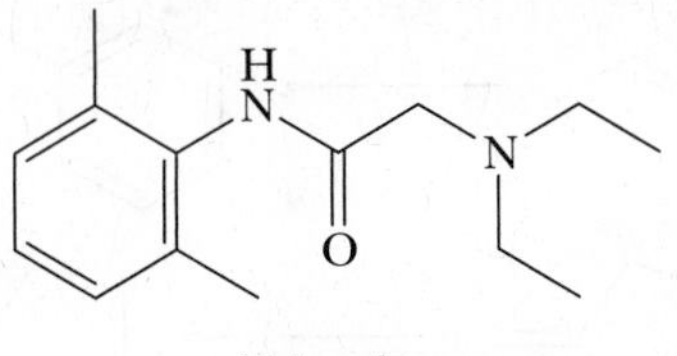

Lidocaine
(Xylocaine®)

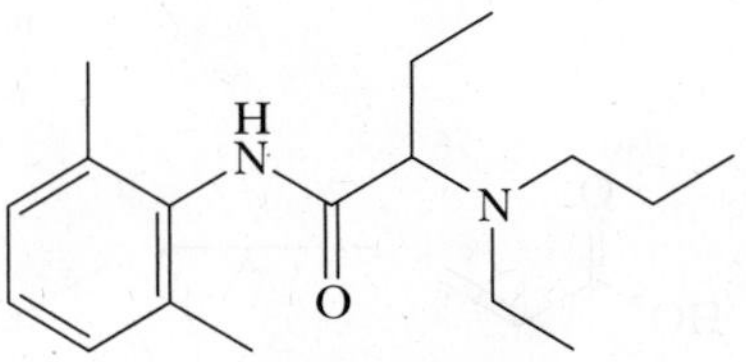

Etidocaine
(Duranest®)

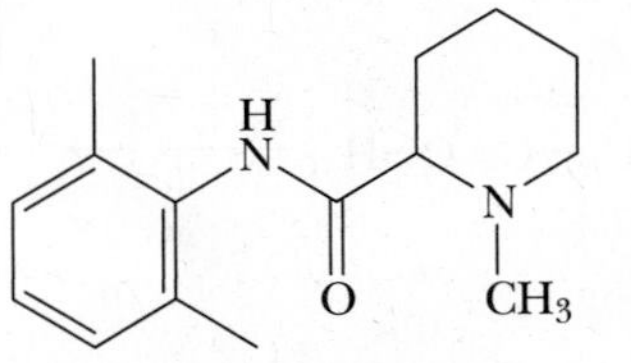

Mepivacaine
(Carbocaine®)

(a) Propose a synthesis of lidocaine from 2,6-dimethylaniline, chloroacetyl chloride ($ClCH_2COCl$), and diethylamine.
(b) Propose a synthesis of etidocaine from 2,6-dimethylaniline, 2-chlorobutanoyl chloride, and ethylpropylamine.
(c) What amine and acid chloride can be reacted to give mepivacaine?

***14.44** Following is the outline of a five-step synthesis for the anthelmintic (against worms) diethylcarbamazine:

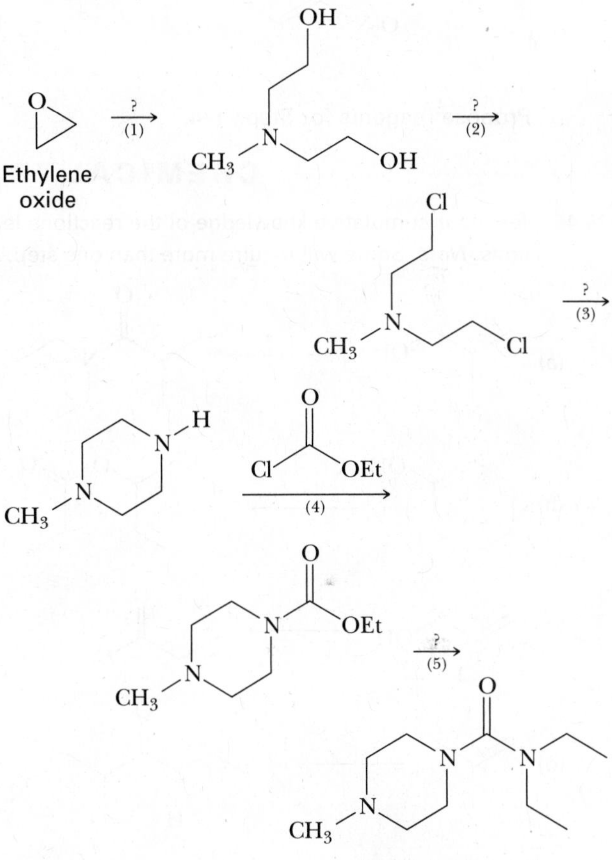

Diethylcarbamazine

Diethylcarbamazine is used chiefly against nematodes, small cylindrical or slender threadlike worms such as the common roundworm, which are parasitic in animals and plants.

(a) Propose a reagent for Step 1. Which mechanism is more likely for this step, S_N1 or S_N2? Explain.
(b) Propose a reagent for Step 2.
(c) Propose a reagent for Step 3.
(d) Ethyl chloroformate, the reagent for Step 4, is both an acid chloride and an ester. Account for the fact that Cl, rather than OCH_2CH_3, is displaced from this reagent.

***14.45** Following is an outline of a multi-step synthesis for methylparaben, a compound widely used as a preservative in foods:

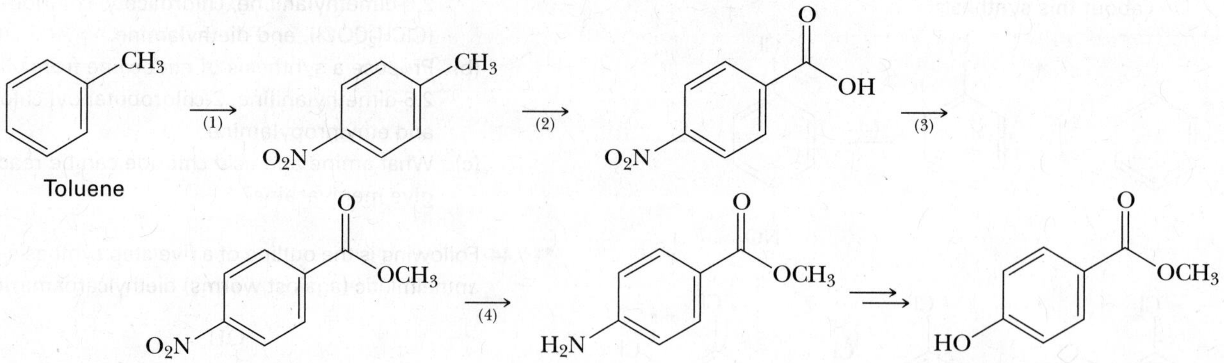

Methyl 4-hydroxybenzoate
(Methylparaben)

Propose reagents for Steps 1–4.

CHEMICAL TRANSFORMATIONS

14.46 Test your cumulative knowledge of the reactions learned thus far by completing the following chemical transformations. *Note*: Some will require more than one step. **(See Examples 14.7, 14.8)**

(a)
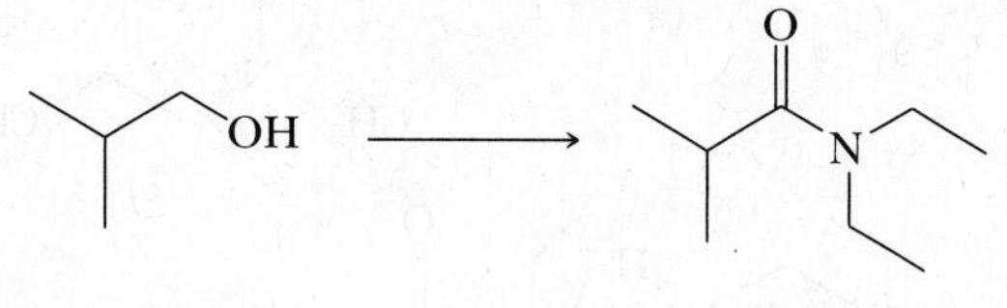

(b)
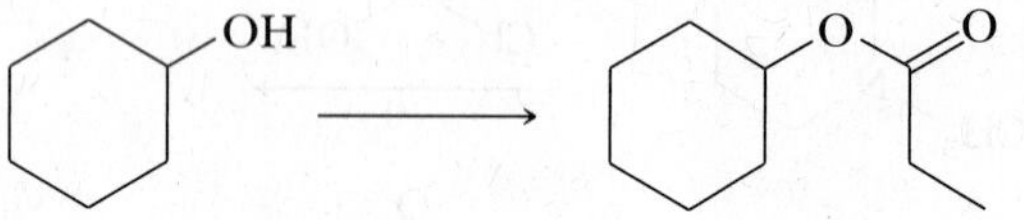

(c)
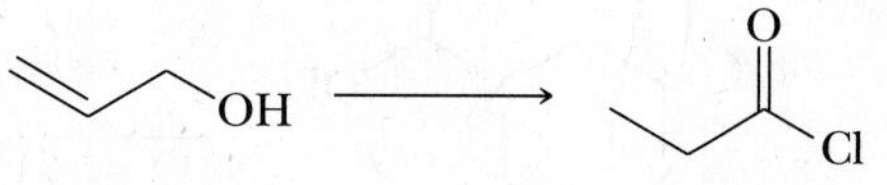

(d)
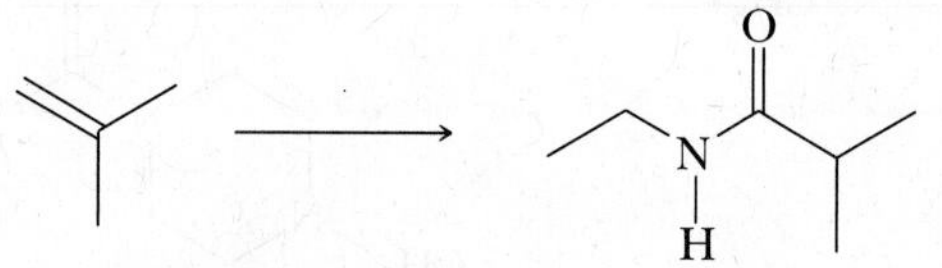

(e)
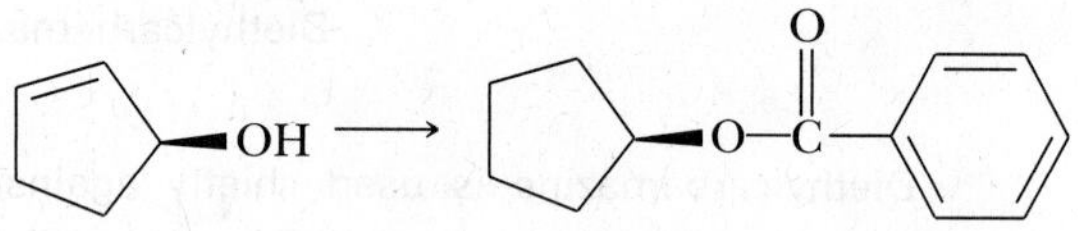

(f)
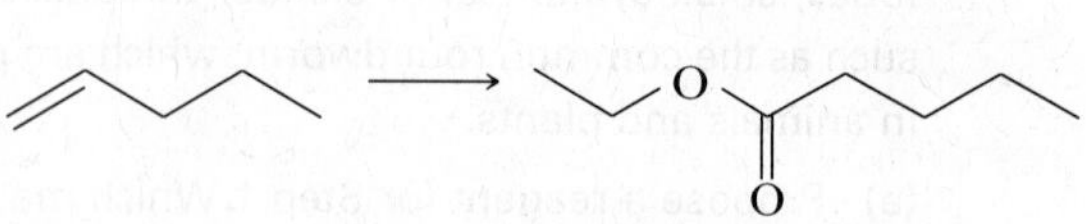

(g)
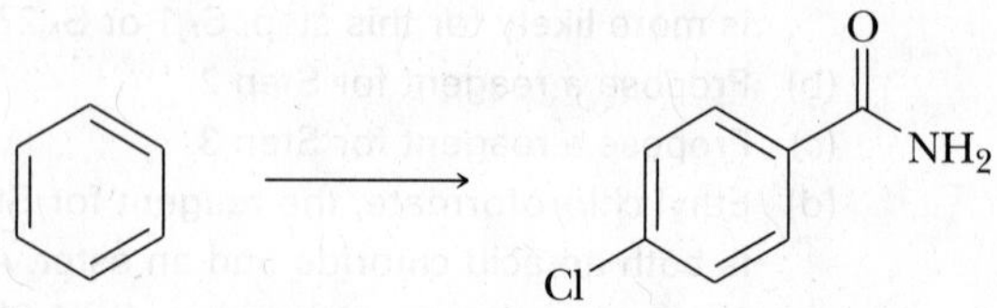

(h)
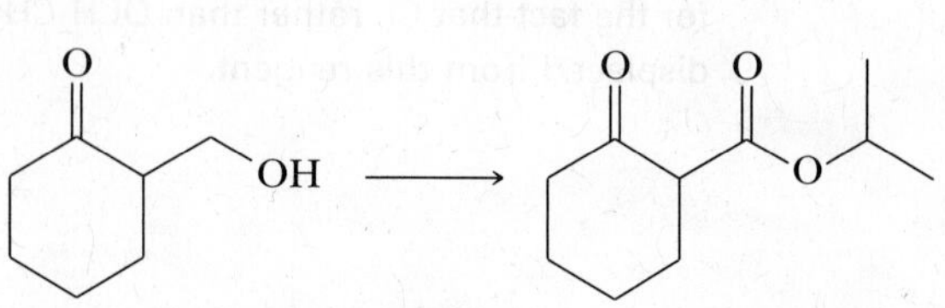

(i)
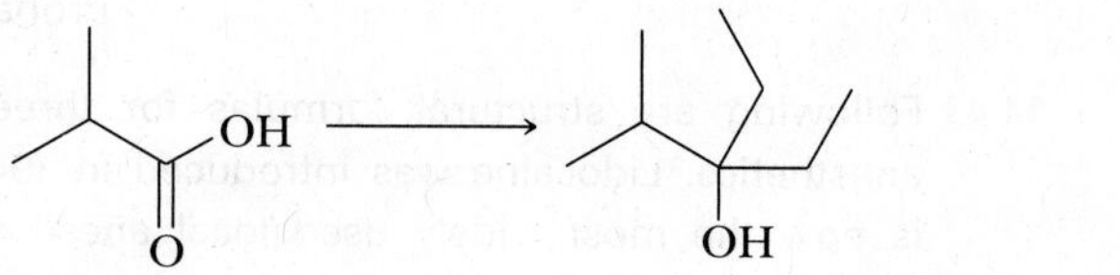

(j)
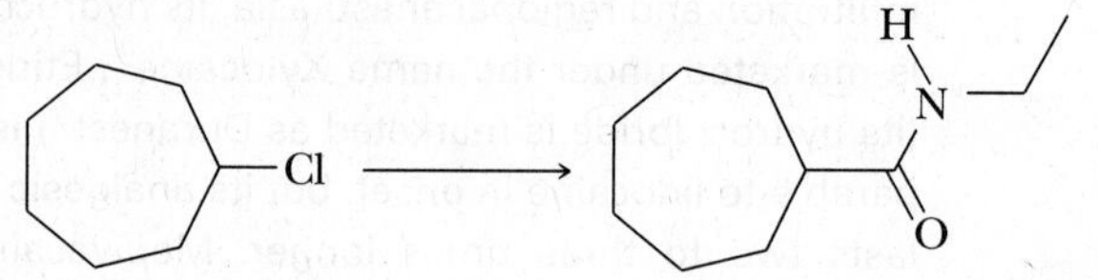

(k)
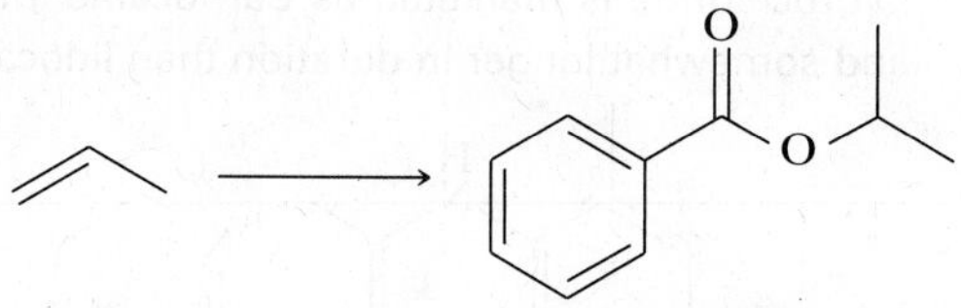

(l)
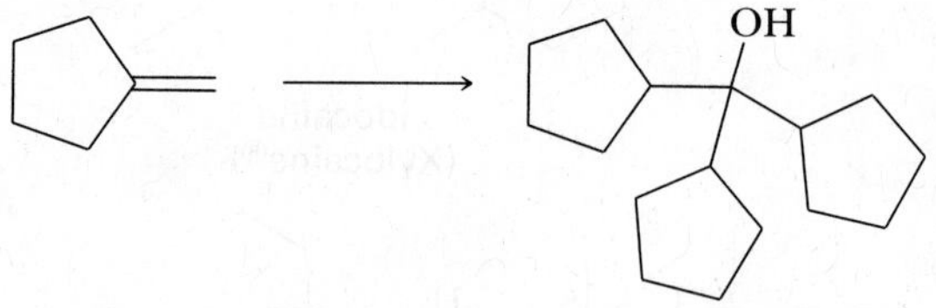

(m)
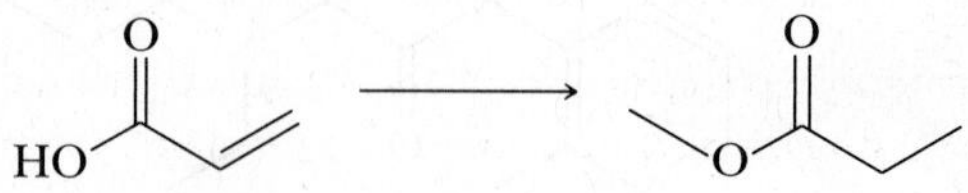

(n)
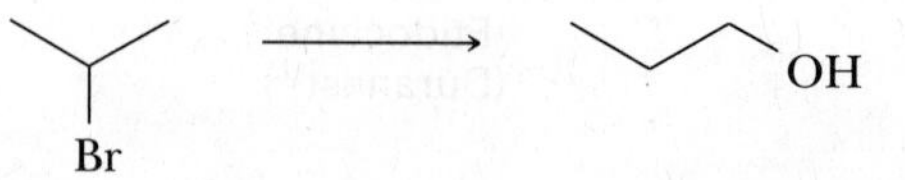

(o)
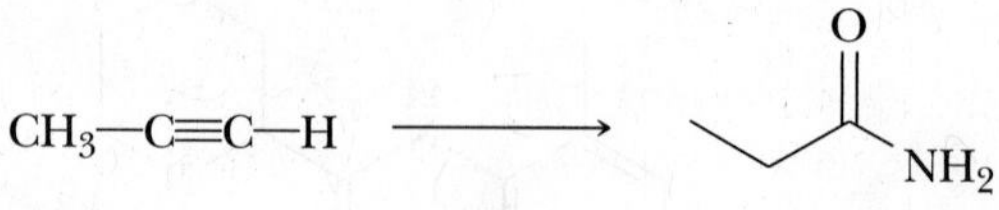

(p)
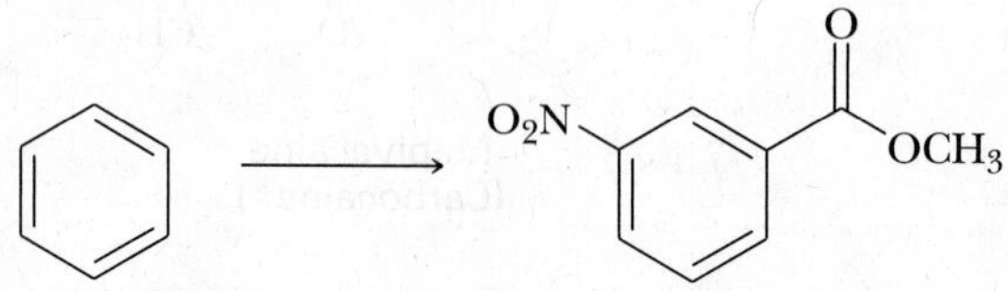

LOOKING AHEAD

14.47 Identify the most acidic proton in each of the following esters:

(a)

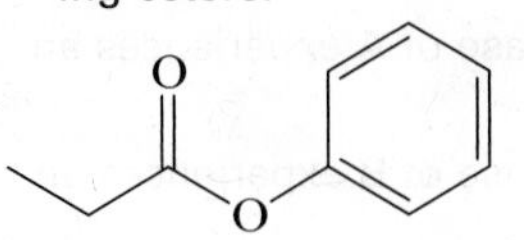

(b)

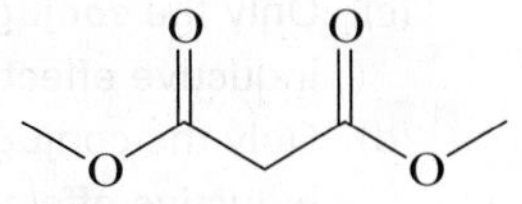

14.48 Does a nucleophilic acyl substitution occur between the ester and the nucleophile shown?

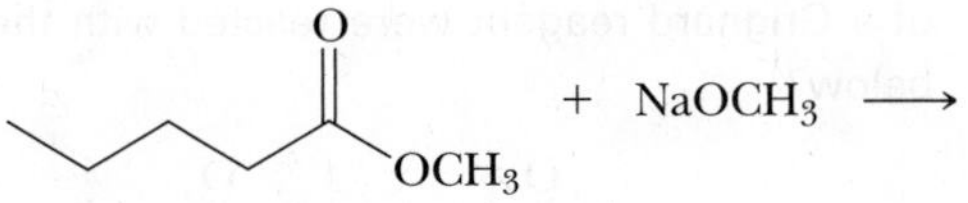

Propose an experiment that would verify your answer.

14.49 Explain why a nucleophile, Nu, attacks not only the carbonyl carbon, but also the β-carbon, as indicated in the following α,β-unsaturated ester:

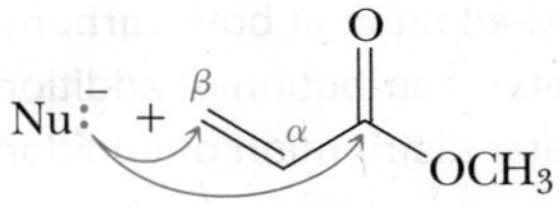

14.50 Explain why a Grignard reagent will not undergo nucleophilic acyl substitution with the following amide:

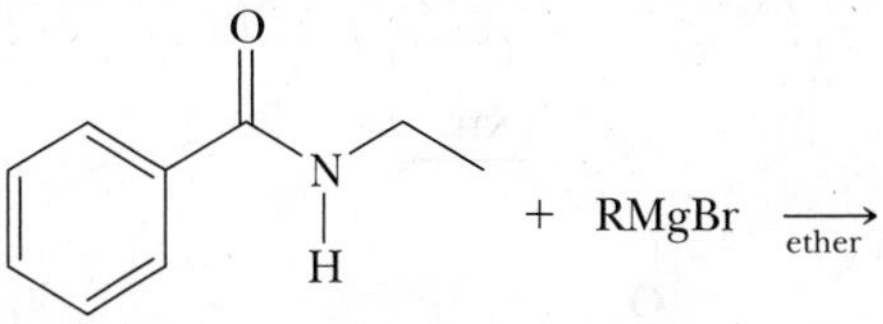

14.51 At low temperatures, the following amide exhibits *cis–trans* isomerism, while at higher temperatures it does not:

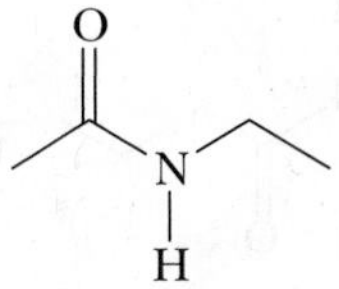

Explain how this is possible.

GROUP LEARNING ACTIVITIES

14.52 Following are two compounds that can also undergo nucleophilic acyl substitution. As a group:

(a) Predict the product if each was treated with NaOH.
(b) Provide a mechanism for each reaction.
(c) Compare the leaving group ability of $^{-}SCH_3$ with that of $^{-}OCH_3$ and of $^{-}CCl_3$ with that of $^{-}CH_3$.

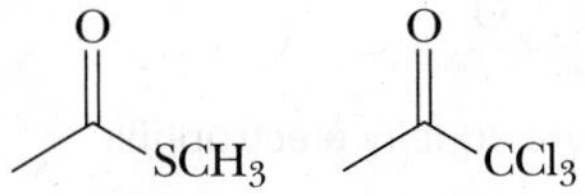

14.53 The mechanism of the reduction of amides to amines by $LiAlH_4$ contains many steps. Work as a group to figure out this mechanism. *Hint*: The carbonyl oxygen is removed as $^{-}OAlH_2$.

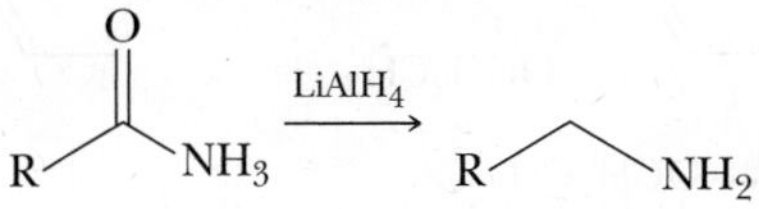

PUTTING IT TOGETHER

The following problems bring together concepts and material from Chapters 12–14. Although the focus may be on these chapters, the problems will also build upon concepts discussed throughout the text thus far.

Choose the best answer for each of the following questions.

1. Which of the following statements is true concerning the following two carboxylic acid derivatives?

A

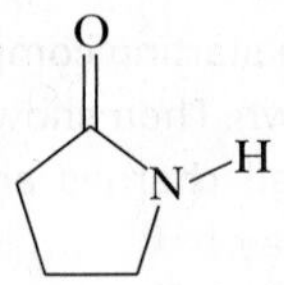

B

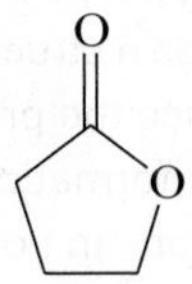

(a) Only molecule **A** can be hydrolyzed.
(b) Only molecule **B** can be hydrolyzed.
(c) Both molecules are hydrolyzable, but **A** will react more quickly than **B**.
(d) Both molecules are hydrolyzable, but **B** will react more quickly than **A**.
(e) **A** and **B** are hydrolyzed at roughly the same rate.

2. How many unique reaction products are formed from the following reaction?

$$CH_3CH_2-\overset{\overset{\Large O}{\|}}{C}-CH_2CH_2-\overset{\overset{\Large O}{\|}}{C}-OCH_3 \xrightarrow[H_2O]{H^+}$$

(a) one (b) two (c) three (d) four (e) five

3. What sequence of reagents will accomplish the following transformation?

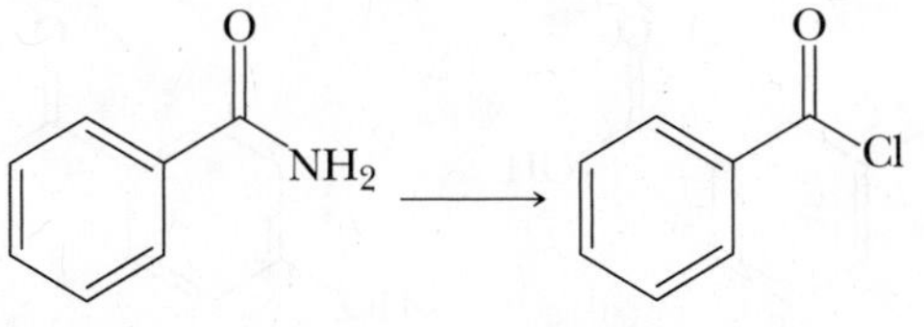

(a) 1) $SOCl_2$
(b) 1) H_2O_2, $SOCl_2$
(c) 1) H_2O_2, HCl
(d) 1) H^+/H_2O_2 2) $SOCl_2$
(e) All of the above

4. Which of the following reactions will not yield butanamide?

(a) 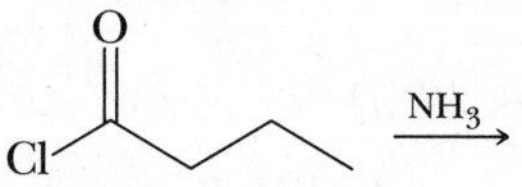
(b) 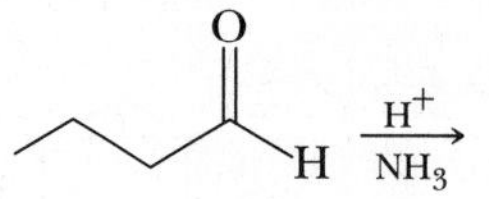
(c) 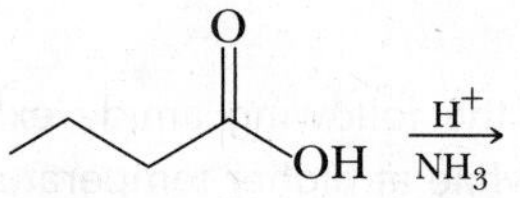
(d) 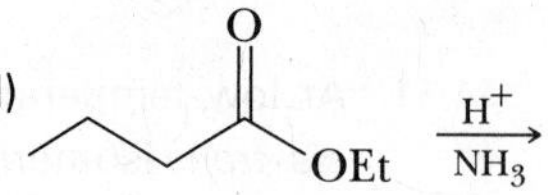
(e) 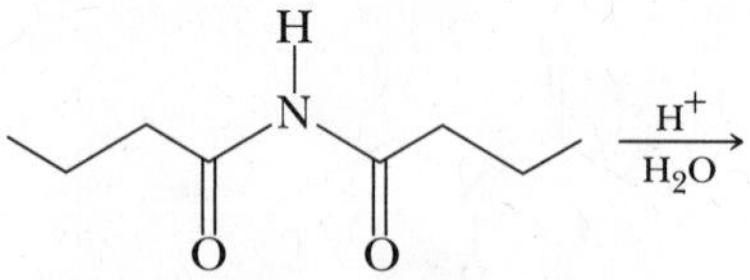

5. Which of the following is the tetrahedral carbonyl addition intermediate (TCAI) for the Fischer esterification of ethanol and benzoic acid?

(a) 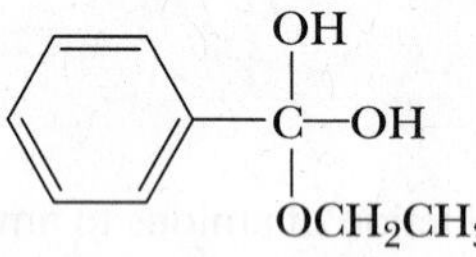
(b) 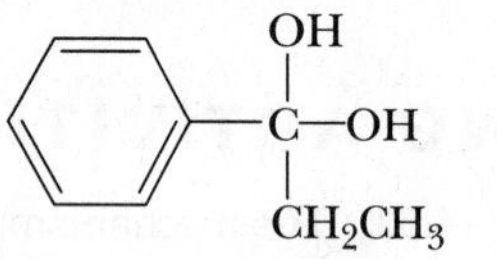
(c) 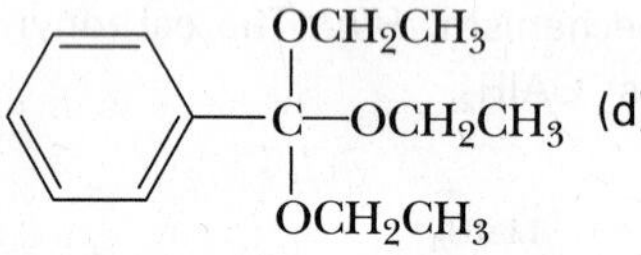
(d) 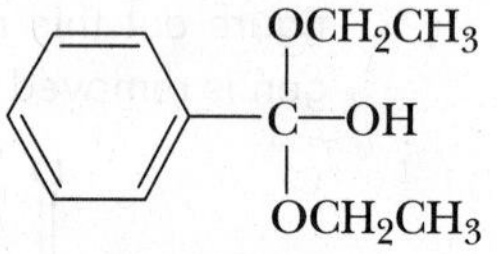
(e) 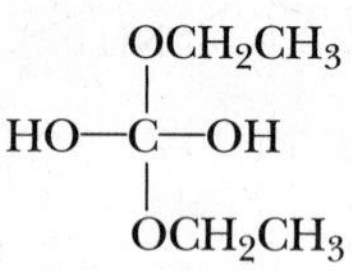

6. Which of the following is the enol intermediate in the decarboxylation of ethylpropanedioic acid?

(a) 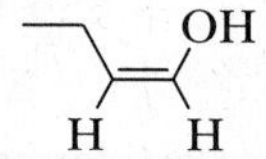
(b) 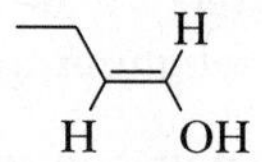
(c) 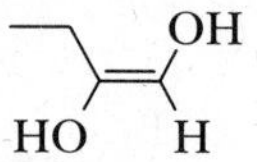
(d) 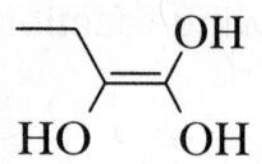
(e) 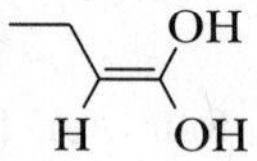

7. Which of the following statements is true concerning the two carboxylic acids shown?

A 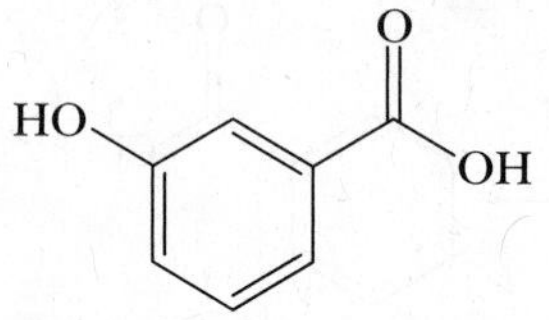
B 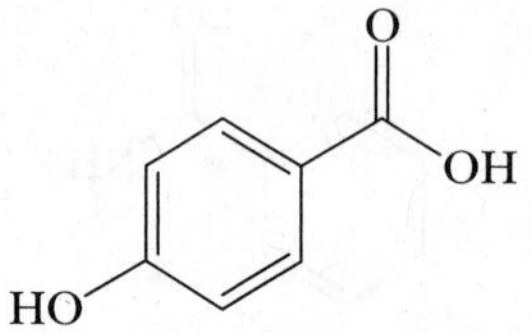

(a) **A** is more acidic than **B** because of an additional resonance effect.
(b) **B** is more acidic than **A** because of an additional resonance effect.
(c) Only the conjugate base of **A** experiences an inductive effect.
(d) Only the conjugate base of **B** experiences an inductive effect.
(e) None of the above.

8. What would be the expected outcome if one equivalent of a Grignard reagent were reacted with the molecule below?

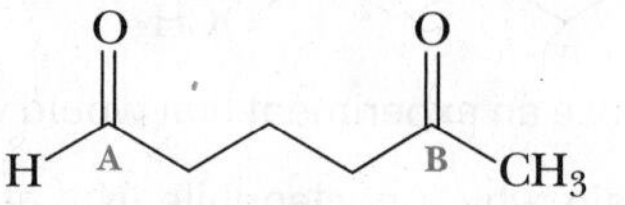

(a) 100% addition at carbonyl **A**.
(b) 100% addition at carbonyl **B**.
(c) Equal addition at both carbonyls.
(d) Greater distribution of addition at **A**.
(e) Greater distribution of addition at **B**.

9. Which of the following carbonyl carbons would be considered the most electrophilic?

(a) 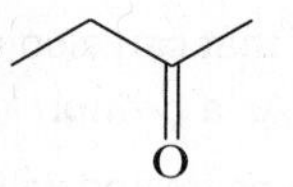
(b) 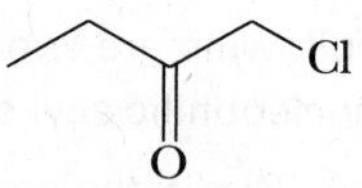
(c) 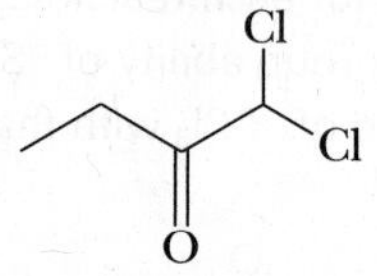
(d) 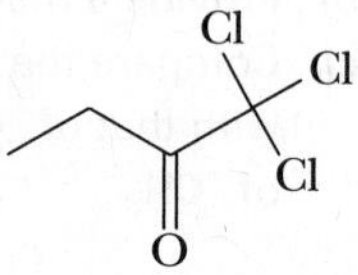
(e) All are equally electrophilic.

10. The following reaction will occur as shown:

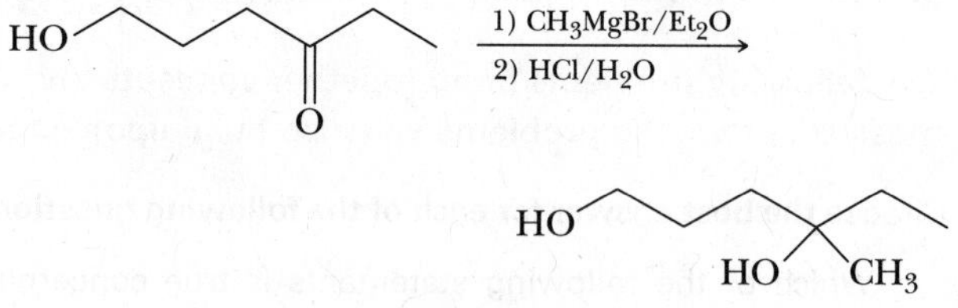

(a) True (b) False

11. Provide a structure for the starting compound needed to produce the product shown. Then show the mechanism of its formation. Show all charges and lone pairs of electrons in your structures.

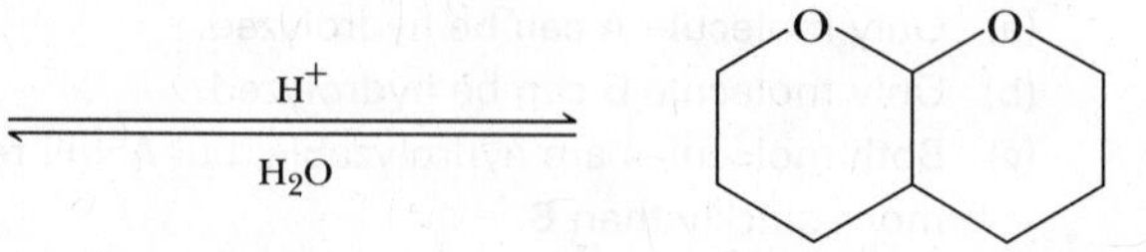

12. Rank the following from most to least reactive with EtOH. Provide a rationale for your ranking.

(a) 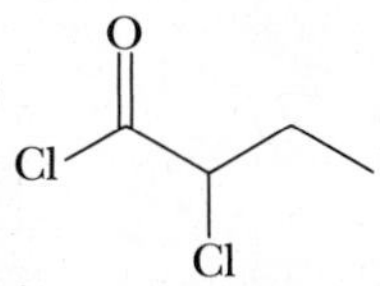 (b) 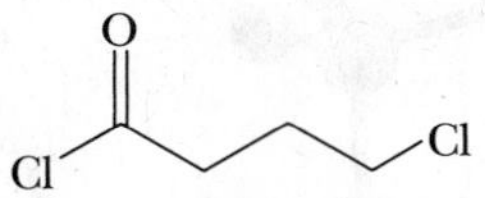

(c) 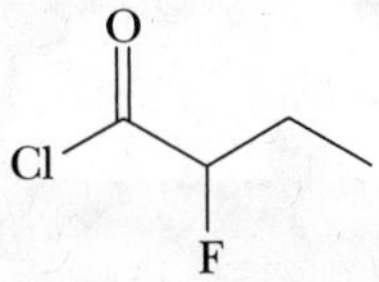 (d) 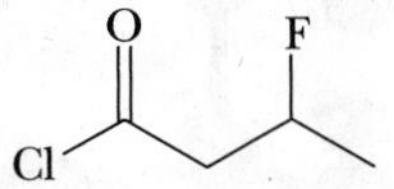

(e) 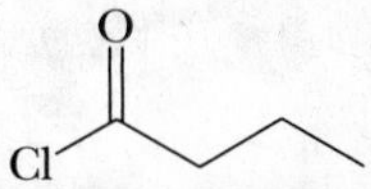

13. Provide IUPAC names for the following compounds.

(a) 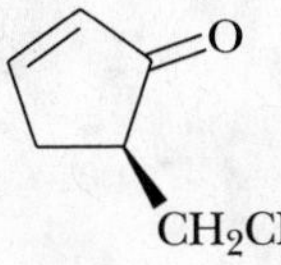 (b) 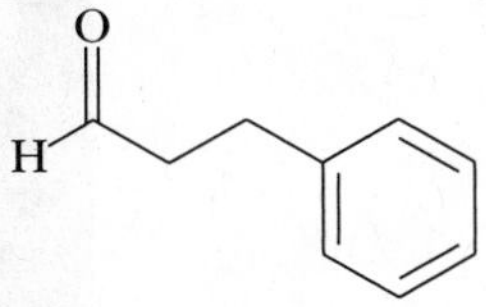

(c) 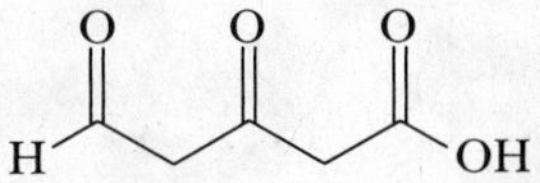

14. Provide a mechanism for the following reaction. Show all charges and lone pairs of electrons in your structures, as well as the structures of all intermediates.

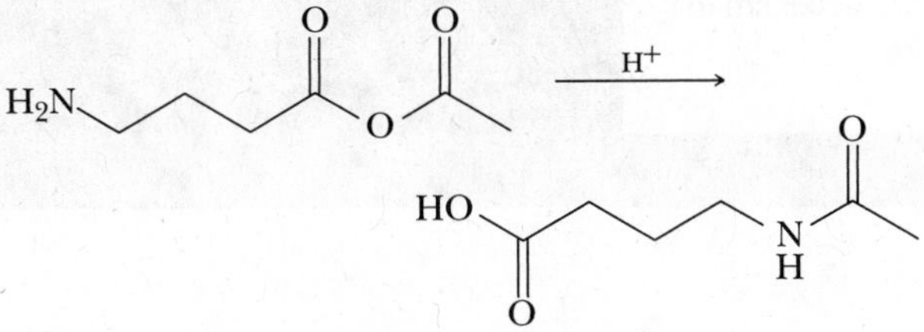

15. Predict the major product of each of the following reactions.

(a) 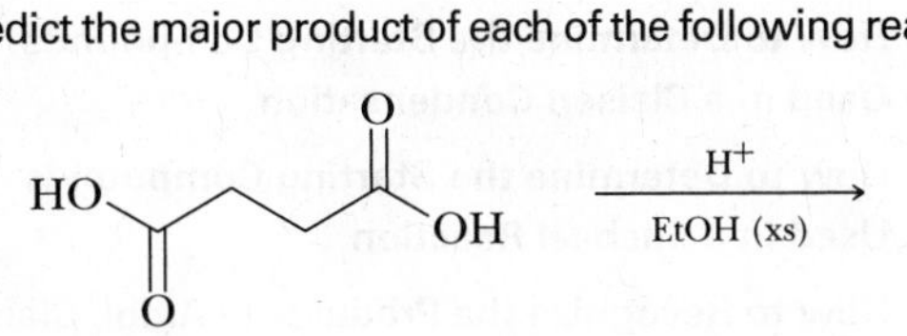

(b) 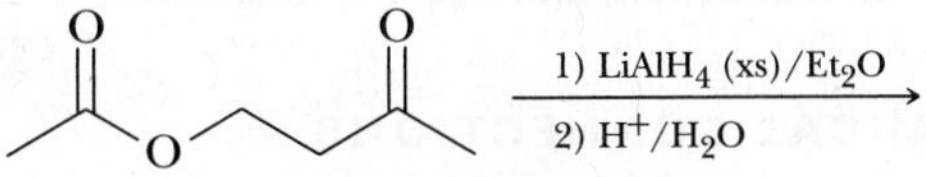

(c) 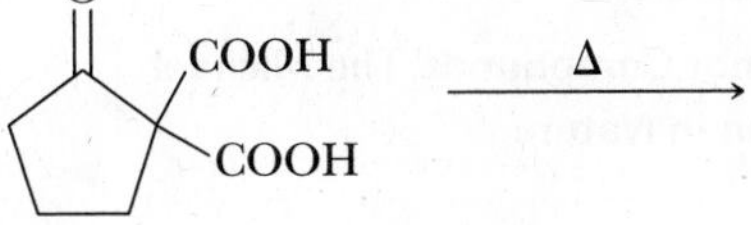

(d) 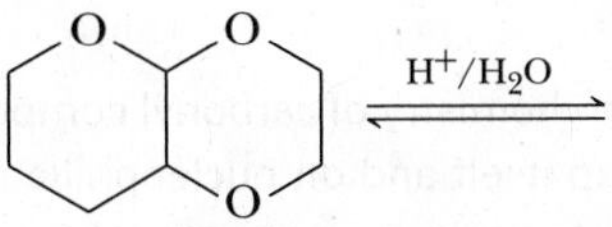

(e) 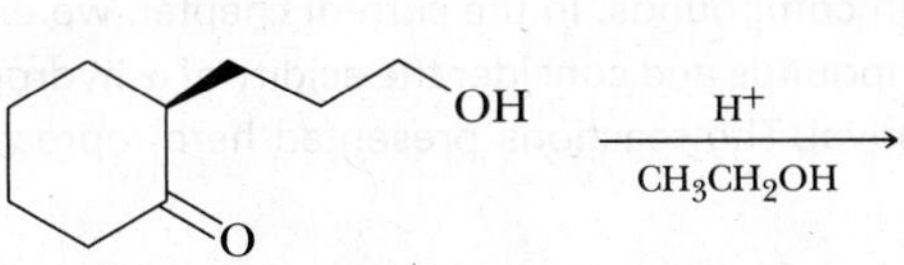

16. Complete the following chemical transformations.

(a) 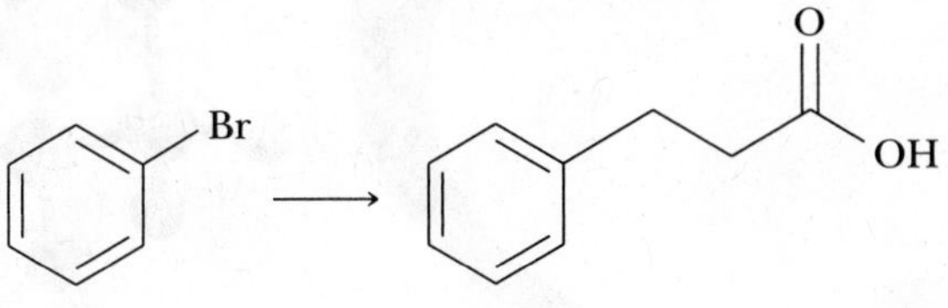

(b) 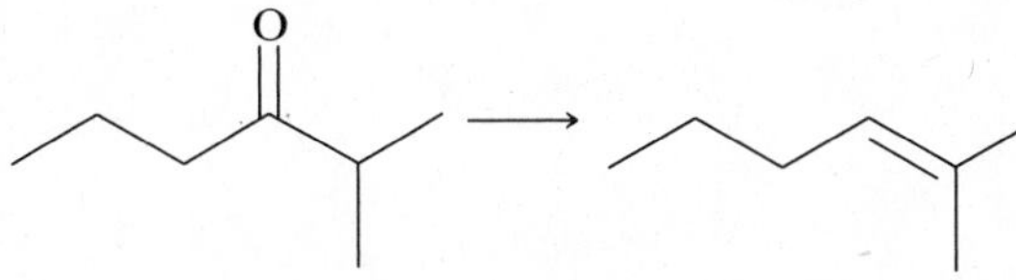

(c) 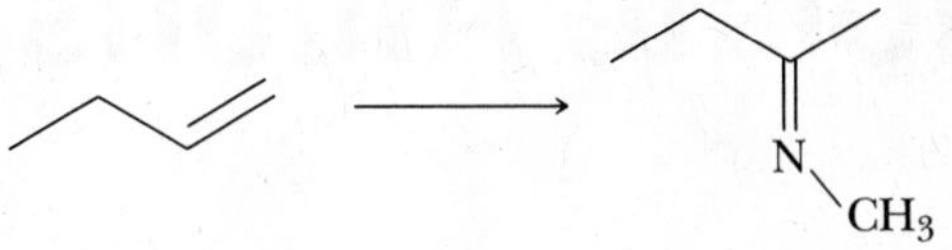

(d) 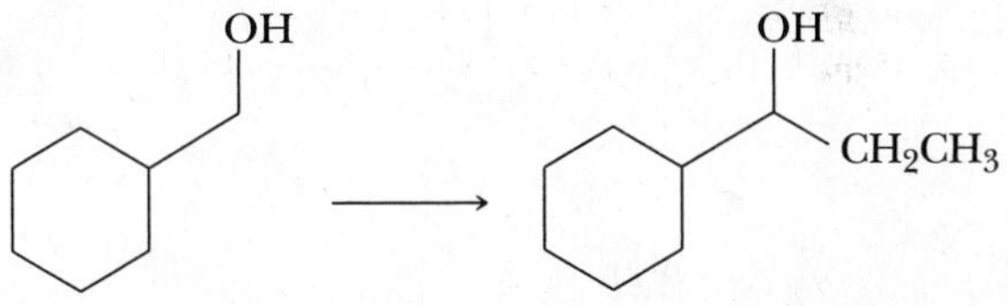

(e) 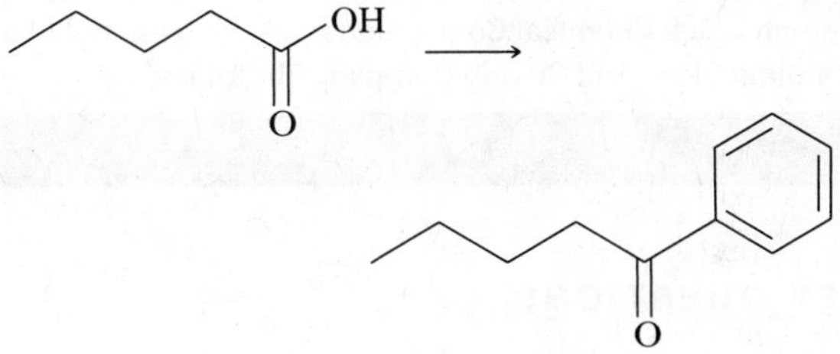

(f) 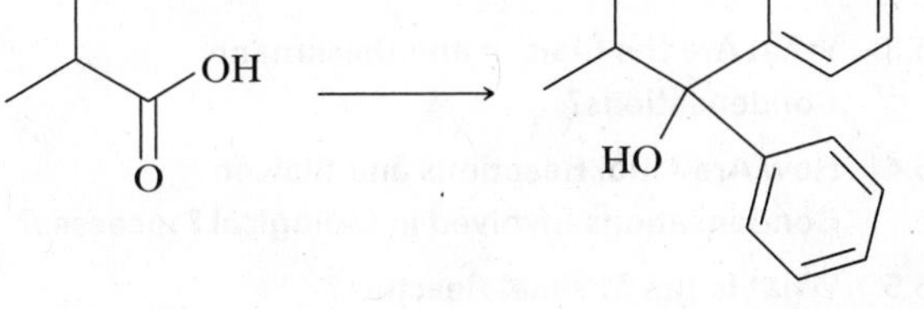

(g) 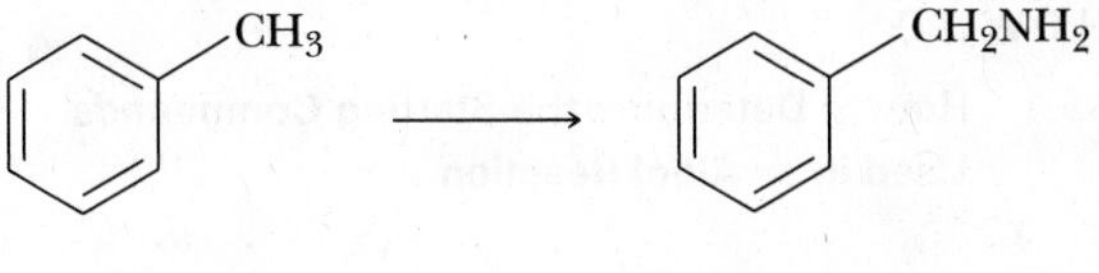

(h) 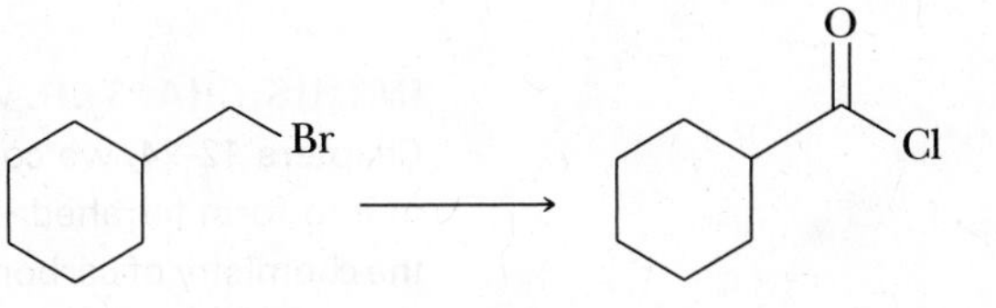

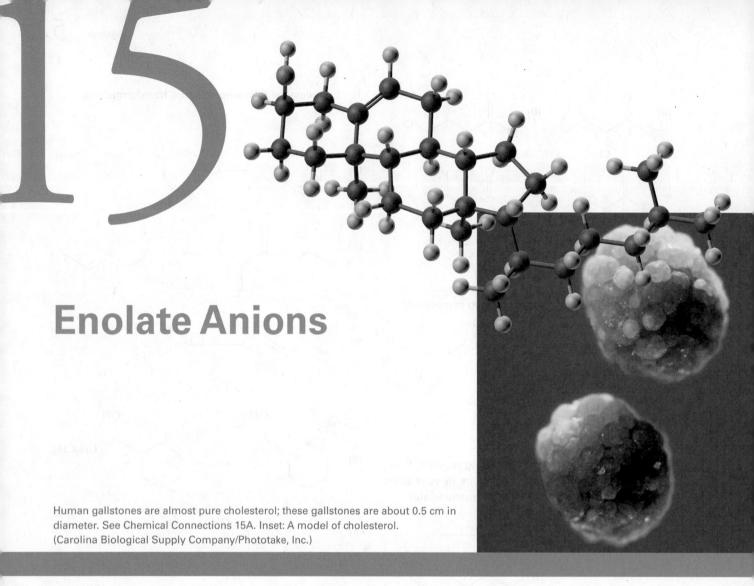

15 Enolate Anions

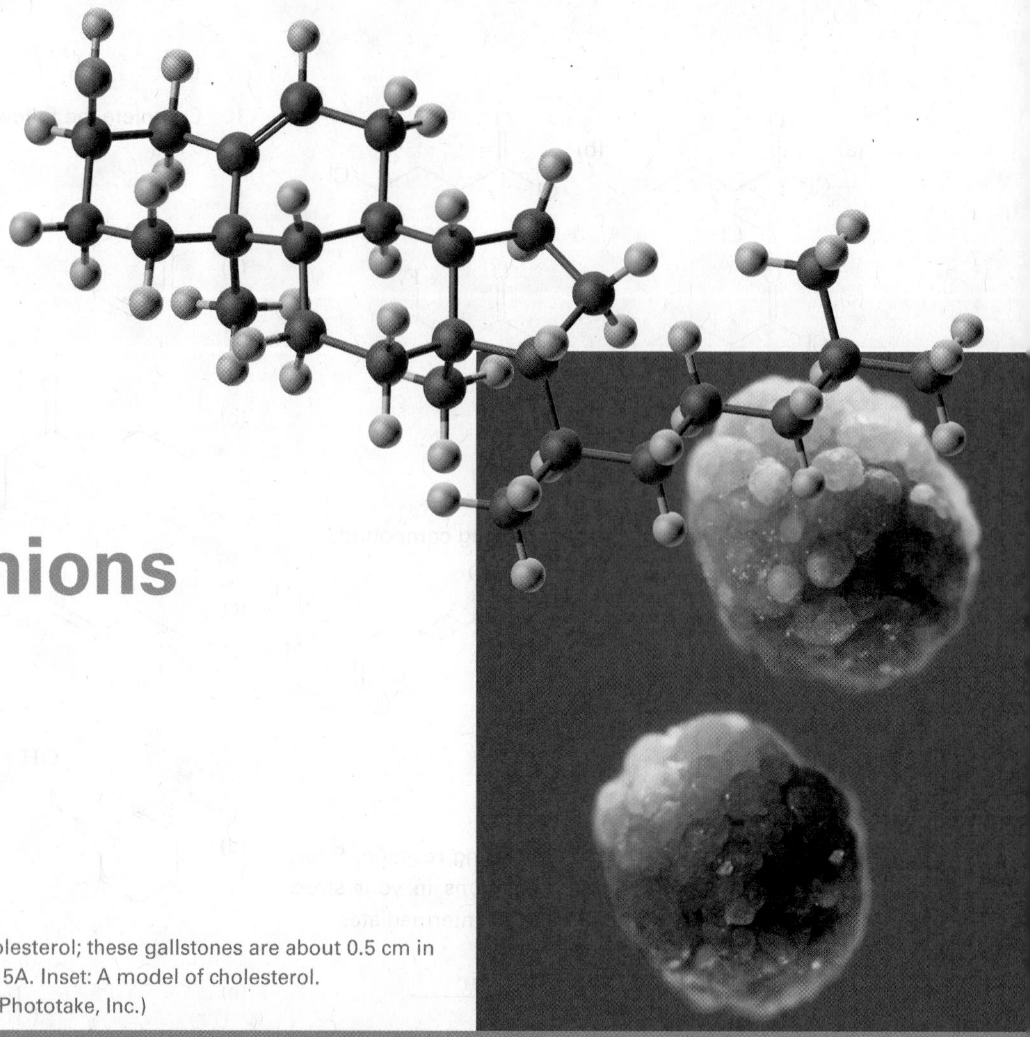

Human gallstones are almost pure cholesterol; these gallstones are about 0.5 cm in diameter. See Chemical Connections 15A. Inset: A model of cholesterol. (Carolina Biological Supply Company/Phototake, Inc.)

KEY QUESTIONS

15.1 **What Are Enolate Anions, and How Are They Formed?**

15.2 **What Is the Aldol Reaction?**

15.3 **What Are the Claisen and Dieckmann Condensations?**

15.4 **How Are Aldol Reactions and Claisen Condensations Involved in Biological Processes?**

15.5 **What Is the Michael Reaction?**

HOW TO

15.1 **How to Determine the Starting Compounds Used in an Aldol Reaction**

15.2 **How to Determine the Starting Compounds Used in a Claisen Condensation**

15.3 **How to Determine the Starting Compounds Used in a Michael Reaction**

15.4 **How to Recognize the Products of Aldol, Claisen Condensation, and Michael Reactions**

CHEMICAL CONNECTIONS

15A **Drugs That Lower Plasma Levels of Cholesterol**

15B **Antitumor Compounds: The Michael Reaction in Nature**

IN THIS CHAPTER, we continue our discussion of the chemistry of carbonyl compounds. In Chapters 12–14, we concentrated on the carbonyl group itself and on nucleophilic additions to it to form tetrahedral carbonyl addition compounds. In the current chapter, we expand on the chemistry of carbonyl-containing compounds and consider the acidity of α-hydrogens and the enolate anions formed by their removal. The reactions presented here represent some of the most important reactions in organic chemistry because they involve the formation of carbon–carbon bonds, allowing the construction of larger molecules from smaller, readily available starting materials.

15.1 What Are Enolate Anions, and How Are They Formed?

A. Acidity of α-Hydrogens

A carbon atom adjacent to a carbonyl group is called an ***α*-carbon**, and a hydrogen atom bonded to it is called an ***α*-hydrogen**:

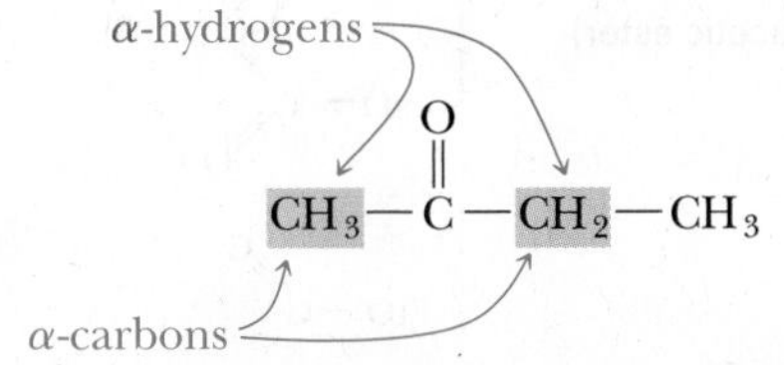

Because carbon and hydrogen have comparable electronegativities, a C—H bond normally has little polarity, and a hydrogen atom bonded to carbon shows very low acidity (Section 2.3). The situation is different, however, for hydrogens that are alpha to a carbonyl group. As Table 15.1 shows, α-hydrogens of aldehydes, ketones, and esters are considerably more acidic than alkane and alkene hydrogens, but less acidic than the hydroxyl hydrogen of alcohols. The table also shows that hydrogens that are alpha to two carbonyl groups—for example, in a β-ketoester and a β-diester—are even more acidic than alcohols.

B. Enolate Anions

Carbonyl groups increase the acidity of their alpha hydrogens in two ways. First, the electron-withdrawing inductive effect of the carbonyl group weakens the bond to the alpha hydrogen and promotes its ionization. Second, the negative charge on the resulting **enolate anion** is delocalized by resonance, thus stabilizing it relative to the anion from an alkane or an alkene:

Enolate anion An anion formed by the removal of an α-hydrogen from a carbonyl-containing compound.

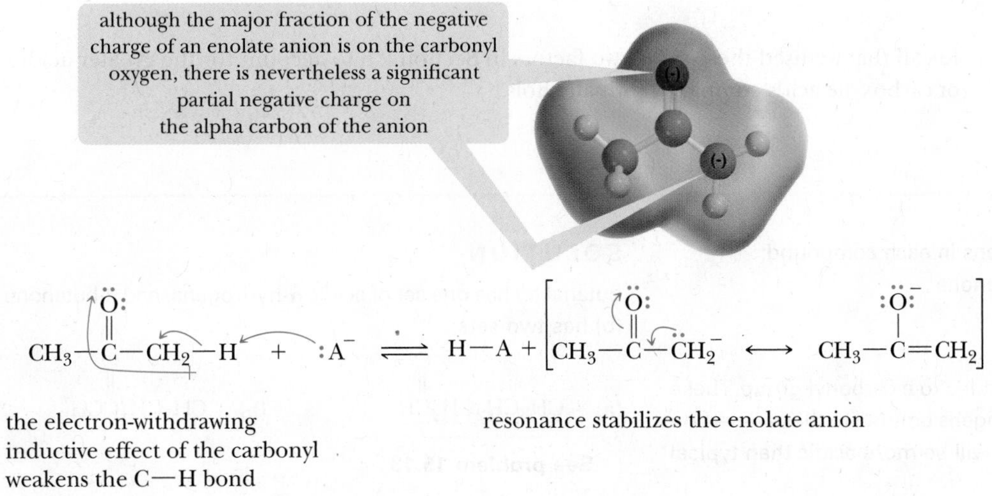

TABLE 15.1 The Acidity of Hydrogens Alpha to a Carbonyl Group Relative to Other Organic Hydrogens

Class of Compound	Example	pK_a
β-Diketone	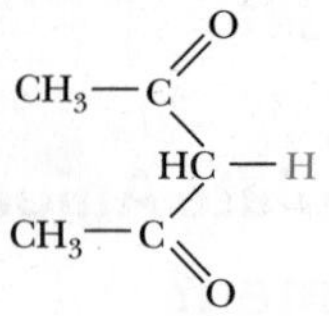	9.5
Phenol	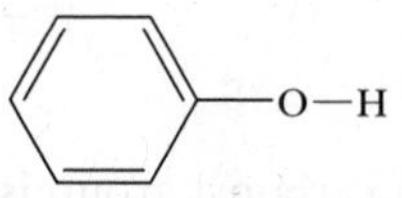	10
β-Ketoester (an acetoacetic ester)	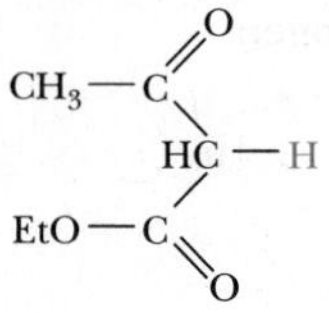	10.7
β-Diester (a malonic ester)	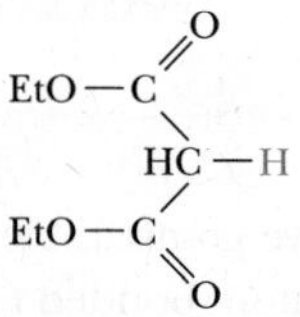	13
Water	HO—H	15.7
Alcohol	$CH_3CH_2O—H$	16
Aldehyde or a ketone	$CH_3C(=O)CH_2—H$	20
Ester	$EtOC(=O)CH_2—H$	22
Terminal alkyne	R—C≡C—H	25
Alkene	$CH_2{=}CH—H$	44
Alkane	$CH_3CH_2—H$	51

Increasing acidity

Recall that we used these same two factors in Section 2.5 to account for the greater acidity of carboxylic acids compared with alcohols.

EXAMPLE 15.1

Identify the acidic α-hydrogens in each compound:
(a) Butanal **(b)** 2-Butanone

STRATEGY

Identify all carbon atoms bonded to a carbonyl group. These are the α-carbons. Any hydrogens bonded to these α-carbon atoms are α-hydrogens and will be more acidic than typical alkane or alkene hydrogens.

SOLUTION

Butanal (a) has one set of acidic α-hydrogens, and 2-butanone (b) has two sets:

(a)  **(b)** 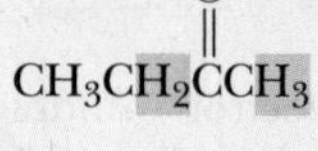

See problem 15.13

PROBLEM 15.1

Identify the acidic α-hydrogens in each compound:

(a) 2-Methylcyclohexanone (b) Acetophenone (c) 2,2-Diethylcyclohexanone

Enolate anions can be formed either quantitatively or under equilibrium conditions. Use of a base that is much stronger than the ensuing enolate anion results in the quantitative removal of an α-hydrogen.

$$CH_3-\overset{O}{\overset{\|}{C}}-CH_3 + NaNH_2 \longrightarrow CH_3-\overset{O}{\overset{\|}{C}}-\ddot{C}H_2^- + Na^+ + NH_3$$

pK$_a$ 20 (stronger acid)	Sodium amide (stronger base)	Enolate (weaker base)	pK$_a$ 38 (weaker acid)

the left side of each equation contains a much stronger acid and base. For this reason both reactions proceed quantitatively

pK$_a$ 9 (stronger acid)	Sodium hydroxide (stronger base)	Enolate (weaker base)	pK$_a$ 15.7 (weaker acid)

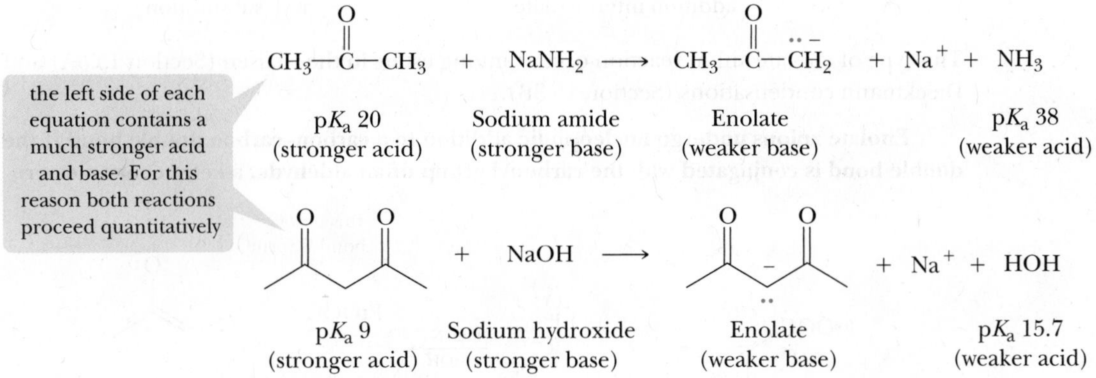

Use of a base that is weaker than the ensuing enolate anion results in an equilibrium in which the enolate exists in very small concentrations.

the stronger acid and base reside on the right side of the equation, causing the equilibrium to favor the reactants

$$CH_3-\overset{O}{\overset{\|}{C}}-CH_3 + NaOH \rightleftharpoons CH_3-\overset{O}{\overset{\|}{C}}-\ddot{C}H_2^- + Na^+ + HOH$$

pK$_a$ 20	Sodium hydroxide	Enolate	pK$_a$ 15.7

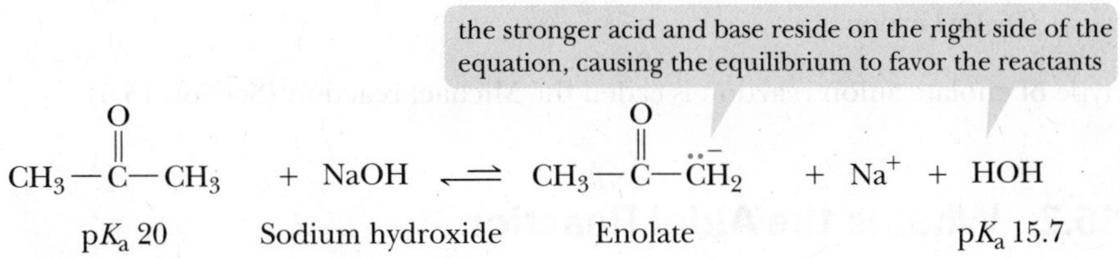

C. The Use of Enolate Anions to Form New C—C Bonds

Enolate anions are important building blocks in organic synthesis, and we will study their use as nucleophiles to form new carbon–carbon bonds. In overview, they participate in three types of nucleophilic reactions.

Enolate anions function as nucleophiles in carbonyl addition reactions:

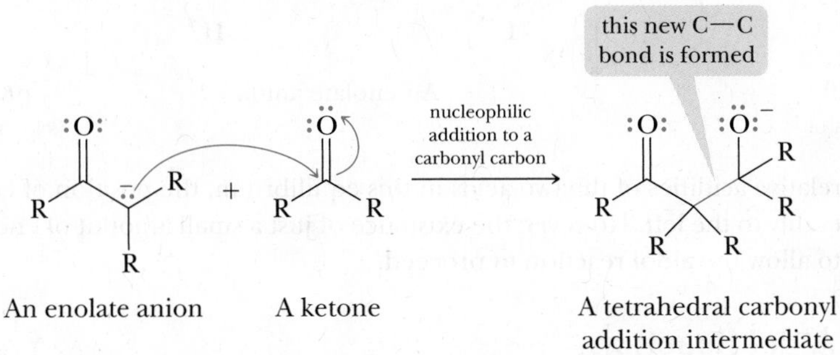

This type of enolate anion reaction is particularly useful among reactions of aldehydes and ketones in the aldol reaction (Section 15.2).

Enolate anions function as nucleophiles in nucleophilic acyl substitution reactions:

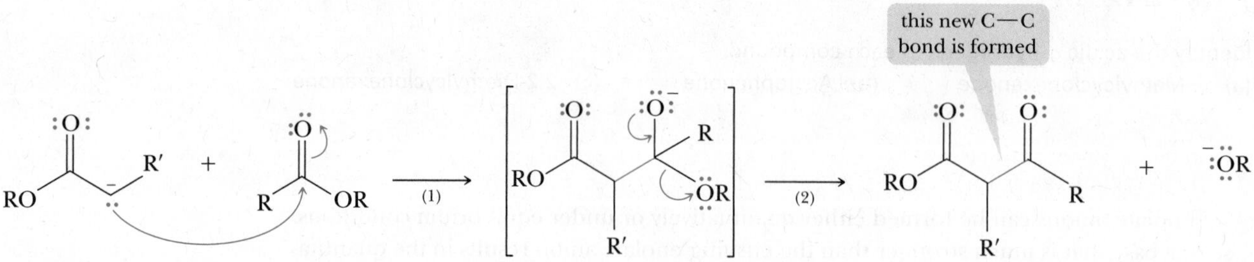

An enolate anion | An ester | A tetrahedral carbonyl addition intermediate | Product of nucleophilic acyl substitution

This type of enolate anion reaction occurs among esters in the Claisen (Section 15.3A) and Dieckmann condensations (Section 15.3B).

Enolate anions undergo nucleophilic addition to a carbon–carbon double bond if the double bond is conjugated with the carbonyl group of an aldehyde, a ketone, or an ester:

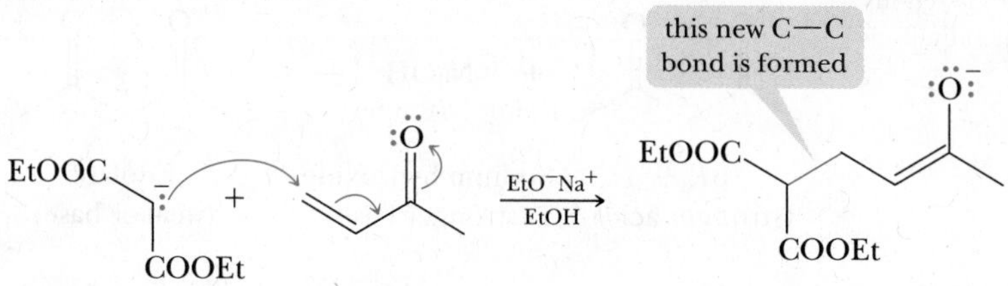

Enolate anion of diethyl propanedioate (Diethyl malonate) | 3-Buten-2-one (Methyl vinyl ketone)

This type of enolate anion reaction is called the Michael reaction (Section 15.5).

15.2 What Is the Aldol Reaction?

A. Formation of Enolate Anions of Aldehydes and Ketones

Treatment of an aldehyde or a ketone containing an acidic α-hydrogen with a strong base, such as sodium hydroxide or sodium ethoxide, gives an enolate anion as a hybrid of two major contributing structures:

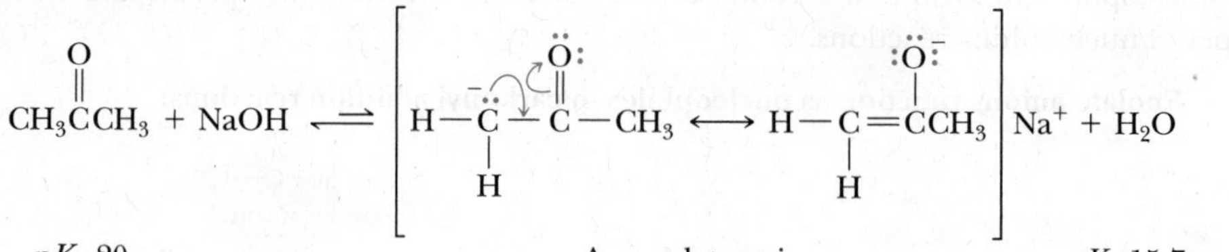

$$\underset{\substack{pK_a\ 20 \\ \text{(weaker acid)}}}{CH_3\overset{O}{\overset{\|}{C}}CH_3} + NaOH \rightleftharpoons \underset{\text{An enolate anion}}{\left[H-\underset{H}{\underset{|}{\ddot{C}^-}}-\overset{:\ddot{O}:}{\overset{\|}{C}}-CH_3 \longleftrightarrow H-\underset{H}{\underset{|}{C}}=\overset{:\ddot{O}:^-}{\overset{|}{C}}CH_3 \right]} Na^+ + \underset{\substack{pK_a\ 15.7 \\ \text{(stronger acid)}}}{H_2O}$$

Given the relative acidities of the two acids in this equilibrium, the position of equilibrium lies considerably to the left. However, the existence of just a small amount of enolate anion is enough to allow the aldol reaction to proceed.

B. The Aldol Reaction

Addition of the enolate anion derived from an aldehyde or a ketone to the carbonyl group of another aldehyde or ketone is illustrated by these examples:

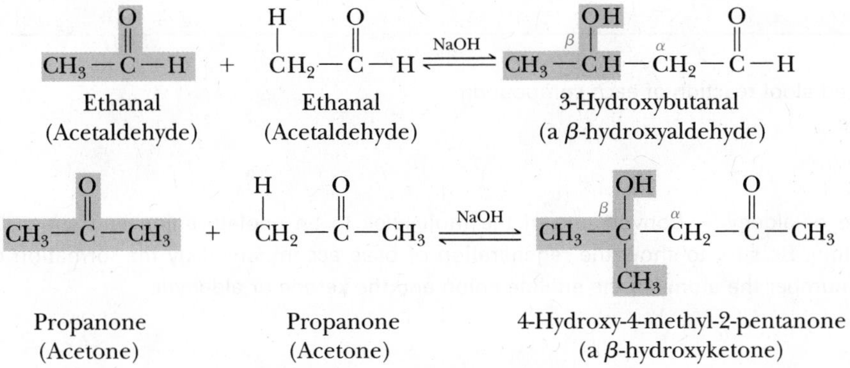

The common name of the product derived from the reaction of acetaldehyde in base is **aldol**, so named because it is both an **ald**ehyde and an alcoh**ol**. *Aldol* is also the generic name given to any product formed in this type of reaction. The functional group of the product of an **aldol reaction** is a β-hydroxyaldehyde or a β-hydroxyketone.

Aldol reaction A carbonyl condensation reaction between two aldehydes or ketones to give a β-hydroxyaldehyde or a β-hydroxyketone.

The key step in a base-catalyzed aldol reaction is nucleophilic addition of the enolate anion from one carbonyl-containing molecule to the carbonyl group of another carbonyl-containing molecule to form a tetrahedral carbonyl addition intermediate. This mechanism is illustrated by the aldol reaction between two molecules of acetaldehyde. Notice that OH^- is a true catalyst: An OH^- is used in Step 1, but another OH^- is generated in Step 3. Notice also the parallel between Step 2 of the aldol reaction and the reaction of Grignard reagents with aldehydes and ketones (Section 12.5) and the first step of their reaction with esters (Section 14.7). Each type of reaction involves the addition of a carbon nucleophile to the carbonyl carbon of another molecule.

Mechanism

Base-Catalyzed Aldol Reaction

STEP 1: Take a proton away. The removal of an α-hydrogen by base gives a resonance-stabilized enolate anion:

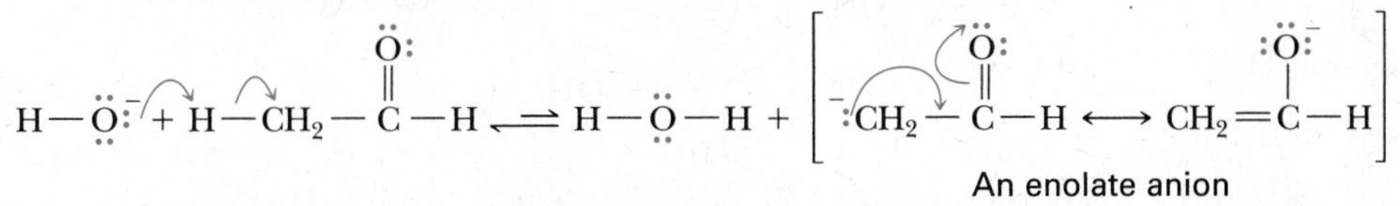

STEP 2: Reaction of an electrophile and a nucleophile to form a new covalent bond. Because the equilibrium favors the left in Step 1, there is plenty of unreacted aldehyde (or ketone) remaining in the reaction mixture. Nucleophilic addition of the enolate anion to the carbonyl carbon of an unreacted molecule of aldehyde (or ketone) gives a tetrahedral carbonyl addition intermediate:

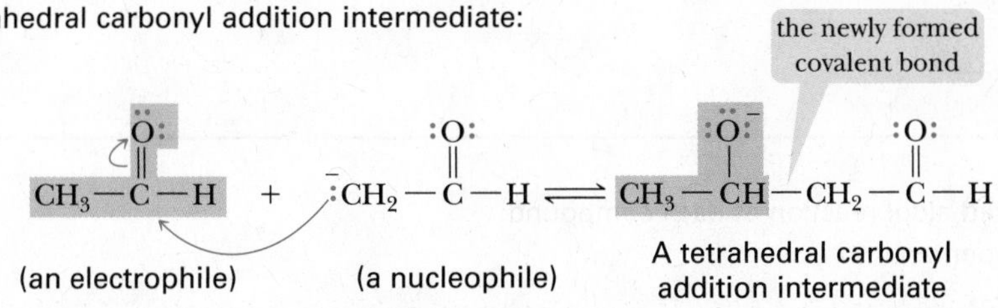

STEP 3: Add a proton. Reaction of the tetrahedral carbonyl addition intermediate with a proton donor gives the aldol product and generates another hydroxide ion:

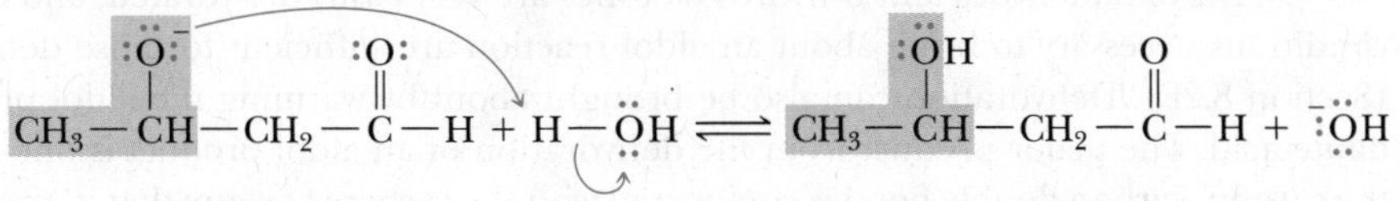

EXAMPLE 15.2

Draw the product of the base-catalyzed aldol reaction of each compound:
(a) Butanal (b) Cyclohexanone

STRATEGY

Draw two molecules of each ketone or aldehyde. Convert one of the molecules to an enolate anion and show it adding to the carbonyl carbon of the other. Be sure to show the regeneration of base accompanied by the formation of the β-hydroxycarbonyl. It often helps to number the atoms in the enolate anion and the ketone or aldehyde.

SOLUTION

The aldol product is formed by the nucleophilic addition of the α-carbon of one compound to the carbonyl carbon of another:

(a)

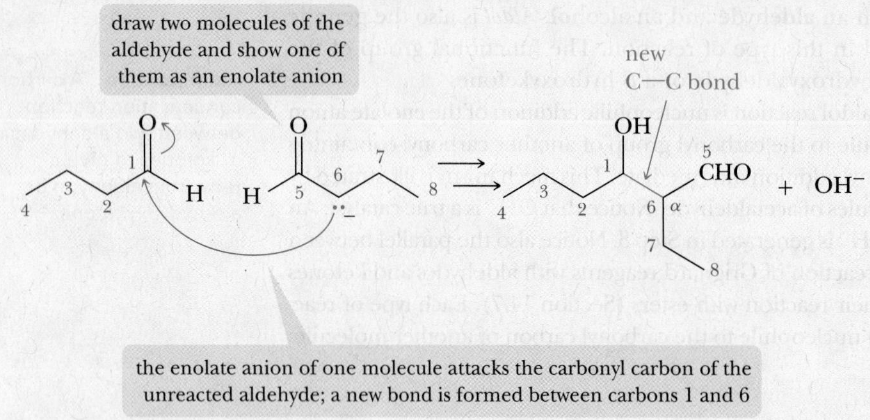
draw two molecules of the aldehyde and show one of them as an enolate anion
new C—C bond
OH
CHO
+ OH⁻
the enolate anion of one molecule attacks the carbonyl carbon of the unreacted aldehyde; a new bond is formed between carbons 1 and 6

(b)

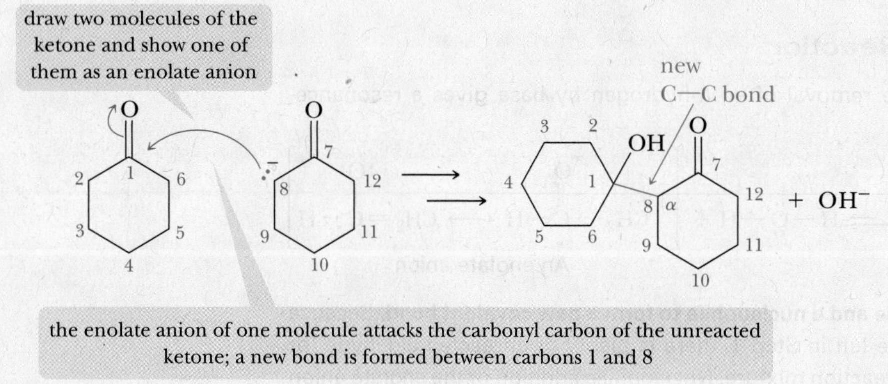
draw two molecules of the ketone and show one of them as an enolate anion
new C—C bond
OH
+ OH⁻
the enolate anion of one molecule attacks the carbonyl carbon of the unreacted ketone; a new bond is formed between carbons 1 and 8

See problems 15.17, 15.20, 15.21

PROBLEM 15.2

Draw the product of the base-catalyzed aldol reaction of each compound:
(a) Acetophenone (b) Cyclopentanone

β-Hydroxyaldehydes and β-hydroxyketones are very easily dehydrated, and often the conditions necessary to bring about an aldol reaction are sufficient to cause dehydration (Section 8.2E). Dehydration can also be brought about by warming the aldol product in dilute acid. The major product from the dehydration of an aldol product is one in which the carbon–carbon double bond is conjugated with the carbonyl group; that is, the product is an **α,β-unsaturated aldehyde or ketone** (so named because the site of unsaturation, the double bond, is between the α and β carbons).

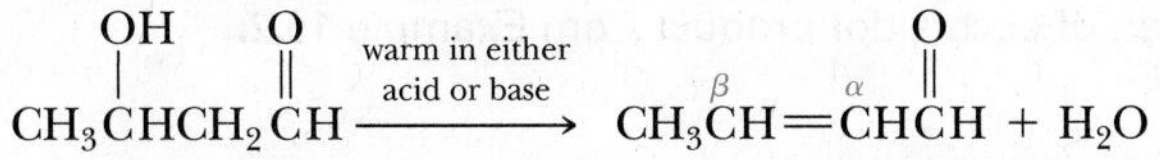

Product of an aldol reaction

An α,β-unsaturated aldehyde

Base-catalyzed aldol reactions are readily reversible, and generally little aldol product is present at equilibrium. Equilibrium constants for dehydration, however, are usually large, so that, if reaction conditions are sufficiently vigorous to bring about dehydration, good yields of product can be obtained.

Mechanism

Base-Catalyzed Dehydration of an Aldol Product

We can write the following two-step mechanism for the base-catalyzed dehydration of an aldol product:

STEP 1: Take a proton away. An acid–base reaction removes an α-hydrogen to give an enolate anion.

STEP 2: Break a bond to form a stable molecule. The enolate anion ejects hydroxide ion, regenerating the base and giving the α,β-unsaturated carbonyl compound.

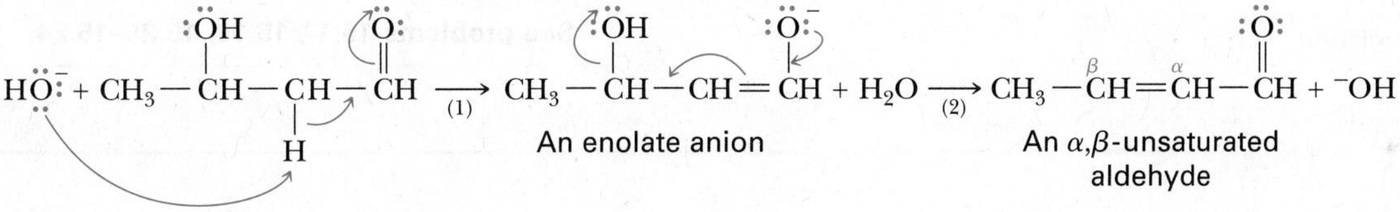

Mechanism

Acid-Catalyzed Dehydration of an Aldol Product

The acid-catalyzed dehydration of an aldol product also takes place in two steps:

STEP 1: Add a proton. An acid–base reaction protonates the β-hydroxyl group.

STEP 2: Take a proton away and break a bond to form a stable molecule. Water acts as a base to abstract an α-hydrogen and eject H_2O as a leaving group, giving the α,β-unsaturated carbonyl compound and regenerating the acid.

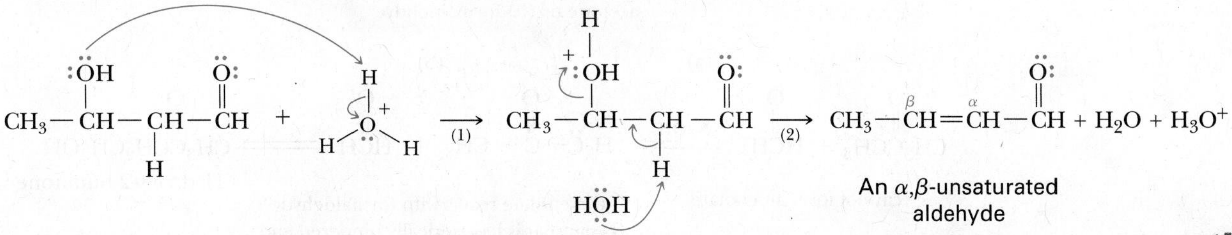

EXAMPLE 15.3

Draw the product of the base-catalyzed dehydration of each aldol product from Example 15.2.

STRATEGY

The product of dehydration of an aldol product is always an α,β-unsaturated carbonyl compound. The C—C double bond always forms between the α-carbon and the carbon that was once bonded to the —OH group.

SOLUTION

Loss of H_2O from aldol product (a) gives an α,β-unsaturated aldehyde, while loss of H_2O from aldol product (b) gives an α,β-unsaturated ketone:

(a)

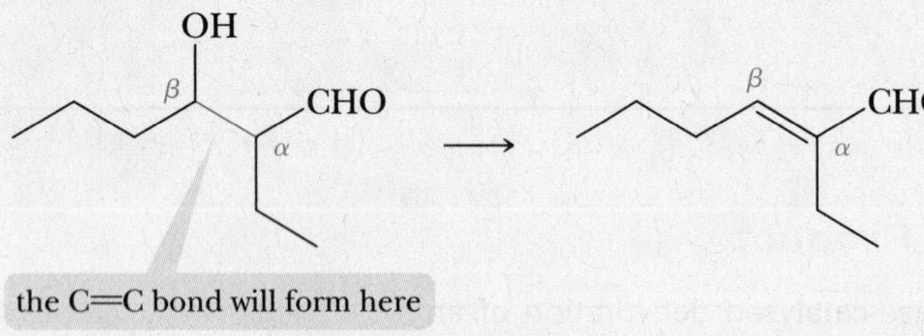

(b)

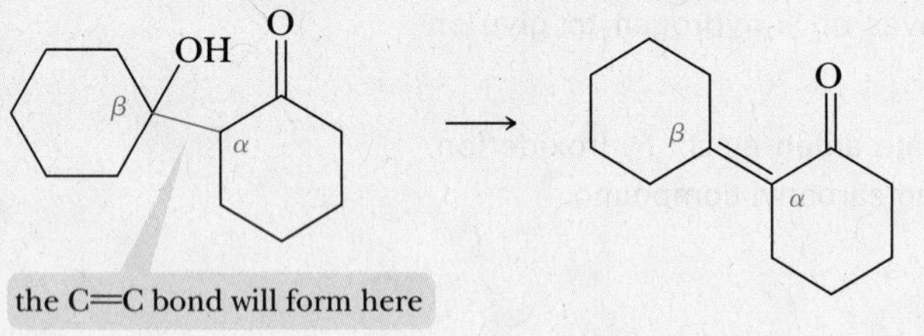

See problems 15.17, 15.18, 15.20–15.24

PROBLEM 15.3

Draw the product of the base-catalyzed dehydration of each aldol product from Problem 15.2.

C. Crossed Aldol Reactions

Crossed aldol reaction An aldol reaction between two different aldehydes, two different ketones, or an aldehyde and a ketone.

The reactants in the key step of an aldol reaction are an enolate anion and an enolate anion acceptor. In self-reactions, both roles are played by one kind of molecule. **Crossed aldol reactions** are also possible, such as the crossed aldol reaction between acetone and formaldehyde. Because it has no α-hydrogen, formaldehyde cannot form an enolate anion. It is, however, a particularly good enolate anion acceptor because its carbonyl group is unhindered. Acetone forms an enolate anion, but its carbonyl group, which is bonded to two alkyl groups, is less reactive than that of formaldehyde. Consequently, the crossed aldol reaction between acetone and formaldehyde gives 4-hydroxy-2-butanone:

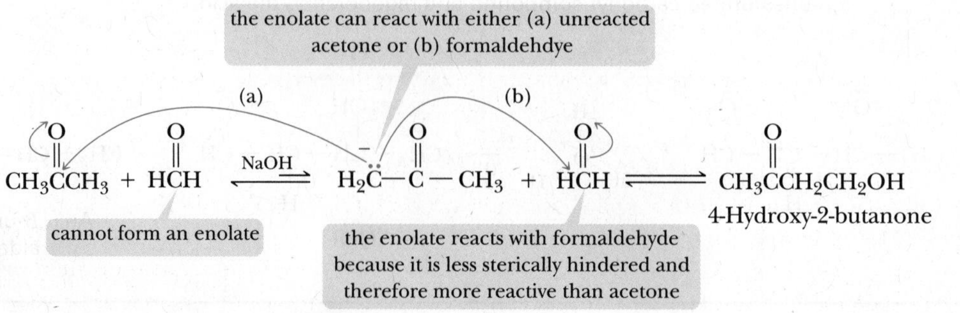

As this example illustrates, for a crossed aldol reaction to be successful, one of the two reactants should have no α-hydrogen, so that its enolate anion does not form. It also helps if the compound with no α-hydrogen has the more reactive carbonyl—for example, an aldehyde. Following are examples of aldehydes that have no α-hydrogens and that can be used in crossed aldol reactions:

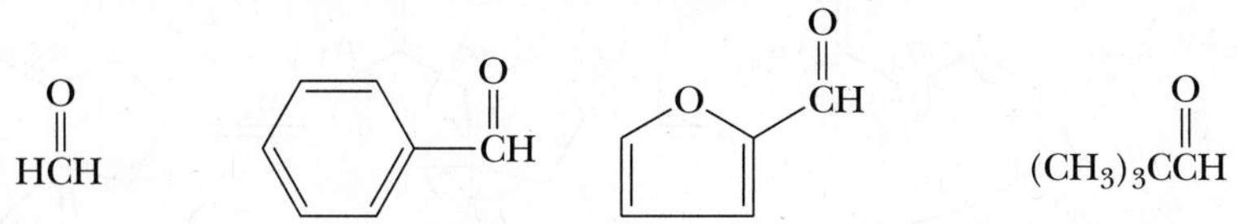

Formaldehyde Benzaldehyde Furfural 2,2-Dimethylpropanal

EXAMPLE 15.4

Draw the product of the crossed aldol reaction between furfural and cyclohexanone and the product formed by its base-catalyzed dehydration.

STRATEGY

Determine which carbonyl compound possesses an abstractable α-hydrogen and draw its enolate anion. Decide which carbonyl compound would be more reactive toward the enolate anion (aldehydes are more reactive than ketones) and show the enolate anion adding to its carbonyl carbon to form a β-hydroxycarbonyl. It often helps to number the atoms in the enolate anion and the ketone or aldehyde. The product of dehydration of an aldol product is always an α,β-unsaturated carbonyl compound. The C—C double bond always forms between the α-carbon and the carbon that was once bonded to the —OH group.

SOLUTION

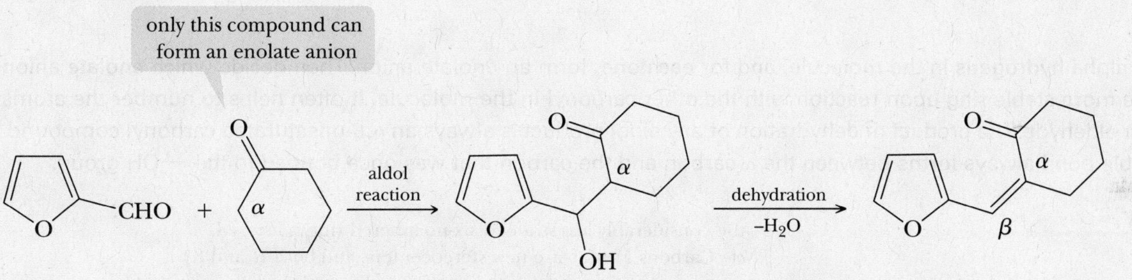

Furfural Cyclohexanone Aldol product

See problems 15.18, 15.19

PROBLEM 15.4

Draw the product of the crossed aldol reaction between benzaldehyde and 3-pentanone and the product formed by its base-catalyzed dehydration.

D. Intramolecular Aldol Reactions

When both the enolate anion and the carbonyl group to which it adds are in the same molecule, aldol reaction results in formation of a ring. This type of **intramolecular aldol reaction** is particularly useful for the formation of five- and six-membered rings. Because they are the most stable rings, and because the equilibrium conditions under which these reactions are performed are driven by stability, five- and six-membered rings form much more readily than four- or seven- and larger-membered rings. Intramolecular aldol reaction of 2,7-octanedione via enolate anion α_3, for example, gives a five-membered ring, whereas intramolecular aldol reaction of this same compound via enolate anion α_1

would give a seven-membered ring. In the case of 2,7-octanedione, the five-membered ring forms in preference to the seven-membered ring:

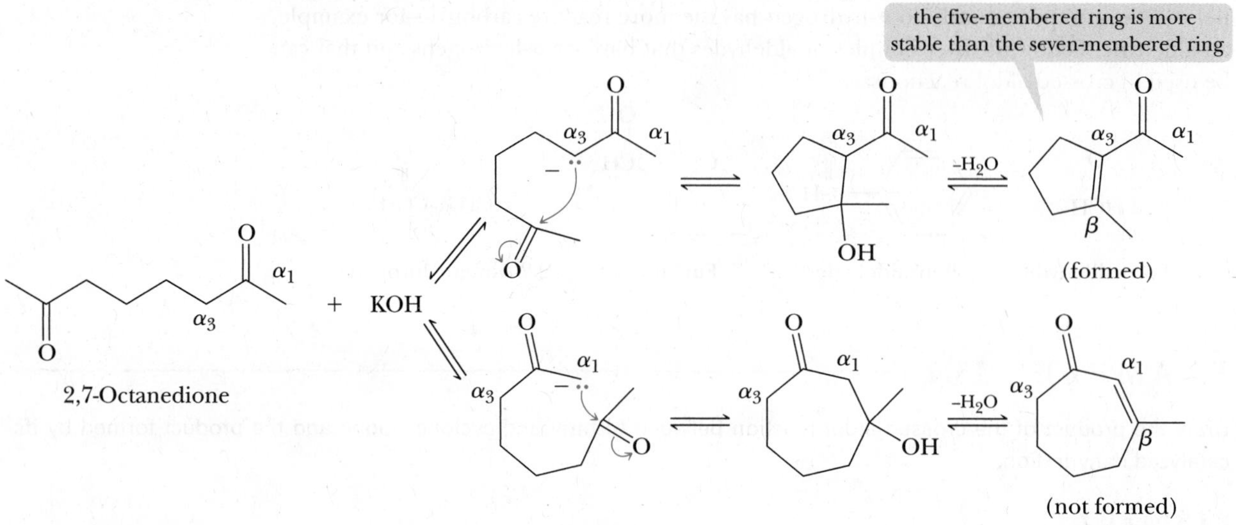
the five-membered ring is more stable than the seven-membered ring
2,7-Octanedione
+ KOH
$-H_2O$
(formed)
(not formed)

EXAMPLE 15.5

Draw the dehydration product of the following intramolecular aldol reaction.

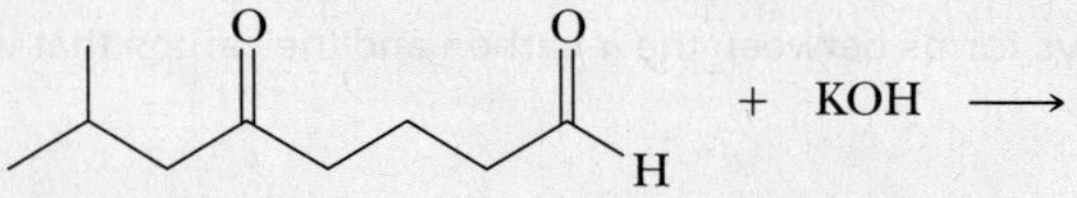
+ KOH

STRATEGY

Identify all the alpha hydrogens in the molecule, and for each one, form an enolate anion. Then decide which enolate anion would form the more stable ring upon reaction with the other carbonyl in the molecule. It often helps to number the atoms in the ketone or aldehyde. The product of dehydration of any aldol product is always an α,β-unsaturated carbonyl compound. The C—C double bond always forms between the α-carbon and the carbon that was once bonded to the —OH group.

SOLUTION

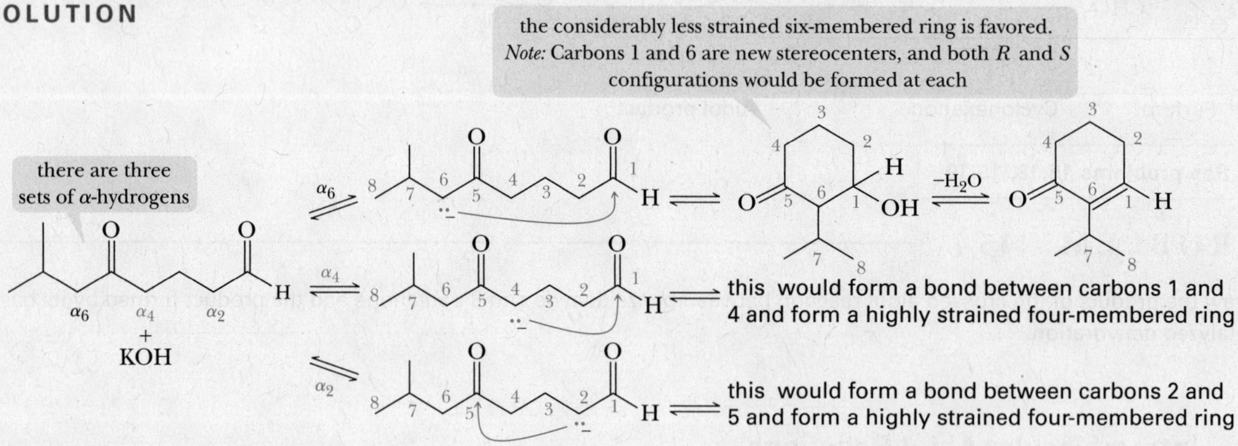
the considerably less strained six-membered ring is favored.
Note: Carbons 1 and 6 are new stereocenters, and both R and S configurations would be formed at each
there are three sets of α-hydrogens
+ KOH
$-H_2O$
this would form a bond between carbons 1 and 4 and form a highly strained four-membered ring
this would form a bond between carbons 2 and 5 and form a highly strained four-membered ring

See problems 15.22–15.24

PROBLEM 15.5

Draw the dehydration product of the following intermolecular aldol reaction.

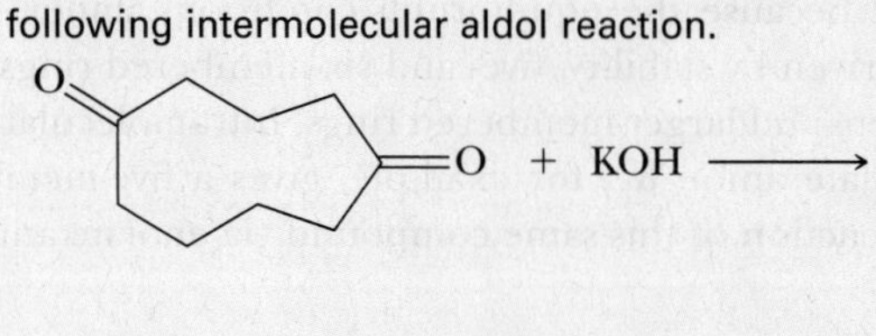
+ KOH

HOW TO 15.1 Determine the Starting Compounds Used in an Aldol Reaction

It will sometimes be necessary to work retrosynthetically (How To 14.2) from the product of an aldol reaction. Following are the steps for determining the starting compounds used in an aldol reaction.

(a) Locate the carbonyl and identify the α- and β-carbons. An aldol product will contain a carbonyl of a ketone or an aldehyde and either an OH group or a C—C double bond. Once the carbonyl is found, label the carbons using the Greek alphabet in the direction of the OH group or C—C double bond:

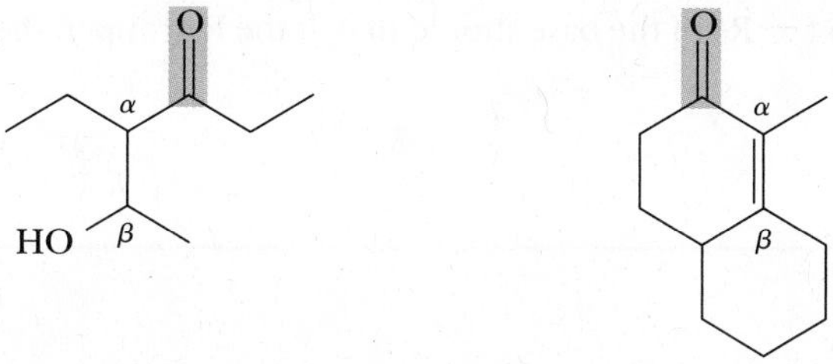

(b) Erase the bond between the α- and β-carbons and convert the carbon labeled β to a carbonyl group (the oxygen of an —OH group bonded to the β-carbon becomes the oxygen atom of the carbonyl). Note that a hydrogen is added to the carbon labeled α, although it is usually unnecessary to show this in a line-angle formula:

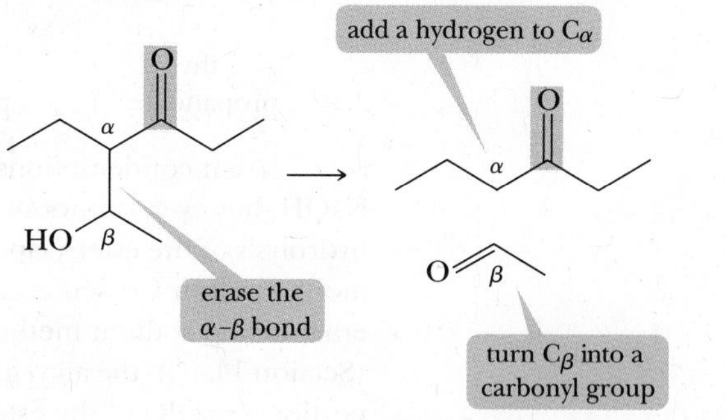

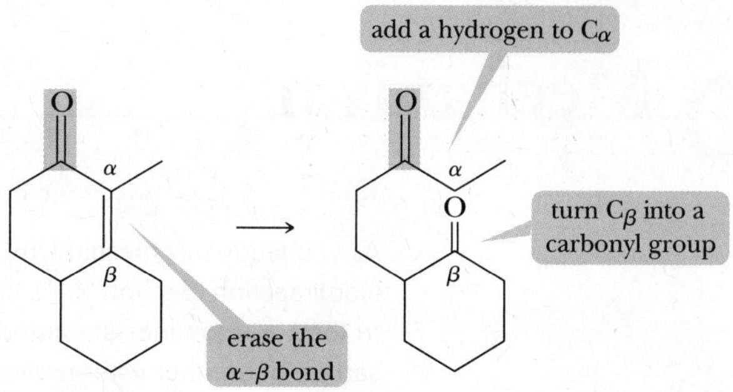

15.3 What Are the Claisen and Dieckmann Condensations?

A. Claisen Condensation

In this section, we examine the formation of an enolate anion from one ester, followed by the nucleophilic acyl substitution of the enolate anion at the carbonyl carbon of another ester. One of the first of these reactions discovered was the **Claisen condensation**, named after its discoverer, German chemist Ludwig Claisen (1851–1930). We illustrate a Claisen condensation by the reaction between two molecules of ethyl acetate in the presence of sodium ethoxide, followed by acidification, to give ethyl acetoacetate (note that, in this and many of the equations that follow, we abbreviate the ethyl group as Et):

Claisen condensation A carbonyl condensation reaction between two esters to give a β-ketoester.

$$2\,CH_3\overset{\overset{\displaystyle O}{\|}}{C}OEt \xrightarrow[2)\ H_2O,\ HCl]{1)\ EtO^-\ Na^+} CH_3\overset{\overset{\displaystyle O}{\|}}{C}CH_2\overset{\overset{\displaystyle O}{\|}}{C}OEt + EtOH$$

Ethyl ethanoate (Ethyl acetate) — Ethyl 3-oxobutanoate (Ethyl acetoacetate) — Ethanol

The functional group of the product of a Claisen condensation is a **β-ketoester**:

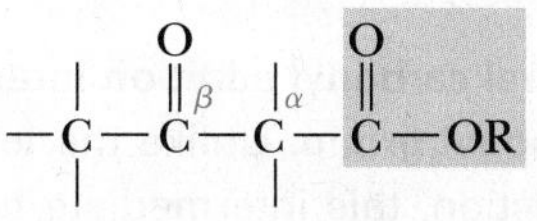

A β-ketoester

The Claisen condensation of two molecules of ethyl propanoate gives the following β-ketoester:

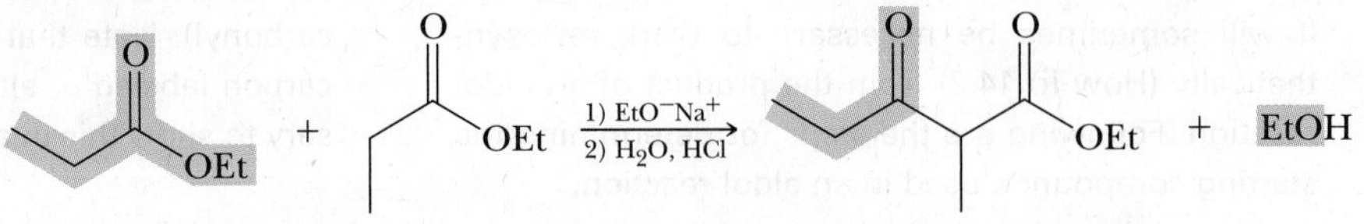

Ethyl propanoate | Ethyl propanoate | Ethyl 2-methyl-3-oxopentanoate

Claisen condensations, like the aldol reaction, require a base. Aqueous bases, such as NaOH, however, cannot be used in Claisen condensations because they would bring about hydrolysis of the ester (saponification, Section 14.3C) instead. Rather, the bases most commonly used in Claisen condensations are nonaqueous bases, such as sodium ethoxide in ethanol and sodium methoxide in methanol. Furthermore, to prevent transesterification (Section 14.4C), the alkyl group (—R) of the base should match the R group in the alkoxyl portion (—OR) of the ester.

Mechanism

Claisen Condensation

As you study this mechanism, note how closely its first two steps resemble the first steps of the aldol reaction (Section 15.1). In each reaction, base removes a proton from an α-carbon in Step 1 to form a resonance-stabilized enolate anion. In Step 2, the enolate anion attacks the carbonyl carbon of another ester molecule to form a tetrahedral carbonyl addition intermediate.

STEP 1: Take a proton away. Base removes an α-hydrogen from the ester to give a resonance-stabilized enolate anion:

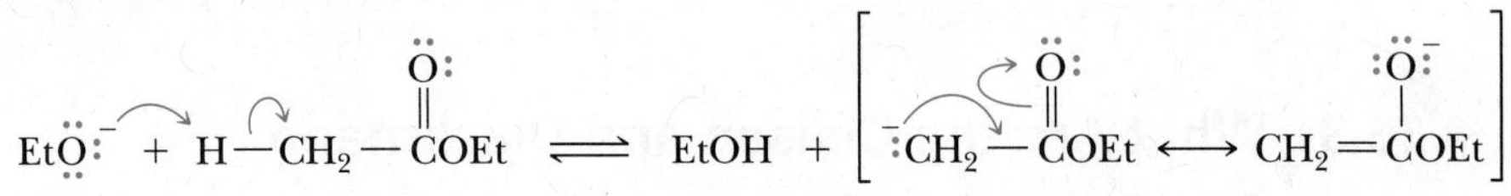

(weaker base) | pK_a 22 (weaker acid) | pK_a 15.9 (stronger acid) | Resonance-stabilized enolate anion (stronger base)

Because the α-hydrogen of the ester is the weaker acid and ethoxide is the weaker base, the position of this equilibrium lies very much toward the left.

STEP 2: Reaction of an electrophile and a nucleophile to form a new covalent bond. Attack of the enolate anion on the carbonyl carbon of another ester molecule gives a tetrahedral carbonyl addition intermediate:

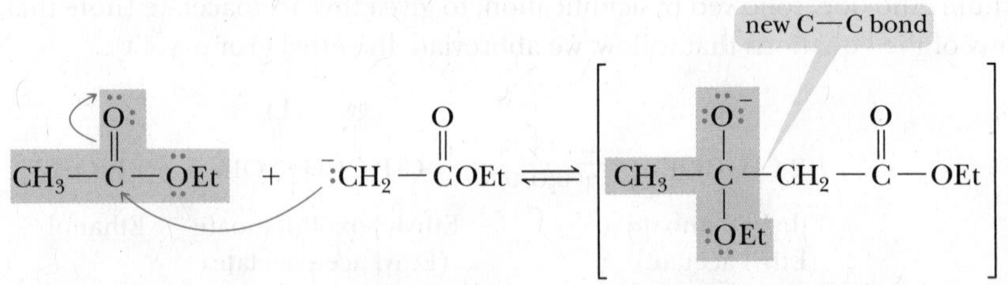

(an electrophile) | (a nucleophile) | A tetrahedral cabonyl addition intermediate

STEP 3: Collapse of the tetrahedral carbonyl addition intermediate to eject a leaving group and regenerate the carbonyl group. Unlike the tetrahedral carbonyl addition intermediate in the aldol reaction, this intermediate has a leaving group (the ethoxide ion). Collapse of the tetrahedral carbonyl addition intermediate by ejection of the ethoxide ion gives a β-ketoester:

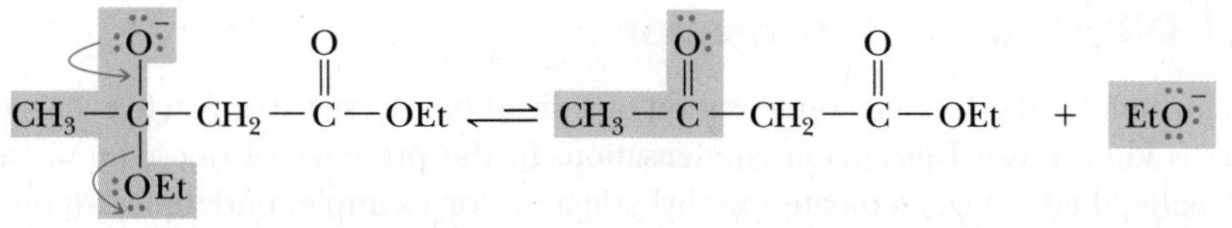

STEP 4: Take a proton away. Formation of the enolate anion of the β-ketoester drives the Claisen condensation to the right. The β-ketoester (a stronger acid) reacts with ethoxide ion (a stronger base) to give ethanol (a weaker acid) and the anion of the β-ketoester (a weaker base):

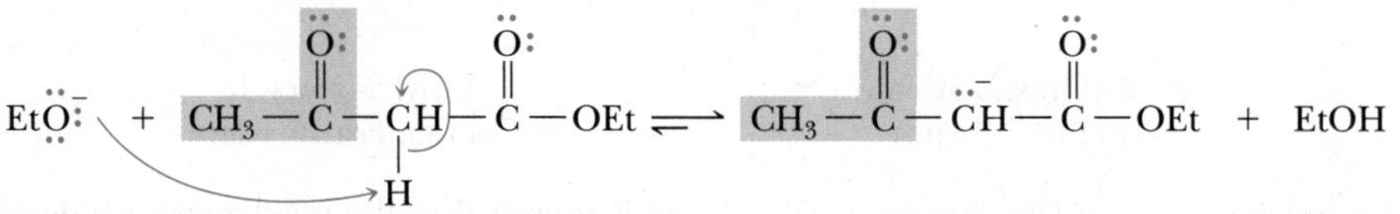

(stronger base) pK_a 10.7 (stronger acid) (weaker base) pK_a 15.9 (weaker acid)

The position of equilibrium for this step lies very far toward the right.

STEP 5: Add a proton. Acidification of the enolate anion gives the β-ketoester:

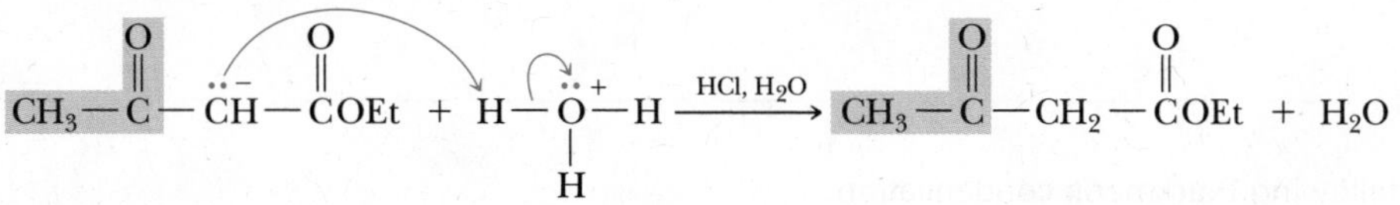

EXAMPLE 15.6

Show the product of the Claisen condensation of ethyl butanoate in the presence of sodium ethoxide followed by acidification with aqueous HCl.

STRATEGY

Draw two molecules of ethyl butanoate. Convert one of the molecules to an enolate anion and show it adding to the carbonyl carbon of the other. Because Claisen condensations occur with nucleophilic acyl substitution, the —OR group of the carbonyl being attacked is eliminated from the final product. It often helps to number the atoms in the enolate anion and the ester being attacked.

SOLUTION

The new bond formed in a Claisen condensation is between the carbonyl group of one ester and the α-carbon of another:

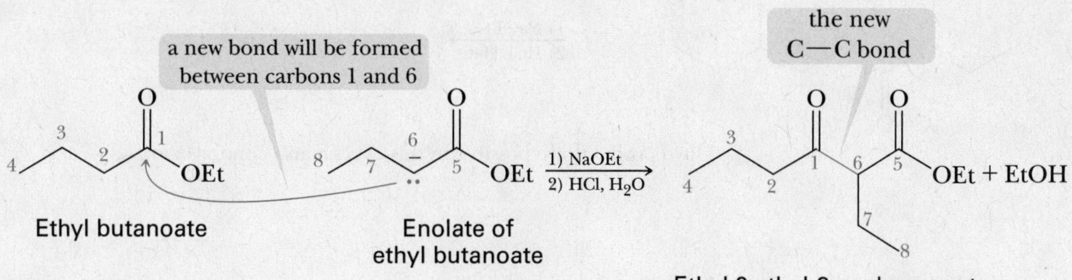

Ethyl butanoate — Enolate of ethyl butanoate — Ethyl 2-ethyl-3-oxohexanoate

See problem 15.27

PROBLEM 15.6

Show the product of the Claisen condensation of ethyl 3-methylbutanoate in the presence of sodium ethoxide.

B. Dieckmann Condensation

Dieckmann condensation An intramolecular Claisen condensation of an ester of a dicarboxylic acid to give a five- or six-membered ring.

An intramolecular Claisen condensation of a dicarboxylic ester to give a five- or six-membered ring is known as a **Dieckmann condensation**. In the presence of one equivalent of sodium ethoxide, diethyl hexanedioate (diethyl adipate), for example, undergoes an intramolecular condensation to form a five-membered ring:

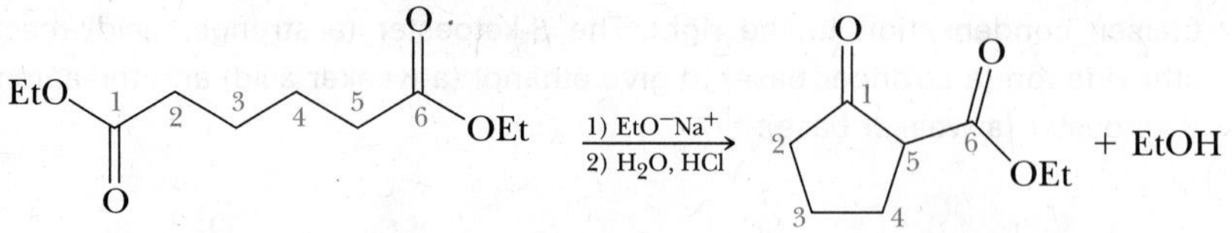

Diethyl hexanedioate (Diethyl adipate) — Ethyl 2-oxocyclopentanecarboxylate

The mechanism of a Dieckmann condensation is identical to the mechanism we described for the Claisen condensation. An anion formed at the α-carbon of one ester in Step 1 adds to the carbonyl of the other ester group in Step 2 to form a tetrahedral carbonyl addition intermediate. This intermediate ejects ethoxide ion in Step 3 to regenerate the carbonyl group. Cyclization is followed by formation of the conjugate base of the β-ketoester in Step 4, just as in the Claisen condensation. The β-ketoester is isolated after acidification with aqueous acid.

EXAMPLE 15.7

Complete the equation for the following Dieckmann condensation:

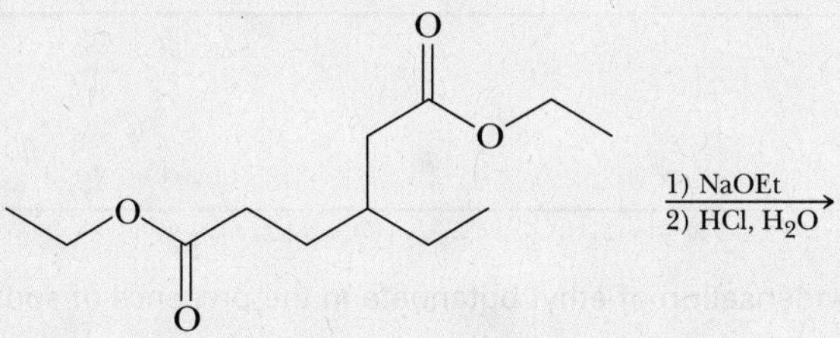

STRATEGY

Identify the α-carbon for each ester group. Convert one of the α-carbons to an enolate anion and show it adding to the other carbonyl carbon. Because Dieckmann condensations occur with nucleophilic acyl substitution, the —OR group of the carbonyl being attacked is eliminated from the final product. It often helps to number the atoms in the enolate anion and the ester being attacked.

SOLUTION

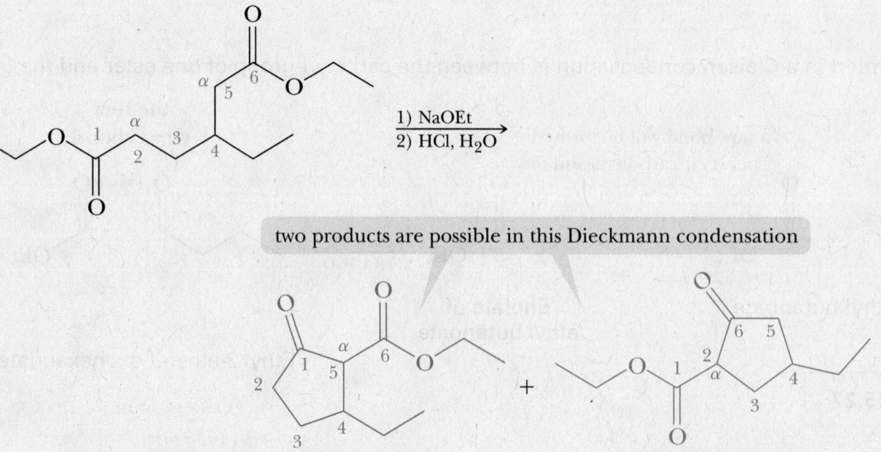

Product from enolate at C_5 — Product from enolate at C_2

See problem 15.33

PROBLEM 15.7

Complete the equation for the following Dieckmann condensation:

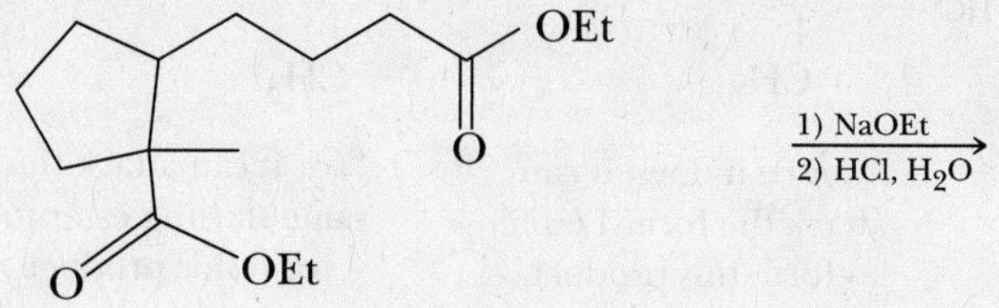

C. Crossed Claisen Condensations

In a **crossed Claisen condensation** (a Claisen condensation between two different esters, each with its own α-hydrogens), a mixture of four β-ketoesters is possible; therefore, crossed Claisen condensations of this type are generally not synthetically useful. Such condensations are useful, however, if appreciable differences in reactivity exist between the two esters, as, for example, when one of the esters has no α-hydrogens and can function only as an enolate anion acceptor. These esters have no α-hydrogens:

Crossed Claisen condensation A Claisen condensation between two different esters.

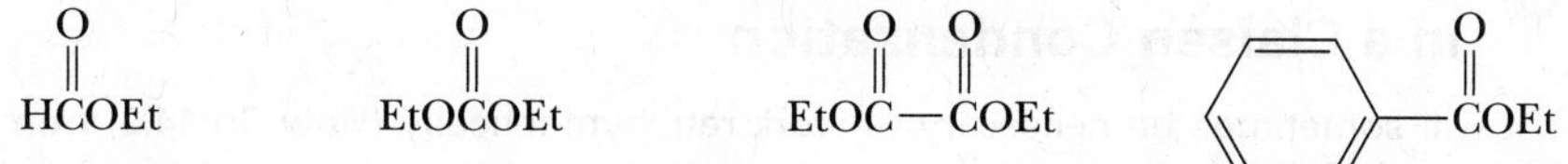

Ethyl formate | Diethyl carbonate | Diethyl ethanedioate (Diethyl oxalate) | Ethyl benzoate

Crossed Claisen condensations of this type are usually carried out by using the ester with no α-hydrogens in excess. In the following illustration, methyl benzoate is used in excess:

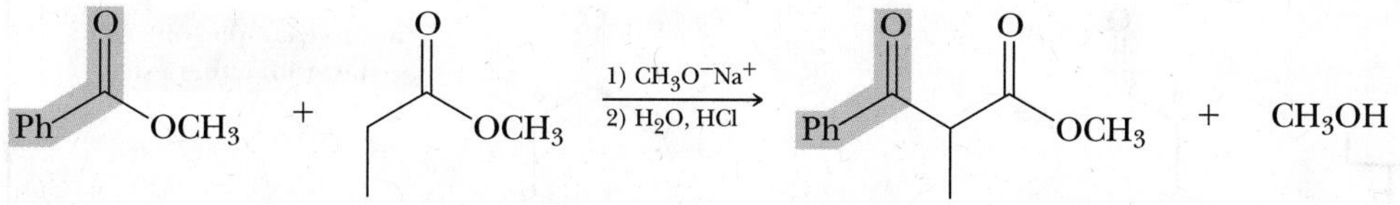

Methyl benzoate | Methyl propanoate | Methyl 2-methyl-3-oxo-3-phenylpropanoate

EXAMPLE 15.8

Complete the equation for this crossed Claisen condensation:

$$\overset{O}{\overset{\|}{HC}}OEt + CH_3CH_2\overset{O}{\overset{\|}{C}}OEt \xrightarrow[2)\ H_2O,\ HCl]{1)\ EtO^-Na^+}$$

STRATEGY

Identify the α-carbon(s) for each ester. Convert one of the α-carbons to an enolate anion and show it adding to the other carbonyl carbon. Repeat this for all α-carbons and ester molecules. Remember that the enolate anion can attack the other ester or an unreacted molecule of itself if equal amounts of ester are used. Because Claisen condensations occur with nucleophilic acyl substitution, the —OR group of the carbonyl being attacked is eliminated from the final product. It often helps to number the atoms in the enolate anion and the ester being attacked.

SOLUTION

$$\text{HCOEt} + \text{CH}_3\text{CH}_2\text{COEt} \xrightarrow[\text{2) H}_2\text{O, HCl}]{\text{1) EtO}^-\ \text{Na}^+} \text{HCCHCOEt}\ (\text{CH}_3) + \text{CH}_3\text{CH}_2\text{CCHCOEt}\ (\text{CH}_3) + \text{EtOH}$$

only this ester can become an enolate...

...once it does, it can attack the formyl ester to form this product...

...or it can attack the same starting ester to form this product

See problems 15.29–15.31

PROBLEM 15.8

Complete the equation for this crossed Claisen condensation:

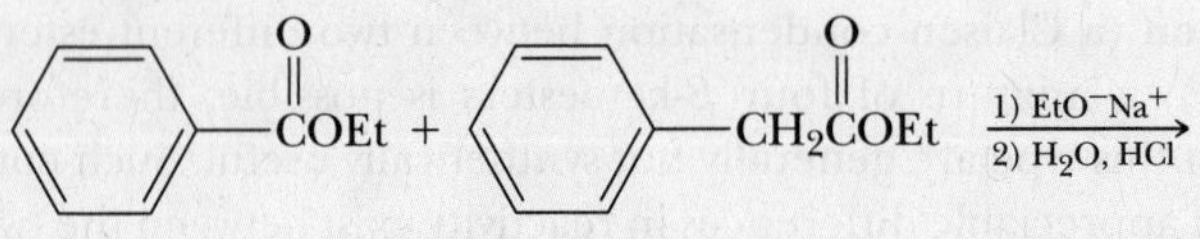

HOW TO 15.2

Determine the Starting Compounds Used in a Claisen Condensation

It will sometimes be necessary to work retrosynthetically (How To 14.2) from the product of a Claisen condensation. Following are the steps for determining the starting compounds used in a Claisen condensation.

(a) Locate the carbonyl of an ester and identify the α- and β-carbons. A Claisen condensation product will contain a carbonyl of an ester and another carbonyl of either an aldehyde, a ketone, or another ester. Once the carbonyl of the ester is found, label the carbons using the Greek alphabet in the direction of the other carbonyl group:

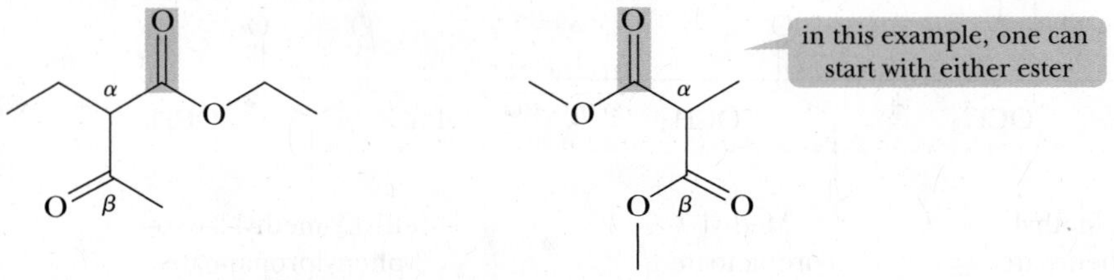

(b) Erase the bond between the α- and β-carbons:

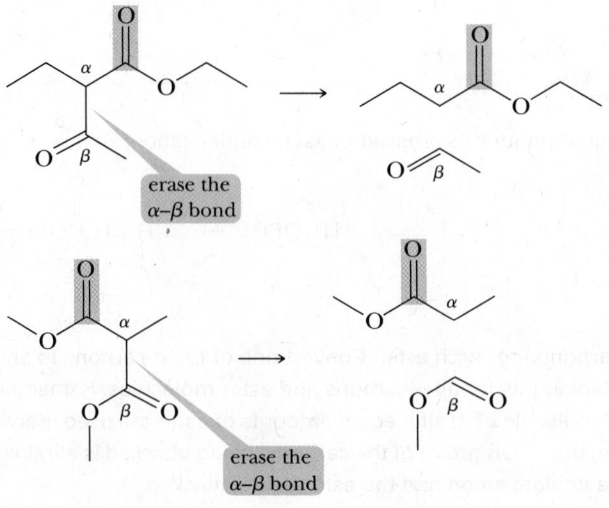

(c) Add a hydrogen to the carbon labeled α and add an —OR group to the carbon labeled β. The type of alkyl group in —OR should match the alkyl group of the other ester:

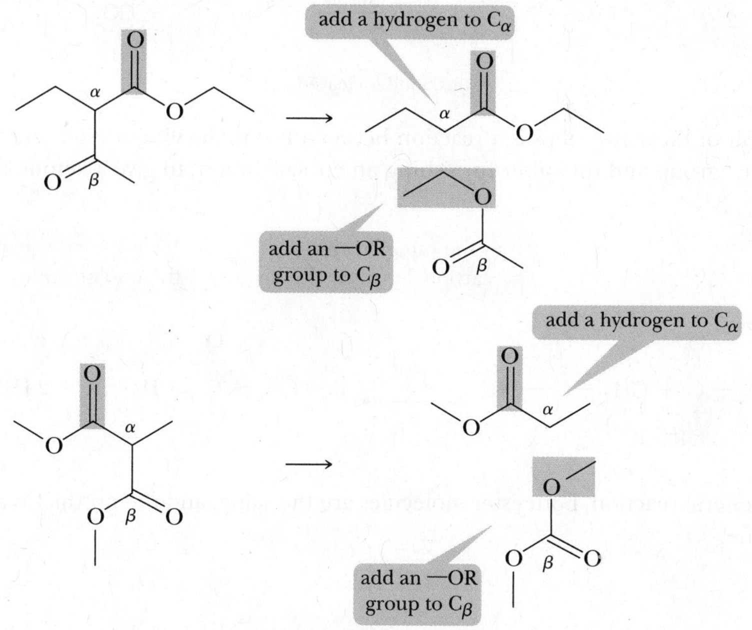

D. Hydrolysis and Decarboxylation of β-Ketoesters

Recall from Section 14.3C that the hydrolysis of an ester in aqueous sodium hydroxide (saponification), followed by acidification of the reaction mixture with HCl or other mineral acid, converts an ester to a carboxylic acid and an alcohol. Recall also from Section 13.8 that β-ketoacids and β-dicarboxylic acids readily undergo decarboxylation (lose CO_2) when heated. The following equations illustrate the results of a Claisen condensation, followed by saponification, acidification, and decarboxylation:

Claisen condensation:

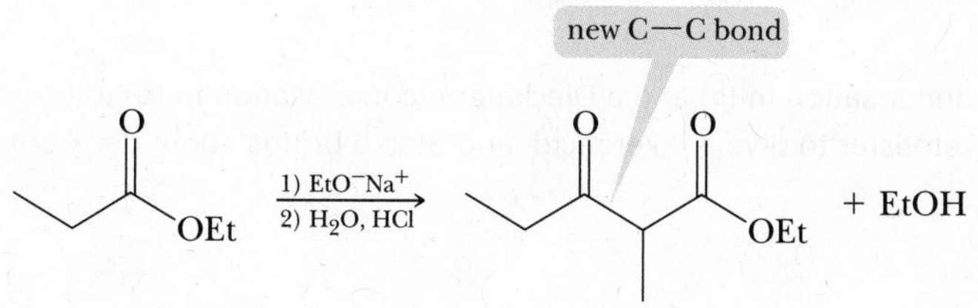

Saponification followed by acidification:

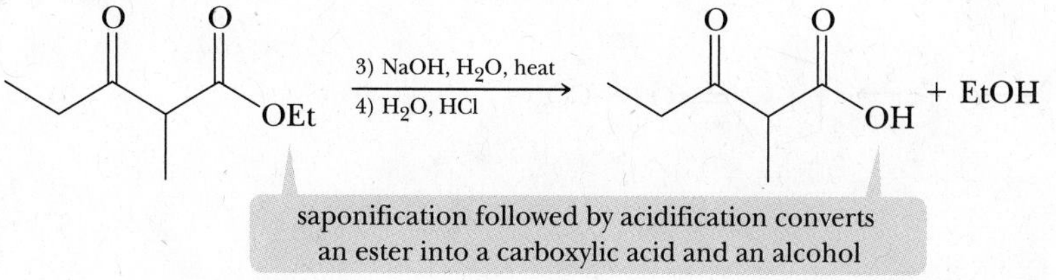

Decarboxylation:

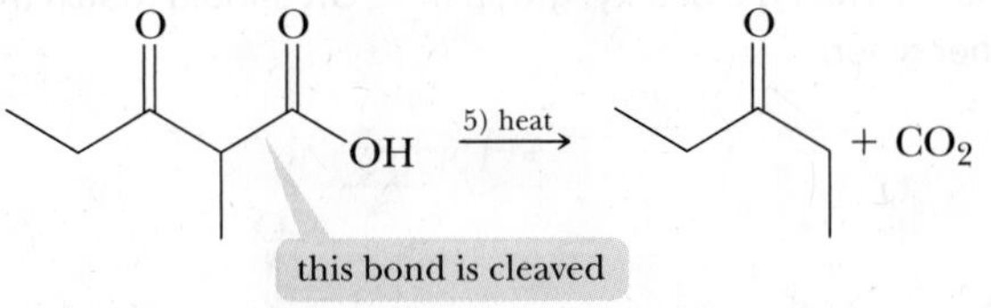

The result of these five steps is a reaction between two molecules of ester, one furnishing a carbonyl group and the other furnishing an enolate anion, to give a ketone and carbon dioxide:

from the ester furnishing the carbonyl group — from the ester furnishing the enolate anion

$$R{-}CH_2{-}\overset{O}{\overset{\|}{\underset{OR'}{\underset{|}{C}}}} + \underset{R}{\underset{|}{CH_2}}{-}\overset{O}{\overset{\|}{C}}{-}OR' \xrightarrow{\text{several steps}} R{-}CH_2{-}\overset{O}{\overset{\|}{C}}{-}CH_2{-}R + 2\,HOR' + CO_2$$

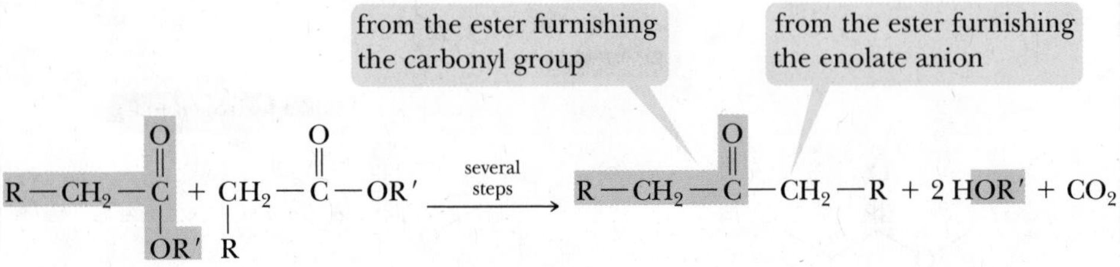

In the general reaction, both ester molecules are the same, and the product is a symmetrical ketone.

EXAMPLE 15.9

Each set of compounds undergoes (1, 2) Claisen condensation, (3) saponification followed by (4) acidification, and (5) thermal decarboxylation:

(a) $Ph\overset{O}{\overset{\|}{C}}OEt + CH_3\overset{O}{\overset{\|}{C}}OEt$ **(b)** Draw a structural formula of the product after completion of this reaction sequence.

STRATEGY

Proceed with a variation of the Claisen condensation (Ex. 15.6–15.8) and arrive at the final decarboxylated product by removing the carbonyl ester group and replacing it with a hydrogen.

SOLUTION

Steps 1 and 2 bring about a crossed Claisen condensation in (a) and a Dieckmann condensation in (b) to form a β-ketoester. Steps 3 and 4 bring about hydrolysis of the β-ketoester to give a β-ketoacid, and Step 5 brings about decarboxylation to give a ketone:

(a) $\xrightarrow{1,2} Ph\overset{O}{\overset{\|}{C}}CH_2\overset{O}{\overset{\|}{C}}OEt \xrightarrow{3,4} Ph\overset{O}{\overset{\|}{C}}CH_2\overset{O}{\overset{\|}{C}}OH \xrightarrow{5} Ph\overset{O}{\overset{\|}{C}}CH_3 + CO_2$

(b)

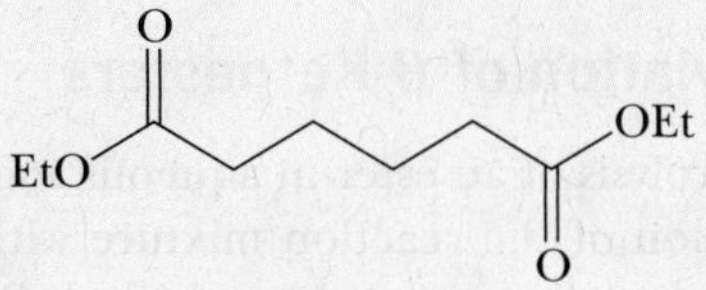

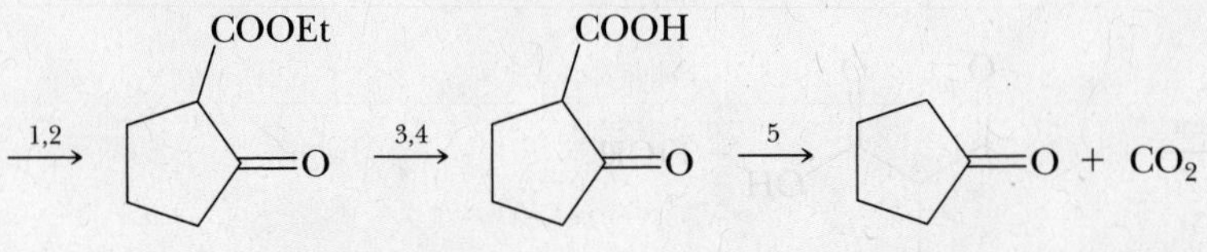

See problems 15.28, 15.32, 15.34

PROBLEM 15.9

Show how to convert benzoic acid to 3-methyl-1-phenyl-1-butanone by using a Claisen condensation at some stage in the synthesis:

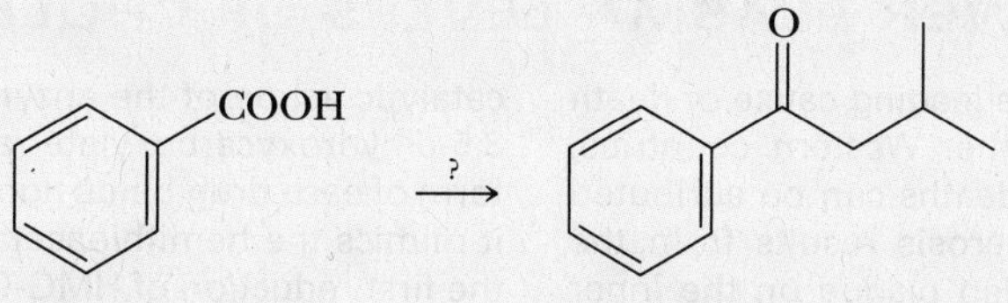

Benzoic acid 3-Methyl-1-phenyl-1-butanone

15.4 How Are Aldol Reactions and Claisen Condensations Involved in Biological Processes?

Carbonyl condensations are among the most widely used reactions in the biological world for the assembly of new carbon–carbon bonds in such important biomolecules as fatty acids, cholesterol, and steroid hormones. One source of carbon atoms for the synthesis of these biomolecules is **acetyl-CoA**, a thioester of acetic acid and the thiol group of coenzyme A. The function of the coenzyme A group of acetyl-CoA is to anchor the acetyl group on the surface of the enzyme systems that catalyze the reactions we examine in this section. In the discussions that follow, we will not be concerned with the mechanism by which each enzyme-catalyzed reaction occurs. Rather, our concern is with recognizing the type of reaction that takes place in each step.

In the Claisen condensation catalyzed by the enzyme thiolase, acetyl-CoA is converted to its enolate anion, which then attacks the carbonyl group of a second molecule of acetyl-CoA to form a tetrahedral carbonyl addition intermediate. Collapse of this intermediate by the loss of CoA-SH gives acetoacetyl-CoA. The mechanism for this condensation reaction is exactly the same as that of the Claisen condensation (Section 15.3A):

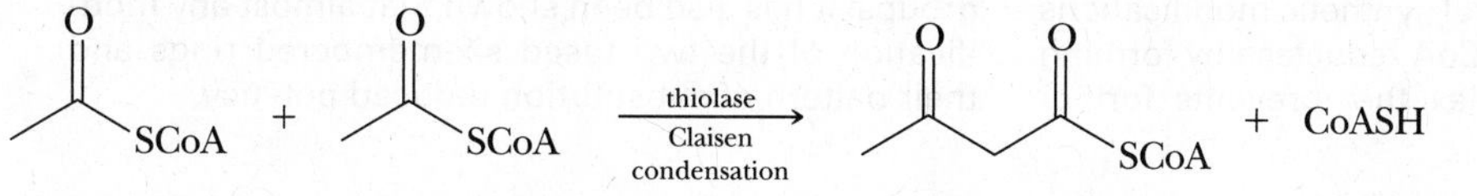

Acetyl-CoA Acetyl-CoA Acetoacetyl-CoA Coenzyme A

An enzyme-catalyzed aldol reaction with a third molecule of acetyl-CoA on the ketone carbonyl of acetoacetyl-CoA gives (*S*)-3-hydroxy-3-methylglutaryl-CoA:

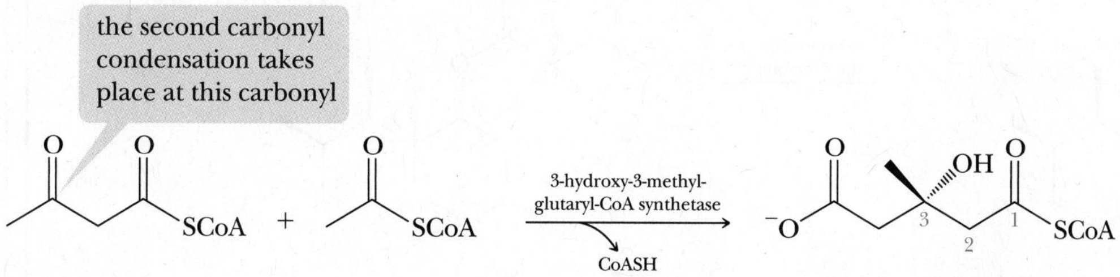

(*S*)-3-Hydroxy-3-methylglutaryl-CoA

Note three features of this reaction. First, the creation of the new stereocenter is stereoselective: Only the S enantiomer is formed. Although the acetyl group of each reactant is achiral, their condensation takes place in a chiral environment created by the enzyme 3-hydroxy-3-methylglutaryl-CoA synthetase. Second, hydrolysis of the thioester group of

Chemical Connections 15A

DRUGS THAT LOWER PLASMA LEVELS OF CHOLESTEROL

Coronary artery disease is the leading cause of death in the United States and other Western countries, where about one half of all deaths can be attributed to atherosclerosis. Atherosclerosis results from the buildup of fatty deposits called plaque on the inner walls of arteries. A major component of plaque is cholesterol derived from low-density-lipoproteins (LDL), which circulate in blood plasma. Because more than one half of total body cholesterol in humans is synthesized in the liver from acetyl-CoA, intensive efforts have been directed toward finding ways to inhibit this synthesis. The rate-determining step in cholesterol biosynthesis is reduction of 3-hydroxy-3-methylglutaryl-CoA (HMG-CoA) to mevalonic acid. This reduction is catalyzed by the enzyme HMG-CoA reductase and requires two moles of NADPH per mole of HMG-CoA.

Beginning in the early 1970s, researchers at the Sankyo Company in Tokyo screened more than 8,000 strains of microorganisms and in 1976 announced the isolation of mevastatin, a potent inhibitor of HMG-CoA reductase, from culture broths of the fungus *Penicillium citrinum*. The same compound was isolated by researchers at Beecham Pharmaceuticals in England from cultures of *Penicillium brevicompactum*. Soon thereafter, a second, more active compound called lovastatin was isolated at the Sankyo Company from the fungus *Monascus ruber*, and at Merck Sharpe & Dohme from *Aspergillus terreus*. Both mold metabolites are extremely effective in lowering plasma concentrations of LDL. The active form of each is the 5-hydroxycarboxylate anion formed by hydrolysis of the δ-lactone.

These drugs and several synthetic modifications now available inhibit HMG-CoA reductase by forming an enzyme-inhibitor complex that prevents further catalytic action of the enzyme. It is reasoned that the 3,5-dihydroxycarboxylate anion part of the active form of each drug binds tightly to the enzyme because it mimics the hemithioacetal intermediate formed by the first reduction of HMG-CoA.

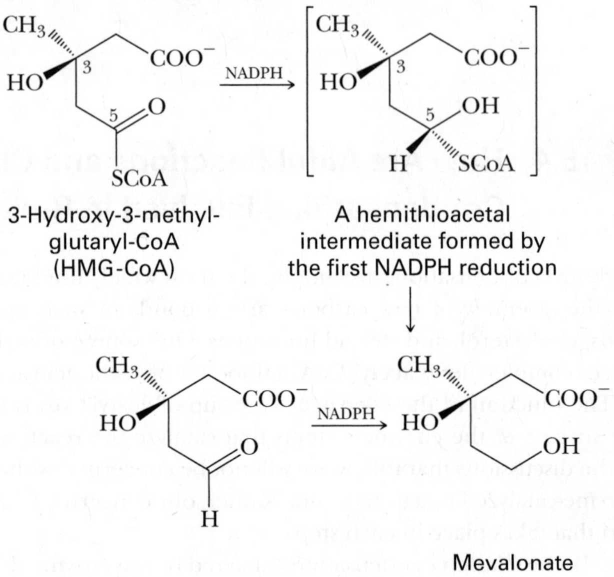

3-Hydroxy-3-methylglutaryl-CoA (HMG-CoA)

A hemithioacetal intermediate formed by the first NADPH reduction

Systematic studies have shown the importance of each part of the drug for effectiveness. It has been found, for example, that the carboxylate anion ($-COO^-$) is essential, as are both the 3-OH and 5-OH groups. It has also been shown that almost any modification of the two fused six-membered rings and their pattern of substitution reduced potency.

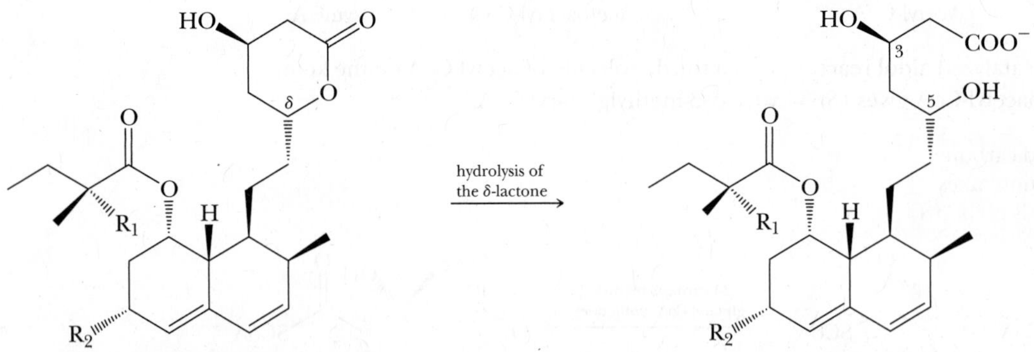

$R_1 = R_2 = H$, mevastatin
$R_1 = H$, $R_2 = CH_3$, lovastatin (Mevacor)
$R_1 = R_2 = CH_3$, simvastatin (Zocor)

The active form of each drug

Question
Which of the biomolecules in the above reaction scheme could be the product of an aldol reaction?

acetyl-CoA is coupled with the aldol reaction. Third, the carboxyl group is shown as it is ionized at pH 7.4, the approximate pH of blood plasma and many cellular fluids.

Enzyme-catalyzed reduction of the thioester group of 3-hydroxy-3-methylglutaryl-CoA to a primary alcohol gives mevalonic acid, shown here as its anion:

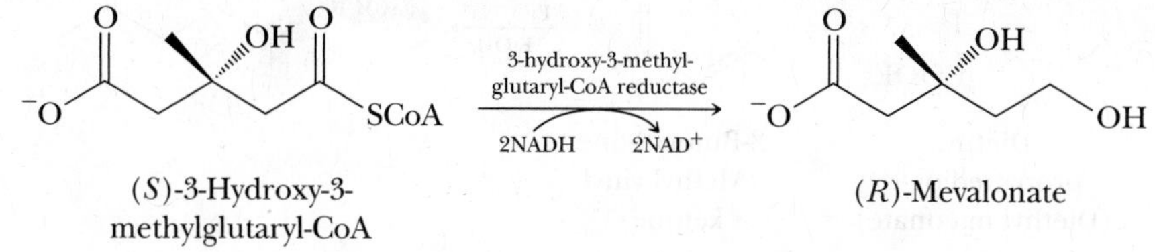

The reducing agent for this transformation is nicotinamide adenine dinucleotide, abbreviated NADH. This reducing agent is the biochemical equivalent of $LiAlH_4$. Each reducing agent functions by delivering a hydride ion ($H:^-$) to the carbonyl carbon of an aldehyde, a ketone, or an ester. Note that, in the reduction, a change occurs in the designation of configuration from S to R, not because of any change in configuration at the stereocenter, but rather because of a change in priority among the four groups bonded to the stereocenter.

Enzyme-catalyzed transfer of a phosphate group from adenosine triphosphate (ATP, Section 20.1) to the 3-hydroxyl group of mevalonate gives a phosphoric ester at carbon 3. Enzyme-catalyzed transfer of a pyrophosphate group (Section 14.1B) from a second molecule of ATP gives a pyrophosphoric ester at carbon 5. Enzyme-catalyzed β-elimination from this molecule results in the loss of CO_2 and PO_4^{3-}, both good leaving groups:

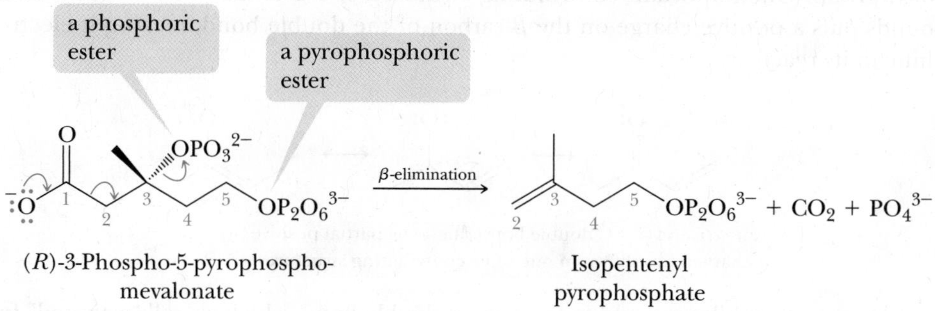

15.5 What Is the Michael Reaction?

Thus far, we have used carbon nucleophiles in two ways to form new carbon–carbon bonds:

1. Addition of organomagnesium (Grignard) reagents to the carbonyl groups of aldehydes, ketones, and esters.
2. Addition of enolate anions derived from aldehydes or ketones (aldol reactions) and esters (Claisen and Dieckmann condensations) to the carbonyl groups of other aldehydes, ketones, or esters.

Addition of an enolate anion to a carbon–carbon double bond conjugated with a carbonyl group presents an entirely new synthetic strategy. In this section, we study a type of **conjugate addition** involving nucleophilic addition to an electrophilic double bond.

A. Michael Addition of Enolate Anions

Michael reaction The conjugate addition of an enolate anion or other nucleophile to an α,β-unsaturated carbonyl compound.

Nucleophilic addition of enolate anions to α,β-unsaturated carbonyl compounds was first reported in 1887 by the American chemist Arthur Michael. Following are two examples of **Michael reactions**. In the first example, the nucleophile is the enolate anion of diethyl malonate. In the second example, the nucleophile is the enolate anion of ethyl acetoacetate:

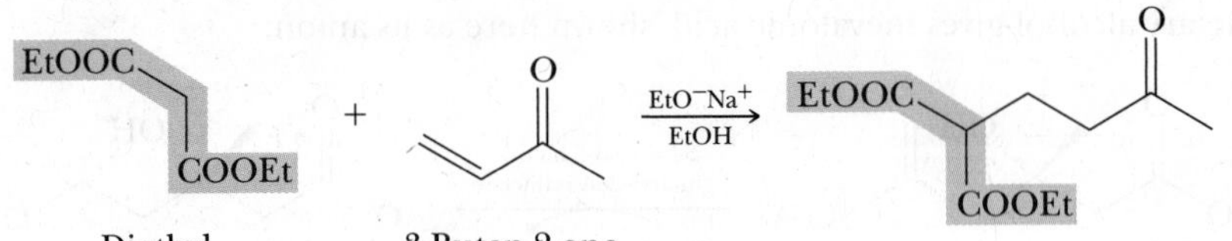

Diethyl propanedioate (Diethyl malonate)

3-Buten-2-one (Methyl vinyl ketone)

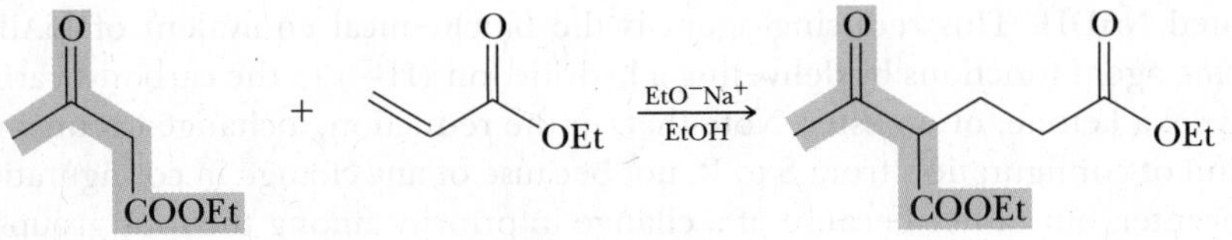

Ethyl 3-oxobutanoate (Ethyl acetoacetate)

Ethyl 2-Propenoate (Ethyl acrylate)

Recall that nucleophiles don't ordinarily add to carbon–carbon double bonds. Rather, they add to electrophiles (Section 5.2). What activates a carbon–carbon double bond for nucleophilic attack in a Michael reaction is the presence of the adjacent carbonyl group. One important contributing structure of α,β-unsaturated carbonyl compounds puts a positive charge on the β-carbon of the double bond, making it electrophilic in its reactivity:

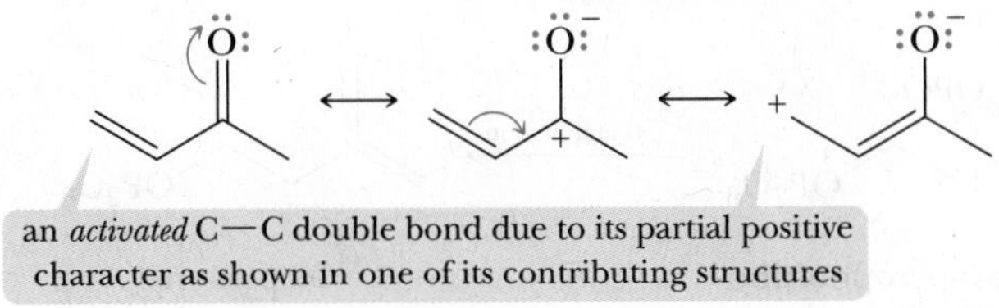

Thus, nucleophiles can add to this type of double bond, which we call "activated" for that reason.

Table 15.2 lists the most common combinations of α,β-unsaturated carbonyl compounds and nucleophiles used in Michael reactions. The most commonly used bases are metal alkoxides, pyridine, and piperidine.

TABLE 15.2 Combinations of Reagents for Effective Michael Reactions

These Types of α,β-Unsaturated Compounds Are Nucleophile Acceptors in Michael Reactions		These Types of Compounds Provide Effective Nucleophiles for Michael Reactions	
$CH_2{=}CHCH{=}O$	Aldehydes	$CH_3C(=O)\ddot{C}^{-}HC(=O)CH_3$	Enolates of β-Diketones
$CH_2{=}CHC(=O)CH_3$	Ketones	$CH_3C(=O)\ddot{C}^{-}HC(=O)OEt$	Enolates of β-Ketoesters
$CH_2{=}CHC(=O)OEt$	Esters	$EtOC(=O)\ddot{C}^{-}HC(=O)OEt$	Enolates of β-Diesters
		RNH_2, R_2NH	Amines

We can write the following general mechanism for a Michael reaction:

Mechanism

Michael Reaction—Conjugate Addition of Enolate Anions

STEP 1: Take a proton away. Treatment of H—Nu with base gives the nucleophile, Nu:⁻.

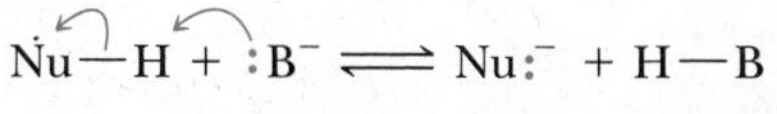

Base

STEP 2: Reaction of an electrophile and a nucleophile to form a new covalent bond. Nucleophilic addition of Nu:⁻ to the β-carbon of the conjugated system gives a resonance-stabilized enolate anion:

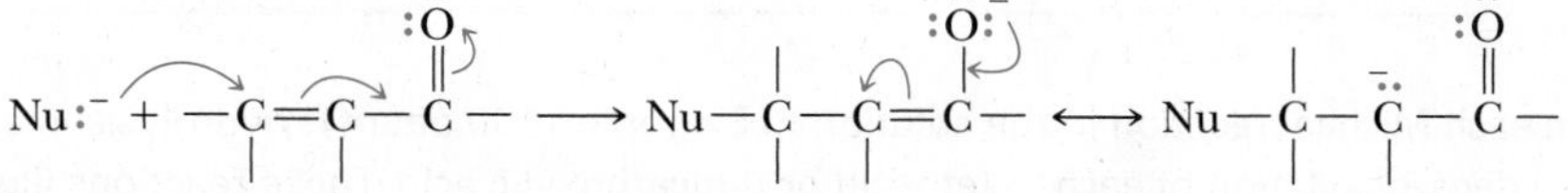

(a nucleophile) (an electrophile) A resonance-stabilized enolate anion

STEP 3: Add a proton. Proton transfer from H—B gives the enol and regenerates the base:

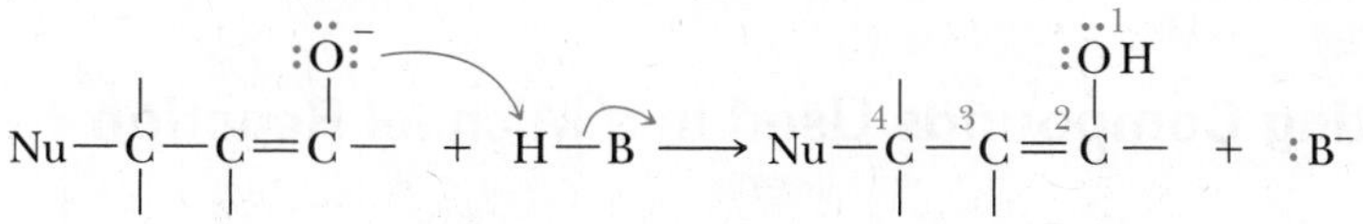

An enol
(a product of 1,4-addition)

Note that the enol formed in this step corresponds to 1,4-addition to the conjugated system of the α,β-unsaturated carbonyl compound. It is because this intermediate is formed that the Michael reaction is classified as a 1,4-, or conjugate, addition. Note also that the base, B:⁻, is regenerated, in accordance with the experimental observation that a Michael reaction requires only a catalytic amount of base rather than a molar equivalent.

STEP 4: Tautomerism (Section 12.8A) of the less stable enol form gives the more stable keto form:

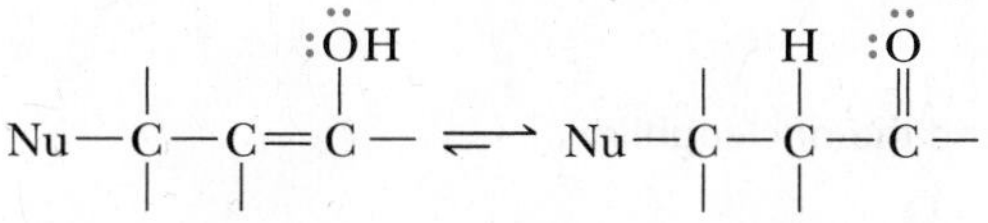

Enol form (less stable) Keto form (more stable)

EXAMPLE 15.10

Draw a structural formula for the product formed by treating each set of reactants with sodium ethoxide in ethanol under conditions of the Michael reaction:

(a)

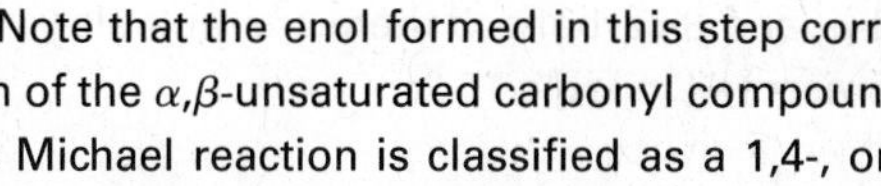

(b)

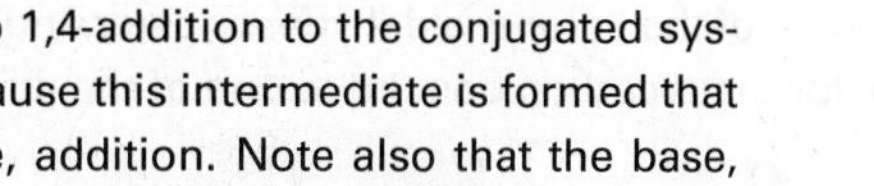

STRATEGY

The net result of a Michael reaction is the addition of a nucleophile to the β-carbon of an α,β-unsaturated carbonyl compound and the addition of a hydrogen to the α-carbon.

SOLUTION

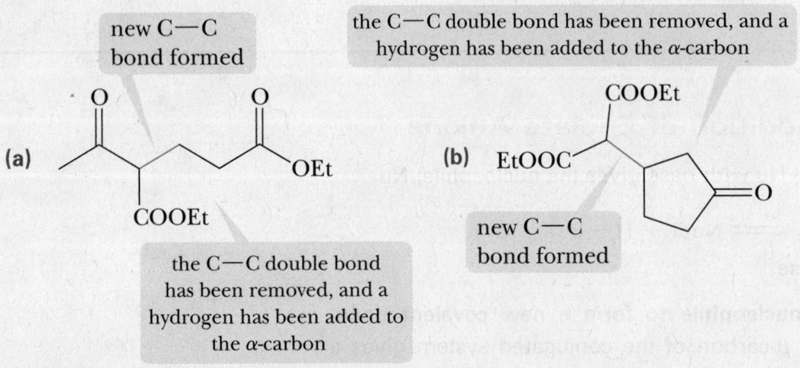
new C—C bond formed
the C—C double bond has been removed, and a hydrogen has been added to the α-carbon
(a)
O
O
OEt
COOEt
(b)
EtOOC
COOEt
O
new C—C bond formed
the C—C double bond has been removed, and a hydrogen has been added to the α-carbon

See problems 15.35, 15.36

PROBLEM 15.10

Show the product formed from each Michael reaction in the solution to Example 15.10 after (1) hydrolysis in aqueous NaOH, (2) acidification, and (3) thermal decarboxylation of each β-ketoacid or β-dicarboxylic acid. These reactions illustrate the usefulness of the Michael reaction for the synthesis of 1,5-dicarbonyl compounds.

HOW TO 15.3 Determine the Starting Compounds Used in a Michael Reaction

It will sometimes be necessary to work retrosynthetically (How To 14.2) from the product of a Michael reaction. Following are the steps for determining the starting compounds used in a Michael reaction.

(a) Locate the carbonyl of the ketone, aldehyde, or ester and identify the α- and β-carbons. If there are multiple carbonyls, look for the β-carbon bonded to one of the nucleophiles presented in Table 15.2:

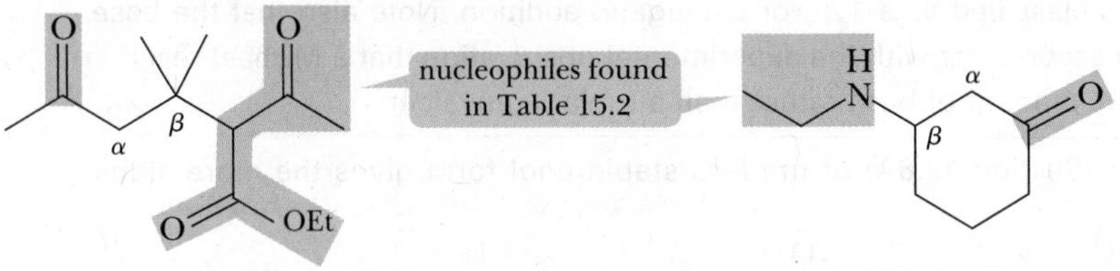
O
O
α
β
O
OEt
nucleophiles found in Table 15.2
H
N
α
β
O

(b) Erase the bond between the β-carbon and the nucleophile:

O
α
β
O
O
OEt
NH
α
β
O

(c) Draw a C—C double bond between the α- and β-carbons. The nucleophile should be drawn as negatively charged (in the case of carbon) or as a neutral amine (in the case of nitrogen).

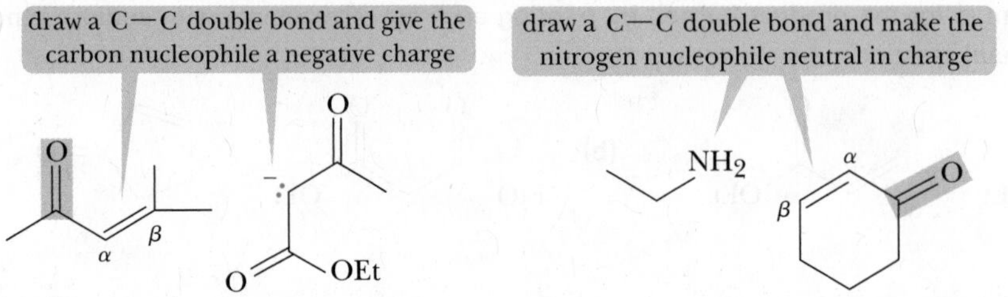
draw a C—C double bond and give the carbon nucleophile a negative charge
draw a C—C double bond and make the nitrogen nucleophile neutral in charge
O
α
β
O
O
OEt
NH2
α
β
O

EXAMPLE 15.11

Show how the series of reactions in Example 15.10 and Problem 15.10 (Michael reaction, hydrolysis, acidification, and thermal decarboxylation) can be used to prepare 2,6-heptanedione.

STRATEGY

The key is to recognize that a COOH group beta to a ketone can be lost by decarboxylation. Once you find where that COOH group might have been located, you should see which carbons of the target molecule can be derived from the carbon skeleton of ethyl acetoacetate and which carbons can be derived from an α,β-unsaturated carbonyl compound.

SOLUTION

As shown here, the target molecule can be constructed from the carbon skeletons of ethyl acetoacetate and methyl vinyl ketone:

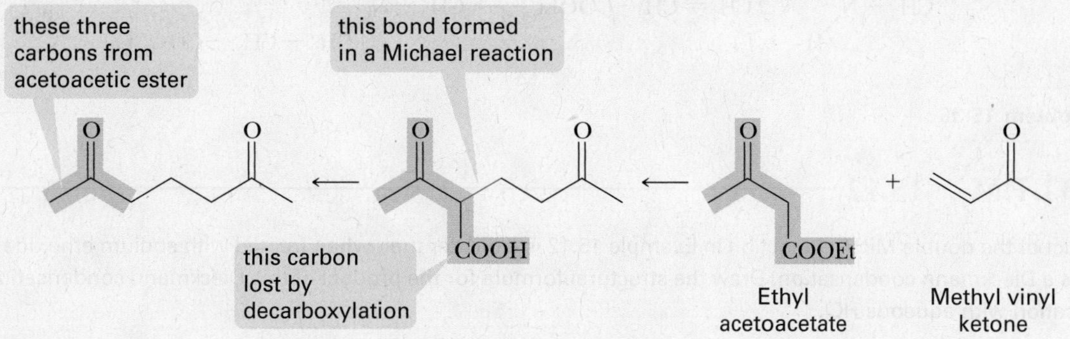

Following are the steps in their conversion to 2,6-heptanedione:

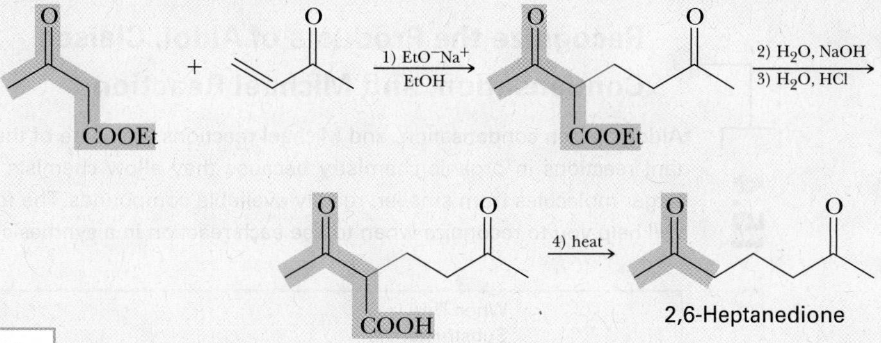

See problem 15.37

PROBLEM 15.11

Show how the sequence consisting of Michael reaction, hydrolysis, acidification, and thermal decarboxylation can be used to prepare pentanedioic acid (glutaric acid).

B. Michael Addition of Amines

As Table 15.2 shows, aliphatic amines also function as nucleophiles in Michael reactions. Diethylamine, for example, adds to methyl acrylate, as shown in the following equation:

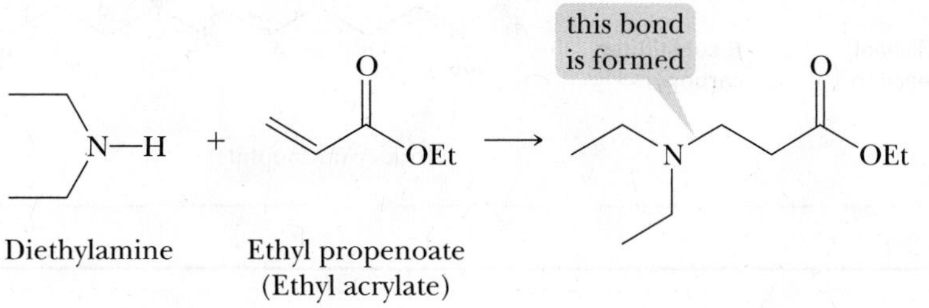

EXAMPLE 15.12

Methylamine, CH_3NH_2, has two N—H bonds, and 1 mole of methylamine undergoes Michael reaction with 2 moles of ethyl acrylate. Draw a structural formula for the product of this double Michael reaction.

STRATEGY

Perform the first Michael reaction with 1 mole of ethyl acrylate. Then treat the product of that reaction with the second mole of ethyl acrylate.

SOLUTION

$$CH_3-NH_2 + 2\,CH_2{=}CH-COOEt \longrightarrow CH_3-N(CH_2-CH_2-COOEt)_2$$

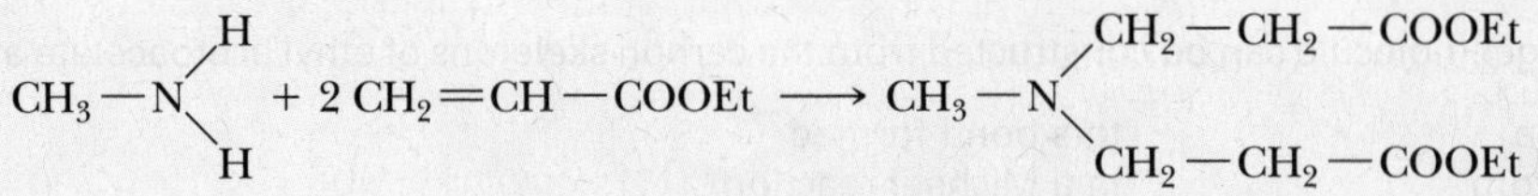

See problem 15.36

PROBLEM 15.12

The product of the double Michael reaction in Example 15.12 is a diester that, when treated with sodium ethoxide in ethanol, undergoes a Dieckmann condensation. Draw the structural formula for the product of this Dieckmann condensation followed by acidification with aqueous HCl.

HOW TO 15.4

Recognize the Products of Aldol, Claisen Condensation, and Michael Reactions

Aldol, Claisen condensation, and Michael reactions are some of the most important reactions in organic chemistry because they allow chemists to synthesize larger molecules from smaller, readily available compounds. The following table will help you to recognize when to use each reaction in a synthesis problem.

Reaction to Use	When This Substructure Is Needed in the Final Product	Example
Aldol reaction	β-hydroxy carbonyl or α,β-unsaturated carbonyl	
Claisen condensation	β-ketoester	
Michael reaction	β-substituted carbonyl	

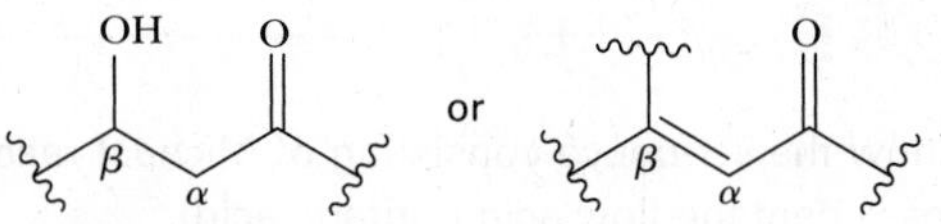

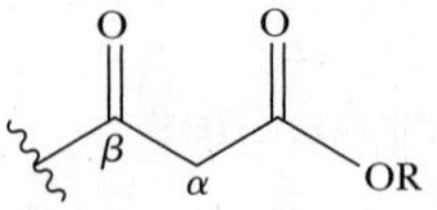

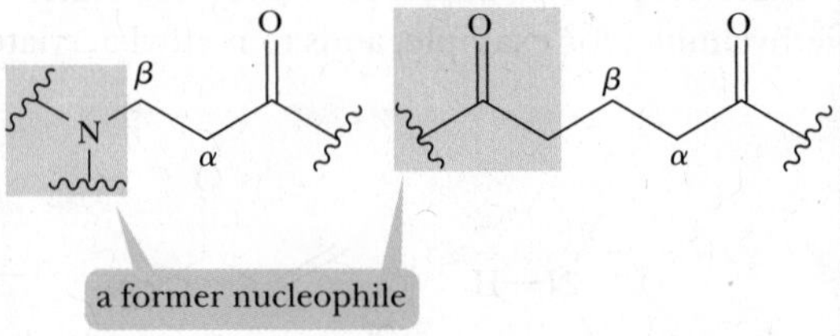

Chemical Connections 15B

ANTITUMOR COMPOUNDS: THE MICHAEL REACTION IN NATURE

K.C. Nicolaou, The Scripps Research Institute and University of California, San Diego

In 1987, a scientist happened upon a red rock (see photo) during a hike while vacationing in Texas. Thinking that there might be interesting chemicals within the organisms growing on the rock, the scientist brought the rock back to his laboratory at Wyeth (formerly Lederle Labs). It was subsequently found that a compound known as calicheamicin could be extracted from the bacteria *Micromonospora echinospora*, which was growing on the rock. The chemical turned out to be bioactive. After the compound's toxicity to cells was further researched, it was found to be among the most potent of all anticancer compounds. The mode of action of calicheamicin was elucidated, and the Michael reaction was found to play a crucial part in the mechanism for reactivity. In Step 1 of the mechanism, a trisulfide group on the molecule (a) is biochemically reduced to the anion of a thiol group. This, in turn, acts as a nucleophile and attacks the α,β-unsaturated ketone of the molecule (b). The product of this intramolecular Michael reaction (c) is thought to place great strain on the enediyne portion of calicheamicin, causing a rearrangement to occur that creates a benzene ring with two unpaired electrons (radicals) that are para to each other on the ring (d). This highly reactive structure acts to cleave both strands of DNA (Section 20.2B), which is the process that makes calicheamicin so damaging to tumor cells. By modifying the sugar unit of the calicheamicin so that it could be bonded to cancer-specific antibodies, this chemical, found by a curious chemist on vacation, has become a promising drug for cancer therapy.

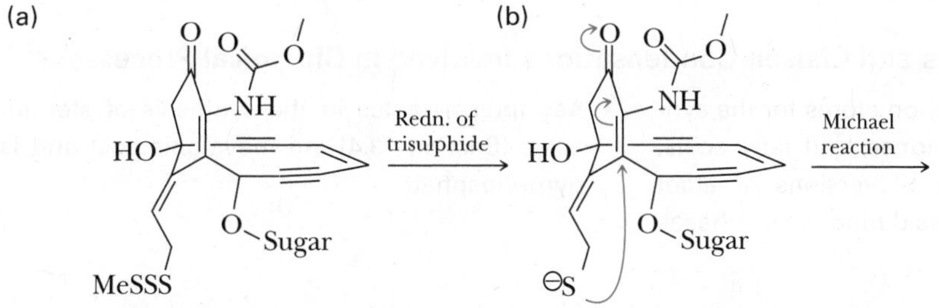

Abbreviated structure of calicheamicin

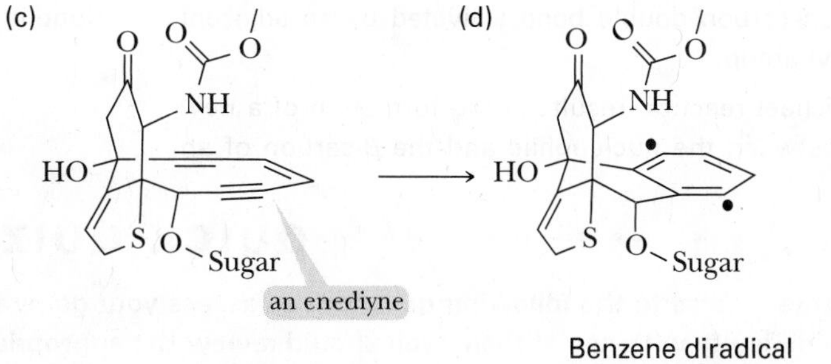

Benzene diradical (DNA cleaving agent)

Question

Provide a complete mechanism for the Michael reaction of b to produce c. Using fishhook arrows, provide a mechanism for the rearrangement of c to produce d.

SUMMARY OF KEY QUESTIONS

15.1 What Are Enolate Anions, and How Are They Formed?

- An **enolate anion** is an anion formed by the removal of an **α-hydrogen** from a carbonyl-containing compound.
- Aldehydes, ketones, and esters can be converted to their enolate anions by treatment with a metal alkoxide or other strong base.

15.2 What Is the Aldol Reaction?

- An **aldol reaction** is the addition of an enolate anion from one aldehyde or ketone to the carbonyl carbon of another aldehyde or ketone to form a **β-hydroxyaldehyde** or **β-hydroxyketone**.
- Dehydration of the product of an aldol reaction gives an **α,β-unsaturated aldehyde** or **ketone**.
- **Crossed aldol reactions** are useful only when appreciable differences in reactivity occur between the two carbonyl-containing compounds, such as when one of them has no α-hydrogens and can function only as an enolate anion acceptor.
- When both carbonyl groups are in the same molecule, aldol reaction results in the formation of a ring. These **intramolecular aldol reactions** are particularly useful for the formation of five- and six-membered rings.

15.3 What Are the Claisen and Dieckmann Condensations?

- A key step in the **Claisen condensation** is the addition of an enolate anion of one ester to a carbonyl group of another ester to form a tetrahedral carbonyl addition intermediate, followed by the collapse of the intermediate to give a β-ketoester.
- The **Dieckmann condensation** is an intramolecular Claisen condensation.

15.4 How Are Aldol Reactions and Claisen Condensations Involved in Biological Processes?

- **Acetyl-CoA** is the source of the carbon atoms for the synthesis of cholesterol, steroid hormones, and fatty acids. Various enzymes catalyze biological versions of aldol reactions and Claisen condensations during the syntheses of these compounds.
- Key intermediates in the synthesis of steroids and bile acids (Section 19.4) are mevalonic acid and isopentenyl pyrophosphate.

15.5 What Is the Michael Reaction?

- The **Michael reaction** is the addition of a nucleophile to a carbon–carbon double bond activated by an adjacent carbonyl group.
- The Michael reaction results in the formation of a new bond between the nucleophile and the β-carbon of an α,β-unsaturated carbonyl compound. The C—C double bond is converted to a C—C single bond in the reaction.

QUICK QUIZ

Answer true or false to the following questions to assess your general knowledge of the concepts in this chapter. If you have difficulty with any of them, you should review the appropriate section in the chapter (shown in parentheses) before attempting the more challenging end-of-chapter problems.

1. All ketones and aldehydes with a carbon atom alpha to the carbonyl group can be converted to an enolate anion by treatment with a catalytic amount of base. (15.1)
2. A Dieckmann condensation favors seven- and eight-membered rings over four-, five-, and six-membered rings. (15.3)
3. An intramolecular aldol reaction favors five- and six-membered rings over four-, seven-, and eight-membered rings. (15.2)
4. A hydrogen that is alpha to two carbonyls is less acidic than a hydrogen that is alpha to only one carbonyl. (15.1)

5. The product of a Claisen condensation is a β-hydroxyester. (15.3)
6. The mechanism of a Michael reaction involves enol–keto tautomerization. (15.5)
7. An enolate anion can act as a nucleophile. (15.1)
8. An aldol reaction involves the reaction of an enolate anion with a ketone or an aldehyde. (15.2)
9. The product of an aldol reaction is a β-hydroxyester. (15.2)
10. Aldol reactions and Claisen condensations can be catalyzed by enzymes. (15.4)
11. A crossed aldol reaction is most effective when one of the carbonyl compounds is more reactive toward nucleophilic addition and cannot form an enolate anion. (15.2)
12. Hydrogen atoms alpha to a carbonyl are many times more acidic than vinyl or alkyl hydrogens. (15.1)
13. The Claisen condensation is a reaction between an enolate anion and an ester. (15.3)
14. The α-hydrogen of an ester is more acidic than the α-hydrogen of a ketone. (15.3)
15. An enolate anion is stabilized by resonance. (15.1)
16. All carbonyl compounds with an alpha hydrogen can be converted to an enolate anion by treatment with a catalytic amount of base. (15.1)
17. A crossed Claisen condensation is most effective when one of the carbonyl compounds can only function as an enolate anion acceptor. (15.3)
18. An enolate anion can participate in a Michael reaction. (15.5)
19. The product of an aldol reaction can be dehydrated to yield an α,β-unsaturated carbonyl compound. (15.2)
20. The Michael reaction is the reaction of a nucleophile with the β-carbon of an α,β-unsaturated carbonyl compound. (15.5)
21. An enolate anion can act as a base. (15.1)
22. The product of a Claisen condensation can be hydrolyzed and decarboxylated to form a ketone. (15.3)
23. An amine can participate in a Michael reaction. (15.5)

Answers: (1) F (2) F (3) T (4) F (5) F (6) T (7) T (8) T (9) F (10) T (11) T (12) T (13) T (14) F (15) T (16) F (17) T (18) T (19) T (20) T (21) T (22) T (23) T

Detailed explanations for many of these answers can be found in the accompanying Solutions Manual.

KEY REACTIONS

1. The Aldol Reaction (Section 15.2B)

The aldol reaction involves the nucleophilic addition of an enolate anion from one aldehyde or ketone to the carbonyl carbon of another aldehyde or ketone to give a β-hydroxyaldehyde or β-hydroxyketone:

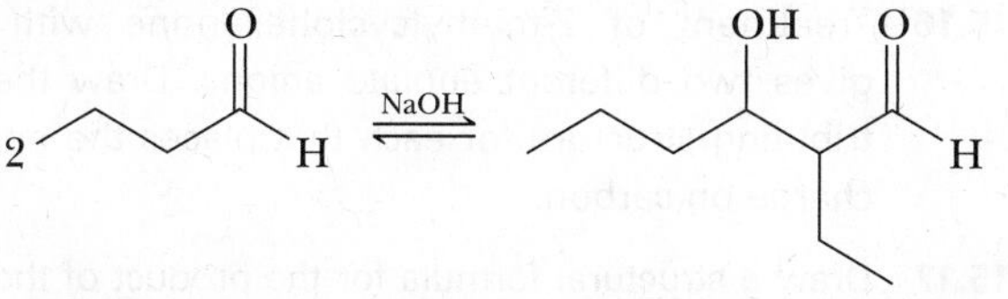

2. Dehydration of the Product of an Aldol Reaction (Section 15.2)

Dehydration of the β-hydroxyaldehyde or ketone from an aldol reaction occurs readily and gives an α,β-unsaturated aldehyde or ketone:

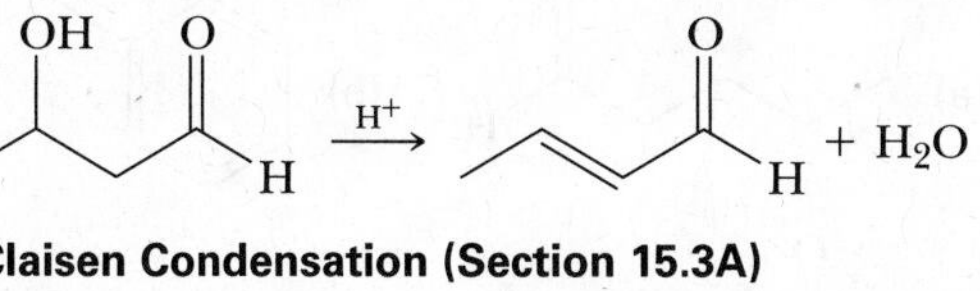

3. The Claisen Condensation (Section 15.3A)

The product of a Claisen condensation is a β-ketoester:

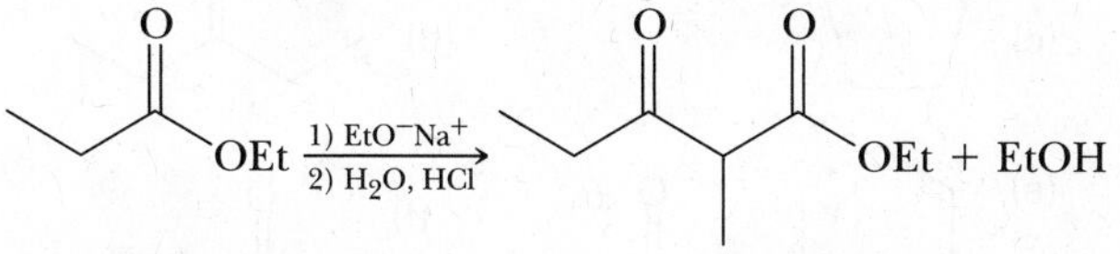

Condensation occurs by nucleophilic acyl substitution in which the attacking nucleophile is the enolate anion of an ester.

4. The Dieckmann Condensation (Section 15.3B)

An intramolecular Claisen condensation is called a Dieckmann condensation:

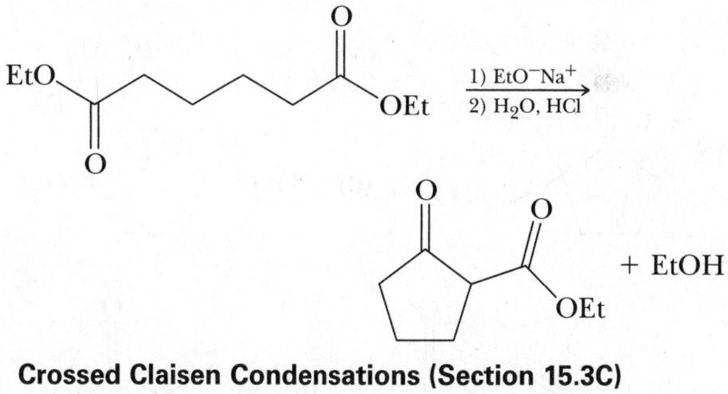

5. Crossed Claisen Condensations (Section 15.3C)

Crossed Claisen condensations are useful only when an appreciable difference exists in the reactivity between the two esters. Such is the case when an ester that has no α-hydrogens can function only as an enolate anion acceptor:

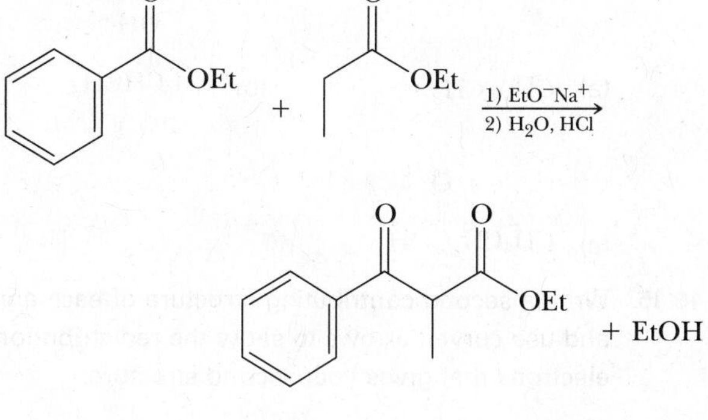

6. Hydrolysis and Decarboxylation of β-Ketoesters (Section 15.3D)

Hydrolysis of the ester, followed by decarboxylation of the resulting β-ketoacid, gives a ketone and carbon dioxide:

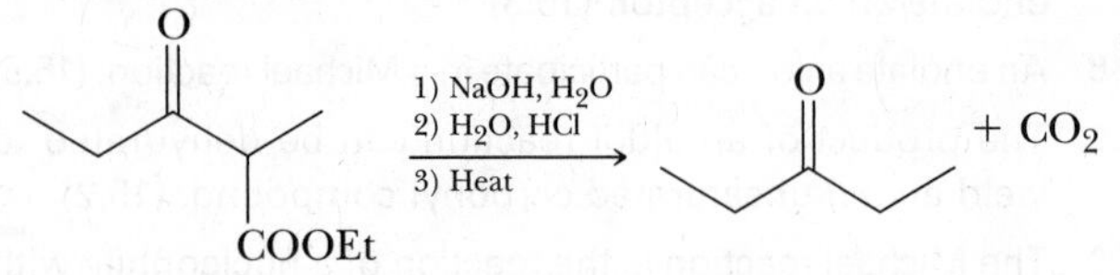

7. The Michael Reaction (Section 15.5)

Attack of a nucleophile at the β-carbon of an α,β-unsaturated carbonyl compound results in conjugate addition:

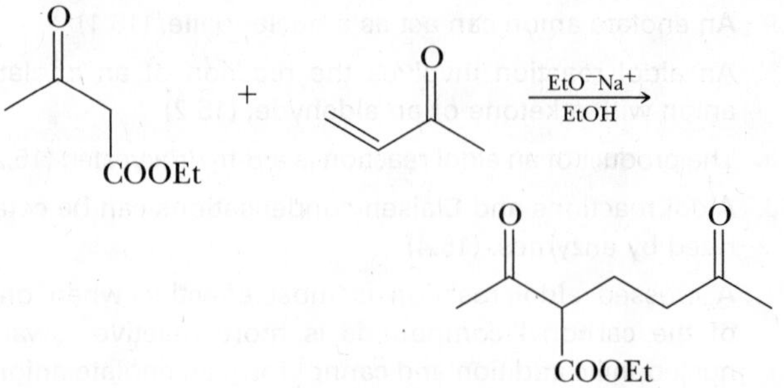

PROBLEMS

A problem marked with an asterisk indicates an applied "real-world" problem. Answers to problems whose numbers are printed in blue are given in Appendix D.

Sections 15.1 and 15.2 The Aldol Reaction

15.13 Identify the most acidic hydrogen(s) in each compound: **(See Example 15.1)**

(a) 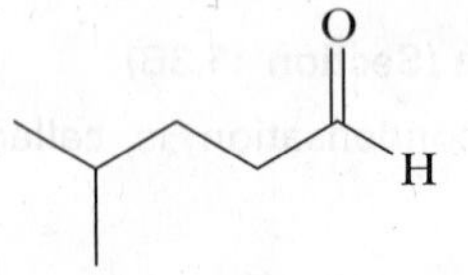

(b) 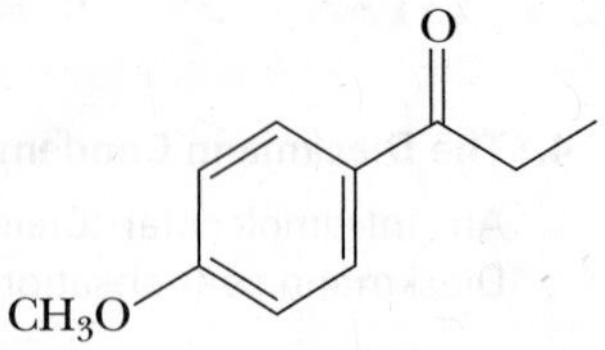

(c) 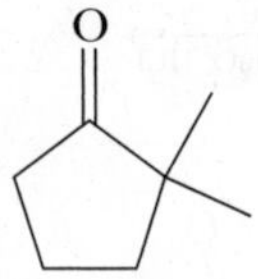

(d) 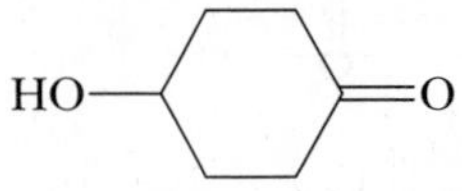

(e) 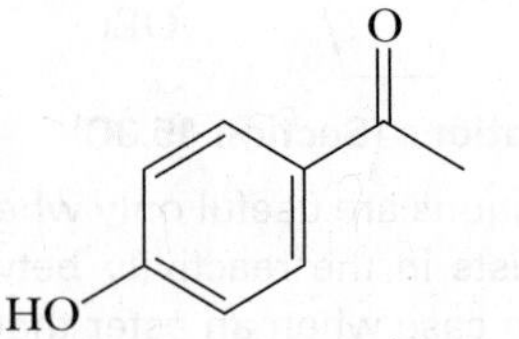

(f) 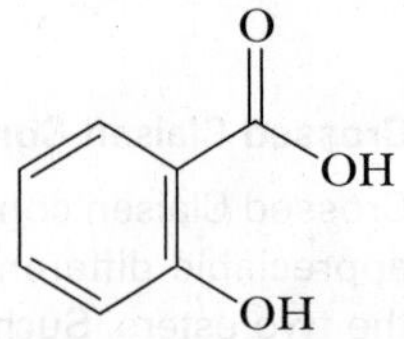

15.14 Estimate the pK_a of each compound and arrange them in order of increasing acidity:

(a) $CH_3\overset{\overset{O}{\|}}{C}CH_3$ (b) $CH_3\overset{\overset{OH}{|}}{C}HCH_3$

(c) $CH_3CH_2\overset{\overset{O}{\|}}{C}OH$

15.15 Write a second contributing structure of each anion, and use curved arrows to show the redistribution of electrons that gives your second structure:

(a) $CH_3CH_2\overset{\overset{:\ddot{O}:^-}{|}}{C}{=}CHCH_3$

(b) 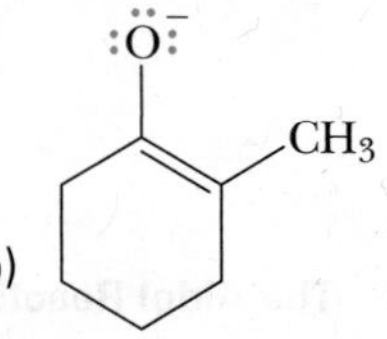

(c) 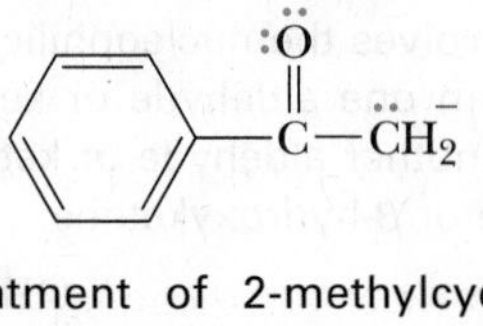

15.16 Treatment of 2-methylcyclohexanone with base gives two different enolate anions. Draw the contributing structure for each that places the negative charge on carbon.

15.17 Draw a structural formula for the product of the aldol reaction of each compound and for the α,β-unsaturated aldehyde or ketone formed by dehydration of each aldol product: **(See Examples 15.2, 15.3)**

(a) 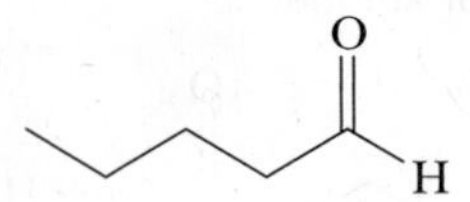

(b) 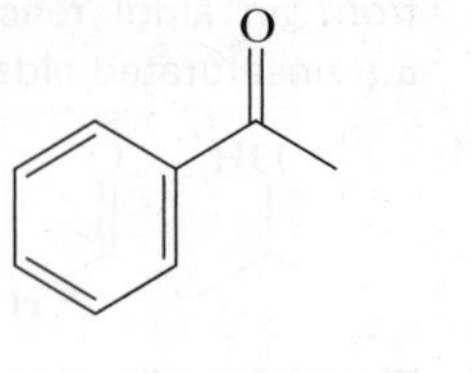

(c) 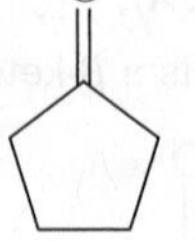

(d) 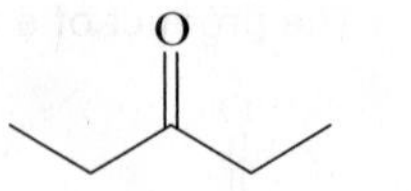

(e) 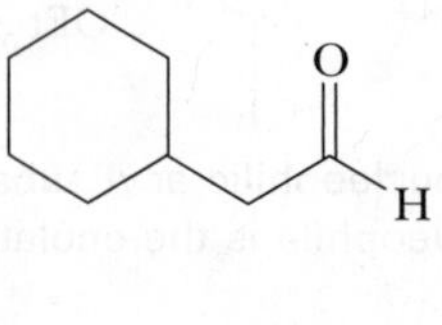

(f) 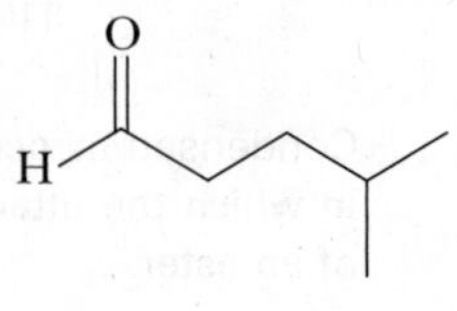

15.18 Draw a structural formula for the product of each crossed aldol reaction and for the compound formed by dehydration of each aldol product: **(See Examples 15.3, 15.4)**

(a) $(CH_3)_3\overset{O}{\overset{\|}{C}}H + CH_3\overset{O}{\overset{\|}{C}}CH_3$

(b) 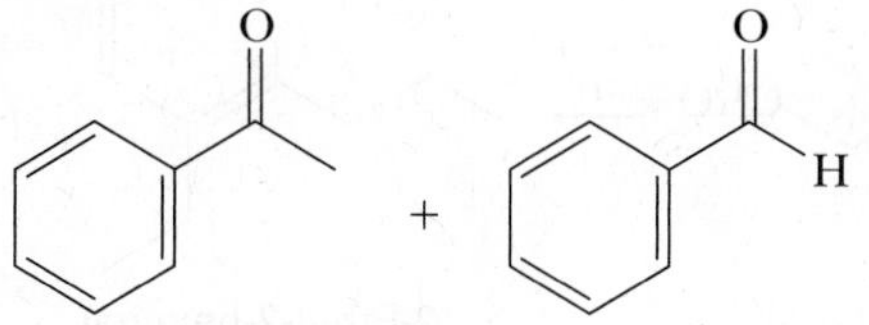

(c) 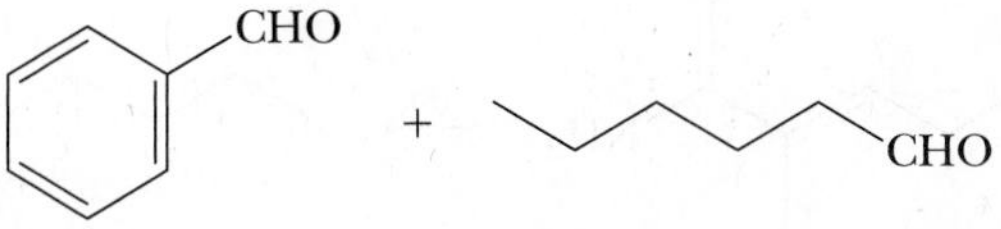

(d) 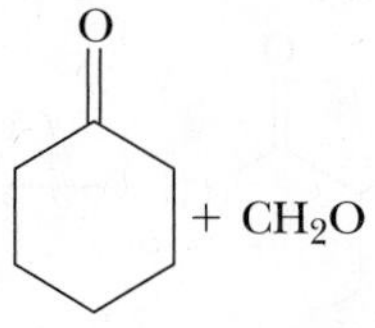

15.19 When a 1:1 mixture of acetone and 2-butanone is treated with base, six aldol products are possible. Draw a structural formula for each. **(See Example 15.4)**

Acetone 2-Butanone

15.20 Show how to prepare each α,β-unsaturated ketone by an aldol reaction followed by dehydration of the aldol product: **(See Examples 15.2, 15.3)**

(a) 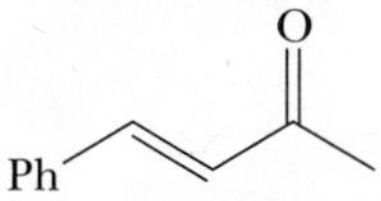

(b) 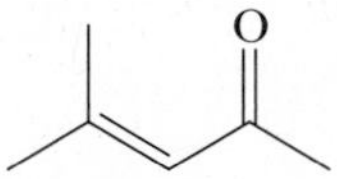

15.21 Show how to prepare each α,β-unsaturated aldehyde by an aldol reaction followed by dehydration of the aldol product: **(See Examples 15.2, 15.3)**

(a) 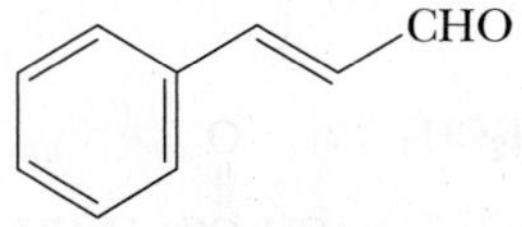

(b) 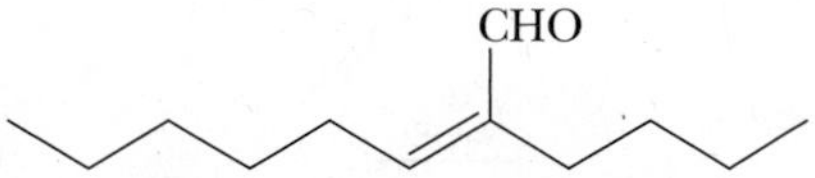

15.22 When treated with base, the following compound undergoes an intramolecular aldol reaction, followed by dehydration, to give a product containing a ring (yield 78%): **(See Examples 15.3, 15.5)**

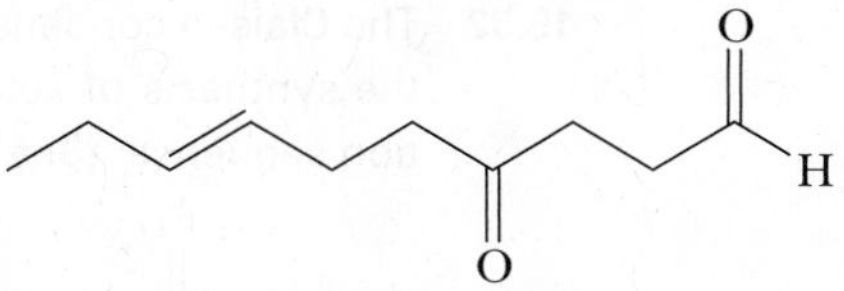

$\xrightarrow{\text{base}} C_{10}H_{14}O + H_2O$

Propose a structural formula for this product.

15.23 Propose a structural formula for the compound with the molecular formula $C_6H_{10}O_2$ that undergoes an aldol reaction followed by dehydration to give this α,β-unsaturated aldehyde: **(See Examples 15.3, 15.5)**

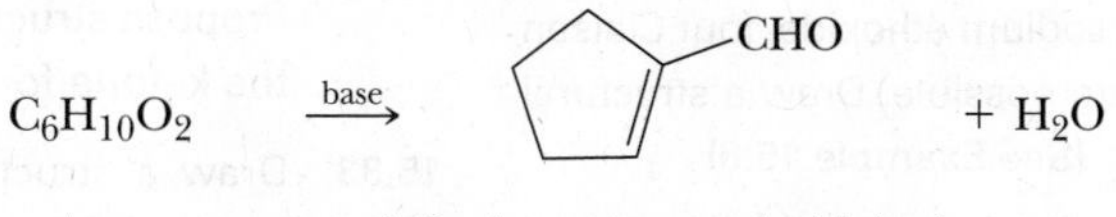

1-Cyclopentenecarbaldehyde

15.24 Show how to bring about this conversion: **(See Examples 15.3, 15.5)**

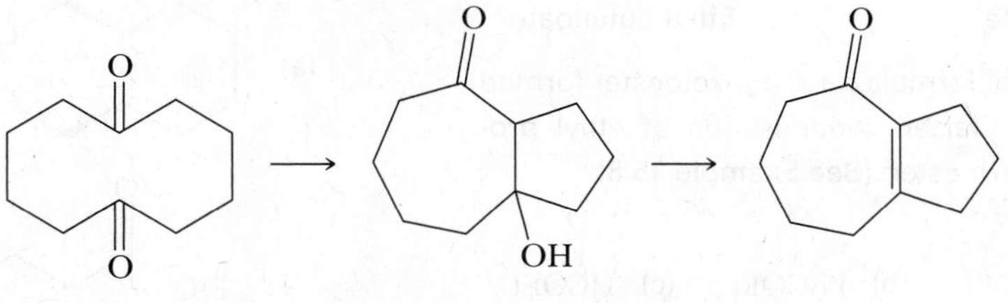

***15.25** Oxanamide, a mild sedative, is synthesized from butanal in these five steps:

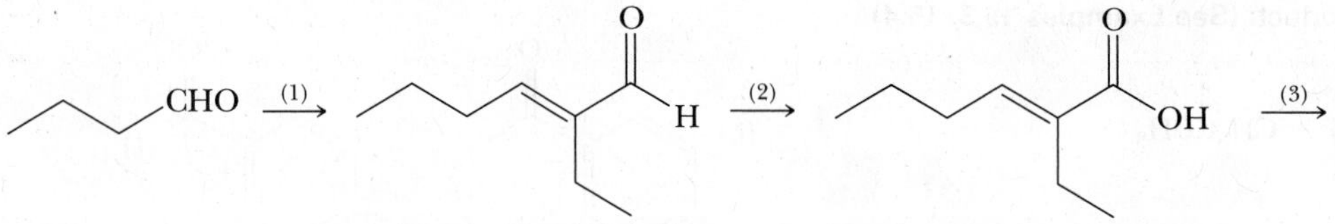

Butanal — 2-Ethyl-2-hexenal — 2-Ethyl-2-hexenoic acid

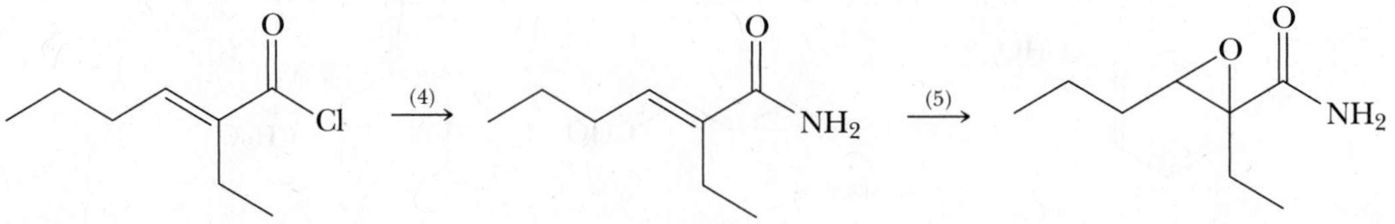

2-Ethyl-2-hexenoyl chloride — 2-Ethyl-2-hexenamide — Oxanamide

(a) Show reagents and experimental conditions that might be used to bring about each step in this synthesis.

(b) How many stereocenters are in oxanamide? How many stereoisomers are possible for oxanamide?

15.26 Propose structural formulas for compounds A and B:

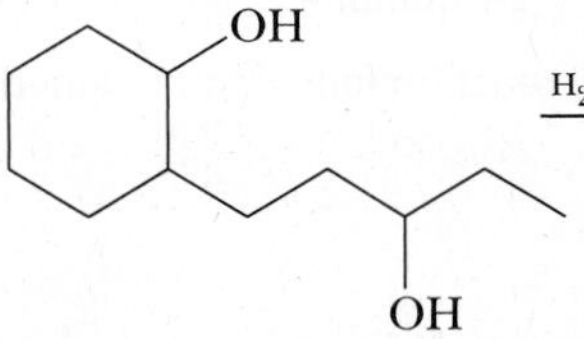

$\xrightarrow{H_2CrO_4}$ A($C_{11}H_{18}O_2$) $\xrightarrow[EtOH]{EtO^-Na^+}$ B($C_{11}H_{16}O$)

Section 15.3 The Claisen and Dieckmann Condensations

15.27 Show the product of the Claisen condensation of each ester: **(See Example 15.6)**

(a) 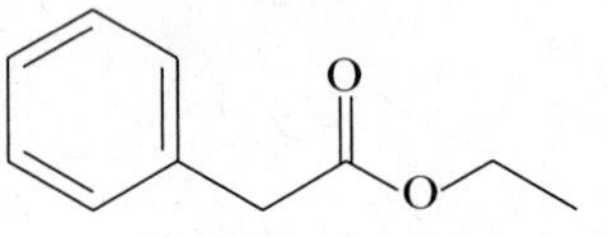 $\xrightarrow{NaOEt}$

(b) 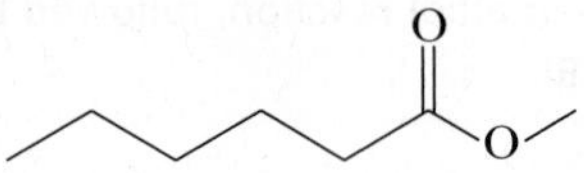 $\xrightarrow{NaOCH_3}$

(c) 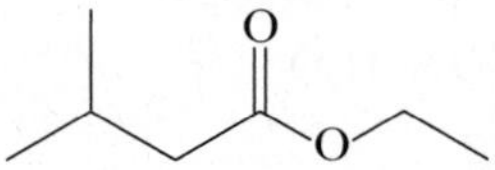 $\xrightarrow{NaOEt}$

15.28 Draw a structural formula for the product of saponification, acidification, and decarboxylation of each β-ketoester formed in Problem 15.27. **(See Example 15.9)**

15.29 When a 1:1 mixture of ethyl propanoate and ethyl butanoate is treated with sodium ethoxide, four Claisen condensation products are possible. Draw a structural formula for each product. **(See Example 15.8)**

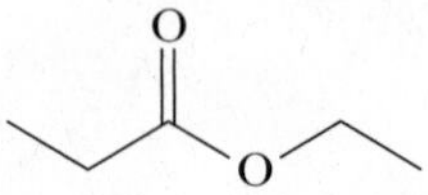

Ethyl propanoate

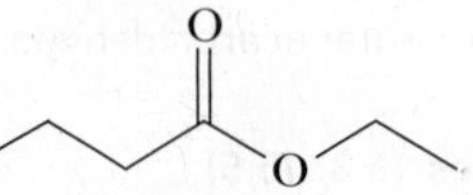

Ethyl butanoate

15.30 Draw a structural formula for the β-ketoester formed in the crossed Claisen condensation of ethyl propanoate with each ester: **(See Example 15.8)**

(a) $EtO\overset{O}{\overset{\|}{C}}-\overset{O}{\overset{\|}{C}}OEt$ (b) $Ph\overset{O}{\overset{\|}{C}}OEt$ (c) $H\overset{O}{\overset{\|}{C}}OEt$

15.31 Complete the equation for this crossed Claisen condensation: **(See Example 15.8)**

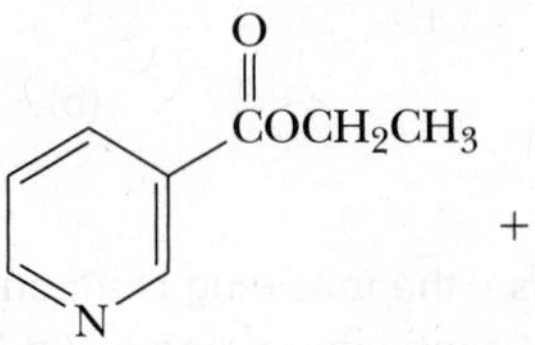

$+ CH_3\overset{O}{\overset{\|}{C}}OCH_2CH_3 \xrightarrow[2)\ H_2O,\ HCl]{1)\ EtO^-Na^+}$

15.32 The Claisen condensation can be used as one step in the synthesis of ketones, as illustrated by this reaction sequence: **(See Example 15.9)**

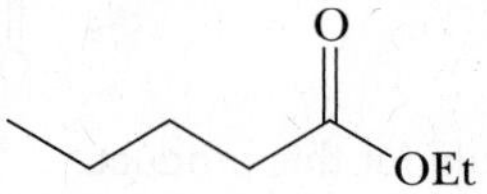

$\xrightarrow[2)\ HCl,\ H_2O]{1)\ EtO^-Na^+}$ A $\xrightarrow[heat]{3)\ NaOH,\ H_2O}$

B $\xrightarrow[5)\ heat]{4)\ HCl,\ H_2O}$ $C_9H_{18}O$

Propose structural formulas for compounds A, B, and the ketone formed in the sequence.

15.33 Draw a structural formula for the product of treating each diester with sodium ethoxide followed by acidification with HCl (*Hint:* These are Dieckmann condensations): **(See Example 15.7)**

(a) 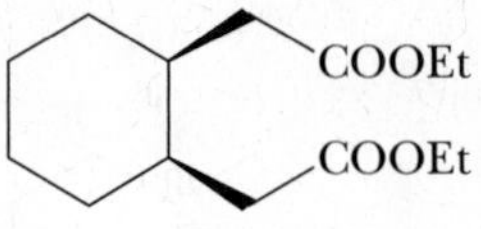

(b) 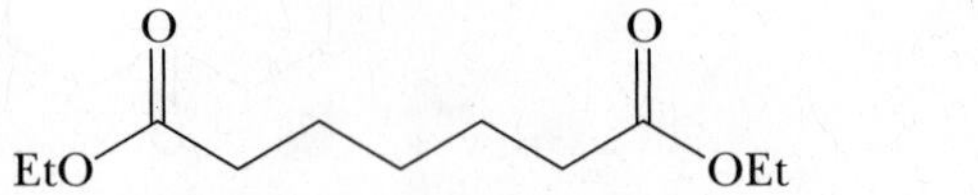

15.34 Claisen condensation between diethyl phthalate and ethyl acetate, followed by saponification, acidification, and decarboxylation, forms a diketone, $C_9H_6O_2$. Propose structural formulas for compounds A, B, and the diketone: **(See Example 15.9)**

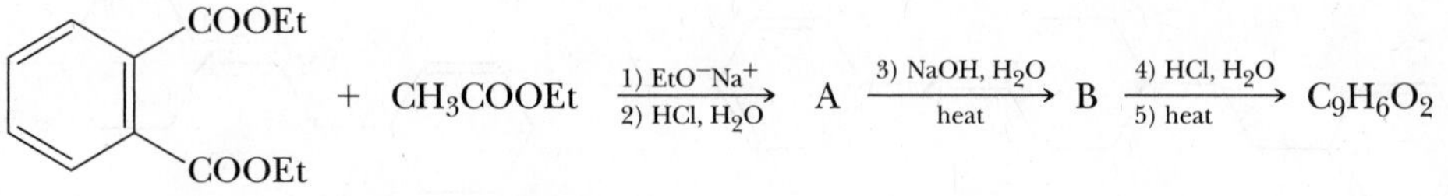

Diethyl phthalate   Ethyl acetate

***15.35** The rodenticide and insecticide pindone is synthesized by the following sequence of reactions: **(See Example 15.10)**

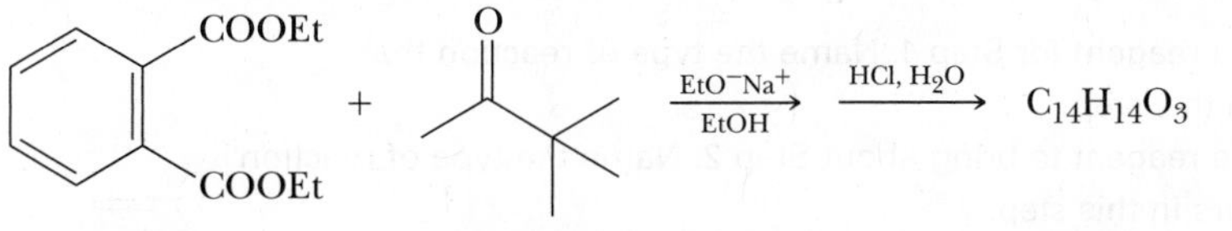

Diethyl phthalate   3,3-Dimethyl-2-butanone   Pindone

Propose a structural formula for pindone.

Section 15.5 The Michael Reaction

15.36 Show the product of the Michael reaction of each α,β-unsaturated carbonyl compound: **(See Examples 15.10, 15.12)**

(a)

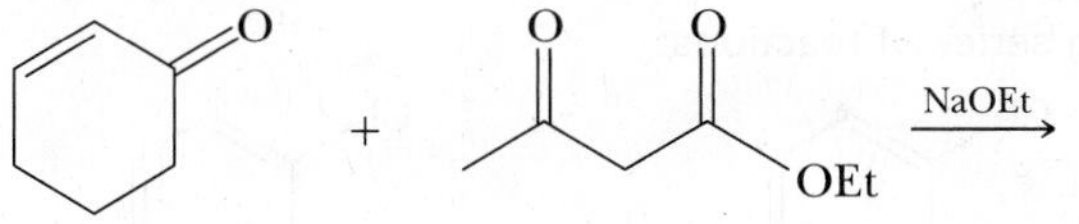

(b)

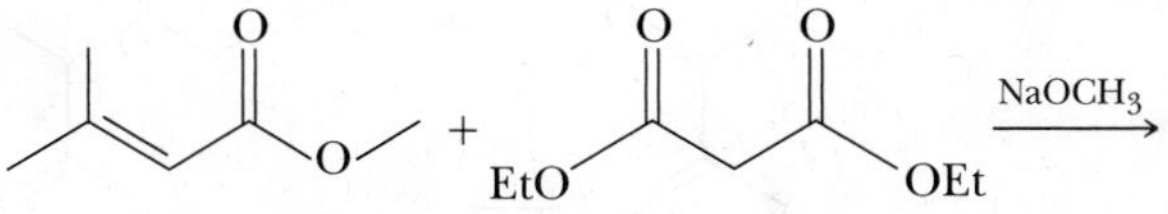

(c)

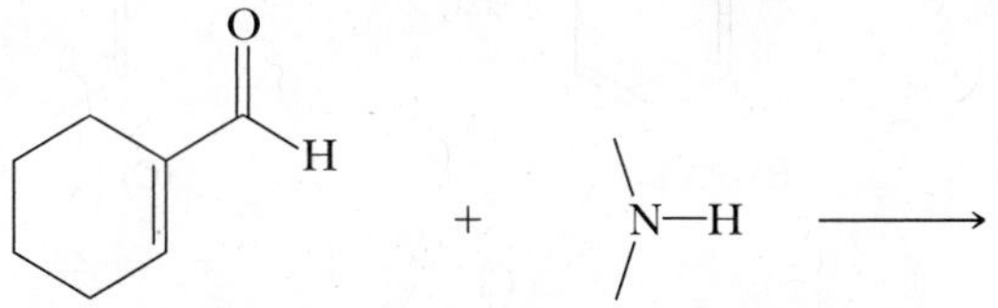

***15.37** Show the outcomes of subjecting the Michael reaction products in Problems 15.36a and 15.36b to hydrolysis, followed by acidification, followed by thermal decarboxylation. **(See Example 15.11)**

***15.38** The classic synthesis of the steroid cortisone, a drug used to treat some types of allergies, involves a Michael reaction in which 1-penten-3-one and the cyclic compound shown are treated with NaOH in the solvent dioxane. Provide a structure for the product of this reaction.

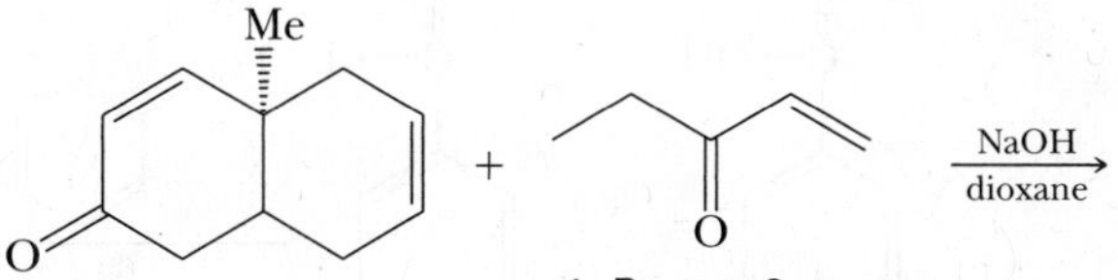

1 -Penten-3-one

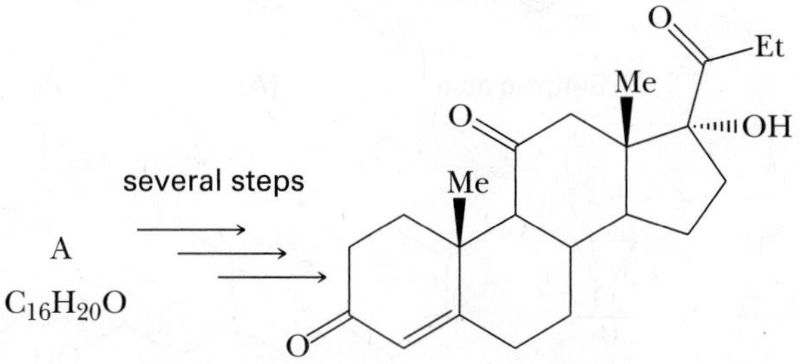

Cortisone

Synthesis

***15.39** Fentanyl is a nonopoid (nonmorphinelike) analgesic used for the relief of severe pain. It is approximately 50 times more potent in humans than morphine itself. One synthesis for fentanyl begins with 2-phenylethanamine:

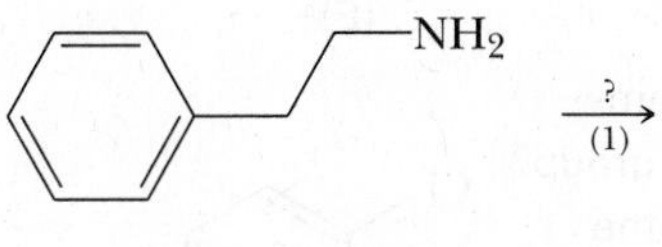

2-Phenylethanamine

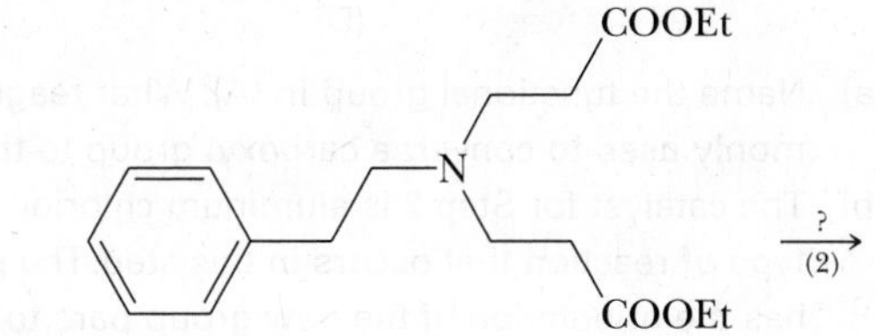

(A)

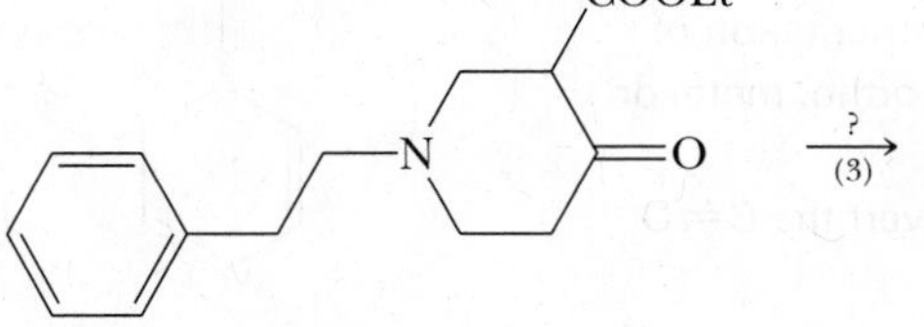

(B)

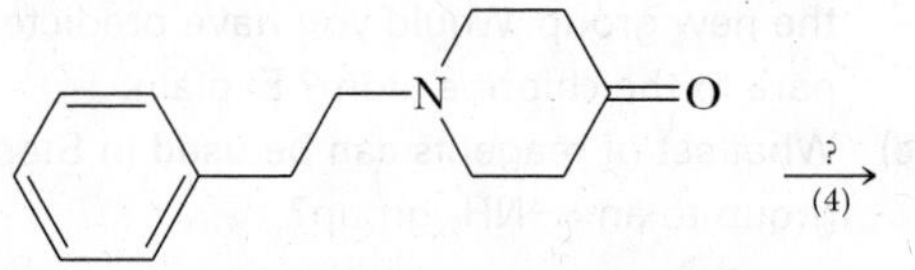

(C)

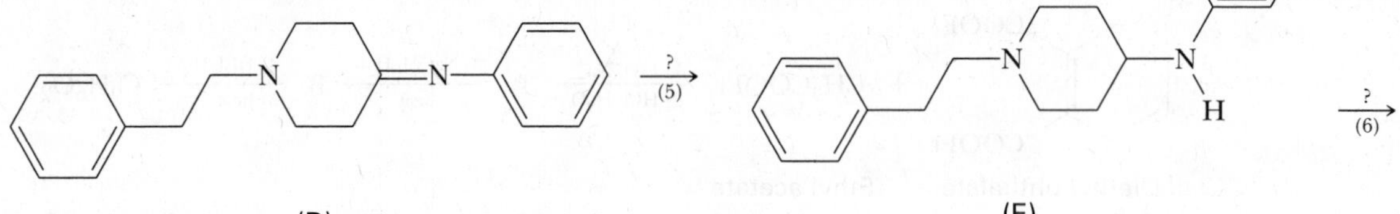

(D) (E)

(a) Propose a reagent for Step 1. Name the type of reaction that occurs in this step.
(b) Propose a reagent to bring about Step 2. Name the type of reaction that occurs in this step.
(c) Propose a series of reagents that will bring about Step 3.
(d) Propose a reagent for Step 4. Identify the imine (Schiff base) part of Compound D.
(e) Propose a reagent to bring about Step 5.
(f) Propose two different reagents, either of which will bring about Step 6.
(g) Is fentanyl chiral? Explain.

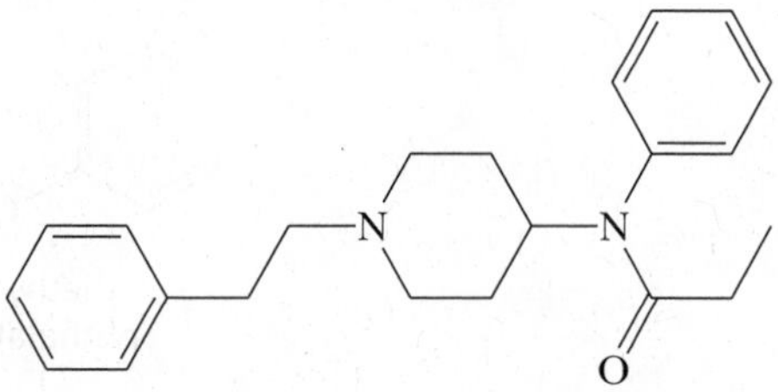

Fentanyl

***15.40** Meclizine is an antiemetic. (It helps prevent or at least lessen the vomiting associated with motion sickness, including seasickness.) Among the names of the over-the-counter preparations of meclizine are Bonine®, Sea-Legs, Antivert®, and Navicalm®. Meclizine can be produced by the following series of reactions:

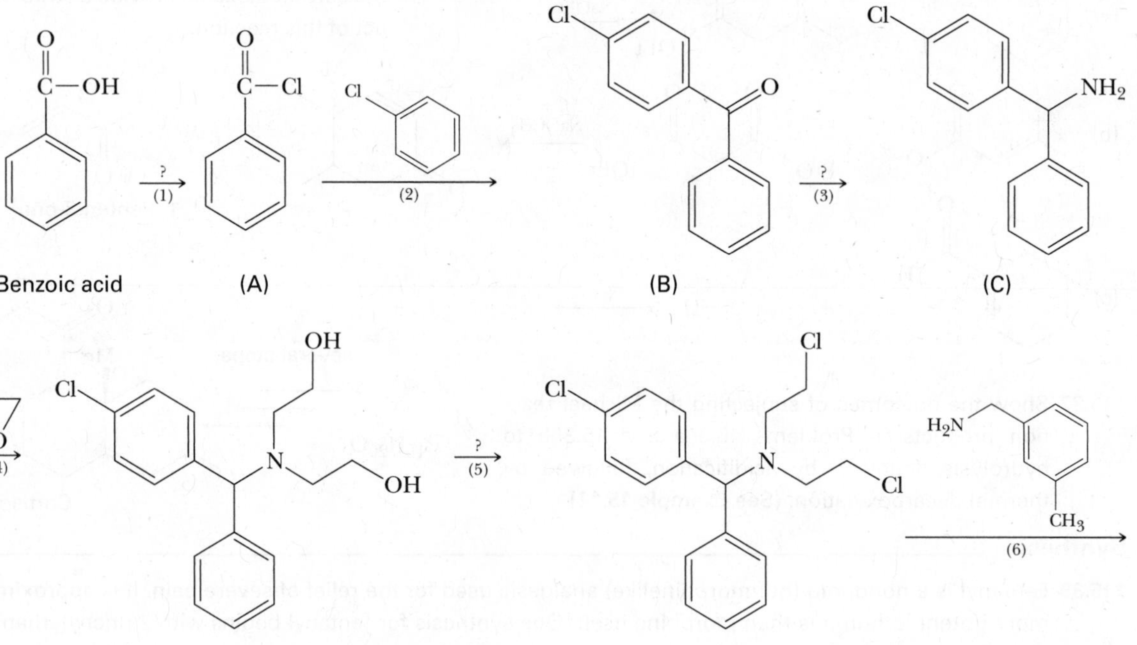

Benzoic acid (A) (B) (C)

(D) (E)

(a) Name the functional group in (A). What reagent is most commonly used to convert a carboxyl group to this functional group?
(b) The catalyst for Step 2 is aluminum chloride, $AlCl_3$. Name the type of reaction that occurs in this step. The product shown here has the orientation of the new group para to the chlorine atom of chlorobenzene. Suppose you were not told the orientation of the new group. Would you have predicted it to be ortho, meta, or para to the chlorine atom? Explain.
(c) What set of reagents can be used in Step 3 to convert the C=O group to an —NH_2 group?

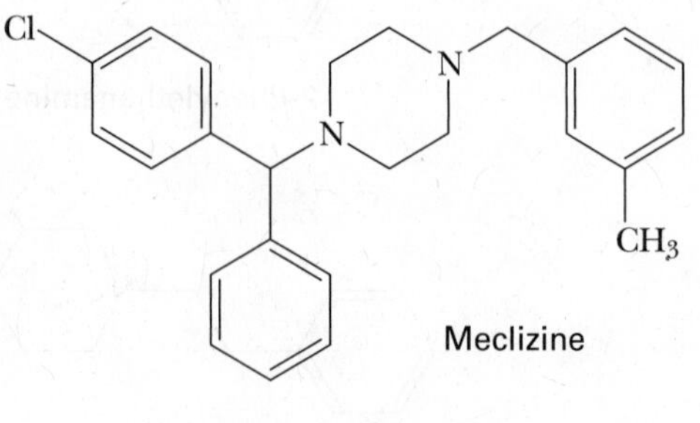

Meclizine

(d) The reagent used in Step 4 is the cyclic ether ethylene oxide. Most ethers are quite unreactive to nucleophiles such as the 1° amine in this step. Ethylene oxide, however, is an exception to this generalization. What is it about ethylene oxide that makes it so reactive toward ring-opening reactions with nucleophiles?

(e) What reagent can be used in Step 5 to convert each 1° alcohol to a 1° halide?

(f) Step 6 is a double nucleophilic displacement. Which mechanism is more likely for this reaction, S_N1 or S_N2? Explain.

***15.41** 2-Ethyl-1-hexanol is used for the synthesis of the sunscreen octyl *p*-methoxycinnamate. (See Chemical Connections 14A.) This primary alcohol can be synthesized from butanal by the following series of steps:

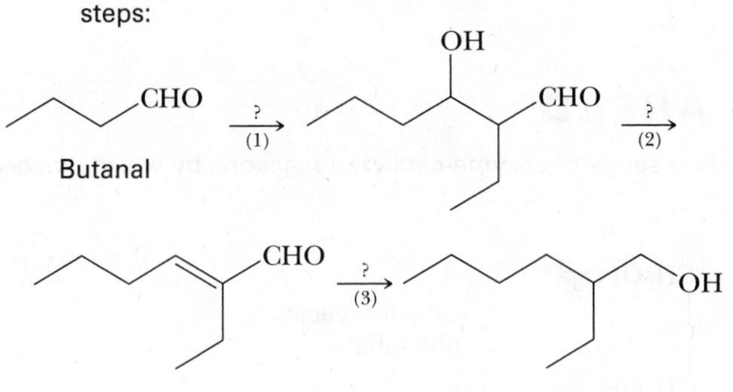

Butanal

2-Ethyl-1-hexanol

(a) Propose a reagent to bring about Step 1. What name is given to this type of reaction?

(b) Propose a reagent for Step 2.

(c) Propose a reagent for Step 3.

(d) Following is a structural formula for the commercial sunscreening ingredient:

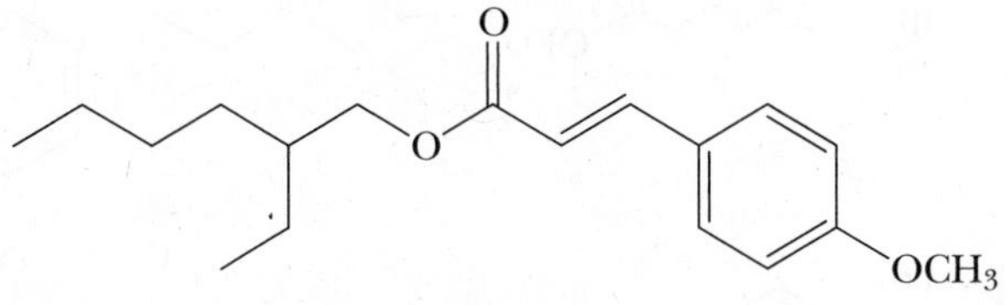

Octyl *p*-methoxycinnamate

What carboxylic acid and alcohol would you use to form this ester? How would you bring about the esterification reaction?

CHEMICAL TRANSFORMATIONS

15.42 Test your cumulative knowledge of the reactions learned thus far by completing the following chemical transformations. *Note:* Most will require more than one step.

(a) 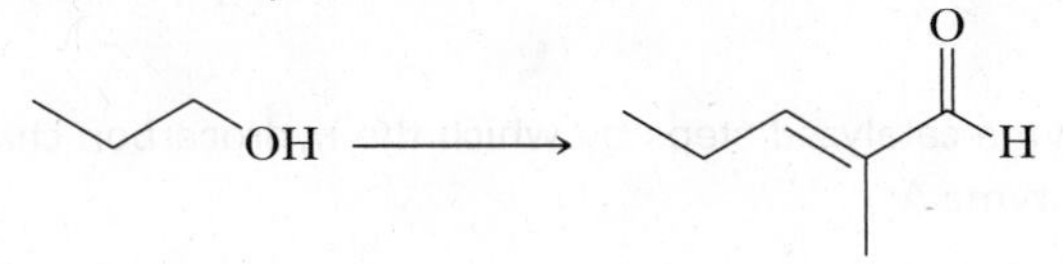

(b) 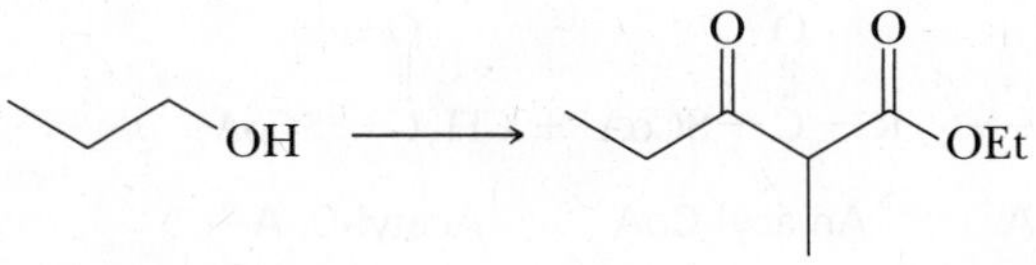

(c) 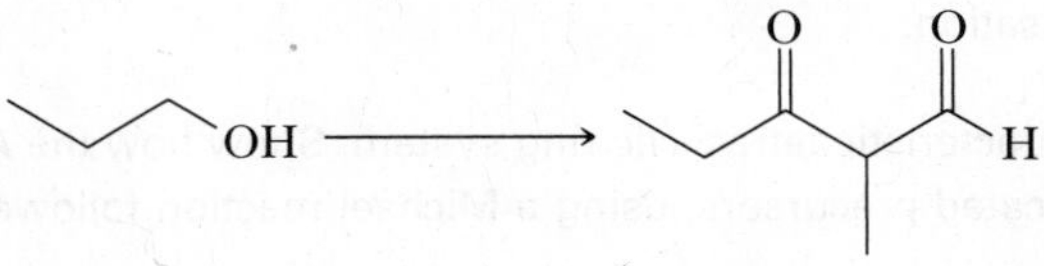

(d) 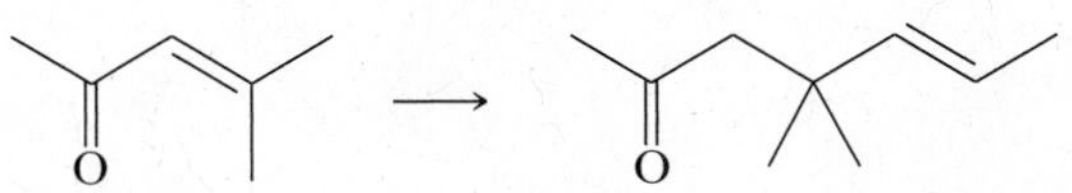

(e) 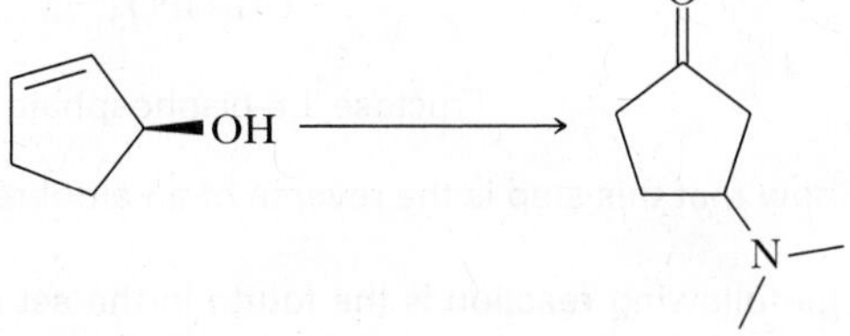

(f) 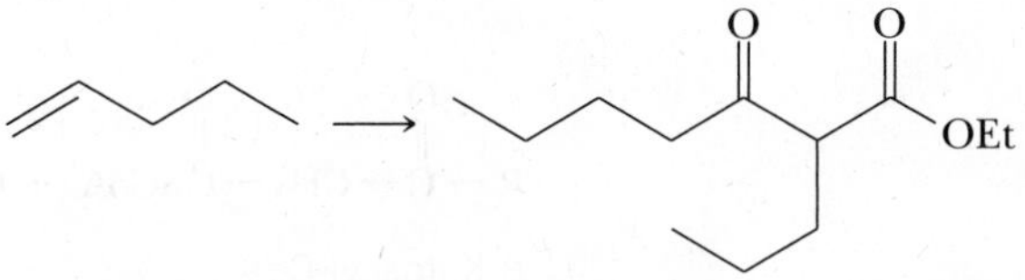

(g) 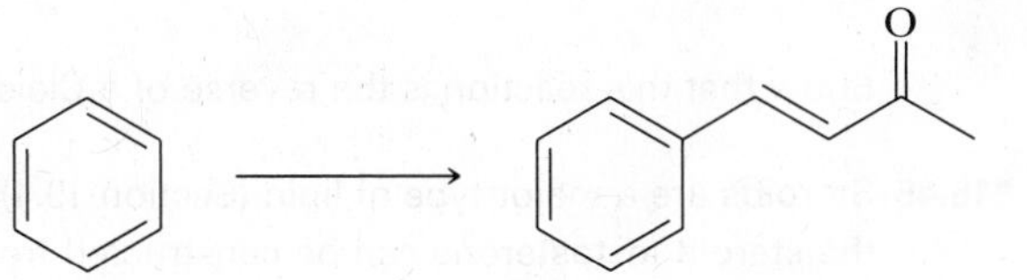

(h) 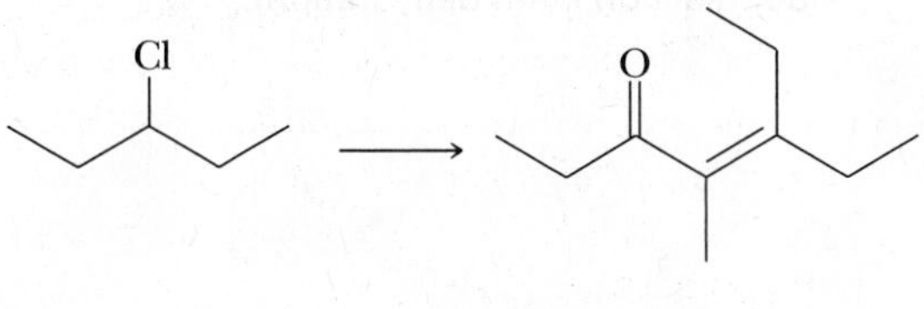

(i) 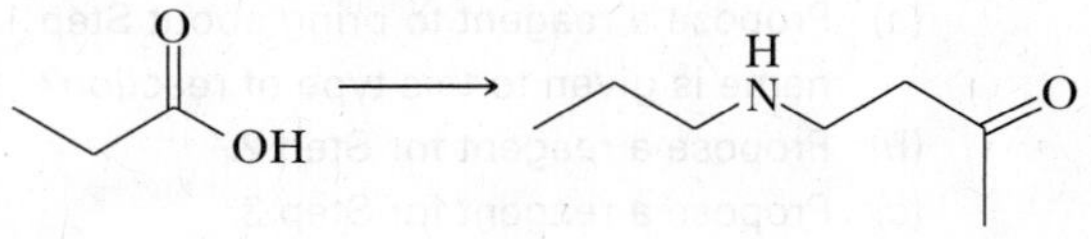

(l) 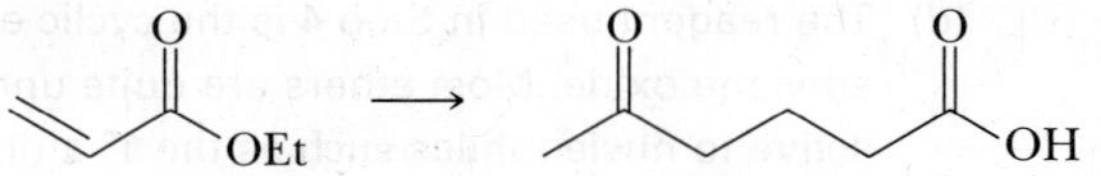

(j) 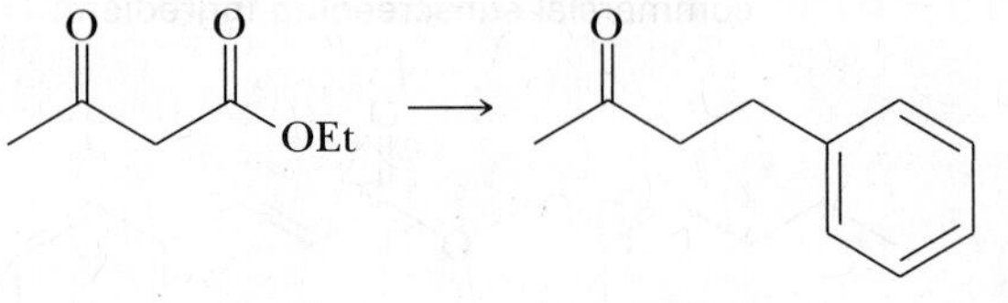

(m) 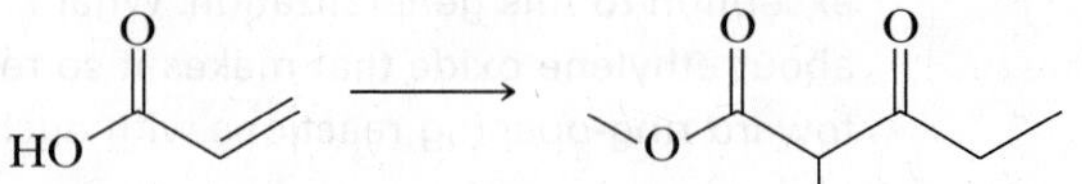

(k) 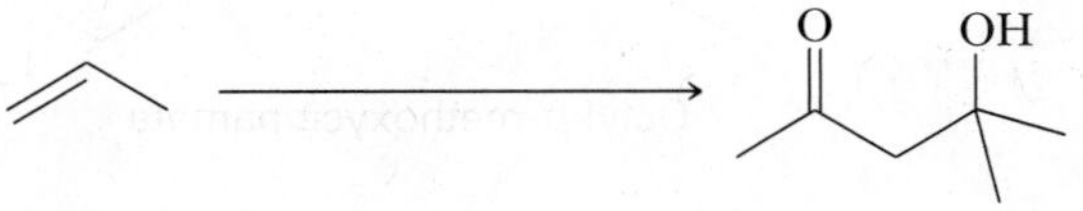

(n) 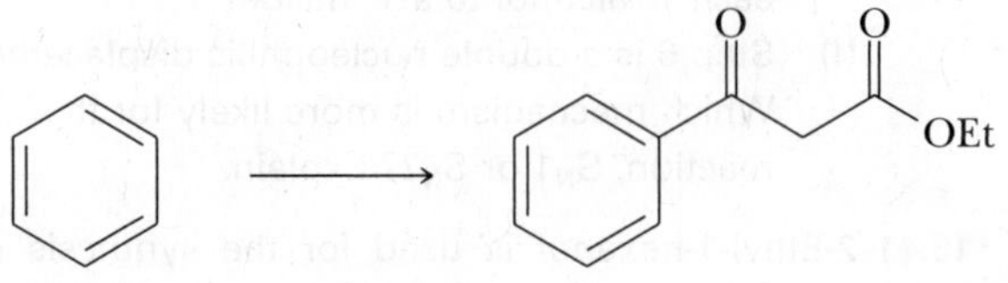

LOOKING AHEAD

***15.43** The following reaction is one of the 10 steps in glycolysis, a series of enzyme-catalyzed reactions by which glucose is oxidized to two molecules of pyruvate:

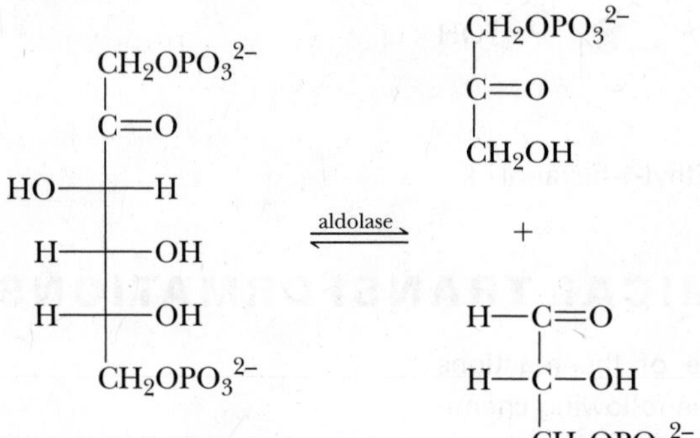

Fructose 1,6-bisphosphate

Dihydroxyacetone phosphate

Glyceraldehyde 3-phosphate

Show that this step is the reverse of an aldol reaction.

***15.44** The following reaction is the fourth in the set of four enzyme-catalyzed steps by which the hydrocarbon chain of a fatty acid is oxidized, two carbons at a time, to acetyl-coenzyme A:

$$R-\overset{O}{\overset{\|}{C}}-CH_2-\overset{O}{\overset{\|}{C}}SCoA + CoA-SH \longrightarrow R-\overset{O}{\overset{\|}{C}}-SCoA + CH_3\overset{O}{\overset{\|}{C}}-SCoA$$

β-Ketoacyl-CoA Coenzyme A An acyl-CoA Acetyl-CoA

Show that this reaction is the reverse of a Claisen condensation.

***15.45** Steroids are a major type of lipid (Section 19.4) with a characteristic tetracyclic ring system. Show how the **A** ring of the steroid testosterone can be constructed from the indicated precursors, using a Michael reaction followed by an aldol reaction (with dehydration):

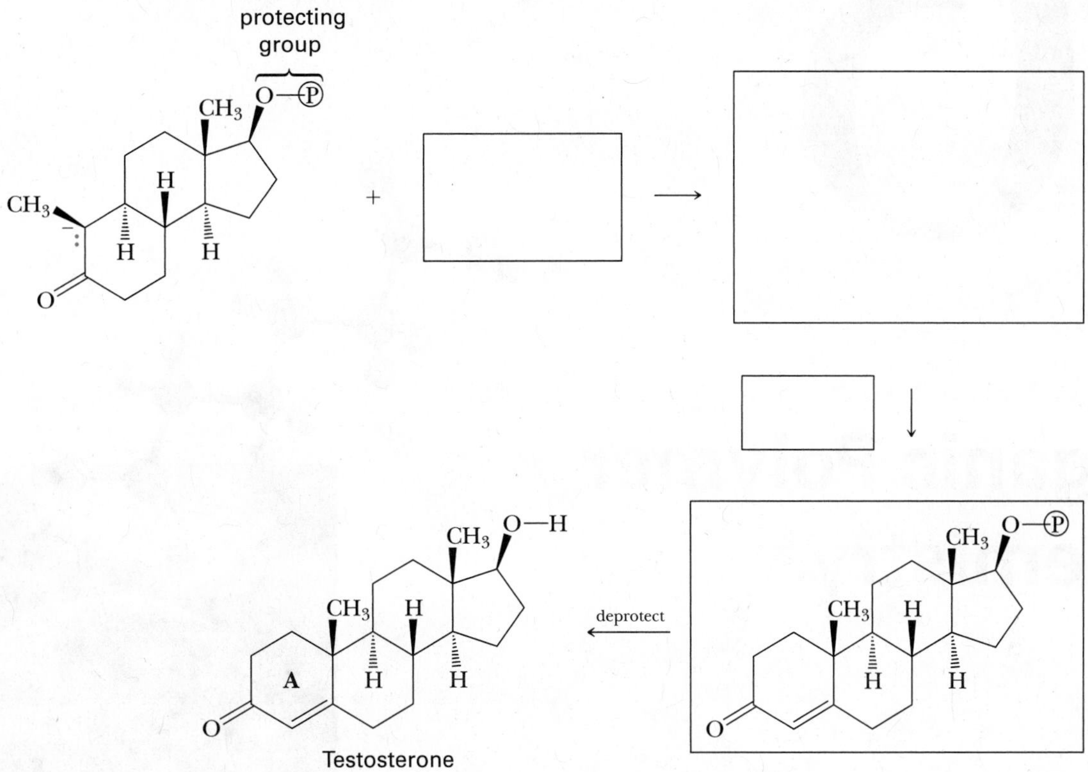

Testosterone

***15.46** The third step of the citric acid cycle involves the protonation of one of the carboxylate groups of oxalosuccinate, a β-ketoacid, followed by decarboxylation to form α-ketoglutarate:

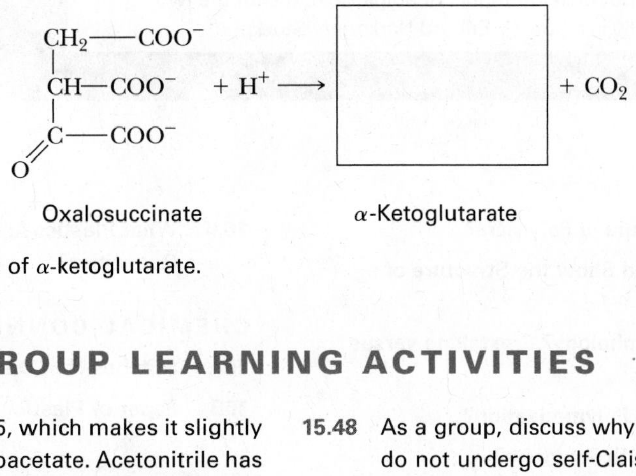

Oxalosuccinate $\qquad$ α-Ketoglutarate

Write the structural formula of α-ketoglutarate.

GROUP LEARNING ACTIVITIES

15.47 Nitroethane has a pK_a of 8.5, which makes it slightly more acidic than ethyl acetoacetate. Acetonitrile has a pK_a of 25, which makes it comparable in acidity to most esters. Account for the acidities of nitroethane and acetonitrile. As a group, decide whether the conjugate bases of these compounds could act similarly to enolates by drawing examples of such reactions.

$CH_3-CH_2-NO_2$ $\qquad$ $CH_3-C{\equiv}N$

Nitroethane $\qquad$ Acetonitrile

15.48 As a group, discuss why the two compounds shown do not undergo self-Claisen condensation reactions. Refer to Section 15.3D if needed.

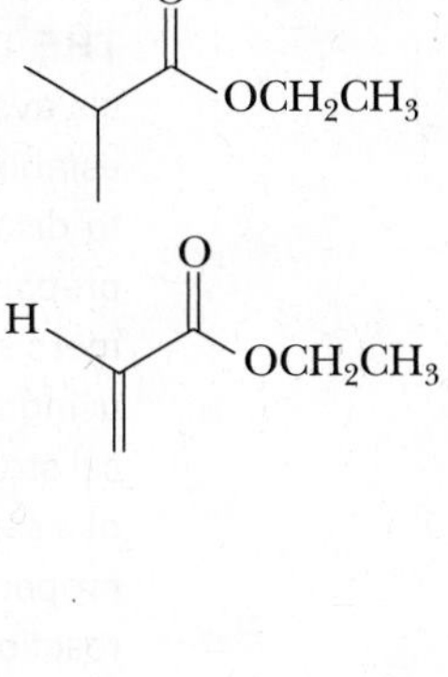

16

Organic Polymer Chemistry

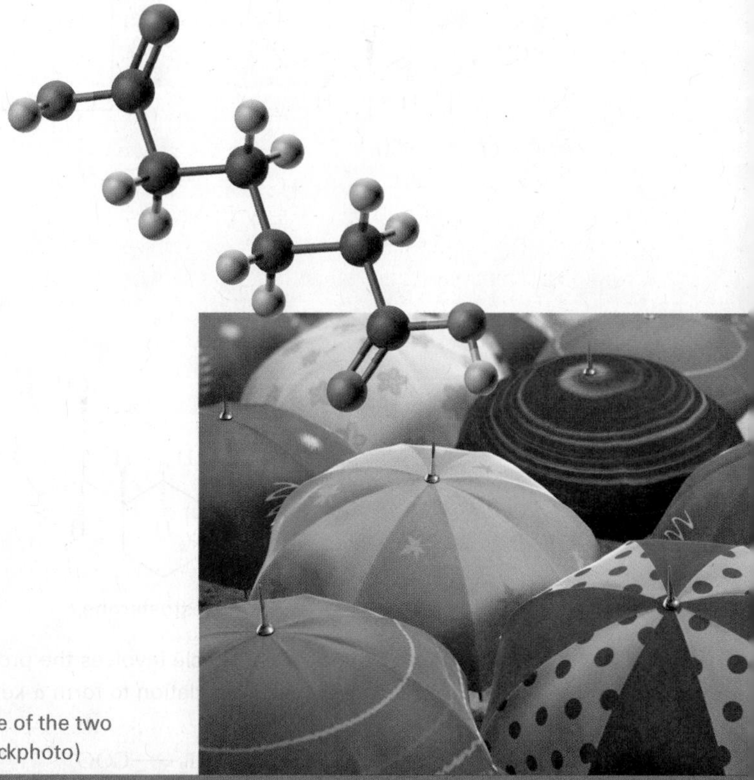

A sea of umbrellas on a rainy day. Inset: A model of adipic acid, one of the two monomers from which nylon 66 is made. (© Eduard Harkonen/iStockphoto)

KEY QUESTIONS

16.1 What Is the Architecture of Polymers?

16.2 How Do We Name and Show the Structure of a Polymer?

16.3 What Is Polymer Morphology? Crystalline versus Amorphous Materials

16.4 What Is Step-Growth Polymerization?

16.5 What Are Chain-Growth Polymers?

16.6 What Plastics Are Currently Recycled in Large Quantities?

CHEMICAL CONNECTIONS

16A Stitches That Dissolve

16B Paper or Plastic?

THE TECHNOLOGICAL ADVANCEMENT of any society is inextricably tied to the materials available to it. Indeed, historians have used the emergence of new materials as a way of establishing a time line to mark the development of human civilization. As part of the search to discover new materials, scientists have made increasing use of organic chemistry for the preparation of synthetic materials known as polymers. The versatility afforded by these polymers allows for the creation and fabrication of materials with ranges of properties unattainable using such materials as wood, metals, and ceramics. Deceptively simple changes in the chemical structure of a given polymer, for example, can change its mechanical properties from those of a sandwich bag to those of a bulletproof vest. Furthermore, structural changes can introduce properties never before imagined in organic polymers. For instance, using well-defined organic reactions, chemists can turn one type of polymer into an insulator (e.g., the rubber sheath that surrounds electrical cords). Treated differently, the same type of polymer can be made into an electrical conductor with a conductivity nearly equal to that of metallic copper!

The years since the 1930s have seen extensive research and development in organic polymer chemistry, and an almost explosive growth in plastics, coatings, and rubber technology has created a worldwide multibillion-dollar industry. A few basic characteristics account for this phenomenal growth. First, the raw materials for synthetic polymers are derived mainly from petroleum. With the development of petroleum-refining processes, raw materials for the synthesis of polymers became generally cheap and plentiful. Second, within broad limits, scientists have learned how to tailor polymers to the requirements of the end use. Third, many consumer products can be fabricated more cheaply from synthetic polymers than from such competing materials as wood, ceramics, and metals. For example, polymer technology created the water-based (latex) paints that have revolutionized the coatings industry, and plastic films and foams have done the same for the packaging industry. The list could go on and on as we think of the manufactured items that are everywhere around us in our daily lives.

16.1 What Is the Architecture of Polymers?

Polymers (Greek: *poly* + *meros*, many parts) are long-chain molecules synthesized by linking **monomers** (Greek: *mono* + *meros*, single part) through chemical reactions. The molecular weights of polymers are generally high compared with those of common organic compounds and typically range from 10,000 g/mol to more than 1,000,000 g/mol. The architectures of these macromolecules can also be quite diverse: There are polymer architectures with linear and branched chains, as well as those with comb, ladder, and star structures (Figure 16.1). Additional structural variations can be achieved by introducing covalent cross-links between individual polymer chains.

Polymer From the Greek *poly*, many and *meros*, parts; any long-chain molecule synthesized by linking together many single parts called monomers.

Monomer From the Greek *mono*, single and *meros*, part; the simplest nonredundant unit from which a polymer is synthesized.

In polymer chemistry, the term **plastic** refers to any polymer that can be molded when hot and that retains its shape when cooled. **Thermoplastics** are polymers which, when melted, become sufficiently fluid that they can be molded into shapes that are retained when they are cooled. **Thermosetting plastics**, or thermosets, can be molded when they are first prepared, but once cooled, they harden irreversibly and cannot be remelted. Because of their very different physical characteristics, thermoplastics and thermosets must be processed differently and are used in very different applications.

Plastic A polymer that can be molded when hot and retains its shape when cooled.

Thermoplastic A polymer that can be melted and molded into a shape that is retained when it is cooled.

Thermosetting plastic A polymer that can be molded when it is first prepared, but, once cooled, hardens irreversibly and cannot be remelted.

The single most important property of polymers at the molecular level is the size and shape of their chains. Shorter chains tend to form softer and more brittle materials, while longer chains form stronger and more flexible materials. These vastly different properties arise directly from the difference in size and molecular architecture of the individual polymer chains.

16.2 How Do We Name and Show the Structure of a Polymer?

We typically show the structure of a polymer by placing parentheses around the **repeating unit**, which is the smallest molecular fragment that contains all the structural features of the chain. A subscript n placed outside the parentheses indicates that the unit repeats n

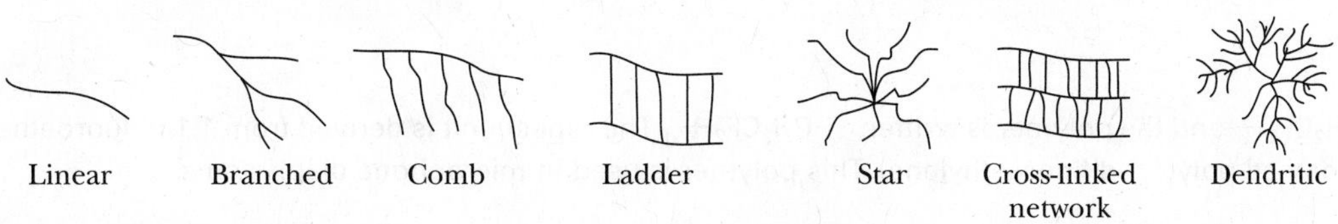

FIGURE 16.1
Various polymer architectures.

Average degree of polymerization, *n* A subscript placed outside the parentheses of the simplest nonredundant unit of a polymer to indicate that the unit repeats *n* times in the polymer.

times. Thus, we can reproduce the structure of an entire polymer chain by repeating the enclosed structure in both directions. An example is polypropylene, which is derived from the polymerization of propylene:

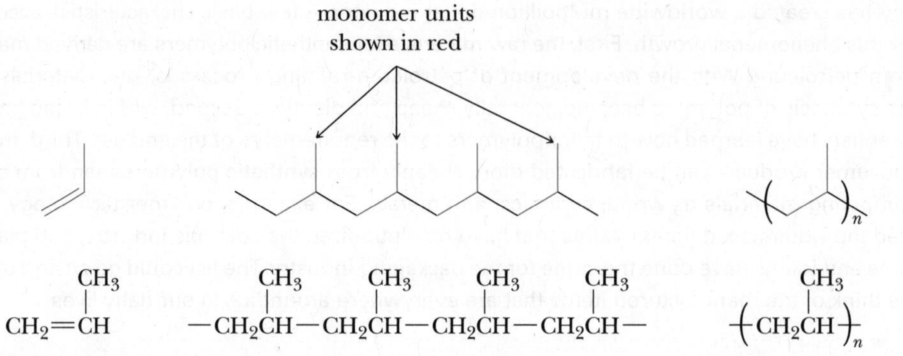

The monomer (propylene) | Part of an extended chain of polypropylene | The repeating unit of polypropylene

The most common method of naming a polymer is to add the prefix **poly-** to the name of the monomer from which the polymer is synthesized. Examples are polyethylene and polystyrene. In the case of a more complex monomer or when the name of the monomer is more than one word (e.g., the monomer vinyl chloride), parentheses are used to enclose the name of the monomer:

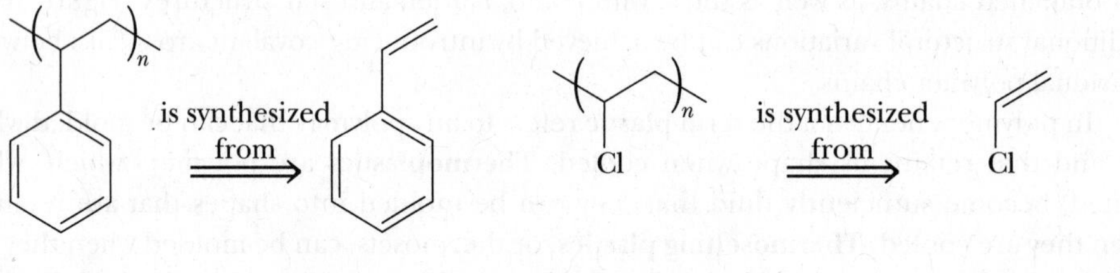

Polystyrene | Styrene | Poly(vinyl chloride) (PVC) | Vinyl chloride

EXAMPLE 16.1

Given the following structure, determine the polymer's repeating unit; redraw the structure, using the simplified parenthetical notation; and name the polymer. Assume that the monomer unit is an alkene:

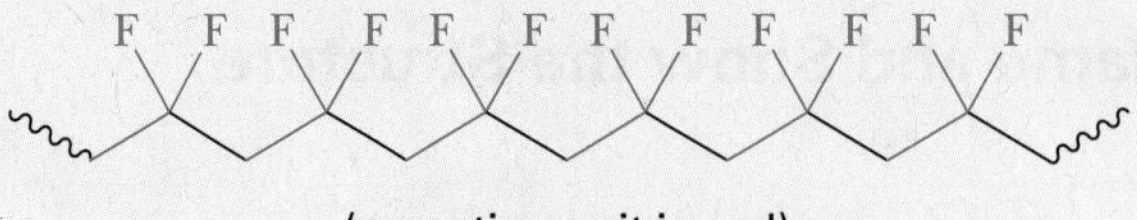

(repeating unit in red)

STRATEGY

Identify the repeating structural unit of the chain and place parentheses around it. Add the subscript *n* to indicate that this unit repeats *n* times.

SOLUTION

The repeating unit is $-CH_2CF_2-$ and the polymer is written $\left(CH_2CF_2\right)_n$. The repeat unit is derived from 1,1-difluoroethylene and the polymer is named poly(1,1-difluoroethylene). This polymer is used in microphone diaphragms.

See problems 16.9, 16.10

PROBLEM 16.1

Given the following structure, determine the polymer's repeat unit; redraw the structure, using the simplified parenthetical notation; and name the polymer:

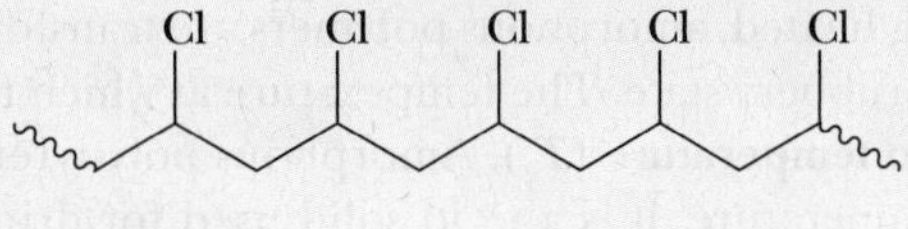

16.3 What Is Polymer Morphology? Crystalline versus Amorphous Materials

Polymers, like small organic molecules, tend to crystallize upon precipitation or as they are cooled from a melt. Acting to inhibit this tendency is the very large size of their molecules, which tends to inhibit diffusion, and their sometimes complicated or irregular structures, which prevent efficient packing of their chains. The result is that polymers in the solid state tend to be composed of both ordered **crystalline domains** (crystallites) and disordered **amorphous domains** (Figure 16.2). The relative amounts of crystalline and amorphous domains differ from polymer to polymer and frequently depend on the manner in which the material is processed (Figure 16.3). We often find high degrees of crystallinity in polymers with regular, compact structures and strong intermolecular forces, such as hydrogen bonding.

Crystalline domains Ordered crystalline regions in the solid state of a polymer; also called crystallites.

Amorphous domains Disordered, noncrystalline regions in the solid state of a polymer.

Arrangement of crystalline polymer chains | Case made of polyethylene, a crystalline polymer | Arrangement of amorphous polymer chains | Rubber bands made of latex rubber, an amorphous polymer

FIGURE 16.2
Examples of various polymer morphologies.

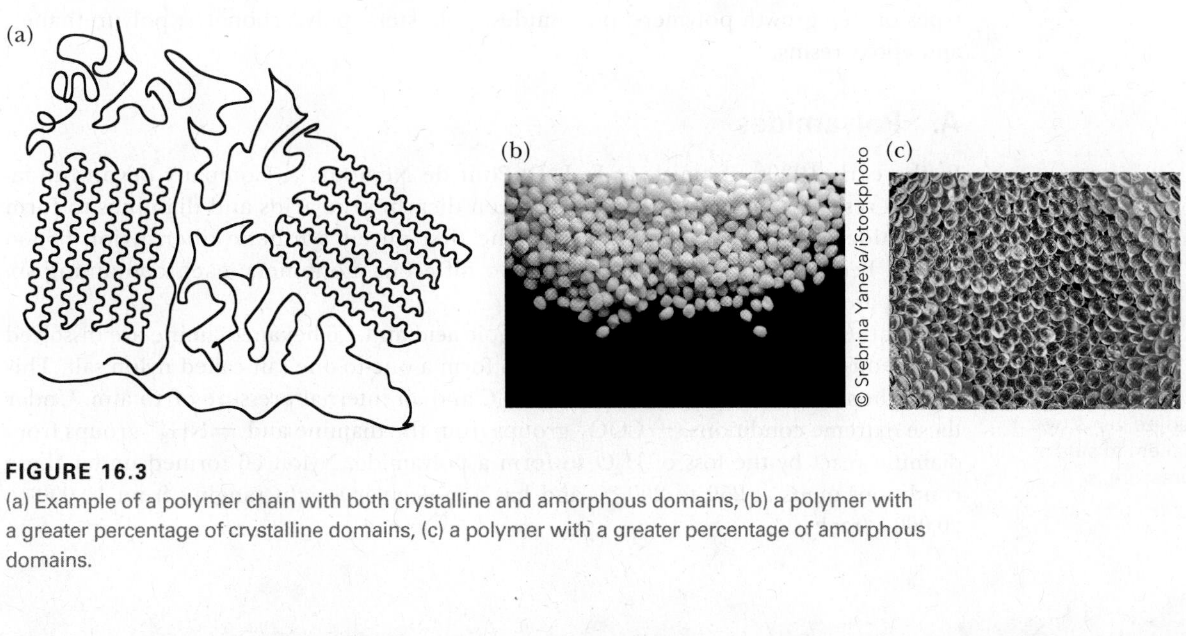

FIGURE 16.3
(a) Example of a polymer chain with both crystalline and amorphous domains, (b) a polymer with a greater percentage of crystalline domains, (c) a polymer with a greater percentage of amorphous domains.

Amorphous domains have little or no long-range order. Highly amorphous polymers are sometimes referred to as **glassy** polymers. Because they lack crystalline domains that scatter light, amorphous polymers are transparent. In addition, they are typically weak polymers, in terms of both their high flexibility and their low mechanical strength. On being heated, amorphous polymers are transformed from a hard, glassy state to a soft, flexible, rubbery state. The temperature at which this transition occurs is called the **glass transition temperature (T_g)**. Amorphous polystyrene, for example, has a T_g = 100 °C. At room temperature, it is a rigid solid used for drinking cups, foamed packaging materials, disposable medical wares, tape reels, and so forth. If it is placed in boiling water, it becomes soft and rubbery.

Elastomer A material that, when stretched or otherwise distorted, returns to its original shape when the distorting force is released.

Rubber materials must have low T_g values in order to behave as **elastomers (elastic polymers)**. If the temperature drops below its T_g value, then the material is converted to a rigid glassy solid and all elastomeric properties are lost. A poor understanding of this behavior of elastomers contributed to the *Challenger* spacecraft disaster in 1985. The elastomeric O-rings used to seal the solid booster rockets had a T_g value around 0 °C. When the temperature dropped to an unanticipated low on the morning of the launch of the craft, the O-ring seals dropped below their T_g value and obediently changed from elastomers to rigid glasses, losing any sealing capabilities. The rest is tragic history. The physicist Richard Feynman sorted this out publicly in a famous televised hearing in which he put a *Challenger*-type O-ring in ice water and showed that its elasticity was lost!

16.4 What Is Step-Growth Polymerization?

Step-growth polymerization A polymerization in which chain growth occurs in a stepwise manner between difunctional monomers, for example, between adipic acid and hexamethylenediamine to form nylon 66. Also referred to as condensation polymerization.

Polymerizations in which chain growth occurs in a stepwise manner are called **step-growth** or **condensation polymerizations**. Step-growth polymers are formed by reaction between difunctional molecules, with each new bond created in a separate step. During polymerization, monomers react to form dimers, dimers react with monomers to form trimers, dimers react with dimers to form tetramers, and so on.

There are two common types of step-growth processes: (1) reaction between A—M—A and B—M—B type monomers to give $\text{-(}A—M—A—B—M—B\text{)-}_n$ polymers and (2) the self-condensation of A—M—B monomers to give $\text{-(}A—M—B\text{)-}_n$ polymers. In this notation, "M" indicates the monomer and "A" and "B" the reactive functional groups on the monomer. In each type of step-growth polymerization, an A functional group reacts exclusively with a B functional group, and a B functional group reacts exclusively with an A functional group. New covalent bonds in step-growth polymerizations are generally formed by polar reactions between A and B functional groups—for example, nucleophilic acyl substitution. In this section, we discuss five types of step-growth polymers: polyamides, polyesters, polycarbonates, polyurethanes, and epoxy resins.

A. Polyamides

Polyamide A polymer in which each monomer unit is joined to the next by an amide bond, as for example nylon 66.

Autoclave An instrument used to sterilize items by subjecting them to steam and high pressure.

In the early 1930s, chemists at E. I. DuPont de Nemours & Company began fundamental research into the reactions between dicarboxylic acids and diamines to form **polyamides**. In 1934, they synthesized the first purely synthetic fiber, nylon 66, so named because it is synthesized from two different monomers, each containing six carbon atoms.

In the synthesis of nylon 66, hexanedioic acid and 1,6-hexanediamine are dissolved in aqueous ethanol, in which they react to form a one-to-one salt called nylon salt. This salt is then heated in an **autoclave** to 250 °C and an internal pressure of 15 atm. Under these extreme conditions, $—COO^-$ groups from the diamine and $—NH_3^+$ groups from diamine react by the loss of H_2O to form a polyamide. Nylon 66 formed under these conditions melts at 250 to 260 °C and has a molecular weight ranging from 10,000 to 20,000 g/mol:

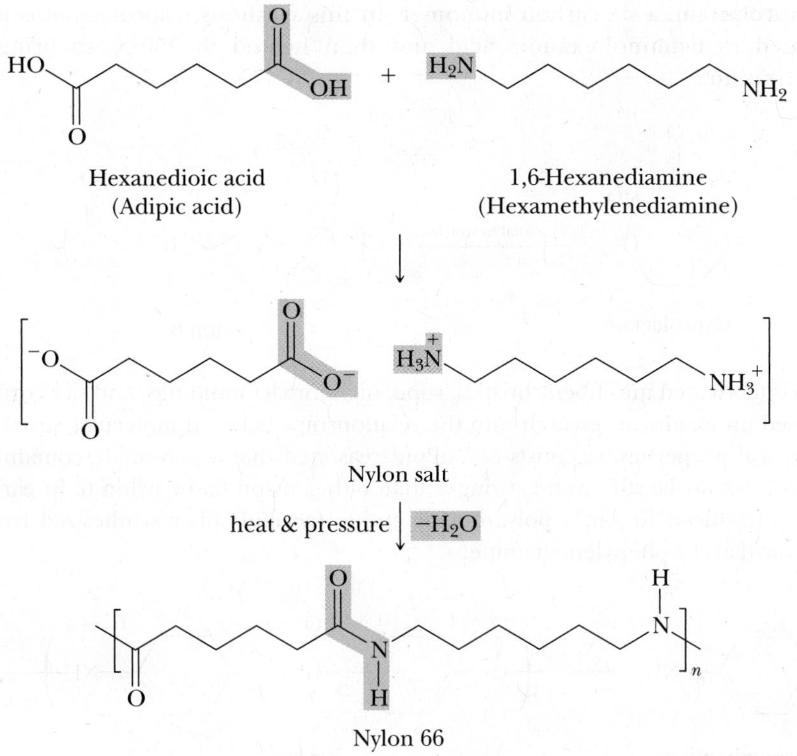

In the first stage of fiber production, crude nylon 66 is melted, spun into fibers, and cooled. Next, the melt-spun fibers are **cold drawn** (drawn at room temperature) to about four times their original length to increase their degree of crystallinity. As the fibers are drawn, individual polymer molecules become oriented in the direction of the fiber axis, and hydrogen bonds form between carbonyl oxygens of one chain and amide hydrogens of another chain (Figure 16.4). The effects of the orientation of polyamide molecules on the physical properties of the fiber are dramatic—both tensile strength and stiffness are increased markedly. Cold drawing is an important step in the production of most synthetic fibers.

The nylons are a family of polymers, the members of which have subtly different properties that suit them to one use or another. The two most widely used members of the family are nylon 66 and nylon 6. Nylon 6 is so named because it is synthesized

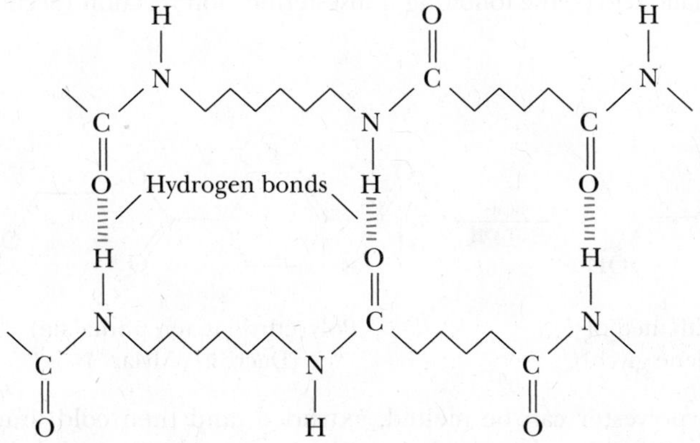

FIGURE 16.4
The structure of cold-drawn nylon 66. Hydrogen bonds between adjacent polymer chains provide additional tensile strength and stiffness to the fibers.

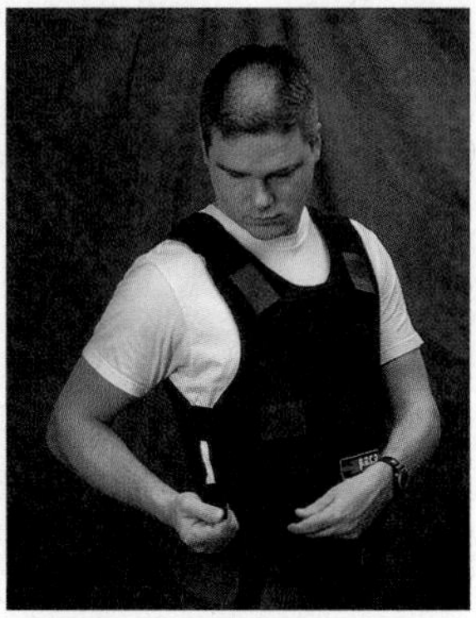
Charles D. Winters

Bulletproof vests have a thick layer of Kevlar.

Aramid A polyaromatic *amide*; a polymer in which the monomer units are an aromatic diamine and an aromatic dicarboxylic acid.

from caprolactam, a six-carbon monomer. In this synthesis, caprolactam is partially hydrolyzed to 6-aminohexanoic acid and then heated to 250 °C to bring about polymerization:

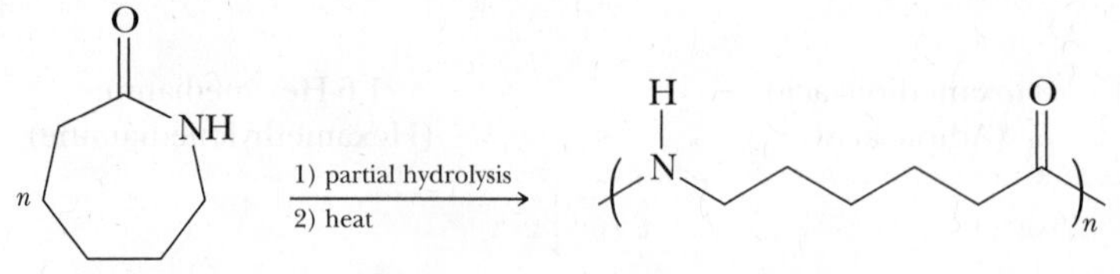

Caprolactam Nylon 6

Nylon 6 is fabricated into fibers, bristles, rope, high-impact moldings, and tire cords.

Based on extensive research into the relationships between molecular structure and bulk physical properties, scientists at DuPont reasoned that a polyamide containing aromatic rings would be stiffer and stronger than either nylon 66 or nylon 6. In early 1960, DuPont introduced Kevlar, a polyaromatic amide **(aramid)** fiber synthesized from terephthalic acid and *p*-phenylenediamine:

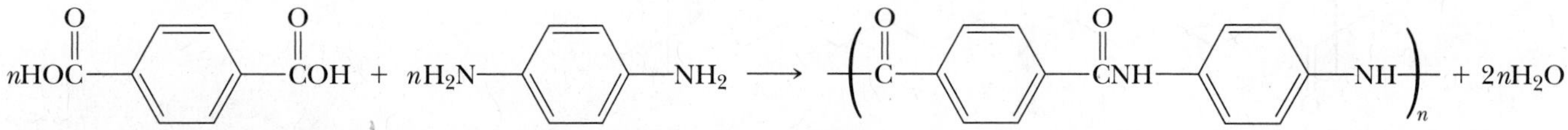

1,4-Benzenedicarboxylic acid (Terephthalic acid) 1,4-Benzenediamine (*p*-Phenylenediamine) Kevlar

Ken Karp for John Wiley & Sons

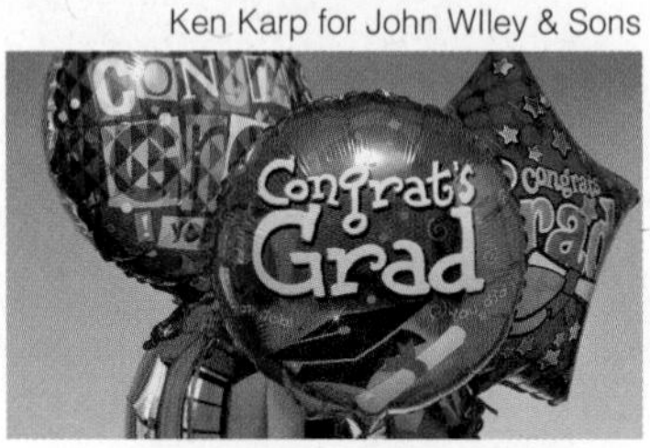

Because Mylar film has very tiny pores, it is used for balloons that can be inflated with helium; the helium atoms diffuse only slowly through the pores of the film.

One of the remarkable features of Kevlar is its light weight compared with that of other materials of similar strength. For example, a 7.6-cm (3-in.) cable woven of Kevlar has a strength equal to that of a similarly woven 7.6-cm (3-in.) steel cable. However, whereas the steel cable weighs about 30 kg/m (20 lb/ft), the Kevlar cable weighs only 6 kg/m (4 lb/ft). Kevlar now finds use in such articles as anchor cables for offshore drilling rigs and reinforcement fibers for automobile tires. Kevlar is also woven into a fabric that is so tough that it can be used for bulletproof vests, jackets, and raincoats.

B. Polyesters

The first **polyester**, developed in the 1940s, involved the polymerization of benzene 1,4-dicarboxylic acid (terephthalic acid) with 1,2-ethanediol (ethylene glycol) to give poly(ethylene terephthalate), abbreviated PET. Virtually all PET is now made from the dimethyl ester of terephthalic acid by the following transesterification reaction (Section 14.4C):

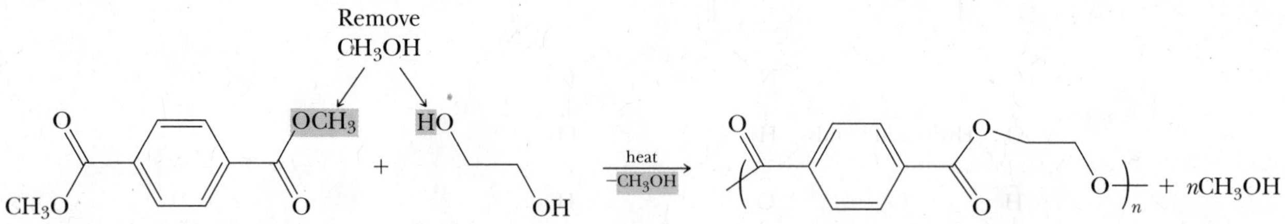

Dimethyl terephthalate 1,2-Ethanediol (Ethylene glycol) Poly(ethylene terephthalate) (Dacron®, Mylar®)

Polyester A polymer in which each monomer unit is joined to the next by an ester bond as, for example, poly(ethylene terephthalate).

The crude polyester can be melted, extruded, and then cold drawn to form the textile fiber Dacron® polyester, the outstanding features of which are its stiffness (about four times that of nylon 66), very high strength, and remarkable resistance to creasing and wrinkling. Because the early Dacron® polyester fibers were harsh to the touch, due to their stiffness, they were usually blended with cotton or wool to make acceptable textile fibers. Newly developed fabrication techniques now produce less harsh Dacron® polyester textile fibers. PET is also fabricated into Mylar® films and recyclable plastic beverage containers.

C. Polycarbonates

Polycarbonate A polyester in which the carboxyl groups are derived from carbonic acid.

Polycarbonates, the most familiar of which is Lexan®, are a class of commercially important engineering polyesters. Lexan® forms by the reaction between the disodium salt of bisphenol A (Problem 9.33) and phosgene:

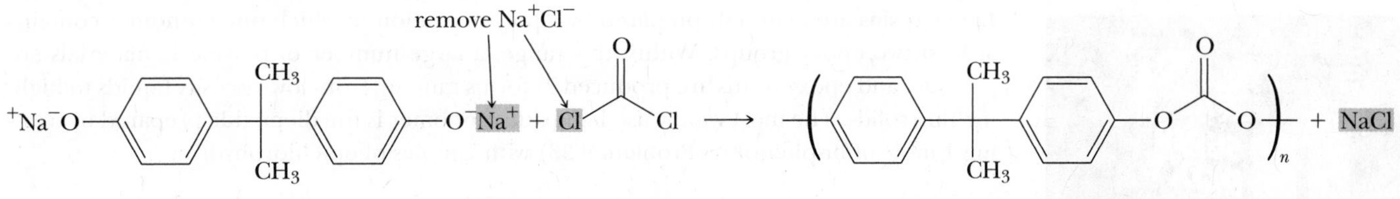

Disodium salt of bisphenol A — Phosgene — Lexan® (a polycarbonate)

Note that phosgene is the diacid chloride (Section 14.1A) of carbonic acid; hydrolysis of phosgene gives H_2CO_3 and 2HCl.

Lexan® is a tough, transparent polymer with high impact and tensile strengths that retains its properties over a wide temperature range. It is used in sporting equipment (for helmets and face masks), in the production of light, impact-resistant housings for household appliances, and in the manufacture of safety glass and unbreakable windows.

Charles D. Winters

A polycarbonate hockey mask.

D. Polyurethanes

A urethane, or carbamate, is an ester of carbamic acid, H_2NCOOH. Carbamates are most commonly prepared by treating an isocyanate with an alcohol. In this reaction, the H and OR′ of the alcohol add to the C=N bond in a reaction comparable to the addition of an alcohol to a C=O bond:

$$\underset{\text{An isocyanate}}{RN{=}C{=}O} + R'OH \longrightarrow \underset{\text{A carbamate}}{RNH\overset{\overset{\large O}{\|}}{C}OR'}$$

Polyurethane A polymer containing the —NHCOO— group as a repeating unit.

Polyurethanes consist of flexible polyester or polyether units (blocks) alternating with rigid urethane units (blocks) derived from a diisocyanate, commonly a mixture of 2,4- and 2,6-toluene diisocyanate:

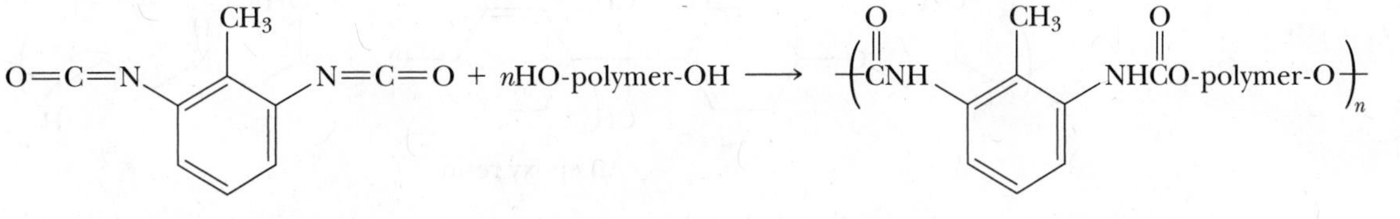

2,6-Toluene diisocyanate — Low-molecular-weight polyester or polyether with OH groups at each end of the chain — A polyurethane

The more flexible blocks are derived from low-molecular-weight (MW 1,000 to 4,000) polyesters or polyethers with —OH groups at each end of their chains. Polyurethane fibers are fairly soft and elastic and have found use as spandex and Lycra®, the "stretch" fabrics used in bathing suits, leotards, and undergarments.

Polyurethane foams for upholstery and insulating materials are made by adding small amounts of water during polymerization. Water reacts with isocyanate groups to form a carbamic acid that undergoes spontaneous decarboxylation to produce gaseous carbon dioxide, which then acts as the foaming agent:

$$RN{=}C{=}O + H_2O \longrightarrow \left[RNH-\overset{\displaystyle O}{\overset{\|}{C}}-OH \right] \longrightarrow RNH_2 + CO_2$$

An isocyanate — A carbamic acid (unstable)

Epoxy resin A material prepared by a polymerization in which one monomer contains at least two epoxy groups.

Charles D. Winters

An epoxy resin kit.

E. Epoxy Resins

Epoxy resins are materials prepared by a polymerization in which one monomer contains at least two epoxy groups. Within this range, a large number of polymeric materials are possible, and epoxy resins are produced in forms ranging from low-viscosity liquids to high-melting solids. The most widely used epoxide monomer is the diepoxide prepared by treating 1 mole of bisphenol A (Problem 9.33) with 2 moles of epichlorohydrin:

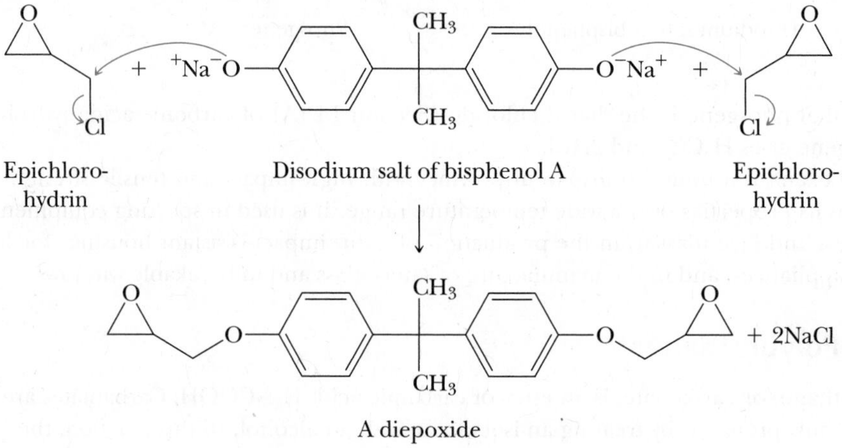

To prepare the following epoxy resin, the diepoxide monomer is treated with 1,2-ethanediamine (ethylene diamine):

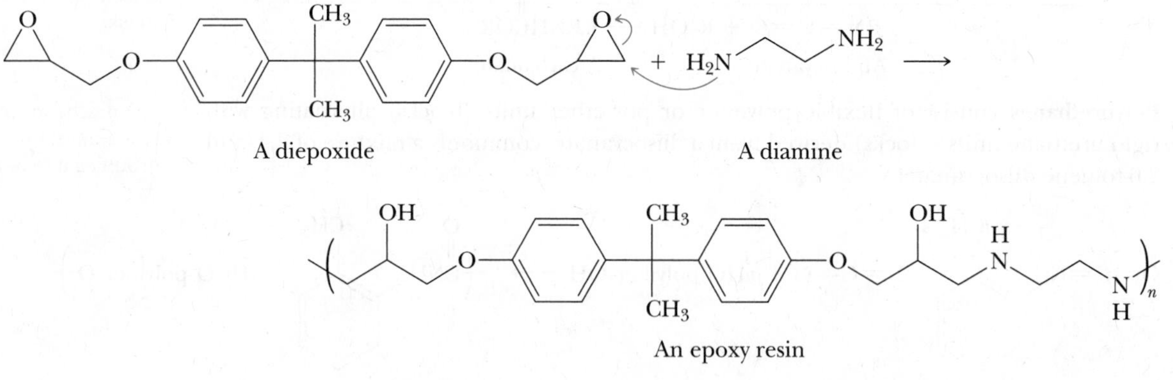

Ethylene diamine is usually labeled the catalyst in the two-component formulations that you buy in hardware or craft stores; it is also the component with the acrid smell. The preceding reaction corresponds to nucleophilic opening of the highly strained three-membered epoxide ring (Section 8.4C).

Epoxy resins are widely used as adhesives and insulating surface coatings. They have good electrical insulating properties, which lead to their use in encapsulating electrical components ranging from integrated circuit boards to switch coils and insulators for power transmission systems. Epoxy resins are also used as composites with other materials, such as glass fiber, paper, metal foils, and other synthetic fibers, to create structural components for jet aircraft, rocket motor casings, and so on.

EXAMPLE 16.2

By what type of mechanism does the reaction between the disodium salt of bisphenol A and epichlorohydrin take place?

STRATEGY

Examine the mechanism on the previous page and you will see by the curved arrows that an oxygen anion of bisphenol A displaces a chlorine atom from the primary carbon of epichlorohydrin. The phenoxide ion of bisphenol A is a good nucleophile, and chlorine on the primary carbon of epichlorohydrin is the leaving group.

SOLUTION

The mechanism is an S_N2 mechanism.

PROBLEM 16.2

Write the repeating unit of the epoxy resin formed from the following reaction:

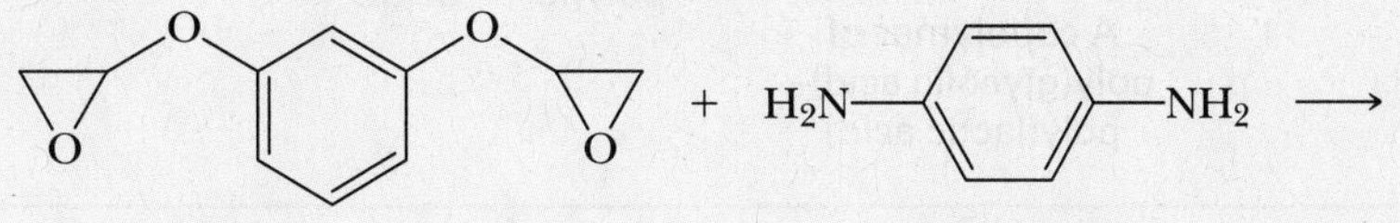

A diepoxide A diamine

16.5 What Are Chain-Growth Polymers?

From the perspective of the chemical industry, the single most important reaction of alkenes is **chain-growth polymerization**, a type of polymerization in which monomer units are joined together without the loss of atoms. An example is the formation of polyethylene from ethylene:

Chain-growth polymerization A polymerization that involves sequential addition reactions, either to unsaturated monomers or to monomers possessing other reactive functional groups.

$$n\mathrm{CH_2{=}CH_2} \xrightarrow{\text{catalyst}} \mathrm{\left(CH_2CH_2\right)}_n$$

Ethylene Polyethylene

The mechanisms of chain-growth polymerization differ greatly from the mechanism of step-growth polymerizations. In the latter, all monomers plus the polymer end groups possess equally reactive functional groups, allowing for all possible combinations of reactions to occur, including monomer with monomer, dimer with dimer, monomer with tetramer, and so forth. In contrast, chain-growth polymerizations involve end groups possessing reactive intermediates that react only with a monomer. The reactive intermediates used in chain-growth polymerizations include radicals, carbanions, carbocations, and organometallic complexes.

Chemical Connections 16A

STITCHES THAT DISSOLVE

As the technological capabilities of medicine have grown, the demand for synthetic materials that can be used inside the body has increased as well. Polymers have many of the characteristics of an ideal biomaterial: They are lightweight and strong, are inert or biodegradable (depending on their chemical structure), and have physical properties (softness, rigidity, elasticity) that are easily tailored to match those of natural tissues. Carbon–carbon backbone polymers are resistant to degradation and are used widely in permanent organ and tissue replacements.

Even though most medical uses of polymeric materials require biostability, applications have been developed that use the biodegradable nature of some macromolecules. An example is the use of glycolic acid/lactic acid copolymers as absorbable sutures:

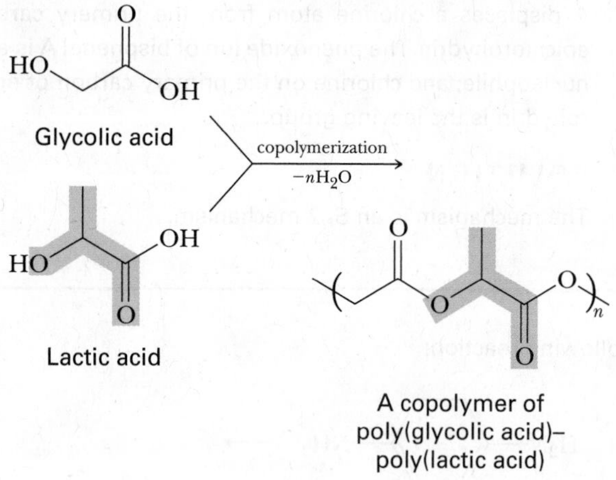

Traditional suture materials such as catgut must be removed by a health-care specialist after they have served their purpose. Stitches of these hydroxyester polymers, however, are hydrolyzed slowly over a period of approximately two weeks, and by the time the torn tissues have fully healed, the stitches are fully degraded and the sutures need not be removed. Glycolic and lactic acids formed during hydrolysis of the stitches are metabolized and excreted by existing biochemical pathways.

Question

Propose a mechanism for the hydrolysis of one repeating unit of the copolymer of poly(glycolic acid)-poly(lactic acid).

The number of monomers that undergo chain-growth polymerization is large and includes such compounds as alkenes, alkynes, allenes, isocyanates, and cyclic compounds such as lactones, lactams, ethers, and epoxides. We concentrate on the chain-growth polymerizations of ethylene and substituted ethylenes and show how these compounds can be polymerized by radical and organometallic-mediated mechanisms.

Table 16.1 lists several important polymers derived from ethylene and substituted ethylenes, along with their common names and most important uses.

A. Radical Chain-Growth Polymerization

Radical Any molecule that contains one or more unpaired electrons.

The first commercial polymerizations of ethylene were initiated by radicals formed by thermal decomposition of organic peroxides, such as benzoyl peroxide. A **radical** is any molecule that contains one or more unpaired electrons. Radicals can be formed by the cleavage of a bond in such a way that each atom or fragment participating in the bond

TABLE 16.1 Polymers Derived from Ethylene and Substituted Ethylenes

Monomer Formula	Common Name	Polymer Name(s) and Common Uses
$CH_2{=}CH_2$	Ethylene	Polyethylene, Polythene; break-resistant containers and packaging materials
$CH_2{=}CHCH_3$	Propylene	Polypropylene, Herculon; textile and carpet fibers
$CH_2{=}CHCl$	Vinyl chloride	Poly(vinyl chloride), PVC; construction tubing
$CH_2{=}CCl_2$	1,1-Dichloroethylene	Poly(1,1-dichloroethylene); Saran Wrap® is a copolymer with vinyl chloride
$CH_2{=}CHCN$	Acrylonitrile	Polyacrylonitrile, Orlon®; acrylics and acrylates
$CF_2{=}CF_2$	Tetrafluoroethylene	Polytetrafluoroethylene, PTFE; Teflon®, nonstick coatings
$CH_2{=}CHC_6H_5$	Styrene	Polystyrene, Styrofoam™; insulating materials
$CH_2{=}CHCOOCH_2CH_3$	Ethyl acrylate	Poly(ethyl acrylate); latex paints
$CH_2{=}C(CH_3)COOCH_3$	Methyl methacrylate	Poly(methyl methacrylate), Lucite®, Plexiglas®; glass substitutes

Chemical Connections 16B

PAPER OR PLASTIC?

Any audiophile will tell you that the quality of any sound system is highly dependent on its speakers. Speakers create sound by moving a diaphragm in and out to displace air. Most diaphragms are in the shape of a cone, traditionally made of paper. Paper cones are inexpensive, lightweight, rigid, and nonresonant. One disadvantage is their susceptibility to damage by water and humidity. Over time and with exposure, paper cones become weakened, losing their fidelity of sound. Many of the speakers that are available today are made of polypropylene, which is also inexpensive, lightweight, rigid, and nonresonant. Furthermore, not only are polypropylene cones immune to water and humidity, but also their performance is less influenced by heat or cold. Moreover, their added strength makes them less prone to splitting than paper. They last longer and can be displaced more frequently and for longer distances, creating deeper bass notes and higher high notes.

© perets/iStockphoto

Question

Paper speaker cones consist of mostly cellulose, a polymer of the monomer unit known as D-glucose (Chapter 17). Propose why one type of polymer is susceptible to humidity while the other type, polypropylene, is resistant to humidity.

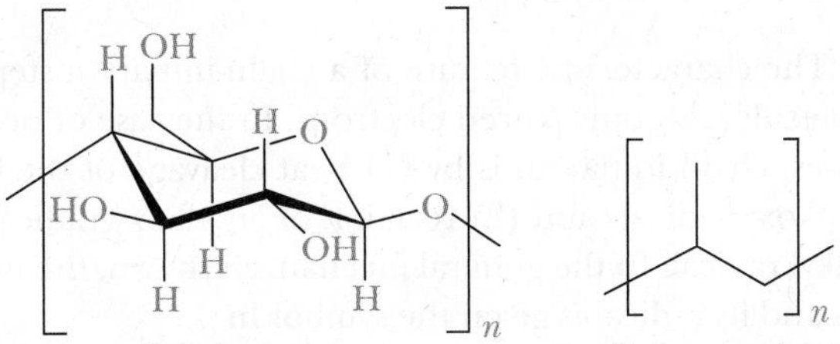

Cellulose   Polypropylene

retains one electron. In the following equation, **fishhook arrows** are used to show the change in position of single electrons:

Fishhook arrow A single-barbed, curved arrow used to show the change in position of a single electron.

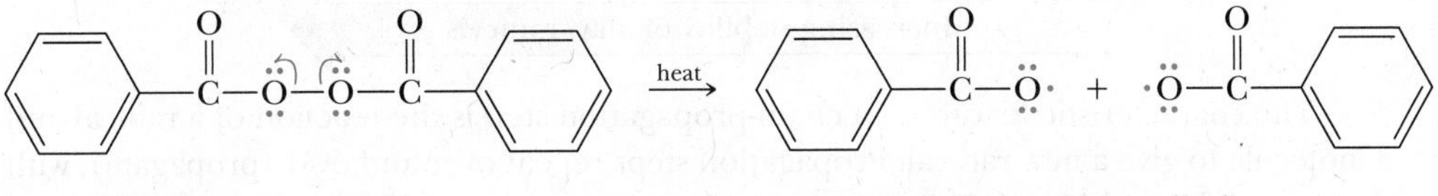

Benzoyl peroxide   Benzoyloxy radicals

Radical polymerization of ethylene and substituted ethylenes involves three steps: (1) chain initiation, (2) chain propagation, and (3) chain termination. We show these steps here and then discuss each separately in turn.

Mechanism

Radical Polymerization of Ethylene

STEP 1: Chain initiation—formation of radicals from nonradical compounds:

$$\text{In—In} \xrightarrow[\text{or light}]{\text{heat}} 2\text{In}\cdot$$

In this equation, In-In represents an initiator that, when heated or irradiated with radiation of a suitable wavelength, cleaves to give two radicals (In·).

Chain initiation In radical polymerization, the formation of radicals from molecules containing only paired electrons.

Chain propagation In radical polymerization, a reaction of a radical and a molecule to give a new radical.

STEP 2: Chain propagation—reaction of a radical and a molecule to form a new radical:

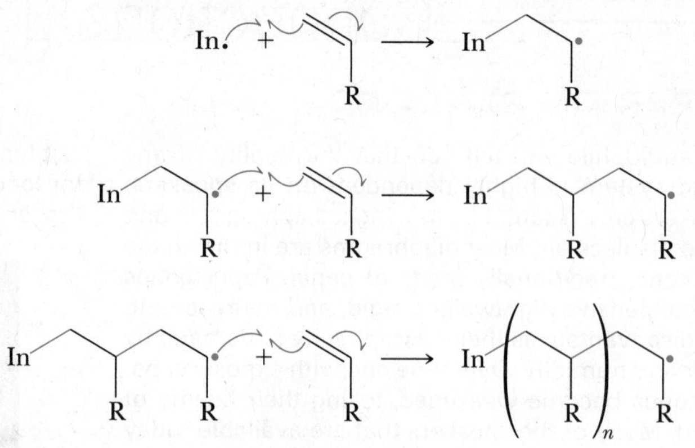

Chain termination In radical polymerization, a reaction in which two radicals combine to form a covalent bond.

STEP 3: Chain termination—destruction of radicals:

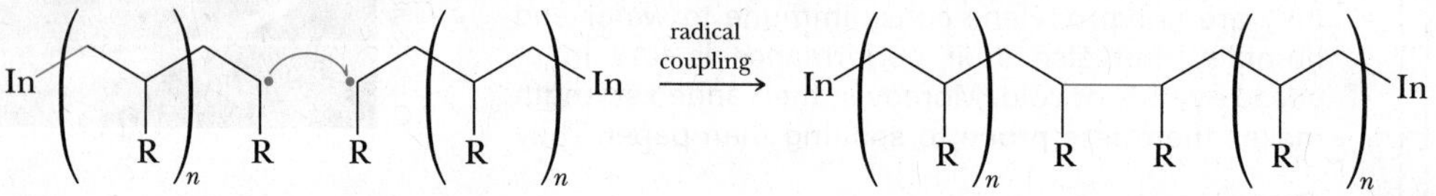

The characteristic feature of a chain-initiation step is the formation of radicals from a molecule with only paired electrons. In the case of peroxide-initiated polymerizations of alkenes, chain initiation is by (1) heat cleavage of the O—O bond of a peroxide to give two alkoxy radicals and (2) reaction of an alkoxy radical with a molecule of alkene to give an alkyl radical. In the general mechanism shown, the initiating catalyst is given the symbol In-In and its radical is given the symbol In·.

The structure and geometry of carbon radicals are similar to those of alkyl carbocations. They are planar or nearly so, with bond angles of approximately 120° about the carbon with the unpaired electron. The relative stabilities of alkyl radicals are similar to those of alkyl carbocations because they both possess electron-deficient carbons.

$$\text{methyl} < 1° < 2° < 3°$$

Increasing stability of alkyl radicals

The characteristic feature of a chain-propagation step is the reaction of a radical and a molecule to give a new radical. Propagation steps repeat over and over (propagate), with the radical formed in one step reacting with a monomer to produce a new radical, and so on. The number of times a cycle of chain-propagation steps repeats is called the **chain length** and is given the symbol ***n***. In the polymerization of ethylene, chain-lengthening reactions occur at a very high rate, often as fast as thousands of additions per second, depending on the experimental conditions.

Radical polymerizations of substituted ethylenes almost always give the more stable (more substituted) radical. Because additions are biased in this fashion, the polymerizations of substituted ethylene monomers tend to yield polymers with monomer units joined by the head (carbon 1) of one unit to the tail (carbon 2) of the next unit:

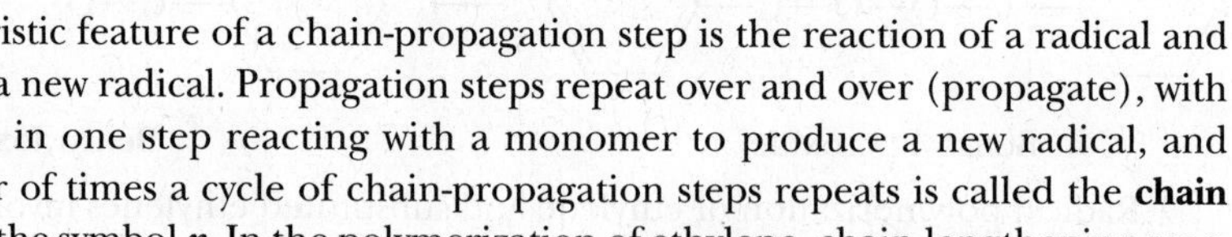

Substituted ethylene monomer

Head-to-tail linkages

In principle, chain-propagation steps can continue until all starting materials are consumed. In practice, they continue only until two radicals react with each other to terminate the process. The characteristic feature of a chain-termination step is the destruction of radicals. In the mechanism shown for radical polymerization of the substituted ethylene, chain termination occurs by the coupling of two radicals to form a new carbon–carbon single bond.

The first commercial process for ethylene polymerization used peroxide catalysts at temperatures of 500 °C and pressures of 1,000 atm and produced a soft, tough polymer known as **low-density polyethylene (LDPE)** with a density of between 0.91 and 0.94 g/cm^3 and a melt transition temperature (T_m) of about 115 °C. Because LDPE's melting point is only slightly above 100 °C, it cannot be used for products that will be exposed to boiling water. At the molecular level, chains of LDPE are highly branched.

Chain-transfer reaction In radical polymerization, the transfer of reactivity of an end group from one chain to another during a polymerization.

The branching on chains of low-density polyethylene results from a "back-biting" reaction in which the radical end group abstracts a hydrogen from the fourth carbon back (the fifth carbon in the chain). Abstraction of this hydrogen is particularly facile because the transition state associated with the process can adopt a conformation like that of a chair cyclohexane. In addition, the less stable 1° radical is converted to a more stable 2° radical. This side reaction is called a **chain-transfer reaction**, because the activity of the end group is "transferred" from one chain to another. Continued polymerization of monomer from this new radical center leads to a branch four carbons long:

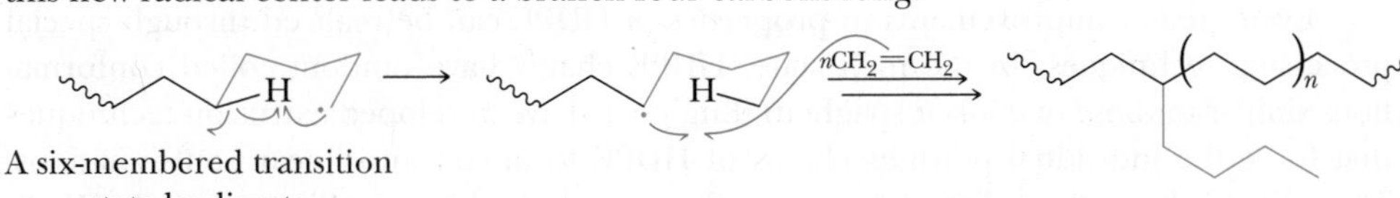

A six-membered transition state leading to 1,5-hydrogen abstraction

Approximately 65% of all LDPE is used for the manufacture of films by a blow-molding technique illustrated in Figure 16.5. LDPE film is inexpensive, which makes it ideal for packaging such consumer items as baked goods, vegetables, and other produce and for trash bags.

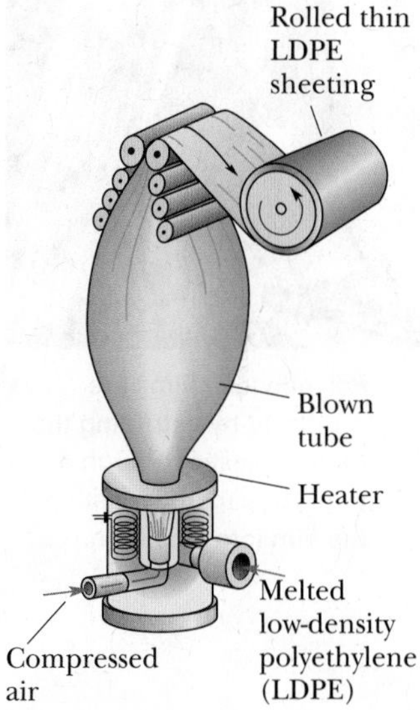

FIGURE 16.5 Fabrication of an LDPE film. A tube of melted LDPE along with a jet of compressed air is forced through an opening and blown into a giant, thin-walled bubble. The film is then cooled and taken up onto a roller. This double-walled film can be slit down the side to give LDPE film, or it can be sealed at points along its length to make LDPE bags.

B. Ziegler–Natta Chain-Growth Polymerization

In the 1950s, Karl Ziegler of Germany and Giulio Natta of Italy developed an alternative method for the polymerization of alkenes, work for which they shared the Nobel Prize for chemistry in 1963. The early Ziegler–Natta catalysts were highly active, heterogeneous materials composed of an $MgCl_2$ support, a Group 4B transition metal halide such as $TiCl_4$, and an alkylaluminum compound—for example, diethylaluminum chloride, $Al(CH_2CH_3)_2Cl$. These catalysts bring about the polymerization of ethylene and propylene at 1–4 atm and at temperatures as low as 60 °C.

The catalyst in a Ziegler–Natta polymerization is an alkyltitanium compound formed by reaction between $Al(CH_2CH_3)_2Cl$ and the titanium halide on the surface of a $MgCl_2/TiCl_4$ particle. Once formed, this alkyltitanium species repeatedly inserts ethylene units into the titanium–carbon bond to yield polyethylene.

Mechanism

Ziegler–Natta Catalysis of Ethylene Polymerization

STEP 1: Formation of a titanium–ethyl bond:

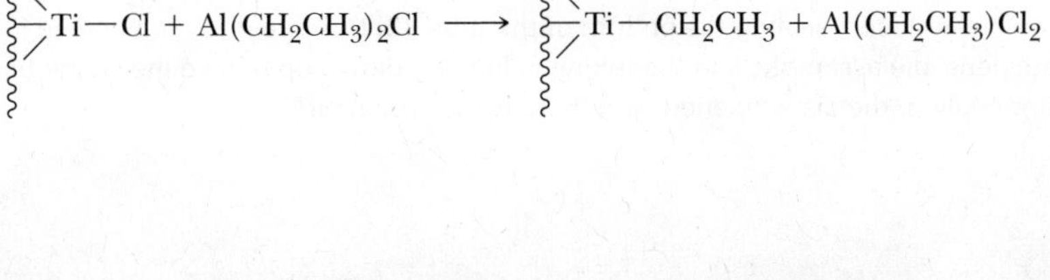

STEP 2: Insertion of ethylene into the titanium–carbon bond:

$$\text{Ti}-CH_2CH_3 + CH_2{=}CH_2 \longrightarrow \text{Ti}-CH_2CH_2CH_2CH_3$$

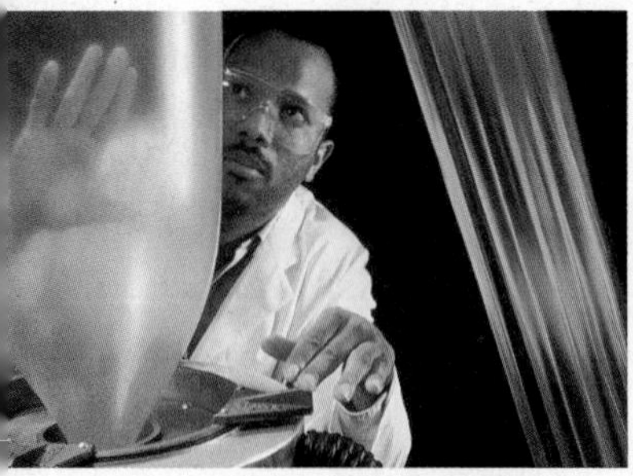

Polyethylene films are produced by extruding the molten plastic through a ring-like gap and inflating the film into a balloon.

Over 60 billion pounds of polyethylene are produced worldwide every year with Ziegler–Natta catalysts. Polyethylene from Ziegler–Natta systems, termed **high-density polyethylene (HDPE)**, has a higher density (0.96 g/cm^3) and melt transition temperature (133 °C) than low-density polyethylene, is 3 to 10 times stronger, and is opaque rather than transparent. The added strength and opacity are due to a much lower degree of chain branching and a resulting higher degree of crystallinity of HDPE compared with LDPE. Approximately 45% of all HDPE used in the United States is blow molded (Figure 16.6).

Even greater improvements in properties of HDPE can be realized through special processing techniques. In the melt state, HDPE chains have random coiled conformations similar to those of cooked spaghetti. Engineers have developed extrusion techniques that force the individual polymer chains of HDPE to uncoil into linear conformations. These linear chains then align with one another to form highly crystalline materials. HDPE processed in this fashion is stiffer than steel and has approximately four times its tensile strength! Because the density of polyethylene ($\approx$1.0 g/cm^3) is considerably less than that of steel (8.0 g/cm^3), these comparisons of strength and stiffness are even more favorable if they are made on a weight basis.

FIGURE 16.6
Blow molding of an HDPE container. (a) A short length of HDPE tubing is placed in an open die, and the die is closed, sealing the bottom of the tube. (b) Compressed air is forced into the hot polyethylene–die assembly, and the tubing is literally blown up to take the shape of the mold. (c) After cooling, the die is opened, and there is the container!

16.6 What Plastics Are Currently Recycled in Large Quantities?

Our society is incredibly dependent on polymers in the form of plastics. Durable and lightweight, plastics are probably the most versatile synthetic materials in existence; in fact, their current production in the United States exceeds that of steel. Plastics have come under criticism, however, for their role in the current trash crisis. They make up 21% of the volume and 8% of the weight of solid waste, most of which is derived from disposable packaging and wrapping. Of the 1.5×10^8 kg of thermoplastic materials produced in the United States per year, less than 2% is recycled.

If the durability and chemical inertness of most plastics make them ideally suited for reuse, why aren't more plastics being recycled? The answer to this question has more to do with economics and consumer habits than with technological obstacles. Because curbside pickup and centralized drop-off stations for recyclables are just now becoming common, the amount of used material available for reprocessing has traditionally been small. This limitation, combined with the need for an additional sorting and separation step, rendered the use of recycled plastics in manufacturing expensive compared with virgin materials. The increase in environmental awareness over the last decade, however, has resulted in a greater demand for recycled products. As manufacturers adapt to satisfy this new market, the recycling of plastics will eventually catch up with that of other materials, such as glass and aluminum.

Charles D. Winters

Some common products packaged in high-density polyethylene containers.

Six types of plastics are commonly used for packaging applications. In 1988, manufacturers adopted recycling code numbers developed by the Society of the Plastics Industry (Table 16.2). Because the plastics recycling industry still is not fully developed, only PET and HDPE are currently being recycled in large quantities. LDPE, which accounts for about 40% of plastic trash, has been slow in finding acceptance with recyclers. Facilities for the reprocessing of poly(vinyl chloride) (PVC), polypropylene (PP), and polystyrene (PS) exist but are rare.

The process for the recycling of most plastics is simple, with separation of the desired plastics from other contaminants the most labor-intensive step. For example, PET

TABLE 16.2 Recycling Codes for Plastics

Recycling Code	Polymer	Common Uses	Uses of Recycled Polymer
1 PET	Poly(ethylene terephthalate)	Soft-drink bottles, household chemical bottles, films, textile fibers	Soft-drink bottles, household chemical bottles, films, textile fibers
2 HDPE	High-density polyethylene	Milk and water jugs, grocery bags, bottles	Bottles, molded containers
3 V	Poly(vinyl chloride), PVC	Shampoo bottles, pipes, shower curtains, vinyl siding, wire insulation, floor tiles, credit cards	Plastic floor mats
4 LDPE	Low-density polyethylene	Shrink wrap, trash and grocery bags, sandwich bags, squeeze bottles	Trash bags and grocery bags
5 PP	Polypropylene	Plastic lids, clothing fibers, bottle caps, toys, diaper linings	Mixed-plastic components
6 PS	Polystyrene	Styrofoam™ cups, egg cartons, disposable utensils, packaging materials, appliances	Molded items such as cafeteria trays, rulers, Frisbees™, trash cans, videocasettes
7	All other plastics and mixed plastics	Various	Plastic lumber, playground equipment, road reflectors

soft-drink bottles usually have a paper label and adhesive that must be removed before the PET can be reused. The recycling process begins with hand or machine sorting, after which the bottles are shredded into small chips. An air cyclone then removes paper and other lightweight materials. Any remaining labels and adhesives are eliminated with a detergent wash, and the PET chips are then dried. PET produced by this method is 99.9% free of contaminants and sells for about half the price of the virgin material. Unfortunately, plastics with similar densities cannot be separated with this technology, nor can plastics composed of several polymers be broken down into pure components. However, recycled mixed plastics can be molded into plastic lumber that is strong, durable, and resistant to graffiti.

An alternative to the foregoing process, which uses only physical methods of purification, is chemical recycling. Large amounts of PET film scrap are salvaged by a transesterification reaction. The scrap is treated with methanol in the presence of an acid catalyst to give ethylene glycol and dimethyl terephthalate, monomers that are purified by distillation or recrystallization and used as feedstocks for the production of more PET film:

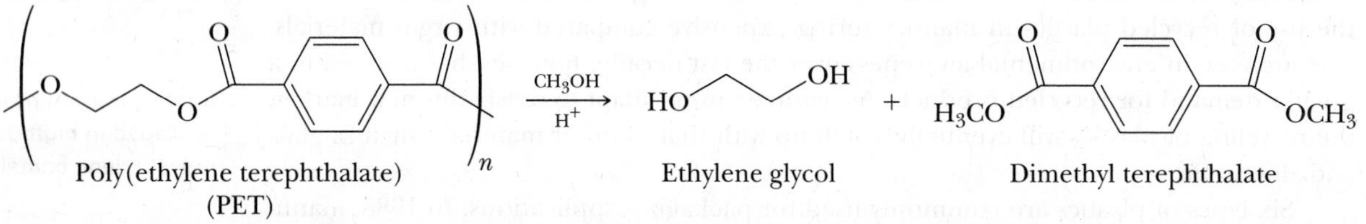

SUMMARY OF KEY QUESTIONS

16.1 What Is the Architecture of Polymers?

- **Polymerization** is the process of joining together many small **monomers** into large, high-molecular-weight **polymers.**
- **Polymers** are long-chain molecules synthesized by linking monomers through chemical reactions. The molecular weight of polymers is generally high compared with those of common organic compounds, and typically range from 10,000 g/mol to more than 1,000,000 g/mol.
- **Thermoplastics** are polymers that can be molded when hot and that retain their shape when cooled.
- **Thermosetting plastics** can be molded when they are first prepared, but once cooled, they harden irreversibly and cannot be remelted.

16.2 How Do We Name and Show the Structure of a Polymer?

- The **repeat unit** of a polymer is the smallest unit that contains all of the structural features of the polymer.
- To show the structure of a polymer, enclose the repeat unit in parentheses and place a subscript *n* outside the parentheses to show that this structural unit repeats *n* times in a polymer chain.
- An entire polymer chain can be reproduced by repeating the enclosed structural unit in both directions.
- The most common method of naming a polymer is to add the prefix **poly**- to the name of the monomer from which the polymer is synthesized. If the name of the monomer is two or more words, enclose its name in parentheses.

16.3 What Is Polymer Morphology? Crystalline versus Amorphous Materials

- The properties of polymeric materials depend on the structure of the repeat unit, as well as on the **chain architecture** and **morphology** of the material.
- Polymers, like small organic molecules, tend to crystallize upon precipitation or as they are cooled from a melt.
- Acting to inhibit crystallization are the facts that polymer molecules are very large, which inhibits their diffusion, and that their structures are sometimes complicated and irregular.
- Polymers in the solid state tend to be composed of both ordered **crystalline domains** (crystallites) and disordered **amorphous domains**.

- The temperature at which a polymer undergoes the transition from a hard glass to a rubbery state corresponds to the **glass transition temperature (T_g)**.
- As the degree of crystallinity of a polymer increases, the polymer becomes more opaque because of the scattering of light by its crystalline domains. With an increase in crystallinity comes an increase in strength and stiffness.
- Amorphous polymers have little or no long-range order. Because they lack crystalline domains that scatter light, amorphous polymers are transparent. In addition, they tend to be highly flexible and have low mechanical strength.

16.4 What Is Step-Growth Polymerization?

- **Step-growth polymerizations** involve the stepwise reaction of difunctional monomers.
- The two most common types of step-growth polymerizations involve (1) reaction between A-M-A and B-M-B monomers to give –(A-M-A-B-M-B)$_n$- polymers, where A and B are reactive functional groups, and (2) self-condensations of A-M-B monomers to give –(A-M-B)$_n$- polymers.
- Important commercial polymers synthesized through step-growth processes include polyamides, polyesters, polycarbonates, polyurethanes, and epoxy resins.

16.5 What Are Chain-Growth Polymers?

- **Chain-growth polymerization** proceeds by the sequential addition of monomer units to an active chain end-group.
- **Radical chain-growth polymerization** consists of three stages: chain initiation, chain propagation, and chain termination.
- **Alkyl radicals** are planar or almost so with bond angles of approximately 120° about the carbon with the unpaired electron.
- In **chain initiation**, radicals are formed from nonradical molecules.
- In **chain propagation**, a radical and a monomer react to give a new radical.
- **Chain length** is the number of times a cycle of chain propagation steps repeats.
- In **chain termination**, radicals are destroyed.
- **Ziegler–Natta chain-growth polymerization** involves the formation of an alkyl-transition metal compound and then the repeated insertion of alkene monomers into the transition metal-to-carbon bond to yield a saturated polymer chain.

16.6 What Plastics Are Commonly Recycled in Large Quantities?

- The six types of plastics commonly used for packaging applications have been assigned recycling codes with values 1 through 6.
- Currently, only (1) poly(ethylene terephthalate), PET, and (2) high-density polyethylene (HDPE) are recycled in large quantities.

QUICK QUIZ

Answer true or false to the following questions to assess your general knowledge of the concepts in this chapter. If you have difficulty with any of them, you should review the appropriate section in the chapter (shown in parentheses) before attempting the more challenging end-of-chapter problems.

1. Radicals can undergo chain-growth polymerization. (16.5)
2. A thermosetting plastic cannot be remelted. (16.1)
3. Chain-transfer reactions can lead to branching in polymers. (16.5)
4. Polymers that have low glass transition temperatures can behave as elastomers. (16.3)
5. A highly crystalline polymer will have a glass transition temperature. (16.3)
6. Polymers can be named from the monomeric units from which they are derived. (16.2)
7. Only compounds that have two or more functional groups can undergo step-growth polymerization. (16.4)
8. The propagation step of a radical polymerization mechanism involves the reaction of a radical with another radical. (16.5)
9. A radical is a molecule with an unpaired electron and a positive charge. (16.5)
10. The term *plastics* can be used to refer to all polymers. (16.1)
11. The mechanism of a radical polymerization reaction involves three distinct steps. (16.5)
12. Hydrogen bonding will usually weaken the fibers of a polymer. (16.4)
13. A secondary radical is more stable than a tertiary radical. (16.5)

14. A thermoplastic can be molded multiple times through heating and cooling. (16.1)
15. Ziegler–Natta polymerization uses a titanium catalyst. (16.5)

Answers: (1) T (2) T (3) T (4) T (5) F (6) F (7) T (8) F (9) F (10) F (11) T (12) F (13) F (14) T (15) T

Detailed explanations for many of these answers can be found in the accompanying Solutions Manual.

KEY REACTIONS

1. Step-growth polymerization of a dicarboxylic acid and a diamine gives a polyamide (Section 16.4A)

In this equation, M and M′ indicate the remainder of each monomer unit:

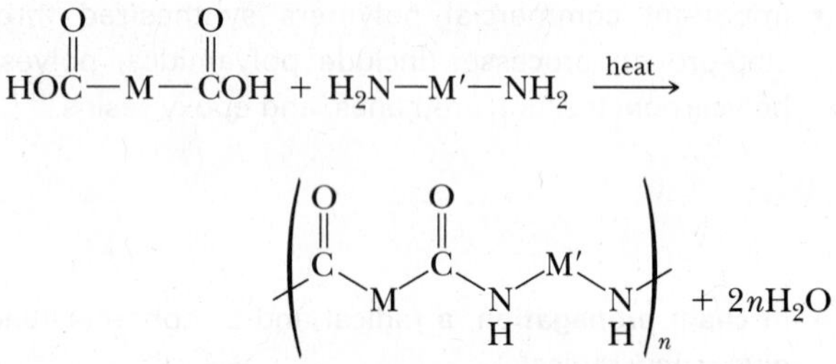

2. Step-growth polymerization of a dicarboxylic acid and a diol gives a polyester (Section 16.4B)

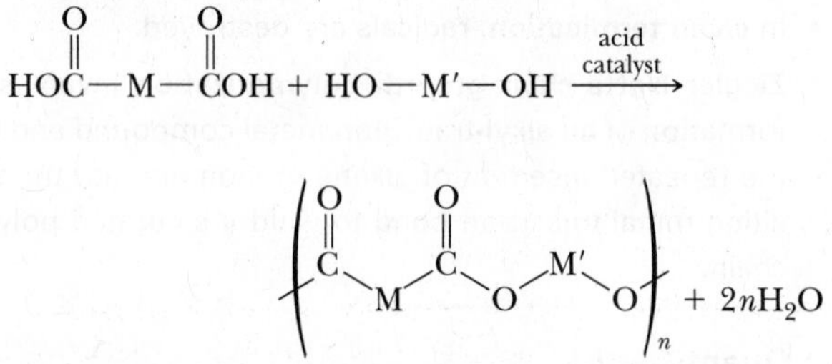

3. Step-growth polymerization of phosgene and a diol gives a polycarbonate (Section 16.4C)

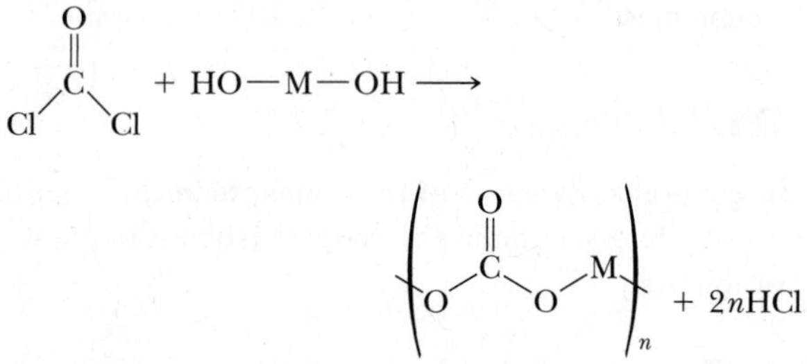

4. Step-growth polymerization of a diisocyanate and a diol gives a polyurethane (Section 16.4D)

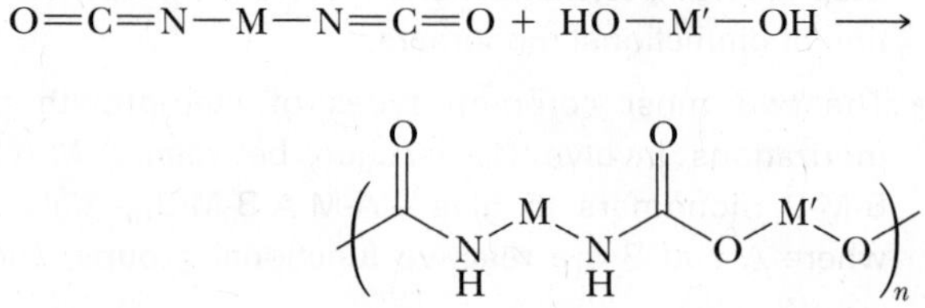

5. Step-growth polymerization of a diepoxide and a diamine gives an epoxy resin (Section 16.4E)

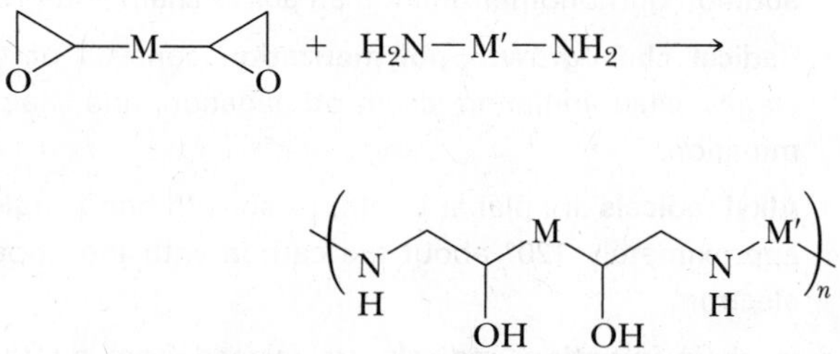

6. Radical chain-growth polymerization of ethylene and substituted ethylenes (Section 16.5A)

$$n\text{CH}_2{=}\text{CHCOOCH}_3 \xrightarrow[\text{heat}]{\text{peroxide}} \left(\text{CH}_2\overset{\text{COOCH}_3}{\overset{|}{\text{CH}}}\right)_n$$

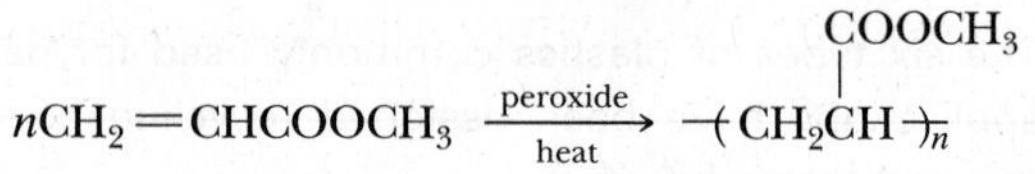

7. Ziegler–Natta chain-growth polymerization of ethylene and substituted ethylenes (Section 16.5B)

$$n\text{CH}_2{=}\text{CHCH}_3 \xrightarrow[\text{MgCl}_2]{\text{TiCl}_4/\text{Al(C}_2\text{H}_5)_2\text{Cl}} \left(\text{CH}_2\overset{\text{CH}_3}{\overset{|}{\text{CH}}}\right)_n$$

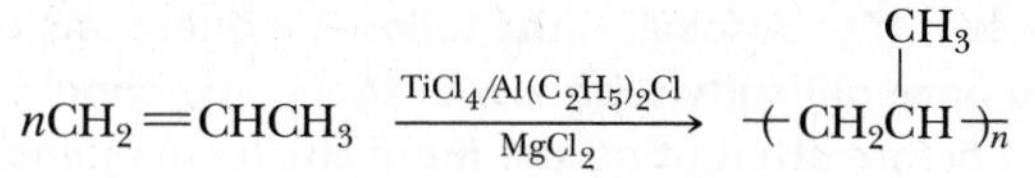

PROBLEMS

A problem marked with an asterisk indicates an applied "real-world" problem. Answers to problems whose numbers are printed in blue are given in Appendix D.

Section 16.4 Step-Growth Polymers

*16.3 Identify the monomers required for the synthesis of each step-growth polymer:

(a) Kodel™
(a polyester)

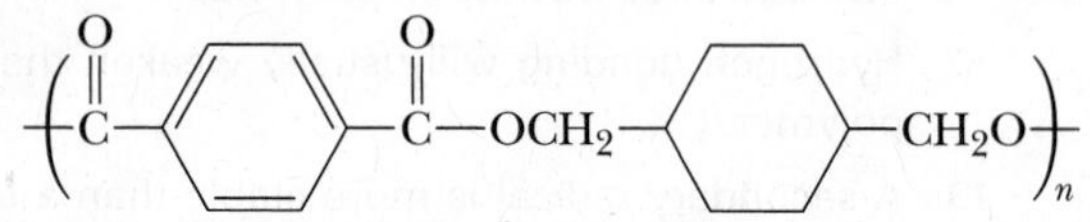

(b) 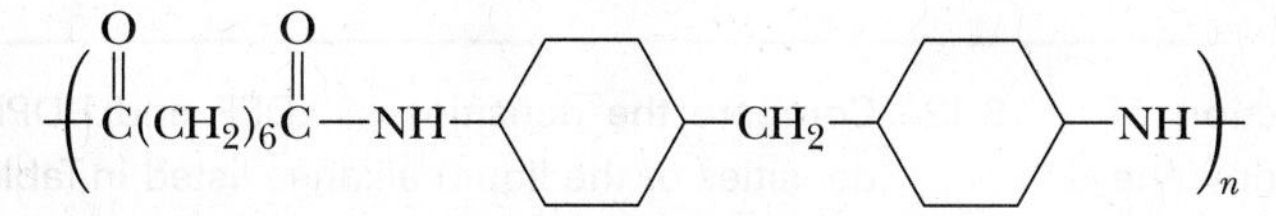

Quiana™
(a polyamide)

(c) 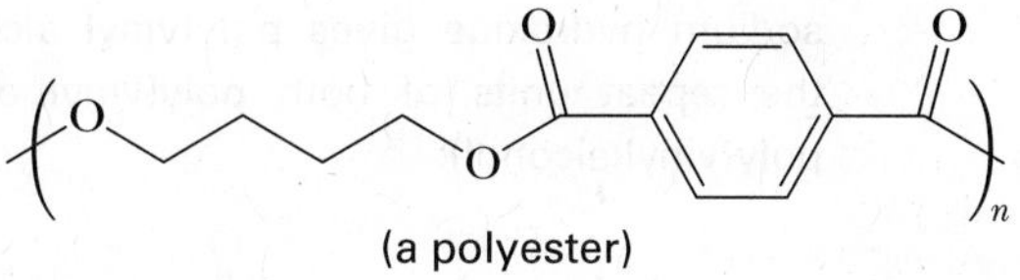

(a polyester)

(d) 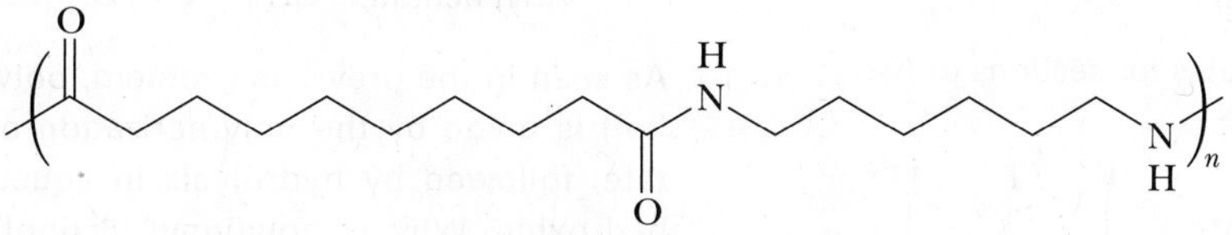

Nylon 6,10
(a polyamide)

16.4 Poly(ethylene terephthalate) (PET) can be prepared by the following reaction:

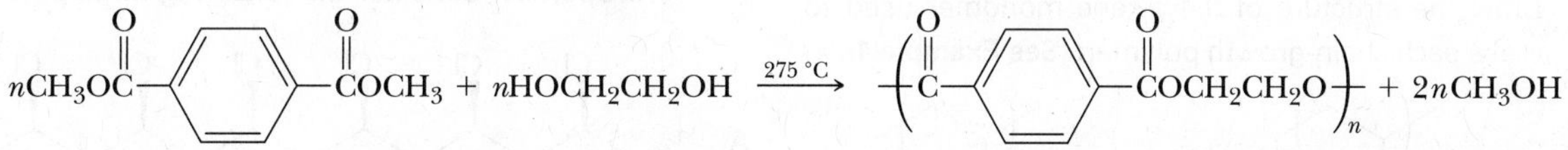

Dimethyl terephthalate — Ethylene glycol — Poly(ethylene terephthalate) — Methanol

Propose a mechanism for the step-growth reaction in this polymerization.

***16.5** Currently, about 30% of PET soft-drink bottles are being recycled. In one recycling process, scrap PET is heated with methanol in the presence of an acid catalyst. The methanol reacts with the polymer, liberating ethylene glycol and dimethyl terephthalate. These monomers are then used as feedstock for the production of new PET products. Write an equation for the reaction of PET with methanol to give ethylene glycol and dimethyl terephthalate.

***16.6** Nomex® is an aromatic polyamide (aramid) prepared from the polymerization of 1,3-benzenediamine and the acid chloride of 1,3-benzenedicarboxylic acid:

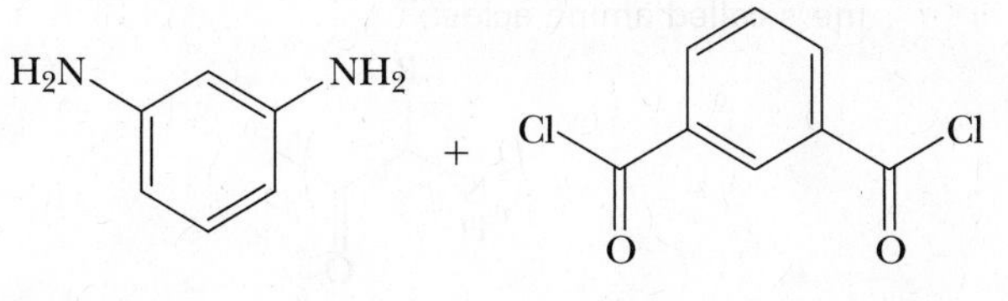

1,3-Benzenediamine — 1,3-Benzene-dicarbonyl chloride

$\xrightarrow{\text{polymerization}}$ Nomex

The physical properties of the polymer make it suitable for high-strength, high-temperature applications such as parachute cords and jet aircraft tires. Draw a structural formula for the repeating unit of Nomex.

16.7 Nylon 6,10 [Problem 16.3(d)] can be prepared by reacting a diamine and a diacid chloride. Draw the structural formula of each reactant.

Section 16.5 Chain-Growth Polymerization

16.8 Following is the structural formula of a section of polypropylene derived from three units of propylene monomer:

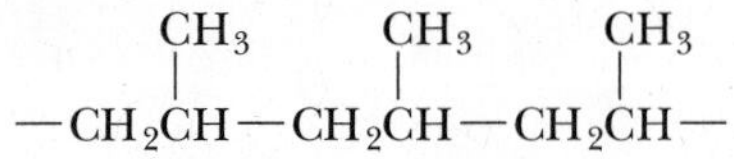

Polypropylene

Draw a structural formula for a comparable section of

(a) Poly(vinyl chloride)
(b) Polytetrafluoroethylene (PTFE)
(c) Poly(methyl methacrylate)

16.9 Following are structural formulas for sections of two polymers: **(See Example 16.1)**

(a) 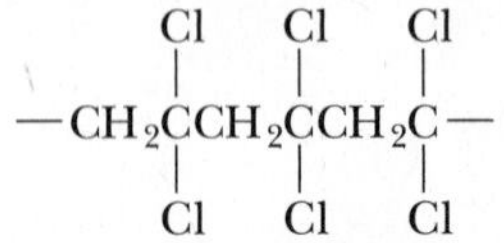 (b) 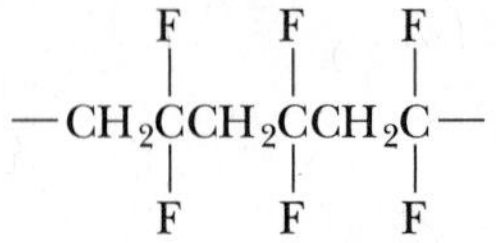

From what alkene monomer is each polymer derived?

16.10 Draw the structure of the alkene monomer used to make each chain-growth polymer: **(See Example 16.1)**

(a) 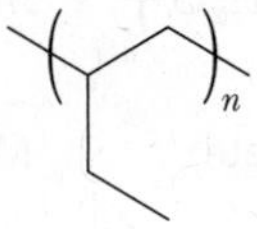 (b) 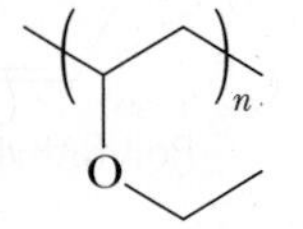

(c) 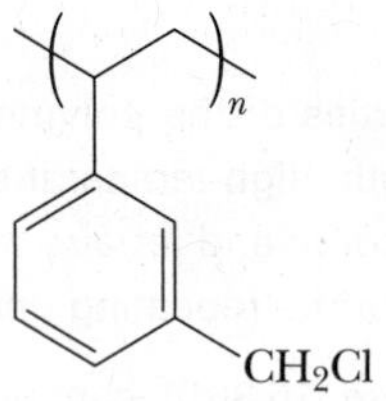 (d) 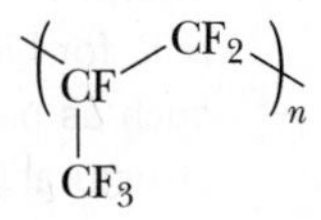

16.11 LDPE has a higher degree of chain branching than HDPE. Explain the relationship between chain branching and density.

16.12 Compare the densities of LDPE and HDPE with the densities of the liquid alkanes listed in Table 3.4. How might you account for the differences between them?

16.13 The polymerization of vinyl acetate gives poly(vinyl acetate). Hydrolysis of this polymer in aqueous sodium hydroxide gives poly(vinyl alcohol). Draw the repeat units of both poly(vinyl acetate) and poly(vinyl alcohol):

Vinyl acetate 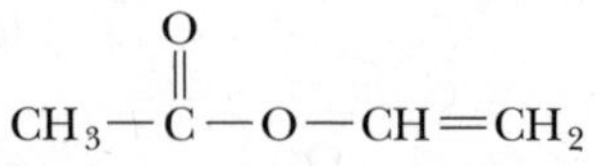

16.14 As seen in the previous problem, poly(vinyl alcohol) is made by the polymerization of vinyl acetate, followed by hydrolysis in aqueous sodium hydroxide. Why is poly(vinyl alcohol) not made instead by the polymerization of vinyl alcohol, $CH_2{=}CHOH$?

16.15 As you know, the shape of a polymer chain affects its properties. Consider the following three polymers:

A 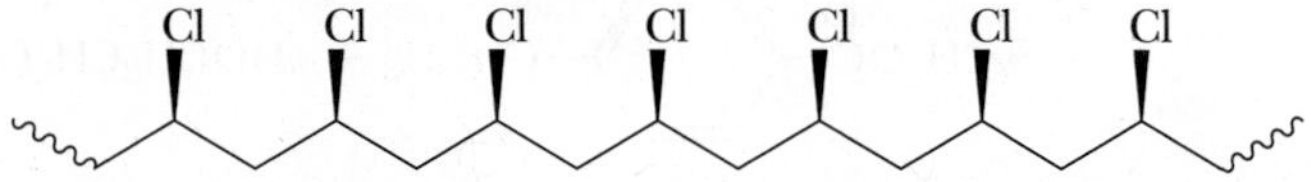

B 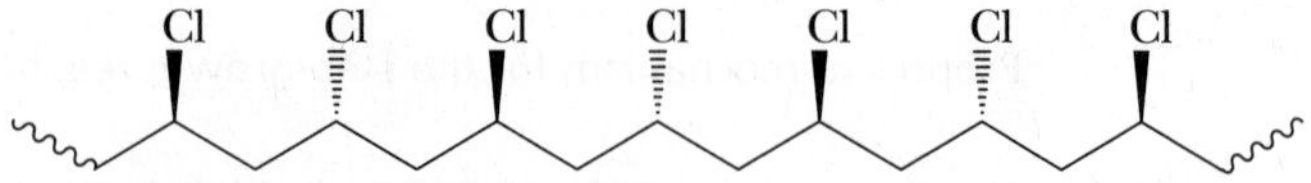

C 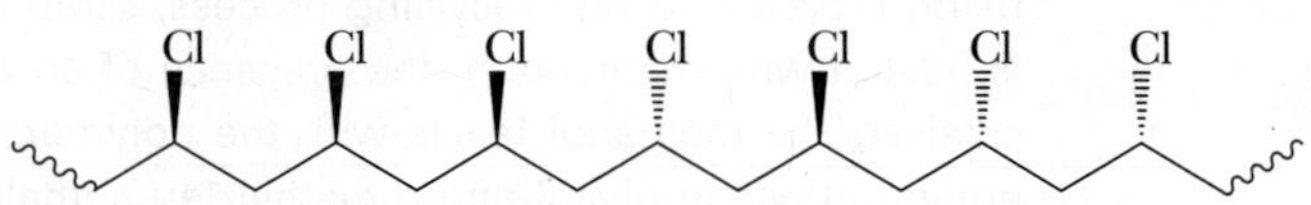

Which do you expect to be the most rigid? Which do you expect to be the most transparent? (Assume the same molecular weights.)

LOOKING AHEAD

16.16 Cellulose, the principal component of cotton, is a polymer of D-glucose in which the monomer unit repeats at the indicated atoms:

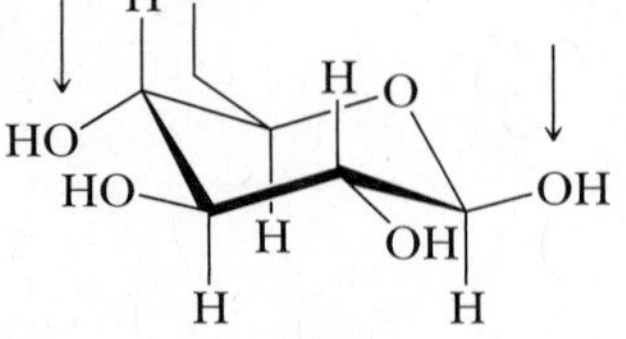

D-Glucose

Draw a three-unit section of cellulose.

16.17 Is a repeating unit a requirement for a compound to be called a polymer?

16.18 Proteins are polymers of naturally occurring monomers called amino acids:

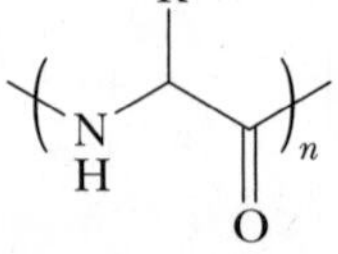

a protein

Amino acids differ in the types of R groups available in nature. Explain how the following properties of a protein might be affected upon changing the R groups from $-CH_2CH(CH_3)_2$ to $-CH_2OH$:

(a) solubility in water (b) melting point
(c) crystallinity (d) elasticity

GROUP LEARNING ACTIVITIES

16.19 Only certain kinds of polymers are readily biodegradable; that is, only certain types have chemical bonds that are easily broken in the process of composting. Chief among these polymers are those that contain ester bonds because ester bonds are readily broken by esterases, microbial enzymes that catalyze the hydrolysis of esters. For this reason, all presently available biodegradable polymers are polyesters. Following are structural formulas for three such biodegradable polyesters. As a group, draw structural formulas and write names for the monomer units present in each. Provide a mechanism for the acid-catalyzed hydrolysis of all hydrolyzable bonds in Ecoflex.

(a) 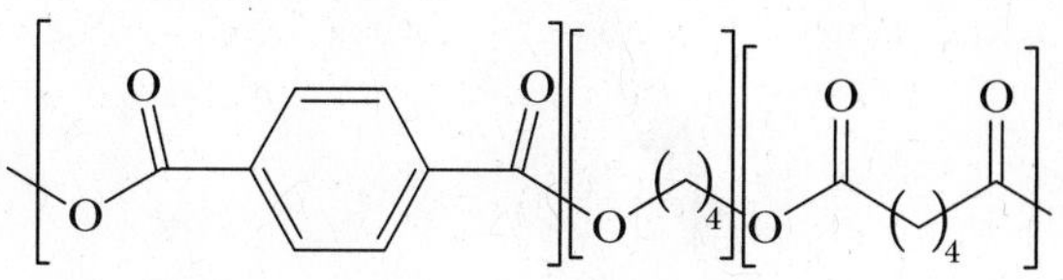

Ecoflex (BASF)

(b) 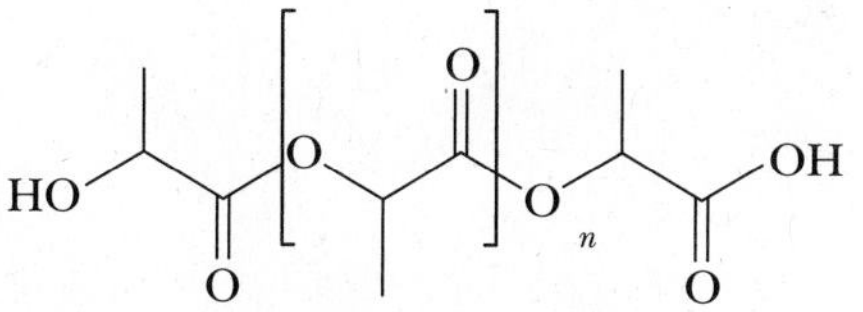

Ingeo (Nature Works)

(c) 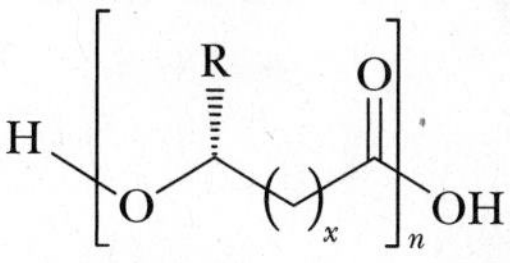

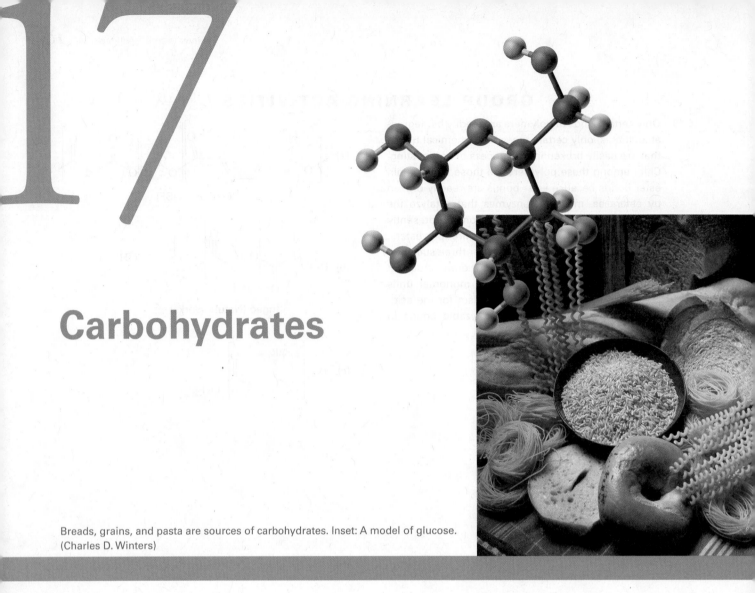

KEY QUESTIONS

- 17.1 What Are Carbohydrates?
- 17.2 What Are Monosaccharides?
- 17.3 What Are the Cyclic Structures of Monosaccharides?
- 17.4 What Are the Characteristic Reactions of Monosaccharides?
- 17.5 What Are Disaccharides and Oligosaccharides?
- 17.6 What Are Polysaccharides?

HOW TO

- 17.1 Determine the Stereochemistry of OH Groups in Cyclic p-Monosaccharides
- 17.2 Determine If a Carbohydrate Is a Reducing Sugar

CHEMICAL CONNECTIONS

- 17A Relative Sweetness of Carbohydrate and Artificial Sweeteners
- 17B A, B, AB, and O Blood-Group Substances

17.1 What Are Carbohydrates?

Carbohydrates are the most abundant organic compounds in the plant world. They act as storehouses of chemical energy (glucose, starch, glycogen); are components of supportive structures in plants (cellulose), crustacean shells (chitin), and connective tissues in animals (acidic polysaccharides); and are essential components of nucleic acids (p-ribose and 2-deoxy-p-ribose). Carbohydrates account for approximately three-fourths of the dry weight of plants. Animals (including humans) get their carbohydrates by eating plants, but

they do not store much of what they consume. In fact, less than 1% of the body weight of animals is made up of carbohydrates.

The word *carbohydrate* means "hydrate of carbon" and derives from the formula $C_n(H_2O)_m$. Two examples of carbohydrates with molecular formulas that can be written alternatively as hydrates of carbon are

- glucose (blood sugar), $C_6H_{12}O_6$, which can be written as $C_6(H_2O)_6$, and
- sucrose (table sugar), $C_{12}H_{22}O_{11}$, which can be written as $C_{12}(H_2O)_{11}$.

Not all carbohydrates, however, have this general formula. Some contain too few oxygen atoms to fit the formula, whereas some contain too many. Some also contain nitrogen. But the term *carbohydrate* has become firmly rooted in chemical nomenclature and, although not completely accurate, it persists as the name for this class of compounds.

At the molecular level, most **carbohydrates** are polyhydroxyaldehydes, polyhydroxyketones, or compounds that yield them after hydrolysis. Therefore, the chemistry of carbohydrates is essentially the chemistry of hydroxyl and carbonyl groups and of acetal bonds (Section 12.6A) formed between these two functional groups.

Carbohydrate A polyhydroxyaldehyde or polyhydroxyketone or a substance that gives these compounds on hydrolysis.

17.2 What Are Monosaccharides?

A. Structure and Nomenclature

Monosaccharides have the general formula $C_nH_{2n}O_n$, with one of the carbons being the carbonyl group of either an aldehyde or a ketone. The most common monosaccharides have from three to nine carbon atoms. The suffix *-ose* indicates that a molecule is a carbohydrate, and the prefixes *tri-*, *tetr-*, *pent-*, and so forth, indicate the number of carbon atoms in the chain. Monosaccharides containing an aldehyde group are classified as **aldoses**; those containing a ketone group are classified as **ketoses**.

Monosaccharide A carbohydrate that cannot be hydrolyzed to a simpler compound.

Aldose A monosaccharide containing an aldehyde group.

Ketose A monosaccharide containing a ketone group.

There are only two **trioses**—glyceraldehyde, which is an aldotriose, and dihydroxyacetone, which is a ketotriose:

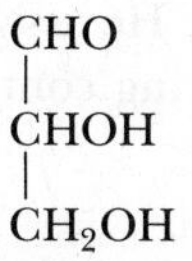

Glyceraldehyde (an aldotriose) Dihydroxyacetone (a ketotriose)

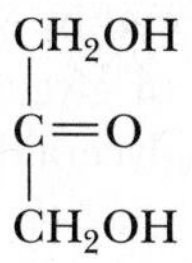

Often the designations *aldo-* and *keto-* are omitted, and these molecules are referred to simply as trioses, **tetroses**, and the like. Although these designations do not tell the nature of the carbonyl group, at least they indicate that the monosaccharide contains three and four carbon atoms, respectively.

B. Stereoisomerism

Glyceraldehyde contains one stereocenter and exists as a pair of enantiomers. The stereoisomer shown on the left has the *R* configuration and is named (*R*)-glyceraldehyde, while its enantiomer, shown on the right, is named (*S*)-glyceraldehyde:

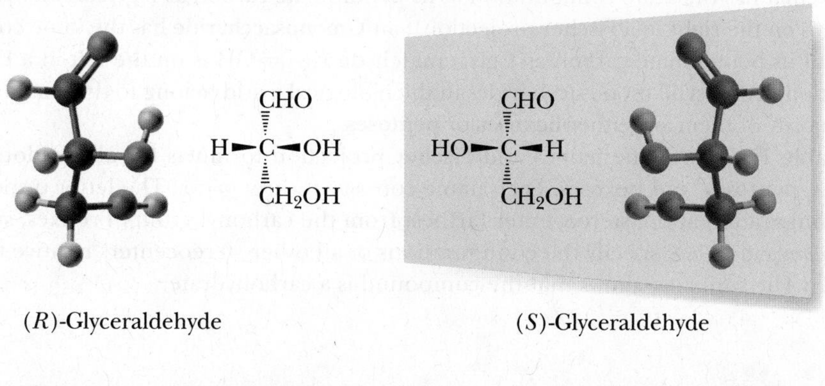

(*R*)-Glyceraldehyde (*S*)-Glyceraldehyde

C. Fischer Projection Formulas

Fischer projection A two-dimensional representation showing the configuration of a stereocenter; horizontal lines represent bonds projecting forward from the stereocenter, whereas vertical lines represent bonds projecting to the rear.

Chemists commonly use two-dimensional representations called **Fischer projections** to show the configuration of carbohydrates. To draw a Fischer projection, draw a three-dimensional representation with the most oxidized carbon toward the top and the molecule oriented so that the vertical bonds from the stereocenter are directed away from you and the horizontal bonds from it are directed toward you. Then write the molecule as a two-dimensional figure with the stereocenter indicated by the point at which the bonds cross. You now have a Fischer projection.

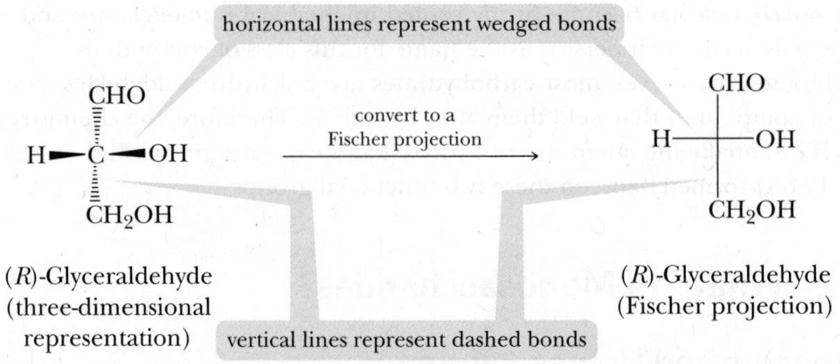

The two horizontal segments of this Fischer projection represent bonds directed toward you, and the two vertical segments represent bonds directed away from you. The only atom in the plane of the paper is the stereocenter.

D. D- and L-Monosaccharides

Even though the *R,S* system is widely accepted today as a standard for designating the configuration of stereocenters, we still commonly designate the configuration of carbohydrates by the D,L system proposed by Emil Fischer in 1891. He assigned the dextrorotatory and levorotatory enantiomers of glyceraldehyde the following configurations and named them D-glyceraldehyde and L-glyceraldehyde, respectively:

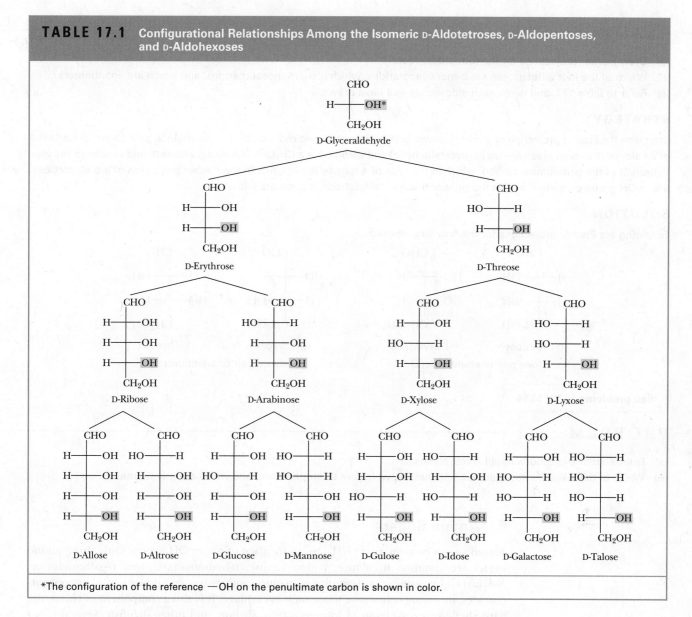

D-Glyceraldehyde $[\alpha]_D^{25} = +13.5°$ L-Glyceraldehyde $[\alpha]_D^{25} = -13.5°$

Penultimate carbon The stereocenter of a monosaccharide farthest from the carbonyl group—for example, carbon 5 of glucose.

D-Monosaccharide A monosaccharide that, when written as a Fischer projection, has the —OH on its penultimate carbon to the right.

L-Monosaccharide A monosaccharide that, when written as a Fischer projection, has the —OH on its penultimate carbon to the left.

D-glyceraldehyde and L-glyceraldehyde serve as reference points for the assignment of relative configurations to all other aldoses and ketoses. The reference point is the stereocenter farthest from the carbonyl group. Because this stereocenter is the next-to-the-last carbon on the chain, it is called the **penultimate carbon.** A **D-monosaccharide** is a monosaccharide that has the same configuration at its penultimate carbon as D-glyceraldehyde (its —OH is on the right in a Fischer projection); an **L-monosaccharide** has the same configuration at its penultimate carbon as L-glyceraldehyde (its —OH is on the left in a Fischer projection). Almost all monosaccharides in the biological world belong to the D series, and the majority of them are either **hexoses** or **pentoses**.

Table 17.1 shows the names and Fischer projection formulas for all D-aldotrioses, tetroses, pentoses, and hexoses. Each name consists of three parts. The letter D specifies the configuration at the stereocenter farthest from the carbonyl group. Prefixes, such as *rib-*, *arabin-*, and *gluc-*, specify the configurations of all other stereocenters relative to one another. The suffix *-ose* shows that the compound is a carbohydrate.

TABLE 17.1 Configurational Relationships Among the Isomeric D-Aldotetroses, D-Aldopentoses, and D-Aldohexoses

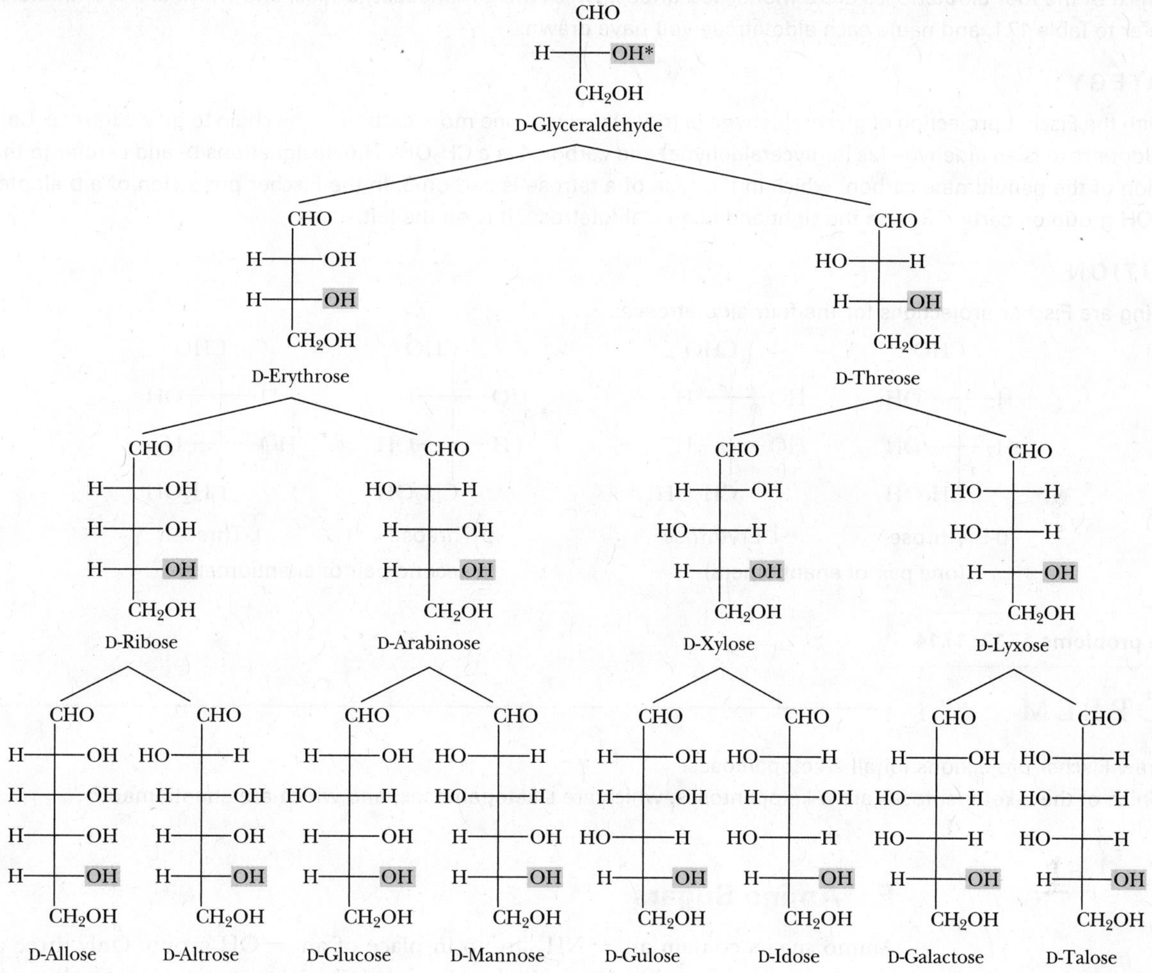

*The configuration of the reference —OH on the penultimate carbon is shown in color.

The three most abundant hexoses in the biological world are D-glucose, D-galactose, and D-fructose. The first two are D-aldohexoses; the third, fructose, is a D-2-ketohexose. Glucose, by far the most abundant of the three, is also known as dextrose because it is dextrorotatory. Other names for this monosaccharide include *grape sugar* and *blood sugar*. Human blood normally contains 65–110 mg of glucose/100 mL of blood. D-Fructose is one of the two monosaccharide building blocks of sucrose (table sugar, Section 17.7A):

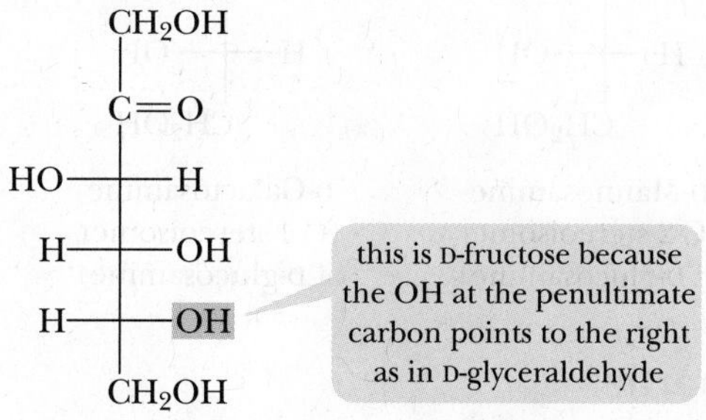

D-Fructose

EXAMPLE 17.1

(a) Draw Fischer projections for the four aldotetroses.
(b) Which of the four aldotetroses are D-monosaccharides, which are L-monosaccharides, and which are enantiomers?
(c) Refer to Table 17.1, and name each aldotetrose you have drawn.

STRATEGY

Start with the Fischer projection of glyceraldehyde (a triose) and add one more carbon to the chain to give a tetrose. Carbon-1 of an aldotetrose is an aldehyde (as in glyceraldehyde) and carbon 4 is a CH_2OH. The designations D- and L- refer to the configuration of the penultimate carbon, which in the case of a tetrose is carbon 3. In the Fischer projection of a D-aldotetrose, the —OH group on carbon 3 is on the right and in an L-aldotetrose, it is on the left.

SOLUTION

Following are Fischer projections for the four aldotetroses:

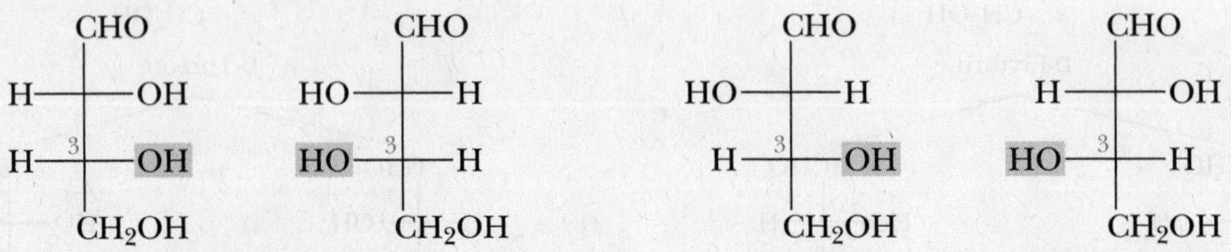

D-Erythrose L-Erythrose D-Threose L-Threose

(one pair of enantiomers) (a second pair of enantiomers)

See problems 17.13, 17.14

PROBLEM 17.1

(a) Draw Fischer projections for all 2-ketopentoses.
(b) Which of the 2-ketopentoses are D-ketopentoses, which are L-ketopentoses, and which are enantiomers?

E. Amino Sugars

Amino sugars contain an $—NH_2$ group in place of an —OH group. Only three amino sugars are common in nature: D-glucosamine, D-mannosamine, and D-galactosamine. *N*-Acetyl-D-glucosamine, a derivative of D-glucosamine, is a component of many polysaccharides, including connective tissue such as cartilage. It is also a component of chitin, the hard shell-like exoskeleton of lobsters, crabs, shrimp, and other shellfish. Several other amino sugars are components of naturally occurring antibiotics.

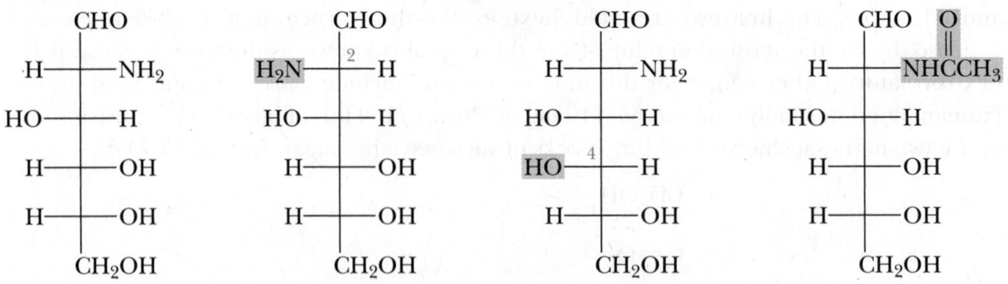

D-Glucosamine D-Mannosamine (C-2 stereoisomer of D-glucosamine) D-Galactosamine (C-4 stereoisomer of D-glucosamine) *N*-Acetyl-D-glucosamine

F. Physical Properties

Monosaccharides are colorless, crystalline solids. Because hydrogen bonding is possible between their polar —OH groups and water, all monosaccharides are very soluble in water.

They are only slightly soluble in ethanol and are insoluble in nonpolar solvents such as diethyl ether, dichloromethane, and benzene.

17.3 What Are the Cyclic Structures of Monosaccharides?

In Section 12.6, we saw that aldehydes and ketones react with alcohols to form **hemiacetals**. We also saw that cyclic hemiacetals form very readily when hydroxyl and carbonyl groups are parts of the same molecule and their interaction can form a five- or six-membered ring. For example, 4-hydroxypentanal forms a five-membered cyclic hemiacetal. Note that 4-hydroxypentanal contains one stereocenter and that a second stereocenter is generated at carbon 1 as a result of hemiacetal formation:

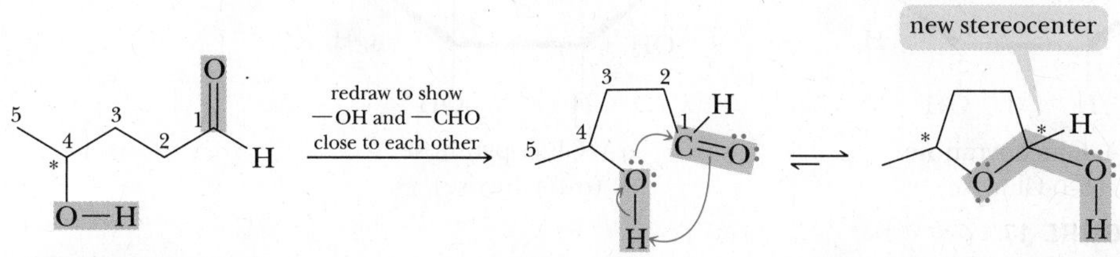

4-Hydroxypentanal
A cyclic hemiacetal

Because monosaccharides have hydroxyl and carbonyl groups in the same molecule, they exist almost exclusively as five- and six-membered cyclic hemiacetals.

A. Haworth Projections

A common way of representing the cyclic structure of monosaccharides is the **Haworth projection**, named after the English chemist Sir Walter N. Haworth, Nobel laureate of 1937. In a Haworth projection, a five- or six-membered cyclic hemiacetal is represented as a planar pentagon or hexagon, respectively, lying roughly perpendicular to the plane of the paper. Groups bonded to the carbons of the ring then lie either above or below the plane of the ring. The new stereocenter created in forming the cyclic hemiacetal is called the **anomeric carbon**. Stereoisomers that differ in configuration only at the anomeric carbon are called **anomers**. The anomeric carbon of an aldose is carbon 1; in D-fructose, the most common ketose, it is carbon 2.

Typically, Haworth projections are written with the anomeric carbon at the right and the hemiacetal oxygen at the back right (Figure 17.1).

As you study the open chain and cyclic hemiacetal forms of D-glucose, note that, in converting from a Fischer projection to a Haworth structure,

- Groups on the right in the Fischer projection point down in the Haworth projection.
- Groups on the left in the Fischer projection point up in the Haworth projection.
- For a D-monosaccharide, the terminal $—CH_2OH$ points up in the Haworth projection.
- The configuration of the anomeric —OH group is relative to the terminal $—CH_2OH$ group: If the anomeric —OH group is on the same side as the terminal $—CH_2OH$, its configuration is β; if the anomeric —OH group is on the opposite side, it is α.

A six-membered hemiacetal ring is shown by the infix **-pyran-**, and a five-membered hemiacetal ring is shown by the infix **-furan-**. The terms **furanose** and **pyranose** are used because monosaccharide five- and six-membered rings correspond to the heterocyclic compounds pyran and furan:

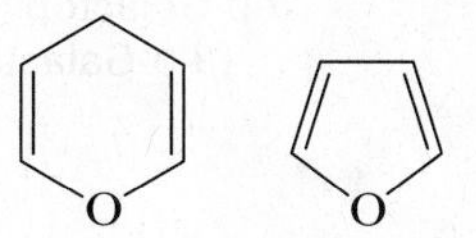
Pyran Furan

Haworth projection A way of viewing the furanose and pyranose forms of monosaccharides. The ring is drawn flat and viewed through its edge, with the anomeric carbon on the right and the oxygen atom of the ring in the rear to the right.

Anomeric carbon The hemiacetal carbon of the cyclic form of a monosaccharide.

Anomers Monosaccharides that differ in configuration only at their anomeric carbons.

Furanose A five-membered cyclic hemiacetal form of a monosaccharide.

Pyranose A six-membered cyclic hemiacetal form of a monosaccharide.

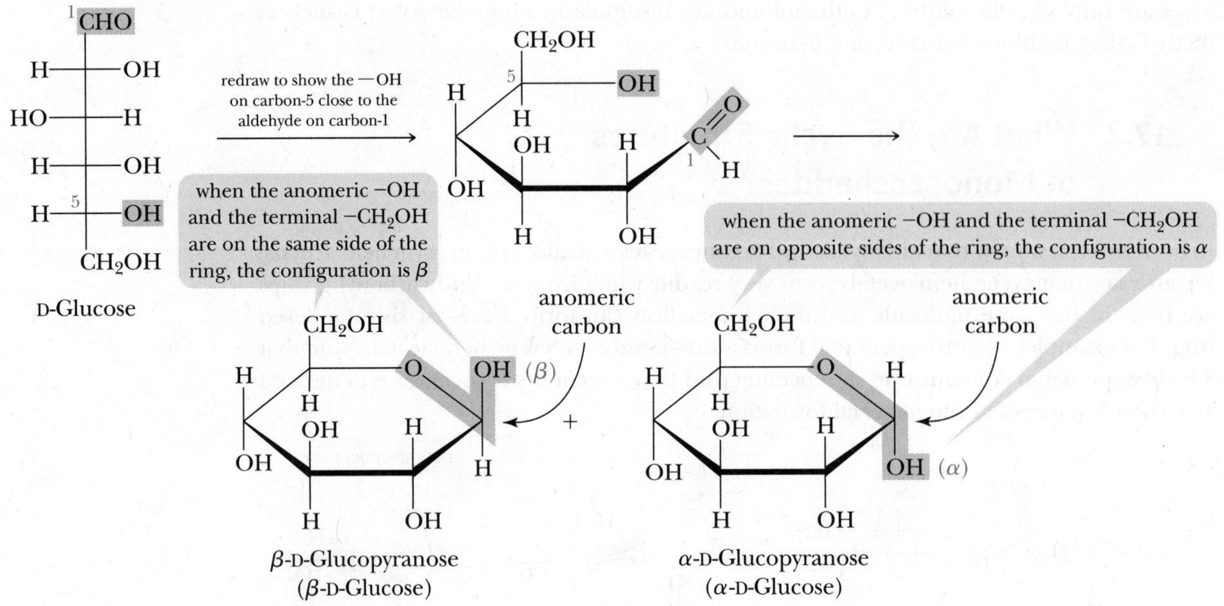

FIGURE 17.1
Haworth projections for β-D-glucopyranose and α-D-glucopyranose.

Because the α and β forms of glucose are six-membered cyclic hemiacetals, they are named α-D-glucopyranose and β-D-glucopyranose, respectively. The designations *-furan-* and *-pyran-* are not always used, however, in names of monosaccharides. Thus, the glucopyranoses are often named simply α-D-glucose and β-D-glucose.

You would do well to remember the configuration of groups on the Haworth projection of both α-D-glucopyranose and β-D-glucopyranose as reference structures. Knowing how the Fischer projection of any other monosaccharide differs from that of D-glucose, you can then construct the Haworth projection of that other monosaccharide by reference to the Haworth projection of D-glucose.

EXAMPLE 17.2

Draw Haworth projections for the α and β anomers of D-galactopyranose.

STRATEGY

One way to arrive at the structures for the α and β anomers of D-galactopyranose is to use the α and β forms of D-glucopyranose as a reference and to remember (or discover by looking at Table 17.1) that D-galactose differs from D-glucose only in the configuration at carbon 4. Thus, you can begin with the Haworth projections shown in Figure 17.1 and then invert the configuration at carbon 4.

SOLUTION

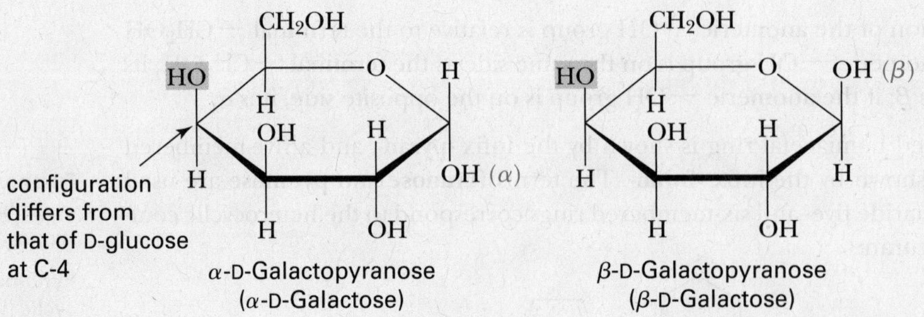

See problems 17.23, 17.26

PROBLEM 17.2

Mannose exists in aqueous solution as a mixture of α-D-mannopyranose and β-D-mannopyranose. Draw Haworth projections for these molecules.

Aldopentoses also form cyclic hemiacetals. The most prevalent forms of D-ribose and other pentoses in the biological world are furanoses. Following are Haworth projections for α-D-ribofuranose (α-D-ribose) and β-2-deoxy-D-ribofuranose (β-2-deoxy-D-ribose):

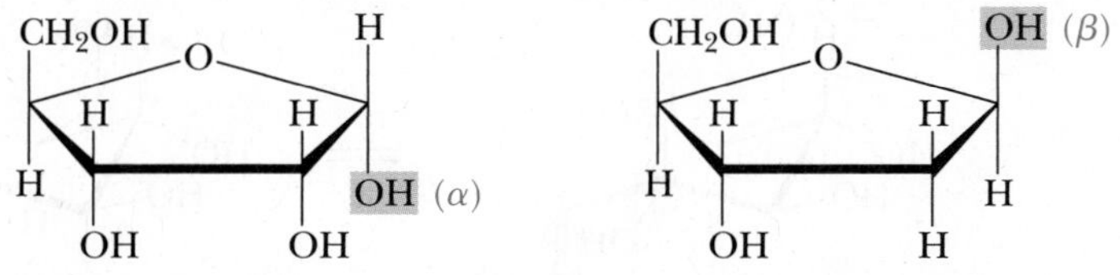

α-D-Ribofuranose
(α-D-Ribose)

β-2-Deoxy-D-ribofuranose
(β-2-Deoxy-D-ribose)

The prefix 2-deoxy indicates the absence of oxygen at carbon 2. Units of D-ribose and 2-deoxy-D-ribose in nucleic acids and most other biological molecules are found almost exclusively in the β-configuration.

Fructose also forms five-membered cyclic hemiacetals. β-D-Fructofuranose, for example, is found in the disaccharide sucrose (Section 17.7A).

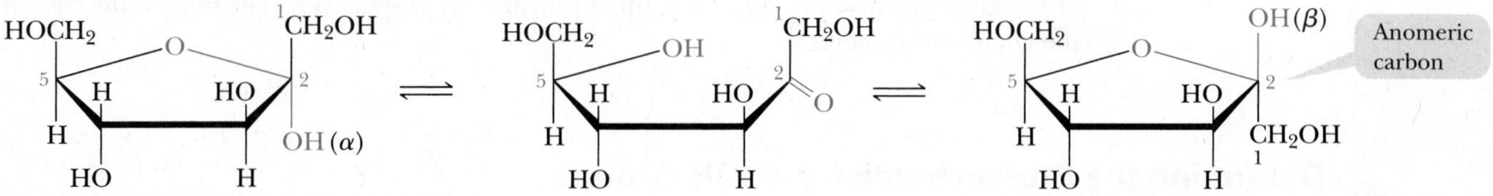

α-D-Fructofuranose
(α-D-Fructose)

β-D-Fructofuranose
(β-D-Fructose)

B. Conformation Representations

A five-membered ring is so close to being planar that Haworth projections are adequate to represent furanoses. For pyranoses, however, the six-membered ring is more accurately represented as a **chair conformation** in which strain is a minimum (Section 3.6B). Figure 17.2 shows structural formulas for α-D-glucopyranose and β-D-glucopyranose, both drawn as chair conformations. The figure also shows the open-chain, or free, aldehyde form with which the cyclic hemiacetal forms are in equilibrium in aqueous solution. Notice that each group, including the anomeric —OH, on the chair conformation of β-D-glucopyranose is equatorial. Notice also that the —OH group on the anomeric carbon in α-D-glucopyranose is axial. Because of the equatorial orientation of the —OH on its anomeric carbon, β-D-glucopyranose is more stable than the α-anomer and therefore predominates in aqueous solution.

At this point, you should compare the relative orientations of groups on the D-glucopyranose ring in the Haworth projection and chair conformation:

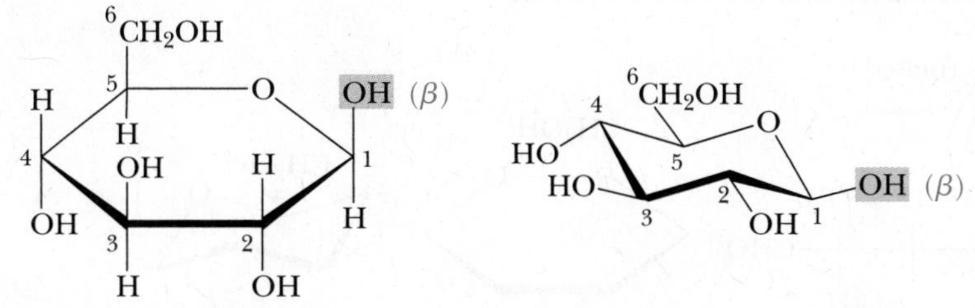

β-D-Glucopyranose
(Haworth projection)

β-D-Glucopyranose
(chair conformation)

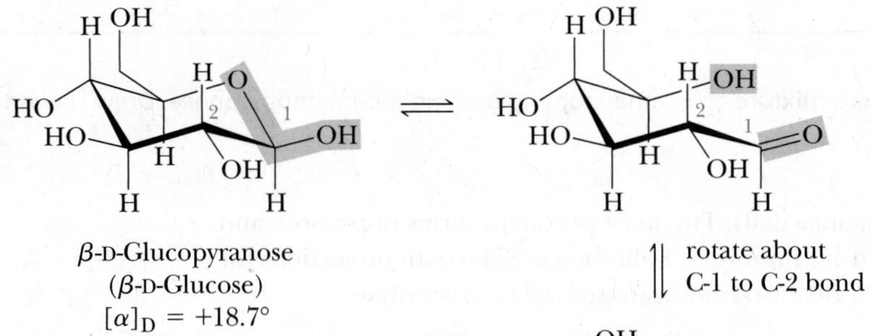

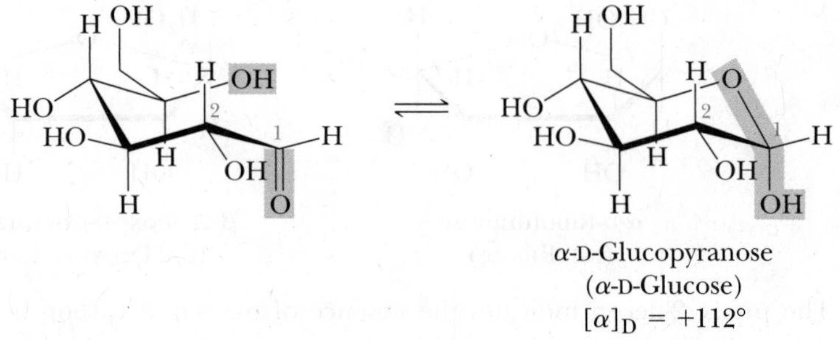

FIGURE 17.2 Chair conformations of α-D-glucopyranose and β-D-glucopyranose. Because α-D-glucose and β-D-glucose are different compounds (they are anomers), they have different specific rotations.

Notice that the orientations of groups on carbons 1 through 5 in the Haworth projection of β-D-glucopyranose are up, down, up, down, and up, respectively. The same is the case in the chair conformation.

HOW TO 17.1

Determine the Stereochemistry of OH Groups in Cyclic D-Monosaccharides

There is another way to determine the stereochemistry of OH groups in the D-series of monosaccharides if you forget the structure of glucopyranose:

(a) Draw the Haworth or chair form of the ring and number the corresponding carbon atoms (don't forget to situate the ring oxygen in the correct position):

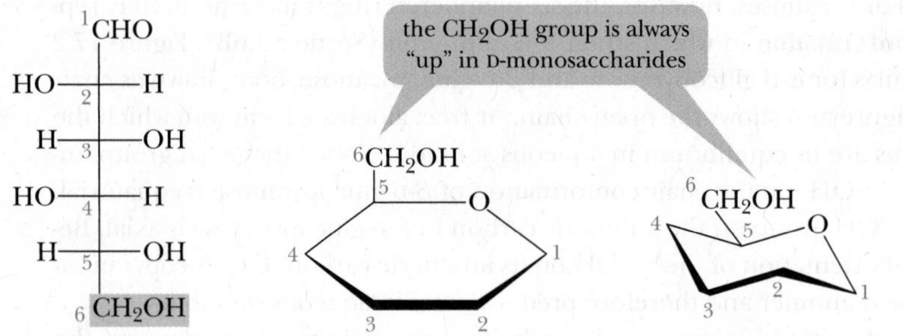

D-Idose

(b) Rotate the drawing of the acyclic monosaccharide clockwise by 90°:

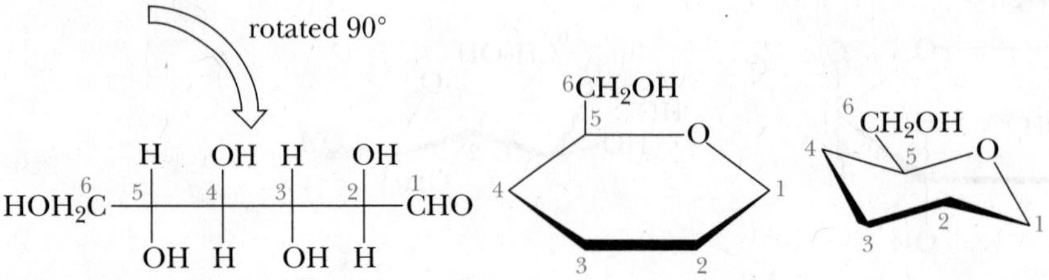

D-Idose

(c) The direction (up or down) of the OH group on the rotated structure is the direction the OH group should be in on the cyclic monosaccharide:

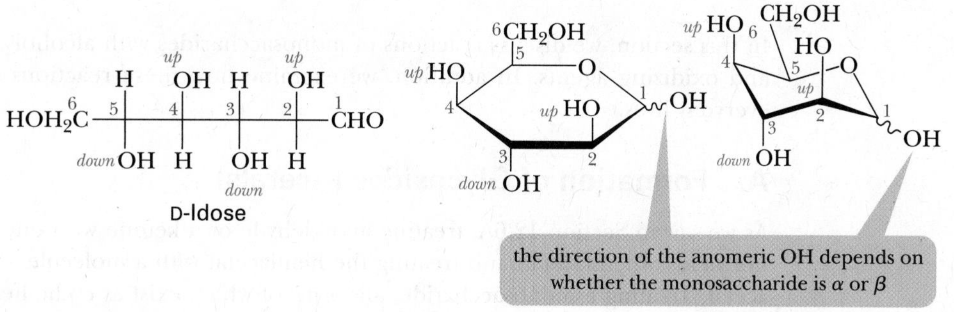

EXAMPLE 17.3

Draw chair conformations for α-D-galactopyranose and β-D-galactopyranose. Label the anomeric carbon in each cyclic hemiacetal.

STRATEGY

The configuration of D-galactose differs from that of D-glucose only at carbon 4. Therefore, draw the α and β forms of D-glucopyranose and then interchange the positions of the —OH and —H groups on carbon 4.

SOLUTION

Shown are the requested α and β forms of D-galactose. Also shown are the specific rotations of each anomer.

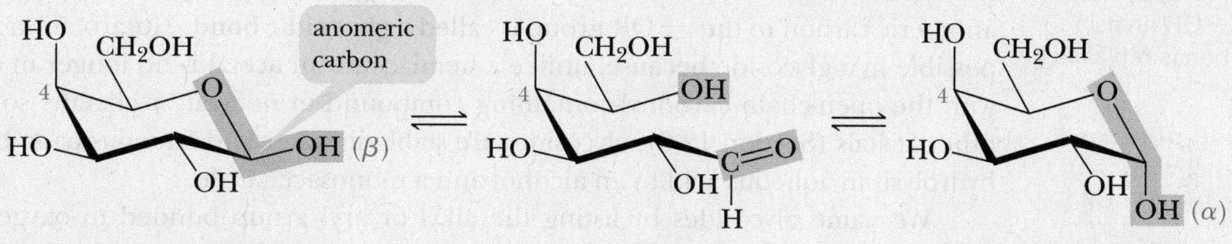

β-D-Galactopyranose (β-D-Galactose) $[\alpha]_D = +52.8°$

D-Galactose

α-D-Galactopyranose (α-D-Galactose) $[\alpha]_D = +150.7°$

See problem 17.26

PROBLEM 17.3

Draw chair conformations for α-D-mannopyranose and β-D-mannopyranose. Label the anomeric carbon atom in each.

C. Mutarotation

Mutarotation is the change in specific rotation that accompanies the interconversion of α- and β-anomers in aqueous solution. As an example, a solution prepared by dissolving crystalline α-D-glucopyranose in water shows an initial rotation of +112° (Figure 17.2), which gradually decreases to an equilibrium value of +52.7° as α-D-glucopyranose reaches an equilibrium with β-D-glucopyranose. A solution of β-D-glucopyranose also undergoes mutarotation, during which the specific rotation changes from an initial value of +18.7° to the same equilibrium value of +52.7°. The equilibrium mixture consists of 64% β-D-glucopyranose and 36% α-D-glucopyranose and contains only traces (0.003%) of the open-chain form. Mutarotation is common to all carbohydrates that exist in hemiacetal forms.

Mutarotation The change in optical activity that occurs when an α or β form of a carbohydrate is converted to an equilibrium mixture of the two forms.

17.4 What Are the Characteristic Reactions of Monosaccharides?

In this section, we discuss reactions of monosaccharides with alcohols, reducing agents, and oxidizing agents. In addition, we examine how these reactions are useful in our everyday lives.

A. Formation of Glycosides (Acetals)

As we saw in Section 12.6A, treating an aldehyde or a ketone with one molecule of alcohol yields a hemiacetal, and treating the hemiacetal with a molecule of alcohol yields an acetal. Treating a monosaccharide, all forms of which exist as cyclic hemiacetals, with an alcohol gives an acetal, as illustrated by the reaction of β-D-glucopyranose (β-D-glucose) with methanol:

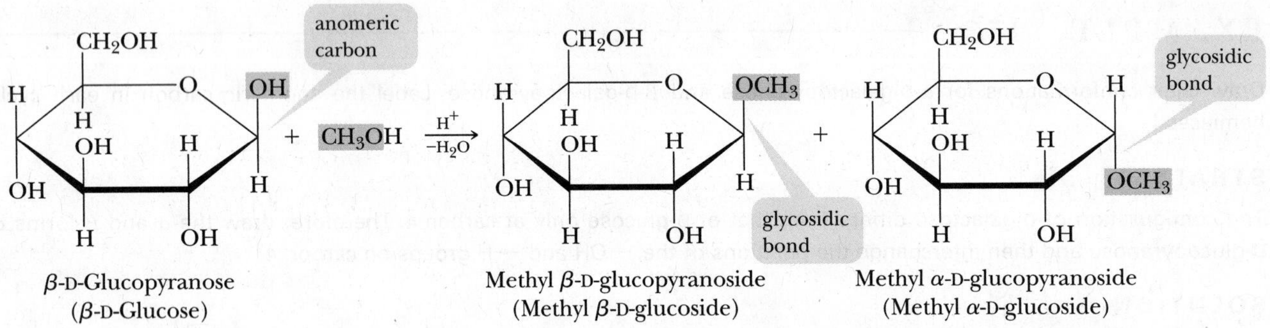

Glycoside A carbohydrate in which the —OH on its anomeric carbon is replaced by —OR.

Glycosidic bond The bond from the anomeric carbon of a glycoside to an —OR group.

A cyclic acetal derived from a monosaccharide is called a **glycoside**, and the bond from the anomeric carbon to the —OR group is called a **glycosidic bond**. Mutarotation is no longer possible in a glycoside because, unlike a hemiacetal, an acetal is no longer in equilibrium with the open-chain carbonyl-containing compound in neutral or alkaline solution. Like other acetals (Section 12.6), glycosides are stable in water and aqueous base, but undergo hydrolysis in aqueous acid to an alcohol and a monosaccharide.

We name glycosides by listing the alkyl or aryl group bonded to oxygen, followed by the name of the carbohydrate involved in which the ending **-e** is replaced by **-ide**. For example, glycosides derived from β-D-glucopyranose are named β-D-glucopyranosides; those derived from β-D-ribofuranose are named β-D-ribofuranosides.

EXAMPLE 17.4

Draw a structural formula for methyl β-D-ribofuranoside (methyl β-D-riboside). Label the anomeric carbon and the glycosidic bond.

STRATEGY

Furanosides are five-membered cyclic acetals. The anomeric carbon is carbon 1, and the glycosidic bond is formed to carbon 1. For a β-glycosidic bond, the —OR group is above the plane of the ring and on the same side as the terminal $-CH_2OH$ group (carbon 5 of a furanoside).

SOLUTION

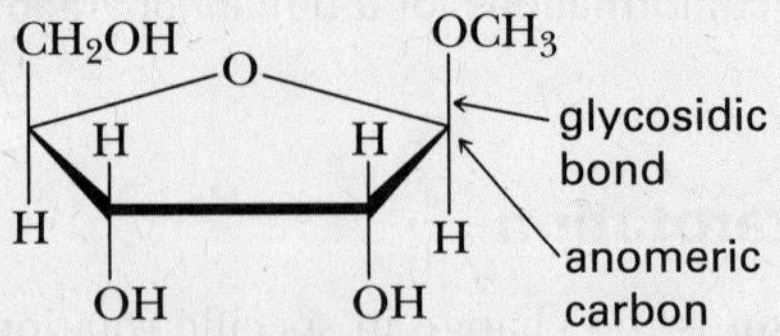

See problems 17.30–17.32

PROBLEM 17.4

Draw a structural formula for the chair conformation of methyl α-D-mannopyranoside (methyl α-D-mannoside). Label the anomeric carbon and the glycosidic bond.

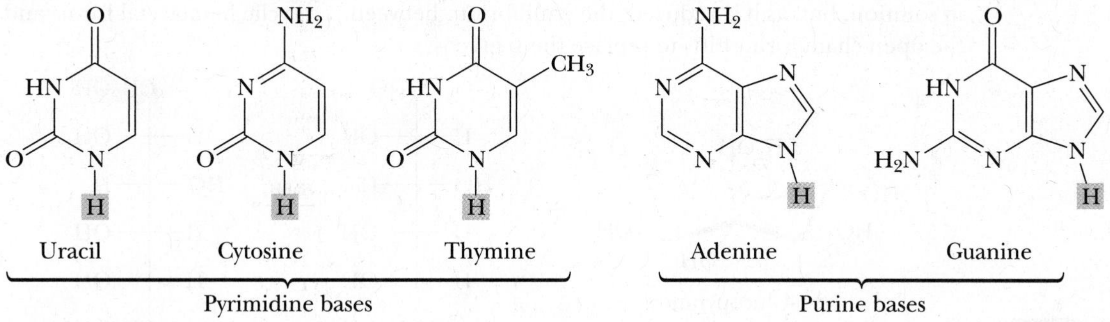

FIGURE 17.3
Structural formulas of the five most important purine and pyrimidine bases found in DNA and RNA. The hydrogen atom shown in color is lost in the formation of an *N*-glycoside.

Just as the anomeric carbon of a cyclic hemiacetal undergoes reaction with the —OH group of an alcohol to form a glycoside, it also undergoes reaction with the —NH group of an amine to form an *N*-glycoside. Especially important in the biological world are the *N*-glycosides formed between D-ribose and 2-deoxy-D-ribose (each as a furanose), and the heterocyclic aromatic amines uracil, cytosine, thymine, adenine, and guanine (Figure 17.3). *N*-Glycosides of these compounds are structural units of nucleic acids (Chapter 20).

EXAMPLE 17.5

Draw a structural formula for the β-*N*-glycoside formed between D-ribofuranose and cytosine. Label the anomeric carbon and the *N*-glycosidic bond.

STRATEGY

Start with the Haworth projection of β-D-ribofuranose. Locate the anomeric carbon (carbon 1). Remove the —OH group from carbon 1 and in its place, bond the appropriate nitrogen atom of cytosine (see Figure 17.3) to give the β-*N*-glycosidic bond.

SOLUTION

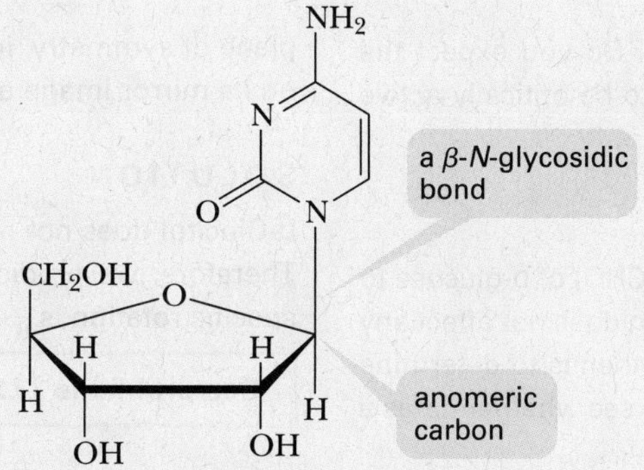

See problem 17.33

PROBLEM 17.5

Draw a structural formula for the β-*N*-glycoside formed between β-D-ribofuranose and adenine.

B. Reduction to Alditols

The carbonyl group of a monosaccharide can be reduced to a hydroxyl group by a variety of reducing agents, including $NaBH_4$ (Section 12.10B). The reduction products are known as **alditols**. Reduction of D-glucose gives D-glucitol, more commonly known as D-sorbitol. Here, D-glucose is shown in the open-chain form, only a small amount of which is present

Alditol The product formed when the C=O group of a monosaccharide is reduced to a CHOH group.

in solution, but, as it is reduced, the equilibrium between the cyclic hemiacetal forms and the open-chain form shifts to replace the D-glucose:

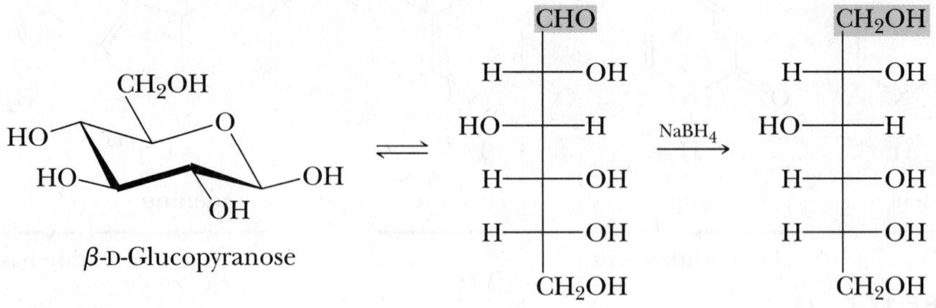

β-D-Glucopyranose D-Glucose D-Glucitol (D-Sorbitol)

Andy Washnik

Many "sugar-free" products contain sugar alcohols, such as D-sorbitol and xylitol.

We name alditols by replacing the *-ose* in the name of the monosaccharide with *-itol.* D-Sorbitol is found in the plant world in many berries and in cherries, plums, pears, apples, seaweed, and algae. It is about 60% as sweet as sucrose (table sugar) and is used in the manufacture of candies and as a sugar substitute for diabetics. Among other alditols common in the biological world are erythritol, D-mannitol, and xylitol, the last of which is used as a sweetening agent in "sugarless" gum, candy, and sweet cereals:

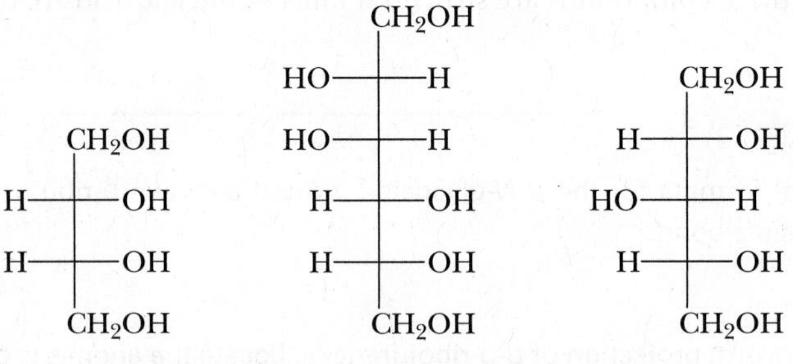

Erythritol D-Mannitol Xylitol

EXAMPLE 17.6

$NaBH_4$ reduces D-glucose to D-glucitol. Do you expect the alditol formed under these conditions to be optically active or optically inactive? Explain.

STRATEGY

$NaBH_4$ reduces the aldehyde group (—CHO) of D-glucose to a primary alcohol (—CH_2OH). Reduction does not affect any other group in D-glucose. The problem then is to determine if D-glucitol is chiral and, if it is chiral, to see whether it has a plane of symmetry, in which case it would be superposable on its mirror image and, therefore, optically inactive.

SOLUTION

D-Glucitol does not have a plane of symmetry and is chiral. Therefore, we predict that D-glucitol is optically active. Its specific rotation is −1.7°.

See problems 17.34–17.39

PROBLEM 17.6

$NaBH_4$ reduces D-erythrose to erythritol. Do you expect the alditol formed under these conditions to be optically active or optically inactive? Explain.

C. Oxidation to Aldonic Acids (Reducing Sugars)

We saw in Section 12.9A that several agents, including O_2, oxidize aldehydes (RCHO) to carboxylic acids (RCOOH). Similarly, under basic conditions, the aldehyde group of an aldose can be oxidized to a carboxylate group. Under these conditions, the cyclic form of the aldose is in equilibrium with the open-chain form, which is then oxidized by the mild oxidizing agent. D-Glucose, for example, is oxidized to D-gluconate (the anion of D-gluconic acid):

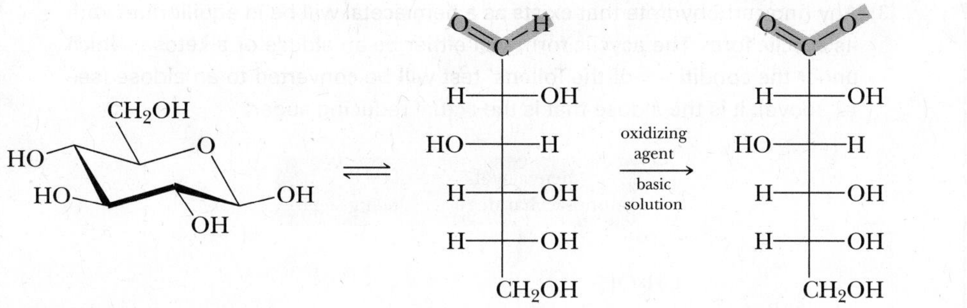

β-D-Glucopyranose (β-D-Glucose) — D-Glucose — D-Gluconate (anion of an aldonic acid)

Any carbohydrate that reacts with an oxidizing agent to form an aldonic acid is classified as a **reducing sugar**. (It reduces the oxidizing agent.)

Reducing sugar A carbohydrate that reacts with an oxidizing agent to form an aldonic acid.

HOW TO 17.2

Determine If a Carbohydrate Is a Reducing Sugar

Following are three commonly encountered features in carbohydrates that are reducing sugars.

(1) Any carbohydrate that is an aldehyde is a reducing sugar.

(2) Any ketose that is in equilibrium with its aldehyde is a reducing sugar. This is because under the basic conditions of the Tollens' test, keto–enol tautomerism occurs and converts the ketose to an aldose (it is the aldose that is the actual reducing sugar):

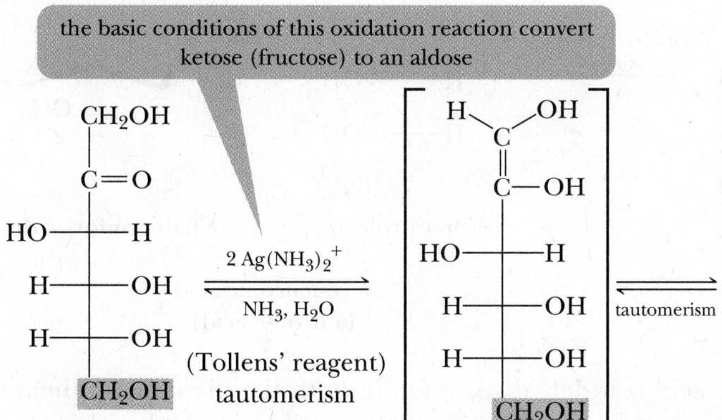

D-Fructose (keto form)

(Enol form)

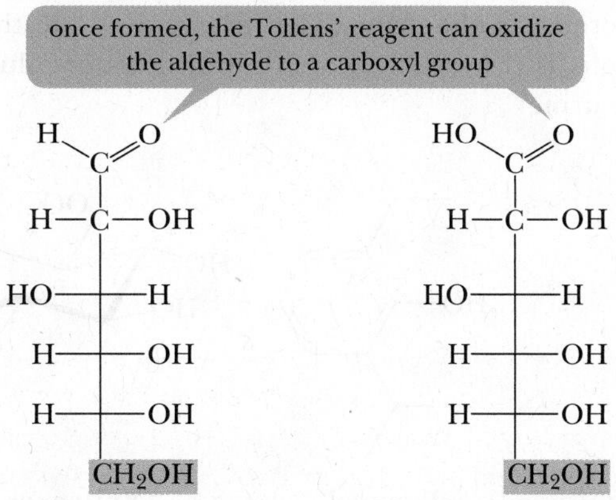

(Keto form)

(3) Any ring carbohydrate that exists as a hemiacetal will be in equilibrium with its acyclic form. The acyclic form will either be an aldose or a ketose, which under the conditions of the Tollens' test will be converted to an aldose (see #2 above). It is the aldose that is the actual reducing sugar:

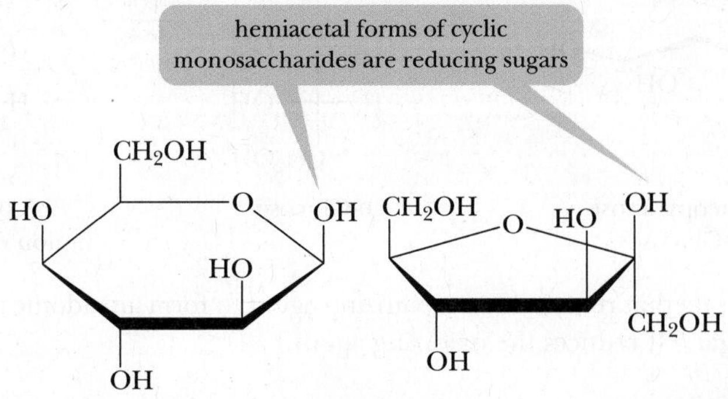

D. Oxidation to Uronic Acids

Enzyme-catalyzed oxidation of the primary alcohol at carbon 6 of a hexose yields a **uronic acid**. Enzyme-catalyzed oxidation of D-glucose, for example, yields D-glucuronic acid, shown here in both its open-chain and cyclic hemiacetal forms:

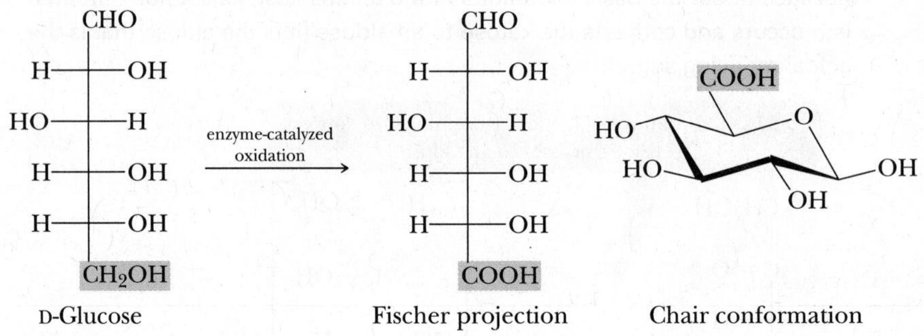

D-Glucuronic acid
(a uronic acid)

D-Glucuronic acid is widely distributed in both the plant and animal worlds. In humans, it is an important component of the acidic polysaccharides of connective tissues. The body also uses it to detoxify foreign phenols and alcohols. In the liver, these compounds are converted to glycosides of glucuronic acid (glucuronides), to be excreted in the urine. The intravenous anesthetic propofol (Problem 10.43), for example, is converted to the following water-soluble glucuronide and then excreted in the urine:

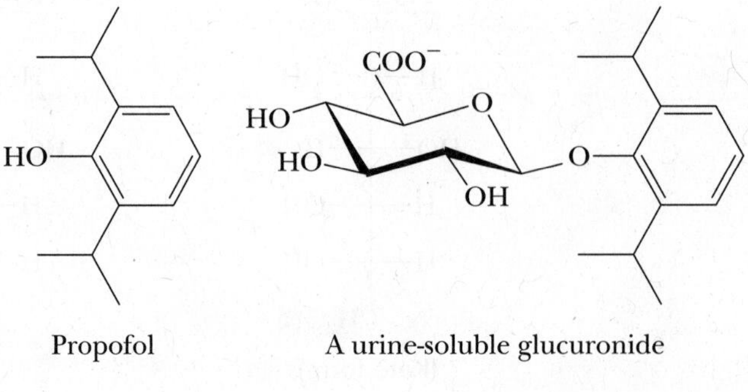

Propofol　　A urine-soluble glucuronide

17.5 What Are Disaccharides and Oligosaccharides?

Most carbohydrates in nature contain more than one monosaccharide unit. Those that contain two units are called **disaccharides**, those that contain three units are called **trisaccharides**, and so forth. The more general term, **oligosaccharide**, is often used for carbohydrates that contain from 6 to 10 monosaccharide units. Carbohydrates containing larger numbers of monosaccharide units are called **polysaccharides**.

In a disaccharide, two monosaccharide units are joined by a glycosidic bond between the anomeric carbon of one unit and an —OH of the other. Sucrose, lactose, and maltose are three important disaccharides.

Disaccharide A carbohydrate containing two monosaccharide units joined by a glycosidic bond.

Oligosaccharide A carbohydrate containing from 6 to 10 monosaccharide units, each joined to the next by a glycosidic bond.

Polysaccharide A carbohydrate containing a large number of monosaccharide units, each joined to the next by one or more glycosidic bonds.

A. Sucrose

Sucrose (table sugar) is the most abundant disaccharide in the biological world. It is obtained principally from the juice of sugarcane and sugar beets. In sucrose, carbon 1 of *α*-D-glucopyranose bonds to carbon 2 of D-fructofuranose by an *α*-1,2-glycosidic bond:

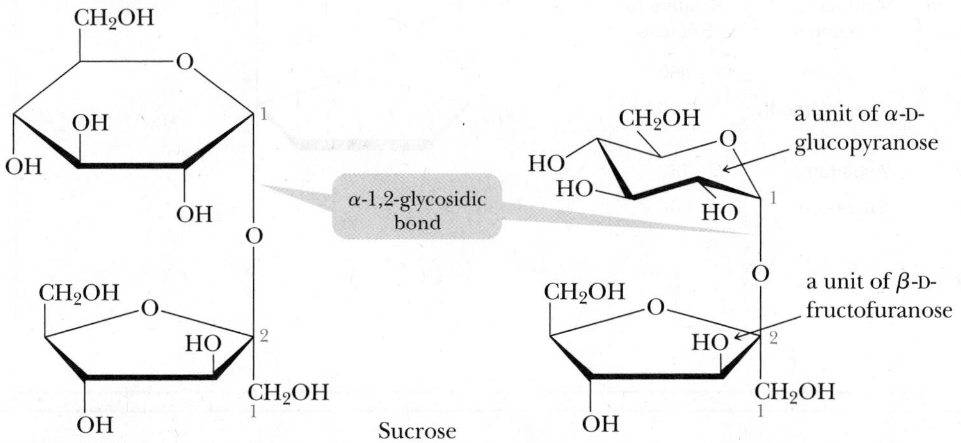

Sucrose

Charles D. Winters

These products help individuals with lactose intolerance meet their calcium needs.

Because the anomeric carbons of both the glucopyranose and fructofuranose units are involved in formation of the glycosidic bond, neither monosaccharide unit is in equilibrium with its open-chain form. Thus, sucrose is a nonreducing sugar.

B. Lactose

Lactose, the principal sugar present in milk, accounts for 5 to 8% of human milk and 4 to 6% of cow's milk. This disaccharide consists of D-galactopyranose, bonded by a *β*-1,4-glycosidic bond to carbon 4 of D-glucopyranose:

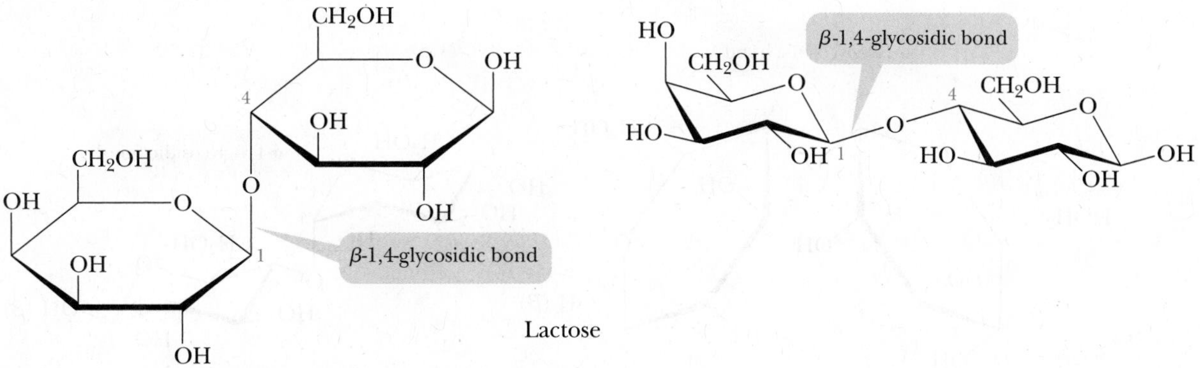

Lactose

Lactose is a reducing sugar, because the cyclic hemiacetal of the D-glucopyranose unit is in equilibrium with its open-chain form and can be oxidized to a carboxyl group.

Chemical Connections 17A

RELATIVE SWEETNESS OF CARBOHYDRATE AND ARTIFICIAL SWEETENERS

Among the disaccharide sweetening agents, D-fructose tastes the sweetest—even sweeter than sucrose. The sweet taste of honey is due largely to D-fructose and D-glucose. Lactose has almost no sweetness and is sometimes added to foods as filler. Some people cannot tolerate lactose well, however, and should avoid these foods. The following table lists the sweetness of various carbohydrates and artificial sweeteners relative to that of sucrose:

Carbohydrate	Sweetness Relative to Sucrose	Artificial Sweetener	Sweetness Relative to Sucrose
Fructose	1.74	Saccharin	450
Sucrose (table sugar)	1.00	Acesulfame-K	200
Honey	0.97	Aspartame	180
Glucose	0.74	Sucralose	600
Maltose	0.33		
Galactose	0.32		
Lactose (milk sugar)	0.16		

Question

Following is the structure of the artificial sweetener sucralose. Indicate all the ways in which it differs from sucrose.

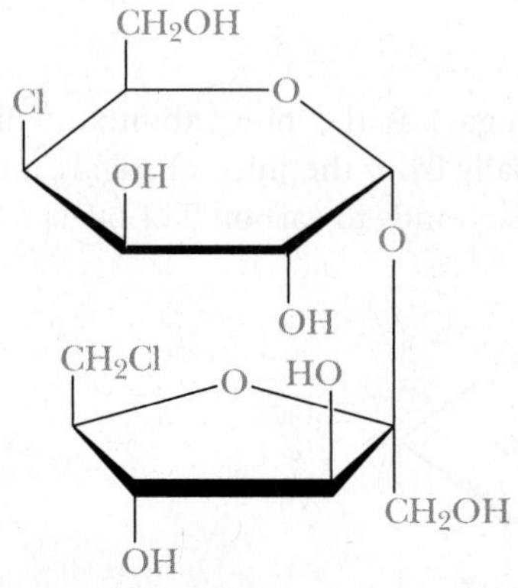

Sucralose

C. Maltose

Maltose derives its name from its presence in malt, the juice from sprouted barley and other cereal grains. Maltose consists of two units of D-glucopyranose, joined by a glycosidic bond between carbon 1 (the anomeric carbon) of one unit and carbon 4 of the other unit. Because the oxygen atom on the anomeric carbon of the first glucopyranose unit is alpha, the bond joining the two units is called an α-1,4-glycosidic bond. Following are a Haworth projection and a chair conformation for β-maltose, so named because the —OH group on the anomeric carbon of the glucose unit on the right is beta:

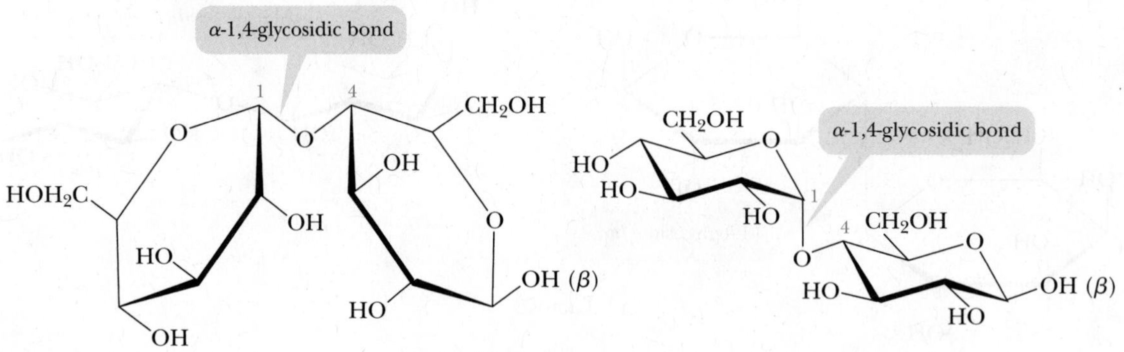

Maltose

Chemical Connections 17B

A, B, AB, AND O BLOOD-GROUP SUBSTANCES

Membranes of animal plasma cells have large numbers of relatively small carbohydrates bound to them. In fact, the outsides of most plasma cell membranes are literally sugarcoated. These membrane-bound carbohydrates are part of the mechanism by which the different types of cells recognize each other; in effect, the carbohydrates act as biochemical markers (antigenic determinants). Typically, the membrane-bound carbohydrates contain from 4 to 17 units consisting of just a few different monosaccharides, primarily D-galactose, D-mannose, L-fucose, *N*-acetyl-D-glucosamine, and *N*-acetyl-D-galactosamine. L-Fucose is a 6-deoxyaldohexose:

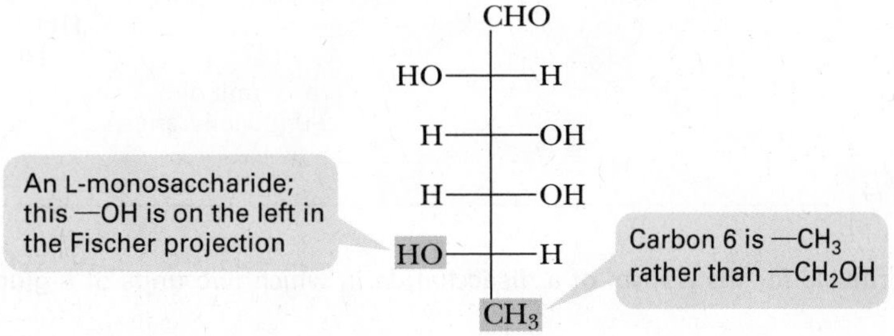

L-Fucose

Among the first discovered and best understood of these membrane-bound carbohydrates are those of the ABO blood-group system, discovered in 1900 by Karl Landsteiner (1868–1943). Whether an individual has type A, B, AB, or O blood is genetically determined and depends on the type of trisaccharide or tetrasaccharide bound to the surface of the person's red blood cells. The monosaccharides of each blood group and the type of glycosidic bond joining them are shown in the following figure (the configurations of the glycosidic bonds are in parentheses):

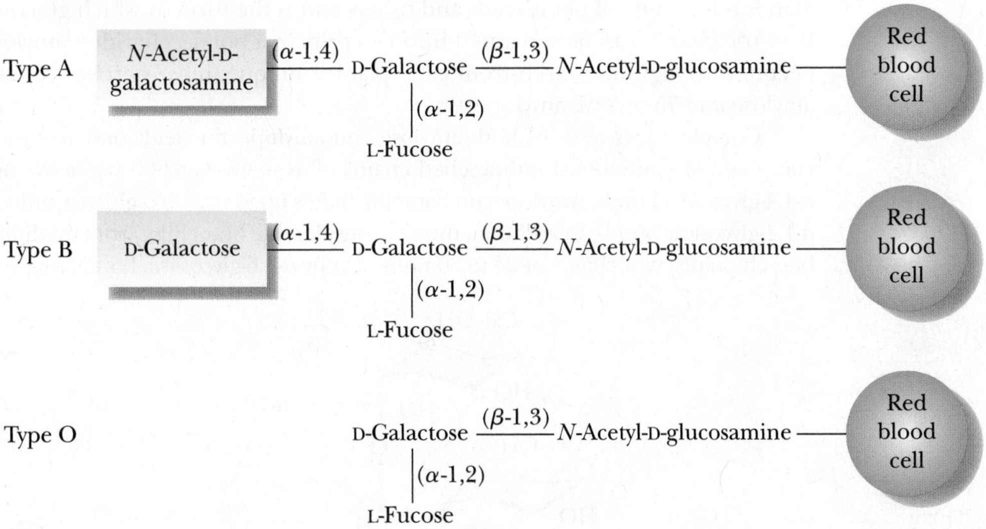

Question

Draw the two pyranose forms of L-fucose.

EXAMPLE 17.7

Draw a chair conformation for the β anomer of a disaccharide in which two units of D-glucopyranose are joined by an α-1,6-glycosidic bond.

STRATEGY

First draw a chair conformation of α-D-glucopyranose. Then bond the anomeric carbon of this monosaccharide to carbon 6 of a second D-glucopyranose unit by an α-glycosidic bond. The resulting molecule is either α or β, depending on the orientation of the —OH group on the reducing end of the disaccharide.

See problem 17.48

SOLUTION

The disaccharide shown here is β:

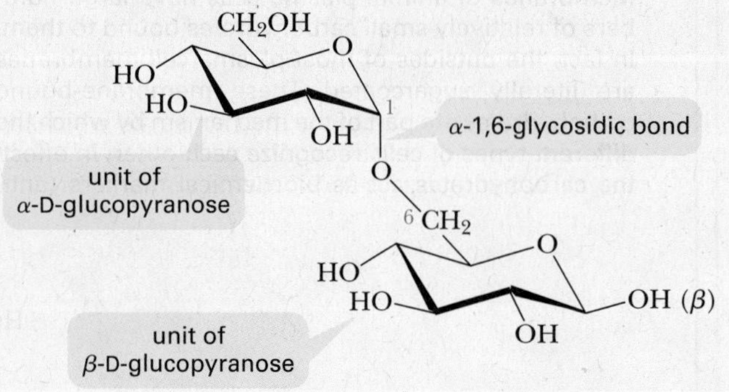

PROBLEM 17.7

Draw Haworth and chair formulas for the α form of a disaccharide in which two units of D-glucopyranose are joined by a β-1,3-glycosidic bond.

17.6 What Are Polysaccharides?

Polysaccharides consist of a large number of monosaccharide units joined together by glycosidic bonds. Three important polysaccharides, all made up of glucose units, are starch, glycogen, and cellulose.

A. Starch: Amylose and Amylopectin

Starch is found in all plant seeds and tubers and is the form in which glucose is stored for later use. Starch can be separated into two principal polysaccharides: amylose and amylopectin. Although the starch from each plant is unique, most starches contain 20 to 25% amylose and 75 to 80% amylopectin.

Complete hydrolysis of both amylose and amylopectin yields only D-glucose. Amylose is composed of continuous, unbranched chains of as many as 4,000 D-glucose units, joined by α-1,4-glycosidic bonds. Amylopectin contains chains up to 10,000 D-glucose units, also joined by α-1,4-glycosidic bonds. In addition, there is considerable branching from this linear network. At branch points, new chains of 24 to 30 units start by α-1,6-glycosidic bonds (Figure 17.4).

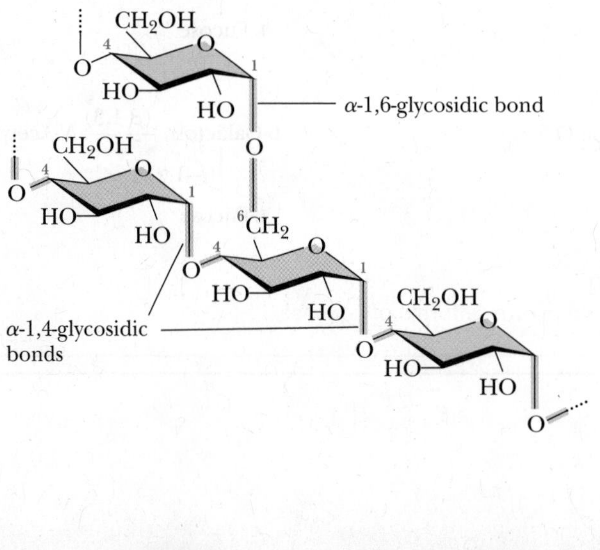

FIGURE 17.4 Amylopectin is a highly branched polymer of D-glucose. Chains consist of 24 to 30 units of D-glucose, joined by α-1,4-glycosidic bonds, and branches created by α-1,6-glycosidic bonds.

Why are carbohydrates stored in plants as polysaccharides rather than monosaccharides, a more directly usable source of energy? The answer has to do with **osmotic pressure**, which is proportional to the molar *concentration*, not the molecular weight, of a solute. If 1,000 molecules of glucose are assembled into one starch macromolecule, a solution containing 1 g of starch per 10 mL will have only 1 one-thousandth the osmotic pressure relative to a solution of 1 g of glucose in the same volume. This feat of packaging is a tremendous advantage because it reduces the strain on various membranes enclosing solutions of such macromolecules.

B. Glycogen

Glycogen is the reserve carbohydrate for animals. Like amylopectin, glycogen is a branched polymer of D-glucose containing approximately 10^6 glucose units, joined by α-1,4- and α-1,6-glycosidic bonds. The total amount of glycogen in the body of a well-nourished adult human being is about 350 g, divided almost equally between liver and muscle.

C. Cellulose

Cellulose, the most widely distributed plant skeletal polysaccharide, constitutes almost half of the cell-wall material of wood. Cotton is almost pure cellulose.

Cellulose, a linear polymer of D-glucose units joined by β-1,4-glycosidic bonds (Figure 17.5), has an average molar mass of 400,000 g/mol, corresponding to approximately 2,800 glucose units per molecule.

Cellulose molecules act much like stiff rods, a feature that enables them to align themselves side by side into well-organized, water-insoluble fibers in which the OH groups form numerous intermolecular hydrogen bonds. This arrangement of parallel chains in bundles gives cellulose fibers their high mechanical strength and explains why cellulose is insoluble in water. When a piece of cellulose-containing material is placed in water, there are not enough —OH groups on the surface of the fiber to pull individual cellulose molecules away from the strongly hydrogen-bonded fiber.

Humans and other animals cannot use cellulose as food, because our digestive systems do not contain β-glucosidases, enzymes that catalyze the hydrolysis of β-glucosidic bonds. Instead, we have only α-glucosidases; hence, the polysaccharides we use as sources of glucose are starch and glycogen. By contrast, many bacteria and microorganisms do contain β-glucosidases and can digest cellulose. Termites are fortunate (much to our regret) to have such bacteria in their intestines and can use wood as their principal food. Ruminants (cud-chewing animals) and horses can also digest grasses and hay because β-glucosidase-containing microorganisms are present within their alimentary systems.

D. Textile Fibers from Cellulose

Both **rayon** and acetate rayon are made from chemically modified cellulose and were the first commercially important synthetic textile fibers. In the production of rayon, cellulose fibers are treated with carbon disulfide, CS_2, in aqueous sodium hydroxide. In this reaction, some of the —OH groups on a cellulose fiber are converted to the sodium

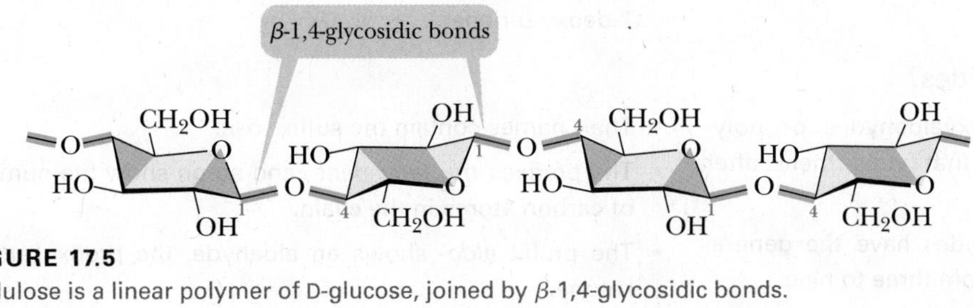

FIGURE 17.5
Cellulose is a linear polymer of D-glucose, joined by β-1,4-glycosidic bonds.

salt of a xanthate ester, which causes the fibers to dissolve in alkali as a viscous colloidal dispersion:

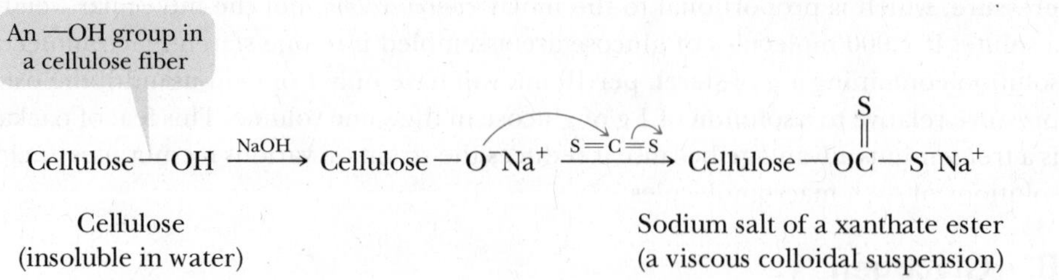

An —OH group in a cellulose fiber
Cellulose—OH
NaOH
Cellulose—O⁻Na⁺
S=C=S
Cellulose—OC—S⁻Na⁺
S
Cellulose (insoluble in water)
Sodium salt of a xanthate ester (a viscous colloidal suspension)

The solution of cellulose xanthate is separated from the alkali-insoluble parts of wood and then forced through a spinneret (a metal disc with many tiny holes) into dilute sulfuric acid to hydrolyze the xanthate ester groups and precipitate regenerated cellulose. Regenerated cellulose extruded as a filament is called viscose rayon thread.

In the industrial synthesis of **acetate rayon**, cellulose is treated with acetic anhydride (Section 14.4B):

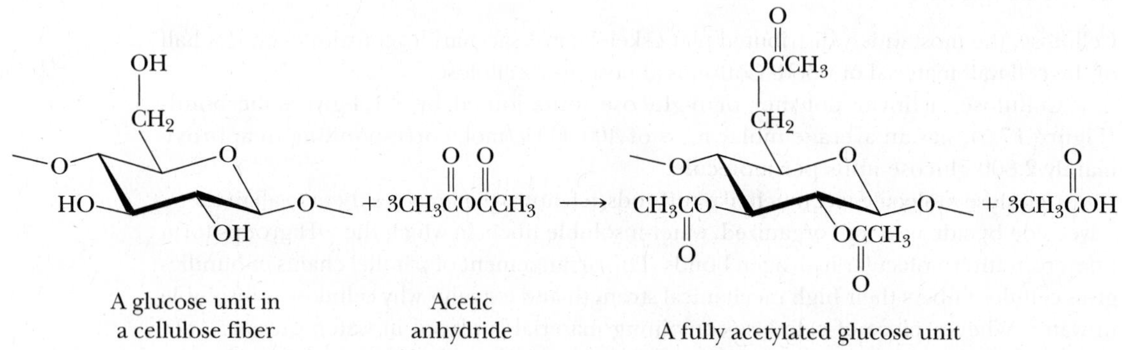

Acetylated cellulose is then dissolved in a suitable solvent, precipitated, and drawn into fibers known as acetate rayon. The fibers are smooth, soft, resistant to static cling, and dry quickly. One of acetate rayon's most valuable properties is its ability to behave as a thermoplastic (Section 16.1). This allows clothing made from acetate rayon to be heated and permanently pleated upon cooling.

SUMMARY OF KEY QUESTIONS

17.1 What Are Carbohydrates?

Carbohydrates are

- the most abundant organic compounds in the plant world.
- storage forms of chemical energy (glucose, starch, glycogen).
- components of supportive structures in plants (cellulose), crustacean shells (chitin), and connective tissues in animals (acidic polysaccharides).
- essential components of nucleic acids (D-ribose and 2-deoxy-D-ribose).

17.2 What Are Monosaccharides?

- **Monosaccharides** are polyhydroxyaldehydes or polyhydroxyketones or compounds that yield them after hydrolysis.
- The most common monosaccharides have the general formula $C_nH_{2n}O_n$ where *n* varies from three to nine.
- Their names contain the suffix *-ose*.
- The prefixes *tri-*, *tetr-*, *pent-*, and so on show the number of carbon atoms in the chain.
- The prefix *aldo-* shows an aldehyde, the prefix *keto-* a ketone.

- In a **Fischer projection** of a monosaccharide, the carbon chain is written vertically, with the most highly oxidized carbon toward the top. Horizontal lines show groups projecting above the plane of the page and vertical lines show groups projecting behind the plane of the page.
- A monosaccharide that has the same configuration at its penultimate carbon as D-glyceraldehyde is called a **D-monosaccharide**; one that has the same configuration at its penultimate carbon as L-glyceraldehyde is called an **L-monosaccharide**.
- An amino sugar contains an $-NH_2$ group in place of an $-OH$ group.

17.3 What Are the Cyclic Structures of Monosaccharides?

- Monosaccharides exist primarily as cyclic hemiacetals.
- The new stereocenter resulting from cyclic hemiacetal formation is referred to as an **anomeric carbon**. The stereoisomers thus formed are called **anomers**.
- A six-membered cyclic hemiacetal form of a monosaccharide is called a **pyranose**; a five-membered cyclic hemiacetal form is called a **furanose**.
- Furanoses and pyranoses can be drawn as **Haworth projections**.
- Pyranoses can be drawn as Haworth projections or as strain-free **chair conformations**.
- The symbol $\boldsymbol{\beta}$- indicates that the $-OH$ on the anomeric carbon is on the same side of the ring as the terminal $-CH_2OH$.
- The symbol $\boldsymbol{\alpha}$- indicates that $-OH$ on the anomeric carbon is on the opposite side of the ring from the terminal $-CH_2OH$.
- **Mutarotation** is the change in specific rotation that accompanies the formation of an equilibrium mixture of α- and β-anomers in aqueous solution.

17.4 What Are the Characteristic Reactions of Monosaccharides?

- A **glycoside** is a cyclic acetal derived from a monosaccharide.
- The name of the glycoside is composed of the name of the alkyl or aryl group bonded to the acetal oxygen atom followed by the name of the parent monosaccharide in which the terminal *-e* has been replaced by *-ide*.
- An **alditol** is a polyhydroxy compound formed by reduction of the carbonyl group of a monosaccharide to a hydroxyl group.
- An **aldonic acid** is a carboxylic acid formed by oxidation of the aldehyde group of an aldose.
- Any carbohydrate that reduces an oxidizing agent is called a **reducing sugar**.
- Enzyme-catalyzed oxidation of the terminal $-CH_2OH$ group of a monosaccharide to a COOH group gives a **uronic acid**.

17.5 What Are Disaccharides and Oligosaccharides?

- A **disaccharide** contains two monosaccharide units joined by a **glycosidic bond**.
- Terms applied to carbohydrates containing larger numbers of monosaccharides are **trisaccharide, tetrasaccharide**, etc.
- An **oligosaccharide** is a carbohydrate that contains from six to ten monosaccharide units.
- **Sucrose** is a disaccharide consisting of D-glucose joined to D-fructose by an α-1,2-glycosidic bond.
- **Lactose** is a disaccharide consisting of D-galactose joined to D-glucose by a β-1,4-glycosidic bond.
- **Maltose** is a disaccharide of two molecules of D-glucose joined by an α-1,4-glycosidic bond.

17.6 What Are Polysaccharides?

- **Polysaccharides** consist of a large number of monosaccharide units bonded together by glycosidic bonds.
- **Starch** can be separated into two fractions given the names amylose and amylopectin. **Amylose** is a linear polymer of up to 4,000 units of D-glucopyranose joined by α-1,4-glycosidic bonds. **Amylopectin** is a highly branched polymer of D-glucose joined by α-1,4-glycosidic bonds and, at branch points, by α-1,6-glycosidic bonds.
- **Glycogen**, the reserve carbohydrate of animals, is a highly branched polymer of D-glucopyranose joined by α-1,4-glycosidic bonds and, at branch points, by α-1,6-glycosidic bonds.
- **Cellulose**, the skeletal polysaccharide of plants, is a linear polymer of D-glucopyranose joined by β-1,4-glycosidic bonds.
- **Rayon** is made from chemically modified and regenerated cellulose.
- **Acetate rayon** is made by the acetylation of cellulose.

QUICK QUIZ

Answer true or false to the following questions to assess your general knowledge of the concepts in this chapter. If you have difficulty with any of them, you should review the appropriate section in the chapter (shown in parentheses) before attempting the more challenging end-of-chapter problems.

1. An acetal of the pyranose or furanose form of a sugar is referred to as a glycoside. (17.4)
2. A monosaccharide can contain the carbonyl of a ketone or the carbonyl of an aldehyde. (17.2)
3. Starch, glycogen, and cellulose are all examples of oligosaccharides. (17.6)
4. An L-sugar and a D-sugar of the same name are enantiomers. (17.2)
5. Alditols are oxidized carbohydrates. (17.4)
6. D-Glucose and D-ribose are diastereomers. (17.2)
7. A pyranoside contains a five-membered ring. (17.3)
8. All monosaccharides dissolve in ether. (17.2)
9. Monosaccharides exist mostly as cyclic hemiacetals. (17.3)
10. A polysaccharide is a glycoside of two monosaccharides. (17.5)
11. α and β in a monosaccharide are used to refer to the positions 1 and 2 carbons away from the carbonyl group. (17.3)
12. Carbohydrates must have the formula $C_n(H_2O)_n$. (17.1)
13. Mutarotation is the establishment of an equilibrium concentration of α and β anomers of a carbohydrate. (17.3)
14. D-Glucose and D-galactose are diastereomers. (17.2)
15. Only acyclic carbohydrates that contain aldehyde groups can act as reducing sugars. (17.4)
16. A methyl glycoside of a monosaccharide cannot act as a reducing sugar. (17.4)
17. The penultimate carbon of an acyclic monosaccharide becomes the anomeric carbon in the cyclic hemiacetal form of the molecule. (17.3)
18. A Fischer projection may be rotated 90°. (17.2)

Answers: (1) T (2) T (3) F (4) T (5) F (6) F (7) F (8) F (9) T (10) F (11) F (12) F (13) T (14) T (15) F (16) T (17) F (18) F

Detailed explanations for many of these answers can be found in the accompanying Solutions Manual.

KEY REACTIONS

1. Formation of Cyclic Hemiacetals (Section 17.3)

A monosaccharide existing as a five-membered ring is a furanose; one existing as a six-membered ring is a pyranose. A pyranose is most commonly drawn as a Haworth projection or a chair conformation:

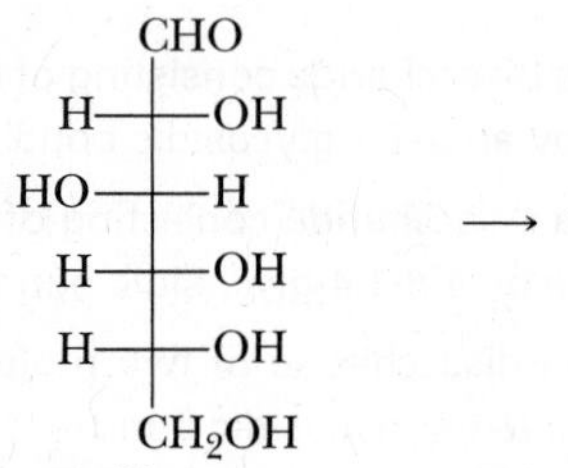

D-Glucose

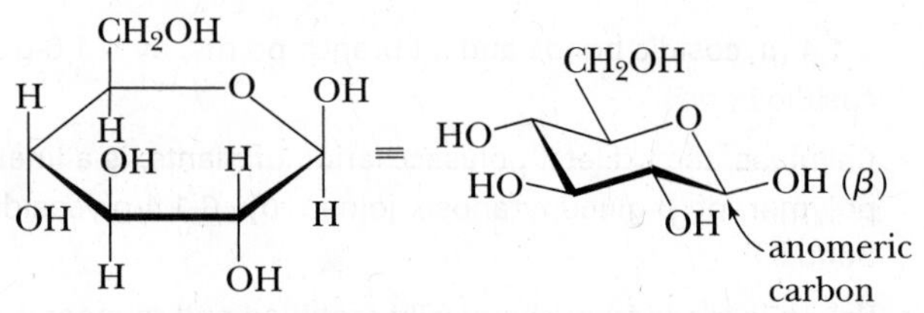

β-D-Glucopyranose
(β-D-Glucose)

2. Mutarotation (Section 17.3C)

Anomeric forms of a monosaccharide are in equilibrium in aqueous solution. Mutarotation is the change in specific rotation that accompanies this equilibration:

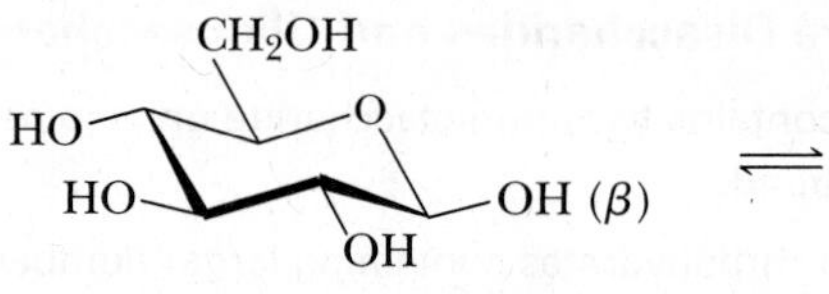

β-D-Glucopyranose
$[\alpha]_D^{25}$ + 18.7°

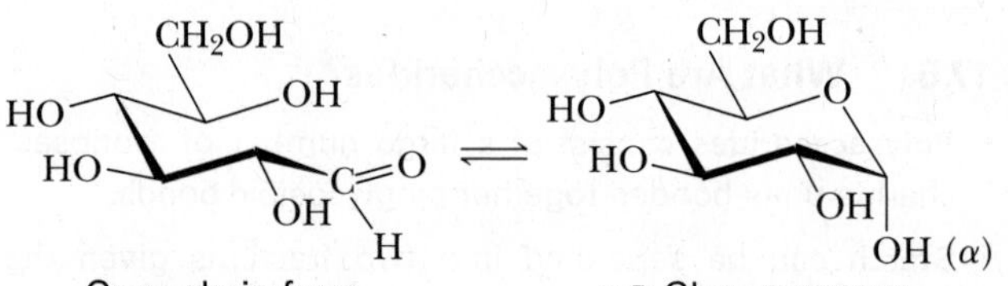

Open-chain form

α-D-Glucopyranose
$[\alpha]_D^{25}$ + 112°

3. **Formation of Glycosides (Section 17.4A)**

   Treatment of a monosaccharide with an alcohol in the presence of an acid catalyst forms a cyclic acetal called a glycoside:

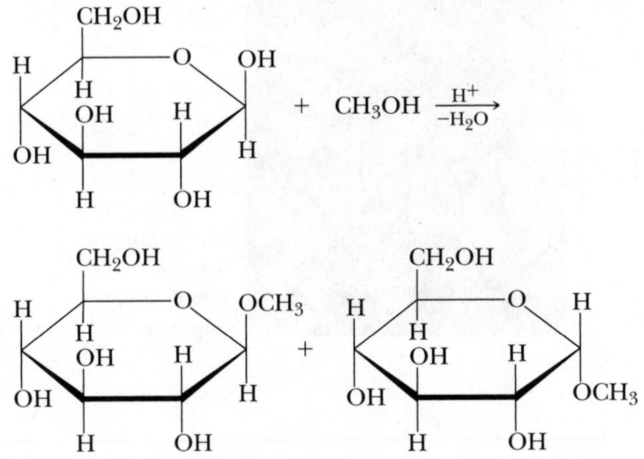

   The bond to the new —OR group is called a glycosidic bond.

4. **Reduction to Alditols (Section 17.4B)**

   Reduction of the carbonyl group of an aldose or a ketose to a hydroxyl group yields a polyhydroxy compound called an alditol:

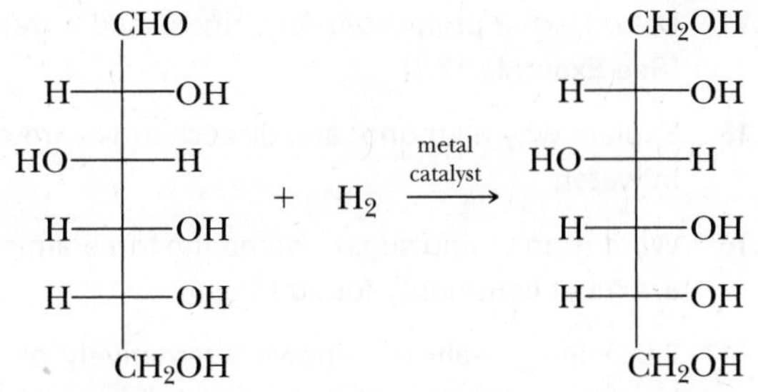

D-Glucose → D-Glucitol (D-Sorbitol)

5. **Oxidation to an Aldonic Acid (Section 17.4C)**

   Oxidation of the aldehyde group of an aldose to a carboxyl group by a mild oxidizing agent gives a polyhydroxycarboxylic acid called an aldonic acid:

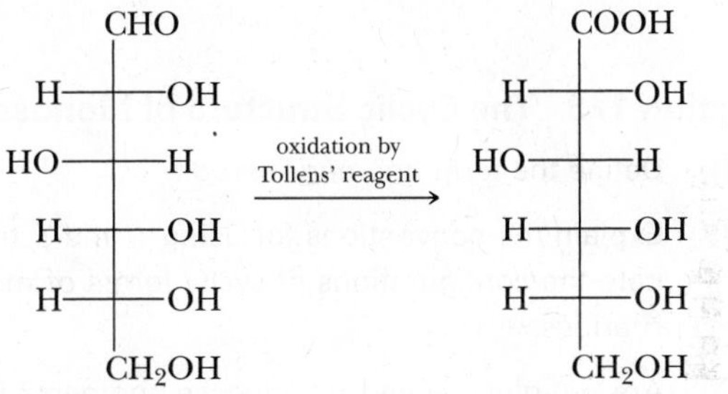

D-Glucose → D-Gluconic acid

PROBLEMS

A problem marked with an asterisk indicates an applied "real-world" problem. Answers to problems whose numbers are printed in blue are given in Appendix D.

Section 17.2 Monosaccharides

17.8 What is the difference in structure between an aldose and a ketose? Between an aldopentose and a ketopentose?

17.9 Which hexose is also known as dextrose?

17.10 What does it mean to say that D- and L-glyceraldehydes are enantiomers?

17.11 Explain the meaning of the designations D and L as used to specify the configuration of carbohydrates.

17.12 How many stereocenters are present in D-glucose? In D-ribose? How many stereoisomers are possible for each monosaccharide?

17.13 Which compounds are D-monosaccharides and which are L-monosaccharides? **(See Example 17.1)**

(a)

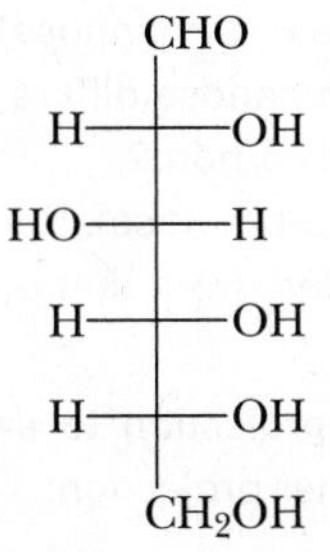

(b)

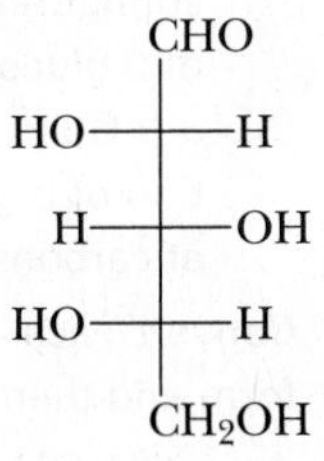

(c)

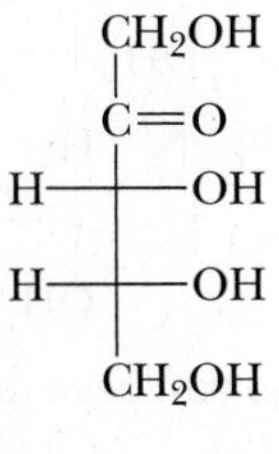

(d)

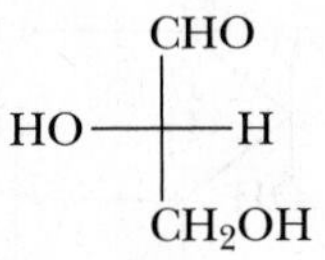

17.14 Draw Fischer projections for L-ribose and L-arabinose. **(See Example 17.1)**

17.15 Explain why all mono- and disaccharides are soluble in water.

17.16 What is an amino sugar? Name the three amino sugars most commonly found in nature.

*17.17 2,6-Dideoxy-D-altrose, known alternatively as D-digitoxose, is a monosaccharide obtained from the hydrolysis of digitoxin, a natural product extracted from purple foxglove *(Digitalis purpurea)*. Digitoxin has found wide use in cardiology because it reduces the pulse rate, regularizes heart rhythm, and strengthens the heartbeat. Draw the structural formula of 2,6-dideoxy-D-altrose.

© Yixin Chen/iStockphoto

The foxglove plant produces the important cardiac medication digitalis.

Section 17.3 The Cyclic Structure of Monosaccharides

17.18 Define the term *anomeric carbon.*

17.19 Explain the conventions for using α and β to designate the configurations of cyclic forms of monosaccharides.

17.20 Are α-D-glucose and β-D-glucose anomers? Explain. Are they enantiomers? Explain.

17.21 Are α-D-gulose and α-L-gulose anomers? Explain.

17.22 In what way are chair conformations a more accurate representation of molecular shape of hexopyranoses than are Haworth projections?

17.23 Draw α-D-glucopyranose (α-D-glucose) as a Haworth projection. Now, using only the following information, draw Haworth projections for these monosaccharides: **(See Example 17.2)**

(a) α-D-Mannopyranose (α-D-mannose). The configuration of D-mannose differs from that of D-glucose only at carbon 2.

(b) α-D-Gulopyranose (α-D-gulose). The configuration of D-gulose differs from that of D-glucose at carbons 3 and 4.

17.24 Convert each Haworth projection to an open-chain form and then to a Fischer projection:

(a) 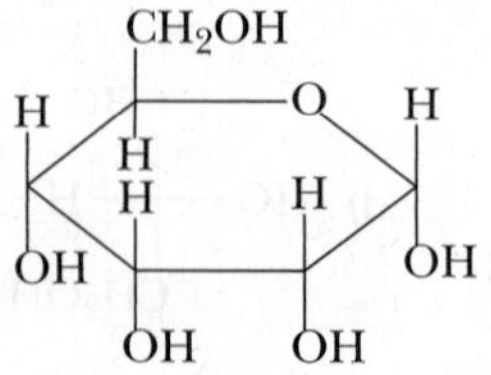

(b) 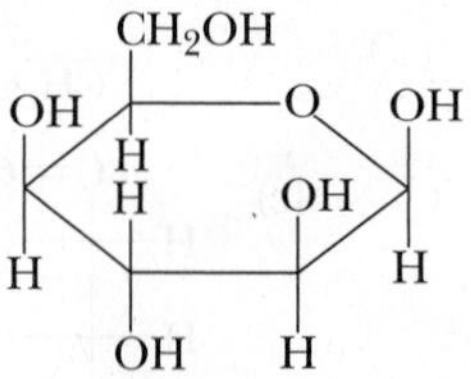

Name the monosaccharides you have drawn.

17.25 Convert each chair conformation to an open-chain form and then to a Fischer projection:

(a) 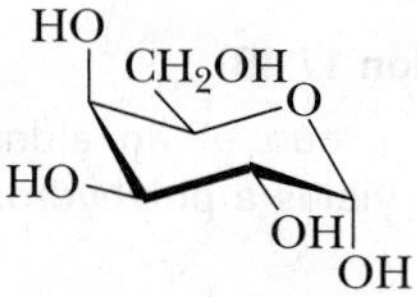

(b) 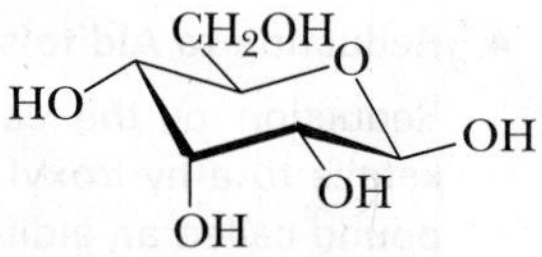

Name the monosaccharides you have drawn.

17.26 The configuration of D-arabinose differs from the configuration of D-ribose only at carbon 2. Using this information, draw a Haworth projection for α-D-arabinofuranose (α-D-arabinose). **(See Examples 17.2, 17.3)**

17.27 Explain the phenomenon of mutarotation with reference to carbohydrates. By what means is mutarotation detected?

17.28 The specific rotation of α-D-glucose is $+112.2°$. What is the specific rotation of α-L-glucose?

17.29 When α-D-glucose is dissolved in water, the specific rotation of the solution changes from $+112.2°$ to $+52.7°$. Does the specific rotation of α-L-glucose also change when it is dissolved in water? If so, to what value does it change?

Section 17.4 Reactions of Monosaccharides

17.30 Draw the structural formula for ethyl α-D-galactopyranoside (ethyl α-D-galactoside). Label the anomeric carbon and the glycosidic bond. **(See Example 17.4)**

17.31 Draw the structural formula for methyl β-D-mannopyranoside (methyl β-D-mannoside). Label the anomeric carbon and the glycosidic bond. **(See Example 17.4)**

17.32 Show the two possible products of each reaction. Label the α and β anomers in each reaction. **(See Example 17.4)**

(a)

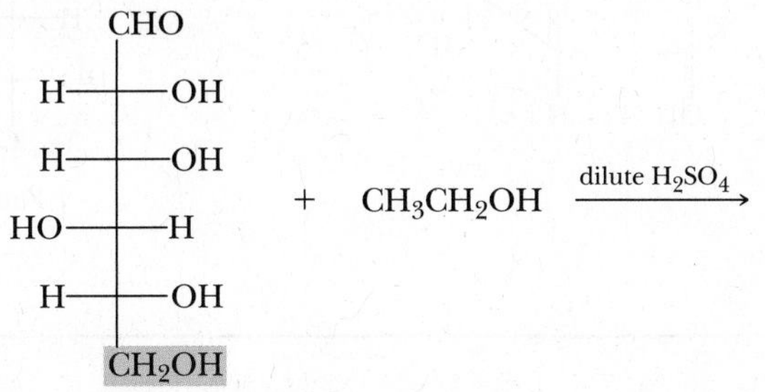

D-Gulose

(b)

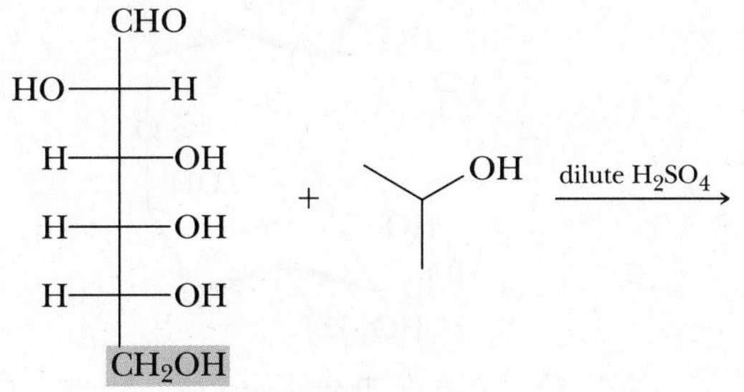

D-Altrose

(c)

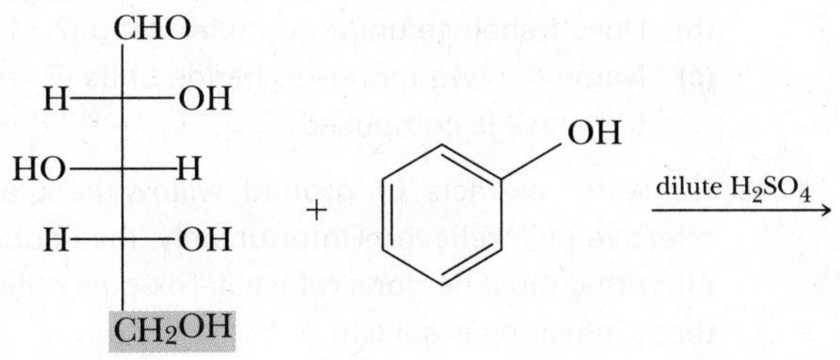

D-Xylose

17.33 Draw a structural formula for the β-*N*-glycoside formed between (a) D-ribofuranose and thymine and (b) D-ribofuranose and guanine. Label the anomeric carbon and the *N*-glycosidic bond. **(See Example 17.5)**

17.34 Draw Fischer projections for the product(s) formed by the reaction of D-galactose with the following compounds, and state whether each product is optically active or optically inactive: **(See Example 17.6)**

(a) $NaBH_4$ in H_2O

(b) $AgNO_3$ in NH_3, H_2O

17.35 Repeat Problem 17.34, but using D-ribose in place of D-galactose. **(See Example 17.6)**

17.36 The reduction of D-fructose by $NaBH_4$ gives two alditols, one of which is D-sorbitol. Name and draw a structural formula for the other alditol. **(See Example 17.6)**

17.37 There are four D-aldopentoses (Table 17.1). If each is reduced with $NaBH_4$, which yield optically active alditols? Which yield optically inactive alditols? **(See Example 17.6)**

17.38 Account for the observation that the reduction of D-glucose with $NaBH_4$ gives an optically active alditol, whereas the reduction of D-galactose with $NaBH_4$ gives an optically inactive alditol. **(See Example 17.6)**

17.39 Which two D-aldohexoses give optically inactive (meso) alditols on reduction with $NaBH_4$? **(See Example 17.6)**

***17.40** L-Fucose, one of several monosaccharides commonly found in the surface polysaccharides of animal cells (Chemical Connections 17B), is synthesized biochemically from D-mannose in the following eight steps:

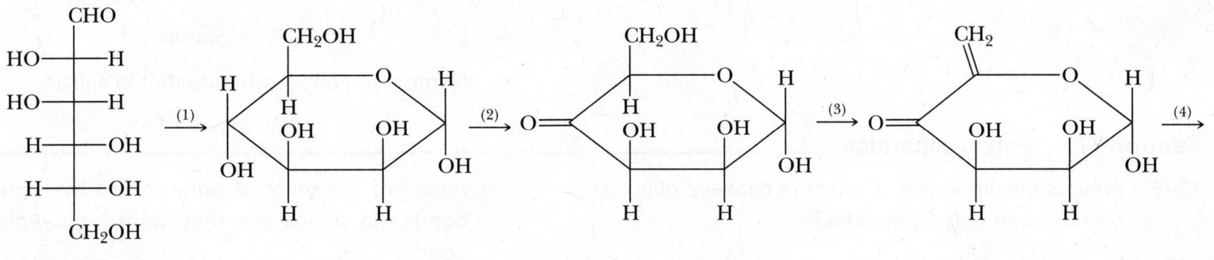

D-Mannose

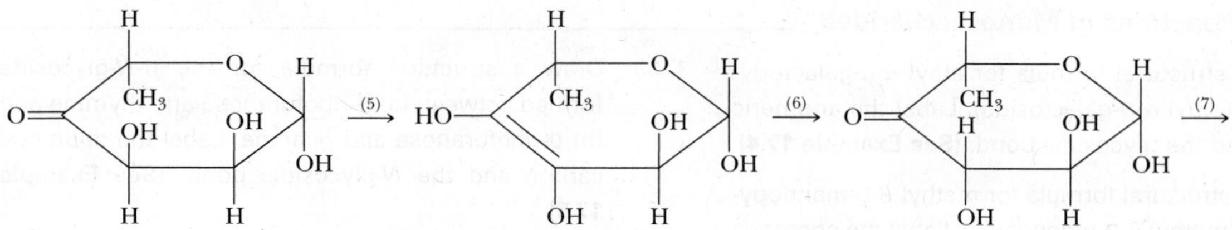

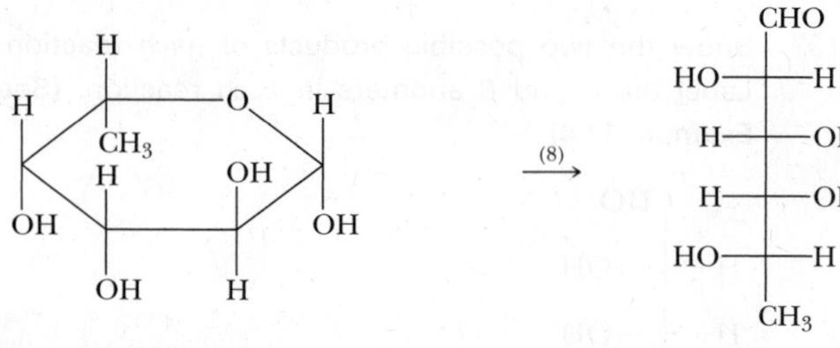

L-Fucose

(a) Describe the type of reaction (oxidation, reduction, hydration, dehydration, or the like) involved in each step.

(b) Explain why this monosaccharide, which is derived from D-mannose, now belongs to the L series.

Section 17.6 Disaccharides and Oligosaccharides

17.41 Define the term *glycosidic bond.*

17.42 What is the difference in meaning between the terms *glycosidic bond* and *glucosidic bond*?

17.43 Do glycosides undergo mutarotation?

*17.44 In making candy or syrups from sugar, sucrose is boiled in water with a little acid, such as lemon juice. Why does the product mixture taste sweeter than the starting sucrose solution?

17.45 Which disaccharides are reduced by $NaBH_4$?
(a) Sucrose
(b) Lactose
(c) Maltose

17.46 Draw Haworth and chair formulas for the β form of a disaccharide in which two units of D-glucopyranose are joined by a β-1,4-glycosidic bond. **(See Example 17.7)**

*17.47 Trehalose is found in young mushrooms and is the chief carbohydrate in the blood of certain insects. Trehalose is a disaccharide consisting of two D-monosaccharide units, each joined to the other by an α-1,1-glycosidic bond:

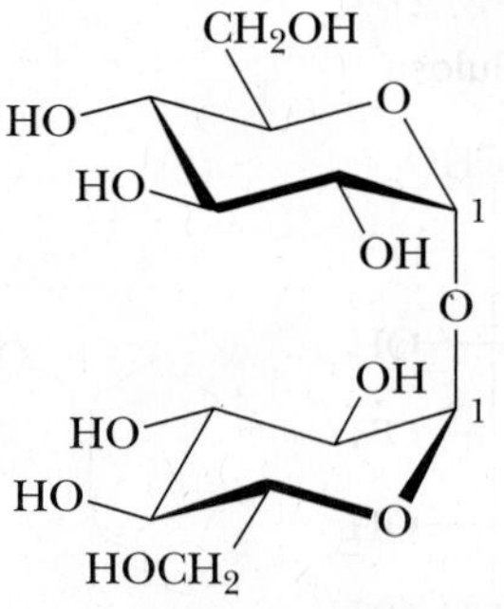

Trehalose

(a) Is trehalose a reducing sugar?
(b) Does trehalose undergo mutarotation?
(c) Name the two monosaccharide units of which trehalose is composed.

*17.48 Hot-water extracts of ground willow bark are an effective pain reliever. Unfortunately, the liquid is so bitter that most persons refuse it. The pain reliever in these infusions is salicin:

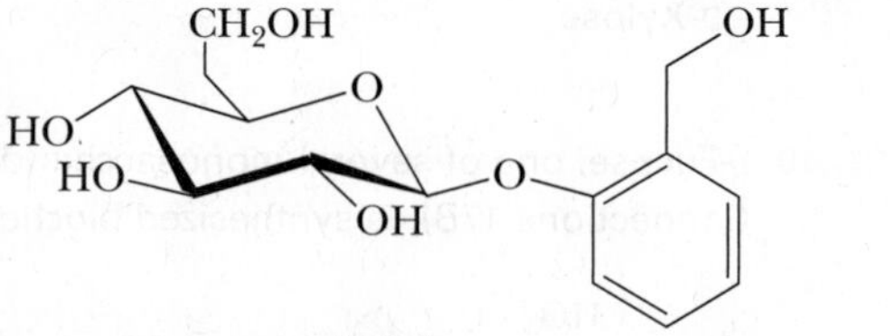

Salicin

Name the monosaccharide unit in salicin.

Section 17.7 Polysaccharides

17.49 What is the difference in structure between oligosaccharides and polysaccharides?

17.50 Name three polysaccharides that are composed of units of D-glucose. In which of the three polysaccharides are the glucose units joined by α-glycosidic bonds? In which are they joined by β-glycosidic bonds?

17.51 Starch can be separated into two principal polysaccharides: amylose and amylopectin. What is the major difference in structure between the two?

*17.52 A Fischer projection of *N*-acetyl-D-glucosamine is given in Section 17.2E.

(a) Draw Haworth and chair structures for the α- and β-pyranose forms of this monosaccharide.

(b) Draw Haworth and chair structures for the disaccharide formed by joining two units of the pyranose form of *N*-acetyl-D-glucosamine by a β-1,4-glucosidic bond. If your drawing is correct, you have the structural formula for the repeating dimer of chitin, the structural polysaccharide component of the shell of lobsters and other crustaceans.

*17.53 Propose structural formulas for the repeating disaccharide unit in these polysaccharides:

(a) Alginic acid, isolated from seaweed, is used as a thickening agent in ice cream and other foods. Alginic acid is a polymer of D-mannuronic acid in the pyranose form, joined by β-1,4-glycosidic bonds.

(b) Pectic acid is the main component of pectin, which is responsible for the formation of jellies from fruits and berries. Pectic acid is a polymer of D-galacturonic acid in the pyranose form joined by α-1,4-glycosidic bonds.

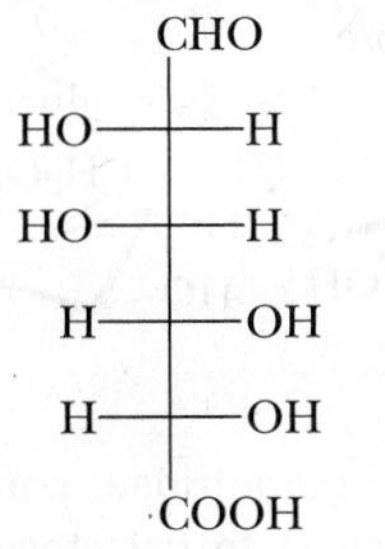

D-Mannuronic acid

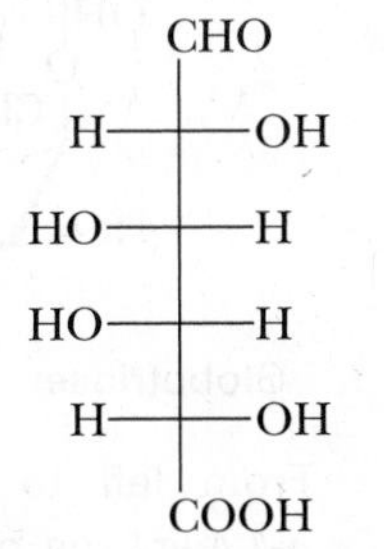

D-Galacturonic acid

*17.54 The first formula is a Haworth projection, and the second is a chair conformation for the repeating disaccharide unit in chondroitin 6-sulfate:

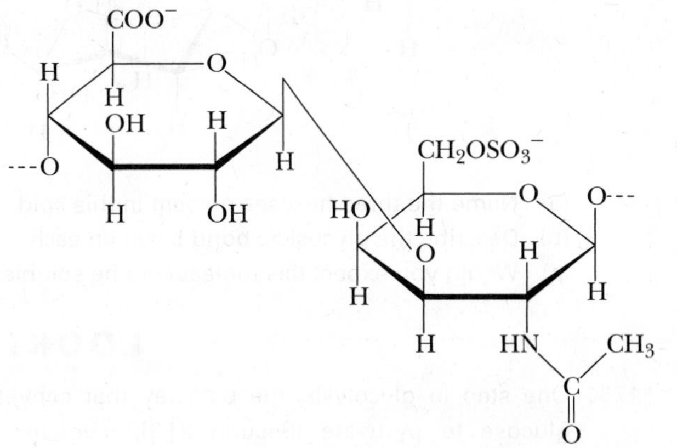

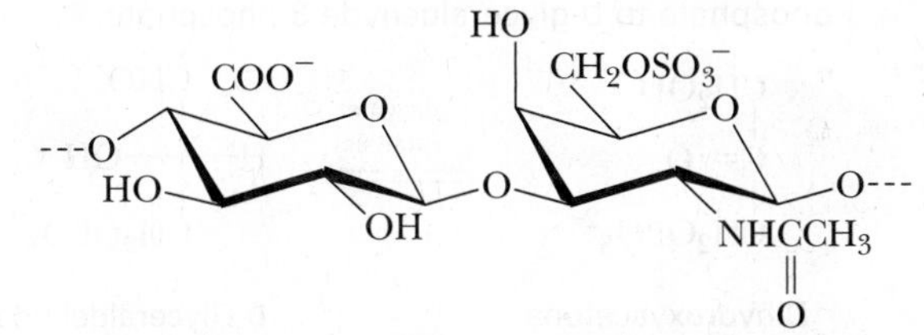

This biopolymer acts as a flexible connecting matrix between the tough protein filaments in cartilage and is available as a dietary supplement, often combined with D-glucosamine sulfate. Some believe that the combination can strengthen and improve joint flexibility.

(a) From what two monosaccharide units is the repeating disaccharide unit of chondroitin 6-sulfate derived?

(b) Describe the glycosidic bond between the two units.

*17.55 Certain complex lipids are constantly being synthesized and decomposed in the body. In several genetic diseases classified as lipid storage diseases, some of the enzymes needed to decompose the complex lipid are defective or missing. As a consequence, the complex lipids accumulate and cause enlarged liver and spleen, mental retardation, blindness, and in certain cases early death. At present no treatment is available for these diseases. The best way to prevent them is genetic counseling. Some of them can be diagnosed during fetal development.

The following is the structure of the lipid that accumulates in Fabray's disease. The genetic defect in this case is that the enzyme α-galactosidase is either missing or defective. This enzyme catalyzes the hydrolysis of the glycosidic bonds formed by α-D-galactopyranose.

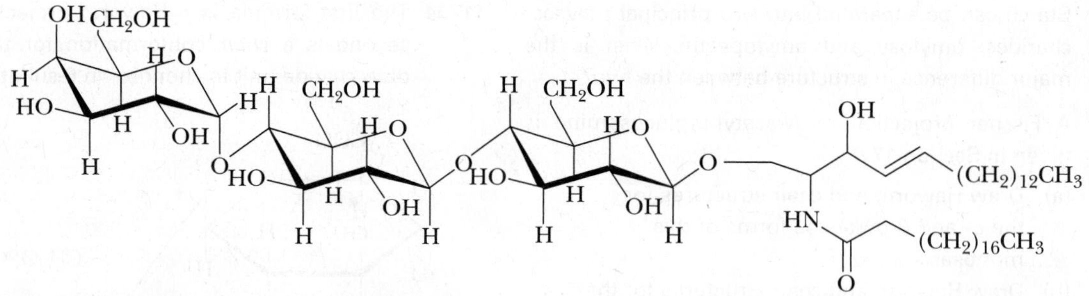

(a) Name the three hexoses present in this lipid.
(b) Describe the glycosidic bond between each.
(c) Would you expect this molecule to be soluble or insoluble in water? Explain.

LOOKING AHEAD

***17.56** One step in glycolysis, the pathway that converts glucose to pyruvate (Section 21.3), involves an enzyme-catalyzed conversion of dihydroxyacetone phosphate to D-glyceraldehyde 3-phosphate:

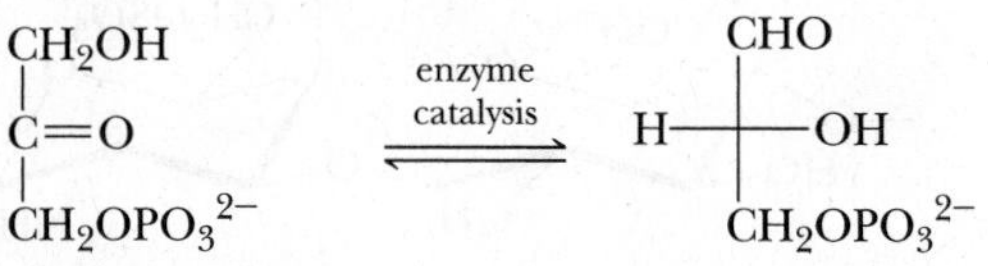

Dihydroxyacetone phosphate — D-Glyceraldehyde 3-phosphate

Show that this transformation can be regarded as two enzyme-catalyzed keto–enol tautomerizations (Section 12.8).

***17.57** One pathway for the metabolism of glucose 6-phosphate is its enzyme-catalyzed conversion to fructose 6-phosphate:

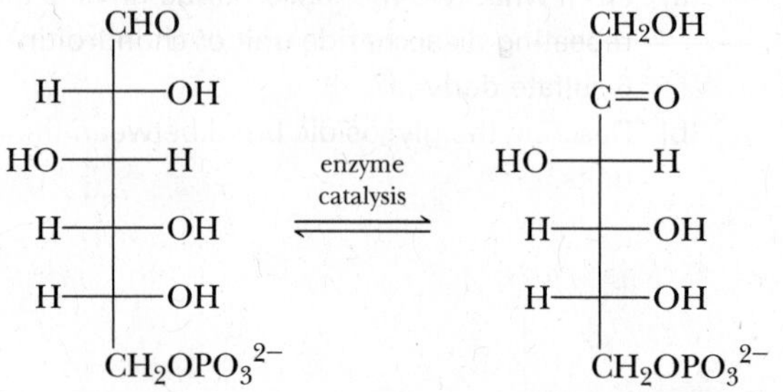

D-Glucose 6-phosphate — D-Fructose 6-phosphate

Show that this transformation can be regarded as two enzyme-catalyzed keto–enol tautomerizations.

17.58 Epimers are carbohydrates that differ in configuration at only one stereocenter.

(a) Which of the aldohexoses are epimers of each other?
(b) Are all anomer pairs also epimers of each other? Explain. Are all epimers also anomers? Explain.

***17.59** Oligosaccharides are very valuable therapeutically and are especially difficult to synthesize, even though the starting materials are readily available. Shown is the structure of globotriose, the receptor for a series of toxins synthesized by some strains of *E. coli:*

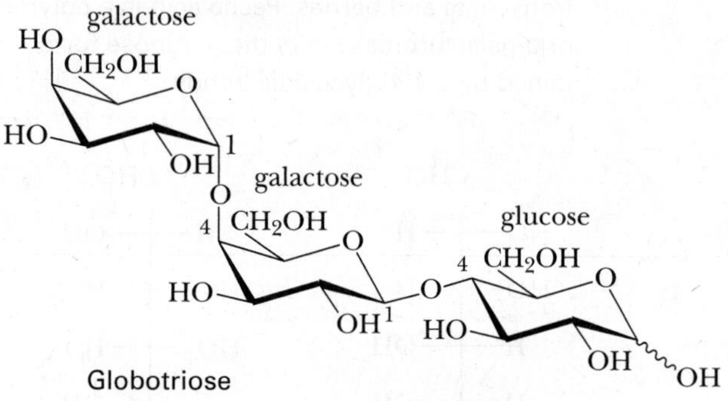

Globotriose

From left to right, globotriose consists of an α-1,4-linkage of galactose to galactose that is part of a β-1,4-linkage to glucose. The squiggly line indicates that the configuration at that carbon can be α or β. Suggest why it would be difficult to synthesize this trisaccharide, for example, by first forming the galactose–galactose glycosidic bond and then forming the glycosidic bond to glucose.

GROUP LEARNING ACTIVITIES

17.60 Pair up with another student. Each of you should select an aldohexose (refer to Table 17.1 for some possibilities). Decide whether the two carbohydrates you selected are:

(a) epimers
(b) enantiomers
(c) diasteromers
(d) D/L isomers

17.61 Discuss how nature settled upon the D form of carbohydrates as the sole stereoisomeric form in living systems. Use the Internet to learn about different scientific theories applicable to this question and debate the merits of each.

17.62 Work as a group to provide the mechanism for the reaction shown below. *Hint:* Each step is a mechanistic pattern we have covered in this or previous chapters.

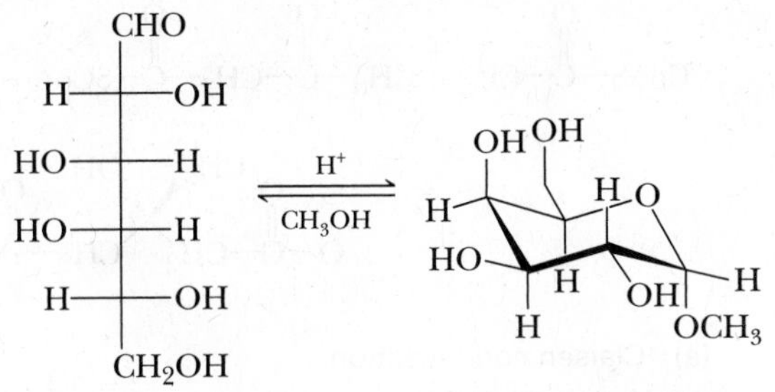

17.63 The structural formula of L-ascorbic acid (vitamin C) resembles that of a monosaccharide. Humans do not have the enzyme systems required for the synthesis of L-ascorbic acid; therefore, for us, it is a vitamin. Approximately 66 million kilograms of vitamin C are synthesized every year in the United States. Ascorbic acid contains four hydroxyl groups. With your group, determine which —OH group is most acidic and debate the merits of your selection. Recall from Section 2.5 that various structural features can enhance the stability of a conjugate base, thus increasing the acidity of the original acid.

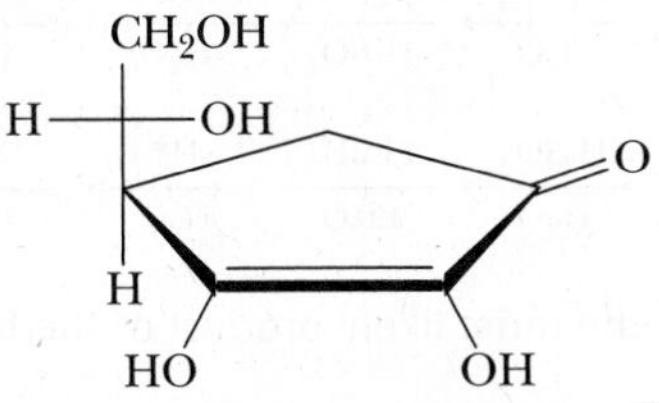

L-Ascorbic acid
(Vitamin C)

PUTTING IT TOGETHER

The following problems bring together concepts and material from Chapters 15–17. Although the focus may be on these chapters, the problems will also build upon concepts discussed throughout the text thus far.

Choose the best answer for each of the following questions.

1. Which carbon on β-maltose will be oxidized by Tollens' reagent?

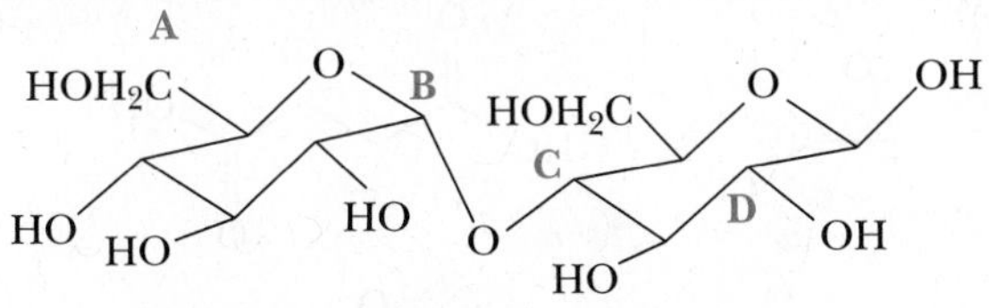

β-Maltose

(a) **A** (b) **B** (c) **C**
(d) **D** (e) **none of the above**

2. What sequence of reagents will accomplish the following transformation?

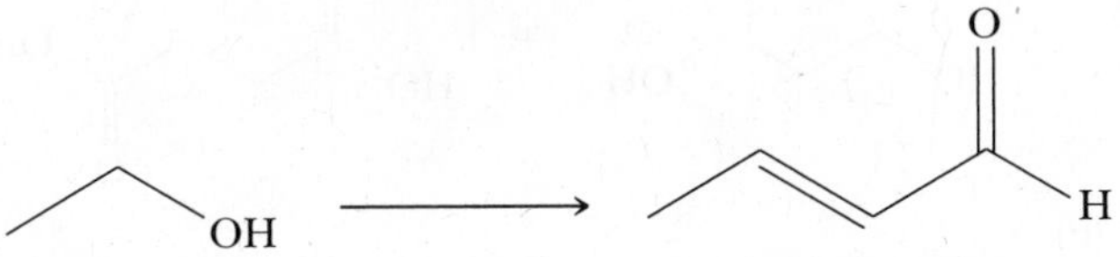

(a) 1) PCC/CH_2Cl_2
2) $NaOH/H_2O$
3) H^+/H_2O

(b) 1) H_2CrO_4/H_2SO_4
2) $NaOH/H_2O$
3) H^+/H_2O

(c) 1) $NaOH/H_2O$
2) H_2CrO_4/H_2SO_4
3) $NaOH/H_2O$
4) H^+/H_2O

(d) 1) $LiAlH_4/Et_2O$
2) H^+/H_2O
3) $NaOH/H_2O$

(e) 1) $NaBH_4/EtOH$
2) H^+/H_2O
3) $NaOH/H_2O$

3. Assuming that the following two polymers are manufactured in similar ways, which of the following statements is *true*?

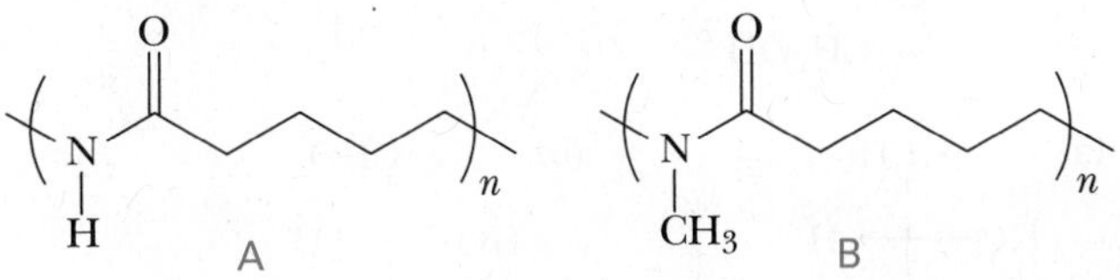

(a) Polymer **A** will be easier to synthesize than polymer **B**.
(b) Polymer **A** will be more amorphous than polymer **B**.
(c) Polymer **A** will be weaker than polymer **B**.
(d) Polymer **A** will have a higher T_g than polymer **B**.
(e) None of the above.

4. Which of the following carbohydrates does *not* undergo mutarotation?

(a)

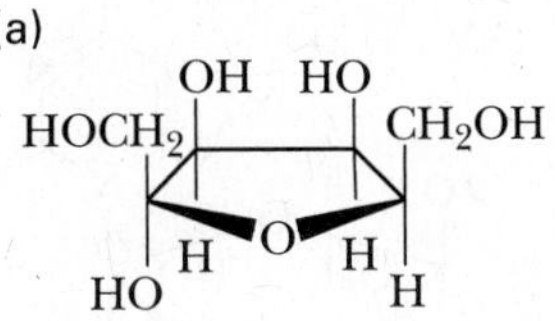

(b)

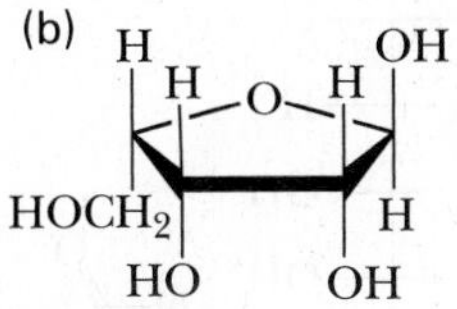

(c)

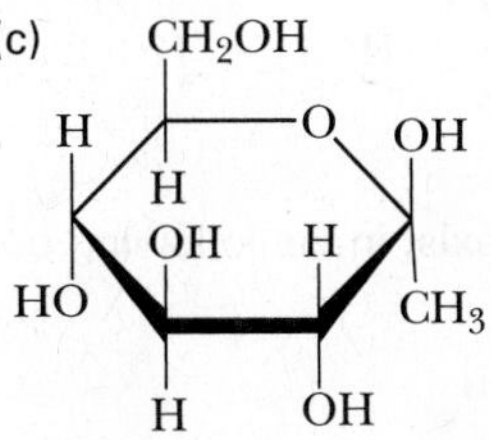

(d)

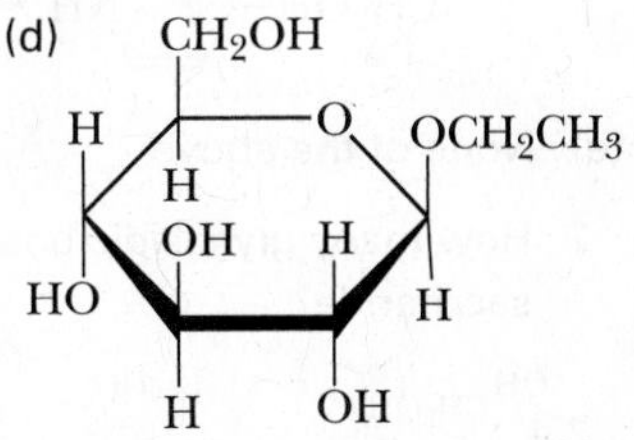

(e) All of these

5. What sequence of reagents will accomplish the following transformation?

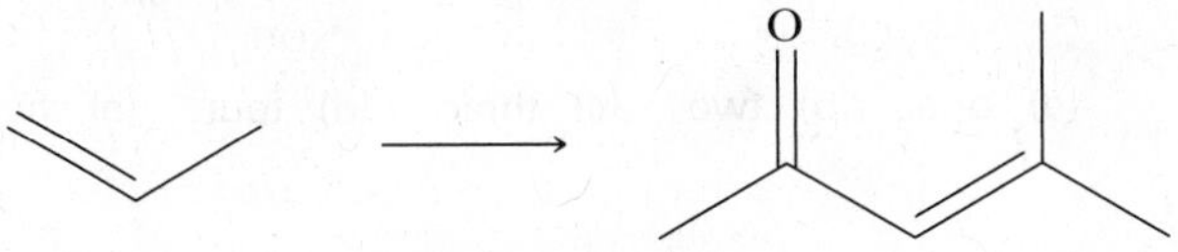

(a) $\xrightarrow{HBr}$ $\xrightarrow[H_2SO_4]{H_2CrO_4}$ $\xrightarrow[H_2O]{NaOH}$

(b) $\xrightarrow[H_2O]{NaOH}$ $\xrightarrow[H_2O]{H^+}$

(c) $\xrightarrow[H_2SO_4]{H_2CrO_4}$ $\xrightarrow[H_2O]{NaOH}$ $\xrightarrow[H_2O]{H^+}$

(d) $\xrightarrow[H_2O]{H_2SO_4}$ $\xrightarrow[H_2SO_4]{H_2CrO_4}$ $\xrightarrow[H_2O]{NaOH}$ $\xrightarrow[H_2O]{H^+}$

(e) $\xrightarrow[H_2O]{H_2SO_4}$ $\xrightarrow[Et_2O]{LiAlH_4}$ $\xrightarrow[H_2O]{H^+}$ $\xrightarrow[H_2O]{NaOH}$ $\xrightarrow[H_2O]{H^+}$

6. Select the most likely product of the following reaction.

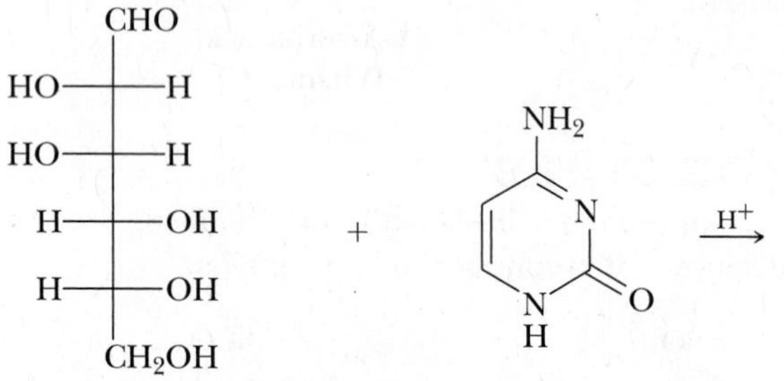

(a)

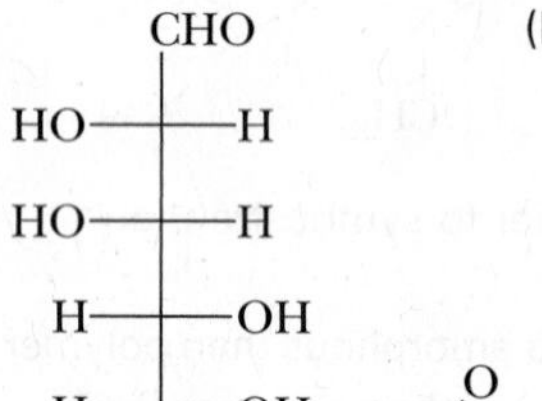

(b)

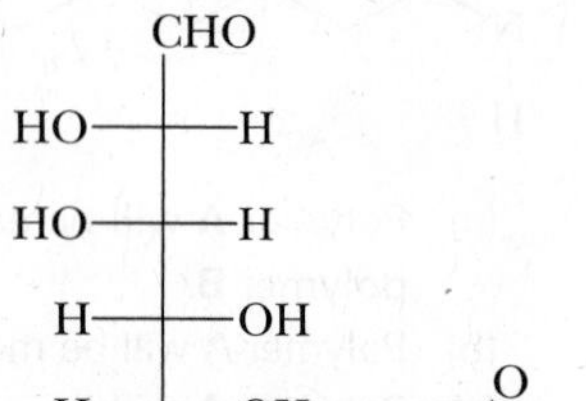

(c)

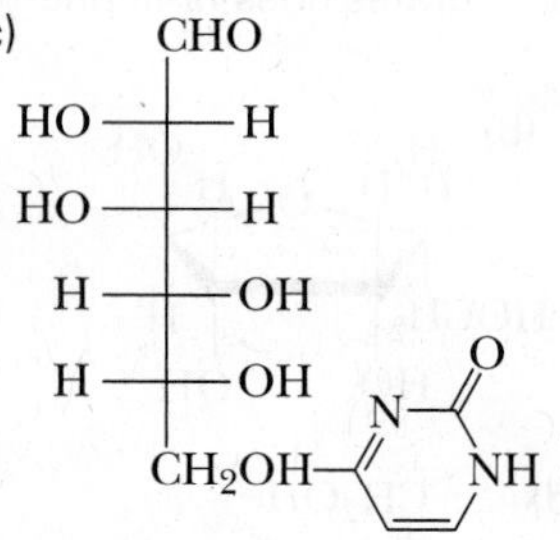

(d)

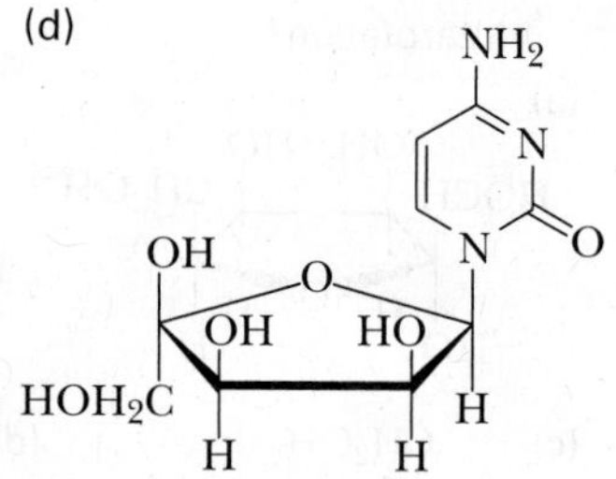

(e) None of the above

7. How many glycosidic bonds exist in the following polysaccharide?

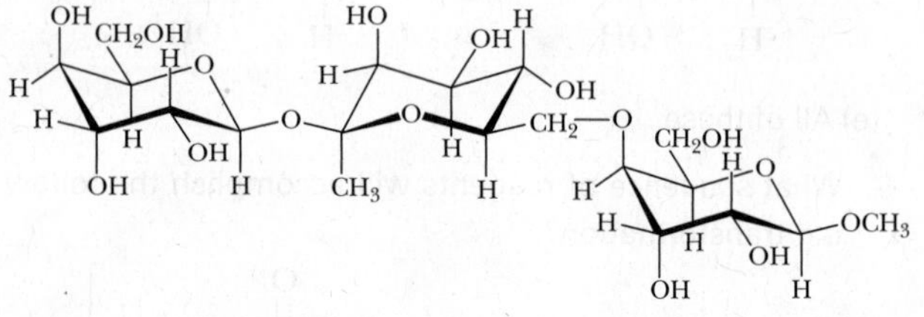

(a) one (b) two (c) three (d) four (e) five

8. Which of the following best classifies the following biological process?

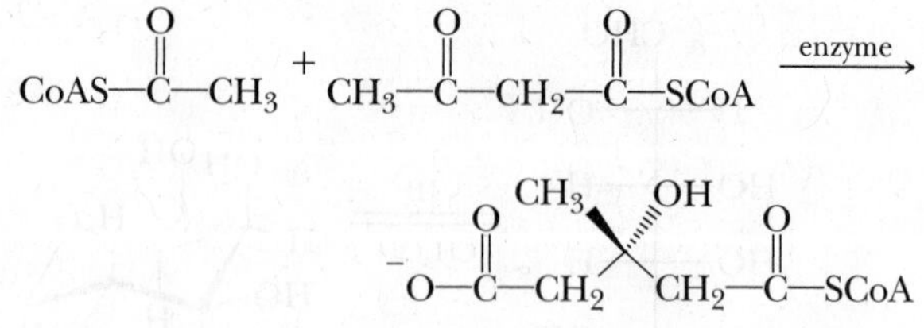

(a) Claisen condensation
(b) Aldol reaction
(c) Nucleophilic acyl substitution
(d) β-elimination
(e) Both **A** and **C**

9. Identify the monomer(s) required for the synthesis of the following polymer:

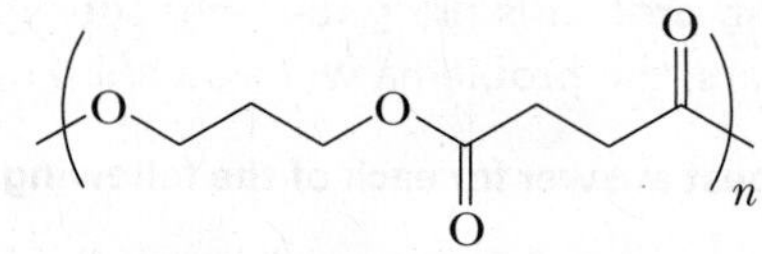

(a)

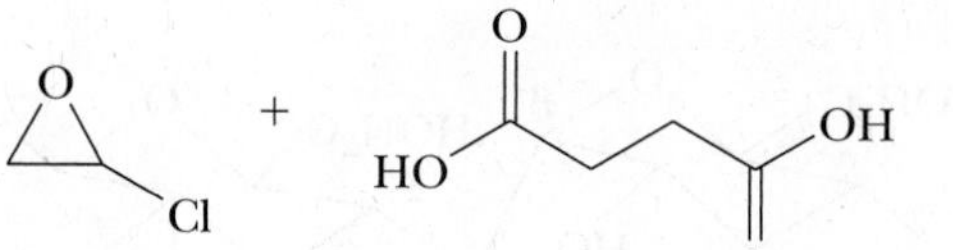

(b)

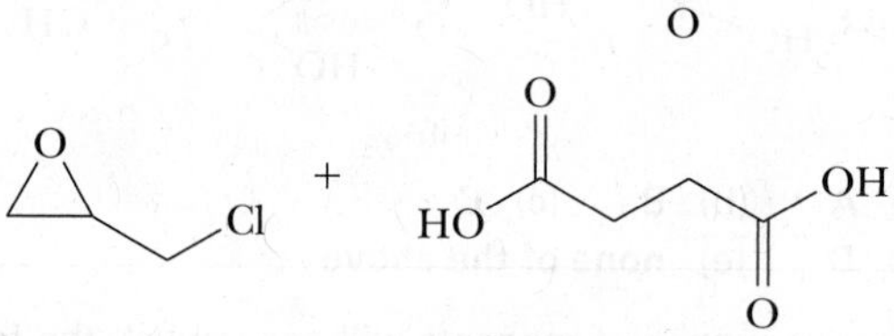

(c)

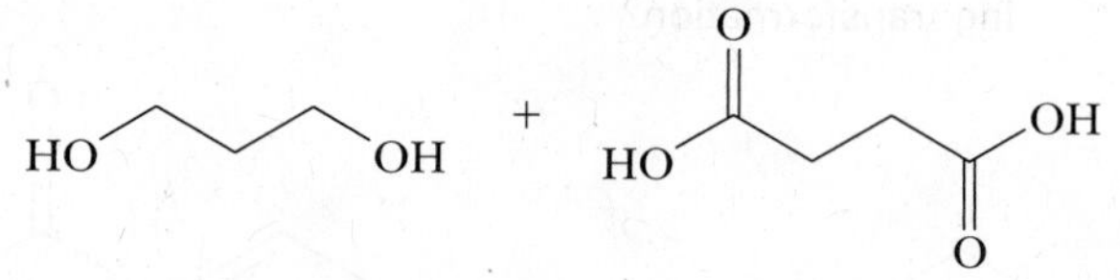

(d)

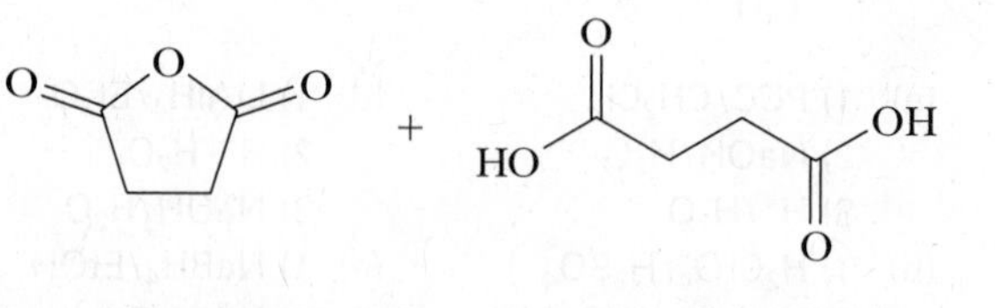

(e) None of these

10. An unknown carbohydrate is placed in a solution of $NaBH_4$/EtOH. After isolating the product, it was discovered that no alditol products were formed. Which of the following carbohydrates could be the unknown?

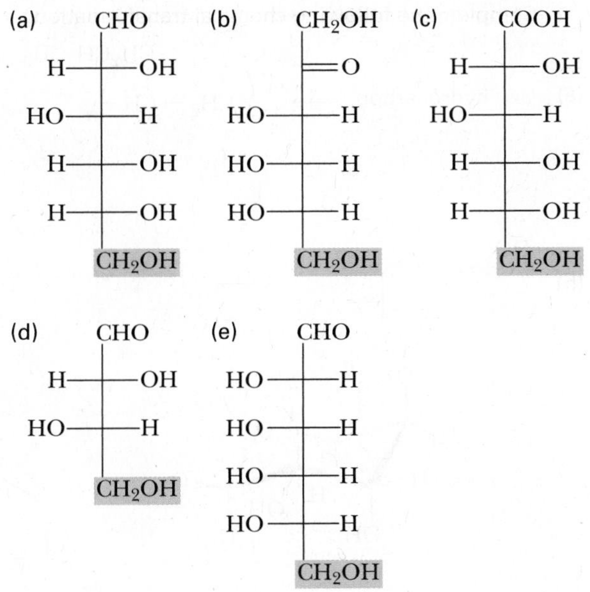

11. Each of the products shown can be made by the reaction indicated under the arrow. Provide a structure for the starting compound(s) needed to produce the product shown. Then show the mechanism of its formation. Show all charges and lone pairs of electrons in your structures.

(a)

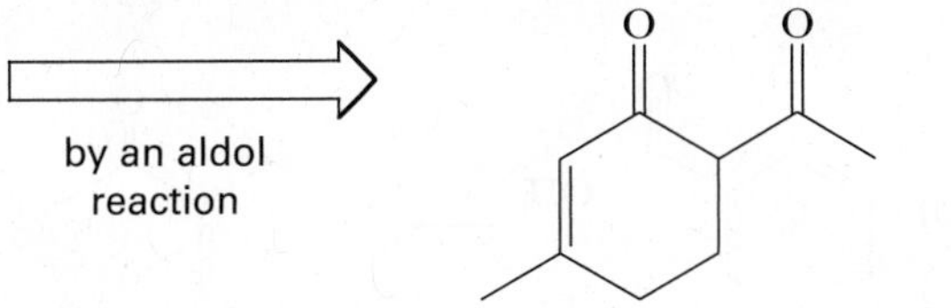

(b)

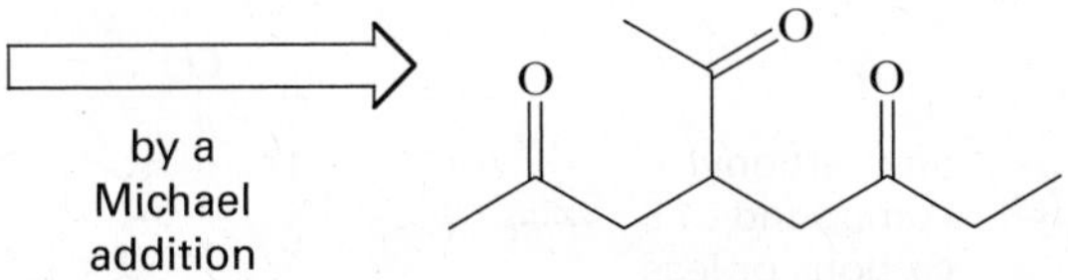

12. NAD^+ is a coenzyme found in all living cells. It acts to carry electrons during biological reactions.

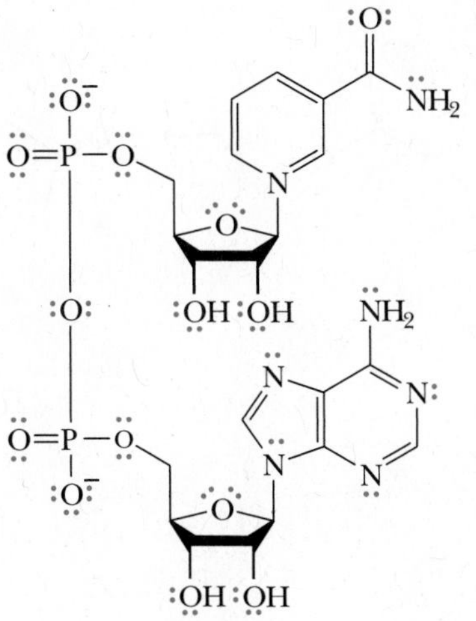

NAD^+

(a) Assign the formal charge in NAD^+ to the appropriate atom.
(b) Is NAD^+ a reducing sugar?
(c) Identify the glycosidic bonds in NAD^+.
(d) From what naturally occurring sugar(s) is NAD^+ derived?
(e) Are the two monosaccharide units α-anomers or β-anomers?
(f) Does NAD^+ undergo mutarotation?

13. Redraw each polymer using the notation in which parentheses are placed around the repeating unit. Identify each as chain-growth or step-growth polymers and identify the monomers required for its synthesis.

(a)

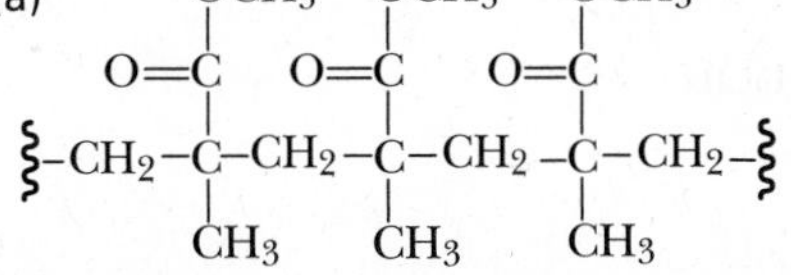

(b)

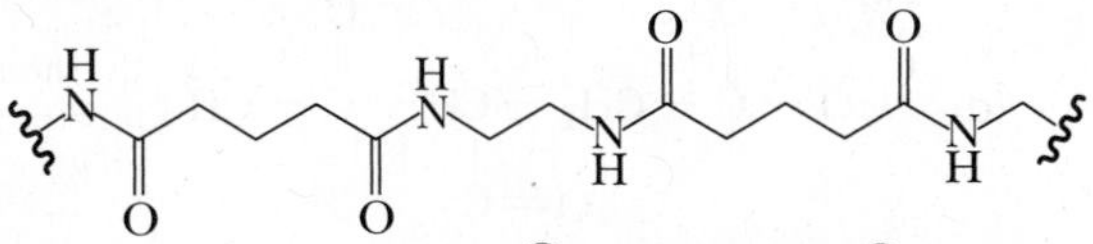

(c)

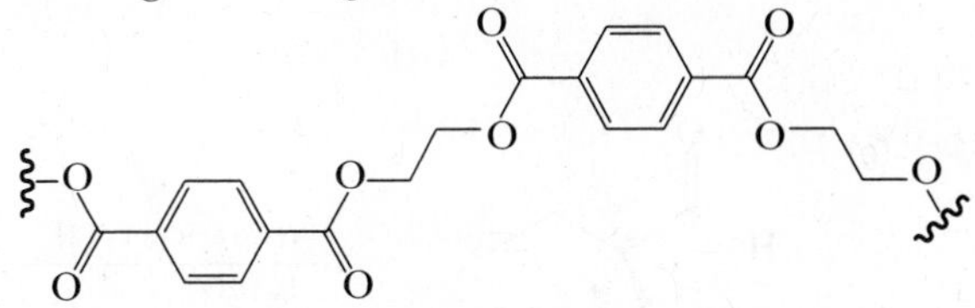

14. Provide a mechanism for the following series of reactions. Show all charges and lone pairs of electrons in your structures as well as the structures of all intermediates.

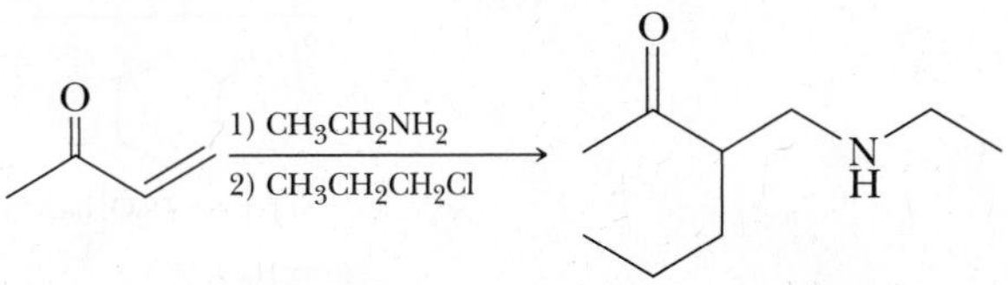

15. Select the polymer from each pair that would have the higher glass transition temperature and provide an explanation for selection.

(a)

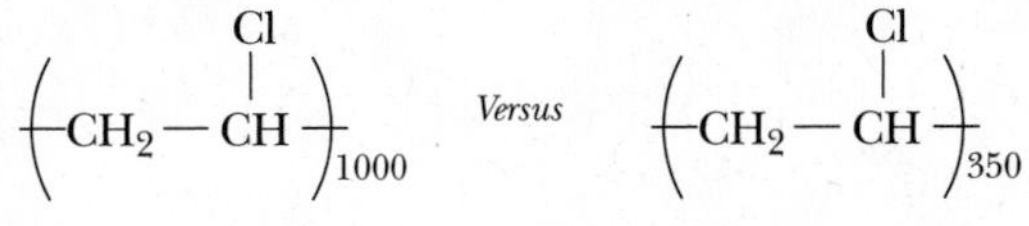

(b)

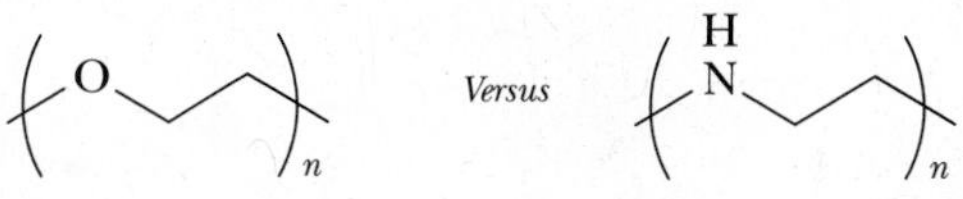

16. Predict the major product of each of the following reactions.

(a)

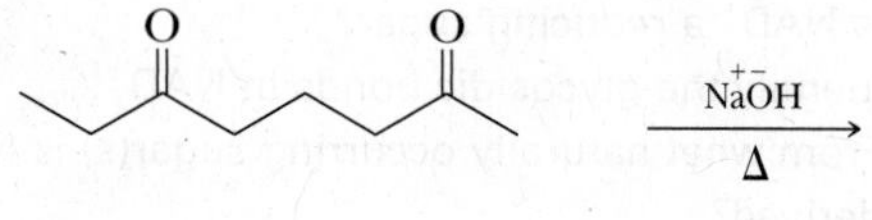

(b)

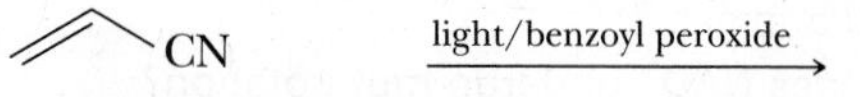

(c)

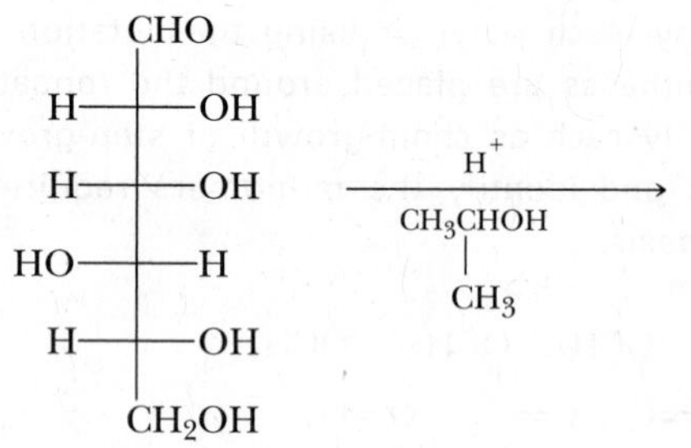

(d)

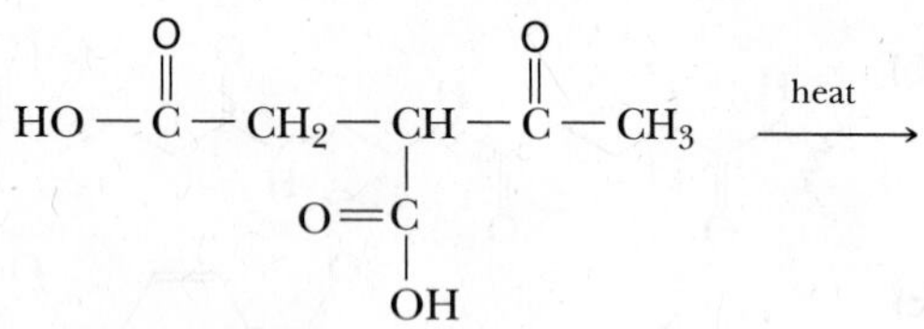

(e)

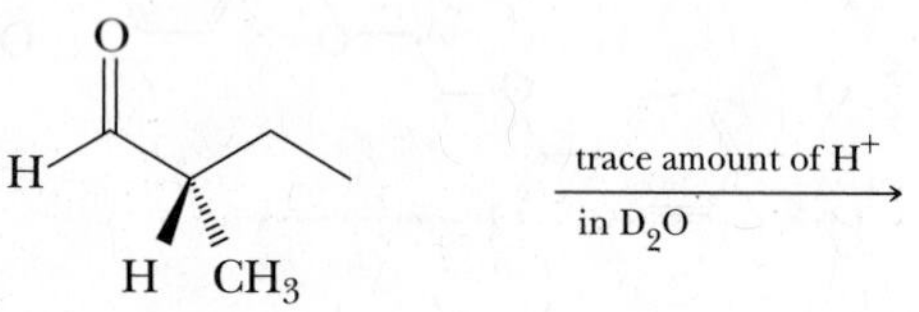

(f)

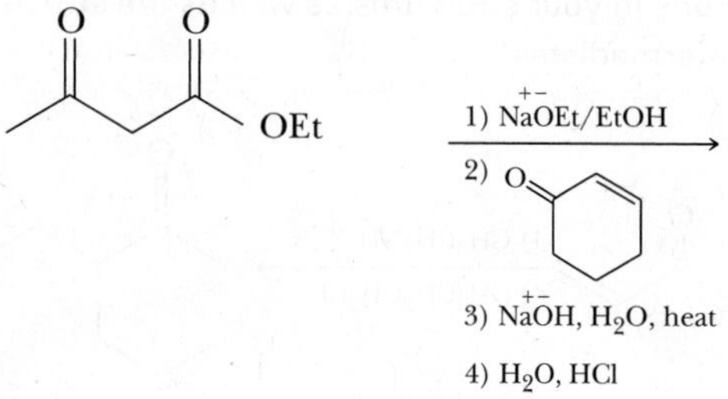

17. Complete the following chemical transformations.

(a) any hydrocarbon

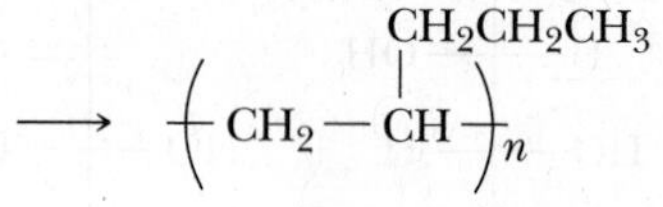

(b)

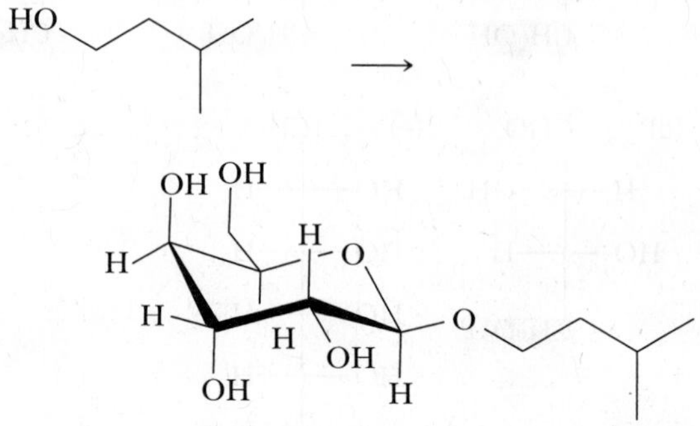

(c)

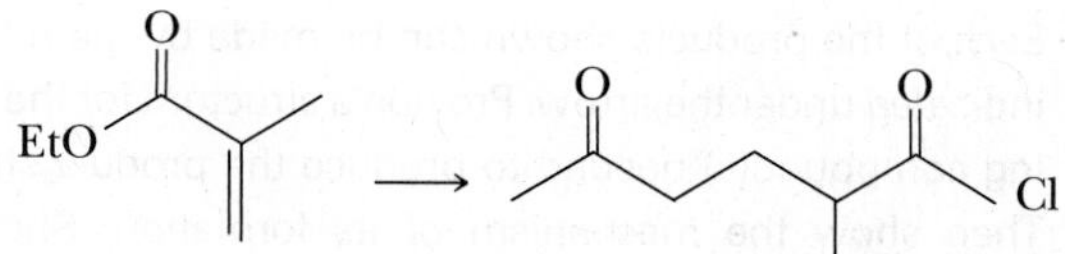

(d)

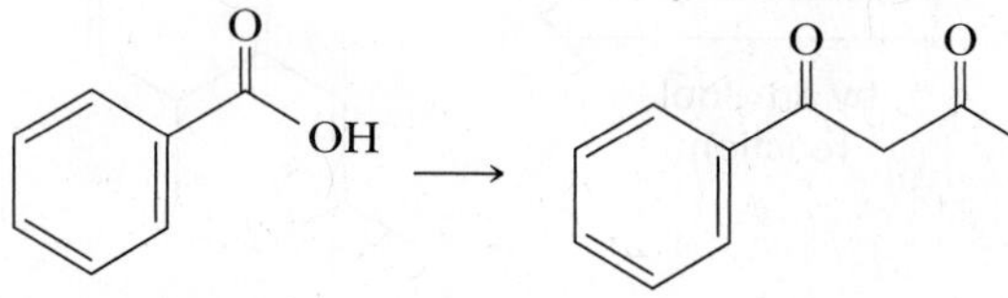

(e) any carbonyl compound of 5 carbons or less

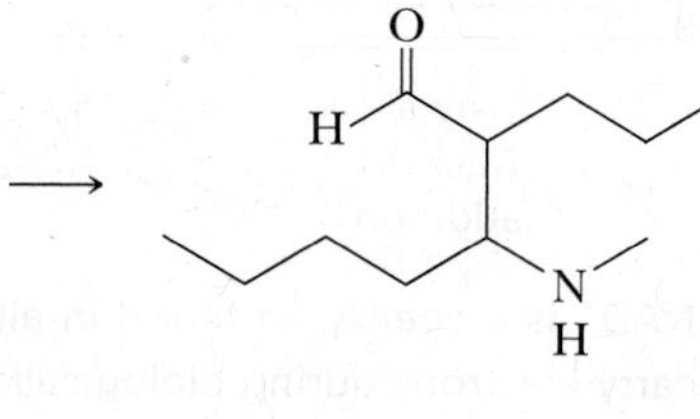

(f)

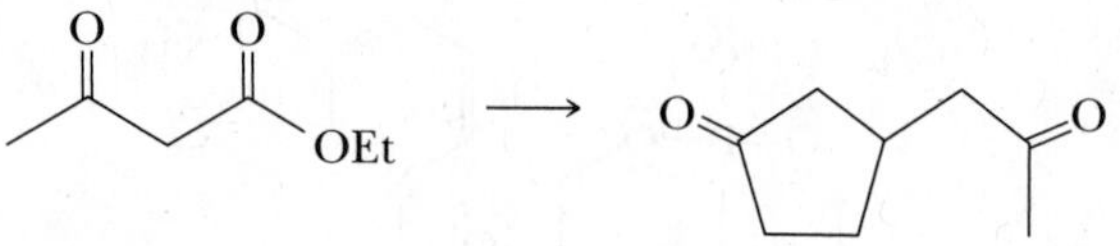

18

Amino Acids and Proteins

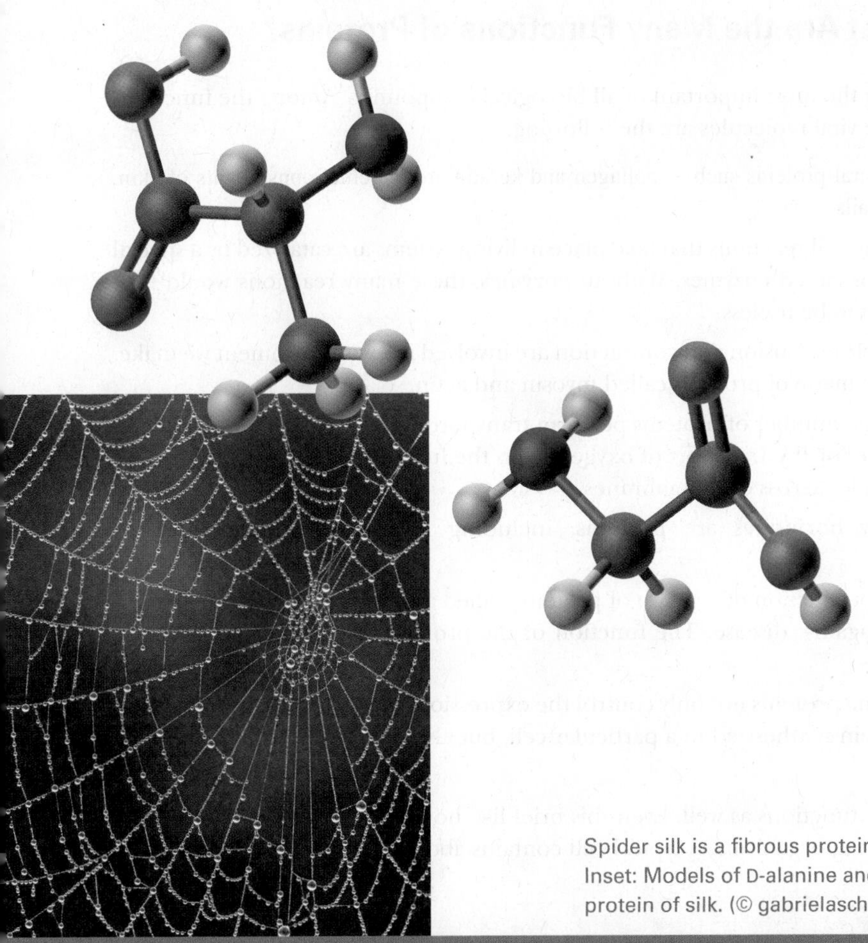

Spider silk is a fibrous protein that exhibits unmatched strength and toughness. Inset: Models of D-alanine and glycine, the major components of the fibrous protein of silk. (© gabrielaschaufelberger/iStockphoto)

KEY QUESTIONS

18.1 **What Are the Many Functions of Proteins?**

18.2 **What Are Amino Acids?**

18.3 **What Are the Acid–Base Properties of Amino Acids?**

18.4 **What Are Polypeptides and Proteins?**

18.5 **What Is the Primary Structure of a Polypeptide or Protein?**

18.6 **What Are the Three-Dimensional Shapes of Polypeptides and Proteins?**

HOW TO

18.1 **Approximate the Charge of an Amino Acid at Any Given pH**

CHEMICAL CONNECTIONS

18A **Spider Silk: A Chemical and Engineering Wonder of Nature**

WE BEGIN THIS CHAPTER with a study of amino acids, compounds whose chemistry is built on amines (Chapter 10) and carboxylic acids (Chapter 13). We concentrate in particular on the acid–base properties of amino acids because these properties are so important in determining many of the properties of proteins, polymers of amino acids that have many functions in living organisms. With this understanding of the chemistry of amino acids, we then examine the structure of proteins themselves.

18.1 What Are the Many Functions of Proteins?

Proteins are among the most important of all biological compounds. Among the functions performed by these vital molecules are the following:

- *Structure*—Structural proteins such as collagen and keratin are the chief constituents of skin, bones, hair, and nails.
- *Catalysis*—Virtually all reactions that take place in living systems are catalyzed by a special group of proteins called enzymes. Without enzymes, these many reactions would take place so slowly as to be useless.
- *Movement*—Muscle expansion and contraction are involved in every movement we make. Muscle fibers are made of proteins called myosin and actin.
- *Transport*—A large number of proteins perform transport duties. The protein hemoglobin is responsible for the transport of oxygen from the lungs to tissues. Other proteins transport molecules across cell membranes.
- *Hormones*—Many hormones are proteins, including insulin and human growth hormone.
- *Protection*—The production of a group of proteins called antibodies is one of the body's major defenses against disease. The function of the protein fibrinogen is to promote blood clotting.
- *Regulations*—Some proteins not only control the expression of genes, thereby regulating the kind of protein synthesized in a particular cell, but also dictate when such synthesis takes place.

Proteins have other functions as well. Even this brief list, however, should convince you of their vital role in living organisms. A typical cell contains about 9000 different proteins.

18.2 What Are Amino Acids?

A. Structure

Amino acid A compound that contains both an amino group and a carboxyl group.

α-Amino acid An amino acid in which the amino group is on the carbon adjacent to the carboxyl group.

Zwitterion An internal salt of an amino acid.

An **amino acid** is a compound that contains both a carboxyl group and an amino group. Although many types of amino acids are known, the **α-amino acids** are the most significant in the biological world because they are the monomers from which proteins are constructed. A general structural formula of an α-amino acid is shown in Figure 18.1.

Although Figure 18.1(a) is a common way of writing structural formulas for an amino acid, it is not accurate because it shows an acid ($-COOH$) and a base ($-NH_2$) within the same molecule. These acidic and basic groups react with each other to form an internal salt (a dipolar ion) [Figure 18.1(b)]. This internal salt is given the special name **zwitterion**. Note that a zwitterion has no net charge; it contains one positive charge and one negative charge.

Because they exist as zwitterions, amino acids have many of the properties associated with salts. They are crystalline solids with high melting points and are fairly soluble in water, but insoluble in nonpolar organic solvents such as ether and hydrocarbon solvents.

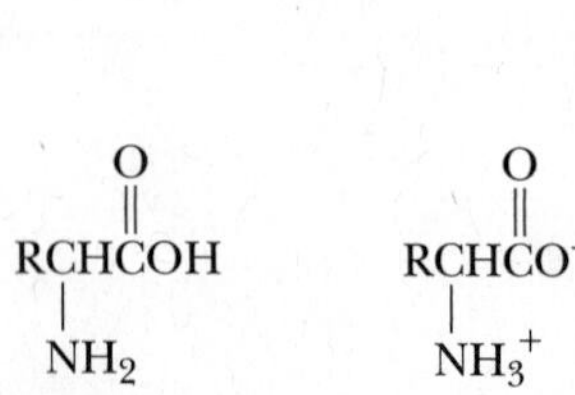

(a) (b)

FIGURE 18.1
An α-amino acid. (a) Un-ionized form and (b) internal salt (zwitterion) form.

B. Chirality

With the exception of glycine, H_2NCH_2COOH, all protein-derived amino acids have at least one stereocenter and therefore are chiral. Figure 18.2 shows Fischer projection formulas for the enantiomers of alanine. The vast majority of carbohydrates in the biological world are of the D-series (Section 17.2), whereas the vast majority of α-amino acids in the biological world are of the L-series.

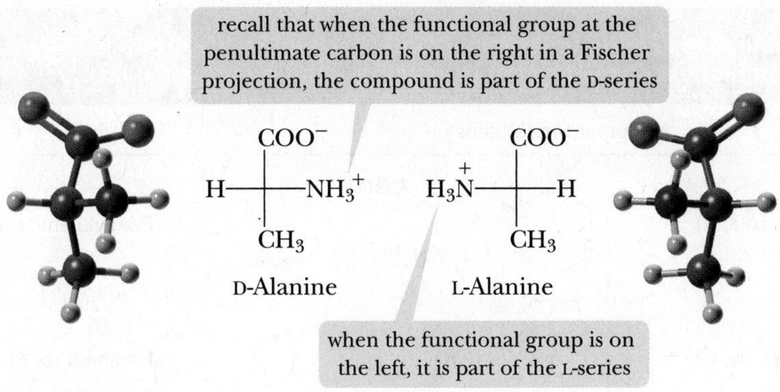

FIGURE 18.2
The enantiomers of alanine. The vast majority of α-amino acids in the biological world have the L-configuration at the α-carbon.

C. Protein-Derived Amino Acids

Table 18.1 gives common names, structural formulas, and standard three-letter and one-letter abbreviations for the 20 common L-amino acids found in proteins. The amino acids shown are divided into four categories: those with nonpolar side chains; those with polar, but un-ionized, side chains; those with acidic side chains; and those with basic side chains. As you study the information in this table, note the following points:

1. All 20 of these protein-derived amino acids are α-amino acids, meaning that the amino group is located on the carbon alpha to the carboxyl group.
2. For 19 of the 20 amino acids, the α-amino group is primary. Proline is different: Its α-amino group is secondary.
3. With the exception of glycine, the α-carbon of each amino acid is a stereocenter. Although not shown in the table, all 19 chiral amino acids have the same relative configuration at the α-carbon. In the D,L convention, all are L-amino acids.
4. Isoleucine and threonine contain a second stereocenter. Four stereoisomers are possible for each amino acid, but only one of the four is found in proteins.
5. The sulfhydryl group of cysteine, the imidazole group of histidine, and the phenolic hydroxyl of tyrosine are partially ionized at pH 7.0, but the ionized form is not the major form present at that pH.

EXAMPLE 18.1

Of the 20 protein-derived amino acids shown in Table 18.1, how many contain (a) aromatic rings, (b) side-chain hydroxyl groups, (c) phenolic —OH groups, and (d) sulfur?

STRATEGY

Study the structural formulas of the amino acids given in Table 18.1.

SOLUTION

(a) Phenylalanine, tryptophan, tyrosine, and histidine contain aromatic rings.

(b) Serine and threonine contain side-chain hydroxyl groups.

(c) Tyrosine contains a phenolic —OH group.

(d) Methionine and cysteine contain sulfur.

See problems 18.14, 18.15

PROBLEM 18.1

Of the 20 protein-derived amino acids shown in Table 18.1, (a) which contain no stereocenter and (b) which contain two stereocenters?

TABLE 18.1 The 20 Common Amino Acids Found in Proteins (*Note:* Each ionizable group is shown in the form present in highest concentration in aqueous solution at pH 7.0.)

Nonpolar Side Chains			
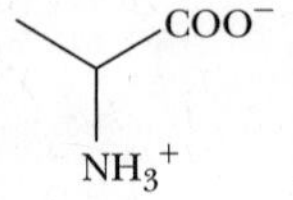	Alanine (Ala, A)	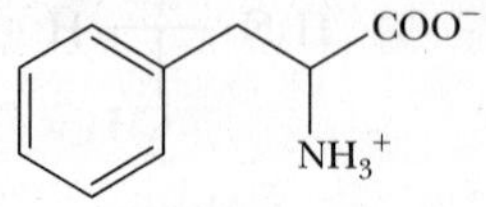	Phenylalanine (Phe, F)
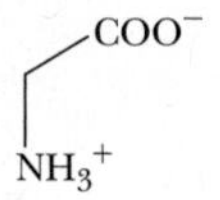	Glycine (Gly, G)	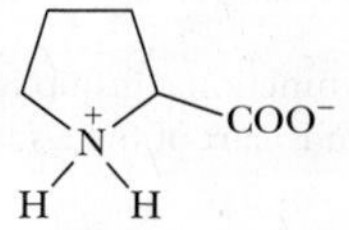	Proline (Pro, P)
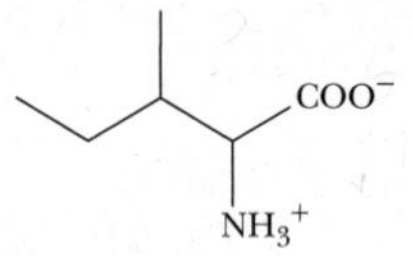	Isoleucine (Ile, I)	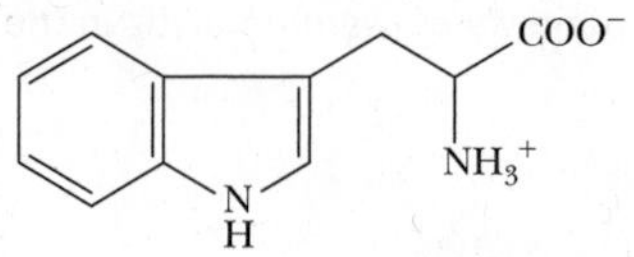	Tryptophan (Trp, W)
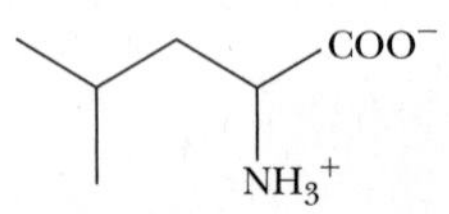	Leucine (Leu, L)	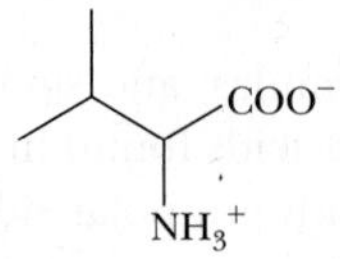	Valine (Val, V)
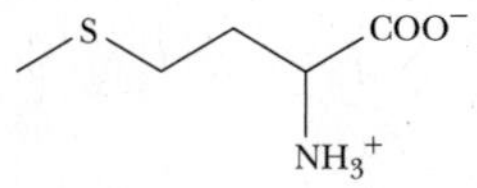	Methionine (Met, M)		
Polar Side Chains			
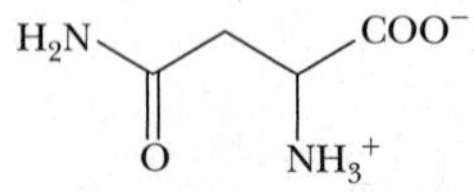	Asparagine (Asn, N)	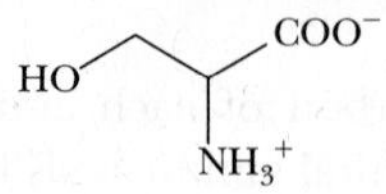	Serine (Ser, S)
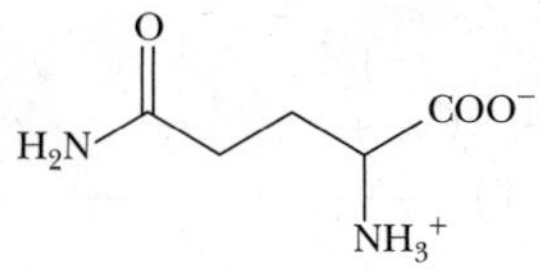	Glutamine (Gln, Q)	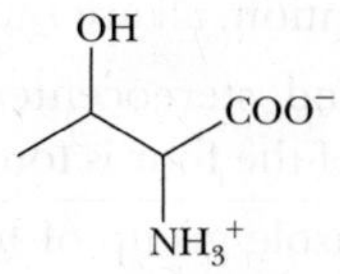	Threonine (Thr, T)
Acidic Side Chains		**Basic Side Chains**	
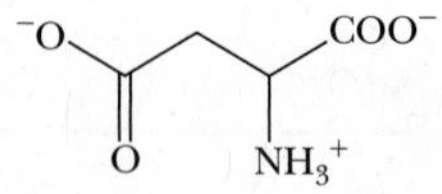	Aspartic acid (Asp, D)	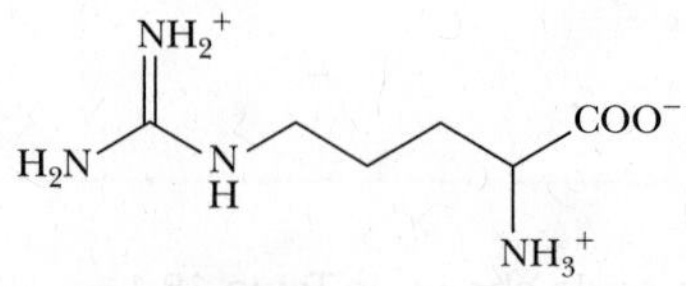	Arginine (Arg, R)
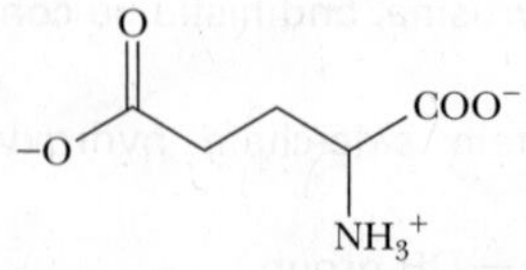	Glutamic acid (Glu, E)	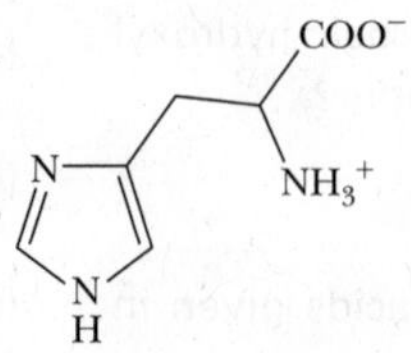	Histidine (His, H)
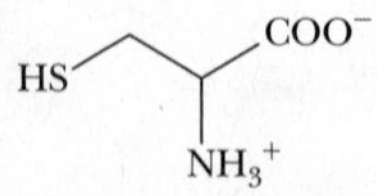	Cysteine (Cys, C)	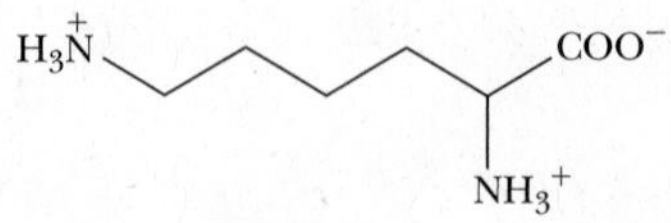	Lysine (Lys, K)
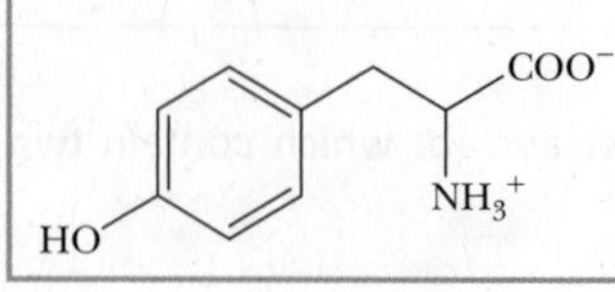	Tyrosine (Tyr, Y)		

D. Some Other Common L-Amino Acids

Although the vast majority of plant and animal proteins are constructed from just these 20 α-amino acids, many other amino acids are also found in nature. Ornithine and citrulline, for example, are found predominantly in the liver and are integral parts of the urea cycle, the metabolic pathway that converts ammonia to urea:

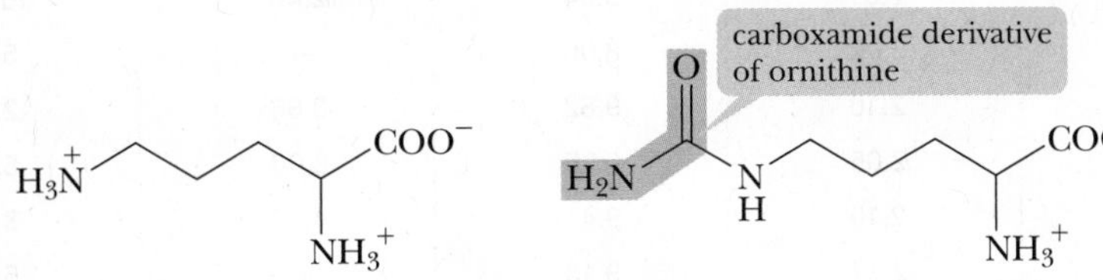

Ornithine Citrulline

Thyroxine and triiodothyronine, two of several hormones derived from the amino acid tyrosine, are found in thyroid tissue:

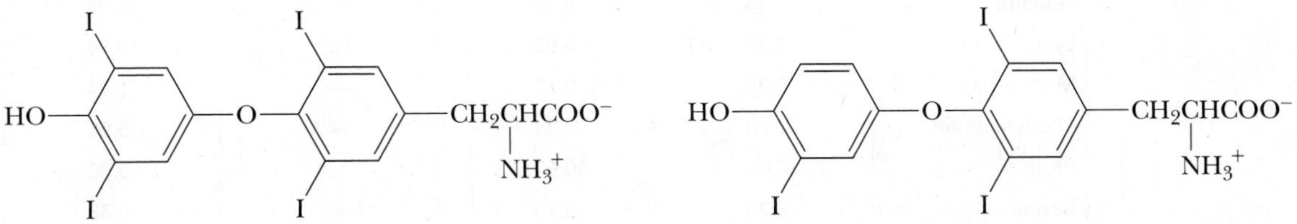

Thyroxine, T_4 Triiodothyronine, T_3

The principal function of these two hormones is to stimulate metabolism in other cells and tissues.

4-Aminobutanoic acid (γ-aminobutyric acid, or GABA) is found in high concentration (0.8 mM) in the brain, but in no significant amounts in any other mammalian tissue. GABA is synthesized in neural tissue by decarboxylation of the α-carboxyl group of glutamic acid and is a neurotransmitter in the central nervous system of invertebrates and possibly in humans as well:

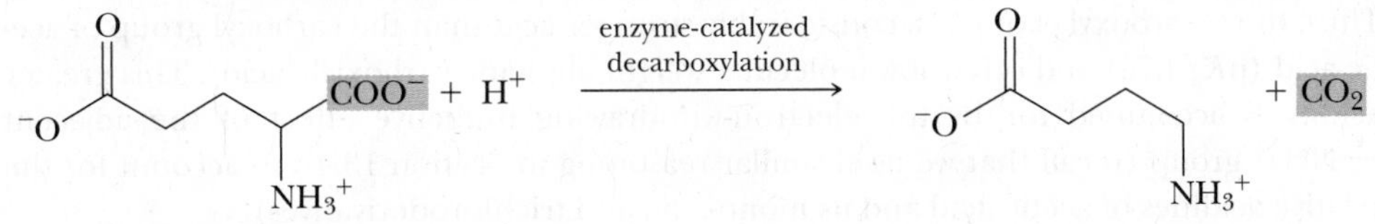

Glutamic acid 4-Aminobutanoic acid (γ-Aminobutyric acid, GABA)

Only L-amino acids are found in proteins, and only rarely are D-amino acids a part of the metabolism of higher organisms. Several D-amino acids, however, along with their L-enantiomers, are found in lower forms of life. D-Alanine and D-glutamic acid, for example, are structural components of the cell walls of certain bacteria. Several D-amino acids are also found in peptide antibiotics.

18.3 What Are the Acid–Base Properties of Amino Acids?

A. Acidic and Basic Groups of Amino Acids

Among the most important chemical properties of amino acids are their acid–base properties. All are weak polyprotic acids because of the presence of both —COOH and $—NH_3^+$ groups. Given in Table 18.2 are pK_a values for each ionizable group of the 20 protein-derived amino acids.

TABLE 18.2 pK_a Values for Ionizable Groups of Amino Acids

Amino Acid	pK_a of α-COOH	pK_a of α-NH_3^+	pK_a of Side Chain	Isoelectric Point (pI)
Alanine	2.35	9.87	—	6.11
Arginine	2.01	9.04	12.48	10.76
Asparagine	2.02	8.80	—	5.41
Aspartic acid	2.10	9.82	3.86	2.98
Cysteine	2.05	10.25	8.00	5.02
Glutamic acid	2.10	9.47	4.07	3.08
Glutamine	2.17	9.13	—	5.65
Glycine	2.35	9.78	—	6.06
Histidine	1.77	9.18	6.10	7.64
Isoleucine	2.32	9.76	—	6.04
Leucine	2.33	9.74	—	6.04
Lysine	2.18	8.95	10.53	9.74
Methionine	2.28	9.21	—	5.74
Phenylalanine	2.58	9.24	—	5.91
Proline	2.00	10.60	—	6.30
Serine	2.21	9.15	—	5.68
Threonine	2.09	9.10	—	5.60
Tryptophan	2.38	9.39	—	5.88
Tyrosine	2.20	9.11	10.07	5.63
Valine	2.29	9.72	—	6.00

Note: Dash indicates no ionizable side chain.

Acidity of α-Carboxyl Groups

The average value of the pK_a for an α-carboxyl group of a protonated amino acid is 2.19. Thus, the α-carboxyl group is a considerably stronger acid than the carboxyl group of acetic acid (pK_a 4.76) and other low-molecular-weight aliphatic carboxylic acids. This greater acidity is accounted for by the electron-withdrawing inductive effect of the adjacent $-NH_3^+$ group (recall that we used similar reasoning in Section 13.4A to account for the relative acidities of acetic acid and its mono-, di-, and trichloroderivatives):

the ammonium group has an electron-withdrawing inductive effect that delocalizes the negative charge and stabilizes the ion

$$\underset{NH_3^+}{RCHCOOH} + H_2O \rightleftharpoons \underset{NH_3^+}{RCHCOO^-} + H_3O^+ \quad pK_a = 2.19$$

$$\underset{R}{RCHCOOH} + H_2O \rightleftharpoons \underset{R}{RCHCOO^-} + H_3O^+ \quad pK_a = 4.5$$

without an ammonium group, there is no electron-withdrawing inductive effect

Acidity of Side-Chain Carboxyl Groups

Due to the electron-withdrawing inductive effect of the α-NH_3^+ group, the side-chain carboxyl groups of protonated aspartic acid and glutamic acid are also stronger acids than acetic acid (p K_a 4.76). Notice that this acid-strengthening inductive effect decreases with increasing distance of the —COOH from the α -NH $_3$ ⁺. Compare the acidities of the α -COOH of alanine (p K_a 2.35), the γ -COOH of aspartic acid (p K_a 3.86), and the δ -COOH of glutamic acid (p K_a 4.07).

Acidity of α-Ammonium Groups

The average value of pK_a for an α -ammonium group, α -NH $_3$ ⁺, is 9.47 compared with an average value of 10.76 for primary aliphatic ammonium ions (Section 10.4). Just as the $-NH_3$ ⁺ group exerts an inductive effect on the carboxylate group, the electronegative oxygen atoms of the carboxylate group exert an electron-withdrawing inductive effect on the $-NH_3$ ⁺ group. This increases the electron deficiency of the ammonium group, making it more likely to donate a proton to become an uncharged $-NH_2$ group. Thus, the α -ammonium group of an amino acid is a slightly stronger acid than a primary aliphatic ammonium ion. Conversely, an α -amino group is a slightly weaker base than a primary aliphatic amine.

the electron-withdrawing effect of the carboxylate oxygens increases the positive character of the ammonium group, making the ion less stable and more likely to give up a proton

$$\overrightarrow{RCHCOO}^- + H_2O \Longrightarrow \overrightarrow{RCHCOO}^- + H_3O^+ \quad pK_a = 9.47$$

$$\downarrow NH_3^+ \qquad NH_2$$

$$R-CH-R + H_2O \Longrightarrow R-CH-R + H_3O^+ pK_a = 10.60$$

 $NH_3^+ NH_2$

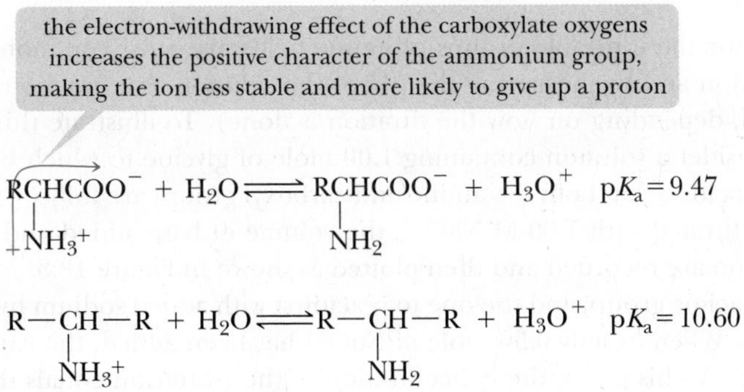

Basicity of the Guanidine Group of Arginine

The side-chain guanidine group of arginine is a considerably stronger base than an aliphatic amine is. As we saw in Section 10.4, guanidine (p K_b 0.4) is the strongest base of any neutral compound. The remarkable basicity of the guanidine group of arginine is attributed to the large resonance stabilization of the protonated form.

$$\vec{\text{RNH}} - \vec{\text{C}} \longleftrightarrow \vec{\text{RNH}}_2^+ \longleftrightarrow \vec{\text{RNH}} - \vec{\text{C}} \longleftrightarrow \vec{\text{RNH}}_2^+ \longleftrightarrow$$

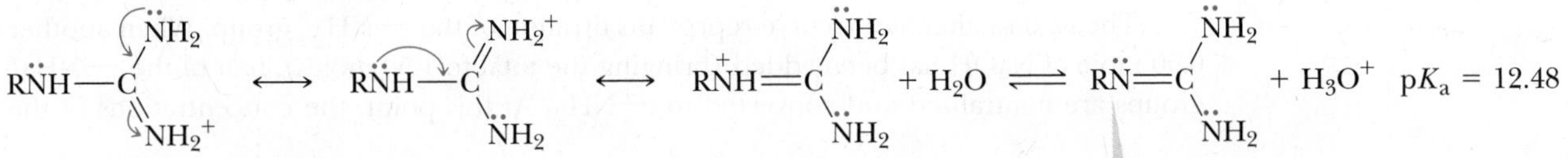

The protonated form of the guanidinium ion side chain of arginine is a hybrid of three contributing structures

the resonance stabilization of the guanidinium ion makes the guanidine nitrogen more basic than an aliphatic amine

no resonance stabilization
$$H - \stackrel{\frown}{N} - R + H_2O \Longrightarrow \stackrel{\frown}{N} - R + H_3O^+ pK_a = 10.5$$

Ammonium ion Aliphatic amine

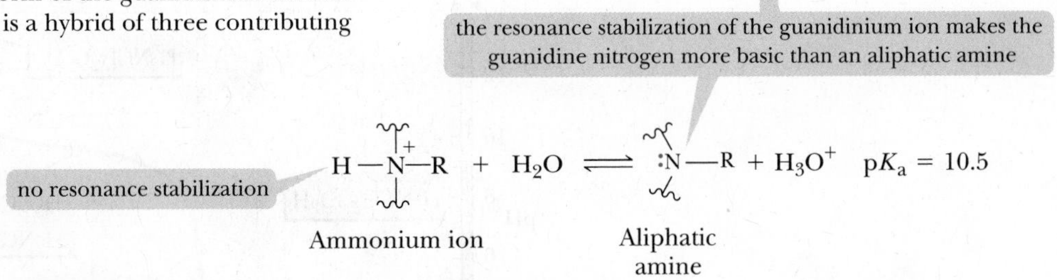

Basicity of the Imidazole Group of Histidine

Because the imidazole group on the side chain of histidine contains six π electrons in a planar, fully conjugated ring, imidazole is classified as a heterocyclic aromatic amine (Section 9.2). The unshared pair of electrons on one nitrogen is a part of the aromatic sextet, whereas that on the other nitrogen is not. It is the pair of electrons that is not part of the aromatic sextet that is responsible for the basic properties of the imidazole ring. Protonation of this nitrogen produces a resonance-stabilized cation:

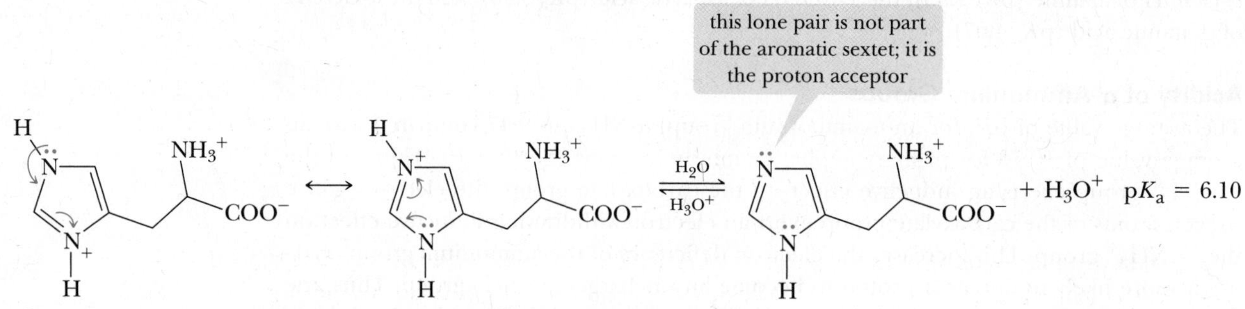

Resonance-stabilized imidazolium cation

B. Titration of Amino Acids

Values of pK_a for the ionizable groups of amino acids are most commonly obtained by acid–base titration and by measuring the pH of the solution as a function of added base (or added acid, depending on how the titration is done). To illustrate this experimental procedure, consider a solution containing 1.00 mole of glycine to which has been added enough strong acid so that both the amino and carboxyl groups are fully protonated. Next, the solution is titrated with 1.00 M NaOH; the volume of base added and the pH of the resulting solution are recorded and then plotted as shown in Figure 18.3.

The most acidic group, and the one to react first with added sodium hydroxide, is the carboxyl group. When exactly 0.50 mole of NaOH has been added, the carboxyl group is half neutralized. At this point, the concentration of the zwitterion equals that of the positively charged ion, and the pH of 2.35 equals the pK_a of the carboxyl group (pK_{a1}):

$$\text{At pH} = pK_{a1} \qquad [H_3\overset{+}{N}CH_2COOH] = [H_3\overset{+}{N}CH_2COO^-]$$

Positive ion — Zwitterion

The end point of the first part of the titration is reached when 1.00 mole of NaOH has been added. At this point, the predominant species present is the zwitterion, and the observed pH of the solution is 6.06.

The next section of the curve represents titration of the $—NH_3^+$ group. When another 0.50 mole of NaOH has been added (bringing the total to 1.50 moles), half of the $—NH_3^+$ groups are neutralized and converted to $—NH_2$. At this point, the concentrations of the

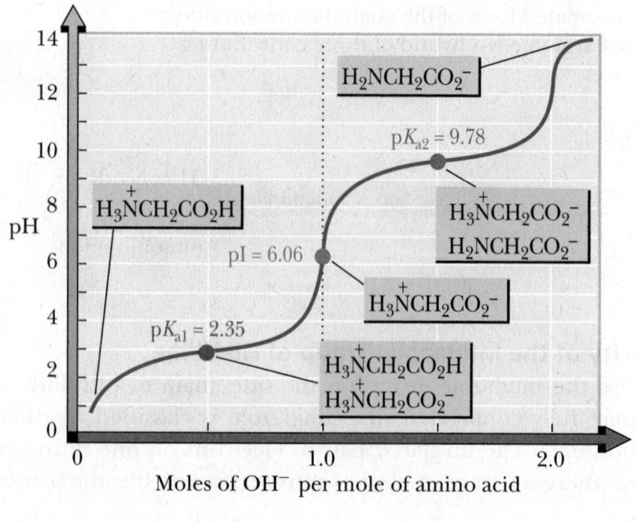

FIGURE 18.3 Titration of glycine with sodium hydroxide.

zwitterion and negatively charged ion are equal, and the observed pH is 9.78, the pK_a of the amino group of glycine (pK_{a2}):

$$\text{At pH} = \text{p}K_{a2} \qquad [H_3\overset{+}{N}CH_2COO^-] = [H_2NCH_2COO^-]$$

Zwitterion Negative ion

The second end point of the titration is reached when a total of 2.00 moles of NaOH have been added and glycine is converted entirely to an anion.

C. Isoelectric Point

Titration curves such as that for glycine permit us to determine pK_a values for the ionizable groups of an amino acid. They also permit us to determine another important property: the **isoelectric point, pI**—the pH at which most of the molecules of the amino acid in solution have a net charge of zero. (They are zwitterions.) By examining the titration curve, you can see that the isoelectric point for glycine falls halfway between the pK_a values for the carboxyl and amino groups:

Isoelectric point (pI) The pH at which an amino acid, a polypeptide, or a protein has no net charge.

$$\text{pI} = \frac{1}{2}(\text{p}K_a\ \alpha\text{-COOH} + \text{p}K_a\ \alpha\text{-NH}_3^+)$$

$$= \frac{1}{2}(2.35 + 9.78) = 6.06$$

At pH 6.06, the predominant form of glycine molecules is the dipolar ion; furthermore, at this pH, the concentration of positively charged glycine molecules equals the concentration of negatively charged glycine molecules.

When estimating the pI for arginine, aspartic acid, glutamic acid, histidine, and lysine (amino acids that contain either two carboxyl or two ammonium groups), we use the pK_a's of the two groups that are closest in value. For example, the pI of lysine would be determined as follows:

$$\text{pI} = \tfrac{1}{2}\ (\text{p}K_a\ \alpha\text{-}\overset{+}{N}H_3 + \text{p}K_a\ \text{side chain-NH}_3^+)$$

$$= \tfrac{1}{2}\ (8.95 + 10.53) = 9.74$$

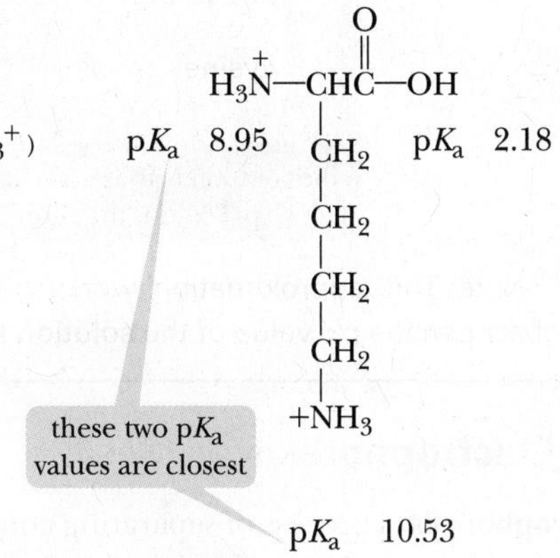

Given a value for the isoelectric point of an amino acid, it is possible to estimate the charge on that amino acid at any pH. For example, the charge on tyrosine at pH 5.63, the isoelectric point of tyrosine, is zero. A small fraction of tyrosine molecules is positively charged at pH 5.00 (0.63 unit less than its pI), and virtually all are positively charged at pH 3.63 (2.00 units less than its pI). As another example, the net charge on lysine is zero at pH 9.74. At pH values smaller than 9.74, an increasing fraction of lysine molecules is positively charged.

At pH values greater than pI, an increasing fraction of its molecules have a net negative charge. To summarize for any amino acid:

$$\underset{\underset{\text{(net charge = +)}}{\text{pH < pI}}}{\underset{NH_3^+}{RCHCOOH}} \underset{H_3O^+}{\overset{OH^-}{\rightleftharpoons}} \underset{\underset{\text{(net charge = 0)}}{\text{pH = pI}}}{\underset{NH_3^+}{RCHCOO^-}} \underset{H_3O^+}{\overset{OH^-}{\rightleftharpoons}} \underset{\underset{\text{(net charge = −)}}{\text{pH > pI}}}{\underset{NH_2}{RCHCOO^-}}$$

HOW TO 18.1

Approximate the Charge of an Amino Acid at Any Given pH

The pH of a solution is a measure of its acidity. The pK_a value of an ionizable functional group is a measure of the acidity of a proton on that functional group. In your study of general chemistry, you learned that the Henderson-Hasselbalch equation $\left(pH = pK_a + \log\frac{[A^-]}{[HA]}\right)$ allows us to relate the pH of a solution to the pK_a of an acid. The equation can be summarized as follows:

(a) If the pH of the solution is lower than the pK_a of an acidic group, the solution behaves as an acid to the group and the group remains protonated.

(b) If the pH of the solution is higher than the pK_a of an acidic group, the acidic group behaves as an acid to the solution and the group is deprotonated.

We use lysine as an example. At pH 5, the charge on lysine will be +1:

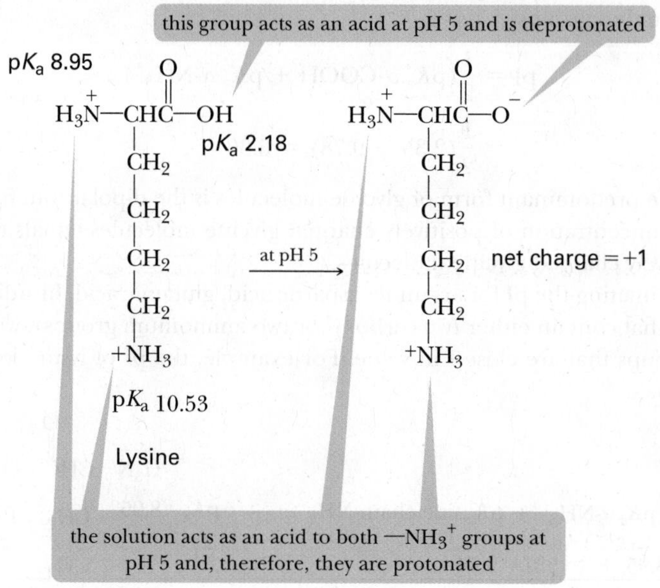

*Note: This approximation works best when there is a difference of 1 unit between the pH value of the solution and the pK_a value of each ionizable group.

D. Electrophoresis

Electrophoresis The process of separating compounds on the basis of their electric charge.

Electrophoresis, a process of separating compounds on the basis of their electric charges, is used to separate and identify mixtures of amino acids and proteins. Electrophoretic separations can be carried out with paper, starch, agar, certain plastics, and cellulose acetate used as solid supports. In paper electrophoresis, a paper strip saturated with an aqueous buffer of predetermined pH serves as a bridge between two electrode vessels (Figure 18.4). Next, a sample of amino acids is applied as a colorless spot on the paper strip. (The amino acid

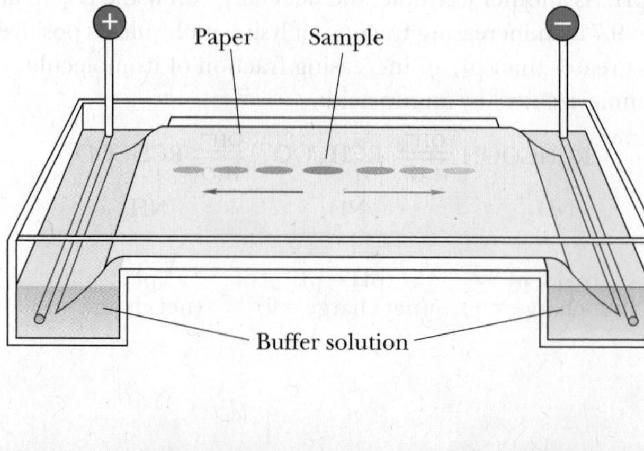

FIGURE 18.4 Electrophoresis of a mixture of amino acids. Those with a negative charge move toward the positive electrode; those with a positive charge move toward the negative electrode; those with no charge remain at the origin.

mixture is colorless.) When an electrical potential is then applied to the electrode vessels, amino acids migrate toward the electrode carrying the charge opposite to their own. Molecules having a high charge density move more rapidly than do those with a lower charge density. Any molecule already at its isoelectric point remains at the origin. After the separation is complete, the paper strip is sprayed with a dye that transforms each amino acid into a colored compound, making the separated components visible.

A dye commonly used to detect amino acids is ninhydrin (1,2,3-indanetrione monohydrate). Ninhydrin reacts with α-amino acids to produce an aldehyde, carbon dioxide, and a purple-colored anion:

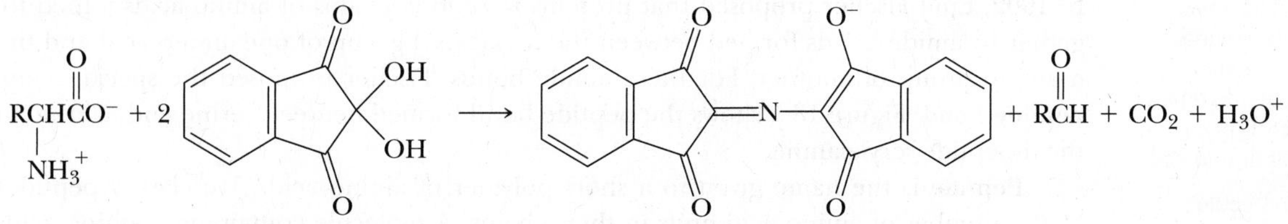

An α-amino acid — Ninhydrin — Purple-colored anion

This reaction is commonly used in both qualitative and quantitative analysis of amino acids. Nineteen of the 20 protein-derived α-amino acids have primary amino groups and give the same purple-colored ninhydrin-derived anion. Proline, a secondary amine, gives a different, orange-colored compound.

EXAMPLE 18.2

The isoelectric point of tyrosine is 5.63. Toward which electrode does tyrosine migrate during paper electrophoresis at pH 7.0?

STRATEGY

At its isoelectric point, a molecule of an amino acid has no net charge. In a solution in which pH > pI, its molecules have a net negative charge, and in a solution in which pH < pI, its molecules have a net positive charge. Therefore, in this problem, the important point is to compare the pH of the solution and the pI of the amino acid.

SOLUTION

During paper electrophoresis at pH 7.0 (more basic than its isoelectric point), tyrosine has a net negative charge and migrates toward the positive electrode.

See problems 18.22, 18.23, 18.25, 18.26, 18.32, 18.33

PROBLEM 18.2

The isoelectric point of histidine is 7.64. Toward which electrode does histidine migrate during paper electrophoresis at pH 7.0?

EXAMPLE 18.3

The electrophoresis of a mixture of lysine, histidine, and cysteine is carried out at pH 7.64. Describe the behavior of each amino acid under these conditions.

STRATEGY

Compare the pI of each amino acid to the pH of the solution in which it is dissolved and determine the net charge on each at that pH. If the pI of the amino acid is identical to the pH of the solution in which it is dissolved, the amino acid will not migrate from the origin. If the pH of the solution is greater than its pI, an amino acid will migrate toward the positive electrode. If the pH of the solution is less than its pI, an amino acid will migrate toward the negative electrode.

SOLUTION

The isoelectric point of histidine is 7.64. At this pH, histidine has a net charge of zero and does not move from the origin. The pI of cysteine is 5.02; at pH 7.64 (more basic than its isoelectric point), cysteine has a net negative charge and moves toward the positive electrode. The pI of lysine is 9.74; at pH 7.64 (more acidic than its isoelectric point), lysine has a net positive charge and moves toward the negative electrode.

See problem 18.34

PROBLEM 18.3

Describe the behavior of a mixture of glutamic acid, arginine, and valine during paper electrophoresis at pH 6.0.

18.4 What Are Polypeptides and Proteins?

Peptide bond The special name given to the amide bond formed between the α-amino group of one amino acid and the α-carboxyl group of another amino acid.

Dipeptide A molecule containing two amino acid units joined by a peptide bond.

Tripeptide A molecule containing three amino acid units, each joined to the next by a peptide bond.

Polypeptide A macromolecule containing 20 or more amino acid units, each joined to the next by a peptide bond.

***N*-Terminal amino acid** The amino acid at the end of a polypeptide chain having the free $-NH_3^+$ group.

***C*-Terminal amino acid** The amino acid at the end of a polypeptide chain having the free $-COO^-$ group.

In 1902, Emil Fischer proposed that proteins were long chains of amino acids joined together by amide bonds formed between the α-carboxyl group of one amino acid and the α-amino group of another. For these amide bonds, Fischer proposed the special name **peptide bond**. Figure 18.5 shows the peptide bond formed between serine and alanine in the dipeptide serylalanine.

Peptide is the name given to a short polymer of amino acids. We classify peptides by the number of amino acid units in their chains. A molecule containing 2 amino acids joined by an amide bond is called a **dipeptide**. Those containing 3 to 10 amino acids are called **tripeptides**, **tetrapeptides**, **pentapeptides**, and so on. Molecules containing more than 10, but fewer than 20, amino acids are called **oligopeptides**. Those containing several dozen or more amino acids are called **polypeptides. Proteins** are biological macromolecules with molecular weight 5,000 or greater and consisting of one or more polypeptide chains. The distinctions in this terminology are not at all precise.

By convention, polypeptides are written from left to right, beginning with the amino acid having the free $-NH_3^+$ group and proceeding toward the amino acid with the free $-COO^-$ group. The amino acid with the free $-NH_3^+$ group is called the ***N*-terminal amino acid**, and that with the free $-COO^-$ group is called the ***C*-terminal amino acid**:

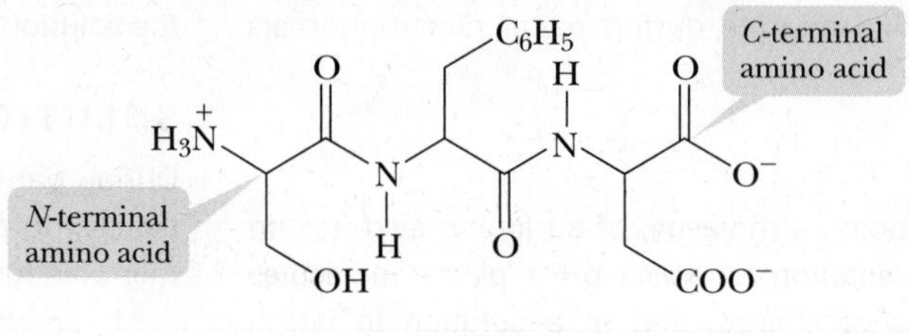

Ser-Phe-Asp

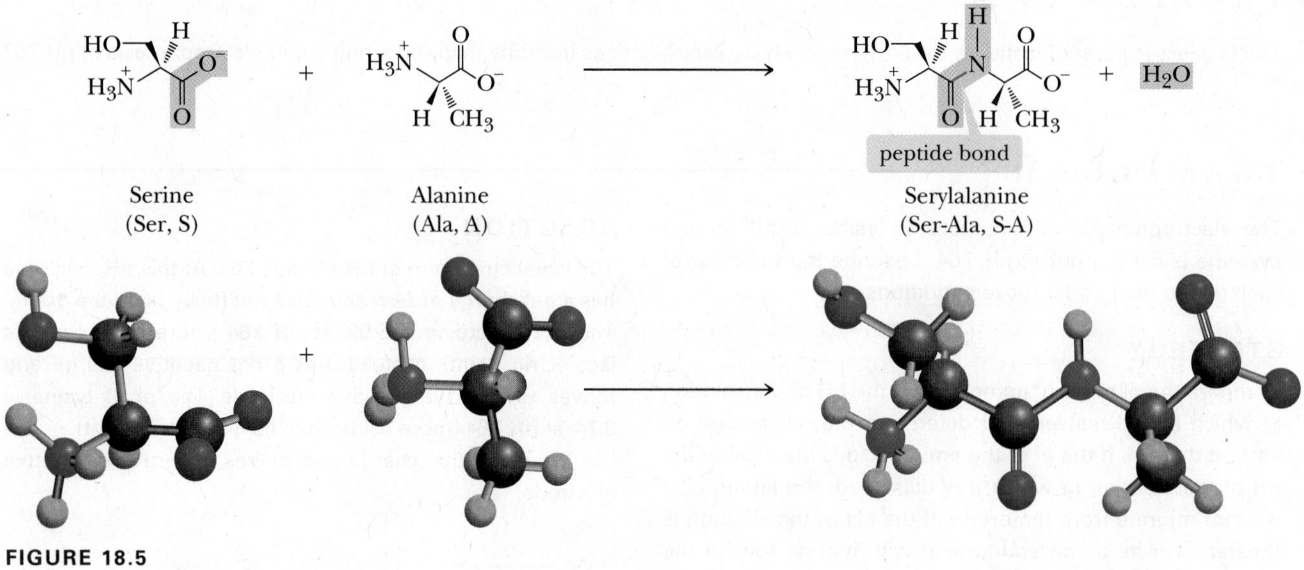

FIGURE 18.5
The peptide bond in serylalanine.

EXAMPLE 18.4

Draw a structural formula for Cys-Arg-Met-Asn. Label the *N*-terminal amino acid and the *C*-terminal amino acid. What is the net charge on this tetrapeptide at pH 6.0?

STRATEGY

Begin by drawing the zwitterion form of each amino acid in order from cysteine to asparagine, each oriented with its α-ammonium group on the left and its α-carboxylate group on the right. Then form peptide bonds by removing a water molecule from between $-COO^-$ and $^+H_3N-$ groups that are next to each other. To determine the net charge on this tetrapeptide, consult Table 18.2 for the pK_a value of the ionizable group on the side chain of each amino acid.

SOLUTION

The backbone of Cys-Arg-Met-Asn, a tetrapeptide, is a repeating sequence of nitrogen-α-carbon-carbonyl. The net charge on this tetrapeptide at pH 6.0 is +1. The following is a structural formula for Cys-Arg-Met-Asn:

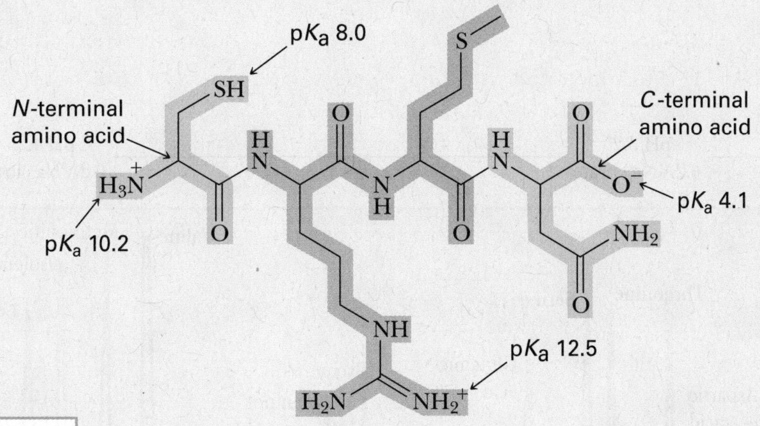

See problems 18.37, 18.41

PROBLEM 18.4

Draw a structural formula for Lys-Phe-Ala. Label the *N*-terminal amino acid and the *C*-terminal amino acid. What is the net charge on this tripeptide at pH 6.0?

18.5 What Is the Primary Structure of a Polypeptide or Protein?

The **primary (1°) structure** of a polypeptide or protein is the sequence of amino acids in its polypeptide chain. In this sense, the primary structure is a complete description of all covalent bonding in a polypeptide or protein.

Primary (1°) structure of proteins The sequence of amino acids in the polypeptide chain; read from the *N*-terminal amino acid to the *C*-terminal amino acid.

In 1953, Frederick Sanger of Cambridge University, England, reported the primary structure of the two polypeptide chains of the hormone insulin. Not only was this a remarkable achievement in analytical chemistry, but also it clearly established that the molecules of a given protein all have the same amino acid composition and the same amino acid sequence. Today, the amino acid sequences of over 20,000 different proteins are known, and the number is growing rapidly.

A. Amino Acid Analysis

The first step in determining the primary structure of a polypeptide is hydrolysis and quantitative analysis of its amino acid composition. Recall from Section 14.3D that amide bonds are highly resistant to hydrolysis. Typically, a sample of a protein is hydrolyzed in 6 M HCl in a sealed glass vial at 110 °C for 24 to 72 hours. (This hydrolysis can be done in a microwave oven in a shorter time.) After the polypeptide is hydrolyzed, the resulting mixture of amino acids is analyzed by ion-exchange chromatography. In this process, the mixture of amino acids is passed through a specially packed column. Each of the 20 amino acids requires a different time to pass through the column. Amino acids are detected by reaction with ninhydrin as they emerge from the column (Section 18.3D), followed by absorption spectroscopy. Current procedures for the hydrolysis of polypeptides and the analysis of amino acid mixtures have been refined to the point where it is possible to determine the amino acid composition from as little as 50 nanomoles (50×10^{-9} mole) of a polypeptide. Figure 18.6 shows the analysis of a polypeptide hydrolysate by ion-exchange chromatography. Note that, during hydrolysis, the side-chain amide groups of asparagine and glutamine are hydrolyzed, and these amino acids are detected as aspartic acid and glutamic acid. For each glutamine or asparagine hydrolyzed, an equivalent amount of ammonium chloride is formed.

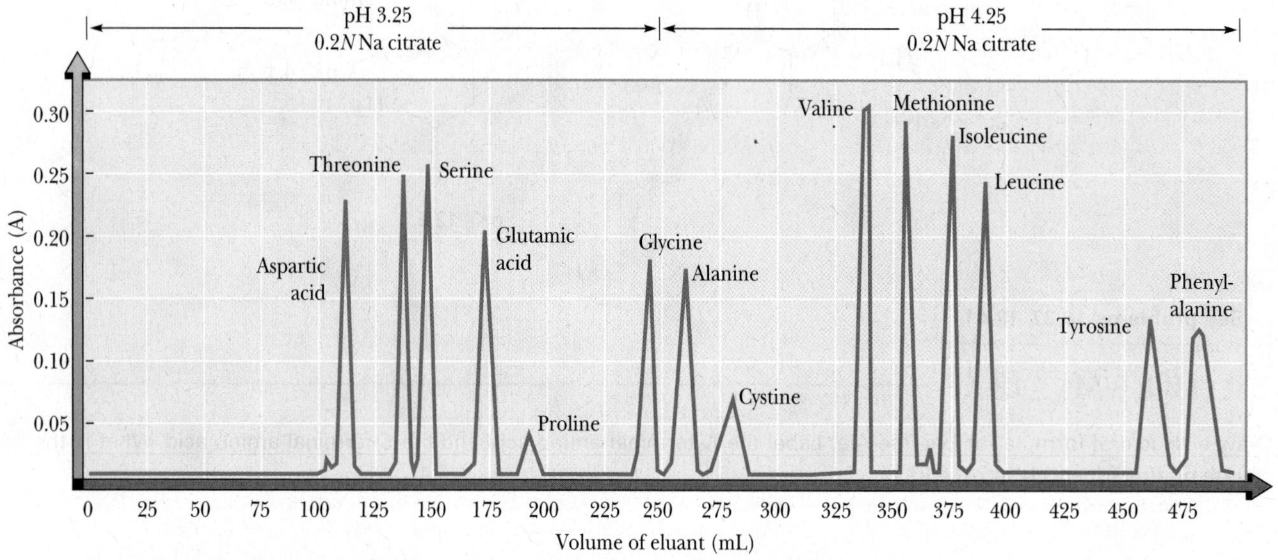

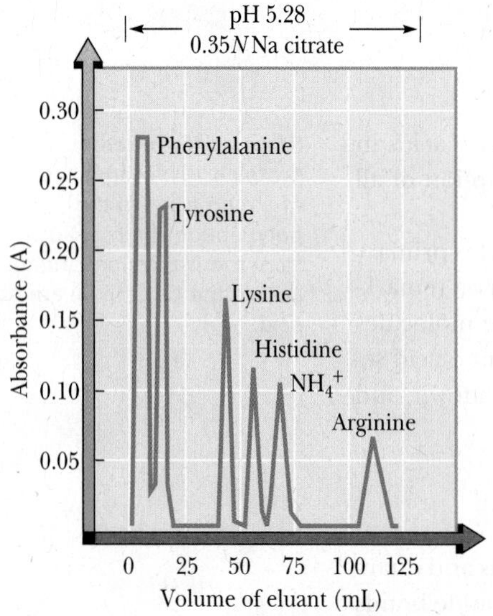

FIGURE 18.6

Analysis of a mixture of amino acids by ion-exchange chromatography using Amberlite IR-120, a sulfonated polystyrene resin. The resin contains phenyl-SO_3^- Na^+ groups. The amino acid mixture is applied to the column at low pH (3.25), under which conditions the acidic amino acids (Asp, Glu) are weakly bound to the resin and the basic amino acids (Lys, His, Arg) are tightly bound. Sodium citrate buffers of two different concentrations and three different values of pH are used to elute the amino acids from the column. Cysteine is determined as cystine, Cys-S-S-Cys, the disulfide of cysteine.

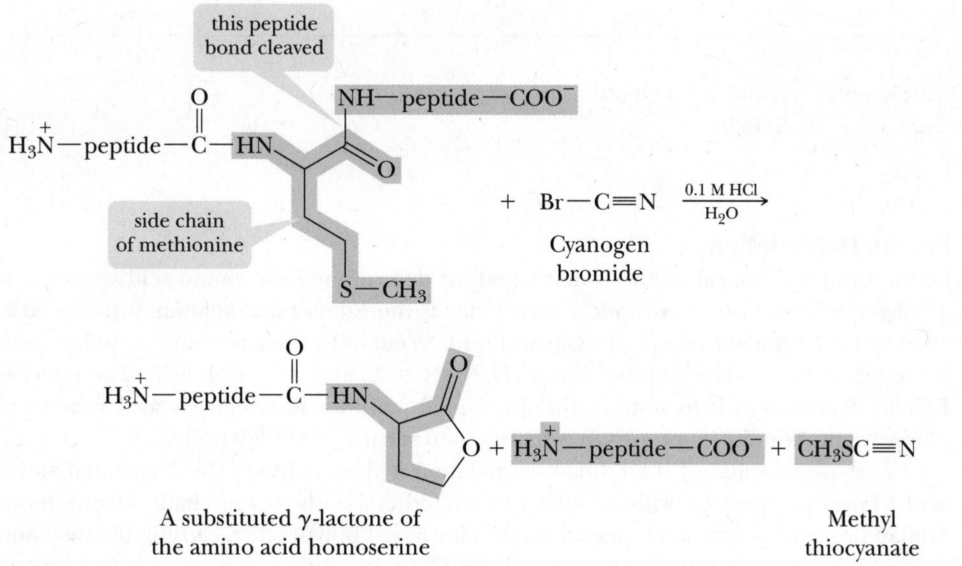

FIGURE 18.7 Cleavage by cyanogen bromide, BrCN, of a peptide bond formed by the carboxyl group of methionine.

B. Sequence Analysis

Once the amino acid composition of a polypeptide has been determined, the next step is to determine the order in which the amino acids are joined in the polypeptide chain. The most common sequencing strategy is to (1) cleave the polypeptide at specific peptide bonds (by using, for example, cyanogen bromide or certain proteolytic enzymes), (2) determine the sequence of each fragment (by using, for example, the Edman degradation), and then (3) match overlapping fragments to arrive at the sequence of the polypeptide.

Cyanogen Bromide

Cyanogen bromide (BrCN) is specific for the cleavage of peptide bonds formed by the carboxyl group of methionine (Figure 18.7). The products of this cleavage are substituted γ-lactones (Section 14.1C), derived from the *N*-terminal portion of the polypeptide, and a second fragment containing the *C*-terminal portion of the polypeptide.

Enzyme-Catalyzed Hydrolysis of Peptide Bonds

A group of proteolytic enzymes, including trypsin and chymotrypsin, can be used to catalyze the hydrolysis of specific peptide bonds. Trypsin catalyzes the hydrolysis of peptide bonds formed by the carboxyl groups of Arg and Lys; chymotrypsin catalyzes the hydrolysis of peptide bonds formed by the carboxyl groups of Phe, Tyr, and Trp.

EXAMPLE 18.5

Which of these tripeptides are hydrolyzed by trypsin? By chymotrypsin?

(a) Arg-Glu-Ser **(b)** Phe-Gly-Lys

STRATEGY

Trypsin catalyzes the hydrolysis of peptide bonds formed by the carboxyl groups of Lys and Arg. Chymotrypsin catalyzes the hydrolysis of peptide bonds formed by the carboxyl groups of Phe, Tyr, and Trp.

SOLUTION

(a) The peptide bond between Arg and Glu is hydrolyzed in the presence of trypsin.

$$\text{Arg-Glu-Ser} + H_2O \xrightarrow{\text{trypsin}} \text{Arg} + \text{Glu-Ser}$$

Because none of these three aromatic amino acids is present in tripeptide (a), it is not affected by chymotrypsin.

(b) Tripeptide (b) is not affected by trypsin. Although Lys is present, its carboxyl group is at the *C*-terminal end and not involved in peptide bond formation. Tripeptide (b) is hydrolyzed in the presence of chymotrypsin.

$$\text{Phe-Gly-Lys} + H_2O \xrightarrow{\text{chymotrypsin}} \text{Phe} + \text{Gly-Lys}$$

See problem 18.39

PROBLEM 18.5

Which of these tripeptides are hydrolyzed by trypsin? By chymotrypsin?
(a) Tyr-Gln-Val (b) Thr-Phe-Ser (c) Thr-Ser-Phe

Edman degradation A method for selectively cleaving and identifying the *N*-terminal amino acid of a polypeptide chain.

Edman Degradation

Of the various chemical methods developed for determining the amino acid sequence of a polypeptide, the one most widely used today is the **Edman degradation**, introduced in 1950 by Pehr Edman of the University of Lund, Sweden. In this procedure, a polypeptide is treated with phenyl isothiocyanate, $C_6H_5N{=}C{=}S$, and then with acid. The effect of Edman degradation is to remove the *N*-terminal amino acid selectively as a substituted phenylthiohydantoin (Figure 18.8), which is then separated and identified.

The special value of the Edman degradation is that it cleaves the *N*-terminal amino acid from a polypeptide without affecting any other bonds in the chain. Furthermore, Edman degradation can be repeated on the shortened polypeptide, causing the next amino acid in the sequence to be cleaved and identified. In practice, it is possible to sequence as many as the first 20 to 30 amino acids in a polypeptide by this method, using as little as a few milligrams of material.

Most polypeptides in nature are longer than 20 to 30 amino acids, the practical limit on the number of amino acids that can be sequenced by repetitive Edman degradation. The special value of cleavage with cyanogen bromide, trypsin, and chymotrypsin is that, at specific peptide bonds, a long polypeptide chain can be cleaved into smaller polypeptide fragments, and each fragment can then be sequenced separately.

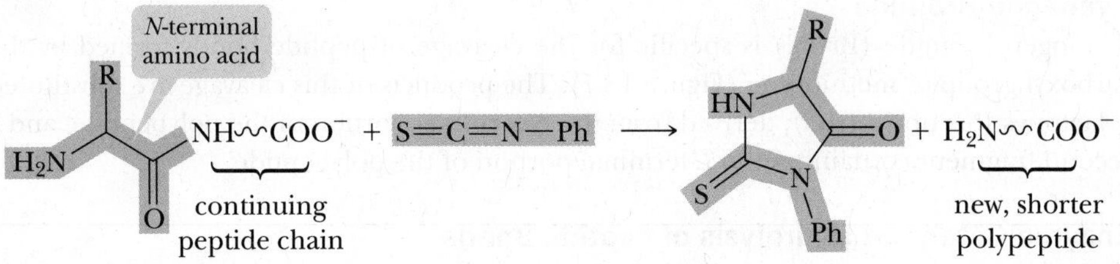

FIGURE 18.8 Edman degradation. Treatment of a polypeptide with phenyl isothiocyanate followed by acid selectively cleaves the *N*-terminal amino acid as a substituted phenylthiohydantoin.

EXAMPLE 18.6

Deduce the amino acid sequence of a pentapeptide from the following experimental results (note that, under the column "Amino Acids Determined from Procedure," the amino acids are listed in alphabetical order; in no way does this listing give any information about primary structure):

Experimental Procedure	Amino Acids Determined from Procedure
Amino Acid Analysis of Pentapeptide	Arg, Glu, His, Phe, Ser
Edman Degradation	Glu
Hydrolysis Catalyzed by Chymotrypsin	
Fragment A	Glu, His, Phe
Fragment B	Arg, Ser
Hydrolysis Catalyzed by Trypsin	
Fragment C	Arg, Glu, His, Phe
Fragment D	Ser

STRATEGY

Review the specificity of each method of degradation:

- Edman degradation: Selectively cleaves the *N*-terminal amino acid.
- Chymotrypsin: Cleaves the peptide bonds formed by the carboxyl groups of Phe, Tyr, and Trp.
- Trypsin: Cleaves the peptide bonds formed by the carboxyl groups of Arg and Lys.

SOLUTION

Edman degradation cleaves Glu from the pentapeptide; therefore, glutamic acid must be the *N*-terminal amino acid, and we have

Glu- (Arg, His, Phe, Ser)

Fragment A from chymotrypsin-catalyzed hydrolysis contains Phe. Because of the specificity of chymotrypsin, Phe must be the *C*-terminal amino acid of fragment A. Fragment A also contains Glu, which we already know is the *N*-terminal amino acid. From these observations, we conclude that the first three amino acids in the chain must be Glu-His-Phe, and we now write the following partial sequence:

Glu-His-Phe-(Arg, Ser)

The fact that trypsin cleaves the pentapeptide means that Arg must be within the pentapeptide chain; it cannot be the *C*-terminal amino acid. Therefore, the complete sequence must be

Glu-His-Phe-Arg-Ser

See problems 18.38, 18.40

PROBLEM 18.6

Deduce the amino acid sequence of an undecapeptide (11 amino acids) from the experimental results shown in the following table:

Experimental Procedure	Amino Acids Determined from Procedure
Amino Acid Analysis of Undecapeptide	Ala, Arg, Glu, Lys_2, Met, Phe, Ser, Thr, Trp, Val
Edman Degradation	Ala
Trypsin-Catalyzed Hydrolysis	
Fragment E	Ala, Glu, Arg
Fragment F	Thr, Phe, Lys
Fragment G	Lys
Fragment H	Met, Ser, Trp, Val
Chymotrypsin-Catalyzed Hydrolysis	
Fragment I	Ala, Arg, Glu, Phe, Thr
Fragment J	Lys_2, Met, Ser, Trp, Val
Treatment with Cyanogen Bromide	
Fragment K	Ala, Arg, Glu, Lys_2, Met, Phe, Thr, Val
Fragment L	Trp, Ser

18.6 What Are the Three-Dimensional Shapes of Polypeptides and Proteins?

A. Geometry of a Peptide Bond

In the late 1930s, Linus Pauling began a series of studies aimed at determining the geometry of a peptide bond. One of his first discoveries was that a peptide bond is planar. As shown in Figure 18.9, the four atoms of a peptide bond and the two α-carbons joined to it all lie in the same plane.

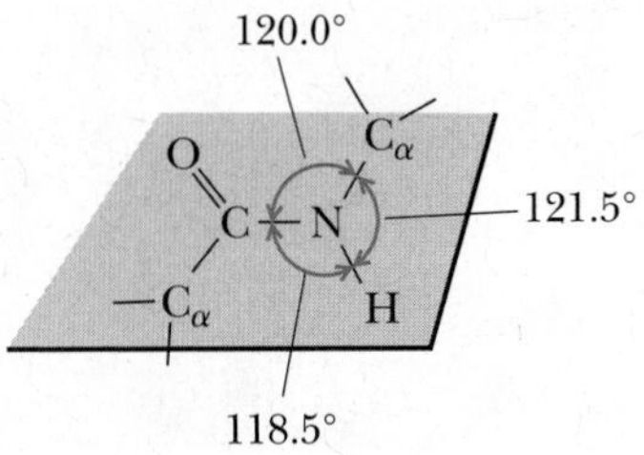

FIGURE 18.9 Planarity of a peptide bond. Bond angles about the carbonyl carbon and the amide nitrogen are approximately 120°.

Had you been asked in Chapter 1 to describe the geometry of a peptide bond, you probably would have predicted bond angles of 120° about the carbonyl carbon and 109.5° about the amide nitrogen.

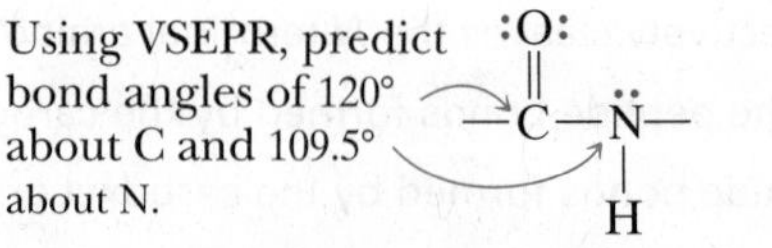

An amide bond

This prediction agrees with the observed bond angles of approximately 120° about the carbonyl carbon. It does not agree, however, with the observed bond angles of 120° about the amide nitrogen. To account for the observed geometry, Pauling proposed that a peptide bond is more accurately represented as a resonance hybrid of these two contributing structures:

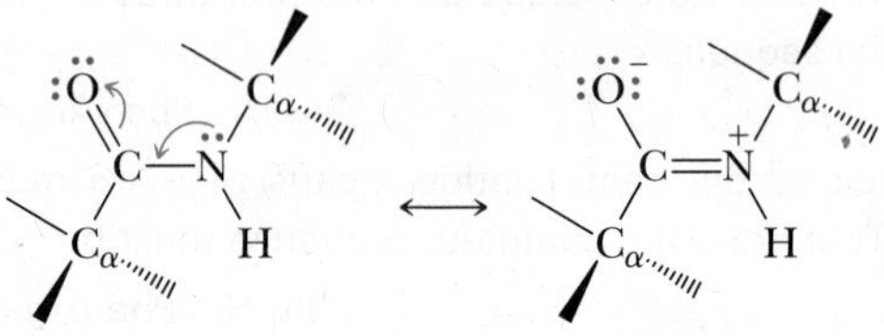

(1) (2)

Contributing structure (1) shows a carbon–oxygen double bond, and structure (2) shows a carbon–nitrogen double bond. The hybrid, of course, is neither of these. In the real structure, the carbon–nitrogen bond has considerable double-bond character. Accordingly, in the hybrid, the six-atom group of the peptide bond and the two attached α-carbons are planar.

Two configurations are possible for the atoms of a planar peptide bond. In one, the two α-carbons are *cis* to each other; in the other, they are *trans* to each other. The *trans* configuration is more favorable because the α-carbons with the bulky groups bonded to them are farther from each other than they are in the *cis* configuration. Virtually all peptide bonds in naturally occurring proteins studied to date have the *trans* configuration.

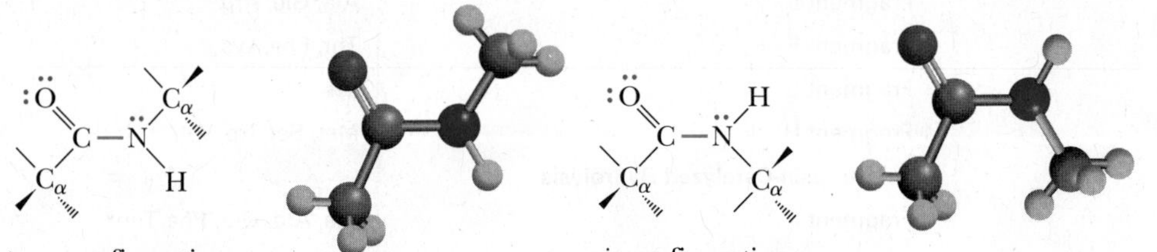

trans configuration *cis* configuration

B. Secondary Structure

Secondary (2°) structure of proteins The ordered arrangements (conformations) of amino acids in localized regions of a polypeptide or protein.

Secondary (2°) structure is the ordered arrangement (conformation) of amino acids in localized regions of a polypeptide or protein molecule. The first studies of polypeptide conformations were carried out by Linus Pauling and Robert Corey, beginning in 1939. They assumed that, in conformations of greatest stability, all atoms in a peptide bond lie in the same plane and there is **hydrogen bonding** between the N—H of one peptide bond and the C=O of another, as shown in Figure 18.10.

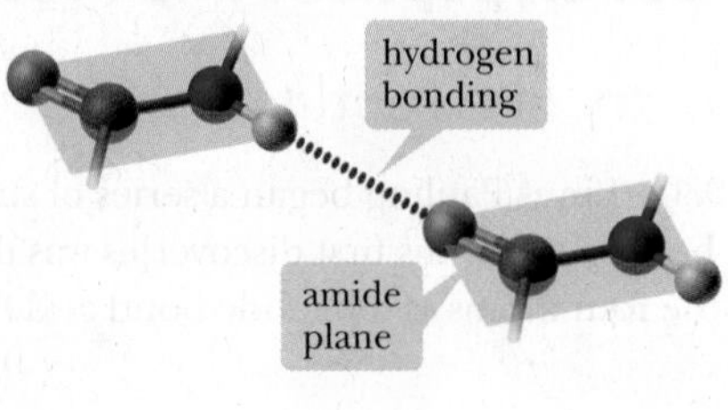

FIGURE 18.10 Hydrogen bonding between amide groups.

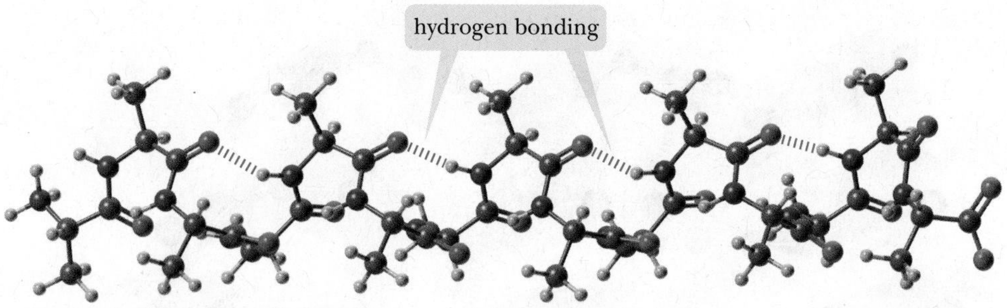

FIGURE 18.11
An α-helix. The polypeptide chain is repeating units of L-alanine.

On the basis of model building, Pauling proposed that two types of secondary structure should be particularly stable: the α-helix and the antiparallel β-pleated sheet.

The α-Helix

In the ***α*-helix** pattern, shown in Figure 18.11, a polypeptide chain is coiled in a spiral. As you study this section of the α-helix, note the following:

1. The helix is coiled in a clockwise, or right-handed, manner. *Right-handed* means that if you turn the helix clockwise, it twists away from you. In this sense, a right-handed helix is analogous to the right-handed thread of a common wood or machine screw.
2. There are 3.6 amino acids per turn of the helix.
3. Each peptide bond is *trans* and planar.
4. The N—H group of each peptide bond points roughly downward, parallel to the axis of the helix, and the C=O of each peptide bond points roughly upward, also parallel to the axis of the helix.
5. The carbonyl group of each peptide bond is hydrogen bonded to the N—H group of the peptide bond four amino acid units away from it. Hydrogen bonds are shown as dotted lines.
6. All R— groups point outward from the helix.

α-Helix A type of secondary structure in which a section of polypeptide chain coils into a spiral, most commonly a right-handed spiral.

The star cucumber, *Sicyos angulatus*, uses left-handed helical tendrils to attach itself to climbing vines. Its helical pattern is analogous, but in reverse, to the right-handed α-helix of polypeptides.

Almost immediately after Pauling proposed the α-helix conformation, other researchers proved the presence of α-helix conformations in keratin, the protein of hair and wool. It soon became obvious that the α-helix is one of the fundamental folding patterns of polypeptide chains.

The β-Pleated Sheet

An antiparallel ***β*-pleated sheet** consists of an extended polypeptide chain with neighboring sections of the chain running in opposite (antiparallel) directions. In a parallel β-pleated sheet, the neighboring sections run in the same direction. Unlike the α-helix arrangement, N—H and C=O groups lie in the plane of the sheet and are roughly perpendicular to the long axis of the sheet. The C=O group of each peptide bond is hydrogen bonded to the N—H group of a peptide bond of a neighboring section of the chain (Figure 18.12).

As you study this section of β-pleated sheet in Figure 18.12 note the following:

1. The three sections of the polypeptide chain lie adjacent to each other and run in opposite (antiparallel) directions.
2. Each peptide bond is planar, and the α-carbons are *trans* to each other.
3. The C=O and N—H groups of peptide bonds from adjacent sections point at each other and are in the same plane, so that hydrogen bonding is possible between adjacent sections.
4. The R— groups on any one chain alternate, first above, then below, the plane of the sheet, and so on.

β-Pleated sheet A type of secondary structure in which two sections of polypeptide chain are aligned parallel or antiparallel to one another.

The β-pleated sheet conformation is stabilized by hydrogen bonding between N—H groups of one section of the chain and C=O groups of an adjacent section. By comparison,

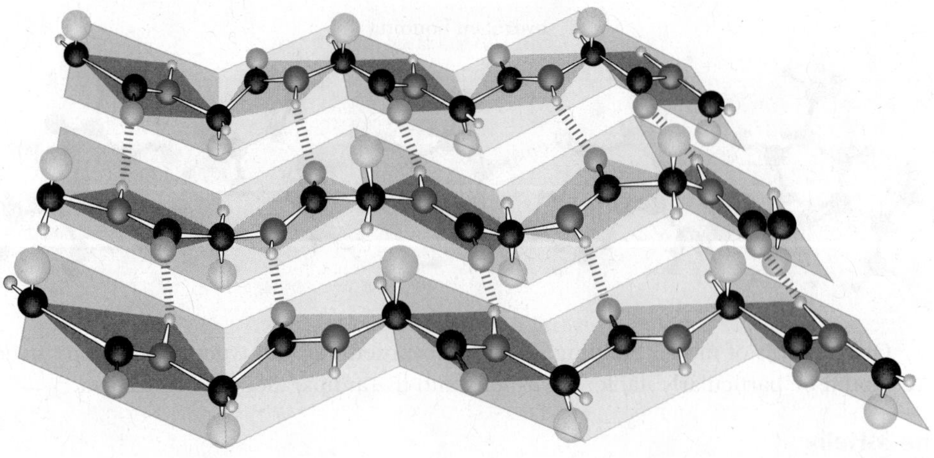

FIGURE 18.12
β-Pleated sheet conformation with three polypeptide chains running in opposite (antiparallel) directions. Hydrogen bonding between chains is indicated by dashed lines.

the α-helix is stabilized by hydrogen bonding between N—H and C=O groups within the same polypeptide chain.

C. Tertiary Structure

Tertiary (3°) structure of proteins The three-dimensional arrangement in space of all atoms in a single polypeptide chain.

Tertiary (3°) structure is the overall folding pattern and arrangement in space of all atoms in a single polypeptide chain. No sharp dividing line exists between secondary and tertiary structures. Secondary structure refers to the spatial arrangement of amino acids *close to one another* on a polypeptide chain, whereas tertiary structure refers to the three-dimensional arrangement of *all* atoms in a polypeptide chain. Among the most important factors in maintaining 3° structure are disulfide bonds, hydrophobic interactions, hydrogen bonding, and salt bridges.

Disulfide bond A covalent bond between two sulfur atoms; an —S—S— bond.

Disulfide bonds play an important role in maintaining tertiary structure. Disulfide bonds are formed between side chains of two cysteine units by oxidation of their thiol groups (—SH) to form a disulfide bond (Section 8.6B). Treatment of a disulfide bond with a reducing agent regenerates the thiol groups:

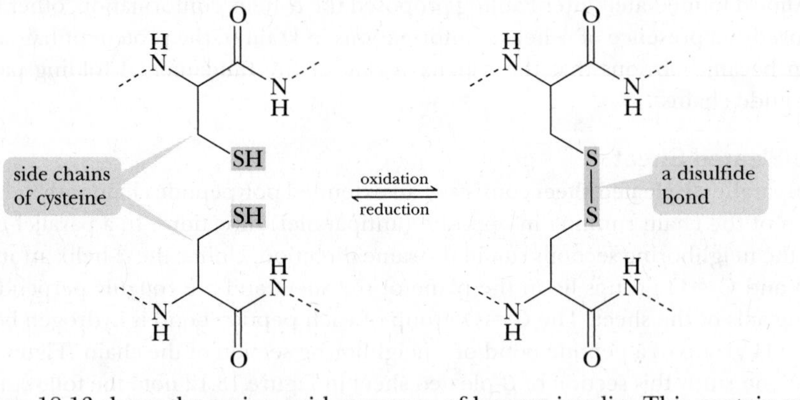

Figure 18.13 shows the amino acid sequence of human insulin. This protein consists of two polypeptide chains: an A chain of 21 amino acids and a B chain of 30 amino acids.

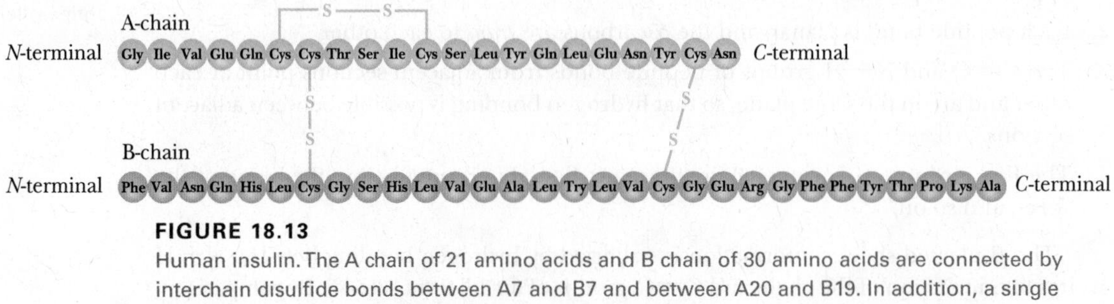

FIGURE 18.13
Human insulin. The A chain of 21 amino acids and B chain of 30 amino acids are connected by interchain disulfide bonds between A7 and B7 and between A20 and B19. In addition, a single intrachain disulfide bond occurs between A6 and A11.

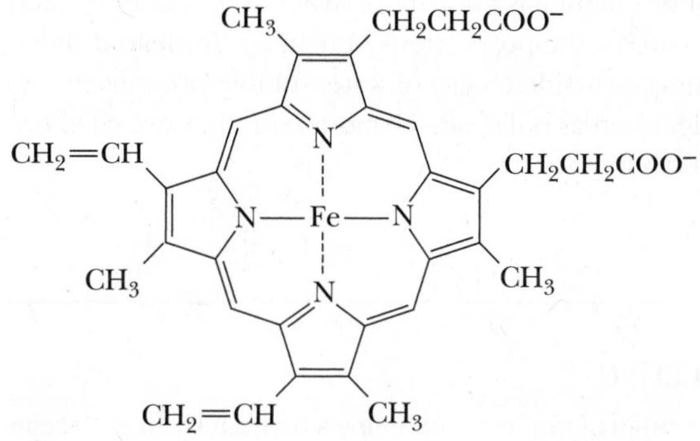

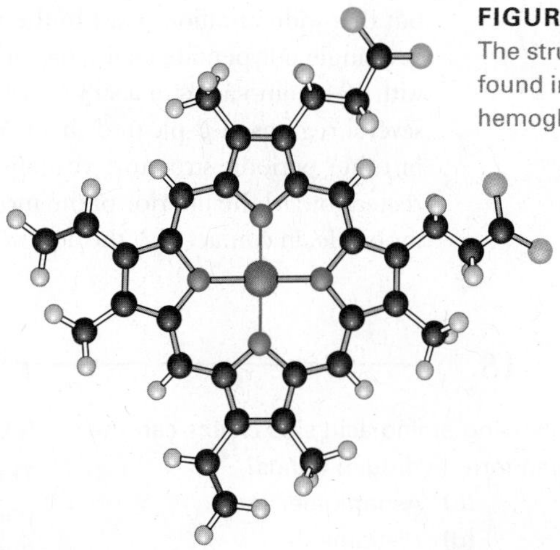

FIGURE 18.14
The structure of heme, found in myoglobin and hemoglobin.

The A chain is bonded to the B chain by two interchain disulfide bonds. An intrachain disulfide bond also connects the cysteine units at positions 6 and 11 of the A chain.

As an example of 2° and 3° structure, let us look at the three-dimensional structure of myoglobin, a protein found in skeletal muscle and particularly abundant in diving mammals, such as seals, whales, and porpoises. Myoglobin and its structural relative, hemoglobin, are the oxygen transport and storage molecules of vertebrates. Hemoglobin binds molecular oxygen in the lungs and transports it to myoglobin in muscles. Myoglobin stores molecular oxygen until it is required for metabolic oxidation.

© Rod Kaye/iStockphoto

The humpback whale relies on myoglobin as a storage form of oxygen.

Myoglobin consists of a single polypeptide chain of 153 amino acids. Myoglobin also contains a single heme unit. Heme consists of one Fe^{2+} ion, coordinated in a square planar array with the four nitrogen atoms of a molecule of porphyrin (Figure 18.14).

Determination of the three-dimensional structure of myoglobin represented a milestone in the study of molecular architecture. For their contribution to this research, John C. Kendrew and Max F. Perutz, both of Britain, shared the 1962 Nobel Prize for Chemistry. The secondary and tertiary structures of myoglobin are shown in Figure 18.15. The single polypeptide chain is folded into a complex, almost boxlike shape.

Important structural features of the three-dimensional shape of myoglobin are as follows:

1. The backbone consists of eight relatively straight sections of α-helix, each separated by a bend in the polypeptide chain. The longest section of α-helix has 24 amino acids, the shortest has seven. Some 75% of the amino acids are found in these eight regions of α-helix.
2. Hydrophobic side chains of phenylalanine, alanine, valine, leucine, isoleucine, and methionine are clustered in the interior of the molecule, where they are shielded from contact with water. **Hydrophobic interactions** are a major factor in directing the folding of the polypeptide chain of myoglobin into this compact, three-dimensional shape.
3. The outer surface of myoglobin is coated with hydrophilic side chains, such as those of lysine, arginine, serine, glutamic acid, histidine, and glutamine, which interact with the aqueous environment by **hydrogen bonding**. The only polar side chains that point to the interior of the myoglobin molecule are those of two histidine units, which point inward toward the heme group.
4. Oppositely charged amino acid side chains close to each other in the three-dimensional structure interact by electrostatic attractions called **salt bridges**. An example of a salt bridge is the attraction of the side chains of lysine ($-NH_3^+$) and glutamic acid ($-COO^-$).

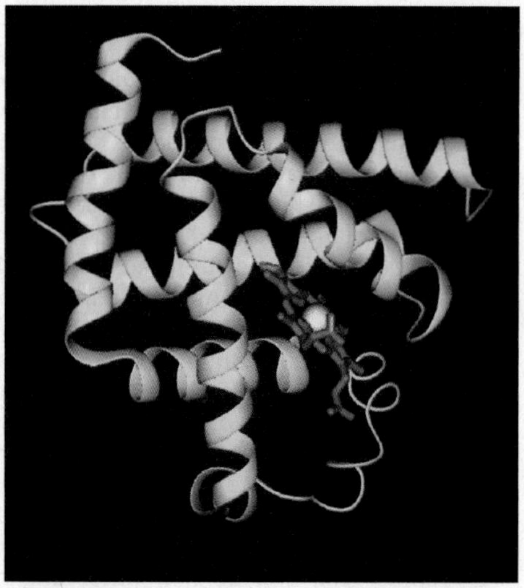

FIGURE 18.15
Ribbon model of myoglobin. The polypeptide chain is shown in yellow, the heme ligand in red, and the Fe atom as a white sphere.

The tertiary structures of hundreds of proteins have also been determined. It is clear that proteins contain α-helix and β-pleated sheet structures, but that wide variations exist in the relative amounts of each. Lysozyme, with 129 amino acids in a single polypeptide chain, has only 25% of its amino acids in α-helix regions. Cytochrome, with 104 amino acids in a single polypeptide chain, has no α-helix structure but does contain several regions of β-pleated sheet. Yet, whatever the proportions of α-helix, β-pleated sheet, or other periodic structure, virtually all nonpolar side chains of water-soluble proteins are directed toward the interior of the molecule, whereas polar side chains are on the surface of the molecule, in contact with the aqueous environment.

EXAMPLE 18.7

With which of the following amino acid side chains can the side chain of threonine form hydrogen bonds?

(a) Valine (b) Asparagine
(c) Phenylalanine (d) Histidine
(e) Tyrosine (f) Alanine

STRATEGY

Analyze the types of side chains of these amino acids and then look for potential interactions between them by hydrogen bonding.

SOLUTION

The side chain of threonine contains a hydroxyl group that can participate in hydrogen bonding in two ways: (1) Its oxygen has a partial negative charge and can function as a hydrogen bond acceptor; (2) its hydrogen has a partial positive charge and can function as a hydrogen bond donor. Therefore, the side chain of threonine can form hydrogen bonds with the side chains of tyrosine, asparagine, and histidine.

See problem 18.47

PROBLEM 18.7

At pH 7.4, with what amino acid side chains can the side chain of lysine form salt bridges?

Chemical Connections 18A

SPIDER SILK: A CHEMICAL AND ENGINEERING WONDER OF NATURE

Many of society's technological innovations have been inspired by nature. Velcro, for example, is modeled after plant burrs. The water-repellent swimsuits that revolutionized the sport of swimming were modeled after the skin of sharks. And hundreds of medicines are based on natural products. However, one product of nature that for centuries has been difficult to harness or imitate is spider silk. A strand of spider silk is almost five times stronger than a strand of steel of the same diameter. In addition to its strength, a strand of spider silk can be stretched up to 30–40% of its length without breaking. As shown in the following graphic of its secondary structure, a strand of spider silk consists of oriented amorphous regions (**A**), crystalline regions (**B**), and completely amorphous regions (**C**). The oriented amorphous regions are held together by hydrogen bonds and give spider silk its elasticity. The crystalline regions are mostly responsible for the strength of spider silk. They consist of β-pleated sheets and are highly hydrophobic, which also makes spider silk insoluble in water and resistant to rain and dew.

For centuries, spider silk has been highly sought after for its properties. Unfortunately, spiders are solitary animals and, unlike silkworms, cannot be domesticated. This leaves only one option for harnessing the utility of spider silk: its reproduction using artificial means. Research thus far has revealed the detailed structure of spider silk. However, it is a testament to the elegance of nature that despite the fact that spider silk consists mostly of alanine and glycine, researchers have yet to find a way to assemble a strand of spider silk in the laboratory. Incidentally, after a spider web has lost its stickiness, most spiders "recycle" the protein by eating their webs, leaving nary a trace of this chemical and engineering wonder of nature.

© AngelaArenal/iStockphoto

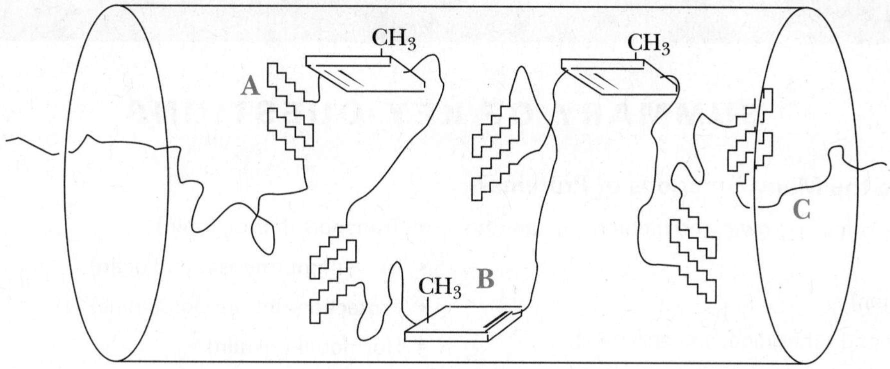

Question
Draw two pentapeptide strands of polyalanine and show how they can hydrogen-bond to each other.

D. Quaternary Structure

Most proteins with molecular weight greater than 50,000 consist of two or more noncovalently linked polypeptide chains. The arrangement of protein monomers into an aggregation is known as **quaternary (4°) structure**. A good example is hemoglobin (Figure 18.16), a protein that consists of four separate polypeptide chains: two α-chains of 141 amino acids each and two β-chains of 146 amino acids each.

The major factor stabilizing the aggregation of protein subunits is the **hydrophobic effect**. When separate polypeptide chains fold into compact three-dimensional shapes to expose polar side chains to the aqueous environment and shield nonpolar side chains from water, hydrophobic "patches" may still appear on the surface, in contact with water. These patches can be shielded from water if two or more monomers assemble so that their hydrophobic patches are in contact. The numbers of subunits of several proteins of known quaternary structure are shown in Table 18.3.

Quaternary (4°) structure of proteins The arrangement of polypeptide monomers into a noncovalently bonded aggregation.

Hydrophobic effect The tendency of nonpolar groups to cluster in such a way as to be shielded from contact with an aqueous environment.

FIGURE 18.16
Ribbon model of hemoglobin. The α-chains are shown in purple, the β-chains in yellow, the heme ligands in red, and the Fe atoms as white spheres.

TABLE 18.3 Quaternary Structure of Selected Proteins

Protein	Number of Subunits
Alcohol dehydrogenase	2
Aldolase	4
Hemoglobin	4
Lactate dehydrogenase	4
Insulin	6
Glutamine synthetase	12
Tobacco mosaic virus protein disc	17

SUMMARY OF KEY QUESTIONS

18.1 What Are the Many Functions of Proteins?

Proteins have many roles in growth and metabolism, among which are:

- Structural (collagen)
- Catalytic (trypsin and other digestive enzymes)
- Transport (hemoglobin)
- Movement (myosin and actin)
- Protection (immunoglobulins)
- Hormonal (insulin)

18.2 What Are Amino Acids?

- **α-Amino acids** are compounds that contain an amino group alpha to a carboxyl group.
- Each amino acid has an acid (a —COOH group) and a base (an —NH_2 group) that undergo an acid–base reaction to form an internal salt given the special name **zwitterion.** A zwitterion has no net charge because it contains one positive charge and one negative charge.
- With the exception of glycine, all protein-derived amino acids are chiral.
- Whereas most monosaccharides in the biological world have the D-configuration, the vast majority of naturally occurring α-amino acids have the L-configuration at the α-carbon. D-amino acids are rare.
- Isoleucine and threonine contain a second stereocenter, and four stereoisomers are possible for each.
- The 20 protein-derived amino acids are commonly divided into four categories: nine with nonpolar side chains, four with polar but un-ionized side chains, four with acidic side chains, and three with basic side chains.

18.3 What Are the Acid–Base Properties of Amino Acids?

- Amino acids are weak polyprotic acids because of their —COOH and —NH_3^+ groups.
- The average value of pK_a for an α-carboxyl group of a protonated amino acid is 2.19. Thus the α-carboxyl group is a considerably stronger acid than the carboxyl group of acetic acid (pK_a 4.76), a fact due to the electron-withdrawing inductive effect of the nearby —NH_3^+ group of the α-amino acid.
- The average value of pK_a for an α-ammonium group is 9.47, compared to an average value of 10.76 for a primary aliphatic ammonium ion. Thus, the α-ammonium group of an amino acid is a slightly stronger acid than a primary aliphatic amine.
- The side-chain guanidine group of arginine is a considerably stronger base than an aliphatic amine. This remarkable basicity is attributed to the large resonance stabilization of the protonated form relative to the neutral form.
- The **isoelectric point, pI**, of an amino acid, polypeptide, or protein is the pH at which the majority of its molecules have no net charge.
- **Electrophoresis** is the process of separating compounds on the basis of their electric charge. Compounds with a higher charge density move more rapidly than those with a lower charge density.
- Any amino acid or protein in a solution with a pH that equals the pI of the compound remains at the origin. One with a net negative charge moves toward the positive electrode, and one with a net positive charge moves toward the negative electrode.

18.4 What Are Polypeptides and Proteins?

- A **peptide bond** is the special name given to the amide bond formed between α-amino acids.
- A **polypeptide** is a biological macromolecule containing 20 or more amino acids joined by peptide bonds.
- By convention, the sequence of amino acids in a polypeptide is written from the ***N*-terminal amino acid** toward the ***C*-terminal amino acid.**
- A **peptide bond** is planar; that is, the four atoms of the amide bond and the two α-carbons bonded to it lie in the same plane.
- Bond angles about the amide nitrogen and the carbonyl carbon of a peptide bond are approximately 120°.

18.5 What Is the Primary Structure of a Polypeptide or Protein?

- The **primary (1°) structure** of a polypeptide or protein refers to the sequence of amino acids in its polypeptide chain.
- The first step in determination of primary structure is hydrolysis and quantitative analysis of amino acid composition by **ion-exchange chromatography**.

- **Cyanogen bromide** is specific for the cleavage of peptide bonds formed by the carboxyl group of methionine.
- **Trypsin** catalyzes the hydrolysis of peptide bonds formed by the carboxyl groups of arginine and lysine.
- **Chymotrypsin** catalyzes the hydrolysis of peptide bonds formed by the carboxyl groups of phenylalanine, tyrosine, and tryptophan.
- The **Edman degradation** selectively cleaves the *N*-terminal amino acid without affecting any other peptide bonds in a polypeptide or protein.

18.6 What Are the Three-Dimensional Shapes of Polypeptides and Proteins?

- The four atoms of a peptide bond and the two α-carbons bonded to it all lie in the same plane; that is, a peptide bond is planar.
- **Secondary (2°) structure** refers to the ordered arrangement (conformations) of amino acids in localized regions of a polypeptide or protein. The two most prevalent types of secondary structure are the α-helix and the β-pleated sheet, both of which are stabilized by hydrogen bonding.
- In an **α-helix**, the carbonyl group of each peptide bond is hydrogen-bonded to the N—H group of the peptide bond four amino acids away from it.
- In an **antiparallel β-pleated sheet**, neighboring sections of a polypeptide chain run in opposite (antiparallel) directions, and the C=O group of each peptide bond is hydrogen-bonded to the N—H group of a peptide bond in a section of the neighboring antiparallel chain.
- In a **parallel β-pleated sheet**, the neighboring sections of the polypeptide chain run in the same (parallel) directions, and the C=O of each peptide bond is hydrogen-bonded to the N—H group of a peptide bond in a neighboring section of the chain.
- **Tertiary (3°) structure** refers to the overall folding pattern and arrangement in space of all atoms in a single polypeptide chain.
- **Quaternary (4°) structure** is the arrangement of individual polypeptide chains into a noncovalently bonded aggregate. A major factor stabilizing quaternary structure is hydrophobic interaction created when separate polypeptide chains fold into compact three-dimensional shapes that expose their polar side chains to the aqueous environment and shield their nonpolar side chains from the aqueous environment. Any remaining exposed hydrophobic patches can be shielded from water if two or more polypeptide chains assemble so that their hydrophobic patches are in contact.

QUICK QUIZ

Answer true or false to the following questions to assess your general knowledge of the concepts in this chapter. If you have difficulty with any of them, you should review the appropriate section in the chapter (shown in parentheses) before attempting the more challenging end-of-chapter problems.

1. The isoelectric point of an amino acid is the pH at which the majority of molecules in solution have a net charge of −1. (18.3)
2. Proteins can protect an organism against disease. (18.1)
3. Titration of an amino acid can be used to determine both the pK_a of its ionizable groups and its isoelectric point. (18.3)
4. Hydrogen bonding, salt bridges, hydrophobic interactions, and disulfide bonds can each be categorized as stabilizing factors in a protein. (18.6)
5. A polypeptide chain is read from its *C*-terminal end to its *N*-terminal end. (18.5)
6. The majority of naturally occurring amino acids are from the D-series. (18.2)
7. The amino group of an α-amino acid is more basic than the amino group of an aliphatic amine. (18.3)
8. Lysine contains a basic side chain. (18.2)
9. Electrophoresis is the process of creating a synthetic protein. (18.3)
10. A peptide bond exhibits free rotation at room temperature. (18.6)
11. In Edman degradation, a polypeptide is shortened one amino acid at a time using the reagent phenyl isothiocyanate. (18.5)
12. Phenylalanine contains a polar side chain. (18.2)
13. The side chain of arginine shows enhanced basicity because of resonance stabilization of the ion that results after protonation. (18.3)
14. α-Helices and β-pleated sheets are examples of the tertiary structure of a protein. (18.6)
15. The majority of amino acids in proteins are β-amino acids. (18.2)
16. Proteins can act as catalysts in chemical reactions. (18.1)
17. In electrophoresis, species with a net negative charge will move toward the negative electrode. (18.3)
18. All naturally occurring amino acids are chiral. (18.2)
19. Cyanogen bromide, trypsin, and chymotrypsin each act to cleave peptide bonds at specific amino acids. (18.5)

20. The carboxyl group of an α-amino acid is more acidic than the carboxyl group of an aliphatic carboxylic acid. (18.3)

21. The amino acid sequence of a protein or polypeptide is known as its secondary structure. (18.5)

22. The 20 common, naturally occurring amino acids can be represented by both three- and one-letter abbreviations. (18.2)

23. The side chain of histidine shows enhanced basicity because of the electron-withdrawing inductive effects that stabilize the ion that results after protonation. (18.3)

24. The quaternary structure of a protein describes how smaller, individual protein strands interact to form the overall structure of a protein. (18.6)

25. An amino acid with a net charge of +1 is classified as a zwitterion. (18.2)

26. The side chain in serine is polar and can undergo hydrogen bonding. (18.2)

Detailed explanations for many of these answers can be found in the accompanying Solutions Manual.

Answers: (1) F (2) T (3) T (4) T (5) F (6) F (7) F (8) T (9) F (10) F (11) T (12) F (13) T (14) F (15) F (16) T (17) F (18) F (19) T (20) T (21) F (22) T (23) T (24) T (25) F (26) T

KEY REACTIONS

1. Acidity of an α-Carboxyl Group (Section 18.3A)

An α-COOH (pK_a approximately 2.19) of a protonated amino acid is a considerably stronger acid than acetic acid (pK_a 4.76) or other low-molecular-weight aliphatic carboxylic acid, due to the electron-withdrawing inductive effect of the α-NH_3^+ group:

$$\underset{\underset{NH_3^+}{|}}{RCHCOOH} + H_2O \rightleftharpoons \underset{\underset{NH_3^+}{|}}{RCHCOO^-} + H_3O^+ \qquad pK_a = 2.19$$

2. Acidity of an α-Ammonium Group (Section 18.3A)

An α-NH_3^+ group (pK_a approximately 9.47) is a slightly stronger acid than a primary aliphatic ammonium ion (pK_a approximately 10.76):

$$\underset{\underset{NH_3^+}{|}}{RCHCOO^-} + H_2O \rightleftharpoons \underset{\underset{NH_2}{|}}{RCHCOO^-} + H_3O^+ \qquad pK_a = 9.47$$

3. Reaction of an α-Amino Acid with Ninhydrin (Section 18.3D)

Treating an α-amino acid with ninhydrin gives a purple-colored solution:

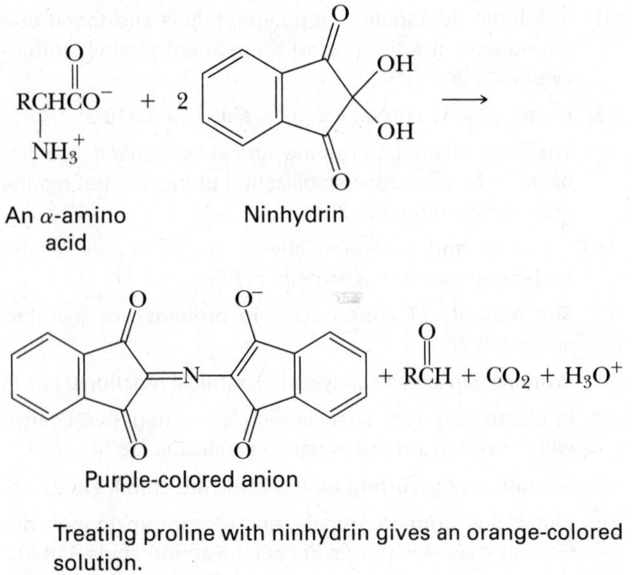

An α-amino acid

Ninhydrin

Purple-colored anion

Treating proline with ninhydrin gives an orange-colored solution.

4. Cleavage of a Peptide Bond by Cyanogen Bromide (Section 18.5B)

Cleavage is regioselective for a peptide bond formed by the carboxyl group of methionine:

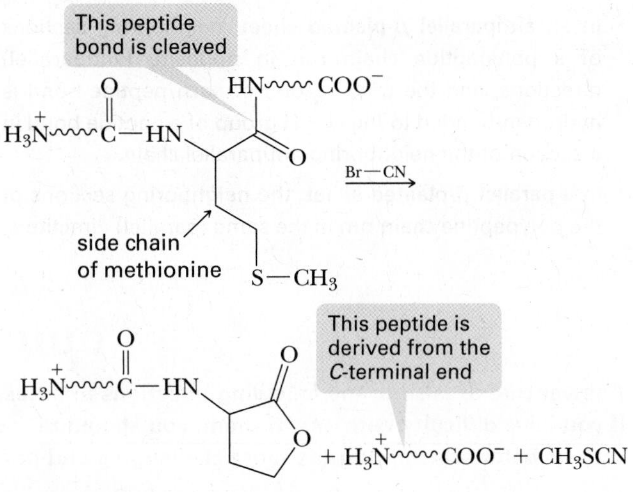

A substituted γ-lactone of the amino acid homoserine

5. Edman Degradation (Section 18.5B)

Treatment with phenyl isothiocyanate followed by acid removes the *N*-terminal amino acid as a substituted phenylthiohydantoin, which is then separated and identified:

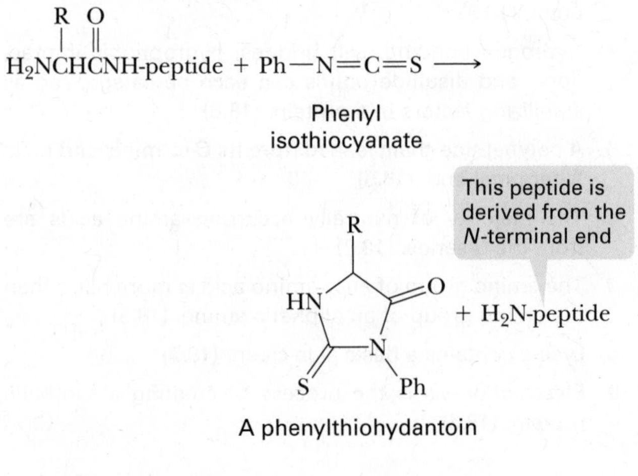

Phenyl isothiocyanate

A phenylthiohydantoin

PROBLEMS

A problem marked with an asterisk indicates an applied "real-world" problem. Answers to problems whose numbers are printed in blue are given in Appendix D.

Section 18.2 Amino Acids

18.8 What amino acid does each abbreviation stand for?

(a) Phe (b) Ser (c) Asp (d) Gln
(e) His (f) Gly (g) Tyr

18.9 The configuration of the stereocenter in α-amino acids is most commonly specified using the D,L convention. The configuration can also be identified using the *R,S* convention (Section 6.3). Does the stereocenter in L-serine have the *R* or the *S* configuration?

18.10 Assign an R or S configuration to the stereocenter in each amino acid:

(a) L-Phenylalanine (b) L-Glutamic acid
(c) L-Methionine

18.11 The amino acid threonine has two stereocenters. The stereoisomer found in proteins has the configuration 2*S*,3*R* about the two stereocenters. Draw a Fischer projection of this stereoisomer and also a three-dimensional representation.

18.12 Define the term *zwitterion.*

18.13 Draw zwitterion forms of these amino acids:

(a) Valine (b) Phenylalanine
(c) Glutamine

18.14 Why are Glu and Asp often referred to as acidic amino acids? **(See Example 18.1)**

18.15 Why is Arg often referred to as a basic amino acid? Which two other amino acids are also referred to as basic amino acids? **(See Example 18.1)**

18.16 What is the meaning of the alpha as it is used in α-amino acid?

***18.17** Several β-amino acids exist. A unit of β-alanine, for example, is contained within the structure of coenzyme A (Section 22.1D). Write the structural formula of β-alanine.

***18.18** Although only L-amino acids occur in proteins, D-amino acids are often a part of the metabolism of lower organisms. The antibiotic actinomycin D, for example, contains a unit of D-valine, and the antibiotic bacitracin A contains units of D-asparagine and D-glutamic acid. Draw Fischer projections and three-dimensional representations for these three D-amino acids.

***18.19** Histamine is synthesized from one of the 20 protein-derived amino acids. Suggest which amino acid is the biochemical precursor of histamine, and name the type of organic reaction(s) (e.g., oxidation, reduction, decarboxylation, nucleophilic substitution) involved in its conversion to histamine.

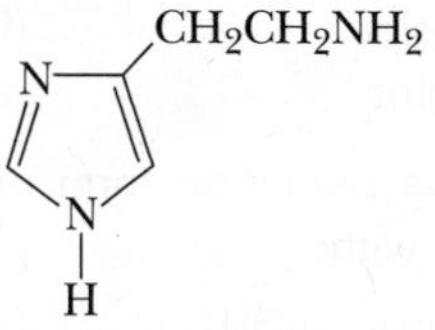

Histamine

***18.20** Both norepinephrine and epinephrine are synthesized from the same protein-derived amino acid:

(a)

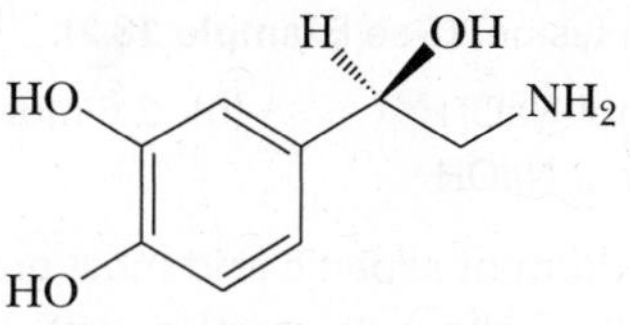

Norepinephrine

(b)

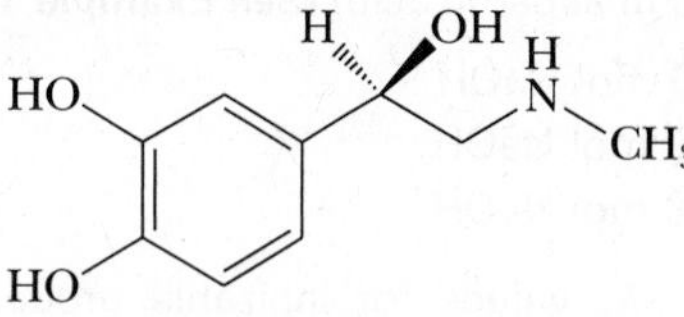

Epinephrine
(Adrenaline)

From which amino acid are the two compounds synthesized, and what types of reactions are involved in their biosynthesis?

***18.21** From which amino acid are serotonin and melatonin synthesized, and what types of reactions are involved in their biosynthesis?

(a)

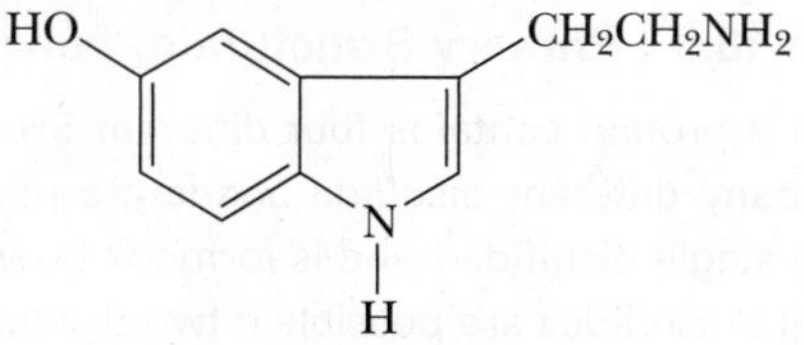

Serotonin

(b)

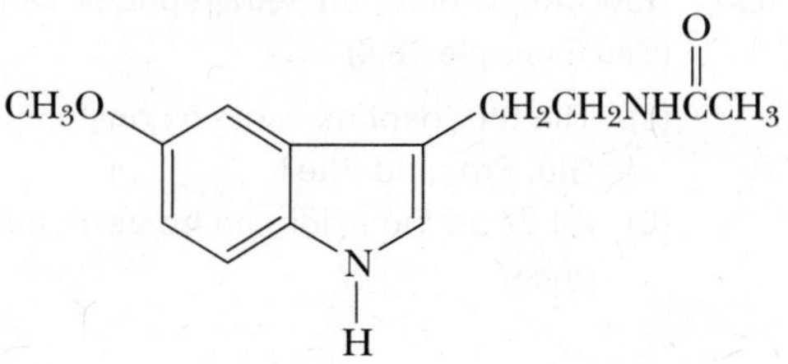

Melatonin

Section 18.3 Acid–Base Behavior of Amino Acids

18.22 Draw a structural formula for the form of each amino acid most prevalent at pH 1.0 **(See Example 18.2)**:

(a) Threonine (b) Arginine
(c) Methionine (d) Tyrosine

18.23 Draw a structural formula for the form of each amino acid most prevalent at pH 10.0 **(See Example 18.2)**:

(a) Leucine (b) Valine
(c) Proline (d) Aspartic acid

18.24 Write the zwitterion form of alanine and show its reaction with:

(a) 1.0 mol NaOH (b) 1.0 mol HCl

18.25 Write the form of lysine most prevalent at pH 1.0, and then show its reaction with each of the following (consult Table 18.2 for pK_a values of the ionizable groups in lysine) **(See Example 18.2)**:

(a) 1.0 mol NaOH (b) 2.0 mol NaOH
(c) 3.0 mol NaOH

18.26 Write the form of aspartic acid most prevalent at pH 1.0, and then show its reaction with the following (consult Table 18.2 for pK_a values of the ionizable groups in aspartic acid) **(See Example 18.2)**:

(a) 1.0 mol NaOH
(b) 2.0 mol NaOH
(c) 3.0 mol NaOH

18.27 Given pK_a values for ionizable groups from Table 18.2, sketch curves for the titration of (a) glutamic acid with NaOH and (b) histidine with NaOH.

18.28 Draw a structural formula for the product formed when alanine is treated with each of the following reagents:

(a) Aqueous NaOH (c) CH_3CH_2OH, H_2SO_4
(b) Aqueous HCl (d) $CH_3C(O)Cl$

18.29 Account for the fact that the isoelectric point of glutamine (pI 5.65) is higher than the isoelectric point of glutamic acid (pI 3.08).

18.30 Enzyme-catalyzed decarboxylation of glutamic acid gives 4-aminobutanoic acid (Section 18.2D). Estimate the pI of 4-aminobutanoic acid.

18.31 Guanidine and the guanidino group present in arginine are two of the strongest organic bases known. Account for their basicity.

***18.32** At pH 7.4, the pH of blood plasma, do the majority of protein-derived amino acids bear a net negative charge or a net positive charge? **(See Example 18.2)**

18.33 Do the following compounds migrate to the cathode or the anode on electrophoresis at the specified pH? **(See Example 18.2)**

(a) Histidine at pH 6.8
(b) Lysine at pH 6.8
(c) Glutamic acid at pH 4.0
(d) Glutamine at pH 4.0
(e) Glu-Ile-Val at pH 6.0
(f) Lys-Gln-Tyr at pH 6.0

18.34 At what pH would you carry out an electrophoresis to separate the amino acids in each of the following mixtures? **(See Example 18.3)**

(a) Ala, His, Lys
(b) Glu, Gln, Asp
(c) Lys, Leu, Tyr

***18.35** Examine the amino acid sequence of human insulin (Figure 18.13), and list each Asp, Glu, His, Lys, and Arg in this molecule. Do you expect human insulin to have an isoelectric point nearer that of the acidic amino acids (pI 2.0–3.0), the neutral amino acids (pI 5.5–6.5), or the basic amino acids (pI 9.5–11.0)?

Section 18.5 Primary Structure of Polypeptides and Proteins

18.36 If a protein contains four different SH groups, how many different disulfide bonds are possible if only a single disulfide bond is formed? How many different disulfides are possible if two disulfide bonds are formed?

18.37 How many different tetrapeptides can be made if **(See Example 18.4)**

(a) The tetrapeptide contains one unit each of Asp, Glu, Pro, and Phe?
(b) All 20 amino acids can be used, but each only once?

18.38 A decapeptide has the following amino acid composition: **(See Example 18.6)**

Ala_2, Arg, Cys, Glu, Gly, Leu, Lys, Phe, Val

Partial hydrolysis yields the following tripeptides:

Cys-Glu-Leu + Gly-Arg-Cys + Leu-Ala-Ala
+ Lys-Val-Phe + Val-Phe-Gly

One round of Edman degradation yields a lysine phenylthiohydantoin. From this information, deduce the primary structure of the given decapeptide.

***18.39** Following is the primary structure of glucagon, a polypeptide hormone with 29 amino acids: **(See Example 18.5)**

1 5 10
His-Ser-Glu-Gly-Thr-Phe-Thr-Ser-Asp-Tyr-Ser-Lys-Tyr-
15 20 25
Leu-Asp-Ser-Arg-Arg-Ala-Gln-Asp-Phe-Val-Gln-Trp-
29
Leu-Met-Asn-Thr

Glucagon

Glucagon is produced in the α-cells of the pancreas and helps maintain the blood glucose concentration within a normal range. Which peptide bonds are hydrolyzed when glucagon is treated with each reagent?

(a) Phenyl isothiocyanate (b) Chymotrypsin
(c) Trypsin (d) Br-CN

18.40 A tetradecapeptide (14 amino acid residues) gives the following peptide fragments on partial hydrolysis **(See Example 18.6)**:

Pentapeptide Fragments	Tetrapeptide Fragments
Phe-Val-Asn-Gln-His	Gln-His-Leu-Cys
His-Leu-Cys-Gly-Ser	His-Leu-Val-Glu
Gly-Ser-His-Leu-Val	Leu-Val-Glu-Ala

From the information shown, deduce the primary structure of the given polypeptide. Fragments are grouped according to size.

18.41 Draw a structural formula of each of the following tripeptides: marking each peptide bond, the *N*-terminal amino acid, and the *C*-terminal amino acid: **(See Example 18.4)**

(a) Phe-Val-Asn (b) Leu-Val-Gln

18.42 Estimate the pI of each tripeptide in Problem 18.41.

***18.43** Glutathione (G-SH), one of the most common tripeptides in animals, plants, and bacteria, is a scavenger of oxidizing agents:

Glutathione $H_3N^+CHCH_2CH_2\overset{O}{\overset{\|}{C}}NHCH\overset{O}{\overset{\|}{C}}NHCH_2COO^-$ (with COO^- on the first CH and CH_2SH on the second CH)

In reacting with oxidizing agents, glutathione is converted to G-S-S-G.

(a) Name the amino acids in this tripeptide.
(b) What is unusual about the peptide bond formed by the *N*-terminal amino acid?
(c) Is glutathione a biological oxidizing agent or a biological reducing agent?
(d) Write a balanced equation for the reaction of glutathione with molecular oxygen, O_2, to form G-S-S-G and H_2O. Is molecular oxygen oxidized or reduced in this reaction?

***18.44** Following is a structural formula for the artificial sweetener aspartame:

(a) Name the two amino acids in this molecule.
(b) Estimate the isoelectric point of aspartame.
(c) Draw structural formulas for the products of the hydrolysis of aspartame in 1 M HCl.

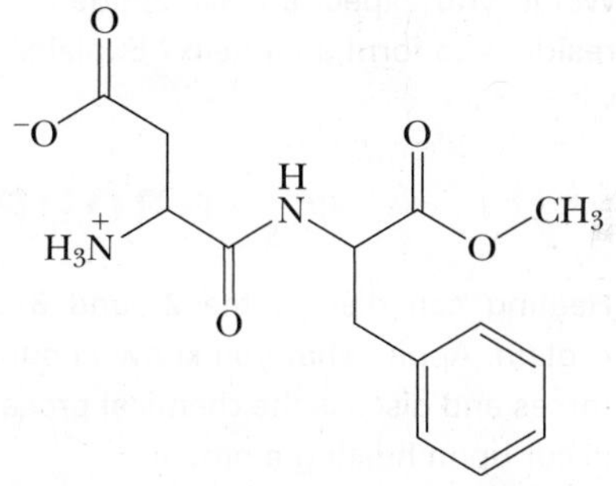

Aspartame

Section 18.6 Three-Dimensional Shapes of Polypeptides and Proteins

18.45 Examine the α-helix conformation. Are amino acid side chains arranged all inside the helix, all outside the helix, or randomly?

18.46 Distinguish between intermolecular and intramolecular hydrogen bonding between the backbone groups on polypeptide chains. In what type of secondary structure do you find intermolecular hydrogen bonds? In what type do you find intramolecular hydrogen bonding?

***18.47** Many plasma proteins found in an aqueous environment are globular in shape. Which of the following amino acid side chains would you expect to find on the surface of a globular protein, in contact with the aqueous environment, and which would you expect to find inside, shielded from the aqueous environment? **(See Example 18.7)**

(a) Leu (b) Arg (c) Ser (d) Lys (e) Phe

Explain.

LOOKING AHEAD

18.48 Some amino acids cannot be incorporated into proteins because they are self-destructive. Homoserine, for example, can use its side-chain OH group in an intramolecular nucleophilic acyl substitution to cleave the peptide bond and form a cyclic structure on one end of the chain:

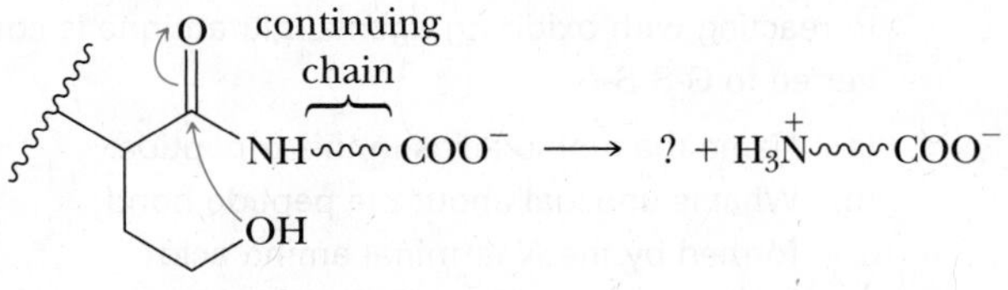

Homoserine residue

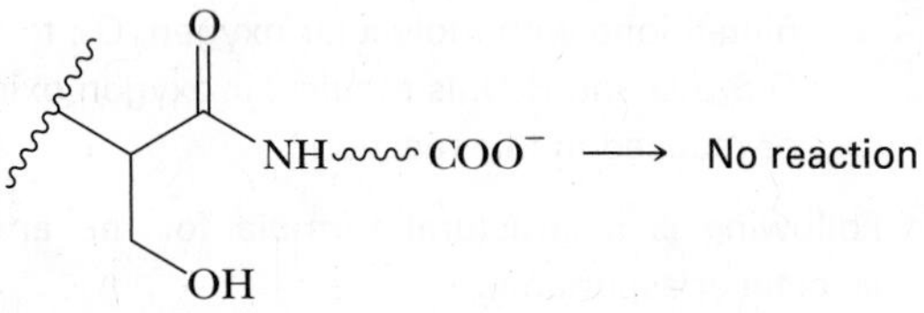

Serine residue

Draw the cyclic structure formed and explain why serine does not suffer the same fate.

18.49 Would you expect a decapeptide of only isoleucine residues to form an α-helix? Explain.

18.50 Which type of protein would you expect to bring about the following change?

Reaction A

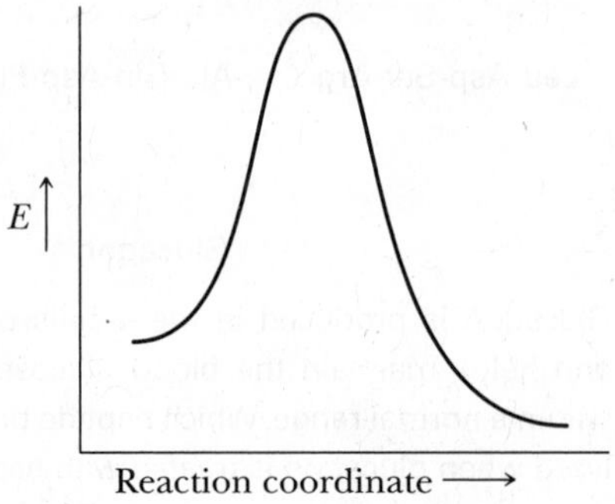

Reaction A + protein

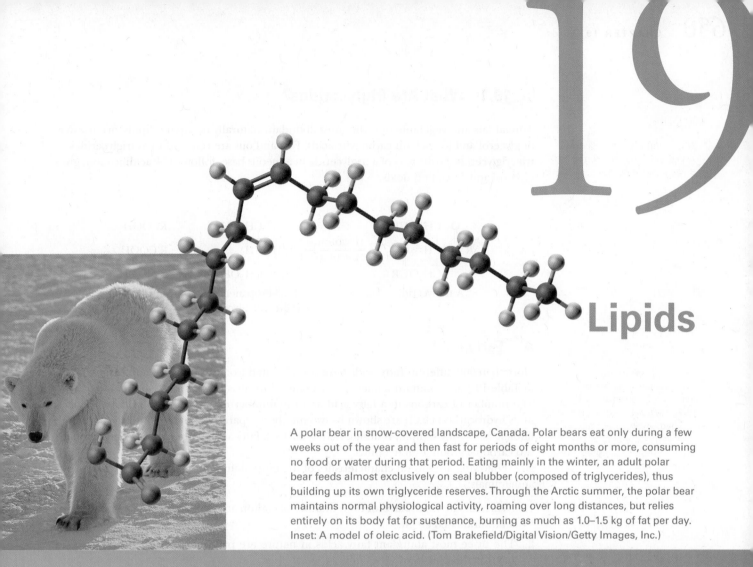

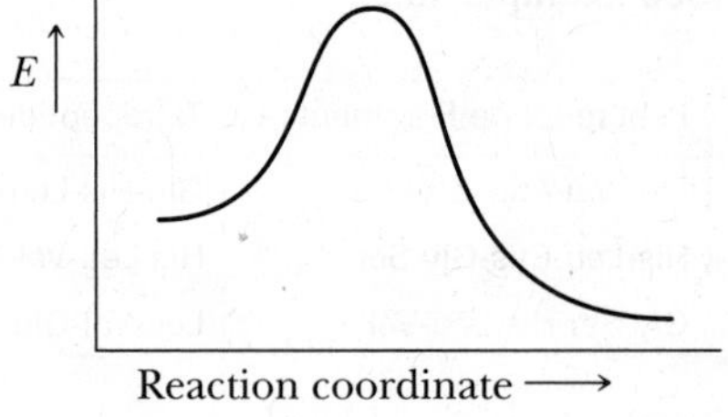

GROUP LEARNING ACTIVITIES

18.51 Heating can disrupt the 2° and 3° structure of a protein. Apply what you know about intermolecular forces and discuss the chemical processes that could occur upon heating a protein.

18.52 Enzymes are examples of proteins. Discuss why enzymes lose their catalytic activity at higher than physiological temperatures.

18.53 Denaturation is the loss of secondary, tertiary, and quaternary structure of a protein by a chemical or physical agent and the resulting loss of function. The previous two problems revealed that heat can cause denaturation. As a group, discuss other physical or chemical agents that could cause denaturation and explain the processes that would effect denaturation.

19

Lipids

A polar bear in snow-covered landscape, Canada. Polar bears eat only during a few weeks out of the year and then fast for periods of eight months or more, consuming no food or water during that period. Eating mainly in the winter, an adult polar bear feeds almost exclusively on seal blubber (composed of triglycerides), thus building up its own triglyceride reserves. Through the Arctic summer, the polar bear maintains normal physiological activity, roaming over long distances, but relies entirely on its body fat for sustenance, burning as much as 1.0–1.5 kg of fat per day. Inset: A model of oleic acid. (Tom Brakefield/Digital Vision/Getty Images, Inc.)

KEY QUESTIONS

CHEMICAL CONNECTIONS

LIPIDS ARE A HETEROGENEOUS group of naturally occurring organic compounds, classified together on the basis of their common solubility properties. Lipids are insoluble in water, but soluble in relatively nonpolar aprotic organic solvents, including diethyl ether, dichloromethane, and acetone.

Lipid A class of biomolecules isolated from plant or animal sources by extraction with relatively nonpolar organic solvents, such as diethyl ether and acetone.

Lipids play three major roles in human biology. First, they are storage depots of chemical energy in the form of triglycerides (fats). While plants store energy in the form of carbohydrates (e.g., starch), humans store it in the form of fat globules in adipose tissue. Second, lipids, in the form of phospholipids, are the water-insoluble components from which biological membranes are constructed. Third, lipids, in the form of steroid hormones, prostaglandins, thromboxanes, and leukotrienes, are chemical messengers. In this chapter, we describe the structures and biological functions of each group of lipids.

19.1 What Are Triglycerides?

Triglyceride (triacylglycerol) An ester of glycerol with three fatty acids.

Animal fats and vegetable oils, the most abundant naturally occurring lipids, are triesters of glycerol and long-chain carboxylic acids. Fats and oils are referred to as **triglycerides** or **triacylglycerols**. Hydrolysis of a triglyceride in aqueous base, followed by acidification, gives glycerol and three fatty acids:

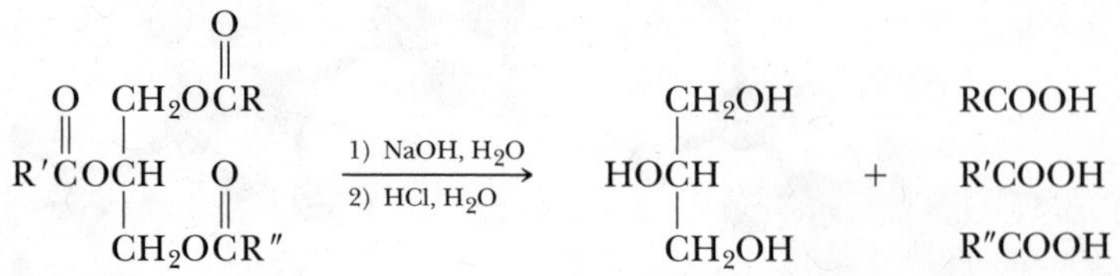

A triglyceride — 1,2,3-Propanetriol (Glycerol, glycerin) — Fatty acids

A. Fatty Acids

Fatty acid A long, unbranched-chain carboxylic acid, most commonly of 12 to 20 carbons, derived from the hydrolysis of animal fats, vegetable oils, or the phospholipids of biological membranes.

More than 500 different **fatty acids** have been isolated from various cells and tissues. Given in Table 19.1 are common names and structural formulas for the most abundant of them. The number of carbons in a fatty acid and the number of carbon–carbon double bonds in its hydrocarbon chain are shown by two numbers separated by a colon. In this notation, linoleic acid, for example, is designated as an 18:2 fatty acid; its 18-carbon chain contains two carbon–carbon double bonds.

Following are several characteristics of the most abundant fatty acids in higher plants and animals:

1. Nearly all fatty acids have an even number of carbon atoms, most between 12 and 20, in an unbranched chain.
2. The three most abundant fatty acids in nature are palmitic acid (16:0), stearic acid (18:0), and oleic acid (18:1).

Charles D. Winters

Some vegetable oils.

TABLE 19.1 The Most Abundant Fatty Acids in Animal Fats, Vegetable Oils, and Biological Membranes

Carbon Atoms/ Double Bonds*	Structure	Common Name	Melting Point (°C)
Saturated Fatty Acids			
12:0	$CH_3(CH_2)_{10}COOH$	lauric acid	44
14:0	$CH_3(CH_2)_{12}COOH$	myristic acid	58
16:0	$CH_3(CH_2)_{14}COOH$	palmitic acid	63
18:0	$CH_3(CH_2)_{16}COOH$	stearic acid	70
20:0	$CH_3(CH_2)_{18}COOH$	arachidic acid	77
Unsaturated Fatty Acids			
16:1	$CH_3(CH_2)_5CH{=}CH(CH_2)_7COOH$	palmitoleic acid	1
18:1	$CH_3(CH_2)_7CH{=}CH(CH_2)_7COOH$	oleic acid	16
18:2	$CH_3(CH_2)_4(CH{=}CHCH_2)_2(CH_2)_6COOH$	linoleic acid	−5
18:3	$CH_3CH_2(CH{=}CHCH_2)_3(CH_2)_6COOH$	linolenic acid	−11
20:4	$CH_3(CH_2)_4(CH{=}CHCH_2)_4(CH_2)_2COOH$	arachidonic acid	−49

*The first number is the number of carbons in the fatty acid; the second is the number of carbon–carbon double bonds in its hydrocarbon chain.

3. In most unsaturated fatty acids, the *cis* isomer predominates; the *trans* isomer is rare.
4. Unsaturated fatty acids have lower melting points than their saturated counterparts. The greater the degree of unsaturation, the lower is the melting point. Compare, for example, the melting points of these four 18-carbon fatty acids:

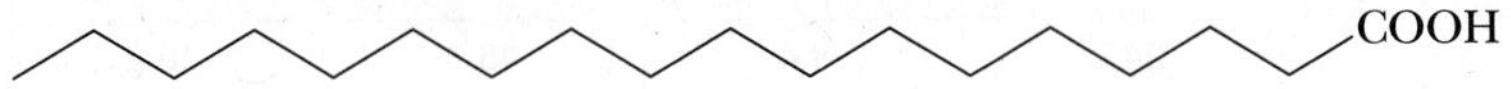

Stearic acid (18 : 0)
(mp 70 °C)

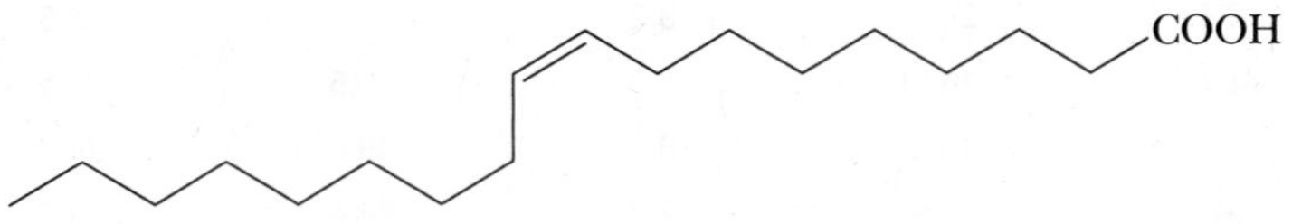

Oleic acid (18 : 1)
(mp 16 °C)

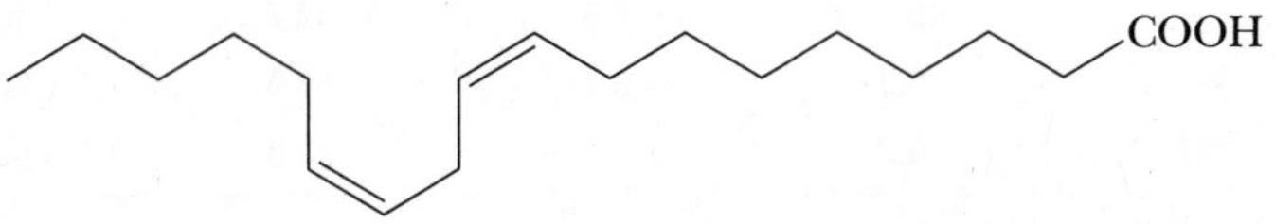

Linoleic acid (18 : 2)
(mp –5 °C)

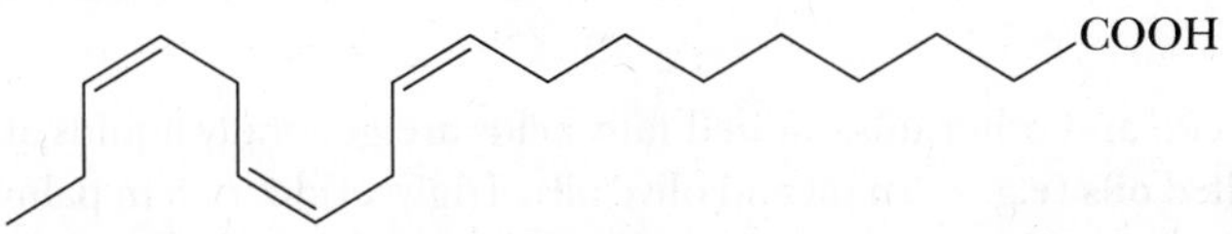

Linolenic acid (18 : 3)
(mp –11 °C)

EXAMPLE 19.1

Draw the structural formula of a triglyceride derived from one molecule each of palmitic acid, oleic acid, and stearic acid, the three most abundant fatty acids in the biological world.

STRATEGY

A triglyceride is a triester of glycerol (a triol) so that each of the three —OH groups of glycerol will form an ester with a carboxylic acid. There are six triglycerides possible using three different fatty acids.

SOLUTION

In this structure, palmitic acid is esterified at carbon 1 of glycerol, oleic acid at carbon 2, and stearic acid at carbon 3:

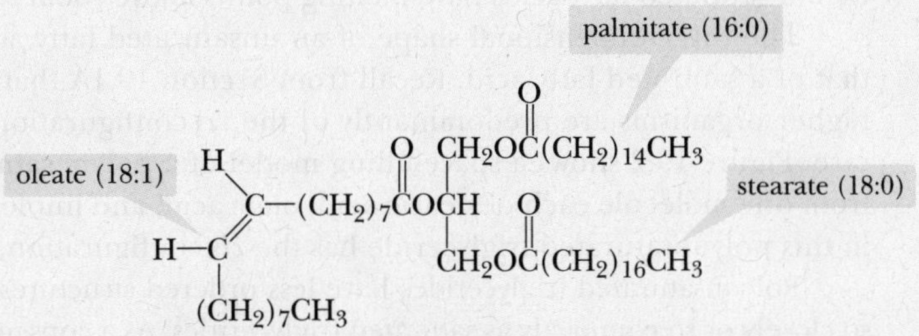

A triglyceride

See problem 19.8

PROBLEM 19.1

(a) How many constitutional isomers are possible for a triglyceride containing one molecule each of palmitic acid, oleic acid, and stearic acid?

(b) Which of the constitutional isomers that you found in part (a) are chiral?

B. Physical Properties

The physical properties of a triglyceride depend on its fatty-acid components. In general, the melting point of a triglyceride increases as the number of carbons in its hydrocarbon chains increases and as the number of carbon–carbon double bonds decreases. Triglycerides rich in

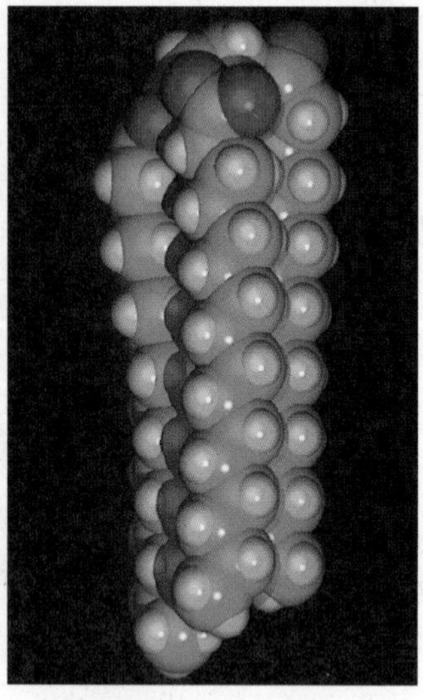

FIGURE 19.1
Tripalmitin, a saturated triglyceride.

TABLE 19.2 Grams of Fatty Acid per 100 g of Triglyceride of Several Fats and Oils*

Fat or Oil	Saturated Fatty Acids: Lauric (12:0)	Palmitic (16:0)	Stearic (18:0)	Unsaturated Fatty Acids: Oleic (18:1)	Linoleic (18:2)
Human fat	—	24.0	8.4	46.9	10.2
Beef fat	—	27.4	14.1	49.6	2.5
Butter fat	2.5	29.0	9.2	26.7	3.6
Coconut oil	45.4	10.5	2.3	7.5	trace
Corn oil	—	10.2	3.0	49.6	34.3
Olive oil	—	6.9	2.3	84.4	4.6
Palm oil	—	40.1	5.5	42.7	10.3
Peanut oil	—	8.3	3.1	56.0	26.0
Soybean oil	0.2	9.8	2.4	28.9	50.7

*Only the most abundant fatty acids are given; other fatty acids are present in lesser amounts.

oleic acid, linoleic acid, and other unsaturated fatty acids are generally liquids at room temperature and are called **oils** (e.g., corn oil and olive oil). Triglycerides rich in palmitic, stearic, and other saturated fatty acids are generally semisolids or solids at room temperature and are called **fats** (e.g., human fat and butter fat). Fats of land animals typically contain approximately 40% to 50% saturated fatty acids by weight (Table 19.2). Most plant oils, on the other hand, contain 20% or less saturated fatty acids and 80% or more unsaturated fatty acids. The notable exception to this generalization about plant oils are the **tropical oils** (e.g., coconut and palm oils), which are considerably richer in low-molecular-weight saturated fatty acids.

Oil A triglyceride that is liquid at room temperature.

Fat A triglyceride that is semisolid or solid at room temperature.

Polyunsaturated triglyceride A triglyceride having several carbon–carbon double bonds in the hydrocarbon chains of its three fatty acids.

The lower melting points of triglycerides that are rich in unsaturated fatty acids are related to differences in the three-dimensional shape between the hydrocarbon chains of their unsaturated and saturated fatty-acid components. Figure 19.1 shows a space-filling model of tripalmitin, a saturated triglyceride. In the model, the hydrocarbon chains lie parallel to each other, giving the molecule an ordered, compact shape. Because of this compact three-dimensional shape and the resulting strength of the dispersion forces (Section 3.8B) between hydrocarbon chains of adjacent molecules, triglycerides that are rich in saturated fatty acids have melting points above room temperature.

The three-dimensional shape of an unsaturated fatty acid is quite different from that of a saturated fatty acid. Recall from Section 19.1A that unsaturated fatty acids of higher organisms are predominantly of the *cis* configuration; *trans* configurations are rare. Figure 19.2 shows a space-filling model of a **polyunsaturated triglyceride** derived from one molecule each of stearic acid, oleic acid, and linoleic acid. Each double bond in this polyunsaturated triglyceride has the *cis* configuration.

Polyunsaturated triglycerides have less ordered structures and do not pack together so closely or so compactly as saturated triglycerides. As a consequence, intramolecular and intermolecular dispersion forces are weaker, with the result that polyunsaturated triglycerides have lower melting points than their saturated counterparts.

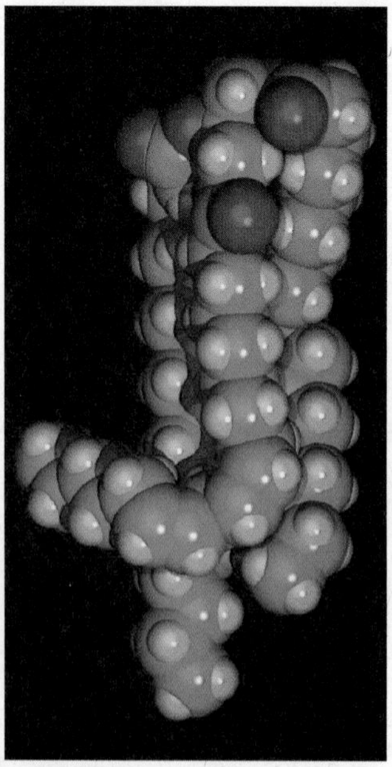

FIGURE 19.2
A polyunsaturated triglyceride.

C. Reduction of Fatty-Acid Chains

For a variety of reasons, in part convenience and in part dietary preference, the conversion of oils to fats has become a major industry. The process is called **hardening** of oils and involves the catalytic reduction (Section 5.8) of some or all of an oil's carbon–carbon double bonds. In practice, the degree of hardening is carefully controlled to produce fats of a desired consistency. The resulting fats are sold for kitchen use (as Crisco®, Spry®, and others). **Margarine** and other butter substitutes are produced by partial hydrogenation of polyunsaturated oils derived from corn, cottonseed, peanut, and soybean oils. To the hardened oil are added β-carotene (to give it a yellow color and make it look like butter), salt, and about 15% milk by volume to form the final emulsion. Vitamins A and D may be added as well. Finally, because the product to this stage is tasteless, acetoin and diacetyl, two compounds that mimic the characteristic flavor of butter, are often added:

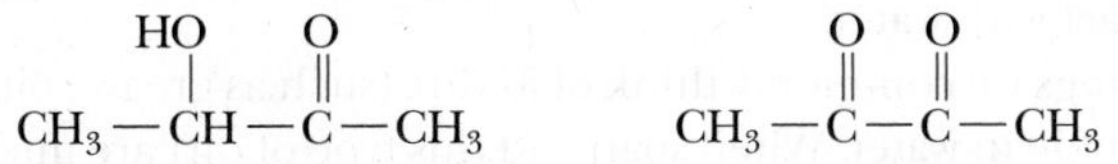

3-Hydroxy-2-butanone (Acetoin) — 2,3-Butanedione (Diacetyl)

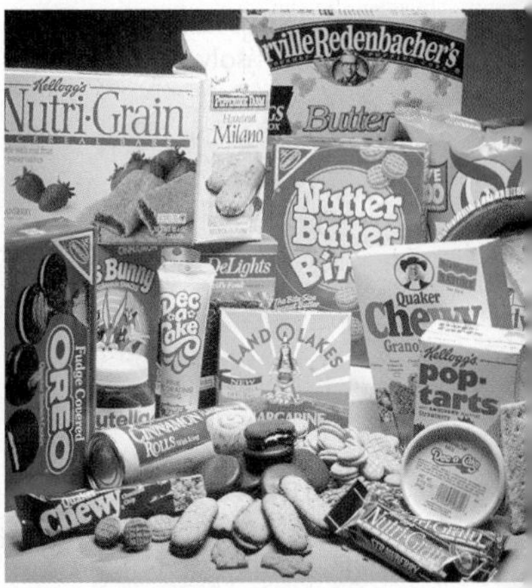

Charles D. Winters

Some common products containing hydrogenated vegetable oils.

19.2 What Are Soaps and Detergents?

A. Structure and Preparation of Soaps

Natural **soaps** are prepared most commonly from a blend of tallow and coconut oils. In the preparation of tallow, the solid fats of cattle are melted with steam, and the tallow layer that forms on the top is removed. The preparation of soaps begins by boiling these triglycerides with sodium hydroxide. The reaction that takes place is called *saponification* (Latin: *saponem*, soap):

A triglyceride — 1,2,3-Propanetriol (Glycerol; glycerin) — Sodium soaps

Soap A sodium or potassium salt of a fatty acid.

Micelle A spherical arrangement of organic molecules in water solution clustered so that their hydrophobic parts are buried inside the sphere and their hydrophilic parts are on the surface of the sphere and in contact with water.

At the molecular level, saponification corresponds to base-promoted hydrolysis of the ester groups in triglycerides (Section 14.3C). The resulting soaps contain mainly the sodium salts of palmitic, stearic, and oleic acids from tallow and the sodium salts of lauric and myristic acids from coconut oil.

After hydrolysis is complete, sodium chloride is added to precipitate the soap as thick curds. The water layer is then drawn off, and glycerol is recovered by vacuum distillation. The crude soap contains sodium chloride, sodium hydroxide, and other impurities that are removed by boiling the curd in water and reprecipitating with more sodium chloride. After several purifications, the soap can be used as an inexpensive industrial soap without further processing. Other treatments transform the crude soap into pH-controlled cosmetic soaps, medicated soaps, and the like.

B. How Soap Cleans

Soap owes its remarkable cleansing properties to its ability to act as an emulsifying agent. Because the long hydrocarbon chains of natural soaps are insoluble in water, they tend to cluster in such a way as to minimize their contact with surrounding water molecules. The polar carboxylate groups, by contrast, tend to remain in contact with the surrounding water molecules. Thus, in water, soap molecules spontaneously cluster into **micelles** (Figure 19.3). A micelle is a

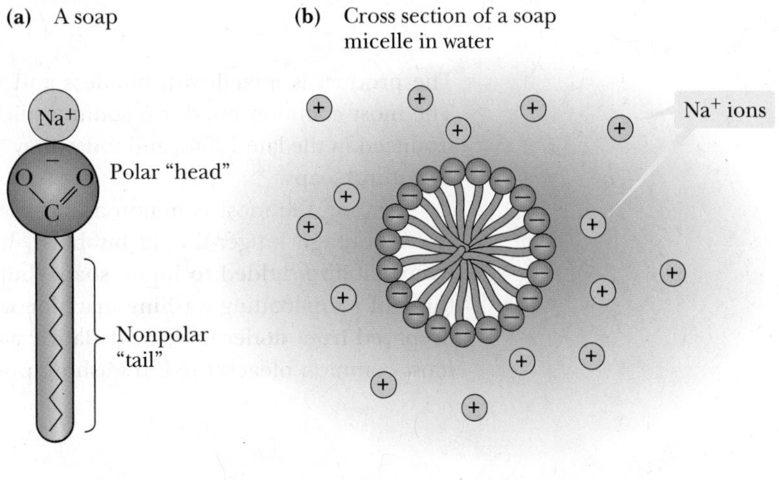

FIGURE 19.3
Soap micelles. Nonpolar (hydrophobic) hydrocarbon chains are clustered in the interior of the micelle, and polar (hydrophilic) carboxylate groups are on the surface of the micelle. Soap micelles repel each other because of their negative surface charges.

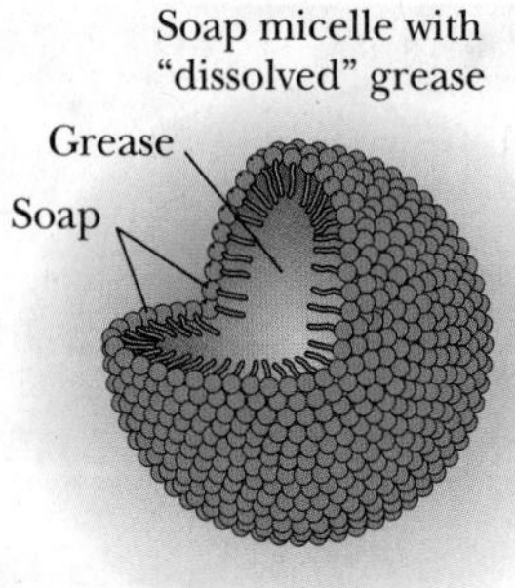

FIGURE 19.4
A soap micelle with a "dissolved" oil or grease droplet.

spherical arrangement of organic molecules in water solution clustered so that their **hydrophobic** parts are buried in the sphere and their **hydrophilic** parts are on the surface of the sphere and in contact with water.

Most of the things we commonly think of as dirt (such as grease, oil, and fat stains) are nonpolar and insoluble in water. When soap and this type of dirt are mixed together, as in a washing machine, the nonpolar hydrocarbon inner parts of the soap micelles "dissolve" the nonpolar dirt molecules. In effect, new soap micelles are formed, this time with nonpolar dirt molecules in the center (Figure 19.4). In this way, nonpolar organic grease, oil, and fat are "dissolved" and washed away in the polar wash water.

Soaps, however, have their disadvantages, foremost among which is the fact that they form water-insoluble salts when used in water, which contains Ca^{2+}, Mg^{2+}, or Fe^{3+} ions (hard water):

$$2CH_3(CH_2)_{14}COO^-Na^+ + Ca^{2+} \longrightarrow [CH_3(CH_2)_{14}COO^-]_2Ca^{2+} + 2Na^+$$

A sodium soap (soluble in water as micelles) — Calcium salt of a fatty acid (insoluble in water)

These calcium, magnesium, and iron salts of fatty acids create problems, including rings around the bathtub, films that spoil the luster of hair, and grayness and roughness that build up on textiles after repeated washings.

C. Synthetic Detergents

After the cleansing action of soaps was understood, chemists were in a position to design a **synthetic detergent**. Molecules of a good detergent, they reasoned, must have a long hydrocarbon chain—preferably, 12 to 20 carbon atoms long—and a polar group at one end of the molecule that does not form insoluble salts with the Ca^{2+}, Mg^{2+}, or Fe^{3+} ions that are present in hard water. These essential characteristics of natural soaps, they recognized, could be produced in a molecule containing a sulfonate ($-SO_3^-$) group instead of a carboxylate ($-COO^-$) group. Calcium, magnesium, and iron salts of alkylsulfonic acids, $R–SO_3H$, and arylsulfonic acids, $ArSO_3H$, are much more soluble in water than comparable salts of fatty acids.

The most widely used synthetic detergents today are the linear alkylbenzene sulfonates (LAS). One of the most common of these is sodium 4-dodecylbenzenesulfonate. To prepare this type of detergent, a linear alkylbenzene is treated with sulfuric acid to form an alkylbenzenesulfonic acid (Section 9.6B), followed by neutralization of the sulfonic acid with NaOH:

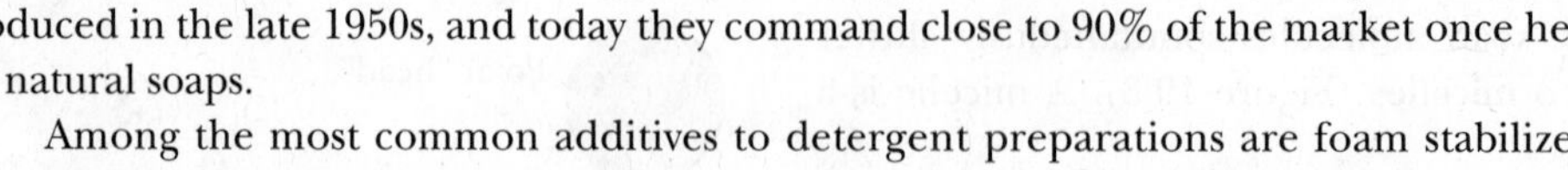

Dodecylbenzene — Sodium 4-dodecylbenzenesulfonate (an anionic detergent)

The product is mixed with builders and spray dried to give a smooth, flowing powder. The most common builder is sodium silicate. Alkylbenzenesulfonate detergents were introduced in the late 1950s, and today they command close to 90% of the market once held by natural soaps.

Among the most common additives to detergent preparations are foam stabilizers (to encourage longer-lasting bubbles), bleaches, and optical brighteners. A common foam stabilizer added to liquid soaps, but not laundry detergents (for obvious reasons: think of a top-loading washing machine with foam spewing out of the lid!), is the amide prepared from dodecanoic acid (lauric acid) and 2-aminoethanol (ethanolamine). The most common bleach used in washing powders is sodium perborate tetrahydrate, which decomposes at temperatures above 50 °C to give hydrogen peroxide, the actual bleaching agent:

$$CH_3(CH_2)_{10}\overset{\overset{\large O}{\|}}{C}NHCH_2CH_2OH \qquad O{=}B{-}O{-}O^-Na^+ \cdot 4H_2O$$

N-(2-Hydroxyethyl)dodecanamide (a foam stabilizer) — Sodium perborate tetrahydrate (a bleach)

Also added to laundry detergents are optical brighteners (optical bleaches). These substances are absorbed into fabrics and, after absorbing ambient light, fluoresce with a blue color, offsetting the yellow color caused by fabric as it ages. Optical brighteners produce a " whiter-than-white" appearance. You most certainly have observed their effects if you have seen the glow of white T-shirts or blouses when they are exposed to black light (UV radiation).

Effects of optical bleaches: (*above*) ordinary light; (*below*) black light.

19.3 What Are Phospholipids?

A. Structure

Phospholipids, or phosphoacylglycerols, as they are more properly named, are the second most abundant group of naturally occurring lipids. They are found almost exclusively in plant and animal membranes, which typically consist of about 40% to 50% phospholipids and 50% to 60% proteins. The most abundant phospholipids are derived from a **phosphatidic acid** (Figure 19.5).

The fatty acids that are most common in phosphatidic acids are palmitic and stearic acids (both fully saturated) and oleic acid (with one double bond in the hydrocarbon chain). Further esterification of a phosphatidic acid with a low-molecular-weight alcohol gives a phospholipid. Several of the most common alcohols found in phospholipids are given in Table 19.3.

Phospholipid A lipid containing glycerol esterified with two molecules of fatty acid and one molecule of phosphoric acid.

All of these products contain lecithin.

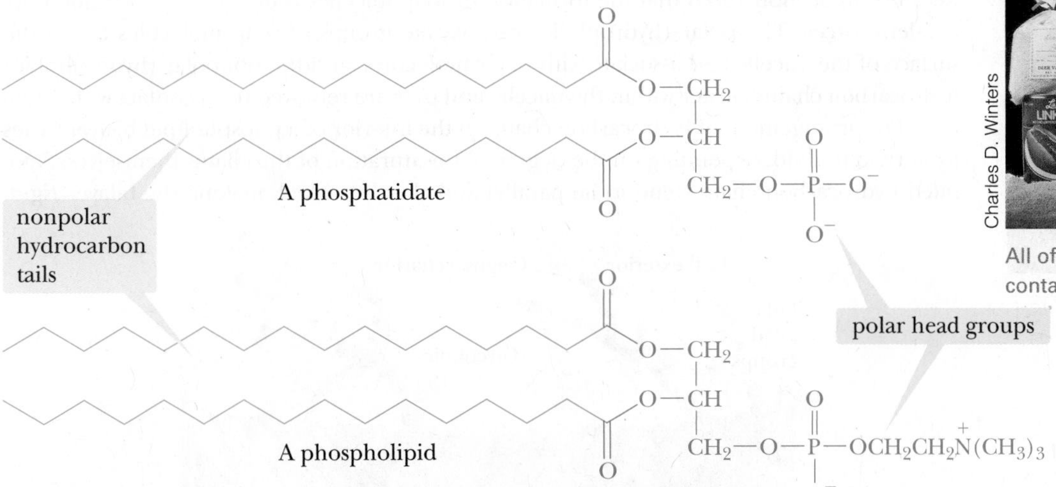

FIGURE 19.5
A phosphatidic acid and a phospholipid. In a phosphatidic acid, glycerol is esterified with two molecules of fatty acid and one molecule of phosphoric acid. Further esterification of the phosphoric acid group with a low-molecular-weight alcohol gives a phospholipid. Each structural formula shows all functional groups as they are ionized at pH 7.4, the approximate pH of blood plasma and of many biological fluids. Under these conditions, each phosphate group bears a negative charge and each amino group bears a positive charge.

TABLE 19.3 Low-Molecular-Weight Alcohols Most Common to Phospholipids

Alcohols Found in Phospholipids		
Structural Formula	Name	Name of Phospholipid
$HOCH_2CH_2NH_2$	Ethanolamine	Phosphatidylethanolamine (cephalin)
$HOCH_2CH_2\overset{+}{N}(CH_3)_3$	Choline	Phosphatidylcholine (lecithin)
$HOCH_2CH(NH_3^+)COO^-$	Serine	Phosphatidylserine
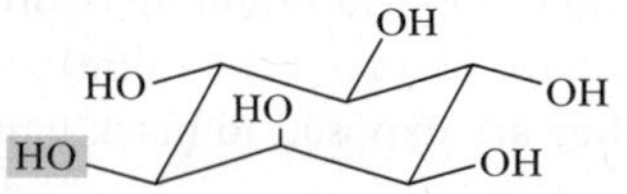	Inositol	Phosphatidylinositol

B. Lipid Bilayers

Lipid bilayer A back-to-back arrangement of phospholipid monolayers.

Figure 19.6 shows a space-filling model of a lecithin (a phosphatidycholine). It and other phospholipids are elongated, almost rodlike molecules, with the nonpolar (hydrophobic) hydrocarbon chains lying roughly parallel to one another and the polar (hydrophilic) phosphoric ester group pointing in the opposite direction.

Placed in aqueous solution, phospholipids spontaneously form a **lipid bilayer** (Figure 19.7) in which polar head groups lie on the surface, giving the bilayer an ionic coating. Nonpolar hydrocarbon chains of fatty acids lie buried within the bilayer. This self-assembly of phospholipids into a bilayer is a spontaneous process, driven by two types of noncovalent forces:

1. **hydrophobic effects**, which result when nonpolar hydrocarbon chains cluster together and exclude water molecules, and
2. **electrostatic interactions**, which result when polar head groups interact with water and other polar molecules in the aqueous environment.

Recall from Section 19.2B that the formation of soap micelles is driven by these same noncovalent forces. The polar (hydrophilic) carboxylate groups of soap molecules lie on the surface of the micelle and associate with water molecules, and the nonpolar (hydrophobic) hydrocarbon chains cluster within the micelle and thus are removed from contact with water.

The arrangement of hydrocarbon chains in the interior of a phospholipid bilayer varies from rigid to fluid, depending on the degree of unsaturation of the chains themselves. Saturated hydrocarbon chains tend to lie parallel and closely packed, making the bilayer rigid.

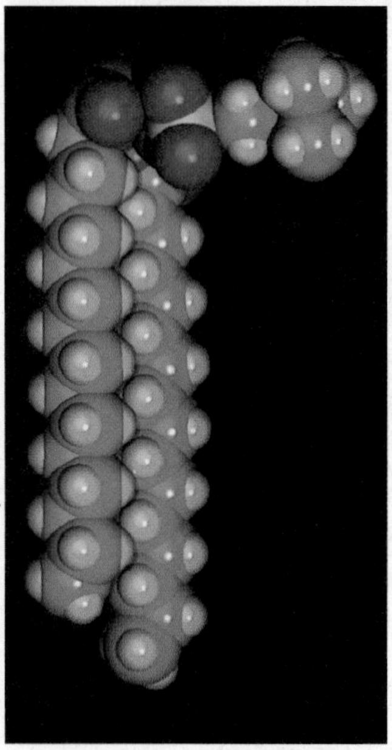

Brent Iverson, University of Texas

FIGURE 19.6
Space-filling model of a lecithin.

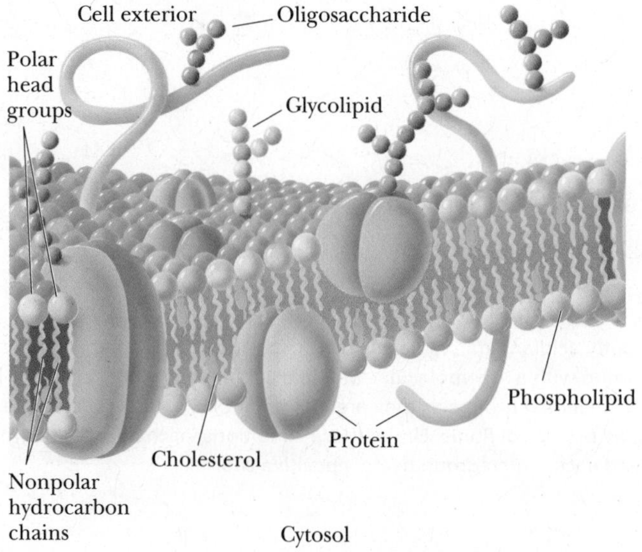

FIGURE 19.7
Fluid-mosaic model of a biological membrane, showing the lipid bilayer with membrane proteins oriented on the inner and outer surfaces of the membrane, and penetrating the entire thickness of the membrane.

Chemical Connections 19A

SNAKE VENOM PHOSPHOLIPASES

The venoms of certain snakes contain enzymes called phospholipases that catalyze the hydrolysis of carboxylic ester bonds of phospholipids. The venom of the eastern diamondback rattlesnake (*Crotalus adamanteus*) and that of the Indian cobra (*Naja naja*) both contain phospholipase PLA_2, which catalyzes the hydrolysis of esters at carbon 2 of phospholipids. The breakdown product of this hydrolysis, a lysolecithin, acts as a detergent and dissolves the membranes of red blood cells, causing them to rupture:

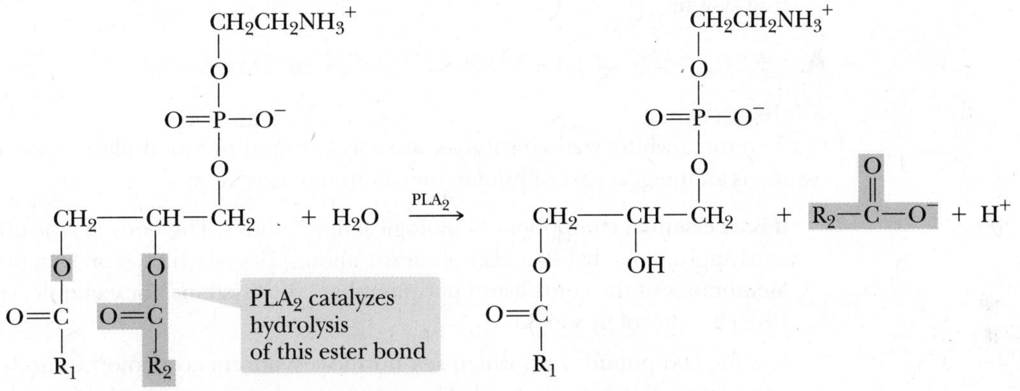

A phospholipid

A lysolecithin

Indian cobras kill several thousand people each year.

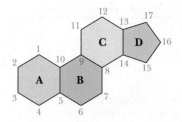

© Marije Pama/Alamy Limited

Milking an Indian cobra for its venom.

Question
How is a lysolecithin able to act as a detergent?

Unsaturated hydrocarbon chains, by contrast, have one or more *cis* double bonds, which cause "kinks" in the chains, so they pack neither as closely nor as orderly as saturated chains. The disordered packing of unsaturated hydrocarbon chains leads to fluidity of the bilayer.

Biological membranes are made of lipid bilayers. The most satisfactory model for the arrangement of phospholipids, proteins, and cholesterol in plant and animal membranes is the **fluid-mosaic model** proposed in 1972 by S. J. Singer and G. Nicolson. The term *mosaic* signifies that the various components in the membrane coexist side by side, as discrete units, rather than combining to form new molecules or ions. "Fluid" signifies that the same sort of fluidity exists in membranes that we have already seen in lipid bilayers. Furthermore, the protein components of membranes "float" in the bilayer and can move laterally along the plane of the membrane.

Fluid-mosaic model A model of a biological membrane consisting of a phospholipid bilayer, with proteins, carbohydrates, and other lipids embedded in, and on the surface of, the bilayer.

19.4 What Are Steroids?

Steroids are a group of plant and animal lipids that have the tetracyclic ring system shown in Figure 19.8.

Steroid A plant or animal lipid having the characteristic tetracyclic ring structure of the steroid nucleus, namely, three six-membered rings and one five-membered ring.

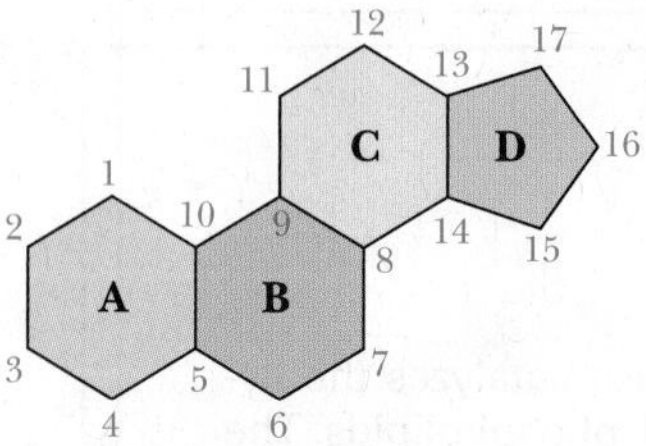

FIGURE 19.8
The tetracyclic ring system characteristic of steroids.

The features common to the tetracyclic ring system of most naturally occurring steroids are illustrated in Figure 19.9.

1. The fusion of the rings is *trans*, and each atom or group of atoms at a ring junction is axial. (Compare, for example, the orientations of —H at carbon 5 and $-CH_3$ at carbon 10.)
2. The pattern of atoms or groups along the points of ring fusion (carbons 5 to 10, 10 to 9, 9 to 8, 8 to 14, and 14 to 13) is nearly always *trans*–anti–*trans*–anti–*trans*.
3. Because of the *trans*–anti–*trans*–anti–*trans* arrangement of atoms or groups along the points of ring fusion, the tetracyclic steroid ring system is nearly flat and quite rigid.
4. Many steroids have axial methyl groups at carbon 10 and carbon 13 of the tetracyclic ring system.

A. Structure of the Major Classes of Steroids

Cholesterol

Cholesterol, a white, water-insoluble, waxy solid found in blood plasma and in all animal tissues, is an integral part of human metabolism in two ways:

1. It is an essential component of biological membranes. The body of a healthy adult contains approximately 140 g of cholesterol, about 120 g of which is present in membranes. Membranes of the central and peripheral nervous systems, for example, contain about 10% cholesterol by weight.
2. It is the compound from which sex hormones, adrenocorticoid hormones, bile acids, and vitamin D are synthesized. Thus, cholesterol is, in a sense, the parent steroid.

Cholesterol has eight stereocenters, and a molecule with this structural feature can exist as 2^8, or 256, stereoisomers (128 pairs of enantiomers). Only the stereoisomer shown here on the right is present in human metabolism:

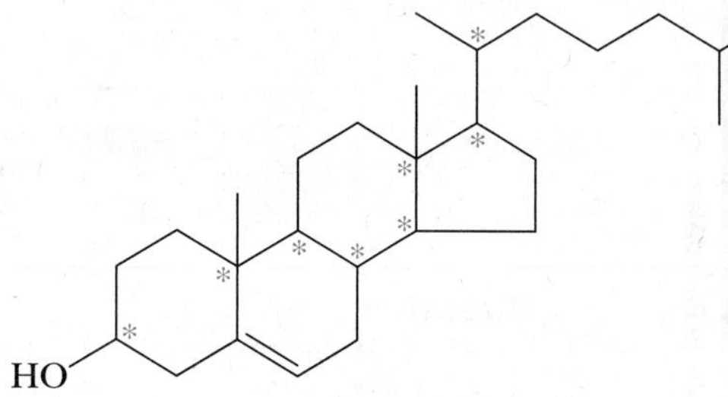

Cholesterol has eight stereocenters; 256 stereoisomers are possible

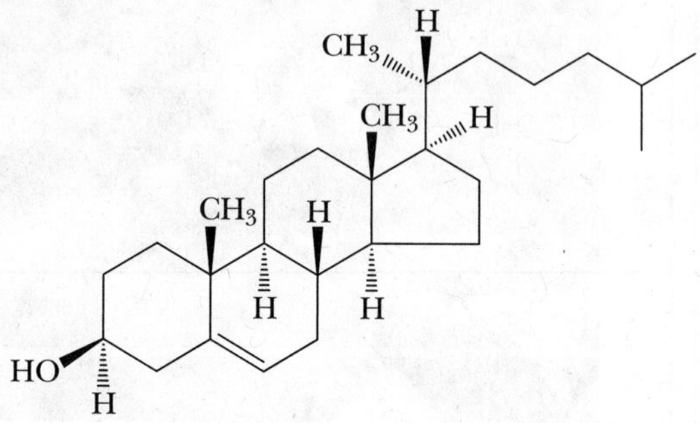

This is the stereoisomer found in human metabolism

Low-density lipoprotein (LDL) Plasma particles, of density 1.02–1.06 g/mL, consisting of approximately 25% proteins, 50% cholesterol, 21% phospholipids, and 4% triglycerides.

High-density lipoprotein (HDL) Plasma particles, of density 1.06–1.21 g/mL, consisting of approximately 33% proteins, 30% cholesterol, 29% phospholipids, and 8% triglycerides.

Cholesterol is insoluble in blood plasma, but can be transported as a plasma-soluble complex formed by cholesterol with proteins called lipoproteins. **Low-density lipoproteins (LDL)** transport cholesterol from the site of its synthesis in the liver to the various tissues and cells of the body where it is to be used. It is primarily cholesterol associated with LDLs that builds up in atherosclerotic deposits in blood vessels. **High-density lipoproteins (HDL)**

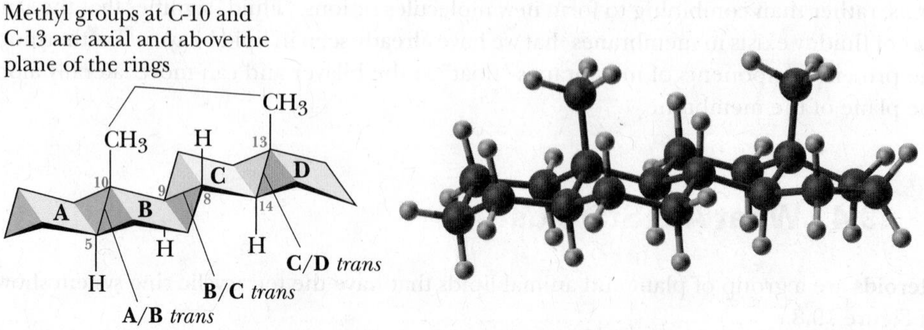

FIGURE 19.9
Features common to the tetracyclic ring system of many steroids.

transport excess and unused cholesterol from cells back to the liver to be degraded to bile acids and eventual excretion in the feces. It is thought that HDLs retard or reduce atherosclerotic deposits.

Estrogen A steroid hormone, such as estradiol, that mediates the development and sexual characteristics of females.

Androgen A steroid hormone, such as testosterone, that mediates the development and sexual characteristics of males.

Steroid Hormones

Shown in Table 19.4 are representatives of each major class of steroid hormones, along with their principal functions. Female steroid sex hormones are called **estrogens**, and male steroid sex hormones are called **androgens**.

After scientists understood the role of progesterone in inhibiting ovulation, they realized its potential as a contraceptive. Progesterone itself is relatively ineffective when taken orally. As a result of a massive research program in both industrial and academic laboratories,

TABLE 19.4 Selected Steroid Hormones

Structure	Source and Major Effects
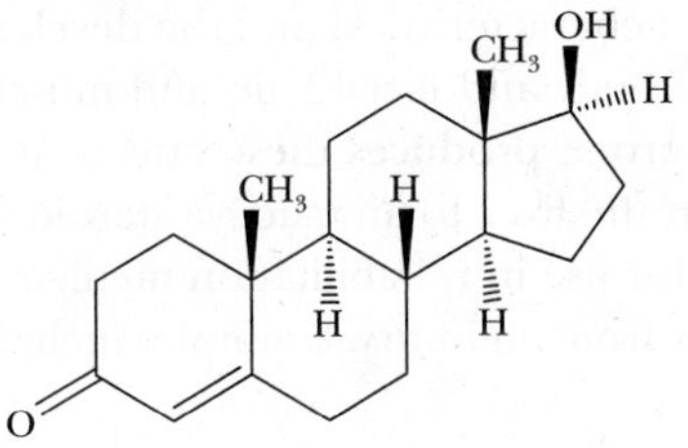 Testosterone 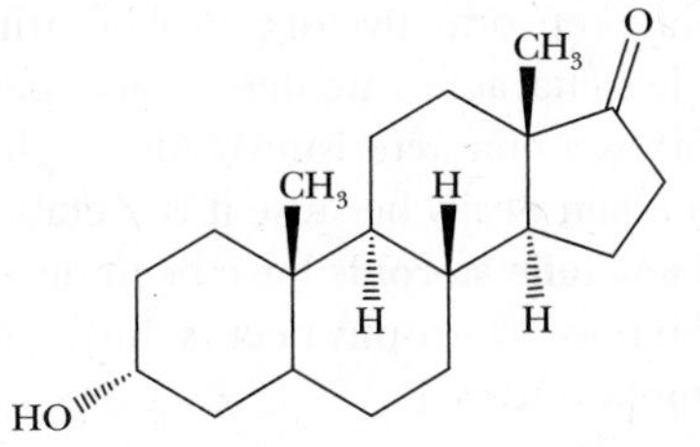 Androsterone	Androgens (male sex hormones): synthesized in the testes; responsible for development of male secondary sex characteristics
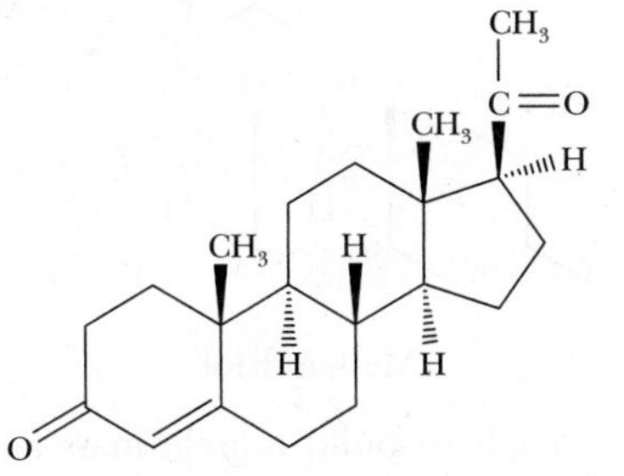 Progesterone 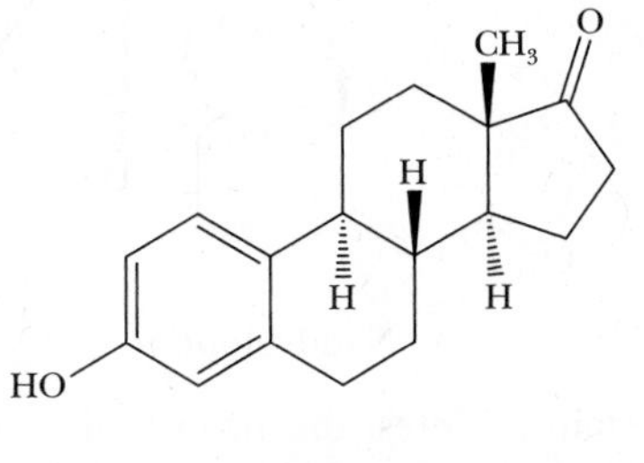 Estrone	Estrogens (female sex hormones): synthesized in the ovaries; responsible for development of female secondary sex characteristics and control of the menstrual cycle
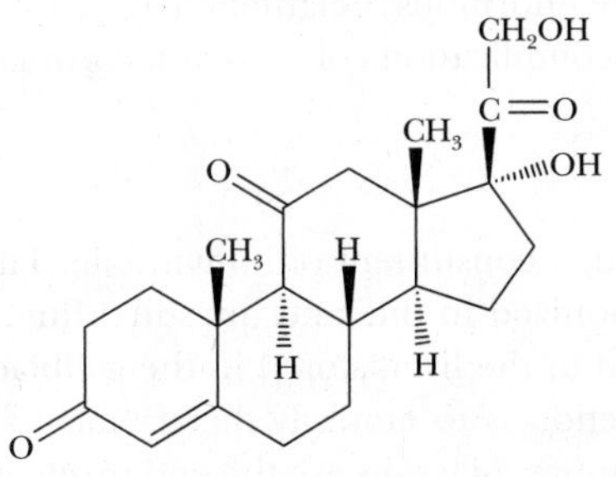 Cortisone 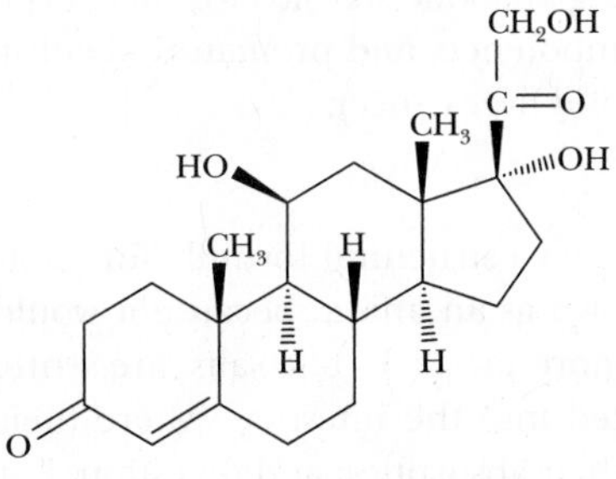 Cortisol	Glucocorticoid hormones: synthesized in the adrenal cortex; regulate metabolism of carbohydrates, decrease inflammation, and involved in the reaction to stress
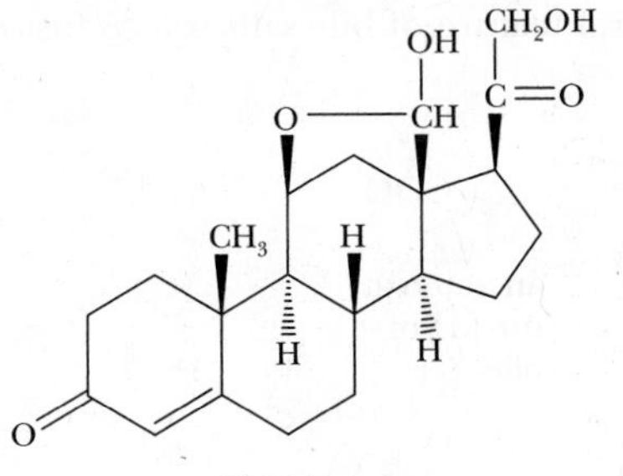 Aldosterone	A mineralocorticoid hormone: synthesized in the adrenal cortex; regulates blood pressure and volume by stimulating the kidneys to absorb Na^+, Cl^-, and HCO_3^-

many synthetic progesterone-mimicking steroids became available in the 1960s. Taken regularly, these drugs prevent ovulation yet allow women to maintain a normal menstrual cycle. Some of the most effective preparations contain a progesterone analog, such as norethindrone, combined with a smaller amount of an estrogenlike material to help prevent irregular menstrual flow during the prolonged use of contraceptive pills.

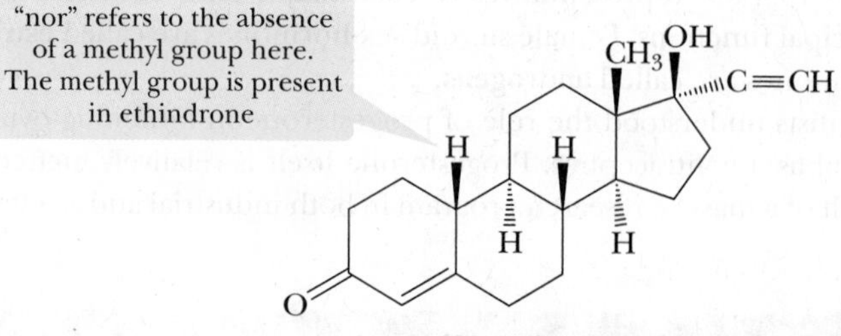

Norethindrone
(a synthetic progesterone analog)

The chief function of testosterone and other androgens is to promote the normal growth of the male reproductive organs (the primary sex characteristics) and the development of the male's characteristic deep voice, pattern of body and facial hair, and musculature (secondary sex characteristics). Although testosterone produces these effects, it is not active when taken orally because it is metabolized in the liver to an inactive steroid. A number of oral **anabolic steroids** have been developed for use in rehabilitation medicine, particularly when muscle atrophy occurs during recovery from an injury. Examples include the following compounds:

Anabolic steroid A steroid hormone, such as testosterone, that promotes tissue and muscle growth and development.

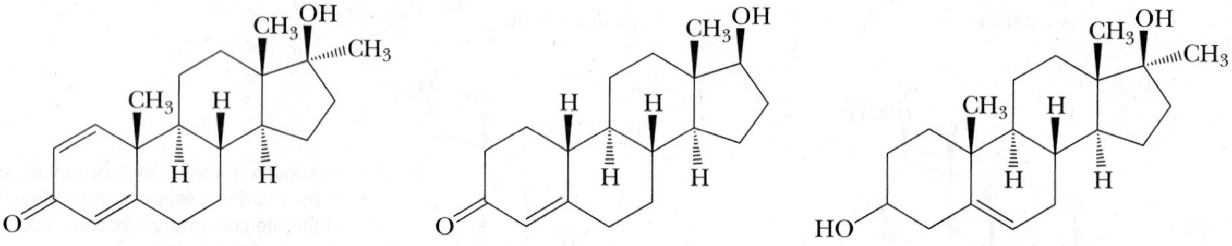

Methandrostenolone   Nandrolone   Methandriol

Among certain athletes, the misuse of anabolic steroids to build muscle mass and strength, particularly for sports that require explosive action, is common. The risks associated with abusing anabolic steroids for this purpose are enormous: heightened aggressiveness, sterility, impotence, and premature death from complications of diabetes, coronary artery disease, and liver cancer.

Bile Acids

Figure 19.10 shows a structural formula for cholic acid, a constituent of human bile. The molecule is shown as an anion, because it would be ionized in bile and intestinal fluids. **Bile acids**, or, more properly, bile salts, are synthesized in the liver, stored in the gallbladder, and secreted into the intestine, where their function is to emulsify dietary fats and thereby aid in their absorption and digestion. Furthermore, bile salts are the end products of the metabolism of cholesterol and, thus, are a principal pathway for the elimination of that substance from the body. A characteristic structural feature of bile salts is a *cis* fusion of rings A/B.

Bile acid A cholesterol-derived detergent molecule, such as cholic acid, that is secreted by the gallbladder into the intestine to assist in the absorption of dietary lipids.

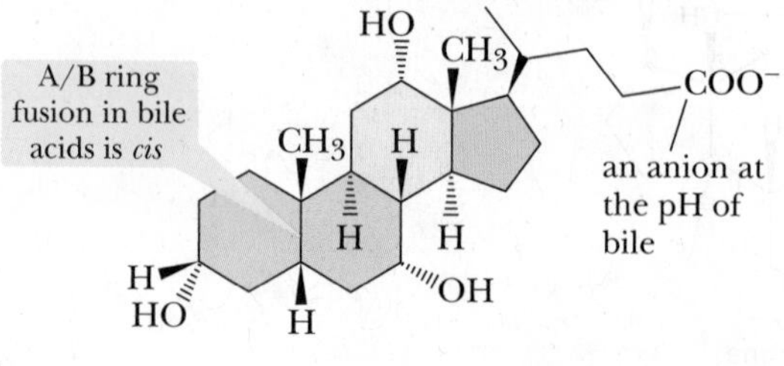

FIGURE 19.10
Cholic acid, an important constituent of human bile.

Chemical Connections 19B

NONSTEROIDAL ESTROGEN ANTAGONISTS

Estrogens are female sex hormones, the most important of which are estrone, estradiol, and estriol (of the three, β-estradiol is the most potent). (*Note:* As per convention in steroid nomenclature, the designation *beta* means "toward the reader," on the topside as the rings are viewed in the accompanying diagram; *alpha* means "away from the reader," on the bottom side.)

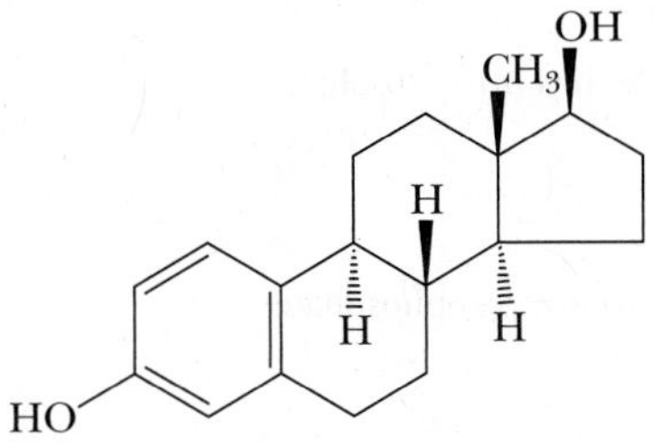

β-Estradiol

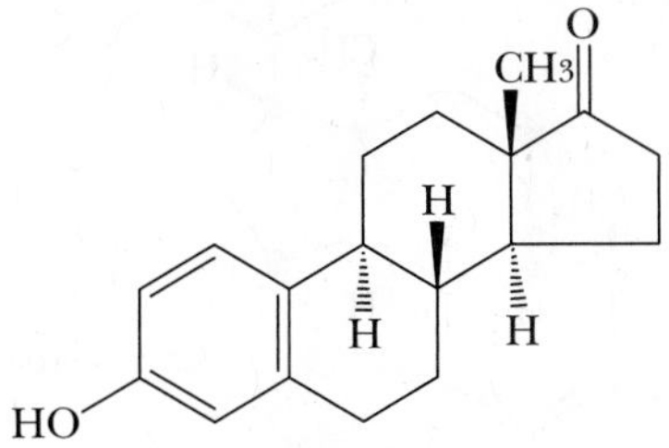

Estrone

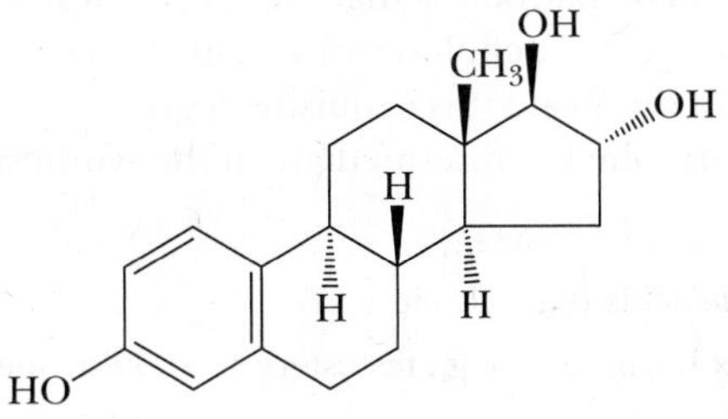

Estriol

As soon as these compounds were isolated in the early 1930s and their pharmacology was studied, it became clear that they are extremely potent. In recent years, there have been intense efforts to design and synthesize molecules that will bind to the estrogen receptor. One target of this research has been nonsteroidal estrogen antagonists—compounds that interact with estrogen receptors as antagonists (i.e., compounds that will block the effect of endogenous or exogenous estrogens). A feature common to many that have been developed is the presence of a 1,2-diphenylethylene, with one of the benzene rings bearing a dialkylaminoethoxyl substituent. The first nonsteroidal estrogen antagonist of this type to achieve clinical importance was tamoxifen, now an important drug in the prevention and treatment of breast cancer:

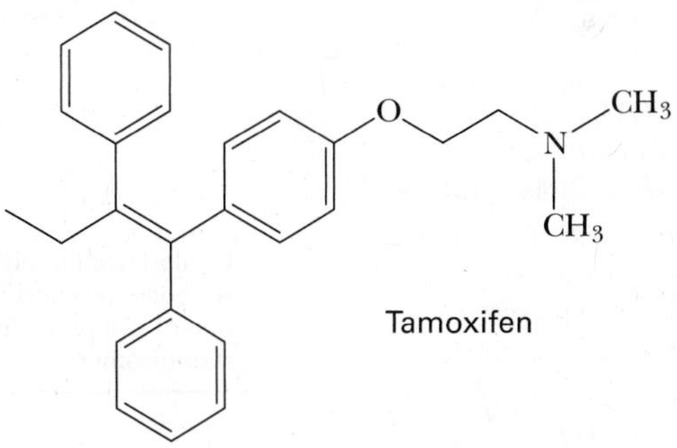

Tamoxifen

Questions

Determine the E/Z configuration of the carbon–carbon double bond in tamoxifen.

What is the role of progesterone and similar compounds in contraceptive pills?

B. Biosynthesis of Cholesterol

In building large molecules, one of the common patterns in the biological world is to begin with one or more smaller subunits, which are then joined by an iterative process and chemically modified by oxidation, reduction, cross-linking, addition, elimination, or related processes to give a biomolecule with a unique identity.

The building block from which all carbon atoms of steroids are derived is the two-carbon acetyl group of acetyl-CoA. Konrad Bloch of the United States and Feodor Lynen of Germany showed that 15 of the 27 carbon atoms of cholesterol are derived from the methyl group of acetyl-CoA; the remaining 12 carbon atoms are derived from the carbonyl group of acetyl-CoA (Figure 19.11). For their discoveries, the two shared the 1964 Nobel Prize in Physiology or Medicine.

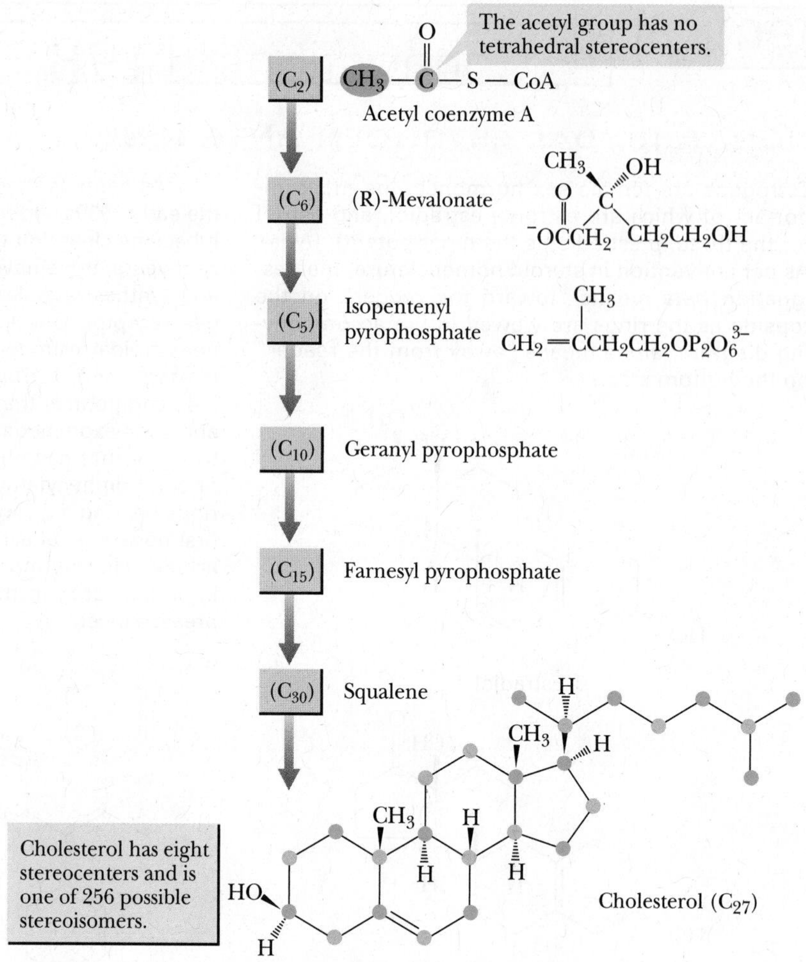

FIGURE 19.11 Several key intermediates in the synthesis of cholesterol from acetyl groups of acetyl-CoA. Eighteen moles of acetyl-CoA are required for the synthesis of 1 mole of cholesterol.

A remarkable feature of this synthetic pathway is that the biosynthesis of cholesterol from acetyl-CoA is completely stereoselective; cholesterol is synthesized as only one of 256 possible stereoisomers. We cannot duplicate this exquisite degree of stereoselectivity in the laboratory. Cholesterol is, in turn, the key intermediate in the synthesis of all other steroids:

cholesterol →
- bile acids (e.g., cholic acid)
- sex hormones (e.g., testosterone and estrone)
- mineralocorticoid hormones (e.g., aldosterone)
- glucocorticoid hormones (e.g., cortisone)

19.5 What Are Prostaglandins?

Prostaglandin A member of the family of compounds having the 20-carbon skeleton of prostanoic acid.

The **prostaglandins** are a family of compounds having in common the 20-carbon skeleton of prostanoic acid:

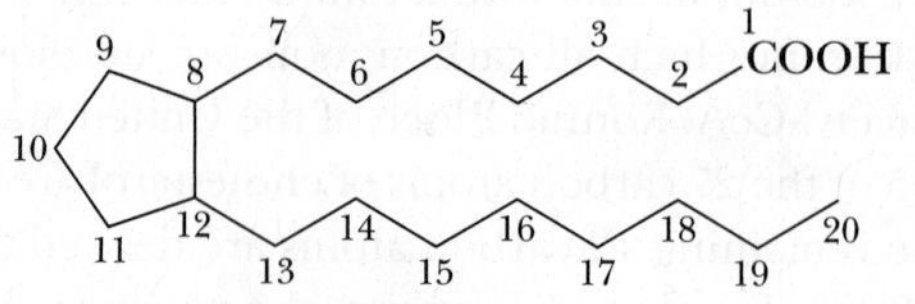

Prostanoic acid

The story of the discovery and structure determination of these remarkable compounds began in 1930 when gynecologists Raphael Kurzrock and Charles Lieb reported that human seminal fluid stimulates the contraction of isolated uterine muscle. A few years later, Ulf von Euler in Sweden confirmed this report and noted that, when injected into the bloodstream, human seminal fluid also stimulates the contraction of intestinal smooth muscle and lowers the blood pressure. Von Euler proposed the name *prostaglandin* for the mysterious substance(s) responsible for these diverse effects, because it was believed at the time that they were synthesized in the prostate gland. Although we now know that prostaglandin production is by no means limited to the prostate gland, the name has stuck.

Prostaglandins are not stored as such in target tissues. Rather, they are synthesized in response to specific physiological triggers. Starting materials for the biosynthesis of prostaglandins are polyunsaturated fatty acids with 20 carbon atoms, stored until they are needed as membrane phospholipid esters. In response to a physiological trigger, the ester is hydrolyzed, the fatty acid is released, and the synthesis of prostaglandins is initiated. Figure 19.12 outlines the steps in the synthesis of several prostaglandins from arachidonic acid. A key step in this biosynthesis is the enzyme-catalyzed reaction of arachidonic acid with two molecules of O_2 to form prostaglandin G_2 (PGG_2). The anti-inflammatory effect of aspirin and other nonsteroidal anti-inflammatory drugs (NSAIDs) results from their ability to inhibit the enzyme that catalyzes this step.

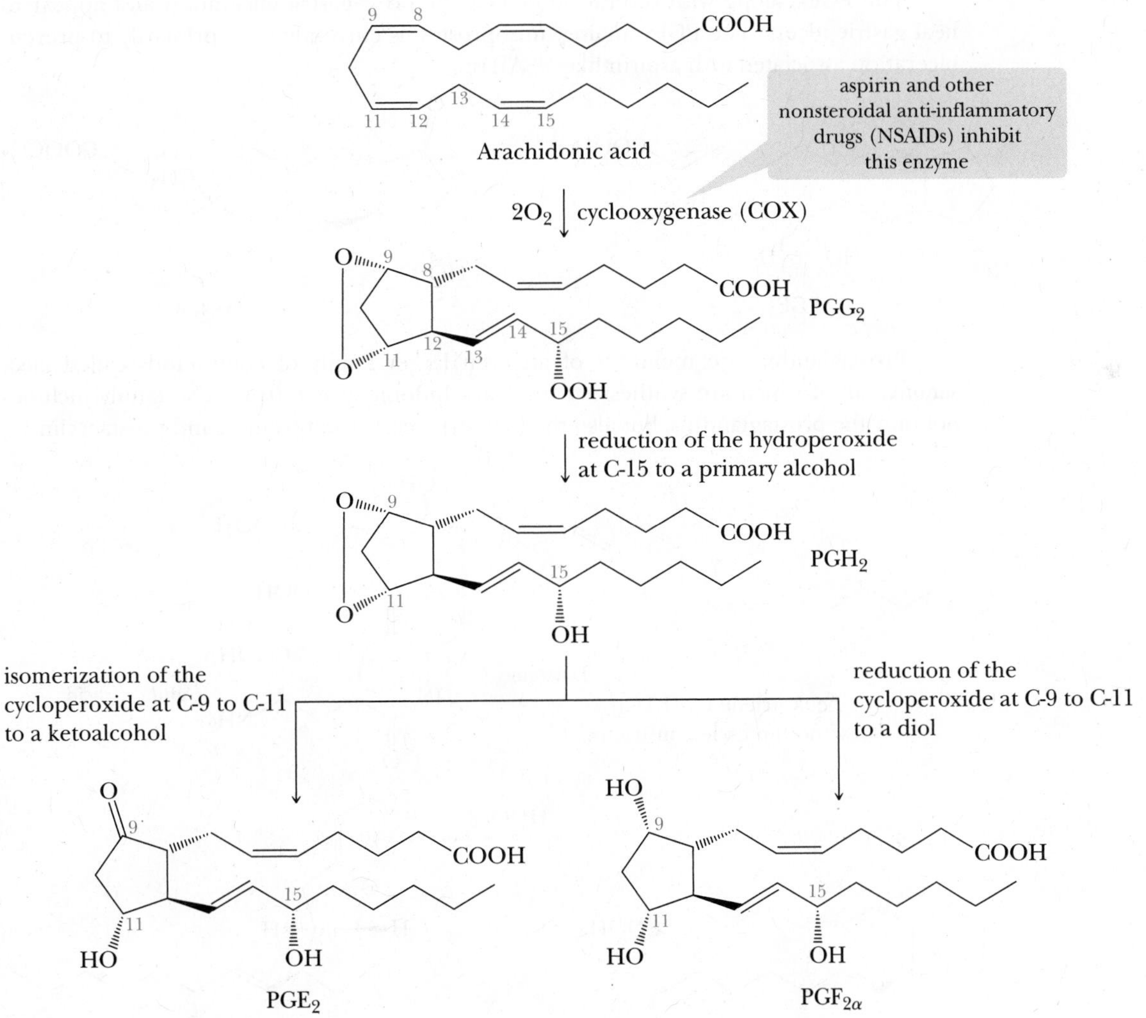

FIGURE 19.12
Key intermediates in the conversion of arachidonic acid to PGE_2 and $PGF_{2\alpha}$. PG stands for prostaglandin. The letters E, F, G, and H are different types of prostaglandins.

Research on the involvement of prostaglandins in reproductive physiology and the inflammatory process has produced several clinically useful prostaglandin derivatives. The observation that $PGF_{2\alpha}$ stimulates contractions of uterine smooth muscle led to a synthetic derivative that is used for therapeutic abortions. A problem with the use of the natural prostaglandins for this purpose is that they are rapidly degraded within the body. In the search for less rapidly degraded prostaglandins, a number of analogs have been prepared, one of the most effective of which is carboprost. This synthetic prostaglandin is 10 to 20 times more potent than the natural $PGF_{2\alpha}$ and is only slowly degraded in the body:

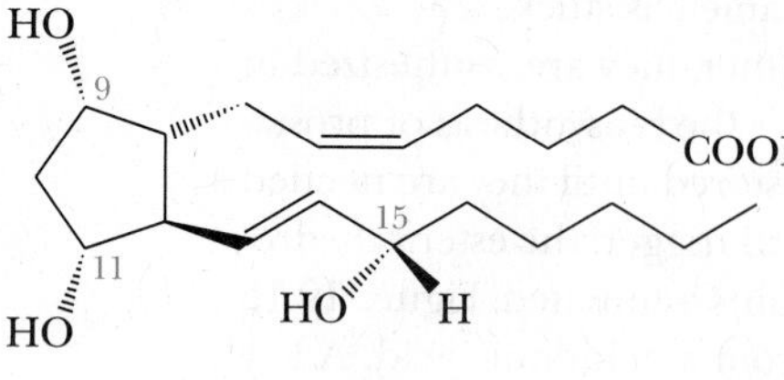

$PGF_{2\alpha}$

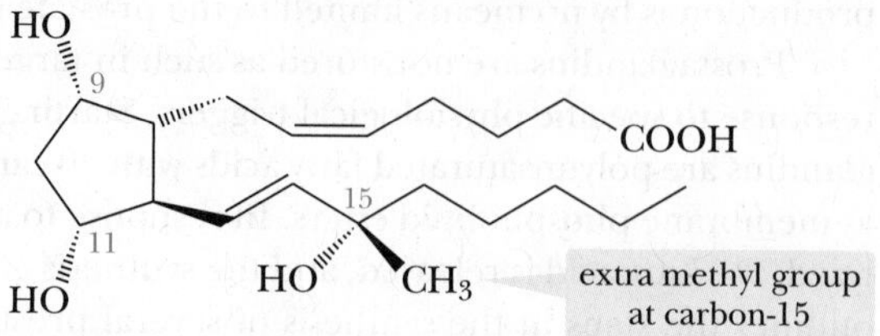

Carboprost
(15*S*)-15-Methyl-$PGF_{2\alpha}$

A comparison of these two prostaglandins illustrates how a simple change in the structure of a drug can make a significant change in its effectiveness.

The PGEs, along with several other PGs, suppress gastric ulceration and appear to heal gastric ulcers. The PGE_1 analog, misoprostol, is currently used primarily to prevent ulceration associated with aspirin-like NSAIDs:

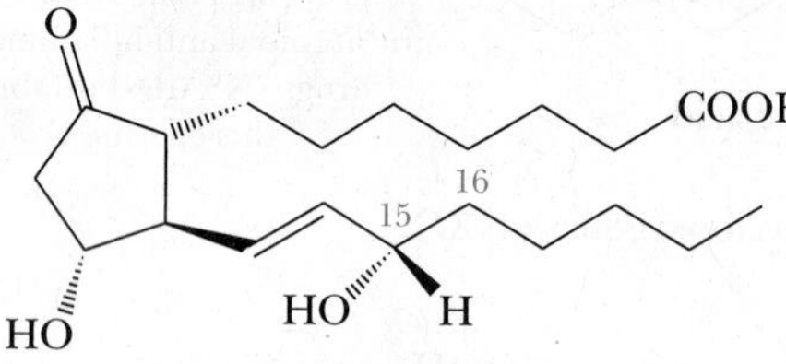

PGE_1

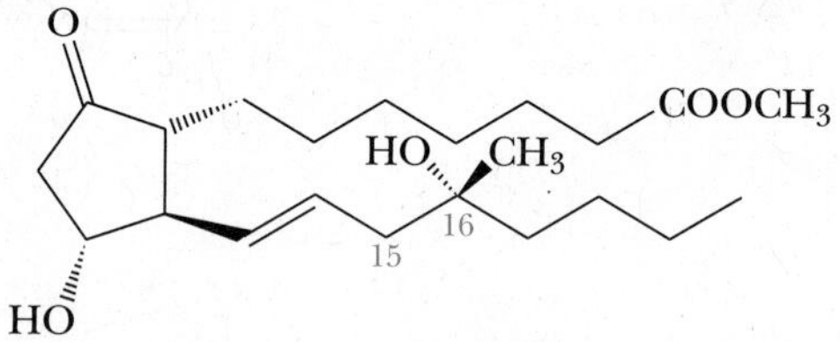

Misoprostol

Prostaglandins are members of an even larger family of compounds called **eicosanoids**, all of which are synthesized from arachidonic acid (20:4). The family includes not only the prostaglandins, but also the leukotrienes, thromboxanes, and prostacyclins:

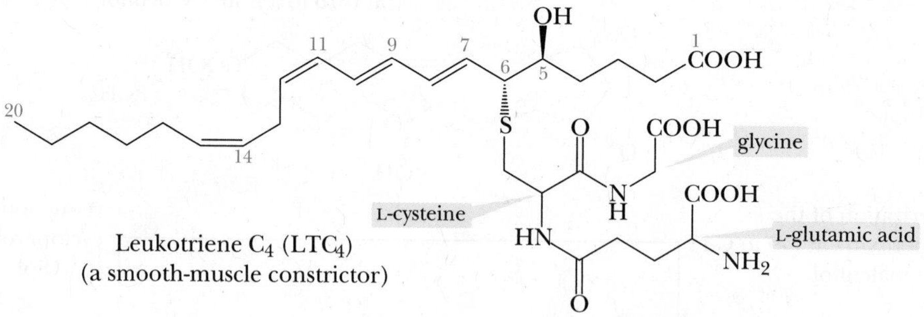

Leukotriene C_4 (LTC_4)
(a smooth-muscle constrictor)

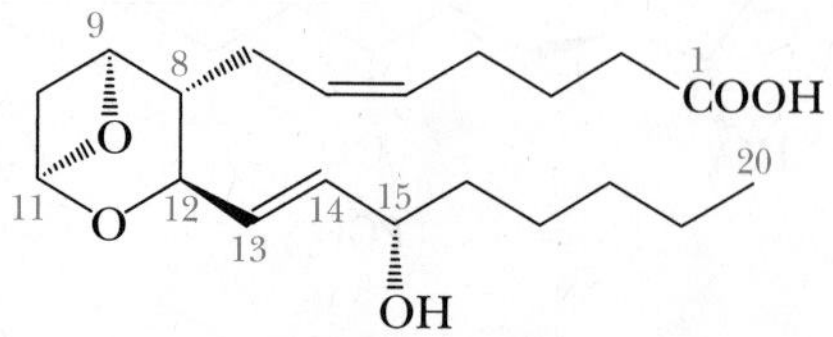

Thromboxane A_2
(a potent vasoconstrictor)

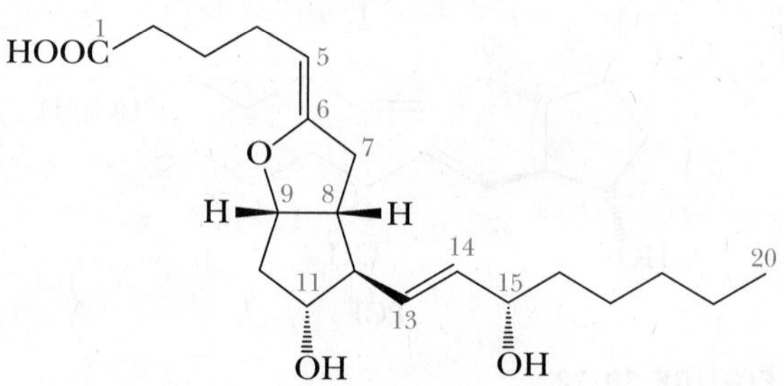

Prostacyclin
(a platelet aggregation inhibitor)

The eicosanoids are extremely widespread, and members of this family of compounds have been isolated from almost every tissue and body fluid.

Leukotrienes are derived from arachidonic acid and are found primarily in leukocytes (white blood cells). Leukotriene C_4 (LTC_4), a typical member of the family, has three conjugated double bonds (hence the suffix *-triene*) and contains the amino acids L-cysteine, glycine, and L-glutamic acid (Section 18.2). An important physiological action of LTC_4 is the constriction of smooth muscles, especially those of the lungs. The synthesis and release of LTC_4 is prompted by allergic reactions. Drugs that inhibit the synthesis of LTC_4 show promise for the treatment of the allergic reactions associated with asthma.

Thromboxane A_2, a potent vasoconstrictor, is also synthesized in the body from arachidonic acid. Its release triggers the irreversible phase of platelet aggregation and the constriction of injured blood vessels. It is thought that aspirin and aspirin-like drugs act as mild anticoagulants because they inhibit cyclooxygenase, the enzyme that initiates the synthesis of thromboxane A_2 from arachidonic acid.

19.6 What Are Fat-Soluble Vitamins?

Vitamins are divided into two broad classes on the basis of their solubility: those that are fat soluble (and hence classed as lipids) and those that are water soluble. The fat-soluble vitamins are A, D, E, and K.

A. Vitamin A

Vitamin A, or retinol, occurs only in the animal world, where the best sources are cod-liver oil and other fish-liver oils, animal liver, and dairy products. Vitamin A in the form of a precursor, or provitamin, is found in the plant world in a group of tetraterpene (C_{40}) pigments called carotenes. The most common of these is β-carotene, abundant in carrots, but also found in some other vegetables, particularly yellow and green ones. β-Carotene has no vitamin A activity; however, after ingestion, it is cleaved at the central carbon–carbon double bond to give retinol (vitamin A):

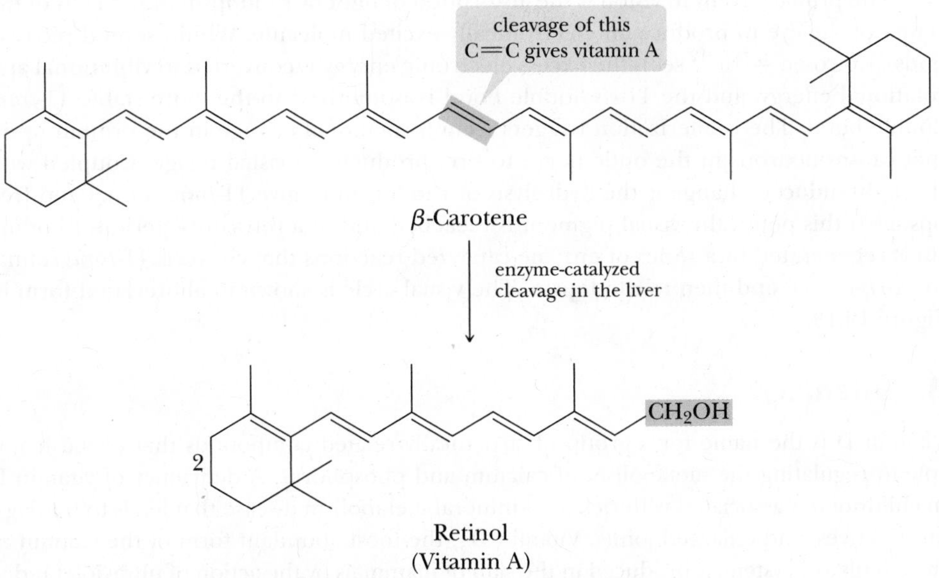

Probably the best understood role of vitamin A is its participation in the visual cycle in rod cells. In a series of enzyme-catalyzed reactions retinol undergoes (1) a two-electron

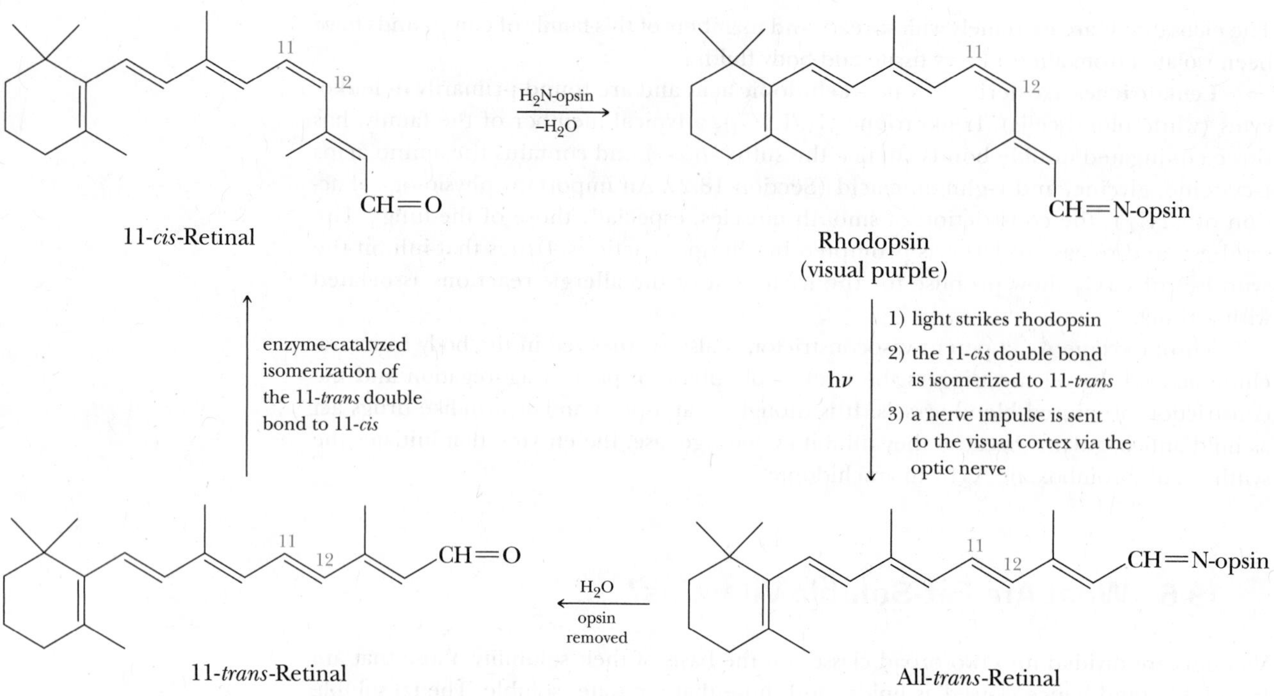

FIGURE 19.13
The primary chemical reaction of vision in rod cells is the absorption of light by rhodopsin, followed by the isomerization of a carbon–carbon double bond from a *cis* configuration to a *trans* configuration.

oxidation to all-*trans*-retinal and (2) isomerization about the carbon 11 to carbon 12 double bond to give 11-*cis*-retinal, (3) thereby forming an imine (Section 12.7A) with the $-NH_2$ from a lysine unit of the protein opsin. The product of these reactions is rhodopsin, a highly conjugated pigment that shows intense absorption in the blue-green region of the visual spectrum.

The primary event in vision is the absorption of light by rhodopsin in rod cells of the retina of the eye to produce an electronically excited molecule. Within several picoseconds (1 picosec $= 10^{-12}$ sec), the excess electronic energy is converted to vibrational and rotational energy, and the 11-*cis* double bond is isomerized to the more stable 11-*trans* double bond. The isomerization triggers a conformational change in the protein opsin that causes neurons in the optic nerve to fire, producing a visual image. Coupled with this light-induced change is the hydrolysis of rhodopsin to give 11-*trans*-retinal and free opsin. At this point, the visual pigment is bleached and in a refractory period. Rhodopsin is regenerated by a series of enzyme-catalyzed reactions that converts 11-*trans*-retinal to 11-*cis*-retinal and then to rhodopsin. The visual cycle is shown in abbreviated form in Figure 19.13.

B. Vitamin D

Vitamin D is the name for a group of structurally related compounds that play a major role in regulating the metabolism of calcium and phosphorus. A deficiency of vitamin D in childhood is associated with rickets, a mineral-metabolism disease that leads to bowlegs, knock-knees, and enlarged joints. Vitamin D_3, the most abundant form of the vitamin in the circulatory system, is produced in the skin of mammals by the action of ultraviolet radiation on 7-dehydrocholesterol (cholesterol with a double bond between carbons 7 and 8). In the liver, vitamin D_3 undergoes an enzyme-catalyzed, two-electron oxidation at carbon 25 of the side chain to form 25-hydroxyvitamin D_3; the oxidizing agent is molecular oxygen, O_2.

25-Hydroxyvitamin D_3 undergoes further oxidation in the kidneys, also by O_2, to form 1,25-dihydroxyvitamin D_3, the hormonally active form of the vitamin:

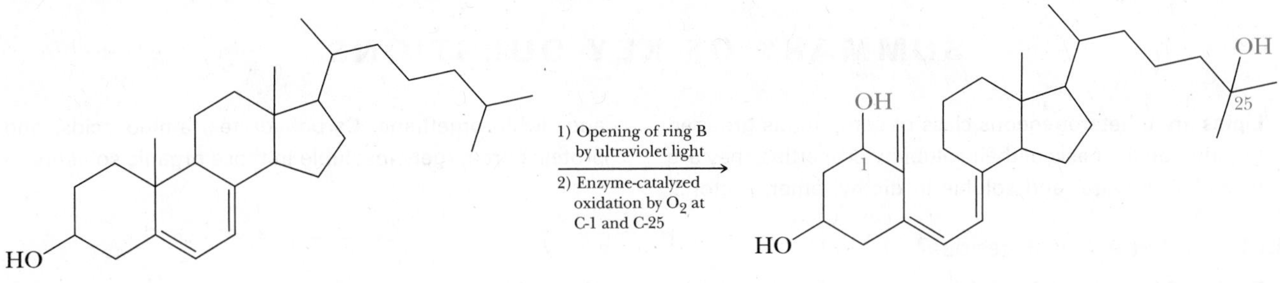

7-Dehydrocholesterol 1,25-Dihydroxyvitamin D_3

C. Vitamin E

Vitamin E was first recognized in 1922 as a dietary factor essential for normal reproduction in rats—hence its name *tocopherol*, from the Greek *tocos*, birth, and *pherein*, to bring about. Vitamin E is a group of compounds of similar structure, the most active of which is α-tocopherol:

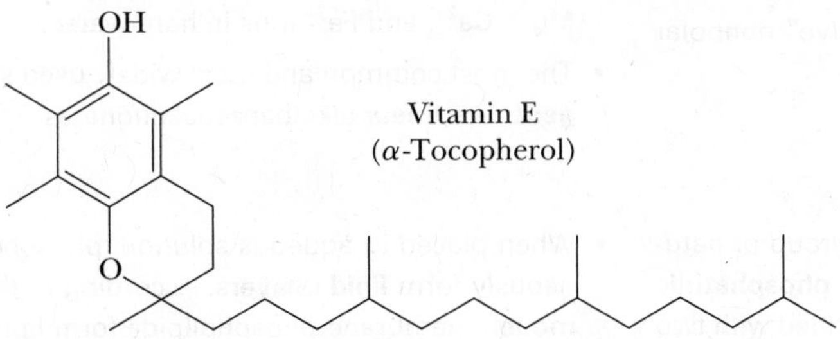

Vitamin E
(α-Tocopherol)

Vitamin E occurs in fish oil; in other oils, such as cottonseed and peanut oil; and in leafy, green vegetables. The richest source is wheat germ oil.

In the body, vitamin E functions as an antioxidant, trapping peroxy radicals of the type HOO· and ROO· formed as a result of enzyme-catalyzed oxidation by molecular oxygen of the unsaturated hydrocarbon chains in membrane phospholipids. There is speculation that peroxy radicals play a role in the aging process and that vitamin E and other antioxidants may retard that process. Vitamin E is also necessary for the proper development and function of the membranes of red blood cells.

D. Vitamin K

The name of this vitamin comes from the German word *koagulation*, signifying its important role in the blood-clotting process. A deficiency of vitamin K results in slowed blood clotting. Natural vitamins of the K family have, for the most part, been replaced in vitamin supplements by synthetic preparations. Menadione, one such synthetic material that exhibits vitamin K activity, has a hydrogen in place of the alkyl chain:

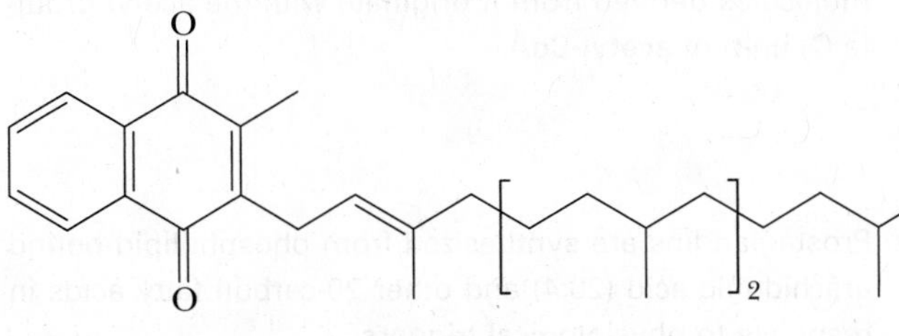

Vitamin K_1

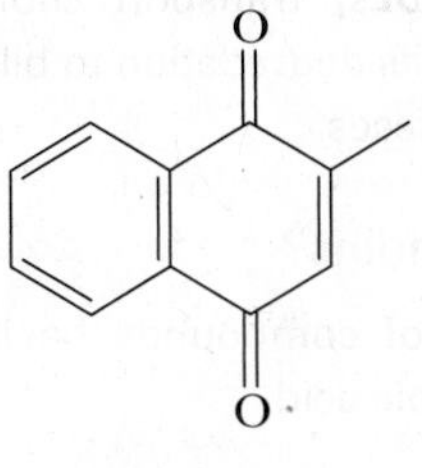

Menadione
(a synthetic vitamin K analog)

SUMMARY OF KEY QUESTIONS

- **Lipids** are a heterogeneous class of compounds grouped together on the basis of their solubility properties; they are insoluble in water and soluble in diethyl ether, acetone, and dichloromethane. Carbohydrates, amino acids, and proteins are largely insoluble in these organic solvents.

19.1 What Are Triglycerides?

- **Triglycerides (triacylglycerols)**, the most abundant lipids, are triesters of glycerol and fatty acids.
- **Fatty acids** are long-chain carboxylic acids derived from the hydrolysis of **fats**, **oils**, and the **phospholipids** of biological membranes.
- The melting point of a triglyceride increases as (1) the length of its hydrocarbon chains increases and (2) its degree of saturation increases.
- Triglycerides rich in saturated fatty acids are generally solids at room temperature; those rich in unsaturated fatty acids are generally oils at room temperature.

19.2 What Are Soaps and Detergents?

- **Soaps** are sodium or potassium salts of fatty acids.
- In water, soaps form **micelles**, which "dissolve" nonpolar organic grease and oil.
- Natural soaps precipitate as water-insoluble salts with Mg^{2+}, Ca^{2+}, and Fe^{3+} ions in hard water.
- The most common and most widely used **synthetic detergents** are linear alkylbenzenesulfonates.

19.3 What Are Phospholipids?

- **Phospholipids**, the second most abundant group of naturally occurring lipids, are derived from **phosphatidic acids**—compounds containing glycerol esterified with two molecules of fatty acid and a molecule of phosphoric acid.
- Further esterification of the phosphoric acid part with a low-molecular-weight alcohol—most commonly, ethanolamine, choline, serine, or inositol—gives a phospholipid.
- When placed in aqueous solution, phospholipids spontaneously form **lipid bilayers**. According to the **fluid-mosaic model**, membrane phospholipids form lipid bilayers with membrane proteins associated with the bilayer as both peripheral and integral proteins.

19.4 What Are Steroids?

- **Steroids** are a group of plant and animal lipids that have a characteristic tetracyclic structure of three six-membered rings and one five-membered ring.
- **Cholesterol**, an integral part of animal membranes, is the compound from which human sex hormones, adrenocorticoid hormones, bile acids, and vitamin D are synthesized.
- **Low-density lipoproteins (LDLs)** transport cholesterol from the site of its synthesis in the liver to tissues and cells where it is to be used.
- **High-density lipoproteins (HDLs)** transport cholesterol from cells back to the liver for its degradation to bile acids and eventual excretion in the feces.
- **Oral contraceptive** pills contain a synthetic progestin (e.g., norethindrone) that prevents ovulation, yet allows women to maintain an otherwise normal menstrual cycle.
- A variety of synthetic **anabolic steroids** are available for use in rehabilitation medicine to treat muscle tissue that has weakened or deteriorated due to injury.
- **Bile acids** differ from most other steroids in that they have a *cis* configuration at the junction of rings A and B.
- The carbon skeleton of cholesterol and those of all biomolecules derived from it originate with the acetyl group (a C_2 unit) of **acetyl-CoA**.

19.5 What Are Prostaglandins?

- **Prostaglandins** are a group of compounds having the 20-carbon skeleton of prostanoic acid.
- Prostaglandins are synthesized from phospholipid-bound arachidonic acid (20:4) and other 20-carbon fatty acids in response to physiological triggers.

19.6 What Are Fat-Soluble Vitamins?

- **Vitamin A** occurs only in the animal world. The carotenes of the plant world are tetraterpenes (C_{40}) and are cleaved into vitamin A after ingestion. The best-understood role of vitamin A is its participation in the **visual cycle**.
- **Vitamin D** is synthesized in the skin of mammals by the action of ultraviolet radiation on 7-dehydrocholesterol. This vitamin plays a major role in the regulation of calcium and phosphorus metabolism.
- **Vitamin E** is a group of compounds of similar structure, the most active of which is α-tocopherol. In the body, vitamin E functions as an antioxidant.
- **Vitamin K** is required for the clotting of blood.

QUICK QUIZ

Answer true or false to the following questions to assess your general knowledge of the concepts in this chapter. If you have difficulty with any of them, you should review the appropriate section in the chapter (shown in parentheses) before attempting the more challenging end-of-chapter problems.

1. Prostaglandins are formed in response to certain biological triggers. (19.5)
2. A fatty acid consists of a carboxyl group on the end of a long hydrocarbon chain. (19.1)
3. Vitamin D is synthesized from a steroid. (19.6)
4. All steroids have the same tetracyclic ring system in common. (19.4)
5. Fatty acids with high melting points are called oils, while fatty acids with low melting points are called fats. (19.1)
6. Steroids are achiral molecules. (19.4)
7. Synthetic detergents are based on fatty acids where the carboxylate group has been replaced by a sulfonate group. (19.2)
8. According to the fluid-mosaic model, proteins in lipid bilayers are stationary and cannot move around. (19.3)
9. Phospholipids organize into micelles in aqueous solution. (19.2)
10. The greater the degree of unsaturation in a fatty acid, the higher is its melting point. (19.1)
11. The function of both low- and high-density lipoproteins is to transport cholesterol throughout the body. (19.4)
12. A fatty acid that has been deprotonated and coordinated with a sodium ion can act as a soap. (19.2)
13. Bile acids differ from most other steroids in the number of their rings. (19.4)
14. Treatment of a triglyceride with aqueous base followed by acidification yields glycerol and up to three fatty acids. (19.1)
15. Vitamin A can be synthesized from β-carotene. (19.6)
16. In fatty acids with C—C double bonds, the *trans* form of each double bond predominates. (19.1)

Detailed explanations for many of these answers can be found in the accompanying Solutions Manual.
Answers: (1) T (2) T (3) T (4) T (5) F (6) F (7) T (8) F (9) F (10) F (11) T (12) T (13) F (14) T (15) T (16) F

PROBLEMS

A problem marked with an asterisk indicates an applied "real-world" problem. Answers to problems whose numbers are printed in blue are given in Appendix D.

Section 19.1 Fatty Acids and Triglycerides

19.2 Define the term *hydrophobic.*

19.3 Identify the hydrophobic and hydrophilic region(s) of a triglyceride.

19.4 Explain why the melting points of unsaturated fatty acids are lower than those of saturated fatty acids.

19.5 Oleic acid has a melting point of 16 °C. If you were to convert the *cis* double bond to a *trans* double bond, what would happen to the melting point?

19.6 Which would you expect to have the higher melting point, glyceryl trioleate or glyceryl trilinoleate?

19.7 Which animal fat has the highest percentage of unsaturated fatty acids? Which plant oil has the highest percentage of unsaturated fatty acids?

19.8 Draw a structural formula for methyl linoleate. Be certain to show the correct configuration of groups about each carbon–carbon double bond. **(See Example 19.1)**

***19.9** Explain why coconut oil is a liquid triglyceride, even though most of its fatty-acid components are saturated.

***19.10** It is common now to see "contains no tropical oils" on cooking-oil labels, meaning that the oil contains no palm or coconut oil. What is the difference between the composition of tropical oils and that of vegetable oils, such as corn oil, soybean oil, and peanut oil?

*19.11 What is meant by the term *hardening* as applied to vegetable oils?

19.12 How many moles of H_2 are used in the catalytic hydrogenation of 1 mole of a triglyceride derived from glycerol, stearic acid, linoleic acid, and arachidonic acid?

19.13 Characterize the structural features necessary to make a good synthetic detergent.

*19.14 Following are structural formulas for a cationic detergent and a neutral detergent:

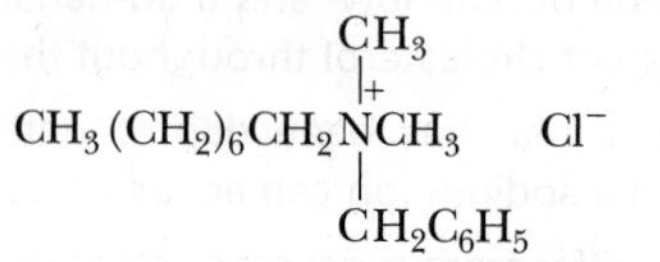

Benzyldimethyloctylammonium chloride
(a cationic detergent)

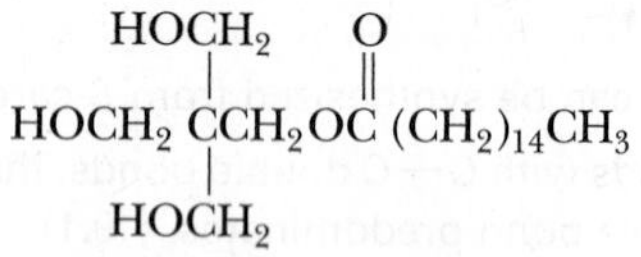

Pentaerythrityl palmitate
(a neutral detergent)

Account for the detergent properties of each.

*19.15 Identify some of the detergents used in shampoos and dishwashing liquids. Are they primarily anionic, neutral, or cationic detergents?

19.16 Show how to convert palmitic acid (hexadecanoic acid) into the following:

(a) Ethyl palmitate
(b) Palmitoyl chloride
(c) 1-Hexadecanol (cetyl alcohol)
(d) 1-Hexadecanamine
(e) *N*,*N*-Dimethylhexadecanamide

*19.17 Palmitic acid (hexadecanoic acid, 16:0) is the source of the hexadecyl (cetyl) group in the following compounds:

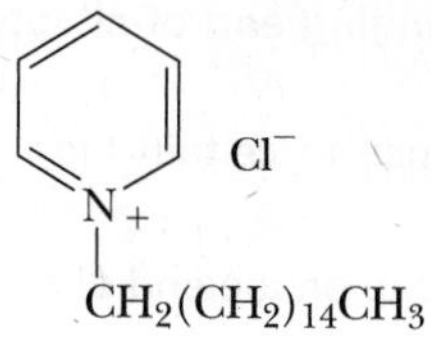

Cetylpyridinium chloride

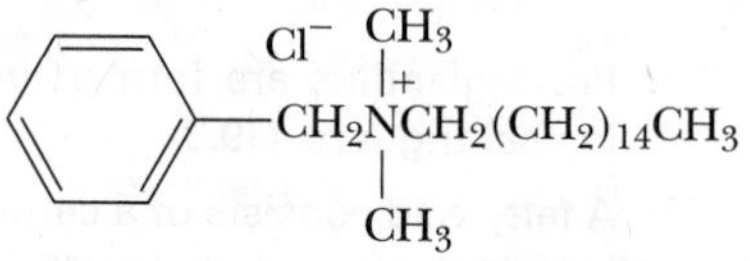

Benzylcetyldimethylammonium chloride

Each compound is a mild surface-acting germicide and fungicide and is used as a topical antiseptic and disinfectant.

(a) Cetylpyridinium chloride is prepared by treating pyridine with 1-chlorohexadecane (cetyl chloride). Show how to convert palmitic acid to cetyl chloride.
(b) Benzylcetyldimethylammonium chloride is prepared by treating benzyl chloride with *N*,*N*-dimethyl-1-hexadecanamine. Show how this tertiary amine can be prepared from palmitic acid.

Section 19.3 Phospholipids

19.18 Draw the structural formula of a lecithin containing one molecule each of palmitic acid and linoleic acid.

19.19 Identify the hydrophobic and hydrophilic region(s) of a phospholipid.

*19.20 The hydrophobic effect is one of the most important noncovalent forces directing the self-assembly of biomolecules in aqueous solution. The hydrophobic effect arises from tendencies of biomolecules (1) to arrange polar groups so that they interact with the aqueous environment by hydrogen bonding and (2) to arrange nonpolar groups so that they are shielded from the aqueous environment. Show how the hydrophobic effect is involved in directing

(a) The formation of micelles by soaps and detergents.
(b) The formation of lipid bilayers by phospholipids.
(c) The formation of the DNA double helix.

19.21 How does the presence of unsaturated fatty acids contribute to the fluidity of biological membranes?

*19.22 Lecithins can act as emulsifying agents. The lecithin of egg yolk, for example, is used to make mayonnaise. Identify the hydrophobic part(s) and the hydrophilic part(s) of a lecithin. Which parts interact with the oils used in making mayonnaise? Which parts interact with the water?

Section 19.4 Steroids

19.23 Draw the structural formula for the product formed by treating cholesterol (a) with H_2/Pd; (b) with Br_2.

*19.24 List several ways in which cholesterol is essential for human life. Why do many people find it necessary to restrict their dietary intake of cholesterol?

19.25 Both low-density lipoproteins (LDL) and high-density lipoproteins (HDL) consist of a core of triacylglycerols and cholesterol esters surrounded by a single phospholipid layer. Draw the structural formula of cholesteryl linoleate, one of the cholesterol esters found in this core.

*19.26 Examine the structural formulas of testosterone (a male sex hormone) and progesterone (a female sex hormone). What are the similarities in structure between the two? What are the differences?

*19.27 Examine the structural formula of cholic acid, and account for the ability of this bile salt and others to emulsify fats and oils and thus aid in their digestion.

19.28 Following is a structural formula for cortisol (hydrocortisone):

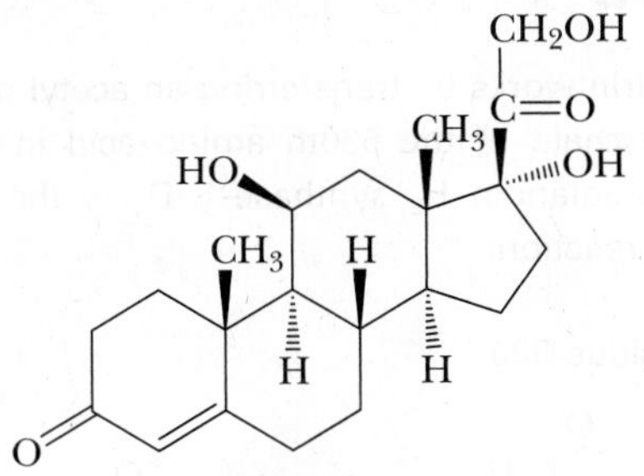

Cortisol
(Hydrocortisone)

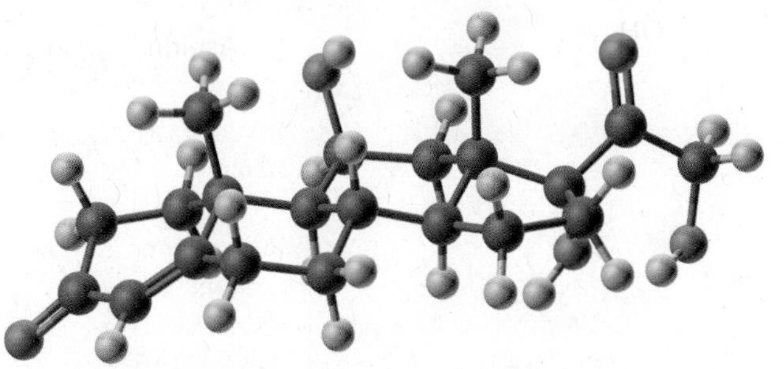

Draw a stereorepresentation of this molecule, showing the conformations of the five- and six-membered rings.

*19.29 How does the oral anabolic steroid methandrostenolone differ structurally from testosterone?

*19.30 Because some types of tumors need estrogen to survive, compounds that compete with the estrogen receptor on tumor cells are useful anticancer drugs. The compound tamoxifen is one such drug. To what part of the estrone molecule is the shape of tamoxifen similar?

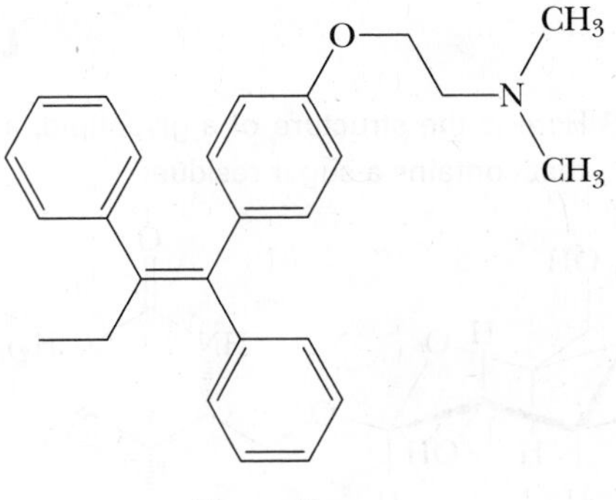

Tamoxifen

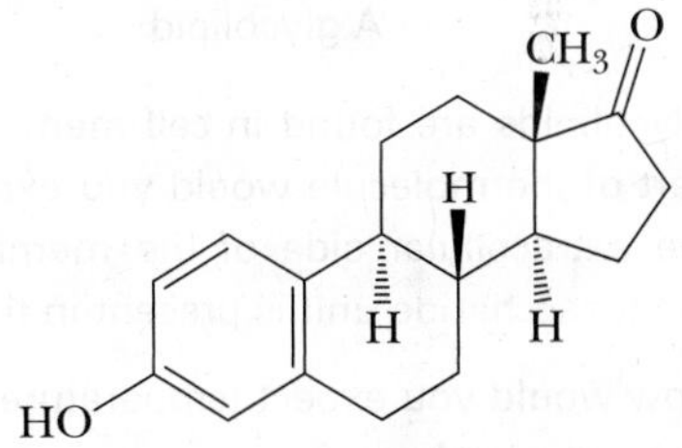

Estrone

19.31 Estradiol in the body is synthesized from progesterone. What chemical modifications occur when estradiol is synthesized?

Section 19.5 Prostaglandins

19.32 Examine the structure of $PGF_{2\alpha}$, and

(a) identify all stereocenters.

(b) identify all double bonds about which *cis,trans* isomerism is possible.

(c) state the number of stereoisomers possible for a molecule of this structure.

*19.33 Following is the structure of unoprostone, a compound patterned after the natural prostaglandins (Section 19.5):

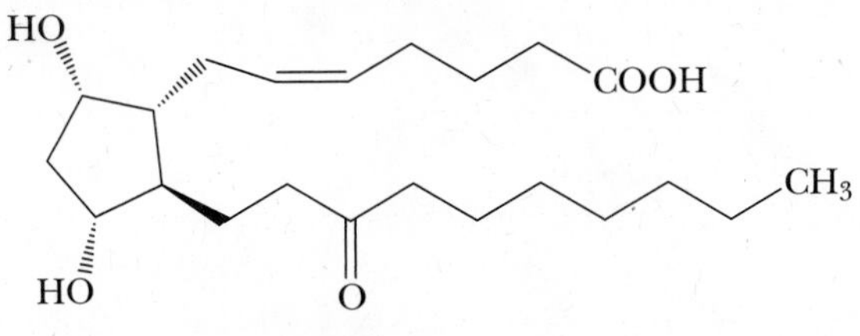

Unoprostone
(antiglaucoma)

Rescula, the isopropyl ester of unoprostone, is an antiglaucoma drug used to treat ocular hypertension. Compare the structural formula of this synthetic prostaglandin with that of $PGF_{2\alpha}$.

*19.34 How does aspirin, an anti-inflammatory drug, prevent strokes caused by blood clots in the brain?

Section 19.6 Fat-Soluble Vitamins

19.35 Examine the structural formula of vitamin A, and state the number of *cis,trans* isomers that are possible for this molecule.

*19.36 The form of vitamin A present in many food supplements is vitamin A palmitate. Draw the structural formula of this molecule.

*19.37 Examine the structural formulas of vitamin A, 1,25-dihydroxy-D_3, vitamin E, and vitamin K_1. Do you expect these vitamins to be more soluble in water or in dichloromethane? Do you expect them to be soluble in blood plasma?

LOOKING AHEAD

*19.38 Here is the structure of a glycolipid, a class of lipid that contains a sugar residue:

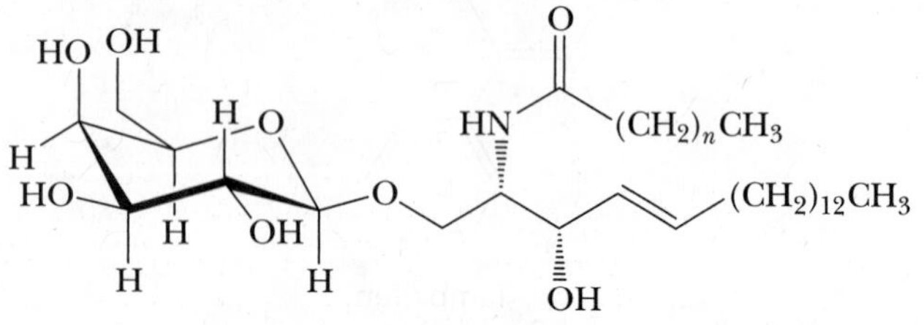

A glycolipid

Glycolipids are found in cell membranes. (a) Which part of the molecule would you expect to reside on the extracellular side of the membrane? (b) What monosaccharide unit is present in this glycolipid?

19.39 How would you expect temperature to affect fluidity in a cell membrane?

19.40 Which type of lipid movement, A or B, is more favorable in cell membranes? Explain.

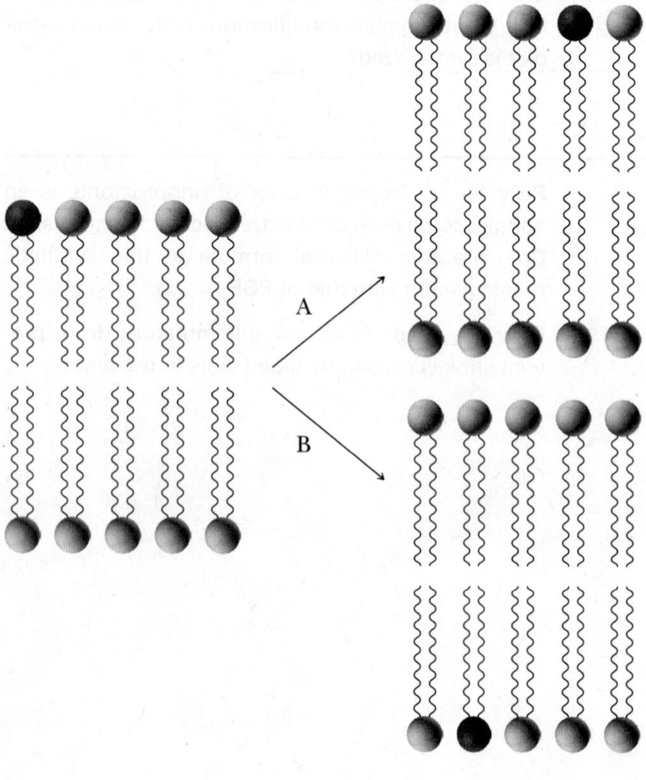

*19.41 Aspirin works by transferring an acetyl group to the side chain of the 530th amino acid in the protein prostaglandin H_2 synthase-1. Draw the product of this reaction:

Residue-530

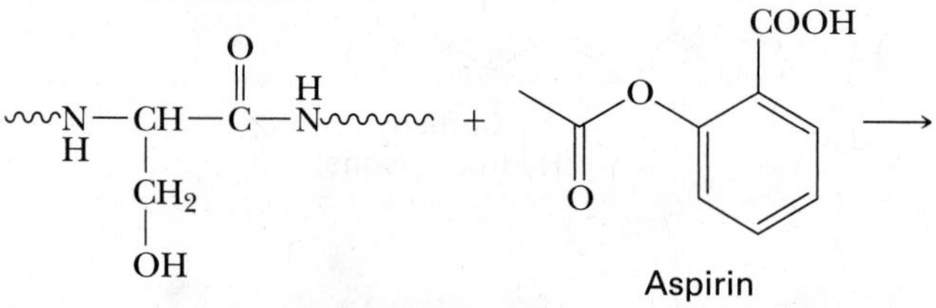

Aspirin

GROUP LEARNING ACTIVITIES

19.42 Bisphenol A, commonly known as BPA, has been widely used as a monomer to make polycarbonates (Section 16.4C).

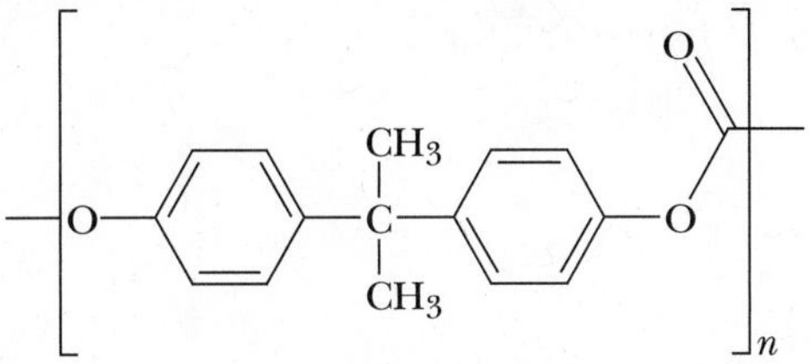

Polycarbonate of BPA

Plastics made with BPA are clear and durable, and for this reason, are ideal for making items such as drinking bottles and other food containers. However, it has recently been suggested that plastic containers made with BPA can react with strong detergents under acidic or heated conditions, causing BPA to leach into the very foods or liquids that the containers are designed to hold. Discuss the following questions as a group:

(a) Provide a structure for BPA by drawing the mechanism for the acid-catalyzed hydrolysis of its polycarbonate.

(b) BPA acts as an endocrine disruptor by mimicking estrogen in the body. Compare the structure of BPA to the three estrogens in Chemical Connections 19B. How are they different? How are they similar? Which part of estrogen do you think binds to hormone receptors in the body?

19.43 Levonorgestrel is the active ingredient in the "morning after pill," an oral contraceptive that has been approved by the FDA. Discuss the following questions about levonorgestrel with your study group:

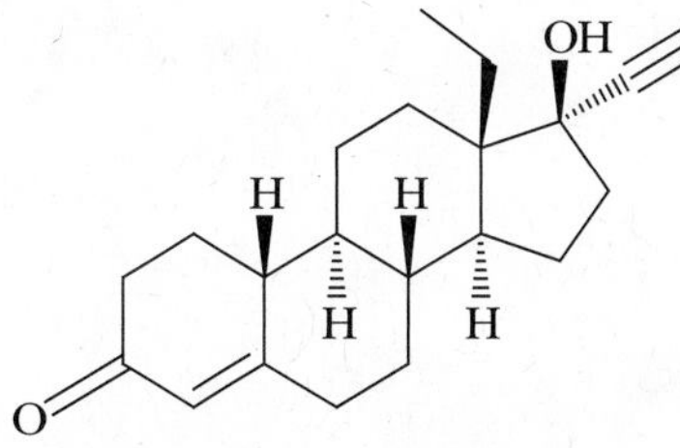

Levonorgestrel

(a) What class of organic compound is levonorgestrel? Describe its similarities with some of the compounds discussed in this chapter.

(b) What does the first part of the name, "levo," suggest about the drug?

(c) Levonorgestrel contains an alcohol. Suggest how this alcohol could have been synthesized from a ketone.

(d) Levonorgestrel contains an α,β-unsaturated ketone. Suggest how this part of the compound could have been synthesized from a Michael reaction followed by an aldol reaction.

Acid Ionization Constants for the Major Classes of Organic Acids

Class and Example	Typical pK_a	Class and Example	Typical pK_a
Sulfonic acid 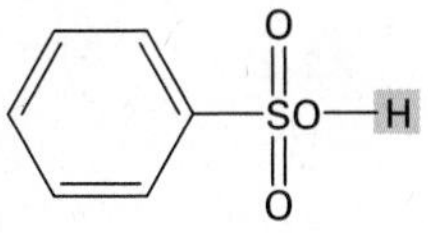	(−3)–(−2)	Alcohol $CH_3CH_2O{-}H$	15–19
Carboxylic acid $CH_3\overset{\overset{O}{\|}}{C}O{-}H$	3–5	α-Hydrogen of an aldehyde or ketone $CH_3\overset{\overset{O}{\|}}{C}CH_2{-}H$	18–20
Arylammonium ion 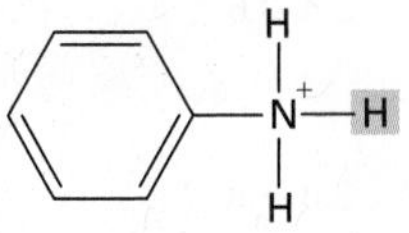	4–5	α-Hydrogen of an ester $CH_3CH_2O\overset{\overset{O}{\|}}{C}CH_2{-}H$	23–25
Thiol $CH_3CH_2S{-}H$	8–12	Terminal alkyne $CH_3{-}C{\equiv}C{-}H$	25
Phenol 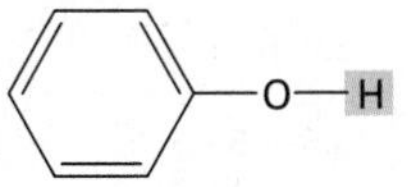	9–10	Aliphatic amine $(CH_3CH_2)_2N{-}H$	36
β-Diketone $CH_3{-}\overset{\overset{O}{\|}}{C}{-}\overset{\overset{H}{\mid}}{C}H{-}\overset{\overset{O}{\|}}{C}CH_3$	10	Allylic hydrogen of an alkene $CH_2{=}CHCH_2{-}H$	43
Alkylammonium ion $(CH_3CH_2)_3\overset{+}{N}{-}H$	10–12	Alkene $CH_2{=}CH{-}H$	50
β-Ketoester $CH_3{-}\overset{\overset{O}{\|}}{C}{-}\overset{\overset{H}{\mid}}{C}H{-}\overset{\overset{O}{\|}}{C}OCH_2CH_3$	11	Alkane $(CH_3)_2CH{-}H$	>51
Water $HO{-}H$	15.7		

APPENDIX 2

Characteristic ¹H-NMR Chemical Shifts

Type of Hydrogen (R = alkyl, Ar = aryl)	Chemical Shift (δ)*	Type of Hydrogen (R = alkyl, Ar = aryl)	Chemical Shift (δ)*
$(CH_3)_4Si$	0 (by definition)	$RC(=O)CH_2R$	2.2–2.6
RCH_3	0.8–1.0	$RC(=O)OCH_3$	3.7–3.9
RCH_2R	1.2–1.4	$RC(=O)OCH_2R$	4.1–4.7
R_3CH	1.4–1.7	RCH_2I	3.1–3.3
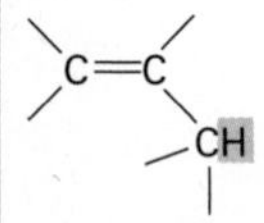	1.6–2.6	RCH_2Br	3.4–3.6
$RC\equiv CH$	2.0–3.0	RCH_2Cl	3.6–3.8
$ArCH_3$	2.2–2.5	RCH_2F	4.4–4.5
$ArCH_2R$	2.3–2.8	ArOH	4.5–4.7
ROH	0.5–6.0	$R_2C{=}CH_2$	4.6–5.0
RCH_2OH	3.4–4.0	$R_2C{=}CHR$	5.0–5.7
RCH_2OR	3.3–4.0	ArH	6.5–8.5
R_2NH	0.5–5.0	$RC(=O)H$	9.5–10.1
$RC(=O)CH_3$	2.1–2.3	$RC(=O)OH$	10–13

*Values are relative to tetramethylsilane. Other atoms within the molecule may cause the signal to appear outside these ranges.

APPENDIX 3

Characteristic ^{13}C-NMR Chemical Shifts

Type of Carbon	Chemical Shift (δ)	Type of Carbon	Chemical Shift (δ)
R**C**H_3	0–40	R**C**≡**C**R	65–85
R**C**H_2R	15–55	R_2**C**=**C**R_2	100–150
R_3**C**H	20–60	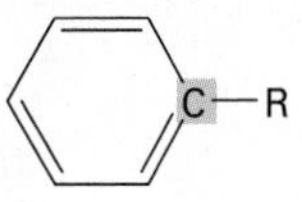	110–160
R**C**H_2I	0–40	R**C**(=O)OR	160–180
R**C**H_2Br	25–65	R**C**(=O)NR_2	165–180
R**C**H_2Cl	35–80	R**C**(=O)OH	175–185
R_3**C**OH	40–80	R**C**(=O)H, R**C**(=O)R	180–210
R_3**C**OR	40–80		

4 APPENDIX

Characteristic Infrared Absorption Frequencies			
Bonding	Functional Group	Frequency (cm^{-1})	Intensity*
C—H	alkane	2850–3000	w–m
	—CH_3	1375 and 1450	w–m
	—CH_2—	1450	m
	alkene	3000–3100	w–m
		650–1000	s
	alkyne	3270–3330	w–m
		1600–1680	w–m
	aromatic	3000–3100	s
		690–900	s
	aldehyde	2700–2800	w
		2800–2900	w
C=C	alkene	1600–1680	w–m
	aromatic	1450 and 1600	w–m
C—O	alcohol, ether,	1050–1100 (sp^3 C—O)	s
	ester, carboxylic		s
	acid, anhydride	1200–1250 (sp^2 C—O)	s
C=O	amide	1630–1680	s
	carboxylic acid	1700–1725	s
	ketone	1705–1780	s
	aldehyde	1705–1740	s
	ester	1735–1800	s
	anhydride	1760 and 1800	s
O—H	alcohol, phenol		
	free	3600–3650	m
	H-bonded	3200–3500	m
	carboxylic acid	2400–3400	m
N—H	amine and amide	3100–3500	m–s

*w = weak, m = medium, s = strong

GLOSSARY

α-Amino acid An amino acid in which the amino group is on the carbon adjacent to the carboxyl group.

α-Carbon A carbon atom adjacent to a carbonyl group.

Acetal A molecule containing two —OR or —OAr groups bonded to the same carbon.

Aceto group A $CH_3C(=O)$ group.

Achiral An object that lacks chirality; an object that has no handedness and is superposable on its mirror image.

Acid halide A derivative of a carboxylic acid in which the —OH of the carboxyl group is replaced by a halogen—most commonly, chlorine.

Activating group Any substituent on a benzene ring that causes the rate of electrophilic aromatic substitution to be greater than that for benzene.

Activation energy The difference in energy between reactants and the transition state.

Acyl halide A derivative of a carboxylic acid in which the —OH of the carboxyl group is replaced by a halogen—most commonly, chlorine.

α-Helix A type of secondary structure in which a section of polypeptide chain coils into a spiral, most commonly a right-handed spiral.

α-Hydrogen A hydrogen on an α-carbon.

Alcohol A compound containing an —OH (hydroxyl) group bonded to an sp^3 hybridized carbon.

Alcoholic fermentation A metabolic pathway that converts glucose to two molecules of ethanol and two molecules of CO_2.

Aldehyde A compound containing a carbonyl group bonded to hydrogen (a CHO group).

Alditol The product formed when the C=O group of a monosaccharide is reduced to a CHOH group.

Aldol reaction A carbonyl condensation reaction between two aldehydes or ketones to give a β-hydroxyaldehyde or a β-hydroxyketone.

Aldose A monosaccharide containing an aldehyde group.

Aliphatic amine An amine in which nitrogen is bonded only to alkyl groups.

Aliphatic hydrocarbon An alternative term to describe an alkane.

Alkane A saturated hydrocarbon whose carbon atoms are arranged in an open chain.

Alkene An unsaturated hydrocarbon that contains a carbon–carbon double bond.

Alkoxy group An —OR group, where R is an alkyl group.

Alkyl group A group derived by removing a hydrogen from an alkane; given the symbol R-.

Alkyl halide A compound containing a halogen atom covalently bonded to an sp^3 hybridized carbon atom; given the symbol RX.

Alkyne An unsaturated hydrocarbon that contains a carbon–carbon triple bond.

Amino acid A compound that contains both an amino group and a carboxyl group.

Amino group An sp^3 hybridized nitrogen atom bonded to one, two, or three carbon groups.

Amorphous domains Disordered, noncrystalline regions in the solid state of a polymer.

Anabolic steroid A steroid hormone, such as testosterone, that promotes tissue and muscle growth and development.

Androgen A steroid hormone, such as testosterone, that mediates the development and sexual characteristics of males.

Angle strain The strain that arises when a bond angle is either compressed or expanded compared with its optimal value.

Anion An atom or group of atoms bearing a negative charge.

Anomeric carbon The hemiacetal carbon of the cyclic form of a monosaccharide.

Anomers Monosaccharides that differ in configuration only at their anomeric carbons.

Anti stereoselectivity Addition of atoms or groups of atoms from opposite sides or faces of a carbon–carbon double bond.

Aprotic solvent A solvent that cannot serve as a hydrogen bond donor as, for example, acetone, diethyl ether, and dichloromethane.

Aramid A polyaromatic *amide;* a polymer in which the monomer units are an aromatic diamine and an aromatic dicarboxylic acid.

Arene A compound containing one or more benzene rings. An aromatic hydrocarbon.

Aromatic amine An amine in which nitrogen is bonded to one or more aryl groups.

Aromatic compound A term used to classify benzene and its derivatives.

Ar— The symbol used for an aryl group, by analogy with R— for an alkyl group.

Arrhenius acid A substance that dissolves in water to produce H^+ ions.

Arrhenius base A substance that dissolves in water to produce OH^- ions.

Aryl group A group derived from an aromatic compound (an arene) by the removal of an H; given the symbol Ar—.

Autoclave An instrument used to sterilize items by subjecting them to steam and high pressure.

Average degree of polymerization, *n* A subscript placed outside the parentheses of the simplest nonredundant unit of a polymer to indicate that the unit repeats *n* times in the polymer.

Axial bond A bond on a chair conformation of a cyclohexane ring that extends from the ring parallel to the imaginary axis of the ring.

β-Elimination reaction The removal of atoms or groups of atoms from two adjacent carbon atoms, as for example, the removal of H and X from an alkyl halide or H and OH from an alcohol to form a carbon–carbon double bond.

Benzyl group $C_6H_5CH_2$—, the alkyl group derived by removing a hydrogen from the methyl group of toluene.

Benzylic carbon An sp^3 hybridized carbon bonded to a benzene ring.

β-Oxidation of fatty acids A series of four enzyme-catalyzed reactions that cleaves carbon atoms, two at a time, from the carboxyl end of a fatty acid.

β-Pleated sheet A type of secondary structure in which two sections of polypeptide chain are aligned parallel or antiparallel to one another.

Bile acid A cholesterol-derived detergent molecule, such as cholic acid, that is secreted by the gallbladder into the intestine to assist in the absorption of dietary lipids.

Bimolecular reaction A reaction in which two species are involved in the reaction leading to the transition state of the rate-determining step.

Boat conformation A puckered conformation of a cyclohexane ring in which carbons 1 and 4 of the ring are bent toward each other.

Bonding electrons Valence electrons shared in a covalent bond.

Brønsted–Lowry acid A proton donor.

Brønsted–Lowry base A proton acceptor.

Carbanion An anion in which carbon has an unshared pair of electrons and bears a negative charge.

Carbocation A species containing a carbon atom with only three bonds to it and bearing a positive charge.

Carbohydrate A polyhydroxyaldehyde or polyhydroxyketone or a substance that gives these compounds on hydrolysis.

Carbonyl group A C═O group.

Carboxyl group A —COOH group.

Carboxylic anhydride A compound in which two acyl groups are bonded to an oxygen.

Cation An atom or group of atoms bearing a positive charge.

Chain-growth polymerization A polymerization that involves sequential addition reactions, either to unsaturated monomers or to monomers possessing other reactive functional groups.

Chain initiation In radical polymerization, the formation of radicals from molecules containing only paired electrons.

Chain propagation In radical polymerization, a reaction of a radical and a molecule to give a new radical.

Chain termination In radical polymerization, a reaction in which two radicals combine to form a covalent bond.

Chain-transfer reaction In radical polymerization, the transfer of reactivity of an end group from one chain to another during a polymerization.

Chair conformation The most stable puckered conformation of a cyclohexane ring; all bond angles are approximately 109.5°, and bonds to all adjacent carbons are staggered.

Chemical shift, δ The position of a signal on an NMR spectrum relative to the signal of tetramethylsilane (TMS); expressed in delta (δ) units, where 1 δ equals 1 ppm.

Chiral center An atom, such as carbon, with four different groups bonded to it.

Chiral From the Greek *cheir*, meaning hand; objects that are not superposable on their mirror images.

Chromatin A complex formed between negatively charged DNA molecules and positively charged histones.

Circular DNA A type of double-stranded DNA in which the 5′ and 3′ ends of each strand are joined by phosphodiester groups.

Cis A prefix meaning "on the same side."

***Cis–trans* isomerism** Isomers that have the same order of attachment of their atoms, but a different arrangement of their atoms in space due to the presence of either a ring (Chapter 3) or a carbon–carbon double bond (Chapter 4).

Cis–trans isomers Isomers that have the same order of attachment of their atoms, but a different arrangement of their atoms in space, due to the presence of either a ring or a carbon–carbon double bond.

Claisen condensation A carbonyl condensation reaction between two esters to give a β-ketoester.

Codon A triplet of nucleotides on mRNA that directs the incorporation of a specific amino acid into a polypeptide sequence.

Coenzyme A low-molecular-weight, nonprotein molecule or ion that binds reversibly to an enzyme, functions as a second substrate for the enzyme, and is regenerated by further reaction.

Conformation Any three-dimensional arrangement of atoms in a molecule that results by rotation about a single bond.

Conjugate acid The species formed when a base accepts a proton.

Conjugate base The species formed when an acid donates a proton.

Constitutional isomers Compounds with the same molecular formula, but a different order of attachment of their atoms.

Covalent bond A chemical bond resulting from the sharing of one or more pairs of electrons.

Crossed aldol reaction An aldol reaction between two different aldehydes, two different ketones, or an aldehyde and a ketone.

Crossed Claisen condensation A Claisen condensation between two different esters.

Crystalline domains Ordered crystalline regions in the solid state of a polymer; also called crystallites.

C-Terminal amino acid The amino acid at the end of a polypeptide chain having the free $—COO^-$ group.

Curved arrow A symbol used to show the redistribution of valence electrons.

Cyclic ether An ether in which the oxygen is one of the atoms of a ring.

Cycloalkane A saturated hydrocarbon that contains carbon atoms joined to form a ring.

Deactivating group Any substituent on a benzene ring that causes the rate of electrophilic aromatic substitution to be lower than that for benzene.

Decarboxylation Loss of CO_2 from a carboxyl group.

Dehydration Elimination of a molecule of water from a compound.

Dehydrohalogenation Removal of —H and —X from adjacent carbons; a type of β-elimination.

Dextrorotatory Rotating the plane of polarized light in a polarimeter to the right.

Diastereomers Stereoisomers that are not mirror images of each other; the term refers to relationships among objects.

Diaxial interactions Interactions between groups in parallel axial positions on the same side of a chair conformation of a cyclohexane ring.

Dieckmann condensation An intramolecular Claisen condensation of an ester of a dicarboxylic acid to give a five- or six-membered ring.

Dipeptide A molecule containing two amino acid units joined by a peptide bond.

Disaccharide A carbohydrate containing two monosaccharide units joined by a glycosidic bond.

Dispersion forces Very weak intermolecular forces of attraction resulting from the interaction of temporary induced dipoles.

Disulfide bond A covalent bond between two sulfur atoms; an —S—S— bond.

D-Monosaccharide A monosaccharide that, when written as a Fischer projection, has the —OH on its penultimate carbon to the right.

Double-headed arrow A symbol used to connect contributing structures.

Double helix A type of secondary structure of DNA molecules in which two antiparallel polynucleotide strands are coiled in a right-handed manner about the same axis.

Doublet A signal that is split into two peaks; the hydrogens that give rise to the signal have one neighboring nonequivalent hydrogen.

Downfield A term used to refer to the relative position of a signal on an NMR spectrum. Downfield indicates a peak to the left of the spectrum (a weaker applied field).

3′ End The end of a polynucleotide at which the 3′-OH of the terminal pentose unit is free.

5′ End The end of a polynucleotide at which the 5′-OH of the terminal pentose unit is free.

E From the German *entgegen*, meaning opposite; specifies that groups of higher priority on the carbons of a double bond are on opposite sides.

Eclipsed conformation A conformation about a carbon–carbon single bond in which the atoms on one carbon are as close as possible to the atoms on the adjacent carbon.

Edman degradation A method for selectively cleaving and identifying the *N*-terminal amino acid of a polypeptide chain.

Elastomer A material that, when stretched or otherwise distorted, returns to its original shape when the distorting force is released.

Electromagnetic radiation Light and other forms of radiant energy.

Electronegativity A measure of the force of an atom's attraction for electrons it shares in a chemical bond with another atom.

Electrophile An electron-poor species that can accept a pair of electrons to form a new covalent bond; alternatively, a Lewis acid (Section 2.6).

Electrophilic aromatic substitution A reaction in which an electrophile, E^+, substitutes for a hydrogen on an aromatic ring.

Electrophoresis The process of separating compounds on the basis of their electric charge.

Enantiomers Stereoisomers that are nonsuperposable mirror images; the term refers to a relationship between pairs of objects.

Endothermic reaction A reaction in which the energy of the products is higher than the energy of the reactants; a reaction in which heat is absorbed.

Energy diagram A graph showing the changes in energy that occur during a chemical reaction; energy is plotted on the *y*-axis, and the progress of the reaction is plotted on the *x*-axis.

Enol A molecule containing an —OH group bonded to a carbon of a carbon–carbon double bond.

Enolate anion An anion formed by the removal of an α -hydrogen from a carbonyl-containing compound.

Epoxide A cyclic ether in which oxygen is one atom of a three-membered ring.

Epoxy resin A material prepared by a polymerization in which one monomer contains at least two epoxy groups.

Equatorial bond A bond on a chair conformation of a cyclohexane ring that extends from the ring roughly perpendicular to the imaginary axis of the ring.

Equivalent hydrogens Hydrogens that have the same chemical environment.

Estrogen A steroid hormone, such as estradiol, that mediates the development and sexual characteristics of females.

Ether A compound containing an oxygen atom bonded to two carbon atoms.

Exothermic reaction A reaction in which the energy of the products is lower than the energy of the reactants; a reaction in which heat is liberated.

E,Z system A system used to specify the configuration of groups about a carbon–carbon double bond.

Fat A triglyceride that is semisolid or solid at room temperature.

Fatty acid A long, unbranched-chain carboxylic acid, most commonly of 12 to 20 carbons, derived from the hydrolysis of animal fats, vegetable oils, or the phospholipids of biological membranes.

Fingerprint region The portion of the vibrational infrared region that extends from 1000 to 400 cm^{-1} and that is unique to every compound.

Fischer esterification The process of forming an ester by refluxing a carboxylic acid and an alcohol in the presence of an acid catalyst, commonly sulfuric acid.

Fischer projection A two-dimensional representation showing the configuration of a stereocenter; horizontal lines represent bonds projecting forward from the stereocenter, whereas vertical lines represent bonds projecting to the rear.

Fishhook arrow A single-barbed, curved arrow used to show the change in position of a single electron.

Flavin adenine dinucleotide (FAD) A biological oxidizing agent. When acting as an oxidizing agent, FAD is reduced to $FADH_2$.

Fluid-mosaic model A model of a biological membrane consisting of a phospholipid bilayer, with proteins, carbohydrates, and other lipids embedded in, and on the surface of, the bilayer.

Formal charge The charge on an atom in a molecule or polyatomic ion.

Frequency (ν) A number of full cycles of a wave that pass a point in a second.

Functional group An atom or a group of atoms within a molecule that shows a characteristic set of physical and chemical properties.

Furanose A five-membered cyclic hemiacetal form of a monosaccharide.

Glycol A compound with two hydroxyl (—OH) groups on different carbons.

Glycolysis From the Greek *glyko*, sweet, and *lysis*, splitting; a series of ten enzyme-catalyzed reactions by which glucose is oxidized to two molecules of pyruvate.

Glycoside A carbohydrate in which the —OH on its anomeric carbon is replaced by —OR.

Glycosidic bond The bond from the anomeric carbon of a glycoside to an —OR group.

Grignard reagent An organomagnesium compound of the type RMgX or ArMgX.

Ground-state electron configuration The electron configuration of lowest energy for an atom, molecule, or ion.

Halonium ion An ion in which a halogen atom bears a positive charge.

Haworth projection A way of viewing the furanose and pyranose forms of monosaccharides. The ring is drawn flat and viewed through its edge, with the anomeric carbon on the right and the oxygen atom of the ring in the rear to the right.

Heat of reaction The difference in energy between reactants and products.

Hemiacetal A molecule containing an —OH and an —OR or —OAr group bonded to the same carbon.

Hertz (Hz) The unit in which wave frequency is reported; s^{-1} (read *per second*).

Heterocyclic amine An amine in which nitrogen is one of the atoms of a ring.

Heterocyclic aromatic amine An amine in which nitrogen is one of the atoms of an aromatic ring.

Heterocyclic compound An organic compound that contains one or more atoms other than carbon in its ring.

High-density lipoprotein (HDL) Plasma particles, of density 1.06–1.21 g/mL, consisting of approximately 33% proteins, 30% cholesterol, 29% phospholipids, and 8% triglycerides.

Histone A protein, particularly rich in the basic amino acids lysine and arginine, that is found associated with DNA molecules.

Hybrid orbital An orbital produced from the combination of two or more atomic orbitals.

Hydration Addition of water.

Hydride ion A hydrogen atom with two electrons in its valence shell; $H:^-$.

Hydrocarbon A compound that contains only carbon atoms and hydrogen atoms.

Hydrogen bonding The attractive force between a partial positive charge on hydrogen and partial negative charge on a nearby oxygen, nitrogen, or fluorine atom.

Hydrophilic From the Greek, meaning "water loving."

Hydrophobic effect The tendency of nonpolar groups to cluster in such a way as to be shielded from contact with an aqueous environment.

Hydrophobic From the Greek, meaning "water hating."

Hydroxyl group An —OH group.

Imine A compound containing a carbon–nitrogen double bond; also called a Schiff base.

Index of hydrogen deficiency The sum of the number of rings and pi bonds in a molecule.

Inductive effect The polarization of electron density transmitted through covalent bonds caused by a nearby atom of higher electronegativity.

Inversion of configuration The reversal of the arrangement of atoms or groups of atoms about a reaction center in an S_N2 reaction.

Ionic bond A chemical bond resulting from the electrostatic attraction of an anion and a cation.

Isoelectric point (pI) The pH at which an amino acid, a polypeptide, or a protein has no net charge.

Ketone A compound containing a carbonyl group bonded to two carbons.

Ketose A monosaccharide containing a ketone group.

Lactam A cyclic amide.

Lactate fermentation A metabolic pathway that converts glucose to two molecules of lactate.

Lactone A cyclic ester.

Levorotatory Rotating the plane of polarized light in a polarimeter to the left.

Lewis acid Any molecule or ion that can form a new covalent bond by accepting a pair of electrons.

Lewis base Any molecule or ion that can form a new covalent bond by donating a pair of electrons.

Lewis structure of an atom The symbol of an element surrounded by a number of dots equal to the number of electrons in the valence shell of the atom.

Line-angle formula An abbreviated way to draw structural formulas in which each vertex and each line ending represents a carbon atom and a line represents a bond.

Lipid A class of biomolecules isolated from plant or animal sources by extraction with relatively nonpolar organic solvents, such as diethyl ether and acetone.

Lipid bilayer A back-to-back arrangement of phospholipid monolayers.

L-Monosaccharide A monosaccharide that, when written as a Fischer projection, has the —OH on its penultimate carbon to the left.

Low-density lipoprotein (LDL) Plasma particles, of density 1.02–1.06 g/mL, consisting of approximately 25% proteins, 50% cholesterol, 21% phospholipids, and 4% triglycerides.

Markovnikov's rule In the addition of HX or H_2O to an alkene, hydrogen adds to the carbon of the double bond having the greater number of hydrogens.

Mercaptan A common name for any molecule containing an —SH group.

Meso compound An achiral compound possessing two or more stereocenters.

Messenger RNA (mRNA) A ribonucleic acid that carries coded genetic information from DNA to ribosomes for the synthesis of proteins.

Meta (*m*) Refers to groups occupying positions 1 and 3 on a benzene ring.

Meta director Any substituent on a benzene ring that directs electrophilic aromatic substitution preferentially to a meta position.

Micelle A spherical arrangement of organic molecules in water solution clustered so that their hydrophobic parts are buried inside the sphere and their hydrophilic parts are on the surface of the sphere and in contact with water.

Michael reaction The conjugate addition of an enolate anion or other nucleophile to an α,β-unsaturated carbonyl compound.

Mirror image The reflection of an object in a mirror.

Molecular spectroscopy The study of the frequencies of electromagnetic radiation that are absorbed or emitted by substances and the correlation between these frequencies and specific types of molecular structure.

Monomer From the Greek *mono*, single and *meros*, part; the simplest nonredundant unit from which a polymer is synthesized.

Monosaccharide A carbohydrate that cannot be hydrolyzed to a simpler compound.

Multiplet A signal that is split into multiple peaks, often of an irregular pattern, due to the presence of more than one type of neighboring hydrogens.

Mutarotation The change in optical activity that occurs when an α or β form of a carbohydrate is converted to an equilibrium mixture of the two forms.

(n + 1) rule The ^{1}H-NMR signal of a hydrogen or set of equivalent hydrogens with n other hydrogens on neighboring carbons is split into (n + 1) peaks.

Newman projection A way to view a molecule by looking along a carbon–carbon bond.

Nicotinamide adenine dinucleotide (NAD^+) A biological oxidizing agent. When acting as an oxidizing agent, NAD^+ is reduced to NADH.

Nonbonding electrons Valence electrons not involved in forming covalent bonds, that is, unshared electrons.

Nonpolar covalent bond A covalent bond between atoms whose difference in electronegativity is less than approximately 0.5.

***N*-Terminal amino acid** The amino acid at the end of a polypeptide chain having the free $—NH_3^+$ group.

Nucleic acid A biopolymer containing three types of monomer units: heterocyclic aromatic amine bases derived from purine and pyrimidine, the monosaccharides D-ribose or 2-deoxy-D-ribose, and phosphate.

Nucleophile An atom or a group of atoms that donates a pair of electrons to another atom or group of atoms to form a new covalent bond.

Nucleophilic acyl substitution A reaction in which a nucleophile bonded to a carbonyl carbon is replaced by another nucleophile.

Nucleophilic substitution A reaction in which one nucleophile is substituted for another.

Nucleoside A building block of nucleic acids, consisting of D-ribose or 2-deoxy-D-ribose bonded to a heterocyclic aromatic amine base by a β-*N*-glycosidic bond.

Nucleotide A nucleoside in which a molecule of phosphoric acid is esterified with an —OH of the monosaccharide, most commonly either the 3′-OH or the 5′-OH.

Observed rotation The number of degrees through which a compound rotates the plane of polarized light.

Octet rule The tendency among atoms of Group 1A–7A elements to react in ways that achieve an outer shell of eight valence electrons.

Oil A triglyceride that is liquid at room temperature.

Oligosaccharide A carbohydrate containing from 6 to 10 monosaccharide units, each joined to the next by a glycosidic bond.

Optically active Showing that a compound rotates the plane of polarized light.

Optically inactive Showing that a compound or mixture of compounds does not rotate the plane of polarized light.

Orbital A region of space where an electron or pair of electrons spends 90 to 95% of its time.

Order of precedence of functional groups A system for ranking functional groups in order of priority for the purposes of IUPAC nomenclature.

Organometallic compound A compound containing a carbon–metal bond.

Ortho (*o*) Refers to groups occupying positions 1 and 2 on a benzene ring.

Ortho–para director Any substituent on a benzene ring that directs electrophilic aromatic substitution preferentially to ortho and para positions.

Oxonium ion An ion that contains an oxygen atom that bears a positive charge and with three bonds to oxygen.

Para (*p*) Refers to groups occupying positions 1 and 4 on a benzene ring.

Peak (NMR) The units into which an NMR signal is split—two peaks in a doublet, three peaks in a triplet, and so on.

Penultimate carbon The stereocenter of a monosaccharide farthest from the carbonyl group—for example, carbon 5 of glucose.

Peptide bond The special name given to the amide bond formed between the α-amino group of one amino acid and the α-carboxyl group of another amino acid.

Phenol A compound that contains an —OH group bonded to a benzene ring.

Phenyl group $C_6H_5—$, the aryl group derived by removing a hydrogen from benzene.

Phospholipid A lipid containing glycerol esterified with two molecules of fatty acid and one molecule of phosphoric acid.

Pi (π) bond A covalent bond formed by the overlap of parallel p orbitals.

Plane of symmetry An imaginary plane passing through an object and dividing it such that one half is the mirror image of the other half.

Plane-polarized light Light vibrating only in parallel planes.

Plastic A polymer that can be molded when hot and retains its shape when cooled.

Polar covalent bond A covalent bond between atoms whose difference in electronegativity is between approximately 0.5 and 1.9.

Polarimeter An instrument for measuring the ability of a compound to rotate the plane of polarized light.

Polyamide A polymer in which each monomer unit is joined to the next by an amide bond, as for example nylon 66.

Polycarbonate A polyester in which the carboxyl groups are derived from carbonic acid.

Polyester A polymer in which each monomer unit is joined to the next by an ester bond as, for example, poly(ethylene terephthalate).

Polymer From the Greek *poly*, many and *meros,* parts; any long-chain molecule synthesized by linking together many single parts called monomers.

Polynuclear aromatic hydrocarbon A hydrocarbon containing two or more fused aromatic rings.

Polypeptide A macromolecule containing 20 or more amino acid units, each joined to the next by a peptide bond.

Polysaccharide A carbohydrate containing a large number of monosaccharide units, each joined to the next by one or more glycosidic bonds.

Polyunsaturated triglyceride A triglyceride having several carbon–carbon double bonds in the hydrocarbon chains of its three fatty acids.

Polyurethane A polymer containing the —NHCOO— group as a repeating unit.

Primary (1°) structure of proteins The sequence of amino acids in the polypeptide chain; read from the *N*-terminal amino acid to the *C*-terminal amino acid.

Primary (1°) structure of nucleic acids The sequence of bases along the pentose– phosphodiester backbone of a DNA or RNA molecule, read from the 5′ end to the 3′ end.

Prostaglandin A member of the family of compounds having the 20-carbon skeleton of prostanoic acid.

Protic solvent A hydrogen bond donor solvent as, for example, water, ethanol, and acetic acid. We define hydrogen bond donors as compounds containing hydrogens that can participate in H-bonding.

Pyranose A six-membered cyclic hemiacetal form of a monosaccharide.

Quartet A signal that is split into four peaks; the hydrogens that give rise to the signal have three neighboring nonequivalent hydrogens that are equivalent to each other.

Quaternary (4°) structure of proteins The arrangement of polypeptide monomers into a noncovalently bonded aggregation.

R From the Latin *rectus*, meaning right; used in the R,S system to show that the order of priority of groups on a stereocenter is clockwise.

R- A symbol used to represent an alkyl group.

Racemic mixture A mixture of equal amounts of two enantiomers.

Racemization The conversion of a pure enantiomer into a racemic mixture.

Radical Any molecule that contains one or more unpaired electrons.

Rate-determining step The step in a reaction sequence that crosses the highest energy barrier; the slowest step in a multistep reaction.

Reaction coordinate A measure of the progress of a reaction, plotted on the *x*-axis in an energy diagram.

Reaction intermediate An unstable species that lies in an energy minimum between two transition states.

Reaction mechanism A step-by-step description of how a chemical reaction occurs.

Rearrangement A reaction in which a carbon or hydrogen atom has shifted its connectivity to another atom within the molecule.

Reducing sugar A carbohydrate that reacts with an oxidizing agent to form an aldonic acid.

Reductive amination The formation of an imine from an aldehyde or a ketone, followed by the reduction of the imine to an amine.

Regioselective reaction A reaction in which one direction of bond forming or bond breaking occurs in preference to all other directions.

Relative nucleophilicity The relative rates at which a nucleophile reacts in a reference nucleophilic substitution reaction.

Resolution Separation of a racemic mixture into its enantiomers.

Resonance The absorption of electromagnetic radiation by a spinning nucleus and the resulting "flip" of its spin from a lower energy state to a higher energy state.

Resonance contributing structures Representations of a molecule or ion that differ only in the distribution of valence electrons.

Resonance energy The difference in energy between a resonance hybrid and the most stable of its hypothetical contributing structures.

Resonance hybrid A molecule or ion that is best described as a composite of a number of contributing structures.

Resonance signal A recording of nuclear magnetic resonance in an NMR spectrum.

Restriction endonuclease An enzyme that catalyzes the hydrolysis of a particular phosphodiester bond within a DNA strand.

Ribosomal RNA (rRNA) A ribonucleic acid found in ribosomes, the sites of protein synthesis.

R,S system A set of rules for specifying the configuration about a stereocenter.

S From the Latin *sinister,* meaning left; used in the R,S system to show that the order of priority of groups on a stereocenter is counterclockwise.

Sanger dideoxy method A method, developed by Frederick Sanger, for sequencing DNA molecules.

Saponification Hydrolysis of an ester in aqueous NaOH or KOH to an alcohol and the sodium or potassium salt of a carboxylic acid.

Saturated hydrocarbon A hydrocarbon containing only carbon–carbon single bonds.

Schiff base An alternative name for an imine.

Secondary (2°) structure of proteins The ordered arrangements (conformations) of amino acids in localized regions of a polypeptide or protein.

Secondary (2°) structure of nucleic acids The ordered arrangement of strands of nucleic acid.

Shell A region of space around a nucleus where electrons are found.

Shielding In NMR spectroscopy, electrons around a nucleus create their own local magnetic fields and thereby shield the nucleus from the applied magnetic field.

Sigma (σ) bond A covalent bond in which the overlap of atomic orbitals is concentrated along the bond axis.

Signal splitting Splitting of an NMR signal into a set of peaks by the influence of neighboring nuclei.

Singlet A signal that consists of one peak; the hydrogens that give rise to the signal have no neighboring nonequivalent hydrogens.

Soap A sodium or potassium salt of a fatty acid.

Solvolysis A nucleophilic substitution reaction in which the solvent is the nucleophile.

Specific rotation Observed rotation of the plane of polarized light when a sample is placed in a tube 1.0 dm long at a concentration of 1.0 g/mL.

***sp* Hybrid orbital** A hybrid atomic orbital produced by the combination of one *s* atomic orbital and one *p* atomic orbital.

sp^2 Hybrid orbital An orbital produced by the combination of one *s* atomic orbital and two *p* atomic orbitals.

sp^3 Hybrid orbital An orbital produced by the combination of one *s* atomic orbital and three *p* atomic orbitals.

Staggered conformation A conformation about a carbon–carbon single bond in which the atoms on one carbon are as far apart as possible from the atoms on the adjacent carbon.

Step-growth polymerization A polymerization in which chain growth occurs in a stepwise manner between difunctional monomers, for example, between adipic acid and hexamethylenediamine to form nylon 66. Also referred to as condensation polymerization.

Stereocenter An atom at which the interchange of two atoms or groups of atoms bonded to it produces a different stereoisomer.

Stereoisomers Isomers that have the same molecular formula and the same connectivity, but different orientations of their atoms in space.

Stereoselective reaction A reaction in which one stereoisomer is formed or destroyed in preference to all others that might be formed or destroyed.

Steric hindrance The ability of groups, because of their size, to hinder access to a reaction site within a molecule.

Steric strain The strain that arises when atoms separated by four or more bonds are forced abnormally close to one another.

Steroid A plant or animal lipid having the characteristic tetracyclic ring structure of the steroid nucleus, namely, three six-membered rings and one five-membered ring.

Strong acid An acid that is completely ionized in aqueous solution.

Strong base A base that is completely ionized in aqueous solution.

Tautomers Constitutional isomers that differ in the location of hydrogen and a double bond relative to O, N, or S.

Tertiary (3°) structure of proteins The three-dimensional arrangement in space of all atoms in a single polypeptide chain.

Tertiary (3°) structure of nucleic acids The three-dimensional arrangement of all atoms of a nucleic acid, commonly referred to as supercoiling.

Thermoplastic A polymer that can be melted and molded into a shape that is retained when it is cooled.

Thermosetting plastic A polymer that can be molded when it is first prepared but, once cooled, hardens irreversibly and cannot be remelted.

Thioester An ester in which the oxygen atom of the —OR group is replaced by an atom of sulfur.

Thiol A compound containing an —SH (sulfhydryl) group.

Torsional strain (also called eclipsed interaction strain) Strain that arises when atoms separated by three bonds are forced from a staggered conformation to an eclipsed conformation.

Trans A prefix meaning "across from."

Transfer RNA (tRNA) A ribonucleic acid that carries a specific amino acid to the site of protein synthesis on ribosomes.

Transition state An unstable species of maximum energy formed during the course of a reaction; a maximum on an energy diagram.

Triglyceride (triacylglycerol) An ester of glycerol with three fatty acids.

Tripeptide A molecule containing three amino acid units, each joined to the next by a peptide bond.

Triplet A signal that is split into three peaks; the hydrogens that give rise to the signal have two neighboring nonequivalent hydrogens that are equivalent to each other.

Unimolecular reaction A reaction in which only one species is involved in the reaction leading to the transition state of the rate-determining step.

Upfield A term used to refer to the relative position of a signal on an NMR spectrum. Upfield indicates a peak to the right of the spectrum (a stronger applied field).

Valence electrons Electrons in the valence (outermost) shell of an atom.

Valence shell The outermost electron shell of an atom.

Vibrational infrared The portion of the infrared region that extends from 4000 to 400 cm^{-1}.

Wavelength (λ) The distance between two consecutive identical points on a wave.

Wavenumber ($\bar{\nu}$) A characteristic of electromagnetic radiation equal to the number of waves per centimeter.

Weak acid An acid that only partially ionizes in aqueous solution.

Weak base A base that only partially ionizes in aqueous solution.

Z From the German *zusammen*, meaning together; specifies that groups of higher priority on the carbons of a double bond are on the same side.

Zaitsev's rule A rule stating that the major product from a β-elimination reaction is the most stable alkene; that is, the major product is the alkene with the greatest number of substituents on the carbon–carbon double bond.

Zwitterion An internal salt of an amino acid.

CHAPTER 1 Covalent Bonding and Shapes of Molecules

Problems

1.1 The two elements in each pair have the same number of electrons in the outermost shell of orbitals (valence shell).
(a) Carbon = $1s^22s^22p^2$ Silicon = $1s^22s^22p^63s^23p^2$
(b) Oxygen = $1s^22s^22p^4$ Sulfur = $1s^22s^22p^63s^23p^4$
(c) Nitrogen = $1s^22s^22p^3$ Phosphorus = $1s^22s^22p^63s^23p^3$

1.2 The electron configuration of the sulfur atom is $1s^22s^22p^6\mathbf{3s^23p^4}$. When sulfur gains two electrons to form S^{2-}, the electron configuration becomes $1s^22s^22p^6\mathbf{3s^23p^6}$. The valence shell has a full octet and corresponds to the configuration of the noble gas Ar.

1.3 (a) Li (b) N (c) C

1.4

Bond	Type of bond
S—H	nonpolar covalent
P—H	nonpolar covalent
C—F	polar covalent
C—Cl	polar covalent

1.5 (a) $\overset{\delta+}{C}$—$\overset{\delta-}{N}$ (b) $\overset{\delta+}{N}$—$\overset{\delta-}{O}$ (c) $\overset{\delta+}{C}$—$\overset{\delta-}{Cl}$

1.6 (a) 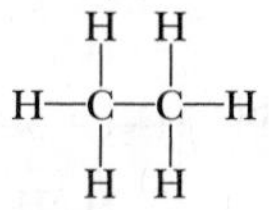 (b) 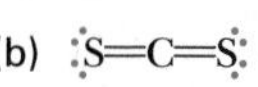

(c) H—C≡N:

1.7 (a) 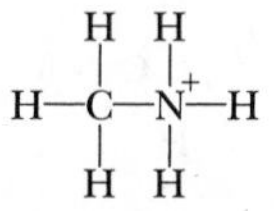 (b) 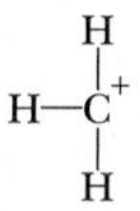

1.8 CH_3OH: all 109.5°
CH_2Cl_2: all 109.5°
H_2CO_3: 109.5° and 120°

1.9 The linear shape of CO_2 results in a cancellation of the dipole moments. In SO_2, which has a bent shape, the dipole moments do not cancel out.

1.10 Pair (a) only.

1.11 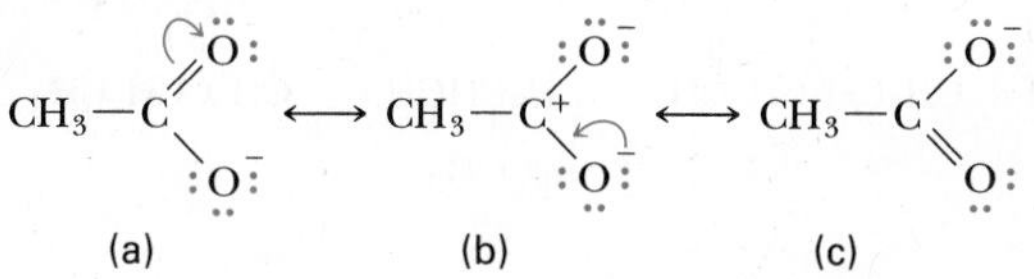

(a) (b) (c)

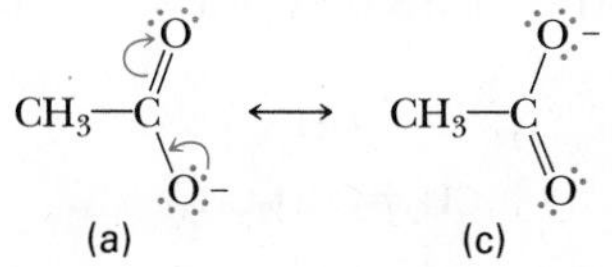

(a) (c)

1.12 (a) 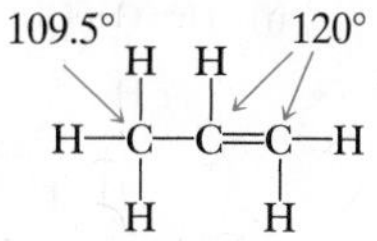 (b) 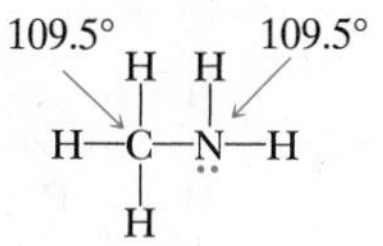

1.13 $CH_3CH_2CH_2CH_2OH$ (1°) 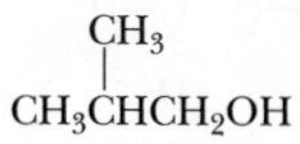 (1°)

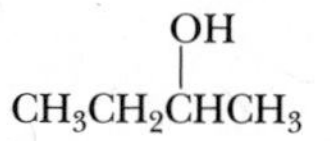 (2°) 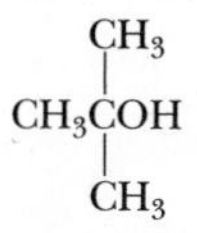 (3°)

1.14 $CH_3CH_2NHCH_2CH_3$ $CH_3CH_2CH_2NHCH_3$ 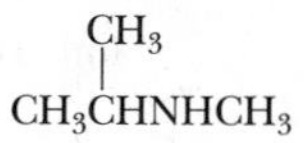

1.15 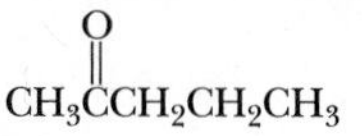 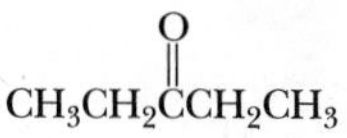 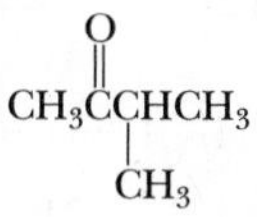

1.16 $CH_3CH_2CH_2COOH$ 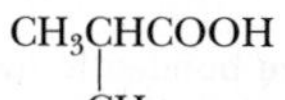

End-of-Chapter Problems

Electronic Structure of Atoms

1.17 (a) Sodium = $1s^22s^22p^63s^1$
(b) Magnesium = $1s^22s^22p^63s^2$
(c) Oxygen = $1s^22s^22p^4$
(d) Nitrogen = $1s^22s^22p^3$
(e) Potassium = $1s^22s^22p^63s^23p^64s^1$
(f) Aluminum = $1s^22s^22p^63s^23p^1$
(g) Phosphorus = $1s^22s^22p^63s^23p^3$
(h) Argon = $1s^22s^22p^63s^23p^6$

1.19 (a) S (b) O

1.21 The *valence shell* of an atom is the outermost shell that can be occupied by electrons in the ground state. The valence shell generally has the highest principal quantum number (*n*). A *valence electron* is an electron that is situated in the valence shell. Valence electrons are more important because they are the electrons involved in bond formation.

1.23 (a) 0 (b) 2 (c) 8 (d) 6

Lewis Structures

1.25

(a) Li—F	ionic
(b) C—F	polar covalent
C—H	nonpolar covalent
(c) Mg—Cl	polar covalent
(d) H—Cl	polar covalent

1.27
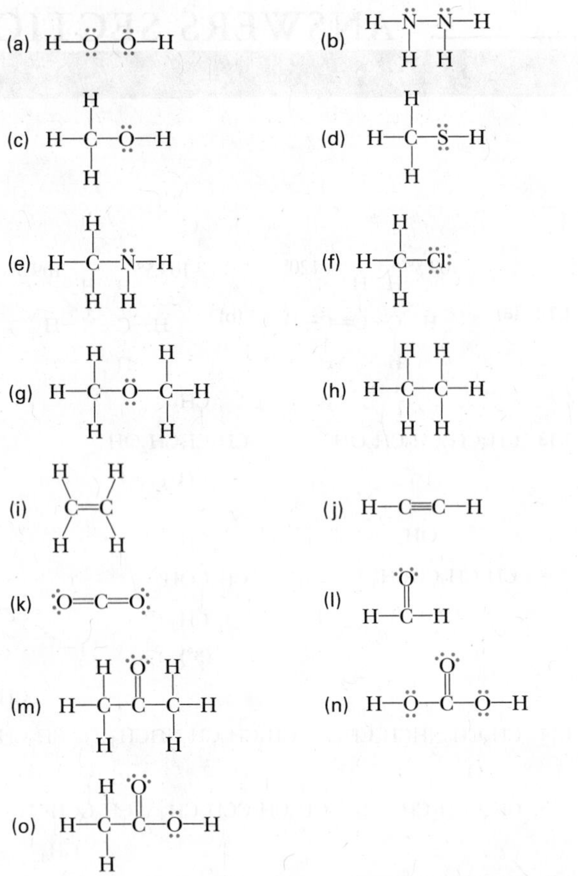

1.29 (a) If carbon were bonded to five hydrogen atoms, the octet rule would be violated. Furthermore, each hydrogen atom can only bond with one other atom, so there is no stable connectivity of the formula CH_5.
(b) Each hydrogen atom can only bond with one other atom, so a single hydrogen atom cannot be bonded to both carbons.
(c) The proton, H^+, does not contain any electrons, so it is not possible to form a bond between two protons.

1.31
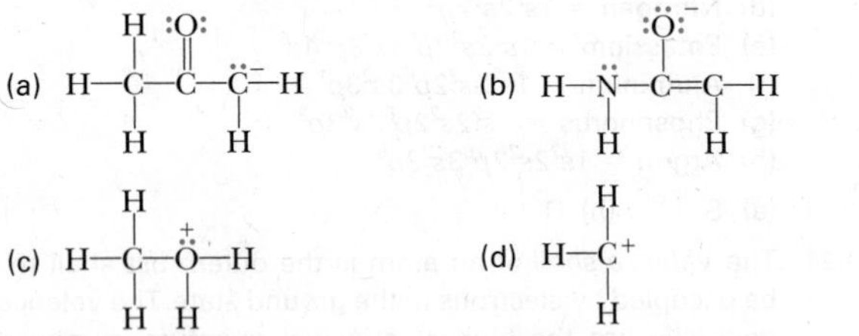

1.33 Given the electronegativity difference between Ag and O, the bonding is polar covalent

1.35 a

1.37 (a) C—H < N—H < O—H
(b) C—I < C—H < C—Cl
(c) C—C < C—N < C—O
(d) C—Hg < C—Mg < C—Li

1.39 (a) O—H (b) C—F (c) O—H

Bond Angles and Shapes of Molecules

1.41
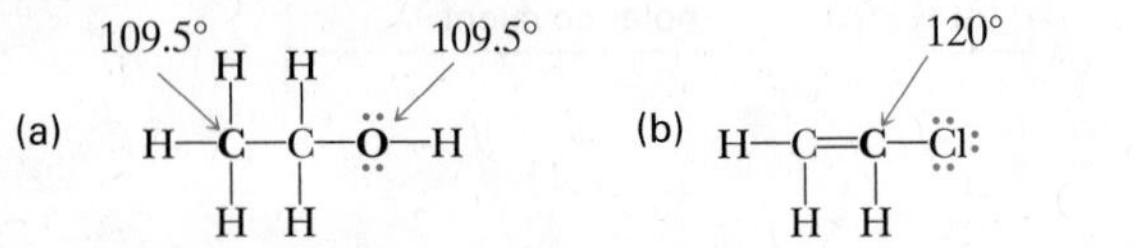

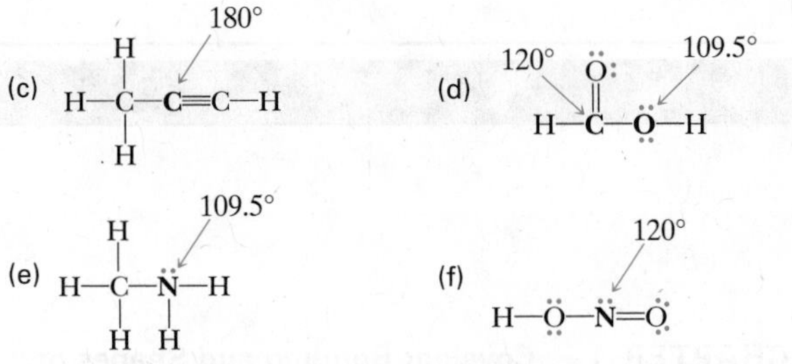

1.43 109.5°

Polar and Nonpolar Molecules

1.45
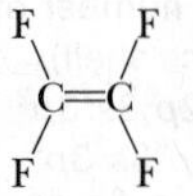

Contributing Structures

1.47 a, b, d, e, f, and g

1.49 The bond angle of the carbon atom involved in resonance remains at 120° and does not change from one contributing structure to another. The carbon atom in the CH_3 group of pair (c) has a bond angle of 109.5°.

Hybridization of Atomic Orbitals

1.51
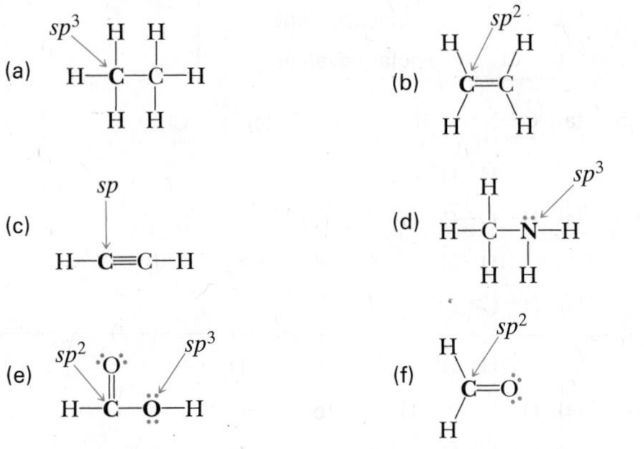

Functional Groups

1.53
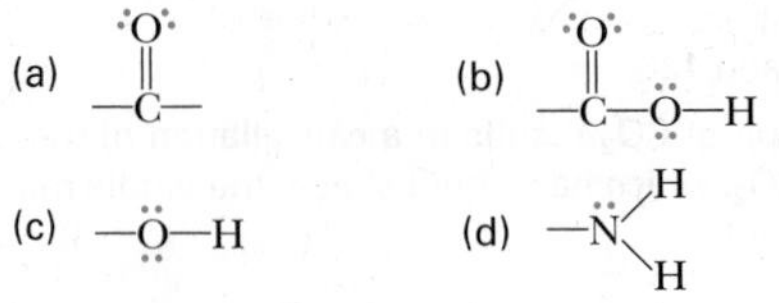

1.55 (a)
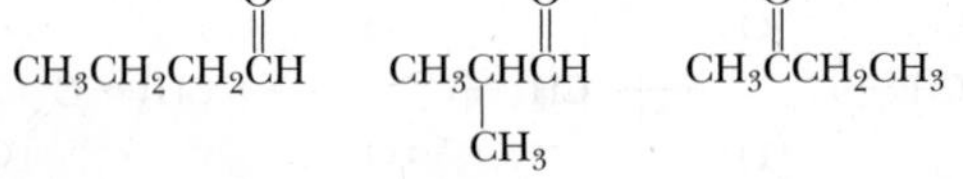

(b)
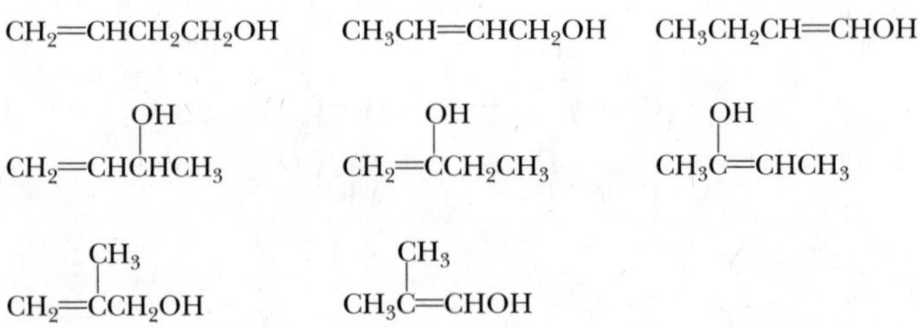

1.57 (a)

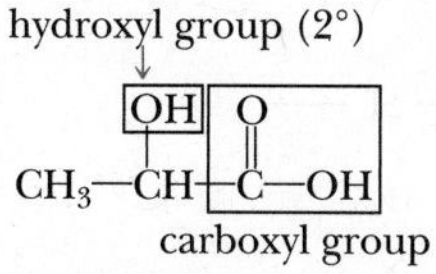

(b)

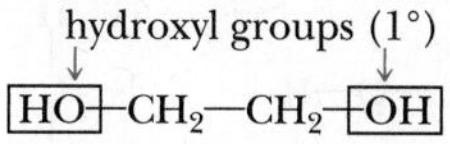

(c)

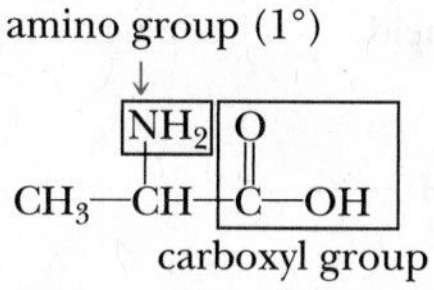

(d)

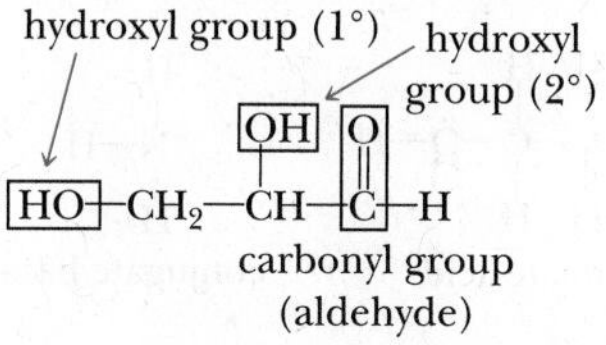

(e)

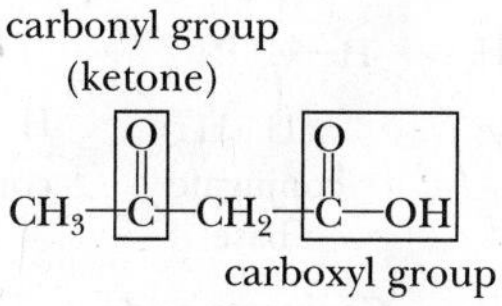

(f)

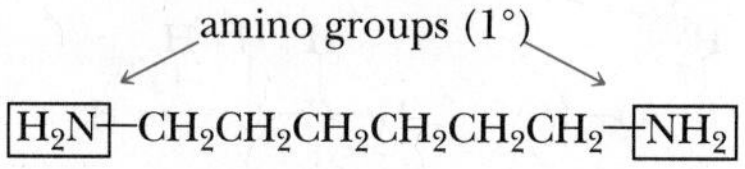

1.59

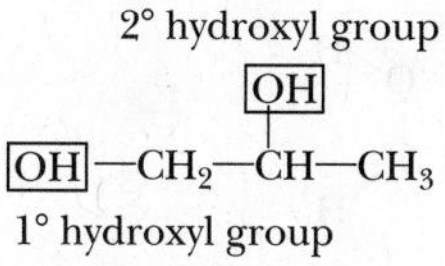

1.61 CO_2 is linear, while O_3 is bent. All atoms in both molecules are *sp*²-hybridized.

Looking Ahead

1.63 The two terminal carbon atoms are *sp*²-hybridized. Although the carbon chain is linear and the two terminal carbon atoms are trigonal planar, the molecule is not flat.

1.65 (a) 6 (b) 120° (c) *sp*²

1.67 (a) 120° (b) *sp*² (c) planar

CHAPTER 2 Acids and Bases

Problems

2.1 (a)

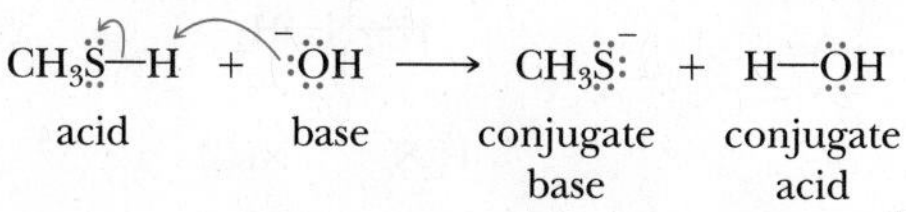

(b)

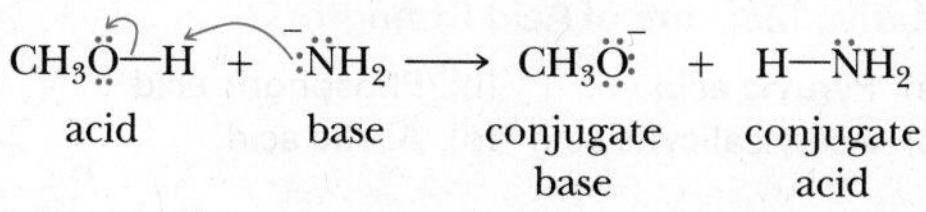

2.2 (a) Acetic acid pK_a = 4.76
(b) Water pK_a = 15.7
Acetic acid is a stronger acid.

2.3 (a) $CH_3NH_2 + CH_3COOH \rightleftharpoons CH_3NH_3^+ + CH_3COO^-$

Methylamine	Acetic acid	Methylammonium ion	Acetate ion
stronger base	stronger acid	weaker acid	weaker base
	pK_a = 4.76	pK_a = 10.6	

(b) $CH_3CH_2O^- + NH_3 \rightleftharpoons CH_3CH_2OH + NH_2^-$

Ethoxide ion	Ammonia	Ethanol	Amide ion
weaker base	weaker acid	stronger acid	stronger base
	pK_a = 38	pK_a =15.9	

2.4 (a) 2 > 1 > 3 (b) 3 > 1 > 2

2.5

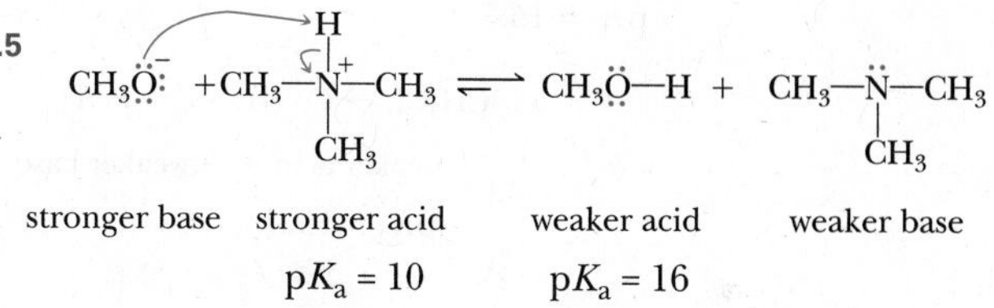

2.6 (a)

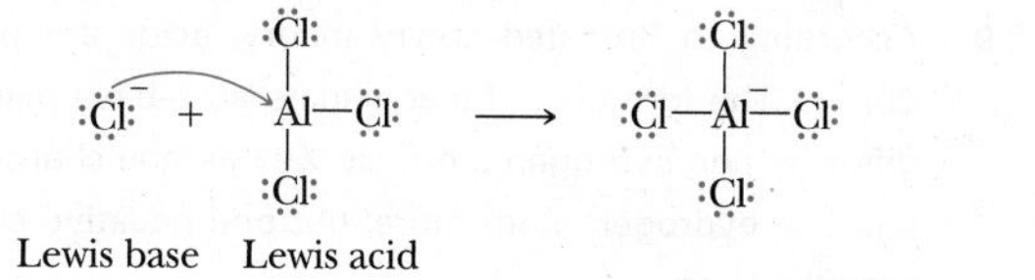

(b)

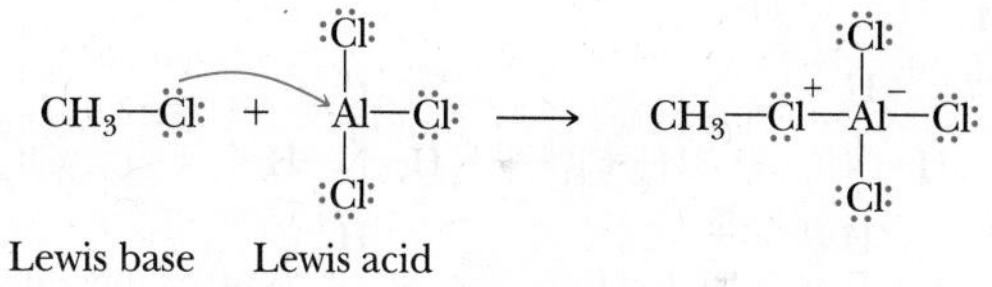

End-of-Chapter Problems

Arrhenius Acids and Bases

2.7

(a)

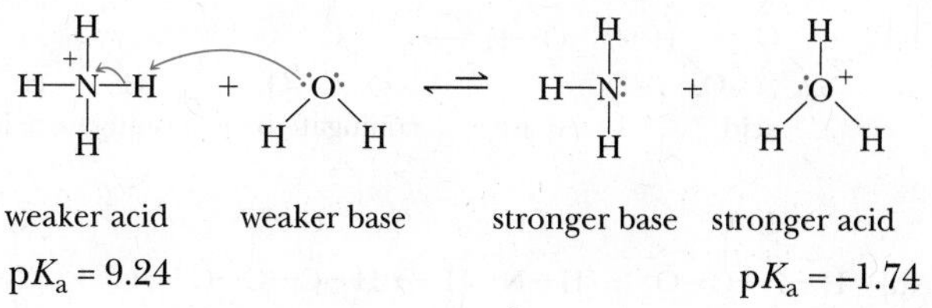

(b)

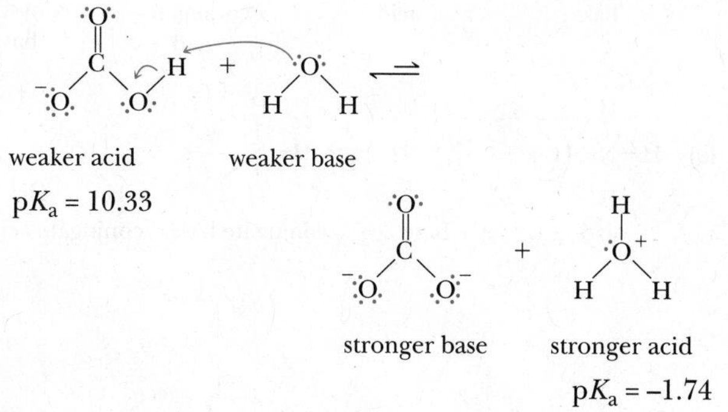

(c) 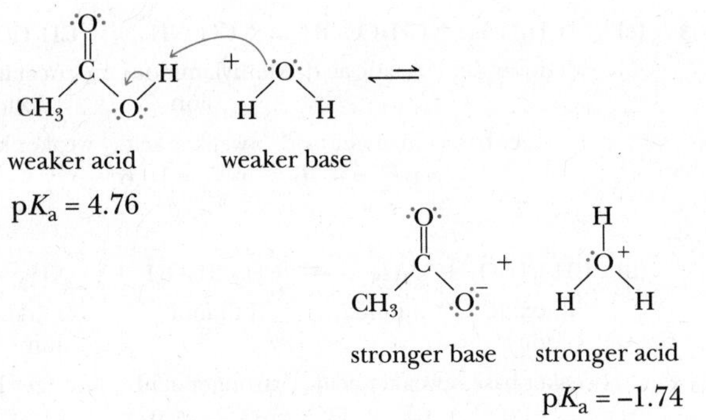

weaker acid — weaker base — $pK_a = 4.76$

stronger base — stronger acid — $pK_a = -1.74$

(d) 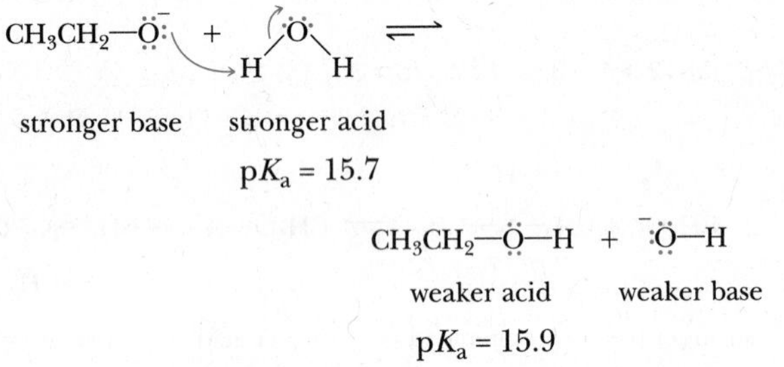

stronger base — stronger acid — $pK_a = 15.7$

weaker acid — weaker base — $pK_a = 15.9$

Brønsted–Lowry Acids and Bases

2.9 According to Brønsted–Lowry theory, acids are proton (H^+) donors. The formulas of a conjugate acid–base pair therefore differ by one hydrogen atom, as well as one charge. The acid has one hydrogen atom more, but one negative charge less, than the base.

2.11

(a) 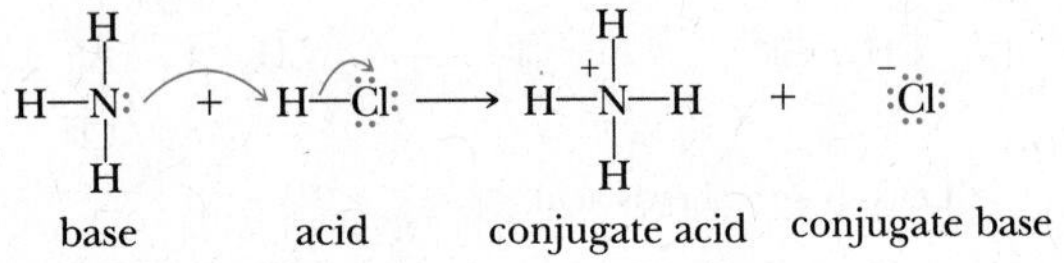

base — acid — conjugate acid — conjugate base

(b) 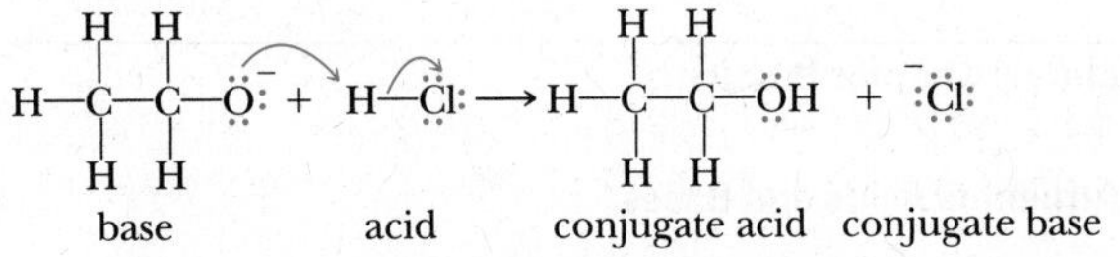

base — acid — conjugate acid — conjugate base

(c) 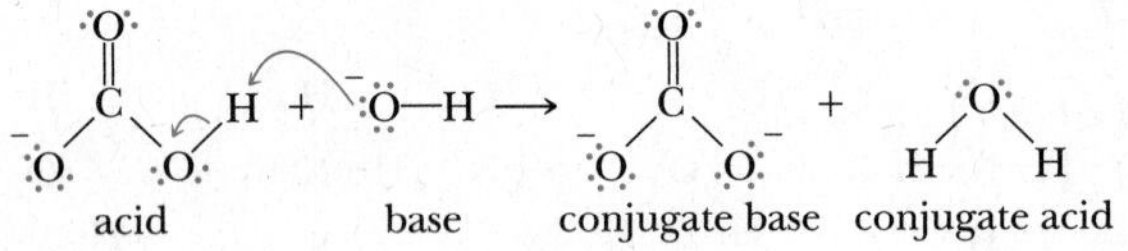

acid — base — conjugate base — conjugate acid

(d) 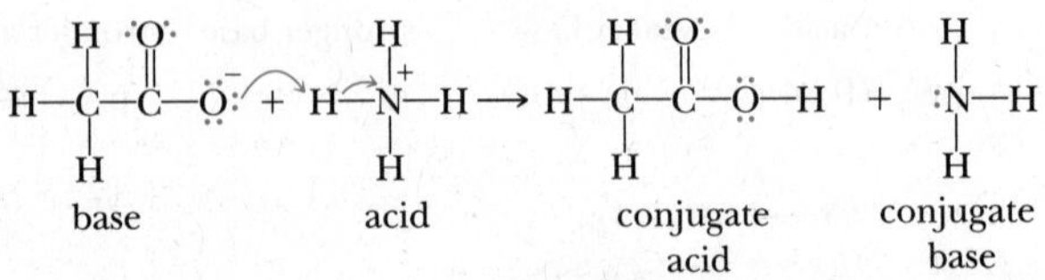

base — acid — conjugate acid — conjugate base

(e) 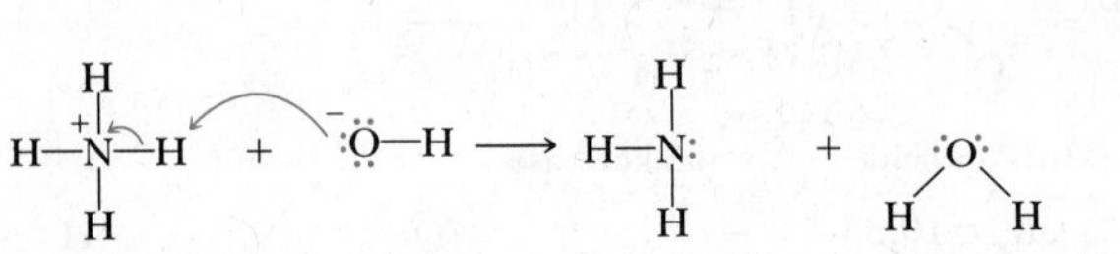

acid — base — conjugate base — conjugate acid

(f) 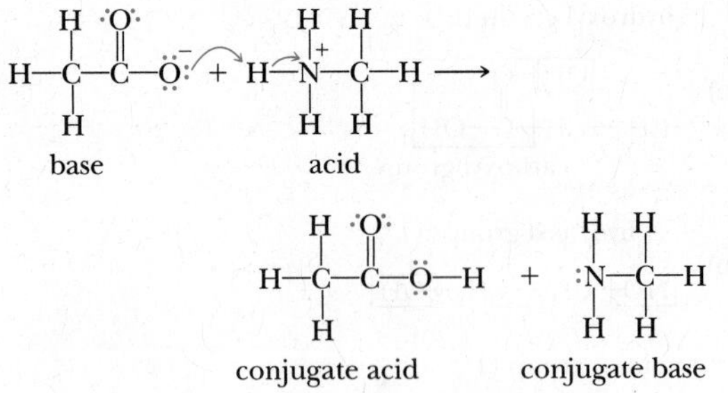

base — acid — conjugate acid — conjugate base

(g) 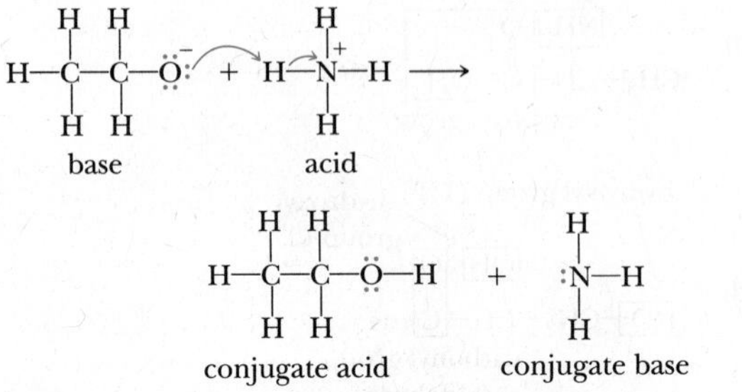

base — acid — conjugate acid — conjugate base

(h) 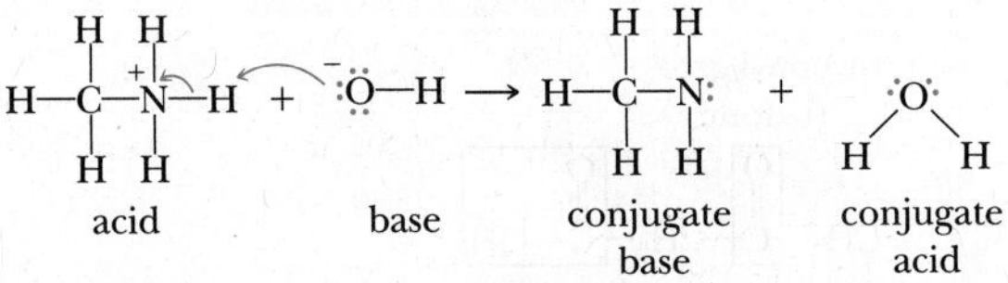

acid — base — conjugate base — conjugate acid

2.13 **Bases** — **Conjugate acids**

(a) (b) (c) (d)

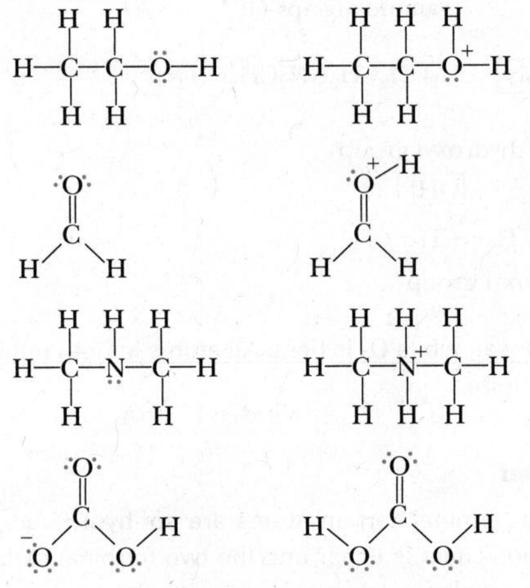

2.15 (a) H_b is the most acidic proton.

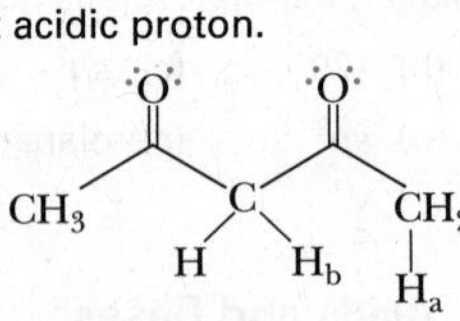

(b) H_a is the most acidic proton.

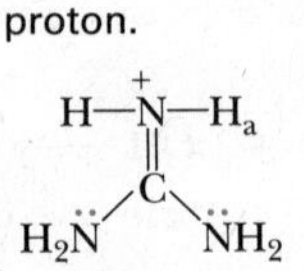

Quantitative Measure of Acid Strength

2.17 (a) Pyruvic acid (b) Phosphoric acid
(c) Acetylsalicylic acid (d) Acetic acid

2.19 (a) $HOC(=O)O^- < NH_3 < CH_3CH_2O^-$

(b) $CH_3C(=O)O^- < HOC(=O)O^- < HO^-$

(c) $H_2O < CH_3C(=O)O^- < NH_3$

(d) $CH_3C(=O)O^- < OH^- < NH_2^-$

2.21 H_2S ionizes to form a conjugate base (HS^-) that is more stable than the conjugate base of H_2O (HO^-).

Position of Equilibrium in Acid–Base Reactions

2.23 $HOC(=O)OH \longrightarrow CO_2 + H_2O$

2.25 (a) $CH_3COOH + HCO_3^- \rightleftharpoons CH_3COO^- + H_2CO_3$
pK_a = 4.76   pK_a = 6.36

(b) $CH_3COOH + NH_3 \rightleftharpoons CH_3COO^- + NH_4^+$
pK_a = 4.76   pK_a = 9.24

(c) $CH_3COOH + H_2O \rightleftharpoons CH_3COO^- + H_3O^+$
pK_a = 4.76   pK_a = −1.74

(d) $CH_3COOH + OH^- \rightleftharpoons CH_3COO^- + H_2O$
pK_a = 4.76   pK_a = 15.7

2.27 In acid–base equilibria, the position of the equilibrium favors the reaction of the stronger acid and stronger base to give the weaker acid and weaker base.

Relationship Between Acidity and Basicity and Molecular Structure

2.29 (a) The oxygen of the carbonyl group is more basic because it has a partial negative charge.

(b) For the same reason as (a), the N is more basic. However, in this case, there is an additional effect: Because N is lower in electronegativity than O, the N is even more likely to accept a proton.

(c) The carbon on the left is more basic because the carbon on the right is stabilized by resonance. Furthermore, the delocalization of the negative charge of the carbon on the right increases the negative charge of the carbon on the left.

(d) The amine is more basic than the alcohol because nitrogen has a lower electronegativity than does oxygen.

Lewis Acids and Bases

2.31

(a)

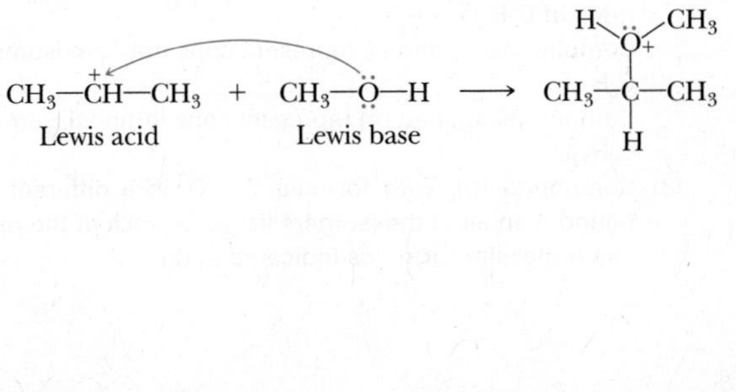

(b)

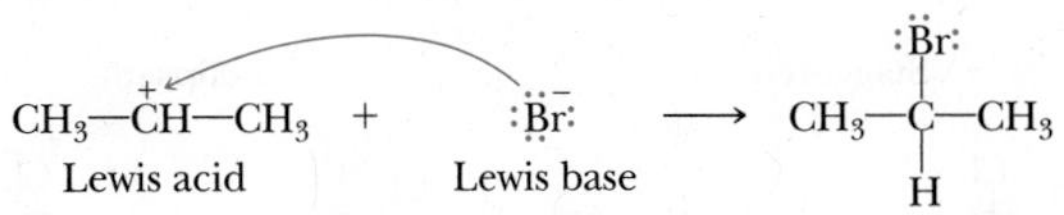

(c)

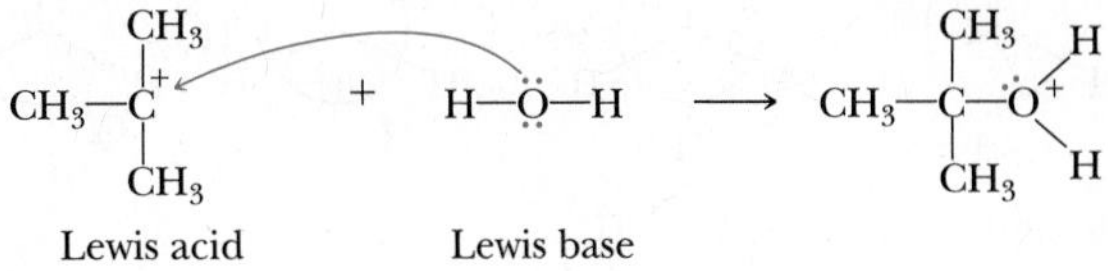

Looking Ahead

2.33 (a) $CH_3CH_2OH + HCO_3^- \rightleftharpoons CH_3CH_2O^- + H_2CO_3$
pK_a = 15.9   pK_a = 6.36

(b) $CH_3CH_2OH + OH^- \rightleftharpoons CH_3CH_2O^- + H_2O$
pK_a = 15.9   pK_a = 15.7

(c) $CH_3CH_2OH + NH_2^- \rightleftharpoons CH_3CH_2O^- + NH_3$
pK_a = 15.9   pK_a = 38

(d) $CH_3CH_2OH + NH_3 \rightleftharpoons CH_3CH_2O^- + NH_4^+$
pK_a = 15.9   pK_a = 9.24

2.35 Benzoic acid will dissolve in all three solutions.

2.37 The conjugate base of dimethyl ether is a highly unstable C^- ion that is stabilized by only the inductive effect of the electronegative oxygen atom. As a result, dimethyl ether is not very acidic.

2.39 Amino acids are bifunctional in that they contain both basic (amino) and acidic (carboxyl) groups. These groups undergo an intramolecular acid–base reaction to give structural formula (B), which is the better representation of alanine.

CHAPTER 3 Alkanes and Cycloalkanes

Problems

3.1 (a) Constitutional isomers (b) Same compound

3.2

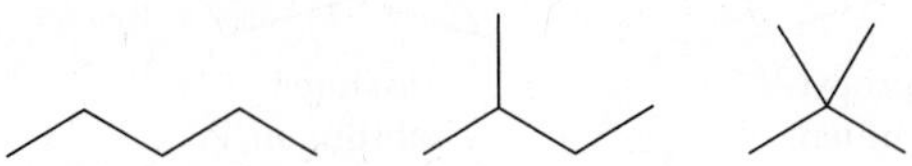

3.3 (a) 5-Isopropyl-2-methyloctane
(b) 4-Isopropyl-4-propyloctane
(c) 4-Ethyl-2,3-dimethylheptane
(d) 4,6-Diisopropyl-2-methylnonane

3.4 (a)

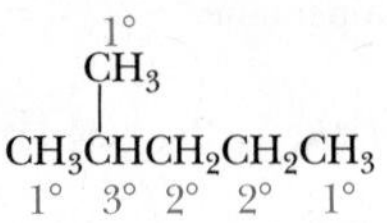

(b)

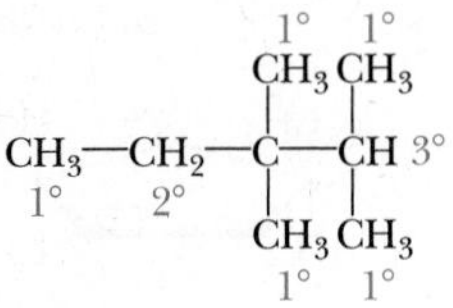

3.5 (a) C_9H_{18} Isobutylcyclopentane
(b) $C_{11}H_{22}$ *sec*-Butylcycloheptane
(c) C_6H_{12} 1-Ethyl-1-methylcyclopropane

3.6 (a) Propanone (b) Pentanal
(c) Cyclopentanone (d) Cycloheptene

3.7

Staggered **Eclipsed**

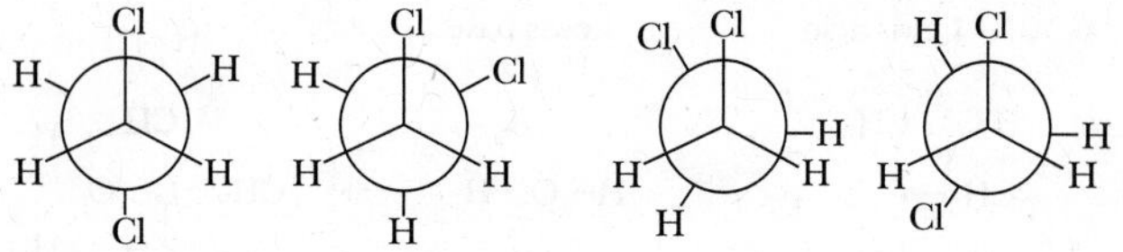

3.8 (a)

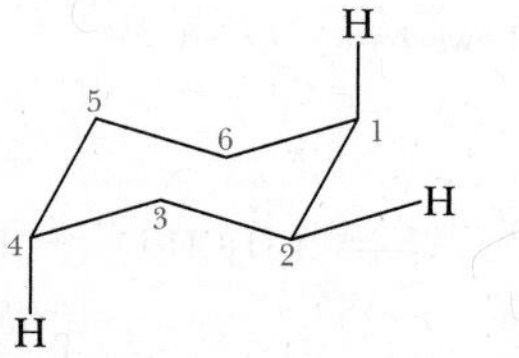

(b) The hydrogen on carbon 2 is equatorial, and the hydrogens on carbons 1 and 4 are axial.

(c)

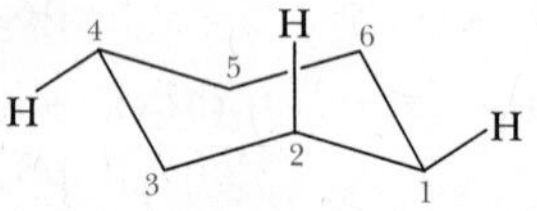

The hydrogen atom on carbon 1 is now equatorial, the hydrogen atom on carbon 2 is now axial, and the hydrogen atom on carbon 4 is now equatorial.

3.9 An axial *tert*-butyl group will always have a $-CH_3$ group directed at the other axial substituents, while the methyl, ethyl, and isopropyl groups of the other three compounds can adopt a conformation where the $-CH_3$ groups face away from the other axial positions.

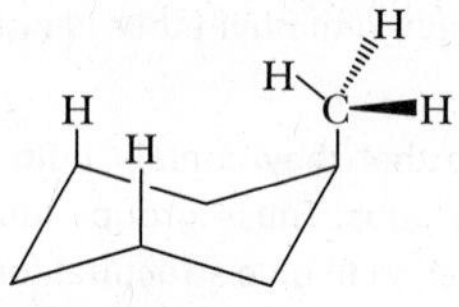

methyl substituent

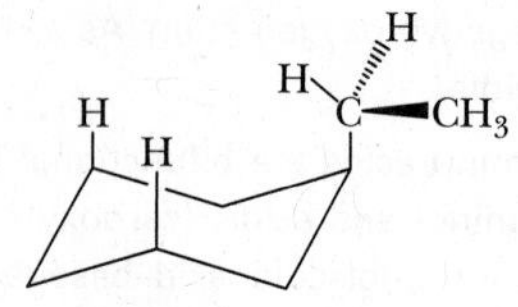

ethyl substituent

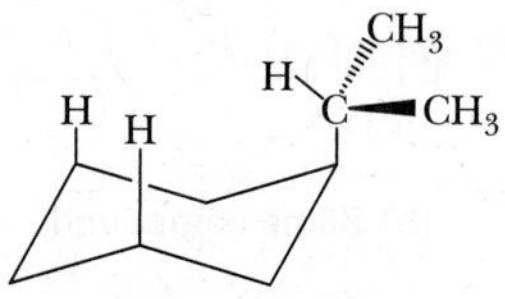

isopropyl substituent

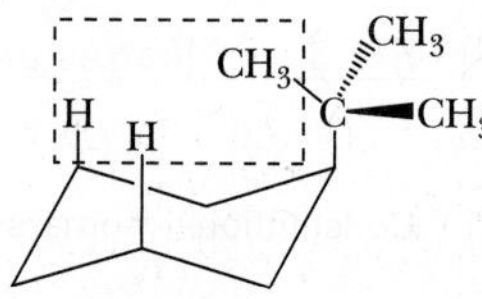

tert-butyl substituent

3.10 (a)

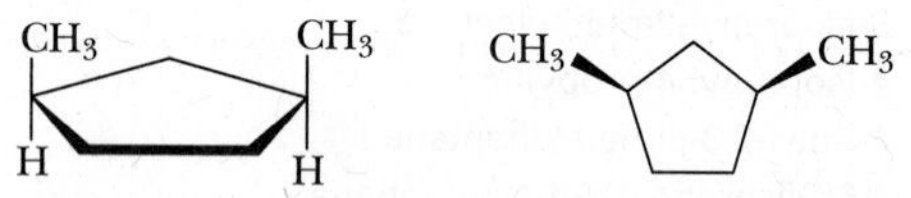

cis-1,3-Dimethylcyclopentane

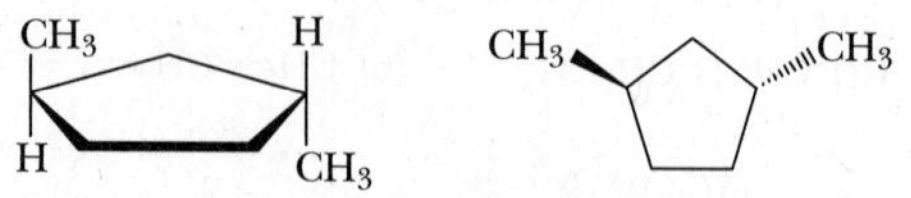

trans-1,3-Dimethylcyclopentane

(b) *cis-trans* isomerism is not possible.

(c)

cis-1-Ethyl-2-methylcyclobutane

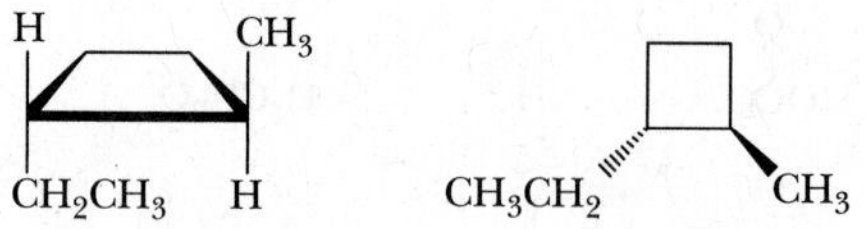

trans-1-Ethyl-2-methylcyclobutane

3.11

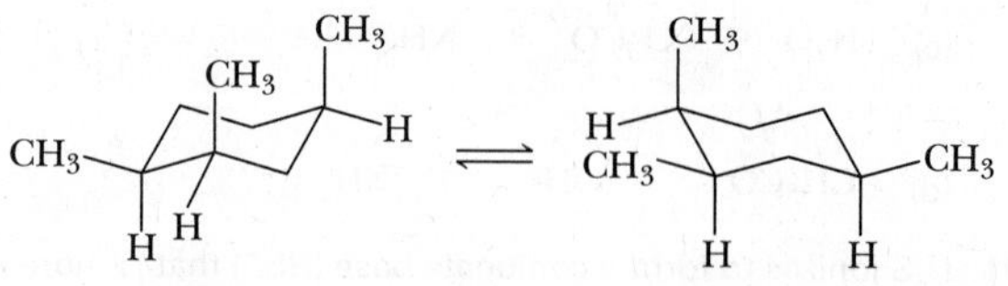

less stable more stable

3.12 (a) 2,2-Dimethylpropane < 2-Methylbutane < Pentane
(b) 2,2,4-Trimethylhexane < 3,3-Dimethylheptane < Nonane

End-of-Chapter Problems

Structure of Alkanes

3.13 (a)

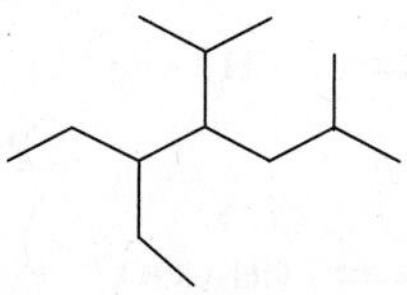

(b)

(c)

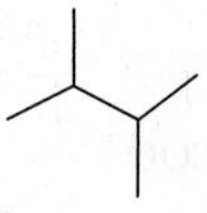

(d)

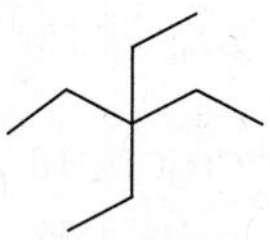

(e)

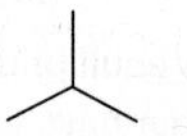

(f)

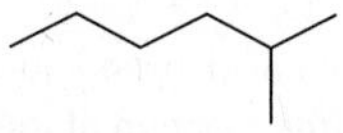

3.15 (a) $CH_3(CH_2)_4CH(CH_3)_2$ (b) $HC(CH_2CH_2CH_3)_3$

(c) $CH_3C(CH_2)_4CH_3$ with two $(CH_2)_2CH_3$ groups on the C (one drawn above, one below)

Constitutional Isomerism

3.17 (1) Compounds (a) and (g) represent the same compound. Compounds (d) and (e) represent the same compound.
(2) Compounds (a = g), (d = e), and (f) represent constitutional isomers of $C_4H_{10}O$.
Compounds (b) and (c) represent constitutional isomers of C_4H_8O.
(3) The isomers of $C_4H_{10}O$ [(a = g) and (d = e)] are different compounds from the isomers of C_4H_8O [(b) and (c)], and all are different from compound (h).

3.19 (1) None of the compounds are the same.
(2) Compounds (a), (d), and (e) represent constitutional isomers of C_4H_8O.
Compounds (c) and (f) represent constitutional isomers of $C_5H_{10}O$.
Compounds (g) and (h) represent constitutional isomers of $C_6H_{10}O$.
(3) Compound (b), with formula C_5H_8O, is a different compound than all of the isomers listed for each of the respective molecular formulas indicated in (2).

3.21

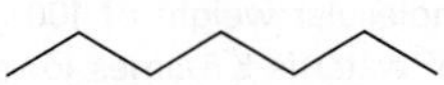

Heptane

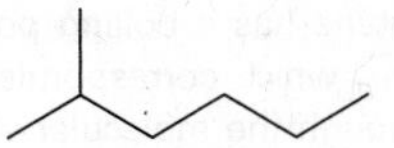

2-Methylhexane

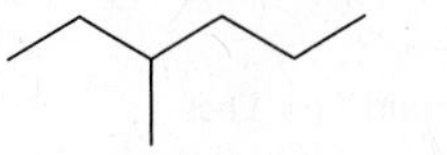

3-Methylhexane

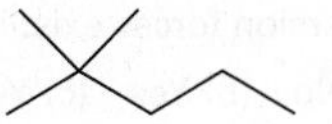

2,2-Dimethylpentane

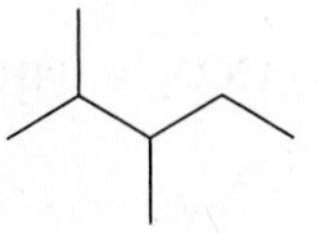

2,3-Dimethylpentane

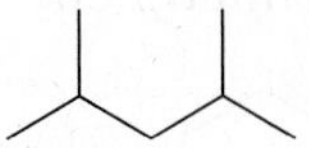

2,4-Dimethylpentane

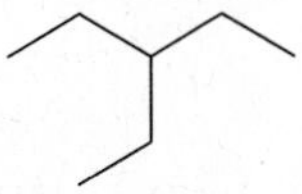

3-Ethylpentane

3,3-Dimethylpentane

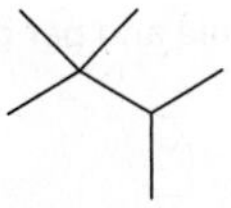

2,2,3-Trimethylbutane

3.23

(a)

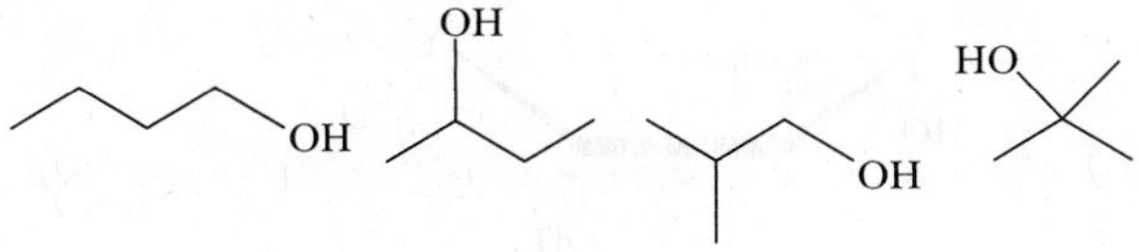

(b)

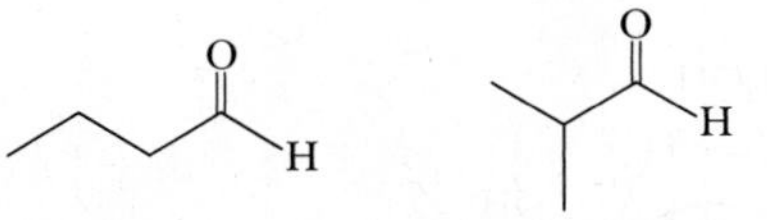

(c)

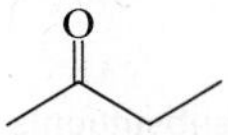

(d)

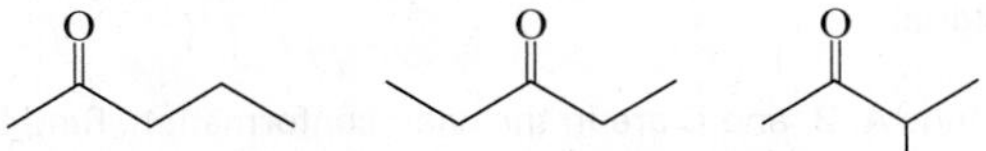

(e)

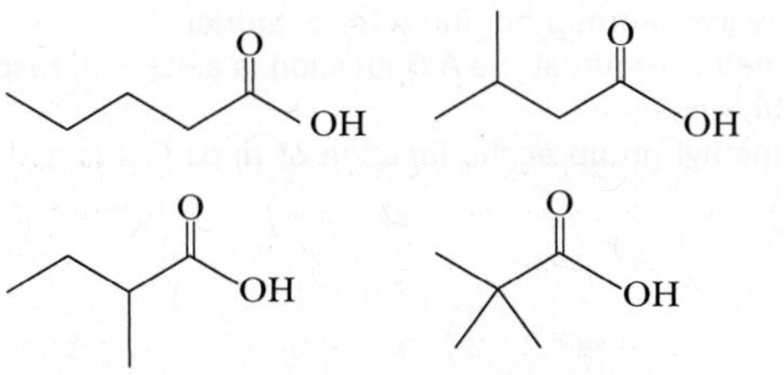

Nomenclature of Alkanes and Cycloalkanes

3.25 (a)

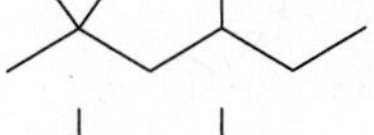

(b)

(c)

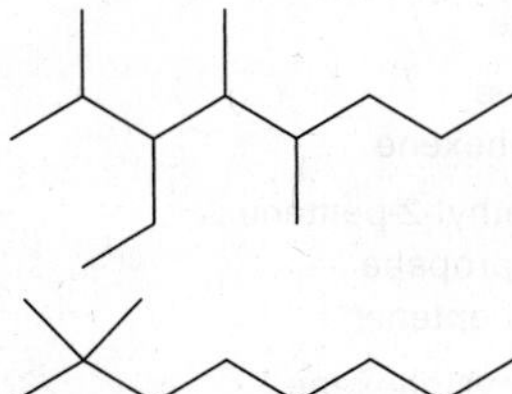

(d)

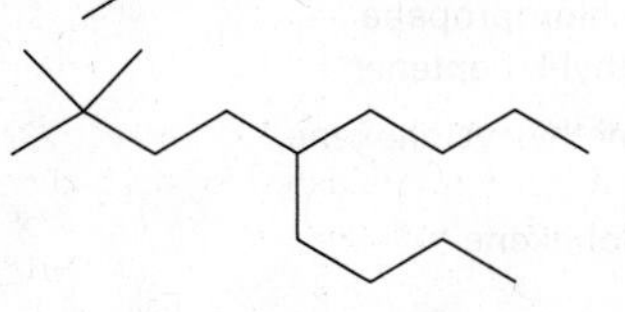

(e)

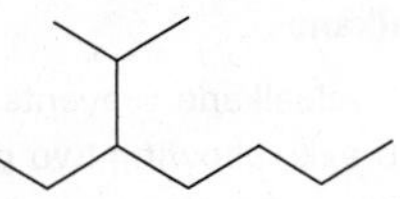

(f)

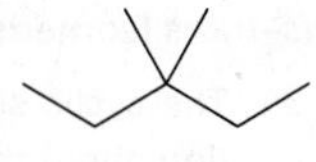

(g)

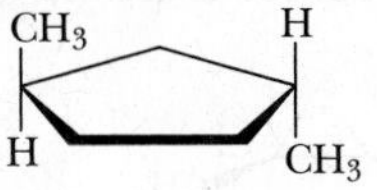

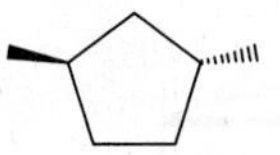

(h)

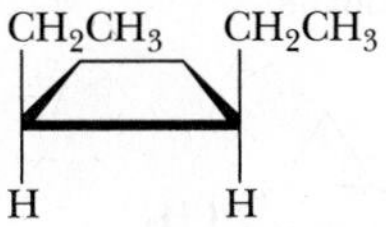

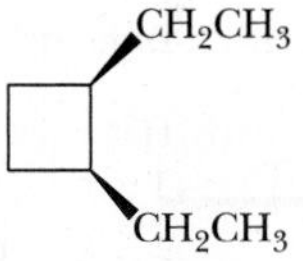

3.27

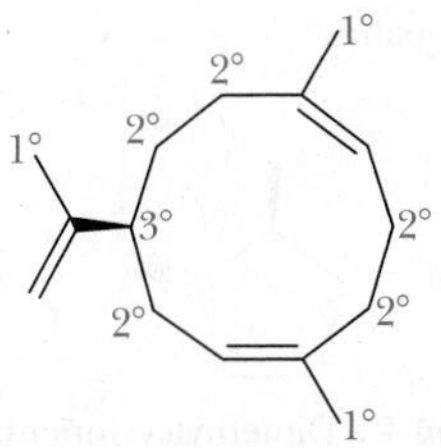

3.29 (a) CH_3CH_2OH (b) $CH_3\overset{O}{\overset{\|}{C}}H$

(c) $CH_3\overset{O}{\overset{\|}{C}}OH$ (d) $CH_3\overset{O}{\overset{\|}{C}}CH_2CH_3$

(e) $CH_3CH_2CH_2\overset{O}{\overset{\|}{C}}H$ (f) $CH_3CH_2CH_2\overset{O}{\overset{\|}{C}}OH$

(g) $CH_3CH_2\overset{O}{\overset{\|}{C}}H$ (h)

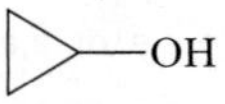

(i)

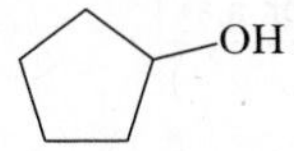

(j)

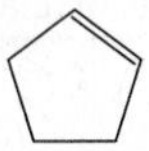

(k)

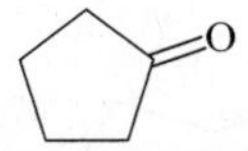

Conformations of Alkanes and Cycloalkanes

3.31 2-Methylpropane has only one staggered conformation and one eclipsed conformation.

3.33 (a) Although the molecule is in a staggered conformation, the two methyl groups are next to one another, increasing steric strain.

(b) Being an eclipsed conformation, the molecule experiences high torsional strain.

(c) The methyl and *tert*-butyl groups are in close proximity, increasing steric strain.

(d) The ethyl and isopropyl groups, which are the two largest groups, are in close proximity.

3.35 (b)

3.37 (a)

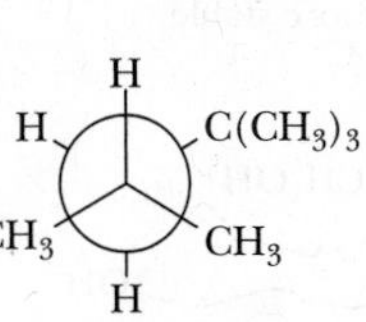

(b)

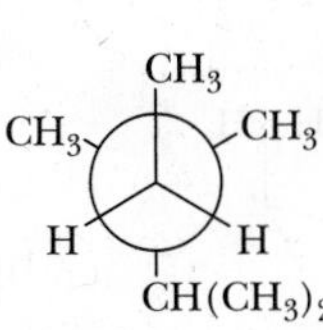

(c)

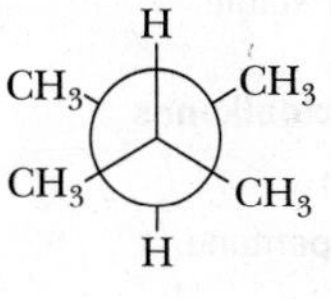

(d)

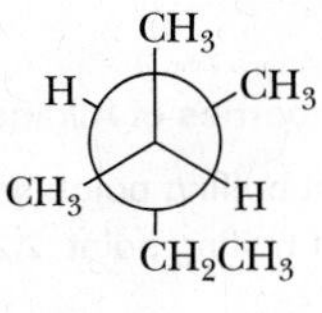

cis–trans Isomerism in Cycloalkanes

3.39 The cyclic structure of a cycloalkane prevents full 360° rotation about the C—C bond axis, allowing two possible spatial orientations of the substituents bonded to each sp^3 carbon.

3.41

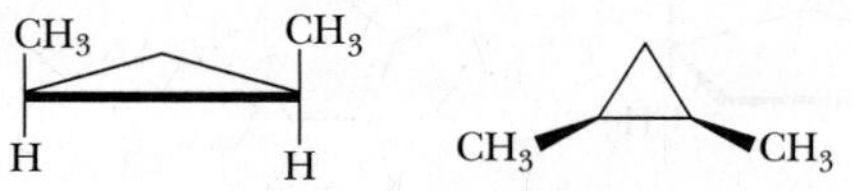

cis-1,2-Dimethylcyclopropane

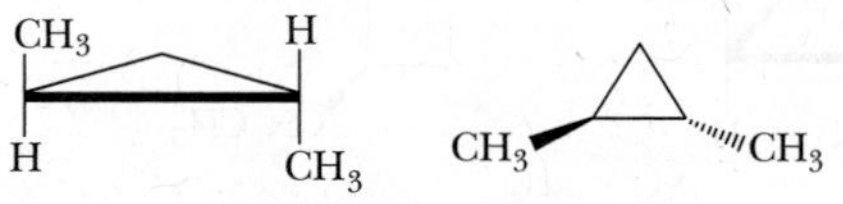

trans-1,2-Dimethylcyclopropane

3.43

(a)

cis-1,2-Dimethylcyclopentane *trans*-1,2-Dimethylcyclopentane

(b)

cis-1,3-Dimethylcyclopentane *trans*-1,3-Dimethylcyclopentane

3.45

Position of substitution	*cis*	*trans*
1,2-	a,e or e,a	e,e or a,a
1,3-	e,e or a,a	a,e or e,a
1,4-	a,e or e,a	e,e or a,a

3.47

(a)

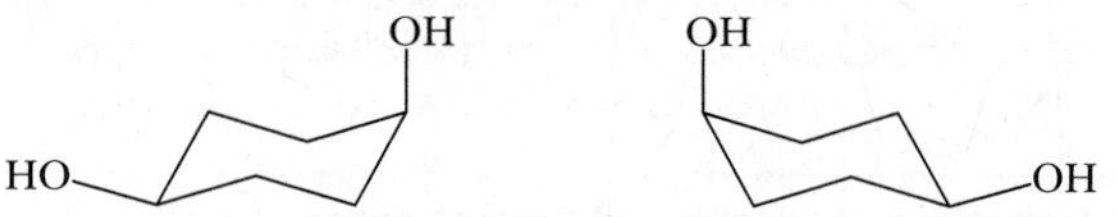

chairs are of equal stability

(b)

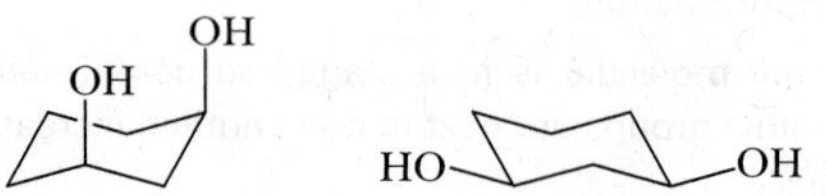

more stable

(c)

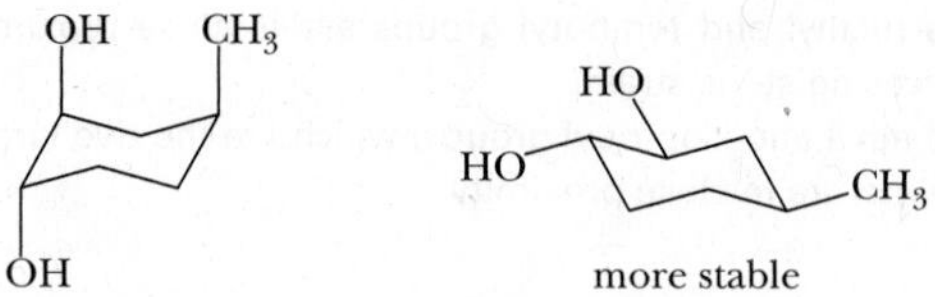

more stable

(d)

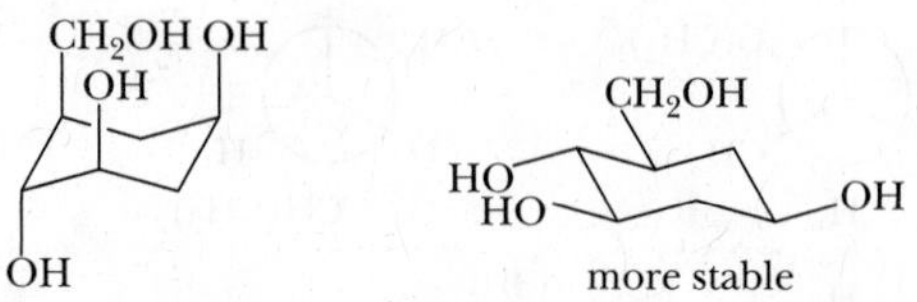

more stable

Physical Properties of Alkanes and Cycloalkanes

3.49 Highest boiling point: heptane
Lowest boiling point: 2,2-dimethylpentane

3.51 Heptane has a boiling point of 98 °C. Its molecular formula is C_7H_{16}, which corresponds to a molecular weight of 100 g/mol. Although the molecular weight of water is 5.5 times lower, the relatively strong hydrogen bonding forces hold the molecules of liquid water together. On the contrary, only the relatively weak dispersion forces exist in heptane.

3.53 (a) No (b) Yes (c) Yes (d) Liquid (e) Less

Reactions of Alkanes

3.55 (a) $2CH_3(CH_2)_4CH_3 + 19O_2 \longrightarrow 12CO_2 + 14H_2O$

(b) 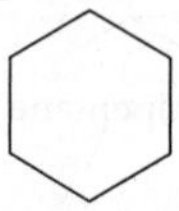 $+ 9O_2 \longrightarrow 6CO_2 + 6H_2O$

(c) $2CH_3\overset{CH_3}{\overset{|}{C}}HCH_2CH_2CH_3 + 19O_2 \longrightarrow 12CO_2 + 14H_2O$

3.57 2,2,4-trimethylpentane on both a per mole and per gram basis

Looking Ahead

3.59 (a)

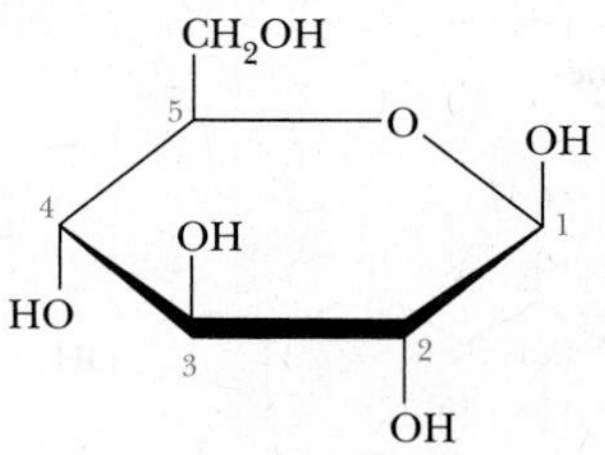

(b)

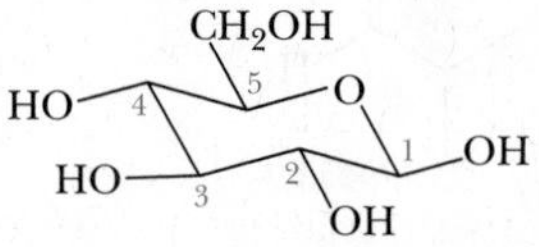

All the hydrogens are axial, and all the other substituents are equatorial.

3.61 (a) Rings A, B, and C are in the chair conformation. Ring D, a cyclopentane ring, is in an envelope conformation.
(b) The hydroxyl group on ring A is equatorial.
(c) The methyl group at the A/B junction is axial with respect to both rings.
(d) The methyl group at the junction of rings C/D is axial to ring C.

CHAPTER 4 Alkenes and Alkynes

Problems

4.1 (a) 3,3-Dimethyl-1-pentene
(b) 2,3-Dimethyl-2-butene
(c) 3,3-Dimethyl-1-butyne

4.2 (a) *cis*-4-Methyl-2-pentene
(b) *trans*-2,2-Dimethyl-3-hexene

4.3 (a) (*E*)-1-Chloro-2,3-dimethyl-2-pentene
(b) (*Z*)-1-Bromo-1-chloropropene
(c) (*E*)-2,3,4-Trimethyl-3-heptene

4.4 (a) 1-Isopropyl-4-methylcyclohexene
(b) Cyclooctene
(c) 4-*tert*-Butylcyclohexene

4.5

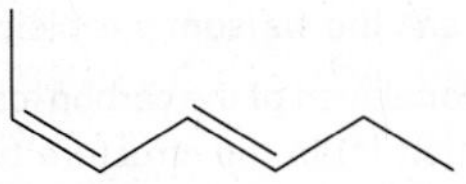

cis,trans-2,4-Heptadiene

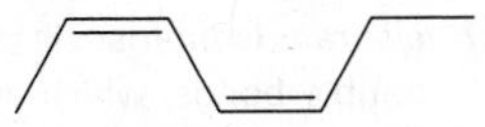

cis,cis-2,4-Heptadiene

4.6 4

End-of-Chapter Problems

Structure of Alkenes and Alkynes

4.7 (a) The alkene will dissolve in cyclohexane, forming a homogeneous solution.
(b) When nonpolar *trans*-3-heptene is added to ammonia, an immiscible mixture is formed.

4.9 A compound that is *saturated* does not contain any carbon–carbon π bonds. Compounds that are *unsaturated* contain one or more carbon–carbon π bonds.

4.11 (a)

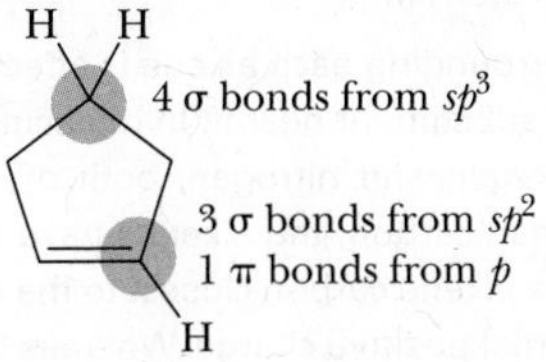

(b)

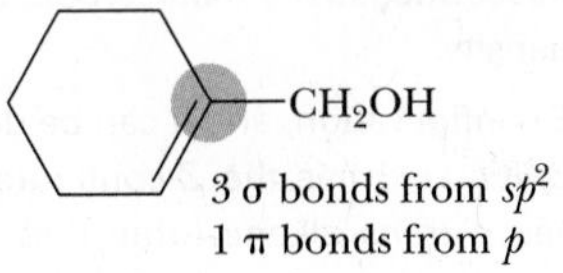

(c)

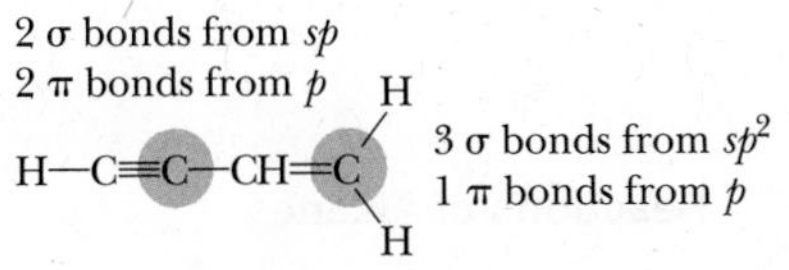

(d)

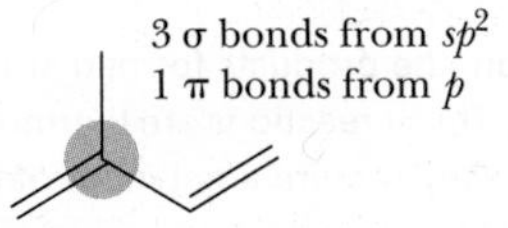

4.13 (a)

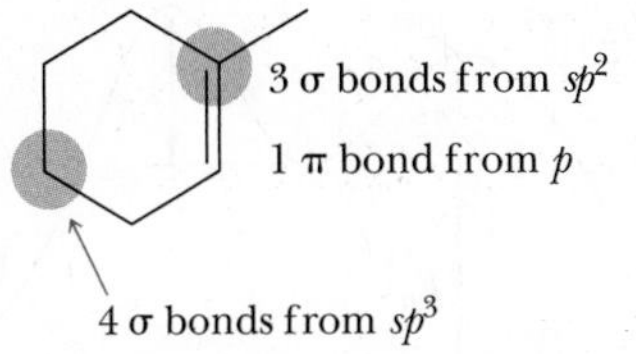

(b)

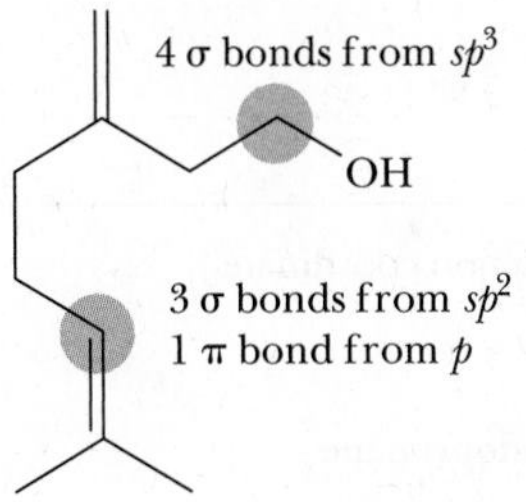

(c)

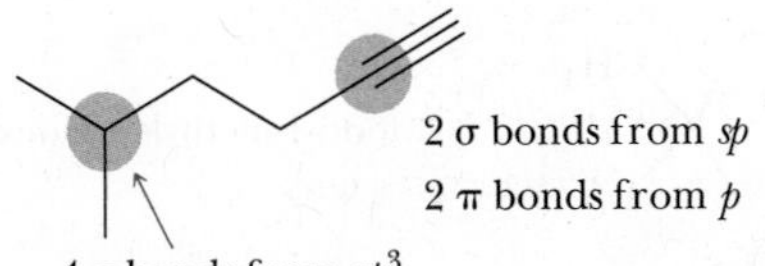

(d)

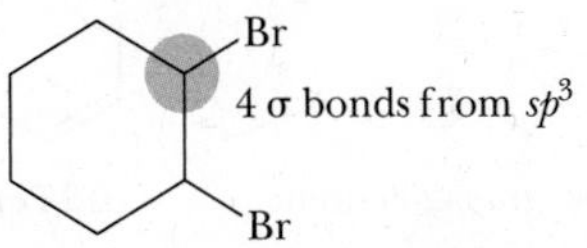

Nomenclature of Alkenes and Alkynes

4.15 (a)

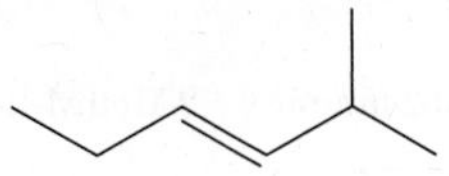

(b)

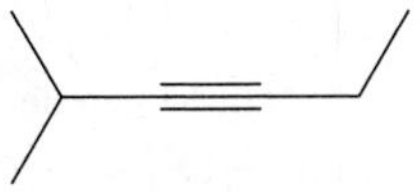

(c)

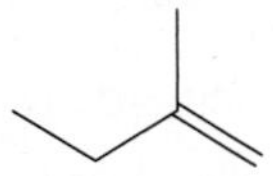

(d)

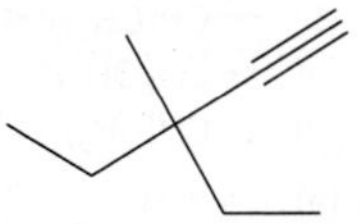

(e)

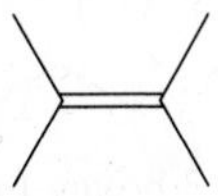

(f)

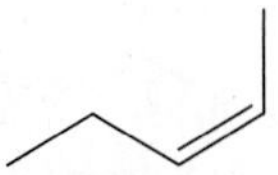

(g)

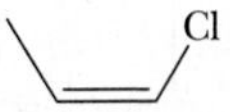

(h)

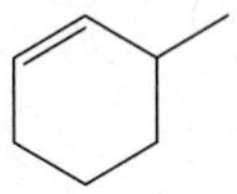

4.17 (a) 1,2-Dimethylcyclohexene
(b) 4,5-Dimethylcyclohexene
(c) 1-*tert*-Butyl-2,4,4-trimethylcyclohexene
(d) (*E*)-1-Cyclopentyl-2-methyl-1-pentene

4.19 (a) The parent chain is four carbons long, and it is also necessary to indicate the configuration (*E* or *Z*). Correct name: 2-butene
(b) The numbering of the chain is incorrect, and it is also necessary to indicate the configuration (*E* or *Z*). Correct name: 2-pentene
(c) The numbering of the ring is incorrect. Correct name: 1-methylcyclohexene
(d) It is necessary to indicate the position of the carbon–carbon double bond. Correct name: 3,3-dimethyl-1-pentene
(e) The numbering of the chain is incorrect. Correct name: 2-hexyne
(f) The parent chain is five carbons long, and it is also necessary to indicate the configuration (*E* or *Z*). Correct name: 3,4-dimethyl-2-pentene

Cis–Trans (E/Z) Isomerization in Alkenes and Cycloalkenes

4.21 (b)

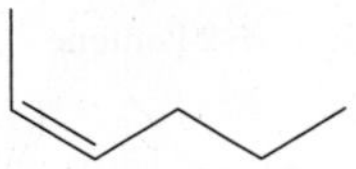

cis-2-Hexene

trans-2-Hexene

(c)

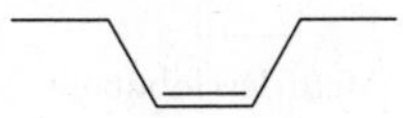

cis-3-Hexene

trans-3-Hexene

(e)

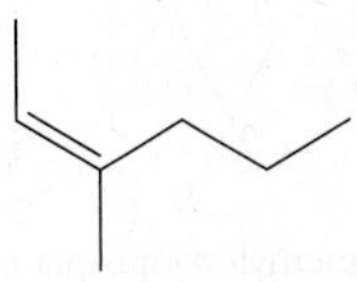

cis-3-Methyl-2-hexene

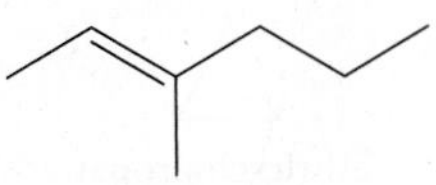

trans-3-Methyl-2-hexene

4.23 (b)

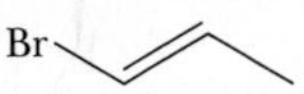

(*E*)-1-Bromopropene

(d)

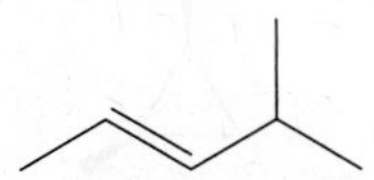

(*E*)-4-Methyl-2-pentene

4.25

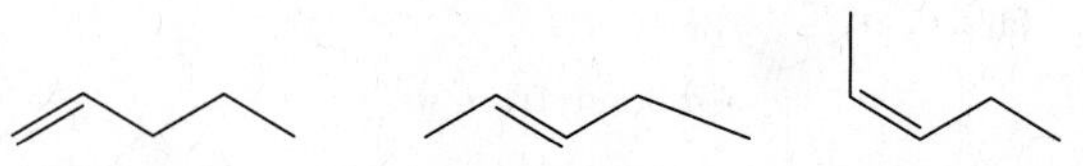

1-Pentene *trans*-2-Pentene *cis*-2-Pentene

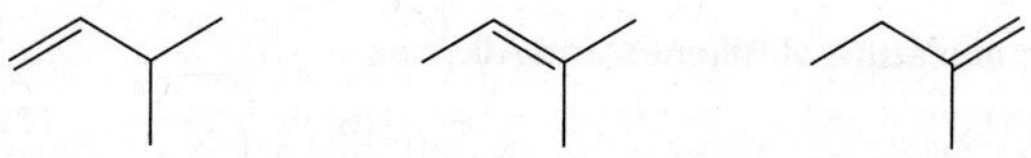

3-Methyl-1-butene 2-Methyl-2-butene 2-Methyl-1-butene

4.27 (a) $-CH_3 < -CH_2CH_3 < -Br$

(b) $-CH(CH_3)_2 < -CH_2CH_2NH_2 < -OCH_3$

(c) $-CH_2OH < -COOH < -OH$

(d) $-CH(CH_3)_2 < -CH{=}CH_2 < -CH{=}O$

4.29 (a)

(*E*)-2-Bromo-2-pentene (*Z*)-1-Bromo-1-pentene

(b)

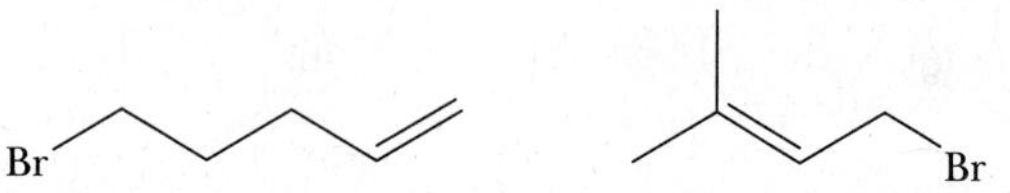

5-Bromo-1-pentene 1-Bromo-3-methyl-2-butene

4.31 (b) (d)

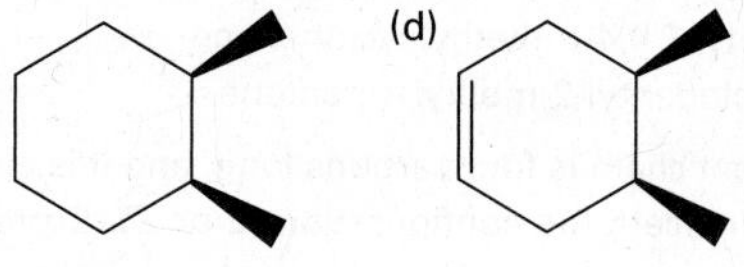

4.33 (a)

1-Pentene 2-Methyl-2-butene

3-Methyl-1-butene 2-Methyl-1-butene

(b)

trans-2-Pentene *cis*-2-Pentene

(c)

Cyclopentane Methylcyclobutane

Ethylcyclopropane 1,1-Dimethylcyclopropane

(d)

cis-1,2-Dimethylcyclopropane *trans*-1,2-Dimethylcyclopropane

4.35 The *trans* isomer is elaidic acid, and the *cis* isomer is oleic acid.

4.37 *cis-trans* Isomerism is possible for eleven of the carbon–carbon double bonds, which are indicated (*) in the structure below. All of these double bonds have the *E* configuration.

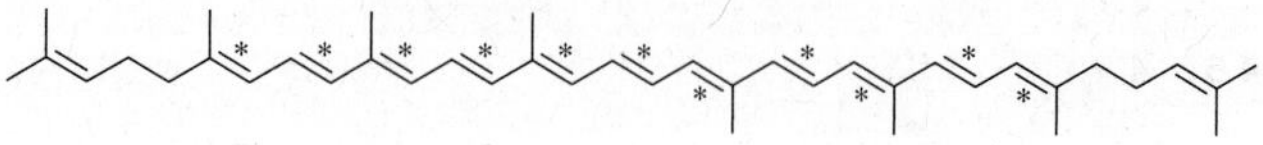

4.39 (a) *E* (b) 4

Looking Ahead

4.41 The indicated bond in 1,3-butadiene is formed by the overlap of two sp^2-hybridized carbons, while the indicated bond in 1-butene is formed by the overlap of one sp^3-hybridized and one sp^2-hybridized carbon. sp^2-Hybridized orbitals are smaller because they have greater s character (an s orbital holds its electrons closer to the nucleus of an atom), so the bond made from two sp^2 hybrids is shorter.

4.43 The electron density surrounding each alkene is affected by the electronegativity of the substituent near it. In molecules (a) and (b), the presence of oxygen and nitrogen, both of which are more electronegative than carbon, the alkenes have a reduced electron density, and the alkene carbon closest to the oxygen or nitrogen atom has a partial positive charge. Whereas the silicon atom in (c) is lower in electronegativity than carbon, the alkene has a higher electron density.

4.45 Fumaric acid has the *E* configuration, and it can be designated as a *trans* alkene. Aconitic acid has the *Z* configuration, and it can be designated as a *trans* alkene (note that while the two COOH groups are *cis* to each other, the C_5 parent chain is *trans*).

CHAPTER 5 Reactions of Alkenes

Problems

5.1 In an endothermic reaction, the products formed are higher in energy than the reactants. These reactions are thermodynamically unfavorable because they require a net input of heat.

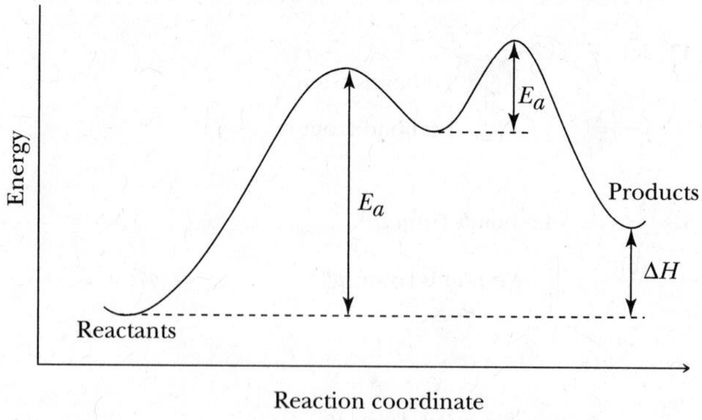

5.2 (a)

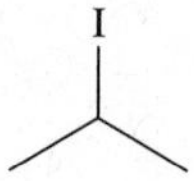

2-Iodopropane

(b)

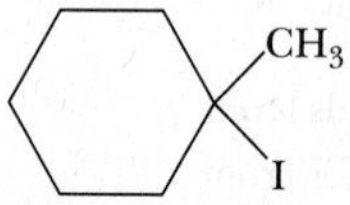

1-Iodo-1-methylcyclohexane

5.3 (a) > (b) > (c)

5.4 Step 1:

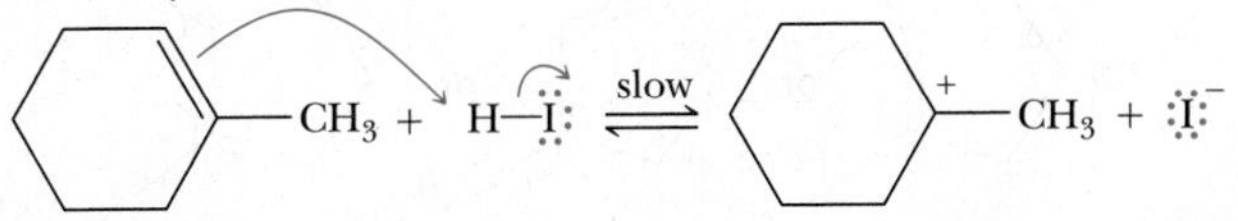

Step 2:

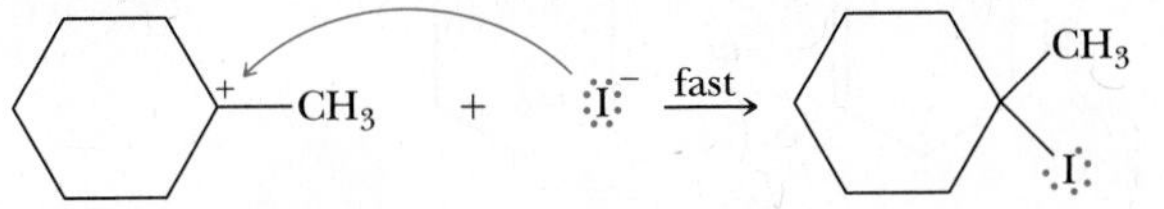

5.5 (a) 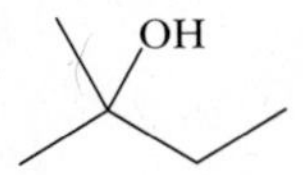 (b) 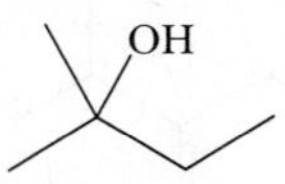

5.6 Step 1:

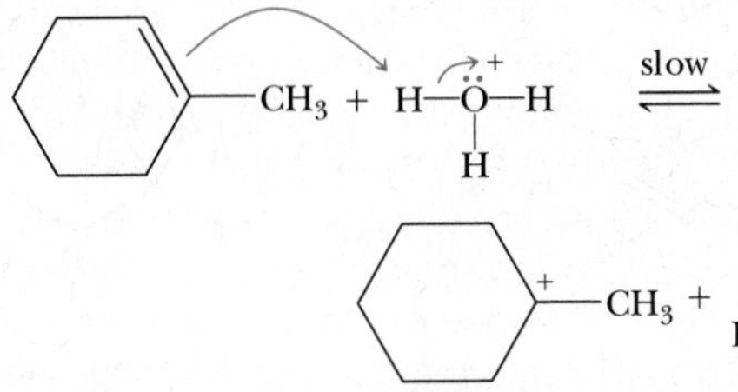

Step 2:

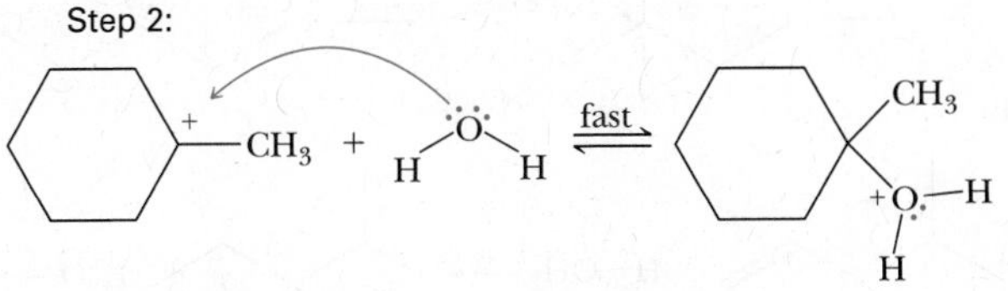

Step 3:

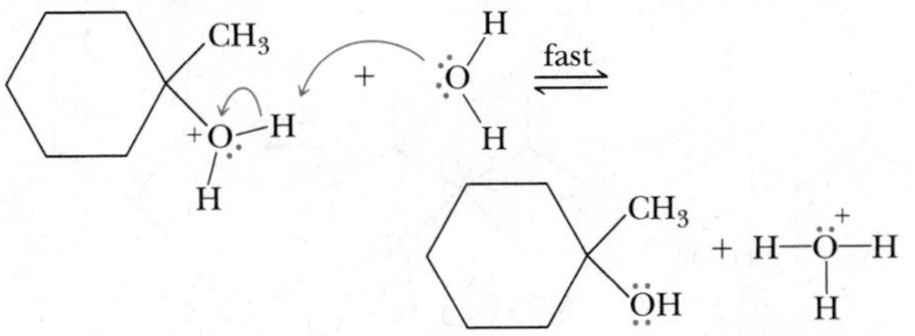

5.7 (a) 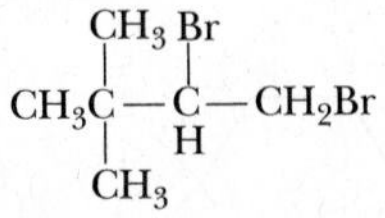 (b) 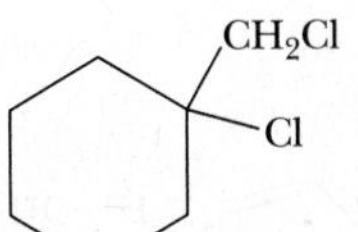

5.8 Step 1:

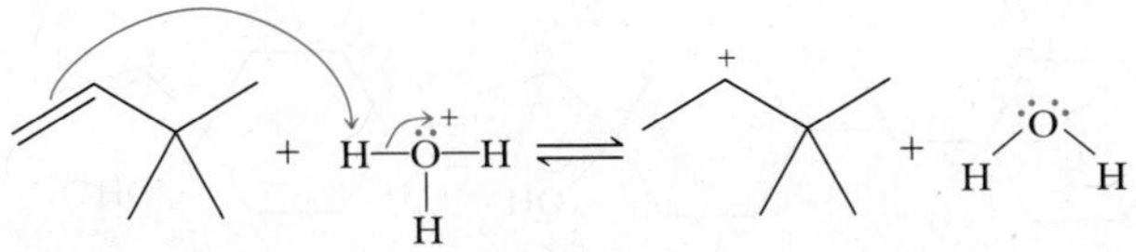

Step 2:

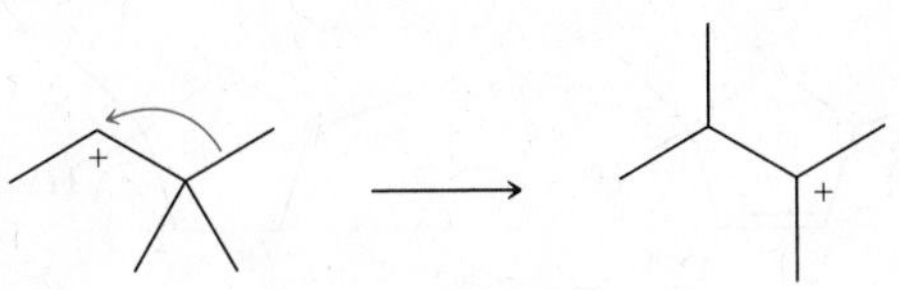

Step 3:

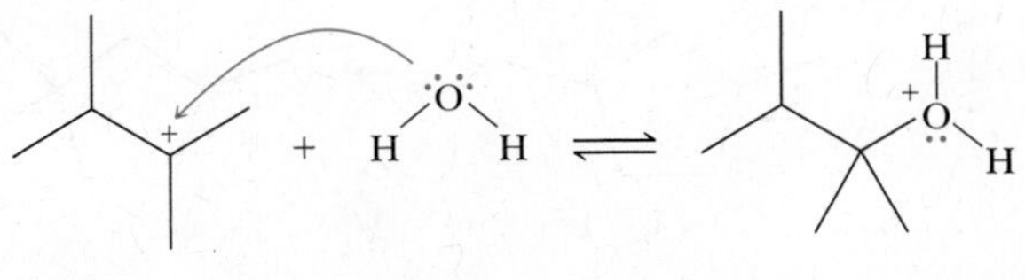

Step 4:

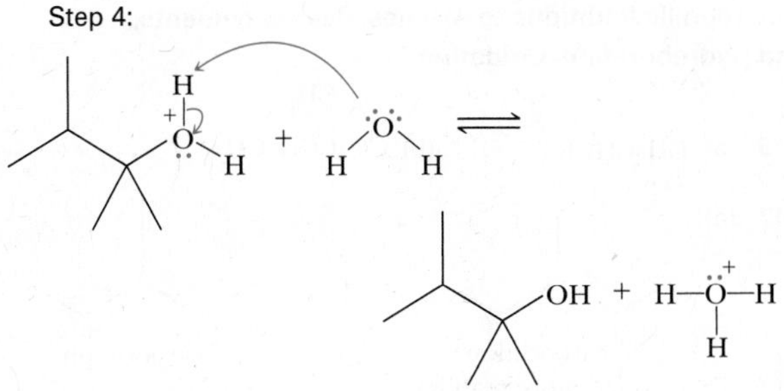

5.9 (a) 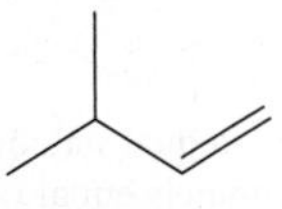 (b) 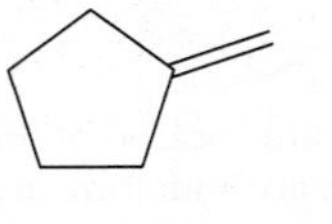

5.10 (a) 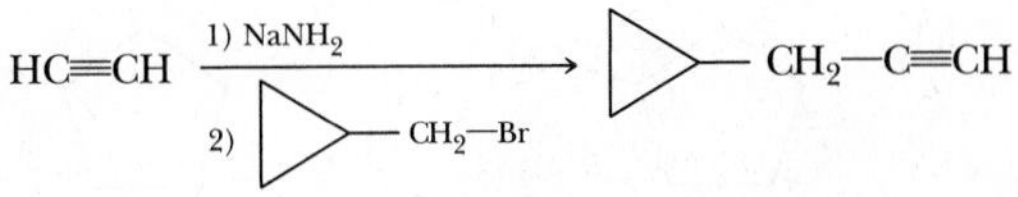

(b) 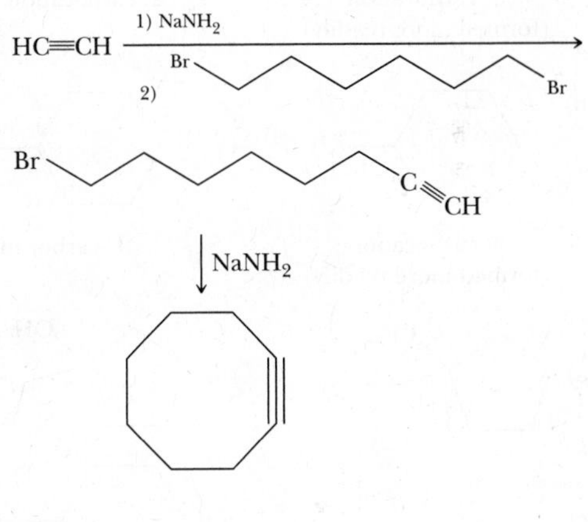

End-of-Chapter Problems

Energy Diagrams

5.11 A transition state is a point on the reaction coordinate where the energy is at a maximum. Because a transition state is at an energy maximum, it cannot be isolated and its structure can only be postulated. A reaction intermediate corresponds to an energy minimum between two transition states, but the energy of the intermediate is usually higher than the energies of the products or the reactants.

5.13 A two-step reaction has two transition states and one intermediate. The intermediate corresponds to the product of the first step and the reactant for the second step.

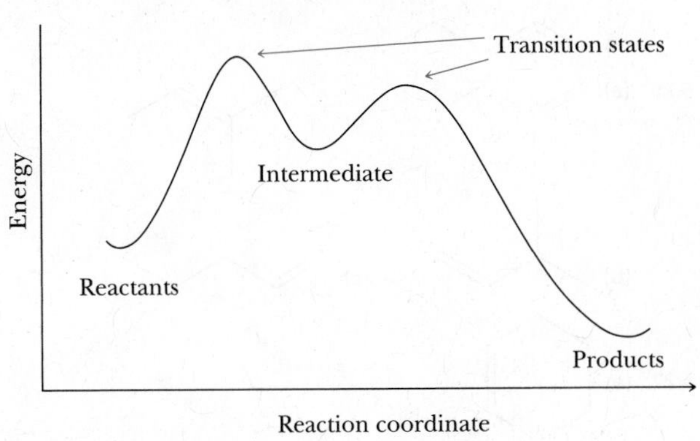

Electrophilic Additions to Alkenes, Rearrangements, and Hydroboration–Oxidation

5.15 (a) $CH_3\overset{+}{C}HCH_3$ (b) $CH_3\underset{+}{\overset{CH_3}{\overset{|}{C}}}CH_2CH_3$

5.17 (a)

3° carbocation (formed more readily) + 2° carbocation

(b)

Both are 2° carbocations and are of equal stability, so they are both formed at approximately equal rates

(c)

3° carbocation (formed more readily) + 2° carbocation

(d)

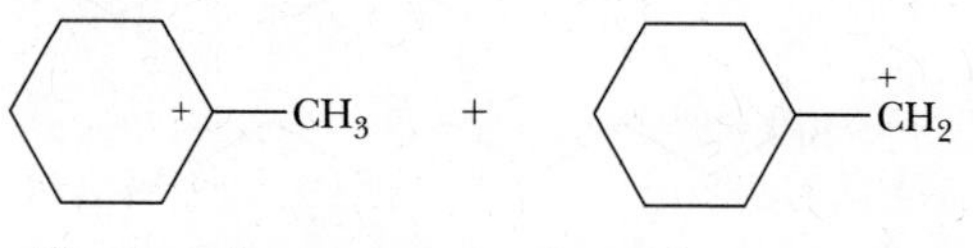

3° carbocation (formed more readily) + 1° carbocation

5.19 (a)

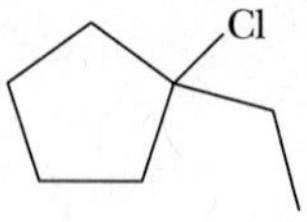

(b)

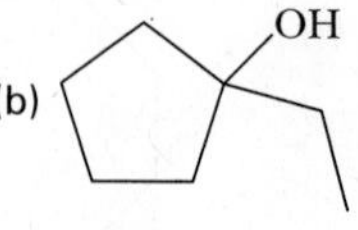

(c)

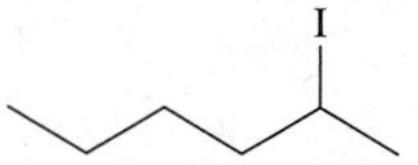

(d)

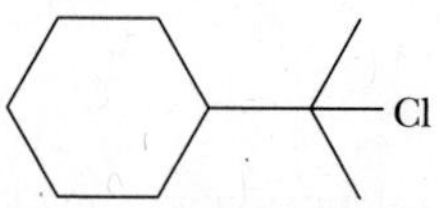

(e)

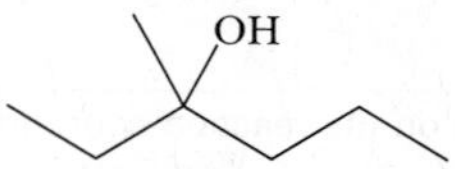

(f)

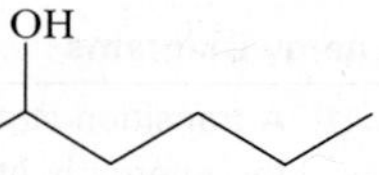

5.21 (a)

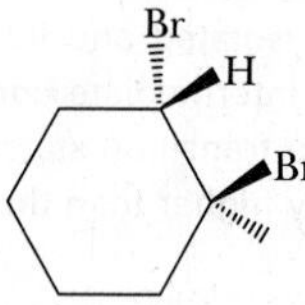

(b)

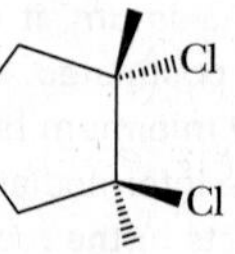

5.23 (a)

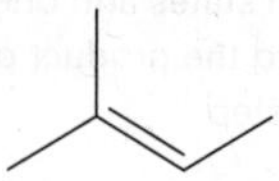

(b)

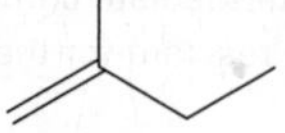

(c)

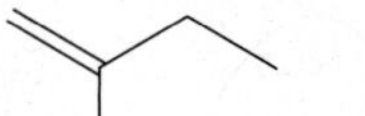

5.25 (a)

or

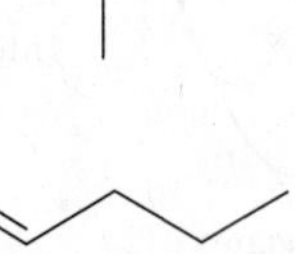

(b)

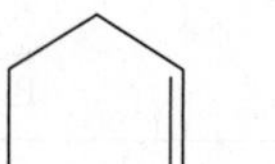

(c)

5.27 (a)

(b)

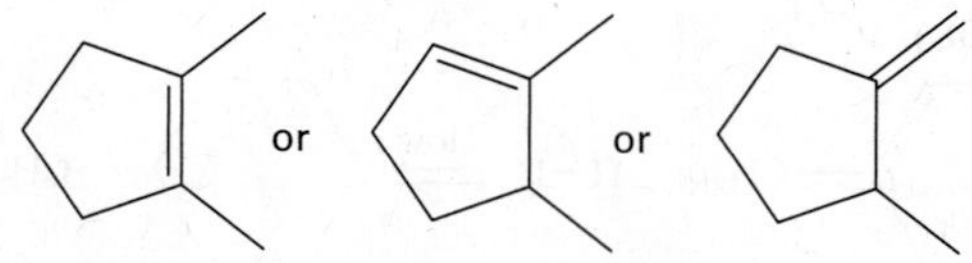

(c)

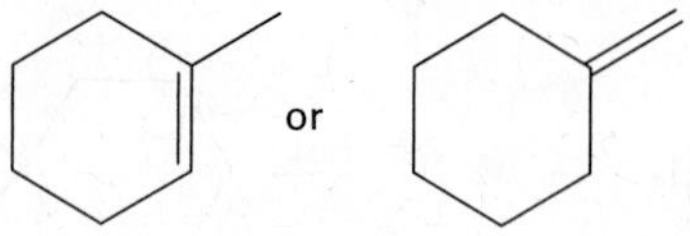

(d)

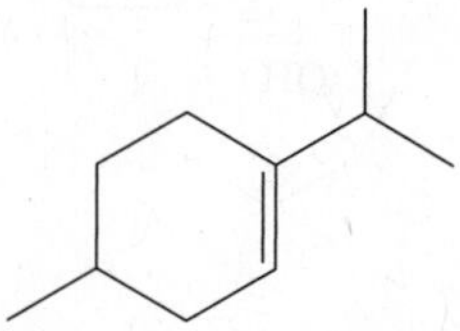

5.29 (a)

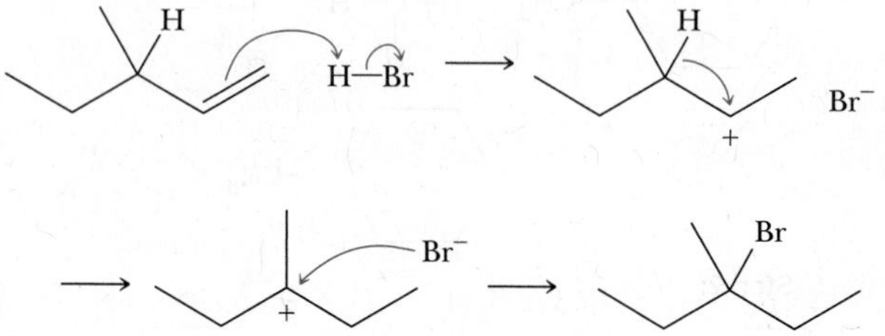

(b)

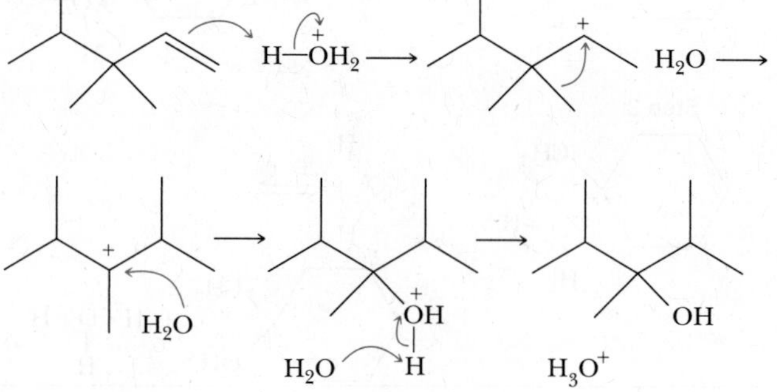

(c)

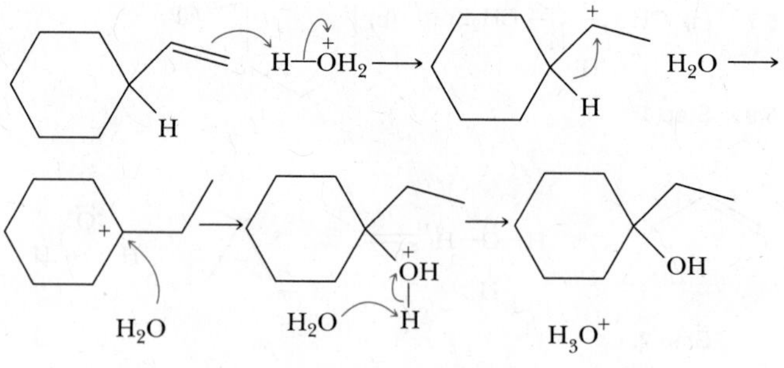

(d)

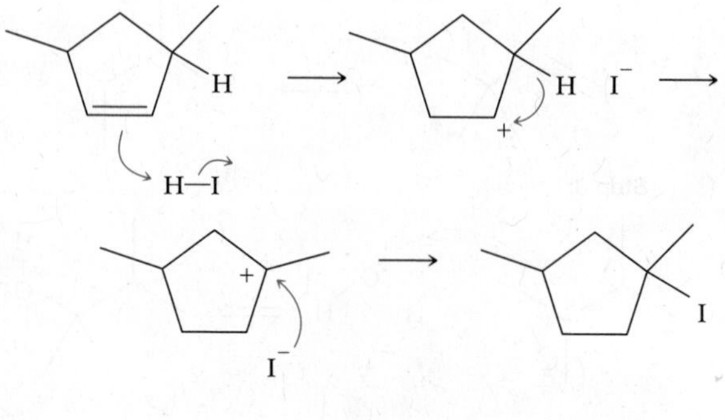

(e)

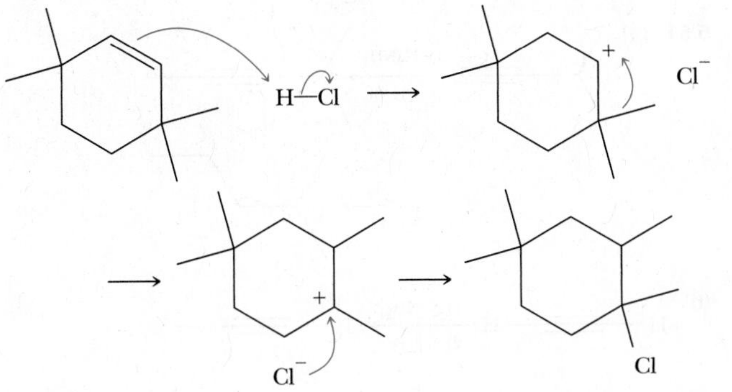

(f)

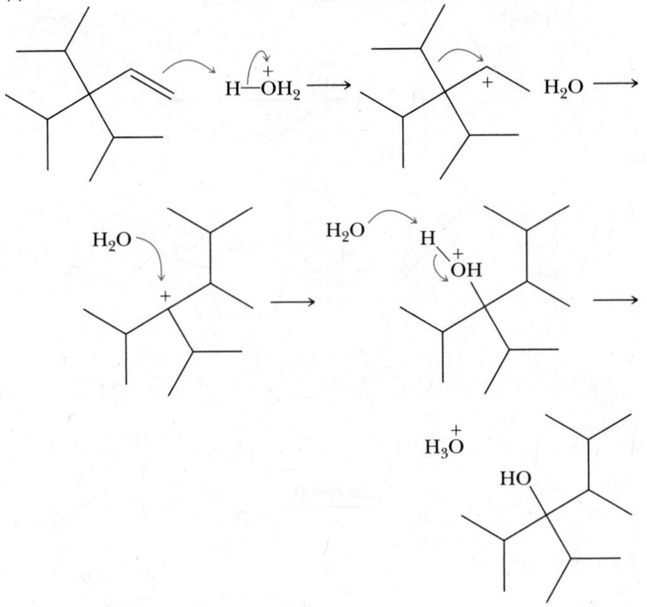

5.31 (a)

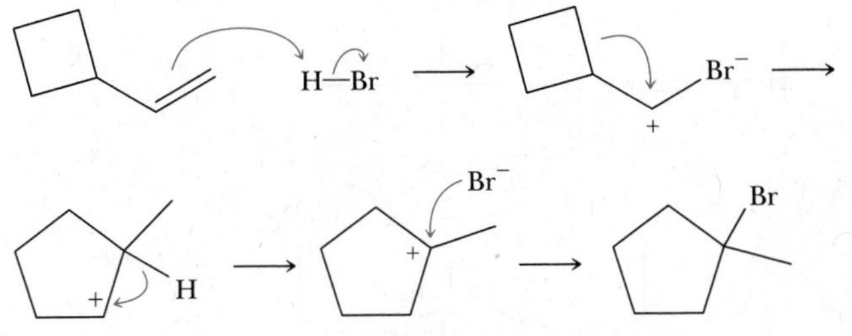

(b)

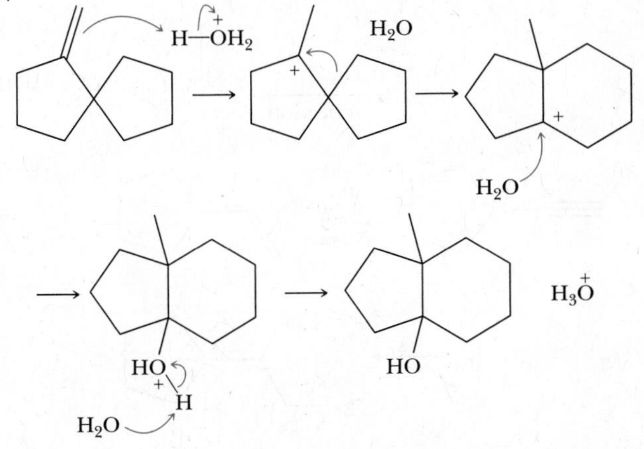

5.33

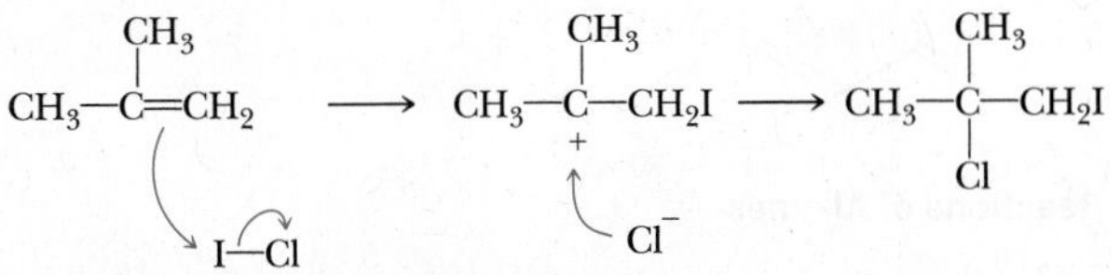

5.35 In the presence of two acids, HBr and acetic acid, the stronger acid (HBr) is more likely to protonate cyclohexene.

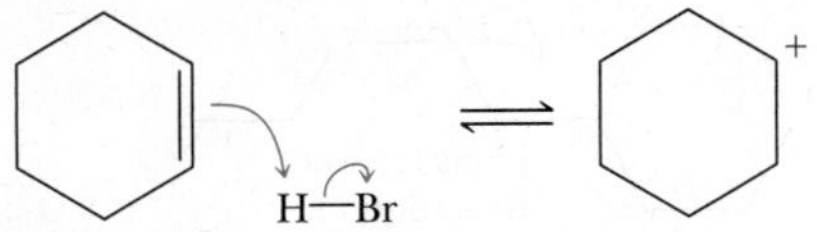

Bromocyclohexane is formed from the nucleophilic attack of the carbocation by Br^-,

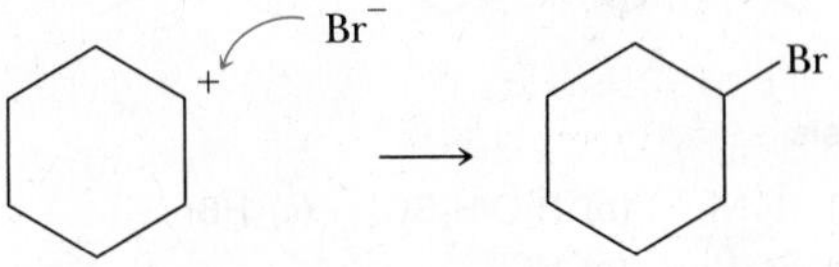

whereas nucleophilic attack by acetic acid followed by deprotonation results in the formation of cyclohexyl acetate.

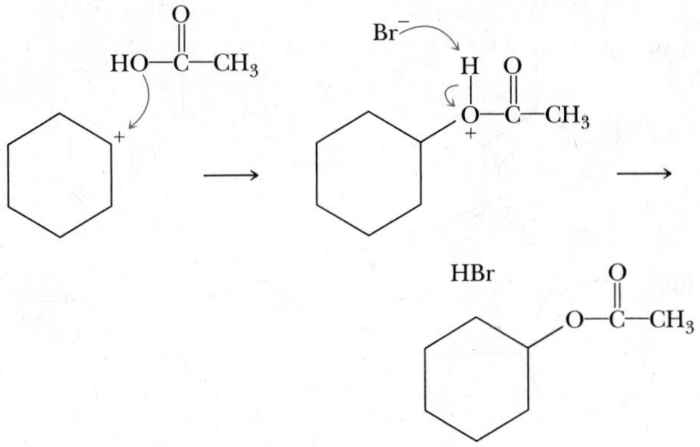

5.37

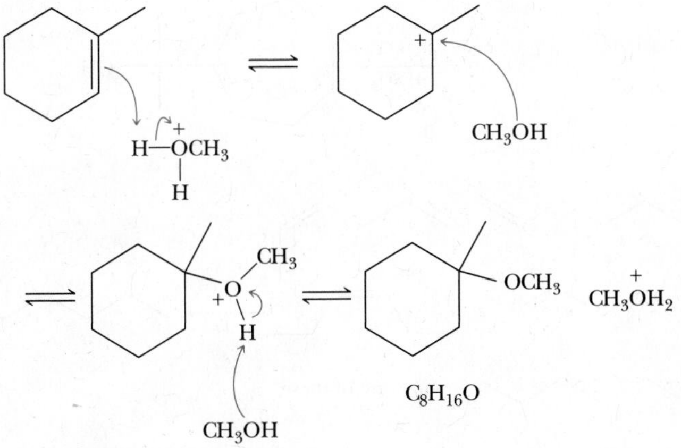

Oxidation–Reduction

5.39

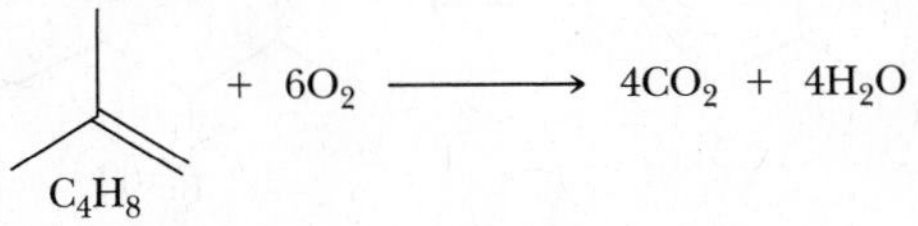

5.41

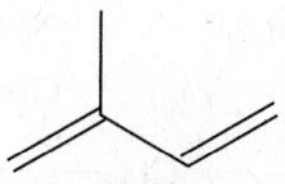

Reactions of Alkynes

5.43 (a)

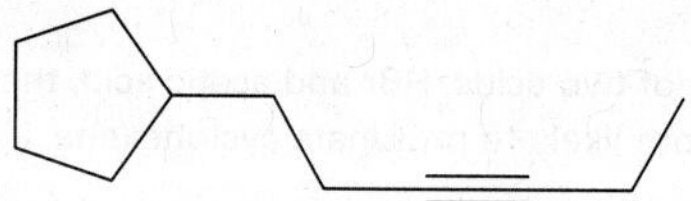

(b)

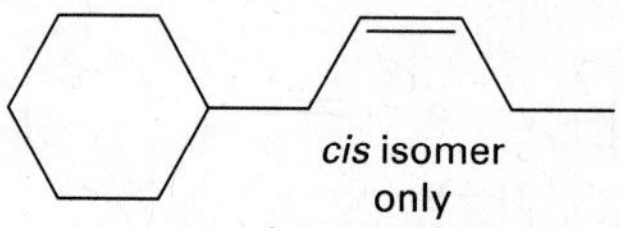

cis isomer only (stereoselective)

(c)

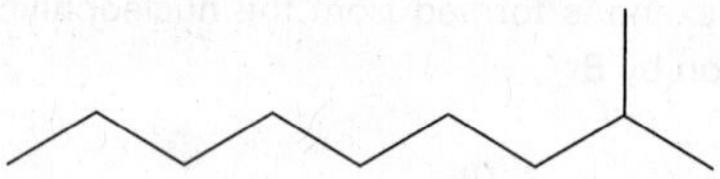

Synthesis

5.45 (a) H_2/Ni (b) H_2O/H_2SO_4 (c) HBr
(d) Br_2 (e) HCl

5.47 (a) 1) BH_3 2) H_2O_2, NaOH
(b) H_2O/H_2SO_4
(c) H_2/Ni

5.49 (a)

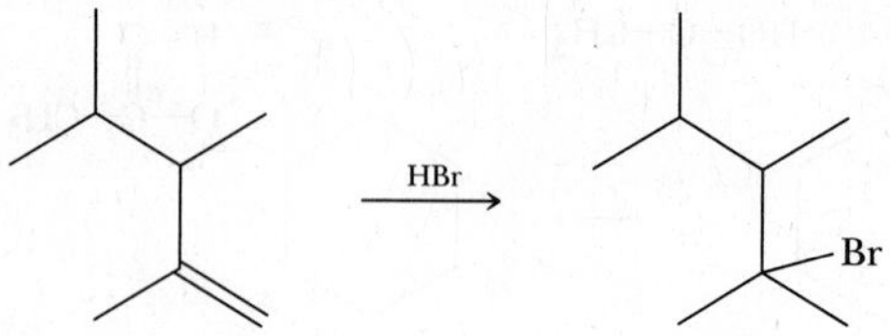

(b)

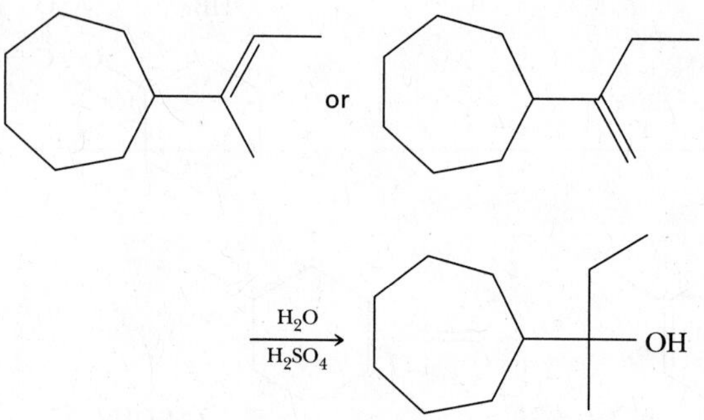

(c)

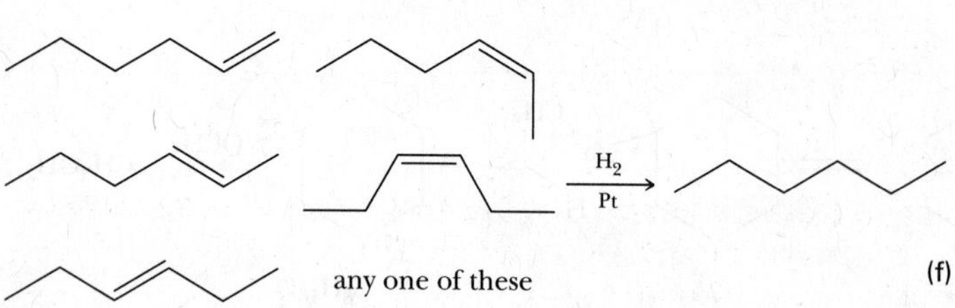

(d)

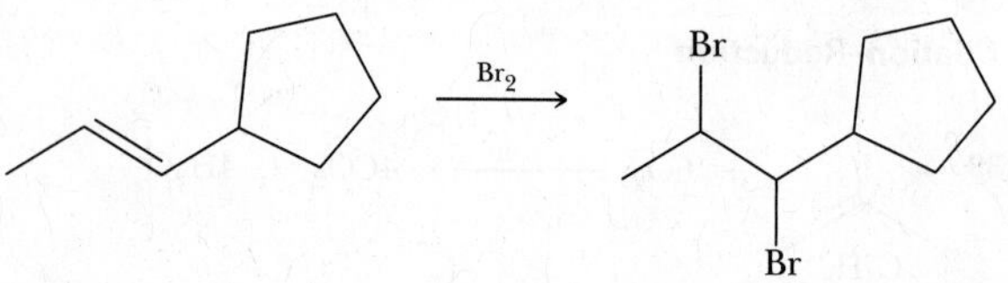

Chemical Transformations

5.51 (a)

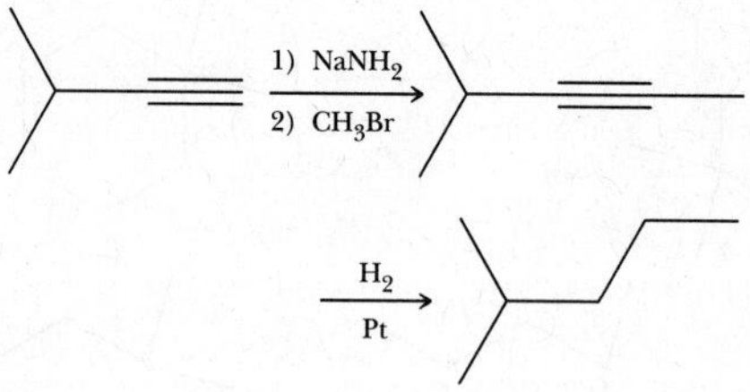

(b)

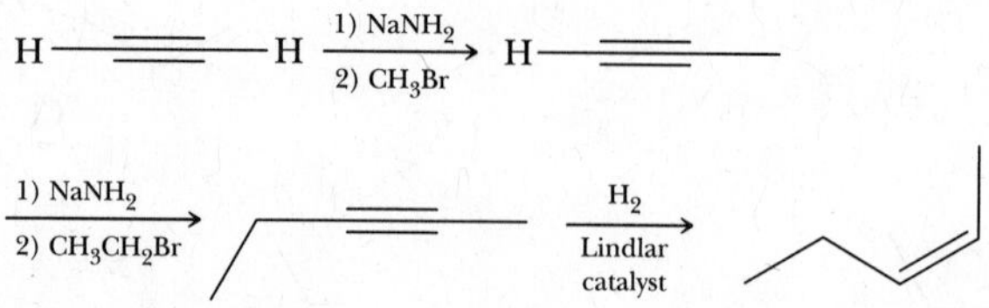

(c)

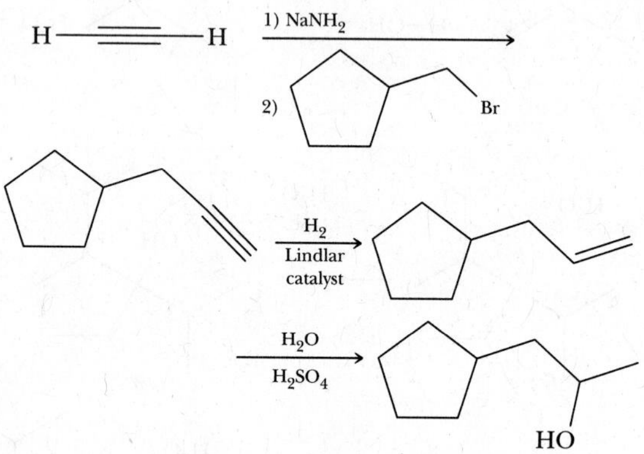

(d)

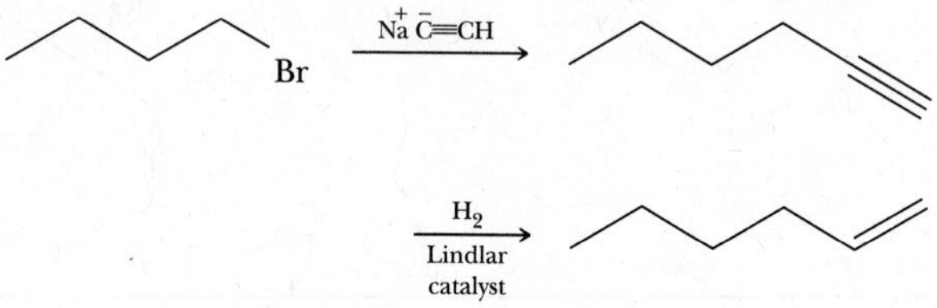

(e)

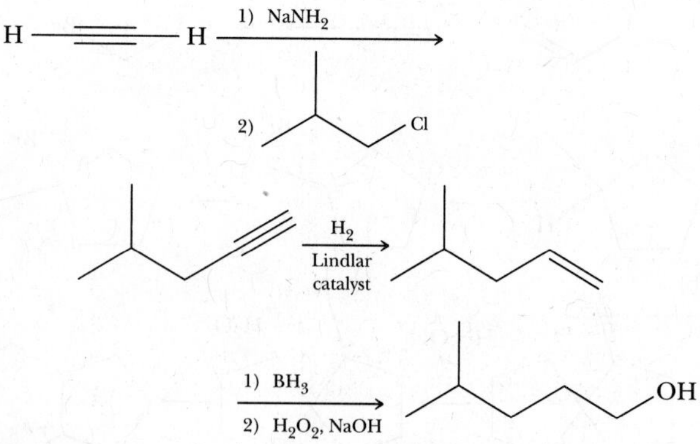

(f)

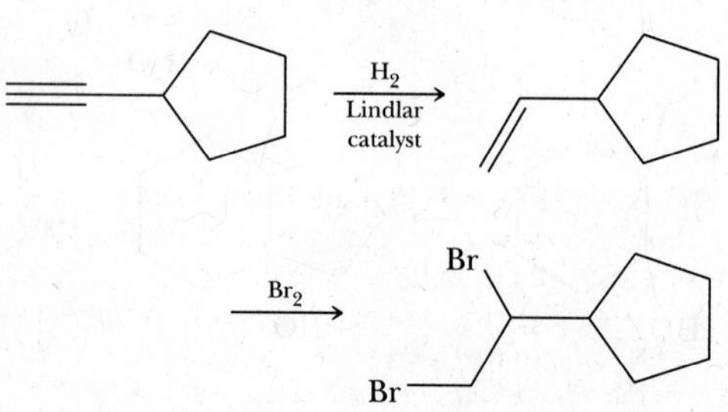

Looking Ahead

5.53 (a)

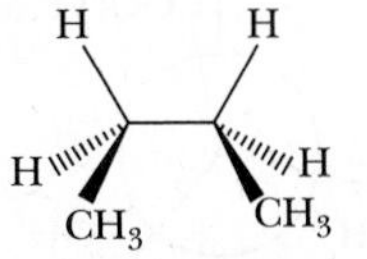

(b)

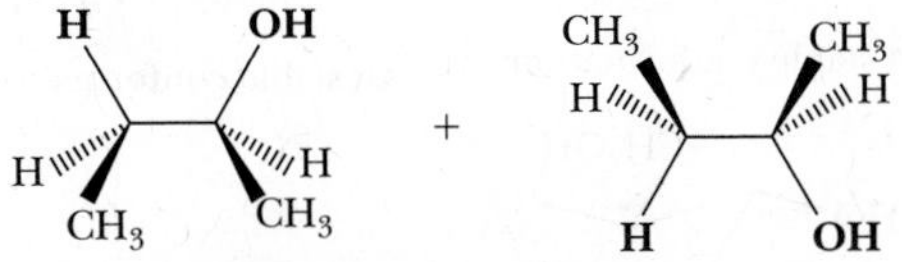

(c)

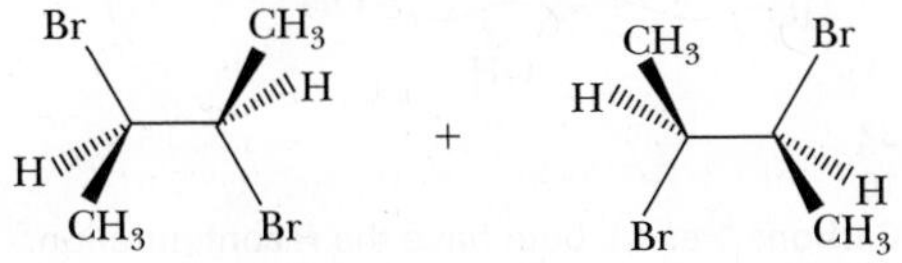

CHAPTER 6 Chirality

Problems

6.1 (a)

(b)

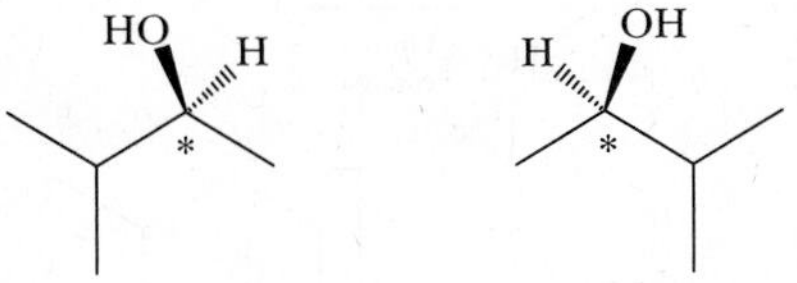

(c)

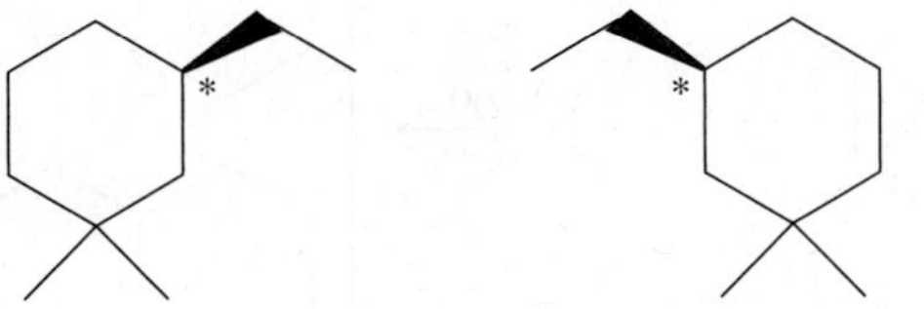

6.2 (a) *S* (b) *S* (c) *R*

6.3 (a) (1) and (3), and (2) and (4)
(b) (1) and (2), (1) and (4), (2) and (3), and (3) and (4)

6.4 (a) (2) and (3) (b) (1) and (4) (c) (2) and (3)

6.5 3

6.6 2

End-of-Chapter Problems

Chirality

6.7 Stereoisomers are compounds that have the same molecular formula and the same atom connectivity (i.e., they are of the same constitutional isomer) but have different, noninterconverting orientations of their atoms or groups in three-dimensional space.

Four types of stereoisomers include:

- Enantiomers
- Diastereomers
- *cis-trans* isomers
- Meso isomers

6.9 *Conformation* refers to the different, interconverting arrangements of atoms, in three-dimensional space, that are the result of rotation about single bonds. *Configuration* also refers to the different spatial arrangement of atoms, but these spatial arrangements are noninterconverting and cannot be made the same by rotation about single bonds.

6.11 A spiral with a left-handed twist will have a left-handed twist when viewed from either end.

6.13 This of course depends on the manufacturer of the pasta. However, in any given box of spiral pasta, usually every piece of pasta is of the same twist because the entire box was manufactured using the same machine.

Enantiomers

6.15 (a), (c), and (d)

6.17

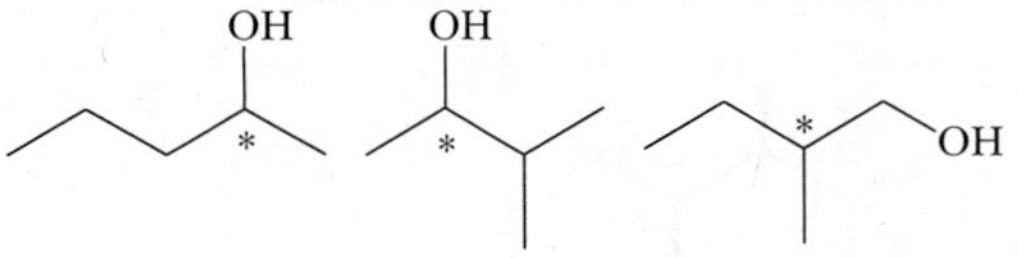

6.19 (a)

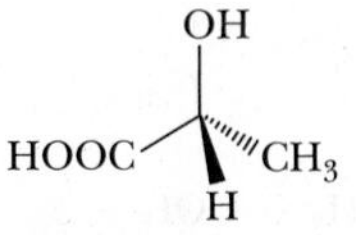

(b)

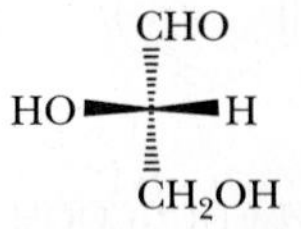

(c)

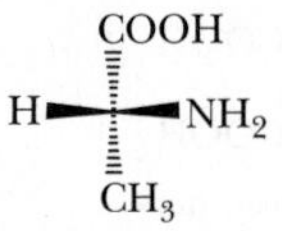

(d)

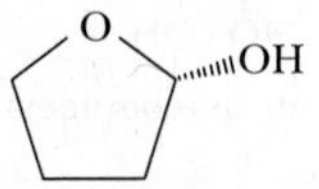

(e)

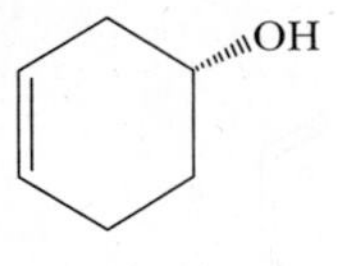

(f)

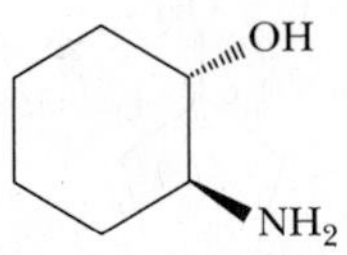

(g)

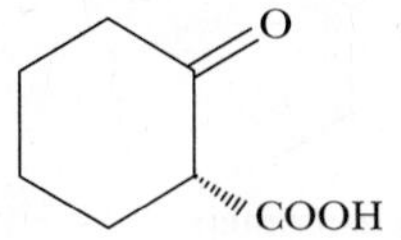

(h)

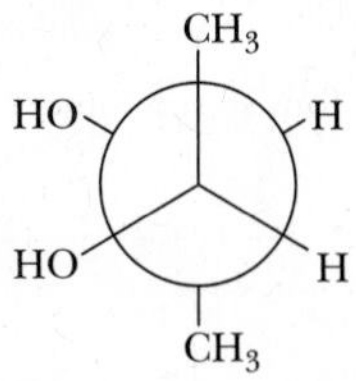

(i)

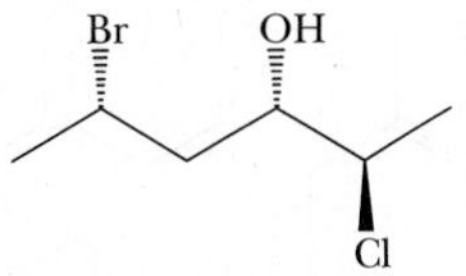

(j)

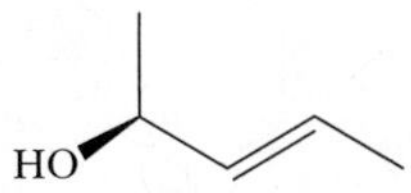

(k)

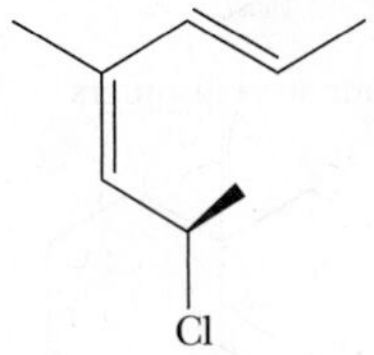

(l)

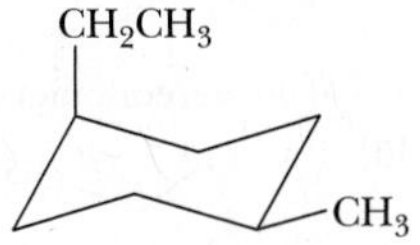

6.21 (b)

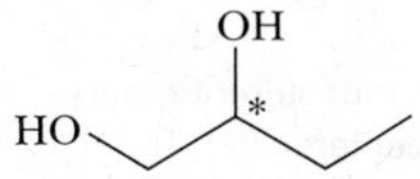

(c)

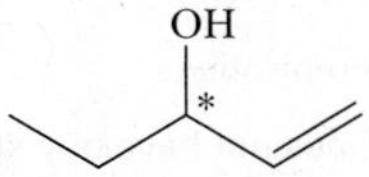

6.23 Structures (b), (c), (d), and (f) are identical to (a). Structures (e), (g), and (h) are mirror images of (a).

Designation of Configuration: The R,S Convention

6.25 (c) and (d)

6.27 (a) (*S*)-2-Butanol (b)

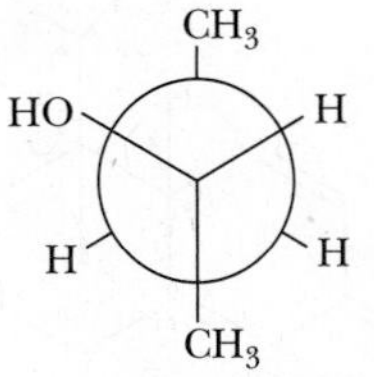

(c)

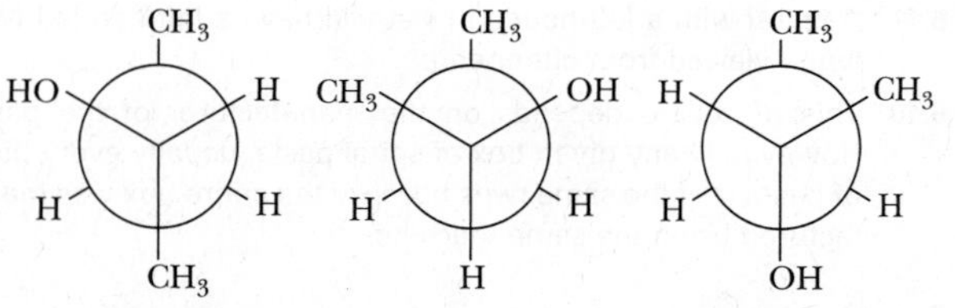

more stable more stable

Molecules with Two or More Stereocenters

6.29

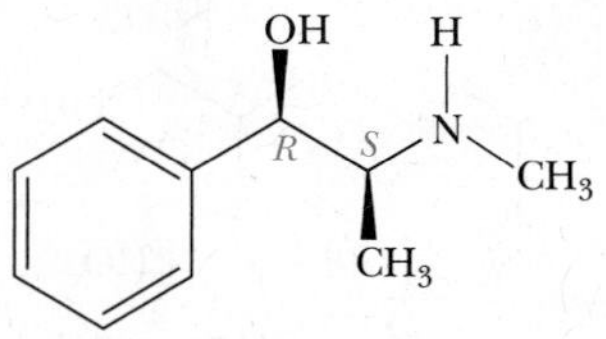

6.31

(a)

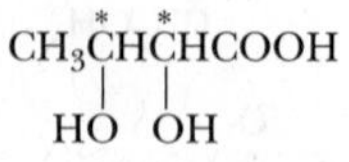

four stereoisomers

(b)

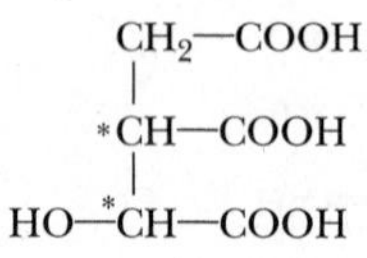

four stereoisomers

(c)

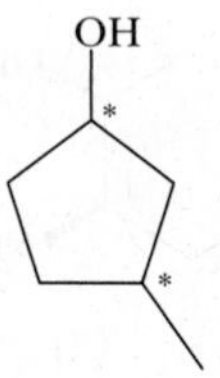

four stereoisomers

(d)

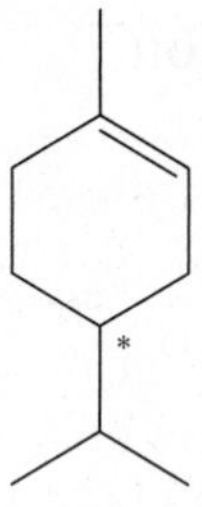

two stereoisomers

(e)

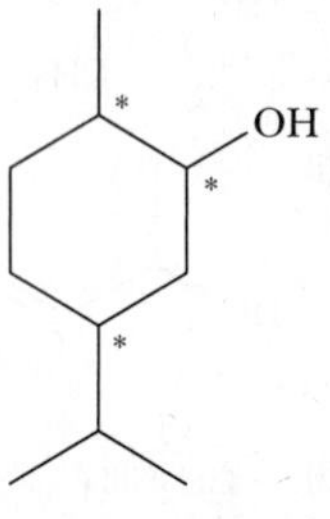

eight stereoisomers

(f)

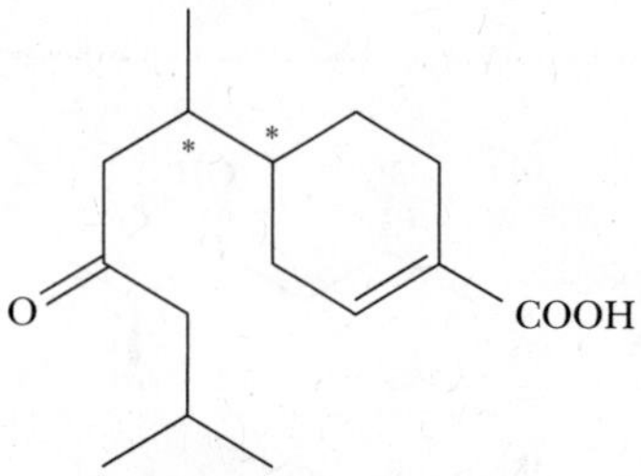

four stereoisomers

(g)

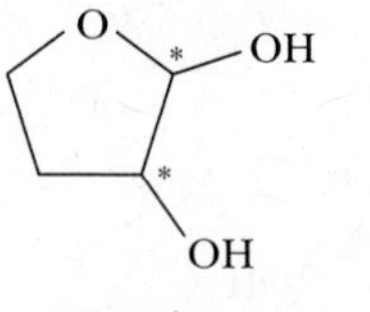

four stereoisomers

(h)

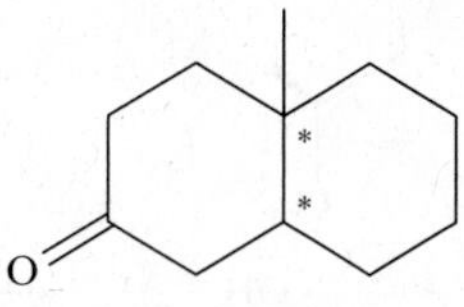

four stereoisomers

6.33 (a) Does not have any stereocenters

(b) Two stereoisomers

6.35 (a)

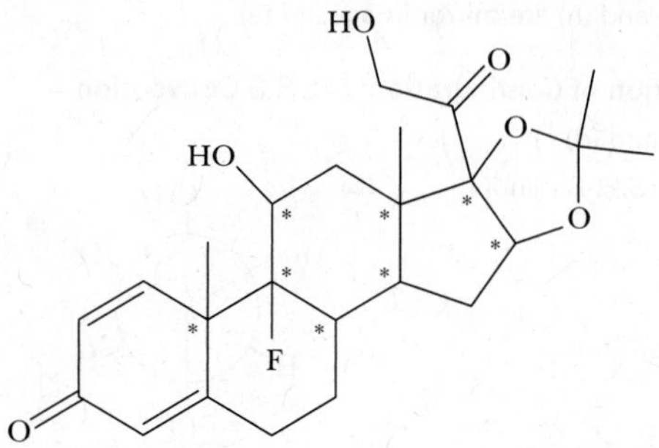

(b) 256

6.37

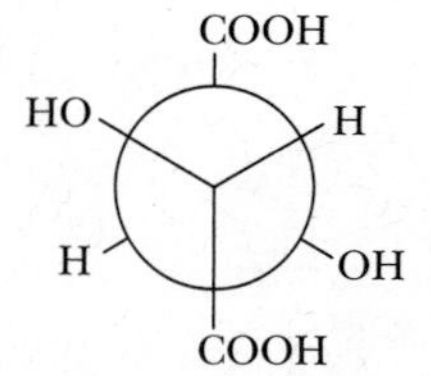

most stable conformation

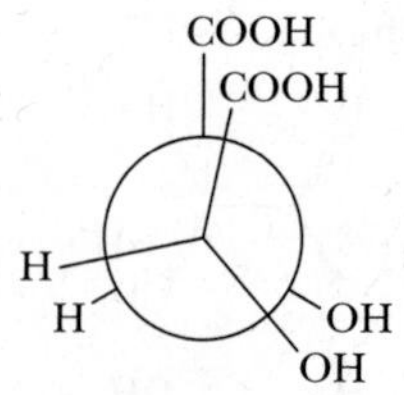

least stable conformation

6.39 (a)

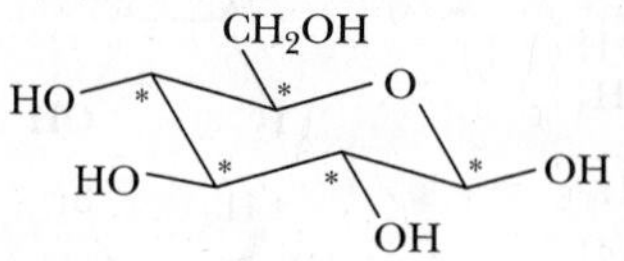

(b) 32

(c) 16

(d) Carbons 1 and 5 both have the *R* configuration.

Chemical Transformations

6.41 (a)

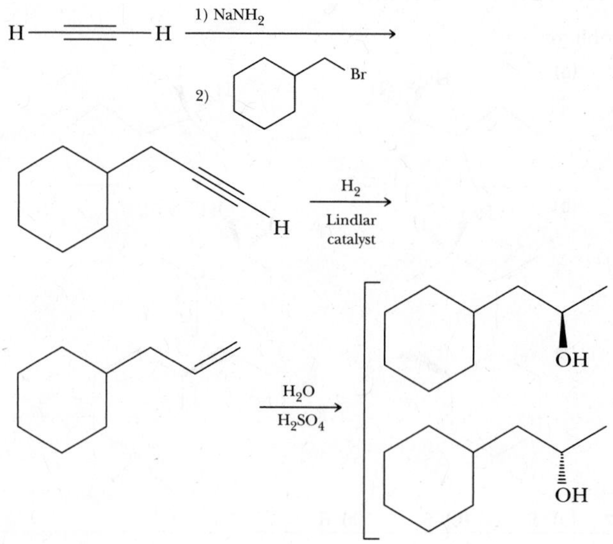

(b)

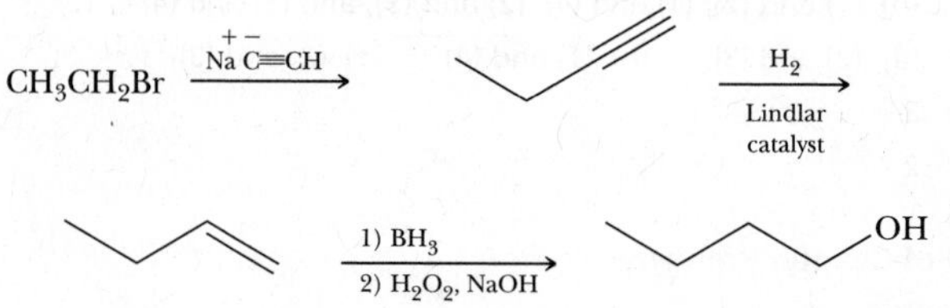

(c)

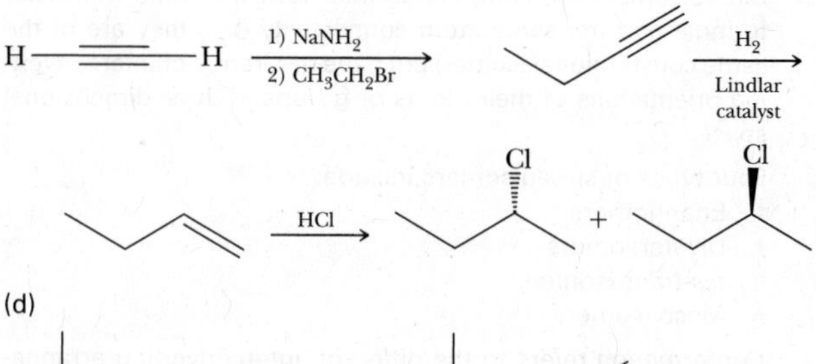

(d)

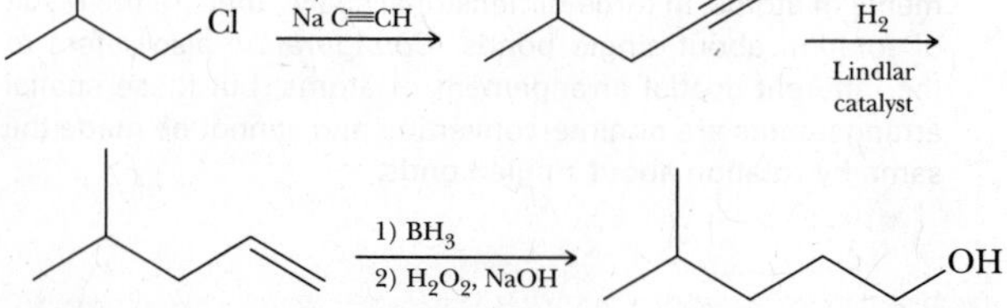

(e)

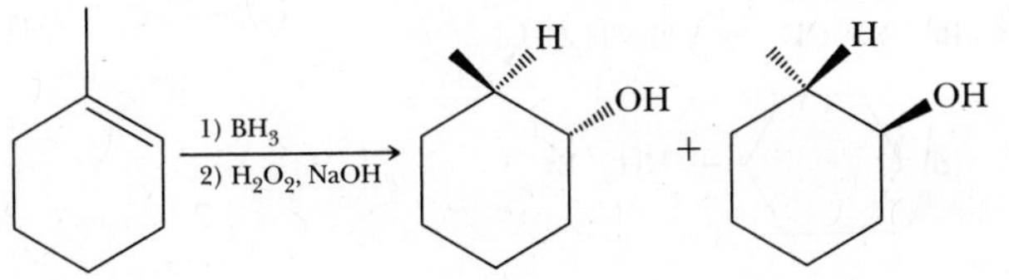

(f)

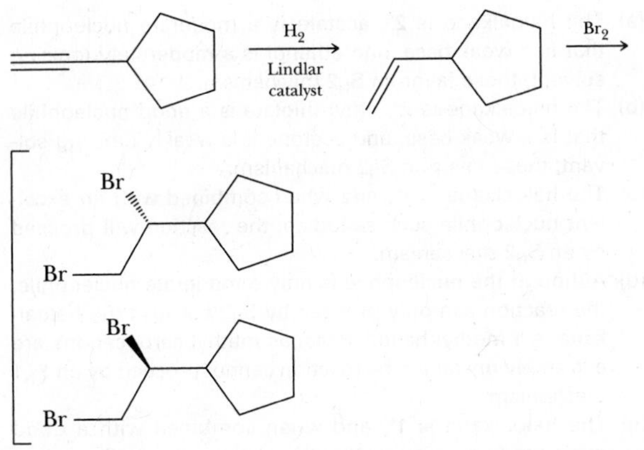

(g)

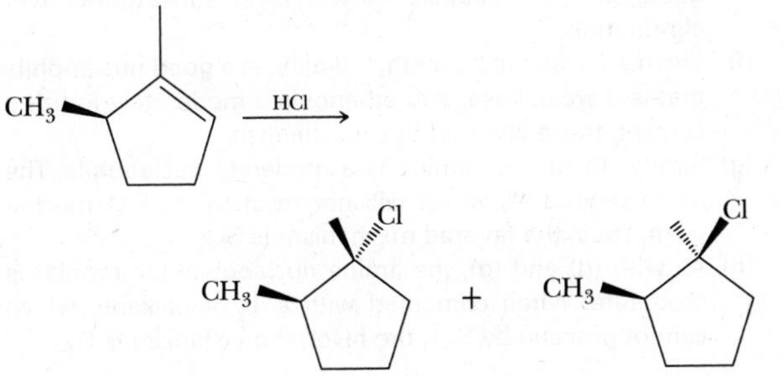

(h)

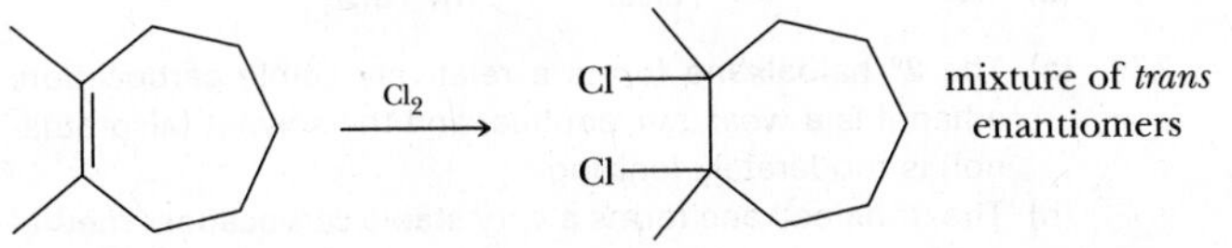

(i)

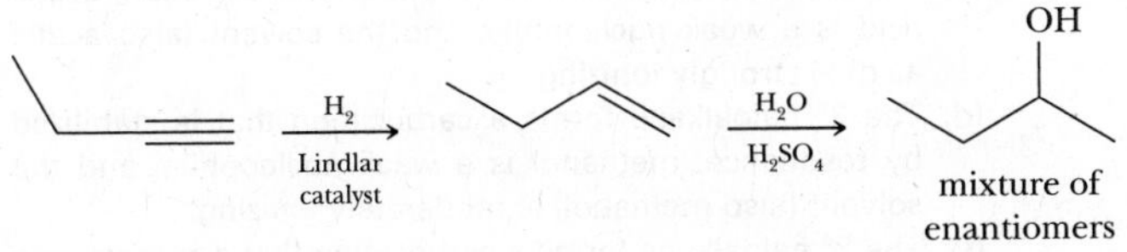

(j)

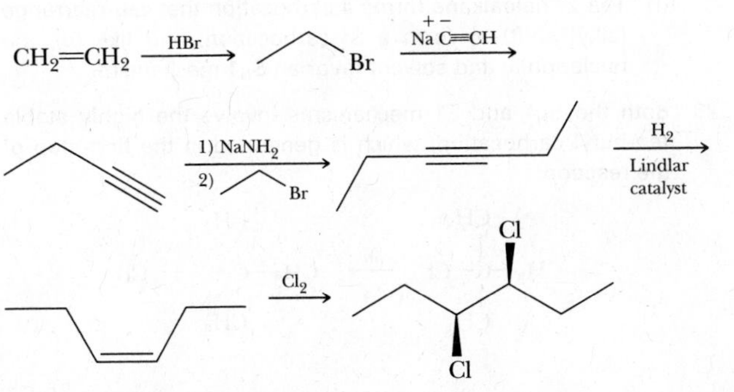

Looking Ahead

6.43 (a)

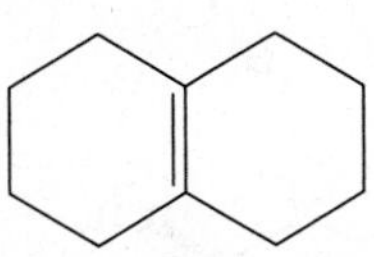

(b)

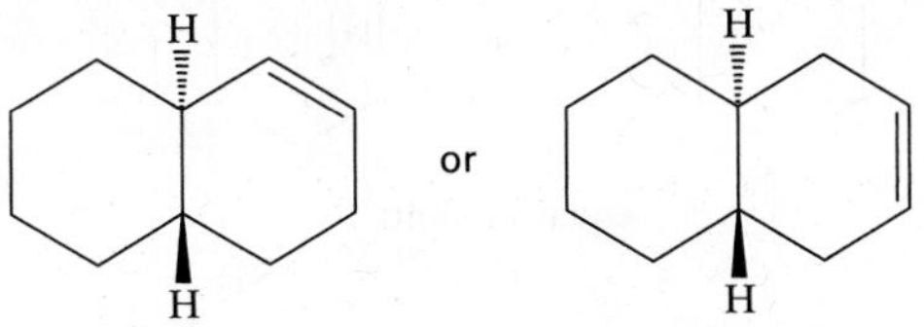

6.45

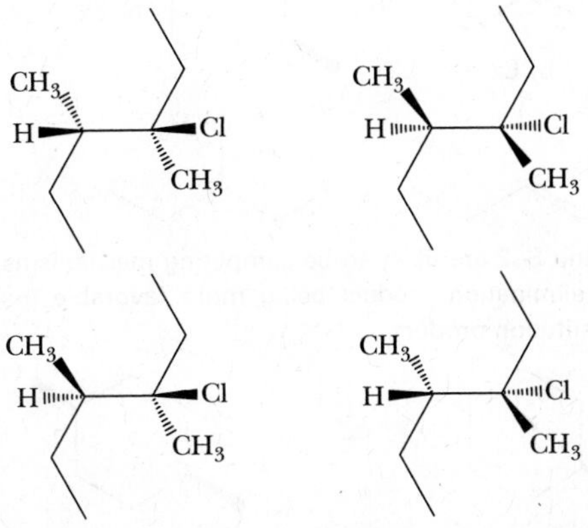

The reaction produces four different stereoisomers. If the goal of the synthesis is to selectively synthesize one of the four stereoisomers, this method is not very useful.

CHAPTER 7 Haloalkanes

Problems

7.1 (a) 1-Chloro-3-methyl-2-butene
(b) 1-Bromo-1-methylcyclohexane
(c) 1,2-Dichloropropane
(d) 2-Chloro-1,3-butadiene

7.2 (a) Substitution
(b) Both substitution and elimination

7.3 (a)

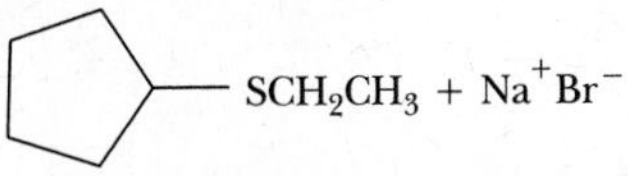

(b)

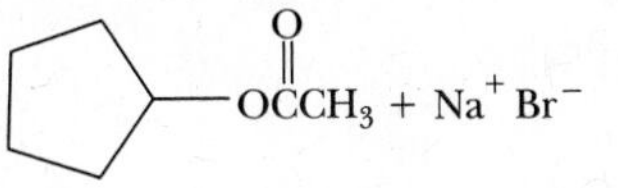

7.4 (a) S_N2
(b) Compound A is more able to undergo S_N2. Both compounds A and B have about the same reactivity toward S_N1.

7.5 (a)

(b)

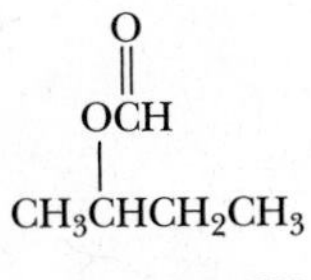

racemic mixture by S_N1

7.6 (a)

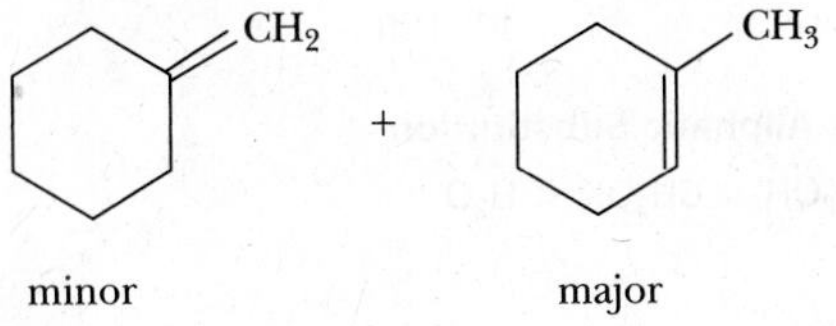

(b)

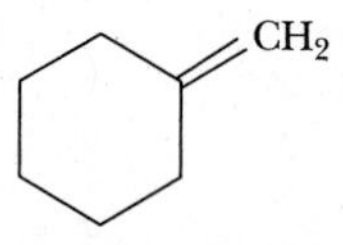

(c)

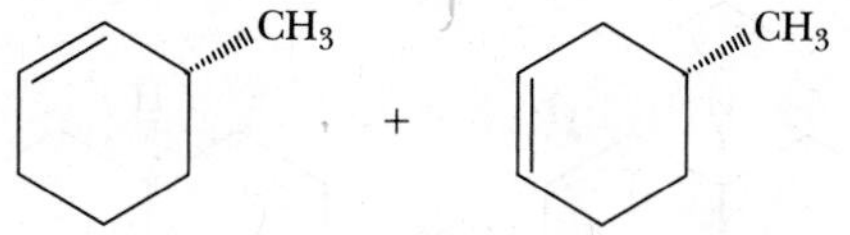

equal amounts

7.7 (a)

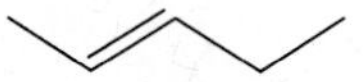

by E2

(b)

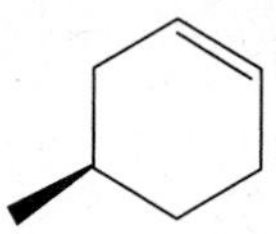

by E2

7.8 (a)

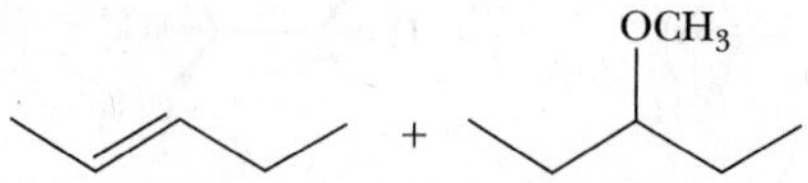

E2 and S_N2 are likely to be competing mechanisms, with the elimination product being more favorable than the substitution product.

(b)

E2 and S_N2 are likely to be competing mechanisms.

End-of-Chapter Problems

Nomenclature

7.9 (a) 1,1-Difluoroethene
(b) 3-Bromocyclopentene
(c) 2-Chloro-5-methylhexane
(d) 1,6-Dichlorohexane
(e) Dichlorodifluoromethane
(f) 3-Bromo-3-ethylpentane

7.11 (a)

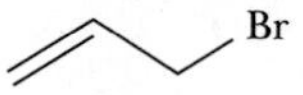

(b)

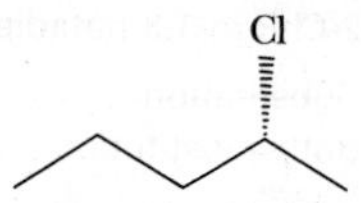

(c)

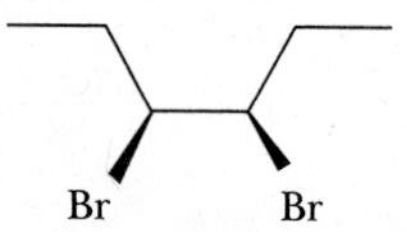

(d)

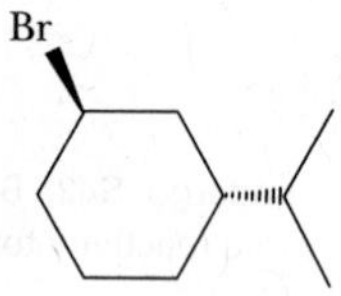

or

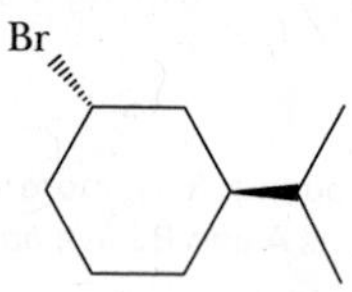

(e)

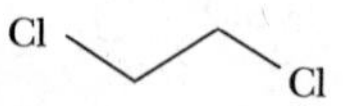

(f)

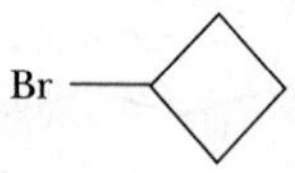

7.13 (b) and (c)

Synthesis of Alkyl Halides

7.15 (a) HCl (b) HI
(c) HCl (d) HBr

Nucleophilic Aliphatic Substitution

7.17 $CH_3CH_2OH < CH_3OH < H_2O$

7.19 (a) OH^- (b) OH^- (c) CH_3S^-

7.21 (a) $Na^+Cl^- + CH_3CH_2CH_2I$

(b)

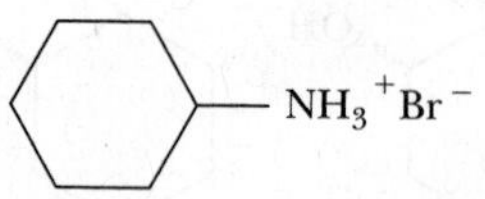

(c) $Na^+Cl^- + CH_2{=}CHCH_2OCH_2CH_3$

7.23 (a) The haloalkane is 2°, acetate is a moderate nucleophile that is a weak base, and ethanol is a moderately ionizing solvent; these favor an S_N2 mechanism.
(b) The haloalkane is 2°, ethyl thiolate is a good nucleophile that is a weak base, and acetone is a weakly ionizing solvent; these favor an S_N2 mechanism.
(c) The haloalkane is 1°, and when combined with an excellent nucleophile such as iodide, the reaction will proceed by an S_N2 mechanism.
(d) Although the nucleophile is only a moderate nucleophile, the reaction can only proceed by S_N2 because the haloalkane is a methyl halide. Because methyl carbocations are extremely unstable, the reaction cannot proceed by an S_N1 mechanism.
(e) The haloalkane is 1°, and when combined with a good nucleophile such as methoxide, the reaction will proceed by an S_N2 mechanism. Although methoxide is also a good base, 1° haloalkanes will favor substitution over elimination.
(f) The haloalkane is 2°, methyl thiolate is a good nucleophile that is a weak base, and ethanol is a moderately ionizing solvent; these favor an S_N2 mechanism.
(g) Similar to (d), the amine is a moderate nucleophile. The haloalkane is 1°, which will not react by an S_N1 mechanism. Thus, the favored mechanism is S_N2.
(h) As with (d) and (g), the amine nucleophile (ammonia) is moderate. When combined with a 1° haloalkane, which cannot proceed by S_N1, the favored mechanism is S_N2.

7.25 (a) False. (b) False. (c) True.
(d) True. (e) False. (f) False.

7.27 (a) The 2° haloalkane forms a relatively stable carbocation, ethanol is a weak nucleophile, and the solvent (also ethanol) is moderately ionizing.
(b) The 3° haloalkane forms a very stable carbocation, methanol is a weak nucleophile, and the solvent (also methanol) is moderately ionizing.
(c) The 3° haloalkane forms a very stable carbocation, acetic acid is a weak nucleophile, and the solvent (also acetic acid) is strongly ionizing.
(d) The 2° haloalkane forms a carbocation that is stabilized by resonance, methanol is a weak nucleophile, and the solvent (also methanol) is moderately ionizing.
(e) The 2° haloalkane forms a carbocation that can rearrange (hydride shift) to form a 3° carbocation, and like (a), the nucleophile and solvent favor an S_N1 mechanism.
(f) The 2° haloalkane forms a carbocation that can rearrange (alkyl shift) to form a 3° carbocation, and like (c), the nucleophile and solvent favor an S_N1 mechanism.

7.29 Both the S_N1 and E1 mechanisms involve the highly stable *tert*-butyl carbocation, which is generated in the first step of the reaction:

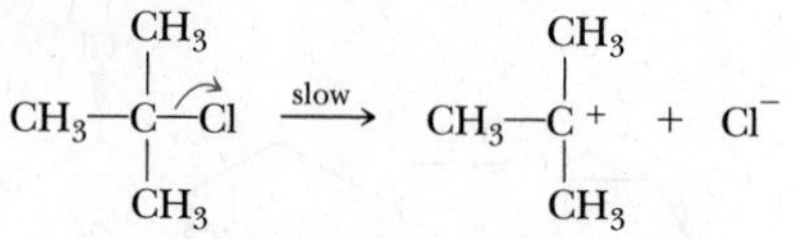

Attack of the carbocation by ethanol gives the ether product:

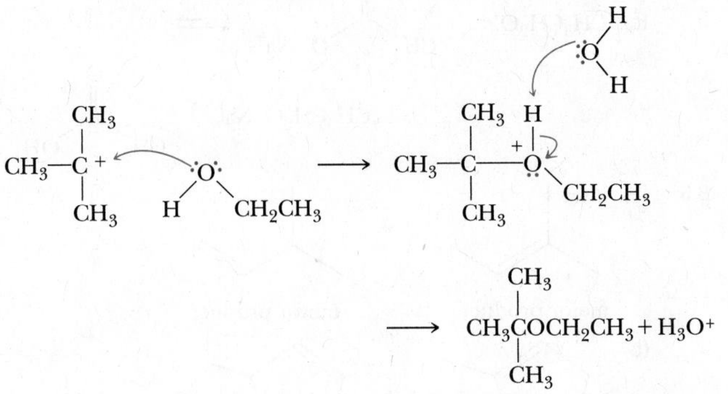

In a similar fashion, nucleophilic attack of the carbocation by water results in the alcohol:

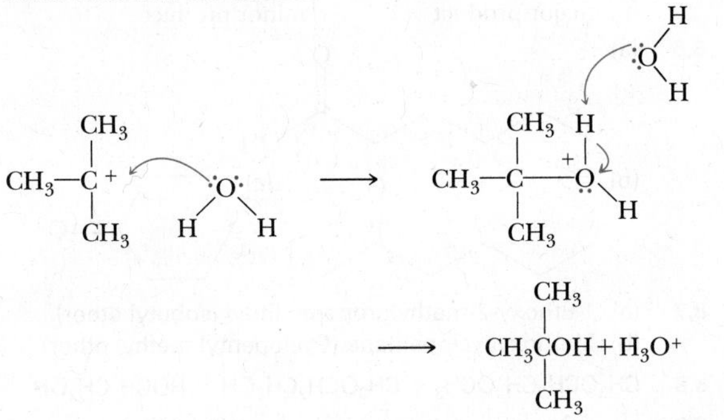

Deprotonation of the carbocation by the solvent (water or ethanol) gives the alkene:

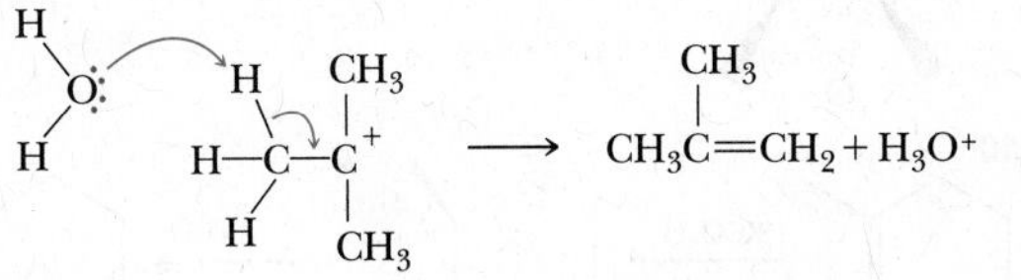

7.31 (a)  (b) 

(c) 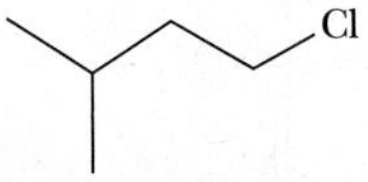 (d) 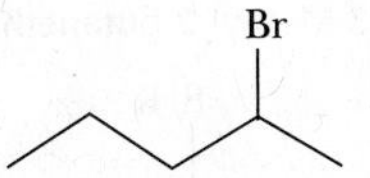

7.33 Haloalkenes fail to undergo S_N1 reactions because the alkenyl carbocations produced through ionization of the carbon-halogen bond are too unstable. They fail to undergo S_N2 reactions because the planar geometry of the alkene does not allow backside attack, and the electron-rich nature of the alkene does not attract nucleophiles.

7.35 (a) 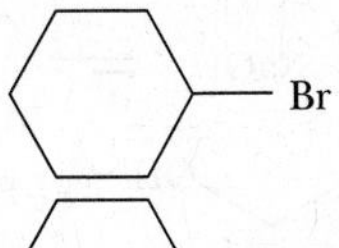 + $2NH_3$

(b) 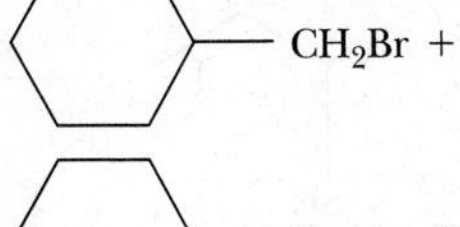 + $2NH_3$

(c) 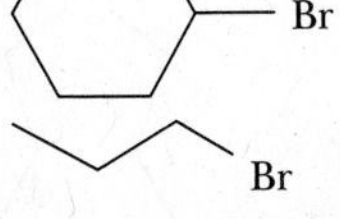 + CH_3COONa

(d) 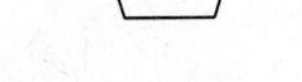 + $NaSCH_2CH_2CH_3$

(e) + CH_3COONa

(f) $CH_3(CH_2)_2CH_2Br$ + $NaOCH_2(CH_2)_2CH_3$

β-Eliminations

7.37 (c) and (d)

7.39 (a) 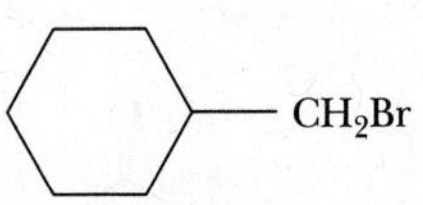 (b) 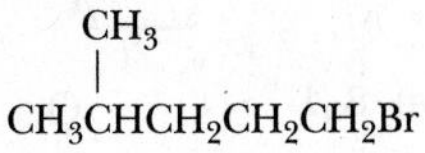

7.41 (a)

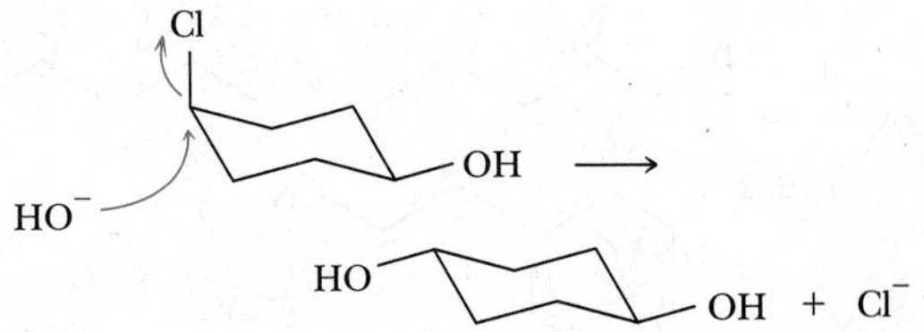

(b)

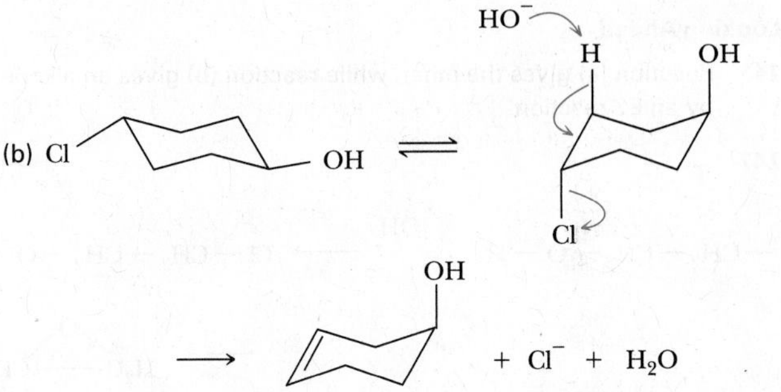

(c) With *trans*-4-chlorocyclohexanol, the nucleophilic atom is created by deprotonating the hydroxyl group. The resulting alkoxide is properly oriented to initiate a backside attack, whereas the alkoxide nucleophile generated from *cis*-4-chlorocyclohexanol is situated on the same side as the leaving group and cannot initiate a backside attack.

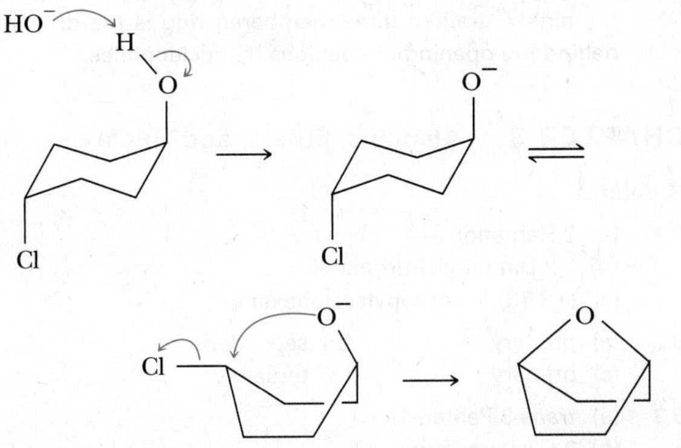

Synthesis and Predict the Product

7.43 (a) S_N1 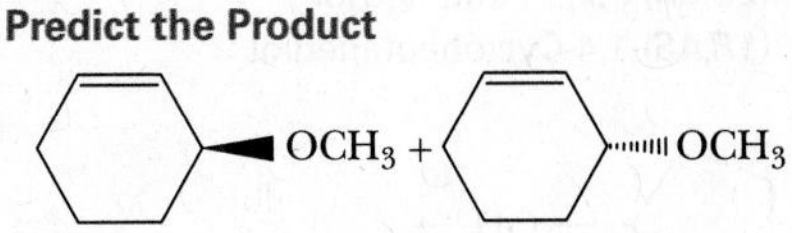

(b) S_N2 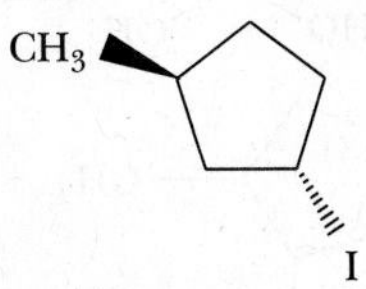

(c) E2 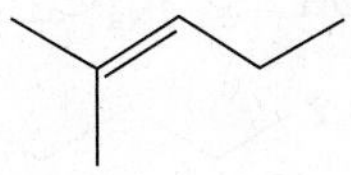

(d) E2

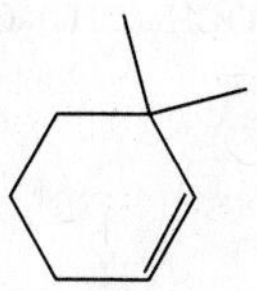

(e) S_N1

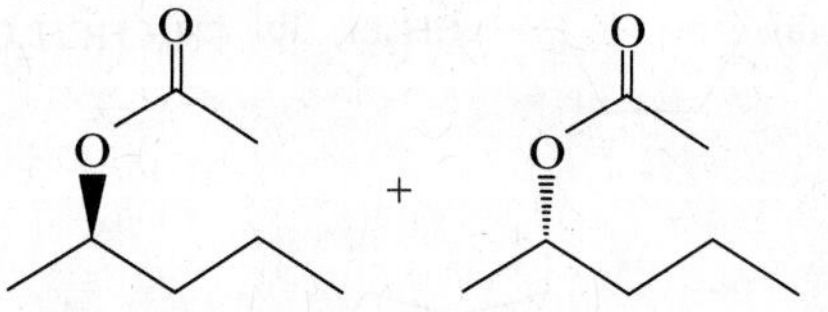

(f) S_N2

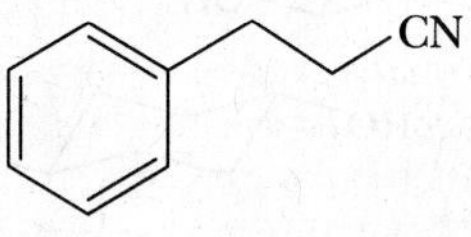

Looking Ahead

7.45 Reaction (a) gives the ether, while reaction (b) gives an alkene by an E2 reaction.

7.47

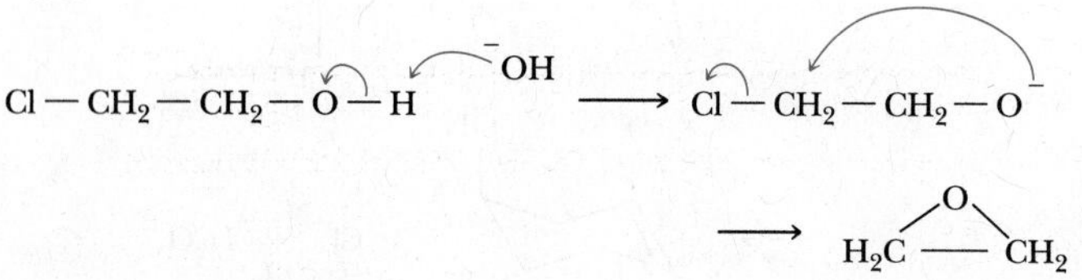

7.49 Over time, an equilibrium mixture consisting of equal amounts of both enantiomers is formed.

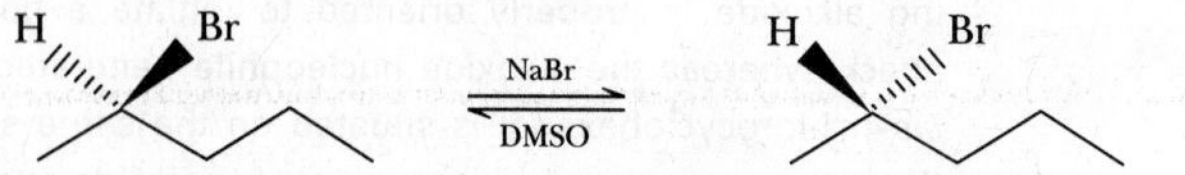

7.51 Although alkoxides are poor leaving groups, the opening of the highly strained three-membered ring is the driving force behind the opening of epoxides by nucleophiles.

CHAPTER 8 Alcohols, Ethers, and Thiols

Problems

8.1 (a) 2-Heptanol
(b) 2,2-Dimethyl-1-propanol
(c) (1*R*,3*S*)-3-Isopropylcyclohexanol

8.2 (a) primary (b) secondary
(c) primary (d) tertiary

8.3 (a) *trans*-3-Penten-1-ol
(b) 2-Cyclopentenol
(c) (2*S*,3*R*)-1,2,3-Pentanetriol
(d) (1*R*,4*S*)-1,4-Cycloheptanediol

8.4 (a)

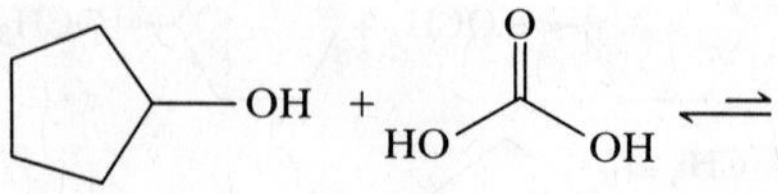

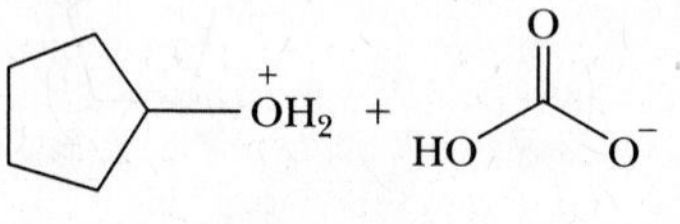

(b)

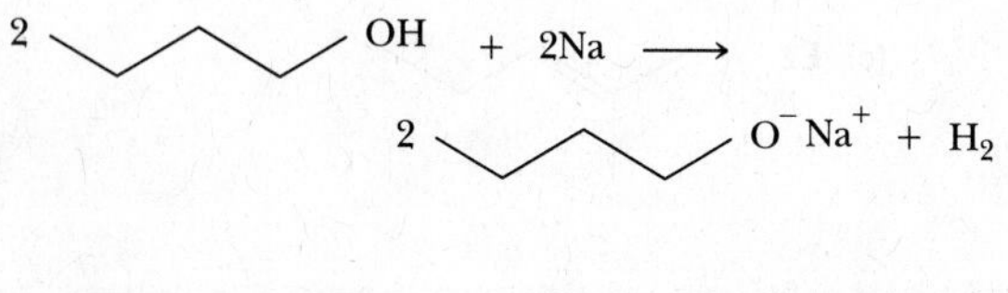

(c)

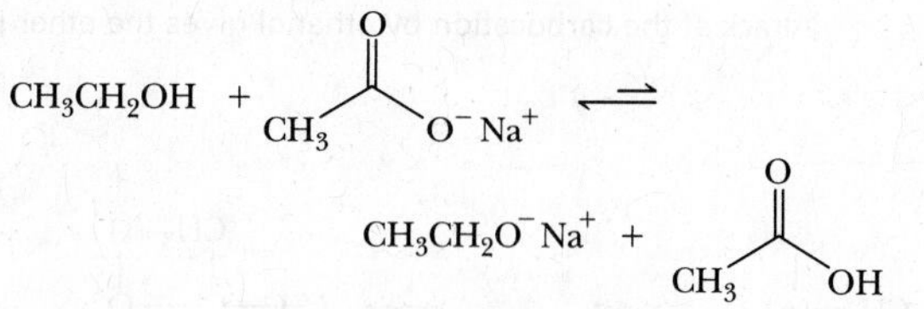

8.5 (a)

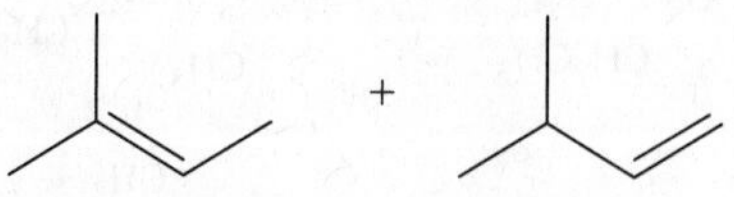

major product minor product

(b)

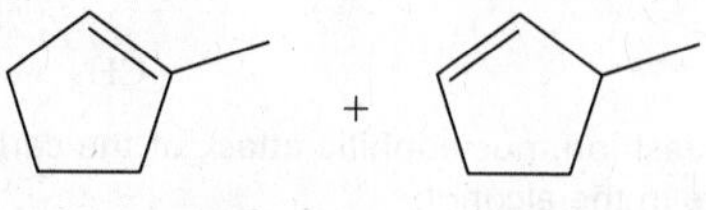

major product minor product

8.6 (a)

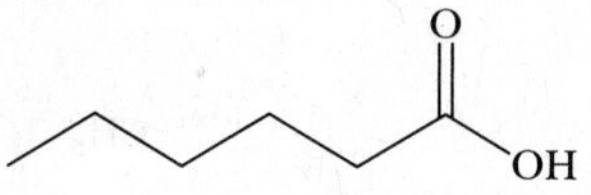

(b)

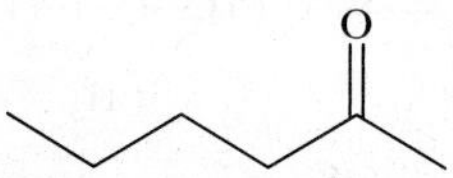

(c)

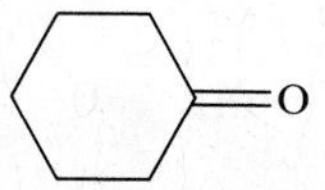

8.7 (a) 1-Ethoxy-2-methylpropane (Ethyl isobutyl ether)
(b) Methoxycyclopentane (Cyclopentyl methyl ether)

8.8 $CH_3OCH_2CH_2OCH_3 < CH_3OCH_2CH_2OH < HOCH_2CH_2OH$

8.9

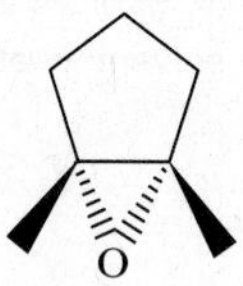

8.10

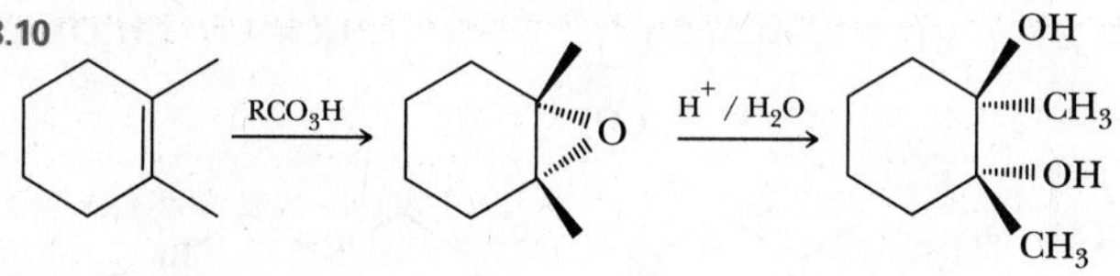

8.11 (a) 3-Methyl-1-butanethiol
(b) 3-Methyl-2-butanethiol

8.12 (a)

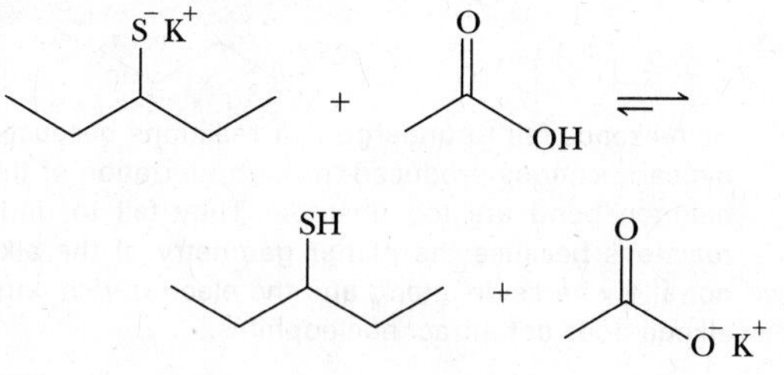

(b)

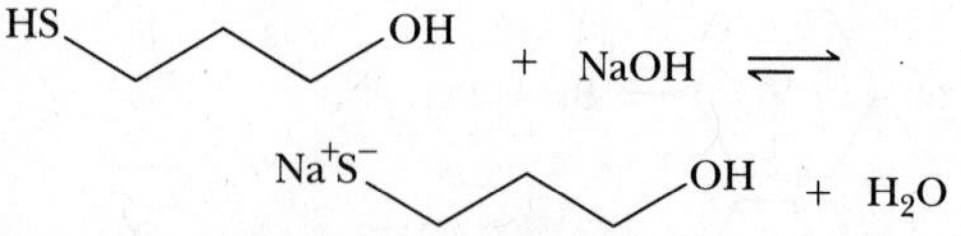

(c)

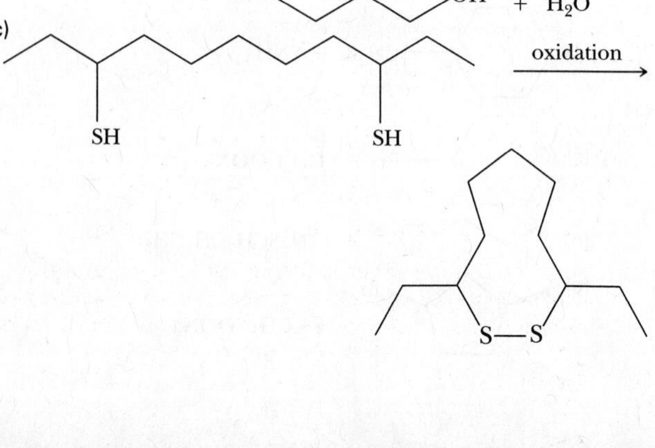

End-of-Chapter Problems

Structure and Nomenclature

8.13 (a) 3° (b) 3° (c) 1° (d) 3°
(e) 2° (f) 2° (g) 3° (h) 2°

8.15

(a) 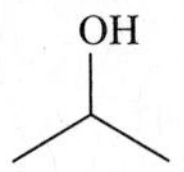

(b) 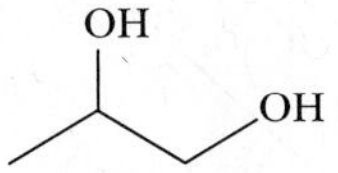

(c) 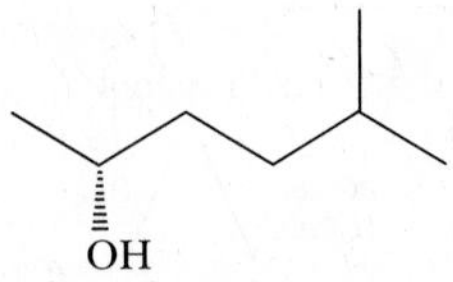

(d) 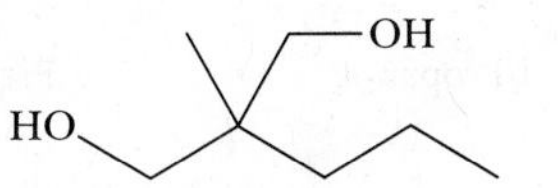

(e) 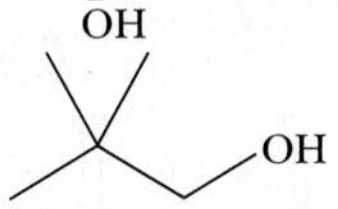

(f) 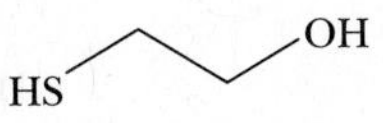

(g) 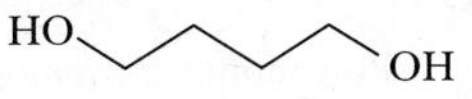

(h) 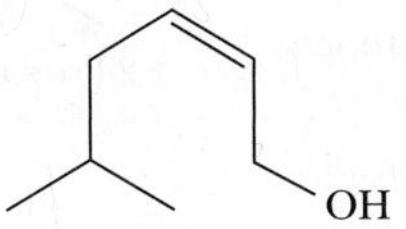

(i) 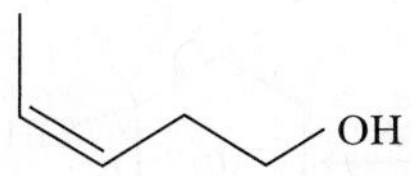

(j) 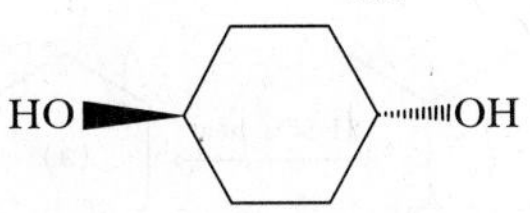

8.17

1-Pentanol

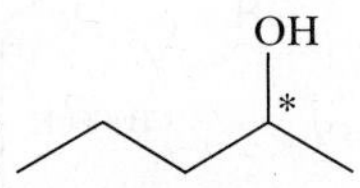

2-Pentanol (chiral)

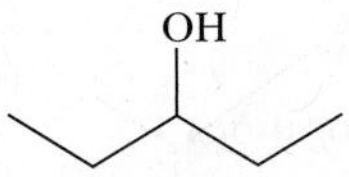

3-Pentanol

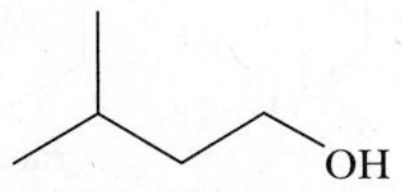

3-Methyl-1-butanol

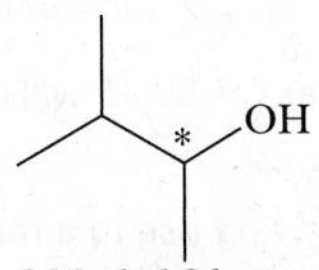

3-Methyl-2-butanol (chiral)

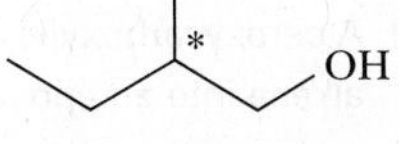

2-Methyl-1-butanol (chiral)

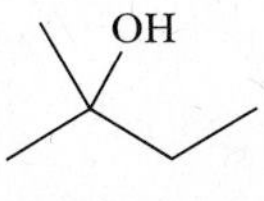

2-Methyl-2-butanol

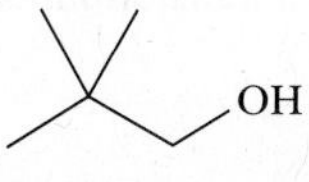

2,2-Dimethyl-1-propanol

Physical Properties

8.19 $CH_3CH_2CH_3 < CH_3OCH_3 < CH_3CH_2OH < CH_3COOH$

8.21

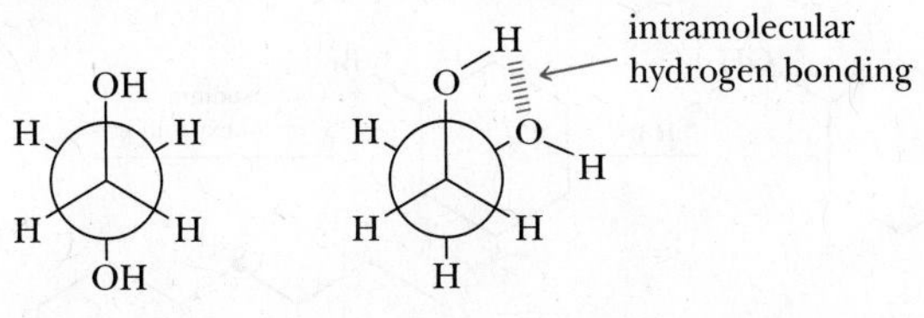

Intramolecular hydrogen bonding can occur between the hydroxyl groups. The strength of the hydrogen bond is greater than 4.2 kJ/mol, so the net result is that the conformation with the larger groups closest to each other is more stable.

8.23 (a) CH_3OH (b) $CH_3\overset{O}{\overset{\parallel}{C}}CH_3$
(c) NaCl (d) $CH_3CH_2CH_2OH$
(e) $CH_3CH_2\overset{OH}{\overset{|}{C}}HCH_2CH_3$

8.25 (a) CH_3CH_2OH (b) CH_3CH_2OH
(c) $CH_3\overset{O}{\overset{\parallel}{C}}CH_3$ (d) $CH_3CH_2OCH_2CH_3$

Synthesis of Alcohols

8.27 The two reactions are stereoselective and result in *trans* products because they both involve an intermediate consisting of a three-membered ring. To open the ring, the nucleophile preferentially attacks from the least-hindered side, which is the side opposite (anti) to that of the three-membered ring. The key ring-opening steps are shown below.

Acid-catalyzed hydrolysis of epoxide:

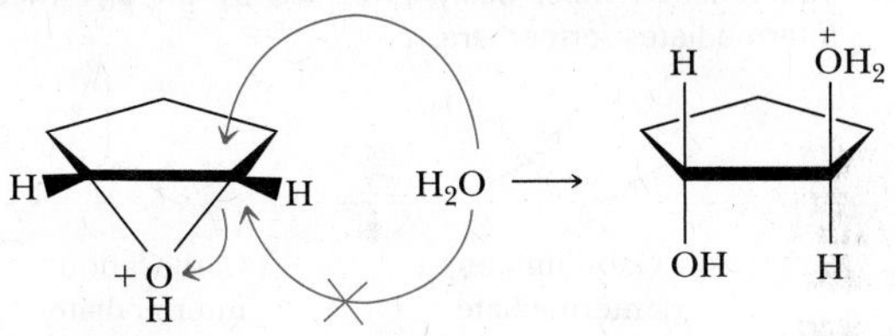

protonated epoxide

Bromination:

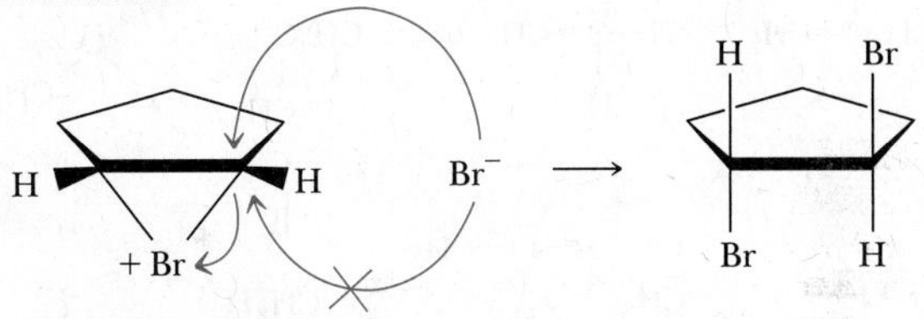

cyclic brominium ion

Acidity of Alcohols and Thiols

8.29 $CH_3CH_2CH_2OH < CH_3CH_2CH_2SH < CH_3CH_2\overset{O}{\overset{\parallel}{C}}OH$

8.31 (a) $CH_3CH_2O^- + HCl \rightleftharpoons CH_3CH_2OH + Cl^-$

stronger base	stronger acid	weaker acid	weaker base

The equilibrium lies far to the right.

(b) $CH_3\overset{O}{\overset{\parallel}{C}}OH + CH_3CH_2O^- \rightleftharpoons CH_3\overset{O}{\overset{\parallel}{C}}O^- + CH_3CH_2OH$

stronger acid	stronger base	weaker base	weaker acid

The equilibrium lies far to the right.

Reactions of Alcohols

8.33 Both cyclohexanol and cyclohexene are colorless. However, cyclohexene will decolorize an orange-red solution of bromine dissolved in CCl_4 (the solvent), while cyclohexanol does not react with bromine.

8.35

(a) 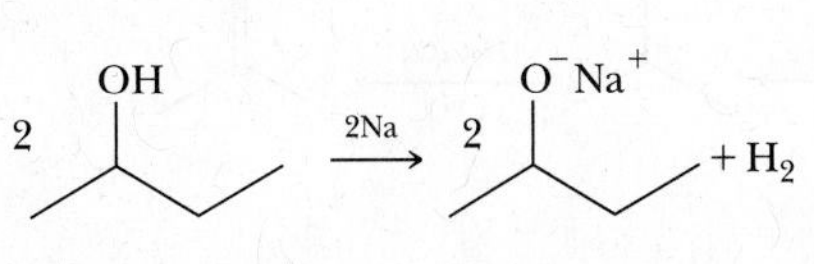

(b)

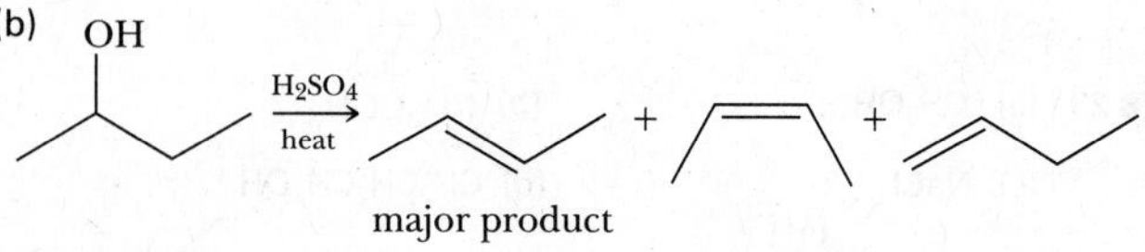

(c)

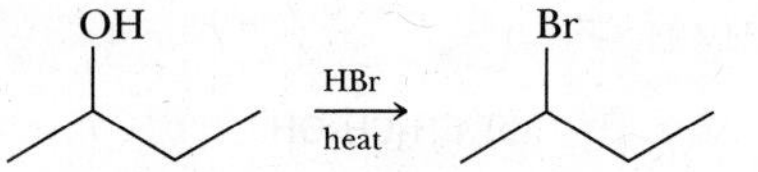

(d)

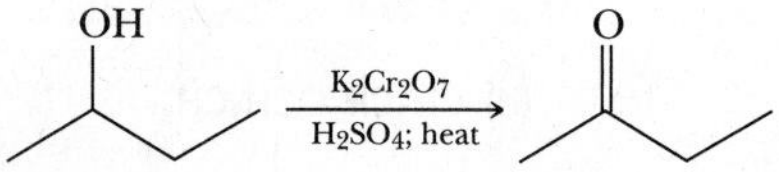

(e)

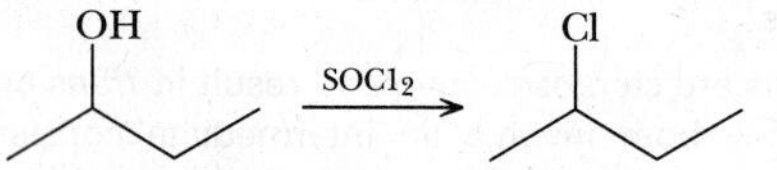

(f)

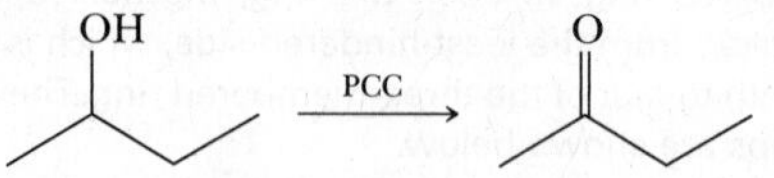

8.37 The reaction most likely proceeds by an S_N1 mechanism. Intermediates formed are:

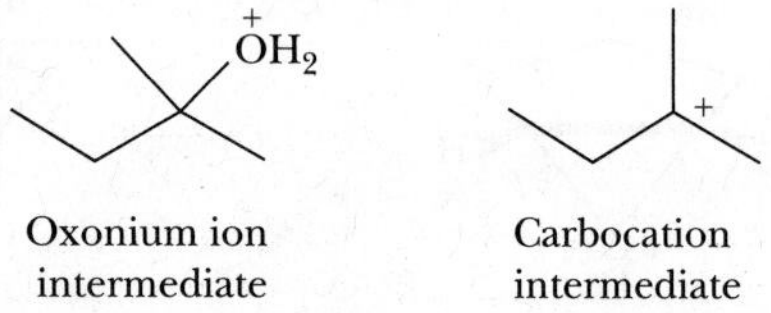

8.39

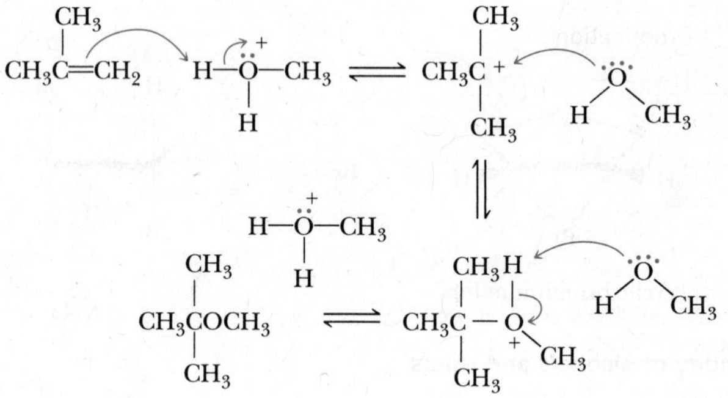

Syntheses

8.41 (a)

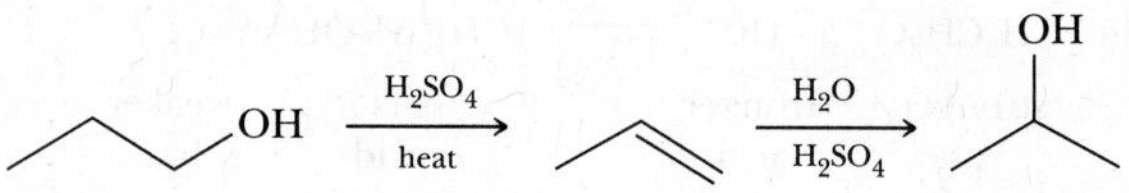

(b)

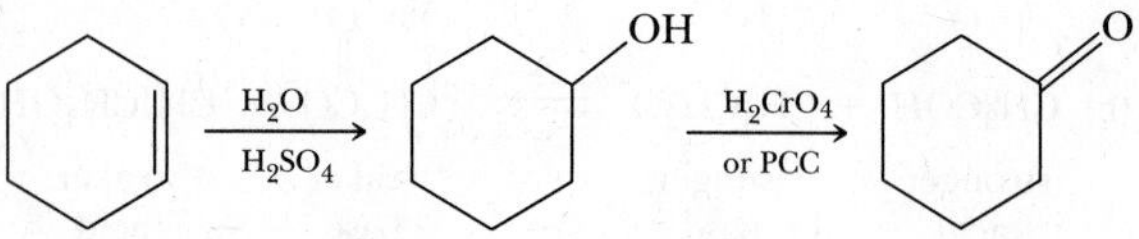

(c)

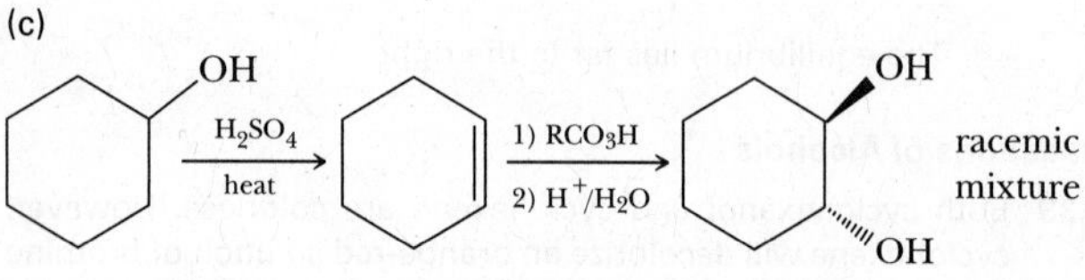

(d)

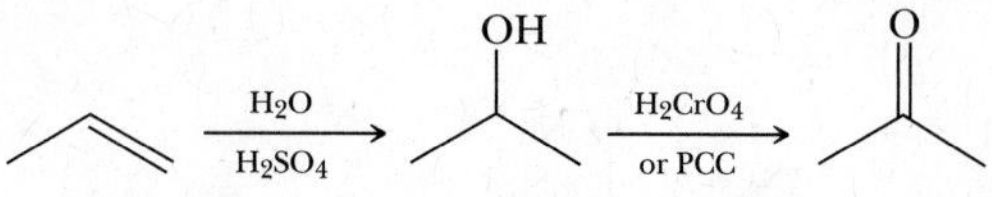

8.43

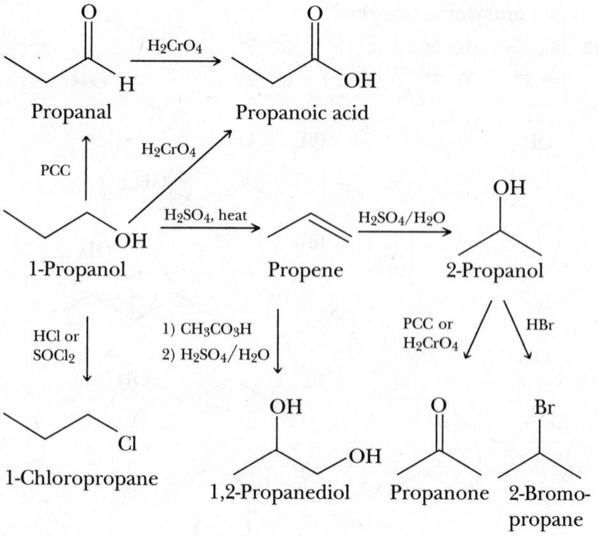

8.45

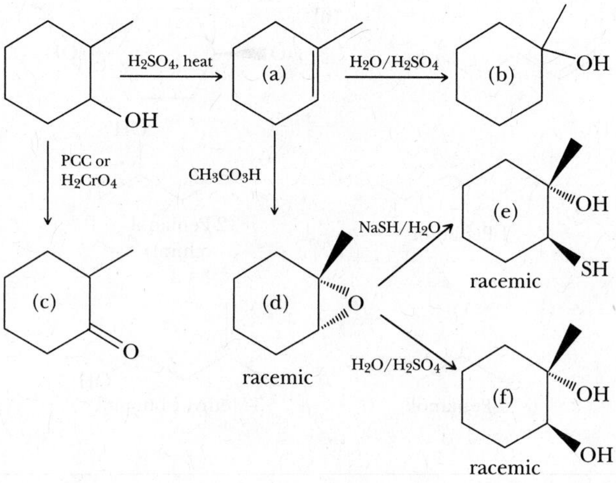

8.47 (a) A peroxycarboxylic acid, such as CH_3CO_3H, will convert the alkene into an epoxide.

(b) There are two stereocenters, giving rise to a maximum of $2^2 = 4$ stereoisomers. However, only two are formed due to the stereoselectivity of the epoxidation reaction.

Chemical Transformations

8.49

(a)

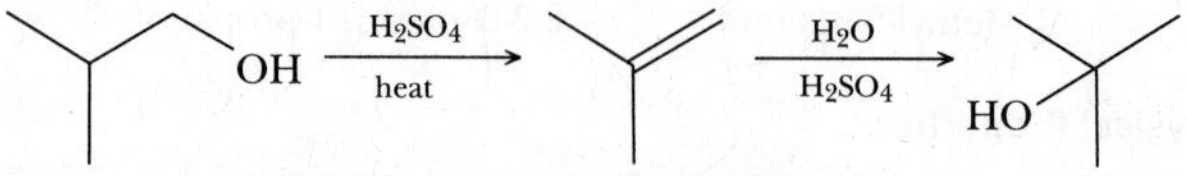

(b)

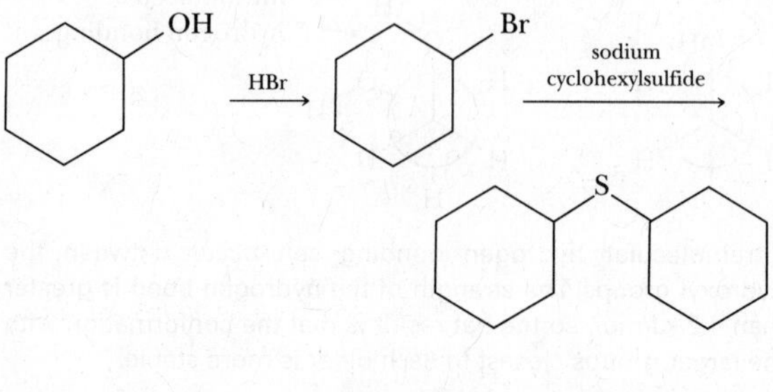

(c)

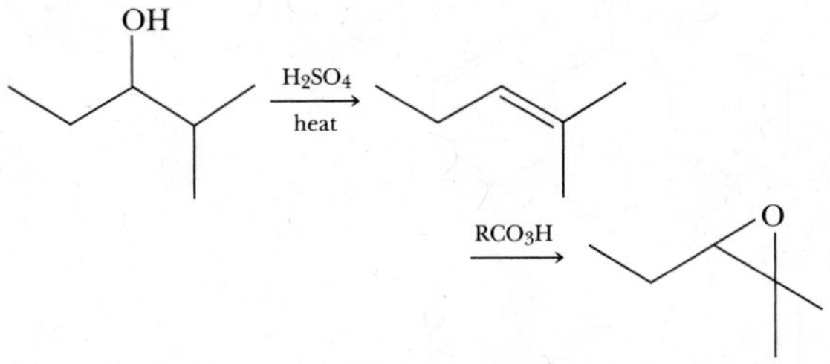

(d)

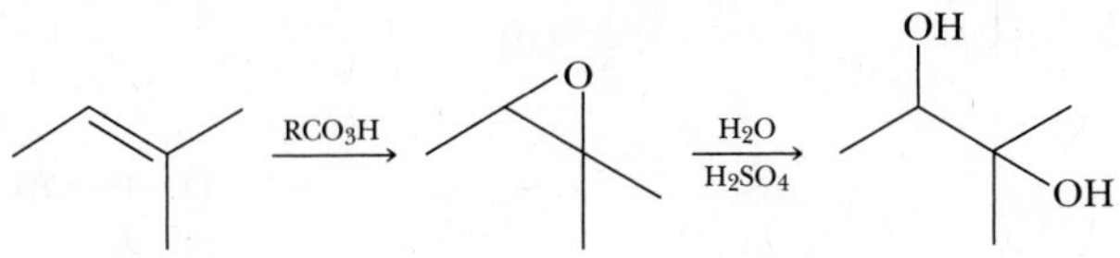

(e)

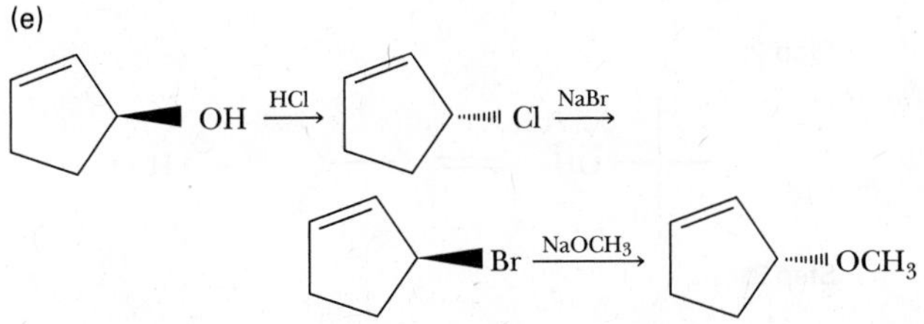

(f)

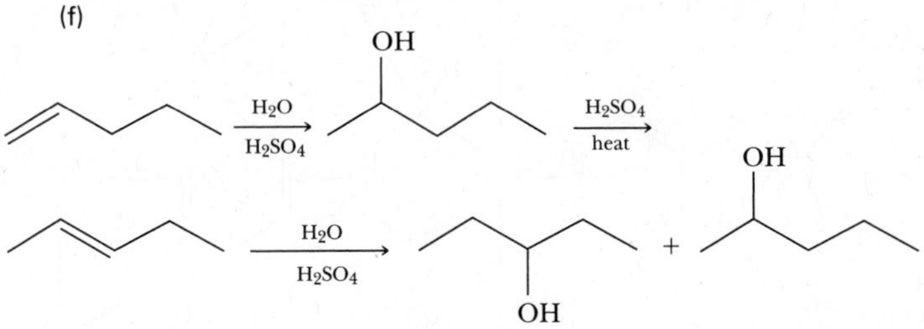

(g)

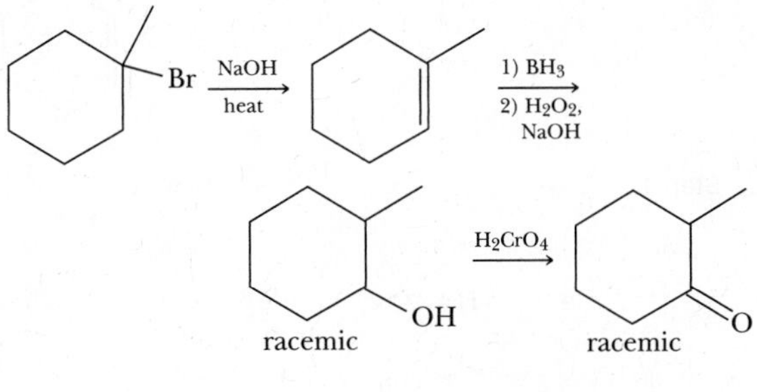

(h)

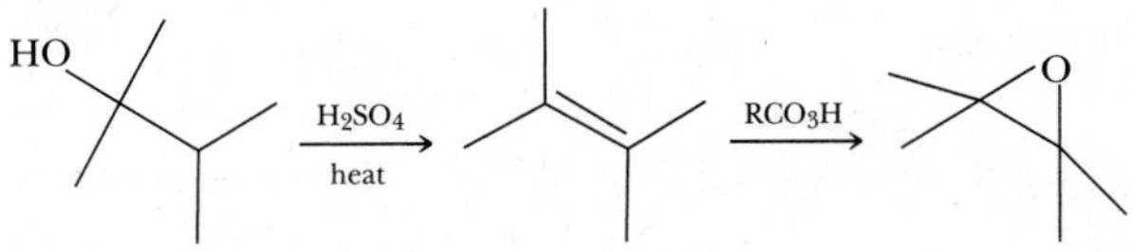

(i)

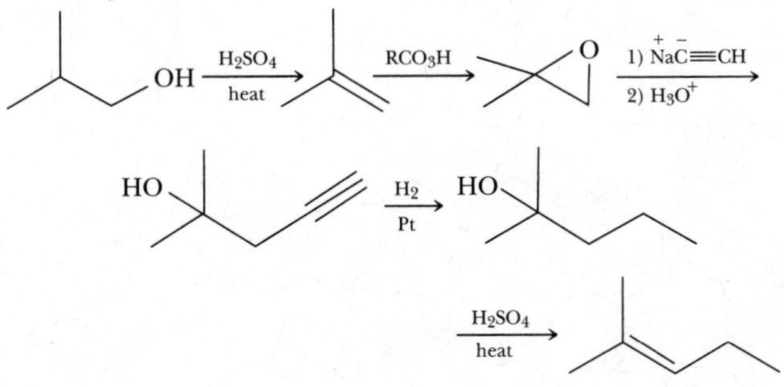

(j)

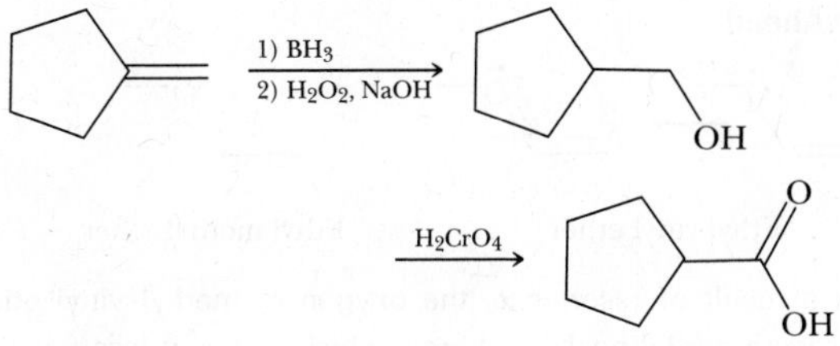

(k)

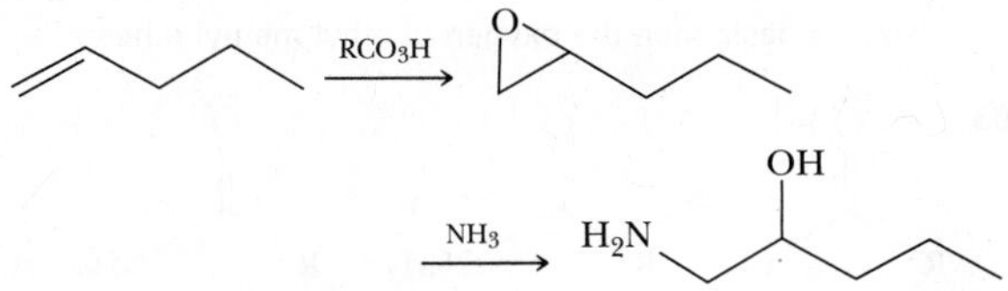

(l)

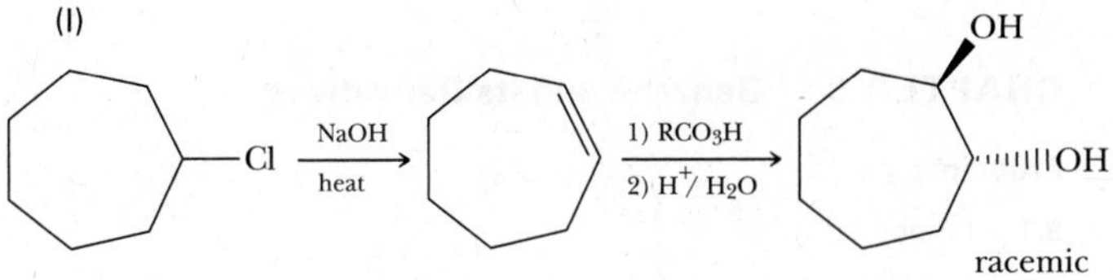

(m)

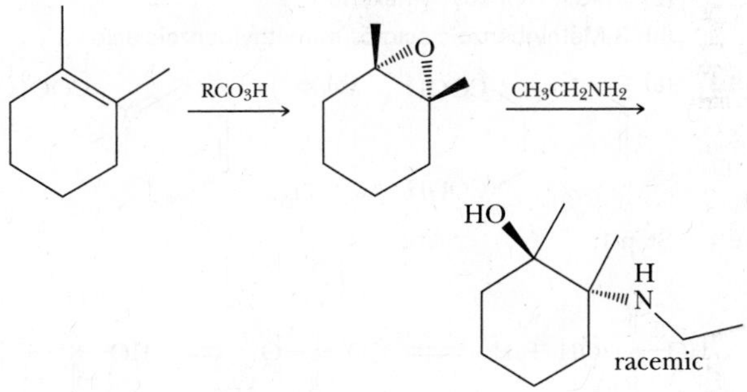

(n)

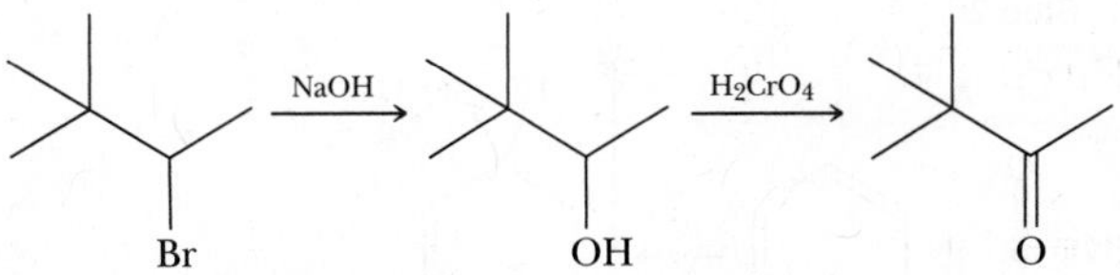

(o)

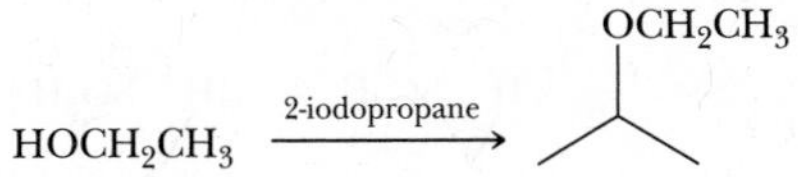

(p)

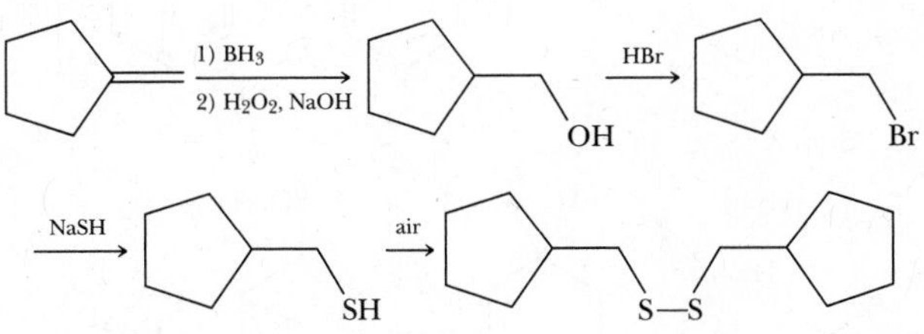

(q)

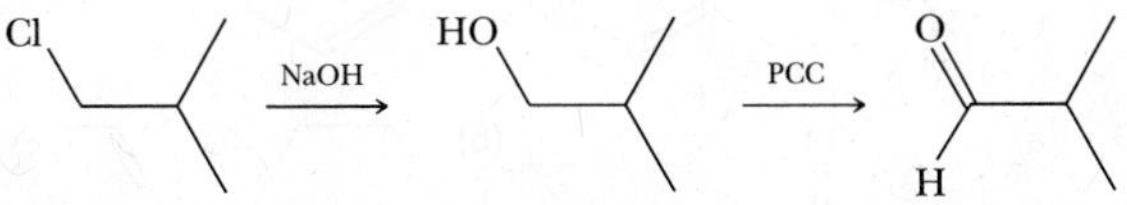

(r)

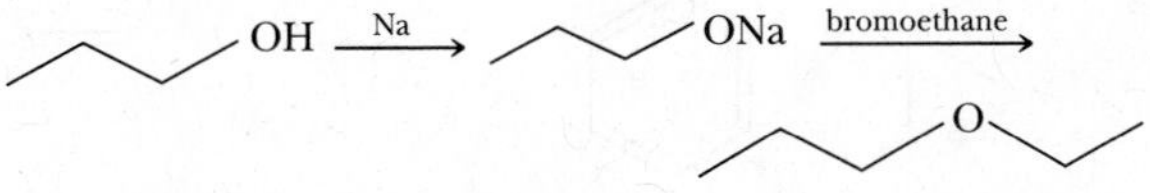

Looking Ahead

8.51

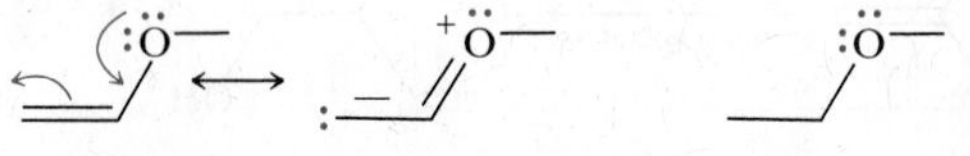

Ethyl vinyl ether Ethyl methyl ether

As a result of resonance, the oxygen of methyl vinyl ether carries a partial positive charge, which makes it less reactive toward an electrophile. The oxygen of methyl vinyl ether is also less basic than the oxygen of ethyl methyl ether.

8.53

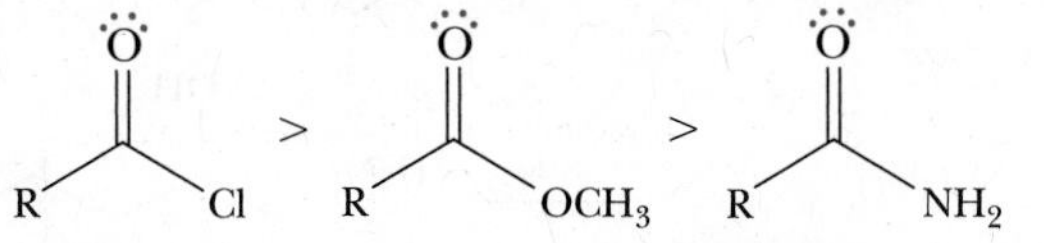

CHAPTER 9 Benzene and Its Derivatives

Problems

9.1 (a) and (c)

9.2 (a) 2-Phenyl-2-propanol
(b) (*E*)-3,4-Diphenyl-3-hexene
(c) 3-Methylbenzoic acid or *m*-methylbenzoic acid

9.3 (a)

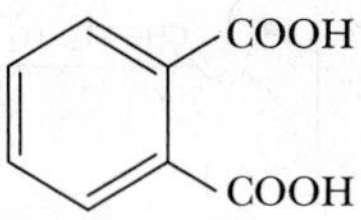

(b)

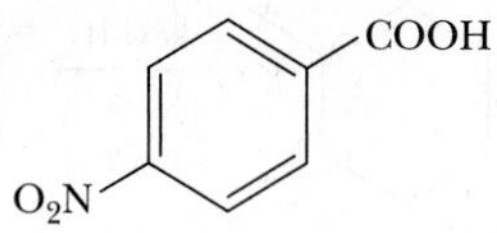

9.4 Step 1:

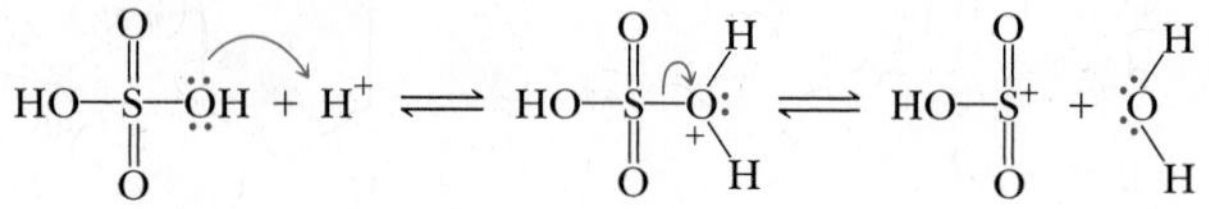

Step 2:

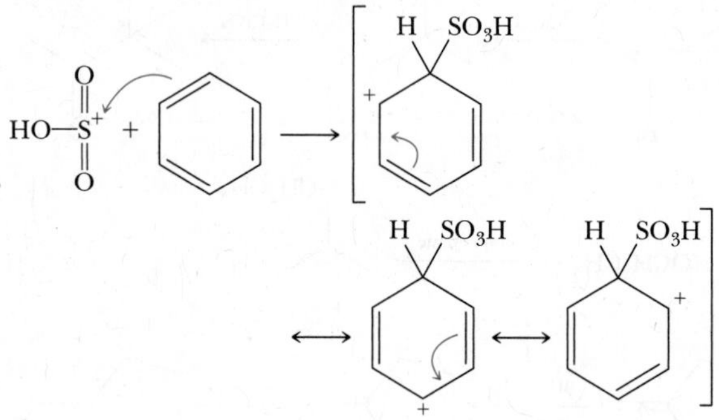

Step 3:

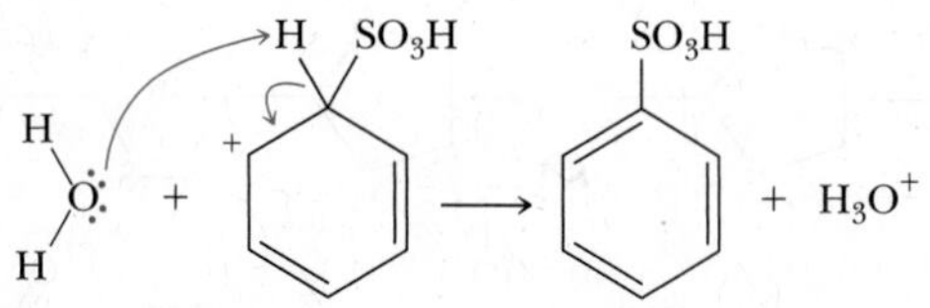

9.5 (a)

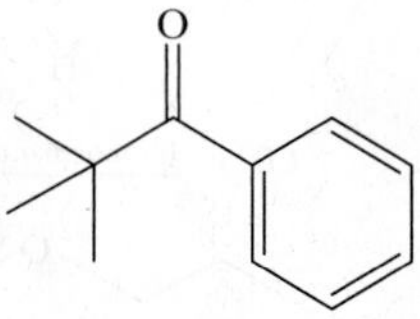

(b)

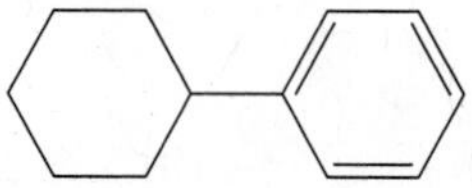

(c)

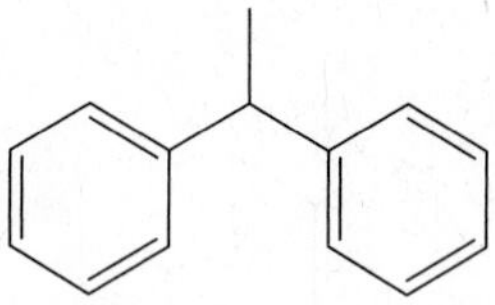

9.6 Step 1:

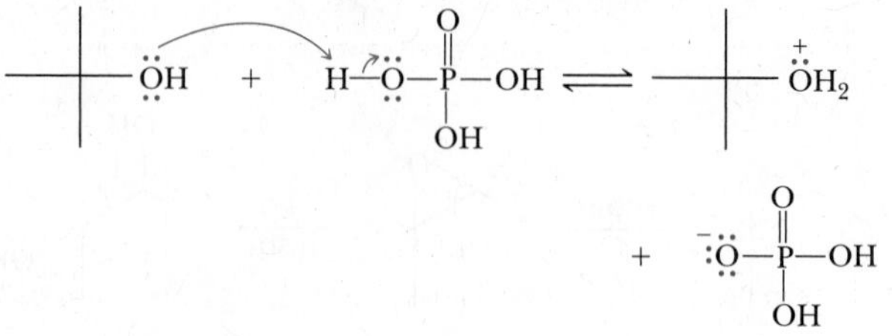

Step 2:

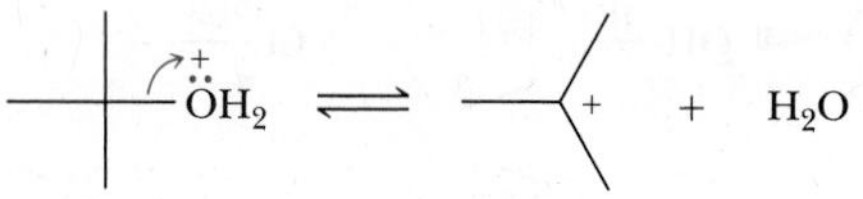

Step 3:

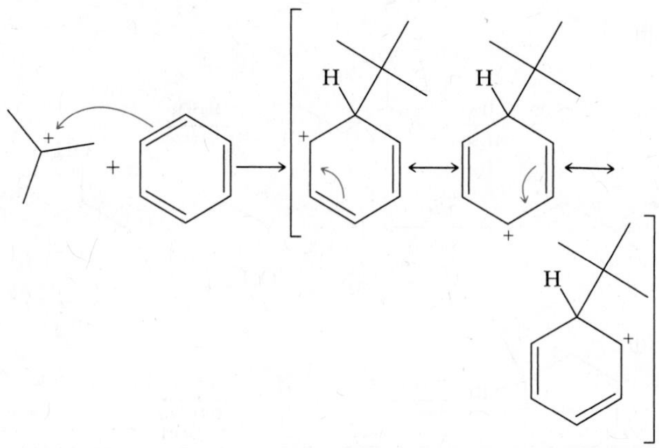

Step 4:

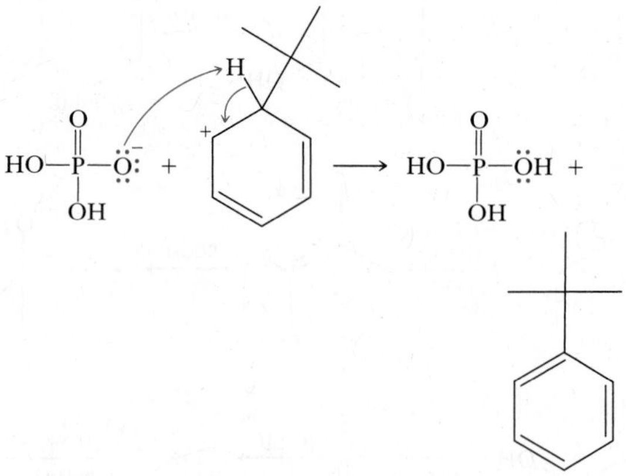

9.7 (a)

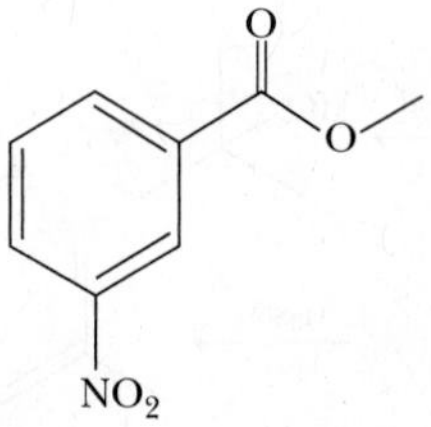

(b)

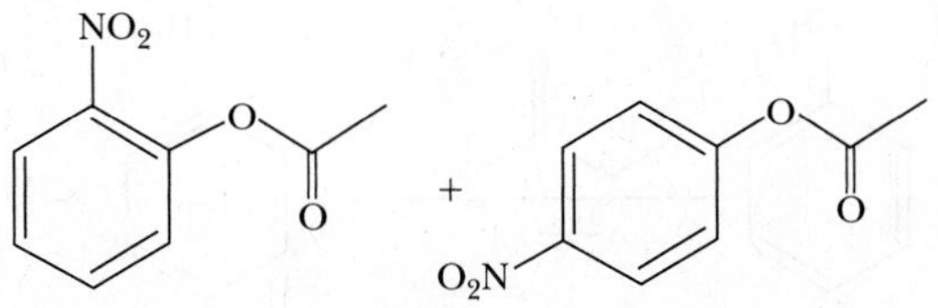

9.8 If the electrophile is added ortho or para, it is possible to draw a contributing structure that places the positive charge directly adjacent to the partially positive carbon atom of the carbonyl group. This interaction destabilizes the carbocation, which in turn disfavors ortho-para attack of the electrophile.

On the other hand, if the electrophile is added meta, no contributing structure places the carbocation directly adjacent to the carbon atom of the carbonyl group. Because there are no destabilizing interactions, meta attack is more favorable.

9.9 (a)

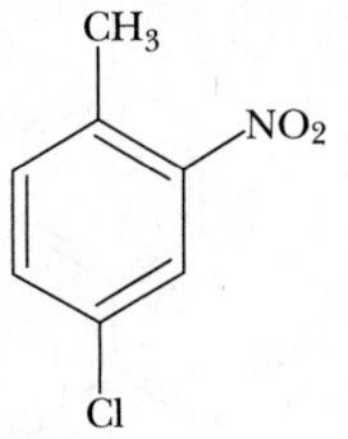

(b)

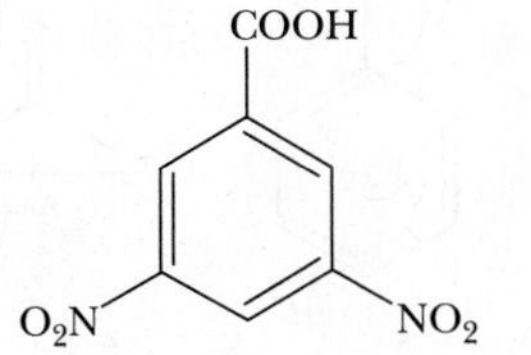

9.10

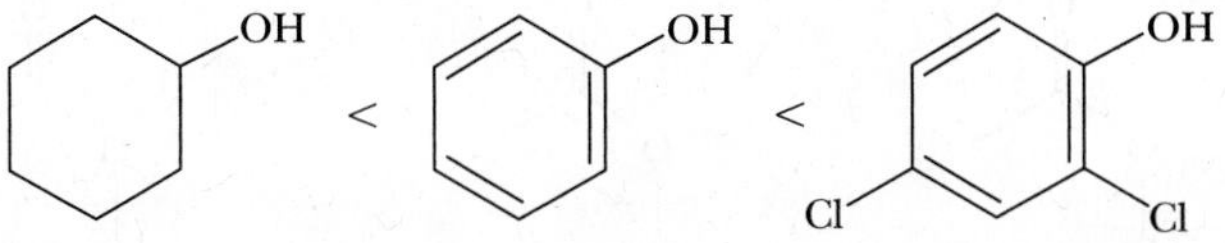

End-of-Chapter Problems

Aromaticity

9.11 (c), (d), (e), (g), (j), (k), (l)

Nomenclature and Structural Formulas

9.13 (a) 1-Chloro-4-nitrobenzene (*p*-Chloronitrobenzene)
(b) 1-Bromo-2-methylbenzene or 2-bromotoluene or *o*-bromotoluene
(c) 3-Phenyl-1-propanol
(d) 2-Phenyl-3-buten-2-ol
(e) 3-Nitrobenzoic acid or *m*-nitrobenzoic acid
(f) 1-Phenylcyclohexanol
(g) (*E*)-1,2-Diphenylethene or *trans*-1,2-diphenylethene
(h) 2,4-Dichloro-1-toluene or 2,4-dichlorotoluene
(i) 4-Bromo-2-chloro-1-ethylbenzene
(j) 1-Fluoro-3-isopropyl-5-vinylbenzene or 3-fluoro-5-isopropylstyrene
(k) 1-Amino-2-chloro-4-ethylbenzene or 2-chloro-4-ethylaniline
(l) 1-Methoxy-4-vinylbenzene or *p*-methoxystyrene

9.15

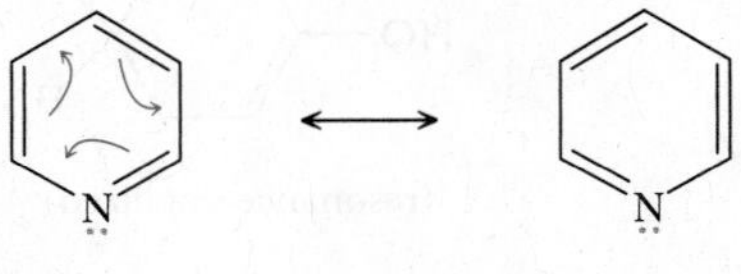

9.17

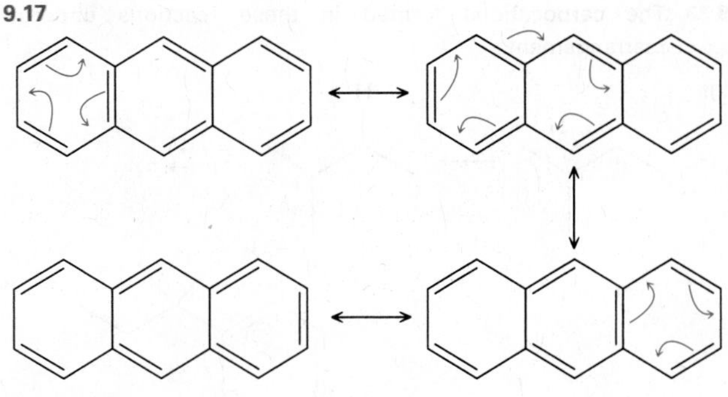

Electrophilic Aromatic Substitution: Monosubstitution

9.19 (1) 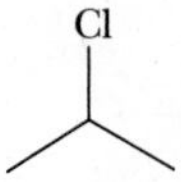 + $AlCl_3$ (2) 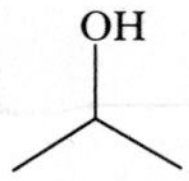 + H_2SO_4 (or H_3PO_4)

(3) 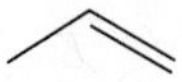 + H_2SO_4 (or H_3PO_4)

9.20 2

9.21

Step 1:

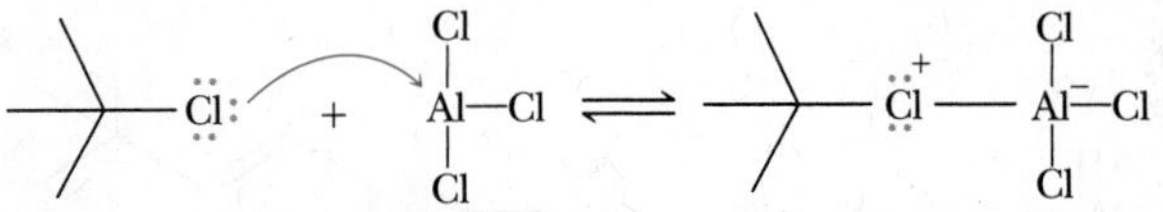

Step 2:

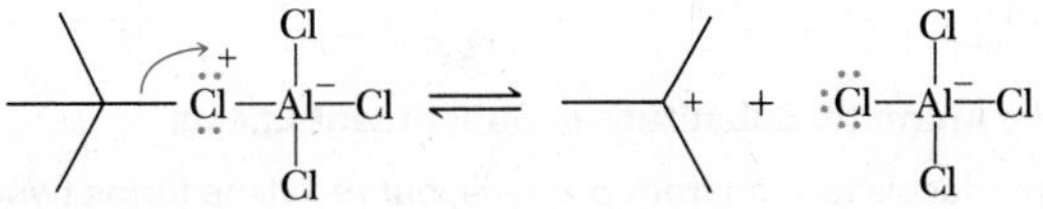

Step 3:

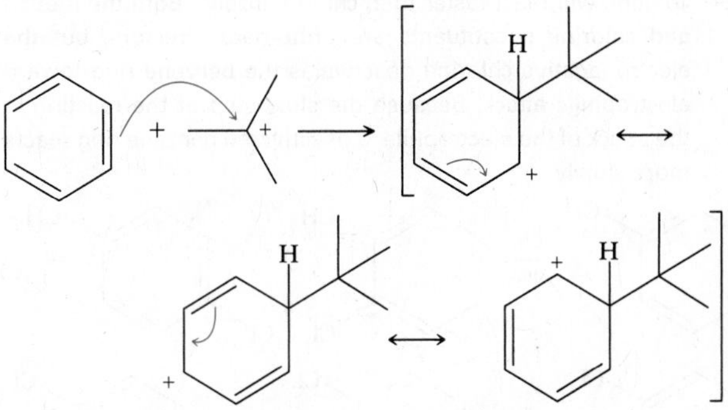

Step 4:

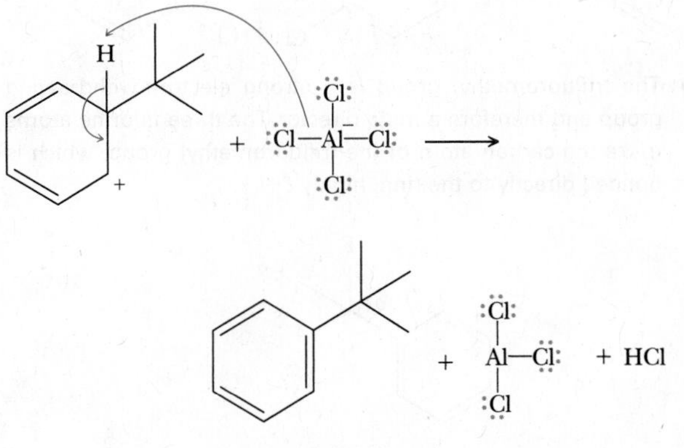

9.23 The carbocations formed in these reactions undergo rearrangement.

(a)

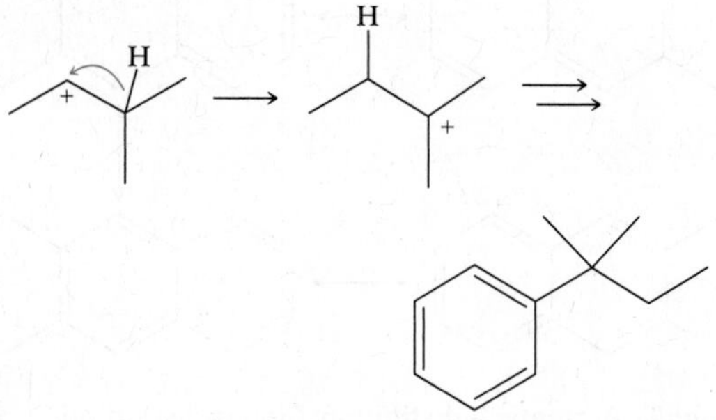

(b)

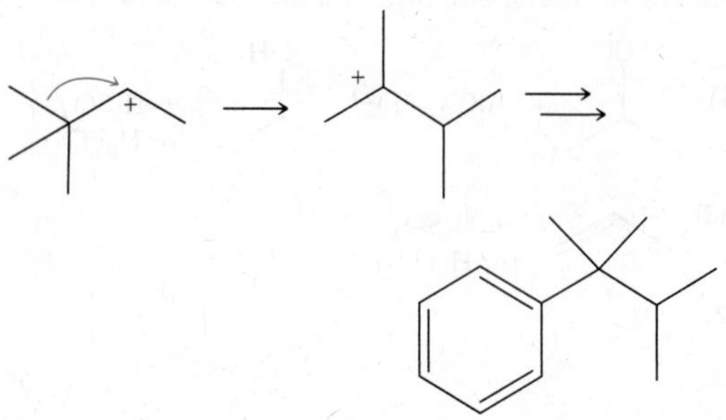

(c)

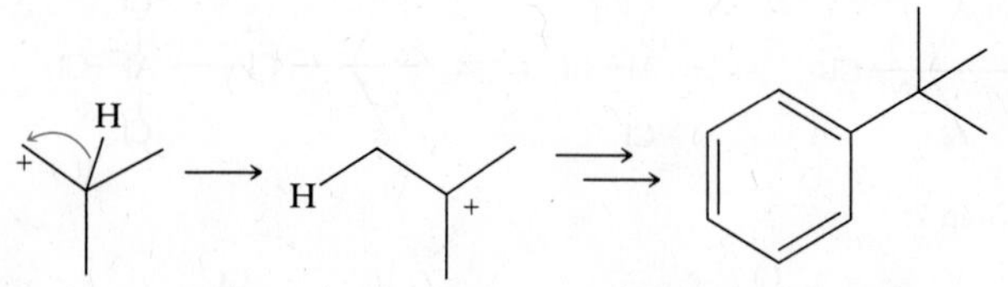

Electrophilic Aromatic Substitution: Substituent Effects

9.25 One product is formed from *p*-xylene, but *m*-xylene forms two products.

9.27 Toluene will react faster than chlorobenzene. Both the methyl and chlorine substituents are ortho-para directors, but the electronegative chlorine deactivates the benzene ring toward electrophilic attack. Because the slow step of the reaction is the attack of the electrophile, a deactivated benzene ring reacts more slowly.

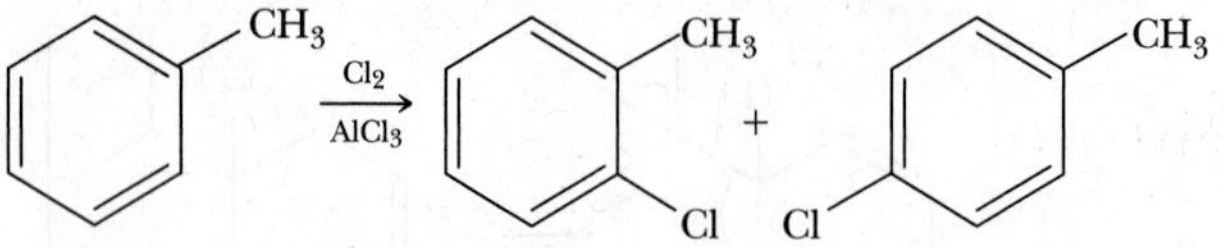

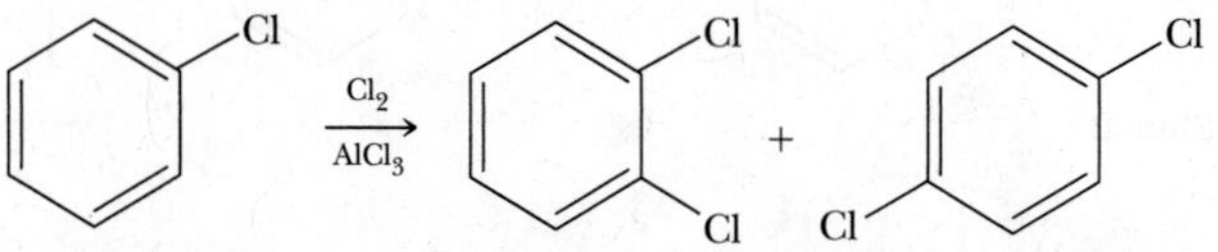

9.29 The trifluoromethyl group is a strong electron-withdrawing group and therefore a meta director. The three fluorine atoms make the carbon atom of the trifluoromethyl group, which is bonded directly to the ring, highly $\delta+$.

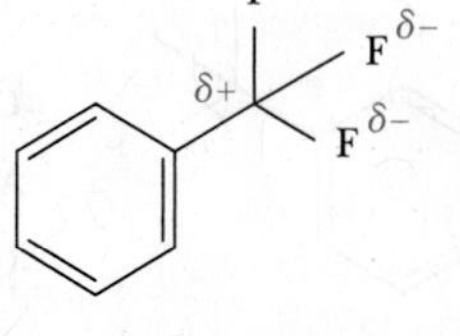

9.31 (a)

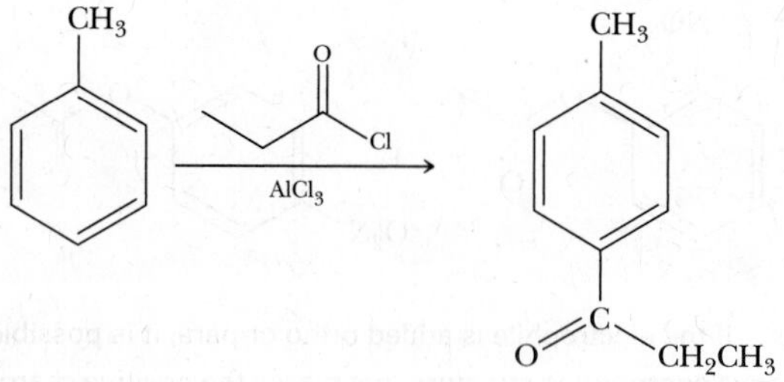

(b)

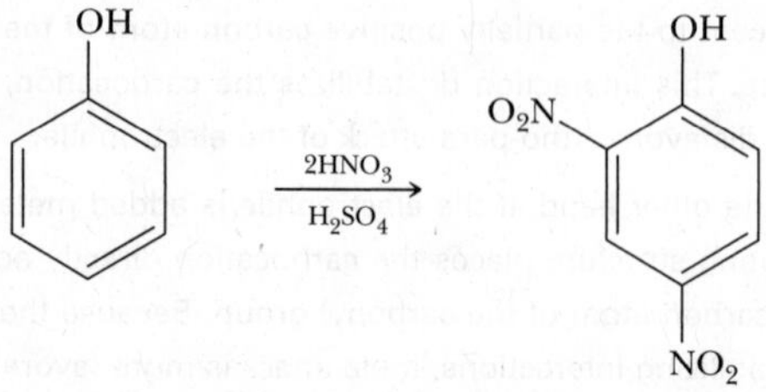

(c)

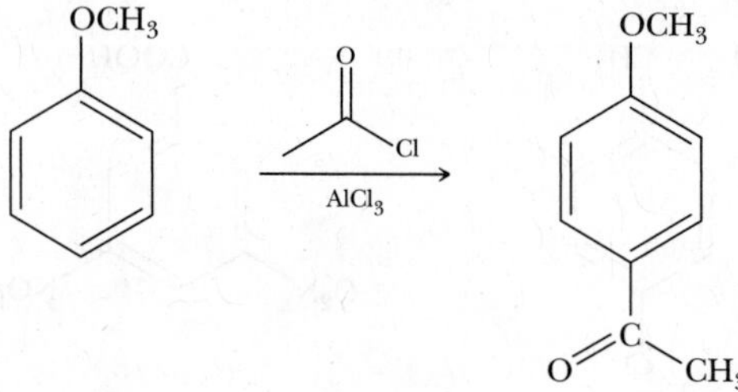

(d)

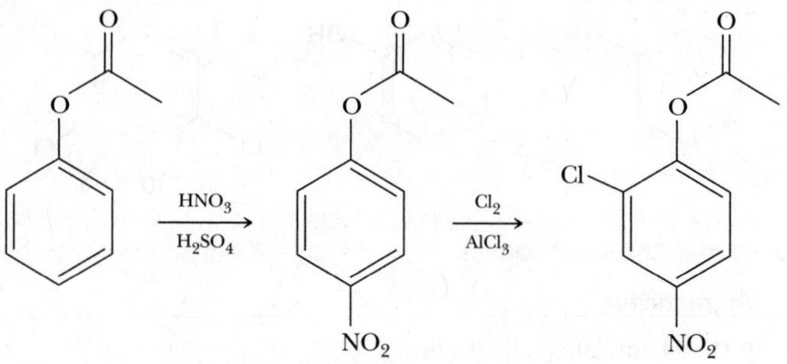

9.33 Step 1:

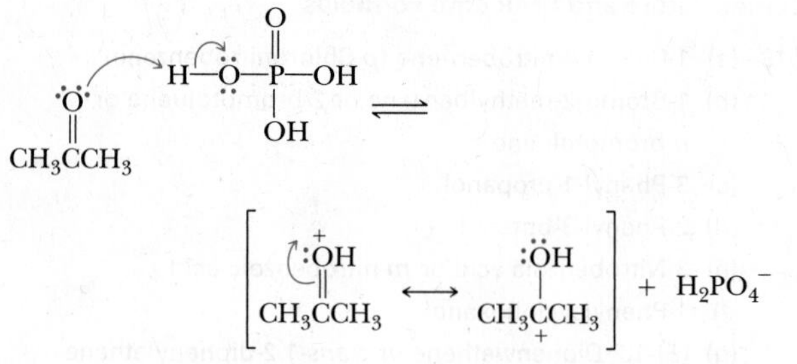

Step 2:

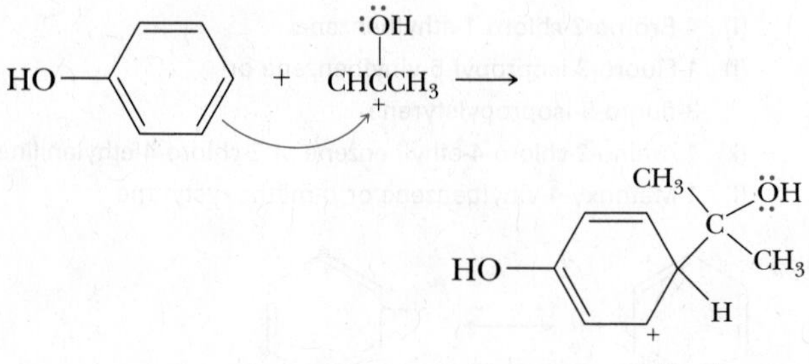

(resonance-stabilized)

Step 3:

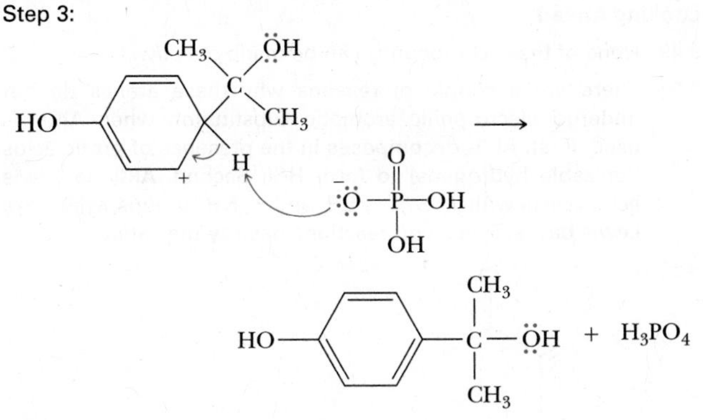

Step 4:

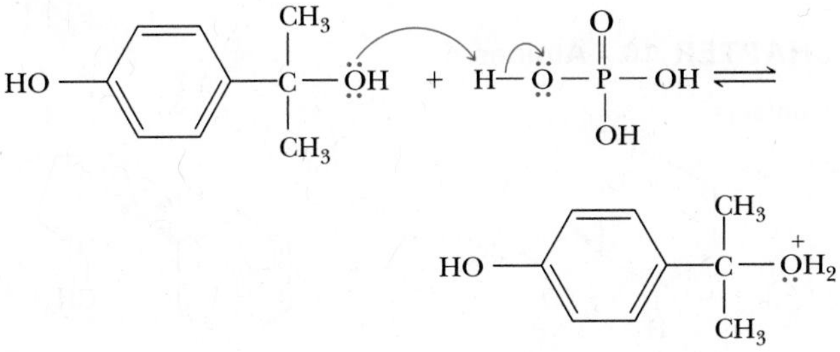

Step 5:

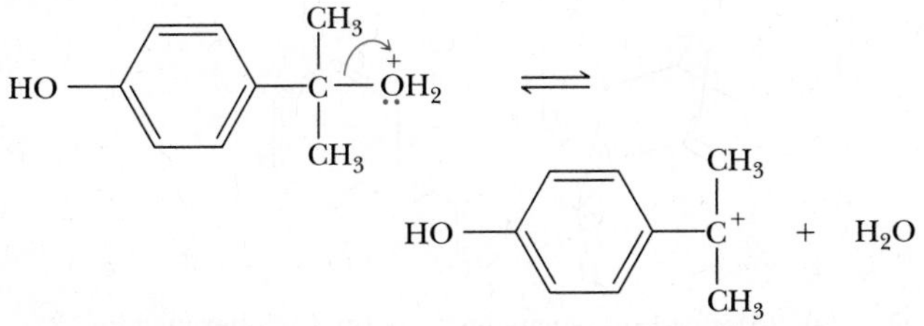

Step 6:

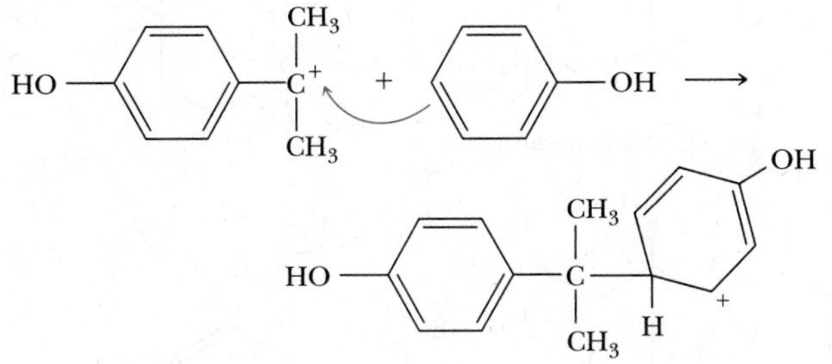

(resonance-stabilized)

Step 7:

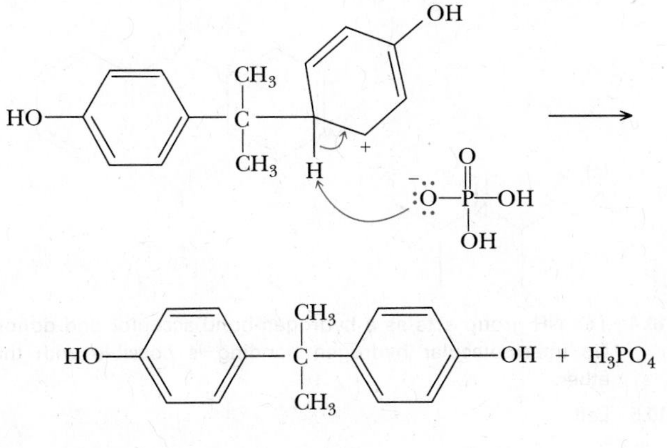

9.35

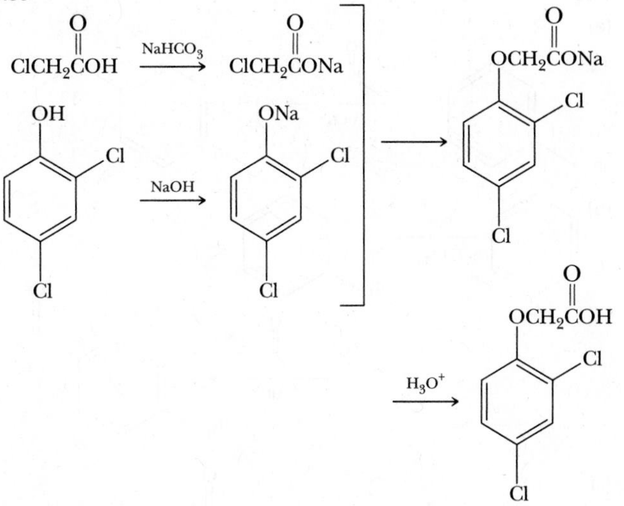

Acidity of Phenols

9.37

(a)

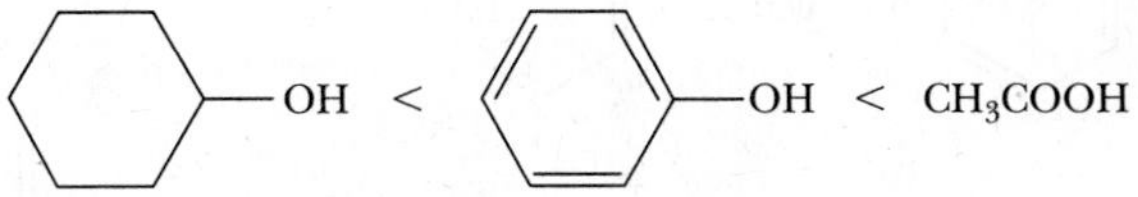

(b)

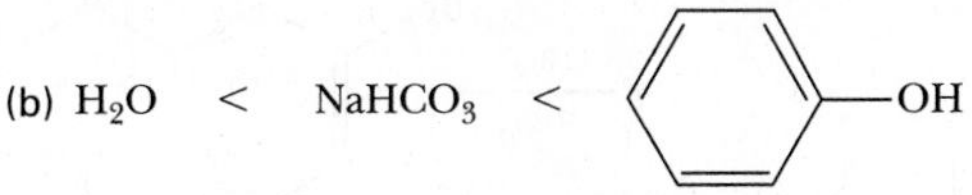

(c)

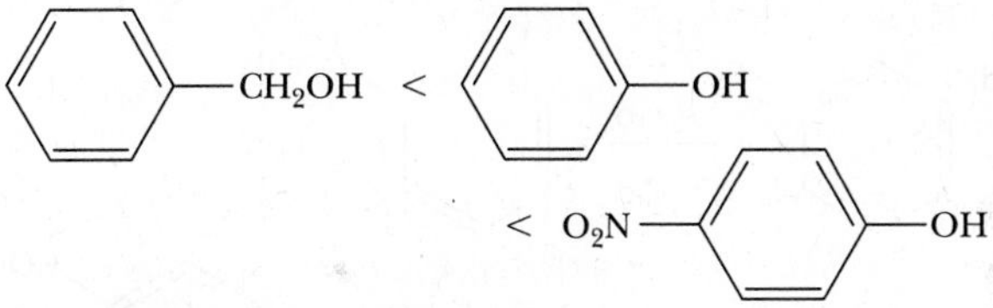

9.39 The gas formed is carbon dioxide, which arises from the decomposition of carbonic acid.

$$H_2CO_3 \longrightarrow CO_2 + H_2O$$

Carbonic acid (pK_a = 6.36) is formed when HCO_3^- acts as a base. A carboxylic acid is a stronger acid than carbonic acid, so the bicarbonate ion is a strong enough base to deprotonate a carboxylic acid. However, because a phenol is a weaker acid than carbonic acid, bicarbonate is not a strong enough base to deprotonate phenol.

Syntheses

9.41

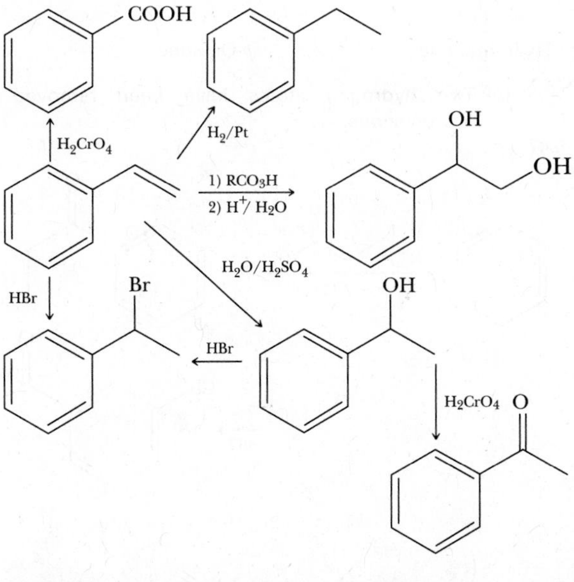

9.43

(a)

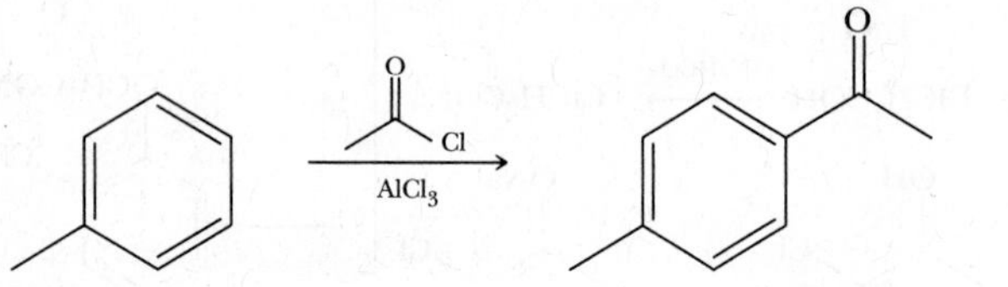

(b)

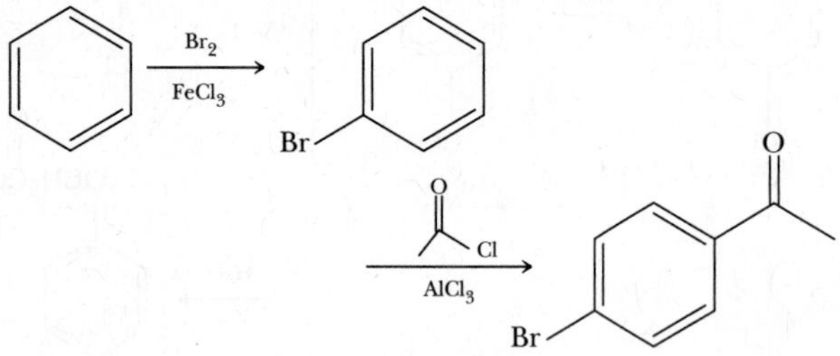

(c)

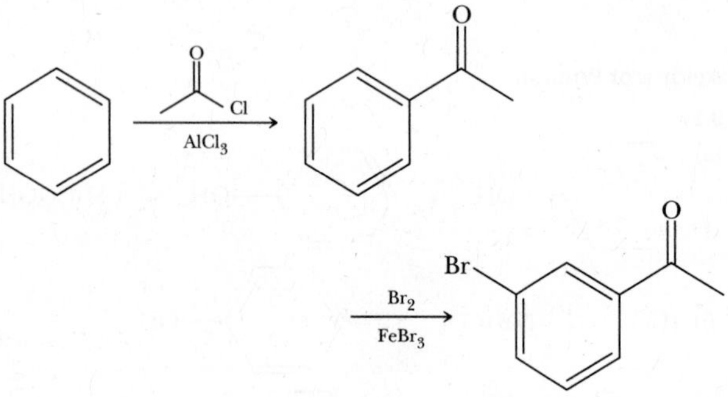

(d)

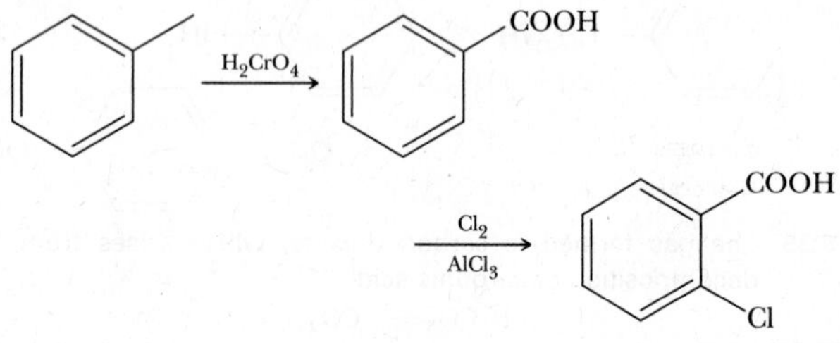

9.45 (a)

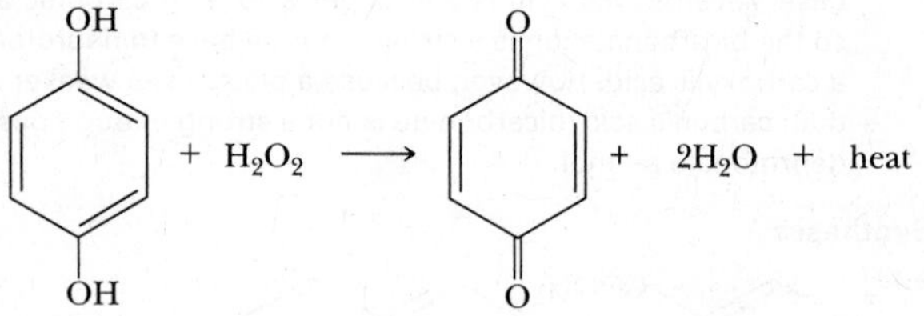

Hydroquinone *p*-Quinone

(b) Two hydrogen atoms have been removed from hydroquinone.

9.47

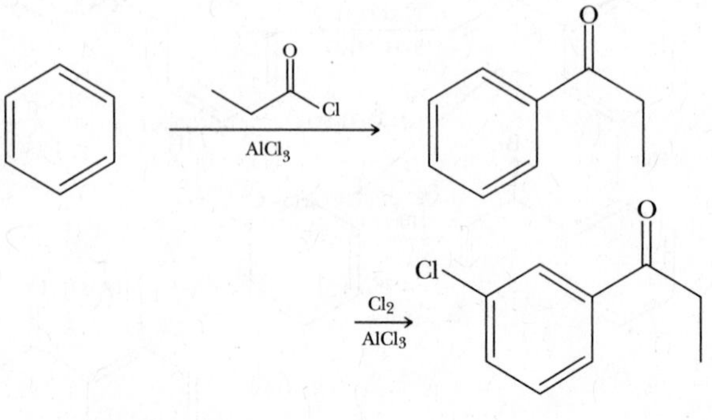

Looking Ahead

9.49 None of these compounds can be made *directly*.

9.51 There are a couple of reasons why these arenes do not undergo electrophilic aromatic substitution when $AlCl_3$ is used. First, $AlCl_3$ decomposes in the presence of protic acids (ionizable hydrogens) to form HCl. Second, $AlCl_3$ (a Lewis acid) reacts with —OH, —SH, and —NH_2 groups, which are Lewis bases. These two reactions destroy the catalyst.

9.53

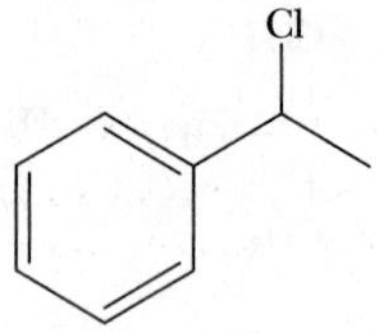

CHAPTER 10 Amines

Problems

10.1 (a)

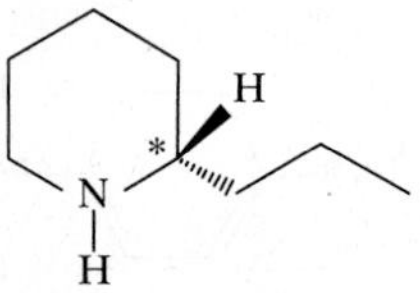

(b)

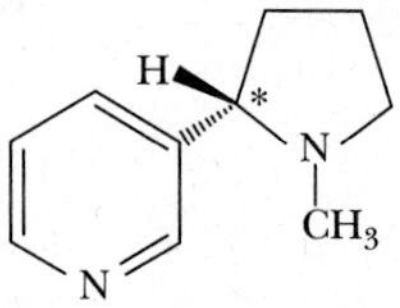

(c)

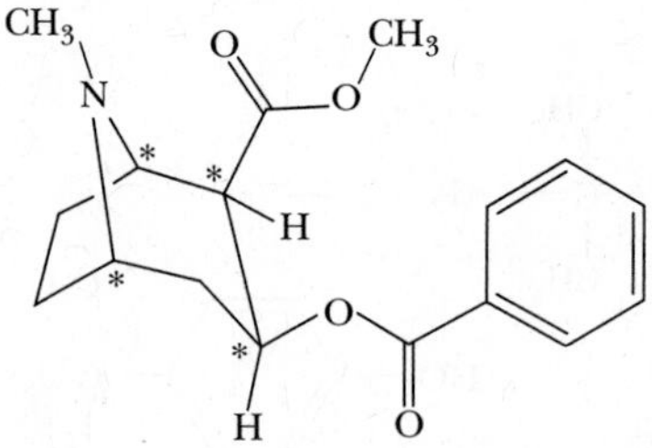

10.2 (a) 2-Methyl-1-propanamine

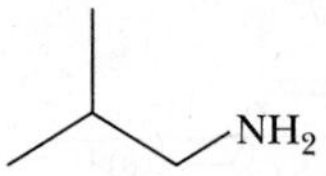

(b) Cyclohexanamine

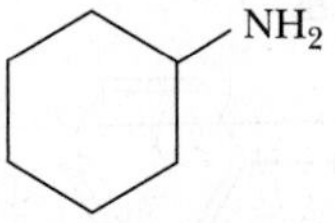

(c) (*R*)-2-Butanamine

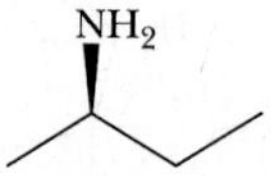

10.3 (a)

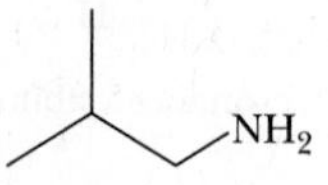

(b)

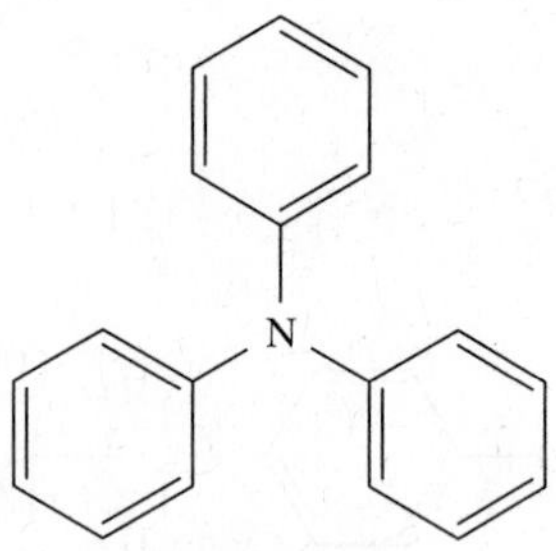

(c)

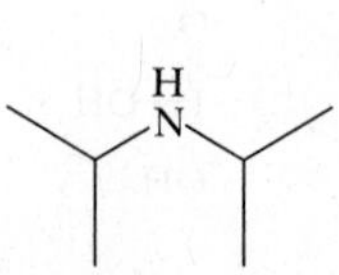

10.4 The NH group acts as a hydrogen-bond acceptor and donor. No intermolecular hydrogen bonding is possible with the ether.

10.5 Left

10.6 (a)
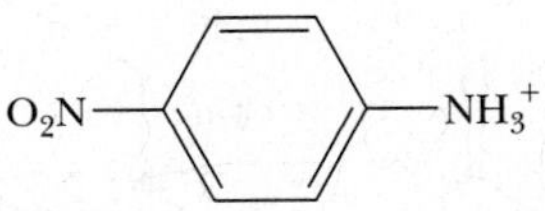

(b)
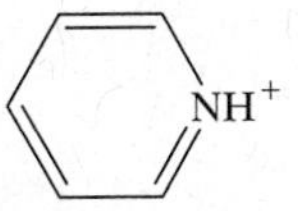

10.7 (a) $(CH_3CH_2)_3NH^+Cl^-$ Triethylammonium chloride

(b)
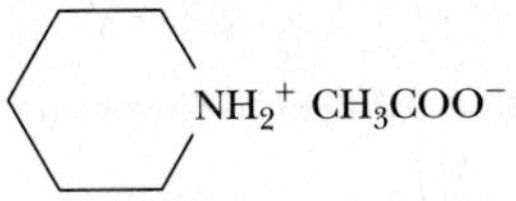

Piperidinium acetate

10.8 (a)
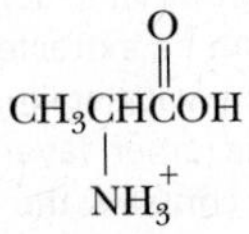

(b)
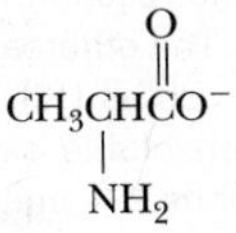

10.9
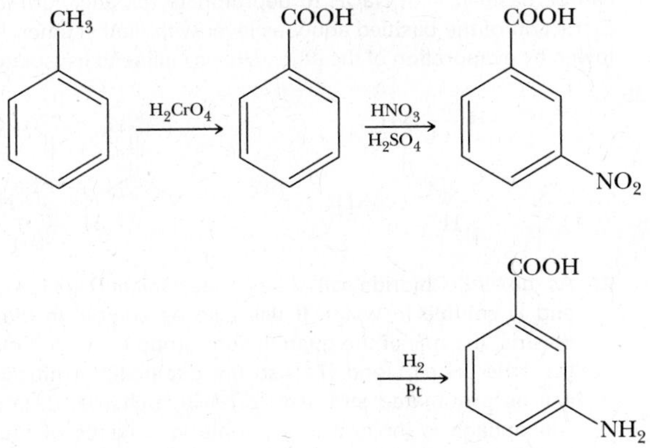

10.10
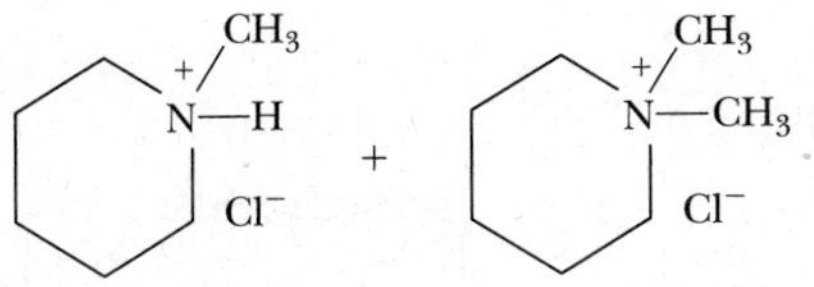

End-of-Chapter Problems

Structure and Nomenclature

10.11 (a)
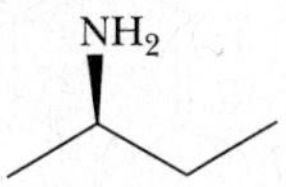

(b) $CH_3(CH_2)_6CH_2NH_2$

(c)

(d)
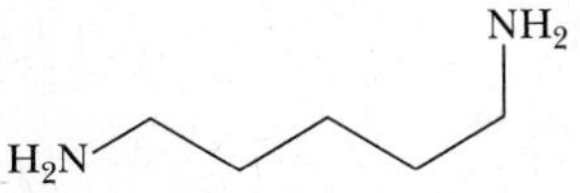

(e)
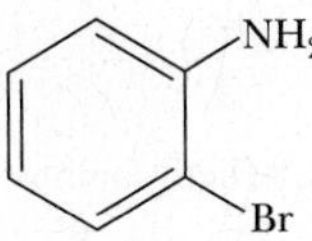

(f) $(CH_3CH_2CH_2CH_2)_3N$

(g)
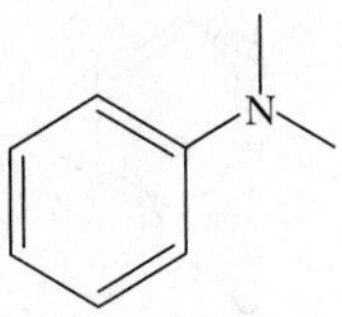

(h)
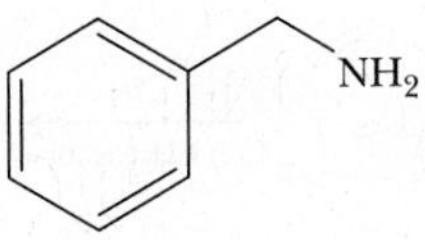

(i)
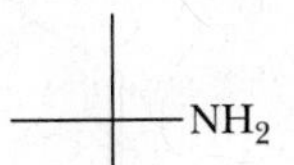

(j)
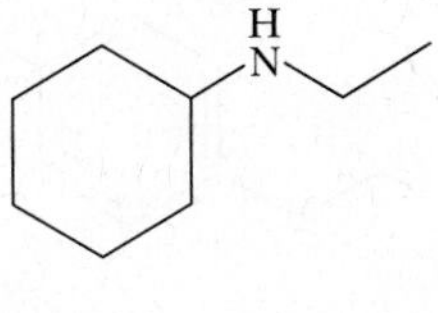

(k)
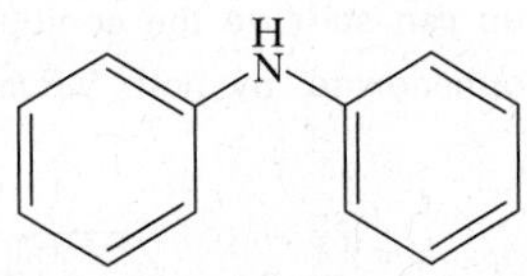

(l)
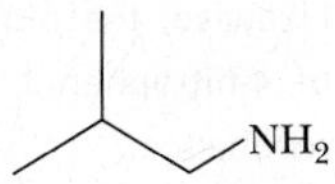

10.13 Amines are classified by the number of carbon substituents bonded to the nitrogen atom, whereas alcohols are classified by the number of carbon substituents bonded to the carbon bearing the —OH group.

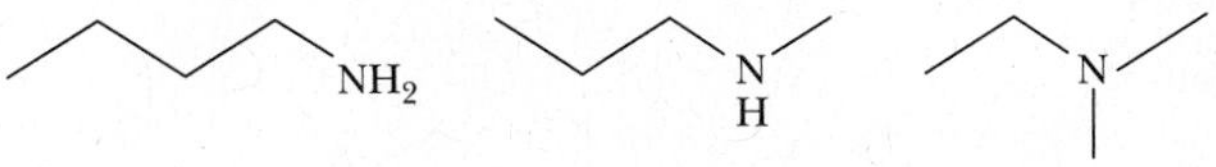

1° amine 2° amine 3° amine

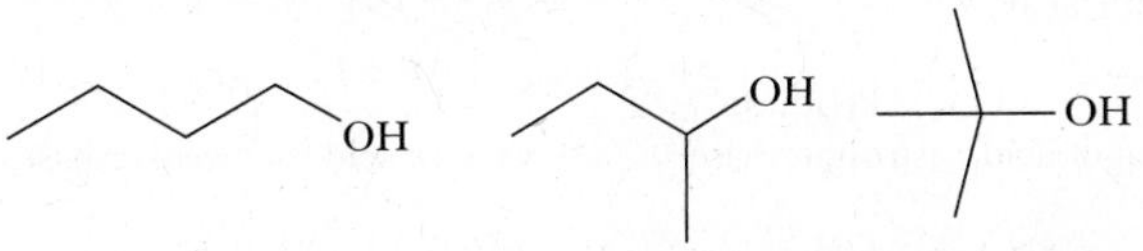

1° alcohol 2° alcohol 3° alcohol

10.15 (a) Both amino groups are secondary.
(b) Both compounds contain the same basic framework and have the same configuration at the stereocenter. Differences are the *tert*-butyl and $-CH_2OH$ groups in (*R*)-albuterol versus the methyl and —OH groups in (*R*)-epinephrine, respectively.

10.17 (a)
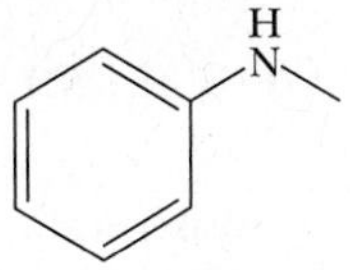

(b)
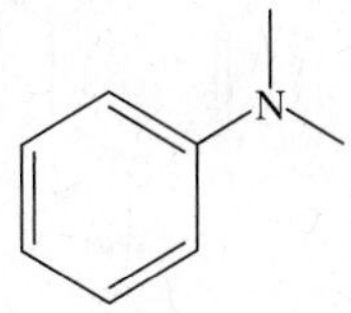

(c)
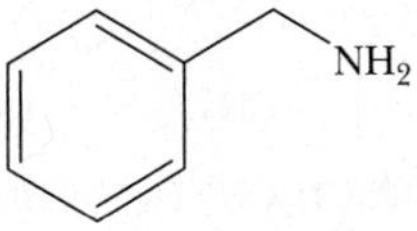

(d)
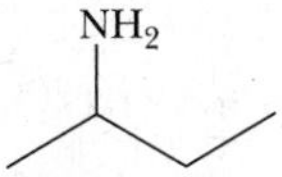

(e)
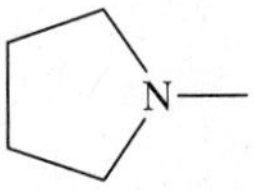

(f)
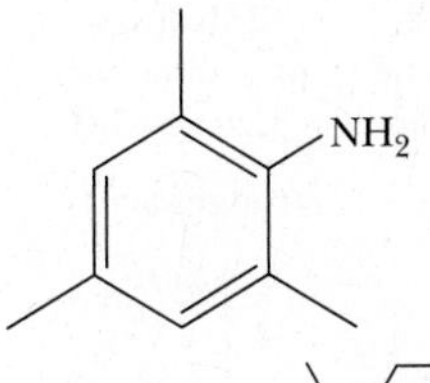

\+ isomers

(g)
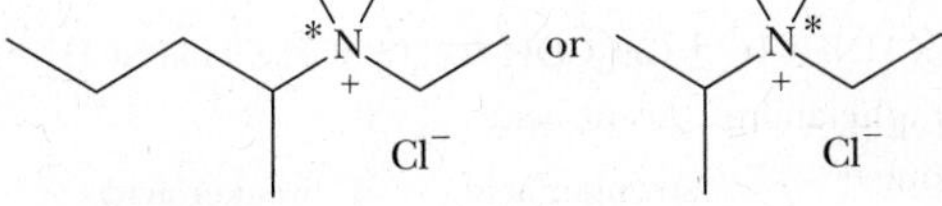

Physical Properties

10.19 1-Butanol has a higher boiling point because an O—H---O hydrogen bond is stronger than an N—H---N hydrogen bond.

Basicity of Amines

10.21 Nitrogen is less electronegative than oxygen.

10.23 The nitro group is an electron-withdrawing group. In addition, it is able to stabilize the lone pair of electrons on the nitrogen atom in 4-nitroaniline by resonance.

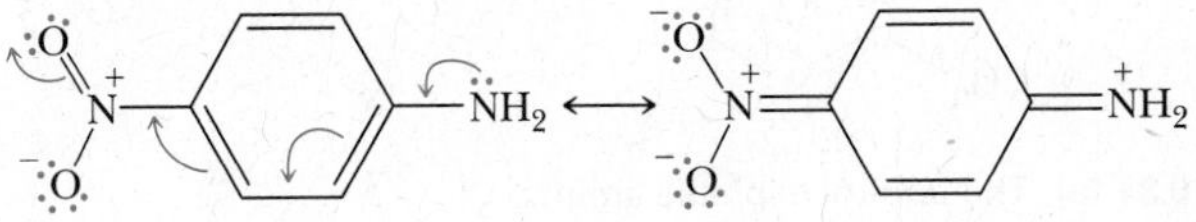

Likewise, the nitro group can stabilize the conjugate base of 4-nitrophenol, 4-nitrophenoxide, by both induction and resonance.

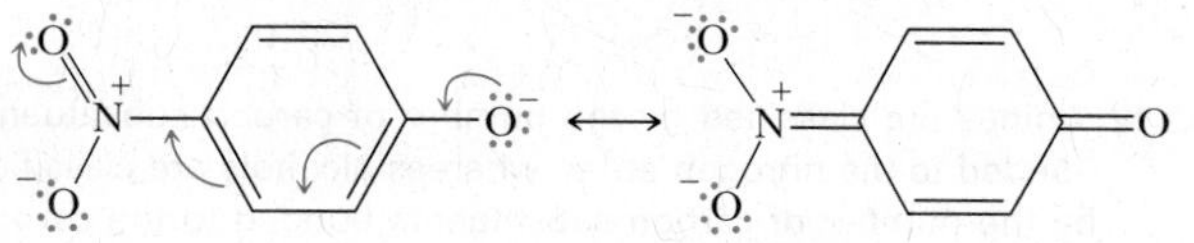

10.25

(a)

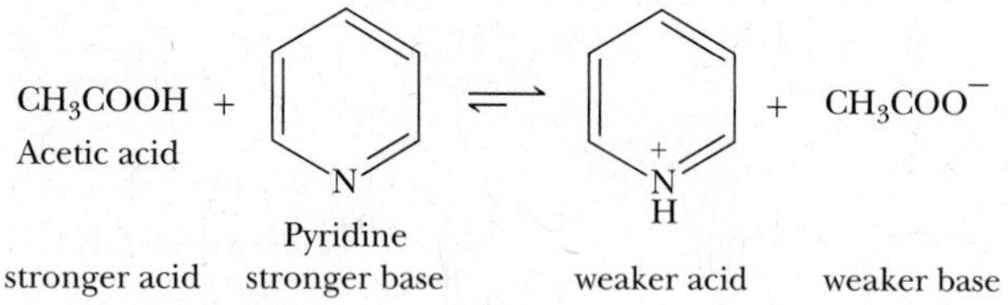

(b)

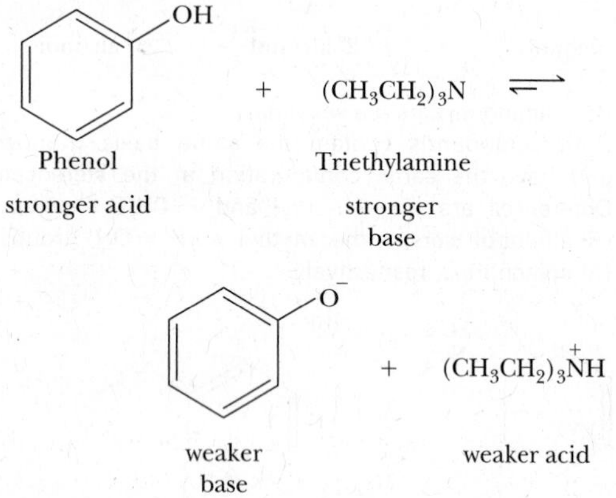

(c)

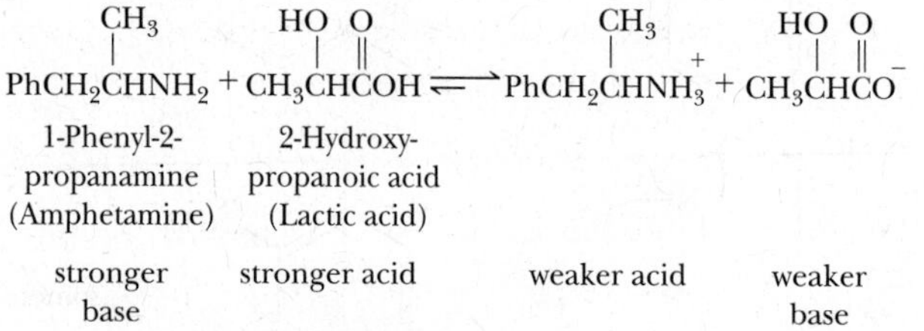

(d)

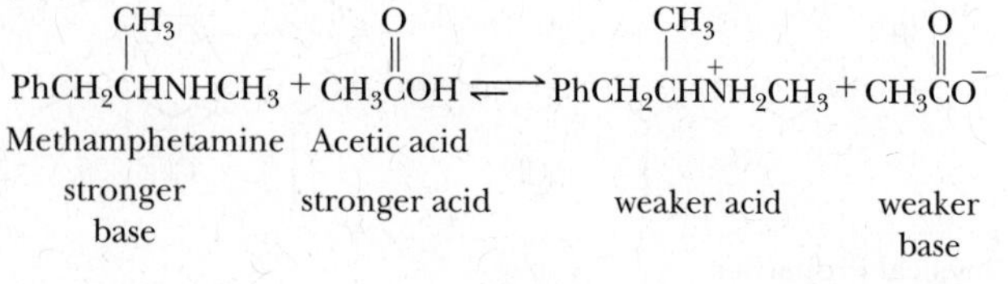

10.27 1:2500

10.29 (a) The primary aliphatic amine.

(b)

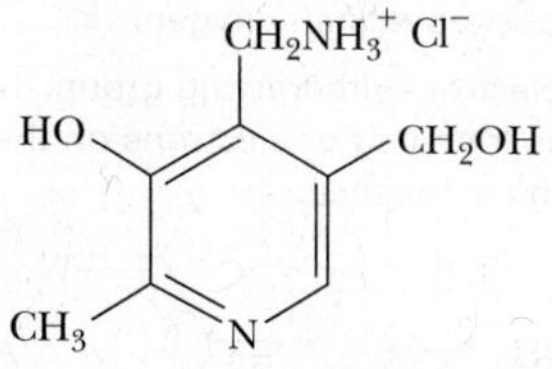

10.31 (a) The tertiary aliphatic amine.

(b)

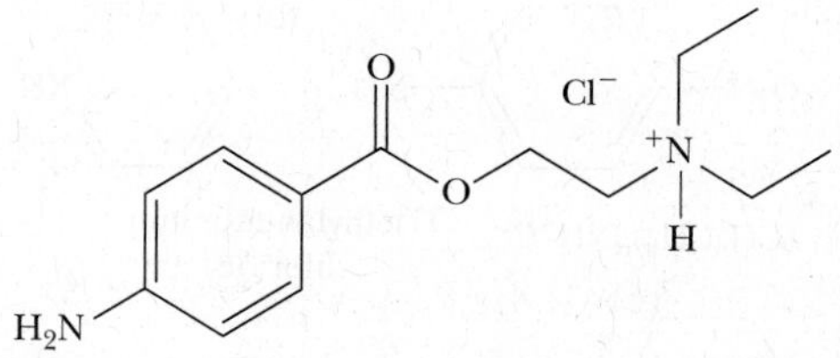

(c) Procaine is not chiral. A solution of Novocaine would be optically inactive.

10.33 First, dissolve the reaction mixture in an organic solvent such as diethyl ether. The ethereal solution can be extracted with an aqueous acid, such as HCl, which reacts with aniline, a base, to form a water-soluble salt. Thus, the ether layer contains nitrobenzene while the aqueous layer contains the anilinium salt. After separating the two layers, the acidic aqueous layer can be basified with NaOH to deprotonate the anilinium ion. Extraction of the basified aqueous layer with diethyl ether, followed by evaporation of the ether, allows aniline to be isolated.

10.35 (a)

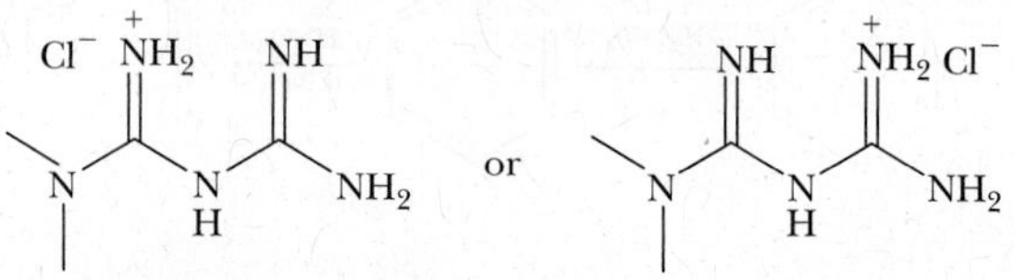

(b) As the hydrochloride salt of an amine, Glucophage is ionic and is soluble in water. It will also be soluble in blood plasma; the pK_a of the guanidinium group is much higher than the pH of blood (7.4), so the guanidinium nitrogen will be protonated and carry a positive charge. Because Glucophage is ionic, it is insoluble in solvents of much lower polarity, such as diethyl ether or dichloromethane.

Synthesis

10.37

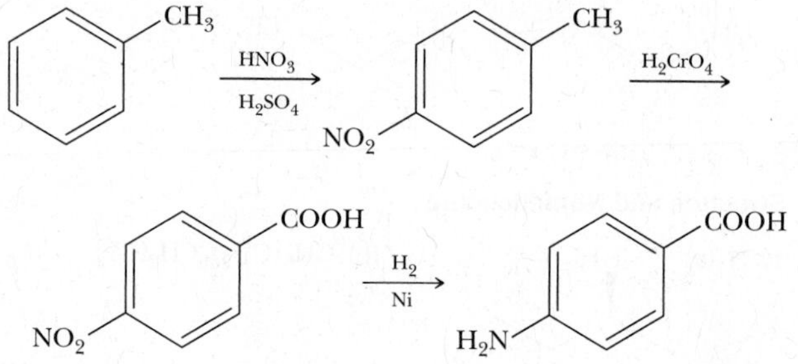

10.39

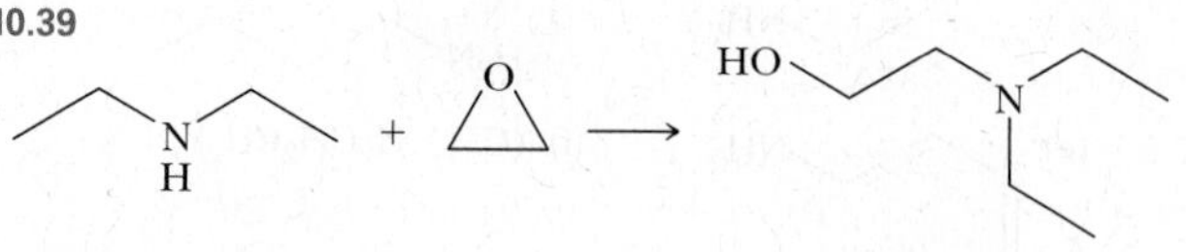

2-Diethylaminoethanol

10.41

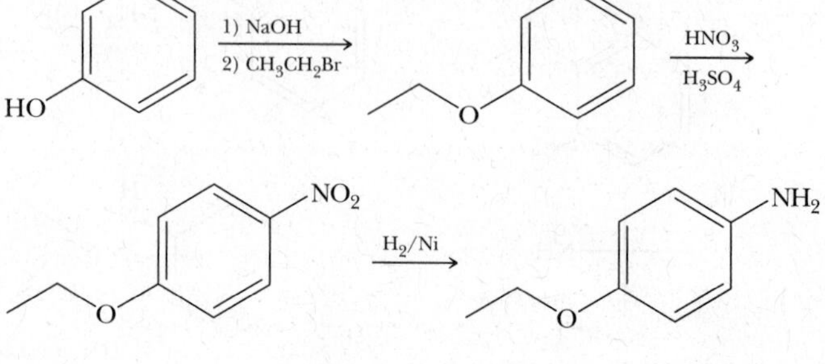

10.43

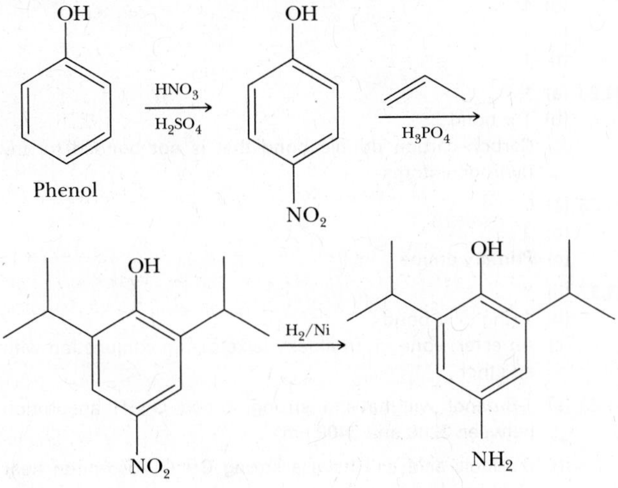

Looking Ahead

10.45 All of the nitrogen atoms are sp^2.

10.47

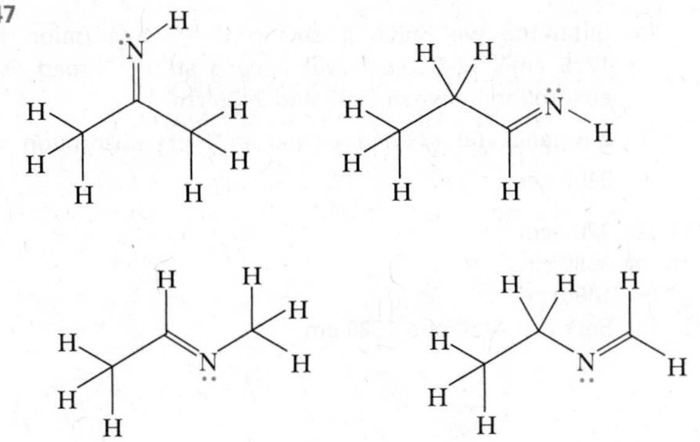

CHAPTER 11 Infrared Spectroscopy

Problems

11.1 The energy of red light (680 nm) is 176 kJ/mol (42.1 kcal/mol) and is higher than the energy from infrared radiation of 2500 nm (47.7 kJ/mol or 11.4 kcal/mol).

11.2 Carboxyl group

11.3 Propanoic acid will have a strong, broad OH absorption between 3200 and 3500 cm^{-1}.

11.4 The wavenumber is directly related to the energy of the infrared radiation required to stretch the bond. Bonds that require more energy to stretch are stronger bonds.

11.5 Cyclohexene has one ring and one π bond, so it has an IHD of two.

11.6 Each index of hydrogen deficiency could be a ring or a π bond. Niacin contains one ring and four π bonds.

11.7 The $C_8H_{10}O$ compounds that would have the same spectrum as the C_7H_8O compounds are shown below. IR spectroscopy only provides functional group information and is not effective for the determination of the actual structure of a compound.

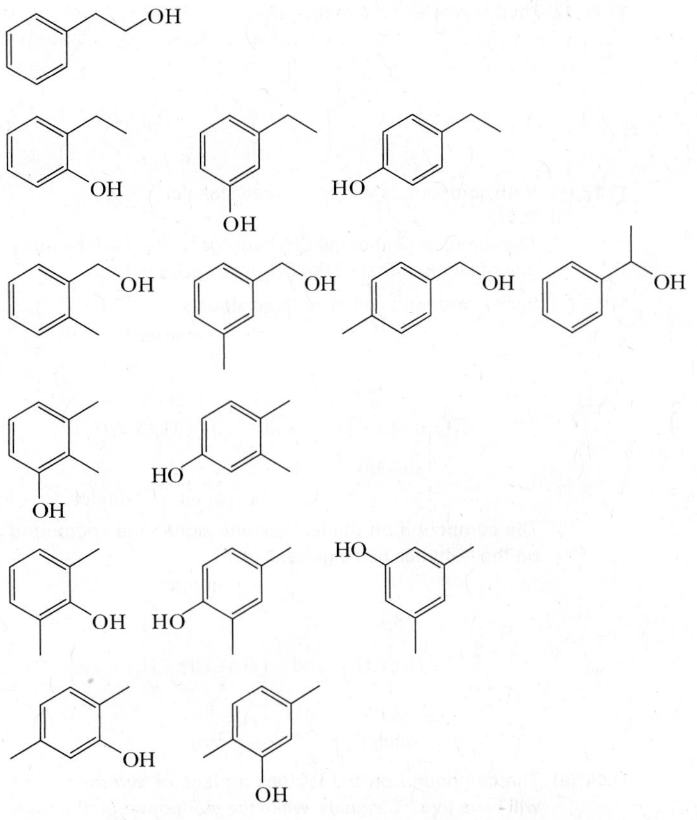

11.8 (a) and (b)

11.9 (a) 3-Methylpentane has four sets of equivalent hydrogens. The number of hydrogens in each set are 6, 4, 3, and 1, which are respectively labeled a, b, c, and d.

(b) 2,2,4-Trimethylpentane has four sets of equivalent hydrogens. The number of hydrogens in each set are 9, 6, 2, and 1, which are respectively labeled a, b, c, and d.

(c) 1,4-Dichloro-2,5-dimethylbenzene has two sets of equivalent hydrogens. The number of hydrogens in each set are 6 and 2, which are respectively labeled a and b.

(a)

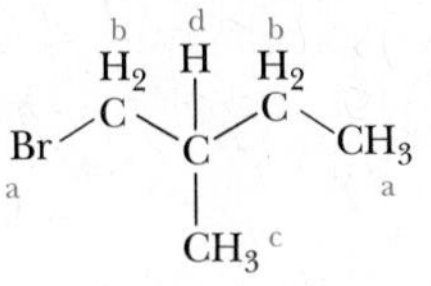

(b)

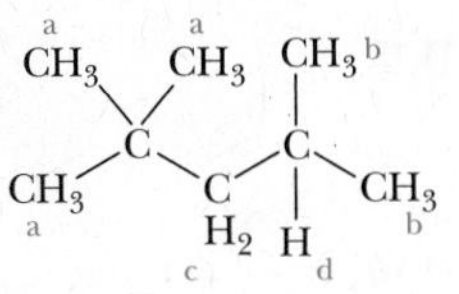

(c)

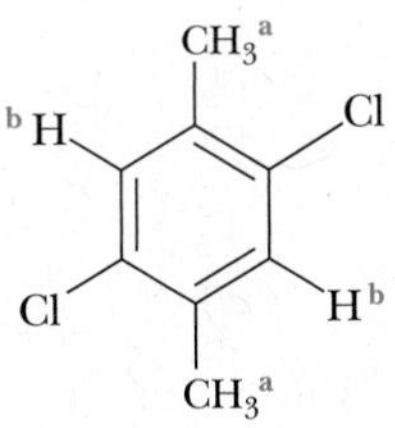

11.10 (a)

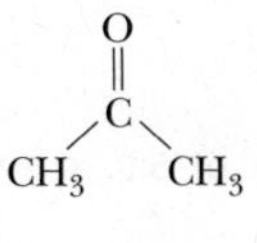

(b)

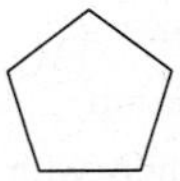

(c)

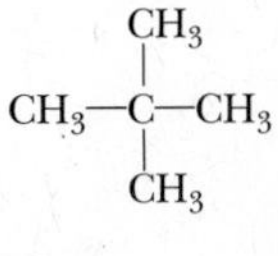

(d)

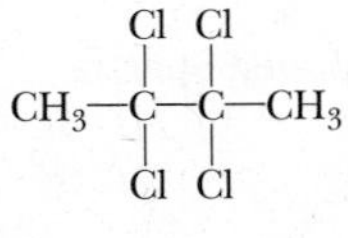

11.11 12 *a* hydrogens and 2 *b* hydrogens.

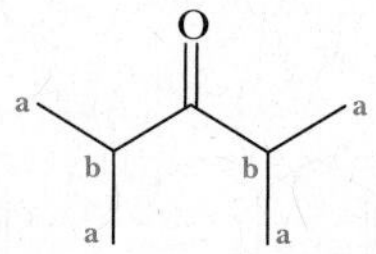

11.12 (a) Both compounds will have three signals.
(b) 3:3:2
(c) The chemical shift of the CH_2 hydrogens in (1) will be more downfield than that of the CH_2 hydrogens in (2).

11.13 (a) Each compound will have three signals.

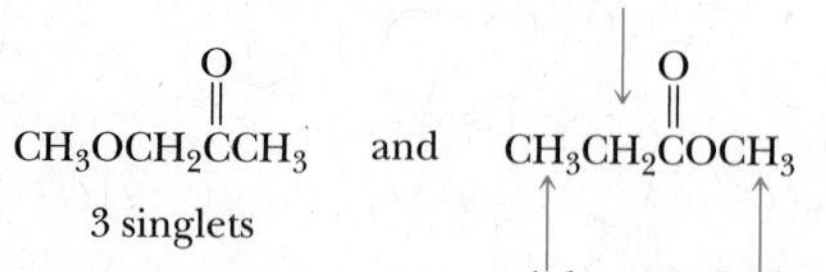

(b) The compound on the left has one signal; the compound on the right has two signals.

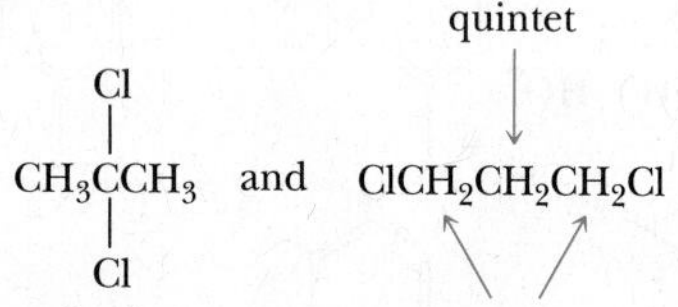

11.14 (a) The compound on the left has a plane of symmetry and will have five ^{13}C signals, while the compound on the right will have seven signals.

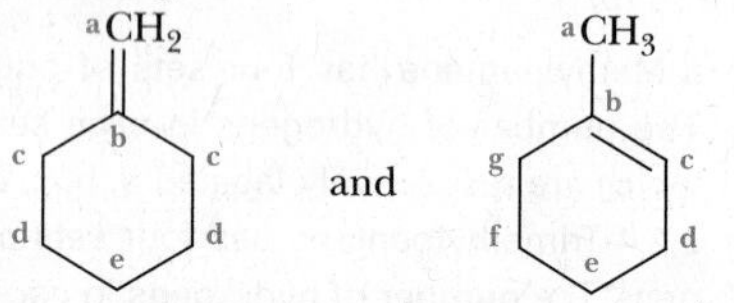

(b) The compound on the left will have six ^{13}C signals, while the compound on the right, which has a plane of symmetry, will have three signals.

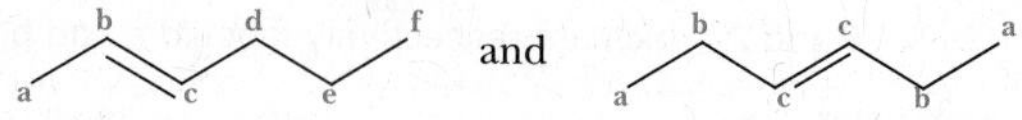

11.15

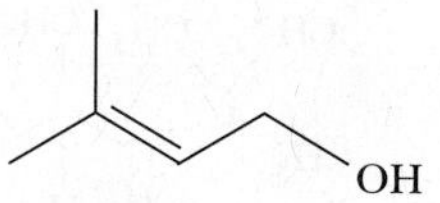

11.16

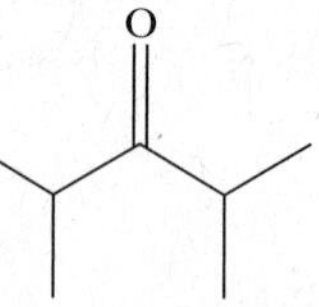

11.17

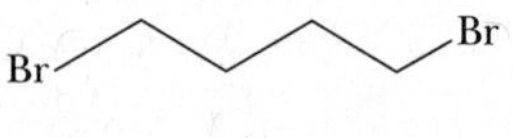

End-of-Chapter Problems

Electromagnetic Radiation

11.19 Microwave radiation with an energy of 5.9×10^{-5} kJ/mol (1.4×10^{-5} kcal/mol)

Interpreting Infrared Spectra

11.21 (a) 6
(b) 3
(c) 4
(d) 1
(e) 5
(f) 1

11.23 (a) 1
(b) 1 π bond
(c) Carbon–carbon double bond that is not bonded to any hydrogen atoms

11.25 (a) 0
(b) 0
(c) Primary amine

11.27 (a) 1
(b) 1 ring or π bond
(c) An ester alone or an aldehyde/ketone in conjunction with an ether

11.29 (a) 1-Butanol will have a strong, broad O—H absorption between 3200 and 3400 cm^{-1}.
(b Butanoic acid will have a strong C=O absorption near 1700 cm^{-1}.
(c) Butanoic acid will have a broad O—H absorption between 2400 and 3400 cm^{-1}.
(d) Butanal will have a strong C=O absorption near 1700 and 1725 cm^{-1}. 1-Butene will have a vinylic =C—H absorption near 3100 cm^{-1}.
(e) Butanone will have a strong C=O absorption near 1725 cm^{-1}. 2-Butanol will have a strong, broad O—H absorption between 3200 and 3400 cm^{-1}.
(f) 2-Butene will have a vinylic =C—H absorption near 3100 cm^{-1}.

11.31 (a) 3200 cm^{-1}
(b) 3050 cm^{-1}
(c) 1680 cm^{-1}
(d) Between 1450 and 1620 cm^{-1}

Equivalency of Hydrogens and Carbons

11.33 (a)

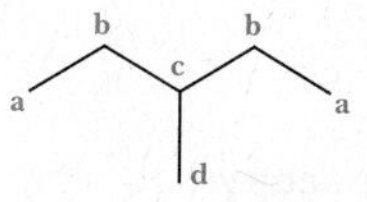

four signals

(b)

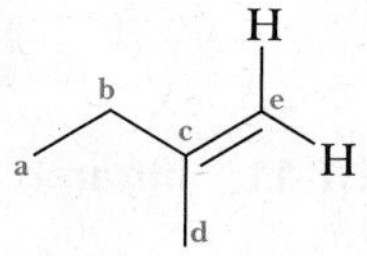

five signals

(c)

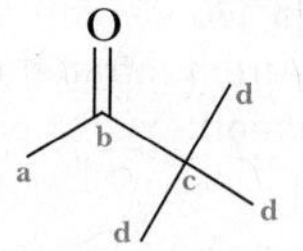

four signals

(d)

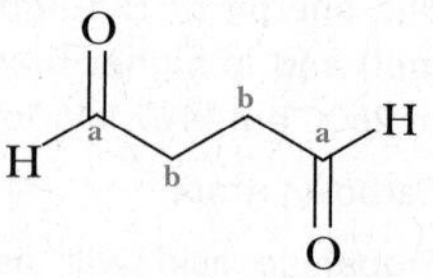

two signals

(e)

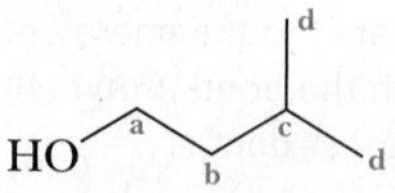

five signals

(f)

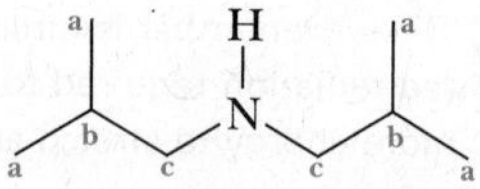

three signals

(g)

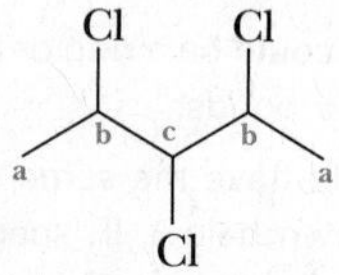

three signals

(h)

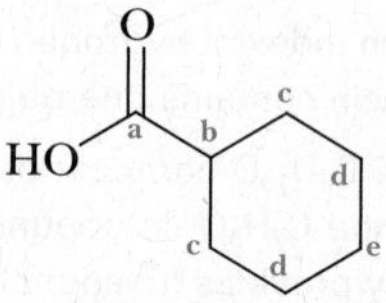

five signals

Interpreting ¹H-NMR and ¹³C-NMR Spectra

11.35

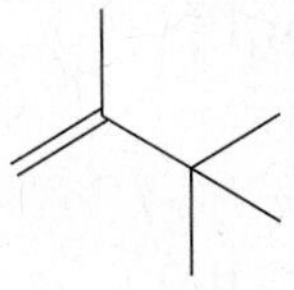

11.37

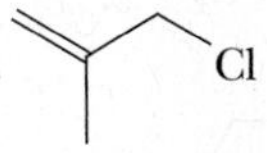

compound L

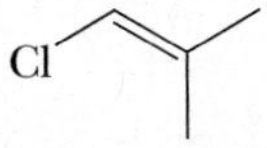

compound M

11.39

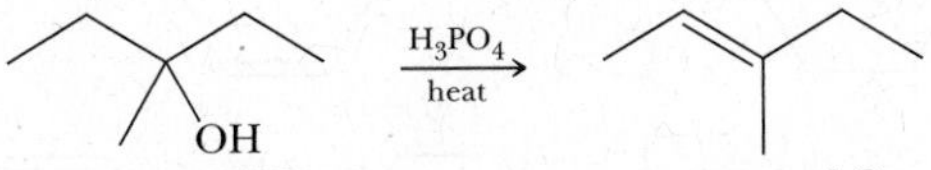

compound N compound O

11.41 (a)

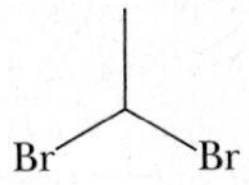

(b)

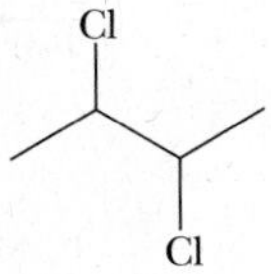

(c)

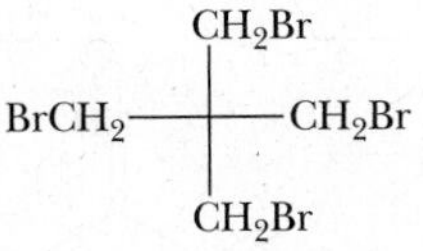

(d)

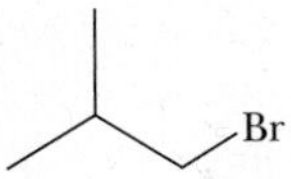

(e)

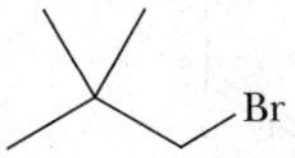

(f)

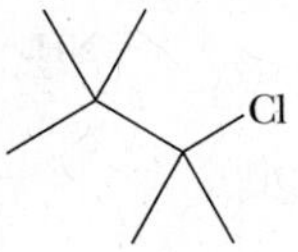

11.43

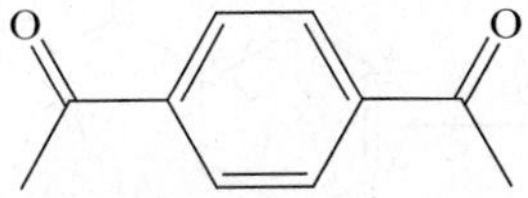

11.45 (a)

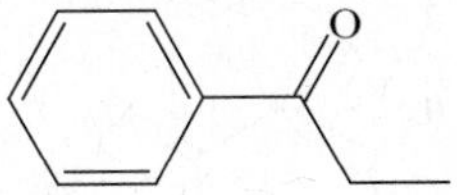

(b)

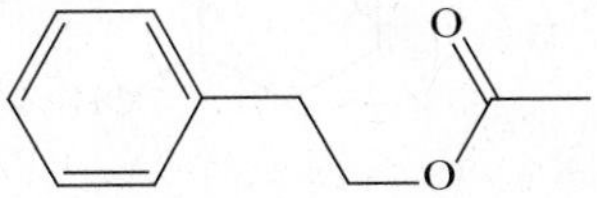

(c)

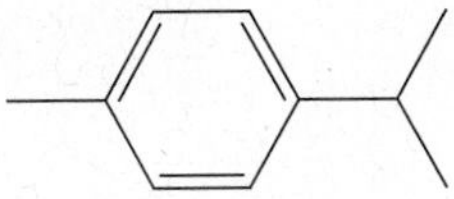

(d)

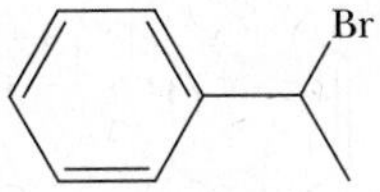

11.47 (a)

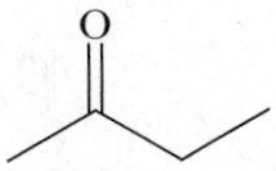

(b)

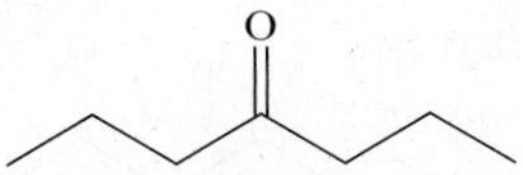

11.49

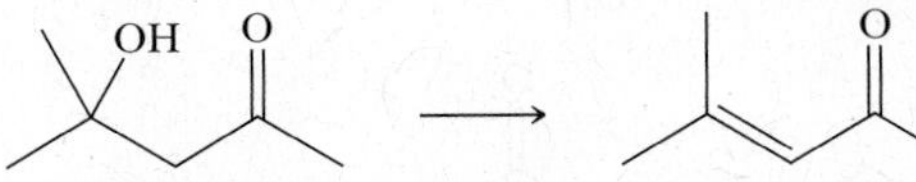

compound Y compound Z

11.51 (a)

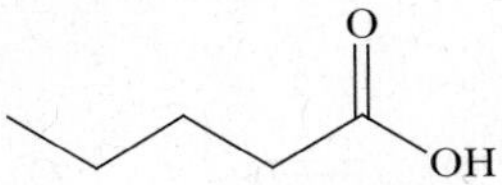

(b)

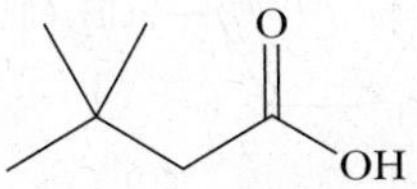

(c)

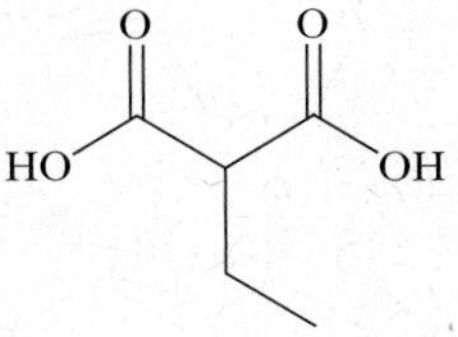

11.53 (a)

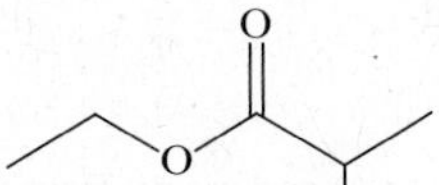

(b)

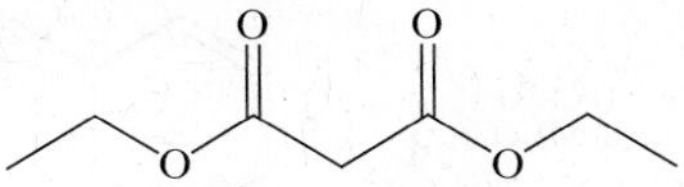

(c)

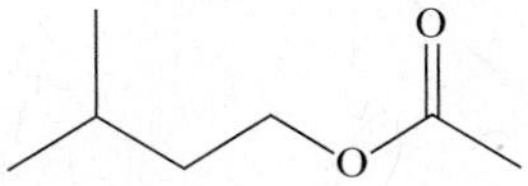

11.55

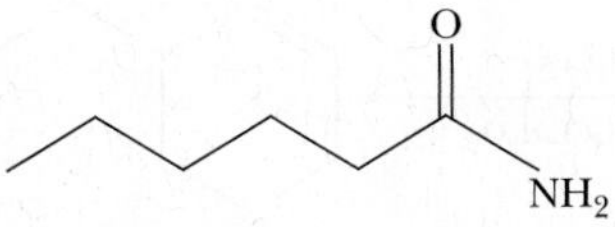

11.57

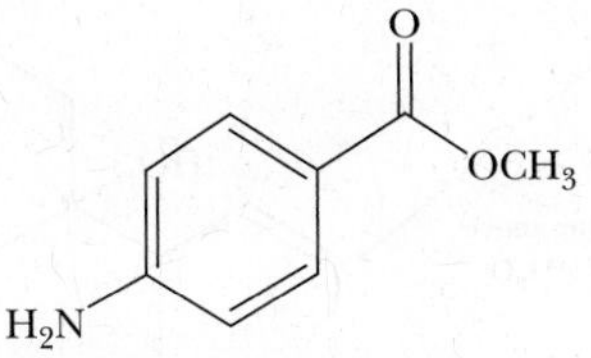

11.59

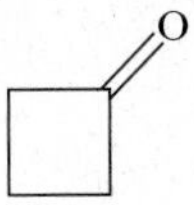

11.61

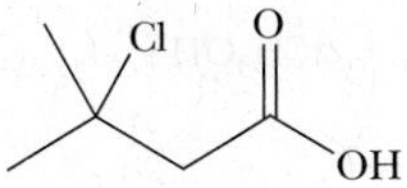

Looking Ahead

11.63 The C=O stretching absorption for acetate will be at a lower wavenumber.

CHAPTER 12 Aldehydes and Ketones

Problems

12.1 (a) 2,2-Dimethylpropanal
(b) (*R*)-3-Hydroxycyclohexanone
(c) (*R*)-2-Phenylpropanal

12.2

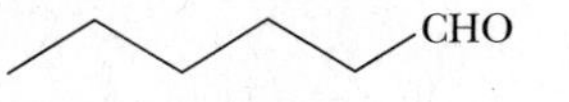

Hexanal

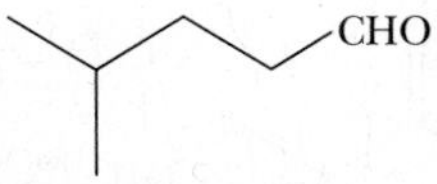

4-Methylpentanal

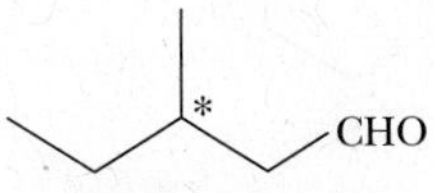

3-Methylpentanal

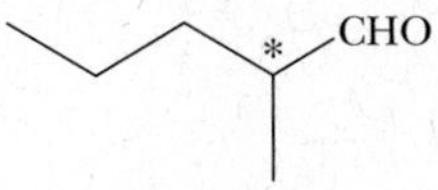

2-Methylpentanal

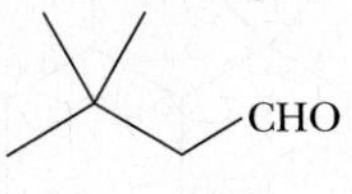

3,3-Dimethylbutanal

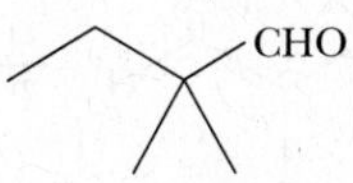

2,2-Dimethylbutanal

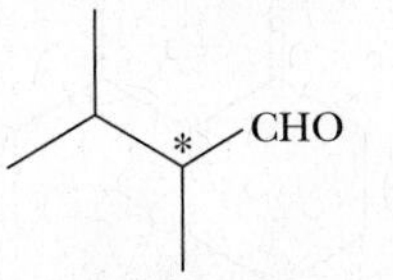

2,3-Dimethylbutanal

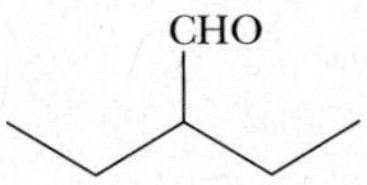

2-Ethylbutanal

12.3 (a) 2-Hydroxypropanoic acid
(b) 2-Oxopropanoic acid
(c) 4-Aminobutanoic acid

12.4 Grignard reagents are highly basic and are destroyed by acids. Both of these reagents contain ionizable hydrogens.

12.5

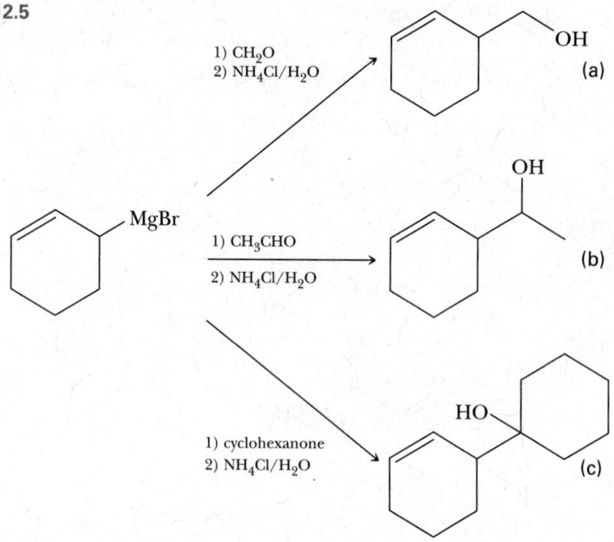

12.6 (a)

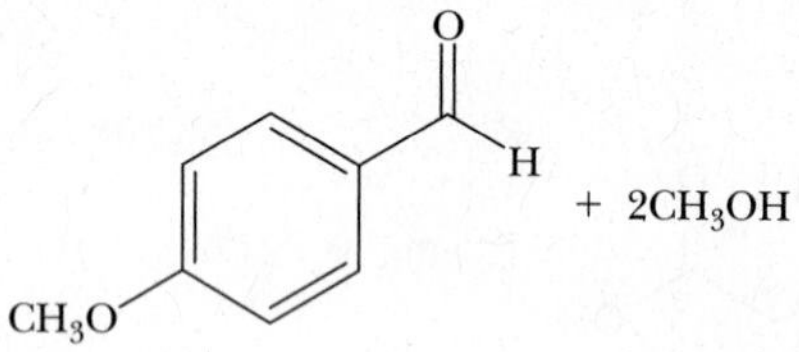

(b)

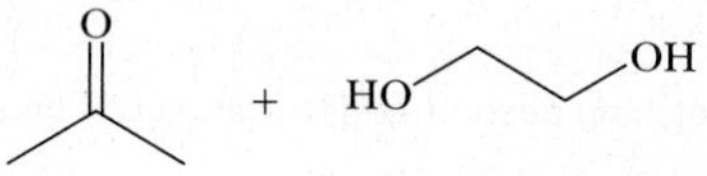

(c)

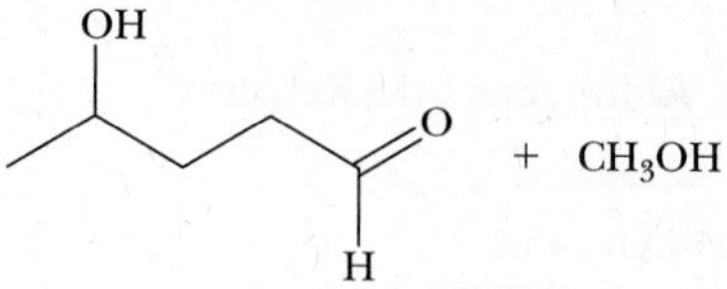

12.7

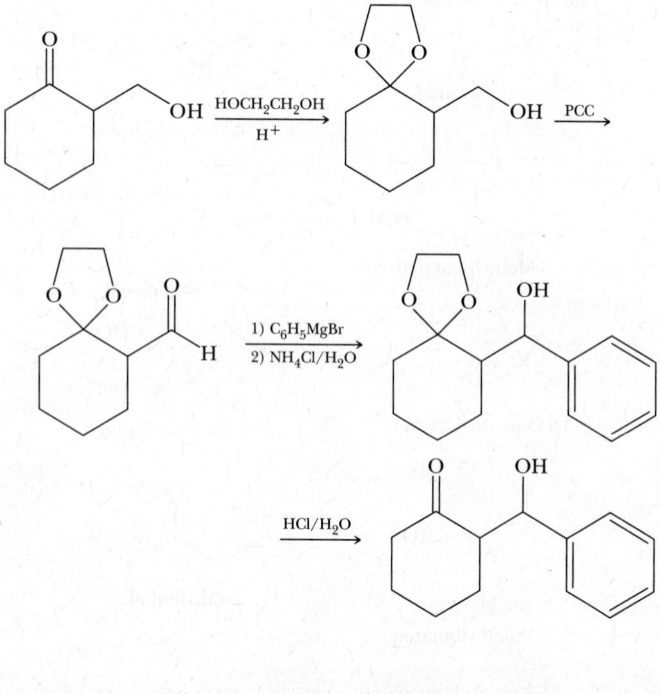

12.8 (a)

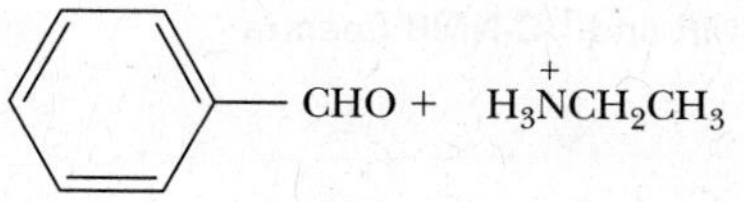

(b)

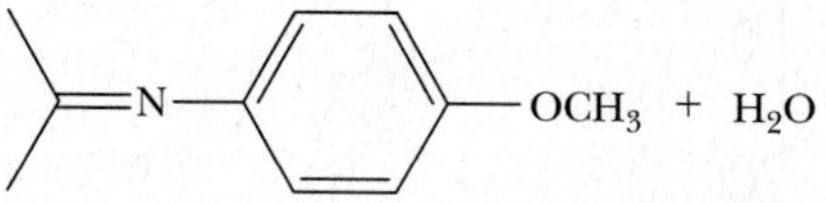

12.9 (a)

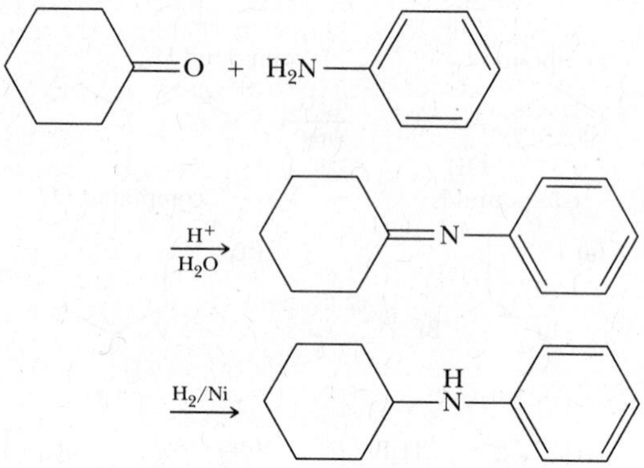

(b)

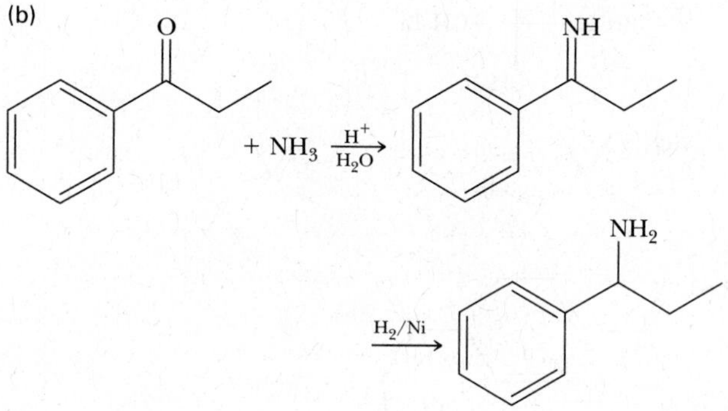

12.10 (a)

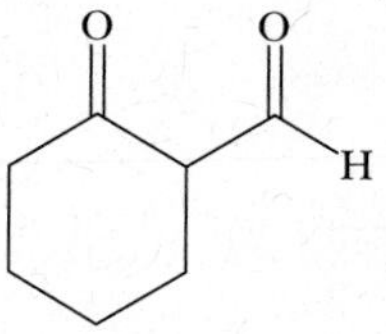

(b)

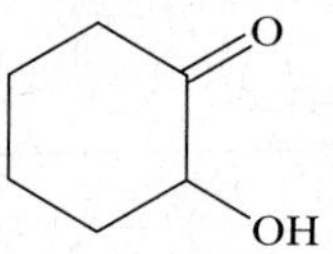

(c)

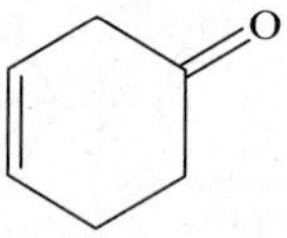

12.11 (a)

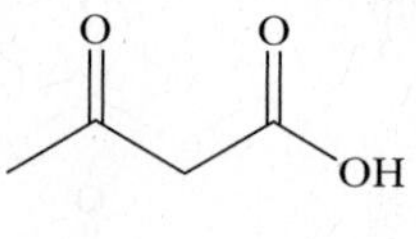

(b)

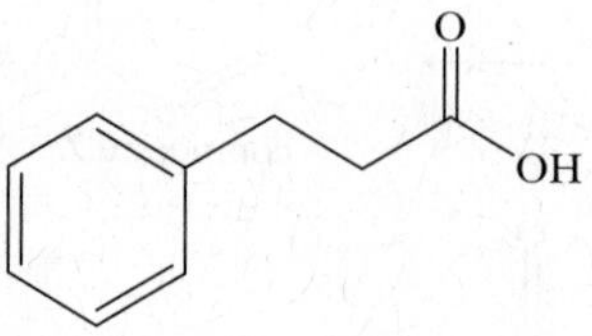

12.12 (a)

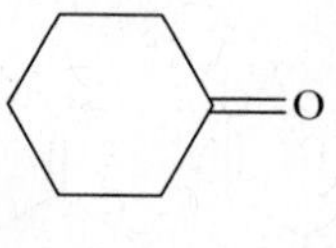

(b)

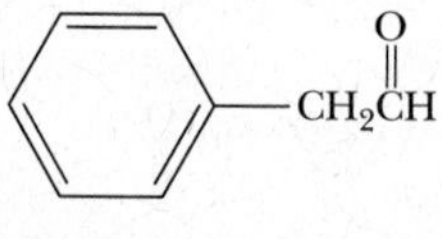

(c)

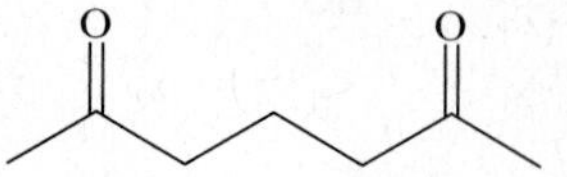

End-of-Chapter Problems

Preparation of Aldehydes and Ketones

12.13 (a) 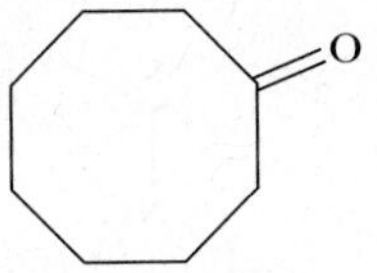 (b) 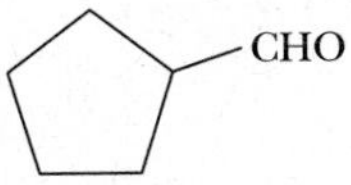

(c) 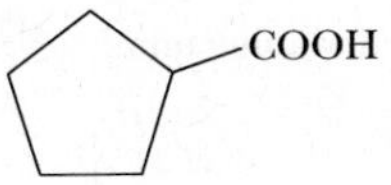 (d) 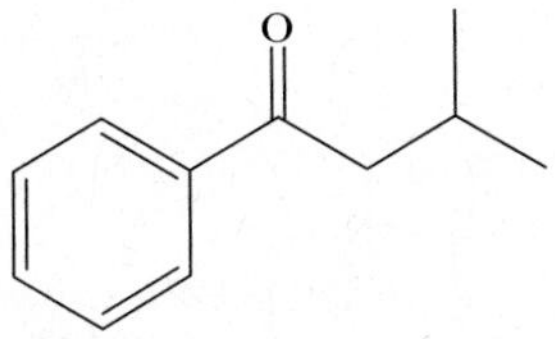

Structure and Nomenclature

12.15 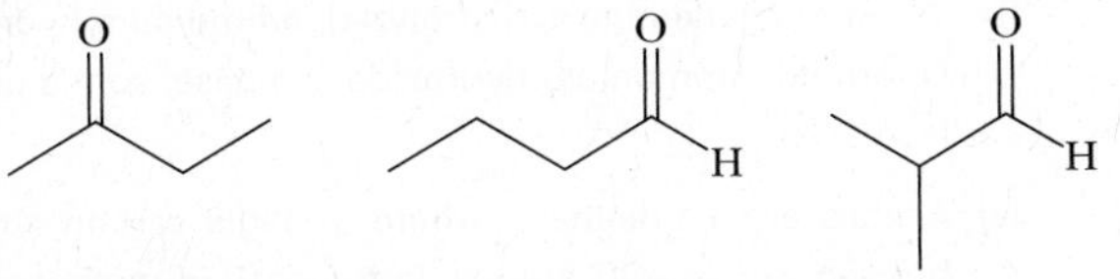

12.17 (a) 4-Heptanone
(b) (*S*)-2-Methylcyclopentanone
(c) (*Z*)-2-Methyl-2-pentenal
(d) (*S*)-2-Hydroxypropanal
(e) 2-Methoxyacetophenone
(f) 2,2-Dimethyl-3-oxopropanoic acid
(g) (*S*)-2-Propylcyclopentanone
(h) 3,3-Dimethyl-5-oxooctanal

Addition of Carbon Nucleophiles

12.19 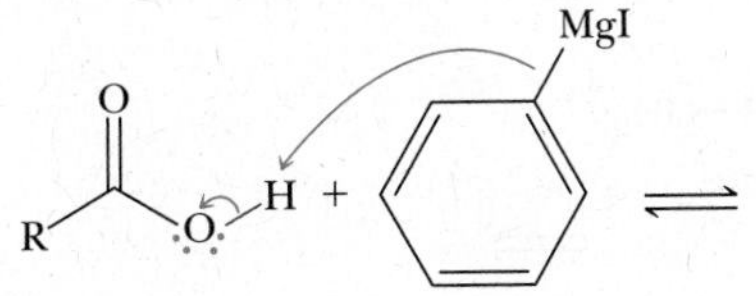

pK_a = 5 — stronger acid; stronger base

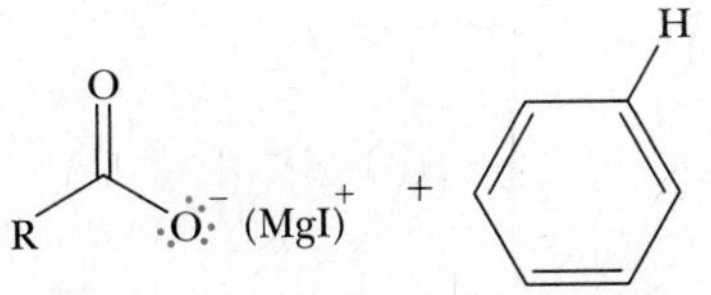

weaker base; pK_a = 43 — weaker acid

12.21 (a) 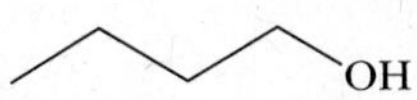 (b) 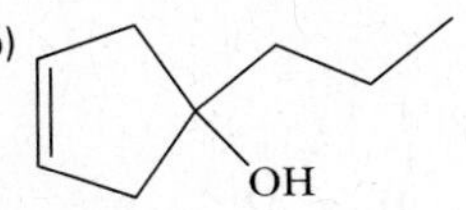

(c) 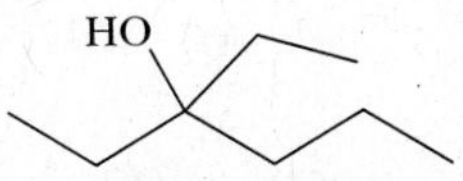
racemic

(d) 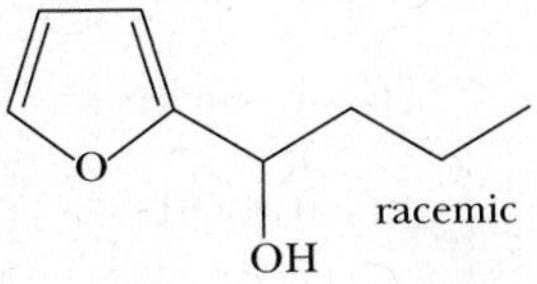
racemic

(e) 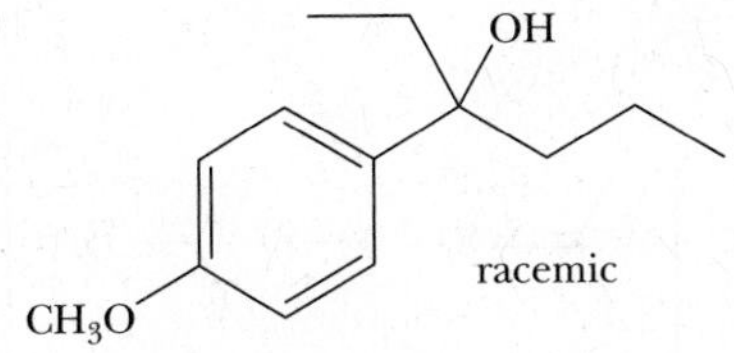
racemic

Addition of Oxygen Nucleophiles

12.23 (a) 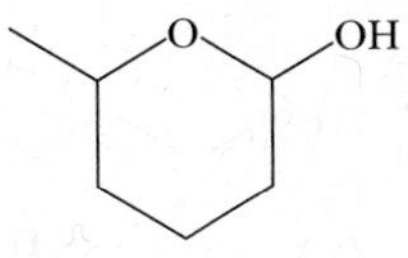 (b) 2 (c) 4

(d) and (e)

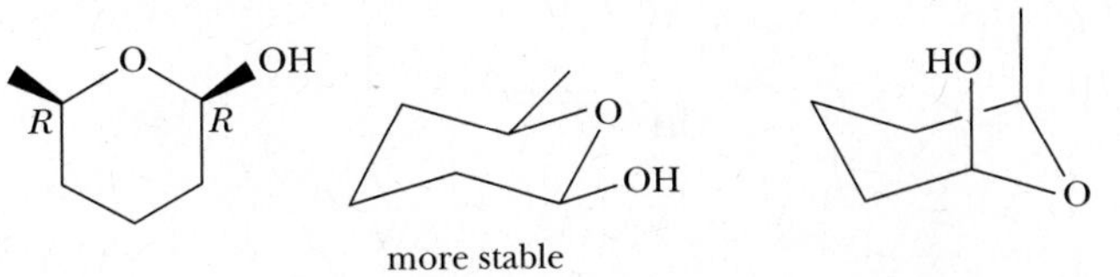

more stable

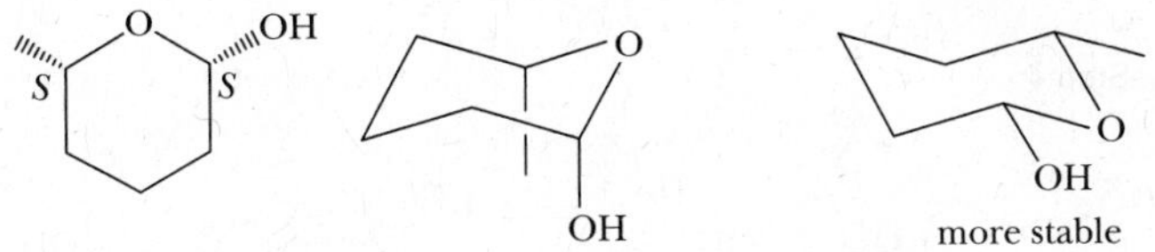

more stable

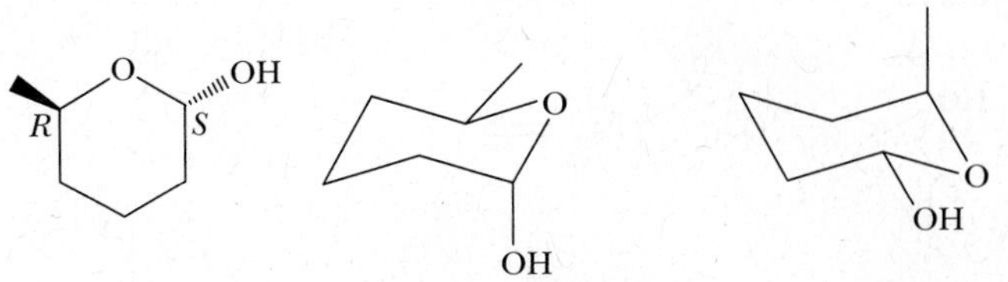

Both are approximately the same stability.

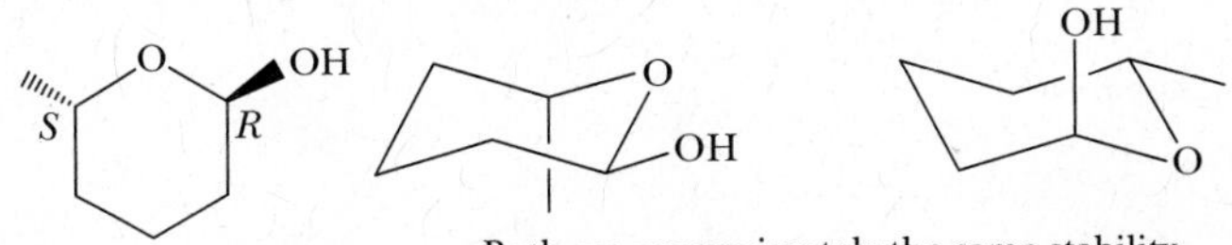

Both are approximately the same stability.

12.25 (a) 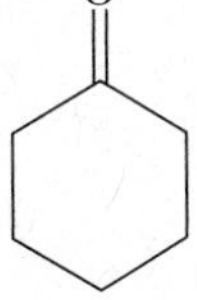 + $2CH_3OH$

(b) 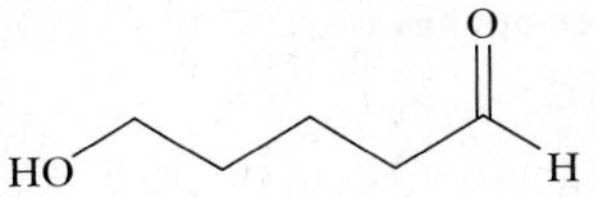 + CH_3OH

(c) 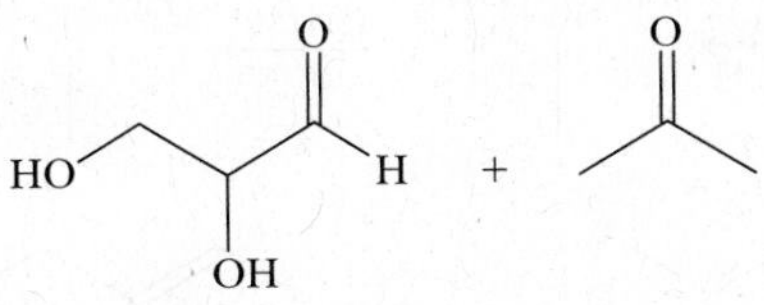

(d) 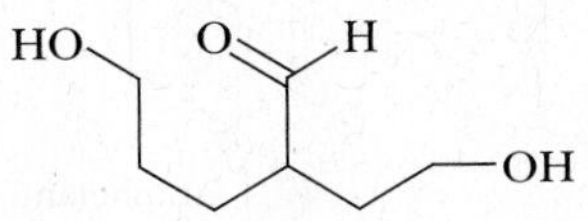

12.27

Step 1:

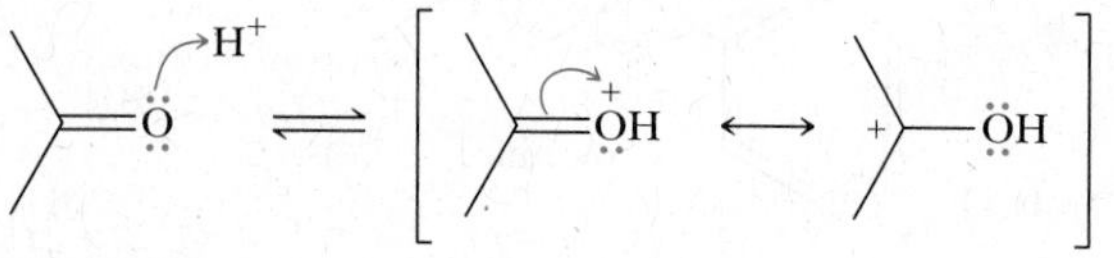

Step 2:

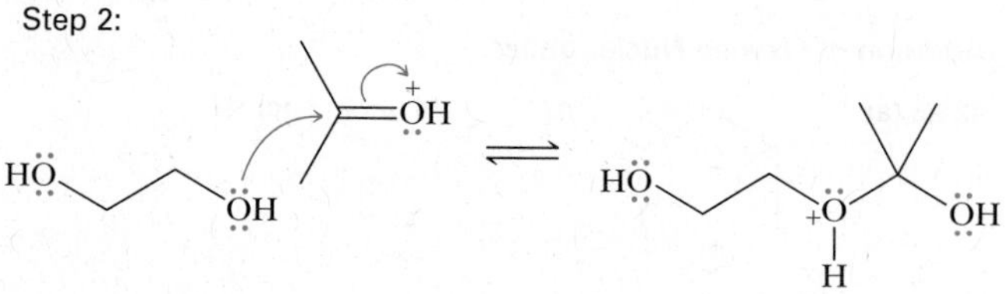

Step 3:

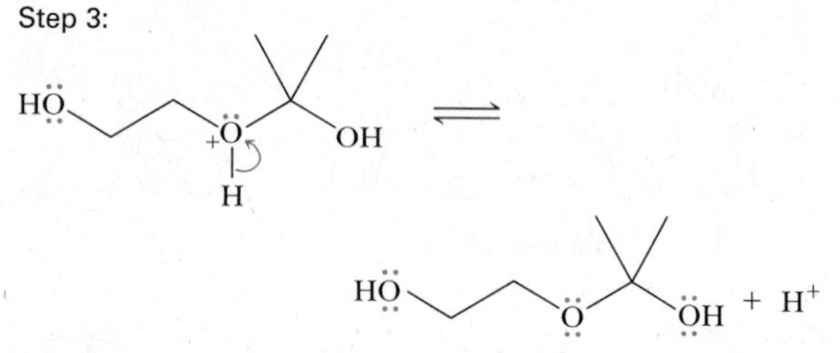

Step 4:

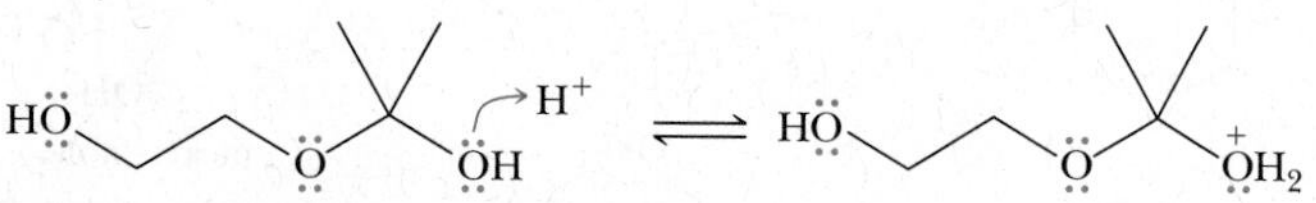

Step 5:

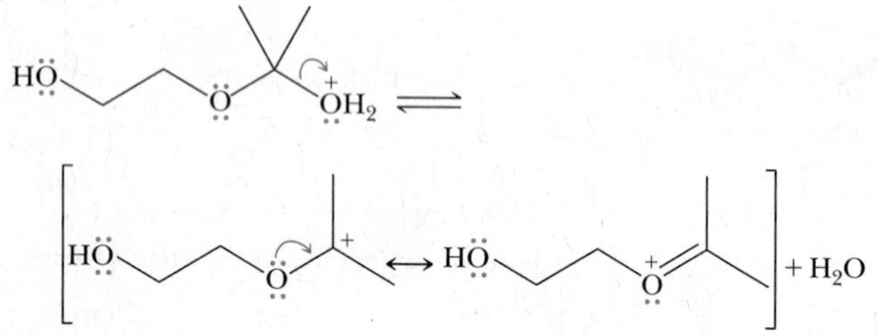

Step 6:

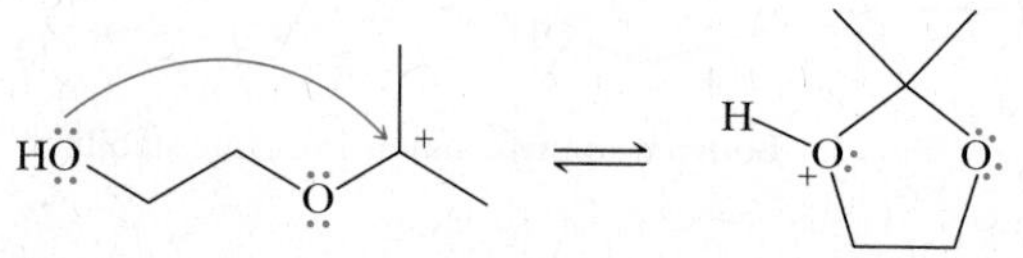

Step 7:

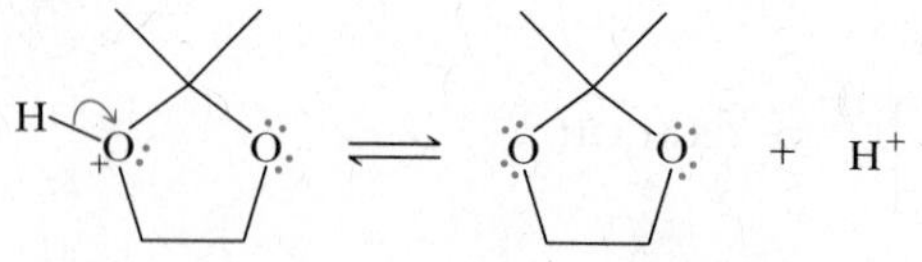

Addition of Nitrogen Nucleophiles

12.29

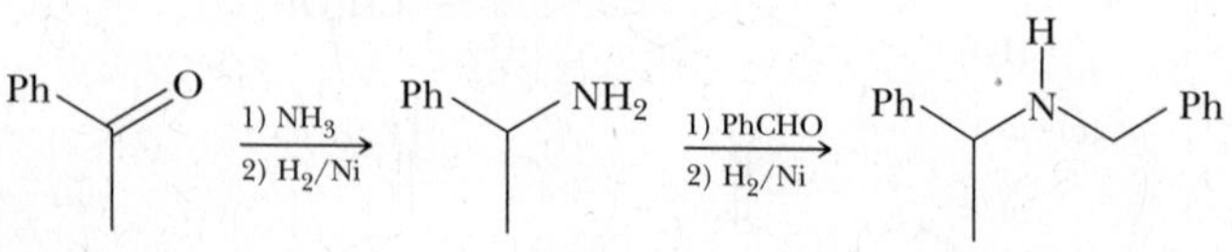

12.31 (a)

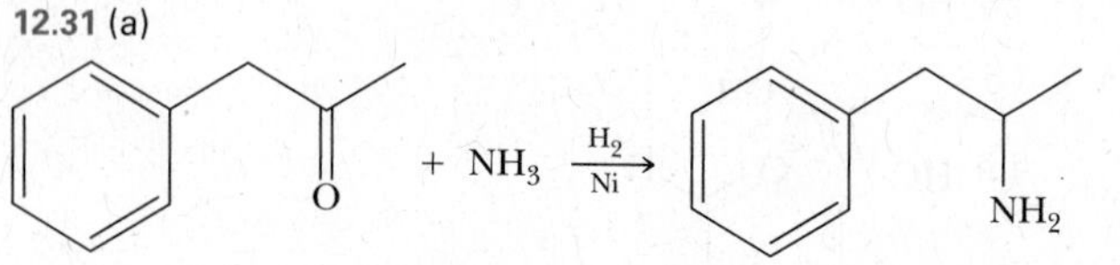

Amphetamine

(b)

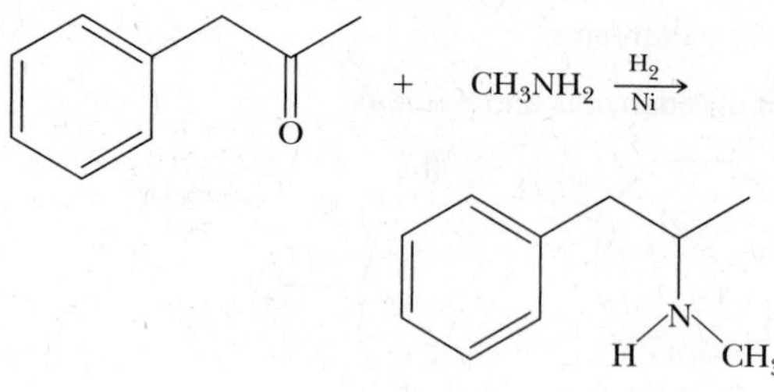

Methamphetamine

12.33 (a)

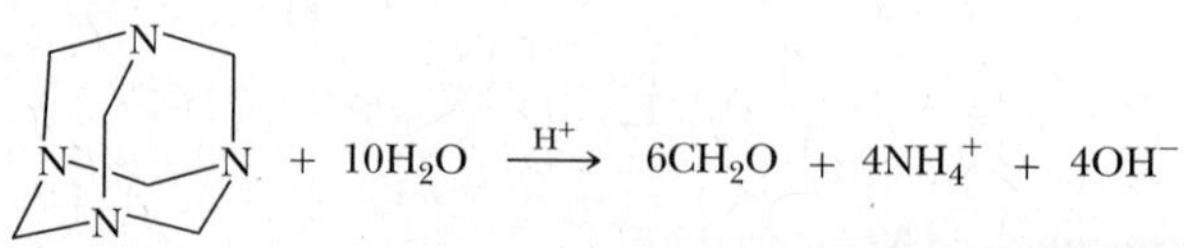

(b) When methenamine is hydrolyzed, ammonium hydroxide is formed. Ammonium hydroxide is a base, so the pH will increase.

(c) Acetals are 1,1-diethers, where a single carbon atom is bonded to two –OR groups. In the case of methenamine, each carbon atom is bonded to two amine functional groups.

(d) The pH of blood plasma is slightly basic (pH of 7.4), but the pH of the urinary tract is acidic. Acetals (and methenamine, which is a nitrogen analog of an acetal) require acidic conditions for hydrolysis to occur, but they are stable under basic conditions.

Keto–Enol Tautomerism

12.35

Step 1:

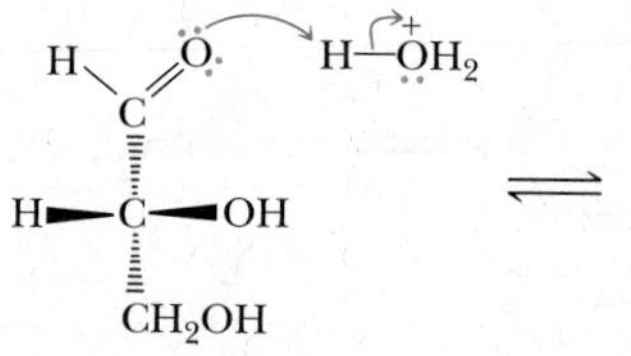

(*R*)-Glyceraldehyde

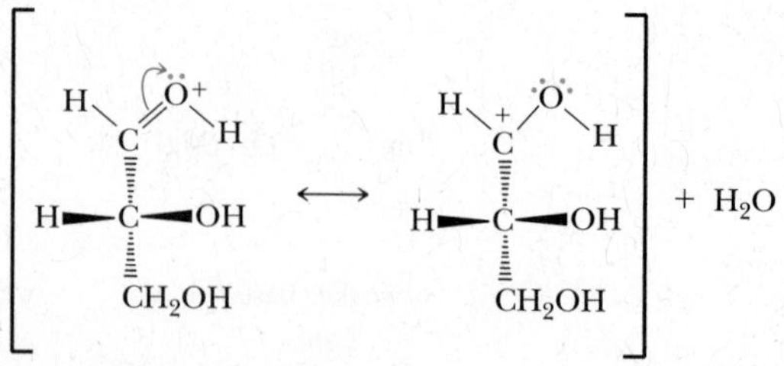

Step 2:

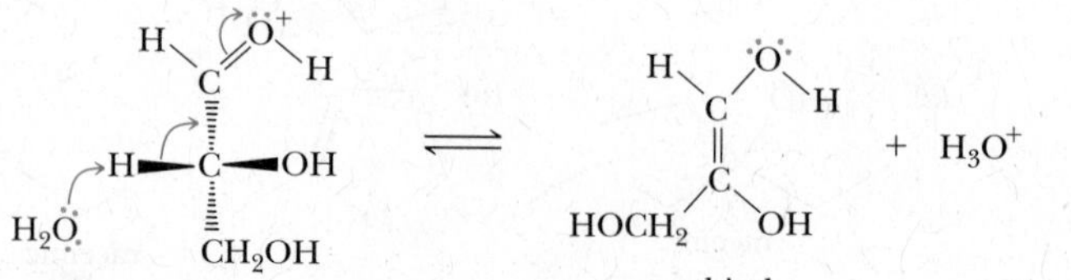

achiral

Step 3:

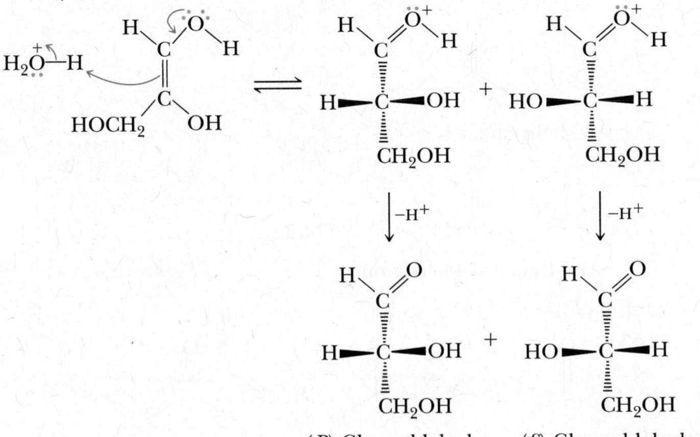

(*R*)-Glyceraldehyde (*S*)-Glyceraldehyde

Step 4:

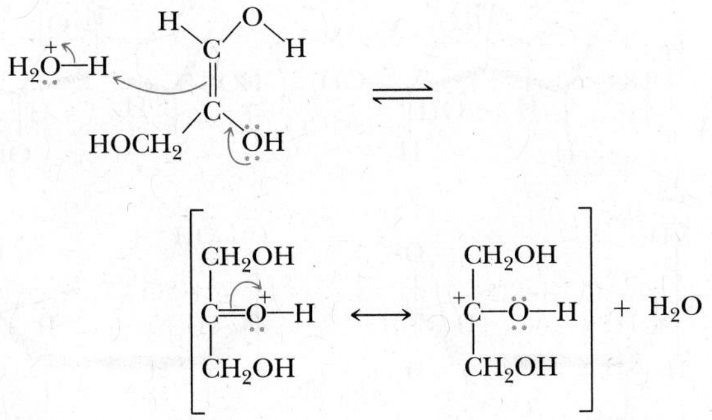

Step 5:

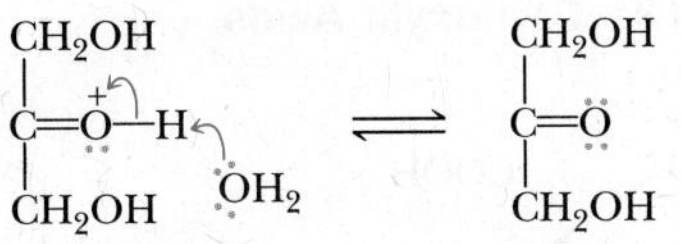

Oxidation/Reduction of Aldehydes and Ketones

12.37

(a), (b), (c):

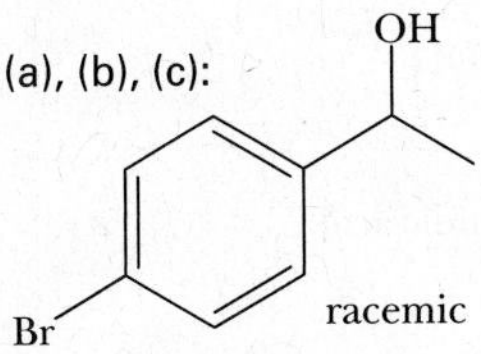

racemic

(d), (e): no reaction

(f)

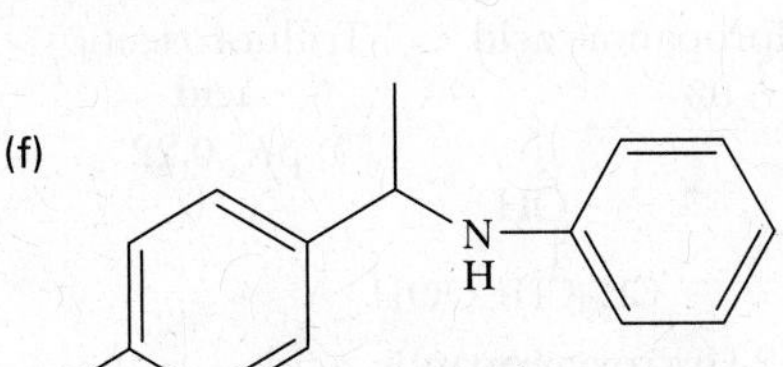

racemic

Synthesis

12.39

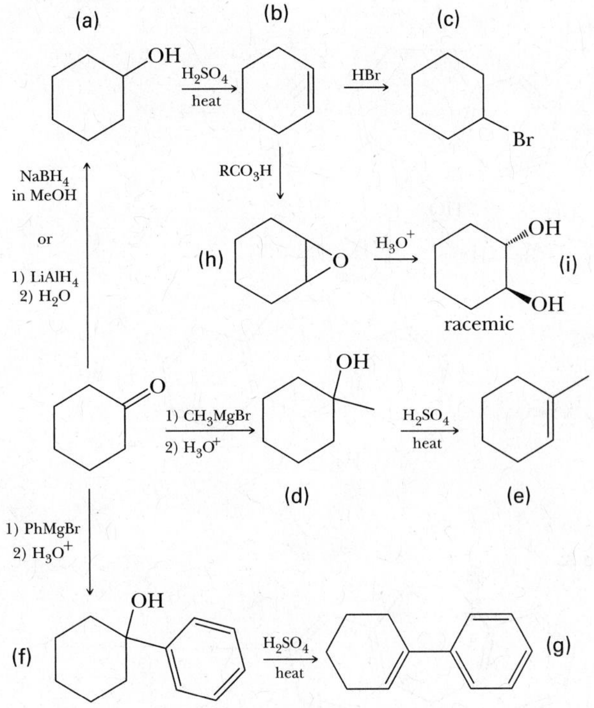

12.41 (a) 2 (b) *Z*

(c)

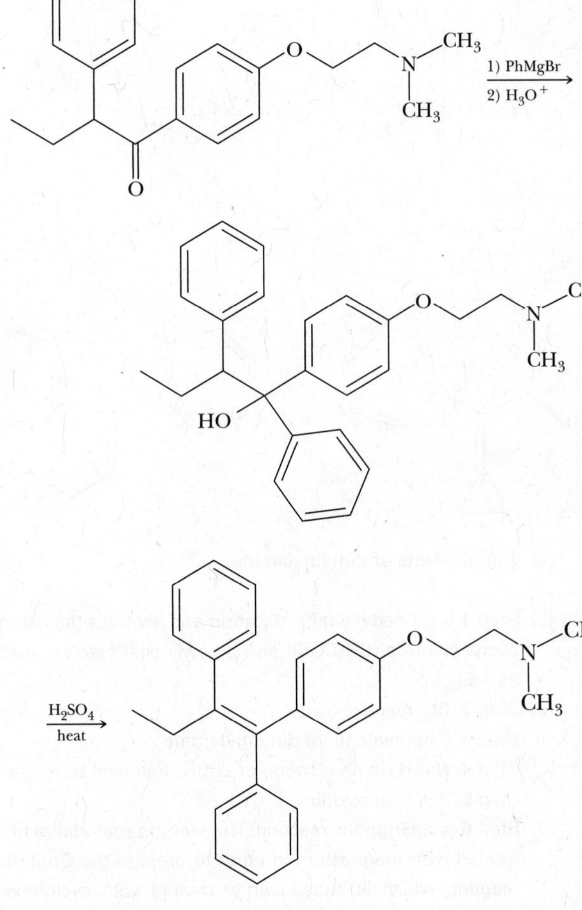

12.43 (a) Cyclopropylmagnesium bromide followed by acid treatment

(b)

Step 1:

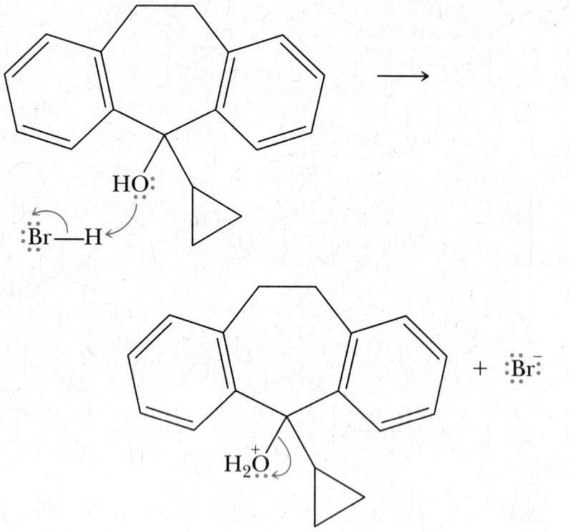

Step 2:

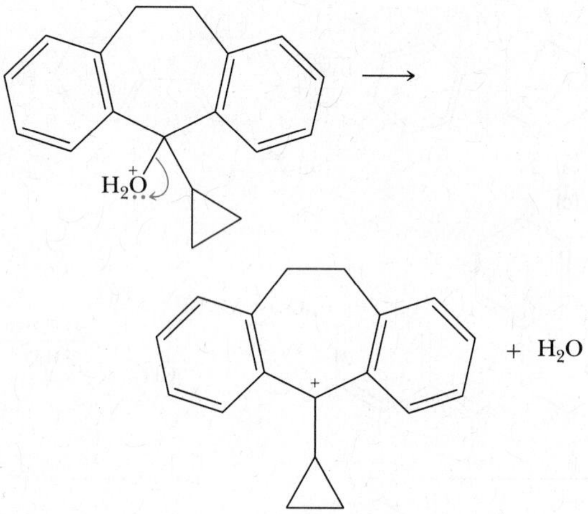

Step 3:

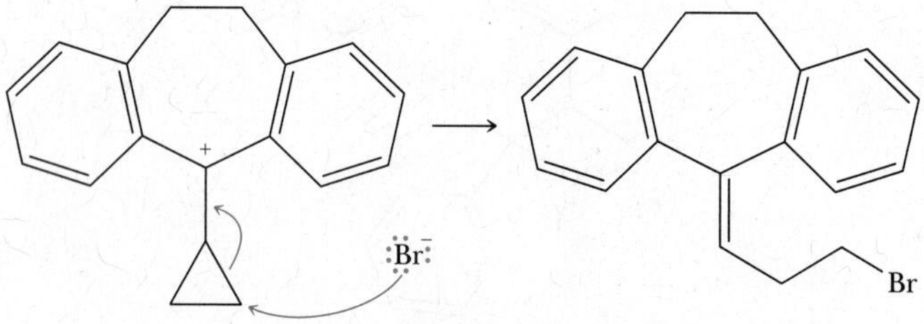

(c) 2 equivalents of dimethylamine

12.45 (a) Step 1 is a Friedel-Crafts acylation and involves the use of acetyl chloride (CH_3COCl) and a Lewis acid catalyst, such as $AlCl_3$.

(b) Step 2: Cl_2 in acetic acid

Step 3: 2 equivalents of dimethylamine

(c) Step 4: $NaBH_4$ in an alcohol, or $LiAlH_4$ followed by water

Step 5: $SOCl_2$ in pyridine

(d) Step 6 is a Grignard reaction. The starting material is first treated with magnesium in ether to prepare the Grignard reagent, which is subsequently treated with cyclohexanone followed by acid.

Spectroscopy

12.47

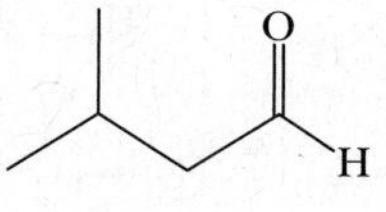

3-Methylbutanal

12.49

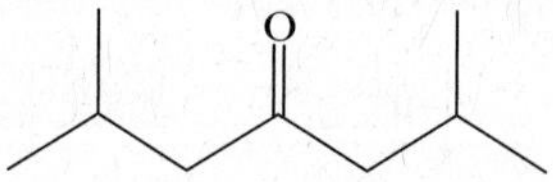

2,6-Dimethyl-4-heptanone

Looking Ahead

12.51

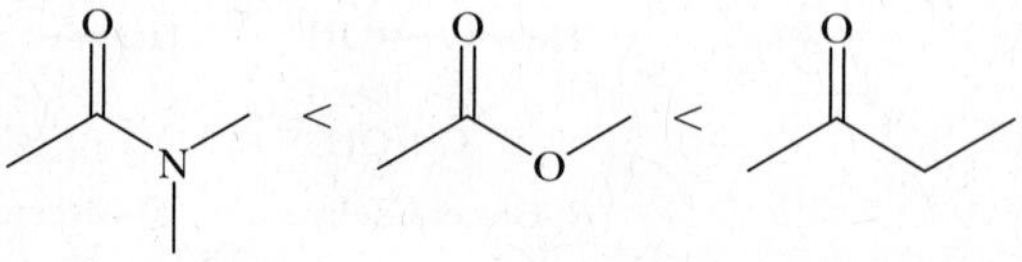

12.53 (a)

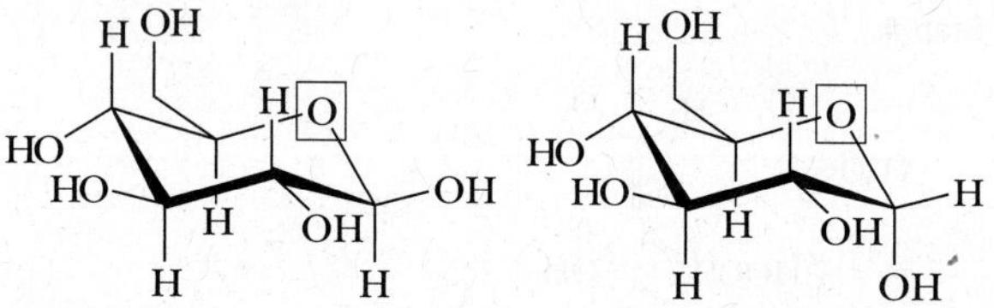

(b)

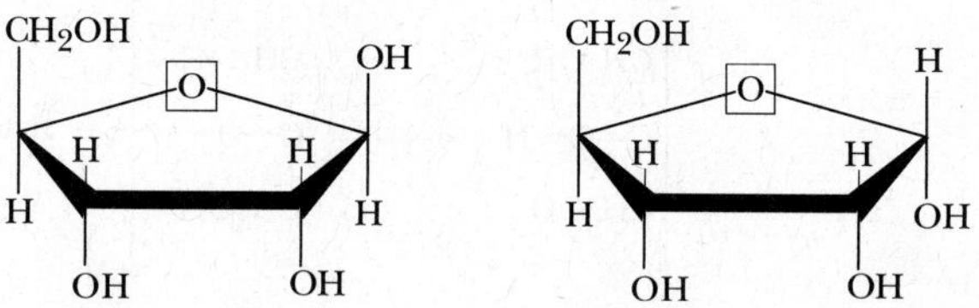

CHAPTER 13 Carboxylic Acids

Problems

13.1

(a)

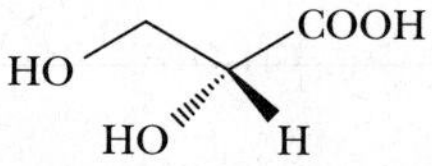

Glyceric acid
(R)-2,3-Dihydroxypropanoic acid

(b)

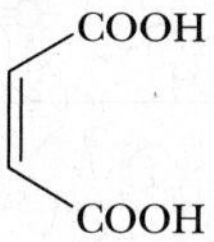

Maleic acid
cis-2-Butenedioic acid
or
(Z)-Butenedioic acid

(c)

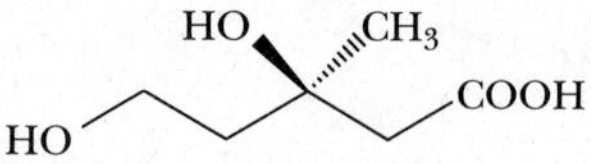

Mevalonic acid
(R)-3,5-Dihydroxy-3-methylpentanoic acid

13.2

CH_3
|
CH_3CCOOH
|
CH_3

2,2-Dimethylpropanoic acid
pK_a 5.03

CF_3COOH

Trifluoroacetic acid
pK_a 0.22

OH
|
$CH_3CHCOOH$

2-Hydroxypropanoic acid
(Lactic acid)
pK_a 3.85

13.3

(a)

Butanoic acid — Ammonium butanoate

(b)

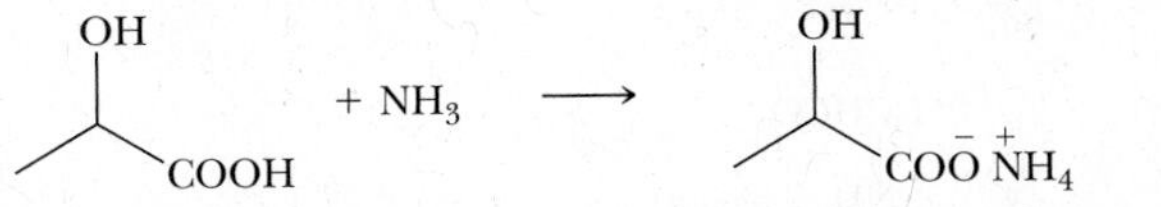

2-Hydroxypropanoic acid (Lactic acid) — Ammonium 2-hydroxypropanoate (Ammonium lactate)

13.4 (a)

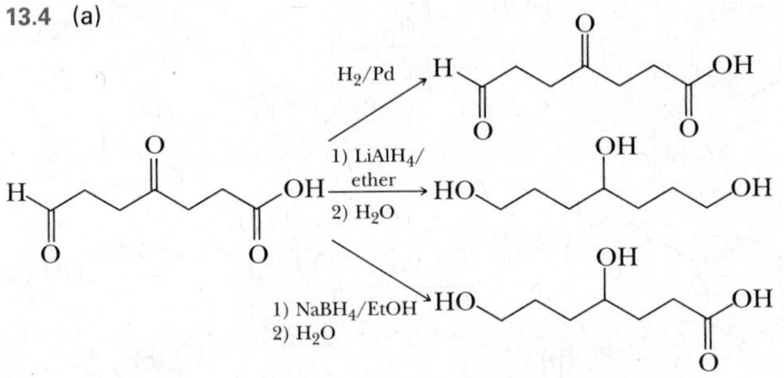

(b)

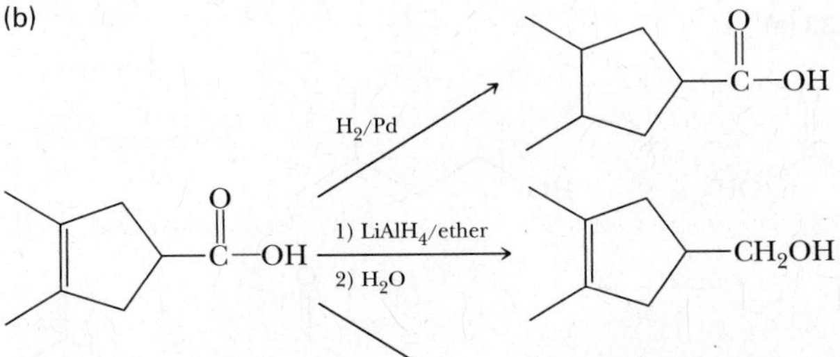

No reaction. Sodium borohydride does not reduce alkenes or acids.

13.5

(a)

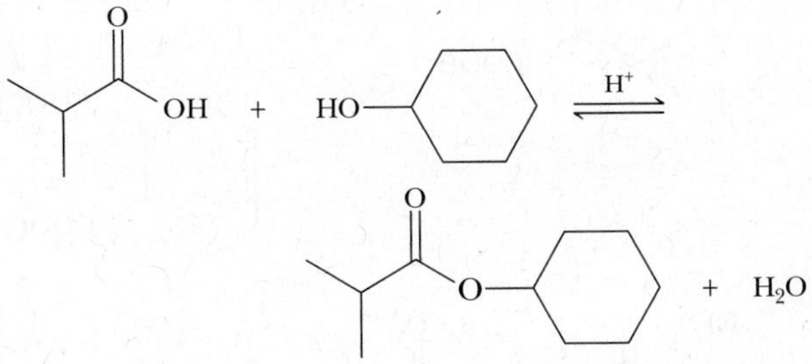

(b)

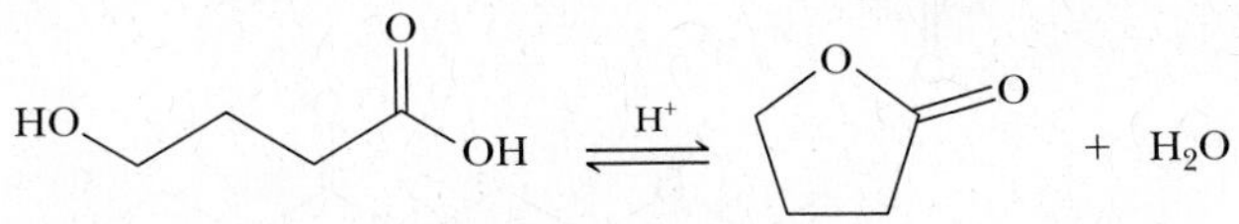

13.6 (a)

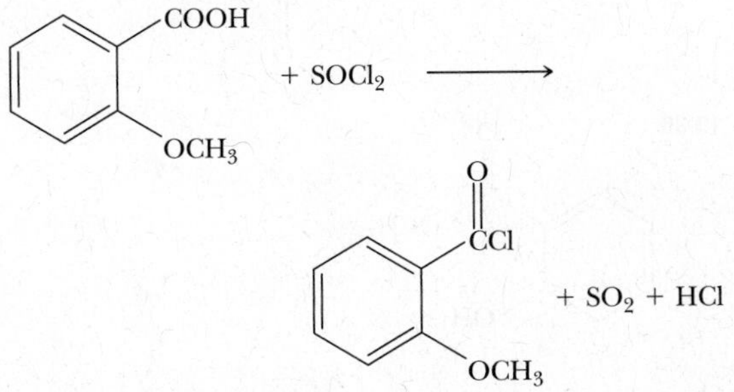

(b)

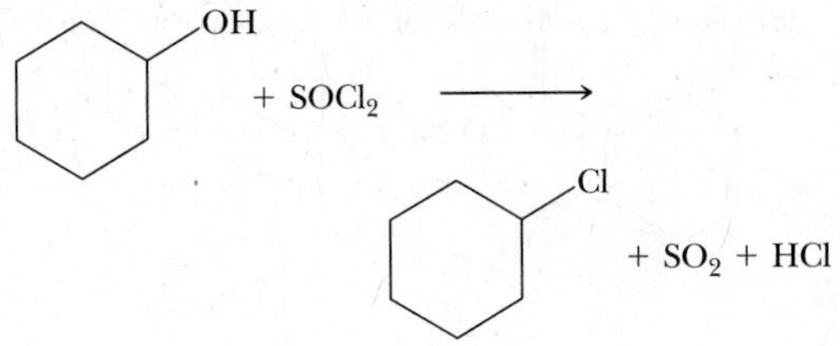

13.7

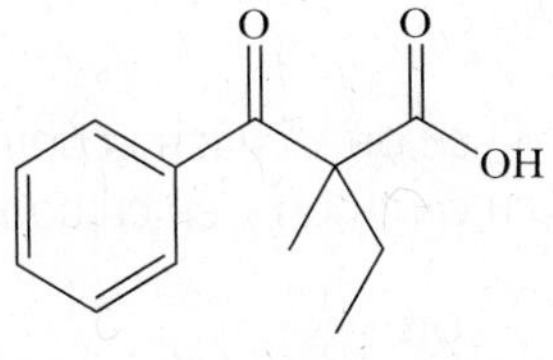

β-Ketoacid

End-of-Chapter Problems

13.9 (a)

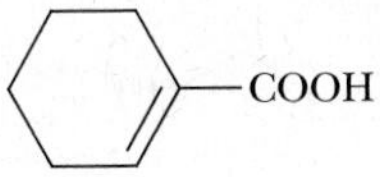

1-Cyclohexenecarboxylic acid

(b)

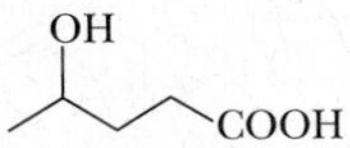

4-Hydroxypentanoic acid

(c)

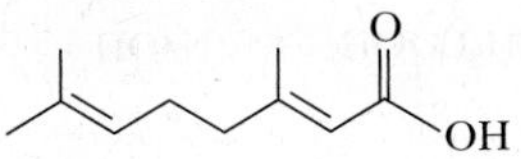

(*E*)-3,7-Dimethyl-2,6-octadienoic acid

(d)

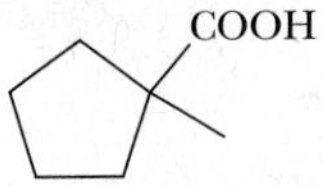

1-Methylcyclopentanecarboxylic acid

(e)

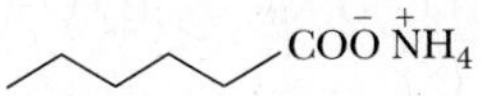

Ammonium hexanoate

(f)

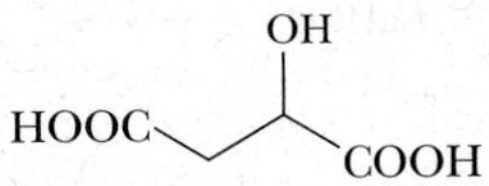

2-Hydroxybutanedioic acid

13.11 (a) 3,5-Tetradecadienoic acid

(b) 4

13.13 (a)

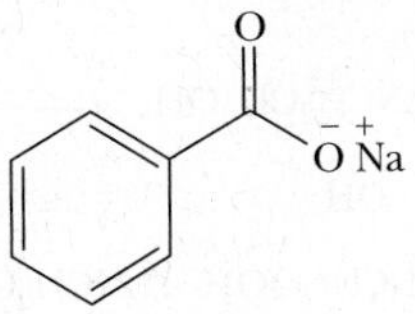

(b)

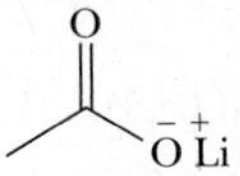

(c)

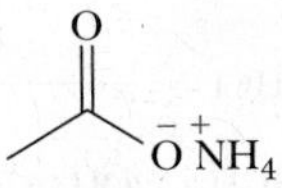

(d)

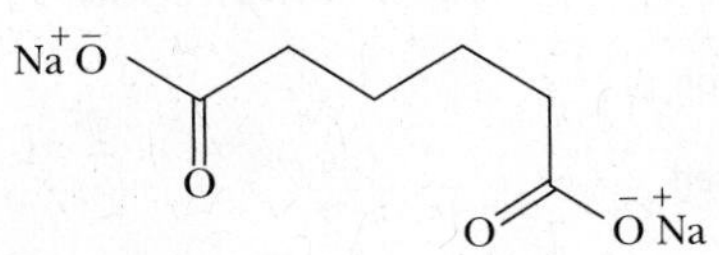

(e)

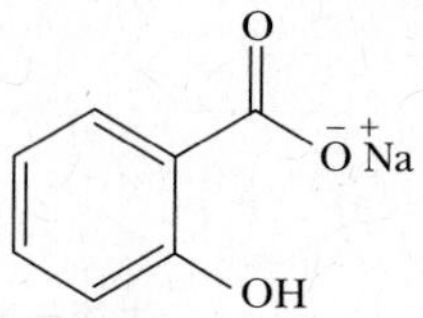

(f)

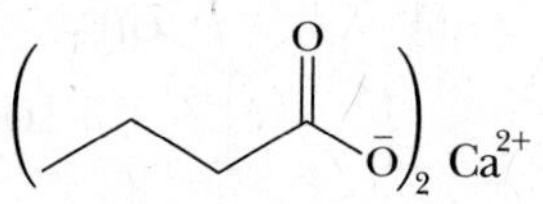

13.15

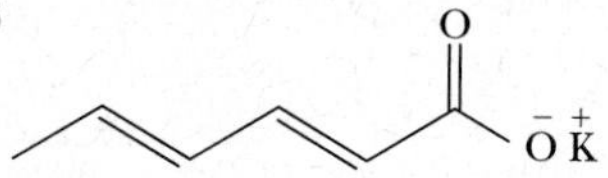

13.17 (a) $CH_3(CH_2)_6CHO < CH_3(CH_2)_6CH_2OH < CH_3(CH_2)_5COOH$

(b) $CH_3CH_2OCH_2CH_3 < CH_3CH_2CH_2CH_2OH < CH_3CH_2COOH$

13.19 (a)

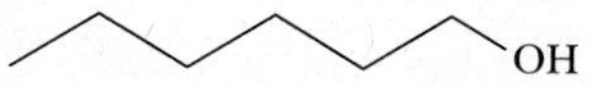

(b)

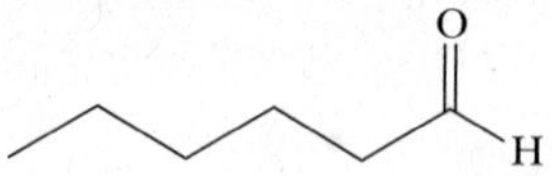

(c)

13.21

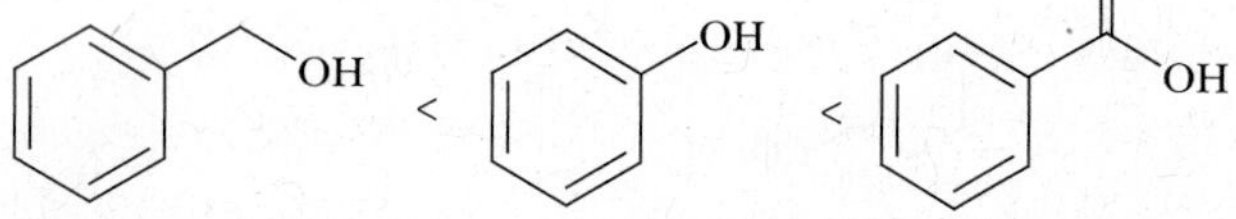

13.23 (a)

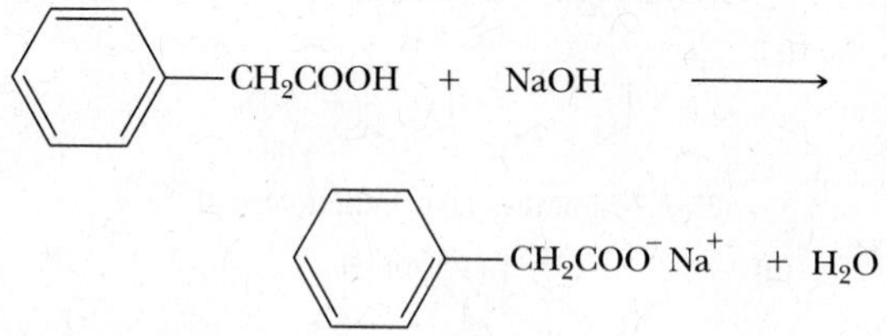

(b) $CH_3CH{=}CHCH_2COOH + NaHCO_3 \longrightarrow CH_3CH{=}CHCH_2COO^-Na^+ + H_2O + CO_2$

(c)

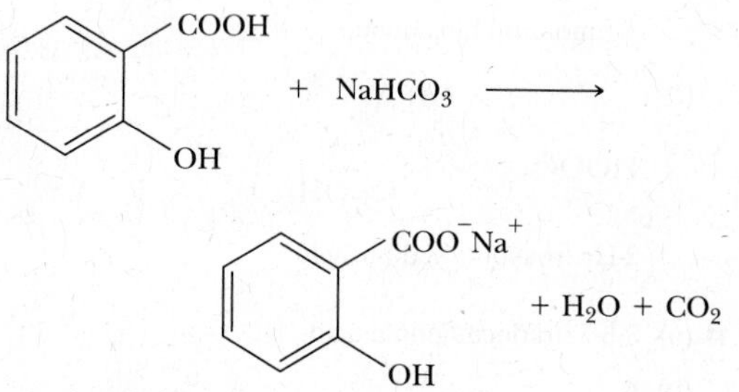

(d) $CH_3CH(OH)COOH + H_2NCH_2CH_2OH \longrightarrow CH_3CH(OH)COOH\ H_3\overset{+}{N}CH_2CH_2OH$

(e) $CH_3CH{=}CHCH_2COO^-Na^+ + HCl \longrightarrow CH_3CH{=}CHCH_2COOH + NaCl$

13.25 Salicylate anion

13.27 Lactic acid itself

13.29 (a) $CH_3CH(\overset{+}{N}H_3)COOH$ (b) $CH_3CH(\overset{+}{N}H_3)COO^-$

(c) $CH_3CH(NH_2)COO^-$

13.31

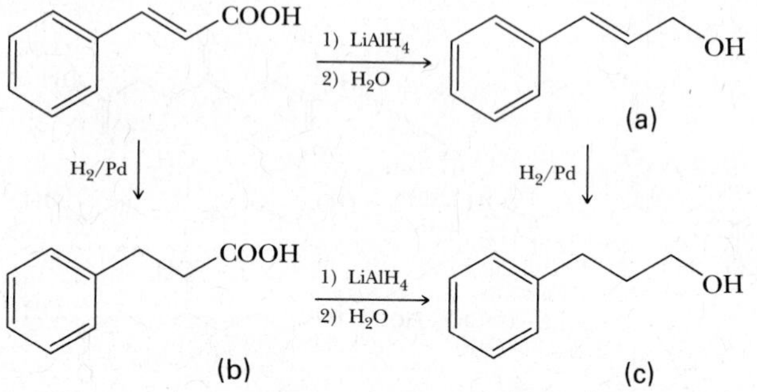

13.33 (a)

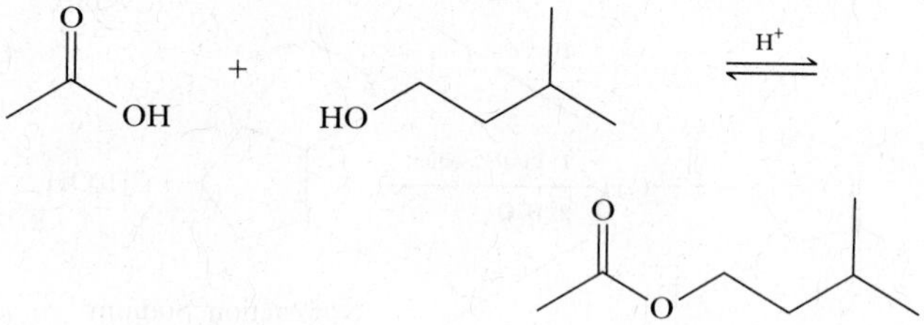

(b)

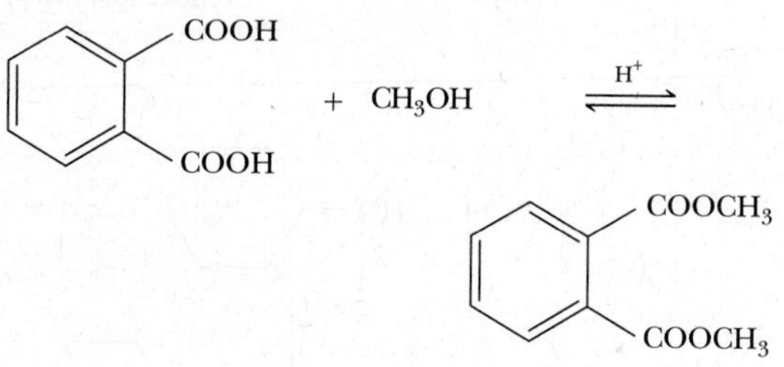

(c)

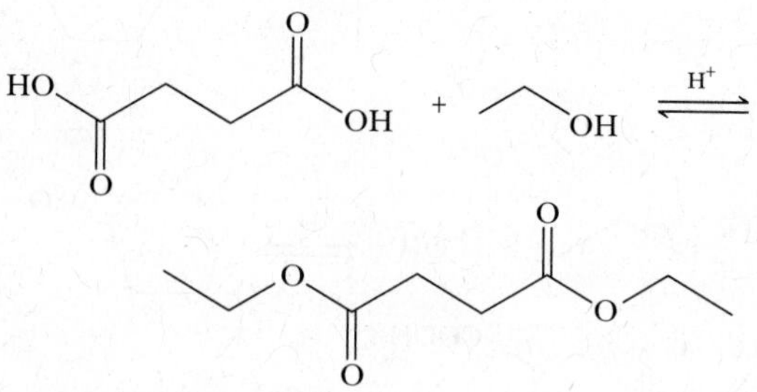

13.35

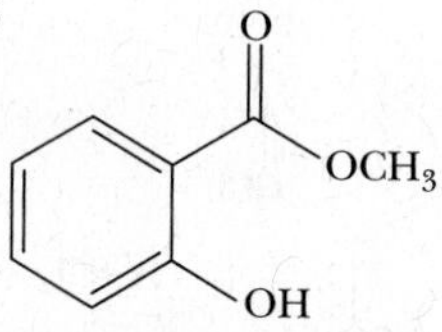

13.37 (a)

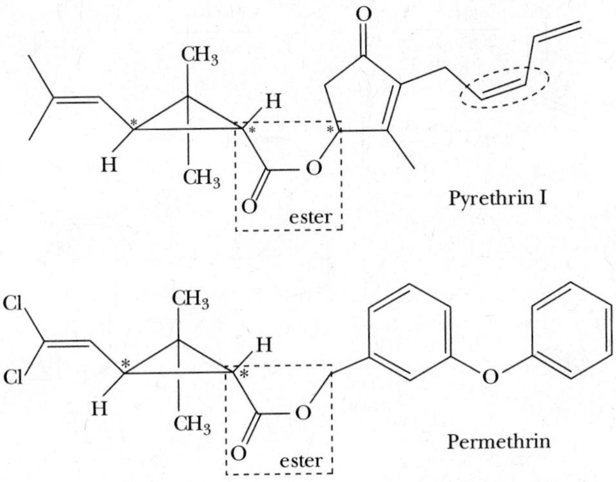

(b) Yes, 16

(c) Yes, 4

13.39 (a)

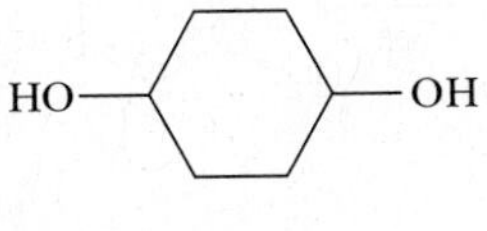

alcohol

$CH_3\overset{O}{\overset{\|}{C}}OH$

carboxylic acid

(b)

CH_3OH

alcohol

$HO\overset{O}{\overset{\|}{C}}CH_2CH_2\overset{O}{\overset{\|}{C}}OH$

carboxylic acid

(c)

CH_3OH

alcohol

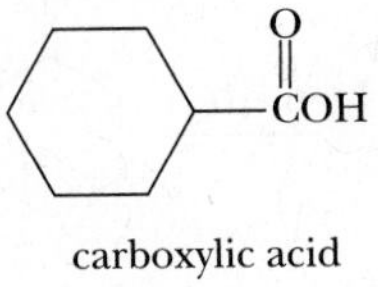

carboxylic acid

(d)

$(CH_3)_2CHOH$

alcohol

$CH_3CH_2CH{=}CH\overset{O}{\overset{\|}{C}}OH$

carboxylic acid

13.41 (a)

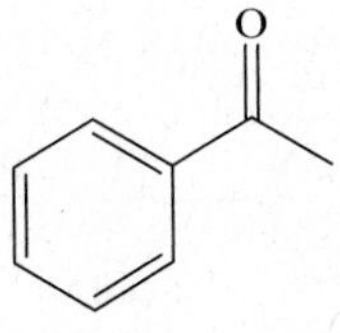

(b)

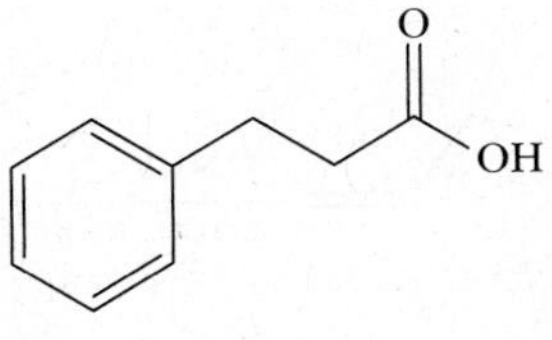

(c)

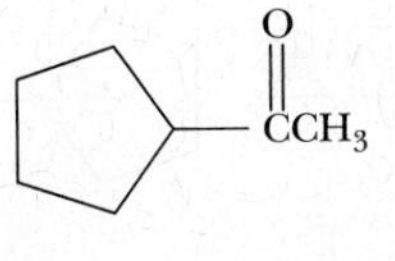

13.43

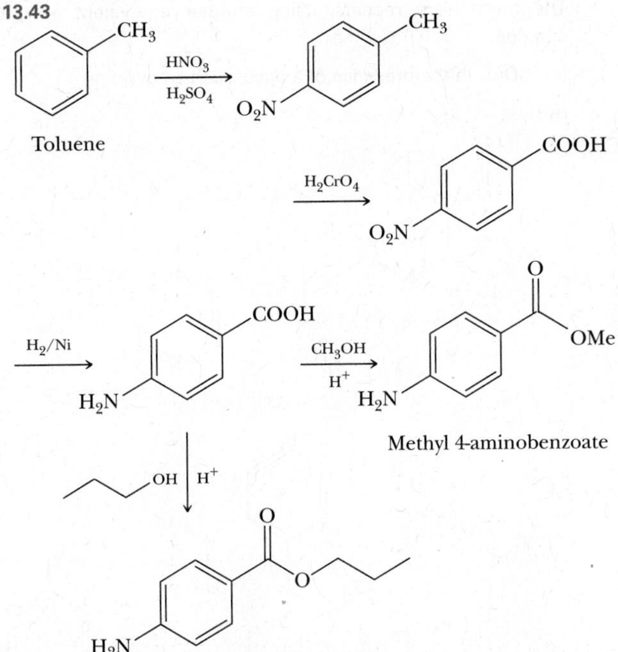

13.45 (a) $SOCl_2$ in the presence of a base, such as pyridine.

(b) Friedel-Crafts acylation

(c) NH_3 followed by catalytic hydrogenation, such as H_2/Pt.

(d)

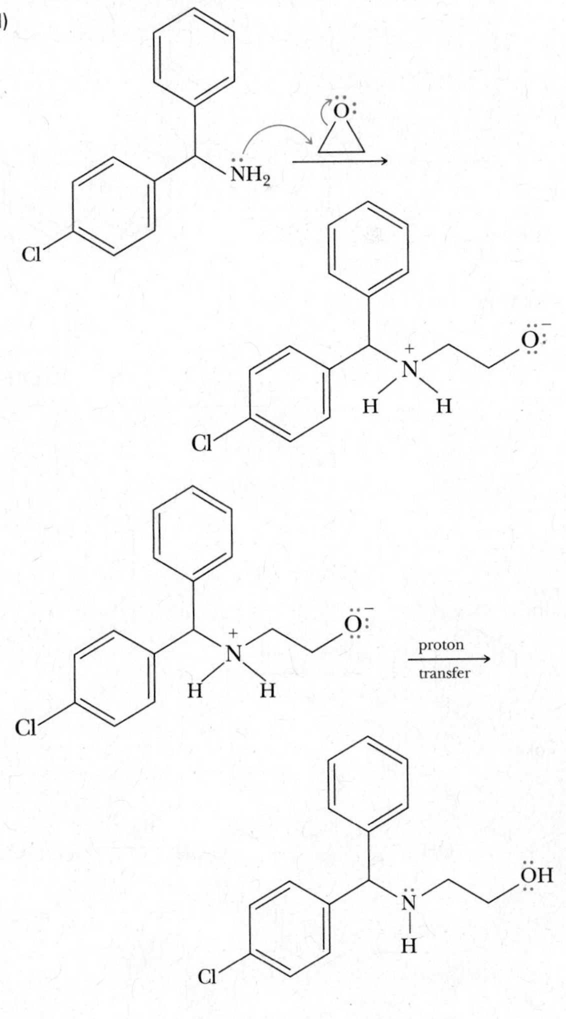

The mechanism repeats, using another equivalent of the epoxide.

(e) $SOCl_2$ in the presence of a base, such as pyridine.

(f)

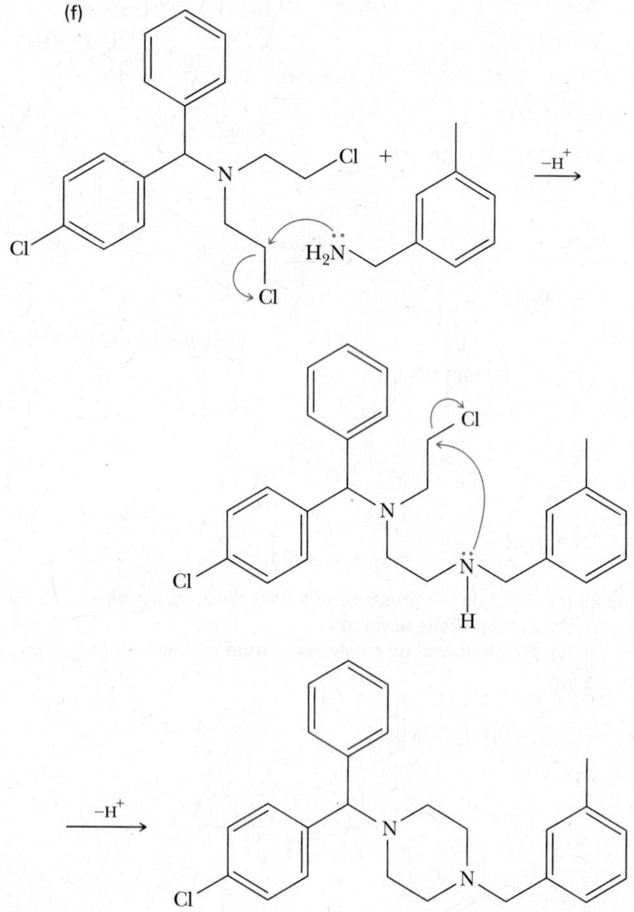

13.47 (a)

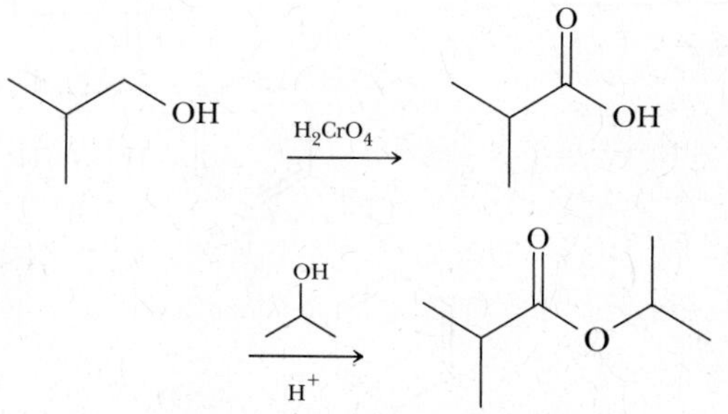

(b)

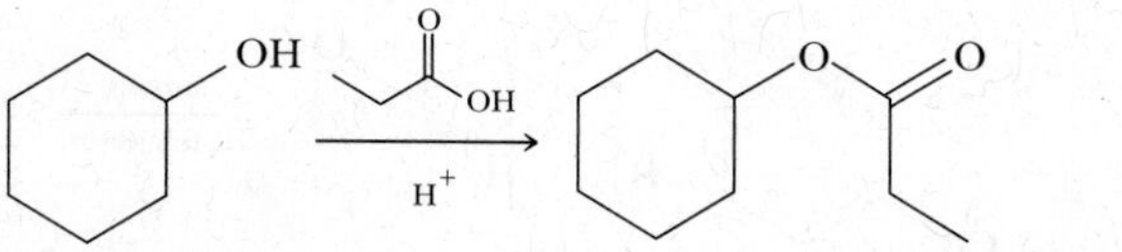

(c)

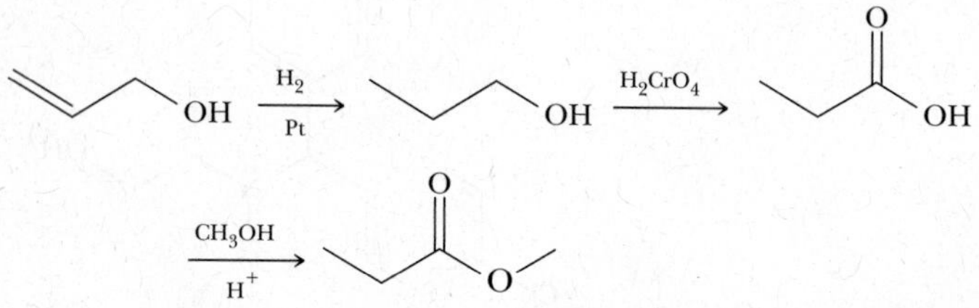

(d)

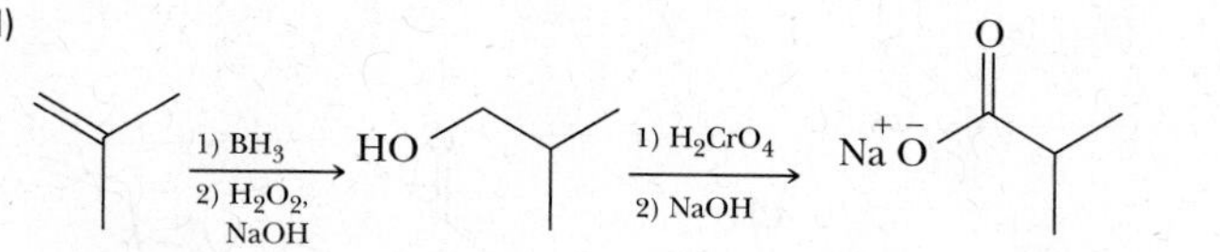

(e)

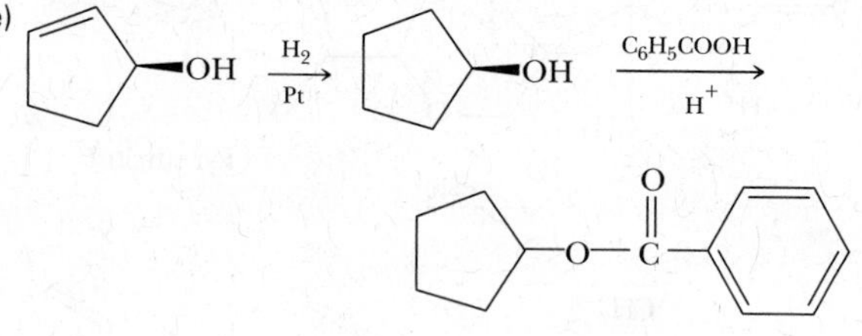

(f)

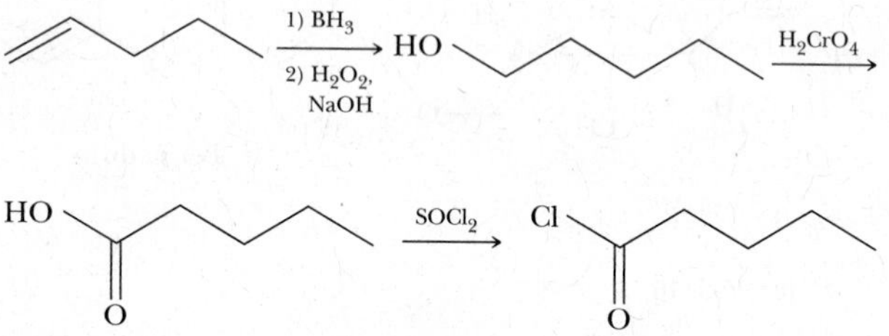

(g)

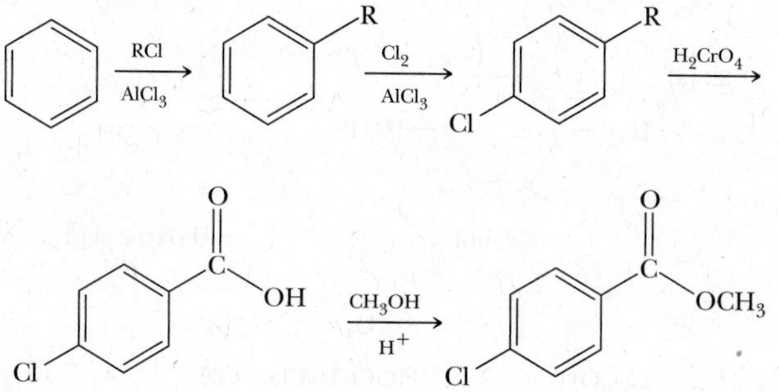

(h)

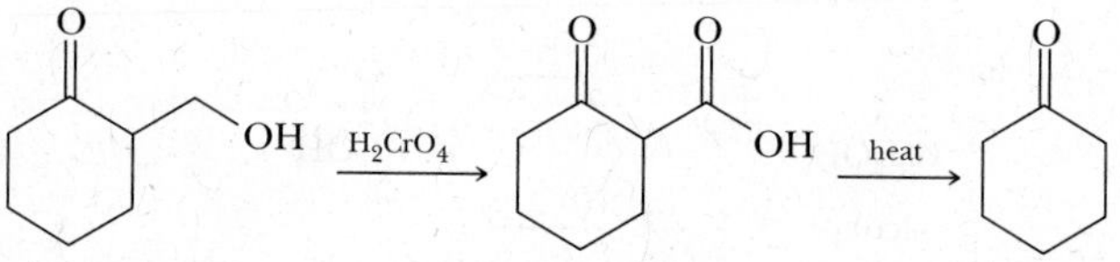

(i)

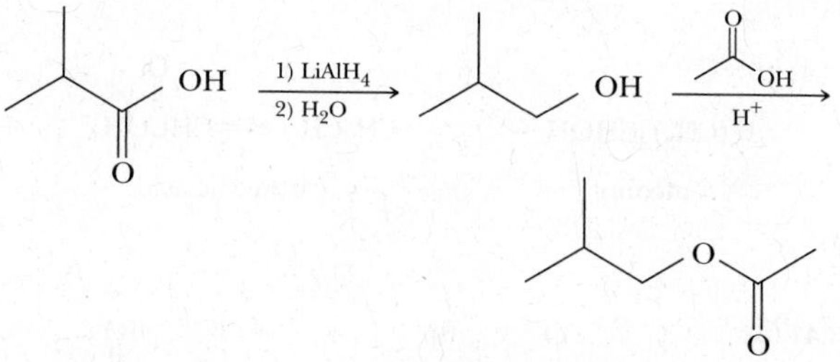

(j)

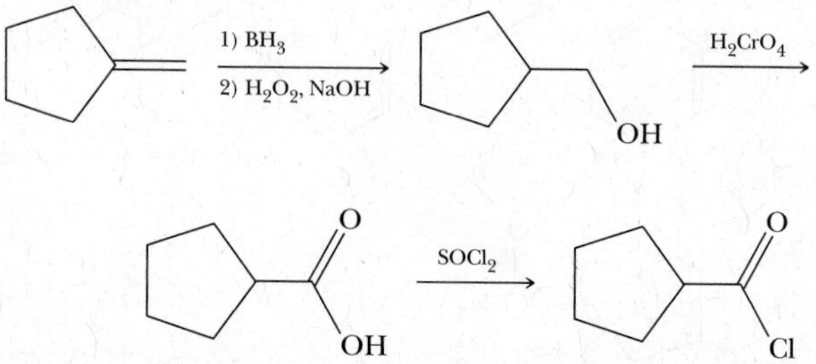

(k)

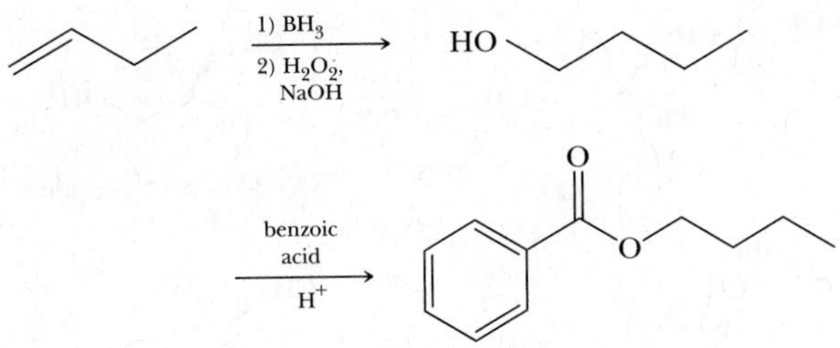

(l)

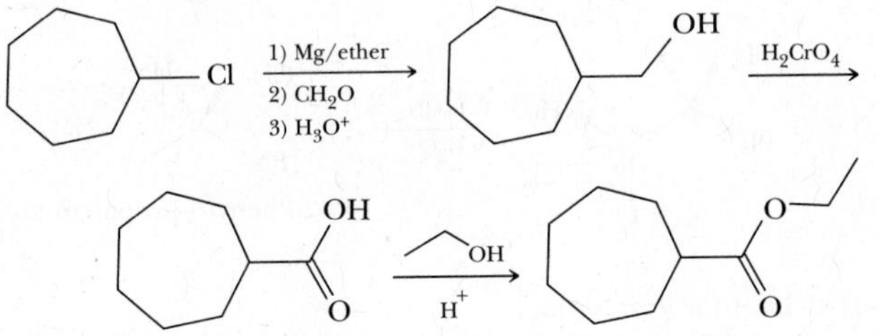

(m)

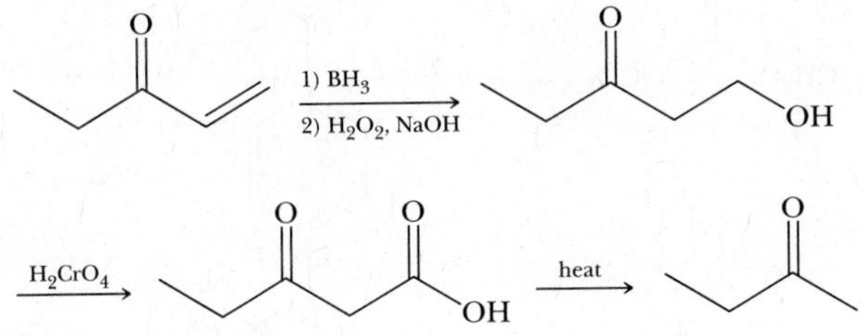

(n)

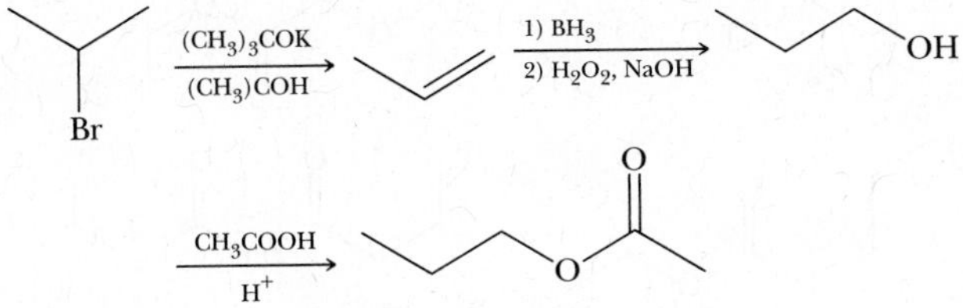

(o)

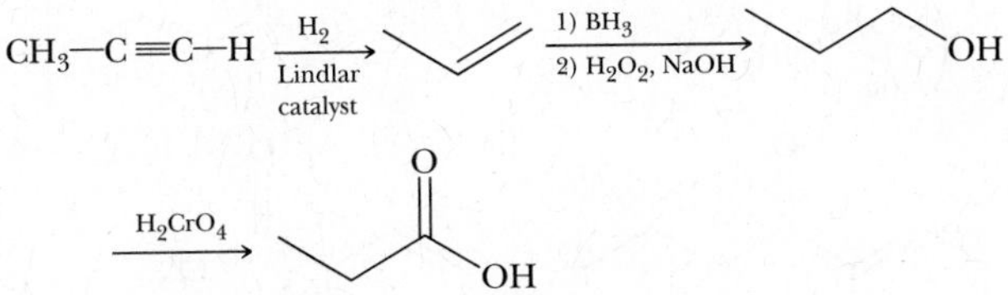

(p)

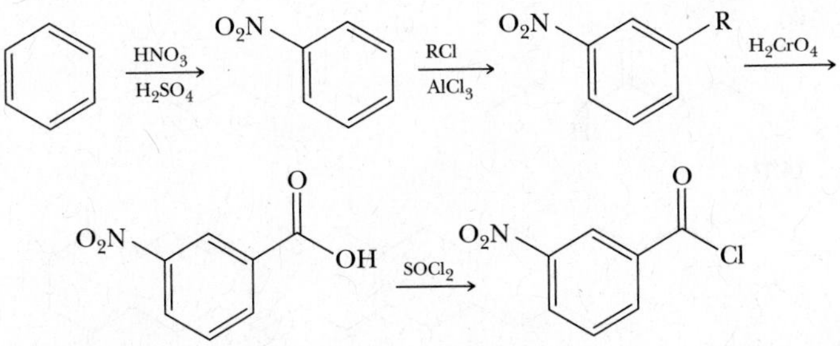

13.49 Carboxylate ion

13.51 No, only with esters

CHAPTER 14 Functional Derivatives of Carboxylic Acids

Problems

14.1 (a)

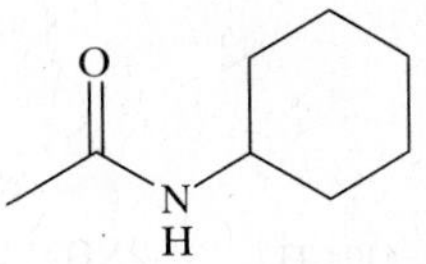

(b)

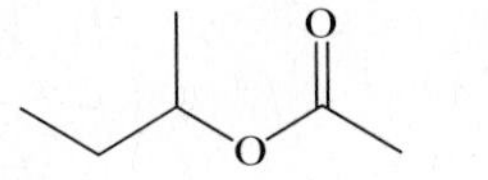

(c)

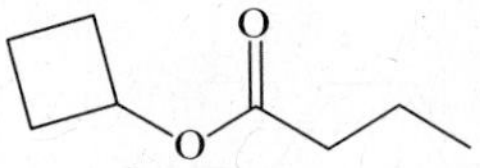

(d)

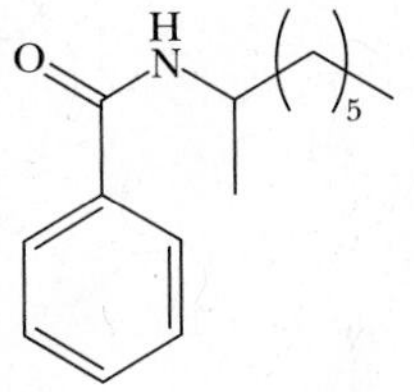

(e)

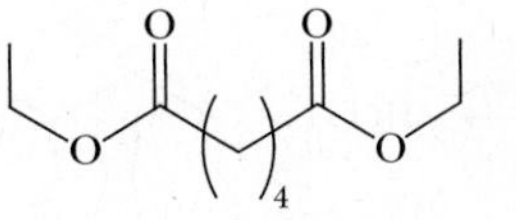

(f)

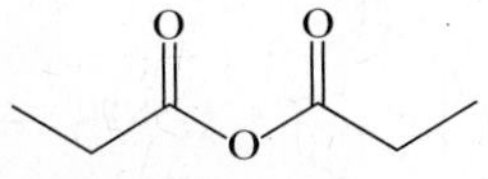

14.2 (a)

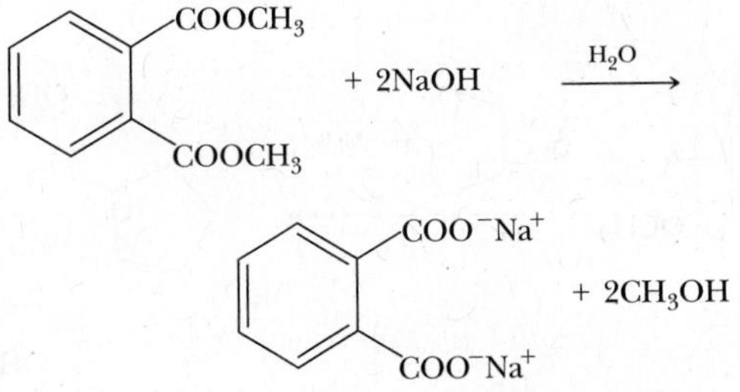

(b)

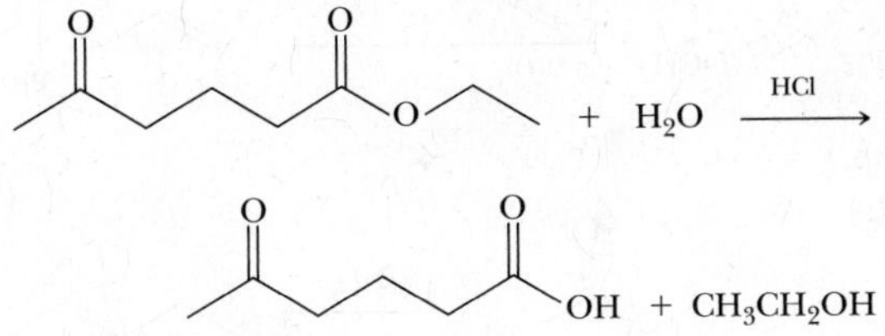

14.3 (a) $CH_3\overset{O}{\overset{\|}{C}}N(CH_3)_2 \xrightarrow[H_2O]{NaOH} CH_3\overset{O}{\overset{\|}{C}}O^-Na^+ + (CH_3)_2NH$

1 mole of NaOH needed for every mole of amide

(b)

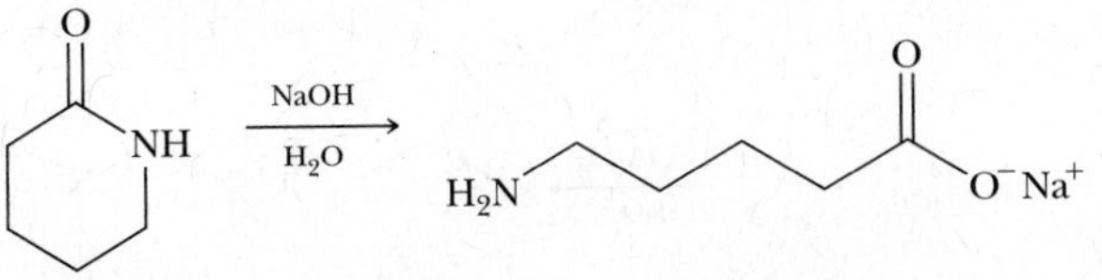

1 mole of NaOH needed for every mole of amide

14.4 (a)

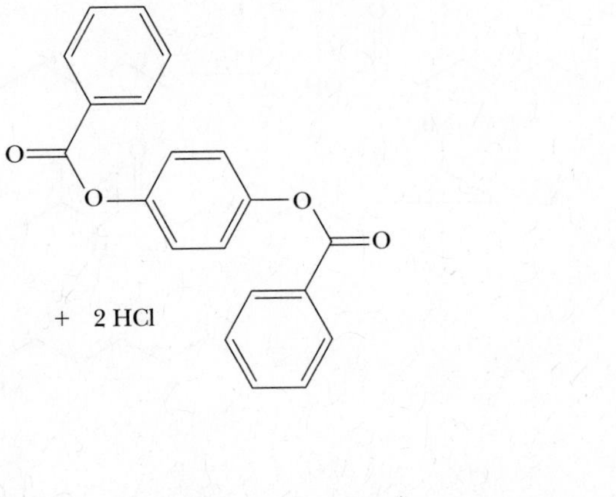

(b)

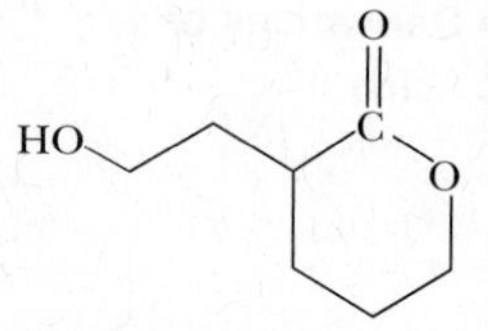

14.5 (a)

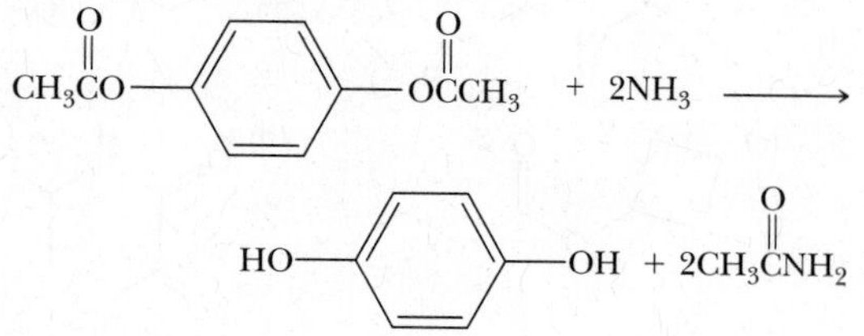

(b)

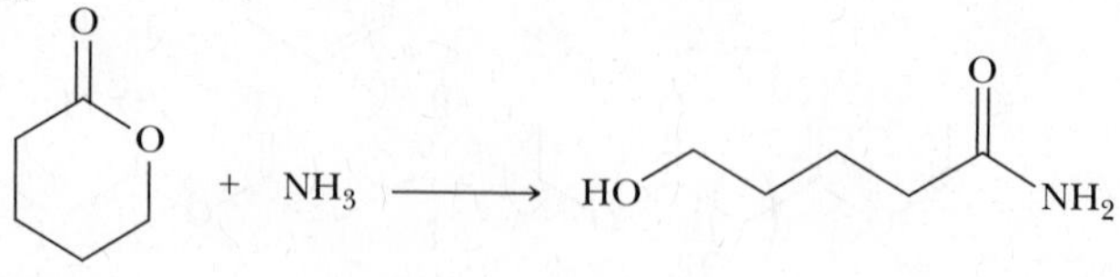

14.6

(a)

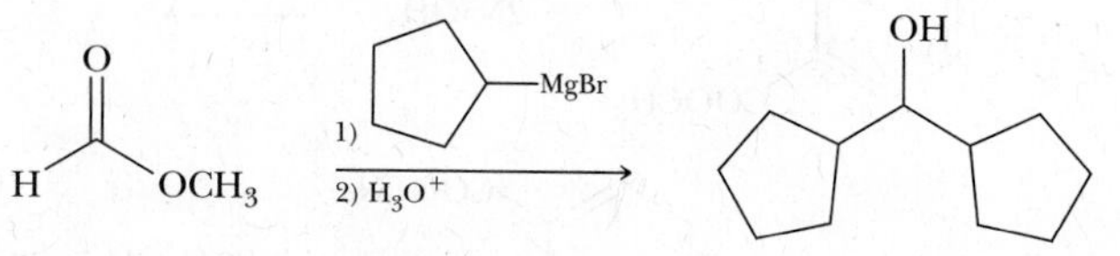

(b)

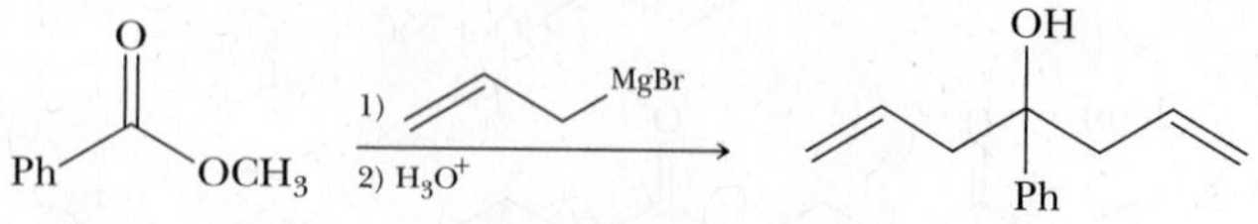

14.7

(a)

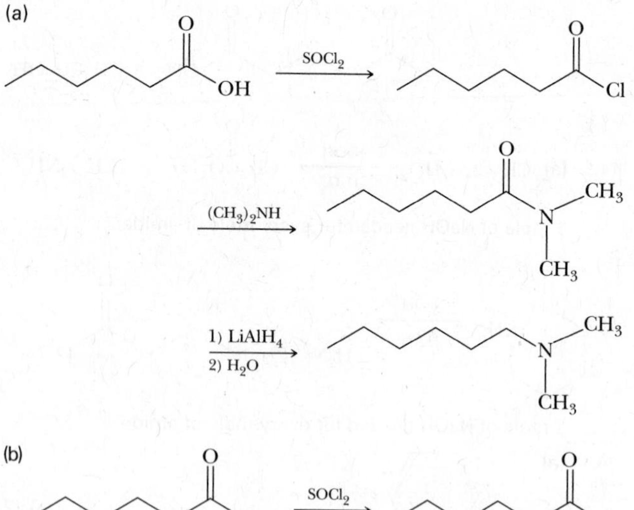

(b)

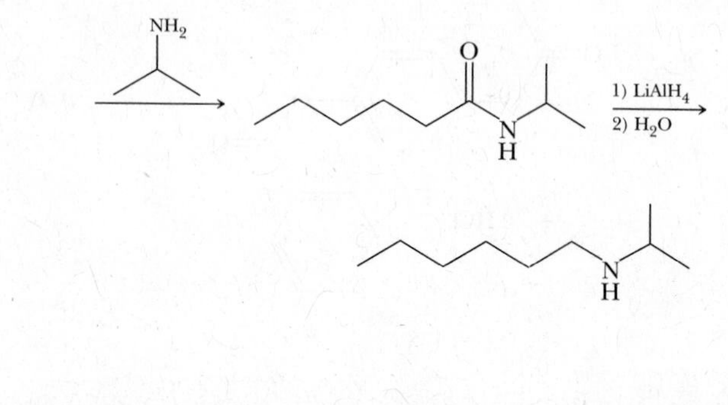

14.8 (a)

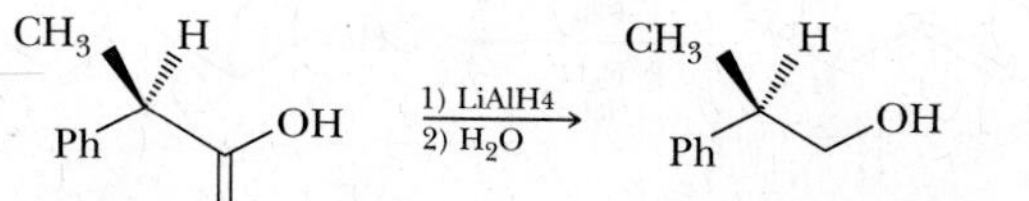

(R)-2-Phenyl-1-propanol

(b)

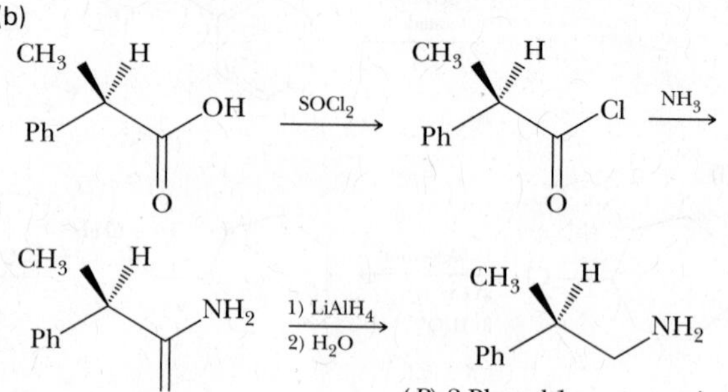

(R)-2-Phenyl-1-propanamine

End-of-Chapter Problems

14.9

(a)

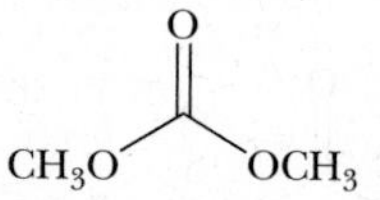

(b)

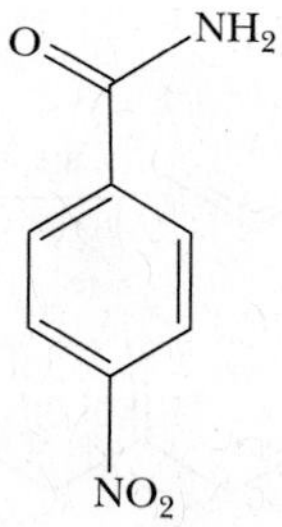

(c)

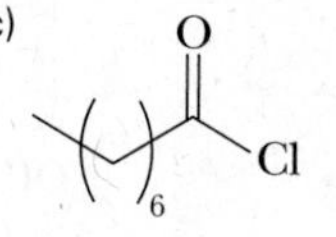

(d)

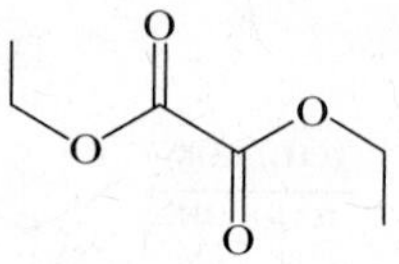

(e)

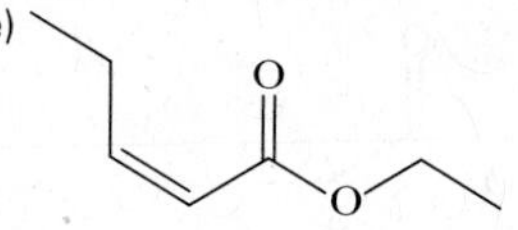

(f)

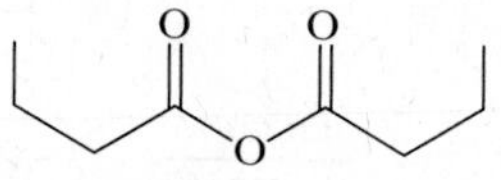

(g)

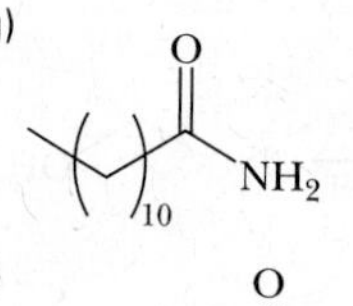

(h)

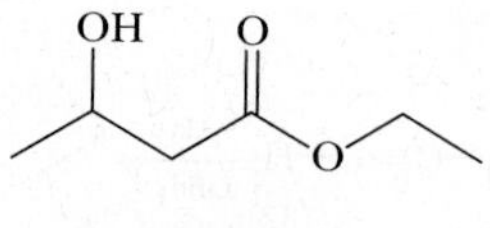

(i)

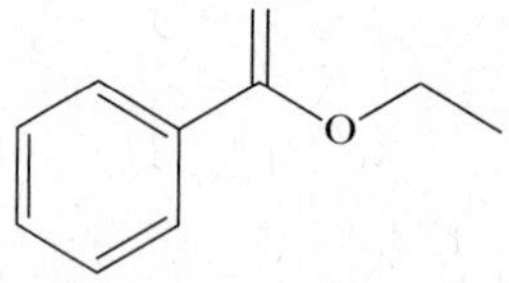

(j)

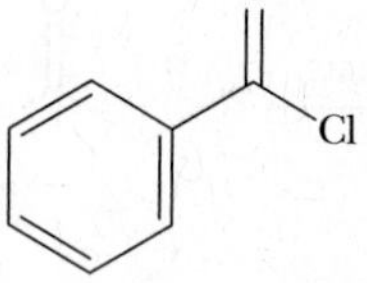

(k)

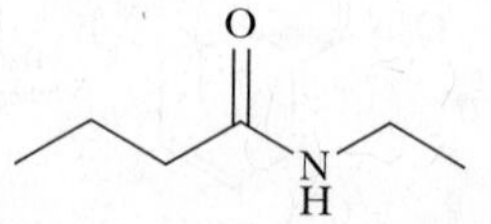

(l)

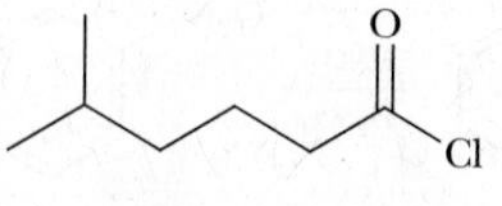

14.11

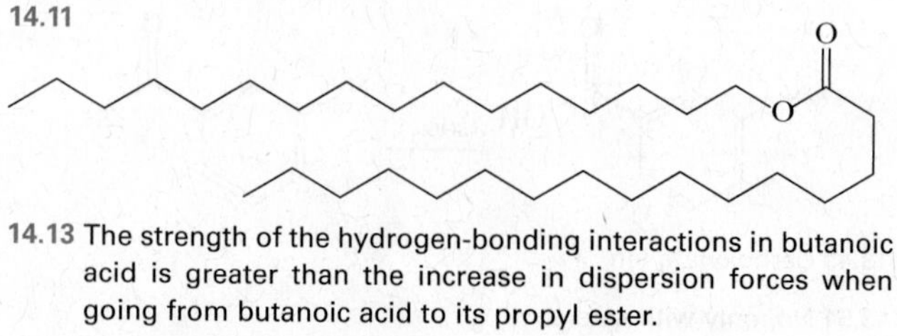

14.13 The strength of the hydrogen-bonding interactions in butanoic acid is greater than the increase in dispersion forces when going from butanoic acid to its propyl ester.

14.15 3 < 1 < 4 < 2

14.17 (a)

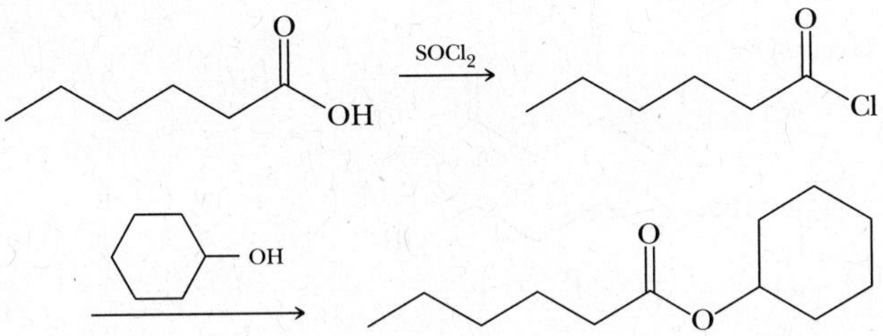

(b)

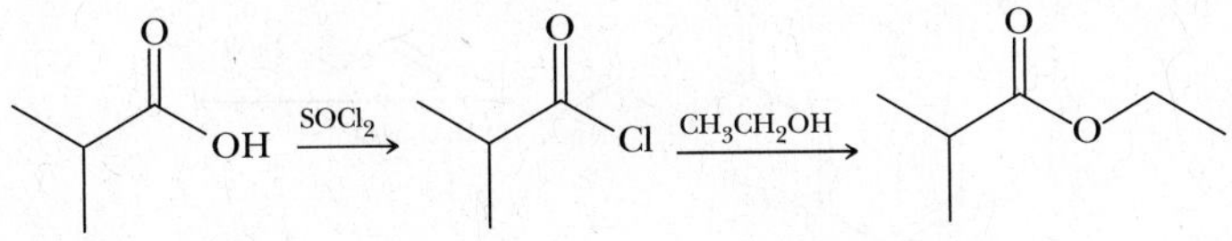

14.19 (a) Step 1:

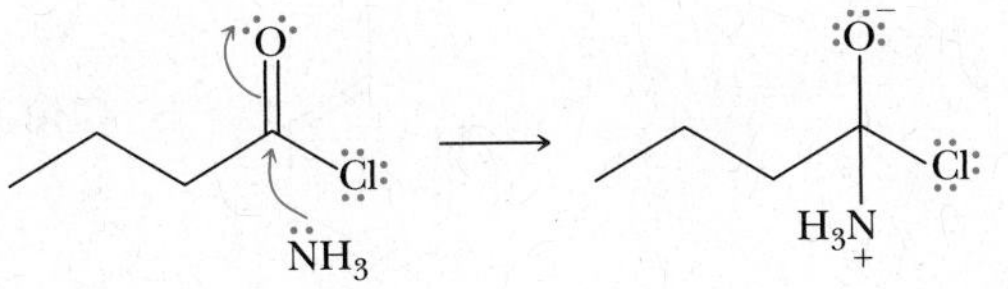

Step 2:

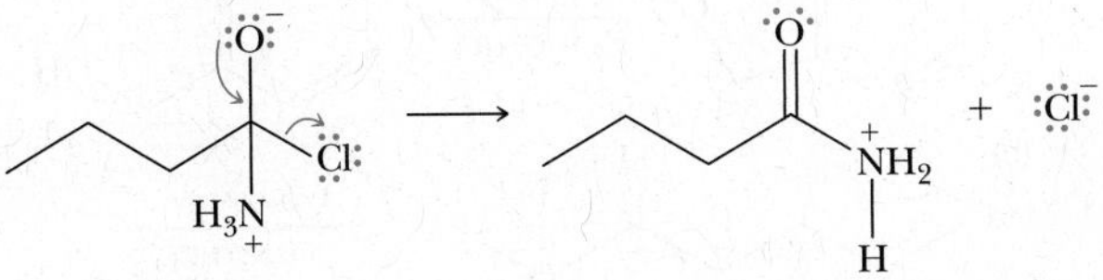

Step 3:

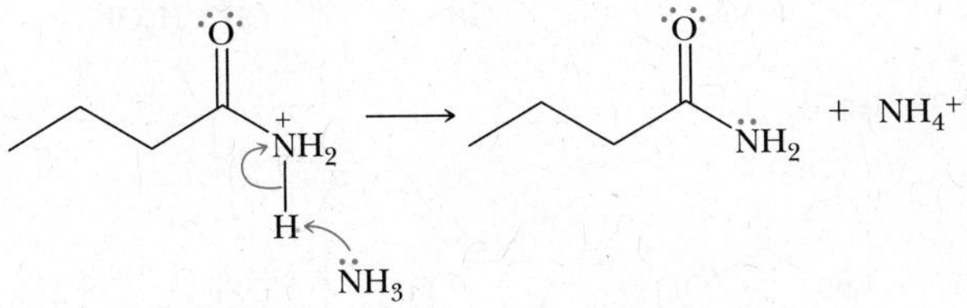

(b) Step 1:

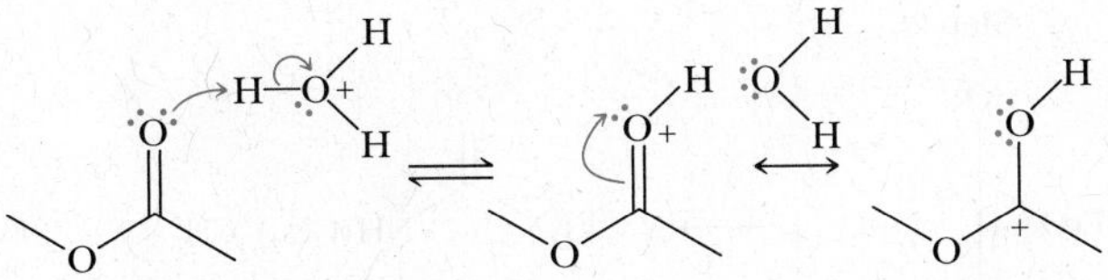

Step 2:

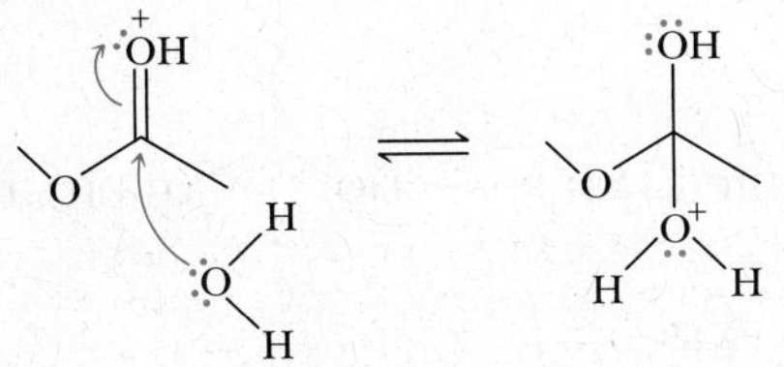

Step 3:

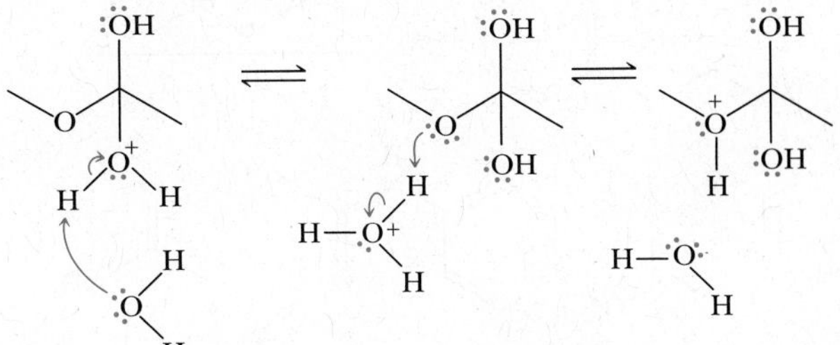

Step 4:

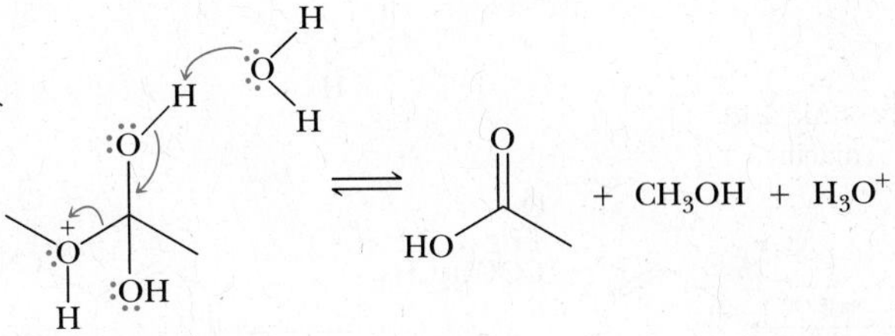

(c) Step 1:

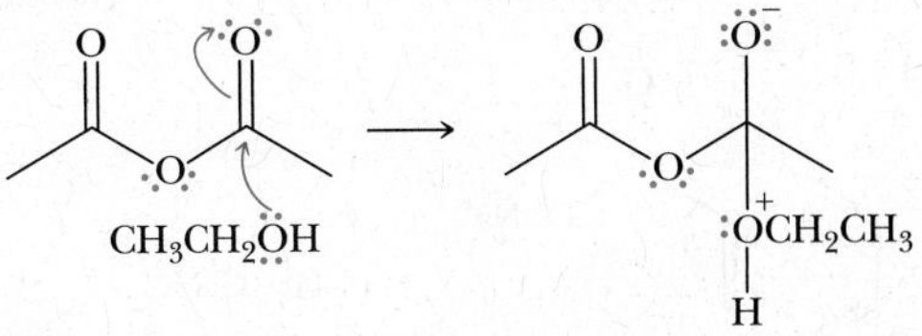

Step 2:

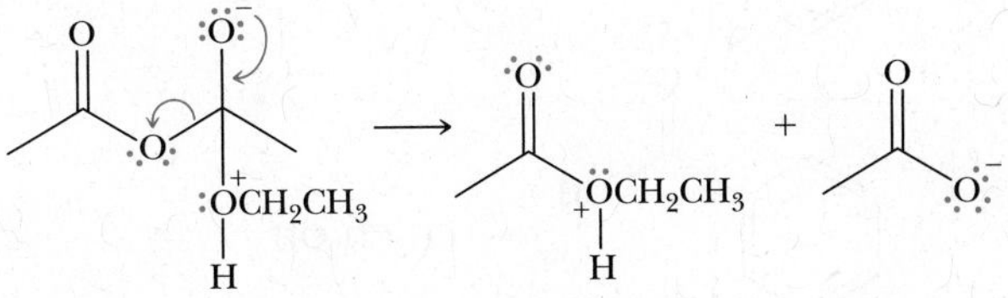

Step 3:

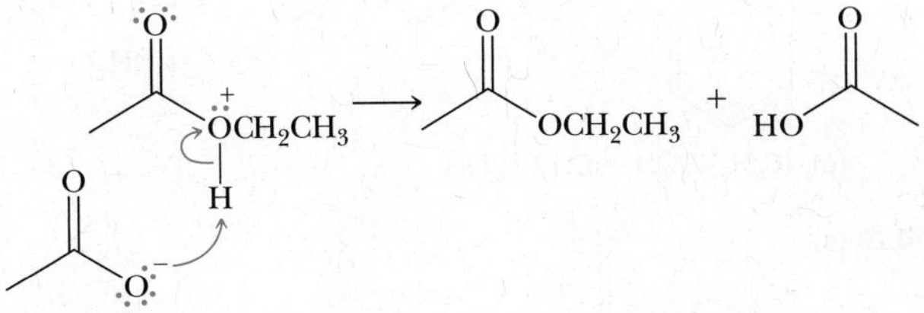

14.21 (a)

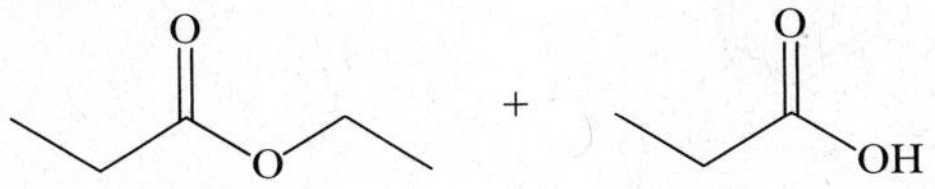

(b)

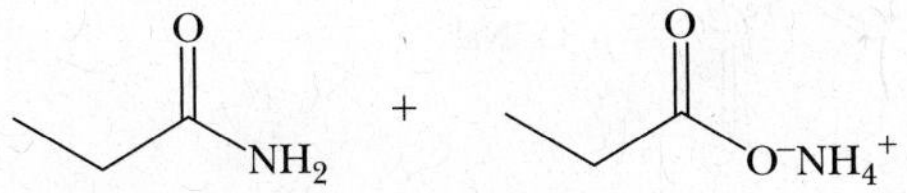

14.23

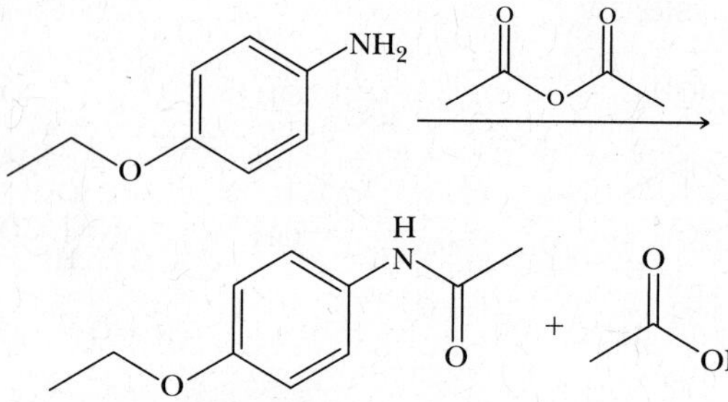

14.25

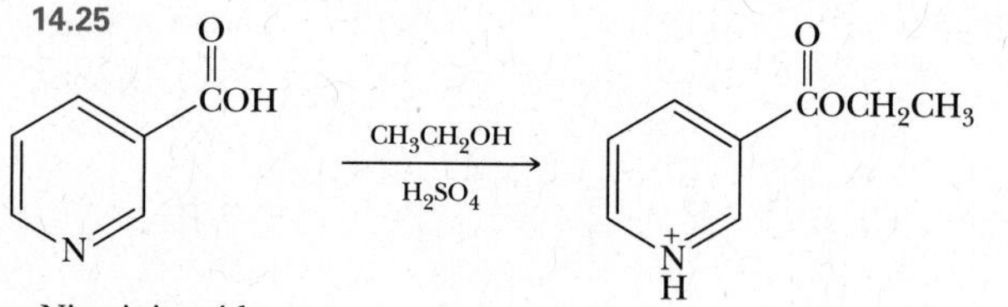

Nicotinic acid (niacin)

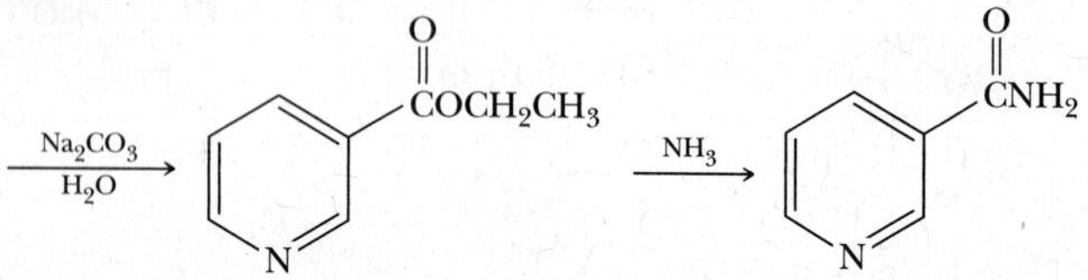

Ethyl nicotinate   Nicotinamide

14.27 (a)

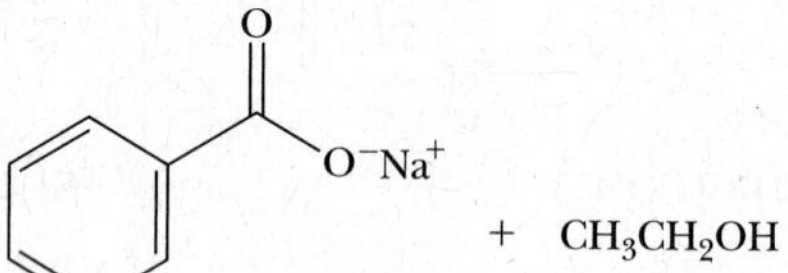

(b)

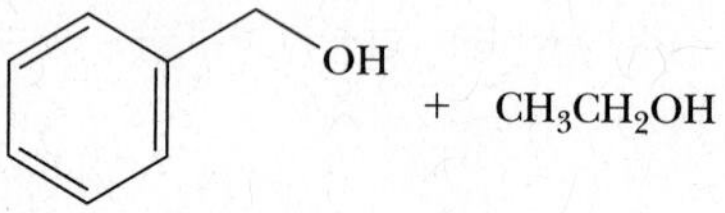

(c)

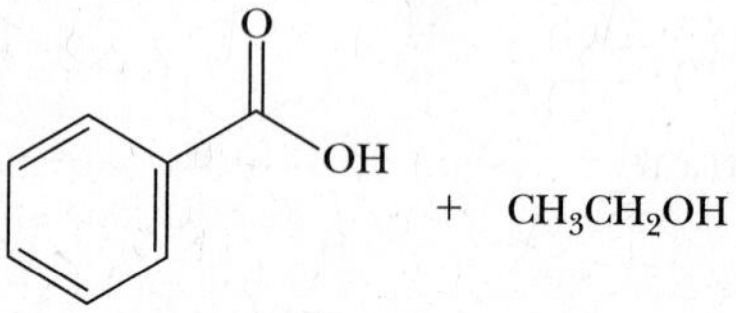

(d)

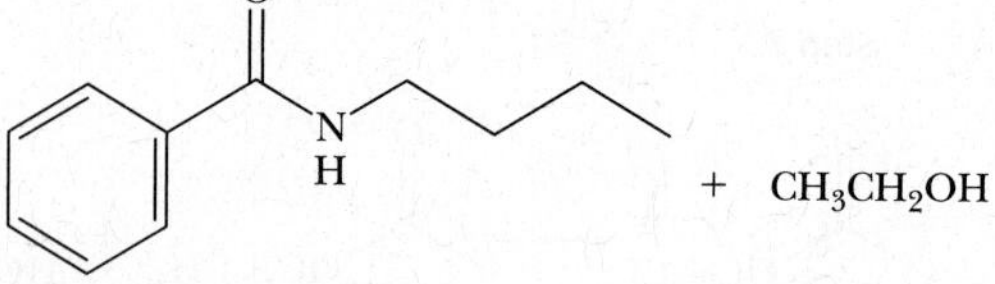

(e) $(C_6H_5)_3COH + CH_3CH_2OH$

14.29 (a)

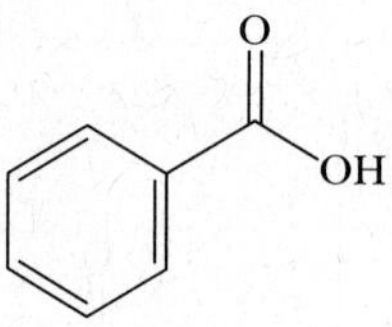

(b)

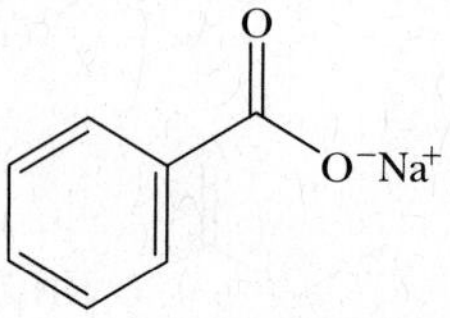

(c)

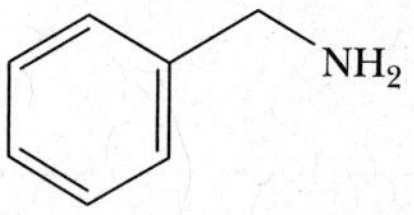

14.31 (a)

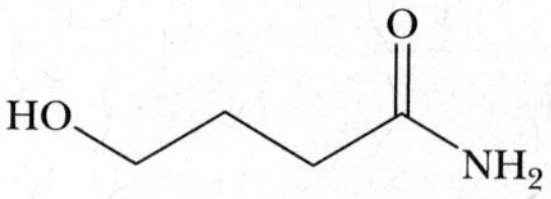

(b)

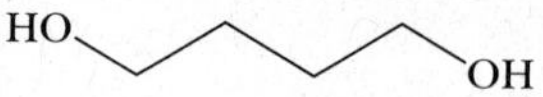

(c)

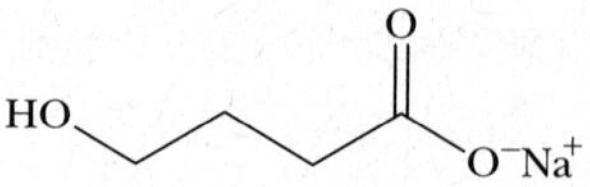

14.33 (a)

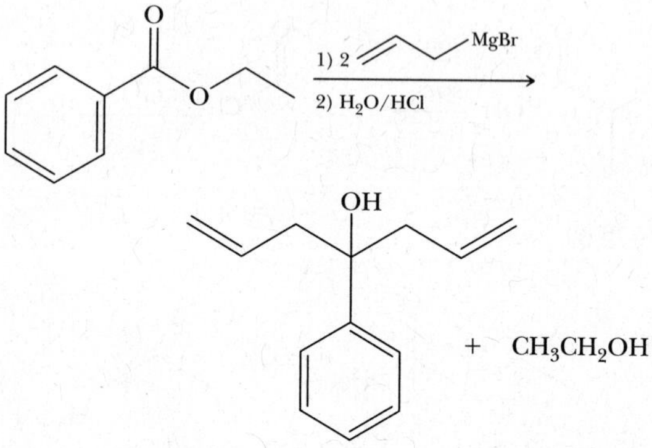

(b)

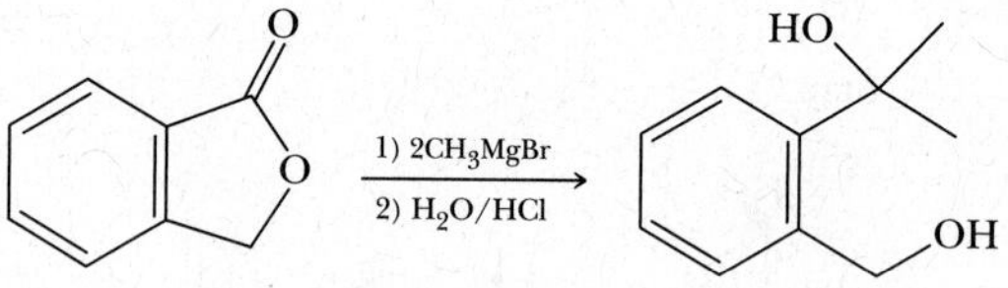

(c)

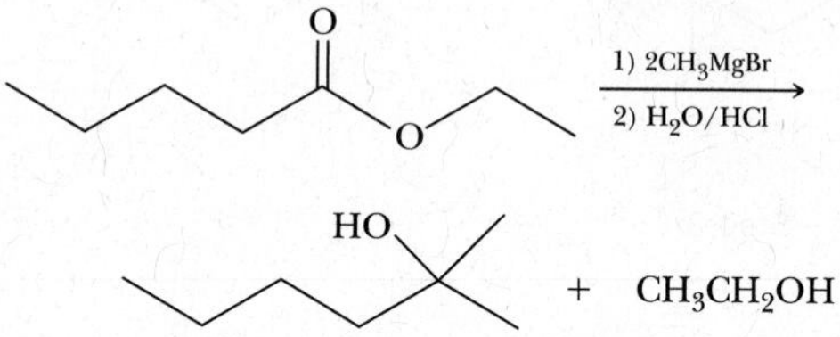

14.35 Step 1:

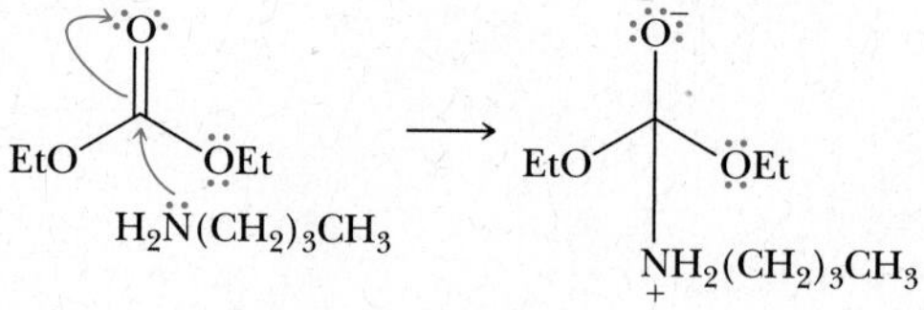

Step 2:

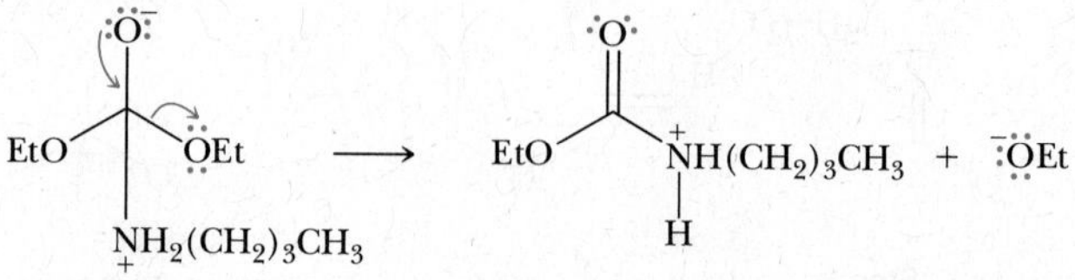

Step 3:

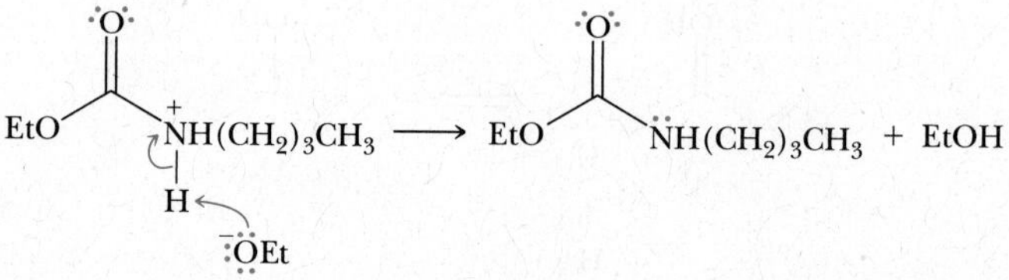

14.37 (a)

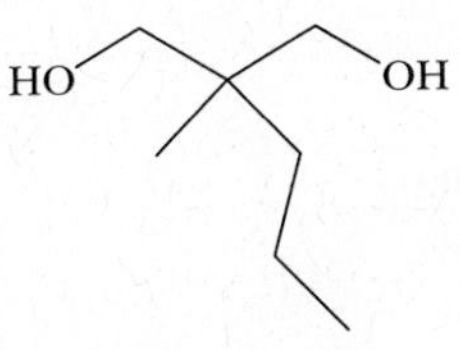

$+\ 2CO_2\ +\ 2NH_4^+$

2-Methyl-2-propyl-1,3-propanediol

(b)

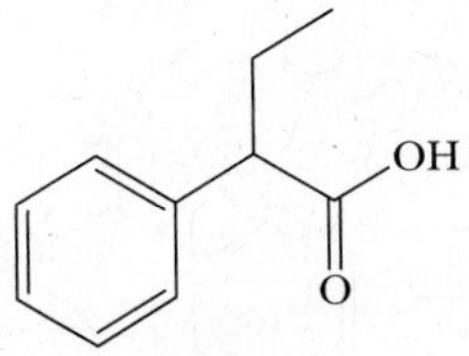

$+\ 2CO_2\ +\ 2NH_4^+$

2-Phenylbutanoic acid

14.39

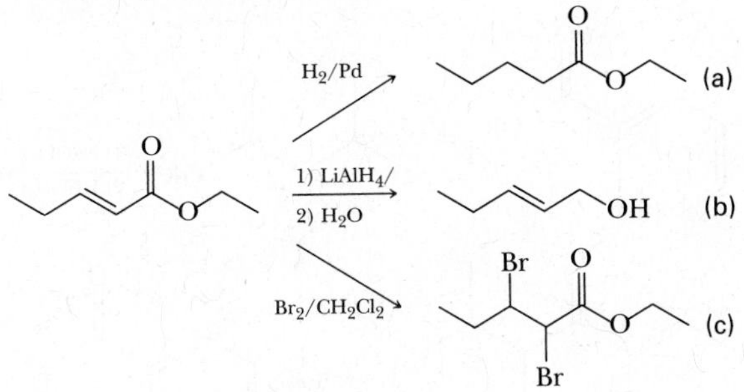

14.41

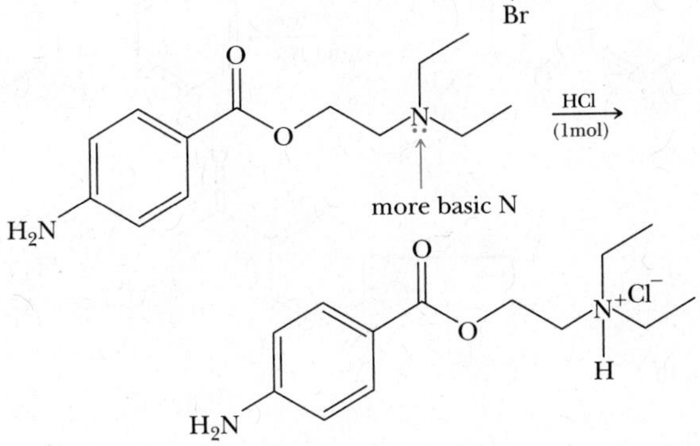

14.43 (a)

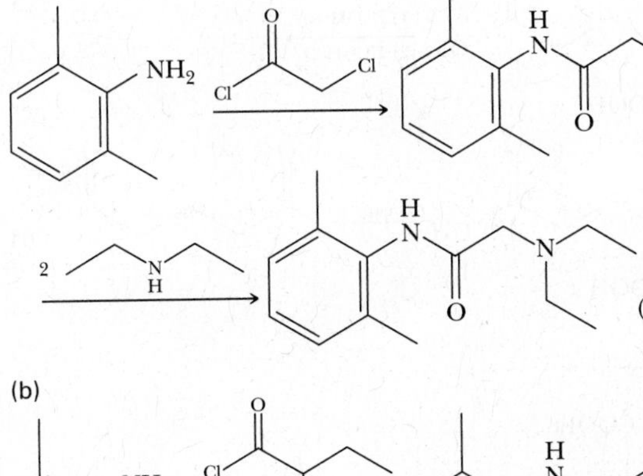

Lidocaine (Xylocaine)

(b)

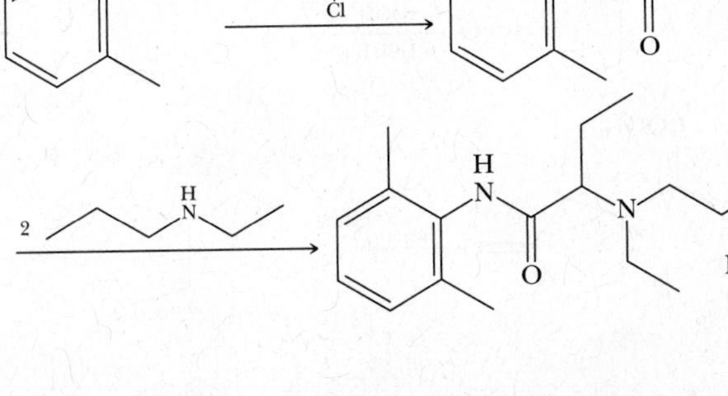

Etidocaine (Duranest)

(c)

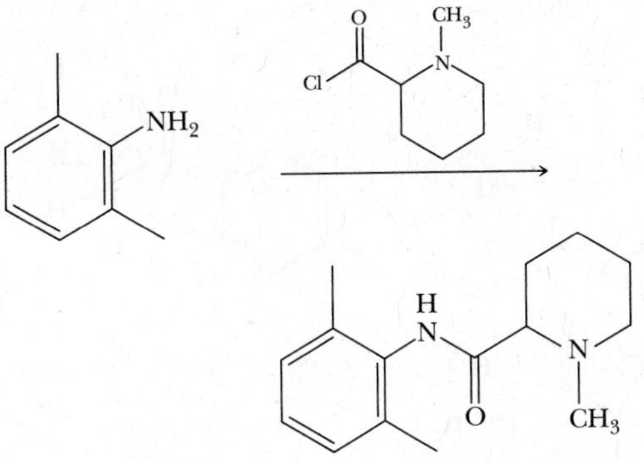

Mepivacaine (Carbocaine)

14.45 1) HNO_3/H_2SO_4 2) H_2CrO_4 3) CH_3OH/H_2SO_4 4) H_2/Ni

14.47 (a)

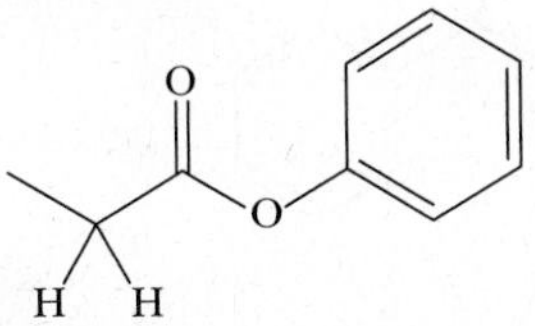

most acidic

(b)

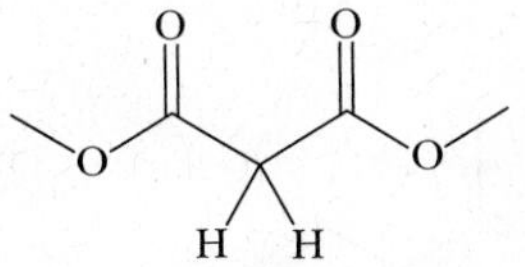

most acidic

14.49 Resonance structures can be drawn to show that the β-carbon is positively charged.

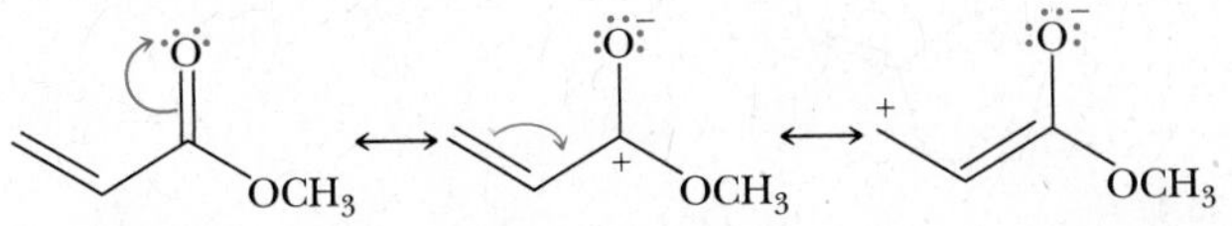

14.51 Amides have partial double-bond character between the carbon and nitrogen atoms.

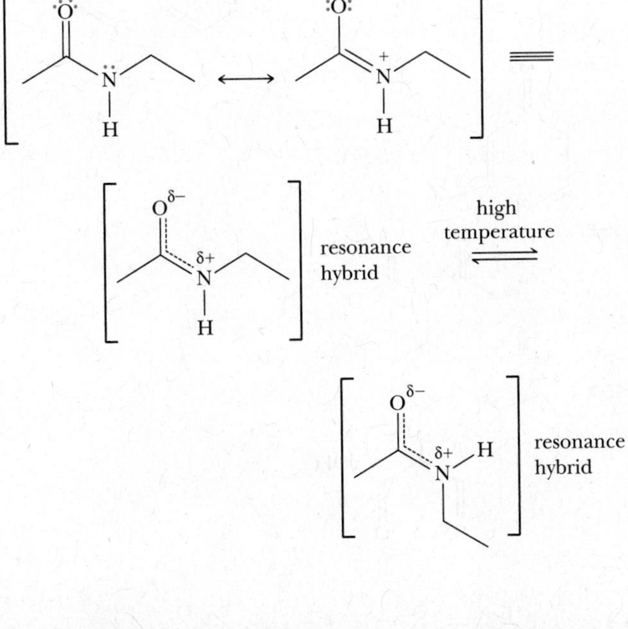

CHAPTER 15 Enolate Anions

Problems

15.1 (a)

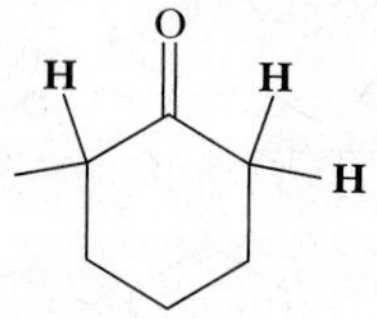

(b)

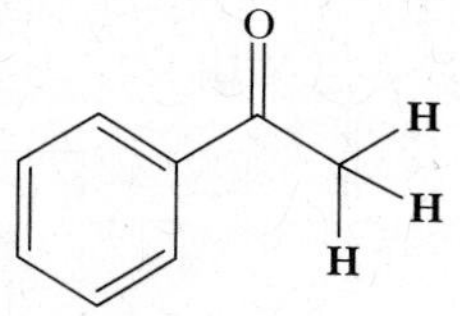

(c)

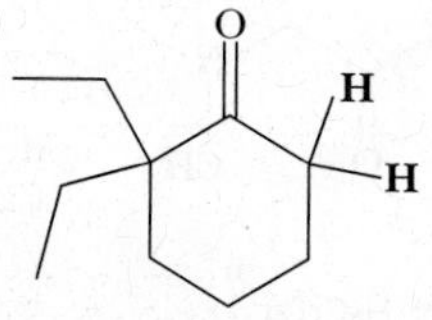

15.2 (a)

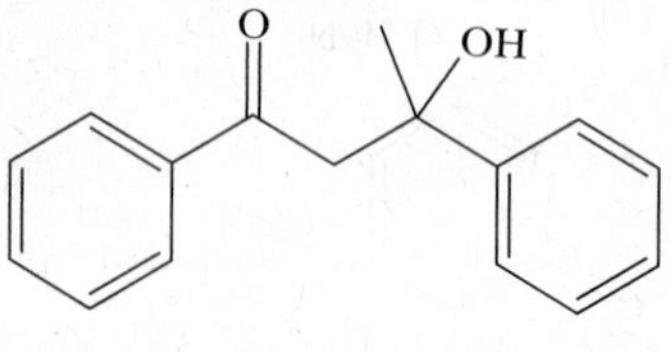

(b)

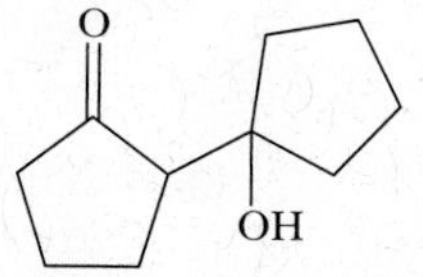

15.3 (a)

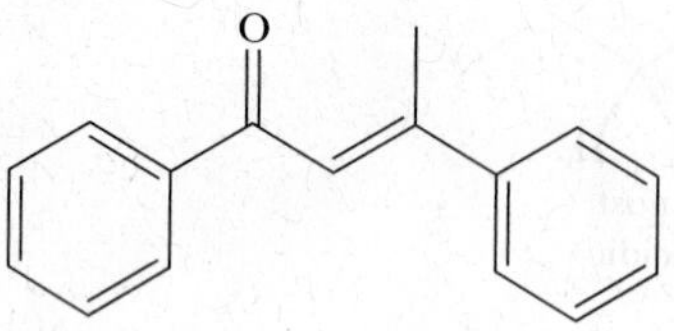

(b)

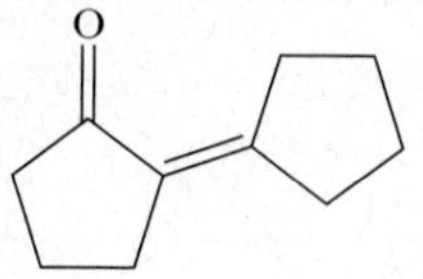

15.4

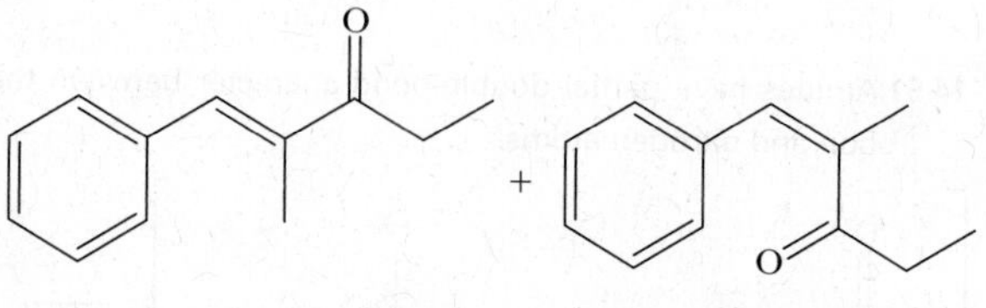

15.5

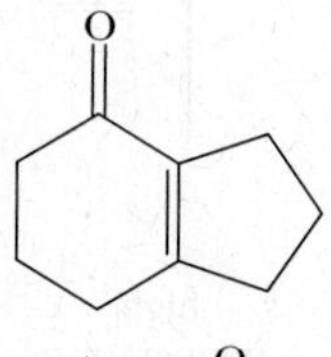

15.6

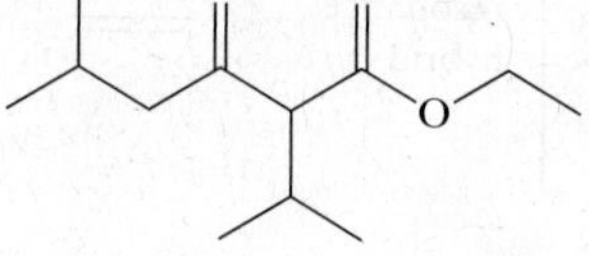

15.7

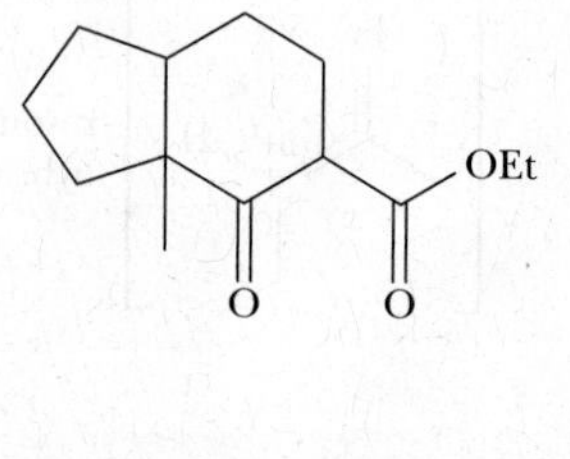

15.8

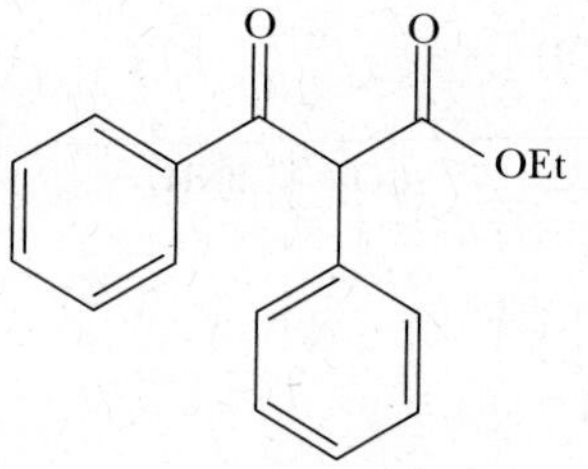

15.9

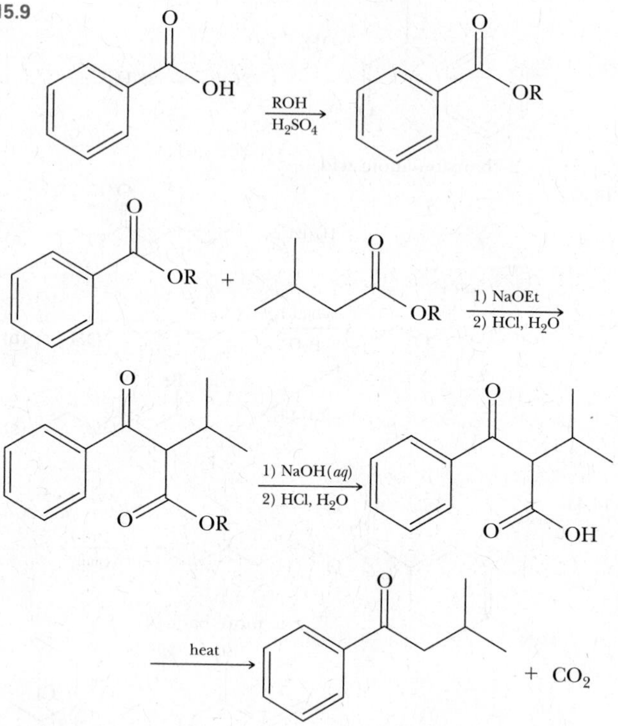

15.10

(a)

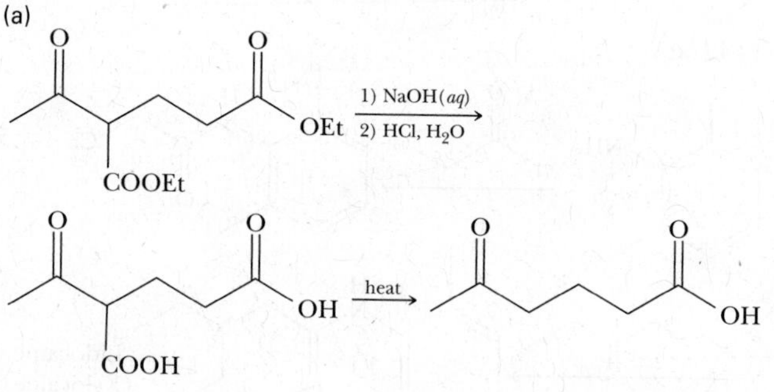

(b)

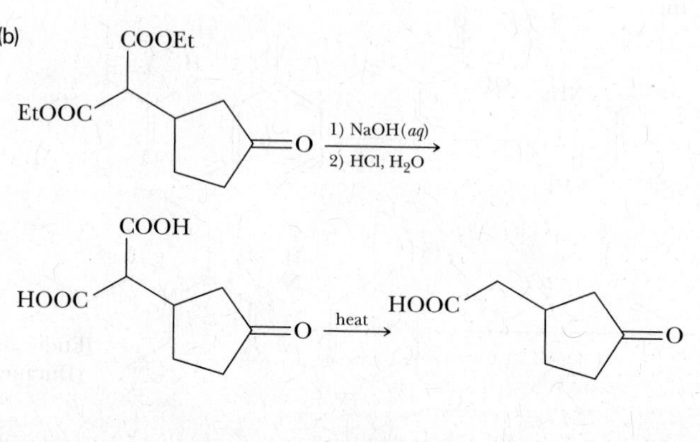

15.11

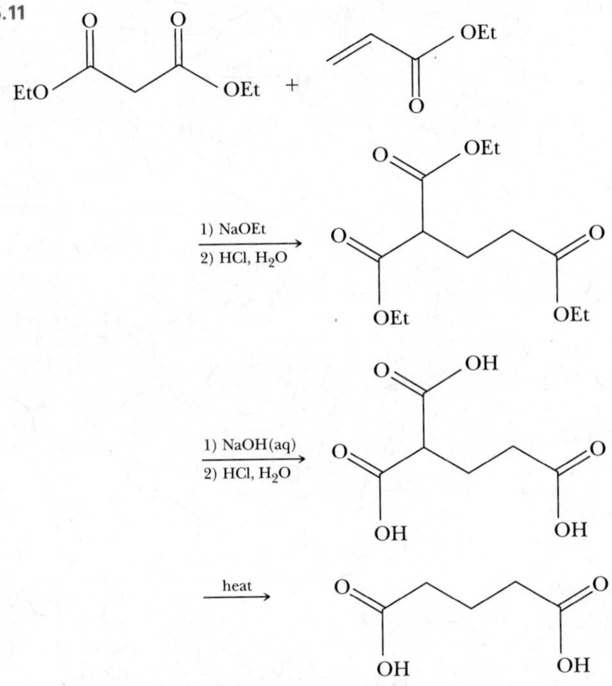

15.12

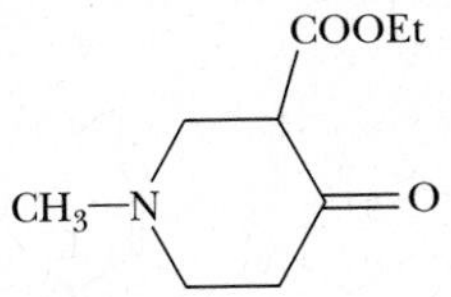

End-of-Chapter Problems

15.13 (a)

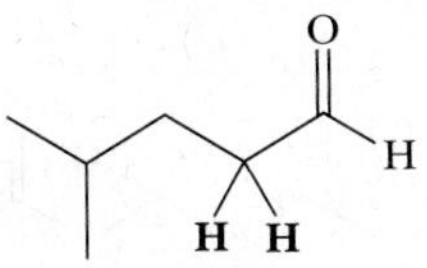

(b)

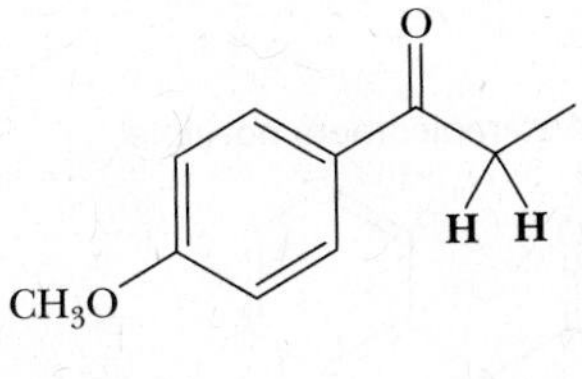

(c)

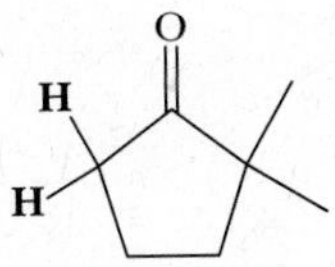

(d)

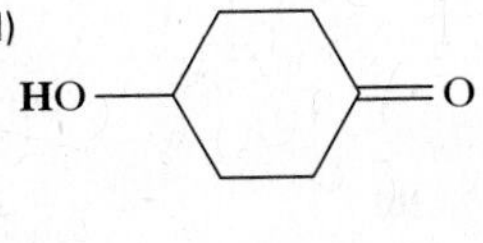

(e)

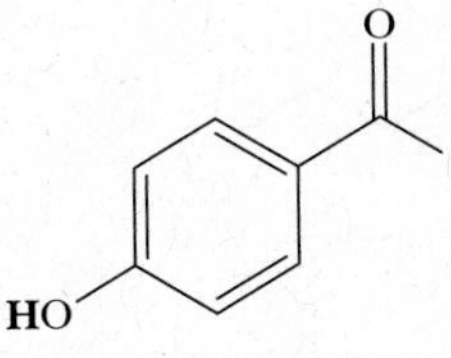

(f)

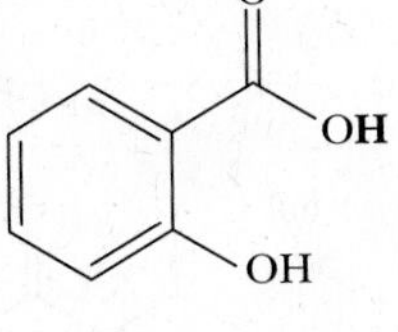

15.15

(a)

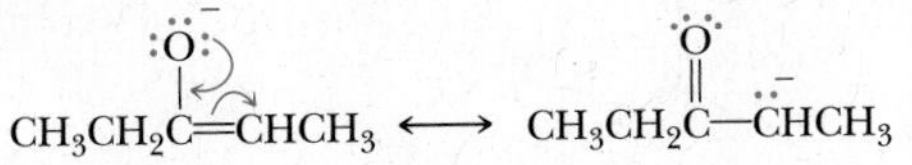

(b)

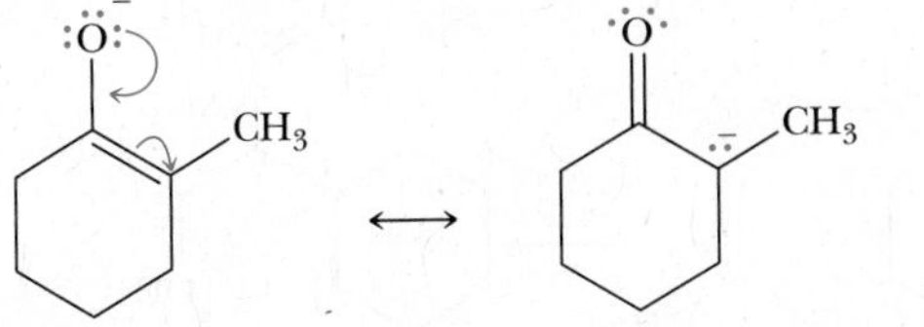

(c)

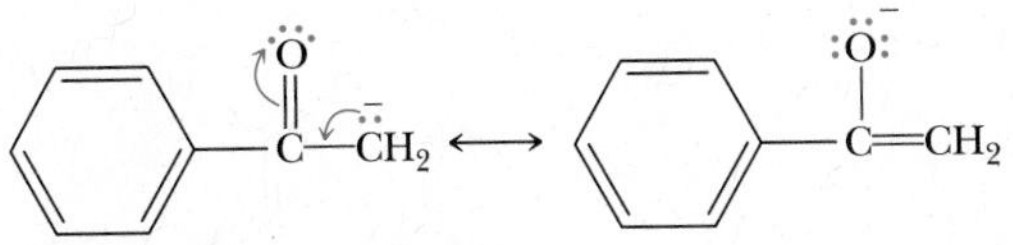

15.17 (a)

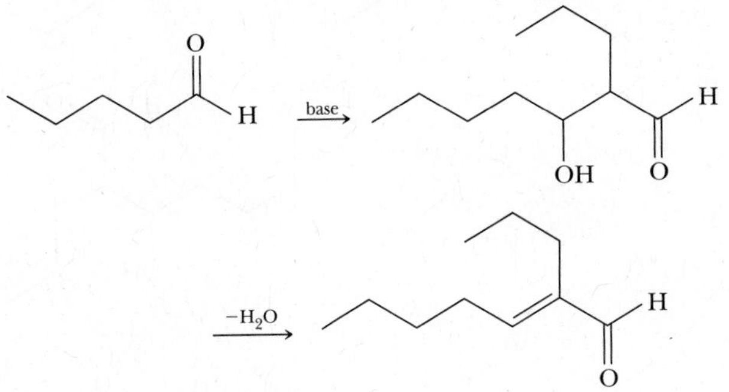

(b)

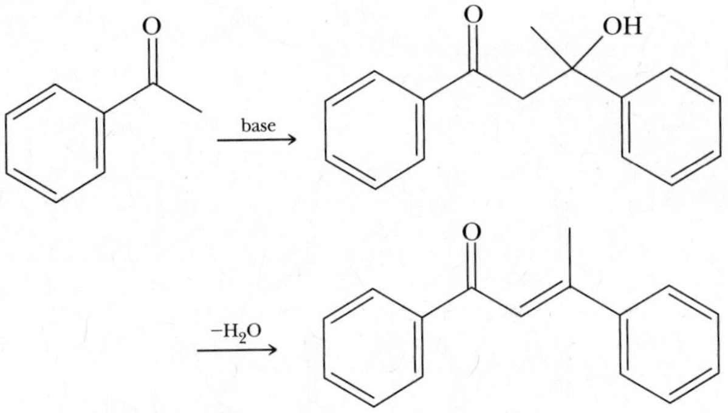

(c)

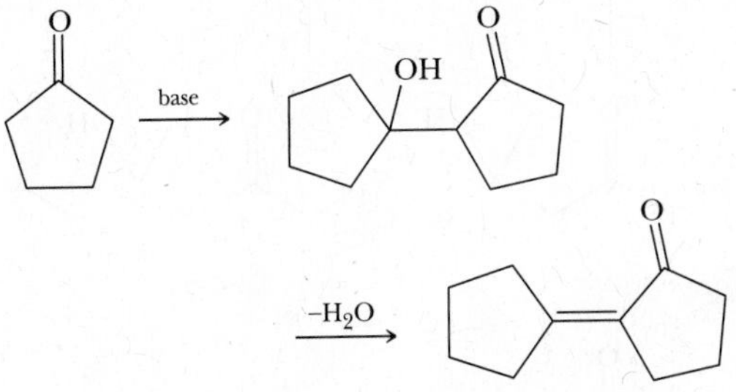

(d)

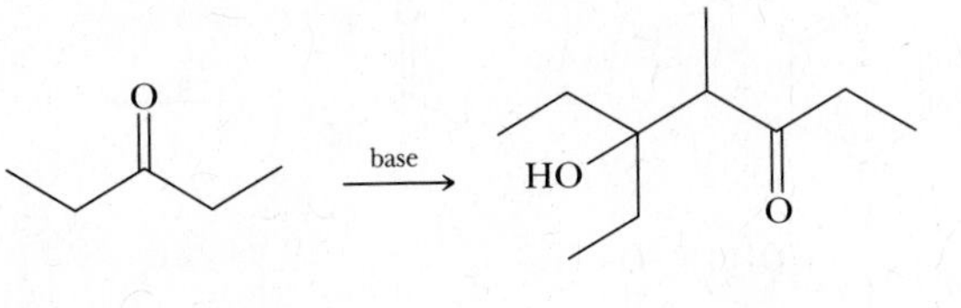

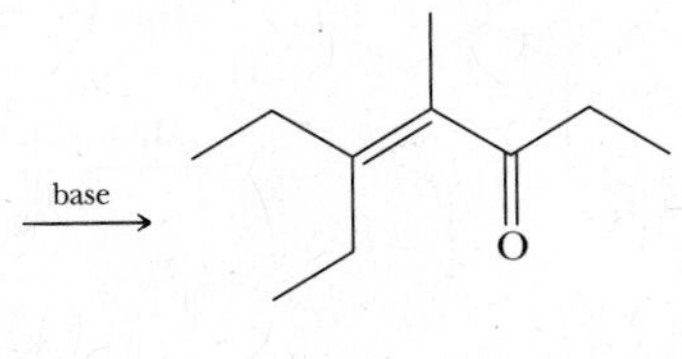

(e)

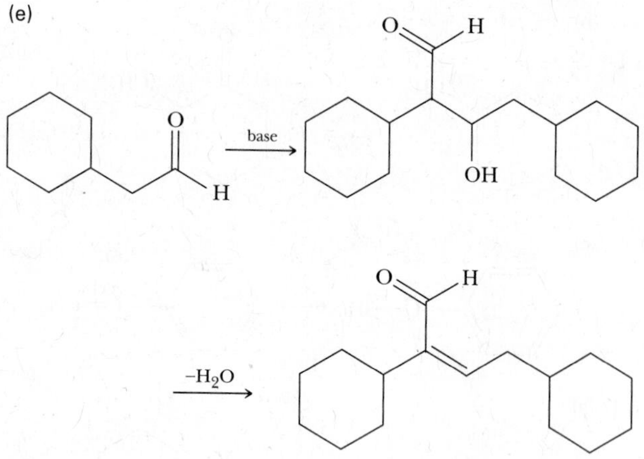

(f)

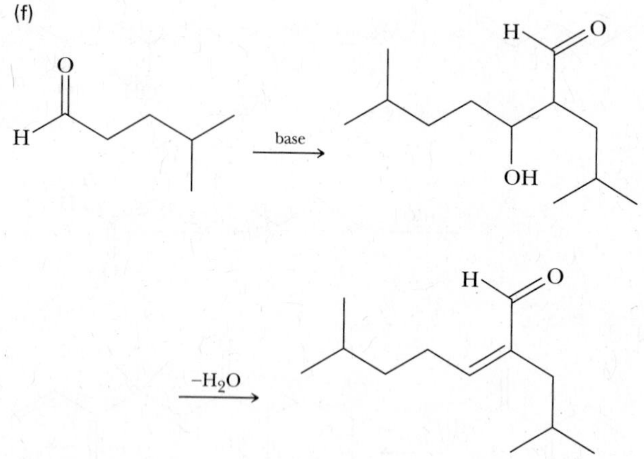

15.19 (a)

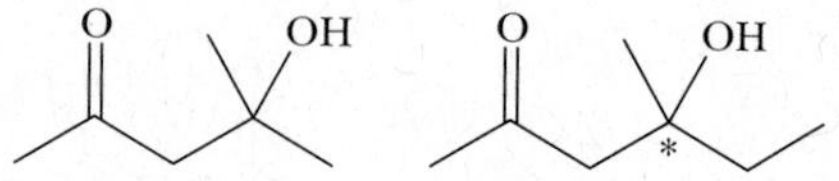

(b)

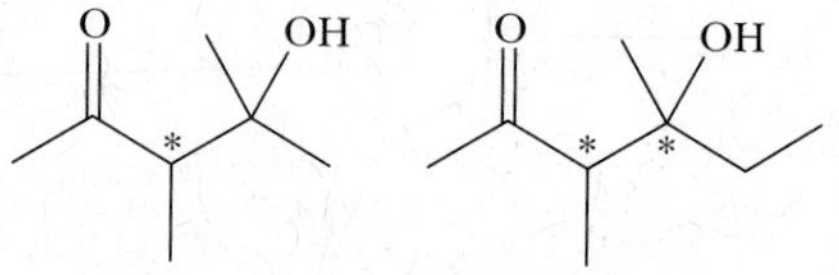

(c)

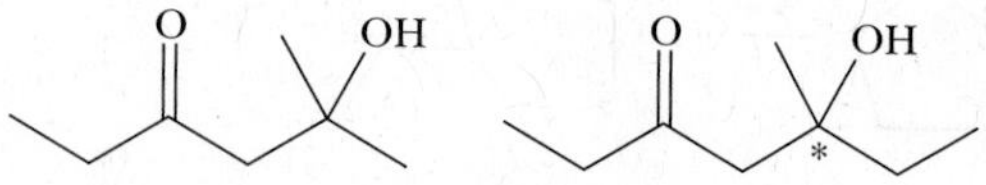

15.21 (a)

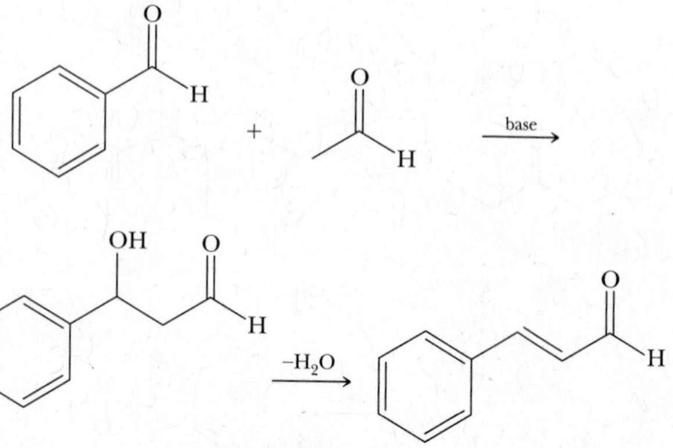

(b)

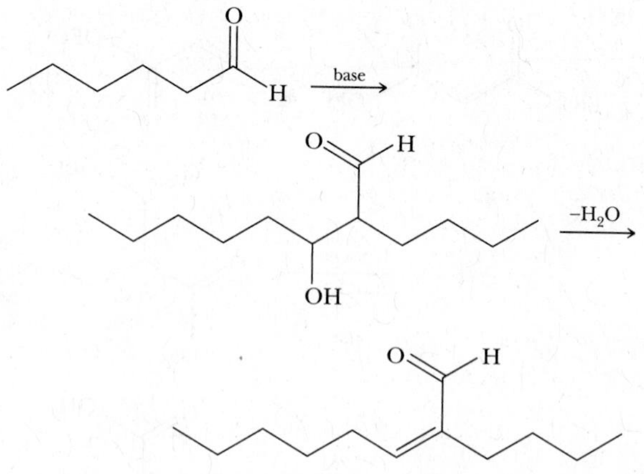

15.23

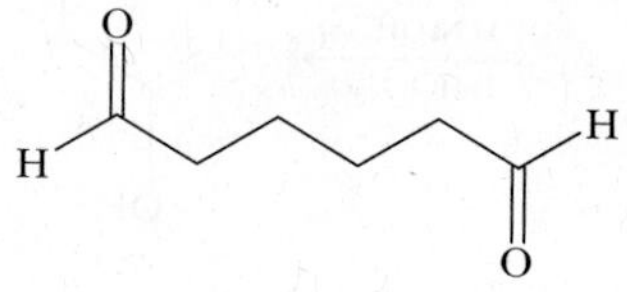

15.25 (a)

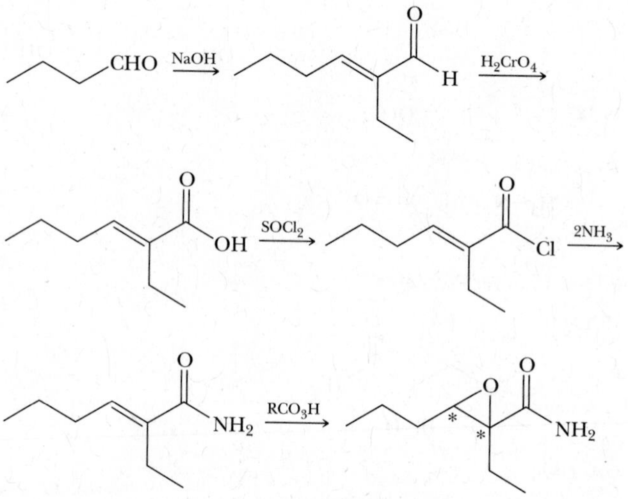

(b) 2 stereocenters, 4 stereoisomers possible

15.27 (a)

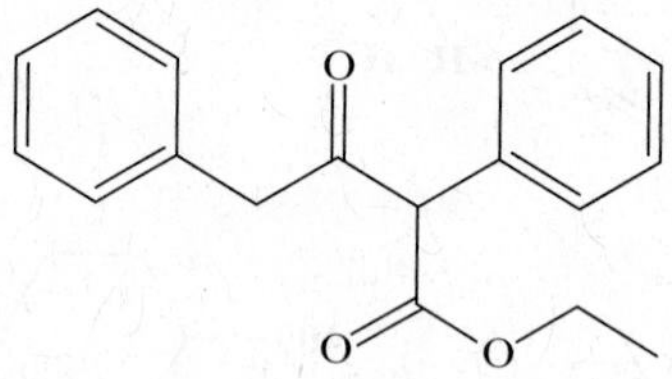

(b)

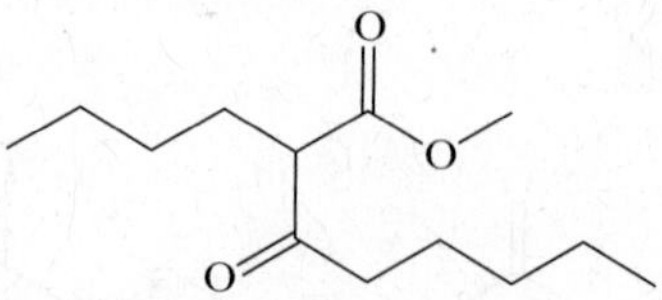

(c)

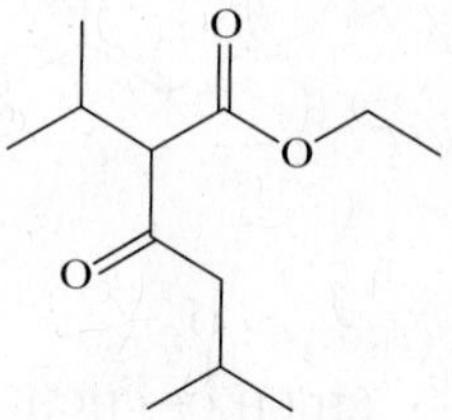

15.29

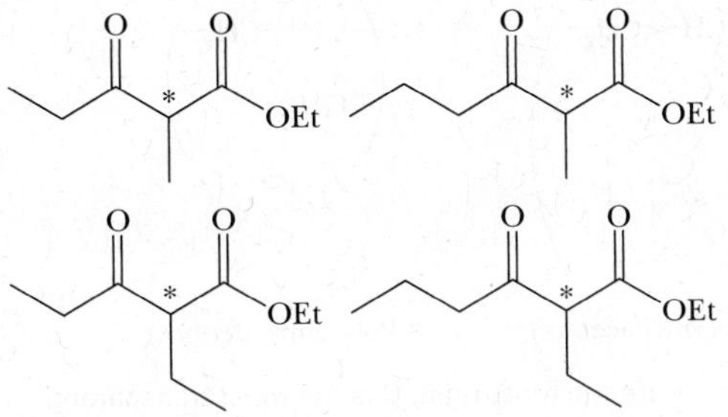

15.31

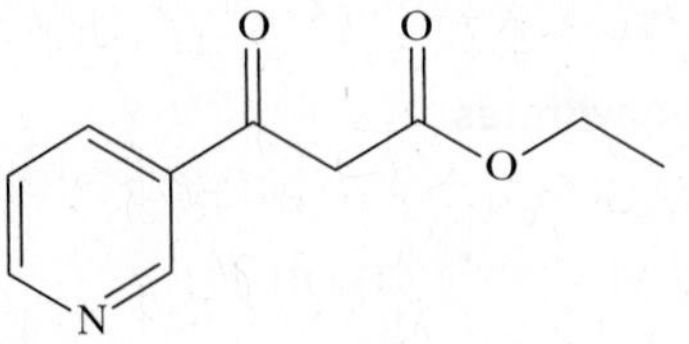

15.33 (a)

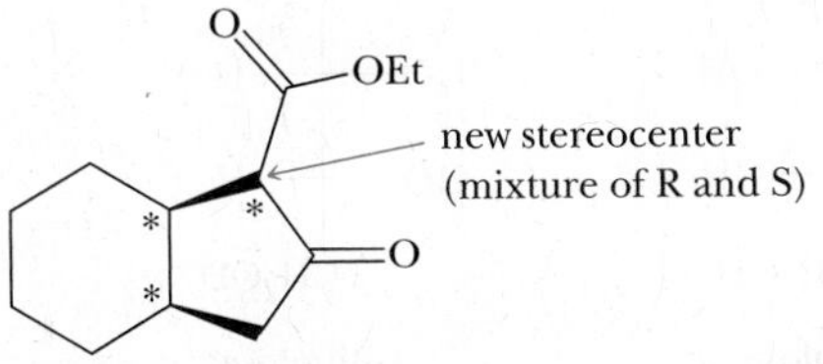

(b)

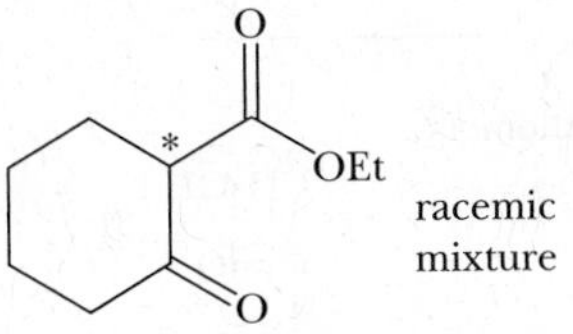

15.35

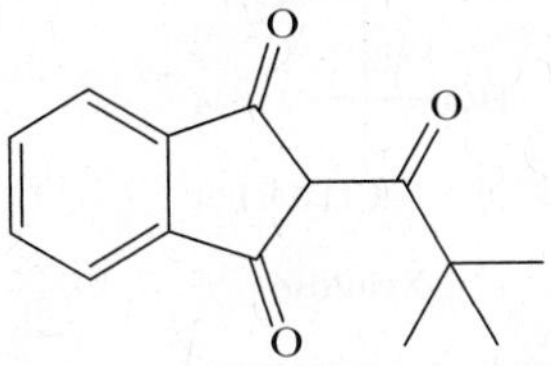

15.37 (a)

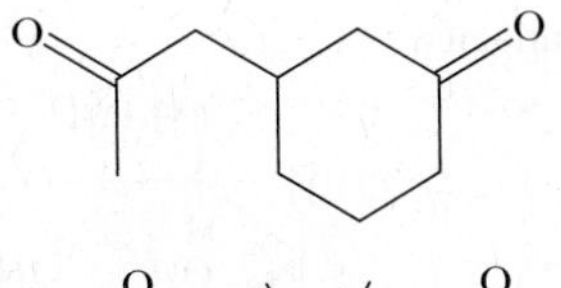

(b)

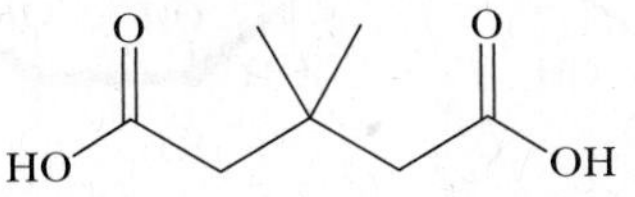

15.39 (a) Ethyl 2-propenoate, Michael addition performed twice

(b) Strong base, Dieckmann reaction, followed by aqueous acid

(c) Saponify the ester with NaOH, treat the carboxylate salt with HCl, and then heat the compound.

(d) Aniline

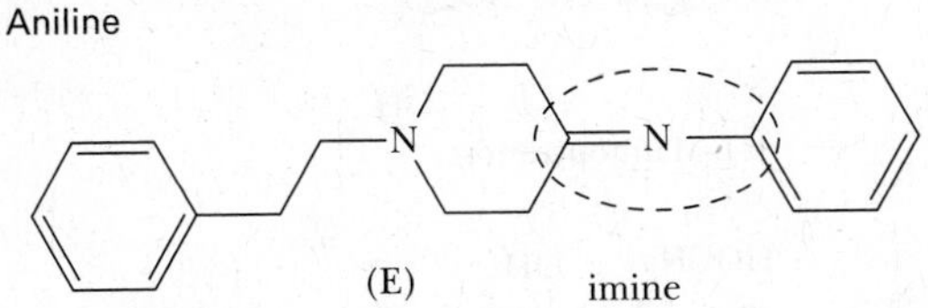

(e) H_2/Pd

(f) An acid chloride, anhydride, or ester

(g) Achiral because it does not have any stereocenters

15.41 (a) NaOH, aldol reaction

(b) Heating in NaOH or H_2SO_4

(c) H_2/Pd

(d) Fischer esterification with *p*-methoxycinnamic acid

15.43

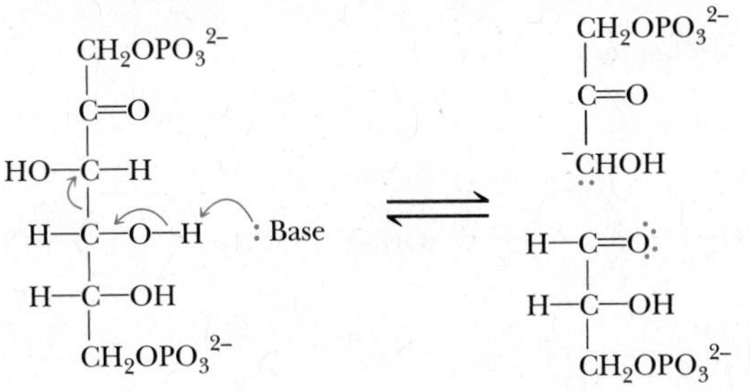

15.45

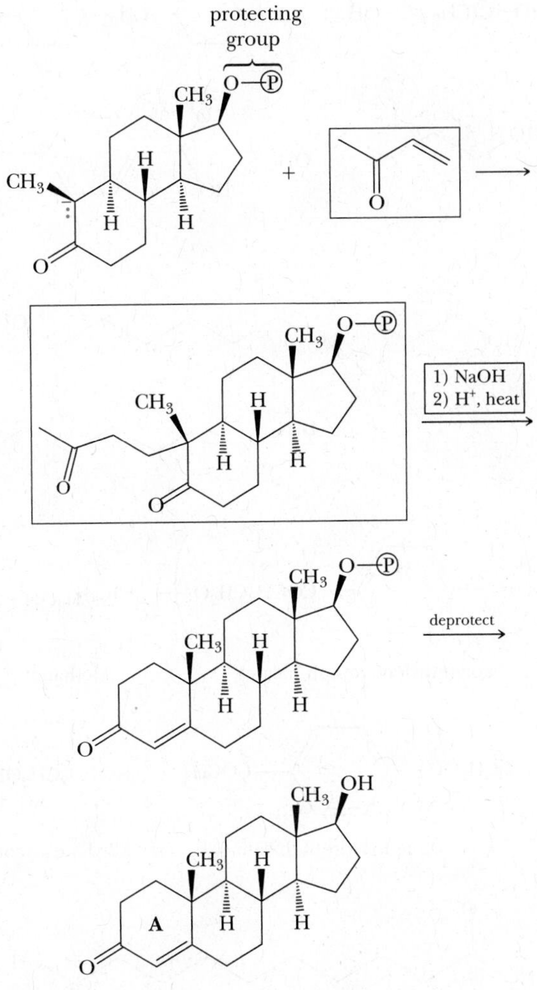

CHAPTER 16 Organic Polymer Chemistry

Problems

16.1

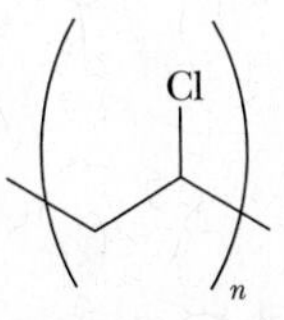

Poly(vinyl chloride)

16.2

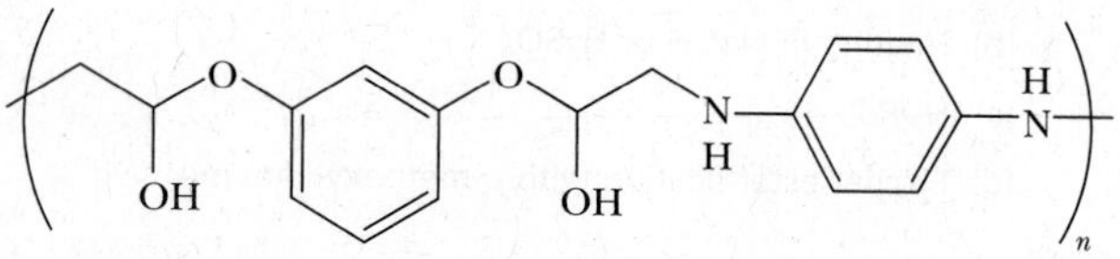

End-of-Chapter Problems

16.3 (a)

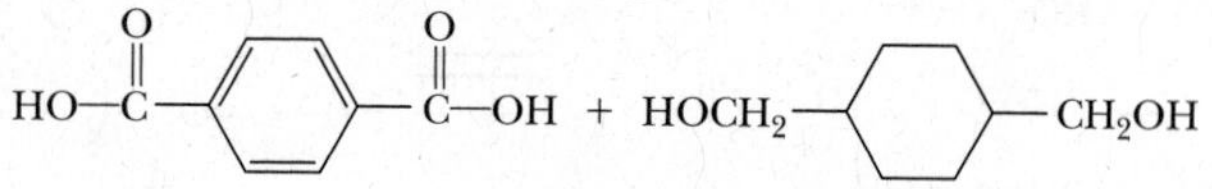

(b)

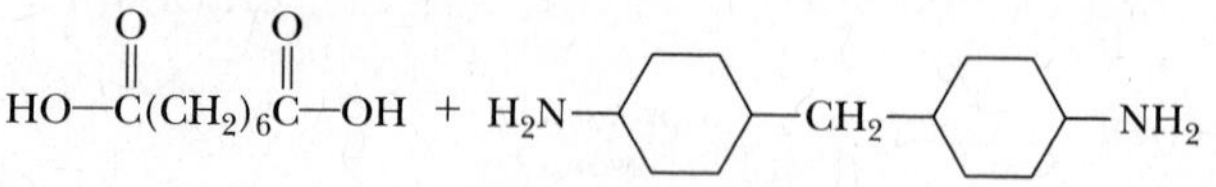

(c)

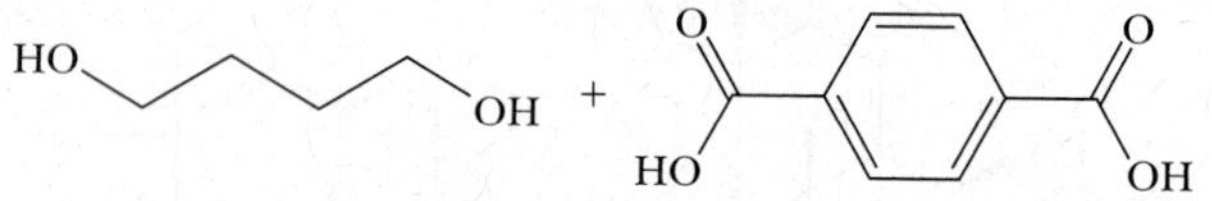

(d)

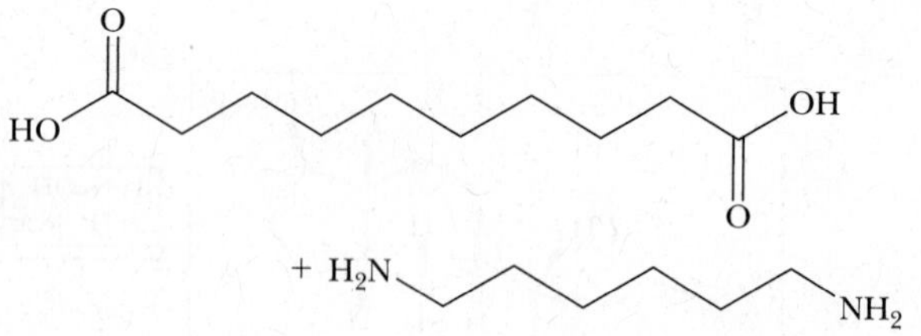

16.5

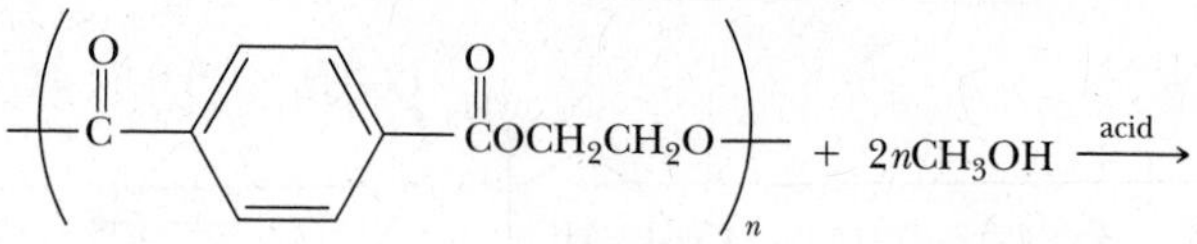

Poly(ethylene terephthalate) Methanol

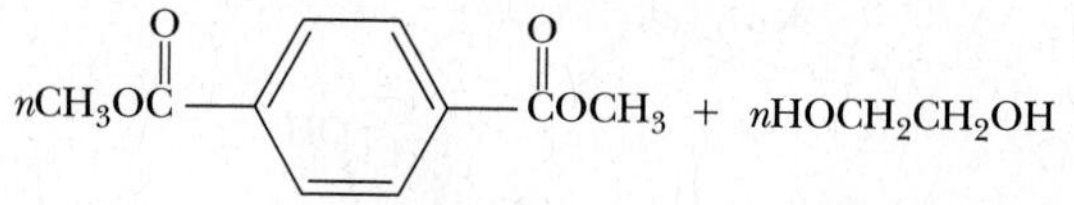

Dimethyl terephthalate Ethylene glycol

16.7

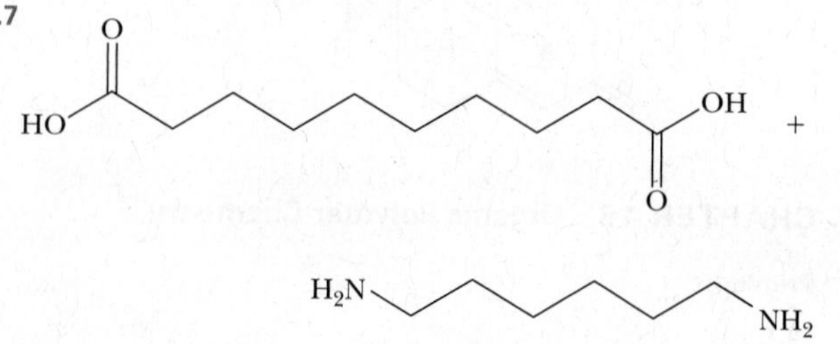

16.9 (a)

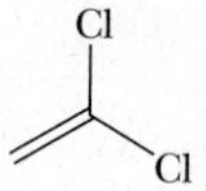

(b)

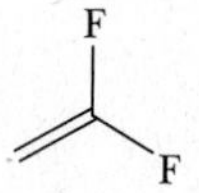

16.11 The chains are less able to pack together in the solid state.

16.13

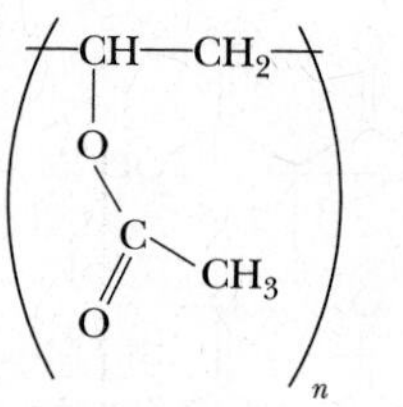

Poly(vinyl acetate)

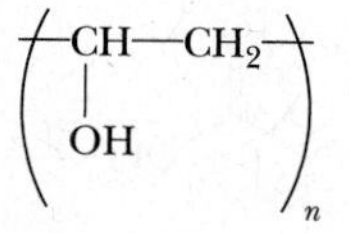

Poly(vinyl alcohol)

16.15 A and B are the most rigid. C is the most transparent.

16.17 Yes

CHAPTER 17 Carbohydrates

Problems

17.1

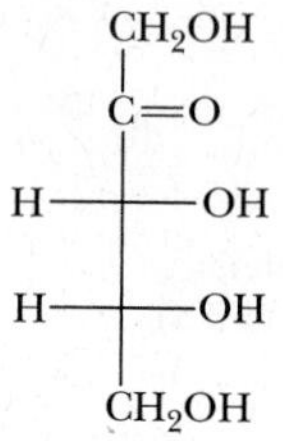

D-Ribulose

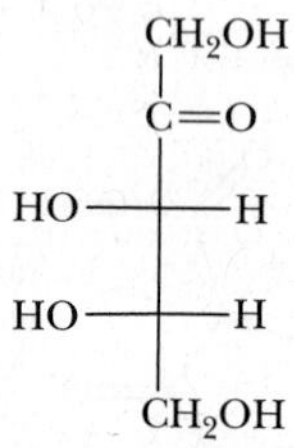

L-Ribulose

enantiomers

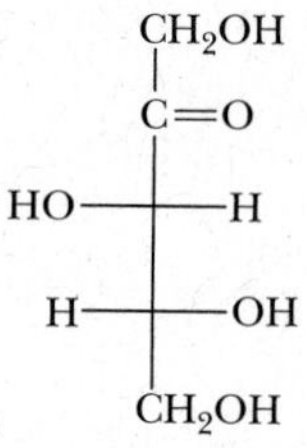

D-Xylulose

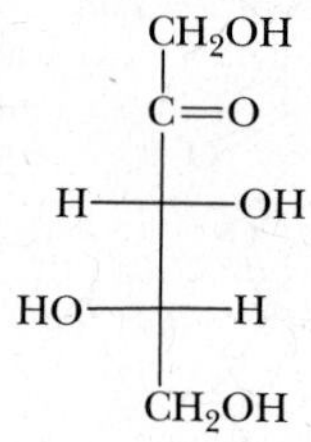

L-Xylulose

enantiomers

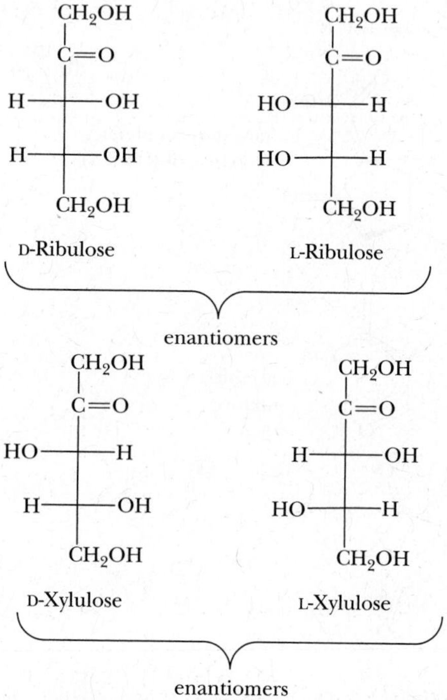

17.2

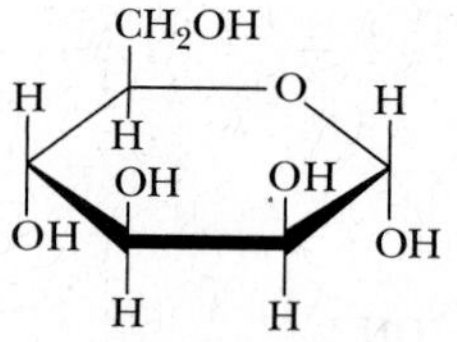

α-D-Mannopyranose
(α-D-mannose)

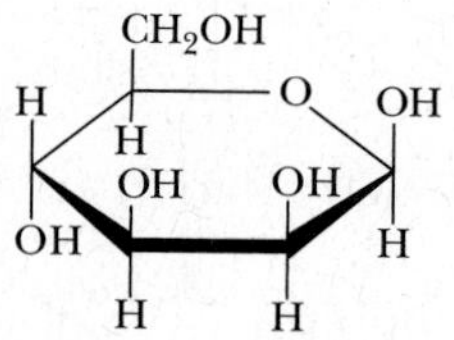

β-D-Mannopyranose
(β-D-mannose)

17.3

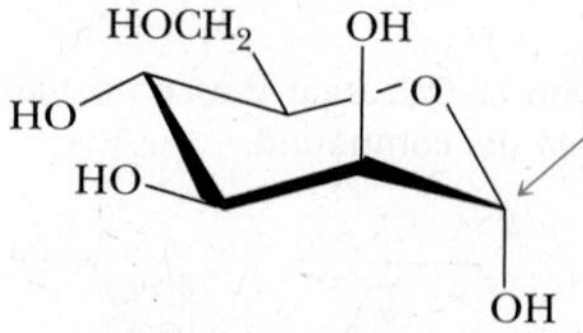

anomeric carbon

α-D-Mannopyranose

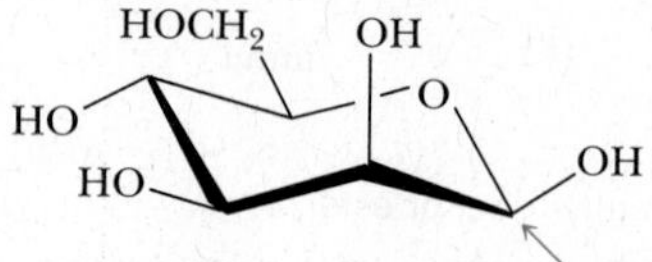

anomeric carbon

β-D-Mannopyranose

17.4 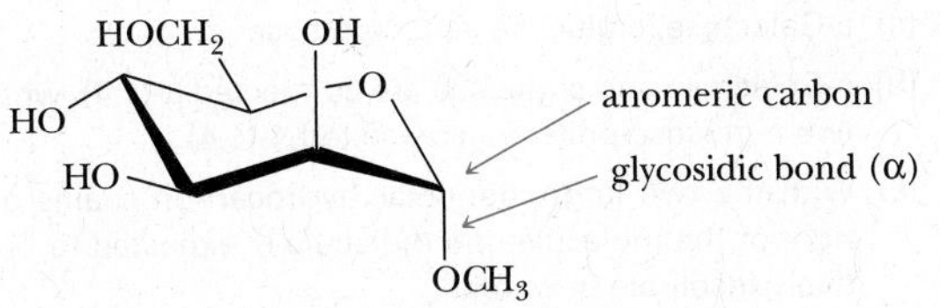

17.5 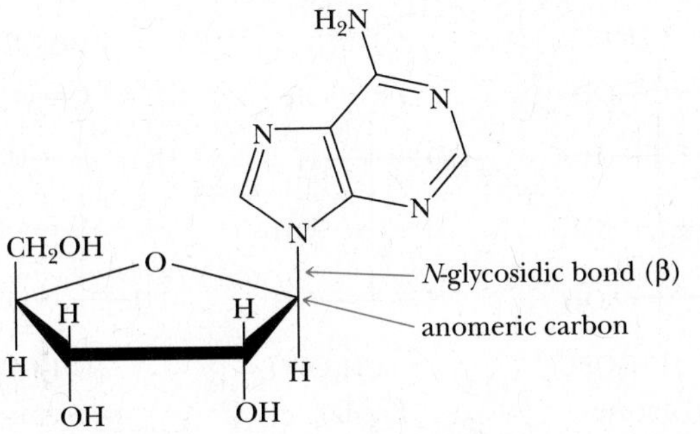

17.6 No, because erythritol is a meso compound

17.7 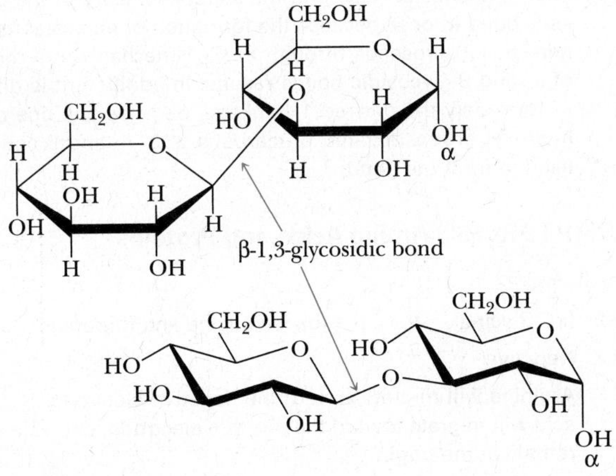

End-of-Chapter Problems

17.9 D-Glucose

17.11 The designations refer to the configuration of the penultimate carbon. If the monosaccharide is drawn as a Fischer projection and the —OH group bonded to this carbon is on the right, the D designation is used; likewise, a monosaccharide is L if the —OH group is on the left.

17.13 (a) and (c) are D-monosaccharides, while (b) and (d) are L-monosaccharides.

17.15 Mono- and disaccharides are polar compounds and are able to participate in hydrogen bonding with water molecules.

17.17 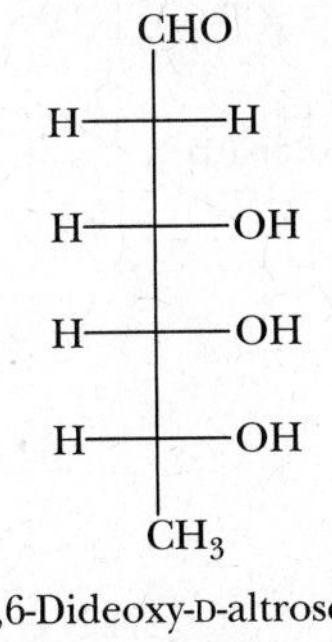

2,6-Dideoxy-D-altrose

17.19 The α and β designations refer to the position of the hydroxyl (—OH) group on the anomeric carbon relative to the terminal —CH_2OH group. If both of these groups are on the same side of the ring (*cis*), a β designation is assigned. If the two groups are on the opposite side of the ring (*trans*), the monosaccharide is assigned α.

17.21 No, because anomers are compounds that differ only in the configuration of the anomeric carbon. These two compounds are enantiomers.

17.23 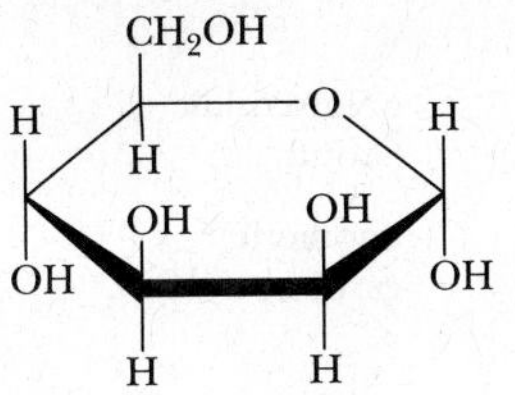

α-D-Mannose

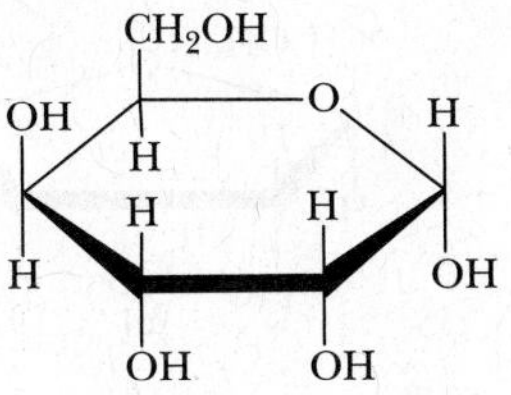

α-D-Gulose

17.25 (a) 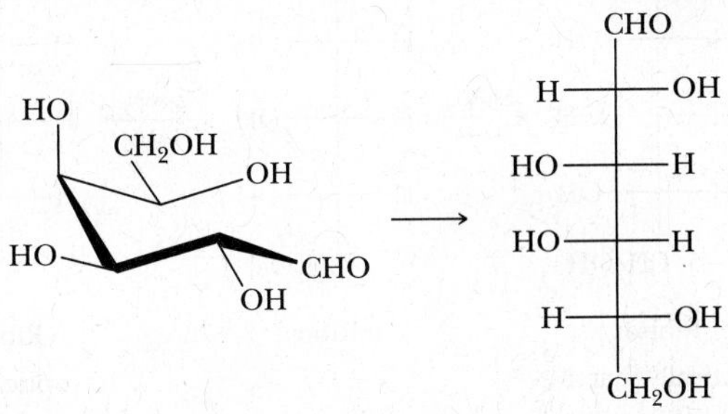

D-Galactose

(b) 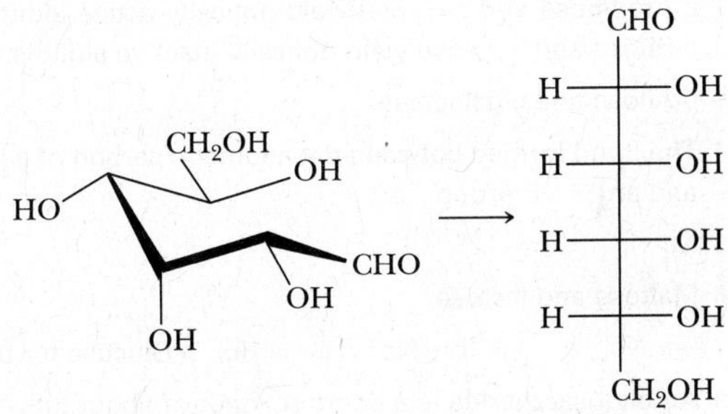

D-Allose

17.27 Mutarotation involves the formation of an equilibrium mixture of the two anomers of a carbohydrate. This process can be detected by observing the change in the optical activity of the solution over time.

17.29 Yes, and the value will change to –52.7° (an equilibrium mixture of α- and β-L-glucose).

17.31 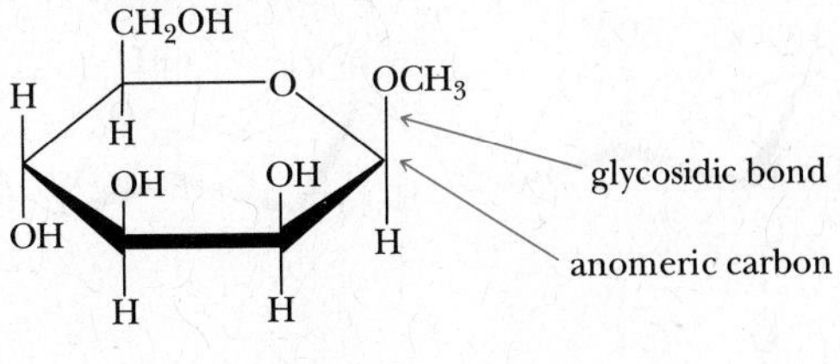

17.33 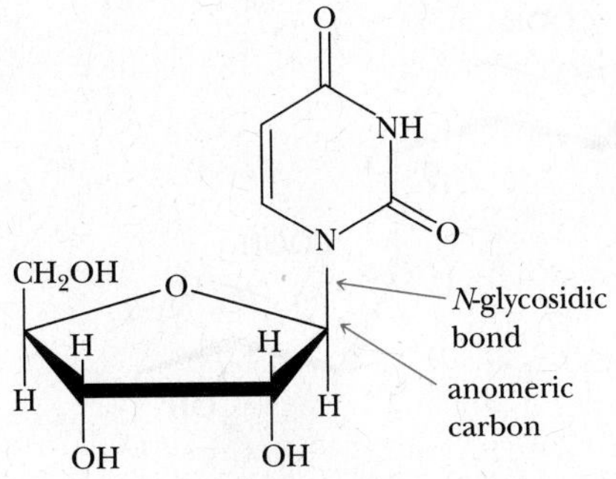

(a)

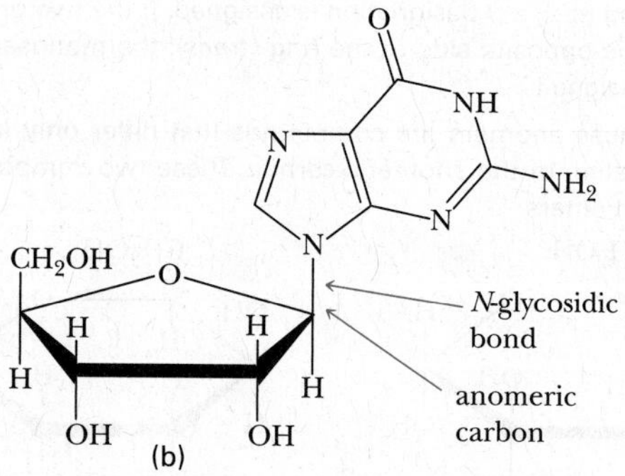

(b)

17.35

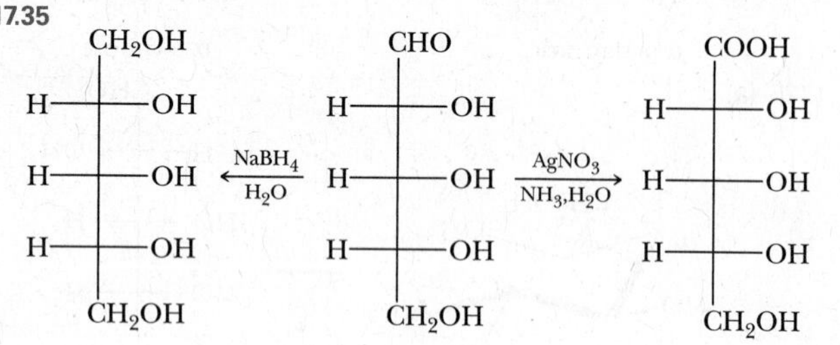

Ribitol — optically inactive (meso)
D-Ribose
D-Ribonic acid — optically active (chiral)

17.37 D-Arabinose and D-lyxose yield optically active alditols, while D-ribose and D-xylose yield optically inactive alditols.

17.39 D-Allose and D-galactose

17.41 The bond formed between the anomeric carbon of a glycoside and an —OR group

17.43 No

17.45 Maltose and lactose

17.47 (a) No (b) No (c) D-Glucose for both

17.49 An oligosaccharide is a short polymer of about 6 to 10 monosaccharides. While there is no definite rule, polysaccharides generally contain more than 10 monosaccharides.

17.51 Both types are composed of D-glucose, and both contain α-1,4-glycosidic bonds. However, amylose is unbranched, while amylopectin contains branches that result from α-1,6-glycosidic bonds.

17.53 (a)

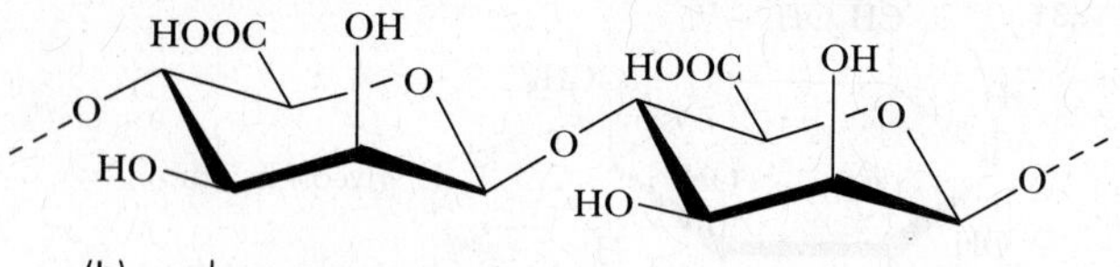

(b)

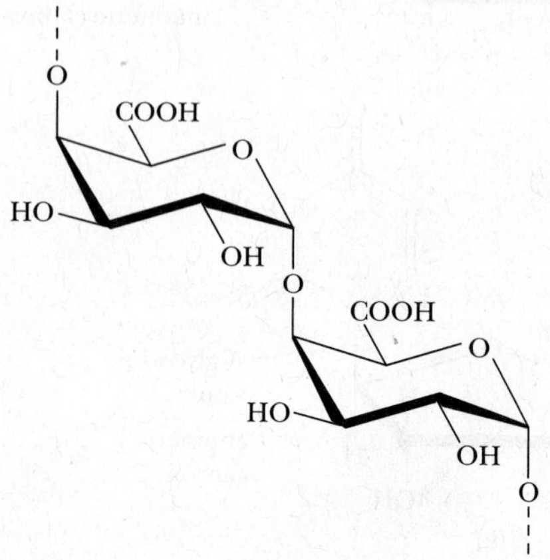

17.55 (a) D-Galactose, D-glucose, and D-glucose

(b) D-Galactose and D-glucose are connected α-(1,4), while the two D-glucose units are connected β-(1,4).

(c) With the two large, nonpolar hydrocarbon chains on the right of the molecule, the molecule is expected to be relatively insoluble in water.

17.57

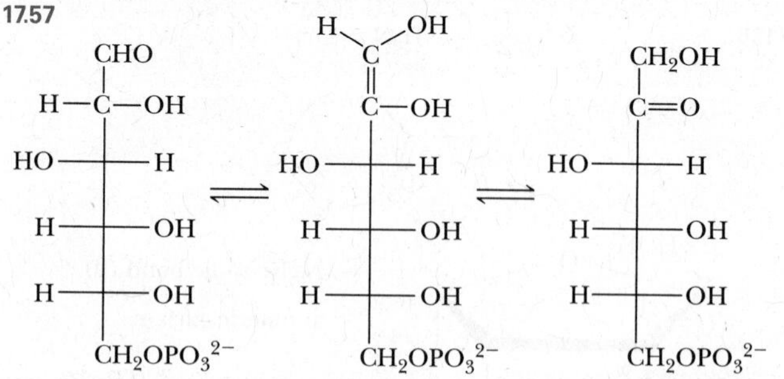

D-Glucose 6-phosphate — Enediol — D-Fructose 6-phosphate

17.59 First, it is difficult to control the stereochemistry of the glycosidic bond (α or β) because the formation of an acetal (from a hemiacetal) proceeds through an S_N1 mechanism; a mixture of α- and β-glycosidic bonds results. In addition, it is difficult to form only the desired 1,4-linkage, because any one of the hydroxyl groups located on carbons 2, 3, 4, and 6 could be used to form the bond.

CHAPTER 18 Amino Acids and Proteins

Problems

18.1 (a) Glycine (b) Isoleucine and threonine

18.2 Negative

18.3 Arginine will migrate toward the negative electrode, glutamic acid will migrate toward the positive electrode, and valine will remain at the origin.

18.4 Net charge is +1.

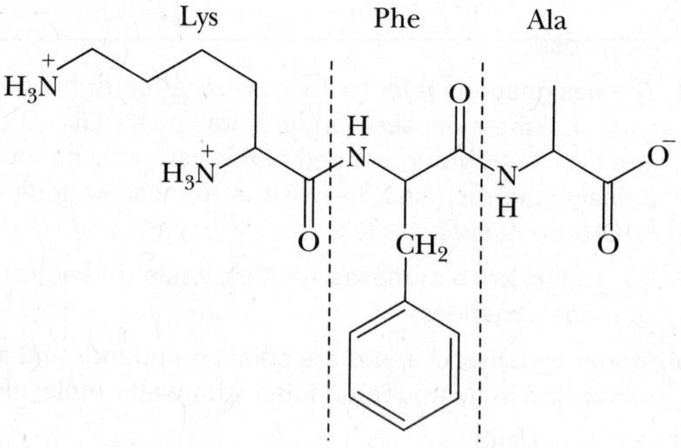

18.5 (a) and (b)

18.6 Ala-Glu-Arg-Thr-Phe-Lys-Lys-Val-Met-Ser-Trp

18.7 Aspartic and glutamic acids

End-of-Chapter Problems

18.9 *S*

18.11

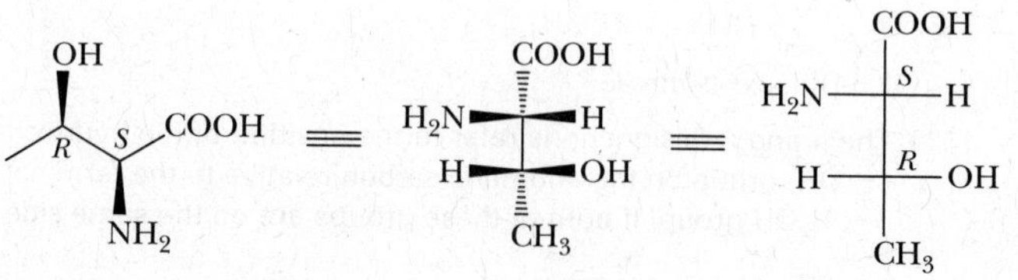

18.13 (a)
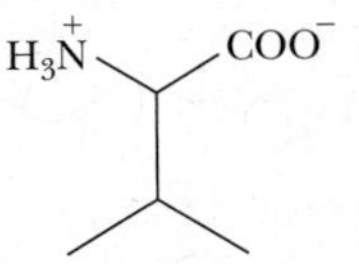
(b)
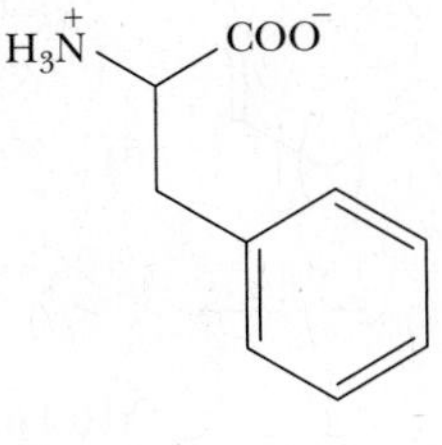
(c)
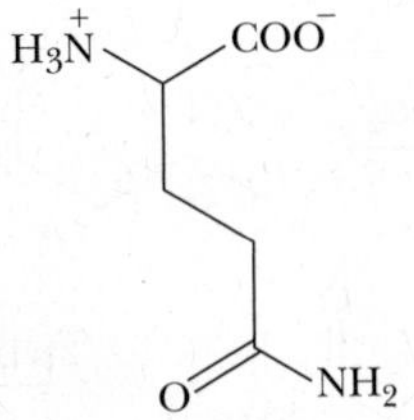

18.15 Arg is a basic amino acid because its side chain is protonated (positively charged) at neutral pH. Lys and His are the other two basic amino acids.

18.17
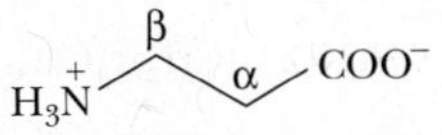
β-Alanine

18.19 The biosynthesis of histamine occurs via the decarboxylation of histidine.

18.21 Serotonin and melatonin are both synthesized from tryptophan. In both cases, the biosynthesis involves a decarboxylation and an oxidation (hydroxylation) of the aromatic ring. In the case of melatonin, there are two more reactions: After the oxidation of the aromatic ring, the hydroxyl group is methylated, and the amino group is acetylated.

18.23 (a)
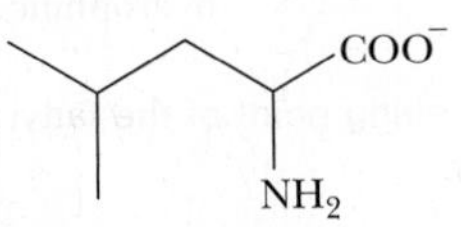
(b)
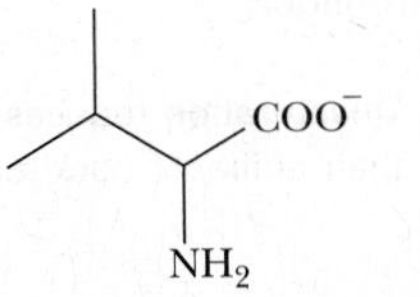
(c)
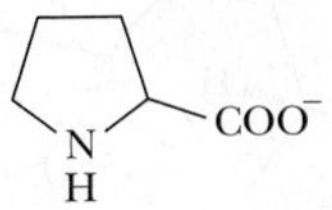
(d)
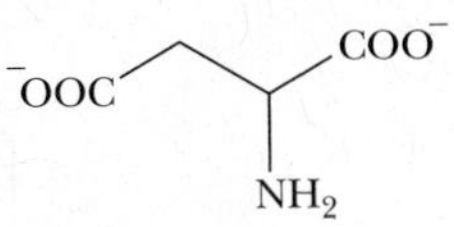

18.25

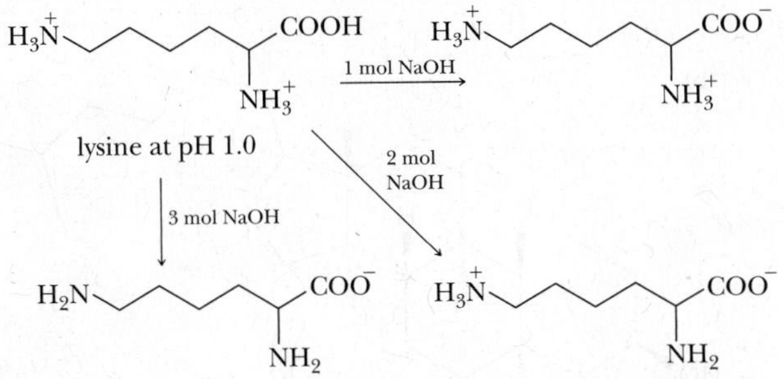

18.27 (a)
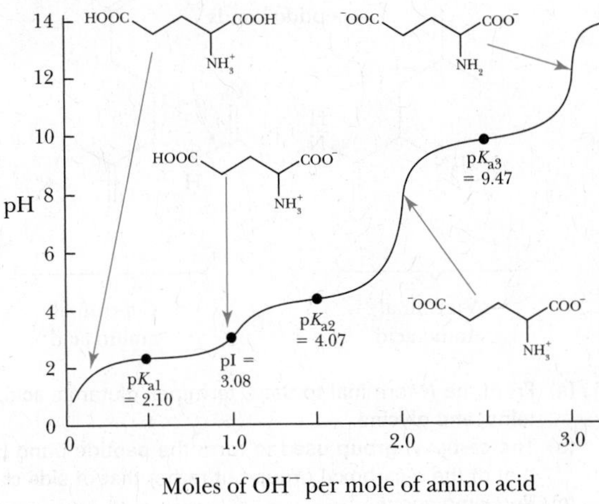

(b)
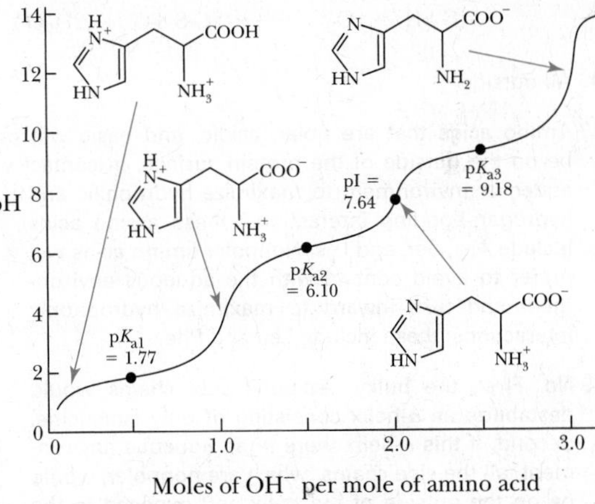

18.29 With glutamine, its pI value is determined by the pK_a values of the only two ionizable groups, the carboxylic acid (pK_a 2.17) and the α-amino group (pK_a 9.03).

18.31 Guanidine and the guanidino group are very strong amine bases due to the resonance stabilization of the conjugate *acid*, the guanidinium group.

18.33 (a) Cathode (b) Cathode (c) Cathode
(d) Anode (e) Anode (f) Cathode

18.35 Neutral amino acids

18.37 (a) 24 (b) 116,280

18.39 (a) Between residues 1 and 2
(b) Between residues 6 and 7, 10 and 11, 13 and 14, 22 and 23, and 25 and 26
(c) Between residues 12 and 13, 17 and 18, and 18 and 19
(d) Between residues 27 and 28

18.41 (a)
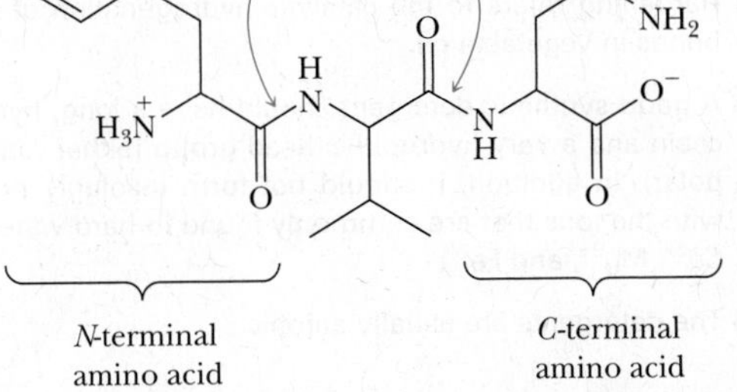

(b)

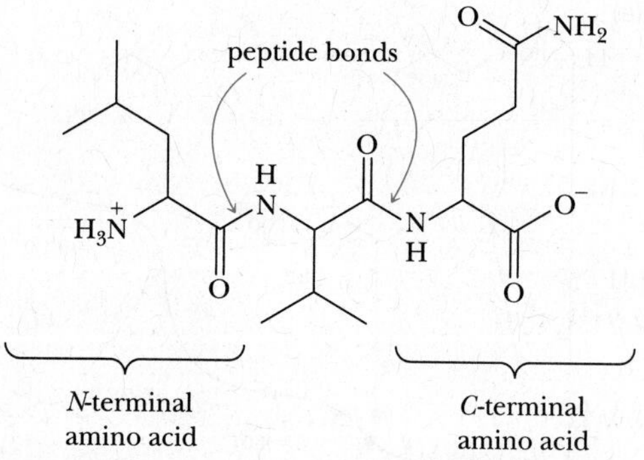

18.43 (a) From the *N*-terminal to the *C*-terminal: glutamic acid, cysteine, and glycine.
(b) The carboxyl group used to form the peptide bond is not that of the α-carboxyl group but rather that of side chain.
(c) Reducing agent
(d) Oxygen is reduced.

$$4\text{G-SH} + O_2 \longrightarrow 2\text{G-S-S-G} + 2H_2O$$

18.45 All outside

18.47 Amino acids that are polar, acidic, and basic will prefer to be on the outside of the protein surface, in contact with the aqueous environment to maximize hydrophilic and hydrogen-bonding interactions; these amino acids include Arg, Ser, and Lys. Nonpolar amino acids will prefer to avoid contact with the aqueous environment and turn inward to maximize hydrophobic interactions; these include Leu and Phe.

18.49 No. First, the bulky *sec*-butyl side chains would destabilize an α-helix consisting of only isoleucine. Second, if this α-helix were in an aqueous environment, all the side chains, which are nonpolar, would be on the outside of the helix and exposed to the aqueous environment.

CHAPTER 19 Lipids

Problems

19.1 (a) 3 (b) All are chiral.

End-of-Chapter Problems

19.3 Each triglyceride contains three hydrophobic regions (the hydrocarbon chains of the fatty acids) and three hydrophilic regions (the ester groups).

19.5 Increase

19.7 Animal fat: human Plant oil: olive

19.9 A very high percentage of the saturated fatty acids have a low molecular weight.

19.11 Hardening refers to the catalytic hydrogenation of the C=C bonds in vegetable oil.

19.13 A good synthetic detergent should have a long, hydrophobic chain and a very hydrophilic head group (either ionic or very polar). In addition, it should not form insoluble precipitates with the ions that are commonly found in hard water, such as Ca^{2+}, Mg^{2+}, and Fe^{2+}.

19.15 The detergents are usually anionic.

19.17 (a)

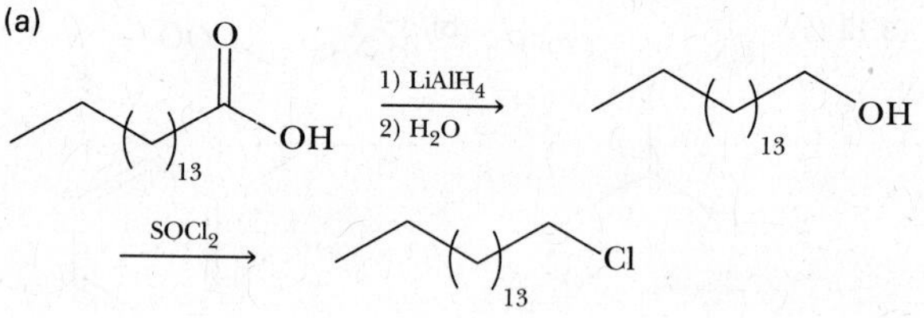

(HCl may also be used)

(b)

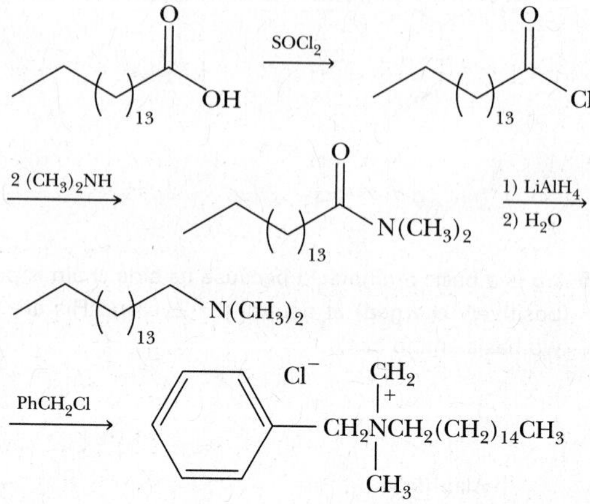

19.19

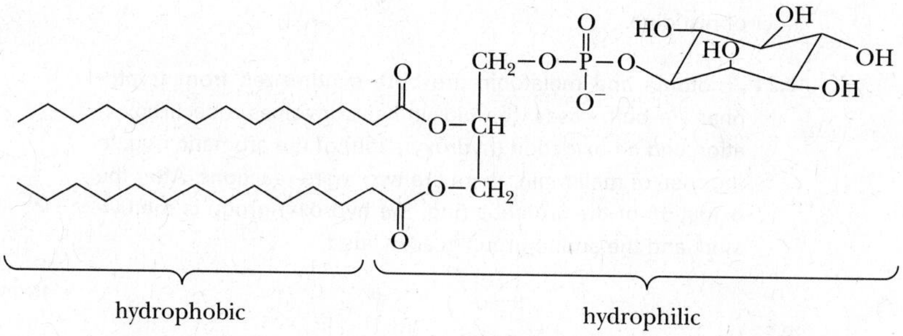

19.21 Unsaturation reduces the melting point of the fatty acids and their ability to pack together.

19.23

(a)

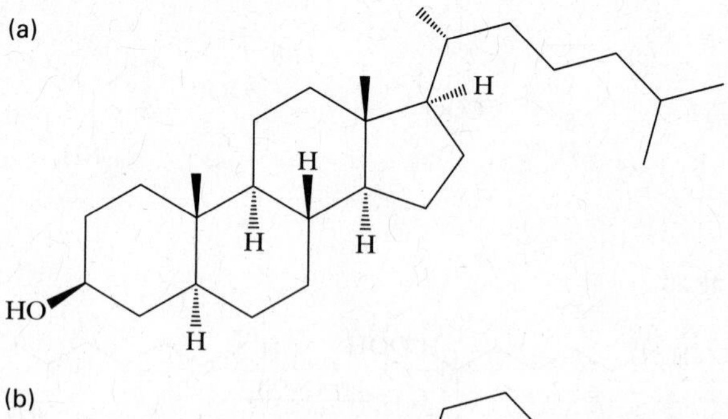

(b)

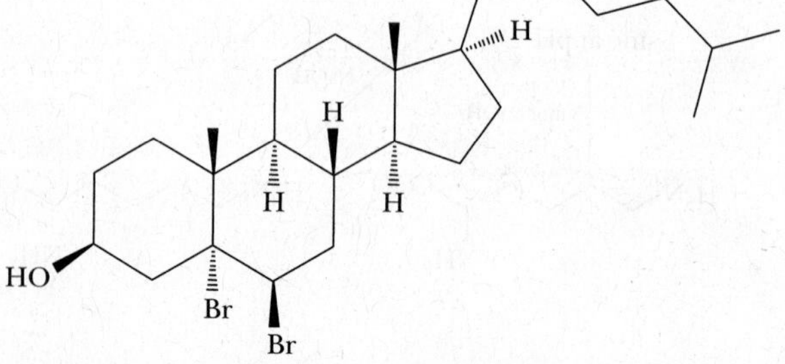

19.25

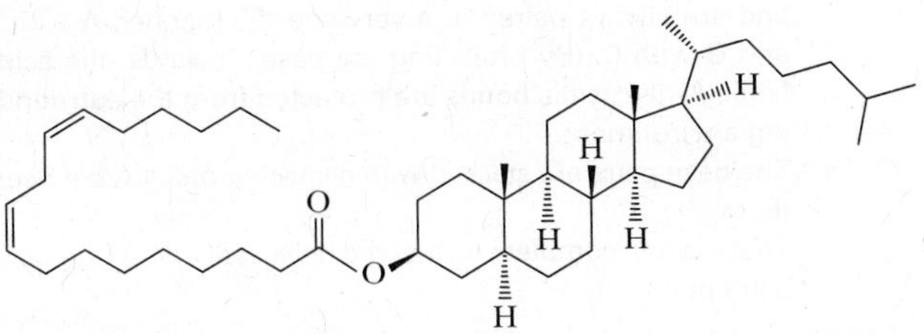

19.27 Cholic acid is able to act as an emulsifier because it contains both hydrophobic and hydrophilic groups.

19.29 Methandrostenolone has an extra carbon–carbon double bond in ring A and a methyl substituent on carbon 17.

19.31 Four chemical modifications occur when progesterone is converted to estradiol: Ring A is converted into an aromatic ring, the ketone of ring A is converted into a phenol, the methyl group on carbon 10 is removed, and the acetyl group on carbon 17 is replaced by a hydroxyl group.

19.33 Unoprostone differs from $PGF_{2\alpha}$ as follows: The double bond between carbons 13 and 14 is reduced, carbon 15 is oxidized from an alcohol to a ketone, and there are two extra carbons (21 and 22) at the end of the molecule.

19.35 16 *cis-trans*

19.37 Not soluble in water or blood plasma, much more soluble in dichloromethane.

19.39 Fluidity increases with increasing temperature.

19.41

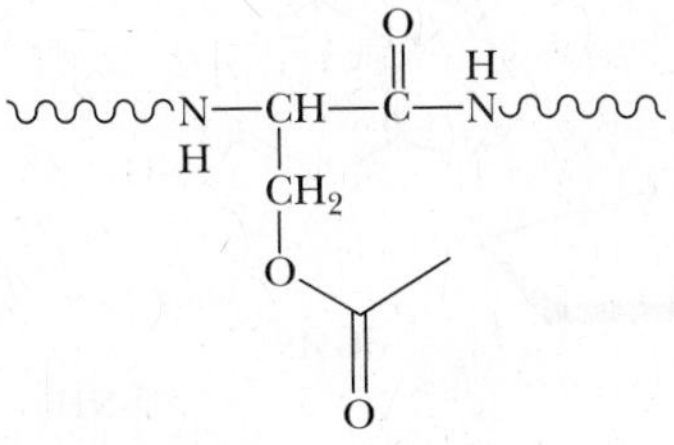

CHAPTER 20 Nucleic Acids

Problems

20.1

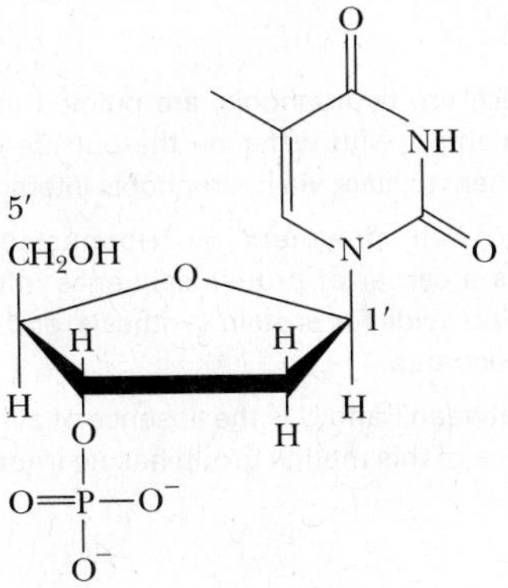

20.2

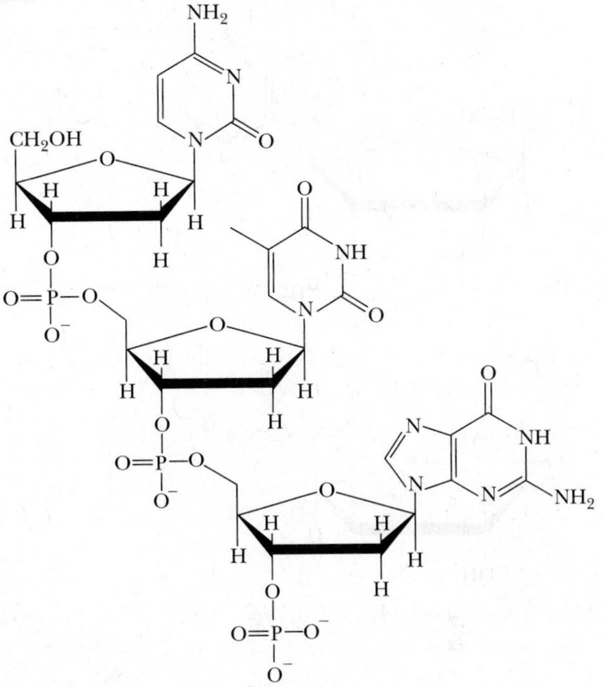

20.3 3′-GGCATGCT-5′

20.4 5′-TGGTGGACGAGTCCGGAA-3′

20.5 (a) 5′-UGC-UAU-AUU-CAA-AAU-UGC-CCU-CUU-GGU-UGA-3′
(b) Cys-Tyr-Ile-Gln-Asn-Cys-Pro-Leu-Gly.

20.6 Restriction endonucleases F*nu*DII and H*pa*II will cleave at the sites indicated below.

5′-ACGTCGGGTCGTCGTCCTCT**CG–C**GTGGTGAGCTT**C–CGG**CTCTTCT-3′
F*nu*DII H*pa*II

End-of-Chapter Problems

20.7

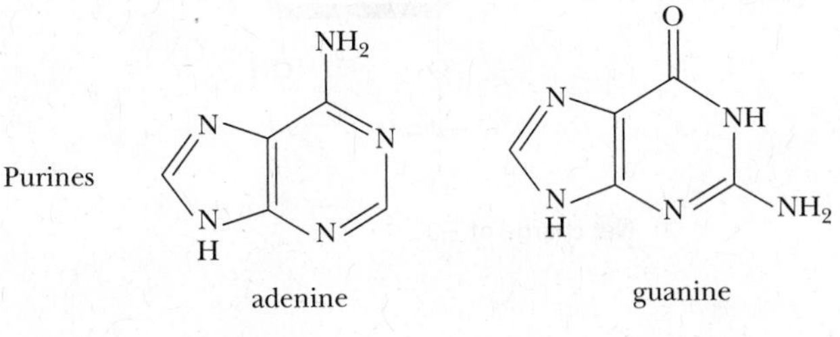

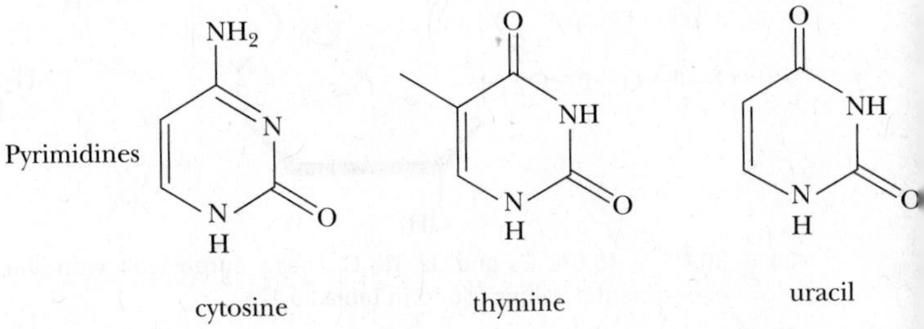

20.9 A nucleoside consists of only a nucleobase and ribose or 2-deoxyribose. A nucleotide is a phosphorylated nucleoside.

20.11 (a)

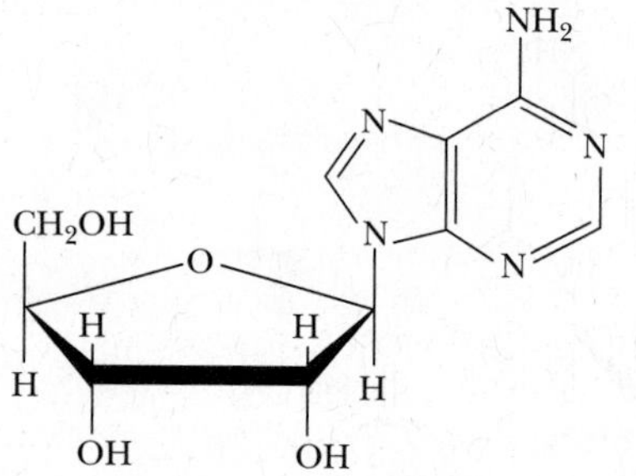

(b)

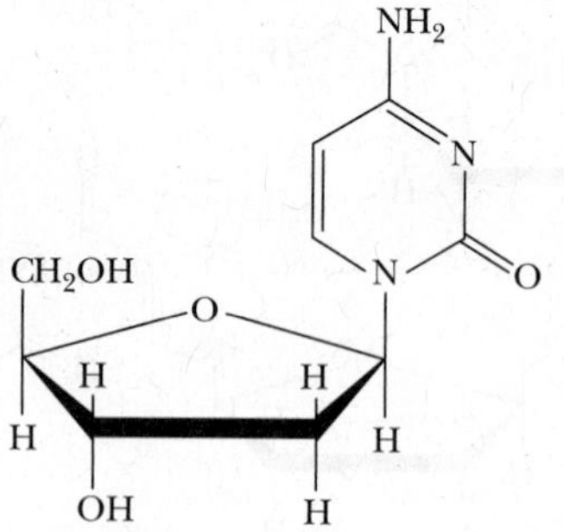

20.13 (a) Net charge of −4

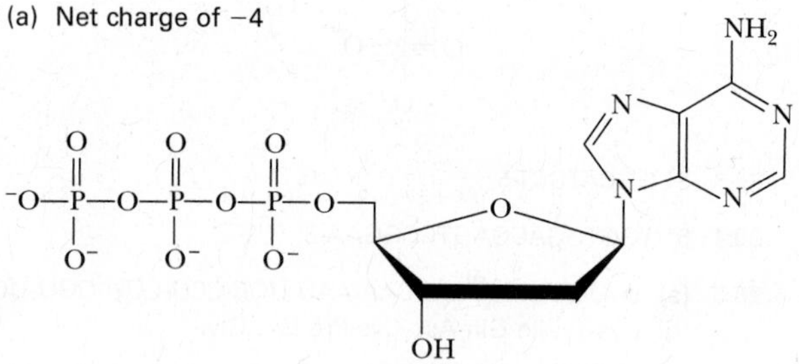

(b) Net charge of −2

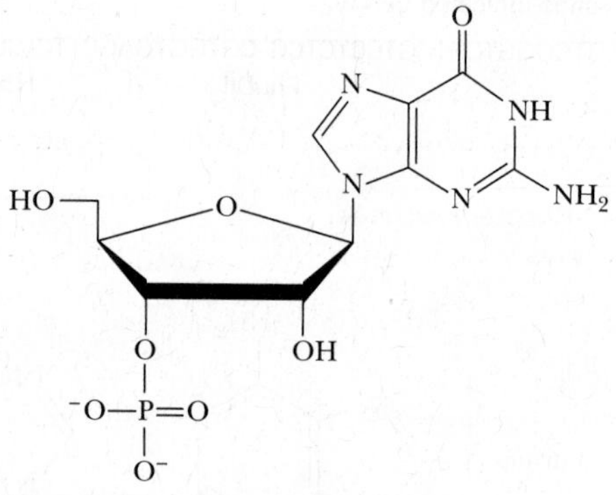

(c) Net charge of −3

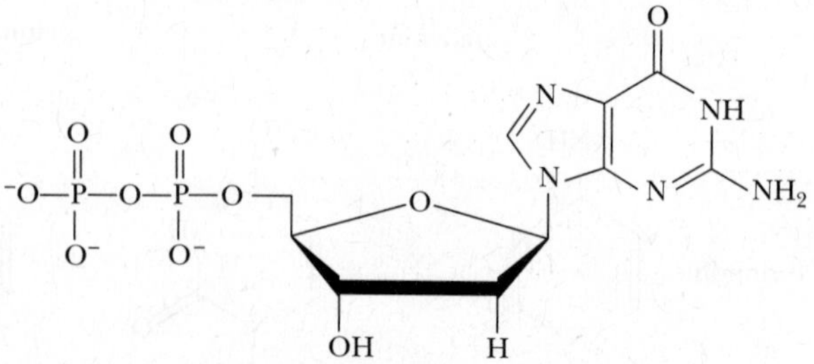

20.15 30.4% T, 19.6% G, and 19.6% C. These agree well with the experimental values found in Table 20.1.

20.17

- DNA consists of two antiparallel strands of polynucleotide that are coiled in a right-handed manner and arranged about the same axis to form a double helix.
- The nucleobases project inward toward the axis of the helix and are always paired in a very specific manner, A with T and G with C. (By projecting the bases inwards, the acid-labile *N*-glycosidic bonds are protected from the surrounding environment.)
- The base pairs are stacked with a spacing of 3.4 Å between them.
- There is one complete turn of the helix every 34 Å (ten base pairs per turn).

20.19 The nucleotides are 2-deoxyadenosine 5′-monophosphate (dAMP), 2-deoxythymidine 5′-monophosphate (dTMP), 2-deoxyguanosine 5′-monophosphate (dGMP), and 2-deoxycytidine 5′-monophosphate (dCMP).

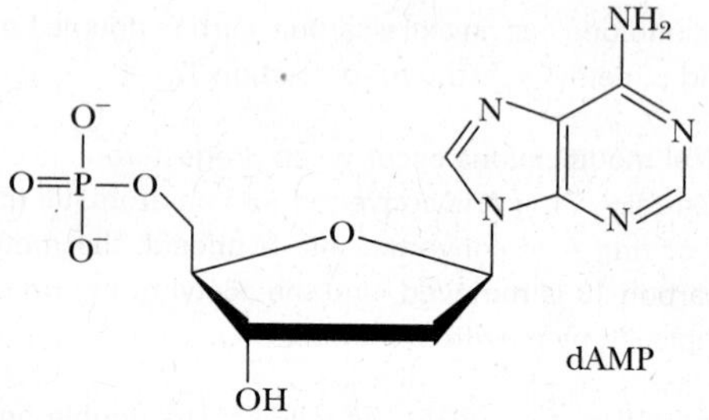

dAMP

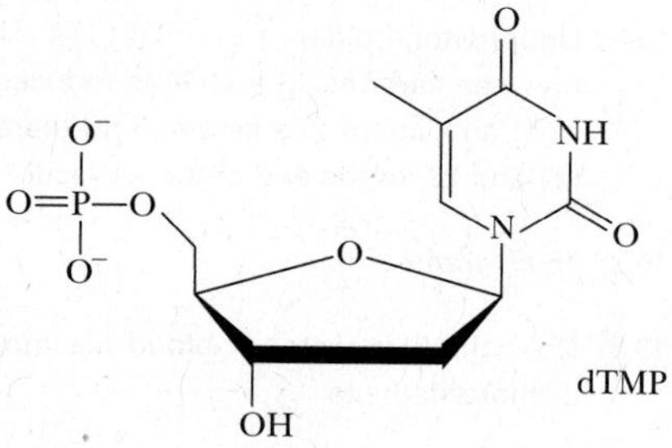

dTMP

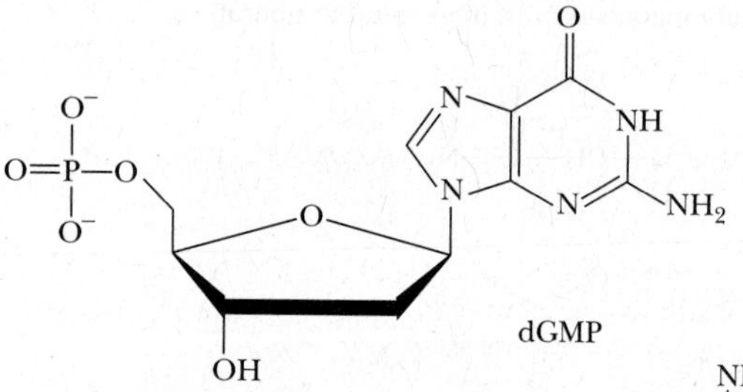

dGMP

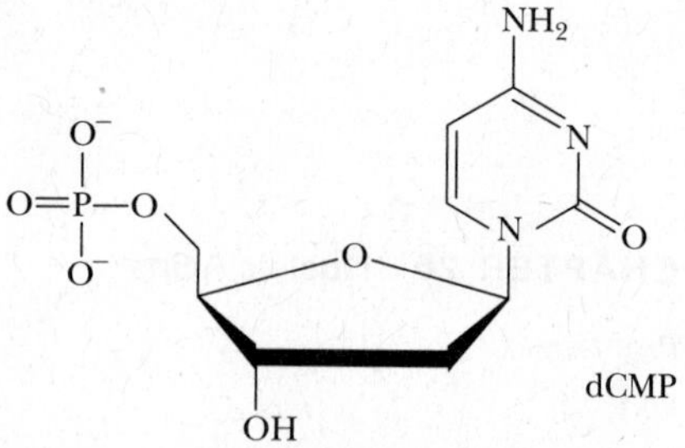

dCMP

20.21 The nucleobases, which are hydrophobic, are pointed inward. This minimizes their contact with water on the outside of the helix and also allows them to stack via hydrophobic interactions.

20.23 Chemically, they are all polymers of ribonucleotides. Functionally, mRNA is a carrier of protein-sequence information, tRNA carries amino acids for protein synthesis, and rRNA is a component of ribosomes.

20.25 The only difference between T and U is the absence of a methyl group in U. The absence of this methyl group has no impact on hydrogen bonding.

20.27 mRNA

20.29 3′-AGUUGCUA-5′.

20.31 There are 20 amino acids that are specified by the genetic code and with three nucleotides, 64 different sequence combinations are possible.

20.33 Stop codons

20.35 3′-TGGCAATTA-5′

20.37 More than one codon can code for the same amino acid.

20.39 Both Phe and Tyr are structurally similar, except that Tyr contains a hydroxyl group on the aromatic ring. The codons for Phe are UUU and UUC, while those for Tyr are UAU and UAC; the codons for the two amino acids differ only in the second position.

20.41 The last base in the codons for Gly, Ala, and Val is irrelevant. Other codons in which the third base is irrelevant include those for Arg (CGX), Pro (CCX), and Thr (ACX).

20.43 With the exception of Trp and Gly, all codons with a purine in the second position code for polar, hydrophilic side chains.

20.45 Each amino acid requires one codon (three nucleotides). Therefore, $3 \times 141 = 423$ bases are required for the amino acids alone, plus another three for the stop codon, giving a total of 426 bases.

20.47

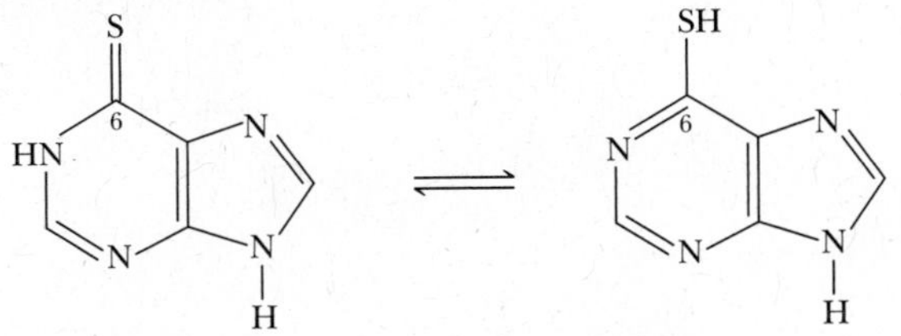

6-Mercaptopurine

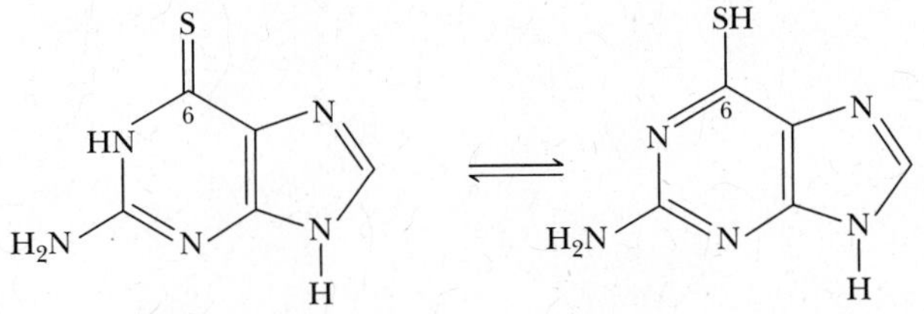

6-Thioguanine

20.49 (a) In the α-helices of proteins, the repeating units are amino acids that are linked by peptide (amide) bonds, whereas the repeating units in DNA are 2′-deoxy-D-ribose linked via 3′,5′-phosphodiester bonds.
(b) The R groups in the α-helices of proteins point outward from the helix, whereas the nucleobases in the DNA double helix point inward and away from the aqueous environment of the cell.

20.51 (a) Cordycepin is missing the 3′-OH group, so it acts as a chain terminator.
(b) The trichlorinated benzimidazole fragment mimics a purine base. This compound likely interferes with RNA polymerase, the enzyme that transcribes RNA from DNA.
(c) It is an analog of adenosine and likely interferes with the enzymes involved in nucleic acid synthesis.

20.53

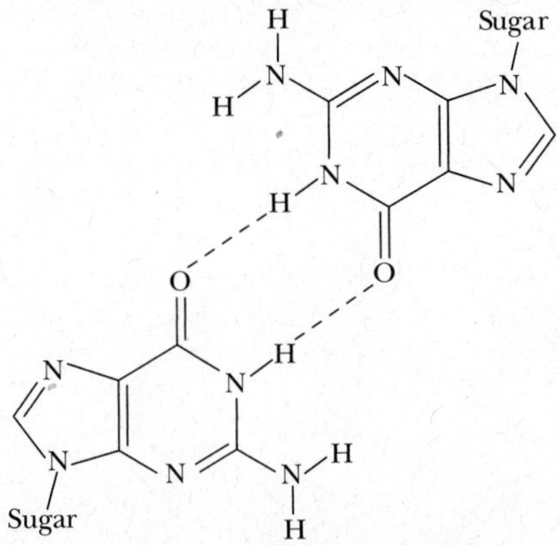

CHAPTER 21 The Organic Chemistry of Metabolism

Problems

21.1 Neither

21.2 Blood pH decreases

End-of-Chapter Problems

21.3 Aspartic acid and glutamic acid; conjugate acids of histidine, lysine, and arginine; and serine and cysteine

21.5 One coenzyme required for glycolysis (the oxidation steps) is nicotinamide adenine dinucleotide (NAD^+), and it is derived from the vitamin niacin.

21.7 6

21.9 Four moles of ethanol and four moles of CO_2

21.11

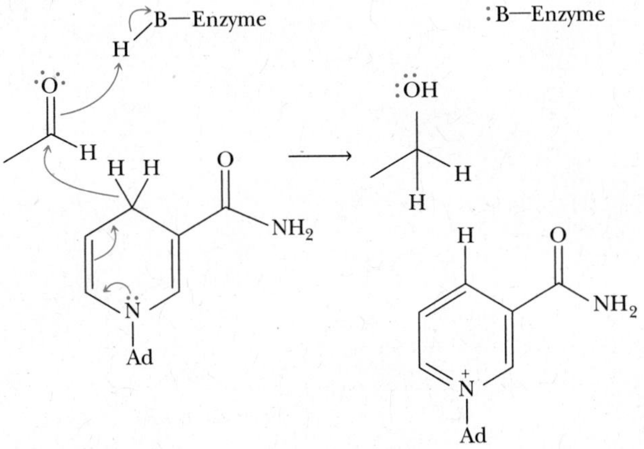

21.13 Hydrogen added to carbonyl carbon

21.15 3 and 4

21.17

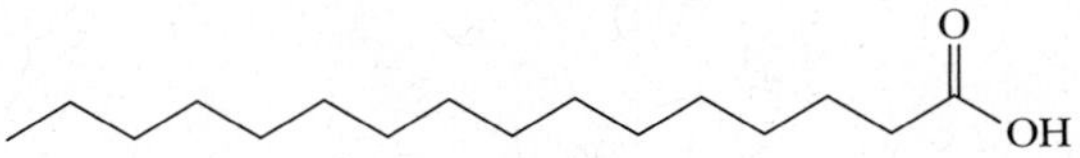

Palmitic acid (C_{16})

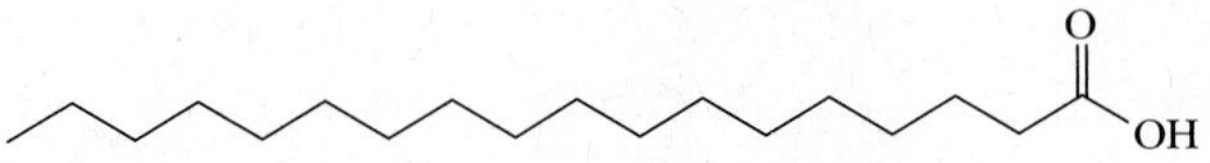

Stearic acid (C_{18})

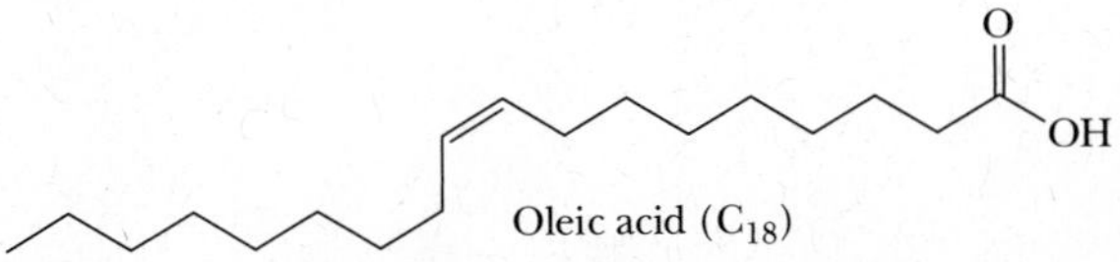

Oleic acid (C_{18})

21.19 FAD (riboflavin), NAD^+ (niacin), and coenzyme A (pantothenic acid)

21.21 To oxidize the two carbon atoms of the acetyl group in acetyl-CoA into carbon dioxide

21.23 None of the intermediates involved in the cycle are destroyed or created in the net reaction.

21.25 (a) $C_6H_{12}O_6 + 6O_2 \longrightarrow 6CO_2 + 6H_2O$
(b) $C_{57}H_{104}O_6 + 80O_2 \longrightarrow 57CO_2 + 52H_2O$ RQ = 0.71
(c) Decrease:
$C_2H_6O + 3O_2 \longrightarrow 2CO_2 + 3H_2O$ RQ = 0.67

21.27 Carbons 1 and 6 of glucose become the methyl groups of acetyl-CoA. The even-numbered carbon atoms of palmitic acid become the methyl groups of acetyl-CoA.

INDEX

A

alkanes (cont.)	heterocyclic aromatic, 333	arginine, 625, 684
nomenclature, 75	hydrogen bonding in, 337	aromatic amine, 333
physical properties of, 87–91	infrared spectroscopy, 371	aromatic compound, 283
reactions, 91	Michael addition, 551	aromaticity, 286–289
sources, 91–94	nomenclature, 334–337	artificial sweeteners, 602
structures, 67–68	as nucleophiles, 347-349	arylamines, 346-347
alkenes, 108	physical properties, 337-340	aryl Grignards, 423
catalytic cracking and, 133	pK_a value for, 341	aryl group, 283
cis-trans isomerism in, 111-112	pK_b value for, 341, 342	aspartic acid, 624–625
cis-trans system, 114-115	reaction with acids, 344-346	aspirin, 365, 466, 467, 665
common names, 114	from reduction of a nitro group to,	atomic orbitals
designating configuration, 114-117	346–347	covalent bond by overlap of, 23
E,Z configuration, 115	separation from nonbasic compounds,	hybridization of, 23, 284
heat of hydrogenation, 154-155	345	order of filling, 3
hydroboration-oxidation of, 150-152	structure, 333	shapes of, 22–23
infrared spectroscopy, 368	amino acids. See also proteins	atomic radii, 52
IUPAC nomenclature, 112–113	acidic and basic groups, 623–626	
naming of, 117	α -, 620	atoms
orbital overlap model, 110–111	analysis, 631–633	electron configuration of, 3–4
physical properties of, 120–122	chirality, 620–621	electronic structure, 2–5
priority rules, 115–116	D-, 623	ground-state electron configuration, 3
reduction to alkanes, 153–155	electrophoresis, 628–629	orbitals of, 2
	그러는 그 모든 그 그리고 있다. 그리고 얼마를 보고 모든 말이 되었다. 그리고 있는 그리고 있는 것이 없는 그리고 있는데 그리고 있다. 네트워크	pairing of electron spins, 3
relative stabilities, 154–155	isoelectric point, 627–628	principal energy levels, 2
shapes of, 110	L-, 623	schematic view of, 2
alkenes, reactions of, 130	polypeptides and, 630–631	shells of, 2
addition of bromine and chlorine,	protein-derived, 621–622	autoclave, 568
144–147	sequence analysis, 633-635	autoxidation, 319-320
addition of hydrogen halides, 136-141	structure, 620	axial-axial interaction, 82-83
addition of water (acid-catalyzed	titration of, 626–627	axial bonds, 79, 80
hydration), 142–144	4-aminobutanoic acid (γ -aminobutyric acid	
alkoxide ion, 247–248	(GABA)), 623	P. Commission of the commissio
alkoxy group, 261	amino group, 30–31	В
alkylamines, 336	amino sugars, 590	ball-and-stick model, 10, 15, 76, 77, 79,
alkylation reaction, 156	α -ammonium groups, acidity of, 625	80, 268, 269, 676
alkylbenzenes, 290	amorphous domains, 567-568	balloon models, to predict bond angles, 14
alkyl group, 69	AMP, 701, 714	base, 41
alkyl halide, 201	amylopectin, 604	Arrhenius definition of, 42
alkynes, 108	amylose, 604	Brønsted-Lowry definition, 43
infrared spectroscopy, 369	anabolic steroids, 660	Lewis definition and, 54-55
IUPAC nomenclature, 113	androgen, 659	as proton acceptor, 43
physical properties of, 120-122	angle strain, 79	strong, 46
reduction to alkenes and alkanes,	aniline, 290, 335, 345	weak, 45, 46
157–158	anion, 5, 7, 52	base ionization constant, 340, 342
structure of, 112	anisidine, 335	base pairing, 682
terminal, 122–123	anisole, 290, 306, 345	batrachotoxin, 338
allyl, 114	nitration, 310	B-DNA, double helix, 682–683
allylic carbon, 319	anomeric carbon, 591	
amides, 488		Benadryl, 268
	anomers, 591	bending motions, 366
hydrolysis, 499–500	anthracene, 292	benzaldehyde, 290, 418
and lactams, 493–494	antibodies, 620	benzene, 282
reaction with alcohols, 502	anti-Markovnikov hydration, 150	activating-deactivating effects theory,
reaction with ammonia and amines, 504	anti selectivity, bromine addition with, 146	312–314
reduction of, 509	anti stereoselectivity, 144	aromaticity, 286–289
amines, 30-31, 331-333	antitumour compounds, 553	directing effects theory,
acid-base properties, 340-344	antiviral drugs, 677	309–312
aliphatic, 333, 342	applied magnetic field, 379	disubstituted, 290-291
aromatic, 333, 342	aprotic solvent, 214, 215	electrophilic aromatic substitutions,
basicity, 340, 342, 343, 345	arachidonic acid, 664, 665	295–306
classification, 333	aramid, 570	Kekulé's model of, 283-284
heterocyclic, 333	arenes, 109, 283	monosubstituted, 289–290

C

D

G

H

I

Q

R

1A	2A
1 **H** Hydrogen 1.0079 [G]	

Atomic number: 92
Symbol: **U** Uranium
Atomic weight: 238.03 [S]

State: [S] Solid, [L] Liquid, [G] Gas, [X] Not found in nature

1A	2A	3B	4B	5B	6B	7B	8B	8B
3 **Li** Lithium 6.941 [S]	4 **Be** Beryllium 9.0122 [S]							
11 **Na** Sodium 22.990 [S]	12 **Mg** Magnesium 24.305 [S]							
19 **K** Potassium 39.098 [S]	20 **Ca** Calcium 40.078 [S]	21 **Sc** Scandium 44.956 [S]	22 **Ti** Titanium 47.867 [S]	23 **V** Vanadium 50.942 [S]	24 **Cr** Chromium 51.996 [S]	25 **Mn** Manganese 54.938 [S]	26 **Fe** Iron 55.845 [S]	27 **Co** Cobalt 58.933 [S]
37 **Rb** Rubidium 85.468 [S]	38 **Sr** Strontium 87.62 [S]	38 **Y** Yttrium 88.906 [S]	40 **Zr** Zirconium 91.224 [S]	41 **Nb** Niobium 92.9064 [S]	42 **Mo** Molybdenum 95.96 [S]	43 **Tc** Technetium (98)* [X]	44 **Ru** Ruthenium 101.07 [S]	45 **Rh** Rhodium 102.91 [S]
55 **Cs** Cesium 132.91 [S]	56 **Ba** Barium 137.33 [S]	57 **La** Lanthanum 138.91 [S]	72 **Hf** Hafnium 178.49 [S]	73 **Ta** Tantalum 180.95 [S]	74 **W** Tungsten 183.84 [S]	75 **Re** Rhenium 186.21 [S]	76 **Os** Osmium 190.23 [S]	77 **Ir** Iridium 192.22 [S]
87 **Fr** Francium (223) [S]	88 **Ra** Radium 226.0254 [S]	89 **Ac** Actinium (227) [S]	104 **Rf** Rutherfordium (265) [X]	105 **Db** Dubnium (268) [X]	106 **Sg** Seaborgium (271) [X]	107 **Bh** Bohrium (270) [X]	108 **Hs** Hassium (277) [X]	109 **Mt** Meitnerium (276) [X]

Lanthanides	58 **Ce** Cerium 140.12 [S]	59 **Pr** Praseodymium 140.91 [S]	60 **Nd** Neodymium 144.24 [S]	61 **Pm** Promethium (145) [X]	62 **Sm** Samarium 150.36 [X]
Actinides	90 **Th** Thorium 232.04 [S]	91 **Pa** Protactinium 231.04 [S]	92 **U** Uranium 238.03 [S]	93 **Np** Neptunium (237) [X]	94 **Pu** Plutonium (244) [S]

* A value in parentheses represents the mass of the most stable isotope.